China
中国

Damian Harper

Marie Cambon	**Bradley Mayhew**
Katja Gaskell	**Korina Miller**
Thomas Huhti	**Mielikki Org**

LONELY PLANET PUBLICATIONS
Melbourne • Oakland • London • Paris

IT

RUSSIA

60°E

80°E

100°E

Ural River

RUSSIA

Omsk

Novosibirsk

Krasnoyarsk

Irtysh River

Yenisey River

250   500km

150   300mi

ASTANA

The external boundaries
of India on this map have not been
authenticated and may not be correct

Qaraghandy

KAZAKHSTAN

PÍNGYÁO
Old walled city boasting some
of China's best-preserved Ming
dynasty buildings

Aral
Sea

Syr Darya River

KASHGAR
Far-flung camel-trading
Central Asian outpost

Balkhash Lake

MONGOLIA

UZBEKISTAN

Almaty

Ürümqi

Amu Darya River

TASHKENT

BISHKEK

Turpan

KYRGYZSTAN

XĪNJIĀNG

Dūnhuáng

TAJIKISTAN

Kashgar

DUSHANBE

Under administration
of China

Qinghai Hu
(Qinghai
Lake)

AFGHANISTAN

Golmud

KABUL

QĪNGHĂI

ISLAMABAD

Rawalpindi

PLATEAU
OF TIBET

Lahore

PAKISTAN

Indus River

HIMALAYA

TIBET

Lhasa

Mt
Everest
(8848m)

Shigatse

DELHI

NEPAL

Karachi

Ganges

KATHMANDU

Jaipur

Agra

THIMPHU

BHUTAN

Lucknow

Patna

River

Varanasi

Ahmedabad

BANGLADESH

INDIA

Calcutta

MYANMAR

DHAKA

Bhubaneswar

Chittagong

Mandalay

Mumbai (Bombay)

Godavari River

Arabian
Sea

Thanlwin River

XĪSHUĀNGBĂNNÀ
Subtropical border region
of minority villages

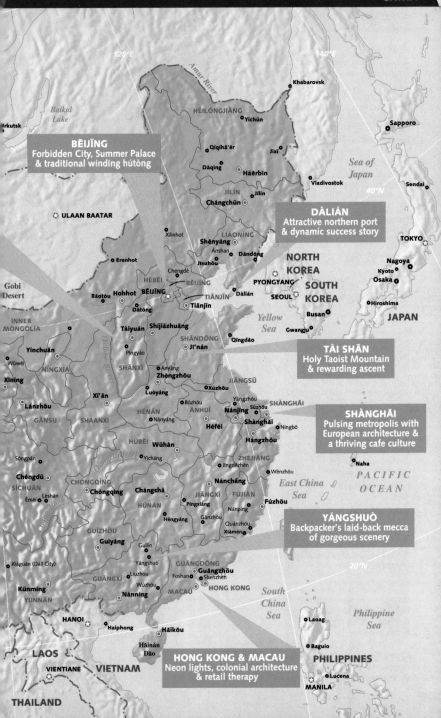

BĚIJĪNG
Forbidden City, Summer Palace & traditional winding hútòng

DÀLIÁN
Attractive northern port & dynamic success story

TÀI SHĀN
Holy Taoist Mountain & rewarding ascent

SHÀNGHǍI
Pulsing metropolis with European architecture & a thriving cafe culture

YÁNGSHUÒ
Backpacker's laid-back mecca of gorgeous scenery

HONG KONG & MACAU
Neon lights, colonial architecture & retail therapy

120°E 140°E

Baikal Lake

Irkutsk

Amur River

Khabarovsk

HĒILÓNGJIĀNG

Yichūn

Qíqíhā'ěr

Dàqìng

Jīxī

Hā'ěrbīn

Sapporo

Vladivostok

Sea of Japan

40°N

Sendai

JÍLÍN

Chángchūn

Jílín

ULAAN BAATAR

Xilinhot

LIÁONÍNG

Shěnyáng

Ānshan Dāndōng

NORTH KOREA

TOKYO

Nagoya

Kyoto

Osaka

Jìnzhōu

Chéngdé

PYONGYANG

SOUTH KOREA

Hiroshima

Erenhot

HÉBĚI BĚIJĪNG

Gobi Desert

Bāotóu Hohhot Běijīng

Dàtóng

SEOUL

Dàlián

TIĀNJĪN

Tiānjīn

JAPAN

Busan

INNER MONGOLIA

Yellow Sea

Gwangju

Tāiyuán Shíjiāzhuāng

Yínchuān

SHĀNDŌNG

Qīngdǎo

Wūwēi

Pingyáo

Jǐ'nán

NÍNGXIÀ

SHĀNXĪ

Xīníng

Ānyáng

Zhèngzhōu

JIĀNGSŪ

Xúzhōu

Lánzhōu

Xī'ān

Luòyáng

Yángzhōu

SHÀNGHǍI

Bózhōu

Nánjīng Sūzhōu

GĀNSÙ

SHAANXI

HÉNÁN

ĀNHUĪ

Shànghǎi

Nányáng

Héféi

Ningbō

HÚBĚI

Wǔhàn

Hángzhōu

Sōngpān

Yíchāng

ZHÈJIĀNG

Jǐngdézhèn

Wēnzhōu

Naha

PACIFIC OCEAN

Chéngdū

CHÓNGQÌNG

Nánchāng

East China Sea

SÌCHUĀN

Lèshān

Chóngqìng Chángshā

JIĀNGXĪ

FÚJIÀN

Émēi

HÚNÁN

Píngxiáng

Fúzhōu

Nánpíng

Héngyáng

Gànzhōu

Quánzhōu

GUÌZHŌU

Xiàmén

Guìyáng

Guìlín

Yángshuò

GUǍNGDŌNG

Xiàguān (Dàlǐ City)

Liǔzhōu

Guǎngzhōu

Kūnmíng

Wúzhōu

Foshan Shenzhen

South China Sea

Philippine Sea

YÚNNÁN

GUǍNGXĪ

Nánníng

MACAU HONG KONG

Laoag

HANOI

Haiphong

Hǎikǒu

Baguio

LAOS

Hǎinán Dǎo

PHILIPPINES

VIENTIANE VIETNAM

Lucena

THAILAND

MANILA

20°N

China
8th edition – August 2002
First published – October 1984

Published by
Lonely Planet Publications Pty Ltd ABN. 36 005 607 983
90 Maribyrnong St, Footscray, Victoria 3011, Australia

Lonely Planet Offices
Australia Locked Bag 1, Footscray, Victoria 3011
USA 150 Linden St, Oakland, CA 94607
UK 10a Spring Place, London NW5 3BH
France 1 rue du Dahomey, 75011 Paris

Photographs
Many of the images in this guide are available for licensing from
Lonely Planet Images.
w www.lonelyplanetimages.com

Front cover photograph
Opera performance in Macau (Michael Aw)

ISBN 1 74059 117 8

text & maps © Lonely Planet Publications Pty Ltd 2002
photos © photographers as indicated 2002

Printed by SNP SPrint (M) Sdn Bhd
Printed in Malaysia

Contents – Text

4 Contents – Text

INDEX 985

MAP LEGEND back page

METRIC CONVERSION inside back cover

Contents – Maps

8 Contents – Maps

MAP INDEX

RUSSIA

KAZAKHSTAN

MONGOLIA

Bu'erjin
p869

Yining p873

KYRGYZSTAN

◉ Ürümqi p843

Turpan p849
Around Turpan
p851

Kashgar p857

XINJIANG

GANSU

Dunhuang
p891

Jiayuguan
p889

Golmud p951

Xining p946 ◉

◉
Lanzhou
p878

Xiahe &
Labuleng Si
p883

QINGHAI

TIBET

Jiuzhai Gou p816 ◉
Songpan p813

SICHUAN   Chengdu p774

Qingcheng Shan
p787

Dujiangyan p789 ◉ ◉

◉ Lhasa p930
Barkhor Area p932

Kangding p802 ◉
Emei Shan p791 ◉
Leshan p796

Shigatse p939

Zhongdian
p741

Tiger Leaping
Gorge p737

NEPAL   BHUTAN

Lijiang p728
Lijiang - Old Town p730
Around Lijiang & Zhongdian p735

INDIA

Baoshan p759
Tengchong p761 ◉

Xiaguan p717
Dali p719
Dali & Erhai Hu
p725

Kunming p698
Around Kunming
(Lake Dian) p711

BANGLADESH

Ruili p766 ◉
Mangshi (Luxi) p765

Shilin
p714

INDIA

YUNNAN

Xishuangbanna p745
Jinghong p748

MYANMAR

Bay of Bengal

LAOS

THAILAND

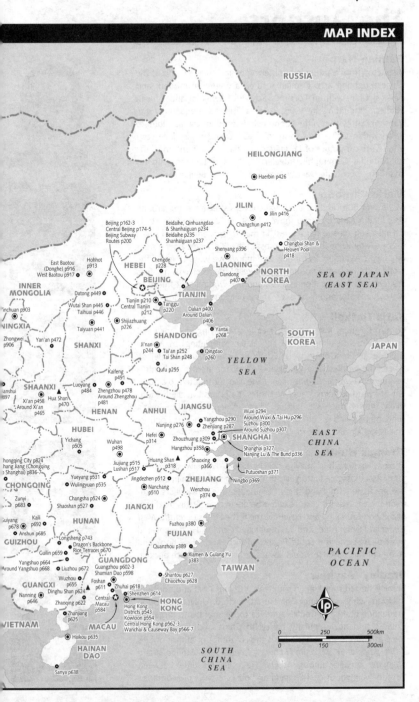

The Authors

Damian Harper

Distracted from a career in bookselling by the arcane world of the Chinese fighting arts, Damian secured a degree in modern and classical Chinese from London's School of Oriental and African Studies, graduating in 1995. After a lifetime subdued by the transport entity that is the London Underground, Damian took to travel within China like a fish to water. Damian has since contributed to a number of LP guides and has done work on China for National Geographic Traveler. He lives in London with his Shāndōng-born wife Dai Min and son, Timothy Benjamin.

Marie Cambon

Marie was born and raised in Vancouver. After travelling around Asia in the early 80s, she moved to Shànghǎi in 1986 to study Chinese and pursue her interest in the city's cinematic and social history. After living in China for most of the 90s, Marie now resides in Vancouver and looks for new and innovative ways to travel the world with the least amount of baggage. Marie received a master's degree in communication in 1993 and has worked as a freelance writer, translator and filmmaker. This is her fourth book for LP.

Katja Gaskell

Born in Belgium, Katja spent her early years living in France and Texas before heading to the UK. After completing an MA in Chinese at the University of Edinburgh she headed to Běijīng where she worked as a writer and editor for an arts and entertainment magazine, *Beijing Scene*. She also contributed to a number of award-winning travel Web sites. Katja has travelled extensively throughout Asia, Europe, North America and the Indian subcontinent and is currently enjoying life in south-east London. This is Katja's first book for LP.

Thomas Huhti

Thomas Huhti hails from Wisconsin in the USA. A university semester in Asia blossomed into years in Taiwan on fellowship in order to flee graduate school and study Chinese. He spent five years bumming the earth as a freelance writer before joining LP. His third tour of duty on *China*, he also co-wrote the first editions of *South-West China* and *Great Lakes* and has researched *Canada*. He has covered most of Asia and the South Pacific, Mexico, and every nook and cranny of the USA. He would always rather be playing ice hockey.

Bradley Mayhew

Bradley started travelling in south-west China, Tibet and northern Pakistan while studying Chinese at Oxford University. Upon graduation he fled to Central America for six months to forget his Chinese and now regularly travels to China's borderlands in a futile attempt to get it back. He is the co-author or author of LP's *Tibet, Pakistan, Karakoram Highway, Central Asia, Mongolia* and *Shanghai* guides, among others. He splits his time between Sevenoaks in south-east England and obscure parts of Montana.

Korina Miller

Korina lived the first 18 years of her life on Vancouver Island. Since then, she hasn't lived in any one place for very long, managing to take in parts of Japan, India, Egypt, Europe, and South and Central America. Along the way she picked up a degree in Communications & Canadian Studies, a MA in Migration Studies and a Limey husband in a Brighton discotheque. A few year ago, she spent six months in Shànghǎi and Lìjiāng researching cooperatives and eco-tourism. She is currently working with an intercultural arts centre in London. This is Korina's third book for LP.

Mielikki Org

Mielikki Org grew up in southern California and discovered there was more to life than the beach at the age of 16, on a trip to Europe. Since then she has worked, studied, and written travel guides in both France and China. She has also studied at Beijing Normal University. A Sino-Finnish linguophile with a penchant for guitar, painting, karate, and flamenco, Mielikki is currently working on a journalism degree from UC Berkeley, where she received BAs in English and French in 1994. This is Mielikki's first book for LP.

FROM THE AUTHORS

Damian

On the rollcall of thanks and appreciation, special mention must go to Dai Ruibin, Liu Meina, Dai Lu, Dajiu, Erjiu, Xiaojiu and Mali Yijia. I raise a glass to Mr Kerry Brown for many an entertaining evening and get down on one knee to Dai Min, for her patience and understanding. To little Long'en, may all your dreams come true.

Marie

Many thanks to all the people along the way. In Shànghǎi, I would like to thank Maria Barbieri, Xiǎo Zhōu, Lǎo Chén, Mary Cao, Tess Johnston, Lily Willens and Filippo Valentini. Raphaele Borie was a great help in Níngbō, (thanks Austen Cambon, former Níngbō resident, for introducing me) as was Hé Jiàn in Shàoxīng. Special thanks to Geoffrey Bowman for corrections on the Hángzhōu Tidal Bore.

Readers' letters were also a great help, but I would like to thank Marilyn McCullough in particular for her exhaustive coverage of Hángzhōu and surrounding areas. Finally, muchos gracias to my parents, and Randy Schuks, who makes life so much easier.

Katja

Thanks must go to Caroline Liou for introducing me to LP, Jocelyn Harewood for sending me to China and Tim Fitzgerald for pre-trip tips. The following people were invaluable for all their help, hospitality and good humour; Lou, John, George and the other folk in Běijīng; Scott and Dodo (Mǔdānjiāng), Dayia and Sarah, Liu Dan (Jílín), Des and Rose (Wēihǎi); Chun Kung Shi, Zhang Lin, Liu Xiuli, Li Haisan and Wang Jing (Jinzhou). Special thanks to my family, Chris, Rhi, John, Laurs and Miss B – you're all so great. Finally I'm grateful to all the people I met on the road who offered help and advice, the readers who contributed letters and all the LP staff who put the China guidebook together.

Thomas

The following grand travel mates accrued huge Elvis points by helping me out (in myriad ways): Tedd Hauptman; the aptly named Paul Wisdom; Paul Simacek (all US); Eyal Rom & Maya Reis (Israel); Miao Yi (Carl; Hong Kong); Parhat (Korla); Gaston & Marie (Netherlands); Aaron Zhang & Ghengis Kane (Xī'ān); Pang Xiaodong (Hohhot); Ali, Peter and Seric (OCTS Ürümqi); Roshni Nirody; Jason Zayl (Canada); Tenzin & Puker Tsering (Xiàhé); Losang and staff (Xiàhé); Niu Xiaojun (Xīníng); and the wonderful Yusuf Qadar (Yarkand) and his family.

My family and colleagues at WESLI: I hope they realise how I treasure them. The art of James Agee and Dou Wei helped pass the lonely hours.

Finally, a shout-out to the wonderful people of China: you make it worthwhile.

Bradley

Thanks again to Calum 'our man in Běijīng' MacLeod for sending steaming loads of China information and for expertise on booze and minorities, travel with children and loads of other great stuff. Special thanks to Andre for his good cheer in difficult circumstances in western Sìchuān. Thanks and love as ever to Kelli.

Korina

Thanks and love to Paul, a fantastic travelling companion, for braving the frozen bus rides, the chunky butter tea and the manic schedule. Thank you to Jocelyn Harewood, Kyla Gillzan, Steve Fallon, Alex English and everyone else at LP who have been supportive and patient – especially with my computer afflictions and Chinese challenged ways. Thanks to Xiao Ning for his help with translations, to Samuel Yue for doling out his knowledge of the region to a writer undercover, and to all of the readers and travellers who shared their insight and experiences. Finally, to the local people I met on the road, thank you for your kindness and for sharing your enthusiasm for your country.

Mielikki

Many who deserve thanks will unfortunately never have the chance to read this book. Thanks to: the many monks, students and bus drivers who made me feel welcome; the Zhuhai Guangdong Regency Hotel staff for discussions about Eminem and hip-hop; Jim and Rebecca for the subversive Bus English lesson in Lúshān; Hu Jian Guo and Qiu Wei Dong at Wǔyí Shān CITS; and Jackie Chan for the company and inspiration on long bus rides.

Thanks to Damian Harper for the advice and humour, my parents for keeping the Feds away, my brother Rikki for cooking for me at home, new and old friends in China – especially Shelley, Linda, and Auntie at Yangshuo's Riverside Retreat, and relatives in Xichang. A special thanks to my partner, Daniel Cota, for his love, humour, and support.

This Book

The 1st edition of this book appeared after Michael Buckley and Alan Samagalski spent many months on the road in China in 1983.

This 8th edition of *China* is the work of a wonderful team of authors, including coordinator Damian Harper.

All those involved in producing this book greatly appreciate the contributions of the travellers who wrote in telling us of their experiences. Your names appear on pages 972 to 974.

From the Publisher

This edition of China was produced in Lonely Planet's Melbourne office. Production was coordinated by Kyla Gillzan (editorial) and Nick Stebbing (cartography/design). Assisting with editing and proofing were Rebecca Hobbs, Anastasia Safioleas, Gina Tsarouhas, Michael Day, Shelley Muir, Nina Rousseau and Elizabeth Swan; and with mapping Meredith Mail, Chris Thomas, Chris Tsismetzis, Clare Capell, Sophie Reed and Rebecca Hobbs. A special thankyou to Rebecca whose expertise was invaluable in editing, mapping and layout, and for answering those endless script and pinyin questions with a smile.

The history section was written by Antonia Finnane. The language chapter was produced by the very organised Quentin Frayne. Matt King coordinated the illustrations. Brush & Ink drawings used throughout this book were drawn by Enjarn Lin. Character derivation drawings were provided by Kieran Grogan. Other illustrations were drawn by Martin Harris, Kelli Hamblet and Jenny Bowman. Aside decorations were drawn by Rebecca Hobbs and Mick Weldon. The etchings used throughout this book were taken from *China, Its Scenery & Social Habits*, Thomas Allom (1843).

Margaret Jung created the cover and Kusnandar generated the climate charts. Thanks to Mark Germanchis for his assistance with layout and Lachlan Ross for creating the colour map.

Thanks also to Leonie Mugavin for airline and other travel information, Jennifer Mundy for compiling the acknowledgements under pressure, Chris Tsismetzis and Agustín Poó y Balbontin for last-minute layout assistance, Bibiana Jaramillo for her help with tricky font issues, and Shu Huadong (Shàoxīng) and Song Jian (Hángzhōu) for coming to the rescue with up-to-date map information.

Corinne Waddell assisted with artwork checks, and the whole process was overseen and brought together by Jocelyn Harewood (editorial) and Tim Fitzgerald (design).

Acknowledgement

Extract from *The Songlines* by Bruce Chatwin published by Jonathan Cape. Used with permission of The Random House Group Limited. Copyright (c) Bruce Chatwin 1987.

THANKS
Many thanks to the travellers who used the last edition and wrote to us with helpful hints, advice and interesting anecdotes. Your names appear in the back of this book.

Foreword

ABOUT LONELY PLANET GUIDEBOOKS

The story begins with a classic travel adventure: Tony and Maureen Wheeler's 1972 journey across Europe and Asia to Australia. There was no useful information about the overland trail then, so Tony and Maureen published the first Lonely Planet guidebook to meet a growing need.

From a kitchen table, Lonely Planet has grown to become the largest independent travel publisher in the world, with offices in Melbourne (Australia), Oakland (USA), London (UK) and Paris (France).

Today Lonely Planet guidebooks cover the globe. There is an ever-growing list of books and information in a variety of media. Some things haven't changed. The main aim is still to make it possible for adventurous travellers to get out there – to explore and better understand the world.

At Lonely Planet we believe travellers can make a positive contribution to the countries they visit – if they respect their host communities and spend their money wisely. Since 1986 a percentage of the income from each book has been donated to aid projects and human rights campaigns, and, more recently, to wildlife conservation.

Although inclusion in a guidebook usually implies a recommendation we cannot list every good place. Exclusion does not necessarily imply criticism. In fact there are a number of reasons why we might exclude a place – sometimes it is simply inappropriate to encourage an influx of travellers.

UPDATES & READER FEEDBACK

Things change – prices go up, schedules change, good places go bad and bad places go bankrupt. Nothing stays the same. So, if you find things better or worse, recently opened or long-since closed, please tell us and help make the next edition even more accurate and useful.

Lonely Planet thoroughly updates each guidebook as often as possible – usually every two years, although for some destinations the gap can be longer. Between editions, up-to-date information is available in our free, quarterly *Planet Talk* newsletter and monthly email bulletin *Comet*. The *Upgrades* section of our website (W www.lonelyplanet.com) is also regularly updated by Lonely Planet authors, and the site's *Scoop* section covers news and current affairs relevant to travellers. Lastly, the *Thorn Tree* bulletin board and *Postcards* section carry unverified, but fascinating, reports from travellers.

Tell us about it! We genuinely value your feedback. A well-travelled team at Lonely Planet reads and acknowledges every email and letter we receive and ensures that every morsel of information finds its way to the relevant authors, editors and cartographers.

Everyone who writes to us will find their name listed in the next edition of the appropriate guidebook, and will receive the latest issue of *Comet* or *Planet Talk*. The very best contributions will be rewarded with a free guidebook.

We may edit, reproduce and incorporate your comments in Lonely Planet products such as guidebooks, websites and digital products, so let us know if you don't want your comments reproduced or your name acknowledged.

How to contact Lonely Planet:
Online: e talk2us@lonelyplanet.com.au, W www.lonelyplanet.com
Australia: Locked Bag 1, Footscray, Victoria 3011
UK: 10a Spring Place, London NW5 3BH
USA: 150 Linden St, Oakland, CA 94607

Introduction

China is not so much a travel destination as a mind-boggling phenomenon. It's home to one of the world's longest continuous civilisations, with an impressive heritage of art, architecture, language and cuisine. It's a country of great contrasts: picturesque rural landscapes and congested cityscapes; and natural beauty that ranges from the untamed to the idyllic – from the windswept plains of the Gobi Desert and the notorious northern face of Mt Everest to Yángshuò's gorgeous karst scenery.

China is huge and wild enough to satisfy your explorer instinct, but criss-crossed with an extensive transportation network so you won't be left high and dry.

Whatever China does to you – entertains, stimulates, appeals or bemuses – you will come away with priceless memories of a country in the throes of reinventing itself. The last decades of the 20th century saw China open up to an eager world that was gazing through the portcullis, visa application in hand.

These past years have been a ceaseless drama of energetic development, economic contortions, an invasion of Western culture and the resurgence of mass inequality. China has never been so transformed, except perhaps when the Mongols passed through with their own blueprints for change.

A light-headedness lingers from the rejection of the austerities and craziness of the Mao era and the effects of that new opiate, carefully named 'socialism with Chinese characteristics'. The currents of change run deep. See for yourself while sipping cappuccinos from Starbucks in Běijīng or perusing the latest fashions in Shànghǎi.

An increasingly confident China knows the importance of engagement with the world. A gold rush of rewards in 2001 has yielded a feel-good factor: China joined the World Trade Organization, Běijīng will stage the 2008 Olympics and the national football team made it to the World Cup for the first time ever.

Domestic tourism is in a state of supernova, showering sights around the land with much-needed investment, and less-needed noise pollution and litter. Sadly, some destinations have been disfigured as the tourist industry swamps them with garish sideshows and commerce, and some previously idyllic locations have perhaps irreversibly lost their magic. Massive investment has brought transport quality a long way over the last 10 years, and routes have become steadily speedier and more comfortable.

The coercive nature of the Chinese State remains, however – placing serious limits on freedoms. China has chosen to embrace modernity without allowing political evolution; dissent is brutally expunged, debate stifled and information carefully controlled. This may not be of great interest to short-term travellers, but will explain why the BBC Web site is blocked (both in English and Chinese), why foreign newspapers are occasionally trimmed of opinion and why there are no demonstrations or political debates on TV.

Also be aware that travel in China can present many difficulties, with language the single most difficult barrier. This guidebook has undertaken to facilitate the ease with which you master some basic Chinese by providing tonal marks to aid pronunciation. Chinese script is also provided where it can come in handy (on maps, to show to taxi drivers, for example). Familiarising yourself with the Chinese words for hotel, restaurant, park, temple, station and so on will make getting around a little easier and, hopefully, will lead to greater interaction with Chinese people.

China is a great rollercoaster ride for anyone with a little time and an instinct for travel. So take a deep breath, plunge in and have a great trip!

Facts about China

HISTORY

History books often claim that China is the world's oldest surviving civilisation. The 'China' of five or six thousand years ago, however, bears little resemblance to the present. The territorial reach of the state, the organisation of society, the content and expressions of culture, how people spoke and dressed, what they produced and ate have all changed beyond recognition.

Confucianism was unknown before the 6th century BC, achieved supremacy only after the 10th century, then in the 20th century lost its once dominant position. The centralised state, a distinguishing feature of the Chinese polity, dates back only to the late 3rd century BC. Even after that time, the unified empire repeatedly broke up into rival states of longer or shorter duration. Rice cultivation did not become widespread until the Tang dynasty, in the 7th to 10th centuries. Cotton, the major fibre used for Chinese clothing in the late imperial era and into the 20th century, was introduced only in the 13th century.

Nonetheless, the history of societies which flourished on Chinese soil in ancient times, together with the remnants of their material culture, forms part of the tale Chinese tell about their own origins. And without this history, the differentiation of north and south, coast and hinterland, Chinese and non-Chinese, would remain unexplained.

High Antiquity: from Archaeology to History

The China story begins with the legend of 'three emperors and five sovereigns', who paved the way for the Xia dynasty of high antiquity. The three emperors were Fu Xi, who pioneered the domestication of animals; Shen Nong, responsible for fashioning farm implements; and Huangdi, warrior and empire-builder, whose queen is accredited with being the first to rear silkworms. These myths encapsulate the agrarian foundations of Chinese civilisation.

While this very early 'history' has no contemporary written record, archaeology confirms the antiquity of human society in China. Excavations at Bànpō, not far from present-day Xī'ān, show that nearly six thousand years ago a sedentary, agricultural society flourished around the future metropolitan region of the early Chinese empire. Bànpō is a site of Yangshao culture, named after Yǎngsháo village in Hénán province. A second early culture was discovered in present-day Shāndōng. Known as Longshan culture it shows the beginning of metallurgy, and appears to have provided the basis of the Bronze Age Shang dynasty.

Shang Dynasty

With the Shang dynasty, textual evidence begins. Bronze vessels from this era, collected and revered for centuries, occasionally carry early forms of characters denoting ownership. In 1899, there was a great leap in recognition of Shang literacy with the discovery of inscribed shells and bones from Ānyáng. The characters inscribed on these bones and shells were the basis for the sophisticated, elaborate writing system still used in China. The written tradition provides China's history with its major line of continuity from the distant past to the present. The focus on ancestor worship in the so-called 'oracle bone' inscriptions shows another line of continuity. The most solemn festival of the year is still Tomb Sweeping Day (Qīng Míng Jié), held in spring, when people visit the graves of their ancestors, sweep them clean, and present food offerings.

Shang culture was spread though much of north China, with sites along both the Huáng Hé (Yellow River) and the Huái Hé (Huái River) valleys. It featured a sacred kingship supported by officials and armies, a skilled artisanry that produced the magnificent bronzeware for which this dynasty is known, and a peasantry that supplied labour for the building of city walls and other public works.

Zhou Dynasty

Around three millennia ago, the last Shang sovereign was defeated and beheaded by the forces of Zhou, from present-day Shaanxi province. The Zhou established rule over an increasingly large territory, reaching up to Běijīng in the north and down to the lower Cháng Jiāng (Yangzi

Chinese Dynasties

dynasty	period	site of capital
Xia	**2200–1700 BC**	
Shang	**1700–1100 BC**	Ānyáng
Zhou	**1100–221 BC**	
Western Zhou	1100–771 BC	Hào (near Xī'ān)
Eastern Zhou	770–221 BC	Luòyáng
Qin	**221–207 BC**	Xiányáng
Han	**206 BC–AD 220**	
Western Han	206 BC–AD 9	Xī'ān
Xin	AD 9–23	Xī'ān
Eastern Han	AD 25–220	Luòyáng
Three Kingdoms	**AD 220–280**	
Wei	AD 220–265	Luòyáng
Shu (Shu Han)	AD 221–263	Chéngdū
Wu	AD 229–280	Nánjīng
Jin	**AD 265–420**	
Western Jin	AD 265–317	Luòyáng
Eastern Jin	AD 317–420	Nánjīng
Southern & Northern Dynasties	**AD 420–589**	
Southern Dynasties		
Song	AD 420–479	Nánjīng
Qi	AD 479–502	Nánjīng
Liang	AD 502–557	Nánjīng
Chen	AD 557–589	Nánjīng
Northern Dynasties		
Northern Wei	AD 386–534	Dàtóng, Luòyáng
Eastern Wei	AD 534–550	Linzhang
Northern Qi	AD 550–577	Linzhang
Western Wei	AD 535–556	Xī'ān
Northern Zhou	AD 557–581	Xī'ān
Sui	**AD 581–618**	Xī'ān
Tang	**AD 618–907**	Xī'ān
Five Dynasties & Ten Kingdoms	**AD 907–960**	
Later Liang	AD 907–923	Kāifēng
Later Tang	AD 923–936	Luòyáng
Later Jin	AD 936–947	Kāifēng
Later Han	AD 947–950	Kāifēng
Later Zhou	AD 951–960	Kāifēng
Liao	**AD 907–1125**	
Song	**AD 960–1279**	
Northern Song	AD 960–1127	Kāifēng
Southern Song	AD 1127–1279	Hángzhōu
Jin	**AD 1115–1234**	Kāifēng, Běijīng
Yuan	**AD 1206–1368**	Běijīng
Ming	**AD 1368–1644**	Nánjīng, Běijīng
Qing	**AD 1644–1911**	Běijīng
Republic of China	**AD 1911–1949**	Běijīng, Nánjīng
People's Republic of China	**AD 1949–present**	Běijīng

River) valley in the south. It held sway over a number of principalities that were centred in walled cities and governed by lords who stood at the apex of a hierarchically organised aristocracy. The Zhou capital moved from a site near Xī'ān to one farther east, near Luòyáng, in the year 771 BC: hence the historical division between the Western and Eastern Zhou.

The period of the Eastern Zhou, ending with the destruction of the Zhou by the Qin is itself divided into the Spring and Autumn (722–481 BC) and Warring States (475–221 BC) periods. During the first of these, the principalities developed greater independence; the lords became kings; law codes were written down; iron was discovered; the fortunes of the landed aristocracy waned, and self-made men achieved places at court; and merchants grew wealthy. The times were troubled, prompting reflection and philosophising on the part of one Master Kong (Kong Fuzi), better known in the West by the Latinised version of his name, Confucius.

Confucius (551–479 BC) was a native of the old state of Lu, in the south of present-day Shāndōng province. The descendant of a minor noble family, he was attached for a while to the court of his home state. Failing to make headway there, he set off in search of an able and righteous ruler who might lead the world back to virtuous paths. In this mission he was doomed to disappointment, and his death in 479 BC was to be followed by an ever keener struggle among the states for supremacy. But he did achieve enormous success as a teacher and moral exemplar. The great body of Confucian books, consisting in part of works by his disciples and commentaries on them, prompted critical interpretations that provided the canon for later generations of Chinese scholars.

Qin Dynasty

Confucius was only one among many philosophers active in the later Zhou, and his teachings were dealt a blow with the creation of the first fully fledged Chinese empire in 221 BC. The long period of the Warring States came to an end in this year, when the western state of Qin, having conquered the Zhou 35 years earlier, succeeded in subduing the remaining states to establish centralised rule. The King of Qin thus went

down in history as the 'The First Emperor of Qin' (Qin Shihuangdi).

Qin Shihuangdi won and ruled by the sword. His ruling philosophy was encapsulated by a legalist doctrine that focused on law and punishment instead of rites and morality. The martial ethos of the dynasty is illustrated in his tomb near Xī'ān, which contains an extraordinary army of clay warriors and horses. He pursued campaigns as far north as Korea and south down to Vietnam. He linked existing defence walls to create the beginnings of the Great Wall.

The 'First Emperor' also laid the foundations for a unified, integrated empire. He introduced a uniform currency, standardised the script, and developed infrastructure through a network of roads and canals. Like some later dynasts, he made the mistake of failing to consolidate his victories by soliciting cooperation with his regime. He is famously said to have 'burnt the books and buried the scholars', a dual feat emulated during the Cultural Revolution by Mao Zedong who was a self-professed admirer of Qin Shihuangdi. A great burning of books took place in 213 BC, but the dynasty fell seven years later, having lasted only 15 years.

Qin Shihuangdi's heir to the imperial throne proved ineffectual and, shaken by rebellion, the Qin capital fell to an army led by the commoner Liu Bang. Liu lost no time in taking the title of emperor and establishing the Han dynasty.

Han Dynasty

With the Han dynasty, the ideal of a unified empire under a single sovereign was consolidated. During the 1st century BC the vassal states of the early Han period were eliminated. Under the energetic Emperor Wu, who reigned from 140 BC to 186 BC, supremacy was established over neighbouring societies to the north and west, able men were recruited to serve the dynasty as officials, and Confucian education was promoted. The examination system, a hallmark of government in the late imperial era, was inaugurated. The Han briefly gave way to the Xin dynasty in AD 9, led by the radical reformer Wang Mang, but it was restored in AD 23, testimony to the legitimacy it had established over a period of more than a century. Due to this interregnum of 14 years the Han is often divided into Former (Western) and Later (Eastern) Han periods.

The reign of Emperor Wu produced two highly influential intellectual figures. One was Dong Zhongshu, who developed a cosmology that identified the human order with the natural elements, predicting a sequence of elemental forces (wood, fire, earth, metal, water) that would determine the rise and fall of dynasties. The other was Sima Qian, whose *Record of History (Shi Ji)* was the first sustained attempt to provide a chronicle of history from antiquity to the present.

Foreign Contacts The expansion of the Han brought the Chinese into contact with the 'barbarians' that encircled their world. As a matter of course, this contact brought both military conflict and commercial gains.

To the north, the Xiongnu (a name given to various nomadic tribes of central Asia) posed the greatest threat to China. Military expeditions were sent against these tribes, initially with much success. This in turn provided the Chinese with access to central Asia, opening up the routes that carried Chinese silk as far afield as Rome.

On the diplomatic front, links were formed with central Asian tribes, and the great Chinese explorer Zhang Qian provided the authorities with information on the possibilities of trade and alliances in northern India. During the same period, Chinese influence percolated into areas that were later to become known as Vietnam and Korea.

Unity and Division

They say the momentum of history was ever thus: the empire, long divided, must unite; long united, must divide.

Thus commences the narrative of *The Romance of the Three Kingdoms,* one of the most popular of China's classical novels, which tells the tale of the wars at the end of the Han period between the states of Wei, Wu and the Shu-Han. With these words, the storyteller sums up a central theme in Chinese history: the idealised unity of the empire, and its cyclical fracturing and reconstruction. The periods of division grew shorter over the centuries, showing the greater integration over time of Chinese territories.

Between the early 3rd century AD and the late 6th, north China was effectively divided between a succession of rival kingdoms that struggled for regional or greater power. The period of disunity, or of 'the 16 kingdoms and six dynasties', showed a marked division between north and south. The north was controlled by non-Chinese rulers and torn by warfare. The south experienced significant economic growth. Migrations from the north intensified and extended Chinese culture into previously non-Chinese territories. Jiankang, later to become Nánjīng, served as capital for a succession of southern dynasties.

The most successful northern regime was the Northern Wei dynasty, known as the Tuoba Wei after the Chinese name for the non-Chinese people who founded it. Originally based in Dàtóng, in the far northern province of Shānxī, the Northern Wei eventually covered a large area of north China down to Huái Hé. Massive population relocations were undertaken to restore devastated lands to productivity. Major administrative innovations such as the 'equal field' system, involving allocation of lands to peasants, and the division of the capital city into wards, well outlasted the dynasty. The Tuoba eventually adopted Chinese language, clothes, and learning. This dynasty in many respects prefigured the more powerful, enduring and successful dynasties of the next millennium: the Jin of the Jurchen, the Yuan of the Mongols, and the Qing of the Manchus.

The period of disunity produced one of the greatest figures in Chinese cultural pantheon, the poet Tao Qian, better known as Tao Yuanming (AD 365–427). Tao's tale of a fisherman coming across Peach Blossom Spring, a peaceful, happy prosperous valley where the trials and tribulations of life in the chaotic outside world were unknown, inspired generations of later utopian writers, painters and even landscape gardeners.

Sui Dynasty

The Tuoba Wei fell in 534. It was succeeded by a series of rival regimes before a nobleman Yang Jian (d. 604), usurping power in the Northern Zhou, swept all before him to establish the Sui dynasty (581–618). The Sui was a short-lived dynasty, but its accomplishments were many.

Yang Jian's great achievement was to bring the south back within the pale of a northern-based empire.

His son, Sui Yangdi, has gone down in the annals as an unsavoury character, given to wine, women and song. The Sui went into rapid decline under his rule.

Despite this unenviable reputation, Yangdi contributed greatly to the unification of south and north through the construction of the Grand Canal, which combined earlier canals and linked the lower Cháng Jiāng valley to Chāng'ān via Huáng Hé. Re-routed and extended northward when Běijīng became capital in the Yuan, the canal remained the empire's most important communication route between south and north till the late 19th century.

However, after three unsuccessful incursions onto Korean soil resulting in disastrous military setbacks and faced with revolt on the streets, Yangdi was assassinated in 618 by one of his high officials.

Tang Dynasty

The Tang is considered a Golden Age in Chinese history, a view grounded partly in its literary productivity. The *Three Hundred Tang Poems*, compiled from over 48,000 poems preserved from this time, provides Chinese conversation with quotable quotes, much as Shakespeare does in English.

Sui Yangdi was succeeded as emperor by the Sui's own leading general Li Yuan, who seized the capital, declared the founding of the Tang dynasty, and within 10 years had eliminated the last of rival claimants to the throne. To discourage the development of regional power bases, the empire was subsequently divided into 300 prefectures *(zhōu)* and 1500 counties *(xiàn)*, establishing a pattern of territorial jurisdiction that persists, with some modifications, to this day.

Li Yuan's achievements were consolidated by his son, the much admired Taizong (626–49). The relationship between Taizong the able ruler, and his wise minister, the official Wei Zheng (580–645), was regarded as a model one by later Confucianists. On the other hand, Taizong's concubine, Wu Zhao, was seen as a good example of what should be avoided in government. Wu wielded increasing influence over the court after Taizong's death, to a point where, in 690, she was able to declare herself ruler of

a new dynasty, the Zhou. The Tang was restored in 705, after one of the most surprising interludes in dynastic history.

It was under Empress Wu that the empire reached its greatest extent. It extended well north of the Great Wall and far west into inner Asia. The rich repository of texts and paintings at Dūnhuáng in Gānsù testifies to the importance of the Silk Route, which linked Chāng'ān to India, Persia, and from there to the Mediterranean. During the 7th and 8th centuries, great cities such as the capital Chāng'ān, the Yangzi port of Yángzhōu and the coastal port Canton, were crowded with foreign merchants. Central Asian cultural influence was pronounced, especially in the north.

Buddhism, introduced into China in the 1st century, flourished during the Sui and Tang dynasties, and was strongly promoted by Empress Wu. The Buddhist monasteries were great centres of learning and cultural activity, as well as economically powerful. They had a pivotal place in the network of communications between China and other parts of Asia. In 639, the great Buddhist master Xuan Zang (602–64) set off for the home place of the Buddha in 639, and toured the whole of India. His travels inspired the Ming dynasty novel *Journey to the West*, featuring one of the best known characters in Chinese culture, the beguiling monkey, Sun Wukong.

Efforts to protect the far-flung frontiers of the empire rebounded in the middle of the 8th century, when the dynasty was nearly destroyed by the An Lushan Rebellion (755–63). An Lushan was a Tang general of Sogdian-Turkic parentage, who took advantage of his command of three military areas in north China to make a bid for imperial power himself. The fighting, which dragged on for around eight years overran the capital and caused massive dislocations of people and millions of death.

His rebellion is regarded as a turning point in Chinese history. Notable developments after it were the decline of the northwestern aristocracy, the rise of a mercenary army to support the imperial house, the rationalisation of taxation, increased dependence by the dynasty on the south, and reduced contact with inner and western Asia. A classical revival paved the way for the Confucian renaissance of the Song dynasty, while Buddhism went from being criticised by the poet Han Yu (768–824) to being proscribed by the emperor Wuzong in 842 to 845. Although the proscription was later modified, Buddhism never regained the power and prestige in China that it had enjoyed for centuries up until that time.

Tang power gradually weakened during the 8th and 9th centuries. In the north-west, Tibetan warriors overran Tang garrisons, while to the south the Nanzhao kingdom centred in Dàlǐ, Yúnnán, posed a serious threat to Sìchuān. Meanwhile, in the Chinese heartland of the Cháng Jiāng region and Zhèjiāng, heavy taxes and a series of calamities engendered wide-ranging discontent that culminated in the Huang Chao rebellion (874–84), which reduced the empire to chaos and resulted in the fall of the capital in 907.

Another period of disunity, the era of 'five dynasties and ten kingdoms', followed the fall of the Tang before the Song dynasty was established in 960.

Song Dynasty

The Song dynasty is conventionally divided into two periods: the Northern Song (960–1127), with its capital in Kāifēng on Huáng Hé, and the Southern Song (1127–1279), with its capital in Hángzhōu. The Northern Song was already a rather small empire, coexisting with the non-Chinese Liao dynasty, which controlled a belt of Chinese territory south of the Great Wall, and rather less happily with another non-Chinese power, the Xi Xia, which pressed hard on the north-western provinces. In 1126, the Song lost its capital, Kāifēng, to a third non-Chinese people, the Jurchen, who had previously allied with the Chinese Song against the Khitan of the Liao. The Song was driven to its southern capital of Hángzhōu for the period of the Southern Song.

The Jurchen, forbears of the Manchus, established the Jin dynasty with a capital near Běijīng. A treaty was drawn up with the Southern Song that divided the empire along the boundary of Huái Hé. The Jin dynasty asserted seniority over the Southern Song, demanding the payment of tribute, which was handed over in the form of silk, tea and silver.

The Song dynasty, North and South, was a time of enormous economic and cultural vitality. Considerable advances were made in archaeology, mathematics, astronomy, geography and medicine. Philosophy, poetry, painting and calligraphy flourished. An increase in agricultural productivity due to the spread of rice cultivation since the 8th century resulted in a surplus of labour that was used for the development of secondary industries such as mining, ceramics, and silk manufacture. The tea-bush and lacquer trees were cultivated and gunpowder and moveable type were invented. Paper making and print technology experienced significant advances, facilitating an increase in the production of books. A busy trade with South-East Asia and Japan sent Song copper currency far afield.

Associated with these developments were increased urbanisation and the rise of commercial classes. Kāifēng, which had served as capital of a series of minor dynasties after the Tang, emerged as the great centre of Northern Song politics, culture and commerce. Many of the restrictions on merchant activities and popular activities observable in Tang cities disappeared and the urban population acquired greater social complexity. The curfew was abolished, and night-life flourished. It was even more the case in Hángzhōu, which underwent a boom as capital of the Southern Song. Hángzhōu was never more than a provincial capital in later dynasties, but it forever retained a name as one of the most beautiful and cultured cities in the empire.

While merchants flourished, the aristocracy effectively disappeared. A scholar-official social stratum, often referred to in English as the gentry or the literati, became a distinguishing feature of Chinese society.

The Song refined and expanded the examination system, selecting officials from the successful candidates. Confucianism achieved a dominance it was to retain till the 19th century. The 'school of human nature and universal order', developed by Zhu Xi (1130–1200) and his followers, became the orthodox Confucian school in the early Ming. Known as Neo-Confucianism in the West, this school featured a dualism between *li* and *qi*, the former naturally good, the latter a force that explains human beings' deviations away from essential goodness. Zhu Xi became a focus of popular as well as scholarly veneration, temples to him eventually rivalling those to Lord Guan, hero of the Three Kingdoms era. Lord Guan was the god of war and also of commerce, and thus represented values rather different to those embodied by Zhu Xi.

While Zhu Xi was speculating about li and qi, Genghis Khan (1167–1227) was beginning to flex his muscles in Mongolia. The son of a chieftain, Genghis commenced his awesome rise to power by avenging his father's murder. In 1206 he was recognised as supreme ruler of the Mongols.

The Mongols, despised for what was considered their ignorance and poverty, occasionally went to war with the Chinese, but had always been defeated. In 1211 Genghis Khan turned his attention on China, penetrated the Great Wall two years later and then took Běijīng in 1215. East he fought the Jin, west he destroyed the Xi Xia and advanced on Russia. Under his descendants a great, although segmented, Mongol empire was formed, stretching from the Ukraine and Persia to Korea and the northern limits of Vietnam.

The Jin fell in 1234. Hángzhōu, the Southern Song capital, was taken in 1276. The court fled, but Southern Song resistance ended in 1279.

Yuan Dynasty

A new emperor, Kublai Khan, grandson of Genghis, now reigned over all China as emperor of the Yuan dynasty.

The fearsome Mongol conquest resulted in a Pax Mongolica in inner Asia. Land routes were reopened and European missionaries and traders made their way across the Eurasian continent. The most famous is Marco Polo, although doubts have been raised as to whether he actually made the journey. The discovery of tombstones engraved in Latin attest, however, to the arrival of other Venetians. Foreigners were easily incorporated into this ethnically complex empire, and religious diversity was tolerated. Despite the continental orientation of the Mongol rulers, the south coast continued to flourish. Its population and wealth were indeed an important resource for the dynasty. Significant diasporas were created in Vietnam and Japan as Chinese fled before the Mongol armies. These may have strengthened maritime trade.

The Mongols controlled China for less than a century. Their capital was Khanbalig,

on the site of present-day Běijīng. The Grand Canal assumed its familiar form when a waterway was cut to join Huái Hé to this northern metropolis. The junction of the canal with Huáng Hé posed technological problems that were only partially overcome in later dynasties. Great though this feat of engineering was, it undoubtedly contributed to the volatility of Huáng Hé. All later rulers struggled with the problem of preventing floods while at the same time keeping the Grand Canal operational.

For purposes of government, the Mongols divided the entire subjected population into categories of Han, Mongol and foreigner. The top administrative posts at metropolitan and provincial levels were reserved for Mongols. The examination system was revived in 1315, but quotas heavily favoured the Mongols and their non-Chinese allies and caused resentment among the Chinese literati. Although they were a mighty military power, the Mongols were undermined by their own weaknesses in political and economic management, and were soon faced with insurmountable opposition. By the middle of the 14th century rebellions raged through central and north China in the last years of Mongol rule. Chief among the rebel groups were the Red Turbans, who were guided in their mission by a belief structure of diverse religious sources, ranging from Buddhism to Manichaeism, Taoism and Confucianism. By 1367 Zhu Yuanzhang, originally an orphan and Buddhist novice, had climbed to the top of the rebel leadership, and in 1368 he established the Ming dynasty and restored Chinese rule.

Ming Dynasty

A man of no great education, Zhu Yuanzhang had considerable leadership abilities and was a strong if harsh ruler. Remembered for his despotism (he had some 10,000 scholars and their families put to death in two paranoid purges of his administration), he was also a strong leader who did much to set China back on its feet in the aftermath of the Yuan collapse. He established his capital in Nánjīng.

In the early 15th century, the court began to move in stages to Běijīng, site of the Yuan capital Khanbalig. A massive reconstruction project was commenced under the emperor Yongle, who reigned from 1403 to 1424, bringing into being the awesome imperial city familiar to later generations of visitors. A great commercial and residential suburb grew up south of the walled city and was itself enclosed by a wall in 1522. In this form the city survived through to the 1950s, retaining its status as capital for all but the 21 years of Nationalist rule in the 20th century.

In the early Ming, relations with inner Asia were at an all-time low. Yongle, after usurping power from his nephew and bringing on a civil war, looked to the world beyond the seas to establish his credentials as ruler. In 1405, he launched the first of seven great maritime expeditions. Led by the eunuch general Zheng He (1371–1433), the fleet consisted of more than 60 large vessels and 255 smaller ones, carrying nearly 28,000 men. The fourth and fifth expeditions, departing in 1413 and 1417 respectively, travelled as far as Aden, on the present Suez Canal. From the perspective of the court, the great achievement of these voyages was to bring tribute missions to the capital, including two embassies from Egypt. As a Muslim, Zheng He was no doubt a good choice of commander for an expedition to the Islamic world.

After the end of the Yongle reign, Ming China retreated into itself. A dramatic invasion by the Mongols in 1439, which resulted in the capture and year-long imprisonment of the then-emperor, appeared to create a fortress mentality. The Great Wall was lengthened by 600 miles in the second half of the century, developing the scale that has made it famous as one of the great building feats of history. The coast was more difficult to defend. In the middle of the 16th century, the coastal provinces were harassed by pirates, who were suppressed only with great effort.

Ships from Europe also arrived in China in the 16th century. In 1557 the Portuguese gained the right to establish a permanent trade base in Macau, on the far south coast. Traders were followed by missionaries. The Jesuits, led by the redoubtable Matteo Ricci, made their way inland, establishing a presence at court. They made a great impression with their skills in astronomy and offered advice to the late Ming emperors on how to cast canons. They were active at court and also in the provinces until their activities were curtailed in the 1720s.

The Portuguese presence linked China directly to trade with the New World. New crops such as potatoes and maize were introduced. New World silver was used to pay for Chinese exports such as tea, porcelain and ceramics. A reform of the tax system under Grand Secretary Zhang Juzheng (1525–82) combined the established grain and labour taxes into a single payment in silver. From the second half of the 16th century, something approaching the great Song revolution was observable in the Ming empire. Commerce became important, facilitated by banks established by merchants from the northwest province of Shānxī; absentee landlordism and tenant farming became common and urbanisation intensified. Publishing and literacy increased, and the corpus of fiction expanded.

Government in the Ming was autocratic but was troubled by the influence of eunuchs at court and by factional struggles between officials. Strong emperors were needed to maintain order, but were few and far between. A low point in imperial prestige was achieved in the early 16th century, when Zhu Houchao, ruler from 1505 to 1521, gave over matters of state to his chief eunuch and devoted his attention to carnal pleasures. In the 1620s, during the Tianqi reign (1621–1628), the government was dominated by the eunuch Wei Zhongxian (1568–1627), responsible for a great purge of officials and a personality cult complete with temples to himself.

By this latter period, able leadership was especially important. North of the border, the Jurchen people were consolidated into a militarised state under the leadership of Nurhaci (1559–1626). By the 1620s, they were carrying out periodic raids, sometimes deep into Chinese territory. Simultaneously, floods and drought devastated large areas of north China, encouraging banditry, which swelled into rebellions.

The Manchus to the north had long been growing in power, and looked with keen interest to the convulsions of rebellion in their huge neighbour. Taking advantage of the turmoil in China, they launched an invasion. Initially held back by the Great Wall, they were allowed to pass by a Ming general, who saw an alliance with the Manchus as the only hope for defeating the peasant rebel armies that now threatened Běijīng itself.

In 1644 Běijīng eventually fell, not to the Manchus but to the peasant rebel Li Zicheng, who sat on the throne for a day before fleeing from the Chinese troops who helped put a Manchu emperor in his place.

Qing Dynasty

The Manchus proclaimed their new dynasty the Qing (1644–1911), although it was to be four decades before they finally cleared the south of Ming loyalist forces and pacified the whole country. Today's 'triads' in China (the modern secret societies generally thought to be involved in criminal activity, especially drug trafficking) are actually the descendants of secret societies originally set up to resist the Manchus.

The Manchu conquest encountered resistance lasting to 1683, when Taiwan was taken. It was marked by acts of great brutality. Massacres in the cities of Yángzhōu and Jiādìng lodged in historical memory and were invoked in anti-Manchu propaganda during Nationalist campaigns at the end of the 19th century. In some ways, however, earlier history had prepared the literati for this northern dynasty, and the Manchus also tuned their policies to indigenous ways.

The new rulers neutralised the inner Asian threat by incorporating into the empire their own homeland as well as that of the Mongols, whom they had subordinated. Their cultural policy involved a careful balance of attention to Chinese, Manchus, Mongols and Tibetans. They courted the literati via the examination system and great literary projects. Their own people were appointed to key positions in the bureaucracy, but matching positions were created for Chinese officials. They also established close relationships with the great merchants, specifically those licensed to trade in the salt monopoly which was a major source of revenue for the imperial government.

At the same time, the Manchus made clear their own ruling position. Chinese men were forced to dress their hair like the Manchus, ie, to shave the front of the head, and braid the remaining hair into a long queue or 'pigtail'. This feature ironically became a sign of Chineseness in countless cartoons in the Western press at a later period.

As an alien dynasty, the Qing was anxious about its own legitimacy. Harsh censorship was practised during the 18th century. A literary inquisition began in the 1770s, and cruel punishments were inflicted on authors of works held to contain anti-Manchu sentiments. An imperial canon of works known as the *Complete Works of the Four Treasuries* was created, and alongside it a register of proscribed books. Despite these efforts at ideological control, scholarship flourished. Classical studies took new directions and local histories proliferated. Drama, phonology, mathematics, hydraulics and geography were all subjected to analysis on the basis of evidential *(kaozheng)* methodology, the hallmark of Qing scholarship.

Women became a site of Chinese cultural resistance to Manchu rule. Chinese women continued to dress in the Chinese way: skirt worn over loose jacket and trousers, as opposed to the one-piece robe worn by Manchu women. Footbinding, in force from perhaps the 10th or 11th centuries, continued under the Qing despite prohibitions of the practice early in the dynasty. The cult of female piety, evident in the practice of widow suicide, affirmed the centrality of Chinese men in their own social order, even if they had to kowtow to a Manchu emperor. The Manchus showed considerable political skill in moving from opposition to endorsement of widow-suicide, awarding honours to women who followed their husbands to the grave.

Some noted Chinese scholars challenged conservative views of the ordained place of women. The poet Yuan Mei had a large number of women students. Novels such as Wu Jingci's *Unofficial History of the Literati*, and Shen Fu's autobiographical *Six Chapters of A Floating Life* provided portraits of companionate marriage. In *A Dream of Red Mansions (Story of the Stone)*, the most famous novel of the Qing, Cao Xueqin provided a complex psychological portrait of a largely female household. The 'woman issue' was to be central to the revolutionary movements from the late 19th century onwards, and in some ways Qing commentaries prepared the way for it.

The Manchu Legacy The Manchus' most significant legacy is the size of the Chinese land mass. When the Manchus entered China, they brought Manchuria with them, and also the lands of the Mongols, who allied with them. Military campaigns in the late 17th and 18th centuries secured large tracts of inner Asia. Although Outer Mongolia was declared a republic in 1924, these territorial gains were mostly retained or restored during the 20th century.

Tibet was made a Chinese protectorate in 1751, enjoying regional autonomy under the watchful eye of a Qing resident. Even before this date, its relations with Běijīng were close. Emperor Yongzheng, who reigned from 1722 to 1735, was a patron of Lamaist Buddhism and turned his own palace into a Lamaist temple. Although never fully integrated into the Chinese administrative system, Tibet was a cornerstone of Qing geopolitical strategy and one of the last military feats of the dynasty was to secure it against the combined threats of the British and Russians.

Xīnjiāng, home to the Muslim Uyghur, was also under special administrative control through the greater part of the Qing. A great rebellion broke out in the 1870s and was defeated only at enormous expense and cost to life on both sides. Regular provincial administration was established and Han settlement encouraged. With the rise of cultural nationalism in the 20th century, however, both Tibetan and Uyghur separatists have challenged Chinese authority.

Taiwan, home to a number of Austronesian peoples, had been colonised by the Dutch in the early 17th century and then occupied by the Ming loyalist Zheng Chenggong (Koxinga; 1624–1662), who defeated the Dutch to make the island his base of resistance against the Manchus. The Manchus conquered Taiwan in 1683, and incorporated it into Fújiàn province. Garrison towns were constructed, evolving into walled cities that housed the Chinese officials dispatched to administer the territory. In 1872, after the island was briefly occupied by the Japanese, the Manchus made it into an independent province in recognition of its strategic vulnerability. In 1895, it was ceded to the Japanese as part of the settlement following the Sino-Japanese War of 1894. Its sinicisation in the course of the Qing meant, however, that the issue of its relationship with the mainland would remain a lasting point of contention.

Another notable legacy of the Qing was the rapid rise in population, which more than doubled from the middle of the 17th century to reach around 350 million at the end of the 18th century. Explanations for this include the introduction of New World crops, which could be grown in relatively harsh conditions, and efficient famine relief and flood control during the 18th century.

One consequence of population growth was increased pressure on the land. The reclamation of alluvial lands meant that drainage basins were increasingly restricted and massive floods ensued in the 19th century. Land-hungry Han migrants pressed farther west and south into lands of aboriginal peoples, leading to the extension of Qing administration and creating ethnic conflict that culminated in rebellions. Suppressing these placed an enormous strains on the imperial treasury, contributing to the dynasty's malaise in the 19th century.

China and the West

The early Qing emperors had shown a relatively open attitude towards Europeans in China, but this changed in the 18th century. Yongzheng, who ruled from 1722 to 1735, banned missionary activity in the provinces, and Qianlong, ruler 1736 to 1795, imposed strict controls on maritime trade, which from 1757 was limited to the single port of Canton. A British embassy under Lord Macartney arrived in Běijīng in 1793 with the aim of establishing a British diplomatic presence and broadening trade relations. Qianlong informed the embassy in nouncertain terms that China did not need foreign goods.

The balance of trade at Canton was in fact a problem for Western merchants, as Chinese exports well exceeded imports. Opium turned the tide of trade in the early 19th century but set the stage for a stand-off between Chinese officials seeking to stem the inflow of opium and foreign traders insisting that the problem lay with the Chinese buyers.

Opium addiction in China skyrocketed in the early 19th century. (Illustration circa 1887.)

In March 1839 Lin Zexiu, an official of great personal integrity, was dispatched to Guǎngzhōu to put a stop to the illegal traffic once and for all. He acted promptly, demanding and eventually getting some 20,000 chests of opium stored by the British in Guǎngzhōu. This, along with several other minor incidents, was just the pretext that hawkish elements in the British government needed to win support for military action against China. In 1840 a British naval force assembled in Macau and moved up the coast to Beihe, not far from Běijīng. The Opium War was on.

For the Chinese, the conflicts centred on the opium trade were a fiasco from start to finish. While the Qing court managed to fob the first British force off with a treaty that neither side ended up recognising, increasing British frustration soon led to an attack on Chinese positions close to Guǎngzhōu.

The resulting treaty ceded Hong Kong to the British and called for indemnities of Y6,000,000 and the full resumption of trade. The furious Qing emperor refused to recognise the treaty, and in 1841 British forces once again headed up the coast, taking Fújiàn and eastern Zhèjiāng. In the spring of 1842, their numbers swollen with reinforcements, they moved up Cháng Jiāng. With British guns trained on Nánjīng, the Qing fighting spirit evaporated, and they reluctantly signed the humiliating Treaty of Nanking.

In the 19th century, the Qing dynasty was under pressure from internal rebellions and outside aggression. The increased presence of missionaries had also fuelled hatred against 'foreign devils', which led to further rebellion throughout the provinces. A growing population combined with the scarcity of arable land added to internal pressures against the Qing rulers.

There was also a decline in the calibre and strength of the emperors, which can be seen by the increasing influence in the period from 1856 to 1908 of the Emperor Xianfeng's favourite consort, Cixi (1835–1908). As the Dowager Empress, Cixi exerted a great deal of influence on politics as coregent for her nephew, Guangxu.

The most serious internal rebellion was the Taiping, which erupted in 1850 in the southern province of Guǎngxī, and commanded forces of 600,000 men and 500,000

Cunning Dowager Empress Cixi held the reigns of Chinese power for more than 40 years.

women. The rebellion raged through central and eastern China, felled Nánjīng, Sūzhōu, Yángzhōu and other great cities of the lower Cháng Jiāng valley, and even threatened Běijīng at one point. Its leader was Hong Xiuquan, a failed examination candidate from Guǎngdōng province (Canton), whose encounters with Western missionaries had led him to believe he was the younger brother of Jesus Christ. The rebellion took tens of millions of lives before being suppressed in 1864.

The Taipings owed much of their ideology to Christianity. They forbade gambling, opium, tobacco and alcohol; advocated agricultural reform; and outlawed foot-binding for women, prostitution and slavery. Ironically, they were defeated by a coalition of Qing and Western forces – the Europeans preferring to deal with a corrupt and weak Qing government than a powerful, united China governed by the Taipings.

One of the effects of the Opium War was to divert trade from Canton to Shànghǎi, the northernmost of the first five Treaty Ports. The loss of employment and economic distress in Canton helped fuel the Taiping Rebellion. While the latter was underway, the foreign powers struck again. The Anglo-French expedition of 1856 to 1860, sometimes called the Second Opium

War, ended with the occupation of Běijīng and the flight of the court to Jehol in the Manchurian homeland. The Treaty of Tianjin resulted in the opening of further Treaty Ports and the establishment of a regular diplomatic corps in Běijīng. While adjusting to these developments the court was simultaneously trying to cope with further massive rebellions: the Nian in central north China, the Panthay in Yúnnán, and the Donggan in the north-west.

In the second half of the 19th century China sent embassies and students to the West and embarked on a campaign of self-strengthening in military technology and industrial development, a belated attempt to learn from the enemy. The Treaty Port cities, especially Shànghǎi, became the face of modernisation in China. Factories, banks, newspapers, new-style schools, bicycles, trains and eventually motor cars, trade unions, chambers of commerce and political parties all made their appearance. In Shànghǎi, the International Concession and the French Concession quickly outgrew the old city. Governed by the Shanghai Municipal Council and the French Consul respectively, these sectors of Shànghǎi experienced enormous increase in population during the Taiping Rebellion.

The Western powers in China were soon joined by Japan, where the Meiji Restoration of 1868 created a climate of competitive nationalism. Initially refused diplomatic status in Běijīng, the Japanese engineered an incident on Taiwan in 1872 and in the ensuing negotiations forced China to surrender any claims to sovereignty over the Liuqiu Islands. These were transformed into present Okinawa province. In 1894, another conflict between China and Japan erupted over rival claims to Korea. China was decisively defeated. The Treaty of Shimonoseki in 1895 ceded Taiwan to Japan, and the Taiwanese entered a 60-year period of Japanese colonialism. The same treaty granted the Japanese (and thence other foreign powers) the right to construct their own factories in Shànghǎi.

In the late 1890s China was in danger of being 'cut up like a melon, divided like a bean', as further leases of land and spheres of influence were ceded to the foreign powers. In 1898 Germany gained a lease in Qìngdǎo, Shāndōng province, after Lutheran missionaries were murdered inland. They commenced building a railway that became the focus of protests by local people upset at the disturbance of *fengshui*. Shāndōng was already in a state of acute economic distress. Conditions fuelled the emergence and spread of the Boxer movement, a martial arts cult that combined physical training with religio-magical beliefs.

The Boxers quickly spread from Shāndōng north into Zhili (present Héběi), where the Treaty Port of Tianjin and the imperial capital, Běijīng, were both located. The number of attacks on railways, churches and foreigners grew rapidly. The Empress Dowager Cixi attempted to use this movement to help her rid the empire of foreigners. In June 1900, the Boxers entered Běijīng en masse, and the court declared war on the Treaty Powers. The foreign legations were placed under siege for fifty-five days before being rescued by the arrival of the troops of the Eight Allied Powers. Lacking support from her own provincial armies in the south, the Empress fled to Xī'ān. In 1901, the Boxer Protocols were signed, imposing a punitive indemnity and forcing the dynasty, too late, into some long overdue reforms.

The Nationalist Century

Southern China, particularly Guǎngdōng province, was an important source of nationalism and political innovation in China. In the 1890s, the two most powerful challenges to the conservative court came from the south. One was issued by the visionary reformer Kang Youwei (1858–1927), with the support of his famous disciple Liang Qichao (1873–1929), both from Guǎngdōng. Kang became a key adviser to the emperor after the debacle of the Sino-Japanese War in 1894. The result was the famous '100 Days Reforms' of 1898, which were expected to set China on the modernising path already taken by Japan. Reforms to the bureaucracy and the examination system were propagated and, simultaneously, social reforms were promotoed. Liang Qichao, especially, championed the education of girls and opposed footbinding. The '100 Days' ended with a palace coup, the house arrest of the emperor by the Empress Dowager, the execution of some reformist activists and the flight of others, including Kang and Liang.

Japan was at that time a hotbed of dissident activity among Chinese exiles and students. Kang and Liang formed the 'protect the emperor society', which was reformist rather than revolutionary in orientation and aimed at the establishment of a constitutional monarchy. A more radical political future was envisaged by Sun Yatsen (1866–1925).

Sun was the source of the other challenge to the court. Born in Guǎngdōng, educated in Hawaii and Hong Kong, a Christian and trained medical practitioner, Sun developed a political program based on the 'Three Principles of the People': nationalism, popular sovereignty, and livelihood. These provided the ideological pillars for the Revolutionary Alliance which he founded in Japan in 1905. The main impulse for his early revolutionary activity, however, was ethno-nationalism directed against the Manchus.

The Revolutionary Alliance spread from Japan into China, infecting the reformed New Armies, which were, ironically, a product of the late Qing reforms.

Fall of the Qing

In 1908 the Empress Dowager died and the two-year-old Emperor Puyi ascended to the throne. The Qing was now rudderless, and quickly collapsed due to the Railway Protection Movement and the Wuchang Uprising of 1911.

Dr Sun Yatsen: enemy of the Qing dynasty and China's most famous revolutionary

The Railway Protection Movement grew out of public anger at new railways being financed and built by foreigners. Plans to construct lines to provincial centres using local funds soon collapsed, and the despairing Qing government adopted a policy of nationalisation and foreign loans to do the work. Opposition by vested interests and provincial leaders soon fanned violence that spread and took on an anti-Qing nature. The violence was worst in Sìchuān, and troops were taken from the Wuchang garrison in Wǔhàn to quell the disturbances.

As it happened, revolutionaries in Wǔhàn, coordinated by Sun Yatsen's Tokyo-based Alliance Society, were already planning an uprising in concert with disaffected Chinese troops. The revolutionaries were quickly able to take control of Wǔhàn and ride on the back of the large-scale Railway Protection uprisings to victory all over China.

Two months later representatives from 17 provinces throughout China gathered in Nánjīng to establish the Provisional Republican Government of China. China's long dynastic cycle had come to an end.

Early Days of the Republic

The Provisional Republican Government was set up on 10 October 1911 (a date that is still celebrated in Taiwan as 'Double Tenth') by Sun Yatsen and Li Yuanhong, a military commander in Wuchang. Lacking the power to force a Manchu abdication, they had no choice but to call on the assistance of Yuan Shikai, the head of the imperial army and the same man that the Manchus had called on to put down the republican uprisings. The republicans promised Yuan Shikai the presidency if he could negotiate the abdication of the Emperor, which he achieved. The favour cost the republicans dearly. Yuan Shikai placed himself at the head of the republican movement and forced Sun Yatsen to stand down.

Yuan lost no time in dissolving the Provisional Republican Government and amending the constitution to make himself president for life.

When this met with regional opposition, he took the natural next step in 1915 of pronouncing himself China's latest emperor. Yúnnán seceded, taking Guǎngxī, Guìzhōu and much of the rest of the south with it. Forces were sent to bring the break-away provinces back into the imperial ambit, and in the confusion Yuan himself passed away.

Between 1916 and 1927, the government in Běijīng lost power over the far-flung provinces and China was effectively frag-mented into semi-autonomous regions gov-erned by warlords.

May 4th Era & Nationalist Revolution

The Nationalist Revolution had its organ-isational roots in Sun Yatsen's tireless ef-forts to follow through what had begun with the 1911 Revolution. It was greatly stimulated by the May 4th Movement, named for demonstrations conducted on 4 May 1919. The catalyst for the demonstra-tions was the decision of the Allies in Ver-sailles to pass defeated Germany's rights in Shāndōng over to the Japanese. The deci-sion inspired a surge of nationalist senti-ment in China.

More broadly, the May 4th Movement refers to a literary and social revolution dating from 1915, when the avant-garde journal *New Youth* was founded by the political radical Chen Duxiu (1879–1942), later a founding member of the Communist Party. *New Youth* mounted a sustained attack on Confucianism and the patriarchal system. In 1917 it featured an essay by prominent liberal reformer, the American-educated Hu Shi (1891–1962), which pointed to the advantages of a vernacular literature. This marked the beginnings of a steady move away from classical prose as the standard form of literary expression. New sorts of romantic, self-conscious po-etry and fiction gave expression to national sentiments and personal life experiences. Love and revolution were increasingly entwined.

Sun Yatsen led the way in the romantic revolution when he divorced the mother of his three children, his wife by an arranged marriage, to marry the young and beautiful Song Qingling (1892–1981). Qingling was effectively China's first 'First Lady'. Her sister, Song Meiling (b. 1897), married Chi-ang Kaishek in 1928. She was Chiang's third wife.

Kuomintang & Communists

By 1920 the Kuomintang (KMT; National-ist Party), had emerged as the dominant pol-itical force in eastern China.

Talks between representatives of the So-viet Communist International (Comintern) – the international body dedicated to world revolution – and prominent Chinese Marx-ists eventually resulted in several Chinese Marxist groups banding together to form a Chinese Communist Party (which became the CCP) at a meeting in Shànghǎi in 1921. Mao Zedong (1893–1976) was present.

Under the advice of the Soviet Comin-tern, the CCP joined a temporary alliance with the Kuomintang, largely to prevent Japanese expansion.

The union was short lived. After Sun Yat-sen's death in 1925 a power struggle emerged in the Kuomintang between those sympathetic to the Communists and those who – headed by Chiang Kaishek – favoured a capitalist state dominated by a wealthy elite and supported by a military dictatorship.

Chiang Kaishek attempted to put an end to growing Communist influence during the 1926 Northern Expedition, which set out to wrest power from the remaining warlords. In 1927 he showed his true colours by ordering the massacre of over 5000 Shànghǎi Com-munists and trade union representatives.

By the middle of 1928 the Northern Ex-pedition had reached Běijīng and a national government was established, with Chiang holding both military and political leader-ship. Nevertheless, only about half of the country was under the direct control of the Kuomintang; the rest was still ruled by local warlords.

China's social problems were many: child slave labour in factories; domestic slavery and prostitution; destitute and starving dying on the streets; and strikes ruthlessly sup-pressed by foreign and Chinese factory own-ers. In the face of such endemic social malaise, Chiang became obsessed with countering the influence of the Communists.

Civil War

After the massacre of 1927, the Commu-nists were divided between an insurrec-tionary policy of targeting large urban centres and one of basing its rebellion in the countryside. After costly defeats in Nánchāng and Chángshā, the tide of opinion started to shift towards Mao Zedong, who, along with Zhu De, had established his forces in Jīnggāng Shān, on the border of Jiāngxī and Húnán, and who advocated rural-based revolt.

Communist-led uprisings in other parts of the country met with some success. However, the Communist armies were still small and hampered by limited resources. It wasn't until 1930 that the ragged Communist forces had turned into an army of perhaps 40,000, which presented such a serious challenge to the Kuomintang that Chiang waged extermination campaigns against them. He was defeated each time, and the Communist army continued to expand its territory.

The Long March

Chiang's fifth extermination campaign began in October 1933, when the Communists suddenly changed their strategy. Mao and Zhu's authority was being undermined by other members of the party who advocated meeting Chiang's troops in pitched battles, but this strategy proved disastrous. By October 1934 the Communists had suffered heavy losses and were hemmed into a small area in Jiāngxī.

On the brink of defeat, the Communists decided to retreat from Jiāngxī and march north to Shaanxi to join up with other Communist armies in Shaanxi, Gānsù and Níngxià.

There was not one 'Long March' but several, as various Communist armies in the south made their way to Shaanxi. The most famous was the march from Jiāngxī province that began in October 1934, took a year to complete and covered 8000km over some of the world's most inhospitable terrain. On the way the Communists confiscated the property of officials, landlords and tax-collectors, redistributed the land to the peasants, armed thousands of peasants with weapons captured from the Kuomintang and left soldiers behind to organise guerrilla groups to harass the enemy.

Of the 90,000 people who started out in Jiāngxī only 20,000 made it to Shaanxi. Fatigue, sickness, exposure, enemy attacks and desertion all took their toll.

The march brought together many people who later held top positions after 1949, including Mao Zedong, Zhou Enlai, Zhu De, Lin Biao, Deng Xiaoping and Liu Shaoqi. It also established Mao as the paramount leader of the Chinese Communist movement; during the march a meeting of the CCP hierarchy recognised Mao's overall leadership, and he assumed supreme responsibility for strategy.

Japanese Invasion

In September 1931 the Japanese took advantage of the confusion in China to invade and occupy Manchuria, setting up a puppet state with the last Manchu emperor, Puyi, as recorded in Bertolucci's film *The Last Emperor*.

Chiang, still obsessed with the threat of the Communists, went ahead with his fifth extermination drive: 'pacification first, resistance later' was his slogan.

The KMT was bitterly criticised for not resisting the Japanese. Its hand was forced in December 1936, when the Manchurian general, Zhang Xueliang (1898–2001), kidnapped President Chiang Kaishek and forced him to agree to a Second United Front with the CCP to resist Japan. Zhang, hero of the hour, afterwards surrendered to the KMT and spent the next half-century under house arrest first in China and then in Taiwan. He was eventually released after Chiang Kaishek's death in 1975.

The rest of China was invaded by Japan in the middle of 1937. The Japanese occupation was marked by the Nánjīng massacre of 1937, human experiments in biological warfare factories in Manchuria, 'burn all, loot all, kill all' campaigns, massive internal migrations, and a process of divide and rule through the establishment of puppet governments. The puppet government in Nánjīng was headed by noted KMT figure Wang Jingwei.

The KMT was forced into retreat by the Japanese occupation. Its wartime capital was Chóngqìng (Chungking), a higgledy-piggledy town piled up on mountains in the upper reaches of Cháng Jiāng in Sìchuān. The city was subjected to heavy Japanese bombardments, but logistical difficulties prevented it being approached by land. Chiang Kaishek's finest hour came when, in the wake of bombings, he toured the ruins of the city giving heart to the beleaguered residents. It is a sign of continuing political sensitivities over the Nationalist legacy that the central monument in Chóngqìng is one

The diverse people of China: (clockwise from top left) a monk throwing prayer tickets in the air, Tibet; a girl doing homework, Macau; an Uyghur girl making carpet, Xīnjiāng; a woman sheltering under a colourful umbrella, Yúnnán; (middle) a baby in a traditional carrier in south-west China.

OLIVER STREWE

BRADLEY MAYHEW

FELICITY VOLK

TOM COCKREM

KEREN SU

China has a great diversity of landscapes: (clockwise from top left) Dragon's Backbone Rice Terraces, Guǎngxī; sunset on Tibet's Northern Plateau; snow-capped mountain scenery in the Himalayas; vast sand dunes in the Taklamakan Desert of Xīnjiāng; stark arid scenery in remote Yúnnán.

celebrating 'liberation' by the Communist Party rather than one to its wartime history.

The major turning point in the war was the entry of the USA after the Japanese bombing of Pearl Harbor on 7 December 1941. After the war, the USA tried to achieve a negotiated settlement of the rivalries between the CCP and the KMT. The CCP had expanded enormously during the war years, filling a vacuum in local government in vast areas behind and beyond Japanese lines, and creating a base from which it would successfully challenge the KMT's claims to legitimacy.

Civil war broke out in 1946. Although the CCP base at Yán'ān was destroyed by the Nationalists, Communist forces were able to outmanoeuvre the KMT on the crucial battle ground of Manchuria. Three great battles were fought in 1948 and 1949 in which the Kuomintang were defeated and thousands of KMT troops joined the Communists. The USA, which from being a hero during the war had become an object of popular vilification in China, was disheartened by the inadequacies of the KMT leadership and refused it further support. The Soviet Union played a two-faced game of alliances early in the post-war period, recognising the Nationalist government but eventually facilitating CCP ambitions.

In Běijīng on 1 October 1949, Mao Zedong proclaimed the foundation of the People's Republic of China (Zhonghua Renmin Gongheguo). Chiang Kaishek fled to the island of Formosa (Taiwan), taking with him the entire gold reserves of the country and what was left of his air force and navy. To prevent an attack from the mainland, President Truman ordered a protective US naval blockade.

The People's Republic of China

The PRC began its days as a bankrupt nation. The economy was in chaos due to rampant inflation and a legacy of economic mismanagement left by the KMT. The country had just 19,200km of railways and 76,800km of useable roads – all in bad condition. Irrigation works had broken down and livestock and animal populations were greatly reduced. Industrial production had fallen during the Japanese bombing and occupation to half that of the prewar period and agricultural output plummeted.

With the Communist takeover, China seemed to become a different country. Unified by the elation of victory and the immensity of the task before them, and further bonded by the Korean War and the necessity to defend the new regime from possible US invasion, the Communists made the 1950s a dynamic period. They embarked upon land reform, recognised the role of women, and restored the economy by curbing inflation.

By 1953 inflation had been halted, industrial production had been restored to prewar levels and the land had been confiscated from the landlords and redistributed to the peasants. On the basis of earlier Soviet models, the Chinese embarked on a massive five-year plan that was successful in lifting production on most fronts.

At the same time, the party increased its social control by organising the people according to their work units (dānwèi) and dividing the country into 21 provinces, five autonomous regions, two municipalities (Běijīng and Shànghǎi) and around 2200 county governments with jurisdiction over around one million party sub-branches.

Hundred Flowers

While the early years of the PRC enjoyed rapid economic development, immense problems remained in the social sphere, particularly with regard to the question of intellectuals. Many Kuomintang intellectuals had stayed on rather than flee to Taiwan, and still more overseas Chinese, many of them highly qualified, returned to China soon after its 'liberation' to help in the enormous task of reconstruction. Returning Chinese and those of suspect backgrounds were given extensive re-education courses in special universities.

Meanwhile, writers, artists and filmmakers were subject to strict ideological controls guided by Mao's writings on art during the Yán'ān period (the time Mao spent in Yán'ān after the Long March).

In the upper echelons of the party itself opinions were divided as to how to deal with the problem of the intellectuals. But Mao, along with Zhou Enlai and other influential figures, felt that the party's work had been so successful that it could roll with a little criticism, and in a closed session Mao put forward the idea of 'letting a hundred flowers bloom' in the arts and 'a hundred schools of thought contend' in the sciences.

It was to be a full year before Mao's ideas were officially sanctioned in April 1957, but once they were, intellectuals around the country responded with glee. Complaints poured in on everything from party corruption to control of artistic expression, from the unavailability of foreign literature to low standards of living; but most of all, criticisms focused on the CCP monopoly on power and the abuses that went with it.

The party quickly had second thoughts about the flowers, and an anti-rightist campaign was launched. Within six months 300,000 intellectuals had been branded rightists, removed from their jobs and, in many cases, incarcerated or sent to labour camps for thought reform.

The Great Leap Forward

The first five-year plan had produced satisfactory results on the industrial front, but growth of agricultural yields had been disappointingly low. The state now faced the problem of how to increase agricultural production to meet the needs of urban populations coalescing around industrialised areas.

As with the question of dealing with intellectuals, the party leadership was divided on how to respond. Some, such as Zhou Enlai, favoured an agricultural incentive system. Mao favoured mass mobilisation of the country and inspirational exhortations that he believed would jump-start the economy into first-world standards overnight.

In the end it was Mao who won the day, and the Chinese embarked on a radical program of creating massive agricultural communes and drawing large numbers of people both from the country and urban areas into enormous water control and irrigation projects. In Mao's view revolutionary zeal and mass cooperative effort could overcome any obstacle and transform the Chinese landscape into a productive paradise. At the same time Mao criticised the earlier emphasis on heavy industry, which had required the support and assistance of Russian engineers, and pushed for small local industry to be developed in the communes, with profits going back into agricultural development.

China embarked on one of the greatest failed economic experiments in human history. The Communists tried to abolish money and all private property, and told everyone to build backyard blast furnaces to increase steel production. Lacking iron ore, peasants had to melt down farm tools, pots and doorknobs to meet their quota of steel 'production'. However, the villages soon discovered that the steel produced was basically worthless.

Despite the enthusiastic forecasts for agricultural production there was little incentive to work in the fields. Large numbers of rural workers engaged in the worthless blast furnaces project resulted in a massive slump in grain output. Bad weather in 1959 and the withdrawal of Soviet aid in 1960 made matters worse.

All effort was made to cover up the ensuing disaster and no foreign assistance was sought. China plunged into a famine of staggering proportions – an estimated 30 million Chinese starved to death (some put the figure at 60 million). As a result of the failure of the Great Leap Forward, Mao resigned his position as head of state, but remained as Chairman of the Communist Party.

Sino-Soviet Split

Droughts and floods were beyond even Mao's ability to control, but he played no small part in the Great Leap Forward and the Sino-Soviet dispute that led to the withdrawal of Soviet aid. Basically Mao's problems with the USSR stemmed from the latter's policy of peaceful coexistence with the USA, Khrushchev's de-Stalinisation speech and what Mao generally felt to be the increasingly revisionist nature of the Soviet leadership. Sino-Soviet relations became ever frostier when Khrushchev reneged on a promise to provide China with a prototype atomic bomb and sided with the Indians in a Sino-Indian border dispute.

In 1960 the Soviets removed all of their foreign experts working in China. In 1969, the Soviet and Chinese armies briefly clashed in a territorial dispute over obscure Zhenbao (Treasure) Island on the border of Siberia and north-east China.

Splitting with the Soviet Union in 1960, the PRC pursued alliances with other countries, sometimes with extraordinary repercussions. Coups in Ghana in 1963 and in Indonesia in 1965 were both directed against China-friendly leaders, Nkrumah and Sukarno respectively. Maoist theories of revolution and warfare were influential on revolutionary movements across the globe, from Algeria to Peru.

The Cultural Revolution

The Cultural Revolution (Wénhuà Dàgémìng; 1966–70), probably the best-known event of the Maoist era, amounted to a reassertion of Mao's leadership and revolutionary vision in face of the stodgy bureaucratism of the Soviet Union and the so-called 'capitalist road' of President Liu Shaoqi and party Secretary-General Deng Xiaoping. Mao's wife, Jiang Qing, and three supporters, Yao Wenyuan, Wang Hongwen, Zhang Chunqiao (known as 'the Gang of Four') were the ginger group for the Cultural Revolution. Premier Zhou Enlai played an enigmatic support role.

Mao's extreme views, his recent disastrous policy decisions and his opposition to bureaucratisation led to his increasing isolation within the party. In response, he set about to cultivate a personality cult with the assistance largely of Lin Biao, the minister of defence and head of the People's Liberation Army (PLA).

In the early 1960s, Lin had a collection of Mao's sayings compiled into a book that was to become known simply as the 'little red book', although its real title was *Quotations from Chairman Mao*. The book became the subject of study sessions for all PLA troops and was extended into the general education system.

The Cultural Revolution began when a play was released, which although set in an earlier era of Chinese history, criticised Mao. This resulted in Mao launching a purge of the arts.

Simultaneously wall posters went up at Beijing University attacking the university administration. Mao officially sanctioned the wall posters and criticisms of party members by university staff and students, and before long students were being issued red armbands and taking to the streets. The Red Guards (*Hóngwèibīng*) had been born. By August 1966 Mao was reviewing mass parades of the Red Guards, chanting and waving copies of his little red book.

Nothing was sacred in the brutal onslaught of the Red Guards as they went on the rampage through the country. Universities and secondary schools were shut down; intellectuals, writers and artists were dismissed, killed, persecuted or sent to labour in the countryside; publication of scientific, artistic, literary and cultural periodicals ceased; temples were ransacked and monasteries disbanded; and many physical reminders of China's 'feudal', 'exploitative' or 'capitalist' past (including temples, monuments and works of art) were destroyed.

Millions of people are estimated to have died in these years through beatings, executions, suicide, or denial of medical care. Violence, social disorder and economic upheaval were most obvious in the cities. The relative stability of rural areas is evidenced by the country's ability at least to feed itself. Destruction of the 'four olds' was a centrepiece of the Cultural Revolution: 'old customs, old habits, old culture, old thinking' were all supposed to be eliminated. Gender equality was promoted but there was little room for personal life. Families were split up. Sex and romance were frowned upon. Clothing codes were as strict as under the most rigid religious regime.

Liu Shaoqi died in prison in 1969, a fact concealed from the public till 1979. Lin Biao plotted a coup in 1971, was exposed, and died in a mysterious plane crash over Mongolia.

Post Cultural Revolution Years

Some measure of political stability returned during the years immediately following the Cultural Revolution. Zhou Enlai exercised the most influence in the day-to-day governing of China and, among other things, worked towards restoring China's trade and diplomatic contacts with the outside world. In the 1970s, China was admitted into the United Nations and engaged in détente with the USA, re-establishing formal diplomatic relations with the latter in 1979.

In 1973, Deng Xiaoping, vilified as China's 'No 2 Capitalist Roader' during the Cultural Revolution, returned to power. Nevertheless, Běijīng politics remained factional and divided. On the one side was Zhou, Deng and a faction of 'moderates' or 'pragmatists', and on the other were the 'radicals', 'leftists' or 'Maoists' led by Jiang Qing. As Zhou's health declined, the radicals gradually gained the upper hand.

Premier Zhou Enlai died in January 1976 and in April a crowd of mourners in Tiānānmén Square erupted into a demonstration that was violently suppressed. Mao's chosen protege was made acting premier and Deng (under attack again from

Madame Mao) disappeared from public view. In July 1976, a great earthquake rocked north China, causing a quarter of a million deaths. The beginning of the end was widely seen to be at hand.

Mao had been a sick man for many years. In 1974 he was diagnosed as having Lou Gehrig's disease, an extremely rare motor-neuron disorder that leads quickly to death. Mao died in September 1976.

Mao's anointed successor was Hua Guofeng, who had started his days in relative obscurity as a party leader in Mao's home county and whom Mao had cultivated and elevated to premier and party chairman.

At first Hua temporised over dealing with the Gang of Four. But when the gang announced their opposition to Hua, he acted with the Politburo to have them arrested on 6 October. There were celebrations throughout China when the news was formally announced three weeks later.

The Gang did not to come to trial until 1980, and when it took place it provided a bizarre spectacle, with the blame for the entire Cultural Revolution falling on their shoulders. Jiang Qing's death sentence was commuted and she lived under house arrest until 1991, when she committed suicide by hanging.

Post-Mao China
In the middle of 1977 Deng Xiaoping returned to power for the third time and was appointed to the positions of vice-premier, vice-chairman of the party and chief of staff of the PLA.

During the last two decades of the 20th century the totalitarian practices of the Communist Government underwent significant modification. Under a 'Four Modernisations' program (agriculture, industry, science, and defence), China under Deng Xiaoping moved towards positive engagement with the capitalist economies of the West. A 'one child' policy was embraced in 1980, and succeeded in slowing population growth.

In rural China, the so-called 'Responsibility System' allowed agricultural households and factories to sell their quota surpluses on the open market. And in coastal China, Special Economic Zones (SEZs) were established at Zhūhǎi (next to Macau), Shēnzhèn (next to Hong Kong) and Shàntóu and Xiàmén (both just across the Taiwan Strait from Taiwan).

Economic growth during the '80s was briefly interrupted by crisis in domestic politics and international relations caused by the Tiānānmén incident in 1989, but resumed strongly in 1993 when Deng Xiaoping frankly proclaimed that 'to get rich is glorious'. Beginning in the 1990s the government began to rationalise state-owned industries. The size of the Chinese market and its growing vitality has encouraged substantial foreign investment, but the closure of many state enterprises has also created unemployment.

With the shift in economic and foreign policy, the party began to lose its ideological grip. Already in 1978 to 1979 demands were heard for a 'fifth modernisation': democracy. These were most notably aired in big character posters on Democracy Wall in Běijīng. Wei Jingsheng, responsible for the catch-cry, was arrested, tried for 'selling state secrets' and sentenced to fifteen years imprisonment, becoming an emblem of opposition to the CCP. In 1986 there were further demands for political reforms and press freedoms in demonstrations in a number of major cities.

Party Secretary-General Hu Yaobang was sidelined within the party for his support for some of these demands. His death in 1989 led directly to the Tiānānmén incident. What began as a mass memorial for Hu in April turned into a popular, peaceful rebellion, workers coming on side with the hundreds of thousands of students who gathered in Tiānānmén Square to press ever-escalating demands for political reform on the beleaguered party leadership. Deng Xiaoping finally sanctioned the forcible dispersal of the demonstrators, hundreds of whom were killed as the tanks of crack troops from the north rolled into the square.

This was the death knell of socialist ideology in China. Since then, the party has relied mainly on patriotism or nationalism for ideology. There has been a revival of established religions from Buddhism to Catholicism, and a flowering of new cults, most notably Falun Gong. Mindful of a long history of heterodox rebellions that have brought down the state, the government regards it as dangerous. In 1999, the Falun Gong attracted world headlines when thousands of practitioners gathered in solidarity outside government headquarters in Běi-jīng. Freedom of religion and the fate of Falun Gong prisoners in China are among the many human rights issues regularly raised by international rights organisations.

Hong Kong & Macau

In 1984 a Sino-British agreement allowed for the reversion of Hong Kong to China in 1997. The original 'unequal' Treaty of Nanking (1842) foisted on China by Britain at the end of the Opium War had ceded Hong Kong to the British 'in perpetuity', but the New Territories adjoining Kowloon were 'leased' to the British for 99 years in 1898. In the event, Britain agreed to hand the entire colony back to China when the lease on the New Territories expired.

The transition of power was not entirely smooth. According to the terms of the 1984 agreement, Hong Kong's transfer to Chinese rule was to take place under the concept of 'one country, two systems'. The implementation of this system was laid out in the Basic Law, which promised the former colony a 'high degree of autonomy' as a Special Administrative Region (SAR). Following the handover, however, the Chinese government scrapped the entire democratically elected Legislative Council (LEGCO) and replaced it with a legislature appointed by Běijīng. This was not entirely unexpected: Běijīng had always maintained that the elections, hastily called by the British after almost a century of completely undemocratic colonial administration, represented a rather hypocritical thumbing of the nose. While not ignoring the differences in the legal and political freedoms enjoyed in the respective countries, one can't help but see Běijīng's point.

Macau was the oldest European settlement in the east until 20 December 1999, when it was returned to the People's Republic of China. As in Hong Kong, a new Basic Law was established for the Macau SAR, enacted by the PRC's National People's Congress, and acts as a mini-constitution, prescribing the systems to be practised in the SAR. Similar to the arrangement with Hong Kong, Macau will govern itself for a period of 50 years and Portuguese will remain one of the official languages. Prior to the handover, Edmund Ho Hau Wah was chosen as Chief Executive.

Taiwan

In the course of 1949, key KMT personnel and then large numbers of troops retreated to Taiwan. After 60 years of Japanese rule, Taiwan had been rejoined to the mainland in 1945. The imposition of KMT rule led to rioting by local people in February 1948 and a massacre of tens of thousands of Taiwanese civilians under the direction of KMT military governor Chen Yi. Known as the '2-28' (ie, February 28) incident, this atrocity became a potent symbol of Taiwanese political dissent. Forty years later, public commemoration of the dead during the period of democratisation was one of the major signs of a change in political culture in Taiwan.

Chiang Ching-kuo, Chiang Kaishek's son and later successor, had Chen Yi arrested and executed before the final flight from the mainland. The KMT regime in Taiwan after 1949 was extremely repressive of Taiwanese, few of whom held any positions of note in government, education or the economy before the 1970s. Economic reforms, particularly land reform, nonetheless secured the government a local support base. The Korean War erupted in 1950, pitching Chinese and US forces against each other and virtually determining that the USA would support Taiwan in face of mainland threats in the 1950s.

This small island with its modest population of around twenty million has untoward importance for China. Its rapid economic growth during the 1970s and 1980s provided an example of what Chinese society could achieve on the world economic stage. The end of military rule and the beginning of full democracy challenged notions that Chinese were better suited to authoritarian, single-party governments. Above all, its continued independence, even within the framework of a 'one China' policy, is a lasting reminder that 'reunification' has yet to be achieved.

The 21st Century

By the beginning of the 21st century, the major challenges facing the Chinese state were still those that had long featured in its history. Unemployment, uneven economic growth, environmental degradation, large-scale migrations of people from poor rural to prosperous urban centres, corruption and crime attendant on economic change, population growth, political opposition in the border regions of Tibet and Xīnjiāng, and the development of alternative mass ideologies such as Falun Gong, are all significant problems for the Communist Party. The sex ratio shows a rising number of males relative to females and may provide a powder keg in future years as millions of young men look around in vain for partners. Already, kidnapping of young women for forced marriage in rural areas is a significant social problem.

Externally, the government has to contend with international critiques of its human rights record, rivalry with Japan for Asian leadership, rejection of its claims to sovereignty over Taiwan and Tibet, and an increasingly confrontational attitude on the part of the USA after the inauguration of George W Bush in 2001. The democratisation of Taiwan has created particular anxiety. In 1996 the Chinese conducted missile tests across the Taiwan Strait just before the first full elections on the island.

President Jiang Zemin, whose rise to power was signalled by his appointment as chairman of the Military Commission after the Tiānānmén incident, can claim popular success in playing the world stage. He presided over the return of Hong Kong and Macau to the Chinese fold, spoke up to Bill Clinton on national television, guided Běijīng to success in the Olympics bid for 2008, oversaw the admission of China into the World Trade Organization, and has played the reunification card for all it is worth. Futuristic scenarios have often portrayed the Taiwan issue as the flash-point for the next major international war, but the terrorist attack on America on 11 September 2001 showed how quickly international relations can change.

GEOGRAPHY

China is bounded to the north by deserts and to the west by the inhospitable Tibet-Qīnghǎi Plateau. The Han Chinese, who first built their civilisation around Huáng Hé (Yellow River), moved south and east towards the sea. The Han did not develop as a maritime people so expansion was halted at the coast; they found themselves in control of a vast plain cut off from the rest of the world by oceans, mountains and deserts.

China is the third largest country in the world, after Russia and Canada, and has an area of 9.5 million sq km. Only half of China is occupied by Han Chinese; the rest is inhabited by Mongols, Tibetans, Uyghurs and a host of other 'national minorities' who occupy the periphery of China. The existence of numerous minority languages is why maps of China often have two spellings for the same place – one spelling being the minority language, the other being Chinese. For example, Kashgar is the same place as Kashi.

From the capital, Běijīng, the government rules 21 provinces and the five 'autonomous regions' of Inner Mongolia, Níngxià, Xīnjiāng, Guǎngxī and Tibet. The 'special municipalities' of Běijīng, Tiānjīn, Shànghǎi and Chóngqìng are administered directly by the central government. Hong Kong and Macau are both termed Special Administrative Zones.

Taiwan is considered by the PRC government to be a province of China. The remote Spratly Islands (Nánshā) in the South China Sea are claimed by China and other countries including the Philippines, Vietnam, Taiwan, Brunei and Malaysia. In 1989 the Chinese forcefully took the Paracel Islands (Xīshā) from Vietnam. China fought and won a border war with India in the 1960s, but the boundary issue remains unresolved and a potential source of further conflict between the two nuclear states.

China's topography varies from mountainous regions with towering peaks to flat, featureless plains. The land surface is like a staircase descending from west to east. At the top are the plateaus of Tibet and Qīnghǎi in the south-west, averaging 4500m above sea level. At the southern rim of the plateau is the Himalayan mountain range, with peaks averaging 6000m high; 40 peaks rise 7000m or more. Mt Everest, known to the Chinese as Zhūmǔlángmǎfēng, lies on the Tibet-Nepal border.

Melting snow and ice from the mountains of western China and the Tibet-Qīnghǎi Plateau provides the headwaters for many of the country's largest rivers: Cháng Jiāng, Huáng Hé, Láncāng Jiāng (Mekong River) and Nù Jiāng (Salween River). The latter runs from eastern Tibet into Yúnnán and on into Myanmar.

The Tarim Basin is the largest inland basin in the world and is the site of the

Xīnjiāng Autonomous Region. Here you'll find the Taklamakan Desert (the largest in China) as well as China's largest shifting salt lake, Lop Nur (Luóbù Pō), where China tested its nuclear bombs. The Tarim Basin is bordered to the north by Tiān Shān.

To the east of this range is the low-lying Turpan Depression, known as the 'Oasis of Fire', which is the hottest place in China. The Junggar Basin lies in the far north of Xīnjiāng province, beyond Tiān Shān.

As you cross the mountains on the eastern edge of this second step of the topographical staircase, the altitude drops to less than 1000m above sea level. Here, forming the third step, are the plains of the Cháng Jiāng valley and northern and eastern China. These plains – the homeland of the Han Chinese, their 'Middle Kingdom' – are the most important agricultural areas of the country and the most heavily populated.

It should be remembered that two-thirds of China is mountain, desert or otherwise unfit for cultivation. If you exclude the largely barren regions of Inner Mongolia, Xīnjiāng and the Tibet-Qīnghǎi Plateau from the remaining third, all that remains for cultivation is a meagre 15% or 20% of land area. Only this to feed 1.3 billion people!

In such a vast country, the waterways took on a central role as communication and trading links. Most of China's rivers flow east. At 6300km long, Cháng Jiāng is the longest.

Huáng Hé, about 5460km long and the second longest river in China, is the birthplace of Chinese civilisation. The third great waterway of China, the Grand Canal, is the longest artificial canal in the world. It originally stretched for 1800km from Hángzhōu in south China to Běijīng in the north. Today, however, most of the Grand Canal is silted over and no longer navigable.

A Tale of Two Rivers

China's two major rivers are Cháng Jiāng (Yangzi River) and Huáng Hé (Yellow River). Cháng Jiāng, surpassed in length only by the Amazon and the Nile, is by far the more important. Commencing in Tanggula Shān in south-west Qīnghǎi near the Tibetan border, it descends in an easterly direction to the sea near Shànghǎi for 6400km. Its watershed of almost 2 million sq km – 20% of China's land mass – supports a population of 400 million people. In the Red Basin area in Sìchuān alone, it nourishes more people than the combined populations of England and France.

Its initial descent from 6000m-high mountains is perilous. When a Chinese photographer called Yao Mao-shu tried to navigate the length of the river from its source in 1985, he completed only one-sixth of the journey before plunging to his death in a steep gorge where the currents run at 60km/h. In the following year, after a further attempt was abandoned, a Chinese team managed to complete the task, but only after four men were lost in the gorges and rapids.

The Middle River, as the central third is called, and the Lower River, below Wǔhàn – the Grain Basket of China, and a popular area for boat tours – have been profoundly important in China's development. Marco Polo travelled in the lower Cháng Jiāng region in the 13th century. He was astonished at the volume of navigation and trading in that area. For centuries, junks, sampans and other vessels have carried commodities such as rice, salt, silk, tea and oil on its waters. Of course, the river's advantages have been offset by problems of floods, which periodically inundate millions of hectares and destroy hundreds of thousands of lives.

The more northerly of the two, Huáng Hé, is a very different river. Whereas Cháng Jiāng is fondly referred to as the Long River, China's Main Street and China's Lifeline, Huáng Hé is called China's Sorrow and the World's Muddiest River. It flows through yellow powdery soil known as loess, which has been deposited by monsoons and cyclones that howl across Inner Asian deserts. Because of its height above the surrounding plains, the east-west section receives no water from tributaries – unlike Cháng Jiāng, which has more than 700 tributaries. As a result, it has flooded frequently and radically changed its course. It has carried little river traffic. Its volume is only one-tenth of that of Cháng Jiāng. The loess soil on its banks can be used to build cave-like housing structures, such as those used by Mao Zedong and his followers between 1936 and 1947, but these are very vulnerable to seismic movement. In 1920, 300,000 people were buried in this area following an earthquake.

CLIMATE

Spread over such a vast area, China is subject to the worst extremes in weather, from the bitterly cold to the unbearably hot. There isn't really an 'ideal' time to visit the country, so use the following information as a rough guide to avoid temperature extremes. In winter the warmest regions are found in areas south and south-west, such as Xīshuāngbǎnnà in Yúnnán, the southern coast and Hǎinán Dǎo. In summer, high spots like Éméi Shān in Sìchuān are a relief from the heat. In both the north and south most of the rain falls during summer.

North

Winters in the north fall between December and March and are incredibly cold. North of the Great Wall, into Inner Mongolia or Hēilóngjiāng, temperatures drop to -40°C (-40°F) and you'll see the curious sight of sand dunes covered in snow. Summer in the north is around May to August.

Spring and autumn are the best times for visiting the north. Daytime temperatures range from 20°C to 30°C (68°F to 86°F) and there is less rain. Although it can be quite hot during the day, nights can be bitterly cold and bring frost.

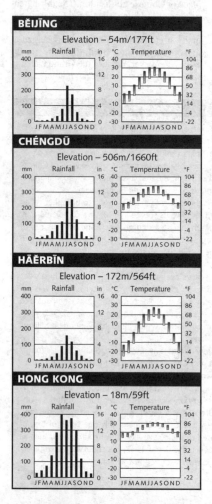

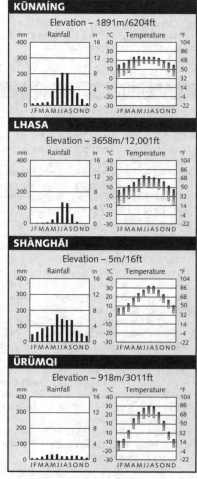

Central

In the Cháng Jiāng valley area (including Shànghǎi) summers are long, hot and humid. Wǔhàn, Chóngqìng and Nánjīng have been dubbed 'the three furnaces' by the Chinese. Expect very high temperatures any time between April and October.

Winters are short and cold, with temperatures dipping below freezing – almost as cold as Běijīng. It can also be wet and miserable at any time apart from summer. While it is impossible to pinpoint an ideal time to visit, spring and autumn are probably best.

South

In the far south, around Guǎngzhōu, the hot, humid periods last from around April to September, and temperatures can rise to 38°C (100°F). This is also the rainy season. Typhoons are liable to hit the south-east coast between July and September.

There is a short winter from January to March. It's nowhere near as cold as in the north, but temperature statistics don't really indicate just how cold it can get, so bring warm clothes.

Autumn and spring can be good times to visit the south, with day temperatures in the 20°C to 25°C (68°F to 75°F) range. However, it can also be miserably wet and cold, with perpetual rain or drizzle, so be prepared for all weather.

North-West

It gets hot in summer, but at least it's dry. The desert regions can be scorching in the daytime. Turpan, which sits in a depression 150m below sea level, more than deserves the title of the 'hottest place in China', with maximums of around 47°C (117°F).

In winter this region is as formidably cold as the rest of northern China. In Ürümqi the average temperature in January is around -10°C (14°F), with minimums down to almost -30°C (-22°F). Temperatures in Turpan are only slightly more favourable to human existence.

Tibet

In Tibet you can easily get the impression that all four seasons have been compressed into one day. Temperatures which can vary from below zero during the evening and early morning can soar to a sizzling 38°C

(100°F) at midday, but it always feels remarkably cool in the shade.

Winter brings intense cold and fierce winds. Snowfall is far less common in Tibet than the name 'Land of Snows' implies – it's an arid place and the sun is quick to melt off snowfalls. Rainfall is scarcest in the north and west of Tibet. Northern monsoons can sweep across the plains for days on end, often whipping up dust storms, sandstorms, snowstorms, or (only rarely) rainstorms.

ECOLOGY & ENVIRONMENT

Like other developing countries, China's economic boom came at the expense of controls on air pollution, land clearing, deforestation, endangered species and rural and industrial waste. China's huge population combined with geographical factors make its environmental problems infinitely more massive than that of other nations.

The floods of 1998 (in large part due to deforestation) in which over 3600 people were killed, brought further attention to the issue. Even Jiang Zemin, state president and CCP general secretary, has publicly called for action on the environment.

Some analysts point to an impending environmental catastrophe, warning that China's greatest challenge will be ecological. Strict measures against environmental degradation are essential to avert disaster, but they could well be too little, too late.

Energy Use & Air Pollution

Nine out of 10 of the world's most polluted cities are found in China, and estimates are that by 2005 China may become the world's largest source of air pollution.

Most major cities lie smothered under great canopies of smog in summer and winter. Běijīng, Xī'ān, Lánzhōu and Jílín are all chronically affected. Tests conducted by the World Health Organization (WHO) and China's National Environmental Protection Agency showed levels of airborne suspended particles average 526 micrograms per sq metre in northern China (WHO recommends a safe limit of 60 to 90 micrograms per sq metre).

The first problem is coal. It provides some 70% of China's energy needs and around 900 million tonnes of it go up in smoke every year. This heavy reliance on coal has lead to an estimated 40% of the country being affected by acid rain. Even Korea and Japan complain about damage to their forests from acid rain that is believed to have come from China.

Despite this, in the late 1990s Premier Li Peng called for further expansion of the coal industry. Běijīng's enthusiasm has, however, been partially dampened by the increasing development of hydroelectric and nuclear power and a spate of coal mining disasters. Dangerous working conditions and inadequate safety controls in local mines have led to a stream of accidents. Coal-rich Shānxī province alone has an annual death rate from mining of over 1000.

Renewable energy use is still in its infancy, with most hope pinned on hydroelectric power such as the Three Gorges Dam and the Xiaowan Lancang River Dam Project in Yúnnán province. The main problem is that renewable energy is uncompetitive against a heavily subsidised coal power industry. China is expected to become a major oil importer as demand rapidly outstrips domestic resources (hence China's interest in the Spratly Islands).

Desertification & Land Use

China has been combating the spread of its deserts for more than 40 years via afforestation programs. They have met with mixed success, as they're continually hampered by the ongoing stress placed on the land by overgrazing and irrigation.

Every year vast, choking dust storms blow across Běijīng, Korea and Japan from China's loess plateau.

The main cause of these storms is the desertification of large parts of northern and western China due to a lack of sustainable land management. Despite afforestation, some experts have suggested that grass should be planted instead to bind the soil more effectively.

During the summer of 2001, north China suffered its worst drought since 1990, with more than 20 provinces being afflicted; Inner Mongolia was badly hit. Běijīng residents were urged to save every drop of water during the drought, which rendered huge amounts of land in north China uncultivable. The problem is expected to worsen over the next few years.

The lower reaches of Huáng Hé have often dried up in recent years, as has the Red Flag Canal. Locust swarms often accompany such conditions. Běijīng is becoming increasingly parched as the water table drops; the imposition of water charges would discourage waste, but have not yet been implemented.

Water & Wetlands

China's rivers and wetlands face great pressure from draining and reclamation, as well as pollution from untreated industrial liquids, domestic sewerage, human waste and chemicals. It is estimated that China annually dumps three billion tonnes of untreated water into the ocean via its rivers. Some reports indicate that half the population is supplied with polluted water. This poor-quality water, coupled with often acute water shortages, is creating significant environmental health hazards.

Drought often hits north and west China while north-east and central China are flooded: waste, silting up of riverbeds, overextraction of water and the general abuse of the environment worsen the situation.

Global Implications

The impact of China's environmental problems doesn't stop at the country's borders – acid rain, desert sand storms, and silted and polluted rivers are all too familiar to China's neighbours. Across the north of China, rampaging natural fires are believed to consume more than 200 million tonnes of coal a year, further exacerbating China's contribution to global warming.

Environment & Education

China has a long tradition of celebrating nature within its frontiers, from landscape paintings to poems dwelling on mountain peaks shrouded in mist. The contradictory China of today eulogises its landscape while simultaneously destroying it.

There is legislation to curb the worst excesses of industry, but these laws are rarely enforced. Corrupt officials are partly to blame but the drag on economic expansion is also cited as a factor.

Compelling economic pressure to exploit the environment has been exacerbated by ignorance on the part of China's citizens. As the Chinese state arrogated responsibilities to itself for almost everything, the nation's citizens became freed from individual responsibility and hence indifferent to ecology. Waking up to this, the government now bombards viewers with green directives on TV, from saving water to planting trees and litter disposal. In the dour 1970s, such environmental concerns were more likely to be dismissed as a bourgeois conspiracy. These days, a growing middle class finds itself wooed by adverts for environment-friendly washing powders and detergents.

There has been an increase in the severity of penalties for violating China's conservation laws, with the death penalty and life sentences not uncommon. However, there is still very little room for debating the issues with gusto in the media.

Culture

The government has long tried to salvage cultural relics that survived the ideological flames of the 1960s and 1970s, although infrastructure priorities may sound the death knell for many of Běijīng's wonderful hútòng, or old alleyways. Heritage protection serves the dual function of luring the tourist dollar and creating a sense of pride among Chinese. Little mention is made of the sheer devastation wrought under Communist control: take the toppling of Běijīng's vast city walls in the 1950s as an example. The administration of what remains is sadly often repackaged with all the kitsch and tastelessness you would expect from a Communist Party that suddenly found itself at the controls of a tourist market economy.

FLORA & FAUNA

China is endowed with an extremely diverse range of natural vegetation and animal life. There are about 30,000 species of seed plants and 2500 species of forest trees, many of which are indigenous to China. Unfortunately, human beings have had a considerable impact and much of China's rich natural heritage is rare, endangered or extinct. Many animals are officially protected, though illegal hunting and trapping continues. A bigger challenge is habitat destruction, caused by encroaching agriculture, urbanisation and industrial pollution. To the government's credit, more than 900 nature reserves have been established protecting about 7% of China's land area.

Flora

One of China's most famous plants must be bamboo. There are actually more than 300 species of bamboo plant covering about 3% of the total forest area in China. Most of this bamboo is located in the sub-tropical zones south of Cháng Jiāng. The plant is not only valued by the giant panda, but cultivated for use as a building material and food.

Many other well-known plants are indigenous to China, including the azalea, rhododendron, lotus flower, magnolia, ginkgo, maple, birch, poplar and spruce. The variety and intermixture of temperate and tropical plants in China is best understood by comparing the vegetation of Jílín province in the semifrigid north and Hǎinán province in the tropical south. It would be difficult to find one common plant species shared by the two provinces with the exception of a few weeds.

China's diversity of ecosystems supports an equivalent range of flora: the tropical forests of south China; the desert and steppe vegetation of north-western China; the taiga coniferous forests of the border areas adjoining Russia; and the mangrove swamps along the shores of the South China Sea. Tropical and temperate coniferous forests with broad-leaved evergreen and deciduous plants prevail in the southern provinces of Hǎinán, Yúnnán and Guǎngxī, whereas vast areas of desolate and very sparse salt-tolerant and drought-resistant vegetation prevails in the arid north-west. Along the borders of the Gobi Desert are wide plains of grasslands and just across to the north-east are the last great tracts of forests in China.

The harvesting of *facai*, a moss-like vegetable that grows wild in the north of China, has been banned due to worries concerning desertification.

Fauna

China's wealth of vegetation and variety of landscapes has fostered the development of a great diversity of fauna.

In spite of the odds against them, a number of rare animals continue to survive in the wild in small and remote areas of China. Notable among such survivors are the small species of alligator in central and eastern China, the giant salamander in western China, the Cháng Jiāng dolphin and the pink dolphin of Hong Kong. The famed giant panda is confined to the fauna-rich valleys and ranges of Sìchuān.

Throughout the Chinese mountains, takin (or goat antelope), wild yaks, argali sheep, numerous species of pheasants, and a variety of laughing thrushes may be found. The extreme north-eastern part of China is inhabited by some interesting mammals, such as reindeer, moose, musk deer, bears, sables and Manchurian tigers.

This region also features considerable birdlife, such as cranes, ducks, bustards, swans and herons. Good bird-watching possibilities exist, especially in the spring. Some good places for this activity include Zhalong Nature Reserve, in Hēilóngjiāng; Qīnghǎi Hú in Qīnghǎi; and Maipo Marsh in Hong Kong.

For sheer diversity of flora and fauna, the tropical south of Yúnnán province, particularly the area around Xīshuāngbǎnnà, is one of the richest in China. This region provides habitats for the parrot, hornbill, slender loris, gibbon, snub-nosed monkey, the Indochina tiger and herds of wild Indian elephants.

If you're interested in delving further into China's flora and fauna, two good books on the subject are *Living Treasures* by Tang Xiyang and *The Natural History of China* by Zhao Ji et al.

Endangered Species

China's endangered plants and animal list is depressingly long. Animals on the list include the giant panda, snow leopard, Cháng Jiāng dolphin, South China tiger, Manchurian tiger, chiru antelope, crested ibis, Asian elephant, golden monkey, red-crowned crane and black-crowned crane, to name just a few.

Intensive farmland cultivation, the reclaiming of wetlands, river damming, industrial and rural waste, and desertification are reducing unprotected forest areas, putting more pressure on isolated populations.

Most of China's endangered species are found in, and adjoining, 900 or so protected nature reserves, whose monitoring and management is complicated by a mechanical bureaucracy.

Perhaps no animal better represents both the beauty and the struggle of wildlife in China than the panda. These splendid animals are endangered by a combination of hunting, habitat encroachment and natural disasters. Through a number of joint programs run by Chinese and overseas agencies, animals like the giant panda and the Cháng Jiāng dolphin are receiving more attention and protection, which will hopefully guarantee their survival.

Chinese news reports in 2001 announced that the pandas in the Giant Panda Breeding Research Base in Chéngdū would forthwith enjoy four-star facilities including air conditioning. The latter is designed to keep the bears, which loath temperatures over 30°C, cool during the summer months.

Nature Reserves

Despite a history of resource, population and pollution pressures, China has an incredibly diverse range of natural escapes scattered across the country. Nature reserves offer the traveller an incredible variety of landscapes and a rich diversity of flora and fauna.

Some notable ones include: Jiǔzhàigōu in Sìchuān province, Zhāngjiājiè in Húnán province and Chángbái Shān in Jílín province. Most of China's sacred mountains (including Pǔtuó Shān, Wǔtái Shān, Éméi Shān, Huá Shān and Jiǔhuá Shān) have also been converted into nature reserves.

Though the prospect for increasing the total number of nature reserves looks good, environmentalists shouldn't cheer too loudly since most of China's parklands are under heavy pressure from commercial development.

GOVERNMENT & POLITICS

Precious little is known about the inner workings of the Chinese government, but what is known is that the entire monolithic structure, from grassroots work units to the upper echelons of political power, is controlled by the Communist Party.

The highest authority rests with the Standing Committee of the CCP Politburo. The Politburo comprises 25 members and below it is the 210-member Central Committee, made up of younger party members and provincial party leaders. At grassroots level the party forms a parallel system to the administrations in the army, universities, government and industries. Real authority is exercised by the party representatives at each level in these organisations. They, in turn, are responsible to the party officials in

NATIONAL PARKS

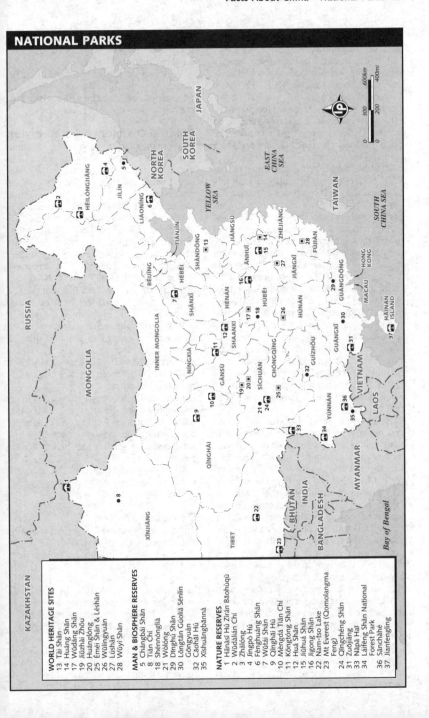

WORLD HERITAGE SITES
13 Tài Shān
14 Huáng Shān
17 Wǔdāng Shān
19 Jiǔzhài Zhōu
20 Huánglóng
25 Éméi Shān & Lèshān
26 Wǔlíngyuán
27 Lúshān
28 Wǔyí Shān

MAN & BIOSPHERE RESERVES
5 Chángbái Shān
8 Tiān Chí
18 Shénnóngjià
21 Wòlóng
29 Dǐnghú Shān
30 Lóngtán Guólà Sēnlín
32 Cǎohǎi Hú
35 Xīshuāngbǎnnà

NATURE RESERVES
1 Hānàsī Hú Zìrán Bǎohùqū
2 Wùdàlián Chí
3 Zhālóng
4 Jìngpō Hú
6 Fènghuáng Shān
7 Wǔtái Shān
9 Qīnghǎi Hú
10 Mèngdá Tiān Chí
11 Kōngtóng Shān
12 Huà Shān
15 Jiǔhuá Shān
16 Jìgong Shān
22 Nam-tso Lake
23 Mt Everest (Qomolangma Feng)
24 Qīngchéng Shān
31 Zuǒjiāng
33 Nàpà Hǎi
34 Làifēng Shān National Forest Park
36 Sānchàhé
37 Jiānfēnglǐng

the hierarchy above them, thus ensuring strict central control.

The day-to-day running of the country lies with the State Council, which is directly under the control of the CCP. The State Council is headed by the premier and beneath the premier are four vice-premiers, 10 state councillors, a secretary-general, 45 ministers and various other agencies. The State Council implements the decisions made by the Politburo.

Rubber-stamping the decisions of the CCP leadership is the National People's Congress (NPC). It comprises a 'democratic alliance' of both party members and non-party members who include intellectuals, technicians and industrial managers. In theory they are empowered to amend the constitution and to choose the premier and members of the State Council. The catch is that all these office-holders must first be recommended by the Central Committee, and thus the NPC is only an approving body.

The Chinese government is also equipped with a massive bureaucracy. The term 'cadre' is usually applied to bureaucrats, and their monopoly on power means that wide-ranging perks are a privilege of rank for all and sundry – from the lowliest clerks to the shadowy puppet masters of Zhongnanhai. China's bureaucratic tradition is a long one.

At grassroots level, the basic unit of social organisation outside the family is the work unit *(dānwèi)*. Every Chinese person is theoretically a member of one, although Chinese nowadays increasingly slip through the net by being self-employed or working in a private operation. For those who are members, tight controls are exercised by the leaders of the unit to which they belong.

The work unit is a perfect organ of social control and little proceeds without it. It approves marriages and divorces and even childbirth. It assigns housing, sets salaries, handles mail, recruits party members, keeps files on each unit member, arranges transfers to other jobs or other parts of the country, and gives permission to travel abroad. The work unit's control extends into every part of the individual's life.

The wild card in the system is the army. Comprising land forces, the navy and the air force, it has a total of around 2.9 million members. China is divided into seven military regions, each with its own military leadership – in some cases with strong regional affiliations.

Whatever the nation's problems may be, Communist-run China is probably infinitely preferable to one ruled by a militaristic general with more warlike ambitions.

Political Dissidence & Repression

Any organised opposition to the Communist Party is ruthlessly extirpated. The events in Tiānánmén Square in 1989 focused world attention on China's political repression.

The Communist Party has succeeded in educating and cautioning the vast majority of citizens against political deviance; they remain 'once bitten twice shy'. University campuses, a comparative hotbed of student idealism in the late 1980s, today have joined in the silence. Repressed anger is discharged at government-sanctioned protests, such as what followed the bombing of the Chinese Embassy in Belgrade.

Resolute, organised dissidence from intellectuals is nipped in the bud through rapid arrests and sentencing; the China Democracy Party, which emerged in 1998, was swiftly uprooted and its organisers packed off to prison.

Many of China's high-profile dissidents live abroad, which suits the PRC fine; others languish in Chinese jails or under house arrest. The dissidents themselves find little common ground and bicker among themselves.

It's fair to say that, for the moment, China has successfully crushed any organised resistance to the government.

Democracy?

The Chinese system of government can be traced back to the legalist, centralised state theories of such philosophers as Han Feizi and the autocratic control of Qinshi Huangdi. In many ways, such models still have a firm grip on today's governance.

Foreign democratic notions only entered China in the late 19th century, and Sun Yat-sen managed to establish a proto-democracy for the rule of China.

With the Communist revolution, however, calls for democracy were quietly chloroformed. Despite the excitement of optimists at village-level democratic elections for local government in China, more pragmatic observers say that true democracy can only accompany some cataclysmic transfer of power.

A full democracy of sorts does, however, exist in the Middle Kingdom. As China sees Taiwan as a rebel province within China, the island can be considered China's first democratic (and wealthiest) state.

Hong Kong also functions as a partial democracy, as does Macau, but the greatest boost to democratic ideals is probably the Chinese government itself.

One party rule in China is an impediment to the development of the nation and the Chinese know this. The government struggles against in-built corruption, yawning inequality, poverty and a constellation of other issues. For many, democracy remains a twinkling solution.

It was fashionable in the 1990s to appease China by agreeing that the nation will find its own way, for the land is somehow different from everywhere else. Not surprisingly, this is also China's line, and rather like 'Socialism with Chinese characteristics', it doesn't actually mean anything at all.

ECONOMY

Under Mao, China's economy was a prisoner to ideology and incompetence. Deng Xiaoping's tenure (essentially 1977 to 1997) was a period of reform, continued in perhaps less dramatic fashion by Jiang Zemin. Deng chose a pragmatic approach to achieving the so-called 'Four Modernisations': namely, modernisation of China's industry, agriculture, defence, and science and technology.

Rural China was the birthplace of Deng's pioneering economic reforms. Unfortunately, rural earnings still lag far behind urban incomes; 70% of the nation's wealth is in the cities, where only 17% of the population live.

A floating population of as many as 150 million to 200 million migrant workers flock to the cities from the countryside in the hope of finding employment – often they end up working long hours in poorly paid factory or construction jobs.

Deng's reform program saw spectacular growth in the eastern and southern seaboard provinces, while the interior trailed behind. The government is now attempting to swing

investment to China's west, partly by sponsoring huge projects in the region.

After two decades of high growth, China's economy is now slowing and unemployment is on the rise. In an attempt to stimulate the economy, the government has turned to pouring money into public works projects. Stimulating domestic demand is also a high priority especially in rural areas, but consumers, worried about lay-offs or uncertain about the future, are holding on to their money.

Corruption sends vast amounts of public money to private bank accounts abroad. Official reports suggest that over 2% of China's GDP is diverted for unlawful purposes.

Reform of the banking sector is urgently needed. Many banks are saddled with huge, non-performing loans to state-owned enterprises. The state's current aim to restructure inefficient state-owned enterprises is costing millions of jobs and is leading to social unrest among laid-off workers.

Chinese leaders are pinning their hopes on WTO membership spurring the economy. In the longer term, it's hoped that it will increase imports and exports, force state industries into the market and revive foreign investment. Pessimists take the view that the government's hesitancy to reform its state enterprises at a faster rate and its unwillingness to nurture the private sector will drive China to crisis point. Optimists point out that China's policy of gradual economic reform has basically worked well so far and has allowed China to come out unscathed from the Asian economic crisis.

In a recent 2001 report, the government admitted to concern at growing demonstrations, especially in rural areas. The report noted that protests involving more than 10,000 people were becoming increasingly widespread. High taxes, levied by corrupt officials, have led to a number of officials being killed.

POPULATION & PEOPLE

Han Chinese make up about 93% of the population; the rest is composed of China's 55 officially recognised ethnic minorities.

Although minorities account for about 7% of the population, they are distributed over some 50% of Chinese-controlled territory, mostly in the sensitive border regions. Minority separatism has always been a threat to the stability of China, particularly among the Uyghurs and the Tibetans, who have poor and often volatile relations with the Han Chinese. The minority regions provide China with the greater part of its livestock and hold vast untapped deposits of minerals.

Maintaining amicable relations with the minorities has been a continuous problem for the Han Chinese. Tibet and Xīnjiāng are heavily garrisoned by Chinese troops, partly to protect China's borders and partly to prevent rebellion among the local population. The Chinese government has also set up special training centres, like the National Minorities Institute in Běijīng, to train minority cadres for these regions.

Tibetan and Uyghur discontent is likely to increase as China mobilises its economy to develop the west. The program may materially benefit the minorities, but at the cost of further Han intrusion and reshaping of the local culture.

China's population has to be fed with the produce of around 15% to 20% of the land they live on – the sum total of China's arable land. Available land is also rapidly shrinking due to industrial and urban encroachment, urbanisation and erosion. The rest is barren wasteland or can only be lightly grazed.

The prospect of an ever-growing population, with an ever-shrinking capacity to feed itself, prompted a limited birth control program in the 1950s, but this was abandoned during the Cultural Revolution.

The one-child policy was railroaded into effect in 1979 without a careful analysis of its logic or feasibility. The original goal was to keep China's population to 1 billion by the year 2000 and then massaged down to an ideal of 700 million by 2050.

The target figure was, however, yanked up over the years, and a figure of 1.25 billion by 2000 somehow emerged. The exact size of China's population was unclear though, as officials downsized numbers in their areas to match birth control aims.

By the end of the 1990s it was assumed that some 30 million people were unaccounted for.

China's current population size outstrips the original goal by almost 30%, so the program has failed to meet the objectives that delivered it in the first place. Current projections depict a population close on 1.5 billion by the year 2010.

The cost and difficulty of enforcing the policy has been massive, and its implementation an unprecedented intrusion by the state into the reproductive rights of its citizens. The policy was originally harshly implemented but rural revolt led to a softer stance; nonetheless, it has generated much bad feeling between local officials and the rural population.

Rural families (the bulk of the population) are now allowed to have two children, but some have upwards of three or four kids, who are unreported and consequently receive no education.

A county in Guǎngdōng province was ordered to perform 20,000 abortions and forced sterilisations before the end of 2001.

Families who do abide by the one-child policy will often go to great lengths to make sure their child is male. This is particularly true in rural China, where the ancient custom of female infanticide continues to this day. In parts of China, this is creating a serious imbalance of the sexes. One survey in Shaanxi province, for example, determined that 145 male infants were being born for every 100 females. The overall average for China is 114 males for every 100 females.

Psychologists also argue that the experiment has created a generation of spoiled children ill prepared to deal with adult life. Growing up as the centre of attention and treated as 'little emperors' *(xiǎo huángdì)* has made the sharp edges of the outside world that much sharper.

The policy is also creating a rapidly aging population. The family structure has become 4-2-1, with one child having to look after two parents and four grandparents. It is estimated that China will be looking after 400 million old people by the year 2040, an aged population that will constitute a huge economic drag.

Supporters of the policy argue that without it China would be dealing with runaway population growth. Others note that alternative, less coercive strategies, such as a national family planning program and improved health care could have afforded better results. Those interested in China's one child policy can check out Ⓦ www.over population.com.

CHINA'S HIGHLIGHTS

SPECTACULAR SIGHTS

With its long and dramatic history, China offers an endless diversity of cultural treasures.

Army of Terracotta Warriors In 1974, an exciting discovery in Shaanxi of underground vaults eventually yielded thousands of life-size terracotta soldiers and their horses in battle formation. The warriors are over 2000 years old and amazingly well preserved.

Grand Buddha In Sìchuān, this is the largest Buddha in the world. It is 71m high, carved into a red sandstone cliff face. Work on this enormous figure took over 90 years and its sheer size and the monumentality of the artistic feat are breathtaking.

Mògāo Caves These caves are set into desert cliffs above a river valley in Gānsù. Some 492 grottoes are still standing and they contain religious art depicting 1000 years of history.

Tombs of Nánjīng Construction of Sun Yatsen's Mausoleum, an immense Ming-style tomb, began a year after his death (in 1925). The finished product in Jiāngsū has become a pilgrimage for people wishing to pay their respects to the father of modern China.

The Great Wall Běijīng is the jumping-off point for the Great Wall, China's awe-inspiring rampart, which stretches from Shānhǎiguān on the east coast to far-flung Jiāyùguān in the Gobi Desert. It was originally built to defend the Middle Kingdom from Mongol attack.

Cloud Ridge Caves These caves are next to the pass near Dàtóng leading to Inner Mongolia. They contain over 50,000 statues and stretch for about 1km east to west. The incredible artwork shows influences of the many foreign craftsmen, from India and central Asia, who worked on the grottoes.

SACRED MOUNTAINS

The sacred mountains of China inspire the climber with a sense of the frailty of human existence. Dotted along the well-marked trails are poems, inscriptions and temples. The chief attraction is sunrise at the summit, where crowds gather to gaze on the 'sea of clouds'.

Wǔtái Shān Centred on the beautiful monastic village of Táihuái in Shānxī, this holy Buddhist area contains some beautiful alpine scenery, architecturally superb temples and peaceful mountain trails.

The Army of Terracotta Warriors standing guard in Shaanxi.
LEE FOSTER

The Great Wall stretches to the horizon; seen at Mùtiányù, Běijīng.
GLENN BEANLAND

Intricate Indian-influenced carvings in the Cloud Ridge Caves, Shānxī.
HILARY SMITH

THOMAS HUHTI

Trek up Éméi Shān to see the sunrise behind the mist over the temples.

JULIET COOMBE

The legendary peaks of Huáng Shān, Ānhuī, are a wonder to behold.

GLENN BEANLAND

Last light warms a hall within the Forbidden City of Běijīng.

Tài Shān Most revered of the five sacred Taoist mountains of China, this mountain in Shāndōng is shrouded in mystique and legend – imperial sacrifices were offered from its summit and upon climbing its heights it's easy to understand why.

Sōng Shān Considered the central peak of the five sacred Taoist mountains, Sōng Shān is also home to the legendary monastic order of Shàolín, whose monks are world famous for their martial arts skills.

Éméi Shān The original temple structures on this mountain in Sìchuān date back as far as the coming of Buddhism to China. The two-day Éméi Shān hike offers beautiful views and spectacular sunsets.

Huáng Shān This mountain in Ānhuī is probably the country's most famous landscape attraction. With its gnarled pines, craggy rocks and a rolling sea of clouds, it's evocative of a Chinese ink painting.

Pǔtuóshān This charming island in Zhèjiāng is also a sacred Buddhist mountain and home to the Goddess of Mercy, Guanyin. It's blessed with ancient temples, pleasant beaches, rolling hills, arched bridges and narrow alleys. The island has no cars so is perfect for exploring on foot.

Héng Shān Kings and emperors once hunted and made sacrifices to heaven and earth at this holy Taoist peak in Húnán. Today, Buddhists and Taoists live here, and there is a smattering of temples amid the picturesque serenity.

HISTORIC ARCHITECTURE

Dynasties have risen and fallen for millenia in China. The spectacular palaces and ruins that remain give an insight into the opulence of China's past.

The Forbidden City This Běijīng palace of Ming and Qing emperors was off-limits to ordinary Chinese citizens for 500 years. What remains is the largest and the best-preserved cluster of ancient buildings in China.

The Summer Palace Most of the buildings of this Běijīng palace date from the late Qing period. Much of the area is lake and parkland, once a royal garden.

Imperial Summer Villa In Chéngdé, Héběi, this imperial retreat is distinguished by an impressive range of regal architecture and Tibetan-flavoured temples. Outside the walls of the imperial gardens are Wàibā Miào, the Eight Outer Temples.

Potala Palace Dominating the skyline of Lhasa in Tibet, this dazzling palace was once the centre of the Tibetan government and the winter residence of the Dalai Lama. The Potala is one of the architectural wonders of the world, standing 13 storeys tall.

The Bund China's most famous street faces Huángpǔ Jiāng in Shànghǎi. An assortment of buildings in neoclassical 1930s styles line the Bund, the European architeture providing a nostalgic echo of a bygone era.

French Concession Shànghǎi's former French Concession turns up some delightful architectural surprises, from Art Deco apartment complexes to neo-classical mansions and villas with quaint balconies and doorways.

Shāmiàn Dǎo Guǎngzhōu, Guǎngdōng, home to China's earliest foreign concession, has an unexpectedly peaceful enclave of European buildings on this island. The colonial buildings, in varying states of decay and shining renovation, make it a great place to wander around.

Gǔlàng Yǔ This car-free, small and hilly island in Xiàmén, Fújiàn is a unique preserve of Mediterranean flavours, charming architecture and peaceful walks.

Tiānjīn In 1858 Tiānjīn became a treaty port for the British. French, Germans, Italians, Belgians and Japanese followed resulting in a remarkable potpourri of architectural styles.

NATIONAL PARKS
China has an incredibly diverse range of natural escapes scattered across the country. The national parks offer a wonderful variety of landscapes and a rich diversity of flora and fauna.

Chángbái Shān This is China's largest nature reserve, covering 210,000 hectares of dense, virgin forest in Jílín. This area is home to a wide variety of animal and plant life. The prime scenic spot is Heaven Pool, a huge volcanic crater lake at the summit of the mountain.

Dīnghú Shān This mountain range in Guǎngdōng offers a myriad of walks amongst dense forest, pools, springs, ponds, temples, nunneries and charming scenery.

Hānàsī Hú Mountains, forests and diverse wildlife surround this alpine lagoon at Xīnjiāng's northernmost tip. The area is inhabited by semi-nomadic Kazakhs and Mongolians and there are plenty of hiking opportunities.

CRAIG PERSHOUSE

A Tibetan stupa is dwarfed by the imposing Potala Palace.

CHRIS MELLOR

Colonial buildings illuminated along the Bund in Shànghǎi at night.

CHRIS MELLOR

Shànghǎi's former French Concession is littered with street cafes.

The glorious alpine scenery of Jiǔzhàigōu in Sìchuān.

Aerial view of Yángshuò with spectacular limestone peaks behind.

The slate rooftops of Lìjiāng Old Town, in Yúnnán.

Jiǔzhàigōu This spectacular nature reserve in Sìchuān is scattered with high alpine peaks, hundreds of clear lakes and lush forests. Jiǔzhàigōu was first settled by ethnic Tibetans and their traditions can still be seen in the shrines, prayer wheels and prayer flags that decorate the region.

Mèngdá Nature Reserve The beautiful and relatively little-visited Heavenly Lake is on the upper reaches of Huáng Hé in Qīnghǎi. The lake is sacred to the local Tibetans and Sala Muslims, and is set in a lush valley of verdant alpine forest.

Sānchàhé Nature Reserve In Xīshuāngbǎnnà, Yúnnán, the dense jungle and rainforest here is home to many endemic species of tropical flora and fauna, including the banyan and umbrella trees, wild tigers, leopards, elephants and golden-haired monkeys.

Zhālóng Nature Reserve This enormous wetlands and bird-watching area in Hēilóngjiāng is the protected breeding area of the red-crowned crane. Some 236 different species of bird are found in the reserve, including storks, swans, geese, ducks, herons, harriers, grebes and egrets.

Wǔlíngyuán (Zhāngjiājiè) Scenic Area This nature reserve in Húnán encompasses dramatic, splintering karst mountain scenery rising from subtropical rainforest. It is home to three minority peoples – the Tujia, Miao and Bai – who maintain their traditional cultures.

GETAWAYS

Tired of big cities and touring the sights? Why not get away for a few days? China has a number of retreats perfect for putting your feet up.

Yángshuò This village is set amid the famous karst scenery of Guìlín in Guǎngxī. The surrounding countryside can be explored by bicycle and there are also river trips along Lí Jiāng, buzzing rural markets and imposing caves to explore.

Lìjiāng Home to the Naxi minority in Yúnnán, Lìjiāng's exotic old town has survived over two centuries and is a picturesque maze of cobbled streets, exquisite old wooden buildings, gushing canals and lively markets.

Xīshuāngbǎnnà On the border with Laos and Myanmar, Xīshuāngbǎnnà is a region of lush rainforest and subtropical weather, and is home to many of Yúnnán's ethnic groups. It's easy to get away from the crowds here and explore the surrounding countryside and villages.

Wives for Sale

In rural China, the sale of wives and children is again part of the rural economy.

Outlawed by Mao and effectively suppressed after 1949, the trafficking of women reappeared in China with Deng Xiaoping's market reforms of the late 1970s. Accurate figures are difficult to obtain, but according to officials 110,000 women and 13,000 children were freed during one crackdown in 2000. Chinese sources further admit that this number probably represents only a small percentage of actual cases. Abductions of women have been increasing by 30% every year, with an annual 15% increase in the abduction of children (largely boys).

Unicef is so concerned that it has set up awareness projects in south-western Yúnnán, one of the worst affected areas.

The demand for wives in rural areas has mushroomed as many women leave poor villages in search of work in nearby cities. The one-child policy and traditional preference for baby boys has led to high rates of selective abortions and infanticide, which has imbalanced the ratio of women to men. In the countryside, a region where it is economically imperative that men find wives and hopefully heirs, there are approximately 130 males for every 100 females. Simple mathematics calculates that brides are bought to make up the shortfall. The trade furthermore exploits women's low social position; in rural China, they grow up with little schooling and have little confidence.

Girls, often under the age of 20 or maybe not even in their teens, are either lured by traffickers with promises of work or abducted at knife-point. Many are drugged, raped and resold a number of times. The increasing number of women escaping (or attempting to) has led to the practice of cutting the tendons in the women's feet and ankles to stop them from running away. The women and children are then sold for between US$450 and US$550 to rural communities. Family members and neighbours often support the buyers by guarding the newly acquired 'wife'. Others are sold to factories for cheap labour or forced into prostitution. It is suspected that shame prevents many of the women from reporting what has happened to them, though in some cases local authorities are in cahoots with the smugglers.

Strong efforts are being made in China to stamp out the practice (in January 2001 eight men were executed for trafficking a total of 140 women) but the roots of the problem lie deep in social policies, economic disparities and traditional attitudes, and that requires profound change.

EDUCATION

China marshals an army of some 14 million teachers in its colossal education drive. On top of trained teachers (guóbān), China also employs around 3 million untrained teachers (mínbān) to educate the nation's 230 plus million schoolchildren.

The Republican period of the 1920s and 1930s sought to modernise education, but the civil war and Japanese invasion thwarted progress. The ensuing Mao era can be blamed for the wholesale deterioration of China's educational system.

Schooling in China still hasn't recovered from the beating it took during the Cultural Revolution, when teachers the land over were beaten and killed, many being replaced with untrained peasants. Education became geared to the great proletarian experiment, becoming a tool of indoctrination.

The Confucian respect afforded to teachers before Mao's anti-intellectualism has been largely restored, but schools are still hugely under-funded and teachers are paid little. An explosion at a local school in Jiāngxī province in March 2001 killed 42 teachers and children. The government blamed a rogue bomber, but local parents accused the school of using the children to manufacture fireworks for the hard-up school.

Rote learning and an absence of open debate on certain issues in the classroom make for an inadequate educational model, a situation that is not helped by a poor record on per capita education spending.

Some academics argue that the difficulties of learning the Chinese script create a huge drag on the educational system. Learning characters certainly takes more time than learning an alphabet, but the issue is probably more one of funding and the quality of teaching; Taiwan and Hong Kong wrestle with an even more complicated script, but manage to educate their citizens.

China records an official literacy rate of 80%, which is above average for a third world country, but still far short of developed country standards. Many minority people cannot read Chinese characters, but may be literate in their own native scripts.

Until very recently, all education right through to university level was 100% state-funded. In return, university graduates had to accept whatever job the state wished to assign them. However, the 1990s saw a new experiment hatching – students could pay their own way through school and were then free to take a job of their own choosing. Of course, most Chinese cannot afford this, but well-connected families have few problems.

China's equivalent of the Boy Scouts is the Red Pioneers, a Communist league for tots.

ARTS

With such a long, unbroken history and culture, China has made one of the greatest artistic contributions to mankind. Sadly, much of China's ancient art treasures have been destroyed in times of civil war or dispersed by invasion or natural calamity. Whatever sidestepped it all to the 20th century walked into the Cultural Revolution and finally called it a day. Many of China's remaining great paintings, ceramics, jade and other works of art were rescued by exile beyond the mainland – in Taiwan, Singapore, Hong Kong and beyond.

The West has also been guilty of ransacking China's heritage, making off with religious art and scriptures from such grottoes as Dūnhuáng (the British Museum has a huge stash). While morally indefensible, some argue that such artwork was fortuitously saved from the Cultural Revolution.

Fortunately since the early 1970s a great deal of work has been done to restore what was destroyed in the Cultural Revolution.

Music

Musical instruments have been unearthed from tombs dating back to the Shang dynasty and Chinese folk songs can certainly be traced back at least this far. Despite their impression of scholastic introspection, Confucian students regularly lent an ear to music. Two books of the Confucian canon, the *Book of Songs (Shījīng)* and the *Book of Rites (Lǐjì)* both dwell on music, the first actually being a collection of songs and

poems, formerly set to music. The large sets of bells often seen in Confucian temples were each rung to maintain their note with that of the *dao*, or 'way'. A concordant pitch would signify all was on an even-keel between Heaven and Earth.

The traditional Chinese music scale differs from its Western equivalent. Traditional Chinese musical instruments include the two-stringed fiddle (*èrhú*), four-stringed banjo (*yuèqín*), two-stringed viola (*húqín*), vertical flute (*dòngxiāo*), horizontal flute (*dízi*), piccolo (*bāngdí*), four-stringed lute (*pípa*), zither (*gǔzhēng*) and ceremonial trumpet (*suǒnà*).

China's ethnic minorities have preserved their own folk song traditions; a trip to Lìjiāng in Yúnnán gives you the chance to appreciate the ancient sounds of the local Naxi orchestra.

Popular Music

The energetic Hong Kong song industry straddles China like a glittering colossus, its twinkle-eyed and pretty emissaries (Aaron Kwok, Faye Wong, Andy Lau, Kelly Chen, Jackie Cheung et al) warbling their catchy, saccharine melodies. Farther north their harmless songs of love and loss impact with the Běijīng rock-face of Cui Jian, bands hacking away at the edifice of rock and metal (Tang dynasty) and punk (Underground Baby, Brain Failure).

China has a thriving music industry, but has been sluggish at developing a market for Western music – largely due to limited airings of tame Western songs on the radio. Generations of Chinese are still convinced that Western music *is* The Carpenters, Richard Clayderman, Kenny G and Lionel Richie – a quite appalling misrepresentation. This is mercifully changing with satellite TV and the popularity of MTV and Channel V.

Literature

China has a rich literary tradition. Unfortunately – barring many years of intensive study – much of it is inaccessible to Western readers. Many of the most important Chinese classics are available in translation, but much of the Chinese literary heritage (particularly its poetry) is untranslatable, although scholars persevere.

The essential point when discussing Chinese literature is that prior to the 20th century there were two literary traditions: the classical and the vernacular. The classical tradition was the Chinese equivalent of a literary canon. The classical canon, largely Confucian in nature, consisted of a core of texts written in ancient Chinese that had to be mastered thoroughly by all aspirants to the Chinese civil service, and was the backbone of the Chinese education system – it was nearly indecipherable to the masses. The *Book of Songs (Shjīng)* is a typical example, supposedly compiled by Confucius. The *I Ching (Yìjīng)*, or *Book of Changes*, is used to predict the future, but is regarded by the Chinese (and New Agers) as an ancient source of wisdom. Both books belong to the five Confucian classics (Wǔjīng).

The vernacular tradition arose in the Ming dynasty and consisted largely of prose epics written for entertainment. For Western readers it is the vernacular texts, precursors of the contemporary Chinese novel and short story, that are probably of more interest. Most of them are available in translation and provide a fascinating insight into life in China centuries past.

Perhaps the three most famous early 'novels' are: *The Water Margin (Shuǐhǔ Zhuàn)*, also translated as *Rebels of the Marsh*; *The Dream of the Red Chamber (Hónglóu Mèng)*, also translated as *The Dream of Red Mansions* and *The Story of the Stone*; and *Journey to the West (Xīyóu Jì)*.

Another classic is the *Plum in the Gold Vase (Jīn Píng Méi)*, a racy story about a wealthy Chinese man and his six wives, available in English. The *Art of War (Bīngfǎ)* by Sun Tzu (Sūnzǐ) was studied by Mao and is still required reading for modern military strategists (and many a middle manager) in the West.

By the early 19th century, Western novels had begun to appear in Chinese translations in increasing numbers. Chinese intellectuals began to look at their own literary traditions more critically, in particular the classical one, which was markedly different in form from the Chinese that was spoken by modern Chinese. Calls for a national literature based on vernacular Chinese rather than the stultifying classical language grew louder.

The first of the major Chinese writers to write in colloquial Chinese as understood by the masses was Lu Xun (1881–1936),

and for this reason he is regarded by many as the father of modern Chinese literature. Most of his works were short stories that looked critically at the Chinese inability to drag its nation into the 20th century. His first set of short stories was entitled *Call to Arms (Nàhǎn)* and included his most famous tale 'The True Story of Ah Q'. His second collection was entitled *Wandering*, and his last collection was called *Old Tales Retold*.

Lao She (1899–1966), another important early novelist, also produced an allegorical work in *Cat City*, but is famous most of all for *The Rickshaw Boy*, a book that has been translated many times into English. It is a social critique of the living conditions of rickshaw drivers in Běijīng. Lao She drowned himself in a Běijīng Lake in 1966, after a dose of Red Guard hounding.

Literary creativity in post-1949 China was greatly hampered by ideological controls. Mao's 'Yan'an Talks on Art & Literature' edict basically reduced literature to the status of a revolutionary tool, and writers were extolled to seek out ideal forms and to find the 'typical in the individual'. Works that did not show peasants triumphing over huge odds were considered not inspirational enough and condemned as bourgeois.

Increased creative freedom in the Chinese literary scene followed the Cultural Revolution, but it remains an area in which the government maintains careful vigilance. Most writers belong to state-sponsored literary guilds and many write on salary. Naturally they are careful not to bite the hand that feeds them.

Wang Meng was born in Běijīng in 1934 and his writings have touched on all sorts of sensitive topics including reform, elections, family, politics and technology. He was labelled a 'rightist' in 1957 because one of his short stories, 'The Young Newcomer in the Organisation Department', mildly criticised bureaucracy. In 1963 he was forced to move to a labour camp in rural Xīnjiāng where he spent the next 16 years. His 'rightist' label was officially removed in 1979 and he was allowed to pick up his pen again. He was given the prestigious job of Minister of Culture in 1986, but was forced to step down in the wake of the 1989 democracy protests in Tiānánmén Square. However, he was later appointed vice-chairman of the Chinese Writers' Association. Wang Meng has authored a number of excellent stories including *The Stubborn Porridge*, *A Winter's Topic*, *The Butterfly* and *Kitty*.

Ba Jin is the penname for Li Feigan, who was born in 1904, studied in Paris and became well known for his novels from the 1930s and 1940s. He was brutally persecuted during the Cultural Revolution, but managed to survive. His best-known works include *Family*, *Autumn*, *Spring*, *Garden of Repose* and *Bitter Cold Nights*.

Shen Congwen (1902–88) lived in Húnán and his fiction reflects the lifestyle in that region. More than 20 of his best stories have been gathered into the book *Imperfect Paradise*, published in English by the University of Hawaii Press.

One of the most interesting writers in contemporary China is Zhang Xianliang, whose book *Half of Man Is Woman* was extremely controversial for its sexual content. His book *Grass Soup* relates his experiences in a *láogǎi* (labour camp).

Wang Shuo is another writer whose work has been translated into English and adapted for film. He is popular with the younger generation. For the authorities, however, his stories about disaffected urban youth, gambling, prostitution and confidence tricksters are considered a bad influence.

Blood Red Dusk by Lao Gui is available in English by Panda (the Chinese publisher). It's a fascinatingly cynical account of the Cultural Revolution years.

Feng Jicai is a writer who has enjoyed great success in China with stories like *The Magic Ponytail* and *A Short Man & His Tall Wife*, which have a satirical magic realist touch to them. His often horrific account of the Cultural Revolution, *Voices from the Whirlwind*, is a collection of anonymous personal accounts of those turbulent years and has recently been published in English by Pantheon Books.

The 2000 Nobel Prize for Literature went to Gao Xingjian, a Chinese author exiled in Paris, for his book *Soul Mountain*. Instead of getting out the red carpet and trumpets, the Chinese government criticised the honour, for the author is persona non grata in Běijīng.

For a recap of some of the latest trends in Chinese literature, look out for a copy of *The Lost Boat: Avant Garde Fiction from China*, edited by Henry YH Zhao (Wellsweep Press, 1994). It has samples from what Zhao identifies as the three main strands in Chinese literature since 1986.

Bookshops Finding any of the above books in non-Chinese editions takes perseverance. The Foreign Languages Bookshops and Friendship Stores in Běijīng and Shànghǎi are the cheapest places to find foreign-language editions of Chinese literature. Some bookshops in Hong Kong also have excellent collections, although prices are higher than elsewhere in China. For information on the exact location of bookshops in China, see the relevant destination chapters in this book.

Taiwan is another good source, although you won't find much there from mainland China. Some made-in-China books are exported to Western countries and sold at vastly inflated prices. You can search in the various Chinatowns around the world, although mostly what you'll find are titles printed in Chinese.

The USA seems to have the most complete collections of English-language books about China, probably because of the large number of ethnic Chinese living there. Some of the US-based bookshops can be accessed online and will do mail orders to other countries.

If you're searching for Chinese literature, you can check out the following:

China
China National Publishing Industry Trading Corporation (☎ 10-6421 5031, 6421 5793, fax 6421 4540 journal subscriptions only) 504 Anhuali, Andingmenwai (PO Box 782), Běijīng, 100011, China

France
L'Harmattan (☎ 1 40 46 79 11, 🅦 www.editions-harmattan.fr) 16 rue des Écoles, in the Latin Quarter Le Tiers Mythe (☎ 1 43 26 72 70) 21 rue Cujas·

Taiwan
Eslite (☎ 02-2773 0095) 2nd floor, 245 Tunhua South Rd, Section 1 (near Jenai Rd), Taipei. This is Taiwan's largest bookshop.
Caves Books (☎ 02-2537 1666) 103 Chungshan North Rd, Section 2, Taipei

UK
Stanford's Bookshop (☎ 020-7836 1321, 🅦 www.standfords.co.uk) 12-14 Long Acre, London WC2E 9LP. It's one of the best shops of its kind in the UK.

USA
The Asia Society's Bookstore (☎ 212-288 6400)
725 Park Ave (at 70th St), New York City, NY
China Books & Periodicals Inc (☎ 415-282
2994, fax 282 0994, Ⓦ www.chinabooks.com)
2929 24th St, San Francisco, CA 94110

Ceramics

China has a well-deserved reputation for producing some of the world's finest ceramics. As many as 8000 years ago Chinese tribes were making artefacts with clay. The primitive Yangshao culture (which existed along Huáng Hé) is noted for its distinctive pottery painted with flowers, fish, animals, human faces and geometric designs. Around 3500 BC the Longshan culture (first found near the village of Lóngshān in Shāndōng) was making white pottery and eggshell-thin black pottery.

Pottery making was well advanced by the Shang period; the most important development occurred around the middle of the dynasty with the manufacture of a greenish glaze applied to stoneware artefacts. During the Han dynasty the custom of glazing pottery became fairly common. However, the production of terracotta items – made from a mixture of sand and clay, fired to produce a reddish-brown colour and left unglazed – continued.

During the Southern and Northern Song dynasties, a type of pottery halfway between Han glazed pottery and true porcelain was produced. The proto-porcelain was made by mixing clay with quartz and the mineral feldspar to make a hard, smooth-surfaced vessel. Feldspar was mixed with traces of iron to produce an olive-green glaze.

Chinese pottery reached its artistic peak under the Song rulers. During this time true porcelain was developed. It was made of fine kaolin clay and was white, thin and translucent. Porcelain was produced under the Yuan, but gradually lost the delicacy and near-perfection of the Song products. However, it was probably during the Yuan dynasty that 'blue-and-white' *qīnghū* porcelain made its first appearance. 'Blue-and-white' was further perfected in the Ming and Qing dynasties. Another noted invention was mono-coloured porcelain in ferrous red, black or dark blue. A new range of mono-coloured vessels was developed under the Qing.

During the Qing period the production of coloured porcelain continued with the addition of new colours and glazes and more complex decorations. This was the age of true painted porcelain, decorated with delicate landscapes, birds and flowers. Elaborate designs and brilliant colouring became the fashion. Porcelain imitations of other materials, such as gold and silver, mother of pearl, jade, bronze, wood and bamboo, also became popular.

Bronze Vessels

Bronze is an alloy whose chief elements are copper, tin and lead. Tradition ascribes the first casting of bronze to the legendary Xia dynasty of 5000 years ago.

Shang dynasty bronzes are marvellous specimens, often fabulously patterned with *tāotiè*, a type of fierce animal design. Zhou dynasty bronze vessels tend to have long messages in ideographic characters; they describe wars, rewards, ceremonial events and the appointment of officials.

Bronze mirrors were used as early as the Shang dynasty and had already developed into an artistic form by the Warring States period. Ceramics gradually replaced bronze utensils by Han times, but bronze mirrors were not displaced by glass mirrors until the Qing dynasty. The backs of bronze mirrors were inscribed with wishes for good fortune and protection from evil influence.

Jade

The jade stone has been revered in China since Neolithic times. Jade *(yù)* was firstly utilised for tools because of its hardness and strength, but later appeared on ornaments and ceremonial vessels for its decorative value. During the Qin and Han dynasties, it was believed that jade was empowered with magical and life-giving properties, and the dead were buried with jadeware. Opulent jade suits, meant to prevent decomposition, have been found in Han tombs, whilst Taoist alchemists, striving for immortality, ate elixirs of powdered jade. Jade was also considered a guardian against disease and evil spirits, and even now pillowcases can be purchased in Chinese department stores with jade squares attached to ward off disease. You occasionally see old Chinese men wearing jade bracelets.

Jade's value lies not just in its scarcity, but depends also on its colour, hardness and the skill with which it has been carved. While the pure white form is the most highly valued, the stone varies in translucency and colour, including many shades of green, brown and black. China's most famous jade comes from Hotan in Xīnjiāng province; much of what is sold in Hong Kong is fake.

Funerary Objects

As early as Neolithic times (9000–6000 BC), offerings of pottery vessels and stone tools or weapons were placed in graves to accompany the departed.

During the Shang dynasty, precious objects such as bronze ritual vessels, weapons and jade were buried with the dead. Dogs, horses and even human beings were sacrificed for burial in the tombs of great rulers, later replaced by replicas (usually in pottery).

Earthenware burial objects were very popular from the 1st to the 8th centuries AD. During the Han dynasty, pottery figures, including attendants, entertainers, musicians, acrobats and so forth were cast in moulds and painted in bright colours after firing.

Close trade links with the west were illustrated among these models by the appearance among funerary objects of the two-humped Bactrian camel, which carried merchandise along the Silk Road.

The cosmopolitan life of Tang China was illustrated by its funerary wares; western and central Asians flocked to the capital at Chāng'ān and were portrayed in figurines of merchants, attendants, warriors, grooms, musicians and dancers.

Guardian spirits are some of the strangest funerary objects. A common one has bird wings, elephant ears, a human face, the body of a lion and the legs and hooves of a deer or horse, all rolled into one.

Architecture

China's architectural history, paralleling that of the Chinese empire and stretching back more than 3000 years, is one of the longest of any civilisation. Despite their long history, however, building forms have remained surprisingly static. The practice of reusing past techniques means that traditionalism has long been a dominant feature of Chinese architecture. Within this traditionalism is however a huge variety of styles, from Běijīng's imperial structures, to Shànghǎi's colonial elegance, to temple architecture, and to modern building forms now seen across China.

Certain basic principles have long been respected, from the lowliest village homestead to the grandest imperial palace. The use of symmetry and axes, and building orientation towards the south, are classic architectural ideas still practiced today. In plan, the basic layout for many building types consists of a walled compound, housing one or more structures. Many different materials and finishes can be seen throughout Chinese architecture – wood, rammed earth, masonry, stone, thatch, tiles, plaster, paint – whose use depended on function, cost, availability and aesthetics.

History Few structures survive from before the 8th century AD. Many early buildings were constructed in wood, which has long since disappeared, with more durable buildings often destroyed by war. Much of what is known has been gathered from references to building in literature, song, and artwork.

Until Qinshi Huangdi became first emperor around 220 BC and unified China under a centralised system, there was no such thing as a Chinese national architecture. Under Qinshi Huangdi's rule large and impressively decorated structures were built, fusing regional architecture into a single imperial style as a sign of national greatness. This period was one of great building accomplishment, including the beginnings of what would later become the Great Wall. This emphasis on monumental building as a symbol of wealth and power continued during the Han dynasty (AD 206–20), not always to the liking of the poor, who still lived under thatch.

After the Han's collapse, a period of decentralisation followed. By the 5th century AD Buddhism had made deep inroads into China, bringing with it foreign decorative influences that can still be seen at Lóngmén and Yúngāng grottoes.

The Sui dynasty (AD 581–618) once again united China at a time when architects were afforded one of the highest civic standings. This era was characterised by expansion and rebuilding, including the restoration of some parts of the Great Wall and the beginnings of the Grand Canal.

Fengshui

Fengshui *(fēngshuǐ)*, literally meaning 'wind and water', is a collection of ancient geomantic principles that sees bodies of water and landforms directing the flow of universal *qi* (vital energy or cosmic currents). With the help of a fengshui master, this qi can be successfully courted to maximise a person's wealth, happiness, longevity and procreation, however, at the same time, a negative flow of qi may invite disaster.

One reason for fengshui's success may be that wealth *(cái)*, happiness *(fú)*, long life *(shòu)* and healthy offspring *(zǐ)* are its four major concerns, paralleling the concerns of the Chinese people.

Pagodas, temples, tombs, houses and even whole cities and villages have been located and built so as to harmonise with the surrounding landscape. Even households will try to maximise their advantage by placing the family's house, tomb, business or furniture in appropriate locations so as to optimise their qi harvest. The positioning of such structures will determine the lasting wellbeing of the inhabitants, with good placement resulting in good fortune.

Fengshui cosmology has been used to select the most auspicious site of cities as far back as the 3rd or 4th century. Yet, fengshui as a tradition has been constantly attacked throughout Chinese history – by imperialists, Nationalists and Communists alike. Despite this century's aggression, it has survived and prospered among the people. While Chinese geomancy is inherently conservative, especially in architecture, peasants have often blamed the state for disturbing the natural balance of fengshui. During the early stages of European and Japanese expansion into China, many Chinese were incensed at the disturbing effects of train line construction and over-shadowing churches on the happy balance of seemingly hidden powers in the surrounding geography. The Chinese called for the removal of the offending steeples and the redirecting of train lines so as to be more in harmony with the local fengshui.

Fengshui has its origins on the mainland of China, but during the last century it has been more closely associated with Singapore, Hong Kong, Taiwan and the overseas Chinese communities. This is mainly due to the way the Communist regime has exploited fengshui as a means of securing power for some, while damaging the fengshui of others. During the Cultural Revolution the authorities classified fengshui as illegal and yet at the same time used it to punish those of a 'bad-class' background, by destroying their ancestors' tombs and bones to truncate the family lines.

A fengshui master or geomancer is normally trained by his father and passes his skills down through the generations. When inspecting a prospective site, the master refers to his compass *(luópán)* and calendar *(nónglì)* and after an inspection of the surrounding landscape and location of the Green Dragon and White Tiger, in the east and west respectively, decides upon the best location. Dates, such as the owner's birthday, are included in the analysis to determine the starting date for construction.

This is a simplistic summary of a trade that draws more on intuition and practical experience than manuals. However, if a geomancer possesses a fengshui manual or calendar then he has an advantage over others who rely purely on oral and practical training.

The geomancer is also often called upon to help determine appropriate marriage and funeral dates, as well as to write 'prayers' to protect and bring good fortune upon a household.

During the past two decades, rural China has seen a building boom that has not only increased the demand for optimal qi sites, but also increased possible disturbances to the fengshui of the neighbours. Fengshui masters are called upon for further duties, for example on how to realign the fengshui of households that have been afflicted by premature death, sickness, poor business performance and even mental disease.

So what do you do if you require the services of a fengshui master? The current situation in mainland China is a lot more tolerant of geomancers and a cash payment would be generally appreciated for services rendered, but don't bargain too hard as it may disturb the fragile qi.

It is from the successive Tang (AD 618–907) and Song dynasties (AD 960–1279) that the first surviving structures appear, many of these square-plan pagodas. The use of colour, both as a decorative and protective element, became more detailed during these dynasties. The Song were overrun by the Mongols of the late 13th century, who contributed little of their own culture to architecture, instead choosing to imitate and rebuild the style of the Chinese.

Běijīng was the long-standing capital during the Ming and Qing dynasties (1368–1911). The Forbidden City, on which construction began in 1406, showcases the architecture of the time. It is also one of the few palaces of any dynasty to survive in relatively intact form. In it we can see the epitome of the traditional Chinese architectural ideas of monumentality and symmetry, with strong use of colour and decoration. The Qing dynasty Manchus largely followed the Chinese architectural style but also left their mark. The coming of the West in the 18th century was to hasten the demise of the last of the dynasties, and led to the entering of a new architectural influence and a profound change in building design and construction.

Western Influence & Modern Architecture

China had early contact with foreign traders along the Silk Road, but it was not until the establishment of Western trading headquarters and banks in the late 18th century that a colonial influence in architecture made its presence felt. The Portuguese, Germans, British, Dutch, Spanish and Russians, among others, established communities and constructed buildings using foreign architects and Chinese craftsmen. These buildings from the late 18th and 19th centuries were often in the Classical Revival style, originally constructed in brick and timber, and later, in steel and concrete.

There are many examples of such architecture from this time (mostly banks, large-scale residences, offices and churches) in Chinese cities such as Shànghǎi, Macau, Guǎngzhōu, Tiānjīn, Hāěrbīn and Qīngdǎo. Although traditional-style Chinese architecture was still retained by the Qing government for use in state and religious buildings and the courtyard house still dominated domestically, Western architecture combined with Chinese decoration began to be used by the Qing for more functional buildings.

It was not until the 20th century, however, that Chinese architects designed Western-style buildings themselves, at first using the Classical Revival style. The first overseas-trained Chinese architects returned to China in the 1920s, bringing with them new ideas. Foreign styles such as the International Style, characterised by sleek, clean lines, flat roofs, and materials such as steel and glass, had appeared in Shànghǎi by the 1940s. There was for some time a push to revive the traditional Chinese style, but this proved uneconomical and was eventually abandoned.

The 1990s especially saw China drawing up an increasingly ambitious building agenda. The Pudong New Area in Shànghǎi is an exciting and brave landscape of high-rises, but it has little to do with Chinese architectural aesthetics. The Western-inspired designs range from the crude Oriental Pearl Tower, to the inspiring Jinmao Building and the extremist stop-start building project of the World Finance Building (all in Shànghǎi). The latter colossus is not due to be completed for many years, if at all (arguments with the Japanese construction group who designed the building included bickering over the design; a huge circular hole at the top of the structure was deemed to resemble the Japanese flag).

High altitude, which was never an objective in traditional Chinese buildings, has become a major design concern in modern Chinese architecture.

Religious Architecture

Places of prayer for Buddhist, Taoist or Confucian worshippers, temples tend to follow a strict schematic pattern, depending on the faith. China is also home to a large number of mosques and churches, testimony to the successful infiltration of such missionary creeds.

Irrespective of faith, all Buddhist, Taoist and Confucian temples are built on a north-south axis, with the main door of each hall facing south. Běijīng's hútòng courtyards were traditionally also constructed on this axis.

A fengshui expert would have been consulted to optimise the exact location of the temple, often positioning them on mountain or hillsides or in forests, places blessed with good fengshui.

Fengshui is also built in to the architectural fabric of temples with the five elements (water, metal, earth, fire and wood) all manifested in the temple in some form. Colours are also significant fengshui symbols: bright red is common and denotes fortune and also fire in the five element theory.

Other commonly used colours are green, yellow and gold, each of which identifies one of the five elements.

The temple may be protected at the front by a spirit screen, designed to deflect bad spirits. Further lines of defence are the door gods and the presence of water (a moat, pool or canal) over which bad spirits cannot traverse.

The Buddhist temple entrance usually gives way to a courtyard with the drum and bell towers to the east and west, often flaming braziers and then a series of halls. The largest hall is generally called the Great Treasure Hall, and typically contains a trinity of Buddhist statues, with a statue of Guanyin facing north at the rear. The eighteen Luohan (Arhats) are often found here, and in other temples they appear in a multitude of 500, housed in a separate hall.

Pagodas are common features of Buddhist temples, built to house Sanskrit sutras, religious artefacts and documents or to store the ashes of the deceased. A number of pagodas stand alone in China, their adjacent temples gone.

Around the 4th century, the construction of Buddhist cave temples began. The caves at Lóngmén near Luòyáng, at Mògāo near Dūnhuáng and at Yúngāng near Dàtóng, are some of the finest examples.

In Taoist temples the main hall is usually called the Hall of the Three Clear Ones, and Taoist motifs are common, such as the circular *bāguà* (eight trigrams) formation, represented in eight-sided pavilions and halls. The *yīn/yáng* diagram is often also present, as are statues of Laotzu and the Yellow Emperor.

Confucius temples are not nearly as active or as colourful as their Taoist or Buddhist cousins, and often have a faded and musty feel. Their courtyards are a forest of steles celebrating local scholars, some supported on the backs of *bìxì* (mythical tortoise-like animals).

A statue of Confucius usually resides in the main hall, overseeing rows of musical instruments and disciples on either side of him. Cypresses are commonly planted in the grounds of Confucian temples.

French and Jesuit missionaries introduced Christian religious architecture to China around the 18th century. Many of the resulting churches utilised the European styles of the Baroque and Gothic, while others blended a Western structure with traditional Chinese decorative styles. Islamic architecture may also be found across China, most of it dating after the 14th century and influenced by Central Asian styles, and again, often combined with local Chinese style.

Gardens

When talking of traditional Chinese gardens we are referring to the combined achievements of garden builders over more than a millennium. As with traditional Chinese architecture, garden design has developed along a relatively consistent theme in the search for perfection. Since the very early days Chinese gardens have been steeped with symbols and meaning, feeding from the rich culture and philosophies of Taoism and Buddhism. Rather than lawn and flowers, they revolve around the more intellectually stimulating *yin* and *yang* of water and stone. Chinese gardens attempt to distill the natural world into the essence of nature. Carefully placed stones, with adequate contemplation, become mountain ranges. To facilitate this illusion, some gardens contain formations that mimic well-known mountains or paintings. Individual stones are also admired for their sculptural form, displayed prominently as works of art created by the forces of nature.

Clear parallels can be drawn between this philosophy in gardening and those in other traditional Chinese arts, such as calligraphy and painting. Minimal but well-planned gestures signify more complex realities. It's no surprise then to see calligraphy, evocative poetic names, references to literary classics and other complementary art forms featured in many Chinese gardens.

Although many are park-like in scale, historically Chinese gardens were nothing like the public parks of today. They were compounds to which only a tiny portion of the population ever had access. The larger and grander of these were imperial, existing to please and entertain the emperor. In prosperous regions, private gardens also proliferated in certain periods. At it's peak Sūzhōu had hundreds of gardens (the city was registered as a Unesco world cultural heritage site in 1997 in recognition of those that remain). The numerous pavilions dotted around the gardens were used for everything from meditating and playing chess to musical performances and banqueting.

Traditional garden styles are still dominant in China. Keeping in tune with Communist ideologies, many historic private and imperial gardens and parks are now open to the public and are well used for everything from badminton and board games to impromptu musical performances. Outside China, an increased interest in Eastern thought and philosophy in recent years has contributed to an international following for traditional Chinese gardens, and subsequently many imitations around the world.

Film

China's 'First Generation' filmmakers emerged in the period between the 1920s and the 1940s. Independently creative films languished in the doldrums after 1949 as cinema increasingly revolved around propagandist story lines. Heroic tales of the revolutionary struggle (gémìng piàn) made filmmaking into a kind of Communist comic strip of beatific peasants and peerless harvests. The Cultural Revolution added its own extremist vision to this surreal cinematography.

The major turning point took place with the graduation of the first intake of students since the end of the Cultural Revolution from the Beijing Film Academy in 1982. This group of adventurous directors, the best known being Zhang Yimou, Chen Kaige, Wu Ziniu and Tian Zhuangzhuang, became known collectively as the 'Fifth Generation'. Signature pieces of this generation are colourful, often luxuriant, historical dramas and tragedies.

Classic films of this generation include Farewell My Concubine (1993), Yellow Earth (1984) by Chen Kaige and Red Sorghum (1987), The One & the Eight (1984), The Story of Qiu Ju (1991), The Old Well (1987), To Live (1994), Ju Dou (1990), Raise the Red Lantern (1991) and Shanghai Triad (1995) by Zhang Yimou. Shāndōng star Gong Li has appeared in most of Zhang's films and was, for a long time his girlfriend.

Tian Zhuangzhuang directed The Blue Kite (1993), a Cultural Revolution tragedy that is banned in China. Huang Jianxin directed Stand Up, Don't Bend Over and The Black Cannon Incident (Hēipào Shìjiàn; 1986). The latter is without a doubt the sharpest satire released by any of the Fifth Generation directors.

The new directors of the 1990s were dubbed the 'Sixth Generation' and include He Jianjun, Jiang Wen, Ning Ying, Wu Wenguang and Zhang Yuan. Their films are far grittier, more urban observations than their Fifth Generation precursors and have not found much of an audience in the West.

Both Fifth- and Sixth-Generation directors have constantly run into problems with the authorities, and the most controversial works get clipped by censors or banned outright. The government has even retaliated against 'troublesome' directors by denying them film to work with, or revoking their passports so they cannot attend foreign film festivals.

Other notable films include: Swan Song, the tragic story of a Cantonese opera composer who dies neglected after his best work is stolen and made famous by a music student; The Horse Thief, a haunting story set in Tibet; and The Women from the Lake of Scented Souls, which portrays the unhappiness of a woman who runs a sesame-oil mill.

Taiwan director Ang Lee's Oscar-winning epic tale Crouching Tiger, Hidden Dragon (2000) caused quite a stir among Western audiences. The Chinese, a public with loftier expectations of cinematic kung fu and death-defying stunts, panned it. Northern Chinese viewers squirmed in their seats at fellow southerners Chow Yun-fat's and Michelle Yeoh's spoken Mandarin. The Western taste was enticed by the film's combination of epic story telling and novel fighting moves but Chinese suspicions were that Ang Lee had shrewdly milked the Western market.

Hong Kong cinema has always been uniquely Chinese – a ramshackle, violent, slapstick, chaotic, vivid and superstitious world. Money, vendettas, ghosts, gambling and romance are endlessly recycled themes. John Woo's gun-toting films are probably the most celebrated of the action films (dòngzuòpiān). The master of slow motion and ultra-violence (Hard Boiled; City On Fire) has been seduced by Hollywood and now works on gargantuan budget spectaculars (Face/Off; Mission Impossible 2). For more information on the Hong Kong film industry, see the boxed text 'From Kung Fu to Cannes' in the Hong Kong chapter.

Theatre

Chinese theatre generally means Chinese opera, the most famous of which is Beijing opera. Opera, with a continuous history of some 900 years, evolved from a convergence of comic and balladic traditions in the Northern Song period. From this beginning, Chinese opera has been the meeting ground for a disparate range of forms: acrobatics, martial arts, poetic arias and stylised dance.

Operas were usually performed by travelling troupes whose social status was very low in traditional Chinese society. In fact, their status was on a par with prostitutes and slaves and their children barred from social advancement by a government decree that made them ineligible to participate in public-service examinations. Chinese law also forbade mixed-sex performances, forcing actors to act out roles of the opposite sex. Opera troupes were frequently associated with homosexuality in the public imagination, contributing further to their 'untouchable' social status.

Despite this, opera remained a popular form of entertainment, although it was considered unworthy of the attention of the scholar class. Performances were considered an obligatory adjunct to Spring Festival celebrations and marriages, and sometimes to funerals and ancestral ceremonies.

Opera performances usually take place on a bare stage, with the actors taking on stylised roles that are instantly recognisable to the audience. The four major roles are the female role, the male role, the 'painted-face' role (for gods and warriors) and the clown.

Spoken drama grew in popularity in the 20th century and is now watched by the young in China in preference to opera. China's most famous modern playwright is probably Cao Yu, author of the tragic *Thunderstorm (Léiyǔ)*, in which a family courts self-destruction, and *Sunrise (Rìchū)*. After 1949, Cao Yu increasingly found his hands tied by political expectations, and manufactured bland drama such as *Bright Skies*.

Calligraphy

Calligraphy has been traditionally regarded in China as the highest form of artistic expression. The basic tools, commonly referred to as 'the four treasures of the scholar's study', are paper, ink, ink-stone (on which the ink is mixed) and brush. These materials, which are shared by Chinese painters, reflect the close relationship between Chinese painting and calligraphy.

Written Chinese is not an alphabetic language but consists rather of characters. Countless calligraphic styles have developed over the years, resulting in a rich variety of graphic forms. Earlier styles of calligraphy, such as the *zhuàn* or Seal Script dating from the Western Zhou dynasty, lean towards a squarer, more formal style. A more flowing, cursive style of calligraphy was later developed to counter the need for a quicker writing style. The later styles of calligraphy, the *kǎishū* (regular script), *xíngshū* (running hand), and *cǎoshū* (grass hand), are sometimes evocatively compared to a person standing, walking and running. Grass hand sees the brush threading the characters together at speed, each pictograph reduced to a squiggle; it is extremely hard to read, and often indecipherable even for Chinese.

Calligraphy is still an extremely popular pastime in China and a major area of study. It can be seen all over China – on documents, artworks, in temples, adorning the walls of caves, and on the sides of mountains and monuments.

Painting

Chinese painting is the art of brush and ink applied onto *xuān* (paper), or silk. The basic tools are those of calligraphy, which has influenced painting in both its style and theory. A painting, like calligraphy, may be achieved in a very short time, but only following much thought and a total conception of the piece in the artist's mind beforehand. The brush line, which varies in thickness and tone, is the important feature of a Chinese painting, along with calligraphy itself, which is usually incorporated in the form of an inscription or poem along with the artist's seal. Shading is regarded as a foreign technique (introduced to China via Buddhist art from central Asia between the 3rd and 6th centuries) and colour plays only a minor symbolic and decorative role.

From the Han dynasty until the end of the Tang dynasty, the human figure occupied the dominant position in Chinese painting, as it did in pre-modern European art. Figure painting flourished against a Confucian background, illustrating moral themes. The practice of seeking places of natural beauty and communing with nature first became popular among Taoist poets and painters, and landscape painting for its own sake started in the 4th and 5th centuries. By the 9th century the interest of artists began to shift away from figures and the separate genre of flower-and-bird painting developed, with a subject matter covering a large range of animals, birds, flowers and fruit. From the 11th century onwards, landscape was to dominate Chinese painting. Later, a group of painters known as the Individualists exerted influence towards the end of the Ming dynasty with unusual compositions and brushwork that diverged from traditional techniques, however it was not until the 20th century that there was any real departure from native traditions.

When the Communists came to power, much of the country's artistic talent was turned to glorifying the revolution and bombarding the masses with political slogans. Colourful billboards of Mao waving to cheering crowds holding up the little red book were popular, as were giant Mao statues standing above smaller statues of enthusiastic workers and soldiers. Since the late 1970s, the Chinese art scene has gradually recovered. The work of traditionally influenced painters can be seen for sale in shops and galleries all over China, while in the major cities a flourishing avant-garde scene has emerged. The work of Chinese painters has been arguably more innovative and dissident than that of writers, possibly because the political implications are harder to interpret by the authorities. Art collecting has become a fashionable hobby among China's new rich, and many of China's young artists have exhibited work overseas to critical acclaim.

SOCIETY & CONDUCT
Traditional Culture

Chinese culture literally took a beating during the Cultural Revolution – the country has yet to recover completely. It should be noted that there is a cultural gap between Hong Kong and Macau and the rest of China. Hong Kong and Macau, while outwardly more modern, are also more traditionally Chinese because the Cultural Revolution didn't have such an effect there.

Some of the more notable aspects of traditional Chinese culture are mentioned below.

Face Loosely defined as 'status', 'ego' or 'self-respect' the concept of 'face' is by no means alien to foreigners. Essentially it's about avoiding being made to look stupid or being forced to back down in front of others.

A negotiated settlement of differences that provides benefits to both parties is always preferable to confrontation. Outright confrontation should be reserved as a last resort (Chinese are not shy of using it) and problems should first be tackled with smiling persistence – if one tack fails, try another.

Handling Paper If you want to impress your Chinese hosts, always use both hands when presenting them with a piece of paper (this includes namecards). This gesture shows respect.

Fortune Telling Being a fortune teller was not a safe occupation during the Cultural Revolution. Most of them either quickly changed their profession or spent 20 years breaking rocks at a labour camp in Qīnghǎi.

It's a different case in Hong Kong and Macau. The lucrative business of fortune telling is how many temples in Hong Kong and Macau pay their bills. Palmists (who also read your face) set up in some of the night markets.

Dos & Don'ts
Speaking Frankly People often don't say what they think, but rather what they think you want to hear or what will save face for them. Thus, for example, a staff member at an airport may tell you that your flight will be here 'very soon' even if they know the flight will be delayed for two days.

Smiling A smile doesn't always mean happiness. Some Chinese people smile when they are embarrassed or worried. This explains the situation where the foreign tourist is ranting and raving at the staff in the hotel lobby, while the person behind the desk stands there grinning from ear to ear.

Guānxì Within their daily life, Chinese people often have to compete for goods or services in short supply and many have been assigned jobs for which they have zero

Up in Smoke

Both Mao Zedong and Deng Xiaoping were chain smokers, and both lived to a ripe old age. Nevertheless, awareness of tobacco's harmful effects is slowly sinking in. The Chinese government is beginning to make good on a long-held promise to do something about public smoking, banning cigarettes in airports and many railway stations. Overall, however, the authorities have a real battle on their hands.

Chinese men smoke like chimneys – China makes up 20% of the world's population, but manages to puff its way through 30% of the world's cigarettes. The Chinese government is also the world's largest manufacturer of cigarettes and does quite nicely out of nationwide tobacco addiction. The health implications for China, however, are enormous and have yet to fully hit, but experts say they will pile up over the next few decades.

You see few Chinese women smokers, and they rarely fumigate their lungs as recklessly as Chinese males. Minimal health education about smoking encourages a deep-rooted complacency concerning the habit.

For smokers, on the other hand, the good news is that cigarettes are cheap (around US$1 per pack for foreign brands; packets of ten do not exist), and you can smoke almost anywhere. Chinese cigarettes can be an acquired taste, but are actually quite flavoursome, albeit dry and rather woody. The cheapest brand can cost Y2, with the most expensive brands (that taste little different) such as Red Pagoda Mountain (Hóngtǎshān) from Yúnnán costing around double the most expensive foreign smokes. You don't see much rolling tobacco in China (apart from the 'Angel Hair' variety in Yúnnán province), so bring your own, along with your own papers.

interest and often no training. Those who have *guānxì* (connections) usually get what they want because the connections network is, of course, reciprocal.

Obtaining goods or services through connections is informally referred to as 'going through the back door' (*zǒu hòu mén*). Cadres and officials are very well placed for this activity, but exploiting *guānxì* can lead to corruption. Typical displays of *guānxì* are lavish banquets, fuelled by *báijiǔ* (white spirit; see the boxed text 'Liquid Lobotomy' in the Běijīng chapter) and the best smokes on the market. As foreign investment in China has grown, gift giving for guānxì has become more and more profuse.

Negotiate Over Dinner If you're planning to cut any business deals in China, you'd best invite the relevant officials or business partners to dinner. Proposals that were 'impossible' a few hours earlier can suddenly become very possible when discussed over a plate of Běijīng duck and a bottle of Johnnie Walker.

Gift Giving This is a complicated issue with the Chinese. It's good manners when visiting people at their homes to bring some sort of gift, especially if you've been invited for a meal. Fruit or flowers are OK, or a box of chocolates. Money would be insulting, but imported goods have much prestige value and will help you win points in the face game.

Tobacco Diplomacy At least in the case of male-to-male relationships, it is always polite to offer a cigarette when meeting somebody. You are under no obligation to smoke, but if refusing always remember to do so politely with a smile and a wave of the hand.

When offering a cigarette to someone, you must extend the open pack with a cigarette protruding from it – it would be impolite to remove a single cigarette from the pack and hand it over.

If you want to butter up your host or make guānxì, prestigious foreign brands like Marlboro and 555 are almost mandatory. The Chinese are obsessive about cigarette brands, and it's really not good form to show up at a banquet with a pack of Tiantan or a local brand that costs Y3. Take along a pack of Marlboro or a famous local brand such as Hongtashan, otherwise there could be embarrassment. A carton of cigarettes for your host is seriously good diplomacy.

The Chinese light up whenever they feel like it at mealtime, so you can as well. Offer your cigarettes around before smoking though.

Treatment of Animals

While China's treatment of animals is not the best, it's not the worst either. Travellers most frequently come up against hard reality when they visit some of the markets, many of which resemble take-away zoos. The southern provinces of Guǎngdōng and Guǎngxī are particularly notable for the wide selection of unusual still-living delicacies on offer – dogs, cats, rats, snakes, monkeys, scorpions, lizards, turtles and other exotica.

The notorious bear-bile extraction industry has come in for particularly virulent condemnation by animal rights activists. After an historic agreement made with Chinese authorities, hope is in sight for many of the 7000 bears incarcerated in the Chinese bear farms. The agreement pledges to work towards eliminating bear farming, and Animals Asia Foundation has already rescued 64 bears from their lives of misery. The bears spend their lives in cages, so bile can be extracted from their gall bladders. The bile is used in medicine, but it can be replaced by herbs and synthetics. Five hundred bears will soon be freed from the worst farms in Sìchuān, at a cost of US$6500 each for veterinary care, rehabilitation and placement in a sanctuary.

There are also periodic reports of rather brutal animal shows used to liven up tourist sights. The 1990s, however, saw a dramatic increase in pet-owners, mainly in the large cities. This is likely to prompt an increasing sentimentality toward animals, but the trickle-down effect may take a long time.

RELIGION

Chinese religion has been influenced by three great streams of human thought: Taoism, Confucianism and Buddhism. Although each has separate origins, all three have been inextricably entwined in popular Chinese religion along with ancient animist beliefs. The founders of Taoism, Confucianism and Buddhism have been deified. The Chinese worship them and their disciples as fervently as they worship their own ancestors and a pantheon of gods and spirits.

Muslims are believed to be the largest identifiable religious group still active in China today, numbering perhaps 2% to 3% of the nation's population. The government has not published official figures of the number of Buddhists, but they must be substantial since most Tibetans, Mongolians and Dai people follow Buddhism. There are around three million Catholics and four million Protestants. It's impossible to determine the number of Taoists, but the number of Taoist priests is very small.

Taoism

It is said that Taoism (Dào Jiào) is the only true 'home-grown' Chinese religion – Buddhism was imported from India and Confucianism is mainly a philosophy. According to tradition, the founder of Taoism was a man known as Laotzu, also known as Laodan, whose name has been variously spelled in Western literature as 'Laotse', 'Laotze' and the pinyin variant 'Lǎozǐ'. He is said to have been born around the year 604 BC, but there is some doubt that he ever lived at all. Almost nothing is known about him, not even his real name. Laotzu translates as the 'Old One' or the 'Grand Old Master'. It's widely believed that Laotzu was the keeper of the government archives in a western state of China, and that Confucius consulted with him.

At the end of his life, Laotzu is said to have climbed on a water buffalo and ridden west towards what is now Tibet, in search of solitude for his last few years. On the way, he was asked by a gatekeeper to leave behind a record of his beliefs. The product was a slim volume of only 5000 characters, the *Tao Te Ching* (*Dao De Jing*) or *The Way & Its Power*. He then rode off on his buffalo. It's doubtful that Laotzu ever intended his philosophy to become a religion.

Zhuangzi (399–295 BC) picked up where Laotzu left off. Zhuangzi (also called Chuangtzu) is regarded as the greatest of all Taoist writers and his collection of stories, *The Book of Zhuangzi*, is still required reading for anyone trying to make sense of Taoism. However, like Laotzu, Zhuangzi was a philosopher and was not actually trying to establish a religion.

Credit for turning Taoism into a religion is generally given to Zhang Daoling, who formally established his Celestial Masters movement in 143 BC.

At the centre of Taoism is the concept of 'dao' (dào). Dao cannot be perceived because it exceeds senses, thoughts and imagination; it can be known only through mystical insight and cannot be expressed with words. The opening lines of Laotzu's

Chinese Zodiac

Astrology has a long history in China and is integrated with religious beliefs. As in the Western system of astrology, there are 12 zodiac signs; however, unlike the Western system, your sign is based on the year rather than the month in which you were born. Still, this is a simplification. The exact day and time of birth is also carefully considered in charting an astrological path.

If you want to know your sign in the Chinese zodiac, look up your year of birth in the chart, though it's a little more complicated than this because Chinese astrology goes by the lunar calendar. The Chinese Lunar New Year usually falls in late January or early February, so the first month will be included in the year before. Future years are included here so you'll know what's coming:

Rat	Ox/Cow	Tiger	Rabbit	Dragon	Snake
1924	1925	1926	1927	1928	1929
1936	1937	1938	1939	1940	1941
1948	1949	1950	1951	1952	1953
1960	1961	1962	1963	1964	1965
1972	1973	1974	1975	1976	1977
1984	1985	1986	1987	1988	1989
1996	1997	1998	1999	2000	2001

Horse	Goat	Monkey	Rooster	Dog	Pig
1930	1931	1932	1933	1934	1935
1942	1943	1944	1945	1946	1947
1954	1955	1956	1957	1958	1959
1966	1967	1968	1969	1970	1971
1978	1979	1980	1981	1982	1983
1990	1991	1992	1993	1994	1995
2002	2003	2004	2005	2006	2007

The Way and its Power advise *'Dào kě dào fēi cháng dào'* which roughly means that the dao that can be expressed is not the real dao. Dao is the way of the universe, the driving power in nature, the order behind all life and the spirit that cannot be exhausted. Dao is the way people should order their lives to keep in harmony with the natural order of the universe.

Taoism today has been much embraced in the West by New Agers, parapsychologists and others who offer their own various interpretations of what Laotzu and Chuangtzu were really trying to tell us. The martial art of *taijiquan* takes Taoism as its principle creed.

Confucianism

Although more a philosophy than a religion, Confucianism (Rújiā Sīxiǎng) has become intertwined with Chinese religious beliefs.

With the exception of Mao, the one name that has become synonymous with China is Confucius. He was born of a poor family around 551 BC in the state of Lu in modern day Shāndōng. His ambition was to hold a high government office and to reorder society through the administrative apparatus. At most he seems to have had several insignificant government posts, a few followers and a permanently blocked career.

At the age of 50 he perceived his divine mission, and for the next 13 years tramped from state to state offering unsolicited advice to rulers on how to improve their governing, while looking for an opportunity to put his own ideas into practice. That opportunity never came, and he returned to his own state to spend the last five years of his life teaching and editing classical literature. He died in 479 BC, aged 72.

The glorification of Confucius began after his death. Mencius (372–289 BC), or Mengzi, helped raise Confucian ideals into the national consciousness with the publication of *The Book of Mencius*.

Eventually, Confucian philosophy permeated every level of Chinese society. To hold government office presupposed knowledge of the Confucian classics, and his words trickled down to the illiterate masses.

During the Han dynasty Confucianism effectively became the state religion – the teachings were made the basic discipline for training government officials and remained so until almost the end of the Qing dynasty in 1911.

In the 7th and 8th centuries temples and shrines were built in memory of Confucius and his original disciples. During the Song dynasty the Confucian bible, the *Analects*, became the basis of all education.

It is not hard to see why Confucianism took hold in China. Confucianism defines codes of conduct and patterns of obedience. Women obey and defer to men, younger brothers to elder brothers, and sons to fathers. Respect flows upwards, from young to old, from subject to ruler. Certainly, any reigning Chinese emperor would quickly see the merits of encouraging such a system.

All people paid homage to the emperor, who was regarded as the embodiment of Confucian wisdom and virtue – the head of the great family-nation. For centuries administration under the emperor lay in the hands of a small Confucian scholar class. In theory anyone who passed the examinations qualified, but in practice the monopoly of power was held by the educated upper classes.

There has never been a rigid code of law, because Confucianism rejected the idea that conduct could be enforced by some organisation; taking legal action implied an incapacity to work things out by negotiation.

The result, however, was arbitrary justice and oppression by those who held power. Dynasties rose and fell, but the Confucian pattern never changed. Indeed, it still holds true in today's China.

The family retains its central place as the basic unit of society; Confucianism reinforced this idea, but did not invent it. Teaming up with traditional superstition, Confucianism reinforced the practice of ancestor worship. The strict codes of obedience were held together by these concepts, as well as by the concept of 'face' – to let down the family or group is a great shame for Chinese.

In its early years, Confucianism was regarded as a radical philosophy, but over the centuries it has come to be seen as conservative and reactionary. Confucius was strongly denounced by the Communists as yet another incorrigible link to the bourgeois past. During the Cultural Revolution, Confucian temples, statues and Confucianists themselves took quite a beating at the hands of rampaging Red Guards. However, in recent years the Chinese government has softened its stance, perhaps recognising that Confucianism can still be an effective instrument of social control. Confucian temples (particularly the ones at Qūfù in Shāndōng province) have been restored.

Buddhism

Buddhism (Fó Jiào) was founded in India by Siddhartha Gautama (563–483 BC) of the Sakyas. Siddhartha was his given name, Gautama his surname and Sakya the name of the clan to which his family belonged.

The story goes that although a prince brought up in luxury, Siddhartha became discontented with the world when he was confronted with the sights of old age, sickness and death. He despaired of finding fulfilment on the physical level, since the body was inescapably subject to these weaknesses.

Around the age of 30 Siddhartha broke from the material world and sought 'enlightenment' by following various yogic disciplines. After several failed attempts he devoted the final phase of his search to intensive contemplation. One evening, sitting beneath a banyan tree, he slipped into deep meditation and emerged having achieved enlightenment. His title 'Buddha' means 'the awakened' or 'the enlightened one'.

Buddha founded an order of monks and preached his ideas for the next four decades until his death. To his followers he was known as Sakyamuni, the 'silent sage of the Sakya clan', because of the unfathomable mystery that surrounded him. It is said that Gautama Buddha was not the first buddha, but the fourth, and will not be the last.

The cornerstone of Buddhist philosophy is the view that all life is suffering. Everyone is subject to the traumas of birth, sickness, decrepitude and death; to what they most dread (an incurable disease or an ineradicable personal weakness); and to separation from what they love.

The cause of suffering is desire – specifically the desires of the body and the desire for personal fulfilment. Happiness can only be achieved if these desires are overcome, and this requires following the 'eightfold path'. By following this path the Buddhist aims to attain nirvana. Volumes have been written in attempts to define nirvana; the *suttas* (discourses of the Buddha) simply say that it's a state of complete freedom from greed, anger, ignorance and the various other fetters of existence.

Buddhism developed in China from the 3rd to 6th centuries AD. In the middle of the 1st century AD the religion gained the interest of the Han emperor Ming. He sent a mission to the west, which returned in AD 67 with Buddhist scriptures, two Indian monks and images of the Buddha.

Centuries later, other Chinese monks such as Xuan Zang journeyed to India and returned with Buddhist scriptures that were then translated from the original Sanskrit. Buddhist monasteries and temples sprang up around China, and played a similar role to the churches and monasteries of medieval Europe – functioning as guesthouses, hospitals and orphanages for travellers and refugees. Gifts from the faithful allowed them to amass considerable wealth and set up money-lending enterprises and pawnshops. These pawnshops functioned as unofficial banks for the poor right up to the mid-20th century.

The Buddha wrote nothing; the Buddhist writings that have come down to us date from about 150 years after his death. By the time these texts came out, divisions had already appeared within Buddhism. Some writers tried to emphasise the Buddha's break with Hinduism, while others tried to minimise it. At some stage Buddhism split into two major schools: Theravada and Mahayana.

The Theravada or 'doctrine of the elders' school (also called Hinayana or 'little vehicle' by non-Theravadins) holds that the path to nirvana is an individual pursuit. It centres on monks and nuns who make the search for nirvana a full-time profession. This school maintains that people are alone in the world and must tread the path to nirvana on their own; buddhas can only show the way. Theravada is the main school of Buddhism in Sri Lanka, Myanmar, Thailand, Laos and Cambodia.

The Mahayana, or 'big vehicle', school holds that since all existence is one, the fate of the individual is linked to the fate of others. The Buddha did not just point the way and float off into his own nirvana, but continues to offer spiritual help to others seeking nirvana. Mahayana is the main school of Buddhism in Vietnam, Japan, Tibet, Korea, Mongolia and China.

Mahayana Buddhism is replete with innumerable heavens, hells and descriptions of nirvana. Prayers are addressed to the Buddha and combined with elaborate ritual. There are deities and Bodhisattvas – a rank of supernatural beings in their last incarnation before nirvana (see the boxed text 'Guanyin' in the Héběi chapter). Temples are filled with images such as the future buddha, Maitreya (often portrayed as fat and happy over his coming promotion) and Amitabha (a saviour who rewards the faithful with admission to a Christian-like paradise). The ritual, tradition and superstition that Buddha rejected came tumbling back in with a vengeance.

In Tibet and areas of Gānsù, Sìchuān and Yúnnán, a unique form of the Mahayana school is practised: Tantric or Lamaist Buddhism (Lǎma Jiào). Tantric Buddhism, often called Vajrayana or 'thunderbolt vehicle' by its followers, has been practised since the early 7th century AD and is heavily influenced by Tibet's pre-Buddhist Bon religion, which relied on priests or shamans to placate spirits, gods and demons.

Generally speaking, it is much more mystical than other forms of Buddhism, relying heavily on *mudras* (ritual postures), *mantras* (sacred speech), *yantras* (sacred art) and secret initiation rites. Priests called *lamas* are believed to be reincarnations of highly evolved beings; the Dalai Lama is the supreme patriarch of Tibetan Buddhism.

Islam

The founder of Islam (Yīsīlán Jiào) was the Arab prophet Mohammed. Strictly speaking, Muslims believe it was not Mohammed who shaped the religion but God, and Mohammed merely transmitted it from God to his people. To call the religion 'Mohammedanism' is also incorrect, since it implies that the religion centres around Mohammed and not around God. The proper name of the religion is Islam, derived from the word *salam*, which primarily means 'peace', and in a secondary sense 'surrender' or 'submission'. The full connotation is something like 'the peace that comes by surrendering to God'. The corresponding adjective is 'Muslim'.

The prophet was born around AD 570 and came to be called Mohammed, meaning 'highly praised'. His ancestry is traditionally traced back to Abraham, who had two wives, Hagar and Sarah. Hagar gave birth to Ishmael, and Sarah had a son named Isaac. Sarah demanded that Hagar and Ishmael be banished. According to Islam's holy book, the Koran, Ishmael went to Mecca, where his line of descendants can be traced down to Mohammed. There have been other true prophets before Mohammed, but he is regarded as the culmination of them and the last.

Mohammed said that there is only one God, Allah. The name derives from joining *al*, which means 'the', with *Llah*, which means 'God'. His uncompromising monotheism conflicted with the pantheism and idolatry of the Arabs. His moral teachings and vision of a universal brotherhood conflicted with what he believed was a corrupt social order based on class divisions.

The initial reaction to his teachings was hostile. He and his followers were forced to flee from Mecca to Medina in 622, where Mohammed built a political base and an army that eventually defeated Mecca and brought all of Arabia under his control. He died in 632, two years after taking Mecca. By the time a century had passed the Arab Muslims had built a huge empire that stretched all the way from Persia to Spain. Although the Arabs were eventually supplanted by the Turks, the strength of Islam has continued to the present day.

Islam was brought to China peacefully. Arab traders who landed on the southern coast of China established their mosques in great maritime cities like Guǎngzhōu and Quánzhōu, and Muslim merchants travelling the Silk Road to China won converts among the Han Chinese in the north of the country. There are also large populations of Muslim Uyghur people (of Turkic descent), whose ancestors first moved into China's Xīnjiāng region during the Tang dynasty.

Christianity

The earliest record of Christianity (Jīdū Jiào) in China dates back to the Nestorians, a Syrian Christian sect. They first appeared in China in the 7th century when a Syrian named Raban presented Christian scriptures to the imperial court at Chāng'ān (present-day Xī'ān). This event and the construction of a Nestorian monastery in Chāng'ān are recorded on a large stone stele made in AD 781, now displayed in the Shaanxi History Museum (Shǎnxī Lìshǐ Bówùguǎn) in Xī'ān.

The next major Christian group to arrive in China were the Jesuits. The priests Matteo Ricci and Michael Ruggieri were permitted to set up base at Zhàoqìng in Guǎngdōng in the 1580s, and eventually made it to the imperial court in Běijīng. Large numbers of Catholic and Protestant missionaries established themselves in China following the intrusion into China by the Western powers in the 19th century. Christians are estimated to comprise about 1% of China's population.

Judaism

Kāifēng in Hénán province has been the home of the largest community of Chinese Jews. Their religious beliefs of Judaism (Yóutài Jiào) and almost all the customs associated with them have died out, yet the descendants of the original Jews still consider themselves Jewish. Just how the Jews got to China is unknown. They may have come as traders and merchants along the Silk Road when Kāifēng was the capital of China, or they may have emigrated from India. For more details, see the Kāifēng section in the Hénán chapter.

Religion & Communism

Today the Chinese Communist government professes atheism. It considers religion to be base superstition, a remnant of old China used by the ruling classes to keep power. This is in line with the Marxist belief that religion is the 'opiate of the people'.

Nevertheless, in an effort to improve relations with the Muslim, Buddhist and Lamaist minorities, in 1982 the Chinese government amended its constitution to allow freedom of religion. However, only atheists are permitted to be members of the CCP. Since almost all of China's 55 minority groups adhere to one religion or another, this rule precludes most of them from becoming party members.

Traditional Chinese religious beliefs took a battering during the Cultural Revolution when monasteries were disbanded, temples were destroyed and the monks were sometimes killed or sent to the fields to labour. While traditional Chinese religion is strong in places like Macau, Hong Kong and Taiwan, in mainland China the temples and monasteries are pale shadows of their former selves.

Since the death of Mao, the Chinese government allowed many temples (sometimes with their own contingent of monks and novices) to reopen as active places of worship. All religious activity is firmly under state control and many of the monks are caretakers within renovated shells of monasteries, which serve principally as tourist attractions.

Confucius has often been used as a political symbol, his role 'redefined' to suit the needs of the time. At the end of the 19th century he was upheld as a symbol of reform because he had worked for reform in his own day. After the fall of the Qing dynasty, Chinese intellectuals vehemently opposed him as a symbol of a conservative and backward China. In the 1930s he was used by Chiang Kaishek and the Kuomintang as a guide to proper, traditional values. Today Confucius is back in favour, with the Chinese government seeing much to be admired in the neo-Confucianist authoritarianism espoused by Lee Kuan Yew of Singapore.

Christianity is still officially frowned upon by the government as a form of spiritual pollution, but nevertheless you can see new churches being built. What the Chinese government does, however, is make it difficult for Chinese Christians to affiliate with fellow Christians in the West. Churches are placed under the control of the government: the Three-Self Patriotic Movement was set up as an umbrella organisation for the Protestant churches, and the Catholic Patriotic Association was set up to replace Rome as the leader of the Catholic churches.

Proselytising is forbidden and Western missionaries are routinely denied visas to enter China – those who enter on tourist visas but are caught proselytising on the sly are unceremoniously booted out.

There is much friction between the government and the Chinese Catholic church because the church refuses to disown the Pope as its leader. For this reason, the Vatican maintains diplomatic relations with Taiwan, much to China's consternation.

Of all people in China, the Tibetan Buddhists felt the brunt of Mao's Cultural Revolution. The Dalai Lama and his entourage fled to India in 1959 when the Tibetan rebellion was put down by Chinese troops. During the Cultural Revolution the monasteries were disbanded (some were levelled to the ground) and the theocracy, which had governed Tibet for centuries, was wiped out overnight. Some Tibetan temples and monasteries have been reopened and the Tibetan religion is still a very powerful force among the people.

In spring 1999, the Communist Party was caught off-guard by a congregation of thousands of practitioners of a quasi-Buddhist health system, Falun Gong (Art of the Wheel of the Law) outside the political headquarters of Zhongnanhai in Běijīng. Falun Gong was branded a cult *(xiéjiào)* and outlawed.

The tussle between the party and Falun Gong quickly relocated to Tiānānmén Square, where followers routinely appeared with banners, only to be pounced upon by patrolling plainclothes police. Some members of Falun Gong even burned themselves alive in the square. Thousands of Falun Gong believers have been sent to prison where human rights watchdogs say many are badly treated or killed.

The party fights a ruthless war against Falun Gong via state media in a bid to extirpate it from society and many say that the group has effectively been menaced into obscurity.

Facts for the Visitor

SUGGESTED ITINERARIES

Unless you have a couple of years up your sleeve and inexhaustible funds, you are only going to be able to see a small part of China on any one trip. It's a good idea to have a loose itinerary to follow. The following suggestions assume you have at least four weeks to play with in China (see the Xīnjiāng chapter for details on the Silk Road).

Běijīng to Tibet via Xī'ān

This route is a favourite among travellers, particularly those arriving overland from Europe by train and heading for Nepal and India via Tibet. The great thing about this route is that it gives you the best of China's historical sights (Běijīng and Xī'ān) and at the same time gives you an opportunity to travel out into China's remote and sparsely populated western regions.

Běijīng, Xī'ān and Lhasa are the main highlights, but en route to Xī'ān, why not visit the Yúngāng grottoes, the mountain temples of Wǔtái Shān and charming Píngyáo? Xīníng is also worth a day or more, mainly for the nearby lamasery of Tǎ'ěr Sì.

From Lhasa, it is possible to travel on to Nepal via the Tibetan temple towns of Gyantse, Shigatse and Sakya, and cross the border at Zhangmu – some travellers make a detour to the Everest base camp. The journey from Lhasa to Kathmandu is a once-in-a-lifetime trip.

Běijīng to Chéngdū, the South-West & Hong Kong/Macau

There are many variations on this route, depending on how much time you have and how much you enjoy travelling on Chinese trains, planes or coaches.

From Chéngdū there are many options: east to Chóngqìng and down Cháng Jiāng (Yangzi River) to Wǔhàn or even Shànghǎi, or south-east to Guìzhōu and Guìlín and then to Hong Kong and Macau. Alternatively, head to Kūnmíng via Lìjiāng and Dàlǐ and explore Yúnnán, arguably the most exotic of China's provinces – rich in culture and some of the best scenery in all China.

Hong Kong to Kūnmíng via Guìlín

This has long been China's most favoured backpacker trail. The standard routine is a brief stay in Guǎngzhōu (one or two nights), followed by a ferry to Wúzhōu, and from there a direct bus to Yángshuò. Many travellers are seduced into spending much longer than they planned in Yángshuò.

Onward travel to Kūnmíng can be undertaken by train or by plane. From Kūnmíng there is a wide range of choices – south to the regional areas of Xīshuāngbǎnnà, west to Déhóng or north-west to Dàlǐ and Lìjiāng (all have airports). Other possibilities include flights from Kūnmíng to Chiang Mai or Bangkok in Thailand, or taking a train to Hanoi in Vietnam.

Cháng Jiāng Routes

Cruises on Cháng Jiāng have long been touted as one of China's premier attractions. In reality they get mixed reports.

The most sublime reaches of Cháng Jiāng lie around the Three Gorges between Chóngqìng and Wǔhàn; you may want to see them before they are submerged for good! The section east of here, between Wǔhàn and Shànghǎi, is of little interest (the river gets so wide you cannot even see its shores).

Gānsù-Sìchuān Route

This scenic route is along the eastern edge of the Tibetan mountains and is usually done in several stages, stopping at Xiàhé, Hézuò, Lǎngmùsì, Zöigê and Sōngpān – a trip taking at least four days. For travel in this area you'll need People's Insurance Company of China (PICC) insurance.

On a highland plateau two hours further south of Gānsù is Zöigê, in Sìchuān, from where it's possible to make a side trip to the national park of Jiǔzhàigōu. Road conditions worsen noticeably once you cross the border from Gānsù into Sìchuān, and from Lǎngmùsì it's a bumpy four hours to Zöigê.

From Zöigê it's a full day's journey by bus south to Chéngdū, although many opt to break up the journey with a stay in Sōngpān. For more information on these areas, see the Sìchuān chapter.

North-East Route

Visit the former Russian port and dynamic metropolis of Dàlián, then head north to what used to be Manchuria and the cities of Shěnyáng, Chángchūn and Hāĕrbīn. It's a region that combines Canadian-style prairies, rust belt heavy industry, leftover traces of Japanese colonialism and undeniable Russian influences. Apart from the cities, you can commune with nature in Chángbái Shān and Zhālóng nature reserves or gaze into alien North Korea from Dāndōng. Winter in the north-east sparkles with ice festivals and -30°C (-22°F) weather, but summers can be fierce. You could keep heading north to the grasslands of Mǎnzhōulǐ in Inner Mongolia and on to Siberia or Europe along the Trans-Siberian Railway.

PLANNING
When to Go

Domestic tourism is in a state of supernova, so getting around and finding accommodation during the peak summer tourist crush can be quite a headache.

Winter's big chill is the quietest time of year and good hotel discounts exist, but the weather in some parts can be prohibitively cold. Spring and autumn are the best months to be on the road.

See the Climate section in the Facts about China chapter for information on seasonal weather variations throughout China.

Major public holidays are to be avoided if possible. Chinese New Year is a terrible time to be travelling; the same applies for the May Day holiday (now a week long from 1 May) and National Day on 1 October (likewise a week long).

Maps

Top-quality maps of almost every Chinese city and many small towns are readily available. Some are very detailed, with bus routes (including names of bus stops), the locations of hotels, shops and so on. City maps normally cost only Y2 to Y4.

Maps are most easily purchased from bookstalls or street vendors around train and bus stations, from branches of the Xinhua Bookshop or from hotel front desks. Unfortunately most maps are only in Chinese. Tourist centres, hotel gift shops, Friendship Stores (Yǒuyì Shāngdiàn) and sometimes foreign-language bookshops stock English versions. Here you may also find Chinese- and English-language atlases of China. The Foreign Languages Bookshop on Wangfujiang Dajie in Běijīng has maps of other Chinese cities, but it's not comprehensive.

Some of the most detailed maps of China available in the West are the aerial survey 'Operational Navigation Charts' (Series ONC). These are prepared and published by the Defence Mapping Agency Aerospace Center, St Louis Air Force Station, Missouri 63118, USA. Cyclists and mountaineers have recommended these highly. In the UK you can obtain these maps from Stanfords Map Centre (☎ 020-7836 1321, 🆆 www.stanfords.co.uk), at 12–14 Long Acre, London WC2E 9LP, or from the Map Shop (☎ freephone 0800 085 4080, 🆆 www.themapshop.co.uk, 🄴 themapshop@btinternet.com), 15 High St, Upton upon Severn, Worcestershire, WR8 OHJ.

Australians can contact Mapland (☎ 03-9670 4383, 🆆 www.mapland.com.au) at 372 Little Bourke St in Melbourne, or the Travel Bookshop (☎ 02-9241 3554) at 20 Bridge St in Sydney.

In France see Ulysse (☎ 01 43 25 17 35) at 26 rue Saint Louis en l'Île, or IGN (☎ 01 43 98 80 00) at 107 rue de la Boetie in Paris.

Lonely Planet publishes *Beijing* and *Hong Kong* city maps. The *Hong Kong Guidebook* by Universal is a first-rate colour map of the city. Nelles publishes good detailed regional maps of China, and Berndtson has an excellent detailed *Beijing* map.

What to Bring

If you are only travelling to a single destination, eg, Běijīng or Shànghǎi, a suitcase will do. For others, a backpack is still the best carrying container. It's worth paying the money for a strong, good-quality pack as it's much more likely to withstand the rigours of Chinese travel.

An alternative is a large, soft, zip bag with a wide shoulder strap. This is obviously not an option if you plan to do any trekking.

If you are undertaking a longer trip, whatever you carry your gear in, the usual budget travellers' rule applies – bring as little as possible.

You can wear pretty much what you want in China, although Hong Kong, Běijīng and Shànghǎi are more fashion-conscious. Shorts and T-shirts are respectable summer wear. Flip-flops (thongs) and sandals are OK. Clothing is one of the best cheap buys in China, so don't feel compelled to bring everything from home.

If you're travelling in the north of China at the height of winter, prepare yourself for incredible cold. Good down jackets are available in China, but it's hard to find good quality boots (at least in larger sizes).

A reasonable clothes list would include:

- swimming gear
- a pair of cotton trousers and shorts
- a long cotton skirt (women)
- lightweight shirts and a sweater
- one pair of sneakers or shoes
- flip-flops (thongs) – hotel slippers are often too small
- lightweight jacket or raincoat
- a hat

Bedding Hotels provide copious bedding during the winter months, as do the sleeper carriages on trains. Nonetheless, a sleeping bag, although a hassle to carry, can come in handy. Some travellers complain of an allergic reaction to some budget hotel blankets – perhaps it's the chemicals they are washed in. You can also use it as a cushion on hard train seats, and as a seat for long waits on railway platforms. If you are planning on camping or spending time in the hills (especially during the cool season) a sleeping bag is essential.

Toiletries Toiletries and sachets of washing powder are readily available. Outside the major cities, some items are hard to find, such as shaving cream, decent razor blades, mosquito repellent, deodorant, dental floss, tampons and contact lens solution. Bring condoms with you, as the quality of locally made condoms may be suspect. Antibacterial hand gel (the kind that you don't need to use with water) comes in handy as some public bathrooms don't have hand-washing facilities.

Miscellaneous Items See the Health section later in this chapter for a medical kit check list. Some handy items to stow away in your pack could include the following:

- a padlock, especially for budget travellers. Having your own sturdy lock on hotel doors does wonders for your peace of mind.
- a knife (preferably Swiss Army)
- insect repellent
- a torch (flashlight) and/or candles
- a voltage stabiliser – for those travellers bringing sensitive electronic equipment
- wet wipes – for your hands and face
- a spare set of glasses and your spectacle prescription
- earplugs and a sleeping mask
- a sun hat, sunglasses and sunscreen
- a water bottle and mug
- a smoke alarm
- international-brand batteries (eg, Duracell) – cheap, local brands run out rapidly
- a sarong – can be used as a bed sheet, an item of clothing, an emergency towel and a pillow
- a pair of binoculars – if you plan to be bird-watching and wildlife-spotting
- a high-pitched whistle – some women carry them as a possible deterrent to would-be assailants
- a compact CD player – a life-saver on long bus or train journeys

You may want to consider taking along gifts for locals you meet in your travels. English books and magazines are appreciated by those who are studying the language. Stamps make good gifts; the Chinese are avid collectors. Odd-looking foreign coins and currency are appreciated.

RESPONSIBLE TOURISM

Common sense and courtesy go a long way when you are travelling. Think about the impact you may be having on the environment and the people who inhabit it. One very simple way of minimising your impact is to reduce the amount of plastic you use. Bring your own cup rather than using disposable plastic ones; recycle plastic bags; try and recycle plastic drinking bottles, or purify your water. Taking your own plastic chopsticks saves trees.

As exotic and tempting as they may be, avoid buying products that further endanger threatened species and habitats.

VISAS & DOCUMENTS
Passport

You must have a passport with you at all times; it is the most basic travel document (all hotels will insist on seeing it). The Chinese government requires that your passport be valid for at least six months after the expiry date of your visa. You'll need at least one entire blank page in your passport for the visa.

Have an ID card with your photo in case you lose your passport; even better, make photocopies of your passport – your embassy may need these before issuing a new one (a process that can take weeks). Also report the loss to the local Public Security Bureau (PSB; Gōngānjú). Long-stay visitors should register their passport with their embassy. Be careful who you pass your passport to (eg, dodgy bike-rental operators as a deposit), as you may never see it again.

Visas

A visa is required for the People's Republic of China (PRC), but at the time of writing, visas were not required for most Western nationals to visit Hong Kong or Macau (including visits of up to six days to neighbouring Shēnzhèn and Zhūhǎi). If you visit Hong Kong or Macau from China, you will need to be on a multiple-entry visa or apply for another visa to re-enter China.

Travellers in transit can stay in China visa-free for up to 24 hours as long as they have an onward air ticket for a flight from China to another destination departing within that time period.

There are five types of visas, as follows:

type	description	Chinese name
L	Travel	lǚxíng
F	Business or Student (less than six months)	fǎngwèn
D	Resident	dìngjū
X	Long-term Student	liúxué
Z	Working	rènzhí

For most travellers, the type of visa is 'L', from the Chinese word for travel (lǚxíng). This letter is stamped right on the visa. The usual length of stay for an 'L' visa is 30 days. Working, student and business visas generally require a letter of invitation from a host unit in China. HIV-negative tests will be required from teachers and students planning to live in China for more than nine months.

Visas are readily available from Chinese embassies and consulates in most other countries. A standard 30-day, single-entry visa from most Chinese embassies abroad can be issued in three to five working days but can take longer; for an extra fee, there should be an express same-day or next day service. Application forms are available from the embassy or consulate or online at Web sites such as W www.cbw.com/tourism. Visa applications require one photo.

The mail service will take up to three weeks (payment generally in cash, postal order or certified cheque only) and an extra charge is often levied. Certain travel agents can also acquire visas on your behalf.

Getting a visa is straightforward in Hong Kong. Thirty-day visas can be obtained from almost any travel agency and some guesthouses and hotels. Visas valid for more than 30 days are often difficult to obtain anywhere other than in Hong Kong. The cheapest visas are available from the Visa Office (☎ 0852-2827 1881), Ministry of Foreign Affairs of the PRC, 5th floor, Low Block, China Resources Building, 26 Harbour Rd, Wanchai. Thirty-day to three-month single-entry visas are HK$100, double-entry visas are HK$150 and multiple-entry visas HK$400. Visas take 24 hours to process; it's HK$150 more for same-day service. US passport holders, unless of Chinese descent, must pay an extra HK$160. It also has a photo service for HK$30. The office is open 9am to 12.30pm and 2pm to 5pm Monday to Friday, and until 12.30pm on Saturday.

If you need more than three months, head to one of the branches of China Travel Service (CTS) in Hong Kong or Macau. Prices range from HK$160 for a single-entry, 90-day visa issued in three days to HK$1300 for a six-month, multiple-entry visa (it also has an express one- or two-day service). Some other Hong Kong travel agencies can also get you 60- and 90-day, and multiple-entry visas. Try Sky Fortune Travel & Tours (☎ 0852-2301 1082), 15th floor, Cameron Centre, 57–59 Chatham Rd South, Tsimshatsui, Kowloon.

Multiple-entry visas allow you to enter and leave the country an unlimited number of times and are available through some travel agencies in Hong Kong and Macau. The cheapest multiple-entry visas cost HK$350 and are valid for 90 days; six-month multiple-entry visas cost HK$500 for next-day pick-up or HK$600 for same day pick-up. The latter are business or short-term student (F) visas.

It is also possible to obtain single-entry visas at the border at Shēnzhèn and Zhūhǎi.

Thirty-day, 60-day and 90-day visas are all activated on the date you enter China, rather than on the date of issue. You must enter within three months of the date of issue, or the visa becomes invalid.

See the Land section in the Getting There & Away chapter for information on visas for travelling on the Trans-Siberian Railway.

Visa Extensions Visa extensions are handled by the Foreign Affairs Branch of the local Public Security Bureau (PSB) – the police force. Government travel organisations, like China International Travel Service (CITS), have nothing to do with extensions, so don't bother asking. Extensions can cost nothing for some, but usually cost between Y100 and Y250.

The situation with visa extensions is constantly in flux. Some travellers report extending their 30-day visa twice (30 days each time, up to 90 days) without any problem while others report difficulty obtaining a second extension. A first extension is generally no problem.

Different PSB offices around China, however, operate at different speeds. In scrupulous Běijīng, you may be told that it could take five days to renew, but you could well have it done in three days in more relaxed Shànghǎi, while other, more remote areas could well give you a stamp on the spot!

The period of extension also differs from city to town as well. Travellers report generous extensions being decided on the spot in provincial towns and backwaters. If you have used up all your options, popping into Hong Kong to apply for a new tourist visa is a reliable option.

It's also possible to get visa extensions through private visa services in Běijīng. Most seem to operate through private connections with the PSB, with questionable legality. They advertise three- to six-month visa extensions and can also arrange letters of introduction. These services are also useful in changing a student X visa to a multiple-entry F visa, which is usually difficult to do. Some foreigners have used these services without incident, but you are taking a risk. Don't hand over your payment until after your visa has been successfully extended. Look in the classified section of expat mags for listings of these services; it's wise to ask around for a personal recommendation from someone who has actually recently used one of the services.

The penalty for overstaying your visa in China is Y500 *per day*! Many travellers have reported having trouble with officials who read the 'valid until' date on their visa incorrectly. For a one-month tourist (L) visa, the 'valid until' date is the date by which you must enter the country, not the date upon which your visa expires. Your visa expires the number of days that your visa is valid for after the date of entry into China.

Travel Permits

Most of China is now open to foreign travellers – the exceptions are militarily sensitive zones and certain remote border areas, especially those inhabited by ethnic minorities.

Most places described in this book are open to foreigners, but one incident (like a riot in Xīnjiāng or Tibet) can cause new permit regulations to be issued overnight. Some small towns in China seem to insist on these permits for the sole reason of extracting fines from any foreigners who show up without one (Kǎilǐ in Húnán province is one such example). To find out about latest restrictions, it's best to check with the police in provincial capitals, or with your nearest Chinese embassy before departure.

To travel to closed places you officially require an Alien Travel Permit (Tōngxíng Zhèng). The police have wide discretion in issuing permits to closed places. However, open places are now so extensive that most travellers won't need to apply. Those bicycling across China may find themselves traversing closed areas; it's worth inquiring up-front, mapping out your route first and sticking to it to avoid run-ins with the authorities. Foreign academics and researchers wanting to poke around remote areas usually need the right credentials or letter of introduction (*jièshào xìn*).

Travel permits can be demanded from you at hotel registration desks, boat or bus ticket offices and unusual areas during spot checks by police. If you're off the track, but heading towards a destination for which you have a permit, the police may stop you and revoke your permit.

The permit also lists the modes of transport you're allowed to take: plane, train, ship or car – if a particular mode is crossed out then you can't use it. If a mode is cancelled it can be reinstated at the next police station, but that may be for only a single trip from point A to point B. You could try and carry on regardless – though if caught, you face losing your permit.

If you manage to get a permit for an unusual destination, the best strategy is to get to that destination as fast as you can (by plane if possible). Local police do not have to honour the permit and can cancel it and send you back. Take your time getting back – you're less likely to be hassled if you're returning to civilisation. Transit points usually don't require a permit, and you can stay the night.

Travel Insurance

Your medical insurance in your own country may not be valid in China; check with your insurance company.

A travel insurance policy to cover theft, loss, trip cancellation and medical problems is sensible. Many travel agents (especially chains like STA or Trailfinders) can sort this out for you. Some policies offer lower and higher medical-expense options; the higher ones are chiefly for countries such as the USA, which have extremely high medical costs. A wide variety of policies exist, so check the small print.

Some policies specifically exclude 'dangerous activities', which can include scuba diving, skiing and even trekking. A locally acquired motorcycle licence is not valid under some policies. Check that the policy covers ambulances or an emergency flight home. If you have to claim later make sure you keep all documentation.

US ISIC (International Student Identity Card) card holders have access to certain insurance benefits including a 24-hour emergency medical, legal and financial emergency hotline. The ITIC (International Teacher Identity Card) provides similar benefits. Some credit-card holders will find they are covered.

Driving Licence

The authorities remain fearful of foreigners with the freedom to roam. Tourists are not permitted to drive between cities in China and can only rent cars to drive within Hong Kong, Macau, Běijīng and Shànghǎi (for the last two cities it's a hassle). To do this you will need an International Driving Permit. Considering the traffic conditions and pile-ups on the roads in mainland China, you won't want to get behind the wheel.

Private visa service companies in Běijīng (see Visa Extensions earlier) also advertise that they can arrange international driving licences and Chinese driving licences. Check the advertising pages of expat mags such as *City Weekend* for car-hire companies and garages.

Student & Youth Cards

An ISIC card is becoming increasingly useful in China, and it carries fringe insurance benefits (see Travel Insurance, previously). It won't work everywhere in China, but you could well get discount entry to many sights. Chinese signs at many sights clearly indicate that students pay half price – so try your luck. It's worth trying to see if you can also get air ticket discounts using your ISIC card; some travellers report success. If you are studying in China, your school will issue you a student card, which is more useful for discounts on admission charges.

Resident Permits

The 'green card' is a residence permit, issued to English teachers, foreign experts and long-term students who live in China. Green cards are issued for one year and must be renewed annually. If you lose your card, you'll have to pay a hefty fee to have it replaced.

A health exam (for which there is a substantial charge) is part of the protocol for acquiring the card. Besides this exam, an ECG and an X-ray, you will be tested for HIV. The staff use disposable syringes for this blood test, which are unwrapped in front of you; if you bring your own syringe they generally refuse to use it unless you adamantly insist. Take along your passport and two photos.

Copies

If you're thinking about working or studying in China, photocopies of university diplomas, transcripts and letters of recommendation could prove helpful.

A photocopy of your passport (data page and visa page) is also a good idea. Married couples should have a copy of their marriage certificate.

These and other important documents (credit cards, travel insurance policy, tickets, driving licence etc) should be photocopied before you leave home. Leave a copy with someone at home and keep another with you, separate from the originals.

It's also a good idea to store details of your vital travel documents in Lonely Planet's free online Travel Vault in case you lose the photocopies or can't be bothered with them. Your password-protected Travel Vault is accessible online anywhere in the world – create it at W www.ekno.lonely planet.com.

EMBASSIES & CONSULATES

Check the Web site W www.embassy world.com for a full listing of Chinese embassies and consulates abroad and foreign embassies in China.

Chinese Embassies & Consulates

Addresses of China's embassies and consulates in major cities overseas include:

Australia (☎ 02-6273 4780/1, W www.china embassy.org.au) 15 Coronation Drive, Yarralumla, Canberra ACT 2600
  Consulates: Melbourne, Perth and Sydney
Canada (☎ 613-789 3434, W www.china embassycanada.org) 515 St Patrick St, Ottawa, Ontario K1N 5H3
  Consulates: Toronto, Vancouver, Calgary
France (☎ 01 47 36 77 90, W www.amb-chine .fr) 9 Avenue V Cresson, 92130 Issy les Moulineaux
Italy (☎ 06-3630 8534, 3630 3856) Via Della Camilluccia 613, 00135 Roma
  Consulate: Milan
Japan (☎ 03-3403 3389, 3403 3065) 3-4-33 Moto-Azabu, Minato-ku, Tokyo 106
  Consulates: Fukuoka, Osaka and Sapporo
Netherlands (☎ 070-355 1515) Adriaan Goekooplaan 7, 2517 JX, The Hague
New Zealand (☎ 04-4721 3823) 2–6 Glenmore Street, Wellington
  Consulate: Auckland

South Korea (☎ 2-319 5101) 83 Myŏng-dong 2-ga, Chunggu, Seoul
UK (☎ 020-7636 9756, W www.chinese-embassy .org.uk) 31 Portland Place, London, W1N 5AG
USA (☎ 202-338 6688, W www.china-embassy .org) Room 110, 2201 Wisconsin Ave NW, Washington, DC 20007
  Consulates: Chicago, Houston, Los Angeles, New York and San Francisco

Embassies & Consulates in China

In Běijīng (area code ☎ 010) there are two main embassy compounds – Jiànguóménwài and Sānlǐtún.

The following are some embassies situated in Jiànguóménwài, east of the Forbidden City:

India (☎ 6532 1908, fax 6532 4684) 1 Ritan Donglu
Ireland (☎ 6532 2691, fax 6532 6857) 3 Ritan Donglu
Japan (☎ 6532 2361, fax 6532 4625) 7 Ritan Lu
Mongolia (☎ 6532 1203, fax 6532 5045) 2 Xiu-shui Beijie
New Zealand (☎ 6532 2731, fax 6532 3424) 1 Ritan Dong Erjie
North Korea (☎ 6532 1186, fax 6532 6056) 11 Ritan Beilu
Philippines (☎ 6532 1872, 6532 2794, fax 6532 3761) 23 Xiushui Beijie
Thailand (☎ 6532 2151, fax 6532 1748) 40 Guanghua Lu
UK (☎ 6532 1961, fax 6532 1937) 11 Guanghua Lu
USA (☎ 6532 3831, fax 6532 6057) 3 Xiushui Beijie
Vietnam (☎ 6532 5414, fax 6532 5720) 32 Guanghua Lu

The Sānlǐtún compound, in the north-east within the third ring road (Dongsanhuan Beilu), is home to the following embassies:

Your Own Embassy

It's important to realise what your own embassy – the embassy of the country of which you are a citizen – can and can't do to help you if you get into trouble. Generally speaking, it won't be much help in emergencies if the trouble you're in is remotely your own fault. Remember that you are bound by the laws of the country you are in. Your embassy will not be sympathetic if you end up in jail after committing a crime locally, even if such actions are legal in your own country.

In genuine emergencies you might get some assistance, but only if other channels have been exhausted. For example, if you need to get home urgently, a free ticket home is exceedingly unlikely – the embassy would expect you to have insurance. If you have all your money and documents stolen, it might assist with getting a new passport, but a loan for onward travel is out of the question.

Some embassies used to keep letters for travellers or have a small reading room with home newspapers, but these days the mail holding service has usually been stopped and even newspapers tend to be out of date.

Australia (☎ 6532 2331, fax 6532 4349)
21 Dongzhimenwai Dajie
Canada (☎ 6532 3536, fax 6532 4311)
19 Dongzhimenwai Dajie
France (☎ 6532 1331, fax 6532 4841)
3 Sanlitun Dongsanjie
Germany (☎ 6532 2161, fax 6532 5336)
17 Dongzhimenwai Dajie
Italy (☎ 6532 2131, fax 6532 4676)
2 Sanlitun Dong Erjie
Kazakstan (☎ 6532 6182, fax 6532 6183)
9 Sanlitun Dongliujie
Myanmar (Burma) (☎ 6532 1584, fax 6532
1344) 6 Dongzhimenwai Dajie
Nepal (☎ 6532 1795, fax 6532 3251)
1 Sanlitun Xiliujie
Netherlands (☎ 6532 1131, fax 6532 4689)
4 Liangmahe Nanlu
Pakistan (☎ 6532 2504, fax 6532 2715)
1 Dong-zhimenwai Dajie
Russia (☎ 6532 2051, fax 6532 4851)
4 Dongzhimen Beizhongjie, west of Sānlǐtún
in a separate compound
South Korea (☎ 6532 0290, fax 6532 6778)
3 Sanlitun Dongsijie

Consulates Hong Kong has consulates for Australia, Canada, France, India, Indonesia, Ireland, Japan, Malaysia, Myanmar, Nepal, New Zealand, Philippines, Singapore, South Africa, South Korea, Taiwan, Thailand, the UK, the USA and Vietnam.

In Shànghǎi there are consulates for Australia, Austria, Canada, France, Germany, India, Italy, Japan, the Netherlands, New Zealand, North Korea, Russia, Singapore, Sweden, Thailand, the UK and the USA.

In Guǎngzhōu, there are consulates for Australia, Canada, France, Germany, Japan, Malaysia, the Netherlands, Thailand, the UK, the USA and Vietnam.

There is a US consulate in Shěnyáng and one in Chéngdū. There are Japanese consulates in Shěnyáng and Dàlián. Kūnmíng has consulates for Laos, Myanmar and Thailand. There is a consulate for Nepal in Lhasa. Qīngdǎo has a consulate for South Korea. These consulates aren't always able (or willing) to issue visas. It's best to get visas for these countries before you leave your home country or in Běijīng. See the relevant destination chapters for details.

CUSTOMS

You're allowed to import 400 cigarettes (600 if you are staying more than six months), four bottles of wine or spirits and a reasonable amount of perfume. Cash amounts exceeding US$5000 (or its equivalent in another currency) should be declared.

Don't bring any cold cuts with you as Chinese law forbids their import. Importation of fresh fruit is prohibited. There are limits to other items, such as herbal medicine, that you can take out of the country. Rare animals and plants also cannot be exported.

Cultural relics, handicrafts, gold and silver ornaments, and jewellery purchased in China have to be shown to customs on leaving. If these items are deemed to be 'cultural treasures', they will be confiscated. All bags are X-rayed.

It's illegal to import any printed material, film, tapes etc 'detrimental to China's politics, economy, culture and ethics'; this includes pornography. But don't be too concerned about what you take to read.

As you leave China, any tapes, books etc 'which contain state secrets or are otherwise prohibited for export' can be seized.

MONEY
Currency

The Chinese currency is known as Renminbi (RMB), or 'People's Money'. Formally the basic unit of RMB is the *yuán*, which is divided into 10 *jiǎo*, which is again divided into 10 *fēn*. Colloquially, the yuán is referred to as *kuài* and jiǎo as *máo*. The fēn has so little value these days that it is rarely used.

The Bank of China issues RMB bills in denominations of one, two, five, 10, 20, 50 and 100 yuán. Coins come in denominations of one yuán, five jiǎo, one jiǎo and five fēn. Paper versions of the coins remain in circulation.

Hong Kong's currency is the Hong Kong dollar and Macau's is the *pataca*. Both currencies are worth about 7% more than Renminbi.

Exchange Rates

Exchange rates for Chinese RMB are:

country	unit		yuán (Y)
Australia	A$1	=	4.41
Canada	C$1	=	5.21
Euro zone	€1	=	7.30
Hong Kong	HK$1	=	1.06
Japan	¥100	=	6.24
New Zealand	NZ$1	=	3.66
UK	UK£1	=	11.90
USA	US$1	=	8.29

Exchange rates fluctuate daily, so try this currency converter to give you the current value of the yuán: **W** www.oanda.com.

Exchanging Money

Foreign currency and travellers cheques can be changed at border crossings, international airports, major branches of the Bank of China, tourist hotels, and some large department stores. Top-end hotels will generally change money for hotel guests only. The official rate is given almost everywhere, so there is little need to shop around for the best deal.

Australian, Canadian, US, UK, Hong Kong, Japanese and most Western European currencies can be changed in China. In some backwaters, it may be hard to change lesser-known currencies – US dollars are still the easiest to change.

Keep at least a few of your exchange receipts. You will need them if you want to exchange any remaining RMB you have at the end of your trip. Those travelling to Hong Kong can change RMB for Hong Kong dollars there.

Cash Counterfeit notes are a problem in China. Very few Chinese will accept a Y50 or Y100 note without first checking to see whether or not it's a fake. Notes that are old and tattered are also sometimes hard to spend. You can exchange notes for new ones at the Bank of China – counterfeits, however, will be confiscated.

Local Chinese have a variety of methods for checking notes, including checking the watermark, the drawn lines (more distinct in fake notes) and colour (more pronounced in counterfeit notes). The texture of a fake note also tends to be smoother than authentic notes. Examine large denomination notes if given to you as change by street vendors; they could well be dumping a forged banknote on you.

Travellers Cheques Take these with you. You should have no problem cashing them at hotels in China. Not only will they protect your money against theft or loss, but the exchange rate for travellers cheques is higher than for cash (around 2% higher). You can make a large saving, especially if you have paid no commission for your travellers cheques in the first place. If cashing

at banks, aim for the larger banks such as the Bank of China or the CITIC Industrial Bank. Bear in mind that most hotels will only cash the cheques of guests. It's a good idea to change your money at the airport when you arrive as the rate there is roughly the same as everywhere else. Keep your exchange receipts so you can change your money back to its original currency when you leave. Cheques from most of the world's leading banks and issuing agencies are now acceptable in China – stick to the major companies such as Thomas Cook, American Express (AmEx) and Visa.

ATMs ATMs (Automated Teller Machines) advertising international bank settlement systems such as GlobalAccess, Cirrus, Maestro, Plus and others are common in Hong Kong and Macau. ATMs can be found in a limited, but growing, number of large banks on the mainland where you can use Visa, MasterCard, Cirrus, Maestro, Plus and AmEx to withdraw cash. The network only applies to sizeable cities at present (such as Běijīng, Shànghǎi, Guǎngzhōu and Shēnzhèn). Useful ATMs include those at large airports such as at Beijing Capital Airport (Bank of China).

For your nearest ATM, consult **W** www .international.visa.com/ps or **W** www.mas tercard.com/cardholderservices/atm; both have comprehensive listings. Most other ATMs in China can only be used for withdrawing Renminbi in domestic accounts. Check the reverse of your ATM card to find which systems work with your card. The exchange rate on ATM withdrawals is similar to credit cards but there is a maximum daily withdrawal amount.

For those without an ATM card or credit card, a PIN-activated Visa TravelMoney card (☎ 1-877-394 2247) gives you access to pre-deposited cash through the ATM network.

Credit Cards Foreign plastic is gradually gaining a foothold in China, and useful cards include Visa, MasterCard, AmEx and JCB. Their use, however, is limited to more upmarket hotels and restaurants, supermarkets and department stores. You still can't use credit cards to buy train tickets, but CAAC offices readily accept international Visa cards for buying air tickets.

Some hotels appear to display Visa signs, but in fact only take Chinese Visa. Check first with your hotel that it takes international cards.

Credit-card cash advances have become fairly routine at head branches of the Bank of China, even in places as remote as Lhasa. Bear in mind, however, that a 4% commission is generally deducted and usually the minimum advance is Y1200. The Bank of China does not charge commission on AmEx cash withdrawals. Certain cards offer insurance and other benefits.

International Transfers Except when in Hong Kong and Macau, having money sent to you in China is a time-consuming and frustrating task that is best avoided. If dealing with the Bank of China, the process can take weeks, although it can be much faster at CITIC Bank.

China Courier Service Corporation (a joint venture with Western Union Financial Services in the USA) is very fast and efficient, albeit quite pricey. In Běijīng, there is a branch (☎ 010-63 18 4313) at 7 Dongdan Jie in Qianmen (in the post office). In Shànghǎi, Shanghai EMS (☎ 021-6356 8129, 1 Sichuan Beilu) acts as an agent for Western Union. Check out ⓦ www.westernunion.com for a more complete list of branches.

Bank Accounts Foreigners can open bank accounts in China – both RMB and US dollar accounts (the latter only at special foreign-exchange banks). You do not need to have resident status – a tourist visa is sufficient. Virtually every foreigner working in China will tell you that CITIC is far better to do business with than the Bank of China. It's basically more efficient and well versed in handling international credit card transactions, including accepting personal cheques against your AmEx.

Black Market Thanks to China's thriving smuggling rings (who need US dollars to carry on their business transactions), you can still change money on the black market in major cities at rates substantially better than those offered by the banks. Your best bet is to ask a foreign resident or someone you trust for a recommendation on a 'reputable' moneychanger. Generally speaking, though, it's inadvisable to change money on the streets given the risk of short-changing, rip-offs and the abundance of counterfeit currency floating about.

Carrying Money

A money belt is essential (for larger sums of cash and your credit cards). Be alert in crowded places such as packed markets and buses. Split up your money and leave a small stash of money (say US$100) in your hotel room or buried in your backpack, with a record of the travellers cheque serial numbers and a photocopy of your passport.

Costs

How much will a trip to China cost? It really depends on how, where, and how long you travel.

Western China remains relatively inexpensive. Popular backpacker getaways such as Yúnnán, Sìchuān, Guǎngxī, Gānsù, Xīnjiāng, Qīnghǎi and Tibet abound in budget accommodation and cheap eats. Generally, keeping costs down to US$25 per day is not too difficult.

Eastern China (between Hēilóngjiāng and Hǎinán Dǎo) is hard to do on a shoestring. Most ultra-cheap hotels are not available to foreigners (this could change) and many cities are devoid of dorm accommodation, putting you into accommodation with rates starting at US$25 to US$35 for a double (singles are rarely available).

Food costs remain reasonable throughout China, and the frugal can eat for as little as US$5 per day. Transport costs can be kept to a minimum by travelling by bus wherever possible or by travelling hard-seat on the train (which can be wearing, but also fun). In other words, travelling through the booming coastal cities of China for less than US$35 per day is quite a challenge.

Mid-range hotel doubles start at around US$35 and it's easy to eat in mid-range restaurants from around US$5.

Train travel is reasonable, and is generally about half the price of flying. For sample train fares see the Getting Around section in the Běijīng chapter, and for domestic airfares see the Getting Around chapter. Flying in China is expensive, but those with less time may have to resort to it to cover potentially vast distances.

Top-end travel in China? You can hit the major attractions of the country stay in five-star hotels (US$100 and up for a double), fly long distances, take taxis to and from airports, dine on Chinese haute cuisine and enjoy a few drinks in the lobby bar in the evenings for between US$200 and US$250 per day. These travellers will find themselves well catered for, unless they venture too far from large cities.

Tipping & Bargaining

In China (including Hong Kong and Macau) almost no-one asks for tips. Tipping used to be refused in restaurants, but nowadays, many middle and top-end eateries include their own (often massive) service charge; cheap restaurants do not expect a tip.

Since foreigners are so often overcharged in China, bargaining is essential. You can bargain in shops, hotels and taxis (unless it's on the meter) – but not everywhere. In large shops where prices are clearly marked, there is usually no latitude for bargaining (although if you ask, the staff sometimes can give you a 10% discount). In small shops and street stalls, bargaining is expected, but there is one important rule to follow – be polite. Keep in mind that entrepreneurs are in business to make money – they aren't going to sell anything at a loss. Your goal should be to pay the Chinese price, as opposed to the foreigners' price – if you can do that, you've done well.

Taxes

Although big hotels and top-end restaurants may add a tax or 'service charge' of 10% or more, all other consumer taxes are included in the price tag.

POST & COMMUNICATIONS
Postal Rates

Postage for domestic letters up to 20g is Y0.80. International airmail postal rates follow:

letters (weight)	international	HK, Macau & Taiwan	Asia Pacific
0–20g	Y5.40	Y2.50	Y4.70
21–100g	Y11.40	Y5.00	Y9.80
101–250g	Y21.80	Y9.50	Y18.60
251–500g	Y40.80	Y17.70	Y34.80
501g–1kg	Y76.70	Y32.70	Y65.30
1–2kg	Y124.00	Y56.80	Y105.00
Postcards	Y4.20	Y2.00	Y3.70
Aerograms	Y5.20	Y1.80	Y4.50

Aerograms are available at post offices (yóujú). There are discounts for printed matter and small packets. Maximum weight is 30kg.

EMS Domestic Express Mail Service (EMS) parcels up to 200g cost Y15; each additional 200g costs Y5. For international EMS, the charges vary according to country. Some sample minimal rates (up to 500g parcels) are as follows:

country/region	cost
Asia (South)	Y255
Asia (South-East)	Y150
Australia	Y195
Europe (Eastern)	Y382
Europe (Western)	Y232
Hong Kong & Macau	Y95
Japan & Korea	Y115
Middle East	Y375
North America	Y217
South America	Y262

Registration Fees The registration fee for letters, printed matter and packets is Y3. Acknowledgment of receipt is Y3 per article.

Sending Mail

The international postal service seems efficient, and airmail letters and postcards will probably take around five to 10 days to reach their destinations. Write the address clearly and if possible, write the country of destination in Chinese for faster delivery. Domestic post is swift – perhaps one or two days from Guǎngzhōu to Běijīng. Intra-city it may be delivered the same day it's sent.

Apart from local post offices, branch post offices can be found in major tourist hotels where you can send letters, packets and parcels, but you may only be able to post printed matter. Other parcels may require a customs form attached at the town's main post office and a contents check. Even at cheap hotels you can usually post letters from the front desk – reliability varies, but in general it's fine.

If you are sending items abroad, take them unpacked with you to the post office to be inspected and an appropriate box/envelope found for you. Most post offices offer materials (for which you'll be charged) for packaging, including padded envelopes, boxes and heavy brown paper. Don't take your own packaging as it will probably be refused.

If you have a receipt for the goods, put it in the box when you're mailing it, since it may be opened again by customs further down the line.

Customs inspections will retain anything suspected of being pirated and you will have to complete a customs declaration form. Post offices are very picky about how you pack things; don't finalise your packing until the item has got its last customs clearance.

Once the box is sealed, you then go to another counter where you pay for the postage. Hang onto your receipt (the one for the postage of the item), as it could be useful for chasing misdirected goods, should this happen.

Private Carriers There are a number of foreign private couriers in China that offer international express posting of documents and parcels. None of these private carriers is cheap, but they're fast and secure. In major cities these companies have a pick-up service as well as drop-off centres, so call their offices for the latest details.

The major players in this market are United Parcel Service, DHL, Federal Express and TNT Skypak.

Receiving Mail

There are fairly reliable poste restante (cúnjú hòu) services in just about every city and town. The collection system is not uniform, but the charge should be Y1 to Y2.30 for each item of poste restante mail you collect. Take your passport along for retrieving letters or parcels.

Some larger tourist hotels will hold mail for their guests, but this is a less reliable option. Receiving a parcel from abroad is a bit complicated. The mail carrier will not deliver the parcel to your address – what you get is a slip of paper (in Chinese only). Bring this to the post office (indicated on the paper) along with your passport – the parcel will be opened and inspected in front of you. Prohibited articles will be seized; the regulations specifically prohibit 'reactionary books, magazines and propaganda materials, obscene or immoral articles'. You also cannot mail Chinese currency abroad or receive it by post.

Telephone

Both international and domestic calls can be made with a minimum of fuss from your hotel room and card phones are increasingly widespread.

Most hotel rooms have phones from which local calls are free. Alternatively, local calls can be made from public pay phones. Also look out for domestic phones at newspaper stands and kiosks – you can make local calls on these for around two jiǎo. Long-distance domestic calls can also be made from phone booths, but not usually international calls. In the lobbies of many hotels, the reception desks have a similar system – free local calls for guests, Y1 for non-guests, and long-distance calls charged by the minute. Calls made between midnight and 7am are 40% cheaper than at other times.

Domestic long-distance rates in China vary according to distance, but are cheap. International calls are quickly becoming cheaper if you use an IP card or a calling card (see Phone Cards following). Phoning direct without a card is, however, expensive. Check expat mags like *City Weekend* for a range of other telephone services and operations offering cheap rates.

If you are expecting a call – either international or domestic – try to advise the caller beforehand of your hotel room number. Hotel operators respond in slow motion when confronted with Western names and some just freeze.

Pager operators don't speak English. They will ask for the number you are calling, your name, your return number and extension, in that order.

The country code to use to access China is ☎ 86.

Phonecards There's a wide range of local and international phonecards. Lonely Planet's eKno Communication Card is aimed specifically at independent travellers and provides budget international calls, a range of messaging services, free email and travel information – for local calls, you're usually better off with a local card. You can join online at **W** www.ekno.lonelyplanet.com, or by phone from China by dialling the local access number, ☎ 10800 140 0208. Check the eKno Web site for access numbers from other countries and updates on super budget access numbers and new features.

International calls on IP (Internet Phone) cards are Y2.40 per minute to the USA or Canada, Y1.50 per minute to Hong Kong, Macau and Taiwan and Y3.20 to all other countries; domestic long-distance calls are Y0.30 per minute. You dial a local number, then punch in your account number, followed by the number you wish to call. English-language service is usually available. The service is available in a large number of cities in China, including Běijīng and Shànghǎi. IP cards come in Y100 increments and can be found at most hotels, news kiosks and Internet cafes. IC cards work on a similar principle, but can only be used domestically.

A calling card from your country's telecom network can also charge call costs to your account from abroad.

Regular card phones are also found in hotel lobbies and in most telecommunications buildings. Calls from them cost about double the price of IP rates and some phonecards can only be used in the province where you buy them. Smartcards can be used throughout China, provided you can find a Smartcard phone.

Direct Dialling and Collect Calls To make international calls from China, the international access code is ☎ 00. Add the country code, then the local area code (omitting the 0 before it) and the number you want to reach. Another option is to dial the home country direct dial number (☎ 108), which puts you straight through to a local operator there. You can then make a reverse-charge (collect) call or a credit-card call with a telephone credit card valid in the destination country.

Dialling codes include:

country	direct dial	country direct
Australia	☎ 00-61	☎ 108-61
Canada	☎ 00-1	☎ 108-1
Hong Kong	☎ 00-852	☎ 108-852
Japan	☎ 00-81	☎ 108-81
Netherlands	☎ 00-31	☎ 108-31
New Zealand	☎ 00-64	☎ 108-64
UK	☎ 00-44	☎ 108-44
USA	☎ 00-1	☎ 108-1*

* For the USA you can dial ☎ 108-11 (AT&T), ☎ 108-12 (MCI) or ☎ 108-13 (Sprint)

Essential Numbers

There are several telephone numbers that are the same for all major cities. However, only international assistance is likely to have English-speaking operators:

directory	number
International assistance	☎ 115
Local directory assistance	☎ 114
Long-distance assistance	☎ 113/173
Police hotline	☎ 110
Fire hotline	☎ 119

To call a number in China from abroad, dial the international access code (☎ 00), the country code for China (☎ 86), then the local area code and the number you're calling. Area codes are located under each main individual city's heading throughout this book.

Mobile Phones Check if your mobile phone has a setting for use in China. Mobile-phone shops *(shǒujīdiàn)* can sell you a phone and a number beginning with 136, which will cost around Y200; you then buy credits on the following denominations of cards: Y50, Y100, Y300 and Y500 (each valid for a limited period). The local per-minute non-roaming city call charge for China Mobile is six jiǎo; intra-provincial calls are Y1.20 per minute, inter-provincial calls Y1.40 per minute. It costs six jiǎo every minute to receive phone calls. Roaming charges cost an additional two jiǎo per minute, but the call receiving charge is the same. Overseas calls can be made for Y4.80 per minute plus the local charge per minute by dialling ☎ 17951, followed by 00, the country code then the number you want to call. Otherwise you will be charged the IDD call charge plus six jiǎo per minute.

Email

Chinese is expected to be the world's largest online language by 2007. Internet cafes are easy to find in cities and many small towns, and you can get online in numerous hotels, universities and libraries. The explosion of Net cafes in China has startled the authorities, with online consoles appearing in hairdressers and even butchers.

[Continued on page 91]

Experience the regional variety and flavours of Chinese cuisine and drink.

Chinese Cuisine

OLIVER STREWE

OLIVER STREWE

CHRIS MELLOR

OLIVER STREWE

BRADLEY MAYHEW

CRAIG PERSHOUSE

Title page: Hedgehog bun (steamed egg custard cream) and green tea, Kowloon. (Photograph by Oliver Strewe.)

Top: Cooking *yóutiáo* (deep fried dough sticks), Hong Kong.

Middle: (Clockwise from left) freshly made noodles, Macau; *zòngzi* (glutinous rice wrapped in bamboo leaves) eaten during the Dragon Boat Festival, Shànghǎi; fried dumplings at a street stall, Shànghǎi; soy beans fermenting to make soy sauce, Hong Kong.

Bottom: An Uyghur woman sells beautifully decorated bread, Kashgar, Xīnjiāng.

GLENN BEANLAND

Whether you're travelling up a mountain, across a desert or through a suburb in China, you'll find people greeting you with *'Chī fànle ma?'* Literally translated as 'Have you eaten rice yet?', this continuous inquiry reveals the significance of food in Chinese culture and, more specifically, the importance of rice in China's history. The phrase is more commonly translated as simply 'Have you eaten yet?' – it's assumed that if you've eaten, you've eaten rice. *Fàn* (rice) may be more loosely translated as 'grain'. The principle that a proper meal is based around a staple grain dates back at least to the Shang dynasty (1700–1200 BC) and remains fundamental to Chinese cuisine wherever it is found.

Fàn sits in opposition to *cài*, literally meaning 'vegetable' and, by extension, any accompaniment to grain in a meal. This dichotomy between fàn and cài shows how the principles of balance and harmony, *yin* and *yang*, are applied in everyday life. Most vegetables and fruits are yin foods, generally moist or soft, and are meant to have a cooling effect, nurturing the feminine aspect of our nature. Yang foods – fried, spicy or with red meat – are warming and nourish the masculine side of our nature. Any meal should harmonise a variety of tastes and provide a balance between cooling and warming foods. Historically, fàn has played a more important role than cài; one of the highest compliments that can be paid to a dish is that it 'helps the rice go down' *(hsai fàn)*.

Cooking in China is divided into four schools: Northern, Eastern, Western and Southern. The differences among them arose not only from geographical, climatic and cultural differences, but also from historical circumstances. It was not until China was under threat from the Jurchen Mongols in the 12th century, when the Song court fled south of the Cháng Jiāng (Yangzi River), that these regional cuisines were distinguished and developed. Widespread urbanisation, made possible by the commercialisation of agriculture and food distribution, gave rise to the restaurant industry, which in turn facilitated the development of the regional cuisines. A further impetus was provided by demand from the merchants and bureaucrats who constantly travelled the kingdom.

The Mongol conquest of the north also precipitated the shift to rice as the main staple. This was significant, as rice is the best source of nutritionally balanced calories and can support more people from a given area than any other crop. Improved communications, notably the building of the Grand Canal to link many of China's waterways, allowed food to be brought from and supplied to any part of the kingdom.

During the Ming dynasty (1368–1644) the restaurant industry continued to flourish. At this time, the court kitchens in the Forbidden City alone are reputed to have employed 5000 people. Giant blocks of ice were cut from northern rivers and lakes in winter and stored in deep caves to use for refridgeration during summer. This allowed further diversification and use of products out of season.

The last significant development in Chinese cuisine took place in the Qing dynasty (1644–1911), when crops were introduced from the New World. Maize, sweet potatoes and peanuts flourished in climates where rice, wheat and millet wouldn't grow, making life possible in formally uninhabitable areas. The other significant import from the New World was red chillies, which are not only a spice, but also a concentrated source of vitamins A and C.

The Northern School

In the north, fàn is traditionally wheat or millet rather than rice. Its most common incarnations are as *jiǎozi* (steamed dumplings) and *chūnjuan* (spring rolls). Arguably the most famous Chinese dish of all, Beijing duck, is also served with typical northern ingredients: wheat pancakes, spring onions and fermented bean paste. The range of cài is limited in the north, so there is a heavy reliance on freshwater fish and chicken; cabbage is ubiquitous and seems to fill any available space on trains, buses and lorries in the winter.

Not surprisingly, the influence of the Mongols is felt most strongly in the north and two of the region's most famous culinary exports – Mongolian barbecue and Mongolian hotpot – are adaptations from Mongol field kitchens. Animals that could be hunted on horseback were cooked with wild vegetables and onions using soldiers' iron shields on top of hot coals. Alternatively, each soldier could use their helmet as a pot, filling it with water, meat, condiments and vegetables. Mutton is now the main ingredient in Mongolian hotpot.

Roasting was once considered rather barbaric in other parts of China, and is still more common in the north. The main methods of cooking in the northern style are steaming, baking and 'explode-frying'. The last of these is the most common, historically because of the scarcity of fuel and, more recently, due to the introduction of the peanut, which thrives in the north and produces an abundance of oil. Although northern-style food has a reputation for being unsophisticated and bland, it has the benefit of being filling and, therefore, well suited to a cold climate.

Provincial dishes of the north include:

Ānhuī 安徽

smoked shad with tea	*máofēng xūn shíyú*	毛峰熏鲥鱼
stewed Mandarin fish with mutton	*yú yǎo yáng*	鱼咬羊
stewed preserved Mandarin fish	*yān xiān guìyú*	腌鲜鳜鱼
steamed crab with roe and shrimp	*xiè huáng xiā zhōng*	蟹黄虾盅
preserved crab in Chinese wine	*túnxī zuì xiè*	屯溪醉蟹
deep-fried mutton	*jiāo zhá yángròu*	焦炸羊肉
blanched smoked chicken	*shēng xūn zǐ jī*	生熏子鸡
chicken wrapped in lotus leaf	*qīngxiāng shā wǔ jī*	清香沙焐鸡
steamed pigeon with yam	*huángshān dùn gē*	黄山炖鸽
deep-fried and stewed bean curd with pork and shrimp	*hóngwǔ dòufu*	洪武豆腐

Shāndōng 山东

steamed shrimp, chicken and dried scallops	*xiùqiú gānbèi*	绣球干贝
stewed sea cucumber with scallion	*cōng shāo hǎishēn*	葱烧海参
hot and sour fish egg and coriander soup	*huì wūgu*	烩乌龟蛋
salty and sour flounder and scallion soup	*kuà dùn mùyú*	侉炖目鱼
deep-fried sweet and sour carp	*tángcù lǐyú*	糖醋鲤鱼

hot and sour Mandarin fish and scallion soup	cù jiāo guìyú	醋椒鳜鱼
stir-fried pork tenderloin with coriander	yuán bào lǐjī	芫爆里脊
stir-fried pig's tripe and kidney	yóu bào shuāng cuì	油爆双脆
spicy braised pig's intestine	jiǔ zhuǎn dàcháng	九转大肠
stir-fried chicken, fish and bamboo shoots	zāo liū sān bái	糟熘三白
steamed and fried pork, shrimp and bamboo shoot balls	sì xǐ wánzi	四喜丸子
stir-fried chicken and jelly fish	chǎo jī sī zhé tóu	炒鸡丝蛰头
stir-fried chicken with egg white	fúróng jī piàn	芙蓉鸡片
stir-fried chicken with bamboo shoots	jiàng bào jī dīng	酱爆鸡丁
steamed bean curd, minced pork and black fungus	bó shān dòufu xiāng	博山豆腐箱
boiled lotus seeds with sugar crystal	bīngtáng liánzǐ	冰糖莲子
deep-fried and stewed bean curd, egg and shrimp	guō tā dòufu hé	锅塌豆腐盒
sliced bean curd with Chinese cabbage	sān měi dòufu	三美豆腐
deep-fried egg yolk with essence of banana	xiāngjiāo guō zhá	香蕉锅炸
sweet and crispy deep-fried apple	básī píngguǒ	拔丝苹果

The Eastern School

The eastern region – blessed with the bounty of Cháng Jiāng and its tributaries, a subtropical climate, fertile soil and a coastline – has long been a mecca for gastronomes. On the banks of Xī Hú (West Lake), with its abundance of fish such as the highly esteemed silver carp, the Southern Song capital of Hángzhōu in Zhèjiāng province is the birthplace of the Chinese restaurant industry. Sūzhōu, the famous garden city in Jiāngsū, is equally famous for its cuisine, which has been eulogised by generations of poets.

A vast variety of ingredients and condiments is available, which has led to a wide diversity of cuisine within the eastern region. Explode-frying is used here, too, but not as much as the form of frying known as archetypally Chinese throughout the world: stir-frying in a wok. Another eastern style of cooking that has been exported to the rest of the world (from Fújiàn via Taiwan) is the red-stew, in which meat is simmered slowly in dark soy sauce, sugar and spices. Indeed, many Fújiàn dishes rely on a heavy, meaty stock for their distinctive flavour. It is also in this region that Chinese vegetarian cuisine reached its apex, partly thanks to the availability of fresh ingredients and partly to the specialisation of generations of chefs. As might be expected, only light seasoning is used to allow the natural flavours of the fresh ingredients to be fully appreciated. The eastern region is also the source of China's best soy sauces and some of the best rice wines.

Jiāngsū 江苏

stir-fried clam, water chestnut and mushroom	tiānxià dìyī xiān	天下第一鲜
steamed crab	qīngzhēng dàxháxiè	清蒸大闸蟹
deep-fried Mandarin fish with shrimp and bamboo shoots	sōngshǔ guìyú	松鼠鳜鱼
hot and sour fish soup	cùliū guìyú	醋溜鳜鱼
boiled fish liver with bamboo shoots	qīngtāng tū fèi	清汤秃肺
fish tail stew	qīngyú shuǎi shuǐ	青鱼甩水
deep-fried and stewed eel	wúxī cuì shàn	无锡脆鳝
carp and water shield	chúncài cuān tángyú piàn	莼菜氽塘鱼片
blanched eel tail	qiàng hǔ wěi	炝虎尾
braised carp head	chāi huì liányú tóu	拆烩鲢鱼头
deep-fried pork with pea shoots	biǎn dǎ kū sū	扁大枯酥
braised pork and crab meat balls	xiè fěn shīzi tóu	蟹粉狮子头
boiled pig's trotters	zhènjiāng yáo ròu	镇江肴肉
salty and sweet stewed spareribs	wúxī ròu gútou	无锡肉骨头
braised duck and pigeon	sān tào yā	三套鸭
roasted hen with ham, pork and mushrooms	jiàohuā jī	叫花鸡
steamed turtle and chicken	bàwáng biē jī	霸王别姬
boiled egg, stewed with minced pork	shénxiān dàn	神仙蛋
stir-fried duck's giblets with chicken	měirén gān	美人肝
shredded chicken with bean curd soup	wénsì dòufu	文思豆腐

Fújiàn 福建

steamed sturgeon	bābǎo fúróng xún	八宝芙蓉鲟
fried eel	jiān zāo mànyú	煎糟鳗鱼
roast Mandarin fish	cōng yóu kǎo yú	葱油烤鱼
fish ball soup with eel, shrimp and pork	qīxīng yú wán tāng	七星鱼丸汤
steamed pork with dried mustard	cài gān kòu ròu	菜干扣肉
stewed frog with mushrooms	yóu mèn shílín	油焖石鳞
steamed bird's nest with shredded chicken	jī sī yànwō	鸡丝燕窝
chicken with glutinous rice	jiā hé cuì pí jī	嘉禾脆皮鸡
chicken skin and mushroom soup	jī pí mógu tāng	鸡皮蘑菇汤

Zhèjiāng (Hángzhōu) 浙江（杭州）

mandarin fish soup with ham and mushrooms	sòngsǎo yú gēng	宋嫂鱼羹
stewed sweet and sour fish	xīhú cù yú	西湖醋鱼
stewed yellowfin croaker with potherb mustard	xuěcài dàtāng huángyú	雪菜大汤黄鱼
stir-fried eel with onion	níng shì shànyú	宁式鳝鱼
stir-fried shrimp in tea	lóngjǐng xiārén	龙井虾仁
stewed pork	dōngpō ròu	东坡肉
steamed pork wrapped in lotus leaf	héyè fěnzhēng ròu	荷叶粉蒸肉
boiled chicken	qīngtāng yuè jī	清汤越鸡
water shield soup	xīhú chúncài tāng	西湖莼菜汤

The Western School

The Western School is most renowned for its use of the red chilli, introduced by Spanish traders in the early Qing dynasty. While northern foods evolved to provide lasting satisfaction in a cold climate, Sìchuān dishes tend to dry out the body through perspiration, which helps it adjust to the intense humidity. Again, with a subtropical climate and the aid of an irrigation system supplied by the Mín Hé (Min River) for over two millennia, fresh ingredients are available year-round, although not in the abundance or variety found in the east or south of the country. Pork, poultry, legumes and soybeans are the most commonly used cài, supplemented by a variety of wild condiments and mountain products, such as mushrooms and other fungi, as well as bamboo shoots. Seasonings are heavy: the red chilli is often used in conjunction with Sìchuān *huājiāo* (flower pepper), garlic, ginger and onions. Apart from its medicinal and nutritional values, fiery seasonings stimulate the palate and help the fàn go down in a province where the choice of cài can be quite limited. Meat, particularly in Húnán, is marinated, pickled or otherwise processed before cooking, which is generally by stir- or explode-frying.

The cuisine of the Western School has a reputation as being down-to-earth, rather like the inhabitants of the region. Mao Zedong hailed from Húnán and remained fond of the hot foods from his native province throughout his life. However it was due to the nationalists in the civil war that Sìchuān cuisine gained international recognition. Fleeing the Japanese in 1937, the nationalist government took refuge in Chóngqìng until the end of the war in Asia. On its return to Nánjīng and Shànghǎi, thousands of Sìchuān chefs were brought along. Most of them continued on to Taiwan when the nationalist government was forced to flee once more, and from there spread out across the globe.

Sìchuān 四川

stewed sea cucumber with pork and soybean sprouts	*jiācháng hǎishēn*	家常海参
stewed carp with ham and hot and sweet sauce	*gānshāo yán lǐ*	干烧岩鲤
stewed eel with garlic	*dàsuàn shàn duàn*	大蒜鳝段
stewed beef with innards in a hot sauce	*fūqī fèi piàn*	夫妻肺片
boiled and stir-fried pork with salty and hot sauce	*huíguō ròu*	回锅肉
boiled pork with minced garlic	*suàn ní bái ròu*	蒜泥白肉
stir-fried pork tenderloin with crispy rice	*guōbā ròu piàn*	锅巴肉片
stir-fried pork, bamboo shoots and black fungus	*yú xiāng ròu sī*	鱼香肉丝
fried and boiled beef, garlic sprouts and celery	*shuǐ zhǔ niúròu*	水煮牛肉
stir-fried beef and celery with chilli	*gānbiān niúròu sī*	干煸牛肉丝
braised oxtail in wine	*qīngdùn niú wěi*	清炖牛尾
boiled chicken in a hot sauce	*bàngbang jī*	棒棒鸡

stir-fried pork or beef tenderloin		
with tuber mustard	*zhàcài ròu sī*	榨菜肉丝
stir-fried chicken with peanuts	*gōngbǎo jī dīng*	宫保鸡丁
stir-fried chicken		
with hot Sìchuān pepper	*huājiāo jī dīng*	花椒鸡丁
chicken and ham soup	*jī dòuhuā*	鸡豆花
stewed chicken wings in red wine	*guìfēi jī chì*	贵妃鸡翅
deep-fried and stewed vermicelli		
and minced beef	*mǎyǐ shàng shù*	蚂蚁上树
stewed bean curd and minced beef	*mápó dòufu*	麻婆豆腐
Chinese cabbage soup	*kāishu báicài*	开水白菜

Húnán 湖南

stir-fried and steamed sea		
cucumber with chicken and duck	*hǎishēn zhēng pén*	海参蒸盆
boiled sliced fish	*húdié piāo hǎi*	蝴蝶飘海
roasted Mandarin fish	*wǎng yóu chāshāo guìyú*	网油叉烧鳜鱼
braised turtle with pork	*dòngtíng jīn guī*	洞庭金龟
steamed pork		
with preserved soybeans	*zǒu yóu dòuchǐ kòu ròu*	走油豆豉扣肉
stewed preserved pork	*xiāngxī suān ròu*	湘西酸肉
steamed dried preserved pork		
with chicken and carp	*làwèi hé zhēng*	腊味合蒸
stir-fried chicken with chilli	*málà zǐ jī*	麻辣子鸡
steamed and stir-fried chestnut		
with cabbage	*bǎnlì shāo càixīn*	板栗烧菜心
lotus seeds and crystal sugar soup	*bīngtáng xiāng lián*	冰糖湘莲

The Southern School

The food from this region is easily the most common form of Chinese food found in the Western world, since most overseas Chinese have their roots in the Guǎngdōng region. The humid climate and heavy rainfall mean that rice has been a staple here since the Chinese first came to the region in the Han era (220–206 BC). Like the Eastern School, the Southern benefits from a cornucopia of ingredients to choose from, yet in the south the choice is even more exotic. Stir-frying is by far the most favoured method of cooking, closely followed by steaming. *Dim sum*, now a worldwide Sunday institution, originated in this region; *yám cha* (Cantonese for 'drink tea') still provides most overseas Chinese communities with the opportunity to get together on the weekend.

Not only are the ingredients more varied than elsewhere in China, methods of preparation also reach their peak of complexity in the south, where the appearance and texture of foods are prized alongside their freshness. Such refinement is a far cry from the austere cuisine of the north and the earthy fare of the west. Consequently, the southerners' gourmandising and exotic tastes – for dogs, cats, raccoons, monkeys, lizards and rats – have earned them a long-standing reputation around China.

Guǎngdōng (Cantonese) 广东

stewed shark's fin with pork and chicken feet	hóngshāo dà qún chì	红烧大群翅
steamed lobster	shēng chuī lóngxiā	生炊龙虾
stir-fried crab with ginger and scallions	jiāng cōng chǎo xiè	姜葱炒蟹
stewed abalone with bamboo shoots and oyster sauce	háoyóu wǎng bào piàn	蚝油网鲍片
blanched prawns with shredded scallion	bái zhuó xiā	白灼虾
stir-fried prawns with coriander and chilli	jiāo yán xiā	椒盐虾
roast pork with sweet syrup	mì zhī chāshāo	蜜汁叉烧
sweet and sour deep-fried pork with pineapple	bōluó gǔlǎo ròu	菠萝咕唠肉
stir-fried beef with bamboo shoots in oyster sauce	háoyóu niúròu	蚝油牛肉
stir-fried beef tenderloin with black pepper	tiěbǎn hēi jiāo niúliǔ	铁板黑椒牛柳
smoked chicken with tea and sugar	tàiyé jī	太爷鸡
salt-baked chicken	dōngjiāng yán jú jī	东江盐焗鸡
stir-fried snake meat with mushrooms and bamboo shoots	wǔcǎi chǎo shé sī	五彩炒蛇丝
stir-fried ham and milk	dàliáng chǎo xiān nǎi	大良炒鲜奶
boiled chicken with scallion and peppercorn	bái qiē jī	白切鸡
boiled chicken with ham and bok choy	jīnhuá yùshù jī	金华玉树鸡
stir-fried dog meat with garlic	yuán bāo gǒu ròu	原煲狗肉
stir-fried and stewed sweet potato leaves and straw mushrooms	hù guó cài	护国菜
steamed white gourd with duck, ham and shrimp	dōngguā zhōng	冬瓜盅
deep-fried and stewed noodles with shrimp and mushrooms	gānshāo yīfǔ miàn	干烧伊府面

Food Etiquette

Eating Chinese-style is well-established in the West and wouldn't faze most people these days. It's a rewarding way to eat for many reasons. For one thing, eating together really does mean sharing food since all diners eat cài from communal bowls, making it much more of a social event than Western-style eating (and arguably contributing to closer family bonds). Also, people can eat as much or as little as they want from each bowl, according to their own taste.

Although Chinese restaurants have a reputation in the West for being noisy, tasteless and basic (Formica tables, tacky calendars and plastic chopsticks), most Chinese consider the quality of the food as paramount. Good restaurants gain a reputation solely for the quality of their food, no matter what the decor and no matter how far out of the way.

There are a few dos and don'ts in Chinese food etiquette, mostly applicable only when you dine with Chinese. Probably the most important is who pays the bill: although you are expected to try to pay, you shouldn't argue too hard, as the one who extended the invitation will inevitably foot the bill. Going Dutch is unheard of except among the closest of friends. Other things to remember are to fill your neighbours' tea cups when they are empty, as yours will be filled by them. You can thank the pourer by tapping your middle finger on the table gently. On no account serve yourself tea without serving others first. Don't place your chopsticks in your rice while you are doing something else; this makes the bowl reminiscent of an offering to the dead and is regarded as very bad form. Finally, in deference to the importance of fàn in Chinese history and culture, it is considered impolite to leave rice in your individual bowl at the end of a meal, especially if all cài dishes have been eaten. Even today, Chinese children are admonished to eat their rice, just as Western children are told to eat their greens.

At the Restaurant 在餐馆

I don't eat dog	*wó bú chī gǒuròu*	我不吃狗肉
I don't want MSG	*wó bú yào wèijīng*	我不要味精
I'm vegetarian	*wǒ chī sù*	我吃素
not too spicy	*bú yào tài là*	不要太辣
(cooked) together	*yíkuàir*	一块儿
restaurant	*cāntīng*	餐厅
menu	*cài dān*	菜单
bill (cheque)	*mǎi dān/jiézhàng*	买单 (结帐)
set meal (no menu)	*tàocān*	套餐
to eat/let's eat	*chī fàn*	吃饭
chopsticks	*kuàizi*	筷子
knife	*dàozi*	刀子
fork	*chāzi*	叉子
spoon	*tiáogēng/tāngchí*	调羹/汤匙

Drinks

Nonalcoholic Drinks Tea is the most commonly served brew in China. The origins of tea-drinking are obscure, but legend has it that it was first cultivated in China about 4000 years ago in the modern-day province of Sìchuān. Although black (fermented) tea is produced in China, principally in the Huáng Shān area (Ānhuī), green (unfermented) is by far the most widely drunk. Indian and Sri Lankan black tea is available only in international supermarkets. Familiar brands of instant coffee are for sale everywhere, but fresh-brewed coffee is still a rarity.

Sugary Chinese soft drinks are cheap and ever-present. Jianlibao is a soft drink made with honey rather than sugar and is a good energy boost, especially if you've venturing up to high-altitudes. Lychee-flavoured carbonated drinks are unique to China and seem to be a favourite with foreign travellers. Peanut-milk is a life-saver after the searing of the Western School dishes.

A surprising treat is fresh sweet yoghurt, available in many parts of China. It's typically sold in what looks like small milk bottles and is drunk with a straw rather than eaten with a spoon. Fresh milk is rare, but you can buy imported UHT milk from supermarkets in big cities.

Coca-Cola, first introduced to China by American soldiers in 1927, is now produced locally. Chinese attempts at making similar brews include TianFu Cola, which has a recipe based on the root of herbaceous peony.

fizzy drink (soda)	qìshuǐ	汽水
Coca-Cola	kěkǒu kělè	可口可乐
mineral water	kuàng quán shu	矿泉水
tea	chá	茶
coffee	kāfēi	咖啡
coffee creamer	nǎijīng	奶精
boiling water	kāi shuǐ	开水
milk	niúnǎi	牛奶
soybean milk	dòujiāng	豆浆
yogurt	suānnǎi	酸奶
fruit juice	guǒzhī	果汁
orange juice	liǔchéng zhī	柳橙汁
coconut juice	yézi zhī	椰子汁
pineapple juice	bōluó zhī	菠萝汁
mango juice	mángguǒ zhī	芒果汁
hot	rède	热的
ice cold	bīngde	冰的
ice cube	bīng kuài	冰块

Alcoholic Drinks If tea is the most popular drink in the PRC, then beer must be number two. By any standards the top brands are good. The best known is Tsingtao, made with a mineral water that gives it a sparkling quality. It's essentially a German beer since the town of Qīngdǎo (formerly spelled 'Tsingtao'), where it's made, was once a German concession and the Chinese inherited the brewery. Experts claim that draft Tsingtao tastes much better than the bottled stuff. Local brews are found in all the major cities of China – notable ones include Zhujiang in Guǎngzhōu and Yanjing in Běijīng. San Miguel has a brewery in Guǎngzhōu, so you can enjoy this 'imported' beer at Chinese prices.

China has cultivated vines and produced wine for an estimated 4000 years. Chinese wine-producing techniques differ from those of the West. While quality-conscious Western wine producers work on the idea that the lower the yield the higher the quality of the wine produced, Chinese farmers cultivate every possible square centimetre of earth, encouraging their vines to yield heavily. The Chinese also plant peanuts between the rows of vines as a cover crop for half the year; however, the peanuts sap much of the nutrient from the soil and in cooler years the large grape crops fail to ripen sufficiently to produce good wine. Western wine producers try to prevent oxidation in their wines, but oxidation produces a flavour that Chinese tipplers find desirable and go to great lengths to achieve. You will inevitably encounter the sweet-smelling, lethal white grape wine, drunk to fend off cold and boredom on long train journeys. Chinese diners are also keen on wines with different herbs and other infusions, which they drink for their health and for restorative or aphrodisiac qualities.

The word 'wine' gets rather loosely translated – many Chinese 'wines' are in fact spirits. Rice wine is intended mainly for cooking rather than drinking. *Hejie jiu* (lizard wine) is produced in the southern province of Guǎngxī; each bottle contains one dead lizard suspended perpendicularly in the clear liquid. Wine with dead bees or pickled snakes is also desirable for its alleged tonic properties – in general, the more poisonous the creature, the more potent the tonic effects.

Tibetans have an interesting brew called *chang*, made from barley. Mongolians serve sour-tasting *koumiss*, made of fermented mare's milk with lots of salt added. *Maotai*, a favourite of Chinese drinkers, is a spirit made from sorghum (a type of millet) and used for toasts at banquets.

beer	*píjiǔ*	啤酒
red grape wine	*hóng pútáo jiǔ*	红葡萄酒
white grape wine	*bái pútáo jiǔ*	白葡萄酒
whisky	*wēishìjì jiǔ*	威士忌酒
vodka	*fútèjiā jiǔ*	伏特加酒
rice wine	*mǐ jiǔ*	米酒
Chinese spirits	*báijiǔ*	白酒

[Continued from page 80]

Be warned that the government periodically shuts swathes of Internet cafes. In summer 2001, after inspecting the country's Internet cafe scene, it ordered the closure of 2000 and the suspension of 6000 cafes. In small Internet cafes around China, you can get connected for as little as Y2 per hour.

One reader wrote:

The proliferation of connections is driving down costs. Overall, the best places to connect are at the China Telecom buildings in various cities. The fee is generally Y3 per hour and the connection is very fast.

Jeff Mahn

Popular places for getting online are marked on the city and town maps of the destination chapters. These are the characters for an Internet cafe (*wǎngbā*):

网吧

Many travellers keep in touch while on the road via free email accounts with Hotmail (W www.hotmail.com) or Yahoo! (W www.yahoo.com), but connections are often agonisingly slow. If you're willing to spend US$15 per year, you can get all your email forwarded to any address of your choice by signing up with Pobox (W www.pobox.com) – this service can also be used to block advertising and mail bombs.

If you are in Běijīng long-term, you can access the Internet just by dialling out (as long as you have a phone number). There is no need to open an account with an Internet Service Provider (ISP) – charges will just appear on your phone bill. China Telecom offers Internet service in most major cities.

You do have to put up with some censorship – the Chinese government blocks access to certain sites with political content deemed unsuitable for the masses (such as the BBC Web site); but newspaper sites strangely tend to be left alone.

INTERNET RESOURCES

The World Wide Web is a rich resource for travellers. You can research your trip, hunt down bargain fares, book hotels, check on weather conditions or chat with locals and other travellers about the best places to visit (or avoid!).

Lonely Planet has information on China on its Internet site at W www.lonely planet.com, as well as the Thorn Tree, where you can post and reply to queries about travel in China and elsewhere. Other recommended China travel, arts and entertainment-related Web sites include:

Art Scene China: Contemporary Chinese Art Gallery Online art gallery featuring a wide selection of artworks by well-established and up-and-coming artists from throughout China.
  W www.artscenechina.com

China Avante-Garde: Contemporary Chinese Art Art advisory service specialising in the acquisition of important works of contemporary Chinese art.
  W www.china-avantgarde.com

China Now – The Ultimate Guide to City Life in China Columns, travel information, nightlife and restaurant listings, and classified ads.
  W www.chinanow.com

Chinese Business World: China Travel Guide Chinese Business World China travel guide with a hotel and flight booking facility.
  W www.cbw.com/tourism

Redbang Compact updated travel info on Běijīng in five different languages, Web, WAP, PDA and SMS accessible.
  W www.redbang.com

Wildchina Wild treks around China, organised within China.
  W www.wildchina.com

Other recommended China-related Web sites worth taking a look at include:

Beijing Language and Culture University Web site of the university that provides foreign students with an education in Chinese language and culture.
  W www.blcu.edu.cn

China Daily Web Site Coverage on economy, politics, social events, culture, life, arts and sport.
  W www.chinadaily.com.cn

Sinopolis Daily China news and information, includes articles translated into English from the Chinese press.
  W www.sinopolis.com

Vegeats.com Lists vegetarian restaurants in Hong Kong and China.
  W www.vegeats.com

World Organizations in China Lists organisations in China.
  W www.chinatoday.com/dip/a2.htm

Zhaopin Huge database of jobs in China.
  W www.zhaopin.com

Zhongwen: Chinese Characters and Culture Includes a pinyin chat room and an online dictionary of Chinese characters.
  W www.zhongwen.com

You can also check out Amnesty International's Web site at **W** www.amnesty.org for its reports on China. Also try Human Rights in China at **W** www.hrichina.org or Human Rights Watch at **W** www.hrw.org and Support Democracy in China at **W** www.christ usrex.org/ww1.sdc. TIN (Tibet Information Network) at **W** www.tibetinfo.net is a comprehensive site of Tibet issues.

BOOKS

Fathoming the enigma of China is such a monumental task that the need for 'China-watchers' and their publications will probably never dry up. Indeed, just keeping up with the never-ending flood of conjecture would be a full-time job in itself.

Most books are published in different editions by different publishers in different countries. As a result a book might be a hardcover rarity in one country while it's readily available in paperback in another. Fortunately, bookshops and libraries search by title or author, so your local bookshop or library is best placed to advise you on the availability of titles. The following is just an abbreviated tour of the highlights.

Lonely Planet

Lonely Planet guides to the region include *Beijing*, *Central Asia*, *Hong Kong & Macau*, *Shanghai*, *South-West China* and *Tibet*. There are phrasebooks covering Mandarin, Cantonese, Tibetan, Central Asian languages and Arabic. Also published by Lonely Planet are *Read This First: Asia & India*, *Healthy Travel Asia & India* and *Chasing Rickshaws*.

Guidebooks

The Hong Kong publisher Odyssey is gradually producing a series of illustrated provincial guides to China. To date there are guides to Yúnnán, Guìzhōu, Sìchuān, Shànghǎi, Xī'ān and Běijīng. There is less emphasis on the kind of practical travel information you find in Lonely Planet guides, but they are attractively packaged and provide good background reading.

It is worth keeping an eye out for reprints of old guidebooks to China. Oxford University Press' *In Search of Old Peking* by LC Arlington and William Lewisohn, is a wonderfully detailed guide to a world that is now long gone. It is out of print now, but you may be able to pick up a used copy.

Travel

From Heaven Lake by Vikram Seth follows Seth's journey from Xīnjiāng to Tibet and on to Delhi. Another possibility is *Danziger's Travels* by Nick Danziger – a good 'Silk Road' book that takes quite a long time to get to China.

China by Bike: Taiwan, Hong Kong, China's East Coast by Roger Grigsby is just what the title implies.

The greatest backpacker of all time was, of course, Marco Polo. Author Ronald Latham published *Marco Polo, The Travels* in 1958, and it's still available as a Penguin reprint.

In Xanadu by William Dalrymple traces Marco Polo's footsteps from Jerusalem to Xanadu and the ruins of Kublai Khan's splendid palace in north China.

History & Politics

The most comprehensive history available is the *Cambridge History of China*. The series runs to 15 volumes and traces Chinese history from its earliest beginnings to 1982.

A far more practical overview for travellers is *The Walled Kingdom: A History of China from 2000 BC to the Present* by Witold Rodzinsky. It should be available in a handy paperback edition of around 450 pages.

A high-quality history of modern China is Jonathan Spence's *The Search for Modern China*. It comprehensively covers China's history from the late Ming dynasty through to the Tiānānmén Massacre, in lively prose that is a pleasure to read.

God's Chinese Son, also by Spence, pursues the Taiping leader, Hong Xiuquan, on his wild Christian quest to put Manchu China to the sword and establish heaven on earth. Relating his tale in the present tense, Spence spares no spadework in the autopsy of his subject.

Burying Mao by Richard Baum is a political history of the Deng years. For anyone seriously interested in China's stop-go reforms of the Deng era, this is the book to read. Merle Goldman also looks at the tortuous course of democratic reform in *Sowing the Seeds of Democracy in China: Political Reform in the Deng Xiaoping Era*.

Jasper Becker's *Hungry Ghosts: Mao's Secret Famine* is perhaps the best book on the disastrous Great Leap Forward. The book focuses on the 1958–62 famine that killed up to 30 million people.

It is worth picking up a copy of *The Soong Dynasty* by Sterling Seagrave for a racy account of the bad old days under the Kuomintang.

The Tiananmen Papers blows away the official smokescreen hanging over the events leading up to June 1989.

General

Insights *Wild Swans* by Jung Chang is one of the more ambitious of the long line of autobiographical 'I survived China, but only just' books. *Life and Death in Shanghai* by Nien Cheng focuses largely on the Cultural Revolution and is also recommended.

Red Azalea by Anchee Min is an account of what it was like to grow up in the Cultural Revolution.

A fine account of life in rural China is *Mr China's Son: A Villager's Life* by He Liuyi.

State-of-the-nation accounts of contemporary Chinese politics and society by Western scholars and journalists are thick on the ground and tend to become repetitive if you read too many of them. *The Chinese* by Jasper Becker is an up-to-date and incisive examination of today's China, and where the author believes the land is headed.

Also recommended is *China Wakes* by Nicholas D Kristof and Sheryl Wudunn.

Another interesting account is Canadian journalist Jan Wong's *Red China Blues*. The book spans the author's experiences from being a pro-Communist foreign student in China during the Cultural Revolution to her stint as a foreign correspondent during the massacre at Tiānánmén.

For an insight into Chinese society, check out Perry Link's *Evening Chats in Beijing*. It's intelligent, well written and packed with illuminating insights and observations drawn from a long career of writing and thinking about China.

China Remembers by Calum MacLeod and Lijia Zhang is an excellent collection of short essays by Chinese whose lives exemplify China in the last 50 years.

The Classic of the Way and its Power by Laotzu may not tell you much about modern China, but it's an essential volume to anyone interested in Chinese philosophy, religion, martial arts, aesthetics, or the *dao*.

The Coming Collapse of China by Gordon G Chang is a bleak look at China's future. Chang sees the land sinking inexorably into a vast quicksand of corruption, banking crises and unemployment, further dragged down by an unwieldy state sector and uninspiring leadership. However conjectural it may be, the title is a useful counterweight to the numerous positive-spin 'China awakes/rises' books available.

Human Rights *Eighteen Layers of Hell: Stories from the Chinese Gulag* by Kate Saunders blows the lid off China's human rights violations.

Harry Wu, imprisoned by Chinese authorities for 19 years, exposes China's *láogǎi* (forced labour camps) in his eloquently written *Bitter Winds: A Memoir of My Years in China's Gulag*. Wu returned to China again in 1995 and was immediately arrested and tried for espionage, but was expelled after intervention by the US congress and President Clinton. He wrote about that experience in his sequel, *Troublemaker: One Man's Crusade Against China's Cruelty*.

The smuggled prison letters of dissident Wei Jingsheng have been collected and published in *The Courage to Stand Alone: Letters from Prison and Other Writings*, edited by Kristina Torgeson.

Some earlier works, now out of print, can be tracked down in libraries. Two such examples are *Prisoner of Mao* (1976) by Bao Ruo-Wang and *Seeds of Fire – Chinese Voices of Conscience* (1989), edited by Geremie Barmé and John Minford.

Biography Biographical appraisals of China's shadowy leaders are immensely popular. Mao, of course, has been the subject of countless biographies. The classic is *Red Star over China* by Edgar Snow, but it was Mao's personal physician, Zhisui Li, who finally exposed the world's most famous dictator cum pop icon. Li's *The Private Life of Chairman Mao* is absolutely compelling in its account of Mao as a domineering manipulator who hypocritically flouted the authoritarian and puritanical rules he foisted on his people – fascinating stuff.

Mao gets similar treatment in *The New Emperors* by Harrison E Salisbury. The book covers the lives of Mao and Deng, but the bulk of the book is devoted to Mao, while Deng remains quite elusive.

Richard Evans has written the excellent *Deng Xiaoping and the Making of Modern China*, which has a particularly good synopsis of the events leading up to the killings in Tiānānmén Square in 1989.

The classic historical investigation *The Hermit of Peking* by Hugh Trevor-Roper relates the story of Wykehamist and Oriental scholar extraordinaire Edmund Backhouse. It's a gripping tale of obsession and intrigue, swirling around the declining Manchu court.

Dragon Empress by Marina Warner is a compelling portrait of the 'Old Buddha', or Empress Dowager Cixi.

Fiction *The Good Earth* by Pearl S Buck has become a classic. Ms Buck lived most of her life in 19th-century China and was a prolific writer. Some of her lesser-known books are still in print, including *Sons – Good Earth Trilogy Volume 2*, *The Big Wave*, *The Child Who Never Grew*, *Dragon Seed*, *East Wind: West Wind*, *A House Divided*, *Imperial Woman*, *Kinfolk*, *The House of Earth Volume 9*, *The Living Reed*, *The Mother*, *Pavilion of Women*, *Peony*, *The Three Daughters of Madame Liang*, *Little Red* and *The Promise*.

Manchu Palaces: A Novel by Jeanne Larsen is the story of Lotus, a woman struggling to secure a job for herself in the Forbidden City during the 18th-century Manchu dynasty.

The work of Jonathan Spence occupies an unusual space somewhere between biography, fiction and history. *The Memory Palace of Matteo Ricci* is a study of the most famous Jesuit to take up residence in China. *The Question of Hu* and *Emperor of China: Self-Portrait of K'ang Hsi* are also highly recommended.

Rose Crossing by Nicholas Jose is a quirky account of a chance encounter between a 17th-century English naturalist and a eunuch of the deposed Ming court on a deserted island.

The Chinese-American writers Maxine Hong Kingston and Amy Tan have both written books about the experiences of immigrant Chinese in the USA. Although their novels are not directly about China, they reveal a great deal about Chinese relationships and customs. Look out for Kingston's *The Woman Warrior* and *China Men*, or Tan's *The Kitchen God's Wife* and *The Joy Luck Club*.

Finally, all of Peter Hopkirk's books are worth reading. None of them deals with China specifically, but in *The Great Game*, *Foreign Devils on the Silk Road* and *Trespassers on the Roof of the World* Hopkirk writes breezily of 19th-century international espionage, exploration, pilfering of lost art treasures and the struggle for territorial domination at the far-flung edges of the Chinese empire in Xīnjiāng (Chinese Turkestan, as it was then known) and Tibet.

FILMS

Movies produced by Westerners and filmed in China are thin on the ground, largely because the Chinese government has a habit of demanding huge fees for the privilege. Still, there are a few that have become well-known classics (see also the discussion of Chinese film in the Facts about China chapter's Arts section).

The definitive classic is *The Last Emperor*, released in 1988 by Columbia Pictures and directed by Bernardo Bertolucci.

American-Chinese author Amy Tan has seen some of her books made into films – *The Joy Luck Club* gives some useful insights into Chinese culture; however, much of the action takes place in California.

On the other hand, documentaries about China are numerous. *The Gate of Heavenly Peace* by Carma Hinton and Richard Gordon covers the democracy protests and bloodshed at Tiānānmén Square in 1989.

NEWSPAPERS & MAGAZINES
Chinese-Language Publications

Newspapers in China contain little hard news. Mostly, they are devoted to sloganeering, selective reporting and editorialising. Papers are quick to censure or endorse, depending on where the party line is at any point in time.

There are more than 2000 national and provincial newspapers in China. The main one is *Renmin Ribao (People's Daily)*, with nationwide circulation. The sports page usually attracts the most interest. Every city in China will have its own local version of the *People's Daily* and, like the banner publication, they tend to serve chiefly as a propaganda vehicle. A relatively good Chinese language paper for international news is *Global Times*.

At the other end of the scale is China's version of the gutter press – hundreds of 'unhealthy papers' and magazines hawked on street corners and bus stations in major cities with nude or violent photos and stories about sex, crime, witchcraft, miracle cures and UFOs. These have been severely criticised by the government for their obscene and racy content. They are also extremely popular.

There are also about 40 newspapers for the minority nationalities.

Foreign-Language Publications

China publishes various newspapers, books and magazines in a number of European and Asian languages. The lifeless *China Daily* is China's official English-language newspaper and is available in most major cities – it even makes its way as far as Lhasa, though usually a couple of weeks out of date. Běijīng, Shànghǎi, Guǎngzhōu, Kūnmíng and other cities have increasingly professional English-language 'what's on' type magazines basically published by and for expats. Another English-language paper to look out for is the *South China Morning Post*.

Imported Publications

In large cities it's not that hard to score copies of popular imported English-language magazines like *Time*, *Newsweek*, *Far Eastern Economic Review* and *The Economist*.

Foreign newspapers like the *Asian Wall Street Journal*, the *Financial Times*, and *The International Herald Tribune* are lifesavers, but usually cost around Y20 or Y30. The best place to look for these are the newspaper shops at five-star hotels, and some Friendship Stores also stock copies. The English-language *The Straits Times* is also available, and it's usually possible to find European magazines such as *Le Point* and *Der Spiegel*.

The government still flinches at a questioning media lens in its face and foreign newspapers such as *The Financial Times* and *The International Herald Tribune* are commonly trimmed of comment, or their distribution within China is limited.

If you find pages missing, demand a discount (generally not given, but make a stand), for you are not receiving a complete product. Usually the whole page, back and front, is removed.

Visit instead online papers for the latest news, for they are generally not blocked; this is probably the best way to get breaking news bar the radio. Certain news media Web sites (such as BBC News Online at W www .news.bbc.co.uk, both English and Chinese) are consistently blocked, but you could try accessing other news media, such as AP (W www.ap.org), AFP (W www.afp.com) and Reuters (W www.reuters.com). Also try going through Yahoo!News.

RADIO & TV

Domestic radio broadcasting is controlled by the Central People's Broadcasting Station (CPBS). Broadcasts are made in *pǔtōnghuà* (standard Chinese speech) plus local dialects and minority languages. English-language programs are also appearing.

There are also broadcasts to Taiwan in pǔtōnghuà and Fujianese, and Cantonese broadcasts for residents of Guǎngdōng, Hong Kong and Macau.

(CRI) is China's overseas radio service and broadcasts in about 40 foreign languages, as well as in pǔtōnghuà and several local dialects.

A short-wave radio receiver (through which you can receive Voice of America and BBC news) is worth bringing with you for world events and breaking news.

The national TV outfit, Chinese Central Television (CCTV), has two English channels – CCTV4 and CCTV9. Major cities may have a second local channel, like Beijing Television (BTV). Sports news can be picked up on CCTV5 (in Chinese); your hotel may have ESPN. Many hotels have their own film channels.

Hong Kong's STAR TV broadcasts via satellite to China and CNN is also available in certain areas.

VIDEO SYSTEMS

China subscribes to the PAL broadcasting standard, the same as Australia, New Zealand, the UK and most of Europe. Competing systems not used in China include SECAM (France, Germany, Luxembourg) and NTSC (Canada, Japan and the USA).

VCD and DVD have rapidly become the standard, rather than video, and you will see many pirate VCDs and DVDs of the latest films for sale on the streets of cities like Běijīng. But be warned, it's a lawless enterprise: that hot-off-the-press summer blockbuster you thought you were buying may turn out to be a blank VCD, *Ishtar* or some other huge disappointment.

PHOTOGRAPHY & VIDEO
Film & Equipment
Processing standards have increasingly improved as Kodak has opened a nationwide chain of film developing outlets. Colour print film can be found everywhere, but it's almost always 100 ASA (21 DIN). Slide film can be found in camera shops in big cities only. B&W film is harder to find, but speciality camera shops sometimes carry it.

Finding the special lithium batteries used by many cameras is generally not a problem.

You're allowed to bring in 8mm movie cameras; 16mm or professional equipment may cause concern with customs. Motion picture film is next to impossible to find in China.

Video
Video cameras were once subject to shaky regulations, but there seems to be no problem now, at least with the cheap camcorders that tourists carry. A large professional video camera might raise eyebrows – the Chinese government is especially paranoid about foreign TV crews filming unauthorised documentaries.

For the average video hobbyist, the biggest problem is recharging your batteries – bring all the adaptors you can, and remember that it's 220V.

Restrictions
Photography from planes and photographs of airports, military installations, harbour facilities and railroad terminals are prohibited; bridges may also be a touchy subject. With the possible exception of military installations, these rules are rarely enforced.

Photography is prohibited in many museums and at certain archaeological sites and temples. There should be a sign in English advising of such restrictions, but ask if you're not sure.

Airport/Railway Security
Most X-ray machines in China's airports are marked 'film safe', and this seems to be the case. However, films with a very high ASA rating could be fogged by repeated exposures to X-rays – you may wish to carry such film by hand rather than have it zapped.

A number of train stations also pass your bags through an X-ray scan before you are allowed to board your train.

TIME
Time throughout China is set to Běijīng time, which is eight hours ahead of GMT/UTC. When it's noon in Běijīng it's also noon in far-off Lhasa, Ürümqi and all other parts of the country. Since the sun doesn't cooperate with Běijīng's whims, people in China's far west follow a later work schedule so they don't have to commute two hours before dawn.

When it's noon in Běijīng the time in other cities around the world is:

Wellington	4pm
Sydney	2pm
Hong Kong	noon
Frankfurt	5am
Paris	5am
Rome	5am
London	4am
Montreal	11pm (previous day)
New York	11pm (previous day)
Los Angeles	8pm (previous day)

ELECTRICITY
Electricity is 220V, 50 cycles AC. For the most part, you can safely travel with two types of plugs – two flat pins (like American plugs, but without the ground wire) and three pronged angled pins (like Australian plugs). Bring along a 120V to 220V converter if needed, as they are scarce here.

Conversion plugs are easily purchased in China's major cities, but are more difficult to find elsewhere. Battery chargers are widely available. Avoid buying cheap Chinese batteries; they run out rapidly.

A torch (flashlight) is useful to take along in case of blackouts.

WEIGHTS & MEASURES
The metric system is widely used in China. However, the traditional Chinese measures are often used for domestic transactions and you may come across them. The following equations will help:

metric	Chinese
1m *(mǐ)*	3 *chi*
1km *(gōnglǐ)*	2 *lǐ*
1L *(gōngshēng)*	1 *gōngshēng*
1kg *(gōngjīn)*	2 *jīn*

LAUNDRY

Almost all tourist hotels have a laundry service, and if you hand in clothes one day you should get them back a day or two later. Hotel laundry services tend to be expensive and you might wind up doing what many travellers do – hand-washing your own clothes.

HEALTH

Although China presents a few particular health hazards that require your attention, overall it's a healthier place to travel than many other parts of the world. Large cities like Běijīng and Shànghǎi have decent medical facilities, but problems can be encountered in isolated areas such as Inner Mongolia, Tibet or Xīnjiāng.

Medical services are generally very cheap in China, although random foreigner surcharges may be exacted meaning that foreigners get better service.

In case of accident or illness, it's best just to get a taxi and go to the hospital directly – try to avoid dealing with the authorities (police and military) if possible.

As elsewhere in Asia, the Chinese do not have Rh-negative blood and their blood banks don't store it.

Predeparture Planning

Immunisations Plan ahead for getting your vaccinations: some of them require an initial shot followed by a booster, while some vaccinations should not be given together. It is recommended you seek medical advice at least six weeks before travel. Note that some vaccinations should not be given during pregnancy or to people with allergies; discuss this with your doctor. Be aware that there is often a greater risk of disease with children and during pregnancy.

Two Web sites that may be helpful are W www.tripprep.com and the Travellers Medical And Vaccination Centre at W www.tmvc.com.au.

It may be useful to record your vaccinations on an International Health Certificate,

available from your doctor or government health department. Discuss your requirements with your doctor, but vaccinations you should consider for this trip include:

Diphtheria & Tetanus Vaccinations for these two diseases are usually combined and are recommended for everyone. After

---

Medical Kit Check List

Following is a list of items you should consider including in your medical kit – consult your pharmacist for brands available in your country.

☐ **Aspirin or paracetamol (acetaminophen in the USA)** – for pain or fever

☐ **Antihistamine** – for allergies, eg, hay fever; to ease the itch from insect bites or stings; and to prevent motion sickness

☐ **Cold and flu tablets, throat lozenges and nasal decongestant**

☐ **Multivitamins** – consider for long trips, when dietary vitamin intake may be inadequate

☐ **Antibiotics** – consider including these if you're travelling well off the beaten track; see your doctor, as they must be prescribed, and carry the prescription with you

☐ **Loperamide or diphenoxylate** – 'blockers' for diarrhoea

☐ **Prochlorperazine or metaclopramide** – for nausea and vomiting

☐ **Rehydration mixture** – to prevent dehydration, which may occur, for example, during bouts of diarrhoea; particularly important when travelling with children

☐ **Insect repellent, sunscreen, lip balm and eye drops**

☐ **Calamine lotion, sting relief spray or aloe vera** – to ease irritation from sunburn and insect bites or stings

☐ **Antifungal cream or powder** – for fungal skin infections and thrush

☐ **Antiseptic (such as povidone-iodine)** – for cuts and grazes

☐ **Bandages, Band-Aids (plasters) and other wound dressings**

☐ **Water purification tablets or iodine**

☐ **Scissors, tweezers and a thermometer** – note that mercury thermometers are prohibited by airlines

☐ **Sterile kit** – in case you need injections in a country with medical hygiene problems; discuss with your doctor an initial course of three injections (usually given in childhood), boosters are necessary every 10 years.

Hepatitis A All travellers to China should be protected against this common disease.

Hepatitis A vaccine (eg, Avaxim, Havrix 1440 or VAQTA) provides long-term immunity (possibly more than 10 years) after an initial injection and a booster at six to 12 months.

Alternatively, an injection of gamma globulin can provide short-term protection against hepatitis A – two to six months, depending on the dose given. It is not a vaccine, but a ready-made antibody collected from blood donations. It is reasonably effective and, unlike the vaccine, it is protective immediately, but because it is a blood product, there are current concerns about its long-term safety.

Hepatitis A vaccine is also available in a combined form, Twinrix, with hepatitis B vaccine. Three injections over a six-month period are required, the first two providing substantial protection against hepatitis A.

Hepatitis B China is one of the world's great reservoirs of hepatitis B infection. The vaccination is recommended (especially for long-term travellers) and involves three injections, with a booster at 12 months. More rapid courses are available if necessary. A combined hepatitis A and B vaccine is available.

Japanese B Encephalitis This mosquito-borne disease is a risk for travellers to rural areas of China. Consider the vaccination if you're spending a month or longer in a high-risk area, making repeated trips to a risky area or visiting during an epidemic (usually associated with the rainy season). It involves three injections over 30 days.

Polio Polio is a very serious, easily transmitted disease, still prevalent in many developing countries. Everyone should keep up to date with this vaccination. A booster every 10 years maintains immunity.

Rabies With rabies, you have the choice of having the immunisation either before you go (called pre-exposure) or just if you're unlucky enough to get bitten (post-exposure).

Pre-exposure vaccination involves receiving a course of three injections over a period of 21 to 28 days. If you then get bitten or scratched by a suspect animal, you will need to have two boosters to prevent rabies developing. Avoid contact with animals – recently an Australian visitor died of rabies after being bitten by a puppy bought in a market in Shànghǎi.

Without pre-exposure vaccination, you will need the full course of rabies vaccination (five injections over a month) as well as an immediate injection of rabies antibodies. However, this can be difficult to obtain in China.

Consider having pre-exposure rabies vaccination if you're going to be travelling through China for more than three months or if you're going to be handling animals. Children are at particular risk of being bitten and may not report a bite, so may need to be vaccinated even if you're going for only a short time.

Tuberculosis The risk of TB to travellers is usually very low. A vaccination is recommended for children living in these areas for three months or more.

Typhoid Travellers to China are at risk for this disease, especially if travelling to smaller cities, villages or rural areas. The vaccine is available either as an injection or as capsules to be taken orally.

Malaria Medication If you're travelling to malarial areas in China (see the Malaria section further on), you'll need to take measures to avoid getting this serious and potentially fatal disease. Expert advice on medication should be sought, as there are many factors to consider, including the area to be visited, the risk of exposure to malaria-carrying mosquitoes, the side effects of medication, your medical history and whether you are a child or an adult or pregnant. Travellers to isolated and high-risk areas may like to carry a treatment dose of medication for use if symptoms occur.

Health Insurance Make sure that you have adequate health insurance. See the Travel Insurance entry under Visas & Documents earlier in this chapter.

Travel Health Guides *Healthy Travel Asia & India* is another comprehensive Lonely Planet title. Lonely Planet's *Travel with Children* gives a rundown on health precautions to be taken with kids, or if you're pregnant and travelling.

There are also a number of excellent travel health sites on the Internet. From the Lonely Planet home page there are links at W www.lonelyplanet.com/weblinks to the World Health Organization and the US Centers for Disease Control & Prevention.

Other Preparations Make sure you're healthy before you start travelling. If you are going on a long trip make sure your teeth are OK. If you wear glasses take a spare pair and your prescription.

If you require a particular medication take an adequate supply, as it may not be available locally. Take part of the packaging showing the generic name, rather than the brand, which will make getting replacements easier. It's a good idea to have a legible prescription or letter from your doctor to show that you legally use the medication to avoid any problems.

Basic Rules

Food It's generally agreed that food, not water, is the most common source of gut troubles in travellers. We can't tell you exactly what to avoid in every situation because there are so many variables, but we can give you some guidelines to help you decide what's likely to be less safe and therefore better avoided:

- How food is prepared is more important than where it's prepared – a plate of noodles cooked in a steaming hot wok in front of you at a street stall is probably safer than food left out on display in an upmarket hotel buffet.
- Heating kills germs, so food that's served piping hot is likely to be safer than lukewarm or cold food, especially food that's been sitting around. Freezing doesn't kill germs.
- Fruit and vegetables are difficult to clean (and may be contaminated where they are grown), but they should be safe if they're peeled or cooked.
- Well-cooked meat and seafood should be OK (but avoid the latter if far from the sea); raw or lightly cooked meat and seafood can be a source of parasites. Steaming does not make shellfish safe for eating.
- Tinned food or milk, or powdered milk, is usually safe (check 'best before' dates if necessary).

- You'll be delighted to know that all forms of bread and cakes are usually safe, although it's best to avoid cream-filled goodies if you can, as microorganisms such as salmonella love cream.
- Popular eating places have an incentive to provide safe food to keep the customers coming.
- Your stomach's natural defences (mainly acid) can cope with small amounts of contaminated foods – if you're not sure about something, don't pig out on it!

And here are a few cautions to bear in mind:

- Good food can be contaminated by dirty dishes or cutlery; blenders used for making fruit juices are often suspect.
- Hot spices don't make food safe, just more palatable.
- Salads are best avoided because they are hard to clean adequately and they are often contaminated with bug-containing dirt.
- Fruit juices and other drinks may be diluted with unsafe water.
- Unpasteurised and unboiled milk and dairy products should be avoided (more likely in rural areas) as unpasteurised milk can transmit diseases (including TB and salmonella); boiling unpasteurised milk makes it safe to drink.
- Be wary of food, including ice cream, that has been kept frozen, and may have thawed and been refrozen.
- Most restaurants use disposable chopsticks, but consider carrying your own chopsticks for the occasional restaurant that doesn't.

Water The number one rule is *be careful of the water* and especially ice. Tap water is not considered safe to drink anywhere in China except Hong Kong. On the other hand, in most cities it's chlorinated and probably won't kill you. You need to be really careful in remote areas like Tibet, especially when drinking surface water. If you don't know for certain that the water is safe, then assume the worst. Bottled water or soft drinks are fine.

Water Purification You've got to pay attention to water purification if you're going to be camping or hiking. The simplest way of purifying water is to boil it thoroughly. Vigorous boiling for a few minutes should be satisfactory; however, at high altitudes water boils at a lower temperature, so germs are less likely to be killed. Boil it longer in these environments.

In China, flasks of boiled water are provided outside most hotel rooms daily. With this you can safely make your own tea.

Consider purchasing a water filter for a long trip. It's very important when buying a filter to read the specifications, so that you know exactly what it removes from the water and what it doesn't.

Simple filtering will not remove all dangerous organisms, so if you cannot boil water it should be treated chemically. Chlorine tablets (Puritabs, Steritabs or other brand names) will kill many pathogens, but not some parasites causing giardiasis and amoebic dysentery.

Iodine is more effective in purifying water and is available in tablet form. Follow the directions carefully and remember that too much iodine can be harmful.

Medical Problems & Treatment

Self-diagnosis and treatment can be risky, so wherever possible seek qualified help. Although we do give drug dosages in this section, they are for emergency use only. Correct diagnosis is vital.

A five-star hotel, embassy or consulate can usually recommend a good place to go for medical advice. In some places medical standards are so low that for some ailments the best advice is to get on a plane and go to Běijīng, Shànghǎi or Hong Kong.

Antibiotics should ideally be administered only under medical supervision. Take only the recommended dose at the prescribed intervals and use the whole course, even if the illness seems to be cured earlier. Stop immediately if there are any serious reactions and don't use the antibiotic at all if you are unsure that you have the correct one. Note that you can pick up antibiotics without a prescription at chemists throughout China.

Some people are allergic to commonly prescribed antibiotics such as penicillin or sulpha drugs; carry this information when travelling (eg, on a bracelet).

Environmental Hazards

Altitude Sickness Lack of oxygen at high altitudes (over 2500m) affects most people to some extent. There are bus journeys in Tibet, Qīnghǎi and Xīnjiāng where the road goes over 5000m. Acclimatising to such extreme elevations takes several weeks at least, but most travellers come up from sea level very fast – a bad move! If you ever experience acute mountain sickness (AMS), you won't forget it.

Symptoms of Acute Mountain Sickness (AMS) usually develop during the first 24 hours at altitude but may be delayed up to three weeks. Mild symptoms include headache, lethargy, dizziness, difficulty sleeping and loss of appetite. AMS may become more severe without warning and can be fatal. Severe symptoms include breathlessness, a dry, irritative cough (which may progress to the production of pink, frothy sputum), severe headache, lack of coordination and balance, confusion, irrational behaviour, vomiting, drowsiness and unconsciousness. There is no hard-and-fast rule as to what is too high: AMS has been fatal at 3000m, although 3500m to 4500m is the usual range.

Treat mild symptoms by resting at the same altitude until recovery, usually a day or two. If symptoms persist or become worse, however, *immediate descent is necessary*; even 500m can help. Drug treatments should never be used to avoid descent or to enable further ascent.

To prevent acute mountain sickness:

* Ascend slowly – have frequent rest days, spending two to three nights at each rise of 1000m. If you reach a high altitude by trekking, acclimatisation takes place gradually and you are less likely to be affected than if you fly directly to a higher altitude.
* It is always wise to sleep at a lower altitude than the greatest height reached during the day. Also, once above 3000m, care should be taken not to increase the sleeping altitude by more than 300m per day.
* Drink extra fluids. The mountain air is dry and cold and moisture is lost as you breathe.
* Eat light, high-carbohydrate meals for more energy.
* Avoid alcohol as it may increase the risk of dehydration.
* Avoid sedatives.

Fungal Infections Occuring more commonly in hot weather, fungal infections are usually found on the scalp, between the toes (athlete's foot) or fingers, in the groin and on the body. You get ringworm (a fungal infection, not a worm) from infected animals or other people. Moisture encourages these infections.

If you do get an infection, wash the infected area daily with a disinfectant or medicated soap and water, and rinse and dry well. Apply an antifungal cream or powder

Everyday Health

Normal body temperature is up to 37°C (98.6°F); more than 2°C (4°F) higher indicates a high fever. The normal adult pulse rate is 60 to 100 per minute (children 80 to 100, babies 100 to 140). As a general rule the pulse increases about 20 beats per minute for each 1°C (2°F) rise in fever.

Respiration (breathing) rate is also an indicator of illness. Count the number of breaths per minute: between 12 and 20 is normal for adults and older children (up to 30 for younger children, 40 for babies). People with a high fever or serious respiratory illness breathe more quickly than normal. More than 40 shallow breaths a minute may indicate pneumonia.

like tolnaftate. Try to expose the infected area to air or sunlight as much as possible and wash all towels and underwear in hot water, change them often and let them dry in the sun.

Heat Exhaustion Dehydration or salt deficiency can cause heat exhaustion. Take time to acclimatise to high temperatures, drink sufficient liquids and do not do anything too physically demanding.

Salt deficiency is characterised by fatigue, lethargy, headaches, giddiness and muscle cramps; salt tablets may help, but adding extra salt to your food is better.

Hypothermia Too much cold can be just as dangerous as too much heat. If you are trekking at high altitudes or simply taking a long bus trip over mountains, particularly at night, be aware. In Tibet it can go from being mildly warm to blisteringly cold in a manner of minutes – blizzards have a way of just coming out of nowhere. If you're out walking, cycling or hitching, this can be dangerous.

It is surprisingly easy to progress from very cold to dangerously cold due to a combination of wind, wet clothing, fatigue and hunger, even if the air temperature is above freezing. It is best to dress in layers; silk, wool and some of the new artificial fibres are all good insulating materials. A hat is important, as a lot of heat is lost through the head. A strong, waterproof outer layer (and a space blanket for emergencies) is essential.

Carry basic supplies, including food containing simple sugars to generate heat quickly and fluid to drink.

Symptoms of hypothermia are exhaustion, numb skin (particularly the toes and fingers), shivering, slurred speech, irrational or violent behaviour, lethargy, stumbling, dizzy spells, muscle cramps and violent bursts of energy. Irrationality may take the form of sufferers claiming they are warm and trying to take off their clothes.

To treat mild hypothermia, first get the person out of the wind and/or rain, remove their clothing if it's wet and replace it with dry, warm clothing. Give them hot liquids – not alcohol – and some high-kilojoule, easily digestible food. The early recognition and treatment of mild hypothermia is the only way to prevent severe hypothermia, which is a critical condition.

Motion Sickness Eating lightly before and during a trip will reduce the chances of motion sickness. If you are prone to motion sickness try to find a place that minimises movement – near the wing on aircraft, close to midships on boats, near the centre on buses. Fresh air usually helps; reading and cigarette smoke don't. Commercial motion-sickness preparations, which can cause drowsiness, have to be taken before the trip commences. Ginger (available in capsule form) and peppermint (including mint-flavoured sweets) are natural preventatives.

Sunburn It's very easy to get sunburnt at high elevations (Tibet), in the deserts (Xīnjiāng) or the tropics (Hǎinán Dǎo). Use a sunscreen, hat, and barrier cream for your nose and lips. Calamine lotion is good for mild sunburn. Protect your eyes with good-quality sunglasses, particularly if you will be near water, sand or snow.

Infectious Diseases

China Syndrome Upper respiratory tract infections (URTIs), or the common cold, are the most common ailment to afflict visitors to China. The Chinese call it *gǎnmào* and it is a particular problem here – transmission rates are high because of the crowding and the cold.

During winter, practically the entire population of 1.3 billion is stricken with gǎnmào. Winter visitors to China should

Acupuncture

Chinese acupuncture (zhēnjiǔ) has received enthusiastic reviews from its many satisfied patients. Of course, acupuncture is unlikely to cure terminal cancer or heart disease, but it is of genuine therapeutic value in the treatment of chronic back pain, migraine headaches, arthritis, asthma and other ailments. It is also widely used in China as an effective anaesthetic, even during surgery.

The therapy employs needles that are inserted into various points of the body. As many as 2000 points for needle insertion have been identified, but only about 150 are commonly used. The oldest Chinese text on acupuncture, the Classic of Acupuncture and Moxibustion, dates from AD 282, although reference to the therapy is made in earlier writings.

The exact mechanism by which acupuncture works is not fully understood. Needles are inserted for anything from a few seconds to thirty minutes or more, each point believed to correspond to a particular organ, joint, gland or other part of the body. These points are connected to the particular area being treated by an 'energy channel', also translated as a 'meridian'. It seems the needle can block pain transmission along the meridian, with the depth of insertion depending on the seriousness and type of ailment.

Acupuncture is practised in hospitals of traditional Chinese medicine, which can be found all over China. And if you need some emergency acupuncture, even hotels (upmarket ones, at least) provide such services at their in-house clinics.

If you're (justifiably) concerned about catching hepatitis or HIV from contaminated acupuncture needles, buy your own before undergoing treatment. Good-quality needles are available in major cities in China. Needles come in a bewildering variety of gauges – try to determine from your acupuncturist which type to buy.

---

bring a few favourite cold remedies. These can easily be purchased from any good pharmacy in Hong Kong or Macau. Such items can be found elsewhere in China, but with considerably more difficulty.

Symptoms of influenza include fever, weakness, sore throat and a feeling of malaise. Any URTI, including influenza, can lead to complications such as bronchitis and pneumonia, which may need to be treated with antibiotics. Seek medical help in this situation.

Diarrhoea Travellers' diarrhoea (lā dùzi) has been around a long time – even Marco Polo had it. A change of water, food or climate can all cause the runs; diarrhoea caused by contaminated food or water is more serious. A few rushed toilet trips with no other symptoms is not indicative of a serious problem.

Dehydration is the main danger with any diarrhoea, which can occur quite quickly in children or the elderly. Under all circumstances *fluid replacement* is the most important thing to remember. Soda water or soft drinks allowed to go flat and diluted 50% with clean water are good. With severe diarrhoea a rehydrating solution is preferable to replace minerals and salts lost.

Commercially available oral rehydration salts (ORS) are very useful; add them to boiled or bottled water. In an emergency you can make up a solution of six teaspoons of sugar and a half teaspoon of salt to a litre of boiled or bottled water. Keep drinking small amounts often. Stick to a bland diet as you recover.

Gut-paralysing drugs such as loperamide or diphenoxylate can be used to bring relief from the symptoms, although they do not actually cure the problem. Only use these drugs if you do not have access to toilets, eg, if you *must* travel. Note that these drugs are not recommended for children under 12 years.

In certain situations antibiotics may be required: diarrhoea with blood or mucus (dysentery), any diarrhoea with fever, watery diarrhoea with fever and lethargy, persistent diarrhoea not improving after 48 hours and severe diarrhoea. In these situations gut-paralysing drugs should be avoided.

A stool test is necessary to diagnose which kind of dysentery you have, so you should seek medical help urgently in this situation. Where this is not possible the recommended drugs for bacterial diarrhoea (the most likely cause of severe diarrhoea in travellers) are norfloxacin 400mg twice daily for three days or ciprofloxacin 500mg twice daily for five days. These are not recommended for children or pregnant women. The drug of choice for children would be co-trimoxazole with dosage dependent on weight. A five-day course is given. Ampicillin or amoxycillin may be given in pregnancy, but medical care is necessary.

Two other causes of persistent diarrhoea in travellers are giardiasis and amoebic dysentery.

Giardiasis This is caused by a common parasite, *Giardia lamblia*. Symptoms include stomach cramps, nausea, a bloated stomach, watery, foul-smelling diarrhoea and frequent gas. Giardiasis can appear several weeks after you have been exposed to the parasite. The symptoms may disappear for a few days and then return; this can go on for several weeks.

Amoebic Dysentery Caused by the protozoan *Entamoeba histolytica*, amoebic dysentery is characterised by a gradual onset of low-grade diarrhoea, often with blood and mucus. Cramping abdominal pain and vomiting are less likely than in other types of diarrhoea, and fever may not be present. It will persist until treated and can recur and cause other health problems.

You should seek medical advice if you think you have giardiasis or amoebic dysentery, but where this is not possible, tinidazole or metronidazole are the recommended drugs. Treatment is a 2g single dose of tinidazole or 250mg of metronidazole three times daily for five to 10 days.

Hepatitis This is a general term for inflammation of the liver. The symptoms are similar in all forms of the illness, and include fever, chills, headache, fatigue, feelings of weakness and aches and pains, followed by loss of appetite, nausea, vomiting, abdominal pain, dark urine, light-coloured faeces, jaundiced (yellow) skin and yellowing of the whites of the eyes.

Hepatitis A is transmitted by contaminated food and drinking water. You should seek medical advice, but there is not much you can do apart from resting, drinking lots of fluids, eating lightly and avoiding fatty foods. **Hepatitis E** is transmitted in the same way as hepatitis A; it can be particularly serious in pregnant women.

There are almost 300 million chronic carriers of **hepatitis B** in the world. It is spread through contact with infected blood, blood products or body fluids. The symptoms of hepatitis B may be more severe than type A and the disease can lead to long-term problems such as chronic liver damage, liver cancer or a long-term carrier state. **Hepatitis C** and **D** are spread in the same way as hepatitis B and can also lead to long-term complications.

There are vaccines against hepatitis A and B, but there are currently no vaccines against the other types of hepatitis. Following the basic rules about food and water (hepatitis A and E) and avoiding risk situations (hepatitis B, C and D) are important preventative measures.

HIV/AIDS Infection with the human immunodeficiency virus (HIV) may develop into acquired immune deficiency syndrome (AIDS).

The disease is often transmitted sexually, but it can be passed through infected blood transfusions; China is notorious for *not* screening blood donors! It can also be spread by dirty needles – vaccinations, acupuncture, tattooing and body piercing can be potentially as dangerous as intravenous drug use. If you do need an injection, ask to see the syringe unwrapped in front of you, or take a needle and syringe pack with you.

Fear of HIV infection should never preclude seeking treatment for serious medical conditions.

Intestinal Worms These parasites are most common in rural, tropical areas. Some may be ingested on food such as undercooked meat (eg, tapeworms) and some enter through your skin (eg, hookworms). Infestations may not show up for some time, and although they are generally not serious, if left untreated some can cause severe health problems later. Consider having a stool test when you return home to check for these and determine the appropriate treatment.

Schistosomiasis Also known as bilharzia, this disease is found in the central Cháng Jiāng basin. It is carried in water by minute worms which infect certain varieties of freshwater snails found in rivers, streams, lakes and particularly behind dams.

China and AIDS

Experts are warning that China could be facing a potential AIDS catastrophe. Ignorance about AIDS is widespread in China, especially in rural areas. This ignorance, coupled with increasing drug use and a liberalising sexual climate provide a perfect environment for the disease to proliferate.

Instead of battling AIDS head-on with mass awareness campaigns, health officials seem to be hoping the problem will just go away. Gao Yaojie, a Chinese doctor who exposed a racket that left thousands in Hénán contaminated with AIDS through tainted blood, was blocked in 2001 from visiting the USA to collect an award at the Global Health Council. Rather than using the issue as a springboard to launch an AIDS-awareness campaign, Hénán health officials muzzled Dr Gao's educational campaign. The scandal reportedly left one Hénán village with a 65% HIV-positive rate. It is also feared that the pooled blood was disseminated to large cities around the country. Conservative estimates suggest around 600,000 Chinese are infected, a figure that is growing at an annual rate of 30%. Some experts speculate that China will have 10 million cases of HIV by 2010.

Travellers who may visit prostitutes or engage in other high-risk activities should be aware of the risks that they are taking (see the Prostitution section later).

The worm enters through the skin and attaches itself to your intestines or bladder. The first symptom may be a general feeling of being unwell, or a tingling and sometimes a light rash around the area where it entered. Weeks later a high fever may develop. Once the disease is established abdominal pain and blood in the urine are other signs. The infection often causes no symptoms until the disease is well established (several months to years after exposure) and damage to internal organs irreversible.

Avoiding swimming or bathing in fresh water where bilharzia is present is the main method of preventing the disease. Even deep water can be infected. If you do get wet, dry off quickly and dry your clothes as well.

A blood test is the most reliable way to diagnose the disease, but the test will not show positive until a number of weeks after exposure.

Sexually Transmitted Diseases HIV/AIDS and hepatitis B can be transmitted through sexual contact. Other STDs include gonorrhoea, herpes and syphilis; sores, blisters or rashes around the genitals and discharges or pain when urinating are common symptoms.

Chlamydia infection can cause infertility in men and women before any symptoms have been noticed. Syphilis symptoms eventually disappear completely but the disease continues and can cause severe problems in later years. While abstinence from sexual contact is the only 100% effective prevention, using condoms is also effective.

The treatment of gonorrhoea and syphilis is with antibiotics. The different sexually transmitted diseases each require specific antibiotics.

Tuberculosis China has traditionally had a high rate of TB infection, and there is now a worldwide resurgence of this severe disease.

It is a bacterial infection, which is usually transmitted from person to person through coughing, but may be transmitted via the consumption of unpasteurised milk. Milk that has been boiled is safe to drink, and the souring of milk to make yogurt or cheese also kills the bacilli.

Travellers are usually not at great risk as close household contact with the infected person is usually required before the disease is passed on. You may need to have a TB test before you travel as this can help diagnose the disease later if you become ill.

Typhoid A dangerous gut infection, typhoid is caused by contaminated water and food. As with cholera, it tends to occur in summer in areas that have had severe flooding. Medical help must be sought.

Early symptoms are a headache, body aches and a fever which rises a little each day until it is around 40°C (104°F) or more. The victim's pulse is often slow relative to the degree of fever present – unlike a normal fever where the pulse increases. There may also be vomiting, abdominal pain, diarrhoea or constipation.

In the second week the high fever and slow pulse continue and a few pink spots

Chinese Herbal Medicine

Chinese medicine encompasses a basic philosophy on life that stresses that it's better to stay healthy than to take medicines. Longevity has been attributed to keeping an even temper, eating a balanced diet, exercising regularly and getting a good sleep. Chinese herbal medicine *(zhōng yào)* is also 'holistic' in that it seeks to treat the whole body rather than focusing on a particular organ or disease. Herbal medicine, along with acupuncture, is the most common medical system in China.

While the origins of Chinese medicine lie in legend, evidence of early medical practices have been found on bones inscribed during the Shang dynasty and on treatises excavated from ancient tombs. A pharmaceutical system was established in the Song dynasty that standardised the practice of medicine, and Chinese medicine made early headway into immunology by developing a method of immunisation against smallpox during the 17th century.

Today, it's common to see herbalists' shops lined with small drawers filled with various ingredients ranging from the ordinary (such as ginseng) to the exotic (snake gall bladder or powdered deer antler). The ingredients all undergo preparation such as baking, roasting or simmering before being consumed – the precise process being determined by the disease.

Chinese medicine seems to work best for the relief of unpleasant symptoms (pain, sore throat etc) and for some long-term conditions that resist Western medicines, such as migraine headaches, asthma and chronic backache.

Another benefit of Chinese medicine is that there are relatively few side effects. Nevertheless, herbs are still medicines, not candy – in fact, some herbs are mildly toxic and if taken over a long period of time can actually damage the liver and other organs.

Before shopping for herbs, keep in mind that although a broad-spectrum remedy, such as snake gall bladder, may be good for treating colds, there are many different types of colds. The best way to treat a cold with herbal medicine is to see a Chinese doctor and get a specific prescription. However, if you can't get to a doctor, you can just try your luck at the pharmacy.

If you visit a Chinese doctor, you might be surprised by what he or she discovers about your body. For example, the doctor will almost certainly take your pulse as it's believed that your pulse indicates the state of your health. They may then tell you that you have a slippery pulse or perhaps a thready pulse. Chinese doctors have identified more than 30 different kinds of pulses. The doctor may then examine your tongue to see if it is slippery, dry, pale or greasy, or has a thick coating or maybe no coating at all. The doctor, having discovered that you have wet heat, as evidenced by a slippery pulse and a red greasy tongue, will prescribe the herbs for your condition.

The Chinese usually deal with motion sickness, nausea and headaches by smearing liniments on their stomach or head. Look for White Flower Oil *(Bái Huā Yóu)*, probably the most popular brand. A variation on the theme are salves, the most famous being Tiger Balm, which originated in Hong Kong. And should you strain yourself carrying a heavy backpack around, try applying 'sticky dog skin plaster' *(gŏupí gāoyào)* to your sore muscles. You might be relieved to know that these days it's no longer made from real dog skin.

Beware of quackery – there is one Chinese herbal medicine, for instance, which pregnant women take to ensure that their foetus develops into a boy. Other herbal tonics promise to boost your IQ or sexual prowess. Counterfeiting is another problem. Everything gets copied in China, and the problem extends even to medications. If the herbs you take seem to be totally ineffective, it may be because you've bought sugar pills. Some herbal formulas may list, for example, rhinoceros horn as an ingredient. Rhinoceros horn, widely acclaimed by herbalists as a cure for fever, is practically impossible to buy (and in any case, the rhino is a rare and endangered species). Any formula listing rhinoceros horn may, at best, contain water buffalo horn.

may appear on the body; trembling, weight loss, delirium, weakness and dehydration may occur. Complications such as pneumonia, perforated bowel or meningitis may occur.

Insect-Borne Diseases

Filariasis, dengue fever, Japanese B encephalitis, leishmaniasis and typhus are all insect-borne diseases, but they do not pose a great risk to travellers.

Malaria This disease is spread by mosquito bites. Symptoms range from fever, chills and sweating, headache, diarrhoea and abdominal pains to a vague feeling of ill-health. Seek medical help immediately if malaria is suspected. Without treatment malaria can rapidly become more serious and can be fatal.

Malaria has been nearly eradicated in China and is not generally a risk for travellers visiting the cities. It is found predominantly in rural areas in the south-western region – principally Guǎngdōng, Guìzhōu, Yúnnán, Hǎinán, Sìchuān and Fújiàn.

Transmission occurs mainly during summer in most risk areas, but occurs year-round in Hǎinán and Yúnnán. If you are travelling to rural Hǎinán or peripheral Yúnnán it is important to take antimalarial tablets and to take steps to avoid mosquito bites.

If medical care is not available, malaria tablets can be used for treatment. You need a malaria tablet that is different from the one you were taking when you contracted malaria. The standard treatment dosages are Mefloquine (two 250mg tablets and another two six hours later), Fansidar (single dose of three tablets). If you were previously taking Mefloquine and cannot obtain Fansidar, then alternatives are Malarone (atovaquone-proguanil; four tablets once daily for three days), Halofantrine (three doses of two 250mg tablets every six hours) or quinine sulphate (600mg every six hours). There's a greater risk of side effects with these dosages than in normal use if used with Mefloquine, so medical advice is preferable.

Halofantrine is no longer recommended by the WHO as emergency stand-by treatment, because of side effects. It should only be used if no other drugs are available.

Travellers are advised to prevent mosquito bites at all times. The main messages are:

- wear light-coloured clothing
- wear long pants and long-sleeved shirts
- use mosquito repellents containing the compound DEET on exposed areas (prolonged overuse of DEET may be harmful, especially to children, but its use is considered preferable to being bitten by disease-transmitting mosquitoes)
- avoid wearing perfumes or aftershave
- use a mosquito net impregnated with mosquito repellent (permethrin) – it may be worth taking your own
- impregnating clothes with permethrin effectively deters mosquitoes and other insects

Cuts, Bites & Stings

Bedbugs & Lice Bedbugs live in various places, but particularly in dirty mattresses and bedding, evidenced by spots of blood on bedclothes or on the wall. Bedbugs leave itchy bites in neat rows. Calamine lotion or a sting-relief spray may help.

All lice cause itching and discomfort. They make themselves at home in your hair (head lice), your clothing (body lice) or in your pubic hair (crabs). Powder or shampoo treatment will kill the lice and infected clothing should then be washed in very hot, soapy water and left in the sun to dry.

Insect Bites & Stings People who are allergic to ant bites and bee and wasp stings may develop severe breathing difficulties and require urgent medical attention. They should carry a kit containing an antihistamine and adrenaline.

Ticks You should always check all over your body if you have been walking through a potentially tick-infested area as ticks can cause skin infections and other more serious diseases. Walkers in tick-infested areas should consider having their boots and trousers impregnated with benzyl benzoate and dibutylphthalate.

If a tick is found attached, press down around the tick's head with tweezers, grab the head and gently pull upwards. Avoid pulling the rear of the body as this may squeeze the tick's gut contents through the attached mouth parts into the skin, increasing the risk of infection and disease.

Snakes China has a variety of poisonous snakes, the most famous being cobras. Snakes are most common in forested areas, where they have far more to eat. *All* sea snakes are poisonous and are readily identified by their flat tails.

Snakes are not generally aggressive with creatures larger than themselves. Always wear boots, socks and long trousers when walking through undergrowth where snakes may be present. Don't put your hands into holes and crevices, and be careful when collecting firewood.

Snake bites do not cause instant death and antivenins are usually available. Immediately wrap the bitten limb tightly, and then attach a splint to immobilise it. Keep

Mosquito Repellents

A variety of anti-mosquito devices can be bought in China, from coils *(wénxiāng)* that you burn to electronic vaporisers *(qūwénqì)* and lotions. The most popular coils are 'lizipai' and 'sanxingpai', which should cost you around Y7 for a pack of 20. They can be a fire hazard, though, so be careful where you place them; some users may be as stifled by the odour as the mosquitoes are. Odourless coils, manufactured by Baygon (Bàigāo) and Raid (Leida), are more expensive. Vaporisers are effective and models from Raid and Baygon can be found in cities across China. Many hotels provide anti-mosquito vaporisers and the tablets *(qūwénpiān)* that go in them, but ask if you can't find one in your room. Some hotel rooms come equipped with mosquito nets. A cheap Chinese mosquito repellent is called *liùshén*, a green liquid that you can smear liberally on exposed skin. Check out **W** www.mosquito.com.

the victim still and seek medical help, if possible with the dead snake for identification. Don't attempt to catch the snake if there is a possibility of being bitten again. Tourniquets and sucking out the poison are now comprehensively discredited.

Less Common Diseases

Cholera China does not have a serious problem with this, but there can be outbreaks during floods (the Huáng Hé basin is notorious). Floods and corresponding cholera outbreaks are generally widely reported, so you can avoid such problem areas.

Fluid replacement is the most vital treatment – the risk of dehydration is severe as you may lose up to 20L a day. If there is a delay in getting to hospital then begin taking tetracycline. The adult dose is 250mg four times daily. It is not recommended for children under nine nor for pregnant women.

Tetracycline may help to shorten the illness, but adequate fluids are required to save lives.

Dengue Fever Occurring in parts of southern China, this viral disease is transmitted by mosquitoes and is fast becoming one of the top public health problems in the tropical world. Unlike the malaria mosquito, the *Aedes aegypti* mosquito, which transmits the dengue virus, is most active during the day, and is found mainly in urban areas, in and around human dwellings.

Signs and symptoms of dengue fever include a sudden onset of high fever, headache, joint and muscle pains (hence its old name, 'breakbone fever') and nausea and vomiting. A rash of small red spots sometimes appears three to four days after

the onset of fever. In the early phase of illness, dengue may be mistaken for other infectious diseases, including malaria and influenza. Minor bleeding such as nosebleeds may occur in the course of the illness, but this does not necessarily mean that you have progressed to the potentially fatal dengue haemorrhagic fever (DHF). This is a severe illness, characterised by heavy bleeding, which is thought to be a result of second infection due to a different strain (there are four major strains) and usually affects residents of the country rather than travellers. Recovery even from simple dengue fever may be prolonged, with tiredness lasting for several weeks.

You should seek medical attention as soon as possible if you think you may be infected. There is no specific treatment for dengue. Aspirin should be avoided, as it increases the risk of haemorrhaging. The best prevention is to avoid mosquito bites at all times by covering up, using insect repellents containing the compound DEET and mosquito nets – see the Malaria section earlier for more advice on avoiding mosquito bites.

Filariasis This is a mosquito-transmitted parasitic infection found in many parts of Africa, Asia, Central and South America and the Pacific. Possible symptoms include fever, pain and swelling of the lymph glands; inflammation of lymph drainage areas; swelling of a limb or the scrotum; skin rashes; and blindness. Treatment is available to eliminate the parasites from the body, but some of the damage already caused may not be reversible. Medical advice should be obtained promptly if the infection is suspected.

Japanese B Encephalitis This viral infection of the brain is transmitted by mosquitoes. Most cases occur in rural areas as the virus exists in pigs and wading birds.

Symptoms include fever, headache and alteration in consciousness. Hospitalisation is needed for correct diagnosis and treatment. There is a high mortality rate among those who have symptoms; of those who survive many are intellectually disabled.

Leishmaniasis This is a group of parasitic diseases transmitted by sandfly bites. Cutaneous leishmaniasis affects the skin tissue, causing ulceration and disfigurement, and visceral leishmaniasis affects the internal organs. Seek medical advice as laboratory testing is required for diagnosis and correct treatment.

Avoiding sandfly bites is the best precaution. Bites are usually painless, itchy and are yet another reason to cover up and apply repellent.

Rabies See under pre-departure planning.

Tetanus This disease is caused by a germ that lives in soil and in the faeces of horses and other animals. It enters the body via breaks in the skin. The first symptom may be discomfort in swallowing, or stiffening of the jaw and neck; this is followed by painful convulsions of the jaw and whole body. The disease can be fatal. It can be prevented by vaccination.

Typhus This disease is spread by ticks, mites or lice. It begins with fever, chills, headache and muscle pains followed a few days later by a body rash. There is often a large painful sore at the site of the bite and nearby lymph nodes are swollen and painful. Typhus can be treated under medical supervision. See under ticks, earlier.

Women's Health
Gynaecological Problems Antibiotic use, synthetic underwear, sweating and contraceptive pills can lead to fungal vaginal infections, especially when travelling in hot climates. These may cause a rash, itch and discharge and can be treated with a vinegar or lemon-juice douche, or with yogurt. Nystatin, miconazole or clotrimazole pessaries or vaginal cream are the usual treatment.

Wearing loose-fitting clothes and cotton underwear may help prevent infection.

Sexually transmitted diseases are a major cause of vaginal problems. Symptoms include a smelly discharge, painful intercourse and sometimes a burning sensation when urinating. Medical attention should be sought and male sexual partners must also be treated. For more details see the section on Sexually Transmitted Diseases earlier. Besides abstinence, the best thing is to practise safe sex using condoms.

Pregnancy It is not advisable to travel to some places while pregnant as some vaccinations normally used to prevent serious diseases are not advisable during pregnancy (eg, yellow fever). In addition, some diseases are much more serious for the mother (and may increase the risk of a stillborn child) in pregnancy (eg, malaria).

The first and last three months should be spent within reasonable distance of good medical care and pregnant women should avoid all unnecessary medication, although vaccinations and malarial prophylactics should still be taken where needed.

TOILETS
Travellers on the road relate China toilet tales to each other like comparing old war wounds. Despite proud claims to have invented the first flushing toilet, China really does have some wicked loos. The capital has made a start on making the city's toilets less of an assault course of foul smells and primitive appliances, but they can still be pungent and sordid. Steer towards fast-food outlets, hotels or department stores for cleaner alternatives.

Public toilets can often be found in train stations and side streets of cities and towns – many charge a fee of around four or five jiǎo; others are free. Some have very low partitions (without doors) between the individual holes and some have none. Toilet paper is never provided – always keep a stash with you.

Rural toilets are just a hole in the ground or a ditch over which you squat.

While it takes some practice to get proficient at balancing yourself over a squat toilet, at least you don't need to worry about whether the toilet seat is clean. Furthermore, experts who study such things claim

Words & Pictures

Nǚ: woman, female, feminine

女 The character for woman, or feminine, has changed over time. Earlier versions depicted more submissive poses. In the modern version, tradition prevails, but the submissiveness has vanished. A woman, unlike her husband and sons, is still to be found around the house, where she can be seen striding around doing household chores, often with a baby strapped to her back.

Nán: man, male, masculine

男 The character for male, or masculine, is a combination of the characters for field (above) and strength (below). Traditionally, the males of the household would exert their strength in the fields. Their daily tasks included planting and harvesting crops, and tending to their livestock.

that the squatting position is better for your elimination system. Some hotels are still connected to ancient, narrow sewer pipes that easily block; in that case, there will be a wastebasket next to the toilet where you should throw the toilet paper. Also, in rural areas there is no sewage treatment plant – the waste empties into a septic tank and toilet paper will really create a mess in there. Be considerate and throw the paper in the wastebasket. Oh, and good luck.

WOMEN TRAVELLERS

Principles of decorum and respect for women are deeply ingrained in Chinese culture. Despite the Confucianist sense of superiority accorded men, Chinese women often call the shots and wield tremendous influence (especially within marriage). Chinese males are not macho, and there is a strong sense of balance between the sexes.

In general, foreign women are unlikely to suffer serious sexual harassment in China, but there have been reports of problems in Xīnjiāng. Wherever you are, it's worth noticing what local women are wearing and how they are behaving and making a bit of an effort to fit in, as you would in any other foreign country. Try to stick to hotels in the

centre, rather than the fringes of town. Taking a whistle or alarm with you would offer a measure of defence in any unpleasant encounter. As with anywhere else, you will be taking a risk if you travel alone. If you have to travel alone, consider arming yourself with some self-defence techniques.

GAY & LESBIAN TRAVELLERS

In 2001 the Chinese Psychiatric Association no longer classified homosexuality as a mental disorder.

Greater tolerance exists in the big cities than in the more conservative countryside. However, even in urban China it is not recommended that gays and lesbians be too open about their sexual orientation in public, even though you will see Chinese same-sex friends holding hands or putting their arms around each other. The situation is changing slowly as an increasing number of gay singers and actors in China are 'outed', but the police periodically crack down on gay meeting places.

On the other hand, there are many recognised gay discos, bars and pubs in the big cities that appear to function without official harassment, although they tend to keep a fairly low profile (see individual city entries for listings of these venues).

Check out W www.utopia-asia.com/tips chin.htm for loads of tips on travelling in China and a complete listing of gay bars nationwide. You can also contact the International Gay and Lesbian Travel Association (☎ +1-954-776 2626, fax 776 3303, W www .iglta.com) in the USA for more information. Club Exotika (W www.clubexotika .com) also does gay and lesbian packages and tours to China.

DISABLED TRAVELLERS

China has few facilities geared for the disabled. But that doesn't necessarily put it out of bounds for those with a physical disability (and a sense of adventure). On the plus side, most hotels have lifts, so booking ground-floor hotel rooms is not essential. In bigger cities, some hotels at the four- and five-star level have specially designed rooms for people with physical disabilities.

The roads and pavements make things very difficult for the wheelchair-bound or those with a walking disability. Pavements can often be crowded, in an appalling and dangerous condition and with high kerbs. People whose sight, hearing or walking ability is impaired must be extremely cautious of the traffic, which almost never yields to pedestrians. Travelling by car or taxi is probably the safest transport option.

Not surprisingly, Hong Kong is more user-friendly to the disabled than the rest of China. However, Hong Kong presents some substantial obstacles of its own such as the stairs at the subway stations, numerous overhead walkways and steep hills.

Get in touch with your national support organisation (the 'travel officer' if there is one) before leaving home. They often have travel literature for holiday planning and can put you in touch with travel agents who specialise in tours for the disabled.

In the UK the Royal Association for Disability & Rehabilitation (☎ 020-7250 3222, fax 7250 0212, W www.radar.org.uk), at 12 City Forum, 250 City Rd, London EC1V 8AF, produces three holiday fact packs for disabled travellers.

In the USA, contact the Society for Accessible Travel & Hospitality (SATH; ☎ 212-447 7284, W www.sath.org) at Suite 601, 347 Fifth Ave, New York, NY 10016.

In France try the CNFLRH (☎ 01 53 80 66 66) at 236 bis rue de Tolbiac, Paris.

SENIOR TRAVELLERS

In China, older people are revered. To be called elderly is a compliment, a tribute to your maturity and wisdom. You won't be short of things to do in China, even if you are not as young as you once were. Try getting up early in the morning to dabble in some *taijiquan* (tai chi) and other Chinese exercises. If you go to parks on weekends, you will hear the elderly singing Chinese songs. You may return to your own country realising that old age is not something to be pessimistic about.

The senior traveller who is adventurous and healthy should not find China too daunting, and may relish the opportunity. But a few precautions and preparations will make your trip more pleasant.

In China, you need to be aware of the sheer number of squat toilets, which you may have encountered if you have travelled in other parts of Asia. If not, and you are less flexible in your joints than you used to be, you should limit your first visit to China to the large cities, and stay in hotels that

have international-style toilets. When you venture out, however, you may have to use squat toilets and not always in private.

China can also be spartan and difficult to navigate, depending on where you travel; consequently, you may consider taking part in a tour for senior travellers. Elderhostel (W www.elderhostel.org), in the USA, organises escapades around China for those over 55. Saga Holidays (W www.saga holidays.com), in the UK, specialises in tours for seniors.

Lonely Planet's *Read this First: Asia and India* has chapters on Niche Travellers (including Senior Travellers) and on Health. Consult your doctor about vaccinations before you go to China, but don't worry, the larger cities are reasonably safe and healthy places.

First-class travel on trains is comfortable, and taxis are an alternative to crowded buses and subways. You should aim to travel in the shoulder season, when the tourist areas are less crowded, and the weather is more benign. Běijīng and Shànghǎi can be uncomfortably hot in the middle of summer and unpleasantly cold in winter.

TRAVEL WITH CHILDREN

One of the greatest advantages of travelling with children is that the Chinese find foreign children fascinating. This opens up the way to conversing with the Chinese and understanding them, even if all they want is to have an opportunity to play with your kids.

Chinese are still very curious about foreigners and more so about foreign children. Don't be surprised if a complete stranger picks up your child or takes them from your arms. Children are almost seen as common property for all to share.

Travelling with a young child or baby can often make life a lot easier in China. People will give up seats, help you through a crowd, make extra allowances and in general treat you as a VIP.

Chinese cities tend to have zoos, spacious parks with rowing boats and amusement parks with lots of cotton candy, Ferris wheels, flashing lights and merry-go-rounds. For older children, travellers' centres like Yángshuò – with everything from watching video movies in the cafes to floating down the river in truck inner tubes – will probably be the highlight of a China visit.

Chinese food seems to go down all right with most foreign children. Try and take them to Chinese restaurants before your trip so that they can get used to flavours, especially to hot spices like chilli. Also consider taking along dry foods to provide a sense of continuity and comfort, and a set of plastic cutlery for each child – coping with chopsticks could well be overwhelming. Western food is also widely available in China.

Baby food is available, but the Chinese prefer the sweeter varieties and nearly everything is processed and has had sugar added. Breast-feeding is the safest and best way to get around; milk powder is available in supermarkets in large towns and cities. Virtually no cheap restaurants have baby chairs and finding baby-changing rooms is next to impossible.

Basics like nappies (diapers), baby wipes, bottles, creams, medicine, clothing, dummies (pacifiers) and other paraphernalia are available in all larger provincial capitals. Remember that you don't need a prescription for drugs if you need a medicine like penicillin. Check the health section, earlier, for information on recommended immunisations for your child.

Travel in China tends to be uncomfortable and slow, involving long distances by train, often in hard-seat carriages where people smoke and spit. As one travelling parent suggested, fly occasionally to overcome the enormous distances; children under the age of two can fly for 10% of the full price and those aged between two and 11 get half-price tickets. Most taxis do not have rear seat belts.

Probably the biggest dangers are the roads (look both ways and watch out for holes), the profusion of dangerous objects (open electric wires) and the flu. If you can avoid these, then your child will come away with very fond and enjoyable memories of their China sojourn.

Many museums and attractions have a cheaper rate for children, usually applying to children under 1.3m, so ask.

USEFUL ORGANISATIONS

English-language cultural and social organisations are thin on the ground in China, as are counselling services. For counselling services, try a medical centre that provides services to foreigners. The embassies and consulates sometimes sponsor cultural events. Business-related organisations are more prolific (see Doing Business, later). Useful organisations include: Alcoholics Anonymous (☎ 010-6437 6305), which meets three times a week in Běijīng; and China Brief (☎ 010-8652 1309, W www.chinadevelopmentbrief.com), 24 Xiehe Hutong, Waijiao Bujie, Běijīng 10005, which publishes a newsletter on development projects in China as well as a directory of NGOs in China.

DANGERS
Crime
Travellers are more often the victims of petty economic crime, such as theft, rather than serious crime. Foreigners are natural targets for pickpockets and thieves, but as long as you keep your wits about you and make it difficult for thieves to get at your belongings, you shouldn't have any problems. Certain cities and places are worse than others – Guǎngzhōu, Guìyáng and Xī'ān are notorious. Kāngdìng in western Sìchuān has also seen a spate of violent robberies.

Two Chinese-Americans were killed in 1999 and 2000, in separate, violent incidents at nightclubs, one in Qīngdǎo, the other in Běijīng – such attacks are rare, however.

High-risk areas in China are train and bus stations, city and long-distance buses (especially sleeper buses) and hard-seat train carriages. Hard-seat carriages of trains in particular can become very anarchic with the onset of darkness – they are sometimes worked by gangs who use knives to persuade travellers to hand over their valuables. Some foreign travellers who have tried to resist have been stabbed in incidents such as these.

Be careful in public toilets – quite a few foreigners have laid aside their valuables, squatted down to business, and then straightened up to find someone has absconded with the lot.

Hotels are generally safe. There are attendants on every floor keeping an eye on the rooms and safeguarding the keys. Dormitories obviously require more care. Don't be overly trusting of your fellow travellers – many of them are considerably less than honest. All hotels have safes and storage areas for valuables – use them. Don't leave anything you can't do without (passport, travellers cheques, money, air tickets etc) lying around in dormitories.

Small padlocks are useful for backpacks and some dodgy hotel rooms. Bicycle chain locks (preferably not Chinese-made) are handy not only for hired bikes, but for attaching backpacks to railings or luggage racks (especially if you are sleeping on long-distance train journeys).

Carry just as much cash as you need and keep the rest in travellers cheques. Fanny bags are definitely *not* advisable for valuables. Always take a money belt for larger sums of cash along with your passport and credit cards. Street tailors are skilled at sewing inside pockets to trousers, jackets and shirts usually for a few yuán, and these can even be sealed with zippers.

Con artists are widespread in China. Ostensibly friendly types invite you for tea, then order food and say they have no money, leaving you to foot the bill, while practising their English on you.

Don't leave any of your belongings with someone you do not know well. Moneychangers are notorious for using various devices to rip off customers. The opening economy in China has also spawned a plague of dishonest businesses and enterprises. The travel agent you phoned may just operate from a cigarette smoke-filled hotel room.

Another scam is for a pedestrian to bump into a Western traveller, dropping a bag in the process with some cheap porcelain inside, and then open it up to expose the fragments to the stunned tourist, followed by demands for compensation.

A worrying trend is the increasing number of reports of foreigners attacked or even killed for their valuables, especially in more rural locations (a Western tourist was recently killed on Moon Hill in popular Yángshuò); so be vigilant at all times. It's always advisable to travel with someone else or in a small group; individual travellers have to accept they are taking a risk.

Loss Reports If something of yours is stolen, you should report it immediately to the nearest Foreign Affairs Branch of the PSB. Staff will ask you to fill in a loss report before investigating the case and sometimes even recovering the stolen goods.

If you have travel insurance (highly recommended), it is essential to obtain a loss report so you can claim compensation. Be warned, however: many travellers have found Foreign Affairs officials very unwilling to provide one. Be prepared to spend many hours, perhaps even several days, organising it.

Violence
Street fighting in China is common, yet it seldom leads to serious injury – mostly there's just lots of arm-waving, screaming and threats.

The reasons are generally simple enough – people are pushing and shoving their way to the front of a queue, the traffic is forever noisily colliding and finally someone just flips out. Don't get involved.

The triads of Macau and Hong Kong are altogether different, but their ultra-violent domain is generally well off the tourist trail. (Tourist figures to Macau nonetheless dropped off in 1997/98 due to the triad civil war there.)

Many Chinese males carry knives but these are seldom used for anything other than slicing bread. That said, there have been cases of armed robbery by gangs on trains – knives are the usual weapons. The chance of it happening to you is small and you need not let this deter you from riding the train, but it's a good idea to be aware that it can happen. Guns are impossible to buy legally.

Terrorism
You are unlikely to be a victim of terrorist activity in China, because foreigners are not specific targets. However, the past 10 years has seen an increase in bombings throughout China (some reports state that over 2000 bombs exploded in China in 1998). A bomb in Shíjiāzhuāng in 2001 killed scores of people. It is often difficult to ascertain who is behind such attacks, but the official version is that unemployed criminals, blackmailers and suicidal individuals are to blame. Xīnjiāng Uyghur separatists have been linked to a few bus bombings in cities

ANNOYANCES
Lǎowài!
Get outside the cosmopolitan centres of Guǎngzhōu, Shànghǎi and Běijīng and you will hear the exclamation *'lǎowài'*, or

alternatively 'Hello, lǎowài, hello'. You'll probably hear this a couple of dozen times a day. *Lǎo* means 'old' in Chinese and is a mark of respect; *wài* means 'outside'. Together they constitute the most polite word the Chinese have for 'foreigner'.

Chinese speakers will hear it used in many ways – sometimes with a thick overlay of irony that undermines the respect implied in the word – but generally it is used in startled surprise at suddenly encountering a foreigner in a world that is overwhelmingly Chinese.

There is no point getting annoyed by it. If you answer by saying hello, they (the audience) will as often as not break into hysterical laughter.

Noise

In recent years the Chinese government has launched an anti-noise pollution campaign. The government is on a loser with this one, but a number of cities have banned the use of car horns within the city. The Chinese are generally much more tolerant of noise than most foreigners. People watch TV at ear-shattering volumes, drivers habitually lean on the horn, and much of China seems to wake uncomplainingly to the sound of jack-hammers and earth-moving vehicles. If it's peace and quiet you want, head for a remote part of China – try the desert in Xīnjiāng, or a mountain-top in Tibet.

Spitting

When China first opened to foreign tourism, many foreign travellers were shocked by the spitting, which was conducted noisily by everyone everywhere. Campaigns to stamp out the practice have been reasonably successful in the major urban centres – there is less public spitting in Guǎngzhōu, Shànghǎi and Běijīng these days (some areas impose a Y50 fine), but in the country, the phlegm still flies thick and fast.

Apart from the fact that it is very unpleasant to be stuck in, say, a bus with 50 people who feel compelled to pave the floor with gob, spitting also spreads the flu (see the Health section for further details).

Racism

Racism in China is a knotty problem. Most Chinese will swear blind that there is no racism in China. But then very few Chinese you meet will have thought very deeply about the issue, and the Chinese government doesn't allow public debate on China's racist policies and attitudes. But, of course, as in most other countries around the world, racism is alive and kicking in China.

The Chinese are a proud people. Being Chinese links the individual to a long historical lineage, for the most part of which, Chinese believe, their country was the centre of the world. Being Chinese is often defined by blood, not nationality (and where does that leave China's ethnic minorities?). China does not accept refugees from any other country unless they are of Chinese blood. The old dual-pricing system for foreigners was fundamentally racist – but most Chinese wouldn't see this as racist – to them, it was simply the rules.

Then there's the interesting case of non-Chinese Hong Kong residents. There are many 'foreigners' who were born in Hong Kong and hold Hong Kong passports, and in fact have never lived anywhere else. Some are one-half Chinese or one-quarter Chinese, but Běijīng flatly refused to grant citizenship to anyone who was not of 'pure Chinese descent'. In other words, racial purity was the deciding factor, not place of birth. This rendered all these people stateless in July 1997.

Politics and science aside, foreigners in China are generally treated well. It is very unusual to encounter direct racism in the form of insults (although it does happen) or be refused service in China. It does help, however, if you are from a predominantly white and prosperous nation. Other Asians and blacks often encounter discrimination in China. The most famous outright racist incident occurred in 1988 when Chinese students in Nánjīng took to the streets to protest black overseas students dating local Chinese women.

Queues

In China a large number of people with a common goal (a bus seat, a train ticket, purchasing a mobile phone etc) generally form a surging mass, although elements of queuing are appearing. It is one of the more exhausting parts of China travel, and sometimes it is worth paying extra in order to be able to avoid train and bus stations. Otherwise, take a deep breath and leap in with everyone else.

Beggars

In major cities, beggars often target Westerners and are found in areas where they congregate (such as near the Silk Market and Sānlǐtún in Běijīng). Children, probably under the supervision of a nearby adult who will collect the cash, are often the most aggressive.

Prostitution

Prostitution has become a massive industry in China over the past decade, most noticeably in Zhūhǎi and Shēnzhèn (and Macau). The further you stray from Běijīng, the more organised the profession, but it flourishes in the capital as well – look at most of the small 'hairdressers' that have sprung up and you'll get the message (or massage). The industry has become so rampant that many waitresses at restaurants throughout China now dislike being addressed as *'xiǎojie'* (literally 'Miss') because of its newfound and dubious connotations.

Single foreign men staying in two- to three-star hotels can expect their phone to ring like a hotline, a prostitute on the other end. This is one of the unadvertised extras that hotels have been running the past 10 years or so (another one is the all-night karaoke).

Sometimes the prostitute calls at 3am, at other times she calls every five minutes. If you want sleep, just unplug your phone.

EMERGENCIES

See the Post & Communications section earlier in this chapter for a list of emergency telephone numbers.

If you are arrested or run into legal problems you should contact your embassy or consulate for assistance.

LEGAL MATTERS
Legal System

China's legal system has improved significantly since opening up began in the late 1970s. When the People's Republic of China was founded in 1949, its new government claimed to establish a new legal system for the whole people. However, the Chinese Communist Party's internal political movements during the first 30 years of the PRC interrupted the drafting of new laws. For instance, during the Cultural Revolution from 1966 to 1976, there was a legal vacuum in China as its law enforcement agencies were smashed. Judges and lawyers either changed their professions or were sent to the countryside for 're-education'. Drafting of new laws and establishing the legal system were only re-started after the end of the Cultural Revolution.

China's legal system is closer to a Civil Law System than a Common Law System as its creative law-making is undertaken by legislature, not by judges. In the past few decades many pieces of law have been enacted covering contract, labour, intellectual property, foreign exchange control, customs, taxation, banking, consumer protection, bankruptcy, dispute resolution etc. Chinese people are relying more and more on laws to govern their civil and commercial activities as legal concepts become more understood. Before the economic and legal reforms, individual Chinese people were not allowed to engage in commercial activities such as opening their own businesses or selling their own hand-made or home-grown products directly in the market. Nowadays, enacted legislation, courts, arbitration commissions and private law firms play dominant roles in resolving civil and commercial disputes in China.

China uses the death penalty liberally and is the world's greatest executioner of criminals. Around 80 offences are punishable with the death penalty, and the number has increased over recent years.

Amnesty International estimated that 1700 alleged criminals were put to death in the three months before the decision was made to grant the 2008 Olympics to Běijīng. This figure is more than the executions in all other countries over the previous three years added together.

Foreign-Related Legal Matters

In China's court system, there are four levels hierarchically. At local county or district level is the basic people's court. At municipal level, there are intermediate people's courts, and at the provincial level is the higher people's court. At the top, is the supreme people's court. If a foreigner is involved in a legal dispute, he or she can take the matter to an intermediate people's court at municipal level or above. A people's court at basic level has no jurisdiction over a matter related to foreigners. If foreigners run into legal troubles in China, they should contact their embassies or consulates in China for assistance. Lawyers skilled in Chinese law also advertise their services in classified pages of expat mags. If foreign investors are involved in legal disputes, they should contact their lawyers in their home country and in China for legal advice.

Over 100 foreign law firms had received permits to open offices in China by 1999. Most of these foreign law firms are in Běijīng or Shànghǎi and mainly focus on civil and commercial matters. Foreign lawyers are not permitted to act on behalf of their clients in the people's courts, but they are permitted to act on behalf of their clients in the arbitration proceedings of an arbitration commission. In addition, parties can appoint foreigners as their arbitrators. The proceeding can be conducted in a foreign language as well. For instance, the proceedings of the China International Economic and Trade Arbitration Commission can be conducted completely in English or any other foreign language chosen by the parties. Interpreters and translators may not be necessary in foreign language arbitration proceedings. From these points of view, it is advisable to take your disputes to an arbitration commission or a conciliation centre for resolution rather than taking the matter to a court.

Travellers should take extra care to comply with Chinese law as it may not be wholly complete or transparent. Inconsistencies exist between the national law and regional regulations and corruption occurs in the judicial system, which affects law enforcement. Sometimes, judges and lawyers may protect illegitimate local interests by ignoring national law, which grants equal treatment to both Chinese and foreigners in China. Therefore, sometimes the written law is not enforced properly or consistently.

Drugs

Since reform and opening up, drugs and drug control have become a big issue in China. According to statistics from the Public Security Bureau, by the end of 2000, there were 860,000 drug users registered in China, an increase of 26.3% over 1999. According to the International Narcotics Control Board's annual report, China is the only country that has witnessed a rise in heroin

seizures, from 3.8 tons in 1994 to 7.0 tons in 1998. If this trend continues, China may become one of the world's biggest consumers of heroin. International trends have also pumped up the use of ice, methamphetamines and other stimulants such as ecstasy.

China has become both a conduit for international drug trafficking and a consumer of drugs. Intravenous drug use is also one of the main arteries for the spread of the HIV virus around China.

The Chinese government places great emphasis on fighting drugs and drug-related crimes. It is making an effort to involve and support international cooperation in controlling drugs. The government's other major task is to help drug addicts quit their habit by establishing and expanding drug rehabilitation centres. In 2000, China took measures to compulsorily stop 243,000 drug users from taking drugs, and 60,000 new drug users entered a re-education scheme along with some 120,000 being re-educated in special clinics. Some measures are more extreme: over 50 people were executed for drug crimes on one day alone, after swift sentencing, to mark UN anti-drugs day in June 2001.

If a traveller is arrested with drugs, he or she will be punished in accordance with the provisions of the Criminal Code of the PRC (Section 7 of Chapter 6 of Part II of the Criminal Code). Depending upon the seriousness of the case, the offender can be sentenced to three to 15 years imprisonment for trafficking, selling, transporting or manufacturing drugs. Some serious offenders will be jailed for life or even subjected to the death sentence. Conditions vary in different prisons. Most prisons are located in rural or isolated areas. Prisoners engage in labour work daily.

Alcohol

Avoid rowdy displays of public drunkenness. The loud, drunken lager lout at large wins no brownie points and could lead to a run-in with the police. The consummate New York, London or Paris hobo staggering wide-legged down the road, strong brew in hand, shouting at the moon doesn't have his equivalent in China. Chinese hard-core drinkers sociably congregate in packs and are the last to be bundled out of restaurants as the shutters crash down.

PSB

The Public Security Bureau (PSB; Gōngānjú) is the name given to China's police, both uniformed and plainclothes. Its responsibilities include suppression of political dissidence, crime detection, mediating family quarrels and directing traffic. A related force is the Chinese People's Armed Police Force (CPAPF), which was formed to absorb cuts in the People's Liberation Army (PLA). The Foreign Affairs Branch (Wài Shì Kē) of the PSB deals with foreigners. This branch (also known as the 'entry-exit' branch) is responsible for issuing visa extensions and Alien Travel Permits.

The PSB is responsible for introducing and enforcing regulations concerning foreigners. So, for example, it bears responsibility for exclusion of foreigners from certain hotels (a practice that should end soon). If this means you get stuck for a place to stay, it can offer advice. Don't pester the PSB with trivia or try to 'use' it to bully a point with a local street vendor. Do turn to it for mediation in serious disputes with hotels, restaurants, taxi drivers etc.

BUSINESS HOURS

China officially has a five-day work week although some businesses stretch to six days. Offices and government departments are normally open Monday to Friday. As a rough guide only, they are open between about 8.30am and 5pm or 6pm, with some closing for one to two hours in the middle of the day. Most museums stay open on weekends and make up for this by closing on Monday and/or another day mid-week.

Travel agencies, department stores, banks and foreign-exchange counters in tourist hotels have similar opening hours, but generally do not close for lunch and are usually open Saturday and Sunday as well (at least in the morning).

Many parks, zoos and monuments have similar opening hours and are also open on weekends and often at night.

Many Chinese restaurants shut from around 2pm to 5pm; note that the Chinese tend to eat earlier than Westerners, eating dinner at around 6pm.

Long-distance bus stations and train stations open their ticket offices around 5am or 5.30am, before the first trains and buses pull out. They stay open until midnight, with maybe a one- or two-hour break in the middle of the day.

PUBLIC HOLIDAYS & SPECIAL EVENTS

The PRC has nine national holidays, as follows (Hong Kong and Macau have different holidays):

public holiday	date
New Year's Day	1 January
Spring Festival (Chinese New Year)	usually February
International Women's Day	8 March
International Labour Day	1 May
Youth Day	4 May
International Children's Day	1 June
Birthday of the Chinese Communist Party	1 July
Anniversary of the founding of the PLA	1 August
National Day	1 October

The 1 May holiday has been drawn out into a week-long holiday, as has National Day on 1 October. The Chinese New Year is also a week-long holiday for many; it's not a great idea to arrive in China or go travelling during these holidays as things tend to grind to a halt. Firecrackers *(bàozhú)* have been banned in most Chinese cities for announcing the Chinese New Year. Notable times when temples are at their liveliest include:

February

Spring Festival (Chūn Jié) This is also known as Chinese New Year and starts on the first day of the first month in the lunar calendar. Many people take a week off work. Be warned: this is China's biggest holiday and all transport and hotels are booked solid. Although the demand for accommodation skyrockets, many hotels close down at this time and prices rise steeply. If you can't avoid being in China at this time, then book your room in advance and sit tight until the chaos is over! The Chinese New Year will fall on the following dates: 1 February 2003 and 22 January 2004.

Lantern Festival (Yuánxiāo Jié) It's not a public holiday, but it is very colourful. People make (or buy) paper lanterns and walk around the streets in the evening holding them. It falls on the 15th day of the first moon, and will be celebrated on the following dates: 16 February 2003 and 6 February 2004.

March/April

Guanyin's Birthday (Guānshìyīn Shēngrì) The birthday of Guanyin, the Goddess of Mercy, is a fine time to visit Buddhist temples, many of which have halls dedicated to the divinity. Guanyin's birthday is the 19th day of the second moon and will fall on the following dates: 21 March 2003, 9 March & 8 April 2004.

April

Tomb Sweeping Day (Qīng Míng Jié) A day for worshipping ancestors; people visit and clean the graves of their departed relatives. They often place flowers on the tomb and burn ghost money for the departed. The festival falls on 5 April in the Gregorian calendar in most years, or 4 April in leap years.

Water-Splashing Festival (Pō Shuǐ Jié) Held in the Xīshuāngbǎnnà in Yúnnán, this event falls around mid-April (usually 13 to 15 April). The purpose is to wash away the dirt, sorrow and demons of the old year and bring in the happiness of the new. The event gets staged virtually daily now for tourists.

April/May

Mazu's Birthday (Māzǔshēngrì) Mazu, Goddess of the Sea, is the friend of all fishing crews. She's called Māzǔ in Fújiàn province and Taiwan. She is also called Tiānhòu (pronounced 'Tin Hau' in Hong Kong) and Niángniang. Her birthday is widely celebrated at Taoist temples in coastal regions as far south as Vietnam. Mazu's birthday is on the 23rd day of the third moon, and will fall on the following dates: 24 April 2003 and 11 May 2004.

June

Dragon Boat Festival (Duānwǔ Jié) This is the time to see dragon boat races and eat triangular glutinous rice dumplings wrapped in reed leaves (zòngzi). It's a fun holiday despite the fact that it commemorates the sad tale of Qu Yuan, a 3rd-century BC poet-statesman who hurled himself into the mythological Mi Lo river in Húnán to protest against the corrupt government. This holiday falls on the fifth day of the fifth lunar month, which corresponds to the following dates: 4 June 2003 and 22 June 2004.

August

Ghost Month (Guǐ Yuè) The devout believe that during this time the ghosts from hell walk the earth and it is a dangerous time to travel, go swimming, get married or move house. If someone dies during this month, the body will be preserved and the funeral and burial will be performed the following month. The Chinese government officially denounces Ghost Month as a lot of superstitious nonsense. The Ghost Month is the seventh lunar month, or really just the first 15 days. The first day of the Ghost Month will fall on the following dates: 9 August 2002, 29 July 2003 and 16 August 2004.

September/October

Mid-Autumn Festival (Zhōngqiū Jié) This is also known as the Moon Festival, and is the time to gaze at the moon and eat tasty moon cakes (yuèbǐng) and it's also a traditional holiday for lovers. The festival takes place on the 15th day of the eighth moon, and will be celebrated on the following dates: 21 September 2002, 11 September 2003 and 28 September 2004.

September

Birthday of Confucius (Kǒngzi Shēngrì) The great sage has his birthday on 28 September of the Gregorian calendar. This is an interesting time to visit Qūfù in Shāndōng, the birthplace of Confucius, although getting a hotel room may be tricky. A ceremony is held at the Confucius Temple starting around 4am and other similar temples around China will observe the event.

ACTIVITIES
Adventure Sports & Hiking

A whiff of the tourist dollar has sent Chinese entrepreneurs scrambling up the rock face of the adventure sport economy. Even in and around Běijīng alone you've got a mushrooming choice: paragliding, hang-gliding, rock climbing, diving with sharks, skiing, bungee jumping, horseback riding and more.

The most exciting mountaineering terrain lies in western China. Individual mountaineering is not, however, a sensible option as you could well have a run-in with the authorities. Foreigners have been asked for outrageous sums of money for mountaineering and rafting permits. The amount demanded varies considerably depending on who you're dealing with, and the price is always negotiable.

As opposed to mountaineering (which requires equipment such as ropes and ice axes), normal hiking activities can usually be pursued without permits. Outfits in China itself like Wildchina (W www.wildchina.com) offer a host of dramatic treks. It's probably worth arranging your climb, hike or trek through such an outfit, as it can take care of all the legalities; and it's all-inclusive.

Hikers can also clamber up either all or some of China's nine sacred mountains. You won't need ropes as there are steps and handrails. You may have to ferret around to find solitude, but the mountains are beautiful. Those stimulated by either Taoism or

Chinese Martial Arts

Kung fu is commonly used as a collective term for the many variations of Chinese martial arts. However, the actual term kung fu does not itself mean martial arts but a skill obtained through dedication and hard work; the correct term for martial arts is *wu shu* or *kou shu* meaning martial or national arts.

In China today the various martial art styles that exist number into the hundreds; many still not known to the Western world, and each style reflecting its own fighting philosophy and spirit. You can take your pick according to your persuasion: drunken boxing, white crane boxing, white eyebrow boxing, monkey boxing, tiger boxing, five ancestors boxing and many, many more. The following is a thumbnail sketch of a few of the arts that you may see while travelling in China.

Shaolin Boxing

Shaolin boxing is one of the major branches of Chinese martial arts. The art is said to have originated at Shàolín Sì on Sōng Shān in Hénán province. Shàolín monk fighters were trained to help protect the temple's assets. The martial art routines of Shàolín Sì were not organised into a complete system until some 30 to 40 years later when an Indian monk Bodhidharma (Da Mo in Chinese) visited the site. Bodhidharma brought a new type of Buddhism to China, that of Chan (Zen) Buddhism, which spread rapidly within China.

Bodhidharma taught the monks various kinds of physical exercises to limber up the joints and build a good physique. These movements were expanded over time and a complicated series of Chinese boxing (or forms) evolved. By the Sui and Tang dynasties, Shaolin boxing was widely known.

The fighting styles originating from Shàolín Sì are based on five animals: dragon, snake, tiger, leopard and crane. Each animal represents a different style, each of which is used to develop different skills.

The temple's famous forms have had a profound influence on many of today's martial arts, and the temple is still being utilised today (see the Hénán chapter for more information).

Taijiquan (Shadow Boxing)

Taijiquan or tai chi is a centuries-old Chinese discipline promoting flexibility, circulation, strength, balance, relaxation and meditation. While the art is seen by many outside China as a slow-motion form of gentle exercise, it is traditionally practised as a form of self defence. Taijiquan aims to dispel the opponent without the use of force, and with minimal effort. It is based on the Taoist idea that the principle of softness will ultimately overcome hardness. According to legend, it is derived from the movements of animals.

A major part of studying taijiquan is the development of *qi*, or life energy that can be directed to all parts of the body with the help of mental training. Qi must flow and circulate freely in the body.

There is no single founder of taijiquan as the art has been developed over many centuries by countless people. Due to different needs and environments various styles of taijiquan evolved. The most popular form of taijiquan is the Yang style, which is not too difficult to learn in its simplified form (though the full form has 108 postures) and is not strenuous. Other styles, such as the Chen style, call for a wider array of skills as the postures are painfully low and the kicks high, so endurance and flexibility are important. Chen style is popular with younger exponents and clearly has its roots in Shaolin, mixing slow movements with fast, snappy punches. Other styles include the Sun and Wu styles.

Wing Chun

Legend has it that the originator of *wing chun* was Ng Mui, a Buddhist nun who lived near Shàolín Sì. She was involved in researching fighting techniques with other monks in the hope of developing a more streamlined approach. The origin of wing chun is said to have followed a chance encounter with a snake and crane locked in combat. Observing them, Ng Mui admired their fighting methods, and began to incorporate the unique tactics into her already well-developed martial skills, creating a remarkable new method. Later, in the village below, she met Yim Yee and his daughter Yim Wing-Chun. Wing-Chun's beauty attracted the attention of a local bully who tried to force Wing-Chun to marry him. Ng Mui learned of this and agreed to teach Wing-Chun fighting skills in the mountains so she could protect herself. When Wing-Chun returned home she challenged her oppressor to an unarmed battle and needless to say won.

The acknowledged grandmaster of modern-day wing chun and the man responsible for spreading the art to the West was Yip Man, who learned the fundamental aspects of wing chun from an early age. Yip Man taught wing chun to Bruce Lee, who used wing chun as a fundamental principle to Jeet Kune Do.

Wing chun emphasises speed rather than strength. Evasion, subterfuge and rapid strikes are its hallmarks. The theory of wing chun is enshrined in its 'centre-line theory', which draws an imaginary line down the human body and centres all attacks and blocks on that line. The line runs through the sensitive regions: eyes, nose, lips, mouth, throat, heart, solar plexus and groin. Any blow that lands on any of these points is debilitating and dangerous.

Bagua Zhang (Eight-Trigram Boxing)

Bagua zhang fighters were feared among Chinese boxers for their ferocity and unorthodox moves. The practitioner wheels around in a circle, changing speed and direction, occasionally kicking or thrusting out a palm strike.

The motifs of this martial art style are the skills of subterfuge, evasion, speed and unpredictability. Force is generally not met with force, but deflected by circular movements. A further hallmark of the style is the exclusive use of the palm instead of the fist as the main striking weapon. This may appear strange and even ineffectual, but in fact the palm can transmit a surprising amount of power. The palm can also be better protected than the fist, as it is cushioned by muscle.

The art of bagua zhang is deeply esoteric and almost off-limits to non-Chinese. There are practitioners who teach foreigners, but they are not nearly as prolific as teachers of bagua's sister art, taijiquan. Anyone who finds a teacher of worth must be prepared for an intense schooling in a difficult art. Those who do become proficient in bagua zhang will inherit a disappearing legacy of old China.

Xingyi Quan (Body-Mind Boxing)

Xingyi quan is often mentioned in the same breath as taijiquan, despite being different in many ways. Like taijiquan the training emphasises the development of qi; however, the movements of xingyi quan are dynamic and powerful, and the fighting philosophy is not passive, like that of taijiquan.

Possibly the oldest martial art still in existence in China, xingyi quan was developed in imitation of the fighting techniques and spirits of twelve animals. There are different schools of xingyi quan, which promote different animal styles, but the standard form consists of the dragon, tiger, horse, monkey, chicken, harrier, Chinese ostrich, swallow, eagle, bear, water lizard and snake. Each animal must be understood in terms of its shape and intention or idea.

The student starts with the five punches. Each punch represents one of the five elements – *pi* (metal), *beng* (wood), *zuan* (water), *pao* (fire) and *heng* (earth). The punches reflect the cycle of conquest and creation implicit in the life of the five elements: fire conquers metal, metal conquers wood, wood conquers earth, earth conquers water and water conquers fire. Alternatively, fire produces earth, earth produces metal, metal produces water, water produces wood and wood produces fire.

Xingyi quan is performed in a relaxed state, emphasising a calm but observant mind. The movements are quick and direct. Training in the art is punishing and consists of many postures that must be held for a long time in order to develop qi. Attacks are generally met with force rather than with evasive manoeuvring. Like bagua zhang, teachers of xingyi quan are hard to find and are often reticent about the art.

Philosophy and Health

Many martial arts of the East have their foundations deeply entwined with the philosophies, doctrines, concepts and religious beliefs of Confucianism, Buddhism, Taoism and Zen. It is certainly true that most of the martial art systems in existence today owe their development and ultimate dissemination to the monks and priests who taught and transferred such knowledge over much of Asia throughout history.

In Chinese wushu a distinction is made between 'external' and 'internal' martial arts. In addition to external training to achieve a strong body and nimble limbs, there is also an internal training to adjust body and mind, strengthen internal organs, and increase circulation of qi.

Buddhism will make a beeline for these peaks and the temples that rise above their plunging cliffs.

Camel & Horse Riding

Camel rides for tourists have become popular pastimes in places like Inner Mongolia, Xīnjiāng and the deserts. There's a growing number of equestrian clubs in the large cities; check the classified or entertainment pages of expat mags for details.

There are chances for beautiful horse-riding trips in the mountains of Xīnjiāng, or for that matter in the hills west of Běijīng. Costs are negotiable, but in general, the further away from a big city you are, the cheaper it gets. Sōngpān in Sìchuān also offers some exciting horse treks.

Exercise & Gymnasiums

Quality gyms, health clubs and weight-training rooms used to be limited to smart hotels. In the large cities of Guǎngzhōu, Shēnzhèn, Shànghǎi, Dàlián, Běijīng etc, Western-style health clubs are becoming more common. Hong Kong and Macau are well equipped with health clubs. Check the classified pages of expat mags for adverts.

For a fee, most hotels in big cities like Běijīng permit non-guests to join their 'health club', which entitles you to use the workout rooms, pools, saunas or tennis courts. This is not a bad idea if you're staying for a month or more – monthly membership fees typically start at around Y850 and there are discounts for married couples and families. Larger discounts exist if you sign up for six months or more.

Massage

Massage has traditionally been performed by blind people in China. The Chinese can take credit for developing many of the best massage techniques that are still employed today.

Most five-star hotels have massage services at five-star prices (typically Y300 per hour). Rates are around Y50 per hour at small specialist massage clinics, but you'll need a Chinese person to direct you to one.

In some budget hotels ànmó (massage) is politely used to describe services performed by prostitutes. If genuine massage is really what you want, try and ascertain that's actually what is on offer.

Winter Sports

Winter can be a great time to see China, if the cold doesn't faze you, and there's a growing list of winter sports available. North-east China is a venue for downhill skiing, snowboarding and cross-country skiing, but the principle slopes are mainly suitable for beginners. There are even a number of ski resorts in Héběi within reach of Běijīng that are open during the winter months. Outdoor skating becomes feasible in Běijīng and the north when lakes freeze over (for example at the Summer Palace).

More adventurous travellers wanting something different and more challenging should book skiing tours through outfits like China Ski Corporation (W www.chinaski.com) who offer a range of adventurous holidays. Such 10-day plus tours take decent skiers and snowboarders on trips to Tibet and Qīnghǎi where few people have skied. They also arrange snowriding adventures in the north-east and north-west – walking, horse riding and low-altitude skiing jaunts, plus 4WD vehicle touring over rough roads; mountain biking is also on the agenda.

Golf

Golf courses have invaded the suburbs of Běijīng, Shànghǎi, Guǎngzhōu and beyond. There were 12 courses in Běijīng alone in 2001, with four more under construction. In Běijīng the game can only be played from spring to autumn; winter is too frigid. Be warned: fees are often ridiculous, and milk foreigners and their companies (over Y1000 per hour), so phone around before reaching for your clubs. For organised golfing tours or information on tournaments in China, call Golfing China (☎ 010-6417 1828/29/30).

Other Sports

Glance at the expat rags in Běijīng, Guǎngzhōu and Shànghǎi and you'll see a host of sporting activities. Running, mountain biking, frisbee throwing, horse riding, rugby, football, swimming, bowling, rock climbing, indoor ice skating, skateboarding, water-skiing, windsurfing and more can all be found.

COURSES

Most universities welcome fee-paying foreign students. Most courses offered are Chinese-language study, but you have a great choice of other courses, including Chinese medicine, *wǔshù* (martial arts), acupuncture, music, calligraphy, brush painting and more.

A bottom-end quote for four hours of instruction per day, five days a week, is around US$1200 per semester, and perhaps half that for a six-week summer session. For these rates, the teacher-to-student ratio is typically 1:25. A semester lasts about four months, with the spring semester starting just after Chinese New Year and the autumn semester starting in mid-September. Dormitory housing starts at around US$15 a day for a private room, or half that amount to share.

If possible, don't pay anything in advance and check the place over beforehand. If you show up a day or two before classes begin you'll usually be allowed to register. An exception to this is Beijing University and Beijing Language and Culture University, where classes fill up early, so registration is necessary. Once you've handed over the cash, don't expect a refund.

If you want real language immersion, then you will probably find there are too many English-speaking Westerners at colleges like Beijing Normal University.

Students argue till they're blue in the face about the merits of learning simplified or full-form Chinese – but the fact is that once you have learned one set, you'll have more than enough time to learn the other if you want to, if you're attending for a semester or more.

Courses aren't restricted to Běijīng; you can attend courses all round China, including Hángzhōu, Nánjīng and Shànghǎi.

An increasing number of private Chinese-language courses have emerged that may offer more professional teaching. These are useful if you find work in China and want to study Chinese in your spare time. Their advertisements litter the classified pages of the expat rags.

If you want to learn Cantonese *(Guǎngdōnghuà)*, then you'll want to be down south in Guǎngzhōu (cheap) or Hong Kong (not cheap).

Consult Ⓦ www.ciee.org/index.cfm for more information on studying in China.

WORK

A growing number of work opportunities exist in China, although some require language skills and you will need a work visa. Consult the classified pages of the expat mags in Běijīng, Shànghǎi and Guǎngzhōu for a listing of work opportunities. These include English teaching, marketing, travel agents, creative English writers (for polishing and rewriting English documents and articles), editors, proofreaders, translators, bar staff and secretarial positions.

Teaching English

English-language teaching is big business in China. Opportunities abound for those who want to teach the language (and to a

Babble-on

Despite the ascendancy of *pǔtōnghuà* (standard Chinese speech), China is still a huge Babel of often mutually unintelligible dialects. Mandarin acts as a general-purpose glue binding the mishmash together, from far-flung camel traders in Kashgar to Hong Kong bank managers. But for both, Mandarin is an awkward fit – it's an off-the-shelf lingo and not the nicely tailored language they grew up with.

As a general rule of thumb, the further one strays from Běijīng within China, the shoddier the spoken Mandarin, although south and west China take the cake. The Hong Kong Chinese are notorious for pummelling *pǔtōnghuà* beyond recognition, but the dialect gets a bruising just about everywhere, in pretty much the same way that English suffers worldwide.

Very average foreign speakers of Mandarin bump into repeated praise in China's south for their mastery of the vernacular, but the acid test is Běijīng. If you can't cut the mustard in the capital, it's back to the drawing board.

The Běijīng dialect, though, is itself quite different from standard *pǔtōnghuà*, despite Mandarin being based on it. Listen to the news announcer on CCTV – that's standard Mandarin. Now listen to the sounds emanating from your Běijīng cabdriver hunched over his wheel – that's Běijīnghuà, and a world divides the two. But the Běijīng accent has excellent cachet the land over – no foreigner aspires to speak *pǔtōnghuà* with, say, a Fúzhōu accent.

lesser extent other languages), or even other technical skills if you're qualified. You can expect to earn around Y100 to Y150 per hour or more if you join a private language school or business in a large city like Běijīng or Shànghǎi. Some schools require that you have a TEFL (Teaching of English as a Foreign Language) certificate or equivalent qualification; others only require that you have a university degree or possess native English-language skills.

If you are employed as a teacher by a university, a voluntary or charitable organisation, you can expect to be paid far, far less than this. In less laissez-faire institutions such as these, a maximum teaching load should be 20 hours per week and you can insist on no more than 15 (although some teachers get away with 10). Certain topics, such as politics and religion, are taboo in such educational frameworks, so avoid discussing them.

For information on teaching in China, consult W www.ciee.org/index.cfm, and for voluntary work in China, have a look at W www.globalvolunteers.org and the Web site of VSO, W www.vso.org.uk, the largest volunteer organisation in the world.

Doing Business

Doing business in China has long been fraught for Westerners, since Lord Macartney's turkey of a mission to Chéngdé in 1793 to develop trade relations.

Things are easing up rapidly, but even simple things can still be difficult. Getting licences, hiring employees and paying taxes can generate mind-boggling quantities of red tape. Many foreign businesspeople who have worked in China say that success is usually the result of dogged persistence and finding cooperative officials. Many a Western business, lured by the Chinese market, has been beached and not many have made any money.

Even when you think you've got everything all agreed to on paper, things can go awry when agreements are put into practice. Your Chinese joint-venture partner may change the terms of the agreement once business has commenced. Your copyrights, patents and trademarks may be pirated.

Your Chinese employees (who know your company's secrets) may walk out and start working for a new company just across the street producing exactly the same goods as you do. With China joining the WTO, the land should become less of a business minefield.

Anyone thinking of doing serious business in China is advised to do a lot of preliminary research. In particular, talk to other foreigners who are already doing business in China. Alternatively, approach a firm of business consultants for advice.

Many nations have their own organisations that promote China trade; these include:

Canada-China Trade Council (☎ 010-6512 6120) 18-2 CITIC Building, 19 Jianguomenwai Dajie, Běijīng
China-Britain Business Council (W www.cbbc .org)
The China Council for the Promotion of International Trade (☎ 010-6801 3344) 1 Fuxingmenwai Dajie, Běijīng
United States-China Business Council (☎ 010-8526 3920) 1-10F CITIC Building, 19 Jianguomenwai Dajie, Běijīng

You can also try the following Chambers of Commerce:

American Chamber of Commerce (☎ 010-8519 1920, W www.amcham-china.org.cn) Suite 1903, China Resources Bldg, 8 Jianguomen Beijie, Běijīng 10005. Provides a forum for foreign businesses in China and publishes an annual directory of individual and corporate members.
British Chamber of Commerce (☎ 010-6593 2150, W britaininchina.com) 2nd floor, Technical Club, 15 Guanghuali, Běijīng. Offers its members assistance in doing business in China and publishes a directory of individual and corporate members.
French Chamber of Commerce & Industry (☎ 010-8451 2071) S123, Office Building, Lufthansa Center, 50 Liangmaqiao Lu, Běijīng.

A couple of Web sites worth checking out are W www.business-in-asia.com/china3.html and W www.angel-pacific.com/business.

MOVING TO/FROM CHINA

If you're going to be moving heavy items like furniture or all your household goods, you will need the services of an international mover or freight forwarder.

In Běijīng you can try China King (☎ 800 8100 300, e chinaking@chinakingmoving .com) or Crown Worldwide (☎ 010-6585 0640/41/43, fax 6585 0648, W www.crown

worldwide.com). Many outfits can move offices, arrange door-to-door moves, storage and warehousing.

In Hong Kong there's Asian Express (☎ 0852-2893 1000) and Jardine International (☎ 0852-2563 6653).

In Shànghǎi you can try calling Crown Worldwide (☎ 021-6472 0254, [e] cnshg @crownworldwide.com). Most of these companies have branch offices serving other major cities in China.

ACCOMMODATION

In China's more developed regions, it's no cheaper than travelling in Europe or the USA. More isolated regions like Inner Mongolia or Qīnghǎi are still pretty cheap, but prices are rising everywhere. The government is aiming to develop the laggardly western regions – the writing could well be on the wall for budget hotels nationwide.

Budget quality has improved – rooms are better and service is not so tight-lipped as hotel staff are more used to dealing with foreigners than a few years ago. Even so, foreigners can still find themselves overcharged and staying in some unhygienic, noisy and grim rooms. Mid-range and up-wards, accommodation is generally of reasonable quality, and there is no shortage of five-star hotels in the major cities.

When registering at a hotel, the registration form will ask what type of visa you have. For most travellers, your visa will be 'L'. For a full list of visa categories, see the Visas & Documents section earlier in this chapter.

Reservations

It's possible to book rooms in advance at up-market hotels through overseas branches of CITS, CTS, other travel agencies or online (see Internet Resources, earlier). Often you actually get a discount by booking through an agency – and these can be substantial, up to 40% to 50% off the walk-in rate. Airports at major cities often have hotel-booking counters that offer discounted rates.

Camping

You have to get a long way from civilisation before camping becomes feasible in China. Camping within sight of a town or village in most parts of China would probably result in a swift visit by the PSB. Wilderness camping is more appealing, but

---

Words & Pictures

宾馆 **Bīnguǎn: guesthouse, hotel, restaurant**

The top of this character is a roof, and underneath it is the character for soldier. It has been suggested that all *bīnguǎn* (guesthouses and hotels) are guarded by a soldier under a small roof. The first part of *guǎn* means food. The second part originally meant official residence (notice the roof) and later came to mean any public building. A building open to the public that serves food is another way of expressing the idea of restaurant or hotel.

饭店 **Fàndiàn: restaurant, hotel**

Fàn, meaning cooked rice, comes from the character for food in combination with the phonetic for 'to return', a reference to a hand returning to the mouth in the process of eating. In earlier times, a *diàn* was an earth platform in a hall, used at banquets to put empty goblets and food on. The earth platform forms part of a building, so the top of the character is a type of house. Underneath is the actual platform with things placed on it. As a *diàn* is somewhere people put things, a place to display goods is also called diàn, as in *shāngdiàn* (shop). A *fàndiàn*, literally a food shop, may even offer you a bed!

餐厅 **Cāntīng: restaurant, dining hall**

This is an amalgamation of two characters: *cān*, meaning food, meal or eat, and *tīng*, meaning hall or room. In ancient times, the top left part of cān meant tongue and mouth, and the top right was like a hand. The bottom part of the character represents a food bowl; thus the hand is putting food into the mouth. In the traditional writing for tīng, the top of the character meant a cliff or cave where people reside. The bottom part of this character means person(s). Thus, tīng is a place where people gather, for example, to hold functions.

most such areas in China require special permits and are difficult to reach. Many travellers have camped successfully in Tibet and remote north-western Sìchuān.

The trick is to select a couple of likely places about half an hour before sunset, but keep moving (by bicycle, foot or whatever) and then backtrack so you can get away from the road at the chosen spot just after darkness falls. Be sure to get up around sunrise and leave before sightseeing locals take an interest.

Hostels

An International Youth Hostel Federation card is of limited use in China. At the time of writing, you can only use it in Hong Kong, Macau, Běijīng and parts of Guǎngdōng province. Dormitories *(duō rén fáng)* exist in most of China's major tourist destinations but many cities are devoid of them.

Hotels

There is no shortage of hotels in China. The problem comes if you are on a budget. In many parts of China, finding a room for less than US$25 a night can be an ordeal. Foreigners are still barred from staying at the very cheap guesthouses *(zhāodàisuǒ)* – WTO entry should slowly change this – but have a shot if you've good Chinese-language skills.

For all overseas Chinese travelling in China: when looking for a cheap place to stay in just any place, walk around the city-centre and look for a sign that says 'zhāodàisuǒ' and ask for prices inside. Quality differs from dirty to 3-star, but they are all cheaper than hotels. We don't know if it works for foreigners, but we could always get by waving our student IDs. We managed to get doubles with bathroom for Y40 a person. Beware that most of these places close after 11pm. If you know you'll come in late, tell them beforehand or you'll end up yelling 'qǐng kāi mén' in the midst of the night.

Mei-Ping Yee & Fili Lou

Note that certain temples and monasteries (especially on China's sacred mountains) can provide accommodation. They can be very cheap, but extremely ascetic, with no running water or electricity.

For travellers on mid-range budgets, China's hotels have improved immensely. Service standards are better, and you may even get a minibar. Unless you are in a four-

or five-star joint venture, however, it is wise not to expect too much, no matter how much you are spending.

Most budget and mid-range hotels have an attendant on every floor, who keeps an eye on hotel guests, primarily for security and perhaps to stop you from bringing locals back for the night.

A budget hotel irritant: the leaking toilet cistern. Just turn it off at the inlet pipe at night and turn it back on the next morning. If this doesn't work, change rooms.

To conserve energy, in some cheaper hotels hot water for bathing is available only in the evening and sometimes only for a few hours. Ask when the hot water will be turned on.

Something to be prepared for in budget hotels is lack of privacy; the room attendants may casually wander in at any time.

Some definitions of hotel terminology are in order. The vast majority of rooms in China are 'twins', which means two single beds placed in one room. A 'single room' (one bed per room) is a rarity, although you may occasionally stumble across one. The Western concept of a 'double room' (a room with one double bed shared by two people) is also extremely rare in China. In most cases, your choice will be between a twin room *(shuāng rén fáng)* or a suite *(tàofáng)*, the latter obviously being more expensive. However, in most cases two people are allowed to occupy a twin room for the same price as one person, so sharing is one good way to cut expenses.

The policy at every hotel in China is that you check out by noon to avoid being charged extra. If you check out between noon and 6pm there is a charge of 50% of the room price – after 6pm you have to pay for another full night.

Almost every hotel has a left-luggage room *(jìcún chù or xínglǐ bǎoguān)*, and in many hotels there is such a room on every floor. If you are a guest in the hotel, use of the left-luggage room should be free.

In big cities, it's wise to phone first to check if there's a vacant room; the reception desk may not speak English. Ask the hotel operator for the *zǒng fúwù tái* (service desk) and then ask *'Yǒu méiyǒu kōng fángjiān?'* (Do you have a vacancy?), to which they'll either reply *yǒu* (have) or *méiyǒu* (don't have).

It may be advisable to take your own smoke alarm for peace of mind – hotel fires are quite common in China. Such conflagrations get the upper hand because of faulty hotel smoke alarms and locked fire exits (check the exits on your floor and complain if they are locked). Remember to take out the battery when on the move as the alarm tends to go off if crammed into a tightly packed rucksack.

The Chinese method of designating floors is the same as that used in the USA, but different from, say, Australia's. What would be the ground floor in Australia is the 1st floor in China, the 1st is the 2nd, and so on.

University Accommodation

In theory, university dormitories are for students, teachers and their guests, or others with business at the university. In practice, universities are trying to make money, and they are simply entering into the hotel business just like many other state-run organisations.

Especially along China's east coast and in major cities, staying in a university dorm can often be one of your cheapest options. Many universities will rent out vacant dorm rooms in the foreign student dormitory. Universities also sometimes have actual hotels, although the prices are usually on a par with regular budget hotels. On the negative side, university dormitories may have certain restrictions such as the main door locking early and a non-central location. On the plus side, many have on-site 24-hour Internet cafes and are surrounded by decent restaurants and bars.

Rental Accommodation

In the big cities, foreigners are encouraged to stay in or purchase 'foreigner-approved' apartments, and local apartments are generally put beyond reach. There is a certain amount of flexibility, and you will find foreigners staying in local apartments; it can be a precarious perch, however, and the police could ask them to leave at a moment's notice.

Living in Chinese housing or with a Chinese family and paying rent means you should be registered with the local PSB (or you can expect a fine of up to Y10,000 per person). In Běijīng expect to pay per month as little as Y1200 for a small one-bedroom up to Y4500 or more for a larger place.

Families typically charge around Y1000 for a room. Although policies exist allowing foreigners to legally live in Chinese housing, landlords often refuse to register their foreign tenants (either they aren't aware of the laws or are distrustful of them). If your landlord does not register you, you will be subjected to periodic sweeps during which your landlord will warn you to stay away for a few days. Of course, none of the above applies in Hong Kong and Macau where you are mostly free to live where you like.

Foreigner-approved housing is generally first-rate, with expensive management fees, 24-hour security, guards, sports facilities, swimming pools and kindergartens. Rates for foreigner-approved housing are generally stratospheric, with rents reaching US$9500 per month for a four-bedroom flat in Běijīng. If you live in a hotel, you might be able to negotiate a discount for a long-term stay, but that's not guaranteed.

If you're going to be working for the Chinese government as a teacher or other type of foreign expert, then you'll almost certainly be provided with low-cost housing. Conditions probably won't be luxurious, but it will be cheap or even free.

Foreign students are also usually offered decent accommodation by their schools, although the price can vary from very reasonable to totally ridiculous.

If you're visiting Chinese friends for any length of time, their work unit may be able to provide you with temporary accommodation at low cost. Alternatively, you could live with your Chinese friends – in the past this was prohibited, but now it seems to be OK almost everywhere in China.

Considering the sky-high rents, buying a flat or villa might seem like a good idea for companies with the cash. It is actually possible, but the rules vary from city to city. In most cases, buying actually means that you nominally own the property for 75 years, after which it reverts to the state (which still, in reality, owns all property in China).

ENTERTAINMENT

In China's big cities, an enterprising entertainment scene has developed. For the latest in art exhibitions, concerts, live performances, theatre, cinema, comedy, nightclubs and more, check the entertainment section of the expat magazines.

Cinemas

Apart from Hong Kong, which has the latest films in auditoriums throughout the territory, it's difficult to catch movies in English in China. Decent hotels have in-house movie channels. Big cities like Běijīng have VCD, DVD and VHS rental outfits; check the relevant chapters. If you have a VCD or DVD Walkman in your baggage, keep an eye out for English-language DVD and VCD titles available on the streets and in shops (see Video Systems, previously); the dialogue is usually kept in English with Chinese subtitles. If you understand Chinese, you'll be spoilt for choice by cinemas in China.

Discos

Cities like Guǎngzhōu, Shànghǎi and Běijīng have pulsing nightclub complexes with up-to-the-minute sounds. See the entertainment entries for Guǎngzhōu, Shànghǎi and Běijīng for some suggestions.

Karaoke

Much maligned by Westerners, karaoke (kǎlā OK) can be fun with enough drinks under your belt and with the right people. It's not unusual for inebriated Westerners who claim to hate karaoke to have to be pried loose from the microphone once they get going.

Warning One thing to watch out for in karaoke parlours is rip-offs. In some heavily touristed areas, young women work as touts. You may not even realise that they are touts – they will 'invite' any likely looking male to join them at a nearby karaoke bar, but no sooner than the bottle of XO is ordered the woman 'disappears' and the hapless male is presented with a bill for US$200.

It is not sensible to accept invitations to clubs from young women on the streets. In clubs themselves, if you invite a hostess to sit with you, it is going to cost you money – the same rules apply in China as anywhere else in the world of paid entertainment and sex.

SPECTATOR SPORTS

The Chinese enjoy watching and playing a wide range of sports, including table tennis (at which they excel), badminton, basketball, snooker, athletics and, increasingly, golf; but they reserve most of their passion for just one thing: football. Religiously covered on several TV channels, domestic league games are rigorously dissected and international tournaments endlessly repeated.

China put all its efforts into qualifying for the World Cup, finally succeeding in 2001. A number of players now have international experience (including Sun Jihai and Fan Zhiyi in the English Premier League for Crystal Palace), but the team lacks the skill and experience of European and Latin American sides. Chinese football spectators are renowned for being extremely lively.

If you want to see Chinese league teams competing, this is possible in any large city during the football season.

Although it hasn't quite fired the Chinese imagination the way football has, basketball does provide entertainment during the long winter when playing outdoors means risking frostbite. China's professional league, the China Basketball Association (CBA), even recruits players from the USA.

SHOPPING

The Friendship Stores you will encounter in China's larger cities are an anachronistic echo from an earlier epoch when imported luxury goods were hoarded under one roof for the privileged few. Some Friendship Stores can still be useful for English literature and magazines, and there are usually some staff who speak a little English. However, you are probably better off visiting markets or smaller shops.

Hotel gift shops should be avoided, unless you want to pick up newspapers, magazines or books. Don't ever buy paintings of antiques from such shops – visit local markets, otherwise you'll be hit with a vastly inflated price.

Five-star hotel arcades are often the place to go for top-brand-name shopping, but expect to pay a hefty whack. Also some five-star hotels have attached residential apartment blocks (like the China World Trade Center in Běijīng) with their own multilevel shopping malls.

The explosion of shopping malls and department stores, feeding the consumer revolution in China, has been a slap in the face to Communist-era service standards. Market forces have jolted sleeping sales staff awake, but you may still meet a defiant clique of the old guard: slumped comatose on the counter or yacking to each other, oblivious to customers shrieking at them.

More Than Meets the Eye...

Once upon a time in China you got what you paid for. If the sales clerk said it was top-quality jade then it was top-quality jade. Times have changed – now cheap forgeries and imitations flood the market, from Tibetan jewellery to Qing coins and phony Marlboro cigarettes, from pirate DVDs, VCDs, CDs and fake computer software to bogus Nike, Burberry, Gucci, train tickets and so on: you name it, the Chinese will fake it. The reason why Chinese TV is stuck showing US films from the '70s and '80s is probably because the pirate DVD market brings you the very latest, without the adverts in between.

Wherever you voyage in China, you'll be cursing the number of forgeries, then snapping them up when you glance at the price tag. Despite all the government's bluster and periodic CCTV footage of steamrollers grinding fake Rolexes and CDs, the pirating industry is in fine fettle. Fake goods just reappear in force after hitting the deck for a while. If China joins the WTO, more heavy duty solutions will be called for.

Take care if you are forking out a large sum for something. Watch out for counterfeit Y100 notes. And if you are after genuine antiques, try to get an official certificate of verification – just make sure the ink is dry.

But the place to go to really roll up your sleeves and get to grips with local rock-bottom prices is the local markets. Blankets spread on the pavement and pushcarts in the alleys – this is where you find the lowest prices. In street markets, all sales are final; forget about warranties and, no, they don't accept AmEx. Nevertheless, the markets are interesting, but be prepared to bargain hard.

While journeying the land, don't get too weighed down with souvenirs and trinkets – there's nothing worse than buying a replica Buddha statue in Dūnhuáng, only to spot exactly the same one in a Běijīng market on the day before you fly home.

It's sensible to save your shopping for imported electronic consumer items for Hong Kong and Macau – import duties are still too high in the rest of China.

Some shopping tips: make sure you keep receipts and try and hang on to the bag of the shop where you bought each item in case you need to return the item. When returning something, try to return to the original store where you bought it; be as firm as possible, as perseverance often pays off. If returning clothes, the sales tags should still be on them and there should be no signs that you have worn the item. Exchanging items is easier than getting a refund. Find out what the time limit is for returning goods bought at the store. Some stores, such as the clothing outlet Esprit, have a no-quibble refund policy; others won't refund or exchange goods.

Antiques

There are very few antiques of real worth left in China, apart from those which remain sealed in tombs, temples, in private hands or museums – basically beyond reach. Most of the antiques that you find in markets and shops around the land are replicas or ersatz. The quality of replication technology can be quite dazzling, but that monochrome Qing Guangxu Imperial Yellow Bowl in your hands is far more likely to be a Jiang Zemin dynasty imitation. It's also worth bearing in mind that even auction houses get caught out quite regularly, and experts assume that a considerable percentage of material that passes under the gavel is of dubious authenticity.

The best places to try your luck at antique shopping are the street markets. Professional antique hunters will need to have a real nose for the business – you'll need to know the culture intimately, which means you probably won't be reading this book. For your average traveller, take everything with a pile of salt.

Only antiques that have been cleared for sale to foreigners are permitted to be taken out of the country. When you buy an item over 100 years old it will come with an official red wax seal attached. However, bear in mind that this seal does *not* necessarily indicate that the item is an antique. You'll get a receipt of sale, and you have to show this to customs when you leave the country; otherwise customs will confiscate the antique.

Stamps & Coins

China issues quite an array of beautiful stamps that are generally sold at post offices in the hotels. Outside many of the post offices you'll find amateur philatelists with books full of stamps for sale; it can be extraordinarily hard bargaining with these enthusiasts! Stamps issued during the Cultural Revolution make interesting souvenirs, but these rare items are no longer cheap. Check out **W** www.cpi.com.cn/cpi-e, a Web site on Chinese philately. Old coins are often sold at major tourist sites, but many are forgeries.

Paintings & Scrolls

Watercolours, oils, woodblock prints, calligraphy – there is a lot of art for sale in China. Tourist centres like Guìlín, Sūzhōu, Běijīng and Shànghǎi are good places to look out for paintings. Convincing imitation oils of the Níngbō-born artist Chen Yifei can be found everywhere, along with copies of other contemporary artists. Don't buy these from hotel shops, however, as you will be massively ripped off.

Much calligraphy is very so-so and some is downright bad; you will have to know your subject, and don't take anybody's word for the quality of the brushwork.

Oddities

If plaster statues are to your liking, the opportunities to stock up in China are abundant. Fat buddhas appear everywhere, along with statues of Guanyin. There's no need to look for musical Chairman Mao cigarette lighters; they will come to you. One interesting oddity sold in 2001 from blankets-on-the-ground around Tiānānmén Square were phone-tapping devices.

Lots of shops sell medicinal herbs and spices. Export tea is sold in extravagantly decorated tins – you can often get a better deal buying the same thing at train stations.

Getting There & Away

AIR
Airports & Airlines

Hong Kong, Běijīng and Shànghǎi are China's main international air gateways. In the past the cheapest way to get to China was via Hong Kong, but these days there is not that much variation in fares to Hong Kong and Chinese mainland cities. A lot of money is being invested in China's international airports, with a smart new terminal at Běijīng's Capital Airport and the new international Pudong Airport in Shànghǎi.

The Civil Aviation Administration of China (CAAC; Zhōngguó Mínháng) acts as China's civil aviation authority. Although it operates a few uneconomical services, most flights are run by one of China's 30 or so airlines, only a handful of which operate international flights. Their safety record has been fairly poor in the past, but it is improving. Air China, China's national flag carrier, celebrated a 46-year safe-flying record in 2001.

Buying Tickets

Stiff competition has resulted in widespread discounting on air tickets. Passengers flying in economy can usually manage some sort of discount, but unless you buy carefully and flexibly, it is still possible to end up paying exorbitant amounts for a journey. Discounts of some form or other are generally available for students, those under 26 and the elderly. Seasonal fluctuations see ticket prices peaking between June and September. The cheapest tickets are round trip; one-way tickets work out to be more expensive if returning to your point of departure by air.

For long-term travel there are plenty of discount tickets that are valid for 12 months, allowing multiple stopovers with open dates. When you're looking for bargain air fares, go to a travel agent rather than directly to the airline. Airlines do occasionally have promotional fares and special offers, but generally they only sell fares at the official listed price.

Normally, the cheapest tickets to Hong Kong and China can be found in Chinatowns around the world. Other budget and student travel agents offer bargain tickets,

but the real offers are in agents that deal with the Chinese who regularly return home (travelling at festival times such as the Chinese New Year will be more expensive however). A visit to your local Chinatown or a thumb through the *Yellow Pages* should unearth the lowest fares. Beyond Chinatown, firms such as STA Travel, with offices worldwide and Council Travel in the USA offer competitive prices to most destinations.

When purchasing tickets through a travel agent, paying by credit card generally offers protection as most card issuers provide refunds if you can prove you didn't get what you paid for. Similar protection can be obtained by buying a ticket from a bonded agent, such as one covered by the Air Travel Organisers License (ATOL) scheme in the UK. Agents who accept cash only should hand over the tickets straight away; after you've made a booking or paid your deposit, call the airline and confirm that the booking was made. It's generally not advisable to send money (even cheques) through the post unless the agent is very well established.

An increasing number of airlines fly to China, with Air China among the cheapest. The cheapest available airline ticket is called an APEX (Advance Purchase Excursion) ticket, although this type of ticket includes expensive penalties for cancellation and changing dates of travel.

Discounted air courier tickets are a cheap possibility, but they carry restrictions. As a courier, you transport documents or freight internationally and see it through customs. You usually have to sacrifice your baggage and take carry-on luggage. Generally trips are on fixed, round-trip tickets and offer an inflexible period in the destination country. For more information, check out organisations such as the Courier Association (W www.air courier.org) or the International Association of Air Travel Couriers (W www .courier.org).

Other possibilities include standby flights, but you will need a degree of flexibility as to when you want to fly. Agents trading in standby flights will try to get you a ticket for a flight within a certain time frame, but cannot guarantee to have you flying on a particular day.

If you purchase a ticket and later want to make changes to your route or get a refund, you need to contact the original travel agent. Airlines only issue refunds to the purchaser of a ticket – usually the travel agent who bought the ticket on your behalf. Many travellers change their routes halfway through their trips, so think carefully before you buy a ticket that is not easily refunded.

Buying Tickets On Line Many airlines offer excellent fares to Web surfers. They may sell seats by auction or cut prices to reflect the reduced cost of electronic selling. Numerous travel agents around the world have Web sites, which can make the Internet a quick and easy way to compare prices – a good start for when you're ready to start negotiating with your favourite travel agency. Try Council (W www.counciltravel .com) or STA (W www.statravel.com).

To bid for last minute tickets online, one site to try is Skyauction (W www.skyauc tion.com). Priceline (W www.priceline .com) aims to match the ticket price to your budget; you name the price for departure from the USA and they'll get to work (with up to 40% savings, they claim), but they 'screen the brand', so you won't know the airline or the time of travel until after you

have purchased your tickets – requiring flexibility on your part.

Online ticket sales work well if you are doing a simple one-way or return trip on specified dates. However, online superfast fare generators are no substitute for a travel agent who knows all about special deals, has strategies for avoiding layovers and can offer advice on everything from the airline that has the best vegetarian food to the best travel insurance to bundle with your ticket. Some Web sites for airlines are:

Aeroflot W www.aeroflot.org
Air Canada W www.aircanada.ca
Air China W www.airchina.com.cn
Air France W www.airfrance.fr
Air Macau W www.airmacau.com.mo
All Nippon Airways W www.ana.co.jp
Austrian Airlines W www.aua.com
British Airways
    W www.british-airways.com
CAAC W www.caac.cn.net
Cathay Pacific W www.cathaypacific.com
China Southern Airlines
    W www.cs-air.com
Dragonair W www.dragonair.com
Japan Airlines W www.jal.co.jp
KLM-Royal Dutch Airlines
    W www.klm.nl
Korean Air W www.koreanair.com
Lufthansa Airlines W www.lufthansa.com
Malaysia Airlines
    W www.malaysia-airlines.com.my
Northwest Airlines W www.nwa.com
Qantas Airways W www.qantas.com.au
Scandinavian Airlines
    W www.scandinavian.net
Singapore Airlines
    W www.singaporeair.com
Thai Airways International
    W www.thaiairways.com
United Airlines W www.ual.com

Departure Tax

If leaving China by air, the departure tax is Y90. This must be paid in local currency, so be sure you have enough yuán to avoid a last-minute scramble at the airport money-changing booth.

The USA

Discount travel agents in the USA are known as consolidators (although you won't notice a sign on the door saying Consolidator). San Francisco is the ticket-consolidator capital of America, although some good deals can also be found in Los

Angeles, New York and other big cities. Consolidators can be found through the *Yellow Pages* or the travel sections of major daily newspapers.

Council Travel (☎ 1-800-266-8624), America's largest student travel organisation, has loads of offices in the USA. You can call the ☎ 1-800 number for the office nearest you or visit their Web site at W www.counciltravel.com. STA Travel (☎ 800-781-4040) has offices in most major US cities. Call the toll-free ☎ 800 number for office locations or visit W www.sta travel.com.

Other sites that are worth taking a look at include W www.ticketplanet.com, W www.lowestfare.com, W www.bestfares.com and W www.travelzoo.com. Another useful Web site with good deals on flights from Canada and the USA to China is Fly China at W www.flychina.com.

From the US west coast, low-season return fares to Hong Kong or Běijīng start at around US$600. Fares increase dramatically during summer and the Chinese New Year. From New York to Běijīng or Hong Kong, low-season return fares start at around US$700.

Canada

Canadian discount air ticket sellers are also known as consolidators and their air fares tend to be about 10% higher than those sold in the USA. Check out travel agents in your local Chinatown for some real deals. Travel CUTS (☎ 800-667 2887) is Canada's national student travel agency and has offices in all major cities. Check out its Web site at W www.travelcuts.com.

From Canada, fares to Hong Kong are often higher than those to Běijīng. Air Canada, Air China and China Eastern Airlines sometimes run super-cheap fares. Return low-season fares between Vancouver and Běijīng start at around US$650.

Australia

Two well-known agents for cheap fares are STA Travel and Flight Centre. STA Travel (☎ 1300 360 960) has offices in all major cities and on many university campuses. Call the ☎ 1300 number Australia-wide for the location of your nearest branch or visit W www.statravel.com.au. Flight Centre (☎ 131 600) also has dozens of offices

throughout Australia. Check its Web site at W www.flightcentre.com.au.

From Australia, Hong Kong is a popular destination and is also the closest entry point into China. Although it's a shorter flight, fares from Australia to Hong Kong are generally not that much cheaper than fares to Běijīng or Shànghǎi. Low-season return fares to either Shànghǎi or Běijīng from the east coast of Australia start at around A$1000, with fares to Hong Kong starting from A$913.

New Zealand

Flight Centre (☎ 0800 243 544) has many branches throughout the country. Check its Web site W www.flightcentre.co.nz for details. STA Travel (☎ 0800 874 773) has offices in Auckland, Newmarket, Hamilton, Palmerston North, Wellington, Christchurch and Dunedin. Their Web site is W www.sta travel.com.

International airlines such as Malaysia Airlines, Thai Airways International and Air New Zealand have return fares from Auckland to Hong Kong for around NZ$1499 during the low season. Return low-season fares to Běijīng start at NZ$1599.

The UK

Discount air travel is big business in London. Advertisements for many travel agencies appear in the travel pages of the weekend broadsheet newspapers, in *Time Out*, the *Evening Standard* and in the free magazine *TNT*.

For students or travellers under 26 years a popular travel agency in the UK is STA Travel (☎ 0870-160 0599, W www.sta travel.co.uk), which has offices throughout the country. This agency sells tickets to all travellers but caters especially to young people and students.

Other recommended bucket shops include: Trailfinders (☎ 0207-938 3939, W www.trailfinder.com), 194 Kensington High St, London W8 7RG; Bridge the World (☎ 0870-444 7474, W www.bridgetheworld.com), 4 Regent Place, London W1R 5FB; and Flightbookers (☎ 0870-010 7000, W www.ebookers.com). Flight Centre also have branches in the UK (☎ 0870-566 6677, W www.flightcentre.co.uk). You can turn to the Air Travel

Advisory Bureau (☎ 0207-636 5000, W www.atab.co.uk) for a list of approved bucket shops and travel agents.

Travel agents in London's Chinatown that regularly deal with flights to China include Jade Travel (☎ 0207-734 7726, W www.jadetravel.co.uk), 5 Newport Place, London WC2H 7JR; and Sagitta Travel Agency (☎ 0207-287 4081, fax 0207-287 0089), 12-13 Little Newport St, London WC2H 7JJ.

For further agents, look at W www.china town-online.co.uk, which also includes a list of travel agents outside London that specialise in tickets to China.

From the UK, the cheapest low-season return fares to Běijīng start at around UK£350 with British Airways; flights to Hong Kong are a little bit pricier.

Western Europe

Though London is the travel-discount capital of Europe, there are several other cities where you will find a range of good deals. Generally there is not much variation in air fare prices from the main European cities. The major airlines and travel agents generally have a number of deals on offer, so shop around.

STA Travel has offices throughout the region. Check out their Web site at W www.statravel.com for office locations and contact details.

USIT World (W www.usitworld.com) has branches in Brussels, Frankfurt, Lisbon, Madrid, Paris, Vienna and other European cities.

Nouvelles Frontières (W www.nouvelles-frontieres.com) also have branches throughout the world.

France has a network of student travel agencies that can supply discount tickets to travellers of all ages. OTU Voyages (☎ 0820 817 817, W www.otu.fr) and Voyageurs du Monde (☎ 01 42 86 16 40, W www.vdm.com) have branches throughout the country and offer some of the best services and deals.

Recommended agencies in Germany include STA Travel (☎ 01805 456 422, W www.statravel.de), who have branches in major cities across the country. Usit Campus (☎ 01805 788 336, www.usitcampus.de), also has several offices throughout Germany.

In Italy, CTS Viaggi (☎ 840 501 150, W www.cts.it) is a student and youth specialist with branches in major cities.

In Spain, recommended agencies include Usit Unlimited (☎ 902 25 25 75, W www.unlimited.es), with branches in major cities; and Barcelo Viajes (☎ 902 116 226, W www.barcelo-viajes.es), which also has branches in major cities.

Return fares to Běijīng from major Western European cities start at around €873 with Lufthansa, Air France and SAS. Flights to Hong Kong are slightly more expensive, return fares starting from €998.

Cambodia

China Southern Airlines has two flights a week from Phnom Penh to Guǎngzhōu for US$349/665 one way/return.

Hong Kong

Dragonair has four flights a day from Běijīng to Hong Kong (US$645 return), although it's cheaper to fly to Guǎngzhōu or Shēnzhèn and then take the train or bus to Hong Kong. Dragonair also has seven flights a day from Shànghǎi to Hong Kong (US$456 return).

Iran

Iran Air has a weekly flight from Běijīng to Tehran (US$600).

Israel

Elal Israel Airlines has twice-weekly flights between Běijīng and Tel Aviv (US$630).

Japan

STA Travel has branches in Tokyo (☎ 03-5391 3205) and Osaka. Their Web site at W www.statravel.co.jp includes an English page.

Numerous flight options exist for travel between Japan and China. Japan Airlines flies daily between Běijīng and Tokyo (US$850), as does Air China (US$850), and All Nippon Airways (US$775). There are five Japan Airlines flights a week between Běijīng and Osaka (US$630), and All Nippon Airways fly the same route twice a week (US$590). Between Shànghǎi and Tokyo, Air China and Japan Airlines have daily flights, All Nippon Airways has two flights a week and Northwest Airlines three. All Nippon Airways and Japan

Airlines also have daily flights from Shànghǎi to Osaka. Prices quoted above are all one-way fares. There are also flights from Japan to other major cities in China, including Dàlián and Qīngdǎo.

Kazakhstan

Xinjiang Airlines has two flights per week between Ürümqi and Almaty.

Macau

Air Macau has a daily flight between Běijīng and Macau and two flights a day between Shànghǎi and Macau (US$274/520 one-way/return).

Malaysia

Malaysia Airlines has five flights a week between Běijīng and Kuala Lumpur (US$839 return) and four flights a week between Shànghǎi and Kuala Lumpur (US$695 return).

Mongolia

MIAT-Mongolian Airlines and Air China run three flights a week between Běijīng and Ulaan Baatar (US$274/520 one way/return) and two flights per week to Ulaan Baatar from Hohhot (US$198/379 one way/return). It can sometimes take a week to get a ticket and schedules are reduced in the winter months.

Myanmar (Burma)

Air China has two flights a week from Yangon to Běijīng, with a stopover in Kūnmíng (US$694 one way). In the reverse direction, you can join the flight in Kūnmíng, but you must have a visa for Myanmar – available at the Myanmar consulate in Kūnmíng.

Nepal

Royal Nepal Airlines operates two flights per week between Kathmandu and Shànghǎi (US$195/376 one way/return) and three flights between Hong Kong (US$190/360 one way/return).

China Southwest Airlines operates flights between Kathmandu and Lhasa – twice weekly in the low season and three times a week in the high season.

Individual travellers cannot buy air tickets from the China Southwest Airlines office without a Tibetan Tourism Board permit.

Your only option is to buy a three- to eight-day package tour through a travel agency

At the time of research, the cheapest of these tours was a three-day tour for around US$360. This included the flight ticket (US$275), airport transfer to Kathmandu and Lhasa, TTB permits and dormitory accommodation for three nights in Lhasa.

Flights between Kathmandu and Lhasa may be cancelled at the slightest whiff of trouble and may also be shut down during the winter months.

North Korea

There are two flights weekly between Běijīng and Pyongyang with Koryo Air and China Northern Airlines (US$161/305 one way/return).

Pakistan

Air China has a weekly flight to Karachi (US$820 return) and Pakistan International Airlines has a weekly flight from Běijīng to Islamabad (US$450 one way). There is one weekly flight between Ürümqi and Islamabad on Xinjiang Airlines (US$280 one way).

Russia

Air China and Aeroflot have direct flights connecting Běijīng and Moscow (US$379 /586 one way/return). MIAT-Mongolian Airlines has two flights a week from Ürümqi to Moscow (US$599/1399 one way/return). Air China also has flights from Shànghǎi to Moscow, via Běijīng (US$1157 return).

Singapore

In Singapore, STA Travel's Head Office (☎ 737 7188, W www.statravel.com.sg) is at 33a Cuppage Rd, Cuppage Terrace. Singapore, like Bangkok, has hundreds of travel agents offering competitive discount fares for Asian destinations and beyond. Chinatown Point Shopping Centre, on New Bridge Rd, has a good selection of travel agents.

Fares to Běijīng are around US$450 return, while fares to Hong Kong start at US$350; there are also daily flights to Shànghǎi.

South Korea

Discount travel agencies in Seoul include: Joy Travel Service (☎ 776 9871, fax 756 5342), 10th floor, 24-2 Mukyo-dong, Chung-gu, Seoul (directly behind City

Hall); and discounters on the 5th floor of the YMCA building on Chongno 2-ga (next to Chonggak subway station).

Air China, Asiana Airlines and Korean Air have daily flights between Běijīng and Seoul (US$310/593 one way/return). Flights to Shànghǎi with China Eastern Airlines and Asiana Airlines are the same price. Seoul is also connected by air to Hong Kong, Shěnyáng and Qīngdǎo.

Thailand

Khao San Rd in Bangkok is the budget-travellers headquarters. Bangkok has a number of excellent travel agents but there are also some suspect ones; ask the advice of other travellers before handing over your cash. STA Travel (☎ 02-236 0262, W www .statravel.co.th), Room 1406, 14th floor, Wall Street Tower, 33/70 Surawong Rd, is a good and reliable place to start.

One-way fares from Bangkok to Běijīng with Thai International or Air China are around US$240 or US$480 return. Other one-way fares from Bangkok include Hong Kong for around US$200, Chéngdū for US$255 and Shànghǎi for US$180.

Uzbekistan

From Běijīng there are twice-weekly flights to Tashkent with Uzbekistan Airways (US$580/650 one way/return).

Vietnam

China Southern Airlines and Vietnam Airlines fly between Ho Chi Minh City and Běijīng (US$175/350 one way/return). China Southern Airlines flights are via Guǎngzhōu. From Běijīng to Hanoi there are two flights per week with either China Southern Airlines or Vietnam Airlines (US$175/350 one way/return).

LAND

If you're starting from Europe or Asia, it's possible to travel all the way to China by land. Numerous interesting routes include the Trans-Siberian Railway trek from Europe or the border crossings of China-Vietnam, Tibet-Nepal, Xīnjiāng-Pakistan and Xīnjiāng-Kazakhstan.

Border Crossings

China shares land borders with 14 countries: Afghanistan, Bhutan, India, Kazakhstan, Kyrgyzstan, Laos, Mongolia, Myanmar, Nepal, North Korea, Pakistan, Russia, Tajikistan and Vietnam. China also has official border crossings between its special administrative regions, Hong Kong and Macau. The borders with Afghanistan, Bhutan and India are closed.

Kazakhstan

A year-round road crosses from Ürümqi in China to Almaty via the border post at Khorgos and Zharkent (formerly Panfilov). Buses run Monday to Saturday in each direction, taking about 24 hours (see the Ürümqi Getting There & Away section for details); crossing the border shouldn't really be a problem as long as you have a valid Kazakhstan or China visa.

Two trains a week also run between Ürümqi and Almaty (see the Ürümqi Getting There & Away section for details).

There are two other China-Kazakhstan crossings farther north, at Tacheng (Bakhty in Kazakhstan) and Jeminay (Maykapchigay on the Kazak side), although neither is particularly reliable.

Kyrgyzstan

From at least June to September it's possible to cross the dramatic 3752m Torugart Pass on a rough road from Kashgar to Bishkek. Even the most painstaking arrangements however, can be thwarted by logistical gridlock on the China side or by unpredictable border closures (eg, for holidays or snow). Ensure you have a valid Kyrgyzstan visa. See the Kashgar Getting There & Away section for details.

Another warm-weather crossing is now open for commerce, from Kashgar via Irkeshtam to Osh, but so far not for individual tourists.

Laos

From the Měnglà district in China's southern Yúnnán province it is legal to enter Laos via Boten in Luang Nam Tha province if you possess a valid Lao visa. From Boten there are morning and afternoon buses onward to the provincial capitals of Luang Nam Tha and Udomxai, three and four hours away respectively. See the Měnglà section in the Yúnnán chapter for more information.

The majority of travellers from Kūnmíng go via Jǐnghóng to Měnglà and then on to the border at Mohan. As the bus journey from Jīnghóng will take the better part of the day, you will probably have to stay overnight at Měnglà.

Lao visas can be obtained in Běijīng; alternatively, the Lao consulate in Kūnmíng issues both seven-day transit and 15-day tourist visas for Laos. See the Kūnmíng section in the Yúnnán chapter for more information on visas.

Myanmar (Burma)

Originally built to supply the forces of Chiang Kaishek in his struggle against the Japanese, the famous Burma Road runs from Kūnmíng, in China's Yúnnán province, to the city of Lashio. Nowadays the road is open to travellers carrying permits for the region north of Lashio, although you can legally cross the border in only one direction – from the Chinese side (Ruìlì) into Myanmar via Mu-se in the northern Shan State. This appears to be possible only if you book a visa-and-transport package from a Chinese travel agency in Kūnmíng. Once across the border at Mu-se, you can continue on to Lashio and farther south to Mandalay and Yangon. See the Yúnnán chapter for details on visas (not good for land crossings) to Myanmar.

A second route, a little farther northwest, from Lwaigyai to Bhamo, is also open in the same direction. You cannot legally leave Myanmar by either route.

Nepal

The 920km road connecting Lhasa with Kathmandu is known as the Friendship Hwy. It's a spectacular trip over high passes and across the Tibetan plateau, the highest point being Gyatso-la Pass (5220m). By far the most popular option for the trip is renting a 4WD through a hotel or travel agency and then organising a private itinerary with the driver.

Visas for Nepal can be obtained in Lhasa, or even at the Nepalese border (see the Lhasa section in the Tibet chapter for details). When travelling from Nepal to Lhasa, foreigners must arrange transport through tour agencies in Kathmandu. If you already have a Chinese visa, you could try turning up at the border and organising a permit in Zhangmu. This is a gamble, however, as

the rules and regulations change hourly – it's far better to join an economy tour to Lhasa in Kathmandu. The occasional traveller slips through (even a couple on bicycles). At Zhangmu you can hunt around for buses, minibuses, 4WDs or trucks heading towards Lhasa.

North Korea

Visas are difficult to arrange to North Korea and at the time of writing it was totally impossible for US and South Korean citizens. Those interested in travelling to North Korea from Běijīng should get in touch with Koryo Tours (**W** www.koryo group.com), who can get you there (and back).

There are twice-weekly trains and flights between Běijīng and P'yŏngyang.

Pakistan

The exciting trip on the Karakoram Hwy, over the 4800m Khunjerab Pass and what is said to be the world's highest public international highway, is an excellent way to get to or from Chinese Central Asia. There are regular bus and 4WD services when the pass is open – normally May to early November. See the Xīnjiāng chapter in this book or Lonely Planet's *Karakoram Highway* guide for more information.

Russia

The Russian border is 9km from Mǎnzhōulǐ and is quite busy and reliable. Officially, the only public transport that crosses the border is the Trans-Manchurian, but there are also ample opportunities for picking up a lift in Mǎnzhōulǐ or at the border. A taxi to the border from Mǎnzhōulǐ will cost you Y10.

Tajikistan

There are grand plans to build a road from near Murgab in eastern Tajikistan to near Bulunkul on the China side, to link up with the Karakoram Hwy to Pakistan. It will take years (if not decades) for this to happen and even then, for the first few years at least, this will be for local traffic only.

Vietnam

Travellers used to require a special visa for entering Vietnam overland from China. However, this is no longer the case and travellers can use a standard visa to enter Vietnam overland from China. Vietnamese visas no longer require that you specify the correct exit point.

Exiting from Vietnam to China is also simple. The Chinese don't require anything more than a standard tourist visa, and Chinese visas do not indicate entry or exit points.

The Vietnam-China border crossing is open from 7am to 4pm, Vietnam time, or 8am to 5pm, China time. Set your watch when you cross the border – the time in China is one hour later than in Vietnam. Neither country observes daylight savings time. There are currently two border checkpoints, detailed below, where foreigners are permitted to cross between Vietnam and China.

Friendship Pass The busiest border crossing is at the Vietnamese town of Dong Dang, 164km north-east of Hanoi. The closest Chinese town to the border is Píngxiáng in Guǎngxī province, but it's about 10km north of the actual border gate. The crossing point (Friendship Pass) is known as Huu Nghi Quan in Vietnamese or Yǒuyì Guān in Chinese.

Dong Dang is an obscure town. The nearest city is Lang Son, 18km to the south. Buses and minibuses on the Hanoi–Lang Son route are frequent. The cheapest way to cover the 18km between Dong Dang and Lang Son is to hire a motorbike for US$1.50.

There are also minibuses cruising the streets looking for passengers. Just make sure they take you to Huu Nghi Quan and not to the other nearby checkpoint – Huu Nghi Quan is the only one where foreigners can cross.

There is a customs checkpoint between Lang Son and Dong Dang. Sometimes there are long delays here while officials gleefully rip apart the luggage of Vietnamese and Chinese travellers. For this reason, a motorbike might prove faster than a van since you won't have to wait for your fellow passengers to be searched. Note that this is only a problem when you're heading south towards Lang Son, not the other way.

There is a walk of 600m between the Vietnamese and Chinese border posts.

On the Chinese side, it's a 20-minute drive from the border to Píngxiáng by bus or share taxi – the cost for the latter is US$3. Píngxiáng is connected by train to Nánníng, capital of China's Guǎngxī province. Trains to Nánníng depart Píngxiáng at 8am and 1.30pm. More frequent are the buses (once every 30 minutes), which take four hours to make the journey and cost US$4.

A word of caution – because train tickets to China are expensive in Hanoi, travellers sometimes buy a ticket to Dong Dang, walk across the border and then buy a Chinese train ticket on the Chinese side. This isn't the best way because it's several kilometres from Dong Dang to Friendship Pass, and you'll have to hire someone to take you by motorbike. If you're going by train, it's better to buy a ticket from Hanoi to Píngxiáng, and then in Píngxiáng buy a ticket to Nánníng or beyond.

Trains on the route from Hanoi to Dong Dang run according to the following schedule:

train no	depart Dong Dang	arrive Hanoi
HD4	8.30am	8.00pm
HD2	5.40pm	1.50am

train no	depart Hanoi	arrive Dong Dang
HD3	5.00am	1.30pm
HD1	10.00pm	5.10am

There is also a twice-weekly international train that runs between Běijīng and Hanoi, and which stops at the Friendship Pass. You can board or exit the train at a number of stations in China. The entire Běijīng-Hanoi run is 2951km and takes approximately 55 hours, which includes a three-hour delay (if you're lucky) at the border checkpoint.

Schedules are subject to change, but at present train No 5 departs Běijīng at 10.51am on Monday and Friday, arriving in Hanoi at 11.30am on Wednesday and Sunday, respectively. Going in the other direction, train No 6 departs Hanoi at 2pm on Wednesday and Saturday, arriving in Běijīng at 5.18pm on Thursday and Sunday, respectively. Following is the complete schedule.

station	to Hanoi train no 5	to Běijīng train no 6
Běijīng	10.51am	5.18pm
Shíjiāzhuāng	1.30pm	2.35pm
Zhèngzhōu	5.25pm	10.38am
Hànkǒu (Wǔhàn)	10.42pm	5.25am
Wǔchāng (Wǔhàn)	11.03pm	4.58am
Chángshā	2.56am	1.06am
Héngyáng	5.05am	10.58pm
Yǒngzhōu	7.12am	8.50pm
Guìlín North	10.35am	5.38pm
Guìlín	10.54am	5.18pm
Liǔzhōu	1.21pm	3.02pm
Nánníng	5.22pm	11.02pm
Píngxiáng	12.15am	12.56am
Dong Dang	3.30am*	8.30pm*
Hanoi	11.30am*	2.00pm*

* Vietnamese time

Lao Cai-Hékǒu A 762km metre-gauge railway, inaugurated in 1910, links Hanoi with Kūnmíng. The bordertown on the Vietnamese side is Lao Cai, 294km from Hanoi. On the Chinese side, the bordertown is Hékǒu, 468km from Kūnmíng.

There is an international train service that runs between Hanoi and Kūnmíng; but at the time of writing, the service had been suspended.

Domestic trains run daily on both sides of the border. On the Chinese side, Kūnmíng-Hékǒu takes about 16 hours. Trains depart and arrive at Kūnmíng's north train station according to the following schedule:

train no	depart Kūnmíng	arrive Hékǒu
L933	9.50pm	2.15pm

train no	depart Hékǒu	arrive Kūnmíng
L934	3.34pm	9.04am

Mong Cai-Dōngxīng Vietnam's third, but little known, border crossing is at Mong Cai in the north-east corner of the country, just opposite the Chinese city of Dōngxīng. Officially only Vietnamese and Chinese citizens may cross here.

TRANS-SIBERIAN RAILWAY

The Trans-Siberian Railway and connecting routes comprise one of the most famous, romantic and potentially enjoyable of the world's great train journeys. Rolling out of Europe and into Asia, through eight time zones and over 9289km of taiga, steppe and desert, the Trans-Siberian makes all other train rides seem like once around the block with Thomas the Tank Engine.

There is some confusion of terms here as there are, in fact, three railways. The 'true' Trans-Siberian line runs from Moscow to Vladivostok. But the routes traditionally referred to as the Trans-Siberian Railway are the two branches that veer off the main line in eastern Siberia to make a beeline for Běijīng.

Most readers of this book will not be interested in the first option since it excludes China – your decision is basically between the Trans-Manchurian or the Trans-Mongolian; however, it makes little difference. The Trans-Mongolian (Běijīng-Moscow, 7865km) is marginally faster, but requires you to purchase an additional visa and endure another border crossing, although you do at least get to see the Mongolian countryside roll past your window. The Trans-Manchurian is longer (Běijīng-Moscow, 9004km).

Trans-Mongolian Railway

This branch line has been open since the mid-1950s and is the rail route most synonymous with the 'Trans-Siberian' tag.

The five-day journey, which leaves Běijīng every Wednesday at 7.40am (arrives in Moscow on Monday at 2.10pm), travels north to the Mongolian border at Erenhot, 842km from Běijīng. The train (No 3) continues to Ulaan Baatar before reaching the last stop in Mongolia, Sukhe Bator. From Moscow, the train leaves at 9.03pm every Tuesday for Běijīng.

From the Russian border town of Naushki, the train travels to Ulan Ude, where it connects with the Trans-Siberian line.

Trans-Manchurian Railway

Departing from Běijīng every Saturday at 11.10pm (arriving in Moscow on Friday at 6.09pm), this train (No 19) travels north through the cities of Shānhǎiguān, Shěnyáng and Hāěrbīn before arriving at the border post Mǎnzhōulǐ, 935km from Běijīng. Zabaykal'sk is the Russian border post and the train continues from here to Tarskaya, where it connects with the Trans-Siberian line. The train leaves Moscow on Friday at 8.25pm for the six-day journey to Běijīng.

Classes of Travel

The Trans-Mongolian train No 3 has three classes of carriage, and there are two on all other trains. First class is divided into two categories: two- and four-bed cabins. Second-class cabins have four comfortable beds and bedding is clean. It is often possible to upgrade to first class. The real luxury comes with Chinese deluxe class, which has roomy, wood-panelled two-berth compartments with a sofa, and a shower cubicle shared with the adjacent compartment (available on train No 3).

Except for in the deluxe class on the Chinese train, there are no showers in any category.

Costs

The standard price for a Běijīng-Moscow ticket is Y1602 for 2nd class on the Trans-Mongolian, and Y1825 on the Trans-Manchurian route. Travel insurance should be taken out.

Visas

Trans-Siberian travellers will need Russian and Mongolian visas if they take the Trans-Mongolian, as well as a Chinese visa. It's safer to obtain all visas in your home country before setting out. Some tour companies arrange visas as part of their package.

Russian A transit visa issued in Běijīng is valid for 10 days if you take the train, and will only give you three or four days in Moscow at the end of your journey. In Běijīng, the Russian embassy (☎ 010-6532 2051, visa section ☎ 6532 1267) is at 4 Dongzhimennei Beizhongjie, just off Dongzhimennei Dajie.

A transit or tourist visa costs US$50 and takes one week to process; US$80 for a three-day express service; or US$120 for a one-day service. There is a consular fee on top of the standard processing charge that varies dramatically with citizenship. You will need one photo, your passport and the exact amount in US dollars. For a transit visa, you will also need a valid entry visa for a third country plus a through ticket from Russia to the third country. Consular hours are Monday to Friday from 9.30am to 12am.

Mongolian If you are travelling on the Trans-Mongolian train, you will need some kind of Mongolian visa. These come in two forms: transit or tourist. A transit visa (valid for seven days) is easy enough to get (just present a through-ticket and a visa for your onward destination). The situation regarding visas changes regularly, so check with a Mongolian embassy or consulate.

In Běijīng, the Mongolian embassy (☎ 010-6532 1203) is at 2 Xiushui Beijie, Jianguomenwai. The visa section is open Monday to Friday from 9am to noon.

A transit visa generally costs US$30 and takes three days to issue, or US$60 for same-day or next-day service. Tourist visas (90 days) cost US$40, or US$60 for express service. Visas are free for Finnish and Indian nationals. All Mongolian embassies shut down for the week of National Day (Naadam), which officially falls around 11 to 13 July.

Books and Info

The Trans-Siberian Handbook by Bryn Thomas covers in some detail the major settlements along the line. Also recommended is *Red Express* (out of print) by Michael Cordell & Peter Solness, a lavish photo album produced to accompany the Australian TV series of the same name. It examines life in ex-Communist realms from East Berlin to China, following the route of the railway. It's really worth picking up a copy of the Thomas Cook Overseas Timetable, available from branches of Thomas Cook (or order online from W www .thomascookpublishing.com). The book lists all train times for Russia, China and Mongolia and other useful info relating to the trip. Also take a look at the Monkey Business (see Buying Tickets from China section) Web site at W www.monkey shrine.com for further, colourful info.

What to Bring

The list of extra travelling essentials for a Trans-Siberian jaunt includes toilet paper, plug for the toilet sink, some soft, slip-on footwear like thongs (flip-flops) or Chinese cloth sandals, and loose, comfortable pants like tracksuit or shell-suit trousers. You won't need a sleeping bag. Take along some good reading material.

Boiling water is always available at the end of each carriage. There's a dining car attached to most long-distance trains, and at each stop you'll find clusters of kiosks and locals selling home produce, so it isn't necessary to bring too much in the way of food. Juice or water in a plastic bottle is a good idea.

Baggage Space

There is a luggage bin underneath each of the lower berths and there is a limit of 35kg per passenger. Passengers with excess baggage should present it (along with passport, ticket and customs entry declaration) the day before departure at the Luggage Shipment Office, which is on the right-hand side of the main train station in Běijīng. The excess is charged at about US$11 per 10kg, with a maximum excess of 40kg allowed.

Time Zones

Officially, China and Mongolia only have one time zone, five hours later than Moscow time. Local time is thus unchanged from Běijīng to Irkutsk, except in late April or early May and again in September, when you may find a one-hour shift at the border. This is because of differences in switching to daylight-saving time.

Food & Drink

The dining cars are changed at each border, so en route to Moscow you get Russian, Chinese and possibly Mongolian versions. There's no menu and no choice, but you usually get a number of stir-fried dishes with rice for about US$6. Dining cars are open from approximately 9am to 9pm local time.

In the dining car there's often a table of pot noodles, chocolate, beer, juice and the like being peddled by the staff. The prices are inflated and there's nothing that isn't available from the station kiosks.

Border Formalities

Border stops can take anything from one to six hours as customs officials go through the travelling warehouses that are the Chinese traders' compartments. For foreign travellers the procedure is uncomplicated: passports, visas and currency forms are examined, and baggage searches are rare (for this reason you may be approached by a trader and asked to carry their bag across the border – this is not a good idea).

At the Chinese-Mongolian and Chinese-Russian borders, about two hours are spent hoisting the train aloft so that its bogies can be changed (the old Soviet Union used a wider gauge of track than its neighbours). If you're riding the Trans-Mongolian and want to witness this odd operation, stay on the train when it disgorges its passengers at Erlian station, on the Chinese side of the China-Mongolia border. The train then pulls into a large shed 500m away. Get off before the staff lock the doors. It's OK to walk around and take photos, then stroll back down the line to the station.

Safety

Common sense applies. Don't leave valuables lying about, and don't leave hand luggage unattended in a compartment while you get off at a station. A few years ago the Trans-Mongolian had quite a bad reputation, but militia now ride the trains and matters have improved. For added safety, lock your cabins from the inside.

Buying Tickets

Intourist Travel (**W** www.intourist.com) has branches in the UK, USA, Canada, Finland and Poland and offers a range of Trans-Manchurian and Trans-Mongolian tours and packages including flights to and from Moscow, 2nd class travel and accommodation in Moscow, Běijīng and Irkutsk. See their Web site for branch locations and further details.

From the USA White Nights (☎/fax 916-979 9381, **W** www.wnights.com, **e** wnights @concourse.net), 610 Sierra Dr, Sacramento, CA 95864, offers Moscow-Běijīng (trans-Manchurian) tickets for US$311/442 2nd/1st class, Moscow-Běijīng (trans-Mongolian) for US$330/540 2nd/1st class and Běijīng-Irkutsk tickets for US$252/369 2nd/1st class. Tickets can also be bought for Haĕrbīn-Vladivostok (US$150, 2nd class). The company also offers visa support.

From Canada Intours Corporation (☎ 416-766 4720, fax 416-766 8507, e intours @on.aibn.com), West Suite 308, 2150 Bloor Street, Toronto, Ontario M6S, offer a number of tours and packages on both the Trans-Siberian and Trans-Mongolian. A typical 13-day Moscow-Beijing Trans-Mongolian tour will cost C$2,199 (2nd class), including hotel accommodation (Moscow, Irkutsk and Ulaan Baatar), city tours and excursions en route (eg, to Lake Baikal).

From Australasia In Australia, Gateway Travel (☎ 02-9745 3333, w www.rus sian-gateway.com.au), 48 The Boulevarde, Strathfield, NSW, 2135, offers 2nd-class through-tickets on the Trans-Manchurian and the Trans-Mongolian for A$750 (A$1100 1st-class) and A$750 (A$1100 1st-class), respectively, as well as some stopover packages.

The New Zealand–based operator SUN Ridge Travel (☎ 09-525 3074, w www .suntravel.com), 407 Great South Rd, PO Box 12-424, Penrose, Auckland, has 'basic express packages'. A 17-day trip from Běijīng to St Petersburg, with stays along the way, costs NZ$2573 on the Trans-Mongolian and NZ$2299 on the Trans-Manchurian.

From the UK The Russia Experience, Research House, Fraser Rd, Perival, Middlesex UB6 7AQ (☎ 020-8566 8846, w www.trans-siberian.co.uk) has a great choice of tickets and are in the know (they are also the people to get in touch with for trips to Mongolia and Russia). They plan to offer a unique Trans-Siberian trip to Moscow for £210 plus three nights hotel accommodation from 2002, but you'll have to make your way out of China to Blagoveshcensk in Russia to get on board (May–Sept). They also offer a range of trips including hotel accommodation, transfers and documentation, eg, Moscow-Vladivostok-Hāěrbīn (UK£364) and Moscow-Irkutsk-Běijīng (UK£499). Full details and prices are in their downloadable Web site brochure.

From Germany Lernidee Reisen (☎ 030-786 0000, w www.lernidee-reisen.de), Dudenstrasse 78, D-10965 Berlin, sells 2nd-class tickets: Běijīng-Moscow (DM775), Moscow-Běijīng (DM735), Běijīng–Ulaan Baatar (DM335), Ulaan Baatar–Běijīng (DM295), Ulaan Baatar–Moscow (DM540) and Moscow–Ulaan Baatar (DM585).

Travel Service Asia (☎ 7351-37 3210, w www.tsa-reisen.de), Schmelzweg 10, D-88400 Biberach/Riss, offers package tours and tickets on the Trans-Mongolian and Trans-Manchurian routes. Typical prices are DM710 (US$320) for Běijīng-Moscow (2nd class) on the Trans-Mongolian and DM795 (US$360) for Běijīng-Moscow (2nd class) on the Trans-Manchurian. They also offer a trip from Běijīng along the Silk Road to Kashgar and onto Almaty in Kazakhstan, Uzbekistan and Russia.

From China In Běijīng, Monkey Business have an infocentre on the 1st floor of the Hidden Tree bar (☎ 010-6591 6519, w www.monkeyshrine.com), 12 Dong Daqiaoxie Lu, Nan Sanlitun, and can book tickets and packages. Also included in the ticket is free transport from the Běijīng office to the railway station. The company has a lot of experience in booking Trans-Siberian trains for independent travellers. A basic, 2nd-class, nonstop ticket from Běijīng to Moscow, including the first night in Moscow, costs US$385 (plus the cost of the visa, which varies according to nationality) on the Trans-Manchurian or US$345 (plus the cost of the visa) on the Trans-Mongolian. Monkey Business also offers various packages with stopovers in destinations along the way. For example, a one-night stopover in Mongolia, two nights in Irkutsk and time at Lake Baikal will cost you US$595, with upgrading possible. If you book a package with Monkey Business, you'll get a 100-page info-pack for the trip.

Alternatively, you can purchase tickets through the Beijing Tourism Group (BTG; Běijīng Lǚxíngshè; ☎ 010-6515 8562/8844, ground floor, Beijing Tourist Bldg, 28 Jianguomenwai Dajie) behind the New Otani Hotel and near Scitech Plaza.

Monkey Business also has an office in Hong Kong known as Moonsky Star (☎ 852-2723 1376, w www.monkeyshrine.com), Flat 6, 4th floor, E-block, Chungking Mansions, 36–44 Nathan Rd, Tsimshatsui, Kowloon.

There are other ticket agencies in Hong Kong worth calling. You might try Time Travel (☎ 852-2366 6222, fax 2739 5413), Block A, 16th floor, Chungking Mansions, 40 Nathan Rd, Tsimshatsui, Kowloon.

From Russia The Travellers Guesthouse/ IRO Travel (☎ 095-971 4059, ☎ 280 8562, e tgh@glasnet.ru), Ulitsa Bolshaya Pere-yaslavskaya 50, 10th floor, Moscow 129401, sells Trans-Mongolian tickets for Moscow-Běijīng for US$200, plus US$20 for each stopover. Along the route, it also offers homestays in Russia and hostels in Mongolia for US$15 to US$25 a night.

SEA
Hong Kong
Some ships still ply the waters between Hong Kong and the mainland, but numbers and destinations have been cut back: vessels still make the trip to Guǎngzhōu and Zhūhǎi. See the Getting There & Away section of the Hong Kong chapter for details.

Japan
Osaka/Kōbe/Yokohama to Shànghǎi
The Japan-China International Ferry service has a once-weekly boat connection between Osaka and Shànghǎi and a twice-monthly Tuesday service from Kōbe to Shànghǎi (from US$200). Boats to Osaka (US$150 to

US$1700; 47 hours) leave from Shànghǎi's international passenger terminal every Tuesday at noon, while departures from Japan are every Friday (arriving Shànghǎi at 10am). In Osaka, for information call the Shanghai Ferry Company (☎ 06-62-436345). For the Kōbe route call Tokyo (☎ 03-54-894800) or Shànghǎi (☎ 021-6535 1713). The address of the shipping office in Shànghǎi is at 1 Jinling Donglu. The Shanghai Ferry Co also runs a boat from Shànghǎi at 1pm on Saturdays for Osaka or Yokohama (each city on alternate weeks); the cheapest ticket is US$155.

Kōbe to Tiānjīn Another ship runs weekly from Kōbe to Tánggū (from US$200), near Tiānjīn. Departures from Kōbe are every Friday at noon, arriving in Tánggū 48 hours later; for Kōbe, the boat departs on Mondays at 11am. The food on this boat gets poor reviews so bring a few emergency munchies. Buses ferry passengers from Tánggū to Tiānjīn and Běijīng.

Tickets can be bought in Tiānjīn from the shipping office (☎ 022-2420 5777) next to the railway station, or at the port in Tánggū (☎ 022-2570 6728). Tickets can also be bought in Běijīng (☎ 010-6512 0507). In Kōbe, the office is at the port (☎ 078-321 5791, fax 078-321 5793).

Qīngdǎo to Shimonoseki Boats run every two weeks between Shimonoseki and Qīngdǎo (US$140, 39 hours).

Korea
Travelling from Korea, international ferries connect the South Korean port of Inch'ŏn with Wēihǎi, Qīngdǎo, Tiānjīn, Dàlián, Shànghǎi and Dāndōng.

The Weidong Ferry Company runs boats on the routes to Wēihǎi (three per week in each direction) and Qīngdǎo (two per week in each direction) in Shāndōng province.

They can be contacted at 1005 Sungji Building, 10th floor, 585 Dohwa-dong, Mapo-gu, Seoul (☎ 02-3271 6713, W www.weidong.com); International Passenger Terminal, 71-2 Hang-dong, Inch'ŏn (☎ 032-886 6171); 48 Haibin Beilu, Wēihǎi (☎ 0631-522 6173); 4 Xin-jiang Lu, Qīngdǎo (☎ 0532-280 3574). Check their Web site for the latest time-tables and prices.

SEA ROUTES

CHINA

◉BĚIJĪNG

Tianjin◉ ○

Tanggu   Dalian ○

NORTH KOREA

SEA OF JAPAN

Weihai ○

◉ SEOUL
Inch'ŏn

Qingdao ◉ ○

SOUTH KOREA

YELLOW SEA

0   200   400km
0   100   200mi

JAPAN

To Kobe

Shanghai ◉ ○

To Kobe, Osaka Yokohama & Shimonoseki

Boats to Tiānjīn are run by the Jinchon Ferry Company. They can be contacted in Seoul (☎ 822-517 8671); Inch'ŏn (☎ 032-888 7911); and Tiānjīn (☎ 022-2331 1657).

In Seoul, tickets for any boats to China can be bought from the International Union Travel Agency (☎ 822-777 6722), Room 707, 7th floor, Daehan Ilbo Bldg, 340 Taepyonglo 2-ga, Chung-gu, Seoul. Prices range from US$88 to US$300, and depending on the destination, boats leave anywhere from once a week to three times a week.

For the Tiānjīn ferry you can also get tickets in Seoul from Taeya Travel (☎ 822-514 6226), in Kangnam-gu by the Shinsa subway station. In China, tickets can be bought cheaply at the pier, or from China International Travel Service (CITS; Zhōngguó Guójì) – for a very *steep* premium. The cheapest price is Y888 for a dorm bed.

To reach the International Ferry Terminal from Seoul, take the Seoul-Inch'ŏn commuter train (subway line 1 from the city centre) and get off at the Tonginch'ŏn station. The train ride takes 50 minutes. From Tonginch'ŏn station it's either a 45-minute walk or five-minute taxi ride to the ferry terminal.

Inch'ŏn to Wēihǎi Departures from Inch'ŏn are on Monday, Thursday and Saturday at 9am. Departures from Wēihǎi are Wednesday, Friday and Sunday at 8am. Tickets range from US$100 (second class) to US$180 (royal class) and can only be bought on the day of travel between 8am and 10am from the office opposite the passenger ferry terminal on Haibin Lu in Wēihǎi. The trip takes approximately 16 hours.

Inch'ŏn to Qīngdǎo Boats for Qīngdǎo leave Inch'ŏn on Tuesday and Thursday at 4pm. Boats for Inch'ŏn leave on Monday and Thursday at 5pm. The trip takes 19 hours and tickets cost between US$110 and US$145.

Inch'ŏn to Tiānjīn The schedule for this ferry is a little irregular, and at the time of writing was leaving on Thursdays and Sundays at 11am for Inch'ŏn (from US$115 to US$230; 24 to 26 hours). Departures from Inch'ŏn to Tiānjīn are at 1pm.

As with boats from Japan, the boat does not dock at Tiānjīn proper, but rather at the nearby port of Tánggū, where there are buses to speed you to either Tiānjīn or Běijīng.

Inch'ŏn to Shànghǎi There are weekly ferries to Inch'ŏn from Shànghǎi (US$120 to US$400; 40 hours), departing from the international passenger terminal north of the Bund. The boat departs Inch'ŏn for Shànghǎi on Wednesdays at 7pm; it leaves Shànghǎi for Inch'ŏn on Saturdays at 10am. Contact China Shipping in Seoul (☎ 02-777 8080), Inch'ŏn (☎ 032-886 9090) or Shànghǎi (☎ 021-6596 6003).

Inch'ŏn to Dàlián A boat leaves for Inch'ŏn in South Korea on Tuesday and Friday at 12pm (Y867 to Y1513, 18 hours) from Dàlián; tickets can be bought at the ferry terminal. Boats leave Inch'ŏn for Dàlián on Wednesday and Saturday at 7pm. Contact Da-In Ferry in Seoul (☎ 02-3218 6550), Inch'ŏn (☎ 032-888 2611) or Dàlián (☎ 0411-270 5082).

ORGANISED TOURS

There are literally hundreds of tour operators who can organise tours to China. If your time is limited but your budget isn't, tours can save you a lot of time and energy.

Tours organised in China with CITS get recommended by only a few, but they are worth considering for day trips and excursions or getting to places that have limited transport options.

There are also an increasing number of private tour companies operating in China, giving you a few more choices. There's little between them, but you can see what's available online at the very useful W www .budgettravel.com/china.htm. Alternatively, consult the pages of the expat mags in Běijīng and Shànghǎi or check them online at W www.thatsbeijing.com and W www .thatsshanghai.com. If you're interested in biking tours, check out Bike China, a company based in Yúnnán with a Web site at W www.bikechina.com.

While there are many companies that can organise straightforward sightseeing tours of China, listed here are some companies that offer more adventurous or special interest tours.

Australia

Intrepid Adventure Travel (☎ 1300 360 667, W www.intrepidtravel.com.au) 11 Spring St, Fitzroy, Victoria 3065, offers small, off-the-usual-tourist-track group tours.

Peregrine Adventures (☎ 03-9662 2700, W www.peregrine.net.au) 258 Lonsdale Street, Melbourne, Victoria 3000; also has offices in Sydney, Brisbane, Perth and Adelaide. Offers walking, hiking and cycling tours.

World Expeditions (☎ 1300 720 000, W www.worldexpeditions.com.au) Level 5, 71 York St, Sydney, NSW 2000; also has offices in Melbourne, Brisbane and Perth. Offers adventure and cultural tours for small groups.

UK

Explore Worldwide (☎ 012-5276 0000, W www.explore.co.uk) 1 Fredrick St, Aldershot, Hampshire GU11 1LQ, offers small group adventure tours.

Imaginative Traveller (☎ 020-8742 8612, W www.imaginative-traveller.com) 1 Betts Ave, Martlesham Heath, Suffolk IP5 3RH, offers cycling and walking tours.

Naturetrek (☎ 019-6273 3051, W www.naturetrek.co.uk) Cheriton Mill, Cheriton, Alresford, Hampshire SO24 0NG, offers birdwatching and botanical tours.

World Expeditions (☎ 020-8870 2600, W www.worldexpeditions.com.au) 3 Northfields Prospect, Putney Bridge Road, London SW18 1PE.

USA

Boojum Expeditions (☎ 1-800-287-0125, W www.boojumx.com) 14543 Kelly Canyon Rd, Bozeman, MT 59715, offers horseback and cycling trips in Mongolia and Tibet.

Earth River Expeditions (☎ 800-643-2784, W www.earthriver.com) 180 Towpath Rd, Accord, NY 12404, has rafting and trekking tours.

Voyagers International (☎ 800-633-0299, W www.voyagers.com) PO Box 915, Ithaca, NY 14851, offers photography tours.

Overseas Adventure Travel (☎ 800-955-1925, W www.oattravel.com) tours place an emphasis on culture and wilderness.

REI (☎ 800-426-4840, W www.rei.com) has offices throughout the country and offers hiking and cycling tours.

Wilderness Travel (☎ 800-368-2794, W www.wildernesstravel.com) 1102 Ninth St, Berkeley, CA 94710, offers Silk Road tours.

Chinese Travel Agents Abroad

For information on offices in Hong Kong and Macau see the relevant chapters.

CNTO Outside China and Hong Kong, the China National Tourist Office (CNTO) has the following offices:

Australia CNTO (☎ 02-9299 4057, W www.cnto.org.au) 19th floor, 44 Market St, Sydney, NSW 2000

Canada CNTO (☎ 416-599 6636, fax 599 6382) Suite 806, 480 University Ave, Toronto, Ontario M5G 1V2

Denmark (☎ 3-3910 400, W www.cits.dk) Ved Vestport 4, DK-1612, Copenhagen

France Office du Tourisme de Chine (☎ 1-5659 1010, fax 1-5375 3288) 15 Rue de Berri, 75008 Paris

Germany Fremdenverkehrsamt der VR China (☎ 069-520 135, fax 528 490) Ilkenhansstrasse 6, D-60433 Frankfurt am Main

Israel CNTO (☎ 03-522 6272, fax 522 6281) 19 Frishman St, PO Box 3281, Tel Aviv 61030

Japan China National Tourist Administration (☎ 3-3591 8686, fax 3-3591 6886) 2-5-2 Air China Bldg, Toranomon, Minato-ku, Tokyo; also CNTA Osaka Office (☎ 06-635 3280, fax 635 3281) 1-4-1, Fourth floor, OCAT Bldg, Minatomachi, Naniwa-ku, Osaka

Singapore CNTO (☎ 221 8681/8682, fax 221 9267) 1 Shenton Way, No 17-05 Robina House, Singapore 068803

Spain China National Tourist Office Madrid (☎ 01-548 0011, 548 0597) Gran Via 88, Grupo 2, Planta 16, Madrid, 28013

Sweden CNTO (☎ 8-7022280 fax 8-7022330) Gotgatan 41, 1tr 11621

Switzerland Fremdenverkehrsamt der VR China (☎ 01-201 8877, fax 201 8878) Genfer-Strasse 21, Ch-8002, Zurich

UK CNTO (☎ 020-7935 9787, fax 7487 5842) 4 Glenworth St, London NW1 5PG

USA CNTO (☎ 212-760 8218, fax 212-760 8809) Suite 6413, 350 Fifth Ave, Empire State Bldg, New York NY 10118; (☎ 818-545 7505, fax 818-545 7506) Suite 201, 333 West Broadway, Glendale CA 91204

Getting Around

For information on Hong Kong and Macau see those chapters.

AIR

While trundling around China in buses or sweeping across the land by train is great on occasion, China is a country of vast distances. If you don't have the time or inclination for a long drawn-out land campaign, take to the air.

Airports are being built and upgraded all over the land, making air transport increasingly appealing, with new airports including Shànghǎi's Pudong Airport, Běijīng's new Capital Airport terminal and Hong Kong's spiffing Chek Lap Kok Airport.

The Civil Aviation Administration of China (CAAC; Zhōngguó Mínyòng) is the civil aviation authority for numerous airlines, including Air China (W www.airchina.com.cn), China Eastern (W www.cea.online.sh.cn), China Southern (W www.cs-air.com), China Northern (W www.cna.ln.cninfo.net), China Southwest (W www.cswa.com), China Northwest, Shanghai, Yunnan and others.

CAAC publishes a combined international and domestic timetable in both English and Chinese in April and November each year. This timetable can be bought at some airports and CAAC offices in China. Individual airlines also publish timetables. You can buy these from ticket offices throughout China.

Round-trip prices are simply double the single price. You'll need to show your passport when reserving or purchasing a ticket.

Business-class tickets cost 25% more than economy-class tickets, and 1st-class tickets cost an extra 60%. Children over 12 are charged adult fares; kids between two and 12 pay half-price. Toddlers under the age of two pay 10% of the full fare. You can use credit cards at most CAAC offices and travel agents.

Travel agents charge you full fare, plus extra commission for their services. The service desks in better hotels (three-star and up) can reserve and even purchase air tickets for you with a little advance notice. Buying tickets during the Chinese New Year, and the 1 May and 1 October week-long holidays is near impossible, so plan early. There is an airport tax of Y50 on domestic flights.

Cancellation fees depend on how long before departure you cancel. On domestic flights, if you cancel 24 to 48 hours before departure you lose 10% of the fare; if you cancel between two and 24 hours before the flight you lose 20%; and if you cancel less than two hours before the flight you lose 30%. If you don't show up for a domestic flight, you are entitled to a refund of 50%.

When purchasing a ticket, you may be asked to buy insurance (Y20). It's not compulsory and the amount you can claim is very low.

You need to arrive at the airport at least 30 minutes before departure.

On domestic and international flights the free baggage allowance for an adult passenger is 20kg in economy class and 30kg in 1st class. You are also allowed 5kg of hand luggage, though this is rarely weighed. The charge for excess baggage is 1% of the full fare for each kilogram. Baggage reclamation facilities are rudimentary at the older airports and waits can be long; lost baggage compensation is Y40 per kilogram.

Planes vary in style and comfort. The more regularly travelled routes between cities employ Boeing or Airbus, more far-flung regions still depend on Soviet-built passenger jets. You may get a hot meal, or just a small piece of cake and an airline souvenir. On-board announcements are delivered in Chinese and English if there are foreigners on board.

BUS

Long-distance buses are one of the best means of getting around the country. Services are extensive and main roads are rapidly improving. Buses stop every so often in small towns and villages, so you get to see parts of the countryside you wouldn't see if you travelled by train, although breakdowns can be a problem. Another plus is that it's easier to secure bus tickets than train tickets and they are often cheaper.

Routes between large cities are sporting a larger, cleaner and more comfortable fleet of private buses; shorter and more far-flung routes still rely on rattling minibuses. Some

DOMESTIC AIRFARES

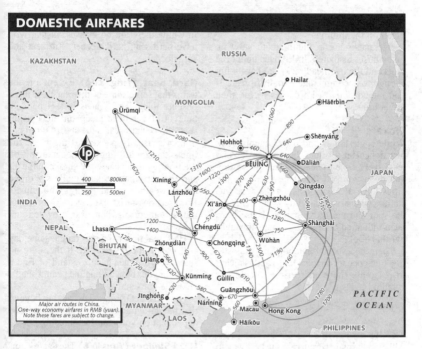

Major air routes in China.
One-way economy airfares in RMB (yuan).
Note these fares are subject to change.

parts of the land (especially in China's south-west, Tibet and the northwest) present formidable challenges to travellers – precipitous drops, pot holes, dangerous road surfaces and reckless drivers. Accidents in black-spot areas such as parts of Sìchuān are common.

Long-distance bus journeys can be cramped and noisy: buses have speakers that entertain with ear-popping music. Other routes loop violent Hong Kong films on overhead TVs with three dimensional sound. The driver leans on the horn at the slightest detection of a vehicle in front.

Mostly bus travel is a slow means of transport, although the increasing number of major highways can make travel faster than trains. It's safe to estimate times for bus journeys on non-highway routes by calculating the distance against a speed of 25km/h. Also factor in driving techniques – drivers are loathe to change gears and appear to prefer to almost stop on a slope rather than changing from third into second.

If taking buses to high altitude destinations in winter, make sure you take plenty of warm clothes. A breakdown in frozen conditions can prove lethal for those unprepared.

Classes

It's a good idea to weigh up the variety of buses plying the route you intend to take. Besides that bone-rattling tin creature that you are being shoved onto by ticket operators, a plush, air-con (albeit slightly more expensive) coach could well be heading to the same location.

Night buses are quite common. Such services get mixed reviews – they are more dangerous and it's difficult to sleep on a crowded jolting bus. Sleeper buses (wòpù qìchē) ply more popular routes – they are usually double the price of a normal bus service, but many travellers swear by them. Some have comfortable reclining seats, while others have two-tier bunks. Watch out for your belongings on them, however.

Privately owned minibuses are increasingly competing with public buses on medium-length routes. They can be infuriating, however, waiting until the last passenger is wedged inside before leaving. All available space is used – this is very dangerous and leaves little room to escape the vehicle in case of an accident. Drivers will sometimes try to make you pay extra for bulky luggage. Generally you buy your ticket on the minibus.

Backpacks are a nightmare to stow on many buses as there's little space under the seats and the overhead racks are hardly big enough to accommodate a loaf of bread. If you intend doing a lot of bus travel, then travel light!

Tickets

While some hotels and travel agents book bus tickets, it's often cheaper, easier and less error-prone to head for the bus station and do it yourself. Most large towns and cities have at least one long-distance bus station where you can buy your ticket on the spot and get on your bus. These have been indicated on the street maps throughout this book.

There is a special symbol for a bus station that appears on local maps and is meant to resemble the bus steering wheel. The symbol is:

TRAIN

Although crowded, trains are the best way to get around in reasonable speed and comfort. The network covers every province except Tibet, but engineers are working on that last mountainous bastion. There is an estimated 52,000km of railway lines in China, most of which was built after 1949.

The safety record of the train system is good. The new fleet of trains is also a vast improvement on the old models – they are much cleaner and are equipped with air-con.

Many train stations require that luggage be x-rayed before entering the waiting area.

Just about all train stations have left-luggage rooms (*jìcún chù*) where you can safely dump your bags for about Y2 to Y4.

Most trains have dining cars where you can find passable food. Railway staff also regularly walk by with pushcarts offering *miàn* (instant noodles), *miànbāo* (bread), *héfàn* (boxed rice lunches), *huǒtuǐ* (ham), *píjiǔ* (beer), *kuàng quán shuǐ* (mineral water) and *qìshuǐ* (soft drinks). After about 8pm, when meals are over, you can probably wander back into the dining car. The staff may want to get rid of you, but if you just sit down and have a beer it may be OK.

Classes

In China there are no classes; instead you have hard seat, hard sleeper, soft seat and soft sleeper.

Hard Seat (Yìng Zuò) Except on the trains that serve some of the branch or more obscure lines, hard seat is in fact padded, but you'll get little sleep on the upright seats. Since hard seat is the cheapest rail option, it's usually packed to the gills, the lights stay on all night, passengers spit on the floor, you can carve the smoke in the air and the carriage speakers endlessly drone news, weather, good tidings and music. Hard seat on tourist, express trains or newer trains is more pleasant, less crowded and there could be air-con.

Hard seat tickets bought on the same day will usually be unreserved. If there are no seats, you'll either have to stand or find a place for your bum among the peanut shells, cigarette butts and spittle.

Hard seat is OK for a day trip, but beyond that the enjoyment of your journey will be dependent on your comfort threshold.

Hard Sleeper (Yìng Wò) These are comfortable and only a fixed number of people are allowed in the sleeper carriage. The carriage has doorless compartments with six bunks in three tiers. Sheets, pillows and blankets are provided. There is a small price difference between berths, with the lowest bunk (*xiàpù*) the most expensive and the top-most bunk (*shàngpù*) the cheapest. You may wish to take the middle bunk (*zhōngpù*) as all and sundry invade the lower berth to use it as a seat during the day, while the top one has little headroom and puts you near the speakers (tall passengers may prefer the top bunk as the beds are short and passengers in the aisle bash into their overhanging feet). When you buy your ticket you will be asked which level you want, and this will be on your ticket.

Lights and speakers in hard sleeper go out at around 9.30pm to 10pm. Competition for hard sleepers has become keen in recent years, and you'll be lucky to get one on short notice.

Soft Seat (Ruǎn Zuò) On shorter journeys (such as Shēnzhèn to Guǎngzhōu) some trains have soft seat carriages. The seats are comfortable and overcrowding is not permitted. Smoking is prohibited, but if you want to smoke you can do so by going out into the corridor between cars. Soft seat costs about the same as hard sleeper. Unfortunately, soft seat cars are a rarity.

Soft Sleeper (Ruǎn Wò) Soft sleeper is luxurious travel, with four comfortable bunks in a closed compartment, wood panelling, potted plants, lace curtains, teacups, clean washrooms, carpets and air-con.

Soft sleeper costs twice as much as hard sleeper, and sometimes as much as flying. It's usually easier to purchase soft rather than hard sleeper because few ordinary Chinese can afford it.

Train Types

Train composition varies from line to line and from day to night, and largely depends on the demand for sleepers on that line. If the journey time is more than 12 hours then the train qualifies for a dining car. The dining car often separates the hard seat from the hard sleeper and soft sleeper carriages.

The conductor is in a little booth in a hard seat carriage in the middle of the train – usually carriage No 7, 8 or 9 (all carriages are numbered on the outside). Coal-fired samovars are found in the ends of the hard-class sections, and from these you can draw a supply of hot water. However, on long trips the water often runs out.

Different types of trains are usually recognisable by the train number. All trains beginning with the letter 'T' are 'special express' trains *(tèkuài)*. They have all classes and there is a surcharge for speed and superior facilities. This class of train is the quickest, most luxurious and most expensive. With a few exceptions, the international trains are included in this group. All trains beginning with the letter 'K' are 'fast speed' *(kuàisù)* trains.

Train numbers starting with the letter 'Y' are tourist trains *(lǚyóu)*. All other train numbers not beginning with a T, K or Y are normal speed trains *(pǔkuài)*. Sleepers can be found on all long-distance trains.

Numbers indicate the destination of the train. As a general rule, the outbound and inbound trains have matching numbers; thus train Nos K79 and K80 divide into No K79 leaving Shànghǎi and travelling to Kūnmíng, and No K80 leaving Kūnmíng and travelling to Shànghǎi.

Reservations & Tickets

Buying hard seat tickets at short notice is usually no hassle, but you will not always be successful in getting a reserved seat.

If you try to buy a sleeper ticket at the train station and the clerk says *méi yǒu* (not have), turn to your hotel travel desk or China International Travel Service (CITS; Zhōngguó Guójì Lǚxíngshè), China Travel Service (CTS; Zhōngguó Lǚxíngshè), China Youth Travel Service (CYTS; Zhōngguó Qīngnián Lǚxíngshè). However, many CITS and CTS offices no longer do rail bookings. Most hotels have an in-house travel agent which can obtain train tickets. You'll pay a service charge of around Y20.

Tickets for sleepers can usually be obtained in major cities, but not in quiet backwaters. There is a five-day, advance-purchase limit.

Buying hard sleeper tickets in train stations can be very trying. Large stations like Beijing Train Station have special ticket offices for foreigners where procuring tickets is straightforward. Otherwise it can be a fraught experience should you decide to queue up and get your ticket at the station. Plan ahead and buy your ticket two or three days in advance, especially if you are heading to popular destinations. Some stations are surprisingly well run, but others are bedlam. The best stations now have computers that spit out tickets quickly and efficiently, resulting in queues that move faster.

Touts swarm around train stations selling black market tickets; this can be a way of getting scarce tickets, but foreigners frequently get ripped off. As with air travel, buying tickets around the Chinese New Year and the 1 May and 1 October holidays can be impossible.

If you can't get a ticket for a popular route, you could try buying a ticket for somewhere two or three stops after your intended destination. Ask the ticket seller to write a note to the conductor, asking them to give you your ticket back early (this is necessary in sleeper trains, where the conductor exchanges your ticket for a plastic or metal chit; you get your original ticket back to exit the train station). You may be asked to show your ticket before leaving the destination station.

Platform Tickets An alternative to all the above is not to bother with a ticket at all and simply walk on to the train. To do this, you need to buy a platform ticket *(zhàntái piào)*. These are available from the station's information booth for a few *jiǎo*. You then buy your ticket on the train.

It's only really worth doing this if you arrive at the station without enough time to buy a ticket as it's generally more hassle than it's worth.

Upgrading If you get on the train with an unreserved seating ticket, you can seek out the conductor (who will usually be in the first hard seat car) and upgrade *(bǔpiào)* yourself to a hard sleeper, soft seat or soft sleeper if there are any available. If you get to the upgrade conductor before that train departs, leave your name on a list of those waiting to upgrade. Once the train departs the conductor will hand out tickets in list order. On some trains it's easy to do, but others are notoriously crowded. A lot of intermediary stations along the railway lines can't issue sleepers, making upgrading the only alternative to hard seat.

If the sleeper carriages are full then you may have to wait until someone gets off. That sleeper may only be available to you until the next major station, but you may be able to get several hours of sleep. The price will be calculated for the distance that you travelled in the sleeper.

If upgrading fails and you can't bear the thought of hard seat, head for the dining car.

Ticket Validity Tickets are valid for three days, depending on the distance travelled. On a cardboard ticket the number of days is printed at the bottom left-hand corner. If you go 250km it's valid for two days; 500km, three days; 1000km, four days; 2000km, six days; and 2500km, seven days.

If you miss your train, your ticket is not refundable. However, if you return your ticket at least two hours before departure, you should be able to get an 80% refund. If you're travelling two weeks before or after the Spring Festival (the high season), you must return your ticket at least six hours before departure for a 50% refund.

Timetables
There are train timetables in Chinese, but no matter how fluent your Chinese, the timetables are excruciatingly detailed and it's an effort working your way through them. Thinner versions listing the main trains can sometimes be bought at major train stations. Hotel reception desks and CITS offices have copies of the timetable for trains out of their city or town.

CAR & MOTORCYCLE
For those who'd like to tour China by car or motorbike, the news is bleak. It's not like India, where you can simply buy a motorbike and head off. The authorities prevent tourists from driving between cities, so if you're hoping to ship in your motorcycle or car or to buy one when you get to China and drive around independently, you can forget about it. Even if you could casually buy a car, prices are ludicrously high. Cars can be hired in Hong Kong, Macau, Shànghǎi and Běijīng for local use. Although road conditions in China should abolish any remaining desire to get behind the wheel. For information on licences, see the Driving Licence section in the Facts for the Visitor chapter. Foreigners can drive motorcycles if they are residents in China and have a Chinese motorcycle licence.

On the other hand, it's easy enough to book a car with a driver. Basically, this is

Navigating Cities on Foot

At first glance, Chinese street names can be a little bewildering, with name changes common every few hundred metres. The good news is that there is some logic to it, and a little basic Chinese will help to make navigating much easier.

Many road names are compound words made up of a series of directions that place the road in context with all others in the city. Compass directions are particularly common in road names. The directions are: *běi* (north), *nán* (south), *dōng* (east) and *xī* (west). So Dong Lu literally means East Road.

Other words which regularly crop up are *zhōng* (central) and *huan* (ring, as in ring road). If you bring them together with some basic numerals, you could have Dongsanhuan Nanlu, which literally means 'east third ring south road' or the south-eastern part of the third ring road.

Words & Pictures – Directions

 Běi: north
This character is a representation of two people back-to-back, and literally means 'in the opposite direction'. The derivation is from a representation of a defeated army, in which the vanquished soldiers were depicted in the act of turning around and running away. In ancient times south was named first; the opposite of south was consequently called, simply, opposite: *běi*.

 Nán: south
The top of this character was formerly a representation of grass or trees growing. When plants face the sun, they grow lush and vigorously and, since China is in the northern hemisphere, in Chinese thinking the south faces the sun. Thus, the character means south.

 Dōng: east
Each day, without fail, the sun rises from the east. It is no surprise, then, that when the ancient Chinese were looking for a way to represent east, the sun made up part of the picture (in the full form – here it is simplified). The other component of the character for east means tree: as the sun rises, it can be seen through the trees.

 Xī: west
The original pictograph for west showed a bird's nest since, as the sun sets in the west, birds can be seen settling in to roost. Over time, the character came to show a bird sitting atop its nest rather than the nest alone. It's easy to see how the modern character was derived from this ideograph.

Zhōng: centre, middle
This character has been through some modifications over the centuries, but essentially remains the same as the original pictograph. It shows an arrow hitting the bull's-eye of a target and passing right through the centre.

just a standard long-distance taxi. Travel agencies like CITS or even hotel booking desks can make the arrangements. They generally ask excessive fees – the name of the game is to negotiate. If you can communicate in Chinese or find someone to translate, it's not particularly difficult to find a private taxi driver to take you wherever you like for less than half CITS rates.

Road Rules
You're more likely to get fined for illegal parking than speeding. Indeed, with China's gridlock traffic, opportunities for speeding are swiftly vanishing, except on the highways. Even if you are a skilled driver, you will be unprepared for the performance on China's roads; cars lunge from all angles and chaos abounds.

If you travel much around China, you'll periodically encounter road blocks where the police stop every vehicle and impose arbitrary fines for driving with sunglasses, driving without sunglasses etc. The fine must be paid on the spot or the vehicle will be impounded.

Highway tolls are excessive in China: driving between Běijīng and Shànghǎi for example, will cost around Y530 in toll fees alone for an average four seat car; then you've got to think of the petrol. You might as well take the train, it'll cost you less and it's much more fun.

Rental
Tourists are permitted to rent vehicles in Hong Kong, Macau, Běijīng and Shànghǎi, but you will be restricted to driving around

within the perimeters of each city. You will need to come armed with an International Driving Permit (see the Driving Licence section in the Facts for the Visitor chapter).

Purchase

Only legal residents of China can purchase a motor vehicle. The whole procedure is plagued by bureaucracy, with lots of little fees to be paid along the way. Unless you import from abroad, you'll have to settle for an inelegant box on wheels. If you want something with style, you'll have to pay through the nostrils for it: the on-the-road price for a bottom-rung Porsche in 2001 was Y1.15 million (sorry, no road tests). That's before you weigh in the insurance.

The licence plates issued to foreigners are different from those issued to Chinese, and this is a big hassle. Since the licence plates go with the car, this essentially means that a foreigner wanting to buy a used car must buy it from another foreigner.

BICYCLE

Probably the first time the Chinese saw a pneumatic-tyred bicycle was when a pair of Americans called Allen and Sachtleben bumbled into Běijīng around 1891 after a three-year journey from Istanbul. They wrote a book about it called *Across Asia on a Bicycle*. The novelty was well received by the Qing court, and the boy-emperor Puyi was given to tearing around the Forbidden City on a cycle.

Today there are over 300 million bikes in China, more than can be found in any other country. Some are made for export, but most are for domestic use. They are an excellent method for getting around China's cities or patrolling tourist sights (see the boxed text 'On Your Bike' in the Běijīng chapter).

The traditional Chinese bicycle and tricycle were the tubular steel workhorses, used to carry anything up to a 100kg slaughtered pig or a couch. More fleet-foot are the multi-gear lightweight mountain bikes and racers that you can buy all over the land.

In most larger towns and cities bicycles should be parked at designated places on the pavement. This will generally be a roped-off enclosure, and bicycle-rack attendants will give you a token when you park

there. It can cost from 1 jiǎo to Y1. If you don't use this service, you may return to find that your bike has been 'towed' away or stolen. Confiscated, illegally parked bicycles make their way to the police station. There will be a fine in retrieving it, although it shouldn't bankrupt you.

In Western countries, travel agencies organising bicycle trips advertise in cycling magazines. Bicycle clubs can contact CITS (or its competitors) for information about organising a trip. See Organised Tours in the Getting There & Away chapter for a list of tour operators.

Rental

There are bicycle hire shops that cater to foreigners in most traveller centres. These are often heavy-going models, but mountain bikes and even tandems can be found (the latter are popular in Běidàihé). The majority of hire places operate out of hotels, but there are also independent hire shops and bike-hire collection points. Surprisingly, medium-size cities and towns (eg, Sūzhōu) often have better bicycle-rental facilities than large metropolises.

Day hire, 24-hour hire or hire by the hour are the norm. It's possible to hire for a stretch of several days, so touring is possible if the bike is in good condition. Rates for Westerners are typically Y2 per hour or Y10 to Y20 per day – the price depends more on competition than anything else. Note that big hotels typically charge ridiculous rates so it's worth looking around.

If you hire over a long period you should be able to reduce the rate. Most hire places will ask you for a deposit of anything up to Y500 (get a receipt) and to leave some sort of ID. Sometimes the staff will ask for your passport. Give them some other ID instead, like a student card or a drivers' licence.

If you're planning to stay in one place for more than about five weeks, it's probably cheaper to buy your own bike and either sell it or give it to a friend when you leave.

Before taking a bike, check the brakes, get the tyres pumped up hard and make sure that none of the moving parts are about to fall off. Get the saddle raised to maximise leg power. It's also worth tying something on the bike – a handkerchief, for example – to identify your bicycle amid the zillions at the bicycle racks.

A bike licence is obligatory for Chinese, but many don't bother and it's not necessary for a foreigner. Outdoor bicycle-repair stalls are found on every other corner in larger cities, and repairs are very cheap – from three jiǎo to pump up your tyres to Y10 to fix a bent wheel rim.

Purchase

Buying a bike in China is straightforward and a range of bikes can be found. For information on specific shops see the Hong Kong, Shànghǎi and Běijīng chapters. Be aware that buying a flashy mountain bike is an invitation to theft (commonplace). Most hired bicycles have a lock around the rear wheel that can be pried open with a screwdriver in seconds. It would be better buying and using a cable lock, widely available from shops in China.

Touring

The legalities of cycling from town to town are open to conjecture. There is no national law in China that prohibits foreigners from riding bicycles. Basically, the problem is that of 'open' and 'closed' areas. It's illegal for foreigners to visit closed areas without a permit. Fair enough, but foreigners can transit a closed area – that is, you can travel by train or bus through a closed area as long as you don't exit the vehicle in this 'forbidden zone'. The question is: Should riding a bicycle through a closed area be classified as 'transiting' or 'visiting' it?

Chinese law is as clear as mud on this issue. Most of the time, the police won't bother you.

If you get caught in a closed area, it is unlikely to be while you are on the road. The law keeps firm tabs on transients via hotels. If you're staying overnight in an open place, but you are suspected of having passed through a closed area, the police may pull a raid on your hotel. You can be hauled down to the police station where you have to submit to a lengthy interrogation, sign a confession and pay a fine. Fines vary from Y50 to whatever they think you can afford. There is some latitude for bargaining in these situations, and you should request a receipt *(shōujù)*. Don't expect police to give you any tips on which areas are closed and which are open – they seldom know themselves.

Words & Pictures

路 **Lù: road, street, way, path**
In ancient times, the left side of this character meant both leg and foot, although it refers only to foot now. The upper part of the right side of the character also meant foot in times gone by, while the lower part referred to a special location. Thus the character as a whole can be interpreted as 'feet heading towards a special place'. How do they get there? By finding a path or road.

街 **Jiē: road, street**
The radical of this character, the two parts of which appear at the side, means to go. Sandwiched between them the repeated phonetic, which means soil, suggests the ground on which one goes; that is, a street or road.

Camping is possible if you can find a spare blade of grass. The trick is to select a couple of likely places about half an hour before sunset, keep pedalling and then backtrack so you can pull off the road at the chosen spot just after darkness falls.

It's essential to have a kickstand for parking. A bell, headlight and reflector are good ideas. Make sure everything is bolted down, otherwise you'll invite theft. Adhesive reflector strips get ripped off.

Hazards

Driving standards in China are appalling and night riding is particularly hazardous. In rural areas, many drivers in China only use their headlights to flash them on and off as a warning for cyclists up ahead to get out of the way. On country roads, look out for those UFO-style walking tractors, which often have no headlights at all.

Your fellow cyclists are another factor in the hazard equation. Be prepared for cyclists to suddenly swerve in front of you, to come hurtling out of a side road or even to head straight towards you against the flow of the traffic. Chinese bicycles are rarely equipped with lights.

Off the Road

Most travellers who bring bikes take at least a couple of breaks from the rigours of the road, during which they use some other means of transport. The best option is the bus. It is generally no problem stowing bikes on the roofs of buses and there is seldom a charge involved. Air and train transport are more problematic.

Bikes are not cheap to transport on trains: they can cost as much as a hard seat fare. It's cheaper on boats, if you can find one. Trains have quotas for the number of bikes they may transport. As a foreigner you will get preferential treatment in the luggage compartment and the bike will go on the first available train. But your bike won't arrive at the same time as you unless you send it on a couple of days in advance. At the other end it is held in storage for three days free, and then incurs a small charge.

The procedure for putting a bike on a train and getting it at the other end is as follows:

- Railway personnel would like to see a train ticket for yourself (not entirely essential).
- Go to the baggage transport section of the station. Get a white slip and fill it out to get the two or three tags for registration. Then fill out a form (it's in Chinese, but just fill it out in English) that reads: 'Number/to station x/send goods person/receive goods person/total number of goods/from station y'.
- Take the white slip to another counter, where you pay and are given a blue slip.
- At the other end (after delays of up to three days for transporting a bike) you present the blue slip and get a white slip in return. This means your bike has arrived. The procedure could take from 20 minutes to an hour depending on who's around. If you lose that blue slip you'll have trouble reclaiming your bike.

The best bet for getting your bike on a bus is to get to the station early and put it on the roof. Strictly speaking, there should not be a charge for this, but in practice the driver will generally try to get you to pay.

Transporting your bike by plane can be expensive, but it's often less complicated than by train. Some cyclists have not been charged; others have had to pay 1% of their fare per kilogram of excess weight.

HITCHING

Hitching is never entirely safe in any country in the world, and we don't recommend it. Travellers who decide to hitch should understand that they are taking a small but potentially serious risk. People who do choose to hitch will be safer if they travel in pairs and let someone know where they are planning to go.

Many people have hitchhiked in China, and some have been amazingly successful. It's not officially sanctioned and the same dangers that apply elsewhere in the world also apply in China. Exercise caution, and if you're in any doubt as to the intentions of your prospective driver, say no.

Hitching in China is rarely free, and passengers are expected to offer at least a tip. Some drivers might even ask for an unreasonable amount of money, so try to establish a figure early to avoid problems later. Even when a price is agreed upon, don't be surprised if the driver raises it when you arrive at your destination and creates a big scene (with a big crowd) if you don't cough up the extra cash. Indeed, he or she may even pull this scam halfway through the trip, and if you don't pay up then you get kicked out in the middle of nowhere.

In other words, don't think of hitching as a means to save money – it will rarely be any cheaper than the bus. The main reason to do it is to get to isolated outposts where public transport is poor. There is, of course, some joy in meeting the locals this way, but communicating is certain to be a problem if you don't speak Chinese.

The best way to get a lift is to head out to main roads on the outskirts of town. There are usually lots of trucks on the roads, and even postal trucks and army convoys are worth trying. There is no Chinese signal for hitching, so just try waving down the trucks.

BOAT

For better or worse, China's boats are disappearing fast. Many services have been cancelled – victims of improved bus and air transport. In coastal areas, you're most likely to use a boat to reach offshore islands like Pǔtuó Shān or Hǎinán Dǎo. Hong Kong employs a veritable navy of vessels that connect with the territory's myriad islands. The Yāntái-Dàlián ferry will likely survive because it saves hundreds of kilometres of overland travel. For the same reason, the Shànghǎi-Níngbō service will probably continue to operate, but elsewhere the outlook for coastal passenger ships is not too good.

There are also several inland shipping routes worth considering, but these are also vanishing. For details of each trip see the appropriate sections in this book.

The best-known river trip is the three-day boat ride along Cháng Jiāng (Yangzi River) from Chóngqìng to Wǔhàn. The Lí Jiāng boat trip from Guìlín to Yángshuò is a popular tourist ride. You can also travel the Grand Canal from Hángzhōu to Sūzhōu on a tourist boat.

There are still a number of popular boats between Hong Kong and the rest of China, but services are getting fewer. See the Getting There & Away section of the Hong Kong chapter for details.

LOCAL TRANSPORT

Long-distance transport in China is not really a problem – the dilemma occurs when you finally make it to your destination. Hiring a car is often impractical or impossible and hiring a bike may be inadequate. Unless the town is small, walking is not usually recommended, since Chinese cities tend to be very spread out.

Bus

Apart from bikes, buses are the most common means of getting around in the cities. Services are fairly extensive and buses go to most places. The problem is that they are almost always packed. If an empty bus pulls in at a stop then a battle for seats ensues. Even more aggravating is the slowness of the traffic. You just have to be patient, never expect anything to move rapidly, and allow lots of time to get to the train station to catch your train. Improvements in bus quality have been matched by increased congestion on the roads. One consolation is that buses are cheap – rarely more than Y1. Bus routes at bus stops are generally listed in Chinese only, without pinyin.

Good maps of Chinese cities and bus routes are readily available and are often sold by hawkers outside the train stations. When you get on a bus, point to where you want to go on the map, and the conductor (who is seated near the door) will sell you the right ticket. They usually tell you where to get off, provided they remember.

Subway

Going underground is highly preferable to taking the bus, as there are no traffic jams, but this transportation option is only possible

in a handful of cities: Hong Kong, Běijīng, Shànghǎi, Guǎngzhōu and Tiānjīn.

By far the best and most comprehensive is Hong Kong's funky system; Běijīng's network is small. Shànghǎi and Guǎngzhōu have new and efficient systems, while Tiānjīn's system is antiquated.

Taxi

Taxis cruise the streets in most large cities, but elsewhere they may simply congregate at likely spots (such as bus stations).

You can always summon a taxi from tourist hotels, which sometimes have separate booking desks. You can hire them for a single trip or on a daily basis – the latter is worth considering if there's a group of people who can split the cost. Some tourist hotels also have minibuses on hand.

While most taxis have meters, they are often only switched on in larger towns and cities. If the meter is not used (on an excursion out of town for example), a price should be negotiated before you get into the taxi, and bargaining employed. Write the price down if you have to and secure an agreement, so that the price is not suddenly upped when you arrive.

Chinese cities impose limitations on the number of passengers that a taxi can carry. The limit is usually four, though minibuses can take more, and drivers are usually unwilling to break the rules and risk trouble with the police.

It is practically impossible to find rear seat belts in China's taxi fleet, and the front passenger seat belt is so rarely used that they leave a strip of dust across your shirt. Be prepared for bad driving and try and position yourself so you don't lose an eye on one of the sharp corners and edges of the security cage the driver sits in if he suddenly halts (or crashes). Watch out for tired drivers – they work long and punishing shifts.

Motorcycle Taxi

The deal is that you get a ride on the back of someone's motorcycle for about half the price of what a regular four-wheeled taxi would charge. If you turn a blind eye to the hazards, this is a quick and cheap way of getting around. You must wear a helmet – the driver will provide one. Obviously, there is no meter, so fares must be agreed upon in advance.

Motor-Tricycle

The motor-tricycle *(sānlún mótuōchē)* – for want of a better name – is an enclosed three-wheeled vehicle with a driver at the front, a small motorbike engine below and seats for two passengers behind. They tend to congregate outside the train and bus stations in larger towns and cities. Some of these vehicles have trays at the rear with bench seats along the sides so that four or more people can be accommodated.

Pedicab

A pedicab *(sānlúnchē)* is a pedal-powered tricycle with a seat to carry passengers. Chinese pedicabs have the driver in front and passenger seats in the back.

Pedicabs are gradually disappearing in China, victims of the combustion engine. However, pedicabs congregate outside train and bus stations or hotels in parts of China. In a few places, pedicabs cruise the streets in large numbers (Lhasa, for example).

Unfortunately, some drivers are aggressive. A reasonable fare will be quoted, but when you arrive at your destination it'll be multiplied by 10. Another tactic is to quote you a price like Y10 and then demand US$10 – the driver claims that you 'misunderstood'. Yet another tactic is for the driver to bring you halfway and demand more payment to bring you to your destination.

ORGANISED TOURS

Some one-day tours are reasonably priced and might be worth the cost as they can save you a lot of trouble: they can solve your transport and accommodation hassles, and make it all a lot cheaper than tackling each stop individually. Some remote spots are difficult to reach and a tour might well be your only option.

Some tours are very informal and even popular with budget travellers. For example, at Turpan in Xīnjiāng province, many travellers do a one-day tour by minibus of the surrounding countryside. The minibus drivers hang around the hotels and solicit business, so there is no need to get involved with CITS or other agencies.

There are an increasing number of expat-run tour companies in China such as Wild-china (W www.wildchina.com), which do a number of more exciting expeditions through China's wilder and more rugged

---

Pedicabs Versus Rickshaws

A rickshaw is a two-wheeled passenger cart pulled by a man on foot. It was invented in Japan, where the word *jin-rikusha* means 'human-powered vehicle'. It was introduced into China in the late 19th century, where it was called *yángchē* (foreign vehicle).

The rickshaw eventually became a symbol of human exploitation – one person pulling another in a cart – and disappeared from China in the 1950s. Its replacement, the pedicab – sometimes mistakenly called a rickshaw – is a tricycle with a seat for one or two passengers.

---

reaches. Check out the expat magazines in Shànghǎi, Běijīng or Guǎngzhōu for further listings.

A low-cost option is to go on a tour with a local Chinese group. A number of travellers use this option in Běijīng, for example, to reach the Great Wall. The tour bus could be an old rattletrap and you'll get to visit tacky souvenir shops (which invariably pay under-the-table commissions to the bus drivers), but these tours can be interesting if you keep a sense of humour about it. Don't expect the guides to speak anything but Chinese – possibly just the local dialect.

Sometimes the buses will whiz through interesting spots and make long stops at dull places for the requisite photo sessions. You might have difficulty getting a ticket if your Chinese isn't good and they think you're too much trouble. The Chinese tours are often booked through hotel service desks or from private travel agencies. In some cases, there is an established tour bus meeting spot – you just roll up in the morning and hop on board.

CITS

China International Travel Service (CITS; Zhōngguó Guójì Lǚxíngshè) deals with China's foreign tourist hordes, and mainly concerns itself with organising and making travel arrangements for group tours. CITS existed as far back as 1954, when there were few customers; now they're inundated with a couple of hundred thousand foreign tourists a year. Unfortunately, after almost half a century of being in business, CITS has still not gotten its act totally together.

Nowadays, travellers make their way around China without ever having to deal with CITS. In many remote regions, CITS does not offer much in the way of services. In other places, CITS may sell hard-to-get-hold-of train tickets or tickets for the opera or acrobatics or perhaps provide tours of rural villages or factories. It really all depends on where you are.

There will usually be a small service charge added on to the price of any train, boat or plane tickets purchased through CITS.

CITS is a frequent target of ire for all kinds of reasons: rudeness, inefficiency, laziness and even fraud. Bear in mind, however, that service varies enormously from office to office. Expect the worst, but be prepared to be pleasantly surprised.

CTS

The China Travel Service (CTS; Zhōngguó Lǚxíngshè) was originally set up to handle tourists from Hong Kong, Macau and Taiwan and foreign nationals of Chinese descent. These days your gene pool and nationality make little difference – CTS has now become a keen competitor with CITS.

Many foreigners use the CTS offices in Hong Kong and Macau to obtain visas and book trains, planes, hovercraft and other transport to China.

CTS can sometimes get you a better deal on hotels booked through their office than you could obtain on your own (of course, this does not apply to budget accommodation such as backpackers' dormitories).

CYTS

The name China Youth Travel Service (CYTS; Zhōngguó Qīngnián Lǚxíngshè) implies that this is some sort of student organisation, but these days CYTS performs essentially the same services as CITS and CTS. Being a smaller organisation, CYTS seems to try harder to compete against the big league. This could result in better service, but not necessarily lower prices.

CYTS is mostly interested in tour groups, but individual travellers could find it useful for booking air tickets or sleepers on the trains.

Běijīng 北京

Telephone code: ☎ 010
Population: 13.8 million
Area: 16,800 sq km

Běijīng, capital of the People's Republic of China (PRC), is where they move the cogs and wheels of the Chinese universe. Those who have slugged it out in hard-seat trains and ramshackle buses through the poverty-stricken interior of China appreciate the creature comforts of Běijīng. The city boasts some of China's best restaurants and recreation facilities, and palatial hotels fit for an emperor. Foreigners who have passed their time only in Běijīng without seeing the rest of China come away with the impression that everything is hunky-dory in the PRC.

Whatever impression you come away with, Běijīng is a cosmetic showcase and not a realistic window on China. For the past twenty years, the city has undergone relentless modernisation. It is now gearing up for the mother of all facelifts in preparation for the 2008 Olympics. But look beyond the wide boulevards, glittering hotels and high-rises and you'll still find many historical and cultural treasures.

HISTORY

History records that Běijīng was first settled around 1000 BC. It began as a frontier trading town for the Mongols, Koreans and tribes from Shāndōng and central China, and by the Warring States period had grown to be the capital of the Yan kingdom. The town underwent a number of changes as it acquired new warlords – the Khitan Mongols and the Manchurian Jurchen tribes among them. During the Liao dynasty, Běijīng was referred to as Yanjing (Capital of Yan), which is still the name of Běijīng's most popular beer.

Běijīng's history really gets under way in AD 1215, the year Genghis Khan set fire to Yanjing and slaughtered everything in sight. From the ashes emerged Dadu (Great Capital), alias Khanbaliq, the Khan's town. By 1279 Genghis Khan's grandson Kublai had made himself ruler of most of Asia, and Khanbaliq was his capital. With a lull in the fighting from 1280 to 1300, foreigners

Highlights

- The Forbidden City, China's centre of power for more than 500 years
- The Temple of Heaven, a perfect example of Ming architecture and the symbol of Běijīng
- The Summer Palace, the lovely gardens of China's imperial rulers in a stunning setting beside Kūnmíng Hú
- The Great Wall, ancient China's greatest public works project and now the nation's leading tourist attraction
- Hútòng, Běijīng's traditional neighbourhoods and alleyways

managed to drop in along the Silk Road for tea with the Great Khan. The mercenary Zhu Yanhang led an uprising in 1368, taking over the city and ushering in the Ming dynasty. The city was renamed Beiping (Northern Peace) and for the next 35 years the capital was shifted south to Nánjīng.

In the early 1400s Zhu's son Yongle shuffled the court back to Beiping and renamed it Běijīng (Northern Capital). Many of Běijīng's historic structures, such as the Forbidden City and the Temple of Heaven, were built in Yongle's reign.

A change of government came with the Manchus, who invaded China and established the Qing dynasty. Under them, and

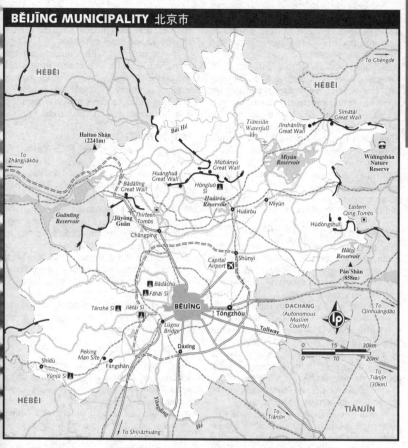

BĚIJĪNG MUNICIPALITY 北京市

particularly during the reigns of the emperors Kangxi and Qianlong, Běijīng was expanded and renovated, and summer palaces, pagodas and temples were built.

In the last 120 years of the Qing dynasty, Běijīng, and subsequently China, was subjected to power struggles and invasions, and the chaos they caused. The list is long: the Anglo-French troops who in 1860 burnt the Old Summer Palace to the ground; the corrupt regime of Empress Dowager Cixi; the Boxers; General Yuan Shikai; the warlords; the Japanese occupation of 1937; and the Kuomintang.

Běijīng changed hands one last time when, in January 1949, the People's Liberation Army (PLA) entered the city. On 1 October of that year Mao proclaimed a 'People's Republic' to an audience of some 500,000 citizens in Tiānānmén Square.

Like the emperors before them, the Communists significantly altered the face of Běijīng to suit their own image. Down came the commemorative arches, while whole city blocks were reduced to rubble to widen major boulevards. From 1950 to 1952 the city's magnificent outer walls were levelled in the interests of traffic circulation. Soviet experts and technicians poured in, leaving their own Stalinesque touches.

The capitalist-style reforms of the past quarter century have transformed Běijīng into a modern city, with an array of skyscrapers, slick shopping malls and heaving flyovers. The once flat skyline is now crenellated with vast apartment blocks and office buildings.

Recent years have seen a convincing beautification of Běijīng: from a toneless and unkempt city to a greener, cleaner and more pleasant place.

Běijīng's successful bid for the 2008 Olympics is set to further transform the capital. The city's already manic construction drive has been ratcheted up another gear: a gargantuan expanse of land in the north of the city will become the 1215-hectare Olympic Green, boasting an Olympic Village capable of housing close to 18,000 people.

In a bid to sweep away the summer smog that chokes the city, officials trumpet a target of 90% of buses and 70% of taxis running on natural gas by 2007, while polluting industries will be elbowed into the suburbs.

ORIENTATION

With a total area of 16,800 sq km, Běijīng municipality is roughly the size of Belgium.

Though it may not appear so to the visitor in the turmoil of arrival, Běijīng is a city of very orderly design. Think of the city as one giant grid, with the Forbidden City at its centre. As for the street names: Chongwenmenwai Dajie means 'the avenue (dajie) outside (wai) Chongwen Gate (Chongwenmen)' – that is, outside the old wall – whereas Chongwenmennei Dajie means 'the avenue inside Chongwen Gate'. It's an academic exercise since the gate and the wall in question no longer exist.

A major boulevard can change names six or even seven times along its length. Streets and avenues can also be split along compass points: Dong Dajie (East Avenue), Xi Dajie (West Avenue), Bei Dajie (North Avenue) and Nan Dajie (South Avenue). All these streets head off from an intersection, usually where a gate once stood.

Officially, there are four 'ring roads' around Běijīng, circling the city centre in concentric rings. A fifth ring road exists on paper, but construction has yet to begin.

Maps

Lonely Planet publishes a waterproof colour Beijing fold-out City Map, with Chinese script. English-language maps of Běijīng are generally handed out free at the big hotels. They're often part of an advertising supplement for various companies whose locations are, of course, also shown on the map. It's better to fork out a few

yuán for a bilingual map that shows bus routes. These are available from the Friendship Store and hotel gift shops.

If you can deal with Chinese-language maps, you'll find a wide variety from which to choose. You can pick these up at train stations or at any streetside news stalls for Y3. Map-laden hawkers patrol Wángfǔjǐng and the area around Tiānānmén Square.

INFORMATION

Běijīng is well serviced by expat mags, which include *That's Beijing*, *Jianwen Guide*, *Beijing Journal*, *City Weekend*, *Beijing this Month* and *Metrozine*. All the bars in the Sānlǐtún area carry them; also try top-end hotels. Expat maps offer extensive and up-to-date listings for bars, restaurants and clubs, and carry classified adverts, personal columns, housing info, reviews and travel columns. On the net, your best bet is W www.chinanow.com for daily updated travel and entertainment news relating to the capital.

Unless otherwise indicated, all of the places mentioned below appear on the Central Běijīng map.

Tourist Offices

Your hotel should offer a number of tours within and around Běijīng. Many travel agents advertise their services in the expat mags; these can be useful for single or multi-day tours around Běijīng and China. Phone around to find one that can reliably converse in English. For a list of travel agents in Běijīng, consult W www.chinatour .com/agt/a.htm.

You can book rail and plane tickets and tours at the main government-run Beijing Tourism Group (BTG; Běijīng Lǚxíngshè; ☎ 6515 8562) on the ground floor of the Beijing Tourist Building at 28 Jianguomenwai Dajie, near Scitech Plaza. This is also where you can pick up Trans-Manchurian and Trans-Mongolian train tickets, as well as information about the city.

The Beijing Tourist Administration Bureau's Panda Tours (☎ 6803 6963, e bjpanda@public.bta.net.cn) have English-speaking guided tours from numerous major hotels. Sights include the Great Wall, Chinese acrobatics, the Summer Palace, the Forbidden City and farther afield destinations such as Chéngdé.

There is an English-speaking 24-hour Beijing Tourism Hotline (☎ 6513 0828). It can answer questions and hear complaints.

Embassies

Běijīng is not a bad place to stock up on visas. There are two major embassy neighbourhoods: Jiàngúoménwài and Sānlǐtún. For a list of embassies in Běijīng with addresses and phone numbers, see the Facts for the Visitor chapter earlier in this book.

The Jiàngúoménwài embassy area is in the vicinity of the Friendship Store, east of the city centre. The Sānlǐtún embassy cluster is several kilometres to the north-east, near the Great Wall Sheraton hotel.

Money

All hotels – even most budget ones – can change travellers cheques or US dollars.

If you want to cash travellers cheques and receive US dollars in return (necessary if you're going to Russia or Mongolia), this can be done at CITIC at the International Building (Guójì Dàshà), adjacent to the Friendship Store at 19 Jianguomenwai Dajie. On major international credit cards CITIC will advance cash. There's a useful branch of the Bank of China in Sundongan Plaza, east of the Forbidden City on Wangfujing Dajie.

The following international credit card companies have representative offices in Běijīng: Visa International (☎ 10 800 110 2911); The American Express Service Center (☎ 6505 2888); Diners Club International (☎ 6510 1833, 24-hour hotline ☎ 6606 2227).

Major bank addresses in Běijīng include: CITIC Industrial Bank (☎ 6554 2388, 6621 9988) Block C, Fuhua Mansion, 8 Chaoyangmen Dajie; Hong Kong and Shanghai Banking Corporation (☎ 6526 0668) Ground Floor, Block A, COFCO Plaza, 8 Jianguomennei Dajie.

ATMs

Growing numbers of Bank of China branches have ATM machines where you can draw from international accounts. The ATM at Capital Airport is extremely useful. Another handy wall-mounted ATM accepting Visa, MasterCard, Plus and Cirrus is at the Bank of China on Wangfujing Dajie. Some upmarket hotels (eg, Lower Level 2, The Palace Hotel and Swissôtel) and department stores (eg, the Lufthansa Center)

have ATMs. The Hong Kong and Shanghai Banking Corporation (see previously) has a 24-hour ATM where you can draw money from your overseas HSBC account.

Post & Communications

The International Post & Communications Building (☎ 6512 8120, Ⓦ www.bipto.com.cn) is on Jianguomen Beidajie. It's open Monday to Friday from 8am to 6pm and 9am to 5pm for international package pick-up (be sure to bring your passport). All letters and parcels marked 'Poste Restante, GPO Beijing' will wind up here. The staff even file poste restante letters in alphabetical order, a rare occurrence in China, but you pay for all this efficiency – there is a Y1.5 fee charged for each letter received.

There are a number of private couriers that offer international express posting of documents and parcels. The major ones are:

United Parcel Service (☎ 6593 2932) Unit A, 1st floor, Tower B, Beijing Kelun Bldg, 12a Guanghua Lu, Chaoyang District
DHL (☎ 6466 2211, fax 6467 7826) 45 Xinyuan Jie, Chaoyang District. There are also branches in the Kempinski Hotel and China World Trade Centre.
Federal Express (☎ 800 810 2338, 6561 2003) Hanwei Bldg, 7 Guanghua Lu, Chaoyang District. There's also a branch in the Golden Land Bldg, next to the 21st Century Hotel.
TNT Skypak (☎ 6465 2227, fax 6462 4018) 8a Xiangheyuan Zhongli, Chaoyang District

---

Běijīng Climate

The capital's seasons are very distinct, each with their own mood. The city can be visited in any season, with autumn probably the most pleasant. Winter can be bitingly cold (-10°C), the thermometer dips from late October onwards. Spring is pleasant, apart from the (worsening) sand clouds that sweep in from Inner Mongolia. The season also sees the snow-like 'liuxu' (Willow catkins) wafting through the air and collecting in drifts; from May onwards the mercury can surge well over 30°C. Spring is acutely arid, and there's loads of static electricity; summer brings rainstorms. Autumn is often *'tiāngāo qìshuǎng'*, literally 'the sky is high and the air is fresh' – with clear skies and breezy days. Note that air pollution can be very harsh in both summer and winter.

Email & Internet Access Běijīng is well served with Internet cafes. The most organised is Sparkice, at a number of locations: 2nd floor, China World Trade Centre, 1 Jianguomenwai Dajie (☎ 6505 2288 ext 80206), open 24 hours, and Unit S118, East Wing, Lufthansa Center, 50 Liangmaqiao Lu (☎ 6465 3388 ext 4530), charging Y8 per hour 10am to 8pm and Y12 per hour 10pm to 1am. Beijing Normal University (Běijīng map) has a popular Internet cafe on the 1st floor of the Foreign Students Building, 19 Xinjiekou Waidajie (Liúxuéshēng Lóu; ☎ 6220 9220), which is open 24 hours and charges Y5 per hour. You can also try 11 Fans, B, Full Link Plaza (☎ 6588 0399), also open 24 hours and charging Y10 per hour. Check the expat rags for further listings.

Libraries/Information Centres

The massive Beijing Library (☎ 6841 5566, W www.nlc.gov.cn), at 39 Baishiqiao Lu, Haidian District, west of the Beijing Zoo, has foreign periodicals and foreign books reading rooms. Although foreigners aren't allowed to check books out, you can buy a day pass for Y1 on the 3rd floor. You can also access the Internet here. The library is open 9am to 5pm daily.

Various embassies also have small libraries. The American Center for Educational Exchange (☎ 6597 3242), at Room 2801, Jingguang Centre, Hujialou, in the Chaoyang district, has a useful library. The British Council (Cultural and Education Section of the British Embassy; ☎ 6590 6903, e enquiry@britishcouncil.org.cn) on the

4th floor of the Landmark Bldg Tower 1, 8 Dongsanhuan Beilu, next to the Great Wall Sheraton, also has a useful information centre.

PSB

The Public Security Bureau (PSB; Gōngānjú; ☎ 6404 7799) has an office at 2 Andingmen Dongdajie, about 300m east of the Lama Temple. It's open 8.30am to noon and 1pm to 5pm Monday to Saturday. The visa office is on the 2nd floor.

Medical Services

Beijing International SOS Clinic (☎ 6462 9112, 24-hour alarm centre ☎ 6462 9100, W www.internationalsos.com) is at 1 Xingfu Sancun Beijie, behind the German embassy. It has a high-quality clinic with English-speaking staff. It's open Monday to Friday 9am to 6pm, with 24-hour emergency medical care. International SOS also has a dental clinic (☎ 6462 0333). The Beijing International Medical Centre (☎ 6465 1561/1562/1563, fax 6465 1961) is at Room 106 in the Regus Office Building, Lufthansa Center, at 50 Liangmaqiao Lu. It is open 24 hours and has English-speaking staff; pharmacy, dental service and counselling is also available.

The Hong Kong International Medical Clinic (☎ 6501 2288 ext 2345/6, fax 6502 3426) is on the 3rd floor of the Hong Kong Macau Center at Swissôtel. It has a 24-hour medical and dental clinic, with obstetrical/gynaecological services, and staff can also do immunisations. Prices are more reasonable than at SOS and the International

The Power of Eunuchs

An interesting feature of the Ming dynasty, and a principal reason for its eventual decline, was the ever-increasing number, and power, of eunuchs in the imperial court. Eunuchs, generally castrated at a young age by their families in the hope that they would attain the court, had been employed by Chinese emperors as early as the Han dynasty. Traditionally, their role was to serve the needs of the emperor and his harem in parts of the imperial palace that were off limits to all adult males barring the emperor himself.

By the early Ming, the number of eunuchs in the service of the emperor was already 10,000 and, despite imperial edicts forbidding their access to political power, they continued to swell in numbers and influence throughout the Ming. In the late years of the dynasty, eunuchs probably numbered somewhere between 70,000 and 100,000 and exercised enormous control over the nation. Certain eunuchs – perhaps the most infamous of whom was Wei Zhongxian, who practically ruled all of China in the 1620s – assumed dictatorial power and siphoned off massive fortunes.

One of Běijīng's bustling fruit and veg markets.

Resting against a wall of the Forbidden City.

Boat on the north shore of Kūnmíng Hú. The lake covers three-quarters of the Summer Palace park.

China World Trade Centre is host to a variety of restaurants and shops.

Artist, Tiānānmén Sq.

The glorious Qing architecture of the Summer Palace, Běijīng.

Kite flying in Tiānānmén Square is a popular pastime.

Directing traffic.

A 19th century etching of Běijīng's Forbidden City: The palatial realm of Ming & Qing emporers.

Medical Centre. Note for all of the afore-mentioned that it's much cheaper just to ask what medicines you need and then buy them at a pharmacy on the street.

Chinese hospitals that cater to foreigners are cheaper than international clinics. Beijing Union Medical Hospital (Xiéhé Yīyuàn; ☎ 6529 6114, emergency 6529 5284), at 53 Dongdan Beidajie, is a first-rate hospital set in a wonderful building near Wángfǔjǐng. There is a foreigners and high-level cadres-only wing in the back building. It's open 24 hours and has the full range of facilities for inpatient and out-patient care, as well as a pharmacy.

Also try the Beijing United Family Hospital (Běijīng map; ☎ 6433 3960, Ⓦ www.beijingunited.com) at 2 Jiangtai Lu, an American joint venture open 24 hours with a comprehensive range of inpatient and outpatient care.

NATIONAL BUILDINGS & MONUMENTS
Forbidden City 紫禁城
Zǐjìn Chéng
The Forbidden City (☎ 6513 2255; admission Y40-60; open 8.30am-4pm May-Sept, 8.30am-3.30pm Oct-Apr), so called because it was off limits for 500 years, is the largest and best-preserved cluster of ancient buildings in China. It was home to two dynasties

of emperors, the Ming and the Qing, who didn't stray from this pleasure dome unless they absolutely had to.

The Běijīng authorities insist on calling this place the Palace Museum (Gǔgōng). Two hundred years ago the admission price would have been instant death, but today a ticket will do. The last admission tickets are sold 30 minutes before closing. Rental of a cassette tape for a self-guided tour (record-ed by Roger Moore of *007* fame) is another Y30 plus a deposit (such as your passport). For the tape to make sense you must enter the Forbidden City from the south gate and exit from the north. The tape is available in a large number of languages.

It's a good idea to get to the palace early in the morning to avoid the crowds.

Don't confuse the Forbidden City entrance with the gate, Tiānānmén – keep heading north until you can't walk any farther with-out paying. This is Wumen, the entrance to the Forbidden City proper. Wumen swarms with guides latching onto foreign visitors but you can learn much more from the tape and by following your own schedule.

The basic layout for the city was estab-lished between 1406 and 1420 by Emperor Yongle, who commanded battalions of up to a million labourers. From this palace the emperors governed China, often rather erratically as they tended to become lost in

Fragrant Hills
Botanical Gardens

Yùquán Shān

Fúhǎi
Hú
2

Yiheyuan Lu 颐和园路

Qinghua
University

Chengfu

Shuangqing Lu

To
Xiāngshān
Gōngyuán
(500m)

Yuquanshan Lu

1

Künmíng
Hú

Beijing
University

3

4

5 Zhongguancun Lu 中关村路

Haidian Lu

Haidian
Lu
海淀路

Xilu 北三环西路

7

PLACES TO STAY & EAT

6 Friendship Hotel
   友谊宾馆
8 Tianwaitian
   天外天烤鸭店
11 Holiday Inn Lido
   丽都假日饭店;
16 Shangri-La Hotel
   香格里拉饭店
21 Lihua Hotel
   丽华饭店
22 Jinghua Youth Hostel
   京华饭店
23 Sea Star Hotel
   海兴大酒店

OTHER

1 Summer Palace
   颐和园
2 Old Summer Palace
   圆明园遗址
3 Solutions
   解决
4 Arthur M. Sackler Museum of
   Art & Anthropology
5 Zhōngguǎncūn Bus Stop
   中关村(公共汽车站)
7 Dàzhōng Sì
   大钟寺
9 Beijing Normal University
   北京师范大学
10 Běijiāo (Déshèngmén)
   Long-Distance Bus Station
   北郊(德胜门)长途汽车站
12 Beijing United Family Hospital
   和睦家医院
13 Cherry Lane Movies

14 The Big Easy
   快乐站
15 Drag On
17 Military Museum
   军事博物馆
18 Liánhuāchí Bus Station
   莲花池长途汽车站
19 Memorial Hall of the War
   of Resistance Against Japan
   抗日战争纪念馆
20 Marco Polo Bridge
   卢沟桥
24 Hǎihùtún Long-Distance
   Bus Station
   海户屯公共汽车站
25 Zhàogōngkǒu Bus Station
   赵公口汽车站

HAIDIAN
DISTRICT

Wanquanhe Lu

Beiwucun Lu 北坞村路

Kūnmíng
Nánlù

Xīn jǐng
Lù

Bǎnjín Lu

Beisanhuan

6

Gaoliangqiao

Beijing
Zoo

Zizhuyuan Lu

Zizhúyuán
Gōngyuán
紫竹院路

16

Baishiqiao Lu

Xizhimenwai Daj

Xisanhuan Beilu

Fushi Lu

Yùyuāntán
Gōngyuán

公主坟
Gōngzhùfén

17

Jūnshìbówùguǎn
军事博物馆

Fifth Ring Road

Xiàngshān Nánlù 香山南路

Shijingshan Lu 石景山路

Fuxing Lu 复兴路

Bājiǎocūn
八角村

Bābǎoshān
八宝山

Yùquánlù
玉泉路

Wǔkēsōng
五棵松

Wànshòulù
万寿路

Fuxingmenwai Daj
复兴门外大街

Liánhuāchí
Gōngyuán

Beijing West
Train Station

Liùlǐ
Bridge

18

Fengtai Lu

京石高速公路 Beijing-Shijiazhuang Expressway

Niúbùlù

Fengtai Lu

FENG TAI
DISTRICT

Third Ring Road

Xisanhuan Nanlu

西三环南路

Jingkai Lu

0   1   2km
0   0.5   1mi

19

20

Fengtai
Train Station

To
Shíjiāzhuāng

this self-contained little world and allocate real power to the court eunuchs. One emperor devoted his entire career to carpentry – when an earthquake struck (an ominous sign for an emperor) he was delighted, since it gave him a chance to renovate.

The buildings that stand today are mostly post-18th century, as with a lot of historic structures around Běijīng. The palace was constantly going up in flames; a lantern festival combined with a sudden gust of wind from the Gobi desert would easily do the trick, as would a fireworks display. Fires were also deliberately lit by court eunuchs and officials, who could get rich off the repair bills. The moat around the palace, now used for boating, came in handy since the local fire brigade was considered too lowly to quench the royal flames. In 1644 the Manchus stormed in and burned the palace to the ground.

It was not just the buildings that went up in smoke, but rare books, paintings and scrolls. In this century there have been two major lootings of the palace: first by Japanese forces, and second by the Kuomintang, who, on the eve of the Communist takeover in 1949, removed thousands of crates of relics to Taiwan, where they are now on display in Taipei's National Palace Museum. The gaps have been filled by treasures (old, newly discovered and fake) from other parts of China. Of these treasures, only a small percentage is on display. Plans are afoot to construct an underground museum in order to exhibit more of the collection.

Beyond the northern palace gate of Shenwumen, there were two further gates that were pulled down in 1931 to make way for the road that now lies south of Jǐngshān Gōngyuán. Previously, this piece of ground between the palace and the park was for imperial use only. It's a fine idea to leave the Forbidden City by Shenwumen and clamber up to the top of Jǐngshān Gōngyuán, which affords a magnificent view over the whole of the palace.

Tiānānmén Square 天安门广场
Tiānānmén Guǎngchǎng

This vast desert of pavement is Mao's creation and the heart of Běijīng. During the Cultural Revolution, the chairman, wearing a Red Guard armband, reviewed parades of up to a million people here. In 1976 another million people jammed the square to pay their last respects to Mao. The square became a household name in the West in 1989, when army tanks and soldiers cut down pro-democracy demonstrators. More recently, members of the banned Falun Gong regularly protested here, only to be bundled into waiting PSB vans.

If the weather is conducive, the square is a place for people to lounge around in the evening and for kids to fly decorated kites.

Surrounding and studding the square is a mishmash of monuments past and present: Tiānānmén, the Chinese Revolution History Museum, the Great Hall of the People, the Front Gate, the Mao Mausoleum and the Monument to the People's Heroes. At the time of writing the Beijing Opera House (due for completion in 2002) was being built to the west of the Great Hall of the People. The egg-like design by French architect Paul Andreu has sparked controversy and even Běijīng residents have joined in the heckling.

If you get up early you can watch the **flag-raising ceremony** at sunrise, performed by a troop of PLA soldiers drilled to march at precisely 108 paces per minute, 75cm per pace. The same ceremony in reverse gets performed at sunset, but you can hardly see the soldiers for the throngs gathered to watch. A digital sign on the square announces the times for the sunrise ceremony for the next two days. Super megawatt light bulbs now light up the square at night, so be sure to bring along your sunglasses.

Bicycles cannot be ridden across Tiānānmén Square, but you can walk your bike. One-way traffic runs along north-south avenues on either side of the square.

Tiānānmén 天安门
Gate of Heavenly Peace

Tiānānmén (☎ 6309 9386; admission Y15; open 8.30am-4.30pm daily) is a national symbol. The gate was built in the 15th century and restored in the 17th. From imperial days it functioned as a rostrum for proclaiming to the assembled masses. There are five doors to the gate, and in front of it are seven bridges spanning a stream. Each of these bridges was restricted in its use and only the emperor could use the central door and bridge.

Words & Pictures

Mén: door, gate

The former character is easily recognisable as a double door that swings open from the middle, reminiscent of the half-doors of saloons in old westerns. The modern character for door represents an open door or doorway – easier to write, but perhaps also indicating the importance of charity in these acquisitive, get-ahead times.

It was from the gate that Mao proclaimed the People's Republic on 1 October 1949. The dominating feature is the gigantic portrait of Mao – the required backdrop for any photo the Chinese take of themselves here. To the left of the portrait is a slogan 'Long Live the People's Republic of China' and to the right 'Long Live the Unity of the Peoples of the World'.

According to locals, one of the two lions that stand in front of the gate has a bullet hole in its belly – allegedly the work of the guns of the allied force that entered Běijīng in 1900 during the Boxer Rebellion.

You pass through Tiānānmén on your way to the Forbidden City (assuming you enter from the southern side). There is no fee for walking through the gate (the admission fee is for climbing up into the gate to look over the square).

Front Gate 前门
Qián Mén

Silent sentinel to the changing times, the Front Gate (☎ 6525 3176; admission Y5; open 8am-4pm daily) sits on the southern side of Tiānānmén Square. The Front Gate guarded the wall division between the ancient Inner City and the outer suburban zone and dates back to the reign of Emperor Yongle in the 15th century. With the disappearance of the city walls, the gate sits out of context, but it's still impressive.

The Front Gate actually consists of two gates. The southern one is called Arrow Tower (Jiàn Lóu) and the northern one is called Zhèngyáng Mén or Chéng Lóu.

Great Hall of the People 人民大会堂
Rénmín Dàhuìtáng

The Great Hall of the People (☎ 6309 6668; admission Y15; open 9am-2pm daily) is the venue of the rubber-stamp legislature, the National People's Congress. It's open to the public when the Congress is not sitting. These are the halls of power, many of them named after provinces and regions of China and decorated appropriately. You can see the 5000-seat banquet room where US President Richard Nixon dined in 1972, and the 10,000-seat auditorium with the familiar red star embedded in a galaxy of lights in the ceiling. There's a sort of museum-like atmosphere in the Great Hall, with *objets d'art* donated by the provinces, plus a snack bar and a restaurant.

Monument to the People's Heroes 人民英雄纪念碑
Rénmín Yīngxióng Jìniànbēi

North of Mao's Mausoleum, the Monument to the People's Heroes was completed in 1958 and stands on the site of the old Outer Palace Gate.

The 36m obelisk, made of Qīngdǎo granite, bears bas-relief carvings of key revolutionary events (one relief shows the Chinese destroying opium in the 19th century), as well as appropriate calligraphy from Mao Zedong and Zhou Enlai. It is illuminated at night.

Mao Zedong Mausoleum
毛主席纪念堂
Máo Zhǔxí Jìniàntáng

Chairman Mao died in September 1976 and his mausoleum (☎ 6513 2277; admission free; open 8.30am-11.30am Tues, Thur & Sat, 8.30am-11.30am & 2pm-4pm Mon, Wed & Fri) was constructed shortly thereafter.

However history judges Mao, his impact on its course was enormous. Easy as it now is to vilify his deeds and excesses, many Chinese show deep respect when confronted with the physical presence of the man. CITS guides freely quote the old 7:3 ratio on Mao that first surfaced in 1976 – Mao was 70% right and 30% wrong (what, one wonders, are the figures for CITS itself?) and this is now the official Party line.

Though entry is free, you have to pay Y10 to check your bags and camera at the entrance; you will also need to bring your passport. Join the enormous queue of Chinese sightseers, but don't expect more than a quick glimpse of the body as you file past the sarcophagus. At certain times of the year the body requires maintenance and is not on view.

Whatever Mao might have done to the Chinese economy while he was alive, sales of Mao memorabilia are certainly giving the free market a boost these days. During the peak season souvenir stalls near the mausoleum are littered with Chairman Mao key rings, thermometers, face towels, handkerchiefs, sun visors, address books and cartons of cigarettes (a comment on his chain-smoking?).

Summer Palace 颐和园
Yíhéyuán

One of the finest sights in Běijīng, the Summer Palace *(Běijīng map; ☎ 6288 1144, Yiheyuan, Haidian District; admission Y20-40 Nov-Mar, Y30-50 Apr-Oct; open 8.30am-5pm daily)* deserves at least a day of your attention.

Teeming with summer tour groups, this dominion of palace temples, gardens, pavilions, lake and corridors was once a playground for the imperial court. Royalty came here to elude the insufferable summer heat that roasted the Forbidden City. The site had long been a royal garden and was considerably enlarged and embellished by Emperor Qianlong in the 18th century.

The park was later abandoned, but Empress Dowager Cixi began rebuilding in 1888 with money supposedly intended for the construction of a modern navy. One nautical acquisition was the marble boat that sits immobile at the northern edge of the lake: it was fitted out with several large mirrors and the empress used to dine there at the lakeside.

In 1900 foreign troops, incensed by the Boxer Rebellion, ransacked the place. Restorations took place a few years later. A major renovation occurred after 1949, by which time the palace had once again fallen into disrepair.

Three-quarters of the park is occupied by Kūnmíng Hú, and most items of structural interest are towards the eastern gate or on Wànshòu Shān (Longevity Hill).

The main building, where the emperor handled state affairs and received envoys, is the **Benevolence and Longevity Hall** *(Rénshòudiàn)*, just off the lake towards the east gate. It houses a hardwood throne and the courtyard's bronze animals include a splendid *qilin*, a mythical hybrid animal.

Along the north shore of the lake is the **Long Corridor** *(Chángláng)*, which runs for more than 700m and is decorated with mythical scenes.

On artificial Wànshòu Shān are a number of temples. The **Cloud Dispelling Hall** *(Páiyún Diàn)* on the western slopes is one of the few structures to escape the attention of Anglo-French forces. At the top of the hill sits the **Huìhǎi Sì** *(Sea of Wisdom Temple)*, made of glazed tiles; good views of the lake can be had from here.

The ornate surroundings of Běijīng's palaces were as impressive as the buildings themselves.

The 17-arch bridge spans 150m to **Nánhú Dǎo** *(South Lake Island)* and nearby on the mainland side stands a beautiful bronze ox. You can see the hills of Jade Spring Mountain off to the west of Kūnmíng Hú, capped by the Yufeng Pagoda.

Also note the **Jade Belt Bridge** *(Yùdài Qiáo)* on the mid-west side of the lake and the **Harmonious Interest Garden** *(Héqù Yuán)*, which is a copy of a Wúxī garden, at the north-eastern end. **Sūzhōu Jiē**, a mock Jiāngsū replica to the north, is a picturesque vignette of shops, eateries and waterways.

Other sights are largely associated with Empress Cixi, like the **Hall of Jade Billows**, where she kept Emperor Guangxu under house arrest.

The **Wenchang Gallery** *(☎ 6288 1144 ext 224; admission Y10; open 8.30am-4.30pm*

On Your Bike

It's Běijīng's broad avenues, tree-lined side streets and narrow *hútòng* (atmospheric, winding alleyways, some of which date back 500 years) that lend the city its unique character. A taxi goes either too quickly for you to catch the details, or too slowly to sustain interest; chronic traffic jams can make bicycle travel not just more adventurous, but more efficient as well.

Běijīng is a sprawling metropolis…but it is flat and ideal for cycling. Much of Běijīng life is lived on the street, too. For an evening's entertainment, people fly kites or throw frisbees in Tiānānmén Square. Elsewhere, under the Imperial Palace walls, young people dance to rock, and older ones gather for ballroom dancing. Clusters of neighbours squat under streetlights to gossip and play cards. Street stalls offer kitchenware, silk, vegetables, noodles and even banquets. Repairmen, upholsterers and house painters jostle on footpaths with their toolboxes.

You may cycle past dentists extracting teeth, barbers doing short-back-and-sides, teenage boys shooting pool, old men taking constitutionals, caged birds in hand. Magicians, 'miracle medicine' salesmen and all sorts of other street performers compete for attention. Tables spill out of restaurants onto the pavement, and brawlers tumble out of bars and karaoke clubs.

Cars, trucks, motorcycles and buses caught in the hideous traffic jams of the inner city rev their motors impatiently. Tempers flare and great bouts of cursing add to the commotion.

The bustle can seem daunting. But you quickly work out how to weave around the horse-drawn carts and negotiate the buses and trams that seem to dip into the bike lanes from nowhere. You learn that crossing large intersections is best done in clusters: opportunistic alliances that are tight as the traffic policemen's white gloves. You find that, unless it's very late, there's almost nowhere you can break down, or get a flat, that's too far from the roadside stand of an itinerant bicycle repairman. With luck, you won't discover that the easiest way to get into a fight in Běijīng is to run into another bicycle.

There are places in Běijīng that really only ought to be seen by bicycle; places of such magic that only the breeze on your face convinces you they're for real. One is the moat around the Forbidden City, traversable around the eastern side of the palace. On one side of the path the clay-red wall of the Imperial Palace, with its crenellated battlements, rears up. Ornamental guard towers with flying eaves and roofs of gold jag into view at each corner. On the other side, through weeping willows, you see lotuses, and fishermen lounging as pleasure boats stir up ripples on the still water of the moat. Fabulous by day, the moat is enchanting by night. If you start at the front of the palace, by Tiānānmén Square, when you come out the back you're just a short ride to the even more spectacular 'back lakes' – Hòuhǎi and Qiánhǎi.

Villas that once belonged to princes (now the abodes of the communist nomenklatura) line these man-made lakes, along with sprawling dazayuar, labyrinthine courtyard houses shared by dozens of families. The majestic Drum Tower, where once imperial timekeepers beat out the hours of the day, looms over the scene. In summer, the paths are lively with strollers, lovers and locals trying their luck with rod and reel. In winter, a blanket of snow freshens the Běijīng grey; no sooner does the lake freeze over than it swarms with skaters.

Linda Jaivin

 Linda Jaivin is a writer and translator. Her books include *Confessions of an S&M Virgin, Eat Me* and *Rock n Roll Babes from Outer Space*

daily) to the left and rear of the entrance of the Summer Palace is a quiet escape from the hordes rampaging through the palace. The galleries, set in a clean and engaging pocket of repro-Qing architecture, comprise a porcelain exhibition (save your sighs for the Shanghai Museum), a jade gallery and an unusual selection of Qing artefacts including some of the 'Old Buddha' Cixi's calligraphy, plus some decent bronzes.

You can get around the lake by hiring a small motorboat or rowing boat. Boating and swimming are popular pastimes for the locals, and skating is possible in winter.

The park is about 12km north-west of the centre of Běijīng. You can get there by taking the subway to Xīzhímén (close to the zoo), then a minibus. A number of buses can get you to the Summer Palace, including Nos 303, 330, 332, 333, 346, 362, 375, 801, 808 (from the Front Gate) and 817. You can also get there by bicycle; it takes about 1½ to two hours from the centre of town. Cycling along the road following the Běijīng-Mìyún Diversion Canal is more pleasant than taking the main roads.

Old Summer Palace 圆明园遗址
Yuánmíng Yuán Yízhǐ
Located north-west of the city centre, the original Summer Palace *(Běijīng map; ☎ 6262 8501; admission Y10-15; open 7am-7pm daily)* was laid out in the 12th century. Resourceful Jesuits were later employed by Emperor Qianlong to fashion European-style palaces for the gardens, with elaborate fountains and baroque statuary.

During the Second Opium War (1860), British and French troops destroyed the palace and sent the booty abroad. Much went up in flames, but a melancholic array of broken columns and marble chunks remain.

Trot through the southern stretch of hawkers and arcade games to the more subdued ruins of the European Palace in the **Eternal Spring Garden** *(Chángchūn Yuán)* to the north-east. Alternatively enter by the east gate that leads to the palace vestiges. It's here that you can find the **Great Fountain Ruins**, considered the best-preserved relic in the palace.

West of the ruins you can lose your way in an artful reproduction of a former labyrinth, the **Garden of Yellow Flowers**.

The gardens cover a huge area – some 2.5km from east to west – so be prepared for some walking. Besides the ruins, there's the western section, the **Perfection and Brightness Garden** *(Yuánmíng Yuán)* and the southern compound, the **10,000 Spring Garden** *(Wànchūn Yuán)*. To get to the Old Summer Palace, take minibus No 375 from the Xīzhímén subway station. Minibuses also connect the new Summer Palace with the old one, or a taxi will take you for Y10.

Xiāngshān Gōngyuán 香山公园
Fragrant Hills Park
Easily within striking distance of the Summer Palace is Xī Shān (Western Hills), another former villa-resort of the emperors. The part of Xī Shān closest to Běijīng is known as **Xiāng Shān** *(Běijīng map; admission Y5; open 6am-7pm daily)*. This is the last stop for the city buses – if you want to go farther into the mountains, you'll have to walk, cycle or take a taxi.

You can either scramble up the slopes to the top of **Incense-Burner Peak** *(Xiānglú Fēng)* or take the chairlift (Y30/50 one way/return), which operates from 8.30am to 5pm daily. From the peak you get an all-embracing view of the countryside.

Near the North Gate of Xiāngshān Gōngyuán is **Bìyún Sì** *(Azure Clouds Temple; ☎ 6259 1155 ext 470; admission Y10; open 8am-5pm daily)*, which dates back to the Yuan dynasty. It took a hammering during the Cultural Revolution and reopened in 1979. The Mountain Gate Hall contains two vast protective deities: 'Heng' and 'Ha'. Next is a small courtyard containing a drum and bell towers, leading to a hall with a wonderful statue of Milefo: it's bronze, but coal black with age. Only his big toe shines from numerous inquisitive fingers.

The next hall contains statues of Sakyamuni and Bodhisattvas Manjushri, Samantabhadra and Avalokiteshvara (Guanyin), plus 18 Luohan; a marvellous golden carved dragon soars above Sakyamuni. A statue of Guanyin stands at the rear, atop a fish.

The Hall of Bodhisattvas contains Wenshu, Guanyin, Dashizhi, Puxian and Dizang, plus further immortals. The Sun Yatsen Memorial Hall contains a statue and a glass coffin donated by the USSR on the death of Mr Sun.

At the very back is the marble Vajra Throne Pagoda where Sun Yatsen was interred after he died and before his body was moved to its final resting place in Nánjīng. The Hall of Arhats contains 500 statues of the Luohan.

There are a few ways to get to Xiāng Shān by public transport: you can take bus No 333 from the Summer Palace, bus No 360 from the zoo or bus No 318 from Píngguǒyuán (the very last stop west on the subway).

Fragrant Hills Botanical Gardens
香山植物园
Xiāngshān Zhíwùyuán
The well-tended and clean Botanical Gardens *(Běijīng map; ☎ 6259 1283; admission Y5; open 6am-8pm daily)*, set against the backdrop of Xī Shān and 2km east of Xiāngshān Gōngyuán, make for a pleasant outing among bamboo fronds, pines and lilacs. The **Beijing Botanical Gardens Conservatory** *(admission Y40)*, built in 1999, contains 3000 different types of plants and a rainforest house.

Within the grounds and about a 15-minute walk from the front gate (follow the signs) is the **Wòfó Sì** *(Temple of the Reclining Buddha; ☎ 6259 1561; admission Y5; open 8am-5pm daily)*. First built in the Tang dynasty, the temple's centrepiece is a huge reclining effigy of Sakyamuni weighing 54 tonnes, which apparently 'enslaved 7,000 people' in its casting.

On each side of Buddha are sets of gargantuan shoes, gifts to Sakyamuni from various emperors in case he went for a stroll. Above him are the apt characters *'Zìzai Dàdé'*, meaning, 'great accomplishment comes from being at ease'. Other halls include effigies of Milefo and Weituo, the Four Heavenly Kings, Golden Buddhas and Guanyin. The temple is near the Magnolia Garden, which flowers profusely in spring.

Zhōngshān Gōngyuán 中山公园
This lovely little park *(☎ 6605 4594; admission Y3; open 6am-9pm daily)* sits to the south-west of the Forbidden City, with a section hedging up against the palace moat. Clean, quiet and tidy, it's a refreshing prologue or conclusion to the magnificence of the adjacent imperial residence.

Jǐngshān Gōngyuán 景山公园
Prospect Hill Park
North of the Forbidden City, Jǐngshān Gōngyuán *(☎ 6403 3225; admission Y2; open 6am-9.30pm daily)*, also called Coal Hill in legation days, was shaped from the earth excavated to create the palace moat. Clamber to the top of this regal pleasure garden for a magnificent panorama of the capital and a great overview of the russet roofing of the Forbidden City.

On the eastern side of the park a locust tree stands in the place where the last of the Ming emperors, Chongzhen, hanged himself as rebels swarmed at the city walls. The hill supposedly protects the palace from the evil spirits – or dust storms – from the north.

Běihǎi Gōngyuán 北海公园
North Sea Park
Approached by four gates, Běihǎi Gōngyuán *(☎ 6407 1415; admission Y5; open 6am-9pm daily)* is largely made up of Běihǎi Hú (North Sea Lake).

The park, covering an area of 68 hectares, was the former playground of the emperors. **Jade Islet** in the lower middle is composed of the heaped earth excavated to create the lake – some attribute this to Kublai Khan.

The site is associated with the Great Khan's palace, the navel of Běijīng before the creation of the Forbidden City. All that remains of the Khan's court is a large jar made of green jade, in the Round City near the southern entrance.

Dominating Jade Islet, the 36m-high **White Dagoba** was originally built in 1651 for a visit by the Dalai Lama and was rebuilt in 1741. On the north-eastern shore of the islet is the handsome, double-tiered **Painted Gallery** *(Huàláng)*. Near the boat dock is Fángshàn Fànzhuāng (see Places to Eat later in this chapter), a restaurant that dishes up imperial recipes that were favoured by Empress Cixi. She liked 120-course dinners with about 30 kinds of desserts.

The **Xītiān Fànjǐng** *(admission free with Běihǎi Gōngyuán ticket)*, on the northern shore, is one of the city's most captivating temples. The Dàcízhēnrú Hall contains three huge Buddhist images; the golden statue of Guanyin at the rear is sadly unapproachable. The nearby **Nine Dragon Screen** *(Jiǔlóng Bì)*, a 5m-high and 27m-long spirit wall, is a glimmering stretch of coloured glazed tiles.

Běihǎi Gōngyuán is a relaxing place to take a stroll, grab a snack, sip a beer, rent a rowing boat or, as the Chinese do, cuddle on a bench in the evening. It's crowded on weekends. In winter there's ice skating.

Tiāntán Gōngyuán 天坛公园
Temple of Heaven Park

The most perfect example of Ming architecture, the **Temple of Heaven** *(Tiāntán; ☎ 6702 2242, Tiantan Donglu; admission low season Y10-30, high season Y15-35; park open 6am-9pm, sights open 8am-6pm daily)* has come to symbolise Běijīng. It appears in countless pieces of tourist literature and as a brand name for a wide range of products from Tiger Balm to plumbing fixtures. It is set in the 267-hectare Tiāntán Gōngyuán, with four gates at the compass points and bounded by walls to the north and east. It originally functioned as a vast stage for solemn rites performed by the Son of Heaven, who came here to pray for good harvests, seek divine clearance and atone for the sins of the people.

The temples, seen in aerial perspective, are round and the bases are square, deriving from the ancient Chinese belief that heaven is round, and the earth is square. Thus the northern end of the park is semi-circular and the southern end is square.

The 5m-high **Round Altar** *(Yuánqiū)* was constructed in 1530 and rebuilt in 1740. It is composed of white marble arrayed in three tiers, and its geometry revolves around the imperial number nine. Odd numbers were considered heavenly, and nine is the largest single-digit odd number. The top tier, thought to symbolise heaven, has nine rings

of stones, each composed of multiples of nine stones, so that the ninth ring has 81 stones. The number of stairs and balustrades are also multiples of nine. If you stand in the centre of the upper terrace and say something, the sound waves are bounced off the marble balustrades, amplifying your voice.

Just north of the altar, surrounding the entrance to the Imperial Vault of Heaven, is the **Echo Wall** *(Huíyīnbì)*, 65m in diameter. A whisper can travel clearly from one end to your friend's ear at the other – that is, if there's not a tour group in the middle.

The octagonal **Imperial Vault of Heaven** was built at the same time as the Round Altar, and is structured along the lines of the older Hall of Prayer for Good Harvests. It used to contain tablets of the emperor's ancestors, which were used in the winter solstice ceremony.

The dominant feature of the whole complex is the **Hall of Prayer for Good Harvests** *(Qínián Diàn)*, a magnificent piece mounted on a three-tiered marble terrace. Amazingly, the wooden pillars support the ceiling without nails or cement – for a building 38m high and 30m in diameter, that's quite an accomplishment. Built in 1420, the hall was hit by a lightning bolt during the reign of Guangxu in 1889 and a faithful reproduction based on Ming architectural methods was erected the following year.

MUSEUMS & GALLERIES
National Museum of Chinese History 中国历史博物馆
Zhōngguó Lìshǐ Bówùguǎn

The National Museum of Chinese History *(☎ 6512 8321)* is one of Běijīng's largest museums. However, at the time of writing it had been closed for some time, probably not to reopen until some time in 2003. It is housed in a sombre building on Tiānānmén Square. There are actually two museums here – the **Museum of History** and the **Chinese Revolution History Museum** *(Zhōngguó Gémìng Lìshǐ Bówùguǎn)*.

Military Museum 军事博物馆
Jūnshì Bówùguǎn

Wandering into the Military Museum *(Běijīng map; ☎ 6851 4441, 9 Fuxing Lu; admission Y5; open 8.30am-5pm daily)* you are greeted by a statue of Mao and his car plus huge portraits of fellow travellers

Lenin, Marx and Stalin. Beyond are Cold War-era F-5 fighters (as featured in parks all over China), the much larger F-7 and F-8, tanks and near the stairs two large HQ-2 (Red Flag-2) surface-to-air missiles. Upstairs bristles with more weaponry and a heavy going gallery of statues of military and political top brass. Farther upstairs, two large halls tackle historic wars, including the Korean War. The top floor has exhibitions detailing the Opium War, the Taiping and the Boxers. There are limited English captions only in the upper gallery. Take the subway to its namesake Jūnshì Bówùguǎn stop. Last entry is at 4pm.

Natural History Museum 自然博物馆
Zìrán Bówùguǎn

The main entrance hall to the overblown, creeper-laden 1950s building that is the Natural History Museum (☎ 6702 3096, 126 Tianqiao Nandajie; admission Y15; open 8.30am-5pm daily) is hung with portraits of great natural historians, including Darwin and Linnaeus (here spelled Linnacus).

Some exhibits, such as the spliced human cadavers and genitalia, are best seen on an empty stomach. Check out the dinosaurs that used to roam China, such as the possibly beer-drinking Tsingtaosaurus (Qingdaolong) named after the beach resort. Other exhibition halls offer a ghastly menagerie of creatures suspended in formaldehyde.

Coming at you in the human evolution chamber upstairs is a posse of apemen in Socialist Realist pose. Exhibits have limited English captions.

The Arthur M Sackler Museum of Art & Anthropology

Tucked away in Beijing University, this museum (Běijīng map; ☎ 6275 1667; admission Y5; open 9am-4.30pm daily) is one of the capital's more stimulating museums. There's a fine collection of ancient pottery and some excellent examples of porcelain from later dynasties.

Madam Song's Residence
宋庆龄故居
Sòng Qìnglíng Gùjū

Madam Song was the second wife of Dr Sun Yatsen, who went on to become the first president of the Republic of China. After 1981, Madam Song's large residence

was transformed into a museum (☎ 6404 4205, 46 Houhai Bei'an; admission Y10; open 9am-4.30pm Tues-Sun). The beautiful residence is set in a charming area of hútòng, but the exhibits are hampered by a dearth of English captions.

Former Home of Lao She
老舍纪念馆
Lǎo Shě Jìniànguǎn

This little courtyard museum (19 Fengfu Hutong; admission Y5; open 9am-5pm Tues-Sun) is dedicated to one of Běijīng's most famous writers of the 20th century. Author of Rickshaw Boy and Tea House, Lao She (1899–1966) tragically committed suicide by throwing himself into a Běijīng lake during the Cultural Revolution 'after suffering gross injustice and persecution from extreme left-wing forces', as a current guide puts it. There are no English captions and the museum is located off Dengshikou Xijie.

Art Galleries

The art scene in Běijīng has really surfaced, and an exciting choice of galleries offloads art into the hands of a growing monied class. The following should give you an idea of current directions in Chinese art.

The **China Art Gallery** (Zhōngguó Měishùguǎn; ☎ 6401 7076, 1 Wusi Dajie; admission Y4; open 9am-5pm Tues-Sun) has a range of progressive paintings and occasional photographic exhibitions. The museum building could do with a revamp and is outshone by the often colourful and vivid works on view. Foreign pieces seem somewhat naive, but the Chinese works are fresh and invigorating. There are no English captions, but it's still a first rate place to see modern Chinese art, and maybe just as importantly, to watch the Chinese looking at art. Last entry is at 4pm.

The **Red Gate Gallery** (*Hóngmén Huàláng;* ☎ *6525 1005,* W *www.china .redgate-gallery.com, Levels 1&4, Dongbianmen Watchtower; open 10am-5pm Tues-Sun*) has a selection of inventive art works from China's increasingly inventive garret community.

The **Courtyard Gallery** (*Sìhéyuàn;* ☎ *6526 8882, 95 Donghuamen Dajie; open 10am-7pm daily*) has avant-garde exhibits nestled next to the moat of the very un-avant-garde Forbidden City. It has a good restaurant The Courtyard (see Places to Eat, later). The **Kebab Cafe Gallery** is another cafe (see Places to Eat) featuring an art gallery.

Just around the corner from the Forbidden City, the **Wan Fung Art Gallery** (*Yúnfēng Huàyuàn;* ☎ *6523 3320,* W *www.wanfung .com.cn, 136 Nanchizi Dajie*) is set in a gorgeous courtyard annex to the imperial palace. It features exciting and colourful art.

TEMPLES & MOSQUES
Lama Temple 雍和宫
Yōnghé Gōng

The Lama Temple (☎ *6404 9027, 12 Yonghegong Dajie; admission Y15; open 9am-4.30pm daily*) is by far the most colourful temple in Běijīng – beautiful rooftops, stunning frescoes, tapestries, incredible carpentry and a great pair of Chinese lions. Get to this one before you're 'templed out' – the complex is simply vast.

The Lama Temple is the most renowned Tibetan Buddhist temple outside Tibet. North-west of the city centre overlooking Andingmen Dongdajie, it became the official residence of Count Yin Zhen after extensive renovation. There was nothing unusual in that, but in 1723 he was promoted to emperor and moved to the Forbidden City. His name was changed to Yong Zheng, and his former residence became Yonghe Palace. In 1744 it was converted into a lamasery and became a residence for large numbers of monks from Mongolia and Tibet.

The temple's most prized possession is its 55-foot high sandalwood statue of the Maitreya Buddha in the Wanfu Pavilion. An absorbing exhibition at the rear displays numerous Tibetan items and chronicles the lineage of the Dalai Lamas.

To get to the temple, get off at the Yōnghégōng subway station.

Kǒng Miào & Imperial College
孔庙
Confucian Temple & Guózǐjiān

Just down the hútòng opposite the gates of the Lama Temple is Kǒng Miào (☎ *8401 1977, 13 Guozijian Jie; admission Y10; open 8.30am-5pm daily*), the second-largest Confucian temple in China after the one at Qūfù, and the Imperial College.

The temple feels forlorn and untended (someone should really take a feather duster to it), but it's a quiet sanctuary from Běijīng's congested streets and snarling traffic. It may not be worth a trip in itself, but its proximity to the Lama Temple makes for a useful escape from the crowds at the latter.

The grounds are home to cypresses and hundreds of steles that record the names of successful candidates of the highest level of the official Confucian examination system. One of Běijīng's last remaining *páilou*, or ornamental arches, bravely survives in the hútòng outside, awaiting its denouement with future road-widening schemes.

The Imperial College was the place where the emperor expounded the Confucian classics to an audience of thousands of kneeling students, professors and court officials – an annual rite.

Dōngyuè Sì 东岳寺

Běijīng hasn't many temples dedicated to Laotzu, but this abode (☎ *6553 2184, Chaoyangmenwai Dajie; admission Y10; open 6am-7pm Tues-Sun*) of the Taoist spirit world is a triumphant restoration. Its roots are somewhere in the Yuan dynasty, and what's above ground level has been recently revived with care, attention and a huge cash injection. The temple is an active place where Taoist monks attend to a world entirely at odds with the surrounding glass and steel high rises.

The huge courtyard of Dōngyuè Sì is surrounded on all sides with heavenly departments, each in charge of different aspects of existence. Worried about your finances? Make a deposit at the Department for Bestowing Material Happiness. Concerned about China's environment? Pay a visit to the Department of the Preservation of

Wilderness. Life-sized painted clay figures – many of which are half animal, painted in garish colours, donning menacing expressions and brandishing painful-looking weapons – depict each department. There are also English explanations of each department's function.

Dàzhōng Sì 大钟寺
Great Bell Temple

Dàzhōng Sì (*Běijīng map;* ☎ *6255 0819, 31a Beisanhuan Xilu; admission Y10; open 8.30am-4.30pm daily*) houses the biggest bell in China, 6.75m tall and weighing a hefty 46.5 tonnes. The bell is inscribed with Buddhist sutras, comprising over 227,000 Chinese characters, and decorated with Sanskrit incantations. Clamber up to the circular hall (admission Y2), where there's a small exhibition on bell casting (some English) and chuck a coin through the opening in the top of the bell for luck.

The bell was cast in 1406 during the reign of Ming Emperor Yongle, and the tower was built in 1733. Getting the bell from the foundry to the temple proved difficult: a shallow canal was built and when it froze over in winter the bell was moved across the ice by sled.

Also on view in one of the other halls is a collection of bells from the Marquis Zeng of Yi, similar to those at the Hubei Provincial Museum in Wǔhàn. Take bus No 302, 300 or 367.

Miàoyīng Temple White Dagoba
妙应寺白塔
Miàoyīng Sì Báitǎ

The Yuan dynasty white dagoba of Miàoyīng Sì (☎ *6616 0211, 171 Fuchengmennei Dajie; admission Y10; open 9am-4pm daily*) is similar to that in Běihǎi Gōngyuán. The highpoint of a visit here is an absolutely fascinating collection of thousands of Tibetan Buddhist statues. There's liberal use of English captions. Take bus No 13, 101, 102 or 103 to the Báitǎ Sì stop.

Guǎngjì Sì 广济寺
Universal Rescue Temple

The Guǎngjì Sì (☎ *6616 0907, cnr Xisi Beidajie & Fuchengmennei Dajie; admission free; open 8.30am-4.30pm daily*) is the headquarters of the Chinese Buddhist Association. With a history of over 800 years,

the temple has an assortment of steles in its tree-shaded courtyard and Buddhist gifts from numerous nations.

Niújiē Lǐbài Sì 牛街礼拜寺
Cow Street Mosque

This fascinating mosque (☎ *6353 2564, 88 Niu Jie; admission Y10, Muslims free; open 8am-sunset daily*) was designed in a Chinese temple style. With a history dating back to the 10th century AD, the mosque is the largest in town, and is also the burial site for a number of Islamic clerics. The temple is given over to a profusion of greenery, trees, flourishes of Arabic, the main prayer hall (you can only enter if you are Muslim), the women's quarters and the Wàngyuèlóu 'Building for Observing the Moon', from where the lunar calendar was calculated. Dress appropriately (no shorts or short skirts).

Fǎyuán Sì 法源寺
Source of Law Temple

This bustling temple (☎ *6353 3966, 7 Fayuansi Qianjie; admission Y5; open 8.30am-11.20am & 1.30pm-3.30pm Thur-Tues*) was originally constructed in the 7th century and is still going strong. It's now the China Buddhism College. A visit here is like going to a college campus – students playing table tennis during the break and hanging out and chatting – except the students are monks dressed in Buddhist yellow robes. Don't miss the hall at the very back of the temple, which houses an unusual copper Buddha seated upon a thousand-petal lotus flower. From the entrance of Niújiē Lǐbài Sì, walk left 100m then turn left into the first hútòng. Follow the hútòng for about 10 minutes and you'll arrive at Fǎyuán Sì.

White Cloud Temple 白云观
Báiyún Guàn

White Cloud Temple (☎ *6346 3531, Baiyun Lu; admission Y8; open 8.30am-4.30pm daily May-Sept, 8.30am-4pm daily Oct-Apr*), once the Taoist centre of northern China, was founded in AD 739. This fascinating temple complex, tended by distinctive Taoist monks and the centre of operations for the Quanzhen School, has a number of halls and shrines, and a pool. Walk south on Baiyun Lu and cross the moat. Continue south along Baiyun Lu and turn into a curving street on the left; follow it for 250m to the temple entrance.

To Summer Palace
& Beijing University

Second Ring Road

Zhongguancun Nandajie

Third Ring Road

Gaoliangqiao Lu

Deshengmen Xidajie

Beijing North
Train Station

1

Zizhuyuan Lu

Xisihuan Beilu

积水潭
Jīshuǐtán

XICHENG
DISTRICT

3

后海
Hòuhǎi
Hú

4

Zizhúyuàn
Gōngyuán

Beijing
Zoo

Beijing
Exhibition
Centre

西直门
Xīzhímén

Xizhimennei Dajie

Xinjiekou Nandajie

Dershengmennei Dajie

Xizhimenwai Dajie 西直门外大街

Xizhimen Nandajie

2

Chegongzhuang Xilu

Chegongzhuang Dajie

Ping'anli Xidajie

Di'anmen Xidajie

Chēgōngzhuāng
车公庄

M

Zhenguang Lu

Sanlihe Lu

Zhanlanguan Lu

Zhaodengyu Lu

Xisi Beidajie

Xishiku Dajie

Fucheng Lu

Fuchengmenwai Dajie

55

阜城门
Fùchéngmén

54

53

Fuchengmennei Dajie 阜成门内大街

Xianmen Dajie

Zhōngnánhǎ

56

Yùyuāntán
Gōngyuán

Yùyuāntán
Hú

Yuètán
Gōngyuán

Fuchengmen Dajie

西单北大街

Bayi Hú

Sanlihe Donglu

复兴门
Fùxīngmén

西单
Xīdān

Xidan Beidajie

107 106

Gōngzhǔfén

M

Fuxingmenwai Dajie

南礼士路
Nánlǐshìlù

Sanlihe Donglu

Bayun Lu

Fuxingmennei Dajie 复兴门内大街

105

Xisihuan Zhonglu

Jūnshìbówùguǎn

Mùxidi
木樨地

M

108

Xichang'an Jie

Fuxingme Dajie

Xuanwumennei Dajie

和平门
Hépíngmén

109

Lianhuachi Donglu

Chángchūnjiē
长春街

M

Xuānwǔmén
宣武门

M

110

Beijing West
Train Station
北京西火车站

Lianhua
Pond

Lianhuachi
Gōngyuán

Guang'anmenwai Dajie

Guang'anmennei Dajie 广安门内大街

Luomashi Dajie

119

Guang'an Lu

XUANWU
DISTRICT

Niu Jie

122

120

121

Nanheng Xijie

Guang'anmen Binhe Lu

0   0.5   1km
0   0.25   0.5mi

Grand View
Garden

Táorántíng
Gōngyuán

124

You'anmen Dongbinhe Lu 友安门东滨河路
123

Fengtai Beilu

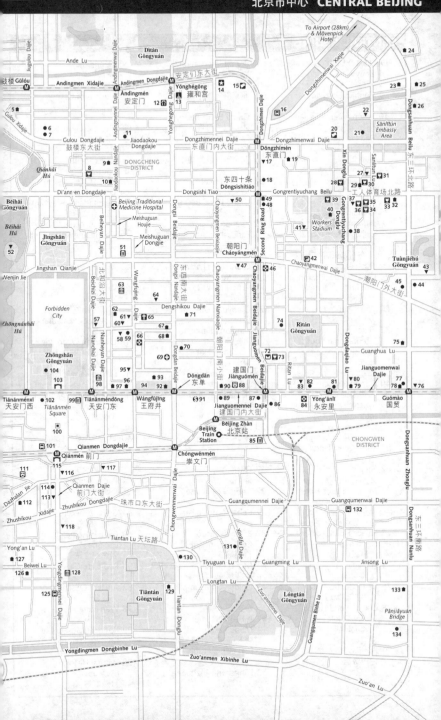

BEIJING

CENTRAL BĚIJĪNG

PLACES TO STAY

5 Zhúyuán Bīnguǎn
竹园宾馆
9 Yǒuhǎo Bīnguǎn
友好宾馆
10 Lǔsōngyuán Bīnguǎn
侣松园宾馆
19 Red House
23 Kūnlún Fàndiàn
昆仑饭店
24 Hilton Hotel;
Louisiana
希尔顿大酒店；
路易斯安娜
25 Kempinski Hotel;
Lufthansa Center;
Beijing International
Medical Centre
凯宾斯基酒店；
燕沙商城
26 Great Wall Sheraton;
The British Council
长城饭店
29 Youyi Youth Hostel
友谊青年酒店
32 Zhaolong
International Youth
Hostel; Zhaolong
Hotel
兆龙青年旅舍
40 Gōngtǐ Bīnguǎn
工体宾馆
49 Swissôtel; Hong Kong
International Medical
Clinic
瑞士酒店
55 State Guest Hotel
国宾酒店
62 Fangyuan Hotel
芳园宾馆
67 Novotel Peace Hotel;
Le Coffee Shop
北京诺富特和平宾
馆；光临咖啡厅
68 Palace Hotel; Fortune
Garden
王府饭店
71 Hǎoyuán Bīnguǎn
好园宾馆
75 Kerry Centre Hotel
嘉里中心饭店
78 China World Hotel;
Trader's Hotel
中国大饭店；
国贸饭店
79 Jianguo Hotel
建国饭店

90 Beijing International
Youth Hostel; Beijing
International Hotel
北京国际青年旅舍；
北京国际饭店
92 Grand Hyatt Beijing
北京东方君悦大酒店
93 Eastern Morning Sun
Youth Hostel
北京东方晨光青年
旅馆
96 Beijing Hotel
北京饭店
97 Grand Hotel Beijing
贵宾楼饭店
112 Yuǎndōng Fàndiàn;
Far East Youth Hostel
远东饭店
119 Jianguo Hotel
Qianmen; Liyuan
Theatre
前门建国饭店；
梨园剧场
123 Qiáoyuán Fàndiàn
侨园饭店
124 Fènglóng Bīnguǎn
凤龙宾馆
126 Xiaoxiang Hotel
潇湘大酒店
127 Běiwěi Fàndiàn
北纬饭店
129 Tiāntán Hàoyuán
Bīnguǎn
天坛昊园宾馆
133 Lèyóu Fàndiàn
乐游饭店

PLACES TO EAT

17 Oasis
静颐洲
22 Green Tea House
紫云茗
27 Kebab Cafe Gallery
画廊
37 Berena's Bistro;
Century Antiques
伯瑞娜酒家
41 Metro Cafe
美特糕
43 Golden Cat Dumpling
City
金猫饺子城
47 A Fun Ti Hometown
Music Restaurant
阿凡提乡音乐餐厅
50 Red Capital Club
新红资
52 Fāngshān Fànzhuāng
芳山饭店

56 Néngrénjū
能仁居
57 The Courtyard;
Courtyard Gallery
四合院；
四合院画廊
58 Hong Kong Food City
香港美食城
60 Dōnghuámén Yèshì
东华门夜市
61 Starbucks
星巴克
64 Green Tianshi
Vegetarian Restaurant
绿天食饭店
76 Jinshancheng
Chongqing Restaurant
金山城重庆菜馆
80 Bleu Marine
83 Makye Ame
玛吉阿米
95 Wángfǔjǐng
Xiǎochījiē
王府井小吃街
113 First Floor Restaurant
第一楼饭店
116 Qianmen Quanjude
Roast Duck Restaurant
前门全聚德烤鸭店
117 Lìchún Kǎoyādiàn
利纯烤鸭店
118 Gongdelin Vegetarian
Restaurant
功德林素菜馆

MUSEUMS & GALLERIES

3 Madam Song's
Residence
宋庆龄故居
4 Prince Gong's
Residence
恭王府
51 China Art Gallery
中国美术馆
63 Former Home of
Lao She
老舍纪念馆
85 Red Gate Gallery
红门画廊
87 Ancient Observatory
古观象台
98 Wan Fung Art Gallery
云峰画苑
99 National Museum of
Chinese History
中国历史博物馆
128 Natural History
Museum
自然博物馆

CENTRAL BĚIJĪNG

OTHER PLACES TO SEE
Prince Gong's Residence 恭王府
Gōngwáng Fǔ

Reputed to be the model for the mansion in Cao Xueqin's 18th-century classic, *A Dream of Red Mansions,* this place (☎ 6616 8149, 14 Liuyin Jie; admission Y5; open 8.30am-4.30pm daily) is one of Běijīng's largest private residential compounds. Despite skulking ice cream sellers, it's a quiet and introspective place. This remains one of Běijīng's more attractive retreats, decorated with rockeries, plants, pools, pavilions, corridors and elaborately carved gateways. Guided tours are available and performances of Beijing opera are held regularly.

Drum Tower & Bell Tower 鼓楼, 钟楼
Gǔ Lóu & Zhōng Lóu

The Drum Tower (☎ 6401 2674, Gulou Dongdajie; admission Y6, with Bell Tower Y10; open 9am-4.30pm daily) was originally built in 1273, marking the centre of the old Mongol capital. It was rebuilt in 1420. Stagger up the incredibly steep steps for views over the Běijīng rooftops. The drums were beaten to mark the hours of the day – in effect the Big Ben of Běijīng. Time was kept with a water clock.

Behind the Drum Tower, down an alley farther north, is the Bell Tower (☎ 6401 2674; admission Y6, with Drum Tower Y10; open 9am-4.30pm daily). This tower was built at the same time as the Drum Tower, but burnt down. The present structure dates from the 18th century. Both towers can be reached on bus No 5, 58 or 107 – get off at the namesake Gǔ Lóu stop.

Ancient Observatory 古观象台
Gǔguān Xiàngtái

Běijīng's quirky Ancient Observatory (☎ 6512 6923; admission Y10; open 9.30am-11.30am & 1pm-4.30pm Wed-Sun), mounted on the battlements of a watchtower, forlornly overlooks the traffic-clogged Second Ring Rd near Jianguomennei Dajie.

The observatory dates back to Kublai Khan's days, but the present building was built from 1437 to 1446.

Enter a courtyard on your right scattered with astronomical instruments. There are some inspiring pieces here featuring dragon designs – the mystical meets the scientific.

The equipment continues on the roof of the tower itself. Most specimens are of Chinese design, although the Azimuth Theodolite is clearly European, the work of Jesuits.

St Joseph's Church 东堂
Dōng Táng

One of the four principal churches in Běijīng, St Joseph's Church (74 Wangfujing Dajie; open 6.30am-7am Mon-Sat, 6.30am-8am Sun) is also called the East Cathedral. Originally built during the reign of Shunzhi in 1655, it was damaged by an earthquake in 1720 and rebuilt. The luckless church also caught fire in 1807, was destroyed again in 1900 during the Boxer Rebellion, and restored in 1904, only to be shut in 1966. The cathedral has been fully repaired and is now a more sublime feature of Wángfǔjǐng's commercial facelift. A large square in front swarms with children playing, as Chinese models in bridal outfits pose for magazine covers at the entrance. You can take in the church through the steam of a cappuccino at the coffee shop opposite.

Marco Polo Bridge 卢沟桥
Lúgōu Qiáo

Described by the great traveller himself in his writings, the 266m-long grey marble Marco Polo Bridge (Běijīng map; ☎ 8389 3919, 88 Lugouqiaochengnei Xijie; admission Y6; open 8am-5pm daily), is host to 485 carved stone lions. Each animal is different, with the smallest only a few centimetres high.

Dating from 1189, the stone bridge is Běijīng's oldest, and spans the river Yǒngdìng Hé near the little town of Wǎnpíng.

Long before CITS, Emperor Qianlong did his bit to promote the bridge, composing calligraphy now engraved into stone tablets on the site.

Despite the praises of Marco Polo and Emperor Qianlong, the bridge wouldn't have rated more than a footnote in Chinese history were it not for the famed Marco Polo Bridge Incident, which ignited a full-scale war with Japan. On 7 July 1937, Japanese troops illegally occupied a railway junction outside Wǎnpíng. Japanese and Chinese soldiers exchanged fire, and that gave Japan enough of an excuse to attack and occupy Běijīng.

The **Memorial Hall of the War of Resistance Against Japan** is a gory glance back at Japan's occupation of China, but the lack of English captions renders much of it meaningless. Also on the site are the **Wanping Castle**, the **Daìwáng Sì** and a tourist hotel.

The bridge and Memorial Hall are 16km south-west of the city centre and getting there is difficult. You can reach the bridge by taking bus No 339 from Liánhuāchí bus station (Běijīng map). Another option is bus No 309, which can be picked up at Liùlǐ Bridge; get off the bus at Xīdàokǒu and the bridge is just ahead.

Beijing Zoo 北京动物园
Běijīng Dòngwùyuán
All zoos are animal prisons, but Beijing Zoo (☎ 6832 1960, Xizhimenwai Dajie; admission with/without pandas Y7/5; open 7.30am-5.30pm daily) seems like death row. Most of the design features date from the 1950s – concrete and glass cells. At least the pandas have plusher living quarters (for good behaviour?).

The polar bears must pin all their hopes on graduating from their concrete hell to the marvellous **Beijing Aquarium** (adult/child Y100/50; open 9am-6pm daily summer, 9am-5.30pm daily rest-of-year), a first class addition in the northeast corner of the zoo – it's the largest inland aquarium in the world. On view are an imaginative Amazon rainforest area (complete with piranha), coral reefs, a shark aquarium (where you can go for dives), whales, dolphins and a marine mammal pavilion. The latter host lively aquatic animal displays. If you've kiddies in tow and they reckon the Temple of Heaven is a colossal bore, bring them here – they'll love it. Getting to the zoo is easy enough – take the subway to the Xīzhímén station. From there, it's a 15-minute walk to the west or a short ride on any of the trolleybuses.

PLACES TO STAY
If you arrive in town without hotel reservations and are planning to stay in a midrange or top-end hotel, stop by the airport hotel reservations counter, which has been known to give discounts of up to 50% off rack rates. The counter is located just outside the arrivals area, after you pass through customs.

PLACES TO STAY – BUDGET
Běijīng's budget options used to be badly located in the far-flung south, but bettersituated contenders have emerged. For the sake of definition, any hotel where a double can be had for less than Y200 in the high season is considered 'budget'. Dorm beds in the high season average around Y35.

Central Běijīng
The following places all appear on the Central Běijīng map.

Beijing International Youth Hostel (Běijīng Guójì Qīngnián Lǚshè; ☎ 6512 6688 ext 6145, fax 6522 9494, 10th floor, rear bldg, Beijing International Hotel, 9 Jianguomennei Dajie) Beds in 6- to 8-bed dorms with/without hostel card Y50/60, doubles with/without hostel card Y80/90. This hotel is a clean, bright, fresh and quiet addition to the budget circuit. It has an excellent central location and long views over the Běijīng rooftops at the rear. Washing machines (Y10), bike rental (Y300 deposit, Y5 per hour) and Internet access (Y20 per hour) are available. Showers and toilets are communal, but they're clean.

Zhaolong International Youth Hostel (Zhàolóng Qīngnián Lǚshè; ☎ 6597 2299, e zlh@zhaolonghotel.com.cn, 2 Gongrentiyuchang Beilu) Beds in 2-/3- to 6-bed dorms members Y60/50, non-members Y70/60. This is a first-rate place with clean rooms and access to the health centre and entertainment facilities of the 4-star Zhaolong Hotel behind. It has communal showers and is well-positioned for the nearby bars at Sānlǐtún.

Far East Youth Hostel (☎ 6301 8811, fax 6301 8233, 90 Tieshuxie Jie, Qianmenwai) Dorm beds low/high season Y45/60. This hostel is located in a wonderful historic courtyard at Yuǎndōng Fàndiàn (see Places to Stay – Mid-Range). It has four- and six-bed dorms and is exceptionally clean and well run, with polite staff, washing machines, bike rental and Internet access.

Lǚsōngyuán Bīnguǎn (☎ 6404 0436, fax 6403 0418, 22 Banchang Hutong) Dorm beds/singles/doubles Y98/284/450. North of the Forbidden City, this hútòng hotel has real character. Built by a Mongolian general in the Qing dynasty, it is an excellent base for exploring the city. Staff are friendly and there is bike rental for Y30 per day. For a double bed, book ahead as the hotel only has two (the other rooms have two single beds). There is a small sign (in English) on Jiaodaokou Nandajie. The hotel is about 50m down the alley. Take bus No 104 from Běijīng train station to the Běibīngmǎ Sì bus stop. Walk a short distance south then turn right down the first alley.

Youyi Youth Hostel (*Yǒuyì Qīngnián Jiǔdiàn;* ☎ *6417 2632, fax 6415 6866, 43 Beisanlitunnan)* Dorm beds Y70, singles or doubles Y180. This place is well located behind Kirin Plaza in the Sānlǐtún bar ghetto and has Internet service at Y10 per hour and free breakfast.

Red House (*Ruìxiù Bīnguǎn;* ☎ *6416 7500,* ⓦ *www.redhouse.com.cn, 10 Taiping Zhuangcun Xilu)* Dorm beds Y70, suites with kitchen & cable TV from Y300. Red House has Internet access (Y10 per hour), free breakfast, laundry and is near Běijīng's expat area, Sānlǐtún.

Fangyuan Hotel (*Fāngyuán Bīnguǎn;* ☎ *6525 6331, fax 6513 8549, 36 Dengshikou Xijie)* Singles/doubles Y126/198. In a fine central location off Wangfujing Dajie, this hotel has a business centre, restaurant, ticketing and laundry service. It is reasonably clean and efficient but there's no air-con.

Fènglóng Bīnguǎn (*Fenglong Youth Hostel;* ☎ *6353 6415, fax 6353 6452, 5 You'anmen Dongjie)* Dorm beds Y25-40, singles Y100-180, doubles Y158-220. This simple, fusty specimen is located on the south-eastern corner of the pleasant Tāoràntíng Gōngyuán.

Qiáoyuán Fàndiàn (*Qiaoyuan Hotel;* ☎ *6301 2244, fax 6303 0119, 135 You'anmen Dongbinhe Lu)* Beds in 2-/4-/10-bed north-block dorms Y40/25/15. Pricier doubles are available in the more attractive south block. This place has bike rental (Y5), a laundry service, Internet access plus a backpacker info office (☎ *8315 1553)*. It is, however, hobbled by a rather isolated location.

Gōngtǐ Bīnguǎn (☎ *6501 6655, fax 6501 2368, Workers Stadium)* Doubles with/without bath Y278/146. Located in the east side of the Workers Stadium, near Sānlǐtún's bar scene, this place is an OK budget option. It's a bit run down, but good value. Of course, if a sports match or concert is taking place in the stadium, prepare for much noise.

Eastern Morning Sun Youth Hostel (*Běijīng Dōngfāng Chénguāng Qīngnián Lǚguǎn;* ☎ *6528 4347,* ⓦ *www.addoil.com, Floor B4, 8-16 Dongdansantiao, Oriental Plaza)* Singles/twins/triples Y80/120/180. This place is slapbang in the centre of town. Besides its ideal location, it's fresh, neat with air-con, and there's a bar and travel service. It has communal showers and toilets. However, despite the name and hostel prices, it's not an official youth hostel and staff are unsure about admitting foreigners.

South Běijīng

The following places all appear on the Běijīng map.

Jinghua Youth Hostel (*Jīnghuá Fàndiàn;* ☎ *6722 2211, fax 6721 1671, Nansanhuan Zhonglu)* Beds in 6-/20-bed dorms Y40/25, twins with bath Y140-230. This place has travel information, bike rental (Y10), Great Wall trips and Internet access (Y10 per half hour). Bus No 66 from the Front Gate drops you off at nearby Yángqiáo. The hotel is east of a small river near a McDonald's.

Sea Star Hotel (*Hǎixīng Dàjiǔdiàn;* ☎ *6721 8855, fax 6722 7915, 166 Haihutun)* Dorm beds/twins Y35/180. This so-so hotel is just around the corner from the Jinghua Youth Hostel with rooms that tend to fill up fast.

Lihua Hotel (*Lìhuá Fàndiàn;* ☎ *6756 1144, fax 6721 1367, 71 Majiapu Donglu)* Dorm beds/twins Y35/198. This is a well-established backpacker's haven. Bus No 14 from Xīdān and Hépíngmén subway stations is the easiest way to get there.

PLACES TO STAY – MID-RANGE

Following are hotels with twin rooms in the Y200 to Y600 range. If you can, stay in a courtyard hotel, which mostly fall within this range (also see Places to Stay – Budget earlier), for a more traditional experience buried quietly away amid Běijīng's remaining hútòng.

Bargaining for a room is possible in some cases – politely ask for a 'discount'. Many travellers negotiate discounts of 30% or more, at least during the winter low season.

The following hotels appear on the Central Běijīng map.

Hǎoyuán Bīnguǎn (*Haoyuan Guesthouse;* ☎ *6512 5557, fax 6525 3179, 53 Shijia*

Hutong) Twins Y360-450. This quiet courtyard hotel is a 10-minute walk from Wángfǔjǐng's main drag, and has comfortable, clean rooms. Walk north on Dongdan Beidajie and about 25m before Dengshikou Dajie you'll see a small alley – Shijia Hutong – off to the right. The hotel is about 200m down the alley on your left; look out for a set of red gates and two stone lions.

Tiāntán Hàoyuán Bīnguǎn (☎ 6711 3388, fax 6711 5388, 9a Tiantan Donglu) Twins Y260. This well-kept, stylish courtyard hotel is in the first hútòng on your right (you'll see a large páilou) south of the east gate of Tiāntán Gōngyuán. It was being renovated at the time of writing.

Zhúyuán Bīnguǎn (Bamboo Garden Hotel; ☎ 6403 2229, W www.bbgh.com.cn, 24 Xiaoshiqiao Hutong) Singles/doubles/suites Y300/380/1200. This cozy, intimate and tranquil courtyard hotel is in a hútòng not far from the Drum and Bell towers. The buildings date back to the late Qing dynasty, while the gardens belonged to a eunuch from Empress Cixi's entourage. The hotel gets good reviews and offers a genuine, historical angle from which to view China's capital. Stays of four days or more warrants free airport pickup and drop-off.

Yuǎndōng Fàndiàn (Far East Hotel; ☎ 6301 8811, fax 6301 8233, 90 Tieshuxie Jie) Doubles Y410, twins Y310-398. With a fine location among the hútòng, this hotel is at the western end of Dàshílàr.

Běiwěi Fàndiàn (☎ 6301 2266, fax 6301 1366, 11 Xijing Lu) Singles/doubles Y349/630. To the west of Tiāntán Gōngyuán, this recently renovated place has clean rooms. Ask for discounts.

Xiaoxiang Hotel (Xiāoxiāng Dàjiǔdiàn; ☎ 8316 1188, fax 6303 0690, 42 Beiwei Lu) Singles Y580. This is a clean, well-kept and fresh three-star hotel very close to the west gate of the Temple of Heaven in Tiāntán Gōngyuán. It also has a restaurant specialising in fiery Húnán cuisine. Discounts trim the price for a single to Y380.

Lèyóu Fàndiàn (☎ 6771 2266, fax 6771 1636, 13 Dongsanhuan Nanlu) Doubles from Y320. Just around the corner from Pānjiāyuán market (aka the Dirt Market), this small hotel is nothing special, but rooms are clean and in good shape. Rates include breakfast.

Yǒuhǎo Bīnguǎn (☎ 6403 1114, fax 6401 4603, 7 Houyuansi Hutong) Singles/doubles Y296/392. In a hútòng just off Jiaodaokou Nandajie, this was once the residence of Chiang Kaishek, and after 1949 the site of the Yugoslav Embassy. Today it's a nice but slightly run-down courtyard hotel.

Jianguo Hotel Qianmen (Qiánmén Jiànguó Fàndiàn; ☎ 6301 6688, fax 6301 3883, 175 Yong'an Lu) Singles/doubles Y725/848. This popular, large hotel is well situated for Tiānānmén Square and the Temple of Heaven. It is home to the Liyuan Theatre with its regular performances of Beijing opera. Rates include breakfast.

PLACES TO STAY – TOP END

Běijīng has fine international-standard hotels. None can really be called 'great hotels' of breathtaking character – but some are crafty imitations. Most are modern, history-free capsules from the recent construction boom era. Facilities and standards of accommodation are however, generally high. English is generally only spoken well at the superior establishments.

For definition purposes, anything costing over Y700 for a standard twin room is called 'top end'. Listed are a selection of Běijīng's top five-star hotels, followed by good-value, centrally located three- and four-star hotels. There is usually a 15% service charge on top of the room rate. As with mid-range hotels, discounts of 30% or more are often available if you ask. Unless otherwise indicated, all hotels appear on the Central Běijīng map.

Grand Hyatt Beijing (☎ 8518 1234, W www.hyatt.com, 1 Dongchang'an Jie) Doubles US$300. This gorgeous hotel is at an exclusive address overlooking Oriental Plaza, with top-notch design, splendid interior, exemplary service and undeniable opulence. It is right in the shopping district of Wángfǔjǐng – the Forbidden City is a 10-minute walk away – and opened late 2001. Ask for promotional prices.

Beijing Hotel (Běijīng Fàndiàn; ☎ 6513 7766, W www.chinabeijinghotel.com, 33 Dongchang'an Jie) Twins US$160, suites US$300-350. Opened in 1900, this is Běijīng's oldest hotel. After a fine refit, this hotel is set to reclaim its crown as one of the capital's best. Outfitted in shimmering marble, lacquer and polished wood flooring, the hotel is perched on Wángfǔjǐng's southern extremity.

Palace Hotel (*Wángfǔ Fàndiàn;* ☎ *6559 2888,* W *www.peninsula.com, 8 Jinyu Hutong*) Doubles US$300. Owned by the Peninsula Group, the Palace Hotel is a consummate residence while in the capital. It boasts four excellent restaurants, a sparkling, multi-tiered, shopping mall, a fine location off Wanfujing Dajie and luxurious styling. Palace Club floors feature an executive lounge with complimentary breakfast and evening cocktails. Promotional prices usually take the sting out of the tariff, bringing it down to around US$190.

State Guest Hotel (*Guóbīn Jiǔdiàn;* ☎ *6800 5588,* W *www.stateguesthotel.com, 9 Fuchengmenwai Dajie*) Doubles US$175. This recently opened five-star luxury hotel with a choice range of services and facilities is geared to the business traveller.

Grand Hotel Beijing (*Guìbīnlóu Fàndiàn;* ☎ *6513 7788,* W *www.grandhotelbeijing .com, 35 Dongchang'an Jie*) Twins US$200, with palace view from US$300. This hotel has unparalleled views over its imperial neighbour the Forbidden City. But while the location is splendid, the experience is marred by a drab and unimpressive interior. Up to 40% discounts are available spring through to summer.

China World Hotel (*Zhōngguó Dàfàndiàn;* ☎ *6505 2266,* W *www.shangri-la .com, 1 Jianguomenwai Dajie*) Doubles US$250. This excellent five-star hotel has all the hallmarks of the Shangri-La chain (reliability and style) and everything you need in the China Word Trade Center. It is well suited to the executive traveller; an extra degree of excellence awaits on Horizon Club floors. The tariff includes free airport limousine transfer, free laundry, dry-cleaning and complimentary breakfast.

Novotel Peace Hotel (*Běijīng Nuòfùtè Hépíng Bīnguǎn;* ☎ *6512 8833,* W *www .novotel.com, 3 Jinyu Hutong*) Twins US$80. This efficient, inviting, refurbished four-star hotel has a fresh and cosmopolitan touch and fantastic central location.

Kerry Centre Hotel (*Jiālǐ Zhōngxīn Fàndiàn;* ☎ *6561 8833,* W *www.shangri-la .com, 1 Guanghua Lu*) Doubles from US$230. Aimed at the business traveller, this modern, slick and stylish hotel has

trendy decor and smart dining options. The adjacent Kerry Mall is a very useful shopping stop.

Trader's Hotel (*Gúomào Fàndiàn;* ☎ *6505 2277, 6505 0818, 1 Jianguomenwai Dajie*) Doubles from US$170. This four-star hotel is a good, lower-priced alternative to staying at the China World Hotel, which is next door.

Hilton Hotel (*Xīěrdùn Fàndiàn;* ☎ *6466 2288,* W *www.hilton.com, 1 Dongfang Lu*) Twins US$118. This typical up-market hotel has a well-equipped gym and an excellent Cajun restaurant, Louisiana (see Places to Eat later).

Kūnlún Fàndiàn (☎ *6590 3388,* W *www .hotelkunlun.com, 2 Xinyuan Nanlu*) Twins US$120. The top floor of this place has a revolving restaurant and bar with excellent views of the city.

Kempinski Hotel (*Kǎibīnsījī Fàndiàn;* ☎ *6465 3388,* W *www.kempinski-beijing .com, Lufthansa Centre, 50 Liangmaqiao Lu*) Twins from US$230. This hotel has a great location, next door to the Lufthansa shopping centre. It also has one of Běijīng's best gyms and a good deli and bakery. There is a possible discount of around US$140.

Great Wall Sheraton (*Chángchéng Fàndiàn;* ☎ *6590 5566,* W *www.sheratonbei jing.com, 10 Dongsanhuan Beilu*) Twins US$220. Note that this hotel, one of the city's first international hotels, often has a much cheaper promotional room rate.

Swissôtel (*Ruìshì Jiǔdiàn;* ☎ *6501 2288,* W *www.swissotel-beijing.com, 2 Chaoyangmen Beidajie*) Doubles from US$115. Just outside Dōngsìshítiáo subway station, this hotel has an excellent gym and swimming pool. A bank of China with an international access ATM is on the 2nd floor.

Jianguo Hotel (*Jiànguó Fàndiàn;* ☎ *6500 2233,* W *www.hoteljianguo.com, 5 Jianguomenwai Dajie*) Twins from US$92. This four-star hotel has a reputation for being good value for money and has a very cosy, slightly yesteryear atmosphere.

Holiday Inn Lido (*Lìdū Jiàrì Fàndiàn; Běijīng map;* ☎ *6437 6688,* W *www.lidoplace .com, cnr Jichang Lu & Jiangtai Lu*) Twins from US$76. This hotel is on the road to the airport, and therefore a bit stranded. Even so, it's a highly popular, first-rate establishment with excellent amenities and a shopping mall.

Friendship Hotel (*Yōuyí Bīnguǎn; Běijīng map;* ☎ *6849 8888, fax 6849 8825, 3 Baishiqiao Lu*) Twins from US$70. Built in the 1950s to house 'foreign experts', this sprawling garden-style hotel has managed to retain its old-style charm. It boasts a great outdoor swimming pool.

Shangri-La Hotel (*Xiānggé Lǐlā Fàndiàn; Běijīng map;* ☎ *6841 2211,* Ⓦ *www .shangri-la.com, 29 Zizhuyuan Lu, Haidian District*) Rooms from US$130. This hotel is located in west Běijīng and is well positioned for trips to the Summer Palace. The Shangri-La has a top-notch selection of restaurants, bars and shops as well as a fine spread of rooms.

Mövenpick Hotel (*Guódū Dàfàndiàn; Běijīng map;* ☎ *6456 5588, fax 6456 5678, Capital Airport*) Twins from US$135. Amenities in this four-star hotel include some excellent tennis courts, a great gym and a large outdoor swimming pool.

PLACES TO EAT
Ballooning incomes in the capital and the droves of foreigners coming to town have provoked a Cultural Revolution of sorts in Běijīng's restaurant scene. The city's increasingly adventurous diners are catered for by an equally imaginative restaurant industry. If it's Chinese you want, you can't choose a better place to start, for chefs from all over the land are in town. And don't fret if you crave more variety, China's open door policy kicked open the kitchen hatch to world food long ago. Just about any fickle fancy meets its match, with cuisine from all over the world. So dive in and start twiddling those chopsticks – some of your best Běijīng memories could well be tabletop ones. Despite the rich aromas around town, you won't pay through the nose for it all – some truly fantastic cheap eats await. And if you don't mind spending a bit more – well, the sky's the limit.

For a comprehensive list of restaurants, check the expat mags.

Chinese Food
Northern cuisine specialities include Beijing duck, Mongolian hotpot, Muslim barbecue and imperial dishes, but the rest of China gets a look-in too, from the snortingly hot dishes of Sìchuān to the ethnic Dai dishes of clement Yúnnán and beyond.

Snacks and Cheap Eats Off the main roads and in Běijīng's alleyways is a world teeming with food stalls and small eateries. Breakfast can be easily catered for with a *yóutiáo* (deep-fried dough stick) and a bowl of porridge *(zhōu)*. Other snacks include the pancake-like and filling *jiānbǐng,* and the heavy meat filled *ròubǐng,* cooked bread filled with finely chopped pork. *Dàbǐng* can be found everywhere – a chunk of round, unleavened bread sprinkled with sesame seeds – and of course there's *mántou* (steamed bread). Also look out for *ròu jiamò,* a scrumptious open-your-mouth-wide bun filled with diced lamb, chilli and garlic shoots.

Worth checking out is the *food mall* in the basement of the Oriental Plaza on Wángfǔjǐng. It's a squeaky-clean fast food emporium of Cantonese, Yúnnán, Sìchuān, teppanyaki, clay pot and porridge outlets plus loads of other types of Asian cuisine.

Markets A sight in itself, the bustling *Dōnghuámén Yèshì* night market at the northern end of Wángfǔjǐng near Sundongan Plaza is a veritable food zoo: lamb kebabs, beef and chicken skewers, corn on the cob, smelly tofu, cicadas, grasshoppers, kidneys, quail's eggs, squid, fruit, porridge, fried pancakes, strawberry kebabs, bananas, Inner Mongolian cheese, stuffed aubergines, chicken hearts, pitta bread stuffed with meat, shrimps…and that's just the start. *Lǎowài* (foreigners) go all slack-jawed at the marvels on view. The market is open every day of the year apart from the Spring Festival; 5.30pm to 10pm.

Another fascinating spectacle is the *Wángfǔjǐng Xiǎochījiē (Wangfujing Snack Street)* south of the night market. Fronted by an ornate *páilou,* the quadrant is a bright and cheery corner of restaurants and stalls overhung with colourful flags and bursting with character and flavour.

Beijing Duck The capital's most famous invention is now a production line of sorts. Your meal starts at one of the farms around Běijīng, where the duck is fattened with grain and soybean paste. The duck carcass is lacquered with molasses, pumped with air, filled with boiling water, dried, and then roasted over a fruitwood fire. The result is delicious. The duck is served in stages. First comes boneless meat and crispy skin with a side dish of shallots, plum sauce and crepes, then duck soup made of bones and all the other parts of the duck except the quack.

Lìchún Kǎoyādiàn (Lichun Roast Duck Restaurant; ☎ 6702 5681, Beixiangfeng Hutong) Roast duck Y68. Tucked in a hútòng in east Qián Mén, this tiny restaurant is squeezed into a typical Běijīng courtyard house. It's worth coming here for the atmosphere alone, and the duck isn't bad either. It only has a few tables and the owners insist that you make reservations. If you get lost, ask the locals to point you in the right direction – just ask for the *Kǎoyādiàn*.

Qianmen Quanjude Roast Duck Restaurant (Qiánmén Quánjùdé Kǎoyādiàn; ☎ 6511 2418, 32 Qianmen Dajie) Duck Y108 or Y168. Otherwise known as the 'Old Duck', this is one of the oldest restaurants in the capital, dating back to 1864. It remains one of the city's best places for roast duck. There is another branch nearby (☎ *6301 8833, 14 Qianmen Xidajie)* and one just off Wángfǔjǐng (☎ *6525 3310, 9 Shuaifuyuan Hutong)*.

Tianwaitian (Běijīng map) is a reliable chain of Beijing Duck specialists dotted around town. The chefs do a fine job on the tasty morsels, served up alongside a thick wad of pancakes. Order beer by the pint *(zhāpí);* the *méicài kǒuròu* is a delicious dish of melt-in-the-mouth strips of fatty pork atop a small mound of méicài cabbage.

Dumplings When in Běijīng, do as Běijīngers do: gobble down dumplings *(jiǎozi)* by the bowl. Small steamed or boiled bite-size parcels of meat and vegetables in pastry envelopes, jiǎozi arrive scalding at the table, to be doused in a small dish of soy sauce and vinegar and chomped.

First Floor Restaurant (Dìyīlóu Guàntāng Xiǎolóngbaozi; ☎ 6303 0268, 83 Qianmen Dajie) Dumplings Y3-9. This restaurant has the best *tāng bāo* (soup buns) around, for only Y9 per bamboo steamer. Other typical, simple Běijīng dishes to try are *xiǎo cōng bàn dòufu* (scallion tofu; Y3) and *liáng bàn huáng guā* (cold cucumber; Y4).

Golden Cat Dumpling City (Jīn Māo Jiǎozichéng; ☎ 8598 5011) Dishes around Y3.5. Open 24 hours. Come here whenever the unpredictable mood for dumplings grabs you, day or night. This courtyard eatery,

near the east gate of Tuánjiéhú Gōngyuán, serves over 20 varieties of dumplings: from the standard pork-filled, through to pumpkin, aubergine, donkey-meat and beyond. Order dumplings by the *liǎng* (about Y3.5 for five dumplings).

Imperial Imperial food *(gōngtíng cài* or *mǎnhàn dàcān)* is food fit for an emperor and will clean your wallet out very quickly. In 1982 a group of Běijīng chefs set about reviving the imperial pastry recipes, and even went so far as to chase up the last emperor Pu Yi's brother to try out their creations.

Fāngshān Fànzhuāng (Fangshan Restaurant; ☎ 6401 1889, Běihǎi Gōngyuán) Set menus from Y100-500 per person. Běijīng's most elaborate imperial cuisine is served up in this restaurant, in a pavilion overlooking the lake in Běihǎi Gōngyuán (enter through the west or south gate). All dishes are elaborately prepared, and range from delicately filled pastries to sea cucumber with deer tendon, peppery inkfish's egg soup and camel paw with scallion (no, it's not a real camel paw). The Y500 menu will get you rare delicacies such as bird's nest soup, abalone and turtle meat. Reservations are a must.

Mongolian Hotpot Mongolian hotpot is ideally a winter dish, but once you get in the spirit, you'll be sweating over it even in mid-July. Hearty patrons dip slivers of lamb into the seething broth for a swift scalding before twiddling the meat in sesame-based sauces and consuming. Cabbage, mushrooms, tofu and potatoes are also used.

Néngrénjū (☎ 6601 2560, 5 Taipingqiao, Baitasi) Hotpot from Y18. Běijīng's most renowned hotpot restaurant is packed with loyal patrons in winter, so come early.

Sìchuān A couple of restaurants specialising in Sichuanese cuisine are:

Jinshancheng Chongqing Restaurant (Jīnshānchéng Chóngqìng Càiguǎn; ☎ 6581 1598, 2nd floor, Zhongfu Bldg, Chaoyang) Dishes from Y25. The fiery *làzi jī* (pepper chicken) here is smokingly hot – nuggets of chicken tossed with crisp, red chillies. Squadrons of diners also nod in appreciation at the *mápo dòufu* (spicy bean curd), the *sōngshǔ guìyú* (deep-fried squirrelfish with sweet-and-sour sauce) and the *gānbiān sìjìdòu* (crisp-fried green beans).

Berena's Bistro (*Bóruìnà Jiǔjiā;* ☎ *6592 2628, 6 Gongrentiyuchang Donglu, Sanlitun*) Dishes around Y25. Approving expats by the table load douse their smouldering tongues with German beers. English menus prevent misunderstandings with the kitchen staff. There is another branch (☎ *6417 4890, 2 Xingfucun Zhonglu*).

Uyghur Wēigōngcūn, off Baishiqiao Lu in Haidian, is where Běijīng's Uyghur minority congregates. It is a pleasant street lined with tiny, family-owned restaurants. It's an authentic part of town and affords a priceless (albeit good value) occasion to sample Uyghur food: *náng* (flatbread), *sānpào tái* or *bābǎo chá* (sweet Uyghur tea), vegetable dishes, *lāmiàn* (noodles) and *ròuchuàn* (kebabs). The street also has a couple of Dai restaurants.

A Fun Ti Hometown Music Restaurant (*Āfántí Jiāxiāng Yīnyuè Cāntīng;* ☎ *6527 2288, 2 Houguaibang Hutong*) Meals Y80-90. Xīnjiāng is maybe a three-day train trip away, but forgo the bunion inducing hard-seat for the fun and frolics of table dancing, belly dancers and the Uyghur sounds of the A Fun Ti Band. Sample some *yángròu chuànr* (lamb kebabs) sprinkled with *zīranfen* (cumin) and *làjiāo* (chilli) and size-up the first-rate *kǎoyángtuǐ* (roasted lamb leg). Stomach-swelling nosh and a fine time all round before the heavy-belly waddle home.

Vegetarian Some options for vegetarians include:

Gongdelin Vegetarian Restaurant (*Gōngdélín Sùcàiguǎn;* ☎ *6511 2542, 158 Qianmen Nandajie*) Meals Y25-Y40. Open 10.30am-8.30pm daily. Still Běijīng's best bloodless dining experience, restore your karma with dishes of bogus meat that taste better than the real thing. A poet's been to work on the menu ('the fire is singeing the snow-capped mountains') and there's a culinary genius at work in the kitchen. Not to be missed.

Green Tianshi Vegetarian Restaurant (*Lǜ Tiānshí Fàndiàn;* ☎ *6524 2349, 57 Dengshikou Dajie*) Dishes from Y40. Serving similar fare to the Gongdelin, this vegie restaurant has cleaner, brighter, more peaceful surroundings (and slightly higher prices). Mount the staircase to the restaurant

on the 2nd floor and photos of famous vegetarians – Socrates, Einstein, Plato, Darwin and Paul Newman, will greet you. Specialties include Beijing duck, meatballs and broccoli, and sweet and sour fish with pine nuts (all fashioned purely with vegetables). Be sure to check the prices on the menu (in English) before letting the staff make suggestions for the best dishes.

Cantonese No self-respecting tourist hotel in Běijīng is without a Cantonese restaurant dishing up dim sum to their Hong Kong clientele.

Hong Kong Food City (*Xiānggǎng Měishíchéng;* ☎ *6525 7349, 18 Donganmen Dajie*) Dishes from Y20. This pricey, vast and popular *yuècaì* (Cantonese) restaurant near Wangfujing Dajie is often full, so reservations are recommended.

Fortune Garden (☎ *6559 2888 ext 7900; Palace Hotel, 8 Jinyu Hutong*) Nearby Food City in the Palace Hotel, a more intimate get together can be had here to the accompaniment of live Chinese *zhēng* (zither) musicians.

Be There Or Be Square (*Bú Jiàn Bú Sàn;* ☎ *8518 6518, BB71 Oriental Plaza, Wangfujing;* ☎ *6518 6515, Level 2, Henderson Center*) 2-person meal Y60. Tired of linen napkins and snobbish waiting staff? Try this excellent chain that really does the business on *cha siu, siu ngap, cha siu bao* and other Canto favourites (they even do a great spag bol). It's all good value, trendy, and you can go online at the Oriental Plaza outlet.

Shànghǎi Běijīng's newfangled nemesis, Shànghǎi, prefers softer flavours.

Oasis (*Jīngyí Zhōu;* ☎ *6418 1073, 2nd floor, Bldg B, East Gate Plaza, 29 Dongzhongjie*) Meals Y100. Oasis is a relaxed, civilised welcome to travellers in need of more southern, Yangzi-delta fare. Try the vegetarian duck, or marinated chicken in wine sauce. Oasis is quiet, restrained ambience, albeit a tad pricey.

Fusion If you're looking for upscale dining, Běijīng has a few exceptional restaurants worth trying. The following all serve Chinese-influenced food, but with a modern twist (hence the subheading). Reservations are necessary.

The Courtyard (☎ 6526 8883, 95 *Donghuamen Dajie*) Meals from Y200. Dining here is a marvellous experience – the view of the Forbidden City a peerless backdrop to the culinary achievements from the kitchen. There's also a trendy modern art gallery downstairs and a cosy cigar room upstairs.

Red Capital Club (*Xīnhóngzī Jùlèbù;* ☎ 6402 7150 day, 8401 8886 night & weekend, 66 *Dongsi Jiu Tiao*) Dishes Y200. Hidden away down a quiet hútòng is this meticulously restored courtyard house with traditional Chinese decor. The bar is made up to resemble a post-liberation Politburo reception room, but it's all rather pricey. There is an English menu.

Chinese Beer

Despite a large beer market, the residents of the Middle Kingdom can only claim to be newborns in the art of beer drinking. The hops, yeast, tinkerings and general goings on at the turn of the 19th-century German Qīngdǎo brewery would have raised a constellation of local eyebrows and set many a curtain twitching.

Even in the 1970s, the liquid was still derided as *mǎniào* (horse piss) and shelved in favour of the local rocket fuel *(báijiǔ)*. But these days, the *yánghuò* (foreign product) known here as *píjiǔ* is pretty much the drink of choice for a get-together, outselling *báijiǔ* for the first time in 1998.

Flavour-wise, Chinese beer is rather drab, but can be lauded as a remarkable feat of socialist standardisation, for it tastes the same pretty much wherever you go.

But Chinese beer is cheap. Depending on where you shop, you can pick up a bottle for Y1.5, with a deposit of five máo on the bottle (vendors will etch this fact into you). Cheap restaurants usually charge around Y3 for a bottle; but they hang on to the deposit. If you want a cold beer, ask for *'liáng píjiǔ'*, and if you want it really arctic, *'bīngzhèn píjiǔ'*.

It isn't strong, at a watery 3.4% proof, and experienced beer drinkers will drink bathloads of the stuff. You may still, however, get the occasional dodgy bottle that seems to bring on a hangover all by itself – and watch out for explosive bottles during the heat of summer.

Green Tea House (☎ 6468 5903, 54 *Tayuancun*) Dishes from Y100. This tiny Chinese-style teahouse in Sānlǐtún is lavishly decorated, with exceptional dishes and (exorbitant) teas. But the real reason to come here is the food presentation – true works of art. It's a beautiful little place for lunch or dinner.

Non-Chinese Food

Metro Cafe (☎ 6552 7828, 6 *Gongti Xilu*) Meals from Y100. If you're craving Italian food, this cafe won't let you down. It has a fine selection of delicious homemade pastas and sauces at reasonable (but not cheap) prices.

Louisiana (☎ 6466 2288 ext 7420, 2nd *Floor, Hilton Hotel, 1 Dongfang Lu*) Meals Y200. Not to be outshone by what is a very famous wine list, the kitchen staff here work hard to dish up excellent Cajun and Creole cuisine; centrepiece dishes are the steaks and seafood. In the Hilton, this place is not cheap, but it's a class act.

Taj Pavilion (☎ 6505 2288 ext 8116, *China World Trade Centre, West Wing Office, Level 1*) Meals from Y100. You'll find mild-mannered service and some mild and not so-mild curries here. For creamy textures and subtle flavourings try the *palak panir* (a creamy spinach dish with cottage cheese). This place has an excellent menu and delightful food.

Le Coffee Shop (☎ 6512 8833, *Novotel Peace Hotel, 3 Jinyu Hutong*) Buffet lunch or dinner Y98. Le Coffee Shop in the Novotel Peace Hotel does an amazingly popular all-you-can-eat buffet. It has stylish surroundings and some terrific food: reach for the ladle and tongs and shovel immodest portions onto your plate.

Bleu Marine (☎ 6500 6704, 5 *Guanghua Xili*) Meals from Y200. There's a daily French menu offering tempting treats like *salade de saumon fume* (smoked salmon salad), *fricasse de volaille sauce au vin rouge* (chicken breast with red wine sauce) and a decent selection of cheeses and wines here.

Makye Ame (*Mǎjí Āmǐ,* ☎ 6507 9966 ext 208, 2nd *floor, Xiushui Nanjie*) Dishes from Y20. This Tibetan restaurant and bar is tucked in behind the Friendship Store. It has a comfy upper room with atmosphere, an excellent menu and a generous crop of

Tibetan ornaments. Go all out for the lamb ribs, the champa and yoghurt, butter tea and cooling salads.

Rainforest Cafe *(Rèdài Sēnlín Cāntīng, ☎ 8518 6851, BB88 Oriental Plaza No 1, Dongchang'an Jie)* Set lunches Y30. You can tuck into burgers beneath a rainforest canopy with an elephant at your shoulder here; a really fun place for the little ones. It has great ribs and grilled salmon. Periodic rainforest lightning storms are sandwiched between jazz and Latino American rhythms; and there are busy and efficient rainforest explorer-type waiting staff.

Cafes In the poor old days, Bĕijīng residents drank *báikāi shuǐ* (hot water), *chá* (tea) or even *hē xīběifēng* (literally 'drank the north-west wind', or 'too poor to have anything to eat'). Now they pay through the nose for roasts from Starbucks *(Xīngbāke)*, the chain that even had the pluck to unveil a branch in the Forbidden City. Some Chinese complain of the influx of Western culture – can you honestly blame them?

Starbucks branches include: 1st floor, Friendship Store, 17 Jianguomen Waidajie; 1st floor, Oriental Plaza; 183 Wangfujing Dajie; 1st floor, Scitech Tower, 22 Jianguomenwai Dajie.

Kebab Cafe Gallery *(KK Huàláng; ☎ 6415 5812, Sanlitun Beilu)* This popular cafe, heavily patronised by Westerners who bask in the sun out front, is situated in Sānlǐtún, serves up European dishes, and features an art gallery

Fast Food The nation's diet has changed dramatically over the past 20 years. Beef was seldom eaten because of its strong flavour, but is now consumed by the herd-load at McDonald's *(Màidānglào)*. With scores of branches in the capital, you'll be hard pressed to elude Ronald's inane countenance.

KFC *(Kěndéjī)* has spawned itself just as relentlessly, while a host of other chains take up the rear.

Despite allegations that Marco Polo took the recipe back to Italy from China, Pizza has boomeranged back, with extra topping. Pizza Hut *(Bìěngkè)*, Domino's *(Dameile)* and others battle it out. *The Pizza Factory* *(☎ 6518 6840, Henderson Center, Dongchang'an Jie)* delivers satisfactory pizza from 7am to 10pm.

Supermarkets A steady influx of capital and expats have ushered in a number of well-stocked supermarkets.

On the eastern fringe of Jiànguóménwài is the China World Trade Centre, where you will find a very well-stocked *CRC Supermarket (open 9.30am-9.30pm daily)*. Adjacent is a *vintner* with a fine selection of wines. There is another branch of CRC in the basement of the Kerry Mall *(Shop B25; open 8.30am-10.30pm daily)*, next to the Kerry Centre Hotel.

The Henderson Center, opposite the Beijing International Hotel, also has a fine *supermarket* in the basement. Full Link Plaza, 18 Chaoyangmen Beidajie, has a branch of *Park N Shop* in the basement.

Just north of the Great Wall Sheraton is the enormous Lufthansa Center – yes, it is a ticket office for a German airline, but also a multi-storey shopping mall. There is a decent *supermarket* in the basement chock-a-block with imported goods.

Carrefour have a number of huge branches in the city, including 6 Beisanhuan Donglu, Chaoyang *(☎ 8460 1030; open 8am-9.30pm daily)* and 15 Zone 11, Fengtai *(☎ 6760 9911; open 8.30am-9.30pm daily)*. Branches take credit cards, have ATM machines and a home delivery service.

Pub Grub For a taste of home, most foreigners are drawn to a collection of pubs in the Sānlǐtún and Jiànguóménwài areas. Since these are great socialising spots, often with outdoor tables, live music and closing times around 2am, we've listed these places in the following Entertainment section.

ENTERTAINMENT

Check out one of the Bĕijīng expat magazines for the latest on entertainment in the capital. Unless otherwise indicated, all venues appear on the Central Bĕijīng map.

Bars

Referred to by locals as 'Bar Street', and shrugging off threats by the authorities to sweep away the whole shebang, Sānlǐtún forms the hub of expat drinking life in town. Sānlǐtún is divided into two streets – the increasingly Chinese-occupied Sanlitun Lu and Sanlitun Nanlu, running to the south. The latter is an alley of expat watering holes, live music venues, microbars and pubs.

BEIJING

Hidden Tree (*Yǐnbìdeshù;* ☎ 6509 3642, 12 Dong Da Qiao) Looking for a Trappist monastery-brewed Chimay, a Leffe or a Duvel to flush away that sour flavour of the local beer? Look no farther, Hidden Tree has a cellar of Belgian beers for closet Europhiles. A beer garden is open from late spring.

Tanewha (☎ 6594 4868) Open 6pm-2am. Understated Tanewha is a popular Kiwi-themed outfit, its relaxing pace due to soft candlelight, bare-wood floors and the passing of time measured by the click of pool balls.

Havana Cafe (☎ 6586 6166, Gongti Beilu) Swinging to a signature Latino beat with regular live music, Havana Cafe has taken Cuban cuisine to Běijīng with gusto. On the north gate of the Workers Stadium, it has a back patio, bar and dance moves till 3am.

Public Space (☎ 6416 0759, 50 Sanlitun Lu) Open 10am-2pm. Right in the middle of Sanlitun Lu, this place is the street's first pacesetter and long-term survivor. Amazingly, it's still trendy and attracts a hip crowd. Evenings see the lights dimming as the in-house DJ spins his magic. The menu includes sandwiches and salads.

John Bull Pub (*Zūnbó Yīngshì Jiǔbā;* ☎ 6532 5905, 44 Guanghua Lu) This is an embassy district English-style pub with not half-bad steak and kidney pie and two pints of Fosters for the price of one during happy hour (5pm to 8pm). It has a snug weeknight atmosphere, comfy furniture, pool and pleasant staff.

Passby Bar (☎ 8403 8004, ⓔ passby_bar @sina.com, 108 Nanluogu Xiang) A converted courtyard house complete with polished beams, an inviting mezzanine and Tibetan motifs, Passby Bar is a must. Sociable travel buffs, who can run tips past you along with some fine coffee, are at the helm and a library of travel books take up the rear. You can find it on the corner of Banchang Hutong and Nanluogu Xiang in one of Běijīng's most historic reaches.

Gay/Lesbian Bars

There are a number of gay and lesbian bars and venues in Běijīng; for gay/lesbian events contact ⓔ cafm@263.net.

Half and Half (☎ 6416 6919, Bldg 15, Sanlitun Beilu) Open 6pm-2am. Just off Gongti Beilu in an alley, this is Běijīng's most popular gay venue.

On/Off Bar (☎ 6415 8083, Lianbao Apartment, Xingfucun Zhonglu, Chaoyang) This quiet and seductive outfit is well-managed by a squad of helpful staff. An hour's free Internet access is delivered with every drink. Otherwise just come here for the relaxed pace and spacious layout. Although largely straight, gay nights are held – phone for details.

Drag On (☎ 6594 8083, 73 Zheng Jie) This place has dance acts, live music and is along the road south of Hard Rock Cafe in the Chaoyang district; *New Man* (*Běijīng map;* ☎ 6468 8273) is near the Holiday Inn Lido Hotel.

Discos & Clubs

The Sānlǐtún area has a handful of places that kick on till late.

Vogue (*Number 88;* ☎ 6416 5316, 88 Xin Donglu) Admission Y50 Fri & Sat. Open 7pm-late. Despite some sobering bar prices (Y40), Vogue remains Běijīng's premier nightspot with a heaving dancefloor and a feverish weekend rush of clubbers.

Solutions (*Hélùshén; Běijīng map;* ☎ 6255 8877) Admission Y20 Fri & Sat. Across from the west gate of Beijing University, this place has a weekend crush of foreign students swaying till 4am to cheap drinks, R&B and hip hop.

The Loft (*Cángkù Jiǔbā;* ☎ 6501 7501, 4 Gongrentiyuchang Beilu) Admission Y40. Clamber into the Loft and access its world of live jazz, tech and house (Fridays), funky TV screens, and art space. The menu is European-fusion.

Live Music

China's increasingly brazen capital nods its head to many sounds: scruffy punk, twangy country, smooth jazz, lumpen rock, cultured classical, edgy alternative plus occasionally unidentifiable, malformed strains.

Nashville (*Xiāngyáo Jiǔbā;* ☎ 6502 4201, Sanlitun Nanlu) This is an expat assembly point in the bar heartland of Sānlǐtún, with all rustic wood and stone floors. It has country, folk, blues and rock merchants on stage from 9:30pm. Happy hour is from 6pm to 8pm.

The Big Easy (*Běijīng map; Kuàilèzhàn;* ☎ 6508 6776, 8 Chaoyang Gongyuan Lu) Patrons munch Cajun and Creole food here to much-loved slices of blues and jazz from

Liquid Lobotomy

Tang poet Li Bai wrote some of his most lucid material on the stuff, until drowning in the Yangzi River on a mind bender. At banquets, it leaves your teeth smoking and your host gloating. Often followed by a ball of harsh cigarette smoke into the lung, *báijiǔ* (white spirit) is many a Chinese person's best friend. But unless you have the liver of an ox, go easy on it.

Westerners wince or wipe tears from their eyes after a whiff of the stuff, but to the Chinese, we are on sacred turf. Drinkers lovingly smell and taste báijiǔ in the same way a wine taster savours a fine vintage. The fiercest Báijiǔ used to pack a 74° proof (!) punch to the guts; today's strongest is a tad tamer, but at 65° will still have you snorting.

Erguotou is the nation's favourite brand and comes in handy 5L plastic drums. It is 65° proof and so cheap you'll be walking into lampposts without spending Y10.

Red Star Erguotou (annual production 100,000 tons) from Bĕijīng is China's best seller, sweeping 25% of the land's drinkers before it; plans are hatching to export in large quantities to the West. The name 'Erguotou' (literally 'two pots') refers to the double pot distilling, condensing and purifying method that converts the hooch into a venomously pure tipple.

Maotai is the best known abroad, but it's also spectacularly expensive for what is essentially the same beverage in a fancier bottle; and anyway, after a few shots, the distinction becomes meaningless.

regulars the Big Easy Band. There is an outdoor terrace. The Big Easy is near the south gate of Cháoyáng Gōngyuán.

Sanwei Bookshop & Teahouse (☎ 6601 3204, 60 Fuxingmennei Dajie) Admission Y30. The Sanwei has a small bookshop on the ground floor, but hidden on the 2nd floor is a charming Chinese teahouse. Chinese classical music is provided 8.30pm to 10.30pm Saturday night.

Cinema

Lycée Francais de Pékin (Fǎguó Xuéxiào Diànyǐngyuàn; ☎ 6532 3498, 13 Dongsi Jie) You can see French films here in the Sānlǐtún area, around the corner from the Public Space bar.

Cherry Lane Movies (Zhōngrì Qīngnián Jiāoliú Zhōngxīn; Bĕijīng map; ☎ 6461 5318, W www.cherrylanemovies.com.cn, Sino-Japanese Youth Exchange Center, 40 Liangmaqiao Lu) Admission Y50. On three Friday evenings per month you can catch up on the latest Chinese cinema here, with English sub-titles. The cinema is located 2km east of the Kempinski Hotel.

Beijing Opera

At most well-known Beijing opera venues, shows last around 90 minutes and are generally performed by major opera troupes such as the China Peking Opera House. English translations can be a bit off the wall. Westerners tend to see versions that are noisy and

strong on acrobatics and wǔshù routines, rather than the more sedate traditional style.

Zhengyici Theatre (Zhèngyǐcí Dàxìlóu; ☎ 6303 3104, 220 Xiheyan Dajie) Tickets from Y50. Originally an ancient temple, this ornately decorated building is the oldest wooden theatre in the country and is the best place in the city to experience this traditional art form. The theatre was restored by a private businessman with an interest in reviving the dying art, and reopened in 1995 after a long period of disrepair. Performances are 7.30pm to 9pm daily.

Huguang Guild Hall (Húguǎng Huìguǎn; ☎ 6351 8284, 3 Hufangqiao Lu) Tickets Y60-180. Traditionally styled, with balconies surrounding the canopied stage, this theatre is the site where the Kuomintang was established in 1912. Performances are 7.15pm to 9pm daily.

Chang'an Grand Theatre (Cháng'ān Dàxìyuán; ☎ 6510 1309, Chang'an Bldg, 7 Jianguomennei Dajie) Tickets Y20-120. This theatre offers a more genuine experience, with an erudite audience chattering knowledgeably among themselves during weekend matinee full-length classics and evening performances.

Liyuan Theatre (Líyuán Jùchǎng; ☎ 6301 6688 ext 8860, 175 Yongan Lu) Tickets Y30-150. Staple on the foreigner-in-town front, this theatre in the Jianguo Hotel Qianmen holds regular performances, but the setting isn't so traditional.

Beijing Opera

It used to be the Marx Brothers, the Gang of Four and the Red Ballet – but it's back to the classics these days. Beijing opera (*píngjù*) is the most famous of the many forms of the art, but it only has a short history. The year 1790 is the key date: in that year a provincial troupe performed before Emperor Qianlong on his 80th birthday. The form was popularised in the West by the actor Mei Lanfang (1894–1961) who is said to have influenced Charlie Chaplin.

Beijing opera bears little resemblance to its European counterpart. The mixture of singing, dancing, speaking, mime, acrobatics and dancing can go on for five or six hours, but two hours is more usual.

There are four types of actors' roles: the *sheng, dan, jing* and *chou*. The sheng are the leading male actors and they play scholars, officials, warriors and the like. The dan are the female roles, but are usually played by men (Mei Lanfang always played a dan role). The jing are the painted-face roles, and they represent warriors, heroes, statesmen, adventurers and demons. The chou is basically the clown.

Language is often archaic Chinese and the screeching music is searing to Western ears, but the costumes and make-up are magnificent. The action that really catches the Western eye is a swift battle sequence – trained acrobats leap, twirl, twist and somersault into attack. It's not unlike boarding a Běijīng bus during rush hour.

Catching at least one Beijing opera is almost mandatory for visitors to the capital.

Prince Gong's Residence is also a good place to enjoy Beijing Opera while taking in one of Běijīng's historic courtyards.

Acrobatics

Two thousand years old, and one of the few art forms condoned by Mao, Chinese acrobatics (*zájì biǎoyǎn*) is a breathtaking spectacle of joint-popping contortion, tumbling, tricks and gravity-defying balancing acts.

Poly Plaza (Bǎolì Dàshà Jùyuàn; ☎ 6500 1188 ext 5127, 14 Dongzhimennan Dajie) Admission Y80. This is a good place to catch the China Acrobatics Troupe, which performs nightly. Shows are at 7.15pm daily.

Chaoyang Theatre (Cháoyáng Dàjùchǎng; ☎ 6507 2421, 36 Dongsanhuan Beilu) Admission Y80. Performances here are 7.15pm to 8.20pm daily.

Classical Music Venues

Classical music can be appreciated at a few venues around town, including *Beijing Concert Hall (☎ 6605 5812, 1 Beixinhua Jie; tickets Y10-200)* and *The Forbidden City Concert Hall (☎ 6559 8294, Zhongshan Park; tickets Y30-180)*. Tickets for concerts, plays etc can be ordered on the toll-free hotline ☎ 800 8100 443. Check the expat mags for the latest listings.

SHOPPING

Běijīng is an excellent place to pick up souvenirs, trawl through markets and browse among elegant malls.

Wángfǔjǐng 王府井

This prestigious shopping street is east of the Forbidden City. It's a solid stretch of stores and a favourite haunt of locals and tourists. The pedestrianised area is an excellent place to window shop and take in a coffee or beer at one of the outside stands in summer.

At the south-eastern end is the huge and impressively designed *Oriental Plaza (Dōngfāng Guǎngchǎng)*, a vast mall of restaurants, boutiques and stores. Starbucks, Pierre Cardin, Lego, Clarks, Hush Puppies, The Rainforest Cafe – they're all here.

The *Palace Hotel* also has a splendid shopping arcade on a number of levels replete with designer clothing and stylish outlets.

Líulíchǎng 琉璃厂

Líulíchǎng is Běijīng's antique street, south of Hépíngmén subway station. In imperial Běijīng, shops and theatres were not permitted near the city centre, but Líulíchǎng was outside the gates. Many of the city's oldest shops can be found along or near this crowded hútòng.

It has been a shopping area for quite some time and has stores designed to look like an ancient Chinese village. Prices are mostly outrageous, but Líulíchǎng is worth a look – some of the art books and drawings are a good deal and not easily found elsewhere. This is a good place to buy a chop; with some bargaining you can get one for Y30 and have it engraved for Y10. Most shops are open from 9am to 6pm daily.

Dàshílàr (Dàshílàn) 大栅栏

Dàshílàr is a hútòng running west from the northern end of the Front Gate, near Tiānānmén Square. It's a heady jumble of silk shops, department stores, theatres, herbal medicine, food and clothing specialists and some unusual architecture.

Xiùshuǐ Silk Market 秀水市场
Xiùshuǐ Shìchǎng

This market, on the northern side of Jiàngúoménwài between the Friendship Store and the Jianguo Hotel, is awash with the silkworm's finest, and top brand and designer labels such as Gucci, Burberry and North Face (largely fake). Bargaining is imperative, although it's often a struggle because of all the foreign tourists willing to throw money around like water. Rumours abound of the market being shut down and moved indoors, but at the time of writing it was still thriving. Be extra vigilant against pickpockets in the crowded quadrants; your wallet could well be talking a walk as you haggle hard.

Markets

Pānjiāyuán Market (Pānjiāyuán Jiǔhuò Shìchǎng; Dirt Market; ☎ 6775 2405) Open 4.30am-5pm Sat-Sun. This market is a must-visit, and the earlier you get there the better, as many vendors start packing up around noon. For sale in the covered section are all kinds of 'antiques' (most are reproductions) and knick-knacks: ceramics, wooden chests, Yíxīng teapots, Cultural Revolution memorabilia, Mao alarm clocks, Tibetan carpets, scrolls, reproductions of 1920s cigarette ads, Chinese furniture etc, but you have to bargain for everything here. Outside the covered section anything goes. Those on the hunt for true antiques usually start here; this is where countryfolk hawk all kinds of things, and collectors dream of lifting a true antique

---

Mao Mania

Although he's been dead for 20 years, the legacy of Mao Zedong continues to play a major role in the contemporary political life of China and, indeed, for many mainland Chinese Mao has made the leap from emperor to god-like status.

What is more intriguing, perhaps, is how Mao has captivated the imagination beyond China's borders in a guise that is far less politically defined: 'Like, wouldn't it be cool to have matching Mao earrings?'. Maybe it all began with Andy Warhol's 1972 silkscreen portrait after Nixon's visit to China, for it can't be denied that the Mao image today, along with other artefacts associated with the Cultural Revolution, has a certain trendy cachet in Hong Kong, Japan and the West. Of course, China experienced its own resurgence of Maoist kitsch in the early 90s, yet this was seen as a nostalgic and even spiritual response to disillusionment with the current leadership and uncertainty about changes brought by the economic reforms.

The fascination with Mao outside of the local context is a little more baffling, especially when seen in the light of historical realities. How can anybody with more than a passing understanding of Mao's role in Chinese history really feel comfortable walking around wearing a Mao T-shirt? It's difficult to see a similar currency among tourists for souvenirs featuring Hitler or Stalin. Perhaps the difference is that the international community, and most certainly the mainland Chinese government, have not repudiated Mao's value as the leader of China after 1949, but this does not make his crimes against humanity any less abhorrent.

Not many foreign tourists seemed interested in buying a Deng Xiaoping T-shirt after the crackdown on demonstrators in the 1989 Tiānānmén Massacre. Yet that single incident pales almost into insignificance when one considers many of the events that occurred under Mao's leadership.

The complete demystification of Mao may never take place in China and no doubt he will occupy a sacred place for many years to come. Outside of China, however, Mao's image might have less appeal as an item of popular recognition if there was a greater awareness about his role in Chinese history. No matter how compelling he may appear in the official portrait hanging above the entrance to the Forbidden City, there's nothing like a few Mao stories to turn you off the chairman forever.

from an unsuspecting farmer for next to nothing. To get here head south on Dongsanhuan Zhonglu (if you're coming from, say, the Jiàngúoménwài area) and exit just before Pānjiāyuán Bridge. The market, surrounded by a tall wall, is about 100m west, on your right.

Hóngqiáo Market (*Pearl Market;* ☎ *6711 7429, 16 Hongqiao Lu*) Open 8.30am-7pm daily. If you can't make it to Pān-jiāyuán, this is a good alternative. Hóngqiáo is where you can find real pearls (of varying quality) dirt-cheap. The pearl vendors are on the 3rd floor. The 2nd floor has a huge selection of fake designers, including Prada, Gucci and Louis Vuitton. The 1st floor has every conceivable everyday item, from nail clippers to pots and pans.

Yábăo Lù Clothing Market (*Yábăo Lù Shìchăng; Yabao Lu*) Open 9.30am-4pm daily. Now open on two fronts, the old Russian market on Yabao Lu is a hectic sprawl of silk and fur; its new wing a gargantuan confusion of clothes, jewellery, electronics, and odds and ends.

Books

Lufthansa Center (*Yànshā Zhōngxīn;* ☎ *6465 3388, 50 Liangmaqiao Lu*) The 6th floor here is the well-stocked World of Books. When last visited, a large selection of Lonely Planet titles were featured.

Foreign Languages Bookshop (☎ *6512 6911, 235 Wangfujiang Dajie*) This place has a reasonable selection of English-language novels and carries a small selection of travel books. Also check out the range on the 3rd floor of the Foreign Imports Bookshop next door.

Friendship Store (*Yŏuyì Shāngdiàn;* ☎ *6500 3311, 17 Jianguomenwai Dajie*) The largest store of this type in the land, this place stocks both tourist souvenirs and everyday useful items. It's been superseded by newer shopping malls, but the book and magazine section is a gold mine for travellers starved of anything to read.

Xidan Bookshop (*Xīdān Túshū Dàshà;* ☎ *6607 8477, 17 Xichang'an Jie*) This vast shop is worth checking out. The only problem is the titles are largely in Chinese.

Department Stores

Běijīng's department stores are plentiful. *Oriental Plaza*, at the south-eastern end of Wángfŭjǐng, is Běijīng's most imposing mall; it's fun around here but prices are high. Nearby, *Sundongan Plaza* (☎ *6527 6688, 138 Wangfujing Dajie*) is a huge, but far scruffier, alternative. *Full Link Plaza* (☎ *6588 1997, 18 Chaoyangmen Beidajie*) is another slick array of top brand names, restaurants, cafes and a supermarket.

The *Lufthansa Center* (☎ *6465 3388, 50 Liangmaqiao Lu*) is an excellent store with a great reputation; and a small range of silk carpets on the fifth floor. The *China World Shopping Mall* (☎ *6505 2288, 1 Jianguomenwai Dajie*), adjacent to the China World Hotel, is where Běijīng's well-heeled come to be seen shopping. It's a lavish and potently snobbish display – the shops are usually empty of customers, alienated by its exclusivity. It must be seen though, and kiddies will love the ice rink!

The *Friendship Store* (☎ *6500 3311, 17 Jianguomenwai Dajie*) smacks of yesteryear, but a last-minute perusal may throw up a souvenir or two from its hordes of shiny trinkets, carvings and silks.

Miscellaneous

For sunscreen, beauty creams, tampons, condoms and vitamins, visit *Watson's* (*Qūchénshì*), in Oriental Plaza (*shops CC17, CC19, CC21 & CC23*), Full Link Plaza (*1st Floor*) or the Holiday Inn Lido.

For over-the-counter Zopiclone sleeping pills, Prozac, Flixonase, Propanalol, Amoxycillin or you name it try *Wànwéiěrkāng Dàyàodiàn* (☎ *6559 5763, 62 Dongdan Beidajie*) on the road parallel to the east of Wángfŭjǐng. The name outside the chemist is in Chinese, but it's bright green.

For antique silk Chinese, Tibetan and Xinjiang carpets, try the *Qianmen Carpet Factory* (☎ *6715 1687, 44 Xingfu Dajie*) – don't forget to bargain. A quality range of Chinese antiques can be perused at *Century Antiques* (☎ *6595 0998, A6 Gongrentiyuchang Donglu*), near Berena's Bistro in Sānlǐtún.

For outdoor gear, *Extreme Beyond* (☎ *6506 5121, 15 Gongrentiyuchang Donglu*) sells high-quality, real (ie, not fake) goods, including brand-name backpacks, Gore-Tex jackets, money belts, sleeping bags and hiking boots. Prices are a little steep, but well below what you'd pay at home. Even though it's a shop, you can bargain.

Běijīng's Hútòng

Step back in time and lose yourself in Běijīng's ancient alleyways.

Běijīng's Hútòng

If you want to plumb Běijīng's homely interior, and move beyond the must-see sights and shopping-mall glitz of town, voyage into the land of the city's *hútòng* (narrow alleyways). Many of these charming alleyways remain, criss-crossing east-west across the city and linking up to create a huge, enchanting warren.

These humble passageways were originally built in the Mongol Yuan dynasty, after Genghis Khan's army had reduced the city to rubble. It was redesigned with hútòng, and by the Qing dynasty there were over 2000, leaping to around 6000 by the 1950s. They are now the stamping ground of a quarter of Běijīng's residents, although recently many have been coming down in clouds of dust as road-widening schemes alter the map of Běijīng. Historic hútòng, protected by the Beijing Cultural Relics Protection Association, are safe from the wrecking ball – but the clock ticks for others.

Living conditions have changed over the past 20 years, and many Běijīngers have forsaken hútòng for the dubious charms of the high-rises (*gāolóu*). Those that stay in hútòng pooh-pooh the high-rise fad, pointing out that they are alienating places with no sense of community. Hútòng instead preserve a powerful sense of togetherness, where everyone helps each other out. As the Chinese say: '*yuǎnqīn bùrú jìnlín*' (close neighbours are better than distant relatives).

Homes in the hútòng may be blisteringly cold in winter (though many are now snugly equipped with central heating) but in summer they stay comparatively cool. Hútòng dwellers also swear blind their Qing-dynasty structures will survive an earthquake.

GLENN BEANLAND

Title page: A hútòng during the celebration of the PRC's 50th anniversary. (Photograph by Caroline Liou.)

Left: Běijīng's fast disappearing hútòng offer a glimpse of times past.

Sìhéyuàn Old walled courtyards *(sìhéyuàn)* are the building blocks of this world. The more historic hútòng have the oldest sìhéyuàn.

Most of the old courtyards date from the Qing dynasty, while a few have struggled through from the Ming; the more functional, utilitarian sìhéyuàn are post-1949 and have little or no ornamentation. Particularly historic and noteworthy sìhéyuàn boast a white-marble plaque near the gates identifying them as being protected.

More venerable courtyards are fronted by large, thick, red doors, outside of which perch either a pair of Chinese lions or drum stones *(bǎogǔshí,* two circular stones resembling drums, each on a small plinth and occasionally topped by a miniature lion or a small dragon head). A courtyard which is particularly notable may be graced with a number of gates accessed by a set of steps and topped with and flanked by ornate brick carvings. The generosity of detail indicates the social clout of the courtyard's original inhabitants. Many of these courtyards were the residences of officials, wealthy families and even princes – Prince Gong's mansion is one of the more celebrated examples.

A number of old courtyards have been preserved as museums, but many are still lived in and hum with activity. From spring to autumn, men collect outside their gates, drinking beer, playing chess, smoking and chewing the fat. Inside, trees soar aloft, providing shade and nesting sites for birds.

The gates are closed at around 10pm for security, and a family in the larger courtyards is paid to act as gatekeeper *(chuándáshì);* they earn around Y150 per month to keep an eye on things and to check out any strangers wandering in or out. This is not to say that courtyards are unsafe: the powerful sense of community creates an extremely secure environment for inhabitants.

Courtyards used to house just one family of the noblesse, but today many belong to the 'work unit', or *dānwèi,* which apportions living quarters to its workforce. Others belong to private owners (although the state still owns all property in China). A lot of the old courtyard houses have been divided into smaller units, but many of their historical features remain, especially their roofs. Courtyard communities are served by small shops *(xiǎomàibù)* and restaurants strung out along hútòng. Children gather at local kindergartens.

Foreigners *(lǎowài)* have cottoned on to the charm of courtyards and have breached this very conservative bastion, however others have been repelled by poor heating, no hot water, dodgy sanitation and no place to park the four-wheel drive. Many hútòng homes still lack toilets and this explains the huge number of malodorous public loos

BĚIJĪNG'S HÚTÒNG

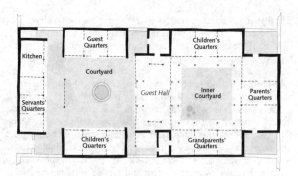

Left: Courtyard houses have been built to a traditional design, which has hardly altered since the Han dynasty.

strung out along the alleyways. Other homes have been thoroughly modernised and sport varnished wood floors, fully fitted kitchens, Jacuzzi and air-con.

Fengshui Hútòng run east-west to ensure that the main gate faces south, satisfying fengshui requirements. This south-facing aspect guarantees a lot of sunshine and protection from more negative forces from the north. This positioning also mirrors the layout of all Chinese temples, nourishing *yáng* (the male and light aspect), while checking *yīn* (the female and dark aspect).

Little connecting alleyways that run north-south link the main alleys. The rectangular waffle-grid pattern that results stamps the points of the compass on the Běijīng psyche. You may hear a local saying, for example, *'wǒ gāoxìng de wǒ bú zhī běi le'*, meaning 'I was so happy, I didn't know which way was north' (an extremely disorientating state of joy).

Many courtyards used to be further protected by rectangular stones bearing the Chinese characters for Tài Shān (Mount Tai), to vanquish bad omens. Some courtyards still preserve their screen walls – fēngshuǐ devices erected in front of the main gate to deflect roaming spirits.

Trees provide *qì* (energy), as well as much-needed shade, and most old courtyards have a locust tree at the front, which would have been planted when its sìhéyuàn was constructed.

Names Hútòng names spring from many roots. Some are christened after families, such as Zhaotangzi Hutong, meaning 'Alley of the Zhao

Family'. Others simply took their name from historical figures, or local features, while others have more mysterious associations, such as Dragon Whiskers Ditch Alley. Others reflect the merchandise plied at local markets, such as Dry Flour Alley (Ganmian Hutong), or Dried Flower Lane and Chrysanthemum Lane.

Hútòng Dimensions Despite an attempt at standardisation, Běijīng's alleys have their own personalities. The longest alley extends for several kilometres, while the shortest – unsurprisingly called One Foot Street (Yichi Dajie) – is a very brief 10m. Some hútòng are wide and leafy boulevards, while others are more claustrophobic: Little Trumpet Alley (Xiaolaba Hutong) is a squeeze at 50cm, while chubby wayfarers could well get wedged in Qianshi Hutong not far from Qianmen – its narrowest reach is a mere 40cm.

Hútòng Tour A perusal of Běijīng's hútòng is an unmissable experience. Trips can be made with Hutong Tours (☎ 6615 9097, 6400 2787), which leaves from opposite the North Entrance to Běihǎi Gōngyuán – watch out for bogus pedicab tours and go for the original. The tour costs Y180 and takes in the Drum Tower and Prince Gong's mansion. Also ask at your hotel.

Alternatively, hire a bike and delve into this historic world yourself. The alleyways can be found all over town, but it's best to limit yourself to historic areas, such as around the Drum Tower, the area around the Lǚsōngyuán Bīnguǎn (see Places to Stay) or east and west off Chaoyangmen Nanxiaojie, east of Wángfǔjǐng.

Those who want to get a taste of courtyard life while staying in Běijīng can check into a number of hotels that occupy sìhéyuàn – check out the Places to Stay section for details.

For many hútòng, Běijīng's 2008 Olympic bid was the kiss of death – get here before the next phase of road-widening schemes again reshape the city.

BĚIJĪNG

GETTING THERE & AWAY
Air

Běijīng has direct air connections to most major cities in the world. Many travellers make use of the direct Běijīng–Hong Kong flights on CAAC or Dragonair. Economy class one-way/return tickets cost Y2800/4500. Flights tend to be heavily booked, especially on Dragonair. It's cheaper to fly from Guǎngzhōu (one way Y1510) or Shēnzhèn (one way Y1550), which are both near Hong Kong and have daily direct flights to Běijīng.

For more information about international flights to Běijīng, see the Getting There & Away chapter earlier in this book.

The CAAC aerial web spreads out in every conceivable direction, with daily flights to most destinations. For the most current information, get a CAAC timetable. Domestic flights connect Běijīng to the following cities:

Bāotóu (Y540, one hour, Wednesday), Chángchūn (Y890), Chángshā (Y1120, two hours, daily), Chéngdū (Y1300, two hours and 20 minutes, daily), Chóngqìng (Y1400, 2¼ hours, daily), Dàlián (Y640, one hour and 10 minutes, daily), Dāndōng (Y580), Dūnhuáng (Y1650), Fúzhōu (Y1390, 2½ hours, daily), Guǎngzhōu (Y1510, two hours and 50 minutes, daily), Guìlín (Y1580, 4¼ hours, daily), Guìyáng (Y1530), Hāěrbīn (Y890), Hǎikǒu (Y1950, three hours and 40 minutes), Hǎilǎěr (Y1060, two hours, four times weekly), Hángzhōu (Y1050, 50 minutes, daily), Héféi (Y910), Hong Kong (Y2800, three hours, daily), Hohhot (Y460, one hour, daily), Huángshān (Y1000), Jílín (Y880), Jì'nán (Y500, one hour, daily), Kūnmíng (Y1600, four hours, daily), Lánzhōu (Y1220), Lhasa (Y2040), Luòyáng (Y630), Nánchāng (Y1190, two hours, daily), Nánjīng (Y930, one hour and 35 minutes, daily), Nánníng (Y1790, three hours and 25 minutes, daily), Níngbō (Y1080, two hours and 10 minutes, daily), Qīngdǎo (Y660), Shànghǎi (Y1040, two hours, daily), Shàntóu (Y1610, three hours, daily), Shěnyáng (Y640, one hour, daily), Shēnzhèn (Y1550, three hours, daily), Shíjiāzhuāng (Y180), Tàiyuán (Y540, 50 minutes, daily), Ürümqi (Y2080), Wēnzhōu (Y1390, two hours, daily), Wǔhàn (Y990, two hours, daily), Xiàmén (Y1520, 2½ hours, daily), Xī'ān (Y970, 1½ hours, daily), Xilinhot (Y340, 50 minutes, twice weekly), Xīníng (Y1310), Yánān (Y800), Yanji (Y900, one hour and 40 minutes, four times weekly), Yāntái (Y630), Yíchāng (Y1190), Zhèngzhōu (Y630, one hour and 10 minutes, daily)

CAAC goes by a variety of aliases (Air China, China Eastern Airlines etc), but you can buy tickets for all of them at the Aviation Building (Mínháng Dàshà; ☎ 6601 3336 for domestic, ☎ 6601 6667 for international) at 15 Xichang'an Jie, south-west of Zhōngnánhǎi Hú. You can purchase the same tickets at any travel agent or business centre. Domestic plane ticket prices are regulated so they're the same price no matter where you buy them.

The offices of other airlines are:

Aeroflot (☎ 6500 2266 ext 8300) 1st floor, Jinglun Hotel, 3 Jianguomenwai Dajie
Air Canada (☎ 6468 2001) Unit C201, Lufthansa Centre, 50 Liangmaqiao Lu
Air France (☎ 6588 1388) Room 512, 5th floor, Full Link Plaza, 18 Chaoyangmenwai Dajie
Air Macau (☎ 6515 8988) Room 807, Scitech Tower, 22 Jianguomenwai Dajie
British Airways (☎ 6512 4070) Room 210, 2nd floor, Scitech Tower, 22 Jianguomenwai Dajie
China Northwest Airlines (☎ 6601 7755 ext 2141) Aviation Bldg, 15 Xichang'an Jie
China Sichuan Airlines (☎ 6601 7755 ext 2265) Aviation Bldg, 15 Xichang'an Jie
China Southern Airlines (☎ 6601 7596) Aviation Bldg, 15 Xichang'an Jie
China Xinjiang Airlines (☎ 6601 7755) Aviation Bldg, 15 Xichang'an Jie
Dragonair (☎ 6518 2533) Room 1710, Bldg A, Henderson Center, 18 Jianguomennei Dajie
Japan Airlines (☎ 6513 0888) 1st floor, Changfugong Office Bldg, 26A Jianguomenwai Dajie
Korean Air (☎ 6505 0088) Room 401, West Wing, China World Trade Centre, 1 Jianguomenwai Dajie
Lufthansa Airlines (☎ 6465 4488) C202, Lufthansa Center, 50 Liangmaqiao Lu
Malaysia Airlines (☎ 6505 2681) W115a/b Level 1, West Wing, China World Trade Centre, 1 Jianguomenwai Dajie
MIAT-Mongolian Airlines (☎ 6507 9297) 1st floor, China Golden Bridge Plaza, 1a Jianguomennei Dajie
Northwest Airlines (☎ 6505 3505) Room 104, China World Trade Centre, 1 Jianguomenwai Dajie
Qantas Airways (☎ 6467 4794/3337) Room S120, Lufthansa Center, 50 Liangmaqiao Lu
Thai Airways International (☎ 6460 8899) Room S102B, Lufthansa Center, 50 Liangmaqiao Lu
United Airlines (☎ 6463 8551) Lufthansa Center, 50 Liangmaqiao Lu

Bus

Besides being cheaper than the train, it's also easier to book a seat. Sleeper buses are widely available and certainly recommended for long overnight journeys. In general, arriving by bus is easier than departing, mainly because when leaving it's hard to figure out which bus station has the bus you need.

The basic rule is that long-distance bus stations are on the perimeter of the city in the direction you want to go. The major ones are at Xīzhímén (☎ 6218 3454) in the west and Dōngzhímén (☎ 6467 4995) in the north-east. Other important ones are at Zhàogōngkǒu bus station (Běijīng map; ☎ 6722 9491) in the south, useful for buses to Tiānjīn and Qīngdǎo, and Yǒngdìngmén (☎ 6303 4307) next to Beijing south train station (Běijīng map).

Other long-distance bus stations include Hǎihùtún (Běijīng map), Běijiāo (Běijīng map; also called Déshèngmén), and Mǎjuàn. The Tiānqiáo bus station (western side of Tiāntán Gōngyuán) and Líanhūachí bus station (Běijīng map; ☎ 6345 4027) are two places where you can get buses to sites south-west of Běijīng.

In addition, there are a few small bus stations where tour buses and minibuses gather (usually just in the morning) looking for passengers heading to the Great Wall and other sites in the outlying areas. The most important of these is the Qián Mén bus station (which has two parts) just to the south-west of Tiānānmén Square.

Train

Travellers arrive and depart by train at Beijing train station (Běijīng huǒchē zhàn; ☎ 6563 3262/3242), which is located south-east of the Forbidden City, or Beijing west train station (Běijīng xī zhàn; ☎ 6321 6253), which is near Líanhūachí Gōngyuán. International trains to Moscow, Pyongyang and Ulaan Baatar arrive at and leave Beijing train station; trains for Hong Kong and Vietnam leave from Beijing west train station.

There are also two other stations of significance in the city: Beijing south train station (Yǒngdìngmén huǒchē zhàn; Běijīng map; ☎ 6563 5222) and Beijing north train station (Běijīng běizhàn; ☎ 6563 6122/6223) on the Second Ring Rd.

Avoid buying tickets in the main ticket hall. There is a ticketing office for foreigners at Beijing train station on the 1st floor, accessed through the soft seat waiting room (guìbīn hǔochēshì). (There is also a foreigners ticketing office on the second floor of Beijing west train station.) You can book return tickets here as well as tickets for trains departing from other cities, eg, from Nánjīng to Shànghǎi, as long as there are seats available. Tickets can be booked five or six days in advance. Your chances of getting a sleeper (hard or soft) are good if you book ahead.

If you can read Chinese, you can check out train schedules and order tickets for trains from Běijīng online at Ⓦ www.piao .com. This could be useful – but you need to book five to 10 days in advance. Tickets are delivered (delivery fee Y10-20) and must be paid for in cash. You can theoretically book train tickets over the phone (☎ 6321 7188), but you need to be able to speak Chinese and be both patient and persistent.

A new train (T21/22) boasting the 'standards of a four-star hotel' (China Daily) should be shuttling between Běijīng and Shànghǎi by the time you read this. It'll be cheaper than flying, but more expensive than taking the usual proletariat train. Soft sleeper couchettes will be fitted with showers, boast liquid crystal TV sets and space for laptops.

See the table for approximate travel times and train fares out of Běijīng for hard seat, hard sleeper and soft sleeper. Variations may arise because of alternative routes taken by different trains: For example, the journey to Shanghai can take between 14 and 21 hours depending on the train.

GETTING AROUND
To/From the Airport

Beijing Capital International Airport (Shǒudū Jīchǎng; ☎ 6456 2580) is 28km north-east of the centre of Běijīng.

At the airport you'll be presented with a bewildering choice of buses all congregating by the main exit. In fact, almost any bus that gets you to a subway station will do; they travel fast along the highway but often run into congestion once in the city proper. All buses into town cost Y16.

The CAAC 'Airbus' operates two routes. Route A goes to and from the International

BĚIJĪNG

Travel Times & Train Fares from Běijīng

destination	soft sleeper (Y)	hard sleeper (Y)	hard seat (Y)	approx travel time (hours)
Bāotóu	-	181	97	14
Běidàihé	-	-	62	3
Chángchūn	379	249	137	14
Chángshā	529	345	191	16
Chéngdé	-	-	41	5
Chéngdū	642	418	231	28
Chóngqìng	658	430	238	30
Dàlián	373	269	147	10
Dāndōng	400	263	143	14
Dàtóng	159	93	46	5
Fúzhōu	705	458	253	35
Guǎngzhōu	705	458	253	24
Guìlín	658	429	237	24
Hāěrbīn	442	290	158	13
Hángzhōu	554	363	200	16
Hohhot	254	170	92	11
Hong Kong	1027	662	-	28
Jǐ'nán	205	128	73	5½
Kūnmíng	890	578	320	44
Lánzhōu	371	235	118	29
Luòyáng	184	117	53	10
Nánjīng	417	274	150	12
Nánníng	770	499	276	31
Qīngdǎo	326	215	116	10
Qíqíhā'ěr	529	345	191	16
Shànghǎi	499	327	179	14
Shěnyáng	286	191	103	9
Shēnzhèn	720	467	257	30
Shíjiāzhuāng	-	-	40	4
Sūzhōu	472	309	170	14
Tài'ān	241	149	92	7
Tàiyuán	224	149	79	11
Tiānjīn	-	-	25	1.5
Ürümqi	1006	652	363	49
Xiàmén	715	465	256	43
Xī'ān	417	274	150	14
Xīníng	658	430	238	33
Yínchuān	292	188	94	21
Zhèngzhōu	264	175	94	8

Hotel; this is probably the most popular bus with travellers. Route B goes to the Xīnxīng Fàndiàn, on the western side of town near Yùyuántán Líanhuāchí. Buses run every 30 minutes 5.30am to 7pm daily.

Another CAAC shuttle bus (Y16) departs from the terminal building, making a number of hotel stops en route to the Aviation Building in the centre of town. The bus operates from 5.30am to 8.30pm daily. Other routes are to Zhōngguāncūn in north-west Běijīng and to the China Art Gallery, north of the central shopping area of Wángfǔjīng.

Some hotels have their own shuttle bus, so ask if you have booked ahead or if you are booking a room form the airport hotel reservations counter outside arrivals.

A taxi (using its meter) should cost about Y85 from the airport to the town centre (depending on the type of taxi). Beware of rip-off taxi drivers who approach you inside the terminal and ask for something like Y250 for the trip – don't even talk to them, just go outside and get in the taxi queue outside the arrival area. Drivers will also expect you to pay the Y10 toll if you take the airport expressway.

Bus

A mind-boggling number of buses navigate Běijīng's traffic-choked boulevards. Destinations are written in Chinese only and figuring out the system will take patience – it's considerably easier if you score a bus map. The buses are packed at the best of times, and during the rush hour it's armpits and elbows all round.

Buses run from 5am to 11pm daily or thereabouts, and the stops are few and far between. It's important to work out how many stops you need to go before boarding.

Buses are routed through landmarks and key intersections, and if you can pick out the head and tail of the route you can get a good idea of where you are heading. Major stations are situated near long-distance junctions: the main Beijing train station, Dōngzhímén, Hǎihùtún, Yǒngdìngmén and the Front Gate. Beijing Zoo has the biggest pile-up, with about 15 bus lines, since it's where inner and outer Běijīng converge.

One- and two-digit bus numbers are city core; 100-series buses are trolleys and 300-series are suburban lines. Minibuses follow the main bus routes, and are slightly more expensive. Some buses are air-conditioned and a rapidly increasing number run on natural gas. If you work out how to combine bus and subway connections the subway will speed up part of the trip.

The following routes hit major points around the city:

1 Beijing west train station, heading east on Fuxingmen Dajie, Xichang'an Jie, Dongchang'an Jie, Jianguomennei Dajie, Jianguomenwai Dajie, Jianguo Lu and terminating at a major bus stop called Bawangfen (intersection of Jianguo Lu and Xidawang Lu)

2 The Front Gate, north on Dongdan Beidajie, Dongsi Nandajie, Dongsi Beidajie, Lama Temple, Ethnic Minorities Park, Asian Games Village

3 Jijia Temple (the south-west extremity of the Third Ring Rd), Grand View Garden, Lèyóu Fàndiàn, Jingguang New World Hotel, Tuánjiéhú Gōngyuán, Agricultural Exhibition Centre, Lufthansa Center

4 Beijing Zoo, Exhibition Centre, Second Ring Rd, Holiday Inn Downtown, Yuetan Gōngyuán, Fuxingmen Dajie flyover, Qianmen Xidajie, Front Gate

6 Guofang University, Agricultural University, Beijing University, Qinghua West Gate, People's University, Wēigōngcūn, Ethnic Minorities Park, Beijing Library, Ganjiakou, Yùyuāntán, Military Museum, Beijing west train station

Subway

The subway (dì tiě), which debuted in 1969, is probably the best way to travel around. The Underground Dragon can move at up to 70km/h – a jaguar compared with the lumbering buses. The system is modest and trains are showing their age, but the system will be given a Herculean makeover with some five new subway lines planned to take the strain off the roads before the 2008 Olympics.

There are two established lines, the Circle line and the East-West line. The fare is a flat Y2 on the Circle line and Y3 on the East-West line, regardless of distance.

Trains run at a frequency of one every few minutes during peak times. It can get very crowded, but it sure beats the buses! The carriages have seats for 60 and standing room for 200. The subway runs from 5am to 11pm daily; platform signs are in Chinese characters and pinyin.

To recognise a subway station (dì tiě zhàn), look for the subway symbol, which is a blue English capital 'D' with a circle around it.

Circle Line This 16km train line presently consists of 18 stations: Běijīng zhàn, Jiànguómén, Cháoyángmén, Dōngsìshítiáo, Dōngzhímén, Yōnghégōng, Āndìngmén, Gǔlóu, Jīshuǐtán, Xīzhímén (the north train station and zoo), Chēgōngzhuāng, Fùchéngmén, Fùxīngmén, Chàngchūnjiē, Xuānwǔmén, Hépíngmén, Qiánmén and Chóngwénmén.

BEIJING

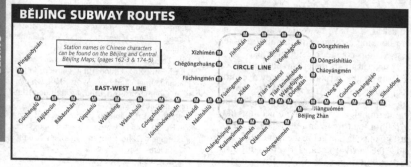

BĚIJĪNG SUBWAY ROUTES

Station names in Chinese characters can be found on the Běijīng and Central Běijīng Maps, (pages 162-3 & 174-5)

Pīnggǔoyuán

CIRCLE LINE

Xīzhímén   Jīshuǐtán   Gǔlóu   Āndìngmén   Yōnghégōng   Dōngzhímén

Chēgōngzhuāng   Dōngsìshítiáo

Fùchéngmén   Cháoyángmén

EAST-WEST LINE

Gǔchénglù   Bābǎoshān   Yùquánlù   Wǔkēsōng   Wànshòulù   Gōngzhǔfén   Jūnshìbówùguǎn   Mùxīdì   Nánlǐshílù   Fùxīngmén   Xīdān   Tiān'ānméndōng   Tiān'ānménxī   Wángfǔjǐng   Dōngdān   Yǒng'ānlǐ   Jiànguómén   Guómào   Dàwàngqiáo   Sìhuìxī   Sìhuìdōng

Běijīng Zhàn

Chángchūnjiē   Xuānwǔmén   Hépíngmén   Qiánmén   Chóngwénmén

East-West Line This line has 23 stations and runs from Sìhuìdōng to Pīnggǔoyuán, a western suburb of Běijīng. The stops are Sìhuìdōng, Sìhuìxī, Dàwàngqiáo, Guómào, Yǒng'ānlǐ, Jiànguómén, Dōngdān, Wángfǔjǐng, Tiān'ānméndōng, Tiān'ānménxī, Xīdān, Fùxīngmén, Nánlǐshílù, Mùxīdì, Jūnshìbówùguǎn, Gōngzhǔfén, Wànshòulù, Wǔkēsōng, Yùquánlù, Bābǎoshān, Bājiǎocūn, Gǔchénglù and Pīnggǔoyuán. The Circle line intersects with the East-West line at Fùxīngmén and Jiànguómén.

Taxi

Taxis are everywhere, and finding one is only a problem during rush hours and rainstorms.

Taxis come in different classes. Red Xiali taxis are the most economical at Y1.2 per kilometre (Y10 for the first 3km). Next are the larger Y1.6 taxis (Y10 for the first 4km), many of these are red Citroens; it pays to take these if you are going a short distance. Top of the line are Volkswagen Santana 2000 taxis that cost Y12 for the first 4km and Y2 for each kilometre thereafter.

Don't expect rear seat belts in any but the best cabs. It's a good idea to have your destination in writing. Taxis are required to switch on the meter for all journeys; if the driver doesn't use the meter, you are under no legal obligation to pay. Between 11pm and 6am there is a 20% surcharge added to the flagfall metered fare. There's a small red sticker on the side rear window of every taxi that tells you how much it is per kilometre.

Bicycle

Getting around Běijīng by bike is an excellent idea, as the city is flat and there are ample bicycle lanes. The increase in traffic in recent years has made biking along major thoroughfares more dangerous and nerve-racking, however. Cycling through Běijīng's hútòng is still an experience not to be missed (see the boxed text 'On Your Bike').

Budget hotels are the place to rent bicycles, which cost around Y10 per day (plus a deposit); rental at upmarket hotels is far more expensive. Rental shops are scarce. When renting a bike it's safest to use your own lock(s) in order to prevent bicycle theft, a common problem in Běijīng. Parking your bike in one of the more secure pavement bike parking lots all over town is around Y0.2.

Good quality bikes can be bought from Giant (☎ 6403 4537) at 77 Jiaodaokou Dongdajie.

Around Běijīng

THE GREAT WALL 长城
Cháng Chéng

'It sure is a great wall.'
US president Richard Nixon, visiting the wall in 1972

Also known to the Chinese as the '10,000 Lǐ Wall' (one lǐ is roughly 500m), the Great Wall stretches from Shānhǎiguān on the east coast to Jiāyùguān in the Gobi Desert.

Standard histories emphasise the unity of the wall. The 'original' wall was begun during the Qin dynasty (221–207 BC), when China was unified under Emperor Qin Shihuang. Separate walls, constructed by independent kingdoms to keep out marauding nomads, were linked up. The effort required hundreds of thousands of workers, many of them political prisoners, and 10 years of hard labour under General Meng Tian. An estimated 180 million cubic metres of rammed earth were used to form the core of the original wall, and legend has it that one of the building materials used was the bodies of deceased workers.

The wall never really did perform its function as a defence line. As Genghis Khan supposedly said, 'The strength of a wall depends on the courage of those who defend it'. Sentries could be bribed. However, it did work very well as a kind of elevated highway, transporting men and equipment across mountainous terrain. Its beacon tower system, using smoke signals generated by burning wolves' dung, quickly transmitted news of enemy movements back to the capital. To the west was Jiāyùguān, an important link on the Silk Road, where there was a customs post of sorts and where unwanted Chinese were ejected through the gates to face the terrifying wild west.

During the Ming dynasty a determined effort was made to rehash the whole project, this time facing it with bricks and stone slabs – some 60 million cubic metres of them. This project took over 100 years, and the cost in human effort and resources was phenomenal.

The wall was largely forgotten after that. Lengthy sections of it have returned to dust and the wall might have disappeared totally had it not been rescued by the tourist industry. Several important sections have been rebuilt, kitted out with souvenir shops,

restaurants and amusement park rides, and formally opened to the public. The most touristed area of the wall by far is Bādálǐng; a magnetic levitation train is already in the planning stages. Also renovated but less touristed are Sīmǎtái and Jīnshānlǐng. But to truly appreciate the wall's magnificence, seeing the wall *au naturel*, such as at Huánghuāchéng, is well worth the effort.

Bādálǐng 八达岭

Most visitors see the Great Wall's most artificial incarnation at Bādálǐng (☎ *6912 1338/1423/1520; admission Y35; open 8.30am-8pm daily*), 70km north-west of Běijīng at an elevation of 1000m. Come here if you want that fairground feel and the companionship of tourist squads surging over the ramparts. A cable car exists for the weary (Y50 round trip). A winter trip is recommended if you want a more solitary inspection of the masonry.

The restored section crawls for about 1km before nobly disintegrating into ruins; unfortunately you cannot realistically explore these more authentic fragments.

Apart from the pristine battlements, you can be conveyed back into history via 15-minute films about the Great Wall at the **Great Wall Circle Vision Theatre** (*admission Y25*), a 360-degree amphitheatre. The admission fee also gets you into the China Great Wall Museum.

Conserving the Great Wall

Built to defend the Middle Kingdom from Mongol attack, the Great Wall north of Běijīng is now under modern attack, from hordes of day trippers riding in Jettas and Santanas, tossing their picnic garbage, letting off earth-shaking fireworks and etching their inglorious names on its 400-year-old history.

No longer self-protected by its inaccessibility – most sections are within three-hour's drive for Běijīng's 750 thousand private car owners – the arrival of the fun-seeking nouveau riche at once-forgotten sections of wall has made tourism development a high priority of local farmers and township bureaucrats eager to impress the party elite with their ability to 'relieve poverty'. Each would like their section of wall to become the next Bādálǐng, but only bigger and 'better', with more cablecars and tourist kitsch, the trademarks of domestic tourism.

But the Great Wall not only belongs to China, someone cries, it is a Unesco World Heritage Site, and surely that ensures its preservation? In theory yes, but in reality, the designation shrouds the wall under a false cloak of security. The Great Wall is the world's most extensive outdoor museum – without a curator. It is neither protected by any specific laws, nor managed as a relic or resource by any special office.

William Lindesay
William Lindesay is author of *Hiking on History: Exploring Beijing's Great Wall* (Oxford University Press)

BĚIJĪNG

Getting There & Away CITS, CTS, big hotels and everyone else in the tourist business does a tour to Bādálǐng. Prices border on the ridiculous, with some hotels asking over Y300 per person.

Probably the cheapest way to get to Bādálǐng is to take bus No 919 (Y7) from Déshèngmén (next to the Jīshuǐtán subway stop). Buses leave regularly from 5.30am; the last bus leaves Bādálǐng for Běijīng at 6.30pm.

Big tour buses leave for Bādálǐng and Thirteen Tombs (see that section later) from the south-west corner of Tiānānmén Square between 6.30am and 10am daily (Y50).

Tour bus Nos 1 and 5 go to Bādálǐng from the north-east corner of the Front Gate, tour bus No 2 takes you to Bādálǐng from Beijing train station and tour bus No 4 will get you there from the zoo. All leave between 6am and 10am and cost Y36. Allow about nine hours for the whole trip. Inexpensive Chinese tour buses also run to Bādálǐng, although they usually combine Bādálǐng with a visit to Thirteen Tombs as well as painful detours to herbal medicine or souvenir shops.

A taxi to the wall and back will cost a minimum of Y400 for an eight-hour hire with a maximum of four passengers.

Mùtiányù 慕田峪

The section of wall at Mùtiányù (☎ 6162 6873; admission Y21; open 6.30am-5.30pm daily), 90km north-east of Běijīng, dates from the Ming dynasty, built upon an earlier Northern Qi dynasty conception. It was restored as an alternative to Bādálǐng, provoking Japanese tour buses to decamp here en masse. Despite the hawking and tourist clutter, this stretch of wall is notable for its numerous guard towers and stirring views. The wall is equipped with a cable car (Y50 round trip).

Getting There & Away From Dōngzhímén bus station take bus No 916 to Huáiróu (Y5, one hour), then change for a minibus (Y20) for Mùtiányù. Tour bus No 6 from Xuānwǔmén runs at weekends to Mùtiányù (Y43, 6.30am to 8.30am).

Jūyōng Pass 居庸关
Jūyōng Guān

Originally constructed in the 5th century and rebuilt by the Ming, this section of the wall (☎ 6977 1665; admission Y25; open 6am-4pm daily) was considered one of the most strategically important because of its position as a link to Běijīng. However, this section has been thoroughly renovated to

Standing for over 2000 years, the Great Wall is China's most spectacular attraction.

the point where you don't feel as if you're walking on a part of history. Still, if you're in a hurry, it's the closest section of the wall to Běijīng. You can do the steep and somewhat strenuous circuit in under two hours.

Getting There & Away Approximately 50km northwest of Běijīng, Jūyōng Pass is on the road to Bādálǐng. Any of the buses listed in the Getting There & Away section for Bādálǐng can get you there – but tell the bus driver you want to be dropped off at Jūyōng Guān Chángchéng.

Sīmǎtái 司马台

In Mìyún country near the town of Gǔběikǒu, the stirring remains at Sīmǎtái (☎ 6903 5025; admission Y20; open 8am-5pm daily) make for a more exhilarating Great Wall experience. Built during the reign of Ming dynasty emperor Hongwu, the 19km undulating stretch is punctuated with watchtowers, steep plunges and scrambling ascents.

It's not for the faint-hearted: this rough section of the wall is very steep. A few slopes have a 70-degree incline and you need both hands free, so bring a day-pack to hold your camera and other essentials. One narrow section of footpath has a 500m drop, so it's no place for acrophobics. The steepness and sheer drops, however, do help keep out the riffraff. The cable car (Y50 round trip) could be an alternative to a sprained ankle. Take strong shoes with a good grip.

Sīmǎtái has some unusual features, like 'obstacle-walls' – walls-within-walls used for defending against enemies who'd already scaled the Great Wall. Small cannons have been discovered in this area, as well as evidence of rocket-type weapons such as flying knives and flying swords. A further peculiar feature is the toboggan ride (Y30).

Unfazed by the dizzying terrain, hawkers make an unavoidable appearance, but you won't be shortchanged by the views.

Getting There & Away Sīmǎtái is 110km north-east of Běijīng. From Dōngzhímén bus station take a minibus to Mìyún (1¼ hours; Y6). From Mìyún take a minibus to Sīmǎtái (another 75 minutes) or a taxi (round trip Y100). At weekends, tour bus No 12 leaves for Sīmǎtái from Xuānwǔmén (Y50, 7am to 8.30am).

Injuries on the Great Wall

Never in his most disturbing dreams could the Great Wall's first architect Qin Shihuang imagine barbarians wobbling around his masterpiece in 'I climbed the Great Wall T-shirts'. His edifice occasionally retaliates, however, against ill-prepared or over-adventurous tourists.

Despite being a generally hazard-free outing for most day-trippers, more elderly or unfit travellers can drag a twisted ankle or even a broken leg back with them through customs. Certain parts of the rampart, especially the steeper reaches, can exhaust the unfit and the steps are often uneven. Remember to take bottled water and shoes with a good grip.

Sīmǎtái can be precarious and Huánghuā, with its wilder sections, can be quite treacherous; a traveller recently fell off a section of this wall, ending up with severe injuries. Fortunately, he was part of a group; if he had been alone he might not have been found.

For budget travellers, the best deal around is offered through the Jīnghuá Fàndiàn – Y60 for the return journey by minibus (not including ticket). Hiring a taxi from Běijīng for the day costs about Y400.

Jīnshānlǐng 金山岭

Though not as steep (and therefore not as impressive) as Sīmǎtái, the Great Wall at Jīnshānlǐng (admission Y40) is considerably less developed than any of the sites previously mentioned.

Jīnshānlǐng is the starting point for a hike to Sīmǎtái. You can do the walk in the opposite direction, but getting a ride back to Běijīng from Sīmǎtái is easier than from Jīnshānlǐng. Of course, getting a ride should be no problem if you've made arrangements with your driver to pick you up (and didn't pay him in advance). The distance between Jīnshānlǐng and Sīmǎtái is only about 10km, but it takes nearly four hours because the trail is steep and stony.

Getting There & Away From Dōngzhímén bus station, take a minibus to Mìyún (Y6, 1¼ hour), change to a minibus to Gǔběikǒu, and get off at Bākèshíyíng (Y6). If you are heading to Chéngdé (see the Héběi chapter), you will pass Jīnshānlǐng en route.

Huánghuā

For a genuine wall experience close to Běijīng, the Huánghuā section is ideal. The Great Wall at Huánghuā lies in two sections, clinging to hillsides adjacent to a reservoir. Around 60km north of Běijīng, Huánghuā is a classic and well-preserved example of Ming defence with high and wide ramparts, intact parapets and sturdy beacon towers.

It is said that one Lord Cai masterminded this section, employing meticulous quality control. Each inch of the masonry represented one labourer's whole day's work. When the Ministry of War got wind of the extravagance, Cai was beheaded for his efforts. In spite of the trauma, it's said his decapitated body stood erect for three days, before toppling. Years later, a general judged Lord Cai's wall to be exemplary and he was posthumously rehabilitated.

The section to the east, accessed across the dam and via a ticket collector (Y1) rises abruptly from a solitary watchtower *(dílóu)*. Be warned that it's both steep and crumbling – there are no guard rails here and it's unrenovated. There are further tickets ahead, depending on how far you venture. It's possible to make it all the way to the Mùtiányù section of the wall, but it'll take you a few days and some hard clambering (pack a sleeping bag). Local hawkers have got wind of foreigners in town, but they won't follow you up the wall.

The section of wall immediately to the west is in bad shape, so you'll have to clamber up the hillside from the south. Alternatively (and for ticket-free access and a great walk), walk south and take the first turning (about 500m down) on the right, walk through the village, keep going until the river bends to the right and take the right fork following the river. Keep bearing right all the way (you'll pass fading Cultural Revolution characters on a corner that proclaim 'Long Live Chairman Mao' and just around the corner 'The Red Heart Faces the Communist Party'). Soon you'll see a watchtower ahead – the path leads up to it.

The whole jaunt should take 45 minutes, and you can continue along the wall. Be warned that the wall here can be quite narrow and perilous, so don't carry on unless you feel confident (see the boxed text 'Injuries on the Great Wall').

Places to Stay & Eat A number of places have sprung up offering beds.

Xiaohong's Shop (☎ 6165 1393, e *damat thewall@hotmail.com)* Beds up to Y35. This is a shack at the entrance which is simple, but clean.

Cāngpōfú Lǐdiàn (☎ 6165 2377) Beds Y20. South of the entrance, this place also has neat quads.

Yínglínlóu Jiǔjiā (☎ 6165 1078) Beds Y35. Farther up on the left-hand side of the road north is this small place that looks like a restaurant, but has beds in clean rooms. All of these places double as restaurants, and none of the bedrooms have bathrooms.

Jīntāng Shānzhuāng (☎ 6499 4812/ 4813) Doubles/triples Y258/288. This is a more upmarket, resort-style establishment overlooking the reservoir, north of Yínglínlóu Jiǔjiā. It's fine, if you like the white-tile effect and security guards.

Getting There & Away You can reach Huánghuā by taking bus No 961 (Y8, two hours, two am and pm departures) from the Dōngzhímén long-distance bus station. The last bus back to Běijīng is at 2.50pm. Ask for Huánghuāchéng and don't get off at the smaller Huánghuāzhèn by mistake. Also from Dōngzhímén long-distance bus station, bus No 916 to Huáiróu leaves every 15 minutes from 5.30am to 6.30pm (Y4) and takes just over an hour to get to Huáiróu. Same number minibuses run the route a little quicker for Y5. From Huáiróu you can take a minibus directly to Huánghuāchéng (Y4, 40 minutes) or hire a *miàndì* (yellow taxi minivan) from Huáiróu to Huánghuāchéng (Y60 round trip). For another Y60, you can hire a miàndì all the way back to the third ring road in Běijīng (most miàndì aren't allowed to enter Běijīng).

THIRTEEN TOMBS 十三陵
Shísān Líng

About 50km north-west of Běijīng, at the Ming Tombs (☎ 6076 1156; admission Y20 per tomb; open 8am-5.30pm daily), lies the final resting place of 13 of the 16 Ming emperors. The Confucian layout and design may intoxicate more erudite visitors, but many find the place lifeless and ho-hum. Confucian shrines lack the vibrancy and colour of Buddhist or Taoist temples, and their motifs can be bewilderingly inscrutable.

Open to the public are three renovated tombs – Cháng Líng, Dìng Líng and Zhāo Líng. Cháng Líng and Dìng Líng are surrounded by sprawling concrete parking lots inundated with big tour buses. Zhāo Líng is quieter, while the rest of the tombs are in various stages of dilapidation, and are sealed off by locked gates.

The road leading up to the tombs is a 7km stretch called the 'Spirit Way'. It starts with a triumphal arch, then goes through the Great Palace Gate, where officials once had to dismount, and passes a giant *bìxì* (tortoise-like animal), which bears the largest stele in China. This is followed by a guard of 12 sets of stone animals.

Getting There & Away

Tour buses usually combine a visit to the Ming Tombs with a visit to the Great Wall at Bādálǐng. Tour bus No 1 (Y36) leaves between 6am and 10am daily from the Front Gate to take in both Bādálǐng and the Ming Tombs. Big tour buses leave from across the street from the south-west corner of Tiānānmén Square between 6.30am and 10am daily, heading for Bādálǐng and the Ming Tombs (Y50). Plan about nine hours for the trip.

If you want to go independently, take minibus No 345 from Déshèngmén to Chāngpíng (Y6, one hour); wave down the mini-bus just outside the Jīshuǐtán subway exit. Take the bus to the Dōngguān stop and change to bus No 314 for the tombs. Alternatively, take a taxi from Chāngpíng (Y20). Chāngpíng can also be reached by train from Beijing train station. Or you can take a large air-con bus (No 845) from Xīzhímén (just outside the Xīzhímén subway stop) to Chāngpíng (Y7). It's about a 10-minute ride from Chāngpíng to the entrance of the tombs.

EASTERN QING TOMBS 清东陵
Qīng Dōng Líng

The area of the Eastern Qing Tombs (admission Y55; open 8am-5pm daily) could be called Death Valley, housing as it does five emperors, 14 empresses and 136 imperial consorts. In the mountains ringing the valley are buried princes, dukes, imperial nurses and more.

Emperor Qianlong (1711–99) started preparations for his tomb when he was 30, and by the time he was 88 he had used up 90 tonnes of his silver building it. His resting place covers half a square kilometre. Some of the beamless stone chambers are decorated with Tibetan and Sanskrit sutras, and the doors bear bas-relief bodhisattvas.

Empress Dowager Cixi also got a head start. Her tomb, Dingdong, was completed some three decades before her death. The phoenix (symbol of the empress) appears above that of the dragon (the emperor's symbol) in the artwork at the front of the tomb – not side by side as on other tombs. Both tombs were plundered in the 1920s.

Located in Zūnhuà county, 125km east of Běijīng, the Eastern Qing Tombs offer a lot more to see than the Thirteen Tombs, although you may be a little jaded after the Forbidden City.

Getting There & Away

Unfortunately, getting to the Eastern Qing Tombs by public bus is difficult and involves changing buses a few times along the way. Weekend tour buses, however, leave from Xuānwǔmén at 7am (Y70) and take around two hours to get there. It is also possible to go from Tiānjīn.

TÁNZHÈ SÌ 潭柘寺
Cudrania Pool Temple

About 45km west of Běijīng is Tánzhè Sì (☎ 6086 2505, Tánzhè Shān; admission Y20; open 8.30am-6pm daily), the largest of all the capital's temples. The Buddhist complex is also Běijīng's oldest, dating back to the 3rd century (Jin dynasty), begetting the Chinese dictum 'First there was Tánzhè Temple, then there was Běijīng'.

Its great age leaves the temple graced with a number of features – dragon decorations, mythical animal sculptures and grimacing gods – no longer found in temples in the capital.

BEIJING

The temple takes its name from its proximity to the Dragon Pool (Lóng Tán) and some rare cudrania *(zhè)* trees. Locals come to the Dragon Pool to pray for rain during droughts. The cudrania trees nourish silkworms and provide a yellow dye. The bark of the tree is believed to cure women of sterility, perhaps explaining why so few of these trees survive at the temple entrance.

Getting There & Away
Take the subway to Píngguǒyuán and then take bus No 931 to the temple. Tour bus No 7 (Y42) from the Front Gate runs to the temple, departing between 6am and 8pm.

PEKING MAN SITE
Zhōukǒudiàn Běijīng Yúanrén Yízhǐ
A Unesco World Heritage Site, the Peking Man Site *(☎ 6930 1272; admission Y20; open 8am-4.30pm daily)* is the site where remains of primitive people who lived here half a million years ago were excavated. Sadly, the site is poorly maintained and has fallen into neglect; Běijīng apparently is unwilling to foot the estimated US$650,000 that is needed to get it back into shape.

Getting There & Away
The Peking Man Site is 48km south-west of Běijīng. Bus 917 from Tiānqiáo bus station (western side of Tiāntán Gōngyuán) goes to Fángshān (one hour) from where you can take a bus (No 2) or taxi to the site (6km). If combined with a trip to Tánzhè Sì and Marco Polo Bridge, approaching the site by taxi is not unreasonable.

SHÍDÙ 十渡
About 110km south-west of Běijīng city, Shídù is Běijīng's answer to Guìlín. Its pinnacle-shaped **rock formations**, pleasant rivers and general beauty make it a favourite with expats. Shídù means '10 ferries' or '10 crossings': before the new road and bridges were built, travellers had to cross the Juma River 10 times while going along the gorge from Zhāngfāng and Shídù village.

Places to Stay
Yíshūlóu Fàndiàn (☎ 6134 9988, Shidu Village) Rooms Y30 per person. In the town of Shídù, this hotel can be found along the main road about 1.5km from the train station. When you see a two-storey building with red lanterns in front you've found it. It's on the 2nd floor, above the restaurant.

Shānguāng Lóu (☎ 6134 0762, Badu Village) Rooms Y280. You'll find this large hotel down near Jiǔdù (Ninth Ferry), next to the bungee jumping platform. There's also a camping ground here, conveniently located on a flood-plain.

Dōngzhèng Bīnguǎn (☎ 6134 0791, Liudu Village) Rooms Y200-240. Nicely located in Liùdù on the river and away from any amusement facilities, this hotel has clean standard rooms.

Getting There & Away
Trains (Y12, two hours) run from Beijing south train station (Yǒngdìngmén) for Shídù at 6.36am, 7.30am and 5.40pm. Trains leave Shídù for Běijīng at 9.36am, 3.50pm and 7.40pm. If you take the morning train, the trip can be done in one day.

Tiānjīn 天津

Telephone code: ☎ 022
Population: 10.4 million
Area: 11,300 sq km

Like Běijīng, Shànghǎi and Chóngqìng, Tiānjīn belongs to no province – it's a special municipality, which gives it a degree of autonomy, but it's also closely administered by the central government. The city is nicknamed 'Shànghǎi of the North', a reference to its history as a foreign concession, its heavy industrial output, its large port and its European architecture. Foreigners who live in the municipality sometimes call it 'TJ' – an abbreviation that mystifies the Chinese.

Tiānjīn is often overlooked by travellers in their rush to get to Běijīng. However, Tiānjīn has developed an intriguing individual style and laissez-faire attitude that makes it a rewarding stopping point for a few days. For business folk, the big event of the year is the Tianjin Export Commodities Fair held every March. Those interested in attending should contact China International Travel Service (CITS; Zhōngguó Guójì Lǚxíngshè), or the exhibition committee (☎ 2835 2222) well in advance.

The hotels tend to be expensive, but you can travel down to Tiānjīn from Běijīng in less than 1½ hours for a day trip.

HISTORY

The city's fortunes are, and always have been, linked to those of Běijīng. When the Mongols established Běijīng as the capital in the 13th century, Tiānjīn rose to prominence as a grain-storage point. Pending remodelling of the Grand Canal by Kublai Khan, the grain was shipped along Cháng Jiāng (Yangzi River), out into the open sea, up to Tiānjīn, and then through to Běijīng. With the Grand Canal fully functional as far as Běijīng, Tiānjīn was at the intersection of both inland and port navigation routes. By the 15th century, the town was a walled garrison.

For the sea-faring Western nations, Tiānjīn was a trading post too good to be passed up. In 1856 Chinese soldiers boarded the *Arrow,* a boat flying the British flag, ostensibly in search of pirates. This was just the excuse the British and the

Highlights

- Tiānjīn's Antique Market, one of China's most outstanding – particularly on Sunday
- Tiānjīn's 19th-century European buildings, poignant reminders of a not-too-distant past
- Strolling, shopping and eating

French needed. Their gunboats attacked the forts outside Tiānjīn, forcing the Chinese to sign the Treaty of Tianjin (1858), which opened the port up to foreign trade and also legalised the sale of opium.

The English and French settled in, and were joined by the Japanese, Germans, Austro-Hungarians, Italians and Belgians between the years 1895 and 1900. Each of these concessions was a self-contained world with its own prison, school, barracks and hospital.

This life was disrupted only in 1870 when locals attacked the French-run orphanage and killed, among others, 10 of the nuns – apparently the Chinese thought the children were being kidnapped. Thirty years later, during the Boxer Rebellion, the foreign powers levelled the walls of the old Chinese city.

Meanwhile, the European presence stimulated trade and industry, including salt, textiles and glass manufacture. Heavy

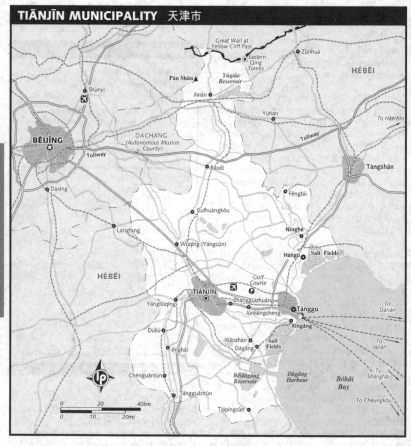

TIĀNJĪN MUNICIPALITY 天津市

silting of Hǎi Hé (Sea River) led to the construction of a new harbour 50km downstream at Tánggū. The opening of this new harbour meant that Tiānjīn lost its bustling-port character.

Since 1949 Tiānjīn has been a centre for major industrialisation and it produces a wide range of consumer goods. Brand-name products from Tiānjīn are favoured within China for their quality – from Flying Pigeon bicycles to Seagull watches.

ORIENTATION

Like Běijīng, Tiānjīn is a large, sprawling municipality of which most is rural. The population of Tiānjīn's city and suburbs is some five million, although the municipality itself takes in a total of more than 10 million.

INFORMATION

The CITS office (Map A; ☎ 2835 8309, fax 2835 2619) is at 22 Youyi Lu (opposite the Friendship Store), and the Tianjin Tourism Bureau (☎ 2835 4860, fax 2835 2324) is next door.

The Public Security Bureau (PSB; Gōngānjú; Map B; ☎ 2311 8951) is at 30 Tangshan Dao. The Bank of China (Map B) is at 82 Jiefang Beilu. On the ground floor of the International Building (Map B) is an ATM accepting Cirrus, Plus, MasterCard and Visa cards.

Post & Communications

The Dongzhan Post Office (Map B) is next to the main train station and another post office can be found on Jiefang Beilu, a short walk north of the New World Astor Hotel.

BĚIJĪNG TO SHÀNGHĂI

Internet cafes are found in abundance on the Nankai and Tianjin university campuses.

THINGS TO SEE & DO
Antique Market 古玩市场
Gǔwán Shìchǎng

The antique market *(Map B; Shandong Lu; open 7.30am-3pm Sat & Sun)* at the corner of Jinzhou Dao, is one of the best sights in Tiānjīn. In every direction, vendors spread blankets along the *hútòng* (narrow alleyways) making it a fascinating place to stroll around. Among the many items on sale are stamps, silverware, porcelain, clocks, Mao iconography and Cultural Revolution memorabilia.

According to the locals, much of what is on display was seized during the Cultural Revolution and warehoused – the government is now slowly selling the stuff off to vendors who, in turn, resell it in Tiānjīn. These goods supposedly come from all over China. Many of the items carry stickers on the back indicating when, where and from whom the goods were seized.

Just why everything wasn't immediately destroyed is subject to speculation – possibly it was to be used as evidence at political trials, or maybe some official was a closet antique buff. Of course, not all that you see is real – there are fake antiques, fake stickers and so on.

The market is best on Sunday. A few diehard vendors set up shop during the week for real antique enthusiasts. Get there early for the best selection.

Gǔwénhuà Jiē 古文化街
Ancient Culture Street

This street *(Map A)* is a recreation of an ancient Chinese street scene. Besides the traditional buildings, the road is lined with vendors plugging every imaginable type of cultural goody including Chinese calligraphy, paintings, tea sets, paper cuts, clay figurines and chops (name seals).

Within the confines of the street is the **Heaven Queen Temple** *(Tiānhòu Gōng; admission Y3; open 9am-4.30pm daily)*. Tianhou, or the Heaven Queen, is the Goddess of the Sea, and is known by various names (Tianhou, Matsu, Linmo and Niang Niang) throughout China. This is supposedly the biggest Tianhou temple in China and was built in 1326, but it has seen a lot of

renovation since then. Street operas are held in the temple and along Gǔwénhuà Jiē on the 23rd of the third month of the lunar calendar to celebrate Tianhou's birthday.

Entrance to the street is off Shizilin Jie, not far from the north-east bus station.

Wén Miào 文庙
Confucius Temple

Wén Miào *(Map A; ☎ 2727 2812, 1 Dongmennei Dajie; admission Y4; open 9.30am-4.30pm Tues-Sun)*, one block west of Gǔwénhuà Jiē, was built in 1463 during the Ming dynasty. The temple, along with Confucianists in general, took a beating during the Cultural Revolution. In 1993 the buildings were restored and opened to the public.

Mosque 清真寺
Qīngzhēnsì

Although distinctly Chinese in style, this large mosque *(Map A; 6 Dasi Qian)* is an active place of worship for the Muslim community. It's not officially open to the public and unless you're Muslim, you are unlikely to be allowed in. If you want to try, make sure you're suitably attired. The area surrounding the mosque is an intriguing maze of hútòng that are well worth exploring.

Monastery of Deep Compassion 大悲禅院
Dàbēichán Yuàn

One of the city's largest and best preserved temples, the Monastery of Deep Compassion *(Map A; ☎ 2626 1769, 40 Tianwei Lu; admission Y4; open 9am-4pm daily)* was built between 1611 and 1644, expanded in 1940, battered during the Cultural Revolution and finally restored in 1980. It continues to be active today. It's in the northern part of the city, a short walk from the Tianjin Holiday Inn Hotel.

Catholic Church
Xīkāi Tiānzhǔ Jiàotáng

This is the largest church in Tiānjīn and was built by the French in 1917. Serious damage during the Cultural Revolution caused it to close for a number of years. Services are permitted again and are held daily at 6am and 7.30am, when you can look around inside. The church is at the southern end of Binjiang Dao (Map B), but you will spot the twin onion domes a mile off.

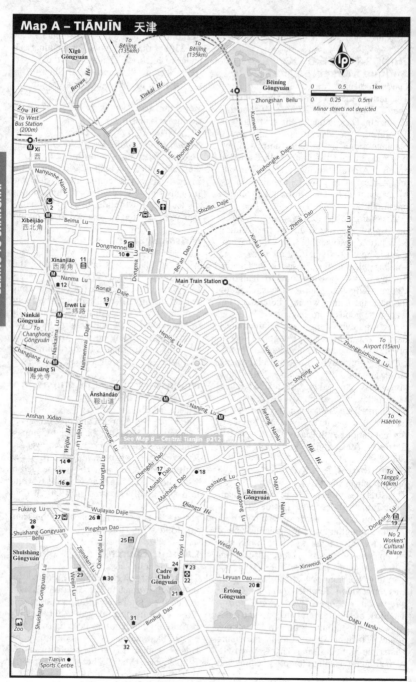

Map A – TIĀNJĪN 天津

Map A – TIĀNJĪN

PLACES TO STAY
5 Tianjin Holiday Inn Hotel
   假日饭店
12 Cairnhill Hotel
   金禧大酒店
20 Park Hotel
   乐园饭店
21 Crystal Palace Hotel
   水晶宫饭店
26 Caesar's Palace Hotel
   凯撒皇宫大酒店
30 Sheraton Hotel
   喜来登大酒店
31 Dickson Hotel
   带城酒店

PLACES TO EAT
13 Shípǐn Jiē
   食品街
15 Alibaba Restaurant; Nuts
   阿里巴巴酒家
17 Broadway Cafe
   贵宾楼西餐厅

23 Cosy Cafe & Bar
   客思特西餐酒吧
32 Geno Bakery

OTHER
1 West Train Station
   西火车站
2 Mosque
   清真寺
3 Monastery of Deep Compassion
   大悲禅院
4 North Train Station
   北火车站
6 Seaview Tower Church
   望海楼教堂
7 North-East Bus Station
   东北角发车站
8 Gǔwénhuà Jiē
   古文化街
9 Wén Miào
   文庙
10 Carrefour
   家乐福

11 Guangdong Guild Hall
   广东会馆
14 Tianjin University
   天津大学
16 Nankai University
   南开大学
18 Foreign Language Institute
   外国语学院
19 History Museum
   历史博物馆
22 Friendship Store
   友谊商店
24 CITS; Tianjin Tourism Bureau
   中国国际旅行社
25 Natural History Museum
   自然博物馆
27 South Bus Station
   八里台发车站
28 Zhou Enlai Memorial Hall
   周恩来级念馆
29 TV Tower
   电视塔

BEIJING TO SHANGHAI

Earthquake Memorial 抗震纪念碑
Kàngzhèn Jìniànbēi

Opposite the Friendship Hotel on Nanjing Lu is a curious, pyramid-shaped memorial. The memorial is a pointed reminder of the horrific events of 28 July 1976, when an earthquake registering eight on the Richter scale struck north-east China. The epicentre was at Tángshān, and Tiānjīn was severely affected – the city was closed to tourists for two years. More than 240,000 people were killed (a fifth of Tángshān's population) and 160,000 seriously injured. It was the greatest natural disaster of the decade.

Hǎihé Gōngyuán 海河公园
Sea River Park

Stroll along the banks of Hǎi Hé (a popular pastime with the locals) and see fishing, early-morning tai chi, old men toting bird-cages, and opera practice. The Hǎi Hé esplanades have a peculiarly Parisian feel, in part because some of the railing and bridge-work is French.

The river water isn't so pure that you'd want to drink it, but it has been cleaned up, and trees have been planted along the embankments. Tiānjīn's industrial pollution horrors are further downstream and are not included in the tour.

There are tourist boat cruises along Hǎi Hé to Tánggū (Y68 to Y88, eight hours) that leave from a dock opposite the train station. The boats cater more to Chinese tourists so run mainly during summer weekends and other holiday periods. Ring ☎ 2331 3158 for information.

At the northern end of town are half a dozen smaller rivers and canals that branch off Hǎi Hé. One vantage point is at the **Xīgū Gōngyuán** *(Map A)* in the north-west of the city. Take bus No 5 from near the main train station.

Shuǐshàng Gōngyuán 水上公园
Water Park

This large park *(Map A; admission Y5; open 5am-9pm daily)* is in the south-western corner of town, not far from the Zhou Enlai Memorial Hall. As its name implies, more than half the park's surface area is covered in water. The park is one of the more relaxed places in Tiānjīn (although locals descend at the weekend) and the most popular activity here is cruising the lake in pedal boats.

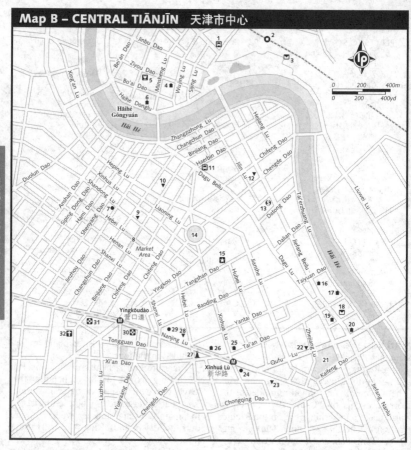

Map B – CENTRAL TIĀNJĪN 天津市中心

To get to the park catch bus No 94 or 98 from the city centre, or No 8 from the main train station.

Museums

There are a number of museums in Tiānjīn, the best of which is the **Natural History Museum** (Zìrán Bówùguǎn; Map A; ☎ 2335 1895 ext 2046, 206 Machang Dao; admission Y25; open 9am-5pm daily). This museum is especially popular with kids, with its large collection of dinosaur skeletons and the amphibians' hall, home to pythons and crocodiles. Bus No 13 runs from the main train station. Last entry is at 4pm.

The **History Museum** (Lìshǐ Bówùguǎn; Map A; ☎ 8429 6460, Guanghua Lu;

admission Y5; open 9am-11.30am & 1.30pm-4pm daily) is in the south-east of the city, within the triangular park called the **No 2 Workers' Cultural Palace** (Dì Èr Gōngrén Wénhuà Gōng). This museum gives an overview of Tiānjīn's history and includes a waxwork display of major personages in the city since the May 4th movement in 1919.

The **Guangdong Guild Hall** (Guǎngdōng Huì Guǎn; Map A; ☎ 2727 3443, 31 Nanmenli Dajie), also known as the Museum of Opera, was built in 1907 and was the last traditional opera house to be constructed in China before the modern opera house took over. It is also of historical relevance because Dr Sun Yatsen gave an important speech here in 1912.

Map B – CENTRAL TIĀNJĪN

PLACES TO STAY

4 Tiānhé Dàjiǔdiàn
天河大酒店

6 Ocean Hotel
远洋宾馆

16 Imperial Palace Hotel
天津皇宫饭店

17 New World Astor Hotel
利顺德大饭店

19 Tianjin First Hotel
天津第一饭店

20 Hyatt Hotel
凯悦饭店

25 Friendship Hotel East Building
友谊宾馆东楼

26 Friendship Hotel
友谊宾馆

PLACES TO EAT

9 Gǒubùlǐ
狗不理总店

10 Dengyinglou Grand Restaurant
登瀛楼饭店

12 Sgt Pepper's Music Hall Grill & Bar
沙金音乐西餐厅

22 Kiessling's Bakery
天津起士林西式餐厅

23 City Slicker Saloon
老外牛仔餐厅

28 Ěrduǒyǎn Zhágāodiàn
耳朵眼炸糕店

OTHER

1 Buses (to Běijīng)
往北京汽车站

2 Main Train Station
天津火车站

3 Dongzhan Post Office
东站邮局

5 Kānghǎo
康好娱乐城

7 Antique Market
古玩市场

8 Shopping Area
购物区

11 Bus Station No 1 (to Tānggū)
一路汽车站(往塘沽)

13 Bank of China
中国银行

14 Zhōngxīn Gōngyuán
中心公园

15 PSB
公安局外事科

18 Post Office
邮局

21 Xiǎobǎi Lóu
小白楼

24 International Building
国际大厦

27 Earthquake Memorial
抗震级念碑

29 CAAC
中国民航

30 International Market
国际商场

31 Isetan Department Store
伊势丹百货

32 Catholic Church
西开教堂

BĚIJĪNG TO SHÀNGHǍI

Zhou Enlai Memorial Hall
周恩来纪念馆
Zhōu Ēnlái Jìniànguǎn

Zhou Enlai grew up in Shàoxīng, Zhèjiāng province, but he attended school in Tiānjīn, so his classroom desk and schoolbooks are enshrined. The memorial *(Map A; ☎ 2352 9257, 1 Shuishang Gongyuan Beilu; admission Y10; open 8.30am-5pm daily)* charts the life of Zhou and his wife Deng Yingchao through photos and memorabilia. A large section of the museum is given over to Deng, a pioneer and leader of the women's liberation movement in China and who's work included drafting the Marriage Law, which ended arranged unions. Zhou's aeroplane is on display outside and you can have a look around for a further Y10.

The memorial hall is next to Shuǐshàng Gōngyuán. Take bus No 8 to Bālǐ Tái from the main train station, and then bus No 54 to the memorial hall.

Seaview Tower Church 望海楼教堂
Wànghǎilóu Jiàotáng

Although this church *(Map A; cnr Haihe Donglu & Shizilin Dajie)* is not open (either to the public or for services), it's a noteworthy attraction simply for the fact it still exists. Built in 1869 by the French, the church was burnt to the ground by locals in 1870, killing 10 nuns in the process. The Qing government rebuilt it in 1897, only to have it destroyed three years later during the Boxer Rebellion. It was restored again in 1904 and stood until the 1976 earthquake when it suffered serious damages. The last lot of reparations took place in 1983 and, so far, it's still standing.

Streetscapes

Tiānjīn itself is a museum of European architecture from the turn of the 20th century. One minute you're in little Vienna, turn a corner and you could be in a London street, hop off a bus and you're looking at some vintage French wrought-iron gates or a neo-Gothic cathedral. Of course, things have been renamed, and anyone with a sense of humour will be amused by some of the uses to which these European flourishes have been put. Unfortunately, recent postmodern architectural horrors are starting to impact on Tiānjīn's skyline. However, the streets around Munan Dao, just south of the city centre, or around Jiefang Lu are still particularly pleasant areas to stroll around.

Chinatown

Sorry, but we couldn't resist this misnomer. The old Chinese sector can easily be identified on the bus map as a rectangle with buses running around the perimeter. Roughly, the boundary roads are: Beima (North Horse), Nanma (South Horse), Xima (West Horse) and Dongma (East Horse). Originally there was one main north-south street, crossing an east-west one within that walled rectangle.

Explore the lanes and side streets where traditional architecture remains, and perhaps even find a dilapidated temple or two. Basically, though, this is a people-watching place where you can catch glimpses of daily life through doorways. Along the way are opportunities to shop and eat to your heart's content.

PLACES TO STAY – BUDGET

Tiānjīn has many reasonably priced hotels, but the PSB has deemed most of these off limits to foreigners. Budget deals open to foreigners can be found at the guesthouses at Nankai and Tianjin universities.

Tianjin University Experts Building (Tiānjīn Dàxué Zhuānjiā Lóu; Map A; ☎ 2740 7508, fax 2335 8714, Beiyang Dao) Doubles/quads Y196/420. Situated at the edge of the lake, this is the most upmarket accommodation on either University campus.

Tianjin University Foreign Students' Dormitory (Tiānjīn Dàxué Liúxuéshēng Lóu; Map A; ☎ 2740 4373, Beiyang Dao) Rooms with/without bath Y126/100. Tucked away behind the Expert Building, the rooms here are spartan but clean.

School of International Education Friendship Garden (Guójì Jiàoyù Xuéyuàn Yǒuyuán; Map A; ☎ 2740 4372, e iso@ tju.edu.cn, 92 Weijin Lu) Rooms Y80. This newly opened dormitory has excellent-value singles. All rooms come with private bathroom, air-con and simple kitchen facilities.

The foreign students' dormitories at Nankai University are not as well kept as at its neighbours', but 50% discounts on rooms are not uncommon.

Nankai University Foreign Guesthouse (Nánkāi Dàxué Wàibīn Zhāodàisuǒ; Map A; ☎ 2350 1832, Youyi Lu) Doubles Y150-240. This building is to your right as you enter the main university gate. The cheaper rooms in Building Two (Èrhàolóu) are old and look it, newer rooms in Building Four (Sìhàolóu) are small but comfortable.

Tiānhé Dàjiǔdiàn (Map B; ☎ 2403 2540, 7 Ziyou Dao) Doubles Y148-190. This hotel is near the train station and has very decent, recently renovated rooms.

PLACES TO STAY – MID-RANGE

All rooms are in addition to a 15% service charge. Discounts are common in most hotels.

Imperial Palace Hotel (Tiānjīn Huánggōng Fàndiàn; Map B; ☎ 2319 0888, fax 2319 0222, 177 Jiefang Beilu) Doubles with breakfast from Y420. Look no further than this hotel; housed in a beautiful, cosy building that was built by a British merchant in 1923. A fantastic Thai dinner buffet is held daily from 6pm to 10pm for Y38 per person.

Park Hotel (Lèyuán Bīnguǎn; Map A; ☎ 2830 9818, fax 2830 2042, 1 Leyuan Dao) Singles/doubles from Y316/480. Not surprisingly, this hotel is next to a park. The rooms smell a bit musty but the permanent 55% discount may be reason enough to stay.

Caesar's Palace Hotel (Kǎisā Huánggōng; Dàjiǔdiàn; Map A; ☎ 2337 5995, fax 2337 4922, 46 Qixiangtai Lu) Doubles Y336-458. Although it's not as glitzy as its Las Vegas namesake, the bedrooms at this place are fairly glam.

Friendship Hotel (Yǒuyì Bīnguǎn; Map B; ☎ 2331 0372, fax 2331 0616, 94 Nanjing Lu) Doubles from Y600. This place has large standard rooms, some overlooking the Earthquake Memorial.

Friendship Hotel East Building (Yǒuyì Bīnguǎn Dōnglóu; Map B; ☎ 2331 0372 ext 2102, 174 Xinhua Lu) Doubles Y300. Try here for more affordable luxury, though scruffier rooms than the Friendship Hotel. The East building is located behind the Friendship Hotel proper.

Tianjin First Hotel (Tiānjīn Dìyī Fàndiàn; Map B; ☎ 2330 9988, fax 2312 3000, 158 Jiefang Beilu) Rooms/suites Y664/913. This hotel boasts a lot of old world charm, enormous bright rooms and even bigger bathrooms.

Cairnhill Hotel (Jīnxī Dàjiǔdiàn; Map A; ☎ 2735 1688, fax 2735 4784, 2 Sanma Lu) Doubles/suites Y338/488. The corridors are grubby but the rooms comfortable, in particular the vinyl loveseats by the window. The hotel is a short walk from the Xīnánjiǎo subway station.

Ocean Hotel (Yuǎnyáng Bīnguǎn; Map B; ☎ 2420 5518, W www.tjoceanhotel.com, 5 Yuanyang Guangchang) Doubles from Y400. This gleaming high-rise to your right as you exit the train station has nautical-themed rooms, some with views over Hǎi Hé.

PLACES TO STAY – TOP END

All rooms have an additional 15% service charge.

Hyatt Hotel (Kǎiyuè Fàndiàn; Map B; ☎ 2331 8888, W www.hyatt.com, 219 Jiefang Beilu) Doubles/suites US$138/250. Rooms in this hotel fall short of the Hyatt's usual high standard.

New World Astor Hotel (Lìshùndé Dàfàndiàn; Map B; ☎ 2331 1688, e astorbc @mail.zlnet.com.cn, 33 Tai'erzhuang Lu) Twins/suites from Y1105/1700. This hotel retains the feel of foreign concession days. The ground floor has some interesting memorabilia on display including Emperor Puyi's gramophone.

Crystal Palace Hotel (Shuǐjīnggōng Fàndiàn; Map A; ☎ 2835 6666, W www .tcph.com, 28 Youyi Lu) Rooms from Y1380. This swish hotel has first-rate rooms and service.

Sheraton Hotel (Xǐláidēng Dàjiǔdiàn; Map A; ☎ 2334 3388, W www.sheraton .com, Zijinshan Lu) Doubles/suites from US$108/160. The Sheraton is an excellent hotel with monthly promotions that make a stay here affordable to even those on a modest budget. Rates include a buffet breakfast.

Tianjin Holiday Inn Hotel (Jiàrì Fàndiàn; Map A; ☎ 2628 8888, fax 2628 6666, 288 Zhongshan Lu) Doubles from Y1079. The Holiday Inn provides calm from the construction storm outside. Good service and regular promotions are simply more reasons to stay.

Dickson Hotel (Dàichéng Jiǔdiàn; Map A; ☎ 2836 4888, fax 2836 5018, 18 Binshui Dao) Doubles from Y747. This is another upmarket hotel with new looking rooms and a frequent generous discount.

PLACES TO EAT
Chinese

The upmarket *Shípǐn Jiē* (Food Street; Map A) is a covered alley with two levels of restaurants. Old places close and new ones open all the time, but there are some 40 to 50 restaurants housed under this one roof. Make sure you check prices – some of the food stalls are dirt cheap, but a few upmarket restaurants are almost absurdly expensive. This is the place to come if you want a taste of the exotica. You can try snake (expensive), dog meat (cheap) and eels (mid-range). Tiānjīn's sweet specialities such as 18th Street Dough Twists can also be found here.

Shípǐn Jiē is a couple of blocks south of Nanma Lu, about 1km west of the city centre. Just one block north of Shípǐn Jiē is *Rongji Dajie*, an alley that boasts its fair share of restaurants.

Gǒubùlǐ (Map B; ☎ 2730 2540, 77 Shandong Lu) Set menu Y13-18. Located between Changchun Dao and Binjiang Dao, this is the king of dumpling shops with a century-old history. The house speciality is *bāozi* (steamed dough bun), filled with high-grade pork, spices and gravy. You can also get bāozi with special fillings like chicken, shrimp or their delicious vegie version *shūcài bāozi*. What's more, Gǒubùlǐ's bāozi aren't greasy (a rarity in these parts). You'll find another Gǒubùlǐ restaurant on the ground floor of Shípǐn Jiē and another, next to the ticket office at the main train station, is open 24 hours.

Dengyinglou Grand Restaurant (Map B; ☎ 2730 3757, 94 Binjiang Dao) Dishes from Y10. This restaurant is not quite a century old (it started in 1913) but it is another Tiānjīn institution. It specialises in Shāndōng cuisine, including roast duck. Breakfast starts at 6am so come for a greasy slap-up Tiānjīn style. Specialities include *cùjiāo huóyú* (live fish hot and sour soup) and *fúróng xièhuáng* (crab roe mixed with egg white).

Érduǒyǎn Zhágāodiàn (Eardrum Fried Cake Shop; Map B; 96 Nanjing Lu) Cakes Y1. This chain got its name from its proximity to Eardrum Lane when it first opened over 80 years ago. It specialises in cakes made from rice powder, sugar and bean paste, all fried in sesame oil called (you guessed it) 'eardrum fried cake'. Other specialities include the wonderfully named *kāikǒu xiàobǐng* (open your mouth and laugh cakes). There are branches all over town; this one is near the Friendship Hotel.

Another Tiānjīn speciality is the 18th Street Dough Twists *(Shíbā Jiē Máhuā)*. The dough twists are made from sugar, sesame, nuts and vanilla (with variations on sweet and savoury) and can be bought all over town – try the train station. *Guìfā Xiáng Máhuādiàn (☎ 2830 9298, 568 Dagu Nanlu)*, in the south-east of the city is the original store.

Kiessling's Bakery (Qǐshìlín Xīshì Cāntīng; Map B; 33 Zhejiang Lu) Cakes from Y5, milkshakes Y12. Mr Kiessling, the former chef of the German Emperor William II established this bakery in 1918. The original structure is still standing and the bakery has grown to include an ice-cream parlour, coffee shop and self-service restaurant. The cakes are distributed all around the city at various shops and restaurants.

Sheraton Hotel (see Places to Stay earlier) Buffet Y120. Open 11am-2pm Sun. Foreign residents of Tiānjīn with a bit of cash like to pig out here every Sunday.

Should you wish to fortify a main meal, Tiānjīn produces a variety of liquid substances. There's Kafeijiu, which approximates to Kahlua, and Sekijiu, which is halfway between vodka and rocket fuel.

International

There are a number of restaurants in Tiānjīn serving Western-style cuisine.

Broadway Cafe (Guìbīnlóu Xīcāntīng; Map A; ☎ 2330 0541, 74 Munan Dao) Mains from Y40. The Broadway reels punters in with hearty Western fares such as steaks and pizzas.

City Slicker Saloon (Lǎowài Niúzǎi Cāntīng; Map B; ☎ 2313 0278, 55 Nanjing Lu) Starters/mains from Y20/50. Leave your cowboy boots at the door (they do) at this friendly Tex-Mex restaurant. Dishes include fajitas, chilli dogs, and excellent tacos.

Cosy Cafe & Bar (Kèsītè Xīcān Jiǔbā; Map A; ☎ 2837 2349, 21 Youyi Lu) Starters/mains from Y20/60. This place is so popular it had to move from its original small location to a larger one near the Friendship store. It's an expat haven: the atmosphere is very Western, the menu is in English and you can watch MTV. A Filipino band takes to the stage every night from 8.30pm.

Sgt Pepper's Music Hall Grill & Bar (Shājūn Yīnyuè Xīcāntīng; Map B; ☎ 2312 8138, 62 Jiefang Beilu) Mains from Y50. Open 6pm-2am daily. You can get Western-style bar food here, but you're better off coming for the drinks and live music. It's packed to the doors at weekends.

Alibaba Restaurant (Ālǐbābā Jiǔjiā; Map A; ☎ 2350 5613, 7 Tiannan Jie) Dishes Y10-30. This unusual and small restaurant is on the Nankai University campus, not far from the foreign students' dormitories. The menu features an eclectic selection of food including Iraq Salad, Irish Stew and Canadian Putine, and you can eat to the sounds of groovy tunes. It doubles as an unofficial pub for foreigners studying in Tiānjīn and stays open until late.

Capitalist Road

Advertising for the foreign market is one area in which the Chinese still stumble. A Chinese-produced TV advertisement shown in Paris for Chinese furs treated viewers to the bloody business of skinning, and to refrigerated cadavers, before the usual parade of fur-clad models down the catwalk.

It would be fun to handle the advertising campaigns for China's more charming brand names. There's Pansy underwear (for men), or you can pamper your stud with Horse Head facial tissues. You can start your breakfast with a glass of Billion Strong Pulpy C Orange Drink, or finish your meal with a cup of Imperial Concubine Tea. Stay away from White Elephant batteries, but you might try the space-age Moon Rabbit variety. Long March car tyres should prove durable, but what about the ginseng product with the fatal name of Gensenocide?

The characters for Coca-Cola translate as 'tastes good, tastes happy', but the Chinese must have thought they were really on to something good when the 'Coke Adds Life' slogan got mistranslated and claimed that it could raise the dead. And as a sign of the times, one enterprising food vendor has started a chain store named 'Capitalist Road'.

Condoms provide fertile ground for creative name-branding. Asia Good Oil is an inventive local product name, while Huan Bao Multifunction Condoms gets you thinking.

Geno Bakery (Map A; 11 Binshui Dao) Pastries from Y2, coffee Y12. Pastries, coffee, ice cream floats and birthday cakes are on offer at this bakery/coffee shop.

The Sheraton Hotel has a small *grocery shop* that sells such rare items as pesto, cereal and Diet Coke. It's not in the main building, so go into the lobby and ask.

ENTERTAINMENT

Sgt Pepper's Music Hall Grill & Bar (see Places to Eat earlier) This is the most popular bar in town, with an in-house Filipino band that packs in a mixed crowd, from well-heeled locals to expats and foreign students. There's no cover charge, but there's a minimum charge of Y60 per person, which is not strictly enforced. *City Slicker Saloon, Cosy Cafe* and *Alibaba* (see Places to Eat) are also lively nightspots.

Nuts (Map A; ☎ 2350 8457, Tiannan Jie) Drinks Y15-20. Around the corner from Alibaba is this hip little hole in the wall especially popular with foreign students at Nankai and Tianjin universities.

Kānghǎo (Map B; ☎ 2353 4791, 47 Minzu Lu) Admission women/men Y10/20. Still going strong is this popular disco that is packed to the hilt at weekends with Tiānjīn's finest.

SHOPPING

Tiānjīn is a shopper's paradise and a trip here will dispel any doubts about China's commitment to the textile trade. Only Hong Kong can match Tiānjīn for the amount of clothing on sale, and much of Hong Kong's supply originates here. The shopping is as varied as Běijīng and significantly cheaper.

The shopping streets to stroll along are *Binjiang Dao* and *Heping Lu*. Including alleyways and other commercial streets in the area, there is something like eight blocks of concentrated shopping to be found here. The area is particularly lively after 5pm when the streets are thronged with shoppers.

At the southern end of Binjiang Dao, running parallel to the street is a clothing market with over 100 stalls. Also at the southern end is *Isetan*, Tiānjīn's most upmarket department store.

One of the more unusual shopping areas is *Xiǎobǎi Lóu*, a market area off Qufu Lu. In addition to the brand-name shops and market stalls housed along the lanes, there

is the *Foreign Goods Market (Bǎihuò Shìchǎng)*. This is a fantastic (and very unusual for China) market selling secondhand clothes imported from Europe, Japan and Korea. The enormous selection includes leather flying jackets, 70s-style suits and retro dresses that can be picked up for as little as Y10. Running parallel to the Foreign Goods Market is a well-stocked, inexpensive *fabric market*.

For supermarkets try *Carrefour*, a branch of the French supermarket chain on Dongma Lu, near Wén Miào, or the supermarket on the ground floor of the *Friendship Store (Yǒuyì Shāngdiàn; Map A; 21 Youyi Lu)* at the southern end of town.

Carpets

Tiānjīn is considered famous for its carpets. If you're serious about carpets (and that's serious money!) the best bet is to get to a factory outlet. There are eight carpet factories in the Tiānjīn municipality. Making the carpets by hand is a long and tedious process – some of the larger ones can take a proficient weaver over a year to complete. Patterns range from traditional to modern.

Tianjin Carpets Import-Export Corporation (☎ 2830 0894, 45 Baoding Dao) and *Tianjin Carpet Corporation (☎ 2830 0894, 5 Xinweidi Dao)* are two place to try. Visits to these and other outlets can also be arranged through CITS.

Clay Figurines

Clay figurines are another local speciality. The brightly coloured figures originated in the 19th century with the work of Zhang Mingshan and today his fifth-generation descendants continue to train new craftspeople.

Nírén Zhāng Cǎisù Gōngzuòshì (Zhang Caisu Clay Figure Workshop; ☎ 2337 4085, 270 Machang Dao) is where the statues are made today. The small figures take themes from human or deity sources and the emphasis is on realistic emotional expressions.

Master Zhang was reputedly so skilful that he carried clay up his sleeves on visits to the theatre and came away with clay opera stars in his pockets. In 1900, during the Boxer Rebellion, Western troops came across satirical versions of themselves correct down to the last detail in uniforms. Not surprisingly, they ordered these voodoo dolls to be removed from the marketplace immediately!

Spring Festival Posters

Tiānjīn is also known for its Spring Festival posters, which first appeared in the 17th century in the town of Yángliŭqīng, 15km west of Tiānjīn. Woodblock prints are hand-coloured, and are considered to bring good luck and happiness when posted on the front door during the Spring Festival – OK if you like Day-Glo pictures of fat babies. Harder to find are the varieties that have historical, deity or folk-tale representations.

GETTING THERE & AWAY
Air

Civil Aviation Administration of China (CAAC; Zhōngguó Mínháng; Map B; ☎ 2330 1543) is at 103 Nanjing Lu. Korean Air (☎ 2319 0088), Dragon Air (☎ 2311 0191) and JAL (☎ 2313 9766) all have booking offices in the International Building (Guójì Dàshà; Map B) at 75 Nanjing Lu. The Tianjin Air-Sales Agency (☎ 2330 1098), which can book flights on most airlines, and an IATA office (☎ 2330 3480) are also within the International Building. CITS can also book flights.

Korean Air flies to Seoul. Dragonair and CAAC both offer daily direct flights between Hong Kong and Tiānjīn. JAL flies to Osaka and Nagoya. For flights to Tokyo you must fly from Běijīng. You can fly to most major cities in China from Tiānjīn.

Bus

The Běijīng-Tiānjīn Expressway has made bus travel a good alternative to taking the train. Buses to Běijīng (Y25, 1½ hours) depart from in front of Tiānjīn's main train station and from near the Xiǎobái Lóu market on Qufu Lu. In Běijīng, catch the bus to Tiānjīn from the Zhàogōngkǒu bus station on the southern side of town, but make sure you get a bus to Tiānjīn train station (Tiānjīn huǒchē zhàn) and not to the outlying districts of Kāifā or Tánggū (unless you want to go to Tánggū). Buses run roughly every half hour throughout the day. Express buses also leave from outside Běijīng's main train station (Y25, 1½ hours).

There are four long-distance bus stations in Tiānjīn. Bus station No 1 (Yīlù qìchēzhàn; Map B) is at the corner of Haerbin Dao and Dagu Beilu. Bus No 815

leaves from here for Tánggū (Y5, one hour).

Other bus stations are located at intervals along the direction of travel. The south bus station (bālǐtái qìchēzhàn) south-west of the city centre is where you catch buses going south. The west bus station (xī qìchēzhàn) is at 2 Xiqing Dao, near Tiānjīn's west train station.

The north-east bus station (dōngbĕijiǎo qìchēzhàn) has the most destinations. From here buses leave to Jìxiàn and Wǔqīng. If you're the sort of person who likes to see everything along the way, it's worth considering a road trip from Tiānjīn to Běijīng via Jìxiàn. The bus station is very close to Gǔwénhuà Jiē, just west of Hǎi Hé. Bus No 24 from the city centre will drop you in the general vicinity.

Train

Tiānjīn is a major north-south train junction with frequent trains to Běijīng, extensive links with the north-eastern provinces, and lines southwards to Jǐ'nán, Nánjīng, Shànghǎi, Fúzhōu, Héféi, Yāntái, Qīngdǎo and Shíjiāzhuāng.

There are three train stations in Tiānjīn: main, north and west. For most trains you'll want the main train station. Some trains stop at both the main and west stations, and some only go through the west train station (particularly those originating in Běijīng and heading south). Trains heading for north-eastern China often stop at the north train station.

If you have to alight at the west train station, bus No 24 will connect you to the main train station.

The main train station has a 'soft-seat booking office' that foreigners can use even for buying hard-seat tickets. To find it, enter the main station entrance (by the X-ray machines) and go up the escalator to the 2nd floor – it's off to the right underneath the green and gold archway. There are usually no queues.

There are 10 daily express trains to Běijīng (Y30 to Y35, 1½ hours). Local trains take about two hours. The last train leaves Tiānjīn at 5.51pm.

Boat

Tiānjīn's harbour is Tánggū, 50km (30 minutes by train or one hour by bus) from

Tiānjīn. See the Tánggū section later in this chapter for details of arriving and departing by boat.

GETTING AROUND
To/From the Airport
From the city centre, it's about 15km to Tiānjīn's Binhai International airport. Taxis ask for Y40 or more for the trip, and there is a bus from the CAAC ticket office. For airport information call ☎ 2490 2950.

Minibuses for Běijīng's airport leave from the CAAC every 30 minutes between 5am and 6pm (Y70, 2½ hours).

Bus
Key local transport junctions are the areas around the three train stations. The main train station has the biggest collection: bus Nos 24, 27 and 13, and farther out toward the river are Nos 2, 5, 25, 28 and 96. At the west train station are Nos 24, 10 and 31 (Nos 11 and 37 run past the west train station); and at the north train station are Nos 1, 7 and 12.

Another major bus station point is around Zhōngxīn Gōngyuán, at the edge of the central shopping district. From here you can get bus Nos 11 and 94, and nearby are bus Nos 9, 20 and 37. To the north of Zhōngxīn Gōngyuán are bus Nos 1, 91, 92 and 93.

A useful bus to know is the No 24, which runs between the main and west stations 24 hours a day. Also noteworthy is bus No 8 – it starts at the main train station then zigzags down to the south-west of town. From the main train station bus No 13 passes by Sgt Pepper's, the Hyatt, the Foreign Language Institute, the Friendship Store and the Crystal Palace Hotel.

With the exception of bus No 24, buses run from 5am to 11pm.

Train
The subway (*dìtiě*) can be useful – it runs all the way from Nanjing Lu to the west train station and costs Y1 per journey. Tiānjīn's subway opened in 1982 but has seen little improvement since then; the rickety cars shuttle back and forth on a single track, but it saves some trauma with the buses.

Taxi
Readily found near the train station and around tourist hotels, the base fare for a taxi is Y5.

Around Tiānjīn

Tiānjīn can be used as a staging point for trips directly north to Jìxiàn and to the Great Wall at Yellow Cliff Pass, as well as Zūnhuà, Tángshān and Běidàihé in Héběi. It's also a launching pad for roaring into the north-east (Manchuria).

TÁNGGŪ 塘沽
There are three harbours on the Tiānjīn Municipality stretch of coastline: Hàngū (north), Tánggū-Xīngǎng (centre) and Dàgǎng (south). Tánggū is about 50km from Tiānjīn, and is one of China's major international seaports. The Japanese began the construction of an artificial harbour during their occupation (1937–45) and it was completed by the Communists in 1952, with further expansions in 1976 for container cargo. The Tánggū-Xīngǎng port now handles one of the largest volumes of goods of any port in China.

As for sightseeing, the best advice we can give is to go no further than the ferry pier. Tánggū is a forest of cranes, containers and smokestacks – it's no place to linger.

Nevertheless, you will find foreigners lingering here – not travellers, but business people. Tánggū is booming and many export-oriented industries have set up shop here. The chief focus of all this activity is the **Tianjin Economic & Development Area** (*Jīngjì Jìshù Kāifāqū*), or TEDA (Tàidà). This area, in the northern part of Tánggū, is full of factories, expensive residences and shops catering predominantly for foreign and overseas Chinese investors and technical experts.

If you insist on seeking out some touristy sights, the city's most famous 'scenic spot' is **Dagu Fort** (*Dàgū Pàotái;* ☎ 2588 8544; admission Y5; open 8am-6pm daily), on the southern bank of Hǎi Hé. The fort was built towards the end of the Ming dynasty, some time between 1522 and 1567. The purpose was to protect Tiānjīn from foreign invasions. It may have worked for a while, but it was not exactly a smashing success. There is a small museum chronicling the various invasions by foreign imperialists and a collection of large iron cannons – you can have a go firing a smaller version for

Y10. Bus No 110 from the train station drops you at the end of the road, from here it's a 5 or 10 minute walk to the fort.

The best sight in Tánggū is **Cháoyīn Sì** (*Sound of Tide Temple*; ☎ *2531 1882, 1 Chaoyinsi Dajie; admission Y2; open 8am-5pm daily*). The original temple was built in 1404 by fishermen to pray to the Goddess of Mercy, Guanyin, for safe passages at sea. It's a lovely temple that features a number of interesting goddesses, including Songzi Guanyin to whom women pray if they have trouble getting pregnant. In the hall to your right as you enter the temple sits Wangsan Grandmother (Wángsān Nǎinai), a figure from local folklore who it is believed can cure ailments. Bus No 110 or 617 will get you here.

The liveliest area of town is **Yanghuo Market** (*Yánghuò Shìchǎng*) on Zhongxin Beilu. Near the train station, this sprawling market sells everything including squid on a stick, 'designer' bags and watches, 'antiques' and penis pumps (no joke!). If you need to catch a quick meal or fritter away some time while waiting for a boat this is the place to come.

An infinitely more refined place to while away some time is the **TEDA Contemporary Art Museum** (*Tàidà Dāngdài Yìshù Bówùguǎn*; ☎ *2532 0088 ext 817; open 10am-4pm Tues-Sat*). This small gallery, on the 3rd floor, has occasional exhibits featuring some of China's up-and-coming contemporary artists. Call ahead to ensure there is an exhibition.

Tánggū has a very heavy public security presence. Many of the cops are in plain clothes, but you'll notice the PSB vehicles – they have long, white licence plates with black lettering, except for the first two letters, which are red. There is a local rumour that Tánggū is the PSB headquarters.

Places to Stay

As in Tiānjīn, dormitories and cheap hotels are no-go areas for foreigners. If arriving in Tánggū by ship, it's best to hop on the first train to Běijīng or Běidàihé.

Kāngdà Fàndiàn (*Kangda Hotel*; ☎ *2579 5941, Xingang Erhao Lu*) Doubles Y100. This is the only budget option within the vicinity of the ferry pier – it's the red brick building across the train tracks. Rooms are

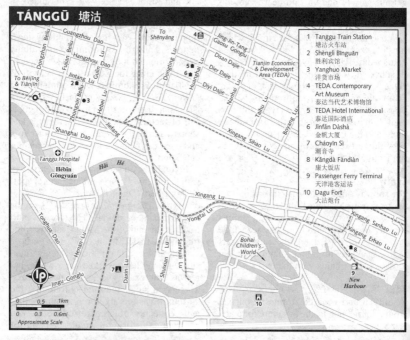

TÁNGGŪ 塘沽

1 Tanggu Train Station
   塘沽火车站
2 Shènglì Bīnguǎn
   胜利宾馆
3 Yanghuo Market
   洋货市场
4 TEDA Contemporary
   Art Museum
   泰达当代艺术博物馆
5 TEDA Hotel International
   泰达国际酒店
6 Jīnfān Dàshà
   金帆大厦
7 Cháoyīn Sì
   潮音寺
8 Kāngdà Fàndiàn
   康大饭店
9 Passenger Ferry Terminal
   天津港客运站
10 Dagu Fort
   大沽炮台

fairly grotty, but tolerable; try for a room facing into the courtyard.

Shènglì Bīnguǎn *(Victory Hotel;* ☎ *2534 5833, fax 2534 4570, 11 Jintang Lu)* Singles Y188-298, doubles Y248-398. This is the closest hotel to the main train station that accepts foreigners, and offers standard, uninspired rooms.

Jīnfān Dàshà *(Golden Sail Hotel;* ☎ *2532 6666, fax 2532 4992, 49 Diyi Dajie)* Doubles Y280-380, triples Y580. Rooms are average and overpriced but this hotel often has discounts of up to 50%.

TEDA Hotel International *(Tàidà Guójì Jiǔdiàn;* ☎ *2532 6000, fax 2532 6216, 8 Dier Dajie)* Doubles from US$100 plus 15% service charge. This bizarre castle-like building is Tánggū's most unattractive but most upmarket hotel. Amenities include a golf simulator, ice-skating rink and swimming pool.

Getting There & Away
From Tiānjīn, buses to Tánggū leave from bus station No 1. In Tánggū you can catch minibuses from outside the train station and the Yanghuo Market. The occasional bus leaves from outside the passenger ferry terminal.

The main railway line to north-eastern China runs from Běijīng to Hāěrbīn via Tiānjīn and Tánggū. In other words, it's a heavily travelled route with frequent services. Although less frequent than the buses, there are regular trains to Tiānjīn (Y3.5 to Y10, 30 minutes to one hour), and to Běidàihé (Y38, three hours).

Tánggū's harbour has been renamed New Harbour (Xīngǎng) – you catch ferries at the New Harbour passenger ferry terminal (Xīngǎng kèyùn zhàn).

From Tánggū, there are daily boats to Dàlián (Y167 to Y697, 13 to 16 hours) at 3pm and 3.30pm. The boats are usually packed with people so it's wise to stick to 4th class or higher. The liners are comfortable, can take up to 1000 passengers, and are equipped with a bar, restaurant and movies.

Tickets can be purchased at the passenger ferry terminal (☎ 2570 6728), but if you're in Tiānjīn it's safer to buy in advance at 1 Pukou Dao (☎ 2339 4290). Difficult to find, Pukou Dao is a short distance south of the Hyatt and runs west off Tai'erzhuang Lu; it

is roughly on the same latitude as the enormous smokestack that stands on the opposite side of the river.

There is a weekly ferry to Kobe, Japan that leaves on Mondays at 11am (tickets from Y1625, 48 hours). And a boat leaves on Thursday and Sunday at 11am for Inch'ŏn, South Korea (tickets from Y935, 24 to 26 hours).

When arriving by boat you will find that buses to Tiānjīn and Běijīng are waiting when you dock. Tickets for these buses can be bought on board and this is by far the easiest way to get out of Tánggū.

JÌXIÀN 蓟县
Rated as one of the 'northern suburbs' of Tiānjīn, although it's actually 120km from Tiānjīn city, the Jìxiàn area is about 90km due east of Běijīng.

Near the city's west gate is the 1000 year-old **Dúlè Sì** *(Temple of Solitary Joy; admission Y10; open 8am-6pm daily).* The temple was first built during the Tang dynasty (618–907) and is one of the oldest wooden structures in China. The main multi-storey wooden structure, the Guanyin Hall, houses a 16-metre-high statue of the Goddess of Mercy, Guanyin. Ten small Guanyin heads were later added to the top of the statue's head to represent her immense power. The statue is therefore known as the Eleven-faced Guanyin.

Getting There & Away
From Běijīng you can join a tour to the Eastern Qing Tombs (Qīng Dōng Líng) in Zūnhuà county (see the Around Běijīng section in the Běijīng chapter for details), which stops in Jìxiàn for lunch. There are also regular long-distance buses from Běijīng.

From Tiānjīn's north-east bus station there are five daily buses to Jìxiàn (Y21, three to four hours). There is also a direct Tiānjīn-Jìxiàn train link (Y28, 3½ hours).

PÁN SHĀN 盘山
To the north-west of Jìxiàn is Pán Shān, a collection of hills ranked among the 15 famous mountains of China. Emperor Qianlong was claimed to have been so taken with the place that he swore he never would have gone south of Cháng Jiāng had he known Pán Shān was so beautiful.

BEIJING TO SHANGHAI

The area consists of five peaks with **Moon Hanging Peak** (*Guìyuè*) being the tallest. On the summit sits Dingguang Stupa and on clear days the peak commands views of the Great Wall and the Taihang mountains. It is a lovely area, dotted with trees, springs, streams, temples and pavilions.

The hills are 12km north-west of Jìxiàn. Buses run to Jìxiàn from Tiānjīn's north-east bus station. In Jìxiàn, you can catch a bus to Pán Shān, 30 minutes away.

GREAT WALL AT YELLOW CLIFF PASS 黄崖关长城

At the very northern tip of Tiānjīn municipality (bordering Héběi) is Yellow Cliff Pass (Huángyá Guān). This section of the wall is 41km long before it crumbles away on each end – the part open to tourists was restored in 1984.

Some new features have been added to the original structures, including the **Eight Diagrams Labyrinth** (*Bāguà Chéng*), **Great Wall Museum** (*Chángchéng Bówùguǎn*), **Forest of Steles** (*Shíkèbēi Lín*) and **Water Pass** (*Shuǐ Guān*).

Getting There & Away
Yellow Cliff Pass is 140km north of Tiānjīn city. Direct buses tend to go to the wall on weekends, with early-morning departures from Tiānjīn's north-east bus station or sometimes from the main train station. Alternatively, take a bus to Jìxiàn, and then change for a bus headed to the Wall (Y2, 30 minutes).

WŬQĪNG 武清
Within Wǔqīng county is the town of Wǔqīng (also called Yángcūn). It is nothing to get too excited about although of possible interest is the **International Shooting Range** (*Guójì Shèjī Chǎng;* ☎ 2934 5757, *Jinjing Hwy; open 8am-6pm daily*), east of the crossroad. Weaponry choices include fully automatic Kalashnikovs and M16 assault rifles. Prices are according to choice of gun and ammunition; pistol rounds are a mere Y4 while special ammunition can cost up to Y8 a shot.

A more benign activity practised here is table tennis, and Wǔqīng was the host of the 43rd World Table Tennis Championships.

Hébĕi 河北

Capital: Shíjiāzhuāng
Population: 64.9 million
Area: 190,000 sq km

Wrapping itself around the centrally administered municipalities of prospering Běijīng and the manufacturing hub of Tiānjīn is the province of Héběi. The province is often seen as an extension of Běijīng and Tiānjīn, which is not far off the mark since, geographically speaking, they both take up a fair piece of the pie. In fact, the former capital of Héběi was Tiānjīn, before that honour was ceded to the next largest city, Shíjiāzhuāng.

Topographically, Héběi falls into two distinct parts: the mountain tableland to the north, where the Great Wall runs, and the monotonous southern plain. The region's agriculture, which is mainly wheat and cotton, is hampered by dust storms, droughts and flooding. It should come as no surprise then that it's scorching and humid in summer, and freezing in winter, with dust fallout in spring and heavy rains in July and August.

Héběi's highlights are the clean and pleasant beach resort of Běidàihé and marvellous Chéngdé, with its grand palaces, sacred temples and park. Zhèngdìng, near the capital Shíjiāzhuāng, is a fascinating accumulation of ancient temples. East along the coast, the walled town of Shānhǎiguān marks the terminus of the Great Wall with the sea, and there are pockets of historic charm.

SHÍJIĀZHUĀNG 石家庄
☎ 0311 • pop 8,600,000

Shíjiāzhuāng is a railway junction about 250km south-west of Běijīng and, in spite of being the provincial capital, is a bit of a cultural desert. At the turn of the 20th century it was just a small village with 500 inhabitants and a handful of buildings. The railway network constructed last century brought the town relative prosperity and a consequent population explosion.

Shíjiāzhuāng has the biggest People's Liberation Army (PLA) officer training school in China; the school is about 2km west of the city. For an industrial city known

Highlights

- The awesome multi-armed statue of Guanyin, the Goddess of Mercy, at Pǔníng Sì in Chéngdé, the temple-studded 18th-century imperial resort

- The ancient walled town of Zhèngdìng with its splendid crop of temples, Tang dynasty pagodas and historic charm

- The breezy beachside resort of Běidàihé where Běijīng residents retreat to escape the stifling summer heat

BĚIJĪNG TO SHÀNGHǍI

chiefly for its smokestacks, Shíjiāzhuāng also attracts hordes of itinerant beggars who swarm in the district around the railway station. For some travellers Shíjiāzhuāng might be a useful transit point, while for most the real treat is the old walled town of Zhèngdìng to the north.

Information

There is a post office just west of the train line on Zhongshan Xilu and China International Travel Service (CITS; Zhōngguó Guójì Lǚxíngshè) and China Travel Service (CTS; Zhōngguó Lǚxíngshè) offices in Héběi Bīnguǎn on Yucai Jie.

The huge Yuǎndōng Wǎngluò Jiāyuán Internet cafe (☎ 699 5812), on the 3rd floor of the Yuandong Tongxin Cheng at 5 Likang

Jie, has endless banks of terminals and is very cheap at Y2 per hour with speedy connections. It's not easy to find: it's on the left up a small alley on the north side of Zhongshan Donglu just west of an Esprit shop.

Revolutionary Martyrs' Mausoleum 烈士陵园
Lièshì Língyuán

The Revolutionary Martyrs' Mausoleum (☎ 702 2904, 343 Zhongshan Xilu; admission Y3; open 7.30am-6pm daily) is a pleasant tree-shaded park fronted with an obelisk graced with calligraphy from Mao Zedong, Deng Xiaoping, Jiang Zemin and others. Among the shrines to Communist martyrs is the tomb of the Canadian guerrilla doctor Norman Bethune (1890–1939). Bethune served as a surgeon with the Eighth Route Army in the war against Japan, and is eulogised in a Mao Zedong Thought – 'We must all learn the spirit of absolute selflessness from Dr Norman Bethune' (inscribed in Chinese on his tomb). A nostalgic relic of a bygone era.

Hebei Provincial Museum
河北省博物馆
Héběi Shěng Bówùguǎn

This large museum (☎ 604 5642, Zhongshan Donglu; admission Y5; open 8am-11.30am & 2pm-5.30pm Tues-Sun) has many historical displays, but unfortunately no English captions. At the time of writing a new Science and Technology Museum was being constructed just to the east.

HÉBĚI 河北

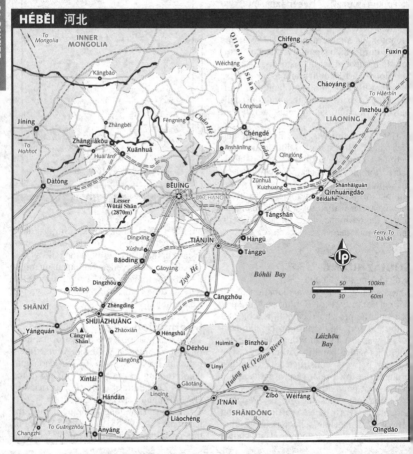

Places to Stay

Bǎilín Dàshà *(Bailin Hotel;* ☎ *702 1398, fax 702 1887, 24 Chezhan Jie)* Singles Y150-198, doubles Y220-260, triples Y298-420. The Y198 doubles here are clean and of excellent quality. The TV video channel shows all the latest films and the staff are courteous; other unexpected touches include telephones in the bathrooms. Rates include breakfast.

Yínquán Fàndiàn *(Silver Spring Hotel;* ☎ *702 7506, fax 702 6360, 12 Zhanqian Jie)* Doubles/quads Y200/280. This hotel has decent rooms and features an oxygen bar if Shíjiāzhuāng's exhaust fumes get too much.

International Trading Holiday Hotel *(*☎ *703 8888, fax 703 2945, 125 Zhongshan Xilu)* Doubles Y198-258, suites Y550. This hotel looks like it should be far more expensive. The bargain rooms are no great shakes, but the facilities and the ambience are a cut above the rest. The Y258 doubles have some nice little extras, including a minibar. The hotel also has a ticket booking office.

Hebei Century Hotel *(Hébĕi Shìjì Dàfàndiàn;* ☎ *703 6699, fax 703 8866, 145 Zhongshan Xilu)* Doubles/suites Y590/1100. This four-star hotel is the best in town and features a slick foyer, coffee shop, international cuisine and a certain measure of elegance, despite the bland exterior.

Guójì Dàshà *(International Hotel;* ☎ *604 8708, fax 603 4787, 301 Zhongshan Donglu)* Doubles/suites Y230/720. The International has long been a haven for tour groups, and the rooms are good value. Rates include breakfast.

Places to Eat

Jinshancheng Chongqing Hotpot *(Jīnshānchéng Chóngqìng Huǒguō;* ☎ *608 0573, 85 Zhongshan Donglu)* This place has hotpots to fend off blisteringly cold winters or bring you out in a torrent of sweat in any other season.

Close to Yínquán Fàndiàn is a long commercial street called **Yǒng'ān Shìchǎng**. Here you'll find lots of good eats at rock-bottom prices from Sìchuān, Lánzhóu, Wēnzhōu, Hui and Qīngzhēn street stalls and restaurants. You can pick up a meal around here for under Y30.

Getting There & Away

Shíjiāzhuāng is connected by air to Chóngqìng, Guǎngzhōu, Hohhot, Kūnmíng, Nánjīng, Qínhuángdǎo, Shànghǎi, Shēnzhèn, Wēnzhōu and Xiàmén.

The city is also a major rail hub with comprehensive connections, including regular trains to Bĕijīng (express Y30, 2½ hours), Chéngdé (Y86), Tiānjīn (Y26), Qínhuángdǎo (Y41), Tàiyuán (Y16), Dàtóng (Y38), Shĕnyáng (Y59), Tài'ān (Y23) and Zhèngzhōu (Y26).

From the central long-distance bus station there are connections to Bĕijīng (Y69, 3½ hours), Tiānjīn (Y80), Qínhuángdǎo (Y130, seven hours), Zhèngzhōu (Y42), Jì'nán (Y53) and Yāntái (Y127).

Getting Around

To/From the Airport Shíjiāzhuāng's airport is 40km north-east of town. Civil Aviation Administration of China (CAAC; Zhōngguó Mínháng) buses (Y15) depart from the CAAC office (☎ 505 4084) at 471 Zhongshan Donglu. The bus schedule changes daily, so check with the office for departure times.

There are two or three buses per day, with the first leaving at around 5.40am and the last leaving at around 5pm. A taxi to the airport will take about an hour and cost Y100.

AROUND SHÍJIĀZHUĀNG
Zhèngdìng 正定
☎ 0311

This prettified old wall town, 18km north of Shíjiāzhuāng, is the highlight of the area. The Chinese nicknamed Zhèngdìng the town of 'nine towers, four pagodas, eight great temples and 24 golden archways'. It still retains many of its temples and pagodas, and some of the archways *(páilou)* have been colourfully restored. Its once imposing city wall has sadly crumbled away, but the grand main gates remain in the south, north and west.

Things to See Of Zhèngdìng's many monasteries, the most famous is Lóngxīng Sì, more popularly known as **Dàfó Sì** *(*☎ *878 6560, Zhongshan Donglu; admission Y30; open 8am-6pm daily),* located in the east of town. Tape guides are available, but only in Chinese.

SHÍJIĀZHUĀNG 石家庄

Dating back to the Sui dynasty, most of the temple has been restored. You are met in the first hall by the corpulent Milefo, or Laughing Buddha, here called the 'Monk with a Bag'. The four Heavenly Kings flanking him in pairs are typically vast and disconcerting.

In the Buddhist Altar Hall is a rather unusual bronze two-faced Buddha that was cast in the Ming dynasty.

Rising up in the **Pavilion of Great Mercy** (*Dàbēi Gé*) is an absolute colossus of a bronze statue of Guanyin, the Goddess of Mercy. At 21.3m high, cast in AD 971 and sporting a third eye, the effigy lacks the beauty and artistry of her sibling in Chéngdé's Pǔníng Sì, but is still impressive. You can climb all the way up into the galleries surrounding Guanyin for Y5. The wooden hall in which the Goddess is housed was rebuilt in 1999 with consultation of Song dynasty architecture manuals.

Tiānníng Sì (*admission Y5*), west of Dàfó Sì in an alleyway off Zhongshan Donglu, is very peaceful and is graced with an attractive front courtyard. The 41m-high Tang-dynasty **Língxiāo Tǎ** (*Lofty Pagoda*) is in fine condition and typical of Tang brickwork pagodas.

Kāiyuán Sì (*Yanzhao Nandajie; admission Y10*) also sports a very well-preserved early Tang dynasty pagoda, formerly called

Wild Goose Pagoda, like its brethren in Xī'ān. The round arched doors are particularly attractive, as are the carvings on the base. The Bell Tower is also from Tang times and you can clamber up inside.

Other temples include **Línjì Sì** (*Linji Lu*), south-east of Kāiyuán Sì, and **Guǎnghuì Sì**, farther south, which has a very unusual pagoda decorated with numerous animal motifs. There is also a Confucian temple, **Wén Miào,** in town.

Part of Zhèngdìng's main street (Yanzhao Dajie) has been restored and gentrified and is now a pleasant stretch of traditional Chinese roofing and brickwork. Called the **Zhengding Historical Culture Street** (*Zhèngdìng Lìshǐ Wénhuà Jiē*), at the time of writing scores of restaurants and souvenir shops were waiting for the paint to dry on the final touches. At the southern end of the street is **Chánglè Gate** (*Chánglè Mén),* one of Zhèngdìng's ancient gates, which can be climbed for Y5.

Place to Stay One place we recommend is:

Lóngxīng Sì Bīnguǎn (☎ 878 6767) Singles with/without bath Y198/120. This hotel has an excellent location in the alley just to the east of Dàfó Sì – there's no English sign, but go to the end of the alley and it's the building through the gate on your right.

SHÍJIĀZHUĀNG

PLACES TO STAY & EAT
2 Hebei Century Hotel
河北世纪大饭店
3 International
Trading Holiday
Hotel
国贸假日酒店
6 Bǎilín Dàshà
柏林大厦
9 Yínquán Fàndiàn
银泉饭店
11 Jinshancheng
Chongqing
Hotpot
金山城重庆火锅
14 Guójì Dàshà
国际大厦

OTHER
1 Revolutionary
Martyrs' Mausoleum
烈士陵园
4 Dongfang City Plaza
Shopping Center
东方城市广场购物
中心
5 Post Office
邮局
7 Train Station
火车站
8 Yǒng'ān Shìchǎng
永安市场
10 Central Long-Distance
Bus Station
长途汽车站

12 Yuǎndōng Wǎngluò
Jiāyuán (Internet)
远东网络家园
13 Mao Zedong Statue
毛泽东像
15 Hebei Provincial
Museum
河北省博物馆
16 CITS; CTS
(Héběi Bīnguǎn)
中国国际旅行社;
中国旅行社
(河北宾馆)
17 Hua Xia Long-
Distance Bus
Station
华夏长途汽车站

BEIJING TO SHANGHAI

Getting There & Away Bus No 201 runs regularly between Shíjiāzhuāng train station and Dàfó Sì (Y10, one hour). Regular train services also run through Zhèngdìng from Shíjiāzhuāng.

Getting Around Zhèngdìng is not huge and walking is relatively easy as the sights are largely clustered together. Taxis within Zhèngdìng are around Y10; three-wheel motorcycles are Y4 for anywhere in town. Bus No 1 runs from the bus station to Dàfó Sì and bus No 3 runs to the train station.

Zhàozhōu Bridge 赵州桥
Zhàozhōu Qiáo

This bridge (admission Y10) is in Zhàoxiàn county, about 40km south-east of Shíjiāzhuāng and 2km south of Zhàoxiàn town. It has spanned Jiāo Hé for 1400 years and is China's oldest standing bridge. The world's first segmental bridge (ie, its arch is a segment of a circle, as opposed to a complete semi-circle), it predates other bridges of this kind throughout the world by 800 years.

Zhàozhōu Bridge is exceptional in that not only does it still stand but it's in remarkable shape. It is 50m long and 9.6m wide, with a span of 37m. Twenty-two stone posts are topped with carvings of dragons and mythical creatures, with the centre slab featuring a magnificent taotie (an offspring of a dragon). Credit for this daring piece of engineering goes to Li Chun, but according to legend the master

mason Lu Ban constructed it overnight. Several more old stone bridges can be found in Zhàoxiàn county.

From Shíjiāzhuāng's central long-distance bus station take bus No 3 to the Hua Xia long-distance bus station. From there take a minibus to Zhàoxiàn town (Y7, one hour). From Zhàoxiàn there are no public buses to the bridge, but there are plenty of taxis willing to take you (Y15 return).

Cāngyán Shān 苍岩山
About 60km south-west of Shíjiāzhuāng, Cāngyán Shān is a scenic area of woods, valleys and steep cliffs dotted with pagodas and temples. The novelty here is a bizarre, double-roofed hall sitting on a stone-arch bridge spanning a precipitous gorge. It is known as the **Hanging Palace**, and is reached by a 300-step stairway. The palace dates from the Sui dynasty. On the surrounding slopes are other ancient halls. Morning buses (Y10) leave for Cāngyán Shān from Shíjiāzhuāng's Dongfang bus station (Dōngfāng zhàn) by the intersection of Xinhua Lu and Youyi Beidajie.

CHÉNGDÉ 承德
☎ 0314 ● pop 200,000
Chéngdé is an 18th-century imperial resort area 255km north-east of Běijīng. Once known as Jehol, it boasts the remnants of the largest regal gardens in China.

Chéngdé was an obscure town until 1703 when Emperor Kangxi began building a summer palace with a throne room and the

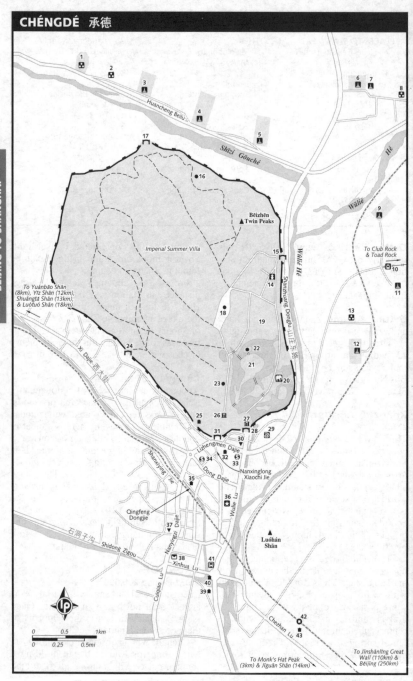

CHÉNGDÉ 承德

Huancheng Beilu

Shīzi Gōuché

Wǔliè Hé

Wǔliè Hé

To Club Rock
& Toad Rock

Imperial Summer Villa

Běizhèn
▲ Twin Peaks

Shanzhuang Donglu 山庄东路

To Yuánbǎo Shān
(8km), Yīz Shān (12km),
Shuāngtǎ Shān (13km),
& Luótuó Shān (18km)

Xī Dàjiē 西大街

Lizhengmen Dajie

Shanyingzi Jie

Dong Dajie

Nanxinglong
Xiaochi Jie

Qingfeng
Dongjie

Wulie Lu

Nanyingzi Dajie

Shidong Zigou
石洞子沟

Cuiqiao Lu

Xinhua Lu

Luóhàn
Shān

Chezhan Lu

To Monk's Hat Peak
(3km) & Jīguān Shān (14km)

To Jīnshānlǐng Great
Wall (110km) &
Běijīng (250km)

0   0.5   1km
0   0.25   0.5mi

CHÉNGDÉ

PLACES TO STAY
25 Qǐwànglóu
   Bīnguǎn
   绮望楼宾馆
32 Mountain Villa
   Hotel
   山庄宾馆
35 Dàyǔ Fàndiàn
   大禹饭店
39 Yúnshān Fàndiàn
   云山饭店
40 Diànlì Bīnguǎn
   电力宾馆
43 Jīngchéng
   Fàndiàn
   京承饭店

PLACES TO EAT
30 Huángchéng
   Dàjiǔdiàn
   皇城大酒店
37 Hénghéxiáng
   Kǎoyādiàn
   恒和祥烤鸭店

OTHER
1 Arhat Hall Ruins
   (Luóhàn Táng)
   罗汉堂
2 Guǎng'ān Sì
   (Ruins)
   广安寺
3 Shūxiàng Sì
   殊像寺
4 Pǔtuózōngchéng
   Zhī Miào
   普陀宗乘之庙

5 Xūmǐfúshòu Zhī Miào
   须弥福寿之庙
6 Pǔníng Sì
   普宁寺
7 Pǔyòu Sì
   普佑寺
8 Guǎngyuán Sì (Ruins)
   广缘寺
9 Ānyuǎn Sì
   安远庙
10 Chairlift to Club &
   Toad Rocks
   棒槌峰索道
11 Pǔlè Sì
   普乐寺
12 Pǔrén Sì
   溥仁寺
13 Pǔshàn Sì
   (Ruins)
   溥善寺
14 Yǒngyòusì Tǎ
   永佑寺塔
15 Huìdíjí Gate
   惠迪吉门
16 Ancient Pavilion (Gǔjù
   Tíng)
   古俱亭
17 North-West Gate
   (Xīběi Mén)
   西北门
18 Wénjīn Chamber
   文津阁
19 Forest Grove
   (Wànshù Yuán)
   万树园
20 Zoo
   动物园

21 Ideal Island
   (Rúyì Zhōu)
   如意洲
22 Misty Rain Tower
   雨楼
23 Fragrant Garden
   House
   (Fāngyuánjū)
   芳园居
24 Bìfēng Gate
   碧峰门
26 Front Palace
   正宫
27 East Palace
   (Dōng Gōng)
   东宫
28 Déhuì Gate
   德汇门
29 Tiānchéng Diànnǎo
   Wǎngbā (Internet)
   天成电脑网吧
31 Lìzhèng Gate
   丽正门
33 Bank of China
   中国银行
34 Bank of China
   中国银行
36 PSB
   公安局
38 Post Office
   邮局
41 Long-Distance Bus
   Station
   长途汽车站
42 Train Station
   火车站

full range of court trappings. Chéngdé became a sort of government seat, since wherever the emperor went his seat went too. Kangxi called his summer creation the Imperial Summer Villa or Fleeing-the-Heat Mountain Villa (Bìshǔ Shānzhuāng).

By 1790, during the reign of Kangxi's grandson Qianlong, it had grown to the size of Běijīng's Summer Palace and the Forbidden City combined. Qianlong extended an idea started by Kangxi, to build replicas of minority architecture in order to make envoys feel comfortable. In particular he was keen on promoting Tibetan and Mongolian Lamaism. The Mongolian branch of Lamaism required one male in every family to become a monk – a convenient method of channelling manpower and damaging the Mongol economy.

This explains the Tibetan and Mongolian features of the monasteries north of the Imperial Summer Villa; one of them is a replica of the Potala Palace in Lhasa.

In 1793 British emissary Lord Macartney arrived and sought to open trade with China. Qianlong dismissed him with the statement that China possessed all things and had no need for trade.

During the Cultural Revolution, the priceless remnants of Qing dynasty culture were allowed to go to seed.

It is all now being slowly restored, in some cases from the base up, in the interests of promoting tourism. Chéngdé is on Unesco's World Heritage list, but this sadly does not guarantee a program of full restoration and some features are gone for good.

Today, Chéngdé's population is engaged in mining, light industry and tourism.

The town of Chéngdé is unexciting, but the park and temples are fine and if you catch some fair weather during your visit the place can be fantastic, with some inspiring views. Grab a bike, pedal through some enchanting countryside and make sure you take in the jaw-dropping statue of Guanyin at Pǔníng Sì – one of Buddhist China's most incredible accomplishments.

Visiting Chéngdé in autumn is an option, as most tourists descend on the place in summer. Autumn adds its own rich colours to the landscape and remains warm enough to be comfortable.

Information

There are two Bank of China branches in town and the post office can be found at the southern end of Nanyingzi Dajie. The Public Security Bureau (PSB; Gōngānjú; ☎ 202 2352) is on Wulie Lu; there is no number, but the office is south of the Fucheng Hotel.

Walking east of Déhuì Gate along Shanzhuang Donglu and over the bridge brings you to a row of shops, where you can find the small Tiānchéng Diànnǎo Wǎngbā Internet cafe. There's no English sign but it's open 24 hours and you can get online for a very cheap Y2 per hour.

Imperial Summer Villa 避暑山庄
Bìshǔ Shānzhuāng

This fanciful park (☎ 216 3761, 202 5918; admission Y50; open 5.30am-6.30pm daily) covers a huge 590 hectares and is bounded by a splendid 10km wall. Emperor Kangxi decreed that there would be 36 'beauty spots' in Jehol (the old name for Chéngdé); Qianlong decreed 36 more. Rampaging warlords and Japanese subsequently took their toll on the park, and even the forests have suffered cutbacks. Even so, the park is a great place to stroll in the shade of the trees and slowly take in the scale of the place.

With some imagination you can perhaps detect traces of the original scheme of things, with landscaping borrowed from the southern gardens of Sūzhōu, Hángzhōu and Jiāxīng, and from the Mongolian grasslands.

Passing through Lìzhèng Gate, the main gate, you arrive at the Front Palace (Zhèng Gōng), containing the main throne hall and the refreshingly cool Hall of Simplicity &

Sincerity, built of an aromatic hardwood called nánmù, and displaying a carved throne; a gorgeous fragrance emanates from the wood. The emperor's bedrooms are fully furnished. Around to the side is a door without an exterior handle (to ensure privacy and security for the emperor), through which the lucky bed partner for the night was ushered before being stripped and searched by eunuchs. Other halls display exhibitions of ceramics, drum stones and calligraphy.

The double storey Misty Rain Tower (Yǔ Lóu), on the north-western side of the main lake, was an imperial study. Further north is the Wénjīn Chamber (Wénjīn Gé), built in 1773 to house a copy of the Sikuquanshu, a major anthology of classics, history, philosophy and literature commissioned by Qianlong. The anthology took 10 years to put together. Four copies were made, but three have disappeared; the fourth is in Bĕijīng.

In the east, tall Yǒngyòusì Tǎ soars above the fragments of its vanished temple. Wander around the pagoda and inspect the temple layout that was levelled by the Japanese.

About 90% of the compound is taken up by lakes, hills, mini-forests and plains (where visitors now play football), with the odd vantage-point pavilion. At the northern part of the park the emperors reviewed displays of archery, equestrian skills and fireworks. Horses were also chosen and tested here before hunting sorties.

The Shānzhuāng Zoo (Dòngwùyuán; admission Y10), in the south-east, is one of the cleanest and prettiest zoos in China, although it is very small. Decked out with flowers and regularly swept, the zoo houses some well-kept animals, including a marvellous Siberian tiger (and its cubs), a great lioness, bears, yaks, ostriches and monkeys.

Just beyond the Front Palace is a ticket office (☎ 203 7720) for tourist buggies that whiz around the grounds (Y40).

Wàibā Miào 外八庙
Eight Outer Temples

The Eight Outer Temples, lying to the north and north-east of the walls of the Imperial Summer Villa, are some of China's finest examples of religious architecture. The number of temples is down on its original compliment and some remain closed, but there are enough to keep you busy.

The surviving temples were all built between 1750 and 1780. The most popular (and most crowded) temples are Pǔtuózōngchéng Zhī Miào and Pǔníng Sì. The temples and monasteries are between 3km and 7km of the Lìzhèng Gate; bus No 6 taken to the northeastern corner of the Imperial Summer Villa will drop you in the vicinity – going by bike is an excellent idea (see Getting Around later). Some of the temples are described in more detail, following.

Pǔníng Sì 普宁寺
Temple of Universal Tranquillity

Pǔníng Sì *(Puningsi Lu; admission Y30; open 8am-5.30pm daily)* is a Chinese-style *(hànshi)* temple at the front, with chubby Milefo (Laughing Buddha) welcoming visitors and more Tibetan-style *(zàngshì)* features at the rear. It was built to commemorate Qianlong's victory over Mongol tribes.

The absolute highlight of a trip here is the heart-arresting golden statue of **Guanyin**, Goddess of Mercy, in the Mahayana Hall. The effigy is totally astounding: it's over 22m high (the highest of its kind in the world) and radiates a powerful sense of divinity.

Mesmerising in its scale, this labour of love is hewn from five different kinds of wood (pine, cypress, fir, elm and linden). Guanyin has 42 arms, with each palm bearing an eye and each hand holding instruments, skulls, lotuses and other Buddhist devices. Tibetan features include the pair of hands in front of the Goddess, below the two clasped in prayer, the right one holding a sceptre-like *dorje,* a masculine symbol, and the left a *dril bu* (bell), a female symbol.

You can clamber up to the first gallery (Y10) for a closer inspection of Guanyin; torches are provided to cut through the gloom and pick out the uneven stairs (take care).

Pǔtuózōngchéng Zhī Miào
普陀宗圣之庙
Pǔtuózōngchéng Temple

This temple *(Shizigou Lu; admission Y20; open 8am-6pm daily),* the largest of the Chéngdé temples, is a mini-facsimile of Lhasa's Potala Palace. It was built for the chieftains from Xīnjiāng, Qīnghǎi, Mongolia and Tibet to celebrate Qianlong's 60th birthday and is a solid-looking fortress.

Guanyin

The boundlessly compassionate countenance of Guanyin, the Buddhist Goddess of Mercy, can be encountered in temples all over China. The Goddess (more strictly a Bodhisattva or a Buddha-to-be) goes under a variety of aliases: Guanshiyin, literally meaning 'Observing the Cries of the World', is her formal name, but she is also called Guanzizai, Guanyin Dashi and Guanyin Pusa or, in Sanskrit, Avalokiteshvara. In Japan, she is known as Kannon and in Cantonese as Guanyam. Guanyin shoulders the grief of the world and dispenses mercy and compassion. Christians will note a semblance to the Virgin Mary in the aura surrounding the Goddess.

In Tibetan Buddhism, her earthly presence manifests itself in the Dalai Lama, and her home is the Potala Palace in Lhasa. In China, her abode is the island mount of Pǔtuóshān in Zhèjiāng province, whose first two syllables derive from the name of her palace in Lhasa.

In temples throughout China, Guanyin is often found at the very rear of the main hall, facing north (most of the other divinities, apart from Weituo, face south). She typically has her own little shrine and stands on the head of a big fish, holding a lotus in her hand. On other occasions, she has her own hall, which is generally towards the rear of the temple.

The Goddess (who in earlier dynasties appears to be male rather than female) is often surrounded by little effigies of the Luohan (Arhat, those freed from the cycle of rebirth), who scamper about (the Guanyin Temple in Dàlǐ is a good example of this). Guanyin also appears in a variety of forms, often with just two arms, but sometimes also in a multi-armed form (a statue of the Goddess in Xīyuán Sì in Sūzhōu bristles with arms). The 11-faced Guanyin, the horse head Guanyin, the Songzi Guanyin (literally 'Offering Son Guanyin') and the Dripping Water Guanyin are all manifestations, and there are many more. She was also a favourite subject for white Dehua porcelain figures, which are typically very elegant.

Among the many exhibits on view are displays of Tibetan Buddhist objects and instruments, including a *kapala* bowl, made from the skull of a young girl (captions all in Chinese). The main hall is housed at the very top, surrounded by several small pavilions (most of which now house souvenir stalls); the climb to the top is worth it for the views. The temple's sacred aura is sadly ruined by graffiti and plastic bottles.

Xūmǐfúshòu Zhī Miào 须弭福寿之庙
Temple of Sumeru, Happiness and Longevity

Xūmǐfúshòu (Shizigou Lu; admission Y20; open 8am-5.30pm daily) was built in honour of the sixth Panchen Lama, who stayed here in 1781. It incorporates elements of Tibetan and Han architecture and is an imitation of a temple in Shigatse, Tibet. At the highest point is a hall with eight gilded copper dragons commanding the roof ridges, behind which sits a glazed-tile pagoda.

Pǔlè Sì 普乐寺
Temple of Universal Happiness

Pǔlè Sì (admission Y20; open 8am-6pm daily) was built in 1776 for visits of minority envoys (Kazaks among them). At the rear of the temple is the unusual Round Pavilion, reminiscent of Bĕijīng's Temple of Heaven.

It's a 30-minute hike to **Club Rock** (Bàngchuí Fēng) from Pǔlè Sì – the rock is said to resemble a club used for beating laundry dry. Nearby is **Toad Rock** (Hámá Shí). There is pleasant hiking, good scenery and commanding views of the area. You can save yourself a steep climb to the base of the rocks by taking the chairlift, but it's more fun to walk if you're reasonably fit. Bus No 10 from Wulie Lu will take you to Pǔlè Sì.

Other Temples

Ānyuǎn Sì (Far Spreading Peace Temple; admission Y10; open 8am-5.30pm daily) is a copy of the Gurza temple in Xīnjiāng. Only the main hall remains and it contains Buddhist frescoes in a very sad state. Neither **Pǔrén Sì** nor **Shūxiàng Sì** are open to the public; just to the west of the latter is a military zone off limits to foreigners, so don't go wandering around. **Pǔyòu Sì** (admission Y10; open 8am-6pm daily) is in a sad state, apart from its plentiful contingent of merry gilded Luohan in the side wings.

Other Hills

Other hills regarded as famous beauty spots (possibly climbable) include: **Luóhàn Shān** (Arhat Hill), almost in the centre of town;

Monk's Hat Peak (Sēngguān Fēng), 4km south of town; **Jīguān Shān** (Cockscomb Hill), 15km to the south-east; **Yuánbǎo Shān** (Ingot Hill), 10km south-west of town; **Shuāngtǎ Shān** (Twin Pagoda Hill), 15km to the south-west; **Yǐzi Shān** (Chair Mountain), 14km to the south-west; and **Luòtuó Shān** (Camel Mountain), 20km to the south-west.

Jīnshānlǐng 金山岭

It's a good 1½-hour, 113km drive from the centre of Chéngdé to the Great Wall at Jīnshānlǐng (admission Y40), but it's in the direction of Bĕijīng, so if you're travelling by car or bus you could stop off here on a Bĕijīng-Chéngdé excursion.

It is possible to hike (about four hours) along the wall between Jīnshānlǐng and Sìmǎtái. For information about the Great Wall at Jīnshānlǐng, see the Bĕijīng chapter.

Organised Tours

The only practical way to see all the sights in one day is to take a tour by minibus, most of which start out at 8am. The cheapest bus tours cost around Y30 (check at the Mountain Villa Hotel), but are Chinese-speaking only; a personal tour costs about Y100, excluding admission prices. Most hotels run tours.

Places to Stay

As soon as you arrive at the train station, hotel touts will be waiting for you. If you go with them you'll get a free ride to your hotel; at the hotel you pay the standard rate and the touts get a commission.

Mountain Villa Hotel (Shānzhuāng Bīnguǎn; ☎ 202 3501, fax 202 2457, 127 Lizhengmen Dajie) Doubles Y140, twins Y240-480. This is a really great place to rest for the night: clean, cheap rooms and pole position for a trip inside the Imperial Summer Villa. The best deal is the doubles in the back part of the hotel. The more expensive rooms are large enough to hold a party in – perhaps that's why they come equipped with *mahjong* tables. Take bus No 7 from the train station and from there it's a short walk.

Jīngchéng Fàndiàn (☎ 202 2077) Beds in quads without bath Y30, doubles Y200. This is a reasonably clean, friendly and good-value place near the station.

Diànlì Bīnguǎn (☎ *217 3735, Daqiao-tou)* Beds in 5-/4-/2-bed dorms with air-con Y40/50/80; singles/doubles with air-con Y200/120. This place has clean, simple and functional tile-floor rooms, and hot water between 7pm and 11pm.

Yúnshān Fàndiàn (☎ *215 6171, fax 215 4551, 6 Nanyuan Donglu)* Doubles Y440. One of the better hotels in town, this place has neat and clean doubles, but the bellowing ground-floor karaoke may put you off.

Qīwànglóu Bīnguǎn (☎ *202 4385, fax 202 1904, 1 Bifengmen Donglu)* Twins from Y400. This Qing-style hotel west of the Lìzhèng Gate has pleasant gardens with peacocks and a quiet atmosphere. Jiang Zemin stayed here, if that's anything to go by.

Places to Eat

Chéngdé's local specialty is wild game – deer *(lùròu)* and pheasant *(shānjī)* – which you can find all over town.

Hénghéxiáng Kǎoyādiàn (☎ *207 5568, 2 Wenjiagou)* Roast duck Y60, deer Y30. This small, clean and well-decorated restaurant is on the right of a small alley to the west of Nanyingzi Dajie. The slightly spicy deer *(gānpēng lùròu)* is tasty and filling and fried in a crisp coating of batter; deep-fried pheasant *(qīngzhá shānjī)* is also good. You can wash it down with a Yanjing Chrysanthemum beer.

Huángchéng Dàjiǔdiàn (☎ *202 5757, 98 Xiaonanmen)* Dishes Y40. If you're in the vicinity of the Déhuì Gate, this restaurant cooks up local favourites.

For street food, try the restaurants along *Shanxiying Jie*, at the northern end of Nanyingzi Dajie, or *Nanxinglong Xiaochi Jie*, across from the Lìzhèng Gate. You can get all kinds of local dishes, including pheasant and dog meat, as well as many of China's staple dishes. The restaurant owners are a highly vocal crowd.

Qingfeng Dongjie, at the northern end of Nanyingzi Dajie, has a brightly lit and colourful spread of restaurants – you can't miss the lights at night.

Getting There & Away

Bus To Chéngdé buses leave from Běijīng's Dōngzhímén long-distance bus station (Y45, four hours); to Běijīng buses leave every 20 minutes from the Chéngdé's long-distance bus station (☎ 202 3476). Other useful routes

from Chéngdé include Qínhuángdǎo (Y64), Tiānjīn (Y60) and Shíjiāzhuāng (sleeper Y50, 9pm). The long-distance bus station has a luggage deposit facility.

Train There are regular trains between Chéngdé and Běijīng. The fastest trains take four hours and cost Y41; slower trains, although cheaper, take around seven hours. There are also connections to Shěnyáng, Dāndōng (17 hours, 6.46pm) and a sleeper to Shíjiāzhuāng (Y86, 10 hours, 9.42pm).

The schedule is as follows:

Běijīng-Chéngdé

train no	depart	arrive
7155	7.20am	11.18pm
2251	1.22pm	6.22pm
7153	4.28pm	11.16pm

Chéngdé-Běijīng

train no	depart	arrive
2252	6.31am	11.40am
7154	7.20am	2.12pm
7156	12.40pm	8.16pm
K710	2.40pm	6.38pm

Shěnyáng-Chéngdé

train no	depart	arrive
2066	7.25am	8.28pm

Chéngdé-Shěnyáng

train no	depart	arrive
2065	7.01am	8.34pm

Getting Around

Taxis and motor-tricycles are widely available – bargaining is necessary, especially with the tricycles. Taxis are Y5 at flagfall, which should get you to most destinations in town. The most useful minibus route is the No 6 to the farther members of Wàibā Miào. The service is infrequent – you might have to wait 30 minutes or more.

A great way to get around town and to Wàibā Miào is on a bicycle. You can rent bicycles at numerous hotels, including the Mountain Villa Hotel and Yúnshān Fàndiàn (it may just be a case of staff renting theirs to you). There's also a bike rental outfit at the train station (Y5 per day, Y200 deposit).

BĚIDÀIHÉ, QÍNHUÁNGDĂO & SHĀNHĂIGUĀN
北戴河、秦皇岛、山海关

BĚIDÀIHÉ 北戴河
☎ 0335

A 35km stretch of coastline on China's east coast, the Běidàihé, Qínhuángdǎo and Shānhǎiguān region borders the Bó Sea (Bó Hǎi). The summer seaside resort of breezy Běidàihé was cobbled together by Westerners, but the Chinese are the main sun seekers today. The innocent fishing village was transformed when English railway engineers stumbled across it in the 1890s. Diplomats, missionaries and business people from the Tiānjīn concessions and the Běijīng legations hastily built villas and cottages in order to indulge in the new bathing fad.

The original golf courses, bars and cabarets have disappeared, but some of the old villas remain, hidden behind crumbling walls. Cash is being pumped into prettifying the town.

The cream of China's leaders congregate at summer villas, continuing a tradition that has starred such personalities as Jiang Qing and Lin Biao. Li Peng and Jiang Zemin currently have heavily guarded residences along the seaside on the road between Běidàihé and Nándàihé.

During the summer high season (May to October) Běidàihé comes alive with vacationers who crowd the beaches, eat at the numerous outdoor seafood restaurants and stroll the night markets.

The average June temperature is 21°C (70°F). In January, by contrast, temperatures rest at -5°C (23°F).

Information
Běidàihé has a Bank of China near the corner of Dongjing Lu and Binhai Dadao and a post office on Haining Lu.

There's a telephone office at 76 Dongjing Lu. It's open from 8am to noon and 3pm to 6.30pm, and has an Internet service for Y0.3 per minute. You can also pick up IP and IC cards here.

Things to See & Do
Wandering the streets and seafront of Běidàihé is thoroughly enjoyable, but it's even better to hire a bike or a tandem (shuāngzuò zìxíngchē) and whiz around the beachfront roads. Bikes can be rented on Zhonghaitan Lu (Y10 per hour) east of Bao Erlu. Otherwise, fork out for a rubber ring,

BĚIDÀIHÉ 北戴河

1	Bus Station 海滨汽车站	6	Telephone Office 邮电局	10	Bank of China 中国银行
2	Buses to Běijīng 去北京的汽车站	7	Kiessling's Restaurant 起士林餐厅	11	Tiějiàn Dùjiàcūn 铁建度假村
3	Post Office 邮局	8	Guesthouse for Diplomatic Missions 外交人员宾馆	12	Yòuyīgōng Bīnguǎn 又一宫宾馆
4	Train Ticket Office 火车票售票处	9	Jiāohǎi Bīnguǎn 交海宾馆	13	Běidàihé Yǒuyì Bīnguǎn 北戴河友谊宾馆
5	Yuèhuá Bīnguǎn 悦华宾馆			14	Bìluó Tǎ 碧螺塔

BEIJING TO SHANGHAI

inner tube and swimming trunks from one of the street vendors and plunge into the sea (after elbowing through the crowds).

Tiger Rocks (*Lǎohǔshí*) are popular with children and fishermen and those who gather to watch the sunrise (unless the sea fog gets in the way).

There are various hikes to vantage points with expansive views of villas or the coast. The **Sea-Viewing Pavilion** (*Wànghǎi Tíng*) is on Liánfēngshān Gōngyuán, the hilly park halfway between Běidàihé and Nándàihé. The tide at the **East Beach** (*Dōng Hǎitān*) recedes dramatically, when tribes of kelp collectors and shell-pickers descend upon the sands.

Always be on the look-out for Běidàihé's peculiar revolutionary emblems and seaside kitsch, including a **statue of Gorky** (*Gāoěrjī*) surrounded by outsized seashells. For those in pursuit of bad taste, Běidàihé comes up trumps with its **Bìluó Tǎ** (*Emerald Shell Tower*) – it's quite ghastly.

Places to Stay

Most budget hotels in Běidàihé only take Chinese. As a result, many foreign travellers give the resort a miss or stay in nearby Shānhǎiguān. Furthermore, the resort is only fully open during the summer season (May to October) and all hotels in town are a long way from the train station. Prices quoted are high season; low-season prices are cheaper, and haggling helps.

Those who speak Chinese can try the Chinese guesthouses. Otherwise the choice is limited.

Běidàihé Yǒuyì Bīnguǎn (*Beidaihe Friendship Hotel;* ☎ *404 8558, fax 404 1965, 1 Yingjiao Lu*) Doubles Y300-580. Set in huge, grassy green grounds in the east of town, this hotel is a good deal with tidy doubles and singles. The cheaper (also clean) doubles are at the rear in stone terraced houses. You can exit the rear entrance, mosey down the road and straight onto the beach.

Guesthouse for Diplomatic Missions (*Wàijiāo Rényuán Bīnguǎn;* ☎ *404 1287, fax 404 1807, 1 Bao Sanlu*) Doubles/triples Y650/300. Open Apr-Oct. This guesthouse remains an appealing place to stay and has outdoor porches, so relax in the breeze and enjoy the hotel's beach. There's also tennis and weekend barbecues.

Yòuyīgōng Bīnguǎn (☎ *404 1353, 8 Yingjiao Lu*) Doubles/triples/suites Y360/ 200/480. This hotel is a cheaper, mustier and more somnolent alternative. You could argue the price down if you can find the hotel (no English sign) and handle the bright red carpets.

Yuèhuá Bīnguǎn (*Yuehua Hotel;* ☎ *404 0470, 100 Dongjing Lu*) Doubles Y450. Smack in the centre of town, this hotel is a reasonably smart and convenient option.

Jiāohǎi Bīnguǎn (*Jiaohai Hotel;* ☎ *404 1388, fax 404 1388, 97 Dongjing Lu*) Doubles/suites Y680/980. This clean, modern and centrally located three-star hotel is newer than many of the others and has a swimming pool.

Tiějiàn Dùjiàcūn (*Tiejian Holiday Village;* ☎ *404 9020, fax 403 3359, Haibin Dong Erlu*) Doubles or triples/suites Y480/680. This is an average-looking Chinese seafront hotel catering to hordes of out-of-towners.

Places to Eat

Finding fine eats in town is easy in summer. A whole string of *seafood restaurants* (*hǎixiāndiàn*) are strung out along Bao Erlu, near the beach; you can't miss them or their vocal owners. Choose your meal from the slippery knots of mysterious sea creatures kept alive in buckets on the pavement.

There's another lively, colourful stretch of *dumpling restaurants* (*jiǎozidiàn*) and *seafood restaurants*, in the market on Hongshi Lu, north of Dongjing Lu. In the evening, check out the tiny *kebab restaurants* (*shāokǎodiàn*) on the eastern side of Haining Lu north of the post office; lamb kebabs (*yángròuchuàn*) are around Y1 each. Grab a bottle of the local Bull Ice or Bull King beer (Y4), sit outside and watch the world go by.

Also look out for one of the ubiquitous *fruit sellers* wheeling their harvest around on bicycles, selling grapes, peaches, bananas, peanuts etc.

Kiessling's Restaurant (*Qǐshílín Cāntīng;* ☎ *404 1043, Dongjing Lu*) Open June-Aug. Kiessling's is a relative of the Tiānjīn branch. It serves both Chinese and international food (although there's no English menu) and has some pleasant outdoor seating.

SHĀNHǍIGUĀN 山海关

Shānhǎiguān is where the Great Wall meets the sea. In the 1980s this part of the wall had nearly returned to dust, but it has been rebuilt and is now a first-rate tourist drawcard. Its proximity to Běidàihé guarantees it a summer tourist bonanza. The town is very poor and a ragged reminder that the benefits of economic reform remain unevenly spread. Facilities for Western visitors are, as a result, basic at best.

Shānhǎiguān was a garrison town with a square fortress, four gates at the compass points and two major avenues running between the gates. Considerable charm remains within the old walled enclosure despite its dilapidation. Part of its appeal lies in its manageable size, its grid-like streets and tenacious sense of history. Sadly, much has been replaced with functional brick and tile structures or uninspired imitations of the old style.

The Wall

There are three places to walk on the wall in the Shānhǎiguān vicinity. Unfortunately, the remains have largely been dressed up for tour groups. It is possible to walk on some unrenovated parts of the wall, although you'd have to drive two hours northeast of the city.

First Pass Under Heaven 天下第一关
Tiānxià Dìyī Guān

At First Pass Under Heaven (*admission Y30 May-Oct, Y20 Nov-Apr; open 6am-7pm daily*), also known as the East Gate (Dōng Mén), tattered flags flap along the wall, which affords views of factories off to the east and decayed sections of battlements trailing off into the hills. This Ming-dynasty structure is topped with a two-storey, double-roofed tower and was rebuilt in 1639.

The calligraphy at the top (attributed to the scholar Xiao Xian) reads 'First Pass Under Heaven', words that reflect the Chinese custom of dividing the world into civilised China and the 'barbarians'. The barbarians (Manchus) got the upper hand when they stormed this gate in 1644 and enslaved China for 250 years. Hordes of souvenir sellers and loud, piped music make further mockery of the wall's fading nobility.

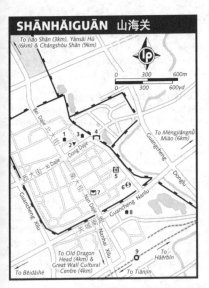

SHĀNHĂIGUĀN 山海关

To Jiǎo Shān (3km), Yànsāi Hú
(6km) & Chángshòu Shān (9km)

To Mèngjiāngnǚ
Miào (6km)

Bei Dajie

Dong Dajie

西大街 – Xi Dajie

Guancheng Xilu

Guangcheng

Dong Dajie

南大街 – Nan Dajie

天城南街 – Nanhai Xilu

Guancheng Nanlu

Donglu

To Old Dragon
Head (4km) &
Great Wall Cultural
Centre (4km)

To Běidàihé

To Hǎěrbīn

To Tiānjīn

SHĀNHĂIGUĀN

1 Běijiē Zhāodàisuǒ
   北街招待所
2 Lìdá Hǎixiān Jiǔlóu
   丽达海鲜酒楼
3 Jīngshān Bīnguǎn
   京山宾馆
4 First Pass Under Heaven
   天下第一关
5 Great Wall Museum
   长城博物馆
6 Bank of China
   中国银行
7 Post Office
   邮局
8 Shānhǎiguān Dàjiǔdiàn
   山海关大酒店
9 Train Station
   火车站

Down the street the **Great Wall Museum** (*Chángchéng Bówùguǎn; Diyiguan Lu; admission included in First Pass Under Heaven ticket; open 8am-6.30pm daily*) is in many ways a more interesting way to commune with the wall through its collection of photographs and mementos. Sadly, there are no English captions.

Old Dragon Head 老龙头
Lǎolóngtóu

Old Dragon Head (*admission Y35; open 8am-5.30pm daily*), 4km south of Shānhǎiguān, was the serpentine conclusion of the Great Wall as it made a grand finale at the sea's edge. What you see now was reconstructed in the late 1980s – the original wall has long since crumbled away. The name derives from the legendary carved dragon head that once faced the waves.

There are beaches on either side of the wall where you can swim and there's also the skirtable **Great Wall Cultural Centre** (*admission Y20; open 8am-5.30pm daily*) on the approach. Minibuses speed to Old Dragon Head from Guancheng Nanlu, as do bus Nos 13 and 23.

Jiǎo Shān 角山
Horned Hill

A 4km walk (taxi Y10; motor tricycle Y5) from the town centre brings you to a steep

section of rebuilt masonry, where the Great Wall mounts its first high peak, Jiǎo Shān (*admission Y10; open 5am-sunset daily*). It's a trying 20-minute clamber from the base, but a cable car can yank you up for Y20. The views are fantastic on a clear day. The path behind the hills to the **Qixian Monastery** (*admission Y5*), can be traversed in an hour, but is thorny and it's easy to lose the trail, which often peters out. However the tranquillity is peerless; the monastery, perched on a hill way beyond the terminus of the cable car, is said to have once served as a retreat for scholars.

Yànsāi Hú
Yànsāi Lake

Just 6km to the north-west of Shānhǎiguān, Yànsāi Hú is also known as Stone River Reservoir (*Shíhé Shuǐkù*). The reservoir is 4km to 5km long and boat trips are available for tourists who marvel at geological manifestations of animals and spirits. Take the No 24 bus from Guancheng Nanlu.

Chángshòu Shān 长寿山
Longevity Mountain

This area has interesting rock formations and potential as a nice place for a hike. However, as with other Shānhǎiguān sights, it's been transformed into a tourist spectacle with stone statues carved into rock faces and concrete paths herding tourists around the various rock formations. It's 9km north-east of Shānhǎiguān; take bus No 26 from Guancheng Nanlu.

Mèngjiāngnǚ Miào 孟姜女庙

Mèngjiāngnǚ Miào *(admission Y10; open 7am-5.30pm daily)* is a Song-Ming reconstruction 6km east of Shānhǎiguān. It has coloured sculptures of Lady Meng and her maids and calligraphy on Looking for Husband Rock. The story is famous in China:

Meng's husband, Wan, was press-ganged into wall building because his views conflicted with those of Emperor Qin Shihuang. When winter came Meng Jiang set off to take her husband warm clothing, only to discover that he had died from the backbreaking labour. Meng tearfully wandered the Great Wall, thinking only of finding Wan's bones to give him a decent burial. The wall, a sensitive soul, was so upset that it collapsed, revealing the skeleton entombed within. Overcome with grief, Meng hurled herself into the sea from a boulder.

The temple itself is washed out and a little tacky. Take bus No 23 from Guancheng Nanlu; a taxi should cost around Y12.

Places to Stay

Shānhǎiguān has a limited number of hotels.

Běijiē Zhāodàisuǒ (North Street Hotel; ☎ 505 1680, 2 Mujia Hutong) Dorm beds Y30, doubles with bath Y120-160. This is a simple courtyard hotel in need of renovation, but not without some charm. The rooms don't have phones, and the heating is dodgy in cold weather.

Jīngshān Bīnguǎn (Jingshan Hotel; ☎ 505 1130, Dong Dajie) Twins Y140-300. There are more creature comforts, but not so much charm in this fairly large hotel, built in imitation traditional Chinese style. The hotel is located west of Shānhǎiguān's premier chunk of Great Wall, so there are plenty of tour buses and souvenir hawkers. Rates include breakfast.

Shānhǎiguān Dàjiǔdiàn (Shanhaiguan Hotel; ☎ 506 4488, Guancheng Nanlu) Doubles Y288. This hotel, just south-east of the city walls, offers reasonable rooms and rates.

Places to Eat

Lìdà Hǎixiān Jiǔlóu (Lida Restaurant; Dong Dajie) Mains Y35. This is a cheerful, colourful eatery with local, northern fare, plus some Sichuanese dishes including stir-fried chicken with peanuts *(gōngbào jīdīng)*. The black rice *(hēimǐ)* is also tasty.

Come sundown, gregarious *kebab sellers* set up barbecue ovens outside many of the shops along Nan Dajie, where you can feast on five lamb kebabs *(yángroùchuàn)* for Y1 and pick up cheap beers (Y2).

Getting There & Away

Air Qínhuángdǎo's little airport has flights to Cháoyáng, Dàlián, Nánjīng, Shànghǎi, Tàiyuán and Yāntái.

Train The Běidàihé, Qínhuángdǎo and Shānhǎiguān train stations are accessible from Běijīng, Tiānjīn or Shěnyáng (Liáoníng). The trains are frequent, but don't always stop at all three stations or arrive at convenient hours.

One factor to consider is that the hotels at Shānhǎiguān are within walking distance of the train station, whereas at Běidàihé the nearest hotel is at least 10km from the station. This is no problem if you arrive during daylight or early evening – minibuses meet incoming trains at Běidàihé train station. However, you can't count on this at night and a taxi is around Y20 into town. If you're going to arrive in the dead of night, it's better to do so at Shānhǎiguān.

The fastest trains (double deckers) take under three hours to Běidàihé from Běijīng (Y70), allow a bit longer for Shānhǎiguān. Shěnyáng to Shānhǎiguān (Y70) is a five-hour trip. Tiānjīn to Shānhǎiguān (Y42) is around four hours. In Běidàihé you can buy train tickets from a ticket office at the corner of Haining Lu and Dongjing Lu.

Alternatively, you can get a train that stops at Qínhuángdǎo and then take a minibus from there to Běidàihé or Shānhǎiguān.

Bus Although there are long-distance buses between all three towns and Běijīng, most travellers go by train. A convenient place to pick up a bus in Běidàihé is from the east side of Haining Lu just south of the kebab outlets: buses leave here for Běijīng at 6am, noon and 4pm during the summer season (Y70, three hours). Comfortable buses also leave for Běijīng from Qínhuángdǎo (Y75, three hours). You can also take direct buses from Qínhuángdǎo to Chéngdé (Y60, seven hours), departing at 6am, 7am and 8am.

Boat Every even-numbered day at 6pm, passenger boats leave from the port in

Qínhuángdǎo to Dàlián, arriving in Dàlián at 7am. Fares range from Y100 to Y629, depending on how fancy a cabin you choose.

Getting Around

Bus Minibuses are fast and cheap and can be flagged down easily. Minibuses speed from Bĕidàihé train station to town – look for one that screams '*hǎibīn*' (the beach). To be more specific, tell the driver you want to get off at the Bĕidàihé bus station (Hǎibīn qìchē zhàn). The fare varies, but should be around Y3; alternatively, take bus No 5 (see later).

On all other minibuses the fare is Y2. The main routes are Bĕidàihé bus station to Qínhuángdǎo train station, and Qínhuángdǎo train station to Shānhǎiguān.

Buses connect all three towns. They generally run every 30 minutes from around 6am to 6.30pm. Some of the useful public bus routes are No 5 from Bĕidàihé train station to Bĕidàihé bus station (30 minutes), No 34 from Bĕidàihé bus station to Qínhuángdǎo (Y2), and Nos 33 and 25 from Qínhuángdǎo to Shānhǎiguān (Y2).

Taxis The cheapest taxis in Bĕidàihé, Qínhuángdǎo and Shānhǎiguān are all Y5 flagfall and Y1.2 per km after that.

Motor-Tricycles These are popular in Shānhǎiguān. It's Y2 to anywhere within town.

Bicycle Shānhǎiguān and Bĕidàihé are good places to explore by bike. Bikes and tandems are available along Zhonghaitan Lu in Bĕidàihé (see Things to See & Do in the Bĕidàihé section). Ask at your hotel in Shānhǎiguān about bike rental outlets.

Shāndōng 山东

Capital: JĪ'nán
Population: 90.8 million
Area: 153,000 sq km

Across the Yellow Sea from South Korea, Shāndōng has a history that can be traced back to the origins of the Chinese state: Confucius. China's great social philosopher was born here and lived out his days in Lǔ, one of the small states in the south of today's province (the Chinese character for Lǔ is still associated with Shāndōng). His ideas were further championed by the great Confucian philosopher Mencius, who hailed from the same region.

From the earliest record of civilisation in the province (furnished by the black pottery remains of the Lóngshān culture), Shāndōng has had a tumultuous history. It was victim to the capricious temperament of the oft-flooding Huáng Hé (Yellow River), which finishes its long journey from tributaries in Qīnghǎi here, emptying into the Bo Sea (Bó Hǎi). The consequences included mass death, starvation and a ruined provincial economy. In more recent years, Shāndōng has suffered the humiliation of foreign encroachment upon its territory.

In 1899 Huáng Hé (also aptly named 'China's Sorrow') flooded the entire Shāndōng plain; a sad irony in view of the two scorching droughts that had swept the area that same year and the year before. The flood followed a long period of economic depression, a sudden influx of demobilised troops in 1895 after China's humiliating defeat by Japan in Korea, and droves of refugees from the south moving north to escape famines, floods and drought.

To top it all off, the Europeans arrived; Qīngdǎo was snatched by the Germans, and the British obtained a lease for Wēihǎi. Their activities included the building of railroads and some feverish missionary work, which the Chinese believed angered the gods and spirits.

All this created the perfect breeding ground for rebellion, and in the closing years of the 19th century the Boxers arose out of Shāndōng, armed with magical spells and broadswords, which they thought would protect them from the West's hail of bullets.

Highlights

- Tài Shān, a sacred peak worth climbing for the sunrise
- Qūfù, the best place to soak up the wisdom of Confucius
- Qīngdǎo, home to remnant colonial architecture and China's most famous brew
- Chéngshān Cape, the most eastern point in China

The port of Qīngdǎo fell into the clutches of the Germans in 1898. They added an industrial infrastructure, cobbled streets and Bavarian architecture. This development still gives Qīngdǎo an economic momentum. Today, JĪ'nán, the provincial capital, plays second fiddle to Qīngdǎo's tune. Other economic focuses in the province include Shengli Oilfield, which is China's second-largest producer of oil. By 1994 Shāndōng was ranked among the top four provincial economies in China (alongside Guǎngdōng, Jiāngsū and Sìchuān).

The sights of Qūfù and Tài Shān, the most revered of China's sacred mountains, are worth a look, although you'll have to share them with droves of tourists. If you want to sink a decent beer, scoff excellent seafood, breathe the sea air and wander the streets filled with colonial relics, then make a beeline to Qīngdǎo on the coast.

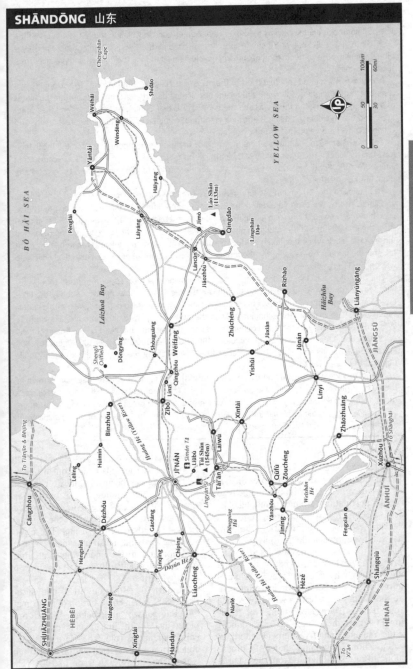

BĚIJĪNG TO SHÀNGHǍI

The Fists of Righteousness & Harmony

The popular movement known as the Boxer Rebellion erupted in China in the last few years of the 19th century. The Boxers, or Yihetuan (loosely translated as the Fists of Righteousness and Harmony), were a loose confederation of anti-foreign elements that took their beliefs and practices from secret societies.

Many reasons spurred the Boxers on to the massacres they were to perform. The strongest was resentment of foreigners, following the recent humiliating defeats for the Qing court at the hands of the foreign powers. But there was also the general dislike of Christian missionaries and their practices, and the widespread feeling that China was about to be sliced up among the 'barbarians' and Chinese culture trampled underfoot.

The Boxers arose in Shāndōng where they quickly found support among the poor and those reeling from the Huáng Hé floods in 1899. Their attacks on missionaries and their families became more and more daring until feelings ran so high that they promised to wipe out all foreigners, or 'hairy men' (and women) altogether.

The policy of the Qing court (as represented by Cixi, the Empress Dowager) toward the Boxers vacillated. At first the court considered the Boxers to be no different from the usual peasant uprisings, but later viewed them as an ally in its agenda to fight back against the foreign powers and restore the integrity of the Manchu administration. The aspirations of the Qing court soon paralleled those of the rebels when the Boxers started to attack and massacre foreigners at random in the capital, and the famous 50-day siege of the foreign legations in Běijīng began. Cixi effectively declared war on the foreign powers on 21 June 1900.

The folly of this alliance was recognised by most provincial authorities, who refused to rally behind the court knowing the weakness of a China pitted against the powers, and doubting the Boxers claims to be impervious to Western bullets (the Boxers protected themselves with charms, superstitions and martial arts techniques). Thus the movement was limited in scale, allowing the Westerners the chance to focus attacks on the capital, Běijīng, and the heart of the Boxers' cause. An international relief force of 8000 Japanese, 4800 Russians, 3000 British, 2100 Americans, 800 French, 58 Austrians and 53 Italians descended on Běijīng, lifting the siege of the legations, while Cixi and the court fled to Xī'ān.

The Boxers were destroyed and China found itself the recipient of a huge indemnity known as the Boxer Protocol. Among the 12 conditions included in the protocol was a bill of 450 million taels of gold (to be paid off yearly with interest), which effectively crippled China's economy for many years. This indemnity contributed to the eventual collapse of the Manchu court and the Qing dynasty.

JǏ'NÁN 济南

☎ 0531 • pop 5,921,700

Jǐ'nán, the capital of Shāndōng province, is for most travellers a transit point on the road to other destinations around Shāndōng. The city is not unattractive, and at night offers a pleasant selection of night markets, hole-in-the-wall restaurants and atmosphere.

Jǐ'nán is most commonly noted for its springs, however after a visit to them you may wonder why. Downplayed in Jǐ'nán's tourist pitch, but perhaps of more interest, are the Chinese celebrities who have come from Jǐ'nán. Bian Que, founder of traditional Chinese medicine, Zou Yan, founder of the Yin and Yang five element school, as well as Zhou Yongnian, founder of Chinese public libraries, all herald from these parts.

A number of nationally and internationally recognised writers also hail from Jǐ'nán.

The area has been inhabited for at least 4000 years, and some of the earliest reminders of this are the eggshell-thin pieces of black pottery unearthed in the town of Lóngshān, 30km east of Jǐ'nán. These provide the first link in an unbroken chain of tradition and artistic endeavour that culminated in the beautifully crafted ceramics of later dynasties.

Modern development in Jǐ'nán stems from 1899, when construction of the Jǐ'nán-Qīngdǎo railway line began. When completed in 1904, the line gave the city a major communications role. The Germans had a concession near the train station after Jǐ'nán was opened to foreign trade in 1906. The

huge German building on Jing Yilu opposite Shāndōng Bīnguǎn now houses a railway sub-office; it is made of the same
stone, and in the same style, as much of the
architecture in Qīngdǎo.

Information

Money The Bank of China is at 22 Lu-
oyuan Dajie, south of Black Tiger Spring.
There is a foreign exchange desk on the
ground floor of the Silver Plaza Shopping
Centre (Yínzuò Shāngchéng) next to the
Sofitel Silver Plaza Hotel.

Post & Communications The main post
office is at 162 Jing Erlu, on the corner of
Wei Erlu. The telephone office is located at
12 Gongqingtuan Lu.

Travel Agencies China International
Travel Service (CITS; Zhōngguó Guójì
Lǚxíngshè; ☎ 292 7071, e sdcitsaa@public
.jn.sd.cn) has moved three times in as many
months and has yet to find a permanent address; the phone number and email address
remain the same.

China Travel Service (CTS; Zhōngguó
Lǚxíngshè; ☎ 296 7401, fax 296 5261) can
be found at 9 Qianfoshan Dong Erlu. To
reach the CTS office take bus No 51 to Jing
Shilu and then transfer to bus No 68.

PSB The Public Security Bureau (PSB;
Gōngānjú; ☎ 691 5454, ext 2459 visa enquiries) is at 145 Jing Sanlu on the corner
of Wei Wulu. It's open from 8am to noon
and 2.30pm to 6pm Monday to Friday.

Qiānfó Shān 千佛山
Thousand Buddha Mountain

Many of the statues in this park to the south-
east of the city centre (admission Y15; open
6am-7pm daily) were disfigured or disappeared during the Cultural Revolution, but
new ones are gradually being added. There's
also a **grotto** (admission Y15) with copies of
the four famous Buddhist caves in China.

A cable car (one way/return Y15/25) runs
up the mountain from where you can descend via a fantastic **summer slide** (admission Y20). Bus Nos 2 and K51 go to the
park from the train station. Bus No 31 goes
from the east side of Dàmíng Hú to the
Provincial Museum, from where it is a short
walk to the east gate.

Shandong Provincial Museum
东省博物馆
Shāndōng Shěng Bówùguǎn

This museum (14 Jingshiyi Lu; admission
Y20; open 8am-noon & 2.30pm-6pm Mon-
Fri, 9am-5pm Sat-Sun) gives you a quick
overview of the history of Shāndōng, as
well as a taste of some local art. There is
also an interesting exhibit of traditional
musical instruments and more bizarrely, a
stuffed six-legged calf. The museum is a
short walk from the Qiānfó Shān east gate.

Dàmíng Hú 大明湖
Big Brilliant Lake

The park (admission Y15; open 6am-10pm
daily) surrounding this lake has small temples, gardens, lily ponds, an amusement
park and, for military aircraft enthusiasts,
the preserved shell of a MiG fighter. It's a
pleasant area to wander or peddle around
the lake in small duck-shaped boats (Y18).

The park has three gates: in the north-east
on Daminghu Beilu, the south-west, and the
south on Daminghu Lu. Ferry boats (Y3.5)
shuttle across the lake connecting the various entrances and islands.

Springs

Jǐ'nán's 100-plus springs were once the main
attraction of the city. Nowadays however,
the springs splutter rather than gush and the
only time you'll see any vestige of activity is
during the rainy season in August.

The three main springs are **Five Dragon
Pool** (Wǔlóng Chí), **Bàotū Spring** (Bàotū
Quán) and **Black Tiger Spring** (Hēihǔ Quán).

Bàotū Quán Gōngyuán (Bàotū Spring
Park; admission Y15; open 7am-7pm daily)
is home to Jǐ'nán's oldest and most famous
spring of the same name.

Those who visit Jǐ'nán on a Sunday
should take an early morning trip to Black
Tiger Spring for the **English Corner** (Yīngyǔ
Jiǎo). Locals of all ages and backgrounds
meet weekly from 7am to 12pm to chat and
practice their English. Visitors, especially
foreigners, are always warmly welcomed.

Li Qingzhao Memorial Hall
李清照祠
Lǐ Qīngzhào Cí

A native of Jǐ'nán, Li Qingzhao remains a
popular cult figure in Chinese literary circles; she is seen as the most significant and

BEIJING TO SHANGHAI

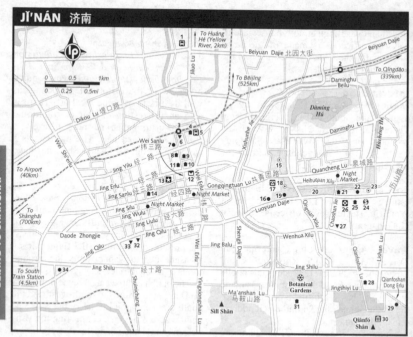

most famous female poet of the Song dynasty (see the boxed text 'The Song Poet').

The memorial hall is within a traditional Chinese courtyard inside Bàotū Quán Gōngyuán, near the east gate. The hall houses a statue of Li and extracts of her work engraved on tablets along the walkways.

Places to Stay

Shāndōng Bīnguǎn (☎ 605 5286, *92 Jingyi Lu*) Singles/doubles/triples from Y120/150 /210. You'll recognise this hotel by the traditional arched doorway. The rooms are large and the location convenient.

Shāndōng Lóngqiāntán Jiǔdiàn (☎ 605 7777, fax 605 5678, *11-15 Wei Sanlu*) Doubles Y180-280. This is a great hotel – small and cosy with excellent value rooms and shiny modern bathrooms.

Xíxíjū Jiēdàichù (☎ 605 7886, *24 Wei Sanlu*) Doubles Y168-200. An atmosphere of neglect hangs over this hotel that even the friendly staff can't shift.

Jǐ'nán Fàndiàn (☎ 793 8981, fax 793 2906, *240 Jing Sanlu*) Doubles Y160-220, triples Y240. The rooms are average but the setting within a small wooded garden is a

blessing for those suffering from a concrete overdose. Reception is in Building No 4.

Jǐ'nán Tiělù Dàshà Jiǔdiàn (*Jinan Railway Hotel;* ☎ 601 2118, fax 601 2188) Doubles Y280-380. Next door to the main train station is one of the plushest railway hotels you will probably come across. Perks include late checkout until 2pm.

Guìdū Dàjiǔdiàn (☎ 690 0888, fax 690 0999, *1 Shengping Lu*) Doubles/suites Y498/880 plus 10% service charge. Rooms here are pleasant but overpriced. Laptop owners can get online in their rooms; otherwise the hotel disco has Internet booths.

Nánjiāo Bīnguǎn (☎ 295 3931, fax 295 3957, *2 Ma'anshan Lu*) Doubles/suites Y480/680. This grand hotel is south of the Botanical Gardens and was apparently constructed for an impending visit by Mao, who then decided to skip Jǐ'nán. Staff are quick to remind guests that despite the Chairman's rejection, many other leaders have spent the night here.

Yínzuò Quánchéng Dàfàndiàn (*Silver Plaza Spring City Hotel;* ☎ 692 1911, fax 692 3187, *2 Nanmen Dajie*) Doubles/suites from Y380/480 plus 10% service charge.

JǏ'NÁN

PLACES TO STAY
4   Jǐ'nán Tiělù Dàshà
    Jiǔdiàn
    济南铁路大厦酒店
8   Shāndōng Bīnguǎn
    山东宾馆
9   Guìdū Dàjiǔdiàn
    贵都酒店
10 Xíxíjū Jiēdàichù
    习习居接待处
11 Shāndōng
    Lóngqiāntán
    Jiǔdiàn
    山东龙千潭酒店
14 Jǐ'nán Fàndiàn
    济南饭店
21 Yínzuò Quánchéng
    Dàfàndiàn
    银座泉城饭店
25 Sofitel Silver Plaza
    Hotel
    素菲特银座大饭店
28 Qílǔ Bīnguǎn
    齐鲁宾馆
31 Nánjiāo Bīnguǎn
    南郊宾馆

PLACES TO EAT
6   Tiānlóng Kuàicān
    天龙快餐

27 Guórén Làmiàn
    国人辣面
32 Yuèdū Jiǔlóu
    粤都酒楼
33 Xīběi Jiǎozi Chéng
    西北饺子城

OTHER
1   Long-Distance
    Bus Station
    长途汽车站
2   East Train Station
    火车东站
3   Main Train
    Station
    济南火车站
5   Bus Station
    汽车站
7   China Railway
    International
    Travel Service
    中铁国路
12 Main Post Office
    邮局
13 PSB
    公安局外事科
15 Five Dragon Pool
    五龙潭公园
16 CAAC
    中国民航

17 Telephone Office
    中国电信
18 Gushing-from-the-
    Ground Spring
    趵突泉
19 Li Qingzhao
    Memorial Hall
    李清照纪年堂
20 Spring City Square
    泉城广场
22 Shandong Airlines
    山东航空公司
23 Black Tiger Spring;
    English Corner
    黑虎泉；英语角
24 Bank of China
    中国银行
26 Silver Plaza
    Shopping Centre
    银座商城
29 CTS
    中国旅行社
30 Shandong Provincial
    Museum
    山东省博物馆
34 China Eastern
    Airlines
    东方航空公司

BĚIJĪNG TO SHÀNGHǍI

Surrounded by the parched springs of Jǐ'nán is this three-star hotel. Rooms come with a huge selection of TV channels.

Qílǔ Bīnguǎn (☎ 296 6888, fax 296 7676, *8 Qianfoshan Lu*) Doubles/suites Y400/500. This four-star hotel is next to Qiānfó Shān. In anticipation of its five-star branch opening next door, all room prices have dropped significantly and permanently. Take bus No K51 from the main train station.

Sofitel Silver Plaza Hotel (*Sùfěitè Yínzuò Dàfàndiàn;* ☎ 606 8888, fax 606 6666, *66 Luoyuan Dajie*) Doubles/suites from Y457/822 plus 15% service charge. In the heart of the commercial district is the Sofitel Hotel with the usual comfortable rooms and attentive service.

Places to Eat

Jǐ'nán is full of good restaurants. The area around the main train station is the best place to seek out cheap eats. The greasy chopstick cafe *Tiānlóng Kuàicān* opposite the train station specialises in cheap and oily grub. Fill up for under Y10.

Yuèdū Jiǔlóu (☎ 792 3581, 588 Jing Qilu) Dishes Y8-25. If you're having trouble ordering from Chinese menus head to the Yuèdū on the corner of Wei Balu, where dishes (prepared but uncooked) lie on chilled shelves. Point and choose from the enormous selection – you know what you're getting and it tastes good.

Xīběi Jiǎozi Chéng (☎ 794 5567, cnr Jing Qilu & Wei Balu) Dumplings/dishes from Y20/15. Almost next door to the Yuèdū Jiǔlóu is this fantastic dumpling restaurant that offers a selection of more unusual fillings including a melon and shrimp concoction.

Guórén Làmiàn (60 Chaoshan Jie) Cold dishes Y1-10. This upmarket fast-food joint has enormous bowls of spicy noodles for Y5.

Try the ***night markets*** for spicy lamb kebabs and other tempting snacks (*xiǎo chī*). The alley off Jing Wulu, between Wei Erlu and Wei Sanlu, is a good place to go. Also try Nanmen Dajie off Quancheng Lu in the commercial district.

Getting There & Away

Air Flights to Hong Kong (Y1940) leave every Sunday, Tuesday and Friday. Daily domestic destinations include Běijīng (Y500), Shànghǎi (Y700) and Guǎngzhōu (Y1420).

An office of the Civil Aviation Administration of China (CAAC; Zhōngguó Mínháng; ☎ 601 0333) at 198 Luoyuan Dajie, opposite the southern entrance to Bàotū

Quán Gōngyuán, is open from 8am to 8pm daily. The phone line is open 24 hours for ticket booking. A China Eastern Airlines office (☎ 796 4445) is at 408 Jing Shilu and a Shandong Airlines office (☎ 691 6737) is opposite the Silver Plaza Shopping Centre on Luoyuan Jie. Larger hotels can also issue airline tickets.

Bus Jǐ'nán has at least three bus stations. The two most useful for travellers are the long-distance bus station (chángtú qìchē zhàn) in the north of town and the bus station opposite the main train station.

The long-distance bus station has frequent buses to Běijīng (Y96, 6½ hours). Buses to Qīngdǎo (Y92, 3½ hours) leave every 40 minutes. There are also regular departures for Yāntái (Y92, 4½ hours) and Wēihǎi (Y139, six hours).

From opposite the main train station there are minibuses every 20 minutes to Tái'ān (Y8 to Y13, one to two hours) and every 30 minutes to Qūfù (Y21, 2½ hours) until 7pm. Slow buses to Běijīng (Y72, nine hours) and Shànghǎi (Y169, 20 hours) also leave from here. There are six departures a day to Yāntái and buses every hour to Qīngdǎo (Y95, 4½ hours) until 7pm.

Train Be aware that there are two train stations in Jǐ'nán: most trains use the main train station (Jǐ'nán huǒchē zhàn), but a handful arrive and depart from the east train station (huǒchē dōngzhàn).

Jǐ'nán is a major link in the east China rail system. From here there are direct trains to Běijīng (Y73 to Y128, four to seven hours), Shànghǎi (Y136 to Y215, 11 to 15 hours) and Qīngdǎo (Y48 to Y66, four to eight hours). A night train runs to Zhèngzhōu (Y83, nine hours) and to Xī'ān (Y149, 17 hours).

You can buy train tickets from the China Railway International Travel Service (Zhōngtiě Guólǚ; ☎ 242 4134) at 16 Chezhan Jie, near the train station. It's open from 8am to 5.30pm daily. There is an additional Y25 service charge per ticket.

Getting Around

To/From the Airport The Xijiao airport is 40km west of the city and the freeway makes it possible to cover the distance in just 40 minutes. An airport bus leaves from

The Song Poet

Li Qingzhao is famed for her elegant language, strong imagery and, perhaps most importantly, her ability to remain unpretentious in her poetry. Only 70 of Li's poems have survived despite the fact that she wrote continuously throughout her lifetime. As the most celebrated female poet of the Song dynasty, she has a large following of literary buffs, especially in her hometown of Jǐ'nán.

Born in 1084 into the privileged world of a scholar's family, Li Qingzhao was able to cultivate her love for poetry from a young age. Her early poems are characterised by her carefree leisure and love for beauty and life.

In 1126 Li's life changed dramatically. Having fled with her family from the advancing Jin army, and with the death of her husband at the same time, Li was forced to leave her life of luxury behind. Although her writing becomes dark and melancholy, it was during this period that she created some of her most powerful work.

Alone in the Night
The warm rain and pure wind
Have just freed the willows from
The ice. As I watch the peach trees,
Spring rises from my heart and blooms on
My cheeks. My mind is unsteady,
As if I were drunk. I try
To write a poem in which
My tears will flow together
With your tears. My rouge is stale.
My hairpins are too heavy.
I throw myself across my
Gold cushions, wrapped in my lonely
Doubled quilt, and crush the phoenixes
In my headdress. Alone, deep
In bitter loneliness, without
Even a good dream, I lie,
Trimming the lamp in the
passing night.

the CAAC ticket office and from the Silver Plaza Shopping Centre. Check with CAAC for times. A taxi will cost around Y150.

Bus & Taxi Bus No 33 connects the long-distance bus station with the main train station. Bus No 51 runs from the main train station through the centre of town and then south past Bàotū Quán to Qiānfó Shān. Bus No 11 will take you from the train station to Dàmíng Hú. Taxis cost Y7 for the first 3km.

AROUND JǏ'NÁN
Sìmén Tǎ 四门塔
Four Gate Pagoda

Near the village of Liùbù, 33km south-east of Jǐ'nán, are some of the oldest Buddhist structures in Shāndōng. Shentong Monastery holds Sìmén Tǎ (☎ 284 3051; admission Y10; open 8am-6pm daily), which dates back to the 6th century and is possibly the oldest stone pagoda in China. The surrounding hills are old burial grounds for the monks of the monastery.

Lónghǔ Tǎ (Pagoda of the Dragon and the Tiger) was built during the Tang dynasty. It stands close to the Shentong Monastery and is surrounded by stupas. Higher up is Qiānfó Yá (Thousand Buddha Cliff), which displays carved grottoes containing Buddhas.

To reach Sìmén Tǎ, catch bus No 22 (Y4, 1½ hours) from near the corner of Jing Silu and Wei Erlu. CTS can also arrange tours.

TÀI SHĀN 泰山

Southern Chinese say they have 'myriad mountains, rivers and geniuses' while those from Shāndōng retort that they have 'one mountain, one river and one saint', with the implication that they have the last word on each: Tài Shān, Huáng Hé and Confucius. Tài Shān is the most revered of the five sacred Taoist mountains of China. Once upon a time, imperial sacrifices to heaven and earth were offered from its summit. Only five of China's emperors ever climbed Tài Shān, although Emperor Qianlong of the Qing dynasty scaled it 11 times. From its heights Confucius uttered the dictum 'The world is small'; Mao lumbered up and commented 'The East is Red'. You too can climb up and say 'I'm knackered'.

Tài Shān is a unique experience – its supernatural allure (see the boxed text 'Tài Shān') drags in the Chinese in droves. Bixia, the Princess of the Azure Clouds, a Taoist deity whose presence permeates the temples dotted along the route, is a powerful cult figure for the rural women of Shāndōng and beyond. Tribes of wiry grandmothers trot up the steps with surprising ease, their target the cluster of temples at the summit where they burn money and incense, praying for their progeny. It's said that if you climb Tài Shān you'll live to be 100. Sun-worshippers – foreign and Chinese – also muster wide-eyed on the peak, straining for the first flickers of dawn. In ancient Chinese tradition, it was believed that the sun began its westward journey from Tài Shān.

Tài Shān is 1545m above sea level, with a climbing distance of 7.5km from base to summit on the central route. The elevation change from Midway Gate to Heaven (Zhōngtiān Mén) to the summit is approximately 600m. The mountain is not a major climb, but with 6660 steps to the summit, it can be gruelling. One wonders how many backs were broken in the building of the temples and stone stairs on Tài Shān – a massive undertaking accomplished without any mechanical aids.

Climate

Bear in mind that weather conditions on the mountain vary considerably compared with Tài'ān. Clouds and mist frequently envelop the mountain, particularly in summer. The best times to visit are in spring and autumn when the humidity is low, although old-timers say that the clearest weather is from early October onwards. In winter the weather is often fine, but very cold. The tourist season peaks from May to October.

Due to weather changes, you're advised to carry warm clothing with you, no matter what the season. The summit can be very cold, windy and wet; army overcoats are available there for rental and you can buy waterproof coats from one of the ubiquitous vendors.

Climbing Tài Shān

The town of Tài'ān lies at the foot of Tài Shān and is the gateway to the mountain (see the Tài'ān section in this chapter).

BĚIJĪNG TO SHÀNGHǍI

Entry costs Y60 off-season (January, February, November and December) and Y82 the remainder of the year. The admission fee includes Y2 insurance.

On Foot It's possible to spend the night at Midway Gate to Heaven halfway up the mountain, or on the summit. Allow two hours for climbing between each of these points – a total of eight hours for the round trip, at the minimum. Allowing several more hours would make the climb less strenuous and give you more time to look around.

If you want to see the sunrise, then dump your gear at the train station or at a guesthouse in Tài'ān and time your ascent so that you'll reach the summit before sundown. Stay overnight at one of the summit guesthouses and get up early the next morning for the famed sunrise, which may or may not make its appearance. It's possible to scale the mountain at night and some Chinese do this, timing it so that they arrive before sunrise. The way is lit by lamps, but it is advisable to take a torch, as well as warm clothes, food and water.

There are two main paths up the mountain: the central route and the western route, converging midway at Midway Gate to Heaven. Most people slog up the central route (once the imperial route and littered with cultural relics) and head down (usually by bus) along the western route. Other trails run through orchards and woods.

By Minibus & Cable Car From Tiānwài Village (Tiānwài Cūn), at the foot of the western route, minibuses (one way/return Y16/31, 20 minutes) run regularly between 4am and 8pm to Midway Gate to Heaven, halfway up Tài Shān. Bus No 3 runs to Tiānwài Village from Tài'ān's train station. Frequent buses come down the mountain; however, as this is the favoured option for getting back to Tài'ān, you may have to wait several buses for a seat.

It's about a five-minute walk from Midway Gate to Heaven to the cable car (kōngzhōng suǒdào; one way/return Y45/90), which holds 30 passengers and takes 10 minutes to travel from Midway Gate to Heaven to **Moon View Peak** (Yùeguān Fēng), near South Gate to

Heaven (Nántiān Mén). Be warned, if you climb Tài Shān in the high season or on weekends, the queues may force you to wait for up to two hours for a cable car.

The same applies when you want to descend from the summit; fortunately, there is another cable car (one way/return Y45/90) that only carries six passengers and is as regular as clockwork. It takes you from north of South Gate to Heaven down to **Peach Blossom Park** (Taóhūa Yuán), a scenic area behind Tài Shān that is also worth exploring. From here you can take a minibus to Tài'ān (Y15, 40 minutes). You can reverse this process by first taking a minibus from Tài'ān train station to Peach Blossom Park and then ascending by cable car.

TÀI SHĀN

PLACES TO STAY

5 Nántiānmén
  Bīnguǎn
  南天门宾馆
6 Xiānjū Fàndiàn
  仙居饭店
8 Shénqì Bīnguǎn
  神憩宾馆
16 Yùyèquán Bīnguǎn
  玉液泉宾馆

OTHER

1 Rear Temple
  (Hòushí Wù)
  后石坞
2 TV Tower
  电视塔
3 North Prayer Rock
  拱北石
4 Jade Emperor
  Temple; Wordless
  Monument
  玉皇顶；无字碑
7 South Gate to
  Heaven
  南天门
9 Azure Clouds
  Temple
  碧霞祠
10 Archway to
   Immortality
   开仙坊
11 Bridge of the Gods
   (Xiānrù Qiáo)
   仙人桥

12 Zhānlǔ Tái (Terrace)
   占鲁台
13 Opposing Pines
   Pavilion; Welcoming
   Pine
   对松亭；迎客松
14 Five Pine Pavilion
   五松亭
15 Cloud Bridge
   (Yúnbù Qiáo)
   云步桥
17 Midway Gate to
   Heaven; Cable Car
   中天门；空中索道
18 Skywalk Bridge
   (Bùtiān Qiáo)
   步天桥
19 Hútiān Gé
   (Pavilion)
   壶天阁
20 Rock Valley
   Scripture
   经石峪
21 Dǒumǔ Hall
   斗母宫
22 Longevity Bridge;
   Black Dragon Pool
   长寿桥；黑龙潭
23 Ticket Booth
   售票处
24 Tiānwài Village;
   Ticket Booth and
   Bus Station for
   Western Route
   天外村；售票处

25 Trailhead for
   Western Route
26 Feng Yuxiang
   Língmù (Tomb);
   Everyman's Bridge
   (Dàzhòng Qiáo)
   冯玉祥陵墓；
   大众桥
27 Pǔzhào Sì
   普照寺
28 Jiniàn Sì
   纪念寺
29 Monument to
   Revolutionary
   Heroes
   (Gémìng Lièshì
   Jìniànguǎn)
   革命烈士纪念馆
30 10,000 Immortals
   Pavilion
   (Wànxiān Lóu)
   万仙楼
31 Red Gate Palace
   红门
32 Guāndì Miào
   关帝庙
33 No 1 Archway
   Under Heaven;
   Ticket Booth
   天下第一门；售票处
34 Trailhead for Central
   Route
35 Cloud Empress Pool
   (Yúnmǔ Chí)
   云母池

Central Route On this route you'll see a bewildering catalogue of bridges, trees, rivers, gullies, towers, inscriptions, caves, pavilions and temples. Tài Shān functions as an outdoor museum of calligraphic art, with the prize items being the **Rock Valley Scripture** (*Jīng Shíyù*) along the first section of the walk and the **North Prayer Rock** (*Gǒngběi Shí*), which commemorates an imperial sacrifice, at the summit. Lost on most foreigners are the literary allusions, word games and analogies spelt out by the calligraphy decorating the journey.

The climb proper begins at **No 1 Archway Under Heaven** (*Tiānxià Dìyīmén*), at the mountain base. Behind that is a stone archway overgrown with wisteria and inscribed with 'the place where Confucius began to climb'. **Red Gate Palace** (*Hóng Mén*), with its wine-coloured walls, is the first of a series of temples dedicated to the Princess of the Azure Clouds. Following the temple is **Dǒumǔ Hall** (*Dǒumǔ Guān*), first constructed in 1542 and given the more magical name of 'Dragon Spring Nunnery'.

Continuing through the tunnel of cypresses known as Cypress Cave is **Húimǎ Peak** (*Húimǎ Lǐng*), where Emperor Zhenzong had to dismount and continue by sedan chair because his horse refused to go further.

Midway Gate to Heaven This is the second celestial gate. A little way on is **Five Pine Pavilion** (*Wǔsōng Tíng*) where, in 219 BC, Emperor Qin Shihuang was overtaken by a violent storm and was sheltered by the pine trees. He promoted them to the 5th rank of minister.

From here set out upon **The Path of Eighteen Bends** that will eventually lead you to the summit. En route you'll pass **Opposing Pines Pavilion** *(Dùisōng Tíng)* and the **Welcoming Pine** *(Yíngkè Sōng)*, with a branch extended as if to shake hands. Beyond that is the **Archway to Immortality** *(Kāixiān Fáng)*. It was believed that those passing through the archway would become celestial beings. From here to the summit, emperors were carried in sedan chairs.

The final stretch takes you to **South Gate to Heaven**, the third celestial gate.

On arrival at the *dàidǐng* (summit) you will see **Diànshì Tǎ** *(Wavelength Pavilion)*, which is a radio and weather station, and the **Journey to the Stars Gondola** (essentially a cable car). If you continue along Paradise Rd, you'll come to **Sunview Peak**.

The march ends at the **Azure Clouds Temple** *(Bìxiá Cí)*, where small offerings of one sort or another are made to a bronze statue in the main hall, once richly decorated. The iron tiling on the buildings is intended to prevent damage by strong winds, and on the bronze eaves are *chīwěn* (ornaments meant to protect against fire). The temple is absolutely splendid, with its location in the clouds, but its guardians are a trifle touchy about you wandering around, and parts of it are inaccessible.

Perched on the highest point (1545m) of the Tài Shān plateau is the **Jade Emperor Temple** *(Yùhuáng Dǐng)*, with a bronze statue of a Taoist deity. In the courtyard is a rock inscribed with the elevation of the mountain. In front of the temple is the one piece of calligraphy that you really can

Tài Shān

Tài Shān's place in the hearts and minds of the Chinese people is deeply rooted in their most ancient creation myth – the story of Pan Gu. In the beginning when all was chaos, and heaven and earth were swirling together, Pan Gu was born and promptly set about separating the ground and the sky. With each day that passed he grew taller, the sky grew higher and the earth grew thicker, until, after 18,000 years, the two were fully separated and Pan Gu died of exhaustion. As his body disintegrated his eyes became the sun and the moon, his blood transformed into rivers, his sweat fell as rain and his head and limbs became the five sacred mountains of China, Tài Shān among them.

Maybe because it sprung from Pan Gu's head, or perhaps because of its location in the dominant east (which signifies birth and spring), Tài Shān is the most revered of these five sacred peaks. The throngs of modern visitors are but recipients of a tradition of pilgrimage and worship that stretches back to earliest historical times.

For nearly 3000 years emperors have paid their homage, a few reaching the summit, all contributing to the rich legacy of temples, trees, pavilions and calligraphy. Originally made for sacrifices, these visits soon acquired a political significance: it was thought heaven would never allow an unworthy ruler to ascend, so a successful climb indicated divine approval.

Emperors aside, China's three most prominent schools of thought also hold Tài Shān dear. A second legend has it there once lived a she-fox on Tài Shān, who, by living a strict Taoist existence, transformed into a goddess named Bi Xia (Azure Clouds). There she remained happily until the arrival of Sakyamuni, the founder of Buddhism, who fell in love with the place and asked her to leave. Bi Xia refused and Sakyamuni was forced to flee when he tried unsuccessfully to trick her into leaving. Today, Bi Xia is venerated as the protectress of peasant women and as the bringer of dawn. A Taoist monk named Lang established the first temples on the mountain in 351 BC, and the most influential are still those dedicated to Bi Xia.

Thus Tài Shān has become a repository of Chinese culture, spanning dynasties and religions, and prompting the modern Chinese scholar Guo Moruo to describe the mountain as 'a partial miniature of Chinese culture'. Indeed, it is probably best to bear this analogy in mind when you visit, as modern China is definitely leaving its mark. Even by the Qing dynasty there were several hundred thousand visitors each year, and on the Labor Day public holiday in 2001, an estimated 60,000 people crowded onto the summit. With the invasion of Polaroid photographers, karaoke stands, porters and hawkers, and even an annual race to the summit, the sacred peak of Tài Shān might just become a victim of its own popularity.

appreciate – the **Wordless Monument** *(Wúzì Bēi)*. One story goes that it was set up by Emperor Wu 2100 years ago – he wasn't satisfied with what his scribes came up with, so he left it to the viewer's imagination.

The main sunrise vantage point is the **North Prayer Rock** *(Gǒngbēi Shí);* if you're lucky, visibility extends to over 200km, as far as the coast. The sunset slides over the Huáng Hé side. At the rear of the mountain is the **Rear Rocky Recess**, one of the better known spots for viewing pine trees; there are some ruins tangled in the foliage. It's a good place to ramble and lose the crowds for a while.

Western Route The most popular way to descend the mountain is by bus via the western route. The footpath and road intercept at a number of points and are often one and the same. Given the amount of traffic, you might prefer to hop on a bus rather than inhale its exhaust. If you do hike down, the trail is not always clearly marked. (Note that buses will not stop for you once they have left Midway Gate to Heaven.)

Either by bus or foot, the western route treats you to considerable variation in scenery, with orchards, pools and flowering plants that make traditional Chinese paintings seem incredibly realistic. The major scenic attraction along this route is the **Black Dragon Pool** *(Hēilóng Tán)*, which is just below the **Longevity Bridge** *(Chángshòu Qiáo)* and is fed by a small waterfall. Swimming in the waters are rare, red-scaled carp, which are occasionally cooked for the rich. Mythical tales revolve around this pool, which is said to be the site of underground carp palaces and of magic herbs that turn people into beasts.

An enjoyable way to end the hike is with a visit to **Pǔzhào Sì** *(admission Y5)*. This monastery was founded 1500 years ago along the base of the mountain.

Places to Stay & Eat
Yùyèquán Bīnguǎn (Spring Guesthouse; ☎ 822 674) Dorm beds Y50. This is a halfway house at the Midway Gate to Heaven – the only one that accepts foreigners. The rooms are cheap but nothing special.

The summit of Tài Shān is rapidly turning into a town in its own right with restaurants, shops and hotels.

Nántiānmén Bīnguǎn (☎ 823 9984) Doubles/triples Y120/140. At weekends during the high season the prices of these so-so rooms jump to Y240/420. This hotel is to your right as you pass through the South Gate to Heaven.

Xiānjū Fàndiàn (☎ 823 9984, fax 822 6877) Beds in 3-/4-bed dorms Y80/60, doubles Y100-300. This hotel is to the east of South Gate to Heaven and has a much better selection of rooms.

Shénqì Bīnguǎn (☎ 822 3866, Ⓦ www .shenqihotel.com)* Beds in 4-bed dorms/ doubles/presidential suite Y160/580/8800. This is the only three-star hotel on the summit. The hotel provides extra blankets and rents out People's Liberation Army-style overcoats. There's even an alarm bell that tells you when to get up for sunrise.

There is no fear of a food shortage on Tài Shān; the central route is dotted with *teahouses, stalls, vendors* and *restaurants*. Your pockets are likely to feel emptier than your stomach, but keep in mind that all supplies are carried up by foot and that the prices rise as you do.

TÀI'ĀN 泰安
☎ 0538 • pop 5,334,600
Tài'ān is the gateway town to the sacred Tài Shān. You'll probably need the better part of a day to take in the mountain, so be prepared to spend the night.

On an incidental note, Tài'ān is the home town of Jiang Qing, Mao's fourth wife, ex-actress and notorious spearhead of the Gang of Four, on whom all of China's ills are sometimes blamed. She was later airbrushed out of Chinese history and committed suicide in May 1991.

Orientation & Information
The Xinhua Bookshop at 80 Qingnian Lu has a selection of Tài'ān and Shāndōng maps. Street vendors sell numerous Tài Shān maps, none of which are in English.

The main branch of the Bank of China is at 48 Dongyue Dajie. The main post and telephone office is at 9 Dongyue Dajie. There is also a small post office at 240 Daizhong Dajie.

The CTS office (☎ 821 1754) is at 145 Hushan Lu. The CITS office (☎ 822 8797, fax 833 2240) is at 22 Hongmen Lu, just north of Dàizōng Archway. Both offices can

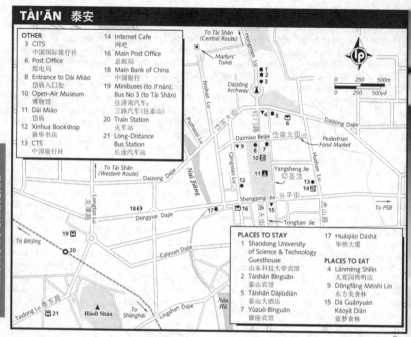

TÀI'ĀN 泰安

OTHER
3 CITS
中国国际旅行社
6 Post Office
邮电局
8 Entrance to Dài Miào
岱庙入口处
10 Open-Air Museum
博物馆
11 Dài Miào
岱庙
12 Xinhua Bookshop
新华书店
13 CTS
中国旅行社

14 Internet Cafe
网吧
16 Main Post Office
总邮局
18 Main Bank of China
中国银行
19 Minibuses (to Jǐ'nán);
Bus No 3 (to Tài Shān)
往济南汽车;
三路汽车 (往泰山)
20 Train Station
火车站
21 Long-Distance
Bus Station
长途汽车站

PLACES TO STAY
1 Shandong University
of Science & Technology
Guesthouse
山东科技大学宾馆
2 Tàishān Bīnguǎn
泰山宾馆
3 Tàishān Dàjiǔdiàn
泰山大酒店
7 Yùzuò Bīnguǎn
御座宾馆

17 Huáqiáo Dàshà
华侨大厦

PLACES TO EAT
4 Lánmèng Shílín
大观园烤鸭店
9 Dōngfāng Měishí Lín
东方美食林
15 Dà Guānyuán
Kǎoyā Diàn
蓝梦食林

arrange tours, air and train tickets. Near the CTS office, at 135 Hushan Lu, is an unnamed Internet bar (☎ 821 7200). It charges Y2 per hour and is open from 8.30am to 11pm daily.

The PSB office for foreigners (☎ 822 5264) can be found to the east end of Dongyue Dajie. It's open from 8am to 11.30am and 2.30pm to 6.30pm Monday to Friday but is a fair hike out of town and is best approached by taxi.

Dài Miào 岱庙

This huge temple complex (☎ 822 3491, Daibeng Lu; admission Y20; open 7.30am-6.30pm daily) is in the centre of town, with Tài Shān as its background. Traditionally a pilgrimage stop on the road to the sacred mountain, the temple was also the site of huge sacrifices to the god of Tài Shān. The main hall is the yellow-eaved **Temple of Heavenly Blessing** (Tiankuang), dating back to AD 1009.

The Temple of Heavenly Blessing was the first of the 'big three' halls to be built (the others being Hall of Supreme Harmony at the Forbidden City and Dacheng Hall at Qūfù). The poorly lit interior has a 62m-long fresco

from the Song dynasty depicting Emperor Zhenzong as the god of Tài Shān. Zhenzong 'raised' the god of Tài Shān to a status equal to his own. You'll find a 7m-high stele to celebrate this in the western courtyard.

The fresco has been painstakingly retouched by artisans of succeeding dynasties but is still in poor shape – a majestic concept nonetheless.

The temple complex now functions as an open-air museum with a forest of 200-odd steles. One inscribed stone, originally at the summit of Tài Shān, is believed to be over 2000 years old (Qin dynasty). It can be seen at the Eastern Imperial Hall.

Around the courtyards are ancient, twisted cypresses, gingkos and acacias. Some of the cypresses appear partially ossified.

There is a cypress in front of Temple of Heavenly Blessing under which visitors can indulge in a game of luck. A person is blindfolded and made to walk around a rock three times anticlockwise and three times clockwise. Then they try to touch the fissure on the south side of the cypress, 20 steps away. Those who succeed are considered lucky, but participants invariably miss every time.

Entrance to the temple is at the southern end of Hongmen Lu.

Places to Stay

Shandong University of Science & Technology Guesthouse (Shāndōng Kējì Dàxué Bīnguǎn; ☎ 622 6485, fax 622 6179, 30 Hongmen Lu) Doubles Y160. The rooms here are old and shabby and the bathrooms seem to date back even further, but the location is convenient for an early morning mountain assault.

Tàishān Bīnguǎn (☎ 822 5888, fax 822 1432, 26 Hongmen Lu) Doubles Y300-420. Next door to the guesthouse is this three-star hotel. To get here, take bus No 3 from the train station. Get off just before the Dàizōng Archway.

Yùzuò Bīnguǎn (☎ 822 3852, fax 822 3180, 3 Daimiao Beijie) Doubles Y280. This comfortable three-star hotel is next door to Dài Miào and has small but welcoming rooms.

Tàishān Dàjiǔdiàn (Taishan Grand Hotel; ☎ 829 1216, 210 Daizhong Dajie) Doubles/triples/suites from Y150/180/680. This hotel has two buildings, Yíngbīn Lóu has the cheaper options. Rooms in the main building are impressive and some have views of Dài Miào.

Huáqiáo Dàshà (Overseas Chinese Hotel; ☎ 822 8112, fax 822 8171, 15 Dongyue Dajie) Doubles/suites from Y480/780. This is supposed to be the poshest gig in town but it's actually quite shabby.

Places to Eat

Tài'ān doesn't have a huge choice of restaurants but there is some good food around. Remember that everything seems to pack up around 9pm.

Dōngfāng Měishí Lín (☎ 827 1996, 20 Damiao Beijie) Dishes from Y10. The food here is excellent. Try the *wǎguàn* (clay pot) specialities. A choice of beef, tofu, vegetables or fish is cooked in a clay pot with noodles and spices. Look for the San Miguel beer sign outside the restaurant.

Lánmèng Shílín (☎ 833 4062, 18 Hongmen Lu) Dumplings Y8. This is a cheap and cheerful dumpling shop.

Dà Guānyuán Kǎoyā Diàn (Duck Restaurant; ☎ 826 0664, Shengping Jie) Roast duck Y50, dishes from Y12. The duck here is not the best you'll ever have but it makes a welcome break from noodles. The restaurant's large plastic duck sits opposite the south entrance of Dài Miào.

Getting There & Away

Bus Tài'ān can be approached by road from either Jǐ'nán or Qūfù and is worth combining with a trip to the latter. Buses to Qūfù (Y13.5, one hour) leave every 20 minutes from the long-distance bus station south of the train station.

Although there are a few large public buses connecting Tài'ān to Jǐ'nán, these are overcrowded horrors and you're better off travelling by minibus (Y20, 70 minutes) that leave every 30 minutes between 6am and 6.30pm from a station north of the train station.

There are four daily departures to Qīngdǎo (Y60, six hours) leaving at 5.40am, 6am, 7.20am and 8.30am.

Train There are more than 20 express trains running daily through Tài'ān including links to Běijīng (seven hours), Hāěrbīn (20 hours), Jǐ'nán (1¼ hours), Nánjīng (nine hours), Qīngdǎo (5½ hours), Shànghǎi (9½ hours), Shěnyáng, Xī'ān (17 hours) and Zhèngzhōu (11 hours). Some special express trains from Jǐ'nán don't stop at Tài'ān. Check schedules to avoid arriving at some unpleasant hour.

Getting Around

Getting around is easy as most destinations can be reached on foot. The long-distance bus station is just south of the train station, so all local transport is directed towards these two terminals.

There are three main bus routes. Bus No 3 runs from the Tài Shān central route trailhead to the western route trailhead via the train station. Bus Nos 1 and 2 also end up near the train station. Minibuses run on the same routes.

Taxis and yellow minivan cabs can be found outside the train station. Taxis start at Y5.

AROUND TÀI'ĀN
Língyán Sì 灵岩寺
Divine Rock Temple

At the northern foot of Tài Shān is this temple (admission Y35), 30km from Tài'ān. It used to be a large monastery that served

BĚIJĪNG TO SHÀNGHǍI

many dynasties (the Tang, Song and Yuan, among others) and housed 500 monks in its heyday. On view is a forest of 200 stupas and a nine storey octagonal pagoda, as well as the **Thousand Buddha Temple** *(Qiānfó Diàn)*, which contains 40 fine, highly individualised clay arhats – the best Buddhist statues in Shāndōng.

Buses to Língyán Sì depart from in front of the train station in Tài'ān. Catch one that is heading to Jǐ'nán and ask the driver to let you off at the temple. You'll be dropped off about 30 minutes up the road from the temple from where it's a 15-minute taxi ride (Y10).

QŪFÙ 曲阜
☎ 0537

Of monumental significance to the Chinese is Qūfù, birthplace of Confucius, with its harmonies of carved stone, timber and fine imperial architecture. Following a 2000-year-old tradition, there are two fairs a year in Qūfù – in spring and autumn – when the place comes alive with craftspeople, healers, acrobats, peddlers and peasants. It also hosts a huge party on 28 September to mark Confucius' birthday.

Information

The post office is at 8-1 Gulou Beijie, just north of the Drum Tower (Gǔ Lòu) and the Bank of China is around the corner at 96 Dongmen Dajie.

You'll find CITS (☎ 448 8491) at the back of Lǚyóu Bīnguǎn, at 1 Dacheng Lu. More useful and better located is the Qufu Tourist Information Centre (☎ 465 5777) at 4 Gulou Beijie. The PSB (☎ 449 4523) at 1 Wuyuntan Lu is south of town and best reached by taxi. It's open from 8am to 12pm and 2.30pm to 6.30pm Monday to Friday.

Small Internet bars can be found around the university area in the western part of town.

Kǒng Miào 孔庙
Confucius Temple

The temple *(☎ 441 2235; admission Y30; open 8am-5pm daily)* started out as a simple memorial hall and mushroomed into a complex one-fifth the size of the Qūfù town centre. Huge extensions during the Ming and Qing dynasties are mainly responsible for its present scale. The main entrance is in the south and leads through a series of portals emblazoned with calligraphy. The third entrance gateway, **Arch of the Spirit of the Universe**, has four bluish painted figures that refer to the doctrines of Confucius as heavenly bodies that move in circles without end.

Magnificent gnarled, twisting pines occupy the courtyards in Kǒng Miào along with over 1000 steles, with inscriptions dating from Han to Qing times – the largest such collection in China. The creatures bearing the tablets of praise are *bìxì* (mythical tortoise-like animals), legendary for their strength.

The tablets at Qūfù are noted for their fine calligraphy; a rubbing once formed part of the dowry for a descendant of Confucius. In earlier dynasties, women were not allowed to set foot in the temple grounds; one tablet records the visit of Emperor Wuzong of the Yuan dynasty who brought his sister along – the first woman ever to enter Kǒng Miào.

Roughly halfway along the north-south axis is the **Great Pavilion of the Constellation of Scholars**, a triple-roofed, Jin dynasty wooden structure of ceremonial importance. Further north through Dacheng Gate and to the right is a juniper planted by Confucius. The small Xingtan Pavilion commemorates the spot where Confucius is said to have taught under the shade of an apricot tree.

The core of the Confucian complex is **Dacheng Hall**, which, in its present form, dates from 1724; it towers 31m on a white marble terrace. The Kong family imported glazed yellow tiling for the halls in Kǒng Miào, and special stones were brought in from Xīshān. The craftspeople carved the dragon-coiled columns so expertly that they had to be covered with red silk when Emperor Qianlong came to Qūfù lest he felt that the Forbidden City's Taihe Hall paled in comparison. The superb stone they are carved from is called 'fish roe stone'.

The hall was used for unusual rites in honour of Confucius. At the beginning of the seasons and on the great sage's birthday, booming drums, bronze bells and musical stones sounded from the hall as dozens of officials in silk robes engaged in 'dignified dancing' and chanting by torchlight. The rare collection of musical instruments is displayed, but the massive stone statue of the bearded philosopher has disappeared – presumably another casualty of the Cultural Revolution.

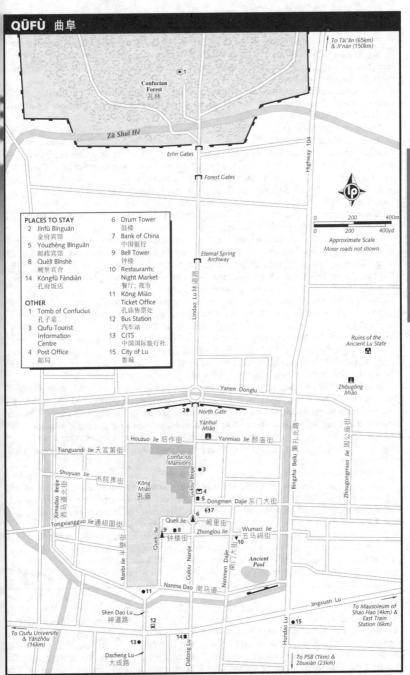

QŪFÙ 曲阜

To Tài'ān (65km)
& Jǐ'nán (150km)

Confucian
Forest
孔林

Zū Shuǐ Hé

Erlin Gates

Highway 104

Forest Gates

0   200   400m
0   200   400yd

Approximate Scale
Minor roads not shown

Eternal Spring
Archway

Ruins of the
Ancient Lu State

Lindao Lu 林道路

Zhōugōng
Miào

PLACES TO STAY
2 Jīnfǔ Bīnguǎn
   金府宾馆
5 Yóuzhèng Bīnguǎn
   邮政宾馆
8 Quèlǐ Bīnshè
   阙里宾舍
14 Kǒngfǔ Fàndiàn
   孔府饭店

OTHER
1 Tomb of Confucius
   孔子墓
3 Qufu Tourist
   Information
   Centre
4 Post Office
   邮局

6 Drum Tower
   鼓楼
7 Bank of China
   中国银行
9 Bell Tower
   钟楼
10 Restaurants;
   Night Market
   餐厅; 夜市
11 Kǒng Miào
   Ticket Office
   孔庙售票处
12 Bus Station
   汽车站
13 CITS
   中国国际旅行社
15 City of Lu
   鲁城

Yanen Donglu

North Gate

Yánhuì
Miào

Houzuo Jie 后作街   Yanmiao Jie 颜庙街

Tianguandi Jie 天官第街

Shuyuan Jie

Confucius
Mansions

Gulou Beijie

Bingzha Beilu 秉礼北路

Zhouggongmiao Jie 周公庙街

书院界街

Xīmàdào Beijie

Kǒng
Miào
孔庙

Dongmen Dajie 东门大街

Tongxiangguo Jie 通相国街

Quelí Jie

Queli Jie

Banbi Jie 半壁街

Zhonglou Jie

Wumaci Jie
五马祠街

Gulou Nanjie

Nanmen Dajie 南门大街

Ancient
Pool

Nanma Dao 南马道

Jingxuan Lu

To Mausoleum of
Shao Hao (4km) &
East Train
Station (6km)

Shen Dao Lu
神道路

Hundao Lu

To Qufu University
& Yǎnzhōu
(16km)

Dacheng Lu
大成路

Datong Lu

To PSB (1km) &
Zōuxiàn (23km)

Confucianism

Qūfù is the birth and death place of the sage Confucius (551–479 BC) whose impact was not felt during his own lifetime. He lived in abject poverty and hardly put pen to paper, but his teachings were recorded by dedicated followers in *The Analects of Confucius*. His descendants, the Kong family, fared considerably better.

Subsequent rulers adopted Confucian ethics to keep the populace in line and Confucian temples were set up in numerous towns. Qūfù acquired the status of a holy place, with the direct descendants of Confucius as its guardian angels.

The original Confucian temple at Qūfù (dating from 478 BC) was enlarged, remodelled, added to, taken away from and rebuilt. The majority of the present buildings are from the Ming dynasty. In 1513 armed bands sacked the temple and the Kong residence, resulting in walls being errected around the town from 1522 to 1567 to fortify it. These walls were recently removed, but vestiges of Ming town planning, like the Drum and Bell towers, remain.

More a code that defined hierarchical relationships than a religion, Confucianism has had a great impact on Chinese culture. It teaches that son must respect father, wife must respect husband, commoner must respect official, official must respect ruler, and so on. The essence of its teachings are obedience, respect, selflessness and working for the common good.

You would think that this code would have fitted nicely into the new order of communism; however, it was swept aside because of its connections with the past. Confucius was seen as a kind of misguided feudal educator, and clan ties and ancestor-worship were viewed as a threat. In 1948 Confucius' direct heir, the first-born son of the 77th generation of the Kong family, fled to Taiwan, breaking a 2500-year tradition of Kong residence in Qūfù.

During the Cultural Revolution the emphasis shifted to the youth of China (even if they were led by an old man). A popular anti-Confucian campaign was instigated and Confucius lost face. Many of the statues at Qūfù also lost face (literally) amid cries of 'Down with Confucius, down with his wife!'. In the late 1960s a contingent of Red Guards descended on the sleepy town of Qūfù, burning, defacing and destroying. Other Confucian edifices around the country were also attacked. The leader of the guards who ransacked Qūfù was Tan Houlan. She was jailed in 1978 and was not tried until 1982. The Confucius family archives appear to have survived intact.

In 1979 the Qūfù temples were reopened and millions of yuán were allocated for renovations and repairs. Tourism is now the name of the game; if a temple hasn't got fresh paint, new pillars, replaced tiling or stonework, and a souvenir shop or photo merchant with a great sage cardboard cutout, they'll get around to it soon. Some of the buildings even have electricity, with speakers hooked up to the eaves playing soothing flute music. One fifth of Qūfù's residents are again claiming to be descendants of the great sage, though incense-burning, mound-burial and ancestor-worship are not consistent with the party line.

While the current popularity of the great sage is undeniable, it is debatable as to what extent his teachings are taking fresh root in China. The majority of devotees around Qūfù are middle-aged or elderly, suggesting that the comeback of Confucianism is more likely a re-emergence of beliefs never effectively squashed by the Communists. Nevertheless, Confucian ethics (though not by that name) are finding their way back into the Shāndōng school system, presumably to instil some civic mindedness. Students are encouraged once again to respect their teachers, elders, neighbours and family.

Chinese scholars are also making careful statements reaffirming the significance of Confucius' historical role and suggesting that the 'progressive' aspects of his work were even cited in the writings of Mao Zedong. Confucius too, it seems, can be rehabilitated.

At the extreme northern end of Kǒng Miào is **Shengji Dian**, a memorial hall containing a series of stones engraved with scenes from the life of Confucius and tales about him. They are copies of an older set that date back to 1592.

In the eastern compound of Kǒng Miào, behind the Hall of Poetry & Rites, is **Confucius' Well** (a Song-Ming reconstruction) and the **Lu Wall**, where the ninth descendant of Confucius hid the sacred texts during the book burning campaign of Emperor Qin

Shihuang. The books were discovered again during the Han dynasty (206 BC–AD 220) and led to a lengthy scholastic dispute between those who followed a reconstructed version of the last books and those who supported the teachings in the rediscovered ones.

Confucius Mansions 孔府

Kǒng Fǔ

Next door to Kǒng Miào is the Confucius Mansions (☎ 441 2235; admission Y20; open 8am-5pm daily), which dates from the 16th century (Ming dynasty), with more recent renovations. The place is a maze of 450 halls, rooms, buildings and side passages, and getting around requires a compass.

The Confucius Mansions is the most sumptuous aristocratic lodgings in China, which is indicative of the Kong family's former great power. From the Han to the Qing dynasties, the descendants of Confucius were ennobled and granted privileges by the emperors. They lived like kings themselves, with 180-course meals, servants and consorts. Confucius even picked up some posthumous honours.

Qūfù grew around the Confucius Mansions and was an autonomous estate administered by the Kongs, who had powers of taxation and execution. Emperors could drop in to visit – the Ceremonial Gate near the south entrance was opened only for this event. Because of this royal protection, huge quantities of furniture, ceramics, artefacts, customary and personal effects survived and some may be viewed. The Kong family archives are a rich legacy and also survived.

The Confucius Mansions is built on an 'interrupted' north-to-south axis. Grouped by the south gate are the former administrative offices (taxes, edicts, rites, registration and examination halls). To the north on the axis is the **Nèizhái Gate** (Nèizhái Mén), a special gate that seals off the residential quarters (used for weddings, banquets and private functions). East of the Nèizhái Gate is the **Tower of Refuge**, where the Kong clan could gather if the peasants turned nasty. It has an iron-lined ceiling on the ground floor, and a removable staircase to the 1st floor. Grouped to the west of the main axis are former recreational facilities (studies, guestrooms, libraries and small temples). To the east is the odd kitchen, ancestral temple and the family branch apartments. Far to the north is a spacious garden with rockeries, ponds and bamboo groves. Kong Decheng, the last of the family line, lived in the Confucius Mansions until 1948, when he hightailed it to Taiwan.

Confucian Forest 孔林

Kǒng Lín

North of town on Lindao Lu is the Confucian Forest (admission Y20; open 7.30am-6pm daily), the largest artificial park and best preserved cemetery in China.

The pine and cypress forest of over 100,000 trees (it is said that each of Confucius' students planted a tree from his birthplace) covers 200 hectares and is bounded by a wall 10km long. Confucius and his descendants have been buried here over the past 2000 years, and are still being buried here today. Flanking the approach to the **Tomb of Confucius** are pairs of stone panthers, griffins and larger-than-life guardians. The Confucian barrow is a simple grass mound enclosed by a low wall and faced with a Ming dynasty stele. His sons are buried nearby. Scattered through the forest are dozens of temples and pavilions.

Electronic golf carts scuttle around the forest (included in the admission fee) stopping at more important tombs en route.

To reach the forest takes about 30 minutes by foot, 15 minutes by taxi, or you can attempt to catch the infrequent bus No 1. From the ticket gate, the route to the forest passes through the **Eternal Spring Archway**; its stone lintels are decorated with coiled dragons, flying phoenixes and galloping horses dating from 1594. Visitors, who needed permission to enter the Confucian Forest, had to dismount at the **Forest Gates** (Dàlín Mén).

Words & Pictures

Lín: forest

The modern character for tree is very close to its original pictograph. Thus, two trees together signify a grove or forest, while a really dense forest might have another tree added.

Mausoleum of Shao Hao 少昊陵
Shào Hào Líng

Shao Hao was one of the five legendary emperors supposed to have ruled China 4000 years ago. His pyramidal tomb *(admission Y5; open 8am-5pm daily)*, 4km north-east of Qūfù, dates from the Song dynasty. It is made of large blocks of stone, 25m wide at the base and 6m high, and has a small temple on top. Some Chinese historians believe that Qūfù was built on the ruins of Shao Hao's ancient capital, but evidence to support this is weak. Today the temple is deserted but the atmosphere is serene.

From the bus station, take a minibus marked 'Jiu Xian'. The bus will drop you 300m south of the tomb.

City of Lu 鲁城
Lǔ Chéng

The City of Lu *(☎ 449 2942, Hundao Lu; admission Y20; open 8am-4.30pm winter, 7am-4.30pm summer)* is an artificial town supposedly representing life at the time of Confucius. Here you can wander the 'old' lanes lined with mock gambling dens, butchers (with polystyrene pigs), and barber shops; or participate in a traditional Confucian ceremony. This is one of Qūfù's more entertaining sites.

Places to Stay

There are cheap guesthouses in Qūfù that may take you, but they are fickle and difficult to find (they only display Chinese signs). Try one of the touts lingering near the bus station.

Kǒngfǔ Fàndiàn (Confucius Mansions Hotel; ☎ 441 1783, fax 441 3786, 1 Datong Lu) Beds in 3-bed dorms Y60, doubles Y120. This is the poor Confucius Mansions and not a bad option if you're on a budget. There is hot water after 7.30pm.

Quèlǐ Bīnshè (☎ 441 1300, fax 441 2022, 15 Zhonglou Jie) Singles/doubles Y298/398. The traditional Chinese architecture of this hotel blends in with adjacent Kǒng Miào and it is the more upmarket option in town.

Yóuzhèng Bīnguǎn (Post Hotel; ☎ 448 3888, 8 Gulou Beijie) Doubles/triples Y260/160. Overlooking the real Confucius Mansions the Post Hotel has lovely rooms and the service is first rate.

Jīnfǔ Bīnguǎn (Gold Mansions Hotel; ☎ 441 3469, fax 441 3209, 1 Beimen Dajie) Doubles/triples Y240/300. North of town, en route to the Confucian Forest, is this hotel with very twee rooms.

Places to Eat

There is plenty of good food in Qūfù. Wumaci Jie, east of Gulou Nanjie, turns into a huge **night market** in the evenings. If you're struggling to order from Chinese menus then you'll enjoy eating here. Point and choose from a delicious selection of seafood, watch your chosen dishes being cooked up and then tuck in with a cold Sankong (Three Confucius) beer. Agree on a price before the stall owners start cooking. The market continues south onto Nanmen Dajie where less fancy food stalls dish up cheap eats such as fried noodles for Y2.5.

Quèlǐ Bīnshè (see Places to Stay) Mains Y30-100. The Quèlǐ Bīnshè restaurant at the back of the hotel offers good, if somewhat pricey, evening meals of local culinary specialities. The larger dining hall has a buffet for Y40 to Y100 per person.

Yóuzhèng Bīnguǎn (see Places to Stay) Mains Y20. The ground floor restaurant here serves fantastic food including a large choice of reasonably priced local specialities – try the fish.

Getting There & Away

Bus Minibuses to the train station in nearby Yǎnzhōu (Y3, 20 minutes) leave every 15 minutes from the bus station in the south of town until 5.30pm.

Buses leave every 30 minutes to Tài'ān (Y13, one hour) and every 20 minutes to Jǐ'nán (Y21, 2½ hours) until 5.30pm. A bus leaves every hour to Qīngdǎo (Y61, seven hours) from 8am to 4.30pm.

To find the minibus station in Yǎnzhōu, walk straight ahead as you exit the train station, cross the parking lot and turn right. The station is 50m down the road on the left.

Train When a railway project for Qūfù was first discussed, the Kong family petitioned for a change of routes, claiming that the trains would disturb Confucius' tomb. They won and the nearest tracks were routed to Yǎnzhōu, 16km to the west of Qūfù.

Eventually, the railway builders constructed another station about 6km east of Qūfù, but only slow trains stop here, so it is more convenient to go to Yǎnzhōu.

When buying tickets, ask for a Qūfù ticket and if the clerk says he doesn't have any *(méi yǒu)*, try 'Yǎnzhōu'. Yǎnzhōu is on the line from Běijīng to Shànghǎi and destinations include Tài'ān (two hours), Jǐ'nán (three hours) and Kāifēng (nine hours). Some special express trains don't stop here; others arrive at inconvenient times like midnight.

Getting Around

There are only two bus lines and service is not frequent. Probably most useful for travellers is bus No 1, which travels along Gulou Beijie and Lindao Lu, connecting the bus station with the Confucian Forest. Bus No 2 travels from east to west along Jingxuan Lu.

Yellow minivans and motor-tricycles swarm around, but expect to haggle. There are also decorated tourist horse-carts (Y10 to Y15) that will take you on a 30-minute tour.

ZŌUXIÀN 邹县

Zōuxiàn is a good place to visit and it's more relaxed than Qūfù. This is the home town of Mencius (372–289 BC), who is regarded as the first great Confucian philosopher. He developed many of the ideas of Confucianism, as they were later understood.

Zōuxiàn's **Mèng Miào** *(Mencius Temple; admission Y20; open 8am-6pm daily)* and **Mencius Mansions** *(Mèng Fǔ)* are at the southern end of town, about a 20-minute walk from the bus station. Excellently restored, these two quiet temples are almost empty save for the storks in the garden.

The temples are next door to one another. To reach them, head out of the bus station and take the first right and then the first left until you reach a T-junction. Turn right at the T-junction and then left onto Yashengmiao Jie. En route you'll pass through a lively *food market*.

Zōuxiàn is 23km south of Qūfù and can be visited as a day trip by train from Yǎnzhōu or by bus from Qūfù. From Qūfù, buses leave every 15 minutes (Y3.5) from the bus station for the 35-minute ride.

QĪNGDǍO 青岛

☎ 0532 • pop 7,494,200

Perched on the southern seaboard of the Shāndōng peninsula, the picturesque town of Qīngdǎo (Green Island) is a welcome breather from the clogging conformity of socialist town planning. Its German legacy more or less intact, Qīngdǎo takes pride in its Bavarian appearance – the Chinese call the town 'China's Switzerland'. With its cool sea breezes, (relatively) clear air, balmy evenings (in summer) and excellent seafood, this is where party cadres come to build sand castles, lick ice cream and dream of retirement.

Qīngdǎo was a simple fishing village until the Kaiser Wilhelm II set his sights on it. When two German missionaries were killed in the Boxer Rebellion, the Kaiser jumped on the opportunity to declare an international crisis. The obvious solution was for China's Manchu government to hand over Qīngdǎo. In 1898 China ceded the town to Germany for 99 years. Under German administration, the famous Tsingtao Brewery opened in 1903, electric lighting was installed, missions and a university were established, the railway to Jǐ'nán was built, a garrison of 2000 men was deployed, and a naval base was established.

In 1914 the Japanese moved into town after the successful joint Anglo-Japanese naval bombardment of the port. Japan's position in Qīngdǎo was strengthened by the Treaty of Versailles and they held the city until 1922 when it was ceded back to the Kuomintang. The Japanese returned in 1938, after the start of the Sino-Japanese war, and occupied the town until defeated in 1945.

Qīngdǎo is now China's fourth-largest port and the second largest city in Shāndōng. Booming industry and an entrepreneurial spirit have successfully carried the city into the 21st century.

Orientation

Qīngdǎo is situated on a peninsula with numerous small bays and beaches along the southern coastline. These coastal areas and the central district are charming. The northern and eastern districts are industrial zones and the west is home to the shipping industry.

BĚIJĪNG TO SHÀNGHǍI

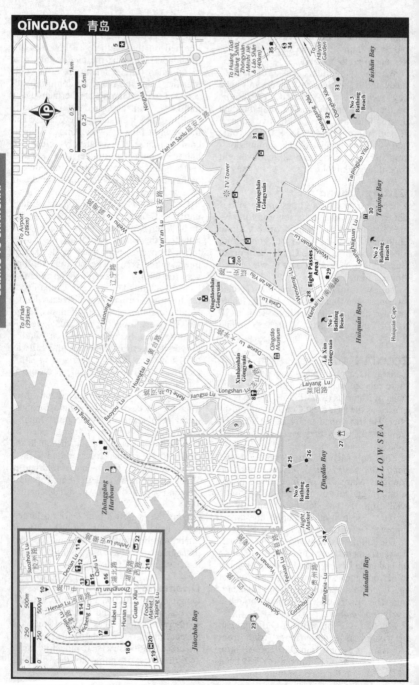

QĪNGDǍO 青岛

QĪNGDǍO

PLACES TO STAY
1 Hépíng Bīnguǎn
 和平宾馆
2 Yǒuyì Bīnguǎn
 友谊宾馆
7 Qīngdǎo Yíng
 Bīnguǎn
 青岛迎宾馆
14 Tiānqiáo Bīnguǎn
 天桥宾馆
15 Qīngdǎo Fàndiàn
 青岛饭店
17 Fótáo Bīnguǎn
 佛桃宾馆
21 Zhànqiáo Bīnguǎn
 栈桥宾馆
29 Yínhǎi Huāyuán
 Fàndiàn
 银海花园饭店
32 Hǎitiān Dàjiǔdiàn;
 Korean Air; All Nippon
 Airways
 海天大酒店；大韩航空；
 全日空航空公司
35 Shangri-la Hotel
 香格里拉大酒店

PLACES TO EAT
10 Chǔnhélóu Fàndiàn
 春和楼饭店

11 Les Bains Douches
 乐邦都市西餐吧
19 California Beef Noodles
 King USA
 美国加州牛肉面
24 Yángguāng Jiàrì
 Hǎishàng Huánggōng
 Diàn
 阳光假日海上皇宫店

OTHER
3 Passenger Ferry
 Terminal
 青岛港客运站
4 Tsingtao Brewery
 青岛啤酒厂
5 PSB
 公安局
6 Qingdao Hill Fort
 青岛山炮台遗址
8 Protestant Church
 基督教堂
9 Guānhǎishān Gōngyuán
 观海山公园
12 Catholic Church
 天主教堂
13 Post Office
 邮电局
16 CAAC
 中国航空公司

18 Train Station; Tiědào
 Dàshà
 火车站；铁道大厦
20 Long-Distance Bus
 Station
 长途汽车站
22 Main Post Office
 and Telephone
 Office; Internet
 邮局；中国电信网吧
23 Local Ferry
 青岛轮渡站
25 Zhàn Bridge
 栈桥
26 Huílán Pavilion
 回澜阁
27 Xiǎo Qīng Dǎo
 Lighthouse
 小青岛
28 CITS (Huiquan
 Dynasty Hotel)
 中国国际旅行社
30 Huāshí Lóu
 花石楼
31 Zhànshān Sì
 湛山寺
33 Outdoor Sculpture
 Park
34 Bank of China
 中国银行

BĚIJĪNG TO SHÀNGHǍI

Information

Money The main branch of the Bank of China is east of town in the World Trade Centre at 6 Xianggang Zhonglu; you can also change money in any of the large hotels.

Post & Communications The main post and telephone office is at 5 Anhui Lu. There is another post office at 51 Zhongshan Lu, opposite the large Parkson Building. A small Internet bar can be found opposite the main post and telephone office, at 6 Anhui Lu. It charges Y2.5 per hour and is open from 8.30am to 12am.

Travel Agencies CITS (☎ 288 0390), at 9 Nanhai Lu, is in the run-down building behind the Huiquan Dynasty Hotel. The office has helpful English-speaking staff. Here you can book tours of the brewery, locomotive factory and Láo Shān.

PSB The PSB office for foreigners (☎ 579 2555 ext 2860) has moved and is now inconveniently located in the east of the city

at 272 Ningxia Lu. It's open from 9am to 11.30am and 1.30pm to 4.30pm Monday to Friday. Bus No 301 goes from the train station and stops outside the terracotta-coloured building (stop no 14).

Things to See

The wonderful castle-like villa is **Huāshí Lóu** (*18 Huanghai Lu; admission Y5; open 7.30am-7pm daily*). It was originally the home of a Russian aristocrat and later the German governor's retreat for fishing and hunting. The Chinese call it the 'Chiang Kaishek Building' as the generalissimo secretly stayed here in 1947. Apparently Chiang was staying at the villa when he heard of the Communist's victory and fled to Taiwan from here.

To the right of Xìnhàoshān Gōngyuán remains one of Qīngdǎo's most astounding pieces of German architecture, **Qīngdǎo Yíng Bīnguǎn** (*Qīngdǎo Yíng Hotel; admission Y10; open 8.30am-4.30pm daily*). This is the former German governor's residence and a replica of a German palace. Built in

1903, it is said to have cost 2,450,000 taels of silver. When Kaiser Wilhelm II got the bill, he immediately recalled the extravagant governor and sacked him.

Around the back is a terrace where the governor used to play tennis with his lackeys and the garage where they used to park the Mercedes.

In 1957 Chairman Mao stayed here with his wife and kids on holiday. A meeting of the CCP Political Bureau was also held and this time with Zhou Enlai, Liu Shaoqi and Deng Xiaoping all present. Their meeting room and bedrooms are on display.

The twin-spired **Catholic Church** (*Tiānzhǔ Jiàotáng;* ☎ *591 1400, 15 Zhejiang Lu; admission Y5; open 8am-5pm Mon-Sat, 9am-5pm Sun*), up a steep hill off Zhongshan Lu, is an imposing edifice with a cross on each spire. The church was badly damaged during the Cultural Revolution and the crosses were torn off. God-fearing locals rescued them however, and buried them in the hills. It re-opened in 1981 and holds Sunday services at 7am and 6pm.

The cobbled streets surrounding the church are rich in architectural textures and worth exploring. A daily **fish market**, featuring colourful exotica from the depths, sets up on Feicheng Lu, which leads up to the church from Zhongshan Lu.

The other main church is the **Protestant Church** (*Jīdū Jiàotáng; admission Y3; open 8.30am-4.30pm daily*), opposite the southwestern entrance to Xìnhàoshān Gōngyuán. This German structure is simple yet attractive; the white clock face on the green tower is still inscribed with the manufacturer's name. Climb up the bell tower for an impressive view of the city.

For a colourful and exhaustive account of Qīngdǎo's historic architecture, turn to *Far from Home: Western Architecture in China's Northern Treaty Ports* by Tess Johnston & Deke Erh.

Beaches

Qīngdǎo is famous for its six beaches, which are extremely popular with the Chinese. The beaches are not bad, but don't go expecting a surfers' paradise. June to September is the main swimming season, when a ridiculous 60,000 to 70,000 sunseekers fight for towel space. The beaches are sheltered and are equipped with changing sheds. Shark nets, lifeguards, lifeboat patrols and medical stations provide safety.

Close to the train station is the **No 6 Bathing Beach**. This is a lively area in the morning, jostling with tai chi practitioners, frisbee throwers and joggers. This beach neighbours the **Zhàn Bridge** (*Zhàn Qiáo*), a pier that reaches out into the bay and has the eight-sided **Huílán Pavilion** (*Huílán Gé*), at its end. The pier is a famous landmark that crops up on the label of Tsingtao beer. Beyond, you can see the **lighthouse** on Xiǎo Qīng Dǎo (Little Green Island). Next to the jetty there are boat ticket vendors for tours around the bay and beyond (Y15, 40 minutes).

Continuing east, around the headland and the lighthouse, is the leafy **Lǔ Xùn Gōngyuán**, named after the father of Chinese modern literature.

The sand of **No 1 Bathing Beach** is coarse-grained, engulfed in seaweed and bordered by concrete beach huts and bizarre statues of dolphins. Past the Huiquan Dynasty Hotel is **Eight Passes Area** (*Bādàguān*), well known for its sanatoriums and exclusive guesthouses. The spas are scattered in lush wooded zones off the coast, and each street is lined with a different tree or flower, including maple, myrtle, peach, snowpine or crab apple. This is a lovely area in which to stroll.

As you head out of Eight Passes Area, Nos 2 and 3 bathing beaches are just east, and the villas lining the headlands are exquisite. **No 2 Bathing Beach** is cleaner, quieter and more sheltered than No 1 Bathing Beach.

Parks

Qīngdǎo has a splendid collection of parks that are worth exploring. The charm of **Guānhǎishān Gōngyuán** lies in finding it – the route winds up a small hill through restful lanes; the park is at the top. Although small, the park used to be a golf course for the Germans. The white trigrams marked on the paving stones at the top are for the practise of a secretive martial art called *bāguà zhàng* (eight-trigram boxing; see the boxed text 'Chinese Martial Arts' in the Facts Visitor chapter).

Down the hill and to the east is **Xìnhàoshān Gōngyuán**, whose summit is graced with the carbuncular towers known as the *mógu lóu* (mushroom buildings). Minibus No 26 can take you to the park.

North of the Huiquan Dynasty Hotel is **Zhōngshān Gōngyuán**, which covers 80 hectares, has a teahouse and temple and in springtime is a heavily wooded profusion of flowering shrubs and plants. Bus Nos 25 and 26 travel to Zhōngshān Gōngyuán.

The mountainous area north-east of Zhōngshān Gōngyuán is called **Tàipíngshān Gōngyuán**, an area of walking paths, pavilions and the best area in town for hiking. In the centre of the park is the **TV Tower** *(Diànshì Tǎ)*, which has an express lift up to fabulous views of the city (Y30). You can reach the tower via cable car (Y20). Also within the park is Qīngdǎo's largest temple, **Zhànshān Sì** *(admission Y5)*. Built in 1934, it is the latest Tiantai Buddhist temple in China and is currently used by the growing number of practising Buddhists in Qīngdǎo as well as by the 20 monks in residence. The temple has a number of dramatic, sandalwood Buddhas covered in gold foil and is well worth the entry fee.

Just west of Tàipíngshān Gōngyuán is **Qīngdǎoshān Gōngyuán**. A notable feature of this hilly park is **Qingdao Hill Fort** *(Qīngdǎoshān Pàotái; admission Y8; open 8.30am-11.30am & 1.30pm-4.30pm daily)*, built by Germans in 1899. All that remains of the fort today is the underground command post – the Germans destroyed the fort in 1914 when they lost to the Japanese. Visitors can take a look around the old living quarters, boiler room and canteen, three storeys underground.

Running along Donghai Xilu is an outdoor **Sculpture Park**. The sculptures, carved by artists from all over China, run from the corner of Donghai Xilu and Taipingjiao Liulu and follow the coastal road until **Hǎiyùn Garden** *(Hǎiyùn Yuán)* and the **Qingdao Sculpture Museum**.

Tsingtao Brewery 青岛啤酒厂
Qīngdǎo Píjiǔchǎng

The brewery is tucked in the industrial part of town, inland and east of the Zhōnggǎng harbour.

The brewery was established in 1903 by the Germans who still supply the parts for modernisation of the system. The flavour of the finest brew in China comes from the mineral waters of nearby Láo Shān. Tsingtao beer has gained a worldwide following. Unfortunately, unless you are on a tour it's almost impossible to get into the brewery for a look. Tours can be booked at CITS in Qīngdǎo and cost around Y60 per person.

Special Events

The summer months see Qīngdǎo overrun with tourists, particularly in the second and third weeks of July, when the annual trade fair and ocean festival is held. Another festival to look out for is the beer festival in August. Gardeners may be interested to note that Qīngdǎo's radish festival is in February, the cherry festival in May and the grape festival in September (Qīngdǎo is a major producer of wine).

Places to Stay – Budget

If you arrive during the summer months, prepare to be forced into expensive accommodation. Also be warned that some of the hotels shut down during winter. All prices quoted are high season; bargain hard if you arrive off-season.

Fótáo Bīnguǎn (☎ 287 1581, 13 Tai'an Lu) Singles/doubles/triples Y50/100/120, with bath Y160/210/220. This hotel is north of the train station and has windowless shoeboxes for rooms. There is hot water after 7pm.

Yǒuyì Bīnguǎn (Friendship Hotel; ☎ 282 3381, 12 Xinjiang Lu) Beds in 4-bed dorms Y50, doubles/triples Y180/270, with bath Y268/330. The corridors of this hotel look like a hospital but the rooms are much cleaner. The public bathrooms are not for the modest. You'll find the hotel next to the passenger ferry terminal.

Hépíng Bīnguǎn (Peace Hotel; ☎ 283 0154, fax 282 7691, 10 Xinjiang Lu) Doubles/triples/quads Y80/100/120, doubles with bath Y170-220. Next door to the Yǒuyì Bīnguǎn is this hotel with decent rooms. The 'Lucky Seamen' disco opposite should warn off light sleepers.

Tiānqiáo Bīnguǎn (☎ 285 8705, 51 Feicheng Lu) Dorm beds/doubles/triples Y90/280/380. Newly opened near the train station, this place has rooms that are unbelievably small and some without windows. Guests can hire bikes.

BEIJING TO SHANGHAI

Places to Stay – Mid-Range

Tiědào Dàshà (*Railway Hotel;* ☎ 286 9963, fax 286 9631, 2 Tai'an Lu) Doubles/triples/suites Y320/480/880. Located at the train station, Tiědào Dàshà has gone upmarket, ridding itself of all dorm rooms and providing instead over-priced doubles. Discounts are not uncommon – even during summer months.

Qīngdǎo Fàndiàn (☎ 289 1888, fax 286 2464, 53 Zhongshan Lu) Singles/doubles/triples from Y178/230/380. Lower-end rooms are small but clean and the more you pay the bigger everything gets (beds included). The hotel's entrance is on Qufu Lu.

Zhànqiáo Bīnguǎn (☎ 287 0502, fax 287 0936, 31 Taiping Lu) Rooms Y298-598. Ideally situated on the beachfront is this charming hotel where Sun Yatsen stayed when he visited Qīngdǎo in 1912.

Yínhǎi Huāyuán Fàndiàn (*Yinhai Garden Hotel;* ☎ 296 7556, 5 Nanhai Lu) Doubles Y268-388. This smaller hotel with ocean views is near Lǔ Xùn Gōngyuán and No 1 Bathing Beach.

Places to Stay – Top End

Qīngdǎo is swarming with top-end accommodation, most of it overpriced.

Hǎitiān Dàjiǔdiàn (☎ 387 1888, fax 387 1777, 48 Xianggang Xilu) Singles/doubles US$100/130. This hotel offers good value for money and some rooms have ocean views. Rates include airport shuttle and newspapers.

Shangri-La Hotel (*Xiānggélǐlā Jiǔdiàn;* ☎ 388 3838, ⓦ www.shangri-la.com, 9 Xianggang Zhonglu) Singles/doubles US$175/195 plus 15% service charge. East of town is the splendid Shangri-La. Rooms are plush and the service is excellent.

Qīngdǎo Yíng Bīnguǎn (☎ 288 9888, fax 286 1985, 26 Longshan Lu) Rooms Y660-680. Probably the hotel with the most character and history is this converted German mansion. The hotel is next to the former German governor's house and is splendid inside and out. The hotel closes during the low season (October to May) so call ahead to make certain that someone is around.

Places to Eat

Qīngdǎo is overrun with good food. The locals are crazy about kebabs, which is understandable as they are delicious! You can buy them for Y1.5 from the ubiquitous *street stalls*. There are *zhūròuchuàn* (pork kebabs) or sometimes *yángròuchuàn* (lamb kebabs) and they come either *là* (spicy) or *búlà* (not spicy). Another local favourite is *diànkǎo yóuyú* (squid on a stick). Go for the popular stalls where the crowds gather (especially on Zhongshan Lu).

The waterfront area is brimming with *restaurants*, from No 6 Bathing Beach almost all the way to No 1 Bathing Beach. The area around No 1 Bathing Beach is the best place to find cheap eats. Any of the seaside restaurants serve up fresh seafood. The *gǎ la* (mussels) are excellent and a plate will cost only about Y12.

The *night market* (*Taiping Lu*) is a great place to go for a cheap seafood dinner. Aquatic delights include squid, oysters and even starfish. The market is down a narrow lane west of McDonald's, across from No 6 Bathing Beach.

California Beef Noodles King USA (*Měiguó Jiāzhōu Niúròumiàn; 20 Feixian Lu*) Noodles Y6. This branch of the popular noodle chain is near the long-distance bus station.

Chūnhélóu Fàndiàn (☎ 282 4346, 146 Zhongshan Lu) Downstairs is a busy help-yourself-to-as-much-as-you-can-eat type diner with dumplings from Y7 and stacks of kebabs for Y4. Upstairs is a bit classier, but the prices are still reasonable.

Yángguāng Jiàrì Hǎishàng Huánggōng Diàn (*Sunshine Holiday Seaside Palace;* ☎ 265 2323, 2 Xilingxia Lu) Dishes Y30-200. Looking just like Australia's Opera House, this chic restaurant has fresh and fancy seafood. Don't wear your flip-flops.

Shangri-La Hotel (*see Places to Stay earlier*) Buffet Y52 per person plus 15% service charge. The hotel offers a weekend dim-sum buffet breakfast from 8am to 10am.

Huáng Tǔdì Záliáng Shífǔ (*Yellow Earth Grain Restaurant;* ☎ 567 2386, 31 Xianggang Zhonglu) Dishes from Y20. This Sìchuān restaurant serves delicious food among Cultural Revolution memorabilia. The restaurant is one of many within a small courtyard – also worth trying is the *hotpot restaurant* to your right as you enter.

The lively street *Zhōngyuàn Měishí Jiē* is packed with seafood restaurants. Entrance is off Xianggang Zhonglu, east of Carrefour.

Les Bains Douches (Lèbāng Dùshì; ☎ 280 2860, 32 Pingdu Lu) Drinks Y20, dishes from Y25. This groovy tapas bar is the ideal place to come and escape. The food is very good and the drink selection huge.

Getting There & Away

Air CAAC (☎ 289 5577) is at 29 Zhongshan Lu. A second office is at 30 Xianggang Lu (☎ 577 5555). Korean Air and All Nippon Airways are in Hǎitiān Dàjiǔdiàn (see Places to Stay earlier). Large hotels also have airline ticket offices. The Qīngdǎo airport inquiries number is ☎ 471 5139.

There are five flights a week between Qīngdǎo and Hong Kong (Y2400) and daily flights to Seoul (Y1170) with Korean Air. All Nippon Airways has four flights a week to both Osaka (Y3950) and Fukuoka (Y3350).

National destinations include daily flights to Shànghǎi (Y670), Běijīng (Y650), Hāěrbīn (Y870), Shěnyáng (Y1070), Kūnmíng (Y1600) and Dàlián (Y430).

Bus Both buses and minibuses depart from the area next to the massive Hualian Building, across from the train station. The ticket offices are in the small pastel-coloured huts.

There are minibuses every 15 minutes to Yāntái (Y31, 3½ hours) until 6pm. Iveco buses leave every hour for Jǐ'nán (Y95, four hours) between 10am and 5pm, slower buses leave every 15 minutes (Y51, six hours). Buses to Wēihǎi (Y41, four hours) leave every 16 minutes until 6pm.

There are daily sleeper buses to Shànghǎi (Y200, 11 hours) that depart at 5pm, 6pm and 7pm. A bus to Běijīng (Y120, 18 hours) leaves at 10am on even days of the month.

Train All trains from Qīngdǎo go through the provincial capital of Jǐ'nán, except for the direct Qīngdǎo to Yāntái trains. There are two trains a day to Yāntái (Y22, 3½ hours), and regular services to Jǐ'nán (Y28 to Y32, four to six hours). Three trains leave daily for Běijīng (Y215, 10 to 12 hours). A train departs for Shànghǎi (Y289, 19 hours) at 1.48pm and there are connections to Guǎngzhōu (Y301, 36 hours) and Zhèngzhōu (Y215, 15 hours).

Sleeper tickets can be hard to come by during peak season so it's best to buy your ongoing ticket as soon as you arrive.

Boat There are boats to Inch'ŏn in South Korea on Monday and Thursday at 2pm (Y920 to Y1180, 19 hours). There are three boats to Shimonoseki, Japan (Y1160, 39 hours) every two weeks. Phone the passenger ferry terminal (☎ 282 5001) to confirm days. Boats to Shànghǎi and Dàlián have been discontinued. The best way to get to Dàlián is to take the train or bus to Yāntái and then continue by boat (see the Yāntái section later in this chapter for details).

Getting Around

To/From the Airport Qīngdǎo's antiquated airport is 30km north of the city. Taxi drivers ask Y100 (or whatever they think you might possibly pay) for the journey. Buses leave regularly from the CAAC office between 6am and 5pm (Y10).

Bus Most transport needs can be catered for by the bus No 6 route, which starts at the northern end of Zhongshan Lu, runs along it to within a few blocks of the train station and then east to the area above No 3 Bathing Beach. Bus No 26 from the train station runs along the coast and past Zhōngshān Gōngyuán before heading north at the end of No 3 Bathing Beach. Minibuses also follow these routes (Y2).

Taxi Qīngdǎo taxis are among the cheapest in China; Y10 will get you almost anywhere around town.

AROUND QĪNGDĂO
Láo Shān 崂山

Láo Shān *(admission winter/summer Y30/50)*, 40km east of Qīngdǎo, is a famous Taoist retreat with temples, waterfalls and secluded walking trails. Covering some 400 sq km, this is where Láo Shān mineral water starts its life. The mountain is associated with Taoist legend and myth, with the central attraction being the Song dynasty **Great Purity Palace** *(Tàiqīng Gōng; admission Y10)*. The first Song Emperor established the palace as a place to perform Taoist rites to save the souls of the dead. It's located a third of the way up Láo Shān, just below the entrance to the first cable car, and just off the main walking path. Due north of the Great Purity Palace is Jiǔ Shuǐ, noted for its numerous streams and waterfalls.

BEIJING TO SHANGHAI

From the Great Purity Palace, there are paths leading to the summit of Láo Shān. Three quarters of the way up, at the top of the second cable car, you have the option of ascending either through a cave or by stairs. The cave is amazing but requires you to crawl, climb steep ladders and cross narrow suspension bridges – all of this in the pitch black together with masses of tourists. Bring a torch. If you suffer vertigo or claustrophobia, you'd be better off taking the stairs.

The cable car up the first half of the mountain costs Y30 (Y50 return) and a ride up the second half costs Y20. From Qīngdǎo, bus No 304 runs to Láo Shān (Y6.5, one to two hours). The first bus leaves from Taiping Lu at around 6.30am and will drop you off at the entrance to the first cable car in Láo Shān. Returning, the last bus leaves Láo Shān at 5pm.

Tour buses to Láo Shān (Y25 return) ply the streets of Qīngdǎo from 6am onwards but visit at least four other 'sites' on the way to the mountain. If you did want to stay the night at Láo Shān, there are a number of guesthouses to choose from. *Zhànqiáo Bīnguǎn* (☎ 794 8100) has a smaller guesthouse at Láo Shān or inquire at the hotel in Qīngdǎo.

About 30 minutes by boat from Qīngdǎo and a further 30 minutes by bus is the beach of **Huáng Dǎo** (*Yellow Island*). Once the secret of locals, it is quickly becoming popular with tour groups. It remains, however, quieter and cleaner than Qīngdǎo's beaches. The ferry (Y10) leaves from the Qīngdǎo local ferry terminal (Qīngdǎo lúndùzhàn) to the west of the train station. The first departure is at 6.30am with the final boat returning at 9pm. Once you reach the island, take bus No 1 to its terminus (Y2.5).

YĀNTÁI 烟台
☎ 0535 • pop 6,635,700

Yāntái is a busy ice-free port on the northern coast of the Shāndōng peninsula. The town started life as a defence outpost and fishing village. Its sleepy existence came to an abrupt halt in the late 19th century when the Qing government, following defeat in the Opium War, handed Yāntái over to the British who established a treaty port. Several nations, Japan and the USA among

them, had trading establishments here and the town was something of a resort area at one time.

Today Yāntái is one of the top three most prosperous and fast developing cities in Shāndōng (along with Qīngdǎo and Wēihǎi). It is also quickly becoming the new summer destination for holidaying Chinese. More relaxed and less crowded than Qīngdǎo, the town sees a steady stream of visitors flocking for its sunny beaches, friendly locals, and good seafood.

The name Yāntái literally means Smoke Terrace; wolf-dung fires were lit on the headland during the Ming dynasty to warn fishing fleets of approaching pirates.

Information

The main branch of the Bank of China is at 166 Jiefang Lu. You can also exchange US dollars in the branch next to the International Seamen's Club opposite the train station.

The main post office can be found on the corner of Nan Dajie and Dahaiyang Lu, and a second branch at 172 Nan Dajie. The telephone office has an Internet cafe of sorts at 29 Haigang Lu, where you can surf the net for free (maximum one hour; open 8am to 5pm Monday to Friday). You must register your passport.

There is a branch of the CTS (☎ 608 5654) at 96 Beima Lu, near the train station, where you can book ferry and airline tickets. The main CTS office (☎ 622 4431) is the dilapidated building behind Huáqiáo Bīnguǎn. CITS (☎ 661 0661) is at 181B Jiefang Lu.

The PSB (☎ 624 5817) at 90 Tongshi Lu is in the southern end of town and a little tricky to find. The office dealing with foreign affairs is the white-tiled building up a small incline. The office is on the 3rd floor; ascend via the outside spiral staircase. It's open from 8am to 11.30am and 1.30pm to 5.30pm Monday to Friday.

Yantai Museum 烟台博物馆
Yāntái Bówùguǎn

The Yantai Museum (*257 Nan Dajie; admission Y5; open 8.30am-12pm & 1.30pm-5.30pm daily*) is definitely worth a visit, but more for the architecture than the exhibits housed within it. It can be found within the guild hall built by merchants and sailors of Fújiàn as a place of worship to

Tianhou (Heaven Queen), Goddess of the Sea. Tianhou (also known as Matsu, Linmo and Niang Niang) was a strong cult figure of the 18th century. It is believed she appeared as a vision to fishermen who were lost at sea, leading them safely to shore.

The main hall of the museum is known as the 'Hall of Heavenly Goddess'. It was designed and finished in Guǎngzhōu and then shipped to Yāntái for assembly. Beyond the hall, at the centre of the courtyard, is the museum's most spectacular piece of architecture: a brightly and intricately decorated gate. Supported by 14 pillars, the gate is a collage of hundreds of carved and painted figures, flowers, beasts, phoenixes and animals. The carvings depict battle scenes and folk stories including *The Eight Immortals Crossing the Sea*.

At the southern end of the museum is a theatrical stage that was first made in Fújiàn and then shipped to Yāntái. Apparently Tianhou wasn't particularly fond of that stage as it was lost at sea during transportation and had to be reconstructed in Yāntái. The stage continues to be used for performances to celebrate Tianhou's birthday and anniversary of deification. On these days you can join the celebrations.

Parks

Yāntái has a number of parks of which **Nánshān Gōngyuán** *(admission Y3)*, south of town, is the largest and most popular. It has a zoo, amusement park and pond.

For a more peaceful retreat, try **Yùhuángdǐng Gōngyuán** *(admission Y6)* in the city centre, with its quiet trails, 600-year-old Taoist temple, archway, pavilion and pagoda. The park is known as Lesser Penglai – and that it is: less money, people and noise!

On the north coast is **Yàntáishān Gōngyuán**, where you can hang out with the local fisherfolk.

Other Sites

There are two beaches in Yāntái, **No 1 Beach** *(Dìyī Hǎishuǐ Yùchǎng)* and **No 2 Beach** *(Dìèr Hǎishuǐ Yùchǎng)*. No 1 Beach is the better of the two; a long stretch of soft sand pads a calm bay area that is ideal for swimming. The coastal road that lines the waterfront is populated with hotels and restaurants and gets busy in the evenings.

No 2 beach is less crowded but more polluted. Both beaches can be reached by bus No 17.

Yāntái is home to Asia's first ever **bowling alley**, built by the British in 1865. The lanes are still open for games (five/10 balls Y30/50). The alley is in the basement of the former British consulate, now a mediocre seafood restaurant, **Tàihé Hǎixiānfǎng Jiǔdiàn** *(☎ 622 1507, 34 Hai'an Lu)*. In the building are some black and white photos of Yāntái at the turn of the century.

Places to Stay

Like Qīngdǎo, Yāntái does not have a lot to offer budget travellers.

International Seamen's Club *(Hǎiyuán Jùlèbù; ☎ 624 3425, 68 Beima Lu)* Dorm beds Y80-100. Across from the train station is this reasonable hotel with decent rooms. You can't miss the large sign on the roof.

Beach Hotel *(Hǎibīn Lóu; ☎ 622 5388, fax 622 5388, Binhai Lu)* Doubles/triples from Y260/268. This popular hotel is along the waterfront and the rooms with sea views get snapped up quickly. A barbecue is held on the terrace most summer evenings.

Yóudiàn Bīnguǎn *(Post and Telecom Hotel; ☎ 628 8888, fax 624 4934, 73 Beima Lu)* Doubles/suites Y320/428. The rooms here are small and pricey, but discounts are not uncommon. The hotel is opposite the train station.

Yāntái Tiědào Dàshà *(Yantai Railway Mansion; ☎ 626 1391, 135 Beima Lu)* Doubles Y240-280. The rooms here are similar to those in Yóudiàn Bīnguǎn but with a strong floral theme to them.

Huáqiáo Bīnguǎn *(Overseas Chinese Guesthouse; ☎ 620 8888, 30 Huanshan Lu)* Doubles Y380-580. On a small hill in the east of town is this hotel whose rooms are fresh and breezy with sea views. The hotel can be reached by bus No 7.

Jīnhǎiwān Jiǔdiàn *(Golden Gulf Hotel; ☎ 622 4491, fax 621 6313, 34 Haian Lu)* Doubles Y520-890. This is a pleasant hotel with homely rooms and rock-solid beds.

Yantai Marina Hotel *(Yāntái Jiàrì Jiǔdiàn; ☎ 666 99990, ⓔ Marinaht@public .ytptt.sd.cn, Binhai Beilu)* Doubles Y600-780. The Yantai Marina is the newest and most upmarket hotel in Yāntái. Take a trip in the external glass elevator for fantastic views over the bay.

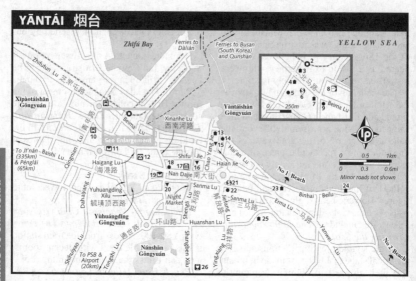

YĀNTÁI 烟台

Places to Eat

In the summer months a *night market* sets up along Shengli Lu, good for cheap kebabs and beer.

Hǎoxiānglái Cāntīng (☎ 662 7588, *51 Shifu Jie*) Set meals Y25. Open 24 hours. This is a bright and busy restaurant serving Chinese and international cuisine, including succulent sirloin steak meals.

Dumpling King of New Sun (*Xīntài Jiǎoziwáng;* ☎ 662 3328, *227 Xinanhe Lu*) Dumplings from Y12. This is a popular and cheap dumpling joint.

Dagama Brazilian BBQ Bar (*Dájiāmǎ Bāxī Kǎoròudiàn;* ☎ 1395 358 6118 mobile, *23 Haian Jie*) Lunch/evening BBQ Y28/30 per person. Open 11.30am-2.30pm & 5.30pm-late daily. For an alternative to seafood, try the tender barbequed meat in this unique South American-themed restaurant. Get there early for first cuts.

Yāntái Jiǎrì Jiǔdiàn (see Places to Stay) has a daily seafood buffet for Y78 in the revolving restaurant on the 25th floor. All drinks are included.

Entertainment

One place to try for a night out is:

Jazz Bar (*Juéshì Ba;* ☎ 609 1573, *52 Shangben Xilu*) Spirits Y35, beers Y10. Open 1.30pm-2am daily. This mellow two-storey bar is popular for its swings, pottery wheels (Y18 to make your own masterpiece), live music and fine drinks selection.

Getting There & Away

Air Flight bookings can be made at CTS or at the CAAC office (☎ 625 3777) at 6 Dahaiyang Lu. Shandong Airlines' (☎ 662 2737) main booking office is at 236 Nan Dajie and China Southwest Airlines (☎ 627 0919) is at the western end of Yāntái Tiědào Dàshà (see Places to Stay earlier).

Flights leave on Wednesday, Saturday and Sunday for Hong Kong (Y1940) and daily for Seoul (Y1260). There are daily flights to Běijīng (Y630) and Shànghǎi (Y720) and flights to Guǎngzhōu (Y1690) on Monday and Thursday.

Bus From Yāntái buses depart from the long-distance bus station on Qingnian Lu and from outside the train station – the latter being the more convenient place to catch a ride. You can catch buses to Jǐ'nán (Y65, 5½ hours) and Wēihǎi (Y16, 1½ hours) from outside the train station. Sleeper buses depart for Běijīng (Y130, 13½ hours) and Shànghǎi (Y230, 16 hours).

There are frequent minibuses between Yāntái and Qīngdǎo (Y30 to Y38, 3½ hours), which depart about every half hour. In both cities, buses park in front of the train stations and depart when full. Minibuses to

YĀNTÁI

PLACES TO STAY	PLACES TO EAT	
3 Yāntái Tiědào Dàshà; China Southwest Airlines 铁道大厦; 西南航空公司	15 Dagama Brazilian BBQ Bar 達加马巴西烤肉店	10 Long-Distance Bus Station 长途汽车站
4 Yóudiàn Bīnguǎn 邮电宾馆	16 Hǎoxiānglái Cāntīng 好香来餐厅	11 Main Post Office 电信大楼
7 International Seamen's Club 国际海员俱乐部	20 Dumpling King of New Sun 新太饺子王	12 Telephone Office; Internet Cafe 中国电信; 网吧
13 Jīnhǎiwān Jiǔdiàn 金海湾酒店	**OTHER**	14 Bowling Alley 保龄球
23 Beach Hotel 海滨楼	1 Buses (to Pénglái) 去蓬莱车站	17 Yantai Museum 烟台博物馆
24 Yantai Marina Hotel 烟台假日酒店	2 Train Station 火车站	18 Shandong Airlines 山东航空公司
25 Huáqiáo Bīnguǎn; CTS 华侨宾馆; 中国旅行社	5 CAAC 中国民航	19 Post Office 邮局
	6 Bank of China 中国银行	21 Bank of China 中国银行
	8 Passenger Ferry Terminal 烟台港客运站	22 CITS 中国国际旅行社
	9 CTS 中国旅行社	26 Jazz Bar 爵士吧

Pénglái (Y8 to Y10, 1½ hours) depart every 15 minutes from the bus station on the corner of Beima Lu and Qingnian Lu, about a five-minute walk west of the train station.

Train The Yāntái to Qīngdǎo train (Y22, 3½ hours) departs daily at 8am. A train leaves daily at 9.30pm for Jǐ'nán (Y86, 8½ hours), 10.12pm for Běijīng (Y145, 15 hours) and at 2pm for Shànghǎi (Y190, 24 hours).

Boat At the passenger ferry terminal (☎ 674 1774) you can buy tickets for express boats to Dàlián (Y192, 3½ hours) departing daily at 8.30am, 10am, 12.30pm and 2pm; tickets can only be purchased on the day of travel. There are also eight slow boats to Dàlián (Y111 to Y242, seven hours) every day. The ferry service to Tiānjīn has been discontinued.

Boats to Busan in South Korea (tickets from Y1020) leave every Wednesday at 5pm. Another destination in Korea is Qunshan; boats leave every Monday, Wednesday and Friday at 5pm (tickets from Y800).

The terminal is down a small lane off Beima Lu, not far from the train station.

Getting Around
The airport is approximately 20km south of town. Airport buses (Y10, 30 minutes) leave regularly from the CAAC office.

Bus No 7 runs through the city from east to west, passing Yùhuángdǐng Gōngyuán, Nánshān Gōngyuán and Huáqiáo Bīnguǎn. Bus No 3 does a loop of town, running past the train station, south down Xinanhe Lu and west on Yuhuangding Xilu. Bus No 17 runs between the two beaches. Taxis start at Y5.

PÉNGLÁI 蓬莱
About 65km north-west of Yāntái is Pénglái and the coastal castle of **Pénglái Gé** (☎ 564 8106; admission Y55; open 7am-6.30pm daily), a place of the gods often referred to in Chinese mythology. China's ancient legend of the Eight Immortals Crossing the Sea originated here. Pénglái Gé is perched on a cliff top overlooking the sea and is about 1000 years old. Here you can discover a fascinating array of castles and temples, and enjoy wonderful views of fishing boat flotillas. Many of the temples, walls and pavilions are delightfully overgrown with ivy and creepers. It's popular with tour groups, so you need to be in the mood for crowds to enjoy a day here. The castle now has a cable car, laser-gun park and theatre. There is no entry after 5.50pm.

Besides the castle, Pénglái is famous for an **optical illusion** that the locals claim appears every few decades. The last full mirage seen from the castle was in July 2001 and lasted for 20 minutes. On June 17th

1988 this phenomenon occurred and lasted for more than five hours. Two islands appeared with roads, trees, buildings, people, bridges and vehicles and was captured on camera by Shandong Television. You can watch the video recording for Y3.

Péngxiáng Dàshà (☎ 565 6788, fax 564 6737, 135 Beiguan Lu) Doubles/triples Y340/360. If you decide to stay the night in Pénglái. this place is not far from the bus station and has spotless rooms.

Cheaper guesthouses line the road to the main gate of Pénglái Gé. They don't technically allow foreigners but if you arrive off-season you will probably find a bed.

Pénglái is easily visited as a day trip from Yāntái. The last bus returning to Yāntái leaves at 6.30pm.

WĒIHǍI 威海
☎ 0631 • pop 2,597,000

About 60km east of Yāntái is the booming port city of Wēihǎi, which was the site of China's most humiliating naval defeat. In 1895 the entire Qing navy, despite being armed with advanced European warships, was slaughtered by a smaller – and weaker – Japanese fleet.

The British had a concession here until 1930, though today little remains to remind you of its colonial heritage.

Today visitors are drawn to Wēihǎi for its golden coastline, Líugōng Dǎo and to catch the passenger ferry to Korea.

Information
The Bank of China is at 9 Qingdao Beilu, attached to the International Financial Hotel, and China Post is at 40 Xinwei Lu, opposite the Weihaiwei Mansions.

You'll find the CITS (☎ 581 8616) at 96 Guzhai Dong Lu on the 3rd floor. Take bus No 12 from the long-distance bus station. The PSB (☎ 521 3620) is at 111 Chongqing Jie.

Líugōng Dǎo 刘公岛
Líugōng Dǎo lies 5km off the coast in the Wēihǎi Gulf. The island was established as a stronghold during the Ming dynasty, to guard against Japanese pirates. Later the Qing government made Líugōng Dǎo their naval base and after their crushing defeat at the hands of the Japanese the island was occupied by Japanese troops for three years.

In 1898 the British wrestled control of the area and governed for 32 years. During this time they built schools, churches and even tea-houses, transforming the island into a summer resort for the British Navy. In 1948 Chiang Kaishek and his troops arrived, shortly followed by the Communists.

Today the island's main attraction is the **Museum of the 1894–1895 Sino-Japanese War** *(Jiǎwǔ Zhànzhēng Bówùguǎn; admission Y25; open 7am-5.30pm daily).* The museum is to your left as you exit the ferry terminal, housed in the old offices of the North Sea Fleet commanders. Displays include photographs and artefacts salvaged from warships. The hilly island also provides some ideal hiking trails.

Regular ferry services run to Líugōng Dǎo (Y25 return, 20 minutes) between 7am and 3.30pm from the passenger ferry terminal (☎ 523 1985) on Bingong Beilu. The last ferry returning to Wēihǎi leaves the island at 5.30pm. There is no accommodation on the island so keep an eye on the time.

Other Sights
Wēihǎi's **International Beach** draws large crowds for its long stretch of golden sand, comparably clean waters and large swimming area. There is a shallow swimming pool for children and a mini-amusement park. Showers and lockers are also available. Sleeping on the beach is an option with battered tents for hire for Y100 per night.

Places to Stay
Shāndōng Dàxué Liúxuéshēng Sùshè (Shandong University Foreign Students Dormitory; ☎ 568 8328, 180 Wenhua Xilu) Dorm beds Y25, doubles with/without air con Y160/120. This is the best option for a budget bed and is a short walk from the beach. The dorm rooms fill up quickly in the summer. Doors shut at 11pm.

Wēihǎi Dàfàndiàn (Weihai Hotel; ☎ 523 3888, fax 523 3422, 9 Dongping Jie) Singles/doubles/suites Y198/228/348. This hotel is located down a quiet alley and while the rooms are not generous in size, they are very clean

Yángguāng Dàshà (Sunshine Hotel; ☎ 520 8999, fax 522 7206, 88 Tongyi Lu) Doubles Y360-420. Huge rooms, some with sea views, and excellent service can be found here.

Places to Eat

There is a great variety of food on offer in Wēihǎi.

Tàipíngyáng Jiǎozi Wáng (☎ 520 6844, 1 Gongyuan Lu) Try this place for good dumplings, a Shāndōng speciality.

Kim's Mexican Chicken and Pizza (☎ 522 9234, 32-7 Xinwei Lu) Pizzas Y30-90. This is one of the more kitsch restaurants in town: eat fried chicken (Y50 for a whole chicken) while listening to the crooning of Korea's answer to Elvis. You'll find more traditional Korean restaurants along Guangming Lu.

Yángguāng Dàshà (see Places to Stay) Try the 2nd-floor restaurant for the all-you-can-eat seafood hotpot deal for Y48, drinks included.

Jīngyǎ Dàjiǔdiàn (☎ 532 9888, Haibin Zhonglu) This glittering seafood restaurant was opened by a man who once sold dumplings on the roadside. The decor is incredible and the seafood delicious.

Getting There & Away

Unless travelling to South Korea, it's best to get to and from Wēihǎi by bus. From the long-distance bus station there are connections to Yāntái every eight minutes (Y16, 1½ hours) between 5.45am and 6.30pm. There is one direct bus to Pénglái at 8am (Y24, two hours). Volvo buses make the trip to Jǐ'nán (Y139, 6½ hours) five times daily and to Qīngdǎo (Y68, three hours) at 8am and 9.30am. Slower buses leave for Qīngdǎo (Y42.5, 4½ hours) every 15 minutes. Buses depart for Běijīng (Y142, 19 hours) at 10am and 2pm.

The train station has poor connections. Trains to Jǐ'nán (Y152, 9½ hours) leave twice daily. A train for Běijīng (Y213, 16½ hours) leaves at 9.28pm.

There is a ferry service to Inch'ŏn in South Korea on Wednesday, Friday and Sunday at 4pm; the trip takes 16 hours. Tickets range from Y881 to Y1480 and can only be bought on the day of travel between 8am and 10am from the office opposite the passenger ferry terminal on Haibin Lu. Boats to Dàlián leave daily at 8.30am, 9.30am, 8pm and 9pm (Y82 to Y800, 7½ hours). Tickets should be bought from the International building adjacent to the passenger ferry terminal.

AROUND WĒIHǍI
Chéngshān Cape 成山头

Often referred to as 'China's Cape of Good Hope', Chéngshān Cape (*Chéngshān Tóu;* ☎ 783 6888; admission Y50) is located on the tip of the Jiaodong peninsula, the most eastern point in China.

The first emperor of China, Qin Shihuang, reportedly visited the cape twice and was so overcome by its beauty and power he was convinced that the area held the secret to eternal life. The only temple in China dedicated to Qin Shihuang can be found here.

The dramatic rock formations are stunning and visitors can scramble along the outcroppings by the sea. If you want to stay the night and see the sun rise, there is a hotel within the main gate.

Chéngshān Tóu Jiēdài Chù (Chengshan Cape Hostel) Beds in 4-bed dorms Y48, doubles Y188. This is the large tiled building towards the cliff edge. The rooms are old but very clean and the doubles have sea views. Check your room first as some of them leak.

Getting There & Away

Minibuses run to Chéngshān Cape (Y10, 1½ hours) every 30 minutes from 6.15am and 5.10pm from the bus station adjacent to the long-distance bus station in Wēihǎi. Returning to Wēihǎi, buses depart from Chéngshān Cape roughly every hour from outside the main gate. The last bus leaves at 4.30pm. A taxi will do the round trip for Y120 to Y150.

Jiāngsū 江苏

Capital: Nánjīng
Population: 78.1 million
Area: 102,600 sq km

Blessed with China's most productive land, Jiāngsū is symbolic of agricultural abundance and has long been known as 'the land of fish and rice' – the original Chinese character for the province contained these two pictographs. The southern part of Jiāngsū lies within the Cháng Jiāng (Yangzi River) Basin, a tapestry landscape of greens, yellows and blues contrasting with whitewashed farmhouses. Together with the northern part of Zhèjiāng this region is known as Jiāngnán, a cultural and geographical entity on the southern side of Cháng Jiāng. Woven into this countryside is a dense concentration of towns and cities with one of the highest levels of industrial output in China.

As far back as the 16th century, the towns on the Grand Canal (Dà Yùnhé) set up industrial bases for silk production and grain storage, and are still ahead of the rest of the nation. While heavy industry is based in Nánjīng and Wúxī, the other towns concentrate more on light industry, machinery and textiles. They're major producers of electronics and computer components, and haven't been blotted out by the scourges of coal mining or steelworks.

Today, southern Jiāngsū is increasingly being drawn into the ever-expanding economy of nearby Shànghǎi, aided in part by an expressway between Nánjīng and Shànghǎi. It's one of the most rapidly developing provinces in China, evident in the fast rate of construction in the major cities.

The stretch from Nánjīng down to Hángzhōu in Zhèjiāng is heavily touristed. North of Cháng Jiāng is a complete contrast, with comparatively snail-paced development that has left it lagging behind the rest of the province. In the north the major port is situated at Liányúngǎng and there's a large coal works in Xúzhōu.

Jiāngsū is hot and humid in summer, yet has overcoat temperatures in winter (when visibility can drop to zero). Rain or drizzle can be prevalent in winter, but it's a gentle rain, and adds a misty, soft touch to the

Highlights

- Nánjīng's Zǐjīn Shān (Purple Mountain), with its wealth of historical sights
- Sūzhōu, a city of canals and beautiful traditional gardens, despite the ravages of redevelopment
- Zhōuzhuāng, a beautifully preserved riverside village known as the new Venice of China and recognised as an International Heritage Site in 1998

land. The natural colours can be brilliant in spring. Heavy rains fall in spring and summer, but autumn is fairly dry.

NÁNJĪNG 南京
☎ 025 • pop 5,320,200

Nánjīng is one of China's more attractive major cities. It sports a long historical heritage and has twice served briefly as the nation's capital, first in the early years of the Ming dynasty (AD 1368–1644) and second as the capital of the Republic of China in the early years of the 20th century. Most of Nánjīng's major attractions are reminders of the city's former glory under the Ming.

Like many other major Chinese cities, Nánjīng is developing fast; vast construction projects are visible everywhere. Nánjīng is home to several colleges and

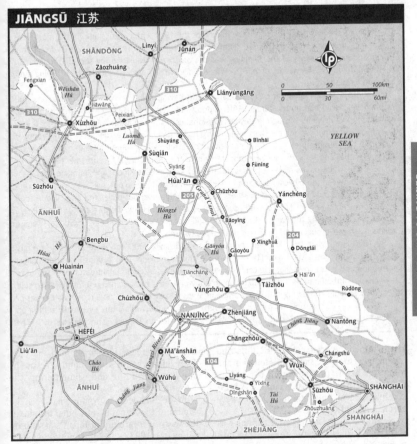

JIĀNGSŪ 江苏

universities and a large foreign student population. There are many international-style restaurants, a lively nightlife and access to just about any amenity from around the world.

Just east of the city is Zǐjīn Shān (Purple Mountain), where it's possible to spend a pleasant day hiking around the many historical sites.

History

The Nánjīng area has been inhabited for about 5000 years, and a number of prehistoric sites have been discovered in or around the city. Recorded history, however, begins in the Warring States period (453–221 BC), when Nánjīng emerged as a strategic object of conflict. The arrival of a victorious Qin dynasty (221–207 BC) put an end to this, allowing Nánjīng to prosper as a major administrative centre.

The city's fortunes took a turn for the worse in the 6th century when it was successively rocked by floods, fires, peasant rebellions and military conquest. With the advent of the Sui dynasty (AD 589–618) and the establishment of Xī'ān as imperial capital, Nánjīng was razed and its historical heritage reduced to ruins. Although it enjoyed a period of prosperity under the long-lived Tang dynasty, it gradually slipped into obscurity.

Then in 1356, a peasant rebellion led by Zhu Yuanzhang against the Mongol Yuan dynasty (AD 1271–1368) was successful. The peasants captured Nánjīng and 12 years

The Heavenly Kingdom of the Taiping

The Taiping Rebellion that occurred in the middle of the 19th century ranks among the most frenzied and calamitous periods in Chinese history. What made it more remarkable was its creed: that Hong Xiuquan, the leader of the Taipings, was the brother of Jesus and the son of God. He had been sent down to exterminate 'demons' – who (coincidentally) were personified by the Qing dynasty and its supporters.

Born into a Hakka family in eastern Guǎngxī and having failed the official examinations that would have placed him on the career ladder among the Qing elite, Hong Xiuquan first came into contact with Christianity through Protestant missionaries in Canton in the mid-1830s. After failing the official examinations for the third time, Hong had a dream of a bearded man and a younger man who he later interpreted, in a flash of realisation after reading some Christian tracts, as being God the Father and Jesus, his son. He repeatedly read the character for his surname 'Hong' in the Chinese translation of the bible he possessed; the character means 'flood' and he made strong associations between the biblical flood and his mission on earth to wipe out evil.

Collecting around him a flock of believers attracted by his zeal, self-belief and drive, Hong soon had a formidable army of faithful who sought to establish the Heavenly Kingdom of Great Peace on Earth, overthrowing the Qing in the process. God was the one true god and traditional Chinese beliefs (such as Confucianism) were heretical and wayward.

By 1850 Hong Xiuquan's followers numbered more than 20,000 and were a capable military force, regimented by a strict morality that forbade opium smoking, took serious measures against corruption and established separate camps to divide the sexes. A communal treasury was set up to take charge of the finances of the Taiping community and legal and agrarian reforms followed suit.

Led by capable and daring officers, the Taiping army dispatched itself on a remarkable series of conquests that took it through Húnán, Húběi and Ānhuī, eventually setting up the Taiping capital in Nánjīng, which fell to the rebels in March 1853. The

later claimed the Yuan capital, Běijīng. Zhu Yuanzhang took the name of Hongwu and took over as the first emperor of the Ming dynasty, with Nánjīng as its capital. A massive palace was built and huge walls were erected around the city.

Nánjīng's glory as imperial capital was short-lived. In 1420, the third Ming emperor, Yongle, moved the capital back to Běijīng. From on, Nánjīng's fortunes variously rose and declined as a regional centre, but it was not until the 19th and 20th centuries that the city again entered the centre stage of Chinese history.

In the 19th century, the Opium Wars brought the British to Nánjīng and it was here that the first of the 'unequal treaties' were signed, opening several Chinese ports to foreign trade, forcing China to pay a huge war indemnity, and officially ceding the island of Hong Kong to Britain. Just a few years later, Nánjīng became the Taiping capital during the Taiping Rebellion (1851–64), which succeeded in taking over most of southern China. In 1864, the combined forces of the Qing army, British army and various European

and US mercenaries surrounded the city. They laid siege for seven months, before finally capturing it and slaughtering the Taiping defenders.

In the 20th century, Nánjīng has been the capital of the Republic of China, the site of the worst war atrocity in Japan's assault on China (the 1937 'Rape of Nanjing' in which as many as 300,000 people may have died), and the Kuomintang capital from 1928 to 1937 and 1945 to 1949 before the Communists 'liberated' the city and made China their own.

Orientation

Nánjīng lies entirely on the southern bank of Cháng Jiāng, bounded in the east by Zǐjīn Shān. The centre of town is a roundabout called Xīnjiēkǒu, which has a bronze statue of Sun Yatsen, giving the street a somewhat patrician air rarely felt in cities on the Chinese mainland. This is where some of the hotels, including Jīnlíng Fàndiàn, and most tourist facilities are located. Nánjīng train station and the main long-distance bus station are in the far north of the city.

The Heavenly Kingdom of the Taiping

Manchu population of Nánjīng was slaughtered in affirmation of Hong's plan to rid China, and the world, of demons.

For 11 years the Taiping held sway over their conquered domain, with Hong ruling over all as the Heavenly King. Hong further regimented the rules governing the Taiping faithful, creating a society ordered by spartan and inflexible decrees all intent on eliminating inequality. However, the forces that were to destroy the Heavenly Kingdom soon emerged in a power struggle among the leadership of the Taiping. Eventually this resulted in the murder of those in positions of great influence, along with their supporters. Hong reasserted his authority, but in doing so eliminated his most useful advisers.

The Taiping's failure to take Peking (Běijīng) and Shànghǎi was partly because the foreign powers (suspicious of Hong's heretical strain of Christianity) failed to respond to Hong's faith that they would not support the Qing. The Taiping's economic strategies similarly failed, and the strict codes of conduct left many bitter and complaining; Hong also failed to align himself and his cause with other contemporaneous anti-Qing rebellions. All of these factors led to an erosion of the power and influence of the Taiping.

Qing soldiers, led by Zeng Guofan, eventually retook Nánjīng in 1864, soon after Hong Xiuquan's death. Zeng Guofan reported to the emperor that none of the 100,000 rebels in Nánjīng surrendered, but instead took their own lives.

The fanaticism of the Taiping was incredible, and despite its strongly anti-Manchu character, the event clearly questions the theory that Christianity has no place in China. Even though Hong arrogated upon himself the heretical (to Protestants and Catholics) title of Son of God, the Taiping were responsible for, among other things, a vast translation and publishing program of Christian scriptures and writings, and it was their aim to spread these ultimately to the four corners of the earth.

The historical sights, including the Sun Yatsen Mausoleum, Línggǔ Sì and the tomb of the first Ming emperor Hongwu, are on Zǐjīn Shān.

The city has experienced long periods of prosperity, evident in the numerous buildings that successive rulers built – their tombs, steles, pagodas, temples and niches lay scattered throughout the city. If you can get hold of a copy, *In Search of Old Nanking* by Barry Till & Paula Swart (Joint Publishing Company, Hong Kong, 1982) will give you a thorough rundown. Unfortunately, much has been destroyed or allowed to crumble into ruins.

Maps Several different versions of local maps are available from the Foreign Language Bookshop, as well as newspaper kiosks and street hawkers around Nánjīng. Many of these maps contain local bus routes. Some of the upscale hotels give out free English-language maps of the city.

Information

Money The main branch of the Bank of China is at 29 Hongwu Lu, just south of Zhongshan Donglu. You can also change money at many top-end hotels.

Post & Communications The main post office is at the corner of Beijing Donglu and Zhongyang Lu. Upmarket tourist hotels also offer postal services. The main telephone office is on the north-east corner of the Drum Tower roundabout and is open daily from 8am to 6pm.

China Telecom has an Internet cafe on the 2nd floor at 1 Yunnan Lu. It charges Y4 per hour and is open from 10am to 10pm daily. The Nanjing University Foreign Students Dormitory also runs an Internet bar on the ground floor. It's open from 9am to 1.30am daily and costs Y2 per hour.

Travel Agencies China International Travel Service (CITS; Zhōngguó Guójì Lǚxíngshè; ☎ 342 3070, fax 342 1960) at 202/1 Zhongshan Beilu, can arrange air and train tickets.

PSB The Public Security Bureau (PSB; Gōngānjú; ☎ 442 0004) is on a small lane called Sanyuan Xiang down a maze of streets west off Zhongshan Nanlu.

NÁNJĪNG 南京

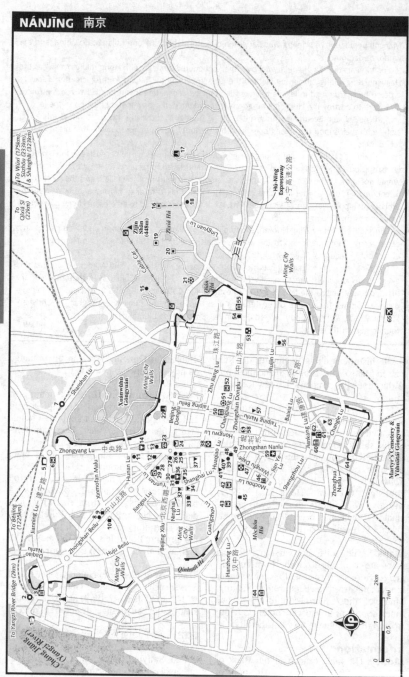

NÁNJĪNG

PLACES TO STAY

9 Hóngqiáo Fàndiàn
虹桥饭店

10 Nánjīng Fàndiàn
南京饭店

12 Jiāngsū Dàjiǔdiàn
江苏大酒店

28 Ramada Plaza
华美达怡华酒店

30 Jīnglì Jiǔdiàn
晶丽酒店

31 Nanjing University
Foreign Students
Dormitory
南京大学外国
留学生宿舍

33 Nanjing Normal
University Nanshan
Hotel
南京师范大学南山宾馆

45 Sheraton Nanjing
Kingsley Hotel
金丝利大酒店

48 Jīnglíng Fàndiàn
金陵饭店

54 Hilton Hotel
希尔顿饭店

62 Zhuàngyuánlóu Jiǔdiàn
状元楼酒店

PLACES TO EAT

32 Kèjiāfú Kǎodiàn
可家福烤店

34 Skyways Bakery & Deli
云中食品店

35 Jack's Place; Italian
Pizza Express
杰克地方；
意大利比萨餐厅

37 Wúzhōu Jiǔjiā
梧州酒家

40 City Garden
Coffee Shop
城市花园咖啡店

41 Henry's Home Cafe
亨利之家

57 Sichuān Jiǔjiā
四川酒家

63 Wǎnqíng Lóu
晚晴楼

MUSEUMS & GALLERIES

3 Nanjing Treaty History
Museum
南京条约史料陈列馆

50 Jiangsu Art Gallery
江苏美术馆

55 Nanjing Museum
南京博物馆

60 Taiping Heavenly
Kingdom History
Museum
太平天国历史博物馆

TEMPLES & TOWERS

13 Bell Tower
钟楼

17 Línggǔ Sì
灵谷寺

22 Jīmíng Sì; Bǎiwèizhāi
鸡鸣寺

27 Drum Tower;
Castle Bar
鼓楼；古堡神曲

61 Fūzǐ Miào; Imperial
Examinations History
Museum
夫子庙；
江南共院历史陈列馆

TRANSPORT

1 No 6 Dock
六号码头

2 Nanjing West Train
Station
南京西站

6 Zhōngyāng Mén Long-
Distance Bus Station
中央门长途汽车站

7 Nanjing Train Station
南京火车站

25 Advance Booking
Office (Train & Boat
Tickets)
火车船售票处

26 Huaxia Air Ticket
Service
华夏旅行社

42 Minibus to Airport
小公共汽车往机场

43 Hanzhong Lu Bus
Station
汉中路汽车站

49 Xīnjiēkǒu
Roundabout
新街口

52 Hanfu Jie Bus Station
汉府街汽车站

56 CAAC
中国民航

65 Nanjing Airport
南京机场

OTHER

4 Monument to the
Crossing of the
Yangzi River
渡江纪念碑

5 Centre Gate
中央门

8 CITS
中国国际旅行社

11 Foreign Language
Bookshop
外文书店

14 Scarlet Bar
乱世佳人酒吧

15 Zǐjīnshān Observatory
紫金山天文台

16 Sun Yatsen Mausoleum
中山陵

18 Sun Yatsen Mausoleum
Music Terrace
中山陵音乐台

19 Tomb of Hongwu
Scenic Area
明孝陵风景区

20 Tomb of Hongwu
明孝陵

21 Botanical Gardens
植物园

23 Telephone Office
中国电信

24 Main Post Office
邮电局

29 China Telecom
Internet Cafe
中国电信网吧

36 Blowing in the
Wind Bar
答案酒吧

38 Zhongshan
Department Store
中山大厦

39 World Trade Centre;
Dragonair Office
世贸中心

44 Memorial Hall of the
Nanjing Massacre
大屠杀纪念馆

46 Heaven Dynasty
Palace; Jiangsu
Kunju Theatre
朝天宫；江苏省昆剧院

47 GE International
Shopping Centre
金鹰国际购物中心

51 Balmy Garden
煦园

53 Ming Palace Ruins
明故宫

58 Bank of China
中国银行

59 PSB
公安局

64 Zhōnghuá Gate
中华门

Ming City Wall

Nánjīng enjoyed its golden years under the Ming dynasty and there are numerous remnants of the period. One of the most impressive is the Ming city wall measuring over 33km – the longest city wall ever built in the world. About two-thirds of it still stands. It was built between 1366 and 1386, by more than 200,000 labourers.

The layout is irregular, an exception to the usual square walls of these times, as much of it is built on the foundations of earlier walls, which took advantage of strategic hills. Averaging 12m high and 7m wide at the top, the wall was built of bricks supplied from five Chinese provinces. Each brick had stamped on it the place it came from, the overseer's name and rank, the brick-maker's

Broken as Jade

'How could historical facts written in blood be concealed by lies written in ink?' questioned a Chinese commentator in 1982. His article continued:

Your 'samurai' forebears used innocent Chinese to test bacteriological warfare, used them as living targets. They dismembered and chopped up Chinese captives who were tied to trees. You forced Chinese to dig holes and bury themselves alive. You adopted such savage means as the 'iron maiden', pulling out fingernails, branding, belly cutting, electric grinding and flesh eating to persecute Chinese compatriots.

The article was published as part of a Chinese protest against the approval and publication of Japanese school textbooks that severely downplayed Japan's brutality during its invasion into China between 1937 and 1945, in particular, its attack on Nánjīng. As part of the Chinese protest, a media campaign of photos and reports was launched. This campaign rekindled fear and hostility towards the Japanese both in those Chinese who had survived the invasion as well as in younger generations.

In 1937, with the Chinese army comparatively weak and under-funded and the Japanese army on the horizon, the invasion into and occupation of Nánjīng by Japan appeared imminent. As it packed up and fled, the Chinese government encouraged the people of Nánjīng to stay, saying: 'All those who have blood and breath in them must feel that they wish to be broken as jade rather than remain whole as tile.' To reinforce this statement, the gates to the city were locked, trapping over half a million citizens inside. Nevertheless, thousands of civilians attempted to follow the retreating government by escaping through Xiaguan Gate, the only gate in the city wall that remained unlocked. Leading up to the gate was a 70-foot tunnel inside of which reigned panic and mayhem. In the resulting chaos and collisions, thousands of people were suffocated, burned or trampled to death.

What followed in Nánjīng was six weeks of continuous, unfathomable victimisation of civilians to an extent that had yet to be witnessed in modern warfare. During Japan's occupation of Nánjīng, between 300,000 and 400,000 Chinese civilians were killed, either in group massacres or individual murders. Within the first month, at least 20,000 women between the ages of 11 and 76 were brutally raped. Women who attempted to refuse or children who interfered were often bayoneted or shot. It has been reported by those involved that the atrocities committed in Nánjīng were condoned and encouraged by the Japanese officers in command as acceptable and expected military procedure.

The Japanese, however, underestimated the courage and strength of the Chinese people. Instead of breaking the people's will, the invasion only served to fuel a sense of identity and determination. Those who did not die – broken as jade – survived to fight back.

Given the brutality of Japan's invasion into Nánjīng, it is not at all surprising that the Chinese protested it being airbrushed from Japanese textbooks. Equally disturbing as Japan's misrepresentation of the brutality is the rest of the world's apparent aversion to it. The Rape of Nanjing is conspicuously absent from many world history books. Despite this, it is hoped that a growing awareness of the horrific event will help to prevent such atrocities from occurring again. As the ancient Chinese proverb says, 'Past experience, if not forgotten, is a guide for the future' ('Qián shì bù wàng hòu shì zhī shī').

name and sometimes the date. This was to ensure that the bricks were well made; if they broke they had to be replaced.

Ming City Gates

Some of the original 13 Ming city gates remain, including the **Centre Gate** (*Zhōngyāng Mén*) in the north and **Zhōnghuá Gate** (*Zhōnghuá Mén; admission Y8*) in the south. The city gates were heavily fortified; Zhōnghuá Gate has four rows of gates, making it almost impregnable, and could house a garrison of 3000 soldiers in vaults in the front gate building. Today some of these vaults are used as souvenir shops.

Ming Palace Ruins 明故宫
Míng Gùgōng

Built by Hongwu, the Ming Palace Ruins (*Zhongshan Donglu; admission Y1; open 6.30am-11pm daily*) is said to have been a magnificent structure after which the Imperial Palace in Běijīng was modelled. Virtually all that remains of it are five marble bridges lying side by side, known as the **Five Dragon Bridges** (*Wǔlóng Qiáo*), the old ruined Wú Gate (*Wú Mén*) and the enormous column bases of the palace buildings.

The palace suffered two major fires in its first century and was allowed to fall into ruins after the Ming court moved to Běijīng. It was later looted by the Manchus and then, during the Taiping Rebellion, bombardments by Qing and Western troops finished it off.

You can reach the Ming Palace Ruins by catching bus No Y1 from the Nanjing train station or Zhongyang Lu.

Early Remains

Nánjīng has been inhabited since prehistoric times. Remains of a prehistoric culture have been found at the site of today's Drum Tower in the centre of the city and in surrounding areas. About 200 sites of small clan communities, mainly represented by pottery and bronze artefacts dating back to the late Shang and Zhou dynasties, were found on both sides of Cháng Jiāng.

In AD 212, towards the end of the Eastern Han period, the military commander in charge of the Nánjīng region built a citadel on Qīngjīng Shān in the west of Nánjīng. At that time the mountain was

---

Words & Pictures

Měishùguǎn: gallery

美术馆

Měi, meaning beautiful or admirable, is itself an amalgamation of the characters for big and sheep. While not perhaps in line with modern Western thinking, in traditional Chinese thinking a grown-up who has learned the gentle manner of a sheep is regarded as admirable. Another interpretation is the idea that having lots of sheep to eat means survival, which is a beautiful thing. Take your pick.

The traditional form for *shù* (skills, art) is, 術 from which only the middle part remains in the simplified character. If we take out 木 from the traditional form, it becomes, 行 which is like a crossroads. As anyone visiting Běijīng or Shànghǎi will testify, the ability to cross the road in heavy traffic is a type of skill, or to some extent an art form!

---

referred to as Shítou Shān (Stone Mountain) and so the citadel became known as the Stone City (Shítou Dūshì). The wall measured over 10km in circumference. Today, some of the red sandstone foundations are still visible.

Drum Tower 鼓楼
Gǔ Lóu

Built in 1382, the Drum Tower (☎ *442 1495, 6 Zhongyang Lu; admission free; open 8am-midnight daily*) lies roughly in the centre of Nánjīng, on a roundabout. Drums were usually beaten to give directions for the change of the night watches and, in rare instances, to warn the populace of impending danger. Only one large drum remains today.

Bell Tower 钟楼
Zhōng Lóu

North-east of the Drum Tower, the Bell Tower (*Beijing Donglu; admission free; open 8.30am-5.30pm daily*) houses an enormous bell, cast in 1388 and originally situated in a pavilion on the western side of the Drum Tower. The present tower dates from 1889 and is a small two-storey pavilion with a pointed roof and upturned eaves. A garden and teahouse surround the tower and remain open late into the evening.

Heaven Dynasty Palace 朝天宫
Cháotiān Gōng

This palace (☎ 446 6460; admission Y15; open 8am-5pm daily), off Mochou Lu, was originally established in the Ming dynasty as a school for educating aristocratic children in court etiquette. Most of today's buildings, including the centrepiece of the palace, a Confucian temple, date from 1866 when the whole complex was rebuilt. Today the buildings are used for a range of endeavours, including an artisan market.

To reach the palace, take bus No 4 from the Xīnjiēkǒu roundabout and get off two stops to the west.

Taiping Heavenly Kingdom History Museum 太平天国历史博物馆
Tàipíng Tiānguó Lìshǐ Bówùguǎn

Hong Xiuquan, the leader of the Taipings, had a palace built in Nánjīng, but the building was completely destroyed when Nánjīng was taken in 1864.

The museum (☎ 220 1849, 128 Zhanyuan Lu; admission Y10; open 8am-6pm daily) was originally a garden complex, built in the Ming dynasty, which housed some of the Taiping officials before their downfall. There are displays of maps showing the northward progress of the Taiping army from Guǎngdōng, Hong Xiuquan's seals, Taiping coins, weapons, and texts that describe the Taiping laws on agrarian reform, social law and cultural policy. Other texts describe divisions in the Taiping leadership, the attacks by the Manchus and foreigners, and the fall of Nánjīng in 1864. Most of the original literature is kept in Běijīng.

Bus No Y2 goes to the museum from the Ming Palace Ruins or Taiping Nanlu.

Nanjing Museum 南京博物馆
Nánjīng Bówùguǎn

Just inside the eastern city walls, this museum (☎ 480 0421, 321 Zhongshan Donglu; admission Y20; open 9am-5.30pm daily) houses an array of artefacts from Neolithic times right through to the Communist period. The main building was constructed in 1933 in the style of an ancient temple with yellow-glazed tiles, red-lacquered gates and columns. A brand-new complex, similar in design to the first, recently opened.

The museum houses an interesting exhibit of a burial suit made of small rectangles of jade sewn together with silver thread, dating from the Eastern Han dynasty (AD 25–220) and excavated from a tomb discovered in the city of Xúzhōu in northern Jiāngsū. Other exhibits include bricks with the inscriptions of their makers and overseers from the Ming city wall, drawings of old Nánjīng, an early Qing mural of Sūzhōu and relics from the Taiping Rebellion.

Nanjing Treaty History Museum 南京条约史料陈列馆
Nánjīng Tiáoyuē Shǐliào Chénlièguǎn

This museum (☎ 880 0255, 116 Chao Yue Lou; admission Y4; open 8.30am-5pm daily) houses a small collection of photographs, maps and newspaper clippings (no English captions) related to the Nánjīng Treaties. It's in Jìnghǎi Sì near the west train station, off Rehe Lu. To get there catch bus No 16 from Zhongshan Lu.

Memorial Hall of the Nanjing Massacre 大屠杀纪念馆
Nánjīng Dàtúshā Jìniànguǎn

The exhibits at this museum (☎ 661 2230, 418 Shuiximen Dajie; admission Y10; open 8am-5.30pm daily) document the atrocities committed by Japanese soldiers against the civilian population during the occupation of Nánjīng in 1937 (see the boxed text 'Broken as Jade'). They include pictures of actual executions – many taken by Japanese army photographers – and a gruesome viewing hall built over a mass grave of massacre victims. Captions are in English, Japanese and Chinese but the photographs, skeletons and displays tell their own haunting stories without words.

The exhibits conclude on a more optimistic note, with a final room dedicated to the post-1945 Sino-Japanese reconciliation. It's in the city's south-western suburbs on bus No Y4 from Zhōnghuá Gate or the west train station.

Monument to the Crossing of the Yangzi River 渡江纪念碑
Dùjiāng Jìniànbēi

In the north-west of the city on Zhongshan Beilu, this monument, erected in April 1979 commemorates the crossing of the river on 23 April 1949 and the capture of Nánjīng from the Kuomintang by the Communist army. The characters on the monument are in the calligraphy of Deng Xiaoping. To get there catch bus No 31 from Taiping Lu.

Yangzi River Bridge 南京长江大桥
Nánjīng Cháng Jiāng Dàqiáo

One of the great achievements of the Communists, and one of which they are justifiably proud, is the Yangzi River Bridge at Nánjīng. Opened on 23 December 1968, it's one of the longest bridges in China – a double-decker with a 4500m-long road on top and a train line below. There are some wonderful socialist realist sculptures on the approaches.

Apparently the bridge was designed and built entirely by the Chinese after the Russians marched out and took the designs with them in 1960. Given the immensity of the construction it's an impressive engineering feat, before which there was no direct rail link between Běijīng and Shànghǎi. Probably the easiest way to get up on the bridge is to go through the Dàqiáo Gōngyuán (Bridge Park; ☎ 582 2455; admission Y9; open 7.30am-6.30pm daily). Catch bus No 67 from Jiangsu Lu, north-west of the Drum Tower, to its terminus opposite the park.

Fūzǐ Miào 夫子庙
Confucian Temple

This ancient Confucian temple (☎ 662 8639, Gongyuan Jie; admission Y12; open 8am-9pm daily) is located in the south of the city in a pedestrian zone. This was a centre of Confucian study for more than 1500 years. Fūzǐ Miào has been damaged and rebuilt repeatedly; what you see here today are newly restored late Qing dynasty structures or wholly new buildings reconstructed in traditional style. The main temple is behind the small square in front of the canal.

Across from the temple complex to the east is the Imperial Examinations History Museum (Jiāngnán Gòngyuàn Lìshǐ Chénlièguǎn; ☎ 662 6556, 1 Jinling Lu; admission Y6; open 8am-6pm daily). This is a recent reconstruction of the building where scholars once spent months – or years – in tiny cells studying Confucian classics in preparation for civil service examinations.

Today, the area surrounding Fūzǐ Miào has become Nánjīng's main amusement quarter and is a particularly lively and crowded place on weekends and public holidays with restaurants and rows upon rows of souvenir shops. The whole area is lit up at night, adding to the kitsch ambience.

Catch bus No 1 from Xīnjiēkǒu and get off at the last stop.

Balmy Garden 煦园
Xù Yuán

After the Taiping took over Nánjīng, they built the Mansion of the Heavenly King (Tiānwáng Fǔ) on the foundations of a former Ming dynasty palace. This magnificent place did not survive the fall of the Taipings but there is a reconstruction and a classical Ming garden, now known as the Balmy Garden (Zǒngtǒng Fǔ; ☎ 664 1131, 292 Changjiang Lu; admission Y20; open 8am-5.30pm daily). Other buildings on the site were used briefly as presidential offices (zǒngtǒng fǔ) by Sun Yatsen's government in 1912 and by the Kuomintang from 1927 to 1949.

Jiangsu Art Gallery 江苏美术馆
Jiāngsū Měishùguǎn

This gallery (☎ 664 1962, 266 Changjiang Lu; admission Y5; open 8am-11.30am & 2pm-5pm daily), displays works of local painters in frequently changing exhibitions.

Martyr's Cemetery 烈士墓地
Lièshì Mùdì

This pleasant park (Yǔhūa Tái; ☎ 241 1523, Yuhuatai Lu; admission Y10; open 7am-10pm daily) is in the south of the city. Once the Kuomintang's execution grounds, the Communists turned it into a garden dedicated to revolutionaries who lost their lives here. Along with a large monument, there's an English-captioned museum (open 8am-5.30pm daily) with a history of the period before 1949 and biographies of revolutionaries.

Zǐjīn Shān 紫金山
Purple Mountain

Most of Nánjīng's historical sights are scattered over the southern slopes of this forested hill at the city's eastern fringe. A half-hour cable car ride (one way/return Y25/40) goes to the top of the 400m hill for a panoramic, if somewhat hazy, view of Nánjīng, or you can walk up the stone path that runs beneath the cable cars. An **observatory** (admission Y10; open daylight hours) is located 350m up the hill, with bronze astronomical instruments from the Ming dynasty on display.

Bus No 9 or Y1 goes from the city centre to the Sun Yatsen Mausoleum at the centre of Zǐjīn Shān. From here, bus No 20 runs between all of the sites on the hill, operating from 8am to 5pm and costing Y2 per ride.

Sun Yatsen Mausoleum 中山陵
Zhōngshān Líng

As the crowds of tourists indicate, for many Chinese, a visit to the Sun Yatsen Mausoleum (☎ 444 6111 ext 2175; admission Y25; open 6.30am-6.30pm daily) is something of a pilgrimage. Sun is recognised by the Communists and Kuomintang alike as the father of modern China. He died in Běijīng in 1925, leaving behind an unstable Chinese republic. He had wished to be buried in Nánjīng, no doubt with greater simplicity than the Ming-style tomb that his successors built for him. Nevertheless, less than a year after his death, construction of this immense mausoleum began.

The tomb itself lies at the top of an enormous stone stairway, 323m long and 70m wide. At the start of the path stands a stone gateway built of Fújiàn marble, with a roof of blue-glazed tiles. The blue and white of the mausoleum symbolise the white sun on the blue background of the Kuomintang flag.

The crypt is at the top of the steps at the rear of the memorial chamber. A tablet hanging across the threshold is inscribed with the 'Three Principles of the People', as formulated by Dr Sun: nationalism, democracy and people's livelihood. Inside is a seated statue of Dr Sun. The walls are carved with the complete text of the *Outline of Principles for the Establishment of the Nation* put forward by the Nationalist government. A prostrate marble statue of Sun seals his coffin.

Tomb of Hongwu 明孝陵
Míng Xiàolíng

The tomb of Hongwu (☎ 444 6111 ext 2024; admission Y15; open 6.30am-6.30pm daily) lies on the southern slope of Zǐjīn

Shān. Construction began in 1381 and was finished in 1383; the emperor died at the age of 71 in 1398.

The first section of the avenue leading up to the mausoleum is lined with stone statues of lions, camels, elephants and horses. There's also a mythical animal called a *xièzhì*, which has a mane and a single horn on its head; and a *qílín*, which has a scaly body, a cow's tail, deer's hooves and one horn.

As you enter the first courtyard, a paved pathway leads to a pavilion housing several steles. The next gate leads to a large courtyard with **Línghún Tǎ** (*Altar Tower or Soul Tower*) – a mammoth rectangular stone structure. Behind the tower is a wall, 350m in diameter, surrounding a huge earth mound. Beneath this mound is the tomb vault of Hongwu, which has not been excavated.

The area surrounding the tomb is the **Tomb of Hongwu Scenic Area** (*Míng Xiàolíng Fēngjǐngqū*). A tree-lined, stone pathway winds around pavilions and picnic grounds and ends at **Zǐxiá Hú** (*Purple Clouds Lake*), a small lake that you can swim in – a very relaxing way to spend a hot afternoon.

Línggǔ Sì 灵谷寺

This large temple complex (☎ 444 6111 ext 2060; admission Y10; open 6.30am-6.30pm daily) has one of the most interesting buildings in Nánjīng – the **Beamless Hall** (*Wúliáng Diàn*). In 1381, when Hongwu was building his tomb, he had a temple on the site torn down and rebuilt a few kilometres to the east. Of this temple only the Beamless Hall (so called because it is built entirely of bricks and contains no beam supports) remains. The structure has an interesting vaulted ceiling and a large stone platform where Buddhist statues once sat. In the 1930s the hall was turned into a memorial to those who died in the 1926–28 revolution. One of the inscriptions on the inside wall is the old Kuomintang national anthem.

A road runs on both sides of the Hall and up two flights of steps to the **Sōngfēng Gé** (*Pine Wind Pavilion*), originally dedicated to the Goddess of Mmercy as part of Línggǔ Sì. Today it houses a small shop and teahouse.

Línggǔ Sì itself and the memorial hall to Xuan Zang are close by; after you pass through the Beamless Hall, turn right and follow the pathway. Xuan Zang was the Buddhist monk who travelled to India and brought back the Buddhist scriptures. Inside the memorial hall is a 13-storey wooden pagoda model that contains part of his skull, a sacrificial table and a portrait of the monk.

Nearby is **Línggǔ Tǎ**. This nine-storey, 60m-high, octagonal pagoda was built in the 1930s under the direction of a US architect as a memorial to Kuomintang members who died in the 1926–28 revolution.

Botanic Gardens 植物园
Zhíwù Yuán

These gardens (☎ 443 2075; admission Y10; open 8.30am-4.30pm daily) were established in 1929. Covering over 186 hectares, more than 3000 plant species including roses, medicinal plants and bonsai gardens are on display.

Places to Stay – Budget
Nanjing University Foreign Students Dormitory (Nánjīng Dàxué Wàiguó Liúxuéshēng Sùshè; ☎ 359 3589, fax 359 4699, 20 Jinyin Jie) Doubles with/without bath Y140/100. This 20-storey white-tiled building has the best budget accommodation in Nánjīng. Rooms are clean and secure. Take bus No 13 from the train station or the Zhōngyāng Mén long-distance bus station and get off at the intersection of Beijing Xilu and Shanghai Lu.

Nanjing Normal University Nanshan Hotel (Nánjīng Shīfàn Dàxué Nánshān Bīnguǎn; ☎ 371 6440 ext 6060, fax 373 8174, 122 Ninghai Lu) Singles Y100, doubles Y100-170. Despite its pleasant location in the middle of the campus, the cheaper rooms here can be damp and grotty. Make sure you check the room before taking one. To get there from the Nanjing University dorm, walk south along Shanghai Lu. Turn right into the second or third alleyway, then take the first road left to the main gate of Nanjing Normal University (next to a McDonald's). The dormitory is inside the campus compound, to the left up the hill.

Places to Stay – Mid-Range
Most Nánjīng accommodation is middle- to top-end in price.

Jīnglì Jiǔdiàn (☎ 331 0818, fax 663 6636, 7 Beijing Xilu) Singles/doubles Y420/545. Located on a pretty, tree-lined street close to Nanjing University this place offers all the amenities of a luxury hotel. Discounts of 20% to 30% are available.

Jiāngsū Dàjiǔdiàn (☎ 332 0888, fax 330 3308, 28 Zhongshan Beilu) Doubles Y420-520. This place has the amenities of an up-market hotel, but is a little cheaper with 35% discounts available.

Hóngqiáo Fàndiàn (☎ 340 0888, fax 342 0756, 202 Zhongshan Beilu) Doubles Y480-580. This hotel caters largely to tour groups and is beside the garish Orgies nightclub. Doubles can be discounted to Y298.

Places to Stay – Top End
Nánjīng Fàndiàn (☎ 341 1888, fax 342 2261, 259 Zhongshan Beilu) Singles or doubles Y608, older doubles Y398. A charming place built in 1936, it's set on pleasant grounds away from the street. The more expensive rooms are newly renovated and cheaper rooms are in a separate building. Discounts of 30% make this place quite a good deal.

Zhuàngyuánlóu Jiǔdiàn (Mandarin Garden Hotel; ☎ 220 2555, W www.mandaringarden-hotel.com, 9 Zhuangyuan Lu) Singles/doubles Y860/990. The five-star rooms here are good value with a 40% discount. Doubles are available for Y380 in the three-star section.

Jīnlíng Fàndiàn (☎ 471 1888, W www.jinlinghotel.com, Xinjiekou) Doubles/suites Y1410/1535. This 36-storey establishment is one of Nánjīng's best hotels. Discounts of 40% are sometimes available.

Hilton Hotel (☎ 480 8888, W www.hilton.com, 319 Zhongshan Donglu) Singles/doubles US$180/200. Don't be too alarmed by these prices – doubles are often discounted to Y599.

Ramada Plaza (☎ 330 8888, fax 330 9999, 45 Zhongshan Beilu) Doubles US$120-140. This place is very good value when discounts of 50% are offered. It has a great location near the Drum Tower.

Sheraton Nanjing Kingsley Hotel (☎ 666 8888, W www.sheraton.com, 169 Hanzhong Lu) Doubles US$155. One of Nánjīng's newer luxury hotels, rooms here are available for Y688 during discount periods.

Places to Eat

Some of Nánjīng's livelier eating houses are in the Fūzǐ Miào quarter though one of the more famous establishments, Lǎozhèngxīng Càiguǎn, was recently replaced by a KFC (the shape of things to come?). There's still lots of variety in traditional Chinese fare from the many food stalls and restaurants in the area.

Wǎnqíng Lóu (☎ 230 6950, *Dashiba Jie)* Dim sum feast Y60. This restaurant is on the opposite side of the river from Fūzǐ Miào's main square and there's another branch beside the McDonald's. Here you can try delicious Nánjīng dim sum – a pre-set, 20-dish feast is definitely good value. A number of teahouses above the shops in this area offer excellent night views of Fūzǐ Miào.

If you want to forget all about local delicacies, head over to one of the cluster of restaurants around Nanjing University catering to adventurous locals and foreign students.

Italian Pizza Express (Famous Grouse Bar; ☎ 323 1353, *19 Jinyin Jie)* Mains Y30-60. Open 10am-10pm daily. Don't let the shabby exterior of this bar and restaurant deter you. The decor inside is comfortable and clean and there are delicious pasta dishes and pizza.

Jack's Place (☎ 332 3616, *160 Shanghai Lu)* Mains Y20-30. Open 9am-2am daily. Jack's now has three branches in Nánjīng, including one opposite Nanjing Normal University. They have a sign saying they're recommended by Lonely Planet, but not all readers agree. Nevertheless, it's cheap and the Western breakfast for Y12 is a bargain.

Many small restaurants are found in the streets around the two universities.

Kèjiāfú Kǎodiàn (☎ 331 2678, *38 Yinyang Ying)* Mains Y10-50. Open 11am-midnight daily. A spotlessly clean and popular place, this Korean restaurant serves huge bowls of spicy cold noodle dishes for Y10. There's an English menu.

Skyways Bakery & Deli (☎ 663 4834, *3-6 Hankou Xilu)* Breakfast and lunch specials Y15-20. Open 9am-9.30pm daily. There's good sandwiches, pastries and coffee here.

Henry's Home Cafe (☎ 470 1292, *33 Huaqiao Lu)* Mains Y40-80. Open 9.30am-10.30pm daily. Henry's Home Cafe serves pasta, pizza, *fajitas* (Mexican tortilla wraps) and steak dishes and has very friendly service.

City Garden Coffee Shop (Chéngshì Huāyuán Kāfēidiàn; ☎ 471 3515, *87 Guanjia Qiao)* Mains Y30-70. Open 9am-2am daily. This is a large, clean place serving set meals of rice and meat dishes (Y35) and sandwiches (Y30). The menu is in English and Chinese.

Wúzhōu Jiǔjiā (Tree House; ☎ 332 2006, *22 Xiaofen Qiao)* Mains Y20-40. Open 11am-2pm & 5pm-9pm daily. This is a popular place with foreigners and locals; the food is cheap and there's an English menu.

Bǎiwèizhāi (Vegetarian Restaurant; ☎ 771 3690, *Jimingsi Lu)* Mains Y20. Open at noon. Connected to **Jīmíng Sì** *(admission Y4; open 7am-5.30pm daily)* this vegetarian restaurant may be worth visiting more for the view overlooking Xuánwǔhú Gōngyuán than for its food, served only at lunch.

Sìchuān Jiǔjiā (☎ 664 4541, *171 Taiping Nanlu)* Mains Y25-50. Open 11am-2pm & 5pm-9pm daily. Despite the name, this is also a good place to sample local specialities. Here, Nánjīng pressed duck *(yánshuǐ yā)* is slathered with roasted salt, steeped in clear brine, baked dry and then kept under cover for some time; the finished product should have a creamy-coloured skin and red, tender flesh. The Sìchuān-style dishes are also good and spicy. A *snack place* occupies the ground floor and the main restaurant is on the 2nd floor. There's no English sign or menu; look for the large red lanterns beside the KFC.

Entertainment

Jiangsu Kunju Theatre (Jiāngsū Shěng Kūnjùyuàn; ☎ 446 5873, *2 Chaotian Gong)* Tickets Y50. Excellent – if rather infrequent – performances are held here. The theatre is next to the eastern entrance of the Heaven Dynasty Palace. *Kūnjù* or *kūnqǔ* is a regional form of classical Chinese opera that developed in the Sūzhōu-Hángzhōu-Nánjīng triangle. It's similar to, but slower than, Peking opera and is performed with colourful and elaborate costumes. To reach the theatre, take bus No 4 from the Xīnjiēkǒu roundabout and get off two stops to the west.

Nánjīng has an active nightlife and a range of bars, pubs and discos to choose from. The best place to ask about entertainment is at the foreign student dormitories where you'll find advertisements and posters.

Blowing in the Wind (☎ 323 2486, 13 Jinyin Jie) Beer Y15-20. Open 7pm-2am daily. This unpretentious place has live music and a relaxed atmosphere.

Castle Bar (☎ 361 9190, 6 Zhongyang Lu) Beer Y16. Open 7pm-2am daily. Inside the Drum Tower complex, this is another good place to go for live and house music. The dance floor can get pretty crowded once the DJs get going.

Scarlet Bar (☎ 335 1916, 29 Gulou Chezhan Dongxiang) Beer Y10. Open 6pm-3am daily. Named after Scarlet in *Gone With The Wind*, this small place is on a lane off Zhongyang Lu. Popular with a younger, local crowd, the dancing starts around 10pm.

Shopping

There's little you can't buy in Nánjīng – from designer clothing to trinket souvenirs. Hunan Lu has a late night market and is lined with shops and stalls. It's good for clothes shopping during the day too. The area surrounding Fūzǐ Miào is a pedestrian zone with souvenirs and antiques for sale. Around Hanzhong Lu and Zhongshan Lu you'll find a number of major department stores.

Zhongshan Department Store (Zhōngshān Dàshà; ☎ 336 1888, 200 Zhongshan Lu) Open 9.30am-9.30pm daily. This older establishment is a good place to go for a whole range of products.

GE International Shopping Centre (Jìnyíng Guójì Gòuwù Zhōngxīn; ☎ 470 8899, 89 Hanzhong Lu) Open 9am-9pm daily. A little more upmarket, this centre is aimed at a younger crowd with more disposable income.

Getting There & Away

Air Nánjīng has regular air connections to all major Chinese cities. There are also daily flights to/from Hong Kong (Y1500).

The main office for the Civil Aviation Administration of China (CAAC; Zhōngguó Mínháng; ☎ 448 5131) is at 50 Ruijin Lu (near the terminus of bus route No 37), but you can also buy tickets at CITS and China Travel Service (CTS; Zhōngguó Lǚxíngshè) offices or at most top-end hotels. Another convenient ticketing office is the Huaxia Air Ticket Service (☎ 331 1747)

near the Drum Tower at 1-1 Beijing Xilu. Dragonair (☎ 471 0181) has daily flights to Hong Kong and there's an office in Room 751–53 in the World Trade Centre.

Bus There are many long-distance bus stations in Nánjīng. In the north, Zhōngyāng Mén long-distance bus station is south-east of the wide-bridged intersection with Zhongyang Lu. Buses from here go to Shànghǎi (Y88, four hours), Héféi (Y38, 2½ hours) and Sūzhōu (Y64, 2½ hours). Another useful station is on Hanzhong Lu, where buses go to Zhènjiāng (Y21, 1½ hours) and Yángzhōu (Y26, two hours). The Hanfu Jie bus station on Changjiang Lu also has buses to Hángzhōu (Y97, five hours). All three stations cover most other major destinations.

Take local bus No 13 north to reach Zhōngyāng Mén bus station and south to reach the Hanzhong Lu station. Bus No Y1 from the train station via Zhongyang Lu goes near the Hanfu Jie station.

Train Nánjīng is a major stop on the Běijīng-Shànghǎi train line, and the station is mayhem; there are several trains a day in both directions. Heading eastwards from Nánjīng, the line to Shànghǎi connects with Zhènjiāng, Wúxī and Sūzhōu.

Four daily express trains run between Nánjīng and Shànghǎi (Y47, three hours). Other trains to Shànghǎi take four hours stopping in Zhènjiāng (Y11, one hour) and Sūzhōu (Y26, 2½ hours). Some of the express trains also stop in Zhènjiāng and Sūzhōu.

There are trains to Hángzhōu (Y63, five hours) and a slow train to Guǎngzhōu (Y401, 32 hours) via Shànghǎi. There's a direct train to the port of Wúhú on Cháng Jiāng which continues on to Huáng Shān (Y54, seven hours) in Ānhuī province.

You can buy train tickets at CITS for a Y5 to Y10 service charge. You can also buy train tickets at the advance booking office at 293 Zhongshan Beilu, open daily from 8am to 12pm and 1.30pm to 5pm.

Boat Several ferries depart daily from Nánjīng's Cháng Jiāng port down river (eastward) to Shànghǎi and upriver (westward) to Wǔhàn (two days); a few boats also go to Chóngqìng (five days). The passenger dock is in the north-west of the city at No 6 dock (liùhào mǎtóu). You can book boat tickets at the advance booking office at 293 Zhongshan Beilu. For full details on Cháng Jiāng cruises, see the Chóngqìng chapter.

Getting Around

To/From the Airport Nánjīng airport is approximately one hour south of the city. A minibus service departs from opposite the Sheraton Nanjing Kingsley Hotel on Hanzhong Lu. Tickets cost Y25. Many of the hotels also have hourly shuttle buses that run to and from the airport. A taxi will cost around Y150.

Local Transport Taxis cruise the streets of Nánjīng and are very cheap – most destinations in the city are Y7, but make sure that the meter is switched on. Motor-tricycles are also common; be sure to agree on a price beforehand.

You can get to Xīnjiēkǒu, in the heart of town, by jumping on bus No 13 from the train station or the Centre Gate. There's also tourist bus routes that visit many of the sites. Bus No Y1 goes from the train and bus station through the city to the Sun Yat-sen Mausoleum. Bus No Y2 starts in the south at the Martyr's Cemetery, passes Fūzǐ Miào and terminates halfway up Zǐjīn Shān.

Many local maps contain bus routes. Normal buses cost Y1 and tourist buses cost Y2.

AROUND NÁNJĪNG
Qīxiá Sì 栖霞寺
Morning of Birds Temple
This temple (☎ 576 1706; admission Y10; open 7am-5.30pm daily) on Qīxiá Shān 22km north-east of Nánjīng, was founded by the Buddhist monk Ming Sengshao during the Southern Qi dynasty, and is still an active place of worship. Qīxiá Sì has long been one of China's most important monasteries, and even today is one of the largest Buddhist seminaries in the country. There are two main temple halls: the **Maitreya Hall**, with a statue of the Maitreya Buddha sitting cross-legged at the entrance, and behind this the **Vairocana Hall**, housing a 5m-tall statue of Vairocana.

Behind the temple is the **Thousand Buddha Cliff** (Qiānfó Yá). Several small caves housing stone statues are carved into the hillside, the earliest of which dates from the Qi dynasty (AD 479–502), although there are others from succeeding dynasties through to the Ming. There is also a small stone pagoda, **Shělì Tǎ**, built in AD 601, and rebuilt during the late Tang period. The upper part has engraved sutras and carvings of Buddha; around the base, each of the pagoda's eight sides depicts Sakyamuni.

You can reach Qīxiá Sì from Nánjīng by a public bus (Y3, one hour) that departs from opposite the train station.

Yangshan Quarry 阳山碑材
Yángshān Bēicái
This quarry (☎ 411 0582; adult/child Y11/5.50; open 7.30am-dusk daily) at Yángshān, 25km east of Nánjīng, was the source of most of the stone blocks cut for the Ming Palace Ruins and statues of the Ming tombs. The attraction here is a massive tablet partially hewn from the rock. Had the tablet been finished it would have been almost 15m wide, 4m thick and 45m high! The base stone was to be 6.5m high and 13m long.

One story goes that Ming dynasty emperor Hongwu wished to place the enormous tablet on the top of Zǐjīn Shān. The gods had promised their assistance to move it, but when they saw the size of the tablet, even they gave up and Hongwu had to abandon the project.

It's not the easiest place to get to. Your best bet is to get on a bus leaving from the train station to the hot springs resort of Tāngshān (Y4, one hour) and from there you can get a bus for the short trip to Yángshān (Y1).

ZHÈNJIĀNG 镇江
☎ 0511 • pop 2,890,000
Just an hour from Nánjīng, Zhènjiāng is known for its production of vinegar, a lingering aroma of which floats over the streets, especially near the train station. The city's main attraction is Jīnshān Gōngyuán, where an active Buddhist temple attracts large crowds of worshippers.

The oldest part of the city is found around Daxi Lu, which is an interesting area to wander around, especially beyond the western end of the street. A new promenade along the shores of Cháng Jiāng is also a pleasant place for a stroll.

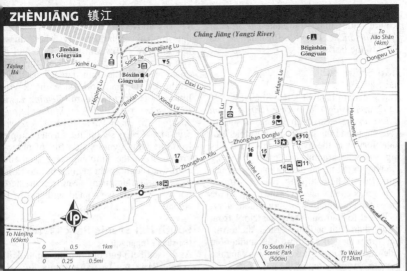

ZHÈNJIĀNG

PLACES TO STAY & EAT
4 Dàhuángjiā Jiǔdiàn
大皇家酒店
5 Yànchūn Jiǔlóu
宴春酒楼
12 International Hotel
国际饭店
15 Zuìxiānlóu Jiǔjiā
醉仙楼酒家
16 Jīngkǒu Fàndiàn
京口饭店
17 Zhènjiāng Bīnguǎn
镇江宾馆

MUSEUM & TEMPLES
1 Jīnshān Sì
金山寺

2 Revolutionary History
Museum
革命历史博物馆
3 Zhenjiang Museum
镇江博物馆
6 Gānlù Sì
甘露寺

OTHER
7 Main Post &
Telephone Office
中国电信
8 Zhènjiāng Wénwù
Shāngdiàn
镇江文物商店
9 Post Office
邮局

10 Main Bank of China
中国银行
11 Express Bus Station
快客气车站
13 PSB
公安局
14 South Gate Long-
Distance Bus Station
南门汽车站
18 Long-Distance Bus
Station; Bank of China
长途汽车站；中国银行
19 Train Station
火车站
20 Yánggǔ Fàndiàn
Ticket Service
阳谷饭店售票处

Information

The main Bank of China is on Zhongshan
Lu, just east of the intersection with Jiefang
Lu. There's also a branch attached to the
new long-distance bus station beside the
train station. The main telephone and post
office is on Dianli Lu, on the corner of
Xinma Lu. The PSB (☎ 531 6192) is at 24
Shizheng Lu.

The International Hotel (see Places to
Stay later) gives out free English maps, or
you can buy the Chinese version at the train
or bus stations.

Jīnshān Gōngyuán 金山公园
Gold Hill Park

This park (☎ 551 2992, 62 Jinshan Xilu;
*adult/child Y25/12.50; open 6am-6pm
daily*) packs in the crowds who fill the
flights of stairs leading up through a Buddhist temple, **Jīnshān Sì**, to the seven-storey
octagonal pagoda, **Císhòu Tǎ**.

The temple gains its name from a Zen
master who is said to have come into copious amounts of gold *(jīn)* after opening the
gates at the entrance of the park. There are
four caves at the mount; of these **Buddhist**

Sea (*Fáhǎi*) and **White Dragon** (*Báilóng*) feature in the Chinese fairy tale *The Story of the White Snake*. To get to Jīnshān take bus No 2 to the last stop.

Jiāo Shān 焦山
Jiāo Hill

The green foliage on Jiāo Shān (☎ *881 5502; admission Y20; open 7.15am-5.30pm daily*), to the east of Zhènjiāng, is said to give the island the impression of a piece of jade floating in the river. There's good hiking here with a number of pavilions along the way to the top of the 150m-high mountain, from where **Xījiāng Tower** (*Xījiāng Lóu*) gives good views over the river. At the base of the mountain is an active monastery.

To get to Jiāo Shān take bus No 4 from Zhongshan Xilu or Jiefang Lu to the terminal. From there it's a short walk and a boat ride (included in the ticket), or you can take a cable car to the top of the hill (Y15).

Běigùshān Gōngyuán 北固山公园
North Hill Park

Also on the No 4 bus route, this park (☎ *881 2169, 3 Dongwu Lu; admission Y15; open 7am-7pm daily*) is home to **Gānlù Sì**, which features an iron pagoda first built in the Tang dynasty. Once 13m high, the pagoda has since suffered damage from fire, lightning and overzealous Red Guards during the Cultural Revolution.

Zhenjiang Museum 镇江博物馆
Zhènjiāng Bówùguǎn

Between Jīnshān Gōngyuán and the centre of town is the old British consulate, built in 1890 and now converted into a museum (☎ *528 6517, 85 Boxian Lu; adult/child Y10/5; open 9am-12pm & 2pm-5.30pm daily*). It houses pottery, bronzes, gold, and silver found in excavations around Zhènjiāng. There are English captions and the building has been nicely restored. To get there catch bus No 2 from Zhongshan Lu.

Daxi Lu & Song Jie Area

It's well worth exploring the old area surrounding the museum. Winding cobblestone alleys pass through an ancient neighbourhood and meander down to boat docks on Cháng Jiāng.

The staircase to the east of the museum leads around to a narrow street known as

Song Jie. A small stone pagoda, **Zhāoguān Tǎ**, sits above an archway and is said to date from the Yuan dynasty. There are a few *antique stores* and *stalls* here and if you keep following the street all the way down and past the train tracks, you'll hit Xinhe Lu. On the north side the **Revolutionary History Museum** (*Gémìng Lìshǐ Bówùguǎn*; ☎ *527 9697, 60 Xinhe Lu; admission Y3; open 9am-11.30am & 2pm-5pm Mon-Fri*) is set up in a former temple from the Qing dynasty. It's full of photographs from the Sino-Japanese war and civil war fought in the region, but no English captions. Not many visitors come here but you will be welcomed with warm if somewhat puzzled smiles.

South Hill Scenic Park 南山风景区
Nánshān Fēngjǐngqū

At the southern end of town the South Hill Scenic Park (☎ *441 7210, Zhulin Lu; admission Y15; open 7.30am-5.30pm daily*) contains **Zhúlín Sì** (*Bamboo Forest Temple*). As temples go, it won't qualify as the biggest or best in China, but its setting among the trees and hills makes it a relaxing spot. To get there take bus No 15 from Zhongshan Lu.

Places to Stay

Unfortunately, Zhènjiāng's funkiest hotel, the **Dàhuángjiā Jiǔdiàn** (*Royal Hotel; 35 Boxian Lu*), with its bizarre neo-classical decor and great location in the old section of town, was closed indefinitely at the time of writing. If you're looking for reasonable rates, catch bus No 2 and check to see if it's open.

Jīngkǒu Fàndiàn (☎ *522 4866, fax 523 0056, 407 Zhongshan Donglu*) Doubles Y120-480. One of the cheapest options around although the cheaper (and older) rooms are often full. A 50% discount is available for the Y480 doubles and the rooms are fine.

Zhènjiāng Bīnguǎn (☎ *523 3888*, ⓔ *zj hotel@public.zj.js.cn, 92 Zhongshan Xilu*) Doubles Y300-580. Close to the train station, this hotel has newer rooms in the front building with slight discounts available.

International Hotel (*Guójì Fàndiàn*; ☎ *502 1888, fax 502 1777, 218 Jiefang Lu*) Doubles Y560-730. This four-star hotel looks incredibly ugly from the outside, but has the most upmarket standard rooms in town and caters to international tourists and business people.

Places to Eat
The best places to look for restaurants are on the streets off Zhongshan Donglu, west of the intersection with Jiefang Lu.

Zuìxiānlóu Jiǔjiā (☎ 523 3960, 50 Jiankang Lu) Mains Y20-30. Open 9am-9pm. This small place is doing so well it recently opened a second branch *(69 Jiefang Lu)*. Very reasonable dishes, like the sautéed beef and green pepper *(jiānjiāo niúliǔ)* for Y25 and delicious braised eggplant *(yóumèn qiézi)* for a paltry Y6 are a steal. There's no English menu but the staff are friendly.

Yànchūn Jiǔlóu (☎ 527 1615, 17 Renmin Lu) Snacks downstairs Y5-10. Mains upstairs Y25-40. Open 1st floor 6am-12.30pm & 3pm-6.30pm, 2nd floor 11am-1.30pm & 5pm-8.30pm. Once the most famous restaurant in town, this place has seen better days. But if you're walking around the old town and feel like a quick snack, the downstairs area has cheap dumplings, noodles and wonton *(húntun)* soup. The 2nd floor serves more substantial meals.

Shopping
Zhènjiāng Wénwù Shāngdiàn (Zhenjiang Antique Shop; ☎ 501 2335, 191 Jiefang Beilu) Open 8.30am-6pm daily. There's a lot of choice in this large shop that stocks embroidery, porcelain, jade and other crafts as well as antiques.

Getting There & Away
Bus Most buses from the south gate long-distance bus station are slow buses. Express buses leave from the express bus station (kuàikè zhàn) across the street. Buses leave for Nánjīng (Y22, 1½ hours), Shànghǎi (Y64, 3½ hours), Wúxī (Y28, two hours) and Sūzhōu (Y37, two hours). Buses for major destinations also leave from the new long-distance bus station near the train station. Frequent buses leave here for Yángzhōu (Y12.5, one hour), which includes a short ferry ride.

Train Zhènjiāng is on the main Nánjīng-Shànghǎi train line. It's a little over three hours to Shànghǎi (Y38) and an hour to Nánjīng (Y13). Although some of the special express trains don't stop at Zhènjiāng, there's still a grand choice of schedules. Most hotels offer a train booking service. The business centre at the International Hotel will book sleepers for a Y30 service charge but it's fairly easy to book sleepers in advance either at the train station or the ticket outlet at Yánggǔ Fàndiàn. They charge Y5 to book sleepers.

Getting Around
Almost all the transport (local buses, pedicabs and motor-tricycles) is close to the train station. Taxis start at Y6.

Bus No 2 is a convenient tour bus. It travels east from the station along Zhongshan Lu to Jiefang Lu. It then swings west to the museums and continues on to the terminus at Jīnshān Gōngyuán. Bus No 4, which crosses the No 2 route in the city centre on Jiefang Lu, runs past Běigùshān Gōngyuán and terminates at Jiāo Shān in the east.

YÁNGZHŌU 扬州
☎ 0514 • pop 4,461,400

Yángzhōu, near the junction of the Grand Canal and Cháng Jiāng, was once an economic and cultural centre of southern China. It was home to scholars, painters, storytellers, poets and merchants in the Sui and Tang dynasties.

Today Yángzhōu is a pleasant, small city with broad, tree-lined boulevards dotted with canals, bridges and gardens. It's more attractive and cleaner than Zhènjiāng and is a worthwhile break from Jiāngsū's bigger centres of Nánjīng and Sūzhōu. The main tourist sight, Shòuxī Hú, tends to get swamped with tour groups but the other places remain quiet enough. Yángzhōu has enough to keep one busy for a couple days or can be visited on a day trip from Nánjīng.

Information
CITS (☎ 734 6474), at 10 Fengle Shangjie, books train and air tickets. The main Bank of China is at 279 Wenchang Zhonglu and the post office is at 162 Wenchang Zhonglu. A telephone office is on the corner of Huaihai Lu and Siwangting Lu. Yángzhōu's PSB (☎ 734 2097) is at 1 Huaihai Lu.

There's an Internet bar, Huìténg Wǎngbā, at 34 Liuhu Lu that's open 24 hours a day and charges Y1.5 per hour.

BEIJING TO SHANGHAI

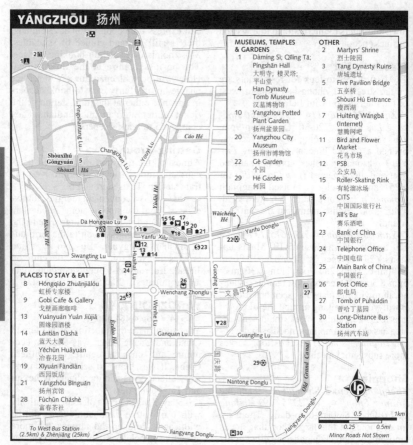

YÁNGZHŌU 扬州

MUSEUMS, TEMPLES & GARDENS

1	Dàmíng Sì; Qīlíng Tǎ; Píngshān Hall	大明寺; 栖灵塔; 平山堂
4	Han Dynasty Tomb Museum	汉墓博物馆
10	Yangzhou Potted Plant Garden	扬州盆景园
20	Yangzhou City Museum	扬州市博物馆
22	Gè Garden	个园
29	Hé Garden	何园

OTHER

2	Martyrs' Shrine	烈士陵园
3	Tang Dynasty Ruins	唐城遗址
5	Five Pavilion Bridge	五亭桥
6	Shòuxī Hú Entrance	瘦西湖
7	Huìténg Wǎngbā (Internet)	慧腾网吧
11	Bird and Flower Market	花鸟市场
12	PSB	公安局
15	Roller-Skating Rink	有轮滑冰场
16	CITS	中国国际旅行社
17	Jill's Bar	赛乐酒吧
23	Bank of China	中国银行
24	Telephone Office	中国电信
25	Main Bank of China	中国银行
26	Post Office	邮电局
27	Tomb of Puhaddin	普哈丁墓园
30	Long-Distance Bus Station	扬州汽车站

PLACES TO STAY & EAT

8	Hóngqiáo Zhuānjiālóu	虹桥专家楼
9	Gobi Cafe & Gallery	戈壁画廊咖啡
13	Yuányuán Yuán Jiǔjiā	圆缘园酒楼
14	Lántiān Dàshà	蓝天大厦
18	Yěchūn Huāyuán	冶春花园
19	Xīyuán Fàndiàn	西园饭店
21	Yángzhōu Bīnguǎn	扬州宾馆
28	Fùchūn Cháshè	富春茶社

To West Bus Station (2.5km) & Zhènjiāng (25km)

0   0.5   1km
0   0.25   0.5mi
Minor Roads Not Shown

Canals

Yángzhōu once had 24 stone bridges spanning its network of canals. Although the modern bridges are concrete, they still offer good vantage points to view canal life.

As the Grand Canal actually passes a little to the east of Yángzhōu, you might like to investigate the environs a short way out of town. The bus No 2 station in the northeast is a boat dock on the river. Bus Nos 4 and 9 run over a bridge on the canal. There are also two ship locks to the south of Yángzhōu.

Gè Garden 个园

Gè Yuán

This garden (☎ 734 7428, 10 Yanfu Dong Lu; admission Y15; open 8am-6pm daily)

was built by a salt merchant as his garden residence during the Qing dynasty and highlights the use of bamboo and the convoluted rockeries typical of classical Chinese gardens. Its design features four separate components to represent the four seasons.

Hé Garden 何园

Hé Yuán

This garden (☎ 722 2353, 77 Xuningmen Jie; admission Y15; open 7.30am-6pm daily) was built in 1883. It contains rockeries, ponds, pavilions and walls inscribed with classical poetry. It's a little out of the way, but worth visiting if you're interested in Chinese gardens. Bus No 1 from Yanfan Xilu stops nearby on Nantong Donglu.

The Grand Canal

The world's longest canal, the Grand Canal once meandered the almost 1800km from Běijīng to Hángzhōu and is a striking example of China's sophisticated engineering prowess. Today perhaps half of it remains seasonally navigable. The party claims that since liberation, large-scale dredging has made the navigable length 1100km. However, canal depths are up to 3m and canal widths can narrow to less than 9m. Putting these facts together and thinking about some of the old stone bridges spanning the route, you come to the conclusion that it's restricted to fairly small, flat-bottomed vessels in some places.

The Grand Canal's construction spanned many centuries. The first 85km were completed in 495 BC, but the mammoth task of linking Huáng Hé (Yellow River) and Cháng Jiāng (Yangzi River) was undertaken during Sui times by a massive conscripted labour force between AD 605 and 609. It was developed again during the Yuan dynasty (1271–1368). The canal enabled the government to capitalise on the growing wealth of the Cháng Jiāng basin and to ship supplies from south to north.

Sections of the canal have been silted up for centuries, however, the canal comes into its own south of Cháng Jiāng, where concern for tourism has ensured year-round navigation. The Jiāngnán section of the canal (Hángzhōu, Sūzhōu, Wúxī and Chángzhōu) is a skein of canals, rivers and branching lakes.

Passenger services on the canal have dwindled to a trickle; they are unpopular with locals now that there are faster ways to get around. If you want a canal journey, the only option (apart from chartering your own boat) is the overnight service that travels between Hángzhōu and Sūzhōu or Wúxī. By all accounts it's a very pleasant trip, and improvements have been made on the much-maligned sanitation front. (See the Sūzhōu and Wúxī Getting There & Away sections in this chapter for more details.)

Yangzhou Potted Plant Garden
扬州盆景园

Yángzhōu Pénjǐng Yuán

Don't be put off by the name. This garden (☎ 734 5247, 12 Youyi Lu; admission Y30; open 7am-6pm daily) offers a quiet escape along a small canal dotted with birds and blossoms, archways, bridges, pavilions and a marble boat. There are hundreds of bonsai-style potted plants on display as well as a **bonsai museum**. The entrance fee is a bit steep, but is well worth the price and a must for garden-lovers.

Shòuxīhú Gōngyuán 瘦西湖公园
Slender West Lake Park

The top scenic spot in Yángzhōu stretches north from Da Hongqiao Lu up towards Dàmíng Sì. **Shòuxī Hú** (Slender West Lake; ☎ 734 1324, 28 Da Hongqiao Lu; admission Y30; open 6.30am-6pm daily) is a slim version of Xī Hú (West Lake) in Hángzhōu. Mass local tourism has helped restore this garden and it's a worthwhile trip if you're lucky enough to visit on a quiet day. The highlight is the triple-arched, **Five Pavilion Bridge** (Wǔtíng Qiáo), built in 1757.

Emperor Qianlong's fishing platform is also in the park. Supposedly, local divers used to put fish on the emperor's hook so he'd think it was good luck and provide more funding for the town.

There's an entrance on Da Hongqiao Lu and another entrance at the Five Pavilion Bridge on bus route No 5 from Wenhe Lu.

Dàmíng Sì 大明寺
Great Brightness Temple

Dàmíng Sì (☎ 734 0720, 1 Pingshan Tang; admission Y18; open 7.30am-5pm daily) has been an important centre for Buddhism since ancient times. Founded more than 1000 years ago, the complex was subsequently destroyed and rebuilt. Then it was destroyed right down to its foundations during the Taiping Rebellion; what you see today is a 1934 reconstruction. The nine-storey **Qīlíng Tǎ** (Dwelling of the Soul Pagoda), nearby, was completed in 1996.

The original temple is credited to the Tang dynasty monk Jianzhen, who studied sculpture, architecture, fine arts and medicine, as well as Buddhism. In AD 742 two Japanese monks invited him to Japan for missionary work, which turned out to be mission impossible – Jianzhen made five attempts to get there, failing due to storms. On the fifth attempt he ended up in Hǎinán. On the sixth trip, aged 66, he finally arrived.

He stayed in Japan for 10 years and died there in AD 763. Later, the Japanese made a lacquer statue of Jianzhen, which was sent to Yángzhōu in 1980.

The Chinese have a wooden copy of this statue on display at the **Jianzhen Memorial Hall**. Modelled after the chief hall of the Toshodai Temple in Nara (Japan), the Jianzhen Memorial Hall was built in 1974 at Dàmíng Sì and was financed by Japanese contributions. Special exchanges are made between Nara and Yángzhōu; even Deng Xiaoping, returning from a trip to Japan, came to the Yángzhōu temple to strengthen renewed links between the two countries.

Near the temple is **Píngshān Hall** (*Píngshān Táng*), the former residence of the Song dynasty writer Ouyang Xiu. A **Martyrs' Shrine** is also nearby. To the east of Dàmíng Sì you'll find some Tang dynasty ruins and the **Han Dynasty Tomb Museum** (*Hànmù Bówùguǎn;* ☎ *761 0650, 16 Xiangbie Lu; admission Y15; open 8.30am-4.30pm daily*).

You can reach Dàmíng Sì by taking bus No 5 along Wenhe Lu to the last stop. The temple is a short walk north of the here.

Tomb of Puhaddin 普哈丁墓园
Pǔhādīng Mùyuán

This tomb (☎ *722 2214, 17 Jiefang Nanlu*) contains documentation of China's contact with the Muslims. It's on the eastern bank of a canal on the bus No 2 route. Puhaddin came to China during the Yuan dynasty (AD 1271–1368) to spread the Muslim faith. There's also a mosque but casual visitors are only allowed to enter the grounds from 6am to 12pm and you need special permission to visit the tomb.

Yangzhou City Museum 扬州市博物馆
Yángzhōu Shì Bówùguǎn

This museum (☎ *734 4585, 2 Fengle Shanglu; admission free; open 8am-5pm daily*) is in a temple originally dedicated to Shi Kefa, a Ming dynasty official who refused to succumb to his new Qing masters and was executed.

Large wooden coffins dating to the Han and Northern Song dynasties, a 1000-year-old wooden boat and a Han dynasty jade funeral suit are on display. Inside the grounds, the museum is surrounded by an antique market.

Places to Stay
Hóngqiáo Zhuānjiālóu (*Hongqiao Foreign Experts Building;* ☎ *797 5275, fax 731 9142, 8 Liuhu Lu*) Singles Y180, doubles Y160-260, triples Y180. The rooms here aren't great but its location on the campus of the Yangzhou Teacher's College is great. From the bus station take bus No 5 to Da Hongqiao Lu and then walk west.

The town's two main hotels are both located behind the museum:

Xīyuán Fàndiàn (☎ *734 4888, fax 723 3870, 1 Fengle Shanglu*) Doubles Y280-620. This huge place is said to have been constructed on the site of Qianlong's imperial villa, and the surrounding grounds are certainly appealing. Rooms are good value with discounts of 30%, especially the cheaper doubles in the back building.

Yángzhōu Bīnguǎn (☎ *734 2611, fax 734 3599, 5 Fengle Shanglu*) Doubles Y388-480. This is another large hotel but not quite as nice as Xīyuán Fàndiàn, though the 40% discounts are attractive.

Lántiān Dàshà (☎ *736 0000, fax 731 4101, 159 Wenhe Beilu*) Singles/doubles Y360/420. Very centrally located, this place is clean, friendly and offers lots of diversions, such as a bowling alley. Doubles are sometimes discounted to Y300 and singles are available for Y280.

Places to Eat
One of Yángzhōu's most famous culinary exports is Yángzhōu fried rice (*Yángzhōu chǎofàn*) and, as most travellers who have tried it will confirm, it tastes just like fried rice. There are lots of restaurants in Yángzhōu, so competition is keen and the prices are reasonable.

Fùchūn Cháshè (*Fuchun Teahouse;* ☎ *733 2572, 35 Desheng Qiao*) Mains Y10-30. Open 6am-2pm & 3.30pm-7.30pm daily. One of Yángzhōu's oldest teahouses, this place is on a lane just off Guoqing Lu, in an older section of town. Popular with Japanese visitors, it's the place to go to sip tea and eat local snacks. The *jiǎozi* (dumplings) for Y5 are delicious. A newer branch of the Fùchūn Cháshè is next to the Gè Garden.

Yěchūn Huāyuán (*Yechun Teahouse;* ☎ *736 8018, 8 Fengle Xialu*) Mains Y10-30. Open 6am-10.30am, 11.30am-1.30pm & 4.30pm-9pm daily. This is another place that's good for early morning dimsum as well as dinner. The location is pleasant, down near the small canal just below the museum.

Yuányuán Yuán Jiǔjiā (☎ 735 8033, 24 Siwangting Lu) Mains Y15-35. Open 9.30am-10.30pm daily. This lively place has an unbelievable deal of Y18 for Beijing duck (*kǎoyā*). Their Yángzhōu fried rice for Y12 is good too. It's among the hundreds of restaurants on Siwangting Lu. There's no English menu.

Entertainment

Jill's Bar (The Cellar Bar; ☎ 736 7713, 8 Fengle Shangjie) The sign outside says there's interesting people to meet here and Jill the owner speaks English. A good place to hang out and play a game of pool after a hard day's sightseeing in Yángzhōu.

Before heading to Jill's Bar, (or after a few pints of beer) try roller skating at the *outdoor rink* (open 7pm-11pm daily) down the street. Skate rental is Y5.

Gobi Cafe & Gallery (☎ 734 3725, 26 Da Hongqiao Lu) Drinks Y12-30. Open 2pm-12.30am daily. For more sedate entertainment, try this cafe on Da Hongqiao Lu. Paintings and sculptures from local artists hang on the walls and there's a delicious variety of snacks, tea, coffee and other drinks. It also has board games, magazines, jazz and a mellow crowd and is a wonderful place to while away a couple of hours.

Shopping

Cheap clothing stores line both sides of Guoqing Lu. A number of stalls sell cooking knives down the alley towards Fùchūn Cháshè (see Places to Eat earlier).

True to its image as a city of gardens, Yángzhōu also has a lively *bird and flower market*. If you feel the need to stock up on plants, vases and bird cages, this is the place to do it. It's full of people from early morning until dusk.

Getting There & Away

The nearest airport is in Nánjīng and the closest train station is in Zhènjiāng. From the Yángzhōu long-distance bus station south of the city centre there are buses to Shànghǎi (Y81, 4½ hours) and Hángzhōu (Y78, five hours). Buses to Nánjīng (Y26, two hours) and Zhènjiāng (Y12.5, one hour) depart from the west bus station, south-west of the city. Buses cross over Cháng Jiāng by ferry.

Getting Around

Most of the sights are at the edge of town. Taxis are cheap and start at Y6, the smaller ones are Y5. The area from the southern entrance of Shòuxīhú Gōngyuán on Da Hongqiao Lu to the City Museum can easily be covered on foot and it's a pleasant walk.

Bus No 8 runs from the west bus station to the long-distance bus station, then up Guoqing Lu to the north of the city. Bus No 5 takes you from the long-distance bus station to Huaihai Lu, Youyi Lu then terminates near Dàmíng Sì.

WÚXĪ & TÀI HÚ 无锡、太湖
☎ 0510 ● pop 4,310,000

Wúxī and Tài Hú are possible stopovers between Sūzhōu and Nánjīng. Wúxī itself has little to recommend it and nearby Tài Hú continues to be an extremely popular destination for tourists, though its sights are more than a little overrun.

Tài Hú is a freshwater lake with a total area of 2200 sq km and an average depth of 2m. There are some 90 islands, large and small, and more than 30 varieties of fish. Despite some major water pollution problems, the fishing industry here is still active.

Orientation

The city centre of Wúxī is ringed by Jiefang Lu. The train station and long-distance bus station are about a 10-minute walk north of Jiefang Beilu. A network of canals, including the Grand Canal, cuts through the city.

Information

The Bank of China is on the corner of Zhongshan Nanlu and Renmin Zhonglu and looks like a stunted version of the Bank of China building in Hong Kong. The main post office is nearby on Renmin Zhonglu. A China Telecom office at the western end of the post office has Internet services for Y4 per hour. It's open daily from 7.30am to 11.30pm.

CTS (☎ 230 8335, fax 230 8331) is in the basement of Zhōnglǚ Dàjiǔdiàn (see Places to Stay later). The office beside the hotel entrance sells train and air tickets and transport to Shànghǎi's Hongqiao Airport. English maps are available at the hotel's business centre for Y5.

The PSB (☎ 270 5678 ext 2215) is at 54 Chongning Lu.

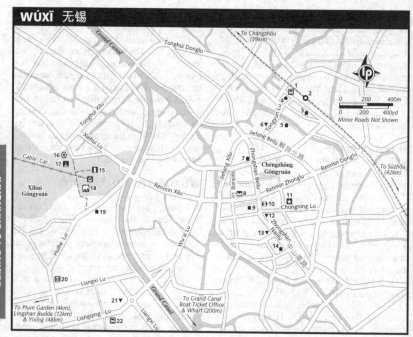

WÚXĪ 无锡

Xīhuì Gōngyuán 锡惠公园

The highest point in this park (☎ *587 3001, Huihe Lu; admission Y10; open 5am-6pm daily*), Xī Shān (West Hill) is 75m above sea level. If you climb **Lóngguāng Tǎ** (*Dragon Light Pagoda*), the seven-storey octagonal structure at the top of the hill, you'll be able to take in a panorama of Wúxī and Tài Hú. The brick and wood pagoda was built during the Ming dynasty, burned down during the Qing dynasty and rebuilt years later. For an even greater view, take the cable car (Y22), which is 1km into **Huì Shān** (*Hill of Benevolence*).

There's a total of 18 historical and cultural sights within the park, including the **Huìshān Sì**, once a Buddhist monastery, an azalea garden with over 300 different species, and the famous Ming-style **Jìchàng Garden** (*Jìchàng Yuán*).

The park also includes an **amusement ground**, complete with children's rides, games, loud speakers, souvenir stalls and a small zoo. Explore the western section if you're looking for some peace and quiet.

To get to Xīhuì Gōngyuán, take bus No 2 or 10.

Plum Garden 梅园
Méi Yuán

Once a small peach garden built during the Qing dynasty (☎ *551 6739, Huyi Gonglu; adult/child Y15/8; open 6am-6pm daily*), Plum Garden has since been renovated, re-landscaped and expanded. It's renowned for its thousands of plum trees that blossom in spring. The highest point is **Méi Tǎ** (*Plum Pagoda*), with views of Tài Hú. The garden is opposite the bus No 2 terminus on the highway to Yíxīng.

Turtle Head Isle 鼋头渚
Yuán Tóuzhǔ

Turtle Head Isle (☎ *555 1974; adult/child Y50/25; open 6.30am-6pm daily*) is not actually an island, but a peninsula. This is a scenic strolling area where you can walk a circuit of the park and take in the views of Tài Hú. A monorail (Y10) does the circuit if you don't feel like walking.

The entrance at the southern end of the park is just north of the **Bǎojiè Bridge** (*Bǎojiè Qiáo*). This end of the park is peaceful with a lovely narrow road leading up to the **Brightness Pavilion** (*Guāngmíng Tíng*),

WÚXĪ

PLACES TO STAY	PLACES TO EAT	
3 Zhōnglǚ Dàjiǔdiàn; CTS 中旅大酒店; 中国旅行社	6 Lóushànglóu Miànguǎn 楼上楼面馆	8 Main Post Office; China Telecom Office; Internet Cafe 市邮电局；中国电信；电信网吧
5 Jīnhuá Dàfàndiàn 锦华大饭店	12 Wúxī Kǎoyāguǎn 无锡烤鸭馆	10 Bank of China 中国银行
7 Sheraton Hotel 喜来登大饭店	13 Wángxìngjì 王兴记	11 PSB 公安局
9 New World Courtyard Marriott Hotel 新世界万怡酒店	21 Hánguó Shāokǎo 韩国烧烤	15 Lóngguāng Tǎ 龙光塔
14 Liángxī Fàndiàn 梁溪饭店	**OTHER**	16 Jìchàng Garden 寄肠园
19 Qinggongye University Foreign Experts Hotel 轻工业大学专家楼	1 Long-Distance Bus Station 无锡汽车站	17 Huìshān Sì 惠山寺
	2 Train Station 火车站	18 Zoo 动物园
	4 Bicycle Rental 租自行车店	20 Wuxi Museum 无锡博物馆
		22 West Bus Station 无锡汽车站

BĚIJĪNG TO SHÀNGHǍI

the highest point of Turtle Head Isle, offering all-round vistas. The northern end of the park has *restaurants, souvenir stalls* and a pier with ferries to Sānshān. From here, the **Perpetual Spring Bridge** (*Chángchūn Qiáo*) leads across a small pond to a rocky vantage point on the lake. At the teahouse *Clear Ripples Hall* (*Chénglán Táng*) you can enjoy some tea while viewing the lake.

Bus No 820 goes to Bǎojiè Bridge from the train station. The Wúxī sightseeing bus goes to the northern entrance from the train station. Speedboats take people out on the lake from the pier at the northern entrance for Y20.

Sānshān 三山
Three Hills Isles
Sānshān is an island park a couple of kilometres south-west of Turtle Head Isle. Vantage points at the top look back toward Turtle Head Isle, so you can work out if it really does look like a turtle head. The islands have a number of pavilions and temples as well as three large Buddha statues, the smallest measuring over 16m high. Watch out for the monkeys here. Ferries to the islands are included in the entry ticket to Turtle Head Isle.

Wuxi Museum 博物馆
Wúxī Bówùguǎn
This museum (☎ 586 7674, 2nd floor, 71 Huihe Lu; admission Y5; open 8am-11am & 1.30pm-4.30pm daily) contains over 200 historical articles and craft works from the past 6000 years, which look at the development of the local culture and its interaction with neighbouring counties. The best part is what's lying around outside. There's some old British textile machinery from the 1920's on display – reminders of Wúxī's development as a major textile centre. There's also some Qing dynasty cannons and a stone statue excavated from the grave of a minor official, discovered when the freeway was put through to Nánjīng.

Língshān Buddha 灵山大佛
Língshān Dàfó
There's a curious mixture of the (mostly) tacky and the sublime driving Wúxī's tourist development. The latest tourist attraction is the completion of the **Língshān Buddha** (☎ 568 9393, Lingshan Lu; adult/child Y50/25; open 6.30am-6pm daily), an 88m-high bronze Buddha south-west of the city. Take bus No 88 from the train station.

Places to Stay – Budget
Qinggongye University Foreign Experts Hotel (*Qīnggōngyè Dàxué Zhuānjiālóu;* ☎ 586 1034, 170 Huihe Lu) Singles/doubles with breakfast Y100/110. The rooms here are somewhat dreary but comfortable. From the train station take bus No 2 and get off at the second stop over the Grand Canal. The hotel is 200m farther down, on the opposite side of the street.

Jīnhuá Dàfàndiàn (☎ 232 3888, fax 230 6092, 9 Liangxi Lu) Singles Y160, doubles Y200-280. Rooms here are slightly run-down, but clean and affordable, especially with a 35% discount.

Places to Stay – Mid-Range
Liángxī Fàndiàn (☎ 272 3798, fax 271 9174, 63 Zhongshan Nanlu) Doubles Y200-680. This friendly place has a whole range of rooms and very pleasant grounds, while still situated close to the city centre. Cheaper doubles have 20% discounts and more expensive rooms are up to 50% off. Take bus No 201 from the train station.

Tài Hú Lǔnéng Dàjiǔdiàn (Tai Hu Lake Resort; ☎ 555 9888, fax 555 9666, Turtle Head Isle) Singles/doubles/triples Y388/398/458. If you want to stay closer to the lake, this hotel is clean and quiet and has 30% discounts. The disadvantage is you have to pay the Y50 park entrance fee to get in the first time. Take the Wúxī sightseeing bus from the train station.

Places to Stay – Top End
Zhōnglǔ Dàjiǔdiàn (CTS Grand Hotel; ☎ 230 0888, fax 230 2213, 88 Chezhan Lu) Doubles Y480-628. Run by the CTS, this fairly new hotel is convenient and the cheaper doubles are good value with 40% discounts.

New World Courtyard Marriott Hotel (☎ 276 2888, 🅦 www.courtyard.com, 335 Zhongshan Lu) Doubles US$70-80. Right in the city centre, this hotel offers all the amenities expected in an international hotel. Standard rooms are often discounted to Y438.

Sheraton Hotel (☎ 272 1888, 🅦 www .sheraton.com, 443 Zhongshan Lu) Doubles with breakfast from Y1100. This new hotel in the city centre has immaculate rooms. Standard rooms are discounted to Y888.

Places to Eat
Wúxī has no shortage of restaurants.

Lóushànglóu Miànguǎn (☎ 232 0777, 61 Tongyun Lu) Mains Y5-10. Open 6.30am-2pm & 4.30pm-9pm daily. On the ground floor of this large, attractive place cheap noodle and fried rice dishes are available. More substantial meals are upstairs.

Wángxìngjì (☎ 272 6484, 221 Zhongshan Lu) Mains Y10-20. Open 7am-8pm daily. Close to the city centre, this is a long-established Wúxī restaurant, though you wouldn't know it from the plastic decor. It's famous for *húntun* (wonton soup) and delicious *xiǎolóngbāo* (steamed dumplings filled with meat or seafood) for Y8.

Wúxī Kǎoyāguǎn (Wuxi Roast Duck; ☎ 270 3210, 222 Zhongshan Lu) Mains Y20-60. Open 11am-1.30pm & 5pm-8.30pm daily. This place has delicious

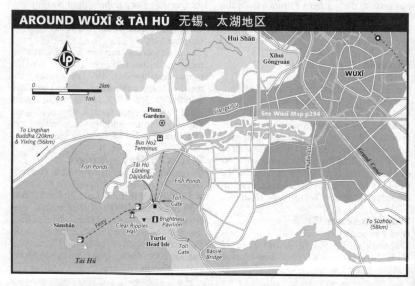

AROUND WÚXĪ & TÀI HÚ 无锡、太湖地区

kǎoyā (Beijing duck) for Y45 (Y30 for half a duck). Although a bit expensive, it's a comfortable and popular place to eat with a wide variety of dishes.

A number of hole-in-the-wall restaurants are clustered around the entrance to the Qinggongye University (see Places to Stay), popular with students for their cheap meals. There's also a string of restaurants and bars on Liangxi Lu near the intersection with Liangqing Lu.

Hánguó Shāokǎo *(Korean BBQ;* ☎ *580 1285, 3 Liangxi Lu)* Mains Y30-50. Open 5.30pm-10pm daily. Nestled between the bars on Liangxi Lu, this attractive place serves Japanese and Korean dishes that you can cook yourself over a grill.

Shopping

Silk products and embroidery are good buys. Also look out for the clay figurines known as *Huì Shān Nírén*. A local folk art, the figurines take many forms and shapes, but are most commonly modelled after famous opera stars. The models of obese infants are symbols of fortune and happiness.

Getting There & Away

Most long distance buses depart from the long-distance bus station next to the train station. The west bus station is on Liangqing Lu but has fewer services. Frequent buses to Yíxīng (Y10, 1½ hours) leave from both the long-distance and west bus stations. For Dīngshān change buses in Yíxīng.

Direct buses go to Shànghǎi (Y36, two hours), Sūzhōu (Y18, 45 minutes) and Nánjīng (Y52, 2½ hours).

Wúxī is on the Běijīng-Shànghǎi train line and has frequent services. There are trains to Sūzhōu (Y10, 30 minutes), Shànghǎi (Y20, 1½ hours) and Nánjīng (Y26, two hours) every two hours or so.

CTS books sleepers for a Y30 service charge but there are numerous ticket agents around the long-distance bus station that book train tickets.

Overnight passenger boats travel between Wúxī and Hángzhōu on the Grand Canal. Departure is at 5.30pm from the wharf off Hubin Lu. You can book tickets at the wharf. Two-person cabins are Y114 per person and four-person cabins are Y82 per person. The trip takes 13 hours.

Getting Around

It's fairly easy getting around Wúxī by bus. Bus No 2 runs from the train station, along Jiefang Lu, across two bridges to Xīhuì Gōngyuán, then out to Plum Garden. Bus No 201 heads from the train station down Zhongshan Lu to the city centre. The Wúxī sightseeing bus is very useful, stopping at all the major sights. There's no number, but it's in the first row of buses to the right as you exit the train station. Tickets are Y3 or Y2 depending on the distance.

Bikes are a good way to tour Wúxī, though the traffic is quite congested. The lane directly across the street from the north bus station has a couple of rental shops. They charge Y1 per hour.

Taxis start at Y8.

YÍXĪNG COUNTY 宜兴县
Yíxīng Xiàn

Yíxīng county is famous for its tea utensils, in particular its pots. Delicious tea can be made in an aged Yíxīng teapot simply by adding hot water, or so it's claimed. The potteries of Yíxīng, especially in Dīngshān, are a popular excursion for Chinese tourists but see very few foreign visitors.

The town of Yíxīng is *not* an attraction, although most visitors end up passing through the place to catch a bus to Dīngshān and the nearby karst caves.

Karst Caves 石灰岩洞
Shíhuī Yándòng

There are karst caves to the south-west of Yíxīng township, and if you're in the area, it's worth visiting one of them. Despite the standard selection of coloured neon lighting up the interior of the caves, you may need to rent a rather useless torch (flashlight) for Y10, although it's far better to bring your own. The caves are cold and slippery so take a jacket and wear sturdy footwear.

To reach the caves from Yíxīng, hop on a bus to Dīngshān and indicate to the driver that you want to get off at the crossroads to the caves. You can also hire a minivan taxi in Dīngshān for Y25 to Y75, depending on how many caves you want to visit.

Shànjuǎn Cave This cave *(Shànjuǎn Dòng;* ☎ *739 4870; adult/child Y38/19; open 7am-5.30pm daily)* is embedded in Lúoyán Shān (Snail Shell Hill), 25km south-west of Yíxīng. It covers an area of roughly 5000 sq metres. Entry is via the middle cave, a stone hall with a 1000m floor space. From here you can mount a staircase to the 'snail's shell', the upper cave, or wander down to the lower caves and the water cave. In the water cave, a rowing boat takes people for a 120m ride to the exit called 'Suddenly See the Light'.

The turn-off road for the cave is about 10 minutes' south of Yíxīng by bus on the route to Dīngshān. From the turn-off road, catch a minibus heading west. It's about 15km to the cave.

Zhānggōng Cave Nineteen kilometres south of Yíxīng town, Zhānggōng Cave (*Zhānggōng Dòng; ☎ 747 0468; adult/child Y30/15; open 7.30am-5.30pm daily*) is the most impressive of the three caves. It's similar in scale to Shànjuān Cave, but offers more possibilities to explore smaller caves.

From inside you scale a small hill called Yúfēng Shān then emerge at the top amid a temple where there's a splendid view of the surrounding countryside with hamlets stretching as far as Tài Hú.

The cave is a short minibus ride west from the crossroads just past the Yíxīng Ceramics Museum on the road from Yíxīng to Dīngshān.

Línggǔ Cave Three kilometres down the road from Zhānggōng Cave, Línggǔ Cave (*Línggǔ Dòng; ☎ 747 0468; adult/child Y30/15; open 7.30am-5.30pm daily*) is the largest and least explored of the three caves. It features six large halls arrayed in a rough semicircle.

Near Línggǔ Cave is the **Yanxian Tea Plantation** (*Yánxiàn Cháchǎng; ☎ 747 0796; admission free*), with bushel-lots laid out like fat caterpillars stretching to the horizon. The trip is worth it for the tea fields alone.

Línggǔ Cave is a five-minute ride farther down the road from Zhānggōng Cave.

Ceramics Museum 宜兴陶瓷博物馆
Yíxīng Táocí Bówùguǎn

On the road to Dīngshān, a couple of minutes walk from the turn off for Zhānggōng Cave, this museum (*☎ 718 8308, 150 Dingshan Beilu; admission Y15; open 7.30pm-5pm daily*) displays examples of Yíxīng

pottery from 6000 years ago to the present day. Workshops near the entrance have ceramic artisans at work.

Dīngshān 丁山
Dīngshān is the pottery centre of Yíxīng county and has enjoyed that reputation since the Qin and Han dynasties; some of the scenes here, especially at the loading dock that leads into Tài Hú, are timeless.

Almost every local family is engaged in the manufacture of ceramics and at least half of the houses are made of the stuff. It's extremely dusty (and probably not recommended for people with respiratory problems). Everywhere you look vehicles are hauling rocks from the mountains outside of town.

Judging a Yíxīng Teapot

Buying a teapot in Dīngshān or the surrounding area can be a memorable experience. To help convince you of the high quality of their teapots, shopkeepers can be extremely animated. You'll encounter shopkeepers standing on the pot, blowing through its spout, striking a match on it, showing you that the inside is the same colour as the outside or rubbing their hand against the side and showing you your palm. Unfortunately, none of these antics give you much of an indication of whether a pot is good quality.

So what should you look for? First, make sure the teapot is stable – the body, spout, handle, lid and knob should all be balanced. Also, the lid should be deep-seated and firm (it shouldn't rattle or jam). The clay should be naturally shiny and slightly rough rather than glazed smooth. Finally, (and this is the most important thing) ask if you can put water in the pot – the water should shoot out straight from the spout instead of dribbling.

Prices can range wildly, from just a few yuán to US$20,000 for a pot made by a renowned artist. Some say that unless you are buying a teapot made by a well-known artist, don't pay more than Y30. You may want to visit the Yíxīng Ceramics Museum, located between Yíxīng and Dīngshān, to view high-quality teapots before venturing to the market across the street where a dizzying variety of generally low-quality teapots are for sale.

Dīngshān, about 15km south of Yíxīng town, has two dozen ceramics factories producing more than 2000 varieties of pottery – quite an output for a population of 100,000. Among the products are the ceramic tables and garbage bins you find around China, jars used to store oil and grain, the famed Yíxīng teapots, and glazed tiling and ceramic frescoes that are desperately needed as spare parts for tourist attractions – the Forbidden City in Běijīng is a customer. The ornamental rocks that you see in Chinese gardens are also made here.

Places to Stay
It's easy to visit this area on a day trip from Wúxī but you can also stay overnight.

Yíxīng Shànghǎi Bīnguǎn (☎ *740 1811, fax 740 4896, Gongyuan Lu*) Doubles Y300-360. This is a nice enough hotel to stay the night and 30% discounts make it a reasonable deal.

Shopping
If you've taken all the trouble to get here, don't leave without buying some pottery. There's a lot of variety, not just the standard Yíxīng style, and it's very cheap. The best place to go is a huge *pottery market (lóngxī táocí shìchǎng),* across the highway from the ceramics museum. There's a number of *stores* and small *stalls* with literally tonnes of pottery. Mid-size teapots range in price from Y20 to Y300 and they also have wonderful goldfish bowls on elongated stems for Y150 that would make great bird baths if you could get them home. The market is open daily from 7.30am to 7pm.

Getting There & Away
Frequent buses go from Wúxī to Yíxīng (Y10, 1½ hours). From Yíxīng minibuses go back and forth to Dīngshān (Y3, 20 minutes).

SŪZHŌU 苏州
☎ 0512 • pop 5,749,900
Jiāngsū's most famous attraction, Sūzhōu, is a famed silk production centre and a celebrated retreat brimming with gardens and canals. Unfortunately, this hasn't done anything to hold back the tide of urban renewal. Much of the city's charm has been swept away by new road, housing and hotel developments. Nevertheless, a wander through the charming gardens and what

remains of its cobbled alleys makes a visit to Sūzhōu worthwhile.

Sūzhōu's gardens are looked upon as works of art – a fusion of nature, architecture, poetry and painting designed to ease, move or assist the mind.

History
Dating back some 2500 years, Sūzhōu is one of the oldest towns in the Yangzi Basin. With the completion of the Grand Canal in the Sui dynasty, Sūzhōu found itself strategically located on a major trading route, and the city's fortunes and size grew rapidly.

Sūzhōu flourished as a centre of shipping and grain storage, bustling with merchants and artisans. By the 12th century it had attained its present dimensions and layout.

The city walls, a rectangle enclosed by moats, were pierced by six gates (north, south, two in the east, and two in the west). Crisscrossing the city were six north-south canals and 14 east-west canals. Although the walls have largely disappeared and a fair proportion of the canals have been plugged, central Sūzhōu retains some of its 'Renaissance' character. The Wàichéng Hé moat still encircles the city.

A legend was spun about Sūzhōu through tales of beautiful women with mellifluous voices, and through the famous proverb 'In heaven there is paradise, on earth Sūzhōu and Hángzhōu'. The story picks up when Marco Polo arrived in 1276. He added the adjectives 'great' and 'noble', although he reserved his finer epithets for Hángzhōu.

By the 14th century Sūzhōu had established itself as China's leading silk producer and aristocrats, pleasure-seekers, famous scholars, actors and painters were attracted to the city, constructing villas and garden retreats for themselves.

At the height of Sūzhōu's development in the 16th century, the gardens, large and small, numbered over 100. If we mark time here, we arrive at the town's current tourist formula – 'Garden City, Venice of the East', a medieval mix of woodblock guilds and embroidery societies, whitewashed housing, cobbled streets, tree-lined avenues and canals.

The wretched workers of the silk sweatshops, protesting against paltry wages and the injustices of the contract hire system, were staging violent strikes back in the 15th century, and the landlords shifted as a result.

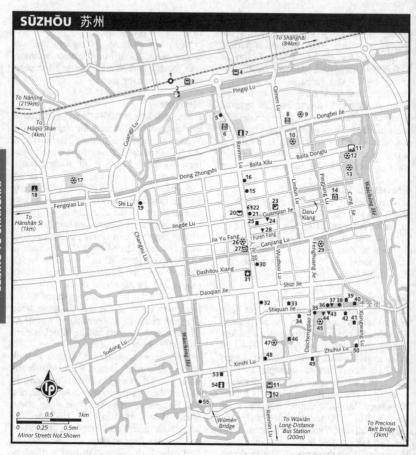

SŪZHŌU 苏州

In 1860 Taiping troops took the town without a blow. In 1896 Sūzhōu was opened to foreign trade, with Japanese and international concessions. During WWII, it was occupied by the Japanese and then by the Kuomintang. Somehow it slipped through the worst ravages of the Cultural Revolution relatively unscathed. These days Sūzhōu is a popular alternative to Shànghǎi for foreign companies investing in hi-tech and light industrial manufacturing.

Orientation

Besides the numerous small canals, Sūzhōu is surrounded by a large, rectangular outer canal (Wàichéng Hé). The main thoroughfare, Renmin Lu, bisects the city into western and eastern halves, while another

large canal, cuts across the middle. The train and main bus stations are at the northern end of town, on the north side of the outer canal. A large boat dock and another long-distance bus station are at the southern end.

Information

Tourist Offices Sūzhōu's CITS (☎ 520 3250) is on the 3rd floor at 1 Daichengqiao Lu. There's also an office beside Lèxiāng Fàndiàn.

Money The main Bank of China is at 490 Renmin Lu. Major tourist hotels also have foreign-exchange counters.

Post & Communications The main post office is on the corner of Renmin Lu and

SŪZHŌU

PLACES TO STAY
25 Lèxiāng Fàndiàn; CITS
    乐乡饭店;
    中国国际旅行社
33 Nánlín Fàndiàn
    南林饭店
34 Nányuán Bīnguǎn
    南园宾馆
39 Yíngfèng Bīnguǎn
    迎风宾馆
40 Dōngwú Fàndiàn
    东吴饭店
41 Gūsū Fàndiàn
    姑苏饭店
42 Sūzhōu Fàndiàn
    苏州饭店
46 Cānglàng Bīnguǎn
    沧浪宾馆
49 Yǒuyì Bīnguǎn
    友谊宾馆
50 Xiāngwáng Bīnguǎn
    相王宾馆
53 Sheraton Suzhou
    Hotel & Towers
    苏州吴宫喜登大酒店

PLACES TO EAT
24 Sōnghè Lóu
    松鹤楼
28 Sicily Pub
    & Restaurant
    西西里餐厅
37 Yángyáng
    Shuǐjiǎoguǎn
    洋洋水饺馆
43 Héxiāng Cūn
    禾香村餐厅
44 Yonghe Soya-Bean
    Milk Shop
    永和豆浆

GARDENS
9   Humble
    Administrator's
    Garden
    拙政园
10 Lion Grove
    狮子林

12 East Garden
    东园
13 Couple's Garden
    耦园
17 Garden for
    Lingering In
    留园
26 Garden of Harmony
    怡园
29 Twin Pagodas
    双塔院
45 Garden of the
    Master of the Nets
    网师园
47 Blue Wave Pavilion
    沧浪亭

**MUSEUMS TEMPLES
& PAGODAS**
6   Suzhou Silk
    Museum
    丝绸博物馆
7   Běisì Tǎ
    北寺塔
8   Suzhou Museum
    苏州博物馆
14 Museum of Opera
    & Theatre
    戏曲博物馆
18 Xīyuán Sì
    西园寺
23 Temple of Mystery
    玄妙观
54 Ruìguāng Tǎ
    瑞光塔

TRANSPORT
1   Train Station
    火车站
2   Foreign Travellers
    Transportation
    Company Pier
    游船游览
3   Local Buses
    当地汽车
4   North Long-Distance
    Bus Station
    气车北站

5   Yángyáng Chēháng
    Bicycle Rental
    租自行车店
16 Lianhe Ticket Centre
    联合售票处
30 China Eastern Airlines
    Booking Office
    东方航空售票处
35 CITS
    中国国际旅行社
38 Bicycle Rental
    租自行车店
51 South Long-Distance
    Bus Station
    汽车南站
52 Grand Canal Boats;
    Ticket Office
    轮船码头; 售票处

OTHER
11 Zoo
    动物园
15 Dōngwú Sīchóu
    Shāngdiàn
    东吴丝绸商店
19 Shi Lu Night Market
    石路夜市场
20 Main Post Office
    邮局
21 Suzhou Food Centre
    苏州食品大厦
22 Main Bank of China
    中国银行
27 China Telecom
    Internet
    电信网吧
31 PSB
    公安局
32 Library
    图书馆
36 Mystery Holy
    Things Shop
    优藏阁工艺店
48 Foreign Language
    Bookshop
    外文书店
55 Coiled Gate
    盘门

Jingde Lu. China Telecom has a pleasant Internet cafe at 333 Renmin Lu. Called Wǎngyǒu Kōngjiān, it has fast connections and charges Y4 per hour. It's open 9.30am to 9pm daily.

Sūzhōu has a stunning new library complex on Renmin Lu. Internet services are on the 2nd floor, but you need a library card to access them.

Bookshops Sūzhōu's Foreign Language Bookshop is at 44 Renmin Lu, and has both English and Chinese maps of Sūzhōu and around.

PSB The PSB (☎ 522 5661 ext 20593) is at 201 Renmin Lu. Look for the lane called Dashitou Xiang by the main gate. The visa office is about 200m down the lane.

Běisì Tǎ 北寺塔
North Temple Pagoda

Běisì Tǎ (☎ 753 1197, 652 Renmin Lu; adult/child Y10/5; open 7.30am-6pm daily) is the tallest pagoda south of Cháng Jiāng – at nine storeys it dominates the area. Climb it for a fine aerial view of the town and the farmland beyond, where tea, rice and wheat are grown. The factory chimneys (the new pagodas of Sūzhōu) loom on the outskirts, hovering in the haze and smoke they create.

The temple complex goes back 1700 years and was originally a residence. The pagoda has been burnt, built and rebuilt. Off to the side is **Nánmù Guānyīn Hall** (Nánmù Guānyīn Diàn), which was rebuilt in the Ming dynasty with some of its features imported from elsewhere. There's a teahouse with a small garden out the back.

Suzhou Museum 苏州博物馆
Sūzhōu Bówùguǎn

The Suzhou Museum (☎ 754 1534, 204 Dongbei Jie; admission Y5; open 8am-4pm daily) was once the residence of Taiping leader Li Xiucheng.

The museum offers some interesting old maps, including those of the Grand Canal, Sūzhōu, and heaven and earth. It also houses Qing dynasty steles forbidding workers' strikes, and relics such as funerary objects, porcelain bowls and bronze swords unearthed or rescued from various sites around the Sūzhōu district. Unfortunately, there are few English captions.

Suzhou Silk Museum 苏州丝绸博物馆
Sūzhōu Sīchóu Bówùguǎn

Highly recommended, this museum (☎ 753 6538, 661 Renmin Lu; admission Y7; open 9am-5.30pm daily) houses a number of fascinating exhibitions that give a thorough history of Sūzhōu's silk industry over the past 4000 years. Exhibits include a section on old looms and weaving techniques and a room with live silk worms in various stages of life. A second building displays clothing made of silk from the early 1900s. Many of the captions are in English.

Temple of Mystery 玄妙观
Xuánmiào Guàn

This Taoist temple (☎ 727 6948, Guanqian Jie; admission Y10; open 7.30am-5.30pm daily) seems almost an anomaly, plunked in the middle of the rampant commercialism that is Guanqian Jie. This area was the heart of what was once the Sūzhōu Bazaar, so maybe the McDonald's and KFC's aren't out out of place after all. Perhaps only the Taoists have the answer.

The temple was founded and laid out during the Jin dynasty in the 3rd century AD, with additions in the Song dynasty. From the Qing dynasty on, the bazaar fanned out from the temple with tradespeople and travelling performers using the grounds.

The enormous temple hall, **Sānqīng Diàn**, is supported by 60 pillars and capped by a double roof with upturned eaves. It dates from 1181 and was burnt and seriously damaged in the 19th century. During the Cultural Revolution the Red Guards squatted here and it was later transformed into a library. For an extra Y5 you can listen to music performed by the Taoist priests, usually in the morning.

Museum of Opera & Theatre
戏曲博物馆
Xìqǔ Bówùguǎn

In the old city of Sūzhōu, this small museum (☎ 727 3741, 14 Zhongzhangjia Xiang; admission Y3; open 8.30am-4pm daily) is worth going to for the surrounding small cobblestone lanes lined with stalls selling vegetables and inexpensive snacks. The museum features the history of kūnqǔ, the opera style of this region, and the singing and storytelling art form sung in Sūzhōu dialect known as píngtán. It houses a moveable stage, old musical instruments, costumes and photos of famous performers. They also put on occasional performances of kūnqǔ and píngtán.

Humble Administrator's Garden
拙政园
Zhuózhèng Yuán

Many consider the Humble Administrator's Garden (☎ 751 0286, 178 Dongbei Jie; adult/child Y32/16; open 7.30am-5.30pm daily) to be one of Sūzhōu's best, second only to the Garden of the Master of the Nets.

Dating back to the early 1500s, this garden's five hectares feature streams, ponds, bridges and islands of bamboo. There's also a teahouse and a small museum that explains Chinese landscape gardening concepts.

Blue Wave Pavilion 沧浪亭
Cānglàng Tíng

A bit on the wild side with winding creeks and luxuriant trees, this one-hectare garden (☎ 519 4375; admission Y8; open 8am-4.30pm daily), off Renmin Lu, is one of the oldest in Sūzhōu. The buildings date from the 11th century, although they have been rebuilt on numerous occasions since.

Originally the home of a prince, the property passed into the hands of the poet and scholar Su Shunqin (Su Zimei), who gave it its name. The designers have tried to create optical illusions with the scenery both outside and inside – you look from the pool immediately outside to the distant hills. **Enlightenment Hall** (*Míngdào Táng*), the largest building, is said to have been a site for delivery of lectures during the Ming dynasty. Close by, on the other side of Renmin Lu, is the former Confucian Temple.

The entrance is signposted as 'Surging Wave' Pavilion.

Garden of the Master of the Nets 网师园
Wǎngshī Yuán

Off Shiquan Jie, this is the smallest garden (☎ 520 3514; admission Y10; open 8am-5pm daily) in Sūzhōu – half the size of the Blue Wave Pavilion and one-tenth the size of the Humble Administrator's Garden. It's small but well worth a visit as it's better than all the others combined.

The garden was laid out in the 12th century, abandoned, then restored in the 18th century as part of the residence of a retired official. According to one story, he announced that he'd had enough of bureaucracy and would rather be a fisherman. Another explanation of the name is that it was simply near Wangshi Lu. The eastern part of the garden is the residential area – originally with side rooms for sedan-chair lackeys, guest reception and living quarters. The central section is the main garden. The western section is an inner garden where a courtyard contains the **Spring Rear Cottage** (*Diànchūn Yí*), the master's study. This section, including the study with its Ming-style furniture and palace lanterns, was duplicated and unveiled at the Metropolitan Museum of Art in New York in 1981.

The most striking feature of this garden is its use of space. Despite its size, the scale

---

Sūzhōu's Gardens

The key elements of these famous gardens are rocks and water. Just like the Zen gardens of Japan, there are surprisingly few flowers, and no fountains. Although the gardens were designed to perfection, they were intended to give the illusion of a natural scene consisting of only moss, sand and rock. These microcosms were laid out by master craftspeople and have changed hands many times over the centuries.

The gardens suffered a setback during the Taiping Rebellion in the 1860s, and under subsequent foreign domination of Sūzhōu. Efforts were made to restore them in the 1950s, but during the so-called Horticultural Revolution gardeners downed tools, as flowers were frowned upon.

In 1979 the Suzhou Garden Society was formed, and an export company was set up to promote Sūzhōu-designed gardens. A number of the gardens have been renovated and opened to the public.

BĚIJĪNG TO SHÀNGHǍI

---

of the buildings is large, but nothing appears cramped. A section of the buildings is used by a co-operative of woodblock artists.

There are two entrances to the entry gate, with English signs and souvenir stalls marking the way. You can enter the alley next to the *Yonghe Soya-Bean Milk Shop (Yǒnghé Dòujiāng)* on Shiquan Jie or an alley off Daichengqiao Lu. There are also music performances in the evening (see the Entertainment section later).

Garden for Lingering In 留园
Liú Yuán

Extending over an area of three hectares, the Garden for Lingering In (☎ 533 7903, 79 Liuyuan Lu; adult/child Y16/8; open 7.30am-5pm daily) is one of the largest gardens in Sūzhōu, noted for its adroit partitioning with building complexes. The garden dates from the Ming dynasty and managed to escape destruction during the Taiping Rebellion.

A 700m covered walkway connects the major scenic spots, and the windows have carefully selected perspectives. The walkway is inlaid with calligraphy from celebrated masters and the garden has a wealth of potted plants. In the north-east section of the garden, there's a particularly large example of a sculptured rock from Tài Hú; at 6.5m high you couldn't miss it if you tried.

The garden is about 4km west of the city centre. Tourist bus No Y2 goes there from the train station or Renmin Lu.

Xīyuán Sì 西园寺
West Garden Temple

A short distance west of the Garden for Lingering In, Xīyuán Sì (☎ 551 7114, *Xiyuan Lu; admission Y10; open 7.30am-5.30pm daily*) was built on the site of a garden laid out at the same time as the Garden for Lingering In, and then donated to the Buddhist community. The temple was destroyed in the 19th century and entirely rebuilt; it contains some expressive Buddhist statues.

Hánshān Sì 寒山寺
Cold Mountain Temple

About 3km west of the Garden for Lingering In, this temple (☎ 723 2891, *24 Hanshansi Long; admission Y10; open 7.30am-5pm daily*) was named after the poet-monk Han Shan, who lived in the 7th century. It was repeatedly burnt down and rebuilt, and was once the site of local trading in silk, wood and grain. Not far from its saffron walls lies the Grand Canal. Today, the temple holds little of interest except for a stele by poet Zhang Ji immortalising both the nearby Maple Bridge and the temple bell (since removed to Japan). However, the fine walls and the humpback bridge are worth seeing.

Tourist bus No Y3 takes you from the train station to Hánshān Sì.

Hǔqiū Shān 虎丘山
Tiger Hill

In the far north-west of town, Hǔqiū Shān (☎ 723 2305, *Huqiu Lu; adult/child Y20/10; open 7.30am-6pm daily*) is extremely popular with local tourists. The hill itself is artificial and is the final resting place of He Lu, founding father of Sūzhōu. He Lu died in the 6th century BC and myths have coalesced around him – he is said to have been buried with a collection of 3000 swords and to be guarded by a white tiger.

Built in the 10th century, the leaning **Yúnyán Tǎ** (*Cloud Rock Pagoda*) stands atop Hǔqiū Shān. The octagonal seven-storey pagoda, also known as Hǔqiū Pagoda, is built entirely of brick, an innovation in Chinese architecture at the time. The pagoda began tilting over 400 years ago, and today the highest point is displaced more than 2m from its original position.

Tourist buses Nos Y1 and Y2 from the train station go to Hǔqiū Shān.

Coiled Gate 盘门
Pán Mén

In the south-west corner of the city, straddling the outer moat, this stretch of the city wall has Sūzhōu's only remaining original city gate (☎ 519 3054, *1 Dongda Jie; admission Y15; open 8am-5pm daily*). It's one of the nicest areas of the city to visit. The exquisite arched bridge **Wúmén Bridge** (*Wúmén Qiáo*), crosses the canal just to the east. From the top of the gate there are good views of the moat, surrounding houses and **Ruìguāng Tǎ** (*Auspicious Light Pagoda*), the oldest pagoda in Jiāngsū, dating from the 3rd century AD. You can climb the pagoda (Y6) for a view of Sūzhōu.

To get there, take tourist bus No Y5 from the train station or Changxu Lu.

Boat Tours

By the canal south of the train station, a boat tour (Y50 per person) goes north to Hǔqiū Shān or west to Hánshān Sì. Either trip takes about an hour. Boats depart from the Foreign Travellers Transportation Company Pier (Wàishì Lǚyóu Chēchuán Gōngsī Mǎtou; ☎ 753 9985) on Chezhan Lu.

Places to Stay

Sūzhōu has little to offer in the way of cheap accommodation. It's often possible to bargain room prices down, however, so don't be immediately deterred by the posted rates.

Hotel touts outside Sūzhōu's train station, especially those with pedicabs, can be extremely aggressive. They may offer a ridiculously cheap fare to your destination and then, once you are loaded into their pedicab, claim that the hotel you have chosen has been bulldozed or burnt to the ground. They will then insist on taking you to a hotel of their choice. The problem is that their choice is often not as cheap as they claim or doesn't accept foreigners.

A couple of hours later you may still not have found a place to stay and instead be stuck with a large taxi bill.

Places to Stay – Budget

Dōngwú Fàndiàn (☎ 519 4437, fax 519 4590, 24 Wuyachang) Doubles with shared bath & air-con Y100, with private bath Y180-280. This clean place, off Shiquan Jie, is run by the Suzhou University International Cultural Exchange Institute.

Yíngfēng Bīnguǎn (☎ 530 0907, 39 Wuyachang) Doubles with bath Y230. This hotel, off Shiquan Jie, is over a small footbridge opposite Sūzhōu Fàndiàn. Don't be put off by the hotel's grotty exterior or drab lobby; rooms are clean and quite nice, some looking onto a central garden. At a discount the doubles go for Y180.

Cānglàng Bīnguǎn (☎ 520 1557, fax 510 3285, 53 Wuqueqiao Lu) Doubles Y180. This place is a little drab but liveable if nothing else is available.

Xiāngwáng Bīnguǎn (☎ 529 1162, fax 529 1182, 118 Zhuhui Lu) Doubles Y220-280. This hotel is a little exposed to busy Zhuhui Lu, but the discounted rooms at Y150 to Y180 make it a budget option.

Places to Stay – Mid-Range

Yǒuyì Bīnguǎn (Friendship Hotel; ☎ 529 1601, fax 520 6221, 243 Zhuhui Lu) Singles Y380, doubles Y240-400. This hotel offers good mid-range accommodation. The more expensive rooms are in the newer west building and 10% discounts are sometimes available.

Nánlín Fàndiàn (☎ 519 6333, fax 519 1028, 20 Gunxiufang) Doubles Y270-600. Nánlín Fàndiàn, off Shiquan Jie, has pleasant gardens and caters to foreign tour groups. Doubles are in a new building and the suites are upmarket. Discounted rooms may go for Y178.

Lèxiāng Fàndiàn (☎ 522 2815, fax 524 4165, 18 Dajing Xiang) Singles Y380, doubles Y480-580. Close to the city centre, this hotel has been recommended by readers. It's been recently renovated and is a bit pricey, though discounts are available and singles at Y300 are good value.

Places to Stay – Top End

Gūsū Fàndiàn (☎ 520 0566, fax 519 9727, 5 Xiangwang Lu) Doubles Y480-560. This pleasant, smaller hotel is close to Shiquan Jie and offers 35% discounts.

Sūzhōu Fàndiàn (☎ 520 4646, fax 520 4015, 115 Shiquan Jie) Doubles Y500-600.

This is a sprawling place that does a brisk trade in tour groups. Discounts bring the prices down slightly but both Nánlín Fàndiàn and Nányuán Bīnguǎn have nicer grounds.

Nányuán Bīnguǎn (Nanyuan Guesthouse; ☎ 519 7661, fax 519 8806, 249 Shiquan Jie) Doubles Y436-600. This place is inside an exquisite, large, walled garden compound with many different buildings to stay in. Discounts of 30% make it very good value.

Sheraton Suzhou Hotel & Towers (☎ 510 3388, Ⓦ www.sheraton.com, 388 Xinshi Lu) Doubles US$180. A notable example of corporate culture masquerading as refined Chinese classicism, this hotel is absolutely the best and most expensive hotel in Sūzhōu. Beautifully designed, it shows how far the Sheraton has come since the first monstrosity was built in Běijīng two decades ago.

Places to Eat

Sūzhōu is a tourist town and consequently there's no shortage of places dishing up local and tourist cuisine. Shiquan Jie, between Daichengqiao Lu and Xiangwang Lu, is lined with bars, restaurants and bakeries.

Yonghe Soya-Bean Milk Shop (Yǒnghé Dòujiāng; ☎ 510 5918, 191 Shiquan Jie) Mains Y5-15. Open 24 hours. This place serves tasty rice, noodle and soup dishes; for breakfast there's the house specialty, *dòujiāng* (sweetened soy milk), and *yóutiáo* (fried dough sticks).

Héxiāng Cūn (183 Shiquan Jie) Mains Y15-25. Open 8am-2am daily. This small place serves cheap, delicious meals and the draught beer is only Y5 a pint. Try the *yúxiāng dòufu* (spicy tofu slices) for Y16.

Yángyáng Shuǐjiǎoguǎn (Authentic Chinese Dumpling House; ☎ 519 2728, 144 Shiquan Jie) Mains Y5-25. Open 7am-3am daily. This very popular restaurant has fresh dumplings, snails and vegie dishes for very reasonable prices – a dozen *shuǐjiǎo* (boiled dumplings) are Y5. You can't miss it because there's a sign on the door saying 'recommended by Lonely Planet' – rest assured no one got a free meal out of this. Try upstairs for more seating if downstairs is full.

If you're on a tight budget, try the *food courts* of the new department stores at the southern end of Renmin Lu as well as the area around Shi Lu.

Sōnghè Lóu (☎ 727 7006, 141 Guanqian Jie) Mains Y20-40. Open 5pm-8pm daily. If money is no object, try this restaurant, rated as the most famous in Sūzhōu; Emperor Qianlong is said to have eaten here. Like many famous restaurants in China, it's huge and overwhelming. Among the large variety of dishes is *sōngshǔ guìyú* (squirrel fish) – fish cooked in sweet and sour sauce. The entrance is around the corner on Taijian Lu. Travellers give the restaurant mixed reviews.

Sicily Pub & Restaurant (☎ 523 2393, 1 Shaomozhen Xiang) Mains Y15-30. Open 11am-2am daily. This is a nice, intimate place to go if you feel like a beer and some Western food in pleasant surroundings. Sandwiches are Y12 and a meal of baked chicken is Y25.

Entertainment

Garden of the Master of the Nets (☎ 520 3514) Tickets Y60. Open 7.30pm-9.30pm daily. These shows, where the audience moves from pavilion to pavilion to watch a variety of traditional Chinese performing arts, are quite popular with tour groups. Visiting the garden at night shows it in a different light but travellers have complained that it's so crowded you can't really appreciate the performances. Try going late in the evening.

Shopping

Sūzhōu-style embroidery, calligraphy, paintings, sandalwood fans, writing brushes and silk underclothes are for sale nearly everywhere. For good quality items at competitive rates, shop along Shiquan Jie, east off Renmin Lu. The street is lined with shops and markets selling souvenirs.

Mysterious Holy Things Shop (☎ 519 9915, 146-1 Shiquan Jie) Open 9am-10.30pm daily. This small shop has jewellery and art items from China's minority areas.

A lively **night market** takes place every evening near Shi Lu from about 6.30pm to 9.30pm, selling food, clothing and all kinds of stuff.

The northern part of Renmin Lu has a number of large silk stores.

Dōngwú Sīchóu Shāngdiàn (☎ 770 6650, 540 Renmin Lu) Open 8am-10pm daily. This shop is attached to a silk factory and has clothes, material and bedding. Wonderful silk duvets go for Y320.

Suzhou Food Centre (Sūzhōu Shípǐn Dàshà; ☎ 523 8672, 246 Renmin Lu) Open 8.30am-9pm daily. This place sells all kinds of local, traditional specialities and teas in bulk.

Getting There & Away

Air Sūzhōu does not have an airport, but China Eastern Airlines (Dōngfāng Hángkōng Gōngsī; ☎ 522 2788) has a ticket office at 192 Renmin Lu for booking flights out of Shànghǎi. For international tickets, you can also try the CITS beside Lèxiāng Fàndiàn. Buses leave frequently for Hóngqiáo Airport in Shànghǎi. Tickets are Y45.

Bus Sūzhōu has three long-distance bus stations. The main one is at the northern end of Renmin Lu, next to the train station, and a second is at the southern end of Renmin Lu. Both have connections to just about every major place in the region, including Shànghǎi (Y30, 1½ hours), Hángzhōu (Y75, three hours), Wúxī (Y18, 30 minutes), Nánjīng (Y64, 2½ hours) and Zhōuzhuāng (Y15, 1½ hours).

A third station, the Wúxiàn long-distance bus station (Wúxiàn chēzhàn), farther south on Renmin Lu, has similar connections with other buses that are slightly cheaper, but run less frequently than from the other two stations.

Travelling by bus on the Nánjīng-Shànghǎi freeway takes about the same amount of time as the train, but tickets are generally slightly more expensive.

Train Sūzhōu is on the Nánjīng-Shànghǎi train line. The fastest train to Shànghǎi (Y13) takes about 45 minutes; more frequent trains take one hour. There are also trains to Wúxī (Y10, 30 minutes) and Nánjīng (Y26, 2½ hours). CITS will book sleepers for a Y30 service charge or you can book train tickets on the 2nd floor of the Lianhe Ticket Centre (Liánhé Shòupiàochù) at 556 Renmin Lu. A Y5 service charge is added for sleepers. It's open daily from 8.30am to 5pm.

Boat Overnight passenger boats travel along the Grand Canal to Hángzhōu and many travellers enjoy this experience. The boat departs daily at 5.30pm and arrives the next morning at 7am. You can purchase tickets at the dock at the southern end of Renmin Lu or at the Lianhe Ticket Centre (see the Train section for details). Tickets in a four-person cabin cost Y60 or Y88 per person, or Y130 per person for a two-person cabin.

Getting Around

Bus Sūzhōu has some convenient tourist buses that visit all the sites and cost Y2. They all pass by the train station. Bus No Y5 goes around the western and eastern sides of the city. Bus No Y2 travels from Hǔqiū Shān south to the Coiled Gate and along Shiquan Jie. Bus Nos Y1 and Y4 run the length of Renmin Lu. Bus Nos Y3 and Y4 also pass by Hánshān Sì.

Taxi There are plenty of taxis in Sūzhōu. They start at Y10 and drivers generally use their meters. Pedicabs hover around the tourist areas and, like elsewhere in China, can be fairly aggressive. Expect to barter hard.

Bicycle Riding a bike is absolutely the best way to tour Sūzhōu. Search out the quieter streets and travel along the canals to get the most of what this city has to offer.

There are a couple of bicycle rental shops near the Silk Museum and on Shiquan Jie near the entrance to Sūzhōu Fàndiàn. The charge is Y10 per day and a deposit is required. We recommend the rental shop called Yángyáng Chēháng at 673 Renmin Lu, about 300m north of the Silk Museum.

AROUND SŪZHŌU
Grand Canal 大运河
Dà Yùnhé

The Grand Canal proper cuts to the west and south of Sūzhōu, within a 10km range of the town. Suburban bus Nos 13, 14, 15 and 16 will get you there. In the north-west, bus No 11 follows the canal for a fair distance, taking you on a tour of the enchanting countryside. Hop off the bus once you find yourself a nice bridge on which you can perch and watch the world of the canal float by. Parking yourself for too long could make you the main attraction.

Precious Belt Bridge 宝带桥
Bǎodài Qiáo

With 53 arches, this is considered one of China's best bridges. It straddles the Grand Canal, and is a popular spot with fisherfolk. The three central humpbacks of the bridge are larger to allow boats through. It recently had some extensive maintenance done but is no longer used for traffic – a modern one has been built alongside it.

Precious Belt Bridge is thought to be a Tang dynasty construction named after Wang Zhongshu, a local prefect who sold his precious belt to pay for the bridge's construction for the benefit of his people.

The bridge is 4km south-east of Sūzhōu. You can get there by taxi or a 30-minute bike ride. Head south on Renmin Lu, over Wáichéng Hé. Turn left on Nanhuan Donglu after you pass the Wúxiàn long-distance bus station. Head east until you hit the canal on Dongqing Lu then south to the bridge.

Tài Hú Area

The towns surrounding Sūzhōu provide ample opportunity for a visit to Tài Hú and the countryside beyond the lake.

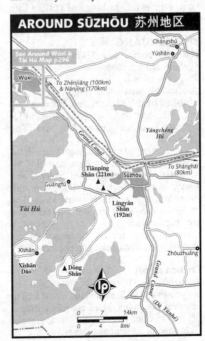

AROUND SŪZHŌU 苏州地区

All of the following destinations can be reached by long-distance bus from Sūzhōu's southern or Wúxiàn long-distance bus stations.

Língyán Shān (☎ 626 1095, Lingtian Lu; admission Y1; open 6.30am-4.30pm daily), 11km south-west of Sūzhōu, is home to an active Buddhist monastery; **Tiānpíng Shān** (Heavenly Peace Hill; ☎ 626 1382, Lingtian Lu; admission Y6; open 8am-5.30pm daily), 13km west of Sūzhōu, is famous for its medicinal spring waters; and **Guāngfú**, 22km west of Sūzhōu, borders the lake with an ancient seven-storey pagoda.

Tourist bus No Y4 goes to Língyán Shān and Tiānpíng Shān.

Dōng Shān (East Hill; ☎ 628 1236; admission Y15; open 7.30am-5pm daily), 37km south-west of Sūzhōu, is surrounded by the lake on three sides and noted for its gardens and the **Purple Gold Nunnery** (Zǐjīn'ān), which contains 16 coloured clay icons. To see eroded Tài Hú rocks 'harvested' for landscaping, visit **Xīshān Dǎo** (Xīshān Island), located 33km south-west of Sūzhōu.

Head 44km north-east to **Chángshú**, known for its lace making and **Yúshān** with its nine-storey Song Pagoda.

ZHŌUZHUĀNG 周庄

Set in the countryside 32km south-east of Sūzhōu, Zhōuzhuāng offers a step back in time into what is known as a water town, bisected by canals and stone bridges. Established over 900 years ago, Zhōuzhuāng has 14 bridges and over 60% of its buildings are from the Yuan, Ming and Qing dynasties.

Zhōuzhuāng also has a huge tourism industry and is extremely popular with Chinese tourists. Despite the crowds and souvenir stalls, a day walking through Zhōuzhuāng is definitely worthwhile. The bridges and cobbled lanes of the Old Town are picturesque and it's long been a favourite place for art students who sit alongside the canals with their easels.

Orientation

Zhōuzhuāng's Old Town is quite small and it's possible to walk around the whole area in less than two hours. Maps are sold throughout the town and have English names for the sights and more famous bridges.

Information

Zhōuzhuāng is not a convenient town to change money; to be on the safe side, have enough cash before arriving.

Things to See

The entrance to Zhōuzhuāng's **Old Town** (☎ 721 1655, Quangong Lu; admission Y60; open 7.30am-6pm daily) is at the western end of Quangong Lu. The admission includes the entry fee for all the exhibits inside.

Quánfú Tǎ (Pagoda of Total Well-Being; Quanfu Lu) was built in 1987 to hide the water tower in preparation for the tourism boom promoted by the provincial government. The campaign seems to have been an enormous success, with Zhōuzhuāng recently declared an International Heritage Site by the United Nations in 1998.

From the pagoda it's a short walk south to the **Ancient Memorial Arch** (Gǔbēi Lóu). Inside the Old Town there are 10 sights including temples, gardens and the former homes of officers from the Qing and Ming dynasties. No vehicles are allowed on the narrow cobbled alleys of the Old Town.

The **Hall of Zhang's Residence** (Zhāng Tíng) dates from the Ming dynasty and has six courtyards and over 70 rooms. Running through the back of the residence is a small waterway that allowed access to the house by boat.

South of here, the **Hall of Shen's Residence** (Shěn Tíng) is considered the best residence in Zhōuzhuāng, containing seven courtyards and over 100 rooms, each connected to a main hall.

At the southern end of town, **Quánfú Sì** (Temple of Total Well-Being) contains 21 gold Buddhas plus one large bronze Buddha measuring over 5m in height. The temple is surrounded by pagodas and courtyard buildings, extending into **South Lake Garden** (Nán Hú Yuán). The garden was built for Zhang Jiying, a literary man of the Jin dynasty, and consists of bridges crisscrossing over the water.

The **Zhouzhuang Museum** (Zhōuzhuāng Bówùguǎn) is home to nearly 1000 artefacts including items from the local fishing and artisan industries.

South of the museum is the **Chéngxū Temple** (Chéngxū Dàoyuàn), a Taoist temple built during the Song dynasty.

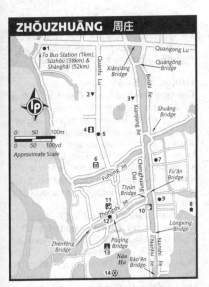

ZHŌUZHUĀNG 周庄

PLACES TO STAY & EAT

2 Vegetable Market
   蔬菜市场
3 Páilóu Càiguǎn
   牌楼菜馆
8 Fengdan Double Bridge Resort
   枫丹双桥度假村

MUSEUM & RESIDENCES

6 Zhouzhuang Museum
   周庄博物馆
7 Hall of Zhang's Residence
   张厅
9 Hall of Shen's Residence
   沈厅

OTHER

1 Old Town Entry Ticket Office
   古镇旅游售票处
4 Quánfù Tǎ
   全福塔
5 Ancient Memorial Arch
   古碑楼
10 Boat Tours
   游船游览
11 Chéngxū Temple
   澄虚道院
12 Shuixiang Pearl Mill
   水乡珍珠坊
13 Quánfù Sì
   全福寺
14 South Lake Garden
   南湖园

Almost all signs and captions within the sights are in Chinese only but you're more than likely to be befriended by a number of Chinese tourists who may be willing to be your tour guides.

It's fun to take a **boat tour** through the canals. The ticket office and wharf are just south of **Fù'ān Bridge** (*Fu'an Qiáo*) across **Tiyún Bridge** (*Tīyún Qiáo*). You can't miss the cluster of boats. Half-hour trips in an eight-seater cost Y60 per boat. Speedboats are available for hire to another nearby water town, **Tónglǐ**. Tickets are Y250 return.

Wooden sailboats tour around **Nán Hú** (*South Lake*) for Y40. Tickets are sold at an office at the southern end of Nanshi Jie. The trip lasts about 30 minutes.

Places to Stay

Zhōuzhuāng can easily be visited on a day trip from either Sūzhōu or Shànghǎi or as a stopover between the two.

Fengdan Double Bridge Resort (*Fēngdān Shuāngqiáo Dùjiàcūn;* ☎ 721 1549, fax 721 1490, Daqiao Lu) Doubles Y220-240. This hotel has 20% discounts on weekdays. The rooms are somewhat shabby but the location in the Old Town with a view of the water more than make up for it. To find the hotel, head south on Nan Shijie and take the first alley left after the Hall of Shen's Residence.

Places to Eat

The central area of the Old Town has many nondescript *restaurants* catering to tour groups at astronomical prices. For more reasonable prices try the north end of town along the main canal on Xianjiang Jie.

Páilóu Càiguǎn (*23 Xianjiang Jie*) Mains Y20-50. Open 7am-8pm daily. This small courtyard restaurant gets you out of the pedestrian traffic, though there are other restaurants across the lane that look over the canal if you prefer a view. Zhōuzhuāng's local specialty is *wànsāntí* a large, fatty dish of stewed pork knuckle. Expect to pay Y40.

The south-west part of the Old Town is quieter and Zhongshi Jie has some nice *teahouses* along the canal.

Shopping

A number of local specialities are available in Zhōuzhuāng, including woven goods, carved wooden buckets and utensils, sweets, lace and Yíxīng teapots. Locally harvested fresh water pearls are available at reasonable prices in every form from traditional jewellery to animal and pagoda shapes and even face powder.

Shuixiang Pearl Mill (*Shuĭxiāng Zhēnzhūfáng;* ☎ *721 2019, Zhongshi Jie*) Open 8.30am-5.30pm. The souvenir stalls sell pearls, but this is a reputable shop with fixed prices. Pearl necklaces range from Y120 to Y650.

Getting There & Away
Public buses let you off at the new bus station north-west of town and it's a bit of a hike across the Zhōuzhuāng Bridge and down to the entrance of the Old Town. Some buses cross the bridge and drive right up to the entry gate. If you take the tourist sightseeing bus from Shànghǎi it parks in a lot on the east end of Quangong Lu.

Frequent buses run between Sūzhōu's north long-distance bus station and Zhōuzhuāng (Y15, 1½ hours). The first leaves Sūzhōu at 7.10am with the last bus returning to Sūzhōu at 4.40pm.

One of the easiest ways to get to Zhōuzhuāng from Shànghǎi, especially for a day trip, is the tourist bus from Shanghai stadium (see the Shànghǎi chapter for details). Tickets are Y100 and include the entry ticket and return trip. From Shànghǎi, three buses depart daily from the bus station at 80 Gongxing Lu.

CHÚZHŌU 楚州 (淮安)
☎ 0517
The small town of Chúzhōu, until more recently known as Huái'ān, is situated in the centre of Jiāngsū province and is the birthplace of Zhou Enlai. If you're heading to northern Jiāngsū you might consider stopping here. His former home is open to the public and there's a large memorial and museum complex dedicated to the much-loved leader. Chúzhōu is also an interesting contrast to Sháoshān, Mao's birthplace in Húnán province. While the former premier Zhou Enlai is revered, his hometown is strikingly free of the tourist trappings of Sháoshān. If Mao achieved an overblown god-like status in both life and death, Zhou

Enlai is remembered in less extreme terms. The late premier died in 1976 and was cremated. He would probably be horrified at even this tribute to his memory.

Things to See
The main thing to see in Chúzhōu is Zhou Enlai's former home and the memorial but it's also a pleasant town to explore, especially the market area and narrow streets north of Zhenhuailou Lu and east of Zhou Enlai's former home. The **Grand Canal** passes to the west of town and is within walking distance (the first canal you come to is actually an offshoot, the Grand Canal is a bit farther west).

A narrow alley off Xichang Jie takes you to **Zhou Enlai's Former Residence** (*Zhōu Ēnlái Gùjū;* ☎ *591 2517, 7 Fuma Lane; admission Y10; open 7am-6pm daily*). It's a pleasant, courtyard residence and offers some insight into the gentry class of the early 1900's. Unfortunately, there are few captions in English.

The large and somewhat monolithic **Zhou Enlai Memorial** (*Zhōu Ēnlái Jìniànguǎn;* ☎ *591 2365; admission Y15; open 7.30am-6pm daily*) is north-east of town. It's surrounded by a large lake with a **museum** on the north shore.

Places to Stay
Chúzhōu has a few hotels but some of them don't take foreigners.

Huái'ān Bīnguǎn (☎ *591 2757, fax 591 3799, 2 Youyi Lu*) Doubles Y100-300. This hotel is set on beautiful grounds close to the western gate entrance to the Zhou Enlai Memorial. The cheapest doubles aren't very nice; better to go for the Y300 rooms discounted to Y200.

Getting There & Away
To add to the confusion of the city's name change to Chúzhōu, the larger city 17km north of the town has changed its name from Huáiyīn to Huái'ān.

Chúzhōu is just off the main northern freeway and there are frequent buses from Nánjīng (Y41, three hours) and less frequent buses from Yángzhōu (Y31, two hours) and Shànghǎi (Y61, five hours).

Ānhuī 安徽

Capital: Héféi
Population: 61.5 million
Area: 139,000 sq km

The historical and tourist sights of Ānhuī are concentrated in the south, and are more accessible from Hángzhōu or Shànghǎi than from the provincial capital, Héféi. For travellers cruising Cháng Jiāng (Yangzi River), the ports of Guìchí and Wúhú are convenient jumping-off points to southern destinations.

The provincial borders of Ānhuī were defined by the Qing government and, except for a few changes to the boundary with Jiāngsū, have remained unchanged. Northern Ānhuī forms part of the North China Plain, which the Han Chinese settled in large numbers during the Han dynasty. Cháng Jiāng cuts through the southern quarter of Ānhuī and the area south of the river was not settled until the 7th and 8th centuries.

HÉFÉI 合肥
☎ 0551 • pop 4,223,100
Prior to 1949 Héféi was a quiet market town but has since boomed into an industrial centre. It's a pleasant, friendly city with lively markets. While there are few cultural or historical attractions, the parks and lakes circling the city centre are ideal for relaxing walks.

Héféi is home to the University of Science and Technology (Zhōngguó Kēxué Jìshù Dàxué), where one of China's more famous dissidents, Fang Lizhi, was vice president until he sought asylum in the West after the 1989 massacre in Tiānānmén Square.

Orientation
Shengli Lu leads down to Nánféi Hé then meets up with Shouchun Lu. Changjiang Zhonglu is the main commercial street and cuts east-west through the city. Between these two streets, Huaihe Lu has been made into a pedestrian street to Huancheng Donglu.

Accommodation is available in the city centre and near the bus stations as well as on Meishan Lu and the university area south-west of the city centre.

Highlights

- Huáng Shān, a mountain considered by many Chinese as definitive of natural beauty
- Shèxiàn and Yīxiàn, Ming and Qing dynasty residential architecture in a scenic rural setting
- Jiǔhuá Shān, a Buddhist sacred mountain and a good antidote to the crowds at Huáng Shān

BĚIJĪNG TO SHÀNGHĂI

Information
The Bank of China is at 155 Changjiang Lu. Ānhuī Fàndiàn and the Holiday Inn (see Places to Stay later) will also change money. The main post office is on Changjiang Lu, next to the City Department Store. Internet access (Y2 per hour; 8am to midnight) is available on the 2nd floor of the post office.

China International Travel Service (CITS; Zhōngguó Guójì Lǚxíngshè; ☎ 281 1909) is in a tiled building at 8 Meishan Lu, beside Ānhuī Fàndiàn. Staff members are helpful and speak English.

The Public Security Bureau (PSB; Gōngānjú; ☎ 265 1776) is on the north-west corner of the intersection of Shouchun Lu and Liu'an Lu.

Things to See & Do
Héféi has some pleasant parks. In the north-east, **Xiāoyáojīn Gōngyuán** (*Shouchun Lu; admission Y5; open 6am-7pm daily*)

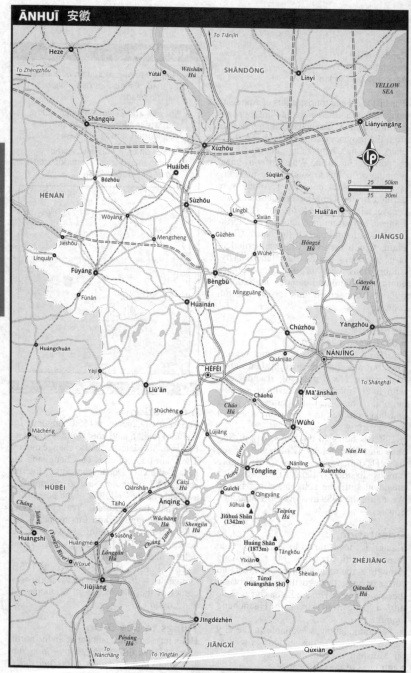

ĀNHUĪ 安徽

is the largest and has a small, rather depressing zoo. **Bāohé Gōngyuán** is nicer and contains the splendid **Lord Bao's Tomb** (*Bāo Gōng Mùyuán;* ☎ 288 7011, 58 Wuhu Lu; admission Y15; open 8am-6pm daily). Lord Bao was (that rare thing in government) an upright and conscientious official during the Northern Song dynasty, and died in 1062. The tombs were excavated in 1973 and restored at this site in 1987.

Small **Míngjiào Sì** (*Bright Teaching Temple; Huaihe Lu; admission Y5; open 7am-6pm daily*) sits 5m above ground. Built in early AD 500, the temple saw military skirmishes a few centuries later when troops from the Wu and Wei kingdoms fought in the area.

Finally, the **Anhui Provincial Museum** (*Ānhuī Shěng Bówùguǎn;* ☎ 282 3529, 268 Anqing Lu; admission Y10; open 8.30am-11.30am, 2.30pm-5pm Tues-Sun*) chronicles the history of Ānhuī with some good displays of bronzes, Han dynasty tomb rubbings and some fine examples of the wooden architectural style found around Huáng Shān.

Places to Stay

Two inexpensive hotels near the bus station accept foreigners:

Yínlù Dàjiǔdiàn (☎ 429 6303, fax 429 5506, 1 Shouchun Lu) Doubles with bath Y128-188. The cheaper rooms here are large but a little grubby. It's near the Holiday Inn – about a 10-minute walk from the long-distance bus station.

Xīnjìyuán Jiǔdiàn (☎ 429 7954, 317 Mingguang Lu) Singles/doubles/triples without bath Y35/40/60, doubles with bath Y100-160. Though far from the city centre, this place is a bargain.

Cháng Jiāng Fàndiàn (☎ 265 6441, fax 262 2295, 262 Changjiang Zhonglu) Doubles Y100-160. This large hotel is centrally located. The Y160 rooms are good value. Bus No 1 goes right by it.

Foreign Experts' Building (*Zhuānjiālóu;* ☎ 360 2881, fax 363 2579, 96 Jinzhai Lu) Singles Y150, doubles Y180-240. Comfortable and clean rooms are available in the park-like campus setting of the University of Science and Technology. Take bus No 1 from the train station to the university bus stop, which is opposite the north gate of the university entrance. Enter here, turning

left at the first road past the pond. Reception is in the large building on the north side of the pond.

Huáqiáo Fàndiàn (*Overseas Chinese Hotel;* ☎ 265 2221, fax 264 2861, 68 Changjiang Zhonglu) Singles Y260-440, doubles Y300-440. This hotel is centrally located with 50% discounts for the more expensive rooms.

Ānhuī Fàndiàn (☎ 281 1818, ℮ anhuihtl @mail.hf.ah.cn, 18 Meishan Lu) Rooms Y660-930. Ānhuī Fàndiàn is an elegant four-star establishment that has a health centre and bowling alley. Prices are subject to a 15% service charge, though 40% discounts are available.

Fùháo Dàjiǔdiàn (☎ 281 8888, fax 282 2581, 18 Meishan Lu) Singles/doubles with bath Y138/188. This clean hotel is within the grounds of Ānhuī Fàndiàn. Rates include buffet breakfast.

Holiday Inn (☎ 429 1188, ℮ hihfe@pub lic.hf.ah.cn, 1104 Changjiang Donglu) Doubles Y920. This has all you would expect in an international hotel, complete with swimming pool and health club. Half-price discounts are often available.

Places to Eat

Huáishàng Jiǔjiā (☎ 265 8551, 104 Changjiang Zhonglu) Mains Y20-30. Open noon-2pm & 5pm-midnight daily. A clean, lively place on the 2nd floor overlooking Changjiang Zhonglu, this place has standard dishes found throughout east China, but spiced up a bit, Ānhuī-style.

Xīnjìyuán Jiǔdiàn (see Places to Stay earlier) Mains Y10-20. Open 9am-2pm & 4.30pm-9pm daily. The small restaurant attached to this hotel has good, cheap meals.

Outdoor *restaurants* abound near the long-distance bus station and on Changjiang Donglu near the Holiday Inn. Choose from the ingredients on display – fish, meat, vegetables etc. Depending on your choice, meal prices range from Y20 to Y60.

Getting There & Away

Air Héféi has daily flights to Běijīng (Y910), Shànghǎi (Y580), Guǎngzhōu (Y950), Hángzhōu (Y420), Wǔhàn (Y330), Xī'ān (Y790) and (except Friday) Huáng Shān (Y330), plus less-regular flights to Chéngdū (Y1110), Fúzhōu (Y580), Kūnmíng (Y1480) and Hong Kong (Y1810).

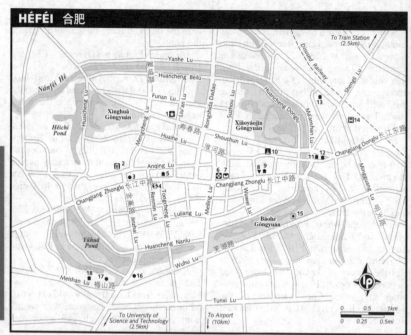

HÉFÉI 合肥

HÉFÉI

PLACES TO STAY & EAT	18	Ānhuī Fàndiàn; Fùháo	6	City Department Store
5	Cháng Jiāng		Dàjiǔdiàn		市百货大楼
	Fàndiàn		安徽饭店；富豪大酒店	7	Main Post Office
	长江饭店				市邮电局
8	Huáishàng Jiǔjiā	**OTHER**		10	Míngjiào Sì
	淮上酒家	1	PSB		明教寺
9	Huáqiáo Fàndiàn		公安局	14	Long-Distance Bus Station
	华侨饭店	2	Anhui Provincial		合肥汽车站
11	Holiday Inn		Museum	15	Lord Bao's Tomb
	古井假日酒店		省博物馆		包公墓园
12	Yínlù Dàjiǔdiàn	3	Train Ticket Office	16	China Eastern Airlines
	银路大酒店		火车预售票处		东方航空售票处
13	Xīnjìyuán Jiǔdiàn	4	Bank of China	17	CITS
	新纪元酒店		中国银行		中国国际旅行社

Bookings can be made at the China Eastern Airlines office (☎ 282 2357) at 246 Jinzhai Lu. Reservations are also possible through CITS and at the train-ticket booking office on the north side of Changjiang Zhonglu at the Jinzhai Lu intersection.

Taking a taxi (Y20, 30 minutes) is the best way to the airport, which is about 11km south of the city centre.

Bus A number of long-distance bus stations are located north of the Changjiang Donglu and Mingguang Lu intersection in the city's east and it can be a bit confusing. Your best bet is to go to the Héféi long-distance bus station (Héféi qìchē zhàn) at 168 Mingguang Lu. There are daily departures to Hángzhōu (Y150, eight hours), Wǔhàn (Y140, 10 hours) and Huáng Shān (Y55, seven hours).

The freeway to Nánjīng has shortened travel times considerably; air-con buses take 2½ hours to Nánjīng (Y38) and six hours for the trip to Shànghǎi (Y145). The freeway connection south to Jiǔjiāng (Y70), in Jiāngxī, allows for an eight-hour journey. Frequent minibuses also depart for Wúhú (Y27, 2½ hours).

Train The train station is 4km north-east of the city centre. Trains go to Shànghǎi (Y160, 8½ hours), Běijīng (Y255, 12 hours), Zhèngzhōu (Y97, 9½ hours, via Kāifēng) and Bózhōu (Y29, 4½ hours).

Tickets are available at the train station, but it's much better to get them at the ticket booking office at 216 Changjiang Zhonglu on the north-east side at the intersection with Jinzhai Lu. You can book sleepers five days in advance and it's open 24 hours a day.

Getting Around

Héféi is easy to get around. Bus No 1 runs from the train station down Shengli Lu to the city centre on Changjiang Zhonglu then south along Jinzhai Lu towards the university. Taxis are cheap, starting at Y5.

BÓZHŌU 亳州
☎ 0558

Bózhōu lies in Ānhuī's far north-west, near Hénán. It's known as one of the most important trading centres for traditional medicine in central China, attracting merchants and Chinese herbalists from a wide area.

Things to See

Bózhōu's main attraction is its **Medicinal Market** (*Zhōngyào Shìchǎng; Mulan Lu*). You'll see mounds of pressed herbs, roots, rocks, minerals, wasp nests, animal skins, tortoise shells, dried insects and snakes here. The market is in a large, white-tiled exhibition hall, near the train station. Things slow down in the afternoon, so it's best to visit before noon.

The **Underground Tunnel** (*Cáocāo Yùnbīngdào*; ☎ 552 1854, 49 Renmin Zhonglu; admission Y12; open 8am-6pm daily) is a 600m-long subterranean passageway parallel to Renmin Zhonglu. The famous Han general Cao Cao built it as a secret route for soldiers to surprise the enemy.

The **Flower Theatre** (*Huā Xìlóu*) features an ornate tiled gate built in the Qing dynasty. There's a small **museum** (☎ 555 2493, 1 Xianning Jie; admission Y10; open 8am-6pm daily), in the town's north east, featuring a Han dynasty burial suit made from pieces of jade sewn together with silver thread.

It's worthwhile walking from the Flower Theatre south towards Renmin Zhonglu through the old part of the city, with its narrow stone-flagged streets and ancient buildings.

Places to Stay & Eat

Most places here seem willing to accept foreigners.

Bózhōu Bīnguǎn (☎ 552 3987, 8 Banjie Lu) Doubles Y240. This place is off Xinhua Lu. It's possible for rooms to be discounted down to Y138, though they aren't that great.

Lìdū Dàshà (☎ 552 3008, 50 Xinhua Lu) Doubles with bath Y60, suites Y100. This clean hotel is about 100m north of Bózhōu Bīnguǎn.

Zhōnghuá Dàjiǔdiàn (☎ 552 1766, 7 Qiaoling Lu) Singles/doubles Y88/168. Newly opened in 2001, this is Bózhōu's best hotel by far and has a good restaurant.

There's a cluster of ***restaurants*** along the sidewalk at the intersection of Heping Lu and Qiaoling Lu, beside Zhōnghuá Dàjiǔdiàn. A steaming bowl of delicious *jiǎozi* (stuffed dumplings) and bottle of beer will set you back Y5.

Getting There & Away

Daily buses leave for Zhèngzhōu (Y50, five hours), Kāifēng (Y35, four hours), Héféi (Y50, five hours) and Xúzhōu (Y30, five hours).

Bózhōu is on the Zhèngzhōu-Héféi train line though most trains stop here at inconvenient hours – either very early in the morning or around midnight. One useful train leaving at a reasonable time and going south is to Wēnzhōu (Y317, 22 hours), passing through Nánjīng, Shànghǎi and Hángzhōu.

There's a daily train to Héféi (Y29, 4½ hours). The train station is about 4km south-east of the city.

HUÁNG SHĀN 黄山
Yellow Mountain
☎ 0559 ● elevation 1873m

Huáng Shān is the name of the 72-peak mountain range in Ānhuī's south, 280km west of the coastal city of Hángzhōu. For the Chinese, Huáng Shān, along with Guìlín, is probably the country's most famous landscape attraction.

Orientation & Information

Buses from Túnxī drop you off in Tāngkǒu, the main village at the mountain's foot, or at the terminal near **Yellow Mountain Gate** (*Huángshān Mén*) in upper Tāngkǒu. Maps, raincoats, food and accommodation are available here.

There's also accommodation near the hot springs, which are 4km farther up the valley. If you'd like to soak your weary body after coming down the mountain, hot spring baths are next to Huángshān Bīnguǎn at **Huángshān Hot Springs** (*Huángshān Wēnquán;* ☎ 558 5808; *private/communal bath Y80/30; open 8am-11pm daily*). There's also a swimming pool, with bathing suits available, but it closes at 9.30pm.

The road ends halfway up the mountain at the Cloud Valley Temple cable car station, 890m above sea level, where the eastern steps begin. Other hotels are scattered on trails around the summit area.

Another cable car goes from the **Jade Screen Peak** (*Yùpíng Fēng*) area to just above the hot springs resort. A third cable car, which at 3709m claims to be the longest in Asia, approaches Huáng Shān from the north-west going to **Pine Forest Peak** (*Sōnglín Fēng*) and is accessible from the southern side of Tàipíng Reservoir.

The Bank of China is next to Huángshān Bīnguǎn in the hot springs area. Táoyuán Bīnguǎn can also change money.

Guides

Guides are unnecessary because the mountain paths are easy to follow, with abundant English signs. However, CITS can organise an English-speaking guide for around Y500 per day. Private individuals sometimes offer their services as guides, but often speak no English beyond 'hello'. The truly decadent might make their ascent in a sedan chair strung between bamboo poles and bounced (literally) along by two porters. The price? Around Y400 one way or Y1000 for the day, depending on your bargaining skills.

Routes to the Summit

There are three basic routes to the top: the short, hard way (eastern steps); the longer, harder way (western steps); and the very short, easy way (cable car). The eastern steps lead up below the Cloud Valley Temple cable car line and the western steps lead up from the parking lot near **Cíguāng Gé** (*Mercy Light Temple*), about 3km above the hot springs. The Jade Screen Peak cable car also goes from here to the Jade Screen Peak area, bringing you about halfway up the mountain.

Regardless of how you ascend Huáng Shān, you'll have to pay a Y82 entrance fee. Pay at the eastern steps near the Cloud Valley Temple cable car station or where the western steps begin. Minibuses run to both places from Tāngkǒu for Y10.

Make sure to pack enough water, food and appropriate clothing before you take your first step toward the summit. Bottled water and food prices increase the higher you go. The market under the stone bridge in Tāngkǒu has a good selection of food at affordable prices.

Eastern Steps The 7.5km eastern steps route can be climbed comfortably in about three hours. It's a killer if you push yourself too hard, but it's definitely easier than the western steps.

Purists can extend the eastern steps climb by several hours by starting from Yellow Mountain Gate, where a stepped path crosses the road at several points before connecting with the main eastern steps trail at the Cloud Valley Temple cable car station.

If you have time, the recommended route is a 10-hour circuit hike taking the eastern steps to the top and descending to the hot springs resort via the western steps. Don't underestimate the hardship involved. While cut-stone stairways make climbing a little easier, the extremely steep gradients can wreak havoc on your knees.

Western Steps The 15km western steps route has some stellar scenery, following a precarious route hewn out of the sheer rock cliffs. But it's twice as long and strenuous as the eastern steps and much easier to enjoy if you're clambering down rather than gasping your way up.

The western steps descent begins at the **Flying Rock** (*Fēilái Shí*), a rectangular boulder perched on an outcrop half an hour from Běihǎi Bīnguǎn, and goes over **Bright Summit Peak** (*Guāngmíng Dǐng*), where there is an odd-shaped weather station and a hotel.

Huáng Shān – A Tradition of Tranquillity and Inspiration

In good weather Huáng Shān is truly spectacular, and the surrounding countryside, with its traditional villages and patchwork paddy fields, is among the most beautiful in China. Huáng Shān has a 1200-year history as a tourist attraction. Countless painters and poets have trudged around the range, seeking inspiration and bestowing the peaks with fanciful names such as Nine Dragons, Taoist Priest, Ox Nose, Fairy Capital and Hunchback.

Today, the reclusive artists seeking an inspirational retreat from the hustle and bustle of the temporal world have been replaced by crowds of tourists, who bring the hustle and bustle with them. Still, with a little effort, you might be rewarded with a small moment of tranquillity, and the views are quite breathtaking.

Some travellers have escaped the well-trodden tourist trails and returned thrilled with what they discovered. It is also worth noting that, given the amount of people who pass through this area, the park management does a commendable job trying to keep the place litter-free.

 The highest peak is Lotus Flower Peak (Liánhuā Fēng) at 1873m, followed by Bright Summit Peak (Guāngmíng Dǐng) and Heavenly Capital Peak (Tiāndū Fēng). Some 30 peaks rise above 1500m.

Highlights on the western steps include the ascent to the highest summit, **Lotus Flower Peak** (*Liánhuā Fēng*), which is located above Yùpínglóu Bīnguǎn, and the exhilaratingly steep and exposed stairway leading to the **Heavenly Capital Peak** (*Tiāndū Fēng*). Young lovers bring locks engraved with their names up here and fix them to the chain railings. This symbolises that they are 'locked' together. It can get quite crowded on this narrow stairway, however, and if you're afraid of heights it might be better to skip this one. The sheer amount of human traffic on Huáng Shān has resulted in restricting access to Heavenly Capital Peak for maintenance and repair, but it should be open by the time you read this. It is possible that Lotus Flower Peak may be closed for maintenance.

The western path continues past **Bànshān Sì** (*Mid-Level Temple*) and back to the hot springs resort. Halfway between Bànshān Sì and the hot springs resort is a parking lot with minibuses. For Y10, you can skip the last 1½ hours of walking and get a lift to the hot springs resort.

Cable Car The least painful way up is by taking the **Cloud Valley Temple Cable Car** (*Yúngǔsì Suǒdào;* ☎ *556 1730; adult/child Y66/36; open 6.30am-4pm daily*). For Y10, minibuses take you from the Yellow Mountain Gate to the station. Either arrive very early or late (if you're staying overnight). Queues of more than one hour are the norm. In high season, many people wait up to three hours for a ride – you may as well walk.

The **Jade Screen Peak Cable Car** (*Yùpíng Fēng Suǒdào;* ☎ *558 5728; adult/child Y66/36; open 6.30am-5pm daily*) goes from just below Yùpínglóu Bīnguǎn to the parking lot above the hot springs resort.

Accessing Huáng Shān from the north via the **Tàipíng Cable Car** (*Tàipíng Suǒdào;* ☎ *558 3218; adult/child Y66/33; 6.30am-5pm daily*) is also an option. Minibuses (Y15, 30 minutes) run from Tàipíng to the station. The cable runs to the Pine Forest Peak area.

On the Summit

Many people find that the highlight of Huáng Shān is the Běihǎi sunrise: a 'sea' of low clouds blanketing the valley to the north with 'island' peaks hazily reaching for the heavens. **Refreshing Terrace** (*Qīngliáng Tái*) is located five minutes from Běihǎi Bīnguǎn and attracts sunrise crowds (hotels supply thick padded jackets for the occasion). It's communal sightseeing at its best. The noise generated by several hundred tourists is almost as incredible as the sunrise itself. Fortunately, most people return to eat breakfast shortly afterwards, leaving you to enjoy the mountains in peace.

If you're seeking some solitude, head for the area around **Purple Cloud Peak** (*Dānxiá Fēng*). The views may not be quite as spectacular, but at least you can enjoy them alone and in relative silence.

HUÁNG SHĀN

PLACES TO STAY
2 Shīlín Fàndiàn
   狮林饭店
3 Běihǎi Bīnguǎn
   北海宾馆
4 Xīhǎi Bīnguǎn
   西海宾馆
5 Páiyúnlóu
   Bīnguǎn
   排云楼宾馆
7 Báiyúnlóu
   Bīnguǎn
   白云楼宾馆
8 Tiānhǎi
   Shānzhuāng
   天海山庄

9 Yùpínglóu Bīnguǎn
   玉屏楼宾馆
10 Yúngǔ
   Shānzhuāng
   云谷山庄
13 Huángshān Bīnguǎn;
   Huángshān Hot
   Springs; Bank of
   China
   黄山宾馆；黄山温泉；
   中国银行
14 Táoyuán Bīnguǎn
   桃源宾馆
15 Yìyuán
   Shānzhuāng
   忆园山庄

OTHER
1 Refreshing Terrace
   清凉台
6 Flying Rock
   飞来石
11 Bànshān Sì
   半山寺
12 Cíguāng Gé
   慈光阁
16 Yellow Mountain Gate
   黄山门
17 Long-Distance Bus Station
   长途汽车站
18 Liáhuā Fàndiàn
   Ticket Centre
   莲花饭店售票处

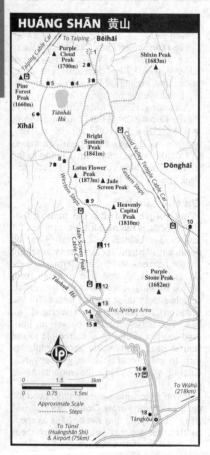

HUÁNG SHĀN 黄山

Places to Stay & Eat

Huáng Shān has five locations where hotels and restaurants can be found. Prices and bed availability vary according to season.

Tāngkǒu There are affordable hotels here, making Tāngkǒu ideal for a Huáng Shān assault.

Xiāoyáo Bīnguǎn (Free and Unfettered Hotel; ☎ *556 2571, fax 556 1679)* Dorm beds Y25, beds in triples with/without bath Y60/40, doubles/triples with bath & air-con Y220/300. Dorm accommodation here is in rooms with four and five beds. The staff are friendly and speak some English. Be adamant here, or you may get an expensive room.

Tāngkǒu Bīnguǎn (☎ *556 2400, fax 556 2687)* Beds in quads without bath Y35, doubles with air-con Y200. This place is up the hill about 300m, to your left as you leave Xiāoyáo Bīnguǎn.

There's plenty of food in Tāngkǒu, many places specialising in expensive local treats such as frogs and preserved meats. Watch out for overcharging – simple dishes should cost Y15 to Y20. For cheap eats, try the makeshift *restaurants* under the main bridge.

Dōngfāng Hóng Cānguǎn Mains Y20-30. Open 6am-late daily. Run by the helpful Mr Cheng, who speaks English, this small place has an English menu (but unfortunately no English sign) and serves large portions. It's located about 200m north from under the main bridge.

Hot Springs The hot springs area, 4km farther uphill, is an attractive place to stay, but most of the accommodation is expensive.

Yìyuán Shānzhuāng (☎ 558 5666, fax 558 5377) Doubles Y280-340. This small hotel has large, clean rooms with discounts of 35%.

Huángshān Bīnguǎn (☎ 558 5808, fax 558 5818) Doubles Y340-420. Discounts of up to 30% are available for this slightly up-market place. Guests can also use the hotel-run hot spring next door.

Táoyuán Bīnguǎn (Peach Blossom Hotel; ☎ 556 2666, fax 556 2888) Doubles Y486-580. Prices have come down here and it's the most luxurious place in the vicinity. The Y580 doubles have a balcony and may be discounted to Y280.

All the hotels have *restaurants* and, as in Tāngkǒu, restaurant touts look for hungry travellers. Watch out for overcharging.

Cloud Valley Temple Cable Car Station This is a secluded, if somewhat inconvenient, setting within the pine and bamboo forest.

Yúngǔ Shānzhuāng (Cloud Valley Hotel; ☎ 556 2444, fax 556 2466) Doubles Y580. This is probably the best place to stay if you have the money. Government officials stay here when they're visiting Huáng Shān. It's down the steps from the car park in front of the cable car station.

Summit Area Ideally, a Huáng Shān visit should include a stay on the summit.

Shílín Fàndiàn (☎ 558 4040) Dorm beds Y150, doubles with bath Y850. This is a good place to be near the summit and the dorms are adequate.

Běihǎi Bīnguǎn (☎ 558 2555, fax 558 1996) Dorm beds Y150, beds in 4-6-bed dorms with bath Y180, doubles Y700-850. This hotel is overpriced but comfortable, and provides the best location for seeing the sunrise.

Xīhǎi Bīnguǎn (☎ 558 8888, fax 558 8988) Doubles Y960-1280. This is a real 'mountain hotel' designed by Swedish architects. All rooms have heating and 24-hour hot water. It caters to international tour groups.

Páiyúnlóu Bīnguǎn (☎ 558 3208, fax 558 3999) Beds in 4-/6-bed dorms with bath Y150, doubles/triples Y800/880. This hotel

is up from Tiānhǎi Hú (Heavenly Sea Lake). It's a little out of the way, but the dorms are good value.

Xīhǎi Bīnguǎn and Běihǎi Bīnguǎn have *bars* and *restaurants* serving international and Chinese food, but as these tend to cater to tour groups, it's sometimes difficult to get service outside meal times. There are cheaper *restaurants* nearby.

Western Steps There are a few accommodation options on this route.

Tiānhǎi Shānzhuāng (☎ 556 1848) Dorm beds Y65, doubles with bath Y125. There are bunk beds crammed in every available space in this rambling collection of buildings just off the main trail. Facilities are spartan and crowded.

Báiyúnlóu Bīnguǎn (☎ 556 1708, fax 556 1602) Dorm beds with bath Y150, doubles Y800. This place (not to be confused with Páiyúnlóu Bīnguǎn mentioned earlier) offers more luxury and privacy than Tiānhǎi Shānzhuāng. Take the turn-off to the right from the main path (if heading down the mountain) and continue past Tiānhǎi Shānzhuāng. It's secluded and set on the mountain's edge.

Yùpínglóu Bīnguǎn (Jade Screen Tower Hotel; ☎ 556 2317, fax 556 2258) Dorm beds/doubles Y150/680. Farther down the mountain, this hotel is perched on a spectacular 1660m-high lookout with a view of Heavenly Capital Peak. The rates and conditions reflect its relative inaccessibility. Washing arrangements are basic and be prepared for water shortages.

There are few eating options on this route. Yùpínglóu Bīnguǎn has a cheap *dining hall* beside its courtyard, and a better *restaurant* upstairs.

Getting There & Away
Buses from Túnxī (Huángshān Shì) take around 1½ hours to reach Yellow Mountain Gate. Minibuses to Túnxī leave from the bridge area in Tāngkǒu; tickets are Y13.

In summer, direct buses to Tāngkǒu come from Héféi (Y63, six hours), Nánjīng (Y75, six hours) and Shànghǎi (Y153, 11 hours). Other buses go to Jiǔhuá Shān (Y40, four hours) and the Cháng Jiāng ports of Wúhú (Y50, four hours) and Guìchí (Y50, five hours). Most buses leave Tāngkǒu very early in the morning. The long-distance bus station is just below the Yellow Mountain Gate but closes early. Try booking bus tickets at your hotel or Liánhuā Fàndiàn in Tāngkǒu, where you can also book train and plane tickets. It's on the highway leading to the Yellow Mountain Gate across from the main bridge area.

One route to Huáng Shān that's worth investigating is a trip starting from Hángzhōu. Take a bus to Qiāndǎo Hú (Y30, four hours) and from there take a boat to the south-west tip of the lake, where a road connects up to a highway going from Zhèjiāng to Huáng Shān.

There are both air and train connections to Túnxī; see the following Túnxī section for details.

Getting Around

Minibuses are the easiest and cheapest way to get around Huáng Shān, though they usually don't budge until enough people are on board. In the morning, they ferry people to the eastern and western steps. You can usually find minibuses on Tāngkǒu's streets or on the highway across the bridge. Likewise, minibuses wait at the bottom of mountain routes in the afternoon. Minivan taxis abound; you'll have to bargain.

TÚNXĪ 屯溪

☎ 0559 • pop 1,510,000

The old trading town of Túnxī (Huángshān Shì) is roughly 70km south-east of Huáng Shān. As its other name implies (meaning Huángshān City), Túnxī is the main springboard for Huáng Shān. It's also a pleasant town to explore for a day.

Information

The Bank of China is at 9 Xinan Lu, opposite the Xinhua Bookshop.

CITS (☎ 252 6184, ⓔ citseu@huangshan guide.com) is at 6 Xizhen Jie, on the 3rd floor of the building opposite Huāxī Fàndiàn. It can arrange English-speaking guides for tours of Huáng Shān and the surrounding area.

The PSB (☎ 231 5429) is in the eastern section of Túnxī, at 108 Changgan Lu.

Places to Stay & Eat

Several Túnxī hotels, especially the cheaper ones, don't accept foreigners.

Jiāngnán Dàjiǔdiàn (☎ 251 1067, fax 251 2192, 25-27 Qianyuan Beilu) Singles Y150, doubles Y180-280. The cheaper rooms are very small and cramped but convenient for the train and bus stations. It's located on the corner of the first intersection you meet coming out of the train station.

Huángshān Jīngwěi Jiǔdiàn (☎ 234 5188, fax 234 5098, 18 Qianyuan Beilu) Doubles Y360-480. Across from Jiāngnán Dàjiǔdiàn, this three-star hotel is a good deal with 30% discounts.

Huāxī Fàndiàn (☎ 251 4312, fax 251 4990, 1 Xizhen Jie) Doubles Y380-680. To the west of town, directly across the bridge where the two rivers, Héng Jiāng and Xīn'ān Jiāng meet, this huge hotel has clean rooms and friendly staff; the best part is its location close to the old part of town.

Huangshan International Hotel (*Huángshān Guójì Dàjiǔdiàn;* ☎ 252 6999, fax 251 2087, 31 Huashan Lu) Doubles Y680. This is the best place to stay if you have the cash and are looking for comfort. Discounts of up to 15% are available.

Lǎo Jiē Dìyīlóu (☎ 253 9797, 247 Lao Jie) Mains Y15-30. Open 6.30pm-2am daily. At the eastern end of Lao Jie, this is one of Túnxī's most popular restaurants. Try the delicious *jīxiāng xiǎopái* (deep-fried sweet pork spare-ribs) for Y15 a plate.

There are numerous cheap *restaurants* and *food stalls* around the train station and down Qianyuan Beilu. The Huangshan International Hotel has a Western restaurant.

Shopping

Running a block in from the river, *Lao Jie (Old Street)* is a souvenir street lined with wooden shops and buildings from the Song dynasty, open 7.30am to 10.30pm daily. Besides the usual trinkets, you can also buy goods similar to those in the Shànghǎi antique markets – prices may be lower here, especially for antique furniture.

While tourists swarm the area during the high season, an early morning stroll through this narrow pedestrian and commercial street can be like stepping into China's past.

Getting There & Away

Air There are flights from Túnxī to Běijīng (Y990, twice weekly), Guǎngzhōu (Y880, daily), Héféi (Y330, daily), Shànghǎi (Y460, daily), Hong Kong (Y1880, twice weekly) and less frequent flights to other cities.

Civil Aviation Administration of China (CAAC; Zhōngguó Mínháng; ☎ 953 4111) is on Huangshan Lu beside the Huangshan International Hotel. The 5km taxi ride to the airport will cost about Y25. You can book airline tickets at outlets near the train station.

Bus The long-distance bus station is 400m east of the train station. Buses run between Túnxī and Tāngkǒu (Y13, 1½ hours). Buses also go to Shànghǎi (Y83, nine hours), Hángzhōu (Y55, six hours), Héféi (Y65, six hours) and Jǐngdézhèn (Y28, four hours).

Train Trains from Běijīng (Y323, 21 hours), Shànghǎi (Y97, 11½ hours) and Nánjīng (Y54, seven hours) stop at Túnxī. Some trains heading south also stop here, such as to Xiàmén (Y217, 32 hours) and Jǐngdézhèn (Y25, 3½ hours). For better connections to southern destinations, first go to Yīngtán (Y51, five hours) in Jiāngxī and change trains there. Book your ticket early. CITS may have difficulty booking sleepers on short notice. Hotels will usually book train tickets for a service charge.

AROUND TÚNXĪ
Shèxiàn & Yīxiàn
☎ 0559

The dazzling and romantic landscape around Huáng Shān abounds with crop fields, road-side markets and classical Chinese residential architecture. The towns of Shèxiàn and Yīxiàn, near Túnxī, are famous for old, narrow streets, memorial arches (*páifāng*) and merchant homes with open courtyards and exquisite wood carvings.

Formerly known as Huīzhōu, this region produced many wealthy merchants who returned with trade profits to build houses in their home towns during the Ming and Qing dynasties. Both Shèxiàn and Yīxiàn can be visited as day trips from Túnxī, although to see Yīxiàn's sights, you ostensibly need a travel permit (Y60) from either the PSB in Túnxī, or one arranged by CITS. The easiest and cheapest way is to get the permit from CITS then arrange your own transport. Many taxi drivers in Túnxī insist that foreigners can still get into the sites without permits, but that will depend on your luck and powers of persuasion.

The **Memorial Arches of Tangyue** (*Tángyuè Páifāng Qún; admission Y35; open 7am-6pm daily*) are imposing structures 1.5km off the highway on the way to Shèxiàn. Get off the bus and walk or take a motor-tricycle.

In Shèxiàn, the street area known as Doushan Jie, in the old town centre, has a fine collection of houses in narrow, stone-lined alleys. There's a good guided tour (☎ 651 1557) for Y10 that takes you inside the houses.

At Yīxiàn there are three main villages worth visiting for their architecture and decorative detailing dating back to the Ming and Qing dynasties. Each village is located outside the main town of Yīxiàn. The best way to get around is to hire a minivan taxi in Yīxiàn.

The first village you come to before Yīxiàn is **Xīdì** (☎ 515 4030; admission Y38; open 6.30am-7pm daily). Nine memorial arches once stood here, which must have been quite a sight. All were destroyed during the Cultural Revolution, except one which survived because it was covered with Mao slogans.

Maze-like **Nánpíng** (☎ 516 4723; admission Y20; open 7.30am-6pm daily) is surrounded by rice fields and was the location for Zhang Yimou's acclaimed 1990 film *Judou*. The set has been preserved for tourists, along with photographs of the production. Several houses have beautiful wood carvings, although many of the human figures were decapitated by Red Guards during the Cultural Revolution.

Hóngcūn (☎ 554 1158; admission Y30; open 7.30am-6pm daily) has similar architecture but the best part is the exterior view of the buildings rising up beside a large pond, whose waterways flow around and through the village and are meant to outline the shape of a cow.

Getting There & Away
From Túnxī, Shèxiàn is 15km north-east and Yīxiàn is 35km north-west.

Minibuses go to both towns from Túnxī bus station or near the roundabout in front of the train station, where the ticket collectors lean out the doors of passing buses and call out the town names. Tickets to Shèxiàn are Y4 and the trip takes 30 minutes. The Y8 journey to Yīxiàn takes one hour. A minivan taxi will take you there and back for Y150.

JIǓHUÁ SHĀN 九华山
Nine Brilliant Mountains
☎ 0566 • elevation 1342m

To avoid Huáng Shān's carnival crowds, skip it in favour of Jiǔhuá Shān, a holy mountain with less spectacular scenery but a quieter and more spiritual atmosphere.

With 99 peaks, Jiǔhuá Shān is one of China's four sacred Buddhist mountains (the others are Pǔtuóshān in Zhèjiāng, Éméi Shān in Sìchuān and Wǔtái Shān in Shǎnxī). Third-century Taoist monks built thatched temples at Jiǔhuá Shān, but with the rise of Buddhism, stone monasteries gradually replaced them.

Jiǔhuá Shān owes its importance to Kim Kiao Kak (Jīn Qiáojué), a Korean Buddhist disciple who arrived in China in AD 720 and founded a worshipping place for Ksitigarbha, the guardian of the earth. Pilgrims flock to Jiǔhuá Shān for the annual festivities held on the anniversary of Kim's death, which falls on the 30th day of the seventh lunar month. The mountain apparently received its name after the poet Li Bai was so moved by seeing nine peaks that he wrote that they help hold the world and heaven together.

In its heyday, during the Tang dynasty, as many as 3000 monks and nuns, living in more than 150 monasteries, worshipped at Jiǔhuá Shān. Today only 70 temples and monasteries remain, but a palpable feeling of spirituality still permeates the place, something often lacking at China's other 'holy' sites.

Jiǔhuá Shān is also an important place for believers to come and bless the souls of the recently deceased to ensure them a passage to Buddhist heaven.

Orientation & Information
Jiǔhuá is a village that lies 600m above sea level, about halfway up the mountain (or, as the locals say, at roughly navel height in a giant Buddha's potbelly). The bus stops below the main gate where you pay an entrance fee (Y60 between March and November; Y45 the rest of the year).

From here the narrow main street heads south up past restaurants, souvenir stalls and hotels, then turns east towards temples.

China Travel Service (CTS; Zhōngguó Lǚxíngshè; ☎ 501 1588) has an office on the 3rd floor of 135 Beimai Xintun Lu, near a school field, and offers tours for Y200 per day, though guides are not really necessary. The Bank of China is at 65 Huachen Lu, near Dàbēi Lóu.

Things to See & Do
Hiking up the ridge behind Qíyuán Sì, at the bottom of Jiuhua Jie, leads you to the **Longevity Palace** (Bǎisuì Gōng; ☎ 501 1293; admission Y5; open dawn-dusk daily). This is an active temple built in 1630 to consecrate the buddhist monk Wu Xia, whose shrunken, embalmed body is on display. If you don't feel like hiking, take the new funicular tram (up/down Y28/18) up to the ridge.

From the top, walk south along the ridge until you reach two paths, a western one that leads to town or an eastern one that dips into a pleasant valley and continues to **Tiāntái Zhèng Peak** (Tiāntái Zhèng Dǐng). The walk to the peak is about four hours and along the way small temples, nunneries and restaurants line the path.

From the valley, a cable car (up/down Y30/20) whisks passengers to the peak. Shuttle buses take people back to Jiǔhuá Shān from here for Y5. Chinese-language maps are available that outline the mountain paths. Exploring the village, talking to the monks and listening to their soothing chanting can be very relaxing.

Places to Stay & Eat
Qíyuán Sì (☎ 501 1281) Dorm beds Y5-20. This beautiful palace-style monastery sits at the bottom of the village. Its beds range from basic to more comfortable. You may have difficulty staying here if you can't speak Chinese.

Fójiào Bīnguǎn (Buddhism Hotel; ☎ 501 1608, fax 501 1325) Doubles Y100-130. The clean rooms here are good value; it's up the road about 100m from the monastery.

Jùlóng Bīnguǎn (☎ 501 1368, fax 501 1022) Doubles Y280-580. Across from the monastery this hotel has been newly renovated and has nice rooms. Try for a discount.

Nányuàn Lǚguǎn (☎ 501 1122, 26 Furong Lu) Beds in doubles/triples without bath Y50, with bath & air-con Y100/150. This friendly, family run hotel has expanded its rooms to include bathrooms and is a great place to stay if it's not full. Meals are also served. It's up a small trail at the south end of the main street.

On the path to Tiāntái Zhèng Peak it's possible to stay in the small village at the bottom of the valley near the cable car.

Fènghuángsōng Mǐnyuán Shānzhuāng (☎ 501 1146) Doubles/triples with bath Y200/150, doubles without bath Y80. This very small, clean, family run hotel is the most luxurious accommodation here.

Qīng Yǎ Fàndiàn (☎ 501 1700) Beds Y10-20. Although there's other accommodation here, this place is the most rustic and charming, 1km farther up the hill. Washing facilities are basic.

Jiǔhuá Shān has numerous restaurants.

Gōngxiāo Dàjiǔdiàn (☎ 501 2118, 24 Furong Lu) Mains Y10-40. Open 6am-11pm daily. Located away from the main street, this unpretentious place serves good meals. It also has more expensive 'speciality' dishes like *tiāntái shuāngdōng* (bamboo shoots and mushrooms) for Y35. You will find it about 50m west down the first lane off the main street south of Nányùan Lǚguǎn.

Cheap, delicious noodles are served at the *noodle stall* at the southern end of the main street.

Getting There & Away

Two buses go to Jiǔhuá Shān daily from Tāngkǒu via Qīngyáng (Y40, four hours) following the road alongside the Tàipíng Reservoir. There are also buses to Shànghǎi (Y80, eight hours), Nánjīng (Y54, four hours), Wúhú (Y35, three hours) and Guìchí (Y9, one hour).

WÚHÚ 芜湖
☎ 0553 • pop 490,500

Wúhú is a Cháng Jiāng port and railway junction. Railway lines branch off south to Túnxī, east to Shànghǎi (via Nánjīng) and, from the northern bank of the river, north to Héféi. There are also buses from Wúhú to Huáng Shān (five hours) and Jiǔhuá Shān (three hours).

GUÌCHÍ 贵池
☎ 0566

The Cháng Jiāng port of Guìchí is west of Wúhú and has buses to Huáng Shān (five hours) and Jiǔhuá Shān (one hour). Ferries also go between Wúhú and Guìchí. The trip takes about five hours. (For details on Cháng Jiāng cruises, see the Chóngqìng chapter).

Shànghǎi 上海

Telephone code: ☎ 021
Population: 13.2 million
Area: 6340 sq km

Whore of the Orient, Paris of the East; city of quick riches, ill-gotten gains and fortunes lost on the tumble of dice; the domain of adventurers, swindlers, gamblers, drug runners, idle rich, dandies, tycoons, missionaries, gangsters and backstreet pimps; the city that plots revolution and dances as the revolution shoots its way into town – Shànghǎi was a dark memory during the long years of forgetting that the Communists visited upon their new China; the city's seductive aura that so beguiled the Western mind was snuffed out.

Shànghǎi put away its dancing shoes in 1949. The masses began shuffling to a different tune – the dour strains of Marxist-Leninism and the wail of the factory siren; and all through these years of oblivion, the architects of this social experiment firmly wedged one foot against the door on Shànghǎi's past, until finally the effort started to tell.

Today Shànghǎi has reawakened and is busy snapping the dust off its cummerbund. This is a city typifying the huge disparities of modern China – monumental building projects push skywards, glinting department stores swing open their doors to the stylish elite, while child beggars, prostitutes and the impoverished congregate among the champagne corks and burst balloons of the night before. History is returning to haunt Shànghǎi and, at the same time, put it squarely back on the map.

As the pulse of this metropolis quickens, its steps are firmer, and at this point we make an apology. A lot of what you read in this guide will have changed by the time you have the book in your hands. The booming metropolis of Shànghǎi is evolving at a pace so unmatched by any other Chinese city that even the morning ritual of flinging open one's hotel curtains reveals new facets to the skyline and new sounds on the streets. Shànghǎi is racing full-speed towards the future and has little time for yesterday.

Shànghǎi's population figure is deceptive since it takes into account the whole

Highlights

- The Bund, the single most evocative symbol of the 'Paris of the East'
- Nanjing Lu, where socialism with Chinese characteristics shakes hands with shop-till-you-drop commercialism
- Getting lost on the backstreets of Frenchtown
- Yu Gardens Bazaar, tacky but fun, with some delicious lunch time snacks

municipal area of 6340 sq km as well as a migrant population of 3 million. Nevertheless, the central core of some 220 sq km has more than 7.5 million people, which must rate as one of the highest population densities in China, if not the world.

The best times to visit Shànghǎi are spring and autumn. In winter temperatures can drop well below freezing and there is often a blanket of drizzle. Summers are hot and humid with temperatures as high as 40°C (104°F).

HISTORY

As anyone who wanders along the Bund or through the backstreets of Frenchtown can see, Shànghǎi (the name means 'by the sea') is a Western invention. As the gateway to Cháng Jiāng (Yangzi River), it was an ideal trading port. When the British opened their first concession in 1842, after the first Opium War, it was little more than a small town supported by fishing and weaving. The British changed all that.

The French followed in 1847, an International Settlement was established in 1863 and the Japanese arrived in 1895 – the city was parcelled up into autonomous settlements, immune from Chinese law. By 1853 Shànghǎi had overtaken all other Chinese ports. Mid-18th century Shànghǎi had a population of just 50,000; by 1900 the figure had jumped to one million. By the 1930s the city had 60,000 foreign residents and was the busiest international port in Asia. There were more motor vehicles than in the rest of China put together and the largest buildings in the East.

This city that was built on the trade of opium, silk and tea, also lured the world's great houses of finance, who erected grand palaces of plenty. Shànghǎi became a byword for exploitation and vice; its countless opium dens, gambling joints and brothels managed by were at the heart of Shànghǎi life. Guarding it all were the American, French and Italian marines, British Tommies and Japanese bluejackets.

After Chiang Kaishek's coup against the Communists in 1927, the Kuomintang co-operated with the foreign police and the Shànghǎi gangs, and with Chinese and foreign factory owners, to suppress labour unrest.

The settlement police, run by the British, arrested Chinese labour leaders and handed

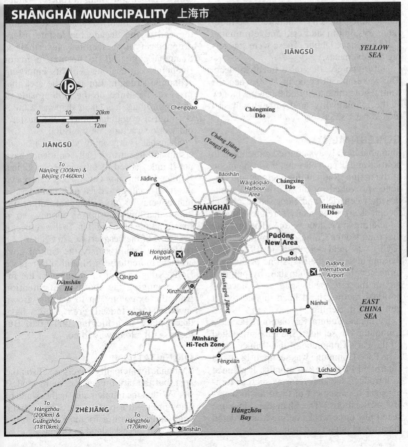

SHÀNGHǍI MUNICIPALITY 上海市

them over to the Kuomintang for imprisonment or execution, and the Shànghǎi gangs were repeatedly called in to 'mediate' disputes inside the settlement.

If it was the Chinese who supported the whole giddy structure of Shànghǎi, worked as beasts of burden and provided the muscle in Shànghǎi's port and factories, it was simultaneously the Chinese who provided the weak link.

Exploited in workhouse conditions, crippled by hunger and poverty, sold into slavery, excluded from the high life and the parks created by the foreigners, the poor of Shànghǎi had a voracious appetite for radical opinion. The Chinese Communist Party (CCP) was formed here in 1921 and, after numerous setbacks, 'liberated' the city in 1949.

The Communists eradicated the slums, rehabilitated the city's hundreds of thousands of opium addicts, and eliminated child and slave labour. These were staggering achievements.

Unfortunately, they also put it to sleep. The wake-up call came in 1990 when the central government started throwing money at the municipality, and Shànghǎi hasn't looked back since.

GOVERNMENT

Shànghǎi has always courted extremism in politics and been a barometer for the mood of the nation. Radical intellectuals and students, provoked by the startling inequalities between rich and poor, were perfect receptacles for the many foreign opinions circulating in the concessions. The meeting that founded the Chinese Communist Party (CCP) was held here back in 1921. Mao Zedong also cast the first stone of the Cultural Revolution in Shànghǎi, by publishing in the city's newspapers a piece of political rhetoric he'd been unable to get published in Běijīng.

During the Cultural Revolution, a People's Commune was set up in Shànghǎi, modelled on the Paris Commune of the 19th century. (The Paris Commune was set up in 1871 and controlled Paris for two months. It planned to introduce socialist reforms such as turning over management of factories to workers' associations.) The Shànghǎi commune lasted just three weeks before Mao ordered the army to put an end to it.

The so-called Gang of Four (see History in the Facts about China chapter) had its power base in Shànghǎi. The campaign to criticise Confucius and Mencius (Mengzi) was started here in 1969, before it became nationwide in 1973 and was linked to Lin Biao.

The city's influence now ripples through the whole of the party apparatus to the top: President Jiang Zemin is Shànghǎi's ex-party chief and premier Zhu Rongji and minister Wu Bangguo also hail from the municipality. Furthermore, Hong Kong's chief executive, Tung Chee-hwa, is a Shànghǎi man.

ECONOMY

Shànghǎi's long malaise came to an abrupt end in 1990, with the announcement of plans to develop Pǔdōng, on the eastern side of Huángpǔ Jiāng. Property values soared in the early 1990s, but overbuilding created a glut of office space and towards the end of the decade real estate prices dropped in most sectors. Nevertheless, Shànghǎi's goal is to become a major financial centre along with its emerging economic strength. Lùjiāzuǐ, the area that faces off the Bund on the Pǔdōng side of Huángpǔ Jiāng, has taken shape as a modern high-rise counterpoint to the austere, old-world structures on the Bund.

Shànghǎi's burgeoning economy, its leadership and its intrinsic self-confidence have put it miles ahead of other cities in China. Neither Běijīng nor Guǎngzhōu can match the superficial, gilt-edged feel of modernity that covers the city. Shànghǎi authorities know that tourism makes money, so it spends a little bringing it in. In this respect it has some of the best services in China.

Nothing would satisfy the central government more than for Shànghǎi to replace Hong Kong as China's frontier on the future, swinging the spotlight of attention from the ex-colony on to a home-grown success story. Indeed, great strides have taken place in achieving this goal. But there's still a long way to go.

ORIENTATION

Shànghǎi municipality covers a substantial area, but the city proper is a more modest size. Within the municipality is the island of Chóngmíng. It's part of the Cháng Jiāng delta and is worth a footnote because it's the second largest-island in China.

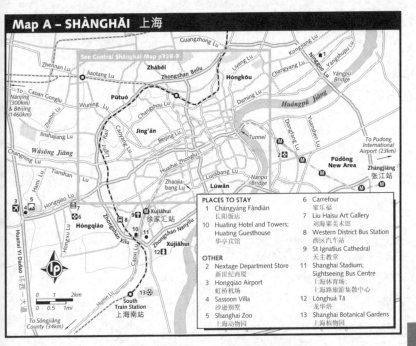

Map A – SHÀNGHǍI 上海

See Central Shànghǎi Map p328-9

PLACES TO STAY
1 Chángyáng Fàndiàn
   长阳饭店
10 Huating Hotel and Towers;
   Huating Guesthouse
   华亭宾馆

OTHER
2 Nextage Department Store
   新世纪广厦
3 Hongqiao Airport
   虹桥机场
4 Sassoon Villa
   沙逊别墅
5 Shanghai Zoo
   上海动物园

6 Carrefour
   家乐福
7 Liu Haisu Art Gallery
   刘海粟美术馆
8 Western District Bus Station
   西区汽车站
9 St Ignatius Cathedral
   天主教堂
11 Shanghai Stadium;
   Sightseeing Bus Centre
   上海体育场;
   上海路旅游集散中心
12 Lónghuá Tǎ
   龙华塔
13 Shanghai Botanical Gardens
   上海植物园

Broadly, central Shànghǎi is divided into two areas: Pǔdōng (east of Huángpǔ Jiāng) and Pǔxī (west of Huángpǔ Jiāng). The First Ring Road does a long elliptical loop around the city centre proper, which includes all of commercial west-side Shànghǎi, the Lùjiāzuǐ Finance and Trade Zone and the Jīnqiáo Export Processing Zone of Pǔdōng.

A second (outer) ring road will link Hongqiao Airport (in the west of town) with the new Wàigāoqiáo Free Trade Zone, a port on Cháng Jiāng in Pǔdōng.

For visitors, the attractions of Shànghǎi are in Pǔxī. Here you will find the Bund, the shopping streets, the former foreign concessions, hotels, restaurants, sights and nightclubs.

In the central district (around Nanjing Lu) the provincial names run north-south, and the city names run east-west. Some roads are split by compass points, such as Sichuan Nanlu (Sichuan South Rd) and Sichuan Beilu (Sichuan North Rd). Encircling Shànghǎi proper, Zhongshan Lu is split by sectors, such as Zhongshan Dong Erlu and Zhongshan Dong Yilu, which mean Zhongshan East 2nd Rd and Zhongshan East 1st Rd.

There are four main areas of interest in the city: the Bund from Wúsōng Jiāng (Sūzhōu Creek) to the Shànghǎi Harbour Passenger Terminal at Shíliùpù Wharf (Shíliùpù Mǎtóu); Nanjing Donglu (a very colourful neighbourhood); Frenchtown, which includes Huaihai Zhonglu and Ruijin Lu (an even more colourful neighbourhood); and Yùfó Sì (Jade Buddha Temple) and the shores along Wúsōng Jiāng.

Maps

English maps of Shànghǎi are available at the Foreign Languages Bookshop (see Bookshops later in this section), the Jin-jiang Hotel bookshop and occasionally from street hawkers. Watch out for the map sellers on the Bund who squawk 'English map' (the only English they know); when you look at them they're usually just a maze of characters.

The best of the bunch is the bilingual *Shanghai Tourist Map*, produced by the Shanghai Municipal Tourism Administration. It's free at hotels and the Tourist Information Centres listed in the Tourist Offices section.

SHÀNGHǍI

West Train Station
上海西站

Chezhan Lu
Caoyang Lu

Jiaotang Lu
Langao Lu
Xincun Lu
Ganquan Lu
Yanchang Lu
Huayin Lu
Huai Lu

Jiaotong Lu

Zhongtan Road
中潭路站

Shiquan Lu

Tāopǔ Hé

0   0.5   1km
0 0.25 0.5mi

Pǔtuó

Moganshan Lu
Aomen Lu
Hengfeng Lu

Langao Xilu

Zhenping Road
镇坪路站

Yichang Lu
Shanxi Beilu
Pǔtuo Lu
Xikang Lu
Tianmu Xilu

Zhongshan Beilu

Caoyang Road
曹样路站

Dongxin Lu
Changde Lu
Changhua Lu
Nanyang Lu

Mellin Beilu
Lanxi Lu
Yangxiaqing Lu
Xindan Lu

Wuning Lu

Anyuan Lu

Haifang Lu

Changping Lu

Changshou Lu

(Sūzhōu Creek)

Shahongbang Lu
Shunyi Lu
Wusong Jiang

Jiaozhou Lu
Kangding Lu

Changde Lu

Mellin Nanlu

Qilianlu Lu
Bahu Lu
Caoyang Lu

Yuyao Lu

Yanping Lu

Xinzha Lu

Jing'ān

Jinshajiang Lu

Jinshajiang Road
金沙江路站

Kanding Lu

Beijing Xilu

41

38
39
40
37
36

Jing'an Temple
静安寺站

Nanjing Xilu

35

Chángfēng
Gōngyuán

49
East China
Normal
University

Light Rail Line

Jiangsu Beilu

Wanghangdu Lu

Wuding Xilu

Wulumuqi Beilu

Tongren Lu

Jing'an
Gōngyuán

Yan'an Zhon...
延安中...

Guanfu Xilu

Zhōngshān
Gōngyuán

Jiangsu Road
江苏路站

Yuyuan Lu

42

Julu Lu
Fumin Lu

43
44

81
80
79
Xin...

Chángníng

Changning Road
长宁路站

Changning Lu

Zhongshan Park
中山路站

Xuanhua Lu
Anhua Lu

Jiangsu Lu

Yan'an Xilu

48

47
46
45
Changle Lu

Huashan Lu
Changshu Lu

Donghu Lu

75

Changshu Road
Road
常熟路站

Yuping Nanlu

Hù Xī
Stadium

Keluan Lu

Wuyi Lu

Zhaohuā Lu

Anfu Lu

71

Dingxiang
Gardens

72

Metro Line
Under Construction

Yuping Nanlu

Tianshan Lu

Zhongshan Xilu

Yanan Road West
延安西路站

Fuxing Xilu

73
Taoyang Lu

74

Loushanguan Lu

Tiānshān
Gōngyuán

Yan'an Xilu

70

67
68
69
64
65

63
62

58
59
60

Gubei Lu

Xianxia Lu

Fahuazhen Lu

Hunan Lu
Wukang Lu
Xingguo Lu
Huashan Lu

66

55

57

56

Hengshan Road

To Hongqiao
Airport (3km)
50

Xinhua Lu

52
51

Anshun Lu

Hongqiao
Road
虹桥路站

Hongqiao Lu

Huaihai Xilu

Panyu Lu

Huaihai Zhonglu
Wanping Lu
Gao'an Lu
Wulumuqi Nanlu

Kangping Lu
Yuqing Lu
Hengshan Lu
Baoqing Lu

53
54

Zhaojiabang Lu

Dong'an...
Xietu L...

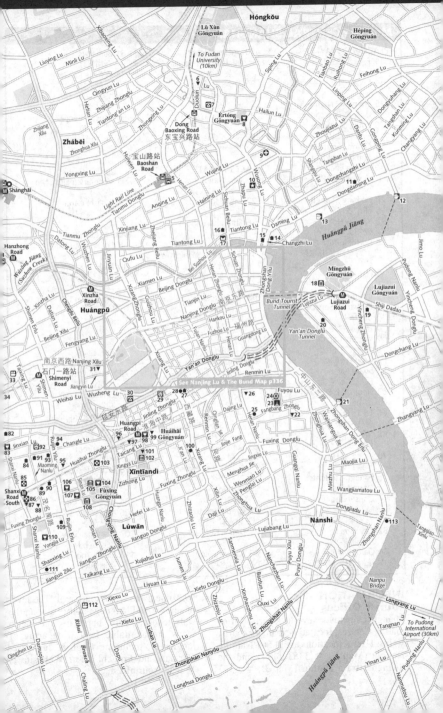

Hóngkǒu

Lǔ Xùn
Gōngyuán

Hépíng
Gōngyuán

To Fudan
University
(10km)

Liuying Lu   Minli Lu

Xiaowong Lu

Qingyun Lu

Zhijiang Zhonglu

Zhongxing Lu

Duolun Lu

Siping Lu

Tianbao Lu

Ruihong Lu

Feihong Lu

Dongguzhuang Lu

Hetian Lu   Tiantong an Lu

6

7

Értóng
Gōngyuán
8

Hailun Lu

Linping Lu

Dongti Lu

Tangshan Lu

Kunming Lu

Changyang Lu

Zhijiang
Xilu

Zhàběi

Dong
Baoxing Road
东宝兴路站

Zhouijiazui Lu

Gongping Lu

Zhonghua Xilu

Huiwon Lu

Baoshan Lu

宝山路站
Baoshan
Road

Wujing Lu

Wuxong Lu

Tangshan Lu

Dongchangzhi Lu

11

12

Yongxing Lu

Light Rail Line   Tianmu Donglu

Henan Lu

Haining Lu

Zhapu Lu

Daming Lu

Dongdaming Lu

13

Huángpǔ Jiāng

M **Shànghǎi**

Xinzha Lu

Anqing Lu

Schuan Beilu

Jimo Lu

Pudong Nanlu

Hanzhong
Road
M

**Wùsōng Jiāng
(Suchow Creek)**

Tianmu Zhonglu

Datong Lu

Wuchen Lu

Xinjiang Lu

Zhejiang Bellu

Tiantong Lu

16

17

Tiantong Lu

15   14

Changzhi Lu

Jinyuan Lu

Qufu Lu

Bei Suzhou Lu

Henan Zhonglu

Schuan Zhonglu

Zhongshan Dong Yilu

18

**Míngzhū
Gōngyuán**

Xinzha
Road
M

Huángpǔ

Xiamen Lu

Beijing Donglu

Xizang Zhonglu

Guizhou Lu

Tianjin Lu

南京东路

Nanjing Donglu

Hankou Lu

Fuzhou Lu 福州路

Guangdong Lu

Lujiazui Lu

Bund Tourist
Tunnel

**Lujiazui
Road**
M

20

19

**Lùjiāzuǐ
Gōngyuán**

Yincheng Donglu

Yincheng Zhonglu

Shiji Dadao

Xinzha Lu

Chengdu Belu

Shimen Erlu

Datian Lu

Beijing Xilu

Fengyang Lu

Yunnan Lu

Fujian Zhonglu

Henan Zhonglu

Yan'an Donglu

Yan'an Donglu
Tunnel

Dongchang Lu

南京西路 Nanjing Xilu

石门一路站
Shimen
Road

31

Jiangyin Lu

Weihai Lu

Wusheng Lu

Jinling Donglu

Renmin Lu

See Nanjing Lu & The Bund Map p336

Fuyou Lu

Zhongshan Dong Erlu

21

Zhangyang Lu

Taixing Lu

33

34

30

28   27

29

26

24

23

25   Fangbang Zhonglu

22

Huangpi
Road
M

Jinling Zhonglu

Huaihai Zhonglu

96

99

97   98

Taicang Lu

**Huáihǎi
Gōngyuán**

Dajing Lu

Qinglian Lu

Henan Lu

Zhonghua lie

Waixianghua lie

Jinxian   94

Ruijin Lu

Changle Lu

82

83

84

91   93

95

Maoming
Nanlu

100

Yan'an Lu

Jinye Fang

Fuxing Donglu

Jingxiu Lu

Maojia Lu

92

Shanxi Nanlu

101

102

103

Xīntiāndì

Zizhong Lu

Fuxing Zhonglu

Menghua lie

Wenmiao Lu

Penglai Lu

Mezhu Lu

Wangjiamatou Lu

85

89

90

106

105

104

107

108

Sinan Lu

**Fuxing
Gōngyuán**

Huangpi Nanlu

Xilin Lu

Zhonghua Lu

Dongjiadu Lu

Shanxi
Road
South
M

86

87

88

Hefei Lu

Nanchang Lu

Daji Lu

Lujiabang Lu

Nánshì

Zhongshan Nanlu

113

Fuxing Zhonglu

109

Lúwān

Jianguo Donglu

Zhizaoju Lu

Puyu Donglu

Nanchezhan Lu

Baodun Lu

110

Yongjia Lu

Shaoxing Lu

111

Jianguo Zhonglu

Jianguo Zilu

Taikang Lu

Xujiahui Lu

Jumen Lu

Liyuan Lu

Xietu Donglu

Sanmenia Lu

Xinchaozhou Lu

Quxi Lu

**Nanpu
Bridge**

Longyang Lu

To Pudong
International
Airport (30km)

112

Xietu Lu

Luban
Branch

Xietu Lu

Quxi Lu

Zhongshan Nanlu

Tangnan

Rihui Lu

Dapu Lu

Chaling Lu

Longhua Donglu

Huángpǔ Jiāng

Yinan Lu

Qingfenan Lu

Damugiao Lu

Yindong Lu

Humatou Lu

Map B – CENTRAL SHÀNGHǍI

PLACES TO STAY

11 E-Best Hotel
一百假日酒店
14 Pujiang Hotel
浦江饭店
15 Shanghai Mansions
上海大厦
16 Xīnyà Dàjiǔdiàn
新亚大酒店
19 Grand Hyatt Hotel;
Jinmao Building;
Eddy's Focus
金贸凯悦大酒店；
金贸大厦；焦点酒吧
20 Pudong Shangri-La
浦东香格里拉大酒店
27 YMCA Hotel
青年会宾馆
36 Portman Ritz-Carlton
波特曼丽思卡尔顿
酒店
43 Hilton Hotel
希尔顿酒店
49 International
Exchange Service
Centre
国际交流服务中心
50 Westin Taipingyang
太平洋大饭店
52 Crowne-Plaza
Shanghai
银星皇冠酒店
53 Héngshān Bīnguǎn
衡山宾馆
66 Tú'ān Dàjiǔdiàn
图安大酒店
68 Nányīng Fàndiàn
南鹰饭店
70 Xingguo Hotel
兴国宾馆
75 Foreign Students'
Dormitory;
Conservatory of
Music
音乐学院留学生楼
82 City Hotel
城市酒店
84 Garden Hotel
花园饭店

90 Jinchen Hotel;
Watson's Pharmacy
金晨大酒店；屈臣氏
91 Jinjiang Hotel;
Grosvenor Villa
锦江饭店
93 Jinjiang Tower
新锦江大酒店
109 Ruijin Guesthouse
瑞金滨馆

PLACES TO EAT

6 Old Time Cafe
老电影咖啡馆
22 Mǎntiānxīng Jiǔlóu
满天星酒楼
26 Shànghǎi Lǎo
Fàndiàn
上海老饭店
31 Gōngdélín Sùshíchù
功德林素食处
39 Irene's Thai
泰国餐厅
48 Da Marco
马可餐厅
54 Keven's Cafe
凯文咖啡
58 Ali YY
阿建餐厅
59 Simply Thai
天泰餐厅
60 Le Garcon Chinois
乐加尔松餐厅
61 Yang's Kitchen
杨家厨房
62 Harn Sheh Teahouse
寒舍泡沫茶坊
63 Sumo Sushi
缘禄寿司
67 Brasil Steak House
巴犀烧烤屋
77 Ooedo
大江户
78 Grape Restaurant
葡萄园
79 Nepali Kitchen
尼泊尔餐厅
80 Bǎoluó Jiǔlóu
保罗酒楼

81 Badlands
百岗餐厅
87 Wùyuè Rénjiā
吴越人家
88 1931 Pub
1931酒吧
95 Wùyuè Rénjiā
吴越人家
96 Sumo Sushi
缘禄寿司
97 Delifrance
德意法兰西
99 Vegetarian Life Style
枣子树
101 Xīnjíshì Cāntīng
新吉士餐厅

BARS & CLUBS

8 Er Ding Mu Bar
二丁目酒吧
40 Malone's American
Cafe
马龙咖啡店
46 Blowing in the Wind
Bar
答案酒吧
51 Goya
戈雅酒吧
55 Real Love
真爱酒吧
72 Cotton Club
棉花俱乐部
73 O'Malley's Bar
欧玛莉酒吧
74 Paulaner Brauhaus
宝莱纳餐厅
83 80% Bar &
Restaurant
满想汇
98 Rojam Disco (Hong
Kong Plaza)
罗尖姆娱乐宫
104 California Club
106 Asia Blue
傲凡酒吧
107 Shanghai Sally's
故乡西餐厅
110 Judy's Too
菊迪酒吧

INFORMATION
Tourist Offices

Shànghǎi operates several Tourist Information Centres, located near major tourist
sights. Useful locations are at 561 Nanjing
Donglu (Map C; ☎ 5353 1117) and the
Shànghǎi train station (Map B; ☎ 6353
9920) near the No 1 south exit. The level
of service and language ability among the
staff tends to vary, but maps and metro
maps are available in a wide array of
languages, including English, Japanese,
German and French. Their Web site is
🆆 www.tourinfo.sh.cn.

SHÀNGHǍI

CENTRAL SHÀNGHǍI – Map B

MUSEUMS & GALLERIES

18 Shanghai History Museum; Oriental Pearl Tower
上海历史博物馆；东方明珠电视塔

35 Shanghai Exhibition Centre
上海展览中心

41 Museum of Chinese Sex Culture
中国古代性文化展览

56 Shanghai Academy of Chinese Painting
上海画院

102 Site of 1st National Congress of CCP
一大会址

105 ShanghART
香格纳画廊

108 Sun Yatsen's Former Residence
孙中山故居

CINEMAS & THEATRES

29 Shanghai Concert Hall
上海音乐厅

32 Majestic Theatre
美琪大戏院

33 Studio City

47 Shanghai Theatre Academy
上海戏剧学院

71 Shanghai Drama Arts Centre
上海话剧中心

92 Lyceum Theatre
兰心大戏院

112 Golden Cinema Haixing
海兴广场

SHOPPING

25 Fangbang Lu Antique Market
方浜路古玩市场

34 Jingdezhen Porcelain Artware Shop
景德镇瓷器店

37 Shanghai Centre; American Express; World Link; The Market; Watsons Pharmacy
上海中心

57 YMCA Bike Shop
青年车行

69 New Ray Photo
新之光摄影图片制作公司

76 Xiangyang Lu Clothes Market
襄阳路市场

85 Parkson Department Store
百盛百货

86 Printemps Department Store
上海巴黎春天百货

89 Huangshan Tea Company
黄山茶业公司

94 Hot Wind Shoe Store
热风鞋业

100 Dongtai Lu Antique Market
东台路古玩市场

103 Isetan Department Store
伊势丹

TRANSPORT

1 Hutai Lu Long-Distance Bus Station
沪太路长途汽车站

2 Longmen Hotel (Train Ticketing Office)
龙门饭店

4 Hengfeng Lu Long-Distance Bus Station
恒丰路客运站

5 Gongxing Lu Long-Distance Bus Station
公兴路长途汽车汽车站

12 Gongpinglu Wharf
公平路码头

13 International Ferry Terminal
外虹桥码头

21 Shíliùpù Wharf
十六浦码头

28 Train Ticket Booking Service
火车预售票处

42 China Eastern Airlines (CAAC)
民航售票处

OTHER

3 Yùfó Sì
玉佛寺

7 Telephone Office
中国电信

9 Shanghai First People's Hospital
上海市第一人民医院

10 PSB
公安局

17 International Post Office
国际邮局

23 Chénghuáng Miào
城隍庙

24 Yu Gardens Bazaar; Nánxiáng Mántoudiàn; Húxīntíng
豫园商城；南翔馒头店；湖心亭

30 Telephone Office
中国电信

38 Main CITS
中国国际旅行社

44 Jing'an Hotel
静安宾馆

45 Huashan Hospital
华山医院

64 US Consulate
美国领事馆

65 Shanghai Library
上海图书馆

111 Old China Hand Reading Room
老汉书店

113 Destination Travel Agency
捷达旅行社

SHÀNGHǍI

The international arrivals hall of Hongqiao Airport has a tourist information booth with staff who give out maps and are very helpful. There was no comprehensive tourist information booth at Pudong International Airport at the time of writing but plans were afoot to install one.

The Tourist Hotline (☎ 6252 0000) has a useful English-language service.

There are a couple of superb Web sites offering up-to-date travel and entertainment information on Shànghǎi. Check out the Shànghǎi sections of **W** www.chinanow.com or **W** www.66cities.com. *That's*

Shanghai is a useful magazine and has a Web site at Ⓦ www.thatsshanghai.com.

Foreign Consulates

There are numerous consulates in Shànghǎi. If you're doing the Trans-Siberian journey and have booked a definite departure date, it's much better to get your Russian visa here than face the queues at the Russian embassy in Běijīng.

Your own country's consulate is worth a visit – not just if you've lost your passport, but also for up-to-date newspapers from home.

Australia (☎ 6433 4604, fax 6437 6669) 71 Fuxing Xilu

Canada (☎ 6279 8400, fax 6279 8401) Suite 604, West Tower, Shanghai Centre, 1376 Nanjing Xilu

France (☎ 6437 7414, fax 6433 9437) 21–23 floor, Qihua Tower, 1375 Huaihai Zhonglu

Germany (☎ 6433 6951, fax 6471 4448) 181 Yongfu Lu

Japan (☎ 6278 0788, fax 6278 8988) 8 Wanshan Lu, Hóngqiáo

New Zealand (☎ 6471 1108, fax 6431 0226) 15a, Qihua Tower, 1375 Huaihai Zhonglu

Russia (☎ 6324 2682, fax 6306 9982) 20 Huangpu Lu

South Korea (☎ 6219 6417, fax 6219 6918) 4th floor, International Trade Centre, 2200 Yan'an Xilu

UK (☎ 6279 7650, fax 6279 7651) 3rd floor, Room 301, Shanghai Centre, 1376 Nanjing Xilu

USA (☎ 6433 6880, fax 6433 4122) 1469 Huaihai Zhonglu

Money

Almost every hotel has money-changing counters. Credit cards are more readily accepted in Shànghǎi than other parts of China.

Most tourist hotels will accept major credit cards such as Visa, American Express, MasterCard, Diners and JCB, as will banks and Friendship Stores (and related tourist outlets like the Shanghai Antique and Curio Shop).

The enormous Bank of China right next to the Peace Hotel (Map C) tends to get crowded, but is better organised than Chinese banks elsewhere around the country (it's worth a peek for its grand interior). A branch of Citibank next door on the Bund is open 24 hours for ATM withdrawal. ATMs at various branches of the Bank of China,

the Industrial and Commercial Bank of China (ICBC) and the China Construction Bank accept most major cards.

American Express (Map B; ☎ 6279 8082) has an office at Room 206, Retail Plaza, Shanghai Centre, 1376 Nanjing Xilu.

Post & Communications

Larger tourist hotels have post offices where you can mail letters and small packages, and this is by far the most convenient option.

The international post office (Map B) is at the corner of Sichuan Beilu and Bei Suzhou Lu on the 2nd floor. Poste restante letters are collected at window No 21. The section for international parcels is in the same building around the corner in another section.

Express parcel and document service is available with several foreign carriers. Contact DHL (☎ 6536 2900), UPS (☎ 6391 5555), Federal Express (☎ 6237 5134) or TNT Skypak (☎ 6421 1111).

Long-distance phone calls can be placed from hotel rooms and don't take long to get through. There's a small China Telecom outlet (Map C) next to the Peace Hotel on Nanjing Donglu. Phonecards, available from many shops as well as China Telecom, are useful but don't usually work with hotel phones.

Email & Internet Access Shànghǎi has many Internet cafes but there's a frequent turnover of locales. Check current listings in *That's Shanghai* magazine.

Many hotels in Shànghǎi provide Internet services, but they're usually a little pricey. The Shanghai Library (Map B), at 1555 Huaihai Zhonglu, has terminals on the ground floor. It's open from 9am to 8.30pm daily and costs Y6 per hour. Bring your passport for ID. The massive Book City (Map C), at 465 Fuzhou Lu, has an Internet cafe on the 2nd floor, charging Y7 per half-hour. It's open daily from 9.30am to 6.30pm and until 9pm from Friday to Sunday.

Travel Agencies

The main office of China International Travel Service (CITS; Zhōngguó Guójì Lǚxíngshè; Map B; ☎ 6323 8749) is at 1277 Beijing Xilu. For train tickets, go to the CITS office (Map C; ☎ 6323 8770) on the 1st floor of the Guangming Building, at 2 Jinling Donglu. There's another CITS office on Nanjing Donglu near the Peace Hotel primarily for booking airline tickets.

CITS may need at least three days to get tickets for destinations further than Hángzhōu or Sūzhōu. A service charge of Y10 is added. If you're in a hurry, try your hotel or one of the other booking options mentioned in the Getting There & Away section later in this chapter.

Travel agencies abound in Shànghǎi, especially since it became easier for people to go abroad as tourists. It's worth shopping around. The staff at Destination Travel Agency (Map B; ☎ 6314 5505, ⓔ irs@uninet.com.cn), at 34 Dongjiadu Lu, speak English and cater to foreign travellers.

Bookshops

Shànghǎi is one of the better places in China to stock up on reading fodder.

The main Foreign Languages Bookshop (Map C) is at 390 Fuzhou Lu. The 1st floor has a good but pricey range of maps and English-language books on China. The 2nd and 4th floors have a good range of Western literature that breaks the usual Jane Austen mould and offers interesting contemporary (but not cheap) English reading material. Fuzhou Lu has traditionally been the bookshop street of Shànghǎi and is well worth a stroll.

The Shanghai Museum bookshop has an excellent range of books on Chinese art, architecture, ceramics and calligraphy and is definitely worth a visit if you're in the museum. It also has a wide selection of cards and slides.

Get a copy of Pan Ling's *In Search of Old Shanghai* for a rundown on who was who and what was what back in the bad old days.

For where they lived, consult *A Last Look: Western Architecture in Old Shanghai* by Tess Johnston & Deke Erh, which offers a fascinating photographic record of buildings in the city. Their latest book on Shànghǎi, *Frenchtown Shanghai,* covers the old French Concession in great detail. These books are usually available at the Shanghai Museum bookshop, the Foreign Languages Bookshop or the Old China

Hand Reading Room (Map B; ☎/fax 6473 2526), at 27 Shaoxing Lu, run by Deke Erh. Besides their series of books on Western architecture in China, the bookshop-cum-cafe has a whole range of books on art, architecture and culture.

Newspapers & Magazines

A small range of foreign newspapers and magazines is available from the larger tourist hotels (eg, Park, Jinjiang, Hilton) and the Foreign Languages Bookshop.

Publications include the *Wall Street Journal, International Herald Tribune, Asiaweek, South China Morning Post, The Economist, Time* and *Newsweek.* They are expensive, however, with *Newsweek* and *Time* usually costing about Y35. You can read foreign magazines and newspapers at the Shanghai Library. Bring your passport.

Back in the late '90s, life for foreigners in Shànghǎi improved considerably with the appearance of entertainment publications edited and compiled by native speakers of English. There were some shaky beginnings and changeovers as the authorities tried to come to terms with these upstart foreigners creating their own publications, which was no small feat in a country that controls its media with an iron fist. Nothing too controversial, of course, but at least they are *interesting* to read.

The most comprehensive is the monthly magazine *That's Shanghai,* followed by the bi-monthly *City Weekend,* published in Běijīng with a Shànghǎi supplement, and the monthly *Shanghai Talk* as well as other English and bilingual magazines. If you want to know what's going on in Shànghǎi, check these out. They're free and available in most of the Western-style bars and restaurants and some hotels.

The two English newspapers with a Shànghǎi focus are the *Shanghai Star* and *Shanghai Daily.*

Medical Services

Shànghǎi is credited with the best medical facilities and most advanced medical knowledge in China. Hospital treatment is available at the Huashan Hospital (Map B; ☎ 6248 9999 ext 1921), at 12 Wulumuqi Zhonglu, which has a Hong Kong joint-venture section catering to those who can afford more luxurious care; and at the

Shanghai First People's Hospital (Map B; ☎ 6324 3852) at 585 Jiulong Lu in Hóngkǒu.

World Link (Map B; ☎ 6279 7688, fax 6279 7698) at Suite 203 in the Shanghai Centre offers private medical care.

PSB

The Public Security Bureau (Gōngānjú; Map B; ☎ 6357 7925) visa office is at 333 Wusong Lu, near the intersection with Kunshan Lu.

THINGS TO SEE & DO
The Bund 外滩
Wàitān

The Bund is an Anglo-Indian term for the embankment of a muddy waterfront. The term is apt: mud bedevils Shànghǎi. Between 1920 (when the problem was first noticed) and 1965, the city sank several metres. Water was pumped back into the ground, but the Venetian threat remains. Concrete rafts are used as foundations for high-rises in this spongy mass.

Its muddy predicament aside, the Bund is symbolic of Shànghǎi. In faraway Kashgar and Lhasa, local Chinese pose for photographs in front of oil-painted Bund facades. Constant throngs of Chinese and foreign tourists pad past the porticos of the Bund's grand edifices with maps in hand. The buildings themselves loom serenely, oblivious to the march of revolutions; a vagabond assortment of neoclassical 1930s downtown New York styles and monumental antiquity thrown in for good measure.

To the Europeans, the Bund was Shànghǎi's Wall Street, a place of feverish trading, of fortunes made and lost. One of the most famous traders was Jardine Matheson & Company. In 1848 Jardine's purchased the first land offered for sale to foreigners in Shànghǎi and set up shop shortly after, dealing in opium and tea. The company grew into one of the great hongs (a 'hong' is literally a business firm), and today it owns just about half of Hong Kong.

At the north-western end of the Bund were the British Public Gardens (now called Huángpǔ Gōngyuán). Famously, a sign at the entrance announced 'No Dogs or Chinese Allowed'. Or that's how posterity remembers it; in actual fact the restrictions on Chinese and dogs were listed in separate clauses of a whole bevy of restrictions on

undesirables. The slight, however, will probably never be forgotten.

The Bund today is in the process of yet another transformation. The building identified by a crowning dome is the old Hongkong & Shanghai Bank, completed in 1921 with much pomp and ceremony. For many years it housed the Shanghai People's Municipal Government and was off-limits to curious travellers. Now it belongs to the **Pudong Development Bank** *(Map C)* and you can take a look inside the magnificent central hall during business hours. Other Bund fixtures have also been fixed up and newly occupied by domestic and foreign companies.

The statues that once lined the Bund no longer exist but you can get an idea of what things used to look like from photos on display at the **Bund History Museum** *(Waitān Lìshǐ Bówùguǎn; Map C; admission free; open 9am-4.30pm daily)*, at the north end of Huángpǔ Gōngyuán.

The Tung Feng Hotel, at the bottom of the Bund near Shíliùpù Wharf, only hints at its former grandeur and conveys nothing of its former exclusivity. It was once home to the Shanghai Club whose membership was confined to upper-crust British males. They sat around the club's 110-foot bar (the longest in the world at the time), sipping chilled champagne and comparing fortunes. The hotel has been closed for the last few years, awaiting new occupants.

Old Shànghǎi

Until recently, Shànghǎi was a vast museum, housing an inheritance of foreign trophies. While state-protected landmark buildings on the Bund and elsewhere are safe from the ball-and-chain, in other parts of town chunks of history have given way to department stores and office blocks.

Shànghǎi is shackled to a past it is both suspicious and proud of, so who knows what the city will look like two decades from now. But as the Chinese saying goes, *'Jiùde bùqù, xīnde bùlái'* (If the old doesn't go, the new won't come).

For the time being, some of old Shànghǎi is still around. The **Chinese city**, for example, is a maze of narrow lanes, lined with closely packed houses and laundry hanging from windows. It lies on the southwestern bank of Huángpǔ Jiāng, bounded to the north by Jinling Donglu and to the south by Zhonghua Lu. The Yu Gardens are in this part of town and well worth a visit. See the Yu Gardens Bazaar section later for details.

The **International Settlement** (*Shànghǎi Zūjiè*), in its time a brave new world of co-operation between the British, Europeans and Americans (the Japanese were also included, but were considered suspect), cuts a broad swathe through the north of the city centre. It extends from the intersection of Yan'an Xilu and Nanjing Xilu north to Wúsōng Jiāng and east to Huángpǔ Jiāng. Nanjing Lu and the Bund shared pride of place in this settlement.

South of Yan'an Lu and squeezed north of the Chinese city was the **French Concession** (*Fǎguó Zūjiè*). Yan'an Lu was known as Avenue Foch in the west, and Avenue Edward VII in the east; the French strip of the Bund (south of Yan'an Lu) was known as the Quai de France. Despite the names, there were never all that many French people in the concession – 90% of the residents were Chinese, and the most numerous foreigners were Russians. Nevertheless, Frenchtown remains one of the most interesting parts of Shànghǎi. The premier district (around the Jinjiang Hotel and on Huaihai Lu) is becoming gentrified, and department stores have opened up everywhere in the last few years. But for Frenchtown at its best, simply strike off on the side streets that head south off Yan'an Zhonglu (see Frenchtown later in this section for more information).

Nanjing Lu & the Central District

Nanjing Donglu, from the Peace to the Park hotels, has long been China's golden mile, though its glamour has slipped a few notches in the last 15 years. Hoping to bring back its former glory, the city began a massive renovation project in the late 1990s, turning Nanjing Lu into a pedestrian-only shopping extravaganza from Xizang Lu to Henan Lu.

Nanjing Donglu becomes Nanjing Xilu at **Rénmín Gōngyuán** (*People's Park; Map C*). The park and the adjacent People's Square were once the site of the Shanghai Racecourse, now occupied by the Shanghai Museum, the Shanghai Grand Theatre, the Shanghai Urban Planning Exhibition Hall

Shanghai Museum

This stunning building (*Shànghǎi Bówùguǎn; Map C; ☎ 6372 3500, 201 Renmin Dadao; adult/child or student Y20/5; open 9am-5pm Sun-Fri, 9am-8pm Sat*) was built in 1994 at a cost of Y570 million, and can be seen as a completely new approach to museum design in China. The museum is symbolic of the many changes that are afoot in China – gone are airy corridors, dry exhibits, yawning security guards and stale air – the new Shanghai Museum is as impressive outside as in.

Designed to recall the shape of an ancient Chinese *dǐng* vessel, this architectural statement is home to one of the most impressive collections of art in China, making it a must-see.

Take your pick from the galleries that house some fantastic specimens – from the archaic green patina of the Ancient Chinese Bronze Gallery through the silent solemnity of the Chinese Sculpture Gallery, from the exquisite beauty of the ceramics in the Zande Lou Gallery to the measured and timeless flourishes captured in the Chinese Calligraphy Gallery. Chinese painting, seals, jade, Ming and Qing furniture, coins and ethnic art are also on offer, intelligently displayed in well-lit galleries. Furthermore, the exhibits are generously spaced out, giving you the opportunity to stroll leisurely and unhurriedly through the galleries.

While guiding you through the craft of millennia, the museum simultaneously takes you through the pages of Chinese history. Expect to spend half if not the whole day here.

and the rather drab municipal government building. Nanjing Xilu itself was previously Bubbling Well Rd, the natural spring having been long sealed over.

The crowds are less intense as you head west along Nanjing Xilu, past the former Shanghai Race Club and previous site of the Shanghai Library, now the Shanghai Art Gallery. Beyond the Chengdu Lu Expressway, which cuts down the centre of Shànghǎi, Nanjing Xilu gives way to office blocks and more shops and hotels, all of which join forces in the impressive Shanghai Centre and Soviet-era Shanghai Exhibition Centre opposite.

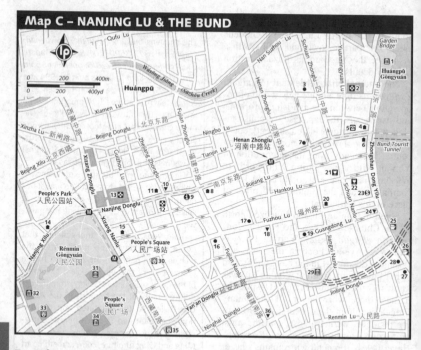

Frenchtown 法国租界
Fǎguó Zūjiè

The core of Frenchtown, the former French Concession, is the area around Huaihai Lu and the Jinjiang Hotel. Huaihai Lu is the shopper's Pǔdōng, a glittering alternative to worn Nanjing Lu, and huge department stores such as Isetan, Printemps and Parkson have gone up. The area around the Jinjiang Hotel and Jinjiang Tower is full of cafes, boutiques and the odd antique shop.

On side streets off Huaihai Lu, from Sinan Lu west to Huashan Lu, is some of the best old architecture, from old Art Deco apartment complexes to neoclassical mansions and villas with quaint balconies and doorways.

Site of the 1st National Congress of the CCP 中共一大会址
Zhōnggòng Yídàhuìzhǐ

The CCP was founded in July 1921 in this French Concession building which is now a museum *(Map B; ☎ 5383 2171, 374 Huangpi Nanlu; admission Y3; open 9am-5pm daily)* Once a modest neighbourhood, this area has been transformed into the upmarket atmos-phere of Xīntiāndì, full of restaurants, bars and shops while preserving the framework of the original *shíkùmén* (stone-framed doorways) low-rise tenement buildings built in the early 1900's. It's a brilliant if ironic juxtaposition for this historical site. The museum has photographs and reconstructions of the historic meeting with English captions.

Sun Yatsen's Former Residence
Sūn Zhōngshān Gùjū 孙中山故居

China is simply brimming with Sun Yatsen memorabilia, and here is one of his former residences *(Map B; ☎ 6437 2954, 7 Xiang-shan Lu; admission Y8; open 9am-4.30pm daily)* on what was formerly the rue Moliére. He lived here for six years, supported by over seas Chinese funds. After Sun's death, his wife, Song Qingling (1893–1981), continued to live here until 1937, constantly watched by Kuomintang plain-clothes and French police. The two-storey house is set back from the street and furnished as it was back in Sun's days, even though it was looted by the Japanese. The entry price gets you a brief tour of the house.

Map C – NANJING LU & THE BUND

PLACES TO STAY

4 Peace Hotel; Bank of China; Citibank; Dragon-Phoenix Hall; Old Jazz Bar
和平饭店；中国银行；花旗银行；龙凤厅

6 Peace Palace Hotel
和平汇中饭店

8 Sofitel Hyland Hotel; Brauhaus 505
上海海仑宾馆

11 Dōngyà Fàndiàn
东亚饭店

14 Park Hotel
国际饭店

15 Yangtze Hotel
杨子饭店

20 Metropole Hotel
新城饭店

PLACES TO EAT

10 Shěndàchéng
沈大成

18 Xìnghuā Lóu
杏花楼

24 M on the Bund; Rollo Di Pollo
米氏西餐厅

36 Juélín Sùshíchù
觉林素食处

SHOPPING

2 Friendship Store
友谊商店

7 Guànlóng Photo Supplies
冠龙照相器材商店

12 Hualian Department Store
华联商厦

13 No 1 Department Store
第一百货

16 Book City
书城

17 Foreign Languages Bookshop
外文书店

19 Shanghai Antique and Curio Shop
上海文物市场

TRANSPORT

3 Train Ticket Booking Service
火车售票处

25 Húangpǔ Jiāng Boat Tour Dock
黄浦上游船

26 Ferries to Pǔdōng
码头（至浦东）

27 Boat Ticketing Office
船售票处

OTHER

1 Bund History Museum
外滩历史博物馆

5 Telephone Office; Gino Cafe
中国电信；季诺意大利餐厅

9 Tourist Information Centre
上海市旅游咨询服务中心

21 Tropicana Bar & Restaurant

22 Fest Beer House
外滩啤酒总汇

23 Pudong Development Bank
浦东发展银行

28 CITS
中国国际旅行社

29 Shanghai Natural History Museum
上海自然博物馆

30 Yifu Theatre
逸夫舞台

31 Shanghai Urban Planning Exhibition Hall
上海城市规划展示馆

32 Shanghai Art Gallery
上海美术馆

33 Shanghai Grand Theatre
上海大剧院

34 Shanghai Museum
上海博物馆

35 Great World
大世界

Yu Gardens Bazaar 豫园市场
Yù Yuán Shāngchéng

At the north-eastern end of the old Chinese city, the Yu Gardens Bazaar *(Map B; ☎ 6326 0830, 218 Anren Jie; adult/child Y25/10; open 8.30am-5pm daily)*, is one of Shànghǎi's premier sights. Try not to visit on the weekend, though, as the crowds are pressing to say the least. See the Places to Eat section for details on the bazaar's justifiably famous and delicious snacks.

The Pan family, rich Ming dynasty officials, founded the gardens, which took 18 years (1559–1577) to be nurtured into existence and were snuffed out by a bombardment during the Opium War in 1842. The gardens took another trashing during French reprisals for attacks on their nearby concession by Taiping rebels. Now restored, they are a fine example of Ming garden design.

Adjacent to the bazaar, **Lǎo Jiē** *(Old Street)*, known more prosaically as Fangbang Zhonglu, spills over with *antique* and *souvenir shops*. **Chénghuáng Miào** *(Temple of the Town Gods)* and the street, together with the Yu Gardens Bazaar itself present a rather Disneyland version of historical China. It's a great stop for lunch and also handy for souvenir shopping.

Yùfó Sì 玉佛寺
Jade Buddha Temple

Yùfó Sì *(Map B; ☎ 6266 2668, 170 Anyuan Lu; admission Y10; open 8.30am-5pm daily)* is one of Shànghǎi's few active Buddhist temples. It attracts large numbers of local and overseas Chinese tourists.

Built between 1911 and 1918, the centrepiece is a 2m-high white jade Buddha around which the temple was built. The story goes that a monk from Pǔtuóshān travelled to Myanmar (Burma) via Tibet, lugged the Buddha back to its present site and then went off in search of alms to build a temple for it. During the Spring Festival in January or February, some 20,000 Chinese Buddhists come to worship.

The seated Buddha, encrusted with jewels, is said to weigh 1000kg. A smaller Buddha from the same shipment reclines on a mahogany couch. There's an extra Y5 entry to view the Buddha. No photography is permitted.

A *vegetarian restaurant* on the premises serves lunch for reasonable prices.

The temple is in the north-west of town, near the intersection of Anyuan Lu and Jiangning Lu. One way to get there is to take the metro out to the Shanghai train station and then walk (about 1km) or take a taxi or motor-tricycle.

Bus No 19 runs along Tiantong Lu near Shanghai Mansions, and eventually on past the temple.

Pǔdōng New Area 浦东新区
Pǔdōng Xīnqū

Larger than Shànghǎi itself, the Pǔdōng New Area *(Map A)* is on the eastern bank of Huángpǔ Jiāng. Before 1990 – when development plans were first announced – Pǔdōng constituted 350 sq km of boggy farmland supplying vegetables to Shànghǎi's markets. Now the vegies are grown elsewhere as Pǔdōng has become a Special Economic Zone (SEZ).

Shànghǎi's second metro line opened at the end of 1999 and connects Pǔdōng with Pǔxī. The Wàigāoqiáo harbour area is being upgraded into a major container port and the US$2 billion Pudong International Airport opened as the main international airport in late 1999.

The **Oriental Pearl Tower** *(Dōngfāng Míngzhū Diànshì Tǎ; Map B;* ☎ *5879 8888, 1 Shiji Dadao; adult/child Y50/25; open 8.30am-9.30pm daily),* which resembles an inverted hypodermic, is a uniquely uninspiring piece of architecture, although the views of Shànghǎi from its lookout halfway up are sensational. Unfortunately, you have to queue forever to get into the high-speed elevator and it costs an extra Y50 if you want to go to the top bauble. The nearby **Jinmao Building** *(Jīnmào Dàshà; Map B;* ☎ *5047 0088, 88 Shiji Dadao; adult/child Y50/25; open 8.30am-9pm daily)* also has an observation deck at the 88th floor. You may be better off spending the same amount of money in the coffee shop in the nearby

Grand Hyatt on the 54th floor or, even better, the Cloud Nine Bar on the 87th floor. Next to the Jinmao is the incomplete Shanghai World Finance Building, which when finished will total 90 storeys and 460m (1518 feet).

The **Shanghai History Museum** *(Shànghǎi Lìshǐ Bówùguǎn; Map B;* ☎ *589 1888, 1 Shiji Dadao; admission Y70; open 9am-9pm daily)* is at the base of the Oriental Pearl Tower. Multimedia presentations and imaginative displays re-create the history of Shànghǎi with emphasis on the pre-1949 era. One of the pair of bronze lions that once stood outside the Hongkong & Shanghai Bank is now housed here as are many other artefacts from old Shànghǎi. It's definitely worth visiting, but you have to pay admission to the Oriental Pearl Tower as well, which brings the price to Y70.

There are many ways to get across the river to Pǔdōng but if you're craving a psychedelic experience take the **Bund Tourist Tunnel** *(Wàitān Guānguāng Suìdào; Map C;* ☎ *5888 6000, 300 Zhongshan Dong Yilu; one way/return Y20/30; open 9am-9.30pm Mon-Thur, 9am-10.30pm Fri-Sun).* Futuristic train modules carry passengers through a tunnel of garish lights between the Bund and the opposite shore. The ticket office is in the underpass directly across from the Peace Hotel.

Other Sights
South-west of central Shànghǎi **Lónghuá Tǎ** *(Map A;* ☎ *6457 0098 ext 8113, 2853 Longhua Lu; admission Y5; open 7am-4.30pm daily)* is part of a beautifully restored temple complex said to date from the 10th century. Take the light rail to Longcao Road station and head east along Longshui Beilu for about 1km. Bus No 44 goes there from Xújiāhuì.

The Xújiāhuì area, bordering the western end of Frenchtown, once had a Jesuit settlement with an observatory (which is still in use). **St Ignatius Cathedral** *(Map A;* ☎ *6253 0959, 158 Puxi Lu; open 5.45am-5pm daily)* whose spires were lopped off by Red Guards, was restored and has regular Catholic services. Take the metro to Xujiahui station; it's a short walk south to the church.

Farther south-west of Xújiāhuì the **Shanghai Botanical Gardens** *(Shànghǎi Zhíwùyuán; Map A;* ☎ *6451 3369, 1111*

The Chinese Circus

Circus acts in China go back 2000 years to the original Middle Kingdom. Effects are obtained using simple props such as sticks, plates, eggs and chairs. Apart from the acrobatics, there's magic, vaudeville, drama, clowning, music, conjuring, dance and mime thrown into a complete performance. Happily, it's an art that actually gained from the Communist takeover and did not suffer during the Cultural Revolution. Performers used to have the status of gypsies, but now it's 'people's art'.

Most of the provinces have their own performing troupes, sponsored by government agencies, industrial complexes, the army or rural administrations. About 80 troupes are active in China and they're much in demand. You'll also see more bare legs, star-spangled costumes and rouge in one acrobat show than you'll see anywhere else in China.

Acts vary from troupe to troupe. Some traditional acts haven't changed over the centuries, while others have incorporated roller skates and motorbikes. One time-proven act that's hard to follow is the 'Balancing in Pairs', with one man balanced upside down on the head of another and mimicking every movement of the partner below, mirror image, even drinking a glass of water!

Hoop jumping is another: four hoops are stacked on top of each other and the person going through the very top hoop may attempt a backflip with a simultaneous body twist.

The 'Peacock Displaying Its Feathers' involves an array of people balanced on one bicycle. According to the *Guinness Book of Records*, a Shànghǎi troupe holds the record at 13 people, though apparently a Wǔhàn troupe has done 14.

 The 'Pagoda of Bowls' is a balancing act where the performer, usually a woman, does everything with her torso except tie it in knots, all the while casually balancing a stack of porcelain bowls on foot, head or both – and perhaps also balancing on a partner.

Longwu Lu; admission Y15; open 7am-5pm daily) is a huge area with an exquisite collection of plants, including special pavilions for bonsai and orchids (Y7 entry). It's an ideal place to replenish your oxygen intake for an afternoon.

The **Shanghai Exhibition Centre** *(Shànghǎi Zhǎnlǎn Zhōngxīn; Map B)* is south of the Shanghai Centre. Architectural buffs will appreciate the monumentality and unsubtle, bold Bolshevik strokes – there was a time when Pǔdōng was set to look like this.

Out near Hongqiao Airport the **Shanghai Zoo** *(Shànghǎi Dòngwùyuán; Map A; ☎ 6268 7775, 23 Hongqiao Lu; admission Y15; open 6.30am-5pm daily)* has pandas and South China tigers, and a few thousand other animal species. West of the zoo is the former **Sassoon Villa** *(Map A)*; see the boxed text 'The Cathay Hotel' later. Take bus No 831 from Jingling Donglu at the Bund or bus No 911 from Huaihai Lu.

On the way to the city of Jiāxīng, by rail or road, is Sōngjiāng county (Sōngjiāng xiàn), 30km south-west of Shànghǎi. The place is older than Shànghǎi itself. On Tiānmǎ Shān in the county is **Hùzhū Tǎ**, a pagoda built in AD 1079. It's the leaning tower of China, with an inclination now

exceeding the tower at Pisa by 1.5°. The 19m-high tower started tilting 200 years ago. The nearby hill of Shé Shān is crowned by the beautiful **Basilica of Notre Dame**. This Catholic church was completed in 1935.

Buses to Tiānmǎ Shān and Shé Shān go from the western district bus station (xīqū qìchēzhàn) at 555 Wuzhong Lu. Bus No 113 from the Shanghai train station terminates there.

Huángpǔ Jiāng Trip 黄浦江游览船

Huángpǔ Jiāng offers some remarkable views of the Bund and the riverfront activity. Huángpǔ Jiāng tour boats (Map C; ☎ 6374 4461), 153 Zhongshan Dong Erlu, depart from the dock on the Bund, near Yan'an Lu. The one-hour cruise (Y25 to Y35) takes in Yángpǔ Bridge (Yángpǔ Dà Qiáo); there are also two-hour and 3½-hour cruises that have several classes (Y35 to Y100). More expensive tickets include refreshments. Depending on your enthusiasm for loading cranes, the night cruises are more scenic, though the boat traffic during the day is interesting. The 3½-hour excursion is a 60km round trip, northwards up Huángpǔ Jiāng to the junction with Cháng Jiāng and back again along the same route.

Departure times vary, but there are afternoon and evening departures for all three categories during weekdays, with the addition of morning cruises on weekends.

Shànghǎi is one of the world's largest ports and the tour boat passes an enormous variety of craft – freighters, bulk carriers, roll-on roll-off ships, sculling sampans, giant praying-mantis cranes, the occasional junk and Chinese navy vessels (which aren't supposed to be photographed).

Musuems & Galleries

Shànghǎi has many art galleries, museums and exhibition sites and new venues keep appearing. It's impossible to list everything here, especially venues for art. Check magazine listings for information on what's going in Shànghǎi's art world.

The **Liu Haisu Art Gallery** *(Liú Hǎisù Měishùguǎn; Map A;* ☎ *6270 1018, 1660 Hongqiao Lu; admission Y5; open 9am-4pm Tues-Sun)* is named in honour of the late Liu Haisu, a well-known artist of traditional Chinese painting. It hosts both local and international exhibitions and is located south-west of central Shànghǎi.

The **Shanghai Academy of Chinese Painting** *(Shànghǎi Huàyuàn; Map B;* ☎ *6474 9977 ext 217, 197 Yueyang Lu; adult/child Y10/5; open 9am-11.30am & 1pm-4pm Tues-Sun)* features local and Western artists in its shows.

One of the first places in Shànghǎi to display cutting-edge works by modern Chinese artists, **ShanghART** *(Xiānggénà Huàláng; Map B;* ☎ *6359 3923,* Ⓦ *www.shanghart .com, 2a Gaolan Lu; open 10am-10pm Tues-Sat, 10am-7pm Sun-Mon)* was opened in the late 1990's by Lorenz Helbling, a Swiss art dealer. Located near Fùxīng Gōngyuán, it has new shows roughly every month.

After much anticipation, the **Shanghai Art Gallery** *(Shànghǎi Měishùguǎn; Map C;* ☎ *6327 8593, 325 Nanjing Xilu; admission Y20; open 9am-5pm daily)* opened in its new premises in the former Shanghai Race Club (which used to be the Shanghai Library). It's worth visiting for the building alone.

The **Shanghai Natural History Museum** *(Shànghǎi Zìrán Bówùguǎn; Map C;* ☎ *6321 3548, 260 Yan'an Donglu; admission Y5; open 9am-5pm daily)* has some full-size dinosaur skeletons and just about every species of animal life that ever existed in China.

For a more current display of natural history, visit the **Museum of Chinese Sex Culture** *(Zhōngguó Gǔdài Xìng Wénhuà Zhǎnlǎn; Map B;* ☎ *6230 1243, 1133 Wuding Xilu; admission Y30; open 9am-9pm daily)*. Curated by Liu Darin, a professor of sexology, this museum first opened as a temporary exhibition in 1999 but proved so popular it became permanent, with a convenient location on Nanjing Donglu. Since then, Professor Liu has had to move his museum to a less prominent locale, but it's definitely worth checking out. Exhibits range from the sacred to the profane, and come from Professor Liu's personal collection. For anyone interested in the history of the dildo and bound feet, among other things, there's a treasure trove of interesting stuff here. The bus No 93 terminus is close to the museum. Catch it from Huashan Lu, just west of the Jing'an Temple metro station.

PLACES TO STAY

Unless otherwise stated places listed in this section appear on the Central Shànghǎi map (Map B).

PLACES TO STAY – BUDGET

Shànghǎi has some of the highest real estate values in China, and lower-end accommodation has felt the squeeze for a while now. Oversupply has brought the prices down slightly. While no real cheap hotels exist for foreigners there are a few that represent value for money.

Take note that budget accommodation can be swamped during the summer and on holidays, leaving you with little choice but to upgrade to pricey doubles that cost Y300 or more.

Pujiang Hotel (Pǔjiāng Fàndiàn; ☎ *6324 6388,* Ⓔ *sales@pujianghotel.com, 15 Huangpu Lu)* Dorm beds Y55, doubles from Y300. Built on the site of the Richards Hotel, the Pujiang was originally called the Astor House Hotel, one of Shànghǎi's first grand hotels. Now it's the place for those counting their shekels – it's central, has loads of style and the rooms are vast. Although the galleries upstairs look like they belong in a Victorian asylum, there's a distinguished nobility in the rooms and halls that makes it a bargain and a half. From the Bund, it's a short walk across the Garden Bridge (Wàibáidù Qiáo) and Wúsōng Jiāng.

YMCA Hotel (*Qīngniánhuì Bīnguǎn;* ☎ *6326 1040,* [e] *ymcahtl@isdnnet.sta.net .cn, 123 Xizang Nanlu*) Dorm beds with bath & air-con Y125, singles/doubles Y300/380. This is another budget option with clean dormitories and it's close to the People's Square.

Foreign Students' Dormitory (*Liúxuéshēng Lóu;* ☎ *6437 2577, 20 Fenyang Lu*) Doubles with shared/private bath Y80/200. This old stand-by at the Conservatory of Music has a great location off Huaihai Zhonglu. Unfortunately, it's often fully booked. It's a short walk from the Changshu Road metro station. To find the rooms, walk through the entrance to the conservatory and turn left.

International Exchange Service Centre (*Guójì Jiāoliú Fúwù Zhōngxīn;* ☎ *6257 9241, fax 6257 1813, 3663 Zhongshan Beilu*) Doubles Y150. This foreign student dormitory at East China Normal University also has reasonably priced rooms. The university is west of the city centre, close to Jinshajiang Road light rail station. To find the foreign student building go through the main gate, cross two bridges then turn left.

Chángyáng Fàndiàn (*Map A;* ☎ *6543 4890, fax 6543 0986, 1800 Changyang Lu*) Doubles/triples Y210/270. This excellent hotel in the north-east is a little out of the way. Push for a discount – doubles may come down to Y120. Bus No 22 from the Bund runs right past it.

E-Best Hotel (*Yìbǎi Jiārì Jiǔdiàn;* ☎ *6595 1818,* [e] *ebest@public6.sta.net.cn, 687 Dongdaming Lu*) Singles Y168-188, doubles Y350-400. An older, renovated building, this mid-range place has some budget rooms. It's east of the international ferry terminal in Hóngkǒu. Bus No 22 goes there from the Bund.

PLACES TO STAY – MID-RANGE

Mid-range accommodation in Shànghǎi will cost between Y300 and Y400 for a double, but discounts can often bring these prices down to Y250 or so. If you're landing at Hongqiao Airport, try the list of discounted hotel rooms at the **Shanghai**

Airport Tourism Company (☎ *6268 3683*), which has booths in both the international and domestic arrival halls.

Yangtze Hotel (*Yángzǐ Fàndiàn; Map C;* ☎ *6351 7880,* [e] *sales@e-yangtze.com,* [w] *www.e-yangtze.com, 740 Hankou Lu*) Singles Y360, doubles from Y520. One of the nicest mid-range hotels around, the Yangtze is right behind the Protestant church that faces Rénmín Gōngyuán. Built in 1934, the exterior is largely unchanged, including the wonderful Art Nouveau balconies.

Dōngyà Fàndiàn (*East Asia Hotel; Map C;* ☎ *6322 3233, fax 6322 4598, 680 Nanjing Donglu*) Singles or doubles Y457. This hotel is not as nice as the Yangtze, but is cheaper with rooms available for Y280 when discounted. It's very central but some of the rooms don't have windows. The reception is on the 2nd floor through a clothing shop.

Metropole Hotel (*Xīnchéng Fàndiàn; Map C;* ☎ *6321 3030,* [e] *metropolehotel-sh @China-dirs.com, 180 Jiangxi Nanlu*) Doubles Y400-500. Down near the Bund, this was once a grand old hotel and some of the old touches remain, like the British-style basement bar. The rooms are a little overpriced but the location is unbeatable.

Xīnyà Dàjiǔdiàn (☎ *6324 2210, 6356 6816, 422 Tiantong Lu*) Singles Y440, doubles Y440-500. Near the main post office in Hóngkǒu but also within walking distance of the Bund, is this thirties-era hotel. Extensive renovations inside have taken away some of its historical feel but it's good value with singles discounted to Y288 and doubles for Y320.

Jinchen Hotel (*Jīnchén Dàjiǔdiàn;* ☎ *6471 7000, 795-809 Huaihai Zhonglu*) Singles/doubles Y300/488. Readers have recommended this hotel for its clean rooms and convenient location on bustling Huaihai Zhonglu. Doubles are discounted to Y358.

Nányīng Fàndiàn (☎ *6437 8188, fax 6437 8593, 1720 Huaihai Zhonglu*) Doubles Y388. Near the Shanghai Library, this hotel is very comfortable with rooms often discounted by 30%.

Tú'ān Dàjiǔdiàn (☎ *6445 3810, fax 6445 3002, 1 Gao'an Lu*) Singles/doubles Y260/380. In the same area as Nányīng Fàndiàn, this is a friendly and well-run place that welcomes foreigners. Doubles are discounted to Y300.

PLACES TO STAY – TOP END

Shànghǎi is virtually built up from hotels in the top-end (over Y400) category, though some of them have discounts that bring them into mid-range prices. Top-end hotels generally fall into two categories: the aristocratic hotels of old Shànghǎi and the slick new towers bursting with modern amenities. Most of the hotels listed below add on a 10% or 15% service charge.

Business travellers will probably opt for modern facilities like the Portman Ritz-Carlton, Hilton or the imposing Grand Hyatt in Pǔdōng. Those with a sense of history might want to stay at one of the more urbane options, such as the Peace Hotel, where they can wrap themselves in nostalgia and fumble for the bell-pull in the middle of the night.

Peace Hotel (*Hépíng Fàndiàn; Map C;* ☎ *6321 6888, fax 6329 0300,* ℮ *peace-htl@public.sta.net.cn, 20 Nanjing Donglu*) Doubles US$100, suites from US$350, deluxe suites US$520. Interior renovations have robbed the Park Hotel, Shanghai Mansions and Jinjiang Hotel of character and history, but if there's one place left in Shànghǎi that will give you a sense of the past, it's this hotel, which rises up majestically from the Bund. Previously known as the old Cathay, this 12-storey edifice has a sumptuous lobby, restaurants, shops, a bookshop, bank, barber, bar and rooftop cafe. Some travellers have rightly pointed out, however, that in terms of service, this hotel is way overpriced. The deluxe suites are laid out in 1930s Art Deco style to represent the concessions of the time – French, British, American and Japanese, not to mention Chinese.

Peace Palace Hotel (*Hépíng Huìzhōng Fàndiàn; Map C;* ☎ *6329 1888, fax 6329 7979, 23 Nanjing Donglu*) Doubles Y680. An annexe of the Peace Hotel right across the street, this hotel is older and just slightly cheaper.

Shanghai Mansions (*Shànghǎi Dàshà;* ☎ *6324 6260,* ℮ *sales@broadwaymansions .com,* Ⓦ *www.broadwaymansions.com, 20 Bei Suzhou Lu*) Doubles from Y960. Across Wúsōng Jiāng from the Bund, this old hotel has great views. Formerly called the Broadway Mansions, this was a block of apartments that used to house American officers just after WWII. A 30% discount is available.

Park Hotel (*Guójì Fàndiàn; Map C;* ☎ *6327 5225, fax 6327 6958, 170 Nanjing Xilu*) Singles US$80-100, doubles from US$150. Erected in 1934, this hotel

The Cathay Hotel

The Peace Hotel (Map C) is a ghostly reminder of the immense wealth of Victor Sassoon. From a Baghdad Jewish family, Sassoon made millions out of the opium trade and then ploughed it back into Shànghǎi real estate and horses.

Sassoon's quote of the day was 'There is only one race greater than the Jews, and that's the Derby'. His office-cum-hotel was completed in 1930 and was known as Sassoon House, incorporating the Cathay Hotel. From the top floors Victor commanded his real estate – he is estimated to have owned 1900 buildings in Shànghǎi.

Like the Taj in Bombay, the Stanley Raffles in Singapore and the Peninsula in Hong Kong, the Cathay was *the* place to stay in Shànghǎi. Sassoon himself resided in what is now the VIP section, which is below the green pyramidal tower, complete with Tudor panelling. He also maintained a Tudor-style villa out near Hongqiao Airport, just west of the zoo. The likes of Noel Coward (who wrote *Private Lives* in the Cathay) wined and dined in the hotel's Tower Restaurant.

Back in 1949 the Kuomintang strayed into the place, awaiting the arrival of the Communists. A Western writer of the time records an incident in which 50 Kuomintang arrived, carrying their pots and pans, vegetables and firewood, and one soldier was overheard asking where to billet the mules. After the Communists took over the city, the troops were billeted in places like the Picardie (now Héngshān Bīnguǎn on the outskirts of the city), where they spent hours experimenting with the elevators, used bidets as face-showers and washed rice in the toilets – which was all very well until someone pulled the chain.

In 1953 foreigners tried to give the Cathay to the Chinese Communist Party in return for exit visas. The government refused at first, but finally accepted after the payment of 'back taxes'.

overlooks Rénmín Gōngyuán and is one of Shànghǎi's best examples of Art Deco architecture. Renovations in the last decade, however, robbed the interior of all its old-world charm. The rooms are quite comfortable and the service is efficient. Doubles are discounted to Y780.

Jinjiang Hotel (*Jǐnjiāng Fàndiàn;* ☎ *6258 2582,* [e] *jinjiang@public2.sta.net.cn, 59 Maoming Nanlu*) North-building doubles US$100, south-building singles US$155-195, doubles US$165-205. The south building underwent massive renovations in 1999. Some discounts are available. The hotel also contains luxurious *Grosvenor Villa* (*Guìbīn Lóu*), a separate building that's been meticulously restored. Suites start at US$800.

Jinjiang Tower (*Xīn Jǐnjiāng Dàjiǔdiàn;* ☎ *6415 1188,* [e] *jjtrsv@public.sta.net.cn, 161 Changle Lu*) Doubles from US$190. Adjacent to the older Jinjiang complex, this is an ugly glass skyscraper. Discounts can bring prices down to US$138.

The following are two historical options, both of which have elegant grounds and separate old mansions. Both hotels were offering discounts of 20% to 30% and have large rooms and suites:

Ruijin Guesthouse (*Ruìjīn Bīnguǎn;* ☎ *6472 5222,* [e] *ruijinsh@public7.sta.net.cn, 118 Ruijin Erlu*) Doubles US$140-180, suites US$300-400. This is an historic place, which has elegant grounds and a series of old mansions converted into rooms.

Xingguo Hotel (*Xīngguó Bīnguǎn;* ☎ *6212 9070, fax 6251 2145, 72 Xingguo Lu*) Doubles/suites US$75/220. Doubles with a discount are Y480, which is very good value considering the grounds of the hotel. Suites are discounted to Y1400.

Grand Hyatt Hotel (☎ *5049 1234,* [e] *info@hyattshanghai.com,* [w] *www.hyatt.com, 88 Shiji Dadao*) Doubles from US$280. This is the brightest star on the Shànghǎi hotel horizon. It starts on the 54th floor of the Jinmao Building in Pǔdōng and goes up another 33 storeys. Even the Grand Hyatt has had to offer discounts though, down to US$178.

Pudong Shangri-La (☎ *6882 6888,* [w] *www.shangri-la.com, 33 Fucheng Lu*) Singles/doubles from US$250/270. The Shangri-La doesn't quite have the height, but is equally as elegant as the Hyatt. Promotional discounts are often offered.

Back across Huángpǔ Jiāng there is a whole slew of modern five-star hotels.

Portman Ritz-Carlton (☎ *6279 8888,* [w] *www.ritzcarlton.com, 1376 Nanjing Xilu*) Doubles from US$270. The Ritz-Carlton is in the Shanghai Centre and considered to be one of the best, if not the best, hotel in Shànghǎi.

Garden Hotel (*Huāyuán Fàndiàn;* ☎ *6415 1111,* [e] *garden@online.sh.cn,* [w] *www.gardenhotelshanghai.com, 58 Maoming Nanlu*) Doubles from US$260. The elegant Japanese-run Garden Hotel has similar rates but nicer grounds than the Ritz-Carlton. It is on the site of the old French Club, across from the Jinjiang Hotel.

Hilton Hotel (☎ *6248 0000, fax 6248 3848,* [w] *www.hilton.com, 250 Huashan Lu*) Singles US$230-270, doubles US$250-290. The Hilton offers all the modern amenities, but doesn't have much character. Discounts of 45% are offered.

Huating Hotel and Towers (*Huátíng Bīnguǎn; Map A;* ☎ *6439 1000,* [w] *www.huating-hotel.com,* [e] *huating@prodigycn.com, 1200 Caoxi Beilu*) Singles/doubles from US$215/235. This was the former Sheraton and first 'modern' hotel to appear in Shànghǎi in 1987. It has now been completely handed over to local management. Discounts of 30% are available.

Huating Guesthouse (*Map A;* ☎ *6439 1818, fax 6439 0322, 2525 Zhongshan Xilu*) Doubles Y680. Smaller and cheaper rooms are right next door to the Huating Hotel. The rooms go for Y487 at a discount and some of the suites have kitchens. Note that both places have the same name in Chinese.

Crowne-Plaza Shanghai (☎ *6280 8888,* [e] *cpsha@crowneplaza.com.cn,* [w] *shanghai.crowneplaza.com, 400 Panyu Lu*) Singles US$210-230, doubles US$230-250. Originally a Holiday Inn hotel, this is good value if you must stay in a five-star hotel. Rooms have 50% discounts.

Sofitel Hyland Hotel (*Map C;* ☎ *6351 5888,* [e] *sofitel@hyland-shanghai.com,* [w] *www.sofitel.com, 505 Nanjing Donglu*) Singles US$170-220, doubles US$190-240. Down at the other end of town near the Bund is another good value place with discounts of 45%. Plus there's the advantage of German home-brewed beer on the premises.

There's a cluster of hotels in Hóngqiáo, including:

Westin Taipingyang (☎ 6275 8888, Ⓦ www.westin.com, 5 Zunyi Nanlu) Doubles US$210. This elegant hotel offers discounted rooms for US$126.

Discounts on some of the locally run four-star hotels with prime locations are also good value.

Héngshān Bīnguǎn (☎ 6437 7050, fax 6433 5732, 534 Hengshan Lu) Doubles Y908. The doubles here are overpriced, but worthwhile when rooms are discounted to Y500.

City Hotel (Chéngshì Jiǔdiàn; ☎ 6255 1133, fax 6255 0211, 5-7 Shanxi Nanlu) Doubles US$110. This place is also somewhat overpriced but acceptable when rooms are discounted to Y561.

PLACES TO EAT

Restaurants just keep getting better and better in Shànghǎi. If you're on a tight budget, however, keep to the side streets where small restaurants serve cheap, local food.

Also look out for Shànghǎi's favourite dumpling, *xiǎolóngbāo*, which is copied everywhere else in China, but is only true to form here. For Y5, you should get a steamer with four of these. They are wonderful, but there's an art to eating them. In the Bund area, Sichuan Zhonglu is a good place to look, as are the side streets in the old French Concession.

Unless otherwise stated places in this section appear on the Central Shànghǎi map (Map B).

The Bund Area & Nanjing Donglu

For cheap eats near the Pujiang Hotel try the **Zhapu Lu food street** for all kinds of eats.

There's just about everything near the Bund; Chinese fast food, KFC, bars, coffee shops and a couple of elegant Western restaurants, all staking out territory along the famous skyline.

M on the Bund (Map C; ☎ 6350 9988, 20 Guangdong Lu) Mains Y100-200. Open 11.30am-2.30pm & 6.15pm-12am daily. For the latest trends in international cuisine, Michelle Garnaut has brought her renowned skills from Hong Kong to Shànghǎi to create this restaurant on the 7th floor of the Huaxia Bank. There's a magnificent terrace view of the Bund and if you don't feel like dinner, it's worth having a drink at least. Set lunches are Y98 and the popular weekend brunch is Y188.

Rollo di Pollo (Map C; ☎ 6321 3389) This eatery is also run by M and is in the back section of the same floor serving Italian food and pizza. There's still a bit of a view, and it's cheaper.

Dragon-Phoenix Hall (Lóngfèng Tīng; Map C; ☎ 6321 6888, 20 Nanjing Donglu) Mains Y30-60. Open 11.30am-2pm & 5.30pm-10pm. For good, if somewhat overpriced, generic Chinese food, this place on the 8th floor of the Peace Hotel comes with superb views and unpretentious service.

Xìnghuā Lóu (Map C; ☎ 6355 3777, 343 Fuzhou Lu) Mains Y20-35. Open 11am-2pm & 5pm-11pm. This place serves quality *dim sum* and was established in the reign of the Qing emperor who ruled from 1851 to 1861. The restaurant upstairs has an English menu. It's a big place, not great for an intimate dinner.

Shěndàchéng (Map C; ☎ 6322 5615, 636 Nanjing Donglu) Prices Y10-20. Open 6.30am-10.30pm daily. Shěndàchéng still clings to the corner of Zhejiang Zhonglu and Nanjing Donglu, serving delicious Shànghǎi snacks and dumplings. It gets very busy at lunch time.

Yu Gardens Bazaar Area

If for no other reason than you are hungry, head down to the **Yu Gardens Bazaar** for some excellent snack food that ranks among the best in China.

Shànghǎi Lǎo Fàndiàn (Old Shanghai Restaurant; ☎ 6328 2782, 353 Henan Nanlu) Mains Y35-70. Open 11am-2pm & 5pm-9pm daily. This place is old but still has good food at fairly reasonable prices and there's an English menu.

Certain outlets are famed for a particular snack, and these inevitably have long queues snaking from the counters:

Nánxiáng Mántoudiàn (Nanxiang Steamed Bun Restaurant; ☎ 6326 5265, 85 Yuyuan Lu) Meals Y10-20. Open 7am-10pm daily. At this place on the eastern side of the pond, opposite the Húxīntíng teahouse, you can fill yourself up with more than a dozen xiǎolóngbāo for Y8. You can also order upstairs.

Mǎntiānxīng Jiǔlóu (*All Stars Restaurant;* ☎ 6336 7245, 35 Sanpailou Lu) Mains Y15-30. Open 11am-10pm daily. To get away from the crowds at Yu Gardens and enjoy a quiet lunch, head to this street slightly south-east of the bazaar. A delicious dish of *yángcōng chǎo niúròu* (fried beef and onions) is Y16.

Old French Concession Area

Yang's Kitchen (*Yángjiā Chúfáng;* ☎ 6445 8418, No 3, Lane 9, Hengshan Lu) Mains Y15-30. Open 11am-2pm & 5pm-11pm. Though it's not quite as good as before, Yang's is still recommended for reasonable Chinese food. The *ròumò qiéguā jiābǐng* (stewed eggplant with pork mince, Y18), that you roll up in little pancakes, is out of this world. It's down a lane off Hengshan Lu and has an English menu.

Grape Restaurant (*Pútáo Yuán;* ☎ 5404 0486, 55 Xinle Lu) Meals Y20-40. Open 10am-2am daily. One of the most enduring and reliable private Chinese restaurants from the 1980s, this place still packs in the crowds in its premises beside the old Orthodox church.

Bǎoluó Jiǔlóu (☎ 5403 7239, 271 Fumin Lu) Mains Y20-40. Open 10am-6am daily. This is a fast and furious place that's a favourite with locals and expats for its delicious Shànghǎi-style food.

Wùyuè Rénjiā (☎ 5306 5410, No 10, Lane 706, Huaihai Zhonglu; 2nd floor, 141 Shanxi Nanlu) Meals Y15-25. A good place to slurp noodles is in this immaculate, small restaurant.

Xīnjíshì Cāntīng (☎ 6336 4546, No 4, Lane 169, Taicang Lu) Mains Y20-40. Open 11am-2pm & 5pm-9.30pm daily. Shànghǎi is full of so many excellent Chinese restaurants, it's impossible to list them all. One of the latest new favourites among expats and locals alike is this place in Xīntiāndì.

Western-style restaurants abound, especially around Hengshan Lu.

Keven's Cafe (☎ 6433 5564, 525 Hengshan Lu) Mains Y30-70. Open 7.30am-2am daily. For reasonable and authentic American breakfasts (Y38) as well as other Western and Asian dishes, try this cafe.

Badlands (☎ 6466 7788, 895 Julu Lu) Mains Y20-50. Open 10am-late daily. This bar-cum-restaurant is an old favourite for good-value nachos, tacos and burritos.

Brasil Steak House (☎ 6437 7288, 1582 Huaihai Zhonglu) Lunch Y55, dinner Y66. Open 11am-11pm daily. For carnivores only, this is probably the best deal in the city for an absolutely filling Western meal. Servers come around with hunks of roasted meat on skewers, slicing off bits onto your plate. There's also a buffet salad and dessert bar. It's opposite the Shanghai Library.

Le Garcon Chinois (☎ 6431 3005, No 3, Lane 9, Hengshan Lu) Mains Y100-200. Open noon-2pm & 6pm-1am daily. At the other end of the spectrum, both in price and style, this elegant place has French cuisine on the first floor and Shànghǎi dishes on the second floor. It's tucked down a lane on the way to Yang's Kitchen. The cakes baked on the premises are especially good.

Da Marco (*Mǎkè Cāntīng;* ☎ 6210 4495, 103 Dong Zhu'anbang Lu) Meals Y80-150. Open noon-11.30pm daily. Somewhat removed from the former French Concession area proper, this is one of the best Italian restaurants according to those in the know.

Shànghǎi also has a growing number of Asian restaurants.

Simply Thai (☎ 6445 9551, 5-C Dongping Lu) Mains Y20-60. Open 11.30am-2pm & 6pm-10.30pm daily. Everyone raves about this place for it's delicious, reasonable dishes and comfortable decor.

Irene's Thai (☎ 6247 3579, 263 Tongren Lu) Mains Y30-70. Open 11.30am-2pm & 5.30pm-11.30pm daily. While delicious, there's not much volume to the chicken coconut soup *thom kha gai* (Y40) here. But the decor and atmosphere are worth the somewhat pricey dishes with small portions. This is another exotic escape from the city streets.

Ali Y Y (☎ 6415 9448, 9b Dongping Lu) Meals downstairs Y15-25, upstairs Y150-200. Open noon-2.30pm & 5pm-11pm daily. At this place inexpensive Xīnjiāng-style food such as kebabs, noodles and unleavened bread is served downstairs and more expensive Middle Eastern food upstairs.

Nepali Kitchen (☎ 5404 5077, 178 Xinle Lu) Mains Y30-50. Open 11am-2pm & 6pm-11pm daily. Sitting on the cushions at the low tables upstairs, you're immediately whisked away from Shànghǎi to something more sublime. The simple Nepali dishes are delicious and reasonably priced. Set lunches and dinners are Y50.

Ooedo (*Dà Jiānghù;* ☎ *5403 3332, 30 Donghu Lu*) Buffet Y200. Open 5.30pm-11pm daily. Shànghǎi has too many Japanese restaurants to list here, but one of the best is Ooedo which offers a delicious all-you-can-eat sushi buffet and other dishes.

At the other end of the buffet spectrum, sushi and other snacks of the conveyor-belt variety can also be found in Shànghǎi.

Sumo Sushi (☎ *6466 9419, 29 Dongping Lu;* ☎ *5383 3298, 398 Huaihai Zhonglu*) Buffet Y58 per person, set lunches/dinners Y28/38. Open 11am-11.30pm daily. The second branch is conveniently located across from the Huangpi Road South metro station.

Vegetarian Food

Vegetarianism became something of a snobbish fad in Shànghǎi at one time; it was linked to Taoist and Buddhist groups, then to the underworld, and surfaced on the tables of restaurants as creations shaped like flowers or animals.

Gōngdélín Sùshíchù (*Gongdelin Vegetarian Restaurant;* ☎ *6327 0218, 445 Nanjing Xilu*) Mains Y20-30. Open 11am-2pm & 5pm-8pm daily. This is probably Shànghǎi's most famous vegetarian restaurant. All the food is designed to resemble meat, and is convincingly prepared. The food and atmosphere are worth experiencing, even if you are not a vegetarian.

Juélín Sùshíchù (*Map C;* ☎ *6326 0115, 250 Jinling Donglu*) Mains Y15-25. Open lunch 6am-7.30pm daily. This is another vegetarian restaurant similar to Gōngdélín.

If you're visiting *Yùfó Sì*, you can also have a vegetarian lunch there. Lunch for two costs from Y20 to Y30.

Vegetarian Life Style (*Zǎozi Shù;* ☎ *6384 8000, 77 Songshan Lu*) Mains Y20-30. Open 10.30am-9.30pm daily. A bright place off the street near Xīntiāndì opened by two vegetarians from Táiwān, there's no pretension of making things look like meat here. Hungry vegans in China will find lots of comfort food here. The name translates as 'Jujube Tree' but is also a pun on the characters roughly meaning 'hurry up and become a vegetarian'.

Tea & Coffee Houses

1931 Pub (☎ *6472 5264, 112 Maoming Lu*) Dishes Y20-60. Open 11am-2am daily. One of the nicest places is this small cafe/pub outfitted with a 1930s theme and serving coffee, tea, drinks and meals.

Gino Cafe (*Map C;* ☎ *6361 2205, 66 Nanjing Donglu*) Meals Y20-40. Open 9am-midnight. If you're trekking through the city and need some refreshment, look for a Gino Cafe. There are eight branches in the city and this one's down near the Peace Hotel. Gino's also serves pasta, pizza and Western food.

There's a number of Taiwanese-style teahouses around town.

Harn Sheh Teahouse (*Hánshè Pàomò Cháfáng;* ☎ *6474 6547, 10 Hengshan Lu*) Meals Y15-30. Open 9.30am-4am daily. There's four of these in the city, featuring a cornucopia of bizarre and delicious beverages highlighted by various kinds of bubble tea. Set meals are also served.

Húxīntíng (*Mid-Lake Pavilion Teahouse;* ☎ *6373 6950, Yu Gardens Bazaar*) Meals Y40-60. Open 8.30am-10pm daily. At the Yu Gardens, this ornate spot is one of the best places to sit and look over the mob below and pretend you're part of the scene on a blue willow teacup. Make sure you stay awhile, however, the price is rather steep for a quick pot of tea. On Monday afternoons, musicians get together to play traditional Chinese music from around 2pm to 5pm.

Old Time Cafe (*Lǎodiànyǐng Kāfēiguǎn;* ☎ *5696 4763, 123 Duolun Lu*) Dishes Y10-30. Open 10am-midnight daily. If you're up taking a look at Duolun Lu in Hóngkǒu, recently turned into a pedestrian street (see Shopping section for details), take a break in this quiet three-storey building dedicated to old movies.

Delifrance (☎ *5382 5171, 125 Central Plaza, 381 Huaihai Zhonglu*) Dishes Y10-40. Open 8am-10pm daily. Not a lot of character here, but good croissants and coffee at reasonable rates. Sandwiches, set breakfasts and small meals are also sold here. It's right beside the Huangpi Road South metro station.

There were six Starbucks in Shànghǎi at the time of writing and surely more will come. We'll let you find them.

ENTERTAINMENT

The last few years have seen an explosion of nightlife options, with everything from the incredibly sleazy to the marginally chic.

There's pretty well something for everyone: rock, hip-hop, techno, salsa and early morning waltzes in the People's Square. None of it comes cheaply, however (except for the waltzing, which is free). A night on the town in Shànghǎi is comparable to a night out in Hong Kong or Taipei.

Places listed in this section are on the Central Shànghǎi map (Map B) unless otherwise indicated.

Bars & Clubs

There's a lot to choose from in Shànghǎi's scene, and venues open and close all the time. Check out the Shànghǎi entertainment magazines for guidance. One thing stays the same, however; drinks at most of the popular bars in Shànghǎi are expensive.

Malone's American Cafe (☎ 6247 2400, 257 Tongren Lu) Set lunches Y50. Open 11am-2am daily. This place was started by Canadians, but is strictly an American-style bar. If you want to forget you're in China, turn your back on the window and focus on the TV screen. Beer is Y40.

If you fancy a home-brewed beer there's quite a few places to choose from in Shànghǎi.

Fest Beer House (Map C; ☎ 6321 8447, 11 Hankou Lu) Open 11am-2am daily. Managed by a woman from Sìchuān, an immigrant who has found her place in the big city, this is a pleasant place down near the Bund with delicious beer for Y38.

Brauhaus 505 (Map C; ☎ 6351 5888 ext 4281, 505 Nanjing Donglu) Open 11am-1.30am daily. Enjoy some good German beer here in the Sofitel Hotel.

Paulaner Brauhaus (☎ 6474 5700, 150 Fenyang Lu) Open 5pm-2am daily. This is the grand master of the Shànghǎi microbreweries. A pint of wheat beer will set you back about Y80.

O'Malley's Bar (☎ 6474 4533, 42 Taojiang Lu) Open 11am-1am daily. Although there's no home-brewed beer here, O'Malley's brought up the standards of beer drinking considerably when it introduced draught Guinness and Kilkenny beers to Shànghǎi residents. It remains one of the most popular places to hang out, either on the large lawn in good weather, or inside within the old-world pub atmosphere.

Shanghai Sally's (☎ 5382 0738, 4 Xiangshan Lu) Open 4pm-2am daily. A well-established private bar, Sally's was recently renovated. It's a good place for pub food and beer, plus live music and dancing later on in the evening.

Goya (Gēyǎ Jiǔbā; ☎ 6280 1256, 357 Xinhua Lu) Open 7pm-2am daily. For the cigar and martini set, try this place near the Crowne-Plaza Hotel. Martinis are Y40 to Y50.

Cotton Club (☎ 6437 7110, 1428 Huaihai Zhonglu) Admission free. Open 7.30pm-2am daily. One of the best bars for live music is this comfortable, unassuming place that features mostly blues bands. The music doesn't usually get going until after 9pm.

Blowing in the Wind Bar (☎ 6248 2215, 649 Huashan Lu) Open 2pm-3am daily. Like its namesake in Nánjīng, this bar offers folk, alternative, blues and more and is a welcome addition to Shànghǎi's live venues.

Peace Hotel Old Jazz Bar (Map C; ☎ 6321 6888 ext 6210, 20 Nanjing Donglu) Admission Y50. Open 8pm-2am daily. Home of the ancient jazz band that has been strumming since time immemorial, it's doubtful whether this place is worth the cover charge. If you're feeling nostalgic it's the place to go though.

Shànghǎi has a few places catering to gay patrons, but the locales keep moving around, so check the listings. Men or women, gay or straight, are welcome at the places listed below.

Eddy's Focus (☎ 5049 3058, Level 6, Jinmao Bldg, 88 Shiji Dadao) Open 9am-2am daily. Shànghǎi's pioneering gay bar, one of the city's first, recently moved from Nanjing Lu to Pǔdōng. The new premises in the Jinmao Building are elegant and spacious and attract a mixed crowd.

Er Ding Mu Bar (Èrdīngmù; ☎ 5671 0803, 67 Siping Lu) Open 6.30pm-2am daily. This is another large place, located in Hóngkǒu. It's popular on weekends and can get quite crowded.

80% (☎ 6253 2464, 226 Jinxian Lu) Open 6pm-2am daily. A small, intimate place on the 2nd floor, 80% has restaurant downstairs serving Hunanese food.

Asia Blue (☎ 5382 0680 ext 1999, 18 Gaolan Lu) Open 8pm-2am daily. This is a friendly, medium-sized place with plush red velvet couches for lounging.

SHÀNGHǍI

Discos

Shànghǎi pulls in some top-notch DJs from abroad and there are a lot of dance venues. It's impossible to list everything here. There's also a lot of turnover, so check the magazines. If you're looking for large, pulsating places, try these two:

Rojam Disco (☎ 6390 7181, 4th floor, Hong Kong Plaza, 283 Huaihai Zhonglu) Admission Y28 Sun-Thur, Y35 Fri-Sat. Open 8.30pm-2am daily. This is a popular place for techno on the weekends. The cover charge includes one drink.

Real Love (Zhēn'ài Jiǔbā; ☎ 6474 6830, 10 Hengshan Lu) Admission Y30 Sun-Thur, Y50 Fri-Sat. Open 8.30pm-2am daily. Real Love attracts a young, mainstream local crowd.

These are places offering three different venue styles if you're looking for variety.

Judy's Too (☎ 6473 1417, 176 Maoming Nanlu) A bar during the weekdays, this place is insanely crowded on the weekends, with more of an older crowd, both local and expat. It's a lot of fun. A whole range of music is played throughout the week and house on weekends.

California Club (☎ 6318 0785, 2 Gaolan Lu) Open 6pm-late daily. Owned by the Lan Kwai Fong group and located in the Park 97 complex in Fùxīng Gōngyuán, this club was recently *the* latest place to be seen.

Tropicana Bar & Restaurant (Map C; ☎ 6329 2472, 8th floor, 261 Sichuan Nanlu) Open 6.30pm-2am Tues-Sun. There's a few places to go for Latin dancing or *salsa*, but this restaurant and nightclub probably has the best location eight floors up in an old building near the Bund.

Performing Arts

As with Běijīng, Shànghǎi is one of the great cultural centres of China. Unfortunately, Bejing and Cantonese opera and Chinese drama (often an extravagant display of costumes, make-up and acrobatics) are almost exclusively delivered in Chinese and therefore inaccessible to most foreigners.

Yifu Theatre (Yìfū Wǔtái; Map C; ☎ 6351 4668, 701 Fuzhou Lu) Admission Y10-40. Beijing opera is performed on Saturday and Sunday at 1.30pm. Other regional opera performances are on weekdays at 7.30pm.

Majestic Theatre (Měiqí Dàxìyuàn; ☎ 6217 3311, 66 Jiangning Lu) Admission Y20-300. All kinds of performances are held in this former cinema, such as ballet, local opera and the occasional revolutionary-style opera, which can be great fun to watch, especially for reactions from the audience.

Great World (Dà Shìjìe; Map C; ☎ 6326 3760 ext 40, 1 Xizang Lu) Admission Y25. Open 9am-6pm & 7.30pm-9.30pm daily. For cheaper, if less sophisticated fare, check out this wedding-cake building near the People's Square. It was once the famous and salacious Great World in pre-1949 Shànghǎi. There's a potpourri of performances available on different stages: opera, acrobatics and magic, but nothing too risque yet.

Modern plays in Chinese are staged at the *Shanghai Theatre Academy* (Shànghǎi Xìjù Xuéyuàn; ☎ 6248 2920 ext 3040, 630 Huashan Lu) and the *Shanghai Drama Arts Centre* (Shànghǎi Huàjù Zhōngxīn; ☎ 6473 4567, 288 Anfu Lu) with tickets ranging from Y20 to Y100 depending on the production.

Classical music is performed by the Shanghai Symphony Orchestra (Shànghǎi Jiāoxiǎng Yuètuán) as well as visiting orchestras and local chamber groups.

Shanghai Grand Theatre (Shànghǎi Dà Jùyuàn; Map C; ☎ 6372 8701, 300 Renmin Dadao) Admission from Y120. Look for what's playing at this magnificent venue in the People's Square. It features both national and international opera, dance, music and theatre.

Shanghai Concert Hall (Shànghǎi Yīnyuè Tīng; ☎ 6460 4699, 523 Yan'an Donglu) A classical music venue for smaller local and international orchestras.

Conservatory of Music (Yīnyuè Xuéyuàn; ☎ 6437 2577, 20 Fenyang Lu) Admission Y10. The Conservatory, off Huaihai Zhonglu in Frenchtown, has regular music performances every Sunday at 7.15pm.

Jing'an Hotel (☎ 6248 1888, 370 Huashan Lu) Admission Y20. Chamber music is also played every Sunday evening at 8pm at the Jing'an, located next to the Hilton Hotel.

Cinemas

Foreign movies are generally dubbed into Chinese and Chinese movies very rarely have English subtitles but there are exceptions at the multiplexes *Golden Cinema Haixing* (☎ 6418 7034, Haixing Plaza, 1

Ruijin Nanlu) and **Studio City** (☎ *6218 2173, Westgate Mall, 10th floor, 1038 Nanjing Xilu*). Many of the bars also show movies.

Acrobatics

Chinese acrobatic troupes are among the best in the world, and Shànghǎi is a good place to see a performance. If you've never seen the show, it's not to be missed. The only performing animals present are humans in the shows listed here.

Shanghai Centre (☎ *6279 8663, 1376 Nanjing Xilu*) Admission Y30-60. The Shanghai Acrobatics Troupe (Shànghǎi Zájì Tuán) has performances here every night at 7.30pm.

Lyceum Theatre (☎ *6217 8530, 57 Maoming Nanlu*) Admission Y30-60. Evening acrobatic shows are held here at an old Shànghǎi theatre across from the Jinjiang Hotel.

SHOPPING

Shànghǎi offers a plethora of choice for the shopper: all Chinese products and popular souvenirs find their way here. The city is catching up with commercial centres like Hong Kong and bargains are everywhere. The traditional shopping streets were always Nanjing Lu and Huaihai Lu, but now it seems almost every side street is full of boutiques and shops.

Department Stores

Shànghǎi has some of the best department stores in China, including the flashy Western and Japanese-style outlets that are probably of more interest to residents than to visitors. On the other hand, if you can find your size, there are sometimes good fashion deals in some of the department stores. Because the competition is so fierce, you can even bargain in some department stores depending on the item.

Hualian Department Store (*Húalían Shāngshà; Map C;* ☎ *6322 4466, 635 Nanjing Donglu*) Open 9.30am-10pm daily. Formerly called No 10, and before that the famous Wing On, this place is best for mid- and low-range prices.

No 1 Department Store (*Dìyī Bǎihuò Shāngdiàn; Map C;* ☎ *6322 3344, 830 Nanjing Donglu*) Open 9.30am-10pm daily. This is another good place that caters to the masses.

Nextage (*Xīnshìjì Shāngshà; Map A;* ☎ *5830 1111, cnr Pudong Lu & Zhangyang Lu*) Open 9.30am-10pm daily. Asia's largest department store is located in Pǔdōng and is second in size only to Macy's. There are 150 retail outlets selling from 100,000 sq metres of floor space to countless customers.

Friendship Store (*Map C;* ☎ *5308 0600, 40 Beijing Donglu*) Open 9.30am-9.30pm daily. This is a good place to pick up last-minute souvenirs, and the lack of crowds makes it possible to browse at your leisure.

Supermarkets & Pharmacies

Local supermarkets are in almost every residential area and often stock many Western food items, especially the local chains *Hualian* and *Tops*.

The Market (*Map B;* ☎ *6279 8081, 1376 Nanjing Xilu*) Open 8am-11.30pm daily. If you're craving obscure foods from home or need Western pharmaceutical items in a hurry, this is a convenient place in the Shanghai Centre but items are priced to the hilt. There's a good notice board with job and other miscellaneous ads.

Parkson (*Map B;* ☎ *6415 8818, Parkson Plaza, 918 Huaihai Zhonglu*) Open 10am-10pm daily. The supermarket in the basement of the Parkson department store here has a good selection.

Carrefour (*Jiālèfú; Map A;* ☎ *6209 8899, 268 Shuicheng Nanlu*) Open 8am-10pm daily. This French hypermarket chain has this branch in Gǔběi, plus others in Pǔdōng and elsewhere. It has very reasonable prices for food, clothes and household items and is extremely popular with locals.

Watson's (*Map B;* ☎ *6279 8382, 1376 Nanjing Xilu; 787 Huaihai Zhonglu*) This pharmacy, at the Shanghai Centre, has Western cosmetics, over-the-counter medicines and health products. Watson's has another convenient branch near the Jinchen Hotel and many other outlets around the city. Watson's is not cheap – prices are similar to those you would pay in Hong Kong.

Photographic Supplies

For photographic supplies, check the shops in the major hotels. Shànghǎi is one of the few places in China where slide film is readily available.

Guànlóng (Map C; ☎ 6323 8681, 190 Nanjing Donglu) Open 9am-10pm daily. You can get slide film here at Shànghǎi's foremost photographic supplies shop.

New Ray Photo (Map B; ☎ 6433 0101, 1650 Huaihai Zhonglu) Open 8am-9pm daily. This is another good place to buy slide film, close to the Shanghai Library.

Porcelain

Shanghai Museum (Map C; ☎ 6372 3500, 201 Renmin Dadao) Open 9am-5pm daily. The best place to find decent porcelain is this shop, which sells imitations of the pieces displayed in the Zande Lou Gallery (within the museum). The imitations are fine specimens and far superior to the mediocre pieces you see in the tourist shops. However, be prepared to pay a hefty whack.

Jingdezhen Porcelain Artware Shop (Jǐngdézhèn Cíqì Diàn; Map B; ☎ 6253 8865, 1185 Nanjing Xilu) Open 10am-9pm daily. There's a variety of more prosaic porcelain for sale here and pricey speciality items as well.

Souvenirs & Antiques

Fangbang Lu antique market (Map B; cnr Fangbang Zhonglu & Henan Nanlu) Open 9am-6pm Mon-Fri, 6am-6pm Sat & Sun. On the arts and crafts, souvenirs and antiques front, one of the best places to go is this market in a two-storey building at the Yu Gardens Bazaar. It's full of stalls selling ceramics, 'antique' posters, pocket watches, paintings and a host of other collectibles. Haggle hard as it's all overpriced – if you wander around you will see the same stuff at a variety of prices, which means that a lot of it is fake.

Dongtai Lu antique market (Map B; Dongtai Lu) Open 8.30am-6pm daily. This market, a block west of Xizang Nanlu and within walking distance of Fangbang Lu, is another place to try.

Shanghai Antique and Curio Shop (Shànghǎi Wénwù Shāngdiàn; Map C; ☎ 6321 5868, 192-246 Guangdong Lu) Open 9am-5pm daily. Designated tourist shops like this long-established place are expensive alternatives to the markets. Their range is good, but again, there's a lot of rubbish so you need a shrewd eye.

In the Hóngkǒu district, *Duolun Lu (Map B)* has been turned into a designated 'cultural street' with restored buildings and a pleasant pedestrian-only thoroughfare. Formerly known as Doulean Road, many well-known literary figures, like Lu Xun, Mao Dun and the Japanese bookseller Uchiyama Kanzo, lived around this neighbourhood in the 1930s. Besides the historical references, there are antique shops, art galleries, bookshops and curio stores. Duolun Lu is within walking distance of the Dong Baoxing Road light rail station.

Tea & Teapots

Tea and the dainty teapots and cups used by the Chinese make excellent gifts, and Shànghǎi is a good place to buy them. The *Yu Gardens Bazaar* is one of the best places in Shànghǎi to make purchases.

Huangshan Tea Company (Huángshān Cháyè Gōngsī; Map B; ☎ 6473 8101, 853 Huaihai Zhonglu) Open 9am-10pm daily. Look for this exclusive shop in the heart of the Huaihai shopping district. Prices can be surprisingly reasonable. Yíxīng ware, the most valued of all Chinese teapots, is available here as well as numerous types of tea.

Clothing & Shoes

Tall and large people may have difficulty finding their size in Shànghǎi, but it's a shopping paradise for smaller folk. Unfortunately, the long-established outdoor clothes market on Huating Lu moved to the corner of Xiangyang Lu and Huaihai Lu in October 2000 and the new venue, known as the *Xiangyang Lu clothes market (Map B)*, is a disappointment. The same wares and vendors are here but the layout is confusing and tiring to wander around. It's open during the day from about 10am to 6pm.

Try Maoming Nanlu and Shanxi Nanlu for various *boutiques*, as well as Nanjing Lu and Huaihai Lu of course. Shanxi Nanlu is packed with small *shoe shops* with good prices.

Outdoor Gear

Some of the department stores, street markets and sporting goods stores have backpacks and sleeping bags. More and more individual stores devoted to outdoor gear are sure to emerge as the idea (or at least the look) of exploring the great outdoors becomes fashionable with local consumers.

Hot Wind (*Rèfēng Xiéyè; Map B;* ☎ *6372 1448, 127-133 Ruijin Yilu*) Open 10am-9pm daily. Ostensibly a shoe shop, this shop actually sells all kinds of outdoor gear, including hiking boots and sleeping bags. Just the place to find the climbing carabiner to hold your drinking cup. Prices vary depending on the item and its origin, but most of the gear is fairly expensive.

YMCA Bike Shop (*Qīngnián Chēháng; Map B;* ☎ *6472 9325, 485 Yongjia Lu*) Open 10am-8am daily. If you're cycling through Shànghǎi and need that crucial missing part, call the YMCA Bike Shop, also known as Wolf's Mountain Bike Club.

GETTING THERE & AWAY
Shànghǎi has rail and air connections to places all over China, ferries travelling up Cháng Jiāng, boats along the coast and buses to destinations in adjoining provinces.

Air
Civil Aviation Administration of China (CAAC; Zhōngguó Mínháng; Map B) international destinations include Bangkok, Brussels, Hong Kong, London, Los Angeles, Madrid, Munich, Nagasaki, Nagoya, New York, Osaka, Paris, San Francisco, Singapore, Sydney, Tokyo, Toronto and Vancouver. Dragonair also flies between Shànghǎi and Hong Kong (Y1780). Northwest Airlines and United Airlines fly to the USA, Air Canada can get you to Canada, Qantas Airways can fly you to Australia and Virgin Atlantic can fly you to London. International departure tax is Y90.

Daily (usually several times daily) domestic flights connect Shànghǎi to every major city in China. Prices include Běijīng (Y1030), Guǎngzhōu (Y1160) and Guìlín (Y1190). Minor cities are less likely to have daily flights, but the chances are there will be at least one flight a week, probably more, to Shànghǎi. The domestic departure tax is Y50.

China Eastern Airlines' main office (Map B; ☎ 6247 5953 domestic, ☎ 6247 2255 international), at 200 Yan'an Zhonglu, is open daily from 8.30am to 10pm. Most of the major hotels have ticket sales counters as do the CITS offices in the Guangming building at 2 Jinling Donglu and 66 Nanjing Donglu. The following airlines have offices in Shànghǎi.

Aeroflot (☎ 6279 8033) Shanghai Centre, 1376 Nanjing Xilu

Air France (☎ 6360 6688) Room 1301, Novel Plaza, 128 Nanjing Xilu

All Nippon Airways (☎ 6279 7000) 2nd floor, East Wing, Shanghai Centre, 1376 Nanjing Xilu

Air Canada (☎ 6375 8899) Suite 702, Central Plaza, 227 Huangpi Beilu

Dragonair (☎ 6375 6375) Room 2103, Shanghai Square Tower, 138 Huaihai Zhonglu

Japan Airlines (☎ 6472 3000) 2nd floor, Ruijin Building, 205 Maoming Lu

Korean Air (☎ 6275 6000) 1st floor, Office Tower, Yangtze Hotel, 2099 Yanan Xilu

Lufthansa Airlines (☎ 5830 4400) POS Plaza, 480 Pudian Lu, Pǔdōng

Malaysia Airlines (☎ 6279 8607) Suite 209, East Wing, Shanghai Centre, 1376 Nanjing Xilu

Northwest Airlines (☎ 6279 8009) Suite 204, Level 2, East Building, Shanghai Centre, 1376 Nanjing Xilu

Qantas Airways (☎ 6279 8660) Suite 203a, West Wing, Shanghai Centre, 1376 Nanjing Xilu

Singapore Airlines (☎ 6289 1000) Room 606, Kerry Centre, 1515 Nanjing Xilu

Thai Airways International (☎ 6248 7788) Room 201, West Building, Shanghai Centre, 1376 Nanjing Xilu

United Airlines (☎ 6279 8010) Suite 204, West Building, Shanghai Centre, 1376 Nanjing Xilu

Virgin Atlantic (☎ 5353 4600) Room 221–23, 12 Zhongshan Dong Yilu

Bus
Shànghǎi has a few long-distance bus stations but the most useful is probably the Hengfeng Lu station (Map B) across from the Hanzhong Road metro station. Deluxe buses leave for Hángzhōu (Y54, 2½ hours), Sūzhōu (Y30, 1½ hours), Nánjīng (Y88, four hours), Shàoxīng (Y70, three hours) and Níngbō (Y96, four hours).

Buses also leave from the station on the corner of Hutai Lu and Zhongshan Beilu, north of Shànghǎi train station, and from the western district bus station at 211 Hongqiao Lu, just west of the Xujiahui metro station. Besides the above destinations, buses from the western district bus station also go to Yángzhōu (Y81, 4½ hours) and Wúxī (Y36, two hours). Buses to Sūzhōu, Wúxī, Hángzhōu and Nánjīng also leave from the parking lot directly in front of the domestic arrival hall at the Hongqiao Airport. Tickets are slightly more expensive.

Buses to Běijīng (Y286, 13 hours) depart from the Hengfeng Lu station and travel the new expressway.

There are three buses a day to Zhōuzhuāng (Y21, one hour), but you have to go to the bus station at 80 Gongxing Lu, near the Baoshan Road light rail station (Map B). Bus No 65 from the Bund passes nearby. Buses to Zhōuzhuāng also leave from the Sightseeing Bus Centre (Map A) near the south entrance to the Shanghai Stadium. Tickets are Y100 return, which includes the entrance fee to Zhōuzhuāng.

Buses to Wūzhèn also leave from the Sightseeing Bus Centre for Y128 including the entry and return trip. You can also get to Wūzhèn by taking a bus from Shànghǎi to Jiāxīng (Y31, one hour) and from there take another bus to Wūzhèn (Y8, one hour).

Train

Shànghǎi is at the junction of the Běijīng-Shànghǎi and Běijīng-Hángzhōu train lines and many parts of the country can be reached by direct train from here.

Many options are available for buying train tickets in Shànghǎi. At the Shanghai train station, the easiest is the counter in the soft-seat waiting room for current and next-day tickets. It's open from 7am to 9pm, with breaks for lunch and dinner. Another convenient place is at the Longmen Hotel, a short walk west of Shanghai train station. You can book sleepers up to four days in advance and there's a Y5 service charge.

In town, CITS at Jinling Donglu books tickets for a Y10 service charge. You can also book train tickets across the street at 1 Jinling Donglu (Y5 service charge). Advance booking outlets are at 230 Beijing Donglu and 121 Xizang Nanlu, open daily from 8am to 5pm.

Most trains depart and arrive at the Shanghai train station (Shànghǎi zhàn). Trains to Hángzhōu also leave from the Shanghai south train station (Shànghǎi nánzhàn) in the south-western suburbs, and take one hour and 40 minutes.

The fast train from Shànghǎi to Běijīng does the journey in 14 hours. Hard sleepers are Y327.

Other trains from Shànghǎi are: Fúzhōu (Y274, 21 hours), Guǎngzhōu (Y379, 25 hours), Hángzhōu (Y33, two hours), Huángshān (Y97, 11½ hours), Kūnmíng (Y519, 46 hours), Nánjīng (Y47, three hours), Xī'ān (Y332, 17 hours) and Ürümqi (Y699, 51 hours).

Special double-decker 'tourist trains' operate between Shànghǎi and Hángzhōu, and Shànghǎi and Nánjīng (with stops at Wúxī, Sūzhōu, Hángzhōu and Zhènjiāng). They are comfortable soft-seat trains and smoking is forbidden; attendants bring around drinks and food.

Trains leave for Kowloon (Hong Kong) every other day in the morning and take 28 hours. Hard sleepers are HK$530, though they're more like the soft sleepers on standard Chinese trains. You can get tickets at the advanced ticket booking outlets and CITS.

Boat

Boats are definitely one of the best ways of leaving Shànghǎi and they're often also the cheapest, especially for destinations inland on Cháng Jiāng. Many coastal routes, however, have all but dried up.

Boat tickets can be bought from the ticket office at 1 Jinling Donglu and at the Shíliùpù Wharf (Map B), 111 Zhongshan Dong Erlu, on the Bund.

Weekly ferries to Inch'ŏn in Korea, weekly boats to Osaka and twice-monthly boats to Kobe in Japan depart from the international ferry terminal (Map B) to the east of Shanghai Mansions, at 1 Taiping Lu. Passengers must be at the harbour three hours before departure. Tickets are sold on the 2nd floor of the ticket office at 1 Jinling Donglu. Tickets to Korea (40 hours) range from Y1000 to VIP cabins for Y3250. Tickets to Japan (47 hours) range from Y1300 to Y6500.

Boats to Pǔtuóshān (12 hours) depart from Shíliùpù Wharf every day at 6pm. Tickets cost Y87 to Y347, depending on the class. A five-hour rapid ferry service has buses departing daily from Shíliùpù Wharf and costs Y195 or Y225 deluxe. It's roughly a two-hour bus ride to the wharf at Lúcháo and then a three-hour boat ride.

There are also about four boats a week to Dàlián (36 hours) in Liáoníng province with tickets ranging from Y300 to Y660.

The main destinations of ferries up Cháng Jiāng from Shànghǎi are Nántōng, Nánjīng, Wúhú, Guìchí, Jiǔjiāng and Wǔhàn, with daily departures from Shíliùpù Wharf. From Wǔhàn you can change to another ferry going to Chóngqìng. If you're only heading as far west as Nánjīng, take the train, which is much faster. (For full details on Cháng Jiāng cruises, see the Chóngqìng chapter.)

SHÀNGHǍI

Shànghǎi roadsign in Mandarin and English

The former Shanghai & Hong Kong Bank

The bicycle still rules in Shànghǎi.

Three girls, one boy, one gun, in the streets of Shànghǎi.

Shànghǎi's pulsating restaurant and nightclub district.

The US$2 billion Pudong International Airport.

For a psychedelic experience take the Bund Tunnel.

Glitzy shopping in the Huángpǔ area.

GETTING AROUND

Shànghǎi is not a walker's dream. There are some fascinating areas to stroll around, but new road developments, building sites and shocking traffic conditions conspire to make walking an exhausting and often stressful experience.

The buses, too, are hard work; they're not easy to figure out, and difficult to squeeze into and out of, though things have improved with many routes offering deluxe air-con vehicles (Y2) and some double-decker buses. Once on board, keep your valuables tucked away since pickpocketing is easy under such conditions, and foreigners make easy targets.

The metro system, however, is a dream. The No 1 line does a north-south sprint through central Shànghǎi while the newer No 2 line runs from Zhōngshān Gōngyuán, along Nanjing Lu and across to Pǔdōng. Tickets are between Y2 and Y4 depending on the distance. A light rail system running from Shànghǎi's south train station towards Fudan University has made getting around even easier. Travellers with money to spare can at least hop into a taxi but despite the improvements in roadways, Shànghǎi's traffic is turning into gridlock once again.

Shànghǎi taxis are reasonably cheap and easy to flag down. Fares start at Y10. Most large, opulent hotels have a free shuttle bus to the Bund and the airports for their guests.

To/From the Airport

Hongqiao Airport (Map A; ☎ 6268 8918) is 18km from the Bund; getting there takes about 30 minutes if you're lucky, or over an hour if you're not. You can take bus No 925 from the People's Square all the way to the airport. Bus 806 goes from Xújiāhuì and Bus No 938 stops in front of the Huating Guesthouse on Zhongshan Xilu. A CAAC bus goes from the north-east corner of Yan'an Zhonglu and Shanxi Beilu for Y5. All these buses leave the airport from directly in front of the domestic departure hall.

Major hotels like the Jinjiang have an airport shuttle. Taxis from the centre of town cost approximately Y50, depending on the kind of taxi, the route taken and the traffic conditions.

The new airport in Pǔdōng (☎ 3848 4500) handles most international flights and some domestic flights. Always check your ticket to be sure which airport you're arriving at or departing from. Bus No 1 (Y30) runs between Hongqiao and Pudong airports, bus No 2 (Y20) runs from Pudong International Airport to opposite the Shanghai Centre on Nanjing Xilu and bus No 5 (Y20) goes from Pudong International Airport to the Shanghai train station. A taxi to Pudong International Airport from the city centre will cost around Y140. Give yourself at least an hour to get there.

Tour Bus

If you want to see Shànghǎi in a hurry, or want to go to Pǔdōng, then it's best to jump on one of the Jinjiang Shanghai Tour buses that leave every half-hour from the Jinjiang Hotel on Maoming Nanlu. They are comfortable, speedy and cheap, with a one-day ticket costing Y18. They stop at a number of tourist destinations, including the People's Square, the Oriental Pearl Tower in Pǔdōng and the Nánpǔ Bridge, then return to the Jinjiang Hotel. You can get off, see the sight and wait for the next bus to come and pick you up, using the same ticket.

Bus

Buses are not colour coded. Some useful bus routes are listed below, though the metro lines and light rail may be more convenient.

No 11 Travels the ring road around the old Chinese city.

No 19 Links the Bund area to the Yùfó Sì area. Catch it at the intersection of Beijing Donglu and Sichuan Zhonglu.

No 20 Takes you to the People's Square from the Bund.

No 42 From the Bund at Guangdong Lu passes Renmin Lu close to the Yu Gardens, heads along Huaihai Lu, up Xiangyang Lu then on to Xújiāhuì, terminating at the Shanghai Stadium.

No 61 Starts from just north of the Shanghai Mansions at the intersection of Wusong Lu and Tiantong Lu, and goes past the PSB on its way along Siping Lu. No 55 from the Bund also goes by the PSB.

No 64 Gets you to Shanghai train station from near the Bund. Catch it on Beijing Donglu, close to the intersection with Sichuan Zhonglu. The ride takes 20 to 30 minutes.

No 65 Runs from the north-east of Shanghai train station and goes near the long-distance bus station on Gongxing Lu. It passes the Shanghai Mansions, crosses Garden Bridge, and then heads directly south along the Bund to the end of Zhongshan Lu.

No 71 Takes you to the CAAC airport bus stop on Yan'an Zhonglu; catch it from Yan'an Donglu close to the Bund.

No 112 Zigzags north from the southern end of the People's Square to Nanjing Xilu, down Shimen Erlu to Beijing Xilu then up Jiangning Lu to Yùfó Sì.

No 911 Leaves from Zhonghua Lu near the intersection with Fuxing Zhonglu, close to the Yu Gardens Bazaar, and goes up Huaihai Lu, continuing to the zoo.

Train

Shànghǎi currently has two metro lines and one light rail line. The No 1 line runs from Shanghai train station in the north through the People's Square and down to the Xin Zhuang metro station in the southern part of town.

The No 2 line runs from Zhōngshān Gōngyuán to Longyang Lu in Pǔdōng. Eventually it will extend to both Hongqiao and Pudong airports. The light rail runs on the western perimeter of the city from the Shanghai south train station to the Shanghai train station then north-east past the Hóngkǒu stadium and on to Jiangwan station.

Tickets are between Y2 and Y4 depending on the number of stops. Stored value tickets are available for Y50 and Y100.

Zhèjiāng 浙江

Capital: Hángzhōu
Population: 44.7 million
Area: 101,800 sq km

One of China's smallest provinces, Zhèjiāng's longtime prosperity has always made it more important than its size might indicate.

The region is mainly divided between the area north of Hángzhōu, which is part of the lush Cháng Jiāng (Yangzi River) delta cut with rivers and canals, and the mountainous area to the south, which continues the rugged terrain of Fújiàn. The jagged coastline of Zhèjiāng has 18,000 islands – more than any other province.

Intensely cultivated for a thousand years, northern Zhèjiāng has lost most of its natural vegetation and is a flat, featureless plain with a dense network of waterways, canals and irrigation channels. The Grand Canal (Dà Yùnhé) also ends here – Zhèjiāng was part of the great southern granary from which food was shipped to the depleted areas of the north. The southern Jiāngsū and northern Zhèjiāng region is known as Jiāngnán, 'south of the river'.

The growth of Zhèjiāng's towns was based on their proximity to the sea and to some of China's most productive farmland. Hángzhōu, Níngbō and Shàoxīng have all been important trading centres and ports since the 7th and 8th centuries. Their growth was accelerated when, in the 12th century, the Song dynasty moved court to Hángzhōu in the wake of an invasion from the north.

Níngbō was opened up as a treaty port in the 1840s, only to fall under the shadow of its great northern competitor, Shànghǎi. Chiang Kaishek was born near Níngbō, and in the 1920s Zhèjiāng became a centre of power for the Kuomintang.

Silk was always a popular export and today Zhèjiāng, producing a third of China's raw silk, brocade and satin, is known as the 'land of silk'. The province is also famous for its tea production.

Hángzhōu is the provincial capital. To the south-east of the city are several places you can visit without backtracking. The major destination for travellers, however is the island of Pǔtuóshān, with its monasteries, nunneries, crags, beaches, myths and legends.

Highlights

- Hángzhōu's Xī Hú (West Lake), one of China's most famous attractions
- Pǔtuóshān, a rapidly developing but still magical getaway dotted with temples, pavilions and caves
- Jǐngnìng county, remote villages and countryside make this the perfect rural respite
- Wūzhèn, a restored Qing dynasty water town near the Grand Canal

HÁNGZHŌU 杭州
☎ 0571 • pop 6,114,000

'In heaven there is paradise, on earth Sūzhōu and Hángzhōu'. So runs one of China's oldest tourist blurbs. For the Chinese, Hángzhōu (along with Guìlín) is the country's most famous tourist attraction. Droves of tour groups descend on the city during all seasons, peaking on holidays and weekends. But don't despair: even this tourist excess has not diminished the beauty of Hángzhōu's Xī Hú (West Lake) area.

History

Hángzhōu's history goes back to the start of the Qin dynasty (221 BC). By the time Marco Polo passed through the city in the 13th century he described it as one of the most splendid in the world.

ZHÈJIĀNG 浙江

Although Hángzhōu prospered greatly after it was linked with the Grand Canal in AD 610, it really came into its own after the Song dynasty was overthrown by the invading Juchen, predecessors of the Manchus.

The Song capital of Kāifēng, along with the emperor and the leaders of the imperial court, was captured by the Juchen in 1126. The rest of the Song court fled south, finally settling in Hángzhōu and establishing it as the capital of the Southern Song dynasty.

China had gone through an economic revolution in the preceding years, producing huge and prosperous cities, an advanced economy and a flourishing inter-regional trade. With the Juchen invasion, the centre of this revolution was pushed south from the Huáng Hé (Yellow River) Valley to the lower Cháng Jiāng Valley and to the coast between the Cháng Jiāng and Guǎngzhōu.

While the north remained in the hands of the invaders (who rapidly became Sinicised), in the south Hángzhōu became the hub of the Chinese state, the population of which rose from half a million to 1.75 million by 1275. The city's large population and its proximity to the ocean promoted the growth of river and sea trade, and of other naval industries.

When the Mongols swept into China they established their court at Běijīng. Hángzhōu, however, retained its status as a prosperous commercial city. It did take a beating in the Taiping Rebellion: in 1861 the Taipings laid siege to the city and captured it, but two years later the imperial armies took it back.

These campaigns reduced almost the entire city to ashes, led to the deaths of over half a million of its residents through disease, starvation and warfare, and finally ended Hángzhōu's significance as a commercial and trading centre.

Few monuments survived the devastation, and most of those that did became victims of the Red Guards a century later during the Cultural Revolution. Much of what can be seen in Hángzhōu today is of fairly recent construction.

Orientation

Hángzhōu is bounded to the south by the Qiántáng Jiāng and to the west by hills. Between the hills and the urban area is Xī Hú, the region's premier scenic attraction. The eastern shore of the lake is the developed touristy district; the western shore is quieter.

Information

Tourist Offices There's a tourist office immediately to your left as you exit the train station at the bottom level. They have maps (Y5) in English and Chinese.

Money The main Bank of China is at 320 Yan'an Lu, near Qingchun Lu.

Post & Communications The main post office is at the western end of Jiefang Lu. More convenient post and telephone offices can be found opposite each other on Yan'an Lu. The Tàipíngyáng Internet Cafe on the 2nd floor, 243 Jiefang Lu is open 24 hours a day and charges Y3 per hour to surf the net.

Travel Agencies China International Travel Service (CITS; Zhōngguó Guójì Lǚxíngshè; ☎ 8521 5525) has an office at 1 Beishan Lu in the collection of buildings overlooking the north end of the Báidī Causeway. It deals mainly with tour groups and is not very useful for the individual traveller. The Overseas Travel Agency (Hǎiwài Lǚxíngshè; ☎ 8770 9770) in Huáqiáo Fàndiàn (see Places to Stay later) can book advance train tickets and charges Y40 to book sleepers.

Bookshops The Foreign Languages Bookshop at 34 Hubin Lu has good maps, including some in English, and a good collection of English novels on the 2nd floor.

A Close Shave

Língyǐn Sì might have been razed for good during the Cultural Revolution but for the intervention of Zhou Enlai. Accounts vary as to what exactly happened, but it seems there was a confrontation between those who wanted to save the temple and those who wanted to destroy it.

The matter eventually went all the way up to Zhou, who gave the order to save both the temple and the sculptures on the rock face opposite. This is hardly surprising considering that Zhou gave the final nod of approval way back in 1953 for the carving of the huge Buddha inside the temple, and twice allocated funds for the statue's completion. The monks, however, were sent to work in the fields.

In the early 1970s a few of the elderly and invalid monks were allowed to come back and live out their last few years in a small outbuilding on the hillside behind the temple.

PSB The Public Security Bureau (PSB; Gōngānjú; ☎ 8706 8080) is located at 35 Huaguang Lu.

Língyǐn Sì 灵隐寺
Temple of the Soul's Retreat

Língyǐn Sì (☎ 8796 7426, Lingyin Lu; adult/child Y20/10; open 7am-5pm daily) is one of Hángzhōu's main attractions.

It was built in AD 326 and, due to war and calamity, has been destroyed and restored no fewer than 16 times.

The present buildings are restorations of Qing dynasty structures. The Hall of the Four Heavenly Guardians at the front of the temple is inscribed with the couplet, 'cloud forest Buddhist temple', penned by the Qing emperor Kangxi, a frequent visitor to Hángzhōu, who was inspired by the sight of the temple in the mist and trees.

Behind this hall is the Great Hall, where you'll find the magnificent 20m-high statue of Siddhartha Gautama. Based on a Tang dynasty original, it was sculpted in 1956 from 24 blocks of camphor wood.

Behind the giant statue is a montage of 150 small figures that charts the journey of 53 children on the road to Buddhahood; also represented are Ji Gong, a famous monk who secretly ate meat, and a character known as

EAST CHINA COAST

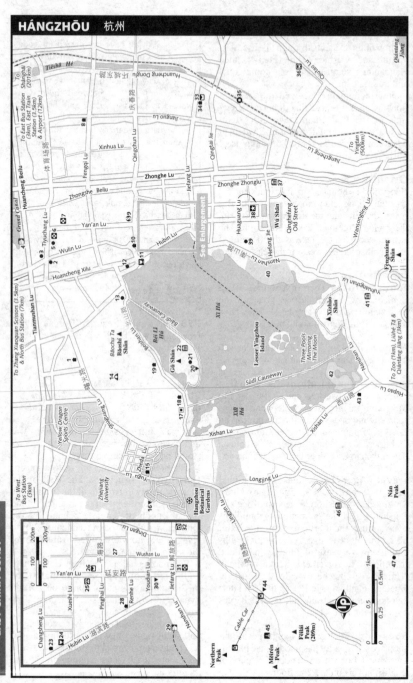

HÁNGZHŌU 杭州

the 'mad monk'. During the time of the Five Dynasties about 3000 monks lived here.

Bus No K7 and tourist bus No 2 (both from the train station), and tourist bus No 1 from the roads circling Xī Hú go to the temple. Behind Língyǐn Sì is the **Northern Peak** (*Běi Gāofēng*), which can be scaled via cable car (Y20). From the summit there are sweeping views across the lake and city.

Zhejiang Provincial Museum
Zhèjiāng Shěng Bówùguǎn 浙江省博物馆
This is an excellent museum (☎ 8797 1177, 25 Gushan Lu; admission Y15; open 8.30am-4.30pm Tues-Sun), with exhibits on the pre-history and history of Zhèjiāng in the main building and other items in the smaller

buildings scattered around the grounds. Captions are in English and Chinese.

Mausoleum of General Yue Fei
Yuè Fēi Mù 岳飞墓
During the 12th century, when China was attacked by Juchen invaders from the north, General Yue Fei (1103–41 BC) was commander of the Song armies.

Despite his successes against the invaders, he was recalled to the Song court where he was executed after being deceived by Qin Hui, a treacherous court official. More than 20 years later, in 1163, Song emperor Gao Zong exonerated Yue Fei and had his corpse reburied at the present site.

HÁNGZHŌU

PLACES TO STAY
1 Yellow Dragon Hotel
  黄龙饭店
8 Holiday Inn
  杭州国际假日酒店
10 Haihua Novotel Hotel
  海华大酒店
15 Zhejiang University Foreign Student Dormitory
  浙大外国留学生楼
18 Shangri-La Hotel
  杭州香格里拉饭店
19 Xīnxīn Fàndiàn
  新新饭店
23 Huáqiáo Fàndiàn; Overseas Travel Agency
  华侨饭店;
  海外旅行社
28 Xīhú Fàndiàn
  西湖饭店
34 Zhèhuá Fàndiàn
  浙华饭店
43 Huāgǎng Fàndiàn
  花港饭店

PLACES TO EAT
16 Shānwàishān Càiguǎn
  山外山菜馆
20 Lóuwàilóu Càiguǎn
  楼外楼菜馆
30 Kǎoyā Diàn
  烤鸭店
44 Tiānwàitiān Càiguǎn
  天外天菜馆

OTHER
2 Train Ticket Booking Office
  火车售票处
3 CAAC
  民航售票处
4 Passenger Wharf
  客运码头
5 Dragonair (Radisson Plaza Hotel)
  雷迪森广场酒店
  (港龙航空公司)
6 International Department Store
  国际大厦
7 Yintai Department Store
  银泰百货大楼
9 Bank of China
  中国银行
11 Casablanca Country Pub
  卡萨布兰卡乡村俱乐部
12 Foreign Languages Bookshop
  外文书店
13 CITS
  中国国旅行社
14 Yellow Dragon Cave
  黄龙洞
17 Yue Fei Mausoleum
  岳飞墓
21 Zhongshan Gōngyuán
  中山公园
22 Zhejiang Provincial Musuem
  浙江省博物馆
24 Paradise Rock Bar & Restaurant
  天上人间酒吧
25 Telephone Office
  中国电信

26 Post Office
  邮局
27 Night Market
  夜市场
29 Boats to Three Pools Mirroring the Moon
  船至三潭印月
31 Jiefang Lu Department Store
  解放路百货商店
32 Tàipíngyáng Internet Cafe
  太平洋网吧
33 Main Post Office
  邮电局
35 Train Station
  火车站
36 South Bus Station
  长途汽车南站
37 Chinese Medicine Museum
  中药博物馆
38 PSB
  公安局
39 China Academy of Art
  中国美术学院
40 Liǔlàngwényīng Gōngyuán
  柳浪闻莺公园
41 China Silk Museum
  中国丝绸博物馆
42 Red Carp Pond
  花港观鱼
45 Língyǐn Sì
  灵隐寺
46 China Tea Museum
  中国茶叶博物馆
47 Dragon Well Tea Village
  龙井问茶

EAST CHINA COAST

Chinese tourists traditionally cursed and spat upon the iron statues of Qin Hui and his wife, Wang Shi, but now they have to do it surreptitiously since, though this might be hard to believe, spitting is against the law in China.

The **mausoleum** (☎ 8799 6663, Beishan Lu; adult/child Y20/10; open 6.30am-6pm daily) is in a compound bounded by a red-brick wall. It was ransacked during the Cultural Revolution, but has since been restored. Inside is a large statue of the general and the words, 'return the mountains and rivers to us', a reference to his patriotism and resistance to the Juchen.

Liùhé Tǎ 六和塔
Six Harmonies Pagoda

South-west of the city stands an enormous rail-and-road bridge that spans Qiántáng Jiāng. Close by is this 60m-high octagonal pagoda (☎ 8659 1401, 16 Zhijiang Lu; adult/child Y15/7.5; open 6am-6pm daily), which also served as a lighthouse. Up until the Ming dynasty it was a prime place for viewing the Qiántáng Jiāng tidal bore (see the Around Hángzhōu section), but the river channel curved east and the bore is best seen today from the shores near the town of Yánguān. Climbing the pagoda is Y10 extra.

Behind the pagoda is a charming walk through terraces dotted with sculptures, bells, shrines and inscriptions. Take bus No 308 from near the post office on Yan'an Lu.

Xī Hú 西湖
West Lake

There are 36 lakes in China called Xī Hú, but this one is by far the most famous. Indeed, this West Lake is the one from which all other west lakes take their name.

Xī Hú is the symbol of Hángzhōu, and can make for a pleasant outing, though some of its charm has fallen victim to the plundering of tour groups and tacky facilities. Twilight and dawn can be better times to view the lake, especially when it's layered with mist.

Xī Hú was originally a lagoon adjoining Qiántáng Jiāng. In the 8th century the governor of Hángzhōu had it dredged; later a dike was built that cut it off from the river completely. The resulting lake is about 3km long and a bit under 3km wide. Two causeways, the Báidī and the Sūdī, split the lake into sections.

The causeways each have a number of arched bridges, large enough for small boats and ferries to pass under. The sights are scattered around the lake – a motley collection of gardens, bridges and pavilions. Many have literary associations that are unfortunately lost on most foreigners.

The largest island in the lake is **Gǔ Shān** (Solitary Hill Island) – the location of the Zhejiang Provincial Museum, Zhōngshān Gōngyuán and the restaurant Lóuwàilóu Càiguǎn. The island's buildings and garden were part of the holiday palace of Emperor Qianlong in the 18th century. The Báidī causeway links the island to the mainland.

The smaller island in the middle of the lake is known as **Lesser Yingzhou Island** (Xiǎo Yíngzhōu) where you can look over at **Three Pools Mirroring the Moon** (Sāntán Yìnyuè), the three small towers in the water on the south side of the island. Each tower has five holes that release shafts of candlelight on the night of the Mid-Autumn Festival in September, when the moon is full.

Boats are available for hire, along with a boat person who rows from the back. Larger boats also cruise from docks along the eastern and northern sides of the lake.

Red Carp Pond (Huāgǎng Guānyú) is a chief attraction and is home to a few thousand red carp.

Hángzhōu's **Botanic Gardens** (Zhíwùyuán) are very pleasant to wander around and even have a sequoia pine presented by Richard Nixon on his 1972 visit.

Other Sights

There's a lot to see in Hángzhōu and it's not possible to cover everything here. It's best if you can get your hands on an English map, rent a bike and head for the sights that catch your interest.

The **Zoo** (Dòngwùyuán; ☎ 8796 2276, Hupao Lu; adult/child Y10/5; open 9.30am-3.30pm daily) is south of the lake, on the way to Liùhé Tǎ. It has Manchurian tigers, who are larger than their southern counterparts and are protected species.

Travellers have recommended the **China Silk Museum** (Zhōngguó Sīchóu Bówùguǎn; ☎ 8706 2079, 73-1 Yuhuangshan Lu; admission Y10; open 8.30am-4.30pm daily). There are good displays of silk samples, and exhibits explaining the history and process of silk production. English-speaking tour guides are available. Bus No 38 from Zhongshan Beilu or Nanshan Lu goes by the museum.

Tea is another one of Hángzhōu's specialties and you'll find all you need to know at the **China Tea Museum** (*Zhōngguó Cháyè Bówùguǎn;* ☎ 8796 4221, *Longjing Lu; admission Y10; open 8am-5pm daily*). Tourist bus No 3 or bus No 27 from Beishan Lu will take you there. Farther up the road you can enjoy one of Hángzhōu's most famous teas at the **Dragon Well Tea Village** (*Lóngjǐng Wènchá; admission Y35*), named after the spring where the pattern in the water resembles a dragon. Tourist bus No 3 will take you there.

Like many other Chinese cities, Hángzhōu has resurrected some of its older sections into tourist attractions. At the south end of Zhonghe Zhonglu, **Qinghefang Old Street** (*Qīnghéfāng Gǔjiē*) has undergone extensive restoration. It's the location of the **Húqìng Yútáng Chinese Medicine Museum** (*Zhōngyào Bówùguǎn;* ☎ 8702 7507, *95 Dajing Gang; admission Y10; open 8.30am-6pm daily*), which is an actual dispensary and clinic. Originally established by the Qing dynasty merchant Hu Xueyan in 1874, the medicine shop and factory retain the typical style of the period. Occasionally the museum has demonstrations on medicinal preparations.

Places to Stay – Budget

Accommodation in Hángzhōu is not cheap and it's a good idea to avoid the high season, weekends and holidays. Unfortunately, one of the best budget places, the China Academy of Art Foreign Student Dormitory (Zhōngguó Měishù Xuéyuàn Wàishì Zhaōdàisuǒ; 220 Nanshan Lu) was wiped off the face of the earth, literally, for the construction of a new campus, which may be completed by the time you read this.

Zhejiang University Foreign Student Dormitory (*Zhèjiāng Dàxué Liúxuéshēng Lóu;* ☎ 8799 6092) Doubles with bath Y100. This dormitory is outside the gate of Zhejiang University and the rooms aren't great but it's cheap. There's also a cheap restaurant with an English menu. Look for the white four-storey building down a small lane off Zheda Lu. Bus No K21 from the train station or No K16 from Pinghai Lu stop close by.

Xīhú Fàndiàn (☎ 8706 6933, *fax 8706 6151, 80 Renhe Lu*) Singles/doubles/triples with shared bath & fan Y100/140/180, singles/doubles with air-con Y120/170, singles/doubles with air-con & bath Y220/280. This hotel has a myriad of different rooms and is a cheap option.

Zhèhuá Fàndiàn (☎ 8780 2366, *fax 8780 7440, 5 Jiefang Lu*) Beds in triples with shared bath Y50, singles Y300, doubles with bath Y138-360. Though away from the lake, this hotel is a good budget option close to the train station. The cheapest doubles are noisy; the standard rooms are a better option, with discounts of 50%.

Places to Stay – Mid-Range

Hángzhōu's accommodation is pretty much priced in the mid-range to top-end bracket. As always, ask for a discount.

Huāgǎng Fàndiàn (☎ 8799 8899, *fax 796 2481, 4 Xishan Lu*) Set on beautiful grounds on the western side of Xī Hú, this hotel was undergoing renovation at the time of writing but expect something in the range of Y400 to Y600.

Xīnxīn Fàndiàn (☎ 8798 7101, *fax 8705 3263, 58 Beishan Lu*) Singles Y500, doubles Y260-528. Lakeview rooms here are more expensive and the cheapest doubles are in the old building. Discounts of 30% are available.

Huáqiáo Fàndiàn (*Overseas Chinese Hotel;* ☎ 8707 4401, ⓔ hq_hotel@mail .hz.zj.cn, *15 Hubin Lu*) Doubles Y544-603. This hotel was recently renovated and, while a little overpriced, is in a convenient location and has good facilities.

Places to Stay – Top End

Shangri-La Hotel (☎ 8707 7951, Ⓦ www .shangri-la.com, *78 Beishan Lu*) Singles US$180-290, doubles US$200-310, plus 15% service charge. There's plenty of top-end hotels in Hángzhōu, but this one is the most elegant and romantic, surrounded by spacious forested grounds. Discounts of 35% are not unknown. Even if you can't afford to stay, go there for a drink or a wander around.

Haihua Novotel Hotel (☎ 8721 5888, Ⓦ www.novotel.com, *298 Qingchun Lu*) Doubles Y1056. This comfortable and efficient hotel is very good value with discounts of nearly 50% available. Some rooms have a lake view. The restaurants are excellent and the facilities superb.

EAST CHINA COAST

Holiday Inn (☎ 8527 1188, e hihz@ mail.hz.zj.cn, 289 Jianguo Beilu) Doubles US$130. The newest of Hángzhōu's luxury hotels offers substantial discounts.

Yellow Dragon Hotel (Huánglóng Fàndiàn; ☎ 799 8833, fax 799 8090, 11 Shuguang Lu) Doubles Y1300. This is a massive place with an overwhelming lobby, but can be good value with discounts of at least 50% available for older rooms.

Places to Eat

Lóuwàilóu Càiguǎn (☎ 8796 9023, 30 Gushan Lu) Mains Y30-100. Open 6.45am-9am, 11am-2pm & 5pm-7pm daily. Right on Xī Hú, this place has been around since 1848 and is probably Hángzhōu's most famous restaurant. The local speciality is *xīhú cùyú* (poached fish in sweet vinegar sauce; Y35) and as long as you stay away from fancy dishes, it's a reasonable place to eat. An English menu is available.

Tiānwàitiān Càiguǎn (☎ 8796 5450, 2 Lingying Tianzhu Lu) Mains Y30-90. Open 10.30am-8.30pm daily. Run by the same group who own Lóuwàilóu Càiguǎn is this nondescript restaurant. Dishes to look out for are *dōngpō ròu* (fatty pork slices flavoured with Shàoxīng wine; Y45), named after the Song dynasty poet Su Dongpo, and *jiàohuàzi jī* (Y85), known in English as 'beggar's chicken', wrapped up and baked in charcoal.

Shānwàishān Càiguǎn (☎ 8799 6621, 8 Yuquan Lu) Mains Y40-80. Open 10.30am-8.30pm daily. Set amid the lush vegetation of the Botanical Gardens, this sprawling place is another Hángzhōu 'famous' restaurant. Bring mosquito repellent if you plan to eat dinner on the veranda.

For Chinese cheap eats, check out Yan'an Lu. The Hangzhou and Yintai Department Stores at the northern end of the street also have good food courts on their upper levels. Farther east, Wushan Lu is a haven for bargain restaurants with snappy service; there are a few popular *dumpling restaurants*, and a *pizza restaurant* here.

Kǎoyā Diàn (Roast Duck Restaurant; ☎ 8708 7122, 49 Youdian Lu) Mains Y25-60. Open 10.30am-1.30pm & 4.30pm-8pm daily. You can order a la carte cheaply here if you can read the menu. Otherwise ask for Beijing duck (*kǎoyā*; Y55). Half a duck (enough for two) is Y30.

Top-end hotels dish out a wide range of superior cuisine. While pricey, the *coffee shop* dinner buffet (Y180) at the Shangri-La Hotel (see Places to Stay) is excellent. The price doesn't include drinks.

Entertainment

There are a couple of bars on the northeastern side of Xī Hú.

Casablanca Country Pub (☎ 8702 5934, Hubin Da Gongyuan) Open 6pm-late daily. This rustic place on the lakeshore has simple meals and snacks. A pint of draft beer is Y22.

Paradise Rock Bar & Restaurant (☎ 8707 4401, 36 Hubin Lu) Lunch Y45-55, dinner Y35-120. Open 11.30am-2.30am daily. This is an ideal place for a break. Besides coffee and drinks, they also serve Western food. Occasionally, live bands show up to play jazz and blues in the evening.

Shopping

Hángzhōu is well known for its tea, in particular Longjing (Dragon Well) green tea (grown in the Lóngjǐng area, south-west of Xī Hú), as well as silk, fans and, of all things, scissors.

Shops around the lake sell all of these, but at high, touristy prices. One of the best places to look for bargains is the *night market* (Wushan Lu; open 6pm-11pm daily). Stalls are piled high with a fascinating confusion of collectables. Fake ceramics jostle with Chairman Mao memorabilia, ancient pewter tobacco pipes, silk shirts and pirated CDs. Get the gloves off and haggle hard if something catches your eye.

For silk, try the *market* (Xinhua Lu; open 8am-6pm daily) a couple of blocks east of Zhonghe Beilu. The silk area starts on the north side of Fengqi Lu. Most of the shops are geared to textile buyers, but there are some smaller retail outlets, especially at the north end of the street. Make sure you check that the silk is genuine and not a polyester clone (it should feel smooth and soft between your thumb and finger).

Jiefang Lu Department Store (Jiěfàng Lù Bǎihuò Shāngdiàn; ☎ 8701 6888, 211 Jiefang Lu) Open 9am-9pm daily. Another good place to buy silk is on the 2nd floor of this place. A range of prints as well as solid colours cost from Y40 to Y60 per metre.

It's possible to buy Chinese-style scissors all over China, of course, but if you want the product with the most famous trademark (and if you're looking for all kinds of scissors and knives, large and small) go straight to the factory source.

Zhang Xiaoquan Scissors *(Zhāng Xiǎoquán Jiǎndāo;* ☎ *8807 7980, 27 Daguan Lu)* Open 8am-5pm Mon-Fri. This enterprise has been around since the beginning of the Qing dynasty and they also have a small **museum** *(admission Y2)* but phone ahead for an appointment. Take bus No 58 from Tiyuchang Lu.

If you're looking to do some food shopping there's a good international supermarket in the basement of the International Department Store at the northern end of Yan'an Lu.

Getting There & Away

Air Civil Aviation Administration of China (CAAC; Zhōngguó Mínháng; ☎ 8510 7160) is at 390 Tiyuchang Lu. Dragonair (☎ 8506 8388) is on the 5th floor of the Radisson Plaza Hotel at 333 Tiyuchang Lu.

Hángzhōu has regular connections with all major Chinese cities. There are several flights a day to Běijīng (Y1050), Guǎngzhōu (Y960) and Hong Kong (Y1840).

Bus Numerous bus services go to and from Hángzhōu but all three long-distance stations are located outside the city centre. The north bus station on Moganshan Lu has buses to Nánjīng (Y113, five hours), Wǔkāng (Y10, 1½ hours) and other points in Jiāngsū.

Buses for Qiāndǎohú (Y30, four hours) and Huáng Shān (Y55, six hours) leave from the west bus station on Tianmushan Lu.

The east bus station is the most comprehensive with frequent deluxe buses to Shànghǎi (Y54, 2½ hours), Shàoxīng (Y18.5, one hour) and Níngbō (Y42, two hours). Economy buses are cheaper, but slower. Buses to Tiāntái Shān (Y43, six hours) and Hǎiníng (Y20, one hour) also leave from here.

Train Hángzhōu has an impressive new train station that is easily navigable. Some trains arrive and depart from the Hángzhōu east station; check your ticket.

Trains from the main station go south to Xiàmén (Y247, 25 hours), Nánchāng (Y146, 10 hours), Wēnzhōu (Y65, eight hours) and Guǎngzhōu (Y333, 23 hours), and east to Shàoxīng (Y13, one hour) and Níngbō (Y29, 2½ hours). Most trains heading north have to go to Shànghǎi, but there's a direct train to Běijīng (Y363, 16 hours) from Hángzhōu. Express trains from Hong Kong to Shànghǎi also stop at Hángzhōu every second day.

Fast trains from Hángzhōu to Shànghǎi (Y33) make the trip in two hours with some trains continuing through to Sūzhōu. Another convenient way to get to Shànghǎi is to catch a train to the Shànghǎi south station (Y29), which has connections to Shànghǎi's metro and lightrail lines.

It can be difficult to book sleepers at the Hángzhōu train station, especially to Běijīng. The Overseas Travel Agency in Huáqiáo Fàndiàn will book sleepers for a Y40 service charge. A better place for tickets is the train ticket booking office at 199 Wulin Lu, open 8am to 5pm daily.

Boat You can get to both Wúxī and Sūzhōu by boat up the Grand Canal from Hángzhōu. There's one boat daily for Sūzhōu, leaving at 5.30pm, and one leaving for Wúxī at 6pm. Both trips take 13 hours. Economy class in a cabin of four people costs Y60. Deluxe cabins for four people are Y88 per bed and two-person cabins are Y130 per bed. Buy tickets at the passenger wharf just north of Huancheng Beilu and get on the boat at a new facility nearby at 138 Huancheng Beilu.

Travellers have mixed opinions about this trip. Although it's more romantic to arrive in a place by boat, keep in mind that most of the journey is in darkness. Readers have also recommended it's worth getting the mid-price cabins, which are more comfortable than economy.

Getting Around

To/From the Airport Hángzhōu's airport is 15km from the city centre; taxi drivers ask around Y60 for the trip. Shuttle buses leave from the CAAC office and cost Y20.

Bus Very useful is bus No K7, as it connects the main train station to the major hotel area on the eastern side of the lake. Bus Nos 15 and K15 connect the north long-distance bus station to the north-west area of Xī Hú. Bus

No K56 travels from the east bus station to Yan'an Lu. Bus No 27 is useful for getting between the eastern and western sides of the lake. Tourist bus No 1 does a circular route around the lake to Língyǐn Sì and tourist bus No 2 goes from the train station, along Beishan Lu and up to Língyǐn Sì. Tourist bus No 3 travels around Xī Hú to the China Tea Museum, Dragon Well Tea Village, the Zoo and Yùhuáng Shān. Tickets are Y2.

Taxi Metered taxis are ubiquitous and start at Y10; figure on around Y20 to Y25 from the train station to Hubin Lu. Keep a map handy and watch out for lengthy detours.

Bicycle Rentals are available in a couple of places and are the best way to get around. Probably the most convenient place is the outlet beside Huáqiáo Fàndiàn. Rentals are Y6 per hour and a deposit of Y300 to Y400 is required.

Check out the bikes before you take off, especially the brakes.

Boat The boating industry on Xī Hú has been regulated in recent years. Boat operators are dressed in light blue uniforms and charge Y80 per hour. They are on the northern and eastern shores. Hiring a private boat is worth the splurge. Less intimate larger boats leave the eastern shore crossing the lake and visiting the islands en route for Y45.

AROUND HÁNGZHŌU
Mògān Shān 莫干山
☎ 0572
About 60km north of Hángzhōu is Mògān Shān. Pleasantly cool at the height of summer, Mògān Shān was developed as a resort for Europeans living in Shànghǎi and Hángzhōu during the colonial era. It's well worth visiting and staying in one of the old villas. There are the obligatory tourist sights, such as old villas that once belonged to Chiang Kaishek and the Shànghǎi gang leader, Du Yuesheng, but the best thing to do in Mògān Shān is to lose yourself on the paths meandering through stands of bamboo and pine.

Mògān Shān is full of hotels, most of them housed in old villas.

Wǔlíng Fàndiàn (☎ 803 3126, Wuling Cun) Rooms Y160-280. You can even stay here at Chang Kaishek's old place.

Lǜyè Shānzhuāng (☎ 803 3300) Doubles/triples Y150/180 low season. A better choice is this spotlessly clean place. It's an old stone villa that's a 15-minute walk uphill from the main street where the bus stops.

Entry to Mògān Shān is Y40. To get there, take a minibus from Hángzhōu's north bus station to Wǔkāng (Y10, 1½ hours) and from there you can either hire a minivan taxi (Y50) or take a public minibus (Y10, 30 minutes) up the mountain. Frequent buses also go to the village (Mògān Shān Zhèn) below the mountain for Y3, where you should be able to get a minivan taxi up the mountain for Y10.

Qiantang River Tidal Bore
Qiántáng Jiāngcháo 钱塘江朝
A spectacular natural phenomenon occurs when the highest tides of the lunar cycle cause a wall of water to thunder up the narrow mouth of the Qiántáng Jiāng from Hangzhou Bay (Hángzhōu Wān).

Although the tidal bore can be viewed from the riverbank in Hángzhōu, the best place to witness this amazing phenomenon is on either side of the river at Yánguān, a small town about 38km north-east of Hángzhōu. Viewing the bore among the Chinese has traditionally been associated with the Mid-Autumn Festival around the 18th day of the 8th month of the lunar calendar, but you can see it throughout the year when the highest tides occur at the beginning and middle of each lunar month. At the height of the traditional viewing season, it can get quite crowded; people have been swept away from the shore and drowned so it's wise to be cautious.

Hotels and travel agencies offer tours to see the bore during the Mid-Autumn Festival, but you can visit just as easily on your own. Buses to Yánguān leave from Hángzhōu's east bus station for Y20. Depending on the season you may have to pay an entrance fee of Y40 to secure the best vantage spots.

SHÀOXĪNG 绍兴
☎ 0575 • pop 4,289,400
Just 67km south-east of Hángzhōu, Shàoxīng is the centre of the waterway system on the northern Zhèjiāng plain. The waterways, with their rivers (subject to flooding), canals, boats and arched bridges, are part of the city's charm.

Since early times, Shàoxīng has been an administrative centre and an important agricultural market town. It was capital of the Yue kingdom from 770–211 BC.

Shàoxīng is the birthplace of many important intellectual and artistic figures in China's modern history, including the country's first great modern novelist, Lu Xun. It's also the home of Shàoxīng wine, which most travellers would agree is definitely an acquired taste.

Orientation

Encircled by large bodies of water and rivers, and crossed by canals, Shàoxīng is a pleasant place to explore by bicycle, pedicab or foot. One of the nicest walks follows the canal along the lane called Longshan Houjie, south-east of Shàoxīng Fàndiàn. The hill in Fǔshān Gōngyuán behind the hotel is a good place for shady walks. A large city square was recently created that fills up the corner of Shengli Lu and Jiefang Lu.

Information

Major hotels can change money for guests. The main Bank of China branch is at 201 Renmin Zhonglu and there's another one at 472 Jiefang Beilu. Both change travellers cheques.

China Telecom is on Dong Jie near Xinjian Beilu. Xiǎochóng Wǎngbā is an Internet cafe at 365 Shengli Lu. Services are Y2.5 per hour and it's open 24 hours a day.

CITS (☎ 515 3454, fax 517 1549) is grouped with a number of other travel agencies at 368 Fushan Xilu. You can find maps at the Xinhua Bookshop and around the major hotels.

The PSB (☎ 865 1333 ext 2104) is about 2km east of the city centre on Renmin Donglu, near Huiyong Lu.

Lu Xun's Former Residence

Lǔ Xùn Gùjū 鲁迅故居

Lu Xun (1881–1936), one of China's best-known modern writers and author of such stories as *Diary of a Madman* and *Medicine*, was born in Shàoxīng and lived here until he went abroad to study. He later returned to China, teaching at Guǎngzhōu's Zhongshan University in 1927. He was forced to hide out in Shànghǎi's French Concession when the Kuomintang decided his books were too dangerous. His tomb is in Shànghǎi.

You can visit **Lu Xun's Former Residence** (☎ 513 2080, 393 Lu Xun Zhonglu; adult/child Y15/3; open 8am-5.30pm daily) where his living quarters are faithfully preserved. At the same site, is the **Lu Xun Memorial Hall** (Lǔ Xùn Jìniànguǎn). Opposite is the school where he was a pupil (his desk is still there).

This area is a treat, not just for the buildings associated with Lu Xun, but also for its scenic charm; wander around and follow the river south along Fuhe Jie for delightful views of Shàoxīng.

Fuhe Jie is home to the **Tōnglián Antique Market** (Tōnglián Gǔwán Shìchǎng), which consists of rows of antique stalls and shops selling ceramics and calligraphy.

King Yu's Mausoleum

Dà Yǔ Líng

According to legend, the first Chinese dynasty held power from the 21st to the 16th century BC, and its founder was King Yu, who is credited with having engineered massive flood-control projects.

A temple and mausoleum complex to honour the great-grandfather of China was first constructed in the 6th century and has been added to over the centuries. The mausoleum (☎ 836 4559; admission Y15; open 7.30am-5.30pm daily) is about 4km south-east of the city centre and is composed of several parts: the huge 24m-tall Main Hall, the Memorial Hall and the Meridian Gate (Wǔ Mén). A statue of Yu graces the Main Hall.

No 2 bus will get you to King Yu's Mausoleum from the train station area or Jiefang Beilu (get off at the last stop). See the following Dōng Hú entry for boat transport from King Yu's Mausoleum to the lake.

Ancestral Homes

Although he was born in the small town of Huái'ān (now called Chǔzhōu) in Jiāngsū, **Zhou Enlai's ancestral home** (Zhōu Ēnlái Zǔjū; ☎ 513 6943, 369 Laodong Lu; admission Y18; open 8am-5.30pm daily) is here in Shàoxīng.

Other historical figures have also had their family homes turned into museums. One of these is the enlightened educator **Cai Yuanpei's Former Residence** (Cài Yuánpéi Gùjū; ☎ 513 6580, 13 Maofei Long; adult/child Y8/4; open 8am-5pm daily).

EAST CHINA COAST

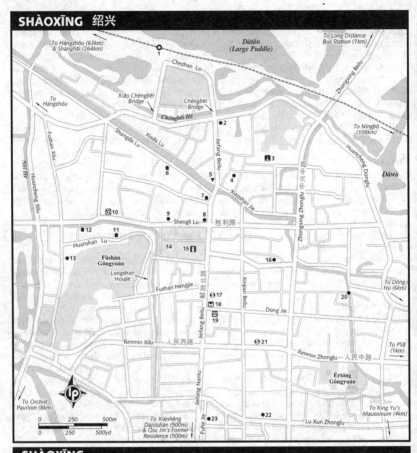

SHÀOXĪNG 绍兴

SHÀOXĪNG

PLACES TO STAY & EAT

5 Food Junction
五福园

6 Huáqiáo Fàndiàn
华侨饭店

7 Shàoxīng Lǚguǎn
绍兴旅馆

11 Shàoxīng Fàndiàn
绍兴饭店

12 Lóngshān Bīnguǎn
龙山宾馆

OTHER

1 Train Station
火车站

2 Bicycle Rental
租自行车店

3 Jièzhū Sì
戒珠寺

4 Cai Yuanpei's Former
Residence
蔡元培故居

8 Xinhua Bookshop
新华书店

9 City Hall
市政府

10 Xiǎochóng Wǎgbā
(Internet)
小虫网吧

13 CITS
中国国际旅行社

14 City Square
城市广场

15 Dàshàn Tǎ
大善塔

16 Zhou Enlai's
Ancestral Home
周恩来祖居

17 Bank of China
中国银行

18 Post Office
邮局

19 Telephone Office
中国电信

20 Eight-Character
Bridge
八字桥

21 Main Bank of China
中国银行

22 Lu Xun's Former
Residence; Lu Xun
Memorial Hall
鲁迅故居；
鲁迅纪念馆

23 Tōnglián Antique
Market
通联古玩市场

Another interesting home to visit is **Qiu Jin's Former Residence** (*Qiū Jǐn Gùjū;* ☎ 806 3369, 35 Hechang Tang; adult/child Y3/1.5; open 8am-5.30pm daily), where the pioneering woman revolutionary, Qiu Jin, was born. Qiu Jin studied in Japan and was active in women's rights and the revolutionary movement against the Qing government. She was executed by Qing authorities at the age of 29. There's a memorial statue of Qiu Jin on Jiefang Beilu, near Fushan Hengjie.

Dōng Hú 东湖
East Lake

Dōng Hú (☎ 864 9560; adult/child Y15/3; open 7am-4pm daily), an attractive place of sculpted rock formations, is around 6km east of the city centre. There's a temple, **Dōnghú Sì**, by the lake. Take bus No 1 from the train station or Jiefang Beilu to the last stop. You can hire a 'pedal boat', a local form of transport, from Dōng Hú to King Yu's Mausoleum and other sights. The trip takes around one hour and costs Y80 to Y100, depending on your bargaining skills.

Places to Stay

Few budget travellers visit Shàoxīng, but it has some of the cheapest accommodation in east China.

Shàoxīng Lǚguǎn (☎ 513 2814, 213 Jiefang Beilu) Singles/doubles/triples with fan & shared bath Y32/50/66, doubles with private bath/air-con Y95/120. This is a clean, basic, and friendly place, the only drawback being the noisy traffic.

Shàoxīng Fàndiàn (☎ 515 5858, fax 515 5565, 9 Huanshan Lu) Singles Y300-450, doubles Y350-550. This hotel has a whole range of options from rather musty doubles to much more pleasant rooms. A 40% discount makes it a good mid-range choice and the grounds and location are hard to beat.

Lóngshān Bīnguǎn (☎ 515 5710, fax 515 5308, 500 Shengli Lu) Singles Y250, doubles Y200-400. This place has a range of rooms in different buildings, some of which are a very good deal with a 40% discount.

Huáqiáo Fàndiàn (Overseas Chinese Hotel; ☎ 513 2323, fax 513 3602, 156 Shangda Lu) Singles with fan & shared bath Y60, doubles Y120-150. The rooms here aren't great but livable if you don't mind the ubiquitous dirty carpet.

Xiánhēng Dàjiǔdiàn (☎ 806 8688, fax 805 1028, 680 Jiefang Nanlu) Doubles Y447, suites Y678-1680. This four-star hotel is located in the southern part of town. Facilities include a tennis court, swimming pool, Western restaurant and coffee shop. A 30% discount is available.

Places to Eat

Food Junction (Wǔfú Yuán; ☎ 513 8598, 177 Jiefang Lu) Mains Y6-12. Open 6am-1am daily. For delicious noodles and cheap meals try this large and bustling place. Don't be put off by the unappetising exterior, which makes it look more like a bus station than a restaurant.

Zhǐyù Lóu (☎ 515 5888) Mains Y25-40. Open 11am-1pm & 5pm-9pm. This restaurant in Shàoxīng Fàndiàn is comfortable and has great food; it's a popular place for locals. There's an English menu and it's in a separate building near the north entrance of the hotel off Shengli Lu.

On the western edge of Shàoxīng's new city square bordering the canal there are a number of *teahouses*.

Getting There & Away

All Hángzhōu-Níngbō trains and buses stop in Shàoxīng. Luxury buses go to Níngbō (Y38, 1½ hours), Hángzhōu (Y18.5, one hour) and Shànghǎi (Y70, three hours) from the long-distance bus station.

Getting Around

The bus system in Shàoxīng is fairly straightforward. Bus No 1 travels from the train station down Jiefang Beilu and then east to Dōng Hú. Bus No 8 travels south down Zhongxing Lu from the long-distance bus station.

Taxis are cheap, starting at Y5, and pedicabs marginally cheaper. The best way to get around is by bicycle, available for rent in a couple of places on Jiefang Beilu. Try the place on the south-east side of Chéngběi Bridge. Rentals are *very* cheap, Y8 per day. A Y300 deposit is required.

AROUND SHÀOXĪNG

Considered one of Shàoxīng's 'must see' spots, the **Orchid Pavilion** (Lán Tíng; ☎ 460 6887; adult/child Y15/3; open 8am-5pm daily) doesn't get many Western visitors, though it has great significance for Chinese and Japanese interested in calligraphy. The history of this sight goes back to the year AD 353 when the calligrapher Wang Xizhi was inspired by a visit to the area. There's a small **museum** on the grounds and a calligraphy festival is held every year on the third day of the third lunar month in commemoration. Even if you're not interested in calligraphy, it's worth visiting for the gardens. The Orchid Pavilion is around 10km south-west of the city and is reached by bus No 3 from Shengli Lu.

NÍNGBŌ 宁波
☎ 0574 • pop 5,350,000

Like Shàoxīng, Níngbō rose to prominence in the 7th and 8th centuries as a trading port. Ships carrying Zhèjiāng's exports sailed from here to Japan, the Ryukyu islands and along the Chinese coast.

By the 16th century the Portuguese had established themselves as entrepreneurs in the trade between Japan and China, as the Chinese were forbidden to deal directly with the Japanese.

Although Níngbō was officially opened to Western traders after the first Opium War, its once-flourishing trade gradually declined as Shànghǎi boomed. By that time the Níngbō traders had taken their money to Shànghǎi and formed the basis of its wealthy Chinese business community.

Today Níngbō is a bustling city with fishing, textiles and food processing as its primary industries. There's not a lot for travellers to see, however, and it's mainly a transit stop on the way to nearby Pǔtuóshān, one of Zhèjiāng's premier tourist attractions.

Information
The main post office is just south of the Xīnjiāng Bridge, where Fènghuà Jiāng forks into the Yúyáo and Yǒng rivers. The main Bank of China is on Yaohang Jie and another smaller branch is on Zhongshan Xilu.

Internet services are available at the BC Net Bar at 38 Long 5-1 Fuqiao Jie. It's open from 8am to late and charges Y3 per hour.

CITS (☎ 8731 9999) have an office on the ground floor of the Mirage Hotel at 129 Yaohang Jie.

The PSB (☎ 8706 2505) is east of town at 658 Zhongxing Lu.

Yuè Hú 月湖
Moon Lake

Yuè Hú is an open park with a wide expanse of green grass and water. Just west of the lake is the **Tiānyī Pavilion** (Tiānyī Gé; ☎ 8736 3526, 10 Tianyi Jie; admission Y20; open 8am-5.30pm daily), an inspired combination featuring a garden pavilion full of books. Built during the Ming dynasty, it's thought to be China's oldest existing private library.

At the northern end of Yuè Hú on Zhongshan Lu there's a restored building known as **Fan's House** (Fàn Zhái) which has antique stalls, painting galleries and bookshops. Across Zhongshan Lu the imposing **Drum Tower** (Gǔ Lóu) marks the entrance to a pedestrian street full of restored buildings housing travel agencies, teahouses, restaurants and other shops.

If you are near the passenger ferry terminal, the old Portuguese **Catholic Church** (Tiānzhǔ Jiàotáng; ☎ 8735 5903, 40 Zhongma Lu; admission free) is well worth a visit. First built in 1628, it was destroyed and rebuilt in 1872. It's an active church (mass is held daily at 6am) with a Mediterranean-style whitewashed interior displaying prints of the fourteen Stations of the Cross, colourful icons and a vaulted ceiling.

Places to Stay
Níngbō is not exactly a Mecca for budget travellers but the large discounts available make it good value for mid-range prices.

Dōngyà Bīnguǎn (☎ 8735 6224, fax 8735 3529, 88-112 Zhongma Lu) Doubles Y168-180. Readers have recommended this hotel for its convenient location by the ferry terminal. Slight discounts are available.

Huáqiáo Fàndiàn (Overseas Chinese Hotel; ☎ 8729 3175, fax 8729 4790, 130 Liuting Jie) Singles Y165-238, doubles Y168-238. There's a wide range of rooms in this large hotel, with the better ones in the back building.

Yúnhǎi Bīnguǎn (☎ 8730 2288, fax 8730 8794, 2 Changchun Lu) Doubles Y318-428. The cheaper doubles are good value, especially with a discount, and the rooms are clean and comfortable.

Níngbō Fàndiàn (☎ 8712 1688, fax 8712 1668, 65 Mayuan Lu) Singles Y288, doubles Y375-660. This large hotel is nicely located by the Húchéng Canal. The cheaper doubles are discounted to Y288 and are the best value.

NÍNGBŌ 宁波

NÍNGBŌ

PLACES TO STAY
4 Dōngyà Bīnguǎn
   东亚宾馆
13 Níngbō Fàndiàn
   宁波饭店
14 Huáqiáo Fàndiàn
   宁波华侨饭店
24 Yúnhǎi Bīnguǎn
   云海宾馆
25 Nányuàn Fàndiàn
   南苑饭店

PLACES TO EAT
8 Wénlán
   Cháyìguǎn
   文澜茶艺馆
15 Wǔyī Dàjiǔdiàn
   五一大酒店
20 Lǎo Fángzi
   Chuānwèiguǎn
   老房子川味馆

OTHER
1 Zhōngshān
   Gōngyuán
   中山公园
2 North Bus Station
   汽车北站
3 Passenger Ferry
   Terminal
   轮船码头
5 Catholic Church
   天主教堂
6 City Hall
   市政府
7 BC Net Cafe
   公元前网吧
9 Drum Tower
   鼓楼
10 Fan's House
   范宅
11 Bank of China
   中国银行

12 Tiānyī Pavilion
   天一阁
16 Main Bank of China
   中国银行
17 CITS (Mirage Hotel)
   中国国际旅行社
   (凯州大酒店)
18 Main Post Office
   邮电居
19 LBB English Bar
   英语酒吧
21 South Bus Station
   汽车南站
22 Train Station
   火车南站
23 Minibuses to Xīkǒu
   往溪口中巴南站
26 CAAC
   中国民航
27 PSB
   公安局

EAST CHINA COAST

Nányuàn Fàndiàn (☎ 8709 5678, fax
8709 7788, 2 Lingqiao Lu) Singles/doubles
Y780/980, cheaper rooms Y298-398. This
five Star hotel may well be the best place
to stay in Níngbō. It is relatively new and
offers all of the usual comforts.

Places to Eat
Wǔyī Dàjiǔdiàn (☎ 8732 5151, 51 Xianxue
Jie) Mains from Y20. Open 12.30pm-
2.30pm & 5pm-8.30pm daily. Níngbō is
famous for its seafood and this is one place
to test its reputation. Menu items, from

clams to turtles, are on display in aquariums so don't worry about getting your order understood.

Lǎo Fángzi Chuānwèiguǎn (141 Leigong Xiang) Mains Y10-30. Open 10am-4am daily. This small, family run restaurant on the east side of Fènghùa Jiāng is a favourite with foreign teachers in Níngbō. The spicy Sìchuān meals are delicious and cheap.

Wénlán Cháyìguǎn (☎ 8728 3312, 63 Gongyuan Lu) Snacks Y5-10. Open 10am-late daily. Different varieties of tea are served here for Y18, but they also have coffee for Y10. Located in the Drum Tower shopping area, it's a nice place for refreshment, with traditional decor and an upstairs seating area.

Nányuàn Fàndiàn has a number of *restaurants* to choose from, including one serving Western food.

Entertainment

LBB English Bar (☎ 8772 1048, 14-1 Dahe Gang) Open 6pm-2am daily. If you're looking for a fun place with great music, try this place. A pitcher of draft beer is Y30 and it's a favourite with foreign teachers and a good place to meet people. Head down the lane next to the Agricultural Bank of China on Zhongshan Lu.

Getting There & Away

Air The CAAC ticket office (☎ 742 7888) is at 91 Xingning Lu. There are daily flights to Hong Kong (Y1680) and air connections with most major Chinese cities.

Bus Deluxe buses leave frequently for Shànghǎi (Y96, four hours), Hángzhōu (Y42, two hours) and Shàoxīng (Y38, 1½ hours) from the south bus station. There are also buses to Wēnzhōu (Y116, six hours) and Tiāntái Shān (Y18.5, three hours).

Minibuses to Xīkǒu (Y8, one hour) depart from a minibus station on the small street running south-east from the train station.

Train Frequent trains run between Shànghǎi and Níngbō but it's still faster to take a deluxe bus. There are trains to Guǎngzhōu (Y351, 26 hours) and Héféi (Y217, 13 hours). It's not too difficult to book tickets at the train station. CITS will book sleepers for a Y20 service charge.

Boat Overnight ferries go to Shànghǎi (12 hours) from the passenger ferry terminal (lúnchuán mǎtou) near the Xīnjiāng Bridge, but only on alternate days. Ticket prices range from Y114 for 2nd class to Y46 for a seat.

Slow boats to Pǔtuóshān depart from the passenger ferry terminal early in the morning and take about five hours; tickets range from Y21 to Y52. Frequent fast boats to Pǔtuóshān take 2½ hours, including a 1½-hour bus ride from the Níngbō passenger ferry terminal to a wharf outside the city. Tickets are Y51, including the bus ride.

The ferry terminal is poorly serviced by public buses. It's best to take a taxi, which will cost about Y25 to most of the hotels.

Getting Around

Níngbō's Lìshè airport is a 20-minute drive from town. Airport buses leave from CAAC and cost Y8. A taxi should cost around Y45.

Taxis around town are fairly cheap, starting at Y8.

PǓTUÓSHĀN 普陀山
☎ 0580

Pǔtuóshān is the China we all dream about, the one we see on postcards and in coffee-table books – temples, pagodas, arched bridges, narrow alleys, fishing boats, artisans and monks. Here you feel miles away from the hustle and bustle that characterise modern Chinese cities.

You pay a Y60 entrance fee to the island upon arrival, which does not include entry fees to other sights.

There's a post office south-west of Pǔjì Temple and a Bank of China farther west down the road.

Pǔtuóshān's temples are shrines for Guanyin, the Buddhist Goddess of Mercy and you will see her image everywhere. A striking landmark is the **Nánhǎi Guānyīn** (☎ 669 8199; admission Y6; open dawn-dusk daily), a 33m high golden statue of Guanyin overlooking the sea at the southernmost tip of the island.

The best way to enjoy the island is to amble about, rather than rush about like the tour groups. While there is no need to see everything, you can also jump aboard one of the numerous minibuses that shuttle people between temples for Y3 to Y6.

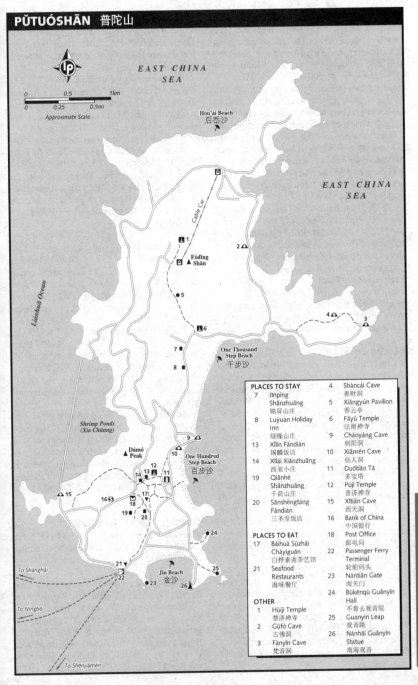

The two large beaches, **One Hundred Step Beach** (*Bǎibùshā*) and **One Thousand Step Beach** (*Qiānbùshā*) on the east of the island, are attractive and largely unspoilt, although you have to pay to get in (Y12). **Fànyīn Cave** (*Fànyīn Dòng;* ☎ 609 1258; admission Y5; open 5.30am-6pm daily) on the far eastern tip of the island, has a temple dedicated to Guanyin perched between two cliffs with a seagull's view of the crashing waves below.

The area around the **Pǔjì Temple** (*Pǔjì Chánsì;* ☎ 609 1236; admission Y5; open 5.30am-6pm daily) is a treat, and from here it is easy to plan an attack on the rest of the island. Most of the minibuses go from the parking lot near here.

The highest point of the island is **Fódǐng Shān**, which is also the site of the **Huìjì Temple** (*Huìjì Chánsì;* ☎ 609 2126; admission Y5; open 5.30am-6.30pm daily). A cable car goes up the back side of the mountain (Y25) and stone steps lead down to sea level and **Fǎyǔ Temple** (*Fǎyǔ Chánsì;* ☎ 609 1540; admission Y5; open 5.30am-6pm daily), a peaceful place surrounded by huge camphor trees. Pilgrims make their way up the steps to the peak, often on their knees.

Places to Stay

It's difficult to provide reliable information on Pǔtuóshān's accommodation as prices vary seasonally and according to demand. Though it's not officially allowed, many travellers find budget accommodation in rooms in people's homes. A barrage of touts meets each ferry and you can always try your luck with them. The arrival hall also has a counter for booking hotels.

Xīlín Fàndiàn (☎ 609 1303, fax 609 1199) Singles/doubles Y308/428. This place has pleasant rooms surrounding a courtyard and it's good value during the weekdays, with discounts of up to 50%. Some of the staff speak English.

Xīlái Xiǎozhuāng (☎ 609 1505, fax 609 1023, 1 Xianghua Jie) Doubles Y460-696. This large place is a little more upscale and has restaurants and shops. Discounts as high as 50% are sometimes offered on weekdays.

Jīnpíng Shānzhuāng (Jinping Mountain Villa; ☎ 609 1500, fax 609 1698, 107 Fayu Lu) Doubles Y290-580. Some of the rooms here have been renovated and the ones with wood floors are nice, available for Y144 on weekdays.

Qiānhé Shānzhuāng (Qianhe Mountain Villa; ☎ 609 1630, 125 Miaozhuangyan Lu) Doubles Y300-480. This place has comfortable rooms and 30% discounts on weekdays but it's often full.

Sānshèngtáng Fàndiàn (☎ 609 1277, fax 609 1140, 121 Miaozhuangyan Lu) Doubles Y214-428. This place is cheap with a discount, but the rooms are damp and the service surly. Best as a last resort.

Luyuan Holiday Inn (Luyuán Shānzhuāng; ☎ 609 2588, fax 609 2537, 61 Fayu Lu) Doubles with sea-view verandas Y650, deluxe singles Y710. The nicest hotel in Pǔtuóshān is located steps from the beach – it's also the best place to go for a romantic getaway. A 20% discount is offered on weekdays.

Places to Eat

Some of the best places to eat in Pǔtuóshān are in the temples, where *vegetarian meals* are usually served at lunch and sometimes at breakfast and dinner for Y2 to Y5. Both the Huìjì and Pǔjì temples have good vegetarian dining.

Xīlín Fàndiàn Restaurant (☎ 609 3133, see Places to Stay) Mains Y20-60. Open 6.30am-9pm daily. If you can stand the looped Kenny G soundtrack, this is a good place to eat. There's not much in the way of atmosphere, but the service is friendly and efficient.

Báihuà Sùzhái Cháyìguǎn (☎ 609 1208) Mains Y10-20. Open 6.30am-7.30pm daily. This vegetarian restaurant and teahouse has an English menu (and a few meat dishes).

Private *seafood restaurants* line the road to the ferry terminal, where you choose your meal from a tub outside. Decide on the price before committing yourself.

Getting There & Away

Pǔtuóshān is accessible by boat from either Níngbō or Shànghǎi, but Níngbō is closer and offers more frequent services.

To Shànghǎi A daily nightboat (two on Sunday) leave Pǔtuóshān at 4.30pm for the 12-hour voyage to Shànghǎi. Tickets range from Y87 to around Y347; it's easy to upgrade once you're on board. A fast boat goes from Pǔtuóshān to Lúcháo, where passengers are then bussed to Shíliùpù Wharf on the Bund. About three hours are spent on the boat and one to two hours on the bus. Tickets are Y195 and Y225. Keep in mind that this can be a rough trip for those prone to seasickness. See the Getting There & Away section of the Shànghǎi chapter for information on how to reach Pǔtuóshān from Shànghǎi.

To/From Níngbō The simplest way to Pǔtuóshān is the fast ferry, with frequent departures from Níngbō's passenger ferry terminal (lúnchuán mǎtou). The trip takes about 2½ hours altogether, which also includes the bus ride from the fast boat wharf outside Níngbō to the Níngbō passenger ferry terminal. Tickets are Y56. A slow boat from Níngbō takes five hours. Tickets range from Y21 to Y52.

Getting Around
Walking around Pǔtuóshān is the most relaxing option if you have time. If not, minibuses zip from the ferry terminal to the Pǔjì Temple (Y3), where you can change to buses going to other sights. If you're walking to the Pǔjì Temple from the ferry terminal, look for the seafood restaurants on your left and the stone path labelled Miaozhuanyan Lu in pinyin. This path heads uphill past tea fields. Keep heading north and you'll pass Sānshèngtáng Fàndiàn and eventually reach the area around the Pǔjì Temple.

WĒNZHŌU 温州
☎ 0577 • pop 7,120,000
Wēnzhōu is an east coast city famous for its people emigrating to France and Italy and, perhaps because of that connection, an abundance of shoe factories. It's a prosperous place, with an emerging skyline of high-rise buildings. For most travellers Wēnzhōu doesn't have a lot to offer in the way of sights, although there are some scenic places to visit outside the city.

Information
There are two Bank of China branches and two post offices near the city centre.

Internet services are available in the China Telecom building at the corner of Liming Xilu and Huancheng Donglu. It's open daily from 8am to 5.30pm and charges Y4 per hour. The HQ City Net Bar is an Internet cafe with fast connections on the corner of Renmin Zhonglu and Jiefang Jie,

beside the McDonald's. It's open 24 hours a day and charges Y4 per hour.

There's a friendly CITS office (☎ 8825 0673) at 107-1 Xiaonan Lu that can book air tickets and arrange tours. The PSB office (☎ 8821 0851) is at the end of a small lane called Xigong Jie, north of Guangchang Lu.

Things to See
The main scenic site is **Jiāngxīn Dǎo** (*Heart of the River Island;* ☎ 8820 1192; *adult/ child Y10/5; open 8am-midnight daily*) in the middle of Ōu Jiāng. The island park is dotted with pagodas, a lake and footbridges. It's easily reached by ferry (Y10) from the Máháng pier (Máháng mǎtou) on Wangjiang Donglu.

Exploring the older streets north and south of Guangchang Lu is worthwhile, though much of the old town has been razed for new developments. There are two active old **churches**, one Protestant (*Chengxi Jie*) and one Catholic (*Zhouzhaici Xiang*). Both were built in the late 19th century.

Places to Stay
Wēnzhōu is a major business centre and has many mid-range hotels, although there are a couple of budget places.

Xìnghuācūn Fàndiàn (☎ 8852 8588, *83 Lucheng Lu*) Doubles Y80, singles/doubles/triples with shared bath & fan Y24/56/60. You'll find clean rooms here and it's certainly a bargain. There's no English sign but look for a grungy white five-storey building, about 100m south-east of the west bus station.

Dōng'ōu Dàshà (☎ 8818 7901, *fax 8818 5875, 1 Wangjiang Donglu*) Singles Y178, doubles Y190-280. Discounts of 20% make this a good budget option. The cheaper doubles are quite small. It's a large 14-storey hotel.

International Seamen's Club (*Wēnzhōu Guójì Hǎiyuán Jùlèbù;* ☎ 8818 2222, *fax 8818 5190, 55 Haitan Shan*) Singles Y220, doubles Y280-380. Located on the hill overlooking the river, the rooms here are fairly new but already look like they get a lot of traffic. Discounts of 20% are available.

Húbīn Fàndiàn (☎ 8822 7961, *fax 8821 0600, 1 Youyongqiao Lu*) Doubles Y300-356. This hotel is a little pricey but very comfortable and in a pleasant location beside the tree-lined Jiǔshān Hé.

There are a number of upmarket hotels in Wēnzhōu:

Wenzhou International Hotel (☎ 8825 1111, **W** www.wzihotel.com, 1 Renmin Zhonglu) Singles/doubles Y530/480. This four-star hotel is one of the best, with restaurants, a swimming pool and in-house movies. Rooms are good value with a 30% discount, though the singles are quite small.

Dynasty Hotel (☎ 8837 8888, **W** www .dynastyhotel.com, 18 Minhang Lu) Doubles Y750. It's less central but this hotel has many amenities, including a good Western-style coffee shop. Discounts of 30% are available.

Places to Eat

Not surprisingly for a port, Wēnzhōu is known for its seafood and there are numerous restaurants near the west bus station.

Cafe de Champselysees (☎ 8825 1318, 2nd floor, Huanqiu Dasha) Mains Y20-60, set meals Y38-48. Open 11am-2am daily. This elegant restaurant has reasonably priced, delicious Western food, coffee and some Asian-style dishes. The French onion soup (Y25) is, without doubt, the best you'll find within 500km. There's an English menu and some of the staff speak English.

Pānjiāhé Guòqiáo Mǐxiàn (☎ 8825 7931, 42 Diyi Qiao) Mains Y10-20. Open 8am-3am daily. This small Yúnnán-style restaurant with an attractive bamboo decor serves across-the-bridge noodles with a Wēnzhōu twist – bits of seafood in the soup. The beef satay at Y1 a skewer, is also good.

Getting There & Away

Air CAAC (☎ 8833 3197) is in the southeast section of town across from the Dynasty Hotel. Wēnzhōu has reasonably good connections with other Chinese cities but the airport is notorious for its heavy fog – pilots often end up flying at ridiculously low altitudes trying to find the runway.

Bus Wēnzhōu has two main bus stations, the west bus station and the new south bus station near the train station. As a general rule, if you're heading south, take the south station; north or west, take the west station. Buses to Fúzhōu (Y145, 10 hours) leave from the south station. For long-haul destinations, you're better off taking the train.

WĒNZHŌU 温州

EAST CHINA COAST

Train The train line from Wēnzhōu connects the city to Hángzhōu (Y65, eight hours), Shànghǎi (Y176, 9½ hours) and Běijīng (Y378, 30 hours). The train station is south of the city. Take bus No 5 or 20 from Renmin Lu. Alternatively, a taxi to the station will cost around Y20.

CITS doesn't book train tickets, but try your hotel, or the little outlet just south of the CITS in an alley off Xiaonan Lu. A Y10 service charge is added.

Getting Around
Wēnzhōu airport is 27km south-west of town and taxis charge between Y100 and Y120 for the trip. A bus goes from CAAC for Y10.

Taxis around town start at Y10.

AROUND WĒNZHŌU
Yàndàng Shān 雁荡山
Along the coast about 80km north-east of Wēnzhōu is Yàndàng Shān, a group of mountains featuring sheer cliffs and peaks similar to the geography of Wǔyí Shān in Fújiàn province. The highest peak, **Bǎigǎng Jiān**, is 1150m above sea level.

The whole area of Yàndàng Shān is huge, about 450sq km, but the most accessible sights are found in three main scenic areas. A long ribbon of water falls into **Big Dragon Pool** (Dàlóng Qiū; ☎ 624 1175; admission Y25; open 5.30am-6.30pm daily), reached

by a winding path passing beneath rock columns towering over 200m above. A breathtaking high-wire act featuring a cyclist making their way between two peaks takes place on the hour.

Walkways and a suspension bridge cling to the **Divine Cliffs** (Líng Yán; ☎ 624 3713; admission Y25; open 5.30am-6.30pm daily), which can also be reached by cable car (Y9). Farther east, **Divine Peaks** (Líng Fēng; ☎ 624 3653; admission Y25; open 5.30am-6.30pm daily) is the largest section and is dotted with caves and more bizarre peaks. It's the best place for longer hikes.

There's lots of accommodation in Yàndàng Shān.

Míngyàn Bīnguǎn (☎ 6224 2577, 15 Buxing Jie) Doubles/triples Y180/200. This is a nice, small family-run place. It's around the corner just north of the bus stop for services from Wēnzhōu.

Buses for Yàndàng Shān leave four times daily from Wēnzhōu's south bus station. Tickets are Y27 and the trip takes 1½ hours.

JĪNGNÌNG COUNTY
Jīngnìng Xiàn
☎ 0578
In southern Zhèjiāng, close to the border of Fújiàn province, Jīngnìng county is a mountainous, undeveloped region full of rushing rivers and old villages. It's home to the She nationality and is the only autonomous

---

WĒNZHŌU

PLACES TO STAY
3　Dōng'ōu Dàshà
　　东瓯大厦
4　International Seamen's
　　Club
　　温州国际海员俱乐部
11　Húbīn Fàndiàn
　　湖滨饭店
14　Xīnghuācūn Fàndiàn
　　杏花村饭店
21　Wenzhou International
　　Hotel
　　温州国大酒店
24　Dynasty Hotel
　　王朝大酒店

PLACES TO EAT
17　Pānjiāhé Guòqiáo Mǐxiàn
　　潘家和过桥米线
18　Cafe de Champselysees
　　香榭丽舍西餐厅

OTHER
1　Ferry to Jiāngxīn
　　Dǎo
　　麻行码头
2　Passenger Ferry
　　Terminal
　　温州港客运站
5　People's Square
　　人民广场
6　PSB
　　公安局
7　City Hall
　　市政府
8　Protestant Church
　　基督教堂
9　Post Office
　　邮电局
10　Catholic Church
　　天主教堂
12　West Bus Station
　　汽车西站

13　Bank of China
　　中国银行
15　Post Office
　　邮局
16　Bank of China
　　中国银行
19　HQ City Net Bar
　　环球网吧
20　China Telecom
　　Internet
　　中国电信
22　CITS
　　中国国际旅行社
23　Train Ticket Booking
　　Office
　　火车预售票处
25　CAAC
　　中国民航

national minority district in east China; the She make up about 10% of the Han-dominated population.

The lure of Jǐngníng county is the lack of tourism and the scenery and unspoiled countryside, which make it an ideal place to visit for some rural respite.

Hèxī, in Jǐngníng county, is a large, sprawling place with modern buildings and little charm. The best thing to do is to hop on a minibus (Y3) heading out of town to Dàjūn, 13km away along the river. From this small village it's possible to float back down the river (Xiǎo Xī) on bamboo rafts to the bridge near Hèxī. The trip takes two hours and costs Y245 per raft. Better yet, take a small boat to the other side of the river and hike around the hills. Chinese maps of the region are available at the Hèxī bus station.

Jǐngníng Bīnguǎn (☎ 508 2760, 85 Renmin Zhonglu) Doubles Y180-300, singles/doubles with fan & bath Y65/100. It's possible to stay in Hèxī here. Another accommodation option is staying with a local family for a small fee.

To get to Hèxī, take a train from Wēnzhōu (Y31, two hours) or Hángzhōu (Y70, six hours) to Lìshuǐ. Then take bus No 3 from the train station to Lìshuǐ's old bus station (lǎo chēzhàn), where you can catch one of the frequent minibuses to Hèxī (Y14, 2½ hours).

TIĀNTÁI SHĀN 天台山
Heavenly Terrace Mountain
☎ 0576

Tiāntái Shān is noted for its many Buddhist monasteries, which date back to the 6th century. While the mountain itself may not be considered sacred, it's the home of the Tiāntái Buddhist sect, which is heavily influenced by Taoism.

From Tiāntái it's a 3.5km hike to Guó-qīng Sì (Guoqing Monastery; ☎ 398 8512; admission Y15; open 7.30am-4pm daily) at the foot of the mountain. A road leads from the monastery 25km to Huàdǐng Peak (Huàdǐng Fēng; ☎ 309 1112; admission Y25; open 8am-4pm daily). The peak is over 1100m high and there's a small village. From here you can continue by foot for 1km or so to Bàijǐngtái Sì (Prayer Terrace Temple) on the summit of the mountain.

Another sight on the mountain is **Shí-liáng Waterfall** (Shíliáng Fēipù; ☎ 309 1169; admission Y30; open 8am-4pm daily). From the waterfall it's a good 5km to 6km walk along a series of small paths to Huàdǐng Peak.

Public transport up to the peak and waterfall is sporadic though you may be able to hook up with a tour bus. Expect to pay about Y20.

There's a CITS (☎ 398 8899) in Tiāntái town at Tiāntái Bīnguǎn.

Buses link the mountain with Hángzhōu, Shàoxīng, Níngbō and Wēnzhōu.

WŪZHÈN 乌镇
☎ 0573

In the north-east corner of Zhèjiāng, the town of Wūzhèn has been around since the late Tang dynasty, but was only recently painstakingly restored and resurrected as a tourist destination. Like Zhōuzhuāng and other places in southern Jiāngsū, Wūzhèn is a water town whose network of waterways and access to the Grand Canal once made it a prosperous place for its trade and production of silk. The ambitious restoration project recreates what Wūzhèn would have been like in the late Qing dynasty. While it's essentially geared toward tourists, residents still live in the old town. Avoid visiting on weekends and holidays when the crowds take away from the experience.

Things to See

Wūzhèn is very small and it's possible to see everything in a few hours. The main street of the **old town**, Dongda Jie, is a narrow path paved with stone slabs and flanked by wooden buildings. You pay an entrance fee at the **main gate** (☎ 871 3991, Daqiao Lu; adult/child Y45/25; open 8am-5pm daily), which covers entry to all of the exhibits. Some of these are workshops, like the **Gongsheng Grains Workshop** (Gōngshēng Zāofāng), an actual distillery churning out a pungent rice wine ripe for the sampling. Next door the **Blue Prints Workshop** (Lán Yìnhuābù Zuòfang) shows the dyeing and printing process for the traditional blue cloth found in the Jiāngnán region. There's a small shop selling the cloth here and it's cheaper than you'll find in Shànghǎi.

Farther down the street and across a small bridge is **Mao Dun's Former Residence** *(Máo Dùn Gùjū)*. Revolutionary writer Mao Dun is a contemporary of Lu Xun and the author of *Spring Silkworms* and *Midnight*. Mao Dun's great-grandfather, a successful merchant, bought the house in 1885 and it's a fairly typical example from the late Qing dynasty. There are photographs, writings and other memorabilia of Mao Dun's life, though not much explanation in English.

At the western end of the old town, around the corner on Changfeng Jie, is an interesting exhibit many visitors miss. The **Huiyuan Pawn House Museum** *(Huìyuán Diǎndàng Bówùguǎn)* was once a famous pawnshop that eventually expanded to branches in Shànghǎi. It's been left intact and despite the lack of English captions, the spartan decor gives a Dickensian feel to the place.

One of the best reasons to visit Wūzhèn is for the live performances of local opera, *Huāgǔ xì* (Flower Drum opera), held throughout the day in the village square and, *píyǐngxì*, the shadow puppet shows in the small theatre beside the square. The puppet shows in particular are great fun and well worth watching.

A good way to enjoy Wūzhèn is to hire a boat at the main gate for Y50.

Places to Stay & Eat
It's possible to see everything in a day trip but if you're on your way between Shànghǎi and Hángzhōu, Wūzhèn is a good stopover.

Zǐyè Dàjiǔdiàn (☎ 871 2401, fax 871 3553, 3 Daqiao Lu) Doubles Y200. Reasonable rooms are available here for Y160 on weekdays. The hotel is south of the old town, a short walk east of the bus station.

There are small *restaurants* clustered near the main gate and at the western end of the old town.

Getting There & Away
If you're coming from Shànghǎi for a day trip, the best way is to take the tour bus from the Shanghai Stadium. The Y128 ticket includes the entrance fee to Wūzhèn and return trip to Shànghǎi (two hours). Alternatively, take a bus from Shànghǎi to Jiāxīng.

Fújiàn 福建

Capital: Fúzhōu
Population: 36.7 million
Area: 120,000 sq km

The coastal region of Fújiàn, known in English as Fukien or Hokkien, has been part of the Chinese empire since the Qin dynasty (221–207 BC), when it was known as Min.

Sea trade transformed the region from a frontier into one of the centres of the Chinese world. During the Song and Yuan dynasties, the coastal city of Quánzhōu was one of the main ports of call on the maritime silk route, which transported not only silk, but textiles, precious stones, porcelain and a host of other valuables. The city was home to more than 100,000 Arab merchants, missionaries and travellers.

Despite a decline in the province's fortunes after the Ming dynasty restricted maritime commerce in the 15th century, the resourcefulness of the Fújiàn people proved itself in the numbers that emigrated to South-East Asia. Ports like Xiàmén were stepping stones for Chinese people heading for Taiwan, Singapore, the Philippines, Malaysia and Indonesia. Overseas links were forged that continue today, contributing much to the modern character of the province.

Most Taiwanese consider Fújiàn to be their ancestral home. The local Fújiàn dialect, Mǐnnánhuà (south-of-the-Min-River-language), is essentially the same as Taiwanese, although both places officially speak Mandarin Chinese. Not surprisingly, the Taiwanese are the biggest investors in Fújiàn and the most frequent visitors.

FÚZHŌU 福州
☎ 0591 • pop 6,500,000

Capital of Fújiàn province, Fúzhōu is an industrial hinterland choked with concrete dust. It can serve as an overnight pit-stop for travellers en route to Xiàmén, Quánzhōu or Wǔyí Shān, but the city itself offers few diversions.

History

Fúzhōu dates back to the 3rd century AD, when it was known as Yěchéng (smelting city). Later it emerged as a major commercial port specialising in the export of tea.

Highlights

- Xiàmén's island of Gǔlàng Yǔ, one of China's most charming pockets of colonial architecture
- Nánpǔtuó Sì, a fascinating temple just outside Xiàmén
- The earth buildings of the Hakka people in remote south-western Fújiàn
- The walled town of Chóngwǔ, not far from Quánzhōu
- Wǔyí Shān, a protected mountain area with scenic rock peaks

Marco Polo, passing through Fúzhōu towards the end of the 13th century, described the city as being so 'well provided with every amenity' as to be a 'veritable marvel'. It is second only to Xiàmén as a centre of Taiwanese investment, and the money that the town has attracted is reflected in a lot of pricey new hotels and restaurants.

Orientation

Fúzhōu's city centre sprawls northward from Mǐn Jiāng. Walking from one end of town to the other will take you more than an hour.

The train station is situated in the northeast of the city, while most of the accommodation is on Wusi Lu, sandwiched between Hualin Lu and Dongda Lu.

FÚJIÀN 福建

Information

The main Bank of China is near the intersection of Wusi Lu and Hudong Lu. It changes travellers cheques and is open weekdays from 8am to 6pm. Another branch is near the KFC on Gutian Lu. The post and telephone office is on the corner of Dong Jie and Bayiqi Lu.

There is an English-friendly China Telecom Internet cafe (☎ 337 3117) located at the intersection of Jintai Lu and Wuyi Beilu. It is open from 8am to 11pm daily, and you will find it on the 2nd floor and charges Y3 per hour.

A large China Travel Service (CTS; Zhōngguó Lǔxíngshè; ☎ 753 6250) is at 128 Wusi Lu, near Huáqiáo Dàshà (see Places to Stay later). It can book plane tickets and has a number of tours to areas around Fújiàn, but it doesn't book train tickets.

The Public Security Bureau (PSB; Gōngānjú; ☎ 782 1104) is at 107 Beihuan Zhonglu, opposite the Sports Centre in the northern part of town.

Things to See

Fúzhōu's sights are minor attractions and the city has few places of historical interest. The areas worth seeing are scattered about the city, which makes travel between them difficult.

In the centre of the city a vast **Mao Ze-dong Statue** (*Máo Zhǔxí Xiàng*), framed by two neon advertisements, presides over a sea of cyclists.

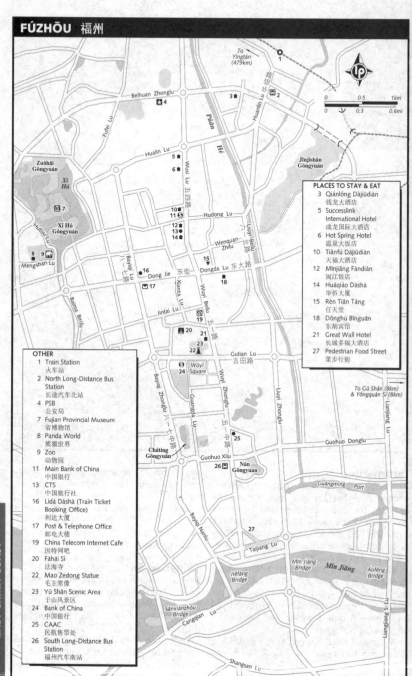

FÚZHŌU 福州

PLACES TO STAY & EAT
3 Qiánlóng Dàjiǔdiàn
钱龙大酒店
5 Successlink
International Hotel
成龙国际大酒店
6 Hot Spring Hotel
温泉大饭店
10 Tiānfú Dàjiǔdiàn
天福大酒店
12 Mǐnjiāng Fàndiàn
闽江饭店
14 Huáqiáo Dàshà
华侨大厦
15 Rèn Tiān Táng
任天堂
18 Dōnghú Bīnguǎn
东湖宾馆
21 Great Wall Hotel
长城多福大酒店
27 Pedestrian Food Street
菜步行街

OTHER
1 Train Station
火车站
2 North Long-Distance Bus
Station
长途汽车北站
4 PSB
公安局
7 Fujian Provincial Museum
省博物馆
8 Panda World
熊猫世界
9 Zoo
动物园
11 Main Bank of China
中国银行
13 CTS
中国旅行社
16 Lìdá Dàshà (Train Ticket
Booking Office)
利达大厦
17 Post & Telephone Office
邮电大楼
19 China Telecom Internet Cafe
因特网吧
20 Fǎhǎi Sì
法海寺
22 Mao Zedong Statue
毛主席像
23 Yú Shān Scenic Area
于山风景区
24 Bank of China
中国银行
25 CAAC
民航售票处
26 South Long-Distance Bus
Station
福州汽车南站

To Yíngtán
(479km)

Beihuan Zhonglu

Huálín Lù

Hualin Lu

Pǔ'ān Hé

Huánlín Lù 华林路

Fúfei Lu

Wusi Lu 五四路

Zuǒhǎi
Gōngyuán

Xī
Hú

Jīnjīshān
Gōngyuán

Xī Hú
Gōngyuán

Hútóu Lu

Hudong Lu

Luyi Beilu 六一北路

Wenquan
Zhilu

Bayiqi Beilu 八一七北路

Mengshan Lu

Dong Jie

Dongda Lu 东大路

Xianta Lu

Jintai Lu

Wuyi Beilu

Baima Beilu

Wúyī
Square

Gutian Lu
古田路

Wuyi
Zhonglu

Luyi
Zhonglu

To Gǔ Shān (8km)
& Yǒngquán Sì (8km)

Bayiqi Zhonglu 八一七中路

Guangda Lu

Wuyi
Zhonglu

Cháting
Gōngyuán

Guohuo Xilu

Nán
Gōngyuán

Guohuo Donglu

Lianjiang Lu

Bayiqi Nanlu

Taijiang Lu

Jiěfàng
Bridge

Guǎngmíng Port

Mǐn Jiāng

Áofēng
Bridge

Sānxiànzhōu
Bridge

Cangqian Lu

Mǐn Jiāng
Bridge

Liangjiang Lu

Shangsan Lu

EAST CHINA COAST

LP

0   0.5   1km
0   0.3   0.6mi

Right behind Mao is the **Yú Shān Scenic Area** *(Yú Shān Fēngjǐngqū)*, which has some remains of the old city walls and is a pleasant place for a stroll.

In the north-west of Fúzhōu is **Xīhú Gōngyuán** *(West Lake Park; admission Y6; open 6am-10pm daily)*. At the time of writing, the park was being re-landscaped and the **Fujian Provincial Museum** *(Fújiàn Shěng Bówùguǎn)*, just inside the park, was closed due to reconstruction.

Next to the lake is the **Zoo** *(Dòng-wùyuán; admission Y6; open 8am-6pm daily)*, home to an unremarkable collection of animals, and **Panda World** *(Xióngmāo Shìjiè; ☎ 372 6522, 88 Shan Gang; admission Y25; open 8.30am-5.30pm daily)* where you can watch this protected species riding bicycles and 'eating Western food'.

About 10km east of the town, on **Gǔ Shān** *(Drum Hill)*, is **Yǒngquán Sì** *(Gushing Spring Monastery; admission Y6; open daily)*. The hill takes its name from a large, drum-shaped rock at the summit that apparently makes a racket when it's stormy. The monastery dates back 1000 years and is said to house a collection of 30,000 Buddhist scriptures, of which 657 are written in blood. You can take bus Nos 7 and 36 (Y2) from Gutian Lu; from there it's a fifteen-minute minivan ride (Y5) or one-hour walk.

Places to Stay – Budget

Hotel prices in Fúzhōu have come down recently and there are now a few budget options. Cheap hotels near the train station don't seem to take foreigners, but you can always try your luck.

Qiánlóng Dàjiǔdiàn *(☎ 759 8888, fax 759 8188, 376 Hualin Lu)* Singles/doubles Y138/338. This reasonable hotel, complete with business centre and nightclub, has clean, bright rooms. It's close to the train station.

Great Wall Hotel *(Chángchéng Duōfú Dàjiǔdiàn; ☎ 752 0388, fax 752 1945, 172 Wuyi Beilu)* Singles/doubles/triples Y148/348/238. Recently renovated, attractive rooms, and a good location near the centre of the city make this hotel a good deal.

Tiānfú Dàjiǔdiàn *(☎ 781 2328, fax 781 2308, 138 Wusi Lu)* Singles/doubles Y198/268. Rooms are attractive and the staff friendly at this three-star hotel.

Places to Stay – Mid-Range

Dōnghú Bīnguǎn *(☎ 755 7755, fax 755 5519, 73 Dongda Lu)* Old doubles Y158, standard doubles Y230-400. This is a large, well-equipped place with a hot spring swimming pool and a whole range of rooms, including old but adequate doubles in its No 2 building. Discounts of 15% are available.

Huáqiáo Dàshà *(Overseas Chinese Hotel; ☎ 755 7603, fax 755 0648, 116 Wusi Lu)* Doubles Y350-465. This hotel is a bit nicer than the Dōnghú, and offers discounts of 25%.

Mǐnjiāng Fàndiàn *(☎ 755 7895, 755 1489, fax 755 1489, 4-5 Wusi Lu)* Doubles Y400-430, suites Y1280. This classy hotel has a range of pleasant rooms and suites. The indoor courtyard features a 'floating bar' with a waterfall and pseudo-bridge, and the tea house is attractively decorated with boat hulls.

Places to Stay – Top End

Successlink International Hotel *(Chénglóng Guójì Dàjiǔdiàn; ☎ 782 2888, fax 782 1888, 252 Wusi Lu)* Standard doubles Y396-578, suites Y880-1288. This well-equipped hotel features a billiard room, Western restaurant, bars, a sauna and a weights room.

Hot Spring Hotel *(Wēnquán Dàfàndiàn; ☎ 785 1818, fax 783 5150, 218 Wusi Lu)* Rooms Y988-1380, suites Y1780-5280. Nearby Successlink, this place has all the facilities expected in a five-star hotel, as well as natural hot spring water in the bathrooms.

Places to Eat

Digging up cheap eats is no problem in Fúzhōu. The best place to head is Wenquan Zhilu, which is full of *restaurants* and *bars*. For cheap noodles and dumplings in a lively nocturnal environment, locals head south to **Taijiang Lu** – an ancient pedestrian street *(cài bùxíngjiē)* lined with Ming dynasty-style wooden buildings and lanterns. Take bus No 51 from Wusi Lu to get there.

Rèn Tiān Táng *(☎ 761 3228, 28 Dongda Lu)* Dishes from Y15. Traditional dishes like *gōngbào jīdīng* (gongbao chicken) and *hóngshāo qiézi* (stir-fried eggplant) are served at this cosy bar/restaurant, which also has an English menu.

Getting There & Away

Air Civil Aviation Administration of China (CAAC; Zhōngguó Mínháng; ☎ 334 5988) has an office on Wuyi Zhonglu. Dōnghú Bīnguǎn also has a large air ticketing centre. Daily flights are available to major destinations such as Běijīng (Y1530, 2½ hours) Guǎngzhōu (Y800, one hour), Shànghǎi (Y730, 70 minutes), Hong Kong (Y1610, 80 minutes) and Wǔyí Shān (Y480, 30 minutes).

Bus There are two long-distance bus stations in town: one in the north near the train station, and one at the southern end of town, down from the CAAC office. Most services are available from both.

There are economy buses to Guǎngzhōu (Y260, 18 hours), Shànghǎi (Y278, 24 hours), Wēnzhōu (Y151, 10 hours), Quánzhōu (Y60, 3½ hours) and Xiàmén (Y50, six hours). Deluxe buses to Guǎngzhōu (Y280, 16 hours) and Shēnzhèn (Y280, 13 hours) depart from the south bus station. Luxury buses travel to Xiàmén (Y80, 4½ hours) and depart from the north bus station and direct buses to Hong Kong (Y334, 15 hours) leave from both stations. Night buses leave the north bus station for Wǔyí Shān (Y90, eight hours).

Train The train line from Fúzhōu heads north-west and connects the city with the main Shànghǎi-Guǎngzhōu line at the Yīngtán junction. Two branch lines split from the Fúzhōu-Yīngtán line and go to Xiàmén and Wǔyí Shān (Y47, seven hours). The rail route to Xiàmén is circuitous, so you're better off taking the bus.

There are direct trains from Fúzhōu to Běijīng, Shànghǎi and Nánchāng. It's fairly easy to buy tickets at the train station, from a spot about 100m to the left of the main train station building, when you are facing it. Many hotels will book train tickets for a service fee and there's also a ticket outlet in town in the entrance of the Lìdá Dàshà building, opposite the post office, which is open from 8am to 5pm daily.

Getting Around

Fúzhōu is a sprawling city, which makes it difficult to get around by foot. Taxi flag fall is Y10. There's a good bus network and bus maps are available at the train station or

hotels. Bus No 51 travels from the train station along Wuyi Lu, and bus No 1 goes to Xī Hú from Bayiqi Lu.

XIÀMÉN 厦门
☎ 0592 • pop 1,250,000
Xiàmén is a bustling, metropolitan city that has a relaxing, coastal charm.

The neighbouring island of Gǔlàng Yǔ is an enchanting retreat of meandering lanes and shaded backstreets, set in an architectural twilight of colonial villas and crumbling remains. It's well worth spending a few days exploring the place.

History

Xiàmén, also known as Amoy, was founded around the mid-14th century, in the early years of the Ming dynasty. A town had been in existence at the site since the Song dynasty, but the Ming built the city walls and established Xiàmén as a major seaport and commercial centre.

In the 17th century it became a place of refuge for the Ming rulers fleeing the Manchu invaders. Xiàmén and nearby Jīnmén were bases for the Ming armies who, under the command of the pirate-general Koxinga, had as their battle-cry, 'resist the Qing and restore the Ming'.

The Portuguese arrived in the 16th century, followed by the British in the 17th century and later by the French and the Dutch, all of whom attempted rather unsuccessfully to establish Xiàmén as a trade port.

The port was closed to foreigners in the 1750s and it was not until the Opium War that the tide turned. In August 1841 a British naval force of 38 ships carrying artillery and soldiers sailed into Xiàmén harbour, forcing the port to open. Xiàmén then became one of the first treaty ports.

Japanese and Western powers followed soon after, establishing consulates and making the island of Gǔlàng Yǔ a foreign enclave. Xiàmén turned Japanese in 1938 and remained that way until 1945.

Just 2km offshore from Xiàmén, the islands of Jīnmén and Xiǎo Jīnmén have been occupied by Taiwanese Nationalist troops since the Communist takeover in 1949. When the People's Liberation Army (PLA) began bombing them in 1958, the USA's mutual security pact with Taiwan very nearly led to war between China and the

XIÀMÉN & GǓLÀNG YǓ 厦门、鼓浪屿

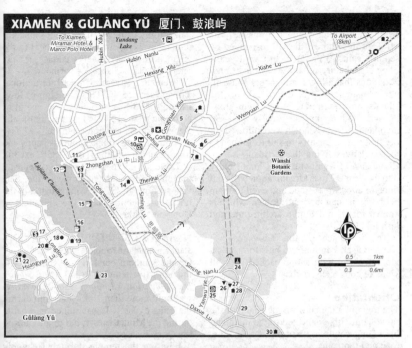

XIÀMÉN & GǓLÀNG YǓ

PLACES TO STAY & EAT

2 Xiamen Plaza Hotel
东南亚大酒店
4 Singapore Hotel
新加坡酒店
6 Xiàmén Bīnguǎn
厦门宾馆
7 Báilù Bīnguǎn
白鹭宾馆
11 Lùjiāng Dàshà
鹭江大厦
14 Holiday Inn; American
Express; Silk Air
假日皇冠海景大酒店
19 Lǜzhōu Jiǔdiàn
绿洲酒店
20 Lìzhīdǎo Jiǔdiàn
丽之岛酒店
26 Dàfāng Sùcàiguǎn
大方素菜馆
27 Gōngdé Sùcàiguǎn
功德素菜馆
28 Xiamen University
Hotel; Fēngyún
Wǎngbā (Internet)
厦门大学国际学术
交流中心；风云网吧

30 Overseas Student
Dormitory
蔡清洁楼

OTHER

1 Long-Distance Bus
Station
长途汽车站
3 Train Station
厦门火车站
5 Zhōngshān Gōngyuán
中山公园
8 PSB
公安局外事科
9 Main Post & Telephone
Office
邮电局
10 Zéyǔ Wǎngbā
(Internet)
泽宇网吧
12 Ferry Terminal (to
Gǔlàng Yǔ)
轮渡码头 (往鼓浪屿)
13 Bank of China; Hong
Kong Bank; CITS
中国银行；香港银行；
中国国际旅行社

15 Hépíng Pier
和平码头
16 Ferry Terminal
(to Xiàmén)
轮渡码头（往厦门）
17 Bank of China
中国银行
18 Xiamen Seaworld
厦门海底世界
21 Koxinga Memorial
Hall
郑成功纪念馆
22 Sunlight Rock;
Rìguāng Yán
Gōngyuán
日光岩；
日光岩公园
23 Statue of Koxinga
郑成功塑像
24 Nánpǔtuó Sì
南普陀寺
25 China Telecom
Internet Cafe
因特网吧
29 Xiamen University
厦门大学

US. Similar tensions resurfaced in early 1996 when China conducted missile tests off Taiwan's shores; the US responded by sending ships to the area. In recent years, more conciliatory relations have led to negotiations that allow mainlanders and Chinese businesses greater access to the islands, now referred to as the 'mini-links' between both countries. In early 2001, 90 mainlanders from Xiàmén were allowed for the first time in history to sail to Jīnmén to meet relatives living there. Businesses in China and Taiwan hope that China's entry into the World Trade Organization will continue to allow freer trade and even tourism between the mainland and Jīnmén, which is known for its old Fujian architecture and lush hiking trails.

The influence of the Taiwanese on Xiàmén itself continues to be strong. It's a vibrant place, with shops packed with all kinds of consumer goodies.

Orientation

The town of Xiàmén is on the island of the same name. It's connected to the mainland by a long causeway bearing a train line, road and footpath.

The interesting part of Xiàmén is the western (waterfront) district, directly opposite the small island of Gǔlàng Yǔ. This is the old area of town, known for its quaint architecture, parks and winding streets.

The central district around the train station and the district farther to the east are soulless places, a jumble of high-rises and featureless, numbing architecture.

Information

The Bank of China is at 10 Zhongshan Lu, near Lùjiāng Dàshà. It has an ATM and is open weekdays from 9am to 5pm. A branch of the Hong Kong Bank with similar hours is also located just behind the Bank of China. There's an American Express office (☎ 212 0268) in Room 212 on the 2nd floor of the Holiday Inn (see Places to Stay later).

Xiàmén's main post and telephone office is on the corner of Xinhua Lu and Zhongshan Lu.

There are Internet cafes scattered around the western district. Zéyǔ Wǎngbā (☎ 207 6300), at 349 Zhongshan Lu, is open until 1am. A China Telecom Internet cafe near Xiamen University, on Yanwu Jie, is open daily from 10am to 11pm. The 24-hour Internet cafe Fēngyún Wǎngbā is next to the Xiamen University Hotel (see Places to Stay later). All cafes charge Y4 per hour.

There are several China International Travel Service (CITS; Zhōngguó Guójì Lǚxíngshè) offices around town. The most convenient (☎ 212 6917) is next door to the Bank of China on Zhongshan Lu.

Xiàmén wants to make tourists happy and has a complaints hotline (☎ 800 8582 ext 36).

There's a large PSB complex opposite the main post and telephone office. The visa section (☎ 226 2203) is located in the north-east section, near the entrance on Gongyuan Xilu.

Nánpǔtuó Sì 南普陀寺
Southern Buddhist Temple

On the southern outskirts of Xiàmén city, this attractive temple (☎ 208 6490, Siming Lu; admission Y3; open 8am-5pm daily) was built more than 1000 years ago during the Tang dynasty. It was ruined in a battle during the Ming dynasty, but rebuilt during the Qing dynasty.

Entering the temple through **Heavenly King Hall** (Tiānwáng Diàn) you are met by Milefo (Laughing Buddha), with the four heavenly kings on either side. The classical Chinese inscription reads: 'When entering, regard Buddha and afterwards pay your respects to the four kings of heaven.'

Behind Milefo is Wei Tuo, a Buddhist deity who safeguards the doctrine. He holds a stick that points to the ground, indicating that the temple is rich and can provide visiting monks with board and lodging (if the stick is held horizontally it means the temple is poor and is a polite way of saying 'find somewhere else to stay').

In front of the courtyard is the **Great Heroic Treasure Hall** (Dàxióngbǎo Diàn), a two-storey building containing three Buddhas that represent Buddha in his past, present and future lives.

The biography of Buddha and the story of Xuan Zang, the monk who made the pilgrimage to India to bring back the Buddhist scriptures, are carved on the lotus-flower base of the Buddha figure. In the corridors flanking the temple are the 18 arhats (monks who reach nirvana) in their customary positions.

Mastering martial arts at Shàolín Sì, Hénán.

Buddha at the Cloud Ridge Caves, Shǎnxī.

A long day in Zhèngzōu, Hénán.

Breath-taking view of Wǔlíng Shān from Tiānzǐshān, Húnán.

Lóngmén Grottoes, Hénán

Tǎyuàn Sì, sacred Buddhist mountain area of Wǔtái Shān, Shānxī.

Xī'ān, Shaanxi, is one of the few cities in China where the ancient city walls are still visible.

It's a long trek up the 2200m-high granite peaks of Huá Shān, Shaanxi.

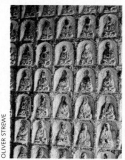

10,000 Buddhas, Lóngmén

The **Great Compassion Hall** *(Dàbēi Dìan)* contains four statues of Guanyin (the Goddess of Mercy). Worshippers cast divining sticks at the feet of the statues to seek heavenly guidance.

The temple has a *vegetarian restaurant* in a nice shady courtyard where you can dine in the company of resident monks.

Take bus No 1 from the train station or No 21 from Zhongshan Lu to reach the temple.

Xiamen University 厦门大学
Xiàmén Dàxué

Xiamen University is next to Nánpǔtuó Sì and was established with overseas Chinese funds. It features an attractive lake and makes for a pleasant stroll. The campus entrance is next to the stop for bus No 1. At the southern entrance to the university there's a pleasant beach, which is also the terminus for bus No 2.

Places to Stay

By far the best area to stay is on Gǔlàng Yǔ (see the Gǔlàng Yǔ section later). It lacks any real budget places but it will make your stay in Xiàmén both memorable and relaxing. In Xiàmén city the western district around the harbour, park or university area has a few decent places to stay.

Lodging becomes expensive and hard to find around the first week of September, when a large investment fair takes place in the city.

Places to Stay – Budget

Overseas Student Dormitory (Càiqīngjié Loú; ☎ 208 4528, fax 208 6774, *Xiamen University)* Doubles/triples Y150/170. Rooms here are usually taken up by foreign students from September to June. To reach the dormitory walk uphill for about 100m from the university's south gate, then take a left and look out for a purple 10-storey building.

Singapore Hotel (Xīnjiāpō Jiǔdiàn; ☎ 202 6668, fax 202 5950, 113-121 *Xian Lu)* Doubles Y190-230. Conveniently located next to Zhōngshān Gōngyuán, this hotel has clean, adequate rooms.

Báilù Bīnguǎn (☎ 202 5201, fax 202 5721, 6 *Huyuan Lu)* Singles/doubles Y180/350. This hotel is also close to Zhōngshān Gōngyuán and has reasonable standard rooms.

Places to Stay – Mid-Range

Most accommodation in Xiàmén is mid-range, shading top end. It's really only worth considering the hotels near the harbour.

Lùjiāng Dàshà (☎ 202 2922, fax 202 4644, 54 *Lujiang Lu)* Singles Y320, doubles Y468-988. This hotel, in a 1940s Chinese-style building, has a prime location opposite the Gǔlàng Yǔ ferry terminal. They often have good deals, and some rooms have ocean views. Add a 10% service charge to your bill.

Xiàmén Bīnguǎn (☎ 202 2265, fax 202 1765, 16 *Huyuan Lu)* Doubles Y214-500. This large, stately place has a certain colonial elegance, and a swimming pool.

Xiamen University Hotel (Xiàmén Dàxué Guójì Xuéshù Jiāoliú Zhōngxīn; ☎ 208 7988, fax 208 6116, *Xiamen University)* Doubles Y310-410. This comfortable hotel, located on the pleasant grounds just inside Xiamen University's north gate, has bright, clean standard rooms. There is sometimes a 20% discount.

Places to Stay – Top End

There is a wide range of top-end accommodation in Xiàmén, but much of it is badly located in the eastern part of town. Most places offer 50% discounts. Add a 12% to 15% service charge to all prices.

Holiday Inn (Jiàrì Huángguān Hǎijǐng Dàjiǔdiàn; ☎ 202 3333, fax 203 6666, 12-8 *Zhenhai Lu)* Doubles US$160-820. The Holiday Inn is the best place to stay. It also has some of the best international and Chinese restaurants in town.

Marco Polo Hotel (Mǎgē Bōluō Dōngfāng Dàjiǔdiàn; ☎ 509 1888, Ⓦ www .marcopolohotels.com, 8 *Jianye Lu)* Rooms US$160-225, suites US$295-980. This posh hotel, on a small street off of Hubin Beilu, tries hard to please the business traveller. Its facilities include a pool, bar, and Chinese and Japanese restaurants.

Xiamen Miramar Hotel (Xiàmén Měilìhuá Dàjiǔdiàn; ☎ 603 1666, fax 602 1814, *Xinglong Lu)* Rooms US$85-168. Although a little austere, the Miramar offers comfortable, reasonable rooms. It's popular with Chinese and Japanese business travellers.

Xiamen Plaza Hotel (Xiàmén Dōngnányà Dàjiǔdiàn; ☎ 505 8888, fax 505 8899, 908 *Xiahe Lu)* Rooms Y918-1330. Beside the train station, the elegant but uncharismatic Xiamen Plaza has standard rooms.

Places to Eat

Xiàmén is brimming with places to eat. All the alleys off Zhongshan Lu harbour cheap eats. Head down Jukou Jie, near the intersection with Siming Lu, which offers a plethora of *Sìchuān restaurants*.

Near the university, good, cheap, attractive restaurants line Siming Nanlu and Yanwu Jie. Two cheap vegetarian restaurants are *Dàfāng Sùcàiguǎn* (☎ 209 3236, 412-4 Siming Nanlu) and *Gōngdé Sùcàiguǎn* (☎ 291 0033, 418-10 Siming Nanlu). Try the monk's vegetables (*luóhàn zhāifàn*).

The *Holiday Inn* has a good coffee shop, a bakery and an Italian restaurant.

Getting There & Away

Air Xiamen Airlines is the main airline under the CAAC banner in this part of China. There are innumerable ticket offices around town, many of which are in the larger hotels like the Holiday Inn.

CAAC has flights to Hong Kong, Kuala Lumpur, Manila, Penang and Singapore. Silk Air (☎ 205 3280) flies to Singapore and has an office in the Holiday Inn. All Nippon Airways (☎ 573 2888) flies to Osaka and has ticketing agents at the Holiday Inn and Lùjiāng Dàshà. Dragonair (☎ 202 5433) is located in the Marco Polo Hotel.

Xiàmén airport has flights to all major domestic destinations around China, including Wǔyí Shān (Y470) four times a week. Airport departure tax is Y90.

Bus Deluxe and economy buses leave from the long-distance bus station and the ferry terminal. Destinations include Fúzhōu (Y80), Quánzhōu (Y32, 1½ hours) and Shàntóu (Y100, five hours). There are also express buses to Guǎngzhōu (Y200, 12 hours), Shēnzhèn (Y180, nine hours) and Hong Kong (Y350, 10 hours). Buses also make trips inland to Lóngyán (Y44, three hours) and Yǒngdìng (Y37, five hours).

Train From Xiàmén there are direct trains to destinations including Hángzhōu (Y250, 23 hours), Shànghǎi (Y300, 25 hours), Běijīng (Y390, 39 hours) and Wǔyí Shān (Y142 sleeper, 14 hours). The train to Fúzhōu takes a circuitous route – the bus is cheaper and quicker. Book tickets at the train station or through CITS who will make bookings for a Y35 service fee.

Boat Unfortunately, the boat to Hong Kong from Xiàmén's Hépíng Pier has been discontinued.

Getting Around

The airport is 15km north-east of the waterfront district, about 8km from the eastern district. From the waterfront, taxis cost around Y35. Bus No 27 travels from the airport to the ferry terminal via the train station.

Frequent minibuses run between the train station and ferry terminal (Y1). Buses to Xiamen University go from the train station (bus No 1) and from the ferry terminal (bus No 2). Taxis start at Y7.

GǓLÀNG YǓ 鼓浪屿

A five-minute boat trip from Xiàmén takes you to this sleepy island of winding paths, creeper-laden trees, Christian cemeteries and almost-Mediterranean flavours. By 1860, the foreign powers had residencies that were well established on Gǔlàng Yǔ and, as the years rolled by, churches, hospitals, post and telegraph offices, libraries, hotels and consulates were built.

In 1903 the island was officially designated an International Foreign Settlement, and a municipal council with a police force of Sikhs was established to govern it. Today, memories of the settlement linger in the charming colonial buildings that blanket the island and the sound of classical piano wafting from shuttered windows. Many of China's most celebrated musicians have come from Gǔlàng Yǔ.

The best way to enjoy the island is to wander along the streets, peeking into courtyards and down alleys to catch a glimpse of colonial architecture seasoned by local life. Most sights and hotels are just a short walk from the ferry terminal.

Things to See

The most prominent attraction on the island is **Sunlight Rock** (*Rìguāng Yán*) – the island's highest point at 93m. On a clear day you can see the island of Jīnmén.

At the foot of the Sunlight Rock is a large colonial building known as the **Koxinga Memorial Hall** (*Zhèngchénggōng Jìniànguǎn; open 8am-11am & 2pm-5pm daily*). The hall has an exhibition partly dedicated to the Dutch in Taiwan, and partly to Koxinga's throwing them out. Both sights are located in **Rìguāng Yán Gōngyuán** *(Sunlight Rock Park; admission Y60; open 8am-7pm daily)*. Locals say you can avoid the entry fee by going before 8am.

Near the ferry terminal is **Xiamen Seaworld** *(Xiàmén Hǎidǐ Shìjiè;* ☎ *206 7668, 2 Longtou Lu; admission Y70; open 8am-6pm daily)*. An impressive collection of penguins, seals, dolphins, and exotic fish swim around in cramped tanks. Their immense shark tank is viewed via a tubular passageway.

Places to Stay & Eat

Lìzhīdǎo Jiǔdiàn (Beautiful Island Hotel of Gulangyu; ☎ *206 3309, fax 206 3311, 133 Longtou Lu)* Singles/doubles Y120/168. This quaintly named hotel is airy, bright and has clean, cosy rooms. The cheapest rooms have no windows.

Lùzhōu Jiǔdiàn (☎ *206 5390, fax 206 5390, 1 Longtou Lu)* Doubles Y198-268, triples Y368. This new hotel, across from the ferry terminal, has bright, spanking clean rooms. Some rooms have ocean views.

Gǔlàng Yǔ is the place to go for seafood. Chinese travellers report that seafood here is fresher and cheaper than places like Hǎinán Dǎo. Meals swim around in buckets and trays outside the restaurants. For budget eats, wander up Longtou Lu towards Lìzhīdǎo Jiǔdiàn, where there are many small *restaurants* and *stalls*.

Getting There & Away

Ferries to Gǔlàng Yǔ leave from the ferry terminal just west of Xiàmén's Lùjiāng Dàshà. Tickets are Y3 going over plus Y1 for the top deck. The return trip from Gǔlàng Yǔ is free, or Y1 for the top.

AROUND XIÀMÉN

The **Jimei School Village** *(Jíměi Xuéxiào Cūn)* is a much-touted tourist attraction on the mainland north of Xiàmén. The school was set up in 1913 by Tan Kahkee, a native of the area who migrated to Singapore and became a wealthy industrialist. He returned some of that wealth to the mother country, and the school now has around 20,000 students. Most tourists head to the surrounding **Memorial Park** *(Jíměi Yuán;* ☎ *610 1713; admission Y10; open 7.30am-5.30pm daily)*. The Chinese pagodas are attractive and the waters in front of the school are the site of a dragon-boat race at the Dragon Boat Festival

Words & Pictures

Cūn: village

村 The left side of this character is *mù*, which means 'trees' or 'wood'; the right side is *cùn*, which means 'inch', 'measurement' or 'regulations'. In ancient China, a household with an acre of land would often be surrounded by mulberry trees grown for silk worms. Thus, a village is somewhere trees are planted according to rules and regulations!

(usually around mid-June). Take bus No 66 or 67 from near the waterfront, on the corner of Zhongshan Lu and Tongwen Lu.

YŎNGDÌNG 永定
☎ 0597

Yŏngdìng is an out-of-the-way place in south-west Fújiàn. Set in a rural area dominated by small mountains and farmland, it wouldn't be worth a footnote, but for its unusual architecture. Known as 'earth buildings' *(tǔlóu)*, these large, circular edifices resemble fortresses and were probably designed for defence. They were built by the Hakka, one of China's ethnic minorities. Some are still inhabited today.

Coming from Hénán in northern China, the Hakka people first moved to Guǎngdōng and Fújiàn to escape severe persecution in their homelands. The name Hakka means 'guests'; today Hakka communities are scattered all over South-East Asia.

There are no tǔlóu in Yŏngdìng itself. One of the main buildings sought out by visitors is the Zhènchénglóu, 43km northeast of Yŏngdìng, in Húkēng. Frequent minibuses travel there from the Yŏngdìng bus station (Y7, 1½ hours). Other buildings are scattered around the villages south-east of Yŏngdìng – Hóngkēng, Xiàyáng, Gǔzhú, and Dàxī – you'll have to hire a driver to get to them. Yŏngdìng is accessed by bus from Guǎngdōng, Xiàmén (Y52, five hours) or Lóngyán (Y7/15 without/with air-con, one hour).

QUÁNZHŌU 泉州

☎ 0595 • pop 7,400,000

Quánzhōu was once a great, international port city and an instrumental stop on the maritime silk route. Marco Polo, back in the 13th century, called it Zaiton and informed his readers that '...it is one of the two ports in the world with the biggest flow of merchandise'. It's slipped a few pegs since then, but Quánzhōu still has a few products of note, including the creamy-white *déhuà* (or 'blanc-de-Chine' as it is known in the West) porcelain figures, and locally crafted puppets.

Prettier and cleaner than Fúzhōu, evidence of Quánzhōu's Muslim population can still be detected among the city's residents and buildings. Quánzhōu's prime attraction is Kāiyuán Sì, which offers a relaxing retreat.

Orientation & Information

The PSB office (☎ 218 0308) and the main post and telephone office are on Dong Jie. There's a Bank of China branch on Jiuyi Jie that also exchanges travellers cheques. It's open weekdays from 9am to 5pm. Quánzhōu's many Internet cafes are clustered together on Wenhua Jie, and charge around Y3 per hour.

Things to See

Kāiyuán Sì (☎ 238 6275, 176 Xi Jie; admission Y4; open 6am-6pm daily) is in the north-west of the city and can be distinguished by its pair of tall pagodas and the huge grounds in which it is set.

Originally called Liánhūa Sì (Lotus Temple), construction began in AD 686. In AD 738, during the reign of the famous Tang emperor Tang Minghuang, the name was changed to Kāiyuán.

The temple reached its peak during Song times when it became home to 1000 monks. The present buildings, including the pagodas and the main hall, are more recent. The main courtyard is the refuge of some huge, ancient trees, one of which has a drooping branch supported by a carved pillar.

Within the grounds of Kāiyuán Sì, behind the eastern pagoda, is a **museum** containing the enormous hull of a Song dynasty seagoing junk, which was recently excavated near Quánzhōu. A ride to the temple by mini-van taxi from the long-distance bus station will cost Y6, or take bus No 2 from Wenling Nanlu.

There are some charming little side streets off Xi Jie; take a pedicab to Kāiyuán Sì from the south of Quánzhōu and the driver will probably take you down the maze of winding streets that lead there.

Quánzhōu is studded with small temples and can make for an interesting ramble. The pleasant **Qīngjìng Sì** (Peaceful Mosque; ☎ 219 3553, 113 Tumen Jie; admission Y2; open 8am-6pm daily) is one of China's only surviving mosques from the Tang dynasty. A small museum with signs in English describes the history of Quánzhōu's once large Muslim community.

Places to Stay

Huáqiáo Zhījiā (Overseas Chinese Home; ☎ 228 3559, fax 228 3560, 147-149 Wenling Nanlu) Singles/doubles Y100/130, triples Y130-180. Rooms at this hotel near the bus station are cheap but on the frumpy side.

Jiànfú Dàshà (☎ 228 3511, fax 218 8850, 150 Wenling Nanlu) Singles Y200, doubles Y320-370, suites Y450. This hotel's clean, comfortable rooms are a pretty good deal. Discounts of up to 50% are possible.

Jīnzhōu Dàjiǔdiàn (☎ 258 6788, fax 257 0057, 106 Quanxiu Jie) Small/large doubles Y200/260. Rooms at this hotel, also near the bus station, are a bit run-down, but adequate. There is a possible 35% discount.

Huáqiáo Dàshà (Overseas Chinese Hotel; ☎ 228 2192, fax 228 4612, Baiyuan Lu) North-building doubles Y350-370, south-building doubles Y190-540, suites Y740. The best value in Quánzhōu is at this three-star property, which has a pool, bowling alley, and restaurants. The south building has nice, recently renovated doubles and some cheaper doubles.

Places to Eat

The are loads of small *restaurants* and *bakeries* in the area surrounding Kāiyuán Sì. A nightly *food market* (Baiyuan Lu) sets up in front of Huáqiáo Dàshà. For some reason, restaurants in the centre of town are hard to find outside of the hotels. For self-catering, try the **Huáxīng Chāoshí supermarket** (1 Quanxiu Jie).

Blue & White (Lánhébái; ☎ 531 8656, 98 Quanxiu Jie) This chain restaurant is

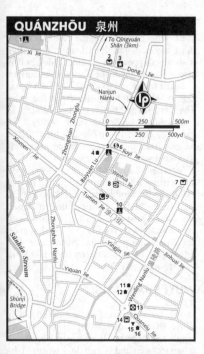

QUÁNZHŌU 泉州

QUÁNZHŌU

PLACES TO STAY & EAT
4 Huáqiáo Dàshà
   华侨大厦
11 Jiànfú Dàshà
   建福大厦
12 Huáqiáo Zhījiā
   华侨之家
15 Blue & White
   篮和白快餐
16 Jīnzhōu Dàjiǔdiàn
   金州大酒店

OTHER
1 Kāiyuán Sì
   开元寺
2 Main Post &Telephone Office
   邮电局
3 PSB
   公安局
5 Tóngfó Sì
   铜佛寺
6 Bank of China
   中国银行
7 Post &Telephone Office
   邮电局
8 Internet Cafes
   因特网吧
9 Qīngjìng Sì
   清净寺
10 Guāndì Miào
   关帝庙
13 Huáxīng Chāoshì (Supermarket)
   华星超市
14 Long-Distance Bus Station
   泉州汽车站

open late and offers cheap, simple, cafeteria-style meat and vegetable dishes.

Huáqiáo Dàshà (see Places to Stay earlier) The restaurant here offers reasonably priced Chinese dishes and traditional Fújiàn specialties like *mínnǎn wǔxiǎngjián*, a dough and pork-filled, deep-fried spring roll.

Getting There, Away & Around

The long-distance bus station is in the southern corner of the city on the intersection of Wenling Nanlu and Quanxiu Jie and serves destinations as far away as Shànghǎi and Guǎngzhōu. Deluxe buses go to Xiàmén (Y32, two hours) and Fúzhōu (Y60, 3½ hours). Slower economy buses are Y18 and Y33.

Trains travel from Quánzhōu to Wǔyí Shān once every few days (Y148 sleeper, 15 hours), leaving from the station 7km east of the city centre.

You can also book tickets for trains originating in Xiàmén or Fúzhōu at two outlets near Tóngfó Sì (Brass Buddha Temple). One is directly across from Huáqiáo Dàshà and the other is across from the Bank of China.

Quánzhōu's most useful bus is No 2 (Y1), which goes from the bus station to Kāiyuán Sì. Minivan taxis can take you to most places for Y6.

AROUND QUÁNZHŌU
Qīngyuán Shān 青原山
Pure Water-Source Mountains
Qīngyuán Shān is a reasonably scenic mountain area 3 km north of Quánzhōu that is scattered with a few caves, tombs and statues.

The **Buddhist Caves** *(Qīngyuán Dòng)* in the mountain were destroyed during the Cultural Revolution, although some people still pray in front of the spaces where the statues used to be.

Also found on the mountain is the 'rock that moves'. It's one of those nicely shaped and balanced rocks that wobbles when you give it a nudge; supposedly to see it move

EAST CHINA COAST

you have to place a stick or a piece of straw lengthways between the rock and the ground and watch it bend as someone pushes on the rock.

The largest statue on the mountain is a stubby Song dynasty effigy of Laozi, legendary founder of Taoism.

Getting There & Away From Quánzhōu, take bus No 3 from the clock tower at the intersection between Xi Jie and Zhongshan Zhonglu.

Chóngwǔ 崇武

One of China's best preserved walled cities, Chóngwǔ is a little-visited marvel, on the coast to the east of Quánzhōu. The granite city walls are around 2.5km long and average 7m in height. Scattered around the walls are 1304 battlements and four gates into the city.

The town wall was built in 1387 by the Ming government as a front line defence against marauding Japanese pirates, and it has survived the last 600 years remarkably well. Koxinga also took refuge here in his battle against Qing forces. The surrounding area is full of stone-carving workshops.

Head up Xinhua Jie to get to the city walls. Along the coast, the **Ancient City Stone Park** *(Gǔchéng Fēngjǐngqū; ☎ 768 3297; admission Y15; open 7am-5pm daily)* consists of over 500 new and ancient statues haphazardly scattered along the cliffs and beach, some of which are eroding attractively into the ocean.

Frequent minibuses depart Quánzhōu's long-distance bus station to nearby Hùi'ān (Y5, 45 minutes). From there minivans departing from the south side of the station go to Chóngwǔ (Y4, 30 minutes).

MÉIZHŌU 湄州
☎ 0594

Halfway between Quánzhōu and Fúzhōu is the county of Pútián. Just offshore is the island of Méizhōu *(admission Y10)*, a peaceful recluse of temples and ocean vistas celebrated by Chinese tourists for its scenic beauty. Taoists credit Méizhōu as being the birthplace of Mazu, Goddess of the Sea. Mazu is known by a number of names: Tin Hau in Hong Kong, Thien Hau in Vietnam, and so on. As protector of sailors and fishing folk, she enjoys VIP status in coastal provinces like Fújiàn.

Mazu's birthday is celebrated according to the lunar calendar, on the 23rd day of the third moon, when the island comes alive with worshippers. In summer, Méizhōu is also a popular spot for Taiwanese tourists.

Māzǔ Miào *(admission Y10)* is a Y2 taxi ride or short uphill walk from the pier. There are several hotels on the island.

Méizhōu Zǔmiào Bīnguǎn *(☎ 509 2319 ext 288, fax 669 4679)* Doubles Y200. Across from the pier this place offers attractive doubles with ocean view.

Méizhōu is a bit inconvenient to visit on a day trip – it might be worth a day or two exploring the temples and beaches. The island is reached by taking a bus to Pútián city from Quánzhōu (Y18, 1½ hours) and then a minibus to Wénjiǎ (Y8, one hour) on the Zhōngwén peninsula. From there, ferries depart hourly between 7am and 6pm (Y6, 15 minutes).

WǓYÍ SHĀN 武夷山
☎ 0599

In the far north-west corner of Fújiàn is Wǔyí Shān, an attractive region of rivers, crags and forests. It recently became a protected area and is certainly worth visiting if you want to get away from towns and cities. Unfortunately, it is also a prime tourist spot and is home to glib-tongued hustlers and would-be guides pursuing tourists in motorised tricycles. It can get crowded during holiday times; the low season (when it's cold) can be a good time to visit.

The scenic area lies on the west bank of Chóngyáng Stream (Chóngyáng Xī), and some of the accommodation is located along its shore. Most of the hotels are concentrated in the resort district *(dùjiàqū)* on the east side of the river. The main settlement is Wǔyíshān city, about 10km to the north-east, with the train station and airport roughly half-way between.

Information
CTS *(☎ 525 2819)* is at the bottom of the driveway leading up to Wǔyí Shānzhuāng (see Places to Stay later), on the west side of the river. It's open daily from 9am to 6pm. CTS and most hotels can book train and plane tickets.

The Bank of China in Wǔyíshān city is on Wujiu Lu and can change travellers cheques. It's open daily from 9am to 5pm. Maps of the Wǔyí Shān area are available at small bookshops in the resort district.

The staff at the CITS (☎ 525 0380) office at 35 Qijianlu Lu, 2nd floor, are also very helpful and can arrange train tickets and tours to surrounding ancient cities. CITS is open from 9am to 4pm Monday to Saturday.

Things to See

The main reason to visit Wǔyí Shān is to walk up to the sheer rock peaks that jut skywards, and take a trip down **Jiǔqū Hé** *(Nine Twists River)* on bamboo rafts. The main entrance is at **Wǔyí Gōng** *(☎ 525 2702; admission Y71; open 6.30am-6.30pm daily)*, about 200m south of the Wǔyí Shānzhuāng, near the confluence of the Chóngyáng and Jiǔqū rivers. The fee includes all other sights, or you can pay individually at each entrance (Y22 to Y30). One way to avoid the fees and the crowds is to visit places at 6am, before the ticket booths open.

A couple of nice walks are the 530m **Great King Peak** *(Dàwáng Fēng)* accessed through the main entrance, and the 410m **Heavenly Tour Peak** *(Tiānyóu Fēng)* where an entrance is reached by road up Jiǔqū Hé. Trails within the scenic area connect all the major sites. At the northern end of the scenic area, the **Water Curtain Cave** *(Shuǐlián Dòng)* is a cleft in the rock about one third of the way up a 100m cliff face. In winter and autumn, water plunges over the top of the cliff creating a curtain of spray.

One of the highlights for visitors is floating down the Jiǔqū Hé. Bamboo rafts (☎ 526 1752), costing Y72 and operating 7am to 5pm daily, are fitted with rattan chairs and depart from Xīngcūn, a short bus ride west of the resort area. The trip down the river takes over an hour.

One of the mysteries of Wǔyí Shān is the cavities carved out of the rock faces at great heights that once held boat-shaped coffins. Scientists have dated some of these artefacts back 4000 years. If you're taking the raft down the river, it's possible to see some remnants of these coffins on the west cliff face of the fourth meander or 'twist', also known as **Small Storing Place Peak** *(Xiǎozàngshān Fēng)*.

Places to Stay

There's a whole range of accommodation in Wǔyí Shān, mostly concentrated on the east side of the river. Consequently, the west side is quieter. Discounts are often available mid-week.

There are a few places scattered on the west bank immediately across from the main bridge spanning Chóngyáng Stream that accept foreigners.

Aǐhú Bīnguǎn (☎ 525 2268, fax 525 2268) Doubles/triples Y160/210. One of the better deals, this quaint, comfortable hotel has a courtyard and rooms with balconies. Turn left just after you cross the river and cross the lawn on your right.

Wǔyí Shānzhuāng (Wuyi Mountain Villa; ☎ 525 1888, fax 525 2567) Doubles Y280-528, suites Y528-1388. Beautiful Chinese fountains, secluded grounds, and a pool make this one of the nicest places in Wǔyí Shān.

The east bank area is packed with hotels: *Yūlín Jiǔdiàn (☎ 525 2206, fax 525 2206)* Singles/triples Y288/368. You can get discounts of up to 45% here if you make the effort to bargain.

Lántíng Fàndiàn (☎ 525 2880, fax 525 2569, Wujiu Lu) Doubles Y360-500. At the southern end of the district, this hotel has comfortable rooms with balconies and scenic views. Discounts of up to 45% are available. There's a good restaurant and an outdoor swimming pool.

Guómaò Dàjiǔdiàn (International Trade Hotel; ☎ 525 2521, fax 525 2891, Wangfeng Lu) Standard doubles Y480-580, suites Y1000. This place has some good amenities, including a Western restaurant, but the surroundings are a little austere.

Getting There & Away

Wǔyí Shān is serviced by flights from Běijīng (Y1100, two hours), Shànghǎi (Y580, one hour), Fúzhōu (Y480, 35 minutes), Xiàmén (Y490, 50 minutes), Guǎngzhōu (Y730, 1½ hours) and Hong Kong (Y1400, two hours).

A bus station (☎ 525 1196) is just in front of Yūlín Jiǔdiàn. Frequent buses go to Xiàmén (Y145), Fúzhōu (Y87), and Shàowǔ (Y15, 1½ hours). The other long-distance bus station is in the north-west part of Wǔyíshān city. Daily buses go south to Fúzhōu (Y90, eight hours), north-east to

Wēnzhōu (Y125, 12 hours), to Nánpíng (Y37, three hours) and north to Shàngráo (Y23, two hours) in Jiāngxī.

Direct trains go to Wǔyí Shān from Fúzhōu, Quánzhōu and Xiàmén. See the Getting There & Away section of those cities for details. CTS can book train tickets for trains stopping in Shàowǔ en route to other destinations such as Shànghǎi and Běijīng.

Getting Around

Minivans or a public bus (Y2) shuttle between Wǔyíshān city and the resort district, and there are minibuses between Wǔyíshān city and Xīngcūn.

Expect to pay about Y10 for a motorised trishaw from the resort district to most of the scenic area entrances. A ride from the train station or airport to the resort district will cost about Y20.

Liáoníng 辽宁

Capital: Shěnyáng
Population: 42.4 million
Area: 145,700 sq km

Once the southernmost province of Manchuria, Liáoníng continues to gleam with a nugget or two of Manchu history. Visitors today, however, are drawn by its beaches, hiking and dynamic city life. Those hoping to get a glimpse into North Korea may also enjoy the pilgrimage to Dāndōng.

The most popular destination for travellers is the enticing refuge of Dàlián. Nicknamed 'the Hong Kong of the North', Dàlián is an innovative and fast-developing city complemented by beautiful historic architecture, clean streets and parkland. This city alone makes a trip to Liáoníng worthwhile.

SHĚNYÁNG 沈阳
☎ 024 • pop 7,200,000
Shěnyáng was a Mongol trading centre as far back as the 11th century, becoming the capital of the Manchu empire in the 17th century. With the Manchu conquest of Běijīng in 1644, Shěnyáng became a secondary capital under the Manchu name of Mukden, and a centre of the ginseng trade.

Industrialisation was introduced by the Russians, who occupied the city at the turn of the century, and continued by the Japanese, the victors of the Russo-Japanese War (1904–05). Throughout its history, Shěnyáng has rapidly changed hands, in turn dominated by warlords, the Japanese (1931), the Russians (1945), the Kuomintang (1946) and the Chinese Communist Party (1948). At the end of WWII, the city was looted of its industrial hardware.

Shěnyáng is, for the most part, a sprawling mass of socialist town planning. Efforts have been made in recent years to beautify the city however, and pedestrian streets such as Zhong Jie are interesting areas to explore, while history buffs will enjoy the well-preserved relics of the Manchu era.

Orientation
Shěnyáng is built on the typical north-south axis of the Qing dynasty, bordered to the

Highlights

- The dynamic port city of Dàlián, with its sea breezes and relaxed atmosphere
- Dāndōng, the gateway to North Korea
- Jǐnzhōu and surrounds, home of the famed feathered dinosaur

south by Hún Hé (Muddy River). Accommodation and sights are scattered all over the city.

Information
Consulates Shěnyáng's US consulate (☎ 2322 1198, visas 2322 2147, fax 2282 0074) is at 52 Shisi Wei Lu in the Heping District. The Japanese consulate (☎ 2322 7530) is next door. There is a North Korean consulate (☎ 8685 2742) in Shěnyáng, however visas are more likely to be obtained in Běijīng. The Russian consulate (☎ 8611 4963) is open from 1.30pm to 3pm, closed Wednesday, Saturday and Sunday, and can be found on the 10th floor of Fènghuáng Fàndiàn (see Places to Stay later).

Money The Bank of China is at 253 Shifu Dalu. There is also a branch in the Traders Shopping Centre. Most large hotels change money.

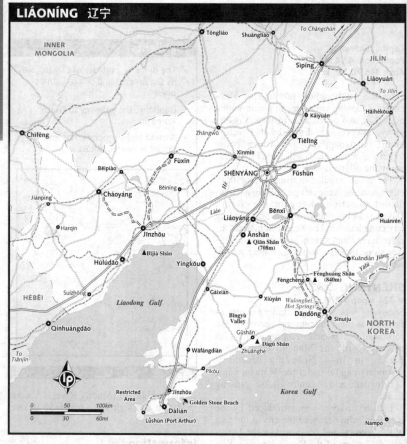

LIÁONÍNG 辽宁

Post & Communications The post office is at 78 Beizhan Lu, right next to Yóuzhèng Dàshà Bīnguǎn (see Places to Stay later). A telephone office can be found at 185 Shifu Dalu. The most convenient Internet cafe is at 25 Zhonghua Lu (☎ 2321 1024), on the corner of Taiyuan Jie. It charges Y2 per hour and is open 24 hours.

PSB The Public Security Bureau (PSB; Gōngānjú; ☎ 2253 4850) can be found at 73 Beizhan Lu, opposite the Gloria Plaza Hotel, on the 4th floor of the Shenyang Service Centre of Foreign Investment.

Travel Agencies You'll find China International Travel Service (CITS; Zhōngguó Guójì Lǚxíngshè; ☎ 8680 9383, fax 8680

8772) at 113 Huanghe Dajie, in a building about 100m north of Fènghuáng Fàndiàn (see Places to Stay later).

Mao Zedong Statue 毛主席像
Máo Zhǔxí Xiàng
The Mao Zedong statue in Zhōngshān Square, at the intersection of Zhongshan Lu and Nanjing Jie, will bring a lump to the throats of art historians, socialist iconographers and students of bad taste. Mao stands aloft, flanked by ecstatic intellectuals, and vociferous peasants, miners and soldiers.

North Tomb 北陵
Běi Líng
The most popular sight in Shěnyáng, the North Tomb (☎ 8689 6294, 12 Taishan Lu;

admission Y13; open 6am-6pm daily) is the burial place of Huang Taiji (1592–1643), the founder of the Qing dynasty (although he did not live to see the conquest of China). Set in a huge park, Běilíng Gōngyuán, the tomb took eight years to build. The impressive animal statues on the approach to the tomb are reminiscent of the Ming tombs and lead up to the central grassy mound known as the Luminous Tomb (Zhāo Líng).

Take bus No 220 from the south train station. Bus No 227 from the Imperial Palace via the east side of the north train station also travels to the North Tomb.

East Tomb 东陵
Dōng Líng
Also known as Fú Líng, this small tomb *(210 Dongling Jie; admission Y10; open 6am-6.30pm daily)* is set in a forested area overlooking a river, 8km from Shěnyáng. Entombed here, along with his mistress, is Nurhachi (1559–1626), grandfather of Emperor Shunzhi, who launched the Manchu invasion of China in 1644.

Take bus No 218 (45 minutes) from the Imperial Palace – see following.

The Imperial Palace 故宫
Gùgōng
The Imperial Palace *(☎ 2282 1999, 171 Shenyang Lu; admission Y35; open 8.30am-5.30pm daily)* is a mini-Forbidden City in layout, although it's far smaller and the features are Manchu. The main structures were started by Nurhachi and completed in 1636 by his son, Huang Taiji.

Straight through the main gate, at the far end of the courtyard, is the main structure: the octagonal Dazheng Hall with its coffered ceiling and elaborate throne. It was here that Emperor Shunzhi was crowned before setting off to cross the Great Wall in 1644.

In the courtyard in front of the hall are the Banner Pavilions, formerly administrative offices used by tribal chieftains.

The central courtyard, west of Dazheng Hall, contains a conference hall, living quarters and some shamanist structures (one Manchu custom was to pour boiling wine into the ear of a sacrificial pig, so that its cries would attract the devotees' ancestors). The courtyard on the western fringe is a residential area added on by Emperor

Qianlong in the 18th century, and the Wensu Pavilion to the rear houses a copy of the Qianlong anthology.

The palace is in the oldest section of the city; take bus No 237 from the south train station, or bus No 227 from the North Tomb via the east side of the north train station.

Běi Tǎ 北塔
North Pagoda
Of the four pagodas that once marked the city boundaries, Běi Tǎ *(27 Beita Jie; admission Y5; open 8.30am-4.30pm daily)* is the best restored.

The pagodas, built in 1643, symbolise the four Buddhist Heaven Kings and were constructed to protect the city and its people.

Within Běi Tǎ, the only original structures to remain are the Great Hall and Falun Temple. The other halls were added in 1984.

The main hall features detailed murals of deities – slightly gruesome but amazing nonetheless, and a wonderful statue of the Sky and Earth Buddha. Within the second hall are two magnificent panelled paintings of city life in the Qing dynasty. They were painted by tutors and students of Shěnyáng's art college in 1984. The final hall contains the Laughing Buddha at his finest – big, gold and jovial with a belly to match.

Bus No 611 or 325 from the north train station, or No 213 from the North Tomb, will drop you in the vicinity of the pagoda.

Wúgòu Jìngguāng Shělì Tǎ
Pagoda of Buddhist Ashes 无垢净光舍利塔
West of the North Tomb, Wúgòu Jìngguāng Shělì Tǎ *(☎ 8678 1651, 22 Taiwan Jie; admission Y5; open 8.30am-5.30pm daily)* is 13m high. This 13-storey brick pagoda dates back to AD 1044. A small museum is also on the grounds and includes relics removed from inside the pagoda. This place is extremely peaceful and is a wonderful escape from the city.

Take bus No 205 from the North Tomb or the south train station and get off at the corner of Taiwan Jie and Ningshan Lu. Walk north, cross the bridge and turn right. The pagoda is a three-minute walk north of here, down an alley on the right. Look for a red gate. Bus No 607 runs from the north train station and bus No 215 from Government Square. Bus No 209 runs from the north train station via Government Square to the pagoda.

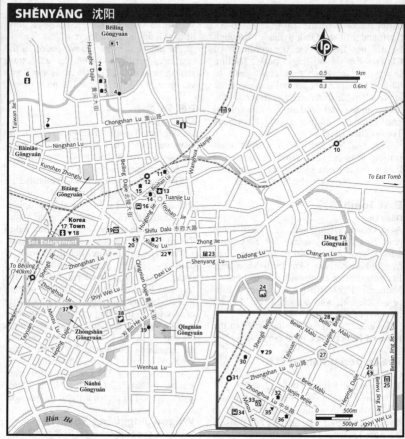

SHĚNYÁNG 沈阳

Liaoning Provincial Museum
Liáoníng Shěng Bówùguǎn
This enormous museum (☎ 2282 2525, 26 Shi Wei Lu; admission Y8; open 9am-4pm Tues-Sun) houses diverse artefacts collected from throughout Liáoníng – from fossils and bones to jade, wall murals and teacups.

On the ground floor is an interesting display of before-and-after photographs of the city – the architecture of Shěnyáng in the early 1900s and the modern delights that have replaced it.

18 September History Museum
Jiǔ Yī Bā Lìshǐ Bówùguǎn 九一八历史博物馆
This museum (☎ 2389 2316, 46 Wanghua Nanjie; admission Y20; open 8.30am-4pm daily) is named after the 18 September

incident, when Shěnyáng was captured by the Japanese on 18 September 1931. The many exhibits explore the Japanese occupation of Manchuria, and although the overall tone is obviously biased, this is the most elaborate and comprehensive museum dedicated to this period of Chinese history.

Gruesome examples of torture on display include a 'rolling cage' (a long metal tube lined with spikes in which prisoners were rolled to death). Not for the faint hearted.

Places to Stay
Yóuzhèng Dàshà Bīnguǎn (Shenyang Post Hotel; ☎ 2522 8717, fax 2252 2369, 78 Beizhan Lu) Doubles Y80-240. This hotel is near the north train station and has new-looking rooms.

SHĚNYÁNG

PLACES TO STAY

3 Fènghuáng Fàndiàn;
   Aeroflot; Russian
   Consulate
   凤凰饭店
5 Liáoníng Dàshà
   辽宁大厦
11 Dōngfāng Dàshà
   东方大厦
14 Gloria Plaza Hotel
   凯莱大酒店
15 Yóuzhèng Dàshà
   Bīnguǎn; Main Post Office
   邮政大厦宾馆；邮电局
21 Méishǎn Bīnguǎn
   梅杉宾馆
30 Hépíng Bīnguǎn
   和平宾馆
32 Traders Hotel; Traders
   Shopping Centre;
   Bank of China
   商贸饭店；商贸中心；
   中国银行
36 New World Courtyard
   新世界酒店

PLACES TO EAT

18 Summer Christmas
   夏日圣诞
22 Xiǎo Tǔdòu
   小土豆
28 Dong Dong Bread House
   东东欧式面包房

29 Lǎobiān Jiǎoziguǎn
   老边饺子馆
35 Food Fair
   美食城

OTHER

1 North Tomb
   北陵
2 CITS
   中国国际旅行社
4 Park Entrance
   公园门口
6 Wúgòu Jìngguāng
   Shělì Tǎ
   无垢净光舍利塔
7 Liaoning University
   辽宁大学
8 Běi Tǎ
   北塔
9 18 September
   History Museum
   九一八历史博物馆
10 East Train Station
   东站
12 North Train Station;
   Shěntiě Dàshà
   北火车站；
   沈铁大厦宾馆
13 PSB
   公安局外事科
16 Long Distance Bus
   Station
   长途汽车站

17 Xī Tǎ
   西塔
19 Telephone Office
   中国电信
20 Bank of China
   中国银行
23 Imperial Palace
   故宫
24 Zoo
   动物园
25 Liaoning Provincial
   Museum
   辽宁省博物馆
26 Bank of China
   中国银行
27 Zhōngshān Square
   毛主席像
31 South Train Station
   火车南站
33 Internet Cafe
   网吧
34 South Long-Distance
   Bus Station
   长途汽车南站
37 IATA
   国际行协航空售票处
38 US Consulate;
   Japanese Consulate
   美国领事馆；
   日本领事馆
39 TV Tower
   电视塔

Shěntiě Dàshà *(Railway Hotel;* ☎ *2252 2888)* Doubles Y120-140, triples Y150. Within the north train station main building, Shěntiě Dàshà has very decent doubles. If you can convince them you're Chinese you can nab a dorm bed for Y15.

Dōngfāng Dàshà *(*☎ *2252 7388, fax 2252 4520, 112 Beizhan Lu)* Doubles/suites Y180/248. Rooms here look expensive but are actually very reasonable.

Méishǎn Bīnguǎn *(*☎ *2273 5538, fax 2272 8048, 48 Xiaoxi Lu)* Singles/doubles Y60/120. This is one of the best places to stay in Shěnyáng; all rooms have wooden floorboards and cosy duvets.

Liáoníng Dàshà *(*☎ *8680 7922, fax 8680 9355, 105 Huanghe Dajie)* Doubles Y180-380. Located near the North Tomb, this enormous Soviet-style building looks like the setting for a Hitchcock film. The creaky floorboards and dripping taps only add to its character.

Fènghuáng Fàndiàn *(Phoenix Hotel;* ☎ *8680 5858,* W *www.phoenixhotel.com.cn, 109 Huanghe Dajie)* Singles/doubles/suites Y415/458/780. Just north of Liáoníng Dàshà, this hotel is a major staging area for tour groups and offers all the modern amenities and prices to go with it.

Gloria Plaza Hotel *(Kǎilái Dàjiǔdiàn;* ☎ *2252 8855,* W *www.gphshenyang.com, 32 Beizhan Yingbinjie)* Doubles Y528. The Gloria is opposite the north train station and offers plush rooms and frequent discounts.

Hépíng Bīnguǎn *(Peace Hotel;* ☎ *2383 3033, fax 2383 7389, 104 Shengli Beijie)* Doubles/triples/quads Y100/120/160. A stone's throw from the south train station, this is a very popular and comfortable hotel.

New World Courtyard *(Xīnshìjiè Jiǔdiàn;* ☎ *2386 9888,* W *www.courtyard.com, 2 Nanjing Nanjie)* Doubles Y500-700. If you've got any spare cash, use it up in this swanky hotel.

Traders Hotel *(Shāngmào Fàndiàn;* ☎ *2341 2288,* Ⓦ *www.shangri-la.com, 68 Zhonghua Lu)* Doubles US$165. The Traders is owned by, and indistinguishable from, the excellent Shangri-La hotel chain.

Places to Eat
Both the north and south train stations are cheap restaurant zones. Stroll along Taiyuan Jie and Zhong Jie for snacks, fruit and evening food stalls.

Nanjing Beijie, off Zhōngshān Square, has a number of ***restaurants*** and ***bakeries,*** including the upmarket ***Dong Dong Bread House*** *(Dōngdōng Ōushì Miànbāofáng; 5 Nanjing Beijie).*

Lǎobiān Jiǎoziguǎn *(Lao Bian Dumpling Restaurant;* ☎ *2383 2406, 55 Shengli Beijie)* Dumplings Y4-12. The Bian family have had time to perfect their delicious dumplings (the restaurant has been going since 1829).

Xiǎo Tǔdòu *(Small Potato; Xiaoxi Lu; open 10am-11pm)* Dishes from Y10. This restaurant is always packed, but the food is well worth the wait.

Head to Xita Jie for the bright lights of ***Korea Town***. Summer evenings see impromptu roadside eateries selling barbecued squid and other snacks. Try the *bulgogi* (Korean barbecue).

Summer Christmas *(Xiàrì Shèngdàn;* ☎ *2347 4704, 99 Xita Jie; open 7am-2am)* Pizzas Y40-80. This bizarrely named restaurant in Korea Town is well known for its excellent pizzas.

Shopping
Traders Shopping Centre *(68 Zhonghua Lu)* Open 9am-8pm daily. This place is next to, and part of, the Traders Hotel. This three-storey emporium is home to international names like Dunhill, Esprit and Sisley.

In the same area is Taiyuan Jie, one of Shěnyáng's major shopping streets. In the evenings a ***night market*** sets up. You'll also find an underground shopping street here that has a decent ***supermarket***. Zhong Jie is another good place to go; even if you're not buying, the Japanese architecture makes it an interesting stroll.

Getting There & Away
Air The IATA ticket office *(Guójì Hángxié Hángkōng Shòupiàochù;* ☎ *2286 7029)* is at 229 Zhonghua Lu. There are a huge number of domestic destinations, including Běijīng (Y640), Shànghǎi (Y1190), Kūnmíng (Y1970) and Guǎngzhōu (Y1600).

Air China has flights to Seoul (Y2160). At the time of writing, flights to Russia were suspended. Inquire at the Aeroflot office (☎ 8610 5447) on the ground floor of Fènghuáng Fàndiàn (see Places to Stay), to see if the situation has changed.

Larger hotels can book airline and train tickets.

Bus If you come out of the south train station and cross over the pedestrian overpass, you'll be confronted with a line of buses; this is the south long-distance bus station. Services include a daily bus to Tiānjīn (seat/sleeper Y60/100; 10 hours) and two departures a day to Běijīng (Y188, 11 hours). There are regular departures to Ānshùn (Y15.5, 1½ hours) and Běnxī (Y12.5, two hours).

The long-distance express bus station (qìchē kuàisù kèyùnzhàn) is on Beizhan Lu, not far from the north train station. From here there are six daily buses to Hāěrbīn (Y130, seven hours), 11 buses to Dàlián (Y99, 4½ hours), and eight buses to Jílín (Y96, 4½ hours). Buses leave every half-hour to Chángchūn (Y70, 3½ hours) and every hour to Jǐnzhōu (Y51, three hours).

Train There are three train stations located in Shěnyáng. The north station (běizhàn) and the south station (nánzhàn) are the most useful for travellers. Arriving in Shěnyáng is not usually a problem, as many trains that arrive at one station will then, after a short stop, travel to the next. However when departing this is not always the case, so be sure to double check as to which station you need.

Buying sleepers anywhere in the northeast is a headache and Shěnyáng is no exception; it is advisable to purchase your ongoing ticket as soon as you arrive.

The south train station includes trains to Hāěrbīn (Y151, eight hours), Chángchūn (Y45, four to five hours), Dāndōng (Y36, four hours), Běijīng (Y150, 10 to 12 hours) and Dàlián (Y119, six to nine hours). Express trains from the north train station travel to destinations including Běijīng, Guǎngzhōu and Shànghǎi.

Getting Around

Although Shěnyáng has lots of buses and routes, the city is sprawling, and getting anywhere by public transport is likely to require at least one transfer. Maps of the bus routes are sold at the train stations.

Bus No 203 runs between the north and south train stations. Bus No 227 runs between the North Tomb , the north train station and the Imperial Palace. Bus No 207 runs east-west across Government Square.

Taxis cost Y7 for the first 4km.

AROUND SHĚNYÁNG
Qiān Shān 千山

These hills are about 80km south of Shěnyáng. The name is an abbreviation of Qiānlián Shān (Thousand Lotuses Mountain) as the 72-sq-km area is composed of approximately 1000 lotus-shaped peaks. You can hike around the hills, which have a scattering of Tang, Ming and Qing temples. Qiān Shān itself gets very crowded on Sunday and public holidays. It is steep in parts and takes about three hours to reach the summit.

At the southern foot of the mountain are the Tānggǎngzi Hot Springs (Tānggǎngzi Wēnquán). The last Qing emperor, Puyi, used to bathe here with his empress. Today Tānggǎngzi's hot springs are piped into ordinary baths for ordinary folk. There is a sanatorium that offers accommodation for those with lingering diseases, as well as for those who just want to linger.

From Shěnyáng's south long-distance bus station there are regular buses covering the 60km journey to Ānshùn (Y12), where you change buses to Qiān Shān. The whole journey takes around 2½ hours.

Maps can be bought from hawkers near the gate or from the ticket office.

Běnxī Water Caves
Běnxī Shuǐdòng 本溪水洞

These aqueous caves (admission Y65; open 8am-5pm daily), 30km east of Běnxī, feature a forest of stalactites and stalagmites. The entry ticket includes a 45-minute boat ride along the 'Milky Way', a 3km-long river that zigzags through caves of differing shapes and sizes. The caves maintain a constant temperature of 10°C (50°F) and coats are provided for the boat journey, but it gets cold so bring some extra layers. The area gets busy on weekends and in the summer.

Buses to Běnxī train station (Y12.5, two hours) depart regularly from Shěnyáng's south long-distance bus station. From Běnxī, minibuses ply the route to the caves (Y6, 40 minutes). A direct bus leaves Shěnyáng at 7.30am and departs the caves at 2.30pm (Y16, two hours).

DÀLIÁN 大连
☎ 411 • pop 5,890,000

Dàlián has been known by several names – Dalny, Dairen, Lüshun and Luda. Today, Lüshun (formerly Port Arthur) is the part farther south, and Lüshun and Dàlián comprise Lüda. A military base is located at Lüshun and considered a 'sensitive zone' – the area is off limits to foreigners.

In the late 19th century the Western powers were busy carving up pieces of China for themselves. To the outrage of Tsar Nicholas II, Japan gained the Liaodong Peninsula under an 1895 treaty (after defeating Chinese battleships off Port Arthur in 1894). Nicholas II gained the support of the French and the Germans, and not only managed to get the Japanese to withdraw from Dàlián, but also to receive it as a Russian concession in 1898. From there, Russia set about constructing a port as an alternative to the only partially ice-free port of Vladivostok.

Itching for a war with Japan (to whip up nationalist feelings at home and distract from internal difficulties), the Tsar pushed the two countries to the brink of war in 1904. However, Nicholas II underestimated the strength of the Japanese navy, who pre-emptively attacked Port Arthur in February 1904, crippling and blockading the Russian fleet. The Russians lurched from one blunder to another, culminating in the serious

> ## Warning
>
> Do not attempt to head south-west, past Xīnghǎi Gōngyuán. This area, including Lüshun (Port Arthur), is considered a sensitive military zone and off limits to all foreigners. While CITS in Dàlián does not seem to be aware of this situation and will encourage you to visit Lüshun, you're likely to see little more than the inside of Lüshun's PSB office, which is not worth the price of the train ticket to get there. If you are tempted to head in this direction, check with the PSB in Dàlián to see if the situation has changed.

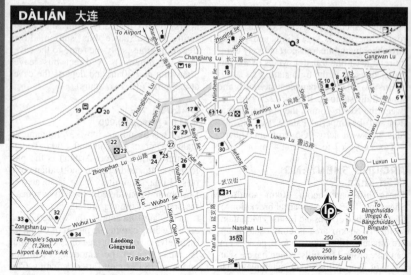

DÀLIÁN 大连

defeat of the Russian Baltic Fleet off Korea in May 1905. The same year, Dàlián passed back into Japanese hands, and the Japanese completed the port facilities in 1930. In 1945, the Soviet Union reoccupied Dàlián and did not withdraw until 10 years later.

Today, Dàlián has the largest harbour in the north-east, and is also one of the most prosperous cities in China. Crisscrossed by old, colourful trams, the city exhibits some wonderful architecture and has refreshing acres of grass and lawns.

Dàlián also harbours a large number of credited 'intellectuals' and an extremely successful and popular soccer team. Next to the sea, the weather in Dàlián tends to be much warmer than in other areas of Liáoníng. Perhaps because of this, Dàlián also has a noticeably relaxed pace and it often feels as if the entire city is on holiday.

Orientation

Dàlián is perched on the Liaodong Peninsula and borders the Yellow Sea to the north. The hub of the city is in the eastern part of town around Zhōngshān Square. The ferry terminal is in the north-east of the city and the Dàlián train station is centrally located.

The main shopping zones and sights are not far from each other and make walking a reasonably easy and enjoyable way to explore the city.

Information

Money The Bank of China is located within the stately green dome-roofed building at 9 Zhongshan Guangchang. Next door to the Shangri-La Hotel, the Hong Kong & Shanghai Banking Corporation has an ATM accepting Cirrus, Plus, MasterCard, Visa and Global Access cards.

Post & Communications The main post and telephone office is at 134 Changjiang Lu, on the corner of Shanghai Lu.

There are a number of small Internet bars around Zhōngshān Square. The Wángzǐ Wǎngbā (☎ 280 5594) is located next to Dàlián Yǒuhǎo Bīnguǎn (see Places to Stay later). It has quick servers available for Y4 per hour and is open 24 hours. There is also an Internet cafe, 21°C (Èrshíyī Shìjìwǎng; ☎ 259 2420), at 45 Qi Qi Jie, near the corner of Jiefang Jie. Servers are Y3 per hour and it's open 24 hours.

Travel Agencies CITS (☎ 368 7843) is at 1 Changtong Jie (4th floor), on the western side of Láodòng Gōngyuán (Workers Movement Park), almost directly opposite the Civil Aviation Administration of China (CAAC; Zhōnguó Míngháng). The Dalian Overseas Tourism Corporation (☎ 368 0857, fax 368 7831), on the 5th floor of the same building, may also be useful.

DÀLIÁN

PLACES TO STAY
1. Dàlián Shènglì Dàjiǔdiàn
   大连胜利大酒店
2. Zàochuán Bīnguǎn
   造船宾馆
8. Dalian Shangri-La Hotel
   大连香格里拉饭店
10. Furama Hotel
    富丽华大酒店
11. Guójì Dàjiǔdiàn
    国际大酒店
13. Dalian Hilton
    大连希尔顿酒店
17. Dàlián Fàndiàn
    大连饭店
21. Bohai Pearl Hotel
    渤海明珠大酒店
24. Dōngfāng Fàndiàn
    东方饭店
26. Dàlián Yǒuhǎo Bīnguǎn;
    Wángzǐ Wǎngbā
    (Internet)
    大连友好宾馆
30. Dàlián Bīnguǎn
    大连宾馆
36. Foreign Experts Hotel;
    University of Foreign
    Languages
    外国语大学

PLACES TO EAT
6. Qúnyīng Lóu
   群英楼
25. Wángmázi
    Dàpáidàng
    王麻子大排档
28. Pizza King Italian
    Restaurant
    比萨王意大利餐厅
29. Shànyī Curry &
    Coffee
    善一餐厅

OTHER
3. East Train Station
   大连东站
4. Ferry Passenger
   Terminal
   大连港客运站
5. JJ's Nightclub
   JJ's 俱乐部
7. ATM
9. Dragonair
   港龙航空
12. Friendship Shopping
    Centre
    友谊商城
14. Bank of China
    中国银行

15. Zhōngshān Square
    中山广场
16. Xinhua Bookshop
    新华书店
18. Post & Telephone
    Office
    邮局
19. Long-Distance Bus
    Station
    长途汽车站
20. Train Station
    大连火车站
22. Victory Square
    胜利广场
23. Shopping Centre
27. Friendship Square
    友好广场
31. PSB
    公安局外事科
32. CAAC
    中国民航
33. All Nippon Airways
    全日空
34. CITS; Dalian Overseas
    Tourism Corporation
    中国国际旅行社
35. 21°C
    二十一世界网络咖啡

Visit Dalian, a free monthly English magazine, lists a range of things to see and do and can be a useful guide. The magazine is available on request from some large hotels, such as the Furama Hotel.

PSB You'll find the PSB (☎ 363 2718) at 16 Yan'an Lu. It's open from 8am to 11.30am and 1pm to 4.30pm Monday to Friday.

Zhōngshān Square 中山广场
Zhōngshān Guǎngchǎng

Zhōngshān Square is the hub of Dàlián – a panorama of grand buildings encircling a huge roundabout. The square (in fact a circle) in the middle comes alive at night with music and lights – half of the city turns up to dance and play badminton. An even larger crowd is drawn to watch the local football team Dàlián Wàndá (the Manchester United of China) on the giant TV screen above Dàlián Bīnguǎn.

The classical edifice opposite Dàlián Bīnguǎn is the People's Cultural Hall. Other historic buildings around the square have been converted to banks, hotels and government offices.

Recently built structures in the area have been designed to harmonise with Zhōngshān Square, testimony to the adulation it receives from locals and architects alike.

People's Square 人民广场
Rénmín Guǎngchǎng

Formerly known as Stalin Square, this is another popular gathering spot at dusk. A small park to the east of the square is where the older folk come to chat, have a haircut or a massage – beds are even brought out.

The residential developments to the north of the square are designed in the Russo-European style that can be seen all over Dàlián. Some truly horrendous crimes against good taste, in the form of government buildings, conspire on either flank.

Bus No 15 travels to the People's Square from Zhōngshān Square. On the way, you will pass the **Friendship Square** *(Yǒuhǎo Guǎngchǎng)*, which has a vast spheroid that's illuminated like a giant disco ball at night.

Northern Warlords

Once known as Manchuria, north-eastern China has historically been a springboard for conquerors.

At the turn of the 20th century, Manchuria was a sparsely populated region rich in untapped resources. Both the Russians and the Japanese eyed it enviously. When the Chinese were defeated in the Sino-Japanese War (1894–95), Liaodong Peninsula was ceded to Japan. Japan's strength alarmed other foreign powers, Russia among them, and Japan was forced to hand the area back to China. As a reward for their intervention, the Russians were permitted to build a railway across Manchuria to their treaty port of Port Arthur (Lüshun), near present-day Dàlián. The Russians moved troops in with the railway and, for the next 10 years, effectively controlled north-east China.

Russia's reign came to an end with the Russo-Japanese War (1904–05) and control of Manchuria moved into the grasp of Zhang Zuolin, a bandit leader in charge of a large and well-organised private army. By the time the Qing dynasty fell, he had full control of Manchuria, and between 1926 and 1928 ran a regional government recognised by foreign powers.

Zhang's policy had been to limit Japan's economic and political expansion, and eventually to break Japan's influence entirely. But by the 1920s the militarist Japanese government was ready to take a hard line on China. Zhang was killed by the Japanese in a bomb attack and his role was taken over by his son, Zhang Xueliang, with the blessing of the Kuomintang.

In September 1931 the Japanese invaded Manchuria and established the puppet state Manchukuo. Zhang Xueliang and his Dōngběi (North-Eastern) Army were forced out of Manchuria and moved into central China to fight with the Kuomintang against the Communists.

Zhang's loyalty to Chiang Kaishek had never wavered. But he came to realise that Chiang's promises not to cede any more territory to Japan and to recover Manchuria were empty. Zhang formed a secret alliance with the Communists and, when Chiang flew to Xī'ān in December 1936 to organise another anti-Communist campaign, Zhang had him arrested. Chiang was released after agreeing to form an alliance with the Communists to resist the Japanese. Chiang never forgave Zhang for his treachery and later had him arrested and taken to Taiwan – he wasn't permitted to leave the island until 1992.

As WWII came to an end, the north-east once more became the battleground for Communist and Kuomintang groups. At the Potsdam Conference, July 1945, it was decreed that Japanese forces in Manchuria and North Korea would surrender to the Soviet army; those stationed elsewhere would surrender to the Kuomintang.

The Hiroshima and Nagaskaki bombings in August 1945 forced the Japanese government to surrender, and Soviet armies moved into Manchuria. With the aid of the Americans, the Kuomintang troops moved north to oversee the surrender of the Japanese and to regain control of north and central China. The US navy stationed 53,000 marines at Qīngdǎo to protect the railways leading to Běijīng and Tiānjīn and the coal mines that supplied those railways.

Despite orders from Chiang to remain put, the Communists marched to Manchuria, picking up arms from abandoned Japanese depots along the way. Other Communist troops headed north by sea from Shāndōng. In November 1945 the Kuomintang attacked the Communists, despite US-organised peace negotiations between the two sides. This attack put an end to all talks.

The Communists occupied the countryside, setting in motion their land-reform policies, which quickly built up support among the peasants. Soon the 100,000 men that had marched into Manchuria had tripled in size as ex-soldiers of the Manchurian armies and peasants eagerly joined the ranks. Within two years the Red Army had grown to 1½ million combat troops and four million support personnel.

On the Kuomintang side, troops numbered three million, with Soviet and US arms and support, but its soldiers were disheartened. Many either deserted or joined the Communists. Chiang's army was also weakened by generals he had chosen for their loyalty to him rather than their military competence.

In 1948, in Manchuria, the Communists made their move. Three great battles led by Lin Biao decided the outcome. In the first battle, in August 1948, the Kuomintang lost 500,000 people. In the second battle from November 1948 to January 1949, whole Kuomintang divisions went over to the Communists. Seven generals were lost through battle, capture or desertion, and seven divisional commanders crossed sides. The final battle was fought in around Běijīng and Tiānjīn. Tiānjīn fell on 23 January and another 500,000 Kuomintang troops switched sides, sealing the fate of the Kuomintang and allowing the Communists to drive southwards.

Láodòng Gōngyuán
Labour Park 劳动公园
This hilly park *(admission Y5; open 7am-7pm daily)* in the city centre is the setting for the annual summer Locust Flower Festival. The park's landmark is a giant football in the middle of the grounds, sure testimony to the popularity of the sport. A cable car (Y40) travels up to the TV Tower, from where there are excellent views of the city. You can descend via the hilarious 'summer slide'.

Places to Stay – Budget
Dàlián has no end of first-class accommodation for those with cash to spend. Unfortunately that choice doesn't extend to those on a budget, and cheapies are generally off limits to foreigners. Prices quoted here are low season – expect prices to rise in the summer.

Dàlián Shènglì Dàjiǔdiàn (Dalian Victory Hotel; ☎ 283 3289, 61 Shanghai Lu) Doubles Y100. This delightful relic of the Russian era has chaotic service and slightly noisy rooms, but the energetic staff make a stay here very amusing.

Zàochuán Bīnguǎn (Shipbuilding Hotel; ☎ 263 3480, 16 Zhuqing Jie) Doubles Y150-180, triples without bath Y105. This is a good hostel with very tidy rooms.

Places to Stay – Mid-Range
Foreign Experts Hotel (Zhuānjiā Gōngyù Bīnguǎn; ☎ 280 1199, fax 263 9958, 110 Nanshan Lu) Doubles Y250-350. Located within the University of Foreign Languages campus at the southern end of town, this hotel has reasonable rooms and a public kitchen on every floor. To reach the hotel take bus No 23 to its terminus and then, heading west (the same direction the bus was heading in), take the second left. The hotel is at the far end of the campus, behind the basketball courts.

Dōngfāng Fàndiàn (☎ 263 4161, fax 263 6859, 28 Zhongshan Lu) This hotel was under renovation at the time of writing but should offer some decent competition (and rates) once it re-opens.

Dàlián Yǒuhǎo Bīnguǎn (Dalian Friendship Hotel; ☎ 263 0010, fax 280 5345, 103 Youhao Lu) Doubles with/without bath Y178/120. The rooms are uninspiring but the location, just off the Friendship Square, is convenient.

Dàlián Fàndiàn (☎ 263 3171, fax 280 4197, 6 Shanghai Lu) Singles/doubles Y200/240. This hotel looks like an old 1930s warehouse from the outside but is sadly lacking in character inside.

Places to Stay – Top End
Prices quoted exclude a 15% service charge.

Dàlián Bīnguǎn (☎ 263 3111, e dlhotel @china.com, 4 Zhongshan Guangchang) Singles/doubles Y400/450. This beautiful hotel was used in a scene in the movie *The Last Emperor* and is easily recognisable by the wrought iron entrance that leads to its fabulous marbled interior.

Guójì Dàjiǔdiàn (International Hotel; ☎ 263 8238, fax 263 0008, 9 Renmin Lu) Doubles/suites Y480/680. This flashy hotel, and all its four-star trimmings, is east off Zhōngshān Square.

Bohai Pearl Hotel (Bóhǎi Míngzhū Fàndiàn; ☎ 265 0888, fax 263 4480, 8 Shengli Guangchang) Singles/doubles/suites Y380/450/780. Tour groups seem to love this hotel, or it could just be the permanently discounted prices they find attractive.

Furama Hotel (Fùlìhuá Dàjiǔdiàn; ☎ 263 0888, e furama@furama.com.cn, w www.furama.com.cn, 60 Renmin Lu) Doubles/suites Y598/1100. The excellent five-star Furama features an executive floor and a presidential suite for a mere Y21,750. Prices include a delicious breakfast.

Dalian Shangri-La Hotel (Dàlián Xiānggé Lǐlā Dàjiǔdiàn; ☎ 252 5000, e slda @shangri-la.com, w www.shangri-la.com, 66 Renmin Lu) Rooms US$190-1200. This branch of the Shangri-La family upholds the company's reputation for excellent service.

Bàngchuídǎo Bīnguǎn (☎ 289 3888, fax 289 2654, 1 Yingbin Lu) Set within enormous lush grounds out of town, this hotel is a favourite with top-ranking party members and cadres who come to relax and play a round of golf on the hotel's own course. The hotel can only be reached by taxi so be sure to call ahead to check for room availability.

Dalian Hilton (Dàlián Xīěrdùn Fàndiàn; ☎ 252 9999, w www.hiltondalian.com.cn, 123 Changjiang Lu) Doubles Y648-948. The newly opened Hilton towers 34 floors above the city and offers some very competitive rates.

Places to Eat

Tianjin Jie is a great place for cheap eats and the area around Youhao Lu is especially popular with students. Bars and restaurants line the roads leading off Zhōngshān Square.

Wángmázi Dàpáidàng (☎ 263 1227, cnr Tianjin Jie & Minsheng Jie) This kebab and hotpot joint is almost always full. For refreshment try Keller (Kǎilóng), Dàlián's local brew, which has a hoppy taste that's a cut above the rest. A second Wángmázi is on Friendship Square.

Qúnyīng Lóu (☎ 274 6029, 2-8 Gangwan Lu) This is Dàlián's oldest and most established seafood restaurant, where you can try a number of weird and wonderful sea creatures such as abalone and sea cucumbers.

Shànyī Curry & Coffee (☎ 282 7111, 63 Baiyu Jie) Curry Y20, coffee Y25. This swish little coffee shop/restaurant serves the unlikely combination of, er, curry and coffee.

Pizza King Italian Restaurant (Yìdàlì Bǐsàbìng Diàn; ☎ 280 6888, 122 Youhao Lu) Pizzas Y20-38, pastas Y26, steaks Y48. Pizza King is a much classier restaurant than its name implies, and offers reasonable Italian food.

Entertainment

Dàlián has enjoyed an increase in bars, pubs and clubs in recent years, with more and more catering to the younger crowd.

The area around Friendship Square, is worth exploring for small bars and late-night coffee shops. You'll find similar places around the University of Foreign Languages. A patio bar on Victory Square serves decent coffees and has Carlsberg and Heineken on tap. Renmin Lu also has a number of bars.

Noah's Ark (Nuóyà Fāngzhōu; ☎ 369 2798, 32 Wusi Lu) This is a very cool bar where local bands play daily. It's behind the People's Square, near the flower market.

JJ's is the place to go for big beats, neon lights and sweaty bodies. The club is at the northern end of Wuwu Lu, not far from the passenger ferry terminal.

Shopping

Tianjin Jie is the main shopping thoroughfare in Dàlián and is a huge jumble of shops and stalls. The five-storey *Xinhua Bookshop* is nearby at 96 Tongxing Jie.

Below Victory Square is an enormous underground *shopping centre*, four floors deep.

The *Friendship Shopping Centre* is on Renmin Lu, off Zhōngshān Square, and stocks expensive brand-name goods.

Getting There & Away

Air International destinations include Hong Kong (Y2740), Osaka (Y2710), Fukuoka (Y2400), Sendai (Y3300), Tokyo (Y3000), and Seoul (Y3000). Domestic flights include Běijīng (Y640), Shànghǎi (Y980) and Guǎngzhōu (Y1790).

The CAAC office (☎ 364 2136) is at 143 Zhongshan Lu, next door to Mínháng Dàshà (Civil Aviation Hotel; also known as the Dalian Royal Hotel), and is open from 8am to 6pm. Shuttle buses to the airport leave regularly, check with CAAC for times.

Dragonair has an office next door to the Furama Hotel. All Nippon Airways is in the Senmao Building, just up the road from CAAC.

Bus The long-distance bus station west of the train station at 20 Anshan Lu. Buses also leave from in front of the train station. Buses leave every hour to Shěnyáng (Y98, four to five hours) until 6pm. A fast bus to Běijīng departs daily at 12pm (Y210, nine hours), and there are regular buses to Dāndōng (Y57, six hours). Other destinations include Tōnghuà leaving at 7am daily (Y73, 12 hours), Běnxī at 9.40am (Y75 to Y90, five hours) and Mǔdānjiāng at 2pm (Y230, 18 hours).

There is a private bus station just next to CITS, where you can book your ticket peacefully. A ticket office for buses to Běijīng and Tiānjīn is behind the Shangri-la Hotel, at 14 Changjiang Lu.

Train Mayhem! There is no information counter at the train station and apparently not nearly enough ticket counters. Have your destination, preferred travel dates and seat-class written down. Armed with this, brave the crowds and buy your ticket as early as possible. Most departures are from Dàlián train station (huǒchēzhàn) rather than from the Dàlián east train station (dōngzhàn).

Regular trains run to Shěnyáng (Y55, four to six hours), the first leaving at 7.30am. There is one overnight train to Dāndōng (Y110) that departs at 7.46pm and arrives at

6.08am. Other destinations include Běijīng (Y131, nine to 10 hours), Hāěrbīn (Y146, 13 hours), Chángchūn (Y116, 9½ hours) and Tōnghuā (Y71, 14 hours).

Boat Ferry tickets can be bought at the terminal in the east of Dàlián. Tickets are also sold at a counter in front of the train station. Boats are a sensible and enjoyable way to leave Dàlián, as the trains and buses are a long haul.

There is an international service to Incheon in South Korea that leaves on Tuesday and Friday at 12pm (Y867 to Y1513, 18 hours).

A boat to Shànghǎi leaves every four days starting on the 6th of each month. Departing at 4pm, the trip takes 37 hours and ticket prices range from Y160 to Y460.

There are four express departures to Yāntái (Y170) daily. Boats sail at 8.30am, 10am, noon and 2pm for the 3½-hour journey. Slower boats also cover the route (Y50 to Y600, six to eight hours). There are three daily boats to Wēihǎi (Y150 to Y190, seven to nine hours), leaving at 9am, 9pm and 9.30pm. Boats to Tánggū (the port of Tiānjīn) depart on even days of the month at 5.30pm (13 hours) and on odd days of the month at 3pm (14 hours). Ticket prices range from Y132 to Y260. Ferry services to Qīngdǎo have been discontinued.

Take bus No 13 from the main train station or bus No 708 from Zhōngshān Square to the passenger ferry terminal.

Getting Around

The central district of Dàlián is not large and can generally be covered on foot. At the time of writing there were no bicycle hire outlets.

The airport is 12km from the city centre and can be reached by bus Nos 701 or 710 from Zhōngshān Square. A taxi from the airport to the city centre will cost about Y30.

The city of Dàlián has splashed out big money upgrading its fleet of buses and they are now among the best in China. Bus No 13 runs from the train station to the passenger ferry terminal. Bus No 23 runs south down Yan'an Lu. Colourful trams also glide around the city until 11pm. Minibuses follow the same routes and charge Y2. A good way to see Dàlián is to take bus No 801 from Victory Square which does a two-hour tour of the city (Y20).

Taxis start at Y8.

AROUND DÀLIÁN
Parks & Beaches

Surrounding parklands, beaches and health resorts are the main reason to visit Dàlián. Five kilometres to the south-east is **Bàngchuídǎo Jǐngqū**, which has an attractive pebbly beach. It's visited mainly by those staying at Bàngchuídǎo Bīnguǎn (see the Dàlián Places to Stay section earlier) but it's worth making the trip out there for its secluded swimming bay.

If the weather's fine you could head out there by taxi and then follow the coastal road on foot to **Lǎohǔtān Lèyuán**. This stretch of coastline provides some excellent views of the ragged cliffs and crashing waves. The walk should take two to three hours. From Lǎohǔtān Lèyuán you can return to Zhōngshān Square by bus Nos 30 or 712.

The best beach for swimming is the small **Fùjiāzhuāng Beach**, which has fine sand, a deep bay and rocky outcrops. The beach is a fair way out of town; take bus No 401 from the corner of Jiefang Lu and Zhongshan Lu.

In the south-west of the city is **Xīnghǎi Gōngyuán**, which has a popular but somewhat dirty beach. Inside the park is Dàlián's **Ocean World** (*☎ 468 5136; admission Y70; open 8.30am-5pm daily)*, with more tourists than fish. Bus No 22 leaves from the corner of Jiefang Lu and Zhongshan Lu and travels to Ocean World. Bus No 406, which leaves from the corner of Jiefang Lu and Zhongshan Lu, and bus No 23 will also get you here.

Golden Stone Beach (*Jīnshítān*), 60km north of Dàlián, has a number of natural scenic wonders and is an attractive beach area with splendid coves and rock formations. There is also a golf course, cross-country motorcycling, an amusement park and hunting grounds within a forest. Buses to Golden Stone Beach leave every 40 minutes from the square in front of the Dàlián train station (Y9).

BĪNGYÙ VALLEY
Bīngyù Gōu

CITS claims this valley is Liáoníng's answer to Guìlín and Yángshuò. It has a number of towering, vertical rock formations with a river meandering between them. It's pretty, but it's not likely to replace Guìlín on the travellers' circuit.

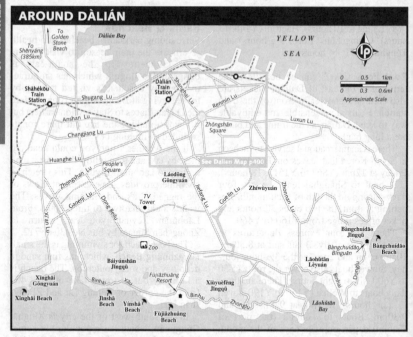

AROUND DÀLIÁN

The valley is 250km north-east of Dàlián. Take a bus from the square in front of the Dàlián train station to Zhuānghé (Y29), a town about two hours east of Dàlián. From there take another bus to **Bīngyù Fēngjǐngqū**, a scenic area a further 1½ hours down the road. Alternatively, you can take a train from Dàlián to Zhuānghé (Y20) and then take a bus.

Furama Hotel (Fùlìhuá Dàjiǔdiàn; ☎ *822 6237)* Doubles Y480. A 15-minute walk from the river, the Furama offers three-star accommodation. Reservations can be made at the Furama Hotel (☎ *263 0888*) in Dàlián. Villas along the river are also available at similar prices; you can ask at the CITS in Dàlián for information and reservations.

DĀNDŌNG 丹东
☎ 0415 • pop 2,390,000
Dāndōng lies at the border of Liáoníng and North Korea. Dāndōng's tourist industry thrives on the views of North Korea across Yālù Jiāng (Green Duck River). Unfortunately, these views only offer what can barely be considered a glimpse into North Korea and many travellers depart from here disappointed.

If you are planning to go to Sinuiju on the other side of Yālù Jiāng, don't get your hopes up. Foreigners can join tour groups to Pyongyang, but are not allowed into Sinuiju. (At the time of writing, American, Israeli and South Korean nationals were not being issued with North Korean visas.) Even going to Pyongyang from Dāndōng via CITS means a wait of anything up to a month for the paperwork to grind its way through the vast cogs of the North Korean bureaucracy. You could try applying for a visa in the North Korean embassy in Běijīng, which will probably prove quicker.

Information
CITS (☎ 213 5854, fax 214 1922), at 1 Zhanqian Guangchang Dalu, is to your right as you exit the train station. The PSB (☎ 210 3138) is at 17 Jiangcheng Dajie and is open from 8am to 12.30pm and 1.30pm to 5.30pm Monday to Friday. You'll find the Bank of China at 60 Jinshan Dajie, on the corner of Sanwei Lu. The post office is at 78 Qiwei Lu.

North Korean Border

Běi Cháoxiǎn Biānjiè 北朝鲜边界

A view of the border can be enjoyed from **Yālùjiāng Gōngyuán** (*admission Y1; open 6.30am-6pm daily*). The park is a favourite spot for Chinese tourists and is peppered with photographers trying to squeeze family members into the standard 'I visited the Sino-Korean border' shot.

The original steel-span bridge was 'accidentally' strafed in 1950 by the Americans, who also accidentally bombed the airstrip at Dāndōng. The Koreans have dismantled this bridge as far as the mid-river boundary line. All that's left is a row of support columns on the Korean side and half a bridge (still showing shrapnel pockmarks) on the Chinese side. You can wander along what's left of it for Y15. Along the way are photographs of the bridge's construction and destruction. The Sino-Korean Friendship Bridge runs parallel to the remains of the old one.

Those without a North Korean visa can get pretty close to the country by jumping onto any number of **boat cruises** (*guānguāng chuán*) along the riverbank. Don't bother with the large boats (Y8, 20 minutes) – you have to wait for them to fill up with passengers (which tends to take forever) and the trip is tedious.

Board one of the speed boats (Y18, 10 minutes) and zip along the river right up along the North Korean side. You are not supposed to take photos, but everyone does. North Korea is largely hidden by an embankment, and apart from some locals and the odd smokestack, there isn't much to see. Nevertheless, if you're wanting to visit North Korea, this may well be as close as you get.

Museum to Commemorate US Aggression 抗美援朝纪念馆

Kàngměi Yuáncháo Jiniànguǎn

With everything from statistics to shrapnel, this museum (*☎ 215 0510; admission Y22; open 8am-4.30pm daily*) offers the Chinese and North Korean perspectives of the war with the United States (1950–53). Almost all captions are in Chinese and Korean, however the visual displays are interesting. Don't miss a look at the Chinese propaganda leaflets that were dropped across enemy lines. The North Korean War Memorial Column that you can see from the road was built 53m high to symbolise the year the war ended.

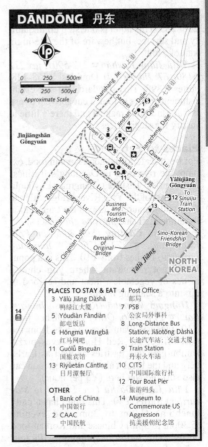

DĀNDŌNG 丹东

PLACES TO STAY & EAT		4	Post Office
3	Yālù Jiāng Dàshà		邮局
	鸭绿江大厦	7	PSB
5	Yóudiàn Fàndiàn		公安局外事科
	邮电饭店	8	Long-Distance Bus
6	Hóngmǎ Wǎngbā		Station; Jiāotōng Dàshà
	红马网吧		长途汽车站; 交通大厦
11	Guólǚ Bīnguǎn	9	Train Station
	国旅宾馆		丹东火车站
13	Rìyuètán Cāntīng	10	CITS
	日月潭餐厅		中国国际旅行社
		12	Tour Boat Pier
OTHER			旅游码头
1	Bank of China	14	Museum to
	中国银行		Commemorate US
2	CAAC		Aggression
	中国民航		抗美援朝纪念馆

Bus No 3 from just north of the train station will drop you off near the stadium. Cross the train tracks and walk west towards the Memorial Column.

Places to Stay

Guólǚ Bīnguǎn (*CITS Hotel; ☎ 212 2166, 1 Zhanqian Guangchang Dalu*) Doubles/triples Y100/120. Run by the friendly folks at the CITS, the rooms are decent but the bathrooms are a little frightening.

Jiāotōng Dàshà (*Traffic Hotel; ☎ 213 2777, fax 213 5242, 4 Jinshan Dajie*) Beds in 4-bed dorms/singles/doubles Y45/160/228. This hotel adjoins the long-distance bus station and has mediocre rooms.

Yóudiàn Fàndiàn (*Post & Telecommunications Hotel; ☎ 216 6888, fax 213 5988,*

78 Qiwei Lu) Singles/doubles/triples Y100/ 218/ 235. This hotel is one step up in quality and service, but beware of the late-night karaoke hall.

Yālù Jiāng Dàshà (☎ 212 5901, fax 212 6180, 87 Jiuwei Lu) Doubles Y368-428, suites Y898. This standard two-star establishment strives to look a cut above the rest, but doesn't quite make it and there's little to justify the steep prices.

Places to Eat

For fresh seafood and good Korean food, explore the riverfront in Dāndōng's Business and Tourism District (Shāngmào Lǚyóuqū) south-west of the Yalu River bridge. Stick to the small restaurants around the train station for authentic Dāndōng *xiǎo chī* (snacks).

Rìyuètán Cāntīng (Sun & Moon Pool Restaurant; ☎ 372 3456, A7 Shangmao Luyouqu) Dishes from Y10. This is a popular hotpot restaurant where you choose dishes of vegetables, meat and seafood to dip into a scalding broth.

Hóngmǎ Wǎngbā (Red Horse Internet Bar; ☎ 214 2886, Qiwei Lu) Dishes from Y10. Open 9.30am-2am. Across from the post office, the Red Horse serves pizza, hamburgers and pastries as well as Carlsberg and the local Yalu River Beer. You can also surf the Net here (Y3 per hour).

Yālù Jiāng Dàshà (see Places to Stay earlier) Buffet Y30. This hotel has a daily lunchtime (11am to 2pm) and evening (5.30pm to 9pm) Chinese and Korean food buffet. The buffet is popular with tour groups however, so arrive early to get your money's worth.

Getting There & Away

Air Flights only leave on Tuesday, Thursday and Saturday. Destinations include Běijīng (Y570), Shànghǎi (Y990), Shēnzhèn (Y1910) and Chéngdū (Y1770). The CAAC office (☎ 212 3427) is at 50 Jinshan Dajie.

Bus The bus station is at 98 Shiwei Lu, near the train station. There are two daily buses to Tōnghuā (Y45, eight hours) at 6.30am and 8.50am. Ten buses leave daily for Dàlián between 5.30am and 2.30pm (Y57, six hours). A bus leaves for Hāěrbīn daily at 10am (Y153, 12 hours), stopping in Chángchūn (Y112) en route. It's best to book long-distance tickets in advance.

Train Direct trains run to Shěnyáng (Y36, four hours), Běijīng (Y263, 14 hours), Chángchūn (Y136, 10 hours), Dàlián (Y110 sleeper, 11 hours) and Qīngdǎo (Y214, 24 hours). The train from Moscow to Pyongyang stops at Dāndōng at 7.24am on Monday, Wednesday, Thursday and Saturday. If you have the necessary visas, you can jump aboard and head for the border for Y160.

AROUND DĀNDŌNG

About 52km north-west of Dāndōng is the town of Fèngchéng. The nearby **Fènghuáng Shān** *(Phoenix Emperor Mountain)* is 840m high and dotted with temples, monasteries and pagodas from the Tang, Ming and Qing dynasties. A mountain temple fair takes place in April and attracts thousands of people. Although the express train does not stop here, it gives you a great view of the mountain from the window. Buses to Fèngchéng leave from Dāndōng's bus station every 10 minutes between 6am and 5.30pm (Y8, one hour).

Dàgū Shān *(Lonely Mountain)* is about 90km south-west of Dāndōng, en route to Dàlián, close to the town of Gūshān. There are several groups of Taoist temples here dating from the Tang dynasty. Buses to Dàgū Shān run every 20 minutes (Y12.5, 2½ hours) from Dāndōng's bus station.

JĪNZHŌU 锦州
☎ 0416

Jīnzhōu is an industrial city situated west of the Liaodong Gulf. Recently, the surrounding areas have been the sites of significant fossils discoveries (see the boxed text 'Feathered Dinosaurs').

Jīnzhōu's main attractions are its fossil museum and nearby **Bǐjiǎ Shān**.

Wényǎ Museum
Wényǎ Bówùguǎn

This is the only privately funded fossil museum in China (☎ 234 3999, 33-13 Block 2, Heping Lu; admission Y5; open 8am-5pm daily) and was opened by Du Wenya in January 2000.

The three-storey museum displays more than 300 rare fossils, the majority of which have come from the surrounding areas. They are the private collection of Mr Du – an amateur collector turned curator. The

Feathered Dinosaurs

In 1996 a local farmer digging for fossils in the village of Sìhétún discovered a dinosaur fossil that rocked the scientific world. The areas of Cháoyáng, Běipiào and Yìxiàn in Liáoníng province had yielded dinosaur fossils before, but what made this discovery so unusual was that the dinosaur had a feather-like downy skin covering. This dinosaur with 'proto-feathers' could be the missing link between dinosaurs and birds – perhaps feathers were first developed for warmth rather than flight.

It's hard to imagine that the barren, arid hills of the Jǐnzhōu fossil sites were once home to lush lakes and fertile land. But about 130 million years ago birds, insects, fish and dinosaurs thrived in this ecosystem. When volcanic storms of fine ash and poisonous gas swept over the area from eruptions in today's inner Mongolia, some of these creatures were blasted into the lakes and covered with layers of fine ash, sealing them into eternal time capsules. The ash preserved minute details; flower petals, insect wings and the hairs or feathers on dinosaurs are all clearly visible.

Since 1997 the fossil sites have been tightly controlled. Local farmers are hired by the Fossil Control Office to excavate specimens, which are then sold to the Control Office for a nominal fee. Rare fossils and those important for scientific research are subsequently sold to scientists or collectors for a handsome return. 'Ordinary' fossils lacking in scientific value are sold for commercial use. With over half the fossil sites still untouched, palaeontologists and scientists are sure the link between dinosaurs and birds lies within the rock slates. But striking a balance between those who depend on fossils for a living – scientists, collectors and local farmers – might prove a more challenging task.

oldest fossil on display is of a bird that is believed to date back 120 million years.

The collection is impressive not only for its size and variety, but for the care with which the fossils are preserved and presented. Even amateur palaeontologists will find this an interesting visit.

The neighbouring fossil sites have been under government control since 1997 and are, in theory, only open to research groups. Those keen to visit the sites should contact Mr Du, who might be able to help.

Places to Stay & Eat

Běishān Bīnguǎn (☎ 416 8144, fax 416 6521, Block 3, 12 Beijing Lu) Singles/doubles/triples Y200/210/220. This hotel offers excellent rooms for bargain prices.

Jǐnzhōu Dàshà (☎ 212 7428, fax 213 1791, Block 3, 58 Zhongyang Dajie) A decent selection of rooms can be found here.

Tiěběi Xiǎo Tiāndì (☎ 414 2915, 24 Block 4, Zhongyang Beijie) Dishes from Y10. For home cooking head to this restaurant, south of Běishān Bīnguǎn, as the food is excellent.

Getting There & Away

Buses leave regularly to Běijīng (Y121, 5½ hours) and Shěnyáng (Y51, three hours)

from Jǐnzhōu's long-distance bus station, opposite the train station. There are two daily buses for Dàlián (Y60, seven hours) at 2pm and 6.30pm.

Jǐnzhōu lies on the Shěnyáng-Běijīng train route, so there are frequent connections to destinations both north and south. Direct trains also run to Dàlián and Chéngdé.

AROUND JǏNZHŌU

Located 37km from Jǐnzhōu is **Bǐjià Shān** (☎ 358 2945; admission Y20), a dramatic island in the Liaodong Gulf. The mountainous island was first settled by a poor monk in the Qing dynasty. Believing the place to have an abundance of feng shui, he set about collecting money to build a temple here. Today there are a number of temples dotted around the island, all made entirely of stone (joints and hinges included). The stone was transported to the island by rolling it across the frozen bay waters during winter months.

A rocky path, **Tiānxià Qíqiáo**, emerges from the sea twice every 23 hours when the tide recedes. At these times you can walk across to the island, otherwise you'll have to take a boat (Y7).

Buses to Bǐjià Shān leave regularly from outside Jǐnzhōu's train station (Y6, one hour).

Jílín 吉林

Capital: Chángchūn
Population: 27.3 million
Area: 187,000 sq km

Bordering Russia, North Korea and Inner Mongolia, Jílín is part of the historic territory of the Manchus, founders of the Qing dynasty (1644–1911). The province was industrialised under the Japanese who seized Manchuria and shaped it into the puppet state of Manchukuo (1931–45). Jílín's main attraction for tourists is the volcanic crater lake Heaven Pool.

CHÁNGCHŪN 长春
☎ 0431 • pop 6,912,000

Chángchūn was the Japanese capital of Manchukuo (known as Hsin-king) between 1933 and 1945. In 1945 the Russians arrived in Chángchūn on a year-long looting spree. When they departed, the Kuomintang moved in only to find themselves surrounded by the Communists who had assembled a formidable array of scrounged and captured weaponry – even former Japanese tanks and US jeeps. The Communists took over the city in 1948.

With Soviet assistance, China's first car-manufacturing plant was set up here in the 1950s, starting with 95-horsepower Jiefang (Liberation) trucks, and moving on to make bigger and better vehicles like the now-defunct Red Flag limousines. If you have ever wondered why so many Volkswagen cars plough China's city streets, the answer is that the company has a factory in Chángchūn (as well as one in Shànghǎi).

Orientation
The city sprawls from north to south, which makes transportation between points tiresome. Roughly bisected from north to south by Yītōng Hé, most of the facilities and places of interest are on the western side of the river. The long-distance bus station and train station are in the north of the city.

Information
Money The Bank of China is in the Yinmao Building at 14 Xinmin Dajie, behind Chángbái Shān Bīnguǎn.

Highlights

- Heaven Pool, a volcanic crater lake in stunning Chángbái Shān – China's largest nature reserve
- Sōnghuā Hú Qīngshān and Běidàhú, two of China's leading ski resort areas
- Korean Autonomous Prefecture, where you can get a taste of Korean culture in rural China

Post & Communications The post office is at 18 Renmin Dajie. Other useful branches are located to the right of the train station and at the western end of Guilin Lu.

Dìqiú Cūn Internet bar (☎ 565 3704), at 47-1 Tongzhi Jie, charges Y2 per hour and is open 24 hours. It sits opposite the Foreign Language Bookshop at 44 Tongzhi Jie.

Travel Agencies China International Travel Service (CITS; Zhōngguó Guójì Lǚxíngshè; ☎ 560 9039, fax 564 5069) is on the 7th floor of the Yinmao Building, which also houses the Bank of China, at 14 Xinmin Dajie and is open from 8.30am to 5pm.

PSB The Public Security Bureau (PSB; Gōngānjú) is on the south-western corner of the People's Square (Rénmín Guǎngchǎng). The office is at the back of the complex in a yellow building left over from the Japanese occupation.

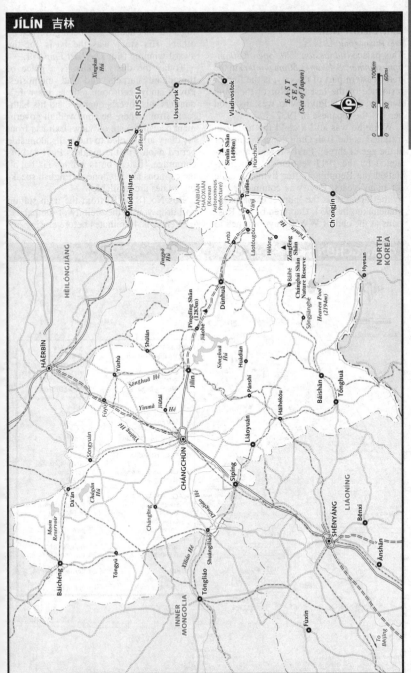

Puppet Emperor's Palace & Exhibition Hall
Wěi Huánggōng 伪皇宫

This palace (admission Y20; open 8.30am-5pm summer, 8.40am-3.50pm winter) in the north-eastern part of the city, is the former residence of the last emperor of the Qing dynasty, Henry Puyi, who was installed here by the Japanese in 1932.

While he was still a child (he had been installed as the 10th Qing dynasty emperor at the age of three), Puyi's reign was interrupted by the 1911 revolution, which installed the Republic. After living in exile for many years, Puyi was commandeered by the Japanese as the 'puppet emperor' of Manchukuo in 1934. Captured by the Russians at the end of WWII, Puyi returned to China in 1959 and died in 1967, thus ending a life that had largely been governed by others. His story was the basis for the award-winning film The Last Emperor.

Today the dusty palace is a place of threadbare carpets and sad memories. Puyi's study, bedroom, temple, his wife's quarters, his lover's quarters and his bathroom (from where he approved all government decisions) are on view. Extracts from his diary are stapled to the walls alongside period photos of the luckless Puyi and his entourage. History buffs will love it, but all the captions are in Chinese (English speaking guides are available).

Bus No 18 or 10 from the train station will drop you in the vicinity of the palace. Last entry is 40 minutes before closing.

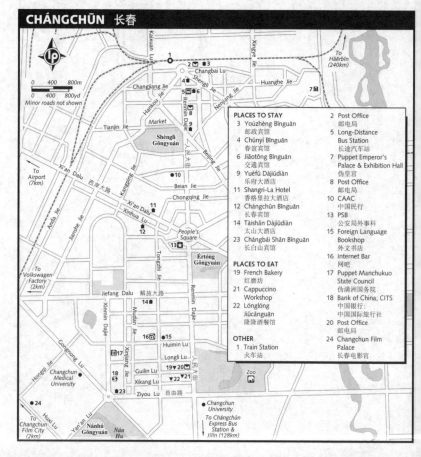

CHÁNGCHŪN 长春

0   400   800m
0   400   800yd
Minor roads not shown

To Hāěrbīn (240km)

To Airport (7km)

To Volkswagen Factory (2km)

To Changchun Film City (2km)

Changchun University
To Chángchūn Express Bus Station & Jílín (128km)

PLACES TO STAY
3 Yóuzhèng Bīnguǎn 邮政宾馆
4 Chūnyí Bīnguǎn 春谊宾馆
6 Jiāotōng Bīnguǎn 交通宾馆
9 Yuèfǔ Dàjiǔdiàn 乐府大酒店
11 Shangri-La Hotel 香格里拉大酒店
12 Chángchūn Bīnguǎn 长春宾馆
14 Tàishān Dàjiǔdiàn 太山大酒店
23 Chángbái Shān Bīnguǎn 长白山宾馆

PLACES TO EAT
19 French Bakery 红磨坊
21 Cappuccino Workshop
22 Lónglóng Jiǔcānguǎn 隆隆酒餐馆

OTHER
1 Train Station 火车站
2 Post Office 邮电局
5 Long-Distance Bus Station 长途汽车站
7 Puppet Emperor's Palace & Exhibition Hall 伪皇宫
8 Post Office 邮电局
10 CAAC 中国民行
13 PSB 公安局外事科
15 Foreign Language Bookshop 外文书店
16 Internet Bar 网吧
17 Puppet Manchukuo State Council 伪满洲国务院
18 Bank of China; CITS 中国银行; 中国国际旅行社
20 Post Office 邮电局
24 Changchun Film Palace 长春电影宫

Changchun Film Palace
Chángchūn Diányǐng Gōng 长春电影宫

This is the original Chángchūn Film Studio (☎ 594 8427, 28 Huxi Lu; admission Y20; open 8am-4.30pm daily). Those expecting Hollywood, or even Bollywood, may vent a few yawns sauntering around the sprawling estate of the film studio. Documentaries and low-budget flicks are still made here, but most of what's on show is a bit stale. The photo exhibit of China's silver screen stars will interest those with a passion for Chinese cinema. Bus No 13 runs from the People's Square.

Changchun Film City
Chángchūn Diànyǐng Chéng 长春电影城

The Film City (☎ 762 8874, Zhengyang Jie; admission Y15-80; open 8am-4.30pm daily) is a comical attempt to create a Universal Studios-style film park. Ticket prices vary according to how many 'movie worlds' you want to visit. Choices include the Adventure Palace, Cyberspace and the dubbing hall where you can participate in the making of movie sound effects. Take bus No 19 from the People's Square or minibus No 262 from the train station.

Puppet Manchukuo State Council
Wěimǎnzhōu Guówùyuàn 伪满洲国务院

This former government building (admission Y5; open 8.30am-6.30pm daily) is built in the shape of the Chinese character wáng, meaning King. It is from here that Puyi first inspected his armies on 6 March 1935. The inspection platform is open to visitors, as is the office of Prime Minister Zhang Jinhui and an elevator made entirely from copper that was installed for use by Puyi and other high-ranking government officials. The entrance to an underground tunnel 12 miles long is somewhere within the building, but is not open to the public.

Today it houses part of the Bethune Medical College, named after the Canadian Doctor Norman Bethune who came to China in 1938 and died a year later. He is regarded as something of a martyr among Chinese folk.

Places to Stay

Follow one of the touts at the train station if you're looking for inexpensive accommodation, but most of Chángchūn's cheap hotels are off limits to foreigners.

Chūnyí Bīnguǎn (☎ 279 9966, W www .chunyihotel.com, 2 Renmin Dajie) Singles/ doubles/triples Y220/220/240. This hotel was built in 1909 for high-ranking Japanese and Manchurian officials and still boasts old-world charm today.

Jiāotōng Bīnguǎn (Traffic Hotel; ☎ 270 3543 ext 3001, 6 Renmin Dajie) Doubles Y108-188, triples Y108-168. This is the tall circular building behind Chūnyí Bīnguǎn. The rooms are old but clean and brightened up with flowering plants.

Yóuzhèng Bīnguǎn (Post Hotel; ☎ 298 7888, fax 294 6577, 21 Changbai Lu) Doubles from Y280. This hotel is to your left as you exit the train station. The rooms are a good deal but the staff's airs and graces might put you off.

Tàishān Dàjiǔdiàn (☎ 563 4991, fax 563 6025, 35 Tongzhi Jie) Doubles Y150-200, suites Y230. Tàishān provides the perfect combination of clean, comfortable, cheerful and cheap rooms.

Chángchūn Bīnguǎn (☎ 892 9920 ext 29, fax 892 2033, 18 Xinhua Lu) Doubles Y160-298. This very reasonable hotel is set within its own resort grounds complete with an outdoor tennis court and swimming pool.

Chángbái Shān Bīnguǎn (☎ 564 3551 ext 9, fax 564 2003, 16 Xinmin Dajie) Doubles from Y360. Near Nánhú Gōngyuán, this is a standard three-star affair popular with Korean tour groups. Take bus No 62 from the train station

Yuèfǔ Dàjiǔdiàn (Paradise Hotel; ☎ 271 7071, e Yfh@Public.cc.jl.cn, 46 Renmin Dajie) Singles/doubles/triples Y248/298/ 398. This is more paradise lost than heaven but the rooms are not bad. Off-season 50% discounts are not uncommon.

Shangri-La Hotel (Xiānggélǐlā Jiǔdiàn; ☎ 898 1818, W www.shangri-la.com, 9 Xi'an Dalu) Doubles US$160. Nothing but luxury awaits those who want to splash out in Chángchūn's most upmarket hotel.

Places to Eat

On the street running along the northern edge of Shènglì Gōngyuán are a number of upscale seafood and hot-pot restaurants. The street itself is a market lined with stalls selling snacks and kebabs.

South of the city, between Renmin Dajie and Xinmin Dajie, is a hotbed of restaurants.

In particular, explore Guilin Lu, a main shopping street and student hang-out for bakeries and bars.

Cappuccino Workshop (☎ *564 6216*) Coffees Y15, pizzas from Y40. Open 9am-11pm. This place is at the eastern end of Guilin Lu. It's obvious the chef isn't Italian, but the pizzas are a welcome respite from a diet of dumplings. A second branch is opposite Tàishān Dàjiǔdiàn (see Places to Stay earlier).

French Bakery (*Hóng Mò Fáng*; ☎ *562 3994, 33 Guilin Lu*) Coffees Y15, pastries Y5. Open 7.30am-10pm. This bakery serves a variety of European coffee-shop treats, including get-you-going espressos and fluffy croissants.

Lónglóng Jiǔcānguǎn (☎ *564 5885, 26 Xikang Lu*) Dishes from Y10. Try the dumplings and a plate of *liáng miàn* (cold noodles), a Jílín speciality. There are several good dōngbĕi *restaurants* along this road. Nearby is Longli Lu, where you'll find a number of popular *bars*.

Getting There & Away

Air Civil Aviation Administration of China (CAAC; Zhōngguó Mínháng; ☎ 298 8888), at 23-1 Shanghai Lu, sits between the train station and Yóuzhèng Bīnguǎn.

There are daily flights to most major domestic cities including Běijīng (Y880), Shànghǎi (Y1430), Shēnzhèn (Y2140) and Dàlián (Y520). A flight leaves for Hong Kong (Y2310) every Tuesday.

Bus The long-distance bus station (kèyùn zhōngxīn) is behind Chūnyí Bīnguǎn at 6 Renmin Dajie. Buses leave every 15 minutes to Jílín (Y14.5, 1½ hours). The express bus to Chángchūn is Y30 (1½ hours), the slow bus is Y14.5 (2½ hours). Other destinations include Shěnyáng (Y70, 3½ hours), Dàlián (Y157, eight hours), Běijīng (Y180) and Hāěrbīn (Y40, 4½ hours). Express buses from Jílín arrive at the Chángchūn express bus station (gāosù gōnglù kèyùn zhàn) in the southern part of town at 219 Renmin Dajie.

Train Regular trains leave for Hāěrbīn (Y61, three to four hours), Jílín (Y26, two hours) and Shěnyáng (Y47, four to five hours). Further destinations include Běijīng (Y217, 14 hours), Dàlián (seat/sleeper Y99 to Y171, 9½ hours) and Shànghǎi (Y285, 28 hours).

Getting Around

Chángchūn's airport is only a few kilometres to the west of the city centre; CAAC provides a shuttle bus (Y5) from its ticket office.

Bus No 62 runs through the centre of town, between the train station and Nánhú Gōngyuán. Bus No 10 runs east from the train station to the Puppet Emperor's Palace & Exhibition Hall and bus No 25 heads south from the station, along the western edge of town.

Taxi fares start at Y5.

JÍLÍN 吉林
☎ 0432 ● pop 4,320,000

The city of Jílín, originally established as a fortress in 1673, was severely damaged during WWII and suffered wholesale looting by Russian soldiers.

Despite the industrial nature of the city, Jílín is noted for its winter scenery, which challenges the backdrop of workers' flats and factories. At any other time of year, unless you are manic about meteorites, there is little to draw you to Jílín.

Information

The Bank of China is at 1 Shenzhen Jie, south of the Línjiāngmén Bridge. The main post office is on Jiangnan Jie, north of the Jílín Bridge, and the PSB (☎ 240 9315) is just north of the Catholic Church at Beijing Lu.

CITS (☎ 243 5819), at 4 Wenmiao Hutong, is near Wén Miào (Confucius Temple) and can organise skiing trips and tours to Chángbái Shān.

A 24-hour Internet bar (☎ 245 6289; Y2 per hour) is at 51 Chongqing Jie.

Ice-Rimmed Trees

Jílín is most attractive during January and February when the branches of the pine and willow trees along the banks of Sōnghuā Jiāng are covered in needle-like hoarfrost creating a spectacular winter wonderland scene. The phenomenon is a result of the Hydroelectric Station in nearby Fēngmǎn. Built by the Japanese, disassembled by the Russians and then reassembled by the Chinese, this station now fuels three large chemical plants. Water passing from artificial Sōnghuā Hú through the power plant becomes a warm, steamy current that merges with Sōnghuā Jiāng and prevents it from freezing. Vapour rising from the river overnight meets the -20°C (-4°F) air temperature, causing the display.

During the Spring Festival Festival (late January to mid-February), hordes of Japanese and overseas Chinese come for the icicle show; the 20km stretch from the lake to the city centre provides ample viewing for all. The best time to catch this sight is in the morning. The stretch of the river in from Dōngguān Bīnguǎn (see Places to Stay later) is a good place to start.

Wén Miào 文庙
Confucius Temple

Temples dedicated to Confucius were built so that the great sage would bestow good luck on local hopefuls taking the notoriously difficult imperial examinations *huìkǎo*. The main hall of this temple *(Wenmiao Hutong; admission Y10; open 8.30am-4pm Mon-Fri, 9am-4pm Sat & Sun)* was built in 1907.

An interesting exhibition details huìkǎo, describing how examinees were confined to solitary cells during examinations. Also on display are ingenious cheating devices, including undershirts covered in minuscule characters (worn despite the risk that the ultimate penalty for cheating was death).

Entrance to the temple is off Jiangwan Lu, next to Jiāngchéng Bīnguǎn (see Places to Stay later). Bus No 13 runs near here from the train station.

Běishān Gōngyuán 北山公园

If you need some exercise, go to Běishān Gōngyuán *(admission Y5)*, a hilly area on the western side of town with temples, pavilions, forests and footpaths. The scenery is mellow enough, although it gets crowded at weekends and holidays, in particular during Běishān's temple fair held annually on the 8th, 18th and 28th of April.

On the western side of the park is Táoyuán Shān, which is worth a short hike. Take bus No 7 from the train station or No 49 from Century Square.

Catholic Church 天主教堂
Tiānzhǔ Jiàotáng

This Catholic Church *(3 Songjiang Lu; open from 5am Mon-Fri, from 8am Sat & Sun)*, built in 1917, has become a symbol of Jílín city. The church was completely ransacked during the Cultural Revolution, and its small library of religious works was also torched. In 1980 the church re-opened and now holds regular services.

Meteorite Shower Museum
Yǔnshí Yǔ Bówùguǎn 陨石雨博物馆

In March 1976 the Jílín area received a heavy meteor shower, and the largest meteor fragment is on view in this museum *(Century Square; admission Y40; open 8.30am-11.30am & 1.30pm-4.30pm daily)*. Apparently it's the largest example of stone meteorite on display anywhere in the world, weighing in at a hefty 1770kg.

Century Square 世纪广场
Shiji Guǎngchǎng

South of Sōnghuā Jiāng is Century Square, a popular hang-out for locals to play badminton, eat ice-cream and join in the latest roller-skating craze. Skates can be hired for Y5 from outside Beiguo Chuntian Department Store on the eastern side of the square.

The large LEGO-type building in the centre of the square is the Century Boat *(admission Y10)*. For views of the city take the elevator to the 12th floor.

Lóngtán Shān Gōngyuán
Lóngtán Mountain Park 龙潭山公园

Far less crowded than Běishān Gōngyuán is this park in the north-eastern section of town that has some ideal walking trails. The park is the site of an ancient fort from the Bohai State and there are a number of dungeons and temples scattered within the grounds. Bus No 49 from Century Square runs to this park.

Festival

Jílín, like Hāěrbīn, has an Ice Lantern Festival *(Bīngdēng Jié)*, held at Jiāngnán Gōngyuán on the southern side of Sōnghuā Jiāng. Locals claim that Jílín invented the Ice Lantern Festival and Hāěrbīn copied it (Hāěrbīn's festival is much more famous though, so it's probably sour grapes).

Places to Stay

It's difficult to find cheap hotels open to foreigners, especially during the winter. Rates quoted are off-season, expect large increases when snowflakes start to fall.

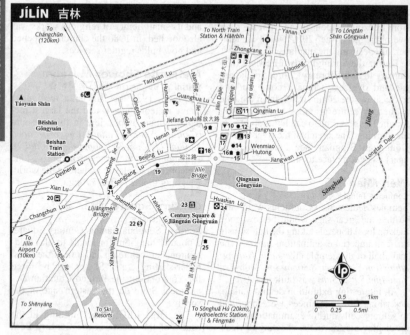

JÍLÍN 吉林

Jiāotōng Bīnguǎn (Traffic Hotel; ☎ 255 8891, fax 253 8149, 6 Zhongkang Lu) Doubles/triples from Y150/240. All rooms here are in good nick.

Dōngguān Bīnguǎn (☎ 245 4272, fax 249 9212, 2 Jiangwan Lu) Doubles Y160-200. These average-looking rooms are second choice to Jiāotōng Bīnguǎn. Take bus No 3 from the train station.

Jiāngchéng Bīnguǎn (☎ 245 7721, W www.jlcta.com.cn, 4 Jiangwan Lu) Doubles Y180-200, suites Y340. The rooms are old but well looked after and the staff is very friendly.

Tiānshǐ Bīnguǎn (Angel Hotel; ☎ 248 1848, fax 248 0323, 2 Nanjing Jie) Singles/doubles/triples Y180/170/180. This comfortable hotel has the best budget deal in town.

Yínhé Dàshà (Milky Way Hotel; ☎ 484 1780, fax 484 1621, 79 Songjiang Lu) Doubles Y340-490, suites Y880. The Milky Way is a reasonable option. However, the hotel is quite a hike from the main train station.

Jílín Guójì Fàndiàn (Jílín International Hotel; ☎ 292 9818, fax 255 3788, 20 Zhongxing Jie) Singles/doubles/triples Y320/ 420/360. This three-star hotel has large and cheery rooms.

The Century Swiss-Belhotel (Shìjì Dà Fàndiàn; ☎ 464 9888, e centswissbel@yun han.com.cn, 77 Jilin Dajie) Doubles from Y800. Recently opened, the Century Swiss brings the ultimate in luxury to Jílín's hotel circuit. Amenities include Shiatsu massages and a Turkish steam bath.

Places to Eat

Jílín is not the capital of epicurean delights but there are still a handful of restaurants worth searching out. During the summer months *night markets* spring up around the city. The biggest and liveliest night market is on Hunchan Jie.

Jǐngfú Gōng (☎ 202 9999, Jiefang Dalu) Dishes from Y25. This Korean restaurant serves very tasty *bànfàn* – a dish of rice, vegetables and egg cooked in a stone pot that comes sizzling to the table. It's on the corner with Niuma Xinglu.

Lùsēnlín Xī Cāntīng (Green Forest European Food Restaurant; 99 Qingnian Lu) Dishes Y6-10. The dishes might have

JÍLÍN

PLACES TO STAY

2 Jílín Guójì Fàndiàn
   吉林国际饭店
3 Jiāotōng Bīnguǎn
   交通宾馆
9 Tiānshǐ Bīnguǎn
   天使宾馆
15 Jiāngchéng Bīnguǎn
   江城宾馆
16 Dōngguān Bīnguǎn
   东关宾馆
21 Yínhé Dàshà
   银河大厦
25 The Century Swiss-
   Belhotel
   世纪大饭店

PLACES TO EAT

5 Night Market
   夜市街
7 Jìngfú Gōng
   竟福宫

10 Lùsēnlín Xī Cāntīng
   绿森林西餐厅
26 Zhuāngjiayuàn
   Fàndiàn
   庄稼院饭店

OTHER

1 Main Train Station
   吉林火车站
4 Long-Distance Bus
   Station (to Hāěrbīn,
   Shěnyáng & Dūnhuā)
   岔路乡汽车站
6 Mosque
   清真寺
8 PSB
   公安局外事科
11 Internet bar
   网吧
12 CITS
   中国国际旅行社
13 Wén Miào
   文庙

14 CAAC
   中国民航
17 Post Office
   邮局
18 Catholic Church
   天主教堂
19 City Hall
   市政府
20 Long-Distance
   Bus Station
   (to Chángchūn)
   汽车站 （往长春）
22 Bank of China
   中国银行
23 Meteorite Shower
   Museum;
   Century Boat
   陨石雨博物馆；
   世纪船
24 Beiguo Chuntian
   Department
   Store
   北国春天百货商城

Western names but the taste is distinctly Chinese – tasty for the price however.

Zhuāngjiayuàn Fàndiàn (☎ 467 8315, *43 Jilin Dajie*) Dishes from Y15. This is a great, if not somewhat surreal, restaurant where you are served by Red Guards and are surrounded by Cultural Revolution memorabilia. The food is traditional *dōngběi* cuisine. Try the raw vegetables wrapped in tofu skins and topped with *nóngjiā jiàng* (a salty sauce unique to Jílín).

Getting There & Away

Air CAAC (☎ 245 4260) is at 1 Chongqing Jie, behind Dōngguān Bīnguǎn. There is a daily flight to Běijīng (Y870). Flights to Shànghǎi (Y1320) and Guǎngzhōu (Y2090) leave on Wednesday and Sunday. A bus to the airport leaves from CAAC at 8.30am and 11.30am (Y10).

Bus There are two long-distance bus stations in Jílín. The bus station in front of the train station has daily departures to Hāěrbīn (2.15pm and 4.30pm, six hours). Buses to Shěnyáng leave every hour between 8am and 10pm and there is a daily bus to Dūnhuā that departs at 9am.

For Chángchūn, buses leave every half hour between 6am and 6pm (Y30, 1½

hours) from Líjiāng bus station (Líjiāng kèyùnzhàn) on Xian Lu just west of the Líjiāngmén Bridge. To get to the Líjiāng bus station take the bright yellow minibus that leaves from the bus stop outside Jílín's train station.

Train The main train station is in the northern part of the city. A regular service runs to Chángchūn (Y26, two hours); last train is at 4pm. There are daily services to Hāěrbīn (Y38, five hours), and Túmén (via Dūnhuā), Shěnyáng (Y108, 7½ hours) and Dàlián (Y181, 15 hours). Overnight trains go to Běijīng (Y238, 17 hours), but tickets should be bought well in advance if you hope to nab a sleeper. It's often easier to go to Chángchūn and organise it there.

Getting Around

Jílín's airport is about 10km west of the city. A taxi will cost around Y50. Shuttle buses (Y5) run from CAAC to the airport twice daily at 8.00am and 11.30am.

Bus No 10 runs to the airport and No 30 runs up Jilin Dajie. A good way to see the city is to take the double-decker bus No 49 which runs between Century Square and Longtán Shān Gōngyuán. Stops are announced in English and Chinese.

Taxi fares start at Y5.

AROUND JÍLÍN
Ski Resorts

Located 25km south-east of Jílín, the slopes of Sōnghuā Hú Qīngshān reach an elevation of 934m. Opened in 1982 with an emphasis on beginners, the ski resort **Sōnghuā Hú Qīngshān Huáxuě Chǎng** *(admission Y50; ski season Dec-Feb)* has progressed in line with its skiers and now offers both intermediate slopes and a 5km section for cross-country fans. The resort has rental equipment, a cafe, restaurant and shopping arcade. Take bus No 9 from Jílín's main train station.

For those who find this all a little too tame, **Tōnghuā** *(admission Y50; ski season Dec-Feb)*, in the southern part of the province, has more challenging ski slopes.

Běidàhú Huáxuě Chǎng *(admission Y50; ski season Dec-Feb)*, 56km from Jílín, is perhaps the best place in China to practise the art of sliding downhill. A day of skiing will cost you around Y500. Ski rental, accommodation and places to eat are available at the resort. Unfortunately the only way to reach Běidàhú is by taxi (Y60).

CHÁNGBÁI SHĀN 长白山
Ever-White Mountains
☎ 0433

Chángbái Shān is China's largest nature reserve *(admission Y40, plus Y29 to get up to Heaven Pool)*, covering 210,000 hectares of dense, virgin forest.

Because of elevation changes there is a wide variation in animal and plant life in the reserve. From 700m to 1000m above sea level there are mixed coniferous and broadleaf trees (including white birch and Korean pines); from 1000m to 1800m, there are cold-resistant coniferous trees such as dragon spruce and fir; from 1800m to 2000m is a third forest belt; and above 2000m the landscape is alpine tundra – treeless and windy.

For the budding natural scientist there's plenty to investigate. Some 300 medicinal plants grow within the reserve (including winter daphne, Asia bell and wild ginseng); and entomologists will have a field day by the shores of Heaven Pool at the end of June, when the snow finally melts and results in an explosion of insect life. Some very shy animal species also make their home in the mountain range (the rarer ones being protected cranes, deer and Manchurian tigers).

CHÁNGBÁI SHĀN & HEAVEN POOL 长白山、天池

WARNING: The North Korean Border is not clearly marked. Avoid walking in the border area.

1 Baishan Skating Rink
  白山冰场
2 Small Heaven Pool
  (Xiǎo Tiānchí)
  小天池
3 Wind Gap (Fēng Kǒu)
  风口
4 Chess Match Cliff (Sàiqí Yá)
  赛棋崖
5 Crest Bridge (Guàn Qiáo)
  冠桥
6 Tianchi Meteorological Observatory
  天池气象站

Heaven Pool 天池
Tiān Chí

Heaven Pool is a volcanic crater lake at an elevation of 2194m and is by far the most popular sight at Chángbái Shān. The lake is 5km from north to south, 3.5km from east to west, and 13km in circumference. It's surrounded by jagged rock outcrops and 16 mountainous peaks; the highest is **White Rock Peak** *(Báiyán Fēng)*, which soars to 2749m. Ěrdàobái Hé runs off the lake, with a rumbling 68m waterfall that is the source of Sōnghuā Jiāng and Túmén Hé. The lake is also said to be home to a monster which was supposedly last sighted in June 2001 (see the boxed text 'Myths and Mists of Heaven Pool').

During the summer months tour buses roll up and disgorge day-trippers who pose heroically for photos in front of the waterfall, gorge on eggs boiled in the natural hot springs, stampede up the mountain (one-hour hike), take a lakeside breather and then rush down again. Yet there are opportunities to leave the crowds behind and spend a couple of peaceful and sublime days hiking around.

Keeping the boxed text 'Beware of the Border' in mind, if you're planning to hike off the beaten tourist trail, it's also advisable to bring dried food, sunscreen lotion and other medical supplies, good hiking gear and to hike in a group. High altitude weather is very fickle; no matter how warm it is in the morning, sudden high winds, rain and dramatic drops in temperature are entirely possible by afternoon. The peaks are often covered in cloud by around the 1000m mark.

Places to Stay

There are a growing number of places to stay in Chángbái Shān, although most are on the pricey side. If you plan to stay for a couple of days, however, staying in a dorm here will likely prove cheaper than basing yourself in Báihé and returning daily.

Chángbái Shān Dùjuān Shānzhuāng (*Mount Changbai Cuckoo Villa*; ☎ 574 6099, fax 574 6098) Dorm beds/doubles/suites Y50/580/980. This place is on the road to the waterfall and has fantastic suites that come with your own private, hot spring bath. Off-season 50% discounts are not hard to negotiate.

Chángbái Shān Guójì Lǚyóu Bīnguǎn (*Mount Changbai International Tourist Hotel*; ☎ 574 6001, fax 574 6002) Doubles Y600. This hotel looks so new it sparkles. Some rooms afford views of the waterfall.

Chángbái Shān Yùndòngyuán Cūn (*Changbai Athletes Village*; ☎ 571 2574, fax 571 2376) Dorm beds/doubles Y50/400. This modest place is not far from the main entrance on the road to the waterfall.

Camping is certainly a possibility although is technically against the rules. Be prepared for thunderstorms and try to find a place far away from curious spectators and the authorities.

Báihé The quiet village of Báihé is a good place to base yourself if you plan to visit Chángbái Shān on a day trip. The village is famous for being the only part of China where you can find a beautiful type of pine tree called a Meiren Song. They are extremely tall, elegant and photogenic.

Báihé has great budget accommodation options for travellers. There appear to be no restrictions for foreigners and so rickety beds can often be found in local households for Y5 to Y10.

> ### Beware of the Border
>
> Hiking at Heaven Pool is limited not only by the sharp peaks but also by the fact that the lake overlaps the Chinese–North Korean border. As recently as 1998, a British tourist was held for a month in a North Korean prison after unknowingly crossing the border while attempting to take a stroll around the circumference of the lake. This is an easy thing to do as the border is either not clearly marked or not indicated at all.
>
> To make matters worse, there are no detailed maps of the area available. Approximately one third of the lake, the south-eastern corner, is on the North Korean side and off-limits. Do not venture east of White Rock Peak or the Lakeside Hot Springs at Heaven Pool's summit. If you have any suspicions that you are nearing the border or are at all unsure as to where exactly it lies, do not proceed any further!

Tiělù Zhāodàisuǒ (☎ 571 1189) Dorm beds/doubles Y20/50. To the right as you exit the train station, this ramshackle place has clean-ish beds and basic washing facilities.

Èrdào Shuìwù Bīnguǎn (☎ 571 2455) Beds in 3-bed dorms Y50. The rooms here are great value and come with private bathroom. The hotel is diagonally accross from the long-distance bus station.

Báiyún Bīnguǎn (☎ 571 2545) Doubles Y260. This clinical looking building is on your left as you exit the train station. The hotel is surrounded by Meiren Song trees but the rooms are overpriced.

Getting There & Away

The best time to tackle Chángbái Shān is from June to early September (when the road from Báihé to the nature reserve isn't iced over). Telephone one of the hotels in the area to get a weather check and status report before you head out.

There are two main directions from which you can reach Chángbái Shān; one is from Shěnyáng to Báihé, via Tōnghuā, and the other is from Dūnhuà or Yánjí to Báihé.

There are two trains daily from Tōnghuā to Báihé, departing at 8.40am and 9.40pm. From Báihé, trains leave for Tōnghuā at 8.02am and 11.40pm (Y78, seven hours). From Tōnghuā, you can catch trains to Běijīng, Chángchūn and Dàlián.

Myths and Mists of Heaven Pool

The enchanting scenery at Heaven Pool would not be complete in the Chinese world without a legend or mystery of some sort. Of the many myths attached to the region, the most intriguing is the origin of the Manchu race.

Three heavenly nymphs descended to the lake in search of earthly pleasure. They took a dip in the lake, and while they were frolicking in the water, along came a magic magpie and dropped a red berry on the dress of one of the nymphs. When she picked it up to smell it, the berry flew through her lips. She became pregnant and gave birth to a handsome boy with an instant gift of the gab. He went on to foster the Manchus and their dynasty.

Dragons and other things that go bump in the night were believed to have sprung from the lake. In fact, they're still believed to do so. There have been intermittent sightings of unidentified swimming objects – China's very own Loch Ness monsters. However, Heaven Pool is the deepest alpine lake in China at a depth estimated at between 200m and 350m. It is frozen over in winter and temperatures are well below zero, so it would take a pretty hardy monster to make this place home (even plankton can't). Sightings from both sides point to a black bear, fond of swimming and oblivious to the paperwork necessary for crossing these tight borders.

On a heartfelt note, Chinese couples throw coins into the lake, pledging that their love will remain as deep and lasting as Heaven Pool.

Trains and buses travel to Dūnhuā from Chángchūn and Jílín. From Dūnhuā there are seven buses daily to Báihé (Y19, four hours), the earliest leaves at 6am. Buses to Jílín (Y25, 4½ hours) and Chángchūn (Y35, seven hours) run from in front of the train station at 7.30am and 9.30am.

Zhōnghuá Yìchūn Bīnguǎn (☎ 623 4075) Doubles Y100. If you get stuck in Dūnhuā for the night, this place is west of the long-distance bus station and has decent rooms.

If you're coming from Hēilóngjiāng, the best (and most enjoyable) option is to take a train to Yánjí from Mǔdānjiāng. In Yánjí there are six buses daily to Báihé (Y24 to Y26, four to six hours) between 6am and 12.20pm. Returning to Yánjí, the last bus leaves Báihé at 1pm. Between June and September there is a direct bus to Chángbái Shān from Yánjí that leaves at 5.30am and returns at 4pm (one way/return Y55/101).

Dōngběiyà Dàjiǔdiàn (*Northeast Asia Hotel;* ☎ *280 8111, fax 282 0970, 109 Changbai Lu*) Doubles Y150. If you want to spend the night in Yánjí, this place next to the long-distance bus station has snug doubles.

In Báihé buses to Dūnhuā and Yánjí leave from the long-distance bus station or from in front of the train station.

Getting Around

Minibuses leave for Chángbái Shān from in front of the train station in Báihé from 6am to noon, although there is no fixed timetable. The return trip should cost around Y50 although prices vary according to the bus driver.

If you want more time to hike around, it's worth hiring a car with a driver for the trip (ask at any of the restaurants in Báihé as some of the restaurant owners provide transport). Hiring a car should cost around Y300, but expect to barter with drivers and always agree on a price before you set out. Both buses and hired cars will drop you off at point where it is still another hour's hike to the lake, however jeeps are available for the final trek for Y80 per person.

No buses cover the route from Báihé when there's snow and ice, but you may find a local driver who can navigate the icy roads with tyre chains. This will probably cost a small fortune and maybe the odd broken rib, followed by the possibility of frostbite, so weigh it up carefully.

AROUND CHÁNGBÁI SHĀN
Korean Autonomous Prefecture
Yánbiān Cháoxiǎn 延边朝鲜

The Korean Autonomous Prefecture has China's greatest concentration of Korean and Hàn-Korean groups. The majority inhabit the border areas north and north-east of Báihé, extending up to the capital Yánjí. While the local people of Korean decent are often indistinguishable in dress and appearance from their Chinese counterparts, many of their traditions continue to link them to their heritage. If you visit this area around mid-August, you can join in the **Old People Festival**.

This area (Yánbiān) is rich in possibilities for shaking off the cities and traipsing through wilderness – and there are certainly some good reasons for doing so, including virgin forest and babbling brooks, and some rough travel and trails. The green mountains here provide more dramatic scenery than Jílín's flatter northern and western areas.

Getting around by train is safer than braving the winding roads by bus. Off the main track, the trains are puffing black dragons – the fittings are old and the trains have no sleepers. Jump on one of these slow beasts that dawdle through small villages and catch glimpses of everyday life off the tourist trail. Most of these villages have at least one basic hostel should you want to stop off at any point.

Apart from public buses, the only other means of vehicle transport is by hiring a private jeep (and driver) or by hitching a lift on a logging truck.

Trains running east from Dūnhuà to Túmén pass through Āntú, Lǎotóugōu and Yánjí from where you can also connect north to Hēilóngjiāng.

Hēilóngjiāng 黑龙江

Capital: Hāěrbīn
Population: 36.9 million
Area: 469,000 sq km

Hēilóngjiāng (Black Dragon River) is China's northernmost province and is known for its subarctic climate. Come January, with its -30°C (-22°F) weather and howling Siberian gales, the locals sensibly huddle round their stoves, swathed in thickly padded clothing, quaffing the local firewater. As a result of living in these conditions, the people of Hēilóngjiāng are hewn from rough material and have a reputation for being hardy and bellicose. Activity slows to a crunch in this snowflake-spitting weather, while the animals bypass the season completely by hibernating.

Welcome, believe it or not, to the tourist season. Inquisitive Hong Kong and Taiwanese tourists fly up to fulfil their childhood ambition of seeing snow, and are reputedly so blown away by the cold that they never set foot north of the tropic of Cancer again. Don't be put off – if you come prepared for weather conditions similar to winter on Pluto, the city of Hāěrbīn offers a sparkling spectacle of ice-encrusted Russian buildings, winter sports and its famous Ice Lantern Festival. The months of May to September open up the rest of the province to exploration.

HĀĚRBĪN 哈尔滨
☎ 0451 • pop 9,271,000

Originally a quiet village on Sōnghuā Jiāng, Hāěrbīn derives its name from *alejin*, the Manchu word for 'honour' or 'fame'.

In 1896 the Russians negotiated a contract to build a railway line from Vladivostok to Hāěrbīn and Dàlián. The Russian imprint on the town remained in one way or another until the end of WWII. By 1904 the 'rail concession' was in place, and with it came other Russian demands on Manchuria. These were stalled by the Russo-Japanese War (1904–05) and, with the Russian defeat, the Japanese gained control of the railway.

In 1917 large numbers of Russian refugees flocked to Hāěrbīn, fleeing the

Highlights

- Hāěrbīn's Ice Lantern Festival, the most spectacular (and coldest) winter event
- The peaceful wetlands of Zhālóng Nature Reserve, home to 236 species of birds
- Jìngpò Hú (Mirror Lake) for its clear reflections, small islands and waterfalls
- The Dàolǐqū district of Hāěrbīn for a look at the city's Russian past

Bolsheviks. The Japanese occupied the city in 1932, and in 1945 the Soviet army wrested it back and held it until 1946 when, as agreed by Chiang Kaishek and Stalin, Kuomintang troops were finally installed.

Hāěrbīn today is largely an industrial city but improving relations with Russia have resulted in flourishing trade and a mini-boom in cross-border tourism. The vast majority of foreign faces on the streets are Russian; the Chinese call them *lǎo máozi* (hairy ones). They will no doubt call you this as well, or speak to you in Russian, whether you are Russian or not.

The Russians generally come over for a holiday and to go shopping. They also bring with them all manner of items that will fetch a price in China, including

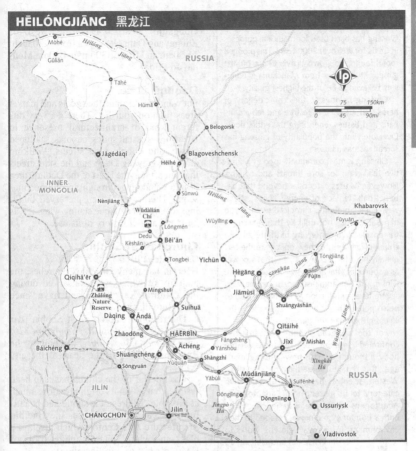

HĒILÓNGJIĀNG 黑龙江

Russian army surplus, such as night-vision goggles.

Hāěrbīn was once a graceful Chinese city and continues to possess a number of architectural gems handed down from the Russian era. The recent success in the tourism industry has spurred the restoration of some of the old Russian neighbourhoods; however, Hāěrbīn's allure is slowly being overwhelmed by giant, glitzy buildings and the fast pace and pollution of city life. Enjoy what's left of its charm while it lasts.

Orientation
In the north is Sōnghuā Jiāng, separating the city from Tàiyángdǎo Gōngyuán (Sun Island Park). The Dàolǐqū district, in the section towards the banks of Sōnghuā Jiāng, houses the main shopping zone and displays most of the historical buildings that give the city its character.

The main train station is in the centre of town, surrounded by a cluster of hotels.

Information
Tourist Office Potentially useful is the China Haerbin Overseas Tourist Corporation (Hǎiwài Lǚyóu Gōngsī; ☎ 461 5846, fax 461 4259) at 89 Zhongyang Dajie. The office is on the 2nd floor of Mǎdié'ěr Bīnguǎn and can arrange all sorts of tours and activities.

Money The Bank of China is at 19 Hongjun Jie. Any of the large hotels will change money.

The Magical Root

Ginseng has been used for medicinal purposes in China for well over 2000 years. This pronged root is found and grown all over China, but the ginseng that comes from Manchuria is popularly believed to be of the highest quality.

Ginseng belongs to the 'chi' category of herbs that are used to restore and rebuild organs and tissues, energising the entire body. Over the years the popularity of ginseng has spread, as has its uses.

Ginseng is most commonly used as a curative tea, good for sore throats and coughs. However, its uses extend far beyond that: fatigue, debility, lack of energy, shock, stress, weakened immunity, chronic diseases…you name it and it's not unlikely that ginseng is the answer. Women giving birth are given a chunk of ginseng to chew on, as are the terminally ill in the belief that the root's power as a source of vital energy will revitalise them. Ginseng is not administered to people with severe fever or infection as the herb is said to be so potent that it will give strength to the illness rather than the patient.

For the sceptical, scientific research has confirmed ginseng's positive effects on the body although exactly how ginseng manages this remains something of a mystery. Western scientists have made up their own category to fit ginseng into: 'adaptogens'. Adaptogens affect the way in which the body's hormones and nerves respond to their environment. In this way, ginseng works to increase the body's ability to adapt to and survive stressful conditions.

Post & Communications The main post office is on the corner of Dong Dazhijie and Fendou Lu. A second office is next to Kūnlún Fàndiàn. The China Telecom office is on Fendou Lu, north of the main post office.

For Internet access try the large Internet bar at 129 Zhongyang Dajie (☎ 457 8002). It is open 8.30am to 10pm daily and charges Y3 per hour for Internet access.

Travel Agencies China International Travel Service (CITS; Zhōngguó Guójì Lǚxíngshè; ☎ 366 1192), at 2 Teilu Jie, is on the 11th floor of the Hushi Dasha building near the train station.

PSB The Public Security Bureau (PSB; Gōngānjú) is at 26 Duan Jie, west off Zhongyang Dajie. It is open from 8.30am to 11.30am and from 1.30pm to 4.30pm Monday to Friday.

Dàolǐqū 道里区

Put wandering around the streets and market areas high on your list. There's a very different kind of architectural presence in Hāěrbīn – Russian spires, cupolas, scalloped turrets and cobblestone streets. Walking along Zhongyang Dajie and the side streets that run off it in the heart of the Dàolǐqū area is like wandering through an outdoor museum. There are thirteen preserved buildings, each with a plaque stating when it was built and a brief history of its use.

Church of St Sophia
Shèng Sùfēiyà Jiàotáng 圣索菲亚教堂

Hāěrbīn has many Orthodox churches, the majority of which were ransacked during the Cultural Revolution and have since fallen into disrepair.

The restored Church of St Sophia *(cnr Zhaolin Jie & Toulong Jie; admission Y10; open 9.30am-5.30pm daily)* was built by the Russians in 1907 in the heart of the city centre.

The interior of the church has also been restored but left in its original state as much as possible. The result is subtle and beautiful. The church now houses the **Haerbin Architecture Arts Centre**, which displays a black-and-white photographic trail of Hāěrbīn's history pre-liberation.

Sīdàlín Gōngyuán 斯大林公园
Stalin Park

Sīdàlín Gōngyuán, a perambulating zone down by the river, is dotted with statues and recreation clubs for the locals. The promenade is constructed along a 42km embankment that was built to curb unruly Sōnghuā Jiāng. The bizarre **Flood Control Monument** *(Fánghóng Shènglì Jìniàntǎ)* was built in 1958 to celebrate the embankment's victory in holding back the river, as well as to commemorate the thousands of people who had previously died in the floods.

A resort feel holds sway in summer, with ice-cream stands, photo booths and boating trips along the river and across to Tàiyángdǎo Gōngyuán.

Sōnghūa Jiāng itself comes alive in winter with **ice-skating**, **ice-hockey**, **tobogganing** and even **ice sailing** (vessels sail on the ice surface, assisted by wind power, and reach speeds of 30km/h). Equipment for each of these sports can be hired. Slightly madder folk astound onlookers by swimming in gaps in the ice.

Tàiyángdǎo Gōngyuán
Sun Island Park 太阳岛公园

A ferry trip away, and facing Sīdàlín Gōngyuán, is Tàiyángdǎo Gōngyuán, a sanatorium/recreational zone covering 3800 hectares and offering gardens, forested areas and a 'water world'. In the summer the area is alive with both flora and tour groups. In the winter it has its own mini-snow sculpture exhibition.

Boat tickets are available in Sīdàlín Gōngyuán. Buy a ticket from one of the government-run boat ticket vendors (*guóyíng chuánpiào*), whose dock is directly north of the Flood Control Monument. These tickets only cost Y2, while the private operators charge around Y10. You can also take a cable car (one-way/return Y35/60) to Tàiyángdǎo Gōngyuán from the end of Tongjiang Jie.

Siberian Tiger Park 东北虎林园
Dōngběi Hǔ Lìnyuán

The mission of the Siberian Tiger Park (☎ 409 0098; adult/child Y50/25; open 8am-4.30pm daily) in Songbeixin district, is to study, breed, release and ultimately save the Manchurian tiger from extinction. However, while you are definitely promised a very up-close look at the 70 captive cats, those who are not too keen on zoos might be best to give this supposed sanctuary a miss. The fenced-off field feels far too small for these bored looking beasts, never mind the touring minibuses whose drivers blare their horns and play chicken with the cats to the delight of the tourists. The drivers continually encourage passengers to buy chunks of meat to throw to the tigers, which makes you wonder how exactly the park is preparing these animals for the wild.

The park is roughly 20km outside the city. Bus No 85 from the corner of Youyi Lu and Zhongyang Dajie will drop you a 15-minute walk, or Y5 pedicab ride, away from the park entrance. Taxis can be hired

and bargaining starts at around Y100 for the round trip. The last tour of the park is conducted at 4pm.

You can combine the trip with a visit to Tàiyángdǎo Gōngyuán from where you can head back to Sīdàlín Gōngyuán via the ferry. Minibuses/taxis running between the gardens and Siberia Tiger Park cost Y10 per person.

Jí Lè Sì 吉乐寺
Temple of Bliss

The deserted feel of Jí Lè Sì (9 Dongda Zhijie; admission Y5; open 9am-4.30pm daily) is defied by the active Buddhist community in residence. Inside the temple are a number of statues including Milefo (Maitreya), the Buddha yet-to-come, whose arrival will bring paradise on earth. If you're already inside when the gates close you can discreetly catch the monks in ceremonial action.

Qījí Fútú Tǎ 七级浮屠塔
Seven-tiered Buddhist Pagoda

Next door to Jí Lè Sì is Qījí Fútú Tǎ (11 Dongda Zhijie; admission Y5; open 9am-4pm daily), the largest temple in Hēilóngjiāng. The complex, built in 1924, features an elegant stone pagoda in the middle of the courtyard. The illustrations along the back wall tell classical stories of filial piety. In spring, the air resonates with the sound of wind chimes and makes for a very peaceful retreat.

Pǔzhào Sì 普照寺
Temple of Universal Light

Pǔzhào Sì is a working monastery next door to Qījí Fútú Tǎ. The monastery is only open to the public on the 1st and 15th of every month for worship. At any other time the doors are shut, but you may find that one of the monks lets you have a peek inside.

All three temples can be reached by bus No 14 from the southern end of Zhongyang Dajie to the bus terminus.

Értóng Gōngyuán 儿童公园
Children's Park

Értóng Gōngyuán (☎ 367 8325, 295 Fendou Lu; adult/child Y2/1; open 5am-9.30pm daily) is a fun place for kids and features the **Children's Railway** (*Értóng Tiělù*), which was built in 1956. It has 2km

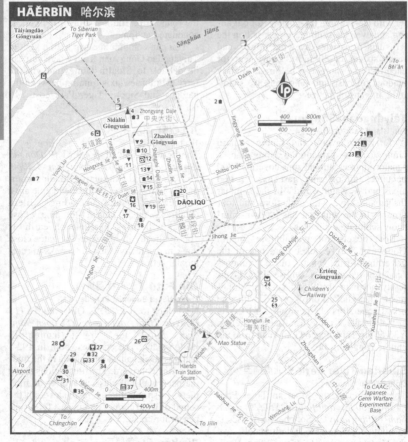

HĀĔRBĪN 哈尔滨

of track that is plied by a miniature diesel engine, pulling seven cars with seating for 200; the round trip from 'Bĕijīng' to 'Hāěrbīn' takes 20 minutes and costs Y5.

Take bus No 8 from the southern end of Zhongyang Dajie and get off at Fendou Lu, or trolleybus No 109 from the station.

Heilongjiang Provincial Museum
Hēilóngjiāng Shĕng Bówùguǎn 博物馆
This museum (☎ 364 4151, 64 Hongjun Jie; admission Y12; open 9am-4pm daily) is one of the better provincial museums you're likely to come across. The Historical Relics Exhibition on the 2nd floor displays some interesting finds from archaeological digs in the province. Included in the exhibition are examples of fish-skin clothing worn by the

Hezhen minority (see the boxed text 'The Hezhen'). The Nature Exhibition has some huge dinosaur skeletons.

Germ Warfare Base
If you haven't visited concentration camps such as Belsen or Auschwitz, a similar lesson in the extreme horrors of war can be learnt at the **Japanese Germ Warfare Experimental Base – 731 Division** (Rìbĕn Xìjūn Shíyàn Jīdì – 731 Bùduì; ☎ 680 4104, cnr Xinjiang Dajie & Xingjian Jie; admission Y10; open 8.30am-11.30am & 1pm-4pm daily).

In 1939 the Japanese army set up a top-secret, germ-warfare research centre in Hāěrbīn. Japanese medical experts experimented on prisoners of war, including

HĀĚRBĪN

PLACES TO STAY

2 Guǒcài Màoyì Dàshà
果菜贸易大厦

3 Sōnghuājiāng
Kǎilái Shāngwù Jiǔdiàn
松花江凯莱商务酒店

7 Haerbin Shangri-La Hotel
哈尔滨香格里拉大饭店

8 Zhōngdà Dàjiǔdiàn
中大大酒店

10 Jīngǔ Fàndiàn
金谷饭店

14 Mǎdiē'ěr Bīnguǎn;
China Haerbin Tourist Corporation
马迭尔宾馆

18 Holiday Inn
万达假日酒店

30 Kūnlún Fàndiàn
昆仑饭店

32 Běiyuàn Fàndiàn
北苑饭店

34 Gōngānjú Zhāodàisuǒ
公安局招待所

35 Tiānzhú Bīnguǎn
天竹宾馆

36 Huáqiáo Fàndiàn; CTS
华侨饭店

PLACES TO EAT

9 Cafe Russia 1914

11 Bālí Miànbāo Fáng
巴黎面包房

13 Portman Bar
波特曼西餐厅

15 Dōngfāng Jiǎozi Wáng
东方饺子王

17 Fùshìshān Rìběn Liàolǐ
福十山日本料理

19 Sweet Chocolate Shop
甜死死巧克力店

OTHER

1 Passenger Ferry Terminal
游船渡

4 Flood Contral Monument
防洪胜利纪念塔

5 Ferries to Tàiyángdǎo
Gōngyuán
太阳岛游览船

6 Cable Car
览车

12 Internet Bar
网吧

16 PSB
公安局外事科

20 Church of St Sophia;
Haerbin Architecture Arts Centre
圣素菲亚教堂

21 Pǔzhào Sì
普照寺

22 Qījí Fútú Tǎ
塔院

23 Jí Lě Sì
吉乐寺

24 Main Post Office
总邮局

25 Bank of China
中国银行

26 Telephone Office
电信局

27 Běiběi Hànbīng Dìtǔ Gāo
北北旱冰迪土高

28 Main Train Station
哈尔滨火车站

29 CITS
中国国际旅行社

31 Post Office
邮局

33 Long-Distance Bus Station
公路客运站

37 Heilongjiang Provincial Museum
省博物馆

Chinese, Soviet, Korean, Mongolian and British prisoners. Over 4000 people were exterminated in bestial fashion: some were frozen or infected with bubonic plague, others were injected with syphilis and many were roasted alive in furnaces.

When the Soviets took back Hāěrbīn in 1945, the Japanese blew up the base. Their secret could have remained buried forever, but a tenacious Japanese journalist dragged out the truth in the 1980s.

The Japanese medical profession was rocked by the news that some of its leading members had a criminal past that had hitherto escaped detection. Another disturbing angle to the story was the claim that the Americans had granted freedom to the perpetrators of these crimes in return for their research data.

The exhibition consists of only two small rooms plus a nearby vestige of the original base. All captions are in Chinese only; if you are unable to read them, it is questionable whether or not the long haul out to the museum is worth it.

The museum is 20km south of the city; take bus No 338 or 343 from the main train station.

Festivals

Hāěrbīn's main attraction is the **Ice Lantern Festival** (*Bīngdēng Jié; admission Y20; open 8am-10pm*), held in Zhàolín Gōngyuán and along Sōnghuā Jiāng. Officially, it's held from 5 January to 15 February, although in reality it may start a week earlier and glisten into March.

Fanciful sculptures are produced in the shapes of animals, plants, buildings or motifs taken from legends. Some of the larger sculptures have included a miniature Great Wall of China and a scaled-down Forbidden City. At night the sculptures are illuminated from the inside with coloured lights, turning the place into a temporary fantasy world.

The main entrance is by the Flood Control Monument. Horse-drawn sleigh rides cost Y10. Drivers will take those with masochistic tendencies to swimming holes for Y100. More enjoyable, perhaps, is the icy slide.

In warmer climes, there's the **Haerbin Music Festival** (*Yīnyuè Jié;* ☎ 360 7724), a 12-day event held annually in July. The festival brings together traditional and modern musicians and performers from all over China. Ticket prices vary from year to year, call ahead or inquire at CITS.

Places to Stay

Hotel prices jump significantly during the Ice Lantern Festival when you can expect a rise of at least 20% in those listed here. In the low season discounts of 30% are not uncommon.

Follow the train station touts if you're looking for a cheap dive. But be warned, these rooms are most often off limits to foreigners and at any moment you may be asked to leave by hotel owners who suddenly remember (or are reminded) that they cannot accommodate foreigners.

Gōngānjú Zhāodàisuǒ *(PSB Hostel;* ☎ 367 7261) Beds in 6-bed dorms/doubles Y40/100. The hotel is in desperate need of a paint job but the rooms are surprisingly tidy. To find the hostel turn left out of the train station and then left past the post office. Be warned: this hotel may sometimes not accept foreigners.

Tiānzhú Bīnguǎn (☎ 363 7261, fax 364 3720, 6 Songhuajiang Jie) Doubles/triples Y120/180. This tower block is on your right as you exit the train station near the Hushi Dasha building. Rooms are decent and include a mediocre breakfast.

Běiyuàn Fàndiàn (☎ 364 2200, 2 Chunshen Jie) Doubles Y150. Directly facing the train station is this hotel with somewhat sorry looking rooms.

Huáqiáo Fàndiàn *(Overseas Chinese Hotel;* ☎ 364 1479, fax 362 3429, 72 Hongjun Jie) Doubles from Y200. Within walking distance of the main train station, this three-star hotel is a refuge of Hong Kong residents and southerners coming to build snowmen; it's often full.

Guǒcài Màoyì Dàshà *(Fruit & Vegetable Trade Hotel;* ☎ 830 7976, 42 Beima Lu)

Species under Threat

Also known as the Amur, Siberian and North-Eastern China tiger, the Manchurian tiger has long been resident in China. Believed to be the ancestor of all tiger species, the Manchurian tiger began its trek south from the Arctic Circle and northern Siberia several million years ago. Today it makes its home in eastern Russia, North Korea and north-eastern China.

The Manchurian tiger is one of the rarest as well as the largest of all tiger sub-species. The average male can grow up to four metres long, with a healthy weight of 300kg. The comforts of captivity can increase this weight to over 500kg. But have no fear – it is extremely unlikely that you will run into one of these beasts in the wilds of China. In 1998 it was estimated that the number of Manchurian tigers had depleted to somewhere between 360 and 406, with only 30 to 35 of those roaming freely in China. Given first-grade protection by the Chinese government and recognised as one of the most endangered species worldwide by the World Wide Fund for Nature, the situation of the Manchurian tiger remains perilous. This is the result of the encroachment of cities and pollution on the tigers' territory as well as the lucrative business of poaching. The bones of the tiger, in particular the thigh bones, are highly prized in traditional Chinese medicine, while tiger skins also fetch a hefty price on the black market. One tiger can earn up to 10 years' income for a Chinese poacher.

In response to the Manchurian tigers' plight, the Chinese government has set up a number of breeding centres, including the Siberian Tiger Park outside Hāěrbīn. Currently home to 70 tigers, the purpose of centres like this one is to restore the natural population of the tigers by breeding them and reintroducing them into the wild. However, conservationists stress the need for minimal human contact with tigers, and for the centres to emulate as much as possible the life that the tigers will face once released. It has been argued that China's breeding centres, which sees bus loads of tourists snapping photos of the cats munching on their dinners of cows and chickens, will produce tigers with a taste for livestock who will associate people and vehicles with feeding time. It is believed that this may render them more suitable for a life of drive-through fast food than one in the great outdoors. Until the first captive tiger is set free, the fate of China's Manchurian tigers – and the local livestock and vehicle owners – remains unknown.

Doubles/triples Y128/188. Good-value, comfortable rooms can be had at this hotel in the Daowai district.

Zhōngdà Dàjiǔdiàn (☎ *463 8888, fax 465 2888, 40 Zongyang Dajie*) Doubles Y190. This excellent budget accommodation in the heart of Dàolǐqū has rooms overlooking Zhongyang Dajie.

Jīngǔ Fàndiàn (☎ *469 8700, fax 469 8458, 185 Zhongyang Dajie*) Doubles Y580. This three-star hotel is minutes away from Sīdàlín Gōngyuán and some rooms have views of Sōnghùa Jiāng.

Mǎdié'ěr Bīnguǎn (*Modern Hotel;* ☎ *461 5846, fax 461 4997, 89 Zongyang Dajie*) Singles/doubles/triples Y220/418/308. This lovely hotel was built in 1906 in the heart of the Dàolǐqū area. The rooms are packed with character and the staff are fantastic. It's best to book in advance.

Sōnghuājiāng Kǎilái Shāngwù Jiǔdiàn (*Songhuajiang Gloria Inn;* ☎ *463 8855, fax 463 8533, 257 Zhongyang Dajie*) Rooms Y588. Half a block from Sīdàlín Gōngyuán, this inn offers plush rooms in a prime location.

Holiday Inn (*Wàndá Jiàrì Jiǔdiàn;* ☎ *422 6666, fax 422 1661, 90 Jingwei Jie*) Doubles Y814. On the cusp of Hāěrbīn's attractive Dàolǐqū district is the four-star Holiday Inn.

Kūnlún Fàndiàn (☎ *360 6688, fax 360 0888, 8 Tielu Jie*) Rooms Y640-1145 plus 15% service charge. To your immediate right as you exit the train station is this pleasant hotel with an indoor pool, sauna and six restaurants.

Haerbin Shangri-La Hotel (*Hāěrbīn Xiānggé Lǐlā Dàjiǔdiàn;* ☎ *285 8888, fax 462 1777, 55 Youyi Lu*) Singles/doubles $175/195 plus 15% service charge. The views from these rooms make this possibly the best place to enjoy the Ice Lantern Festival in Hāěrbīn.

Places to Eat

Lanterns hang above the entrance to every restaurant – a practice almost exclusive to Hāěrbīn. It's actually a rating system – the more lanterns, the higher the standard and price. Red lanterns mean Chinese food, and blue denotes pork-free cuisine from the Muslim Hui minority (mainly lamb dishes).

Hāěrbīn has also long been famous for expensive culinary exotica, such as grilled bear paws, deer nostrils and Siberian tiger testicles. Fortunately, Běijīng now takes a dim view of serving up endangered species.

Sausages are especially popular in Hāěrbīn. This culinary art has developed alongside the growth in Russian tourism and has now become something of a city trademark.

Zhongyang Dajie is a good place to stroll for bakeries, restaurants and bars where you can sample the local beer 'Hapi'.

Dōngfāng Jiǎozi Wáng (*Kingdom of Eastern Dumplings;* ☎ *469 0888, 39 Zhongyang Dajie*) Dumplings Y20. This popular restaurant serves royal helpings of dumplings with a large choice of fillings.

Portman Bar (*Bōtèmàn Xīcāntīng;* ☎ *468 6888, 63 Xiqi Daojie*) Dishes from Y30. The Portman looks like a German beer-house but serves Western cuisine including fresh seafood and pasta. Jugs of red wine are on tap to wash it all down.

Fúshìshān Rìběn Liàolǐ (☎ *427 2851, 132 Jingwei Jie*) Dishes from Y20. Escape the Zhongyang Dajie crowds for sushi and barbecue at this small Japanese restaurant.

Cafe Russia 1914 (☎ *456 3207, 57 Toudao Jie*) Set meals from Y25. For home-cooking Russian-style, including some succulent sausages, head over to this authentic Russian tearoom near Jīngǔ Fàndiàn.

Bālí Miànbāo Fáng (*Paris Cafe;* ☎ *464 9109, 174 Zhongyang Dajie*) Coffees Y15, pastries Y5. For those in need of something stronger than green tea try this cafe for a double-strength espresso and croissants.

Sweet Chocolate Shop (*Tiánsīsī Qiǎokèlì Diàn;* ☎ *469 3350, 45 Zhongyang Dajie*) This is an Aladdin's Cave of all things delicious and has shelves stacked high with imported chocolate, coffee, tea and sweets.

Entertainment

Běiběi Hànbīng Díshìgāo (*Běiběi Dry Ice Disco*) Admission Y20. Open 9am-noon. The pick of Hāěrbīn's entertainment has to be this bar/disco/roller skating rink. It is regularly packed with Hāěrbīn's finest and is a must for anyone with a sense of humour. The Běiběi is in the underground shopping centre opposite the train station – use the entrance outside Běiyuàn Fàndiàn. Admission includes skate hire.

Getting There & Away

Air Civil Aviation Administration of China (CAAC; Zhōngguó Mínháng; ☎ 262 7070) is in the hotel of the same name at 101 Zhongshan Lu. China Travel Service (CTS; Zhōngguó Lǚxíngshè; ☎ 364 0916) has a ticketing office in Huáqiáo Fàndiàn. There are frequent flights to Seoul (Y2680) and twice-weekly flights to Hong Kong (Y2000). CAAC offers international flights to Khabarovsk (Y1350) in Siberia and twice-weekly flights to Vladivostok (Y1430).

A huge number of domestic destinations can be reached from Hāĕrbīn including Běijīng (Y890), Shànghǎi (Y1560), Shēnzhèn (Y2120) and Dàlián (Y770).

Bus The main long-distance bus station is directly opposite the train station. Buses leave every hour to Mǔdānjiāng (Y81, four hours), Jiāmùsī (Y86), Qíqíhā'ěr (Y61) and Shěnyáng (Y130). A daily bus leaves for Wǔdàlián Chí (Y69) at 1.30pm.

Train There is a vast number of destinations including Chángchūn (Y61, three to four hours), Dàlián (seat/sleeper Y125 to Y216, 12 to 14 hours), Běijīng (Y281, 13 hours) and Suífenhé (Y165, 11 hours). Rail connections to Qíqíhā'ěr (Y44) and Mǔdānjiāng (Y52) are regular but slow.

For travellers on the Trans-Siberian Railway, Hāĕrbīn is a possible starting or finishing point, but it is tricky to get hold of tickets. For more information try the Hāĕrbīn Railway International Tourist Agency on the 7th floor of Kūnlún Fàndiàn, which has information on travelling through to Russia. The CITS and the China Haerbin Overseas Tourist Corporation may also be able to help.

Boat Unfortunately all ferry services have been suspended and they are unlikely to resume. Check with the passenger ferry terminal when you arrive in Hāĕrbīn to see if the situation has changed.

Getting Around

To/From the Airport Hāĕrbīn's airport is 46km from town and the journey takes at least one hour. Shuttle buses go to the airport from the CAAC office and cost Y10. Buses leave about 2½ hours before scheduled flight departure times. A taxi will cost around Y100.

Bus Hāĕrbīn's many buses start running at 5am and finish at 10pm (9.30pm in winter). Some useful buses include trolleybus Nos 101 and 103 that run from Sīdàlín Gōngyuán to the train station. Minibuses also follow this route and cost Y2. Trolleybus No 109 runs from the train station to Értóng Gōngyuán. Minibus No 64 goes from Dàolǐqū to the Provincial Museum. Bus Nos 60 and 7 run to the passenger ferry terminal.

Boat The government ferry can take you from Sīdàlín Gōngyuán to Tàiyángdǎo Gōngyuán for Y2 (see Tàiyángdǎo Gōngyuán in this chapter for more information). Tickets are also available in Sīdàlín Gōngyuán for boat cruises up and down Sōnghūa Jiāng (Y30).

AROUND HĀĔRBĪN
Ski Resorts

The **Yùquán hunting grounds** (*admission Y30*), 65km from Hāĕrbīn, offer skiing facilities most appreciated by beginners. If you do want to go hunting, you pay per animal slaughtered (a wild turkey will set you back Y70) in addition to gun rental and a fee of Y5 per bullet shot. From Hāĕrbīn there is a train to the town of Yùquán from where you must take a taxi to the hunting grounds. Inquire in Hāĕrbīn at the China Haerbin Overseas Tourist Corporation or ask at CITS.

Yăbùli, 200km east of Hāĕrbīn, is *the* place to go skiing and has the biggest and best facilitated ski resort in China. **Windmill Village** (*☎ 345 5088, fax 345 5138*) is the ski resort village and was host to the 1996 Asian Winter Games. Dàguōkuī Shān is the actual **ski area** and has 11 ski runs, a 5km cross-country circuit and children's skiing area. The ski season depends on the weather, but can last from the end of November until the beginning of April. Ski passes include equipment and cost Y260/750 for one/three days. In summer the area is popular for hiking.

Information and room bookings can be organised in Hāĕrbīn (☎ 345 5088). The China Haerbin Overseas Tourist Corporation offers some surprisingly good deals on tours to the area that include transport, ski pass and equipment rental and accommodation.

Places to Stay

Fēngchē Shānzhuāng (Windmill Hotel; ☎ *345 5168, fax 345 5138)* Dorm beds low/high season Y240/480. Located in Windmill Village, Fēngchē Shānzhuāng offers three-star accommodation at the bottom of the ski hill. Prices vary with season and day; a double room on a weekday in low season will cost Y340 while on a weekend in high season, the same room will cost Y980. The hotel also has a youth section *(qīngnían gōngyù).*

There are 11 villas in Windmill Village that can sleep 15 to 30 people from Y1000. Contact the Windmill Village reception/general enquiries (☎ 345 5088) for information. Alternatively try one of the smaller hotels in Yàbùli village (not the ski resort) where beds can often be found for Y70.

Getting There & Away

Buses run from Hāěrbīn to Yàbùli at 8am and 1.20pm daily (three hours). From Mǔdānjiāng there are buses every 30 minutes from 6am to 5pm (1½ hours). Yàbùli can also be approached by train from Hāěrbīn (four hours). There are minibuses in Yàbùli village that run to the ski resort.

MǓDĀNJIĀNG 牡丹江

☎ 0453 • pop 570,000

A nondescript city of more than one million people, Mǔdānjiāng's main interest to independent travellers is its function as a staging post for visits to nearby Jìngpò Hú (Mirror Lake) and the Underground Forest.

Information

The Bank of China is two blocks south of the train station, on the eastern side of Taiping Lu. Three blocks south of the bank is the post office and China Telecom is directly behind it on Dongyi Tiaolu.

CITS has an office at 34 Jingfu Jie (☎ 691 1944), which is open 8am to 5pm. The PSB is two blocks east of the train station on Guanghua Jie, and CAAC (☎ 691 6775) is on the corner of Donger Tiaolu and Aimin Jie.

There is an enormous underground Internet bar on Pingan Jie. It is open 24 hours and Internet access costs Y1.5 per hour. Look for the large multicoloured sign.

Places to Stay

Cheaper accommodation options are in the process of being bulldozed so mid-range hotels are all that is available.

Běishān Bīnguǎn (☎ *652 5788, fax 652 4670, 1 Xidiming Jie)* Doubles Y188-280. This hotel is about 1km north of the train station and has large airy doubles, some overlooking the picturesque hotel garden.

Mǔdānjiāng Jiālín Fàndiàn (☎ *653 0888, fax 655 4888, 46 Xinhua Lu)* Doubles Y220. Just south of Běishān Bīnguǎn is this very stylish hotel with all rooms recently renovated.

Both hotels can be reached by bus No 2 or 14 from the train station.

Getting There & Away

The usual approach to Mǔdānjiāng is by rail and there are connections with Hāěrbīn, Suífēnhé, Túmén, Jiāmùsī and Dōngjīng.

Flight destinations include Běijīng (Y950), Shànghǎi (Y1460) and Guǎngzhōu (Y2080). A shuttle bus makes the 10km journey to the airport (Y10) from the CAAC office and departs 1½ hour before flights.

Long distance buses arrive and depart from in front of the train station. Regular departures link Mǔdānjiāng to Túmén, Jiāmùsī, Dōngjīng and Hāěrbīn.

AROUND MǓDĀNJIĀNG
Jìngpò Hú 镜泊湖
Mirror Lake

Covering an area of 90 sq km and 45km in length, Jìngpò Hú *(admission Y22)* was formed on the bend of the Mudan River 5000 years ago by the falling lava of five volcanic explosions. The clear reflections of the tree-lined coast and many small islands within Mirror Lake leave no question as to why it has been so-named. It is extremely popular with visiting Russians and Chinese Party cadres as well as the busloads of Chinese tourists who roll up during the summer months. As a result the area has been developed into a resort with hotels, recreation centres and even a post office.

Apart from speeding about from island to islet by boat (which costs an incredible Y800 per hour), or turning off the beaten path and escaping into the woods that ring the lake, the main visitor pastime is **fishing**. The fishing season is from June to August, and tackle and boats can be hired (prices are negotiable). Different varieties of carp (silver, black, red-tailed and crucian) are the trophies.

Nearby, **Diaoshuilou Waterfall**, spanning 20m in height and 40m in width, is an attractive spectacle that swells in size during the rainy season.

Unfortunately, the area has relinquished much of its majesty to the tourist industry, which has pock-marked the surrounding greenery with resorts and hotels and polluted the air with the screeching sounds of karaoke. Its popularity has also meant a dramatic rise in prices to the extent that the resort is fast becoming a summer playground of the rich.

Visiting the lake during low season, from October to May, however, provides a relatively peaceful getaway. The low season sees the disappearance of not only the majority of vendors and tourists, but also of the PSB. This means your chances of getting a bargain bed are much greater. Be warned, however, that many hotels and restaurants shut down during the low season.

Places to Stay
A number of hotels encircle the lake, all of which fill up quickly during the summer months. Call ahead.

Shānzhuāng Bīnguǎn (Mountain Village Hotel; ☎ *627 0039)* Doubles Y200. The rooms are nothing special but they all come with views of the lake.

Yóudìanjú Bīnguǎn (Post & Communication Hotel; ☎ *627 0096)* Dorm beds/doubles Y60/200. The doubles look a bit battered but the dorms are good value.

Zhōngguó Bīnguǎn (China Hotel; ☎ *627 0030)* Doubles or triples Y300. Situated on the edge of Jìngpò Hú, this new hotel has generous, airy rooms and a large balcony that extends out over the lake.

Getting There & Away
From Mǔdānjiāng there is a direct bus to Jìngpò Hú that leaves from outside the train station at 7am (one way/return Y15/30, 1½ hours) and returns at 3.30pm. Slower minibuses also do the journey (Y17). From Hāěrbīn there is a daily bus to the lake that leaves at 8am and returns at 4pm.

There are regular trains to Dōngjīng (Y10, 1¼ hours) from Mǔdānjiāng, from where it's one hour by minibus (Y10) to the lake. From

June to September, three buses run daily from Mǔdānjiāng train station to Dōngjīng between 6am and 7am (two hours). In Dōngjīng, minibuses *only* run to the lake during these summer months and at all other times you will be forced to take at taxi.

Dōngjīng is connected by slow trains to Suífēnhé, Jiāmùsī and Túmén.

If you are on a tour of the lakes of the north-east, it is possible to take the bus from Báihé, near Tiān Chí in Jílín province, to Dūnhuā and from there take the bus to Dōngjīng. The bus from Dūnhuā will pass Jìngpò Hú, but it is better to carry on to Dōngjīng and backtrack as you will be dropped off miles from any transport at the edge of the lake.

Underground Forest 地下森林
Dìxia Sēnlín
Although called the Underground Forest *(open June-Sept)* by locals, the forest has actually grown within the craters of volcanoes that erupted some 10,000 years ago. There are ten craters in total out of which Crater No 3 is the largest and open to the public. The lush forest is home to a rich variety of plants and animals including the Purple Pine and the Dragon Spruce, and the leopard and black bear.

The forest is 50km from Jìngpò Hú. To reach the forest, take a bus or train from Mǔdānjiāng to Dōngjīng and from there change to a minibus for the forest. Some buses combine a trip to the forest with visits to Jìngpò Hú.

SUÍFĒNHÉ 绥芬河
☎ 0453
This town achieved commercial importance in 1903 with the opening of the South Manchurian Railway, a vital link in the original Trans-Siberian route running from Vladivostok to Moscow via Manchuria. The role of Suífēnhé faded, however, when the railway was later rerouted via Khabarovsk to Vladivostok and Nakhodka.

Suífēnhé has, like other borderland outposts, enjoyed a spasmodic growth in cross-border trade and tourism in recent years. Yet the self-flattering nickname of 'Little Moscow of the East' harbours little, if any, truth. Other than shop signs printed in Russian, one or two dilapidated Russian-style buildings and a whole lot of Russians themselves, you'll be hard pressed to find anything in Suífēnhé to remind you of its pre-revolutionary days.

Unless you're planning on crossing the border into Russia, for which you will need to have organised a Russian visa in Běijīng and, if you plan to re-enter China, a re-entry visa, there is little to justify the long journey needed to reach Suífēnhé.

Information

The Bank of China is at 41 Shancheng Lu, across from the main square. The post office is in a large, Russian relic building on the corner of Jingxin Jie and Guanghua Lu behind the church. The PSB is at 20 Xinkai Jie, uphill from the train station.

Places to Stay

Most hotels in Suífēnhé are of poor quality and often packed with Russian tour groups.

Dōngxīng Dàjiǔdiàn (☎ 392 5430, fax 392 5439, cnr Yingxin Jie & Guanghua Lu) Dorm beds Y50, doubles Y128-300. This is the 'official' foreign guesthouse and has colourless, shoddy rooms. The hotel is up the hill from the train station, just past the church.

Hùdàjiàrì Jiǔdiàn (☎ 392 1630, cnr Tongtian Lu & Xinhua Jie) Doubles Y200-260. This hotel is a five minute walk past the Dōngxīng Hotel. The rooms are more expensive but are much nicer than Dōngxīng Dàjiǔdiàn.

Getting There & Away

The Hāěrbīn to Suífēnhé train leaves Hāěrbīn at 6.30pm, passing through Mǔdānjiāng around 1.30am and arriving in Suífēnhé at 5.49am.

From Suífēnhé to Hāěrbīn there is an overnight train departing at 8.06pm that arrives at 7.26am.

There is a daily international passenger train for Vladivostok. This train passes through Pogranichny (Grodekovo), a small town that borders China near Suífēnhé, 210km from Vladivostok. Pogranichny is also connected with Ussuriysk and Vladivostok by bus and taxi.

WǓDÀLIÁN CHÍ 五大连池
☎ 0456

Wǔdàlián Chí is a nature reserve and health spot that has also been turned into a 'volcano museum'. Despite being voted one of the top 40 sights in China in 1992, Wǔdàlián Chí is still primarily the domain of geologists, volcanologists and the infirm, and sees few tourists apart from the tour groups arriving by the bus load in the summer.

This area, in the north of the province, has a long history of volcanic activity. The most recent eruptions occurred in 1719 and 1720, when lava from craters blocked the nearby Běi Hé (North River) and formed the series of barrier lakes. The malodorous mineral springs are the source of legendary cures and are the main attraction for the hordes of chronically ill people who arrive in the summer to slurp the waters or slap mud onto themselves.

As for the volcanoes themselves, don't come expecting Krakatoa. Basically, the volcano museum has steam fumaroles, hot springs and a little geothermal activity here and there, but not much else. Of the 14 volcanoes in the area, **Hēilóng Shān** (*Black Dragon Mountain; admission Y30; open 7.30am-4.30pm daily*) is the most popular. Taxis or pedicabs will take you half-way up the volcano from where it's a one-hour walk to the summit with awesome views. Within the Hēilóng Shān park area is **Huǒshāo Shān** (*Fire Burnt Mountain*), which you can also scramble up.

To liven up the scenery, there are two underground caves each boasting a year long ice lantern festival. Both the **Crystal Palace** (*Shuǐjīng Gōng; admission Y20; open 8am-4.30pm daily*) and the **White Dragon Cave** (*Báilóng Dòng; admission Y20; open 9am-4.30pm daily*) have a steady temperature of -10°C (14°F), even during summer. The ice sculptures are lit from the inside by fluorescent coloured lights that create a psychedelic effect. There is little difference between the two caves, although the Crystal Palace is slightly bigger.

The sights are best approached by taxi or pedicab as the town has yet to develop a public bus system. Taxis can be hired to do a 20km loop of the area, taking in the lakes, volcanoes and caves. Bargaining begins at Y150.

A 'water drinking festival' is held at the start of May every year by the local Daur minority. The festival lasts for three days and includes music, dancing and unbridled drinking of the local waters.

Places to Stay

Wǔdàlián Chí might look small but there are over 40 sanatoriums in town with beds ranging from Y30 to Y60. Many sanatoriums close during the low season (October to May).

Lóngquán Bīnguǎn (Dragon Spring Hotel; ☎ 722 2426) Dorm beds Y50. Open year-round. This hotel is on the north-east corner of the traffic circle. Rooms have been recently renovated.

Gōngrén Liáoyǎng Yuán (Workers Sanatorium; ☎ 722 1569) Dorm beds Y25. Open May-Nov. This is a popular destination for ailing Russians in the summer, which is not surprising as the rooms are a steal. The hotel is next to the yellow China Telecom building at the traffic circle.

Getting There & Away

To reach Wǔdàlián Chí, take a train from Hāěrbīn or Qíqíhā'ěr to Běi'ān. In Běi'ān, there are five buses departing daily for Wǔdàlián Chí (5.50am, 10.30am, 12.40pm, 3.30pm and 7.30pm). The last bus returning to Běi'ān leaves Wǔdàlián Chí at 3.30pm (Y20, 1½ hours).

Tiānlóng Dàjiǔdiàn (☎ 666 4818, fax 666 4943) Doubles with/without bath Y160/90. If you find yourself stuck in Běi'ān for the night you can stay in this place. The hotel is opposite the train station and has rooms that are really quite nice.

The nearest train station to Wǔdàlián Chí is in Zhānhé, 40km away. A train leaves Zhānhé for Hēihé in the north daily at 2pm (Y33, six hours). Trains also run from Zhānhé to Běi'ān. A minibus leaves Wǔdàlián Chí at 9am for Zhānhé and returns at 2pm. At all other times you will have to take a taxi.

HĒILÓNG JIĀNG BIĀNJÌNG
黑龙江边境

Black Dragon River Borderlands

Much of the north-eastern border between China and Siberia follows the course of Hēilóng Jiāng (Black Dragon River), also known to the Russians as the Amur River. Along the border it is possible to see Siberian forests and the dwindling settlements of northern tribes, such as the Daur, Ewenki, Hezhen and Oroqen.

Currently, most foreigners require permits to visit the area – international borders

and ethnic minority areas are sensitive places. Check the current situation with the PSB. CITS is likely to encourage you to head off regardless. However, this is not advisable unless you are willing to undertake a very long journey at risk of being sent straight back.

Boat tours along Sōnghūa Jiāng have ceased due to the problem with permits. Nevertheless, as areas are continuously falling in and out of restrictions, check with CITS or the China Haerbin Overseas Tourist Corporation to see if the tours have resumed.

Assuming that you have at least two weeks to spare, are flexible about transport and have your permits in order, an independent trip should be viable during the summer – make sure that you take a small medical kit, insect repellent and warm clothing. Hēihé and Mòhé can both be reached by a combination of train and bus transport.

Mòhé 漠河

Mòhé, in northern Hēilóngjiāng, holds the record for China's lowest plunge of the thermometer, a mere -52.3°C (-61.1°F), which was recorded in 1956. Not surprisingly on a normal winter day a temperature of -40°C is common.

Natural wonders are the attraction in China's northernmost town, which is sometimes known as the Artic of China. In mid-June, the sun is visible for as long as 22 hours. The aurora borealis (northern lights) are another colourful phenomenon of Mòhé.

Getting to Mòhé requires a train trip north from Jāgédáqí to Gǔlián, followed by a 34km bus ride.

Hēihé 黑河
☎ 0456 ● pop 69,900

Hēihé's claim to fame is that it borders Russia. Due to the recent thawing in relations between the two countries, there is a steadily increasing amount of cross-border trade and even a fledgling tourist industry. Chinese tour groups are now able to cross the border to Blagoveshchensk, a large Russian port opposite Hēihé.

Unfortunately it is not so easy for foreigners to visit Blagoveshchensk. A Russian tourist visa is needed, as is a re-entry

The Hezhen

The Hezhen minority, spread across the northern plains of Hēilóngjiāng, is the smallest ethnic group in China numbering only 1300. Their lineage can be traced back to the nomadic Nuzhens, a race of Tartar horsemen who ravaged the borders of several Chinese dynasties.

The Hezhen are a people of fish; they hunt fish, eat fish, celebrate fish and even wear fish. They are expert fishermen and legend has it that they can determine what kind of fish is underwater by looking at the bubbles on the water's surface.

Traditionally, the Hezhen make their clothes out of locally caught fish, such as salmon, carp or green pikes. Buttons are made from catfish bones and cuffs and collars are dyed with cloud-shaped patterns. Dresses, trousers, shoes, aprons and gloves can all be made, but you'd have to be a patient fisherman as it apparently takes around 250kg of fish to make one suit.

Having once been restricted to the northern Hēilóngjiāng borders, these fishy designs have recently found themselves making a splash on the international fashion stage. Clothes enthusiasts, in particular from Korea, Japan and the USA are reportedly paying through the gills for the fish skin costumes – one suit is reported to fetch US$660.

Fashion aside, the Hezhen's lifestyle is rapidly changing. Although they continue to maintain their own language and traditions, just how much of Hezhen culture has remained intact is open to some speculation. The official line trumpets stories of wondrous change from a primitive and nomadic lifestyle to a settled consumerism, complete with satellite TV. Some would argue that such change is not a bad thing; not least because the Hezhen can now watch their fish skin creations hit the international catwalks.

visa for China. All this must be arranged in Běijīng, not in Hēihé.

Those without a Russian visa can console themselves with hour-long cruises of Hēilóng Jiāng from Hēihé (Y10), departing from various points along the waterfront promenade. The departing point for Russia and the customs and immigration facilities are on **Dà Hēihé Dǎo** (*Big Black River Island*) at the eastern end of the promenade. This is also where you will find the **Big Heihe Island International Market City** (*Dà Hēihé Guójì Shāngmào Cháng*), where Chinese and Russian traders come to haggle over the price of wholesale shoes and bras. The **Russian Wares Street** (*Éluósí Shāngpǐn Jiē; Hailan Jie*) sells chocolate, coffee and other such stuff from across the river.

Information Train tickets are not bought at the train station but from the ticket office (☎ 823 7296) at 77 Guandu Lu, on the corner with Xinghua Jie. It is open from 8am to 4pm daily.

The PSB is at 145 Hailan Jie, on the corner with Guandu Lu. The Bank of China is at 169 Wenhua Jie, the post office is at 168 Wenhua Jie and China Telecom is next door. There is an Internet bar next to the Bank of China on Wenhua Jie.

CITS (☎ 825 9753) is on the ground floor of the Shangmao Dasha building in the eastern part of town. CITS is open 6.30am to 11.30am and 2pm to 5pm daily.

Places to Stay Options include:

Hēihé Guójì Fàndiàn (*Hēihé International Hotel;* ☎ 822 7025, 48 Wangsu Jie) Doubles from Y268. This is the classiest joint in town with rooms overlooking the river, an Internet bar and a disco popular with visiting Russians.

Zìyún Fàndiàn (*Zìyún Hotel;* ☎ 823 1970, 41 Dongxing Lu*) Doubles Y130. In need of a complete overhaul is this hotel with corridors that smell of cabbage. But it's the cheapest Hēihé has to offer.

Getting There & Away Trains run daily to and from Hāěrbīn (Y153), leaving Hēihé at around 8pm and arriving in Hāěrbīn at 8am the next day. Buses also run to Hāěrbīn, Běi'ān, Wǔdàlián Chí and Qíqíhā'ěr. The passenger ferry service that used to link Hēihé with Mòhé has been discontinued.

QÍQÍHĀ'ĚR 齐齐哈尔
☎ 0452 • pop 5,537,000

Qíqíhā'ěr was established in 1684 and is one of the oldest settlements located in the

---

Rare Cranes Find Sanctuary

The Zhālóng Nature Reserve, one of China's first nature reserves, was set up in 1979. In 1981 the Chinese Ministry of Forestry invited Dr George Archibald (director of the International Crane Foundation – ICF) and Wolf Brehm (director of Vogelpark Walsrode, Germany) to help set up a crane centre at Zhālóng.

Of the 15 species of cranes in the world, eight are found in China and six are found at Zhālóng. Four of the species that migrate here are on the endangered list: the red-crowned crane, the white-naped crane, the Siberian crane and the hooded crane. Both the red-crowned and white-naped cranes breed at Zhālóng (as do the common and demoiselle cranes), while hooded and Siberian cranes use Zhālóng as a stopover.

The centre of attention is the red-crowned crane, a fragile creature whose numbers at Zhālóng (estimated to be only 100 in 1979) were threatened by drainage of the wetlands for farming. The near-extinct bird is, ironically, the ancient symbol of immortality and has long been a symbol of longevity and good luck in the Chinese, Korean and Japanese cultures. With some help from overseas experts, the ecosystem at Zhālóng has been studied and improved, and the number of these rare birds has risen.

Several hand-reared (domesticated) red-crowned and white-naped cranes are kept in a pen at the sanctuary for viewing and study.

On the eve of their 'long march' southwards in October, large numbers of cranes can be seen wheeling around, as if in farewell. The birds have been banded to unlock the mystery of their winter migration grounds (in either Korea or southern China).

Since the establishment of the ICF, George Archibald and Ron Sauey have managed to create a 'crane bank' in Wisconsin, USA, stocking 14 of the 15 known species. They've even convinced the North Koreans to set up bird reserves in the mine-studded demilitarised zone between North and South Korea, and the travel baggage of these two countries includes suitcases full of Siberian crane-eggs picked up in Moscow (on one trip a chick hatched en route and was nicknamed 'Aeroflot'). Last on the egg list for the ICF is the black-necked crane, whose home is in remote Tibet and for whom captive breeding may be the final hope.

---

north-east. It's name is taken from the Daur word for 'borderland'. The town is a gateway to the Zhālóng Nature Reserve, a birdwatching area 35km south-east, rather than a tourist destination itself. There's not much to see in this industrial town – a zoo, mosque, night market and the ice-carving festival held from January to March.

Highest and lowest temperatures of the year achieve a nice symmetry with 39°C (102.2°F) in July and -39°C (-38.2°F) in January.

Information

The Bank of China is on the corner of Bukui Dajie and Longhua Lu; take tram No 14 from the train station. The central post office is diagonally across from the bank at Bukui Dajie and Xinsheng Lu. China Telecom is next door.

CITS (☎ 271 5836) is at the back of Húbīn Fàndiàn, and staff here can advise you about the best times and places for bird watching. They also run tours to the bird reserve (see the Zhālóng Nature Reserve section).

The PSB is on Bukui Dajie, just north of Longhua Lu. It is open 8am to 11.30am and 1.30pm to 5pm Monday to Friday. The CAAC ticket office is at 2 Minhang Jie (☎ 242 4445).

Places to Stay

Húbīn Fàndiàn (☎ 271 3121, fax 271 2062, 4 Wenhua Dajie) Doubles Y280. Set back from the road amongst a lush garden is this very relaxed hotel. Tram No 15 will get you here from the train station.

Tiědaò Fàndiàn (☎ 212 4579, 7 Longhua Lu) Doubles Y120. This friendly and accommodating hotel is situated just opposite the train station.

Báihè Bīnguǎn (White Crane Hotel; ☎ 292 1112, fax 212 7639, 25 Zhanqian Dajie) Doubles Y220. This well-furnished hotel is to your left as you exit the train station. Room prices include three free meals.

Getting There & Away

Qíqíhā'ěr is linked directly by rail to Běijīng (Y262, 21 hours), via Hāěrbīn (Y44, three to five hours). There are also rail connections north to the towns of Běi'ān and Hēihé. A night train leaves for Hēihé at 8pm, passing through Běi'ān at 2.40am. Look after your valuables if travelling this route, as it's notorious for theft.

While it's easier to purchase train tickets, there are also buses to Hāěrbīn. A bus departs at noon for Běi'ān (Y32) from the eastern bus station on Longhua Lu, but the road is in poor condition and the bumpy journey takes eight hours.

There are flights between Qíqíhā'ěr and Běijīng, Dàlián, Guǎngzhōu, Shànghǎi and Shěnyáng.

ZHĀLÓNG NATURE RESERVE

Zhālóng Zìrán Bǎohùqū 扎龙自然保护区

This nature reserve *(admission Y20; open 7am-5pm daily)* is at the north-western tip of a giant marsh, and is made up of about 210,000 hectares of wetlands. It lies strategically on a bird-migration path that extends from the Russian Arctic, around the Gobi Desert and down into South-East Asia. Opened in 1979, the reserve now has some 290 different species of bird, including storks, swans, geese, ducks, herons, harriers, grebes and egrets. The tens of thousands of winged migrants arrive from April to May, rear their young from June to August and depart from September to October.

Birds will be birds – they value their privacy. While some of the red-crowned cranes are more than 1.5m tall, the reed cover is taller. The best time to visit is in spring, before the reeds have a chance to grow; however, as this is low tourist season, it's more difficult (and expensive) to arrange tours.

For the patient binoculared and rubber-booted ornithologist, day tours are offered by CITS in Qíqíhā'ěr (approximately Y100 per person plus Y160 for a return bus). Zhālóng Bīnguǎn (see Places to Stay, following) also offers tours through the freshwater marshes in flat-bottomed boats during the summer months.

Even if you're not a bird fan, a trip into this very peaceful countryside will be bliss to those who have been traipsing around China's cities. Without doing a tour, you can wander the marshes and nearby villages. Be warned: the mosquitoes are almost as big as and definitely more plentiful than the birds – take repellent!

If you are entering by public bus, get off at the main gate and buy your own ticket rather than leaving the task to the driver, who is likely to add an additional commission.

Places to Stay

Zhālóng Bīnguǎn (☎ 452 0024) Doubles low/high season Y100/Y360. This is the only hotel on the reserve grounds and is somewhat run-down. Arriving in low season, you might find that you're the only guest.

As an alternative, you can walk through the nearby villages where locals will sometimes offer beds for Y10 or Y20.

Getting There & Away

Zhālóng is 27km from Qíqíhā'ěr and linked by a good road, but there is not much traffic along it. Minibuses travel to the bird reserve (Y20, 1½ hours) from the west bus station on the corner of Longhua Lu and Xiongying Jie (one block east of the Bank of China). The minibuses tend to leave Qíqíhā'ěr late and Zhālóng early; the schedule is very erratic so show up early if you don't want to miss your bus.

Shānxī 山西

Capital: Tàiyuán
Population: 33.8 million
Area: 156,000 sq km

Shānxī was one of the earliest centres of Chinese civilisation and formed the state of Qin. After Qin Shihuang unified the Chinese states in 221 BC, the northern part of Shānxī became the key defensive bulwark between the Chinese and the northern nomadic tribes.

Despite the Great Wall, the nomadic tribes still managed to break through and used Shānxī as a base for their conquest of the Middle Kingdom.

When the Tang dynasty fell in the 9th century, the political centre of China moved away from the north-west. Shānxī went into a rapid economic decline, although its importance in the northern defence network remained paramount.

It was not until the intrusion of foreign powers into China that industrialisation truly got under way. When the Japanese invaded China in the 1930s they carried out development of industry and coal mining around the capital of Tàiyuán.

After 1949, the Communist government began to exploit Shānxī's mineral and ore deposits, and developed Dàtóng and Tàiyuán as major industrial centres. China's biggest coal mines can be found near these cities, and the province accounts for a third of China's known iron and coal deposits.

Shānxī means West of the Mountains, the mountains being Tàiháng Shān, the range which forms the province's eastern border. To the west it is bordered by Huáng Hé (Yellow River). The province's population of about 31 million people is surprisingly small by Chinese standards, unless you consider the fact that almost 70% of the province is mountainous.

Along with its mineral deposits, Shānxī is rich in history. This is especially true of the northern half, which is a virtual gold mine of temples, monasteries and cave-temples – a reminder that this was once the political and cultural centre of China. Among these, the main attraction for travellers are the Cloud Ridge Caves at Dàtóng, the extant Ming dynasty architecture of Píngyáo, and the Buddhist mountain of Wǔtái Shān.

Highlights

- The Buddhist Cloud Ridge Caves, a stunning array of China's oldest sculptures

- The 1400-year-old monastery Xuánkōng Sì, an architectural feat 75km south-east of Dàtóng

- Táihuái, a peaceful monastic village in picturesque Wūtái Shān

- Píngyáo, a great new backpacker hang-out and funky old walled city with some of China's best-preserved Ming dynasty architecture

TÀIYUÁN 太原
☎ 0351 • pop 2,932,800

Tàiyuán, provincial capital and industrial sprawl often shrouded in fog, has a few attractions, but little to make it worth a special trip. It is, however, more cosmopolitan than its northern neighbour Dàtóng.

The first settlements on the site of modern-day Tàiyuán date back 2500 years. By the 13th century it had developed into what Marco Polo referred to as 'a prosperous city, a great centre of trade and industry'. But it was also the site of constant armed conflict, sitting squarely on the path by which successive northern invaders entered China. There were once 27 temples here dedicated to the God of War.

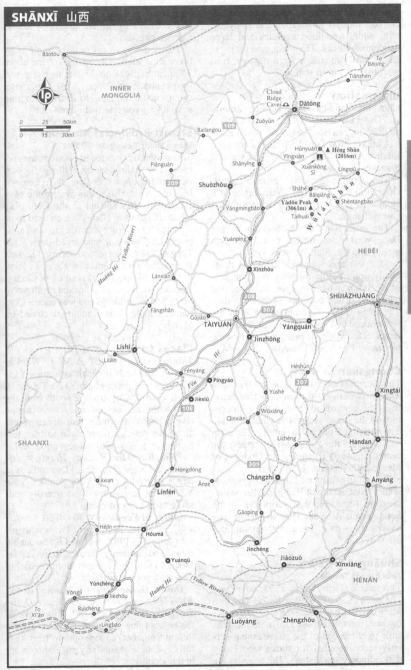

CENTRAL CHINA

Today, the city looks much like its modern counterparts Zhèngzhōu and Luòyáng, with wide, tree-lined avenues and large residential blocks. The main street Yingze Dajie, easily mistaken for a runway, runs west from the train station.

Information

China International Travel Service (Zhōngguó Guójì Lǚxíngshè; CITS; ☎ 407 4209) is at 282 Yingze Dajie, next door to the Bank of China. China Travel Service (Zhōngguó Lǚxíngshè; CTS; ☎ 413 0833) has a few branches downtown.

The Public Security Bureau (PSB; Gōngānjú) has a foreign affairs office at 9 Houjia Lane, near May 1st Square (Wǔyī Guǎngchǎng).

The main Bank of China is on Yingze Dajie, west of Jiefang Lu. You can change money and travellers cheques.

The post and telephone office is diagonally opposite the train station. The post office is open 8am to 8pm daily and the telephone office operates 24 hours a day. The main China Telecom office is at the western end of Yingze Dajie. There is an Internet cafe (wǎngbā) here, but every time we showed up it was closed.

Chóngshàn Sì 崇善寺

This Buddhist monastery (Taiwan Wenmiao Xiang; admission Y4; open 8am-5pm daily) was built towards the end of the 14th century on the site of a monastery that is said to date back to the 6th or 7th century. The main hall contains three impressive statues; the central figure is Guanyin, the Goddess of Mercy with 1000 hands and eyes.

Beautifully illustrated book covers show scenes from the life of Buddha. Also on display are some Buddhist scriptures of the Song, Yuan, Ming and Qing dynasties. The monastery is on a side street running east off Wuyi Lu.

Shuāngtǎ Sì 双塔寺

Twin Pagoda Temple

This temple (Twin Pagoda Park; admission Y6; open 8.30am-5.30pm daily) has two Ming dynasty pagodas, each a 13-storey octagonal structure almost 55m high. It is possible to climb one of the pagodas, but it is only recommended for those who enjoy dark, slippery spiral stairs. The pagodas are built entirely of bricks carved with brackets and cornices to imitate ancient Chinese wooden pagodas.

The best way to get to this temple is by bike. Ride along Chaoyang Jie for about 750m, turn right on Shuangta Beilu and then continue south for 1.5km. Otherwise, catch a taxi (Y6). Bus No 19 from the train station gets you relatively close.

Shanxi Provincial Museum

Shānxī Shěng Bówùguǎn 省博物馆

This museum is located in two separate sections. The main museum (Qifeng Jie; admission Y5; open 8am-7pm daily summer, less rest-of-year) is north-west of the May 1st Square. It's housed in the Chúnyáng Palace (Chúnyáng Gōng), which used to be a temple for offering sacrifices to the Taoist priest Lu Dongbin, who lived during the Tang dynasty. The second section (Taíwān Wénmiào Xiàng; admission Y5; open 9am-noon & 2.30-6pm daily) is south of Chóngshàn Sì. The museum is housed in attractive Ming period buildings and was once a Confucian temple. It is sometimes closed on Monday.

Places to Stay

Tiānhé Dàshà (☎ 407 5054, 11 Gongyu Lane) Dorm beds in quads or triples Y15-27, twins with private bath Y120. This hotel is on a small alley leading south from the train station and has passable rooms, though take a look at the other half-dozen places along the way, as most claim to take foreigners now. You may score a good deal.

Tiělù Bīnguǎn (Railway Hotel; ☎ 404 1522, 18 Yingze Dongdajie) Dorm beds in quads or triples from Y20, doubles Y50-Y298. This largish hotel has friendly staff and a huge array of rooms.

Chángtài Fàndiàn (☎ 403 4960, fax 403 4931, 30 Yingze Dongdajie) Twins with private bath Y78-198. This hotel is reasonably clean and certainly fresher than Tiánhé Dàshà. There are cheaper dorm beds but they may not be available.

Diànlì Dàshà (Electric Power Hotel; 404 1784, fax 404 0777, 39 Yingze Dajie) Singles or twins from Y180. This is one of the better value places in Tàiyuán. Take a look at a number of room options (if it's not full). A couple of similarly priced hotels are in the vicinity.

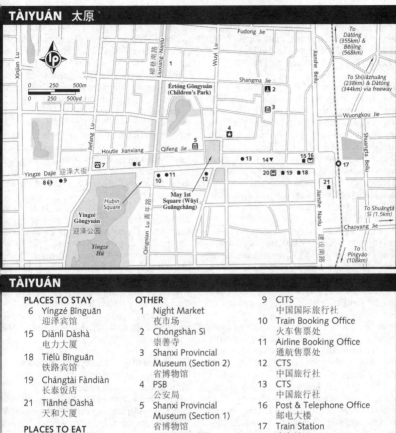

TÀIYUÁN

PLACES TO STAY
6 Yíngzé Bīnguǎn
迎泽宾馆
15 Diànlì Dàshà
电力大厦
18 Tiělù Bīnguǎn
铁路宾馆
19 Chángtài Fàndiàn
长泰饭店
21 Tiānhé Dàshà
天和大厦

PLACES TO EAT
14 Dumpling Shop
饺子店

OTHER
1 Night Market
夜市场
2 Chóngshàn Sì
崇善寺
3 Shanxi Provincial
Museum (Section 2)
省博物馆
4 PSB
公安局
5 Shanxi Provincial
Museum (Section 1)
省博物馆
7 Telephone Office
电信局
8 Bank of China
中国银行

9 CITS
中国国际旅行社
10 Train Booking Office
火车售票处
11 Airline Booking Office
通航售票处
12 CTS
中国旅行社
13 CTS
中国旅行社
16 Post & Telephone Office
邮电大楼
17 Train Station
火车站
20 Long-Distance Bus
Station
长站汽车站

Yíngzé Bīnguǎn (☎ 404 3211, fax 404 3784, 189 Yingze Dajie) Twins with refrigerator & English-language satellite TV Y530 plus 10% service charge. This hotel incorporates two massive buildings. The west block is a glittering four-star hotel, complete with sauna, gym, medical clinic and swimming pool. The east block is only for Chinese guests.

Places to Eat
On the Tàiyuán street-food menu are local favourites like *zhūjiǎo* (pigs' trotters) stewed in cauldrons, and a savoury pancake called *làobǐng*. The local variant of Chinese

noodles, called *liángpí*, is often served in steaming bowls of spicy soup.

There is a good *dumpling shop* (*jiǎozi diàn; Yingze Dongdajie; dishes Y6*) directly opposite the bus station. Here, a plate of dumplings will warm your belly before or after a long bus trip.

Most of Tàiyuán's hotels also have tasty and reasonably priced restaurants. Those craving Western food could try the buffet at Yíngzé Bīnguǎn.

Getting There & Away
Air The airline booking office (☎ 404 2903) is at 158 Yingze Dajie and is open daily

from 8am to 8pm. Useful flights include Běijīng (Y490, daily), Guǎngzhōu (Y1140, daily), Shànghǎi (Y960, daily) and Xī'ān (Y460, daily). There are also flights to most other major domestic destinations.

Bus Iveco buses to Dàtóng (Y53 to Y70, five hours) leave hourly 6.30am to roughly 4pm from the long-distance bus station and from outside the southern end of the train station; a few slower and cheaper (Y35) buses still make the run. There are half-hourly buses to Wǔtái Shān (Y43, four hours) from the bus station leaving 6am to 2.30pm (the earlier, the better). Buses troll maddeningly around the train station area, leaving only when completely full.

From in front of the west side of the long-distance bus station there are express buses travelling to Běijīng (Y120, six hours) every half hour from 7am to 11.20pm; opposite the train station are private expresses running day and night. There are also departures every day to Zhèngzhōu from the bus station and the southern end of the train station.

Train It's fairly easy getting sleeper tickets for trains originating from Tàiyuán, but difficult for trains that don't. For advance purchases go to the train booking office at 138 Yingze Dajie, which is open daily from 8am to 7pm. Services leaving from Tàiyuán include express trains to Běijīng (eight to ten hours), Chéngdū (30 hours), Dàtóng (seven to eight hours), Luòyáng (12 hours), Zhèngzhōu (10 hours) and Shànghǎi (22 hours).

If you're headed to Xī'ān, your best bets are train Nos 1485 and 2535 as they start from Tàiyuán.

AROUND TÀIYUÁN
Jìncí Sì 晋祠寺
This ancient Buddhist temple *(admission Y15; open 8am-6pm daily)* is at the source of Jìn Hé, by Xuánwàng Hill, 25km southwest of Tàiyuán. Take the No 8 minibus from Tàiyuán's train station (Y2, one hour). It's thought that the original buildings were constructed between AD 1023 and 1032, but there have been numerous additions and restorations over the centuries, right up to Qing times.

As you enter the temple compound the first major structure is the Mirror Terrace, a Ming building used as an open-air theatre.

The name is used in the figurative sense to denote the reflection of life in drama.

Zhibo's Canal cuts through the temple complex and lies west of the Mirror Terrace. Spanning this canal is the Huixian (Meet the Immortals) Bridge, which provides access to the Terrace for Iron Statues, which displays figures cast in AD 1097.

Further back is the Goddess Mother Hall, the oldest wooden building in the city and one of the most interesting in the temple complex. Inside are 42 Song dynasty clay figures of maidservants standing around a large seated statue of the sacred lady, said to be the mother of Prince Shuyu of the ancient Zhou dynasty.

Next to the Goddess Mother Hall is the Zhou Cypress, an unusual tree which has supposedly been growing at an angle of about 30° for the last 900 years.

In the north of the temple grounds is the Zhenguan Baohan Pavilion, which houses four stone steles inscribed with the handwriting of the Tang emperor Tai Zong. In the south of the temple grounds is the Sacred Relics Pagoda, a seven-storey octagonal building constructed at the end of the 7th century.

Qiao Family Courtyard House
Qiáo Jiā Dàyuàn 乔家大院
This house *(admission Y28)* is the site where Zhang Yimou's film *Raise the Red Lantern*, starring Gong Li, was filmed. This extensive Qing dynasty courtyard house complex was built by Qiao Guifa, a small-time tea and beancurd merchant who rose to riches. The ornate complex consists of six courtyards, containing over 300 rooms and on display are Qing dynasty curios and furniture.

To get here take any Píngyáo-bound minibus. On the right-hand side of the highway you'll see red lanterns and a large gate marking the complex. It's 40km southwest of Tàiyuán.

PÍNGYÁO 平遥
☎ 0354 • pop 40,000
Surrounded by a completely intact 6km Ming dynasty city wall (claimed to be the last remaining one in China), Píngyáo is an exceptionally well-preserved traditional Han Chinese city. Its ancient temples and courtyard houses offer a rare glimpse into

the architectural styles and town planning of imperial China.

Located on the old route between Běijīng and Xī'ān, Píngyáo was a thriving merchant town during the Ming and Qing dynasties. It was here that China's earliest *tongs* (banks) were set up and Píngyáo rose to be the financial headquarters of all of China during the Qing dynasty. After its heyday the city fell into poverty, and without the cash to modernise, Píngyáo's streets remained unchanged.

Tourism is changing this small town fast. Until a couple of years ago, Píngyáo saw few visitors. Now visitors are arriving in ever increasing numbers, especially domestic tourists. So far general over-restoration has not taken place and several hundred homes have been deemed cultural relics and are thus protected from being demolished or radically altered. It seems weekly that another historic structure is being reopened as a guesthouse or museum (or both in one case!). In 1997 Píngyáo was inscribed as a Unesco World Heritage Site.

A good, although crowded, time to visit Píngyáo is during the Lantern Festival (15 days after Chinese New Year, during the full moon). Red lanterns are hung outside the doors of residences, and every year a small, country-style parade takes place. Locals munching on sugar cane and candied fruit flood the streets and vendors sell *yuán xiāo*, a traditional round white snack (which symbolises the moon) made of glutinous rice flour, filled with a sweet sesame and walnut paste and served in soup.

Things to See & Do

The city's main drag is Nan Dajie, also known as Ming Qing Jie, inside the walls. Several 'antique' shops line the street. The numbers of inns, shops, and restaurants has exploded since the late-1990s. Note that the number of museums and temples greatly exceeds the scope of this book. Almost all entrance fees are Y10 to Y20; some tour agencies near the city walls offer package tours with entrance tickets included, though few people find them of value.

In the middle of the Ming Qing Jie (and marking the centre of town) is the **Town Building** *(Ming Qing Jie; admission Y5; open 9am-5pm daily)*. At a whopping 18.5m, it's the tallest building in the city.

You can see over the tiled roofs of the entire city from the top. The **Furniture Museum** *(109 Ming Qing Jie; admission Y13, plus Y20 for guided tour; open 9am-5pm daily)* is a Qing-style courtyard house with elaborately carved wooden window frames; it's a typical example of a home of a wealthy financier of the time.

Not to be missed is the **Rishengchang Financial House Museum** *(40 Xi Dajie; admission Y10; open 8am-7pm summer, less rest-of-year)*. In the late 18th century a man named Li Daquan opened a small dye shop here. His business prospered and he opened branches as far away as Sìchuān. As sales grew Li introduced a system of cheques and deposits, and the home office in Píngyáo essentially became a financial agent for the company, and eventually, for other businesses, individuals and the Qing government. The bank prospered for over 100 years, and at its height had 57 branches around China. The Japanese invasion and civil strife in the 1930s, along with increased competition from foreign banks, forced its decline and eventual closure. The museum has over 100 rooms, including offices, living quarters and a kitchen, as well as several old cheques.

The ancient **city wall** *(admission Y15)*, originally erected in the Zhou dynasty (827–728 BC), completely surrounds the city. Most of what you'll see now was actually built during the Ming dynasty; notice the stamped bricks below your feet. The outer portion of the wall has a few shell marks, remnants of the Japanese invasion in the 1930s. If you ascend the wall at the north gate, you can hire a pedicab to pedal you around the wall.

Exploring Píngyáo streets, you'll come across several other small museums housed in traditional courtyard houses, temples and even a Catholic church. Museums aside, wandering the streets and back alleyways is the real reason to come here. The main commercial streets are filled with locals selling traditional Chinese snacks – candied or dried fruit, all manner of nuts and seeds, fruit and sugarcane.

Nearby to Píngyáo is the popular **Shuānglín Sì** *(admission Y12)*. This monastery, 7km south-west of Píngyáo (a motorcycle taxi is around Y15 return), is well worth the effort. It contains exquisite painted clay figurines and statues dating from the Song, Yuan, Ming and Qing dynasties. Most of the present buildings date from the Ming and Qing dynasties, while most of the sculptures are from the Song and Yuan dynasties. There are around 2000 figurines in total.

Places to Stay & Eat

There are a few traditional courtyard-style hotels within the city walls; more are opening seemingly every week. Cheapest beds are Y30 in a shared room (you generally can't split the room but some allow it) and this should decrease as competition increases.

Tiānyuánkuí Mínfēng Bīnguǎn (☎ 568 0069, W www.pytyk.com, 73 Nan Dajie) Rooms with private bath Y100-120. This is definitely the most popular place. Rooms are spotless, service is impeccable (some English is spoken) and they even get kudos for getting tough-to-find train tickets (even same-day sleepers to Xī'ān!).

Jīnjǐngloú Bīnguǎn (☎ 568 3751, 29 Nan Dajie) Doubles with shared bath from Y60. This is another friendly place with slightly cheaper but similarly good rooms; they're also amenable to friendly negotiation.

Local fare includes such treats as *shuǐ jiānbāo* (fried pork-filled bread) and *dòu miàn jiānbǐng* (fried pancake with string beans), along with local pastas made and cooked in a seeming infinite variety. Local restaurants make it easy: their dishes are advertised with photos on large posters outside and a few have English menus. The small restaurant opposite Tiānyuánkuí Bīnguǎn is popular.

Getting There & Away

Train Most visitors arrive on a day trip from Tàiyuán, or overnight from Běijīng. Train No 4405 leaves Běijīng west train station daily at 8.41pm and arrives in Píngyáo at 7.31am. Hard sleeper is Y99. Although several trains depart Píngyáo for Běijīng, tickets are extremely limited, so if returning to Běijīng your best bet is to take a minibus to Tàiyuán. Train No K702 departs Tàiyuán for Běijīng at 9pm and arrives at Běijīng train station at 7am. Hard sleeper is Y155.

Loads of trains travel between Tàiyuán and Píngyáo (a good one is train No 4421, which originates in Tàiyuán at 9.45am). It takes less than two hours so even if you don't get a seat it's an easy ride.

From Píngyáo to Xī'ān is also problematic. Some guesthouses have landed sleepers from Píngyáo but don't count on it. You may have to head to Tàiyuán.

Bus Minibuses or faster Iveco buses depart the Tàiyuán bus station or southern end of the train station and leave for Píngyáo as they fill up (Y11 to Y23, 1½ to 3 hours). The faster buses may deposit you on the highway crossroads; from here it's a Y2 motorcycle taxi ride into the old city. The Píngyáo bus 'station' is really just the train station parking lot and the buses from here are in awful shape; to get anywhere it's probably best to head back to the highway crossroads and flag down a bus.

Getting Around

Píngyáo can be easily navigated on foot, or you can rent a bike for the day at one of the shops on Xi Dajie or outside the city walls. Motorcycle taxis average Y2 for local trips; Y15 to Y20 should get you around the countryside.

RUÌCHÉNG 芮城
☎ 0359

At Ruìchéng, 93km south of Yùnchéng, is **Yǒnglè Taoist Temple**, which has valuable frescoes dating from the Tang and Song dynasties. In the 1960s the temple was moved to Ruìchéng from its original site beside Huáng Hé, when the Sānménxià Dam was built. The temple is 3km directly south from the main intersection.

The surrounding area is quite charming, with many people continuing to live in simple cave dwellings.

Places to Stay

Grain Hostel (Shíliáng Zhāodàisuǒ) Dorm beds Y6, rooms with private bath Y30. Opposite the bus station, the Grain Hostel has clean dorms, but the rooms with attached bathrooms are not worth Y30, as there is hardly ever any water.

Closer to the city centre are a number of other more upmarket hotels.

Getting There & Away

From Yùnchéng's long-distance bus station there are half-hourly departures to Ruìchéng (Y8, 2½ hours). On the way, the bus passes Jièzhōu before climbing the cool subalpine slopes of Zhōngtiao Shān. It is also possible to hop on this bus in Jièzhōu, but you will need to catch a motor tricycle back to the main road from Guāndì Miào from where you can just wave the bus down.

From Ruìchéng there are early-morning buses to both Luòyáng and Xī'ān via Huá Shān, starting at 6.30am.

YÙNCHÉNG 运城

☎ 0359 • pop 188,800

Yùnchéng is in the south-western corner of Shānxī, near where Huáng Hé completes its great sweep through far northern China and begins to flow eastwards. The small city is famed for the gutsy little orange tractors that are assembled here and often seen chugging along country roads.

At Jièzhōu, 18km south of Yùnchéng, is large **Guāndì Miào** *(admission Y20)*. This temple was originally constructed during the Sui dynasty, but was destroyed by fire in AD 1702 and subsequently rebuilt. Bus No 11 from Yùnchéng train station terminates at Guāndì Miào. The trip takes 40 minutes and costs Y2.

Places to Stay

Tiědaò Dàshà (☎ 206 8899) Singles with shared bath or beds in triples with private bath Y50. This hotel is to the right as you exit the train station. It has new and clean rooms, and friendly staff.

Huáxià Dàjiǔdiàn (☎ 208 0239) Dorm beds from Y15, twins/triples with private bath Y50/40 per bed. Directly opposite the train station, this hotel has reasonable rooms.

Getting There & Away

Yùnchéng is on the Tàiyuán-Xī'ān train line; all trains, including daily express trains, stop here.

There are direct bus connections from Yùnchéng to Luòyáng (Y20, six hours), leaving every half hour between 7am and 4.30pm from the bus station. If you're lucky you will get an Iveco, which completes the trip in 3½ hours. There are also Iveco buses to Xī'ān (Y35) departing half-hourly. Both the buses and trains to Xī'ān pass by Huá Shān.

The bus station is a five-minute walk south from the train station on the right.

WǓTÁI SHĀN & TÁIHUÁI 五台山

Wǔtái Shān *(Five-Terrace Mountain)*, centred on the beautiful monastic village of Táihuái, is one of China's sacred Buddhist mountain areas. Táihuái lies deep in an alpine valley enclosed by the five peaks of Wǔtái Shān, the highest of which is the 3058m northern Yèdòu Peak (Yèdòu Fēng), known as the roof of northern China. Táihuái itself has 15 or so old temples and monasteries, and some 20 others dot the surrounding mountainsides.

The relative inaccessibility of Wǔtái Shān spared it the worst of the Cultural Revolution. However, improved roads have now made it possible to reach Táihuái in at least five hours from either Dàtóng or Tàiyuán, and the area sees a steady flow of tourists, which rises to a flood in July and August. But at other times of the year Wǔtái Shān is a charming, relaxing spot. Between October and March, temperatures are often below freezing, and even in summer the temperature drops rapidly at night, so make sure that you take appropriate clothing.

WǓTÁI SHĀN 五台山

1	Fēnglín Sì 风林寺	5	Lóngquán Sì 龙泉寺	9	Bus Station 汽车站
2	Bìshān Sì 碧山寺	6	Pǔhuà Sì 普化寺	10	Nánshān Sì 南山寺
3	Qīfó Sì 七佛寺	7	Guānyīn 观音洞	11	Yòuguó Sì 佑国寺
4	Shūxiàng Sì 殊像寺	8	Qīxiángé Bīnguǎn 栖贤阁宾馆	12	Zhènhǎi Sì 镇海寺

To Yèdòu Peak

To Shāhé (50km)

Qīngshuǐ Hé

See Táihuái Map p446

Táihuái

Dàiluó Peak

0   1   2km
0   0.5   1mi

To Tàiyuán (249km)

CENTRAL CHINA

In addition to the temples, the surrounding scenery is great, and there are quite a few mountain trails leading out from near Táihuái.

Information

CITS (☎ 654 3218) has several offices in the area, the most convenient office being the one along Qīngshuǐ Hé right in Táihuái. The staff arrange tours of the outlying temples, but unless you want an English-speaking guide (and CITS doesn't always have one available), you can take one of the Chinese tours from Táihuái for far less money (see Organised Tours later in this section).

If you need to reach the PSB for any reason, talk to the owner of the hotel you're staying at.

The Bank of China can only change major currencies. Some of the expensive tourist hotels south of town have money-changing facilities, but you may have to be a guest to use them, especially if you wish to change travellers cheques.

Temples

You'd have to either be a sincerely devout Buddhist or utterly temple-crazed to take in every temple and monastery in the Wǔtái Shān area. Most people will probably just stroll around Táihuái, although there are some temples outside town that are worth visiting.

Tǎyuàn Sì with its large, white, bottle-shaped pagoda built during the Ming dynasty is the most prominent temple in Táihuái. **Xiàntōng Sì** has seven rows of halls, totalling over 400 rooms. **Luóhòu Sì** contains a large wooden lotus flower with eight petals, on each of which sits a carved Buddhist figure; the big flower is attached to a rotating disk so that when it turns, the petals open up and the figures appear.

Just next door, small **Guǎngrén Sì**, run by Tibetan and Mongolian monks, contains some fine examples of early Qing wood-carvings.

For a more secluded, spiritual visit, try **Cífú Sì**, several hundred metres beyond Púsàdǐng Sì on the ridge overlooking the town. Here there are no hawkers, just a few pleasant monks, one or two of whom speak English.

To get a bird's-eye view of Táihuái, you can make the somewhat strenuous trek up to

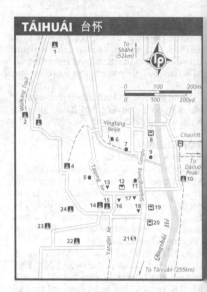

Dàiluó Peak (*Dàiluó Dǐng*), on the eastern side of Qīngshuǐ Hé. If you want to spare your legs, and lighten your wallet, there's a chairlift.

About 2.5km south of Táihuái is sprawling **Nánshān Sì**, which offers nice views of the Wǔtái Shān valley. Just above it, **Yòuguó Sì** contains frescoes of the fable *Journey to the West*.

Other sights include the marble archway of **Lóngquán Sì** and the 26m-high Buddha and carvings of 500 arhats in **Shūxiàng Sì**.

In the summer, free Shanxi opera performances are given during the evenings at 7.30pm (and some mornings around 11.30am) at **Wànfó Sì**.

Organised Tours

Privately operated minibuses make half-day and full-day tours of the outlying temples. For a group of four to six people, this kind of tour costs Y50 per person, but if there is a larger number of tourists taking the same bus you may only have to pay Y40.

Show up at the local tour minibus stop between 7am and 7.30am: after that most of the tourists will be gone, making it hard to join a tour.

Places to Stay

Táihuái is teeming with hostels and hotels that cater mainly to local tourists, officially

TÁIHUÁI

PLACES TO STAY
5 Xiānhé Bīnguǎn
  先禾宾馆
6 Fóguó Bīnguǎn
  佛国宾馆
7 Dōngfēng Bīnguǎn
  东风宾馆
11 Wǔtáishān Bīnguǎn
  五台山宾馆

PLACES TO EAT
13 Railway
  Restaurant
16 Zhìlè Yuàn
  智乐苑
17 Zhèngxīnlián
  净心莲
18 Noodle Stands
  路边面摊

OTHER
1 Cífú Sì
  慈福寺
2 Pǔsàdǐng Sì
  菩萨顶寺
3 Guǎngzōng Sì
  广宗寺
4 Yuánzhào Sì
  圆照寺
8 Public Buses to
  Dàtóng
  大同国营汽车站
9 CITS
  中国国际旅行社
10 Shàncái
  善财洞
12 Post Office
  邮政局

14 Luóhòu Sì
  罗侯寺
15 Guǎngrén Sì
  广仁寺
19 Public Buses to
  Tàiyuán
  太原国营汽车站
20 Local Tour
  Minibuses
  一日游中巴站
21 Bank of China
  中国银行
22 Wànfó Sì
  万佛寺
23 Tǎyuàn Sì
  塔院寺
24 Xiǎntōng Sì
  显通寺

CENTRAL CHINA

and otherwise, although at the time of writing we had no trouble getting in virtually anywhere. Rates for all hotels generally go up around 40% during the high season (July to August).

Dōngfēng Bīnguǎn (☎ 654 2524) Dorm beds Y10 low season, Y20-40 high season, twins with bath Y40/80 low/high season. A popular cheaper option is this blue-tiled building on a small lane north of the creek. Dorms are a little drab, though prices are quite cheap in the low season. The catch: the hotel's water isn't turned on until late April.

Fóguó Bīnguǎn (☎ 654 5962, Zhenjianfang Jie) Dorm beds/doubles from Y30/80. In a warren of back alleys, this isolated place has a very quiet location and clean rooms. Prices are less during the low season.

Xiānhé Bīnguǎn (☎ 654 2531, 25 Taiping Jie) Twins with private bath Y100. Also known as the Gōngyì Měishù Zhāodàisuǒ (Arts & Crafts Hotel), this place has splendidly clean rooms (some of the better bath facilities in the region, perhaps) and friendly staff.

Wǔtáishān Bīnguǎn (No 2 Reception Centre; ☎ 654 2342, Shijuliangcheng Gonglu) Middle-building twins Y100, twins/triples with bath Y160/180, new-building twins or triples Y240. The large Wǔtáishān Bīnguǎn has cosy twins in the middle building, and more comfortable

twins and triples in the new building. Basically, you get what you pay for here; in general, the lower-priced rooms are not much value, but the higher-end rooms are pretty decent.

Wǔtái Shān's luxury hotels are several kilometres south of the village. Every year more are being built.

Qīxiángé Bīnguǎn (☎ 654 2400, fax 654 2183) Doubles/twins/triples with shared bath Y280/380/160, luxury suite Y1080. With a peaceful setting at the foot of the mountains, this hotel is probably the best choice. Rooms are nicely furnished, and if you require a living room and a study to go with your bedroom, there's a luxury suite.

Places to Eat

Táihuái has almost as many small restaurants as it does hotels, and again they are largely similar. Prices tend to be higher here, as nearly all food has to be trucked in from the plains. There are noodle stands just off the main road north of the Tàiyuán bus station serving tasty *liáng pí*, fried noodles, fried rice, dumplings etc. A bowl of noodles should cost around Y3.

Railway Restaurant (☎ 654 3012, 20 Taiping Jie) Dishes from Y5. Railway Restaurant has good food and the prices are pretty reasonable. There is no English sign, but look out for the karaoke/youth club located opposite.

Not surprising given all the Buddhist temples in the village, you'll find two somewhat pricey but excellent vegetarian restaurants in town; both have English menus and staff that speak some English.

Zhìlè Yuàn *(☎ 654 5674, Yanglin Jie)* Dishes from Y6, daily set meal Y15. Here you'll find great service, good food and a decent and not too pricey daily set meal.

Zhèngxīnlián *(Pure Lotus Restaurant, ☎ 654 5202, Yanglin Jie)* Dishes from Y5. Another friendly place, this restaurant has some mistranslated items but a copious menu and good service.

Getting There & Away

There is now a park entrance fee of Y48 (plus an optional Y5 insurance fee) that both Chinese and foreigners have to pay before entering Wǔtái Shān. Genuine card-carrying Tibetan pilgrims are exempt.

From Dàtóng, there are several buses during summer to Wǔtái Shān departing from the new or old bus stations in the early mornings; some days a 1.30pm bus may also do the trip. The trip, via Húnyuán, Shāhé and over the scenic pass near Yèdǒu Peak, takes five hours (Y43).

From Táihuái, buses to Dàtóng (Y43) leave from the northern part of the village. There are three or four departures daily from 6am to 1.30pm. There's no bus stop per se; bus drivers park in the lot of whatever hotel they've got a working deal with. (So don't buy your ticket from your guesthouse as this limits you to only their bus.) Buses used to stop off at **Xuánkōng Sì** *(Hanging Monastery)* for 30 minutes en route, but nowadays you usually have to cajole the driver.

Fast Iveco buses (Y43) and a few slower minibuses (Y25 to Y35) to Tàiyuán leave from a small stop near the middle of the village though there is a proper bus 'station' some 3km south of the village. Most leave in the morning, although sometimes there are afternoon departures. Private buses generally loiter between the two public bus stops.

Getting Around

Táihuái town can be covered on foot, and you can make pleasant day hikes out to some of the temples in the surrounding area.

DÀTÓNG 大同

☎ 0352 • pop 2,696,800

Dàtóng's chief attraction is the nearby Cloud Ridge Caves. The city itself is not very attractive, although it has a few interesting historical sights. An ancient imperial capital, modern Dàtóng has little to show for its former greatness. It's crowded and industrial, but local authorities have been trying to spruce it up recently and it's turning into a pretty lively place, with rows of upmarket shops and restaurants.

In the 5th century AD, the Tuoba, a Turkic-speaking people, succeeded in unifying all of northern China and forming the Northern Wei dynasty. Adopting Chinese ways, they saw trade, agriculture and Buddhism flourish. Their capital was Dàtóng. It remained as such until AD 494, when the court moved to Luòyáng.

Orientation

The pivotal point of Dàtóng is Red Flag Square (Hóngqí Guǎngchǎng) at the intersection of Da Xijie and Xinjian Nanlu. Apart from the Cloud Ridge Caves, the historic sights such as Huáyán Sì and the Nine Dragon Screen are inside the crumbling old city walls. This is where you'll also find most of the shops and nightlife.

At Dàtóng's northern end is the train station. You can pick up tourist maps from hawkers around the train station; some speak a little English.

Information

Dàtóng has two CITS offices: a helpful and friendly branch at the train station (☎ 712 4882), open 6.30am to 6.30pm, and another at Yúngāng Bīnguǎn (☎ 510 1326). The staff broker discounted accommodation, can purchase train tickets and run regular tours of the city and the Cloud Ridge Caves. In addition to informative English-language tours, it also has French-speaking guides.

The Bank of China's main branch on Yingbin Xilu is the only place to change travellers cheques, unless you're staying at Yúngāng Bīnguǎn.

The main post and telephone office is south of Red Flag Square at the intersection of Da Xijie and Xinjian Nanlu.

Internet access is available for Y10 an hour from an Internet cafe opposite Hóngqí Dàfàndiàn or one just west of the train station.

DÀTÓNG

PLACES TO STAY
1 Hóngqí Dàfàndiàn
红旗大饭店
8 Fēitiān Bīnguǎn
飞天宾馆
10 Shuàifǔ Bīnguǎn
帅府宾馆
21 Yúngāng Bīnguǎn;
CITS
云冈宾馆；
中国国际旅行社

PLACES TO EAT
3 Chēzhàn Kuàicān
车站快餐
18 Yǒnghé Dàjiǔdiàn
永和大酒店
23 Yǒnghé Hóngqí
Měishíchéng
永和红旗美食城

OTHER
2 Train Station; CITS
火车站；
中国国际旅行社
4 Post & Telephone
Office
邮电局
5 Internet Cafe
网吧
6 Old (North) Bus Station
汽车北站(旧站)
7 Internet Cafe
网吧
9 New Bus Station
新汽车站
11 PSB
公安局
12 Main Post & Telephone
Office
邮电大楼

13 Huáyán Sì
华严寺
14 Nine Dragon Screen
九龙壁
15 Drum Tower
(Gǔ Lóu)
鼓楼
16 Xīnkāilǐ Bus Station (for
Cloud Ridge Caves)
新开里汽车站
17 Shànhuà Sì
善化寺
19 Datong Stadium
大同体育场
20 Advance Train Booking
Office
火车售票处
22 Bank of China
(Main Branch)
中国银行(大同支行)

CENTRAL CHINA

The PSB office is on Xinjian Beilu, north of the large department store.

Nine Dragon Screen
Jiǔlóng Bì 九龙壁

The Nine Dragon Screen (Da Dongjie; admission Y3; open 8am-6.30pm daily summer, less rest-of-year) is one of Dàtóng's several 'dragon screens' – tiled walls depicting fire-breathing dragons. It was originally part of the gate of the palace of Ming dynasty emperor Ming Taizhu's 13th son, and is 8m high, over 45m long and 2m thick. The Nine Dragon Screen is a short distance east of the intersection of Da Dongjie and Da Beijie. Take bus No 4 from the train station to get here.

Huáyán Sì 华严寺

This monastery (Xiasipo Xiang; bus No 4; admission Y6; open 8am-6.30pm daily) is on the western side of the old city. The original monastery dates back to AD 1140 and the reign of Emperor Tian Ju'an of the Jin dynasty. The entire complex is being developed into a regional museum.

Mahavira Hall is one of the largest Buddhist halls still standing in China. In the centre of the hall are five gilded Ming dynasty Buddhas seated on lotus thrones. Around them stand Bodhisattvas, soldiers and mandarins. The ceiling is decorated with colourful paintings originally dating from the Ming and Qing dynasties, but recently restored.

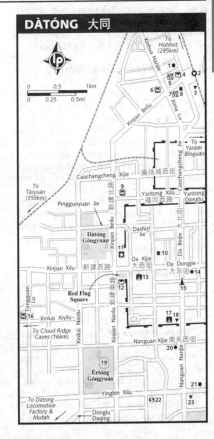

Bojiajiaocang Hall (*Hall for the Conservation of Buddhist Scriptures of the Bojia Order*) is smaller but more interesting than the main hall. It contains 29 coloured clay figures made during the Liao dynasty (AD 907–1125), representing the Buddha and Bodhisattvas.

Huáyán Sì is about 500m east of the post office at the end of Xiasipo Lane, which runs south off Da Xijie.

Shànhuà Sì 善化寺

Built during the Tang dynasty, this temple (*Nansi Jie; admission Y6; open 8.30am-6pm daily*) was destroyed by fire during a war at the end of the Liao dynasty.

In AD 1128 more than 80 halls and pavilions were rebuilt, and further restoration was done during the Ming dynasty. The main hall contains statues of 24 divine generals. There is a small dragon screen within the monastery grounds. Lots of needed renovation was ongoing at the site but enough is accessible to make it a worthwhile visit.

Datong Locomotive Factory
Dàtóng Jīchē Chǎng 大同机车厂

This factory was the last in China to make steam engines for the main train lines. In 1989 it finally switched to diesel and electric engines. However, the factory maintains a museum housing several steam locomotives. After wandering through the factory you enjoy the ultimate train-buff fantasy – a ride in the cabin of one of the locomotives.

The factory is on the city's south-western outskirts. You can only see it as part of a CITS tour. It's rare that large groups wish to go, but CITS will arrange small group tours for about Y100 per person.

Places to Stay

Officially, Dàtóng offers little for the budget traveller. A couple of cheap options exist; you may need to book through CITS at the train station to get a dorm room.

Fēitiān Bīnguǎn (☎ 281 5117, Chezhan Qianjie) Dorm beds Y45, twins with bath Y180-220. This hotel has very average twins available. If you book through CITS you can get a dorm bed though you can usually march in alone and get the same price.

Shàifǔ Bīnguǎn (☎ 206 8950; Dapi Xiang) Dorms Y28, doubles with shared/private bath Y70/98. This is a clean place that's very receptive to foreign guests. To get to this hotel go one block east of Huáyán Sì and turn left.

Yúngāng Bīnguǎn (☎ 502 1601, fax 502 4927, 21 Yingbin Donglu) Singles or doubles Y300. This place used to be *the* backpacker enclave in town with clean dorm rooms. Now it's gentrified into a three-star monster; the rooms and service are very good, but Y300 worth is debatable. The entrance is to the right as you enter the main gate. To get there catch bus No 15 from the train station and get off at shìzhèngfǔ stop and then walk another five minutes east; otherwise catch a taxi for Y10.

Hóngqí Dàfàndiàn (☎ 281 6813, fax 281 6671, Huochezhan Bei) Twins Y170. This is a good mid-range choice with reasonably clean rooms; the price includes breakfast. It also sports a full range of amenities.

Yànběi Bīnguǎn (☎ 602 4116, fax 602 7287, 1 Yuhe Beilu) Twins Y260-400. This clean and modern place is about 2km south-east of the train station (a 10-minute walk). It's Y6 in a taxi. Its isolated spot makes it a bit quieter than the hotels near the train station.

Places to Eat

Yǒnghé Dàjiǔdiàn (☎ 204 7999, Nanguan Nanjie) Dishes from Y15. Dàtóng's locals regard this to be the best restaurant in Shānxī. Lunch and dinner crowds provide a glimpse of Dàtóng's upper crust. Ask for some local specialities (on English menu) or try its delicious Beijing duck.

Yǒnghé Hóngqí Měishíchéng (☎ 510 1555, 3 Yingbin Donglu) Dishes from Y15. The same owner as Yǒnghé Dàjiǔdiàn has this restaurant, also offering an English menu. The decor is glitzy and the prices are fairly stratospheric but it's a good place for a splurge.

Chēzhàn Kuàicān Dishes from Y5. At the opposite end of the spectrum is this tiny, five-table affair serving tasty and cheap noodles and dumplings. A Y12 plate of dumplings is enough for two people.

Hóngqí Dàfàndiàn (*see Places to Stay earlier*) Dishes from Y10. This hotel's restaurant (not the canteen) is pretty good, and is quite reasonably priced. However, it is often booked out on weekends with rowdy wedding banquets that are best avoided.

Getting There & Away

Air Dàtóng's airport is still on the drawing board after the military airport closed due to insufficient demand. If or when it is built, it will be less than 10km south of the city and will have flights to Běijīng, Shànghǎi and Guǎngzhōu.

Bus Dàtóng has two bus stations: the old, or north station, near the train station, and the new station on Yantong Xilu. Departures mostly start from the new station and pass by the old one before heading out, although some routes have separate departures from each station.

Daily buses to Tàiyuán leave the new station; a few leave the old station. About a half-dozen per day depart 6.30am to early afternoon. Slower minibuses take five to six hours (Y50); express air-con Daewoo buses from the new station take four to 4½ hours (Y80).

There are daily morning buses to Wǔtái Shān (Y35 to Y43, five hours) from May to September leaving the new and old stations, most between 6.30am and 8.30am though afternoon departures run in high seasons.

One bus daily makes the run to Hohhot (Y50, 3½ to four hours) from the new station. As trains aren't convenient for this route, it might be better to take the bus.

Train A train line north-east to Běijīng and a northern line to Inner and Outer Mongolia meet in a Y-junction at Dàtóng. Trans-Siberian trains via Ulaan Baatar come through here. It is possible to do Dàtóng as a daytrip from Běijīng using night trains coming and going, but you can never be guaranteed of getting a berth, even going through CITS.

There are daily express trains to Běijīng (5½ to nine hours), Lánzhōu (24 hours), Hohhot (four to seven hours), Tàiyuán (seven to eight hours) and Xī'ān (18 hours). Tickets to Xī'ān can be hard to get, mainly because there's only one direct train, No 1674. To Hohhot one train originates in Dàtóng, so it's possible to reserve tickets; the problem is it's an achingly slow local train so the bus is probably a better option unless you don't mind standing.

Tickets can be hard to get for all trains not originating in Dàtóng. If you want to buy sleeper or advance tickets try the office just south of the main ticket building or the advance booking office at the corner of Nanguan Nanjie and Nanguan Xijie. Failing that, try upgrading once you are on board or contact the staff at CITS who might be able to get you a ticket: they charge a Y40 commission per hard sleeper berth.

AROUND DÀTÓNG
Cloud Ridge Caves 云岗石窟
Yúngāng Shíkū

These caves (*admission Y50 summer; open 8.30am-5.30pm daily*) are the main reason most people make it to Dàtóng. The caves are cut into the southern cliffs of Wǔzhōu Shān, 16km west of Dàtóng, next to the pass leading to Inner Mongolia. The caves contain over 50,000 Buddhist statues and stretch for about 1km east to west.

On top of the mountain ridge are the remains of a huge, mud-brick 17th-century Qing dynasty fortress. As you approach the caves you'll see the truncated pyramids, which were once the watchtowers. Sadly, many of the caves suffer damage from coal and other pollution, largely a result of the neighbouring coal mine. At the time of writing, most of the coal trucks were being diverted to a back road, making the trip more pleasant. East of the caves you can walk to a remnant of the Great Wall.

There are no guides at the caves, but there are good English descriptions and explanations throughout. For details, see the boxed text 'Bodhisattvas, Dragons & Celestial Beings'.

Getting There & Away Minibuses (Y4) run from the bus stop opposite the train station in Dàtóng; these aren't numbered but don't worry, the drivers will find you (look for the *yuàzìshān* bus). Alternatively, bus No 3 (Y1.5) from the terminal at Xīnkāilǐ, on the western edge of Dàtóng, goes past the Cloud Ridge Caves. You can get to Xīnkāilǐ on bus No 4 from the train station or bus No 17 from opposite the main Bank of China. From Xīnkāilǐ it's about a 25-minute ride to the caves.

Many travellers take a CITS tour out to the caves, which costs Y100 per person (minimum of five people). The tour also includes Xuánkōng Sì and a visit to some local cave dwellings and possibly remnants of the Great Wall.

CENTRAL CHINA

Bodhisattvas, Dragons & Celestial Beings

Most of the Cloud Ridge Caves were carved during the Northern Wei dynasty between AD 460 and 494. Cloud Ridge (Yúngāng) is the highest part of Wǔzhōu Shān's sandstone range and is on the north bank of the river of the same name. The Wei rulers once came here to pray to the Gods for rain.

The caves appear to have been modelled on the Mògāo Caves at Dūnhuáng in Gānsù, which were dug in the 4th century AD and are some of the oldest in China. At Dūnhuáng the statues are terracotta since the rock was too soft to be carved, but here at Dàtóng are some of the oldest examples of stone sculpture to be seen in China. Various foreign influences can be seen in the caves: there are Persian and Byzantine weapons, Greek tridents, and images of the Indian Hindu gods Vishnu and Shiva. The Chinese style is reflected in the robust Bodhisattvas, dragons and flying apsaras (celestial beings rather like angels).

Work on the Cloud Ridge Caves fizzled out when the Northern Wei moved their capital to Luòyáng in AD 494. In the 11th and 12th centuries the Liao dynasty, founded by northern invaders, saw to some repairs and restoration. More repairs to the caves were carried out during the Qing dynasty. From east to west the caves fall into three major groups, although their numbering has little to do with the order in which they were constructed.

Caves 1–4

These early caves, with their characteristic square floor plan, are at the far eastern end, and are separated from the others. Caves 1 and 2 contain carved pagodas. Cave 3 is the largest in this group, although it contains only a seated Buddha flanked by two Bodhisattvas.

Caves 5–13

Yúngāng art is at its best in this group, especially in caves 5 and 6, which boast walls of wonderfully carved Buddhist tales and processions. Cave 5 also contains a colossal seated Buddha almost 17m high. Cave 6 contains a richly carved pagoda, and an entrance flanked by fierce guardians. In the centre of the rear chamber stands a two-storey pagoda-pillar about 15m high. On the lower part of the pagoda are four niches with carved images, including one of the Maitreya Buddha (Future Buddha). Gautama Buddha's life story from birth to his attainment of nirvana is carved in the east, south and west walls of the cave and on two sides of the pagoda.

Caves 7 and 8 are linked and contain carvings with Hindu influences. Shiva, with eight arms and three heads, and seated on a bull, is on one side of the entrance to cave 8. On the other side is the multifaced Indra, perched on a peacock. Caves 9 and 10 are notable for their front pillars and figures bearing musical instruments. These instruments appear again in cave 12, while cave 13 has a 15m-high Buddha statue, its right hand propped up by a figurine.

Caves 16–20

These caves were carved in about AD 460 and the Buddha in each one represents an emperor from the Northern Wei dynasty. The Buddha in cave 18 represents Emperor Taiwu, who was once a great patron of Buddhism, but later (through the influence of a minister) came to favour Taoism.

After a revolt that he blamed on the Buddhists, Taiwu ordered the destruction of Buddhist statues, monasteries and temples, and the persecution of Buddhists. This lasted from AD 446 to 452, when Taiwu was murdered. His son is said to have died of a broken heart, having been unable to prevent his father's atrocities, and was posthumously awarded the title of emperor.

Taiwu's grandson (and successor) Emperor Wencheng, who restored Buddhism to the dynasty, is represented by the 14m-high seated Buddha of cave 20.

Cave 21 and onwards are small, in poor condition and can't compare to their better preserved counterparts.

Xuánkōng Sì 悬空寺
Hanging Monastery

This monastery (☎ 832 2142; admission Y36 summer; open 6.30am-7pm daily summer, less rest-of-year) is just outside the town of Húnyuán, 65km south-east of Dàtóng. Built precariously on sheer cliffs above Jīnlóng Canyon, the monastery dates back more than 1400 years. Its halls and pavilions were built along the contours of the cliff face using the natural hollows and outcrops. The buildings are connected by corridors, bridges and boardwalks and contain bronze, iron and stone statues of gods and buddhas.

Notable is the Three Religions Hall where Buddha, Laotzu and Confucius sit side by side. Some long-overdue repairs have been made to the monastery in recent years and some sections have been closed off.

The CITS tour to the Cloud Ridge Caves will include Xuánkōng Sì. Chinese 'tours' costing Y35 and taking four to five hours leave from opposite the old bus station from 7.30am to late morning.

You can also take a public or private bus from Dàtóng to Húnyuán, just 5km from Xuánkōng Sì. Public buses to Húnyuán, leave from the old bus station at 7am, take two hours and cost Y5. Private minibuses leave from near the bus station and cost Y8. A taxi from Húnyuán, to the monastery costs Y30 return. The last bus back from Húnyuán, leaves at around 4pm. Another option is the bus to Wǔtái Shān, which goes directly past the monastery and may stop for half an hour (not likely); getting back to Dàtóng is usually simple, but not as many run to Wǔtái Shān so plan wisely.

Mù Tǎ 木塔
Wooden Pagoda

This 11th-century pagoda at Yìngxiàn, 70km south of Dàtóng, is one of the oldest wooden buildings in the world. It's said that not a single nail was used in the construction of the nine-storey, 97m structure. As of 2001 a massive, US$1 million renovation project was undertaken to relieve damage done by earthquakes and problems from internal weight.

Tours of Xuánkōng Sì sometimes include Mù Tǎ. You can also get there by taking a minibus from near the old bus station in Dàtóng (Y8, two hours).

Shaanxi (Shǎnxī) 陕西

Capital: Xī'ān
Population: 38.3 million
Area: 205,000 sq km

Highlights

- The Army of Terracotta Warriors, one of China's premier attractions
- Huá Shān, one of China's quieter sacred mountains
- Xī'ān, with its cultural sites, great food and interesting mix of Chinese and Islamic cultures
- Yán'ān, where the Communist Party holed up in the hills and planned a revolution

The northern part of Shaanxi is one of the oldest settled regions of China, with remains of human habitation dating back to prehistoric times. This was the homeland of the Zhou people, who eventually conquered the Shang and established their rule over much of northern China. It was also the homeland of the Qin, who ruled from their capital of Xiányáng near modern-day Xī'ān and formed the first dynasty to rule over all of eastern China.

Shaanxi remained the political heart of China until the 9th century. The great Sui and Tang capital of Chāng'ān (Xī'ān) was built there and the province was a crossroads on the trading routes from eastern China to central Asia.

With the migration of the imperial court to pastures farther east, Shaanxi's fortunes declined. Rebellions afflicted the territory from 1340 to 1368, again from 1620 to 1644, and finally in the mid-19th century, when the great Muslim rebellion left tens of thousands of the province's Muslims dead. Five million people died in the famine from 1876 to 1878, and another three million in the famines of 1915, 1921 and 1928.

It was probably the dismal condition of the Shaanxi peasants that provided the Communists such willing support in the province in the late 1920s and during the subsequent civil war. From their base at Yán'ān the Communist leaders directed the war against the Kuomintang and later against the Japanese, before being forced to evacuate in the wake of a Kuomintang attack in 1947.

Some 38 million people live in Shaanxi, mostly in the central and southern regions. The northern area of the province is a plateau covered with a thick layer of wind-blown loess soil, which masks the original landforms. Deeply eroded, the landscape has deep ravines and almost vertical cliff faces.

The Great Wall in the far north of the province is something of a cultural barrier, beyond which agriculture and human existence were always precarious ventures.

Like so much of China, this region is rich in natural resources, particularly coal and oil. Wèi Hé, a branch of Huáng Hé (Yellow River), cuts across the middle of the province. This fertile belt became a centre of Chinese civilisation.

The south of the province is quite different from the north; it's a comparatively lush, mountainous area with a mild climate.

XĪ'ĀN 西安

☎ 029 • pop 6,620,600

Xī'ān once vied with Rome and later Constantinople for the title of greatest city in the world. Over a period of 2000 years Xī'ān has seen the rise and fall of numerous Chinese dynasties. The monuments and archaeological sites in the city and the surrounding plain are a reminder that once upon a time Xī'ān stood at the very centre of the Chinese world.

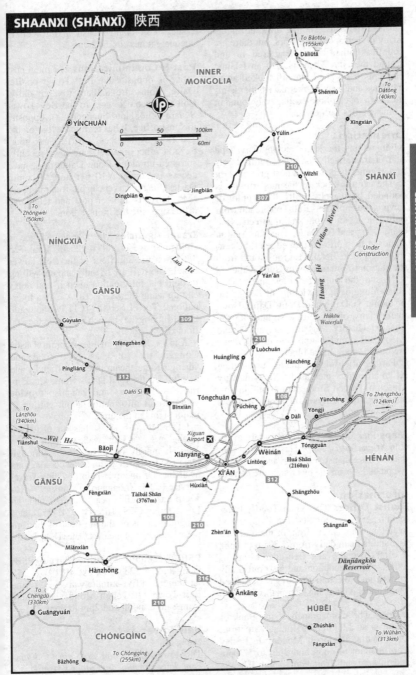

SHAANXI (SHĂNXĪ) 陕西

Today Xī'ān is one of China's major tourist attractions. The big drawcard is the Army of Terracotta Warriors, but there are countless other sights scattered in and around the city. There is also an Islamic element to Xī'ān, found in tucked-away mosques and busy marketplaces, that lends the city a touch of the exotic rarely found in Chinese cities farther east.

Orientation

Xī'ān retains the same rectangular shape that characterised Cháng'ān, with streets and avenues laid out in a neat grid pattern.

The central block of the modern city is bounded by the city walls. The centre of town is the enormous Bell Tower, and from here run Xī'ān's four major streets: Bei, Nan, Dong and Xi Dajie. The train station stands at the north-eastern edge of the central city block. Jiefang Lu runs south from the station to intersect with Dong Dajie.

Most of the tourist facilities can be found either along or in the vicinity of Jiefang Lu or along Xi Dajie and Dong Dajie. However, many of the city's sights like the Shaanxi History Museum, Dàyàn Tǎ and Xiǎoyàn Tǎ, and Bànpō Neolithic Village are outside the central block.

Farther afield on the plains surrounding Xī'ān are sights such as the Xianying City Museum, Fǎmén Sì, the Tomb of Qin Shihuang and the Army of Terracotta Warriors near Líntóng.

Maps Pick up a copy of the widely available *Xi'an Tourist Map*. This bilingual production has exhaustive listings and is regularly updated – even the bus routes are correct.

Information

Tourist Offices The Xi'an Tourist Information Services Centre (☎ 745 5043) is next to Jiěfàng Fàndiàn, in front of the train station and is open daily from 7.30am to 8pm. It offers friendly and free advice on bus routes, accommodation and also runs daily Eastern and Western tours (see Organised Tours under Xiánguáng later in this chapter).

Money The main branch of the Bank of China is at 223 Jiefang Lu, just up from Dong Wulu. It's open Monday to Friday from 8.30am to noon and 2pm to 5.30pm and on weekends from 9am to 3pm. There's

also a branch on Dong Dajie where foreigners can change cash and travellers cheques; it has similar hours.

Post & Communications The main post office is opposite the Bell Tower on Bei Dajie. Hours are 8.30am to 8pm daily. China Telecom is next to the Bell Tower Square (Zhōnglóu Guǎngchǎng), opposite the post office. It has an Internet bar on the 2nd floor with access for Y12 per hour. Several other Internet bars have recently sprouted up along Dong Dajie; most have access for under Y10 per hour. Rénmín Dàshà Gōngyù has cheap but frustrating access. There is another post and telephone office opposite the train station.

Travel Agencies One popular choice is Golden Bridge Travel (☎ 725 7975, fax 725 8863), on the 2nd floor of the Bell Tower Hotel. The staff are friendly and are willing to dole out information even if you don't end up using their services. A China International Travel Service (CITS; Zhōngguó Guójì Lǚxíngshè) branch is also on the 2nd floor of this hotel.

Kane's Kafe is inside Rénmín Dàshà Gōngyù; the cafe has good food and Ghengis Kane, the proprietor, is friendly and helpful. Up the road Dad's Home Cooking run Eastern Tours and can also provide some useful information about getting to major sights in the area.

CITS (☎ 524 1864) has an office on Chang'an Lu, a short walk south of Youyi Xilu. It mainly organises tours, although other services such as rail ticket bookings are available. Or, the ever-helpful China Travel Service (CTS; Zhōngguó Lǚxíngshè; ☎ 526 1760) has an office nearby at 63 Chang'an Lu. A larger CTS office (☎ 324 4352), at 4 Xingqing Lu, is on the 4th floor of the Empress Hotel east of the East Gate (Dōng Mén).

PSB The Public Security Bureau (PSB; Gōngānjú; ☎ 723 4500, ext 51810), at 138 Xi Dajie, is a five-minute walk west of the Bell Tower. It's open Monday to Friday from 8am to noon and 2pm to 6pm.

Bell Tower 钟楼
Zhōng Lóu

This tower (*admission Y15; open 7.30am-7pm daily summer, less other seasons*) is a huge building in the centre of Xī'ān that is entered through an underpass on the north side of the tower. The original tower was built in the late 14th century, but it was rebuilt at the present location in 1739 during the Qing dynasty. A large iron bell in the tower used to mark the time each day, hence the name. There are musical performances inside the tower every afternoon and most mornings.

Drum Tower 鼓楼
Gǔ Lóu

The Drum Tower (Beiyuanmen; admission Y12; open 8am-7pm daily), a smaller building to the west of the Bell Tower, marks the Muslim quarter of Xī'ān. Beiyuanmen is an interesting restored street of traders and craftspeople that runs directly north from the Drum Tower. It's a good spot to see traditional artists and musicians at work.

City Walls 城墙
Chéngqiáng

Xī'ān is one of the few cities in China where old city walls (admission Y8-10; open 8am-10pm daily summer) are still visible. The walls were built on the foundations of the walls of the Tang Forbidden City during the reign of Hongwu, first emperor of the Ming dynasty.

The walls form a rectangle with a circumference of 14km. On each side is a gateway, and over each gateway stand three towers. At each of the four corners is a watch-tower, and the top of each wall is punctuated with defensive towers. The walls are 12m high, with a width at the top of 12m to 14m and at the base of 15m to 18m.

Air-raid shelters were hollowed out of the walls when the Japanese bombed the city, and during the Cultural Revolution caves were dug to store grain. Most sections have been restored or even rebuilt, but others have disappeared completely (although they're still shown on the maps), so unfortunately it's not possible to walk right around Xī'ān along the city walls.

There are a number of access ramps up to the walls, some of which are located just east of the train station, near Heping Lu and at the South Gate (Nán Mén), beside the Forest of Steles Museum. There are also some obscure steps at the eastern end of the south wall.

Dàyàn Tǎ 大雁塔
Big Goose Pagoda

This pagoda (☎ 521 5014, Yanta Lu; admission Y15, plus Y5 to climb pagoda; open 8.30am-7pm daily summer, less other seasons) stands in what was formerly the Temple of Great Maternal Grace in the south of Xī'ān. The temple was built around AD 648 by Emperor Gaozong (the third emperor of the Tang dynasty) when he was still crown prince, in memory of his deceased mother. The buildings that stand today date from the Qing dynasty and were built in a Ming style.

The original pagoda was built in AD 652 with only five storeys, but it has been renovated, restored and added to many times. It was built to house the Buddhist scriptures brought back from India by the travelling monk Xuan Zang, who then set about translating them into 1335 Chinese volumes. The impressive, fortress-like wood-and-brick building rises to 64m. You can climb to the top for a view of the countryside and the city.

Dàyàn Tǎ is at the southern edge of Xī'ān. The entrance is on the southern side of the temple grounds. Take bus No 41 or 610 from the train station.

The **Tang Dynasty Arts Museum** (Tángdài Yìshù Bówùguǎn; ☎ 524 2894; admission Y15; open 8.30am-5.30pm daily), on the eastern side of the temple, has a collection specifically devoted to the Tang period in Xī'ān.

Xiǎoyàn Tǎ 小雁塔
Little Goose Pagoda

Xiǎoyàn Tǎ (Youyi Xilu; admission Y5-10; open 8.30am-5.45pm daily) is in the pleasant grounds of **Jiànfú Sì**. The top of the pagoda was shaken off by an earthquake in the middle of the 16th century, but the rest of the 43m-high structure is intact.

Jiànfú Sì was originally built in AD 684 as a site to hold prayers to bless the afterlife of the late Emperor Gaozong. The pagoda, a rather delicate building of 15 progressively smaller tiers, was built from AD 707 to 709 and housed Buddhist scriptures brought back from India by another pilgrim. You can climb to the top of the pagoda for a panorama of Xī'ān's apartment blocks and smokestacks.

Bus No 3 runs from the train station through the South Gate of the old city and down Nanguan Zhengjie.

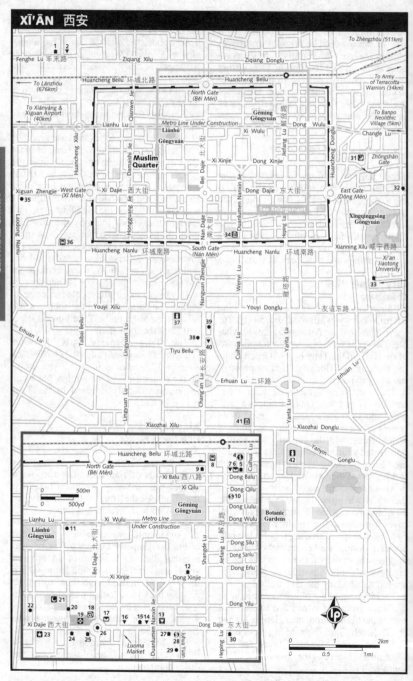

XĪ'ĀN 西安

To Zhèngzhōu (511km)

Fenghe Lu 丰禾路

Ziqiang Xilu

Ziqiang Donglu

To Lánzhōu
(676km)

Huancheng Beilu 环城北路

Huancheng Beilu

To Army
of Terracotta
Warriors (34km)

To Xiányáng &
Xiguan Airport
(40km)

North Gate
(Běi Mén)

Géming
Gōngyuán

To Banpo
Neolithic
Village (5km)

Lianhu Lu

Metro Line Under Construction

Dong Wulu

Changle Lu

Lianhú
Gōngyuán

Xi Wulu

Zhōngshān
Gate

Huancheng Xilu

Muslim
Quarter

Xi Xinjie

Dong Xinjie

31

Xiguan Zhengjie

West Gate
(Xī Mén)

Xi Dajie 西大街

Dong Dajie 东大街

East Gate
(Dōng Mén)

32

35

Xingqìngsōng
Gōngyuán

36

South Gate
(Nán Mén)

Huancheng Nanlu

Huancheng Nanlu 环城南路

Xianning Xilu 咸宁西路

Xi'an
Jiaotong
University

33

Youyi Xilu

Youyi Donglu

友谊东路

37

39

38

40

Tiyu Beilu

Erhuan Lu 二环路

Erhuan Lu

Xiaozhai Xilu

41

Xiaozhai Donglu

3

Huancheng Beilu 环城北路

Yanyin

42

Gonglu

North Gate
(Běi Mén)

4

7 6 5

8

9

Xi Balu 西八路

Dong Balu

0 ――――― 500m
0 ――――― 500yd

Xi Qilu

Dong Qilu

10

Géming
Gōngyuán

Dong Liulu

Lianhu Lu

Xi Wulu

Metro Line
Under Construction

Dong Wulu

Botanic
Gardens

Liánhú
Gōngyuán

11

Dong Silu

Dong Sanlu

Xi Xinjie

12

Dong Xinjie

Dong Erlu

Dong Yilu

22

21

20 18

19

17

16 15 14

13

Xi Dajie 西大街

23

24 25

26

27

28

29

30

Luoma
Market

0   1   2km

0   0.5   1mi

XĪ'ĀN

PLACES TO STAY

1 Rénmín Dàshà
Gōngyù;
Kane's Kafe
人民大厦公寓
5 Jiěfàng Fàndiàn
解放饭店
9 Shàngdé Bīnguǎn
尚德宾馆
12 Rénmín Dàshà
人民大厦
15 YMCA Hotel
青年会宾馆
24 Lìjīng Jiǔdiàn
丽晶酒店
25 Bell Tower Hotel;
Golden Bridge Travel
钟楼饭店
27 Hotel Royal Xi'an
西安皇城宾馆
30 Hyatt Regency Xi'an
西安凯悦饭店
33 No 25 Dormitory
二十五号宿舍

PLACES TO EAT

2 Dad's Home
Cooking
7 Jiěfàng Měishí
Guǎngchǎng
解放美食广场
14 Wángfǔ Cānyǐn
16 Wǔyī Fàndiàn
五一饭店
40 Wèiwèi Jiǎoziguǎn
味味饺子馆

OTHER

3 Train Station
火车站
4 Xi'an Tourist
Information
Services Centre
旅游资问服务中心
6 Post & Telephone
Office
邮电局
8 Long-Distance Bus
Station
长途汽车站
10 Main Bank of China
中国银行
11 Advance Rail Booking
Office; ICBC Bank
铁路售票处;
工商银行
13 1+1 Nightclub
一加一
17 Main Post Office
邮电大楼
18 China Telecom
Internet Bar
中国电信网吧
19 Bell Tower Square;
Century Ginwa
Shopping Centre;
Beer Garden
钟鼓楼广场;
世纪金花
20 Drum Tower
鼓楼
21 Dàqīngzhēn Sì
大清真寺

22 Chénghuáng Miào
Market
城隍庙
23 PSB
公安局外事科
26 Bell Tower
钟楼
28 Bank of China
中国银行
29 Airport Ticket Office
菊花园售票处
31 Temple of the Eight
Immortals
八仙安
32 CTS; Empress Hotel
中国旅行社;
皇后大酒店
34 Forest of Steles
Museum
碑林博物馆
35 China Northwest
Airlines
中国西北航空公司
36 West Bus Station
西安汽车西站
37 Xiǎoyàn Tǎ; Jiànfú Sì
小雁塔; 荐福寺
38 CITS
中国国际旅行社
39 CTS
中国旅行社
41 Shaanxi History
Museum
陕西历史博物馆
42 Dàyàn Tǎ
大雁塔

Dàqīngzhēn Sì 大清真寺

Great Mosque

Dàqīngzhēn Sì (☎ 721 9807, Huajue Xiang; admission Y12; open 8am-8.30pm daily) is among the largest mosques in China. The present buildings only date back to the middle of the 18th century, although the mosque might have been established several hundred years earlier.

The mosque is built in a Chinese architectural style with most of the grounds taken up by gardens. Still an active place of worship, the mosque holds several prayer services each day.

The courtyard of the mosque can be visited, but only Muslims may enter the prayer hall.

Dàqīngzhēn Sì is a five-minute walk from the Drum Tower: go under the arch, then take the second tiny lane leading left to a small side street. From here the mosque is a few steps to the right past a gauntlet of souvenir shops.

Shaanxi History Museum

Shǎnxī Lìshǐ Bówùguǎn 陕西历史博物馆

Built in huge, classical Tang style (though modern-day white tile mania remains predominant), this museum (☎ 525 4727, 90 Xiaozhai Donglu; adult/student Y30/12; open 8.30am-5.30pm daily) was opened in 1992 and is rated as one of the best museums in China. The collection is chronologically arranged and includes material previously housed in the Provincial Museum, although many objects have never been on permanent display before.

The ground floor section deals with China's prehistory and the early dynastic period, starting with Palaeolithic Langtian

Man and the New Stone Age settlements at Líntóng and Bànpō between 7000 and 5000 years ago. Particularly impressive are several enormous Shang and Western Zhou dynasty bronze cooking tripods, Qin burial objects, bronze arrows and crossbows, and four original terracotta warrior statues taken from near the Tomb of Qin Shihuang.

Upstairs, the second section is devoted to Han, Western Wei and Northern Zhou dynasty relics. There are some interesting goose-shaped bronze lamps and a set of forged-iron transmission gears, which are surprisingly advanced for their time.

The third section has mainly artefacts from the Sui, Tang, Ming and Qing dynasties. The major advances in ceramic-making techniques during this period are most evident, with intricately crafted terracotta horses and camels, fine pale-green glazed *misi* pottery and Buddhist-inspired Tang dynasty statues.

The final section, in the basement, is devoted to various exhibitions, which are worthy of a browse, but often lack English explanations.

Photography is allowed but you must deposit (free of charge) any hand luggage in the lockers provided. Foreigners are required to enter through a special entrance (gift shop) to the west. English guided tours are available for Y60 (or free in winter), although most exhibits include labels and explanations in English. Guides are available from an office to the far right of the main entrance. Take bus No 5, 610 or 14 from the train station to get here.

Forest of Steles Museum
Bēilín Bówùguǎn 碑林博物馆

Once the Temple of Confucius, this museum (☎ 721 3868, Shuyuanmen; admission Y30; open 8am-6pm daily) houses a fine collection devoted largely to the history of the Silk Road. Among the artefacts is a tiger-shaped tally from the Warring States period, inscribed with ancient Chinese characters and probably used to convey messages or orders from one military commander to another.

One of the more extraordinary exhibits is the **Forest of Steles** (Bēilín), the heaviest collection of books in the world. The earliest of these 2300 large engraved stone tablets dates from the Han dynasty.

Most interesting is the Popular Stele of Daiqin Nestorianism, which can be recognised by the small cross at the top, engraved in AD 781 to mark the opening of a Nestorian church. The Nestorians were an early Christian sect who differed from orthodox Christianity in their belief that Christ's human and divine natures were quite distinct.

Other tablets include the Ming De Shou Ji Stele, which records the peasant uprising led by Li Zhicheng against the Ming, and the 114 Stone Classics of Kaichen, from the Tang dynasty, inscribed with 13 ancient classics and historical records.

All of the important exhibits have labels in English, or you can pay Y100 for an English guide. The museum entrance is on a side street that runs west off Baishulin Lu, close to the South Gate of the old city wall. The buildings and streets around the museum have been tastefully renovated in Ming style and there are quite a few street stalls selling their wares.

Muslim Quarter

This area near Dàqīngzhēn Sì has retained much of its original character. The backstreets to the north and west of the mosque have been home to the city's Hui community for centuries.

Walking through the narrow laneways lined with old mud-brick houses, you pass butcher shops, sesame oil factories, smaller mosques hidden behind enormous wooden doors and proud, stringy-bearded men wearing white skullcaps. Good streets to explore are Nanyuan Men, Huajue Xiang and Damaishi Jie, which runs north off Xi Dajie through an interesting Islamic food market.

Temple of the Eight Immortals
Bāxiān Ān 八仙安

This is Xī'ān's largest Taoist establishment (Yongle Lu; admission Y5; open 8am-5pm daily) and an active place of worship. Scenes from Taoist mythology are painted around the temple courtyard.

To get there take bus No 10, 11, 28 or 42 east along Changle Lu and get off two stops past the city walls, then continue 100m on foot and turn right (south) under a green-painted iron gateway into a market lane. Follow this, turning briefly right then left again into another small street leading past the temple. The entrance is on the southern side of the temple grounds. You can also reach the temple by following the street running directly east from Zhōngshān Gate (Zhōngshān Mén).

Places to Stay – Budget

For such a major travel destination, Xī'ān has a depressingly limited selection of true budget spots; the good news is that what there is, is *fairly* good. In a pinch, consider one of the many universities in the city.

Rénmín Dàshà Gōngyù (Flats of Renmin Hotel; ☎ 624 0349, 9 Fenghe Lu) Dorm beds Y35-45, twins with bath Y160. For several years this has been the main backpacker crash pad. Located about 4km northwest of the city centre, it's not a convenient location and the hotel's popularity stems solely from its *relatively* cheap dorm beds and the presence of two nearby cafes, where you can meet other travellers and fill up on banana pancakes.

All rooms have air-con, which is a bonus during Xī'ān's sweltering summer. There's supposedly 24-hour hot water, bicycle rental, Internet access, free baggage storage and a relatively cheap laundry service. Rooms aren't particularly clean and the toilets sometimes look like they were last cleaned during the Ming dynasty.

If no-one from one of the restaurants meets you at the station, take bus No 9 from in front of the bus station on Huancheng Beilu and ask to be let off at Fenghe Lu (it should be nine stops). A taxi from the station costs Y10. Minibus No 501 runs from in front of Rénmín Dàshà Gōngyù to the city centre and the Bell Tower (Y1.5).

Shàngdé Bīnguǎn (☎ 742 6164, fax 742 7787, 198 Shangde Lu) Beds in triples/quads with shared bath Y30/25, twins with private bath Y158-178, triples with private bath Y190. This hotel has cheap bicycle rental and a reliable laundry service. It gets extremely mixed reviews from readers but at least you can't beat the location, which also means you may not get a bed.

No 25 Dormitory (Èrshíwǔhào Sùshè; ☎ 326 8813, Ganning Xilu) Twins with TV & air-con Y80-99. This is a foreign student building of Xi'an Jiaotong University (Xī'ān Jiāotōng Dàxué), which offers clean and comfortable rooms. Give it a ring first before you head out here. The university is

just south-east of the city wall. Take bus No 75 from the train station. After you hop off the bus, pass through the main gate of the university and turn right, walk for about 200m and turn left at the long straight road. Walk all the way to the end and the building is on the other side of the basketball court. It's about a 10-minute walk. Taxis are allowed on campus for a gate fee of Y3.

Places to Stay – Mid-Range

Jiěfàng Fàndiàn (☎ 742 8946, fax 742 2617, 321 Jiefang Lu) Twins Y198-320, triples/quads Y280/320. This convenient hotel is diagonally across the wide square to your left as you leave the train station; its location is the deciding factor for some travellers. Take a look at a few rooms – some of the Y198 doubles are actually quite spacious and in pretty good shape, considering the location and price, not to mention the huge guest turnover.

Rénmín Dàshà (People's Hotel; ☎ 721 5111, fax 721 8152, 319 Dong Xinjie) Twins/suites from Y300/650. This enormous hotel was designed in early 1950s Stalinist architectural style (with Chinese characteristics) and has been renovated into a fairly upmarket accommodation option. The hotel sits in between two monolithic derelict buildings on Dong Xinjie.

YMCA Hotel (Qīngniánhuì Bīnguǎn, ☎ 726 2288, fax 723 5479, 339 Dong Dajie) Twins/suites Y268/488. The friendly YMCA is down an obscure lane off Dong Dajie. The staff is generally solicitous and rooms well-maintained but its best draw may be its quiet location, very central but off the main drag. Rates include breakfast.

Lìjīng Jiǔdiàn (☎/fax 728 8731, 6 Xi Dajie) Singles or twins US$48. Opposite the Bell Tower Square, this hotel is very central. Singles are small and twins are very comfy. If you need a place to unwind from the noise and pollution, it has a very pleasant tea garden on the 4th floor. The staff is fairly good here.

Places to Stay – Top End

This is the category most Xī'ān hotels aim for, and there are dozens of choices. Here are some that stand out from the crowd.

Hyatt Regency Xi'an (Kǎiyuè Fàndiàn; ☎ 723 1234, Ⓦ www.hyatt.com, Dong Dajie) Standard/luxury twins US$140/160, regency

CENTRAL CHINA

club rooms US$170, plus 15% service charge. For location and luxury you can't beat the Hyatt Regency. Its service and facilities have garnered it a five-star rating, and it's just a few minutes' walk to Xī'ān's restaurant and nightlife scene. The regency club rooms are better equipped for business travellers. There's also Internet access on the 2nd floor.

Hotel Royal Xi'an (*Xī'ān Huángchéng Bīnguǎn; ☎ 723 5311, e xaroyal@xa .colcom.cn, 334 Dong Dajie*) Twins/suites US$90/200. Enjoying a fine location, and a bit cheaper, is the four-star Hotel Royal, which is a member of Japan's Nikko Hotels group. Room prices are usually discounted to the cheaper rate.

Bell Tower Hotel (*Zhōnglóu Fàndiàn; ☎ 727 9200, e bthotel@pub.xaonline.com, Xi Dajie*) Rooms from Y680 summer, Y550 other times. The prize for best position among Xī'ān's hotels has to go to the Bell Tower, managed by the Holiday Inn group. It's among the more reasonably priced top-end choices and is quite pleasant. The service and amenities don't match the Hyatt or other luxury hotels, but should still make for a comfortable stay.

Places to Eat

There's a lot of good street food in Xī'ān. In winter the entire population seems to get by on endless bowls of noodles, but at other times of the year there are all kinds of delicious snacks.

Much of the local street food is of Islamic origin, and some common dishes are: *fěnrèròu*, made by frying chopped mutton in a wok with finely ground wheat; *héletiáo*, dark brown sorghum or buckwheat noodles; and *ròujiāmó*, fried pork or beef stuffed in pita bread, sometimes with green peppers and cumin.

Another dish worth trying is *yángròu pàomó*, a soup dish that involves breaking (or grating) a flat loaf of bread into a bowl and adding a delicious mutton stock. You will first be served a bowl and one or two pieces of flat bread: try and break the bread into tiny chunks, the better to absorb the broth.

Wǔyī Fàndiàn (*☎ 721 2212, 351 Dong Dajie*) Dishes Y1-10. This cheap ground-floor restaurant is good for staple northern Chinese food like pork dumplings and

hearty bowls of noodles. It's popular with locals and always frenetic and noisy; there's some English on the menu here.

Wèiwèi Jiǎoziguǎn (*61 Chang'an Lu*) Dishes from Y6. Just across the road from CITS, this restaurant serves a good range of tasty dumplings. Two people can eat on Y10 worth of dumplings.

Wǎngfǔ Cānyǐn (*☎ 725 0133, 333 Dong Dajie*) Dishes from Y2. Just to the east, this place is similar to Wǔyī Fàndiàn with point and eat canteen-style food. Head upstairs to the 2nd floor and try some of the specials. The *wǎngfǔ zhásúpái* (home-style ribs), *xiāngjiān yínxuěyú* (fish) and *měiwèi páigǔbāo* (rib soup) are all very tasty.

Jiěfàng Měishí Guǎngchǎng Dishes from Y2. Opposite the train station, this is a convenient place after a long train journey. The food is nothing special, but it's cheap and ordering is easy: just point and choose.

Around Rénmín Dàshà Gōngyù, the travellers' restaurant scene centres on two establishments.

Dad's Home Cooking (*Fenghe Lu*) Dishes from Y3. This is a pleasant place to meet up with other backpackers, trade travellers' tales and knock back more beer than is good for you.

Kane's Kafe (*11 Fenghe Lu*) Dishes from Y3. Located inside the compound of Rénmín Dàshà Gōngyù, lots of weary travellers meet here, sample the good food and quaff the cold beers.

During the warmer months, a beer garden is set up in the Bell Tower Square. It's a pleasant place to rest your weary feet and have a cold drink.

Entertainment

Although not on a par with Běijīng or Shànghǎi, Xī'ān does have an increasingly lively nightlife scene. In addition to the usual karaoke and hostess clubs, a number of small bars featuring live music have sprung up, and are worth popping into. Virtually every week along Dong Dajie east of the Bell Tower a new bar or club opens; at present you'll find five or six popular options. Remember that these places are never cheap.

1+1 (*Yījiāyī; ☎ 721 6265, 285 Dong Dajie*) 1+1 is a very popular nightclub and a long-standing fave that draws large crowds on weekends.

Shopping

Huajue Xiang is a narrow alley running beside Dàqīngzhēn Sì with many small souvenir and 'antique' shops – they're great for browsing. This is one of the best places in China to pick up souvenirs like name chops or a pair of chiming steel balls. Bargaining is the order of the day.

Chénghuáng Miào (City God's Temple) This old-style wooden structure that possibly dates from the early Qing period is an interesting place to visit. It's actually no longer a temple, but now houses a small wares market that looks like the China of the early 1980s: lots of older consumer goods, some interesting porcelain ware, Chinese musical instruments and calligraphy implements. The temple is a 10-minute walk west of the Drum Tower at the end of a long covered market running north off Xi Dajie. There's no English sign, so look for the large red Chinese characters above the entrance.

Around town you'll also find worthy conversation pieces like carved-stone ink trays used in Chinese calligraphy and a wide range of jade products from earrings to cigarette holders. There are plenty of silks too, but you're probably better off buying these closer to their source (Sūzhōu, Shànghǎi etc). Street hawkers sell delicate miniature wire furniture and ingenious little folded bamboo-leaf insects such as crickets and cicadas, which make cheap and attractive souvenirs.

If you're interested in Chinese and Buddhist classical music, there's an interesting selection at Xiǎoyàn Tǎ.

Getting There & Away

Air Xī'ān is one of the best-connected cities in China – it's possible to fly to almost any major Chinese destination, as well as several international ones.

China Northwest Airlines (☎ 870 2299) is somewhat inconveniently located on the south-eastern corner of Xiguan Zhengjie and Laodong Nanlu, 1.5km from the West Gate (Xī Mén). Office hours are 8am to 9pm daily. There are numerous other outlets around town, as well as at most hotels, which normally sell plane tickets and are more centrally located.

A friendly ticket outlet (☎ 772 3663) run by the airport (not CAAC) is found south of the Bank of China along Juhua Yuan. One or two staff speak English and there's usually someone around, even off-hours.

Daily flights include Běijīng (Y970), Chéngdū (Y570), Guǎngzhōu (Y1340) and Shànghǎi (Y1280).

On the international front, there are flights to Hong Kong with both Dragonair and China Northwest (HK$2100). Dragonair (☎ 426 9288) has an office in the lobby of the Sheraton Hotel. Note that most China Northwest flights arrive very late, leaving you with a very pricey taxi ride into town.

China Northwest also has flights to Macau, Seoul, and to Nagoya, Fukuoka, Niigata, and Hiroshima in Japan.

Bus The most central long-distance bus station is opposite Xī'ān's train station. From here you can get buses to Huá Shān (Y15 to Y20, two to three hours) and Yán'ān (Y36 to Y120, six to eight hours, seven departures daily), as well as sleeper buses to more distant destinations such as Zhèngzhōu (Y98, 12 hours), Luòyáng (Y60, 10 hours) and Yínchuān (Y110, 15 hours).

Buses to Zhèngzhōu leave around 9am and to Luòyáng at 9am and 4.30pm, while sleepers to Yínchuān leave hourly from 12.30pm to 6.30pm. Xī'ān's west bus station is on Huancheng Nanlu, west of the South Gate.

If you're headed to Huáshān village, private minibuses leave when full from the east parking lot in front of the train station from 7am to 6pm. If they go via the highway the ride takes 2½ hours and costs Y20. See the Huáshān section for more information.

For more regional destinations like Dàfó Sì (Grand Buddha Temple; see Around Xī'ān), there is a regional bus station (chéngxī kèyùnzhàn) several kilometres west of downtown just off Daqing Lu. Bus No 103 from the train station stops a block away; or bus Nos 223, 301 and 210 go right past.

Train There are direct trains from Xī'ān to Běijīng (hard sleeper, Y274, 14 to 18 hours), Chéngdū (hard sleeper, Y175, 16 to 27 hours), Guǎngzhōu (hard sleeper, Y420, 27 hours), Lánzhōu (hard sleeper, Y140, 13 hours), Héféi, Qīngdǎo, Shànghǎi (hard sleeper, Y250, 22 to 24 hours), Tàiyuán (hard sleeper, Y135, nine to 12 hours), Ürümqi and Wǔhàn. For Chóngqìng and Kūnmíng change at Chéngdū.

CENTRAL CHINA

For travellers to Luòyáng and Zhèng-zhōu, there is a daytime air-con tourist train that only takes 8½ hours to reach Zhèngzhōu.

While you can sometimes get same-day tickets in the main ticket hall, most counters will probably refer you to the foreigners' ticket window on the 2nd level; the stairway is to the west of the main ticket hall. You may need to bring your passport in order to register at the small window at the western end of the 2nd level though this practice seems to have stopped. The ticket clerk will then give you a registration slip that you take to window No 2, at the eastern end of the floor: this is where you actually buy the ticket. The foreigners' window is open from 8.30am to 11am and from 2.30pm to 5.30pm. Be aware that it often closes early, especially on weekends.

There's an Advance Rail Booking Office inside the ICBC Bank on Lianhu Lu, but it only sells tickets for trains starting from Xī'ān. CITS can organise tickets with a minimum of fuss, providing you give two or three days' notice. Some travellers have complained about service (and especially price) from travel agencies.

Getting Around

To/From the Airport Xī'ān's Xiguan Airport is around 40km north-west of Xī'ān. China Northwest Airlines runs shuttle buses hourly from 5am to 6pm between the airport and its Xī'ān booking centre (Y15, 50 minutes), from where you can pick up a taxi or local bus to your hotel.

Don't arrive on a late-night flight: taxis into town charge Y160 to Y180 on the meter!

Xī'ān's packed public buses are a pickpocket's paradise, so watch your wallet when you ride them. More comfortable minibuses run on the same routes and charges are around Y1 or Y2 for most central destinations.

Local buses go to all the major sights in and around the city, such as Bànpō Neolithic Village and the Army of Terracotta Warriors.

Taxis are abundant and reasonably cheap: flag fall is around Y6, although short trips around town are a set Y5.

Bicycle hire is available at Rénmín Dàshà Gōngyù and the Bell Tower Hotel for around Y1 to Y2 per hour.

AROUND XĪ'ĀN

Most of the really interesting sights are outside the city. The two biggest drawcards are the Army of Terracotta Warriors near the Tomb of Qin Shihuang, and the Bànpō Neolithic Village.

Army of Terracotta Warriors

Bīngmǎyǒng 兵马俑

Ranking up there with the Great Wall and the Forbidden City as one of China's top historical sights, the 2000-year-old Army of Terracotta Warriors (☎ 391 1961; admission Y65; open 8.30am-5.30pm daily) remains stunningly well preserved: a perpetually vigilant force standing guard over an ancient imperial necropolis. In 1974 peasants digging a well uncovered what turned out to be perhaps the major archaeological discovery of the 20th century: an underground vault of earth and timber that eventually yielded thousands of life-size terracotta soldiers and their horses in battle formation. In 1976 two other smaller vaults were discovered close to the first one.

The first underground vault measures about 210m east to west and 60m from north to south. The pit varies in depth from 5m to 7m. Walls were built running east to west at intervals of 3m, forming corridors. In these corridors, on floors laid with grey brick, are arranged the terracotta figures. Pillars and beams once supported a roof.

The 6000 terracotta figures of warriors and horses face east in a rectangular battle array. The vanguard appears to be three rows of 210 crossbow and longbow bearers who stand at the easternmost end of the army. Close behind is the main force of armoured soldiers holding spears, dagger-axes and other long-shaft weapons, accompanied by 35 horse-drawn chariots (the latter, made of wood, have long-since disintegrated). Every figure differs in facial features and expressions.

The horsemen are shown wearing tight-sleeved outer robes, short coats of chain mail and wind-proof caps. The archers have bodies and limbs positioned in strict accordance with an ancient book on the art of war. There is speculation that the sculptors used fellow workers, or even themselves, as models for the warriors' faces.

Many of the figures originally held real weapons of the day, and over 10,000 pieces

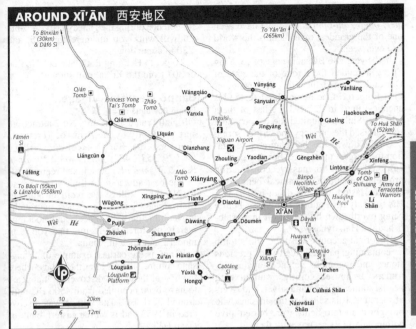

AROUND XĪ'ĀN 西安地区

have been sorted to date. Bronze swords were worn by the figures representing the generals and other senior officers. Surface treatment made the swords resistant to rust and corrosion so that after being buried for more than 2000 years they were still sharp. The weapons are now kept in storage, out of public view.

The second vault, excavated in 1976, contained about 1000 figures. The third vault contained only 68 warriors and one war chariot, and appeared to be the command post for the soldiers in the other vaults. Archaeologists believe the warriors discovered so far may be part of an even larger terracotta army still buried around the Tomb of Qin Shihuang. Excavation of the entire complex and the tomb itself could take decades.

Almost as impressive is a pair of bronze chariots and horses unearthed in 1980 just 20m west of the Tomb of Qin Shihuang and now housed in the small **Qínyǒng Museum** (*Qínyǒng Bówùguǎn*), which is within the enclosure of the warriors site.

Visitors are not permitted to take photos at the site, unless they pay for the privilege. People who break this rule can expect to

have their film confiscated. If you decide to take a few sly shots and get caught, try to remember that the attendants are just doing their job.

The admission price includes entry to the vaults and museum, and a *Circle Vision* documentary on the warriors and excavation. The last admission is at 5pm.

You also can't help but experience the world-famous freneticness of the souvenir hawkers here; their, er, passionate pursuit of tourist yuán leaves many folks breathless.

Getting There & Away You can see the site as part of a tour from Xī'ān (see Organised Tours in the Xiányáng section later). Or it is possible to do it yourself by public bus. From the parking lot just east of the train station take bus No 306 or 307 (Y5/8 one way/return), which travel via Huáqīng Pool. Bus No 307 does the return journey to Xī'ān via Bànpō Neolithic Village.

Tomb of Qin Shihuang
Qín Shǐhuáng Líng 秦始皇陵

It may not amount to much as a tourist attraction, but in its time the Tomb of Qin

Shihuang (☎ 391 2369; admission Y26 summer; open 7am-6pm daily) must have been one of the grandest mausoleums the world had ever seen.

In the year 246 BC, at the age of 13, Ying Zheng ascended the throne of the state of Qin and assumed the title 'Shihuang', or First Emperor. One by one he defeated his enemies, until in 221 BC the last of them fell. Qin Shihuang united the country, and standardised the currency and written script.

On the down side, he acquired a reputation for purges, mass book-burning parties, enforced labour in massive construction projects, and other tyrannical behaviour. His rule lasted until his death in 210 BC. His son only held out for four years, before being overthrown by the revolt that established the Han dynasty.

Historical accounts describe Qin's tomb as containing palaces filled with precious stones and ingenious defences against intruders. It housed ceilings vaulted with pearls, statues of gold and silver, and rivers of mercury. It is said that the artisans who brought it all into being were buried alive within, taking its secrets with them.

Despite the legends and impressive statistics, basically all there is to see nowadays is a mound. If you are interested, the tomb is about 1.5km west of the Army of Terracotta Warriors. Take bus No 306 or 307 from Xī'ān train station.

Huáqīng Pool
Huáqīng Chí 华清池

The Huáqīng Pool (admission Y30; open 7.30am-7pm daily) is 30km east of Xī'ān, at the foot of Lí Shān (Black Horse Mountain). Water from hot springs is funnelled into public bathhouses, which have 60 pools accommodating 400 people.

During the Tang dynasty these natural hot baths were a favoured retreat of emperors and their concubines. However, nowadays the Huáqīng Pool leaves most visitors cold. If you don't fancy strolling around the gardens with swarms of excited tourists, try the museum up the road or take a walk on one of the paths leading up through the forest behind the complex.

There is a Taoist temple on Lí Shān dedicated to the 'Old Mother' Nüwa, who created the human race and also patched up cracks in the sky after a catastrophe. On the

mountain's summit are beacon towers built for defence during the Han dynasty. A cable car will whiz you up there for Y25, and Y20 to come down.

To get to Huáqīng Pool take bus No 306 or 307 from the Xī'ān train station.

Bànpō Neolithic Village
Bànpō Bówùguǎn 半坡博物馆

Officially rated as Xī'ān's No 2 attraction, surpassed only by the Army of Terracotta Warriors, the Bànpō Neolithic Village (☎ 029 353 2482; admission Y20; open 8am-6.30pm daily) gets mixed reports.

The best advice is to limit your visit to the Neolithic Village and avoid the adjacent Matriarchal Clan Village, where matriarchs in Neolithic garb, high heels and stockings merely reinforce the feeling that you're in modern, not ancient, China.

Bànpō is the earliest example of 'Yangshao culture', named after the village where the first of these was discovered. It appears to have been occupied from 4500 BC until around 3750 BC. The village was discovered in 1953 and is on the eastern bank of Chǎn Hé.

A large hall has been built over what was part of the residential area of the village, and there are adjacent buildings housing pottery and other artefacts. Pottery found south of Qínlíng Shān has suggested that even earlier agricultural villages may have existed here.

The Bànpō ruins are divided into three parts: a pottery-manufacturing area, a residential area and a cemetery. These include the remains of 45 houses or other buildings, over 200 storage cellars, six pottery kilns and 250 graves.

The residential part of the village was surrounded by an artificial moat, 300m long, about 2m deep and 2m wide. It protected the village from attacks by wild animals and from the effects of heavy rainfall in what was originally a hot and humid environment. To the east of the residential area is the pottery kiln centre. To the north of the village lies the cemetery, where the adult dead were buried along with funerary objects like earthen pots. The children were buried in earthen pots close to the houses.

The Eastern Tour to the Army of Terracotta Warriors usually includes Bànpō Neolithic Village.

Dàfó Sì 大佛寺
Grand Buddha Temple

This large temple complex *(admission Y8)* is a bit far from Xī'ān at 115km or so to the north-west outside Bīnxiàn. However, it is easy to reach on public transport and better still, it opens up a route to the excellent Taoist temples of Kōngdòng Shān in Píngliáng, Gānsù. The main Buddha is 30m high and 34m wide; the exterior of the grotto is framed by an impressive three-storey fortress tower. Two other caves house nearly 2000 arhats, sculptures, shrines and steles.

Getting There & Away Buses to Bīnxiàn (Y15, three hours) leave from the west bus station in Xī'ān. From Bīnxiàn it's around 7km north to Dàfó Sì; a motorcycle taxi will cost Y10. Or, any bus north toward Chángwǔ or Píngliáng will pass right by the entrance; for Y1 they'll give you a lift. From the temple it's easy to flag down a bus along the highway.

XIÁNYÁNG 咸阳
☎ 0910 • pop 4,730,500

This little town is half an hour's bus ride from Xī'ān. The chief attraction is the **Xianyang City Museum** *(Xiányáng Shì Bówùguǎn; ☎ 096 321 3015, Zhongshan Jie; admission Y20; open 8am-6pm daily)*, which houses a remarkable collection of 3000 miniature terracotta soldiers and horses, excavated from a Han dynasty tomb in 1965. Each figure is about half a metre high.

To get to the Xianyang City Museum from Xī'ān, take bus No 3 or 611 from the Xī'ān train station to the regional bus stop and then get bus No 59. Get off at the bus station in Xiányáng. Up ahead on the left-hand side of the road you'll see a clock tower. Turn right at this intersection and then left at Xining Jie.

The museum is housed in a former Ming dynasty Confucian temple on Zhongshan Jie, which is a continuation of Xining Jie. The entrance is flanked by two stone lions. It's about a 20-minute walk from the bus station.

Imperial Tombs
Apart from the Tomb of Qin Shihuang, a large number of other imperial tombs dot the Guānzhōng plain surrounding Xī'ān. The easiest way to get there is by tour from Xī'ān (see the Organised Tours section later in this section for details).

In these tombs are buried the emperors of numerous dynasties, as well as empresses, concubines, government officials and high-ranking military leaders. Construction of an emperor's tomb often began within a few years of his ascension to the throne and did not finish until he died.

Admission to the tombs varies from Y15 to Y35. Most are open 8.30am to 5pm daily (closing later in summer).

Zhāo Tomb This tomb *(Zhāo Líng)* set the custom of building imperial tombs on mountain slopes, breaking the tradition of building tombs on the plains with an artificial hill over them. This burial ground on Jiǔzong Shān, 70km north-west of Xī'ān, belongs to the second Tang emperor, Taizong, who died in AD 649.

Of the 18 imperial mausoleums on the Guānzhōng plain, this is probably the most representative. With the mountain at the centre, the tomb fans out to the south-east and south-west. Within its confines are 167 lesser tombs of the emperor's relatives and high-ranking military and government officials. Burying other people in the same park as the emperor was a custom dating back to the Han dynasty.

Buried in the sacrificial altar of the tomb were six statues known as the 'Six Steeds of Zhaoling', representing the horses the emperor used during his wars of conquest. Some of the statues have been relocated to museums in Xī'ān.

Qián Tomb This tomb *(Qián Líng)* is one of the most impressive tombs, 85km north-west of Xī'ān, in Liáng Shān. It's the joint resting place of Tang Emperor Gaozong and his wife Empress Wu Zetian.

Gaozong ascended the throne in AD 650 after the death of his father, Emperor Taizong. Empress Wu, actually a concubine of Taizong, also caught the fancy of his son, who made her his empress. Gaozong died in AD 683, and the following year Empress Wu dethroned her husband's successor, Emperor Zhongzong. She reigned as an all-powerful monarch until her death around AD 705.

CENTRAL CHINA

The tomb consists of three peaks; the two on the southern side are artificial, but the higher northern peak is natural and is the main part of the tomb. Walls originally surrounded the tomb, but these are gone. South-west of the tomb are 17 smaller tombs of officials.

The grounds of the imperial tomb boast a number of large stone sculptures of animals and officers of the imperial guard. There are 61 (now headless) statues of the leaders of minority peoples of China and of the representatives of friendly nations who attended the emperor's funeral. The two steles on the ground each stand more than 6m high. The Wordless Stele (Wúzì Bēi) is a blank tablet; one story goes that it symbolises Empress Wu's absolute power, which she considered inexpressible in words.

Prince Zhang Huai's Tomb This is the tomb of Zhang (Zhāng Huái Mù), the second son of Emperor Gaozong and Empress Wu. For some reason the prince was exiled to Sìchuān in AD 683 and died the following year, aged only 31.

Empress Wu posthumously rehabilitated him. His remains were brought to Xī'ān after Emperor Zhongzong regained power. Tomb paintings show horsemen playing polo, but these and other paintings are in a terrible state.

Princess Yong Tai's Tomb Near Prince Zhang Huai's Tomb is the Princess Yong Tai's Tomb (Yǒng Tài Gōng Zhǔ Mù), which features tomb paintings depicting palace servants. The line engravings on the stone outer coffin are extraordinarily graceful.

Yong Tai was a granddaughter of Tang Emperor Gaozong, and the seventh daughter of Emperor Zhongzong. She was put to death by Empress Wu in AD 701, but was rehabilitated posthumously by Emperor Zhongzong after he regained power.

Mào Tomb This tomb (Mào Líng), 40km north-west of Xī'ān, is the resting place of Emperor Wu (d. 87 BC), the most powerful ruler of the Han dynasty. The cone-shaped mound of rammed earth is almost 47m high, and is the largest of the Han imperial tombs. A wall used to enclose the mausoleum, but now only the ruins of the gates on the eastern, western and northern sides remain.

It is recorded that the emperor was entombed clad in jade clothes sewn with gold thread and with a jade cicada in his mouth. Apparently buried with him were live animals and an abundance of jewels.

Fǎmén Sì 法门寺
Doorway Temple
Fǎmén Sì (admission temple/crypt/museum Y15/20/18; open 8am-6pm daily), 115km north-west of Xī'ān, was built during the Eastern Han dynasty in about AD 200.

In 1981, after torrential rains had weakened the temple's ancient brick structure, the entire western side of the 12-storey pagoda collapsed. The subsequent restoration work produced a sensational discovery. Below the pagoda in a sealed crypt (built during the Tang dynasty to contain four sacred finger bones of the Buddha, known as sarira) were over 1000 sacrificial objects and royal offerings, including stone-tablet Buddhist scriptures, gold and silver items and some 27,000 coins. These relics had been completely forgotten for over 1000 years.

A museum housing part of the collection has been built on the site. After the excavations had finished the temple was reconstructed in its original form.

The best way to visit Fǎmén Sì is to take a Western Tour from Xī'ān (see the following Organised Tours section). Some tours don't include the temple so check before you book. Note that the pagoda itself is not open to the public.

Organised Tours
One-day tours allow you to see all the sights around Xī'ān more quickly and conveniently than if you arranged one yourself. Itineraries differ somewhat, but there are two basic tours: a 'Western Tour' and an 'Eastern Tour'. There are also Chinese tours that leave from the square in front of the train station.

Travel agency tours are more expensive than those run by other operators, but the train station operators don't leave until they have enough people and tend to give you less time at each place and more time at other 'attractions'.

Eastern Tour The Eastern Tour (Dōngxiàn Yóulǎn) is the most popular as it includes the Army of Terracotta Warriors as well as the Tomb of Qin Shihuang, Bànpō Neolithic Village and Huáqīng Pool. See Travel Agencies in the Xī'ān section for more contact information; asking around can also have good results.

CITS offers an Eastern Tour (Y280), including lunch, all entry tickets and a visit to Dàyàn Tǎ. The coach leaves Xī'ān around 9am and returns by 5pm. An English-speaking guide is provided and you usually get two hours at the terracotta warriors and Tomb of Qin Shihuang.

The Xi'an Tourist Information Services Centre runs daily Eastern Tours with 10 stops (Y44) that depart from the office at the train station between 7.30am and 8.30am. For a little extra the staff may provide you with an English-speaking guide.

Essentially the same tour can be done for less by taking one of the Chinese minibus tours; you can buy tickets (Y35 to Y40) at a kiosk in front of the train station. Travellers have mixed reports about these tours and have sometimes come away with a deeper understanding of contemporary Chinese culture, rather than Chinese history.

Western Tour The longer Western Tour (Xīxiàn Yóulǎn) includes the Xianyang City Museum, some of the imperial tombs, the Qián Tomb and sometimes also Fǎmén Sì.

It's far less popular than the Eastern Tour and consequently you may have to wait a couple of days for CITS to organise enough people. Otherwise contact the tourist bureau's office at the station, which seems to run the most frequent tours. Its Western Tour visits seven locations and costs Y54.

HUÁ SHĀN 华山

The 2200m-high granite peaks of Huá Shān, 120km east of Xī'ān, tower above the plains to the north, forming one of China's sacred mountain areas. The tough climb to the top rewards you with stunning views.

There are now three different choices for climbing the mountain, all of which meet up at the **North Peak** (Běi Fēng), the first of five summit peaks. Two of these routes start from the eastern base of the mountain at the cable car terminus. If your legs aren't feeling up to the task, an Austrian-built cable car can get you to the North Peak in 10 scenic minutes (Y55/100 one way/return).

The second route works its way under the cable-car route and takes a sweaty two hours; note that two sections of 50m or so are quite literally vertical with nothing but a steel chain to grab onto and tiny chinks cut into the rock for footing – terrifying if you're descending or it's raining.

The third route is the traditional and most popular route and the one that will leave the most memories, both physical and psychological. A 6km path leads to the North Peak from the town of Huáshān. The first 4km are pretty easy going, but after that it's all steep stairs, and from the North Peak on to the other summits it's also fairly strenuous. But the scenery is great; along **Green Dragon Ridge** (Cānglóng Fēng), which connects the North Peak with the **East Peak** (Dōng Fēng), **South Peak** (Nán Fēng) and **West Peak** (Xī Fēng), the way has been cut along a narrow rock ridge with impressive sheer cliffs on either side.

The South Peak is the highest at 2160m, but all three rear peaks afford great views when the weather cooperates.

From Huáshān village, at the base of the mountain, it usually takes between three to five hours to reach the North Peak, and another hour or so to get to any one of the others. Several narrow and almost vertical 'bottleneck' sections can be dangerous when the route is crowded, particularly under wet or icy conditions.

There is accommodation on the mountain, most of it quite basic and overpriced, but it does allow you to start in the afternoon, spend the night, and catch the sunrise from either the East Peak or South Peak. Many tourists actually make the climb at night, aided by torches (flashlights) and countless tea and refreshment stands. The idea is to start off at around 11pm to midnight, which should get you to the East Peak at sunrise. In summer this is certainly a much cooler option, but you do miss the scenery on the way up.

The gate ticket price is Y60. Some travellers have also been asked to register their passport at the main gate. When heading out from Huáshān village, be careful not to hit the trail via the **Yùquán Sì** (Jade Fountain Temple), unless you're interested in seeing it, and paying another Y8 entry fee. There's a path that skirts the temple to the left and reconnects with the main Huá Shān trail.

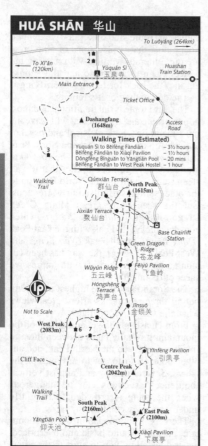

HUÁ SHĀN 华山

To Luòyáng (264km)

To Xi'ān
(120km)

Yùquán Sì
玉泉寺

Huashan
Train Station

Main Entrance

Ticket Office

▲ Dashangfang
(1648m)

Access
Road

Walking Times (Estimated)
Yùquán Sì to Běifēng Fàndiàn – 3½ hours
Běifēng Fàndiàn to Xiàqí Pavilion – 1½ hours
Dōngfēng Bīnguǎn to Yángtiān Pool – 20 mins
Běifēng Fàndiàn to West Peak Hostel – 1 hour

Walking
Trail

Qúnxiān Terrace
群仙台

North Peak
(1615m)

Jùxiān Terrace
聚仙台

Base Chairlift
Station

Green Dragon
Ridge
苍龙岭

Wǔyún Ridge
五云峰

Fēiyú Pavilion
飞鱼岭

Hóngshēng
Terrace
鸿声台

Jīnsuǒ
金锁关

Not to Scale

West Peak
(2083m)

Yīnfēng Pavilion
引凤亭

Cliff Face

Centre Peak
(2042m) ▲

Walking
Trail

South Peak
(2160m)
▲

East Peak
(2100m)

Yángtiān Pool
仰天池

Xiàqí Pavilion
下棋亭

HUÁ SHĀN

PLACES TO STAY

1 Xīyuè Bīnguǎn
西岳宾馆
2 Huáyáng Dàjiǔdiàn
华洋大酒店
3 Hairy Woman Cave Hostel
毛女洞
4 Běifēng Fàndiàn
北峰饭店
5 Diànlì Bīnguǎn
电力宾馆
6 West Peak Hostel
西峰旅社
7 Zhènyuè Gōng Hostel
镇岳宫
8 Dōngfēng Bīnguǎn
东峰宾馆

Places to Stay & Eat

Take your own food or eat well before ascending or you're left with instant noodles and processed meat at the top – a proper meal can be eyepoppingly expensive.

Hairy Woman Cave Hostel Beds in 10-bed dorm/twins with shared bath Y20/45. Just over 4km up the mountain trail, this small hostel is at **Hairy Woman Cave** (*Máonǚ Dòng*). Although rooms are very basic, it's a good place to stop for the night, especially if you arrive at Huáshān later in the day.

Běifēng Fàndiàn (☎ 430 0062) Beds in 30-bed dorms Y30, twins/quads with private bath Y240/280. This place is just below the North Peak. It's spartan and, given the congestion along the three trails that converge here, rarely quiet.

Zhènyuè Gōng Hostel Dorm beds Y30-50. The best-value accommodation is this pleasant hostel at Zhènyuè Gōng, which sits in the valley between the rear peaks. Despite lacking the view, it does receive the morning sun and is centrally located. They tried to extort an insane amount of money from us on a most recent trip, so walk away back over to West Peak if they try it with you.

West Peak Hostel (*Xīfēng Lǚshè*) Beds in dorms/twins Y40/120. This place atop West Peak is very, very clean and the proprietors have been very helpful on a couple of trips; the only downside is a lack of washing facilities. It's one place down from the hotel at the peak.

Diànlì Bīnguǎn (☎ 216 2970) Twins or triples with bath Y980. Providing all the creature comforts, this place on West Peak is also ridiculously priced.

Dōngfēng Bīnguǎn Beds Y60. This place on East Peak charges a usurious Y60 for a mat and blanket in the grimy and draughty attic – there's an awful lot of traffic through here as well. Then again, anything on the east side – given the sunrise – is going to cost more.

There are plenty of cheap places to stay in Huáshān village along the road leading up to the trailhead and Yùquán Sì.

Huáyáng Dàjiǔdiàn (☎ 0913-436 6178) Beds in quads with shared bath Y20. This fairly clean place is 100m from the main intersection on the right heading towards the Huá Shān trailhead. (Look for the English menu items painted onto the window.) The owners' teenage son speaks some English.

Xīyuè Bīnguǎn (*☎ 436 4741, fax 436 4559*) Twins/triples with air-con & bath Y218/320. This place is at the main intersection and has more creature comforts than any other place in town.

Getting There & Away

The nearest train station is at Mèngyuán, on the Xī'ān-Luòyáng line, about 15km east of Huáshān. This station is also referred to as Huáshān, and is served by nearly a dozen trains daily in either direction. To and from Xī'ān takes two to three hours. Minibuses run between the train station and Huáshān village (Y3, 30 minutes) though they're not *that* frequent.

There are minibuses (Y10) direct to the cable car from a separate ticket entrance just east of Huáshān village. A motorcycle taxi to this entrance should only cost Y5. It's a lovely hour's walk down from the cable car to the ticket entrance; it's all downhill and follows the gurgling river.

Minibuses to Xī'ān (Y20, 2½ hours) leave when full from around the main intersection or the eastern ticket entrance from 7am to around 6pm. Coming from Xī'ān, buses leave from the east parking lot in front of the train station but these depart only when full and you may have to haggle the price. Instead, large green public buses (Y18, two hours) depart a few times early in the morning (first bus around 7.30am, every 30 minutes) from the train station square at Jiefang Lu. They depart promptly with no hassle; you have to inform them if you wish to ascend from Huáshān village.

If you are heading east, there are regular buses that pass through Huáshān going to Luòyáng, Ruìchéng and Tàiyuán. The bus station is a few hundred metres west of the main intersection.

YÁN'ĀN 延安
☎ 0911 • pop 117,200

Yán'ān, 270km from Xī'ān in northern Shaanxi, is a small city, but together with Mao's birthplace at Sháoshān it has special significance as a major Communist pilgrimage spot.

Between 1936 and 1947 this was the headquarters of the fledgling Chinese Communist Party. The Long March from Jiāngxī ended in 1936 when the Communists reached the northern Shaanxi town of Wúqí. The following year they moved their base to Yán'ān.

Apart from the revolution history sites, there's not a whole lot to see in Yán'ān, although just making it up to this remote section of the province is in itself pretty interesting.

Orientation

Yán'ān is spread out along a Y-shaped valley formed where the east and west branches of Yán Hé meet. The town centre is clustered around this junction, while the old Communist army headquarters is at Yángjiālǐng on the north-western outskirts of Yán'ān. The train station is at the far southern end of the town, 4.5km from the centre.

For a bird's eye view of Yán'ān head up to the revolving restaurant on the top floor of Yàshèng Dàjiǔdiàn.

Information

The PSB can be found inside Yán'ān Bīnguǎn on Zhongxin Jie. The Bank of China is inconveniently located in the north of town on Beiguan Jie; hours are 9am to noon and 2.30pm to 5pm. The post and telephone office is on Zhongxin Jie. In addition to the usual services there is an Internet bar inside the telephone section. Hours are from 8am to 6pm.

Things to See

During their extended stay, the Communist leadership moved house quite a bit within Yán'ān. As a result there are numerous former headquarters sites.

One of the most interesting is the **Yángjiālǐng Revolution Headquarters Site** (*Yángjiālǐng Gémìng Jiùzhǐ; ☎ 211 2671, Zaoyuan Lu; admission Y11; open 7am-8pm daily summer, less other seasons*), 3km north-west of the town centre. Here you can see the assembly hall where the first Central Committee meetings were held, including the 7th national plenum, which formally confirmed Mao as the leader of the party and the revolution.

Nearby are simple dugouts built into the loess earth where Mao, Zhu De, Zhou Enlai and other senior Communist leaders lived, worked and wrote. Farther uphill are caves that used to house the secretariat, propaganda and personnel offices.

About 1km south-east of here you will find the **Yan'an Revolution Museum** (*Yán'ān Gémìng Jìniànguǎn;* ☎ *238 2161, Zaoyuan Lu; admission Y11; open 8am-6.30pm daily summer, less other seasons*), which has an extensive collection of revolutionary paraphernalia – old uniforms, weaponry and many photographs and illustrations. Unfortunately there are no English labels.

Just a few minutes' walk south is the last site occupied by the Communist leadership in Yán'ān, the **Wángjiāpíng Revolution Headquarters Site** (*Wángjiāpíng Gémìng Jiùzhǐ;* ☎ *238 2161, Zaoyuan Lu; admission Y10; open 7am-dusk daily*). There's not quite as much to see here, although it's interesting to note the improvement in living standards enjoyed by Mao and top-ranking comrades.

All the aforementioned sights can be reached by taking bus No 1, which runs from the train station along the road east of the river and then heads up Zaoyuan Lu. Bus No 3 runs along the other side of the river along Zhongxin Jie; get off when it crosses north over the river. Both of these start at the train station. Just ask the conductor to drop you off at the respective site. Bus No 8 also passes by all these places and can be caught from Dà Bridge.

More accessible from the city is the **Fènghuángshān Revolution Headquarters Site** (*Fènghuángshān Gémìng Jiùzhǐ; admission Y7; open 8am-6pm daily*), about 100m north of the post office. This was the first site occupied by the Communists after their move to Yán'ān, as reflected by the relatively primitive lodgings of the leading cadres. Often someone is around until 8pm.

Bǎo Tǎ (*Treasure Pagoda; admission Y10, plus Y5 to climb pagoda; open 7am-8pm daily*), built during the Song dynasty, stands on a prominent hillside south-east of the river junction.

Qīngliáng Shān (☎ *211 2236; admission Y10; open 7am-8pm daily*) is a pleasant hillside park with some nice trails and a few sights, including **Ten Thousand Buddha Cave** (*Wànfó Dòng*) dug into the sandstone cliff beside the river. The cave has relatively intact Buddhist statues and wall inscriptions.

Places to Stay & Eat

Bǎiyuè Fàndiàn (☎ *211 2159, Zhongxin Jie*) Dorm beds/twins with air-con Y45/160. Just north of the post office is this more modest affair. Actually it's a bit weird – the 'lobby' is actually a China Mobile phone retail outlet. The rooms are adequate at best and you may not get a cheap bed but it's really all there is budget-wise downtown.

Yàshèng Dàjiǔdiàn (☎ *213 2778, fax 213 2779, Erdao Jie Zhongduan*) Twins/suites from Y228/590. Mains from Y20. Located in

YÁN'ĀN 延安

PLACES TO STAY	PLACES TO EAT
7 Jiālíng Bīnguǎn 嘉岭宾馆	4 Zhōngyuàn Dàjiǔdiàn 中苑大酒店
13 Yàshèng Dàjiǔdiàn; Rotating Restaurant 亚圣大酒店	9 Night Market 夜市
15 Bǎiyuè Fàndiàn 百悦饭店	10 Night Market 夜市
17 Yán'ān Bīnguǎn; PSB 延安宾馆；公安局外事科	12 Night Market 夜市

OTHER
1 Yan'an Revolution Museum 延安革命纪念馆
2 Wángjiāpíng Revolution Headquarters Site 王家坪革命旧址
3 Bank of China 中国银行
5 Qīngliáng Shān Entry Gate 清凉山售票口
6 CAAC 民航售票处
8 Long-Distance Bus Station 延安汽车站
11 Bǎo Tǎ 宝塔
14 Post & Telephone Office; Internet Bar 邮电大楼；网吧
16 Fènghuángshān Revolution Headquarters Site 凤凰山革命旧址
18 Train Station 火车站

the centre of town, this used to be Yán'ān's fanciest hotel. It has stylish rooms. The best food in town (both Chinese and Western) is claimed to be found in the rotating restaurant on the top floor of the hotel. The only problem is that it's often booked out.

Yán'ān Bīnguǎn (☎ *211 3122, fax 211 4297, 56 Zhongxin Jie)* Singles/doubles from Y280/320. This is the city's most sybaritic spot – it was totally renovated as of 2001 and is very luxurious (even world leaders stay here). For the money it's decent value, given the laundry list of amenities. The restaurants here are very good but pricey.

Jiālíng Bīnguǎn (☎ *231 5470, Baimi Dadao)* Dorm beds/twins with private bath Y30/158. On the eastern side of town, this hotel is reportedly not supposed to accept foreigners, but they had no problem with us. If so, you can get dorm beds or slightly dingy but comfortable twins.

Zhōngyuàn Dàjiǔdiàn (*Beiguan Jie)* Dishes from Y5. If you have to do any banking, then drop into this popular place just next door. If you can put up with the tacky elevator music, it serves a tasty bowl of *niúròu shāozi,* a kind of spaghetti bolognaise.

Markets set up on both sides of the Dà Bridge during the day and in the evening with lots of tea tables. The locals while away the day here, chewing pumpkin seeds and playing chess. Noodles are the order of the day.

Getting There & Away

Air There are daily flights to Xī'ān (Y380) and Běijīng (Y800) four times a week.

The airline booking office/CAAC (☎ 211 3854) is on Jichang Lu (also known as Baimi Dadao, and diagonally opposite Jiālíng Bīnguǎn, and is open daily from 8am to noon and 2.30pm to 5.30pm. A free bus service connects the office with the airport, 7km north-east of the city.

Bus Heading to Xī'ān, a large variety of buses run every half to one hour from 6am to late afternoon. The ride takes anywhere from six to nine hours and costs Y38 all the way up to Y120 (for an express air-con luxury bus). Iveco vans take seven hours and run every 30 minutes; the express buses leave a handful of times between 9.30am and 2.30pm. Slower buses leave whenever they can trap enough souls aboard. The schedule is roughly the same in the reverse

direction. Otherwise, there are share taxis (Santanas) to Xī'ān that take four hours and cost Y100 or Y120 for the front seat.

From Yán'ān there are Iveco vans and express buses to Yúlín (Y31 to Y45, five to seven hours) roughly hourly from 6.20am to 1pm. Heading west, there are three daily departures to Yínchuān in Níngxià (Y51, 12 hours) at 2.40am, 5.30am and 4.30pm. You can also get to Běijīng and Lánzhōu.

Train A train line links Yán'ān with Xī'ān via an interesting route along Luò Hé. There are daily trains in either direction: an overnight service that leaves both Xī'ān and Yán'ān (7½ hours) was the most convenient but there was word it was to be scrapped; and a day train (No 7551) that departs either station around 9am or 10am (nine hours).

Getting sleeper tickets to Yán'ān is usually no problem, but getting them back can be quite difficult: either get down to the station by 3pm to line up for the overnight train, or try the foyer of the large hotel opposite the bus station at 9am. No advance tickets are sold. A taxi from the train station into town costs Y10.

YÚLÍN 榆林
☎ 0912 • pop 93,700

Yúlín lies on the fringe of Inner Mongolia's Mu Us Desert in far northern Shaanxi. During the Ming dynasty, Yúlín was a fortified garrison town and patrol post serving the Great Wall.

Yúlín's remoteness and relative poverty have kept the old town somewhat insulated from the 'white-tile' trend in Chinese architecture, which is rapidly destroying what remains of the country's older buildings. Along the narrow brick lanes near the unrestored Bell Tower (Zhōng Lóu) are traditional family houses with tiny courtyards hidden behind low enclosure walls and old stone gates. The city's old Ming walls are mainly still standing, although in places their original outer brick layer has been removed.

A large three-tiered **fortress** and **Beacon Tower** (*Zhènběi Tái)* lie 7.5km north of town.

Places to Stay & Eat

Yúlín Bīnguǎn (☎ *328 3971, fax 328 3970, Xinjian Lu)* Beds in twins/triples with shower Y50/40, singles Y160, twins Y120-160. Just north of the city walls, this is the official tour group and conference hotel, and is therefore often full. The hotel's dining hall is not bad and quite cheap.

Yúxī Dàjiǔdiàn (☎ 328 0492, 64 Renmin Xilu) Beds in triples with bath from Y35, twins Y92-130. This place is showing its age so look at several rooms if the first one doesn't strike your fancy. The management has been pretty solicitous in the past.

There's a depressing dearth of interesting food, especially if you're a solo traveller.

Getting There & Away

There are daily flights to Xī'ān (Y590) and there are flights twice weekly to Baōtóu and Běijīng.

The city has two bus stations. If you get off the bus inside the city walls, you're at the south station (the main one); the other is next to Yúxī Dàjiǔdiàn downtown and has mostly regional buses but it's got express buses to Xī'ān too. From the main station there are buses roughly every 90 minutes daily between Xī'ān and Yúlín (Y70 to Y128, 10 to 12 hours), but it's more convenient and less tiring to stop in Yán'ān. There are also six express buses each day between Yán'ān and Yúlín (Y45, six to seven hours) and several morning expresses to Taìyuán.

There is one daily bus at 5.30am to Yínchuān (Y51, 12 hours) following a route close to the Great Wall. There are also half-hourly buses to Dàliǔtǎ, from where you can catch a train to Dōngshèng and Bāotóu in Inner Mongolia.

Hénán 河南

Capital: Zhèngzhōu
Population: 92.6 million
Area: 167,000 sq km

Hénán, or at least its northern tip where Huáng Hé (Yellow River) crosses, is allegedly where it all began. The beginnings of Chinese civilisation can be traced back about 3500 years, when primitive settlements here began to coalesce into a true urban sprawl.

It was long thought that tribes who migrated from western Asia founded the Shang dynasty (c. 1700–1100 BC). Shang dynasty settlement excavations in Hénán, however, have shown these towns to be built on the sites of even more ancient settlements. The Shang probably emerged from a continuous line of development that reaches back into prehistoric times.

The first archaeological evidence of the Shang period was discovered near Ānyáng in northern Hénán. However it is believed that the first Shang capital, perhaps dating back 3800 years, was at Yǎnshī, west of modern-day Zhèngzhōu. Around the mid-14th century BC, the capital is thought to have moved to Zhèngzhōu, where its ancient city walls are still visible. Many Shang settlements have also been found outside the walled area. Later the capital moved to Yīn, near the modern town of Ānyáng to the north.

The only clues as to what Shang society was like are found in the remnants of its cities, in divining bones and in ancient Chinese literary texts. Apart from the Zhèngzhōu walls, all that has survived of its cities are the buildings' pounded-earth foundations, stone-lined trenches where wooden poles once supported thatched roofs, and pits used for storage or as underground houses.

Hénán again occupied centre stage during the Song dynasty (AD 960–1279), but political power deserted it when the government fled south from its capital at Kāifēng following the 12th-century Juchen invasion from the north. Nevertheless, with a large population on the fertile (although periodically flood-ravaged) plains of unruly Huáng Hé, Hénán remained an important agricultural area.

Highlights

- Kāifēng, a delightful blast from the past
- Shàolín Sì, a monastery for those with an interest in kung fu
- Dragon Gate Grottoes, the Buddhist caves near Luòyáng
- Jīgōng Shān, a breezy mountain retreat

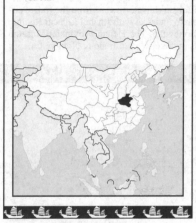

CENTRAL CHINA

Hénán's urban centres dwindled with the demise of the Song dynasty. It was not until the 1949 Communist victory that they again expanded. Zhèngzhōu was transformed into a sizeable industrial city, as was Luòyáng. Kāifēng and Ānyáng, however, have been slower to respond to the call of the hammer and anvil.

Today, Hénán is one of China's smallest provinces but also the most densely populated. Almost 93 million people (about a third the population of the USA) jostle for living space and train tickets.

ZHÈNGZHŌU 郑州
☎ 0371 • pop 6,210,000
Provincial capital of Hénán since 1949, Zhèngzhōu is a sprawling paradigm of ill-conceived town planning. It sports broad, neatly intersecting boulevards, two parks, a towering anachronistic Mao statue and a new provincial museum. It is also valiantly

holding up its end in the latest Chinese revolution with a high-tech science park on the town's outskirts.

Zhèngzhōu is at best an overnight stop en route to more worthwhile attractions.

Orientation

All places of interest to travellers lie east of the railway line.

North-east of the train station, five roads converge at prominent modern Èrqī Tǎ (7 Febraury Pagoda) to form the messy traffic circle 7 February Square (Èrqī Guǎngchǎng) that marks Zhèngzhōu's commercial centre. Erqi Lu runs northward from the traffic circle to intersect with Jinshui Lu near Rénmín Gōngyuán. The Henan Provincial Museum is in the city's north along Nongye Lu.

Information

The Bank of China, located at 16 Huayuankou Lu, is in the northern part of the city. The branch at 8 Jinshui Lu will exchange travellers cheques and cash. The post office is to your right as you exit the train station.

China International Travel Service (CITS; Zhōngguó Guójì Lǚxíngshè; ☎ 392 7758, fax 381 1753, 50 Jingqi Lu) is inconveniently located in the city's north on the 8th floor of the Hǎitōng Dàshà building. It's open 8.30am to 12pm and 2pm to 6.30pm Monday to Friday. The Public Security Bureau (PSB; Gōngānjú; 70 Erqi Lu) is not far from Rénmín Gōngyuán and is open 8.30am to noon and 3pm to 6pm Monday to Friday.

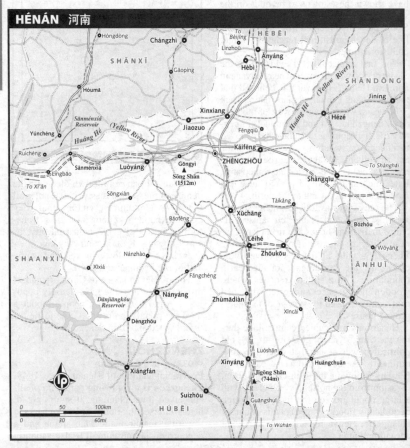

HÉNÁN 河南

Shang Dynasty Ruins
Shāngdài Yízhǐ 商代遗址

On Zhèngzhōu's eastern outskirts lie the remains of an ancient city from the Shang period. Long, high mounds of earth indicate where the city walls used to be. This is one of the earliest relics of Chinese urban life.

Excavations here, and at other Shang sites, suggest that a 'typical' Shang city consisted of a central walled area containing large buildings surrounded by villages. Each village specialised in a product such as pottery, metal-work, wine or textiles. The village dwellings were mostly semi-underground pit houses, while the buildings in the centre were rectangular and above ground.

Excavations have also uncovered Shang tombs. These are rectangular pits with ramps or steps leading down to a burial chamber where the coffin was placed and surrounded with funerary objects, such as bronze weapons, musical instruments, inscribed oracle bones and silk fabrics. Some also contained the skeletons of sacrificial animals and humans. Study of these human skeletons suggests they were of a different ethnic origin from the Shang – possibly prisoners of war. This and other evidence suggests that Shang society was an aristocratic dictatorship with the emperor/father-figure at the apex and did not enslave its own people.

The ruins are at two sites. The portion that still has some of the city wall standing is in the city's south-eastern section at the junction of Chengdong Lu and Chengnan Lu. Bus No 2 stops nearby, get off at the East Gate (Dōng Ménkǒu). Bus No 3 runs near the old Shang city. The other ruins are in Zǐjīngshān Gōngyuán.

Henan Provincial Museum
Hénán Shěng Bówùguǎn 河南省博物馆

The fantastic provincial museum (☎ 351 1237, 8 Nongye Lu; admission Y20; open 8.30am-6pm daily) is housed in a pyramid-shaped building to the north of the city.

The museum traces the origins of Chinese civilisation through artefacts discovered in Hénán. The impressive collection includes relics of the Shang and Zhou dynasties as well as examples of pottery, porcelain, bronze and jade craftsmanship. The 4th floor has a small display of dinosaur-egg fossils discovered in the region. Captions are in Chinese and English.

Take bus No K906, which runs from outside Hóngshānhú Jiǔdiàn (see Places to Stay later) and get off at the seventh stop; the museum is a short walk west of here. There is no entry after 5pm.

Huáng Hé 黄河
Yellow River

Huáng Hé (admission Y25; open 6.30am-sunset daily) is 25km north of Zhèngzhōu. The road passes near Huāyuánkǒu village, where in April 1938 Kuomintang general Chiang Kaishek ordered his troops to blow up the river dikes to halt the Japanese advance. This desperately ruthless tactic was successful for a few weeks; it also drowned about one million Chinese people and left another 11 million homeless and starving.

The United States helped repair the dike in 1947 and today the point where it was breached has an irrigation sluice gate and Mao's instruction, 'Control the Huáng Hé', etched into the embankment. The river has always been regarded as 'China's sorrow' because of its propensity to flood. It carries masses of silt from the loess plains and deposits them on the riverbed, causing the water to overflow the banks. Peasants have built the dikes higher and higher over the centuries and as a result, parts of the river flow along an elevated channel that is sometimes more than 15m in height.

Bus No 16 goes to the river from Erma Lu.

Places to Stay

Jīnyángguāng Dàjiǔdiàn (Golden Sunshine Hotel; ☎ 696 9999, fax 699 9534, 86 Erma Lu) Singles/doubles Y40/60, with bath Y298/328, plus 10% service charge. This hotel is not as upmarket as it may look and the lower level rooms tend to be noisy. It's to your left as you exit the train station.

Zhōngyuán Dàshà (☎ 676 8599, fax 696 8612) Beds in 4-bed dorms/doubles/triples Y25/40/35, with bath Y45/70/50. This cavernous white tower, with recently renovated rooms in two adjoining hotels, requires no cash deposit.

Èrqī Bīnguǎn (☎ 696 1169, fax 696 1268, 168 Jiefang Lu) Dorm beds Y35-40, doubles/triples with bath Y130/180. A definite no frills affair for those who don't mind musty smelling rooms.

ZHÈNGZHŌU 郑州

Hóngshānhú Jiǔdiàn (Red Coral Hotel; ☎ 698 6688, fax 699 3222, 20 Erma Lu) Singles/doubles Y360/388. This marble-festooned hotel offers a free Chinese-style breakfast and there's a swimming pool.

Yǒuyì Bīnguǎn (Friendship Hotel; ☎ 622 8807, fax 622 4728, 97 Jinshui Lu) Doubles/triples without bath Y90/120, with bath Y208/258. This hotel has a generous selection of small rooms and the shared bathrooms are exceptionally clean.

International Hotel (Guójì Fàndiàn; ☎ 595 6600, fax 599 7818, 114 Jinshui Lu) Doubles/suites Y288/398 plus 15% service charge. Although worn around the edges the International still provides welcoming rooms for travellers looking for comfort.

Holiday Inn Crowne Plaza (Huángguān Jiàrì Bīnguǎn; ☎ 595 0055, ⓔ hicpzz@public.zz.ha.cn, 115 Jinshui Lu) Singles/doubles US$98/113. Next door to the International Hotel, this place started life as the Russian Foreign Experts' Hotel back in the 1950s. It is now managed by the Holiday Inn group and offers unbridled luxury.

Hotel Sofitel (Sùfēitè Guójì Fàndiàn; ☎ 595 0088, fax 595 0080, 289 Chengdong Lu) Doubles/suites Y996/1660 plus 20% service charge. The Sofitel is the last in the triangle of top-end hotels and is pretty much perfect.

Places to Eat

Within the train station there is a **canteen** of no discernible name that has noodle, dumpling and rice dishes to choose from behind the counter. Fill up for as little as Y3.

Next to Èrqī Bīnguǎn, is **Hǎo Chī Jiē** (Delicious Food Street; Jiefang Lu), a small market good for cheap snacks. Jinshui Lu is a road worth exploring for its selection of **bars**, **coffee shops** and **restaurants**.

Háoxiǎnglái Zhōngxī Cāntīng (☎ 662 6038, 221 Minggong Lu) Set meals from Y25. Open 24 hours daily. This is a tasty place to go for Chinese-Western food and it includes juicy steaks. There is a second branch (79 Erqi Lu) near the PSB.

Cola Planet (Kělè Xīngqiú Cāntīng; ☎ 397 7155 ext 7777, 159 Jiankang Lu) Dishes Y25-50. This hip bar/restaurant is especially popular with the expat crowd and has regular live music and a DJ at weekends. The menu includes Asian and Western dishes.

ZHÈNGZHŌU

PLACES TO STAY
5 Holiday Inn Crowne
   Plaza
   郑州皇冠假日宾馆
6 International Hotel
   国际饭店
7 Hotel Sofitel
   素菲特国际饭店
8 Yǒuyì Bīnguǎn
   友谊宾馆
13 Èrqī Bīnguǎn
   二七宾馆
15 Hóngshānhú Jiǔdiàn
   红珊瑚酒店
17 Zhōngyuán Dàshà
   中原大厦
18 Jīnyángguāng Dàjiǔdiàn
   金阳光大酒店

PLACES TO EAT
1 Cola Planet
   可乐星球餐厅
2 Target Pub
   目标酒吧
9 Háoxiǎnglái
   Zhōngxī Cāntīng
   豪享来中西餐厅
14 Hǎo Chī Jiē
   好吃街

OTHER
3 Bank of China
   中国银行
4 CAAC
   中国民航售票处
10 PSB
   公安局外事科

11 Advance Booking
   Office
   (Train Tickets)
   火车预售票处
12 Èrqī Tǎ; 7 February
   Square
   二七塔；二七广场
16 Long-Distance
   Bus Station
   长途汽车站
19 Train Station
   火车站
20 Post & Telephone
   Offices
   邮政大楼
21 Shang Dynasty
   Ruins
   商代遗址

CENTRAL CHINA

Target Pub (Mùbiāo Jiǔba; Jingliu Lu)
This laid-back bar that plays Jazz, blues and hip hop is also run by Lao Wang of Cola Planet fame.

Getting There & Away

Air Civil Aviation Administration of China (CAAC; Zhōngguó Mínháng; ☎ 599 1111) has an office at 3 Jinshui Lu. The airport is about 30km south of the city centre. An airport shuttle bus (Y15, 40 minutes) leaves from the CAAC office every hour. A taxi to the airport costs from Y80 to Y100.

There are flights to more than 20 domestic cities. Daily services include Běijīng (Y630), Guǎngzhōu (Y1230), Shànghǎi (Y730), and Guìlín (Y1090). Less frequent services fly to Kūnmíng (Y1150), Wǔhàn (Y450) and Qīngdǎo (Y750). Three flights per week go to Hong Kong (Y1790).

Bus From the long-distance bus station (opposite the train station) Iveco minibuses run every 20 minutes to Luòyáng (Y26.5, two hours). Slow buses (Y18, two to three hours) take the old road and pass through Gongyi City (see the boxed text 'Gǒngyì City' later in this chapter).

Buses leave every 30 minutes to Ānyáng (Y33.5, four hours) and Kāifēng (Y12.5, one hour). Overnight sleeper coaches *(wòpùchē)* go to Běijīng (Y170 to Y190, eight hours) leaving every 30 minutes between 8.30pm and 10pm daily. A bus leaves daily for Shànghǎi (seat/sleeper Y113/181, 21 hours)

and Wǔhàn (Y71, 11 hours). There are three buses per day to Xī'ān (Y107, eight hours).

Minibuses for Shàolín Sì (Y20.5, three hours) depart from in front of the train station. Buses to Dēngfēng (Y10.5, 2½ to three hours) run every 20 minutes from where you can connect to Shàolín, 15 minutes away.

Train Zhèngzhōu is a crucial junction in the Chinese rail network, so you could find yourself here 'in transit' for a few hours, or even days. The train station ticket office is often crowded and tickets are easier to buy at the advance booking office (☎ 697 1920, 134 Erqi Lu), which is open 8.30am to noon and 2.30pm to 5pm daily. CITS and many hotels also book tickets.

Express trains run to Běijīng (Y164, six to seven hours) and Guǎngzhōu (Y330, 20 hours). Other destinations include Luòyáng (Y15, two hours), Shànghǎi (Y224, 11 to 14 hours), Wǔhàn (Y76, six hours) and Tàiyuán (Y140, 12 hours). The Běijīng-Kowloon express train also stops in Zhèngzhōu.

Travellers to Xī'ān are best off taking the faster, two-tiered 'tourist train' (Y113, nine hours) that leaves Zhèngzhōu at 11.02am and arrives in Xī'ān just before 8pm.

Getting Around

Bus is the best way to get around as most sights and tourist facilities are away from the city centre. Bus Nos 2 and 32 run from the train station to Zǐjīngshān Gōngyuán, and bus No 3 runs near the Shang city ruins.

Cave Dwellings

The road between Zhèngzhōu and Luòyáng provides a unique opportunity to see some of China's cave dwellings. Over 100 million Chinese people live in cave houses cut into dry embankments, or in houses where the hillside makes up one or more walls. These are not peculiar to Hénán province: a third of these dwellings are found in the dry loess plain.

Some communities use both caves and houses; the former are warmer in winter and cooler in summer, but also tend to be darker and less ventilated than ordinary houses. Sometimes a large square pit is dug first and then caves are hollowed into the four sides of the pit. A well is sunk in the middle of the yard to prevent flooding during heavy rains. Other caves, such as those at Yán'ān, are dug into the side of a cliff face (see the Yán'ān section in the Shaanxi chapter).

The floors, walls and ceilings of these cave dwellings are made of loess, a fine yellowish-brown soil, which is soft and thick and makes good building material. The front wall may be made of loess, mud-brick, concrete, brick or wood, depending on the availability of materials. Ceilings are shaped according to the quality of the loess. If it is hard then the ceiling may be arched; if not, the ceiling may rise to a point. Besides the doors and windows in the front wall, additional vents may let in light and air.

Bus No K906 travels from Hóngshānhú Jiǔdiàn (see Places to Stay earlier), along Erma Lu towards the museum and bus No 29 runs from outside the Bank of China on the corner of Jinshui Lu and Chengdong Lu to the long-distance bus station, which also services the city's local routes.

Taxis and minivan cabs start at Y7.

SŌNG SHĀN 嵩山
☎ 0371

Three main peaks and two areas – Shàolín Sì and Dēngfēng – comprise Sōng Shān, which rises to 1512m above the sea and sits about 80km west of Zhèngzhōu.

In Taoism, Sōng Shān is considered the central mountain, symbolising earth in the religion's belief that five elements make up the world. Legend says that Taoists searched throughout China for mountains to match these crucial elements. They came up with Héng Shān in Shānxī for wood, Héng Shān in Húnán for fire, Tài Shān in Shāndōng for water and Huá Shān in Shaanxi for metal. Sōng Shān occupies the axis – directly under heaven.

While kung fu's popularity draws crowds to Shàolín Sì during the high season, it's possible to eke out an alternative visit by trekking the area for some peace and quiet.

Shàolín Sì 少林寺

China's most famous martial arts tradition was developed here by Buddhist monks (☎ 274 9204; admission Y42; open 6am-6.30pm daily), 80km west of Zhèngzhōu.

Each year, thousands of Chinese enrol at Shàolín's martial art schools. Arrive early in the morning and you'll see enthusiastic trainees, many as young as five, outside ramming a javelin through their imaginary opponent's body or gracefully kicking into a sparring dummy with enough force to wind an elephant. You can also catch regular performances (admission Y40) within the temple and witness young students demonstrating control of their minds and bodies by smashing bricks over their backs.

Some students have even found stardom; one teacher's young son has struck it big and appears in Hong Kong martial arts movies. Others become police officers, security guards or physical education teachers after graduation.

The origins of Shàolín Sì are unclear but legend has it that it was founded in the 5th century by an Indian monk. Several decades later another monk, Bodhidharma (Damo in Chinese) arrived at the temple preaching Chan (Zen) Buddhism. Apparently, for relief between long periods of meditation, Bodhidharma's disciples imitated the natural motions of birds and animals, developing these exercises over the centuries into a form of physical and spiritual combat.

However, the story goes that when Damo arrived at the temple he was refused entrance and so he retired to a nearby cave where he lived and calmed his mind by resting his brain 'upright' as the religion teaches. To do this, Damo sat and prayed toward a cave wall for nine years; legend says his shadow was left on the cave wall. This 'Shadow Stone' is within Shàolín Sì.

The monks have supposedly intervened continually throughout China's many wars and uprisings – always on the side of righteousness, naturally. Perhaps as a result, their monastery has suffered repeated sackings. The most recent episodes were in 1928, when a local warlord, Shi Yousan, torched almost all the temple's buildings, and in the early 1970s, courtesy of the Red Guards.

Despite fires and vandalism, many of the monastery buildings are still standing, although much of their original charm has been restored out of them. One interesting sight is **Pagoda Forest** (*Shàolín Tǎlín*), a cemetery outside the walls of the temple. Each of the 246 pagodas contains the ashes of an eminent monk.

Nowadays Shàolín Sì is a tourist trap. Arrive in the morning before the busloads of tourists roll up and the area gives way to food stalls, street photographers and souvenir shops.

The main gate ticket includes a 10-minute panoramic film in Chinese that is screened in the building near the entrance.

Trekking It's possible to escape the din of tourists and souvenir hawkers by climbing the mountains and breathing some fresh air. As you face Shàolín Sì, paths on your left lead up **Wǔrǔ Peak** (*Wǔrǔ Fēng*).

At 1512m above sea level, **Shǎoshì Shān** is the area's tallest peak and has a more scenic trek beside craggy rock formations along a path that often hugs the cliff. The trek takes about three hours each way, covers 15km and takes you to the 782-step **Rope Bridge** (*Suǒ Qiáo*).

For safety reasons, monks suggest trekking with a friend. The path starts to the east of the Shàolín cable car (Y20), which takes you to part of Shǎoshì Shān. Maps in Chinese are available at souvenir stalls.

Kung Fu Classes If you're striving to be the next Jackie Chan, you can enrol for classes at almost any of the ten schools in the area. The **Shaolin Monastery Wushu Institute at Tagou** (☎ 274 9627, ⓦ *www.shaolin-kungfu.com*) is supposedly Shàolín's oldest and largest school with 7000 students. It has one-day classes (US$24); the price includes accommodation. Ask at the school's hotel for more information.

A cheaper option is to try one of the smaller schools in the hills where one-day classes cost Y50 (including accommodation). The **Shaolin Temple Secular Disciple's Union** (☎ 274 9172, ⓦ *www.shaolin1500.com*) regularly receives foreign students.

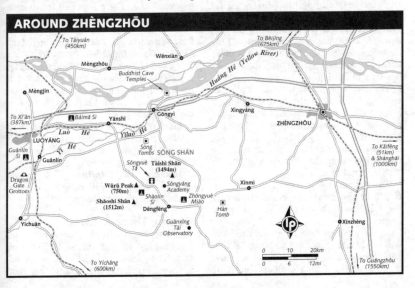

AROUND ZHĒNGZHŌU

Places to Stay It's possible to spend the night at Shàolín and hopefully avoid – at least for a bit – the high season's congested atmosphere.

Tǎgōu Wǔshù Xuéxiào Jiāoxué Bīnguǎn (Tagou Wushu School Hotel; ☎ *274 9617)* Dorm beds/triples/quads Y30/80/60, doubles with bath Y100. Students often occupy the dorm beds so you may be forced to take a double. The school is on your right towards the main gate; 'Dharma Hall' is written above the hotel.

Sōngshān Bīnguǎn (☎ *274 9050)* Doubles Y120. Beside the school, this place has a variety of damp rooms and is often full by the afternoon.

Basic accommodation and washing facilities are available at most of the schools.

Dēngfēng 登封
☎ 0371
About 15 minutes by minibus east of Shàolín Sì lies the peaceful town of Dēngfēng.

The town sits at the foot of Tàishì Shān and is home to some noteworthy historical attractions and enjoyable trekking opportunities. If Shàolín is crowded (and it most likely will be), it's worth basing yourself here and making a day trip to the temple.

CITS (☎ 287 2137) at 48 Zhongyue Dajie has helpful, English-speaking staff.

Things to See & Do Built during the Qin dynasty, **Zhōngyuè Miào** *(admission Y15; open 8am-6.30pm daily)* remains a popular attraction and is modelled after the Forbidden City in Běijīng.

The temple originally served as a place to worship the God of the central mountain Sōng Shān. But the temple's significance eventually meshed with Taoism, whose adherents dubbed Sōng Shān the earth's centre. Inside the elaborate, red temple is a tablet illustrating the location of all of the Taoist sacred mountains.

The temple is 4km east of the city centre. Take the green bus No 2 from near the CITS, which runs along Zhongyue Dajie.

In the town of Gàochéng, 15km southeast of Dēngfēng, is the **Guānxīng Tái Observatory** *(admission Y10; open 8am-6.30pm daily)*, China's oldest surviving observatory. In AD 1276, the emperor ordered two astronomers to chart a calendar by watching the shadows cast by the sun. After observing from the stone tower, they came back in AD 1280 with a mapping of 365 days, five hours, 49 minutes and 12 seconds, which differs from modern calculations by only 26 seconds.

Regular southbound buses from Dēngfēng can take you there; catch them from any large intersection in the south-eastern part of town.

At the foot of Tàishì Shān sits one of China's oldest academies **Sōngyáng Academy** *(Sōngyáng Shūyuàn; admission Y12; open 8am-6.30pm daily)*. In the courtyard are two cypress trees believed to be around 4500 years old – and still alive!

Nearby is **Sōngyuè Tǎ** *(Central High Mountain Pagoda; admission Y10; open 8am-7pm daily)*. Built in AD 509, during the Northern Wei dynasty, it's China's oldest brick pagoda.

Take bus No 2 (the green one that runs along Zhongyue Dajie where CITS is) to the last stop and then a motor-rickshaw to the pagoda; the ride should cost Y10 to Y15. A round-trip to the academy and pagoda by motor-rickshaw is Y20.

North of Dēngfēng the 1494m-high **Tàishì Shān** provides ample trekking opportunities. Area maps show trails leading to the summit. There is a Y10 fee to enter the Tàishì Shān scenic area.

Places to Stay & Eat Options include: *Shàolín Guójì Dàjiǔdiàn (*☎ *286 6188, fax 287 1448, 16 Shaolin Lu)* Doubles Y218-358. This is the most upmarket hotel in town and has comfortable rooms, some with views of Tàishì Shān. The hotel is in the east of the city.

Liángyě Bīnguǎn (☎ *287 1791, 28 Shaolin Lu)* Beds in 2-/3-bed dorms Y68/58. About half a block west is this cheaper option, with old but immaculate rooms.

Yùshàn Zhāi Cāntīng (42 Zhongyue Dajie) Dishes from Y10. Next to CITS, this restaurant serves very tasty food.

Getting There & Away
Regular buses from Zhèngzhōu and Luòyáng go to Shàolín Sì (Y20.5) and Dēngfēng (Y16.5, 15 to 30 minutes). Hotels in these two cities often arrange day tours

(Y40, excluding entrance fees) that include sites along the way.

In Shàolín, Iveco minibuses to Zhèngzhōu and Luòyáng wait for passengers in the parking lot opposite the Pagoda Forest and at the town's major intersection. The last bus leaves at 8pm.

The Dēngfēng bus station is on western Zhongyue Dajie. Orange bus No 1 will get you half-way to Shàolín where you should change for a minibus to the temple (the driver will tell you where to change). The entire journey takes about 30 minutes. Direct minibuses between Shàolín and Dēngfēng also run regularly.

LUÒYÁNG 洛阳
☎ 0379 • pop 6,230,000

Founded during the Xia dynasty, Luòyáng was the capital of 13 dynasties until the Northern Song dynasty moved its capital to Kāifēng in the 10th century AD. In the 12th century Juchen invaders from the north of China stormed and sacked Luòyáng, which never quite recovered.

For centuries it languished with only memories of greatness. By the 1920s it had just 20,000 inhabitants. The Communists brought life back to Luòyáng, constructing an industrial city that now houses more than six million people.

Today, it's hard to imagine that Luòyáng was once the centre of the Chinese world and home to more than 1300 Buddhist temples. Reminders of the city's historical greatness are scattered about town but the main attractions are the Dragon Gate Grottoes 13km out of town.

Orientation

Luòyáng is spread across the northern bank of Luò Hé. The train station (and long-distance bus station) is in the northern part of the city. Luòyáng's chief thoroughfare is Zhongzhou Zhonglu, which meets Jinguyuan Lu leading down from the train station at a central T junction.

The old city is in the town's eastern part, beyond the West Gate (Xī Guǎn) where sections of the original walls can still be seen. Throughout the maze of narrow streets and winding laneways stand many older houses. Using **Wén Fēng Tǎ** as a landmark, it's a great area to explore on foot or by bicycle.

Information

CITS (☎ 432 3212) is on Changjiang Lu, diagonally opposite Xīyuàn Gōngyuán. The PSB is open Monday to Wednesday and Friday, and is located at 1 Tiyuchang Lu, on the corner with Kaixuan Lu.

The Bank of China is at 439 Zhongzhou Zhonglu. The branch opposite the Friendship Store will exchange only US dollars.

You'll find the post office and China Telecom at the T-junction of Zhongzhou Zhonglu and Jinguyuan Lu. A small 24-hour Internet cafe (☎ 330 2912) charging Y2 per hour is on the corner of Jiefang Lu and Kaixuan Lu.

Báimǎ Sì 白马寺
White Horse Temple

Founded in the 1st century AD, Báimǎ Sì (admission Y25; open 7am-6.30pm daily) was the first Buddhist temple built on Chinese soil. Today, Ming and Qing structures stand at the site of the original temple.

Five hundred years before the journey of Xuan Zhuang, the Tang dynasty monk whose travels are fancifully immortalised in the Chinese classic Journey to the West, two envoys of the Han dynasty court went in search of Buddhist scriptures.

In Afghanistan, they met two Indian monks and together they returned to Luòyáng. The story goes that they carried Buddhist scriptures and statues on the backs of two white horses. In due course the temple was founded to house the scriptures and statues, and it was named after the horses.

The temple grounds are lovely although they can get crowded during the summer months. Well worth a look is the unusual **Depository of Magic Weapons Hall** that houses questionable magical gifts from abroad.

The temple is 13km east of Luòyáng. Minibuses run from the area around the train and bus station.

Wángchéng Gōngyuán
King City Park 王城公园

Jiàn Hé runs through this park. Attractions include a tiny, depressing zoo and an **underground 'theme park'** (admission Y15), which has an assortment of polystyrene ghouls.

The **Peony Festival** *(admission Y20)* is centred in Wàngchéng Gōngyuán. The festival is held annually from 15 to 25 April when thousands of tourists descend on Luòyáng to view the peony flowers. If nature fails to provide sufficiently resplendent blooms, fake peonies are attached to the bushes.

Luoyang Museum

Luòyáng Bówùguǎn 洛阳博物馆

This museum *(☎ 393 7107, 298 Zhongzhou Zhonglu; admission Y10; open 8am-6.30pm daily)* houses early bronzes, Tang figurines and implements from the Stone Age. There are some eye-catching pieces, especially in jade. Take bus No 2 from the train station.

LUÒYÁNG

PLACES TO STAY
4 Tiānxiāng Fàndiàn
天香饭店
5 Míngyuán Bīnguǎn
明苑宾馆
16 Peony Hotel
牡丹饭店
17 Huāchéng Fàndiàn
花城饭店
20 Xīn Yǒuyì Bīnguǎn
新友谊宾馆
21 Yǒuyì Bīnguǎn
友谊宾馆

PLACES TO EAT
2 Luòyáng Dàshà
洛阳大厦

7 Zhēn Bù Tóng Fàndiàn
真不同饭店

OTHER
1 Train Station
火车站
3 Long-Distance Bus Station
长途汽车站
6 West Gate
西关
8 Night Market
南大街夜市
9 Wén Fēng Tǎ
文峰塔
10 Post & Telephone Office
邮电局

11 Government Building
12 PSB
公安局
13 Main Bank of China
中国银行
14 Internet Cafe
网吧
15 Luoyang Museum
洛阳博物馆
18 Friendship Store
友谊商店
19 Bank of China
中国银行
22 CITS
中国国际旅行社

Luoyang Museum of Ancient Tombs 洛阳古墓博物馆

Luòyáng Gǔmù Bówùguǎn

The thousands of tombs unearthed by archaeologists in and around Luòyáng form the basis of this museum (admission Y15; open 8.30am-7pm daily). There are 25 restored tombs on view, dating from the Han to the Song dynasties and belonging to different social strata. Burial items and murals showing the exorcising of demons and mortals ascending to heaven are also on display. Captions are in Chinese and English.

The museum is on the road to the airport, north of the city. Bus No 83 runs from opposite the long-distance bus station – ask the driver to let you off at the turn-off to the museum. A motor-rickshaw costs around Y10.

Places to Stay

Míngyuán Bīnguǎn (☎ 390 1377, fax 390 1376, 20 Jiefang Lu) Doubles/triples/suites Y165/150/240. This newly opened hotel is just south of the train station. The rooms are large and clean and the staff is extremely friendly.

Tiānxiāng Fàndiàn (☎ 391 6652, fax 393 7871, 56 Jinguyuan Lu) Dorm beds Y20-50, doubles with bath & air-con Y100. The dorm rooms are OK but the bathrooms are quite alarming. The double rooms are much nicer.

Huáchéng Fàndiàn (☎ 485 7115, 49 Zhongzhou Xilu) Dorm beds Y20-50, doubles with bath Y100-130. The rooms are cheap but you won't want to spend more time here than you have to. Bus Nos 11 and 54 run past this hotel.

Peony Hotel (Mǔdān Dàjiǔdiàn; ☎ 485 6699, fax 485 6999, 15 Zhongzhou Xilu) Doubles Y480-550 plus 5% tax. This high-rise joint venture is popular with foreign tour groups. Be careful when booking a massage, the masseuses are sometimes over-keen in their pursuit of customer satisfaction.

In the western part of town, on Xiyuan Lu, there are two Friendship Hotels.

Yǒuyì Bīnguǎn (Friendship Hotel; ☎ 491 2780, fax 491 3808, 6 Xiyuan Lu) Singles/doubles from Y220/318. The older of the two hotels, this branch is still the better deal with bright rooms and a swimming pool.

Gòngyì City

Gòngyì City (Gòngyì Shì), formerly called Gongxian County, is between Zhèngzhōu and Luòyáng and is home to a fascinating series of Buddhist caves and tombs built by the Northern Song emperors. Construction of the caves began in AD 517 and today there are 256 shrines containing more than 7700 Buddhist figures.

Song Tombs (Sòng Líng; admission Y5) are scattered over an area of 30 sq km, and within them repose seven of the nine Northern Song emperors (the other two were carted off by the Juchen armies who overthrew the Northern Song in the 12th century). Some 800 years on all that remain of the tombs are ruins, burial mounds and the statues which, amid fields of wheat, line the sacred avenues leading up to the ruins. About 700 stone statues are still standing, and together they comprise the main attraction of the tombs. The statues illustrate a progression of styles, from the simplicity of late-Tang forms to the life-like depiction of public figures and animals.

Buses running on the old highway (not the freeway) from Luòyáng to Gòngyì pass by one of these Song Tomb sites. You can get off the bus there and visit the tombs, or you can continue on into Gòngyì and hire a taxi to visit both the tombs and **Buddhist Caves** (Shíkūsì; admission Y5). It's possible to do this in half a day; expect to pay about Y80 for the taxi. If you're coming from the direction of Zhèngzhōu, get off at Gòngyì.

Xīn Yǒuyì Bīnguǎn (New Friendship Hotel; ☎ 491 3770-20, fax 491 2328, 6 Xiyuan Lu) Doubles Y358-458. This place is just down the road from the older branch and has similar, bright rooms; the only difference is the price. Bus No 103 runs to the hotels from the train station (seventh stop).

Places to Eat

Although Luòyáng is not overrun with good restaurants, no visitor should miss sampling its famous Water Banquet. The main dishes of this 24-course meal are soups and are served up with the speed of 'flowing water' – hence the name.

Zhēn Bù Tóng Fàndiàn (One of a Kind Restaurant; ☎ 399 5080, Zhongzhou

Donglu) Dishes Y15-40, budget water banquet from Y60. This is *the* place to come for a water banquet experience. If 24 courses seem excessive, you can pick individual dishes from the menu. They have an up-market branch next door.

The lively **night market** (*cnr Nan Dajie & Zhongzhou Donglu*), in the old city, is a great place for dinner. Barbequed beef and squid, cold dishes and an assortment of bugs can be had for as little as Y2 per dish. Other tasty roadside snacks include *jiǎnpào* (fried pastries filled with chopped herbs and garlic) and *dòushā gāo* (a sweet 'cake' made from yellow peas and Chinese dates).

Opposite the train station, **Luòyáng Dàshà** has a cheap canteen with bowls of beef noodles for Y6. Better 'sit-down' **restaurants** can be found along Zhongzhou Lu.

Getting There & Away

Air Luòyáng is not well connected by air and you would do better to fly into or out of Zhèngzhōu. Luòyáng Dàshà has a ticket booking office on the ground floor.

Flights to Běijīng (Y630) leave daily. Flights to Dàlián (Y850) and Chéngdū (Y780) depart on Thursday and Sunday; and to Guǎngzhōu (Y1280) on Tuesday, Thursday and Saturday.

Bus The long-distance bus station is near the main train station. Iveco buses to Zhèngzhōu (Y26, two hours) run every 20 minutes until 7pm. Slow buses (Y17, 2½ hours) also run regularly. Fast buses to Shàolín (Y15, 1½ hours) depart every half hour until 4.30pm; slow buses (Y10, two hours) run until 6pm and pass through Dēngfēng.

There are frequent buses to Ānyáng (Y48, five hours) and Kāifēng (Y33, 2½ hours). A bus leaves at 10am for Ruìchéng in Shānxī (Y23, eight hours).

Sleeper buses leave in the evening from outside the train station. Destinations include Běijīng (seat/sleeper Y148/188, nine hours), Xī'ān (Y65, 10 hours), Tàiyuán (Y80, 11 hours), Wǔhàn (Y81, 15 hours) and Guǎngzhōu (Y166, 30 hours).

Minibuses to Gōngyì City (Y10, two hours) leave every 15 minutes from outside the train station.

Train Direct trains go to Běijīng (Y185, 10 hours), Shànghǎi (Y245, 14 to 15 hours) and Xī'ān (Y102, six hours). A two-tiered tourist train runs between Zhèngzhōu and Xī'ān daily – it stops in Luòyáng en route at 12.25pm (arriving in Xī'ān around 7pm the same day).

There are some direct trains northbound to Tàiyuán (Y185, 13 hours) and south-bound to Yíchāng (Y151, 10 hours). Yíchāng is a port on Cháng Jiāng (Yangzi River), where you can catch the ferry for Chóngqìng-Wǔhàn.

Getting Around

The airport is 12km north of the city; bus No 83 runs from opposite the long-distance bus station and takes 30 minutes. A taxi from the train station will cost about Y25.

Bicycles can be hired across the street from the train station (Y5 per day, Y100 deposit), but check your bike carefully before setting off as the frames have been known to fall apart within hours.

The bus system runs until 8pm or 9pm, although bus No 5 runs until 11pm. Bus Nos 5 and 41 run to the old city from the train station. Bus No 102 runs in a westerly direction from the train station past Wángchéng Gōngyuán to the Peony Hotel.

Taxis and yellow minivan cabs start at Y6. Motor-rickshaws are a good way to get around and start at Y2.

DRAGON GATE GROTTOES
Lóngmén Shíkū 龙门石窟

In AD 494 the Northern Wei dynasty moved its capital from Dàtóng to Luòyáng. At Dàtóng the dynasty had built the impressive Yúngāng Buddhist Caves (Yúngāng Shíkū). Now in Luòyáng, the dynasty commenced work on the Dragon Gate Grottoes (*admission Y60; open 6am-8pm daily summer, 6.30am-7pm daily winter*). Over the next 200 years, more than 100,000 images and statues of Buddha and his disciples were carved into the cliff walls on the banks of Yī Hé, 16km south of the city. The caves of Luòyáng, Dūnhuáng and Dàtóng represent the peak of Buddhist cave art.

In the 19th and 20th centuries, Western souvenir hunters beheaded almost every figure they could lay their saws on. These heads now grace the museums and private paperweight collections in Europe and North America. Also removed were two murals that today hang in the Metropolitan

Museum of Art in New York and the Atkinson Museum in Kansas City. The Cultural Revolution also took its toll on the caves and the Ten Thousand Buddha Cave was particularly damaged during this period (see the Ten Thousand Buddha Cave section later).

The art of Buddhist cave sculpture largely came to an end around the middle of the 9th century as the Tang dynasty declined. Persecution began of foreign religions in China, with Buddhism a main target. Buddhist art and sculpture continued in China, although it never again reached the heights it had previously enjoyed.

Three Binyang Caves 宾阳三洞
Bīnyáng Sān Dòng
The main Dragon Gate Grottoes honeycomb the cliff face on Yī Hé's western bank and stretch for 1km on a north-south axis. The three Binyang caves are at the northern end, closest to the entrance. Construction began on all three under the Northern Wei dynasty and, although two were finished during the Sui and Tang dynasties, the statues all display the benevolent expressions that characterised the Northern Wei style.

Ten Thousand Buddha Cave
Wànfó Dòng 万佛洞
South of Three Bīnyáng Caves is the Tang dynasty Ten Thousand Buddha Cave, built in AD 680. In addition to the incredible legions of tiny bas-relief Buddhas that give the cave its name, there is a fine, big Buddha and images of celestial dancers.

Lotus Flower Cave
Liánhuā Dòng 莲花洞
This cave was carved in AD 527 during the Northern Wei dynasty and has a large standing Buddha, now faceless. On the ceiling are wispy *apsaras* (celestial nymphs) drifting around a central lotus flower. A common symbol in Buddhist art, the lotus flower represents purity and serenity and can be seen on many of the cave ceilings.

Fèngxiān Sì
Ancestor Worshipping Temple 奉先寺
Carved in the Tang dynasty between AD 672 and 675, this is the largest structure at Lóngmén and contains the best works of art. Today the roof is gone and the figures lie exposed to the elements.

Tang figures tend to be more three-dimensional than the Northern Wei figures, standing out in high relief and rather freer from their stone backdrop. Their expressions and poses also appear to be more natural, but unlike the other-worldly figures of the Northern Wei, the Tang figures are meant to be awesome.

The seated central Buddha is 17m high and said to be Losana. Allegedly, the face was modelled on Empress Wu Zetian of the Tang dynasty who funded the carving of the statue.

To the left as you face the Buddha, are statues of the disciple Ananda and a Bodhisattva wearing a crown, a tassel and a string of pearls.

To the right are statues (or remains) of another disciple, a Bodhisattva, a heavenly guardian trampling on a spirit and a guardian of the Buddha.

Medical Prescription Cave
Yàofāng Dòng 药方洞
South of Fèngxiān Sì is the tiny Medical Prescription Cave. The entrance to this cave is filled with 6th-century stone steles inscribed with remedies for common ailments.

Earliest Cave
Gǔyáng Dòng 古阳洞
Adjacent to the Medical Prescription Cave is the much larger Earliest Cave, carved between AD 495 and 575. It's a narrow, high-roofed cave featuring a Buddha statue and a profusion of sculptures, particularly of flying apsaras. This was probably the first cave of the Lóngmén group to be built.

Carved Cave
Shíkū Dòng 石窟洞
This cave was carved during the Northern Wei dynasty. This is the last major cave in the Lóngmén complex and features intricate carvings depicting religious processions.

Getting There & Away
The Dragon Gate Grottoes are 13km south of town. Bus No 81 runs from Luòyáng's train station and No 60 runs from opposite Yǒuyì Bīnguǎn. Bus No 53 from the Xiguan traffic circle also goes past the caves.

Minibuses run from the train and bus station area for Y2.

Guānlín Sì

North of the Dragon Gate Grottoes is Guānlín Sì (admission Y20; open 8.30am-6pm daily), the burial place of the legendary general Guan Yu of the Three Kingdoms period (AD 220–265). Legend has it that Guan Yu was executed by King Sunquan of the Wu Kingdom who then tried to put the blame on Cao Cao of the Wei Kingdom. Cao Cao saw straight through Sunquan's trickery, and respectfully buried Guan Yu's head in a grave south of Luòyáng.

The temple buildings were built during the Ming dynasty and Guan Yu was issued the posthumous title 'Lord of War' in the early Qing dynasty. Bus No 81 runs past Guānlín from the train station in Luòyáng.

ĀNYÁNG 安阳

☎ 0372 • pop 5,170,000

Ānyáng is north of Huáng Hé near the border for Hénán-Héběi. As a result of significant archaeological discoveries, Ānyáng is now believed to be the site of Yīn, the last capital of the ancient Shang dynasty and one of the first centres of an urban-based Chinese civilisation.

Peasants working near Ānyáng in the late 19th century unearthed pieces of polished bone inscribed with an ancient form of Chinese writing that turned out to be divining bones with questions addressed to the spirits and ancestors. Other inscriptions were found on tortoise shells and on bronze objects, suggesting that the late Shang capital once stood here in the 14th century BC. These are the earliest examples of Chinese characters.

It was not until the late 1920s, however, that excavations uncovered ancient tombs, the ruins of a royal palace, and workshops and houses – proof that the legendary Shang dynasty had indeed existed.

Museum of Yin Ruins

Yīnxū Bówùguǎn 殷墟博物馆

There is a museum (☎ 393 2171; admission Y15; open 8am-6.30pm daily) at Yīn's site, but its collection is disappointingly limited. It includes reassembled pottery, oracle bone fragments and jade and bronze artefacts. There are no English captions, and it's a bit mystifying unless you're really into this stuff.

The museum is a fair way out of town. Bus No 1 from the train station goes past the museum turn-off. You then have to walk across the railway tracks and head along the river for about 10 minutes until you come to the museum.

Tomb of Yuan Shikai

Yuán Shìkǎi Mù 袁世凯墓

A more recent remnant of Chinese history is this tomb (☎ 292 2959, Shengli Lu; admission Y20; open 8am-6pm daily). Yuan Shikai had it built in the style of the tomb of the American Civil War general and president, Ulysses S Grant, with some Chinese touches. It reflects, more than anything else perhaps, the Napoleonic aspirations of this man who started out as a Qing military official. He later supported Sun Yatsen, only to wrest the presidency from him and attempt a restoration of the imperial system, crowning himself emperor in 1916! His coup was short-lived, however, and he was buried shortly afterwards in this tomb of his own design.

The tomb is 3km east of the Yin museum; you can take bus No 2 from the train station. Get off at the bridge and walk in a northerly direction to the site.

Other Sights

It's worth walking around the town's old section, a few blocks east of the train station and south of Jiefang Lu. For a view of the city climb Wén Fēng Tǎ, an ancient Buddhist pagoda.

Places to Stay & Eat

Zhōngyuán Bīnguǎn (☎ 592 3235, 52 Beimen Dongjie) Singles/doubles/triples from Y120/130/240. The rooms here are large and have wooden floorboards. The hotel is located in the lively part of town near the pagoda.

Ānyáng Bīnguǎn (☎ 592 2219, fax 592 2244, 1 Youyi Lu) Doubles Y168. The rooms have been patched up, but the cracks are already showing through. CITS has an office on the 2nd floor (☎ 592 5650; open 8am to 6.30pm) and the hotel has a decent restaurant.

Both hotels can be reached by bus No 2 from the train station; ask the driver where to get off.

The old town is a good place to go for restaurants, in particular along Hongqi Lu near the restored gate tower. The area around Ānyáng Bīnguǎn is busy with road-side restaurants serving Muslim food.

Getting There & Away

Bus From Ānyáng's long-distance bus station there are connections to Zhèngzhōu (Y33, 3½ hours) every 20 minutes, and Kāifēng (Y36, 2½ hours) every 30 minutes until noon and every hour thereafter. There are frequent buses to Lìnzhōu City (Y7, two hours) and Luòyáng (Y48, five hours). A new road to Tàiyuán has reduced the journey time to five hours (Y90).

The long-distance bus station is a large orange-tiled building close to the train station. Turn right after exiting the train station and then take the first left.

Train Ānyáng is on the main Běijīng-Zhèngzhōu railway line and it is easy to get connections to Wǔhàn, Guǎngzhōu and Běijīng, as most express trains stop here.

AROUND ĀNYÁNG

About 50km west of Ānyáng, in the Tài-háng Shān foothills, lies Línxiàn county, although the name of the main town has been changed to Lìnzhōu City (Lìnzhōu Shì).

Línxiàn is a rural area that ranks as one of the 'holy' places of Maoism because of the famous **Red Flag Canal** (Hóngqí Qú). To irrigate the district, a river was rerouted through a tunnel beneath a mountain and then along a new bed built on the side of steep cliffs.

The statistics are impressive: 1500km of canal dug, hills levelled, 134 tunnels pierced, 150 aqueducts constructed and enough earth displaced to build a road 1m high, 6m wide and 4000km long. The Communists insist that this colossal job, carried out during the Cultural Revolution, was done entirely by the toiling masses without the help of engineers and machines.

Buses run from Ānyáng to Chángzhì in Shānxī that go past the canal. Alternatively, take a bus to Lìnzhōu City and then transfer to another bus for the canal.

JĪGŌNG SHĀN 鸡公山

Rooster Mountain
☎ 0376 • elevation 744m

Jīgōng Shān (☎ 691 2044; admission Y40; open daily year-round), on the border for Hénán-Húběi, was developed as a hill station resort by American missionaries in the early 20th century. It soon became popular with Westerners living in Hànkǒu and Wǔhàn as a relief from the hot summers.

Jīgōng Shān is dominated by **Dawn Heralding Peak** (Bàoxiǎo Fēng), a large stone outcrop resembling a crowing rooster. Climb to the top for an awesome view of the surrounding area.

Over 200 European-style stone villas are spread around this breezy mountain retreat. Sites include the well-preserved former **American School** (Měiguóshì Dàlóu), near the main entrance. To the south, near the cable car, **Chiang Kaishek's Air Raid Shelter** (Jiǎng Jièshí Fángkōng Dòng) is part of his former residence and is open to visitors. On the path to the air-raid shelter is the **Meiling Dance Hall** (Měilíng Wǔtīng), named for Chiang Kaishek's wife. The area also provides some good hiking opportunities. The main village in Jīgōng Shān, known as **Nánjiē**, is on the western flank of the mountain.

Places to Stay & Eat

Some hotels close during the winter months, so call before heading out. There are a handful of small, cheap guesthouses off the main road.

Yúnzhōng Bīnguǎn (☎ 691 2025) Doubles/suites Y180/460. This stone castle is ideally located if you plan to catch the sunrise from Dawn Heralding Peak. The suites have fantastic views over the valley.

Yúnzhōng Gōngyuán Zhāodàisuǒ (Yunzhong Park Guesthouse; ☎ 691 2033) Beds in 3-bed dorms Y20. On the road to the main peak past Yúnzhōng Bīnguǎn, this old stone villa has grotty rooms and basic washing facilities.

Yǒuyì Bīnguǎn (Friendship Hotel; ☎ 691 2091) Twins/triples Y220/210. This large Friendship Hotel is near the air-raid shelter. All rooms have a private balcony.

All these hotels have *restaurants* but there are places to eat throughout the village – try the family run teahouse next to the cable car.

Getting There & Away

The train station for Jīgōng Shān (with the same name) is on the railway line for Běijīng-Guǎngzhōu. A train passes through daily at 11.50am heading southbound to Wǔhàn, and a train heading northbound to Zhèngzhōu departs daily at 5.40pm.

The nearest main train station is in Xìnyáng, one hour away. Frequent minibuses run to Xìnyáng (Y5) from the foot of Jīgōng Shān and from the main gate (Y10).

Arriving at Xìnyáng you'll find minibuses to Jīgōng Shān's main gate (Y10) leave from in front of the train station. If you get dropped off at the foot of the mountain you can catch a cab to the main gate for Y20.

There is a cable car that runs down the south-eastern side of the mountain for Y10/20 one way/return.

KĀIFĒNG 开封
☎ 0378 • pop 4,630,000

Established south of Huáng Hé, Kāifēng was once the prosperous capital of the Northern Song dynasty (AD 960–1126). Today however, after centuries of flooding, the city of the Northern Song lies buried eight to nine metres below ground. Between 1194 and 1938 the city was flooded 368 times, an average of once every two years.

One of the reasons you won't see soaring skyscrapers here is because civic planners and engineers are prohibited from constructing buildings requiring deep foundations for fear of destroying the city below.

Although locals may tut with embarrassment about being left behind in China's modernisation drive, for the foreign visitor Kāifēng is a charming city. Kāifēng was the first city in China where Jews settled when they arrived, via India along the Silk Road, during the Song dynasty. A small Christian community also lives here alongside a much larger local Muslim minority.

Orientation

The southern long-distance bus station and the train station are both outside (about 1km south) the old city walls; the rest of Kāifēng is mostly within the walled area. The city's pivotal point is the Sihou Jie and Madao Jie intersection; the famed street market here is particularly lively at night. Many of the wooden restaurants, shops and houses in this area were constructed during the Qing dynasty in the traditional Chinese style.

Information

The Bank of China is at 64 Gulou Jie. Post and China Telecom offices can be found near the corner of Zhongshan Lu and Ziyou Lu, and on the corner of Mujiaqiao Jie and Wushengjiao Jie.

CITS (☎ 398 4593) has an office at 98 Yingbin Lu, next to Dōngjīng Dàfàndiàn (see Places to Stay later). A train-ticket booking office (☎ 396 6888) is next door.

China Travel Service (CTS; Zhōngguó Lǚxíngshè; ☎ 595 5743) is at 98 Dayuan Kengyan Jie and the PSB can be found at 86 Zhongshan Lu.

More information about Jews in the region is available from the Kaifeng Institute for Research on the History of Chinese Jews (☎ 393 2178 ext 8010); its office is at the Kaifeng Museum.

Dà Xiàngguó Sì 大相国寺
Temple of the Chief Minister

This temple (☎ 566 5878, Ziyou Lu; admission Y20; open 8am-6.30pm daily) was founded in AD 555, but frequently rebuilt over the following 1000 years. Dà Xiàngguó Sì was completely destroyed in the early 1640s when rebels opened the Huáng Hé's dikes, destroying the temple and the city.

Within the temple is a Qing dynasty statue of the 1,000 Eye and 1,000 Arm Guanyin. This beautiful sculpture, six metres tall, was carved entirely from one gingko tree. The temple is next door to an enormous market **Temple of the Chief Minister Market** (Dà Xiàngguó Sì Shìchǎng) that sells all manners of goods.

Tiě Tǎ 铁塔
Iron Pagoda

Built in the 11th century, Tiě Tǎ (☎ 286 2279, 210 Beimen Dajie; admission Y20; open 8am-6pm daily) is actually made of normal bricks, but is covered in glazed chocolate-coloured tiles that look like iron. You can climb to the top of this impressive structure for a further Y10 – but the experience is not dissimilar to scaling a narrow chimney.

Take bus No 3 or 18 from near the western long-distance bus station to the route terminus on Beimen Dajie, not far from Tiě Tǎ; it's a short walk east to the park's entrance from here.

Fán Tǎ 繁塔

This unusual pagoda (admission Y5; open 8am-6pm daily) is the oldest Buddhist

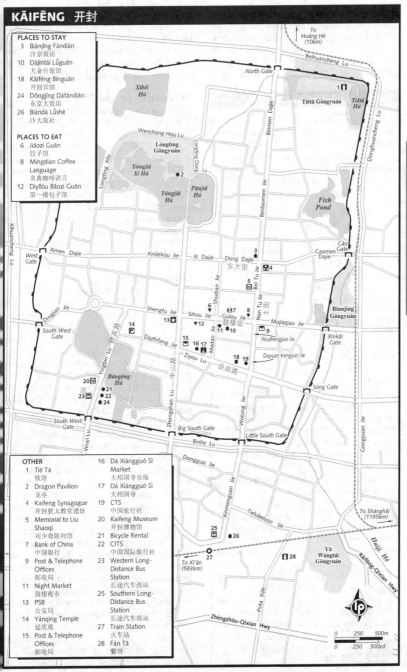

KĀIFĒNG 开封

PLACES TO STAY
3 Biànjīng Fàndiàn
汴京饭店
10 Dàjīntái Lǚguǎn
大金台旅馆
18 Kāifēng Bīnguǎn
开封宾馆
24 Dōngjīng Dàfàndiàn
东京大饭店
26 Biàndà Lǚshè
汴大旅社

PLACES TO EAT
6 Jiǎozi Guǎn
饺子馆
8 Mingdian Coffee Language
名典咖啡语言
12 Dìyīlóu Bāozi Guǎn
第一楼包子馆

OTHER
1 Tiě Tǎ
铁塔
2 Dragon Pavilion
龙亭
4 Kaifeng Synagogue
开封犹太教堂遗址
5 Memorial to Liu Shaoqi
刘少奇陈列馆
7 Bank of China
中国银行
9 Post & Telephone Offices
邮电局
11 Night Market
鼓楼夜市
13 PSB
公安局
14 Yánqìng Temple
延庆观
15 Post & Telephone Offices
邮电局
16 Dà Xiàngguó Sì Market
大相国寺市场
17 Dà Xiàngguó Sì
大相国寺
19 CTS
中国旅行社
20 Kaifeng Museum
开封博物馆
21 Bicycle Rental
22 CITS
中国国际旅行社
23 Western Long-Distance Bus Station
长途汽车西站
25 Southern Long-Distance Bus Station
长途汽车南站
27 Train Station
火车站
28 Fán Tǎ
繁塔

structure in Kāifēng. The original pagoda was a nine-storey hexagonal building, typical of the Northern Song style, although it has seen additions and renovations since then. The pagoda is covered in tiles decorated with 108 different Buddha images.

Kāifēng's Israelites

Father Nicola Trigault translated and published the diaries of the Jesuit priest Matteo Ricci in 1615, and based on these diaries he gives an account of a meeting between Ricci and a Jew from Kāifēng. The Jew was on his way to Běijīng to take part in the imperial examinations, and Trigault writes:

> When he (Ricci) brought the visitor back to the house and began to question him as to his identity, it gradually dawned upon him that he was talking with a believer in the ancient Jewish law. The man admitted that he was an Israelite, but he knew no such word as 'Jew'.

Ricci found out from the visitor that there were 10 or 12 families of Israelites in Kāifēng. A 'magnificent' synagogue had been built there and the five books of Moses had been preserved in the synagogue in scroll form for more than 500 years.

The visitor was familiar with the stories of the Old Testament, and some of the followers, he said, were expert in the Hebrew language. He also told Ricci that in a province which Trigault refers to as 'Cequian' at the capital of 'Hamcheu' there was a far greater number of Israelite families than at Kāifēng. Ricci sent one of his Chinese converts to Kāifēng, where he confirmed the visitor's story.

Today several hundred descendants of the original Jews live in Kāifēng and though they still consider themselves Jewish, the religious beliefs and customs associated with Judaism have almost completely died out. The original synagogue was destroyed in a Huáng Hé flood in 1642. It was rebuilt but destroyed by floods again in the 1850s. This time there was no money to rebuild it. Christian missionaries 'rescued' the temple's scrolls and prayer books in the late 19th century and these are now in libraries in Israel, Canada and the USA.

You'll find the pagoda hidden among the alleyways in the south-eastern part of the city. Cross southward over the railway tracks from Tielubeiyan Jie and take the first alleyway on your left. From here follow the red arrows spray-painted on the walls.

Memorial to Liu Shaoqi

Liú Shàoqí Chénlièguǎn 刘少奇陈列馆

This memorial/museum (☎ 596 5306, 10 Beitu Jie; admission Y10; open 8am-6.30pm daily) is in the house where Liu spent the last month of his life. Liu Shaoqi (1898–1969) was Mao's intended successor until he was purged during the Cultural Revolution. Photos of Liu as a member of the Communist Party and with his family are on display as is a small collection of his things and the bed and room where he died. Photocopies of his medical records and the bill for his cremation are also on view.

Other Sights

The local **Kaifeng Museum** (Kāifēng Bówùguǎn; ☎ 393 2178, 26 Yingbin Lu; admission Y10; open 8.30am-11.30am & 3pm-6pm, Tues-Sun), south-west of Bāogōng Hú, is now virtually empty – 'no money', the staff complain. The museum reputedly has two Jewish steles and other artefacts from early settlers, but these are not open to the public. This is also the location for the **Kaifeng Institute for Research on the History of Chinese Jews** (☎ 393 2178, ext 8010).

Lóngtíng Gōngyuán (☎ 566 0316; admission Y25; open 6.30am-7pm daily) is largely covered by lakes. On its drier northern rim near **Dragon Pavilion** (Lóng Tíng) there's a small children's fun park; old men often sit here playing Chinese chess in the shade. The park is at the northern end of Zhongshan Lu.

Small Taoist **Yánqìng Temple** (Yánqìng Guàn; ☎ 393 1800, Dazhifang Jie; admission Y10; open 6.30am-6.30pm daily) was built in commemoration of Wang Zhe, founder of the True Unity Sect of Taoism. The yurt-shaped Tower of the Jade Emperor was repeatedly buried during the floods but was excavated and repaired in 1985.

Unfortunately there is almost nothing left of the **Kaifeng Synagogue** (see the boxed text 'Kāifēng's Israelites') now the boiler room of the No 4 People's Hospital (59 Beitu Jie; on the route for bus No 3). You can see the remains of an iron cover over an old well, which still has water. The staff at the hospital have seen so many visitors coming through, they'll know what you're looking for.

You can visit **Huáng Hé**, about 10km north of the city, although there isn't much to see because the water level is so low these days. Bus No 6 runs from near Tiě Tǎ to Huáng Hé twice per day. A taxi will cost Y50 to Y60 for the return trip. About 1km east of where the bus terminates, there's a Ming dynasty statue called the **Iron Rhinoceros** (Tiě Niú) which was meant to guard against floods.

Places to Stay

Kāifēng is a place where independent travellers get a wider range of accommodation than those with lots of money to throw around.

Biàndà Lǚshè (☎ 565 3163, 397 Xinmenguan Jie) Singles/twins from Y20/30, with air-con Y50/70. This terrifying hostel is the white building right of the southern bus station and has very grim rooms.

Dàjīntái Lǚguǎn (☎ 595 6677, 17 Gulou Jie) Beds in 2-/3-bed dorms Y30/25, doubles Y160. The Dàjīntái has fantastic rooms and is located next to the night market.

Biànjīng Fàndiàn (☎ 288 6699, fax 288 2449, 109 Dong Dajie). Dorm beds Y30, doubles/triples from Y120/180. The recent hotel face-lift jars with the surrounding architecture, but the rooms here are comfortable. Take bus No 3 from the western long-distance bus station and get off at the sixth stop.

Kāifēng Bīnguǎn (☎ 595 5589, fax 595 3086, 66 Ziyou Lu) Doubles/triples/quads Y180/210/280. This ornate Russian-built hotel, constructed in the style of traditional Chinese architecture, is in the centre of town. The cheaper rooms are small but bright and the more expensive rooms have been entirely renovated.

Dōngjīng Dàfàndiàn (☎ 398 9388, fax 595 6661, 99 Yingbin Lu) Older/newer doubles Y120/288. This gloomy place attempts to bring international comfort to the weary traveller. Better deals can be had elsewhere.

Places to Eat

Kāifēng offers some gastronomical delights, especially at the famed **night market** near the corner of Gulou Jie and Madao Jie. Worth sampling here is *ròuhé*, a local snack of fried vegetables and pork (or mutton) stuffed into a 'pocket' of flat bread. There is also a good vegie version. Another speciality are *chòu gānzǐ* (smelly dried things), which taste as bad as they sound! With a big bottle of beer costing Y2, this is the place to table-hop and try the different small eats *(xiǎo chī)*, such as hand-pulled and shaved noodles, won ton soup and kebabs.

Jiǎozi Guǎn (cnr Shudian Jie & Sihou Jie) This three-storey Chinese building is straight out of a Qing dynasty novel. What's more, the dumplings are tasty and inexpensive.

Dìyīlóu Bāozi Guǎn (☎ 565 0780, 8 Sihou Jie) Dumplings Y5. The *xiǎolóng bāo* (small buns filled with pork) served here are so tasty, the restaurant is always packed.

Mingdian Coffee Language (Míngdiàn Kāfēi Yǔyán; ☎ 597 7606, 56 Gulou Jie). Coffees & teas from Y20. This is the Chinese equivalent to Starbucks.

Getting There & Away

Bus Buses to Zhèngzhōu (Y10 to Y12.5, one to two hours) depart from the western bus station every 20 minutes between 6am and 7pm. To Luòyáng (Y35, 2½ hours), buses leave every hour from 7am to 5pm.

From the southern bus station (in front of the train station) there are buses every hour to Ānyáng (Y36, 3½ hours) from 7.20am until 5pm. One bus leaves daily at noon for Bózhōu (Y24, 4½ hours) in Ānhuī.

Train Kāifēng lies on the railway line between Xī'ān and Shànghǎi and trains are frequent. But tickets (especially for sleepers) can be hard to obtain. You might want to consider leaving from Zhèngzhōu instead. Express trains to Zhèngzhōu take about one hour (Y12); to Shànghǎi 12 hours (Y208); and to Xī'ān 10 hours (Y150). Slow trains heading south-easterly to Bózhōu and Héféi in Ānhuī run from here but departure times are inconvenient.

Getting Around

Buses leaving from both bus stations travel to major tourist areas. Gulou Jie, Sihou Jie and Shudian Jie are all good for catching buses. Pedicabs and taxis are also available and congregate around the bus and train stations. Rickety bicycles can be hired from the shop next door to CITS, on Yingbin Lu, for Y10 per day (Y100 deposit).

Húběi 湖北

Capital: Wǔhàn
Population: 64.2 million
Area: 187,400 sq km

Site of the great industrial city and river port of Wǔhàn, dissected by Cháng Jiāng (Yangzi River) and its many tributaries, and supporting nearly 60 million people, Húběi is one of China's most important provinces. For most travellers, however, it's mainly a transit point, or the end point of the Cháng Jiāng cruise down from Chóngqìng (see the Chóngqìng chapter for full details).

The province actually comprises two quite different areas. The eastern two-thirds is a low-lying plain drained by Cháng Jiāng and its main northern tributary, Hàn Jiāng, while the western third is an area of rugged highlands with small cultivated valleys and basins dividing Húběi from Sìchuān.

The plain was settled by the Han Chinese in 1000 BC. Around the 7th century AD it was intensively settled and by the 11th century it was producing a rice surplus. In the late 19th century it was the first area in the Chinese interior to undergo considerable industrialisation.

WǓHÀN 武汉
☎ 027 • pop 7,940,000

A lot of people pass through Wǔhàn as it's the terminus of the Cháng Jiāng ferries from Chóngqìng. Livelier, less grimy and more modern than Chóngqìng, Wǔhàn is now enjoying a boom in foreign and local investment that may help it catch up to the comparatively sparkling, cosmopolitan citadels of Nánjīng and Shànghǎi.

Greater Wǔhàn is one of China's largest cities, although it's actually a conglomeration of what were once three independent cities: Wǔchāng, Hànkǒu and Hànyáng.

Wǔchāng was established during the Han dynasty, became a regional capital under the Wu kingdom and is now the provincial capital. It used to be a walled city. Hànkǒu was a village and became an important military stronghold during the Song dynasty. By the Ming dynasty it had become one of China's four major commercial cities. The Treaty of Nanjing opened it to foreign trade. There were five foreign concession areas in

Highlights

- Wǔhàn, a major port on Cháng Jiāng (Yangzi River) and probably the most cosmopolitan and lively of China's interior cities

- Yíchāng, access point for the massive Three Gorges Dam project and cruises upriver to Chóngqìng via the soon to be submerged Three Gorges

- Shénnóngjià district, a relatively untravelled mountainous region boasting some of Húběi's wildest scenery

Hànkǒu – British, German, Russian, French and Japanese – all grouped around present-day Zhongshan Dadao.

With the completion of the Běijīng-Wǔhàn railway in 1904, Hànkǒu continued to expand. A reconstruction effort started in 1895, following the Sino-Japanese War, sparked the initial expansion.

Many of the European-style buildings from the concession era have remained – particularly Russian buildings, along Yanjiang Dadao on the north-western bank of Cháng Jiāng, and British, French and German structures, on Zhongshan Dadao. Government offices now occupy what were once the foreign banks, department stores and private residences. These European buildings and the density of development give Hànkǒu an unusually cosmopolitan atmosphere.

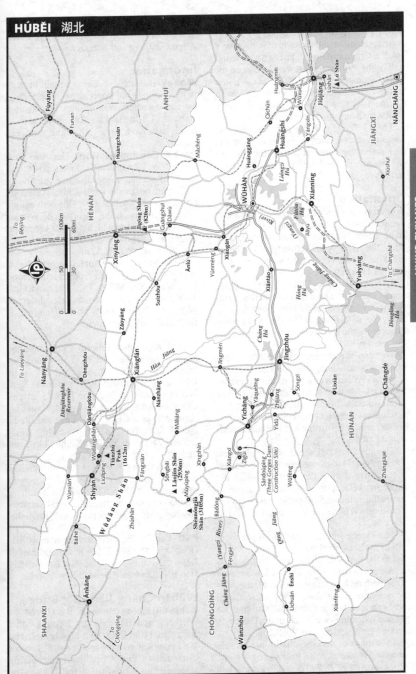

Hànyáng, which dates back to about AD 600, has long been outstripped by neighbouring Hànkǒu and today is the province's smallest municipality. During the second half of the 19th century it was developed for heavy industry, and in 1891 became home to the first modern iron and steel plant in China. This was followed during the early 1900s by a string of riverside factories.

The 1930s depression and the Japanese invasion ruined Hànyáng's heavy industry, and since the Communists gained power the main economic activity has been light industry.

Orientation

Wǔhàn is the only city on Cháng Jiāng that can truly be said to lie on both sides of the river. From Wǔchāng on the south-eastern bank, the city spreads across Cháng Jiāng to Hànkǒu and Hànyáng, the two separated by smaller Hàn Jiāng.

Two bridges cross Cháng Jiāng: an older one in the south and a new one to the north. A shorter bridge spans Hàn Jiāng linking Hànyáng with Hànkǒu. Ferries and speedboats cross the rivers continuously throughout the day.

The city's real centre is Hànkǒu, especially around Zhongshan Dadao, although 'central' Wǔhàn seems to be shifting gradually north-west, across Jiefang Dadao. Most of Hànkǒu's hotels, department stores, restaurants and street markets are within this sector, which is surrounded by quieter residential areas.

The area around the Jianghan Lu and Zhongshan Dadao intersection is lively, particularly during the evening when the night markets open. Hànkǒu has an enormous train station 5km north-west of town. The main Wǔhàn ferry terminal is also in Hànkǒu.

The Tianhe International Airport is about 30km north of Hànkǒu.

On the east side of the river, Wǔchāng is a modern district with long, wide avenues lined with drab concrete blocks of flats, businesses and restaurants. Many recreational areas and the Hubei Provincial Museum are on the Wǔchāng side of the river. The city's second train station is in Wǔchāng.

City maps of varying quality are on sale around Wǔhàn; try the four-storey Xinhua Bookshop (☎ 8378 3952) at 896 Zhongshan

Dadao, which also has an impressive selection of books in English, including titles by Allen Ginsberg and Nietszche.

Information

Money The Bank of China's main branch is in an ornate old concession-era building on the corner of Zhongshan Dadao and Jianghan Lu in Hànkǒu. The major tourist hotels also have money changing services.

Post & Communications The main post office is on Zhongshan Dadao, opposite the Bank of China. Long-distance telephone calls can be made from China Telecom phones throughout the city. One convenient phone office is on the 2nd floor of Wǔhàn Xīn Mínzhòng Lèyuán, a popular shopping centre in a yellow concession-era building at 608 Zhongshan Dadao.

Travellers can use Mínzú Internet (Mínzú Wǎngbā; ☎ 8566 2089) on the second floor of Wǔhàn Xīn Mínzhòng Lèyuán. China Telecom has an Internet cafe, Internet World (☎ 8221 0189), at 38 Tianjin Lu. Both charge Y2 per hour.

Travel Agencies Helpful China International Travel Service (CITS; Zhōngguó Guójì Lǚxíngshè; ☎ 8578 4125) is in Hànkǒu at 26 Taibei Yilu, opposite the New World Courtyard Wuhan. There's an enclosed parking lot outside and the building entrance has a CITS sign. Take the lift to the 7th floor. Bus No 9 stops near the western end of Taibei Yilu on Xinhua Lu; from there it's a five-minute walk.

Across from the Wǔhàn ferry terminal is a China Travel Service (CTS; Zhōngguó Lǚxíngshè; ☎ 8285 5259) at 142 Yanjiang Dadao. The office offers the usual services and has staff members that speak English.

PSB The Public Security Bureau (PSB; Gōngānjú; ☎ 8271 2355) is at 306 Shengli Jie, a 20-minute walk north-east of Jiāng Hàn Fàndiàn (see Places to Stay later).

Wǔhàn Cháng Jiāng Big Bridge

Wǔhàn Chángjiāng Dàqiáo 武汉长江大桥
Wǔchāng and Hànyáng are linked by this enormous 110m-long, 80m-high bridge. The 1957 completion of the bridge marked one of Communist China's first great engineering achievements. Until then all traffic had to be

laboriously ferried across the river. A second bridge, Wǔhàn Chángjiāng Èrqiáo, in northern Wǔhàn was completed in mid-1995.

Hubei Provincial Museum
Húběi Shěng Bówùguǎn 湖北省博物馆

This museum (☎ 8679 4127, 1856 Donghu Lu; admission Y20; open 8.30am-noon & 2pm-4.30pm daily) is a must if you're interested in archaeology and is worth a look even if you're not. In 1999, a new building was opened to house a large collection of artefacts from the Zenghouyi Tomb, which was unearthed in 1978 on the outskirts of the city of Suízhōu, about two-thirds of the way to Xiāngfán from Wǔhàn.

The tomb dates from around 433 BC, when the male internee, whose surname is Yi, was buried with about 7000 of his favourite artefacts, including bronze ritual vessels, weapons, horse and chariot equipment, bamboo instruments, utensils, and gold and jade objects.

One of the most fascinating finds was a two-tone, seven-note scale of bronze bells. The 64 elaborate bells are played using hammer-like objects and poles. The entire bell set has intricate carvings and warrior figures serving as bases and shows that a musical scale existed in ancient China.

There are musical performances throughout the day on duplicate bells, and the Chinese performers introduce each song in English. Various examples of musical recordings are for sale at a museum counter.

The museum has informative photographs and English captions.

The museum is beside Dōng Hú (East Lake) in Wǔchāng, one of the most pleasant areas in Wǔhàn. Take bus No 14 from the Zhōnghuá Lù pier (the dock closest to the old bridge) to the last stop, then walk back along the road for about 10 minutes, turning down a road that's signposted for Mao Zedong Villa (see next).

Day Trip In summer you can do a scenic day trip that includes the museum, taking a ferry from Hànkǒu to the Zhōnghuá Lù pier in Wǔchāng, then boarding bus No 36 to Mó Shān. Take another ferry across the lake to Dōnghú Gōngyuán (East Lake Park), walk to the museum, then get bus No 14 to the Yellow Crane Tower (Huánghè Lóu), and finally get a ferry back to Hànkǒu.

Mao Zedong Villa
Máo Zédōng Biéshù 毛泽东别墅

If you've just arrived from Húnán, you may have had enough of Mao by now. If not, stroll through the Chairman's bucolic hideaway here (☎ 8679 6109, Donghu Lu; admission Y10; open 8am-6pm daily).

The villa tour takes in his living quarters, offices, private swimming pool, bomb shelter and a meeting room where key decisions were made during the Cultural Revolution. Mao stayed here more than 20 times between 1960 and 1974, including nearly 18 months between 1966 and 1969. The pleasant tree-filled grounds have become a haven for a variety of birds. To get there, take bus No 14 from the Zhōnghuá Lù pier to the last stop and walk about 10 minutes farther. There are signs to show you the way.

Wuhan University
Wǔhàn Dàxué 武汉大学

Wuhan University, beside Luòjiā Shān in Wǔchāng, was founded in 1913, and many of the charming campus buildings originate from that period.

The university was the site of the 1967 'Wǔhàn Incident' – a protracted battle during the Cultural Revolution, where machine gun nests were built on top of the library and supply tunnels were dug through the hill. For a bit of Cultural Revolution nostalgia take bus No 12 from Zhōnghuá Lù pier to the terminus.

Other Things to See

Doubling as a curiosity shop and active Buddhist temple, **Guīyuán Sì** (☎ 8484 1434, 20 Cuiwei Lu; admission Y10; open 8am-4.30pm daily) in Hànyáng, has buildings dating from the late-Ming and early-Qing dynasties. The main attractions are statues of Buddha's disciples in an array of comical poses. A few years ago the statues were out in the open, and the incense smoke and sunshine filtering through the sky-lights gave the temple a rare magic. The incense is considered a fire hazard, so now visitors have to make do with unlit offerings.

To get there, take bus No 45 down Zhongshan Dadao and over the Hàn Jiāng bridge; there's a stop near the McDonald's within walking distance of the temple.

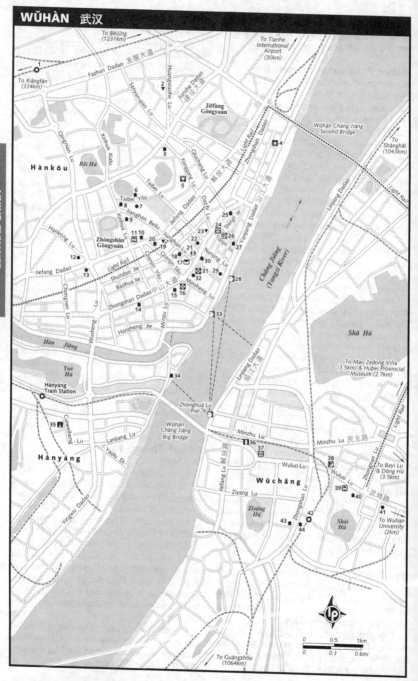

WǓHÀN 武汉

WǓHÀN

PLACES TO STAY
3 Shangri-La Hotel
   香格里拉大酒店
6 New World Courtyard
   Wuhan
   新世界万怡酒店
8 Xīnhuá Jiǔdiàn
   新华酒店
9 Huáxià Dàjiǔdiàn
   华夏大酒店
10 Mèngtiān Hú Bīnguǎn
   梦天湖宾馆
14 Yínfēng Bīnguǎn
   银丰宾馆
15 Dàhuá Fàndiàn
   大华饭店
18 Xuángōng Fàndiàn
   璇宫饭店
20 Holiday Inn
   天安假日酒店
25 Jiāng Hàn Fàndiàn
   江汉饭店
27 Xiélì Bīnguǎn
   协力宾馆
30 Huáyuán Yángguāng
   Jiǔdiàn
   华源阳光酒店
34 Holiday Inn Riverside
   晴川假日酒店
40 Jīnghàn Dàshà
   京汉大厦
43 Hánghǎi Bīnguǎn
   航海宾馆
44 Jiǔzhōu Fàndiàn
   九洲饭店

PLACES TO EAT
2 Kaiwei Beer House
   凯威啤酒室
19 Míngdiǎn Kāfēi Yǔ
   Chá
   名典咖啡与茶
23 Lǎotōngchéng Jiǔlóu
   老通城酒楼

OTHER
1 Hànkǒu Train Station
   汉口新火车站
4 PSB
   公安局外事科
5 Měiměi Jiǔbā
   美美酒吧
7 CITS
   中国国际旅行社
11 Long-Distance Bus
   Station (Hànkǒu)
   长途汽车站
12 China Southern
   Airlines (Hànkǒu)
   中国南方航空公司
13 CAAC
   中国民航售票处
16 Wǔhàn Xīn Mínzhòng
   Lèyuán; Telephone
   Office; Mínzú Internet
   武汉新民众乐园；
   中国电信；民族网吧
17 Main Post Office
   邮局
21 Main Bank of China
   中国银行

22 Advance Booking
   Office (Train Tickets)
   火车预售票处
24 Telephone Office
   中国电信
26 Internet World
   网吧
28 Wǔhàn Ferry Terminal
   武汉港客运站
29 CTS
   中国旅行社
31 Galaxy Shopping Centre
   佳丽广场
32 Xinhua Bookshop
   新华书店
33 Hànkǒu-Wǔchāng
   Ferries
   汉口武昌渡船
35 Guīyuán Sì
   归元寺
36 Yellow Crane Tower
   黄鹤楼
37 Former Headquarters of
   the Wuchang Uprising
   武昌起义纪念馆
38 Chángchūn Temple
   长春观
39 Long-Distance Bus
   Station (Wǔchāng)
   武昌长途汽车站
41 China Southern Airlines
   (Wǔchāng)
   中国南方航空公站
42 Wǔchāng Train Station
   武昌火车站

CENTRAL CHINA

A former military observation post, the **Yellow Crane Tower** (*Huánghè Lóu*, ☎ 8887 5179; *Wuluo Lu*; *admission Y30*; *open 7.30am-6pm daily*) sits at the southern end of the Wǔhàn Cháng Jiāng Big Bridge and is one of Wǔhàn's noted landmarks. Constructed during the Warring States period, the 51m tower used to be a site of inspiration for poets like Li Bai – but that was back when you could actually see the river. The five-level tower is more of a tourist trap today. The double-decker bus No 64 loops the city and stops near the tower; alternatively, take bus No 1, 4 or 10.

At the beginning of Wuluo Lu below the Yellow Crane Tower is a small square with a statue of Sun Yatsen. Behind the statue is a colonial-style red brick building that is the **Former Headquarters of the Wuchang Uprising** (*Xīnhàigémìng Wǔchāng Qǐyì Jìniànguǎn*) of 10 October 1911, which marked the end of the Qing dynasty. Sun Yatsen wasn't even in China at that time, but he returned as president of the new republic. At the time of writing, the building was closed for renovation.

Farther east on Wuluo Lu is the lovely Ming dynasty-style **Chángchūn Temple** (*Chángchūn Guān*; ☎ 8280 1399; *admission Y5*; *open 7.30am-5pm daily*). This Taoist temple dates from the Han dynasty but was subsequently rebuilt during the Tang and Song dynasties. In the middle of the courtyard is a statue of a very sagely looking Laotzu, the founder of Taoism.

Places to Stay – Budget
Many budget places in Wǔhàn have closed their doors to foreigners. Some mid-range hotels, however, offer significant discounts. All rooms have bathroom and air-con unless otherwise noted.

While a bit difficult to get to, accommodation at Wuhan University is the cheapest. Both of the following accept foreigners, but it's best to phone first. They are located in the eastern part of the campus (Féng Yuán) and it's a long 30-minute slog up the hill; take Xuefu Lu to Wenti Lu. You might be better off hiring a motorcycle with side-car at the entrance (Y8). Wuhan University is located to the east of the city centre. Bus No 12 from Zhōnghuá Lù pier will take you there.

Foreign Student Dormitory (*Liúxuéshēnglóu;* ☎ 8768 2813) Dorm beds Y40. This dormitory also has newly renovated, clean, basic doubles. The reception office is housed in an old brick building.

Foreign Experts Guesthouse (*Wàiguó Zhuānjiā Zhāodàisuǒ;* ☎ 8768 2930) Twin rooms Y180. About 200m up the road from the Foreign Student Dormitory, just past an iron gate, this guesthouse has large twin rooms with attached bathroom and air-con.

Hánghǎi Bīnguǎn (*Marine Hotel;* ☎ 8804 3395, fax 8807 8717, 452 Zhongshan Lu) Singles/doubles Y128/138. A far more convenient choice in Wǔchāng is this hotel, diagonally opposite the Wǔchāng train station and underneath the overpass on Zhongshan Lu. Rooms are a bit tattered. The manager, Cheng Hongqing, is friendly and helpful and may give you a tour of the city.

Jīnghàn Dàshà (*Chinese Capital Hotel;* ☎ 8782 5700, fax 8736 7885, 442 Wuluo Lu) Singles or twins Y148. This pleasant and convenient hotel is next to the long-distance bus station in Wǔchāng. They offer some good deals.

Mèngtiān Hú Bīnguǎn (*Mengtian Lake Hotel;* ☎ 8579 6368 ext 8188, fax 8577 2600, 1305 Jiefang Dadao) Singles/doubles with shared bath Y78/118, nicer singles/twins with private bath Y110/158. In Hànkǒu, next to the long-distance bus station, this hotel has cheap, basic rooms with clunky air-conditioners and nicer rooms with floral decor.

Places to Stay – Mid-Range

Huáxià Dàjiǔdiàn (☎ 8579 5688, fax 8577 7490, 294 Xinhua Lu) Doubles Y188-348. Large discounts of up to 50% are given at this hotel. It is about 500m north-west of the Hànkǒu long-distance bus station. Deluxe rooms set around a courtyard on the top floor can go as low as Y208, singles Y108.

Dàhuá Fàndiàn (☎ 8566 3999, 604 Zhongshan Dadao) Economy rooms/singles/doubles/suites Y150/320/620/1080. In the centre of Hànkǒu, this sophisticated hotel has gorgeous rooms – some with balconies.

Huáyuán Yángguāng Jiǔdiàn (*Magnificent Sunshine Hotel;* ☎ 8280 1366, fax 8283 4128, 997 Zhongshan Dadao) Singles or doubles Y288, other rooms Y450. Given its prime location in Hànkǒu, this is a decent place to stay. Discounts of up to 45% are sometimes given.

Xīnhuá Jiǔdiàn (☎ 8579 0333, fax 8577 1967, 162 Jianghan Beilu) Doubles/triples Y68/88, with bath Y158/218, with bath & air-con Y268/348. This renovated property in central Hànkǒu is on a side street off Jianghan Beilu.

Xiélì Bīnguǎn (☎ 8280 3903, 2 Tianjin Lu) Singles/twins Y140/200. Just north of the Wǔhàn ferry terminal, this place has decent twins. It's handy for those late-night Cháng Jiāng cruise arrivals.

Yínfēng Bīnguǎn (☎ 8568 0711, fax 8564 8511, 400 Zhongshan Dadao) Twins Y348-580, suites Y980-1880. A little more expensive but definitely worth it, this hotel has clean wooden floors, sparkling bathrooms and great water pressure for showers. Depending on the season, the hotel may lower its rates.

Jiǔzhōu Fàndiàn (☎ 8804 2120, fax 8804 2784, 651 Zhongshan Lu) Singles/twins Y188/228. This two-star hotel has comfortable, attractive rooms and is located at the far left of the square as you exit the Wǔchāng train station. Discounts of 20% are sometimes available.

Places to Stay – Top End

Most of the top-end places have an additional 15% service charge.

Jiāng Hàn Fàndiàn (☎ 8281 1600, fax 8281 4342, 245 Shengli Jie) Twins US$80, suites US$200-280. This hotel, located near the disused Hànkǒu train station, is the place to stay if you can afford it. Built by the French in 1914, it was originally named the the Demin Hotel. It has been used as a French embassy and is one of the best examples of colonial architecture in this part of China. The interior is impressive. The hotel has its own post office, shops and an excellent restaurant.

Xuángōng Fàndiàn (☎ 6882 2588, W www.xuangonghotel.com, 57 Jianghan Lu) Singles/doubles with balcony Y380/ 480. Located on a pedestrian-only shopping street in Hànkǒu's city centre, this hotel has clean rooms. Discounts of 30% are sometimes given.

New World Courtyard Wuhan (*Xīnshìjiè Wànyí Jiǔdiàn;* ☎ 8578 7968, W www .courtyard.com, 9 Taibei Yilu) Twins US$109. Although inconveniently located, the plain-looking New World offers three-star service. It's a good spot for international food (see Places to Eat following). Discounts of 50% are sometimes given.

Holiday Inn (*Jiàrì Jiǔdiàn;* ☎ 8586 7888, W www.sixcontinentshotels.com, 868 Jiefang Dadao) Standard singles/twins US$120/130, suites $200. This is one of the best hotels in town. Sometimes discounts of 50% are given.

Holiday Inn Riverside (*Qíngchuān Jiàrì Jiǔdiàn;* ☎ 8471 6688, W www.sixcontinents hotels.com, 88 Xima Chang Jie) Standard doubles with river view Y449-599, suites Y888. Accessible only by taxi, this branch of the Holiday Inn in Hànyáng is near an old city gate, on the edge of the river, north of the Cháng Jiāng Big Bridge. This location puts it in rather an isolated area. The hotel attendants and bellboys wear traditional Chinese dress.

Shangri-La Hotel (*Xiānggélǐlā Dàjiǔdiàn;* ☎ 8580 6868, W www.shangri-la .com, 700 Jianshe Lu) Standard doubles $150-195. Although a bit far from central Hànkǒu, the well-equipped Shangri-La Hotel is still popular. Their Western cafe serves excellent cuisine.

Places to Eat

Wǔhàn has some pretty good eating houses in all price ranges. Popular local snacks include fresh catfish from Dōng Hú in the west of the city, and charcoal-grilled whole pigeons served with a sprinkling of chilli. You can try some of these dishes on the *floating restaurants* at the end of Bayi Lu on the shore of Dōng Hú, where you can pick your catfish before they cook it.

The *night markets* on Minsheng Lu and Jianghan Lu in Hànkǒu are good places for food. If you have a craving for Western food, try the Holiday Inn, Shangri-La, or New World Courtyard Wuhan.

Bakeries with crunchy rolls and French bread are also fairly common. There's a good one in the lobby of the Holiday Inn on Jiefang Dadao.

Lǎotōngchéng Jiǔlóu (☎ 8285 9036, 1 Dazhi Lu) Dishes Y4-52. This bustling canteen on the corner of Dazhi Lu and Zhongshan Dadao is a great place to people watch. It serves a tasty snack called *dòupí*, made with a bean curd base – its name translates as 'bean skin' – rolled around a filling of rice and diced meat, vegetables (*shuāngdōng dòupí*) or egg (*dànguāng dòupí*). Dòupí is no great delicacy, but at Y4 a serving you can't go wrong. There is also a restaurant upstairs.

Kaiwei Beer House (*Kǎiwēi Píjiǔwū;* ☎ 8260 5679, 71 Huangxiaohe Lu) Spicy, all-you-can-eat Sichuanese hotpot (Y28) and authentic, German-brewed beer prove to be the ultimate Wǔhàn experience at this popular spot, where Berlin brewmaster Hans has been brewing his own stuff for the past four years. Take bus No 608.

Míngdiǎn Kāfēi Yǔ Chá (*Mingdian Coffee Lounge;* ☎ 8583 2256, 914 Jiefang Dadao) Espresso/cappuccino Y22/28. This upmarket cafe is near the Holiday Inn and rows of teahouses.

Entertainment

There are discos and nightclubs opening all over Hànkǒu, and cafes are also becoming a popular nightspot – there are several at the corner of Tianjin Lu and Yanjiang Dadao.

Měiměi Jiǔbā (*Meimei Bar; 100 Xianggang Lu*) This new place has dancing most nights. From the Xianggang Lu and Jiefang Dadao intersection, walk north for about 10 minutes; the club is on your left.

Getting There & Away

The best way to get to eastern destinations such as Nánjīng and Shànghǎi is by air or river ferry, rather than the circuitous rail route.

Air The main Civil Aviation Administration of China (CAAC; Zhōngguó Mínháng) ticket office is at 151 Liji Beilu in Hànkǒu, but it's better to go to the China Southern Airlines (☎ 8361 1756) outlet at 1 Hangkong Lu. In Wǔchāng there is a China Southern Airlines office (☎ 8764 5121) at 586 Wuluo Lu. The airlines offer air connections to virtually all major cities in China, including daily flights to Běijīng (Y990), Guǎngzhōu (Y850), Kūnmíng (Y1050), Shànghǎi (Y750) and Shēnzhèn (Y780); and several each week to Chéngdū (Y750), Fúzhōu (Y720), Hong Kong (Y1550) and Xī'ān (Y650). It's about 45 minutes to the airport.

You can also find a number of ticket outlets in the area around the Wǔchāng train station.

Bus The main long-distance bus station is in Hànkǒu on Jiefang Dadao, between Xinhua Lu and Jianghan Beilu. From Hànkǒu there are daily departures to Chángshā (Y88, five hours), Nánchāng (Y116, 10 hours), Zhèngzhōu (Y96, 12 hours) and Shànghǎi (Y310, 16 hours). One good way to get to Yíchāng is on a comfortable air-conditioned bus run by the Jielong bus company (Y98, four hours). The Korean bus company Hanguang has buses for Y88. Smaller Iveco buses cost Y72.

Buses to Xiāngfán (Y80, seven hours), en route to Wǔdāng Shān, leave from the Wǔchāng long-distance bus station; sometimes there are direct buses to Wǔdāng Shān (Y87, nine hours). You can also get buses to Yíchāng, Shànghǎi (Y305, 16 hours) and other destinations. The bus station is south-east on Wuluo Lu, and marked by a pedestrian bridge.

For travellers disembarking from the Wǔhàn ferry terminal, long-distance buses are waiting at the terminal's car park and go to Shànghǎi (Y306, 16 hours), Héféi (Y150, seven hours), Jiǔjiāng (Y80, four hours) and Nánjīng (Y190, nine hours) as well as other cities. As you enter the terminal's waiting hall, the booking office is to your right.

Train Wǔhàn is on the main line from Běijīng to Guǎngzhōu; express trains to Kūnmíng, Xī'ān, Hong Kong (Kowloon) and Lánzhōu run via the city. Trains going to major destinations such as these leave from both the Hànkǒu and Wǔchāng train stations. Trains to Shànghǎi, however, leave from Wǔchāng. Most trains going to Shíyàn (Y150, 12 hours) and Liùlǐpíng – cities near Wǔdāng Shān – leave from the Wǔchāng station. At Hànkǒu station, hard and soft sleepers must be booked in the small ticket

office between the waiting hall and the main ticket office.

There is also a train ticket office at 24 Baohua Jie in central Hànkǒu at the intersection with Nanjing Lu. You can book sleepers three days in advance.

Tickets for trains originating from Wǔchāng must be bought at the Wǔchāng station rather than Hànkǒu. Window 18 is for foreigners, but you can go to any window. CITS can book sleepers for a Y50 service charge. You can also book tickets at the Wǔchāng bus station.

The Běijīng-Kowloon express train stops at both Wǔchāng and Hànkǒu.

Some sample hard-sleeper tickets are Běijīng (Y281, 12 hours), Guǎngzhōu (Y257, 17 hours), Guìlín (Y222, 12 hours), Kūnmíng (Y399, 24 hours), Shànghǎi (Y262, seven hours) and Xī'ān (Y215, 16 hours).

Boat You can catch ferries from Wǔhàn along Cháng Jiāng, either east to Shànghǎi (Y1125, 16 hours) or west to Chóngqìng (see the Chóngqìng chapter for full details). Ferries also go to Jiǔjiāng (Y269, 10 hours) in Jiāngxī.

Getting Around

To/From the Airport Buses to Tianhe International Airport (Y10, 40 minutes) leave 12 times a day from the China Southern Airlines office on Hangkong Lu and five times daily from the office on Wuluo Lu in Wǔchāng.

Flag fall for taxis is Y8. A taxi to the airport should cost about Y80 and take 30 minutes; enterprising taxi drivers may try to undercut the airport bus.

Bus & Ferry Bus routes crisscross the city, but getting where you want to go may mean changing at least once. A useful bus is the No 603, which passes Jiāng Hàn Fàndiàn to and from the Hànkǒu train station. Bus No 9 runs from the train station down Xinhua Lu to the Wǔhàn ferry terminal.

In Wǔchāng, bus No 12 runs from Wuhan University to the Zhōnghuá Lù pier, and bus No 503 goes from near the Wǔhàn ferry terminal across to Wǔchāng. Motortricycles and pedicabs wait outside the main train stations and the Wǔhàn ferry terminal, as well as the smaller ferry docks.

The Hànkǒu-Wǔchāng ferries are normally a more convenient, and always a much faster, way of crossing the river during the day. The large boats (Y1) take 20 minutes to make the crossing, while smaller speedboats (Y5) carry around 15 people and do it in five minutes.

WǓDĀNG SHĀN 武当山
☎ 0719

These mountains (entrance gate ☎ 566 7415; admission Y31) stretch for 400km across north-western Húběi and are particularly sacred to Taoists. Situated south-east of Shíyàn, the highest summit is the 1612m **Tiānzhú Peak**, which translates as 'Pillar Propping Up the Sky' or 'Heavenly Pillar Peak'.

Wǔdāng Shān is also famous for the Wǔdāng Shān–style of martial arts developed here and traditionally practiced by Taoist priests. There are numerous schools in and around the town.

A number of Taoist temples were built on the range during the construction sprees of Ming emperors Chengzu and Zhenwu. The most notable temple is the **Golden Hall** (Jīn Diàn; admission Y10; open 8.30am-5pm daily) on Tiānzhú Peak. It was built entirely of gilded copper in 1416; the hall contains a bronze statue of Zhenwu, who became a Taoist deity.

Below, on Soaring Flag Peak (Zhǎnqí Fēng), are two temples. The attractive **Purple Cloud Temple** (Zǐxiāo Gōng; admission Y10; open 7am-6pm daily) originates from the Song dynasty but was renovated during the Ming dynasty. The less remarkable **Nányán Temple** (Nányán Gōng) is at the beginning of the trail used to ascend Tiānzhú Peak.

These temples are about 10km from the entrance gate to the mountain, which is about 1km from town. There are walking paths up from the entrance gate, but most people skip this first part of the walk by taking a minivan taxi up to the parking lot for Y10. From there it's another two-hour hike up to the Golden Hall.

There are a number of other choices. Some people opt to be carried up on chairs (zuòjiào) for Y40. Beware of overcharging. A cable car (Y45) also runs between the Golden Hall and Qióngtǎi, an area north-west of Soaring Flag Peak.

Zhang San Feng

Zhang San Feng was a Wǔdāng Shān monk in the 13th or 14th century, and is reputed to be the founder of the martial-art tàijíquán, or tai chi. A master of Shaolin martial arts, Zhang disliked the 'hard' techniques of the Shaolin style and was searching for something 'softer'. As he was sitting on his porch one day, he was inspired by a battle between a huge bird and a snake. The sinuous snake used flowing movement to evade the bird's attacks. The bird, exhausted, eventually gave up and flew away. There is a close association between tai chi and Taoism, and virtually all of the Taoist priests on Wǔdāng Shān practice some form of the art.

Places to Stay & Eat

Xuánwǔ Dàjiǔdiàn (☎ 566 6013, Hanshi Gonglu) Twins Y70-100, beds in twins with bath Y40. On the main street of Wǔdāngshān town, directly down from the train station, this hotel has nice, newly renovated rooms with squat toilets. They also have a good restaurant. There's no English sign, but keep an eye out for the bus station across the street.

Lǎoyīng Fàndiàn (☎ 566 5347, 1 Hanshi Gonglu) Singles/twins/triples Y70/140/180. Rooms here have spartan furnishings. This hotel is also on the main street, east of the Yongle Lu intersection, near an ornate arch.

Wǔdāngshān Bīnguǎn (☎ 566 5548, 33 Yongle Lu) Twins Y180. This hotel is supposed to be the town's most luxurious, but the rooms are so-so. It's at the end of Yongle Lu.

There is also accommodation available on the mountain.

Jīndǐng Lǚguǎn (☎ 695 0718) Dorm beds in doubles or triples Y44, singles Y88. This simple hotel is just below the temple on Tiānzhù Peak. Bathroom and eating facilities are basic, but there are fantastic views and you might meet the resident Taoist priests.

Bǎihuì Shānzhuāng (☎ 568 9191, fax 568 9088) Twins Y78-120. At the parking lot before the Nányán Temple, this hotel has nice rooms and is the best place to stay on the mountain.

In town, there are a couple of good **private restaurants** on Yongle Lu near its intersection with the main road. *Xuánwǔ Dàjiǔdiàn* also has a good restaurant.

Getting There & Away

The train station is called Wǔdāngshān, but the town used to go by the name of Laǒyíng. Wǔdāngshān is on the railway line from Wǔhàn to Chóngqìng, but few trains stop and you may have to take a bus to/from either Shíyàn (Y5, one hour) or Liùlǐpíng (one hour). There are daily trains from Wǔhàn and Xiāngfán (Y35, two hours). There are also sleeper buses to Wǔhàn (12 hours) leaving from the bus station that is diagonally opposite Xuánwǔ Dàjiǔdiàn.

Minibuses to Shíyàn go up and down the main street collecting passengers.

SHÉNNÓNGJIÀ 神农架
☎ 0719

The Shénnóngjià district in remote northwestern Húběi has the wildest scenery in the province. With heavily forested mountains of fir, pine and hemlock, including something rare in China – old-growth stands – the area is known as a treasure trove of more than 1300 species of medicinal plants. Indeed, the name for the area roughly translates as 'Shennong's Ladder' to commemorate a legendary emperor, Shennong, believed to be the founder of herbal medicine and agriculture. According to the legend, he heard about some special plants growing high on a precipice, so he cut down a great tree and used it as a ladder to reach the plants, which he added to his medicinal collection.

As part of a more modern legend, Shénnóngjià is also famous for the sightings of wild, ape-like creatures – a Chinese equivalent of the Himalayan yeti or the North American bigfoot. The stories are interesting, but the creatures seem to be able to distinguish between peasants and scientists – molesting the former and evading the latter. Nevertheless, there is a small base station set up in the reserve with displays of 'evidence' of sightings. More real, but just as elusive perhaps, are leopards, bears, wild boars and monkeys (including the endangered golden snub-nosed monkey) that reportedly inhabit the area.

Foreigners are allowed into the area of the Shénnóngjià district near the town of Mùyúpíng, 200km north-west of Yíchāng.

There are two high peaks in the area, Shénnóngjià Shān at 3105m and Laǒjūn Shān at 2936m. It's an eight-hour bus ride to Mùyúpíng from Yíchāng (Y80), or you can take a boat to Xiāngxī (five hours) on the Three Gorges (Sānxiá) and from there it's a 90km ride to Mùyúpíng. From Mùyúpíng you will have to hire a car to get into the reserve.

CITS in Yíchāng arranges a three-day tour that includes visits to botanical sites, rafting and Shénnóngjià Shān, but be prepared to pay up to Y1400 per person. The tour includes accommodation, although much of the time is taken up with transportation. Other travel agencies around the train station in Yíchāng also offer tours to Shénnóngjià, but you should specify the Mùyúpíng area unless you want some adventures with the police.

It is now possible to visit Sōngbǎi, an area in the Shénnóngjià reserve that has been off limits to foreigners in the past. In 2001 Yíchāng CITS reported that foreigners were allowed to visit the area, but only when accompanied by tour guides. It may be possible to visit the area independently if you acquire a travel permit for the area – check with CITS or the PSB in Yíchāng or Mùyúpíng for updates. If you travel to the area without a permit, take care: those caught without permits may face a Y1000 fine and be ejected from the area.

YÍCHĀNG 宜昌
☎ 0717 • pop 3,996,700

Just below the famous Three Gorges, Yíchāng is the gateway to upper Cháng Jiāng and was a walled town as long ago as the Sui dynasty. The city was opened to foreign trade in 1877 by a treaty between Britain and China, and a concession area was set up along the riverfront south-east of the old city.

Today Yíchāng is best known as the gateway city to the massive and controversial Three Gorges hydroelectric project being built at Sāndòupíng, 40km upstream. Because it helps generate electricity for the area, the Gezhou Dam on the city's western end has also made Yíchāng noteworthy. A second bridge across Cháng Jiāng was completed in 2001.

A steady flow of Cháng Jiāng tourists passing through town is also swelling local coffers. Unless you have a special fondness

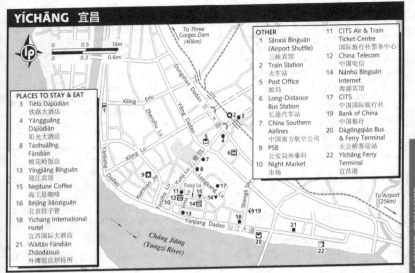

YÍCHĀNG 宜昌

PLACES TO STAY & EAT
3 Tiělù Dàjiǔdiàn
    铁路大酒店
4 Yángguāng
    Dàjiǔdiàn
    阳光大酒店
8 Táohuālǐng
    Fàndiàn
    桃花岭饭店
9 Yíngjiāng Bīnguǎn
    迎江宾馆
15 Neptune Coffee
    海工星咖啡
16 Běijīng Jiǎozuìguǎn
    北京饺子管
18 Yichang International
    Hotel
    宜昌国际大酒店
21 Wàitān Fàndiàn
    Zhāodàisuǒ
    外滩饭店招待所

OTHER
1 Sānxiá Bīnguǎn
    (Airport Shuttle)
    三峡宾馆
2 Train Station
    火车站
5 Post Office
    邮局
6 Long-Distance
    Bus Station
    长途汽车站
7 China Southern
    Airlines
    中国南方航空公司
9 PSB
    公安局外事科
10 Night Market
    市场
11 CITS Air & Train
    Ticket Centre
    国际旅行社票务中心
12 China Telecom
    中国电信
14 Nánhú Bīnguǎn
    Internet
    南湖宾馆
17 CITS
    中国国际旅行社
19 Bank of China
    中国银行
20 Dàgōngqiáo Bus
    & Ferry Terminal
    大公桥客运站
22 Yichang Ferry
    Terminal
    宜昌港

CENTRAL CHINA

for dams, there's really not much worth seeing in Yíchāng, but it's a useful jumping-off point for more interesting places.

Information

You can change money at the Bank of China on Shengli Silu near Longkang Lu. The main post office is at the corner of Yunji Lu and Yiling Dadao.

CITS (☎ 624 1875) is at 18 Longkang Lu, though residents still call the street by its old name, Kangzhuang Lu. CITS offers tours of the Three Gorges that include rafting trips (Y280 per person), but you will need at least four people for a tour.

Across from Neptune Coffee, in Nánhú Bīnguǎn, an Internet cafe (☎ 888 3561) on the second floor at 43 Fusui Lu charges Y2 per hour.

Three Gorges Dam 三峡水力枢纽工程
Sānxiá Shuǐlì Shūniǔ Gōngchéng

Dam enthusiasts (see the boxed text 'The Damned Yangzi' in the Chóngqìng chapter) and people who like being around large rock-crushing equipment will enjoy taking a look at the construction site of the Three Gorges Dam, which is expected to be completed in 2009.

To get there, take yellow minibus No 4 (Y1) from outside the train station until it arrives at the bus No 8 terminus. Bus No 8

(Y18 return) takes 40 minutes to reach the construction site and drops you off at the dam's south-western end. Minibuses (Y20 return) and motorcycle taxis (Y10 return) can take you up the cement road to see the project; alternatively you can walk up the paved road.

Places to Stay

Wàitān Fàndiàn Zhāodàisuǒ (☎ 622 4275, 148 Yanjiang Dadao) Beds Y15-65. Some rooms in this economical place have heating and bathrooms and others don't. The staff only speaks Chinese but is friendly and helpful; look for the hotel's name in red characters on a silver background.

Tiělù Dàjiǔdiàn (Railway Hotel; ☎/fax 644 7530) Doubles Y168-188. Readers recommend this convenient hotel, right next to the train station. Discounts of up to 30% are sometimes available.

Yíngjiāng Bīnguǎn (☎ 623 0743, 55 Erma Lu) Twins Y118-258. Tidy rooms in this place may be dropped to Y80.

Yángguāng Dàjiǔdiàn (Sunshine Hotel; ☎ 644 6075, fax 644 6086, 1 Yunji Lu) Twins Y108-320. Just down the steps from the train station is this good deal with clean, although slightly tattered, rooms.

Táohuālǐng Fàndiàn (☎ 623 6666, fax 623 8888, 29 Yunji Lu) Twins Y398 plus 10%, twins in annex Y140. This recently renovated luxury hotel in the middle of town has nice twins with wooden floors in the main building. Given the location, however, the best deals are the unheated twins with Chinese toilets in an annex building. The hotel also has a bowling alley, swimming pool and lush landscaping.

Yichang International Hotel (*Yíchāng Guójì Dàjiǔdiàn; 622 2888, fax 622 8186, 127 Yanjiang Lu*) Doubles Y428-898. Towering over Cháng Jiāng, this place, with a revolving restaurant at its top, is the city's newest luxury palace.

Places to Eat
Yíchāng has a variety of restaurants around town.

Neptune Coffee (*Hǎiwángxīng Kāfēi; 622 9934, 40 Fusui Lu*) Mains Y8-45. For great coffee, pizza, and salads, visit this popular, Western-style restaurant. It tries to bring a slice of Paris to Yíchāng through fleur-de-lis decor, a wall-sized Renoir imitation, and a good selection of coffees.

Běijīng Jiǎoziguǎn (*624 1691, 28 Longkang Lu*) Mains Y8-40. This bustling place serves up dumplings and an array of northern-style cold dishes.

There is a lively **night market** for dining on Taozhu Lu.

Getting There & Away
Air Yíchāng's airport is 25km south-east of the city centre and has flights to Běijīng (Y1190), Shēnzhèn (Y830), Shànghǎi (Y960) and other cities. There are several ticket offices around town, especially near the train station and ferry terminals. There's a helpful China Southern Airlines office (625 1538) at 21 Yunji Lu.

CITS (622 8915) has a ticket centre that books flights and train tickets at 2 Erma Lu.

Bus The main long-distance bus station is south of the train station along Dongshan Dadao. There are also long-distance services from the two ferry terminals on Yanjiang Dadao. The Korean joint-venture Hanguang air-conditioned bus to Wǔhàn (Y105, four hours) leaves from the long-distance bus station every hour. There is also a daily bus to Mùyúpíng (Y46, six hours). The Jielong bus service to Wǔhàn

(Y98) departs from the Dàgōngqiáo terminal; and Iveco buses to Wǔhàn (Y70) leave from the Yíchāng ferry terminal. Buses to Shànghǎi should cost around Y300 and take about 24 hours.

Train Yíchāng's train station sits atop a tall stairway at the intersection of Dongshan Dadao and Yunji Lu. The ticket office is on your far left as you approach the main building.

Train service has improved in the past few years with trains going to Běijīng (Y330, 22 hours), Zhèngzhōu (Y195, 12 hours), Xī'ān (Y176, 20 hours), Huáihuà (Y69, 11 hours) and Guǎngzhōu (Y335, 25 hours). From Yíchāng, the best way to get to Zhāngjiājiè in Húnán is by train. The seven-hour journey costs Y60.

Boat All passing river ferries stop at the Yíchāng ferry terminal or the Dàgōngqiáo bus and ferry terminal. Travellers often find the two-day trip through the gorges between Chóngqìng and Yíchāng quite long enough, and some disembark or board here rather than spend an extra day on the river between Yíchāng and Wǔhàn.

There is also a hydrofoil service that goes to Wànxiàn in Chóngqìng at the western end of the Three Gorges (Y195, six hours), as well as to Chóngqìng City (Y380, 12 hours). Tickets can be purchased at either of the ferry terminals.

For full details on Cháng Jiāng cruises, see the 'Cruising Downriver' special section in the Chóngqìng chapter. While both ferry terminals sell tickets east and west on Cháng Jiāng, the larger Yíchāng ferry terminal is a better place to purchase tickets because it offers a wider variety of services, especially east to Shànghǎi.

Getting Around
The airport bus (Y20, 30 minutes) leaves from Sānxiá Bīnguǎn (673 9888 ext 8100) at 42 Yanjiang Dadao. A taxi to the airport should cost Y60. Yíchāng's city centre is small enough that you can walk to many places. Bus Nos 3 and 4 (Y1) run from Yunji Lu, near the train station, to the ferry terminals. Motorcycle taxis (Y5) and taxis (Y10) are also available.

Jiāngxī 江西

Capital: Nánchāng
Population: 45.4 million
Area: 166,600 sq km

Tucked between some of China's wealthier cities and provinces, south-eastern Jiāngxī sees few foreign visitors, which is part of its allure for independent travellers.

Jiāngxī entered the Chinese empire at an early date, but remained sparsely populated until the 8th century. Before this the main expansion of Han Chinese had been from the north into Húnán and Guăngdōng. The Grand Canal was built from the 7th century onwards, it opened up the south-eastern regions and made Jiāngxī an important transit point on the trade route from Guăngdōng.

Peasants settled in Jiāngxī between the 8th and 13th centuries. The development of industries such as silver mining and tea growing allowed the formation of a wealthy Jiāngxī merchant class. By the 19th century, however, the province's role as a major transport route from Guăngzhōu was reduced by the opening of coastal ports to foreign shipping, which forced the Chinese junk trade to decline.

Jiāngxī also has Jǐnggāng Shān, one of the most famous Communist guerrilla bases that travellers can visit. It was only after several years of war that the Kuomintang were able to drive the Communists out onto their 'Long March' to Shaanxi.

NÁNCHĀNG 南昌
☎ 0791 • pop 4,078,900

A city of squat, box-like buildings, Nánchāng has a rhythm similar to other crowded metropolises in the new China – congested roads with horns blaring and locals hawking their goods.

The city's characters mean 'southern prosperity', but expensive hotel rooms and a lack of tourist attractions prompt many travellers to use this provincial capital as nothing more than a stopover.

History

In modern Chinese history, Nánchāng is best remembered for the Communist-led uprising of 1 August 1927.

Highlights

- Jǐngdézhèn, China's most famous area for the production of porcelain and ceramics
- Lúshān, a hill resort where mountain vistas have inspired Communist leaders and artists alike

After Chiang Kaishek staged his massacre of Communists in March 1927, what was left of the Communist Party fled underground. At the time, urban revolution dominated Party ideology.

Kuomintang Army troops led by Communist officers happened to be concentrated around Nánchāng at the time, and an opportunity for a successful insurrection appeared possible.

On 1 August (known as bāyī in Chinese) 30,000 troops led by Zhou Enlai and Zhu De seized the city and held it for several days until loyalists to the Nánjīng regime drove them out.

The revolt was largely a fiasco, but the gathering of soldiers marked the beginning of the Communist army in Chinese history. The army retreated south from Nánchāng to Guăngdōng, but Zhu De led some soldiers and circled back to Jiāngxī to join forces with the ragtag army that Mao Zedong had organised in Húnán. From there, they sought refuge in Jǐnggāng Shān (Well-Shaped Ridge Mountains).

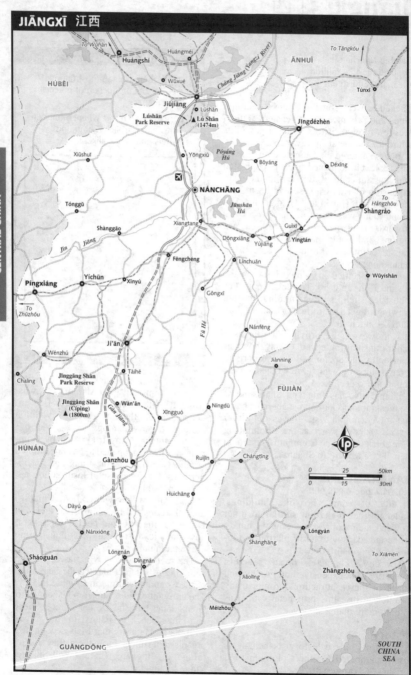

JIĀNGXĪ 江西

Orientation

Gàn Jiāng lies to Nánchāng's north, and Fǔ Hé (Comfort River), which branches off Gàn Jiāng, sits to the city's west. Zhanqian Lu leads directly west from the train station to the Fushan roundabout and overpass.

Bayi Dadao heads north-west from the roundabout and is the main north-south artery through the city; another main strip is Yangming Beilu, which cuts east-west to the old and new Bāyī Bridges over Gàn Jiāng.

Most tourist sights and facilities are on or in the vicinity of Bayi Dadao. The People's Square sits at the town's centre, at the intersection of Bayi Dadao and Beijing Xilu. Maps (Y5) are available from the Xinhua Bookshop on Bayi Dadao (☎ 626 2026), across from the People's Square.

Information

The main Bank of China is opposite Nánchāng Bīnguǎn on Zhanqian Xilu. There's a post office on the corner of Bayi Dadao and Ruzi Lu, just south of the Exhibition Hall. The tiny Daìtián Internet (Daìtián Wǎngbā), just off Minde Lu at 211 Sipu Lu, charges Y1 per hour.

China International Travel Service (CITS; Zhōngguó Guójì Lǚxíngshè; ☎ 626 3437) and the helpful Jiangxi International Tour and Aviation Corporation (☎ 621 5891) share a building at 169 Fuzhou Lu, just in front of Qīngshānhú Bīnguǎn (see Places to Stay later). CITS is on the second floor. Many hotels can also book tickets.

The Public Security Bureau (PSB; Gōngānjú) is about 100m north of Minde Lu, in a cream-tiled high-rise building on Shengli Lu.

Things to See

On Bayi Dadao in the heart of Nánchāng is the **People's Square** (Rénmín Guǎngchǎng). Here you'll find the **Monument to the Martyrs** (Bāyī Jìniàn Tǎ), a sculpture of red-tiled flags and a stone column topped with a rifle and fixed bayonet. Opposite the square is the **Exhibition Hall** (Zhǎnlǎnguǎn), an immense building with a giant red star – a nostalgic tribute to Stalinist architecture now cluttered with advertising billboards.

The city's pride is towering **Téngwáng Gé** (Jumping King Pavilion; 7 Yanjiang Lu; admission Y30; open 8am-5.30pm daily), erected in 1989, allegedly on the site of 28 previous reconstructions. Originally built during the Tang period, the nine-storey granite pavilion overlooks Fǔ Hé and houses exhibition rooms with paintings, teahouses and the inevitable souvenir shop. On the top floor is a traditional Chinese music and dance theatre with performances throughout the day.

North of Dōng Hú, **Yòumín Sì** (177 Minde Lu; admission Y2; open 8am-5.30pm daily) is an attractive Buddhist temple dating from the Liang dynasty. It was destroyed during the Cultural Revolution and rebuilt in 1995.

Other sights include the **Memorial Hall to the Martyrs of the Revolution** (Gémìng Lièshì Jìniànguǎn; ☎ 626 2566, 399 Bayi Dadao; admission Y5; open 8am-11.30am & 2.30pm-5.30pm Mon-Thur), north of the People's Square. The hall's exhibits are in Chinese, but the archival photos from the 1920s to 1940s are worth the admission.

The **Residence of Zhou Enlai & Zhu De** (Zhōu Enlái Hé Zhū Dé Jiùjū; 2 Huawen Jiaojie; admission free; open 9am-3pm daily) is a charming traditional wooden building dating from 1927. It's located in a small alley just off Minde Lu.

The overpriced **Former Headquarters of the Nanchang Uprising** (Bāyī Nánchāng Qǐyì Jìniànguǎn; 380 Zhongshan Lu; admission Y15) houses wartime paraphernalia.

Places to Stay

Xiàngshān Fàndiàn (☎ 678 1402, fax 677 1015, 222 Xiangshan Beilu) Dorm beds Y56, triples with bath Y156, twins Y160-260. Rooms here are cheap but run-down, with tacky green carpets. It's a bit far from the bus and train stations. Take bus No 5 for nine stops from the train station; the bus stop is diagonally opposite the hotel entrance. There's no English sign, but look for a courtyard and the hotel disco (Y28), which the staff say is popular.

Nánchāng Bīnguǎn (☎ 621 9698, fax 622 3193, 16 Bayi Dadao) Twins/triples Y165/198. This is a massive two-star hotel with clean, comfortable rooms. It's at the Fushan roundabout, close to the train and bus stations.

Póyánghú Dàjiǔdiàn (☎ 647 1188, fax 647 1177, 1128 Jinggang Shan Dadao) Twins Y180-295, triples Y180. This hotel, on the roundabout's south-western side, is plush, with marble floors and an exercise room. All rooms have private bath.

Jiāngxī Fàndiàn (☎ *621 2123, fax 621 4126, 356 Bayi Dadao*) Twins Y180-200, older triples behind building Y180. This reasonable three-star hotel has cosy, elegant rooms, a restaurant and a business centre.

Qīngshānhú Bīnguǎn (☎ *622 1162, fax 622 1447, 169 Fuzhou Lu*) Singles or doubles Y230-690. Nánchāng's most well-appointed, four-star hotel features a bar, sauna and swimming pool, shops, and Western and Chinese restaurants. It's across from the north entrance of Rénmín Gōngyuán.

Places to Eat

As usual, the train station area is good for cheap eats. For street snacks try *xiànbǐng* (fried pancakes stuffed with vegetables). The ones cooked in electric fryers are less oily than the deep-fried variety.

The adventurous seekers of local cuisine may want to eat under the Fushan roundabout, where entrepreneurs with woks and tricycles fry up tasty meat, tofu and other vegetable dishes for Y3, and you can sit at tables in the street.

Shíshén Fànzhuāng (☎ *629 7799, 191 Ruzi Lu*) Dishes Y15-40. This rustic Jiāngxī restaurant serves spicy specialties like *kèjiājiǔ zāoyú* (fish stewed in white wine) and *cōngyóuluòbǐng* (fried green onion pancake).

Zìzài Xuāngān Sīlóu (☎ *625 5537, 147 Supu Lu*) Dishes Y5-40. Chinese dishes are served in the ground floor cafeteria, the 2nd-floor restaurant, and on the top floor, where there's casual, open-air dining.

Several Western-style restaurants and bars congregate on Bayi Dadao, just south of the Martyrs of the Revolution memorial. The fast-food restaurant *Donald's Burger* (*Duōlé Hànbǎo;* ☎ *678 2702, 345 Bayi Dadao*) has coffee (Y18) and ice cream (Y15).

Getting There & Away

Air The main office of the Civil Aviation Administration of China (CAAC; Zhōngguó Mínháng; ☎ 627 8246) is at 37 Beijing Xilu, near the People's Square, but the Fushan roundabout and Zhanqian Lu near the train station also have travel agencies. China Eastern Airlines (☎ 627 0881) is at 87 Minde Lu.

The new Chāngběi airport is 28km north of the city. Flights go to Běijīng (Y1256), Guǎngzhōu (Y696), Hong Kong (Y1370), Kūnmíng (Y1296), Níngbō (Y440), Shànghǎi (Y704), Wēnzhōu (Y640) and Xī'ān (Y810).

Bus Nánchāng's long-distance bus station (kèyùn zhōngxīn) is on Bayi Dadao, between the People's Square and the Fushan roundabout. Air-con buses go twice a day to Chángshā (Y75 to Y82, eight hours), Jiǔjiāng (Y35, 1½ hours) and the porcelain-

producing centre of Jǐngdézhèn (Y32, 6½ hours). There are also buses to Jǐnggāng Shān (Y60 to Y74, nine hours) in Jiāngxī's south-western mountains, Lúshān (Y37, 2½ hours) to the north and Guǎngzhōu (Y135, 15 hours). The bus station is open daily from 4am to 10pm.

Minibuses to Jiǔjiāng (Y20) run throughout the day and depart from the train station. Tickets for sleeper buses to various destinations, such as Guǎngzhōu (18 hours) or Shēnzhèn (20 hours) are available on the right as you exit the train station.

Train Nánchāng lies off the main Guǎngzhōu-Shànghǎi railway line, but most trains make the detour north via the city. There are direct trains to Fúzhōu (Y100, 10 hours) once daily. Express trains run daily to Jiǔjiāng (Y22, 2½ hours), although the freeway makes it quicker and cheaper to do the trip by bus.

Boat The small Nanchang Ferry Terminal (☎ 681 2251) is south of the two Bāyī Bridges. An alternate route to Jǐngdézhèn is to catch a 6.30am boat across the lake Póyáng Hú to Bōyáng (Y26, seven hours), then a bus to Jǐngdézhèn (Y8, two hours). There are daily fast boats (Y61, three hours) at 8am and 2pm. In summer, tourist cruise boats also leave from here.

Getting Around

Buses to the airport (Y15, 40 minutes) leave from the main CAAC office. A taxi will cost about Y100.

From the train station, the most useful public transport routes are bus No 2, which goes up Bayi Dadao past the long-distance bus station, and bus No 5, which runs north along Xiangshan Beilu. Motor-tricycles and meter taxis are available.

JǏNGDÉZHÈN 景德镇
☎ 0798 • pop 1,404,700

An ancient town with many narrow streets and wooden buildings, Jǐngdézhèn manufactures the country's much-coveted porcelain. The city continues to be a major ceramics producer and attracts numerous buyers, especially from Hong Kong and Singapore.

Mass production may be compromising quality so purchasing good items depends on which factory made the porcelain and how much money you want to spend. The process of making fine porcelain dates back to the Song dynasty and is quite fascinating to observe.

The city has some charming back alleys but chimney stacks belching out coal from firing kilns dominate the city skyline, making the outskirts depressing.

In the 12th century the Song dynasty fled south after an invasion from the north. The

CENTRAL CHINA

NÁNCHĀNG

PLACES TO STAY
2 Xiàngshān Fàndiàn
  象山宾馆
7 Qīngshānhú Bīnguǎn
  青山湖宾馆
11 Jiāngxī Fàndiàn
  江西饭店
23 Nánchāng Bīnguǎn
  南昌宾馆
25 Póyánghú Dàjiǔdiàn
  鄱阳湖大酒店

PLACES TO EAT
9 Donald's Burger
  多乐汉堡
12 Zìzài Xuāngǎn Sīlóu
  自在轩感思楼
16 Shíshén Fànzhuāng
  食神饭庄

OTHER
1 Nánchāng Ferry Terminal
  南昌港客运站

3 Yòumín Sì
  佑民寺
4 Dàitán Internet
  因特网吧
5 Residence of Zhou
  Enlai & Zhu De
  周恩来和朱德旧居
6 China Eastern Airlines
  中国东方航空公司
8 CITS; Jiangxi
  International Tour &
  Aviation Corporation
  中国国际旅行社
10 Memorial Hall to the
  Martyrs of the Revolution
  革命烈士纪念馆
13 PSB
  公安局外事科
14 Téngwáng Gé
  腾王阁
15 Former Headquarters of
  the Nanchang Uprising
  八一南昌起义纪念馆

17 Xinhua Bookshop
  新华书店
18 People's Square
  人民广场
19 Exhibition Hall
  展览馆
20 CAAC
  中国民航
21 Post Office
  邮电局
22 Long-Distance
  Bus Station
  长途汽车站
24 Main Bank of China
  中国银行
26 Minibuses to Jiǔjiāng
  往九江小型车
27 Train Station
  火车站

CENTRAL CHINA

JǏNGDÉZHÈN

PLACES TO STAY
1 Jǐngdézhèn Bīnguǎn
  景德镇宾馆
9 Jǐngdézhèn Jīnshèng
  Dàjiǔdiàn
  景德镇金盛大酒店
12 Liángyǒu Bīnguǎn
  良友宾馆
15 Wényuàn Dàfàndiàn
  文苑大饭店

PLACES TO EAT
3 Xiǎomáquè Jiǔdiàn
  小麻雀酒店
5 Xiǎomáquè Jiǔdiàn
  小麻雀酒店

OTHER
2 CITS
  中国国际旅行社
4 Museum of Porcelain
  陶瓷馆
6 CAAC Ticket Office
  中国民航
7 Xinhua Bookshop
  新华书店
8 Porcelain Friendship
  Store
  友谊商店
10 Post Office
  邮电局
11 Zhōngkē Diànnǎo
  (Internet)
  中科电脑网吧

13 Porcelain Market
  陶瓷市场
14 Bank of China
  中国银行
16 Train Station; Long-
  Distance Bus Station
  火车站;长途汽车站
17 Long-Distance Bus
  Station
  长途汽车站
18 Main Bank of China
  邮电局
19 Museum of Ceramic
  History; Ancient
  Pottery Factory
  陶瓷历史博物馆;
  古窑瓷厂

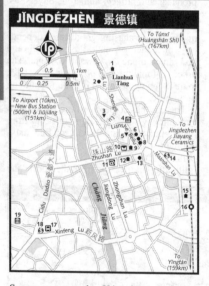

Song court moved to Hángzhōu and the imperial potters moved to Jǐngdézhèn, near Gāolǐng village and the rich supply of Gāolǐng clay. The area also started producing pottery because locals noticed the clay's strength. Folk artists and rivers in the area assisted with production and transportation.

Today, the ceramics industry employs about 60% of Jǐngdézhèn's residents.

Orientation

Most of Jǐngdézhèn is flat and lies on the eastern bank of Cháng Jiāng. The main arteries are Zhongshan Lu and Zhushan Lu.

Maps are available from newspaper stands, the Xinhua Bookshop and around the bus and train stations.

Information

CITS (☎ 822 2939) at 8 Lianhuatang Lu is located in a stone building in a courtyard near Jǐngdézhèn Bīnguǎn. The post office is on Zhushan Lu. There is a Bank of China on Maanshan Lu, towards the train station. Traveller cheques are exchanged at the main branch on 448 Cidu Dadao. The Internet cafe Zhōngkē Diànnǎo (☎ 852 0227) at 50 Zhushan Lu charges Y2 per hour.

Things to See & Do

The tiny side streets leading off Zhongshan Lu, particularly those in the older area between Zhongshan Lu and the river, are good for wandering.

Porcelain and ceramic lovers will enjoy Jǐngdézhèn's museums. Exquisite bowls, vases, plates and sculptures are on display at the **Museum of Porcelain** (*Táocí Guǎn*; ☎ 822 9784 , *21 Lianshe Beilu; admission Y10; open 8am-11am & 2.30pm-5pm daily*). The collection includes pieces from the Song, Ming and Qing dynasties and the post-1949 era.

The **Museum of Ceramic History** (*Táocí Lìshǐ Bówùguǎn*; ☎ 852 1594; *admission Y10; open 8am-5pm daily*) is on the city's western edge. Pleasantly set amidst bamboo groves, its stone-and-wood structures display a few pieces taken from ancient kiln sites. Potters are at work in the various workshops. There's a teahouse in the back near a lake.

Next to the museum, the **Ancient Pottery Factory** (*Gǔyáo Cíchǎng;* ☎ 851 6124; admission Y10; open 8am-5pm daily) is a workshop where craftsmen demonstrate the traditional Qing and Ming porcelain-making technology of moulding and baking.

The process takes about four days and has remained virtually unchanged since its inception. The ancient structures make it fascinating to watch, even though the factory is touristy.

To get there take bus No 3 past the long-distance bus station to the terminus near Cidu Dadao. Walk under the stone gate and follow the road through forest and tea groves for about 800m to the museum entrance. From the city centre, a taxi will cost about Y10.

There are **pottery factories** throughout the city, some of which were government run.

One small factory known for good quality duplicates from the Yuan, Ming and Qing dynasties is **Jingdezhen Jiayang Ceramics** (*Jiāyáng Táocí Yǒuxiàn Gōngsī;* ☎ 844 1200, 356 Chaoyang Lu; admission free; open 8am-6pm daily), in the city's eastern suburbs. Vice Director Huang Yun Peng is the porcelain expert here. You'll need to take a taxi (Y8) to get there.

To better understand porcelain, CITS has helpful English-speaking guides. A half-day tour costs Y100 and is worth it. Tours may include the city's museums, the Art Porcelain Factory (Yìshù Táochǎng), the Porcelain Sculpture Factory (Měidiāo Táochǎng) or the modern Wèimín Porcelain Factory (Wèimín Táochǎng). Confirm with the CITS staff as to where you'll go because you may not see workers at all the factories.

Places to Stay
Wényuàn Dàfàndiàn (*Wen Yuan Grand Hotel;* ☎ 822 4898, Xinfeng Lu) Singles/doubles Y65/90. This inappropriately named hotel is next to the station. There are cheaper rooms, but the staff may refuse to rent them to you. If you're a good negotiator, a bed in a spartan triple is Y40.

Jǐngdézhèn Jīnshèng Dàjiǔdiàn (☎ 823 2728, 29 Zhushan Lu) Twins Y120-190. This is a reasonable, central hotel with clean, attractive rooms. It's a 10-minute walk from the train station. Bus No 1 also runs close by.

Liángyǒu Bīnguǎn (☎ 821 9808, 8 Zhushan Lu) Twins Y198-288. This new

hotel has bright, attractive rooms. It usually attracts business travellers. From the street entrance, walk for about five minutes bearing left to get to the lobby.

Jǐngdézhèn Bīnguǎn (☎ 822 5010, fax 822 6416, 60 Fengjin Lu) Twins Y280-480 with refrigerator & air-con. This three-star guesthouse is near a quiet lake park, about 15 minutes' walk from the town centre. Porcelain-buyers often stay in the hotel and it has restaurants, a post office and a money-changing counter.

Places to Eat
There is no shortage of cheap eats in Jǐngdézhèn, particularly the tasty thick rice noodles known locally as *liángbàn mǐfěn*. At night there's a lively *market area* with restaurants near the Xinhua Bookshop.

Xiǎomàquè Jiǔdiàn (☎ 822 3615, 67 Shengli Lu; ☎ 823 6777, 5 Lianshe Beilu) Dishes Y8-32. This restaurant has two branches; the one on Lianshe Lu specialises in Beijing duck and seafood.

Shopping
Porcelain is sold everywhere, piled on pavements, lined up on street stalls and tucked away in antique shops, particularly those on Lianshe Beilu, towards the museum.

Porcelain Friendship Store (*Yǒuyì Shāngdiàn; 13 Zhushan Lu*) There is a good selection of vases, teapots, and ceramic figures here, but prices are more expensive.

The *market* on the same road as Jǐngdézhèn Jīnshèng Dàjiǔdiàn is a good alternative. Huge blue and white summer teapots sell for Y15 or you can purchase a 2m-high mega-vase for Y1000 and up. Also worth checking out are the hand-painted *cíbǎn* (tiles) that come in a variety of sizes and prices. Dinner sets are also a bargain, ranging from Y60 to Y90.

Getting There & Away
Jǐngdézhèn is a bit of a transportation bottle-neck, but the situation has improved with the Luójiā airport and expanded bus service.

Air Luójiā airport is 10km north-west of the city. There is a CAAC ticket office on Lianshe Beilu just up from the Xinhua Bookshop. Flights only go to Shànghǎi (Y460), Guǎngzhōu (Y790) and Běijīng (Y1140).

Bus In the north of town, the long-distance bus station *(kèyūn zhōngxīn)* has services to Yīngtán (Y25, four hours), Jiŭjiāng (Y25, 4½ hours) and Nánchāng (Y32, 6½ hours), as well as Shànghăi (Y88, 16 hours) and Hángzhōu (Y60, 10 hours). There is an express bus to Jiŭjiāng (Y40, 1½ hrs). Buses to Túnxī (Huángshān Shì) take about four hours (Y30). Another long-distance bus station near the train station has similar routes.

Train Jĭngdézhèn train station is like a deserted crypt, and there is little in the way of tickets available either. Everything but hard-seat tickets, which should suffice for short hauls, is reserved for those with connections with the ticket sellers.

For longer trips, it may be worth calling CITS, where you can organise hard-sleeper and soft-sleeper tickets, although you may have to book a few days in advance.

If you're heading north there are trains to Shànghăi (Y122, 17 hours) and Nánjīng (Y86, seven hours) via Túnxī, the gateway to legendary Huáng Shān (Y13, four hours) and Wúhú (Y31, five hours).

There is train service to Nánchāng (Y22, 5½ hours), but for better connections, go to the railway junction at Yīngtán (Y12, three hours).

Getting Around

There is no direct bus to the airport, but a taxi should cost Y30 from the city centre. Bus No 3 crawls at a snail's pace from the south long-distance bus station to the town centre, along Zhushan Lu. Taxis are reasonable, but you may have to bargain. There are also pedicabs, motor-tricycles and motorcycles for hire. A taxi to the new bus station should be Y5.

JIŬJIĀNG 九江
☎ 0792 • pop 4,376,900

Jiŭjiāng is a stopover on the road to Lúshān; if you're travelling from Nánchāng, you can safely miss the city by taking a bus directly to Lúshān. Travellers arriving in Jiŭjiāng by ferry from Chóngqìng or Shànghăi may need to stay overnight.

Situated close to Póyáng Hú, which drains into Cháng Jiāng, Jiŭjiāng has been a port since ancient times. Once a leading market town for tea and rice in southern China, it opened to foreign trade in 1862. The city

eventually developed into a port serving nearby Húběi and Ānhuī. Today Jiŭjiāng is a medium-sized city, second in importance to Nánchāng on a provincial level.

Orientation

Jiŭjiāng stretches along the southern bank of Cháng Jiāng. Two interconnected lakes divide the older north-eastern part of the city from a newer industrial sprawl to the south. The long-distance bus station is on the city's eastern side, the train station is on the city's southern edge and the main river port is conveniently close to the heart of town.

Information

There's a friendly CITS office (☎ 821 5793) at 28 Nanhu Lu on the 2nd floor of a building in the courtyard of disused Nánhú Bīnguăn. China Travel Service (CTS; Zhōngguó Lǚxíngshè; ☎ 813 7788) is more centrally located at 6 Xunyang Lu. The main Bank of China is at 52 Xunyang Lu, east of Nánmén Hú (South Gate Lake) at the intersection of Nanhu Lu and Xunyang Lu. The post office is close to the intersection of Jiaotong Lu and Xunyang Lu. Hóng Internet (Hóng Wăngbā; ☎ 813 3076) on the 3rd floor at 1 Huancheng Lu charges Y2 per hour for Internet access.

Things to See

Small **Néngrén Sì** *(Benevolent Temple; Yuliang Nanlu)* has a disused Yuan dynasty pagoda and garden. About 20 monks returned to the temple in 1988 after it closed during the Cultural Revolution. On the same street, at the corner of Gantang Nanlu, is an old Catholic church that reopened in 1984.

On a tiny island in Gāntáng Hú, **Misty Water Pavilion** *(Yānshuĭ Tíng; ☎ 822 2168; admission Y5; open 8am-10pm daily)* was most recently rebuilt during the Qing dynasty by a monk. It's near the town centre and a bridge connects it to the shore. A small museum contains some interesting photographs of Jiŭjiāng during the treaty port days.

Places to Stay

Zhígōng Dàshà (☎ 811 1918, 44 Jiaotong Lu) Beds in quads/singles/doubles Y20/40/50. One inexpensive place is super basic Zhígōng Dàshà. As you leave the

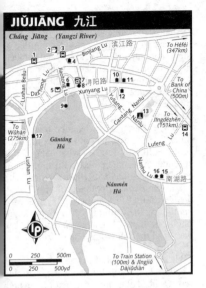

JIǓJIĀNG 九江

Cháng Jiāng (Yangzi River)

To Héféi (347km)

To Bank of China (500m)

To Jǐngdézhèn (151km)

To Wǔhàn (275km)

Gāntáng Hú

Nánmén Hú

To Train Station (100m) & Jǐngjiǔ Dàjiǔdiàn

0   250   500m
0   250   500yd

JIǓJIĀNG

PLACES TO STAY
4   Jiǔjiāng Dàjiǔdiàn
    九江大酒店
6   Zhígōng Dàshà
    职工大厦
10 Lúshān Bīnguǎn
    庐山宾馆
11 Kuānglú Bīnguǎn
    匡庐宾馆
12 Báilù Bīnguǎn
    白鹿宾馆
15 Jiǔjiāng Bīnguǎn
    九江宾馆
17 Jiǔlóng Bīnguǎn;
    CAAC
    九龙宾馆;
    中国民航

OTHER
1   Minibuses to
    Nánchāng
    往南昌小型车

2   Cháng Jiāng Ferry
    Terminal
    轮船客运码头
3   Minibuses to Lúshān
    往庐山小型车
5   Post Office
    邮局
7   Hóng Internet
    红网吧
8   CTS
    中国旅行社
9   Misty Water Pavilion;
    Museum
    烟水亭; 博物馆
13 Néngrén Sì
    能仁寺
14 Long-Distance Bus
    Station
    长途汽车站
16 CITS; Nánhú Bīnguǎn
    中国国际旅行社;
    南湖宾馆

CENTRAL CHINA

ferry terminal, it's a five-minute walk south down Jiaotong Lu.

Jiǔjiāng Dàjiǔdiàn (☎ 898 8333, fax 898 8000, 388 Dazhong Lu) Twins/triples Y200/ 285 with air-con. A short walk east of the ferry terminal, this place is clean and spacious. Discounts of up to 25% are available and their shabbier twins often go for Y150.

Most of the hotels are clustered on Xunyang Lu, about 10 minutes' walk from the ferry terminal.

Kuānglú Bīnguǎn (☎ 822 8893, fax 822 1249, 88 Xunyang Lu) Singles/twins Y100/ 110, triplesY160-210. This clean, modern hotel with 'Roman decor' has great deals.

Lúshān Bīnguǎn (☎ 813 2570, 294 Xunyang Lu) Singles/twins Y220/320. Next door to the Kuānglú Bīnguǎn, rooms at this hotel are less appealing. Up to 60% discounts are sometimes available.

Báilù Bīnguǎn (White Deer Hotel; ☎ 822 2818, fax 822 1915, 133 Xunyang Lu) Twins Y285-365, suites Y485. Across the street from Kuānglú Bīnguǎn is this Chinese version of a three-star luxury hotel. Báilù Bīnguǎn also has tours to Lúshān – see the following Lúshān section for details.

Jiǔlóng Bīnguǎn (☎ 823 6779, fax 822 8634, 75 Lushan Lu) Twins/triples Y220/240. On the west side of Gāntáng Hú, this hotel has clean, standard rooms. Try bargaining for cheaper rates.

Jiǔjiāng Bīnguǎn (☎ 856 0018, fax 856 6677, 30 Nanhu Lu) Standard twins Y380, suites Y500-1280. On the south-eastern shore of Nánmén Hú, this comfortable three-star is the city's best hotel. Foreigners pay a Y100 surcharge.

Jīngjiǔ Dàjiǔdiàn (☎ 856 5918, 366 Changhong Lu) Beds in triples Y30, triples with shared bath Y90, twins with bath Y168. If you arrive late at night by train, this hotel offers inexpensive and clean rooms. It's about a 10-minute walk east of the station.

Getting There & Away
Air Jiǔjiāng's airport closed in 1999, so the closest airport is Nánchāng's Chāngběi airport. There are no direct buses there from Jiǔjiāng; travellers will have to first travel to Nánchāng.

Bus Minibuses for Lúshān leave frequently from the car park next to the ferry terminal. Scheduled public buses to Lúshān leave from the long-distance bus station between 7.30am and 1.30pm. The fare for all Lúshān buses is about Y10.

Several hotels offer guided one-day tours of Lúshān for Y100. You can buy tickets for the same tour from the parking lot in front of the ferry terminal.

Minibuses depart for Jǐngdézhèn (Y25) every half-hour from the long-distance bus station. The 4½-hour trip includes a short ferry ride across Póyáng Hú. There are frequent buses to Nánchāng (Y25, 1½ hours) and to Wǔhàn (Y65, four hours), among other places.

Minibuses to Nánchāng (Y35, 1½ hours) can also be picked up at the car park in front of the ferry terminal and at the train station.

Train There are several Jiǔjiāng-Nánchāng express trains each day (Y22, 1½ hours). Jiǔjiāng's train station is in the city's southern section.

The train to Héféi in Ānhuī province takes four hours.

Boat Most long-distance boats plying the Cháng Jiāng stop in Jiǔjiāng. Tickets upriver to Chóngqìng (10 hours) cost Y700 (2nd class), Y295 (3rd class) and Y215 (4th class); downriver fares to Shànghǎi are Y285 (2nd class), Y147 (3rd class) and Y106 (4th class). First class exists only on the Wǔhàn to Chóngqìng route.

Getting Around
Bus No 1 and minibuses (Y1) ply the route between Xunyang Lu, the long-distance bus station, the Bank of China and the train station. Pedicabs and motor-tricycles are at the bus and train stations and the dock. The fare is around Y3 but this can be negotiated.

LÚSHĀN 庐山
☎ 0792
European and American settlers in the late 19th century established Lúshān, or Kuling as English speakers called it, as a refreshing escape from lowland China's hot and sweaty summers.

They left a fascinating hotchpotch of colonial buildings, from stone cottages reminiscent of southern Germany to small French-style churches and more grandiose hotels built in classical Victorian style.

Lúshān can be cold and shrouded in heavy fog, and tourists swarm the area in summer. But on the right day, the fog can make for a picturesque blanket over the town. If you arrive on a clear, uncrowded day, stay for some trekking and fresh mountain air.

For the Chinese, Lúshān is rich with significance. Its mountain vistas have been the subject of poems and paintings, and it has seen some historical, epoch-making events.

China's post-1949 revolutionaries found Lúshān's cool uplands ideal for Party conferences. In 1959 the Central Committee of the Communist Party held its fateful meeting, which eventually ended in Peng Dehuai's dismissal, sent Mao almost into a political wilderness and provided the seeds for the rise and fall of Liu Shaoqi and Deng Xiaoping.

In 1970, after Mao regained power, another meeting was held in Lúshān, this time of the Politburo. Exactly what happened is shrouded in as much mist as the mountains, but it seems that Lin Biao clashed with Mao, opposed his policies of *rapprochement* with the USA and probably proposed continuing the Cultural Revolution's xenophobic policies. Whatever happened, Lin was dead the following year.

Orientation & Information
The arrival point in Lúshān is the charming resort village of Gǔlǐng, perched 1167m high at the range's northern end. Two kilometres before Gǔlǐng is the entrance gate (☎ 828 3627), where you must pay a Y51 fee.

Gǔlǐng village has shops and restaurants, a post office, bank, Internet cafes and the long-distance bus station. Scores of tourist hotels, sanatoriums and factory work-units' holiday hostels sit in the surrounding hills.

CITS (☎ 828 2497), uphill from Lúshān Bīnguǎn, is well organised and helpful.

Detailed maps showing roads and walking tracks are available from shops and hawkers in Gǔlǐng.

Things to See
Lúshān has enough attractions to keep you there for a couple of days. While it costs Y10 to visit most tourist attractions, an alternative is to skip these and explore the mountain roads and paths on your own.

Built by Chiang Kaishek in the 1930s as a summer getaway, **Měilú Villa** (*Měilú Biéshù; 180 Hedong Lu; admission Y15; open 8am-6pm daily*) was named after the general's wife, Song Meiling. It's not a particularly grand house but interesting to visit. Although the original gardens were probably more spacious and better maintained than today, the villa has been kept much as it was. There are interesting items on display, like the kerosene-operated American fridge.

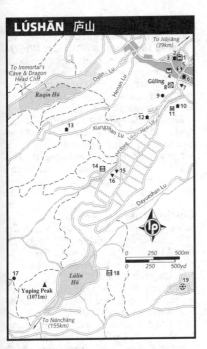

LÚSHĀN 庐山

LÚSHĀN

PLACES TO STAY & EAT
2 Lúshān Fàndiàn
   庐山饭店
6 Gǔlǐng Fàndiàn
   牯岭饭店
7 Zuìshí Dàjiǔdian
   醉石酒家
10 Lúshān Biéshù Cūn
   庐山别墅村
12 Lúshān Bīnguǎn
   庐山宾馆
13 Yúnzhōng Bīnguǎn
   云中宾馆
15 Lúshān Fēngwèi Shānzhuāng
   庐山风味山庄
16 Zhēngfǔ Fàndiàn

OTHER
1 Long-Distance Bus Station
   长途汽车站
3 Jiēxīn Gōngyuán
   街心公园
4 Post Office; Bank
   邮局；银行
5 Bank of China
   中国银行
8 Qīngchéng Internet
   倾城网吧
9 CITS
   中国国际旅行社
11 Měilú Villa
   美庐别墅
14 People's Hall
   人民剧院
17 Three Ancient Trees
   三宝树
18 Lushan Museum
   博物馆
19 Botanical Gardens
   植物园

The **People's Hall** (*Rénmín Jùyuàn; 504 Hexi Lu; admission Y10; open 8am-5.30pm daily*), built in 1936 and the venue for the Communist Party's historic 1959 and 1970 get-togethers, is now a museum. On display are photos of Mao, Zhou and other Party elite taking it easy between meetings.

At Lúshān's north-western rim, the land falls away abruptly to give some spectacular views across Jiāngxī's densely settled plains. A long walking track south around these precipitous slopes passes the **Immortal's Cave** (*Xiānrén Dòng*) and continues to **Dragon Head Cliff** (*Lóngshǒu Yá*), a natural rock platform tilted above a vertical drop of hundreds of metres.

Chinese visitors enjoy the **Three Ancient Trees** (*Sānbǎoshù*), not far by foot from Lúlín Hú. Five hundred years ago Buddhist monks planted a gingko and two cedar trees near their temple. Tourists used to climb the branches to have their photos taken, but a fence now protects the trees.

The **Lushan Museum** (*Lúshān Bówùguǎn*; ☎ 828 2341, 1 Lulin Lu; admission Y10; open 8am-5.30pm daily*) is housed in Mao's drab former residence, beside Lúlín Hú. A photo collection commemorates the historic 1970 Communist Party meeting. Scrolls and inscribed steles displaying Li Bai's poetry and calligraphy are also visible. Unfortunately, the English explanations are limited.

The **Botanical Gardens** (*Zhíwù Yuán*; ☎ 707 9828; admission Y10; open 7.30am-5.30pm daily*) is mainly devoted to sub-alpine tropical plants that thrive in the cooler highland climate. In the open gardens there are rhododendrons, camellias and conifers.

Organised Tours

From Jiǔjiāng, return day trips cost Y100 and give you about five hours in Lúshān; Báilù Bīnguǎn in Jiǔjiāng gives tours. Tours normally include pavilions, a nature hike and the museum and are more enjoyable if you bring a friend.

Places to Stay

Hotel prices vary according to season. During the low season (from October to May), when it's cold, drizzly and miserable, few people stay overnight and there are better deals.

In the height of summer, budget travellers can forget about Lúshān – it's probably cheaper to do a day trip from Jiǔjiāng, unless you want to be based on the mountain.

Most places open to foreigners are more upmarket, but it's worth checking around Gǔlǐng for a bargain; locals will approach you. You can also book villa accommodation through CITS.

Lúshān Fàndiàn (☎ *828 2861, 1044 Zhengjie)* Twins Y120-160, triples Y300. In the town centre, this hotel has the best deals. Rooms are nice but the bathrooms are a tad dank.

Gǔlǐng Fàndiàn (☎ *828 2200, fax 828 2209, 104 Hedong Lu)* Twins with bath Y200/400 low/high season. This centrally located two-star hotel, also in Gǔlǐng village, used to be reasonable, but prices have increased. They may rent a single bed for Y100 during the low season.

These hotels are a short walk from Gǔlǐng.

Lúshān Bīnguǎn (☎ *828 2060, fax 828 2843, 446 Hexi Lu)* Twins Y260-580. This large three-star colonial-era hotel is now managed as a joint venture. Discounts of up to 40% are sometimes available.

Lúshān Biéshù Cūn (☎ *828 2927, fax 828 8946, 182 Hedong Lu)* Suites Y480-3000. This place has cottages scattered throughout a lovely old pine forest. Discounts of up to 20% are available.

Yúnzhōng Bīnguǎn (☎ *828 5420, fax 828 2853, 49 Xiangshan Lu)* Rooms Y360-3000. Yúnzhōng Bīnguǎn rents villas as well as rooms in villas.

Lúshān Fēngwèi Shānzhuāng (*see Places to Eat later)* Rooms Y30-100. Farther away, this restaurant/hotel has basic rooms with squat toilets.

Places to Eat

Remember that Lúshān is a tourist attraction for Chinese, who like to spend big on meals; if you're on a budget, check the prices first. The restaurants listed all serve typical Chinese dishes (Y15 to Y45) and *shíjī* (Lúshān cave frog, Y60).

Zuìshí Dàjiǔdiàn (☎ *828 1531, 102 Hedong Lu)* The name of this popular restaurant means 'drunk stone' and probably alludes to the future state of the many Chinese patrons feasting and *gānbēi*'ing (draining liquor shots) inside.

Zhèngfǔ Fàndiàn (☎ *828 9938)* On the road to the People's Hall, this hotel is housed in a quaint stone building.

Lúshān Fēngwèi Shānzhuāng (☎ *828 5348)* Next door to Zhèngfǔ Fàndiàn, this place is run by Běijīng local Mr Liu and serves a delicious lemon chicken (Y28).

Getting There & Around

In summer, daily buses go to Nánchāng (Y35, two hours), Jiǔjiāng (Y7, one hour), and Wǔhàn (Y65, four hours); from November to late March direct buses to Nánchāng are sporadic.

Minibuses to Jiǔjiāng also congregate opposite the long-distance bus station on the road heading towards Jiǔjiāng.

If you like country walking, exploring Jiǔjiāng on foot is ideal. Paths and small roads crisscross Lúshān, so getting around is easy. If time is short, consider hiring a taxi to visit sights and walking back.

YĪNGTÁN 鹰潭
☎ 0792 • pop 1,025,800

Although most trains make the short detour to Nánchāng (which is north of the Shànghǎi-Guǎngzhōu railway line), you may have to catch some at Yīngtán, a railway junction town. If you're here, the river area near the old town is worth exploring. You might try getting a boat to the other side.

Places to Stay

Huáqiáo Fàndiàn (*Overseas Chinese Hotel;* ☎ *622 1344, fax 622 1149, 21 Zhanjiang Lu)* Standard twins Y288. This adequate hotel is a large 15-storey building on the main street down from the station.

There are also cheaper hotels on the same street.

Getting There & Away

The long-distance bus station is opposite the train station. There are buses to Jǐngdézhèn (Y35, four hours) and Nánchāng (Y35, 2½ hours).

There are trains from Yīngtán to Fúzhōu (9½ hours), Guǎngzhōu (16 hours), Shànghǎi (11½ hours) and Xiàmén (15 hours). Trains to Nánchāng take two hours and there is also a line to Jǐngdézhèn (2½ hours) via Guìxī.

JǏNGGĀNG SHĀN 井冈山
☎ 0792

With its tree-lined streets and misty mountain range, Jǐnggāng Shān provides a welcome respite from China's congested, noisy cities.

But from June to October Jǐnggāng Shān can be packed with tourists who come to view the area's famous mountains (some of which appear on the old Y100 note), tranquil waterfalls and Red Army war sites.

Historically, this remote 500-peak region in Luóxiāo Shān (Clouds on Display Mountains) along the Húnán-Jiāngxī border played a crucial role in the early Communist movement. It's been dubbed the 'Cradle of the Chinese Revolution'.

After suffering a string of defeats in an urban-based revolution, Mao led 900 men into these hills in 1927. Other companies of the battered Communist army led by Zhu De joined them a year later. From here, Mao launched the 'Long March' into Shaanxi.

Orientation & Information

Cípíng (also called Jǐnggāng Shān), the main township, is nestled around a small lake in the mountains, 820m above the sea. Hotels, restaurants and the bus station are within easy walking distance.

The local China Travel Service (CTS; Zhōngguó Lǚxíngshè; ☎ 655 6788) is on 2 Tianjie Lu, across from Jǐnggāngshān Bīnguǎn. Some English is spoken here. The Bank of China is on 6 Nanshan Lu on the lake's south-eastern end.

Emergency phone numbers, including the PSB (☎ 655 2360) and medical help (☎ 655 2595), are listed on roadside signs.

For an English-language tourist brochure (Y3) or a map showing hiking trails in the hills (Y2), try the Xinhua Bookshop in the Cuihu Hotel on Hongjun Nanlu. Hotels also sell maps.

Local companies give tours – expect them to knock on your door. Your hotel may be able to help you hire a van for about Y100 to tour major sites, but be careful of overcharging. CTS provides tours for Y300.

Things to See

Jǐnggāng Shān is a major scenic area with large expanses of natural highland forest and numerous attractions devoted to the civil war. The area has square-stemmed bamboo and some 26 kinds of alpine azaleas that bloom from late April.

At **Five Dragon Pools** (*Wǔlóng Tán;* ☎ 655 6937; admission Y25; open 7am-6pm daily), 7km north-west of town, five cascading waterfalls, as well as vista points and well-marked cement paths, make for a refreshing day-long trek. There's also a cave that Communist troops used as a hospital during the civil war.

If you start early, you'll avoid the tourist onslaught. The total hike can take six hours (three hours each way) and there are signs in English. There is also a cable car (Y50 return).

A reliable transportation option is to hire a van to take you there early in the morning and pick you up in the afternoon. A few sporadic minibuses (Y3) leave from the bus station.

The watching post, **Huángyángjiè** (*admission Y7; open 7am-6pm daily*), sits to the west. At 1300m above sea level, the mountainous scenic area offers stunning views on a clear day. In 1928 the outnumbered Red Army defended the area from nationalist attacks.

Standing 1438m above sea level, **Five Fingers Peak** (*Wǔzhǐ Fēng; admission Y20; open 7am-6pm daily*) is to the south – it features on the back of the old Y100 banknote. Five Dragon Pool has better hiking paths though.

The **Jinggangshan Revolutionary Museum** (*Jǐnggāngshān Gémìng Bówùguǎn;* ☎ 655 2248, 12 Hongjun Nanlu; admission Y8; open 8am-5.30pm daily) is devoted to the Kuomintang and Communists' struggle for control of the Húnán-Jiāngxī area in the late 1920s. Explanations are in Chinese, but the collection is visual enough. A sign in the museum forbids 'spitting and laughing'.

The **Former Revolutionary Quarters** (*Gémìng Jiùzhǐqún; Tongmu Linglu; admission Y5; open 8am-6pm daily*) is a reconstruction of the mud-brick building that served as a Communist command centre between 1927 and 1928, and where Mao lived temporarily.

The town has a **Sculpture Park** *(Diāosù Yuán; ☎ 655 5937, Wugang Lu; admission Y20)*, but the entrance fee is steep unless you like statues of young Communist martyrs.

Adventurous trekkers can venture into the surrounding mountains for self-guided walks on dirt trails. Local maps from the Xinhua Bookshop show trails but are mediocre. You'll have to ask locals where they start.

Places to Stay & Eat

Just about every building in town is a hotel, but only the expensive ones officially accept foreigners. A couple of hotels are willing to unofficially accept foreigners.

As you exit the long-distance bus station, turn left and make a sharp right along Tongmu Linglu, where hotels range from Y45 to Y200 per night.

Yuándǐng Bīnguǎn (☎ 655 2246, 10 Tongmu Linglu) Twins Y180, beds in twins/triples/quads Y70/60/45. First in line on the main street, rooms here are basic and have squat toilets.

Jǐnggāngshān Fàndiàn (☎ 655 2328, 1 Xinshi Chang Lu) Twins Y180-240. A few doors down, clean, basic rooms in this hotel used to be reasonable but prices have gone up.

Túshūguǎn Zhaòdàisuǒ (☎ 655 2276, 22 Hongjun Beilu) Singles or twins Y40-80. Dorm-like rooms with bath are a fantastic deal here, but the staff doesn't speak English. It's a ten-minute walk from the bus station, just past the lake and to the right of a school. Look for a white sign with red lettering.

Jǐnggāngshān Bīnguǎn (☎ 655 2272, fax 655 2551, 10 Hongjun Beilu) Twins Y280-680. A little farther down on the same road, this is where the Party top brass chose to stay – Mao Zedong, Lin Biao, Deng Xiaoping and Li Peng have all stayed here. This hotel is expensive, and there is a mind-boggling variety of rooms and villas. The hotel will be on your left. There's no English sign.

Jǐnggāngshān Dàshà (Jinggangshan Plaza; ☎ 655 2251, fax 655 2428, 31

Hongjun Beilu) Twins or triples Y200-320. Farther down the road from Jǐnggāngshān Bīnguǎn is another monolithic enterprise. This is a huge stone villa. A sign also refers to the hotel as the Jinggangshan Grand Hotel. It's popular with tour groups on government-sponsored jaunts, and rooms are often unavailable. Prices go up by about 20% during the high season. The rooms are stately.

There are good cheap *restaurants* on the main street down from the bus station. The restaurant in Yuándǐng Bīnguǎn is cheap and serves tasty food. For something a bit more romantic, try the place on the island in the middle of the lake.

Shopping

Stalls in the town centre sell different bamboo products – some are tacky – but there are nice summer mats and comfortable rocking chairs. These products can be found all over south-central China, but the chairs are a good buy here, ranging from Y15 to Y70. Mats sell for Y90.

Getting There & Away

From Nánchāng there are direct buses to Jǐnggāng Shān each day (seven to nine hours). It's a pleasant ride with scenes of lush countryside, high bamboo fences, old stone bridges, water buffalo and flocks of ducks in rice paddies.

From Jǐnggāng Shān, there are sleeper buses to Nánchāng at 6.30am and 7.30am daily. The trip costs Y71.

It's possible to take sleeper buses at noon to Chángshā (Y70, 12 hours) and Héngyáng (Y50, 10 hours) in Húnán.

From Jǐnggāng Shān, you may have to transfer buses in Jí'ān in Jiāngxī (Y23 to Y31, three hours). If you arrive in Jí'ān from Chángshā, it's possible to go directly by bus to Jǐnggāng Shān.

Don't be confused with the Jǐnggāng Shān train station, which is in Tàihé, a town south of Jí'ān. From the Tàihé station, you'll have to take a bus or taxi to the town centre and catch a long-distance bus to Jǐnggāng Shān (three hours).

Húnán 湖南

Capital: Chángshā
Population: 70.3 million
Area: 210,000 sq km

Húnán has many notable attractions. The province occupies some of China's richest land. Between the 8th and the 11th centuries the population increased fivefold, spurred on by a prosperous agricultural industry and southerly migration. Under the Ming and Qing dynasties it was one of the empire's granaries, and vast quantities of rice were shipped to the depleted north.

By the 19th century, Húnán began to suffer from the pressure of population. Land shortage and landlordism led to widespread unrest among Chinese farmers and hill-dwelling minorities. This increasingly desperate economic situation led to the massive Taiping Rebellion of the mid-19th century and the Communist movement of the 1920s.

The Communists found strong support among Húnán's peasants and established a refuge on the mountainous Húnán-Jiāngxī border in 1927. Several prominent Communist leaders were born in Húnán. Mao Zedong, Liu Shaoqi, Peng Dehuai and Hu Yaobang. Hua Guofeng, a Shǎnxī native, became an important provincial leader in Húnán.

Most of Húnán's residents are Han Chinese, but hill-dwelling minorities occupy the border regions. They include the Miao, Tujia, Dong (a people related to the Thais and Lao) and Yao. In Húnán's far north, there's a pocket of Uyghurs.

CHÁNGSHĀ 长沙
☎ 0731 ● pop 5,719,100

The site of Chángshā has been inhabited for 3000 years. By the Warring States Period a large town had been established. The town owes its prosperity to its location on the fertile Húnán plains and on Xiāng Jiāng, where it grew as a major agricultural trading centre.

In 1904 the city opened to foreign trade as a result of the 1903 Treaty of Shanghai between Japan and China. The 'most-favoured nation' principle allowed foreigners to establish themselves in Chángshā, and large numbers of Europeans and

CENTRAL CHINA

Americans arrived to build factories, churches and schools. Yale University started a college here, which eventually became a medical centre.

Orientation

Most of Chángshā lies on the eastern bank of Xiāng Jiāng. The train station is in the city's far east. From the station, Wuyi Lu leads to the river, neatly separating the city's northern and southern sections.

From Wuyi Lu, you cross the Xiāng Jiāng bridge to the western bank, passing over Long Island (Júzi Zhōu) in the middle of the river. Most major attractions are located east of the river. City maps are on sale at kiosks around the train station and in hotel shops.

521

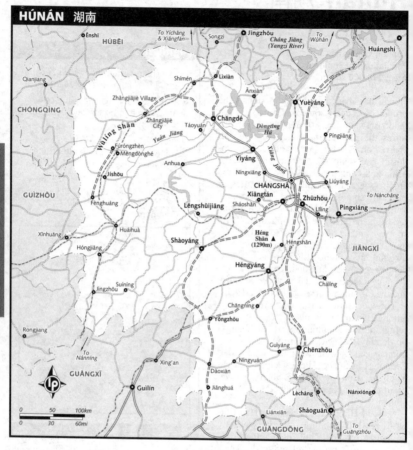

HÚNÁN 湖南

Information

Money The Bank of China (open 8.30am to 5.30pm daily) is next to the Civil Aviation Administration of China (CAAC; Zhōngguó Mínháng) office on Wuyi Donglu. You can also change money at Xiāngjiāng Bīnguǎn and Fúróng Bīnguǎn. There is an ATM in front of Xiāngjiāng Bīnguǎn.

Post & Communications The main post and China Telecom office is on Wuyi Zhonglu near the intersection of Yingbin Lu. There is another post office immediately to your right as you leave the train station.

The business centre of Huá Tiān Dàjiǔdiàn (see Places to Stay later) has Internet access for Y2 per hour, as does Láilái Internet (Láilái Wǎngbā) at 9 Chezhan Lu, next to the train station.

Travel Agencies China International Travel Service (CITS; Zhōngguó Guójì Lǚxíngshè; ☎ 228 0184) in Xiǎoyuán Dàshà is at 46 Wuyi Donglu. Its Europe and America Department (☎ 228 0439, @ citsamer @public.cs.hn.cn) has friendly, multilingual staff and is located on the 11th floor. Another CITS office where English is spoken is next to Fúróng Bīnguǎn. Most hotels can assist with transport bookings.

PSB The Public Security Bureau (PSB; Gōngānjú) is in a cream-tiled building on Huangxing Lu, at the western end of town just south of Jiefang Xilu.

Hunan Provincial Museum

Húnán Shěng Bówùguǎn 湖南省博物馆

This museum (☎ 222 4385, Dongfeng Lu; admission Y17; open 8am-noon & 2.30pm-5pm Mon-Fri, 8.30am-5pm Sat & Sun) is a 20-minute walk from Xiāngjiāng Bīnguǎn. The exhibits chronicle revolutionary history and two buildings are devoted to the 2100-year-old Western Han tombs at Mǎwángduī, some 5km east of the city, which were fully excavated by 1974.

Not to be missed are the mummified remains of a Han dynasty woman. Her preserved body, which was discovered wrapped in more than 20 layers of silk and linen, is housed in the basement. The organs have been removed and are on display. Another building houses the enormous solid outer timber casks.

Large quantities of silk garments and fabrics were found in the tomb, as well as stockings, shoes and gloves. One interesting object is a painting on silk depicting the underworld, earth and heaven. To get here, take bus No 113 or 303 from the train station.

Maoist Pilgrimage Spots

Scattered about the city are Maoist pilgrimage spots. The **Hunan No 1 Teachers' Training School** (Dìyī Shīfàn Xuéxiào; 324 Shuyuan Lu; admission Y6; open 8am-5.30pm daily) is where Mao attended classes between 1913 and 1918; he returned as a teacher and principal from 1920 to 1922. The school was destroyed during the civil war but has since been restored. Follow the arrows for a self-guided tour of Mao's dormitory, study areas, halls where he held some of his first political meetings and an open-air bathing well where he enjoyed taking cold baths. A quote from him above the well states that this was a good way to 'exercise fearlessness'.

The school is still in use, so you can see China's education system in action. To get here, take bus No 1 from the train station.

The **Former Office of the Hunan Communist Party Committee** (Zhōng Gòng Xiāngqū Wěiyuánhuì Jiùzhǐ; 480 Bayi Lu; admission Y10; open 8am-noon & 2pm-5.30pm daily) is now a museum that includes Mao's living quarters, photos, and historical items from the 1920s. Within the museum grounds there's a long wall with Mao's poems, showing his characteristic expansive brushstrokes. Take bus No 1 from the train station.

Lei Feng Memorial Museum

Léi Fēng Jìniànguǎn 雷锋纪念馆

If you're interested in communism or Communist propaganda, visit this museum (☎ 810 5014; admission Y4; open 8am-6pm daily), an hour's bus ride west of Chángshā.

Lei Feng was a soldier who the Communists lionised in 1963, one year after he died in a traffic accident at age 22, as a model worker, party member and all-round Communist citizen. His feats included washing his fellow soldiers' laundry, helping old ladies cross the street and getting people up-to-date on party doctrine.

The museum exhibits a group of photos featuring Lei smiling over a washtub of dirty socks and cartoon-like renderings of him and his parents facing down evil landlords and Japanese invaders.

To get there, take bus No 12 from the train station to the bus terminus at Róngwānzhèn. From there take bus No 315, which makes its final stop just south of the museum.

Other Sights

Yuèlù Gōngyuán (Bottom of the High Mountain Park) and **Hunan University** (Húnán Dàxué) are pleasant places to visit on the western bank of Xiāng Jiāng. The university evolved from the site of the **Yuèlù Academy** (Yuèlù Shūyuàn; Lushan Lu; admission Y14; open 8am-5pm daily), which was established during the Song dynasty for scholars to prepare for civil examinations. In 1903 the Confucian classics were replaced by more practical subjects as the Qing government attempted to reform education to foster modernisation. In 1926 Hunan University was established. The Yuèlù Academy lies on the hillside behind the Mao statue. There's a teahouse inside and a good Chinese bookshop in the back.

From the university you can hike to **Loving Dusk Pavilion** (Àiwǎn Tíng), to get a good view of the town. To get to the university, take bus No 202 from Wuyi Xilu or the train station and get off at the last stop, past the Mao statue.

The only remaining part of the old city walls is **Tiānxīn Gé** (Heart of Heaven Pavilion), off Chengnan Xilu, which is an interesting area to explore.

CHÁNGSHĀ 长沙

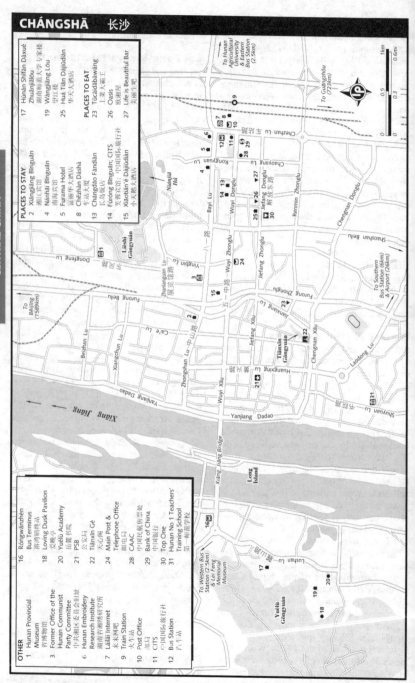

PLACES TO STAY

2	Xiāngjiāng Bīnguǎn 湘江宾馆
4	Nánhái Bīnguǎn 南海宾馆
5	Furama Hotel 华天华大酒店
8	Chēzhàn Dàshà 车站大厦
13	Chángdǎo Fàndiàn 长岛饭店
14	Fúróng Bīnguǎn; CITS 芙蓉宾馆; 中国国际旅行社
15	Xiǎotiān'é Dàjiǔdiàn 小天鹅大酒店

17	Húnán Shīfàn Dàxué Zhuānjiālóu 湖南师范大学专家楼
19	Wǎngjiāng Lóu 望江楼
25	Huá Tiān Dàjiǔdiàn 华天大酒店

PLACES TO EAT

23	Tǔcàidàbǎwáng 土家大阿王
26	Oasis 欧咪叫
27	Life is Beautiful Bar 美丽生吧

OTHER

1	Hunan Provincial Museum 省博物馆
3	Former Office of the Hunan Communist Party Committee 中共湘区委员会旧址
6	Hunan Embroidery Research Institute 湖南省湘绣研究所
7	Lailai Internet 来来网吧
9	Train Station 火车站
10	Post Office 邮电局
11	CITS 中国国际旅行社
12	Bus Station 火车站
16	Róngwǎnzhèn Bus Terminus 荣湾镇终点站
18	Loving Dusk Pavilion 爱晚亭
20	Yuèlù Academy 岳麓书院
21	PSB 公安局
22	Tiānxīn Gé 天心阁
24	Main Post & Telephone Office 邮电局
28	CAAC 中国民航(售票处)
29	Bank of China 中国银行
30	Top One
31	Hunan No 1 Teachers' Training School 第一师范学校

Places to Stay
Unhappily for independent travellers, most city hotels that accept foreigners are up-market. The cheapest option is university accommodation; the only drawback is getting there.

Húnán Shīfàn Dàxué Zhuānjiālóu (Hunan Normal University Foreign Experts' Building; ☎ 887 2211) Beds in twins with bath Y70-80. It's best to phone first because this place is often full. The university is located north of Hunan University, on the western side of the river. Take bus No 202 from Wuyi Xilu or the train station and ask the driver to let you off at shīfàn dàxué. From the university entrance, it's about a 750m slog uphill to a white building with a circular driveway. You might want to take a taxi from the entrance.

Húnán Nóngyè Dàxué Wàibīnlóu (Hunan Agricultural University Guesthouse; ☎ 461 8060) Beds in twins with bath Y60. The rooms here are pleasant and have balconies. Again, it's best to phone about vacancies. The university is located in the eastern outskirts of town, past the eastern bus station. Take bus or minibus No 110 from the south car park beside the train station. The university is the last stop, about a 40-minute ride. From the entrance, walk straight beside the playing field, turn left at the first intersection, then right and left again at the small garden circle. Go straight ahead for about 75m. At the bottom of a flight of stairs there's an English sign for the guesthouse.

Chēzhàn Dàshà (☎ 229 3366, 1 Wuyi Donglu) Twins/triples Y138/148. On the northern side of the train station, this hotel has great rooms, and the staff can book train tickets. The hotel even has a doorway to the platform, just before the exit gate. If you're taking a train, this one is hard to beat.

Nánhǎi Bīnguǎn (☎ 229 7888, fax 229 6771, 1 Rongyuan Lu) Twins Y160-220. Rooms are worn, but this convenient, friendly, navy-run hotel is in the city centre.

Xiāngjiāng Bīnguǎn (☎ 440 8888, fax 444 8285, 36 Zhongshan Lu) Twins Y160-256. You can opt for clean, simple twins or deluxe rooms at this comfortable three-star hotel. To reach it take bus No 1 from the train station.

Chángdǎo Fàndiàn (☎ 446 5133, fax 446 5157, 90 Wuyi Donglu) Twins/triples Y260/307. This hotel's brand-new rooms feature sparkling bathrooms and wood floors. A 35% discount is sometimes available.

Wàngjiāng Lóu (☎ 882 1246, fax 882 4287, Hunan University) Singles Y160, twins/triples with bath Y240/360. Far from the city centre, this quiet option is in a red-brick building on the hillside tucked behind the Yuèlù Academy. It's a good idea to phone ahead.

Fúróng Bīnguǎn (Lotus Hotel; ☎ 440 1749, fax 446 5175, 128 Wuyi Donglu) Singles/twins Y398/458. This fancy hotel offers a 30% discount on its new, clean rooms.

Furama Hotel (Fùlìhuá Dàjiǔdiàn; ☎ 229 8888, fax 229 1979, 88 Bayi Lu) Twins Y500 plus 10% service charge. This fine hotel has immaculate rooms, a pool, restaurants, a disco and shops.

Xiǎotiān'é Dàjiǔdiàn (Cygnet Hotel; ☎ 441 0400, fax 442 3698, 178 Wuyi Zhonglu) Twins Y258-458 plus 14% service charge. This hotel is a three-star joint venture. The hotel has Chinese and Western restaurants and a bowling alley.

Huá Tiān Dàjiǔdiàn (☎ 444 2888, fax 444 2270, 380 Jiefang Donglu) Standard twins/executive suites US$88/318 plus 15% service charge. Business travellers praise this five-star property as the best luxury place in town.

Places to Eat
Hunanese food uses plenty of chilli and hot spices. There are several good fast-food places on Chezhan Lu, just south of the train station, and there are *street-side stalls* at night on Chaoyang Lu, near the CAAC office.

Tǔcàidàbàwáng (☎ 222 0088, 226 Renmin Zhonglu) This serves great Hunanese dishes like *málà zǐjì* (spicy diced chicken, Y25). It's usually packed.

On Jiefang Lu, Western-style establishments offering coffee, international dishes, and imported booze compete for attention. Huá Tiān Dàjiǔdiàn's *coffee shop* has standard fare for reasonable prices.

Oasis (Ōuxiāng Wū; ☎ 411 0532, 378 Jiefang Donglu) This Taiwan-style coffee house offers set meals with tea or coffee for Y35.

Life is Beautiful Bar (Měilìshēng; ☎ 416 0716, 328 Jiefang Donglu) This dark and sultry place has steak (Y35), chips, ice cream, and Guinness beer (Y28).

The adventurous might like to sample *bīnglang* (betel nut), which is sold at street stalls. When chewed, the woody flesh, which has an overpowering, spicy-sweet taste, produces a mild, semi-narcotic effect.

Entertainment

In the new Chángshā, it's possible to check email, relax over a cup of fresh brew and then groove at a flashy disco – all within kilometres of where Mao studied and contemplated the plight of the rich and poor.

For music venues, try the bars on and around Jiefang Lu.

Top One (☎ 413 0452, 137 Jiefang Dong-lu) To boogie the night away with the fashionable set, head to this pub, the city's trendiest disco. There's no cover charge, but you have to purchase Y30 worth of drinks.

Shopping

Hunan Embroidery Research Institute (Húnánshěng Xiāngxiù Yánjiūsuǒ; ☎ 229 1821, 70 Bayi Lu) The institute has exquisite embroidered items from Y20, including pictures of sacred mountains, bamboo scenes and goldfish. The institute is housed in the courtyard. It's geared for tour groups.

Getting There & Away

Air The main office of Civil Aviation Administration of China (CAAC; Zhōngguó Mínháng; ☎ 411 9821) is at 5 Wuyi Donglu, one block west of the train station. Fúróng Bīnguǎn also has a CAAC booking office.

From Chángshā, there are flights almost daily to Běijīng (Y1350), Chéngdū (Y910), Guǎngzhōu (Y680), Kūnmíng (Y1040), Shànghǎi (Y970) and Xī'ān (Y920). There are also daily flights to Hong Kong (Y1600) except for Wednesday and Sunday.

The airport is 26km from the city centre. CAAC shuttle buses leave about two hours before scheduled flights. The fare is Y13.

Bus A bus station across from the train station at 61 Chezhan Lu has buses to major locations including Sháoshān (Y22, 2½ hours), Zhāngjiājiè (Y93, seven to 11 hours) and Zhūzhōu (Y14, two hours); it also sells tickets departing from other stations. The three other long-distance bus stations are all inconveniently located outside the city centre. Buses heading west depart from the western bus station; points east

and north depart from the eastern bus station; and for the south, the southern bus station. From the train station, bus No 126 goes to the eastern bus station, bus No 12 followed by bus No 315 goes to the western station and bus No 103 or 107 goes to the southern bus station.

Buses for Yuèyáng (Y24, 2½ hours), Nánchāng (Y77, eight hours) and Nánjīng (Y256, 20 hours) leave from the eastern bus station. Buses for Huáihuà (Y99, 11 hours) and Zhāngjiājiè leave from the western bus station.

Buses for Sháoshān, Héng Shān (Y21, three hours) and Guǎngzhōu (Y93, 15 hours) leave from the southern bus station. All the stations are open 6am to at least 9pm. Minibuses from the train station to Yuèyáng cost Y20.

Train There are two Guǎngzhōu-Chángshā-Běijīng express trains daily in each direction and a daily train to Shànghǎi (Y300, 20 hours). Other important routes via Chángshā are Běijīng-Guìlín-Kūnmíng and Guǎngzhōu-Xī'ān-Lánzhōu. Not all trains to Shànghǎi, Kūnmíng and Guìlín stop in Chángshā, so it may be necessary to go to Zhūzhōu first and change there.

If you're heading to Hong Kong, you can take an overnight Chángshā-Shēnzhèn air-conditioned express train that gets into Shēnzhèn around 9.10am. A hard-sleeper berth costs around Y300. The Běijīng-Kowloon express train also passes through Chángshā. There is a daily train to Sháoshān (Y17) that leaves at 6.40am. Counter No 6 at the Chángshā train station is for foreigners, but you can also book tickets with CITS for a Y40 service charge.

SHÁOSHĀN 韶山
☎ 0732

Although small, the town of Sháoshān, about 130km south-west of Chángshā, looms large in significance to Chinese communism as Mao Zedong's birthplace. In the 1960s during the Cultural Revolution's headier days, three million pilgrims came here each year, and a railway line and paved road from Chángshā were built to transport them.

After Mao's death the numbers declined. But as memories of the Cultural Revolution's excesses gradually fade, the village has seen a tourist revival. In 1993, Sháoshān celebrated the centenary of Mao's birth.

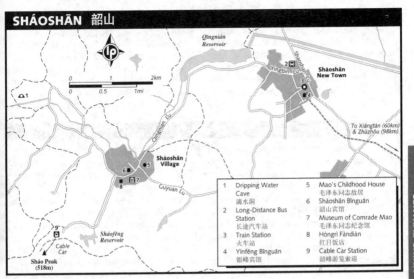

SHÁOSHĀN 韶山

Qīngnián Reservoir

Sháoshān New Town

Yíngbīn Lu

To Xiāngtán (60km) & Zhūzhōu (98km)

Sháoshān Village

Guyuan Lu

Qīngnián Lu

Sháofēng Reservoir

Cable Car

Sháo Peak (518m)

1	Dripping Water Cave 滴水洞	5	Mao's Childhood House 毛泽东同志故居
2	Long-Distance Bus Station 长途汽车站	6	Sháoshān Bīnguǎn 韶山宾馆
3	Train Station 火车站	7	Museum of Comrade Mao 毛泽东同志纪念馆
4	Yínfēng Bīnguǎn 银峰宾馆	8	Hóngrì Fàndiàn 红日饭店
		9	Cable Car Station 韶峰游览索道

CENTRAL CHINA

Considering the tourists who have passed through since it became a national shrine, Sháoshān is hardly typical of Chinese villages. Despite tourism's impact, the countryside has retained its charm. Traditional adobe houses dot this landscape of mountains and lush rice paddies.

Apart from its historical significance, Sháoshān is a great place to get away from big cities.

Orientation

Sháoshān has two parts: the new town clustered around the train and bus stations and the original Sháoshān village about 5km away.

From the train station or the main road there are minibuses to village sites. Motorcycle taxis also meet the train from Chángshā. The minibus to the village should only cost Y1.5, but some drivers may want more money. Normally, they proceed directly to the Dripping Water Cave, so make sure you tell the driver you want to stop at the village. Some minibuses will take you to the key sites for Y10.

Mao's Childhood House

Máo Zédōng Gùjū 毛泽东同志故居

This mud-brick house (*admission free; open 7am-6pm daily*) with a thatched roof and stable is the village's principal shrine. Mao was born here in 1893 and returned to

live here briefly in 1927. It's very similar to other dwellings in China except for its former occupant, its painstaking restoration and the People's Liberation Army guard.

Exhibits include kitchen utensils, original furnishings, bedding and photos of Mao's parents.

Museum of Comrade Mao

Máo Zédōng Jìniànguǎn 毛泽东同志纪念馆

This museum (☎ 568 4957; admission Y7; open 8am-5pm daily) opened in 1967 during the Cultural Revolution. Unfortunately there are no English captions, but the exhibits of Mao's belongings and photos with Communist leaders are graphic enough.

Other Sights

Fancy a Chinese fan that unfolds to reveal a jolly profile of the Chairman? How about a red cigarette lighter with his portrait that plays 'The East is Red' when you flick it open? If you came looking for Mao souvenirs, you can drop your cash at the three *tourist markets*, which are uphill from his childhood house, near Sháoshān Bīnguǎn and at the Dripping Water Cave site. All should satiate any craving for Maoist kitsch. There is also more conventional Maobilia such as badges, rings, busts, statues and the Mao portrait good-luck charms that Chinese drivers attach to their car mirrors.

Some 3km up from Sháoshān village is the **Dripping Water Cave** (Dī Shuǐ Dòng; ☎ 568 4957; admission Y25). Retreating to Sháoshān in June 1966, Mao lived in this cave for 11 days, possibly thinking up new slogans for the Cultural Revolution that had just begun. The Mao clan are entombed nearby.

Buses to the cave leave from the car park opposite Sháoshān Bīnguǎn.

Sháo Peak (Sháo Fēng) is the conical-shaped mountain visible from the village. The summit has a lookout pavilion, and the 'forest of steles' on the lower slopes has stone tablets engraved with Mao's poems. The area is less frequented than other

Mao Zedong

Mao was Húnán's main export. He was born in the Húnánese village of Sháoshān, not far from Chángshā, in 1893. His father was a poor peasant who had been forced to join the army because of heavy debts. After several years of service he returned to Sháoshān and by careful saving, through small trading and other enterprises, managed to buy back his land.

As 'middle' peasants, Mao's family owned enough land to produce a surplus of rice with which they were able to buy more land. This raised them to the status of 'rich' peasants. Mao began studying in the local primary school when he was eight years old and remained at school until the age of 13, while working on the farm and keeping accounts for his father's business.

Several incidents influenced Mao around this time. A famine in Húnán and a subsequent uprising of starving people in Chángshā ended in the execution of the leaders by the Manchu governor. This left a lasting impression on Mao, who '...felt that there with the rebels were ordinary people like my own family and I deeply resented the injustice in the treatment given to them'. He was also influenced by a band of rebels who had taken to the hills around Sháoshān to defy the landlords and the government, and by a radical teacher at the local primary school who opposed Buddhism and wanted people to convert their temples into schools.

At the age of 16 Mao left Sháoshān to enter middle school in Chángshā, his first stop on the path to power. At this time he was not yet an anti-monarchist. He felt, however, even at an early age, that the country was in desperate need of reform. He was fascinated by stories of the ancient rulers of China, and learned something of foreign history and geography.

In Chángshā, Mao was first exposed to the ideas of revolutionaries and reformers active in China, he heard of Sun Yatsen's revolutionary secret society and read about the abortive Canton Uprising of 1911. Later that year an army uprising in Wǔhàn quickly spread and the Qing dynasty collapsed. Yuan Shikai made his grab for power and the country appeared to be slipping into civil war. Mao joined the regular army, but resigned six months later, thinking the revolution was over when Sun handed the presidency to Yuan and the war between the north and south of China did not take place.

Mao became an avid reader of newspapers and from these was introduced to socialism. He decided to become a teacher and enrolled in the Hunan No 1 Teachers' Training School, where he was a student for five years. During his time at the school, he inserted an advertisement in a Chángshā newspaper 'inviting young men interested in patriotic work to make contact with me...'. Among them was Liu Shaoqi, who later became president of the People's Republic of China (PRC); Xiao Chen, who became a founding member of the Chinese Communist Party (CCP); and Li Lisan.

'At this time', said Mao, 'my mind was a curious mixture of ideas of liberalism, democratic reformism and utopian socialism...and I was definitely anti-militarist and anti-imperialist.' Mao graduated from the teachers' training school in 1918 and went to Běijīng, where he worked as an assistant librarian at Beijing University. In Běijīng he met future co-founders of the Chinese Communist Party: the student leader Zhang Guodao, Professor Chen Duxiu and university librarian Li Dazhao. Chen and Li are regarded as the founders of Chinese communism. It was Li who gave Mao a job and first introduced him to the serious study of Marxism.

Mao found in Marxist theory a program for reform and revolution in China. On returning to Chángshā, he became increasingly active in Communist politics. He became editor of the Xiang River Review, a radical Húnán students' newspaper, and took up a post as a teacher. In 1920 he organised workers for the first time and considered him-

Sháoshān sites and has pleasant paths through pine forests and stands of bamboo.

From Sháoshān village you can take a minibus south to the end of the road at the cable car station, or hop aboard a motorcycle taxi for about Y5. Hiking to the top takes about an hour or you can take the cable car for Y20.

Places to Stay & Eat

Sháoshān Bīnguǎn (☎ 568 5080) Doubles/triples Y240/280. This upmarket place is on the main street into town. A hotel extension *(☎ 568 5064)* is around the corner to the right, up a small hill, and has nice grounds, although the reception, with its portraits of Marx, Mao et al, is rather austere.

Mao Zedong

self a Marxist from then on. In 1921 Mao went to Shànghǎi to attend the founding meeting of the Chinese Communist Party. Later he helped organise the first provincial branch of the CCP in Húnán, and by the middle of 1922 the CCP had organised trade unions among the workers and students.

Orthodox Marxist philosophy saw revolution spreading from the cities as it had in the Soviet Union. The peasants, ignored through the ages by poets, scholars and political soothsayers, had likewise been ignored by the Communists; however, Mao took a different stance and saw the peasants as the lifeblood of the revolution. The party had done very little work among them, but in 1925 Mao began to organise peasant trade unions. This aroused the wrath of the landlords and Mao had to flee to Guǎngzhōu (Canton), where the Kuomintang and Communists held power in alliance with each other. Mao proposed a radical redistribution of the land to help the peasants, and supported (and probably initiated) the demands of the Húnán peasants' union to confiscate large landholdings. Probably at this stage he foresaw the need to organise and arm them for a struggle against the landlords.

In April 1927 Chiang Kaishek launched his massacre of the Communists. The party sent Mao to Chángshā to organise what became known as the 'Autumn Harvest Uprising'. By 1 September units of a peasant-worker army had been formed, with troops drawn from the peasantry, Héngyáng miners and rebel Kuomintang soldiers. Mao's army moved south through Húnán and climbed up into the peaks of Jǐnggāng Shān to embark on a guerrilla war against the Kuomintang. This action eventually culminated in the 1949 Communist takeover.

Mao became the new chairman of the PRC, and was to retain the title until his death in 1976. Faced with a country exhausted from civil war, yet jubilant with victory, Mao embarked on a number of radical campaigns to repair his war-ravaged country. During the formative years of the Chinese Communist state, Mao was inclined to conform to the Stalinist model of 'constructing socialism'. In the mid-1950s, however, he and his advisers became more disillusioned with the Soviets and began to implement Mao's preferred peasant-based and decentralised socialist development. The outcome was the ill-fated Great Leap Forward and, later, the Cultural Revolution (for details, see the History section in the Facts about China chapter).

The current regime in Běijīng still remembers Mao as being 70% correct and 30% wrong, and for many Chinese they will never forget both sides of their chairman. The feelings towards Mao today are complex and contradictory. He is hated for the torturous memories and experiences that he dragged many Chinese through, but at the same time, he is revered like a god who united the Chinese people and put China on the map as a world power. For many Chinese he will always be remembered as the 'Great Leader', 'Great Teacher', 'Great Helmsman', 'Great Commander-in-chief' and 'supremely beloved Chairman Mao'.

Despite the ever-present image of Mao looking down upon Tiānānmén Square, Mao is now often found hanging from the rear-view mirror of Běijīng's taxis. As China moves away from its revolutionary past and into its current capitalist zeal, Mao has slowly been replaced by his successors – and has been transformed from the people's idol into a saint who will protect them from a crash or bankruptcy.

Detailed biographies of Mao Zedong include Ross Terrill's *Mao*, Jerome Ch'en's *Mao and the Chinese Revolution* and Stuart R Schram's *Mao Tse-tung*. An interesting account of Mao's earlier years is recorded in Edgar Snow's *Red Star Over China*. The five-volume *Selected Works of Mao Tse-tung* provide an abundant collection of materials on Mao Zedong's thoughts.

CENTRAL CHINA

Hóngrì Fàndiàn Dorm beds Y10, twins with shared bath Y30. Up the road from the Mao statue is this popular backpacker place. It's a small, family run hotel with basic accommodation. The family also dishes up some tasty meals.

Yínfēng Bīnguǎn (☎ 568 1080, 34 Yingxiong Lu) Dorm beds in triples with bath & air-con Y50, twins Y168. In the new town, south of the train station, this place has simple, clean rooms.

Meals are a bit pricey in Sháoshān because food must be shipped in to meet tourist demand. There are *restaurants* on the road across from Sháoshān Bīnguǎn and to the left of Hóngrì Fàndiàn.

Getting There & Away
Bus Chángshā has several buses a day to Sháoshān (Y20, 2½ hours), leaving from the southern bus station from 8am onwards. The Sháoshān long-distance bus station on Yingbin Lu, just north of the train station, has daily buses to Chángshā. There may be others leaving from the village throughout the day; just keep an eye out near Sháoshān Bīnguǎn. There are also frequent minibuses to Xiāngtán (Y6, 1½ hours). From there you can catch a train or bus to Chángshā or Huáihuà. Buses also go to Héng Shān.

Train There is one train daily (Y17, 3½ hours) to Sháoshān from Chángshā. It leaves Chángshā at 6.40am and returns from Sháoshān at 5pm, so you can do the town as a day trip.

ZHŪZHŌU 株州
☎ 0733 • pop 3,656,500
Formerly a small market town, Zhūzhōu underwent rapid industrialisation following the completion of the Guǎngzhōu-Wǔhàn railway line in 1937. As a major railway junction and port city on Xiāng Jiāng, Zhūzhōu developed into an important coal and freight reloading point and manufacturing centre. Most travellers stop here to change trains, but the city has some pleasant areas.

Places to Stay
Qìngyún Bīnguǎn (☎ 822 2222, fax 822 5356, 1 Chezhan Lu) Triples Y165, twins Y180-288. This impressive, reasonable three-star hotel is opposite the train station.

Zhūzhōu Bīnguǎn (☎ 821 9888, fax 821 0399, 2 Yanjiang Zhonglu) Triples Y248, twins with bath Y288. Along the river, this hotel has somewhat overpriced, deluxe rooms. From the train station head right, passing Qìngyún Bīnguǎn, turn left at the next main intersection, and turn right when you get to the river. The hotel is up a slope on your right. It should take 15 minutes from the train station.

Getting There & Away
Zhūzhōu is at the junction of the Běijīng-Guǎngzhōu and the Shànghǎi-Kūnmíng railway lines. From Chángshā it's one hour by express train.

The bus station on Xinhua Xilu has buses to Xiāngtán, which has buses to Sháoshān. It's a 15-minute walk to the train station: turn right and cross the railway bridge, then turn left again at the next intersection.

YUÈYÁNG 岳阳
☎ 0730 • pop 5,103,500
Yuèyáng is a port of call for river ferries plying Cháng Jiāng between Chóngqìng and Wǔhàn. The Wǔhàn-Guǎngzhōu railway passes through this small provincial city, so if you're heading to Guǎngzhōu you can get off the boat here instead of going to Wǔhàn.

Orientation & Information
Yuèyáng is situated south of Cháng Jiāng on the north-eastern shore of Dòngtíng Hú, where the lake flows into the river. Yuèyáng has two separate sections. Yuèyáng proper is the southern section of the city; it's where you'll find the train and bus stations, many hotels and sights. Some 17km away to the north at Chénglíngjī is the city's main port. Most Cháng Jiāng ferries dock here, but there are two smaller local docks in the main (southern) part of Yuèyáng, where long-distance ferries also call in.

CITS (☎ 823 2010) is in the courtyard of Yúnmèng Bīnguǎn, at 25 Chengdong Lu, and can help you book boat and train tickets.

An Internet cafe can be found to the west of town, near Dongting Beilu.

Things to See
Yuèyáng has a port city, working-class atmosphere, and its narrow, old backstreets are a colourful contrast to China's modernisation drive.

YUÈYÁNG

PLACES TO STAY & EAT
2 Xuělián Bīnguǎn
  雪莲宾馆
4 Yuèyáng Lóu
  Bīnguǎn
  岳阳楼宾馆
5 Shénzhōu Bīnguǎn
  神州宾馆
7 Guòqiáo Mǐxiàn
  过桥米线
9 Highsun Hotel
  汉森宾馆

12 Jūngān Xiǎozhāo
  军干小招
13 Yúnmèng Bīnguǎn;
  CITS
  云梦宾馆;
  中国国际旅行社

OTHER
1 Yuèyáng Lóu
  Ferry Dock
  岳阳楼轮船
  客运站

3 Yuèyáng Tower
  岳阳楼
6 Internet Cafe
  网吧
8 Nányuèpō Dock
  南岳坡码头
10 Train Station
  火车站
11 Long-Distance Bus Station
  长途汽车站
14 Cí Shì Tǎ
  慈氏塔

The city's chief landmark is the **Yuèyáng Tower** (*Yuèyáng Lóu; Dongting Beilu; admission Y29; open 7.30am-4.30pm daily*), a temple complex constructed during the Tang dynasty and subsequently rebuilt. Housed within the tower is a gold replica of the complex. The park is something of a Mecca for Japanese tourists, apparently because of a famous poem written in its praise that Japanese kids learn at school. However, it may not be worth the entrance fee.

For a foray into the past, head to **Cí Shì Tǎ** (*Loving Clan Pagoda*), a crumbling brick tower dating back to 1242. To get there, walk or take any bus south on Dongting Nanlu to Baling Lu. Continue south on Dongting Nanlu, keeping to the left so the buildings don't block your view. After about seven minutes, you'll see the pagoda, up a lane to the right in a residential courtyard.

Dongting Nanlu and the old railway area also have some of Yuèyáng's oldest and most interesting streets, with vegetable markets, brown brick buildings and fish drying on poles.

Yuèyáng borders the enormous 3900 sq km **Dòngtīng Hú**, China's second-largest body of fresh water. There are several islands in the lake; the most famous is **Jūnshān Dǎo** (*admission Y10*), where *yínzhēn chá* (silver needle tea) is grown. When the tea is added to hot water, it's supposed to remain on the surface, sticking up like tiny needles and emitting a fragrant odour.

The island is worth a visit for the tea plantations and other farming. Boats leave approximately every two hours for Jūnshān Dǎo (Y32 return, 45 minutes) from the Yuèyáng Tower Ferry Dock (*Yuèyáng Lóu Lúnchuán Kèyùnzhàn*) on Dongting Beilu.

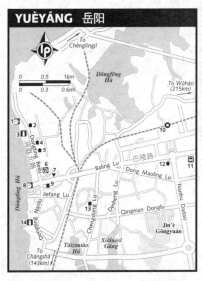

YUÈYÁNG 岳阳

The Nányuèpō Dock (*Nányuèpō Mǎtóu*), located at the end of Baling Lu also has departures, but it's only convenient for groups.

The earliest boats to Jūnshān Dǎo leave around 7.30am, and the last boat from the island departs at 4.30pm.

Places to Stay

Xuělián Bīnguǎn (☎ 832 1633, *Dongting Beilu*) Beds in quads/2nd-floor twins Y35/40, beds in twins with bath Y75-100. This quaint hotel is the best deal in town. The building is of traditional Chinese architecture, with hexagonal windows and wood balconies. It's set in a scenic part of town. Rooms are spartan and the bathrooms have squat toilets. More expensive rooms have heating in winter. There's no English sign, so look for white Chinese characters on a green billboard. From the train station, take bus No 22 to the Yuèyáng Tower and walk north a few minutes.

Jūngān Xiǎozhào (☎ 824 1008, fax 821 9827, 28 Baling Lu) Twins/triples with bath & air-con Y108/118. This reasonable hotel has new, attractive rooms. It's really only convenient if you need to catch an early train.

Yuèyáng Lóu Bīnguǎn (☎ 832 1288, 57 Dongting Beilu) Twins/triples with bath Y148/188. On a side street just off Dongting Beilu, this friendly place has somewhat tattered twins and triples. Bus No 22 will get you there.

Yúnmèng Bīnguǎn (☎ 822 1115, 25 Chengdong Lu) Twins Y200, triples Y190-210. This ornate three-star has good service and pleasant rooms.

Shénzhōu Bīnguǎn (☎ 832 4600, fax 832 4618, 50 Dongting Beilu) Singles/twins from Y168/248. This convenient hotel has decent rooms.

Highsun Hotel (Hànsēn Bīnguǎn; ☎ 831 8888, fax 832 2666, 1 Bailing Lu) Standard twins Y380, suites Y420-880. This hotel is luxurious.

Places to Eat

There are good fish and *seafood restaurants*, particularly on Dongting Beilu, which also has cheap spots for dumplings, noodles and breakfast.

Guòqiáo Mǐxiàn (☎ 832 0288, 11 Baling Lu) Dishes Y10-60. Yúnnán specialities are served at this cafeteria-style restaurant for Y20 to Y25. It also serves sandwiches, pizza, and other Western specialities.

There are also *food stalls* and small *restaurants* near the Nányuèpō Dock, on Dongting Beilu, and just south of the new train station.

Shopping

'Silver needle tea' remains a popular souvenir to amaze friends back home. It's not cheap – the best quality goes for Y120 for 50g – but you can buy the same amount of lesser quality for Y48. It's sold around town, but try the shop across from the Yuèyáng Tower.

Getting There & Away

Yuèyáng is on the main Guǎngzhōu-Běijīng railway line. There are trains to Wǔhàn (Y35, four hours), Chángshā (Y28, two

hours) and Guǎngzhōu (Y200, 12 hours). There are also daily buses to Chángshā (Y33, 2½ hours) and Wǔhàn (Y60, four hours) from the long-distance bus station.

Most of the large Cháng Jiāng ferries dock at Yuèyáng's northern port at Chénglíngjī. Private minibuses to Yuèyáng train station regularly meet arriving boats. Bus No 22, which leaves from an intersection about 200m inland from the ferry terminal, also takes you to the trains.

There are usually four boats daily to Chóngqìng from Chénglíngjī. Boats to Wǔhàn leave twice daily in the morning. The Yuèyáng Tower Ferry Dock usually has one to two departures daily in either direction. Although boats are less frequent, sailing from the Yuèyáng Tower Ferry Dock is more convenient if you're in town, not to mention aesthetically more pleasing.

Upriver to Chóngqìng usually takes four days. Ticket prices from Yuèyáng are: 2nd class Y482, 3rd class Y208, and 4th class Y150. Although not available on all boats, there are also 1st-class cabins for Y955. Sailing to Chóngqìng, prices out of Chénglíngjī are a bit lower.

Downriver to Wǔhàn normally takes under 10 hours. Ticket prices from Yuèyáng are: 2nd class Y105, 3rd class Y52, and 4th class Y40.

You can book train and boat tickets at the Yuèyáng Lóu Bīnguǎn ticket counter and at CITS. For more information on the Chóngqìng to Shànghǎi boat trip, see the 'Cruising Downriver' special section in the Chóngqìng chapter.

HÉNGYÁNG 衡阳
☎ 0734 • pop 6,924,200

Despite its status as Húnán's second largest city, Héngyáng is a particularly unattractive town. But it's on the junction of the Guìlín-Chángshā and Běijīng-Guǎngzhōu lines, so travellers from Guǎngzhōu or Guìlín often find themselves here between train connections.

Héngyáng has important lead and zinc mining industries, but was badly damaged during WWII. Despite post-1949 reconstruction, it still lags noticeably behind its northern neighbour, Zhūzhōu.

CITS (☎ 825 4160) at 206 Huancheng Lu has some obliging English speakers and is around the corner from Yànchéng Bīnguǎn. It can book train tickets and arrange guided visits to Héng Shān.

Places to Stay & Eat

Héngyáng is strict about where foreigners can stay.

Nányuè Dàjiǔdiàn (☎ 833 6999, 5 Guangdong Lu) Twins Y50-100. Rooms at this hotel down the road from the train station are basic but clean.

Jìngyuán Bīnguǎn (☎ 822 2971, fax 822 8814, cnr Jiefang Lu & Zhengxiang Lu) Standard twins Y168. Close to the bus station, this three-star hotel has nice rooms.

Yànchéng Bīnguǎn (☎ 822 6921, 91 Jiefang Lu) Twins Y188-300. Down an alley off the main road, rooms here are just OK. Bus No 1 passes the hotel, but a taxi is the easiest way to find this place.

Try the *restaurant* at the Jìngyuán Bīnguǎn for Chinese and Western dishes starting at Y20. There are plenty of *food stalls* near the train station.

Getting There & Away

Héngyáng is a major railway junction with trains to Wǔhàn, Guǎngzhōu and Guìlín, among other places. Trains to Chángshā take 2½ hours and hard seats cost Y28.

From the bus station, hourly buses go to Chángshā (Y40, three hours) and Nányuè (Héng Shān; Y12, one hour); a bus to Jǐnggāng Shān (Y50, eight hours) in Jiāngxī leaves at 6.20am. To get to the long-distance bus station, take bus No 1 from the train station to the last stop on Jiefang Lu.

HÉNG SHĀN 衡山
☎ 0734

Héng Shān (☎ 566 2571; admission Y40) is one of China's holy mountains, shooting up 1290m above sea level and covering 400km. About 100km south of Chángshā, it is also known as Nányuè Shān (Southern High Mountain), and is where kings and emperors once hunted and made sacrifices to heaven and earth.

Today Buddhists and Taoists live peacefully on the mountain and Chinese tourists flock here, especially during the summer, to pray before the gods. While there are more scenic and famous mountains in China, Héng Shān still makes for an interesting visit.

Words & Pictures

Shān: hill, mountain

This character can be seen either as a mountain range with three peaks or as a mountain in its own right, with its peak in the middle. Either way, it is one of the simplest to remember!

Orientation & Information

Héng Shān's main streets are Zhurong Lu, which runs north to south and Xi Jie, which runs west to east, just in front of the Nányuè Temple. Dengshan Lu is at the north end of the temple. There are a few English-language maps (Y2) on sale; try the Xinhua Bookshop, near the south end of the temple's entrance on Bei Jie. Héngyáng CITS (☎ 825 4160), where English is spoken, can help arrange a guide, but one is not necessary.

As you leave the archway at the foot of Bei Jie, the Bank of China is on your left, at 37 Hengshan Lu. As you enter the archway, the post office is about a block down on your left. The PSB office is at Xi Jie, or about a block south of Dengshan Lu.

Things to See & Do

To get to Héng Shān, follow Dengshan Lu until it curves to your right. Hiking on the paved road or marked paths to **Wishing Harmony Peak** *(Zhùróng Fēng)*, the mountain's highest point, takes four hours by foot and another four hours to descend. The time excludes visiting the monasteries, temples, villas and gardens that dot the mountain.

Wishing Harmony Palace *(Zhùróng Diàn)*, built during the Ming dynasty, sits atop the mountain and is the resting place of Zhu Rong, an official 'in charge of' fire during one of China's early periods. Zhu Rong used to hunt on Héng Shān, and so Taoists selected the mountain to represent fire.

If time is crucial, hire a motorcycle taxi to whiz you to the top (Y30 to Y50). There's also a cable car (Y30) that starts midway on the mountain and goes nearly to the top.

The large, attractive **Nányuè Temple**
(*Nányuè Dàmiào;* ☎ *566 2353; admission*
Y20; open 7am-7pm daily), built during the
Qing dynasty, attracts many Chinese
tourists.

Places to Stay & Eat

Héng Shān's numerous hotels on Dengshan
Lu range from basic to comfortable. The
cheapest option is to sleep in an extra room
over a restaurant.

Jiāchéng Jiǔlóu (*10 Dengshan Lu*) Beds
in 4-bed rooms Y30. This tiny place is inexpensive and serves tasty dumplings and
dishes. The friendly owners don't speak
English, but they'll get the idea if you're
looking for cheap lodging. There's no heating in the basic rooms and you share a
bathroom.

Don't be surprised if other restaurant
owners offer you rooms as you eat.

Fùháo Dàjiǔdiàn (☎ *566 2392, Banbian*
Jie) Twins Y60, triples Y120-210. At Héng
Shān's base, in a dirt lot near souvenir
hawkers, this place has nice twins in its
main building. If those are unavailable, the
staff may put you in more spartan triples for
the same price.

Nóngyè Bīnguǎn (*Agricultural Bank of*
China Hotel; ☎ *566 6492, fax 566 6491, 19*
Zhurong Lu) Triples Y88, twins with bath
Y138. This hotel has decent rooms, the
twins being nicer, and is across the street
from more expensive hotels.

Zǐzhúlín Bīnguǎn (☎ *566 1400*) Dorm
beds Y20-30, twins Y140. Midway up
Héng Shān, this place offers basic twins
with stunning vistas. The plain wood beds
in the dormitory rooms in the back don't
look stable. The guesthouse is near some
restaurants off the main mountain road and
dirt bend. A motorcycle taxi is probably the
best way to get there, and it's best to call
about vacancies.

For food, there are plenty of street-side
restaurants on Dengshan Lu.

Getting There & Away

From the archway on Bei Lu, turn right and
the long-distance bus station is a few minutes' walk across the street on your left. It's
the gateway to Héng Shān and also has
buses to Chángshā (Y28, three hours) and
Héngyáng (Y12, one hour). Arriving buses
may drop you at Dengshan Lu.

HUÁIHUÀ 怀化
☎ 0745 ● pop 4,766,200

Huáihuà is a town built around a railway
junction in western Húnán. Most people use
it as a transit point to or from Zhāngjiājiè
or Liǔzhōu.

Places to stay include the following:

Tiědào Bīnguǎn (*Railway Hotel;*
☎*/fax 225 1888, 8 Huochezhan Kou)* Twins
or triples Y188. This hotel, the first on your
right as you exit the train station, has nice
rooms.

Tiānfù Fàndiàn (☎ *226 4792, 30*
Huochezhan Kou) Twins Y90-240. A much
better deal than Tiědào Bīnguǎn is this
place, which is right beside it.

Lìdū Bīnguǎn (☎ *223 8888, fax 223*
9988, 156 Yingfeng Xilu) Twins Y268. Turn
left at the first intersection off the main
street leading from the train station and walk
about 50m to get here. Rooms are standard.

Getting There & Away

Běijīng-Kūnmíng, Chéngdū-Guǎngzhōu
and Shànghǎi-Chóngqìng express trains run
via Huáihuà. There are also slower trains
from Guìyáng, Guǎngzhōu, Zhèngzhōu and
Liǔzhōu, terminating in Huáihuà.

There is a daily train to Zhāngjiājiè (5½
hours) that leaves at 11.17am. You can also
catch a train to Sānjiāng (5½ hours) in
northern Guǎngxī.

WǓLÍNGYUÁN & ZHĀNGJIĀJIÈ
武陵源、张家界
☎ 0744 ● pop 1,537,700

Parts of Wǔlíng Shān in north-western
Húnán were set aside in 1982 as nature
reserves collectively known as the Wǔlíngyuán Scenic Area (Wǔlíngyuán Fēngjǐngqū), encompassing the localities of Zhāngjiājiè, Tiānzǐshān and Suǒxīyù. Zhāngjiājiè
is the best known, and many Chinese refer
to this area by that name.

The first area of its kind in China,
Wǔlíngyuán is home to three minority
peoples – Tujia, Miao and Bai – who continue to speak their languages and maintain
their traditional cultures.

The mountains have gradually eroded to
form a spectacular landscape of craggy
peaks and huge rock columns rising out of
the luxuriant subtropical forest. There are
waterfalls, limestone caves (including
Asia's largest chamber), fresh clear

streams, and rivers suitable for organised rafting trips. It's a relaxing place to rest and recuperate and there are many short and extended hikes available.

Several towns serve as access points to Wǔlíngyuán, but the most popular are Zhāngjiājiè City (Zhāngjiājiè Shì) and Zhāngjiājiè Village (Zhāngjiājiè Cūn). The city is near the railway line, while the village is situated nearly 600m above sea level in the Wǔlíng foothills, surrounded by sheer cliffs and vertical rock outcrops.

A fee of Y110, good for two days with extension, must be paid at the Zhāngjiājiè forest reserve's main entrance just past the village. Chinese maps showing walking trails, some with sites marked in English, are on sale in Zhāngjiājiè city and village. The scenery is spectacular, but don't expect to view it alone. Wǔlíngyuán is a major national tourist area and is usually swarming with tour groups.

An airport is furthering tourism, and more hotels and karaoke nightspots are being added to the already considerable number both inside and outside the park. Locals who serve as guides will approach you, but you don't really need one. Just follow the crowds up the mountain paths.

Things to See & Do

The highest area closest to Zhāngjiājiè village is **Huángshízhài** and, at 1048m, it's a two-hour hike up 3878 stone steps. There's a cable car (Y48) for anyone who's less physically inclined.

In the northern section of the reserve, **Tiānzǐ Shān** (Tiānzǐ Peak) is another good hike. Like Huáng Shān, every rock, crag and gully has been given an elaborate name.

Organised tours to the park and **Jiǔtiān Cave** (Jiǔtiān Dòng) often include a **rafting trip** (piāoliú), or you can join a tour and just do the rafting trip. While there are good white-water rafting possibilities north-west of Zhāngjiājiè near the Húběi border, you'll have to make special arrangements for the equipment and transport.

In Wǔlíngyuán, most of the rivers covered by the tours are pretty tame, so don't expect great thrills; still, it's a good way to get away from the crowds and the scenery is beautiful. The actual rafting usually lasts

CENTRAL CHINA

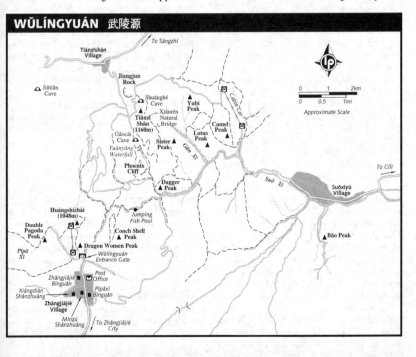

WǓLÍNGYUÁN 武陵源

about two hours with about the same amount of time taken up in travel to the launch area.

You can join tours or arrange your own through the hotels in Zhāngjiājiè or at a travel agency in Zhāngjiājiè city. The **Dongsheng Travel Agency** *(Dōngshēng Lüxíngshè;* ☎ *828 6258)* at 36 Jiefang Lu offers good rates for group tours (Y180 per person). CITS (☎ 822 7111) at 37 Jiefang Lu has English speakers and offers rafting tours (Y300 per person).

Places to Stay

It's more convenient and interesting to stay in Zhāngjiājiè village, but Zhāngjiājiè city hotels also take foreigners.

Dūlè Bīnguǎn *(☎ 822 2872, 1 Renmin Lu)* Twins or triples Y120, twins with bath Y240. This hotel, diagonally opposite the bus station, has spartan economy rooms and nicer, more costly doubles.

Wǔlíng Guójì Jiǔdiàn *(☎ 822 2630, fax 822 2165, 1 Jiefang Lu)* Twins or triples Y228. This hotel, past Pǔguāng Sí, has nice twin rooms.

Xiánglóng Guójì Jiǔdiàn *(Dragon International Hotel;* ☎ *822 6888, fax 822 2935, 46 Jiefang Lu)* Twins in older/newer wing Y477/764, plus 15% service charge. This is a glittering marble and chrome establishment masquerading as a four-star hotel. Rooms are standard.

In Zhāngjiājiè village most places accept foreigners. All of the following hotels are on the main road.

Zhāngjiājiè Bīnguǎn *(☎ 571 2388)* Dorm beds Y75, twins Y150-300. Closest to the park, this hotel has so-so twins. There's a three-star addition next door that offers more upmarket air-con twins. You'll have to push to get the dorm beds. The hotel can also book train tickets three days in advance.

Xiāngdiàn Shānzhuāng *(Xiangdian Mountain Inn;* ☎ *571 2266, fax 571 2172)* Twins or triples Y312, luxury twins Y340. This place, 50m off the main road, is better value than Zhāngjiājiè Bīnguǎn. You have your choice of clean twins and triples or nicer rooms. The hotel is nicely laid out, and some rooms have balconies. It's also quieter (Zhāngjiājiè Bīnguǎn sits amid several karaoke clubs).

Mínzú Shānzhuāng *(☎ 571 2516)* Singles/twins Y100/120. This thatched, Tujia-run

establishment is by far the best in town. The beautiful, Tujia-style wood rooms even have balconies.

Pípāxī Bīnguǎn *(☎ 571 8888, fax 571 2257)* Twins Y280-348, suites Y1200. In a quiet setting, this hotel has somewhat fancy twins as well as suites. Pípāxī Bīnguǎn is one of the last hotels on the road, just outside Zhāngjiājiè village.

For those hiking overnight in Wǔlíngyuán, there are places to stay inside the park along the popular trail routes. Local visitors often do a two- to three-day circuit hike, going in at Zhāngjiājiè village and hiking or bussing it to villages within the park boundaries such as Tiānzǐshān and Suǒxīyù, both of which have a bewildering choice of hotels and hostels. If you're just interested in day hiking, a stay in Zhāngjiājiè will suffice.

Places to Eat

There are simple **eating houses** scattered around the village, and the better hotels, such as Mínzú Shānzhuāng, also have **restaurants**. The places on the other side of the small stream opposite Zhāngjiājiè Bīnguǎn on the road towards the park entrance have good *húndùn* dumplings.

Bābǐ Q Táiwāncūn Cāntīng *(Taiwan Barbecue Village;* ☎ *823 5595, 13 Tianmen Lu)* Dishes Y8-38. At the corner of Jiaochang Lu, this 2nd-floor bar/restaurant has a great atmosphere and good meals featuring barbecued chicken. Beer is available in the afternoon and evening. Mr Ding, who is Tujia, started the restaurant. He was born in Taiwan where his father retreated with Kuomintang troops after 1949.

Shopping

A good buy in Zhāngjiājiè are the tightly woven baskets with a simple black line pattern; Tujia women often carry the baskets on their backs. You can find the baskets at markets in Zhāngjiājiè city and on Huilong Lu. These aren't the coloured baskets sold to tourists but the real thing, and cost about Y20. Also available are other items such as wooden buckets and bamboo cradles.

Getting There & Away

There are flights linking Zhāngjiājiè city with Běijīng (Y1220), Chángshā (Y560), Chóngqìng (Y490), Guǎngzhōu (Y780),

Shànghǎi (Y1160), Wǔhàn (Y480) and Shēnzhèn (Y810).

There are direct trains from Zhāngjiājiè city to Chángshā (Y98, 16 hours), Zhèngzhōu (Y110, 30 hours) and Guǎngzhōu (Y319, 24 hours). A fast train leaves Chángshā around 6.06pm and arrives at Zhāngjiājiè city at 10.55am. You can also get trains from the Cháng Jiāng port of Yíchāng that pass through Zhāngjiājiè on their way to Huáihuà, including the daily train from Xiāngfán in Húběi that passes through Sānjiāng and terminates at Liǔzhōu in Guǎngxī.

China Travel Service (CTS; Zhōngguó Lǚxíngshè; ☎ 822 7718) in Zhāngjiājiè city is opposite Xiánglóng Guójì Jiǔdiàn on Jiefang Lu. The staff can book hard and soft sleepers, as well as air tickets.

Buses leave the Zhāngjiājiè city bus station for Chángshā in the early morning. The seven-hour trip costs Y65, or Y84 for aircon buses. Sleeper buses are also available for Y65, leaving at 6pm and arriving in Chángshā seven hours later.

Minibuses to Zhāngjiājiè village (Y10, one hour) pick up incoming passengers at the car park in front of the train station. The minibuses sometimes stop at the bus station in Zhāngjiājiè city, which lies across the river, 14km from the train station. They then continue on to the Zhāngjiājiè village. At the Zhāngjiājiè city bus station, you can also get buses to Tiānzǐshān and Suǒxīyù.

MĚNGDÒNGHÉ 猛洞河
☎ 0743
An hour and a half south of Zhāngjiājiè by train, Měngdònghé is nestled between the hills and rivers of western Húnán.

From here you can take a 45-minute boat ride to Wáng Cūn, better known as **Fúróngzhèn** (*Hibiscus Town*). It was the location for Xie Jin's 1986 film of the same name. The film, adapted from Gu Hua's novel *A Town Called Hibiscus*, portrayed how the political turbulence of the 1950s and 1960s unsettled the lives of ordinary villagers. The film turned the town into a tourist destination. Wandering up the twisting stone streets and looking at the dilapidated wooden buildings just up from the pier is a trip into the past. On the main street, there's also a worthwhile private **museum** (☎ 585 3363, 60 Hepan Jie; admission Y5;

open 8am-6pm daily) of Tujia culture in an old house.

One reason to visit Fúróngzhèn is for **rafting**. Trips here are better organised than in Zhāngjiājiè and you can buy tickets at the rafting ticket office at the dock. The cost is Y122 and includes transport to the launch site. Be prepared to get drenched, as water warfare between passing rafts, using ladles and bamboo squirt guns, is highly encouraged. There are also swimming opportunities. Flimsy ponchos are sold by vendors and around town.

Places to Stay & Eat
Tiānxià Dìyī Jiǔlóu (First Snail Under Heaven Restaurant; ☎ *585 3418, fax 585 3898, 19 Hepan Lu)* Rooms Y60-288. About 150m up the stone steps from the pier and to your right, this quaintly named hotel/restaurant has nice, airy rooms overlooking the river. There's no English sign, but look for a white and blue sign with red characters across from a wide stairway. The staff can also arrange tickets for the rafting trip, and throw in a free hat as well.

Tīngtāo Shānzhuāng (☎ *585 3372)* Singles/twins with bath Y150/180. This place is hard to get to unless you take a motor taxi *(mánmányoǔ)*. It's on top of a hill across from the river. Rooms are worn.

Xiāngliú Dàjiǔdiàn (☎ *585 3463)* Twins Y100. This is a ten-minute walk uphill; turn left when you can't go up any more and look for a pink building with a stairway. It has nice, basic rooms.

It's obvious where you should go if you enjoy eating snails. Other *restaurants* line the main street.

In the film *Hibiscus Town* the main protagonist is renowned for making *mǐdòufu,* a tasty snack that looks like cubes of tofu, but is actually milled rice flour topped with pickles and chilli sauce. The stalls down by the dock sell it for about Y2.

Getting There & Away
Trains from Zhāngjiājiè, Huáihuà and Liǔzhōu all stop in Měngdònghé. From the train station, walk down the steps towards the ferry boat dock. Bus or boat tickets to Fúróngzhèn are Y4, but beware of overcharging. Boats run infrequently so it's probably easier to take a minibus.

CENTRAL CHINA

Hong Kong 香港

Telephone code: ☎ 0852
Population: 7 million
Area: 1092 sq km

A curious anomaly, Hong Kong is both an energetic paragon of the virtues of capitalism and a part of the largest Communist country in the world. A British colony since the middle of the 19th century, Hong Kong was handed back to China on 1 July 1997 amid much fanfare and anticipation.

While many tourists view Hong Kong as one giant shopping mall, the New Territories and Outlying Islands continue to offer country parks, tranquil village life and clean beaches. At first glance the territory may appear as Western as a Big Mac; however, with 95% of its population ethnic Chinese, many traditions from the Middle Kingdom remain. You'll also find a thriving arts community and a growing number of excellent museums.

Despite its return to the 'motherland', Hong Kong's political and economic systems are still significantly different from those of the People's Republic of China (PRC). Thus, much of the general information you've read elsewhere in this book (about visas, currency, accommodation, international phone calls etc) does not apply to Hong Kong.

Most visitors should have few problems getting around Hong Kong – English is widely spoken and most street signs are bilingual. Although increasingly used since the handover, Mandarin is spoken by less then half the population – most speak Cantonese as their native tongue.

Highlights

- A sampan ride in Aberdeen harbour
- Retail therapy in the many shopping centres
- A hair-raising ride up the Peak Tram to Hong Kong Island's highest point
- Fantastic hiking through forests, up peaks and along white-sand beaches
- A delicious dim sum feast in a top-notch restaurant

HISTORY & POLITICS

European trade with China stretches back over more than 400 years. Trade mushroomed during the 18th century as European demand for Chinese tea and silk grew. However, as the Chinese were largely self-sufficient, the balance of trade was unfavourable to the Europeans – until they began running opium into the country.

While the drug had long been used medicinally in Asia as well as in Europe, addiction swept China like wildfire. The British, with a virtually inexhaustible supply of the drug from the poppy fields of Bengal, developed the trade aggressively and by the start of the 19th century opium formed the basis of most of their transactions with China.

China's attempts to stamp out the trade, including confiscating a huge British store of the drug, gave the British the pretext they needed for military action against China. Two British gunboats were sent in and managed to demolish a Chinese fleet of 29 ships. The ensuing first Opium War went much the same way and, at its close in 1841, the island of Hong Kong was ceded to the British.

Following the Second Opium War in 1860, Britain took possession of Kowloon Peninsula. Finally, in 1898, a 99-year lease was granted for the New Territories. What would happen after the lease ended in 1997 was the subject of considerable speculation.

In late 1984 an agreement was reached: China would take over the entire colony in 1997, but Hong Kong's unique free enterprise economy would be maintained for at

Unequal Treaties

The first of the many unequal treaties foisted on the Chinese by the Europeans (and later the Japanese) was the Treaty of Nanking. It brought the opium wars to a close with a humiliating slap in the face for the Qing court.

According to its terms (there were 12 articles altogether), the ports of Guǎngzhōu, Xiàmén, Fúzhōu, Níngbō and Shànghǎi were to be opened to foreign trade; British consuls were to be established in each of the open ports; an indemnity of 21 million Mexican dollars was to be paid to the British; the Co hong was to be disbanded; and, perhaps most humiliating, Hong Kong was to be ceded to the British 'in perpetuity'.

Unequal treaties followed thick and fast once a precedent had been established in Nánjīng. The Treaty of Tianjin, originating in a Chinese refusal to apologise for having torn a British flag and culminating in a combined British-French occupation of Tiānjīn, provided a further 10 treaty ports and more indemnities.

Subsequent complications led to the burning of the Summer Palace by the British and the ceding of the Kowloon Peninsula. Further unequal treaties won the French the Chinese vassal state of Vietnam, gave the Japanese Taiwan, the Pescadores and the Liaodong Peninsula, and eventually opened 50 treaty ports from as far south as Sīmáo in Xīshuāngbǎnnà to Mǎnzhōulǐ on the Russian frontier.

In the space of some 50 years or so, a spate of unequal treaties effectively turned China into a colony of the imperial forces of the day.

least 50 years. Hong Kong would become a Special Administrative Region (SAR) of China with the official slogan, 'One country, two systems'.

Nervousness grew as the handover date drew near. Both people and capital began to flee to safe havens overseas. A belated attempt by Britain to increase the number of democratically elected members of Hong Kong's Legislative Council (Legco) caused China to threaten to dismiss the council altogether and appoint leaders approved by Běijīng.

And it did just that. On 1 July the new Provisional Legislative Council took office, composed of Hong Kong representatives appointed by Běijīng. Former shipping magnate, Tung Chee-hwa, himself a refugee to Hong Kong after 1949, was given the post of Chief Executive.

The first incident to test the degree of autonomy Hong Kong has from Běijīng occurred in January 1999, when Hong Kong's Court of Final Appeal argued that mainland Chinese applying for residency in Hong Kong could be granted legal status if one of their parents was a Hong Kong resident. The Hong Kong government did not agree, and asked Běijīng for support in disallowing the court's decision. Běijīng complied. Regardless of whether or not immigrants would aid or hinder Hong Kong's prosperity, many observers were concerned that letting Běijīng overrule the court's appeal of the law did not bode well for future issues and judicial procedures based in democratic process.

There's a strong sense of pride among the Hong Kong people that they are no longer a colony of Britain, combined with a new consciousness about being Chinese. The gulf between China and Hong Kong in education, public services, lifestyle, language and economy, however, makes the twinning of these two entities almost absurd. At this point in time, it's very difficult to see what Hong Kong will become, other than to suggest its position as a dynamic city may fade and be gradually overshadowed by Shànghǎi.

ORIENTATION

Hong Kong's 1092 sq km are divided into four main areas – Kowloon, Hong Kong Island, the New Territories and the Outlying Islands.

Hong Kong Island is the economic heart of the colony, but comprises only 7% of Hong Kong's land area. Kowloon is the densely populated peninsula to the north – the southern tip of the Kowloon Peninsula is Tsim Sha Tsui, where herds of tourists congregate. The New Territories, which officially include the more than 230 Outlying Islands, occupy 91% of Hong Kong's land area. Much of it is rural and charming with some clean beaches, opportunities for excellent walks and few tourists.

HONG KONG & MACAU

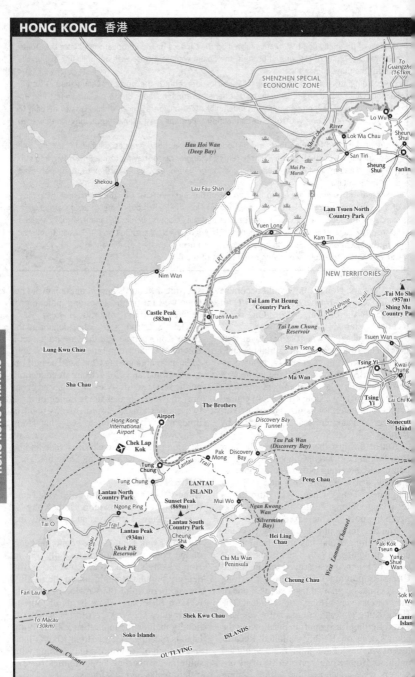

HONG KONG 香港

SHENZHEN SPECIAL ECONOMIC ZONE

To Guangzhou (161km)

Lo Wu

Shenzhen River

Lok Ma Chau

Sheung Shui

Hau Hoi Wan (Deep Bay)

San Tin

Sheung Shui

Fanlin

Shekou

Mai Po Marsh

Lau Fau Shan

Lam Tsuen North Country Park

Yuen Long

Kam Tin

LRT

NEW TERRITORIES

Nim Wan

Tai Lam Pat Heung Country Park

MacLehose Trail

Tai Mo Sh (957m)

Shing Mu Country Pa

Castle Peak (583m)

Tuen Mun

Tai Lam Chung Reservoir

Lung Kwu Chau

Tsuen Wan

Sham Tseng

Tsing Yi

Kwai Chung

Sha Chau

Ma Wan

Tsing Yi

Lai Chi Ke

The Brothers

Discovery Bay Tunnel

Stonecutt Island

Hong Kong International Airport

Airport

Chek Lap Kok

Lantau Trail

Pak Mong

Discovery Bay

Tau Pak Wan (Discovery Bay)

Tung Chung

Peng Chau

Tung Chung

LANTAU ISLAND

Lantau North Country Park

Sunset Peak (869m)

Mui Wo

Ngan Kwong Wan (Silvermine Bay)

Ngong Ping

Lantau South Country Park

Tai O

Trail

Lantau Peak (934m)

Cheung Sha

Hei Ling Chau

Pak Kok Tseun

Yung Shue Wan

Lantau

Shek Pik Reservoir

Chi Ma Wan Peninsula

West Lamma Channel

Sok K Wa

Fan Lau

Cheung Chau

Lamn Islan

To Macau (30km)

Shek Kwu Chau

Lantau Channel

Soko Islands

OUTLYING

ISLANDS

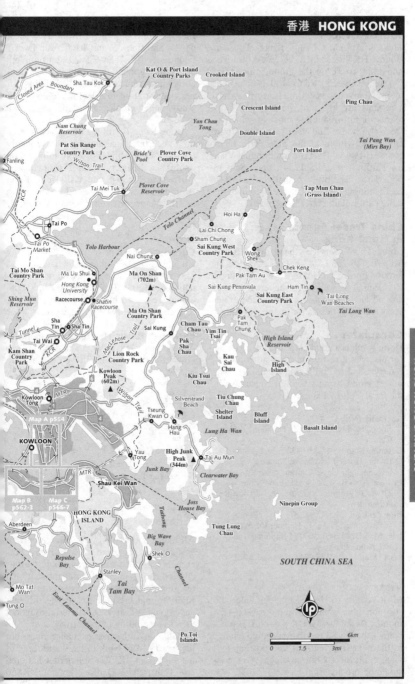

香港 **HONG KONG**

INFORMATION
Tourist Offices

The enterprising Hong Kong Tourism Board (HKTB; Map B; W www.discover hongkong.com), on the ground floor, The Centre, 99 Queen's Rd Central, is open 8am to 6pm daily, and is definitely worth a visit. The staff are efficient, helpful and have reams of information – most of which is free. You'll also find an office at the airport and in Kowloon, at the Star Ferry Concourse (Map A). HKTB's multilingual Visitor Hotline (☎ 2508 1234), open 8am to 6pm daily, is helpful whether you're lost or need shopping advice (including which retailers are reliable HKTB members).

China Travel Agents in Hong Kong

China Travel Service's head office (CTS; Map B; ☎ 2853 3888, fax 2541 9777), Ground floor, CTS House, 78–83 Connaught Rd Central, as well as its numerous outlets around Hong Kong, is a good place to get visas and book tickets for mainland China.

Consulates

Hong Kong is a good place to pick up a visa for elsewhere or to replace a stolen or expired passport. You'll find a complete listing of Hong Kong's foreign consulates in the local Yellow Pages.

Australia (Map C; ☎ 2827 8881) 23rd & 24th floors, Harbour Centre, 25 Harbour Rd, Wan Chai
Canada (Map B; ☎ 2810 4321) 11th–14th floors, Tower I, Exchange Square, 8 Connaught Place, Central
France (Map B; ☎ 2529 4316) 26th floor, Tower II, Admiralty Centre, 18 Harcourt Rd, Admiralty
New Zealand (Map C; ☎ 2877 4488) Room 6508, Central Plaza, 18 Harbour Rd, Wan Chai
UK (Map B; ☎ 2901 3000) 1 Supreme Court Rd, Admiralty
USA (Map B; ☎ 2523 9011) 26 Garden Rd, Central

Visas

Most visitors to Hong Kong can enter and stay for three months without a visa – six months if you have a UK passport. But beware – these visa regulations could change in the next few years. If you do require a visa, apply at a Chinese embassy or consulate before arriving.

For tourist visa extensions, inquire at the Immigration Department (Map C; ☎ 2824 6111), 2nd floor, Wan Chai Tower Two, 7 Gloucester Rd, Wan Chai. Extensions are not readily granted unless there are extenuating circumstances – cancelled flights, illness, registration in a legitimate course of study, legal employment, marriage to a local etc.

Hong Kong is still the best place to pick up a visa for China, and this will probably continue for a while. For more information on this see the Facts for the Visitor chapter.

Be aware that if you visit Hong Kong from China you will need to be on a multiple-entry visa to re-enter China, or else will have to get a new visa.

Money

Currency The unit of currency in Hong Kong is the HK dollar, which is divided into 100 cents. Bills are issued in denominations of $20, $50, $100, $500 and $1000. Coins are issued in denominations of $10, $5, $2, $1, $0.50, $0.20 and $0.10.

Exchange Rates The Hong Kong dollar is pegged to the US dollar at a rate of US$1 to HK$7.80, though it is allowed to fluctuate a little.

country	unit		HK$
Australia	A$1	=	4.15
Canada	C$1	=	4.91
China	Y1	=	0.94
Euro zone	€1	=	6.87
Japan	¥100	=	5.88
New Zealand	NZ$1	=	3.44
Thailand	B1	=	0.18
UK	UK£1	=	11.20
USA	US$1	=	7.80

All major and many minor foreign currencies can be exchanged in Hong Kong. Foreigners can open bank accounts in various currencies (or in gold!), and international telegraphic transfers are fast and efficient. International credit cards are readily accepted and ATMs are scattered throughout the city, including in the airport.

Banks give the best exchange rates, but these vary from bank to bank and three of the biggest – HSBC, Standard Chartered and Hang Seng Bank – levy a HK$50

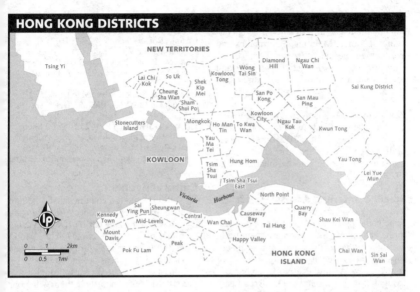

HONG KONG DISTRICTS

commission for each transaction. Licensed moneychangers are abundant in tourist districts and are open late, but they give relatively poor exchange rates. These rates are clearly posted but if you're changing several hundred US dollars or more, you might be able to bargain. Avoid the exchange counters at the airport; they offer some of the worst rates in Hong Kong.

The half-dozen moneychangers operating on the ground floor of Chungking Mansions on Nathan Rd in Tsim Sha Tsui usually offer good rates. Worth trying is Wing Hoi Money Exchange (Map A; ☎ 2723 5948), ground floor, shop No 9B, Mirador Arcade, 58 Nathan Rd, Tsim Sha Tsui. They'll change just about any currency for you as well as travellers cheques.

Costs Hong Kong has become an extremely pricey destination, but if you stay in dormitories and eat budget meals, you can survive (just barely) on HK$250 per day.

In general, tipping is not expected in Hong Kong. Most upmarket restaurants and hotels add a 10% service charge and with taxis the norm is to round up the fare.

If you're shopping in the Tsim Sha Tsui tourist zone, bargaining is essential. In department stores, retail outlets or in the street markets of Mongkok and Sham Shui Po, however, everything has a price tag and bargaining is not accepted. You can always try to bargain for your accommodation if you're staying at a private guesthouse or smaller hotel.

Post & Communications

Post All post offices are open from 8am to 6pm Monday to Friday and 8am to 2pm Saturday. They are closed on Sunday and public holidays.

If you want to receive mail in Hong Kong, have it addressed to GPO Hong Kong, which is just west of the Star Ferry terminal. Poste restante letters are held for two months.

Telephone Local calls in Hong Kong are free on public phones and cost HK$1 per minute on pay phones.

To call Hong Kong from abroad, the country code is ☎ 852. To call abroad from Hong Kong, dial ☎ 001, then the country code, area code and number. Phone rates are cheaper from 9pm to 8am on weekdays and all weekend. You can make international direct-dial calls to almost anywhere in the world from public phones, but you'll need a phonecard. These are available as stored-value cards (HK$70 and HK$100) and as Hello Smartcards (five denominations from HK$50 to HK$500). The latter allow you to call from any phone – public

HONG KONG & MACAU

or private, by punching in a PIN code. You can buy them at 7-Eleven and Circle K convenience stores, Mannings pharmacies and Wellcome supermarkets.

For directory assistance dial ☎ 1081 and for international dialling assistance call ☎ 10013.

Fax Many hotels and even hostels have fax machines and will allow you to both send and receive faxes for a 10% surcharge. If dialling your own fax for an overseas transmission, use the international fax code (☎ 001).

Email & Internet Access Most hotels and plenty of guesthouses have Internet access. If the place you're staying at doesn't, there are plenty of cybercafes scattered throughout the territory and in most places logging on is free if you buy a drink or snack. Try Avanti Network Cybercafe (Map C; ☎ 3101 6363), The Broadway, 54–62 Lockhart Rd, Wan Chai, on Hong Kong Island, where HK$30 buys you an hour online, a drink and a snack. Also try the Pacific Coffee Company, which has a number of cafes around Hong Kong.

Free Internet access is available at most public libraries in Hong Kong. The main library (Map B; ☎ 2921 2555) is in the High Block of City Hall, opposite Queen's Pier in Central. You'll find a list of other branches at Ⓦ www.lcsd.gov.hk.

Travel Agencies
There are lots of travel agencies in Hong Kong. For competitive prices try:

Phoenix Services Agency (Map A; ☎ 2722 7378, fax 2369 8884, ⓔ phoenix1 @netvigator.com) Room A, 7th floor, Milton Mansion, 96 Nathan Rd, Tsim Sha Tsui
Hong Kong Student Travel (☎ 2730 3269) Room 835a, Star House (Map A), 3 Salisbury Rd, Tsim Sha Tsui
Traveller Services (Map A; ☎ 2375 2066, fax 2375 2050, Ⓦ www.traveller.com.hk, ⓔ travelhk@asiaonline.net) 1012 Silvercord Tower One, 30 Canton Rd, Tsim Sha Tsui

Bookshops
Hong Kong is an excellent place to stock up on books, although English-language books are very expensive. The widest selection of shops is on Hong Kong Island.

Bookazine (Map B; ☎ 2521 1649) Pacific House, 20 Queen's Rd Central
Cosmos Books (Map C; ☎ 2866 1677) 30 Johnston Rd, Wan Chai
Dymocks Booksellers (Map B; ☎ 2117 0360) International Finance Centre, 1 Harbour View St, Central
Hong Kong Book Centre (Map B; ☎ 2522 7064) On Lok Yuen Bldg, 25 Des Voeux Rd Central
Kelly & Walsh (Map B; ☎ 2522 5743) Shop 304, Pacific Place, 88 Queensway, Admiralty
Times Books (Map B; ☎ 2525 8797) Shop B, Hong Kong Club Bldg, 3 Jackson Rd, Central

Cultural Events
The HKTB can give you the latest schedule of upcoming events, or check *bc Magazine* (Ⓦ www.bcmagazine.net) or *HK Magazine*. You can pick up free copies at the Hong Kong Book Centre in Central and in various expat gathering places around town.

Book tickets by credit card through Cityline (☎ 2317 6666) or reserve them with your passport number through URBTIX (☎ 2374 9009), open 10am to 8pm daily).

Media
Hong Kong has two local English-language daily newspapers, the *South China Morning Post* and the *Hong Kong Standard*. Also printed in Hong Kong are the *Asian Wall St Journal,* the *International Herald Tribune* and *USA Today International*. Imported news magazines are readily available.

There are two English-language and two Cantonese TV stations. Star TV, a satellite TV broadcaster, has some English programming. There's also a variety of English radio stations to choose from.

Medical Services
Medical care is generally of a high standard in Hong Kong, though public hospital staff are grossly underpaid and facilities stretched. Attendance at out-patient clinics is on a first-come, first-served basis and costs HK$195 per visit. Private hospital treatment is expensive but not exorbitant, and you'll have less of a wait for treatment.

The general inquiry number for hospitals is ☎ 2300 6555. The Hong Kong Medical Association (HKMA) maintains a MediLink hotline (☎ 90000 223 322) with recorded information about access to medical consultation during holiday periods.

Try to keep up with Queens Rd's frenetic pace, Hong Kong.

Dining out in Sok Kwu Wan on Lamma Island, Hong Kong.

The Bank of China Building

The bright city lights of Hong Kong as viewed from the Regent Hotel, Kowloon.

For exotic produce head to Graham St Market.

Double-decker trams in Hong Kong's main drag.

People waiting for take-away drinks at lunchtime near Shelley St, Hong Kong Island.

Private hospitals with 24-hour emergency services include the Matilda & War Memorial (☎ 2849 0700, 24-hour help line ☎ 2849 0123), 41 Mt Kellett Rd, The Peak, Hong Kong Island, and the Baptist (☎ 2339 8888), 222 Waterloo Rd, Kowloon Tong, Kowloon.

Emergency

The general emergency phone number for ambulance, fire and police is ☎ 999. You can dial this on pay phones without a coin.

ACTIVITIES

For a jog with spectacular views, nothing beats the path around Victoria Peak on Harlech and Lugard roads.

Sporting buffs should contact the South China Athletic Association (Map C; ☎ 2577 6932, W www.scaa.org.hk), 88 Caroline Hill Rd, Causeway Bay. Visiting membership costs HK$50.

Another excellent place you can contact is the Hong Kong Amateur Athletic Association (Map C; ☎ 2504 8215, W www.hkaaa.com), Room 2015, Sports House 1, Stadium Path, So Kon Po, Causeway Bay. All sorts of sports clubs have activities here or hold members' meetings.

Windsurfing is extremely popular in Hong Kong, especially after local windsurfer Lee Lai-San won Hong Kong's first Olympic gold medal in 1996. Some popular places to windsurf are Stanley, Shek O, Cheung Chau Island and other beaches in the New Territories. Boards and other equipment are available for rent at the Cheung Chau Windsurfing Centre (☎ 2981 8316/5063), 1 Hak Pai Rd, Tung Wan Beach, open daily from April to December. Board rental is HK$60 to HK$100; it also rents kayaks and offers windsurfing courses. The best months for windsurfing in Hong Kong are September, October and November.

The HKTB (☎ 2508 1234) offers free tai chi lessons from 8.15am to 9.15am on Tuesday, Friday and Saturday in the Garden Plaza of Hong Kong Park, next to Admiralty MTR station.

Hong Kong doesn't usually come to mind when you think of wildlife, but bird enthusiasts might consider visiting Mai Po Marsh, a protected wetland near the mouth of the Shenzhen River at Hau Hoi Wan (Deep Bay). The World Wide Fund for Nature Hong Kong (WWFHK; ☎ 2526 4473, W www.wwf.org.hk) can arrange guided visits to the marsh (three-hour tours Saturday, Sunday and public holidays HK$70; unguided access 9am to 5pm daily HK$100 for permit). Splendid Tours & Travel (☎ 2316 2151, W www.splendidtours.com) also offers five-hour tours (HK$360) every Tuesday, Thursday and Sunday from October to April.

You can also cruise the waters around Hong Kong to observe endangered Chinese white dolphins with Hong Kong Dolphinwatch (☎ 2984 1414, W www.zianet.com/dolphins), 1528a Star House (Map A), 3 Salisbury Rd, Tsim Sha Tsui (2½-hour cruises cost adult/child HK$320/160; tours are conducted on Wednesday, Friday, Saturday and Sunday).

Walking & Hiking Trails

There are numerous trails on Hong Kong Island, the New Territories and the Outlying Islands. There are four main trails in Hong Kong. At 100km, the MacLehose Trail is the territory's longest (see the New Territories section for more details), followed by the Wilson Trail (78km), the Lantau Trail (70km) and the Hong Kong Trail (50km).

The Map Publications Centre (Map A; ☎ 2780 0981, W info.gov.hk/landsd/mapping), 382 Nathan Rd, open from 9am to 6pm Monday to Friday and 9am to 1pm Saturday, has a series of excellent maps, and both the Country and Marine Parks Authority (☎ 2420 0529) and the HKTB (☎ 2508 1234) produce useful hiking leaflets.

ORGANISED TOURS

There are dozens of these, including boat tours. All can be booked through the HKTB, travel agents, large tourist hotels or directly from the tour company.

GETTING THERE & AWAY
Air

More than 60 international airlines operate services between Hong Kong's International Airport and some 120 cities worldwide. Consequently, competition keeps fares relatively low and it's a great place to hunt down discounted tickets; just watch out for swindlers. The most common trick is a request for you to pay a non-refundable deposit on an air ticket, only to be told when you return to pick up the ticket, that the flight has been cancelled and all that's available is a seat on a much pricier flight. The best way is not to pay a deposit, but rather to pay for the ticket in full and get a receipt clearly showing that there is no balance due and that the full amount is refundable if no ticket is issued. It's also wise to go with a reputable business – you can check this with the HKTB.

Tickets are normally issued the day after booking, but for the really cheapie tickets (actually group tickets) you must pick these up yourself at the airport from the 'tour leader' (whom you will never see again once you've got the ticket). Check these tickets carefully; occasionally there are errors, such as being issued a ticket with the return portion valid for only 60 days when you paid for a ticket valid for one year.

You can generally get a good idea of what fares are available by looking in the classified section of the *South China Morning Post,* where courier trips are also advertised.

Some budget return fares available in Hong Kong follow, but please note that these are discounted fares and may have various restrictions upon their use:

destination	HK$
Bangkok	1600
Johannesburg	6000
London	3500
Los Angeles	3500
Moscow	4950
Seoul	2800
Singapore	2100
Sydney	4000
Taipei	1700
Tokyo	3600
Vancouver	4000

Depending on the season, flights into mainland China can be extremely full; try to book in advance. You can make some savings on flights to destinations in China by flying from Guǎngzhōu or Shēnzhèn rather than Hong Kong. Domestic Chinese airlines run numerous direct flights between Hong Kong and every major city in China. Some one-year normal return fares are: Kūnmíng HK$3200, Shànghǎi HK$3300

and Guǎngzhōu HK$1020. You should, however, be able to find better prices. Return flights to Běijīng, for example, can be as low as HK$2300, and to Chéngdū HK$2600.

You can purchase a ticket from a travel agent, or the Civil Aviation Administration of China (CAAC), though you can sometimes get better rates from travel agents especially for popular routes like Hong Kong–Shànghǎi and Hong Kong–Běijīng. The most convenient CAAC ticketing offices in Hong Kong are in the airline list later in this section.

Dragonair typically charges HK$100 less than CAAC on one-way tickets, and double that amount for return tickets, although again it's wise to check around. Dragonair has flights from Hong Kong to 16 cities in China including Běijīng, Chéngdū, Chóngqìng, Dàlián, Guìlín, Kūnmíng, Nánjīng, Qīngdǎo, Shànghǎi, and Xī'ān. In Hong Kong, any travel agent with a computer can book you onto a Dragonair flight, but you can contact the ticketing offices of Dragonair directly.

Airport departure tax is HK$80; sometimes it's included in your ticket. You need to reconfirm your onward or return flight if you break your trip in Hong Kong. This can be accomplished at one of the following airline offices:

Air New Zealand (☎ 2524 9041) 17th floor, Li Po Chun Chambers, 189 Des Voeux Rd, Sheungwan
British Airways (☎ 2822 9000) 24th floor, Jardine House, 1 Connaught Place, Central
CAAC (☎ 2973 3666) Ground floor, 10 Queen's Rd Central; (☎ 2922 1028) 2nd floor, CNT House, 120 Johnston Rd, Wan Chai
China Airlines (Taiwan) (☎ 2868 2299) 3rd floor, St George's Bldg, 2 Ice House St, Central
Dragonair (☎ 2868 6777) Room 4609-11, Cosco Tower, 183 Queen's Rd Central
Northwest Airlines (☎ 2810 4288) 29th floor, Alexandra House, 16–20 Chater Rd, Central
Qantas Airways (☎ 2822 9000) 24th floor, Jardine House, 1 Connaught Place, Central
Singapore Airlines (☎ 2520 2233) 17th floor, United Centre, 95 Queensway, Central
United Airlines (☎ 2810 4888) 29th floor, Gloucester Tower, The Landmark, 11 Pedder St, Central
Virgin Atlantic (☎ 2532 6060) 27th floor, Kinwick Centre, 32 Hollywood Rd, Central

Bus

Shēnzhèn is the city just across the border from Hong Kong where you can get buses (and trains) to other points in Guǎngdōng. The border checkpoint is open from 6am to midnight daily. A new superhighway connects Hong Kong to Guǎngzhōu (Canton) – the bus journey takes three hours and there are a number of different bus companies making the trip.

From Hong Kong's Citybus Terminal (Map A; ☎ 2736 3888, ⓦ www.citybus .com.hk), buses to Guǎngzhōu (HK$110) depart between 7.30am and 9.30am. These buses also call at the station on the ground floor of China Hong Kong City in Tsim Sha Tsui en route to the border.

The Eternal East bus company (Map A; ☎ 2723 2923) at the Hankow Centre, 5–15 Hankow Rd, Tsim Sha Tsui has services to points throughout southern China, including Guǎngzhōu (HK$100), Fóshān (HK$150), Chángshā (HK$320) and Xiàmén (HK$350). Buses also head for Guǎngzhōu between 8am and 10am from City One Shatin on Tak Wing St in Sha Tin.

CTS runs hourly buses to Guǎngzhōu and southern China from Nelson St, opposite its Mong Kok branch at 62–72 Sai Yee St (Map A).

Finally, a number of bus companies, including CTS and Eternal East, run buses from Hong Kong's international airport to destinations throughout southern China, including Guǎngzhōu. Tickets are available in the arrivals hall.

Train

Reaching Shēnzhèn by train is a breeze. Board the KCR train at Hung Hom (1st/2nd class HK$66/33) or any KCR station along the way, and ride it to the border crossing at Lo Wu. China is a couple of hundred metres away. From Shēnzhèn you can take a local train or bus to Guǎngzhōu and beyond.

Alternatively, catch the Kowloon-Guǎngzhōu express train (two hours). Other high-speed trains leave Hung Hom station for Guangzhou east train station daily at 8.25am, 9.25am, 11.05am, 12.10pm, 1.25pm, 2.30pm and 4.45pm. They leave Guǎngzhōu at 8.30am, 9.50am, 11am, 1.36pm, 2.28pm, 3.50pm and 5.20pm (one way 1st/2nd class HK$230/180). There are also direct rail links between Hung Hom

and both Shànghǎi and Běijīng. Trains to Beijing west train station (hard/soft sleeper HK$574/934, 28 hours) depart on alternate days and travel via Guǎngzhōu, Chángshā and Wǔhàn. Trains to Shànghǎi (hard/soft sleeper HK$508/825, 28 hours) also depart on alternate days and pass through Guǎngzhōu and Hángzhōu.

Immigration formalities at Hung Hom are completed before boarding; you won't get on the train without a visa. Passengers are required to arrive at the station 45 minutes before departures. One-way and return tickets can be booked in advance from CTS or the KCR stations in Hung Hom, Kowloon Tong and Sha Tin. Tickets booked by phone (☎ 2947 7888) must be collected at least one hour before departure.

Boat

Due to competition with rail and air transportation, slow coastal boats between Hong Kong and other cities in China have largely been phased out. Those that do remain depart from the China Hong Kong City ferry terminal (Map A) in Kowloon.

Jet-powered catamarans and hovercrafts, however, go between Hong Kong and destinations on the Zhū Jiāng (Pearl River) Delta, as well as to Zhūhǎi and Macau. You can book tickets at the ferry terminals or at CTS, which usually charges a service fee. Boats depart from both the China Hong Kong City ferry terminal and the Hong Kong Macau ferry terminal (Map B) in the Shun Tak Centre in Sheungwan. There is a HK$19 departure tax when leaving Hong Kong by sea, but it's almost always included in the ticket price.

To Macau, there are three separate companies running rapid boat services, with frequent departures from both the Shun Tak Centre and Kowloon. See the Getting There & Away section of the Macau chapter for details.

Hovercrafts and catamarans depart from the China Hong Kong City ferry terminal for Guǎngzhōu (HK$198, two hours) at 7.30am and 2pm, with return sailings at 10.30am and 4.30pm. Once you reach Guǎngzhōu, buses shuttle passengers to major hotels in the city.

Shekou Passenger Ferry Lines (☎ 2526 5305) runs 13 Jetcats between Hong Kong and Shékǒu (HK$90, one hour), a port

HONG KONG & MACAU

From Kung Fu to Cannes

The swashbuckling Hong Kong film industry has developed into reputedly the third largest outside Hollywood and Bombay. It churns out more than 150 each year and has spawned some successful international stars.

During the early years of film production in Hong Kong, films tended to mirror the traditions and conventions of the more classical Shànghǎi cinema, but amid a relatively free business environment and few political constraints, the Hong Kong film industry gradually came into its own.

The unique feature of the cinema of Hong Kong is the successful combination of Hollywood-style audience appeal with high technical standards and the particular circumstances of Hong Kong's urban culture. Instead of being merely derivative, Hong Kong movies are infused with a distinct life of their own that strikes a chord with local viewers.

Many people unfamiliar with Hong Kong film associate it solely with kung fu, which is understandable, given that the first splash on the non-Asian market was via the awesome talent of Bruce Lee. Lee's phenomenal success in movies like *The Big Boss* (1971), which set local box-office history, *Fist of Fury* (1972) and *Return of the Dragon* (1972), shifted the emphasis of kung fu drama to actors with authentic martial arts experience. Lee's death cut short his career, but kung fu films dominated screens in Hong Kong for most of the 1970s and also drew the attention of the US market. Hong Kong was entering a period of economic boom and capitalist expansion and with it Hong Kongers began indulging in thrill-packed trips to the movies. These films drew crowds because they placed action over drama, a sure-fire method that had a lasting influence on Hong Kong film.

Kung fu films later evolved with the talented work of superstar Jackie Chan and more recently Jet Li. Chan's kung fu flicks and cop stories dominated the late 1970s and 1980s and led to his first foray into Hollywood in *Rush Hour* (1998).

Hong Kong's second wave of international notoriety came with the action films of director John Woo. Films like *City On Fire* (1987), *A Better Tomorrow I & II* (1986, 1987) and *The Killer* (1989) found enthusiastic fans in the US, among them Quentin Tarantino. John Woo's modern interpretation of kung fu films replaced sword-fighting with gun-toting and he achieved a specific brand of stylised action and violence. A great example of his technique can be seen in *Hard Boiled* (1992). Woo has gone on to make a number of films in Hollywood including *Face/Off* (1997) and *Mission Impossible 2* (2000), as have other successful Hong Kong directors like Tsui Hark and Ringo Lam.

The essence of Hong Kong cinema lies in more than kung fu and shoot-em-up gangster films. There's a remarkable flexibility between genres, not only between films, but within films and among directors and performers. Chow Yun Fat, Leslie

20km west of Shēnzhèn, between 7.45am and 9pm daily. Eight depart from the China Hong Kong City ferry terminal and the rest from the Hong Kong Macau ferry terminal. Return sailings from Shékǒu are from 7.45am until 9.30pm.

Zhūhǎi can also be reached by ferry. A dozen boats operated by Chu Kong Passenger Transportation Co (☎ 2858 3876) leave Hong Kong daily (HK$177, 70 minutes) from 7.45am to 9.30pm. Departures are from both the China Hong Kong City ferry terminal and the Hong Kong Macau ferry terminal. Return sailings run from 8am until 9.30pm.

High-speed ferries (☎ 2921 6688, W www.turbojet.com.hk) leave the China Hong Kong City ferry terminal for Shēnzhèn airport, via the Fuyong ferry terminal, (HK$189, one hour) eight times daily between 7.30am and 7pm. Return sailings from Fuyong run between 9am and 8.45pm, with the last two terminating at Hong Kong Macau ferry terminal.

For boats to Zhàoqìng and Hǔmén (Tàipíng) see the Guǎngdōng chapter.

GETTING AROUND

To/From the Airport

The days of daredevil landings into Hong Kong's downtown Kai Tak airport ended in 1998 with the opening of the Hong Kong International Airport at Chek Lap Kok, a massive improvement in efficiency and safety. At the airport, you'll find restaurants, left luggage, travel and transport agencies, ATMs, banks, shops, Internet services and even hot showers.

From Kung Fu to Cannes

Cheung and Jackie Chan perform across styles in comic, romantic and heroic roles. Hong Kong's strong crop of women actors, such as Maggie Cheung, Anita Mui and Michelle Yeoh (from *Crouching Tiger, Hidden Dragon*), also play interesting and diverse roles.

The Hong Kong film industry has achieved great success and notoriety through its comedies. There's no other place in Asia that comes close to matching the quality of Hong Kong's humorous and zany flicks. Examples include: *Aces Go Places 1, 2, 3, 4* and *5* from the 1980s; *God of Gamblers 1, 2* and *3* from the early 1990s; *Golden Girls* (1995); *Haunted Cop Shop 2* (1988); *Love on Delivery* (1994); and *Mack the Knife* (1995). These films exude a wacky, manic energy, expressing a surprisingly quirky world-view that shows a side of Hong Kong that is unfamiliar to most foreigners.

There's also a solid tradition of work outside the commercial mainstream. Directors like Ann Hui, Clara Law, Jacob Cheung, Peter Chan and Stanley Kwan are known for their introspective and critical films, whether it's exploring the subject of mainland immigrants in *Comrades, Almost a Love Story* (1996); social issues in *Cageman* (1992); or the effects of the Vietnam War in *The Story of Woo Viet* (1981) and *Boat People* (1982). More recently, the international festival circuit has been beguiled by the lush, dream-like films of Wong Kar-Wai, such as *Chungking Express* (1994) and *Happy Together* (1997), which won him Best Director at Cannes.

During the early 1980s a prominent theme of cinema in Hong Kong was the imminent handover of power to China. The rise of films featuring ghost stories, demons and fantastical scenarios expressed a sense of uncertainty about the future.

By the time of the handover, Hong Kong's film industry had entered a dangerous slump with a decrease in production and poor box office returns. Both the economic downturn and the proliferation of pirated VCDs were blamed. Hong Kong audiences lost confidence in local films and began to turn their attention to Hollywood blockbusters.

In just a few short years, however, the industry has rebounded. Wong Kar-Wai's sublime *In the Mood For Love* (2000) earned its star, Tong Leung Chiu Wai, the Best Actor award at Cannes. *Crouching Tiger, Hidden Dragon* (2000) may have been shot by Taiwan director Ang Lee, but most of the cast are Hong Kong talent.

Along with its successes, Hong Kong (similar to Hollywood and Bollywood) also produces a lot of garbage, much of which seems to end up as videos on those long bus rides you take in mainland China. Ultimately, the best Hong Kong films are like a good *dim sum* lunch: not too heavy, lots of variety and full of tantalising flavours to tickle the mind.

Located off the north side of Lantau Island, the airport is easily reached by a number of rail and bus links. Airport Express trains (☎ 2881 8888) depart from Hong Kong station in Central (Map B) every 10 minutes from 5.50am to 12.48am daily, calling at Kowloon station in Jordan and at Tsing Yi Island (HK$90/80/50 Central/Kowloon/Tsing Yi one way, children and seniors half price). The last train leaves the airport for all three stations at 12.48am. You can purchase return tickets for a slightly better rate and same-day returns are equivalent to a one-way fare. The journey takes 23/20/12 minutes from Central/Kowloon/Tsing Yi. All stations are equipped with flight indicators.

Airport Express runs two shuttle bus routes on Hong Kong Island (H1 and H2) and six in Kowloon (K1 to K6). They run from just after 6am until 11pm. Schedules and routes are available at Airport Express and MTR stations. Information is also available at the HKTB counter in the arrivals lounge.

Airbus also runs a number of shuttles between the airport and downtown Hong Kong and Kowloon, stopping at major hotels and guesthouse areas. These buses are air-conditioned, have lots of luggage room and stops are announced in English. The A series runs from 6am to midnight. The N series of buses follows roughly the same route, running after midnight.

Bus A21 (HK$33) runs from the airport and heads down Nathan Rd passing through Mong Kok, Yau Ma Tei, Jordan and Tsim Sha Tsui, then terminating at Hung Hom station.

Bus A12 (HK$45) goes to Central then through Wan Chai and Causeway Bay, finally terminating in Chai Wan.

Bus A11 (HK$40) goes from the airport to the Hong Kong Macau ferry terminal, on to Central, along Hennessy Rd through Wan Chai, Causeway Bay, terminating at the Tin Hau MTR station.

Buses also go to Lantau Island and destinations in the New Territories. Kiosks in the public arrivals hall have brochures on all the bus services available.

A taxi from the airport to Central will cost about HK$330.

Bus

Hong Kong's extensive bus system is able to take you just about anywhere in the territory. The HKTB has useful leaflets on the major bus routes, which can be downloaded from its Web site (W www.discover hongkong.com). Most buses run from about 6am until midnight although there are a handful of night buses including N121 (running from the Hong Kong Macau ferry terminal to Chatham Rd in Tsim Sha Tsui East and on to eastern Kowloon), N111 (running from Victoria Park to Choi Hung in eastern Kowloon), N122 (running from North Point on Hong Kong Island to Chatham Rd, the northern part of Nathan Road and on to Lai Chi Kok in Kowloon) and N112 (running from Victoria Park to the Prince Edward MTR station in Kowloon).

Fares range from HK$1.20 to HK$45, depending on the destination. Night buses cost from HK$12.80 to HK$23. You need exact change.

Minibus & Maxicabs

Small red minibuses supplement the regular bus services. They cost HK$2 to HK$20 and you pay as you exit. They generally don't run regular routes, but you can get on or off almost anywhere – provided you can get the driver to stop.

Green Maxicabs are just like minibuses except they operate on some 295 regular routes and stop at designated places. Two popular routes are No 6 from the car park in front of the Star Ferry terminal in Central to Ocean Park, and No 1 from Star Ferry Terminal to Victoria Peak. Pay the exact fare as you enter.

Train

Mass Transit Railway (MTR) The MTR (☎ 2881 8888) has five lines that operate from Central, across the harbour and up along Kowloon Peninsula to the New Territories. It is very fast and convenient, but fairly pricey and not great value for short journeys. Ticket prices range from HK$4 to HK$26. The ticket machines give change and single-journey tickets are valid only for the day they are purchased. Once you go past the turnstile, you must complete the journey within 90 minutes or the ticket becomes invalid. The MTR operates from 6am to 1am.

If you use the MTR frequently, it's very useful to buy a stored-value Octopus card, which can also be used on the KCR, Airport Express and some buses and ferries. You can buy them at the MTR station (minimum HK$150, including deposit) and add value to them at automated machines.

Smoking, eating and drinking are not allowed in MTR stations or on trains; fines range from HK$1000 to HK$2000.

Kowloon-Canton Railway (KCR) The KCR (☎ 2602 7799) is a single line running from Hung Hom station in Kowloon to Lo Wu, where you can walk across the border into Shēnzhèn. It's excellent transport to the New Territories and offers some nice vistas. Trains run every five to 10 minutes or every three minutes during rush hour. Fares are cheap (HK$9) unless you go all the way to the border ($HK33). Octopus cards can be used on the KCR, but for Lo Wu station you have to get it zapped at one of the ticket booths at KCR stations.

Tram

There is just one major tram line, in operation since 1904, running east-west along the northern side of Hong Kong Island. As well as being ridiculously picturesque and fun to travel on, the tram is quite a bargain at HK$2 for any distance. You pay as you get off.

Light Rail Transit (LRT)

The LRT (☎ 2468 7788) operates only on routes in the western part of the New Territories, running between the Tuen Mun ferry pier and Yuen Long. Fares are HK$4 to HK$5.80.

Taxi

On Hong Kong Island and Kowloon, the flag fall is HK$15 for the first 2km then HK$1.40 for every additional 200m. In the New Territories, flag fall is HK$12.50, thereafter HK$1.20 for every 200m. There is a luggage fee of HK$5 per bag, but not all drivers insist on this. It also costs an extra HK$5 to book a taxi by telephone.

If you go through either the Cross-Harbour Tunnel, Eastern or Western Harbour Tunnel, or any other tunnels with fees, you'll be charged double the toll (HK$20 for the Cross Harbour Tunnel, HK$60 for the Lantau Link).

Bicycle

Bicycling in Kowloon or Central would be suicidal, but in quiet areas of the islands, in Shek O on Hong Kong Island or the New Territories, a bike can be quite a nice way of getting around. The bike-rental places tend to run out early on weekends.

Flying Ball Bicycle Co (☎ 2381 3661), 201 Tung Choi St, Mong Kok, near the Prince Edward MTR station, is where serious cyclists will find a great selection of bikes and accessories.

At Silvermine Bay (Mui Wo) on Lantau Island, bicycles are available for hire at two central locations, which are both a short distance from the ferry pier: Friendly Bicycle Shop (☎ 2984 2278), Shop 12, Mui Wo Centre, 1 Ngan Wan Rd, just opposite Wellcome, and the nearby King of Bicycles (☎ 2984 9761), Shop 14, Mui Wo Centre, 1 Ngan Wan Rd. Bikes per day cost HK$25 during the week and HK$35 at the weekend; otherwise it's HK$10 per hour. On summer weekends, bikes can also be hired from stalls in front of the Silvermine Bay Beach Hotel in Mui Wo and in Pui O village.

In the New Territories, bicycles can be rented in season from several stalls around Tai Po Market KCR station. There are a number of bicycle shops lining Kwong Fuk Rd north-west of Tai Po Market KCR station.

Boat

With such a scenic harbour and a wide variety of public transport boats, commuting by ferry is the most enjoyable (and cheapest) way of getting around.

Star Ferry

First launched in 1888, Star Ferry services (☎ 2366 2576, W www .starferry.com.hk) are as much a tourist attraction as a mode of transport. There are four routes, but by far the most popular one shuttles between Tsim Sha Tsui and Central, offering some dramatic views on clear nights.

Tsim Sha Tsui–Central Every four to 10 minutes from 6.30am to 11.30pm; HK$1.70/2.20 lower/upper deck
Tsim Sha Tsui–Wan Chai Every eight to 20 minutes from 7.30am to 11pm; HK$2.20
Hung Hom–Central Every 15 to 20 minutes from 7.20am to 7.20pm; HK$5.50
Hung Hom–Wan Chai Every 15 to 20 minutes from 7.08am to 7pm; HK$5.30

Other Cross-Harbour Ferries

Three other ferry companies operate cross-harbour routes: Discovery Bay Transportation Service, New World First Ferry and Fortune Ferry Co. The schedule is as follows:

Central (Queen's Pier)–Tsim Sha Tsui East Every 20 minutes from 7.40am (from 8am Sunday) to 8.20pm daily; HK$4.50
North Point–Hung Hom Every 20 minutes from 7.20am to 7.20pm daily; HK$4.50
North Point–Kowloon City Every 20 minutes from 7.10am to 7.30pm daily; HK$4.50
North Point–Kwun Tong Every 15 to 30 minutes from 7.15am to 7.45pm Monday to Saturday, every 30 minutes from 7am to 7.30pm Sunday; HK$5

Other Boats

A *kaido* is a small- to medium-sized ferry that can make short runs on the open sea. Few kaido routes operate on regular schedules, preferring to adjust their supply according to demand. There is a schedule on popular runs like the trip between Aberdeen and Lamma Island. Kaidos run most frequently on weekends and public holidays when everyone tries to get away from it all.

A *sampan* is a motorised launch that can accommodate only a few people. A sampan is too small to be considered seaworthy, but can safely zip you around typhoon shelters like Aberdeen Harbour.

Bigger than a sampan, but smaller than a kaido, is a *walla walla*. The few that are left operate as water taxis on Victoria Harbour. Most of the customers are sailors living on ships anchored in the harbour.

Outlying Island Ferries New World First Ferry Services (☎ 2131 8181, **w** www.nwff .com.hk) runs boats to the Outlying Islands and the Hong Kong & Kowloon Ferry (☎ 2815 6063, **w** www.hkkf.com.hk) serves destinations on Lamma. Schedules are posted at all ferry piers or you can pick up a copy at the HKTB or on the ferry companies' Web sites. Fares are higher on weekends and public holidays, and the boats can get crowded. From Central, most ferries go from the Outlying Islands piers just west of the Star Ferry terminal on Hong Kong Island. Besides the ordinary ferries, pricier hovercrafts also shuttle to Lantau, Cheung Chau and Peng Chau.

Kowloon

Kowloon (Map A), the peninsula pointing out towards Hong Kong Island, is a riot of commerce and tourism. Its main drag, Nathan Rd, is packed with shops, hotels, bars, restaurants, nightclubs and tourists.

Start your exploration from Kowloon's southern tip, the tourist ghetto known as Tsim Sha Tsui. Adjacent to the Star Ferry terminal is the **Hong Kong Cultural Centre** (☎ 2734 2009, 10 Salisbury Rd; open 9am-11pm Mon-Sat, 1pm-11pm Sun & public holidays) with its controversial windowless facade facing one of the most spectacular views in the world. Forty-minute tours cost HK$10/5 for adults/children, students and seniors. Part of the Cultural Centre complex, the **Hong Kong Museum of Art** (☎ 7221 0116; adult/child or senior HK$10/5; open 10am-6pm Fri-Wed) has six floors filled with antiques, historical photographs and contemporary art.

The **Hong Kong Space Museum** (☎ 2721 0226; admission exhibition halls HK$10, Space Theatre HK$24-32; open 1pm-9pm Mon, Wed-Fri, 10am-9pm Sat, Sun & public holidays) has several exhibition halls and a Space Theatre (planetarium). The Space Theatre shows about seven IMAX films each day. Check film times with the museum.

A site in itself, the lower end of Nathan Rd is known as the **Golden Mile**, a reference to both the price of its real estate and its ability to suck money out of tourist pockets. Halfway up Nathan Rd is **Kowloon Park**, an oasis of greenery after the hustle of Tsim Sha Tsui. Unfortunately, it's becoming less of a park and more of an amusement ground. The **swimming pool** (☎ 2724 3577; admission HK$19; open 6.30am-9pm daily Apr-Oct) is perhaps the park's finest attribute – it's even equipped with waterfalls.

The **Kowloon Mosque** (☎ 2724 0095, 105 Nathan Rd) was opened in 1984 on the site of an earlier mosque constructed in 1896. Unless you are Muslim, you must obtain permission to go inside. It's usually given but make sure you are dressed modestly and have removed your shoes.

The **Hong Kong Science Museum** (☎ 2732 3232; admission HK$25; open 1pm-9pm Tues-Fri, 10am-9pm Sat, Sun & public holidays), in Tsim Sha Tsui East, is a multilevel complex housing more than 500 exhibits.

The **Museum of History** (☎ 2724 9042, 100 Chatham Rd South; admission HK$10, free Wed; open 10am-6pm Tues-Sat, 1pm-6pm Sun & public holidays) takes visitors on an interesting wander through Hong Kong's existence from prehistoric times (about 6000 years ago, give or take a few) to the present.

At the north end of Nathan Rd, the Mong Kok district is home to the exotic **Yuen Po Street Bird Market**. It's a short walk east of the Prince Edward MTR station, which will also take you through the deliciously sensual **Flower Market** (Flower Market Rd). Another market worth checking out is the **Temple Street Night Market**, the liveliest place to bargain for cheap clothes and fake name-brand goods. Just north of here, is the **Jade Market** (Kansu St; open 10am-4pm daily), where hundreds of indoor stalls sell all varieties of jade. Beware: unless you really know your stuff, you'll likely get fleeced.

The **Wong Tai Sin Temple** (Lung Cheung Rd; admission by HK$1 or more donation; open 7am-6pm daily) is a large and active Taoist temple built in 1973. It's right near the Wong Tai Sin MTR station just north of Kowloon. Just below and to the left of the temple is an arcade of fortune tellers; many speak decent English. East of here is the **Chin Lin Nunnery** (5 Chin Lin Drive; admission free; open 9am-4pm Thur-Tues), a large and serene Buddhist complex that's worth a visit. To reach it, take the MTR to Diamond Hill (exit C2).

PLACES TO STAY

Accommodation in Hong Kong is expensive. Solo backpackers may want to seek out dormitories, some of which are very basic. There are a few YHA dormitories, but all are very inconveniently located. The same is true for campsites – they exist, but you'll spend an hour or two commuting to the city. Guesthouses are the salvation for most budget travellers where you can often find dorms or private rooms the size of closets.

The prices for many of Hong Kong's 'mid-range' hotels have dropped to reasonable levels; it's worth checking around for discounts. At mid-range and top-end hotels you can get sizeable discounts (up to 50%) by booking through some travel agencies. The Hong Kong Hotels Association (☎ 2383 8380, fax 2362 2383, e hrc@hkha.org) provides this service at its reservation centre at the airport. Budget travellers can use its free courtesy phone to hunt for vacancies.

Rentals are generally about 20% cheaper if you pay by the week, but stay one night first to scout out noisy neighbours and rats.

PLACES TO STAY – BUDGET

YMCA Salisbury (☎ 2368 7000, W www .ymcahk.org.hk, 41 Salisbury Rd, Tsim Sha Tsui) Dorm beds HK$199. This is not a budget hotel; its 9th-floor four-bed dorm rooms are pricey but plush. Restrictions are plentiful: check in at 2pm, seven-night-stay maximum and walk-in guests are not accepted if they've been staying in Hong Kong for more than 10 days.

Hakkas Guesthouse (☎ 2771 3656, fax 2770 1363, Flat G, 3rd floor, 300 Nathan Rd) Singles or doubles/triples with bath HK$250/300. One of eight guesthouses in New Lucky House, this place has the nicest rooms.

Rent-A-Room (☎ 2366 3011, W www .rentaroomhk.com, Flat A, 2nd floor, Knight Garden, 7-8 Tak Hing St, Yau Ma Tei) Singles/doubles/triples HK$300/350/450. There are 40 immaculate rooms here, with shower, TV and telephone. Local calls are free, as is use of the hotel's washing machine.

YWCA Anne Black Guesthouse (☎ 2713 9211, e annblack@ywca.org.hk, 5 Man Fuk Rd, Yau Ma Tei) Singles/doubles from HK$330/429. This guesthouse welcomes both men and women. It's inconveniently located but the prices are reasonable. It's near Pui Ching and Waterloo Rds, up a hill behind a Caltex petrol station. Expect discounts during the low season.

Caritas Bianchi Lodge (☎ 2388 1111, e cblresv@bianchilodge.com, 4 Cliff Rd, Yau Ma Tei) Singles/doubles/triples HK$360/410/510. Though it's just off Nathan Rd, the rear rooms here are quiet and some have views onto King's Park.

Star Guesthouse (☎ 2723 8951, fax 2311 2275, Flat B, 6th floor, 21 Cameron Rd, Tsim Sha Tsui) and **Lee Garden Guesthouse** (☎ 2367 2284, e charliechan@ iname.com, 8th floor, D Block, 36 Cameron Rd) Singles with shared bath HK$200, doubles/triples with private bath HK$250/400. These two excellent guesthouses have a charismatic owner who can arrange most things for you. Long-term stayers get good discounts.

Chungking Mansions

There is probably no other place in the world like Chungking Mansions (36-44 Nathan Rd), the budget accommodation ghetto of Hong Kong. It's a huge run-down high-rise in the heart of Tsim Sha Tsui with approximately 80 guesthouses. It's divided into five blocks labelled A to E, each with its own sluggish lift. Despite the dilapidated appearance of the building, most of the little guesthouses are OK. Although rooms are the size of cupboards, they generally have air-con and TVs.

With few exceptions, there is little difference in prices for private rooms, although dormitories are of course significantly cheaper.

Travellers' Hostel (☎ 2368 7710, fax 2368 2505, Flat A1, 16th floor, A Block) Dorm beds HK$65, doubles with/without bath HK$130/120. This popular hostel is a landmark in this building, with dorms and cooking facilities available.

Park Guesthouse (☎ 2368 1689, fax 2367 7889, Flat A1, 15th floor, A Block) Singles with shared/private bath HK$120/150, doubles HK$150/200. This guesthouse is clean, air-conditioned and friendly.

Peking Guesthouse (☎ 2723 8320, fax 2366 6706, Flats A1-2, 12th floor, A Block) Singles/doubles/triples with bath HK$150/ 180/300. The spotless Peking has friendly management.

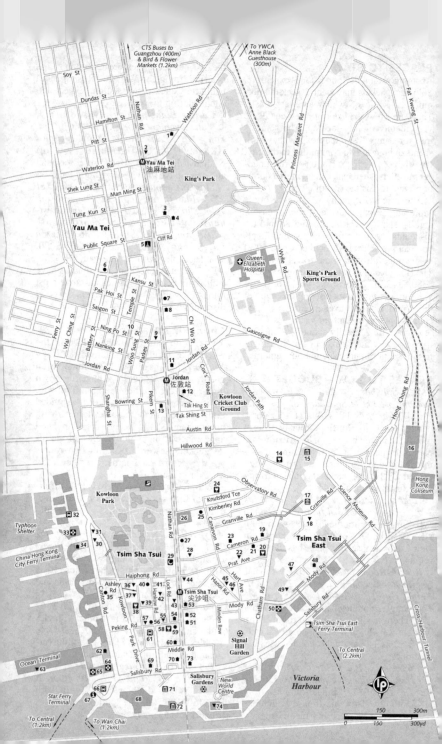

KOWLOON – Map A

PLACES TO STAY
1 YMCA International House
青年會國際賓館
3 Booth Lodge
卜威廉
4 Caritas Bianchi Lodge
明愛白英奇
8 Nathan Hotel
彌敦酒店
11 Hakkas Guesthouse; New Lucky House
嘉應賓館
12 Rent-A-Room
13 Shamrock Hotel
新樂酒店
19 Park Hotel
百樂酒店
21 Lee Garden Guesthouse
利園旅店
23 Star Guesthouse
26 Miramar Hotel
美麗花酒店
34 Royal Pacific Hotel & Towers
皇家太平洋酒店
48 Royal Garden; Royal Garden Chinese Restaurant
帝苑酒店
51 Chungking Mansions
重慶大廈
52 Holiday Inn Golden Mile
金域假日酒店
53 Mirador Arcade
美麗都
54 Hyatt Regency Hotel
60 Kowloon Hotel
九龍酒店
62 Marco Polo Hong Kong Hotel
香港馬哥孛羅酒店
69 YMCA Salisbury
香港基督教青年會
70 Peninsula Hotel
香港半島酒店
73 Sheraton Hong Kong Hotel & Towers
香港喜來登酒店

PLACES TO EAT
2 Joyful Vegetarian
如意素食
9 Miu Gute Cheong Vegetarian Restaurant
妙吉祥素食館

18 Genki Sushi
22 Canton Court
28 Cafe.com
咖啡店
30 Dai Pai Dong
大排档
31 Happy Garden Noodle & Congee Kitchen
36 Fat Angelo's
37 Gaylord
爵樂餐廳
39 Kyo-Zasa
42 Java South East Asian Restaurant
爪哇東南亞餐廳
43 Branto Indian Pure Vegetarian Club
44 Banana Leaf Curry House
蕉葉咖喱屋
45 Biergarten
啤酒花园
46 La Tasca
47 North Sea Fishing Village
49 Woodlands Indian Vegetarian Restaurant
活蘭印度素食
55 First Cup Coffee
57 Three-Five Korean Restaurant
三五亭韓國餐廳
63 Dan Ryan's Chicago Grill
74 Lai Ching Heen; Regent Hotel
麗晶酒店

OTHER
5 Tin Hau Temple
天后廟
6 Jade Market
7 Map Publications Centre
10 Temple Street Night Market
廟街夜市
14 Chemical Suzy
15 Museum of History
香港歷史博物館
16 Hung Hom KCR Terminal
紅磡車站
17 Hong Kong Science Museum
香港科學館
20 Boom Bar & Club

24 Bahama Mama's Caribbean Bar
25 David Chan; Onestop Photo Company
陣烘相機公司；忠誠影音公司
27 Phoenix Services Agency
29 Kowloon Mosque
清真寺
32 China Hong Kong Citybus Station (Buses to China)
33 The Gateway
港威大廈
35 Traveller Services
38 Ned Kelly's Last Stand
力嘉利絲餐廳
40 Ming's Sports Co
名任運動用品
41 Curio Alley
50 Wing On Department Store
永安九龍中心
56 HMV Record Store
58 Delaney's
愛爾蘭餐廳酒吧
59 CTS
中國旅行社
61 Eternal East Bus Company (Buses to China)
64 Marco Polo Hong Kong Hotel Shopping Arcade; Silk Road
65 Star House
星光行
66 Kowloon Star Ferry Bus Terminal
天星碼頭巴士總站
67 HKTB Information Centre
香港旅遊協會
68 Hong Kong Cultural Centre
香港文化中心
71 Hong Kong Space Museum
香港太空館
72 Hong Kong Museum of Art
香港藝術館

HONG KONG & MACAU

Garden Guesthouse *(☎ 2368 0981, Flat C5, 16th floor, C Block)* Singles/doubles with bath HK$150/200. This clean place is favoured by backpackers.

Mirador Arcade

You can avoid the stigma of staying in Chungking Mansions by checking out Mirador Arcade *(58 Nathan Rd)*. There are numerous places here and it's a bit cleaner and less crowded.

Man Hing Lung *(☎ 2722 0678, e mhl hotel@hkstar.com, Flat F2, 14th floor)* Singles HK$120-180, doubles HK$200-250. This place has clean rooms, a good atmosphere and Internet access. If you want a roommate, the friendly management can put you in with another traveller.

Cosmic Guesthouse *(☎ 2739 4952, fax 2311 5260, Flat A2, 12th floor)* Dorm beds HK$60, singles with bath HK$160, doubles HK$200-220. This is a clean, recently refurbished, quiet guesthouse.

First-Class Guesthouse *(☎ 2724 0595, fax 2724 0843, Flat D1, 16th floor)* Singles/doubles HK$150/180. While its name is a little ambitious, this place is clean and bright and the staff friendly. All rooms have attached bathroom.

Ajit Guesthouse *(☎ 2369 1201, fax 2739 0187, Flat F3, 12th floor)* Rooms with shared/private bath HK$150/250. This clean place is deservedly popular with travellers.

PLACES TO STAY – MID-RANGE & TOP END

Nathan Hotel *(☎ 2388 5141, w www .nathanhotel.com, 378 Nathan Rd, Yau Ma Tei)* Singles/doubles/triples from HK$500/600/780. This hotel is surprisingly quiet and pleasant; even the cheapest rooms are spacious and clean. Enter from Pak Hoi St.

Booth Lodge *(☎ 2771 9266, w boothlodge .salvation.org.hk, fax 2385 1140, 11 Wing Sing Lane, Yau Ma Tei)* Rooms with breakfast HK$620-1200. This spotlessly clean place on a quiet street is run by the Salvation Army and is an excellent choice.

Shamrock Hotel *(☎ 2735 2271, w www .yp.com.hk/shamrock, 223 Nathan Rd, Yau Ma Tei)* Rooms HK$650-1200. Long an affordable favourite and conveniently located, the Shamrock has recently undergone a massive facelift. You should be able to get a better deal than the rack rate.

YMCA International House *(☎ 2771 9111, w ymca-hotels.com, 23 Waterloo Rd, Yau Ma Tei)* Singles/doubles from HK$560/680. Though a bit out of the way, this large hotel with all its mod-cons is a steal for what it offers. Book well in advance.

Miramar Hotel *(☎ 2368 1111, w www .miramarhk.com, 118-130 Nathan Rd, Tsim Sha Tsui)* Rooms HK$1100-1800. This landmark central hotel has recently been renovated and comes up trumps.

Park Hotel *(☎ 2366 1371, e park2@ chevalier.net, 1-65 Chatham Rd South, Tsim Sha Tsui)* Singles HK$900-1500, doubles HK$1000-1600, plus 15% tax and service charge. This hotel is busy and congenial with slightly dated but comfortable rooms.

Royal Pacific Hotel & Towers *(☎ 2736 1188, w www.royalpacific.com.hk, China Hong Kong City, 33 Canton Rd, Tsim Sha Tsui)* Rooms HK$1080-2100. This hotel has a great location: there's a walkway to Kowloon Park, leading onto Nathan Rd and the MTR station. At the back, the hotel is connected to the ferry terminal from where boats sail for Macau and China.

Kowloon Hotel *(☎ 2929 2888, e khh@ peninsula.com, 19-21 Nathan Rd, Tsim Sha Tsui)* Singles/doubles from HK$1300/1400. This large hotel has a comically ostentatious lobby and great views of the back of the Peninsula Hotel. Nevertheless, it's popular for its unflappable service and decent rooms.

Marco Polo Hong Kong Hotel *(☎ 2113 0888, w www.marcopolohotels.com, Harbour City, 3 Canton Rd, Tsim Sha Tsui)* Singles/doubles from HK$2300/2400. This hotel has an outdoor pool and plenty of shops. Its two sister hotels have rooms at similar rates.

Sheraton Hong Kong Hotel & Towers *(☎ 2369 1111, w www.sheraton.com, 20 Nathan Rd, Tsim Sha Tsui)* Singles/doubles/suites from HK$2200/2400/3300. The Sheraton offers its usual plush rooms and high service. Rooms in the towers have fantastic views at steeper prices.

Holiday Inn Golden Mile *(☎ 2369 3111, w www.goldenmile.com, 50 Nathan Rd, Tsim Sha Tsui)* Singles/doubles/suites from HK$1000/1050/3500. This business-like hotel's rooms are Holiday Inn-reliable.

Hyatt Regency Hotel (☎ 2311 1234, Ⓦ www.hyatt.com, 67 Nathan Rd, Tsim Sha Tsui) Rooms HK$1250-2500, suites from HK$4400. The Hyatt is lower priced than most of its neighbours and a relaxed kind of hotel.

Peninsula Hotel (☎ 2920 2888, Ⓦ www .peninsula.com, cnr Salisbury & Nathan Rds, Tsim Sha Tsui) Singles & doubles from HK$3000. Elegant rooms in Hong Kong's finest hotel boast faxes, VCRs, CD players and marble bathrooms.

Royal Garden (☎ 2721 5215, Ⓦ www .theroyalgardenhotel.com.hk, 69 Mody Rd, Tsim Sha Tsui East) Singles/doubles/suites from HK$2100/2250/3700. This often overlooked hotel has an impressive garden atrium and a stunning rooftop pool.

PLACES TO EAT
Chinese Cuisine

While in Hong Kong, you should try dim sum at least once, a uniquely Cantonese dish served for breakfast or lunch, but never dinner. Dim sum delicacies are normally steamed in a small bamboo basket and you pay by the number of baskets you order. The baskets are stacked up on pushcarts and rolled around the dining room.

In Cantonese restaurants, tea is often served free of charge, or at most you'll pay HK$1 for a big pot, which can be refilled indefinitely.

Dai Pai Dong (☎ 2317 7728, 70 Canton Rd, Tsim Sha Tsui) Breakfast HK$22-30, noodles & rice dishes from HK$48. Breakfast (bacon and eggs, porridge, instant noodles), lunch and dinner are served here but it's best to come at afternoon tea for such oddities as *yuān yang* (half tea, half coffee), toast smeared with condensed milk and boiled cola with lemon and ginger.

Happy Garden Noodle & Congee Kitchen (☎ 2377 2604, 78-80 Canton Rd, Tsim Sha Tsui) Fill up on noodles at this budget place.

Extremely Good Restaurant (☎ 2394 8414, 148-150 Sai Yeung Choi St South, Mong Kok) Dishes HK$20-36. This busy place is known for its wonton soups and shredded pork noodles with spicy bean sauce.

North Sea Fishing Village (☎ 2723 6843, Basement, Auto Plaza, 65 Mody Square, Tsim Sha Tsui East) Meals from HK$150. This place is celebrated for its inexpensive fish dishes.

Canton Court (☎ 2739 3311 ext 176, Guangdong Hotel, 18 Prat Ave, Tsim Sha Tsui) Meals from HK$200, dim sum 7am-3pm. Excellent dim sum and meals at reasonable prices are available here.

Royal Garden Chinese Restaurant (☎ 2721 5215, Royal Garden Hotel, 69 Mody Road, Tsim Sha Tsui East) Meals from HK$200. This is one of the best places in Hong Kong for dim sum.

Lai Ching Heen (☎ 2721 1211, Regent Hotel, 18 Salisbury Rd, Tsim Sha Tsui) Meals from HK$400. This restaurant has repeatedly won awards for its Cantonese cuisine. The menu changes with each lunar month.

Temple Street Night Market (open 8pm-11pm daily) This is the cheapest place to enjoy authentic Chinese cuisine.

Indian Cuisine

The greatest concentration of cheap Indian restaurants is in Chungking Mansions on Nathan Rd. Despite the grotty appearance of the entrance to the Mansions, many of the restaurants are surprisingly plush inside.

Swagat (☎ 2722 5350, Flat C4, 1st floor, C Block, Chungking Mansions) One of the most popular in the building, this place has great food; the portions huge and it is the only fully licensed restaurant in the Mansions.

Delhi Club (☎ 2368 1682, Flat C3, 3rd floor, C Block, Chungking Mansions) This place does good-value Indian and Nepalese food and offers free delivery.

Taj Mahal Club Mess (☎ 2722 5454, Flat B3, 3rd floor, B Block, Chungking Mansions) The Taj is popular with those who like truly hot curries and don't like to pay a lot for them.

Kyber Pass (☎ 2721 2786, Flat E7, 7th floor, E Block, Chungking Mansions) Inexpensive, delicious food can be found at the Kyber Pass.

Gaylord (☎ 2376 1001, 1st floor, Ashley Centre, 23-25 Ashley Rd) Vegetarian/meat mains from HK$52/78. The first Indian restaurant to open in Hong Kong, this place has fantastic food and live music.

Branto Indian Pure Vegetarian Club (☎ 2366 8171, 1st floor, 9 Lock Rd) Dishes HK$60. This cheap and excellent place is where to go if you want to try sublime south Indian food.

Woodlands Indian Vegetarian Restaurant (☎ 2369 3718, Shops 5 & 6, Mirror Tower, 61 Mody Rd, Tsim Sha Tsui) Dishes about HK$100. If you can't handle the less-than-salubrious surrounds of Chungking Mansions, this place offers inexpensive Indian meals in comfortable surroundings.

Other Asian Cuisine

Java South East Asian Restaurant (☎ 2367 1230, Ground floor, Han Hing Mansion, 38 Hankow Rd, Tsim Sha Tsui) Mains HK$50-70, rijstafel per person HK$140-170. Here you'll get *rijstafel* (literally, rice table), with up to 16 dishes served with a large bowl of rice.

Genki Sushi (☎ 2722 6689, Shop G7-9, East Ocean Centre, 98 Granville Rd, Tsim Sha Tsui East) Sushi HK$9-35. This is cheerful and perhaps the cheapest place for sushi in Hong Kong.

Kyo-Zasa (☎ 2376 1888, 20 Ashley Rd, Tsim Sha Tsui) Dishes HK$48-68. Colourful and cosy, this has fantastic food and the prices are reasonable.

Three-Five Korean Restaurant (☎ 2376 1545, 6 Ashley Rd, Tsim Sha Tsui) Mains HK$88-130. This small place is sizzlingly popular.

Banana Leaf Curry House (☎ 2721 4821, 3rd floor, Golden Crown Court, 68 Nathan Rd, Tsim Sha Tsui) Meals from HK$100. For something with a little more spice, try this curry house. There are five other branches around Hong Kong.

Western Cuisine

Dan Ryan's Chicago Grill (☎ 2735 6111, Shop 200, Ocean Terminal, Zone C, Harbour City, Canton Rd, Tsim Sha Tsui) Mains HK$95-135, ribs HK$132-198. Dan Ryan's has made a name for itself as the place for burgers and ribs in Hong Kong.

Biergarten (☎ 2721 2302, 5 Hanoi Rd, Tsim Sha Tsui) Set lunch HK$65. Head here for pork knuckle, sauerkraut and some excellent beers on tap.

Fat Angelo's (☎ 2730 4788, 33 Ashley Rd, Tsim Sha Tsui) Salads/pasta/mains from HK$30/65/125. This place is generous with its portions and seamless in its service.

La Tasca (☎ 2723 1072, 8 Hanoi Rd, Tsim Sha Tsui) Mains HK$75-95, tapas HK$38-50. This place is famed for its tapas but also does more substantial Spanish main courses.

Vegetarian

See the Indian Cuisine section for more vegetarian options.

Miu Gute Cheong Vegetarian Restaurant (☎ 2771 6218, 31 Ning Po St, Yau Ma Tei) Dishes about HK$50. This cheap and cheerful place is family oriented. The tofu is fresh and firm, the vegetables are the pick of the market and the tea flows freely.

Joyful Vegetarian (☎ 2780 2230, 530 Nathan Rd, Yau Ma Tei) Mains around HK$40-60. The vegetable country-style hotpot here is made with a ravishing range of fungi.

Cafes

Cafe.com (☎ 2721 6623, Shop 5, Tern Plaza, 5 Cameron Rd) Espresso HK$15, sandwiches HK$12-20, salads HK$15. On offer here are 13 different coffee concoctions. There are also teas, including fruit tisanes. Enter from Cameron Lane.

Delifrance (☎ 2629 1845, Shop G101, The Gateway, 25-27 Canton Rd, Tsim Sha Tsui) Sandwiches from HK$25, set lunches HK$29-45. This is a branch of the popular bakery and patisserie chain noted for its pastries, muffins, submarine sandwiches and quiche, not to mention coffee.

First Cup Coffee (☎ 2316 7793, 3 Lock Rd, Tsim Sha Tsui) Coffee HK$9-58. This hole-in-the-wall of a shop serves some excellent gourmet coffees and sweet treats.

ENTERTAINMENT

There's as much to do in Hong Kong in the evening as during the day, but none of it comes cheap and the best places are on Hong Kong Island. It's impossible to list all the bars and clubs here and the following is only a selection: it's best to check out reviews and listings in *bc magazine* or *HK Magazine*.

Pubs & Bars

There are three basic clusters of bars in Tsim Sha Tsui: along Ashley Rd; within the triangle formed by Hanoi, Prat and Chatham Rds; and up along Knutsford Terrace. Tsim Sha Tsui East is the domain of swanky hostess bars and nightclubs.

Delaney's (☎ 2301 3980, Basement, Mary Building, 71-77 Peking Rd, Tsim Sha Tsui) Delaney's has Irish food, live folk music and great beer. Happy hour is from 5pm to 8pm.

Ned Kelly's Last Stand (☎ 2376 0562, 11a Ashley Rd, Tsim Sha Tsui) Open 11am-1am. This place is an authentic Aussie pub, right down to its meat pies. There's often live music.

Bahama Mama's Caribbean Bar (☎ 2368 2121, 4-5 Knutsford Terrace, Tsim Sha Tsui) Admission after 11pm HK$100, Fri & Sat only. Bahama Mama's is a friendly spot and stands apart from most of the other late-night watering holes in this part of town. On Friday and Saturday nights there's a DJ spinning and folks shuffling out on the bonsai-sized dance floor.

Boom Bar & Club (☎ 2172 7282, Shop D, Chevalier House, 45-51 Chatham Rd South, Tsim Sha Tsui) Admission HK$180. The new kid on the block is making a splash, especially with Groove@Boom, a techno and house disco every Wednesday and Friday 11pm to 6am.

Chemical Suzy (☎ 2736 0087, AWT Centre, 2a-b Austin Ave, Tsim Sha Tsui) This is a cyber-groover hide-out with DJs, snacks and a mixed crowd. Thursday is Queer Night from 6pm to 4am.

SHOPPING
Shopping in Kowloon is a bizarre mix of the down at heel and the glamorous; you can find just about anything, if you hunt hard enough. Die-hard shoppers should head for Harbour City, a mall with 700 shops on Canton Rd in Tsim Sha Tsui.

A word of warning: if you're looking for pricey high-tech items like cameras or video recorders, Tsim Sha Tsui is probably not the place to shop; you could be burned in more ways than one. The HKTB advises tourists to shop where they see the HKTB red logo on display, although this is no guarantee. The free *Official Shopping Guide* published by the HKTB is very useful, especially if you're looking for a specific item.

Antiques & Curios
Curio Alley Just south of Haiphong Rd, in an alleyway linking Lock and Hankow roads, this is a fun place to shop for name chops (carved seals that act as signatures), soapstone carvings, fans and other Chinese bric-a-brac.

Silk Road (Level 3, Marco Polo Hong Kong Hotel Shopping Arcade, Zone D, Harbour City, 3 Canton Rd, Tsim Sha Tsui)

Antique shops are concentrated along this corridor; here you can find cloisonne, bronzes, jade, lacquer, ceramics, rosewood furniture and screens.

Stone Village (☎ 2787 0218, 44 Flower Market Rd, Mong Kok) Check out the creative plant pots, pottery figurines and tea sets, plus a lot of beautiful bonsai that you're unfortunately unlikely to be able to take home.

Cameras & Photo Equipment
While Tsim Sha Tsui is not the place to buy cameras, not all dealers should be tarred with the same brush.

David Chan (☎ 2723 3886, Shop 15, Champagne Court, 16 Kimberley Rd, Tsim Sha Tsui) This dealer, one of the most reliable in Hong Kong, sells both new and antique cameras.

Onestop Photo Company (☎ 2723 4668, Shop 2, Champagne Court, 16 Kimberley Rd, Tsim Sha Tsui) Formerly trading as Kimberley Camera Company, this place is reliable.

Clothing
Clothing is the best buy in Hong Kong. The best hunting grounds for streetwear and one-of-a-kinds are generally at the eastern end of Granville Rd and along Austin Ave in Tsim Sha Tsui. You'll find better prices at the street markets on Tong Choi St in Mong Kok and in Apliu St in Sham Shui Po but the selection is not as good.

Department Stores & Emporiums
All big Western-style departments have outlets in Kowloon, some of them much bigger than their counterparts on Hong Kong Island. They include *Lane Crawford* (☎ 2118 3428, Levels 1 & 2, Ocean Terminal, Zone C, Harbour City, Canton Rd, Tsim Sha Tsui) and *Wing On* (☎ 2710 6288, Wing On Plaza, 62 Mody Rd, Tsim Sha Tsui East).

Chinese emporiums sell a range of ceramics, furniture, souvenirs and clothing. Try *Chinese Arts & Crafts* (☎ 2735 4061, Star House, 3 Salisbury Rd, Tsim Sha Tsui).

Music
The *Temple Street Night Market* is the place to pick up cheap CDs, DVDs and video cassettes. You can also try *HMV* (☎ 2302 0122, Sands Bldg, 12 Peking Rd, Tsim Sha Tsui; open 10am-midnight daily).

HONG KONG & MACAU

Sporting Goods

Chamonix Alpine Equipment (☎ 2388 3626, On Yip Bldg, 395 Shanghai St, Mong Kok) This two-floor shop has a wide range of camping, hiking and climbing equipment. The Hong Kong Mountaineering Training Centre (☎ 2384 8190) is also based here. Also try **Mountaineer Supermarket** (☎ 2397 0585, 1st floor, 395 Portland St, Mong Kok) and **Wise Mount Sports** (☎ 2787 3011, 75 Sai Yee St, Mong Kok).

Ming's Sports Co (☎ 2376 1387, 53 Hankow Rd, Tsim Sha Tsui) This is an excellent place to buy diving equipment.

Hong Kong Island

The northern and southern sides of the island have very different characters. The northern side is an urban jungle, while much of the south is still surprisingly rural (but developing fast). The central part of the island is incredibly mountainous and protected from further development by a country park.

NORTHERN SIDE

Central (Map B) is the bustling business centre of Hong Kong. A free shuttle bus from the Star Ferry terminal brings you to the lower station of the famous Peak Tram on Garden Rd. The tram terminates at the top of 552m **Victoria Peak** (one way/return HK$20/30; every 10min 7am-midnight daily). It's worth repeating the peak trip at night as the illuminated view is spectacular if the weather co-operates.

Wander up Mt Austin Rd to **Victoria Peak Garden** or take the more leisurely stroll around Lugard and Harlech roads making a 3.5km loop around the summit. You can walk right down to Aberdeen on the southern side of the island or you can follow Old Peak Rd for a few kilometres to return to Central. The more energetic may want to walk the 50km **Hong Kong Trail**, which traverses four country parks along the top of the mountainous spine of Hong Kong Island from the Peak to Big Wave Bay.

There are many pleasant walks in the **Zoological & Botanical Gardens** (admission free; gardens open 6am-10pm daily, zoo & aviaries 6am-7pm daily, greenhouses 9am-4.30pm daily) with views overlooking Central. This is also a leading centre for the captive breeding of endangered species; unfortunately the animals have less park to enjoy than the visitors. Located at the top of Garden Rd, the gardens are an easy walk from Central.

Dramatically sandwiched between skyscrapers and mountains, **Hong Kong Park** (Cotton Tree Drive; admission free; open park 6.30am-11pm daily, conservatory & aviary 9am-5pm daily) is home to a fantastic **aviary** of over 800 birds. This is also an easy walk from Central.

Linking Des Voeux Rd with Queen's Rd Central, **Li Yuen St East & West** are narrow alleys closed to motorised traffic and crammed with shops selling anything and everything. North-west of here, the four-storey **Central Market** resembles a zoo, selling everything from quail to eels. For more exotic produce, head uphill to the **Graham St Market**. Central Market marks the start of the 800m-long **Central Escalator**, the longest in the world, which transports pedestrians through Central and Soho, as far as Conduit Rd.

In the Sheung Wan district, is **Man Mo Temple** (cnr Hollywood Rd & Ladder St; admission free; open 8am-6pm daily), one of the oldest in Hong Kong. Farther north is the restored indoor **Western Market** (1906), home to Chinese knick-knacks and textile vendors. At the Western Market you can hop on one of Hong Kong's delightfully ancient double-decker trams, which take you east to Wan Chai, Causeway Bay and Happy Valley.

Just east of Central is **Wan Chai** (Map C), known for its raucous nightlife, but relatively dull in the daytime. One thing worth seeing is the **Hong Kong Arts Centre** (☎ 2582 0200, 2 Harbour Rd), which contains the **Pao Sui Loong Galleries** (☎ 2582 0256, 4th & 5th floors; admission free; open 10am-8pm daily during exhibitions), with local and international exhibitions of contemporary art.

The **Hong Kong Convention & Exhibition Centre** (☎ 2582 8888, 1 Expo Drive) is an enormous building on the harbour boasting the world's largest 'glass curtain' – a window seven storeys high. Ride the escalator to the 7th floor for a superb harbour view. The new wing on the waterfront with its distinctive roof is where the handover to China took place at midnight on 30 June 1997.

On the eastern side of Causeway Bay is the large **Victoria Park**, best-visited on

The Hong Kong Orchid

It was late in the 19th century when a few French priests happened upon the purple flowering *Bauhinia blakeana* near Hong Kong's seashore. When no identical tree could be found anywhere else in the world, it was declared a new species of bauhinia (of which there are 250 to 300) and named after Sir Henry Blake, governor of Hong Kong from 1898 to 1903.

Also known as the Hong Kong Orchid, the *Bauhinia blakeana* has spreading branches and broad, heart-shaped leaves. Its delicately scented flowers have five magenta-coloured petals, in blossom from November to March. The tree does not produce seeds and can only be propagated by air-layering, cutting or grafting. Thus all *Bauhinia blakeana* today are direct descendants of that single tree discovered by the priests.

When the British headed home in 1997, they took their Union Jack with them. Finding itself grafted onto China, it's not surprising that Hong Kong chose the *Bauhinia blakeana* for its new flag – a symbol of beauty and uniqueness.

You'll see examples of the *Bauhinia blakeana* throughout the territory, but specific locations include Victoria Park, the Kowloon Walled City Park, Penfold Park in the centre of the Sha Tin Racecourse in the New Territories and along Yu Tong Rd in Tung Chung on Lantau Island.

weekday mornings when it becomes a slow-motion forest of tai chi practitioners. East of here, the tiny, famous **Tin Hau Temple** *(101 Tin Hau Temple Rd)* has been a site of worship for 300 years.

South-east of Causeway Bay, near Happy Valley, is **Tiger Balm Gardens** *(☎ 2890 5365, Tai Hang Rd; admission free; open 9.30am-4pm daily)*, officially known as the Aw Boon Haw Gardens. The gardens are 3 hectares of grotesque statuary. Even if you find it to be in appallingly bad taste, it's a sight to behold. Aw Boon Haw made his fortune from the cure-everything Tiger Balm medication.

SOUTHERN SIDE

The southern side of Hong Kong Island is of a totally different character to the north. The coast is dotted with fine beaches and villas perch on the hillsides overlooking the coast. If you're in a hurry to reach the beach, hop on a No 6 bus to **Stanley** from the Exchange Square bus terminal in Stanley. Otherwise, take the tram from Central to Shau Kei Wan where you can continue south by bus.

The tram marked 'Shau Kei Wan' takes you through the hubbub of Wan Chai and Causeway Bay to the Sai Wan Ho ferry pier at Shau Kei Wan. From there, bus No 14 heads over the central hills to Stanley. Stanley has a good beach where you can rent windsurfers and a busy **market** *(open 10am-6.30pm daily)*.

From Stanley, bus No 73 takes you along the coast by beautiful **Repulse Bay**, which is rapidly developing into high-rises and shopping malls. Towards the eastern end of the bay is the unusual **Kwun Yam Temple**, filled with likenesses of the Goddess of Mercy and an eclectic collection of figures and deities. Crossing the temple's **Longevity Bridge** is said to add three days to your life.

From here, the bus passes **Deep Water Bay**, which has a sandy, relatively quiet beach, and continues to **Aberdeen**. The big attraction here is the boat-filled harbour, many of which are part-time residences for Hong Kong's fishermen and their families. Sampans will take you on a half-hour tour of this floating city for about HK$60 per person (less if there's a group of you). For a free 10-minute tour, hop on one of the shuttle boats heading out to the harbour's floating restaurants. From Aberdeen, a final short ride on bus No 7 takes you back to your starting point, via Hong Kong University.

If you're feeling vigorous, the entrance to **Aberdeen Country Park** and **Pok Fu Lam Country Park** is about a 15-minute walk north along Aberdeen Reservoir Rd. From there you can walk up to Victoria Peak.

To the south-east of Aberdeen, **Ocean Park** *(☎ 2552 0291, Ocean Park Rd; adult/child $150/75; open 10am-6pm daily)* is a huge amusement park, complete with roller coaster, space wheel and octopus. The park is also home to what is reputed to be the world's largest **aquarium** as well as **Middle Kingdom**, a Chinese cultural village. Don't try to include Ocean Park in a tour to Aberdeen – it's worth a full day on its own.

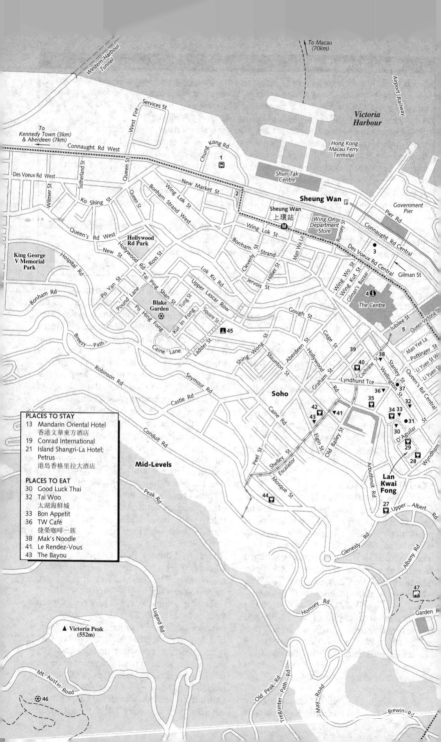

To Macau (70km)

Victoria Harbour

Airport Railway

Hong Kong Macau Ferry Terminal

Western Harbour Tunnel

Services St

West Fire St

Chung Long Rd

To Kennedy Town (3km) & Aberdeen (7km)

Connaught Rd West

1

Shun Tak Centre

Des Voeux Rd West

Sutherland St

Queen St

New Market St

2

Sheung Wan

Government Pier

Des Voeux Rd West

Wilmer St

Ko Shing St

Bonham Strand West

Wing Lok St

Sheung Wan
上環站

Wing On Department Store

Pier Rd

Connaught Rd Central

Queen's Rd West

Queen St

New St

Bonham Strand

Wing Lok St

Main Wai St

Rumsey St

3

Gilman St

Hollywood Rd Park

Hospital Rd

Hollywood Rd

Ross St

Cleverly St

Bonham St

Strand

Hillier St

Jervois St

Wing Wo St

Wing Kut St

Gilman's Bazaar

Des Voeux Rd Central

Queen Victoria St

King George V Memorial Park

Bonham Rd

Po Yan St

Tai Ping Shan St

Pound Lane

Lok Ku Rd

Upper Lascar Row

Tung St

Square St

Gough St

The Centre

4

5

Jubilee St

Mar Yee La

Po Hing Fong

Blake Garden

Kui In Fong

45

Ladder St

Shing Wong St

Staunton St

Aberdeen St

Hollywood Rd

Gage St

Graham St

39

Cochrane St

38

Wellington St

Stanley St

Pottinger St

Li Yuen St W

Li Yuen St E

Queen's Rd Central

Caine Lane

Breezy Path

Robinson Rd

Seymour Rd

Castle Rd

Conduit Rd

Soho

40

Lyndhurst Tce

36

35

37

32

D'Aguilar St

34 33

30

31

29

28

Wyndham

Peel St

Shelley St

Elgin St

Old Bailey St

Caine Rd

42

43

41

Mid-Levels

Mosque St

Escalator

44

Arbuthnot Rd

Lan Kwai Fong

27

Upper – Albert – Rd

Peak Rd

Glenealy Rd

47

Garden

Gleneary Rd

Hornsey Rd

Albany Rd

Lugard Rd

▲ *Victoria Peak (552m)*

Mt. Austin Road

46

Old Peak Path Rd

Tregunter Path Rd

May Road

Brewin Rd

PLACES TO STAY
13 Mandarin Oriental Hotel
   香港文華東方酒店
19 Conrad International
21 Island Shangri-La Hotel;
   Petrus
   港島香格里拉大酒店

PLACES TO EAT
30 Good Luck Thai
32 Tai Woo
   太湖海鮮城
33 Bon Appetit
36 TW Café
   捷榮咖啡一族
38 Mak's Noodle
41 Le Rendez-Vous
43 The Bayou

BARS & CLUBS

27	Zip
28	Post 97
29	The Jazz & Blues Club
34	Club 64
35	Propaganda
40	CE Top
42	Staunton's Wine Bar & Cafe
44	Bruce Lee's Café at Rickshaw

OTHER

1	Buses to Hong Kong & Macau Ferry Terminal
2	Western Market 西港城
3	CTS 中國旅行社
4	Hong Kong Tourism Board
5	Central Market 中環街市
6	Pacific Coffee Company
7	Bus Terminus 汽車站
8	International Finance Centre; Hong Kong Station 國際金融中心; 香港站
9	Dymocks Booksellers
10	Main Post Office 郵局
11	Canadian Consulate 加拿大領事館

12	HKTB Information Office 香港旅遊協會
14	Main Public Library; Internet 中央圖書館; 網吧
15	Times Books 當代圖書中心
16	HMS Tamar Naval Centre 添馬艦
17	Admiralty Centre; French Consulate
18	Pacific Place; Kelly & Walsh 太古廣場
20	British Consulate 英國領事館
22	US Consulate 美國領事館
23	Ocean Optical; Standard Chartered Bank Building
24	Hong Kong Book Centre
25	HMV 音樂無限
26	Bookazine
31	Mountain Folkcraft 高山民藝
37	Everbest Photo Supplies 永佳攝影器材
39	Graham Street Market
45	Man Mo Temple 文武廟
46	Victoria Peak Garden 山頂公園
47	Zoological & Botanic Gardens 動植物公園

See Map C Wan Chai & Causeway Bay Map p566-7

To Tuen Mun (23km)

To Tsuen Wan & Lamma Island (12km)

To Peng Chau (15km); Lantau Island (18km) & Cheung Chau (20km)

To Jordan (2.1km)

To Tsim Sha Tsui (1.2km)

To Hung Hom (3.6km)

To Tsim Sha Tsui East (2.2km)

Pier 5
Pier 6
Pier 7

Man Kwong St
Man Po St
Man Cheong St
Man Yin St

Blake Pier

Airport Express Central Station

Harbour View St

Exchange Square

Chiu Lung St

Connaught Centre

Connaught Pl

Star Ferry Terminal

Edinburgh Pl
Queen's Pier

Memorial Gardens

City Hall

Lung Wui Rd

Theatre La
Pedder St

Central 中環站

Connaught Rd Central

Cenotaph

Chater Rd

Prince of Wales Building

Tim Wa Ave

Landmark Shopping Centre

Duddell St
Ice House St

Statue Square

Chater Garden

Lambeth Walk

Harcourt Rd

Tim Mei Ave

Fenwick Pier St

Performing Arts Avenue

Sin Hua Bank

Bank St
Murray Rd
MTR Tsuen Wan Line

Far East Finance Centre

Drake St

To Wan Chai (600m) & Causeway Bay (1.5km)

Central

Queen's Rd

金鐘站
Admiralty

Harcourt Garden

Queensway

Hennessy Rd

Rodney St

MTR Island Line

Arsenal St

Queen's Rd East

Anton St

Landale St

Beaconsfield House Post Office

Bank of China Tower

Tram

Former Government House

St John's Cathedral

Garden Rd
Battery Path

Flagstaff House Museum

22

Peak Tram Terminus

Cotton Tree Dve

Supreme Court Rd

21

Admiralty

18

19

Justice Dve

20

Star St

Hong Kong Park

Kennedy Rd

Peak Tram

MacDonnell Rd

Borrett Rd

Kennedy Rd

Borrett Rd

0   100   200m
0   100   200yd

To reach Ocean Park, special Citybus vans leave from the bus station next to Admiralty MTR station (adult/child HK$12/6) every 15 to 20 minutes from 9.10am. Ocean Park Citybus leaves the Star Ferry terminal for the same price, with the last bus returning to the ferry at 4.30pm (6.30pm on Sunday). Citybus also sells a package ticket that includes transportation and admission to Ocean Park (adult/child HK$174/87). A cheaper option is bus No 70 from Exchange Square in Central; get off at the first stop past the tunnel and walk 10 minutes to the park entrance. Minibus No 6 from Central's Star Ferry terminal takes you directly to the park but doesn't run on Sunday or public holidays.

On the south-east coast, the village of Shek O has one of the best beaches on Hong Kong Island. Take the MTR or tram to Shau Kei Wan and from there bus No 9 to the last stop. On Sunday and public holidays, Bus No 390 goes directly to Shek O from the Exchange Square terminus.

PLACES TO STAY – BUDGET

Jockey Club Mount Davis Hostel (☎ 2817 5715, W *www.yha.org.hk/mawui.html, Mt Davis Path, Kennedy Town)* Beds per junior/senior from HK$40/64, family rooms HK$250-450. Check-in 7am-11pm daily. On top of Mt Davis, off Victoria Rd in the northwest of Hong Kong Island, is this clean, quiet hotel that was until recently called Mui Wui Hall. There are cooking facilities, a recreation room and secure lockers. The only drawback is reaching it. The easiest way to get there is by the hostel's shuttle bus from the Shun Tak Centre in Sheung Wan (200 Connaught Rd; departures at 9.30am, 7pm, 9pm and 10.30pm). Alternatively, catch bus No 47A from Admiralty or minibus No 54 from the Outlying Islands ferry terminal. Alight at Felix Villas and follow Mt Davis Path (not Mt Davis Rd – look for the YHA sign) for 30 to 40 minutes. Call ahead before you make the trek out here.

Most of the cheaper guesthouses on Hong Kong Island are in Causeway Bay (Map C).

Wang Fat Hostel (☎ 2895 1015, e *wang fath@netvigator.com, Flat A2, 3rd floor, 47 Paterson St, Causeway Bay)* Singles/doubles with shared bath HK$180/200, with private bath HK$220/250. This quiet, clean hostel is perhaps the best deal in the territory. The English-speaking owner is friendly, offers free Internet access and can arrange almost anything for you.

Noble Hostel (☎ 2576 6148, fax 2577 0847, Flat A3, 17th floor, 27 Paterson St, Causeway Bay)* Singles/doubles with shared bath HK$250/300, with private bath HK$300/360. This squeaky clean hostel is also very good value.

Causeway Bay Guesthouse (☎ 2895 2013, fax 2895 2355, Flat B, 1st floor, 44a-d Leighton Rd, Causeway Bay)* Singles/doubles/triples with bath HK$250/350/400. On the south side of Causeway Bay, wedged between a church and a pub, this seven-room guesthouse gets booked up quickly. Airport bus A11 stops very near here. Also on the 1st floor is the *Emerald House* (☎ 2577 2368) with small, clean doubles for HK$450.

Alisan Guesthouse (☎ 2838 0762, e *alisangh@hkstar.com, Flat A, 5th floor, Hoito Court, 275 Gloucester Rd, Causeway Bay)* Singles/doubles/triples HK$280/320/380. Run by friendly, multilingual owners, this spotlessly clean place has 30 rooms with air-con, showers and toilets.

Lung Tin Guesthouse (☎ 2832 9133, Flats F & G, 2nd floor, Central Bldg, 531 Jaffe Rd)* Singles & doubles HK$250. Rooms in this pleasant place have shower, TV and telephone.

PLACES TO STAY – MID-RANGE

Hong Kong Island has fewer mid-range hotels than Kowloon. For deals, it's best to check with travel agents. Many offer weekly and monthly deals. Hotels listed here are on Map C.

New Cathay Hotel (☎ 2577 8211, W *newcathay.gdhotels.net, 17 Tung Lo Wan Rd, Causeway Bay)* Singles/doubles from HK$740/1050, including tax. Cheesy but cheap, this hotel faces the Victoria Park side of the bay, just down the road from Tiger Balm Gardens.

Newton Hotel (☎ 2807 2333, W *www .newtonhk.com, 218 Electric Rd, North Point)* Singles & doubles HK$900-1600, suites from HK$2600. On the corner of Oil St, this hotel is a real find and an easy walk from Causeway Bay through Victoria Park.

Charterhouse Hotel (☎ 2833 5566, W *www.charterhouse.com, 209-219 Wan*

Chai Rd, Wan Chai) Singles/doubles/suites from HK$950/1500/2000. This is a fantastic deal; almost top-end accommodation for mid-range rates.

Empire Hotel *(Map C; ☎ 2866 9111,* **W** *www.asiastandard.com, 33 Hennessy Rd, Wan Chai)* Singles/doubles/suites HK$1400/2000/2200, including tax & service charge. With sunny staff, pleasant rooms and a small swimming pool, the Empire is conveniently located and a great option, with extras such as complimentary apples at the desk. Enter from Fenwick St.

Wesley Hotel *(☎ 2866 6688,* **W** *www .grandhotel.com.hk, 22 Hennessy Rd, Wan Chai)* Singles or doubles HK$700-1800. This large, central hotel is one of the best deals on the island but there are very few facilities and the service is cavalier at best. Enter from Anton St.

Wharney Hotel *(☎ 2861 1000,* **e** *whar ney@wlink.net, 57 Lockhart Rd, Wan Chai)* Singles/doubles from HK$1000/1200. Wharney is popular for its rooftop swimming pool and outdoor whirlpool.

PLACES TO STAY – TOP END

Island Shangri-La *(Map B; ☎ 2877 3838,* **W** *www.shangri-la.com, Pacific Place, Supreme Court Rd, Admiralty)* Rooms HK$2400-3550, suites HK$5800. With fantastic personal service and nice touches like a library and outdoor spa, the sophisticated Shangri-La is bliss.

Conrad International *(Map B; ☎ 2521 3838,* **W** *www.conrad.com.hk, Pacific Place, 88 Queensway, Admiralty)* Rooms HK$1850-2250. A member of the Hilton Hotels group, the elegant Conrad gets enthusiastic reviews from business travellers.

Mandarin Oriental Hotel *(Map B; ☎ 2522 0111,* **W** *www.mandarinoriental .com, 5 Connaught Rd Central)* Singles/doubles HK$2950/4200. With stellar service, this place is the height of old-style luxury, though some people think it's starting to get a bit tattered. Rooms are outfitted with free Internet-capable TVs.

Renaissance Harbour View *(Map C; ☎ 2802 8888,* **W** *www.renaissancehotels .com, 1 Harbour Rd, Wan Chai)* Rooms HK$2100-2500. This spectacular hotel adjoins the Hong Kong Convention & Exhibition Centre. With the largest outdoor pool in town, a well-equipped business centre and informed concierges, it's hard to go wrong here.

PLACES TO EAT

The place to go for reasonably priced eats and late-night revelry is the neighbourhood known as Lan Kwai Fong. However, it's such a conglomeration of pubs and all-night parties that it's covered in the Entertainment section.

Chinese Cuisine

Mak's Noodle *(Map B; ☎ 2854 3810, 77 Wellington St, Central)* Dishes under HK$100. Readers praise this fantastic noodle shop. Get here early; it's shut tight by 8pm.

Tai Woo *(Map B; ☎ 2526 2920, 15b Wellington St, Central)* Dim sum HK$20-23 per serving. Very authentic Cantonese food is served here, with excellent dim sum from 11am to 4.30pm.

Beijing Shui Jiao Wong *(Map C; ☎ 2527 0289, 18 Jaffe Rd, Wan Chai)* Dishes HK$22-33. You won't find better (or cheaper) northern-style dumplings or noodle soup anywhere in Hong Kong.

Liu Yuan Restaurant *(Map C; ☎ 2845 1199, 2nd floor, CRE Bldg, 297-307 Hennessy Rd, Wan Chai)* Meals from HK$250. This superb and quite stylish Shanghai restaurant is well worth spending the extra money on. The crab claws cooked with duck egg and the tiny prawns steamed with tea leaves are superb.

One Harbour Road *(Map C; ☎ 2588 1234, 7th & 8th floors, Grand Hyatt Hotel, 1 Harbour Rd, Wan Chai)* Meals around HK$300. This is probably the classiest hotel Chinese restaurant in town. In addition to the beautiful design and fab harbour view, six pages of gourmet dishes await your perusal.

The two floating restaurants at Aberdeen, ***Jumbo Floating Restaurant*** *(☎ 2553 9111)* and ***Tai Pak Floating Restaurant*** receive bad press for their food but offer good views and a different kind of dining experience.

Other Asian Cuisine

Good Luck Thai *(Map B; ☎ 2877 2971, 13 Wing Wah Lane, Central)* Curries HK$37-55. Somewhat chaotic but full of atmosphere, this is a great place for a cheap fix of Thai food.

Map C – WAN CHAI & CAUSEWAY BAY 灣仔、銅鑼灣

PLACES TO STAY

6 Renaissance Harbour View
9 Alisan Guesthouse 阿里山賓館
10 Lung Tin Guesthouse 龍田小築
12 Wang Fat Hostel 宏發賓館
13 Noble Hostel 高富旅館
16 New Cathay Hotel 新國泰酒店
17 Newton Hotel
22 Causeway Bay Guesthouse 華生旅舍
23 Emerald House 翡翠別墅
26 Charterhouse Hotel 利景酒店
31 Wharney Hotel 華美酒店
37 Empire Hotel 港島皇悦酒店
39 Wesley Hotel 衛蘭軒酒店

PLACES TO EAT

2 One Harbour Road
15 Kung Tak Lam 功德林
24 Isshin 口心
27 Liu Yuan Restaurant 留園飯店
28 Beijing Shui Jiao Wong 北京飯店
32 Simply Healthy 美康膳
33 Saigon Beach 濱海越南小館
36 Healthy Mess Vegetarian Restaurant 康健素食
40 Tan Ta Wan Thai Restaurant 月亮茶餐廳

OTHER

1 Hong Kong Convention & Exhibition Centre Extension 香港會議展覽中心
3 Hong Kong Arts Centre 香港藝術中心
4 Immigration Department 入境事務處裡

5 Hong Kong Convention & Exhibition Centre 香港會議展覽中心
7 Central Plaza; New Zealand Consulate 中環廣場；新西蘭領事館
8 Australian Consulate 澳洲領事館
11 Fashion Walk
14 Clothing Shops
18 Tin Hau Temple 天后廟
19 Tiger Balm Gardens 胡文虎花園
20 South China Athletic Association Stadium 南華體育會運動場
21 Hong Kong Amateur Athletic Association
25 Tower Records
29 Delaney's 愛爾蘭餐廳酒吧
30 Dusk till Dawn
34 Devil's Advocate
35 Avanti Network Cybercafe
38 The Wanch
41 Cosmos Books 天地圖書

To North Point (800m),
Quarry Bay (3km)&
Chai Wan (7.5km)

To Kowloon
(1km)

Cross-Harbour Tunnel

Oil St

Fortress Hill
炮台山 Ⓜ

■17

Fook Yum Rd

Wang On Rd

Electric Rd

Watson Rd

Shell St

King Ming Rd

Whitfield St

Mercury St

Causeway Bay
Typhoon Shelter

Eastern Corridor Island Rd

Wing Hing St

Gordan Rd

Electric Rd

Tsing Fung St

Lau Li St

Victoria Park Rd

Swimming Pool

🖼

Tin Hau Temple Rd

Royal Hong
Kong Yacht
● Club

Noonday
Gun ●

Gloucester Rd

Cleveland St

Tennis Stadium

Tin Hau
天后 Ⓜ

World
Trade
Centre
9 ■

Paterson St

Houston St

■11

Victoria Park

⚓
18

Cannon St

10 ●

Kingston St

Gloucester Rd

Percival St

12 ■

MTR Island Line

**Causeway
Bay**

13 ■

Lockhart Rd

Great George St

Causeway Rd

Causeway Bay Ⓜ
銅鑼灣站

Jardine's Bazaar

Sugar St

15 ▼

Moreton Tce

Tang Lung St

Tram

Kai Chiu Rd

14 ●

Lee Wo St

Shelter St

Tung Lo Wan Rd

Russell St

Pak Sha Rd

Jardine's Cres

Irving St

School St

Pennington St

Tung Lo

King St

Wun Sha St

Times
24
Square
●
25

Matheson St

Percival St

Lee Garden Rd

Lan Fong Rd

Hysan Ave

Hoi Ping Rd

Wan Rd

16 ●

Chun St

23 ■

Leighton Rd

Haven St

Kaning Path

22 ■

Leighton La

Broadwood Link Rd

Leighton Rd

Cotton Path

Caroline Hill Rd

Eastern Hospital Rd

Tai Hang Rd

**Leighton
Hill**

**Caroline
Hill**

21 ●

20

Tai Hang Rd

19 ✿

Sports Rd

Wong Nai Chung Rd

Caroline Hill Rd

Tung Wah
Eastern
Hospital

Happy Valley
Racecourse

To Happy
Valley (600m)

Hong Kong Stadium

Tai Hang

Tai Hang Drive

0   100   200m
0   100   200yd

Tan Ta Wan Thai Restaurant *(Map B; ☎ 2865 1665, Shop 9, Rialto Bldg, 2 Landale St, Admiralty)* Dishes from HK$40. This is perhaps the most authentic Thai food on Hong Kong Island, with great curries (HK$40-50) and seafood dishes (HK$100-145).

Bon Appetit *(Map B; ☎ 2525 3553, 14b Wing Wah Lane, Central)* Snacks HK$18-26, mains HK$26-30. This Vietnamese restaurant serves cheap but tasty meals for those on a tight budget.

Saigon Beach *(Map C; ☎ 2527 3383, 66 Lockhart Rd, Wan Chai)* Noodles & rice HK$26-33, mains HK$58-62. This popular hole-in-the-wall may not impress at first sight, but the affable service and excellent food is well worth sharing a table for – which you'll undoubtedly have to do.

Isshin *(Map C; ☎ 2506 2220, Shop 1304, Food Forum, Times Square, 1 Matheson St, Causeway Bay)* Meals around HK$300. Isshin is not cheap but does rate among the best of Hong Kong's Japanese restaurants.

Western Cuisine

Le Rendez-Vous *(Map B; ☎ 2905 1808, 5 Staunton St, Soho)* Savoury galettes & sweet crepes HK$7-43. This tiny place does baguettes, salads and fantastic crepes. Happy hour at the full bar is from 6pm to 8pm.

TW Café *(Map B; ☎ 2544 2237, Shop 2, Capital Plaza, 2-10 Lyndhurst St, Central)* Afternoon tea HK$34. This tiny place offers more than 20 types of coffee as well as light snacks.

Simply Healthy *(Map C; ☎ 2137 9797, 138 Lockhart Rd, Wan Chai)* Soups HK$10, set breakfast/lunch/dinner HK$18/30/17. Fabulous, affordable food that's just what it claims to be – low in fats, sugar and salt, high in fibre and no MSG.

The Bayou *(Map B; ☎ 2526 2118, 9-13 Shelley St, Soho)* Mains HK$132-168, set lunch HK$100. This popular spot serves authentic New Orleans-style Cajun and Creole cuisine.

Petrus *(Map B; ☎ 2820 8590, 2877 3838, 56th floor, Island Shangri-La Hotel, Pacific Place, 88 Queensway, Admiralty)* 5-/6-course set dinner HK$700/850.With its head in the clouds, this French restaurant is one of the finest in Hong Kong.

Vegetarian

Healthy Mess Vegetarian Restaurant *(Map C; ☎ 2527 3918, 51-53 Hennessy Rd, Wan Chai)* Dim sum HK$2.30-5 per dish, dishes HK$48-60. This strictly Buddhist restaurant offers tasty, filling food.

Kung Tak Lam *(Map C; ☎ 2890 3127, Lok Sing Centre, 31 Yee Wo St, Causeway Bay)* Dishes HK$100. This long-established place is usually packed out for its huge range of inexpensive Shanghai dishes.

ENTERTAINMENT
Central (Map B)

Running off D'Aguilar St in Central is **Lan Kwai Fong**, a narrow, pedestrian alley. Along with neighbouring streets and alleys, this is Hong Kong's hippest eating, drinking, dancing and partying venue, where prices range from economical to outrageous. Another area for bars and restaurants, **Soho** can be found south of Hollywood Rd and is easily accessed by the Mid-Levels escalator link. The following is just a taste of Central's hunting grounds.

Club 64 *(☎ 2523 2801, 12-14 Wing Wah Lane)* This laid-back place is an old favourite. From 2.30pm to 9pm it has one of Hong Kong's better happy hours with pints of draught beer from HK$24 and bottles for HK$21.

Post 97 *(☎ 2186 1817, 1st floor, Cosmos Bldg, 9 Lan Kwai Fong)* Open 9.30am-1am Sun-Thur, 9.30am-3am Fri & Sat. By day this comfortable place is more of a restaurant and coffee shop; you can sit for hours taking advantage of the excellent rack of Western magazines and newspapers. By night it's a popular bar.

Staunton's Wine Bar & Cafe *(☎ 2973 6611, 10-12 Staunton St, Soho)* Staunton's is swish with a lovely terrace upstairs. Happy hour is from 6pm to 9pm.

Bruce Lee's Café at the Rickshaw *(☎ 2525 3977, Basement, 22 Robinson Rd, Mid-Levels)* This club/bar has a swimming pool on the terrace and live music or a DJ on weekdays and a disco on weekends. Happy hour is from 3pm to 9pm. Enter from Mosque St.

CE Top *(☎ 2544 3584, 3rd & 9th floors, 37-43 Cockrane St)* This popular rooftop club features a mix of house, trance, garage, soul and drum n' bass. Enter from Gage St.

The Jazz & Blues Club (☎ 2845 8477, *2nd floor, California Entertainment Bldg, 24-26 D'Aguilar St*) Admission for local acts HK$60-100, overseas bands HK$300. This venue has long been *the* oasis for jazz fans. Jazz greats have graced its small stage as well as blues, rock and folk acts.

Wan Chai (Map C)

Most of the action here is concentrated at the intersection of Luard and Jaffe Rds and kicks on later than any other part of town. Expect to pay a cover charge of HK$100 or more at most of the places mentioned here, although it's often cheaper or free for women, and may include one drink.

Devil's Advocate (☎ 2865 7271, *48-50 Lockhart Rd*) This pleasant newcomer has been luring away trade from other pubs in the area.

Dusk till Dawn (*76-84 Jaffe Rd*) There's live music nightly from 10pm at this extremely popular dance club. It can get packed but the atmosphere is friendly.

The Wanch (☎ 2861 1621, *54 Jaffe Rd*) Just west of Fenwick St, this small live venue has alternative/folk music and beer and wine at low prices, but it can get crowded.

Delaney's (☎ 2804 2880, *2nd floor, One Capital Place, 18 Luard Rd*) This immensely popular Irish pub has a great atmosphere, Irish music and draught Guinness. The food is good too.

Gay Pubs & Bars

Listed previously, *CE Top* has a strong gay following on certain nights and *Post 97* has a gay happy hour from 6pm to 10pm.

Propaganda (Map B; ☎ 2868 1316, *Ground floor, 1 Hollywood Rd, Central*) Admission free Mon-Wed, after 10.30pm Thur HK$80, before/after 10.30pm Fri HK$70/140, before/after 10.30pm Sat HK$150/230. Unbelievably expensive, this is *the* gay club of Hong Kong.

Zip (Map B; ☎ 2523 3595, *2 Glenealy Rd, Central*) Open 6pm-2am. This is a small place that can get very crowded at the weekend.

SHOPPING

As mentioned in the Kowloon section, the HKTB advises tourists to shop where they see the HKTB red logo on display, although this is no guarantee. Central and Causeway Bay are the main shopping districts on Hong Kong Island. If you're shopping for clothes, the two alleys known as Li Yuen St East and Li Yuen St West in Central have some bargains. For antiques and curios, head to Hollywood Rd.

Jardine's Bazaar in Causeway Bay, near the Causeway Bay MTR station, has low-cost garments for those willing to hunt. Also in Causeway, the more upmarket *Fashion Walk* (or Houston St) has more than 30 boutiques.

Mountain Folkcraft (Map B; ☎ 2523 2817, *12 Wo On Lane, Central*) This is one of the nicest shops in Central for folk craft, bolts of batik and sarongs, clothing, and wood carvings.

Everbest Photo Supplies (Map B; ☎ 2522 1985, *28b Stanley St, Central*) For reliable cameras and photography equipment, try this place, patronised by locals. You may find cheaper buys elsewhere, but the rock-solid reputation and honesty is worth paying for.

Eyeglasses are more than likely much cheaper in Hong Kong than wherever you're from. *Ocean Optical* (Map B; ☎ 2868 5670, *Shop 9, Ground floor, Standard Chartered Bank Bldg, 4-4a Des Voeux Rd Central*) is one of the best in the territory.

Know every word to every song on every tape or CD you've got with you? *HMV* (Map B; ☎ 2793 0268, *1st floor, Central Bldg, 1 Pedder St, Central*) and *Tower Records* (Map C; ☎ 2506 0811, *7th floor, Shop 701, Times Square, 1 Matheson St, Causeway Bay*) are good places to restock.

New Territories 新界

The New Territories are so called because they were leased to Britain in 1898, almost half a century after Hong Kong Island and four decades after Kowloon were ceded to the crown. With urbanisation picking up the pace, a trip to NT gives you a glimpse of a society in transition as well as a look at what remains of traditional rural life in the territory. Temples and museums, fabulous mountain walks and sandy beaches abound. With a plethora of bus routes and the KCR and MTR, travel to and around NT is generally efficient and easy. The following sites are listed by location, travelling in a loop from east to west.

Located in **Tsuen Wan**, the **Sam Tung Uk Museum** (☎ 2411 2001, Ⓦ *www.heritage museum.gov.hk, 2 Kwu Uk Lane; admission free; open 9am-5pm Wed-Mon*) is an imaginative museum housed in a restored 18th-century Hakka walled village. Take exit B3 at the Tsuen Wan MTR station and walk five minutes south-east along Sai Lau Kok Rd to Kwu Uk Lane and the museum.

Nearby, **Chuk Lam Sim Yuen** (☎ 2490 3392, *Fu Yung Shan Rd; open 7am-4pm daily*), or 'Bamboo Forest Monastery', is one of the most impressive temple complexes in Hong Kong. To reach the temple, take minibus No 85 from Shiu Wo St, which is two blocks south of Tsuen Wan's MTR station.

In the hills north-east of Tsuen Wan, the **Yuen Yuen Institute** (*Lo Wai Rd; open 7am-5pm daily*) is a colourful Taoist temple complex and a popular tourist destination. Minibus No 81 from Shiu Wo St in Tsuen Wan will bring you here. A short distance away, the **Buddhist Western Monastery** (*Lo Wai Rd; open 7am-4pm daily*) feels relatively comatose, although you may enjoy the respite.

From here you can visit Hong Kong's tallest mountain, 957m **Tai Mo Shan** (*Big Misty Mountain*). The climb to the summit isn't too gruelling and offers impressive views in fine weather. The path is part of the **MacLehose Trail** (100km) that spans from Tuen Mun in the west to Pak Tam Chung on the Sai Kung Peninsula in the east. If you want to hike anywhere along this trail, the MacLehose Trail map is essential, available from the Map Publications Centre (see Walking & Hiking Trails in the Activities section near the start of this chapter).

East of Tai Mo Shan, parts of the MacLehose Trail overlap with the **Wilson Trail** (78km) which stretches from Hong Kong Island (near Stanley) all the way to Shau Tau Kok, near Hong Kong's border with the mainland. For details, get your hands on a good map from the Map Publications Centre.

Due north of **Tuen Mun** town centre, **Miu Fat Monastery** in Lam Tei is one of the most attractive and active Buddhist complexes in the territory. On the 1st floor is a *vegetarian restaurant* (*set meals HK$75*). The monastery is easily reached by taking LRT line No 610 or 615 to Lam Tei station. Bus No 63X from Nathan Rd in Tsim Sha Tsui also stops in front of the monastery.

If you're a birdwatcher, the 300-hectare **Mai Po Marsh** in the north-western New Territories is home to up to 300 species of your feathered friends. See Activities at the beginning of this chapter for details on tours. Bus No 76K, which runs between the town of Yuen Long and the Fanling and Sheung Shui KCR stations, will drop you off at Mai Po Lo Wai, a village along the main road just east of the marsh.

The area around **Kam Tin** (*Brocade Field*), is home to two 16th-century walled villages. Their fortifications serve as reminders of the marauding pirates, bandits and imperial soldiers the Hong Kong's early residents faced. Just off the main road and easily accessible, the tiny **Kat Hing Wai** is the more popular of the two. Drop HK$1 in the donation box at the village's entrance and wander the narrow little lanes. The old Hakka women in traditional clothing will let you take their photograph for the right price. **Shui Tau**, a 17th-century village about a 15-minute walk north of Kam Tin Rd, is famous for its prow-shaped roofs decorated with dragons and fish.

To reach Kam Tin, take bus No 64K, 77K or 54. Alternatively, take minibus No 601 from Fung Cheung Rd in Yuen Long. Kam Tin is also accessible from Tsuen Wan via a scenic route on bus No 51.

The main attraction in **Fanling** is **Fung Ying Sin Temple** (*Pak Wo Rd*), directly opposite the KCR station. This is a huge Taoist complex for the dead with fantastic murals, an orchard terrace, herbal clinic and the *Vegetarian Kitchen* (*meals around HK$60*).

Continue on to Tai Po's KCR Market station and then to the **Hong Kong Railway Museum** (☎ 2653 3455, Ⓦ *www.heritage museum.gov.hk, 13 Shung Tak St; admission free; open 9am-5pm Wed-Mon*), housed in the former Tai Po Market train station (1913). The museum is a 15-minute walk from the station.

From the Tai Po Market station, take bus No 64K to the **Kadoorie Farm & Botanic Garden** (☎ 2488 1317, Ⓦ *www.kfbg.org.hk, Lam Kam Rd; admission free; open 9.30am-5pm daily*). The farm, now a conservation and teaching centre, is home to indigenous birds and animals and there is a refuge centre for injured wildlife and plants. It's best to phone prior to arriving.

The **Chinese University of Hong Kong** overlooks Tolo Harbour and houses an **art museum** (*☎ 2609 7416; admission free; open 10am-4.45pm Mon-Sat, 12.30pm-5.30pm Sun*) displaying 2000-year-old bronze seals and a large collection of jade flower carvings. It is closed on any public holidays.

Sha Tin is popular for its racecourse and **Sha Tin Town Plaza**, one of NT's largest shopping malls. This is also where you begin the climb up to the **Ten Thousand Buddhas Monastery** (*open 9am-5pm daily*), about 500m north-west of Sha Tin KCR station. It actually has some 12,800 miniature statues lining its walls. To reach the monastery, take exit B at Sha Tin KCR station. Do not mistake the modern temple with the tacky pagoda at the end of Pai Tau St as your destination. Instead, carry on and turn left onto Sheung Wo Che St. A series of yellow signs in English will direct you through the food stalls to the steep path leading up to the monastery.

South-west of Sha Tin, in Tai Wai, is Hong Kong's newest and unequivocally best museum. The **Hong Kong Heritage Museum** (*☎ 2180 8188, ⓦ www.heritage museum.gov.hk, 1 Man Lam Rd, adult/senior, student or child HK$10/5; open 10am-6pm Tues-Thur, Sat & Sun, 10am-9pm Fri*) has interactive exhibits on everything from shrimp harvesting to opera to comic books. Prices are for seniors over 60 and children under 12. The museum is closed some public holidays.

The **Sai Kung Peninsula** is one of the least spoilt areas in NT – it's great for hiking and you can get from village to village on boats in Tolo Harbour. The best beaches in the New Territories are around this area, including **Clearwater Bay**. From the Choi Hung MTR station take bus No 91 to Clearwater Bay or No 92 to Sai Kung village.

To explore the eastern side of the peninsula, take bus No 94 from Sai Kung which ends at Wong Shek pier.

PLACES TO STAY

The New Territories' greatest accommodation draws are its fantastic campgrounds and the numerous (though remote) hostels, operated by the Hong Kong Youth Hostel Association (HKYHA; ☎ 2788 1638). All of the hostels require a YHA card which can be bought at the hostels for HK$180 (bring a photo) – otherwise you'll have to pay the nonmembers' price. You are strongly advised to ring first to make sure a bed is available.

Bradbury Lodge (*☎ 2662 5123, ⓦ www .yha.org.hk/bradlodg.html, 66 Ting Kok Rd, Tai Mei Tuk*) Dorm beds per junior/senior HK$30/45, doubles/quads HK$200/260. This is the most accessible hostel, with 96 beds and check in from 7am to 10am and again from 4pm (2pm on Saturday) to 11pm. Take the KCR to Tai Po Market station, then bus No 75K to Tai Mei Tuk (last stop). Walk south for four minutes (the sea will be to your right) to reach the hostel. Camping is not permitted.

Sze Lok Yuen Hostel (*☎ 2488 8188, ⓦ www.yha.org.hk/szelok.html, Tai Mo Shan*) Beds per junior/senior HK$25/35, camping per member/nonmember HK$16/25. This 92-bed hostel, usually open Saturday and on the eve of public holidays only, is in the shadow of Hong Kong's highest peak. At this elevation it can get pretty chilly at night so come prepared. There are cooking facilities but you'll need to bring food supplies with you. Take bus No 51 (Tsuen Wan ferry pier–Kam Tin) at Tsuen Wan MTR station and alight at Tai Mo Shan Rd. Follow Tai Mo Shan Rd for about 45 minutes, pass the car park and turn on to a small concrete path on the right-hand side. This leads directly to the hostel.

Pak Sha O Hostel (*☎ 2328 2327, ⓦ www .yha.org.hk/pakshao.html, Ho Ha Rd*) Beds per junior/senior HK$25/35, camping per member/nonmember HK$16/25. This large hostel is south-west of Hoi Ha Bay and the marine park. It's not open every day so call ahead. To get there, take bus No 92 from the Choi Hung Estate bus station to Sai Kung station and then bus No 94 (last one is at 7pm) towards Wong Shek pier, alighting at Ko Tong village. Walk 100m along Pak Tam Rd to find Hoi Ha Rd on the left; from here it's a 40-minute walk.

Bradbury Hall (*☎ 2328 2458, ⓦ www .yha.org.hk/bradhall.html, Chek Keng*) Beds per junior/senior HK$25/35, camping per member/nonmember HK$16/25. This 92-bed hostel is on the harbour facing Chek Keng pier. In the past it's been open at the weekend and on the eve of public holidays only so telephone in advance to check. To find it, follow the directions to Pak Sha O Hostel but alight from bus No 94 at Pak Tam Au. There's a footpath at the side of the road leading to Chek Keng village (a 45-minute walk).

Ascension House (☎ 2691 4196, **w** *www .achouse.com, 33 Tao Fong Shan Rd*) Dorm beds HK$125. This 11-bed place staffed by Scandinavians is one of the best deals in Hong Kong as the price of a bed includes free laundry service and three meals! To get there, take the KCR to Sha Tin Station, leave via exit B and follow a staircase up on the left. Continue along the path to a roundabout; turn right. About 150m up, you'll come to a small staircase and a sign pointing the way to Ascension House on the right. The walk should take between 15 and 20 minutes.

The Country and Marine Parks Authority (☎ 2420 0529, **w** parks.afcd.gov.hk) manages a number of *campgrounds* in the New Territories including a dozen or so sites on Sai Kung Peninsula and a site at Long Ke Wan, a lovely bay to the south-east of High Island Reservoir.

Outlying Islands 外岛

There are 234 islands dotting the waters around Hong Kong; however, only four have substantial residential communities and are thus readily accessible by ferry. These islands offer great beaches and hiking trails that are tranquil during the week. Weekends are packed out and best avoided.

CHEUNG CHAU ISLAND 长洲
Dumbbell-shaped Cheung Chau island has some 22,000 people crammed onto its 2.5 sq km area. The town sprawls across the narrow neck connecting the two ends of the island. The bay on the western side of the island (where the ferry lands) has a colourful collection of bobbing sampans and fishing boats. The eastern side of the island is where you'll find **Tung Wan Beach**, Cheung Chau's longest. There are a few tiny, remote beaches that you can reach by foot, and at the southern tip of the island is the hideaway cave of the notorious pirate Cheung Po Tsai.

Places to Stay
There is a solid line-up of booths when you come off the ferry pier that offer *flats* and *rooms* for rent, some of which can be very reasonable if you bargain. Expect to pay from HK$200 for a two-person studio during the week and from HK$400 on weekends and public holidays.

Warwick Hotel (☎ 2981 0081, *fax 2981 9174, Cheung Chau Sports Rd, Tung Wan Beach*) Doubles with mountain/sea view HK$690/790, suites HK$1590. This is Cheung Chau's one upmarket place to stay, with wonderful views and a reasonable restaurant.

LAMMA ISLAND 南丫岛
This is the second-largest of the Outlying Islands and the one closest to the city. Lamma has good beaches and excellent hikes and is an island haven for expats. There are two main communities here – Yung Shue Wan in the north and Sok Kwu Wan in the south. Both have ferry services to Central. One of the best things to do here is hike across the island, then have something to eat in one of the island's many seafood restaurants.

Places to Stay & Eat
Jackson Property Agency (☎ 2982 0606, *fax 2982 0636, 15 Main St, Yung Shue Wan*) Studios or apartments per 2 people HK$280 Sun-Fri, HK$500 Sat. This place offers studios and apartments.

Lamma Vacation House (☎ 2982 0427, *29 Main St, Yung Shue Wan*) Rooms from HK$200 Mon-Fri, HK$400 Sat & Sun. This guesthouse, in the thick of the action amid all the bars and restaurants of Main St, is the cheapest place to stay on Lamma.

Concerto Inn (☎ 2982 1668, 2836 3388 *in Hong Kong, 28 Hung Shing Ye Beach*) Standard doubles HK$408 Mon-Fri, HK$680 Sat & Sun, deluxe doubles with sea view HK$528 Mon-Fri, HK$880 Sat & Sun. This beachfront hotel is the fanciest place to stay on Lamma.

Tung O Bay Homestay (☎ 2982 8461, *fax 2982 8424, Tung O*) Dorm beds/doubles HK$100/350. For those really looking to escape, this basic guesthouse on the beach is very secluded. The energetic owner can throw together a cheap dinner if you give advance notice. It's best to phone ahead. Rates include breakfast.

Popular seafood restaurants line the waterfront in Sok Kwu Wan, all offering the same relatively high-quality seafood at similar prices.

Rainbow Seafood Restaurant (☎ *2982 8100, 1a-1b & 16-20 First St*) Dishes HK$150-200. The Rainbow specialises in grouper, lobster and abalone. Book a table and the restaurant will transport you by yacht from Queen's Pier in Central or Aberdeen.

Lamma Hilton Shum Kee Seafood Restaurant (☎ *2982 8241, 26 First St*) Dishes HK$150-200. This is considered by many to be the best seafood restaurant in Sok Kwu Wan.

Lancombe (☎ *2982 0881, 47 Main St*) Dishes HK$100. If you're looking for seafood in Yung Shue Wan, try this place. It's slow but tasty and has great views.

Sampan Seafood Restaurant (☎ *2982 2388, 16 Main St, Yung Shue Wan*) Meals HK$75-180. This is popular with locals.

Bookworm Café (☎ *2982 4838, 79 Main St*) Breakfasts HK$35-60. This vegetarian cafe-restaurant has excellent breakfasts and fruit juices. It is also a second-hand bookshop and an Internet cafe.

Also try the relaxed ***Deli Lamma Café*** (☎ *2982 1583, 36 Main St*), the ***Espresso Banza*** (☎ *2982 0865, 67a Main St*) for coffee and sandwiches and ***Pizza Milano*** (☎ *2982 4848, 2 Back St*).

Keep in mind that many restaurants on Lamma Island are closed on Monday.

LANTAU ISLAND 大嶼山

Twice the size of Hong Kong Island, Lantau has only 45,000 residents and you could easily spend a couple of days exploring its mountainous walking trails and enjoying its uncrowded beaches.

Mui Wo is the major arrival point for ferries. As you exit the ferry, to your right is the road leading to the beach. It passes several eateries and hotels along the way.

From Mui Wo, most visitors board bus No 2 to **Ngong Ping**, a plateau 500m above sea level in the western part of the island. It's here that you'll find the impressive **Po Lin Monastery** (*admission free; open 6am-5.30pm daily*), as much a tourist attraction as a religious centre. Just outside the monastery is the world's largest outdoor bronze Buddha statue, **Tian Tan Buddha** (*open 10am-5.30pm daily*). Vegetarian

lunches are available in the monastery dining hall. You can also spend the night here in order to lumber up **Lantau Peak** (934m) at sunrise.

Another place to visit is **Tai O**, a village at the western end of the island; take bus No 1. The 2km-long **Cheung Sha Wan** on the island is Hong Kong's longest beach. You'll have it to yourself on weekdays, but forget it on weekends.

On Lantau's northern shore is the 19th-century **Tung Chung Fort**, which still has its old cannon pointing out to sea. Just off the coast, Hong Kong's new airport at Chek Lap Kok has transformed this part of the island into a new town development. It's connected to Tsuen Wan by the huge Tsing Ma road and rail bridge. To reach Lantau via the bridge, take bus No E31 from the Tsuen Wan ferry pier and change at Tung Chung, or take the train to Tung Chung from Hong Kong station.

A ritzy housing development in the north-eastern part of the island, **Discovery Bay** has a sandy beach and is serviced by jet-powered ferries to and from Central every 10 to 30 minutes. From Discovery Bay you can walk for one hour southwards along the coastline to find the **Trappist Haven Monastery**, whose monks have taken a vow of absolute silence. Walking about another 1½ hours from there over a dangerously slippery trail brings you out to **Mui Wo**, from where you can get ferries back to Central.

Lantau Trail (70km) is a superb footpath stretching the length of the island, passing over both Lantau Peak and Sunset Peak (869m). Beginning at Mui Wo and then doubling back along the coast at Tai O, it's been divided into a dozen manageable stages. Hikers need to be well equipped with a map, food and water supplies.

Places to Stay & Eat

The Country and Marine Parks Authority (**W** parks.afcd.gov.hk) maintains eight free *campsites* on Lantau. These are listed in the Camp Sites of Hong Kong Country Parks brochure available from the tourist office.

During the summer and on weekends, you'll find kiosks by the ferries renting *holiday rooms* and *apartments*. For a double room expect to pay HK$120 during the week and HK$200 at the weekend.

SG Davis Hostel (☎ 2985 5610, W www .yha.org.hk/sgdavis.html, Ngong Ping) Beds per junior/senior HK$25/35, camping per member/nonmember HK$16/25. Open year-round. This 52-bed hostel is a 10-minute walk from the bus stop in Ngong Ping and is ideal for anyone wanting to climb nearby Lantau Peak in time to catch the sunrise. Check-in is from 7am to 10am and again from 4pm (2pm on Saturday) to 11pm.

Jockey Club Mong Tung Wan Hostel (☎ 2984 1389, W www.yha.org.hk/mong tung.html, Mong Tung Wan) Beds per junior/senior HK$25/35, camping per member/nonmember HK$16/25. This tranquil 88-bed waterfront property on the south-east side of the Chi Ma Wan Peninsula is often open at the weekend and on the eve of public holidays. From Mui Wo, take bus No 7 (or bus A35 from Hong Kong International Airport) to Pui O. Follow the footpath across the fields from the bus stop and continue along Chi Ma Wan Rd until it leaves the sea edge. At a sharp bend in the road at Ham Tin, turn right onto the footpath by the sea and follow it to the hostel. The walk will take about 45 minutes. Alternatively, you can take a ferry to Cheung Chau and hire a sampan (about HK$50) to the jetty at Mong Tung Wan.

Seaview Holiday Resort (☎ 2984 8877, fax 2984 8787, 11 Tung Wan Tau Rd) Doubles HK250/300/500, triples HK$300/350/60 Sun-Thur/Fri/Sat. The Seaview is by far the cheapest place to stay along Silvermine Bay but not the nicest.

Mui Wo Inn (☎ 2984 7225, fax 2984 1916, Tung Wan Tau Rd) Doubles Sun-Fri from HK$280, Sat HK$450-550, twins Sun-Fri from HK$400, Sat HK$650. This is nicer than the Seaview, and includes breakfast.

Tak Juk Kee (Sun Lee) Seafood Restaurant (☎ 2984 1265, 1 Chung Hao Rd) Dishes HK$55-80. Catching sea breezes from Silvermine Bay, this is arguably the best Chinese restaurant in Mui Wo.

China Bear (☎ 2984 7360, Ground floor, Mui Wo Centre, Ngan Wan Rd, Mui Wo) Mains HK$55-85, snacks HK$25-65. This is

the most popular expatriate pub/restaurant in town, with a wonderful open bar facing the water.

Namaste Indian Restaurant (☎ 2984 8491, 31 South Lantau Rd, Pui O) Dishes HK$38-88. This place has curries of every hue and a range of vegetarian dishes.

The Stoep Restaurant (☎ 2980 2699, 32 Lower Cheung Sha Village) Mains HK$55-150. Open Tues-Sun. This Mediterranean-style restaurant facing Lower Cheung Sha Beach has fish dishes and South African barbecue.

The Gallery (☎ 2980 4966/2582, 26 Tong Fuk Village) Mains HK$90-130. Open Wed-Sun. This offers South African food with Middle Eastern overtones.

Tea Garden Restaurant (☎ 2985 5161, Lantau Tea Garden, Ngong Ping) Dishes HK$100. Specialising in seafood, this place is down the path to the left of the Buddha statue just before the SG Davis Hostel.

Fook Moon Lam (☎ 2985 7071, 29 Market St, Tai O) Dishes HK$100. This relatively upmarket place is one of the best in Tai O, a village famous for its seafood.

PENG CHAU ISLAND 坪洲

This is the smallest and most traditionally Chinese of the easily accessible islands. Explore the narrow alleys, the outdoor meat and vegetable market and the **Tin Hau Temple**, built in 1792. A climb to the top of **Finger Hill** (95m) will reward you with a view of the entire island and nearby Lantau.

Peng Chau has two rather popular pub/restaurants; both closed on Monday.

Sea Breeze Club (☎ 2983 8785, 38 Wing Hing St) Starters HK$38-68, mains HK$48-148. The Sea Breeze is known for its fine T-bone steaks, which aren't cheap at HK$148. The place is so popular that Discovery Bay residents hop on the kaido to cross over and dine here.

Jungle Restaurant & Pub (☎ 2983 8837, 38a-c Wing Hing St) Mains HK$49-69. This small but cosy place next door to the Sea Breeze serves popular pub grub like fish and chips, bangers and mash, as well as six different draught beers.

Macau 澳门

Telephone code: ☎ 0853
Population: 438,000
Area: 23.8 sq km

Sixty kilometres west of Hong Kong, on the other side of the mouth of Zhū Jiāng (Pearl River), tiny Macau was the oldest European settlement in the east until 20 December 1999, when the territory was returned to the People's Republic of China. Less than 2% of Macau residents are Portuguese, about 95% Chinese and the rest are Macanese, people with mixed Portuguese, Chinese and/or African blood.

Archaeological finds from digs around Hác Sá Bay on Coloane Island suggest that Macau has been inhabited since Neolithic times. Before the arrival of the Portuguese, Macau was home to relatively small numbers of Cantonese-speaking farmers and Fújiàn fisherfolk under the tutelage of the imperial court.

Portuguese galleons visited Macau in the early 16th century. In 1557, as a reward for clearing out a few pirates, China ceded the tiny enclave to the Portuguese and for centuries it was the principal meeting point for trade with China. However, when the Opium War erupted between the Chinese and the British, the Portuguese stood diplomatically to one side and Macau became the poor relation of the more dynamic Hong Kong.

China's Cultural Revolution spilled over into the territory in 1966–67. The governor at the time reportedly proposed that Portugal should leave Macau forever but, fearing the loss of Macau's foreign trade, the Chinese backed off.

In 1999, under the Sino-Portuguese Pact, Macau was returned to China as a Special Administrative Region (SAR). Like Hong Kong, Macau is to continue to enjoy a 'high degree of autonomy' in all matters except defence and foreign affairs for 50 years.

While Macau is a popular destination for Hong Kong residents lured by the city's many casinos, it has much more to offer than gambling. You'll find a fascinating fusion of Mediterranean and Asian architecture, food, lifestyles and temperaments. Macau is a colourful palette of pastels and ordered greenery and is so tidy, it ranks second only

Highlights

- With pastel villas, fantastic hybrids of Portuguese food and sandy island beaches, Macau is a taste of the Mediterranean on the South China Sea

- The majestic ruins of the Church of St Paul, the symbol of Macau

- The incomparable Macau Museum, the best of the city's wide array of museums

- Gambling, gambling and more gambling

to Singapore as the cleanest city in Asia. There are several new museums, a glittering multilevel cultural centre, a nightlife strip built on reclaimed land, and a phenomenal number of new Portuguese and Macanese restaurants. The Lotus Flower Bridge, connecting China with the islands of Taipa and Coloane, was opened in December 1999 as part of the handover ceremonies.

While both Cantonese and Portuguese are official languages, Cantonese is by far the more widely spoken. About half the population can also speak Mandarin.

ORIENTATION

The lion's share of Macau's sites are on the mainland, the peninsula that juts down from mainland China. Avenida de Almeida Ribeiro (San Ma Lo in Cantonese) is Macau's main thoroughfare, running from

Avenida da Praia Grande to the Inner Harbour. Its extension, Avenida do Infante Dom Henrique, runs south of the Avenida da Praia Grande to the Outer Harbour, just below the landmark Lisboa Hotel.

South of here are the islands of Coloane and Taipa, joined together by a causeway and connected to the mainland by two bridges.

Maps

The Macau Government Tourist Office distributes two versions of the *Macau Tourist Map,* both containing major tourist sights, the islands and streets labelled in both Portuguese and Chinese characters. The larger one is much more detailed with bus routes and other useful information for travellers.

INFORMATION
Tourist Offices

The Macau Government Tourist Office (MGTO; Map B; ☎ 315 566, 513 355, ⓦ www.macautourism.gov.mo) at 9 Largo do Senado is well organised and extremely helpful. Staff have free leaflets on Macau's sights, as well as bilingual maps with a list of public bus routes. Especially good are the *Walking Tours* and the three *Cultural Heritage Tours of Macau* pamphlets.

The MGTO also has information counters at the Guia Lighthouse, the Macau Cultural Centre, the facade of the Church of St Paul, Macau International Airport and the ferry terminal. There are computer terminals with information about the territory placed at strategic locations throughout Macau.

The MGTO tourist assistance unit hotline is ☎ 340 390, open from 9am to 6pm daily. The organisation also maintains tourist offices in Hong Kong, many European and Asian countries, Australia, New Zealand and the USA.

Visas

The vast majority of travellers, including citizens of the European Union (EU), Australia, New Zealand, the USA, Canada and South Africa, are allowed to enter the Macau SAR for one month without a visa. Hong Kong residents with a Hong Kong identity card, permanent identity card or re-entry permit and Portuguese nationals get 90 days.

Travellers who do require visas can get ones valid for 20 days on arrival in Macau. They cost M$100/50 for adults/children

under 12 years old. If you're part of a tour group of 10 people or more, visas are M$50 each, and family visas (one couple plus children under 12) cost M$200.

Travellers from countries that do not have diplomatic relations with China should apply for visas in advance at a Chinese embassy or consulate in a third country.

Be aware that if you visit Macau from China to re-enter China you will need to be on a multiple-entry visa, or else will have to get a new visa.

Visa Extensions Once your permitted length of stay in the Macau SAR has expired, you can obtain a single one-month extension. To apply, you must go in person to the Macau Immigration Office (Map A; ☎ 725 488), Ground floor, Travessa da Amizade. It is open from 9am to 12.30pm and 2.30pm to 4pm Monday to Saturday.

Money

Macau's currency is the *pataca,* normally written as M$, which is divided into 100 *avos.* Bills are issued in denominations of M$20, M$50, M$100, M$500 and M$1000. There are little copper coins worth 10, 20 and 50 avos and silver-coloured M$1 and M$5 ones.

Costs Macau is cheaper than almost anywhere else on the eastern coast of China. However, it's important to avoid weekends when hotel prices double and even the ferries charge more.

As in China, tipping is not the usual custom. Upmarket hotels have a 10% service charge and a 5% 'tourism tax'.

Most stores have fixed prices, but clothing, trinkets and tourist 'treasures' from the street markets offer some scope for bargaining.

Currency The Macau pataca is pegged to the Hong Kong dollar at the rate of M$103.20 to HK$100 so exchange rates are virtually the same. For a table of exchange rates see the Money section in the Hong Kong chapter.

Hong Kong dollars, including coins, are readily accepted throughout Macau and, in big hotels, restaurants and department stores, your change will be returned in that currency. Although you might make a tiny

Easy riding, Hǎikǒu, Hǎinán Dǎo

Cool tracksuits at the fountain in Macau's Senate Square.

Decorations for the Mid-Autumn Festival displayed before St Francis Xavier Chapel, Coloane Village.

Tropical rainstorms drench the streets of Guǎngzhōu, Guǎngdōng.

Kwun Yam tile painting, Macau

Fishing boats moored at the shore on the south-east coast of Guǎngdōng.

The high-rise sprawl of Shēnzhèn, a Special Economic Zone in Guǎngdōng.

Catching up on the goss at the Memorial Garden to the Martyrs, Guǎngdōng.

saving by using patacas, most money-changers and banks will refuse to change them back into Hong Kong dollars, so use up all your patacas before departing Macau.

You can change cash and travellers cheques at the banks lining Avenida da Praia Grande and Avenida de Almeida Ribeiro and at major hotels. Major credit cards are readily accepted at Macau's hotels, larger restaurants and casinos. There are ATMs around the city (in particular, outside the Lisboa Hotel) where you can withdraw cash. Most ATMs allow you to choose between patacas and Hong Kong dollars.

If you want to change money outside banking hours, you'll find moneychangers open 24 hours in the Arrivals Hall of Macau International Airport and in shop G3 of the Lisboa Hotel's Old Wing.

Post & Communications

Post The main post office (Map B; ☎ 574 491), on Avenida de Almeida Ribeiro, is open from 9am to 6pm weekdays and until 1pm on Saturday. Staff are efficient and many speak English. Little red vending machines also dispense stamps throughout Macau and many hotels sell stamps and can post letters and parcels for you.

Poste restante service is available at counter Nos 1 and 2 of the main post office. You can collect letters from 9am to 6pm on weekdays and until 1pm on Saturday.

Telephone Companhia de Telecomunicações (CTM) runs the Macau telephone system, and for the most part the service is good.

Local calls are free from private or hotel telephones while at a public pay phones they cost M$1 for five minutes. All pay phones permit International Direct Dialling (IDD) using coins or a phonecard. Rates are cheaper from 9pm to 8am during the week and all day Saturday and Sunday. You can find public phones around the Largo do Senado and most large hotels have one in the lobby.

The international access code is ☎ 00. For Hong Kong, dial ☎ 01 first plus the number you want, minus Hong Kong's country code (☎ 852). To call Macau from abroad – including Hong Kong – the country code is ☎ 0853.

Some useful phone numbers in Macau include:

Local directory assistance	☎ 185
International directory assistance	☎ 101
Emergency	☎ 999

Fax Most mid-range and top-end hotels have fax machines. You can also send and receive faxes at the main post office.

Email & Internet Access Despite high-tech Hong Kong being so close, email services are not very well developed in Macau and there are no commercial cybercafes at present. The business centres in the more expensive hotels offer pricey email services, often available to non-guests.

CTM's Mobile Zone branch at 18 Rua de São Domingos (Map B) has three terminals on the first floor where you can access emails and surf the Web for free. It's open from 10am to 8pm daily. You can also check emails at the Unesco Centre (Map A; ☎ 727 220) on Alameda Doutor Carlos d'Assumpção in NAPE, and on the ground floor library of the Macau Museum of Art (Map A).

Travel Agencies

Travel agents offer day tours around Macau, and China Travel Service (CTS; Map B; ☎ 709 888, fax 706 611) in the Xinhua Building, Rua de Nagasaki, and a few other agencies do visas for China in 24 hours. You can also get visas for Hong Kong from CTS.

You can book tours of Macau at booths at the jetfoil pier. A typical bus tour of peninsular Macau takes about three hours and costs M$180 per person, including lunch. Bus tours to the islands lasting two hours cost about M$100 per person. The Tour Machine, run by Avis Rent A Car (☎ 336 789) runs a two-hour tour from the Macau Ferry Terminal. Daily departures are at 11am and 3pm and tickets cost M$150/80 for adults/children.

Film & Photography

You can find virtually any type of film, camera and accessory in Macau, and photo-processing is cheap and of a high standard. A good shop for all photographic services, including visa photos, is Foto Princesa (Map B; ☎ 575 959) at 55-59 Avenida do Infante Dom Henrique. Also try Rua do Campo, west of the Vasco da Gama Garden (Map B).

Map A – MACAU PENINSULA 澳門半島

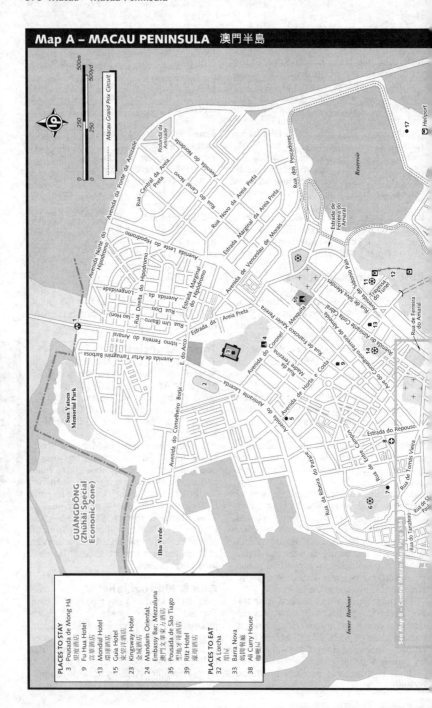

Macau Grand Prix Circuit

GUĂNGDŌNG
(Zhūhǎi Special
Economic Zone)

Ilha Verde

Sun Yatsen
Memorial Park

Inner Harbour

See Map B – Central Macau Map Page 584

PLACES TO STAY
3   Pousada de Mong Há
     望廈酒店
9   Fu Hua Hotel
     富華酒店
13 Mondial Hotel
     環華新酒店
15 Guia Hotel
     東望洋酒店
23 Kingsway Hotel
     金域酒店
24 Mandarin Oriental;
     Embassy Bar; Mezzaluna
     澳門文華東方酒店
35 Pousada de São Tiago
     聖地牙哥酒店
39 Ritz Hotel
     濠璟酒店

PLACES TO EAT
32 A Lorcha
     船屋
33 Barra Nova
     媽閣餐廳
38 Ali Curry House
     咖喱屋

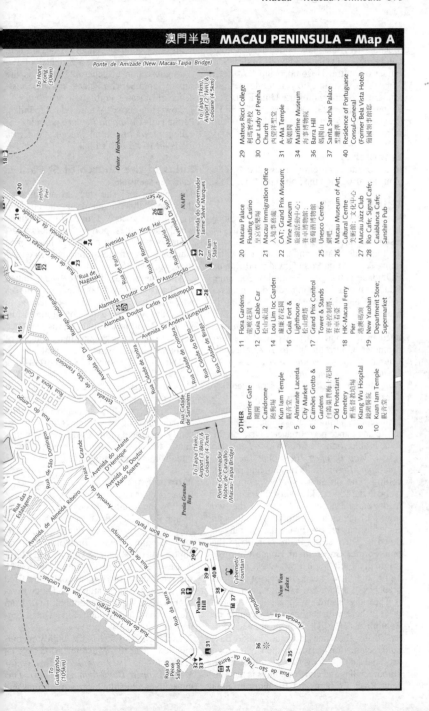

Ponte de Amizade (New Macau-Taipa Bridge)

To Hong
Kong
(30km)

To Taipa (1km) &
Airport (2.1km) &
Coloane (4.5km)

Outer Harbour

Jetfoil
Pier

NAPE

Avenida do Governador
Jaime Silver Marques

Avenida Xian Xing Hai

Avenida de Roma

Avenida de Madrid

Avenida Dr Sun Yat Sen

Rua de Paris

Kun Iam
Statue

Rua de Nagasaki

Alameda Doutor Carlos D'Assumpção

Alameda Doutor Carlos D'Assumpção

Avenida Sir Anders Ljungstedt

Rua Cidade de Sintra

Rua Cidade de Coimbra

Rua Cidade do Porto

Rua Cidade de Braga

Rodrigo Rodrigues

Rua Cidade
de Santarém

Estrada de São Francisco

Avenida do Dr

Avenida de São Francisco

Rua Nova à Guia

Avenida do Campo

Rua de São Domingos

Avenida do Infante D'Henrique

Avenida do Doutor
Mario Soares

Praia Grande – Grande

To Taipa (1km) &
Airport (3.8km) &
Coloane (4.7km)

Ponte Governador
Nobre de Carvalho
(Macau-Taipa Bridge)

Rua das
Estalagens

Avenida de Almeida Ribeiro

Rua da Praia do Bom Parto

Praia Grande
Bay

Cybernetic
Fountain

Nam Van
Lakes

Avenida da República

Penha
Hill

Rua das Lorchas

Avenida do Almirante Sérgio

Rua do Campo

Rua da Barta

Rua de São – Tiago da Barta

To
Guangzhou
(105km)

Rua do Peixe
Salgado

OTHER

1　Barrier Gate
　　關閘
2　Canidrome
　　跑狗場
4　Kun Iam Temple
　　觀音堂
5　Almirante Lacerda
　　City Market
6　Camões Grotto &
　　Gardens
　　白鴿巢賈梅士花園
7　Old Protestant
　　Cemetery
　　舊基督教墳場
8　Kiang Wu Hospital
　　鏡湖醫院
10　Kuan Iam Temple
　　觀音堂

11　Flora Gardens
　　南灣花園
12　Guia Cable Car
　　松山纜車
14　Lou Lim Ioc Garden
　　盧廉若花園
16　Guia Fort &
　　Lighthouse
　　松山燈塔
17　Grand Prix Control
　　Tower & Stands
　　賽車控制塔
18　HK-Macau Ferry
　　Pier
　　港澳碼頭
19　New Yaohan
　　Department Store;
　　Supermarket

20　Macau Palace
　　Floating Casino
　　皇宮娛樂場
21　Macau Immigration Office
　　入境事務組
22　CAT; Grand Prix Museum;
　　Wine Museum
　　旅遊活動中心；
　　賽車博物館；
　　葡萄酒博物館
25　Unesco Centre
　　鋼吧
26　Macau Museum of Art;
　　Cultural Centre
　　文藝館；文化中心
27　Macau Jazz Club
28　Rio Cafe; Signal Cafe;
　　Casablanca Cafe;
　　Sanshiro Pub

29　Mateus Ricci College
　　利瑪竇學校
30　Our Lady of Penha
　　Church
　　西望洋聖堂
31　A-Ma Temple
　　媽閣廟
34　Maritime Museum
　　海事博物院
36　Barra Hill
　　媽閣山
37　Santa Sancha Palace
　　聖珊府
40　Residence of Portuguese
　　Consul-General
　　(Former Bela Vista Hotel)
　　葡國駐華領事邸

Medical Services

Macau's two hospitals both have 24-hour emergency services. The Conde São Januário Central Hospital (Map B; ☎ 313 731) is on Estrada do Visconde de São Januário, south-west of the Guia Fort. The Kiang Wu Hospital (Map A; ☎ 371 333), Rua Coelho do Amaral, is north-east of the ruins of the Church of St Paul.

Emergency

In the event of an emergency, dial ☎ 999. You can also reach the police on ☎ 573 333.

THINGS TO SEE

Macau is packed with historical sites. Since 1992 more than half of Macau's buildings of historic significance have been restored, with the Largo de Senado and the splendid villas lining Avenida da Praia Grande and Rua da Felicidade being good examples. Although Buddhism and Taoism are the dominant religions, Catholicism remains very strong in Macau – as a legacy of the Portuguese.

A good walk is the peninsula route outlined in the tourist office's *Walking Tour* pamphlet. Go up the hill to **St Augustine's Church** *(São Agostinho Igreja; Map B; Largo de Santo Agostinho; open 10am-6pm daily)* built in 1814, and the **Dom Pedro V Theatre** *(Teatro Dom Pedro; Map B; ☎ 939 646, Calçada do Teatro),* a colonnaded, 19th-century building occasionally used for music and dance performances. Next on the route is **St Lawrence's Church** *(São Lourenço Igreja; Map B; open 10am-6pm Tues-Sun, 1pm-2pm Mon)* with its magnificent painted ceiling. The original church was built of wood in the 1560s and reconstructed in stone in the early 19th century. One of the two towers of the church formerly served as an ecclesiastical prison. From the church, go down to Travessa do Padre Narciso to the pink **Former Government House** *(Map B),* originally built for a Portuguese noble in 1849 and now headquarters of various branches of the Macau SAR government.

The oldest section of Macau is just southwest of here with its beautiful **Avenida da República** *(Map A).* This promenade followed the shoreline of Praia Grande Bay; land reclamation has turned the bay into two artificial lakes. Along this stretch of grand colonial villas and civic buildings is the **Mateus Ricci College** and the **Former Bela**

Vista Hotel, which has served as a private mansion, secondary school, WWII refugee shelter and is now the residence of the Portuguese consul-general. Nearby is the superb **Santa Sancha Palace**, erstwhile residence of Macau's Portuguese governors.

Towering above Avenida da República, **Penha Hill** *(Colina da Penha),* provides excellent views of central Macau and across the Pearl River into China.

Ruins of the Church of St Paul

Ruinas de São Paulo

The facade, majestic stairway and mosaic floor are all that remain of this church *(Map B),* built in the early 17th century. With its wonderful statues, portals and engravings, some consider the ruins of the Church of St Paul to be the greatest monument to Christianity in Asia.

The church was designed by an Italian Jesuit and built in 1602 by Japanese refugees who had fled anti-Christian persecution in Nagasaki. After the expulsion of the Jesuits in 1762 a military battalion was stationed here. In 1835, a fire erupted in the kitchen of the barracks, destroying all but what you see.

The small **Museum of Sacred Art** *(Museu de Arte Sacra; ☎ 387 333; Rua de São Paulo; admission free; open 9am-6pm daily)* contains polychrome carved wooden statues, silver chalices and monstrances and oil paintings. In the nearby crypt is the recently unearthed tomb of Alessandro Valignano, the Jesuit who is credited with establishing Christianity in Japan.

Monte Fort

Fortaleza de Monte

Built by the Jesuits between 1617 and 1626, Monte Fort *(Map B; open 6am-7pm daily May-Sept, 7am-6pm daily Oct-Apr)* overlooks the ruins of the Church of St Paul and almost all of Macau. Barracks and storehouses were designed to allow the fort to survive a siege, but the cannons were fired only once: during an attempted Dutch invasion in 1622 when a cannonball fired from the fort conveniently landed in a Dutch gunpowder carrier.

Housed in the fort is the highly recommended **Macau Museum** *(Museu de Macau; ☎ 357 911; adult/child or senior M$15/8; open 10am-6pm Tues-Sun).* This museum exhibits the history, traditions and culture of Macau through a host of CD-ROMs, videos and holograms.

Temples

The 400-year-old **Kun Iam Temple** *(Map A; Avenida do Coronel Mesquita; open 10am-6pm daily)* is Macau's most historic and interesting temple. The likeness of Kun Iam, the Goddess of Mercy, is in the main hall. The first treaty of trade and friendship between the USA and China was signed in the temple's terraced gardens in 1844. To the west is a second **Kun Iam Temple**, which is much smaller but a hive of activity and well-worth visiting.

North of Barra Hill is the **A-Ma Temple** *(Map A; Rue de São Tiago da Barra; open 10am-6pm daily)*. The original temple was probably already standing when the Portuguese arrived, although the present one may only date back to the 17th century. The temple is dedicated to A-Ma, Goddess of Seafarers, better known as Tin Hau. According to legend A-Ma manifested as a beautiful young woman whose presence on a Guǎngzhōu-bound ship saved it from disaster. All the other ships of the fleet, whose rich owners had refused to give her passage, were destroyed in a storm. The boat people of Macau come here on a pilgrimage each year in April or May.

Old Protestant Cemetery

Lord Churchill (great-great uncle of Winston) and the Irish-born artist George Chinnery are buried at this cemetery *(Map A; 15 Praça de Luís de Camões)*. Far more interesting however are the graves of missionaries and their families, traders and seamen – whose epitaphs often provide detailed accounts of their lives and deaths.

The cemetery is behind the small Protestant church, also known as the Morrison Chapel in commemoration of Robert Morrison, the first Protestant missionary to China who is buried here.

Gardens

Macau has a number of pleasant gardens. **Camões Grotto & Gardens** *(Jardim de Luís de Camões; Map A; open 6am-9pm daily)* is dedicated to the one-eyed Luís de Camões who is said to have written part of his epic *Os Lusiadas* in Macau, despite there being little proof that he ever reached the city.

The cool and shady **Lou Lim Ioc Garden** *(Map A; 10 Estrada de Adolfo de Loureiro; admission M$1 Sat-Thur, free Fri; open 6am-9pm daily)* was once the property of a wealthy Chinese merchant, whose ornate mansion now houses a secondary school. The gardens have huge shady trees, lotus ponds, bamboo groves, grottoes and a bridge with nine turns to escape from evil spirits who can only move in straight lines.

Flora Gardens *(Jardim da Flora; Map A; Travessa do Túnel; open 9am-6pm daily)*, Macau's largest, was once the grounds of the Flora Palace, an aristocratic Portuguese family mansion that burned to the ground in 1931. This attractive garden contains a miniature zoo, aviary and a couple of tennis courts. This is also where you catch the mini-cable car to the top of Guia Hill.

Guia Fort
Fortaleza de Guía

This is the highest point on the Macau Peninsula, topped with a 15m-tall lighthouse and 17th-century chapel (Map A). First lit up in 1865, the lighthouse is the oldest on China's coast. There are two popular jogging trails.

The easiest way up is to hop on the little **Guia Cable Car** *(Teleférico da Guia; one way/return adult M$3/5, student or senior M$1/3; open 9am-6pm Tues-Sun)* that runs from Rua do Túnel, near the entrance to the Flora Gardens. To reach the Guia Lighthouse and the chapel, turn south after getting off the cable car, walk up the hill and continue on for another 10 minutes.

Loyal Senate
Leal Senado

This graceful building (Map B) looks over the main town square and is home to the main municipal administrative body. It also houses an **art gallery** *(☎ 387 333; admission free; open 9am-9pm daily)* with rotating exhibits, usually relating to the history of Macau, and the **Senate Library** *(☎ 387 333; admission free; open 1am-7pm Mon-Fri)*, with an extensive collection of books on Asia.

St Dominic's Church
Igreja de São Domingo

Arguably the most beautiful church in Macau, this 17th-century baroque building *(Map B; open 10am-6pm daily)* has an impressive tiered altar.

At the back of the church, the **Treasury of Sacred Art** *(Tresouro de Arte Sacra; ☎ 572 401; admission free; open 10am-6pm daily)* is a treasure trove of ecclesiastical art and liturgical objects exhibited on three floors that reach up to the loft of the church tower.

Museums

The **Maritime Museum** *(Museu Marítimo; Map A; ☎ 595 481, Largo do Pagode da Barra; adult/child or senior M$10/5 Mon & Wed-Sat, M$5/3 Sun; open 10am-5.30pm Wed-Mon)*, has interesting boats and artefacts from Macau's seafaring past, a Hakka fishing village and displays of the long narrow boats raced during the Dragon Boat Festival in June. There's a small aquarium and a motorised junk moored next to the museum that offers 30-minute rides around the Inner Harbour.

Located in the Tourist Activity Centre (CAT), the **Macau Wine Museum** *(Museu do Vinho de Macau; Map A; ☎ 798 4188, 431 Rua de Luís Gonzaga Gomes; adult/student M$10/5; open 10am-6pm Wed-Mon)* is a good place to learn how to tell a Dão from a Douro. The museum displays wine racks, barrels and presses, and has free wine tastings. Children under 11 are admitted free.

Also on the CAT premises is the **Grand Prix Museum** *(Museu do Grande Prémio; Map A; ☎ 798 4108, Basement floor, 431 Rua de Luís Gonzaga Gomes; adult/student M$10/5; open 10am-6pm Wed-Mon)*, which features cars and motorcycles from the Macau Formula 3 Grand Prix. Children under 11 are admitted free.

The **Macau Museum of Art** *(Museu de Arte de Macau; Map A; ☎ 791 9800, Macau Cultural Centre, Avenida Xian Xing Hai; adult/student or senior M$5/3; open 10am-7pm Tues-Sun)* houses visiting exhibits as well as permanent collections of Chinese traditional art and paintings by Western artists who lived in Macau, such as George Chinnery. You'll also find a cafe and Internet access here.

Macau Museums Pass A pass allowing entry to six of Macau's museums over a five-day period is available for M$25/12 for adult/student or senior. Participating museums are the Grand Prix Museum, the Wine Museum, the Maritime Museum, the Macau Museum of Art and the Museum of Macau.

The Islands

Connected to the mainland peninsula by two bridges and joined together by a causeway, Coloane and Taipa remain oases of calm and greenery with striking pastel-coloured colonial villas, quiet lanes and a couple of good beaches. There's ample opportunity for walking and cycling and the Portuguese and Macanese restaurants of Taipa village are worth the trip alone.

Taipa Traditionally an island of duck farms and boat yards, Taipa (population 18,000) now boasts four major hotels, a university, a racecourse and stadium, high-rise apartments and an airport. Despite the construction of Taipa City, a parade of baroque churches and buildings, Taoist and Buddhist temples, overgrown esplanades and lethargic settlements mean it's still easy to experience the traditional charms of the island.

Taipa Village, on the southern shore of the island, is a window to the island's past and old-world charm. Here you'll find the stately **Taipa House Museum** *(☎ 827 012, Avenida da Praia; admission free; open 10am-8pm daily)*, which gives a good sense of how the Macanese middle class lived at the beginning of the 20th century. Also in the village is the **Church of Our Lady of Carmel**, built in 1885, and three small temples: **Tin Hau Temple**, **Pak Tai Temple** and **Kun Iam Temple**. The village **market** is at the end of Rua do Regedor.

At the southern end of the main village street is the main bus stop and several shops where you can rent bikes for M$10 an hour.

Taipa has two hiking trails. The **Little Taipa Trail** *(Trilho de Taipa Pequena)* is a 2km-long circuit around a hill in the northwest of the island and the 2.2km-long **Big Taipa Trail** *(Trilho de Taipa Grande)* rings a 160m hill at the eastern end of the island.

Coloane A haven for pirates until the start of the 20th century, Coloane now attracts large numbers of tourists to its sleepy main fishing village, **Coloane Village** and sandy coastline. The island (population 2500) remains largely unspoiled with just a number of hotels and a golf course giving the local economy a boost. On Avenida de Cinco de Outubro, you'll find the main attraction, the

Chapel of St Francis Xavier (1928). Also in the village is the tiny **Kun Iam Temple**, the larger and more interesting **Tin Hau Temple** and the **Tam Kong Temple**, dedicated to the Taoist God of Seafarers.

About 1.5km from the village is **Cheoc Van Beach** where you can swim in the ocean (there are public changing rooms and toilets) or in the **outdoor pool** (adult/child M$15/5; open 8am-9pm Mon-Fri, 8am-midnight Sat & Sun). Larger and more popular is **Hác Sá Beach** from where, on a clear day, you can just make out the mountaintops on Hong Kong's Lantau Island. The **Hác Sá Sports and Recreation Park** (☎ 882 296; open 8am-9pm Sun-Fri, 8am-11pm Sat) here offers everything from swimming pools to football to mini-golf. There are also places to rent windsurfing boards and jet skis on the beach.

Coloane has several walking and fitness trails. The longest, which begins at Seac Pai Van Park, is the **Coloane Trail** (Trilho de Coloane), a loop of just over 8km that takes you over Macau's highest point.

Getting There & Away The most useful buses from peninsular Macau to both Taipa and Coloane are Nos 21, 21A, 25 and 26A. Bus Nos 22 and 28A travel to and around Taipa only and terminate at the Macau Jockey Club.

SPECIAL EVENTS

The mixing of two very different cultures and religious traditions for over 400 years has left Macau with a unique collection of holidays, festivals and cultural events, still celebrated since the handover to China except for Portugal's Independence Day.

An International Fireworks Festival is held annually in mid-September, the International Music Festival is held in late October and early November, and the Macau Marathon is held in late autumn. The Macau Arts Festival in March features music, drama and dance from both Asia and the West.

The biggest event of the year is the Macau Formula 3 Grand Prix when, on the third weekend in November, the city's streets become a racetrack and accommodation scarce.

Some of the highlights of Chinese, Portuguese and religious festivals and holidays are:

Spring Festival As elsewhere in China, Chinese New Year is a three-day public holiday held in late January or early February.

Lantern Festival Not a public holiday, but alot of fun, this festival occurs two weeks after the Chinese New Year.

Battle of 13 July Celebrated only on the island Coloane, this holiday commemorates the final defeat of pirates in 1910.

Feast of the Drunken Dragon In mid-May, people who make their living by fishing close up shop and take a break to enjoy three days of drinking and feasting. Watch for dancing dragons in the streets.

Dragon Boat Festival As in Hong Kong, this is a major public holiday held in early June.

Winter Solstice Many Macau Chinese consider the Winter Solstice more important than the Chinese New Year. It's not a public holiday but there is plenty of feasting and temples are crammed with worshippers.

PLACES TO STAY

On the weekend, public holidays, festivals or high season, rooms are scarce and hotel prices double or even treble.

With mid- to top-range places you can get discounts of 30% or more by booking through a Hong Kong travel agent. There are many in the Shun Tak Centre (Macau ferry pier) at Sheung Wan, Hong Kong Island. At the ferry pier in Macau you can book rooms.

Unless on Taipa or Coloane Island, or otherwise indicated, the following places can be found on the Central Macau map (Map B).

PLACES TO STAY – BUDGET

Macau's two hostels are located on Coloane Island. Call the hostel(s) or the MGTO (☎ 315 566) about vacancies before you set out. You must have a Hostelling International card or equivalent. Both have separate quarters for men and women.

Pousada de Juventude de Cheoc Van (☎ 882 024, Rue de António Francisco) Beds in dorms/quads/doubles M$40/50/70 Mon-Fri, M$50/70/100 Sat & Sun. This very clean hostel is on the east side of Cheoc Van Bay, below the Pousada de Coloane, and has a small kitchen and garden. Big youth groups fill it during summer and school holidays.

Pousada de Juventude de Hác Sá (☎ 882 701, Estrada Nova de Hac Sa) Beds in dorms/quads/doubles M$40/50/70 Mon-Fri, M$50/70/100 Sat & Sun. In a grey-tiled building at the southern end of Hác Sá Beach, this is more modern.

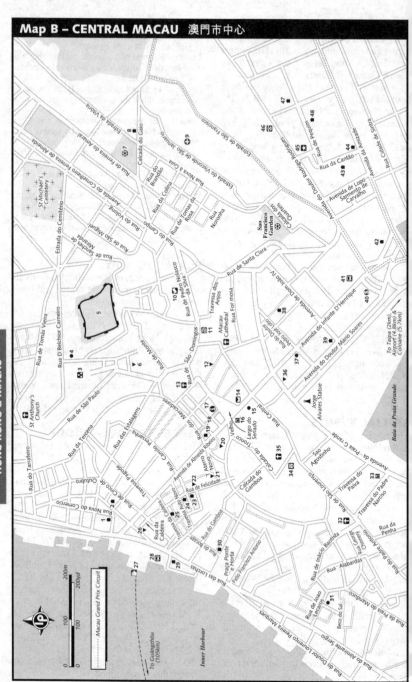

Map B – CENTRAL MACAU 澳門市中心

CENTRAL MACAU – Map B

PLACES TO STAY
1 Vila Capital
  京藝賓館
2 East Asia Hotel
  東亞酒店
8 Royal Hotel
  皇都酒店
19 Central Hotel
  新中央酒店
23 San Va Hospedaria
  新華大旅店
24 Vila Universal; Ko
  Wah Hotel
  世界迎賓館；
  高華酒店
25 Man Va Hotel
  文華酒店
29 Macau Masters
  Hotel
  萬事發酒店
30 Sun Sun Hotel
  新新酒店
38 Pensão Nam In
  南苑酒店
39 Sintra Hotel
  新麗華酒店
42 Lisboa Hotel;
  Lisboa Casino
  葡京酒店
43 Fortuna Hotel;
  Fortuna Lounge
  財神酒店
44 Hotel Presidente; Silla
  Korean Restaurant
  總統酒店
47 Grandeur Hotel
  京澳酒店
48 Holiday Inn Macau;
  Oskar's Pub
  假日酒店

PLACES TO EAT
6 Yes Brazil
  巴西美食

12 Bolo de Arroz
  米饼屋
20 Restaurante Safari
  金池餐廳
21 Sai Nam Restaurant
  西南飯店
22 Fat Siu Lau Restaurant
  佛笑樓大餐廳
26 Food Stalls
  大排檔
36 Solmar
  沙利文餐廳

OTHER
3 Ruins of the Church of
  St Paul; Museum of
  Sacred Art; Crypt
  大三巴牌坊；天主教藝；
  術博物館
4 Escalator to Monte Fort
  and Macau Museum
5 Monte Fort; Macau
  Museum
  中央大炮台；
  澳门博物馆
7 Vasco da Gama Garden
  華士古達嘉馬花園
9 Conde São Januário
  Central Hospital
  山頂醫院
10 Portuguese Consulate
  葡國領事館
11 CTM Mobile Zone
  Internet
  澳門電訊網吧
13 St Dominic's Church;
  Treasury of Sacred Art
  玫瑰堂
14 Main Post Office
  郵電局
15 CTS
  中國旅行社
16 Loyal Senate
  市政廳

17 Macau Government
  Tourist Office
  (MGTO)
  澳門旅遊公司
18 St Dominic's Market
27 Macau-Shenzhen
  Ferry Pier
  深圳客運碼頭
28 Kee Kwan Motor
  Road Co. (Buses to
  Guǎngzhōu)
  岐關車路有限公司
31 St Lawrence City
  Market
32 St Lawerence's
  Church
  聖老楞佐堂
33 Former Government
  House
  澳督府
34 Dom Pedro V
  Theatre
  崗頂劇院
35 St Augustine's
  Church
  聖奧斯堂
37 Foto Princesa
  公主攝影器材行
40 Bank of China
  中銀大廈
41 Buses to Airport &
  Coloane & Taipa
  Islands
45 Main Police Station
  正警署
46 CTM Telephone
  Office
  澳門電訊

There's a *campsite* on Coloane Island at the Colónia Balnear de Hac Sa (☎ 825 170, *Estrada Nova de Hac Sa),* equipped with toilets and showers.

On the mainland peninsula, budget accommodation mostly forms a cluster to the north-west of the Largo do Senado, a lively area between Rua da Caldeira and Rua das Lorchas.

Central Hotel (☎ 373 888, 264 Avenida de Almeida Ribeiro) Singles M$150-188, doubles M$160-280. This hotel is in bad repair but is just what its name says.

Man Va Hotel (☎ 388 655, 3rd floor, 30 Travessa da Caldeira) Singles/doubles from M$172/230. The more expensive rooms in this rather scuzzy place have a fridge.

San Va Hospedaria (☎ 573 701, e sanva @hongkong.com, 67 Rua de Felicidade) Singles/doubles M$70/140. This traditional-style guesthouse has a great deal of character and a homey feel, though the rooms are not very clean and are separated by cardboard partitions.

Ko Wah Hotel (☎ 375 599, 4th floor, 71 Rua de Felicidade) Singles/doubles

M$150/170. This 27-room hotel has friendly management. Take the lift to reception on the 4th floor.

Vila Universal (☎ 573 247, 1st floor, Cheng Peng Bldg, 73 Rua da Felicidade) Singles/doubles M$147/216. This is one of the better budget options.

East Asia Hotel (☎ 922 433, fax 922 430, 1a Rua da Madeira) Singles M$260-340, doubles M$400-500, triples M$500. Women loiter with intent outside this place, housed in a remodelled, classic colonial-style building with spacious rooms with bath; there's a fine restaurant on the 2nd floor.

Vila Capital (☎ 920 154, 920 157, 3 Rua Constantino Brito) Singles/doubles M$230/ 250. This place is seedy but has good-value rooms.

Pensão Nam In (☎ 710 024, 3 Travessa da Praia Grande) Singles/doubles M$110/ 230. In a little alleyway south of the Avenida da Praia Grande, this guesthouse has singles with shared bath and pleasant doubles with bath.

Mondial Hotel (Map A; ☎ 566 866, fax 514 083, 8-10 Rua de António Basto) Singles or doubles HK$200 Mon-Fri, HK$300 Sat & Sun. This large hotel is on the east side of peaceful Lou Lim Ioc Garden.

PLACES TO STAY – MID-RANGE

The prices listed are sometimes halved during the week and in the low season.

Pousada de Coloane (☎ 882 143, fax 882 251, Estrada de Cheoc Van) Singles or doubles M$680-750, triples M$880-950. On Coloane Island, this cosy hotel overlooks Cheoc Van Beach. With a relaxed atmosphere, its own sauna and swimming pool, and a fantastic Sunday lunch buffet, it's an excellent choice.

Sintra Hotel (☎ 710 111, ⓔ bcsintra @macau.ctm.net, Avenida de Dom João IV) Singles or doubles M$860-1260, suites from M$1860. This palace-like hotel has the best service.

Grandview Hotel (☎ 837 788, ⓔ hotelgdv @macau.ctm.net, 142 Estrada Governador Albano de Oliveira) Singles or doubles M$350 Mon-Fri, M$550 Sat & Sun. This large, pleasant hotel is close to the nightlife on Taipa Island. With a swimming pool, sauna and badminton courts, it's a bargain.

Fu Hua Hotel (Map A; ☎ 553 838, fax 527 575, 98-102 Rua de Francisco Xavier Pereira) Singles/doubles/triples M$730/ 830/830, suites from M$1380. This is a modern and bright hotel.

Sun Sun Hotel (☎ 939 393, ⓔ sunsun96 @macau.ctm.net, 14-16 Praça Ponte e Horta) Singles or doubles M$600-980, suites from M$1650. This modern, clean hotel offers big discounts. Rooms on the upper floors have excellent views of the Inner Harbour.

Macau Masters Hotel (☎ 937 572, fax 937 565, 162 Rua das Lorchas) Singles/ doubles/triples M$440/550/1000. This is a smallish hotel with modern rooms and facilities.

Pousada de Mong Há (Map A; ☎ 561 252, Ⓦ www.ift.edu.mo) Singles/doubles M$400/500 Mon-Fri, M$500/600 Sat & Sun, suites M$900. This traditional-style Portuguese inn is run by tourism students. Rates include breakfast. The restaurant is open Monday to Friday for lunch and on Friday night for a Macanese buffet (M$130).

Royal Hotel (☎ 552 222, ⓔ royalmcu @macau.ctm.net, 2-4 Estrada da Vitória) Singles or doubles M$750-1100, suites from M$2200. This large hotel is a bit removed from the action but it has great weekday packages. Its restaurant does a dinner buffet Monday to Thursday (M$78) and a traditional Macanese one (M$118) on Friday and Saturday.

Guia Hotel (Map A; ☎ 513 888, fax 559 822, 1-5 Estrada do Engenheiro Trigo) Singles or doubles M$470-600. Try this place for something a bit more remote.

Kingsway Hotel (Map A; ☎ 702 888, fax 702 828, 230 Rua de Luís Gonzaga Gomes) Singles or doubles M$780-980, suites from M$1180. This place has its own casino, massive sauna and Jacuzzi.

Fortuna Hotel (☎ 786 333, fax 786 363, 63 Rua da Cantão) Singles or doubles M$720-1180, suites from M$1888. This place is equipped with a giant nightclub.

Hotel Presidente (☎ 553 888, Ⓦ www .hotelpresident.com.mo, 355 Avenida da Amizade) Singles or doubles M$660-920, suites from M$2280. Located on a busy road, this hotel has all the modern conveniences and is within walking distance to Macau's nightlife.

PLACES TO STAY – TOP END

During the summer season, many of the top-end places get solidly booked.

Pousada de São Tiago *(Map A; ☎ 378 111, W www.saotiago.com.mo, Fortaleza de São Tiago da Barra, Avenida de República)* Singles or doubles M$1580-1920, suites from M$2200. The 'St James Inn', built into the ruins of a 17th-century fort, commands a splendid view of the harbour and is worth stopping at for a drink on the terrace even if you don't stay. It only has 23 rooms so book well in advance.

Hyatt Regency *(☎ 831 234, W www .macau.hyatt.com, 2 Estrada Almirante Marques Esparteiro)* Singles or doubles M$850-1800, suites from M$2800. More of a resort than a hotel, the Hyatt is on Taipa Island and has tennis courts, squash courts, a nearby golf course, a gym, play areas, heated swimming pool and a casino. The restaurants serve Cantonese, Macanese and Portuguese, and there's a decent delicatessen.

Ritz Hotel *(Map A; ☎ 339 955, e ritzhtlm @macau.ctm.net, Rua Comendador Kou Ho Neng)* Singles or doubles M$980-1380, suites from M$2080. This palace is in a quiet street high above Avenida da República.

Westin Resort *(☎ 871 111, W www .westin.com, 1918 Estrada de Hac Sa)* Singles or doubles M$2000-2350, suites from M$5000. This five-star complex is on Coloane Island, on the east side of Hác Sá Beach. Rooms have large terraces and facilities include a golf course, tennis, squash, and badminton courts, swimming pools, sauna and gym.

Mandarin Oriental *(Map A; ☎ 567 888, W www.mandarinoriental.com, 956-1110 Avenida da Amizade)* Singles or doubles M$1800-2100, suites from M$4600. This is a superb five-star hotel with a huge pool at the harbour's edge. Check for special deals through a travel agent.

Lisboa Hotel *(☎ 377 666, e lisboa @macau.ctm.net, 2-4 Avenida de Lisboa)* Singles or doubles M$1350-2000, suites from M$3800. With over 1000 rooms, this hotel is Macau's most famous landmark with a wonderfully tacky facade straight out of Las Vegas. Inside is one of the best arcades, with shops, restaurants, banks and, for many, the city's only casino worth visiting.

Holiday Inn Macau *(☎ 783 333, W www.holiday-inn.com, 82-86 Rua de Pequim)* Singles or doubles M$1000-1480, suites from M$3300. Service here is somewhat erratic, but the location is excellent.

Grandeur Hotel *(☎ 781 233, W www .hotelgrandeur.com, 199 Rua de Pequim)* Singles or doubles M$1000-1200, suites from M$1850. This 26-storey hotel has a revolving restaurant on the top floor.

PLACES TO EAT

Given its cosmopolitan past, it's not surprising that the food of Macau is an exotic mixture of Portuguese and Chinese. People eat relatively early here; in some restaurants the chef has gone home by 9pm.

Portuguese cuisine is meat-based and uses a viscous form of olive oil, garlic and *bacalhau* (dried salted cod). Popular dishes include: *caldo verde,* a green vegetable and potato soup; *pasteis de bacalhau,* codfish croquettes; *sardinhas grelhadas,* grilled sardines; and *feijoada,* a casserole of beans, pork, spicy sausages, potatoes and cabbage. There's also oxtail, veal and rabbit dishes to have with imported Portuguese red and white wines, port and brandy.

Macanese food borrows from Chinese and other Asian cuisines as well as from those of former Portuguese colonies in Africa and Indian. It is redolent of coconut, tamarind, chilli, jaggery (palm sugar) and shrimp paste. A famous speciality is African chicken, made with coconut and chillies. There's also plenty of seafood: cod, shrimp, crab, squid and sole. From the former Portuguese enclave of Goa are spicy prawns.

Other Macanese favourites include: *casquinha,* stuffed crab; *porco balichão,* a savoury dish of pork cooked with tamarind and shrimp paste; *minchi,* minced beef or pork cooked with potatoes, onions and spices; and baked rice dishes made with seafood. *Serradura* is a Macanese dessert made with crushed biscuits, cream and condensed milk. A dish of that and you'll never leave the table.

Unless situated on Taipa or Coloane Island, or otherwise indicated, the following places can be found on the Central Macau map (Map B).

Portuguese & Macanese

A Lorcha *(Map A; ☎ 313 193, 289a Rua do Almirante Sérgio)* Meals around M$150. Some people refer to this place as the

HONG KONG & MACAU

'quality benchmark' of Portuguese food in Macau. Among the tasty dishes at this much loved restaurant are chicken with onion and tomato, feijoada and raw codfish salad.

Solmar (☎ 574 391, 512 Avenida da Praia Grande) Meals around M$150. Despite the gloomy interior, Solmar is quite an institution in Macau, serving excellent seafood dishes (try the seafood soup).

Barra Nova (Map A; ☎ 965 118, 287 Rua do Almirante Sérgio) Mains M$38-64, fish dishes M$40-158. This small restaurant is in a row of excellent local eateries and serves fantastic Macanese specialities like porco balichão (M$48) and spicy piri-piri prawns (M$50).

Ali Curry House (Map A; ☎ 555 865, 4k Avenida da República) Mains M$38-68. This place serves inexpensive Macanese curries and has outside tables along the waterfront.

Bolo de Arroz (☎ 339 089, 11 Travessa de Santo Domingos) Delectable Macanese pastries and cakes are served here.

Restaurante Estrela do Mar (☎ 825 025, 12 Rua Direita Carlos Eugénio) Mains from M$40. Relocated on Taipa Island, this restaurant serves some of the best old-style Portuguese food in Macau.

Pinocchio (☎ 827 128, 4 Rua do Sol) Meals M$120-150. This place started the rash of fine eateries in Taipa Village. Recommended dishes include grilled squid, fresh sardines and roast lamb.

Fernando's (☎ 882 531, House No 9 Hác Sá Beach) Soups M$22-26, fish & seafood M$55-148, meat dishes M$50-128, rice dishes M$60-66. On Coloane Island, this Portuguese restaurant is famed for its seafood. You'll need to book ahead.

Chinese & Other Asian Cuisines
Rua da Felicidade is a good part of town for both established and hole-in-the-wall Chinese restaurants.

Fat Siu Lau Restaurant (☎ 573 580, 64 Rua da Felicidade) Meals around M$150. The 'House of the Smiling Buddha', established in 1903, is Macau's most famous Chinese restaurant. The speciality is roast pigeon and it also serves Western dishes.

Sai Nam Restaurant (☎ 574 072, 36 Rua da Felicidade) To sample abalone (M$380) at its freshest, try this small, popular restaurant.

Silla Korean Restaurant (☎ 569 039, Mezzanine floor, Hotel Presidente, Avenida da Amizade) Meals around M$200. Head here to satisfy cravings for bulgogi (Korean barbecued beef) and kimchi (fermented vegetables).

Western Cuisine
Mezzaluna (Map A; ☎ 567 888, 2nd floor, Mandarin Oriental, 956-1110 Avenida da Amizade) Meals around M$250-300. This classy restaurant serves pasta and pizzas from wood fired ovens.

Restaurante Safari (☎ 322 239, 14 Patio do Cotovelo) Soups M$14, mains M$22-60, set menus M$50. This friendly place serves coffee-shop snacks and meals. It's at the end of an alleyway off Avenida de Almeida Ribeiro.

Yes Brazil (☎ 358 097, 6a Travessa Fortuna) Mains M$38-68, set menu M$38. This is a tiny, friendly restaurant with excellent feijoada (M$70) and, other Brazilian dishes.

Street Food & Self-Catering
Macau's *food stalls* sell excellent stir-fried dishes; try any of the *dai pai dong* along Rua do Almirante Sérgio near the Inner Harbour, or the stalls in Rua da Escola Commercial, a tiny lane one block west of the Lisboa Hotel and next to a sports field.

You'll find y*uk gon* (dried sweet strips meats) and *hung yan bang* (almond-flavoured biscuits), both Macanese specialities, around Rua da Caldeira and Travessa do Matadouro, near the Inner Harbour.

Two of the largest markets are the ***Almirante Lacerda City Market*** (Mercado Municipal Almirante Lacerda; Map A; 130 Avenida do Almirante Lacerda) in northern Macau and the ***St Lawrence City Market*** (Mercado Municipal de São Lourenço; Rua de João Lecaros) in the south.

The largest ***supermarket*** in Macau is on the 2nd floor of the New Yaohan Department Store (Map A), opposite the ferry terminal.

ENTERTAINMENT
Pubs & Bars
The main place for a pub crawl is the Docks (Map A) where attractive bars line the waterfront area to the south-east opposite the giant, illuminated Kum Iam statue. Try ***Casablanca Cafe***, ***Rio Cafe*** and ***Signal Cafe*** for more posh surroundings, or ***Sanshiro***

Pub for cheap beer by the pitcher. These places are typically open till the wee hours.

Macau Jazz Club (Map A; ☎ 596 014, The Glass House, Avenida Doutor Sun Yat Sen, NAPE) Open 6pm-late Wed-Sun. In a lovely glass building on the waterfront, this place has live jazz at 10.30pm on Friday and Saturday nights.

Embassy Bar (Map A; ☎ 567 888, Mandarin Oriental, 956-1110 Avenida da Amizade) Open from 5pm. This very popular ground floor bar with a live band nightly at 10.30pm, and has a small dance floor.

Fortuna Lounge (Map B; ☎ 786 333, Ground floor, Fortuna Hotel, 63 Rua da Cantão) Most people show up here at some point during the evening.

Oskar's Pub (Map B; ☎ 783 333, Holiday Inn Macau, 82-86 Rua de Pequim) This pub off the main lobby draws a large number of local expats. Happy hour is from 5pm to 9pm.

On Taipa Island, the area just north of the Macau Jockey Club has late-night pubs and bars.

Gambling

A wander through Macau's casinos is an interesting sight. Most casinos require ID and reasonably proper attire. Also, dealers and croupiers take 10% of your winnings for themselves.

Lisboa Casino (Map B; ☎ 375 111) The Lisboa is large and lively, occupying four floors inside the Lisboa Hotel. There's also a Las Vegas-style dancing show – *Crazy Paris* – every night (M$300). Shows start at 8pm and 9.30pm. You must be 18 to enter; buy your tickets in the lobby of the New Wing.

There are also a number of independent casinos such as the *Macau Palace Floating Casino (Map A)*.

The Macau Jockey Club (☎ 821 188, ⓦ www.macauhorse.com, Estrada Governador Albano de Oliveira) Admission M$20. On Taipa Island, this has been Macau's venue for horse racing since 1991. You can watch races from the five-storey, air-conditioned grandstands on Sunday afternoon from 12.30pm and midweek from 7.30pm. For more information call the hotline in Macau (☎ 820 868) or Hong Kong (☎ 800-967 822). Minimum bet is M$10.

Canidrome (Map A; ☎ 261 188, ⓦ www.macaudog.com, Avenida do General Castelo Branco) Admission general/

members' stand M$2/5. Open from 8pm Mon, Thurs, Sat & Sun. This is the largest facility for greyhound racing in Asia. For more information call the hotline in Macau (☎ 333 399) or Hong Kong (☎ 800-903 888).

SHOPPING

Pawnshops are ubiquitous in Macau, and it is possible to get good deals on cameras, watches and jewellery, but you must bargain without mercy. You'll find these shrewd entrepreneurs on the upper stretches of Avenida de Almeida Ribeiro.

Around Macau's back lanes and narrow streets, you'll stumble across bustling markets and traditional Chinese shops selling bird cages, dried herbs, medicines and mahjong sets. Try Rua de Madeira or Rua dos Mercadores, which lead up to Rua da Tercena and its *flea market*, a great place for old Macanese coins. There's another *flea market* near the ruins of the Church of St. Paul. *St Dominic's Market (Map B)* has cheap clothing.

Great streets for antiques, ceramics and curios are Rua de São Paulo, Rua das Estalagens and Rua de São António as well as the lanes leading off them. Watch out for forgeries – especially moulded cement Buddha heads that the vendor has buried for a few months.

Asian Artefacts (☎ 881 022, 25 Rua dos Negociantes) Open 10am-7pm daily. Try this place on Coloane Island for quality antiques.

Reproductions of antique Chinese furniture are much cheaper in Macau than Hong Kong. The shops are concentrated in the tourist area on Rua da Palha and Rua de São Paulo, near the ruins of the Church of St Paul.

Macau's main commercial shopping area is along the Avenida do Infante Dom Henrique and Avenida de Almeida Ribeiro. Also check out Rua da Palha, Rua do Campo and Rua Pedro Nolasco da Silva.

You can pick up wonderful collectors' postage stamps in Macau. Mint sets and first-day covers are available at the main post office; enter from Avenida de Almeida Ribeiro.

Macau is cheap for Portuguese wine, imported cigarettes, cigars and pipe tobacco. However, Hong Kong customs only allow you to bring in 1L of wine and 200 cigarettes duty free.

The MGTO distributes a useful pamphlet called *Shopping in Macau*, which highlights neighbourhoods and their specific wares.

GETTING THERE & AWAY
Air

Ultra-modern Macau International Airport has only a small volume of passenger traffic so it's fast and efficient but airport departure tax is M$130/80 for adults/children for international destinations and M$80/50 for destinations in China.

Air Macau (☎ 396 5555), Dynasty Plaza Building, Avenida da Amizade, NAPE, and several Chinese carriers under the China National Aviation Corporation banner (CNAC; ☎ 788 034), Teng Hou Commercial Centre, Avenida de Dom João, fly to Běijīng (daily), Chóngqìng (three times a week), Fúzhōu (daily), Guìlín (daily), Hǎikǒu (four times a week), Kūnmíng (daily), Nánjīng (twice a week), Shànghǎi (three times daily), Xiàmén (twice daily) and Xī'ān (daily).

EVA Airways (☎ 726 848), Dynasty Plaza Building, Avenida da Amizade, NAPE; Trans Asia Airways (☎ 701 556), 11th floor, Macau Finance Centre, 244-246 Rua de Pequim and Air Macau each have up to six flights a day to and from Taipei.

Air Macau also has flights to Seoul on Thursday and Sunday, direct flights to Bangkok on Monday, Wednesday and Friday and to Manila on Tuesday and Saturday.

Singapore Airlines (☎ 711 728), Room 1001, 10th floor, Luso International Building, 1-3 Rua Dr Pedro Jose Lobo, has daily flights to Singapore.

East Asia Airlines (☎ 727 288, Hong Kong ☎ 2108 4838, W www.helihongkong .com) runs a helicopter shuttle between Macau and Hong Kong (16 minutes, HK$1206 Monday to Friday, HK$1310 Saturday and Sunday). There are up to 22 flights daily from around 9.30am to 10.30pm. Helicopters leave from the roof of the ferry terminal.

Bus

Macau is an easy gateway into China. Simply take bus No 3, 5 or 9 to the Border Gate (Portas de Cerco) and walk across. A second crossing is on the causeway linking Taipa and Coloane. The Cotai Frontier Post allows passengers to cross over the new Lotus Bridge to the Zhuhai SEZ from 9am to 5pm daily. Bus No 26 will drop you off here.

If you want to travel farther afield in China, buses run by the Kee Kwan Motor Road Co (☎ 933 888) leave the small station on Rua das Lorchas, 100m south-west of the end of Avenida de Almeida Ribeiro. Buses for Guǎngzhōu (HK$55) depart about every 15 minutes and for Zhōngshān (about M$20) every 20 minutes. The bus to Guǎngzhōu (six hours) often gets bogged down at customs; it's probably easier to take a bus to the border, walk across and catch a train or minibus to Guǎngzhōu from the other side.

Boat

Most visitors to Macau arrive and depart by boat. If you're coming from Hong Kong, be prepared for long waits at Macau immigration. The jetfoil pier in Macau has left luggage lockers. There's a departure tax of M$19 on anyone leaving by sea for China or Hong Kong, although it's almost always included in the price of the ticket.

Hong Kong The most popular gateway to and from Macau is Hong Kong. Two ferry companies operate services with frequent departures and boats running virtually 24 hours.

TurboJet (☎ 790 7039; in Hong Kong ☎ 2859 3333 information, ☎ 2921 6688 bookings, W www.turbojet.com.hk) runs three types of vessels (55 to 65 minutes; economy/superclass tickets HK$130/232 Monday to Friday, HK$141/247 Saturday, Sunday and public holidays and HK$161/260 at night). Departures are from the Macau ferry pier (Shun Tak Centre, 200 Connaught Rd in Sheung Wan) in Hong Kong and from the Macau Ferry Terminal (☎ 790 7240) in Macau.

The Hong Kong & Yaumatei Ferry Co (HYFCO; ☎ 726 301; in Hong Kong ☎ 2516 9581, W www.nwff.com.hk) operates catamarans hourly from 9.30am to 10.30pm (1¼ hours; day/night HK$113/154 Monday to Friday, HK$134/154 Saturday, Sunday and public holidays).

Tickets can be booked up to 28 days in advance and are available at ferry terminals, CTS branches and travel agents. There is also a stand-by queue before each sailing. On weekends and public holidays, book your return ticket in advance as boats are often full.

China A daily ferry run by the Yuet Tung Shipping Co (☎ 574 478, 331 067) connects Macau with the port of Shékǒu in the Shēnzhèn SEZ. The boat departs from Macau at 2.30pm (1½ hours, adult/child M$100/M$57). Tickets can be bought up to three days in advance from the point of departure, which is pier No 14 in Macau, located just off Rua das Lorchas and 100m south-west of the end of Avenida de Almeida Ribeiro.

Sampans and ferries trip across the Inner Harbour to Wanzai (M$12) on the mainland from a small pier to the south-west, where Rua das Lorchas meets Rua do Dr Lourenço Pereira Marques.

GETTING AROUND
On Macau's peninsula it's relatively easy to walk almost everywhere, however, if you're heading out to Taipa and Coloane, you'll need motorised transport.

To/From the Airport
Airport bus AP1 (M$6) leaves the airport and zips around Taipa before crossing the Macau-Taipa Bridge and heading to the Macau Ferry Terminal and the Border Gate (Portas do Cerco), where it terminates. The bus stops at a number of major hotels en route and departs every 15 minutes from 6.30am to 1.20am.

A taxi from the airport to the centre of town should cost about M$40.

Bus
Public buses and minibuses operate on some 40 routes from 6.45am till midnight, with their destination displayed in Portuguese and Chinese. Fares (M$2.50) can be paid in pataca or Hong Kong dollar coins, however no change is given.

The *Macau Tourist Map* distributed free by the MGTO has a full list of both bus companies' routes. The two most useful buses are Nos 3 and 3A, which run between the ferry terminal and the city centre, near the main post office. No 3 continues up to the border crossing with the mainland, as does No 5. Bus No 12 runs from the ferry

terminal, past the Lisboa Hotel and then up to the Lou Lim Ioc Garden and Kun Iam Temple.

From the Macau Peninsula, the fare to Taipa Island is M$3.30, to Coloane Village it's M$4, and to Hác Sá Beach on Coloane it's M$5. Bus No 21 runs from the A-Ma Temple and along Avenida Almeida Ribeiro to the Lisboa Hotel, over the bridge to Taipa Village and on to Coloane. Bus No 21A follows the same route but carries on to Cheoc Van and Hác Sá Beaches. Bus No 22 runs from the Kun Iam Temple, past the Lisboa Hotel to Taipa Village and then the Macau Jockey Club.

Car
The horrendous traffic and lack of parking space means car rental only makes sense for exploring Taipa and Coloane.

Drivers and front-seat passengers must wear seatbelts, it's illegal to beep the horn in built-up areas and drivers must always stop for pedestrians at a crossing. An International Driver's Permit is usually required, and a deposit of M$4000.

Happy Mokes (☎ 439 393, fax 727 888) in Room 1025 of the Arrivals Hall at the ferry terminal rents four-person Mokes for M$450/500 a day during the week/weekends and six-person ones for HK$500/600.

You can also rent Mokes from Avis Rent A Car (☎ 336 789, fax 314 112) at the Mandarin Oriental Hotel. Avis also rents cheap Subarus (M$400/520 a day during the week/weekend). You can book in advance through the Avis Hong Kong office (☎ 2890 6988, fax 2895 3686), Bright Star Mansion, 93 Leighton Rd, Causeway Bay.

Taxi
Taxi drivers are required to use meters. Flag fall is M$10 for the first 1.5km and M$1 for each additional 250m. There is a M$5 surcharge to go to Taipa and Coloane; travelling between the islands is M$2 extra. Journeys starting from the airport incur an extra charge of M$5.

Taxis can be ordered on ☎ 519 519, ☎ 939 939 or ☎ 398 8800. Hiring a taxi for the day should cost about M$300; both price and itinerary should be agreed on in advance. Many large hotels will help you arrange this.

Pedicab

These three-wheeled trishaws, or *triciclos* in Portuguese, seat two people and are mainly found outside the Lisboa Hotel. Agree on a fare beforehand but expect to pay from M$30 to M$50 for a single ride and M$150 per hour of a very slow tour. Pedicabs cannot negotiate hills, so you'll be limited to the waterfront and some of the narrow alleys.

Bicycle

Bikes can be rented in Taipa Village; see the Taipa and Coloane sections in Things to See for details. You are allowed to cross the Macau-Taipa Bridge on foot but not on a bicycle; the only way to get a bike across to the island is in the boot of a car. Bikes are, however, allowed on the causeway linking Taipa and Coloane.

Guǎngdōng 广东

Capital: Guǎngzhōu
Population: 75.1 million
Area: 186,000 sq km

Guǎngdōng's proximity to Hong Kong has made it a major gateway into China and the country's most affluent province. In the '70s Guǎngdōng was just an economic middleweight, but the high level of economic integration between Guǎngdōng's Zhū Jiāng (Pearl River) Delta and Hong Kong has led to record economic growth – some economists refer to the area as Greater Hong Kong.

The Cantonese, as the people of Guǎngdōng are called, are regarded with a mixture of envy and suspicion by many in the rest of China. Guǎngdōng's topography, unique dialect (Cantonese) and remoteness from traditional centres of authority, coupled with long-standing contact with 'foreign barbarians', has created a strong sense of autonomy and self-sufficiency.

The Cantonese also spearheaded Chinese emigration to the USA, Canada, Australia and South Africa in the mid-19th century, spurred on by the gold rushes in those countries and by the wars and growing poverty in their own. Bustling Chinatowns around the world are steeped in the flavours of Guǎngdōng cuisine and ring with the sounds of the Cantonese dialect and Cantopop melodies. Hong Kong heroes such as Bruce Lee and Jackie Chan are as famous in Guǎngdōng as they are in Hong Kong.

The province has basked in the healthy regional economic climate encompassing Hong Kong, becoming the target for investment by overseas Chinese. Indeed, the manufacturing industries that Hong Kong was once famous for are now located in Guǎngdōng.

Supping at the same table as Hong Kong has both fattened the province and cultivated a regional idiosyncrasy that finds vigorous expression in the burgeoning media industries. When China-watchers worry (or rub their hands in glee) about the possible decentralisation of power in China and the rise of regionalism, it is Guǎngdōng that they look to first. After all, Guǎngdōng was a latecomer to the Chinese empire. While it was integrated in 214 BC (during the Qin

Highlights

- The decaying colonial ambience of Guǎngzhōu's Shāmiàn Dǎo (Sand Surface Island)

- Near Zhūhǎi, Dr Sun Yatsen's Residence is the rustic former home and birthplace of the lionised leader

- The beauty of the countryside around Zhàoqìng, reminiscent of Guìlín, and featuring nearby Dǐnghú Shān

dynasty), it was not until the mid-12th century that large numbers of Han settlers (propelled by the Jurchen invaders) emigrated to the province from northern China. Until then, Guǎngdōng was considered to be a barbaric borderland fit only for exiled officials.

In subsequent years, the province was the site of many rival national governments, which earned it a reputation for unruliness and revolt.

Today Guǎngdōng is an economic powerhouse rather than a sightseeing destination. Most foreigners visiting the province are there on business, or in transit to less-developed parts of China.

GUǍNGZHŌU 广州
☎ 020 • pop 6,664,900
Also known as Canton, Guǎngzhōu is the capital of Guǎngdōng and one of the most prosperous cities in China. To some, the city may seem like one enormous shopping

COASTAL SOUTH

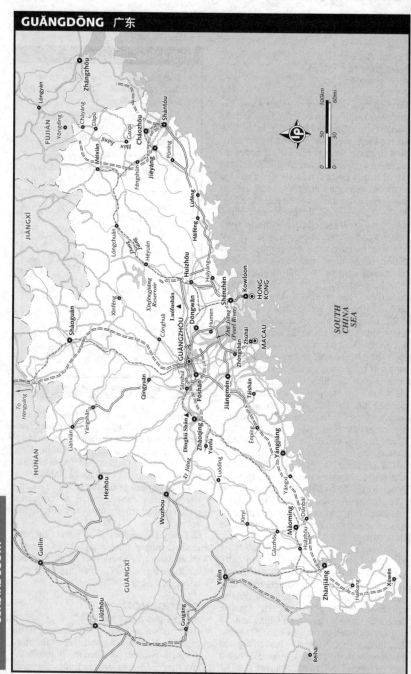

mall. There isn't much by way of sights, but wandering the high-rise- and shop-lined streets – plied by shoppers and farmers alike – provides interesting insight into the extremes of poverty and wealth in China.

Over the last decade, Guǎngzhōu has been busy casting off the yoke of recent history in an effort to catch up with the late 20th century. While there are a few interesting temples and parks and some fine restaurants, shopping centres and crammed textile and clothing stalls dominate the city. Most of the city's charm lingers on in the streets and colonial-style architecture of Shāmiàn Dǎo (Sand Surface Island), a foreign concession that is being gracefully gentrified despite the growing encroachment of tourist shops.

History

The first town to be established on the site of present-day Guǎngzhōu dates back to the Qin dynasty (221–207 BC). The first foreigners to arrive were the Indians and Romans, who appeared as early as the 2nd century AD. By the Tang dynasty (500 years later) Arab traders were visiting, and a sizeable trade with the Middle East and South-East Asia had developed.

The Portuguese arrived in the 16th century hunting for porcelain and silk, and providing Guǎngzhōu with its first contact with a modern European nation; they were allowed to set up base downriver in Macau in 1557. Then the Jesuits came and in 1583 were allowed to establish themselves at Zhàoqìng, a town to the west of Guǎngzhōu, and later in Běijīng.

The first trade overtures from the British were rebuffed in 1625, but the imperial government finally opened Guǎngzhōu to foreign trade in 1685. In 1757, by imperial edict, China's foreign trade was restricted to Guǎngzhōu, and the Co Hong, a Guǎngzhōu merchants' guild, gained exclusive rights to it. Foreigners were restricted to Shāmiàn Dǎo. Trade flourished in China's favour.

In 1773 the British shifted the balance of trade by unloading 1000 chests of Bengal opium at Guǎngzhōu.

In 1839 opium was still the key to British trade in China. The emperor appointed Lin Zexu commissioner of Guǎngzhōu with orders to stamp out the opium trade once and for all. The Chinese war on drugs led to a British military reaction, the first Opium

War. The conflict was ended by the Treaty of Nanking (1842), which ceded Hong Kong Island to the British. A later treaty ceded the island and a piece of Kowloon 'in perpetuity'.

In the 19th century, Guǎngzhōu became a cradle of revolt. The leader of the antidynastic Taiping Rebellion, Hong Xiuquan (1814–64), was born at Huaxian, north-west of Guǎngzhōu, and the early activities of the Taiping centred on this area (see the boxed text 'The Heavenly Kingdom of the Taiping' in the Jiāngsū chapter).

Guǎngzhōu was also a stronghold of the republican forces after the fall of the Qing dynasty in 1911. Sun Yatsen, the first president of the Republic of China, was born at Cùihēng village south-west of Guǎngzhōu. In the early 1920s, Sun headed the Kuomintang (Nationalist Party) in Guǎngzhōu, from where the republicans mounted their campaigns against the northern warlords. Guǎngzhōu was also a centre of activities for the fledgling Communist Party.

Contemporary Guǎngzhōu, however, swings to the tinkle of cash registers rather than the drum roll of protest and revolt. In recent times the Cantonese have usually left the turbulence of politics to their northern compatriots.

Orientation

Central Guǎngzhōu is bounded by a circle road (Huanshi Lu, literally 'circle-city road') to the north and Zhū Jiāng to the south. Most hotels, commercial areas and places of interest lie within this boundary. A larger ring road (the Huancheng Expressway) and numerous inner-city overpasses are still under construction.

Accommodation is clustered around the train station (in the north), on Huanshi Donglu (in the north-east), and in and around the old foreign concession of Shāmiàn Dǎo (in the south). If you don't want to leave with the impression that Guǎngzhōu is one huge construction site, seek sanctuary on Shāmiàn Dǎo, which is by far the quietest and most appealing sector of the city.

According to Chinese convention, Guǎngzhōu's major streets are usually split into numbered sectors (Zhongshan Wulu, which could also be written Zhongshan 5-Lu etc). Alternatively they are labelled by compass points: *běi* (north), *dōng* (east), *nán* (south) and *xī* (west) – as in Huanshi

Donglu, which will sometimes be written in English as Huanshi East Road.

Guǎngzhōu's first subway line opened in July 1999 and runs from the Guǎngzhōu east train station in the north-east to across Zhū Jiāng in the south-west. Another line is under construction that will connect with the north (main) train station; it is expected to be completed in 2003.

Information

A monthly entertainment guide, *South China City Talk*, is produced by foreigners living in the city and is an invaluable resource for what's happening in town and around. It's available at most of the major hotels and international-style bars. Several Internet magazines, including ⓦ www .thatsguangzhou.com, offer up-to-date info on restaurants, clubs, and events.

The Public Security Bureau (PSB; Gōngānjú; ☎ 8338 3731) can renew visas and is at 155 Jiefang Nanlu, just south of Dade Lu. Visa renewals take about a week (Y300).

Travel Agencies China International Travel Service (CITS; Zhōngguó Guójì Lǚxíngshè; ☎ 8666 6889), at 185 Huanshi Lu, is next to the main train station. It books tickets and has a bevy of English speakers. The friendlier China Foreign Trade Guangzhou Travel Service (Guǎngjīaohùi Piàowù Zhōngxīn; ☎ 8669 4550) is at 117 Liuhua Lu. China Travel Service (CTS; Zhōngguó Lǚxíngshè; ☎ 8333 6888) at 10 Qiaoguang Lu, next to the Hotel Landmark Canton, also runs tours and books tickets. Most hotels can help with travel needs as well.

Consulates There are several consulates that can issue visas and replace stolen passports.

Australia (☎ 8335 0909, fax 8335 0718) Room 1509, Main Bldg, GITIC Plaza, 339 Huanshi Donglu
Canada (☎ 8666 0569, fax 8667 2401) Room 801, China Hotel, Liuhua Lu
France (☎ 8330 3302, fax 8330 3437) Room 803, GITIC Plaza, 339 Huanshi Donglu
Germany (☎ 8330 6533, fax 8331 7033) 19th floor, GITIC Plaza, 339 Huanshi Lu
Holland (☎ 8330 2067, fax 8330 3601) Room 905, GITIC Plaza, 339 Huanshi Lu
Japan (☎ 8333 8999) Garden Hotel Tower, 368 Huanshi Donglu
Thailand (☎ 8192 3313, fax 8192 3072) Room 316, White Swan Hotel, Shāmiàn Dǎo
USA (☎ 8188 8911, fax 8186 2341) 1 Shamian Nanjie, Shāmiàn Dǎo

Money Most of the Bank of China branches around town change travellers cheques and have ATMs that take Cirrus, MasterCard, Visa, Plus etc. There's one on the ground floor of the GITIC Plaza, one at the Bank of China near Yǒuyì Bīnguǎn (see Places to Stay later), and another across from the Furama Hotel at the Bank of China on Changdi Lu.

If you're coming from Hong Kong, be warned that Guǎngzhōu's residents are all too happy to receive Hong Kong dollars from you, but they will give you change in *yuán;* change your dollars first to yuán at the bank or at your hotel.

Guǎngzhōu's American Express office (☎ 8331 1771, fax 8331 3535) is on the 8th floor of the GITIC Plaza Hotel.

Post & Communications The major tourist hotels have post offices where you can send letters and packets containing printed matter.

Adjacent to the train station is the main post office, known locally as the Liúhuā post office (Liúhuā yóujú). Overseas parcels can be sent from here.

DHL (☎ 8664 4668) has an office in Guǎngzhōu, as does UPS (☎ 8775 5778) and Federal Express (☎ 8386 2026) at Garden Hotel, Room 1356–7, Garden Tower.

The China Telecom office (☎ 8103 1848) is at 196 Huanshi Xilu, opposite the train station on the eastern side of Renmin Beilu. Most hotels have International Direct Dialling (IDD) – calls to Hong Kong are very cheap. All the main tourist hotels have 'business centres' offering domestic and international telephone, fax and telex facilities.

China Telecom has computers on its 2nd floor and provides cheap and fast Internet access for Y3 per hour plus a Y20 deposit. It's open 8am to 8pm daily. Farther away, Meet Internet Coffee House (☎ 8731 0888), at 83 Nonglin Xilu, has terminals for hire for Y10 per hour. It's open 10am to 1am daily. On Shāmiàn Dǎo, Henan Webmail (☎ 8188 7561) charges a minimum of Y20 for the first hour and Y10 every half hour after. Major hotels also offer Internet access from Y15 to Y25 for 15 minutes.

Bookshops The Foreign Languages Bookshop (☎ 8333 5185) can be difficult to find; head to the back of the store at 326 Beijing Lu and go up the stairway. The selection includes abbreviated classics in English for Chinese students and translations of Chinese classics.

Most major hotels have small bookshops with a smattering of popular novels, as well as current issues of *Time*, *Newsweek*, *The Economist*, *Far Eastern Economic Review*, *Asiaweek* and even some French and German publications.

Medical Services The Guangzhou Red Cross Hospital has an emergency number (Hóngshízìhùi Yīyuàn; ☎ 8441 2035), but the operator may not speak English. For general treatment of non-emergencies, try the medical clinic for foreigners at the Guangzhou No 1 People's Hospital (Dìyī Rénmín Yīyuàn; ☎ 8108 3090 ext 681) at 602 Renmin Beilu. For serious emergencies requiring an English-speaking doctor, it's best to call the Pioneer International Clinic (☎ 8384 8911), at Room 3003, Peace World Plaza, 352 Huanshi Donglu.

If you're staying on Shāmiàn Dǎo or the riverfront, a nearby hospital is the Sun Yatsen Memorial Hospital (Sūn Yìxiān Jìniàn Yīyuàn; ☎ 8133 2415) at 107 Yanjiang Xilu. Not much English is spoken here, but the medical facilities are pretty good and the prices low.

Next to Shāmiàn Dǎo and the Peaceful Market is the Guangzhou Hospital of Traditional Chinese Medicine (Zhōngyī Yīyuàn; ☎ 8188 6504) at 16 Zhuji Lu. If you want to try acupuncture and herbs, this is the place to go. Many foreigners come here to study Chinese medicine.

Shāmiàn Dǎo 沙面岛
Sand Surface Island
This island is a blessed retreat from the bustle of Guǎngzhōu's streets. Everything is conducted in low gear – pedestrians saunter rather than walk, cars sidle rather than drive and lazy tennis matches stretch out into the late afternoon. With its serenity and crumbling history, it's an ideal place to wander around and inhabit the past.

Shāmiàn means 'sand surface', which is all this island was until foreign traders were permitted to set up their warehouses here in the middle of the 18th century. Land reclamation has increased its area to its present size: 900m from east to west, and 300m from north to south. The island became a British and French concession after these nations defeated the Chinese in the Opium Wars, and is covered with decaying colonial buildings that housed trading offices and residences.

The French Catholic **Our Lady of Lourdes Chapel** (*Tiānzhǔjiào Loùshèngmǔ Táng*) has been restored and stands on the main boulevard. The boulevard itself is a gentle stretch of gardens, trees and birdsong. Today most of the buildings are used as offices or apartment blocks.

Slowly but surely the island is being gentrified as new sidewalk cafes, bars and boutiques open to cater to tourists and residents.

Temple of the Six Banyan Trees
Liùróngsì Huātǎ 六榕寺花塔
The six banyan trees of the temple's name are no longer standing, but the temple remains a popular attraction for its octagonal **Huā Tǎ** (*Flower Pagoda; 87 Liurong Lu; admission Y1; open 8am-5pm daily*). The banyan trees were celebrated in a poem by Su Dongpo, a renowned poet who visited the temple in AD 1100.

At 55m, the pagoda is the tallest in the city – from the outside it appears to have only nine storeys, but inside it has 17. The pagoda was constructed in AD 1097. It's worth climbing, although if you are tall you might end up with a collection of bruises as the doorways on the way up are very low.

The temple, which may date as far back as AD 537, was originally associated with Hui Neng, the sixth patriarch of the Zen Buddhist sect. Today it serves as the headquarters of the Guangzhou Buddhist Association. It is an active temple – be sensitive about taking photographs of monks and worshippers. Inside the **Guanyin Temple** is a huge golden effigy of Guanyin, the Goddess of Mercy, to whom women burn incense and pray.

Liurong Lu has a colourful array of souvenir shops selling ceramics, jade and religious ornaments. There is also a bustling fruit and meat market on Ruinan Lu, on the right just before you reach the temple itself.

COASTAL SOUTH

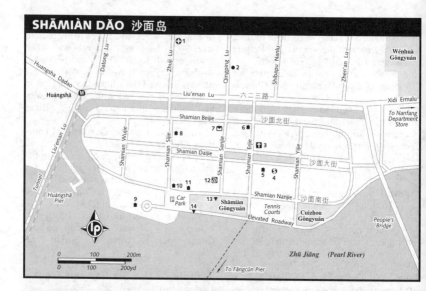

SHĀMIÀN DǍO 沙面岛

PLACES TO STAY
5   Qiáobǎo Huódōng
    Zhōngxīn
    侨胞活动中心
6   Shènglì Bīnguǎn
    (New Annexe)
    胜利宾馆(新楼)
8   Shènglì Bīnguǎn
    胜利宾馆
9   White Swan Hotel
    白天鹅宾馆
10 Guangzhou Youth
    Hostel
    省外办招待所

11 Shāmiàn Bīnguǎn
    沙面宾馆

PLACES TO EAT
13 Lucy's
    露丝酒吧餐厅
14 Rose Garden Club
    玫瑰园俱乐部

OTHER
1   Guangzhou Hospital
    of Traditional Chinese
    Medicine
    中医医院

2   Peaceful Market
    清平市场
3   Our Lady of Lourdes
    Chapel
    天主教露圣母堂
4   Bank of China
    中国银行
7   Post Office
    邮局
12 Henan Webmail

Guāngxiào Sì 光孝寺
Bright Filial Piety Temple

Guāngxiào Sì *(109 Guangzhou Lu; admission Y2; open 6am-5pm daily)* is one of the oldest and most attractive temples in Guǎngzhōu. The earliest Buddhist temple on this site may date to the 4th century AD, perhaps even before the city of Guǎngzhōu was established. The temple has particular significance for Buddhists because Hui Neng of the Zen Buddhist sect was a novice monk here during the 7th century.

The temple buildings are much more recent, the original buildings having been destroyed by fire in the mid-17th century. The main temple houses numerous golden figures, and is an impressive construction of latticed wood windows and splintered wood eaves.

Five Genies Temple
Wǔxiān Guàn 五仙观

This Taoist temple *(☎ 8333 6853, Xizhai Xiang; admission Y5; open 9am-5pm daily)* is held to be the site of the appearance of the five rams and celestial beings in the myth of Guǎngzhōu's foundation (see the entry on Yuèxiù Gōngyuán later).

The large hollow in the rock in the temple courtyard is said to be the impression of a celestial being's foot; the Chinese refer to it as Rice-Ear Rock of Unique Beauty. The

5-tonne bell, cast during the Ming dynasty, is 3m high, 2m in diameter and about 10cm thick, and probably the largest in Guǎng-dōng. It's known as the 'calamity bell', since the sound of the bell, which has no clapper, is a portent of calamity for the city.

At the rear of the main tower stand life-size statues with archaic Greek smiles; these appear to represent four of the five genies. In the temple forecourt are four statues of rams, and embedded in the temple walls are inscribed steles. The temple is just south of Remember the Prophet Mosque at the end of an alley off Huifu Xilu.

Peaceful Market 清平市场
Qīngpíng Shìchǎng

When it first came into existence in 1979, this market (Shāmiàn Dǎo map) was one of the first private markets to flourish as a result of Deng Xiaoping's radical economic (capitalist) reforms.

Although the vast displays of medicinal herbs and spices, semi-toxic mushrooms, dried plant and animal parts, live birds, and tubs of squirming scorpions, snakes, and turtles are now common fixtures in all Chinese cities, this market reached a disturbing zenith in the 1990s when animal traffickers appropriated the spot and used it for the illicit dealing of live (or parts of live) monkeys, dogs, cats, owls, anteaters, and other exotic creatures, often for some form of human consumption. Police cracked down on the smugglers two years ago and dogs and cats are now only sold on the street for adoption.

The market is north of Shāmiàn Dǎo, on the north side of Liu'ersan Lu and spills out into Tiyun Lu, which cuts east-west across Qingping Lu.

Sacred Heart Church 石室教堂
Shí Shì Jiàotáng

The impressive twin-spired Sacred Heart Church is built entirely of granite. Started in 1863 and completed in 1888 (during the reign of emperor Guangxu), it was designed by the French architect Guillemin. The church is an imitation of a European Gothic cathedral and its spires tower to a height of 58m. Four bronze bells suspended in the building to the east of the church were cast in France; the original coloured glass was also made in France, but almost all of it is gone.

Remember the Prophet Mosque
Huáishèngsì Guāngtǎ 怀圣寺光塔

The original mosque on this site is said to have been established in AD 627 by the first Muslim missionary to China.

The present buildings (Guangta Lu) were built in the Qing dynasty (1644–1911), as the original mosque was destroyed in a fire in 1343. Inside the grounds of the mosque is a minaret, which because of its even appearance is known as Guāng Tǎ (Smooth Tower).

At the time of writing, the mosque was not open to the public, but this situation may change.

Hǎizhuàng Gōngyuán 海幢公园

This park (337 Tongfu Zhonglu; admission Y2; open 6am-11pm daily), south of the river, would be unremarkable but for the remains of what was once Guǎngzhōu's largest monastery, Hǎizhuàng Sì. It was founded by a Buddhist monk in 1662, and in its heyday the monastery grounds covered 2.5 hectares. After 1911 the monastery was used as a school and a soldiers' barracks. It was opened to the public as a park in the 1930s.

Religious services stopped at the temple during the Cultural Revolution, but have resumed today. The temple is home to three huge golden Buddhas and in the rear courtyard incense burning and prayers are conducted. An adjacent building houses thousands of miniature shrines, each with a photograph of the deceased.

The temple, the gate to the park and other fixtures are being slowly restored, and the area gradually prettified. During the day the grounds are full of old men chatting, playing cards and chequers, and airing their pet birds. Take bus No 10 from Haizhu Circle.

Yuèxiù Gōngyuán 越秀公园

This is the biggest park (13 Jiefang Beilu; admission Y5; open 9am-6pm daily) in Guǎngzhōu, covering 93 hectares. Its attractions include a few artificial lakes and a huge swimming pool.

Inside the park is the symbol of Guǎngzhōu, the Sculpture of the Five Rams (Wǔyáng Shíxiàng), erected in 1959. It's said that long ago five celestial beings wearing robes of five colours came to Guǎngzhōu riding through the air on rams. Each carried a stem of rice, which they presented to the people as an auspicious sign from heaven that the area would be free from famine forever. Guǎngzhōu means Broad Region, but from this myth it takes its other name, City of Rams, or just Goat City.

The **Zhènhai Tower** (*Zhènhǎi Lóu*), also known as the Five-Storey Pagoda, is the only part of the old city wall that remains. From the upper storeys it commands a view of the city to the south and Báiyún Shān (White Cloud Hills) to the north. The present tower was built during the Ming dynasty upon the highest portion of the northern city wall.

Because of its strategic location it was occupied by the British and French troops at the time of the Opium Wars. The 12 cannons in front of the tower date from this time. The tower now houses the City Museum, with exhibits that describe the history of Guǎngzhōu from Neolithic times until the early part of the 20th century.

You can get to the park on bus Nos 5, 24 and 101.

Wénhuà Gōngyuán 文化公园
Cultural Park

Just north-east of Shāmiàn Dǎo, this park (*37 Xidi Malu; admission Y25, open 9am-5.30pm daily*) opened in 1956. Attractions include dodgem cars, a miniature funfair, a big wheel, a weights room, a theatre and even a flight simulator (about Y5 per ride).

Guangzhou Museum of Art
Guǎngzhōu Yìshù Bówùguǎn 广州艺术博物馆

Guǎngzhōu's new art museum (☎ *8358 9126, 13 Luhu Lu; admission Y30; open 9am-5pm daily*) opened in 2000 and houses an impressive collection of contemporary and modern Chinese art and sculpture, including works by famous Chinese painters Guan Shanyue, Lai Shaoqi, and Lu Xiongcai. Several of the terracotta soldiers from Xī'ān are also on display here. One wing of the museum houses an interesting collection of works by Liao Bing Xiong, a political cartoonist exiled from China shortly after his works were deemed too 'rightist' in 1958.

Southern Yue Tomb Museum
Nányuèwáng Hànmù 南越王汉墓

This is also known as the Museum of the Western Han Dynasty of the Southern Yue King's Tomb (☎ *8666 4920, 867 Jiefang Beilu; admission Y12; open 9.30am-5.30pm daily*). It stands on the site of the tomb of Emperor Wen, the second ruler of the Southern Yue kingdom, dating back to 100 BC. The Southern Yue kingdom is what the area around Guǎngzhōu was called during the Western Han dynasty (AD 206–220).

The tomb was originally 20m under **Xiànggǎng Shān** (*Elephant Hill*) and was discovered in 1983; inside were 15 funerary bodies – including four concubines – and more than 1000 sacrificial objects made of jade. It's an excellent museum, with a great layout and interesting English explanations. More than 500 rare artefacts are on display. Take bus No 5, 24 or 101 to the museum.

Zhū Jiāng Cruises 珠江游览船
Zhūjiāng Yóulǎnchuán

The northern bank of Zhū Jiāng is one of the most interesting areas of Guǎngzhōu – filled with people, markets and dilapidated buildings. By contrast, the southern side takes its inspiration from Victoria Harbour in Hong Kong – a growing forest of huge neon advertisements.

Guangzhou Passenger Ship Company (☎ 8333 0397) has two daily runs at 8am and 1.30pm down Zhū Jiāng (Y38). Boats leave from the Xīdī pier just east of the People's Bridge (Rénmín Qiáo) and head down the river as far as Èrshā Dǎo and then turn around and head back to the People's Bridge. Night cruises depart at 7pm, 8pm, and 9pm. The trip takes 1½ hours.

For more upmarket evening cruises with dinner, check at the White Swan Hotel.

Other Sights

The **Peasant Movement Institute** (*Nóngmín Yùndòng Jiǎngxísuǒ*; ☎ 8333 3936, 42 Zhongshan Silu; admission Y2; open 8.15am-11.30am & 2pm-5pm daily*) was formerly a Ming-dynasty temple-turned-Communist training ground, designed to teach aspiring cadets how to copy good examples set by peasants. The institute is now a revolutionary museum.

Farther up Zhongshan Sanlu, the **Memorial Garden to the Martyrs** (*Lièshì Língyuán*) commemorates the unsuccessful Communist uprising of 11 December 1927; the garden is laid out on Red Flower Hill (Hónghuāgǎng), on Zhongshan Sanlu. North of Huanshi Donglu, **Huánghuāgǎng**

Gōngyuán (*Yellow Flower Park*) is the site of the **Mausoleum of the 72 Martyrs** (*Qīshíèr Lièshì Mù*).

The **Chen Clan Academy** (*Chénjiā Cí; 34 Enlongji Lu; admission Y10; open 8.30am-5pm daily*) is a family shrine housed in a large compound built between 1890 and 1894. The compound encloses 19 traditional-style buildings along with numerous courtyards, stone carvings and sculptures. It's next to the Chénjiācí station, or take bus Nos 102 and 104.

Liúhuāhú Gōngyuán is enormous, containing the largest artificial lake in Guǎngzhōu. Ornithologists may be interested in one of the islands, which is home to thousands of birds.

It was built in 1958, a product of the ill-fated Great Leap Forward. The entrance to the park is on Renmin Beilu and can be reached on bus Nos 7 and 103.

Also built in 1958, **Guangzhou Zoo** (*Guǎngzhōu Dòngwùyuán; ☎ 8775 2702, 122 Xianlie Zhonglu; admission Y10*) is one of the largest and best zoos in China, although that's not saying much. Hippos, bears, leopards, panthers, monkeys, and a lone, miserable giant panda are some of the popular attractions. Next door, **Ocean World** (*Hǎiyángguǎn; ☎ 8761 1250; admission Y30*) features dolphins, penguins and sharks. To reach the zoo, take bus No 220 from Báiyún Bīnguǎn (see Places to Stay – Top End).

Special Events

The invitation-only, 20-day **Guangzhou Trade Fair** (*Zhōngguó Chūkǒu Shāngpǐn Jiāoyì Huì*), also called the Chinese Export Fair, is held twice yearly, usually in April and October. Apart from the Spring Festival (Chinese New Year), this is the biggest event in Guǎngzhōu. This fair is important to travellers because accommodation becomes a real problem while it's on, and many hotels double room prices.

The city is unbearably crowded at the best of times, but during the **Spring Festival**, around February, Guǎngzhōu is even more packed out.

Places to Stay – Budget

Guǎngzhōu is not a great place for budget hotels, but prices have dropped from the dizzy heights of former years. Although a bit risky, if you're getting off the train it might be worth checking out what's offered from the galaxy of touts. They will come rushing at you as you exit the station, waving brochures advertising inexpensive rooms. Some of these places are Chinese-only, but some don't seem to care who they take.

Shāmiàn Dǎo is by far the quietest and most attractive area to stay; you are much more likely to meet other travellers and the bars are better. All rooms listed have bathrooms and air-con unless otherwise noted.

Guǎngdōng Lǚyóu Dàshà (*Guangdong Tourist Hotel; ☎ 8666 6889 ext 3812, fax 8667 9787, 179 Huanshi Xilu*) Dorm beds for HI (International Youth Hostel) members Y50, singles/doubles with shared bath Y118/178, with private bath Y188/248. This convenient hostel/hotel is beside the main train station. The windowless, single rooms, however, reek perpetually of cigarette smoke.

Guangzhou Youth Hostel (*Shěngwàibàn Zhāodàisuǒ; Shāmiàn Dǎo map; ☎ 8188 4298, fax 8188 4979, 2 Shamian Sijie*) Dorm beds Y80, singles/doubles/triples with shared bath Y100/170/210, doubles/triples with private bath Y190/240. By default, this place wins the title of 'backpackers headquarters' in Guǎngzhōu since there is little else in this price range that is open to foreigners. It has clean and comfortable rooms. Train and plane tickets can also be booked here.

Qiáobǎo Huódòng Zhōngxīn (*Overseas Chinese Activity Centre; Shāmiàn Dǎo map; ☎ 8188 5913, fax 8186 8690, 31-33 Shamian Dajie*) Doubles/triples Y190/250. The friendly service compensates for the somewhat claustrophobic rooms at this small hotel on Shāmiàn Dǎo.

Places to Stay – Mid-Range

The vast majority of Guǎngzhōu hotels open to foreigners belong to the mid- and top-end price ranges, but room surpluses have forced many places to offer discounts of 20% to 30%. It's a good idea to get into the habit of asking for discounts (*zhékòu*).

Train Station Area There are a few options in this area:

Yǒuyì Bīnguǎn (*Friendship Hotel; ☎ 8667 9898, fax 8667 8653, 698 Renmin Beilu*) Doubles Y330-480. This hotel is reliable.

GUĂNGZHŌU 广州

PLACES TO STAY
4   Liúhuā Bīnguǎn
    流花宾馆
5   Guǎngdōng Lǚyóu
    Dàshà
    广东旅游大厦
8   Youyi Bīnguǎn; Yìshù
    Bīnguǎn
    友谊宾馆;艺术宾馆
11 Dōngfāng Bīnguǎn
    东方宾馆
12 China Hotel; Hard
    Rock Cafe
    中国大酒店;硬石俱乐部
19 GITIC Plaza Hotel
    广东国际大酒店
22 Garden Hotel
    花园酒店
24 Báiyún Bīnguǎn
    白云宾馆
26 Guótài Bīnguǎn
    国泰宾馆
28 Holiday Inn
    文化假日酒店

55 Báigōng Jiǔdiàn
    白宫酒店
57 Xīnhuá Dàjiǔdiàn
    新华大酒店
58 Xīnyà Jiǔdiàn
    新亚酒店
61 Aiqún Dàjiǔdiàn
    爱群大酒店
63 Furama Hotel
    富丽华大酒店
67 Hotel Landmark Canton
    华厦大酒店

PLACES TO EAT
18 Banana Leaf Restaurant
    蕉叶风味屋
20 Cave Bar
    墨西哥餐厅酒吧
23 Elephant and Castle Pub
    大象堡酒吧
29 Seattle Expresso
    西雅图伊帕苏
32 Cafe Elles
    本字吧

42 Guāngxiào Sùshíguǎn
    光孝素食馆
43 Tsai Ken Hsiang
    Restaurant
    菜根香素菜馆
47 Wǔyáng Huímín
    Fàndiàn
    五羊回民饭店
51 Pànxī Jiǔjiā
    洋溪酒家
53 Táotáojū
    陶陶居
54 Guǎngzhōu Jiǔjiā
    广州酒家
60 Dàtóng Jiǔjiā
    大同酒家

TRANSPORT
1   Long-Distance Bus
    Station
    广东省汽车客运站
3   Liúhuā Bus Station
    流花车站
10 Jīhàn Bus Station
    锦汉车站
38 Buses to Báiyún Shān
    往白云山的汽车站
50 Guǎngfó Bus Station
    (to Fóshān)
    广佛汽车站
68 Train Ticket Booking
    Office
    火车售票处

广州 GUĂNGZHŌU

OTHER

2 Liúhuā Post Office
邮政总局(流花邮局)

6 CITS; CAAC
中国国际旅行社;
中国民航

7 Telephone Office
国际电信大楼

9 China Foreign Trade
Guangzhou Travel
Service
广交会票务中心

13 Southern Yue Tomb
Museum
南越王汉墓

14 Sculpture of the
Five Rams
五羊石像

15 Zhènhǎi Tower
镇海楼

16 Sun Yatsen
Monument
孙中山纪念碑

17 Guangzhou Museum
of Art
广州艺术博物馆

21 Peace World Plaza; Pioneer
International Clinic
好世界广场

25 Nanfang International
Plaza
南方国际商厦

27 Wind Flower Club
南吧国际

30 Mausoleum of the 72
Martyrs
七十二烈士墓

31 Ocean World
广州海洋馆

33 Meet Internet Coffee
House
网吧音乐咖啡室

34 L'Africain
非洲吧

35 Peasant Movement
Institute
农民运动讲习所

36 Foreign Languages
Bookshop
外文书店

37 Guangzhou Department
Store
广州百货大楼

39 Temple of the Six
Banyan Trees
六榕寺花塔

40 Guangzhou No 1
People's Hospital
第一人民医院

41 Guāngxiào Sì
光孝寺

44 Remember the Prophet
Mosque
怀圣寺光塔

45 Five Genies Temple
五仙观

46 Bank of China
中国银行

48 ChenClan Academy
陈家祠

49 Face Club
菲私俱乐部

52 Antique Market
古玩市场

56 Nanfang Department
Store
南方百货

59 Sun Yatsen Memorial
Hospital
孙逸仙纪念医院

62 Bank of China
中国银行

64 Sacred Heart Church
石室教堂

65 PSB
公安局外事科

66 CTS
中国旅行社

69 Guangzhou Red Cross
Hospital
市红十字会医院

Yìshù Bīnguǎn (Art Hotel; ☎ *8667 0255 ext 2100, fax 8667 0255 ext 2678, 698 Renmin Lu)* Standard doubles Y268-328. Newly renovated, directly behind Yǒuyì Bīnguǎn, this is one of the best mid-range deals in this neighbourhood. Discounts of 30% are sometimes available.

Liúhuá Bīnguǎn (☎ *8666 8800, fax 8666 7828, 194 Huanshi Xilu)* Rooms from Y418. This is a large building opposite the train station. Service is a bit complacent because of its prime location, and rooms are a little overpriced. Nevertheless, the lobby is a great place to recuperate after stumbling off a 36-hour train ride. Discounts of up to 60% are available.

Zhū Jiāng Area There are a number of places to try here.

Shāmiàn Bīnguǎn (Shāmiàn Dǎo map; ☎ *8191 8359, fax 8191 1628, 52 Shamian Nanjie)* Doubles Y275-323, triples Y345. This is an attractive, charming and popular hotel just up from Shāmiàn Gōngyuán. It has discounts of up to 20%.

Shènglì Bīnguǎn (Guangdong Victory Hotel; Shāmiàn Dǎo map; ☎ *8186 2622, fax 8186 2413)* On Shāmiàn Dǎo, there are two branches of Shènglì Bīnguǎn that are fairly upmarket, though the branch at 54 Shamian Beijie *(rooms HK$360)* is the cheaper of the two (rooms sometimes go for HK$280). The branch at 53 Shamian Beijie *(doubles/triples HK$530/600)* also accept Renminbi (RMB); ask for discounts. Despite the consecutive number both hotels are on the same side of the road, around five minutes' walk from each other.

Àiqún Dàjiǔdiàn (☎ *8186 6668, fax 8188 3519, 113 Yanjiang Xilu)* Singles Y250, doubles Y320-480. This is a grand old hotel from the 30s that overlooks Zhū Jiāng. Singles are a good deal; the more expensive deluxe doubles options have river views.

Three smaller hotels clustered on Renmin Nanlu cater to Hong Kong visitors and are good value, but the street and overpass above make things very noisy:

Báigōng Jiǔdiàn (☎ *8188 2313, fax 8188 9161, 13-17 Renmin Nanlu)* Singles or doubles Y218-268. This is a pleasant and friendly place.

Xīnyà Jiǔdiàn (New Asia Hotel; ☎ *8188 4722, fax 8188 3733, 10-12 Renmin Nanlu)*

Singles Y230-260, doubles Y280-320. Rooms here are clean and attractive, and the staff tries hard to please. Discounts of 30% are available.

Xīnhuá Dàjiǔdiàn (☎ *8188 9788, fax 8186 8809, 2-6 Renmin Nanlu)* Singles/ doubles/triples/suites Y198/288/450/880. This hotel is the best of the bunch, and prices are reasonable. Some rooms have Chinese-style suites with outside terraces. Discounts of up to 30% are available.

Furama Hotel (Fùlìhuá Dàjiǔdiàn; ☎ *8186 3288, fax 8186 3388, 316 Changdi Nanlu)* Standard doubles Y360. Although normally considered a top-end hotel, the Furama has standard doubles as well as the more expensive rooms.

Places to Stay – Top End
Train Station Area Two places to try are:

China Hotel (Zhōngguó Dàjiǔdiàn; ☎ *8666 6888, fax 8667 7014, Liuhua Lu)* Doubles US$148-298 plus 20% service charge. A long-standing favourite with international business travellers, this place is also a hub for buses heading to Hong Kong and Macau. Discounts of up to 30% are available.

Dōngfāng Bīnguǎn (☎ *8666 2946, fax 8666 2775, 120 Liuhua Lu)* Rooms US$108-301. This place is a little more glitzy than it was in the days when it used to offer Y6 dormitory beds. Discounts of up to 60% are also available.

Zhū Jiāng Area A couple of hotels to try are:

White Swan Hotel (Báitiān'é Bīnguǎn; Shāmiàn Dǎo map; ☎ *8188 6968, fax 8186 2288, 1 Shamian Nanjie)* Standard/deluxe doubles US$148/170, executive suites US$260 plus 20% service charge. This is the best hotel in the area, with an excellent range of rooms and facilities: 11 restaurants and bars, Rolls-Royce rental, an indoor waterfall and a complete shopping arcade.

Hotel Landmark Canton (Huáshà Dàjiǔdiàn; ☎ *8335 5988, fax 8333 6197, Qiaoguang Lu)* Standard rooms Y650-Y1100, low-season rooms from Y500, plus 20% service charge. Conveniently located by Haizhu Circle, this hotel has a wide range of facilities and comfortable rooms on offer.

North-Eastern Area The north-eastern part of the city has the highest concentration of top-end hotels and is probably the best area for business travellers to be based. For the tourist it's a bit bland.

GITIC Plaza Hotel (Guǎngdōng Guójì Dàjiǔdiàn; ☎ *8331 1888, fax 8331 1666, 339 Huanshi Donglu)* Standard rooms Y1410-1730 plus 20% service charge. This five-star property has all the trappings of an international business hotel, including top-notch business services, but lacks character.

Garden Hotel (Huāyuán Jiǔdiàn; ☎ *8333 8989, fax 8335 0467, 368 Huanshi Donglu)* Standard rooms Y1160-4980. Farther east along Huanshi Donglu, the Garden is elegant and spacious.

Báiyún Bīnguǎn (☎ *8333 3998 ext 3128, fax 8334 3032, 367 Huanshi Donglu)* Singles Y398-658, doubles Y508-728, plus 15% service charge. On the opposite side of the street to the Garden, this place is a little easier on the wallet and a wide range of rooms. Discounts of up to 20% are also available.

Guótài Bīnguǎn (Cathay Hotel; ☎ *8386 2888, fax 8384 2606, 376 Huanshi Donglu)* Standard doubles Y500 plus 15% service charge. Rooms here are pleasant and the service is decent. Up to 30% discount is sometimes available.

Holiday Inn (Wénhuà Jiàrì Jiǔdiàn; ☎ *8776 6999, fax 8775 3126, 28 Guangming Lu)* Rooms US$130-260 plus 20% service charge. Farther east, this hotel has standard immaculate rooms, a health club and an Italian restaurant.

Places to Eat

Guǎngzhōu is certainly one of the best places in China to eat and is famous for its old, established restaurants. However travellers on a budget will be better off tracking down the many inexpensive eats that line the streets and back alleys.

Chinese A few recommended restaurants to sample Chinese cuisine are:

Dàtóng Jiǔjiā (☎ *8188 8988, 63 Yanjiang Xilu)* Dim sum Y16-Y22. This is a local favourite for dim sum. The restaurant is an eight-storey building and can seat 1600 customers so don't worry about space. Specialities are *dàtóng cuìpíjī* (crisp-fried chicken) and *kǎo rǔzhū* (roast suckling pig).

Guǎngzhōu Jiǔjiā (☎ *8188 8388, 2 Wenchang Nanlu)* Dishes from Y36. This is probably the most famous eatery in the city. Specialities include shark fin soup with shredded chicken, chopped crabmeat balls and braised dove. This is an expensive restaurant and reservations are sometimes necessary.

Wǔyáng Huímín Fàndiàn (Five Rams Muslim Restaurant; ☎ *8130 3991, 325 Zhongshan Liulu)* Dishes from Y25. This restaurant isn't as big as it used to be, but it still serves excellent Muslim-Chinese cuisine. Try the *shuàn yángròu* (boiled mutton slices) and the *cuìpí huǒé* (crispy goose).

Pànxī Jiǔjiā (☎ *8181 5718, 151 Longjin Xilu)* Dishes from Y15. Pànxī Jiǔjiā is noted for its dumplings, stewed turtle, roast pork, chicken in tea leaves and a crabmeat-sharkfin consommé. Its dim sum is famous and is served from about 5am to 9.30am, noon to 3pm and 5pm to 9.30pm daily.

Táotáojū (☎ *8181 5769, 20 Dishipu Lu)* Dim sum from Y22. This is a very popular restaurant. Originally built as a private academy in the 17th century, it was turned into a restaurant in the late 19th century. Dim sum is the speciality here; you choose sweet and savoury snacks from the trolleys that are wheeled around the restaurant. Other specialities include the trademark *táotáo jiāngcōng jī* (taotao ginger and onion chicken). Taotaoju mooncakes are very popular at the time of the Mid-Autumn Festival.

Vegetarian A couple of options are:

Tsai Ken Hsiang Restaurant (Cài gēnxiāng Sùcàiguǎn; ☎ *8334 4363, 167 Zhongshan Liulu)* Here you can pick and choose from the snacks downstairs (Y12) or head upstairs for delicious tofu and vegetable dishes (around Y20).

Guǎngxiào Sùshíguǎn (☎ *8108 1964, 68 Jinghui Lu)* Dishes Y18-32. No English is spoken at this popular vegetarian restaurant. You can select take-away orders *(dàizǒu)* from the counter or sit down and order specials like deep fried mashed sweet potato *(zàilìyòngyǔ)*.

Pub Grub Guǎngzhōu has a number of international-style bars where you can scoff pizza or burgers, sink a chilled imported beer and put a few yuán into the jukebox.

COASTAL SOUTH

The trouble is keeping up with them – they come and go with annoying regularity.

Lucy's (Shāmiàn Dǎo map; ☎ 8187 4106, 5 Shamian Nanjie) Mains Y30-50. Lucy's is good for American-style food and has beer for Y18 a pint. The pizzas and pasta here are good approximations of the real thing.

Rose Garden Club (Méiguì Yuánjùlèbù; Shāmiàn Dǎo map; ☎ 8192 2808, 3 Shamian Nanjie) Mains Y15-45. This pleasant riverside restaurant/bar serves Western and Chinese specialties and has outdoor seating.

Hard Rock Cafe (Yìngshí Jùlèbù; ☎ 8666 6888) Dishes Y32-62. The Hard Rock Cafe can be found in the basement of the China Hotel, dishing up the usual buffalo wings, steak and chips fare, albeit with hefty price tags for the experience.

Seattle Espresso (Xīyǎtú Yìpàsū; ☎ 8732 2808, 71 Xianlie Lu) Dishes from Y20. In addition to fries, imported beer, and real espresso (Y20), this Western-style cafe and bar serves tasty and reasonable breakfast and lunch/dinner combinations. Spaghetti, a salad and drink cost Y28.

Cave Bar (Mòxīgē Cāntīngjǐubā; ☎ 8386 3660, 360 Huanshi Donglu) Dishes Y18-55. Cave Bar serves Tex-Mex food as well as drinks, and is popular with foreigners.

Elephant and Castle Pub (Dàxiàngbǎo Jǐubā; ☎ 8359 3309, 363 Huanshi Donglu) Dishes Y18 and above. This place is also popular with foreigners.

Cafe Elles (Mùzǐ Bā; ☎ 8761 9909, 2nd floor, Huaxin Bldg, cnr Shuiyin Lu & Huanshi Lu) Mains Y18-60. Live jazz performances and European flair make this cosy dive particularly popular with locals and expatriates. Nicolas, the French owner, even has an authentic crepe-making machine to impress.

Banana Leaf Restaurant (Jiāoyè Fēngwèi Wū; ☎ 8359 1288 ext 3118, Broadcasting & Television Hotel, 8 Luhu Lu) Mains Y30-65. Another popular place with foreigners is the Banana Leaf, part of the Banana Leaf chain. It serves up delicious South-East Asian curries and is a pleasant place to eat.

Guǎngzhōu's major international hotels are also stocked with some excellent restaurants and bars that often have good food.

Entertainment

The entertainment scene in Guǎngzhōu is moving fast, with burgeoning rave and live music scenes, but it is difficult to pin down venues. Check South China City Talk for the latest spots. The large hotels offer a range of late-night drinking holes and nightclubs, but it's all pretty mundane stuff. Try any of the bars listed in the Pub Grub section of Places to Eat for darts, pool, jukebox music and imported beers.

L'Africain (Fēizhōu Bā; ☎ 8762 3336, 707 Dongfeng Donglu) Open 7.30pm-2am Mon-Fri, 7.30pm-4am Sat & Sun. If reggae and bongo beats appeal to you more than techno, you may want to try this place, near the corner of Dongfeng Donglu and Nonglin Xialu. It's a popular gay venue.

Face Club (Fēisī Jùlèbù; ☎ 8388 0688, 191 Dongfeng Xilu) Open 8.30pm-2am daily. DJs from all over the world come to spin trance, techno, and industrial music at this popular club.

Hard Rock Cafe (☎ 8666 6888) Admission Y60. Open 10pm-2am Sun-Thur, 10.30pm-3am Fri & Sat. Hard Rock, in the basement of the China Hotel, features either a DJ or live rock bands, usually from other parts of Asia, nightly. The beer is pricey but the entry fee includes one drink.

Wind Flower Club (☎ 8358 2446, 387 Huanshi Donglu) Drinks Y20-60. The Wind Flower tends to attract Guǎngzhōu's spanglier set, but it still makes for a good place to get into the drinking mood. Music, often of the techno variety, plays nightly.

Shopping

You can hardly walk anywhere in central Guǎngzhōu without stumbling over shop after shop, selling everything under the sun.

The intersection of Beijing Lu and Zhongshan Lu, north-east of Haizhu Circle, was traditionally the principal shopping area in the city and is still a good place to buy clothes and shoes if you can find the right size. A sprawling **night market** sets up after dark. Near Qīngpíng Shìchǎng, there are more **clothing shops** on Xiajiu Lu and Shangjiu Lu, which are closed off to vehicles on the weekends, but it can get incredibly crowded.

Not surprisingly, the large hotels have well-supplied tourist shops, but bear in mind that their prices are astronomical compared to local shops, often 10 times the price on the streets, so it's worth spending some time looking around.

North of Qingping Lu there's an **antique and jade market** near the corner of Wenchang Lu and Changshou Lu. At the western end of Shāmiàn Dǎo, on Shamian Sijie, is a string of **souvenir shops** selling paintings, clothes and calligraphy. The road leading up to the Temple of the Six Banyan Trees is also chock-a-block with souvenir shops bursting with ceramics and jade.

Getting There & Away

Air Civil Aviation Administration of China (CAAC; Zhōngguó Mínháng; 24-hour hotline ☎ 8668 2000) has an office (open 8am to 8pm daily) represented by China Southern (probably China's best-run airline) at 181 Huanshi Lu, on your left as you come out of the train station. You can also book air tickets at various locations around town. China Southern has five daily flights to Hong Kong (Y590 one way, 35 minutes).

The airline also has direct flights between Guǎngzhōu and a number of foreign cities, including Amsterdam, Bangkok, Ho Chi Minh City, Jakarta, Kuala Lumpur, Los Angeles, Manila, Melbourne, Osaka, Penang, Singapore and Sydney. International airport tax is Y80.

Foreign airlines in Guǎngzhōu include:

Garuda Indonesia (☎ 8332 5484) Room 1009, Peace World Plaza, 352 Huanshi Donglu
Japan Airlines (8669 6688) Room A201, China Hotel, Liuhua Lu
Malaysia Airlines (☎ 8335 8828) Shop M04–05, Garden Hotel, 368 Huanshi Donglu
Singapore Airlines (☎ 8335 8868) Mezzanine floor, Garden Hotel, 368 Huanshi Donglu
Vietnam Airlines (☎ 8382 7187) Room 924, East Bldg, Garden Hotel, 368 Huanshi Donglu

You can fly virtually anywhere in China from Guǎngzhōu. Flights to Shànghǎi are Y1250 and to Běijīng Y1750. Domestic airport tax is Y50.

Bus Bus services in Guǎngzhōu are very well developed.

The hassle-free way to get to Hong Kong is by the deluxe buses that ply the Guǎngzhōu-Shēnzhèn super-highway, which can get you there in just over three hours. Most of the major top-end hotels have services, and tickets range between HK$100 and HK$150. Frequent buses also depart from the Jǐnhàn bus station (Jǐnhàn zhàn) across from the China Hotel on Liuhua Lu. Customs procedures are fairly routine, but you have to take all your luggage off the bus.

Direct buses to Macau via Zhūhǎi (Y60, three hours) leave from the China and Garden Hotels, as well as the Jǐnhàn bus station. At Zhūhǎi you have to walk across the border, where shuttle buses will take you to the centre of town.

Deluxe buses to Shēnzhèn (Y65, two hours) leave frequently from three bus stations: the Jǐnhàn station, the Liúhuā bus station (Liúhuā chēzhàn) that straddles the chaotic mess of vehicles across Huanshi Xilu in front of the train station, and from the main long-distance bus station (shěng qìchēzhàn), west of the train station on Huanshi Xilu. They leave every 30 minutes from 7am to 9pm. The Liúhuā bus station also has economy buses (Y27).

Similarly, economy buses (Y35, 2½ hours) depart every half an hour for Zhūhǎi from the Liúhuā bus station, while deluxe buses (Y55, 2½ hours) leave from the long-distance and Jǐnhàn bus stations. They terminate in the Gǒngběi district just on the border with Macau.

Buses to Zhàoqìng (Y30, 1¼ hours) leave from the long-distance bus station. Buses for Guìlín (Y100, sleeper, 13 hours), Nánníng (Y100, 15 hours), Hǎikǒu (air-con sleeper Y140, 16 hours), Shàntóu (Y90, eight hours), Fóshān (every half hour, Y10, 45 minutes) and Zhōngshān (Y25, two hours) leave from the Liúhuā station. Deluxe buses also leave for Shàntóu (Y180, seven hours) from the Jǐnhàn station.

Train Guǎngzhōu's main train station is a constant, seething mass of humanity, gaping road repairs and vehicular traffic that seems to defy all logic. The ongoing construction of a new subway line to the train station – to be finished in 2003 – has compounded the chaos, resulting in mass sit-ins by waiting passengers on the square outside. The Guangzhou east train station, by comparison, is a model of efficiency. Ticketing at east station is fairly straightforward, with separate booths for Kowloon (Hong

Kong) and Shēnzhèn (on the border with Hong Kong). Signs are in English.

Trains to Kowloon (Jiǔlóng) and high-speed trains to Shēnzhèn that do the journey in 55 minutes depart from here. Travel to the Guangzhou east train station has been vastly improved by the opening of the subway line. Bus No 272 also goes between the two stations, as does bus No 271, which departs from the Liúhuā bus station.

Booking train tickets departing from the main Guǎngzhōu train station to other parts of China is a lot more painless than it used to be. Ticket touts swarm around the station area and zero in on foreigners, but it's not worth the risk of being ripped off. There are two separate ticket places at the station itself. A 24-hour ticketing office is in the hall to the left of the large clock as you face the station. It's usually the more crowded of the two. Current, next-day and two-day advance tickets are sold in the pink building just east of the station, open daily from 5.30am to 10.30pm.

CITS nearby will book train tickets up to five days in advance for a service charge of Y20. In town, other travel agencies will book train tickets (see the Information section earlier) for similar charges. You can also book train tickets at the train ticket issuing office at 185 Baiyun Lu, which is open daily from 8am to noon and 1pm to 5pm. There's no English sign, but look for the China railway logo.

Trains head north from Guǎngzhōu to Běijīng (24 hours; arrival at the Beijing west train station), Shànghǎi (27 hours) and every province in the country except Hǎinán Dǎo and Tibet.

The express train between Hong Kong and Guǎngzhōu is comfortable and convenient. It covers the 182km route in a shave under two hours; tickets cost Y209 for ordinary soft-seat class. You'll save more than half that by taking a hard seat to Shēnzhèn, crossing the border and taking the KCR to Hong Kong. Trains departing from the Guangzhou east train station to Hong Kong follow:

train no	departs	arrives
T811	8.30am	10.25am
T815	1.03pm	2.45pm
T817	3.50pm	5.32pm
KTT819	5.20pm	7.17pm

The timetable for trains travelling from Hong Kong to Guǎngzhōu follows:

train no	departs	arrives
TKTT820	8.25am	10.07am
T802	12.10pm	1.42pm
T814	1.25pm	3.22pm
T804	4.45pm	6.17pm

The local train from Shēnzhèn to Guǎngzhōu is cheap and reasonably fast (two hours); five daily high-speed trains leave from the east train station (Y80, 55 minutes). Trains to Zhàoqìng (Y26, two hours) leave from the main train station.

Boat Guǎngzhōu is a major port on China's southern coast. It offers high-speed catamaran services to various destinations, but overnight ferries have almost disappeared as road services improve. Former overnight services to Wúzhōu, Yángzhōu, Hong Kong and Macau have been discontinued and the boat to Hǎikǒu may soon follow suit. Coastal ferries to Shànghǎi and beyond are also the victim of improved land transportation.

The two main departure and ticketing locations are at Zhōutóuzuǐ wharf (Zhōutóuzuǐ kèyùnzhàn; ☎ 8444 8218), on the southern arm of Zhū Jiāng, and Dàshātóu wharf (Dàshātóu kèyùnzhàn; ☎ 8383 3691) on the north shore, east of Beijing Lu.

Zhōutóuzuǐ is easily reached by taxi from the Zhū Jiāng area, or take bus No 31 from Wénhuà Gōngyuàn and ask the driver to let you off at the road leading to the wharf. Bus No 7 goes from the main train station to Dàshātóu.

Hong Kong Jet-cats (jet-powered catamaran) make twice daily trips from the wharf at Píngzhōu, located about 20 miles south-west of Guǎngzhōu. The trip takes 2½ hours and there are two classes of tickets for Y180 and Y220. You can buy tickets at Zhōutóuzuǐ wharf and a free shuttle bus departs for Píngzhōu. Tickets are also available at the White Swan Hotel and Hotel Landmark Canton, both of which also have shuttle buses.

A hovercraft service also makes the trip to Hong Kong in two hours (HK$190) from Húangpǔ, departing at 10.30am and 4.30pm.

Tickets are sold at the Garden Hotel, where there is also a shuttle bus to the wharf.

Hǎikǒu Ferries for Hǎikǒu leave from Zhōutóuzuǐ wharf every other weekday. The service was still operating at the time of writing, but it's probably a good idea to give the wharf a call before trooping out there to buy tickets. Tickets range from Y301, for 2nd class, to Y134, for 5th class. The trip takes 24 hours.

Getting Around
Guǎngzhōu proper extends for 60 sq km, with most of the interesting sights scattered throughout, so seeing the place on foot is impractical. The subway line goes by many of the city's major sights along Zhongshan Lu, and is also a convenient way to get to Shāmiàn Dǎo. Otherwise the only alternative to riding wedged against someone's armpit on one of the public buses is to take a grid-locked taxi and inch through the streets.

Guǎngzhōu's traffic conditions are in a state of mob rule. Be careful when crossing the road and use 360° vision, as vehicles come from all directions.

To/From the Airport Guǎngzhōu's Báiyún airport is 12km out of town near Báiyún Shān. There is a regular airport bus that runs from the CAAC office near the train station to the airport (Y3), departing every 20 minutes.

Just outside the entrance to the airport is a taxi ramp. Taxis leaving from here are metered. Don't go with the taxi touts unless you want to be ripped off. When you get into a taxi, tell the driver *dǎ biǎo* (turn on the meter). The cost should be between Y30 and Y40, depending on the size of the taxi and where you are headed in town.

Bus Guǎngzhōu has an extensive network of motor and electric trolley-buses, which will get you just about anywhere you want to go. Unfortunately the network is still overstretched, though the subway will ease things a bit.

It's worth getting a detailed map of the city (for the bus routes) from one of the hawkers outside the train station or at one of the hotels. Exiting the train station, you'll find a huge cluster of buses (and queues) on

the right. There are too many bus routes to list them all here, but a few of the important routes are:

No 31 Runs along Gongye Dadao Bei, east of Zhōutóuzuǐ wharf, crosses the People's Bridge and goes straight up Renmin Lu to the main train station at the north of the city.
No 30 Runs from the main train station eastwards along Huanshi Lu before turning down Nonglin Xialu to terminate in the far east of the city. This is a convenient bus to take if you want to go from the train station to Báiyún Bīnguǎn and the Garden Hotel.
No 5 Starting from the main train station, this bus takes a similar route to No 31, but instead of crossing the People's Bridge it turns west along Liu'ersan Lu, which runs past the northern side of Shāmiàn Dǎo. Get off here and walk across the small bridge to the island. It terminates at the Huangsha terminal across from the north-west tip of Shāmiàn Dǎo.

Subway Guǎngzhōu's subway runs from the Guangzhou east train station down Tiyudong Lu, then heads west along Zhongshan Lu to the city's western district. The line then runs south along Baohua Lu to the north-west tip of Shāmiàn Dǎo and under Zhū Jiāng. At the time of writing, 16 stations were in operation. Tickets are Y5 for 10 or more stations, Y4 for trips between seven to nine stations, Y3 for four to six stops and Y2 for three or fewer stops.

Taxi Although taxis are abundant on the streets of Guǎngzhōu, demand is great, particularly during the peak hours: from 8am to 9am and during lunch and dinner hours. When taking a taxi from the main train station avoid the touts; look for the line-up of red taxis amid the chaos that defines Guǎngzhōu.

Taxis are equipped with meters and start at Y7. Depending on the vehicle, a trip from the train station to Shāmiàn Dǎo should cost between Y15 and Y20.

Bicycle Shāmiàn Dǎo usually has a place where you can rent a bike. The shifting sands of the bike-rental world on Shāmiàn Dǎo move outlets around, so ask at your hotel for details. Usually rental is Y2 per hour or Y20 per day, plus a large deposit (Y400).

A look at the traffic in Guǎngzhōu might deter you from cycling here. Before hiring a bike, check the brakes.

COASTAL SOUTH

AROUND GUǍNGZHŌU
Báiyún Shān 白云山
White Cloud Hills

These hills, in the north-eastern suburbs of Guǎngzhōu, are an offshoot of Dàyǔ Peak (Dàyǔ Lǐng), the chief mountain range of Guǎngdōng. There are more than 30 peaks that were once dotted with temples and monasteries, although none of any historical significance remains. The brochure describes it as 'the first spectacular scene of Guǎngzhōu' (the lawless traffic conditions are a close second), and it's really not bad in fair weather. It's a good hike up to the top or a leisurely walk down, as well as being a temporary respite from the polluted atmosphere below.

The highest peak in Báiyún Shān is **Star Touching Peak** *(Mōxīng Lǐng)*. On a clear day you can see a panorama of the city – Xīqiáo Shān to one side, Běi Jiāng (North River) and the Fayuan Hills on the other side, and the sweep of the Zhū Jiāng. Unfortunately, clear days are becoming a rarity in Guǎngzhōu.

Locals rate the evening view from White Cloud Evening View (Báiyún Wǎnwàng; formerly known as Cheng Precipice) as one of the eight sights of Guǎngzhōu. The precipice was formerly the site of the oldest monastery in the area.

Famous as a resort since the Tang and Song dynasties, the area is being thematically restored to attract Hong Kong tourists and now sports water slides, a golf course, botanical gardens and a sculpture park, among other sights. One of the more interesting among these is the **Míngchūn Valley Aviary** *(Míngchūngǔ; admission Y10; open 8am-6pm daily)*, which features a wide variety of bird species, albeit in small cages. Watch the performance if you want to hear parrots speak Chinese. The restored **Néngrén Sì** *(admission Y5; open 8am-6pm daily)* is also worth visiting. The serenity here gives some idea of what the area might once have been like, if you can ignore the cable car overhead. The temple is a short walk down from the top.

Getting There & Away Báiyún Shān are about 15km from Guǎngzhōu and make a good half-day excursion. Bus No 285 can take you from Dongfeng Zhonglu, just north of Rénmín Gōngyuán, to the cable car at the bottom of the hill near Lù Hú. The trip takes between half and one hour, depending on traffic, and goes all the way up to the top. The bus stops at the park entrance for the Y5 admission fee. Or, take bus No 24 from the west side of Rénmín Gōngyuán to the Báiyún Shān bus station. Minibuses from there stop at various park locations for Y3.

Liánhuā Shān 莲花山
Lotus Mountain

This mountain is an old Ming dynasty quarry site, 46km south-east of Guǎngzhōu. It's a possible day trip from Guǎngzhōu, though it may be of more interest to Guǎngzhōu residents than to travellers with a busy itinerary.

The stone-cutting at Liánhuā Shān ceased several hundred years ago and the cliffs have eroded to a state where it looks almost natural. On the mountain is an assortment of temples and pagodas, including **Liánhūa Tǎ** *(Old Lotus Tower)* that was built in 1664. During the Opium War, Liánhuā Shān served as a major line of defence against the British forces.

Getting There & Away Boats to Liánhuā Shān depart from Xīdī pier (☎ 8333 0397) just south of the Nanfang department store on Yanjiang Xilu.

There's an individual service that leaves from Xīdī pier at 8am and 1.30pm for Y25, every day except Saturday, but probably the best option is to get the earlier, luxury one-day tour that leaves the same pier at 8am and returns from Liánhuā Shān at 3.15pm. Tickets are Y38 and can be bought at Xīdī pier. The trip takes about one hour.

The major hotels in Guǎngzhōu also run tours to Liánhuā Shān, as does the Guanzhou Tourism Centre (☎ 8668 1022) at 180 Huanshi Lu. Naturally it is cheaper to do it yourself.

Theoretically there should also be a bus to Liánhuā Shān, but good luck finding it!

Fóshān 佛山
☎ 0757 • pop 3,209,600

Fóshān, just 28km south-west of Guǎngzhōu, is remarkable mainly for Zǔ Miào (Ancestor Temple), which has emerged as a popular destination for local and overseas Chinese tourists.

Like all tourist attractions worth their salt in China, there is a legend connected with Fó Shān (Buddha Hill). In this case, the story involves three Buddha statues that mysteriously disappeared only to be rediscovered hundreds of years later during the Tang dynasty (AD 618–907).

Fóshān also has a reputation as a pottery and ceramics centre.

Zŭ Miào Fóshān's No 1 tourist attraction (☎ 229 3723, 21 Zumiao Lu; admission Y20; open 8.30am-7pm daily), this is one of those temples that has been rebuilt so many times that its name and function have drifted apart from each other.

The original 11th-century temple may have been a place of ancestor worship, but from the mid-14th century it has enshrined a 2.5-tonne bronze statue of Beidi, the Taoist God of Water and all its denizens, especially fish, turtles and snakes.

Because southern China is prone to floods, people often tried to appease Beidi by honouring him with temples and carvings of turtles and snakes. Outside the temple is a statue of 'the cast-iron beast of flood easing' – a one-horned buffalo. Statues like this were placed near the river at times of flood to hold back the waters.

Among other historical fragments are caricatures of British imperialists on the stone plinths outside the temple, some examples of ineffectual local cannons cast here during the Opium War and a huge ridge tile covered with ceramic figures.

To get here take bus No 1 from the train station.

Getting There & Away Fóshān is easily visited as a day trip from Guăngzhōu. There are frequent minibuses from the west bus station (guăngfó qìchē zhàn) on Zhongshan Balu. Tickets are Y8.

Frequent minibuses also leave from the Liúhuā bus station near the train station for Y12. If you are in the Shāmiàn Dăo area of Guăngzhōu just wait on Liu'ersan Lu and you will see minibuses heading west, many of which are going to Fóshān (Y10). Put your hand out and they'll stop.

Minibuses take about an hour, but can take longer in Guăngzhōu's horrific traffic.

Minibuses arrive and depart from the Zŭmiào bus station (Zŭmiào chē zhàn) on

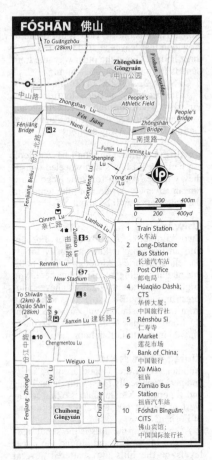

FÓSHĀN 佛山

1	Train Station 火车站
2	Long-Distance Bus Station 长途汽车站
3	Post Office 邮电局
4	Húaqiáo Dàshà; CTS 华侨大厦; 中国旅行社
5	Rénshòu Sì 仁寿寺
6	Market 莲花市场
7	Bank of China; 中国银行
8	Zŭ Miào 祖庙
9	Zŭmiào Bus Station 祖庙汽车站
10	Fóshān Bīnguǎn; CITS 佛山宾馆; 中国国际旅行社

Chengmentou Lu, which is within walking distance of the temple. Buses also depart here for other destinations in Guăngdōng such as Zhūhǎi (Y42/28 with/without aircon), Shēnzhèn (Y50) and Hong Kong (HK$150). The main long-distance bus station is north of town on Fenjiang Beilu. Five buses daily also leave for Hong Kong (3½ hours) from Fóshān Bīnguǎn and Húaqiáo Dàshà. Buses to Xīqiáo Shān (Y10) depart from the main long-distance bus station on Fenjiang Beilu.

Train services between Guăngzhōu and Fóshān (Y16, 30 minutes) are faster than the buses but are only really worth it if you are living in the train station area. If you add on the time getting to the station and queuing for a ticket, it could take a lot longer. There

COASTAL SOUTH

are also direct express trains to/from Hong Kong. There is one service from Fóshān to Kowloon that leaves at 10.43am (HK$220, three hours). Going the other way, the train departs from Kowloon at 2.45pm.

CTS (☎ 222 3828, 14 Zumiao Lu) in Fóshān provides a free shuttle to the Píngzhōu wharf for high-speed catamarans to Hong Kong (see the earlier Guǎngzhōu Getting There & Away section).

Getting Around You won't have to look too hard for Fóshān's two-wheeled taxis – they will be looking for you. Negotiate a fare in advance. A ride from the temple to the train station will be about Y5.

Shíwān 石湾

Two kilometres south-west of Fóshān, Shíwān township is known mostly for its porcelain factories. Although there's nothing of outstanding scenic value here, you might want to take a look if you have an interest in pottery. Bus No 1 goes to Shíwān from the train station, via Zǔ Miào. From Zǔ Miào, a brisk walk would get you to Shíwān in about half an hour.

Xīqiáo Shān 西樵山

Another scenic area, made up of 72 crags and peaks (basically hills) with caves, lakes and waterfalls, Xīqiáo Shān is 62km south-west of Guǎngzhōu and 28km south-west of Fóshān.

At the foot of the hills is the small market town of Xīqiáo, and around the upper levels of the hills are scattered several centuries-old villages, as well as a recently built statue of Guanyin that is visible from the highway. Popular sights among visitors include **White Cloud Cave** (*Báiyún Dòng*) and a waterfall called **Water Flies 1000 Feet** (*Fēiliú Qiānchǐ*). Most of the area is made accessible by stone paths. It's popular with local tourists, but foreigners of any kind are rare.

Getting There & Away Buses to the hills depart from Fóshān's long-distance bus station on Fenjiang Beilu. Ask at your hotel in Guǎngzhōu about a day tour of Guǎngzhōu, Fóshān, Shíwān, Xīqiáo Shān and back to Guǎngzhōu. These tours are usually very good value and are certainly less hassle than doing it all yourself, but the commentary will undoubtedly be delivered in Chinese. Fóshān's CTS also has tours for Y60 per person, but you will need a group of 10 or more people.

SHĒNZHÈN 深圳
☎ 0755 • pop 1,094,600

'You think you're brave until you go to Manchuria, you think you're well read until you reach Běijīng and you think you're rich until you set foot in Shēnzhèn', goes an oft-coined maxim of today's China.

The locals of China's north-east have always been a rough-and-ready lot and Běijīng's residents have a long history of learning, but you can give the knives and broken bottles a miss, forgo the books and the erudition and head straight for Shēnzhèn if you want to be rolling in it.

The name Shēnzhèn refers to three places: Shēnzhèn City (Shenzhen Shì, opposite the border crossing at Lo Wu); Shēnzhèn Special Economic Zone (SEZ); and Shēnzhèn County, which extends several kilometres north of the SEZ. The majority of foreigners who come here are on business. If you are coming from the north, Shēnzhèn City will seem like a tacky introduction to Hong Kong and if you are coming from the south, it may seem like a tacky prologue to China. Most travellers give the place a wide berth, but it is a useful transportation hub if you're coming from Hong Kong.

The northern part of the SEZ is walled off from the rest of China by an electrified fence, to prevent smuggling and to keep back the hordes of people trying to emigrate illegally into Shēnzhèn and Hong Kong. There is a checkpoint when you leave the SEZ. You don't need your passport to leave, but you will need it to get back in, so don't leave it in your hotel if you decide to make a day trip outside Shēnzhèn.

History

Shēnzhèn was no more than a fishing village until it won the equivalent of the National Lottery and was made an SEZ in 1980. Developers added a stock market, glittering hotels, office blocks and a population of two million. Like anyone who's suddenly come into a lot of money, the city has attracted a lot of unwanted friends:

beggars throng the streets and two-thirds of its residents have no permit to live there. Prostitution and sleaze are endemic; the crime rate surged by 66% in the mid-90s.

These days, Shēnzhèn is becoming an extended shopping mall for Hong Kong residents, much to the chagrin of Hong Kong retailers. Shēnzhèn has no doubt been a fabulous commercial success, but it's a place without culture or spirit. In other words, if it's high-rises and the high life you want, stay in Hong Kong and if you want history, anywhere else is an improvement.

Information

Visas It is possible to cross the border from Hong Kong to Shēnzhèn without a visa to China but you are limited to a five-day stay within Shēnzhèn only. The cost is Y100 at the Shēnzhèn border check-point.

The border is open daily from 6.30am to 11.30pm.

Money Shēnzhèn effectively operates with a dual currency system – Chinese yuán and Hong Kong dollars. If you pay in HK dollars, you will get RMB as change and will effectively lose out on every transaction, so change some of your dollars into RMB.

There is a branch of the Hong Kong and Shanghai Bank in the Century Plaza Hotel. The Bank of China is at 23 Jianshe Lu; there's also a branch on the mainland side when you cross the border. Both the Bank of China and the Industrial and Commercial Bank (ICBC) have ATMs that take most international bank cards (Visa, Cirrus etc).

Post & Communications The main post office is at the northern end of Jianshe Lu. Telephone facilities are in a separate building on Shennan Donglu. Their Internet cafe (☎ 233 8822) at 1001 Dongmen Lu charges Y10 per hour and is open daily 9am to 5pm.

For express delivery of packages, phone DHL (☎ 339 5592).

Travel Agencies CITS (☎ 232 6437) is inconveniently located at 1064 Yanhe Lu, east of the train station. CTS has a branch next to the Wah Chung International Hotel (☎ 225 5888-6152) at 3023 Renmin Nanlu. There is also a travel agency in Guǎngxìn Jiǔdiàn. All these agencies can arrange plane and train tickets.

PSB The Foreign Affairs Branch of the PSB (☎ 446 3999) is at 4018 Jiefang Lu.

Dangers & Annoyances Shēnzhèn has had a bad reputation as a mecca for beggars from all over the country, though they are swept off the streets periodically when officials visit town. Beggars mainly congregate on Jianshe Lu and Renmin Nanlu and tenaciously follow foreigners in search of alms. If you do give them money, this is generally the green light for the rest to pursue you.

Places to Stay – Mid-Range

Most of the cheaper hotels have rates that start at Y250 for a standard double, plus a 10% or 15% service charge. Always try to push for a discount. You can try your luck with the hotel touts at the train station, but they usually take you to cheap and tacky sleaze joints.

Rìhuá Bīnguǎn (☎ 558 8530, Shennan Donglu) Singles or doubles Y140-200, triples Y250. This hotel, about a 15-minute walk from the train station, is one of the cheapest hotels in Shēnzhèn. Rooms are a bit tattered but adequate.

Shēntiě Dàshà (☎ 558 4248, fax 556 1409, 63 Heping Lu) Doubles Y258-288. Rooms here are spartan and a bit run-down. They usually offer a 20% discount.

Yúehǎi Jiǔdiàn (Guangdong Hotel, ☎ 222 8339, fax 223 4560, Shennan Donglu) Doubles Y538-1188. Rooms are attractive and comfortable at this three-star hotel, which offers up to a 40% discount.

Shēnzhèn Dàjiǔdiàn (☎ 235 1666, fax 222 4922, 3085 Shennan Donglu) Standard doubles Y328-348. At the intersection of Jianshe Lu and Shennan Donglu, this place isn't much to look at from the outside but has a nice interior with attractive, comfortable rooms. Discounts of 15% are available.

Guǎngxìn Jiǔdiàn (☎ 223 8945, fax 225 5849, 3021 Renmin Nanlu) Doubles Y288, 5-person rooms Y385, family suites Y388. This is a popular place with overseas Chinese travellers on a budget. Discounts of 20% are available.

Zhōngyǒudàhuá Jiǔdiàn (CTS Dawa Hotel; ☎/fax 220 2828, 40 Renmin Nanlu) Singles/doubles Y310/328. Another cheap option is this hotel, which has a 30% discount.

SHĒNZHÈN 深圳

PLACES TO EAT
3 Miàndiǎn Wáng
面点王
18 Miàndiǎn Wáng
面点王
23 Hǎishàng Huáng
Jiǔjiā
海上皇酒家
25 Luóhú Dàjiǔjiā
罗湖酒家
27 Sandra
仙乐都西餐酒廊

OTHER
1 Huálián Dàshà
华联大厦

2 PSB
公安局外事科
5 Post Office
邮局
7 Main Bank of China
中国银行
8 CTS
中国旅行社
11 Oriental New World
Department Store
东方天虹商场
15 Telephone Office
电信大楼
16 Internet Cafe
网吧
17 Bank of China
中国银行

19 Seibu Department Store
东方新世界百货
21 International Trade
Centre
国贸大厦
24 CRC Shop
CRC超市
29 Bank of China
中国银行
30 CITS
中国国际旅行社
33 Train Station
火车站
34 Luóhú Bus Station;
Luóhú Commercial City
长途汽车站;
罗湖商业城

PLACES TO STAY
4 Rìhuá Bīnguǎn
日华宾馆
6 Shēnzhèn Dàjiǔdiàn
深圳酒店
9 Zhōngyoúdàhuā
Jiǔdiàn
中游大花酒店
10 Wah Chung Inter-
national Hotel; CTS
华中国际酒店;
中国旅行社

12 Yúehǎi Jiǔdiàn
粤海酒店
13 Landmark Hotel
14 Hángkōng
Dàjiǔdiàn
航空大酒店
20 Sunshine Hotel;
JJ's; Polka Club
阳光酒店
22 Guǎngxìn Jiǔdiàn
广信酒店

26 Shēntiě Dàshà;
Tiěchéng Jiǔjiā
深铁大厦;
铁城酒家
28 Century Plaza Hotel
新都酒店
31 Shangri-La Hotel;
Henry J Bean
Bar and Grill
香格里拉大酒店
32 Forum Hotel
富临大酒店

Wah Chung International Hotel
(*Huázhōng Guójì Jiǔdiàn;* ☎ 223 8060, fax
222 1439, 3041 Shennan Donglu) Singles/
doubles Y300/350. The Wah Chung is
pricey and a little faded.

Hángkōng Dàjiǔdiàn (Airlines Hotel;
☎ 223 7999, fax 223 7866, 3027 Shennan
Donglu) Singles/doubles Y480/638. This is
an attractive hotel with friendly staff. Discounts of 40% are available.

Places to Stay – Top End

There's no shortage of luxurious accommodation in Shēnzhèn, and competition has
brought some of the prices down.

Shangri-La Hotel (*Xiānggélǐlā Dàjiǔdiàn;* ☎ 223 0888, fax 223 9878, Jianshe Lu)
Singles/doubles Y1750/2000. This is a

prominent landmark near the train station,
with overpriced rooms. Check for discounts.

Century Plaza Hotel (*Xīndū Jiǔdiàn;*
☎ 232 0888, fax 233 4060, Jianshe Lu)
Doubles Y1320-1430. In the luxury hotel
category, the Century Plaza is a better deal
than the Shangri-La and has more comprehensive facilities. Discounts of 50% are
sometimes available.

Landmark Hotel (*Shēnzhèn Fùyuàn
Jiǔdiàn;* ☎ 217 2288, fax 229 0473, 3018
Nanhu Lu) Singles or doubles Y1540-2008.
This hotel offers the best value. It has an en-
thusiastic English-speaking staff and attrac-
tive rooms. Discounts of 60% are available.

Forum Hotel (*Fùlín Dàjiǔdiàn;* ☎ 558
6333, fax 556 1700, 1085 Heping Lu)
Rooms Y1296-1404. This well-equipped,

elegant hotel has comfortable rooms in addition to a pool, fitness centre, and several Chinese restaurants.

Sunshine Hotel (Yángguāng Jiǔdiàn; ☎ 223 3888, fax 222 6719, 1 Jiabin Lu) Doubles Y1600-1800. Rooms are sufficiently upscale, the staff speaks good English, and amenities include a bar, nightclub, and several Western and Chinese restaurants. Discounts of up to 45% are available.

Places to Eat

Shēnzhèn has a thriving upmarket dining scene, but there are also cheap eats available around town. The train station has a number of affordable restaurants on the 3rd floor.

Tiěchéng Jiǔjiā (☎ 558 4248, 63 Heping Lu) Dim sum Y15-68. Beside Shēntiě Dàshà, this eatery has reasonable dim sum served from 6.45am to 5pm daily. An **outdoor restaurant** next door also has cheap dishes.

Dim sum breakfast is available in almost all of the hotels and can usually be found in the restaurants on the 2nd and 3rd floor. Prices are slightly lower than in Hong Kong.

Hǎishàng Huáng Jiǔjiā (☎ 223 9000, 1116 Jianshe Lu) Dishes from Y15. This is one of Shēnzhèn's best seafood restaurants.

Luóhú Dàjiǔjiā (☎ 225 2827, Jianshe Lu) Dishes Y15-70. This popular restaurant, in a traditional building, specialises in northern cuisine. At night it's noticeable a long way off for its decorations and bright lights.

Shēnzhèn is fast-food city and all the usual names are represented.

Miàndiàn Wáng (Noodle King, ☎ 570 2317, 4 Jiefang Lu; ☎ 570 2315, Shennan Donglu) Dishes Y8-15. This popular place has a line-up of chefs from whom you request dishes. Pick and choose from dumplings, noodles, and vegetable dishes.

For self-catering, **CRC Shop** (☎ 516 4289, 49 Renmin Nanlu) is across from the International Trade Center.

Pubs & Entertainment

Sandra (☎ 557 2419, 63 Heping Lu) Foreigners are warmly welcomed at this newly opened bar/restaurant, where a Guinness will set you back Y20 .

Most of the top-end hotels have international-style bars. The **Henry J Bean Bar and Grill** is on the 2nd floor of the Shangri-La Hotel.

Shēnzhèn has several discos, including **JJ's** (☎ 223 3888; admission Y30) and **Polka Club** (☎ 223 3911; admission Y30) flanking the entrance to the Sunshine Hotel.

For more sedate entertainment, one of the best venues is the **revolving restaurant** on the 31st floor of the Shangri-La Hotel. It serves meals and afternoon tea, but unfortunately when we visited the food tends to cost far more than its worth. Better to order the cheapest drink and watch the vista of one of the most intriguing borders in the world unfold below you.

Shopping

On the flyovers to the east of the train station and around the Luóhú Commercial City (Luóhú Shāngyè Chéng) are whole avenues of **stalls** selling ceramics and curios for souvenir and antique hunters. Don't expect to find trophies from the Summer Palace in Běijīng here, but it's a colourful and varied selection.

The shops in the **Luóhú Commercial City** also sell cheap bedding materials and there are some good deals on running shoes. On Youyi Lu near the intersection with Nanhu Lu are a number of **small boutiques** selling a nice assortment of clothing.

There are also **art and antique shops** at the western end of Chungfeng Lu, near the Century Plaza Hotel, with a varied if pricey selection. If you see anything that sparks your interest, either haggle hard or look around for cheaper versions.

Getting There & Away

Air Shēnzhèn's airport (☎ 777 6789) is rapidly becoming one of China's busiest. There are flights to most major destinations around China, but it is often significantly cheaper to fly from Guǎngzhōu.

Air tickets can be purchased from most of the larger hotels, such as Shēntiě Dàshà, and various agencies around town including CITS. The Landmark Hotel and Yúehǎi Jiǔdiàn run shuttles (Y180) to Hong Kong's Chek Lap Kok International Airport.

Bus Services from Hong Kong to Shēnzhèn are run by Citybus, the Motor Transport Company of Guangdong & Hong Kong, and CTS. They depart from the Landmark Hotel four times a day and terminate at China Hong Kong City in Kowloon.

COASTAL SOUTH

Shēnzhèn has a comprehensive and efficient long-distance bus system that makes it one of the best places to head to other destinations in Guǎngdōng or Fújiàn. Deluxe buses leave from the Luóhú bus station (Luóhú qìchēzhàn), underneath the Luóhú Commercial City. There are frequent departures to Shàntóu (Y160, four hours), Cháozhōu (Y180, five hours), Hǔmén (Y40, one hour), Guǎngzhōu (Y60, two hours) and Xiàmén (Y310, nine hours). Economy buses and minibuses to various destinations are slightly cheaper.

Train The Kowloon-Canton Railway (KCR) offers the fastest and most convenient transport to Shēnzhèn from Hong Kong. See the Hong Kong chapter for more details.

There are frequent local trains (Y42, two hours) and high-speed trains (Y80, 55 minutes) between Guǎngzhōu and Shēnzhèn. The former goes to the Guangzhou east train station. It's probably just as quick to take a bus.

Boat There are 13 jet-cat departures daily between Shékǒu (a port on the western side of Shēnzhèn; ☎ 669 5601) and Hong Kong. Four of these go to the China Hong Kong City ferry terminal in Kowloon, while the rest go to the Macau ferry terminal on Hong Kong Island. Ticket prices are HK$110 and the trip takes one hour.

There are eight departures daily to the China Hong Kong City ferry terminal (☎ 777 6241) from the Shēnzhèn Fúyǒng ferry terminal (Fúyǒng kèyùnzhàn) at the airport. The trip takes one hour and 10 minutes; ticket prices are Y180 (economy) and Y261 (1st class).

There is one jet-cat departure daily from Shékǒu to Macau. It departs from Shékǒu at 11am and arrives at noon. Tickets are HK$87. Ferries leave every 15 minutes for Zhūhǎi from Shékǒu, take one hour and cost Y65.

There's a boat to Hǎikǒu from Shékǒu that takes 18 hours and ranges in price from Y453 to Y113.

Getting Around

To/From the Airport Shēnzhèn's airport is 36km west of the city, past Shékǒu. Airport buses leave from the Huálián Dàshà

building on Shennan Zhonglu. Tickets are Y20 and the trip takes about 40 minutes. Bus No 101 goes to the Huálián Dàshà building from the train station. A taxi to the airport will cost about Y130.

Subway A subway that connects to Hong Kong's Kowloon-Canton-Railway (KCR) at Lo Wu and at Lok Ma Chau is under construction and should be completed by 2003.

Bus Shēnzhèn has some of the best public transport in China. The city bus services are cheap and not nearly as crowded as elsewhere. From the large terminus on the north side of the Luohu Commercial City (see Shopping earlier), bus Nos 12 and 101 from the train station pass by Lychee Park. Bus No 204 to Shékǒu leaves from a station just north of the intersection of Jianshe Lu and Jiabin Lu. The trip takes about 15 minutes, depending on traffic.

Taxi Taxis are abundant but expensive, starting at Y12.5. Insist on the driver using the meter. Payment can be made either in RMB or Hong Kong dollars.

AROUND SHĒNZHÈN

At the western end of the SEZ, grouped together near Shēnzhèn Bay, are a collection of tacky attractions possibly of interest if you are stuck in Shēnzhèn.

Splendid China (Jǐnxiù Zhōnghuá; ☎ 660 1008; admission Y30-60) is a hum-drum assembly of China's sights in miniature. Famous monuments of the world get the same treatment at **Window of the World** (Shìjiè Zhī Chuāng; ☎ 660 8000; admission Y30-60), which has rides and is the most interesting and interactive of the three. **China Folk Culture Villages** (Zhōngguó Mínzú Wénhuà Cūn; ☎ 660 1008; admission Y30-60) recreates 24 life-sized ethnic minority villages.

They are all clumped together not far from the Shékǒu ferry terminal on Shennan Dadao and can be reached either by bus No 101 (Y4) or the purple double-decker sightseeing buses (Y10) that leave from the terminus on the north side of the Luohu Commercial City. If you are entering Shēnzhèn by way of Shékǒu, then you could take a taxi.

HǓMÉN 虎门

Also known as Tàipíng, the small city of Hǔmén on Zhū Jiāng is of interest only to history buffs curious about the Opium War that led directly to Hong Kong's creation as a British colony.

After the Treaty of Nanking, there was a British Supplementary Treaty of the Bogue, signed on 8 October 1843. The Bogue Forts (Shājiǎo Pàotái) at Hǔmén are now the site of an impressive museum. There are numerous exhibits, including large artillery pieces and other relics, and the actual ponds in which Commissioner Lin Zexiu had the opium destroyed.

Economy buses to Hǔmén leave from the entrance to the Dàshātoú wharf in Guǎngzhōu. Tickets are Y20 and the trip takes about two hours. From Shēnzhèn, minibuses leave from the Luohu bus station (Y35, one hour). Boats from Hong Kong make the trip in two hours and cost HK$186, departing from the China Hong Kong City ferry terminal in Kowloon.

ZHŪHǍI 珠海

☎ 0756 • pop 673,400

Like Shēnzhèn to the east, Zhūhǎi is doing very well out of the South China Gold Coast. In true rags to riches style, Zhūhǎi was built from the soles up on what was until recently farmland.

Travellers from the 1980s (even *late* 1980s) remember Zhūhǎi as a small agricultural town with a few rural industries and a quiet beach. Well, that's all gone – the Zhūhǎi of today not only has the usual SEZ skyline of glimmering five-star hotels and big-name factories, it has its own 'aerotropolis' to boot (servicing a spotless ultramodern airport).

Zhūhǎi is mainly a business destination offering little in the way of interest to the independent traveller, though its size and relaxed atmosphere make it more attractive than Shēnzhèn. The city is so close to the border with Macau that a visit can be arranged as a day trip; alternatively, you can use Zhūhǎi as an entry or exit point for the rest of China.

Orientation

Zhūhǎi is divided into three main districts. The area nearest the Macau border is called Gǒngběi, the main tourist zone. To the north-east is Jídà, the eastern part of which has Zhūhǎi's Jiǔzhōu Harbour (Jiǔzhōu Gǎng). A mountainous barrier separates these two sections from northern Xiāngzhōu – an area of worker flats and factories. The rest of Zhūhǎi SEZ is to the east and harbours the airport, tacky holiday resorts and infrastructure projects. A huge new complex was built in 1999 at the south end of Yingbin Dadao to celebrate Macau's return to China. This is now the site of the new checkpoint.

Information

The most useful post office is on Qiaoguang Lu in Gǒngběi. You can make IDD calls from your own room in most hotels. The Bank of China beside Yíndū Jiǔdiàn changes travellers cheques, as does another branch on Lianhua Lu. There is a helpful CTS office (☎ 335 3338 ext 8877) next door to Huáqiáo Bīnguǎn. The PSB (☎ 222 2211 ext 22528) is in the Xiāngzhōu district on the south-western corner of Anping Lu and Kangning Lu. The 24-hour Crazy Club Internet Cafe (☎ 828 0589), at 153 Shuiwan Lu, charges Y6 per hour.

It is possible to get a five-day visa (limited to Zhūhǎi) at the Gǒngběi border checkpoint, or Jiǔzhōu Harbour if you arrive by boat.

Things to See

North of the Gǒngběi district is a monumental symbol of where China's tourist industry is headed. The **New Yuan Ming Palace** (*Yuánmíng Xīnyuán;* ☎ 861 0388, *Jiuzhou Dadao and Lanpu Lu; admission Y100; open 9am-7pm daily*) is a reproduction of the original imperial Yuan Ming Palace in Běijīng that was torched by British and French forces during the Second Opium War.

The very impressive entrance gives way to a huge adventure playground of reproduction scenic sights from around China and the world, including the Great Wall of China, Italian and German castles, halls, restaurants, temples and a huge lake.

The colossal scale of the project is reflected in the ticket price. Depending on your taste, you're probably better off spending your money somewhere else. To get there catch bus Nos 1 and 13 from the Gǒngběi area.

COASTAL SOUTH

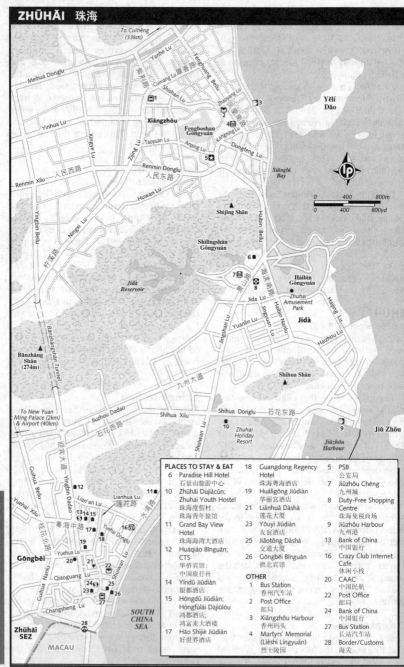

ZHŪHǍI 珠海

PLACES TO STAY & EAT
6   Paradise Hill Hotel
    石景山旅游中心
10 Zhūhǎi Dùjiàcūn;
    Zhuhai Youth Hostel
    珠海度假村;
    珠海青年旅馆
11 Grand Bay View
    Hotel
    珠海海湾大酒店
12 Huáqiáo Bīnguǎn;
    CTS
    华侨宾馆;
    中国旅行社
14 Yíndū Jiǔdiàn
    银都酒店
15 Hóngdū Jiǔdiàn;
    Hóngfúlái Dàjiǔlóu
    鸿都酒店;
    鸿富来大酒楼
18 Hǎo Shìjiè Jiǔdiàn
    好世界酒店

18 Guangdong Regency
    Hotel
    珠海粤海酒店
19 Huálìgōng Jiǔdiàn
    华丽宫酒店
21 Liánhuā Dàshà
    莲花大厦
23 Yǒuyì Jiǔdiàn
    友谊酒店
25 Jiāotōng Dàshà
    交通大厦
26 Gōngběi Bīnguǎn
    拱北宾馆

OTHER
1   Bus Station
    香州汽车站
2   Post Office
    邮局
3   Xiāngzhōu Harbour
    香州码头
4   Martyrs' Memorial
    (Lièshì Língyuán)
    烈士陵园

5   PSB
    公安局
7   Jiǔzhōu Chéng
    九州城
8   Duty-Free Shopping
    Centre
    珠海免税商场
9   Jiǔzhōu Harbour
    九州港
13 Bank of China
    中国银行
16 Crazy Club Internet
    Cafe
    休闲小栈
20 CAAC
    中国民航
22 Post Office
    邮局
24 Bank of China
    中国银行
27 Bus Station
    长站汽车站
28 Border/Customs
    海关

COASTAL SOUTH

Jiŭzhōu Chéng, in Jídà, opposite the duty-free shopping centre, may be worth a look. It's a huge reproduction of classical Chinese architecture that is currently being turned into a museum.

Just up the road and facing the sea, Hăibīn Gōngyuán *(Haibin Nanlu; admission Y1; open 8am-10pm daily)* makes for a pleasant walk with hills on both sides, palms, statues and a windmill. For an overall view of the area, visit Shíjǐngshān Gōngyuán and climb the hill of the same name.

The bustling **markets** and side streets of the Gŏngbĕi area, close to the Macau border, offer a colourful diversion. Lianhua Lu is a lively area of hairdressers, restaurants and family run stores.

Places to Stay – Mid-Range

As in Shēnzhèn, very few travellers stay in Zhūhăi. Most of the accommodation is clustered close to the Macau-Zhūhăi border, an area with some charm. Budget accommodation was elbowed out of Zhūhăi a long time ago, so prices are mid-range to top end.

Zhuhai Youth Hostel (☎ 333 3838, fax 333 3311, Shihua Donglu) Beds Y60. The only budget option is this HI-run hostel, housed in fancy Zhūhăi Dùjiàcūn.

Huálìgōng Jiŭdiàn (☎ 813 1828, fax 813 1299, 116 Yuehua Lu) Singles/doubles Y280/368. Rooms here are clean, yellow and bright, and there are discounts of up to 40%. It's centrally located.

Gŏngbĕi Bīnguăn (☎ 888 6833, fax 888 5686, 8 Shuiwan Lu) Singles/doubles Y460/530. Within walking distance of the border, this fancy hotel offers great discounts (singles Y180, triples Y230) on its nice rooms.

Hóngdū Jiŭdiàn (☎ 813 1188, fax 888 5554, 1138 Yuehai Donglu) Singles/doubles from Y368/478. This three-star hotel's rooms are a great deal, with sleek and cosy furnishings. Discounts of 40% are available.

Hăo Shìjiè Jiŭdiàn (Good World Hotel; ☎ 888 0222, fax 889 2061, 82 Lianhua Lu) Doubles Y300. This place is a bit more downmarket, but is good value at these rates. Discounts of 30% are also available.

Yŏuyì Jiŭdiàn (Friendship Hotel; ☎ 813 1818, fax 813 5505, 2 Youyi Lu) Singles/doubles Y368/418. Also close to

the border crossing, rooms here are just adequate. Discounts of 45% are available.

Jiāotōng Dàshà (Traffic Hotel; ☎ 888 4474, fax 888 4187, 19 Shuiwu Lu) Doubles Y278-380. Rooms here are a bit musty.

Huáqiáo Bīnguăn (Overseas Chinese Hotel; ☎ 888 6288, fax 888 5119, 35 Yingbin Dadao) Doubles Y368-398. This large place has restaurants and an international-style coffee shop. Doubles are standard, and discounts of 30% are sometimes available.

Places to Stay – Top End

Most top-end accommodation in Zhūhăi includes a tax of 10% to 15%, and sometimes a further 10% to 15% for weekends and holidays.

Yíndū Jiŭdiàn (☎ 888 3388, fax 888 3311, Yuehai Lu) Standard rooms Y860. This comfortable five-star hotel is within striking distance of the border. Its services include a coffee shop, bar, shopping arcade, massage centre, sauna and bowling alley. Discounts of 30% are sometimes available.

Guangdong Regency Hotel (Yuèhăi Jiŭdiàn; ☎ 888 8128, fax 888 5063, 30 Yuehai Donglu) Standard doubles Y730. The staff are friendly and rooms sufficiently luxurious at this upscale hotel, which also has a pool. Sometimes discounts of 30% are available.

Grand Bay View Hotel (Zhūhăi Hăiwān Dàjiŭdiàn; ☎ 887 7998, fax 887 8998, Shuiwan Lu) Rooms Y830. Facing the South China Sea, this is one of Zhūhăi's finest. A substantial discount is offered on weekdays. The *Harbour Cafe* is a Western restaurant in the hotel, with a good view.

Paradise Hill Hotel (Shíjǐngshān Lǚyóu Zhōngxīn; ☎ 333 7388, fax 333 3508, 1 Jingshan Lu) Doubles Y680-1800. Competing with the Grand Bay View is this stately place nestled beneath Shíjǐng Shān (Paradise Hill). Rooms are tastefully done, each with a veranda. The hotel has three international-style restaurants, a swimming pool and tennis courts.

Zhūhăi Dùjiàcūn (Zhuhai Holiday Resort; ☎ 333 2038, fax 333 2036, Shihua Lu) Doubles Y880, villas from Y2288. If you're looking for a resort in Zhūhăi with everything from a shooting gallery to go-karts, then this is the place to go. Some of the rooms can be very good value, with doubles going for half price during the low season.

COASTAL SOUTH

Places to Eat

Zhūhǎi is brimming with places to eat. The Gǒngběi area is the best place to seek out restaurants. Try Lianhua Lu for *bakeries* and a couple of restaurants serving cheap Cantonese cuisine. In warm weather many restaurants set up tables outside. There's a collection of these places opposite Huáqiáo Bīnguǎn up on Yingbin Dadao – most of them sell seafood. Most of the top-end hotels in Zhūhǎi have great bakeries.

Liánhuā Dàshà (☎ 818 8057, *72 Lianhua Lu*) Dishes Y5-18. Down an alley off of Lianhua Lu, this cheap restaurant has simple, tasty dishes like *hóngshǎo qiézi* (stir-fried eggplant).

Hóngfūlái Dàjiǔlóu (☎ 828 2693, *1138 Yuehai Donglu*) Dishes from Y15. Next to Hóngdū Jiǔdiàn, this restaurant serves exotic seafood and simple vegetable and meat dishes.

There's a cluster of *fast-food* places at the corner of Yuehai Lu and Yingbin Dadao.

Getting There & Away

Air Zhūhǎi's glimmering new airport has domestic flights to most major cities in China. CAAC (☎ 828 7888) is located on the ground floor of the Zhongzhu building. Zhuhai Airlines has an office opposite Gǒngběi Dàshà. Fares to Běijīng are Y1550 and to Shànghǎi Y1135.

Bus There are connections with Guǎngzhōu, Fóshān, Zhàoqìng, Zhànjiāng and Shàntóu. Buses leave from the main bus station on Youyi Lu near Yǒuyì Bīnguǎn. Buses from Zhūhǎi to Guǎngzhōu depart regularly through the day from 6.30am to 6.30pm, and air-con services cost Y50. Buses to Zhōngshān are Y16. You can also book train tickets originating from Guǎngzhōu at the bus station. Hard-sleeper bookings incur a Y40 service charge.

Buses to Hong Kong (Y130, 2½ hours) leave from the Guangdong Regency Hotel five times daily and pass the major hotels.

Boat Jet-cats between Zhūhǎi and Hong Kong do the trip in about 70 minutes. There are five departures a day from the Jiǔzhōu Harbour (☎ 333 3359) to the China Hong Kong City ferry terminal on Canton Rd, and three a day to Central. Tickets are HK$150.

A high-speed ferry operates between the port of Shékǒu in Shēnzhèn and Jiǔzhōu Harbour. There are departures every 15 minutes between 7.30am and 6pm. The cost is Y65 and the journey takes one hour. Bus Nos 3, 25, 4 and 12 go to the harbour.

Zhūhǎi to Macau Simply walk across the border. In Macau, bus Nos 3 and 10B lead to the Barrier Gate, from where you make the crossing on foot. Taxis from the Hong Kong ferry area cost around HK$22. The Macau-Zhūhǎi border is open from 7.30am to midnight.

Getting Around

To/From the Airport Zhūhǎi's airport is about 43km from the city centre. A taxi will be expensive (more than Y100), so the best option is a CAAC shuttle bus (Y25) that runs reasonably frequently from the CAAC office.

Bus Zhūhǎi has a clean and efficient bus system. The buses are new and the routes are clearly marked on the Zhūhǎi city map. Minibuses ply the same routes and cost Y2 for any place in the city.

Taxi You will mainly use taxis to shuttle between your hotel and the boats at Zhūhǎi's harbour. Taxi drivers cruising the streets use their meters. From the customs area to the Jiǔzhōu Harbour costs around Y20.

AROUND ZHŪHǍI

In **Cuiheng Village** (*Cuìhēng Cūn*), 33 km north of Zhūhǎi, is **Dr Sun Yatsen's Residence** (*Sūn Zhōngshān Gùjū;* ☎ 550 1691, *Cuiheng Dadao; admission Y20; open 8.30am-4.45pm daily*). Sun Yatsen was born here on 12 November 1866. The original house was torn down when a new home was built in 1892. You can see the second house, which is quite interesting, where he came back to live with his parents from 1892 to 1895. There are signs in English. Take bus No 10 from Yingbin Dadao to the terminus, then walk 10 minutes past the gate to the next bus stop. From there take bus No 12.

ZHŌNGSHĀN 中山
☎ 0760

The administrative centre of the county by the same name, this city is also known as Shíqí. An industrial city, there is little to see or do here. If you get stranded here for an hour or so, the one and only scenic spot in town is **Zhōngshān Gōngyuán**, which is pleasantly forested and dominated by Yāndūn Shān, a large hill topped with a pagoda. It's visible from most parts of the city so it's easy to find.

AROUND ZHŌNGSHĀN

The **Zhongshan Hot Springs** resort (*Zhōngshān Wēnquán;* ☎ *668 3888; admission Y100; open 7am-10pm daily*) has over 30 indoor hot springs and a golf course. If you're a real enthusiast of either activity, you might want to spend a night here. Otherwise, you'll probably just want to look around briefly and then head back to Gǒngběi. It's about 25km north of Zhūhǎi, near the town of Sānxiāng.

Zhōngshān Wēnquán Bīnguǎn (Zhongshan Hot Springs Hotel; ☎ *668 3888, fax 668 3333)* Doubles Y460 plus 10% service charge. Accommodation is available here where rooms are adequate.

Buses to Zhōngshān can drop you by the entrance to the resort, then it's a 500m walk to the hotel. For a couple of yuán you can hire someone to carry you on the back of a bicycle. To get back to Gǒngběi, flag down any minibus you see that's passing the resort entrance.

ZHÀOQÌNG 肇庆

☎ 0758 • pop 3,683,400

Zhàoqìng, home to some craggy limestone rock formations similar to those around Guìlín, is rated highly among the attractions of Guǎngdōng. Despite not having the appeal of Yángzhōu, Zhàoqìng is an attractive city with far more character than Guǎngzhōu or Fóshān. The mountainous Dǐnghú Shān area nearby is well worth visiting and features some nice walks among temples, pools, brooks and lush scenery.

Orientation & Information

Zhàoqìng, 110km west of Guǎngzhōu on Xī Jiāng, is bounded to the south by the river and to the north by the lakes and crags that make up Seven Star Crags. The main attractions can be easily seen on foot.

There's a post office on Jianshe Lu and the main Bank of China is on Duanzhou Lu east of Renmin Lu. There's a convenient ATM in the Star Lake Hotel lobby.

Divine Inspiration

Legend has it that the Seven Star Crags were actually seven stars that fell from the sky to form a pattern resembling the Big Dipper.

Another legend dates from Ming dynasty times said that if you stood under Stone House Crag on a clear moonlit night, you could hear the celestial strains of music played by the Jade Emperor, the supreme God of Taoism, as he gave a banquet for the rest of the gods and goddesses.

Furthermore, a tablet known as Horse Hoof Tablet, one of many inscribed tablets in the area, was dented by the hoof of an inquisitive celestial horse as he alighted on the shores of Xīng Hú.

CTS (☎ 222 9908) is on Duanzhou Wulu. The Xinghu Travel Agency (☎ 226 7872) also books tickets and is more friendly. It's a small office squeezed in the corner of Tianning Lu and Duanzhou Lu. The major hotels will book tickets too.

Things to See

Zhàoqìng's premier attraction, the **Seven Star Crags** (*Qīxīng Yán;* ☎ *227 7724; admission Y50; open 8am-5.30pm daily*) is a group of limestone towers – a peculiar geological formation abundant in the paddy fields of Guìlín and Yángshuò.

The crags are home to myriad inscriptions and limestone caves that you can explore. Willows and kapok trees surround Xīng Hú (Star Lake). A boat (Y8) can take you from Gateway Square (Páifáng Guǎngchǎng) at the southern tip of Xīng Hú and speed you across to a bridge that crosses over to the crags.

On Tajiao Lu in the south-east, the nine-storey **Chóngxī Tǎ** was in a sad state after the Cultural Revolution but was restored to its original Song style in the 1980s. On the opposite bank of the river are two similar pagodas.

The Qing dynasty-era **River View Pavilion** (*Yuèjiāng Lóu;* ☎ *223 2968; admission Y10; open 8am-5pm daily*) was rebuilt in 1959. It's a pleasant piece of Chinese architecture, located about 15 minutes' walk north from Chóngxī Tǎ, just back from the waterfront at the eastern end of Zheng Donglu.

COASTAL SOUTH

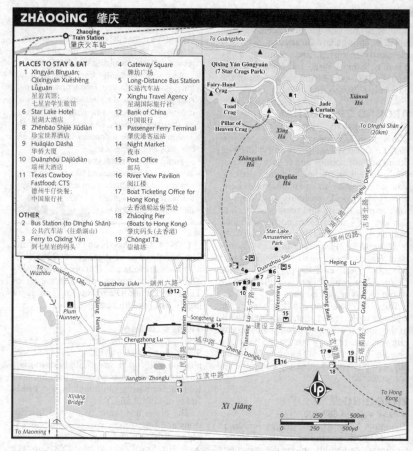

ZHÀOQÌNG 肇庆

PLACES TO STAY & EAT
1 Xīngyán Bīnguǎn;
  Qīxīngyán Xuéshēng
  Lǚguǎn
  星岩宾馆;
  七星岩学生旅馆
5 Star Lake Hotel
  星湖大酒店
8 Zhēnbǎo Shìjiè Jiǔdiàn
  珍宝世界酒店
9 Huáqiáo Dàshà
  华侨大厦
10 Duānzhōu Dàjiǔdiàn
  端州大酒店
11 Texas Cowboy
  Fastfood; CTS
  德州牛仔快餐;
  中国旅行社

OTHER
2 Bus Station (to Dǐnghú Shān)
  公共汽车站（往鼎湖山）
3 Ferry to Qīxīng Yán
  到七星岩的码头

4 Gateway Square
  牌坊广场
5 Long-Distance Bus Station
  长站汽车站
7 Xinghu Travel Agency
  星湖国际旅行社
12 Bank of China
  中国银行
13 Passenger Ferry Terminal
  肇庆港客运站
14 Night Market
  夜市
15 Post Office
  邮局
16 River View Pavilion
  阅江楼
17 Boat Ticketing Office for
  Hong Kong
  去香港船运售票处
18 Zhàoqìng Pier
  (Boats to Hong Kong)
  肇庆码头（去香港）
19 Chóngxǐ Tǎ
  崇禧塔

Places to Stay

The two budget places offer the nicest area to stay, but you'll have to hire a motorbike to get there. Otherwise, Zhàoqìng is not the place for budget accommodation.

Qīxīngyán Xuéshēng Lǚguǎn (Seven Star Crags Student Youth Hostel; ☎ 222 6688, fax 222 4155) Dorm beds Y38, doubles/triples with air-con & bath Y168/198. The only budget place here, this is in a great location within the crags.

Xīngyán Bīnguǎn (Star Crag Hotel; ☎/fax 222 4112) Doubles/triples with bath & air-con Y168/198. This is part of the same complex as the youth hostel.

Duānzhōu Dàjiǔdiàn (☎ 223 2281, fax 222 9228, 77 Tianning Beilu) Singles/doubles/triples Y198/228/348. The elegant,

attractive rooms here are a great deal. Some have views of the lake and 40% discounts are also available.

Zhēnbǎo Shìjiè Jiǔdiàn (☎ 229 1888, fax 222 2333, 76 Tianning Beilu) Standard doubles/triples Y248/328. This place has decent rooms and 30% discounts are sometimes available.

Huáqiáo Dàshà (☎ 223 2952, fax 223 1197, 90 Tianning Beilu) Doubles Y288-Y330. Next door to Duānzhōu Dàjiǔdiàn, this is a little more upmarket and has adequate doubles.

Star Lake Hotel (Xīnghú Dàjiǔdiàn; ☎ 222 1188, fax 223 6688, 37 Duanzhou Silu) Rooms from Y500. This is the nicest place to stay but pricey. There's a full range of near international-class facilities.

Places to Eat

A number of *restaurants* spill out onto the pavements of Wenming Lu, just west of the bus station. You can find some better restaurants on Jianshe Lu around the KFC.

Texas Cowboy Fastfood (*Dézhōuniúzǎi Kuàicān*) Dishes Y8-25. This restaurant serves fried chicken, pizza, hamburgers, French toast and Chinese food.

Shopping

There is a lively *night market* (*yè shìchǎng; Songcheng Lu*) in front of the old city walls. Items on display include curios, antiques, old watches, Qing-dynasty water pipes, woodcarvings, jade ornaments and ceramics. It gets going after 7pm.

Getting There & Away

Bus Frequent air-con buses to Zhàoqìng (Y30) leave from Guǎngzhōu's long-distance bus station near lake on Duanzhou Lu. The trip, most of it by freeway, takes 1½ hours. Minibuses also leave from Guǎngzhōu's west bus station at Zhongshan Balu for Y15. Zhàoqìng's bus station is conveniently located within walking distance of the lake; buses to Guǎngzhōu leave every half hour.

A deluxe bus to Hong Kong leaves daily at 4pm from Huáqiáo Dàshà (HK$160, four hours).

Train The train is a little inconvenient compared to the bus, though marginally quicker if your bus runs into one of Guǎngzhōu's horrendous traffic jams. The fastest train to Guǎngzhōu takes two hours and hard seat tickets are Y26. You can book tickets at CTS, Xinghu Travel Agency and the Star Lake Hotel, but there's a Y15 service charge (Y30 for sleepers if you're heading east to Zhànjiāng).

There's a daily train to and from Hong Kong (HK$235, 4½ hours).

Boat The boat to Zhàoqìng from the Dàshātóu ferry terminal in Guǎngzhōu has been discontinued.

Jet-cats speed from Zhàoqìng to Hong Kong at 2pm, take four hours and cost Y250 for ordinary class. Boats leave from Zhàoqìng pier and tickets can be bought just up the road on Gongnong Nanlu.

Getting Around

The local bus station is on Duanzhou Lu, a few minutes' walk east of the intersection with Tianning Lu and next to Gateway Square. Bus No 1 runs to the ferry dock on Xī Jiāng.

The train station is a long haul, but can be reached on bus No 2, which goes from the local long-distance bus station. A taxi will set you back Y12.

AROUND ZHÀOQÌNG
Dǐnghú Shān 鼎湖山

Twenty kilometres north-east of Zhàoqìng is Dǐnghú Shān (☎ 262 2510, 21 Paifang Lu; admission Y50), one of the most attractive scenic spots in Guǎngdōng and a protected reserve. This easy-to-reach mountainous area offers myriad walks among pools, springs, ponds, temples, nunneries and charming scenery. You can easily spend half a day or more here as there is a lot to cover. Qìngyún Sì is the most famous temple on Dǐnghú Shān. Like many sightseeing spots in China, every geographical feature has been named in a manner to enhance the viewer's imagination. These include Leaping Dragon Pool (Yuèlóng Tán) and Immortal Riding a Crane (Xiānrén Qíhè).

About 300m up from the main gate there's a reserve office where, for a fee of Y20, you can request permission to hike up the west trail that follows the river. You'll need to show your passport. The hike takes about four hours and eventually ends up at Qìngyún Sì. Guides are available, varying in price from Y100 to Y200, but not really necessary. Otherwise it's possible to hike up the road, or take a taxi or motorbike to the top, roughly 7km from the entry gate.

There are a few places to swim – one popular place is at the base of a tall waterfall near the temple, where Sun Yatsen used to swim back in the early '20s.

Dinghu Shan Youth Hostel (*Dǐnghú Shān Guójì Qīngnián Lǚguǎn; ☎ 262 1688, fax 262 1665*) Beds/rooms Y38/152. If you get stranded on the mountain, this hostel has basic rooms and a popular pool.

Bus No 15 goes to Dǐnghú Shān from the southern tip of Zhōngxīn Hú in Zhàoqìng. It drops you off about 500m from the main gate. You can then walk or take a golfcart taxi (Y2).

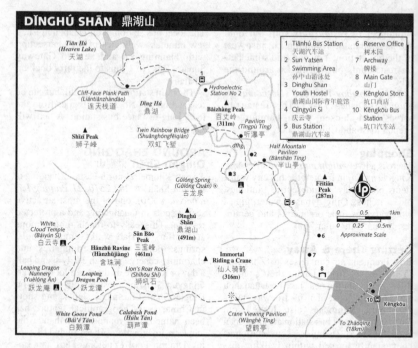

DĪNGHÚ SHĀN 鼎湖山

Tiān Hú
(Heaven Lake)
天湖

Cliff-Face Plank Path
(Liántiānzhàndào)
连天栈道

Dǐng Hú
鼎湖

Hydroelectric
Station No 2

Bǎizhàng Peak
百丈岭
(311m)

Pavilion
(Tīngpù Tíng)
听瀑亭

Shīzǐ Peak
狮子峰

Twin Rainbow Bridge
(Shuānghóngfēiqiàn)
双虹飞堑

dfhg

Half Mountain
Pavilion
(Bànshān Tíng)
半山亭

Gǔlóng Spring
(Gǔlóng Quán)
古龙泉

Fēitiān
Peak
(287m)

White
Cloud Temple
(Báiyún Sì)
白云寺

Dīnghú
Shān
鼎湖山
(491m)

Sān Bǎo
Peak
三宝峰

Hánzhū Ravine
(Hánzhūjiàng)
含珠涧

Immortal
Riding a Crane
仙人骑鹤
(316m)

Leaping Dragon
Nunnery
(Yuèlóng Ān)
跃龙庵

Leaping
Dragon Pool
跃龙潭

Lion's Roar Rock
(Shīhòu Shí)
狮吼石

White Goose Pond
(Bái'é Tán)
白鹅潭

Calabash Pond
(Húlú Tán)
葫芦潭

Crane Viewing Pavilion
(Wànghè Tíng)
望鹤亭

To Zhàoqìng
(18km)

Kēngkǒu

0   0.5   1km
0   0.25 0.5
Approximate Scale

1 Tiānhú Bus Station 天湖汽车站	6 Reserve Office 树木园
2 Sun Yatsen Swimming Area 孙中山游泳处	7 Archway 牌楼
3 Dinghu Shan Youth Hostel 鼎湖山国际青年旅馆	8 Main Gate 山门
4 Qingyún Sì 庆云寺	9 Kēngkǒu Store 坑口商店
5 Bus Station 鼎湖山汽车站	10 Kēngkǒu Bus Station 坑口汽车站

ZHÀNJIĀNG 湛江
☎ 0759 • pop 6,273,200

Zhànjiāng is a major port on the southern
coast of China, and the largest Chinese port
west of Guǎngzhōu. It was leased to France
in 1898 and remained under French control
until WWII.

Today the French are back, but this time
Zhànjiāng is a base for their oil-exploration
projects in the South China Sea. Very few
foreigners come to Zhànjiāng, and when
they do they are usually travelling en route
to Hǎinán Dǎo.

Orientation & Information

Zhànjiāng is split into two districts –
Chìkǎn to the north and Xiáshān to the
south. The harbour, bus station and most of
the hotels are conveniently close together in
the southern part of town.

The Bank of China is in the north part of
town on Renmin Dadao, across from a shopping centre. It changes cash and travellers
cheques and is open daily 8.30am to 7pm.

CITS (☎ 227 0688) is at 20 Renmin
Dadao north of the Canton Bay Hotel and
CTS (☎ 222 2222) is to the south of this

hotel's entrance. The PSB (☎ 331 5651) is in
the Chìkǎn Qū district at 29 Zhongshan Yilu.

Places to Stay & Eat

There's little budget accommodation in
Zhànjiāng.

Cuìyuán Fàndiàn (☎ 228 6633, fax 228
0308, 124 Minzhi Lu) Doubles/triples
Y180/230. Rooms here are basic and the
staff doesn't speak much English. Discounts of 50% are available.

Hǎiwān Bīnguǎn (☎ 222 2266, fax 222
2266 ext 3111, 6 Renmin Nan Dadao) Singles Y168, doubles Y198-280, triples
Y228. This place, near the wharf, has old
but passable rooms. It's also the location of
the International Seamen's Club (Guójì
Hǎiyuán Jùlèbù).

Most of the other hotels that take foreigners are mid-range in price.

Canton Bay Hotel (Guǎngzhōuwān Huáqiáo Bīnguǎn; ☎ 228 1966, fax 228 1347,
16 Renmin Nan Dadao) Singles/doubles
Y218/ 238. This hotel with clean rooms is
well managed and offers the best value in
Zhànjiāng. Sometimes 30% discounts are
available.

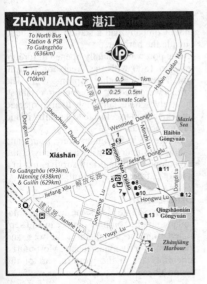

ZHÀNJIĀNG 湛江

Hǎifù Dàjiǔdiàn (Haifu Grand Hotel; ☎ 228 0288, fax 228 0614, 15 Dongdi Lu) Doubles Y220. The more inconvenient Hǎifù tries to masquerade as a fancy hotel. Rooms are nice but those with views overlook the ugly, industrial harbour.

There's a number of small restaurants on Renmin Dadao north of the Canton Bay Hotel.

Coffee Language Cafe (Kāfēi Yǔchá; ☎ 222 3365, 17 Renmin Nan Dadao) Opposite the hotel, this cafe has international-style meals (Y20-28) and an English menu, as well as Chinese food, and coffee and tea.

Getting There & Away

Air CAAC (☎ 338 0439) is at 29 Renmin Dadao Zhonglu, in the north-western section of the city. Tickets are easily booked at CTS.

Flights from Zhànjiāng go directly to Guǎngzhōu (Y530) and Běijīng (Y2180). Flights to Shànghǎi (Y1630) go via Guǎngzhōu.

Bus The long-distance bus station, southeast of the train station, has services to Guǎngzhōu three times daily (Y130, seven hours). Buses to Guǎngzhōu also leave from the wharf. Other useful destinations from the bus station are Hǎi'ān (Y33, three hours), from where you can get a ferry to Hǎinán Dǎo, and Guìlín (Y100, 10 hours).

Air-con Iveco buses travel directly to Hong Kong (Y340, 10 hours) from CTS, daily at 9am.

Train Trains to Guìlín, Nánníng, Fóshān and Guǎngzhōu leave from the southern train station. Overnight air-con fast trains connect with Guǎngzhōu for Y212 (sleeper) and take 10 hours. From Zhànjiāng to Guìlín takes about 13 hours. As well as at the train station, you can purchase tickets outside the customs building at the ferry terminal. CTS and hotels will also book sleepers for a Y20 service charge. Buses going to the train station meet boat arrivals at Zhànjiāng Harbour (Zhànjiāng Gǎng).

Boat You can get combination bus-boat tickets to Hǎikǒu on Hǎinán Dǎo at the bus station. If the weather is favourable, it's more convenient – and not much more expensive – to take the express boat to Hǎikǒu (Y100, four hours); tickets are on sale at the harbour and boats leave at 9am and 2.30pm.

There's also a slow boat that leaves at 8pm and arrives at Hǎikǒu's Xiuying wharf at 6am.

Getting Around

Zhànjiāng's airport is 10km north-east of the city centre. A taxi will cost about Y20.

There are two train stations and two long-distance bus stations, one each in the northern and southern parts of town, but most travellers will only need the southern stations.

Bus No 1 runs between the two districts and bus No 10 travels along Renmin Nan Dadao from the train station. Taxis cost about Y10 for destinations anywhere in the Xiáshān area. There are many motorcycles, some with side cars, cruising the streets; Y5 is enough for trips of a couple of kilometres.

Pedicabs also swarm after foreigners – Y10 will get you almost anywhere on one of these (maybe even to Guǎngzhōu).

SHÀNTÓU 汕头
☎ 0754 • pop 4,130,900

Shàntóu is one of China's four original Special Economic Zones (SEZ), along with Shēnzhèn, Zhūhǎi and Xiàmén. It's a little-visited port with a unique culture.

The local dialect is known as *chaoshan* in Mandarin – a combination of Cháozhōu and Shàntóu – or *taejiu* by the people themselves, and is the language of many of the Chinese who emigrated to Thailand. The language is completely different from Cantonese. Overseas Chinese from Thailand have started to return, and it's not unusual to see Thai script in hotels and on business signs.

Unfortunately, Shàntóu shows all the signs of an SEZ damp squib, with little to recommend it. Evidence of Shàntóu history is also seriously deficient here (although there are a few pockets of interest), and the city is basically a transit point on the little-travelled haul between Guǎngzhōu and Fújiàn.

History

Shàntóu was previously known to the outside world as Swatow. As early as the 18th century, when the town was little more than a fishing village on a mudflat, the East India Company had a station on an island outside the harbour.

The port was officially opened to foreign trade in 1860 with the Treaty of Tianjin, which ended another Opium War. The British were the first foreigners to establish themselves here, although their projected settlement had to relocate to a nearby island due to local hostility.

Before 1870 foreigners were living and trading in Shàntóu town itself. Many of the old colonial buildings still survive, but in a state of extreme dilapidation.

Orientation

Most of Shàntóu lies on a peninsula, bounded in the south by the ocean and separated from the mainland in the west and the north by a river and canals. Most tourist amenities are in the western part of the peninsula.

Information

There are numerous Bank of China branches, but the one at the intersection of Changping Lu and Dongsha Lu changes travellers cheques.

The post and telecommunications building is on Waima Lu just east of Xīnhuá Jiǔdiàn. At 34 Changping Lu, Yīnglián Internet (Yīnglián Wǎngbā; ☎ 854 6859) charges Y4 per hour for Internet access, but you have to buy a card for Y20. CTS (☎ 862 6646) next to Huáqiáo Dàshà sells bus and air tickets.

The PSB (☎ 842 3592) is at 60 Gongyuan Lu, north of Waima Lu.

Things to See

There's not much in the way of sights in Shàntóu. However, the roundabout at the point where Shengping Lu and Anping Lu converge is interesting for its colonial remains, and it's worth looking at the architecture while it's still there.

Places to Stay

Qiáolián Dàshà (☎ 825 9109, fax 861 3721, 39 Shanzhang Lu) Singles/doubles/triples with fan & shared bath Y62/87/98; doubles/ triples with air-con & bath Y168/198. This one-star property has basic but clean rooms – the dorm rooms are a better deal than those with bath. There's

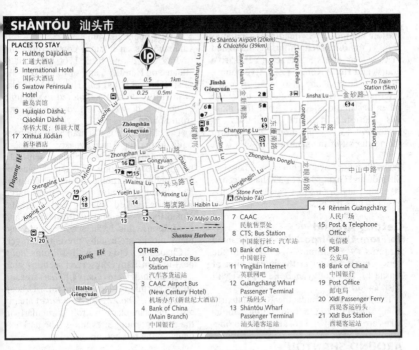

SHÀNTÓU 汕头市

PLACES TO STAY
2 Huìtōng Dàjiǔdiàn
汇通大酒店
5 International Hotel
国际大酒店
6 Swatow Peninsula
Hotel
藏岛宾馆
9 Huáqiáo Dàshà;
Qiáolián Dàshà
华侨大厦；侨联大厦
17 Xīnhuá Jiǔdiàn
新华酒店

OTHER
1 Long-Distance Bus
Station
汽车长货运站
3 CAAC Airport Bus
(New Century Hotel)
机场办车 (新世纪大酒店)
4 Bank of China
(Main Branch)
中国银行

7 CAAC
民航售票处
8 CTS; Bus Station
中国旅行社；汽车站
10 Bank of China
中国银行
11 Yìnglián Internet
英联网吧
12 Guǎngchǎng Wharf
Passenger Terminal
广场码头
13 Shàntóu Wharf
Passenger Terminal
汕头港客运站

14 Rénmín Guǎngchǎng
人民广场
15 Post & Telephone
Office
电信楼
16 PSB
公安局
18 Bank of China
中国银行
19 Post Office
邮电局
20 Xīdī Passenger Ferry
西堤客运码头
21 Xīdī Bus Station
西堤客运站

---

no English sign, but it's down an alley near the corner of Shanzhang Lu and Changping Lu.

Huáqiáo Dàshà (Overseas Chinese Hotel; ☎ 862 9888, fax 825 2223, 41 Shanzhuang Lu) Singles/doubles Y198/228. This huge, rambling place has clean, new and old, overpriced rooms. Rooms with carpets are more expensive, but less attractive.

Xīnhuá Jiǔdiàn (☎ 827 3710, fax 827 1070, 121 Waima Lu) Doubles Y150-170, triples Y220-250. This older hotel has clean and comfortable tiled rooms.

Huìtōng Dàjiǔdiàn (☎ 860 0899, fax 860 2440, 69 Jinsha Lu) Doubles Y198-234. Near the CAAC Airport Bus pick-up location, this hotel has clean, comfortable standard rooms.

Swatow Peninsula Hotel (Túodǎo Bīnguǎn; ☎ 831 6668, fax 825 1013, 36 Jinsha Lu) Rooms Y388-988. The Thai and Chinese-owned Swatow offers pleasant rooms. Discounts of 40% are also available.

International Hotel (Guójì Dàjiǔdiàn; ☎ 825 1212, fax 825 2250, 52 Jinsha Zhonglu) Doubles Y980-1380. The glitzy International is the best top-end hotel. It also has a Western restaurant.

Places to Eat
There are *street markets* that set up at night on many streets and these markets are where you'll find the cuisine Shàntóu is famous for. Rice noodles (called *kwetiaw* locally) are a speciality. Minzu Lu has a number of *stalls* specialising in delicious *húndùn* (wontons).

For more upmarket cuisine, try the *revolving restaurant* on the 23rd floor of the International Hotel, which does reasonable Western food at an affordable price. You'll also find Western fast-food around town.

Getting There & Away
Air Shàntóu airport, about 20km from the city centre, has flights to Bangkok and Hong Kong (twice daily). Domestic flights are available to Běijīng, Guǎngzhōu, Fúzhōu, Guìlín, Hǎikǒu, Nánjīng, Shànghǎi and other cities.

CAAC (☎ 860 4698) is at 46 Shanzhang Lu, a few minutes' walk south of the intersection with Jinsha Lu. CTS, housed in the same building as the bus station, is also a convenient place to get air tickets.

COASTAL SOUTH

Bus Deluxe buses leave from the bus station behind CTS, heading to Guǎngzhōu (Y180, seven hours), Shēnzhèn (Y150, four hours), Xiàmén (Y100, five hours) and Hong Kong (Y210, five hours). Buses to Hong Kong also leave from the International Hotel. Economy buses to other destinations leave from the main bus station. Frequent minibuses to Cháozhōu (Y12, one hour) leave from the north exit of the station.

Train There are overnight services between Shàntóu and Guǎngzhōu (Y230 hard sleeper, 10 hours) and trains to Cháozhōu, but it's easier to take the bus.

Getting Around
To/From the Airport Buses to Shàntóu airport (Y4, 20 minutes) leave from the New Century Hotel at the intersection of Jinsha Lu and Longyan Beilu. A taxi will cost Y40 or Y50.

Bus Nos 2 and 6 make the 10-minute trip along Jinsha Lu to the train station. Motorbikes are plentiful and cost about Y5 a ride.

AROUND SHÀNTÓU
Not far out of the city is **Māyǔ Dǎo**, which makes a good day trip. A boat leaves for the island from the Guǎngchǎng wharf (Guǎngchǎng matou) at 9.30am daily and returns at 2.30pm (Y20 return). Speedboats do the trip in about 15 minutes for Y60 per person.

On an ordinary weekday the boat is filled with people toting bags of food and sacrificial offerings. Follow the crowd from the landing to **Tiānhòu Miào** (*Temple of the Mother of the Heavenly Emperor*), built in 1985 with funds supplied by overseas Chinese.

The site has apparently always been holy to this deity, and this is where the fisherfolk burn incense before they leave in the morning. Evidently the island has been developed to keep pace with the worshippers' enthusiasm; there are hotels and restaurants, as well as marked trails for getting around. There are no cars, and the beaches and views are refreshing after the large Chinese cities.

According to the villagers, the island was settled largely during the Japanese occupation, although there were a few people living here before then.

CHÁOZHŌU 潮州
☎ 0768 • pop 2,362,400
Cháozhōu is an ancient commercial and trading city dating back 1700 years. It is situated on Hán Jiāng and surrounded by Jīn Shān (Golden Hills) and Húlú Shān (Calabash Hills). It can be explored in a couple of hours and is best visited as a day trip from Shàntóu.

The chief sight is **Kāiyuán Sì**, which was built during the Tang dynasty to house a collection of Buddhist scriptures sent here by Emperor Qianlong. This temple was reduced almost to rubble during the Cultural Revolution, but now houses three large Buddhas flanked by 18 golden arhats. Noted for its colourful roof ornaments and decorations, this is an active temple and many monks are usually present at prayer.

Cháozhōu's old city wall still runs along next to Hán Jiāng; preserved sections such as the **Guǎngjǐ Gate** (*Guǎngjǐ Mén*) area are attractive (this is also an area full of cheap *food stalls*). The **Xī Hú** (*West Lake*) area is also a pleasant place to stroll, particularly in the early morning or evening. The park extends up the hill behind the lake.

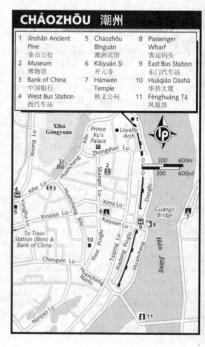

CHÁOZHŌU 潮州

1	Jīnshān Ancient Pine 金山古松	5	Cháozhōu Bīnguǎn 潮洲宾馆
2	Museum 博物馆	6	Kāiyuán Sì 开元寺
3	Bank of China 中国银行	7	Hánwén Temple 韩文公祠
4	West Bus Station 西汽车站		
8	Passenger Wharf 客运码头		
9	East Bus Station 东门汽车站		
10	Huáqiáo Dàshà 华侨大厦		
11	Fènghuáng Tǎ 凤凰塔		

It's also pleasant to walk in the area around the **Jīnshān Ancient Pine** (*Jīnshān Gǔsōng*) at the north end of the city wall. Crossing the river, the **Gǔangjǐ Bridge** (*Gǔangjǐ Qiáo*) was first built in the Song dynasty and was originally joined in the middle by a floating span of boats that could open for barges and other vessels. The present structure dates from 1958, but you can still see remnants of the old bridge. On the west side of the river, the **Hánwén Temple** (*Hánwén Gōng Cí*) commemorates the Tang dynasty poet and philosopher Han Yu, who was exiled to Guǎngdōng for his outspoken views against Buddhism.

South-east of Cháozhōu is the seven-storey **Fènghuáng Tǎ** (*Phoenix Pagoda*), built in 1585.

Places to Stay

It is worthwhile to stay in Cháozhōu for a day or two.

Cháozhōu Bīnguǎn (☎ 226 1168, fax 226 4298, 1 Chaofeng Lu) Doubles Y198. This place is conveniently located opposite the west bus station. Doubles are dingy but adequate. Discounts of 25% are also available.

Huáqiáo Dàshà (*Overseas Chinese Hotel;* ☎ 222 8899, fax 222 3123, 34 Huancheng Xilu) Doubles Y240-280. Closer to the old part of town, this hotel has similar rates to the Cháozhōu, plus suites. Discounts of 40% are available.

Getting There & Away

Minibuses go to Cháozhōu (Y12, one hour) from the bus station behind CTS in Shàntóu. Buses leave from Cháozhōu's west bus station to various destinations around Guǎngdōng and Fújiàn.

There are six trains a day to Guǎngzhōu. The train station in Cháozhōu is 8km west of the town centre. Minivan taxis are cheap, starting at Y6, and will cost about Y15 to the train station.

An interesting way to head into Fújiàn is to take a speedboat up Hán Jiāng to Gāopí (Y50, three hours), then make your way by local bus to Yǒngdìng in Fújiàn via the towns of Dàpǔ and Cháyáng. The route passes through some nice country. Speedboats leave from the wharf opposite the East bus station, but there are no fixed departure times.

Hǎinán Dǎo 海南岛

Capital: Hǎikǒu
Population: 8.2 million
Area: 34,000 sq km

Hǎinán Dǎo is a large tropical island off the southern coast of China. It was administered by the government of Guǎngdōng until 1988, when it became the province of Hǎinán.

With its acres of beaches in the south, dense vegetation, balmy winds and lilting palm trees, Hǎinán is popular as a winter refuge; unless you wish to spend the Yuletide season cheek-by-jowl with the rest of China in pricey hotels, however, miss the rush and go between March and November when you can expect large discounts on hotel accommodation.

Despite mainly catering to tour groups, Hǎinán still manages to tempt with some of the trappings of an island paradise: golden beaches, the promise of a deep tan and the thud of falling coconuts.

HISTORY
Historically, Hǎinán was a backwater of the Chinese empire, a miserable place of exile and poverty. When Li Deyu, a prime minister of the Tang dynasty, was exiled to Hǎinán he dubbed it 'the gate of hell'. According to historical records, only 18 tourists came to Hǎinán of their own volition during the entire Song, Yuan and Ming dynasties (almost 700 years)! That's about the rate per second during winter nowadays.

Times are changing – the entire island of Hǎinán was established as a Special Economic Zone (SEZ) in 1988 and quickly emerged as an enclave of free-market bedlam operating on the periphery of the law. Despite the once heady economic climate, Hǎikǒu's skyline today is punctuated with the shells of unfinished construction, testament to the fickleness of investors and financial overreaching.

Heavy industry is virtually absent, and some 80% of the island's economy is washed ashore by tourism.

ORIENTATION
Hǎikǒu, the capital of Hǎinán, and Sānyà, a port with popular beaches, are the two major urban centres, at opposite ends of the island.

Highlights

- Li and Miao minority villages around Tōngzhá – for the intrepid, Chinese-speaking traveller
- Yàlóng Bay, to the east of Sānyà, a 7km-stretch of beautiful sand and sun

Three highways link the towns: the eastern route via Wànníng (the fastest route); the central route via Túnchāng and Tōngzhá (also known as Tōngshí); and the less popular western route via Dānzhōu (also known as Nàdà), Bāsuǒ (Dōngfāng) and Yīnggēhǎi.

Most visitors to Hǎinán take the eastern or western freeway routes from Hǎikǒu to Sānyà. A highway that replaces the road cutting through the centre of the island may be finished by the time you read this.

The central route takes you through the highlands of Hǎinán and past local villages of the Li and Miao minority groups. However, showcase minority villages for tour groups are not the real thing; the genuine articles lie hidden far away from convenient transport links and take a fair amount of effort to reach.

The best mountain scenery on the island is between Sānyà and Qióngzhōng, but there's little of interest beyond that. This route tunnels through what remains of the mountainous forest regions of Hǎinán; the island was the scene of mass deforestation

COASTAL SOUTH

between 1950 and 1980, when up to half of the natural forest cover was felled to make way for rubber plantations.

To get some idea of what the forested regions of Hǎinán Dǎo used to be like, it's worth making a trip to the Jiānfēnglǐng Nature Reserve, which is near the town of Sānyà. See the Around Sānyà section later in this chapter for details.

HǍIKǑU 海口
☎ 0898 • pop 514,100

Hǎikǒu, Hǎinán's capital, lies on the northern coastline at the mouth of Nándù Jiāng. It's a port town and handles most of the island's commerce with the mainland.

For most travellers, Hǎikǒu is merely a transit point on the way to Sānyà. The city is attractive, but – apart from a sprinkling of temples, and decaying colonial charm in the Sino-Portuguese architecture around Xinhua Lu – there's not much to keep you from hopping on a bus and heading for the surf and sun in the south.

Orientation

Hǎikǒu is split into three separate sections. The western section is the port area. The centre of Hǎikǒu has all the tourist facilities. The district on the southern side of the former airport is of little interest to travellers.

Information

Money The Bank of China is outside the International Financial Centre at 33 Datong Lu. Moneychangers throng the entrance. The

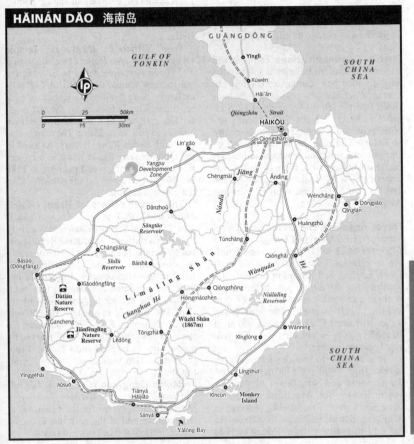

HĂINÁN DĂO 海南岛

Climate

Hǎinán is the southernmost tip of China (Sānyà, in the south, is roughly on the same latitude as the southern reaches of Hawaii), and can be relied on to be warm even when the rest of China is freezing.

At the height of China's frigid winter, average temperatures of 21°C (69.8°F) prevail; the yearly average is 25.4°C (77.7°F). From as early as March through to November, the weather becomes hot and humid.

Typhoons can play havoc with a tight itinerary, crippling all transport and communication with the mainland for several days at a time. They usually descend on the island between May and October and there has been at least one every year for the last 50 years.

branch opposite Huáqiáo Dàshà (see Places to Stay) and the one beside Dōnghú Jiāfēng Dàjiǔdiàn also change travellers cheques.

Post & Communications The post and telecommunications building is south of the long-distance bus station, on Daying Lu. Up the street from the post office, 24-hour Jīnshí Internet (Jīnshí Wǎngbā) at 22 Nanbao Lu charges Y3 per hour. There's another post and telecommunications centre on Jiefang Xilu, near the Xinhua Bookshop. Opposite the post and telecommunications centre on Jiefang Xilu, there is another Internet cafe, with similar rates; it's on the 2nd floor of the Haikou Worker's Cinema (Gōngrén Yīngjù Yùan).

Travel Agencies The main China Travel Service (CTS; Zhōngguó Lǚxíngshè; ☎ 6675 7455, fax 6623 1585) is in the same building as Huáqiáo Dàshà. Some of the staff speak English and are quite helpful. It's worth asking about tours around the island, as these can work out much cheaper than tackling it all yourself. The tour group leader will speak Chinese, unless you are a sizeable group, in which case CTS will supply an interpreter.

There are one- to four-day tours ranging in price from Y400 to Y1780 depending on the duration and what level of comfort you're looking for. The usual package is three days and four nights, taking in Xīnglóng, Sānyà, and back to Hǎikǒu via the odd minority village. Prices include transport, accommodation and meals (ticket prices for sights not included).

Take the time to shop around if CTS is too pricey, as Hǎikǒu has many travel agencies.

PSB One of the friendliest Public Security Bureaus (PSB; Gōngānjú; ☎ 6853 3166 ext 3123) is at 43 Jinlong Lu in the western part of the city. The easiest way to get there is by taxi for Y15 or bus No 12.

Things to See

Hǎikǒu is quite a pleasant city, sporting palm-tree-lined boulevards and a picturesque old quarter.

The city's crumbling colonial remains can be viewed by strolling down Xinhua Lu. Take a couple of detours along Zhongshan Lu and then back to the city centre through the lively market street of Bo'ai Beilu.

Five Officials Memorial Temple (Wǔgōng Cì; 169 Haifu Dao; admission Y15; open 8am-6pm daily) is an attractive but touristy temple dedicated to five officials who were banished to Hǎinán in earlier times. The famous Song dynasty poet, Su Dongpo, was also banished to Hǎinán and is commemorated here. The temple was first built in the Ming dynasty, restored in the Qing dynasty and is home to a collection of ponds, bridges and palm trees. Take bus No 11 or 12 and get off one stop after the east bus station.

The attractive **Tomb of Hairui** (Hǎiruì Mù; ☎ 6892 2060, Shugang Dadao; admission Y5; open 8am-6pm daily) was mostly torn down during the Cultural Revolution, but has since been repaired. Hairui was a compassionate and popular official who lived in the 16th century; the temple has been fully restored and painted in vibrant colours. The ceiling is particularly attractive. The tomb is in western Hǎikǒu, off Haixiu Dadao; take bus No 2 and watch for the west bus station or a turn off marked by a blue sign in English and Chinese. From there it's a 1km-walk along the road heading south.

Hǎikǒu Gōngyuán (Gongyuan Lu; admission Y2; open 7am-10pm daily) is a pleasant place, except for the small zoo at the southern end of the park that houses a sad collection of monkeys and bears.

The Spratly Spat

If it was not such a contentious piece of real estate, very few people would have heard of the Spratly Islands, and their near neighbours the Paracel Islands. To find them on a map, look for a parcel of dots in the South China Sea hemmed in by Malaysia, Brunei, the Philippines, Vietnam and China way to the north. They all claim the islands as their own.

It is tempting to ask what all the fuss is about. After all, this is a collection of 53 specks of land, many of which are reefs and shoals rather than islands. The answer is oil. Not that any oil has been discovered in the region, and some experts dispute that any will ever be found. Yet the very possibility that there might be oil in the Spratly Islands has set all the countries in the region at loggerheads with each other.

China, the most distant of the claimants, sees its territorial rights to the area as being validated by a historical relationship with the islands that dates back to the Han dynasty. The ruins of Chinese temples can still be found on some of the islands. Vietnam has for long been a disputant to this claim, and in 1933 the colonial French government of Vietnam annexed the islands. They lost them to Japan in 1939. With Japan's WWII defeat, the question of the Spratly Islands was left unaddressed. It was not until a Philippine claim in 1956 that the Taiwan-based Kuomintang government reasserted the traditional Chinese claim over the island group by occupying the largest of the islands, Taiping, where they remain. Vietnam followed by hoisting a flag over the westernmost point of the islands. The Chinese struck back in 1988 by sinking two Vietnamese ships and forcibly occupying the islands. In 1996, the Philippine navy destroyed a small Chinese-built radar base on Mischief Reef in the Spratlys. But the Chinese refuse to be dislodged and continue to build more permanent structures on Mischief Reef.

With all the countries of the region embarking on programs of updating their military capabilities, the Spratly Islands remain one of the most potentially destabilising issues in the Asian region.

Places to Stay – Budget

Prices aren't quite as bad in Hǎikǒu as they used to be, but there's not a lot to choose from for budget travellers. All rooms listed here have a bathroom and air-con. Many hotels offer large discounts during the low season.

Wǔhàn Dàshà (☎ 6622 6522, *Xīngǎng*) Singles/doubles/triples Y40/90/120. This place also has grubby, cheap singles with fan and shared bathroom, as well as other rooms. Look for the white-tiled building on the eastern side of the parking lot of the Xīngǎng passenger ferry terminal. The reception is on the 2nd floor.

Hǎidōng Bīnguǎn (☎ 6677 5638 ext 8000, *3 Gongyuan Lu*) Singles/doubles/triples Y158/198/268. This place is down an alley off Gongyuan Lu, and offers a 50% discount for its below-average rooms.

Qiáoyǒu Dàshà (☎ 6676 6852, *18 Gongyuan Lu*) Singles/doubles Y100/120. This hotel is near Hǎidōng Bīnguǎn and has much nicer rooms.

Yǒuyì Dàjiǔdiàn (*Friendship Hotel; ☎ 6622 5566, fax 6621 8200, 2-1 Datong Lu*) Doubles Y138-158. This is one of the best deals in the city centre, with clean, standard rooms. The staff doesn't speak English.

Places to Stay – Mid-Range

Most of Hǎikǒu's hotels are middle to top end, but always push for discounts (*zhékòu*) as sometimes up to 50% is offered.

Huáqiáo Dàshà (*Overseas Chinese Hotel; ☎ 6670 8430, fax 6677 2094, 17 Datong Lu*) Singles Y248-276, doubles Y360. This convenient, three-star hotel has nice rooms.

Hǎinán Mínháng Bīnguǎn (*Hainan Civil Aviation Hotel; ☎ 6677 2608, fax 6677 2610, 9 Haixiu Dadao*) Doubles Y488-888. This hotel is a bit more pricey but is very good value.

Places to Stay – Top End

These hotels offer 40% to 50% discounts in the low season.

Dōnghú Jiāfēng Dàjiǔdiàn (*East Lake Hotel; ☎ 6535 3333, fax 6535 8827, 8 Haifu Dadao*) Doubles Y550. This hotel has a pool and adequate, if somewhat overpriced, standard doubles.

Hǎikǒu Bīnguǎn (☎ 6535 0221, fax 6535 0232, 4 Haifu Lu) Doubles Y588. This

HǍIKǑU

bustling, noisy place is often fully booked with tour groups. Maybe they come for the dazzling video arcade strategically located off the lobby.

Haikou International Commercial Centre *(Hǎikǒu Guójì Shāngyè Dàshà;* ☎ *6679 6999, fax 6677 4751, 38 Datong Lu)* Rooms with kitchenette Y680-1080. This modern structure, catering to business travellers, is in Hǎikǒu's prime location. It offers a health club, tennis courts, banks, shops and restaurants. The staff is efficient and friendly.

Haikou International Financial Centre *(Hǎikǒu Guójì Jīnróng Dàshà;* ☎ *6677 3088, fax 6677 2113, 29 Datong Lu)* Standard/large doubles Y798/928. This red-pillared establishment is similar to the Commercial Centre next door. Amenities include everything from a swimming pool to a bowling alley. The standard doubles are a bit cramped.

Places to Eat

In response to the phalanxes of tour groups that trundle through Hǎikǒu, most restaurants tend to be hotpot affairs. A number of them spill out onto the sidewalk on Jichang Donglu, and at the northern end of Xinhua Lu. Many hotpot restaurants feature dog meat and snake, besides the usual ingredients of *pángxiè* (crab), *mógu* (mushroom), *qīngcài* (cabbage), tofu, sliced pork and lamb, and congealed duck's blood. Expect to pay about Y50 to Y60 for a hearty meal.

A well-known dish from Hǎinán and common in East and South East Asia is *wénchāng jī* (succulent chicken raised on a rice diet). Despite the cornucopia of tropical ingredients available in the market, food in Hǎinán isn't much different from the rest of southern China. The best places for cheap, delicious meals are the informal establishments at ***Xīngǎng passenger ferry terminal.*** There are also a number of cheap ***restaurants*** on Jichang Donglu.

Plenty of street fruit sellers offer bananas, mangoes, and sugar cane. Green coconuts, with their tops chopped off and straws poked in, are delicious and plentiful as a refreshing drink (Y2).

Fēnggé Kāfēidiàn *(*☎ *6623 8890, 2nd floor, 4 Datong Lu)* Mains Y20-30. Tasty reasonable Western and Chinese meals are served in this pleasant cafe/restaurant. Coffee, chips (*tǔdòutiáo*) and beef with noodles (*niúròumiàn*) are each Y10.

Kuàihuólín *(1 Jichang Donglu)* Dishes Y5-20. Pick and choose from dishes like potstickers and green beans from the servers wheeling around trolleys.

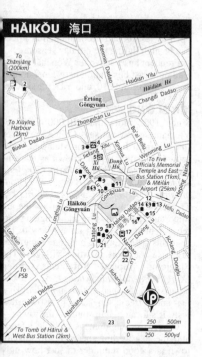

HǍIKǑU 海口

To Zhànjiāng (200km)

To Xiùyīng Harbour (2km)

To PSB

To Tomb of Hǎiruì & West Bus Station (2km)

23   0   250   500m
      0   250   500yd

Yēfēngtáng (Cocowind Restaurant; ☎ *6535 1234, 4 Haifu Lu)* Dishes from Y25. This restaurant serves Hainanese specialties and is located in Hǎikǒu Bīnguǎn (see Places to Stay).

Entertainment

Hǎikǒu's wild reputation has been somewhat tamed in the last few years. Crime rates are down and prostitution isn't quite as visible as it was before. Karaoke parlours are popular and larger hotels have nightclubs and tacky floor shows. There's a disco beside Dōnghú Jiāfēng Dàjiǔdiàn, near the Bank of China. There is a cluster of bars on Jichang Donglu – one of the better ones is *Forever Café (*☎ *6532 4658; 4 Jichang Donglu).*

Getting There & Away

Air Civil Aviation Administration of China (CAAC; Zhōngguó Mínháng; ☎ 6676 3166) is in a large building that houses Hǎinán Mínháng Bīnguǎn. Just a few doors down at 29 Haixiu Dadao is the China Southern Airlines office (☎ 6534 9433). Between them they have regular flights between Hǎikǒu

and many cities including Běijīng (Y2130), Guǎngzhōu (Y620), Kūnmíng (Y1040), Nánníng, Shànghǎi (Y1590) and Shēnzhèn (Y670).

Daily flights travel between Hǎikǒu and Hong Kong (Y1420) on CAAC and Dragonair; China Southern Airlines has flights once a week to Bangkok (Y3344). Dragonair (☎ 677 3088 ext 743) has a representative in Room 201 at the International Financial Centre.

Bus The long-distance and west bus stations have departures to Sānyà and many destinations on the mainland; combination ferry/sleeper buses go to Guǎngzhōu (with/without air-con Y177/157, 16 hours) and Zhànjiāng (Y72, six hours). Sleek aircon buses depart for Sānyà (Y78, three hours), leaving roughly every half hour between 7am and 6.30pm. The ordinary bus (Y49) takes five hours.

The east bus station, near the Five Officials Memorial Temple, has buses to all major destinations on the island. Frequent buses go to Wénchāng (with/without aircon Y15/12, 1½ hours), Tōngzhá (with/without air-con Y41/30, 5½ hours), Sānyà and other destinations.

Boat Hǎikǒu has two harbours but most departures are from the Xīngǎng passenger ferry terminal. Minibus Nos 218 and 212 go to the harbour from the stop opposite Hǎikǒu Bīnguǎn. A taxi costs around Y15. Bus No 3 goes to Xiùyīng harbour.

Ferries depart roughly every 1 ½ hours from Xīngǎng for Hǎi'ān (Y32, 1½ hours) on Léizhōu Peninsula, where there are bus connections to Zhànjiāng (Y30, three hours) and Guǎngzhōu (Y130, 13 hours). If the weather is decent, it's easier to take a boat directly to Zhànjiāng. Fast boats leave from Xīngǎng to Zhànjiāng at 9.30am and 1.30pm (Y105, four hours). There are daily overnight boats from both harbours for Běihǎi in Guǎngxī departing at 6pm. Tickets are sold at both harbours and cost between Y84 for a seat and Y254 for a VIP cabin.

Slower boats to most destinations listed above leave from Xiùyīng harbour. Two slow ferries leave daily for Zhànjiāng (Y33, seven hours). They leave at 9am and 9pm; seat prices range from Y44 to Y123. Boats leave every two days to Guǎngzhōu, and

COASTAL SOUTH

tickets start at Y135 for the bottom class and up to Y303 for a two-person cabin in 2nd class. The journey takes 25 hours. There's also a daily boat to Shékǒu, the harbour port near Shēnzhèn, which takes 18 hours. Tickets are Y113 for a seat to Y453 for VIP class. Tickets for these departures can be bought at the Xiùyīng harbour or in town at the Hǎikǒu harbour passenger ferry ticket office. The office is located opposite Dōnghú Jiāfēng Dàjiǔdiàn, directly under the pedestrian overpass.

There's no passenger train service on Hǎinán, but it's possible to book tickets originating from Zhànjiāng at the ticket booth inside Xīngǎng passenger ferry terminal, on your immediate right as you enter. These include useful trains to Guǎngzhōu and Guìlín. On the ground floor of Wǔhàn Dàshà another office books tickets originating from Guǎngzhōu.

Getting Around

Hǎikǒu's Měilán Airport opened in May 1999 and is located 25km south-east of the city centre. CAAC has an airport shuttle (Y15) that leaves every half hour from in front of Hǎinán Mínháng Bīnguǎn on Haixiu Dadao. A taxi will cost about Y40.

Hǎikǒu's centre is easy to walk around, but there is also a workable bus system (Y1). Taxis are expensive, starting at Y10 for the first 3km.

WÉNCHĀNG 文昌
☎ 0898

Wénchāng is the homeland of a famous chicken dish and the Soong sisters, Meiling and Qingling, the wives of Chiang Kaishek and Sun Yatsen. For the traveller, however, it's **Dōngjiāo Yēlín** and **Jiànhuáshān Yēlín** coconut plantations, with their cool, inviting pathways, and glorious beaches that make Wénchāng attractive.

Minibuses heading to Gālóngwān, which is 10km from Wénchāng's bus station, depart from the riverside in Wénchāng and pass by the turn-off to Qīnglán Harbour (Qīnglán Gǎngwān). It's a five-minute motorbike ride to the harbour, where you can take a ferry (Y45) and motorbike (Y10) to the stands of coconut palms and mile after mile of beach. Another way is to take the direct bus to Dōngjiāo (Y16) from Hǎikǒu's east bus station.

The beaches in this area have been developed as resorts and accommodation prices can be high during the holiday season.

Frequent buses leave for Wénchāng from Hǎikǒu's east bus station between 7am and 7pm. Tickets are Y10, and Y13 for air-con.

XĪNGLÓNG 兴隆

Since 1952 more than 20,000 Chinese-Vietnamese and overseas Chinese refugees (mostly from Indonesia or Malaysia) have settled at a cultural park known as the **Xinglong Overseas Chinese Farm** (*Xīnglóng Huáqiáo Cūn;* ☎ *6225 1888 ext 8811; admission Y38; open 7.30am-6pm daily*). Tropical agriculture, rubber and coffee are important cash crops here and Xīnglóng coffee is famous all over China. Many of the residents speak English and may be able to organise transport to Miao villages. The **Xinglong Tropical Botanical Garden** (*Xīnglóng Rèdài Zhíwùyuán;* ☎ *6225 5900; admission Y15; open 7.30am-6pm daily*) has tea- and coffee-tastings and is also worth a visit. It's located 3km south of the town.

Otherwise, Xīnglóng is of little interest and the nearby hot spring resort east of town is a good reminder of just how ugly tourist resort developments in China can be. The baths at the hotels are typically swimming pool sized, open air and separated into hot and cool, but unless you're in need of such therapy, Xīnglóng is not a place to linger.

From the bus stop to the hotels it costs Y3 on the back of a motorbike, or Y5 for a motor-tricycle. Trips out to the farm or the botanical garden from the city centre are Y5.

XĪNCŪN 新村

Xīncūn is populated almost solely by Danjia (Tanha) minority people, who are employed in fishing and pearl cultivation. The main attraction here is Monkey Island. It's home to a population of Guǎngxī monkeys (*Macaca mulatta*) and it makes a pleasant day trip from Sānyà. Buses travelling the eastern route from Hǎikǒu will drop you off at a fork in the road about 3km from Xīncūn. It should then be easy to get a lift on a passing minibus, or hitch or walk into Xīncūn. Frequent minibuses run to Xīncūn directly from Língshuǐ (15km away) and Sānyà.

Monkey Island 南湾猴岛
Nánwān Hóudǎo

About a thousand macaque monkeys live on this narrow, hilly peninsula near Xīncūn. This park (☎ 6336 1465; admission Y20; open 8am-5pm daily) is under state protection and a special wildlife research centre has been set up to investigate all the monkey business.

The animals are tame and anticipate tourist arrivals for snacks of peanuts. It's all right to feed them (there are bags of peanuts for sale at the park entrance) but don't try to touch the monkeys. Keep a tight grip on your camera, as some wily monkeys are prone to steal and hang them in trees.

Ferries (Y2) from Xīncūn's pier putt-putts from Xīncūn to Monkey Island in 10 minutes, where a bus or hired car can take you to the park entrance. A cable car also runs between Xīncūn and Monkey Island (Y45 return).

For best contact with the monkeys, visit in the morning or evening, otherwise you might have trouble spotting them in the foliage; occasionally a wild, woolly head pops out of the top branches to see what's happening or to scream at you.

The mating season is a much more active time (February to May), however, and the monkeys are, shall we say, over-hospitable and you may have to crowbar them off your leg.

SĀNYÀ 三亚
☎ 0899 • pop 440,600

Sānyà's harbour area is protected to the south-east by the hilly Lùhuítóu Peninsula. Except for the harbour area crammed with fishing boats, however, there's not much to see in Sānyà itself. The main reason to come here is for the surrounding beaches.

On the western outskirts of Sānyà there's a community of around 5000 Hui, the only Muslim inhabitants of Hǎinán.

Information

There's a convenient Bank of China in Dàdōnghǎi that changes travellers cheques, and another one in Sānyà near Fènghuáng Jīchǎng Bīnguǎn. It's open daily from 8.30am to 5.30pm.

The post and telecommunications building is on Jiefang Lu in Sānyà and there's another one at the eastern end of Yuya Dadao

Words & Pictures

Dǎo: island

The unsimplified version of this character is readily identifiable as a bird sitting atop a mountain, with its feet tucked under its body. One can imagine the mountain being partly submerged under water, its peak forming an island in the sea. (The modern character leaves out more details of the bird.)

in Dàdōnghǎi. Just north of the bus station, 24-hour Tiānshān Internet (Tiānshān Wǎngbā; ☎ 8827 5364), on the 2nd floor, 16 Jiefang Lu, charges Y3 per hour.

The area around Dàdōnghǎi Beach (Dàdōnghǎi Hǎitān) in Sānyà is full of travel agencies. For tickets and information, try Dragon Travel Agency (☎ 821 3526) at 11 Luling Lu. They can arrange tickets and tours and may even be able to rustle up a couple of bicycles. The travel agency in Fènghuáng Jīchǎng Bīnguǎn (☎ 8827 7409) has good prices on plane tickets.

Things to See

The popular beaches are Yàlóng Bay, Dàdōnghǎi, Lùhuítóu Peninsula and Tiānyá Hǎijiǎo. The sun is very intense at this latitude from March onwards and if you intend going to the beach, take high sun-factor lotion; sunburn is common.

The best of the lot is **Yàlóng Bay** (Yàlóng Wān; Asian Dragon Bay), to the east of Sānyà, a great beach that features a 7km strip of sand (much longer than the longest beach in Hawaii). The views here are excellent and you can roam about for hours. Take bus No 102 (Y5) from Yuya Dadao.

The crescent-shaped beach at **Dàdōnghǎi** is around 3km south-east of Sānyà and is easily reached by minibus Nos 2 and 4 (Y1), which shuttle between Jiefang Lu in Sānyà and the beach. Dàdōnghǎi is a good

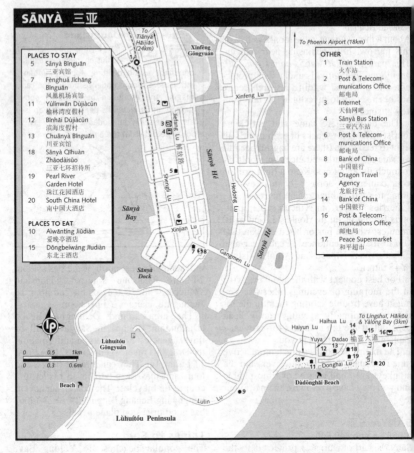

SĀNYÀ 三亚

PLACES TO STAY
5 Sānyà Bīnguǎn
    三亚宾馆
7 Fènghuá Jīchǎng
    Bīnguǎn
    凤凰机场宾馆
11 Yúlínwān Dùjiàcūn
    榆林湾度假村
12 Bīnhǎi Dùjiàcūn
    滨海度假村
13 Chuānyà Bīnguǎn
    川亚宾馆
18 Sānyà Qīhuàn
    Zhāodàisùo
    三亚七环招待所
19 Pearl River
    Garden Hotel
    珠江花园酒店
20 South China Hotel
    南中国大酒店

PLACES TO EAT
10 Aìwǎntíng Jiǔdiàn
    爱晚亭酒店
15 Dōngběiwáng Jiǔdiàn
    东北王酒店

OTHER
1 Train Station
    火车站
2 Post & Telecom-
    munications Office
    邮电局
3 Internet
    天仙网吧
4 Sānyà Bus Station
    三亚汽车站
6 Post & Telecom-
    munications Office
    邮电局
8 Bank of China
    中国银行
9 Dragon Travel
    Agency
    龙旅行社
14 Bank of China
    中国银行
16 Post & Telecom-
    munications Office
    邮电局
17 Peace Supermarket
    和平超市

To Tiānyá Hǎijiǎo (24km)
Xīnfēng Gōngyuán
To Phoenix Airport (18km)
Xinfeng Lu
Jiefang Lu 解放路
Sānyà Hé
Hedong Lu
Shengli Lu
Sānyà Bay
Xinjian Lu
Gangmen Lu
Sānyà Hé
Sānyà Dock
Sānyà Bay
Lùhuítóu Gōngyuán
Haihua Lu
To Lingshuǐ, Hǎikǒu & Yálóng Bay (3km)
Haiyun Lu
Yuya Dadao 榆亚大道
Yuya
Donghai Lu
Dàdōnghǎi Beach
Beach
Lulin Lu
Lùhuítóu Peninsula

0   0.5   1km
0   0.3   0.6mi

---

place to base yourself, but the beach is smaller, more developed and crowded with all the accoutrements of a resort, boat, scuba and snorkelling hire and, of course, trinket-sellers.

The beaches on **Lùhuítóu Peninsula** are poor, but they make for pleasant enough walks.

The beach at **Tiānyá Hǎijiǎo** (literally 'edge of the sky, rim of the sea'), about 24km north-west of Sānyà, is not bad, but is of great interest to local tourists who crowd around the stone immortalised on the back of the Y2 note to have their photo taken. Entry to the beach is Y38. Catch any minibus (Y2, 45 minutes) heading north along the coast road from the No 2 or 4 northern terminus.

Places to Stay – Budget

Even though it's been inundated for years with foreign students studying in China, Sānyà hasn't yet grasped the idea of budget travel. Most of the hotels in and around Sānyà cater mainly to package tourists. Always try to bargain for a discount.

Bīnhǎi Dùjiàcūn (Seaside Holiday Inn Resort; ☎ 8821 3898, fax 8821 2081, Yuya Dadao) Economy rooms with balcony Y160, standard doubles Y320/180 high/low season. If you want to keep costs to a minimum in a good location, your best bet is this place, in Dàdōnghǎi. The economy rooms have tiny, run-down bathrooms.

Chuānyà Bīnguǎn (☎ 8821 2901, fax 8821 3568, Yuya Dadao) Doubles/triples Y298/335. This place is near Bīnhǎi

Population & People

Thirty-nine minority groups live on Hǎinán Dǎo, including the original inhabitants of the island, the Li and Miao, who live in the dense tropical forests covering Límǔlǐng Shān (Mother of the Li Mountain Range), that stretch down the centre of the island. The Li probably settled on Hǎinán 3000 years ago after migrating from Fújiàn, and today number 1 million on the island.

Although there has been a long history of rebellion by the Li against the Chinese, they aided the Communist guerrillas on the island during the war with the Japanese. Perhaps for this reason the island's centre was made an 'autonomous' region after the Communists came to power.

Until recently the Li women had a custom of tattooing their bodies at the age of 12 or 13. Today, almost all Li people except the elderly women wear standard Han dress. However, when a member of the Li dies, traditional Li costume is considered essential if the dead are to be accepted by ancestors in the afterworld.

The Miao (Hmong) people spread from southern China across northern Vietnam, Laos and Thailand. In China they moved south into Hǎinán as a result of the Chinese emigrations from the north, and now occupy some of the most rugged terrain on the island. Today there are some 60,000 Miao living on the island.

The coastal areas of the island are populated by Han Chinese. Since 1949, Chinese from Indonesia, Malaysia and, later, Vietnam have settled here.

Dùjiàcūn and offers 50% discounts. The rooms, however, are nowhere as nice.

Sānyà Qīhuàn Zhāodàisǔo (☎ 8821 5770, *Yuya Dadao*) Rooms with/without bath Y150/100. There's no English sign but this place is located 20m down the lane opposite Chuānyà Bīnguǎn, in an unlikely looking building on the left. The rooms with shared bathroom are small, and expect these rates to double during the holiday season.

Finding a hotel in Sānyà itself will bring costs down slightly, but it's not a very pleasant place to stay.

Sānyà Bīnguǎn (☎ 8827 4819, fax 8827 4758, *2 Jiefang Lu*) Singles/doubles from Y130/180. In the centre of town, the rooms at this hotel are pleasant, although the bathrooms are small. There's a 30% discount in the high season.

Fènghuáng Jīchǎng Bīnguǎn (*Airport Hotel;* ☎ 8825 2763, fax 8825 2763 ext 8888, *1 Jiefang Lu*) Doubles/triples Y180/258. In the southern part of town, the rooms here are a bit run-down, but the staff is friendly, and discounts of 45% are offered.

Places to Stay – Mid Range
There are many other hotels in Dàdōnghǎi (in fact there is really nothing but hotels in Dàdōnghǎi) with high-season room rates hovering around Y350 for a double. Most hotels offer a 50% discount.

Yúlínwān Dùjiàcūn (*Yulin Bay Holiday Resort;* ☎ 8822 7188, fax 8821 2536, *Lulin Lu*) Singles/doubles Y300/410. This place is a good mid-range option; try bargaining for a 50% discount during the low season.

South China Hotel (*Nánzhōngguó Dàjiǔdiàn;* ☎ 8821 9888, fax 8821 4005, *Yuhai Lu*) Doubles Y880. Set right on the beach, this is one of Sānyà's better hotels, with several Western/Chinese restaurants, a pool, and rooms with ocean views.

Pearl River Garden Hotel (*Zhūjiāng Huāyuán Jiǔdiàn;* ☎ 8821 1888, fax 8821 1999, *Donghai Lu*) Standard/ocean-view doubles Y780/1080. This four-star hotel is a more luxurious option; it has a pool and several bars and restaurants.

Places to Stay – Top End
There are three five-star international-style resorts in Yàlóng Bay which offer a great escape for those looking for a little high-priced luxury. See the Getting There & Away section for details on how to get there.

Holiday Inn Yalong Bay (*Yàlóng Hǎiwān Jiàrì Jiǔdiàn;* ☎ 8856 5666, fax 8856 5688 Standard/ocean-view doubles Y1080/1228. The Holiday Inn is located on a beautiful stretch of beach and offers discounts of 40%. Facilities include a lush beachside pool, disco and several bars and restaurants.

Gloria (*Sānyà Kǎlái Dùjià Jiǔdiàn;* ☎ 8856 8855, fax 8856 8533) Doubles

COASTAL SOUTH

Y1308-1438. This hotel has a semi-private beach, several restaurants, a pool, and vast grounds.

Resort Horizon (Tiānyù Dùjià Jiǔdiàn; ☎ 8856 7888, fax 8856 7890) Doubles Y990-1380. This hotel also boasts a semi-private beach, restaurants, and a pool.

Places to Eat
Sānyà and its environs are swarming with restaurants. In Dàdōnghǎi, the small enterprises are cheap and tasty and seem to be exclusively run by Sichuanese migrants. Seafood is big, with live wares displayed in basins along the street. There's plenty of fruit for sale, but you will have to sharpen your bargaining skills. Betel nut *(bīngláng)* abounds, as it does everywhere in Hǎinán, and is worth trying if you want to walk around with a bright red mouth and a peculiar sensation in your gums. The South China Hotel also has a good coffee shop and small bakery. The *Peace Supermarket* (Hépíng Chāoshì; ☎ 8821 3011, 30 Yuya Dadao) has a good supply of items for self-catering.

Dōngběiwáng Jiǔdiàn (King of the Northeast Restaurant; ☎ 8821 2192, Yuya Dadao) Dishes Y8-38. This delicious and reasonable place is by far one of the best restaurants in Dàdōnghǎi. It features dishes from northern China and great service. It also has an English menu. It's beside the Kodak shop on Yuya Dadao.

Aìwǎntíng Jiǔdiàn (☎ 8821 3278, 61 Luling Lu) Mains Y20-45. This famous restaurant serves up spicy Húnán specialties, and it also has a branch in Shànghǎi. It's next to Yùlínwān Dùjiàcūn.

Shopping
Southern Hǎinán is famous for its cultured pearls, but watch out for fakes. Tourists have been known to pay one hundred times the going price for authentic-looking plastic. Other knick-knacks and souvenirs fill the shops in Dàdōnghǎi and, for some peculiar reason, they are snapped up by local tourists.

Getting There & Away
Phoenix airport is open for domestic flights including Shēnzhèn (Y710), Guǎngzhōu (Y640), Běijīng (Y1850) and Shànghǎi (Y1510).

Dàdōnghǎi is full of travel agencies and the major hotels can also book plane tickets.

From Sānyà's bus station there are frequent buses and minibuses to most parts of Hǎinán. Deluxe buses to Hǎikǒu (Y70, three hours) depart frequently and you can also wave them down on Yuya Dadao in Dàdōnghǎi. Buses to Tōngzhá leave roughly every hour (Y13, 2½ hours) and there are three departures daily for Qióngzhōng (Y23, five hours).

One minibus, No 102, goes directly to Yàlóng Bay (Y5). It runs roughly every half hour, and you can catch it at most bus stops on Yuya Dadao. Or, hail any minibus heading east and see if it goes to Tiándú. From there, a motorcycle sidecar costs Y10 out to Yàlóng.

The railway line is used for hauling freight and does not have a passenger service. There are currently no boat services operating from Sānyà; all boat services operate from Hǎikǒu.

Getting Around
The airport is 18km north of Sānyà and the only way there is by taxi. Expect to pay about Y50.

Motorcycle sidecars cruise the streets all day. The real fare is usually half the asking price (Y5 to most places).

Given that Sānyà's attractions are so widely spread out, it is worth getting together with a few people and hiring a vehicle and driver. The minibuses down by the long-distance bus station charge Y200 for a full day, six-destination excursion.

AROUND SĀNYÀ
Two islands, **Xīmaò Zhōu** and **Dōngmaò Zhōu**, are visible off Sānyà's coastline. Only Xīmaò Zhōu is open to visitors. At 2.6 sq km, it's fairly small, but you can hike around or go snorkelling. The Peace Supermarket in Dàdōnghǎi hires out a boat for Y450 return and the trip takes about two hours. Speedboats from the beach take 30 minutes, but are very expensive. A small homestay on the island offers basic accommodation for Y80 per night.

Jiānfēnglǐng Nature Reserve (Jiān fēnglǐng Zìrán Bǎohùqū) is 115km from Sānyà. This lush area is located high above the humidity of the coastal plain and is home to many different species of plants and insects. To really get a feel for the place, it's best to stay overnight and spend the day walking in the reserve and surrounding area.

Tiānchí Shānzhuāng Rooms with bath Y80. This place has basic accommodation in folksy huts in the middle of a man-made lake.

Tiānchí Bishŭ Shānzhuāng (☎ 8572 0162) Rooms Y120-180. Nestled up in the hill west of the lake, this place has pristine rooms.

Getting to Jiānfēng by public transport is a little tiresome. Buses going to Bāsuŏ from Sānyà's bus station will drop you off at the turn-off (there's an English sign). Tickets are Y15, or Y25 for air-con. From the turn-off it's a rough 10km-ride by motorcycle sidecar (Y10) or a public mini-truck (Y1) to the town of Jiānfēng, 16km from the reserve. From there a public bus leaves at mid-morning (Y5) to go up the horrendous road to the mountain. Unfortunately, if you miss the bus you'll have to hire a vehicle for about Y70.

TŌNGZHÁ 通什
☎ 0899

Tōngzhá, also known as Tōngshí, is the capital of the Li and Miao Autonomous Prefecture. It's a pleasant place, somewhat cooler than the humid coast, with a lively market on Jiefang Lu, a modern university and a **museum** (*Mínzú Bówùguǎn;* ☎ 862 2336; admission Y10; open 8.30am-5.30pm daily) that displays Li and Miao artefacts; it's down a palm tree-lined road. For intrepid travellers, Tōngzhá is a good place to start for trips further into the highlands to seek out real Li and Miao villages.

For hikes around Tōngzhá, head out in a north-easterly direction past Tōngzhá Lǚyóu Shānzhuāng, at the head of Shanzhuang Lu, or start climbing some of the hills behind the university past the bus station.

There's a Bank of China near the intersection of Jiefang Lu and Xinhua Lu and the post office is just across the main bridge, on the north-eastern side of the river.

Places to Stay
There are a few hotels in Tōngzhá.

Tōngzhá Mínzú Bīnguǎn (☎ 8662 3082, fax 8662 2870) Doubles/triples Y55/65, with air-con Y100/150. This hotel – the cheapest in the area that accepts foreigners – is perched on the hill near the museum and past the bus station. It's a nice setting, but the rooms aren't well maintained. Off the parking lot there's an outdoor hotpot restaurant that overlooks the town.

Tōngzhá Lǚyóu Shānzhuāng (*Tongzha Resort Hotel;* ☎ 8662 3188, fax 8662 2201, 38 Shanzhuang Lu) Doubles Y388-468, rooms with verandas Y488-588. This hotel is on the north-eastern fringe of town and offers discounts of 60%. The rooms/facilities here are elegant and very pleasant and the rooms have rustic, rattan furniture.

Getting There & Away
Minibuses depart regularly from the Sānyà bus station (Y14, 2½ hours). Frequent buses travel on to Qióngzhōng (Y11, two hours) and Hǎikǒu (Y30, 5½ hours) from Tōngzhá. Air-con buses to Hǎikǒu travel a bit quicker and cost Y40.

To head deep into the highlands, catch the bus to Báishā (Y14, three hours), 94km north-west of Tōngzhá.

AROUND TŌNGZHÁ
Near Tōngzhá, at 1867m, is **Wǔzhǐ Shān** (Five Fingers Mountain), Hǎinán's highest mountain. Climbing the mountain takes about three to four hours, but it's a bit of a scramble. It's possible to stay at the bottom at *Wǔzhǐshān Bīnguǎn*. The rooms here cost between Y100 and Y200, depending on demand.

Buses leave at 10am and 2pm from the parking lot opposite the entrance to the main bridge on the north-eastern side of the river in Tōngzhá. Tickets are Y4 to the town of Wǔzhǐ Shān, 60km north-east of Tōngzhá. From there it's another 5km to the base of the mountain by motorcycle (Y10).

QIÓNGZHŌNG 琼中
☎ 0898

The route between Tōngzhá and Qióngzhōng passes through forested hills and small villages. It's worthwhile starting off early in the day and getting off the bus at one of the villages, such as Hóngmáozhèn, taking a look around, then catching the next bus going through. Qióngzhōng is a small, rather ugly hill town but the surrounding countryside is beautiful. The nearby **waterfall** at Báihuā Shān drops more than 300m and is about 7km from town. Motorcycles go up for about Y15, and it's a nice walk back.

In Qióngzhōng there are two hotels on the main street on either side of the bus station. *Jiāotōng Dàshà (Traffic Building; ☎ 8622 2615, 119 Haiyi Lu)* Singles/doubles with fan & shared bath Y40/60, standard doubles with fan/air-con Y80/120. The rooms here are basic but clean.

Hòngxiāo Dàshà (☎ 8622 1446, 59 Haiyi Lu) Doubles Y80-138. A few stores down westward of Jiāotōng Dàshà, this hotel has slightly fancier rooms.

Besides the road through the central highlands linking Qióngzhōng and Hǎikǒu to the north, and Tōngzhá and Sānyà to the south, you can also take a bus nearer to the coast to Xīnglóng (Y11, two hours) and hook up to the coastal freeway.

Guǎngxī 广西

Capital: Nánníng
Population: 45.9 million
Area: 236,300 sq km

Guǎngxī's best-known attraction is Guìlín. While most travellers also visit the nearby town of Yángshuò, few venture farther afield to explore Guǎngxī's other attractions. For the adventurous, the northern reaches of the province, bordering Guìzhōu, are home to remote minority regions, some accessible only by water. In the south are the less-touristed rock paintings on Zuǒ Jiāng (Left River), not far from Nánníng. Guǎngxī also has an easily accessible border crossing with Vietnam near the town of Píngxiáng.

Guǎngxī first came under Chinese sovereignty when a Qin dynasty army was sent southwards in 214 BC to conquer what is now Guǎngdōng and eastern Guǎngxī; two earlier attempts by Emperor Qin Shi Huang had wrested little effective control away from the Zhuang people. The situation was complicated in the northern regions by the Yao (Mien) and Miao (Hmong) people, who had been driven there from their homelands in Húnán and Jiāngxī by the advance of Han Chinese settlers. Unlike the Zhuang, who were immersed in Chinese customs and eventually assimilated, the Yao and Miao remained in the hill regions and were often cruelly oppressed by the Han. There was continuous conflict between the Chinese and tribes, leading to uprisings in the 1830s and again during the Taiping Rebellion, which began in Guǎngxī.

Today the Zhuang are China's largest minority, with well over 15 million people concentrated in Guǎngxī. In 1955, Guǎngxī province was reconstituted as the Guǎngxī Zhuang Autonomous Region. The Zhuang are, however, virtually indistinguishable from the Han Chinese, the last outward vestige of their original identity being their linguistic links with the Thai people. Besides the Zhuang, Miao and Yao minorities, Guǎngxī is home to smaller numbers of Dong, Maonan, Mulao, Jing (Vietnamese Gin) and Yi peoples. Until very recently, 75% of Guǎngxī's population was non-Han.

Highlights

- Yángshuò, a backpackers' mecca, famed for its gorgeous scenery and laid-back rural atmosphere
- Guìlín, one of China's favourite tourist cities, famous for its karst scenery and Lí Jiāng boat cruise
- Lóngshèng/Sānjiāng, mountain towns and gateways to many minority villages, spectacularly terraced fields and beautiful scenery
- Běihǎi, a sleepy seaside town boasting white-sand beaches

China's first canal was built in Guǎngxī after the emperor gained a foothold in the Qin dynasty, but the scattered Han had little ability to use it to economic advantage and the province remained a comparatively poor one until the 20th century. The first attempts at modernising Guǎngxī were made during 1926 to 1927 when the 'Guangxi Clique' (the main opposition to Chiang Kaishek within the Kuomintang) controlled much of Guǎngdōng, Húnán, Guǎngxī and Húběi. After the outbreak of war with Japan, the province was the scene of major battles and suffered substantial destruction.

Guǎngxī remains one of China's less affluent provinces, though you might be forgiven for not realising this if you only visit the urban centres, where industry, trade, tourism and foreign investment flourish.

GUĂNGXĪ 广西

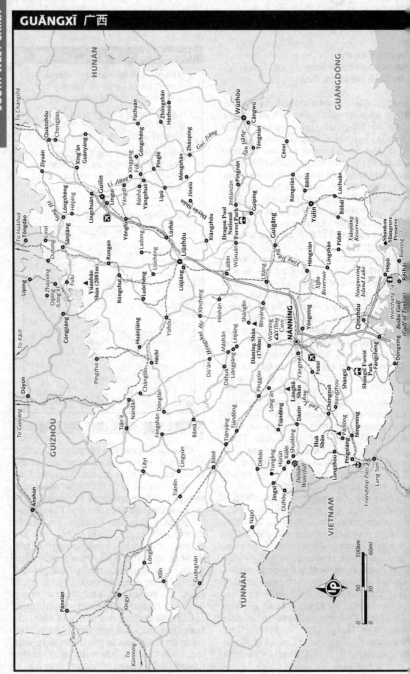

NÁNNÍNG 南宁

☎ 0771 • pop 1.3 million

Nánníng is one of those provincial centres that provide an insight into just how fast China is developing. In recent years, most of the city's main streets and riverbanks have been beautifully landscaped and restored. Since the opening of the Nánkūn Railway in 1998, Nánníng is seeing more visitors who are circumventing Guìlín on the congested Kūnmíng-Yángshuò route.

Apart from the urban expansion that the post-1949 railway induced in the southwest, Nánníng became an important staging post for shipping arms to Vietnam in the 1960s and 1970s. It's now reprising that role, this time in the thriving border trade that has sprung from Běijīng's increasingly friendly ties with Hanoi.

The railway line to the border town of Píngxiáng was built in 1952, and was extended to Hanoi, giving Vietnam a lifeline to China. The link was cut in 1979 with the Chinese invasion of Vietnam but is now reopened. Nánníng is an oft-ignored transit point for travellers moving on to Vietnam; you can even arrange a Vietnam visa here.

Despite the region's rich patchwork of 30 minorities, the only colourful minorities you're likely to pick out in the city crowd are the occasional Miao and Dong people selling silver bracelets and earrings on the pedestrian overpasses near the train station.

Orientation

Nánníng's streets require only a few blocks to work out. In the north are the bus and train stations. The main artery, Chaoyang Lu, runs roughly north-south towards Yōng Jiāng, which bisects the city. Halfway down Chaoyang Lu is Cháoyáng Garden, a good place for people watching and for bus connections to scenic sights.

Maps Nánníng city maps are available in the train and bus stations.

Information

Money The main Bank of China on Minzu Dadao, open from 8am to 6pm daily, changes travellers cheques.

Post & Communications Opposite the main Bank of China is the main post office. You can make international telephone calls

Heading West?

Westerners trying to travel between Guìlín and Kūnmíng soon discover what locals have long since known: everyone else is trying to get there too. In early 1998 the Chinese government finally drove the last spike into its pet project – the Nánkūn Railway, linking Kūnmíng with Nánníng and offering a crucial alternative transportation route between Guǎngxī, Guizhōu, and Yúnnán.

This extraordinary project may seem tame when compared with the schematics of the Three Gorges Dam; nevertheless, it's another perfect representation of the New China 'can-do' spirit. The government poured over 20 billion *yuán* into the project, with a small army of workers toiling away non-stop for over seven years. The resulting all-electric railroad sports all the features they could cram in, including modern sensors built into the track to judge conditions and make adjustments.

Engineers had a field day with the geography; nearly one-third of the route is bridge or tunnel. The train passes through a rough jumble of around 900km of mountain ranges and steep valleys but, thanks to the designers, manages to bypass scenic waterfalls and other natural sights.

The government had a secondary motive for the railroad, which roars through some of the most 'backward' areas in China; already officials have touted that fresh fruit and vegetables are now available year-round in previously isolated villages. The government is also counting on tourism and, more particularly, mining, to boom in the region.

What really concerns most travellers, however, is one other highlight of the train: at the time of writing, hard sleeper tickets were relatively easy to procure, even for next-day travel.

and send faxes from here; it's open from 8.30am to 11pm daily. There's also an Internet cafe on the 2nd floor.

China Telecom's Internet cafe, on the 5th level of the Nanning Department Store, is also a convenient place to surf the Web. Access is Y10 per hour.

Travel Agencies Located in China International Travel Service (CITS; Zhōngguó Guójì Lǚxíngshè; ☎ 280 4960) at 40 Xinmin

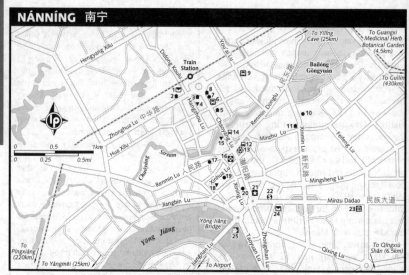

NÁNNÍNG

PLACES TO STAY	OTHER	16 Nanning Department
2 Tiědào Fàndiàn 铁道饭店	1 Post Office 邮局	Store; Internet Cafe 南宁百货大楼; 网吧
3 Yíngbīn Fàndiàn 迎宾饭店	6 Nanning Bus Station	17 Night Market Area 夜市
5 Nánfāng Dàjiǔdiàn 南方大酒店	南宁客运总站	19 Xinhua Bookshop 新华书店
8 Yínhé Dàjiǔdiàn 银河大酒店	7 CAAC 中国民航	20 Bicycle Hire 出租单车
11 Xiángyún Dàjiǔdiàn 翔云大酒店	9 Nanning Passenger Centre 南宁客运中心	21 PSB 公安局
	10 CITS (FIT) 中国国际旅行社	22 Main Bank of China 中国银行
PLACES TO EAT	12 Cháoyáng Garden Bus Stop	23 Guangxi Provincial Museum
4 Fruit Market; Restaurants 杭州路水果市场和餐厅	朝阳花园	广西省博物馆
15 Canine Cuisine District 狗肉区	13 Cháoyáng Garden 朝阳花园	24 Main Post Office 电信大楼
18 Muslim Restaurant 清真饭店	14 Bus to Yángměi	25 Ferry Dock 南宁客运码头

Lu, the Family and Individual Traveller (FIT) department on the 2nd level is open from 8.30am to noon and 2.30pm to 5pm weekdays and is worth a visit.

The English-speaking staff is friendly and can help you get your hands on a one-month Vietnam visa (Y650), although it takes 10 days to process. FIT also offers five-day individual or group tours to Hanoi and Haiphong, and a nine-day tour that takes in Saigon as well.

Bookshops Xinhua Bookshop on Xinhua Lu is one of the largest in China, with four levels jam-packed with books.

PSB The Foreign Affairs office of the Public Security Bureau (PSB; Gōngānjú; ☎ 280 4530) is to the left of the entrance of the main PSB building, at the intersection of Chaoyang Lu and Minzu Dadao. It's open from 8am to noon and 2.30pm to 5pm Monday to Thursday, and 8am to noon Friday.

Guangxi Provincial Museum
Guǎngxī Shěng Bówùguǎn 广西省博物馆
This museum (Minzu Dadao; admission Y3; open 8.30am-noon & 3pm-10.30pm daily) offers a peaceful browse through 50,000 years of Guǎngxī history. There are minority costumes and artefacts, including the world's largest bronze drum collection (although not much is actually displayed). In the tree-filled rear garden sit several full-size examples of Dong and Miao houses and a nail-less bridge. Catch bus No 6 from the train station.

Báilóng Gōngyuán 白龙公园
White Dragon Park
Also known as Rénmín Gōngyuán (admission Y3; open until 10.30pm daily), this park is a pleasant place for a stroll, with a lake, pagodas, botanical gardens, a restaurant and boat hire. Close to the main entrance on Xinmin Lu, a long flight of stairs leads to the remains of a fort, which gives a decent view of the city.

Qīngxiù Shān Scenic Area
This largish 'scenic area' is full of lakes, ponds, pavilions, cable cars, viewing platforms and tour groups. A favourite summer retreat since the Sui and Tang dynasties, the park offers verdant woods, springs and landscaped gardens with modest but scenic peaks of up to 180m that can easily be scaled.

Local bus No 10 heads to the park, but you still have a fair walk to the entrance. Tour buses to the park also depart when full from the northern side of Cháoyáng Garden. They charge Y3 to the front gate or Y11 into the park including admission.

Guangxi Medicinal Herb Botanical Garden 广西药用植物园
Guǎngxī Yàoyòng Zhíwùyuán
Far on the eastern outskirts of town, this fascinating garden (admission Y5) is the largest of its kind in China, with over 2400 species of medicinal plants and more being planted all the time (Guǎngxī alone has 5000 species). The gardens will be especially impressive if you can read Chinese or are lucky enough to tag along with one of the centre's few English speakers. It takes about 30 minutes to get there on bus No 101 or 102 from Cháoyáng Garden.

Dragon Boat Races
Popular throughout this region, Nánníng has dragon boat races on the fifth day of the fifth lunar month (sometime in June), when large numbers of sightseers cheer the decorated rowing vessels along Yōng Jiāng.

Organised Tours
Boats depart at 9.30am (and occasionally at 9.30pm) from a pier off Linjiang Lu, south of the Yōng Jiāng bridge, for two-hour river tours (Y30). The pier is the head of a lovely riverside footpath with teahouses and an excellent 500m-long mural depicting Guǎngxī's history and attractions.

Places to Stay – Budget
Nánníng is getting expensive. While most hotels are pricing themselves out of the backpacker market, there are still a few cheap though noisy picks around the train station.

Tiědaò Fàndiàn (Railway Hotel; ☎ 243 8600, fax 242 2572, 84 Zhonghua Lu) Bed in dorms/doubles Y25/45. This well-run, friendly guesthouse is the top choice in Nánníng. Doubles are spiffy with private bathrooms.

Yíngbīn Fàndiàn (☎ 241 2299 ext 3688) Dorm beds/singles Y18/80, doubles Y28-80. This is probably the cheapest guesthouse open to foreigners in Nánníng. You won't find an English sign and from the outside this place appears rather shabby, but it's clean and friendly all the same. The Y80 singles or doubles are good value and worth the splurge.

Places to Stay – Mid-Range & Top End
Nánfāng Dàjiǔdiàn (☎ 243 1662, e nanfang @nn.col.com.cn) Discounted twins Y138-252, doubles Y254. Rooms here are often discounted by 50%. The luxury twins are comfortable and a better value than the doubles.

Yínhé Dàjiǔdiàn (Milky Way Hotel; ☎ 243 8223 ext 4001, fax 242 0303) Doubles with air-con & bath Y140-150. This hotel has comfortable rooms that are often offered at 50% discounts (yōuhuì).

Xiángyún Dàjiǔdiàn (☎ 210 1999) Singles/twins Y320/380. Less conveniently located, this three-star hotel offers 50% discounts outside summer months.

Places to Eat

Nánníng, like Guìlín and Liǔzhōu, is famous for its dog hotpot (gǒuròu huǒguō). The **Canine Cuisine District**, south of the Cháoyáng Stream along Chaoyang Lu, is teeming in the evenings with roadside stalls.

Zhongshan Lu, at the southern end of the city centre, is the most raucous street for other-than-dog **food stalls**. A variety of tasty local snacks are served up, including juàntǒngfěn (steamed noodle pancake wrap with pork and coriander filling served in steaming broth), lǎoyǒumiàn and lǎoyǒufěn (literally 'old friend' wheat or rice noodles).

Muslim Restaurant (Qīngzhēn Fàndiàn) This place has excellent food, cheap beer, friendly staff and a limited English menu.

Nánníng also specialises in **fast food** like nowhere else in China; there are literally hundreds of restaurants incorporating 'fast' into their name, however the menus are inevitably in Chinese only. There's also a lively row of **restaurants** offering a variety of dishes on the northern end of Hangzhou Lu. This is also where you'll find a **fruit market**, where you can choose from a delicious variety of fruit year-round.

For self-caters, there is a good **supermarket** in the basement of the Nanning Department Store.

Getting There & Away

Air Domestic airlines fly daily to Guǎngzhōu (Y670), Shànghǎi (Y1480), Shēnzhèn (Y710), Kūnmíng (Y580) and Běijīng (Y1790). There are also less frequent flights to Chéngdū (Y820), Chóngqìng (Y700), Guìyáng (Y570), Hǎikǒu (Y560), Wǔhàn (Y1000) and Zhūhǎi (Y740).

International flights include Hong Kong (Tuesday, Friday and Sunday, Y1880) and Hanoi (Hénèi; Monday and Thursday, Y890).

Civil Aviation Administration of China (CAAC; Zhōngguó Mínháng; ☎ 243 1459) at 82 Chaoyang Lu is generally efficient. It may be worth asking some travel agencies as they often sell discounted tickets.

Bus Nánníng has two central bus stations, the Nanning Bus Station (Nánníng Kèyùn Zǒngzhàn) and the Nanning Passenger Centre (Nánníng Kèyùn Zhōngxīn). The bus station should satisfy most travellers; the passenger centre mostly serves regional destinations. Like the rest of the province's bus stations, a left luggage service is available.

Since the advent of highway construction in Guǎngxī, once bumpy rides have been replaced by a growing number of smooth, express bus services (kuàibānchē). These new luxury express buses are equipped with reclining seats, air-con and attendants.

Frequent express buses depart from the Nanning Bus Station to: Bǎisè (Y45, three hours), Běihǎi (Y50, three hours), Guǎngzhōu (Y180, 10 hours), Guìlín (Y80, 4½ hours), Guìpíng (Y40, four hours), Liǔzhōu (Y50, three hours) and Wúzhōu (Y80, six hours). There are still one or two regular snail buses prowling these routes for less, but they are now few and far between.

If you want to head south-west to Píngxiáng (Y60, 4½ hours), then you should consider the infinitely more convenient morning train. Heading towards Détiān Waterfall (on the Vietnam border) and environs, buses leave for Jìngxī at 7.50am (Y50, seven hours), and there is a direct bus to Détiān Waterfall at 8.30am (Y50, four hours).

If the Nanning Bus Station doesn't have the route you're looking for, wander a giant block east of the train station to the round-the-clock Nanning Passenger Centre. It has zillions of departures to mostly regional destinations, and also provides a few long-distance services to places such as Guìzhōu.

Train Since the advent of express buses, the train is most useful for longer hauls. Major destinations with direct rail links with Nánníng include the following:

destination	train no	departure	duration
Běijīng	T6	11.02am	32 hours
Chéngdū	K142	6.57pm	39 hours
Guǎngzhōu	L240	2.12pm	18 hours
Kūnmíng	2005	3.40pm	16 hours
Shànghǎi	1380	5.52pm	36 hours
Xī'ān	1316	7.05am	38 hours

The T6 bound for Běijīng also passes through Liǔzhōu (four hours), Guìlín (six hours), Wǔhàn (18 hours), Zhèngzhōu (24 hours) and Shíjiāzhuāng (27½ hours). The K142 to Chéngdū passes through Guìyáng (19 hours) and Chóngqìng (29 hours).

The T905/M2 from Nánníng to Dong Dang (Tóngdēng) departs at 8.20pm, but think twice before hopping on. It takes forever with lengthy delays in Píngxiáng and at customs.

Getting next-day tickets at the train station doesn't seem to be too problematic. Foreigners can use window 15; window 16 is the place to go to change tickets.

Getting Around
To/From the Airport The most efficient way to reach the airport is by CAAC buses (Y15, 40 minutes), which depart regularly from the CAAC office on Chaoyang Lu.

Local Transport You can hire bicycles at the southern end of Chaoyang Lue from 7am to 11pm for Y0.6 per hour.

There are an abundance of taxis plying the streets as well as motorcycle taxis. Taxi rides usually start at Y10; motorcycle taxis are around Y5.

Buses generally run from 6am to around 11pm and fares start at Y0.7.

AROUND NÁNNÍNG
Yángměi
This beautifully preserved 17th-century town on Lōng Jiāng (26km west of Nánníng) has become a popular day trip from Nánníng for Chinese tourists. While many of the buildings have their history posted outside, it's generally in Chinese. Guides will offer their services upon arrival and you may be lucky to find someone who speaks some English.

The best way to get around the town is to hire an ox-cart for the half-day (Y10).

From Nánníng, boats depart from the wharf near the Yōng Jiāng bridge every Saturday and Sunday at 8.30am and return from Yángměi around 6pm (Y80).

Yílǐng Cave 伊岭岩
Yílǐng Yán
Twenty-five kilometres north of Nánníng, Yílǐng Cave (admission Y25) is a bit of a tourist trap, but fun all the same with stalagmites and galactic lights. About 15 minutes is enough for the caves themselves, but the surrounding countryside is also worth exploring.

Buses for Yílǐng Cave depart from the Nanning Passenger Centre; express buses depart from inside the main gates (Y6). Minibuses run from Cháoyáng Garden on most weekends (especially during summer). The daily Nánníng to Dàmíng Shān bus also passes by the caves at around 4pm (Y8, 1½ hours).

North of Yílǐng Cave is **Língshuǐ Springs**, essentially a large mineral outdoor swimming pool. To reach the springs, continue on the bus past Yílǐng to Wǔmíng, and catch a motorcycle taxi (Y3) the remaining few kilometres.

Dàmíng Shān 大明山
Some 90km north-east of Nánníng is Dàmíng Shān (admission Y8), an impressive mountain with an average elevation of over 1200m. With more than 1700 species of plants, the mountain is a provincially protected zone. The majority of the scenic spots are accessible within a day's hike, however most visitors organise a guide to show them around as paths are poorly marked.

Daming Shan Resort (Dàmíng Shān Dùjiàcūn; ☎ 986 0902) Dorm beds/twins with bath Y25/100. Here you'll find log cabins, a restaurant and a couple of inns for accommodation. Prices are reasonable, but vary depending on the season. Out of season, it's best to ring ahead so they can make appropriate arrangements.

Línyè Zhāodàisuǒ Beds Y15. The Forestry Bureau also has this place with very basic dorm beds.

Coming from Nánníng's Cháoyáng Garden, there is one daily public bus (Y14, 3.10pm) that terminates at **Dàmíngshān**, the small forestry town at the base of the mountain. This is where you'll find the ticket office, accommodation and a small shop. It is, however, another 27km from here to the top (and Daming Shan Resort) and the bus will only continue up if there are enough paying passengers.

If you don't want to walk, consider hopping off 5km earlier in **Léijiāng**, where you can arrange a motorbike (Y50) to take you up to the top early the next day. In Léijiāng, accommodation can be found at the ***Dàmíng Shān Lǚshè***. You can also reach Léijiāng on any Dàhuà, Mǎshān or Liǎngjiāng bound buses from Wǔmíng or Nánníng.

A bus returns to Nánníng from Dàmíng Shān daily at 7.30am with a second service at 2.30pm on weekends.

Lónghǔ Shān 龙虎山

Closer to Nánníng (about 65km west), with both waterfalls and a mountain, Lónghǔ Shān Reserve covers an area of 1000 hectares and is home to more than 1200 plant species and 200 animal species, including about 3000 wild monkeys.

Despite a lack of direct public transport, you can hop on a bus to the small village of Pīngshān just west of the reserve, and arrange local transport from there. Otherwise, from late spring to late summer, tours (Y45) depart from Nánníng's Cháoyáng Garden on weekends at 8.30am, returning around 4.30pm.

ZUǑ JIĀNG SCENIC AREA
Zuǒjiāng Fēngjǐngqū 左江风景区

A boat trip down Zuǒ Jiāng to an area around 190km south-west of Nánníng will take you through karst rock formations and past minority rock paintings.

Of the 80 or so groups of rock paintings here, the largest is in the area of **Huā Shān Bìhuà** *(Flower Mountain; admission Y12),* about 3 hours farther south by boat. Here a fresco 170m high and 90m across depicts some 2000 figures of hunters, farmers and animals. It is now believed that the Luoyue, ancestors of the Zhuang minority, painted these cliffs around 2000 years ago.

Halfway to the site is the cheerful village of **Pānlóng** and the rough, explorable **Lóngruì Nature Reserve** *(Lóngruì Zìrán Bǎohùqū; admission Y6).* The reserve is the only known home of the rare white leaf monkey *(báitóu yèhóu).*

Hua Shan Ethnic Culture Village *(Huā Shān Mínzú Shānzhài Dùjiàcūn;* ☎ *862 8195)* Rooms from Y120. Meals Y25. Behind Pānlóng village, this low-key tourist resort offers decent rooms in Dong-style wooden cabins. A restaurant here serves traditional fare. The resort can also arrange guides for the nearby reserve.

To reach Zuǒ Jiāng Scenic Area, catch a morning Pínxiáng train from Nánníng as far as Nínmíng. Tour operators in Nínmíng are found along the main road, straight out of the train station. They offer Y80 boat tours for one or two people, and Y100 for three or four. Add Y50 if you want to stop overnight in Pānlóng.

If you are pressed for time or dislike puttering boats, a new road runs along the river

from Nínmíng to Pānlóng. A ride in a taxi takes about 20 minutes (Y30).

There are frequent buses connecting Nínmíng with Pínxiáng and Nánníng. You could do the whole trip in one *extremely* long day, minus any exploration of the Lóngruì Nature Reserve.

In Nínmíng, accommodation is available next to the train station at the budget *Tiělù Zhāodàisuǒ* or at the nicer *Huāshān Bīnguǎn*.

PÍNGXIÁNG 凭祥
☎ 0771 • pop 100,000

The staging post for onward transport to Vietnam, Pínxiáng is a trading town rife with bustling markets but there is not much else to see.

Yínxīng Bīnguǎn Twins Y20-45. If you're looking for accommodation, this is the cheapest option in town, located inside the bus station. A slightly more comfortable choice is *Xīnníng Bīnguǎn*, behind the bus station.

There is, however, no real need to stay in Pínxiáng. By early morning bus or train from Nánníng, you'll reach Pínxiáng around midday, from where you should be able to find transport to the Friendship Pass (Yǒuyì Guān) on the Vietnamese border. Minibuses and private vehicles run from near the bus and train stations and cost Y5 to Y20, depending on the number of passengers. From the Friendship Pass it's another 600m to the Vietnamese border post. Onward transport to Hanoi by train or bus is via the Vietnamese town of Lang Son (Liàngshān), 18km from the Friendship Pass. Remember that Vietnam is one hour behind China.

If you're heading into China, catch one of the minibuses into Pínxiáng on the Chinese side of the border, from where you can catch a bus or train to Nánníng.

There are heaps of banks in Pínxiáng, so changing money is no problem.

DÉTIĀN WATERFALL
Détiān Pùbù 德天瀑布

Located at the 53rd boundary marker between China and Vietnam, the Chinese have the earth-shaking majority of Détiān Waterfall *(admission Y30).* The cascade drops only 40m, but makes up for it by a more than modest breadth. July is the best time to visit, although water levels will be fairly high from May through late September. Show up in November or December and be thoroughly underwhelmed. While wandering around, be particularly careful that you don't accidentally cross the border into Vietnam or you may find yourself on a lengthy tour of a prison in one country or the other.

Places to Stay & Eat

Just behind the ticket office is a new *guesthouse* and *restaurant* with a fantastic view. If you want to stay here, ensure to book with their Nánníng (☎ 362 7088) or Dàxīn (☎ 262 4540) office for a discounted rate. If you just turn up at the door, twins/quads cost Y450/680.

Troubled Waters

Uneasy neighbours, China and Vietnam have been at odds, if not actually skirmishing, for over 2100 years. Han dynasty armies conquered the first Vietnamese patriot, Tire Da, in the 2nd century BC, making Vietnam one of many countries devoured by China as it tried to expand its commercial influence. This had a significant cultural and social impact on Vietnam: the introduction of a patriarchal Confucian social and governmental system was a double-edged sword. It made Vietnamese elites more inclined to tolerate Chinese rule, but also gave the Vietnamese the framework to encourage revolt. After dozens of attempts, Vietnam eventually threw off the yoke of imperialism in the 10th century AD.

After WWII, Western forces sent a 200,000-strong force of Chinese Nationalists to northern Vietnam to demobilise Japanese troops. The two nations have regularly been at war ever since, apart from when China supported Vietnam during the (American) Vietnam War.

In 1979, open war broke out after years of sporadic skirmishes. The Chinese were propelled to cross the border for several reasons. In 1978 the Vietnamese had rebuffed China and signed a treaty with (and accepted military and monetary support from) the Soviet Union – another border country with a Chinese love-hate relationship. Vietnam had also invaded Cambodia to topple the Khmer Rouge. Finally, and most importantly, Vietnam had seized the assets of and deported (or forced out) up to 250,000 huáqiáo (overseas Chinese), most of them to the Chinese provinces of Yúnnán and Guǎngxī.

The Chinese say Vietnamese forces crossed the border first, necessitating their own incursion. The Vietnamese of course deny this (most Western sources back their version). Over 16 days, scores of people were killed and five provincial border towns in Vietnam were heavily damaged. Bizarrely, both sides claimed to have won this battle.

It didn't end there, though. The border was sealed and major battles erupted again in 1984 in Láoshān, Zheyoushan, and Balihedong in Yúnnán and along much of Guǎngxī's border. This time the Vietnamese used up to 10 expanded divisions to attack Chinese border forces. They shelled the Chinese with around 10,000 rounds per day and, while they didn't seize any land in this conflict, they did inflict a humiliating lesson on China. It's not uncommon to meet China's own Vietnam veterans when travelling around the south-west provinces.

Things have long since cooled down; border points at Hékǒu in Yúnnán and the Friendship Pass in Píngxiáng, Guǎngxī, hardly show any lingering effects, and the only disagreements for a decade have been between haggling Vietnamese and Chinese traders. All is not exactly cosy, however. In 1997 Vietnam took its protests over China's selling of oil exploration rights in its waters to Asean (which sided with Vietnam), and in January 1998 the Vietnamese daily newspapers ran front-page banner headlines screaming about major Chinese border transgressions. The focal point was a 1km-long river embankment in Guǎngxī, which the Vietnamese said the Chinese had deliberately built 10m into Vietnamese territory and which now floods the Vietnamese side of the river.

The Chinese initially laughed off the accusations. Then, to everyone's surprise, made a concession, agreeing to clear landmines from 10 sq km (at a cost of US$10 million) in Vietnam as a goodwill gesture. Cynics argue China did this as much to facilitate further trade – which had quadrupled from 1992 to 1997 along the border – as to encourage friendly relations. As of May 1998, Chinese troops had cleared three sq km by removing 21,600 mines. Soon after, with hopes to further stabilise relations, Běijīng greeted the first high-level contingent of Vietnamese to visit since 1990. Later that year, historic sites in Dongxing (Guǎngxī) dating Sino-Viet ties to the 19th century were restored and opened to the public. Perhaps most symbolic: in mid-1999, direct postal links – which had previously gone through Singapore – were finally restored through Guǎngxī.

Détiān Bīnguǎn Back towards Shuòlóng, prices at this very average hotel are the same, despite its lack of character or views.

If you get stuck in Shuòlóng, there are a few grubby *guesthouses* at the main intersection.

Getting There & Away

From Nánníng or Píngxiáng, first head to Dàxīn. From Dàxīn, hop on a bus heading to Xiàléi and get off in Shuòlóng (Y8, 1½ hours). In Shuòlóng, you can catch a rattletrap minibus or motorbike taxi for the final 14km (Y2).

When you leave the falls, walk 10 minutes down to the main road towards Shuòlóng. Morning buses leave from a little cluster of stands there. Be forewarned: there isn't much movement after 5pm. From Shuòlóng, buses are hit and miss although semi-regular service is found towards Dàxīn and Nánníng.

If you're heading for Jìngxī, the best thing to do is leapfrog villages. First take a Y2 minibus to Xiàléi in the north-west, and then another Y2 minibus to Húrùn (pronounced Fúyuàn), from where you can get a 'proper' bus for the hour-long ride to Jìngxī. All up, the trip should take around two to three hours.

Jìngxī is a friendly town and home to the Jiuzhou Pagoda and a few cheap places to stay. From Jìngxī, take one of many buses to Baìsè, the largest city in north-west Guǎngxī. The interesting **Baise Uprising Museum** *(Yuèdōng Huìguǎn)* traces every movement of Deng Xiaoping and the Seventh Red Army during the 1920s and 1930s. Baìsè is also home to one of south-west China's largest man-made lakes. From Baìsè it's easy to head into Guìzhōu or Yúnnán via Xīngyì.

BĚIHǍI 北海

☎ 0779 • pop 560,000

This friendly, tree-lined port community, 229km south of Nánníng, is best-known for its ferry to Hǎinán Dǎo and its famous Silver Beach. More than 2000 years old, Běihǎi's harbour area is lined with eye-catching historical architecture. The city was once a major node on the ancient Marine Silk Route and flourished under the Han dynasty. Pearl production later cemented its reputation. Today, the city is home to thousands of Chinese-Vietnamese refugees who landed here after the 1979 Sino-Viet conflict.

Orientation

The northern coast of Běihǎi is home to the bus terminal, most of the population, shops and budget lodging options. The southern strip has the new International Ferry Terminal, a couple of upmarket hotels and that famous stretch of white sand.

Silver Beach

Silver Beach *(Yíntān; admission Y25)*, about 10km south-east of Běihǎi city, has 1.6km of sparkling white sands and fairly clean water. The beach is also home to some of the oddest resort villas you're likely to see in China – Swiss chalets, German castles and the obligatory concrete hulk hotels.

To get there from Běihǎi, walk west from the bus station, bear right at Woping Lu, which branches off behind the Běihǎi Yíngbīnguǎn, and catch bus No 3 at the corner of Jiefang Lu (Y2, 20 minutes). Just behind Silver Beach are a large number of reasonably cheap and simple restaurants and hotels.

Places to Stay

In Town Běihǎi has a few touts hanging about the bus terminal. Most hotels seem amenable to foreign friends; expect to pay as little as Y40 for a double at the more pungent options.

Táoyuán Dàjiǔdiàn (☎ 202 0919) Doubles with air-con Y70. This great mid-range hotel is across the street from the bus station and down a small alley. Rooms are reasonably clean and have 24-hour hot water. Cheaper twins and triples are also available, and there's a good restaurant. Rates include breakfast.

Běihǎi Yíngbīnguǎn (☎ 202 3511) Doubles from Y100. This hotel has clean, quiet rooms and friendly staff.

Shangri-la Hotel (☎ 206 2288, **w** www .shangri-la.com) Doubles Y960. Běihǎi's most luxurious abode, this hotel is oddly located in the northern more dilapidated part of town. Rates are usually heavily discounted.

At the Beach There are a couple of good accommodation choices available close to the beach.

Yíntān Zhāodàisuǒ Dorm beds Y25. If you're wanting to stay at the beach, this is one of a number of hotels available. Rooms here are relatively clean with common showers.

Beach Hotel (*Hǎitān Bīnguǎn;* ☎ 388 8888, e *bhht@bh.gx.cninfo.net*) Doubles Y630. This is a good mid-range option on the beach. Rooms are comfy and offered at almost half price outside of summer.

Places to Eat

Jìnxìng Fàndiàn A five-minute walk west of the bus station (look for the white sign with red letters) this restaurant has some outdoor seating and fantastic *dānghuā rìbén dòufu* (sweet-and-sour beancurd) and *hóngshāo dòufu* (braised beancurd).

Èrgēlǎojī Fàndiàn Around the corner from the bus station, this popular and often rowdy place specialises in *huǒguō* (hotpot), *tángcù páigǔ* (sweet & sour pork ribs) and *bǎisǐjī*, a free-range chicken dish also referred to as *tǔjībǎn*.

Opposite here is a good *market* that has a row of stalls and tents serving local snacks and lots of fresh produce.

Just west of the post office on Woping Lu, is a good little *tea house* serving beverages and small snacks. You'll also find clusters of nondescript *eateries* and *noodle shops* around the bus station.

In the northern section of Yunnan Lu, close to the wharf, is Běihǎi's large *seafood market*. This is the place to come to if you feel the need to stock up on dried squid or any other such delicacies. Bus Nos 2 and 8 pass by the market from in front of the bus station.

Getting There & Away

There is a helpful ticket office (☎ 202 8618) open 8am to 10pm on the ground floor of the Shangri-la Hotel, selling boat, bus, train and plane tickets, and many other travel agencies around town.

Air Major connections with Běihǎi include daily flights to: Běijīng (Y1800), Guǎngzhōu (Y630), Guìyáng (Y730), Hǎikǒu (Y350) and Guìlín (Y480). CAAC buses (Y10, 30 minutes) meet arriving planes and depart two hours before departures from the CAAC building (☎ 305 1899), located in the Mínháng Dàshà building on Beibuwan Xilu.

Bus Express buses connect Běihǎi with Dōngxīng (Y35, three hours), Guǎngzhōu (Y180, 9½ hours), Guìlín (Y150), Liǔzhōu (Y110) and Nánníng (Y50, three hours).

Train Since the completion of the expressway to Nánníng it's much easier to take the bus rather than a train. Nevertheless, train No K140 departs Běihǎi for Chéngdū (hard sleeper Y227, 43 hours), via Nánníng, Guìyáng and Chóngqìng.

Boat Despite its name, the International Ferry Terminal (Guójì Kèyùn Mǎtou) has yet to offer any international departures. Services include Hǎikǒu on Hǎinán Dǎo and the nearby island of Wéizhōu. Boats for the 11 hour journey to Hǎikǒu leave twice daily (7.30am and 6pm) on even days and once only on odd days. Tickets cost from Y100 for a seat to Y250 for a cabin.

Getting Around

To/From the Airport Comfortable buses meet planes at the airport, 21km north of town (Y10, 30 minutes). A taxi should cost about Y50.

Bus Most of Běihǎi's buses congregate on Jiefang Lu north of Zhōngshān Gōngyuán. Here you can catch bus No 3 to Silver Beach and No 2 bus west to the ferry docks and seafood market. Local buses cost Y2.

Motorcycle Taxi A cheap way to get around town in a hurry is by motorcycle taxis. For Y6 you can get to Silver Beach from the town centre.

GUÌPÍNG 桂平
☎ 0775

Midway between Nánníng and Wúzhōu, Guìpíng is known for its gorgeous mountains and famed Xī Shān tea. Most tourists are lured to this friendly town however by **Xī Shān Park** (*admission Y11-31; open 8am-5pm daily*), with a modest mountain climb of 880m.

Only 20km north-west of town is the relatively new **Dragon Pool National Forest & Park** (*Lóngtán Guójiā Sēnlín Gōngyuán*), which gives you the opportunity to delve into rustic wilderness and Guǎngxī's only remaining old-growth forest. Accommodation is available here for about Y25 per night.

Unfortunately, direct transportation to Dragon Pool Park doesn't exist. From Guìpíng, hop on the bus to Jīntiáncūn (Y2) and ask the driver to drop you off at the Dragon Pool Park access road (Lóngtán Lùkǒu). There are usually motorbike taxis waiting at the intersection that will take you to the park for about Y20. It is also possible to organise a tour to the park with the Forestry Department's travel agency, Lǚyóu Liánluòchù (☎ 338 0413), located inside the Forestry building in Guìpíng. A two-day trip including guide, food, transport and accommodation is about Y180.

Just 25km north of Guìpíng is **Jīntiáncūn**, the birthplace of Hong Xiuquan. Hong was a schoolteacher who declared himself a brother of Jesus Christ and eventually led an army of over a million followers against the Qing dynasty in what came to be known as the Taiping Rebellion, one of the bloodiest civil wars in human history. A museum, **Qǐyì Jìniànguǎn** (admission Y3) now stands at the site of Hong's home.

To reach Jīntiáncūn from Guìpíng, take a green bus (Y2, 40 minutes) from inside the bus terminal gates. Backtrack 500m from the bus drop off in Jīntiáncūn to the motorcycle taxis, from where the museum is a farther 4km. The last bus back to Guìpíng departs Jīntiáncūn around 6pm.

Places to Stay
Guìpíng Fàndiàn (☎ 338 2775, fax 338 3919) Beds in 4-bed dorms/singles Y20/45, superior doubles Y250. This enormous hotel is the only accommodation in Guìpíng that's open to foreigners. There is a mind-boggling array of Spartan but pleasant rooms. You'll find the hotel south of the square on Renmin Zhonglu.

Gōngdé Shānzhuāng (☎ 339 3399, fax 339 3618) Doubles Y298. It's also possible to stay at Xī Shān – much more peaceful than in town but also much more pricey. Posh rooms at this hotel are usually offered for a 20% discount, with impeccable service. There are also a few basic inns but they're not officially allowed to accept foreigners.

Getting There & Away
From Guìpíng, express buses leave for Nánníng every three hours (Y50). There are four express buses to Wúzhōu (Y30, three hours) and one daily to Guǎngzhōu at 1pm

(Y90, six hours). If you want to get to Guìlín or Liǔzhōu, head to Guìgǎng (Y12) and change there.

WÚZHŌU 梧州
☎ 0774 • pop 330,000
For most travellers, Wúzhōu is a pit stop on the road between Yángshuò and Guǎngzhōu or Hong Kong. Although it's not one of Guǎngxī's major attractions, Wúzhōu has some pleasant parks and street life.

Wúzhōu was an important trading town in the 18th century. In 1897 the British arrived, setting up steamer services to Guǎngzhōu, Hong Kong and later Nánníng. A British consulate was established, and the town became the launching pad for British and US missionaries for the conversion of the 'heathen' Chinese.

The period after 1949 saw a growth in the city's industrial development but, sadly, Wúzhōu fared badly during the Cultural Revolution.

Today, Wúzhōu has some fine street markets (absolutely everywhere you walk, in fact). Situated at the confluence of Guì Jiāng and Xún Jiāng, the city is effectively divided in two, with the modern and developed Héxī west of the river and the more interesting Dōnghé on the east bank. Wúzhōu is also home to one of Guǎngxī's more unusual sights: the Snake Repository.

Information
The post office and telephone office are on Nanhuan Lu, east of the bridge. Next door and hidden behind is an Internet cafe. The main Bank of China is just to the east of here, on the corner of Zhongshan Lu. Good maps of the city with bus routes are available at the shops inside both bus stations.

Snake Repository 蛇园
Shéyuán
Wúzhōu has what it claims is the world's largest snake repository (admission with/without guide Y10/5; open 8am-6pm daily), a major drawcard for overseas Chinese tourists and a sight that pulls in the occasional Western traveller. More than one million snakes are transported each year to Wúzhōu for export to the kitchens of Hong Kong, Macau and other snake-devouring parts of the world. To get there walk along Shigu Lu for about 2km from the Wúzhōu

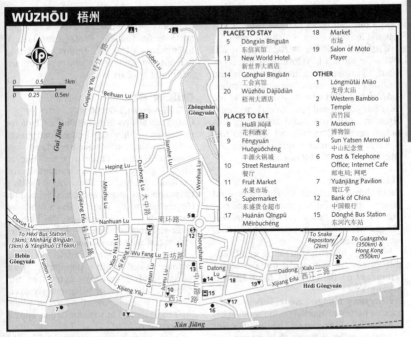

WÚZHŌU 梧州

PLACES TO STAY
5 Dōngxin Bīnguǎn
   东信宾馆
13 New World Hotel
   新世界大酒店
14 Gōnghuì Bīnguǎn
   工会宾馆
20 Wúzhōu Dàjiǔdiàn
   梧州大酒店

PLACES TO EAT
8 Huálì Jiǔjiā
   花利酒家
9 Fēngyuán
   Huǒguōchéng
   丰源火锅城
10 Street Restaurant
   餐厅
11 Fruit Market
   水果市场
16 Supermarket
   东盛货仓超市
17 Huánán Qīngpǔ
   Měiròuchéng

18 Market
   市场
19 Salon of Moto
   Player

OTHER
1 Lóngmǔtài Miào
   龙母太庙
2 Western Bamboo
   Temple
   西竹园
3 Museum
   博物馆
4 Sun Yatsen Memorial
   中山纪念堂
6 Post & Telephone
   Office; Internet Cafe
   邮电局; 网吧
7 Yuānjiāng Pavilion
   鸳江亭
12 Bank of China
   中国银行
15 Dōnghé Bus Station
   东河汽车站

Dàjiǔdiàn. Snake and cat fights are sometimes staged for visiting groups of tourists – something you may wish to avoid.

Zhōngshān Gōngyuán 中山公园
Sun Yatsen Park
This park (admission Y1) is the site of China's earliest memorial hall (1928) for the founder of the Republic of China.

Western Bamboo Temple
Xīzhú Yuán 西竹园
Just north of town, bordering Zhōngshān Gōngyuán, Western Bamboo Temple is home to around 40 Buddhist nuns. Resting above the town, the temple is filled with character and worth a look.

The temple's *vegetarian restaurant*, usually open for lunch on weekends, is highly recommended. The restaurant doesn't keep regular hours, but it seems the earlier you get there, the better.

To reach the temple, continue straight up Wenhua Lu to the top end of Sun Yatsen Park. At the end on the left is a small path that follows a brick wall all the way around to the temple.

Lóngmǔtài Miào 龙母太庙
Dragon Mother Temple
Recently renovated, this temple (admission Y3) was originally constructed during the Northern Song dynasty to honour the dragon mother of a mythical female chieftain.

A good time to visit is during the temple's main festival, held on the seventh and eighth day of the fifth lunar month and the 15th of the eighth lunar month.

Places to Stay
Cheap options are somewhat scarce in Wúzhōu. The rates at official tourist hotels reflect the budgets of the city's steady flow of overseas Chinese and Hong Kong travellers. You may get lucky at one of the cheaper hostels, but don't count on it.

Gōnghuì Bīnguǎn Twins/doubles Y60/78. This hotel is the cheapest option.

Dōngxin Bīnguǎn (☎ 283 8888, fax 282 5461, 28 Wenhua Lu) Doubles/twins/suites Y186/203/350. This is the newest hotel in town. Prices appear permanently discounted by 50%.

New World Hotel (Xīnshìjiè Dàjiǔdiàn; ☎ 282 8222, fax 282 4895) Doubles Y388.

This is a good mid-range option. Rooms are a little old, but clean and are usually discounted to Y195.

Wúzhōu Dàjiǔdiàn (☎ 202 2193, fax 202 4905) Doubles Y118-260. Recently renovated, the rooms here are good value and comfortable. The pricier ones have a fridge.

Mínháng Bīnguǎn If you arrive at the Héxī bus station and have an early morning departure, then you could always try this budget option. Officially off limits to foreigners, they appear willing to bend the rules if you speak a bit of Chinese.

Places to Eat

Huálì Jiǔjiā is one of Wúzhōu's seafood palaces, specialising in game meats and raw fish. A similar fancy eatery is *Huánán Qīngpǔ Měiròuchéng*, offering goat, dog, hotpot and seafood.

For more local flavours at more affordable prices try the small, popular *street restaurant* on the corner of Juren Lu and Xijiang Yilu.

Fēngyuán Huǒguōchéng This is a very popular hotpot restaurant on the waterfront.

Salon of Moto Player This trendy cafe/restaurant offers Western-style cuisine.

For self-caterers, there is a large *supermarket* on the waterfront opposite the Dōnghé bus station. Otherwise there are plenty of *fresh produce markets* along the backstreets.

Getting There & Away

Wúzhōu has two bus stations, Dōnghé and the main bus station in Héxī. In general, buses heading east depart from Dōnghé and those heading west or north depart from Héxī bus station. If your bus is not departing from the station where you buy the ticket, your ticket will be stamped allowing you to hop on the free shuttle bus that runs between the two stations every 40 minutes. Bus No 2 also connects the stations (Y1.2, 20 minutes) or, if you're in a hurry, a taxi costs around Y20.

The most popular destination from Wúzhōu is Yángshuò. The trip takes a bumpy seven hours (Y70), and it's another 1½ hours to Guìlín (Y75). Buses leave from Héxī bus station at 8.40am, 12.30pm, 4.30pm and 11pm.

For Guǎngzhōu, a morning express bus departs at 10am (Y80, 5½ hours) and a

slower bus covers the route at night (Y45, 6½ hours). There are also express bus connections for Liǔzhōu (Y80, seven hours), Shēnzhèn (Y150, six hours, departing 8.30am and 4pm) and every two hours for Nánníng (Y80, six hours).

GUÌLÍN 桂林
☎ 0773 • pop 1,342,000

Guìlín has always been famous in China for its scenery. While rapid economic growth and a booming tourist trade have diminished some of Guìlín's charm it's still one of China's greener, more scenic cities. If you can handle the hectic traffic, most of Guìlín's limestone karst peaks and parks are a short bicycle ride away. There is also a wealth of restaurants – particularly of the outdoor point-and-choose variety – to experiment with, a few with English menus to boot.

Unfortunately, locals don't shy from cashing in on Guìlín's popularity. Most tourist sights levy heavy entry fees and many travellers tell of being grossly overcharged at restaurants throughout town. Near the train and bus stations, touts appear at every turn.

Guìlín prefecture was organised in 214 BC during the Qin dynasty and developed as a transport centre with the building of the Ling Canal, which linked the important Zhū Jiāng and Cháng Jiāng systems. Under the Ming it was a provincial capital, a status it retained until 1914 when the capital was transferred to Nánníng. During the 1930s and throughout WWII, Guìlín was a Communist stronghold with refugees swelling its population from about 100,000 to over one million.

Orientation

Most of Guìlín lies on the west bank of Lí Jiāng. The main artery is Zhongshan Lu, which runs roughly parallel to the river on its western side. At the southern end of this street (Zhongshan Nanlu) is Guìlín's train station. Zhongshan Zhonglu is a rapidly gentrifying stretch of tourist-class hotels, shops and expensive restaurants.

Closer to the centre of town, north-east of Róng Hú and Shān Hú, is Guìlín's new Central Square (Zhōngxīn Guǎngchǎng) and the main shopping and eating district. Farther along Zhongshan Beilu is the main commercial area of the city.

Heading east on Jiefang Donglu and crossing over Liberation Bridge, will bring you to large Qīxīng Gōngyuán, one of the town's chief attractions.

Maps There are a couple of reliable maps of Guìlín. *The Tourist Map of Guilin* (Y4) is a good one that includes a bit of English.

Information

Tourist Offices Several tourist booths can help you with directions and transport and may be able to assist you in booking accommodation or offering tour information (☎ 282 7491). Some staff speak a little English. The main booths are in front of the train station and inside the bus station. Most of the others are located at park entrances and are usually open only during summer.

CITS's FIT department (☎ 286 1623) at 41 Ronghu Beilu has friendly and reasonably helpful staff offering a range of tours including a half-day city tour (Y200) and a full-day Lí Jiāng tour (Y460). They also organise longer trips, but prefer larger groups.

Money The main branch of the Bank of China is on Shanhu Beilu. For changing money and travellers cheques, you can use the branches at the corner of Shanghai Lu and Zhongshan Nanlu – next to the train station – and at Zhongshan Nanlu, near Yinding Lu. Most tourist hotels also have foreign exchange services.

Post & Communications The main post and telephone office is on Zhongshan Beilu. There is a second post office on the north corner of the large square in front of the train station.

A 24-hour Internet cafe sits inside the southern entrance to the Xinhua Bookshop on Zhongshan Zhonglu (Y4 per hour). Another Internet cafe is opposite the main post office and is open from 9am to 10pm daily (Y3 per hour).

Bookshops Guìlín's Xinhua Bookshop, north along Zhongshan Beilu, has a foreign language section that carries a selection of English classics and photo-travel books on Guìlín.

PSB The PSB office (☎ 582 9930) is on the east side of Lí Jiāng, south off Longyin Lu,

and is open from 8.30am to noon and 3pm to 6pm Monday to Friday. They can help with visa extensions.

Solitary Beauty Peak 独秀峰
Dúxiù Fēng

This 152m pinnacle *(admission Y15)* is at the centre of the town. The climb to the top is steep, but offers good views of the town, Lí Jiāng and surrounding hills.

At the foot of the peak is the 14th century **Wáng Chéng**, a palace built by the nephew of a Ming emperor. The restored walls and gates of the palace surround the peak although the site is now occupied by Guangxi Normal University. It's also home to a theatre that holds nightly traditional, **minority performances** *(admission Y35)*, which start at 7.30pm.

You can reach the peak by Bus No 1, 2 or 11 from Guìlín's train station.

Fúbō Shān 伏波山
Wave-Subduing Hill

Close to Solitary Beauty Peak, Fúbō Shān *(admission Y10)* offers a fine view of the town. Just inside the gate, you can still see a rice pot left over from the temple – it's big enough to cook rice for 1000 people at a time.

On the southern slope of the hill is **Returned Pearl Cave** *(Huánzhū Dòng)*. A 1000-year-old Buddha image is etched into the wall somewhere in the cave, along with more than 200 other images of the Buddha, most dating from the Song and Tang dynasties. Somewhere, too, is a portrait and autograph by Mi Fu, a famous calligrapher of the Song dynasty.

Nearby is **Thousand Buddha Cave** *(Qiānfó Yán)*. The name's an exaggeration – there are a couple of dozen statues at most, dating from the Tang and Song dynasties.

There is a pleasant cafe inside the park, overlooking Lí Jiāng. Bus No 2 from the train station runs past the hill.

Other Hills
North of Solitary Beauty Peak is **Diécǎi Shān** *(Folded Brocade Hill; admission Y13)*. Climb the stone pathway that takes you through the cooling relief of Wind Cave, with walls decked with inscriptions and Buddhist sculptures. There are great views from the top of the hill, which can be skirted by taking Bus No 1 or 2.

GUÌLÍN

PLACES TO STAY
8　Jīnfēng Bīnguăn
　　锦丰宾馆
11　Universal Hotel
　　环球大酒店
12　Guilin International
　　Youth Hostel
　　桂林国际青年旅馆
20　Brave Hotel;
　　Dragonair
　　桂林宾馆
24　Golden Elephant
　　金象大酒店
26　Guìlín Fàndiàn
　　桂林饭店
27　Băilèmén Jiŭdiàn
　　百乐门酒店
28　Osmanthus Hotel
　　丹桂大酒店
30　Huali Hotel
　　华丽酒店
37　New City Hotel
　　新城市饭店
38　Nánxī Fàndiàn
　　南溪饭店
40　Overseas Chinese
　　Hotel
　　华侨大厦

PLACES TO EAT
4　Nikodo Plaza
　　微笑堂

6　Good Aunt; Bagui
　　Mansion
　　好大妈；八桂大厦
7　MFW
　　桂林人/旺角
9　MFW
　　桂林人/旺角
10　Chéngdū Xiăochī
　　成都小吃
13　Crescent Mansion
　　月乐楼
16　Coffee-Language
　　110
　　名典
19　Forest of Flowers
　　花之林茶坊
22　Tailian Hotel
　　台联酒店
25　Yíyuán Fàndiàn
　　怡园饭店
32　Dōngběi Fàndiàn; Měishí
　　Wénhuàchéng
　　东北饭店; 美食文化城
33　Shèngfā Fàndiàn
　　胜发饭店

OTHER
1　Main Post & Telephone
　　Office
　　中国电信
2　Internet Cafe
　　网吧

3　Wáng Chéng Palace
　　王城
5　South City Gate
　　南门
14　PSB (Visa Extensions)
　　市公安局出入境管理所
15　Tourist Wharf
　　漓江游览船码头
17　Main Bank of China
　　中国银行
18　Xinhua Bookshop;
　　Internet Cafe
　　新华书店；网吧
21　Guilin Children's
　　Palace
　　桂林少年宫
23　CITS (FIT)
　　中国国际旅行社
29　Main Bus Station
　　汽车总站
31　Bank of China
　　中国银行
34　CAAC
　　中国民航
35　Post Office
　　邮局
36　Tourist Information
　　旅游咨询服务中心
39　Bank of China
　　中国银行

From Fúbō Shān there's a good view of **Lăorén Shān** (*Old Man Hill*), a curiously shaped hill 2km to the north-west. The best way to get there is by bicycle, as buses don't go past it. At the southern end of town, one of Guìlín's best-known sights is **Xiàngbí Shān** (*Elephant Trunk Hill; admission Y15*), which actually does resemble an elephant dipping its snout into Lì Jiāng.

Qīxīng Gōngyuán 七星公园
Seven Star Park
One of China's nicer city parks, Qīxīng Gōngyuán (*admission Y30 summer, Y20-25 rest-of-year; open park 7am-9.30pm daily, caves 8am-5pm daily*) is on the eastern side of Lí Jiāng and covers 137 hectares. The park was one of the original tourist spots in south-west China, first opened to sightseers as far back as the Sui dynasty. It takes its name from its seven peaks, which are supposed to resemble the Ursa Major (Big Dipper) constellation.

Lots of trails wind in and around the hills and you can picnic on the sprawling lawns. Head up to **Round Viewing Pavilion** (*Kuàngguān Tíng*) to get your bearings and a view of the park.

To reach the park, walk across Liberation Bridge or catch bus No 9, 10 or 11 from the train station. From the park, bus No 13 runs across Liberation Bridge, past Fúbō Shān and across to Reed Flute Cave.

Reed Flute Cave 芦笛公园
Lúdí Yán
Some of the most extraordinary scenery Guìlín has to offer is underground at Reed Flute Cave (*admission Y40*), 5km north-west of the city centre. Here multicoloured lighting and fantastic stalactites and stalagmites resemble a set from *Journey to the Centre of the Earth*. At one time the entrance to the cave was distinguished by clumps of reeds used by the locals to make musical instruments, hence the name.

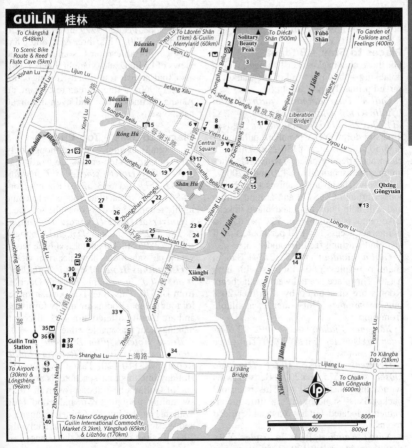

GUÌLÍN 桂林

Inside, the Crystal Palace of the Dragon King alone can comfortably hold about 1000 people, although many more crammed in during the war when the cave was used as an air-raid shelter.

Despite the high entrance price, the cave is worth visiting. Consider some of the other walks around the surrounding park, including ones up to **Half-Hill Pavilion** and across to **Lotus Pond**.

Take bus No 3 (Y1.5) from the train station or Zhongshan Zhonglu to the last stop. Otherwise, it's a pleasant bicycle ride. Follow Lijun Lu, which runs into Xishan Lu and then Taohua Jiang Lu. The latter parallels small Táohuā Jiāng, and winds through fields and karst peaks. At Ludi Lu turn left and continue for another 1.2km back to Zhongshan Beiglu.

Chuān Shān Gōngyuán 穿山公园
Tunnel Hill Park

The cave is here interesting, but the park is quite rundown. From here you can cross Xiǎodōng Jiāng (a small branch of Lí Jiāng) and hike up to a fairly interesting pagoda.

Other Sights

At the southern end of Guìlín, **Nánxī Gōngyuán** *(South Stream Park)* is a pretty place.

There are two lakes near the city centre, **Róng Hú** on the western side of Zhongshan Zhonglu and **Shān Hú** on the eastern side. Róng Hú is named after an 800-year-old banyan tree on its shore. The tree stands by the restored **South City Gate** *(Nán Mén)* originally built during the Tang dynasty.

This area is one of the nicer neighbourhoods in town for a stroll.

Places to Stay – Budget

For those on a backpacker's budget, Guìlín is lacking – the lower end of the market is served primarily by Yángshuò.

Guilin International Youth Hostel *(Guìlín Guójì Qīngnián Lǚguǎn;* ☎ 282 7115, fax 282 7116, 90 Binjiang Lu) Beds in 4-person dorms YHA member/nonmember Y35/50, twins/suites Y150/258. This is a clean and friendly place. Twins and suites are readily discounted to Y120 and Y200 respectively. The hostel organises a number of tours (through CITS) in and around Guìlín and will help book train and plane tickets. Bike rental is available for Y20 per day, as is Internet access for Y10 per hour. You'll also find washing facilities and a cafe.

Guìlín Fàndiàn *(*☎ *282 2754)* Bed in twins or triples Y30, doubles with bath Y140. This place is a tad weary, but cheap. Rooms are discounted by a further 20% outside summer. Hot water is available from 6pm.

Bǎilèmén Jiǔdiàn *(*☎ *282 5492, 42 Nanhuan Lu)* Doubles/twins Y70/80. This place has OK rooms.

Overseas Chinese Hotel *(Huáqiáo Dàshà;* ☎ 383 5753 ext 2001) Beds in twins with/without bath Y70/44. This is an old backpackers' stand-by. It's a little inconveniently located, but has reasonably priced rooms.

Nánxī Fàndiàn Beds in triples Y40, doubles/twins Y100/120. This place has cheap beds in triples, but they may want you to take the whole room. Hot water is available in the evenings from 7pm to 11.30pm.

Places to Stay – Mid-Range

Most of the aforementioned budget places have nicer rooms for Y100 to Y200, but there are also a few mid-range spots for those looking for something a bit cushier.

Huali Hotel *(Huálì Jiǔdiàn;* ☎ 383 6409, fax 382 7103) Twins/doubles/triples Y130/120/150. This quiet and clean hotel is a well-kept secret. Rooms are often discounted to Y100 or less.

Jīnfēng Bīnguǎn *(*☎ *283 8919)* Twins/doubles Y180/214. Down a lane off Central Square, this place offers good mid-range rooms that fill-up quickly.

Golden Elephant *(Jīnxiàng Dàjiǔdiàn;* ☎ 280 8888, fax 280 9999, 36 Binjiang Lu) Doubles Y320. This three-star hotel has very comfortable rooms, some with nice views of Lí Jiāng and Xiàngbí Shān. You'll also find stylish traditional-Korean *ondol* suites (Y960), a fine Korean restaurant, an Asiana Airlines office and even a Korean bathhouse.

Places to Stay – Top End

No shortage of choice here, although only some of Guìlín's top-enders are worth it.

New City Hotel *(Xīnchéngshì Jiǔdiàn;* ☎ 343 2511, fax 383 3340) Rooms from US$60. The immaculate rooms here come highly recommended, as does the service.

Universal Hotel *(Huánqiú Dàjiǔdiàn;* ☎ 282 8228, 1 Jiefang Donglu) Doubles/suites Y380/650. This hotel is a little worn, yet the pleasant rooms have nice river views.

Osmanthus Hotel *(Dānguì Dàjiǔdiàn;* ☎ 383 4300, Zhongshan Zhonglu) Doubles from US$70. This hotel is a popular target for tour groups. Rooms are nicely furnished and are usually offered at a 40% discount, making them reasonable value.

Brave Hotel *(Guìlín Bīnguǎn;* ☎ 282 3950, fax 282 2101, 14 Ronghu Nanlu) Rooms US$110-120. Taken over by the Holiday Inn, this four-star hotel is arguably one of Guìlín's best abodes, with the only swimming pool in town and good food available in the hotel's Chinese, Japanese and Western restaurants. Unfortunately, the 20% discount only negates the service tax.

Places to Eat

Guìlín is traditionally noted for its snake soup, wild cat or bamboo rat, washed down with snake-bile wine. You could be devouring some of these animals into extinction, and we don't recommend that you do. The pangolin (a sort of armadillo) is a protected species but still crops up on restaurant menus. Other protected species include the muntjac (Asian deer), horned pheasant, mini-turtle, short-tailed monkey, and gemfaced civet. Don't be too put off though; generally the most exotic food you should come across is eel, catfish, pigeons and dog.

Since the Qing dynasty, Guìlín has also been known for its white fermented beancurd, most often used to make a sauce for dipping roast pork or chicken in. Sanhua wine, actually more like mellow rice fire-water, is a favourite local drink.

Around Central Square you'll find a good variety of eateries including buffet-style cafeterias, standard restaurants, trendy cafes and small hole-in-the-wall restaurants. All are very popular.

Chéngdū Xiǎochī (cnr Yiren Lu & Zhengyang Lu) Noodles Y3. This restaurant serves up heaps of tasty noodle dishes, including the *dàndan miànlèi* (Sichuanese noodles) and *Chéngdū lěngmiàn* (cold noodles).

MFW Guìlín has two outlets offering good value, Chinese fast food. Photo menus are a help in choosing your meal.

Good Aunt (Hǎodàmā; Zhongshan Zhonglu) This enormous food gallery is on the 4th level of Bagui Mansion. Here you'll find an amazing smorgasbord of provincial specialities from all over China as well as some Western dishes and a Japanese sushi bar.

Coffee-Language 110 (Míngdiǎn; Zhongshan Zhonglu) A trendy cafe with a variety of Chinese and Western food and beverages, prices here are reasonable but not cheap. A set breakfast is available.

Forest of Flowers With a nice eating environment, this cafe/restaurant has an English menu and offers a fusion of Western and Chinese cuisine and drinks. The restaurant is on the 2nd level, opposite Xinhua Bookshop.

Crescent Mansion (Yuèlèlóu) Located in Qīxīng Gōngyuán, this is a good place to head for lunch, and offers lots of vegetarian fare. Try the local specialty, *gūzi miàn* (nun noodles).

Shèngfā Fàndiàn (Zishan Lu) This restaurant is very popular with locals who come to eat *píjiǔyú* (beer fish, Y18), which is wok-fried on your table and usually knocked down with the local Liqun Beer. Noodles are added at the end to mop up the sauce.

Yíyuán Fàndiàn (Nanhuan Lu) Open 11.30am-2.30pm & 5.30pm-9.30pm daily. This outstanding, inexpensive Sichuanese restaurant has no English sign; look for the all-wood exterior.

Tailian Hotel (Táilián Jiǔdiàn) Lunch/dinner Y20/28. Open noon-2pm & 6pm-8pm daily. Considered to be the best place

in town for a dim sum or yum cha buffet, you'll be hard pressed to find any empty seats here on weekends.

Dōngběi Fàndiàn This is one of a dozen restaurants in *Měishí Wénhuàchéng*, a small eateries district near the train and bus stations. Try the tasty dumplings, like *jiǔcài jiǎozi* (with pork and chive) or *guōtiē jiǎozi* (dry fried). They also have *sùshè jiǎozi* (vegetarian dumplings) using chives and egg.

For the self-caterers there are a number of *supermarkets* around town. By far the most convenient is in the basement of Nikodo Plaza.

Entertainment

In addition to the traditional and minority performances at Wáng Chéng theatre there are also shows at *Garden of Folklore and Feelings (Mínsú Fēngqíngyuán; admission Y50)* at 8.30am, 2pm, 7.30pm and 8.30pm daily. Yet another venue is the *Guilin Children's Palace (Guìlín Shàoniángōng; admission Y80)* with performances at 7.30pm daily.

For those looking for a Disneyland with Chinese characteristics, *Guilin Merryland (Guìlín Lèmǎndi Xiūxián Shìjiè; admission Y150)* is Guìlín's answer – a brand new theme park 60km north of the city. If you think you need more than a day of thrills, it's possible to stay the night at *Merryland Resort (☎ 622 9988)*. Express buses depart for Merryland from the main bus station every 40 minutes from 7am to 12.20pm.

On an island in the middle of Lí Jiāng, *Xiāngba Dǎo,* a cultural theme park has traditional minority architecture, performances, crafts and cuisine. Some of the Lí Jiāng tour boats stop off on their way to Yángshuò.

Shopping

Guìlín and its back-alley workshops are purportedly the source of many of southwest China's crafts for tourist consumption. One place you may wish to check out is the enormous *Guilin International Commodity Market*, located in the far southern section of town. To get there, take bus No 11 from Zhongshan Zhonglu to its final stop and walk south towards the whir and whine of small carving tools.

Getting There & Away

Air CAAC has an office (☎ 384 7252) at the corner of Shanghai Lu and Minzhu Lu that's open from 7.30am to 8.30pm. You'll find Dragonair (☎ 282 5588 ext 8895) in the Brave Hotel.

Guìlín is well connected to the rest of China by air. Destinations include Běijīng (Y1580), Chéngdū (Y900), Chóngqìng (Y670), Hǎikǒu (Y710), Guǎngzhōu (Y610), Guìyáng (Y500), Hong Kong (Y1710), Kūnmíng (Y770), Shànghǎi (Y1190) and Xī'ān (Y1000). While Guìlín is one of China's most popular tourist spots, and it's best to purchase tickets in advance, seats may be available for next-day purchase.

International destinations include flights to Seoul (Hànchéng; Monday, Tuesday, Friday and Saturday) and Fukoka, Japan (Fùgāng; Tuesday and Saturday). Tickets cost at least Y2800 one way for either destination.

Bus For short local runs such as Yángshuò (Y6, one hour) and Xīng'ān (11.40am, Y6, two hours), buses depart from in front of the train station as well as from the main bus station.

Guìlín's bus station is north of the train station, on Zhongshan Nanlu. There are hourly buses to Lóngshèng (Y10 to Y15 express, three to four hours). There are several really slow buses to Sānjiāng (Y17) between 6am and 7.30pm and express buses to Quánzhōu every hour (Y10, one hour). Frequent buses leave for Liǔzhōu every 20 minutes (Y40, two hours) and to Nánníng every 20 to 30 minutes (Y80, 4½ hours).

To Guǎngzhōu and Shēnzhèn, express and sleeper buses are available, however, the expresses are usually more reliable and smoother. Express buses head for Guǎngzhōu hourly (Y150, eight hours) and to Shēnzhèn at 8.30am and 8pm (Y180, 10 hours). Buses for Wúzhōu leave at 8.20am, 12.30pm, 4.30pm and 11pm (Y75, 6½ hours).

Train Guìlín is not as convenient as Nánníng or Liǔzhōu for train connections and tickets are harder to come by. Outside national holidays, you should have better luck, but be prepared to wait an extra day or two for hard sleeper tickets. If things aren't going well at the ticket window, try window 5 'for foreigners'.

Direct trains include train No T6 to Běijīng (5.27pm, 24 hours), No 35/38 to Guǎngzhōu (6pm, 14 hours), No 150 to Shànghǎi (12.52pm, 26½ hours) and train No 1316 to Xī'ān (2.24pm, 30 hours). For Chóngqìng and Chéngdū, change trains at Guìyáng.

Train No K154/155 to Kūnmíng (via Guìyáng) departs at 1.55pm and takes 30 hours. If tickets aren't available it might be worth your while to first go to Nánníng and buy a ticket there for the direct Nánkūn line to Kūnmíng (15 hours).

Getting Around

To/From the Airport Guìlín's international airport is 30km west of the city. CAAC runs buses from its Shanghai Lu office (Mínháng Dàshà) to the airport for Y20, leaving half-hourly from 6.30am. A taxi to the airport costs about Y80.

Bus Most of the city buses that stop in front of Guìlín's bus and train station will get you to the major sights, but a bicycle is definitely better, especially in the searing summer heat. Bus No 2 runs from the train station through town, passing Xiàngbí Shān, Liberation Bridge, Fúbō Shān and Diécǎi Shān. Bus No 15 runs a circuit route from the train station to the city's main tourist highlights. Local buses cost between Y1 and Y1.5.

Taxi A taxi ride around town costs around Y20. Motorcycle taxis charge only Y5 per trip and are a good way of getting to the nearby parks.

Bicycle One of the best ways to get around Guìlín is by bicycle. There are plenty of bicycle-hire shops – just look along Zhongshan Zhonglu. You'll find some near the bus and train stations and one next to the Overseas Chinese Hotel. Most charge Y10 to Y20 per day and require Y200 or your passport as security. Try to avoid handing over your passport.

Tours If you would prefer to leave the transport details to someone else, there's no shortage of tour operators offering half- or full-day tours of Guìlín's major sights. They normally charge around Y35, not including entry tickets.

AROUND GUÌLÍN
Líng Canal 灵渠
Líng Qú

The Líng Canal is in Xīng'ān county, about 70km north of Guìlín. It was built from 219 to 214 BC, to transport supplies to the armies of the first Qin emperor, and is considered to be one of the three great feats of Chinese engineering (the others being the Great Wall and the Dū Jiāng irrigation system in Sìchuān). The 34km canal links Xiāng Hé (which flows into Cháng Jiāng) and Lí Jiāng (which flows into the Zhū Jiāng), connecting two of China's major waterways.

You can see the Líng Canal at the market town of **Xīng'ān**. Two branches of the canal flow through the town, one at the northern end and one at the southern end.

From Guìlín, there is one bus daily for Xīng'ān at 11.40am (Y6, two hours) and hourly express buses to Quánzhōu (Y10, one hour). Minibuses to Xīng'ān may also leave from in front of the train station.

Lí Jiāng 漓江
Lí Jiāng runs between Guìlín and Yángshuò and is a major tourist attraction. A popular tourist trip is the boat ride from Guìlín down Lí Jiāng to Yángshuò. Many travellers have been put off by the exorbitant ticket prices, which presently come in at around Y500, including lunch and the bus trip back to Guìlín from Yángshuò. If you don't mind joining a Chinese tour group, then you'll only have to pay around Y180 for the same service, just lacking the English language guide.

Tour boats (Y460) depart from Guìlín from the tourist wharf opposite the Golden Elephant hotel each morning at around 8am, although when the water is low you have to take a shuttle bus to Zhújiāng or Mópánshān wharf downriver. The ticket office is nearby, or you can book through many hotels. The trip lasts all day. It's probably not worth it if you're going to be spending any length of time in Yángshuò, where you can organise personalised trips through villagers and more picturesque boat trips to nearby villages.

YÁNGSHUÒ 阳朔
☎ 0773 • pop 300,000

Just 65km south of Guìlín, Yángshuò has become a legendary backpacker destination. Set amid gorgeous limestone pinnacles, it's a small town growing bigger on the back of its popularity and is the perfect antidote to weeks or months on the road.

Yángshuò is a great, laid-back base from which to explore other small villages in the nearby countryside where you'll still encounter strong local flavours. Many people stay overnight in the villages.

Orientation
You'll likely only need to know two streets. The first, Pantao Lu, forms the south-west perimeter of Yángshuò and is the main artery to/from Guìlín. The second, Xi Jie, is known as 'Foreigner Street'. It runs northeast to Lí Jiāng, and is lined with Western-style cafes, hotels and tourist shops. The further you go from Xi Jie or from Pantao Lu at its intersection with Xi Jie, the closer you get to Chinese group-tour reality. Xi Jie itself has been turned into a pedestrian mall, free from bicycles, traffic and those infamous tractors.

Maps A reasonably good street map of Yángshuò and surrounds is available throughout town (Y2.5). The regional map isn't great but that's okay – half the adventure is finding your way through the rice paddies.

Information
Tourist Offices Most travel agents appear to work for CITS nowadays, or at least use the acronym. Enterprising locals offering guides from cafes are another option. Just be sure to choose your tours carefully. There are reports of aggressive agents not providing the service they've been paid for and one unfortunate group was sent out in death-trap kayaks, and then charged for the sunk vessels.

Money The Bank of China on Binjiang Lu will change cash and travellers cheques, as well as do credit card advances and receive wire transfers, although these can take up to 15 days. It's open from 8am to 5pm weekdays. On weekends, you'll find a small counter operating next to the bank.

Post & Communications The post office on Pantao Lu is open from 8am to 5pm and has English-speaking staff and long-distance phone services. You can also

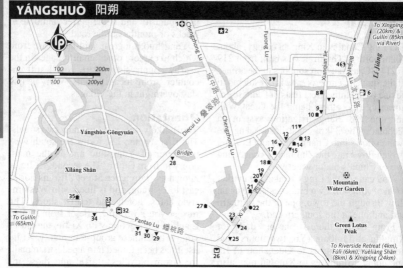

purchase IP cards that only cost Y2.4 to Y3.6 per minute for international calls, rather than the standard Y12 on China Telecom IC cards.

Internet bars are springing up all over town. The standard charge is Y10 per hour. Connection speeds and service vary considerably.

PSB The Yángshuò PSB is well versed in dealing with travellers. That said, reports have been mixed: some people have received an extension pronto, others have been given a serious run-around. Consider getting a friendly cafe representative to act on your behalf if your business is important.

Medical Services The People's Hospital is north of the main tourist centre, not far from the PSB.

There are a number of traditional medicine clinics on the northern side of Pantao Lu offering therapeutic massage, acupuncture and traditional medicine. It is even possible to enrol in brief courses at some of these centres.

Dangers & Annoyances While Yángshuò is relatively safe, it's important to keep your wits about you. Foreigners are seen as wealthy by locals and this alone can invite predators. Yuèliàng Shān (Moon

Hill) is particularly popular with muggers who have wounded their victims with knifes; don't stray off alone. Yángshuò is also the scene of many rip-offs, from hotel 'deposits' to dodgy tours, and many travellers leave town jaded.

Things to See
You can't help but notice the peaks surrounding Yángshuò, and you'll likely work up a big desire to try to hoof it up one or more of them. Get specific instructions from locals before you set off – there's no search and rescue service for foreigners stranded on a karst cliff face.

In the south-eastern corner of town is Yángshuò's main peak, **Green Lotus Peak** (*Bìlián Fēng; admission Y18*). It's also called Bronze Mirror Peak (*Tóngjìng Fēng*) because it has a flat northern face that is supposed to look like an ancient bronze mirror. The peak is next to Lí Jiāng, in the **Mountain Water Garden** (*Shānshuǐyuán*).

Yángshuò Gōngyuán is in the western part of town, and here you'll find **Xīláng Shān** (*Man Hill; admission Y6*), which is supposed to resemble a young man bowing and scraping to a shy young girl represented by **Xiǎogū Shān** (*Lady Hill*). There's a further jungle of hills nearby: **Shīzi Qí Lǐyú Shān** (*Lion Riding Carp Hill*), **Lóngtóu Shān** (*Dragon Head Hill*) and the like.

YÁNGSHUÒ

PLACES TO STAY	PLACES TO EAT	OTHER
8 Hotel Explorer 文化酒店	3 Fresh Produce Market 商贸市场	1 People's Hospital 人民医院
10 Blue Lotus	7 Karst Cafe	2 PSB 公安局
13 Lisa's Cafe	9 Drifter's	4 Bank of China 中国银行
14 Sihai Hotel 四海饭店	11 Red Star Express	5 Tourist Market 旅客市场
17 West Street International Youth Hostel 西街国际青年旅馆	12 Susannah's 15 Le Vôtre Cafe 16 Cafe Under the Moon	6 Wharf 码头
18 Bamboo House Inn & Cafe 竹林饭店	19 Meiyou Cafe 没有饭店	20 Merry Planet Language Club 快乐星球
21 Yangshuo International Youth Hostel 阳朔国际青年旅馆	23 Tent City Market 24 Momozi 25 MC Blues Bar 28 Night Market	22 Buckland School 26 Post Office 邮电局
27 Yangshuo Resort Hotel 阳朔白果来度假饭店	29 Planet Yangshuo 30 Hard Rock Cafe 31 Hard Seat Cafe	32 Main Bus Station 汽车总站 33 Private Buses to Guìlín, Fúlì, Yángdī & Xīngpíng
35 New Century Hotel 新世纪酒店	34 Farmer's Trading Market 农贸市场	往桂林; 福利; 杨堤; 兴坪的班车

It's amazing how many travellers come to Yángshuò and don't really see the town – they're too preoccupied with the karst peaks (and banana pancakes and movies). To the north and west of Pantao Lu are great areas to explore: back alleys, small markets, and throngs of Chinese tourists poking about dozens of shops.

Places to Stay

Despite the seeming plethora of local guesthouses and hotels, tourist numbers are increasing faster than lodging infrastructure can go up, and it can at times take a fair bit of walking to nail down a room. Competition has kept things somewhat sane (at least outside summer), although you couldn't exactly say there are any fantastic steals. Weekly rates seem universally available and you can even use credit cards at many of the cheapies now.

Places to Stay – Budget & Mid-Range

On arrival you will no doubt be met by touts wielding name cards and photo albums of their abodes. You may want to check them out as new places keep springing up and old stand-bys keep on renovating.

The most popular places to stay are on Xi Jie. Most of these also offer very reasonably priced mid-range options, although during summer all rooms become pretty pricey. A number of travellers complain that many of the older hostels suffer from winter damp, and they all suffer the noise of the late-night revellers in the cafes below.

Yangshuo International Youth Hostel (Xījiē Guójì Qīngnián Lǚguǎn; ☎ 882 0933, fax 882 0988, Xi Jie) Dorm beds/twins Y18/80. This is a new addition, offering spotless YHA-standard rooms. Despite appearing a tad sanitary for some travellers, they offer very good value.

West Street International Youth Hostel (☎ 882 0933, fax 882 0988, 102 Xi Jie) Singles with HI card Y24, doubles with/without bath & balcony Y90/70. There are nice rooms and good service at this Hostelling International (HI) branch.

Bamboo House Inn & Cafe (Zhúlín Fàndiàn; ☎ 882 3222) Dorm beds Y15, doubles or triples Y20-25, rooms with air-con Y30-60. Down a small lane off Xi Jie, this place is quiet and pleasant and the staff are reasonably friendly. All rooms have good bathrooms.

Sihai Hotel (Sìhǎi Fàndiàn; ☎ 882 2013, ✉ Sihai@hotmail.com) Dorm beds from Y15, doubles with bath/air-con Y50/80, family room Y200-500. Recently renovated, this labyrinthine hotel is popular for its convenience to the cafes on Xi Jie. Apart from the noise in the evenings, it's a good spot.

Hotel Explorer (Wénhuà Fàndiàn; ☎ 882 8116, fax 882 7816) Dorm beds with/without bath Y45/25, twins Y100-150. This place is a fusion of backpacker and Chinese white tile-style accommodation. Rooms are clean and good value.

Riverside Retreat (☎ 882 7708, ⓦ www .abstraction.org/rr) Singles or doubles Y80. On the road to Yuèliàng Shān, 4km from town, this quiet, family-run guesthouse is on the banks of Yùlóng Hé with 24-hour hot water, clean, heated rooms, Internet access and excellent food.

Lisa's Cafe and the *Blue Lotus* were renovating at the time of research but looked promising, with budget to mid-range rooms.

Places to Stay – Top End

New Century Hotel (Xīnshìjì Jiǔdiàn; ☎ 882 9822, fax 882 9823) Singles or doubles US$60, triples US$75. This new, three-star Chinese-style hotel has good quality rooms and service. They usually discount by 20%.

Yangshuo Resort Hotel (Yángshuò Bǎilèlái Dùjià Fàndiàn; ☎ 882 2109, fax 882 2106) Standard/luxury doubles US$48/110. Also donning three stars, this hotel has a little more ambience and fantastic gardens. The hotel has recently caught onto the renovation craze and rooms are receiving a much needed face-lift. It has a serious slate of amenities, including a fitness centre, swimming pool, satellite TV, pool tables, a business centre, restaurants and lounges.

Places to Eat

Xi Jie teems with tiny cafes offering interesting Chinese/Western fusion cuisine as well as perennial travellers favourites, such as banana pancakes, muesli and pizza. At night, movie junkies are in heaven as almost all the cafes try to woo travellers with Hollywood flicks over dinner.

Red Star Express Pumping out a pretty mean pizza with a good range of toppings (including vegetarian choices), this is a popular choice. The nearby *Drifter's* is another favourite haunt, especially in the evenings. *Meiyou Cafe* promises 'mei you bad service, mei you warm beer' (*méiyǒu* means 'don't have'), and it delivers.

Cafe Under the Moon This place has lots of ambience, friendly service and tasty food. They also have tables on a lovely 2nd-level balcony.

Susannah's Just north-west of the Sihai Hotel off a side street, this was the first Western restaurant in town and continues to draw a steady stream of customers. Do try the *zuì yā* (drunk duck), cooked in a sauce of local red wine.

Karst Cafe This is the place for enthusiastic rock climbers. They not only provide good food and beverages, but also information on climbing possibilities around Yángshuò and climbing guides.

Le Vôtre Cafe While it appears a little grand, this cafe has won the praise of many travellers for its fine French cuisine and delectable bakery.

Other popular places include the cluster of cafes on the corner of Xi Jie and the main road; the Japanese-Chinese *Momozi* and *MC Blues Bar* are here. They all have outdoor seating and are good places to sit and watch the world go by.

Pantao Lu is where some of Yángshuò's original cafes started, and while they don't enjoy the popularity of the Xi Jie strip, cafes like the *Planet Yangshuo*, *Hard Rock Cafe* and the *Hard Seat Cafe* are all friendly spots for a meal or a cup of coffee. There are countless other cafes in town, making for fierce competition.

Don't forget that you *are* in China: wander the labyrinth of back alleys and you'll discover many small *markets* and *restaurants* catering to locals and Chinese travellers.

Farmer's Trading Market (Nóngmào Shìchǎng; Pantao Lu) Through an archway, this place is open all day and late into the evenings. *Píjiǔyú* (beer fish, Y30 per kilo) is Yángshuò's most famous dish and this may be the best and cheapest place to try it. Local Lí Jiāng fish are cooked with chillies, spring onion, tomato, ginger and beer. A good winter alternative is *qīngshuǐyú huǒguō* (Lí Jiāng catfish hotpot). For the more adventurous, there is also *lǎoshǔgān* (fried dried rat with chillies and garlic, Y20). If you like the game meat taste then why not also try *sōngshǔgān* (fried squirrel, Y20). Other interesting cuisine includes *yútóutāng huǒguō* (fish head broth hotpot), *qīngwādàn* (frogs eggs), *zhūcháng* (pig intestines), *tùzi* (wild rabbit) and *yějī* (wild hen).

Fresh Produce Market (Shāngmào Shìchǎng) Here you can choose from a range of small snacks. In the morning there are sticks of *yóutiáo* (deep-fried batter, Y0.5) with *dòujiāng* (soy milk, Y1). Pyramid *zòngzi* (green bean, pork and peanuts wrapped in a lotus leaf with tofu and chilli sauce, Y0.5) are a local winter favourite. You can stock up on fresh or dried fruit here.

Another great **night market** for larger meals starts up from 5.30pm on Diecui Lu. Tasty dishes on offer include *tiánluóniàng* (stuffed field snails, Y15) and *niàng xiānggū* or *niàng làjiāo* (stuffed mushrooms or capsicum). On Xi Jie, approximately a quarter of the way to the river from Pantao Lu, is an evening **tent city** of outdoor grills and woks. Try the local speciality, *mǐfěn* (rice-flour noodles), usually served with crispy fried soy beans and spicy sour pickles.

Shopping

Yángshuò is a good place to do souvenir shopping. Good buys include silk jackets (at much cheaper prices than in Hong Kong), hand-painted T-shirts, scroll paintings and batiks (from Guìzhōu). Name chops are available from Y10 to Y60, but you are expected to bargain for everything; you'll be amazed at how far the prices will drop. Most travellers suggest shopping in the early evening after all the tour groups have left. Don't forget that Yángshuò is not simply Xi Jie; for comparison shopping, wander around the backstreets, especially north around the **tourist market** on Binjiang Lu.

If you are in the market for a chop, bear in mind that it is not the size of the stone that is important in determining a price but the quality of the stone itself. Often the smaller pieces are more expensive than the hefty chunks of rock available.

Work & Study

Merry Planet Language Club on Xi Jie offers brief courses in Chinese language, tai chi or Chinese medicine. It is also possible to enrol in some of the courses offered by the Buckland School, who welcome volunteer teachers in exchange for a bed and food.

Getting There & Away

Air The closest airport is in Guìlín; the numerous CITS outlets and many cafes dispense air tickets relatively cheaply. Check the Guìlín Getting There & Away section earlier in this chapter for details on available flights. Cafes and hotels can organise

taxi rides from Yángshuò directly to the airport (Y75, one hour).

Bus Most travellers arrive in Yángshuò via Guìlín, from where there are good connections to both domestic and international destinations.

Regular buses and minibuses run between Yángshuò and Guìlín throughout the day. Minibuses depart from in front of Yángshuò's bus station as soon as they're full, approximately every five to 15 minutes. The trip takes a little over an hour and the price is Y5 per person, plus Y1 per piece of luggage. Buses also depart regularly from inside the bus station (Y6).

Other options include express buses to Guǎngzhōu (Y150, 7½ hours), Wúzhōu (Y70, six hours), Shēnzhèn (Y180, nine hours) and Hong Kong. If you arrive in Yángshuò on one of the express buses heading from Guìlín, they might deposit you at the petrol station on the edge of town. Don't despair as there will most likely be a welcoming party of hostel touts wielding photo albums to lead or follow you into town.

In times past it was possible to take a bus/boat combination to Guǎngzhōu and Hong Kong via Wúzhōu, however the improvement in buses and road conditions have left the boat by the wayside.

If you're heading for Liǔzhōu, it's quicker to first go to Guìlín and then transfer. See the Guìlín section for more details.

If you're looking for cheaper rates, ancient sleepers still ply most of these routes from the bus station however they're smoky, haphazard and excruciatingly slow.

Train The nearest train station is in Guìlín. Almost any cafe or travel outfit around Yángshuò will organise train tickets. Some offer hard sleepers for high-demand routes like Guìlín to Kūnmíng for around Y270. To get any of these tickets you'll have to book at least two to three days in advance. Outside of national holidays, train tickets to most other destinations are reasonably easy to obtain.

Getting Around

Yángshuò itself is small enough to walk around, but if you want to get farther afield you should hire a bicycle. Look for rows of bikes and signs near the intersection of Xi

Jie and the main road, or ask at the plethora of cafes in town. The charge is about Y10 per day plus a deposit. Before taking a bike out check its gears, brakes, tyres, handle bars, cranks and anything else that could possibly fall off. The farmer's paths around Yángshuò put all bikes to the test and could leave you stranded miles away from your deposit. There have also been some ugly situations when travellers have been accused of returning bikes 'broken'; if this happens, don't expect the PSB to side with you.

AROUND YÁNGSHUÒ
Yuèliàng Shān Area 月亮山

The highway from Guìlín turns southward at Yángshuò and, after a couple of kilometres, crosses Yùlóng Hé. South of the river and just west of the highway is **Yuèliàng Shān** *(Moon Hill; admission Y5),* a limestone pinnacle with a moon-shaped hole. The views from the top (some 1251 steps up, so reports one focused Frenchman) are incredible! You can espy **Moon Hill Village** and the 1500-year-old **Big Banyan Tree** (ask the hawkers to point it out). To reach Yuèliàng Shān by bicycle, take the main

road south out of town towards the river and turn right on the road about 200m before the bridge. Cycle for about 50 minutes – Yuèliàng Shān is on your right.

Black Buddha Cave & Water Cave
Hēifó Dòng & Shuǐ Yán 黑佛洞、水岩

These caves *(admission per cave Y50)* have been opened up not far from Yuèliàng Shān. Both caves are worth a visit although Water Cave is especially popular. It's easy to reach the caves by bike; if you head for Yuèliàng Shān, you will undoubtedly be intercepted by touts. You can also join one of the many tours from Yángshuò.

Chufa Tours is located at Yuèliàng Shān and offers both independent and group tours of the caves. Tours aren't bargains with two to four hours tours from Y78 to Y108, but prices include transport, entry and equipment and all who partake say it's a good adventure.

If you're wanting to stay at Yuèliàng Shān, *Swallow's Guesthouse* comes highly recommended with new, basic rooms and hot showers.

Yùlóng Hé 遇龙河

There are weeks and weeks of possible exploration along Yùlóng Hé for travellers on bike, boat or foot. The scenery along here equals or even beats that of Lí Jiāng. Whether you just meander between the rice paddies or sit by the river and take in the rural and karst landscape, this is the place that usually leaves the biggest impression on most visitors to Yángshuò. Unfortunately, the local tourist bureau has also taken notice of this area's charm and plans are currently underway to develop the valley for tourism.

It is possible to do a full-day tour of the river and neighbouring sights, including **Double Flow Crossing** *(Shuāngliǔdù)*, **Shàngguì Bridge** *(Shàngguì Qiáo)*, nearby **Xīniú Hú** *(Rhinoceros Lake)* and **Dragon Bridge** *(Yùlóng Qiáo)*. This impressive last bridge was built in 1412 and is among Guǎngxī's biggest at 59m long, 5m wide and 9m high.

From Yángshuò, head out towards Yuèliàng Shān (see Yuèliàng Shān Area section earlier). Before crossing the bridge over Yùlóng Hé, turn right down the dirt trail. It is possible to continue along this path all the way to Dragon Bridge and Báishā. Don't be tempted by the Báishā road as it is busy,

AROUND YÁNGSHUÒ 阳朔地区

To Guìlín (30km)

▲ Xiù Shān

Yángdì

Lí Jiāng

0   5   10km
0   3   6mi

To Guìlín (45km)

Jiǔmǎ ▲ Huàshān

Xīngpíng

Pútáo

Pavilion Of Peace

Shīzi Qí Shān ▲

Shangri-La

Dragon Bridge

Báishā

Shàngguì Bridge

Lóngtóu Shān

Fúlì

Xīniú Hú

Jīnbǎo Hé

Double Flow Crossing

Yùlóng Hé

Yángshuò

Liúgōng

Lìmǎ

Riverside Retreat

Lí Jiāng

Big Banyan Tree

Dragon Cave

Three Colours Pond

Yuèliàng Shān ▲

Gāotián

Black Buddha Cave

Water Cave

Puyǐ

To Wúzhōu (215km)

noisy and dusty. A round trip to Dragon Bridge takes a full day, but it's definitely worth it. Pack a lunch and plenty of water.

In Yángshuò, there are also several locals offering guided tours of Yuèliàng Shān, the caves and other famous spots, as well as their home villages. Some now cook lunch or dinner as well. These mini-tours have garnered rave reviews from some travellers and may be worth a try, although you may need to get at least three people together to make it worth your guide's while. Prices vary wildly for these tours – figure Y50 to Y70 for a full day.

River Excursions

There are many villages close to Yángshuò that are worth checking out. A popular riverboat trip is to the picturesque village of Fúlì, a short distance down Lí Jiāng, where you'll see stone houses and cobbled lanes. There are a couple of boats a day to Fúlì from Yángshuò for around Y40, although most people tend to cycle there – it's a pleasant ride and takes around an hour.

Another way to get to Fúlì is by inner tube, available for about Y10 per day. It takes around three or four hours to get to Fúlì this way. Several places also offer rafting trips and kayak hire, popular options in the warm summer months. Ask at your hotel or at one of the restaurants.

Many cafes and travel agents also organise boat trips to Yángdī and Xīngpíng, about three hours upstream from Yángshuò. The mountain scenery around Xīngpíng is breathtaking and you'll spot many caves. Official prices for all boat trips are now Y100 a ride. Local boats charge Y2 for the same trip, but are deemed dangerous and the owners are not allowed to take foreigners.

A good alternative is to ride your bike to Xīngpíng and then put your bike on the boat coming back. Any number of places in Yángshuò or Xīngpíng can organise boat tickets (Y20 to Y45 per person). It's also possible to catch a local bus to Xīngpíng (Y3, one hour) from the minibus car park opposite the bus station in Yángshuò.

Another option is to spend the night in Xīngpíng where there are a growing number of accommodation and cuisine options.

Róngtán Fàndiàn (☎ 870 2248) Room with bath/air-con Y20/30. This is the first hotel up from the wharf on the left.

River View Hotel (*Wàngjiāng Fàndiàn;* ☎ 870 2276) Beds in quads Y25, twins Y80. Next door to Róngtán Fàndiàn, this place is also reasonably priced.

Bamboo Cafe (*Zhúlín Fàndiàn*) Right on the river, this is a good spot for a meal and refreshing drink. Just up from the river is *One World Cafe* and the *Cottage Cafe*, both serving tasty food.

A popular evening activity in Yángshuò is to take part in one of the cormorant fishing tours that begin around 7pm. While it's entertaining, it's mainly a tourist attraction these days as the river supports an ever diminishing supply of fish. Hotels and restaurants usually charge around Y25 per person.

Markets

The villages in the vicinity of Yángshuò are best visited on market days, which operate on a three-day, monthly cycle. Thus, markets take place every three days starting on the first of the month for Báishā (1, 4, 7 etc), every three days starting on the second of the month for Fúlì (2, 5, 8 etc), and every three days starting on the third of the month for Yángshuò and Xīngpíng (3, 6, 9 etc). There are no markets on the 10th, 20th, 30th and 31st of the month.

LÓNGSHÈNG 龙胜
☎ 0773 • pop 170,000

About four hours by bus to the north-west of Guìlín, Lóngshèng is close to the border of Guìzhōu and is home to a colourful mixture of Dong, Zhuang, Yao and Miao cultures. Close by the Dragon's Backbone Rice Terraces and a nearby hot spring (*wēnquán*).

The hot spring is a tacky tourist highlight and can be safely missed, although buses (Y5) running out there pass through rolling hills sculptured with rice terraces and studded with Yao and Zhuang minority villages. It's possible to desert the bus around 6km from the hot spring and take off into the hills for some exploring. Other tourist sights around Lóngshèng include forest reserves and unusual stone formations.

When you return from the day's outing, Lóngshèng offers cheap accommodation and even cheaper food at its lively night market.

Information

The post and telephone office is on Gulong Lu. Just 50m beyond is an Internet cafe that charges Y4 per hour and is open from 9am to midnight daily.

The Longsheng Travel Service (☎ 751 7566) is just next to the bus station and should be able to help you arrange transport, guides and tours to the surrounding sights.

Dragon's Backbone Rice Terraces
Lóngjǐ Tītián 龙脊梯田

Though the region around Lóngshèng is covered with terraced rice fields, in the Dragon's Backbone Rice Terraces (admission Y20) these feats of farm engineering reach all the way up a string of 800m peaks. A half-hour climb to the top delivers an amazing vista.

The Zhuang village of **Píng'ān**, located on the central main ridge of the backbone, is rapidly becoming a small travellers centre and within a couple of years has accumulated a host of guesthouses, bars, restaurants and Internet cafes.

The cause of this boom was the construction of a 6km zigzag road from the riverside at the bottom of the valley up to Píng'ān. In order to build this road, a large number of rice terraces had to be blasted away and serious environmental damage has resulted. In any case, it is still possible to avoid using the road as Píng'ān is only a half-hour's walk up a beautiful stone path from **Huángluò**.

DRAGON'S BACKBONE RICE TERRACES 龙脊梯田

Despite the proliferation of buildings in Píng'ān, the town remains a very attractive place to base yourself for a couple of days and explore the area. Walking possibilities include the one-hour circuit walk from the village to the clearly marked Viewpoint 1 and Viewpoint 2. More extensive day-walks are also possible along the dragon's backbone and down to Hépíng or over the ridge and down into the valley behind. The best time to visit the area is during summer when water is plentiful, although some travellers have remarked at the beauty of the terraces covered in snow. Winter and early spring bring heavy fogs and mist that often shroud the terraces.

Buses to the terraces leave infrequently from 7am to 5.30pm (Y4.5/6.5 to base/top) from Lóngshèng's bus station. The 9.20am, 10.40am and 4pm buses are more regular and usually make the trip to the top, whereas the other buses will drop you off at the base of the terraces and continue on to Shuānghékǒu. The trip is only about 20km, however, some buses stop midway at the town of Hépíng to try to pull in more passengers, dragging the trip out to 1½ hours! Returning to Lóngshèng, buses usually depart from the car park near the beautiful covered bridge at the entrance to Píng'ān at 7.30am, 10.30am and 2pm.

The entrance fee is collected on the main road along the valley bottom and checked just before the covered bridge.

Places to Stay

By far the best choice for accommodation is found in Píng'ān. Most of the other villages in the area also offer accommodation in traditional wooden homes. A basic dorm bed costs Y15 in Píng'ān or Y10 elsewhere. Most of the hostels in Píng'ān have 24-hour hot water and will serve you meals (Y5 to Y10 per meal). The only difference between most of the hostels appears to be their views. Two worth checking out are *Liǎoměilǐ Lǚguǎn* (☎ 758 2542) and *Lóngyíng Lǚguǎn* (☎ 758 2410).

In Lóngshèng you can find accommodation at the following places.

Foreign Trade Hotel (Wàimào Bīnguǎn; ☎ 751 2078) Dorm beds in twins or triples Y10, beds in twins with bath Y25. Follow the many signs around Lóngshèng to this hotel for good value and friendly staff.

Cheaper rooms have toilets, but no hot water; pricier rooms have 24-hour hot water.

Lŭyóu Bīnguăn (☎ *751 7206, Gulong Lu*) Doubles with bath & air-con Y80-100, twins Y100-120, quads Y160. This is a very good mid-range option with clean, newly renovated rooms. Prices are usually discounted by 20% and include 24-hour hot water.

Riverside Hotel (*Kăikăi Lŭshè*) Dorms Y10. Down the road to Guìlín, this hotel is run by an English teacher who seems happy to give travellers information on how to get to the local sights. Rooms are very basic.

There are also plenty of extremely noisy places to stay around the bus station.

Places to Eat

Lóngshèng is not a culinary wonderland, however, in recent years, plenty of restaurants have opened up.

Longsheng Green Food Restaurant (*Lùsè Cháguăn*) North of the Foreign Trade Hotel, this place serves up decent local specialities. There is a photo board to help you order, but check the prices first as some dishes aren't cheap. Try hotpot (Y30 for the basic plus extras) or the tasty *xiānggū ròupiàn*, beef strips with shitake mushrooms and red capsicum.

Up Shengyuan Lu, towards the PSB, is a pleasant, little traditional building with a *tea house* inside serving local teas and snacks.

Just past the bridge on Xinglong Xilu, *street stalls* appear around 8pm, offering point-and-choose meals by lantern light. There are also some *noodle shops* on Xinglong Beilu.

Zhuang-Minority Flavours Restaurant This restaurant offers a wide range of traditional Zhuang snacks, meals and drinks. Traditional performances are also hosted in the restaurant on special occasions.

Getting There & Away

Buses leave the Lóngshèng bus station every 10 to 15 minutes for Guìlín (Y10, four hours) and express buses depart every two hours (Y15, three hours). Buses depart Lóngshèng for Sānjiāng hourly (Y7, two hours).

SĀNJIĀNG 三江

☎ 0772 • pop 330,000

Capital of the Sanjiang Dong Minority Autonomous County (Sānjiāng Dòngzú Zìzhìxiàn), the reason for coming here is to get out and explore. Approximately 20km to the north of town, Chéngyáng Wind and Rain Bridge and the surrounding Dong villages are as peaceful and attractive as Sānjiāng is not.

Chéngyáng Wind & Rain Bridge
Chéngyáng Qiáo 程阳桥

Built in 1912, this 78m-long elegant covered bridge (*admission Y10*) is considered by the Dong to be the finest of the 108 such structures in Sānjiāng county. The bridge is 78m-long and took villagers 12 years to build, theoretically without nails. On the bridge you'll encounter minority women hawking their wares and you can also enjoy views over a lush valley dotted with Dong villages and water wheels. Chéngyáng is a great place to base yourself for a couple of days to explore the surrounding countryside and minority villages.

From the Sānjiāng bus station you can catch hourly buses to Línxī (Y3), which go right past the bridge. Otherwise, catch one of the frequent minivan taxis (Y3) that conglomerate outside the bus station. Bus services stop around 6pm in either direction. The first bus of the day back to Sānjiāng passes by the bridge around 7.40am.

Places to Stay

Chengyang Bridge National Hostel (*Chéngyáng Qiáo Zhāodàisuŏ;* ☎ *861 2444, fax 861 1716*) Dorms/doubles with shared bath Y20/60. Just to the left of the Chéngyáng bridge, on the far side of the river, this is easily the best abode in the area. The hotel is an all wood, Dong-style building and the owners are friendly, informative and welcoming. Even if you don't spend the night, a cup of tea or a simple meal on the hostel's riverside balcony is a great way to enjoy the scenery. The entrance is on the far side of the building.

A couple of other hotels have sprung up around the bridge, including the *Dong Village Hotel*, but they don't really offer any competition.

Guesthouse of the People's Government of the Sanjiang Dong Autonomous County (*Sānjiāng Dòngzú Zìzhìxiàn Rénmín Zhèngfŭ Zhāodàisuŏ*) Doubles with/without bath Y60/40. This is another quiet option in Sānjiāng. To get here, follow the road running between the Department Store Hotel and the bus station uphill, and bear left. The guesthouse is a further 10 minutes on your right, across from a Dong drum tower.

Chengyang Bridge Hotel *(Chéngyáng Qiáo Bīnguǎn)* Rooms from Y100. Down the street from the bus station, this place offers slightly more upmarket rooms.

Getting There & Away

Sānjiāng's bus station has several buses to Guìlín between 7.10am and 2.30pm (Y18.5, five hours) and to Liǔzhōu between 7.50am and 4pm (Y23, six hours). These should pass through Róngshuǐ (Y4.5), a scenic trip of 3½ hours. Buses to Lóngshèng (Y7) leave every 40 to 50 minutes between 6.30am and 5.10pm.

Sānjiāng to Kǎilǐ If you have time on your hands, it's worth considering entering Guìzhōu province through the backdoor. From Sānjiāng take the 6.50am or 2pm bus to Dìpíng (Lóng'é) (Y10), which is just across the Guìzhōu border. Though the journey is only approximately three hours, delays may leave you stranded in Dìpíng for the night. There are frequent buses departing Dìpíng for Lípíng (Y15, five hours).

The journey to Lípíng passes through some beautiful mountains, as well as the fabulous Dong village of Zhàoxīng, the highlight of the trip and definitely worth a visit. For more information on these areas, see the Guìzhōu chapter.

There are also frequent buses from Sānjiāng to Cóngjiāng in Guìzhōu. The road is new and improved but the route isn't as pretty. However, if you're in a hurry to reach Kǎilǐ, there are numerous onward connections from Cóngjiāng.

Another possibility is to take a train to Tōngdào in Húnán province and from there travel onward by bus to Lípíng. Minibuses run every half-hour throughout the day to the train station a few kilometres west of Sānjiāng.

LIǓZHŌU 柳州

☎ 0772 • pop 880,000

Liǔzhōu is the largest city on Liǔ Jiāng (Willow River) and is an important railway junction in south-west China. The place dates back to the Tang dynasty, when it was a dumping ground for disgraced court officials. Liǔzhōu was largely left to its

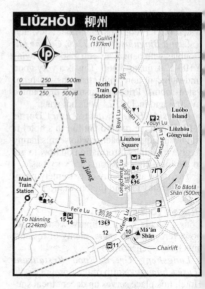

mountain wilds until 1949, when it was transformed into a major industrial city. It has recently received a much needed face-lift, transforming it into a modern Chinese city. Nevertheless, foreigners are still something of a rarity here.

Liǔzhōu is Guìlín's poor cousin, with similar but less impressive karst scenery on the outskirts of town. Most mornings, eagle-eyed travellers can witness tai chi sessions atop the peaks ringing the city.

Information

The main post and telephone office is south of Liuzhou Square and is open from 8am to 8pm. Next door is an Internet cafe that's open until 10pm daily and charges Y3 per hour. The Bank of China has a couple of branches here that can exchange travellers cheques. There is also a useful ticket office on Longcheng Lu selling plane and train tickets.

City Parks

Liǔzhōu may be lacking in big tourist draw-cards, but the city retains a certain charm with its picturesque river banks and urban parks. Pleasant **Liǔzhóu Gōngyuán** has a lake and a small temple erected to the memory of Liu Zongyuan (AD 772–819), a famous scholar and poet. Bus No 2, 5 or 6 will get you there.

LIǓZHŌU

PLACES TO STAY & EAT
1 Time Bar
时间酒吧
4 Lìjīng Dàjiǔdiàn
丽晶大酒店
9 Yúfēng Dàshà
鱼峰大厦
12 Night Market
夜市
15 Jīn'é Dàjiǔdiàn
金鹅大酒店
16 Nánjiāng
Fàndiàn
南疆饭店

17 Tiān'é Fàndiàn
天鹅饭店

OTHER
2 Popular Cafes
& Bars
热闹的酒吧和餐厅
3 Main Post &
Telephone Office;
Internet Cafe
中国电信; 网吧
5 Train & Plane Ticket
Office
售票处

6 Bank of China
中国银行
7 East Gate
东门城楼
8 Ferry Dock
航运码头
10 Yúfēng Gōngyuán
鱼峰公园
11 Main Bus Station
汽车总站
13 Bank of China
中国银行
14 Liuzhou South Bus Station
柳州南站

Along Fei'e Lu, near the main bus station, is **Yúfēng Shān** *(Fish Peak Mountain)*, in **Yúfēng Gōngyuán**. At only 33m high, it derives its name from its resemblance to a 'standing fish'. Climb to the top for a smoggy vista of Guǎngxī's foremost industrial city. You can also ride the cable car (return Y20), which is open until 8pm daily, from Yúfēng Gōngyuán up to the peak of neighbouring **Mǎ'ān Shān** *(Horse Saddle Mountain)*, home to several temples and pavilions and offering better views.

The pleasant **Bǎotǎ Shān** *(admission Y3)* is to the south-east of town with two beautiful seven-storey pagodas perched upon its peaks.

With Liǔzhōu's riverside parks recently landscaped, plans are in place for tourist boats to start making tours along Liǔ Jiāng during summer, departing from the wharf on the river.

Places to Stay
Tiān'é Fàndiàn Beds in a triple/doubles/twins Y30/55/35. More expensive rooms with damp carpet are also available here and are usually discounted by 30%.

Jīn'é Dàjiǔdiàn (☎ 361 1888 ext 2100) Twins/triples from Y50/60. This hotel is a more preferable option. They will also purchase bus, train and air tickets for you for a 20% commission.

Yúfēng Dàshà (☎ 787 8177 ext 3108) Twins/triples/singles Y118/125/130. This is the cheapest 'official' option anywhere near the main bus station, though still quite a trek. Rooms are a little tired but OK for a night.

Nánjiāng Fàndiàn (☎ 361 2988, fax 361 7575) Doubles/twins/family rooms Y153/180/266. This mid-range three-star outfit

has good comfy rooms. There is also a pleasant cafe in the foyer.

Lìjīng Dàjiǔdiàn (☎ 280 8888, fax 280 8828) Twins Y338-418. This is Liǔzhōu's top-end hotel. Rooms are brand new and luxurious. A 20% discount is usually available.

Places to Eat
Your best bet is the lively **night market** across from the main bus station. From around 8pm, numerous stalls serve tasty dumplings and noodles fried with a choice of fresh ingredients. The main train station area also has dumpling and noodle places. There is a string of trendy and popular *cafes* and *bars* on Youyi Lu near the Liuzhou Hotel, serving Western food and cocktails.

Time Bar (Shíjiān Jiǔbā; Beizhan Lu) This is another Western-style bar with a few decent Western dishes and draught beer!

Getting There & Away
Air There is one flight daily to Guǎngzhōu (Y570) at 8.50pm. Tickets for this flight as well as flights departing from Guìlín and Nánníng can be purchased at window No 13 at the main bus station.

Bus The Liǔzhōu south bus station is actually north of the main bus station, but let's not quibble. It's along Fei'e Lu and is much closer to budget lodgings and the train station, so it's likely to become the main terminus for travellers. The other bus station is south of Yúfēng Gōngyuán and a fair hike from the train station. The bus stations have entirely different schedules, so if one doesn't have what you're looking for, check the other.

From the south bus station, frequent express buses depart for Guìlín (Y40, 1½ hours) and hourly buses run to Sānjiāng (Y22, five hours). For Yángshuò, it's quicker to travel to Guìlín and change buses there.

Train Liǔzhōu is a main railway junction connecting Nánníng to Guìlín. There are a number of good connections including Běijīng, Chángshā, Chéngdū, Guǎngzhōu, Guìyáng, Shànghǎi and Xī'ān.

Boat Once upon a time boats connected Liǔzhōu with Wúzhōu and Guǎngzhōu, but now the only services are tour boat cruises on Liǔ Jiāng.

Getting Around

Bus Nos 2 and 24 connect the Liuzhou Square with the train station. Bus Nos 10 and 25 run past the main bus station and go to Liuzhou Square and No 11 goes to the train station.

Guìzhōu 贵州

Capital: Guìyáng
Population: 39.5 million
Area: 170,000 sq km

Terraced crops climb the sides of rolling mountains that eventually stretch out into wide plateaus. These give way to jagged karst hills dotted with giant limestone caves and countless waterfalls plunging to the ground. Within this setting lives a vibrant and colourful mix of people. Around 35% of Guìzhōu's population is made up of over 80 different ethnic minorities. While the majority Han cluster mainly in the province's cities, communities of Miao, Bouyi, Dong, Yi, Shui (Sui), Hui, Zhuang, Bai, Tujia, Gelao and Gejia populate the more remote villages.

Surprisingly, for a province so rich in minority culture, Guìzhōu is still neglected by most travellers. The only attraction to gather relatively large numbers is Huángguǒshù Falls, China's largest.

One reason for this lack of interest is probably the perceived difficulty of travel in this area, perhaps due to Guìzhōu's reputation as one of China's more hard-done-by provinces. In reality though, travel here is no more difficult than in other, more popular regions of the country.

The south-eastern part of Guìzhōu is particularly worth exploring. Around 72% of the population in this region are Miao or Dong or a mixture of other minorities.

HISTORY

Although Chinese rulers set up an administration in the area as far back as the Han dynasty (206 BC to AD 220), they merely attempted to maintain some measure of control over Guìzhōu's non-Chinese tribes. Chinese settlement was confined to the northern and eastern parts of the province and the western areas were not settled until the 16th century, when the native minorities were forced out of the most fertile areas.

It wasn't until the Japanese invasion forced the Kuomintang to retreat to the south-western part of China that the development of Guìzhōu began in earnest: roads to the neighbouring provinces were constructed, a rail link was built to Guǎngxī,

Highlights

- Huángguǒshù Falls, at 74m China's premier cascade; surrounded by scenic countryside
- The south-eastern region, home to remote minority villages of the Miao and Dong and the site of countless festivals
- Zhījīn Cave, China's largest cavern; an endless moonscape of towers, tunnels and huge, open rooms
- Cǎohǎi Hú, a bird-watcher's paradise in Guìzhōu's wild west

and industries were set up in Guìyáng and Zūnyì. Most of this activity ceased with the end of WWII and it wasn't until the Communists began construction of the railways that industrialisation was revived.

Nevertheless, Chinese statistics continue to paint a grim picture of underdevelopment and poverty for Guìzhōu, with eight million of the province's population still living below the national poverty line. The government is attempting to change all this, mostly by laying down roads in every possible place to facilitate travel to Huángguǒshù Falls and by promoting minority cultures as a local attraction.

FESTIVALS

Festivities among the minorities in Guìzhōu offer plenty of scope for exploration.

GUÌZHŌU 贵州

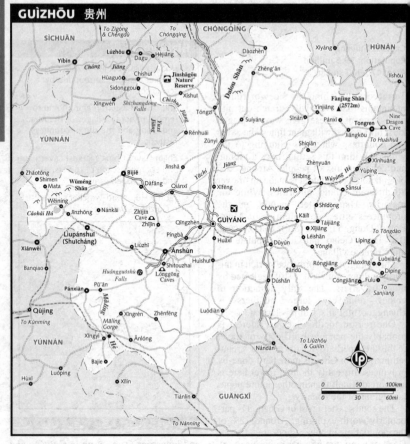

The majority of festivals are held on auspicious lunar dates, such as the third day of the third lunar month or the sixth of the sixth. Most are annual events, though a few are held every few years and some just once a decade. Many of Guìyáng's festivals take place during the first lunar month (usually February or March), fourth lunar month (around May) and sixth lunar month (around July).

A good starting point for festival forays is Kǎilǐ, east of Guìyáng. A profusion of festivals is held in nearby minority areas such as Léishān, Xījiāng, Zhoūxī, Qīngmàn, Pánghǎi and Zhijiāng. China International Travel Service (CITS; Zhōngguó Guójì Lǚxíngshè) in Kǎilǐ is a helpful source for specific dates of festivals in the region.

GUÌYÁNG 贵阳

☎ 0851 • pop 3.5 million z elevation 1070m
Guìyáng, the underappreciated capital of Guìzhōu, has a mild climate all year round.

The city appears to be getting a face-lift, meaning the usual uncountable number of construction sites and mushrooming highrises. Nevertheless, a few of the older neighbourhoods and temples have held on and some of the new areas, including the riverside and Rénmín Square, provide enjoyable areas to wander, mingle and relax. There's also some fantastic food, lively market and shopping areas and a few interesting sights to keep you busy for a day or two.

Guìyáng is Guìzhōu's transport hub, with a brand new, state-of-the-art train station and good bus connections in every direction.

The city is a good jumping-off point for Huángguǒshù Falls, 100km west, or the minority villages to the east around Kǎilǐ.

Orientation

While Guìyáng is somewhat sprawling, it remains a manageable size and is easy enough to get around. The main commercial district is found along Zhonghua Lu and Zhonghua Nanlu, spreading out along the main roads they intersect. In the south of this area you'll find the main Bank of China, China Telecom and China Post. If you continue south you'll reach Zunyi Lu and Rénmín Square. To the east of here is Jiǎxiù Pavilion, a symbol of the city that hovers over Nánmíng Hé.

Information

Tourist Offices CITS (☎ 581 4829) at 20 Yan'an Zhonglu is one of the south-west's most helpful and friendly branches. It's open from 9am to 5pm and the staff has maps, timetables and information on minority areas.

Staff at the Guizhou Overseas Travel Company (GOTC; ☎ 582 5328), next door, are more reliable if you actually want to book travel arrangements.

Near the train station, the Guizhou Railway Travel Service (☎ 575 3505) are also helpful in handing out info on nearby sites and at booking train travel. They also arrange regular tours to Huángguǒshù Falls and nearby minority villages. Nobody here speaks English.

PSB The Public Security Bureau (PSB; Gōngānjú; ☎ 682 1231) is in a white-tiled building on Zhongshan Xilu, quite close to the intersection with Zhonghua Nanlu. This is the place to report thefts or seek visa extensions and travel permits. While the vast majority of Guìzhōu is open to foreign travellers, if you're planning on visiting anywhere extremely remote, in particular along the provincial borders, you might be wise to check on restrictions before heading out. Unfortunately, you need to know your exact destinations as the PSB only has a *long* list of where you can go – not a list of where you are not allowed.

Money The Bank of China has several branches around town with ATMs accepting all major credit and bank cards. A number of the branches exchange money. The main branch on Dusi Lu is the best place to go for credit card advances and wire transfers.

Post & Communications The main post and telephone building is at the intersection of Zunyi Lu and Zhonghua Nanlu. You can make international phone calls from the international and long-distance hall, to the left of the main doors. Collect calls are made from the inquiry desk by the front door.

China Telecom offers Internet access in the office furthest round to the left (north) from the main doors of China Post. Access is available until 5.30pm for Y5 an hour. Across the street, on the 4th floor of the Telecommunication Business Centre, there are more computers where you can get online for the same price until 6.30pm.

A number of private Internet cafes are opening throughout Guìyáng, offering access for Y3 per hour. You'll find two on Wenchang Beilu and another at the southern end of Ruijin Beilu.

Bookshops The Foreign Languages Bookshop on Yan'an Donglu isn't particularly well stocked.

The Xinhua Bookshop, further west along Yan'an Zhonglu on the roundabout, has a wider selection of Chinese-language maps and posters.

Dangers & Annoyances Guìyáng has a reputation among Chinese as one of China's worst cities for theft. Be particularly careful in crowded areas such as the train station, busy streets and on local buses – the favoured haunts of pickpockets.

Walking Tour

Beginning at **Rénmín Square**, north of the train station, you'll find one of China's largest glistening white statues of Mao Zedong, as well as two new Louvre-like glass pyramids. The square itself, extending onto both sides of Zunyi Lu, is a favourite hangout for Guiyangese to fly kites, practise taijiquan or visit in the small gazebos.

Just north of here, a wander along **Yangming Lu** takes you through an interesting market of birds, plants, goldfish, antiques and incense. Take a staircase down, closer to the river, to see herbal medicine sellers peddling their wares.

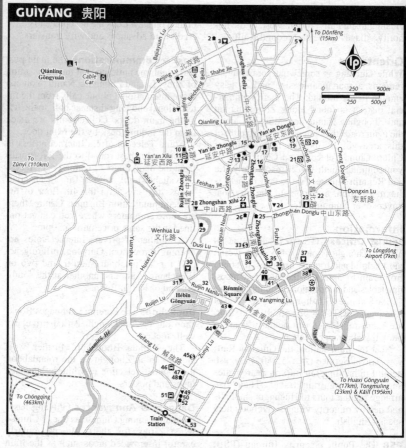

GUÌYÁNG 贵阳

Follow a small alley branching left off Yangming Lu to find Buddhist **Qiánmíng Sì**. Friendly monks and worshippers will welcome you into this peaceful oasis, which has an eclectic collection of Buddha statues.

North of here is **Jiǎxiù Pavilion** *(Jiǎxiù Lóu)*, resting on a bridge over Nánmíng Hé. On the other side of the river is **Cuìwēi Gōngyuán** *(admission Y3)*, a collection of several small pavilions set in a charming garden of bonsai trees, Chinese stones and miniature plum blossoms. The garden was originally a Buddhist abbey built during the Ming dynasty (AD 1425–35), however nowadays it's essentially home to a group of shops selling traditional Miao embroidery; interesting to browse, but pricey.

Backtracking across the bridge and heading north up Wenchang Beilu brings you to **Wénchāng Gé** *(Wénchāng Pavilion)*, now a small coin museum.

Parks

In the north of the city, **Qiánlíng Gōngyuán** *(admission Y2; open 8am-10.30pm)* is worth a visit for its forested walks and for 17th-century Qing dynasty **Hóngfú Sì**, perched near the top of 1300m Qiánlíng Shān. A path winds uphill from inside the entrance gate, or if that seems like hard work, there's a cable car that takes you straight to the top (Y12 one way). The monastery has a vegetarian *restaurant (open 11am-4pm)* in the rear courtyard. From the train station area take a No 2 bus.

GUÌYÁNG

Not far from Rénmín Square is **Hébīn Gōngyuán**, which has benches under shady trees along the river and a Ferris wheel that offers good views of Guìyáng for Y6.

Provincial Museum 省博物馆
Shěng Bówùguǎn

In the northern part of town, the provincial museum *(Beijing Lu)* has good displays on various aspects of the province's minorities, dating from the ancient Yelang kingdom. At the time of writing the museum was closed for renovations, but it should be reopened by the time you read this.

Places to Stay – Budget

There isn't much to choose from when it comes to budget accommodation in Guìyáng.

Míngzhū Fàndiàn (☎ 579 3389) Beds in 3-/5-bed dorms Y35/40, doubles with bath Y120. This is a good choice, especially if you're catching an early morning train. The rooms here are comfortable although not so quiet.

Kebabs & Raisins

On many street corners in Guìyáng, and many other towns in the south-west, you'll see (and smell, long before you see) the occasional hard-nosed entrepreneur grilling delicious mutton kebabs over a crackling rack of coals. On the other side of the street there'll often be another swarthy-looking guy lovingly piling Turpani raisins into a conical mound.

These guys are Uyghurs, Turkic-speaking Muslims from Xīnjiāng in Chinese Central Asia, recognisable by their Mediterranean or Middle Eastern appearance, their black or green skullcaps and the knife that hangs perennially by their side. Uyghurs are only one of 10 Muslim ethnic groups scattered throughout China, which together number 15 million (officially) to 35 million (unofficially). The largest group by far is the Chinese Hui, who you'll also spot throughout the south-west, wearing small white hats and often running fantastic restaurants.

On Saturday in Guìyáng, keep an eye out for *matang*, a wonderful chewy walnut-and-fruit nougat loaf that some Uyghurs sell near the Penshuichi Fountain. It's a bit pricey at Y15 for 500g, but it's worth its weight in gold. If you really want to impress, try out the Muslim greeting *A salaam aleikum*, 'May peace be upon you', or the Turkic *Yakshimisis?*, meaning 'How are you?'. If that doesn't get you cheap kebabs, nothing will.

Gōnglù Dàshà (☎ 599 2524, 12 Ruijin Beilu) Dorm beds Y25, doubles/triples with bath Y148/165. This guesthouse is divided into two; receptions for both are on the ground floor, next to each other. The dorm rooms are on the 13th floor but you will likely be directed to the 5th floor reception with its pricier doubles and triples. (You might not mind being on the 5th floor after 11pm when the elevator stops running.)

Places to Stay – Mid-Range

Tōngdá Fàndiàn (☎ 579 0484, fax 579 0235) Doubles Y148. This hotel has good service and clean, comfortable rooms with heating and new showers. It's great value when you consider how closely these rooms resemble those in many of Guìyáng's top-end hotels. Prices rise with each floor,

however the rooms stay the same. Try to get a room at the back of the hotel where you can't hear the booming train announcements. Rates include breakfast.

Tǐyù Bīnguǎn (☎ 579 8777, fax 579 0799) Doubles with bath Y138. The rooms here are enormous and comfortable. You'll find the hotel on the grounds of Guizhou Gymnasium, next door to the restaurant, at the southern end of the complex.

Jīnqiáo Fàndiàn (☎ 582 9958, fax 581 3867) Doubles Y248. This hotel has OK standards with private balconies.

Báichéng Fàndiàn (☎ 586 6888, fax 582 4985, 246 Zhonghua Donglu) Doubles Y480. Although this four-star hotel's prices are definitely top end, at the time of writing it was permanently offering standard doubles marked down to Y260.

Places to Stay – Top End

Trade-Point Hotel (Bǎidùn Jiǔdiàn; ☎ 582 7888, fax 5823118, Yan'an Donglu) Doubles Y800. While there are loads of top-end hotels in Guìyáng, few are worth the splurge. The Trade-Point Hotel is by far the most tempting. Out of season you may get a room here for Y428.

Guizhou Park Hotel (Guìzhōu Fàndiàn; ☎ 682 2888, fax 682 4397, 66 Beijing Lu) Doubles Y320-680. This hotel has fairly plush standards.

Jinjiang Fresh Flower Hotel (Jǐnjiāng Xiānhuā Dàjiǔdiàn; ☎ 586 7888, fax 587 3010, 1 Zhonghua Nanlu) Singles/doubles Y198/428. Above the Parkson Shopping Centre, you're paying more for location here than anything else. Enter the hotel off Zhongshan Xilu and take the lift up to the 12th-floor reception.

Crown Point Holiday Inn (☎ 677 1888, fax 677 1688, 1 Guikai Lu) Doubles Y750. Here you'll find the Holiday Inn's usual, comfortable rooms.

Places to Eat

Street Snacks Guìyáng, like Kūnmíng, is a great city for snack tracking. Just follow Zunyi Lu up to Zhonghua Nanlu and peer into the side alleys for *noodle, dumpling and kebab stalls*. One alley definitely worth trying is just north-east of the train station. On the first block off Zunyi Lu are lots of fresh noodles and *jiǎozi* (Chinese ravioli). If you take the first left off this alley, towards

Jiefang Lu, you'll find *stalls* with chefs cooking vegies, tofu and meat on huge table-top grills.

There's also a decent, if small, *night market* on Ruijin Lu, just north of Hébīn Gōngyuán. You can select from the local varieties of *shāguō fěn*, a noodle and seafood, meat or vegetable combination put in a casserole pot and fired over a flame of rocket-launch proportions. All of these market stalls offer filling meals for around Y10.

Traditional Restaurants Next door to Tǐyù Bīnguǎn, on the grounds of Guizhou Gymnasium, is a good *restaurant* where attentive staff serve up the traditional form of eight treasures tea (*bābǎo chá*), by swirling hot water from a long-stemmed copper kettle.

Guìzhōu Běijīng Kǎoyādiàn (Guizhou Beijing Duck Restaurant) Whole duck Y60. While many Guìyáng restaurants specialise in duck, this place comes highly recommended. If you like duck it's money well spent.

Miao Nationality Restaurant (Miáo Miáo Zhài) You can try authentic Miao cuisine here. Follow the staircase down to a courtyard.

Júeyuán Cāntīng (Awakening Palace Restaurant; 51 Fushui Beilu). Open 11.30am-2.30pm & 4.30pm-7pm. This Buddhist restaurant, originally constructed in 1862, forms part of the adjacent temple and promises meals 'free of worldly dust'. All food is strictly vegetarian.

Western Restaurants Western restaurants are beginning to sprout up throughout Guìyáng.

New Zealand Western Restaurant (Niǔxīlán Xīcāntīng; ☎ 651 2086, Ruijin Beilu) This restaurant has salads, soups, burgers and pasta, not to mention baked Alaska, for reasonable prices. They also serve a few Japanese dishes, have a full bar and will deliver to your door.

Shakey's (Zhongshan Xilu) Pizzas from Y26. In addition to an amazing number of fried chicken fast-food outlets, Guìyáng now boasts a Shakey's, which serves deep-pan pizzas. You'll find it next to the overpass.

For amazing, freshly baked cinnamon buns, head for the *bakery* at the bottom of Fushui Lu. The *cafe* at the Holiday Inn serves croissants, cheesecake and sells fantastic loaves of banana bread for Y16.

If you're looking for something a little more classy (or filling), try the Western buffet on the 2nd floor of the *Trade-Point Hotel (see Places to Stay)* for Y78.

Entertainment

Cafes & Bars There are quite a few entertainment options:

No-Name Coffee Bar (Wúmíng Kāfēitīng, Ruijin Nanlu) Snacks from Y10. This is a cosy place to lounge for a while. There's a well-stocked bar, and it serves small plates of snacks and coffees.

Norway Forest (Mèngwēi Sēnlín) Open until 2am. This cafe/bar near Jiǎxiù Pavilion has a large array of beer, including Carlsberg, Heineken and Sol, along with Irish coffees and Baileys.

Along Beijing Lu, between Ruijin Beilu and Zhonghua Beilu, are a plethora of bars and cafes including *Legends of the Fall Bar* and *The Little Beer House*. Be forewarned, however, most local Guìzhōu beers have a fairly bad reputation among travellers.

Getting There & Away

Air Civil Aviation Administration of China (CAAC; Zhōngguó Mínháng; ☎ 584 4534 to book, 581 2138 to reconfirm), at 264 Zunyi Lu, is open 8.30am to 9pm. The English-speaking staff is cheerful and helpful. China Southern Air (☎ 582 8429) has a booking office on the corner of Ruijin Nanlu and Zunyi Lu.

Destinations from Guìyáng's shiny Lóngdòng airport, 7km east of town, include Chóngqìng (Y420, Wednesday and Saturday), Guìlín (Y500, Tuesday, Thursday and Sunday) and Xī'ān (Y770, Monday, Wednesday and Friday). There are also daily flights to Chéngdū (Y570), Kūnmíng (Y400), Guǎngzhōu (Y790), Běijīng (Y1530), Shànghǎi (Y1430) and Shēnzhèn (Y860).

Tickets to Hong Kong (Y1850, Tuesday and Friday) and Bangkok (Y1850, Wednesday, Thursday and Sunday) can be booked through China Southwest at its booking office on Beijing Lu and Ruijin Beilu.

Bus There are three main places where you can catch long-distance buses in Guìyáng. The main bus station is quite a long trek from the train station.

From the long-distance bus station on Yan'an Xilu, buses travel between Guìyáng and Ānshùn between 8am and 7pm (Y20, two hours). To Zūnyì, buses leave every 30 minutes from 7am to 9pm. The ride along the new expressway costs Y50 and takes 2½ hours. There is also a morning bus to Zhījīn at 8am (five to six hours) and an evening sleeper heads to Xīngyì at 8pm (Y106).

Buses seem to be leaving continually from the stand just north of the train station. Tickets can be bought on the bus or from the booth at the southern end of the road, nearest the train station. Buses and minibuses head for Zūnyì from 7am until as late as midnight; officially the price is Y49 but shop around, you may be able to find one for around Y30. To Ānshùn (Y23), buses leave from 7am until late and there is a sleeper at 5pm for Xīngyì (Y105).

From the bus stand on Jiefang Lu, buses leave for Kǎilǐ from 8am to 7pm, for Róngjiāng at 4pm and for Ānshùn from 7.30am until 7.30pm.

It's also possible to take tour buses (don't expect much from that first word) to Huángguǒshù Falls and Lónggōng Caves from either the train station, the long-distance bus station or many of the hotels. The tour buses generally only run in the summer, depart in the early morning and cost Y55 to Y68, depending on the type of bus. This does not include admission fees to the various sights. These buses will get you to Huángguǒshù in around three hours, as opposed to the five hours required if you take public transport. If you don't want to stay overnight at Ānshùn or at the falls, this is definitely the most hassle-free way of getting out there. Tōngdá Fàndiàn also offers a daily tour to Zhījīn Cave for Y98 per person.

Train Guìyáng's glossy new train station has a modern, computerised ticket office, making it one of the more pleasant places in China to buy a train ticket.

A direct train runs to Kūnmíng, train No 2079, departing at 6.50pm (hard/soft sleeper Y160/250, 12½ hours). To Chéngdū, train No K922 leaves at 3.40pm (hard/soft sleeper Y170/250, 18 hours), and to Chóngqìng train No 5608 leaves at 7.30pm (hard/soft sleeper Y100/150).

A train departs for Guìlín at 10am (three or four hours) and for Guǎngzhōu at 10.50am (Y240, seven hours).

For a longer haul, train No K112 takes three days to reach Shànghǎi, leaving Guìyáng at 8pm (hard/soft sleeper Y360/400). To Běijīng, catch train No T88, which departs at 10pm and arrives three days later (hard/soft sleeper Y500/650).

There are also connections to Zūnyì (7.07am and noon) and Liùpánshuǐ (9.20am and 5pm). The 7.40am train to Kǎilǐ (Y25) originates in Guìyáng and is therefore the easiest on which to get a seat. Most of the trains to Ānshùn leave Guìyáng in the late evening; it's easier to take the bus.

Getting Around

To/From the Airport Airport buses depart from the CAAC office two hours before flight departures to meet incoming flights (Y10, 20 minutes).

Bus Buses No 1 and 2 do city tour loops from the train station, passing close to the long-distance bus station. Bus No 1 travels up Zhongshan Nanlu and heads westward along Beijing Lu. Buses cost Y1 and recorded announcements in Chinese and English boom out stops.

Taxi Taxis charge a flat Y10 fare to anywhere in the city.

ZŪNYÌ 遵义
☎ 0852 • pop 6.7 million

Around 160km north of Guìyáng, Zūnyì is the site of the famous Zūnyì Conference and something of a mecca for those with an interest in Chinese Communist Party (CCP) history.

History

On 16 October 1934, hemmed into the Jiāngxī soviet by Kuomintang forces, the Communists set out on a Herculean, one-year, 9500km Long March from one end of China to the other. By mid-December they had reached Guìzhōu and marched on Zūnyì, a prosperous mercantile town. Taking the town by surprise, the Communists were able to stock up on supplies and take a breather.

From 15 to 18 January 1935, the top-level Communist leaders took stock of their situation in the now-famous Zūnyì Conference.

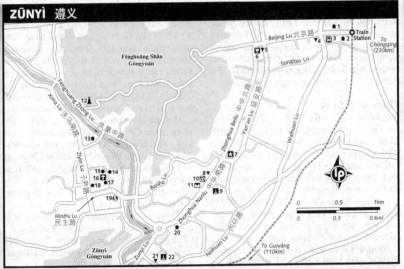

ZŪNYÌ 遵义

ZŪNYÌ

PLACES TO STAY
1 Lántiān Bīnguǎn
  蓝天宾馆
2 Jǐnghóng Dàjiǔdiàn
  金虹大酒店
13 Zūnyì Bīnguǎn
  遵义宾馆
20 Huáhǎi Dàjiǔdiàn
  华海大酒店

PLACES TO EAT
4 Hotpot & Grill Stalls
  火锅烧烤摊
5 Hotpot Restaurants
  火锅餐馆
8 Dōng Dōng Bō
  东东包

21 Hotpot & Grill Restaurants
  火锅烧烤店

OTHER
3 Long-Distance Bus Station
  长途汽车站
6 Bar 1950
7 PSB
  公安局
9 Báiyún Sì
  白云寺
10 China Telecom Internet Cafe
  网吧
11 Post Office
  邮电局

12 Monument to the Martyrs of the Red Army
  红军烈士纪念碑
14 Red Army General Political Department
  红军总政治部旧址
15 Residence of Bo Gu
  博古旧居
16 Catholic Church
  天主教堂
17 State Bank of the Red Army
  红军银行
18 Zunyi Conference Site
  遵义会议会址
19 Bank of China
  中国银行
22 Xiāngshān Sì
  湘山寺

Its resolutions largely reflected the views of Mao Zedong, who was elected a full member of the ruling Standing Committee of the Politburo and Chief Assistant to Zhou Enlai in military planning. This was a pivotal factor in Mao's rise to power.

Things to See

Communist History Sites The most celebrated site is the **Zunyi Conference Site** (*Zūnyì Huìyì Huìzhǐ; admission Y5; open 8.30am-5pm daily*). Open to the public there are rooms filled with CCP memorabilia as

well as the meeting rooms and living quarters of the bigwigs.

Nearby are the original headquarters of the **Red Army General Political Department** (*Hóngjūn Zǒngzhèngzhìbù; admission Y2; open 8.30am-5pm daily*). There are a couple of rooms that are open to the public with displays on the Long March. On the other side of the street the street are two more sites – the **Residence of Bo Gu** and the original home of the **State Bank of the Red Army** (*Huìyìqījiān; admission Y2*), today's Bank of China.

Also worth a visit is peaceful **Xiāngshān Sì**, built in the 1920s and still an active place of worship. Zūnyì also has two parks which provide ample space for a stroll. **Zūnyì Gōngyuán** is in the western part of town and **Fènghuáng Shān Gōngyuán** (*Phoenix Hill Park*) is the huge, green area in the north.

Places to Stay
Jīnghóng Dàjiǔdiàn (☎ 882 2925 ext 30199) Singles/doubles Y30/50, with bath & air con Y80/90. Also known as Zūntiě Dàshà, this place is friendly, comfortable and immaculate. Try to get a room at the back where you won't hear the bus and train station noise all night.

Lántiān Bīnguǎn (☎ 862 2916 ext 9810) Doubles Y138. This place might let you stay but they'll only offer up their over-priced doubles with basic bathrooms.

Huáhǎi Dàjiǔdiàn (☎ 883 7660) Singles/doubles with bath Y100/120, twins without bath Y160. The rooms here are nice enough but the bathrooms need a good cleaning. Look for a sign over the hotel's entrance that reads 'Zunyi Huahai Entertainment Service'.

Zūnyì Bīnguǎn (☎ 822 4902, fax 822 1497) Singles/doubles Y326/388. This is the official three-star tourist hotel. The rooms are spacious and comfortable but overpriced.

Places to Eat
There is nothing to rave about in Zūnyì, culinary-wise. Come dinnertime, Beijing Lu at Waihuan Lu comes alive with *hotpot and grill stalls*. You'll also find similar grills during the day along Zhonghua Nanlu – devoted mainly to meat lovers. The alleys running south-east off Zhonghua Nanlu are crowded with *noodle stalls*.

If you're wanting to eat indoors, try the *hotpot restaurants* at the western end of Beijing Lu or the *hotpot and grill restaurants* along Neihuan Lu.

Dōng Dōng Bō (*Zhonghua Nanlu*) This is a popular noodle restaurant, located near the pedestrian overpass, that makes delicious, fresh, rice noodles and dumplings.

Entertainment
Bar 1950 (*Beijing Lu*) With a well-stocked bar, this pretty close rendition of an American pub is a great place to enjoy a drink.

Getting There & Away
Buses and minibuses zip along the expressway between Guìyáng and Zūnyì from 7am until around midnight; they start to thin out around 6pm. The trip takes 2½ to three hours. Prices range drastically but you should be able to get a seat in a comfy Aveco van for Y30. In Zūnyì, you'll find buses at the main bus station and outside the train station.

Despite government plans to link Guìyáng with Chéngdū via Chóngqìng with new expressways, nothing has yet materialised. Consequently, no bus runs to Chéngdū and only one heads to Chóngqìng (Y80) at 4pm – a 10-hour journey that'll dump you off in the middle of the night. You might be better off on the train.

Zūnyì is on the main northern rail line connecting Guìyáng with Chóngqìng, Chéngdū and the rest of China. Trains depart for Guìyáng (Y10) at 8.04am, 11.49am, 8.35pm and 9pm daily.

To Chóngqìng (Y23), a train passes through at 3.59pm and to Chéngdū (Y60) at 6.32pm.

ĀNSHÙN   安顺
☎ 0853
In addition to giving you fairly easy access to Huángguǒshù Falls and Lónggōng Caves, Ānshùn itself is set in a pleasant karst limestone region. Markets abound and are often host to minority entrepreneurs in traditional dress. Many of these markets are located in the town's narrow streets, which are lined with interesting old wooden buildings.

Once an important tea- and opium-trading centre, Ānshùn remains the commercial hub of western Guìzhōu. Today it's most famous as a producer of batiks, kitchen knives and the lethal Anjiu brand of alcohol. The nearby aviation factory is also well known, and recently diversified production from fighter planes to family hatchbacks.

Orientation
The long-distance bus and train stations are 3km and 4km south of downtown respectively. The main commercial and shopping area is found on Zhonghua Donglu, Minzhu Lu and Zhonghua Nanlu.

Information
Tourist Office Ānshùn lacks a CITS branch, but China Travel Service (CTS;

Zhōngguó Lǚxíngshè; ☎ 322 4379) has an office at the northern end of Tashan Donglu (3rd floor). It organises trips to Huángguǒshù and the surrounding area, and has information on attractions and festivals. Outside the tourist season the office's opening hours can become somewhat sporadic.

Money You can change money at the Bank of China's main branch, across the street from the China Telecom office.

Post & Communications The main China Post is at the corner of Zhonghua Donglu and Zhonghua Beilu. China Telecom is south of here, on the corner of Zhonghua Nanlu and Tashan Donglu.

Next door to its main office, China Telecom offers Internet access for Y5 per hour from 8.30am to 10pm. On the corner of Xingian Lu and Zhonghua Donglu, there are three or four Internet cafes on the 2nd floor, offering access for Y3 per hour.

Things to See & Do

The town's main attraction is **Dōnglín Sì** *(admission Y0.5)*, an active Buddhist temple dating back to the Ming dynasty (AD 1405) and restored in 1668. North of here, **Wén Miào** is a more recent concrete temple, which is dilapidated and deserted. However the narrow market streets which surround it are worth exploring.

Ānshùn has a huge **Sunday market** where you can buy anything – modern or traditional – from dried beef to human hair

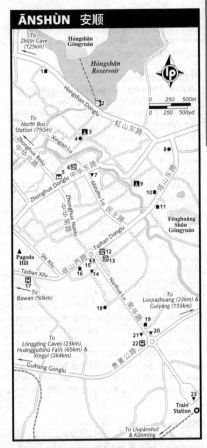

(bought by young Miao women to boost their hairdos). The market completely takes over the centre of town, though the most traditional part lies along Shi Xilu.

Places to Stay

Golden Phoenix Mountain Hotel (Fēnghuǎngshā Dàjiǔdiàn; ☎ 322 5663, Tashan Donglu) Twins without bath Y80, doubles with bath Y180. This place has the best and cheapest rooms in town – clean, wooden and next-to-new. Bus No 1 will take you here from the long-distance bus or train station.

Xīxiùshān Bīnguǎn (☎ 322 3900) Doubles/suites Y98/138. This clean and friendly hotel has rooms at the back with views over a small garden and karst hills.

Huáyóu Bīnguǎn (☎ 322 6020) Doubles Y120-160. This hotel is now open to foreigners, however you won't be let near the cheap rooms. The doubles you will be offered are overpriced.

Mínzú Fàndiàn (☎ 322 2500) Doubles Y180. This is one of Ānshùn's two old standbys, to which you may be directed. The rooms are clean but overpriced and nondescript and the place appears deserted.

Hóngshān Bīnguǎn (☎ 322 3101) Doubles Y200-500. This hotel has been given a new paint job on the outside but inside it's damp, less than clean and severely overpriced.

Places to Eat

If you're hunting down cheap eats, outside the train station are a row of forgettable *noodle stalls* and around the bus station are some friendly *point-and-choose restaurants*, a few of which do hotpot as well. Along many of Ānshùn's streets, vendors sell fried potatoes with onion and chilli, fried bread or meaty barbeques. There is also a popular *bakery* on the corner of Minzhu Lu and Zhonghua Donglu.

Be forewarned: dog is eaten in these parts – lots of dog. You'll see the skinned animals propped up outside restaurants as an enticement to come in for lunch.

Getting There & Away

Bus The trip to Guìyáng takes about two hours along the Guihuang Expressway, built specifically to whisk tourists up to Huángguǒshù Falls. Luxury buses (Y18) and super-luxury Daewoo coaches (Y20) whip along the route every 20 minutes or so from 7.10am until 6.30pm, and drop off at the bus station on Jiefang Lu, near Guìyáng's train station. Private operators run this route until late into the night. Local buses take a lot longer and stop everywhere en route.

There is a 1pm direct sleeper bus to Kūnmíng (Y126, 19 hours) via Pánxiàn. You can also reach Kūnmíng via Xīngyì in Guìzhōu's south-west, from where you can catch a direct bus or train. Buses leave Ānshùn for Xīngyì (Y46) between 8.30am and 11am.

To Huángguǒshù Falls there is a slow 10am bus (Y6); or you can take a Xīngyì-bound bus which will let you off on the highway, about a 15-minute walk from Huángguǒshù village.

If you're headed to Zhījīn Cave, buses depart from Ānshùn's north bus station between 8am and 6pm, more or less hourly (Y20, three hours).

The local bus station on Tashan Xilu has buses to Lónggōng (Y5 to Y8) hourly between 8am and 5pm.

Train It is virtually impossible to get sleeper reservations to Kūnmíng in Ānshùn. If that's what you're after, you may have to backtrack to Guìyáng and make one there. If you are willing to brave a hard seat (Y68) for the 11-hour journey, the train pulls out of Ānshùn at 8.20pm.

Trains for Guìyáng (Y15, one hour 40 minutes) leave at 10.50am and 7.20pm however most people hop on a bus instead.

A train for Liùpánshuǐ (Y16) departs daily at 11.20am. Another leaves at 6.29pm and arrives around 9pm.

Getting Around

The No 1 minibus is the most useful – it zips around town from the train station, up Tashan Donglu and on past Hóngshān Bīnguǎn (see Places to Stay). Bus No 2 travels between the train station and the north bus station. A seat on a bus costs Y1.

AROUND ĀNSHÙN
Lónggōng Caves 龙宫洞
Lónggōng Dòng

About 23km south of Ānshùn, near the Bouyi settlement of Shítou Zhài, is a series of underground caverns called Lónggōng

(*Dragon Palace; admission Y35*), which forms a huge network through 20 hills. At present only 1km of the cave system is open to tourists. While it's dolled up with recorded music and coloured spotlights, on a quiet day a glide through here in a hand-paddled boat can be an impressive and peaceful experience. Admission includes the boat ride.

A second, less impressive site has been opened 4km before Lónggōng, called **Guānyīn Cave** (*admission Y25, with Lónggōng Y50*). It's pleasant but not really worth the admission fee (which also includes the boat ride).

Getting There & Away Local buses to Lónggōng depart hourly from Ānshùn's local bus station on Tashan Xilu, between 8am and 5pm. The trip costs Y5 and takes just under an hour. Buses return hourly until 5pm.

Buses from Ānshùn will more than likely drop you at Guānyīn Cave even if you've asked for Lónggōng. If you aren't planning on visiting Guānyīn Cave, be sure you've been taken all the way to Lónggōng (the final stop) or you'll have a 4km hike ahead of you.

Many of the tours from Guìyáng or Ānshùn to Huángguǒshù also stop in Lónggōng for an hour or so. Unfortunately, there is no public transport between Lónggōng and Huángguǒshù other than via Ānshùn. Private microvans will take you – bargaining begins at Y50.

Zhījīn Cave 织金洞
Zhījīn Dòng

At around 10km long and up to 150m high, Zhījīn Cave (*admission Y60*) ranks as the largest in China and one of the biggest in the world. Located at the edge of a small village some 15km outside Zhījīn, this place is impressive even if you're not a cave fanatic. Small passageways open up into giant room after room, where calcium deposits have created an otherworldly landscape of spectacular shapes and spirals, often reaching from floor to ceiling.

Tickets to the site are steep but include a compulsory tour. If you're not travelling with a posse, this can mean a bit of a wait, as tours depart with a minimum of ten people. While the tour itself is in Chinese

only, you'll likely be glad to have someone around who knows the way back out of the maze of trails. The tour lasts for around three hours, possibly more.

Places to Stay If you're planning to stay overnight here, it would be a good idea to check with CTS in Ānshùn about accommodation.

There is a tourist hotel on the right as you enter the village, however it was closed when we last visited. There are a couple of guesthouses in Zhījīn but the only one open during the off season would not accept foreigners. You're options are likely to be better in the summer months.

Getting There & Away A trip to the cave can be made as a daytrip from Ānshùn – just. Buses depart from Ānshùn for Zhījīn (Y20) between 8am and 6pm and take 2½ to 3½ hours, depending on whether you're on a bus that can reach speeds greater than a lawnmower. Once in Zhījīn a bus can take you to the cave from the local bus station, however it's inconsistent and slow. Shared taxis can do the trip in 20 minutes and cost around Y5 per person, or you can charter a taxi for Y20. The last bus departs Zhījīn for Ānshùn at 6pm.

Tours from Guìyáng also visit Zhījīn Cave. See the Getting There & Away section of Guìyáng.

HUÁNGGUǑSHÙ FALLS
Huángguǒshù Dà Pùbù 黄果树大瀑布

Reaching a width of 81m and plunging 74m down into Rhinoceros Pool, it is not surprising that this huge cascade of water (*admission Y30*) is Guìzhōu's No 1 tourist attraction. The Chinese explored this area in the 1980s, as a preliminary to harnessing the region's hydroelectric potential. They discovered about 18 falls, four subterranean rivers and 100 caves, many of which are now being gradually opened to visitors. The massive waterfall, cave and karst complex covers some 450 sq km, however the area near Huángguǒshù village, home to the massive Huángguǒshù (Yellow Fruit Tree) Falls, is closer to 6km in length and easily explored in an afternoon.

The thunder of Huángguǒshù Falls can be heard for some distance, and during the rainy season (May to October) the mist from the falls carries up to Huángguǒshù village. The falls are most spectacular about four days after heavy rains. The dry season lasts from November to April and during March and April the flow of water can become a trickle.

There are three entrances to the main falls: at the top of the presently closed cable car, next to Huángguǒshù Bīnguǎn and just before Huángguǒshù village. Once inside, you can get up close to the falls, both by trapezing across a stone path over **Rhinoceros Pool** and by visiting **Water Curtain Cave** where, for an extra Y10, you can walk through a tunnel behind the falls and view the water streaming past. During the rainy season, both of these explorations can turn into wades and prove treacherous. Good footwear and waterproof gear are necessary at any time of year.

There are a number of other waterfalls in the area that you can visit. One kilometre above the main falls and a couple of kilometres' walk north of the falls is **Steep Slope Falls** (*Dǒupō Pùbù*), 105m wide and 23m high. Eight kilometres below Huángguǒshù Falls is the **Star Bridge Scenic Area** (*Tiānxīng Qiáo Jǐngqū; admission Y30*), known for its 'potted landscape'. The occasional minibus and motor rickshaw run here from the bus stand. You can haggle the price down to around Y10.

In addition to its impressive falls, the area around Huángguǒshù also provides an excellent chance to ramble on foot through nearby rural minority areas.

Places to Stay & Eat Accommodation options open to foreigners in Huángguǒshù village have recently increased – but so have the prices. The hotels are fairly grim and very overpriced.

Huángguǒshù Bīnguǎn (☎ 359 2110) Doubles in old/new building Y280/380. Halfway between the bus stand and Huángguǒshù village, this hotel is located in two separate buildings. The newer, pricier hotel is on the left of the main road. The older hotel is off to the right of the main road (look for the parking sign) and has somewhat musty rooms in peaceful surroundings with tiptoe views of the falls.

Huángguǒshù Gōngsāng Zhāodàisuǒ (☎ 359 2583) Standard rooms/triples Y160/220. This police-run guesthouse is a little further up the road from Huángguǒshù

Bīnguǎn; it has OK but overpriced rooms. You may be able to cut a deal.

Pùbù Bīnguǎn (☎ 359 2520) Triples without bath Y120, standard rooms with bath Y200. In the centre of the village, this place is also overpriced. The rooms here are clean but extremely basic and bare.

Along the main road in town are several *restaurants* with verandas at the back where you can eat and enjoy a great view of the falls. There are also *snack bars* and souvenir stalls scattered along the path from the bus station to the falls viewing area.

Getting There & Away Unless you're on a tour, Huángguǒshù is easiest to reach from Ānshùn, from where a bus departs daily at 10am (Y6). During the summer months, additional buses as well as tour buses run from the station and some of Ānshùn's major hotels.

Buses from Ānshùn to Xīngyì also pass by Huángguǒshù, leaving you about a 15-minute walk from the highway to the village. If you're coming from Xīngyì, morning buses to Guìyáng will also drop you off at this point. Be sure to let the driver know that you want to get off at the falls.

Coming from Guìyáng, the only direct transport to Huángguǒshù is by tour bus (see Getting There & Away in the Guìyáng section).

Heading out of Huángguǒshù, minibuses and buses for Ānshùn and occasionally for Guìyáng depart between 7am and 7pm. Buses for Xīngyì leave in the morning. Local buses often take the old road to Ānshùn, which stretches out the journey to 1½ hours. If you're headed directly to Ānshùn or Guìyáng, you may want to find a bus taking the expressway.

You can look for tour buses headed for Lónggōng Caves at the bus stand, however there is no public transport from here to Lónggōng except via Ānshùn. Private microvans and even rickshaws will offer to take you – bargaining begins at Y50.

Western Guìzhōu

As the area most recently opened to tourists, Guìzhōu's west is rough and, at times, forbidding. The main attraction is the Nature Reserve at Cǎohǎi Hú. It's also possible to head into Yúnnán from here, passing through some interesting minority territory before heading for Zhāotōng and on to Xīchàng (Sìchuān) or Xuānwēi. This route is for adventurers looking to get off the beaten track.

WĒINÍNG 威宁
☎ 0857

The town of Wēiníng is caked with mud and not likely the most beautiful place you'll visit, however it has an interesting mix of minority peoples. A large **market** is held here every three or four days. At other times there is a quieter market street in the old, eastern part of town. Evidence of the Hui includes a modern mosque in the northern part of town and several Muslim restaurants nearby.

The town's main draw is **Cǎohǎi Hú** (Grass Sea Lake), one of China's premier birdwatching sites and only a 15-minute walk south-west from downtown Wēiníng. This 20 sq km freshwater wetland became a national nature reserve in 1992 and is an important winter site for many migratory birds, the most famous of which is the black-necked crane.

The lake has a fragile history, having been drained during both the Great Leap Forward and the Cultural Revolution with unfulfilled hopes of producing useable farmland. Refilled again in 1980, environmental problems remain and the government is enlisting locals in its attempts to protect the lake.

Trails wrap around the shore, but the best way to see the lake – and the birds – is by 'punts'. Don't worry about finding the boatmen: they'll find you. The best time to visit the lake is from December to March, when the birds are wintering. Bring warm clothes.

Places to Stay
Cǎohǎi Bīnguǎn (☎ 622 1511) Beds in 4-bed dorms Y38, doubles or triples with bath Y58. West of town, this place is convenient to the lake however it's fairly musty and cold and your chance of getting a view is minimal. The doubles and triples have heated blankets.

Hǒngyàn Bīnguǎn (☎ 622 4755) Beds in 3-bed dorms Y20, doubles with bath Y80. In the centre of town, just off the main road and behind China Post, this place is friendly, bright and comfortable. Unfortunately, without heating, it's also cold.

Jiàngōng Bīnguǎn (☎ 622 4438) Doubles/triples without bath Y50/60, singles/doubles with bath Y90/120. Also in the centre of town, east from the main intersection, this hotel's biggest seller is its central heating, which kicks in each night at 8pm. In the centre of town, this place is most easily found by asking a local.

Zhēngfù Zhāodàisuǒ Dorm beds Y15-20, singles/doubles Y70/80. This is the only other place in town that will take foreigners, however it's poorly maintained and not very clean. These prices include bathroom, but don't be fooled by the heaters – they don't work.

Places to Eat
Cǎohǎi Cāntīng About 200m east of Cǎohǎi Bīnguǎn, this restaurant is cheap and friendly.

Shíxiāng Jiǔjiā Next to Jiàngōng Bīnguǎn, this restaurant serves great stir-fried dishes (try the smoked tofu) and also has hotpot.

There are several **point-and-choose restaurants** south of the Xinhua Bookshop and lots of people selling roasted potatoes along the streets. Near the mosque are a number of **Muslim restaurants** that serve good beef noodles.

Getting There & Away
First take a train from Guìyáng to Liùpánshuǐ station, which is actually the station at the forgettable Shuǐchéng city. There are a few daily trains that run to/from Guìyáng via Ānshùn (hard/soft seat Y25/42). Shuǐchéng has a few places to stay.

Xīnlǒng Dàjiǔdiàn (☎ 822 3378 ext 8888) Beds in doubles/triples Y45/35. Across from the train station, this is the most convenient place.

From Shuǐchéng to Wēiníng you can take a comfortable postal bus (Y17, three hours) every day at 7am from the main China Post office. Buy your tickets in advance as the local buses departing from the bus station are crowded, decrepit and cost Y40.

Leaving Wēiníng you can backtrack to Guìyáng or take a minibus north to **Zhāotōng** in Yúnnán (Y30, five hours). From here you can hop over to Xīchàng in southern Sìchuān to connect with the Kūnmíng-Chéngdū train line.

From Wēiníng's main bus station there is a 9am departure for Xuānwēi (Y30) in Yún-nán. There's also a sleeper for Guìyáng (Y100) at 8.30pm.

XĪNGYÌ 兴义
☎ 0859

Underappreciated Xīngyì is mainly a stopover in the far south-western part of Guìzhōu for those travelling between Guìyáng and Nánníng or Kūnmíng. How-ever, with some of the finest weather in Guìzhōu, this place is an interesting town to wander around and has some worthwhile sights, including a good **minorities museum** (admission Y8; open 8.30am-11am & 2.30pm-5.30pm Mon-Fri) and some nearby karst scenery.

The main attraction in the area is the 15km-long **Mǎlíng Gorge** (Mǎlínghé Xiágǔ), which is peaceful and well worth a visit. With stunning scenery, many trav-ellers find it more interesting than Huáng-guǒshù Falls, and you can spend the better part of a day following the winding path into the lush gorge, across bridges and up to and behind high, cascading waterfalls. It's a good idea to bring waterproof gear, sturdy shoes and a torch (flashlight) to light your way through some of the caves.

You can also raft on the river at several points; don't expect white-water rapids, this is a slow descent. Xingyi Travel Service arranges 2½-hour trips for Y98 per person.

To reach the gorge from Xīngyì, you can attempt to catch a Xīngrén- or Dǐngxiào-bound bus. At the time of writing, these buses were being diverted away from the gorge due to construction on the bridge over Mǎlíng Gorge. If this is still the case, taxis will take you the 6km for Y15.

Places to Stay
Pánjiāng Bīnguǎn (☎ 322 3456, Panjiang Lu) Twins/triples without bath Y38/48, doubles with bath Y88-138, triples Y98. As the official tourist hotel, this place is busy and the cheaper rooms are almost always full. This hotel is located just north of the south bus station.

Jīnhuì Bīnguǎn (Pinjiang Lu) Doubles with/without bath Y60/30. Just up the road from Pánjiāng Bīnguǎn, the rooms here are bright and clean. There is no hot water to speak of, however.

Yínhé Jiǔdiàn (☎ 323 2001) Doubles with bath Y90. Down the road from Xingyi Travel Service, prices here are a little steep for what's on offer. There are cheaper rooms but you're unlikely to get near them.

Getting There & Away
Sleeper buses leave for Guìyáng from the eastern bus station at 3pm and 6pm (Y84, eight hours). If you don't want to arrive in the middle of the night, consider taking one of the morning minibuses (Y78) that depart between 6am and 9am. These buses also stop at Huángguǒshù Falls and Ānshùn.

If you're headed west, buses to Kūnmíng (Y91, 10 hours) leave from the western bus station every half hour between 6am and 8am. There is also a sleeper bus that de-parts at 8pm. Buses from Kūnmíng pass by Shílín in Yúnnán, about eight hours from Xīngyì.

Xīngyì is now served by the train line be-tween Nánníng and Kūnmíng, though the train station is 10km away. Buses will take you there for Y10 from outside Xīngyì's eastern bus station. Trains to Kūnmíng de-part at 9.07am and 1.32pm. A train also stops here en route to Nánníng at 1.52pm.

Eastern Guìzhōu

The rich minority areas of south-eastern Guìzhōu are surprisingly unexplored by Western travellers. Technically, in the Qiandongnan Miao and Dong Autonomous Prefecture, over 80 different minorities live in the forested hillsides and river valleys of this region. Many of these minorities con-tinue to hold epic weekly markets and an-nual festivals and retain a unique way of life relatively untouched by China's mod-ernising mania.

Particularly recommended is Xījiāng, China's largest Miao (Hmong) village, only a few hours outside of Kǎilǐ. The remote Dong village of Zhàoxīng, in the south-east, is also well worth a visit and can be incor-porated into a back-door route into Guǎngxī.

Outside Kǎilǐ, there are no places to change money in the area, so bring plenty of cash Renminbi with you.

Traditional Garments

The variety of clothing among the minorities of Guìzhōu provides travellers with a daily visual feast. Clothes are as much a social and ethnic denominator as pure decoration. They also show whether or not a woman is married and are a pointer to a woman's wealth and skills at weaving and embroidery.

Many women in remote areas still weave their own hemp and cotton cloth. Some families, especially in Dong areas, still ferment their own indigo paste as well, and you will also see this for sale in traditional markets. Many women will not attend festivals in the rain for fear that the dyes in their fabrics will run. Methods of producing indigo are greatly treasured and kept secret, but are increasingly threatened by the introduction of artificial chemical dyes.

Embroidery is central to minority costume and is a tradition passed down from mother to daughter. Designs include many important symbols and references to myths and history. Birds, fish and a variety of dragon motifs are popular. The highest quality work is often reserved for baby carriers, and many young girls work on these as they approach marrying age. Older women will often spend hundreds of hours embroidering their own funeral clothes.

Costumes move with the times. In larger towns, Miao women often substitute their embroidered smocks with a good woolly jumper (sweater) and their headdresses look suspiciously like mass-produced pink and yellow Chinese towels.

KǍILǏ 凯里
☎ 0855

About 195km almost directly east of Guìyáng, Kǎilǐ is the gateway to the surrounding minority villages.

Information

Tourist Office The CITS office in Kǎilǐ (☎/fax 822 2506) is located in the Yíngpánpō Mínzú Bīnguǎn complex (see Places to Stay). Helpful English-speaking staff can fill you in on minority destinations and festivals. Organised tours with CITS are on the pricey side, with a day tour of nearby villages without transport costing Y200 per person. Two- or three-day tours either north through Miao areas or south to the Dong region cost Y100 per person per day for the guide, Y2.5 per kilometre for transport, plus meals and accommodation for you, the guide and the driver.

Money The main branch of the Bank of China is near the city's main roundabout, on Beijing Donglu. You can change travellers cheques and money without any fuss. The branch around the corner on Zhaoshan Nanlu now houses the train ticket office but continues to have an ATM outside that accepts MasterCard.

Post & Communications You can post mail, send faxes and make international phone calls until around 7pm from China Post.

You'll see a number of cafes around town where you can access the Internet for Y2 to Y3 per hour.

Things to See & Do

There's not much to see or do in Kǎilǐ other than a visit to **Dàgé Gōngyuán** (*Big Pagoda Park*) or **Jīnquánhú Gōngyuán** at the very southern end of town, which has a Dong minority drum tower built in 1985. There is also a moderately interesting **Minorities Museum** (*Zhōu Mínzú Bówùguǎn; Zhaoshan Nanlu; admission Y10; open 9am-4pm*) which might be open if somebody turns up to unlock the doors. Don't be deterred by what appears to be a furniture shop on the 1st floor; continue upstairs another flight to the museum.

Kǎilǐ also has a good **Sunday market** that swamps the streets with traders from nearby minority villages.

Festivals

Kǎilǐ and the areas around it host a large number of minority festivals – over 130 annually, according to CITS. One of the biggest is **Lúshēng Festival**, held in Zhoūxī from the 11th to the 18th of the first lunar month. The *lúshēng* is a reed instrument used by the Miao people.

A similar festival is held midway through the seventh lunar month in Qīngmàn, to which 20,000 are said to turn up. The Miao new year is celebrated on the first four days of the 10th lunar month in

Kǎilǐ, Guàdīng, Zhōuxī and other Miao areas. CITS in Kǎilǐ should be able to provide you with a list of local festivals and their dates.

Places to Stay

Shíyóu Zhāodàisuǒ (☎ 823 4331) Beds in 5-bed dorms Y12, doubles or triples with bath Y68. This hotel currently has the cheapest beds in town, all with heated blankets. The rooms here are big and clean but freezing cold in the winter.

Jīnxīn Bīnguǎn (☎ 825 1910) Dorm beds/doubles Y40/180. This place is near the museum and has cheap beds in basic, clean rooms in a building out back. The price for the doubles with heating and bathroom are a bit of a jump.

Lántiān Jiǔdiàn (☎ 823 4699) Beds in 3-/4-bed dorms Y30/35, doubles Y168. In the heart of town, this popular hotel has a great location and 24-hour hot water, however you may struggle to get a dorm bed. Instead you'll be offered the heated doubles with a spotless bathroom and a nice view. The hotel's entrance is down the side of the building, off Beijing Xilu.

Zhènhuá Zhāodàisuǒ (☎ 823 4600) Doubles Y60. In the eastern part of town, you'll find nice, refurbished doubles here with heating, hot water and a shower.

Yíngpánpō Mínzú Bīnguǎn (☎ 823 4600) Doubles Y60. This place isn't as good a deal as Zhènhuá Zhāodàisuǒ. The rooms are the same price but somewhat more rundown.

Kǎilǐ Bīnguǎn (☎ 827 5000) Doubles/triples Y218/228. This two-star hotel is working hard to gain its next star. The rooms here are clean and comfortable but really overpriced.

Places to Eat

Kǎilǐ has some fantastic snack stalls lining its streets. Savoury crepes, potato patties, barbeques, tofu grills, noodles, hotpot, *shuǐjiǎo* (steamed *jiǎozi*, or Chinese ravioli) and wonton soup overflow for extremely reasonable prices. Check out Beijing Donglu, east of China Post or Zhaoshan Beilu, especially its night market.

Lǎodìfāng Jiǔjiā *(Yingpan Donglu)* Mains from Y12. This restaurant has OK food and is worth a try if you can get them to unplug the karaoke.

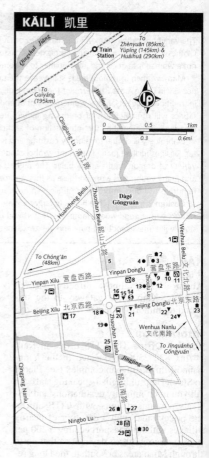

KǍILǏ 凯里

There are a many ***noodle bars*** in Kǎilǐ. A good one is near the museum, and another on Beijing Donglu and one east of the bank.

There is also a plethora of ***bakeries*** throughout town. The one on Beijing Donglu, across from the bank and behind a pedestrian overpass, sells instant hot drinks and cakes in a heated cafe.

Lìxiǎngmiàn Shídiàn This backpacker-friendly cafe has an English menu (with pictures!) and serves Chinese dishes along with some creative takes on Western food, including a pizza that'll stick to your ribs (Y2.2).

Getting There & Away

Bus The Kǎilǐ long-distance bus station has frequent buses to Guìyáng (Y35 to Y50, three hours) between 6.40am and 6pm.

KǍILǏ

PLACES TO STAY

2 Yíngpánpō Mínzú
   Bīnguǎn
   营盘坡民族宾馆
10 Shíyóu Zhāodàisuǒ
   石油招待所
18 Lántiān Jiǔdiàn
   蓝天酒店
23 Zhènhuá Zhāodàisuǒ
   振华招待所
26 Jīnxīn Bīnguǎn
   金鑫宾馆
30 Kǎilǐ Bīnguǎn
   凯里宾馆

PLACES TO EAT

9 Lǎodìfāng Jiǔjiā
   老地方酒家
15 Snack Stalls
   小吃摊
21 Bakery
22 Noodle Bar
   面条店

24 Lǐxiǎngmiàn Shídiàn
   理想面食店
27 Noodle Bar
   面条店

OTHER

1 Long-Distance Bus
   Station
   长途汽车站
3 CITS
   中国国际旅行社
4 Minorities Souvenir
   Shop
   民族纪念品商店
5 Night Market
   夜市
6 Market
   市场
7 Local Bus Station
   汽车站
8 Internet Cafe
   网吧
11 Internet Cafe
   网吧

12 Minorities Souvenir
   Shop
   民族纪念品商店
13 Minorities Souvenir
   Shop
   民族纪念品商店
14 Bank of China
   中国银行
16 Post Office
   邮电局
17 PSB
   公安局
19 Train Ticket Office
   火车售票处
20 Buses to Guàdīng &
   Train Station
   到火车站的中巴
25 Internet Cafe
   网吧
28 Minorities Museum
   贵州民族博物馆
29 Wànbó Local Bus
   Station
   万博汽车站

There are also lots of minibuses and vans leaving for Guìyáng in the morning from the local bus station in the western part of town.

A bus for Chóng'ān departs from the long-distance bus station at 6.50am, however more frequent buses also leave for here from the local western bus station between 6.50am and 5pm.

Buses depart Kǎilǐ's long distance bus station for Léishān (Y9.5, 1½ hours) more or less hourly from 7am to 6pm. Sleepers leave for Cóngjiāng (Y71) at 7pm; you might also find a couple of morning buses along this route, however the schedule is 'flexible'.

Train Kǎilǐ's train station is a couple of kilometres north of town, however you can buy hard-seat tickets from the train ticket office on Zhaoshan Nanlu that is effectively disguised as the Bank of China.

The first of five trains to Guìyáng (Y25) departs Kǎilǐ at 8am. The afternoon trains are faster (four hours), with the final one leaving at 6.30pm.

For longer distances, it's worth stopping in Guìyáng to secure a reservation. Trains to Chóngqìng and to Kūnmíng pass through Kǎilǐ at 5.08pm and 5.30pm respectively. You can't get a sleeper reservation in Kǎilǐ

so you'll have to pray for intervention from a higher power (the conductor guard). The same advice is valid for east-bound services to Běijīng and Shànghǎi.

Getting Around

Bus fares cost Y0.5 in Kǎilǐ and almost all of those buses departing from the train station follow the same route up Qingjiang Lu, past the long-distance bus station, along Beijing Donglu and down Zhaoshan Nanlu to the museum.

AROUND KǍILǏ
Xījiāng 西江

Hidden in the folds of the Léigōng Hills, Xījiāng is thought to be the largest Miao village. It's a superbly picturesque place, set in a natural basin and bordered by paddy fields drenched in green, with wooden houses rising up the hillside. While there really isn't much to do here, the village is a site in itself and there are also plenty of pleasant walks you can take around the hillsides.

Yóudiàn Zhāodàisuǒ (☎ 334 8206) Beds without bath Y15. To find this guesthouse, continue about 200m past the bus drop-off. The rooms here are clean and basic.

There are a couple of small restaurants near the bus drop-off.

Getting There & Away There are one or two direct buses every day to Kǎilǐ (four hours) but it's generally easier to take a minibus to Léishān (Y8, four hours), which runs every hour or two until 4pm, and change there. You could visit Xījiāng as a day trip from Kǎilǐ if you left *really* early, but it's far better to spend at least one night here.

Chóng'ān 重安

Lying about two hours north of Kǎilǐ by bus, this hamlet's claim to fame is its **market**, held every five days. Set along the river, Chóng'ān retains its village size and atmosphere as well as many of its wooden homes and buildings. There are also some good walks along the river and into the Miao villages nearby.

Xiǎojiāngnán Lǚyóu Fàndiàn (☎ 3266) Beds Y20-25. This hotel has two buildings in the western part of the village, one on the riverbank and the other backing onto a fruit garden. The rooms are basic; the owner can arrange local tours.

Getting There & Away Buses between Shībǐng, Huángpíng and Kǎilǐ all pass through Chóng'ān, which means there's a bus almost every half-hour in either direction. Buses to Kǎilǐ run until around 6.30pm.

ZHÀOXÌNG 肇兴

South-east of Kǎilǐ, the road climbs into the hills before finally descending into a sub-tropical basin. In the very south of this region is Zhàoxìng, a lively, traditional Dong minority village with a remarkable total of five drum towers. Zhàoxìng still boasts its traditional wooden structures, including a number of wind and rain bridges and theatre stages. Many of the town's inhabitants continue to wear traditional clothing and speak only their native Dong language. Surrounded by lush fields and hills, Zhàoxìng is a small oasis and well worth a day's stopover.

Wénhuàzhàn Zhāodàisuǒ Beds Y20. East of the main drum tower, this is your best option for accommodation. The wood-panelled rooms are basic but cosy and clean, and still smell of timber. The hotel also gives tours of Zhàoxìng, the surrounding area and nearby villages for extremely reasonable rates (we were quoted Y8 per person).

Food options are limited in Zhàoxīng. Be sure to check on the meat of the day, as rat meat (*lǎoshǔ ròu*) is a common dish in this area. If you plan to do some day walks, it might be a good idea to bring some snacks along.

Getting There & Away

There are no direct buses between Cóngjiāng and Zhàoxīng. From Cóngjiāng, take a Líping bus and change at Pilin for a Líping-Dìping minibus, which passes through Zhàoxīng. These run until around 4pm.

Alternatively, if you're looking to stretch your legs, take a Laoxiang-bound bus from Cóngjiāng, which run from (approximately) 7.30am until 4.30pm (Y11, two hours). From Laoxiang, it's a lovely 1½-hour walk along a dirt road to Zhàoxīng, passing through a number of smaller villages en route.

Cóngjiāng can be reached from Kǎili (see the Getting There & Away section of Kǎilǐ).

Ténglónggé Bīnguǎn (☎ 641 2468) Singles Y70, doubles Y90-130. In Cóngjiāng, this is one accommoation option.

From Zhàoxīng, there is at least one Líping-Sānjiāng bus passing through each way. The trip to Sānjiāng, in Guǎngxī, takes about five hours. From there you can catch an onward bus to Guìlín (see the Guìlín section in the Guǎngxī chapter).

Yúnnán 云南

Capital: Kūnmíng
Population: 43.7 million
Area: 394,000 sq km

Yúnnán is without doubt one of the most alluring destinations in China. It's the most varied of all of China's provinces, with terrain ranging from tropical rainforest to snow-capped Tibetan peaks. It's also the sixth-largest province and home to a third of all China's ethnic minorities (nearly 50% of the province is non-Han) and half of all China's plant and animal species. If you could only go to one province, this might well be it.

Yúnnán is also well known for its mild climate year-round – its name means 'South of the Clouds'. The provincial capital, Kūnmíng, is similarly referred to as the 'Spring City'.

Despite the best government efforts, numerous pockets of the province have successfully resisted Chinese influence and exhibit strong local identities. Even the provincial capital Kūnmíng has a flavour all its own that seems more than half a world away from Běijīng, although this individual identity is in danger of being eroded by rapid economic growth.

Nicknames are affixed to everything in China, and Yúnnán boasts more than its fair share. Since the province contains the nation's highest number of species of flora and fauna – including 2500 varieties of wild flowers and plants – it has been given monikers such as 'Kingdom of Plants (or Animals)', 'Garden of Heavenly Marvellous Flowers', and 'Hometown of Perfume'. Officials are less thrilled with the new tag 'Treasure House of Crude Drugs'.

HISTORY

In the 1960s scientists discovered fragments of human-like teeth dating from 1.75 million to 2.5 million years ago, making 'Yuanmou' man the oldest human remains yet found in China. Yúnnán's other great anthropological discovery was of sophisticated Bronze Age cultures around Lake Diān.

It was not until the days of Qin Shihuang and the Han emperors that imperial China held tentative power over the aboriginal

Highlights

- Kūnmíng, a modern city with great food and good sights
- Lìjiāng's old town, the narrow stone streets of which give a fascinating glimpse into Naxi culture and history
- Tiger Leaping Gorge, a short trek amid dramatic cliffs and waterfalls
- Dàlǐ, one of China's best places to kick back and relax surrounded by wooden buildings and flagstone streets
- Téngchōng, a quaint town with nearby hot springs, Lisu minority villages and dormant volcanoes
- Ruìlì, a sometimes wild border town surrounded by plenty of Dai temples, minority villages and Burmese jade sellers
- Xīshuāngbǎnnà, a taste of tropical South-East Asia and home to the Dai people
- Déqīn, self-proclaimed 'Shangri-la', the next best thing to Tibet

peoples of the south-west, and forged southern Silk Road trade routes to Burma.

By the 7th century AD, however, the Bai people had established a powerful kingdom, Nanzhao, south of Dàlǐ. Initially allied with the Chinese against the Tibetans, this kingdom extended its power until, in the middle

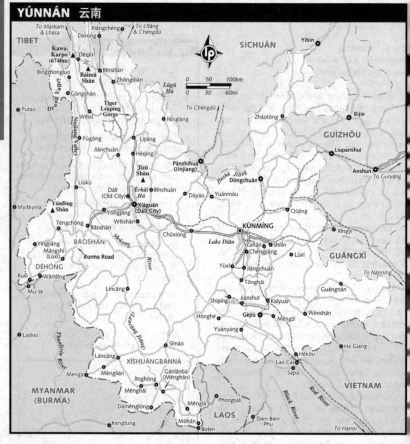

YÚNNÁN 云南

of the 8th century, it was able to challenge and defeat the Tang armies. It took control of a large slice of the south-west and established itself as a fully independent entity, dominating the trade routes from China to India and Burma.

The Nanzhao kingdom fell in the 10th century and was replaced by the kingdom of Dàlǐ, an independent state that lasted until it was overrun by the Mongols in the mid-13th century. After 15 centuries of resistance to northern rule, this part of the south-west was finally integrated into the empire as the province of Yúnnán.

Even so, it remained an isolated frontier region, with scattered Chinese garrisons and settlements in the valleys and basins, a mixed aboriginal population occupying the highlands, and various Dai (Thai) and other minorities along the Mekong River (Láncāng Jiāng).

Like the rest of the south-west, Yúnnán was always one of the first regions to break with the northern government. During China's countless political purges, fallen officials often found themselves exiled here, which added to the province's rebellious character.

Today, however, Yúnnán looks to be firmly back in the Chinese fold. It is a province of over 43 million people, including a veritable constellation of minorities (25 registered): the Zhuang, Hui, Yi, Miao, Tibetans, Mongols, Yao, Bai, Hani, Dai, Lisu, Lahu, Wa, Naxi, Jingpo, Bulang, Pumi, Nu, Achang, Bulang, Jinuo and Drung.

KŪNMÍNG 昆明

☎ 0871 • pop 3,838,200

Once you get off the wide boulevards, Kūnmíng can be a fine place to spend a few days wandering. Unfortunately its charm is under threat from relentless modernisation and the city's quaint back alleyways and fascinating wooden buildings are fast disappearing There are enough pockets still standing to make exploration worthwhile, but it won't be long before the last remnants of old Kūnmíng succumb to the wrecking ball.

At an elevation of 1890m, Kūnmíng has a milder climate than most other Chinese cities, and can be visited at any time of year. Light clothes will usually be adequate, but it's wise to bring some woollies during the winter months when temperatures can suddenly drop, particularly in the evenings – there have even been a couple of light snowfalls in recent years. Winters are short, sunny and dry. In summer (June to August) Kūnmíng offers cool respite, although rain is more prevalent.

History

The region of Kūnmíng has been inhabited for 2000 years. Until the 8th century the town was a remote Chinese outpost, but the kingdom of Nanzhao captured it and made it a secondary capital. In 1274 the Mongols came through, sweeping all and sundry before them.

In the 14th century the Ming set up shop in Yunnanfu, as Kūnmíng was then known, building a walled town on the present site. From the 17th century onwards, the history of this city becomes rather grisly. The last Ming resistance to the invading Manchu took place in Yúnnán in the 1650s and was crushed by General Wu Sangui. Wu in turn rebelled against the king and held out until his death in 1678. His successor was overthrown by the Manchu emperor Kangxi and subsequently killed himself in Kūnmíng in 1681.

In the 19th century the city suffered several bloodbaths, as the rebel Muslim leader Du Wenxiu, the Sultan of Dàlǐ, attacked and besieged the city several times between 1858 and 1868; it was not until 1873 that the rebellion was finally and bloodily crushed.

The intrusion of the West into Kūnmíng began in the middle of the 19th century from British Burma (Myanmar) and French Indochina. By 1900 Kūnmíng, Hékǒu, Sīmáo and Měngzì had been opened to foreign trade. The French were keen on exploiting the region's copper, tin and timber resources, and in 1910 their Indochina train, started in 1898 at Hanoi, reached the city.

Kūnmíng's expansion began with WWII, when factories were established and refugees fleeing the Japanese poured in from eastern China. In a bid to keep China from falling to Japan, Anglo-American forces sent supplies to nationalist troops entrenched in Sìchuān and Yúnnán. Supplies came overland on a dirt road carved out of the mountains in 1937–38 by 160,000 Chinese with virtually no equipment. This was the famous Burma Road, a 1000km haul from Lashio to Kūnmíng. Today, Renmin Xilu marks the tail end of the road.

In early 1942 the Japanese captured Lashio, cutting the supply line. Kūnmíng continued to handle most of the incoming aid during 1942–45 when US planes flew the dangerous mission of crossing the 'Hump', the towering 5000m mountain ranges between India and Yúnnán. A black market sprang up and a fair proportion of the medicines, canned food, petrol and other goods intended for the military and relief agencies were siphoned off into other hands.

The face of Kūnmíng has been radically altered since then, with streets widened and office buildings and housing projects flung up. With the coming of the trains, industry has expanded rapidly, and a surprising range of goods and machinery available in China now bears the 'Made in Yúnnán' stamp. The city's produce includes steel, foodstuffs, trucks, machine tools, electrical equipment, textiles, chemicals, building materials and plastics.

Orientation

The jurisdiction of Kūnmíng covers 6200 sq km, encompassing four city districts and four rural counties (that supply the city with fruit and vegetables). The centre of the city is the roundabout at the intersection of Zhengyi Lu and Dongfeng Xilu. Surprisingly it's still possible to find a few rows of old wooden houses in nearby neighbourhoods.

East of the intersection is Kūnmíng's major north-south road, Beijing Lu. At the southern end is the main train station and the long-distance bus station.

SOUTH-WEST CHINA

KŪNMÍNG 昆明

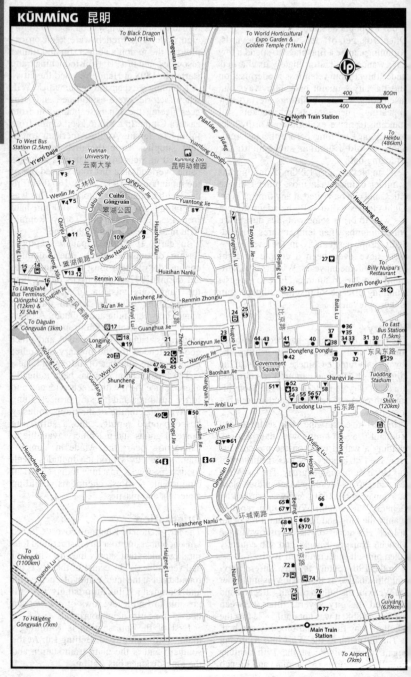

To Black Dragon Pool (11km)

To World Horticultural Expo Garden & Golden Temple (11km)

0   400   800m
0   400   800yd

North Train Station

To Hékǒu (486km)

Pánlóng Jiāng

Longquan Lu

Chuanjin Lu

Huancheng Donglu

To West Bus Station (2.5km)

Yi'eryi Dàjiē

Yunnan University
云南大学

Yuantong Donglu

Kunming Zoo
昆明动物园

6

Wenlin Jie 文林街

Qingyun Jie

Cuihu Beilu

Yuantong Jie

8

7

Qingnian Lu

Taoyuan Jie

Beijing Lu

27

To Billy Nuipai's Restaurant

Cuìhú
Gōngyuán
翠湖公园

11

10

9

Cuihu Xilu

Huashan Xilu

Cuihu Nanlu

Xichang Lu

Qianju Jie

Dongfeng Xilu

15   14

16

13 12

Renmin Xilu

Huashan Nanlu

26

Renmin Donglu

28

To Liàngjiāhé
Bus Terminus,
Qióngzhú Sì
(12km) &
Xī Shān

Ru'an Jie

Minsheng Jie

Renmin Zhonglu

24

25

Baita Lu

37

36

35

34 33

31 30

To East Bus Station (1.5km)

17

Guanghua Jie

Chongyun Jie

Huguo Lu

44 43

41

40

38

39

29

东风东路

Dàguān
Gōngyuán (3km)

Longjing
Jie

18
19

21

22

Nanping Jie

Zhengyi Lu

Wuyi Lu

Government
Square

42

Dongfeng Donglu

32

Tuódōng
Stadium

20

48

47 46 45

Baoshan Jie

Shangyi Jie

To
Shílín
(120km)

Shuncheng
Jie

Xiangyun Jie

51

52
53

55 56 57
54   58

Tuodong Lu 拓东路

Jinbi Lu

Wujing Lu

Heping Lu

Chuncheng Lu

59

49

50

Dongsi Jie

Shulin Jie

Houxin Jie

62   61

64

63

60

Huancheng Xilu

Qingnian Lu

Huancheng Nanlu

65
67

66

68

69
70

71

Chéngdū
(1100km)

Dianchi Lu

Haigeng Lu

环城南路

72

73   74

Beijing Lu 比京路

75

76

To
Guìyáng
(639km)

77

To Hǎigēng
Gōngyuán (7km)

Namba Lu

Main Train
Station

To Airport
(7km)

KŪNMÍNG

PLACES TO STAY

1　Yúndà Zhāodàisuǒ
　　云大招待所
9　Cuìhú Bīnguǎn
　　翠湖宾馆
12　Kunming Harbour Plaza
　　昆明海逸酒店
19　Yúnnán Fàndiàn
　　云南饭店
30　Báiyún Dàjiǔdiàn
　　白云大酒店
31　Camellia Hotel; Lao
　　Consulate; Myanmar
　　Consulate
　　茶花宾馆; 老挝领事馆;
　　缅甸领事馆
37　Kunming Hotel
　　昆明饭店
39　Holiday Inn Kunming;
　　Charlie's Bar
　　樱花假日酒店
46　Chūnchéng Jiǔlóu
　　春城酒楼
50　The Hump
　　驼峰客栈
65　Kūnhú Fàndiàn
　　昆湖饭店
72　King World Hotel;
　　CITS (FIT)
　　锦华大酒店;
　　中国国际旅行社
76　Tiělù Dàshà
　　昆明铁路旅行社

PLACES TO EAT

2　Journey to the East Cafe
　　往东方旅行
3　French Cafe
　　兰白红
4　Paul's; Face to Face Pub
　　堡利; 面对面
5　Teresa's Pizzeria; Dove
　　Email
　　信鸽
7　The Brothers Jiang
　　江氏兄弟
8　Yuquanzhai Vegetarian
　　Restaurant
　　玉泉斋
10　Lǎozhīqīng Shíguǎn
　　老知青食馆
13　Bluebird Cafe
　　青鸟
15　Mengzi Across-the-Bridge
　　Noodles Restaurant
　　蒙自过桥米线
16　Yúnnán Fēngwèi Kuàicān
　　云南风味快餐
32　Xuéchú Fàndiàn
　　学厨饭店

33　City Cafe
　　厦门陈氏小吃
34　Zhènxīng Fàndiàn
　　振兴饭店
35　Ma Ma Fu's 2
　　马马付
43　The Brothers Jiang
　　江氏兄弟
48　Muslim Restaurants
　　清真饭店
51　Mengzi
　　Across-the-Bridge Noodles
　　Restaurant
　　蒙自过桥米线
54　Yuánlóng Fēngweìchéng
　　元龙风味城
56　Yuèlái Píjiǔguǎn
　　悦来啤酒馆
57　Wei's Pizzeria
　　哈哈餐厅
58　Báitǎdǎiwèi Cāntīng
　　白塔傣味餐厅
62　1910 La Gare Du Sud
　　火车南站
67　Mr Ball's
　　利来啤酒馆
71　Dicos
　　得卡斯

TRANSPORT

11　Fat Tyres Bike Shop
14　Xiǎoxīmén Bus Station
　　小西门汽车客运站
18　Buses to Xī Shān &
　　Qióngzhú Sì
　　往西山; 筇竹寺的车
40　Shanghai Airlines
　　上海航空公司
42　China Southern Airlines
　　西南航空公司
47　Kunming United Airlines
　　昆明联合航空公司
55　Yunnan Airlines; CAAC
　　云南航空公司; 中国民航
68　China Southwest Airlines
　　西南航空公司
69　Dragonair; Golden Dragon
　　Hotel
　　港龙航空; 龙饭店
73　Long-Distance Bus Station
　　长途汽车总站
74　Bus Station
　　客运站
75　Sleeper Bus Stand
　　卧铺汽车站
77　Train Ticket Office;
　　Kunming Tour Information
　　Office
　　火车站售票处;
　　昆明旅游咨询中心

OTHER

6　Yuántōng Sì
　　圆通寺
17　Arts Theatre
　　艺术剧院
20　Yunnan Provincial
　　Museum
　　云南省博物馆
21　Flower & Bird Market
　　花鸟市场
22　Nánchéng Mosque
　　南城清真古寺
23　Mosque
　　清真寺
24　Kunming Theatre
　　昆明剧院
25　Bank of China
　　中国银行
26　Main Bank of China
　　中国银行
27　Camel Bar
　　骆驼酒吧
28　Yán'ān Hospital
　　延安医院
29　Tuodong Swimming
　　Pool
　　拓东游泳池
36　Postar Outdoor &
　　Equipment Collection
38　Thai Consulate
　　泰王国总领事馆
41　Post & Telephone
　　Office
　　邮电电信营业厅
44　Climber Outdoors
　　攀登者
45　Kunming Department
　　Store
　　昆明百货大楼
49　Mosque
　　清真寺
52　Tien Fu Famous Teas
　　天福茗茶
53　PSB
　　公安局
59　Kunming City Museum
　　昆明市博物馆
60　International Post
　　Office
　　国际邮局
61　Upriver Club
　　上河会馆
63　Dōngsì Tǎ
　　东寺塔
64　Xīsì Tǎ
　　西寺塔
66　CITS
　　中国国际旅行社
70　Bank of China
　　中国银行

Maps Shop around as there's a great variety of maps, some with a smattering of English names. The *Kunming Tourist Map* has street and hotel names in English and shows bus lines, while the *Yunnan Communications and Tourist Map* has the names of nearly every town in the province – along with bordering countries – written in English.

Information

There is a Kunming Tour Information office opposite the main train station. Kūnmíng has a 'Tourist Complaint and Consultative Telephone' number at ☎ 316 4961.

Consulates Thailand, Myanmar (Burma) and Laos now all have visa-issuing consulates in Kūnmíng – but (sigh) still not Vietnam. Visa details given here are current at time of research but regulations change frequently.

Laos The Lao consulate (☎ 317 6624, 669 2751) is in Room 120 on the ground floor of the main building of the Camellia Hotel (see Places to Stay later). Standard 15-day tourist visas are issued in three working days or you can pay a surcharge for an express 24-hour service. Seven- and 15-day visas cost the same. Fifteen/30-day visas cost Y320/440 for Germans and Americans and Y270/400 for most Western European travellers and Australians. You must bring one photo. None of these visas can be extended and you currently cannot get a Lao visa at the border. Note that Lao visa regulations change frequently. Office hours are 8.30am to 11.30am and 2.30pm to 4.30pm Monday to Friday.

Myanmar The office (☎ 317 6609, fax 317 6309) is on the 3rd floor of Building No 3 of the Camellia Hotel. The consulate can grant you a four-week visa in 72 hours for Y185, in 12 hours for Y235 or in three hours for Y285. There are two catches: first, you are required to change US$300 into Myanmar *kyat* at the government's scandalously low rate; and second, the visas are not good for land crossings – you must fly in via Yangon (Rangoon). The consulate is open 8.30am to noon and 1pm to 4.30pm Monday to Friday.

Thailand The Thai consulate (☎ 316 2033 ext 62105, fax 316 6891), on the ground floor of the building next to the Kunming Hotel, can arrange 60-day visas for Y110 that are normally ready the next day. Travellers from most countries won't need one unless they plan to spend more than 30 days in Thailand. Office hours are 9am to 1.30pm Monday to Friday, closed all Chinese and Thai holidays.

Money The main Bank of China is at 448 Renmin Donglu and is open 9am to noon and 1.30pm to 5.30pm daily. Other branches are on Beijing Lu near Huancheng Nanlu, and on Qingnian Lu (both branches closed weekends). All the main hotels have foreign-exchange counters, but may offer lower rates than the banks.

Post & Communications There is an international post office on the east side of Beijing Lu, halfway between Tuodong Lu and Huancheng Nanlu. It has a very efficient poste restante and parcel service – for poste restante bring some ID. This is the city's Express Mail Service (EMS) and Western Union agent. You can also make telephone calls here.

There is another post and telephone office to the north of this one, at the intersection of Beijing Lu and Dongfeng Donglu. The postal service hours here are 8am to 8pm daily, and the telecommunication service operates from 8am to 5pm daily.

The post and telephone office on the corner of Beijing Lu and Dongfeng Donglu has fast hook-ups and cheap rates – Y10 per hour, once you've handed over a Y20 refundable deposit. It's open 8am to 6.30pm weekdays and 9am to 5pm weekends. Most cafes frequented by travellers also offer email, albeit at slightly higher rates. The Hump (see Places to Stay later) and Dove Email, near Yunnan University, at 47 Wenlin Jie, both charge Y4 per hour.

Travel Agencies China International Travel Service (CITS; Zhōngguó Guójì Lǚxíngshè; ☎ 314 8308) is east of Beijing Lu in a white-tiled building at 220 Huancheng Nanlu. Better for independent travellers is CITS' Family and Independent Traveller (FIT) office (☎ 313 8888, 313 3104) at the King World Hotel, 98 Beijing Lu.

Mr Chen, formerly of Chéngdū, recently moved to the Camellia Hotel and now arranges flight tickets from Zhōngdiàn to Lhasa along with the requisite Tibet Tourism Bureau (TTB) permit and three-day 'tour' in Lhasa. Prices are currently around Y2000 to Y2500 for the package (the ticket is Y1250) but prices and tour requirements change regularly.

PSB The Foreign Affairs Branch of the Public Security Bureau (PSB; Gōngānjú; ☎ 313 0139) is on Beijing Lu and is open weekdays 8am to 11.30am and 1pm to 5.30pm (4.30pm Friday). The officers speak English. First visa extensions are fairly routine now.

Medical Services The Yán'ān Hospital (Yán'ān Yīyuàn), on Renmin Donglu, has a foreigners clinic (☎ 317 7499 ext 311) on the 1st floor of Building No 6, at the back of the compound.

Dangers & Annoyances Kūnmíng is one of the safest cities in China but take special precaution near the train and long-distance bus stations. There are lots of travellers' reports of having a bag razored or pilfered in the train station or on a Dàlǐ-bound bus.

Tang Dynasty Pagodas
To the south of Jinbi Lu are two Tang pagodas. **Xīsì Tǎ** (West Pagoda; Dongsi Jie; admission Y2; open 9am-9pm) is the more interesting and is on a bustling market street. Attached is a compound that is a popular spot for older people to get together, drink tea and play cards and mahjong. You can even get a haircut and a shave at the base of the pagoda.

Dōngsì Tǎ (East Pagoda) was, according to Chinese sources, destroyed by an earthquake; Western sources say it was destroyed by the Muslim revolt. It was rebuilt in the 19th century, but there's little to see.

Yunnan Provincial Museum
Yúnnán Shěng Bówùguǎn 云南省博物馆
This museum (Wuyi Lu; admission Y5; open 9am-5pm Tues-Sun) is divided into three sections covering the province's ancient bronze drums, Buddhist art and ethnic minorities. It's generally worth a visit. Bus No 5 goes here from the Camellia Hotel.

Kunming City Museum
Kūnmíngshì Bówùguǎn 昆明市博物馆
The museum (Tuodong Lu; admission Y5; open 10am-4pm Wed-Sun) focuses on the history of the Lake Diān (Diān Chí) area. Only one room has English translations, but a few rooms, despite the language barrier, offer interesting looks at the history of Kūnmíng, and one room offers a scale model of the city.

Yuántōng Sì 圆通寺
This temple (Yuantong Jie; admission Y4; open 8am-5pm daily) is the largest Buddhist complex in Kūnmíng and a target for pilgrims. It is over 1000 years old and has seen many renovations. Leading up to the main hall from the entrance is an extensive display of flowers and potted landscapes. The central courtyard holds a large square pond intersected by walkways and bridges, and has an octagonal pavilion at the centre.

To the rear of the temple a new hall has been added, enshrining the **statue of Sakyamuni**, a gift from the king of Thailand. There's a great vegetarian restaurant across the main road from the temple entrance (see Places to Eat later).

Kunming Zoo 昆明动物园
Kūnmíng Dòngwùyuán
Close to Yuántōng Sì is the zoo (92 Qingnian Lu; admission Y6; open 9am-6pm daily). The grounds are pleasantly leafy and provide a bird's-eye vista of the city, but most travellers find the animals' living conditions depressing. The main entrance is near the corner of Yuantong Jie and Qingnian Lu.

Cuìhú Gōngyuán 翠湖公园
Green Lake Park
A short distance south-west of the zoo, this park (Ciuhu Nanlu; admission Y2; open 6am-6pm daily) is good for a stroll. Sunday sees it at its liveliest, when it hosts an English Corner, colourful paddleboats and hordes of families at play.

Mosques 清真寺
Qīngzhēnsì
Kūnmíng's Buddhist shrines, devastated by the Cultural Revolution, have been mostly 'rehabilitated' and hum with tourist trade. Now the local officials focus on the left-out Muslim community and their mosques.

Yúnnán's Muslims

Unlike Muslims in other parts of China, who generally settled along trade routes used by Arab traders, Yúnnán's sizeable Muslim population dates back to the 13th century, when Mongol forces swooped into the province to outflank the Song dynasty troops. They were followed by Muslim traders, builders, and craftsmen. Yúnnán was the only region to have been put under a Muslim leader immediately after Kublai Khan's armies arrived, when Sayyid Ajall was named governor in 1274.

All over China mosques were simultaneously raised with the new Yuan dynasty banner. A Muslim was entrusted to build the first Mongol palace in Běijīng. An observatory based on Persian models was constructed in Běijīng, and later copied by the Ming emperor. Dozens of Arabic texts were translated and consulted by Chinese scientists, influencing Chinese mathematics more than any other source. The most famous Yúnnán Muslim was Cheng Ho, the famed eunuch admiral who opened up the Chinese sea lanes to the Middle East.

Ethnically indistinguishable from the Han Chinese, the Hui, as ethnic Chinese Muslims are known, have had an unfortunate history of repression and persecution, a recent low point being the years of the Cultural Revolution. Heavy land taxes and disputes between Muslims and Han Chinese over local gold and silver mines triggered a Muslim uprising in 1855, which lasted until 1873.

The Muslims made Dàlǐ the centre of their operations and laid siege to Kūnmíng, overrunning the city briefly in 1863. Du Wenxiu, the Muslim leader, proclaimed his newly established Kingdom of the Pacified South (Nánpíng Guó) and took the name Sultan Suleyman. But the Muslim successes were short-lived. In 1873 Dàlǐ was taken by Qing forces and Du Wenxiu was captured and executed after a failed suicide attempt. Up to a million people died in Yúnnán alone, the death toll rising to 18 million nationwide. The uprisings were quelled, but they also had the lasting effect of eliciting sympathy from Burma and fomenting a passion for culture among many of south-western China's ethnic minorities, most of whom had supported the Hui.

The oldest of the lot, the 400-year-old **Nánchéng Mosque** (*Nánchéng Qīngzhēn Gǔsì; 51 Zhengyi Lu*), was ripped down in 1997 in order to build a larger version. The new mosque looks vaguely like a bad Las Vegas casino. Not too far away is a lively strip of Muslim restaurants and shops selling skullcaps, Arabic calligraphy and pictures of Mecca. To get to the Muslim area from the Zhengyi Lu roundabout, walk north-eastward past Chūnchéng Jiǔlóu and then bear left a half-block to a small alley.

There's another mosque nearby, wedged between Huguo Lu and Chongyun Jie and another on the corner of Jinbi Lu and Dongsi Jie.

Organised Tours

Several tour outfits cover Kūnmíng and its surrounding sights faster than public minibuses would, but you must be prepared to pay for them. They generally feature a lot of sights that most travellers find rather boring. Some tour operators refuse to take foreigners on their tours, claiming the language barrier causes too much trouble. More central sights like Yuántōng Sì are

just a short bicycle ride away – it hardly makes sense to join a tour to see them.

For tours to Shílín (Stone Forest) see the Shílín section later.

Places to Stay – Budget

Camellia Hotel (*Cháhuā Bīnguǎn;* ☎ *316 3000, 316 2918, fax 314 7033, 154 Dongfeng Donglu*) Dorm beds Y30. Long frequented by budget travellers, the Camellia is still a grand bargain. Building No 3 is in a quiet location and has three floors of dorms, some better than others.

The hotel has bicycle hire, a foreign-exchange counter, poste restante, a decent Y10 breakfast buffet, free luggage and valuables storage, and a reasonably priced laundry service. The staff do a pretty good job with the steady stream of backpacker guests. To get here from the main train station, take bus No 2 or 23 to Dongfeng Donglu, then change to bus No 5 heading east and get off at the second stop.

The Hump (*Tuófēng Kèzhàn;* ☎ *364 4638, 364 4197, Jinbi Lu*) Dorm beds Y15-40. This fresh, new place looks set to shake up Kūnmíng's budget accommodation scene. Beds in eight- and 17-bed dorms come with a locker, and the shared showers are clean (toilets too) and have 24-hour hot water. Best of all is the fine sun terrace on the roof. The bar and restaurant downstairs have cheap beer and should be a good place to pick up some travel tips.

Kūnhú Fàndiàn (☎ 313 3737, 202 Beijing Lu) Dorm beds Y25, singles/doubles with shared bath Y60/68, doubles with private bath Y128. Near the train and bus stations, this hotel attracts many backpackers. Unfortunately the dorm rooms look out onto the street, so they're quite noisy. Some rooms aren't quite worth the price – the doubles with attached bathrooms are dingy. Some travellers have been more than a bit unnerved by the unisex washrooms *and* showers; but they are at least fairly clean. Next door to the hotel are several cafes. The hotel is two stops from the main train station on bus No 2, 23 or 47, though it's easy enough to walk it.

Yúndà Zhaōdàisuǒ (*Yunnan University Chinese Language Centre for Foreign Students;* ☎ 503 3624, fax 514 8513, Sanjia Xiang, Yi'eryi Dajie) Singles with bath Y40-60, doubles with bath Y80-120. Rooms here are clean and good value and it's a good place to meet foreign students who live here long-term.

Places to Stay – Mid-Range
Camellia Hotel (*see Places to Stay – Budget*) Doubles with bath Y140-220. Take a look at the cheaper doubles in the older wing, as they have satellite TV, have been recently spruced up and are a great bargain.

Báiyún Dàjiǔdiàn (*White Cloud Hotel;* ☎ 318 8688, fax 316 2566, 112 Dongfeng Donglu) Old-block doubles Y80-100, new-block doubles Y320-440. The excellent value old-block rooms in this swanky three-star hotel opposite the Tuòdōng Stadium are carpeted and have immaculate bathrooms with 24-hour hot water. Some rooms are better than others.

Chūnchéng Jiǔlóu (*Spring City Hotel;* ☎ 363 3271, fax 363 3191, 11-17 Dongfeng Xilu) Doubles with shared bath Y54, with private bath Y90-128. A trusty stand-by, this hotel has acceptable rooms, which are a quiet alternative to the other budget dorms (the corner rooms are generally the most pleasant). The showers are clean and have

24-hour hot water. Take a look at a few rooms, as we've seen some clunkers as well as some of prime value. The restaurant gets great reviews too.

Tiělù Dàshà (*Railroad Travel Service;* ☎ 313 7667) Doubles with bath Y160-198. Right next to the main train station, this hotel is fairly new, so it's not a bad place to stay as long as you don't mind wading through the train station crowds on your way in and out of the building.

Yúnnán Fàndiàn (☎ 313 7667, Dongfeng Xilu) Singles Y180, doubles with/without bath Y220/80. This establishment, near the Yunnan Provincial Museum, was Kūnmíng's first tourist hotel. Rooms aren't too bad and discounts are offered but you'll probably get better value at the city's other budget hotels.

Places to Stay – Top End
Thanks to the city's hosting of the 1999 World Horticultural Expo, there is now plenty to choose from in this category. Most hotels in this section offer free transfers to and from the airport.

Kunming Hotel (*Kūnmíng Fàndiàn;* ☎ 316 2063, Ⓦ www.kmhotel.com.cn, 50-52 Dongfeng Donglu) Doubles US$66-128. There are useful facilities here that include airline ticket bookings, poste restante, a post office, photocopying, a snooker room, bike hire, several high-end restaurants, including Korean and Cháozhōu (coastal region in eastern Guǎngdōng; light, tasty cuisine with an abundant use of vegetables) eateries, and a couple of shops. Discounts of 20% are available if you book online.

Holiday Inn Kunming (*Yīnghuā Jiàrì Jiǔdiàn;* ☎ 316 5888, fax 313 5189, 25 Dongfeng Donglu) Singles/doubles Y800/950 plus 15% tax. This super-luxury monster is opposite the Kunming Hotel. The rooms come with a Western buffet breakfast. It sports some excellent restaurants (Thai and south-western American/Mexican along with a popular breakfast/lunch buffet), a Western-style pub, a small health club and pool, and a chic disco.

Cuìhú Bīnguǎn (*Green Lake Hotel;* ☎ 515 8888, fax 515 3286, 6 Cuihu Nanlu) Doubles Y280, rooms in newer section US$100. In an older section of Kūnmíng overlooking Cuìhú Gōngyuán, this used to be quiet and quaint, but has lost some of its character with the construction of a 20-floor, four-star addition in the back. The cheaper rooms are not great value; equivalent rooms for Y100 less can be found in town. Ask for discounts. The hotel has a bar, a coffee shop and both Western and Chinese restaurants.

Kunming Harbour Plaza *(Hǎiyì Jiǔdiàn;* ☎ *538 6688,* W *www.harbourplaza .com, 20 Cuihu Nanlu)* Doubles from US$78. This is a reliable hotel that is part of the popular Hong Kong chain.

King World Hotel *(Jīnhuá Dàjiǔdiàn;* ☎ *313 8888,* W *www.kingworld.com.cn, 98 Beijing Lu)* Wing-A/B doubles Y460/625. This luxury hotel features an expensive revolving restaurant (the highest above sea level in China, the hotel proudly points out) on the top floor. Rooms come with fruit baskets. The best rooms even have computer modules, some of the first in China. Doubles can be discounted as low as Y288 and Y388 respectively, including breakfast, making this place particularly good value.

Places to Eat

Chinese Cuisine There are several eating places near the Kunming and Camellia Hotels on Dongfeng Donglu that have bilingual menus.

Xuéchú Fàndiàn *(Cooking School; Dongfeng Donglu)* Dishes from Y10. This place specialises in local fish and vegetable dishes, but it must save its novice chefs for foreigners; it gets mixed reviews.

Zhènxīng Fàndiàn *(Yunnan Typical Local Food Restaurant; cnr Baita Lu & Dongfeng Donglu)* Dishes from Y5. This corner restaurant has a good range of dishes and snacks, including across-the-bridge noodles (Y15 to Y25), and gets good reviews on its food from both locals and foreigners.

Yuèlái Píjiǔguǎn Dishes Y8-20. Off Tuodong Lu, this is one of the best places in town for cheap Chinese food. What's refreshing is that there's an extensive menu of Chinese dishes in English, which enables you to try something different from the usual clueless wander through the kitchen. There's also an extensive list of foreign food like muesli and yogurt and burgers, which the chef learned in Dàlǐ. The mini hotpots are excellent but not on the English menu.

Yúnnán Fēngwei Kuàicān *(Yunnan Flavour Fast Food)* Dishes from Y5. If you want real Yunnanese food real fast, this outstanding option is also known as Xīngfùyú (Happy Fish). It's east of Xiǎoxīmén bus station and set back a bit off Renmin Xilu (look for Yúnnán's first US-based Wal-Mart store – as if you could ever miss one – it's opposite that). You pay first, then just wander along a pan-Yúnnán line of food stations, point, and drool as chefs prepare it in front of you.

Yuánlóng Fēngweìchéng *(King Dragon Food Village; Tuodong Lu)* Dishes from Y5. This is a similar venture, where you pay first, then choose, but it's a bit harder to deal with since the cooks are set far back behind high counters. This place is just west of Yunnan Airlines.

Mengzi Across-the-Bridge-Noodles Restaurant *(Mēngzì Guòqiáo Mǐxiàn; Beijing Lu)* Noodles Y5-20. This is one place specialising in Kūnmíng's favourite noodles that has held out in the face of the city's modernisation drive. You'll find this one near the PSB office; another branch *(Renmin Xilu)* is west of Xiǎoxīmén bus station.

A more recent phenomenon in Kūnmíng is the discovery of ethnic cuisines. At present there are at least two Dai minority restaurants in the city. The food is spicy and uses sticky rice as its staple.

Lǎozhīqīng Shíguǎn *(*☎ *514 0231, 4 Cuihu Nanlu)* Dishes from Y6. Adjacent to the entrance to Cuìhú Gōngyuán, this place is popular with overseas students studying in Kūnmíng.

Báitǎdàiwèi Cāntīng *(Shangyi Jie)* Dishes from Y10. This place has tasty food, an English menu and cold draught beer. The prices are a bit high, but it's a good place to try Dai cuisine – an opportunity that you won't get again unless you head down to Xīshuāngbǎnnà.

1910 La Gare Du Sud *(Huǒchē Nánzhàn;* ☎ *316 9486)* Dishes from Y15. For something a little classier, this new restaurant serves traditional local Yunnanese specialities in a pleasant neo-colonial-style atmosphere. There's no English menu but most dishes are moderately priced. It's hidden down an alley next to the Upriver Club (see Entertainment later), south of Jinbi Lu.

Kūnmíng Food

Kūnmíng has some great food, especially in the snack line. Regional specialities are *qìguōjī* (herb-infused chicken cooked in an earthenware steampot), *xuānwēi huǒtuǐ* (Yúnnán ham), *guòqiáo mǐxiàn* (across-the-bridge noodles), *rǔbǐng* (goat's cheese) and various Muslim beef and mutton dishes. Qìguōjī is served in dark brown casserole pots from Jiànshuǐ county and is imbued with medicinal properties depending on the spices used – caterpillar fungus *(chóngcǎo)* or pseudo-ginseng is one. Some travellers wax lyrical about toasted goat's cheese, another local speciality. It probably depends on how long you've been away from home – the cheese is actually quite bland and sticks to your teeth.

Gourmets with money to burn may perhaps be interested in a whole banquet based on Jizhong fungus (mushrooms) or 30 courses of cold mutton, not to mention fried grasshoppers.

The chief breakfast in Kūnmíng, as throughout most of Yúnnán, is noodles (choice of rice or wheat), usually served in a meat broth with a chilli sauce.

Yúnnán's best-known dish is across-the-bridge noodles. You are provided with a bowl of very hot soup (stewed with chicken, duck and spare ribs) on which a thin layer of oil is floating, along with a side dish of raw pork slivers (in classier places this might be chicken or fish) and vegetables, and a bowl of rice noodles. Diners place all of the ingredients quickly into the soup bowl, where they are cooked by the steamy broth.

Across-the-bridge noodles is the stuff of which fairy tales are made, as the following story proves:

> Once upon a time there was a scholar at the South Lake in Mēngzì (southern Yúnnán) who was attracted by the peace and quiet of an island there. He settled into a cottage on the island, in preparation for official examinations. His wife, meanwhile, had to cross a long wooden bridge over the lake to bring the bookworm his meals. The food was always cold in winter by the time she got to the study bower. Oversleeping one day, she made a curious discovery. She'd stewed a fat chicken and was puzzled to find the broth still hot, though it gave off no steam – the oil layer on the surface had preserved the temperature of the broth. Subsequent experiments showed that she could cook the rest of the ingredients for her husband's meal in the hot broth after she crossed the bridge.

It is possible to try across-the-bridge noodles in innumerable restaurants in Kūnmíng. Prices generally vary from Y5 to Y15 depending on the side dishes provided. It's usually worth spending a bit more, because with only one or two condiments it lacks zest.

Vegetarian Apart from the various temples in and around town, most of the restaurants near Kūnhú Fàndiàn and the Camellia Hotel that cater to Westerners also have vegie selections.

Yuquanzhai Vegetarian Restaurant (Yuantong Jie) Dishes from Y10. This outstanding vegetarian restaurant doesn't have a whole lot of aesthetic charm, and prices are higher than elsewhere, but it's still definitely worth a try. It takes the practice of 'copying' meat-based dishes to a new level, with an encyclopaedic menu. Staff recommend the duck in fermented bean curd. Also check out the *tiěbǎn* (sizzling iron-pot) meals (Y20).

Snacks Kūnmíng used to be a good place for bakeries, but many of these seem to be disappearing. Exploration of Kūnmíng's backstreets might turn up a few lingerers, however.

In the vicinity of the long-distance bus station and in many of the side streets running off Beijing Lu are **roadside noodle shops**. Generally you get a bowl of rice noodles for around Y4 and a bewildering array of sauces with which to flavour the broth – most of them are hot and spicy.

Another place to go snack hunting is Huguo Lu in the centre of town. Also try Shuncheng Jie, an east-west street running south of Dongfeng Xilu near the Chūnchéng Jiǔlóu (see Places to Stay earlier). Here you'll find literally dozens of **Muslim restaurants**, **kebab stalls** and **noodle stands**. Try *bānmiàn* (a kind of spaghetti) or Uyghur *suoman* (fried noodle squares with peppers, tomato and cumin).

The Brothers Jiang (Jiāngshì Kèdì) Noodles Y5-60. This place has good across-the-bridge noodles (ask for *shāoguō mǐxiàn*) and there are several branches, all popular at lunchtime. Pay up-front first at the cash register. One convenient branch *(Dongfeng Donglu)* is opposite Government Square, and another is just south of the zoo on Qingnian Jie.

Western Food Literally dozens of friendly Western-style cafes are found near the Camellia Hotel and Kūnhú Fàndiàn, and especially the new up-and-coming area surrounding Yunnan University.

Ma Ma Fu's 2 (Māmāfù Cāntīng; Baita Lu) Dishes Y5-30. A legendary Lìjiāng cafe, this opened up around the corner east of the Camellia Hotel and is now run by the original Mama and Papa; it's still got the same to-die-for fresh breads and apple pie.

City Cafe (Chéngshì Xiǎochī; Dongfeng Donglu) Dishes Y6-25. This place doesn't look like much from the outside but it serves up good portions of authentic Western food ranging from lasagne to brownies. There are even some Chinese dishes, with a few Fujianese specialities such as fish-ball soup (the owners are from Xiàmén).

Wei's Pizzeria (☎ 316 6189) Dishes from Y12. This excellent cafe down a small alley off Tuodong Lu (look for arrows on the wall), has outstanding Italian food and a pleasant atmosphere of eclectic Western music. The wood-fired pizzas (Y20 to Y25) are unspeakably good and you can also get tasty and good value Chinese dishes, such as good *qìguōjī* (medicinal-herb chicken in a pot). Frosted beer mugs (or try a glass of Yúnnán red wine) top off the effect.

Mr Ball's (Beijing Lu) Dishes Y5-20. This very popular place (it's got a few names actually) serves excellent food, has good service, and has a budget-conscious menu.

The environs of Yunnan University (and nearby Cuìhú Gōngyuán) cater to foreign students and are the best place to find out what's going on where in Kūnmíng. Wenlin Jie houses a host of restaurants, bars, an Internet cafe and even *Paul's (Bǎolì Shāngdiàn; ☎ 535 4210)*, a grocery specialising in Western gourmet and hard-to-find imports.

Teresa's Pizzeria (☎ 537 6725, 40 Wenlin Jie) Dishes Y10-40. This is a delightful place with excellent pizzas, calzones, salads and a great atmosphere. It sits between the university and the park.

The alley that leads north of Wenlin Jie leads to Yunnan University and is crammed with restaurants and bars:

French Cafe (Lán Bái Hóng; ☎ 538 2391, 52 Wenhua Gang) Dishes from Y10. This fine cafe off Wenlin Jie offers hard-to-find goodies like salads, sandwiches, crepes (savoury and sweet) and lots of different teas and coffees, all served up with typical Gallic charm. It's a great place to read during the day and gets lively at night with good music and a nice mix of foreign and Chinese diners. There's Internet access and books for loan.

Journey to the East Cafe (Wàngdōngfāng Lǚxíng) Dishes Y8-20. This is the town's original Western cafe, with good food, email and tons of books. Some travellers have complained of falling standards.

Bluebird Cafe (☎ 531 4071, 150 Cuihu Nanlu) Dishes Y8-25. This is one of the most popular Western-inspired restaurants in town.

Dicos (Dékèshì Huǒjī; Beijing Lu) Dishes from Y8. Kūnmíng hasn't as yet experienced the invasion of KFC a la Chéngdū, but this is a decent local approximation. There are several branches around town.

Billy Niupai's (Bǐlì Niúpái; ☎ 331 1748, 47 Tianyuan Lu) Meals Y50. At this swanky steakhouse, tucked away in the north-eastern Xīnyíng Xiǎoqū district, you can get steaks, burgers, pasta and even tacos that should successfully satisfy a homesick appetite. Much of these Western meals are made with imported ingredients. The decor is strictly American cowboy, but pleasant for all that. It's probably best to take a taxi, if for no other reason than you'll definitely need the taxi driver to help you find the place. The ride should cost around Y15 from Kūnhú Fàndiàn, less from the Camellia Hotel.

Holiday Inn Kunming (see Places to Stay earlier) Breakfast/lunch/dinner buffets Y65/55/86. This is the place to head to for a no-holds-barred buffet blowout – you can eat as much as you can stuff in.

Entertainment

Once restricted to dismal karaoke bars, Kūnmíng is exploding with night-time options, most of the boozing rather than dancing variety. Any of the Western-style cafes mentioned earlier double as drinking holes.

The Hump (see Places to Stay earlier) Beers from Y5. There are no fewer than three bars here, which offer regular drink specials and low-priced domestic beer.

Upriver Club (Shànghé Huìguǎn) Teas/meals from Y20/15. This is a unique coffee/tea shop-cum-art gallery hidden down an alley off Houxin Jie, south of Jinbi Lu. It's got a pleasant outdoor area, Internet access and books, as well as both permanent art displays and visiting exhibits.

Camel Bar (Lùotuo Jiǔbā; ☎ 337 6255, 274 Baita Lu) This bar is run by Li Du, a local rocker of some repute. It's got cheap Tsingtao beer and live music on weekends.

Charlie's Bar (☎ 316 5888, 25 Dongfeng Donglu) This bar, in the annexe of the Holiday Inn, is frequented by Kūnmíng's expat community, but prices are considerably higher than elsewhere (mixed drinks Y80) – stick to beer.

You might be able to chase up minority dancing displays (more often held for the benefit of group tours), travelling troupes or Yunnan opera. CITS sometimes has information on these events. The Song and Dance Ensemble of Yunnan performs most weekdays at 8.30pm at the **Kunming Theatre** (Kūnmíng Jùyuàn).

Shopping

You have to do a fair bit of digging to come up with inspiring purchases in Kūnmíng. Yúnnán specialities are jade, marble (from Dàlǐ), batik, minority embroidery, musical instruments and spotted-brass utensils.

Some functional items make good souvenirs: large bamboo water pipes for smoking angel-haired Yúnnán tobacco, qìguō (ceramic steampots) and local herbal medicines such as Yúnnán Báiyào (Yunnan White Medicine), which is a blend of over 100 herbs and highly prized by Chinese throughout the world.

Yunnanese tea is also an excellent buy and comes in several varieties, from bowl-shaped bricks of smoked green tea called tuóchá, which have been around since at least Marco Polo's time, to leafy black tea that rivals some of India's best. One tea shop worth checking out is **Tien**

Fu Famous Teas (Tiānfù Míngchá), next to the PSB on Beijing Lu.

One of the main shopping drags is Zhengyi Lu, which has numerous department stores. Other shopping areas are Jinbi Lu by the Zhengyi Lu intersection (lots of small speciality shops), and Dongfeng Donglu, between Zhengyi Lu and Huguo Lu (here renamed Nanping Jie).

Flower & Bird Market (Huāniǎo Shìchǎng; Tongdao Jie) This market is definitely worth a visit. It's tucked away on one of numerous little streets and alleys lying between Zhengyi Lu and Wuyi Lu, just north of the Kunming Department Store. Pet supplies, fishing gear and flowers dominate the cramped rows of tiny stalls, but there is a bizarre assortment of other items, such as old coins, wooden elephants, tacky wall murals and so-called 'antiques'. Just walking around here is rewarding: if you actually find something you want to buy, consider it an added bonus.

For antiques it's better to look among the privately run shops on Beijing Lu and Dongfeng Donglu. Outside the Kunming Hotel you will probably be ambushed by women flogging their handiwork – bargain if you want a sane price. Both the **Cuìhú Bīnguǎn** and **Kunming Hotel** sell batik, which you can also find in Dàlǐ. There are a few **herbal medicine shops** at the southern end of Beijing Lu.

If you are heading off to the mountains and need warm clothes or camping equipment try **Climber Outdoors** (Pāndēngzhe; ☎ 313 2783, 20 Dongfeng Donglu), just down an alley next to the Brothers Jiang restaurant, or **Postar Outdoor and Equipment Collection** (Jíxīng; Baita Lu), not far from the Camellia Hotel.

Getting There & Away

Air Yunnan Airlines/CAAC (☎ 316 4270 domestic, 312 1220 international) is the large office on Tuodong Lu. You can buy air tickets for any Chinese airline but the office only offers discounts (of around 20%) on Yunnan Airlines flights. It's open 24 hours, though only the small ticket-window on the left side of the building is open 8pm to 8am. You can pay for tickets with a Visa credit card but there's a 3% surcharge.

Other airline offices in Kūnmíng include:

China Southern Airlines (☎ 310 1831) 433 Beijing Lu

China Southwest Airlines (☎ 353 9702) 160 Beijing Lu

Kunming United Airlines (☎ 362 8592) 13 Dongfeng Xilu

Shanghai Airlines (☎ 313 8502) 46 Dongfeng Donglu

Kūnmíng is well connected by air to the rest of China, and most flights (even within Yúnnán) are on Boeing 737 and 757 jets. Popular destinations include: Běijīng (Y1600), Chéngdū (Y640), Chóngqìng (Y660), Guǎngzhōu (Y1160), Guìlín (Y770), Guìyáng (Y400), Nánjīng (Y1710), Nánníng (Y580), Qīngdǎo (Y2140), Shànghǎi (Y1670), Shēnzhèn (Y1400), Xiàmén (Y1540) and Xī'ān (Y970).

Within the province you can reach Bǎoshān (Y440), Jǐnghóng (Y520), Lìjiāng (Y420), Mángshì/Déhóng (Y530), Xiàguān/Dàlǐ (Y340), Zhāotōng (Y390) and Zhōngdiàn (Y560).

Several carriers have flights to Hong Kong (Y1870, daily), Macau (Y1770), Bangkok (Y1540, daily), Chiang Mai (Y1450), Yangon (Rangoon; Y2190, weekly), Vientiane (Y1520, twice weekly), Osaka (Y4400), Singapore (Y3580, discounted to Y2150, twice weekly) and Seoul (Y5860, discounted to Y4480). It's also possible to fly from Jǐnghóng (Xīshuāngbǎnnà) to Bangkok for Y1300.

Foreign airline offices include the following:

Dragonair (☎ 313 8592) 575 Beijing Lu (in the Golden Dragon Hotel)

JAS (☎ 316 1230) Room 633, 6th floor, 25 Dongfeng Donglu (Holiday Inn Kunming)

Lao Aviation 154 Dongfeng Donglu (entrance to the Camellia Hotel)

Silk Air/Singapore Airlines (☎ 313 2334) 2nd floor, 25 Dongfeng Donglu (Holiday Inn Kunming)

Thai Airways International (☎ 313 3315, fax 316 7351) 28 Beijing Lu, next to the King World Hotel. Flights to Bangkok (Y1750) leave daily; Tuesday, Thursday and Sunday flights stop off in Chiang Mai (Y1450).

Bus There seem to be buses leaving from all over the place in Kūnmíng and bus transport can be a little confusing at first. However, the long-distance bus station on Beijing Lu is the main centre of operations, and this is the best place to organise bus tickets to almost anywhere in Yúnnán or farther afield. Exceptions to this are more local destinations like Lake Diān.

The most popular bus routes from Kūnmíng are to Dàlǐ and Lìjiāng (northwest of Kūnmíng) and Jǐnghóng (south, in Xīshuāngbǎnnà), and Déhóng (west). The long distances to the last two destinations make sleeper buses a popular if not necessary option. The long-distance bus station now has super-fast Korean luxury buses for many destinations.

For information on Dàlǐ, see the Dàlǐ Getting There & Away section later.

Once an unspeakably horrible trip of up to 30 hours, Lìjiāng (Y152) is now just nine hours away on the Korean express buses. Express buses depart at 7.30am, 9.15am, 10.20am and noon. Normal sleeper buses depart in the early morning, or around 7pm, take longer (around 11 hours) and cost Y100.

A daily express bus leaves for Zhōngdiàn (Y171, 12 hours) at 8.20am but most travellers break the trip in Lìjiāng or Dàlǐ.

With road and vehicle improvements, the marathon trip to Jǐnghóng in Xīshuāngbǎnnà now takes only 15 to 22 hours, depending on the bus type, the length of the numerous meal breaks and various unscheduled but inevitable stops. The trip used to include an overnight stop, but now nearly all buses drive straight through. Express buses depart at 4pm and 6.30pm (Y150, 16 hours). A single express bus also departs at 1.30pm from in front of the train station.

Sleepers to Jǐnghóng (Y120, 22 hours) leave between 6pm and 9pm. Many more sleeper buses to Jǐnghóng are found in front of the main train station and fares are often negotiable. These operators also have a few sleepers that bypass Jǐnghóng and go straight to Měnglà (Y138, 24 to 29 hours), the jump-off point for Laos.

Both options for getting to the Déhóng region involve long hauls, so it's worth considering doing at least one leg of the trip by air (to Mángshì). Sleeper buses leave for Bǎoshān (Y97, 14 hours) from the long-distance bus station four times daily between 4.30pm and 6.20pm. An express bus to Bǎoshān leaves sometime between

7.30am and 9am (Y116). Sleeper buses direct to Ruìlì (Y148, 22 to 26 hours) leave six times daily between 10am and 7.30pm. More options are found outside the main train station.

If you're headed to Vietnam, a single express bus runs to the Chinese border town of Hékǒu (Y95, 11 hours) in the morning from the long-distance bus station. There are also overnight sleeper buses (Y83 to Y88, 14 hours), leaving in the early evening.

It is possible to travel by bus to several destinations in neighbouring provinces from the long-distance bus station, including Guìyáng (Y101, 18 hours) in Guìzhōu and Nánníng (Y161) in Guǎngxī; Xīngyì (Y64, 10 hours) in Guìzhōu is the closest.

For information on getting to Shílín see that section later in this chapter.

Train Rail options (all prices listed are for hard sleepers) include trains to Shànghǎi (Y325 to Y518), Běijīng (Y538 to Y577), Chóngqìng (Y212), Guǎngzhōu (Y329; via Guìlín), Xī'ān and Chéngdū (Y193 to Y256). Almost any train headed east (for Běijīng, Chóngqìng, Guǎngzhōu, Shànghǎi etc) passes through Guìyáng. For Éméi Shān take a Chéngdū-bound train; the fastest trains take about 17 hours and cost Y215 to Y230 for a hard sleeper and Y336 to Y351 for a soft sleeper. If you're going to Guìlín, consider the impressive Nánkūn railway to Nánníng.

To Xiàguān (Dàlǐ City) trains depart at 10.10pm (Y75 to Y95 hard sleeper, Y160 soft sleeper, nine hours). Tourist trains also roar to Shílín.

You can also take a daily 4pm train from the north train station down the narrow-gauge line to the border crossing with Vietnam at Hékǒu (Y72 to Y77 hard sleeper, 16 hours); this continues on to Hanoi on Friday and Sunday (Y298 soft sleeper only, 30 hours).

The main train station sells both hard-sleeper and hard-seat tickets from 8.30am, up to eight days in advance. At peak times, especially holidays, you may need to book a few days ahead. The train station ticket office is open from 6.30am to 11pm. The good news is that the station seems to have more hard-sleeper tickets available closer to departure days, sometimes even on the morning of departure.

Getting Around

Bus Bus No 63 runs from the east bus station to the Camellia Hotel and on to the main train station. Bus No 23 runs from the north train station south down Beijing Lu to the main train station. Fares range from Y0.5 to Y4. The main city buses have no conductors and require exact change.

To/From the Airport A super-efficient shuttle bus (Y5) runs between Kūnmíng's airport and the Yunnan Airlines office. Buses run from the airport when full, pretty much every 15 minutes. The driver will normally drop off passengers at the Camellia Hotel and at Kūnhú Fàndiàn.

Alternatively, you can exit the airport, walk past the taxis, a traffic roundabout and a hotel to the main road. Bus No 52 runs along this road to/from the city centre. From Beijing Lu bus No 67 runs to the airport.

Better still, treat yourself to a taxi (approximately Y15) – this is one of the few cheap airport taxi rides in China.

Bicycle The Camellia Hotel carries a decent selection of bikes for hire for Y2 per hour or Y15 for the day (plus a deposit of Y200). Kūnhú Fàndiàn also has a few bikes for hire for Y8 per day, with a deposit of Y100, but they've seen better days.

Fat Tyres Bike Shop (☎ 530 1755), at 61 Qianju Jie, just off Cuihu Nanlu, has superb equipment, including some mountain bikes to rent, and organises Sunday morning bike rides – you need to make reservations ahead of time.

AROUND KŪNMÍNG

Most of the major sights are within a 15km radius of Kūnmíng. Local transport to these places is awkward, crowded and time-consuming; it tends to be an out-and-back job, with few crossovers for combined touring. If you wish to take in everything, it would take something like five return trips, which would consume three days or more.

You can simplify this by pushing the Black Dragon Pool, Ānníng Hot Springs and Golden Temple to the background, and concentrating on the trips of high interest – Qióngzhú Sì and Xī Shān, both of which have decent transport connections. Lake Diān presents some engrossing circular-tour possibilities on its own.

Better still, buy a map, hire a good bicycle and tour the area on two wheels (although there are some steep hills lurking out there…).

Golden Temple 金殿
Jīn Diàn

This Taoist temple *(admission Y15)* is hidden amid a pine forest on Phoenix Song Mountain, 11km north-east of Kūnmíng. The original Ming temple was carted off to Dàlǐ; the present one dates from 1671 and was the brainchild of General Wu Sangui, who was dispatched by the Manchus in 1659 to quell uprisings in the region. Wu Sangui turned against the Manchus and set himself up as a rebel warlord, with the Golden Temple as his summer residence.

The pillars, ornate door frames, walls, fittings and roof tiles of the 6m-high temple are all made of bronze; the entire structure, laid on a white Dàlǐ marble foundation, is estimated to weigh more than 250 tonnes. In the courtyard are ancient camellia trees, one 600 years old. At the back there is a 14-tonne bronze bell, cast in 1423.

To get here, take bus No 10 or 71 from Kūnmíng's north train station. Many travellers ride hired bikes to the temple – it's fairly level-going all the way to the base of the hill. Once you get here, you'll have to climb an easy hill path to the temple compound. A cable car (Y15) runs from the temple to the World Horticultural Expo Garden, or you can take a bus.

World Horticultural Expo Garden
Shìjiè Yuányì Bólǎnyuán 世界园艺博览园

This 218-hectare garden complex (☎ 501 2367; admission before/after 2pm Y100/50; open 8am-5pm daily), 10km north-east of Kūnmíng near the Golden Temple, was built in April 1999 for the World Horticultural Exposition. It's a mix of pleasant Disney-style gardens and strangely pointless exhibits left over from the expo; the place is worth a visit if you are interested in gardens and plants, otherwise give it a miss. The best exhibits are the Grand Greenhouse, which has absorbing displays of Yúnnán's tropical plants and flowers, and the bonsai and vegetable and fruit gardens.

To get here, take bus No 47 from Kūnmíng's main train station or No 71 from the north train station; the same bus continues to the Golden Temple. A cable car at the back of the gardens can take you to the Golden Temple for Y15. Last admission is at 4pm.

Black Dragon Pool
Hēilóng Tán 黑龙潭

This is a rather mediocre garden *(admission Y1)*, 11km north of Kūnmíng, with old cypresses, dull Taoist pavilions and no bubble in the springs. But the view of the surrounding mountains from the garden is inspiring. Within walking distance is the **Kunming Botanical Institute**, where the flora collection might be of interest to specialists. Take bus No 9 from the north train station.

Qióngzhú Sì 筇竹寺
Bamboo Temple

Qióngzhú Sì *(admission Y3)*, 12km north-west of Kūnmíng, dates back to the Tang dynasty. Burned down and rebuilt in the 15th century, it was restored from 1883 to 1890 when the abbot employed master Sichuanese sculptor Li Guangxiu and his apprentices to fashion 500 *luohan* (arhats or noble ones). These life-size clay figures are stunning – either very realistic or very surrealistic – a sculptural *tour de force*. Down one huge wall come the incredible surfing Buddhas, some 70-odd, riding the waves on a variety of mounts – blue dogs, giant crabs, shrimp, turtles and unicorns.

The statues have been constructed with the precision of a split-second photograph – a monk about to chomp into a large peach (the face contorted almost into a scream), a figure caught turning around to emphasise a discussion point, another about to clap two cymbals together, yet another cursing a pet monster. The old, the sick, the emaciated – nothing is spared; the expressions of joy, anger, grief or boredom are extremely vivid.

So lifelike are the sculptures that they were considered in bad taste by Li Guangxiu's contemporaries (some of whom no doubt appeared in caricature), and upon the project's completion he disappeared into thin air.

By far the easiest way to get here is to take a bus from in front of Yúnnán Fàndiàn (see Places to Stay – Mid-Range earlier). Buses run from 7am to around 4.30pm (although the last often goes at around 10am) leaving as soon as they are full. The ride takes 30 minutes and costs around Y8 one way.

Ānníng Hot Springs 安宁温泉

Ānníng Wēnquán

Most travellers sensibly give this place (44km south-west of Kūnmíng) a wide berth as it's not particularly interesting. There are various hotels and guesthouses here that pipe the hot spring water into the rooms, but reports have it that couples are not accepted in some of these – this rule may have changed.

Nearby, and possibly worth a look, is **Cáoxī Sì**. This temple is over the river and a couple of kilometres or so to the south in a bamboo grove on Cong Hill.

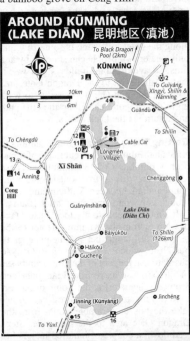

AROUND KŪNMÍNG (LAKE DIĀN) 昆明地区（滇池）

Buses to the springs run approximately every hour from Xiǎoxīmén bus station between 8am and 6pm; the trip costs Y4. Returning, the last bus is at 5pm. There is another bus station west of Xiǎoxīmén that may also have buses.

Lake Diān 滇池

Diān Chí

The shoreline of this lake, to the south of Kūnmíng, is dotted with settlements, farms and fishing enterprises; the western side is hilly, while the eastern side is flat country. The southern end of the lake, particularly the south-east, is industrial.

The lake is elongated – about 40km from north to south – and covers an area of 300 sq km. Plying the waters are *fānchuán*, pirate-sized junks with bamboo-battened canvas sails. It's mainly for scenic touring and hiking, and there are some fabulous aerial views from the ridges at Dragon Gate in Xī Shān (see the Xī Shān section later).

Dàguān Gōngyuán 大观公园

Grand View Park

This park *(admission Y5)* is at the northernmost tip of Lake Diān, 3km south-west of the city centre. It covers 60 hectares and includes a nursery, a children's playground, rowboats and pavilions. A Buddhist temple was originally constructed here in 1862. The **Grand View Tower** *(Dàguān Lóu)* provides good views. Its facades are inscribed with a 180-character poem by Qing poet Sun Ranweng, rapturously extolling the beauty of the lake. Bus No 4 runs to Dàguān Gōngyuán from Yuántōng Sì via the city centre; bus No 52 departs from near the Kunming Hotel.

AROUND KŪNMÍNG

At the north-eastern end of the park is a dock where you may be able to get a boat (Y5, 40 minutes) to Lóngmén village and Hǎigěng Gōngyuán. From Lóngmén village you can hike up the trail to Dragon Gate and Xī Shān, and catch a minibus back into town from near the summit at the Tomb of Nie Er. From Hǎigěng Gōngyuán, take bus No 44 to Kūnmíng's main train station.

Xī Shān 西山
Western Hills

This range spreads out across a long wedge of parkland on the western side of Lake Diān; its hills are also known as the 'Sleeping Beauty Hills', a reference to the hills' undulating contours, which are thought to resemble a reclining woman with tresses of hair flowing into the sea. The path up to the summit passes a series of famous temples – it's a steep approach from the north side. The hike from Gāoyáo bus station, at the foot of the hills, to Dragon Gate takes 2½ hours, though most people take a connecting bus from Gāoyáo to the top section, or take a minibus direct to the Tomb of Nie Er. Alternatively, it is also possible to cycle to the hills from the city centre in about an hour – to vary the trip, consider doing the return route across the dikes of upper Lake Diān.

At the foot of the climb, about 15km from Kūnmíng, is **Huátíng Sì** *(admission Y4)*, a country temple of the Nanzhao kingdom believed to have been constructed in the 11th century, rebuilt in the 14th century, and extended in the Ming and Qing dynasties. The temple has some fine statues, a Buddhist scripture library, and excellent gardens.

The road from Huátíng Sì winds 2km from here up to the Ming dynasty **Tàihuá Sì** *(admission Y3)*. The temple courtyard houses a fine collection of flowering trees, including magnolias and camellias.

Farther along the road, near the minibus and cable car terminus is the **Tomb of Nie Er** *(Nièěr Zhǐmù; admission Y1)*. Nie Er (1912–36) was a talented Yúnnán musician who composed the national anthem of the People's Republic of China (PRC) before drowning in Japan en route for further training in the Soviet Union. From here you can catch a chairlift (Y15) if you want to skip the fairly steep ascent to the summit. Alternatively a tourist tram takes passengers up to the Dragon Gate for Y2. You can also catch a cable car (Y30) here down to Hǎigěng Gōngyuán and Yunnan Nationalities Village.

Sānqīng Gé, near the top of the mountain, was a country villa of a Yuan dynasty prince, and was later turned into a temple dedicated to the three main Taoist deities.

Farther up, near the top of the mountain, is **Dragon Gate** *(Lóng Mén; admission Y20)*. This is a group of grottoes, sculptures, corridors and pavilions that were hacked from the cliff between 1781 and 1835 by a Taoist monk and co-workers, who must have been hanging up there by their fingertips. At least that's what the locals do when they visit, seeking out the most precarious perches for views of Lake Diān. The tunnel along the outer cliff edge is so narrow that only one or two people can squeeze by at a time, so avoid public holidays and weekends! Admission to the Dragon Gate area includes Sānqīng Gé. It's possible to walk up to the Dragon Gate along the cliff path and return via the back routes.

Getting There & Away From Kūnmíng to Xī Shān the most convenient mode of transport is minibus (Y8, 30 minutes). These leave as they fill up from outside the Yúnnán Fàndiàn between 7.30am and 1pm, though you won't find many after 10am.

It's more reliable to use local buses: take bus No 5 from the Kunming Hotel to the terminus at Liǎngjīahé, and then change to bus No 6, which will take you to Gāoyáo bus station at the foot of the hills. Minibuses (Y5 to Y6) also leave from Liǎngjīahé and drop passengers off at the Tomb of Nie Er.

Returning to Kūnmíng you can either take the bus or scramble down from the Dragon Gate area to the lake side. Steps lead down a couple of hundred metres before Dragon Gate and Sānqīng Gé area ticket office and end up in Lóngmén village (Lóngmén cūn), also known as Sānyì Cūn. When you reach the road, turn right and walk about 100m to a narrow spit of land that leads across the lake. Continuing across the land spit, you arrive at a narrow stretch of water and a small bridge. (You could also take the cable car across to Hǎigěng Gōngyuán for Y30.) Proceed by foot through Hǎigěng Gōngyuán to the far entrance, where you can catch bus No 44 to Kūnmíng's main train station.

The tour can easily be done in reverse; start with bus No 44 to Hǎigěng Gōngyuán, either walk to Lóngmén village and climb straight up to Dragon Gate or take the cable car for Y30, then when you are finished make your way down through the temples to Gāoyáo bus station, where you can get bus No 6 back to the Liǎngjīahé terminus and then the No 5 bus to the Kunming Hotel. Note that if you don't want to pay Y8 to walk through Hǎigěng Gōngyuán you'll have to walk 3km or so from the entrance of the Yunnan Nationalities Village or take a taxi.

Alternatively, bus No 33 runs along the western lake shore through Lóngmén village, or you can take a boat from Dàguān Gōngyuán.

Yunnan Nationalities Village
Yúnnán Mínzúcūn 云南民族村

On the north-eastern side of the lake, the local tourist authorities have thrown together a string of model minority villages *(adult/student Y45/25)* with the aim of finally representing all 25 of Yúnnán's minorities. There are also various song-and-dance performances throughout the day. An evening ticket (Y20, issued after 6pm) gets you access to an evening bonfire and song-and-dance performance only.

If you're at all averse to tourist-board fabrications of ethnic cultures, give the place a miss and spend an extra day in Xīshuāngbǎnnà or Déhóng, where you can see the real thing.

With the advent of the Yunnan Nationalities Village, what little remains of **Hǎigěng Gōngyuán** *(admission Y8)* – a narrow strip of greenery along the lakefront – has become a good place to kick back and enjoy the views of the lake.

Bus No 44 runs to Haigeng Lu from one street north of Kūnmíng's main train station.

Yunnan Nationalities Museum
Yúnnán Mínzú Bówùguǎn 云南民族博物馆

A better bet if you have a special interest in China's minority nationalities is to visit this nearby museum *(adult/student Y10/4; open 9am-4.30pm Tues-Sun)*. There are eight main halls that take in festivals, folk art, jewellery, costume, social structure, writing, handicrafts and musical instruments.

The museum has a couple of shops that sell some of the best examples of minority clothing that you'll find in south-western China, though prices are relatively high.

Zhènghé Gōngyuán 郑和公园

At the south-western corner of Lake Diān, this park commemorates the Ming dynasty navigator Zheng He (known as Admiral Cheng Ho outside China). A mausoleum here holds tablets with descriptions of his life and works. Zheng He, a Muslim, made seven voyages to more than 30 Asian and African countries in the 15th century in command of a huge imperial fleet.

From Xiǎoxīmén bus station take the bus to Jìnníng; the park is on a hill overlooking the town. For a change of pace, take a train from the north train station to Hǎikǒu and then a local bus to Jìnníng. You can complete a full circuit by catching a bus on to Jìnchéng and Chénggòng. There's also accommodation in Jìnníng for around Y20 per bed if you feel like moving at a more relaxed pace.

Chénggòng 呈贡县

This is an orchard region on the eastern side of Lake Diān. Flowers bloom all year round, with the 'flower tide' in January, February and March. This is the best time to visit, especially the diminutive Dòunán village nearby. Once one of Yúnnán's poorest villages, it now sells more than 400,000 sprays of flowers *each day*. The village's per capita income went from US$13 to US$415 in four years (even Yunnan Airlines has opened an office to expedite international deliveries).

Many Western varieties of camellia, azalea, orchid and magnolia derive from south-western Chinese varieties. They were introduced to the West by adventuring botanists who carted off samples in the 19th and 20th centuries. Azaleas are native to China – of the 800 varieties in the world, 650 are found in Yúnnán.

During the Spring Festival (January/ February) a profusion of blooms can be found at temple sites in and around Kūnmíng – notably the temples of Tàihuá, Huátíng, Yuántōng and the Golden Temple, as well as at Black Dragon Pool. Take bus No 5 heading east to the terminus at Júhuācūn, and change there for bus No 12 to Chénggòng.

SHÍLÍN 石林
Stone Forest
☎ 0871

Shílín *(admission Y55)*, found around 120km south-east of Kūnmíng, is a massive collection of grey limestone pillars, the tallest 30m high, split and eroded by wind and rain water into their present fanciful forms. Marine fossils found in the area suggest that it was once under the sea. Legend has it that the immortals smashed a mountain into a labyrinth for lovers seeking privacy.

The maze of grey pinnacles and peaks, with the odd pond, is treated as an oversized rockery, with a walkway here, a pavilion there, some railings along paths and, if you look closely, some mind-bending weeds.

Most travellers find Shílín somewhat overrated on the scale of geographical wonders. The important thing, if you venture here, is to get away from the main tourist area – there are some idyllic, secluded walks within 2km of the centre and by moonlight it's otherworldly.

The villages in the Lùnán county vicinity are inhabited by the Sani branch of the Yi tribespeople. Considering that so many other ethnically interesting areas of Yúnnán are now open, you could be disappointed if you make the trip just to see the tribespeople who live in this area. Their craftwork (embroidery, purses, footwear) is sold at stalls by the entrance to the 'forest', and Sani women act as tour guides for groups. English-speaking guides cost Y80 for a 2½-hour tour.

For those keen on genuine village and farming life, well, Shílín is a big place – you can easily get lost. Just take your butterfly net and a lunch box along and keep walking and you'll get somewhere eventually.

There are actually several 'stone forests' in the region. About 8km in a north-easterly direction is a larger (300-hectare) **Nǎigǔ Stone Forest** *(Nǎigǔ Shílín Fēngjǐngqū; admission Y25)*, with karst caves, a large waterfall and an impressive causeway of

SHÍLÍN (STONE FOREST) 石林

To Lùnán (10km)
To Kūnmíng (120km)
Main Walking Circuit
Other Paths
LP
To Nǎigǔ Stone Forest (8km) & Train Station (10km)
0   200   400m
0   200   400yd
Five-Tree Village
Main Entrance
Inscription of Mao Zedong's poem 'Ode to the Plum Blossom' 咏梅石
Shílín Hú
Stage 舞台
Minor Stone Forest
Lion Pond 狮子池
Sweet Water Well 甜水井
Baby Buffalo
Lotus Pond
Monk Tanseng 唐僧石
Stone Prison 石监狱
Open Stage 舞场
Stone Mushroom 灵芝石
Lotus Peak 莲花峰
Stone Bell 石钟
Sword Peak Pond (Jiànfēng Chí) 剑峰池
Major Stone Forest
Moon-Gazing Rhino 犀牛望月
Forest-Circling Hwy
Wife Waiting for Her Husband 望夫石
Area of the Plum Tree Garden
Goddess of Mercy 观音石
Swan Gazing Afar 天鹅远瞩
Old Man Taking a Stroll 漫步从容

SHÍLÍN

PLACES TO STAY & EAT
2 Restaurants
   餐厅饭店
6 Shílín Bīnguǎn (Old Building)
   石林宾馆（老楼）
7 Shílín Bīnguǎn; CITS
   石林宾馆；中国国际旅行社
9 Yúnlín Bīnguǎn
   云林宾馆
10 Shílín Bìshǔyuán Bīnguǎn
   石林避暑园宾馆

OTHER
1 Microbuses to Lùnán;
   Horse Carts
   中巴车到路南；马车
3 Bus Departures
   汽车出发处
4 Buses to the Train Station
   到火车站的汽车
5 Post Office
   邮局
8 PSB
   公安局

black, volcanic blocks. The easiest way to get to Nǎigǔ is to take a microbus (Y15 one way) or a more relaxing horse cart (45 minutes, Y10 return) from the main road.

It's best to take an overnight stop in the forest for further exploration, although if you're just looking at the forest itself a day trip will do.

Places to Stay

Shílín Bīnguǎn (☎ 771 1405) Dorm beds in old building Y30, doubles Y240-300, triples Y350. This is a villa-type place near the main entrance to Shílín, with a souvenir shop and dining hall. The 'Common Room Department' (Pǔtōng Kèfáng), at the rear section of the hotel compound, has basic dormitory accommodation but you don't get a lot for your money here. To find the dorm rooms, follow the circular road clockwise to the other side of the hill.

Shílín Bìshǔyuán Bīnguǎn (☎ 771 1088) Doubles/triples Y300/360. This new hotel, where the main forest trails start, has clean and pleasant rooms with nice bathrooms and views over the Shílín. This is probably the best-value mid-range choice, and doubles/triples are sometimes discounted to Y150/180.

Yúnlín Bīnguǎn (☎ 771 1410) Old-block doubles Y100-150, new-block doubles Y250-350. Rates are a bit cheaper at this hotel than at the others. It's a little less than a kilometre down the road that forks to the right after you cross the main bridge. Reception is in the new block.

Places to Eat

Several restaurants next to the bus terminal specialise in *duck*, roasted in extremely hot clay ovens with pine needles. A whole duck costs Y40 to Y50 and takes about 20 minutes to cook – have the restaurant staff put a beer in their freezer and it'll be just right when the duck comes out.

Near the main entrance is a cluster of *restaurants* and *snack bars* that are open from dawn to dusk. Check all prices before you order as overcharging is not uncommon. The hotels also have decent restaurants.

Entertainment

Sani song-and-dance evenings are organised when there are enough tourists around.

Surprisingly, these events generally turn into good-natured exchanges between Homo Ektachromo and Sani Dollari, and neither seems to come off the worse for wear. Shows normally start at around 8pm at a stage next to the minor stone forest but there are sometimes extra performances so ask at the hotels; performances are free.

There are also Sani performances during the day between 2pm and 3pm. Occasional bullfighting takes place between 1pm and 2pm at a natural outdoor amphitheatre by Hidden Lake at the back of Shílín. Wrestling, bullfighting, singing and dancing are held here during the Torch Festival in July/August.

Getting There & Away

Bus From Kūnmíng's long-distance bus station, buses leave at 7.30am and 8.40am to Shílín (Y18.5). In the afternoon there are usually minibuses waiting at Shílín's car park, leaving when full (Y10 to Y15). In the morning you'll have less choice and you may have to take a horse cart or microbus a couple of kilometres to the main highway and flag down a Kūnmíng-bound bus there.

There are plenty of day tours that leave from in front of Kūnmíng's main train station, and from near the King World Hotel, but choose these with caution as you may well spend the whole morning stopping off at various caves (a national obsession) and souvenir stalls en route.

Train Express tourist trains are probably the most popular way to get to Shílín. Services depart Kūnmíng's main train station at 8.32am, arriving at 10.06am and return from Shílín at 4.30pm, arriving back in Kūnmíng at 6.04pm. Tickets cost Y20/30 one way/return for a hard seat or Y25/40 for a soft seat. Buses meet the trains to take passengers the extra 10km or so to Shílín. The Camellia Hotel normally runs a morning bus from the hotel to catch the morning departure. It's possible to buy your entrance tickets to the forest on the train.

LÙNÁN 路南
☎ 0871

Lùnán is a small market town about 10km from Shílín. It's not really worth making a special effort to visit, but if you are in the area, try and catch a market day (Wednesday or Saturday) when Lùnán becomes a colossal jam of donkeys, horse carts and bikes. The streets are packed with produce, poultry and wares, and the Sani women are dressed in their finest.

Kēxīng Bīnguǎn (☎ 779 6725) Dorm beds Y10, doubles with bath Y50. This place, on the south-western side of the main roundabout, is a decent budget bet, though it's in need of renovation in places.

Stone Forest Hotel (Shílín Dàjiǔdiàn; ☎ 779 8888, fax 779 4887, 2 Longquan Lu) Doubles Y228-368 plus 15% tax. This is a three-star hotel right on the central roundabout. Prices include breakfast and transfer from the train station.

Minibuses shuttle between Lùnán and Shílín regularly (Y2, 10 minutes). In Lùnán, flag down anything heading north of the main traffic circle. At Shílín, minibuses leave from a stand on the main road.

Minibuses to Kūnmíng (Y14, 1½ hours) depart regularly from the western side of Lùnán's main roundabout until around 7pm.

XIÀGUĀN 下关
☎ 0872

Xiàguān lies at the southern tip of Ěrhǎi Hú (Ear-Shaped Lake), about 400km west of Kūnmíng. It was once an important staging post on the Burma Road and is still a key centre for transport in north-west Yúnnán. Xiàguān is the capital of Dàlǐ prefecture and is also referred to as Dàlǐ City (Dàlǐ Shì). This confuses some travellers, who think they are already in Dàlǐ, book into a hotel and head off in pursuit of a banana pancake only to discover they haven't arrived yet. Nobody stays in Xiàguān unless they have an early bus the next morning.

To go straight to Dàlǐ, upon arriving in Xiàguān, turn left out of the long-distance bus station, and at the first intersection turn left. Just up from the corner, diagonally opposite Dàlǐ Fàndiàn, is the station for the No 4 local bus, which runs to the real Dàlǐ (Y1.2, 30 minutes) until around 8pm. If you want to be sure, ask for Dàlǐ Gǔchéng (Dàlǐ Old City). Alternatively, minibuses run from a block west of the bus station (turn right out of the entrance) but you'll spend a lot of time waiting around for other passengers.

Information
The regional PSB office on 21 Tianbao Jie now handles all visa extensions for Xiàguān and Dàlǐ. See the Dàlǐ section for more details.

Things to See
There are good views of the lake and mountains from **Ěrhǎi Gōngyuán** *(Ear-Shaped Lake Park)*. You can reach the park on foot, by motor-tricycle for around Y3, or on bus No 6.

Local travel agents around the bus station also sell tickets for day trips up and down Ěrhǎi Hú, taking in all the major sights. Prices for the all-day tours range from Y60 to Y80.

Places to Stay
Some travellers end up staying a night in Xiàguān in order to catch an early morning bus from the long-distance bus station.

Kèyùn Fàndiàn (☎ 212 5286) Singles/doubles/triples with shared bath Y38/50/48, with private bath Y68/80/90. This hotel next to the long-distance bus station is a bit grim but is probably the cheapest option if you have to stay in Xiàguān.

Xiàguān Bīnguǎn (☎ 217 4933) Main-building singles Y120-168, doubles Y240, west-wing doubles Y60-80, triples Y45-60. Rooms in the glitzy main building are often discounted by up to 40%, making them a good deal. Rooms in the separate west wing come without bathroom, and are OK but still overpriced.

Dàlǐ Fàndiàn (☎ 217 9888) Singles/doubles Y128/168. Near the No 4 bus stop, this hotel has transformed itself into a three-star monster. Rooms are sometimes discounted to Y100.

Getting There & Away
Air Xiàguān's new airport is 15km from town. Flights leave daily to Kūnmíng (Y340) and Xīshuāngbǎnnà/Jǐnghóng (Y540). The Yunnan Airlines ticket office (☎ 216 6588) is next to Dàlǐ Fàndiàn. There are no public buses to the airport; taxis cost Y40 to Y50 from Xiàguān or Y80 from Dàlǐ.

Bus Xiàguān has several bus stations, which throws some travellers. Luckily, the two main ones are both on the same side

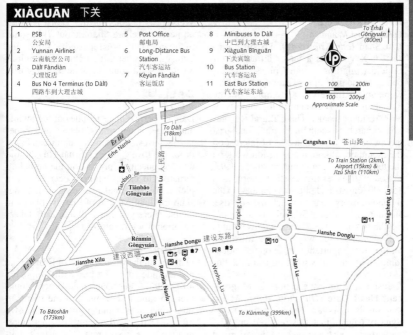

XIÀGUĀN 下关

1	PSB 公安局	5	Post Office 邮电局	8	Minibuses to Dàlǐ 中巴到大理古城
2	Yunnan Airlines 云南航空公司	6	Long-Distance Bus Station 汽车客运站	9	Xiàguān Bīnguǎn 下关宾馆
3	Dàlǐ Fàndiàn 大理饭店	7	Kèyùn Fàndiàn 客运饭店	10	Bus Station 汽车客运站
4	Bus No 4 Terminus (to Dàlǐ) 四路车到大理古城			11	East Bus Station 汽车客运东站

of the street, approximately two blocks apart. You might get dropped off at either one. Both have departures throughout the province, so if the long-distance bus station doesn't have a good departure time for you, wander over to the other one.

The long-distance bus bus station has luxury Royale Express buses and this is the quickest way to travel. Buses to Lìjiāng (Y50, 3½ hours) depart at 8.30am and 9.30am, and at 2pm and 7pm. There are two buses to Zhōngdiàn (Y85, seven hours, via Lìjiāng) at 9am and 3pm. There are express buses to Kūnmíng leaving every 30 minutes between 7.30am and 8.30pm. Fares range from Y89 to Y103 depending on the bus and the journey takes about six hours. There are also plenty of minibuses going to Kūnmíng.

Other bus departures from the long-distance bus station include Bǎoshān (Y26, six hours) and Mángshì (Lúxī; Y50 or Y80 for a sleeper, 12 hours). The Mángshì buses continue to Ruìlì (Y90, 15 hours). Sleeper buses to Téngchōng leave at 7.30pm (Y70).

Normal buses heading north for Lìjiāng leave at 6.40am, 10am and 12.30pm and cost Y40 to Y50 (these stop in Dàlǐ to pick up passengers, and tickets can also be booked in Dàlǐ).

There are occasional direct sleeper buses to Jǐnghóng in Xīshuāngbǎnnà (Y145, 30 hours). Alternatively you could take local buses, breaking the trip at Líncāng and Láncāng. Roads are very bad along this route, and travel times have been known to stretch to three days.

Train The railway link between Kūnmíng and Xiàguān was finally opened in 1999. Overnight sleeper trains leave Kūnmíng's main train station at 10.10pm, arriving in Xiàguān at 6.45am. Hard sleepers are Y75/85/95 for upper/middle/lower berth. A soft sleeper is Y160. Returning to Kūnmíng, trains leave Xiàguān at around 9.30pm.

You can buy train tickets for most destinations (Chéngdū etc) from Kūnmíng at a window at the entrance to the bus station but, stupidly, not for Xiàguān to Kūnmíng. For that you'll have to go to the train station in the eastern suburbs! Bus No 1 goes to the train station from the centre of town.

AROUND XIÀGUĀN
Jīzú Shān 鸡足山
Chicken-Foot Mountain

Jīzú Shān *(admission Y40)*, 110km north-east of Xiàguān, is a major attraction for Buddhist pilgrims – both Chinese and Tibetan. At the time of the Qing dynasty there were approximately 100 temples on the mountain and somewhere in the vicinity of 5000 resident monks. The Cultural Revolution's anarchic assault on the traditional past did away with much that was of interest on the mountain, although renovation work on the temples has been going on since 1979.

Today it is estimated that more than 150,000 tourists and pilgrims clamber up the mountain every year to watch the sun rise. Jīndǐng, the Golden Summit, is at a cool 3240m so you will need some warm clothing.

Sights along the way include **Zhùshèng Sì**, the most important temple on the mountain, about an hour's walk up from the bus stop at Shāzhǐ.

Just before the last ascent is the **Magnificent Head Gate** *(Huáshǒu Mén)*. At the summit is **Lèngyán Tǎ**, a 13-tier Tang-dynasty pagoda that was restored in 1927, and there is basic accommodation at **Jīndǐng Sì** *(Golden Summit Temple)* next to the pagoda – a sleeping bag might be a good idea at this altitude.

A popular option for making the ascent is to hire a pony. Travellers who have done the trip claim it's a lot of fun. A cable car (Y22) to the summit is a good way to cheat, though the ride only starts halfway up.

Places to Stay & Eat Accommodation is available at the base of the mountain, about halfway up and on the summit. Prices average Y10 to Y15 per bed. Food gets fairly expensive once you reach the summit so you may want to consider bringing some of your own.

There are a few hotels in Bīnchuān, 70km north-east of Xiàguān, including the *Bīnchuán Bīnguǎn*, *(dorm beds Y15)*.

Getting There & Away From Xiàguān's east bus station (a 10-minute walk east of the main bus station) take a bus to Bīnchuān, 70km to the north-east (Y10, two hours), from where you'll have to take another bus or minibus to Shāzhǐ at the foot of the mountain (Y10, one hour).

Wēishān 巍山

Wēishān is famous for the Taoist temples on nearby **Wēibǎo Shān**, about 7km south of town. There are reportedly some fine Taoist murals here. It's 61km due south of Xiàguān, so it could be done as a day trip.

DÀLǏ 大理
☎ 0872

Dàlǐ is a perfect place to tune out for a while and forget about trains, planes and bone-jarring buses. The stunning mountain backdrop, the lovely lake of Ěrhǎi Hú, the old city, cappuccinos, pizzas and the herbal alternative to cheap Chinese beer (you can pick it yourself) make it, along with Yángshuò in Guǎngxī, one of the few places in China where you can well and truly take a vacation from travelling.

History

Dàlǐ lies on the western edge of Ěrhǎi Hú at an altitude of 1900m, with imposing 4000m-tall Cāng Shān (Jade Green Mountains) behind it. For much of the five centuries in which Yúnnán governed its own affairs, Dàlǐ was the centre of operations, and the old city still retains a historical atmosphere that is hard to come by in other parts of China.

The main inhabitants of the region are the Bai, who number about 1.5 million. The Bai people have long-established roots in the Ěrhǎi Hú region, and are thought to have settled the area some 3000 years ago. In the early 8th century they grouped together and succeeded in defeating the Tang imperial army before establishing the Nanzhao kingdom.

The kingdom exerted considerable influence throughout south-western China and even, to a lesser degree, South-East Asia, since it controlled upper Burma for much of the 9th century. This later established Dàlǐ as an end node on the famed Burma Road. In the mid-13th century it fell before the invincible Mongol hordes of Kublai Khan.

The influx of Chinese tour groups has started to change Dàlǐ's character. The southern part of town has been radically renovated to create a new 'old Dàlǐ', complete with original gates and renovated city walls. The wrecking balls have inched their way up Fuxing Lu, which is now lined with shops catering to Chinese tourists led around by guides dressed up in Bai costumes. The gentrification has been less successful than Lìjiāng's and some of the city's historical charm and authenticity has sadly been lost.

Orientation

Dàlĭ is a miniature city that has some preserved cobbled streets and traditional stone architecture within its old walls. Unless you are in a mad hurry (in which case use a bike), you can get your bearings just by taking a walk for an hour or so. It takes about half an hour to walk from the South Gate (Nán Mén) across town to the North Gate (Běi Mén). You can also get a good overview of the town and its surroundings by walking around the town walls (renovated in 1998).

Huguo Lu is the main strip for cafes – locals call it Yángrén Jiē (Foreigner's Street) – and this is where to turn to for your cafe latte, burritos, ice-cold beer and other treats.

Maps of Dàlĭ and Ěrhǎi Hú areas are available at street stalls near the corner of Huguo Lu and Fuxing Lu, though none of them is all that useful.

Information

Money The Bank of China is in the centre of town, near the corner of Huguo Lu and Fuxing Lu. Bank staff say that Western credit cards can be used in the ATM just outside the entrance to the bank. The

Industrial & Commercial Bank of China (ICBC), right on Huguo Lu, also changes cash and travellers cheques daily and is open until 9pm – so you really don't have to keep track of what day it is in Dàlĭ.

DÀLĬ

PLACES TO STAY
- 4 Jīnhuā Dàjiǔdiàn
  金花大酒店
- 10 Sunny Garden
  第三招待所
  (桑尼园)
- 11 Yu'an Garden
  第四招待所
  (榆安园)
- 17 No 2 Guesthouse
  第二招待所
- 19 Dàlĭ Bīnguǎn
  大理宾馆
- 20 Jim's Tibetan Peace
  Guesthouse; Jim's
  Peace Café
  和平饭店
- 21 Old Dali Four
  Seasons Inn
  大理四季客栈
- 26 MCA Guesthouse

PLACES TO EAT
- 2 Yunnan Cafe
  云南咖啡馆
- 5 Star Cafe
- 6 Old Wooden House
  如意饭店
- 7 Sunshine Cafe
- 8 Marley's Cafe
  马丽咖啡馆
- 9 Sister's Cafe
- 13 Mr China's Son Cafe
- 15 Cafe De Jack; Tim's
  Internet Shop
  樱花阁; 网吧

OTHER
- 1 North Gate
  北门
- 3 Post & Telephone
  Office
  邮电

- 12 Local Buses to
  Shāpíng
  往沙坪的公共汽车
- 14 Michael's Travel
- 16 Dali Passenger
  Service Ticket Office
  大理客运售票处
- 18 Bank of China
  中国银行
- 22 Wǔhuá Pagoda
  五华楼
- 23 Dali Museum
  大理博物馆
- 24 South Gate
  南门
- 25 Pagoda
  三塔公园

Post & Communications China Post is on the corner of Fuxing Lu and Huguo Lu. This is the best place to make international calls, as it has direct dial and doesn't levy a service charge. It's open until 8.30pm.

A number of cafes offer Internet access for Y10 per hour. One of the most popular and professional places is Tim's Internet Shop at 82 Boai Lu.

PSB Exhausted by a deluge of demands for visa extensions, the Dàlǐ PSB office has finally packed its bags and retreated to the relative safety of Xiàguān. This probably won't affect visa extensions too much; you'll just have to take a bus into Xiàguān.

To get there, take bus No 4 until just after it crosses the river in Xiàguān. The PSB office is a short walk south from here.

Dangers & Annoyances The hike up to Zhōnghé Sì and along the mountain ridges is super, but there have been instances of robbery of solo walkers, and in 1997 one German traveller was killed. Try to find a partner.

Dali Museum 大理博物馆
Dàlǐ Bówùguǎn

This museum (*Wenxian Lu; admission Y5; open 8.30am-5pm*) houses a small collection of archaeological pieces relating to Bai history and has some moderately interesting exhibits on marble handicrafts. A number of marble steles grace one wing.

Sān Tǎ Sì 三塔寺
Three Pagodas

Two kilometres north-west of Dàlǐ, standing on the hillside, the three pagodas look particularly pretty when reflected in the nearby lake. They are among the oldest standing structures in south-western China.

The tallest of the three, Qianxun Pagoda, has 16 tiers that reach a height of 70m. It was originally erected in the mid-9th century by engineers from Xī'ān. It is flanked by two smaller 10-tiered pagodas, each of which are 42m high.

The temple behind the pagodas, **Chóng-shèng Sì** (*admission Y10*), is laid out in the traditional Yunnanese style, with three layers of buildings lined up with a sacred peak in the background. The temple has recently been restored and converted into a museum

chronicling the history, construction and renovation of the pagodas.

Organised Tours & Travel Agencies

Numerous travel agencies and cafes on Huguo Lu have tours to sights around Dàlǐ. Private entrepreneurs run cruises around the lake daily if there is enough demand.

A new activity is horse-riding to waterfalls around the base of Cāng Shān. Horsemen congregate at the main highway and offer escorted horse-riding for Y20 per hour or Y70 per day, though initial offers will start much higher than that.

Jim's Tibetan Peace Cafe and Cafe De Jack both offer a bus trip to a Yi minority market, about a two-hour drive from Dàlǐ, held every 10 days. The interesting trip costs Y40 per person.

Michael's Travel, on Boai Lu, can arrange calligraphy or tai chi lessons for Y40 per hour, as well as almost everything else you could think of, including bus and train tickets.

Special Events

If you don't mind crowds, the best time to be in Dàlǐ is probably during the **Third Moon Fair** (*Sānyuè Jié*), which begins on the 15th day of the third lunar month (usually April) and ends on the 21st day. The origins of the fair lie in its commemoration of a fabled visit by Guanyin, the Buddhist Goddess of Mercy, to the Nanzhao kingdom. Today it's more like an extra-festive market, with people from all over Yúnnán arriving to buy, sell and make merry.

The **Three Temples Festival** (*Ràosān Líng*) is held between the 23rd and 25th days of the fourth lunar month (usually May). The first day involves a trip from Dàlǐ's South Gate to Shèngyúan Sì (Sacred Fountainhead Temple) in Xǐzhōu. Here travellers stay up until dawn, dancing and singing, before moving on to Jīnguì Sì on the shore of Ěrhǎi Hú. The final day involves walking back to Dàlǐ by way of Majiuyi Sì.

The **Torch Festival** (*Huǒbǎ Jié*) is held on the 24th day of the sixth lunar month (normally July). Flaming torches are paraded at night through homes and fields. Other events include fireworks displays and dragon-boat racing.

Markets Usually markets follow the lunar calendar, but shrewd local operators have co-opted it into a regular scheme so tourists know where to go. See Around Dàlĭ for information on the Monday Shāpíng market. Markets then take place in Shuāngláng (Tuesday), Yòusuŏ (Friday, the largest in Yúnnán) and Jiāngwěi (Saturday).

Wāsè also has a popular market every five days with trading from 9am to 4.30pm. Many cafes organise transport for Y20 to Y30 per person.

Places to Stay

The addition of several new, low-budget hotels has greatly improved the accommodation situation in Dàlĭ. Even so, places tend to fill up quickly, and those visiting during the peak summer months may find themselves trekking around town in search of that perfect bed on their first day.

MCA Guesthouse (☎ 267 3666, 700 Wenxian Lu) Dorm beds/singles Y10/30, doubles with bath Y50, doubles at back Y80-120 off season, Y100-150 other times. This self-contained little community has spacious dorms with hardwood floors. The only very minor down side is that the OK bathrooms are across the compound; the showers at least have 24-hour hot water. The bar/restaurant and pool area are pleasant places to hang out in. Mid-range doubles at the back are clean and comfortable and are often discounted.

The guesthouse also has book rental, laundry service (and a washing machine), poste restante, Internet access (free for guests except those in dorms) and bikes for rent (Y10 to Y15 per day). The restaurant is good and weekends feature a Tibetan brunch.

Old Dali Four Seasons Inn (Sìjì Kèzhàn; No 5 Guesthouse; ☎ 267 0382, 51 Boai Lu) Dorm beds Y10-15, singles or doubles with shared bath Y30, doubles with private bath Y125. This hotel has been converted from one of the street's oldest and most distinctive old-style buildings, a former school. Two wings of the two-storey complex face a flower-laden courtyard, which has a gazebo and lots of greenery. A cafe serves good food and the occasional video. The communal squat toilets are fairly clean and the showers have reliable hot water 18 hours per day. Dorm rooms have hard beds

in clean quads; for the extra money you can get the 'luxury dorm', which means a soft bed. Bicycles can be rented here and the laundry service is cheap.

Yu'an Garden (Yú'ān Yuán; No 4 Guesthouse; ☎ 267 2093, 4 Huguo Lu) Dorm beds Y10-15, singles/doubles Y30/50, doubles with bath Y100-150. Still popular and rated highly by travellers, this old favourite has 24-hour hot water, Internet access, mountain-bike hire (Y10 per day), a lovely Thai-style cafe, washing machines, a score of laundry lines, and friendly staff. Double rooms tend to suffer from poor ventilation. Look at a few room options, since there's a wide variety. The only problem with this place is that the best rooms always seem to be full. The rooms with private bathroom are a recent addition.

Sunny Garden (Sāngní Yuán; No 3 Guesthouse; ☎ 267 0213) This place just down from Yu'an Garden was undergoing renovation during our last visit so this might be a good new option (though prices might have risen with standards).

Jim's Tibetan Peace Guesthouse (Jímǔ Hépíng Fàndiàn; Boai Lu) Dorm beds Y15, singles with bath Y50, doubles Y60-80. The dorm beds in triples are a little cramped but the shared bathroom is clean and has a Western toilet. The bathtub in the single room is particularly awesome.

No 2 Guesthouse (Dì'èr Zhāodàisuŏ; New Red Camellia Hotel; ☎ 267 0423, Huguo Lu) Dorm beds Y12-15, singles with shared bath Y30, old-wing doubles with private bath Y80, new-wing doubles Y200-220. Close to the action, this has long been Dàlĭ's official stand-by. Though a bit lacking in charm, it's not a bad place to stay, especially if you get a room on the 2nd or 3rd floor of the old wing. The 1st-floor rooms tend to be damp and dark. The doubles in the old wing are mostly on the 1st floor, and not really worth the money unless you're a pair. The newer ones are decent value.

Dàlĭ Bīnguǎn (☎ 267 0386, fax 267 0551, Fuxing Lu) Doubles with bath Y80-150 low season, Y110-240 other times. It's a bit farther away, but the exercise of walking the ten minutes or so from here to Huguo Lu may give you the illusion of having earned your banana pancake. The rooms are clean and pleasant, making it an acceptable option if all the other places are booked.

Jīnhuā Dàjiǔdiàn (☎ *267 3343, cnr Huguo Lu & Fuxing Lu*) Doubles/triples from Y168/198. Sticking out like a sore thumb, this recently renovated hotel probably won't see much in the way of backpacker traffic, though if you're in the mood for luxury, or are toting the kids around, this might be a good choice. The rooms have air-con and satellite TV. Sporting red-capped doormen, hostesses with colourful and ill-fitting headgear, and a marble staircase, the Jīnhuā definitely seems out of sync with the rest of Dàlǐ.

Places to Eat

Most of the travellers' hang-outs are at the top section of Boai Lu and on Huguo Lu. There are many more restaurants than those listed here, but truthfully many are nothing more than cookie-cutter tedium – not bad, simply unremarkable. So many restaurants have opened up that some reported a tenfold drop in business from one summer to the next. The best advice is to spread your patronage; you'll eventually find one you really like.

You would be surprised how many little, very local places way off the main drags have English menus so get around and experiment.

Marley's Cafe (*cnr Boai Lu & Huguo Lu*) Recently relocated, this is one place that seems certain to keep drawing a steady crowd. Marley herself is a great source of local information and her restaurant is divided into Western and Chinese sections. Hopefully the Sunday Bai food group dinner will continue in this new location (make reservations).

Cafe de Jack (*82 Boai Lu*) The No 1 choice for hip music and a congenial atmosphere, this is known for its amazing chocolate cake with ice cream. It also has good pizza and comfy couch seating worth a mention.

Mr China's Son (☎ *267 8234,* Ⓦ *http://mcs.k12.net.cn, 67-5 Boai Lu*) Dishes from Y8, Bai meals Y13-15. For an interesting afternoon of conversation, try this cafe, opened by a gentleman who has penned an English-language account of his trials and tribulations during the Cultural Revolution. It's worth a visit alone for its thorough collection of maps and tips on Dàlǐ and environs – it's got a minor guidebook of its own.

The food was recently given a real boost and there's now a wide selection of Western dishes, as well as good-value set Bai meals (the more people the better the selection). The cafe also runs cultural tours.

Sunshine Cafe (*Huguo Lu*) Meals from Y10. The friendly folks here serve everything from burritos to doner kebabs and whip up the best brownies in town.

Old Wooden House (*Huguo Lu*) This cafe has good outside seating and its bolognese is definitely worth trying – a roving Italian gave them the recipe.

Yunnan Cafe (☎ *267 9014, 151 Huguo Lu*) This hotel is about a five-minute walk down Huguo Lu from Fuxing Lu, and was formerly called the Coca Cola Restaurant (until the long arm of Coca-Cola Inc sniffed out the use of its name and dispatched warnings to Dàlǐ). It serves consistently good food. Travellers routinely plant themselves on the rooftop sun deck until the night-time chill or closing time drives them away. The cafe also has an extensive CD collection, book exchange and rental service.

Sister's Cafe (*Boai Lu*) If you're a fan of Japanese food, try this place; it serves the Japanese travellers market.

Star Cafe (*Huguo Lu*) This is another good place for Japanese food.

Shopping

Dàlǐ is famous for its marble, and while a slab of the stuff in your backpack might slow you down a bit, local entrepreneurs produce everything from ashtrays to model pagodas in small enough chunks to make it feasible to stow one or two away.

Huguo Lu has become a smaller version of Bangkok's Khao San Rd in its profusion of clothes shops. It won't take you long to decide whether the clothes are for you or not – you could outfit yourself for a time-machine jaunt back to Woodstock here, but bear in mind that the shopkeepers can also make clothes to your specifications, so you're not necessarily just stuck with the ready-made hippie stuff. Prices are very reasonable.

Most of the 'silver' jewellery sold in Dàlǐ is really brass. Occasionally it actually is silver, although this will be reflected in the starting price. The only advice worth giving, if you're in the market for this kind of thing, is to bargain hard. For those roving sales ladies badgering you incessantly, don't feel bad to pay *one-fifth* of their asking price – that's what locals advise. For marble from street sellers, 40% to 50% is fair. In shops, two-thirds of the price is average. And don't fall for any 'expert' opinions; go back later on your own and deal.

Batik wall hangings have also become popular in Dàlǐ. Several places near the No 2 Guesthouse on Huguo Lu have good collections, but don't believe the proprietors when they tell you they make the stuff themselves and start justifying the extortionate prices they charge by telling how many hours they worked on a piece. Most of the batik, as in Yángshuò, comes from Guìzhōu where it can be bought for a song. Some batik is made locally, particularly in Xǐzhōu. Authentic Dàlǐ batik is the blue and white printed on cotton and silk.

Getting There & Away

Xiàguān's new airport has brought Dàlǐ to within 45 minutes' flying time from Kūnmíng. There are flights several times daily to Kūnmíng (Y340) and daily to Jǐnghóng in Xīshuāngbǎnnà (Y540). For any flight after about 9am it's easy enough to catch an early morning local bus to Xiàguān and then take a taxi to the airport from there.

Probably the most popular means of getting to Dàlǐ is the overnight sleeper train from Kūnmíng (hard sleeper Y75 to Y95). For details on train and air options, and for additional bus options see the Xiàguān section earlier.

Bus The golden rule about getting to Dàlǐ by bus is to find out in advance, preferably several times, whether your bus is for Dàlǐ or Xiàguān. Many buses advertised to Dàlǐ actually only go as far as Xiàguān. For information on getting to Dàlǐ from Kūnmíng see the Kūnmíng Getting There & Away section.

Most travellers now take the daytime express buses from Kūnmíng. If you do take the overnight sleeper bus take care, as someone always seems to find a bag pinched or razored; chain them securely and try and cram them under the lower bunk as far back as possible.

Coming from either Xiàguān or Lìjiāng by express bus along the express highway to the east of Dàlǐ, you may find yourself dropped off next to the highway at the eastern end of Dàlǐ. From here it's a 20-minute walk to the main guesthouses, or take a horse cart for around Y5.

Leaving Dàlǐ, the best thing to do is shop around. Plenty of tour and travel agencies means plenty of options and competitive prices. Most buses for Lìjiāng and Kūnmíng depart from Dàlǐ; for other destinations, you can buy tickets in Dàlǐ but must return to Xiàguān to get on the bus.

Buses to Kūnmíng generally leave between 6.30am and 9am. Travel time is around eight hours, depending on traffic and whether your bus really is a direct bus. Most agencies also run sleeper buses, generally leaving in the evening. Prices are flexible and cost from Y40 to Y55 (the latter for a sleeper).

Buses to Lìjiāng leave between 7am and 2.30pm. Tickets for the three-hour trip are Y35 for minibuses and Y40 to Y50 in an express bus, and can be bought from the Dali Passenger Service Ticket Office (see following) or any travel agency on Huguo Lu. You can also catch any one of numerous buses to Lìjiāng that originate in Xiàguān. Buses to Zhōngdiàn pass through Dàlǐ between 7.30am and 10am (Y50, seven hours).

Tickets for public buses are available at the Dali Passenger Service Ticket Office (Dàlǐ Kèyùnzhàn Shòupiàochù) on Boai Lu; this office also sells tickets for the Xiàguān long-distance bus station.

To catch buses to other points, such as Bǎoshān, Ruìlì or Jǐnghóng, you have to go to Xiàguān. The No 4 local bus to Xiàguān starts early enough – around 6.30am – runs every 15 minutes, and there are stops along Boai Lu. The trip takes around 30 minutes and costs Y1.2. If your bus leaves Xiàguān earlier than 7.30am, you'll have to stay overnight there.

Getting Around

A taxi to Xiàguān airport should take around 45 minutes and cost around Y80; to Xiàguān train station it costs Y30.

Bikes are the best way to get around. Prices average Y2 per hour or Y5 per day for clunky Chinese models, Y2 per hour and Y10 per day for better mountain bikes. Most of the guesthouses and several other places on Boai Lu rent bikes.

AROUND DÀLǏ
Ěrhǎi Hú 佴海湖
Ear-Shaped Lake

This 250 sq km lake is a 50-minute walk from town or a 10-minute downhill zip on a bike.

From Cáicūn, a pleasant little lake-side village east of Dàlǐ (Y2 on the No 2 minibus), there's a ferry at 4.30pm to Wāsè on the other side of the lake. You can stay overnight at the *Wāsè Zhāodàisuǒ* and catch a ferry back at 6am. Plenty of locals take their bikes over.

Ferries crisscross the lake at various points, so there could be some scope for extended touring. Close to Wāsè is Pǔtuó Dǎo and Xiǎopǔtuó Sì *(Lesser Putuo Temple)*, set on an extremely photogenic rock island. Other ferries run between Lóngkān and Hǎidōng, and between Xiàguān and Jīnsuō Dǎo. Ferries leave early in the morning (for market) and return around 4pm; timetables are flexible and departures are somewhat unreliable.

Roads now encircle the lake so it would be possible to do a loop (or partial loop) of the lake by mountain bike, taking in Xīzhōu, Zhōuchéng, Shāpíng and Wāsè.

Plenty of cafes can arrange a horse-and-carriage ride to the lake, then a boat ride to Tiānjìng Pavilion and Guānyīn Pavilion, then Jīnsuō Dǎo or whatever you dream up, for around Y30 per day.

Zhōnghé Sì 中和寺

The temple *(admission Y2)* is a long, steep hike up the mountainside behind Dàlǐ. This is a great day trip and offers fantastic vistas of Dàlǐ and Ěrhǎi Hú. You can cheat and take a new chairlift (Y35/15 up/down) up Zhōnghé Shān. Restaurants here serve up some interesting local concoctions.

You could also hike up the hill, a sweaty hour for those in relatively good shape. (See also Dangers & Annoyances in the Dàlǐ section earlier.) No one path leads directly up the hill; instead, oodles of local paths wind and switchback through farm fields, local cemeteries, and even one off-limits military area (there is a sign in English here!). Walk about 200m north of the chairlift base to the riverbed (often dry). Follow the left bank for about 50m and you'll see lots of ribbony trails leading up. Basically, all roads lead to Rome from here, just keep the chairlift in

sight and when in doubt, bear left. You should eventually come upon a well-worn trail and, following that, some steps near the top.

Branching out from either side of the temple is a trail that winds along the face of the mountains, taking you in and out of steep, lush valleys and past streams and waterfalls. From Zhōnghé it's an amazing 11km up-and-down hike south to Gǎntōng Sì or Qīngbì Stream, from where you can continue to the road and pick up a Dàlǐ-bound bus.

Guānyīn Pavilion 观音堂
Guānyīn Táng

This temple is built over a large boulder said to have been placed there by Guanyin, the Buddhist Goddess of Mercy, disguised as an old woman, to block the advance of an invading enemy. It is 5km south of Dàlǐ.

Gǎntōng Sì 感通寺

This temple is not far south of Guānyīntáng village, which is about 6km south of Dàlǐ. From Guānyīntáng follow the path uphill for 3km. Locals will direct you.

Qīngbì Stream 清碧溪
Qīngbì Xī

This scenic picnic spot near the village of Qīlǐqiáo is 3km south of Dàlǐ. After hiking 4km up a path running close to the river, you'll reach three ponds.

Xīzhōu 喜洲

Among the 101 things to do while you're in Dàlǐ, a trip to Xīzhōu would have to rate fairly high. It's an old town around 18km north of Dàlǐ, with even better preserved Bai architecture than Dàlǐ. A local bus bound for Ěryuán would be the easiest option for getting there, but a bicycle trip with an overnight stop in Xīzhōu (there's accommodation in town) is also a good idea. From here, the interesting town of Zhōuchéng is 7km farther north; it too has basic accommodation.

A few intrepid travellers have leap-frogged these lovely villages, made for Shāpíng's market, then continued all the way around the lake for other markets, including Wāsè's, before boating themselves and their bicycles back to Dàlǐ. From Dàlǐ to Wāsè it's around 58km by road.

Shāpíng Market
Shāpíng Gǎnjí 沙坪赶集

Every Monday Shāpíng, about 30km north of Dàlǐ, is host to a colourful Bai market. The market starts to rattle and hum at 10am and ends around 2.30pm. You can buy everything from tobacco, melon seeds and noodles to meat, pots and wardrobes. In the ethnic clothing line, you can look at shirts, headdresses, embroidered shoes and moneybelts, as well as local batik. Expect to be quoted ridiculously high prices on anything you set your eyes on, so get into a bargaining frame of mind, and you should have a good time.

Getting to Shāpíng market from Dàlǐ is fairly easy. Some of the hotels and cafes in town run minibuses out there on market day for Y15 return. Usually they leave at 9am,

DÀLǏ & ĚRHĂI HÚ 大理与洱海湖

although it's a good idea to ask around and book the day before. Alternatively you can walk up Huguo Lu to the main highway and catch a local bus bound for Ěryuán (Y6). Market day is not the ideal time to take a spin on the local buses but generally there are enough buses to cater for the numbers of visitors.

Shíbǎoshān 石宝山

About 110km north-west of Dàlǐ are the **Stone Treasure Mountain Grottoes** (*Shíbǎoshān Shíkū*). There are three temple groups: Stone Bell (Shízhōng), Lion Pass (Shīzi Guān) and Shādēng Village. The grottoes include some of the best Bai stone carvings in southern China and offer insights into life at the Nanzhao court of the 9th century.

To get to Shíbǎoshān, first take a bus to Jiànchuān, 92km north of Dàlǐ on the old Dàlǐ-Lìjiāng road. Get off at the small village of Diànnán, about 8km south of Jiànchuān, where a narrow road branches south-west to the village of Shāxī, 23km away. You'll just have to wait for a bus for this leg. The grottoes are close to Shāxī.

LÌJIĀNG 丽江
☎ 08891 new town, 0888 old town

North of Dàlǐ, bordering Tibet, the town of Lìjiāng is set in a beautiful valley and makes another great spot to while away a few days or weeks. Your initial response when you pull into town and roar toward the bus station might well be: 'Get me out of here!'. It's not until you get into the old town – a delightful maze of cobbled streets, rickety old wooden buildings, gushing canals and the hurly-burly of market life – that you realise Lìjiāng is more than a boring urban sprawl in the middle of nowhere.

There are a number of interesting sights around Lìjiāng, some of which can be reached by bicycle, offering a week or more's worth of excursions.

Apart from the writings of botanist-explorer Joseph Rock (see the boxed text 'Joseph Rock' later in the Around Lìjiāng section), another venerable work on Lìjiāng that's worth reading if you can find it is *The Forgotten Kingdom* by Peter Goulart. Goulart was a White Russian who studied Naxi culture and lived in Lìjiāng from 1940 to 1949.

The Naxi

Lìjiāng has been the base of the 286,000 strong Naxi (also spelt Nakhi and Nahi) minority for about the last 1400 years. The Naxi are descended from ethnically Tibetan Qiang tribes and lived until recently in matrilineal families. Since local rulers were always male it wasn't truly matriarchal, but women still seem to run the show, certainly in the old part of Lìjiāng.

Like the related Mosu people, the Naxi matriarchs maintained their hold over the men with flexible arrangements for love affairs. The *azhu* (friend) system allowed a couple to become lovers without setting up joint residence. Both partners would continue to live in their respective homes; the boyfriend would spend the nights at his girlfriend's house but return to live and work at his mother's house during the day. Any children born to the couple belonged to the woman, who was responsible for bringing them up. The man provided support, but once the relationship was over, so was the support. Children lived with their mothers, and no special effort was made to recognise paternity. Women inherited all property, and disputes were adjudicated by female elders.

There are strong matriarchal influences in the Naxi language. Nouns enlarge their meaning when the word for 'female' is added; conversely, the addition of the word for 'male' will decrease the meaning. For example, 'stone' plus 'female' conveys the idea of a boulder; 'stone' plus 'male' conveys the idea of a pebble.

Naxi women wear blue blouses and trousers covered by a blue or black apron. The T-shaped traditional cape not only stops the basket always worn on the back from chafing, but also symbolises the heavens. Day and night are represented by the light and dark halves of the cape; seven embroidered circles symbolise the stars. Two larger circles, one on each shoulder, are used to depict the eyes of a frog, which until the 15th century was an important god to the Naxi. With the decline of animist beliefs, the frog eyes fell out of fashion, but the Naxi still call the cape by its original name, 'frog-eye sheepskin'.

The Naxi created a written language over 1000 years ago using an extraordinary system of pictographs – the only hieroglyphic language still in use. The most famous Naxi text is the Dongba classic *The Creation*, and ancient copies of it and other texts can still be found in Lìjiāng, as well as in the archives of some US universities. The Dongba were Naxi shamans who were caretakers of the written language and mediators between the Naxi and the spirit world. The Dongba religion, itself an offshoot of Tibet's pre-Buddhist Bon religion, eventually developed into an amalgam of Tibetan Buddhism, Islam and Taoism. The Tibetan origins of the Naxi are confirmed by references in Naxi literature to Lake Manasarovar and Mt Kailash, both in western Tibet.

 Useful phrases: 'hello' in the Naxi language is *nuar lala*; 'thank you' is *jiu bai sai*.

Beyond the Clouds is an excellent nine-hour documentary about Lìjiāng made a few years ago by Britain's Channel 4. It's well worth seeking out.

In 1996 an earthquake measuring over seven on the Richter scale rocked the Lìjiāng area, killing more than 300 people – including one foreign tourist – and injuring 16,000. Damage was estimated at over half a billion US dollars. While much of newer Lìjiāng was levelled, the traditional Naxi architecture held up quite well. The Chinese government took note and sank millions of yuán into rebuilding most of Lìjiāng county with traditional Naxi architecture, replacing cement with cobblestone and wood. The United Nations was so impressed by the survival of Lìjiāng that it placed all of Lìjiāng county on its World Heritage Site list in 1999.

The town's reconstruction coupled with the unveiling of Lìjiāng's new airport has led to a huge increase in tourists. One indirect result has been a cluster of new tourist sights with fairly high admission fees. More worrying is the influx of Han Chinese entrepreneurs running tourist shops and restaurants for Han tourists, and souvenir sellers pushing out Naxi stalls. What used to be the preserve of hardy backpackers is now a major tourist destination.

Orientation

Lìjiāng is separated into old and new towns that are starkly different. The approximate line of division is Shīzī Shān (Lion Hill), he green hump in the middle of town that's topped by a radio mast and Looking at the Past Pavilion, a new pagoda. Everything west of the hill is the new town, and everything east is the old town.

The easiest way into the old town is from the north, along Dong Dajie. This area was largely reconstructed following the 1996 earthquake. From the long-distance bus station head east one block and follow an alley lined with snack bars heading north. The old town is a delightful maze of twists and turns – although it's small, it's easy to get lost in, which, of course, is part of the fun. Enjoy!

Information

Lìjiāng's cafes and backpacker inns are the best source of information. Most have noticeboards and travellers books full of useful tips on surrounding sights, especially the Tiger Leaping Gorge trek.

Books The Xinhua Bookshop on Xin Dajie has postcards, maps of the city and a couple of guidebooks.

Hello Lijiang! by Duan Ping-Hua and Ray Hilsinger is a fairly useful guide to sights around Lìjiāng. It's available for Y30 at the Xinhua Bookshop or at the Grand Lijiang Hotel.

Money The Bank of China on Xin Dajie and a branch on Nanguo Zhonglu in the south of town both give cash advances on your credit card. There is also a small branch next to the entrance of the Lìjiāng Bīnguǎn. All branches will change travellers cheques.

Post & Communications The main post and telephone office is on Minzhu Lu, just south of the turn to the old town. It's open 8am to noon and 2pm to 6pm daily. You should be able to make reverse-charge calls and calling-card calls here; if not, head to one of the backpacker cafes, which charge the same (or less) and keep your beer cold while you dial.

Another post office (for letters and postcards only) is in the old town just north of the Old Market Square.

Loads of places in the old town offer Internet access for between Y10 and Y12 per hour. China Telecom is significantly more expensive at Y18 per hour, though this may change.

Travel Agencies CITS has a Family & Independent Traveller (FIT) office across the street from the entrance to Gǔlùwān Bīnguǎn. The staff are helpful, and should be able to give you ideas for local outings and book plane and even train tickets.

PSB The PSB is opposite the Lìjiāng Bīnguǎn, with an extremely helpful official in charge of visa extensions – let's hope he keeps his job. It's open 8am to noon Monday to Friday though somebody's usually around anytime.

Dangers & Annoyances In 1997 two solo female travellers were robbed at knifepoint in separate incidents atop Xiàng Shān (Elephant Hill) in Hēilóngtán Gōngyuán. Both attacks occurred in broad daylight in the early afternoon, so keep your eyes sharp for people lurking behind you. It would obviously be a good idea to pair up with at least one other traveller.

Old Town

Criss-crossed by canals, bridges and a maze of narrow streets, the old town is not to be missed. The town's web of artery-like canals once supplied the city's drinking water. There are several wells and pools still in use around town. You can see one of the original wells opposite the Well Bistro.

The focus of the old town is the **Old Market Square** (*Sìfāng Jiē*), full of Naxi women in traditional dress. Parrots and plants adorn the front porches, women sell griddle cakes in front of teahouses and players energetically slam down the trumps on a card table in the middle of the street. Unfortunately the Naxi traders are slowly being pushed out by tacky souvenir stalls. For all the controversy regarding what to preserve in the town and how, for now it is extraordinary.

Above the old town is a beautiful park that can be reached on the path leading past the radio mast. Sit on the slope in the early morning and watch the mist clearing as the old town comes to life.

Now acting as sentinel of sorts for the town is **Looking at the Past Pavilion** (*Wànggǔ Lóu; admission Y15*), raised for tourists at a cost of over one million yuán. It's famed for a unique design using dozens of four-storey pillars, but unfortunately these were culled from northern Yúnnán old-growth forests. A path (with English signs) leads from the Old Market Square.

Mu Family Mansion 木氏土司府
Mùshì Shìsīfǔ

This former home of a Naxi chieftain (admission Y35; open 8.30am-6.30pm daily) was heavily renovated (more like built from scratch) after the 1996 earthquake, with funds from the World Bank. There's not much to see at the moment, though it's likely that some kind of museum will be installed before too long. The mansion backs onto Shīzi Shān and you should be able to get access from here to Looking at the Past Pavilion.

Hēilóngtán Gōngyuán
Black Dragon Pool Park 黑龙潭公园

This park (Xin Dajie; admission Y20) is on the northern edge of town. Apart from strolling around the pool – its view of Yùlóng Xuěshān is the most obligatory photo shoot in south-western China – you can visit the Dongba Research Institute (Dōngbā Wénhuà Yánjiūshì), which is part of a renovated complex on the hillside.

At the far side of the pool are renovated buildings used for an art exhibition, a pavilion with its own bridge across the water and the Ming dynasty Five Phoenix Hall (Wǔfèng Lóu).

Trails lead straight up Xiàng Shān to a dilapidated gazebo and then across a spiny ridge past a communications centre and back down the other side, making a nice 45-minute (if you push it) morning hike. See also Dangers & Annoyances earlier.

At the northern entrance of the park is the Museum of Naxi Dongba Culture (Nàxī Dōngbā Wénhuà Bówùguǎn; admission Y5; open 8.30am-5.30pm daily). Displays include Naxi dress and culture, Dongba script, information on Lìjiāng's old town and the dubious claim that the region is the 'real' Shangri-la.

Xuan Ke Museum 宣科住所
Xūan Kē Zhùsuǒ

Xuan Ke, a Naxi scholar who spent 20 years in labour camps following the suppression of the Hundred Flowers movement, has turned his Lìjiāng family home, just west of Dōngbā House, into a small museum (11 Jishan Alley) that's a repository for Naxi and

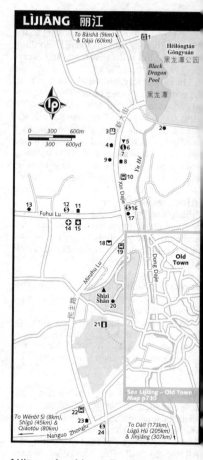

Lìjiāng cultural items. Besides clothing and musical instruments (including an original Persian lute that has been used in Naxi music for centuries), his home displays Dr Joseph Rock's large, handmade furniture and has a small library of out-of-print books on Lìjiāng. Dr Rock was a close family friend.

Xuan Ke speaks excellent English and is always willing to discuss his original ideas about world culture (for example, that music and dance originated as rites of exorcism).

Festivals

The 13th day of the third moon (late March or early April) is the traditional day to hold a Fertility Festival.

July brings the Torch Festival (Huǒbǎ Jié), also celebrated by the Bai in the Dàlì

LÌJIĀNG

PLACES TO STAY & EAT
4 Gǔlùwān Bīnguǎn
  古路湾宾馆
5 Ali Baba's Cafe
  阿里巴巴餐厅
8 Red Sun Hotel
  红太阳酒店
11 Lìjiāng Bīnguǎn
  丽江宾馆
23 Yúnshān Fàndiàn
  云杉饭店

OTHER
1 Museum of Naxi
  Dongba Culture
  东巴博物馆
2 Dongba Research
  Institute
  东巴研究所
3 Cinema
  云岭剧场

6 CITS (FIT); Express Bus
  Station
  中国国际旅行社；
  高块汽车客运站
7 Mao Square
  毛主席广场
9 Lijiang International
  Ethnic Cultural
  Exchange Centre
  丽江国际民族文化交换
  中心
10 Northern Bus Station
  北客运站
12 Bank of China
  中国银行
13 CAAC
  中国民航
14 Hospital
  医院
15 PSB
  公安局

16 Bank of China
  中国银行
17 Xinhua Bookshop
  新华书店
18 Post & Telephone
  Office
  邮电局
19 No 6 Bus to Báishā &
  Yùlóng Xuěshān
  到白沙和玉龙雪山的6路
  公共车
20 Radio Mast
  狮子山
21 Looking at the Past
  Pavilion
  望古楼
22 Long-Distance Bus
  Station
  长途汽车
24 Bank of China
  中国银行

egion and the Yi all over the south-west. The origin of this festival can be traced back to the intrigues of the Nanzhao kingdom, when the wife of a man burned to death by the king eluded the romantic entreaties of the monarch by leaping into a fire.

Places to Stay

Lìjiāng now has half a dozen guesthouses with traditional Naxi architecture. Stroll around – there will be more by the time you read this – and compare.

New Town Places to try in the new town include:

Yúnshān Fàndiàn (☎ 512 1315, Nanguo Zhonglu) Beds in 2-/3-bed dorms Y35/20, doubles with bath Y90/200 off season/other times. Next to the long-distance bus station (south), this is the first place you're likely to come across when you arrive in town. The dorms are good but there's not much reason to stay here.

Red Sun Hotel (Hóngtàiyáng Jiǔdiàn; ☎ 512 1018, Xin Dajie) Dorm beds Y30, doubles Y70-100, with bath Y200. Adjacent to Mao Square, the dorms are large and bright and there's a nice shared shower and wash area. A few travellers have reported ear-shattering karaoke.

Gǔlùwān Bīnguǎn (☎ 512 1446, fax 512 081, Xin Dajie) Old-block dorm beds Y10-20, doubles Y100-200. North of Mao

Square, this hotel doubles as the car park for the northern bus station. Dorms in the old block (also known as the No 2 Guesthouse) are charmless and the shared toilets will make your eyes water but the dorms are cheap. Decent and quiet (due to location), some rooms have a private bathroom. The new block at the end of the driveway has comfortable upmarket rooms.

Lìjiāng Bīnguǎn (☎ 512 1911, fax 512 1223, Fuhui Lu) Doubles with bath Y140-380. The rooms are nicely furnished and you can normally get discounts of 40%, though the location is a bit inconvenient.

Old Town There are a number of options in the old town.

Grand Lijiang Hotel (Gélán Dàjiǔdiàn; ☎ 512 8888, fax 512 7878, Xinyi Jie) Doubles US$55. At the northern edge of the old town, this Sino-Thai joint venture is the best luxury option. Prices include tax and breakfast.

Square Inn (Sìfāng Kèzhàn; ☎ 512 7487) Triples/quads per person Y20/15, doubles with shared bath Y60. Immediately to the rear of the Old Market Square, this is perhaps the best new option. The dorms are a bit dark but pleasant enough; the doubles are comfortable and good value for two people. The shared bathrooms are clean and there's plenty of hot water in the showers (though the barrierless toilets can be a bit disconcerting). There are some nice sitting areas, the staff is very helpful and there's a cheap laundry service.

First Bend Inn (*Dìyīwān Kèzhàn;* ☎ *518 1688*) Doubles/triples/quads with shared bath per person Y40/30/25. This is one of the old town's best-preserved buildings. The rooms are comfortable and carpeted and set on two levels around a lovely courtyard. Little touches include travel information and motion-sensor lights for late-night trips to use the facilities. The bathrooms are quite clean; the showers have reliable hot water in the mornings and evenings. The staff is attentive and friendly and are full of information on local sights.

Ancient Town Youth Hostel (*Gǔchéng Guójì Qīngnián Lǚguǎn;* ☎ *517 5403, 44 Mishi Xiang*) Dorm beds Y15-20, doubles per person with/without bath Y60/30. This new option is affiliated with Youth Hostels International (YHI) and card holders get a small discount. The best value are the bunk-bed dorms, which come with a locker; the doubles are not so good value. Facilities include cheap Internet access, a washing machine (Y10 per hour) and bike hire.

Dongba House (*☎/fax 517 5431, 16 Jishan Xiang*) Dorm beds Y15, doubles/triples with shared bath Y50/90. This new and very well-run place is in the northern part of the old town. The bunk dorm beds are good value. The main down side is that there's only one bathroom/shower and it's not up to much. The place has an attractive sunlit cafe, Internet and bike rental. The friendly Tibetan owner also owns the Tibet Cafe in Zhōngdiàn (and his brother owns the MCA Guesthouse in Dàlǐ).

Prague Cafe (*☎ 512 3757, 80 Mishi Xiang*) Dorm beds with/without set breakfast Y25/10. Mostly a cafe, this place has a couple of rooms round the back that rank as the cheapest in Lìjiāng. It's not a bad choice if you don't mind the communal atmosphere and close quarters. *Sakura Cafe (see Places to Eat later)* runs a similar operation.

Ancient Stone Bridge Inn (*Gǔchéng Dàshíqiáo Kèzhàn;* ☎ *518 4001, 71 Xingren Xiaduan*) Doubles with shared bath Y60-80, with private bath Y80-100. This is a small family run inn in a lovely location. There are a couple of fabulous rooms right on the side of the canals with a shared bathroom and one good upper-floor double; apart from

LÌJIĀNG – OLD TOWN
丽江古城市中心

these the rooms are average. The mai[n] downside is that there is only one toilet.

Old Town Inn (*Gǔchéng Kèzhàn;* ☎ *51[2] 9000, Xinyi Jie*) Doubles with shared bat[h] Y180, with private bath Y200-320. In th[e] northern part of the old town, the lovel[y] courtyard and traditional architecture is th[e] main draw here. The hotel is quite popula[r] with Chinese groups. Discounts are nor[-] mally available.

Sānhé Nàxī Bīnguǎn (*☎ 512 0891, Xiny[i] Jie*) Doubles with bath Y150-180 low sea[-] son, Y380-320 other times. This is anothe[r] mid-range place aimed at groups, which ha[s] rooms around a lovely traditional courtyar[d]

Lìjiāng has many other traditional-styl[e] inns in the backstreets south and east of th[e] old-town centre.

LÌJIĀNG – OLD TOWN

PLACES TO STAY
1 Grand Lijiang Hotel
格兰大酒店
9 Old Town Inn
古城客栈
11 Sānhé Nàxī
Bīnguǎn
三河纳西宾馆
13 Dongba House
东巴豪斯
14 Ancient Town
Youth Hostel
古城国际青年旅馆
15 First Bend Inn
第一湾客栈
25 Sakura Cafe Annexe
27 Ancient Stone
Bridge Inn
古城大石桥客栈
30 Square Inn
四方客栈

PLACES TO EAT
5 Naxi Snack Food
纳西风味小吃

6 Gǔchéng
Jiǔlóu
古城酒楼
8 Snack Bars
小吃店
18 Prague Cafe
布拉格咖啡馆
19 #69
20 Well Bistro
井卓餐馆
22 Ma Ma Fu's
马马付餐厅
23 Sakura Cafe
24 Delta Cafe
29 Old Market Inn
纳西餐厅

OTHER
2 Yùlóng Bridge
& Waterwheel
玉龙桥
3 Fruit Market
水果市场
4 Taxis
出租汽车

7 Máoniúpíng
Booking Office
牦牛坪索道售票处
10 Naxi Ancient Music
House
古乐院
12 Xuan Ke Museum
宣科住所
16 Naxi Music Academy
纳西音乐
17 Dōngbā Palace
21 Stone Bridge
大石桥
26 Post Office
邮电局
28 Old Market Square
四方街
31 Gate
门
32 Mu Family Mansion
木氏土司府
33 Wells
水井
34 Market
市场

Places to Eat

Like Dàlǐ, Lìjiāng has a legion of small, family operated restaurants catering to backpackers. The following run-down is by no means exhaustive.

There are always several 'Naxi' items on the menu, including the famous 'Naxi omelette' and 'Naxi sandwich' (goat's cheese, tomato and fried egg between two pieces of local *bābā*). Bābā is the Lìjiāng local speciality – thick flatbreads of wheat, served plain or stuffed with meats, vegetable or sweets; the *yùmǐ bābā*, corn bābā on a husk, is delicious. Morning is the best time to check out the bābā selection. Try locally produced *yinjiu*, a lychee-based wine with a 500-year history – it tastes like a decent semi-sweet sherry.

Western Food Lìjiāng has an abundance of places serving Western food.

Old Market Inn (*Nàxī Cāntīng; Market Square*) Often mentioned for its atmosphere, this place has seats downstairs that look out onto the market square, allowing you to take in the market sights and sounds over a cold beer or hot Yúnnán coffee.

Prague Cafe (*see Places to Stay earlier*) Meals from Y10. This is a bright, modern place run by a Hong Kong couple and their assorted pets. It's not the cheapest place in town but it does deliver the goods. The pizza, milkshakes and desserts are excellent and there's a computer for Internet access. A major plus in winter is that it catches all the afternoon sun.

Ma Ma Fu's (*Māmāfù Cāntīng*) In a lovely location right along a stream, this is one of Lìjiāng's stalwarts. Now run by a younger Mama Fu, it's still got grand home-baked breads and apple pie (Y7), and an excellent array of dishes.

Sakura Cafe This popular and well-run cafe serves up excellent Korean and Japanese food (the cook is Korean and married to a local). The outstanding *bimbap* (rice, egg, meat and vegetables with hot sauce) set meal is enough for two. The chocolate cake is also well worth the Y7 investment.

Delta Cafe This place has good food and music, heavy on the reggae. The whole street is now pretty much lined with restaurants.

Well Bistro (*Jǐngzhuō Cānguǎn*) This place will likely capture your fancy. The cosy all-wood interiors and tastefully understated decor add to the superb food. Everything is made from scratch, including the bread and to-die-for desserts, which

The Conductor

The village schoolmaster was a chivalrous and energetic man with a shock of glinting blue-black hair, who lived with his childlike wife in a wooden house beside the Jade Stream.

A musicologist by training, he had climbed to distant mountain villages to record the folksongs of the Na-Khi tribe. He believed, like Vico, that the world's first languages were in song. Early man, he said, had learnt to speak by imitating the calls of animals and birds, and had lived in a musical harmony with the rest of Creation.

His room was crammed with bric-a-brac salvaged, heaven knows how, from the catastrophes of the Cultural Revolution. Perched on chairs of red lacquer, we nibbled melon seeds while he poured into thimbles of white porcelain a mountain tea known as 'Handful of Snow'.

He played us a tape of Na-Khi chant, sung antiphonally by men and women around the bier of a corpse: Wooo...Zeee! Wooo...Zeee! The purpose of the song was to drive away the Eater of the Dead, a fanged and malicious demon thought to feast upon the soul.

He surprised us by his ability to hum his way through the mazurkas of Chopin and an apparently endless repertoire of Beethoven. His father, a merchant in the Lhasa caravan trade, had sent him in the 1940s to study Western music at the Kunming Academy.

On the back wall, above a reproduction of Claude Lorrain's *L'Embarquement pour Cythère*, there were two framed photos of himself: one in white tie and tails behind a concert grand; the other, conducting an orchestra in a street of flag-waving crowds – a dashing and energetic figure, on tiptoe, his arms extended upwards and his baton down.

'In 1949,' he said. 'To welcome the Red Army into Kūnmíng.'

'What were you playing?'

'Schubert's *Marche Militaire*.'

For this – or rather, for his devotion to 'Western culture' – he got twenty-one years in jail.

He held up his hands, gazing at them sadly as though they were long-lost orphans. His fingers were crooked and his wrists were scarred: a reminder of the day when the Guards strung him up to the roof-beams – in the attitude of Christ on the Cross...or a man conducting an orchestra.

Bruce Chatwin, *The Songlines* (1987)

change daily. The pizza here without a doubt rivals any in south-western China. There are also lots of good vegetarian options. Hip, eclectic music echoes quietly throughout the day.

#69 Set meals from Y15. This is across the alley from the Well Bistro and is an outstanding place for vegie dishes, such as spinach and mushroom pie or baked vegetables in a pot. The food can be a bit bland but it does come without MSG and salt. The set meals are good value and it has Internet access.

Naxi & Chinese Food If you get tired of pizza and cappuccino, Lìjiāng also has plenty of good snack bars and local restaurants, often in atmospheric surroundings and catering to Chinese tourists.

Naxi Snack Food (Nàxī Fēngwèi Xiǎochī) On the banks of the main canal at the north end of the old town, this place serves local Naxi food and has an English menu of sorts.

There's a row of inviting *snack bars* on Xinyi Jie in the north of the old town. There are also some good *snack bars* south of Dashi Bridge. Many signs are anglicised to read 'Old Town Small Eat' and the like, though the menus aren't yet translated.

Gǔchéng Jiǔlóu Dishes around Y12. Try this place for something a bit more upscale; the restaurant is lit up with dozens of lamps at night giving it a romantic feel.

Ali Baba's Cafe (Mao Square) Good food and friendly people make this a good spot. It's also a good place to find out about details on Tiger Leaping Gorge and Lúgū Hú. The local bus to Dàjù leaves from near here.

Entertainment

One of the few things you can do in the evening in Lìjiāng is attend performances of the *Naxi Orchestra* at the Naxi Music Academy (Nàxī Gǔyuè Huì). Performances are held nightly inside a beautiful old building in the old town, usually from 8pm to 10pm.

Not only are all 20 to 24 members Naxi but they play a type of Taoist temple music (known as *dongjing*) that has been lost elsewhere in China. The pieces they perform are supposedly faithful renditions of music from the Han, Song and Tang dynasties played on original instruments. In most of China such instruments didn't survive the

Cultural Revolution; several of this group hid theirs by burying them underground. This is a rare chance to hear Chinese music as it must have sounded in classical China. They also play plenty of Han Chinese music, so don't be surprised.

Xuan Ke usually speaks for the group at performances – speaks too much, some say – explaining each musical piece and describing the instruments. There are taped recordings of the music available; a set of two costs Y30. If you're interested, make sure you buy the tape at the show – tapes on sale at shops around town, and even in Kūnmíng, are pirated copies.

You can usually turn up on your own and watch a performance, but you should book seats earlier in the day if you want a good seat. Tickets range from Y30 to Y50.

Aware of the popularity of the Naxi Orchestra, several other troupes have hopped on the bandwagon. The *Naxi Ancient Music House* (Nàxī Gǔyuèyuàn; Dong Dajie), next to the cinema, has a 90-minute performance of traditional Naxi music every night at 8pm. Tickets cost Y35.

The government-run *Dongba Palace* (Dong Dajie) has a less authentic song-and-dance show at 8pm (Y35).

Getting There & Away

Air Lìjiāng's airport is 25km to the east of town. Yunnan Airlines now flies several times daily from Lìjiāng to Kūnmíng (Y420) and daily to Jǐnghóng in Xīshuāngbǎnnà (Y610). Direct flights to Guǎngzhōu and Guìlín are rumoured but not yet existent.

In Lìjiāng, tickets can be booked at the Civil Aviation Administration of China (CAAC; Zhōngguó Mínháng) ticket office (☎ 512 0289), which is closed from 11.30am to 2pm, and at Gǔlùwān Bīnguǎn and CITS; the latter two levy a service charge.

Bus Lìjiāng has a northern and a larger main long-distance bus station in the south; many, but not all, buses make stops at both. The key is to make sure exactly where your bus leaves from. The ticket window for the northern station is just south of the Red Sun Hotel, though buses depart from Gǔlùwān Bīnguǎn's car park across the road. Note that schedules on the wall are mostly wrong at both.

Minibuses for Xiàguān (Y31.5) go via Dàlǐ and leave from both stations every half-hour or so until 5.30pm. Express buses depart from the long-distance bus station at 8.20am, 2.30pm and 6.30pm (Y50). Xiàguān buses will either drop you by the main highway or at the eastern edge of Dàlǐ, from where it's a 20-minute walk or five-minute horse cart ride (Y5) into the centre.

For Kūnmíng, an express coach leaves the long-distance bus station at 8.20am (Y154.5, 10 hours). Sleeper buses depart from here between 6pm and 8pm (Y105 to Y115).

If you are headed to Chéngdū you'll need to go to the railhead at Jīnjiāng. Jīnjiāng buses leave at 6.30am (Y51.5, 10 hours) from the long-distance bus station and 6.45am, 7am and 8am from the express bus station in the north of town. Sleepers leave between 5pm and 6pm for Y65.5 from the long-distance and express bus stations. The early bus will allow you to connect with trains to Chéngdū at 6.28pm (No 2152) and 11.05pm (No K114).

Buses to Zhōngdiàn leave from the long-distance bus station every hour or so from 7.30am to 3pm (Y32.5) and pass through Qiáotóu, giving access to Tiger Leaping Gorge.

Getting Around

Yunnan Airlines has a bus service to and from the airport for Y10; taxis cost around Y60.

Taxis start at Y6 flag fall in town. The old town, however, is best seen on foot. Bike hire is available at the Ancient Town Youth Hostel and sometimes from Mao Square. Bikes should cost around Y15 for the day.

AROUND LÌJIĀNG

It is possible to see most of Lìjiāng's environs on your own, but a few agencies do offer half- or full-day tours, starting from Y150; it might be worth it if you take one that includes admission fees.

Monasteries

The monasteries around Lìjiāng are Tibetan in origin and belong to the Karmapa (Red Hat) sect. Most of the monasteries were extensively damaged during the Cultural

Joseph Rock

Yúnnán was a hunting ground for famous, foreign plant-hunters such as Kingdon Ward and Joseph Rock. Rock lived in Lìjiāng between 1922 and 1949, becoming the world's leading expert on Naxi culture and local botany. More than his academic pursuits, however, he will be remembered as one of the most enigmatic and eccentric characters to travel in western China.

Rock was born in Austria, the son of a domineering father who insisted he enter a seminary. A withdrawn child, he escaped into imagination and atlases, discovering a passion for China. An astonishing autodidact – he taught himself eight languages, including Sanskrit – he began learning Chinese at 13 years of age. He somehow wound up in Hawaii, and in time became the foremost authority on Hawaiian flora.

Asia always beckoned and he convinced the US Department of Agriculture, and later Harvard University, to sponsor his trips to collect flora for medicinal research. He devoted much of his life to studying Naxi culture, which he feared was being extinguished by the dominant Han culture. He became *National Geographic* magazine's 'man in China' and it was his exploits in north-western Yúnnán and Sìchuān that made him famous.

He sent over 80,000 plant specimens from China – two were named after him – along with 1600 birds and 60 mammals. Amazingly, he was taking and developing the first colour photographic plates in his field in the 1920s! Tragically, container-loads of his collections were lost in 1945 in the Arabian Sea when the boat was torpedoed.

Rock's caravans stretched for half a mile, and included dozens of servants, including a cook trained in Austrian cuisine (who was fired and rehired on every trip), trains of pack horses, and hundreds of mercenaries for protection against bandits, not to mention the gold dinner service, a battery-powered gramophone player and a collapsible bathtub.

Rock lived in Yùhú village (it was called Nguluko when he was there) outside Lìjiāng. Many of his possessions are now local family heirlooms.

The *Ancient Nakhi Kingdom of Southwest China* (Harvard University Press, 1947) is Joseph Rock's definitive work. Immediately prior to his death, his Naxi dictionary was also finally prepared for publishing. For an insight into the man and his work, take a look at *In China's Border Provinces: The Turbulent Career of Joseph Rock, Botanist-Explorer* (Hastings House, 1974) by JB Sutton or the man's many archived articles for *National Geographic*.

Revolution and there's not much monastic activity nowadays. Nevertheless, it's worth hopping on a bicycle and heading out of town for a look.

Pǔjì Sì This monastery is around 5km north-west of Lìjiāng (on a trail that passes the two ponds to the north of town). The few monks here are usually happy to show the occasional stray traveller around.

Fùguó Sì Not far from the town of Báishā, Fùguó Sì *(admission Y8)* was once the largest of Lìjiāng's monasteries. Much of it was destroyed during the Cultural Revolution. In the monastery compound look out for the **Hufa Hall**; the interior walls have some interesting frescoes.

Yùfēng Sì This small lamasery *(Jade Peak Temple)* is on a hillside about 5km past Báishā. The last 3km of the track require a

steep climb. If you decide to leave your bike at the foot of the hill, don't leave it too close to the village below – the local kids have been known to let the air out of the tyres (or worse)!

The monastery sits at the foot of Yùlóng Xuěshān and was established in 1756. The monastery's main attraction nowadays is the **Camellia Tree of 10,000 Blossoms** *(Wànduǒ Shānchá)*. Ten thousand might be something of an exaggeration, but locals claim that the tree produces at least 4000 blossoms between February and April. A monk on the grounds risked his life to keep the tree secretly watered during the years of the Cultural Revolution.

Wénbǐ Sì To get to Wénbǐ Sì requires a fairly steep uphill ride 8km to the south-west of Lìjiāng. The monastery itself is not that interesting, but there are some good views and pleasant walks in the near vicinity.

AROUND LÌJIĀNG & ZHŌNGDIÀN 丽江、中甸地区

Frescoes

Lìjiāng is famed for its temple frescoes. Most travellers probably won't want to spend a week or so traipsing around seeking them out, but it may be worth checking out one or two.

Most of the frescoes were painted during the 15th and 16th centuries by Tibetan, Naxi, Bai and Han artists. Many of them were restored during the later Qing dynasty. They depict various Taoist, Chinese and Tibetan Buddhist themes and can be found on the interior walls of temples in the area. However, the Red Guards came through here slashing and gouging during the Cultural Revolution, so there's not that much to see.

In Báishā ask around for **Dàbǎojī Palace** *(Dàbǎojī Gōng)*, where the best frescoes are found, and also **Liúlí Temple** *(Liúlí Diàn)* or **Dàdīng Gé**. The Dàbǎojī Palace recently introduced an admission fee. Check the little shop for reasonably priced Naxi scrolls and paintings.

In the lovely nearby village of Lóngquán, frescoes can also be found on the interior walls of **Dàjué Palace** *(Dàjué Gōng)*.

Báishā 白沙

Báishā is a small village on the plain north of Lìjiāng, near several old temples and is one of the best day trips out of Lìjiāng, especially if you have a bike. Before Kublai Khan made it part of his Yuan empire (1271–1368) it was the capital of the Naxi kingdom. It's hardly changed since then and though at first sight it seems nothing more than a desultory collection of dirt roads and stone houses, it offers a close-up glimpse of Naxi culture for those willing to spend some time nosing around.

The star attraction of Báishā will probably hail you in the street. Dr Ho (or He) looks like the stereotype of a Taoist physician and has a sign outside his door: 'The Clinic of Chinese Herbs in Jade Dragon Mountains of Lijiang'. The travel writer Bruce Chatwin propelled the good doctor into the limelight when he mythologised Dr Ho as the 'Taoist physician in the Jade-Dragon Mountains of Lìjiāng'. Chatwin did such a romantic job on Dr Ho that he was to subsequently appear in every travel book (including this one) with an entry on Lìjiāng; journalists and photographers turned up from every corner of the world, and Dr Ho, previously an unknown doctor in an unknown town, has achieved worldwide renown. Look out for the John Cleese quote: 'Interesting bloke; crap tea'.

Báishā is an easy bike ride from Lìjiāng. Otherwise take bus No 6 (Y2) from opposite the post office in Lìjiāng. The village is about 1km off the main road.

Yùlóng Xuěshān 玉龙雪山
Jade Dragon Snow Mountain
Soaring to 5500m, some 35km from Lìjiāng, is Yùlóng Xuěshān, also known as Mt Satseto. Its peak was climbed for the first time in 1963 by a research team from Běijīng.

A chairlift has been built up the mountain. The first section takes you about halfway up, near Love-Suicide Hill, where you can rent horses to ride to a large meadow. The second chairlift, the highest in Asia, takes you to a stunning 4506m, where walkways lead to awesome glacier views. Watch out for the symptoms of altitude sickness here (see the Facts for the Visitor chapter's Health section) – Chinese entrepreneurs sell bags of oxygen to chain-smoking Chinese tourists for around Y30.

Getting out to the mountain will either require hitching, hiring your own van for around Y130, or catching a ride on a minibus to Dàjù or Bǎoshān. A bus is said to depart daily at 8.30am from the bus stop across from the post office. Buses take passengers the 4km from the reception centre on the main road to the cable car.

Local tour operators have prohibitively priced tours taking in the mountain and a whole lot else. Once there, the chairlift ride will cost Y110, the optional horse rental another Y20.

Several other scenic areas have recently opened up. A ski lift has been built at **Yúnshānpíng**, 36km from Lìjiāng. The lift costs Y42 return and takes you up to a plateau at 3300m, from where there are walking trails.

The scenic area of **Yak Meadow** (*Máoniúpíng*) is around 60km from Lìjiāng, where yet another cable car takes tourists up to the meadows at 3500m. Snowflake Lake (Xuěhuā Hǎi) is nearby and there are plenty of hiking opportunities all around. The cable car costs Y60 return and departs from just by the roadside. To get to either site take bus No 6 or any Dàjù- or Bǎoshān-bound bus.

There's a Y40 admission fee to the entire area north of Báishā including Yùlóng Xuěshān, Yúnshānpíng and Yak Meadow. If you enter the region from the north (Bǎoshān or Tiger Leaping Gorge) there's no ticket gate. You don't have to pay the fee if you are just travelling by public bus to Bǎoshān or Dàjù.

Shígǔ & the First Bend of the Yangzi River 石鼓、长江第一湾
Shígǔ & Chángjiāng Dìyīwān
The small town of Shígǔ sits on the first bend of China's greatest river. Shígǔ means 'Stone Drum', referring to the marble plaque shaped like a drum that commemorates a 16th-century Naxi victory over a Tibetan army. The other plaque on the river's edge commemorates the People's Army crossing here in 1936 in the Great March to the north. Kublai Khan is also said to have crossed the river here on inflated sheep skins.

Buses to Shígǔ (Y8, two hours) leave at 10am from Lìjiāng's main bus station. Alternatively, take a 7.30am departure to Wēixī or 8am to Jùdiàn. It's easily visited in a day trip, which is good as all lodgings in town are grotty.

Tiger Leaping Gorge 虎跳峡
Hǔtiào Xiá
After making its first turn at Shígǔ the mighty Yangzi River (at this point known as Jīnshā Jiāng) surges between Hābā Shān and Yùlóng Xuěshān, through one of the deepest gorges in the world. The entire gorge measures 16km, and it's a giddy 3900m from the waters to the snowcapped mountaintops. The best time to come is May and the start of June, when the hills are afire with plant and flower life.

This hike through the gorge has gone from obscure adventure to the can't-miss experience of northern Yúnnán, but you'll still probably only encounter several other travellers on the trail (unless it's peak season, in late summer). All up, plan on three to four days away from Lìjiāng doing the hike. You can do the walk in two days – one maniac walked it in a day – although some travellers, enchanted with Walnut Grove have lengthened the hike to over a week.

The first thing to do is to check with cafes in Lìjiāng for the latest gossip on the mini-trek, particularly the weather and its possibly lethal effects on the trail. Most cafes give away hand-drawn maps of the trek. They show paths, walking times and some places to stay but remember that they aren't to scale.

Transport is easier than it once was. Finishing in Qiáotóu allows for quicker transport back to Lìjiāng, but heading towards Dàjù gives you the option of continuing north to Báishuǐtái or combining a visit to the gorge with a trip to Bǎoshān. Most people take a Zhōngdiàn-bound bus early in the morning, hop off in Qiáotóu, and hike quickly to stay overnight in Walnut Grove.

Development is taking its toll on the gorge. After three years of Herculean blasting and building, a road now leads all the way through the gorge from Qiáotóu to Walnut Grove and a dirt track swings north to Báishuǐtái, joining the road to Zhōngdiàn. Tour buses shuttle up and down the gorge and kitschy stop-off points are being constructed. Buses currently only reach as far as the upper rapids, about halfway through the gorge, but you can expect the fuss to slowly head downstream. This currently isn't too much of an annoyance for trekkers as the high path climbs way above all the activity.

This does mean that you can still see the gorge (if you don't want to trek) by taking a bus to Qiáotóu and then catching one of the ubiquitous microbuses that shuttle people to the main viewpoint 10km away (Y10 per person one way). You could even take a taxi (Y50) the 23km from Qiáotóu to Walnut Grove.

A second road has been built part of the way through the southern side of the gorge, though it remains to be seen what kind of development will follow.

There is an admission fee to the gorge of Y30, which many people have avoided by walking through at 5am or waiting for the guy to go to sleep in front of the TV. There are check posts about 600m after you cross the bridge at Qiáotóu and at the eastern end of Walnut Grove.

Dangers & Annoyances The gorge trek is not to be taken lightly, particularly during the wet months of July and August – or any time it rains, really – when landslides and swollen waterfalls can block the paths. Half a dozen people – including a few foreign travellers – have died in the gorge. Most perished because they wandered off the trail, got lost and/or were unable to return to the trail, or fell. One hiker was buried while trying to scramble over a landslide. Two solo travellers have also reported being assaulted

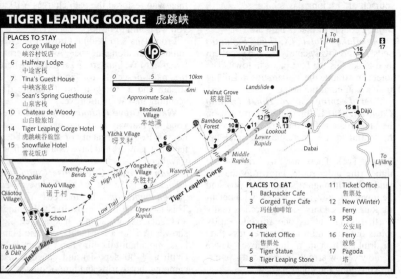

TIGER LEAPING GORGE 虎跳峡

PLACES TO STAY
2 Gorge Village Hotel
    峡谷村饭店
6 Halfway Lodge
    中途客栈
7 Tina's Guest House
    中峡客栈
9 Sean's Spring Guesthouse
    山泉客栈
10 Chateau de Woody
    山白脸客馆
14 Tiger Leaping Gorge Hotel
    虎跳峡谷旅馆
15 Snowflake Hotel
    雪花饭店

- - - Walking Trail

Landslide ●
Walnut Grove
核桃园
Bēndìwān Village
本地湾
Bamboo Forest
Yāchà Village
呀叉村
Lookout
Lower Rapids
Dabai
Middle Rapids
Yǒngshèng Village
永胜村
Waterfall
Twenty-Four Bends
High Trail
To Zhōngdiàn
Nuòyú Village
诺于村
Qiáotóu Village
Low Trail
School
Upper Rapids
Tiger Leaping Gorge
To Lìjiāng & Dàlǐ
Jīnshā Jiāng
To Hābā
To Dàjù
To Lìjiāng

PLACES TO EAT
1 Backpacker Cafe
3 Gorged Tiger Cafe
    玛佳咖啡馆

OTHER
4 Ticket Office
    售票处
5 Tiger Statue
8 Tiger Leaping Stone

11 Ticket Office
    售票处
12 New (Winter) Ferry
13 PSB
    公安局
16 Ferry
    渡船
17 Pagoda
    塔

0   5   10km
0   3   6mi
Approximate Scale

on the trail by locals, although this couldn't be officially confirmed.

On a less severe note, several travellers have reported becoming ill after eating in Qiáotóu or from drinking water along the trek. Speaking of water, one litre of water is *not* enough on this trek. (See also under Health in the Facts for the Visitor chapter.)

Places to Stay & Eat There are accommodation options at either end of the trek.

Qiáotóu Options here include:

Gorge Village Hotel Doubles per person Y20, doubles with bath Y100. An excellent option, this is the best choice if you have to stay overnight. The cheaper doubles come with electric blanket. There are hot showers and it has a decent restaurant.

Backpacker Cafe Across from the bridge in Qiáotóu this has long been the nerve-centre for trail information. It has an English menu, staff speak passable English and there's backpack storage.

Gorged Tiger Cafe This is a new, perhaps more reliable, place to get up-to-date information on the trail, run by the same folks who own Sean's Spring Guesthouse in Walnut Grove. The cafe is just over the bridge on the right-hand side as you walk towards the gorge from Qiáotóu. It's a good place to feed up before a trek or reward yourself after a long day's hike.

Dàjù A couple of places here are:

Snowflake Hotel (*Xuěhuā Fàndiàn*) Beds Y10. A lovely courtyard and excellent food make this the best place in town. The hotel can arrange the 7.30am bus to Lìjiāng to pick you up at the hotel.

Tiger Leaping Gorge Hotel (*Hǔtiào Xiágǔ Lǚguǎn*) If for some bizarre reason the Snowflake is full then try this place by the central square where the buses pick up.

Gorge Trek There are two trails – the higher (the older route, known as the 24-bend path, although it's more like 30), and the lower, the new road, replete with belching tour buses. Only the high trail is really worth hiking but as one traveller aptly points out, 'the high road leaves less time for drinking beer in Walnut Grove'. There are now yellow arrows – a godsend – pointing you along the upper path.

The following description starts at Qiáotóu. To get to the high road, after crossing through the gate, cross a small stream and go 150m. Take a left fork, go through the schoolyard's football pitch, and join the tractor road. Continue until the track ends and then follow the yellow arrows to the right. It's six hours to Běndìwān or a strenuous eight hours to Walnut Grove.

Halfway Lodge (*Zhōngtú Kèzhàn*) Beds Y10-15. In Běndìwān this is an excellent place. There are hot showers on request and some of the best food on the trek. A few years back the owner, a traditional medicine practitioner, was so regularly interrupted by exhausted, dehydrated travellers panicking in the dark outside his modest home that he just opened up a room. He and his ad hoc medicinal herb-and-plant tours proved so popular that he's now had to expand with additional rooms and showers/toilets.

Tina's Guest House (*Zhōngxiá Lǚdiàn*) Beds Y10. After 1½ hours from Běndìwān you descend to the road to this place – budget more time if you are ascending. Tina's is a friendly and convenient place to spend your first night from Dàjù. Many rooms have fine views. A good detour from here leads down 40 minutes to the middle rapids and Tiger Leaping Stone, where a tiger is once said to have leapt across the Yangzi, thus giving the gorge its name. The man who restored the path charges Y10 to take people down it (regardless of whether you want him to or not).

From Tina's to Walnut Grove it is a 40-minute walk along the road. A new alternative trail to Walnut Grove keeps high where the path descends to Tina's, crosses a stream and a 'bamboo forest' before descending into Walnut Grove.

Walnut Grove (*Hútáoyuán*) is a bit beyond the halfway mark and has two guest-houses. Both offer plenty of food and beer, have hot showers and have won praise from travellers.

Sean's Spring Guesthouse (*Shānquán Kèzhàn;* ☎ 0887-880 6300, e adventureti ger@hotmail.com) Dorm beds Y10-15. This is the spot for more lively evenings and socialising. Sean's has a free hot shower (Y5 for a hot bath!), electric blankets, mountain-bike hire for Y10 per hour (with a Y400 deposit) and can organise camping, horse trips and hire of horses.

Chateau de Woody *(Shānbáiliǎn Lǚguǎn)*
Dorm beds Y10-15. This is considered the
quiet alternative but a recent ugly concrete
annexe of cramped rooms has taken some of
the charm. Woody's also has a free hot
shower and Y5 hot bath.

Be aware that in peak times – particularly
late summer – up to 100 people per day can
make the trek, so bed space is short. Both
hotels are planning to expand, but be prepared to sleep in a back room somewhere.
Supplies of bottled water can be chancy;
it's probably best to bring your own.

The next day's walk is slightly shorter at
four to six hours. There are now two ferries
and so two route options to get to Dàjù.
After 45 minutes you'll see a red marker
leading down to the new (winter) ferry (xīn
dùkǒu); the descent includes one particularly hairy section over planks with a sheer
drop below. The ferry costs an extortive
Y10. From here it's a hard climb to the car
park where you should register with the
Lìjiāng PSB. The PSB officer offers a car
to take you into Dàjù for Y10, which
avoids the fairly dull 1½-hour's walk to
Dàjù along the road.

The second, lesser-used option continues
along the road from Walnut Grove until it
reaches the permanent ferry crossing (Y10).
From here paths lead to Dàjù.

If you're doing the walk the other way
round and heading for Qiáotóu, walk north
through Dàjù, aiming for the white pagoda
at the foot of the mountains.

Tiger Leaping Gorge to Báishuǐtái An

adventurous add-on to the gorge trek is to
continue north all the way to Hābā village
and the limestone terraces of Báishuǐtái,
making it a four-day trek from Qiáotóu.
From here you can travel on to Zhōngdiàn.
From Walnut Grove to Hābā, via Jiāngbiān,
it is seven to eight hours. From here to the
Yi village of Sānbà is about the same, following trails. You could just follow the
road and hitch with the occasional truck or
tracker but this way is longer and less
scenic. Some hardy mountain bikers have
followed the trail but this is really only fun
from north to south, elevations being what
they are. The best way would be to hire a
guide in Walnut Grove for Y50 to Y100 per
day, depending on the number of people.
For Y100 to Y120 per day you should be

able to get a horse and guide. Eventually
buses will make the trip but that is still
some time off.

In Hābā most people stay at the ***Haba
Snow Mountain Inn*** *(Hābā Xuěshān
Kèzhàn; beds Y10)* which has toilets and
showers. In Sānbà the ***Shānzhuāng
Lǚguǎn*** is probably the most popular.
From Sānbà there is an 8am bus to
Zhōngdiàn (five hours), or you could get
off at the turn-off to Emerald Pagoda Lake
(Bìtǎ Haǐ) and hike there.

If you plan to try the route alone assume
you'll need all provisions and equipment
for all extremes of weather. Ask for local
advice before setting out.

Getting There & Away From Lìjiāng to
Qiáotóu, buses run to Zhōngdiàn every hour
or so from 7.30am to 3pm from the main
bus station and pass through Qiáotóu (Y13).

From Lìjiāng to Dàjù (Y23.5, four to five
hours) buses leave from Gǔlùwān Bīnguǎn at
7.30am, 9am and 1pm. The drivers can sometimes be persuaded to carry on to the new
ferry crossing for an extra Y5 per person.

Returning to Lìjiāng from Qiáotóu, buses
start running through from Zhōngdiàn between 8am and 9am. The last one rolls
through around 7pm, though 5pm is safer.
It'll cost you between Y10 and Y15. You can
also catch a bus north-west to Zhōngdiàn
until about 5pm.

Returning to Lìjiāng from Dàjù several
buses leave daily at 7.30am. Sometimes
there are buses at 1.30pm and even rarer
buses at 3pm.

Eventually the new highway through the
gorge will link Qiáotóu, Walnut Grove and
the settlement across the river from Dàjù
and then bend north to connect Báishuǐtái,
allowing travellers to get to Zhōngdiàn
from here.

Lúgū Hú 泸沽湖

This remote lake overlaps the Yúnnán-
Sìchuān border and is a centre for several Tibetan, Yi and Mosu (a Naxi subgroup)
villages. The Mosu still practise matriarchy,
and many of the Naxi customs lost in Lìjiāng
are still in evidence here. The lake is fairly
high at 2685m and is usually snowbound
over the winter months. The best times to
visit are April to May, and September to October, when the weather is dry and mild.

There is now a spurious 'entry' fee of Y30 to the lake (on paper a nature reserve) which is collected from tourists at a roadside check post.

Things to See You can visit several islands on the lake via large dugout canoes, which the Mosu call 'pig troughs' (*zhūcáo*). The canoes, which are rowed by Mosu who also serve as guides, generally take you out to **Lǐwùbǐ Dǎo**, the lake's largest island. From here you can practically wade across to a spit of land in Sìchuān. Out to the island and back is around Y15 per person, Y30 if you want to be rowed around the island as well. The canoes can hold around seven people, but the price should be the same regardless of how many of you there are. At these prices you should stretch it into a whole day of picnicking. Canoes leave from near the Mósuōyuàn hotel and a beach area to the south of the hotel strip.

In the outskirts of nearby Yǒngníng is **Zhāměi Sì** (*admission Y1*), a Tibetan monastery with at least 20 lamas in residence. There is also a concrete **hot spring** (*wēnquán*) nearby, about 10km north of town. A private bus costs Y15 a head for the half-hour ride. A bus passes through Luòshuǐ to Yǒngníng for Y5; you could opt to walk the 20km or so through pleasant scenery.

Places to Stay & Eat Buses from Nínglàng drop passengers in Luòshuǐ, where you can stay in Mosu homes for around Y15 per bed. Most of the homes are equipped to take guests, so you won't be short of options. There are no showers. Food is cooked up for you by the Mosu: little fish, potatoes and barbecued hard-boiled eggs are the order of the day. Average prices are Y5 to Y10, depending on how well you want to eat.

Ahkejia Beds Y15. Formerly known as Móānyuán, this is a good place and far away from the clutter.

Mósuōyuán Beds Y20-30. Of the village's guesthouses, this seems to be the centre of action. Occasional Mosu song-and-dance performances are held here.

Husi Teahouse Beds Y15-20. This is a backpacker restaurant and guesthouse owned by immigrants from Chóngqìng. There's little Mosu character here but the rooms are glass-fronted and so offer good views of the lake.

Many travellers are put off by the crowds and crass disregard of minority culture. You could stay with a family on **Lǐgēn Dǎo** on the opposite side of the lake. To get here, don't stop in Luòshuǐ, but continue toward Yǒngníng, 18km north. Ask the driver to let you off where the road branches; from here it's 2km, though it's tough to find at night. A taxi is really expensive.

There are also several guesthouses in Yǒngníng. These make good bases from which to hike out to the nearby hot spring. Beds average around Y20.

Nínglàng, the changeover point between Lìjiāng and Lúgū Hú, also has several hotels:

Kèyùn Zhāodàisuǒ (Bus Station Guesthouse) Triples/doubles per person Y15/20. If you have to stay overnight in Nínglàng, this is probably the most convenient place.

Jiāměi Bīnguǎn Singles/doubles/triples Y30/40/50, doubles with bath Y60. About 100m on your right, as you exit the bus station, this place has better rooms than the Kèyùn Zhāodàisuǒ.

Lúgū Hú Dàjiǔdiàn (☎ 552 2862) Doubles with shared bath Y30-60, with private bath Y160. Diagonally opposite Jiāměi Bīnguǎn and down a small lane, this is the top hotel in town. Rooms with private bath are discounted to Y100.

Getting There & Away From Lìjiāng it's a six-hour bus trip to Nínglàng through some fine scenery. Luxury buses leave Lìjiāng's main bus station at 7.50am and 9am and the fare of Y54 includes the two-hour minibus ride from Nínglàng on to Lúgū Hú. Other buses to Nínglàng depart from Lìjiāng's main bus station and express bus station until 11am and cost Y37.

Leaving Luóshuǐ, buses leave from the courtyard of Mósuō Fàndiàn. An 8am minibus to Nínglàng meets the express bus to Lìjiāng (Y57). There is also a 7.30am departure to Jīnjiāng (Y68).

To get to Yǒngníng (three hours) you'll need to wait at the main road for the bus that passes through from Nínglàng.

Some travellers have tried crossing over to Lúgū Zhèn (also known as Zuǒsuǒ), on the Sìchuān side, from where there is bus transport to Xīchāng on the Kūnmíng-Chéngdū line. But be warned: it's a remote route with no accommodation. You'll need to bring a tent, a warm sleeping bag and all provisions.

One Canadian traveller we met had a frightening experience with locals while hiking this route and headed back to Yǒngníng (though another had a challenging but rewarding experience). Most travellers head back to Lìjiāng the same way they came.

ZHŌNGDIÀN 中甸
☎ 0887

Zhōngdiàn, 198km north-west of Lìjiāng, marks the start of the Tibetan world. At 3200m, this boom town is a principally Tibetan town, known as Gyeltang or Gyalthang in Tibetan. A boom in Shangrila-driven tourism has fuelled the construction of a bland Han Chinese town but there is still an interesting old town. The main reason to come here is to visit the monastery and to get a taste of Tibet if you can't make it to the real thing.

Zhōngdiàn is also the last stop in Yúnnán for more hardy travellers looking at a rough five- or six-day journey to Chéngdū via the Tibetan townships and rugged terrain of western Sìchuān.

In mid-June Zhōngdiàn plays host to a horse-racing festival that sees several days of dancing, singing, eating and, of course, horse-racing. Another new festival – usually in September – features minority artists of south-western China. Accommodation can be a bit tight around these times, so you may want to arrive a day or two early in order to secure a room.

Information
The Bank of China on Changzheng Lu can change money but can't give cash advances from credit cards.

Internet access is available at the China Telecom office on Changzheng Lu for Y8

per hour. The office is open 8.30am to 9pm daily. Internet access is also available at the Tibet Cafe (Y12) and at the restaurant of the Tibet Hotel (Y10).

ZHŌNGDIÀN 中甸

ZHŌNGDIÀN

PLACES TO STAY & EAT
6 Tibetan Art Cafe & Coffee Shop
  金丝咖啡室
10 Díqìng Bīnguǎn
  迪庆宾馆
12 Tibet Cafe
13 Tibet Hotel
  永生旅馆
14 Tiānchéng Zàngshì Jiǔdiàn
  天成藏式酒店

OTHER
1 North Bus Station
  汽车站
2 Market
  市场
3 Bank of China
  中国银行
4 Post Office
  邮电局
5 Market
  市场
7 Central Bus Station
  汽车总站

8 Market
  市场
9 Telephone Office
  中国电信
11 Yunnan Airlines; CAAC
  云南航空公司; 中国民航
15 Scripture Chamber
  中甸古城藏经堂
16 CITS
  中国国际旅行社

CITS (☎ 822 2238) is in the old town and offers pricey trips to remote local sights and overland tours to Tibet.

Dangers & Annoyances Be careful in Zhōngdiàn's bus stations, particularly on the early morning Lìjiāng buses; there's been a spell of push-and-slash bandit bands.

Things to See
About an hour's walk north of town is the **Ganden Sumtseling Gompa** *(Sōngzànlín Sì; admission Y10)*, a 300-year-old Tibetan monastery complex with around 600 monks. The monastery is the most important in south-west China and it is definitely worth the trip to Zhōngdiàn. Bus No 3 runs here from anywhere along Changzheng Lu (Y1).

Much closer to the centre of things, overlooking the old town district, is another monastery with exceedingly friendly monks.

Close to the Tibet Hotel is the **Scripture Chamber** *(Gǔchéng Cángjīngtáng; admission Y5)*, formerly a memorial hall to the Red Army's Long March, and **Guīshān Gōngyuán** *(admission Y3)*, which has a temple at the top with commanding views of the area.

Places to Stay & Eat
Tibet Hotel *(Yǒngshēng Fàndiàn;* ☎ 822 3263, fax 822 3863, Tuanjie Lu) Dorm beds Y20-25, doubles with/without bath Y220/60, with bath low-season Y150. This clean and friendly spot has remained backpacker-friendly and is probably the best budget place in town. All beds come with electric blankets, which is a godsend in winter. Hot showers are available from 8pm to midnight and the shared bathrooms are clean. The hotel also has nice sitting areas and a good restaurant that serves Western and Chinese food, which is a fine place to swap travellers tales. It includes Internet access, money exchange, a pricey laundry service and an impressively ornate Tibetan-style lobby. Bike rental is relatively steep at Y3 per hour. The hotel can be hard to find if you arrive at night so it's worth forking out Y5 on a taxi from the central bus station.

Tiānchéng Zàngshì Jiǔdiàn Triples per person Y30, doubles Y80/160 low season/other times. This is another clean and comfortable place, though the lack of shared showers is a distinct disadvantage.

Díqìng Bīnguǎn *(☎ 822 7599, 11 Changzheng Lu)* Dorm beds Y20, doubles Y150/280 low season/other times. Approximately opposite the bus station and set back a bit, this place looks pretty opulent for offering dorm rooms. Don't get excited, as the rooms are in a dilapidated wing out the back. Lots of more expensive hotels can be found on this road.

Gyalthang Dzong Hotel *(☎ 822 3646, 822 7583,* ⓔ *gylhotel@chengdunet.com)* Doubles Y300. This US joint-venture hotel, built in a Tibetan style, is the best mid-range choice. This hotel is in the outskirts of town, and it runs the region's most professional ecotourism and trekking packages. From November to March rooms are discounted by 50%.

Tibet Cafe *(☎/fax 823 0282, Changzheng Lu)*. Dishes from Y7. Run by the owners of the Dongba House in Lìjiāng, this is aimed squarely at foreigners. There's decent Western and Chinese food and this is a good place to pick up information on local sights.

Tibetan Art Cafe and Coffee Shop *(Jiantang Donglu)* If you fancy a break, try a cup of locally grown Golden Ring Tea *(Jīnsī Xiāngchá)* or yak butter tea at this cafe. The cafe offers courses in Tibetan and is a good place to meet local English speakers. The cafe was planning to add Tibetan food like *thugpa* (noodles) to its sparse menu.

The town's main *markets* are generally worth a visit, especially the one in the northern part of town, which is a good place to get a snack lunch.

Getting There & Away
Air Yunnan Airlines has flights from Zhōngdiàn to Kūnmíng every Tuesday, Thursday, Saturday and Sunday for Y560. China Southwest Airlines recently introduced a weekly Chéngdū-Zhōngdiàn flight, as well as a weekly flight from Chéngdū to Zhōngdiàn via Kūnmíng, and then on to Lhasa in Tibet.

The CAAC office is open 8.30am to noon and 2pm to 5.30pm daily. The airport is 5km from town and a taxi will cost from Y15 to Y20. Zhōngdiàn airport is sometimes referred to as Shangri-la, Díqìng or Deqen – there is currently no airport at Déqīn.

Bus Buses to Lìjiāng (Y29, five hours) depart hourly between 7am and 4pm. Buses pass through Qiáotóu (Y15.5), at the south-western end of the Tiger Leaping Gorge trek.

Sleeper buses back to Kūnmíng (Y141) and Xiàguān (Y57) leave all day and there are also daytime buses for the latter, including a 9am express coach (Y99).

Buses to Déqīn (Y33, seven hours) depart at 7am, 8am and 9am and take in some stunning scenery on a clear day, stopping for lunch in Bēnzìlán.

The long-awaited destination from Zhōngdiàn is Tibet and, who knows, by the time you have this book in your hands the miraculous may have occurred and this route may be open – don't count on it, though. For more information see under Other Routes in the Getting There & Away section of the Tibet chapter.

The route that is now once again legal is the arduous bus-hopping trek to Chéngdū, in Sìchuān. If you're up for this you're looking at a minimum of five to six days' travel at some very high altitudes – you'll need warm clothes. The first stage of the trip is Zhōngdiàn to Xiāngchéng in Sìchuān, a journey of around 12 hours. Buses run only occasionally, maybe every three or four days (Y50 to Y65); travellers on a tight timeframe have had to hire a jeep for this leg. If that's too expensive, one option would be to take the 8am bus north to Dōngwàng, get off where it turns off the main road and hitch from here. From Xiāngchéng, your next destination is Lǐtáng (Y70, 10 hours), though if roads are bad you may be forced to stay overnight in Dàochéng. From Lǐtáng it's 12 hours to Kāngdìng and another 12 hours on to Chéngdū. For more details on these towns see the Western Sìchuān & the Road to Tibet section in the Sìchuān chapter.

Note that roads out of Zhōngdiàn can be temporarily blocked by snow at any time from November to March. If you are travelling at this time bring lots of warm clothes and a flexible itinerary.

AROUND ZHŌNGDIÀN

Some 7km north-west of Zhōngdiàn you'll find the seasonal **Nàpà Lake** *(Nàpà Hǎi)* (part of a nature reserve) surrounded by a large grass meadow. Between September and March budding ornithologists will love the myriad rare species, including the black-necked crane.

Approximately 10km south-east of Zhōngdiàn is the **Tiānshēng Bridge** *(Tiānshēng Qiáo),* a natural limestone formation, and farther south-east, a subterranean **hot spring** *(admission Y5).* If you can arrange transport, en route is **Dàbǎo Sì** *(Great Treasure Temple),* one of the earliest Buddhist temples in Yúnnán.

Emerald Pagoda Lake 碧塔海
Bìtǎ Hǎi
Some 25km east of Zhōngdiàn, the bus to Sānbà (for more details see the following Báishuǐtái section) can drop you along the highway for Emerald Pagoda Lake *(admission Y30),* which is 8km down a trail (ponies are available for hire). You can stay here in basic cabins for Y15 to Y30. Lots of hiking options on foot or ponies can be arranged at the lake. There is a second, southern entrance, from where it is 2km to the lake. It's possible to rent boats between the two ends of the lake.

Leaving Emerald Pagoda Lake you can wait (sometimes forever) for a bus; or hike to one of the entrances or main road and wait for taxis dropping off tourists – these guys need fares back to Zhōngdiàn so bargain hard.

Báishuǐtái 白水台
Báishuǐtái is a limestone deposit plateau 108km south-east of Zhōngdiàn with some breathtaking scenery and Tibetan villages en route. The terraces *(admission Y30)* are resplendent in sunlight, but can be tough to access if rainfall has made trails slippery. There are normally horses for hire.

A couple of *guesthouses* at the nearby towns of Báidì and Sānbà have rooms with beds from Y10 to Y15.

At the time of writing there was a bus to Sānbà (Y20, five hours) leaving Zhōngdiàn daily in summer around 8am. Don't count on this always departing, however. The starting price to charter a microbus from Zhōngdiàn to Báishuǐtái via Emerald Pagoda Lake is Y400 to Y500.

One option is to trek or hitch all the way from Báishuǐtái to Tiger Leaping Gorge. See the Tiger Leaping Gorge section for information.

Bēnzìlán 奔子栏

This laid-back Tibetan village makes an excellent base to explore the wonderful **Dhondrupling Gompa** *(Dōngzhúlín Sì),* 22km heading north-westerly along the main road.

Bēnzìlán has plenty of restaurants and small hotels. All offer decent beds for Y20.

Duōwén Lǚguǎn Beds Y10-20. Perhaps the best choice, around the bend in the northern end of town, is this Tibetan-style place, which has a prayer wheel by the entrance and pleasant rooms.

To get to Bēnzìlán take any bus between Zhōngdiàn and Déqīn; buses pass through town between 11am and noon.

DÉQĪN 德钦
☎ 0887

Some 168km north-west of Zhōngdiàn is the last outpost of Yúnnán before Tibet – Déqīn town and county (part of Díqìng Tibetan Autonomous Prefecture). The county has an average elevation of 3550m and is 80% Tibetan, though a dozen other minorities are found here, including one of the few settlements of non-Hui Muslims in China. For borderholics, east is Sìchuān, west is Tibet, and Myanmar lies south-west. Chinese authorities have christened Déqīn 'Shangri-la' and claim James Hilton's classic *Lost Horizon* used the area for inspiration; they've decided to pump millions of yuán into tourism in coming years.

Getting here is possible on a bus but you're crossing some serious ranges along this route and at any time from mid-October to late spring heavy snows can close the road. Tibet beckons to be sure, but the road is currently closed to foreigners.

Places to Stay & Eat
Deqin Tibet Hotel (*Déxīn Lóu*) Dorm beds Y25, doubles with shared bath per person Y40. This is the best place in town, 200m south of the bus station. Bathroom facilities are barely adequate but there is a hot shower (ask the owner to turn on the electric water heater). There's a nice communal sitting area and an excellent map of the region on the wall. The owners can help arrange transport, such as to Fēilái Sì (Y40 return).

Taizi Mount Hotel (*Tàizifēng Dàjiǔdiàn*) Doubles with shared/private bath Y260/328. This deserted three-star monster is at the southern end of the town.

Around the bus station there are a couple of places serving *shuǐjiǎo* (boiled dumplings) and *bāozi* (steamed savoury buns).

Líshí Fàndiàn About 100m uphill from the Deqin Tibet Hotel, on your left, his doesn't look like much but serves consistently good food.

Shuǐyuán Cāntīng (*Tax Office Restaurant*) This restaurant has decent food and an outside eating area; look for the colourful canopy and pool table.

Getting There & Away
Buses depart for Zhōngdiàn at 7.20am, 8am and 8.40am (Y33, seven hours). There is also a 3pm departure to Bēnzìlán (Y19).

AROUND DÉQĪN
Approximately 10km south-west of Déqīn is small but interesting Tibetan **Fēilaí Sì**.

A farther 800m along the main road brings you to a row of **chörtens** (stupas) and, weather permitting, breathtaking views of Méilǐ Xuěshān range, including 6740m Kawa Karpo (also known as Méilǐ Xuěshān or Tàizi Shān). The more beautiful peak to the south is 6054m-high Miacimu (Shénnǚ in Chinese). Locals come here to burn juniper incense. To get here from Déqīn, get out on the road and flag anything down that moves.

Míngyǒng Glacier
Míngyǒng Bīngchuān

Tumbling off the side of Kawa Karpo Peak is the 12km-long Míngyǒng Glacier *(admission Y60).* For millennia the mountain and glacier has been a pilgrimage site.

Trails to the glacier lead up from Míngyǒng's central square marked by a new chörten. After 45 minutes a path splits off down to the scruffy toe of the glacier. Continuing on, after another 45 minutes you get to Tibetan **Tàizi Miào,** where there is a **guesthouse** *(doubles Y50-60 per person).* A farther 30 minutes along the trail is **Liánhuā Miào** *(Lotus Temple),* which offers fantastic views of the glacier framed by prayer flags and chörtens. Horses can be hired (Y60) up to the glacier.

Places to Stay Beds in all guesthouses are around Y20 and toilet facilities are basic. Electricity is iffy so bring a torch or some candles.

Up some steps from Míngyǒng's main square, where the bus drops you off, is *Míngyǒng Shānzhuāng*, a government-run place with decent dorm rooms.

Heading back along the road towards Déqīn, other choices include the friendly, family run *Nuòbù Sāngmù Kèzhàn* and, a few minutes farther, *Biānmǎdìngzhǔ Kèzhàn*, set in a lovely hamlet.

Getting There & Away From Déqīn, minibuses to Míngyǒng leave from the bridge near the market at the top end of town at 4pm (Y13, two hours) and return to Déqīn the next day at 8am. The road descends into the dramatic Mekong River gorge.

Xīshuāngbǎnnà Region 西双版纳

The region of Xīshuāngbǎnnà (usually called Bǎnnà) is in the deep south of Yúnnán, next to the Myanmar and Lao borders. The name is a Chinese approximation of the original Thai name, Sip Sawng Panna (12 Rice-Growing Districts). The place has a laid-back South-East Asian feel and it's easy to watch the weeks slip by as you make your way around small villages, tropical forests and the occasional stupa.

In recent years Xīshuāngbǎnnà has become China's own mini-Thailand, and tourists have been heading down in droves for the sunshine, Dai minority dancing, water-splashing festivals (held daily nowadays), as well as the ubiquitous tour-group lures, such as the Forest of One Tree (Dúshù Chénglín), the King of Tea Trees and other trees with names suggesting something less prosaic than a mere tree. But it's easy to get away from the crowds and explore the surrounding countryside and villages.

Xīshuāngbǎnnà Dai Autonomous Prefecture, as it is known officially, is subdivided into the three counties of Jǐnghóng, Měnghǎi and Měnglà.

The region has wet and dry seasons. The wet season is between June and August, when it rains ferociously almost every day. From September to February there is less rainfall, but thick fog descends during the late evening and doesn't lift until 10am or

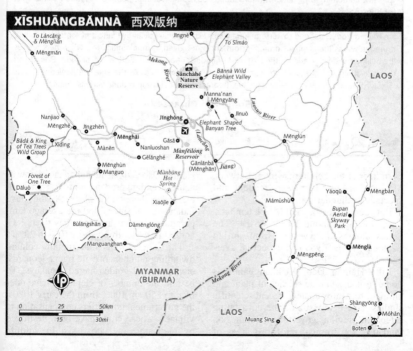

XĪSHUĀNGBǍNNÀ 西双版纳

To Láncāng & Měnglián

Měngmǎn

Jǐngnè

To Sīmáo

Mekong River

Sānchàhé Nature Reserve

Bǎnnà Wild Elephant Valley

LAOS

Manna'nan Měngyǎng

Jinuò

Luosuo River

Nanjiao

Měngzhè

Jǐngzhēn

Jǐnghóng

Elephant Shaped Banyan Tree

Měnghǎi

Gāsǎ

Lánjiāng

Měnglún

Bādá & King of Tea Trees Wild Group

Xiding

Mǎnēn

Nanluoshan

Gělǎnghé

Mànfēilóng Reservoir

Měngbǎn

Měnghǔn

Manguo

Mànbǎng Hot Spring

Gǎnlǎnbà (Měnghǎn)

Jiāng

Yáoqū

Forest of One Tree

Dàluò

Mámǔshù

Bupan Aerial Skyway Park

Xiǎojiē

Bùlǎngshān

Dàměnglóng

Měnglà

Manguanghan

Měngpēng

MYANMAR (BURMA)

Mekong River

Shàngyǒng

LAOS

Muang Sing

Móhān

Boten

0   25   50km
0   15   30mi

LP

The Dai

The Dai are Hinayana Buddhists (as opposed to China's majority Mahayana Buddhists) who first appeared 2000 years ago in the Yangzi Valley and who were subsequently driven southwards by the Mongol invasion of the 13th century. The Dai state of Xīshuāngbǎnnà was annexed by the Mongols and then by the Chinese, and a Chinese governor was installed in the regional capital of Jinglan (present-day Jǐnghóng). Countless Buddhist temples were built in the early days of the Dai state and now lie in the jungles in ruins. During the Cultural Revolution, Xīshuāngbǎnnà's temples were desecrated and destroyed. Some were saved by serving as granaries, but many are now being rebuilt from scratch. Temples are also recovering their role as village schools where young children are accepted for religious training as monks.

The Dai live in spacious wooden houses raised on stilts, to keep themselves off the damp earth, with the pigs and chickens below. The most common Dai foods are sticky rice (khao nio in Dai) and fish. The common dress for Dai women is a straw hat or towel-wrap headdress; a tight, short blouse in a bright colour; and a printed sarong with a belt of silver links. Some Dai men tattoo their bodies with animal designs, and betel-nut chewing is popular. Many Dai youngsters get their teeth capped with gold; otherwise they are considered ugly.

Linguistically, the Dai are part of the very large Thai family that includes the Siamese, Lao, Shan, Thai Dam and Ahom peoples found scattered throughout the river valleys of Thailand, Myanmar, Laos, northern Vietnam and Assam. The Xīshuāngbǎnnà Dai are broken into four subgroups, the Shui (Water) Dai, Han (Land) Dai, Huayao (Floral Belt) Dai and Kemu Dai, each distinguished by variations in costume, lifestyle and location. All speak the Dai language, which is quite similar to Lao and northern Thai dialects. In fact, Thai is often as useful as Chinese once you get off the beaten track, and those with a firm linguistic background might have fun with a Thai phrasebook. The written language of the Dai employs a script that looks like a cross between Lao and Burmese.

In temple courtyards, look for a cement structure looking like a letterbox; this is an altar to local spirits, a combination of Buddhism and indigenous spirit worship. Some 32 separate spirits exist for humans.

Zhang khap is the name of solo narrative opera, for which the Dai have a long tradition. Singers are trained from childhood to perform long songs accompanied by native flute and sometimes a long drum known as the elephant drum. Performances are given at monk initiations, when new houses are built, at weddings, and on the birthdays of important people and often last all night. Even if you do understand Dai, the lyrics are complex if not fully improvised. At the end, the audience shouts 'Shuay! Shuay!' which is close to 'Hip, hip, hooray!' Even courtship is done via this singing.

Some Dai Phrases

Hello	doūzaǒ lǐ
Thank you	yíndií
Goodbye	goīhán

even later at the height of winter. Between May and August there are frequent and spectacular thunderstorms.

Between November and March temperatures average about 19°C (66°F). The hottest months of the year are from April to September, when you can expect an average of 25°C (77°F).

Like Hǎinán Dǎo, Xīshuāngbǎnnà is home to many unique species of plant and animal life. Unfortunately, recent scientific studies have demonstrated the devastating effects of previous government policies on land use; the tropical rainforest areas of

Hǎinán Dǎo and Xīshuāngbǎnnà are now as acutely endangered as similar rainforest areas elsewhere on the planet. Studies have indicated that since 1960 the average temperature of Xīshuāngbǎnnà has risen 1°C, and rainfall has dropped off 10% to 20%.

The jungle areas that remain contain dwindling numbers of wild tigers, leopards, elephants and golden-haired monkeys. To be fair, the number of elephants have doubled to 250, up 100% from the early 1980s; the government now offers compensation to villagers whose crops have been destroyed by elephants, or who assist in wildlife conservation. In 1998 the government - banned hunting or processing of animals, but poaching is notoriously hard to control.

About one-third of the 800,000-strong population of this region are Dai; another third or so are Han Chinese and the rest is made up of minorities that include the Hani, Lisu, Yao and lesser-known hill tribes such as the Aini (a subgroup of the Hani), Jinuo, Bulang, Lahu and Wa.

SPECIAL EVENTS

The **Water-Splashing Festival**, held around mid-April (usually from the 13th to the 15th), washes away the dirt, sorrow and demons of the old year and brings in the happiness of the new. The first day of the festival is devoted to a giant market. The second day features dragon-boat racing, swimming races and rocket launching. The third day features the water-splashing freak-out – be prepared to get drenched all day, and remember, the wetter you get, the more luck you'll receive. In the evenings there's dancing, launching of hot-air paper balloons and game playing.

During the **Tanpa Festival** in February, young boys are sent to the local temple for initiation as novice monks. At approximately the same time (between February and March), **Tan Jing Festival** participants honour Buddhist texts housed in local temples.

The **Tan Ta Festival** is held during the last 10-day period of October or November, with temple ceremonies, rocket launches from special towers and hot-air balloons. The rockets, which often contain lucky amulets, blast off with a curious droning sound, like mini-space shuttles, before exploding high above; those who find the amulets are assured of good luck.

The farming season (from July to October) is the time for the **Closed-Door Festival**, when marriages or festivals are banned. Traditionally this is also the time of year that men aged 20 or older ordain as monks for a period of time. The season ends with the **Open-Door Festival**, when everyone lets their hair down again to celebrate the harvest.

During festivals, booking same-day airline tickets to Jǐnghóng can be extremely difficult – even with 17 flights per day! You can try getting a flight into Sīmáo, 162km to the north, or take the bus. Hotels in Jǐnghóng town are booked solid, but you could stay in a nearby Dai village and commute. Festivities take place all over Xīshuāngbǎnnà, so you might be lucky farther away from Jǐnghóng.

JǏNGHÓNG 景洪
☎ 0691

Jǐnghóng, the capital of Xīshuāngbǎnnà prefecture, lies beside the Mekong River. It's a sleepy but rapidly growing town with streets lined with palms, which help mask the Chinese-built concrete boxes until they merge with the stilt-houses in the surrounding villages. It's more a base for operations than a place to hang out, although it's not without a certain laid-back charm. The town's name means 'City of Dawn' in Dai.

Information
Check out the travellers books at the Mei Mei, Forest and Mekong cafes for the most recent travel tips and for some very detailed trek notes.

Money The Bank of China is on Jinghong Nanlu, next door to the Banna Mansion Hotel. It's open 8am to 11.30am and 3pm to 6pm Monday to Friday. The China Agricultural Bank is east of the PSB and also takes care of travellers cheques and credit-card advances during similar working hours.

Post & Communications The post and telephone office is in the centre of town at the intersection of Jinghong Xilu and Jinghong Nanlu. Postal services are available 8am to 8.30pm, with telecommunication services slightly longer.

Internet access is available at the Mekong Cafe for Y5 per hour, though there's only one computer. The King New Network computer shop next to the Mei Mei Cafe has computers upstairs with Internet access for Y5 per hour.

The telephone office has slow Internet access but it's cheap at Y3 per hour, with a Y50 refundable deposit. It's open 8am to 11pm.

Travel Agencies CITS (☎ 212 4479, 213 0460) has an office across from the entrance to Xīshuāngbǎnnà Bīnguǎn. The staff are friendly, and can provide information on several one-day tours from Y50 to Y100 per person that generally take in one to two towns and sights en route.

JǏNGHÓNG 景洪

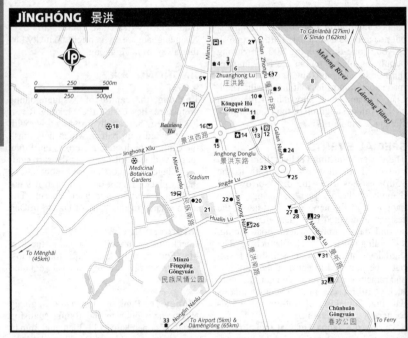

The Mengyuan Travel Agency (☎ 212 5214) at 3 Jinghong Nanlu, next to the Bank of China, can arrange treks. The Forest Cafe and Mekong Cafe can help with trekking information and can put you in touch with English-speaking guides.

PSB The PSB is opposite Kǒngquè Hú Gōngyuán in the centre of town. Staff there are polite enough and visa extensions are fairly straightforward. The office is open 8am to 11.30am and 2pm to 5.30pm.

Dangers & Annoyances There have been two reports (unconfirmed) from travellers regarding drug-and-rob incidents (one successful, one not) on the Kūnmíng-Jǐnghóng bus trip. If true, it marks the first time it's appeared in Yúnnán. Like other countries in South-East Asia, be careful who your friends are on buses, accept nothing, and leave nothing unattended when you hop off on breaks.

Tropical Flower & Plants Garden
Rèdài Huāhuìyuán 热带花卉园
This botanical garden (☎ 212 0493, 28 Jinghong Xilu; admission Y10; open 10am-6pm daily), west of the town centre, is one of Jǐnghóng's better attractions. Admission gets you into a series of gardens, many of them still under construction, where you can view over 1000 different types of plant life. Unless you're a botanist, telling them all apart could be tricky – the only English translations are scientific. Still, it's easy to get a feel for the impressive variety of plants that make up Yúnnán's tropical forests, and the grounds make for a pleasant stroll. Admission also gets you into the **Zhou Enlai Memorial** (Zhōu Ēnlái Zǒnglǐ Jìniànbēi), a contemporary sculpture commemorating a 1961 visit by China's best-loved premier.

Kǒngquè Hú Gōngyuán
Peacock Lake Park 孔雀湖公园
This artificial lake in the centre of town isn't much, but the small park next to it is pleasant. There's also a zoo, but it's not for the squeamish. The English Language Corner takes place here every Sunday evening, so this is your chance to exchange views or to engage with the locals practising their English.

JĪNGHÓNG

PLACES TO STAY
4　Ruìfēng Bīnguǎn
　　瑞丰宾馆
9　Xīshuāngbǎnnà Bīnguǎn
　　版纳宾馆
11　Jǐngyǒng Fàndiàn
　　景咏饭店
15　Banna Mansion Hotel;
　　Bank of China;
　　Mengyuan Travel
　　Agency
　　版纳大厦;
　　中国银行
24　Bǎnnà Jiǔdiàn
　　版纳酒店
28　Dai Building Hotel
　　傣家花苑小楼
30　Dǎijiā Zhāodàisuǒ
　　傣家招待所
33　Tai Garden
　　Hotel
　　傣园酒店

PLACES TO EAT
2　Xīngguāng Jiǔjiā
　　星光酒家
3　Myanmar
　　Mandalay Cafe
　　缅甸瓦城风
　　味冷饮店

5　Burmese Teahouse
　　缅甸茶馆
8　Night Market
　　夜市场
23　Mei Mei Cafe;
　　King New Network
　　(Internet)
　　美美咖啡厅;
　　劲牛网路
25　Forest Cafe
　　森林咖啡厅
27　Mekong Cafe
　　湄公餐馆
31　Barbeque
　　Restaurants
　　干锅餐厅

OTHER
1　Long-Distance
　　Bus Station
　　长途汽车站
6　Jade Market
　　玉市场
7　Bank of China
　　中国银行
10　CITS
　　中国国际旅行社
12　Nationality Song &
　　Dance Theatre
　　歌舞剧院

13　China Agricultural
　　Bank
　　中国业银行
14　PSB
　　公安局
16　Post &
　　Telephone Office
　　邮电大楼
17　No 2 Bus Station
　　第二客运站
18　Tropical Flower & Plants
　　Garden
　　热带花卉园
19　Minibuses to Airport
　　到机场的中巴车
20　Yunnan Airlines;
　　CAAC
　　云南航空公司;
　　中国民航
21　Market
　　市场
22　Blind Massage School
　　盲人按摩
26　Crown Hotel
　　Swimming Pool
　　皇冠大酒店
29　Temple
　　曼景兰金狮佛寺
32　Màntīng Fósì
　　曼听佛寺

Mínzú Fēngqíng Gōngyuán
National Minorities Park 民族风情公园

This park *(admission Y20; open 9am-6.30pm daily)* includes displays on minority customs and houses, a poor zoo and displays (10am and 4pm) of elephant dancing and other things best avoided.

Activities

Jīnghóng's oft-recommended **Blind Massage School** *(Mángrén Ànmó; ☎ 212 5834, Jinghong Nanlu; open 9am-1am daily)* offers massages for Y40 per hour. There are also freelance masseurs around Kǒngquè Hú Gōngyuán. For a foot massage try the south-eastern corner of the park, for back and shoulders try the western side.

Non-guests can use the **swimming pool** at the Crown Hotel (Y10) or Tai Garden Hotel (Y20).

Places to Stay

Xīshuāngbǎnnà Bīnguǎn (Bǎnnà Bīnguǎn; ☎ *212 3679/3559, fax 212 3368, 11 Ganlan Zhonglu)* Doubles/triples with bath per person Y40/30, Riverview Building doubles Y150-240. This used to be one of those rare Chinese hotels that travellers reminisced about after they had left. It's not quite that idyllic any more, but it's still generally solid. The staff are usually attentive and friendly. It's also got 24-hour hot water. Doubles in building Nos 6 and 7 have balconies and TV and are a good deal. Standard doubles in the Riverview Building already seem to be falling apart. If you get a dorm room on the ground floor you may want to leave any valuables with the front desk, as some travellers have had possessions stolen here.

If you're in the market for basic accommodation with a Dai flavour, head down to Manting Lu. It's a long walk from the bus station (around 25 minutes), in the south of town. A taxi should cost Y10.

Dai Building Hotel (Dǎijiā Huāyuán Xiǎolóu; Manting Lu) Dorm beds Y25. People either love or hate this popular backpacker hang-out – one of the first signs you see upon entering the courtyard is for

Etiquette in Dai Temples

Around Dai temples the same rules apply as elsewhere: dress appropriately (no tank tops or shorts); take off shoes before entering; don't take photos of monks or interior shots without permission; leave a donation if you do take any shots and consider a token donation even if you don't, since unlike in Thailand these Buddhists receive no government assistance. Like in Thailand, it is polite to 'wai' the monks as a greeting and remember to never rub anyone's head, raise yourself higher than a Buddha figure or point your feet at anyone. (This last point applies to secular buildings too. If you stay the night in a Dai household it is good form to sleep with your feet pointing towards the door.)

'Cold Beer'. All accommodation is in two- or four-bed bamboo bungalows on stilts. The bathrooms are clean and a new solar-heated shower has been installed. Some travellers have been less than impressed with the occasional rodent visitors and lack of privacy (the bamboo walls are definitely not sound-proof!).

Dǎijiǎ Zhāodàisuǒ (☎ 213 9335, 69 Manting Lu) Beds Y15. The cheapest lodging on the street is this decidedly non-Dai style but cheery guesthouse, just south of the Dai Building Hotel. It provides hard beds in spartan triples. The toilets are pretty grim and you'll need your flip-flops for the mildly warm showers. Its sitting area overlooks Manting Lu.

Bǎnnà Jiǔdiàn (☎ 213 2052, Ganlan Nanlu) Doubles/triples with bath Y50/70. This place is in a good location and has characterless but good-value rooms.

Ruìfēng Bīnguǎn (☎ 213 6449, Minzu Lu) Doubles with bath from Y50. This excellent-value, modern hotel has spotless, carpeted rooms with nice bathrooms.

Jǐngyǒng Fàndiàn (☎ 212 3430, 12 Jinghong Donglu) Beds Y30, doubles with fan/air-con & bath Y80/190. This is a centrally located place with clean rooms and dormitory accommodation in triples.

Banna Mansion Hotel (Bǎnnà Dàshà; ☎ 212 2049, fax 212 7021, cnr Jinghong Xilu & Jinghong Nanlu) Doubles/triples with air-con Y238/316. Right in the heart of town, this is Jǐnghóng's original luxury option – there are literally dozens now.

Tai Garden Hotel (Tàiyuán Jiǔdiàn; ☎ 212 3888, fax 212 6060, 8 Nonglin Nanlu) Singles/doubles US$70/80 plus 15% tax. Probably the top option, this hotel is in the south of town towards the airport. It has quiet grounds replete with its own island, pool, sauna, gym and tennis court.

Places to Eat

As with accommodation, Manting Lu is the place for Dai-style food. The road is lined with restaurants. The majority of these restaurants dish up Dai dance performances along with their culinary specialities. Dai women thump drums at the entrance and the restaurants are filled nearly every night with tourists generally being festive.

Dai dishes include roast fish, eel or beef cooked with lemon grass or served with peanut-and-tomato sauce. Vegetarians can order roast bamboo shoot prepared in the same fashion. Other mouth-watering specialities include fried river moss (better than it sounds and excellent with beer) and spicy bamboo-shoot soup. Don't forget to try the black, glutinous rice.

Mekong Cafe (Méigōng Cānguǎn; ☎ 212 8895, 111 Manting Lu) Near the Dai Building Hotel, this is the best new place by a long way. It's well run and friendly, with sofas, cold beer and excellent travellers books. Owners Vicky and Orchid are good sources of travel information. Food is generally excellent, with a set Hani vegetarian meal for Y20 and plenty of Western, Dai, Japanese and even Thai dishes. You can also use the Internet and hire bikes here. The upstairs balcony is a pleasant place to sit with a beer in the winter and read about the sub-zero temperatures in Běijīng.

Mei Mei Cafe (Měiměi Kāfēitīng; Manting Lu) Dishes from Y5. For good food, strong coffee, really cold beer and (you guessed it) banana pancakes, stop by this pleasant little Akha hole-in-the-wall, just down from the intersection with Jingde Lu. Mei Mei was the first cafe to cater to foreigners and is still one of the most popular. Azhu, the owner, and her staff are delightful and great fun to while away an evening with. You can also get your laundry done and this is the spot to rent a bicycle.

Forest Cafe (Sēnlín Kāfēitīng; Manting Lu roundabout) Another cafe definitely meriting your attention is the Forest. It boasts the greatest hamburger in China and it's pretty good (though the bun could use some work). There are also home-baked speciality breads, good juices, the hippest music and more books than anywhere else. There are several other good **snack bars** next door.

Xīnguāng Jiǔjiā (Ganlan Zhonglu) If you want Dai food in an unpretentious atmosphere, north of the market area, this restaurant is run by one of Xīshuāngbǎnnà's best-known traditional singers. The place is packed at lunchtime.

Street stalls sell kebabs, coconuts, bananas, sugar cane, papayas, pomelos (a type of sweet grapefruit) and pineapples. The pineapples, served peeled on a stick, are probably the best in China.

At night there is a huge *food market* by the new bridge over the Mekong. There are dozens of stalls serving up barbecued everything, from sausages to snails.

The *Myanmar Mandalay Cafe (Zhuanghong Lu)* and the *Burmese Teahouse (Minzu Lu)* sell Burmese-style coffee, and milk tea (Y3). Zhuanghong Lu is lined with dozens of Burmese jade shops and is a fascinating area. Something to look out for is *palatar*, a Burmese crepe served hot and doused in sweetened condensed milk.

Getting There & Away

Air More flights and bigger planes (737s) mean that it's a lot easier to fly to Jǐnghóng from Kūnmíng than it used to be. It's usually even possible to book the day before, if not the same day. In April (Water-Splashing Festival), however, you may need to book several days in advance, as this is a very popular time for tourists to visit. And always be careful if you want to change your flight date on or around a weekend.

There are normally several flights daily to Kūnmíng (Y520) and daily flights to Dàlǐ (Y520), Lìjiāng (Y610) and Bangkok (Y1300). Shanghai Airlines offers a service to Shànghǎi (Y1670), with a 40-minute stop (but not change of plane) in Kūnmíng. Flights can be booked at the Yunnan Airlines booking office (☎ 212 7040) on Jingde Lu, open 8am to noon and 3pm to 6pm daily.

Bus The Jǐnghóng long-distance bus station does have buses to towns around Xīshuāngbǎnnà, but it is most useful for long-distance destinations. To explore Xīshuāngbǎnnà, go to the No 2 bus station, which has frequent buses, minibuses and minivans from 7am to around 5pm. The ticket office is generally very efficient, but if you have problems walk through the station to the parking lot/departure area, wander around and before long you'll find a van waiting for passengers. See the Getting There & Away sections throughout this chapter for details on these buses.

There are daily buses between Kūnmíng and Jǐnghóng (see the Kūnmíng Getting There & Away section for details). From the long-distance bus station, sleepers leave all day (Y120). There is a luxury express coach (seats not berths) at 4pm (Y146, 15 hours). The price includes bottled water and one meal. The No 2 station has a similar service at 6pm, as well as more sleeper services.

If you're torn between the bus and the plane to Kūnmíng, don't worry about missing the scenery on the flight. There are some good views from the bus window, but nothing worth all those hours of inhaling second-hand smoke and bouncing up and down in lieu of sleep.

The Jǐnghóng long-distance bus station also has buses running epic journeys to Xiàguān, Bǎoshān and Ruìlì. The trips to Xiàguān and Bǎoshān shouldn't require any overnight stays if on a sleeper, but don't count on it. Sleepers to Xiàguān (Y150, 28 to 36 hours) leave the long-distance station early in the morning and the No 2 bus station at 1.30pm. Buses to Bǎoshān cost about the same but take 36 hours – and these routes are served by minibuses at times! For the marathon trip (about 40 hours) to Ruìlì, seriously consider breaking the trip in Bǎoshān, if for no other reason than to preserve at least some traces of pink in your lungs. Roads are quite poor on these routes and many travellers have found their two-day trip stretch to three and even four days due to landslides, floods and bus breakdowns. As compensation the scenery can be gorgeous.

Getting Around

The airport is 5km south of the city; CAAC buses (Y2) leave when full, across from the

Yunnan Airlines booking office. A taxi will cost around Y20.

Jǐnghóng is small enough that you can walk to most destinations, but a bike makes life easier. The Xīshuāngbǎnnà Bīnguǎn, Mekong and Mei Mei cafes rent bikes for around Y10 per day, or Y20 for a mountain bike.

AROUND JǏNGHÓNG

The possibilities for day trips and longer excursions out of Jǐnghóng are endless. Some travellers have hiked and hitched from Měnghǎi to Dàměnglóng, some have cycled up to Měnghǎi and Měngzhē on mountain bikes (it's almost impossible on bikes without gears), and one French photographer hitched up with a local medicine man and spent seven days doing house calls in the jungle.

Obviously, it's the longer trips that allow you to escape the hordes of tourists and get a feel for what Xīshuāngbǎnnà is about. But even with limited time there are some interesting possibilities. Probably the best is an overnight (or several nights) stay in Gǎnlǎnbà (also known as Měnghǎn). It's only around 27km from Jǐnghóng, and not that hard to cycle to, even on a local bike. The trip takes two to three hours.

Most other destinations in Xīshuāngbǎnnà are only two or three hours away by bus, but generally they are not much in themselves – you need to get out and about. Note that to get to many villages, you'll often first have to take the bus to a primary village and stay overnight there, since only one bus per day – if that – travels to the tinier villages.

If you're a serious collector of local market experiences, there are plenty to be found in the region. Like anything else, *markets* are subjective things, but most people seem to prefer the Thursday market in Xīdìng, then Měnghùn, followed up by Měnghǎi.

The best advice is to get yourself a bike or some sturdy hiking boots, pick up a map, put down this book and get out of town.

Nearby Villages

Before heading farther afield, there are numerous villages in the vicinity of Jǐnghóng that can be reached by bicycle. Most of them you will happen upon by chance, and it's difficult to make recommendations.

On the other side of the Mekong are some small villages, and a popular jaunt involves heading off down Manting Lu – if you go far enough you'll hit a ferry crossing point on the Mekong (Y1), beyond which there are plenty of Dai temples and villages to explore.

Sānchàhé Nature Reserve

Sānchàhé Zìrán Bǎohùqù 三岔河自然保护区
Sānchàhé, 48km north of Jǐnghóng, is one of five enormous forest reserves in southern Yúnnán. This one has an area of nearly 1.5 million hectares.

The part of the park that most tourists visit is **Bǎnnà Wild Elephant Valley** (*Bǎnnà Yěxiànggǔ; admission Y25*), named after the 40 or so wild elephants that live in the valley. It might be worth a visit if you want to see something of the local forest.

There are two entrances to the reserve. The main southern entrance has accommodation, displays on tropical birds and butterflies, and peacock shows. The other entrance has 'wild' elephant performances for the throngs of shutterbug tourists. A 2km cable car (Y40) leads over the canopy from the main entrance into the heart of the park, or there is a similar-length pathway from the other entrance.

Accommodation at the main entrance ranges from Y20 per person in a concrete triple to Y120, Y180 and Y220 for a decent double room with views over the lake. There are a couple of *restaurants* at both entrances. You can stay in one of 22 carpeted *canopy treehouses* in the heart of the park for Y220.

It is only possible to get off the main paths with a guide and that will cost Y200 per day. Ask about packages that include entry, food and accommodation for a discounted Y150.

Just about any bus travelling north from Jǐnghóng to Sīmáo will pass this reserve (Y10, one hour).

Měngyǎng 勐养

Měngyǎng is 34km north-east of Jǐnghóng on the road to Sīmáo. It's a centre for the Hani, Lahu and Floral-Belt Dai. Chinese tourists stop here to see the **Elephant-Shaped Banyan Tree** (*Xiàngxíng Róngshù*).

From Měngyǎng it's another 19km to **Jīnuò**, which is home base for the Jinuo minority. Travellers have reported a cool reception here, so you'll probably have to stay in Měngyǎng. Some minorities dislike tourists, and if this is the case with the Jinuo they should be left alone.

Gǎnlǎnbà (Měnghǎn) 橄榄坝

Gǎnlǎnbà, or Měnghǎn as it's sometimes referred to, lies on the Mekong south-east of Jǐnghóng. In the past the main attraction of Gǎnlǎnbà was the boat journey down the Mekong from Jǐnghóng. Unfortunately, improved roads sank the popular boat trip (locals prefer to spend an hour on a bus to three hours on the boat), and the only way to travel down the river now is to charter a boat at special tourist prices that most tourists can't afford.

However, Gǎnlǎnbà remains a wonderful retreat from hectic Jǐnghóng. The town itself is fairly forgettable, but if you come on a bike (it is also possible to hire one in Gǎnlǎnbà) there is plenty of scope for exploration in the neighbourhood.

Things to See Following Manting Lu to the south-east (past Gǎnlǎnbà Bīnguǎn) a kilometre or two brings you to the **Měngbàlà Bǎnnà Xīwàng Park** (*Měngbàlà Xīwàng Guǒyuánlín; admission Y20*), where you'll find a couple of gorgeous **pagodas** and pleasant Dai villages. Some travellers have avoided the admission fee by cycling around the north side of the nearby reservoir and entering the back of the park.

There's a couple of old decaying temples on the road into town from Jǐnghóng, and nearby is a huge **tourist market** (*nóngtiè chǎnpǐn gòuwù shìchǎng*), which sells all kinds of regional specialities, from Dai dresses to weird tropical fruit.

Travellers recommend heading to the south of town, taking the ferry over the Mekong by ferry (Y2 with a bike), and then heading left (east). Check the visitors' book in the Sarlar Restaurant for some ideas.

Places to Stay & Eat There are a number of options:

Dai Bamboo House (*Dǎijiā Zhúlóu*) Once this was a good place to stay but it has recently gone downhill fast. It's still possible to stay on a mat on the floor but there's little interest shown in guests. Dai Bamboo

The Jinuo People

The Jinuo, sometimes known as the Youle, were officially 'discovered' as a minority in 1979. The women wear a white cowl, a cotton tunic with bright horizontal stripes and a tubular black skirt. Ear-lobe decoration is an elaborate custom – the larger the hole and the more flowers it can contain the better. The teeth are sometimes painted black with the sap of the lacquer tree, which serves the dual dental purpose of beautifying the mouth and preventing tooth decay and halitosis.

Previously, the Jinuo lived in long houses with as many as 27 families occupying rooms on either side of the central corridor. Each family had its own hearth, but the oldest man owned the largest hearth, which was always the closest to the door. Long houses are rarely used now and the Jinuo seem to be quickly losing their distinctive way of life.

House is on the right-hand side of Jinlun Donglu, the main road, travelling away from Jǐnghóng.

Gǎnlǎnbà Bīnguǎn (☎ 241 1233, Manting Lu) Dorm beds Y30, doubles with bath Y100. More formal lodging than at the Bamboo House is available here, a block farther south. Rooms are decent and there's 24-hour hot water.

Lóngfèng Dàjiǔdiàn Doubles with bath Y40. Across the road from Gǎnlǎnbà Bīnguǎn, this is probably the best-value choice.

Sarlar Restaurant (*Shālā Cāntīng; Jinlun Donglu*) Rooms Y10. This friendly place has a few 'rooms' (though these are little more than a corner of the restaurant partitioned off by a piece of wood) with Dai-style mats on the floor. Check whether the sheets are clean and don't expect to get to sleep early if people are socialising in the restaurant. The bathrooms and shower room are clean. To get here, continue past the Dai Bamboo House until just before the road begins to bend to the right.

If you follow the road south from the intersection near Lóngfèng Dàjiǔdiàn to Manting Lu you'll find several *Dai restaurants* with pleasant wooden balconies. The problem with these is that there's no menu, so you have to point and choose.

Dai Family Restaurant *(Manting Lu)* This place has an English menu on the wall but there are no prices listed, so check before you order as food is a little pricier than elsewhere.

Getting There & Away Microbuses to Gǎnlǎnbà leave from Jǐnghóng's No 2 bus station every 20 minutes (Y7, 45 minutes). Minibuses depart Gǎnlǎnbà for Jǐnghóng and Měnglún from the main intersection in the centre of town.

It's possible to cycle from Jǐnghóng to Gǎnlǎnbà in a brisk two hours or a leisurely three hours, and it's a pleasant ride.

Getting Around If you didn't bring your own bike, you can rent a mountain bike at the Sarlar Restaurant, or at a private shop a few doors down, for about Y10 to Y15 per day. If they're all out, walk back towards town to the main intersection where an elderly bicycle-repair man rents out Chinese bikes for Y10 per day.

Měnglún 勐伦

Měnglún is the next major port of call east of Gǎnlǎnbà. The major attraction is the **Tropical Plant Gardens** *(Rèdài Zhíwùyuán; adult/student Y35/20)*. It's a pleasant enough place, although concrete pathways and guides toting bullhorns dash any hopes of communing with nature. But the gardens are nicely laid out, and the tour groups give it a somewhat festive atmosphere.

To get here, turn left out of the bus station and walk to the first corner. Walk one block and turn left again. You'll come to market hawkers, and a road leading downhill to the right side. Follow this until you reach a footbridge across the Mekong. The ticket booth is just in front of the bridge.

Places to Stay & Eat There are a number of places to stay and eat in Měnglún.

Bus Station Hotel Dorm beds Y10. This is the best-value option. Beds are in comfortable quads and there's a shared bathroom and shower down the hall.

Chūnlín Lǚshè (☎ 871 7172) Doubles from Y30. Take a look at a number of rooms, as this is a huge place with many different options.

There is also budget accommodation within the gardens. After crossing the bridge, follow the main path for about 15 minutes until you arrive at a group of buildings and a fork in the road. Take the left fork and you'll find the grungy hostel ***Zhíwùyuán Zhāodàisuǒ*** *(dorm beds Y20).*

Zhíwùyuán Bīnguǎn *(Botanical Gardens Hotel)* Doubles/triples with bath Y180/210. For a more upmarket stay, take the right fork, go over the hill and to the left of the pond or this damp but clean hotel. Doubles are discounted to Y100.

There are a couple of other mid-range places in town, with rooms for around Y80.

Friendship Restaurant *(Yǒuyì Cāntīng; on main highway)* This place has lots of dishes made from strange vegetables, ferns and herbs only found locally.

Getting There & Away From Jǐnghóng's No 2 bus station there are buses to Měnglún (Y11 to Y13, two hours) every 45 minutes until 3pm. The buses pass through Gǎnlǎnbà. Some travellers have cycled here from Gǎnlǎnbà.

From Měnglún, there are minibuses (Y16, three hours) and faster Iveco buses (Y20, 2½ hours) to Měnglà every 30 minutes or so. Most buses travelling between Jǐnghóng and Měnglà stop here, so you should have no trouble landing a ride in either direction. The last bus back to Jǐnghóng is around 7pm.

Měnglà 孟腊

Měnglà sees an increasing number of travellers passing through en route to Laos via the border crossing at Móhān. As the bus journey from Jǐnghóng, or even Měnglún, will take the better part of the day, you will probably have to stay overnight here.

The Bank of China in the southern half of town changes cash and travellers cheques but won't give cash advances off a credit card. To change Renminbi back into US dollars you'll need your original exchange receipts. The bank is open 8am to 11.30am and 3pm to 6pm Monday to Friday.

The **Bupan Aerial Skyway Park** *(Wàngtiānshù Zǒuláng; admission Y20),* a 45-minute bus ride (Y7) heading north, makes a half-day trip from Měnglà. It has walks along raised, wooden pathways through the forest canopy, featuring the rare Chinese *parashorea* tree (known locally as the 'Looking at the Sky Tree' because of its height and fast growth). To get here take an hourly minibus heading to Měngbàn or Yáoqū. The last bus back is around 5.30pm.

Places to Stay *Nánjiāng Bīnguǎn (Mengla Jie)* Dorm beds with shared bath Y15, singles Y22, doubles with bath Y50-80. There's a range of rooms here; quad dorms are pretty good but doubles are not much value. Try to look at a few rooms.

Měnglà Bīnguǎn Dorm beds Y20, doubles with bath & TV Y60. CITS has an office with at least one or two English-speaking staff at this hotel, about 2km uphill from the bus station. The location is inconvenient, but a pedicab should get you here for Y3 to Y4.

Getting There & Away There are four or five direct buses daily between Jǐnghóng's No 2 bus station and Měnglà (Y25 to Y31, five to seven hours). Jǐnghóng's long-distance bus station also has five daily departures between 6.40am and 5.30pm.

Měnglà has three bus stations. The northern long-distance bus station has buses to Kūnmíng at 6.30am, 8am and 9.30am (Y138, 24 to 29 hours) and many departures to Jǐnghóng via Gǎnlǎnbà (Y26 to Y31). If there's nothing suitable try the northern bus station a couple of hundred metres farther north.

The bus station farther south-east has buses to Móhān (Y10, 1½ hours) on the border, along with other long-distance buses and a few to Jǐnghóng.

LAOS BORDER CROSSING

First off, it is currently impossible to obtain a visa at the border. (See also under Laos in the Land section of the Getting There & Away chapter.) From Měnglà, there are buses to Móhān every 30 minutes or so from 8am. No matter what anyone says, there should be no 'charge' to cross. Once your passport is stamped (double-check all stamps) and you've waved goodbye to the border guards, you can jump on a tractor or truck to take you 3km into Laos for around Y3. If you can't find a bus to Móhān, get on one to Shàngyǒng, and arrange another ride. Whatever you do, go early. Things often wrap up for good around noon on the

Lao side (and don't forget they're an hour ahead) and you won't find a truck if you go later. There are guesthouses on both the Chinese and Lao sides; change money on the Lao side.

DÀMĚNGLÓNG 大勐龙

Dàměnglóng (written just 'Měnglóng' on buses) is about 70km south of Jǐnghóng and a few kilometres from the Myanmar border. It's another sleepy village that is a good base for hikes around the surrounding hills. The village itself is not much (it rouses itself somewhat for the Sunday market), but the surrounding countryside, peppered with decaying stupas and little villages, is worth a couple of days' exploration. You can hire bikes at Dàměnglóng Zhāodàisuǒ for Y15 per day.

The town's laid-back feel may change in the next few years, however. The border crossing point with Myanmar (poetically named 2-4-0) has been designated as the entry point for a planned highway linking Thailand, Myanmar and China. If and when it does open, things should definitely pick up here.

Mànfēilóng Tǎ 曼飞龙塔
White Bamboo Shoot Pagoda

This pagoda *(admission Y5)*, built in 1204, is Dàměnglóng's premier attraction. According to legend, the temple was built on the spot of a hallowed footprint left by Sakyamuni Buddha, who is said to have visited Xīshuāngbǎnnà – if you're interested in ancient footprints you can look for it in a niche below one of the nine stupas. Unfortunately, in recent years a 'beautification' job has been done on the temple with a couple of cans of white paint.

If you're in Xīshuāngbǎnnà in late October or early November, check the precise dates of the Tan Ta Festival. At this time Mànfēilóng Tǎ is host to hundreds of locals whose celebrations include dancing, rocket launchings, paper balloons and so on.

Mànfēilóng Tǎ is easy to get to: just walk back along the main road towards Jǐnghóng for 2km until you reach a small village with a temple on your left. From here there's a path up the hill; it's about a 20-minute walk. There's an admission fee, but many times no-one's around anyway.

Hēi Tǎ 黑塔
Black Pagoda

Just above the centre of town is a Dai monastery with a steep path beside it leading up to Hēi Tǎ – you'll notice it when entering Dàměnglóng. The pagoda itself is actually gold, not black. Take a stroll up, but bear in mind that the real reason for the climb is the superb views of Dàměnglóng and the surrounding countryside.

Places to Stay & Eat

Plenty of cheap options are available for foreigners.

Qìchēzhàn Zhāodàisuǒ (Bus Station Guesthouse) This has quite pleasant-looking rooms. Another cheap place sits at the base of Hēi Tǎ.

Dàměnglóng Zhàodàisuǒ Dorm beds Y10. Formerly the only place for foreigners, beds here are basic and the bathrooms are fragrant but passable. To get here, walk uphill from the main highway to where the local government building sits. The hotel is in the grounds to the left, just past some ornamental frogs. Bicycles can be rented here for Y3 per hour, Y15 per day.

There are a couple of decent *restaurants* down from the bus station, near the steps leading up to Hēi Tǎ, The Chinese signs proclaim them to be Dai restaurants.

Dàměnglóng specialises in *shāokǎo,* skewers of meat wrapped in banana leaves grilled over wood fires.

Getting There & Away

There are buses to Dàměnglóng (Y13, 2½ hours) every 30 minutes (or less) between 7am and 5pm (occasionally until 7pm) from Jǐnghóng's No 2 bus station. Purchase your tickets on the bus – just walk through the station and across the car park to the far left corner, where they congregate. Remember that the 'Da' character won't be painted on the bus window. Buses for the return trip run on a similar schedule, though the last bus tends to leave earlier.

AROUND DÀMĚNGLÓNG

The village of **Xiǎojīe**, about 15km north of Dàměnglóng, is surrounded by Bulang, Lahu and Hani villages. Lahu women shave their heads; apparently the younger ones aren't happy about this any more and hide their heads beneath caps. The Bulang are possibly descended from the Yi of northern Yúnnán. The women wear black turbans with silver decorations; many of the designs are of shells, fish and marine life.

There's plenty of room for exploration in this area, although you're not allowed over the border.

MĚNGHǍI 勐海

This place serves as a centre for trips into the surrounding area. The Sunday market attracts members of the hill tribes and the best way to find it is to follow the early morning crowds. To the north of Měnghǎi there are many pagodas and interesting villages that would make for some fine exploring on bicycle.

Bus Station Hotel Doubles Y80. This flashy place has comfortable doubles, that can be negotiated down to Y60.

Liángyuán Bīnguǎn (Grain Hotel) Beds in triples Y20, doubles Y60. This is across the street from the Bus Station Hotel.

Tiānyuánqín Bīnguǎn (Commercial City Hotel) Doubles with bath Y168. A five-minute walk heading north along the main street, this has comfortable doubles, sometimes discounted to Y80.

Buses run from Jǐnghóng's No 2 bus station to Měnghǎi (Y7, 1½ hours) approximately every 30 minutes between 7.30am and 5.30pm. Měnghǎi's flashy new bus station in the southern part of town has minibuses to Bùlǎngshān at 9am and 2pm and to Xīdìng (Y10, three hours) at 10.40am and 3.30pm, among others.

AROUND MĚNGHǍI
Měnghùn 勐混

This tiny village is about 26km south-west of Měnghǎi. Some prefer the Sunday **market** here to that of Měnghǎi. It all begins buzzing around 7am and lingers on through to noon. The swirl of hill tribespeople and women sporting fancy leggings, headdresses, earrings and bracelets alone makes the trip worthwhile. Although the market seems to be the main attraction, a **temple** and footpaths that wind through the lush hills behind the White Tower Hotel are also worth an extra day or two.

Places to Stay & Eat White Tower Hotel

(Báitǎ Fàndiàn) Beds Y10. This hotel is basic but it is secluded and looks out over a

Trekking in Xīshuāngbǎnnà

Treks around Xīshuāngbǎnnà used to be among the best in China – you'd be invited into a local's home to eat, sleep, and drink *báijiǔ*. Increasing numbers of visitors have changed this in places. Don't automatically expect a welcome mat and a free lunch just because you're a foreigner, but don't go changing the local economy by throwing money around either. Also take care, it's jungle out there, so go prepared, and make sure somebody knows where you are and when you should return. In the rainy season you'll need to be equipped with proper hiking shoes and waterproof gear. At any time you'll need water purification, bottled water or a water bottle able to hold boiling water, as well as snacks and sunscreen.

Dàměnglóng to Bùlǎngshān Trek

The most popular walk is this long two-day-or-more, 48km trek through Dai, Hani, Bulang and Lahu villages. It can be done in either direction. This is a poor area but the people are still friendly and the jungle is relatively pristine. If you do get invited in, try to establish whether payment is expected. If it's not, leave an offering of around Y10 or leave modest gifts such as candles, matches, rice etc – even though the family may insist on nothing.

Start by taking a bus to Dàměnglóng (see Dàměnglóng's Getting There & Away section). From there it's a 10km-or-so walk or hitch on a tractor to the Dai village of Manguanghan. One bus per day should leave Dàměnglóng at noon but this is neither certain nor necessary. Take the path to the right, 200m beyond the end of Manguanghan. It's a steady 12km walk (three to four hours) to Manpo, a Bulang village. As you cross through Guangmin, an Aini village en route, look out for a temple. After staying overnight in a villager's home in Manpo, the next day is a 24km (six hours) walk to Weidong via Nuna (Bulang people), Songeer (Lahu people), and Bannankan (Lahu). In Manpo ask for the right path to Weidong (the path goes down). There are three or four places where you may get off the track and have to backtrack but that's part of the fun. Stay overnight in Weidong and the next day is another leisurely 10km (three hours) to Bùlǎngshān on a good road. If you want to just spend one night on the trail, a family in Songéer offers accommodation and two meals for Y20 per person. From Manpo to Songéer it's a three-hour walk.

From Bùlǎngshān there are minibuses back to Měnghǎi (via Měnghùn) at 8am and 2.30pm. There is a truck stop/karaoke hellhole in Bùlǎngshān with dorm beds, but you'll probably be kept awake by drinking truckers offering you smokes. Try and find a local to put you up.

If you're short of time, on the second day you could get to Bùlǎngshān from Manpo without staying overnight in Weidong. It's an epic day of trekking but the trail is mostly level, with only a minor uphill grade. Those in shape can probably finish in nine hours.

If you time it right you could stop over at Měnghùn's Sunday market on the way back to Jǐnghóng, or start the trek in Bùlǎngshān and visit the market en route to the town.

Guides

One travel agency catering to these treks is the Mengyuan Travel Service in Jǐnghóng (see Travel Agencies in the Jǐnghóng section). For a guide and transport you'll pay a minimum of Y80 to Y100 per person per day. Vicky and Orchid at the Mekong Cafe and Sarah at the Forest Cafe, both in Jǐnghóng, can also put you in touch with a guide. One of the main advantages of taking a guide is to communicate with villagers en route; you won't hear much Mandarin Chinese on the trail, let alone any English.

---

lily pond. From the main intersection, take the road uphill, walk through the archway, then bear left across the basketball court and follow a small path heading downhill; around the corner is the hotel.

Yúnchuān Fàndiàn Rooms Y10-20. Located right in the centre of town, where the buses let you off, this place has basic concrete rooms.

Fènghuáng Fàndiàn (*Phoenix Hotel*) Beds Y5. Farther down from Yúnchuān Fàndiàn on the right-hand side of the street, this hotel is cheaper, but very noisy – you're better off giving it a miss.

The Hani (Akha) People

The Hani (also known in adjacent countries as the Akha) are of Tibetan origin and related to the Yi, but according to folklore they are descended from frogs' eyes. They stick to the hills, cultivating rice, corn and the occasional poppy and are famed for their intricate rice terraces.

Hani women (especially the Aini, a subgroup of the Hani) wear headdresses of beads, feathers, silver rings and coins, some of which are turn-of-the-century French (Vietnamese), Burmese and Indian coins.

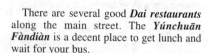

There are several good *Dai restaurants* along the main street. The *Yúnchuān Fàndiàn* is a decent place to get lunch and wait for your bus.

Getting There & Away Buses from Jǐnghóng to Měnghùn (Y11.5, two hours) leave Jǐnghóng's No 2 bus station every 20 minutes between 7am and 5.40pm. Going back to Jǐnghóng you should have just a short wait on the side of the road until a bus passes by. You could visit Jǐngzhēn (see the following section) on the way back – get off at the main crossroads, catch the first transport heading west and get off about 10km later.

If you are headed to Bùlǎngshān, buses pass through Měnghùn at 9.30am and 3pm.

Unless you have a very good bike with gears, cycling to Měnghǎi and Měnghùn is not a real option. The road up to Měnghǎi is so steep that you'll end up pushing the bike most of the way.

Jǐngzhēn 景真

In the village of Jǐngzhēn, about 14km north-west of Měnghǎi, is the **Octagonal Pavilion** *(Bājiǎo Tíng; admission Y10; open daylight hours)*, first built in 1701. The original structure was severely damaged during the Cultural Revolution but renovated in 1978 and the ornate decoration is still impressive. The temple also operates as a monastic school. The paintings on the wall of the temple depict scenes from the Jatatka, the life history of Buddha.

Jǐngzhēn is a pleasant, rural spot for walks along the river or the fish ponds behind the village. Frequent minibuses from the minibus centre in Měnghǎi go via Jǐngzhēn.

Bǎoshān Region 保山

Travellers who pass through the Bǎoshān area tend to do so quickly, generally staying overnight in Bǎoshān town on the way to or from Ruìlì, but the area is worth a bit more time than that. There are some worthwhile historical sights and many distinctive minority groups. The old quarters of Téngchōng and Bǎoshān also make for some good browsing, and the Téngchōng area is rich in volcanic activity, with hot springs and volcanic peaks.

As early as the 4th and 5th centuries BC (two centuries before the northern routes through central Asia were established), the Bǎoshān area was an important stage on the southern Silk Road – the Sìchuān-India route. The area did not really come under Chinese control until the time of the Han dynasty when in AD 69 it was named the Yongchang Administrative District. In 1277 a huge battle was waged in the region between the 12,000 troops of Kublai Khan and 60,000 Burmese soldiers and their 2000 elephants. The Mongols won and went on to take Pagan.

BǍOSHĀN 保山
☎ 0875

Bǎoshān is a small city that's easily explored on foot. There are pockets of traditional wooden architecture still standing and some good walks on the outskirts of town. It has innumerable speciality products, ranging from excellent coffee to leather boots, pepper and silk. Tea aficionados might like to try the Reclining Buddha Baoshan Tea, a brand of national repute.

Information

Shops in the long-distance bus station sell maps of Bǎoshān prefecture that show regional sights in Chinese, with some explanations in English. Otherwise you're pretty much on your own. The Bank of China is next to Yíndū Dàjiǔdiàn, on Baoxiu Donglu, with another branch opposite the Yunnan Airlines office. The post and telephone offices are not far away on Xiagang Jie. You can get slow Internet access (Y3 per hour) at a computer shop on the corner of Shanggang Jie and Yunwen Lu, or at nearby Kele Computer Company (Kèlè Diànnǎogōngsī) for Y5 per hour.

BĂOSHĀN 保山

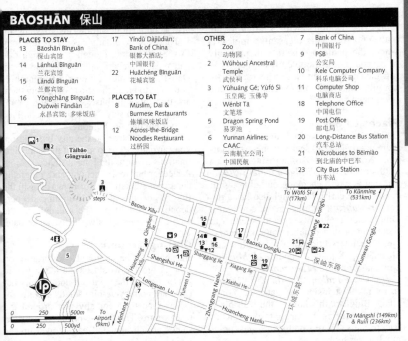

PLACES TO STAY	17	Yíndū Dàjiǔdiàn; Bank of China 银都大酒店; 中国银行	OTHER	7	Bank of China 中国银行
13	Bǎoshān Bīnguǎn 保山宾馆		1	Zoo 动物园	9	PSB 公安局
14	Lánhuā Bīnguǎn 兰花宾馆	22	Huāchéng Bīnguǎn 花城宾馆	2	Wǔhòucí Ancestral Temple 武侯祠	10	Kele Computer Company 科乐电脑公司
15	Lándū Bīnguǎn 兰都宾馆				11	Computer Shop 电脑商店
16	Yǒngchāng Bīnguǎn; Duōwèi Fàndiàn 永昌宾馆; 多味饭店	PLACES TO EAT	3	Yùhuáng Gé; Yùfó Sì 玉皇阁; 玉佛寺	18	Telephone Office 中国电信
		8	Muslim, Dai & Burmese Restaurants 傣缅风味饭店	4	Wénbǐ Tǎ 文笔塔	19	Post Office 邮电局
		12	Across-the-Bridge Noodles Restaurant 过桥园	5	Dragon Spring Pond 易罗池	20	Long-Distance Bus Station 汽车总站
				6	Yunnan Airlines; CAAC 云南航空公司; 中国民航	21	Microbuses to Běimiào 到北庙的中巴车
						23	City Bus Station 市车站

Things to See

Bǎoshān's streets are lively and, in many areas, lined with old, traditional homes. The major sight within easy walking distance of the town centre is **Tàibǎo Shān** and its surrounding park *(admission Y3)*. Just before you head up the steps leading up the hillside you'll see the Ming dynasty **Yùhuáng Gé** *(Jade Emperor Pavilion)* and the attached **Yùfó Sì** *(Jade Buddha Temple)* on your right. At the top of the steps is the small park and the **Wǔhòucí Ancestral Temple**, which has a nice garden and teahouse. It's possible to get here by taxi, following the road that leads around the back of the hill.

There are paths in the park striking off to the north, west and south. The northern path doubles back to the south and eventually takes you past a very mediocre zoo (keep walking). Continuing southbound you will reach **Dragon Spring Pond** *(Yìluó Chí or Lóngquán Chí)*, with views of the 13-tiered **Wénbǐ Tǎ**.

Places to Stay

Huāchéng Bīnguǎn *(☎ 212 2037, Huancheng Donglu)* Doubles/triples with shared bath Y44/60, doubles with private bath Y50-90. This place has clean, bright and generally quiet rooms and is good value. It is popular so you may find it booked out. Deals are available for stays of three or more nights.

Along Baoxiu Xilu there are a few sprawling Chinese-style hotels with little to separate them:

Yǒngchāng Bīnguǎn *(☎ 212 2802, Baoxiu Xilu)* Beds Y10-30, doubles with bath Y80-360. This place is the cheapest in town.

Lánhuā Bīnguǎn *(☎ 212 2803, Baoxiu Xilu)* Beds in 3-bed dorms Y25, doubles/triples with bath 150/180. Discounts of up to 50% are available.

Lándū Bīnguǎn *(☎ 212 1888, fax 212 1990, Baoxiu Xilu)* Doubles Y400, discounted to Y320, 4th-floor rooms Y240, discounted to Y200. This is Bǎoshān's premier accommodation with fine rooms and slavish service. The 4th-floor rooms are cheaper because they have no views.

Yíndū Dàjiǔdiàn *(☎ 212 0948, Baoxiu Donglu)* Doubles Y80. This venture is brought to you by the Bank of China but rooms are tatty and you can do better.

Bǎoshān Bīnguǎn (☎ *212 2804, Shanggang Jie*) Doubles with shared/private bath Y60/160. This pleasant complex is where the pedicab drivers will probably bring you if you stumble off the bus looking dazed and confused. The rooms are not great and the more expensive ones are overpriced.

Places to Eat

Baoxiu Xilu and the road running south of it are good places to seek out cheap restaurants. Next door to Bǎoshān Bīnguǎn is an outdoor *across-the-bridge noodles restaurant* that is worth checking out, although it closes quite early. The hotel also has a decent *restaurant* in the main courtyard. Other hotel restaurants seem to be either in mourning or in a drunken karaoke frenzy. Near the intersection of Baoxiu Xilu and Huancheng Xilu is a handful of *Muslim, Dai,* and *Burmese restaurants*.

Duōwèi Fàndiàn (*Baoxiu Xilu*) Dishes from Y8. Just inside the gates of Yǒngchāng Bīnguǎn, this hole-in-the-wall place is used to serving up cheap, tasty meals to backpackers. There's no menu so just point at whatever looks good.

Getting There & Away

Air You can fly daily between Bǎoshān and Kūnmíng (Y440). The Yunnan Airlines/CAAC office (☎ 216 1747) is inconveniently located at the intersection of Longquan Lu and Minhang Lu. Look for a large yellow-tiled building. The ticket office is on the 1st floor, facing Longquan Lu and is open from 8.30am to 6.30pm daily. The airport is around 9km south of town.

Bus The Bǎoshān long-distance bus station has buses running to a host of destinations around Yúnnán. There are several sleeper departures between 3pm and 8pm to Kūnmíng (Y70 to Y97, 14 hours). One express bus leaves for Kūnmíng at 8am (Y116). Buses for Xiàguān (Dàlǐ) leave every 40 minutes (Y26, five hours). Buses to Téngchōng (Y25, 4½ hours) also leave every 40 minutes or so. Buses on to Yíngjiāng, past Téngchōng, leave at 9.50am and take pretty much forever.

To Ruìlì there are buses at 8.30am and 9am and sleeper buses at 5pm and 7pm (Y36, seven hours). Buses to Ruìlì pass through Mángshì and Wǎndīng. There are also a couple of departures just to Mángshì.

There is also a daily sleeper to Jǐnghóng (Y158, 20 hours), though it's a rough ride and most travellers opt to take the direct Dàlǐ-Jǐnghóng bus or return to Kūnmíng. If you want to break the trip to Jǐnghóng there are two morning buses to Líncāng (Y41) where you can stay overnight and continue onto Mènglián or Jǐnghóng.

Across the street at the city bus station, you can catch a bus to most of the same destinations as from the long-distance station. A sleeper bus to Téngchōng and Yíngjiāng departs at 8.30am. To Ruìlì via Mángshì the first bus departs at 8am. Kūnmíng sleepers depart from 4.30pm. The schedule on the wall of this station is woefully out of date.

Getting Around

Bǎoshān can be explored comfortably on foot. A bicycle would be the ideal way to get to some of the sights around the city but there are no bicycle-hire stands as yet.

Taxis cost Y5 for any ride around the town centre. The three-wheeler motor rickshaws are cheaper but can't travel up the main street, Baoxiu Xilu.

AROUND BǍOSHĀN

Just 17km north of town, **Wòfó Sì** (*Reclining Buddha Temple*) is one of the most important historical sights near Bǎoshān. The temple dates back to the Tang dynasty, with a history of some 1200 years. The reclining Buddha, in a cave to the rear of the temple area, was damaged during the Cultural Revolution and has only recently been restored.

To get to the temple take a microbus from a stand just north of the main bus station to the interesting village of Běimiào and walk or hire a microbus for the rest. A motorcycle with sidecar can take two people there and back from Bǎoshān for Y40. Taxis ask around Y80. It would be a fairly comfortable bicycle trip if you could get hold of a bike.

TÉNGCHŌNG 腾冲
☎ 0875

Not many travellers get to this town on the other side of Gāolígòng Shān mountain range, but it's an interesting place. There are about 20 volcanoes in the vicinity and lots of hot springs (see the Around Téngchōng section later for details). It's

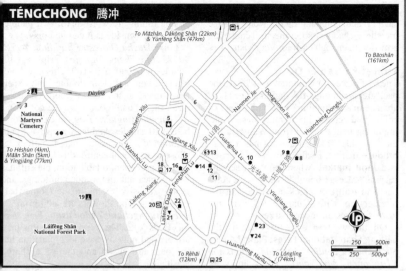

TÉNGCHŌNG 腾冲

TÉNGCHŌNG

also prime earthquake territory, having experienced 71 earthquakes measuring over five on the Richter scale since AD 1500.

The town has preserved, on a larger scale, the kind of traditional wooden architecture that has survived only in pockets in Kūnmíng and Bǎoshān. It's not exactly Dàlǐ, but there's a definite charm to some of the narrow backstreets.

Information

A good English-language map of the town and the surrounding sites is available from the lobby of Téngchōng Bīnguǎn for Y3.

The post and telephone offices are together on Fengshan Lu. China Telecom also has an Internet office on Laifeng Dadao, 100m uphill from the main intersection, open 8am to 10pm. The Bank of China towers over the town's main intersection at Feng-shan Lu and Yingjiang Lu but won't change travellers cheques, so come to Téngchōng armed with enough cash for your visit.

Things to See & Do

The best places for a random wander are the backstreets running off Yingjiang Lu. There are a couple of small markets with plenty of colour and activity in the mornings. Walking along Fengshan Lu from Wanshou Lu, the first side street on the left has a small **produce market**. Farther down on the right is a **Jade market**, where you can see the carving process (though it's a bit tame compared to Ruìlì). A block north-west of the intersection with Guanghua Lu is the town's biggest **produce market**.

On the western edge of town is the **Láifēng Shān National Forest Park** (*Láifēng Shān Gúojiā Sēnlín Gōngyuán; admission Y10; open 8am-7pm*). You can walk through lush pine forests to **Láifēng Sì** or make the sweaty hike up to the summit where a pagoda offers fine views. There are lots of further hiking possibilities.

In the north-western suburbs of town **Xiānlè Sì** (*admission Y5*) is beside the small **Diéshuǐ Waterfall**, which makes a good place for a picnic. On the way to the temple there is a new **Nationalities Cultural Performance Centre** and a memorial to Chinese soldiers lost fighting the Japanese. The area makes a nice destination for a bike ride and you could easily combine it with a trip to Héshùn.

Places to Stay

Téngchōng's accommodation options are fairly spread out:

Gōnglù Zhāodàisuǒ (*Huancheng Dong-lu*) Dorm beds Y10. It's a noisy place here, but it's the closest one just south of the bus station. The hotel has no English sign – look for the ubiquitous bus steering-wheel logo at the top of the entry gate. Dorm beds are in triples and it has other options starting at Y15.

Tōnglìdá Bīnguǎn (☎ 518 7787, *Huancheng Donglu*) Beds with shared bath Y25-30, doubles with private bath Y70. This is a better option than the Gōnglù Zhāodàisuǒ; the beds are in spartan but OK doubles, the shared showers and toilets are clean and hot water is available all day. The

rooms on the 4th floor are the best. Fine double rooms are worth it for two people. The only downside is it can be noisy.

Línyè Dàshà (*Forestry Building;* ☎ 51(4057, *Huancheng Donglu*) Triples Y40(doubles with bath Y70-100. This new hote offers bright and clean doubles and excel lent triples on the fourth floor. There's clean shared bathroom down the corridor.

Téngyún Bīnguǎn (*Yingjiang Xilu*) Dorn beds Y10, singles/doubles with private batl Y40/60, doubles with shared bath Y25 Close to the town centre, this hotel is wel into the process of dilapidation, but still ha beds in pleasant, old wooden buildings, an more expensive rooms in the (somewhat newer wing. The showers are a bit grim.

Fúzhuāngchǎng Zhāodàisuǒ (*Fengshar Lu*) Beds Y12. The very basic rooms her are divided only by a wooden partition bu the beds are cheap and there's a share wash area.

Téngchōng Bīnguǎn (☎ 518 1044 *Huancheng Nanlu*) Dorm beds Y30 singles/doubles with bath Y128/160. Thi sprawling hotel is in a quiet location though far from the bus station (take a tax for Y5). The beds are in clean, carpete dorms, though the shared bathrooms aren' up to much and the showers are a hik away. The rooms at the back are better. It' not exactly the Hilton – the lights in the en tire hotel dim when anyone uses the eleva tor – but it's good value. Singles/double are discounted to Y60/100.

Fèngyuán Cāntīng (*see Places to Eat* Beds Y10, doubles with bath Y50. If yo ask at this restaurant a waiter will take yo to the hotel (*zhaōdàisuǒ*) around the back Beds here are in doubles, which is probabl the best deal in town.

Places to Eat

There are scores of tiny, inviting eaterie housed in Téngchōng's wooden buildings

Ténghé Fàndiàn (*Huancheng Donglu* This is a friendly, family run place and it i convenient if you are staying in Línyè Dàshà nearby. There is an English menu of sorts.

Myanmar Teahouse Stop here, at the en trance to the Téngyún Bīnguǎn, for swee coffee, excellent samosas, Mekong whisk and the likely chance of chatting with som of Téngchōng's itinerant Burmese jew ellery peddlers. There is an English sign ou the front, and usually at least one English speaker within.

Fèngyuán Cāntīng (Laifeng Dadao) Dishes from Y10. This pleasant restaurant is set in a traditional Chinese-style courtyard. Dishes are generally cheap and the atmosphere and service is great.

Getting There & Away

Téngchōng's long-distance bus station must be the only bus station in the whole of the south-west with a board listing information in English. Ignore it – it's completely out of date, though it's a nice thought.

Buses leave hourly to Bǎoshān (Y27, five hours) until 4pm. Directly to Xiàguān (Dàlǐ) there is a bus leaving at 7am (Y70, 12 hours), though it would make sense to stay overnight in Bǎoshān.

Buses to Ruìlì run via Yíngjiāng and Zhāngfēng twice daily (Y27, six hours). Alternatively, take one of the buses that leave every 90 minutes to Yíngjiāng (Y18, four hours), stay overnight there and travel on to Ruìlì by bus the next day (four hours).

There is also a bus to Mángshì at 7.30am (Y20, five hours) and at least one sleeper to Kūnmíng in the mid-morning (Y130 to Y140, around 24 hours).

Buses to local destinations north of Téngchōng, such as Mǎzhàn, Gùdōng, Ruìdián, Diántān or Zìzhì either leave from, or pass through, Dongximen Jie in the north-eastern part of town.

Getting Around

Téngchōng is small enough to walk around, but a bicycle would be useful for getting to some of the closer sights outside town – the surrounding scenery alone justifies a ride. There is a bicycle shop at 79 Guanghua Lu that rents bikes for Y1 per hour, with a deposit of Y100. There's a sign in fractured English out the front, but just look for a mass of bicycles parked in front of a yellow wooden building. It's normally open from 8am to 10pm daily.

AROUND TÉNGCHŌNG

There's a lot to see around Téngchōng but, as in Bǎoshān, getting out to the sights is a bit tricky. Catching buses part of the way and hiking up to the sights is one possibility, while some of the closer attractions can be reached by bicycle.

Your other option is a hired van, which may be affordable if there are several of you. Head down to the minibus stand just off the northern end of Dongximen Jie or where minibuses, in the south-western part of town, leave for the Sea of Heat and where van drivers often wait for business to walk their way.

Some highlights of the region are the traditional villages that are scattered between Téngchōng and Yùnfēng Shān. The relatively plentiful public transport along this route means that you can jump on and off minibuses to go exploring as the whim takes you.

Héshùn 和顺

Just 4km south-west of town is the village of Héshùn. It has been set aside as a retirement village for overseas Chinese, but it's of more interest as a quiet, traditional Chinese village with cobbled streets. There are some great old buildings in the village, providing lots of photo opportunities. The village also has a small **museum** *(aìsìqí gǔjū)* and a famous old **library**.

You could take a minibus from the corner of Wanshou Lu and Fengshan Lu (Y1.5) or take bus No 3 that passes nearby. It's an easy bicycle ride out to the village but the ride back is an uphill slog.

Yúnfēng Shān 云蜂山
Cloudy Peak Mountain

Yúnfēng Shān *(admission Y10)*, 47km north of Téngchōng, is a Taoist mountain dotted with 17th-century temples and monastic retreats. Most people take the cable car (Y32/54 one way/return), from where it's a 20-minute walk to **Dàxióngbǎo Diàn**, a temple at the summit. **Lǚzǔ Diàn**, the temple second from the top, serves up great *vegetarian food* at lunchtime for Y6. It's a quick walk down but it can be hard on the knees.

To get to the mountain go to the Xīmén bus stand and catch a bus to Ruìdián or Diántān and get off at the turnoff to Yúnfēng (Y8). Alternatively, take a bus to Gùdōng (Y6) and then a microbus from here to the turn-off (Y2). From the turn-off you'll have to hitch, which isn't too difficult, or alternatively it's a lovely walk past the Lisu village of Heping to the pretty villages just before the mountain. Gāolígòng Shān's Reserve fills the skyline to the east.

Hiring a vehicle from Téngchōng to take you on a return trip will cost about Y300.

Volcanoes

Téngchōng county is renowned for its volcanoes, and although they have been behaving themselves for many centuries the seismic and geothermal activity in the area indicates that they won't always continue to do so. The closest one to town is **Mǎ'ān Shān** *(Saddle Mountain)*, around 5km to the north-west. It's just south of the main road to Yíngjiāng.

Around 22km to the north of town, near the village of Mǎzhàn, is the most accessible cluster of volcanoes *(admission Y20)*; the main central volcano is known as **Dàkòng Shān** *(Big Empty Hill)*, which pretty much sums it up, and to the left of it is the black crater of **Hēikòng Shān**. You can haul yourself up the steps for views of the surrounding lava fields (long dormant).

Minibuses run frequently to Mǎzhàn (Y5) from along Dongximen Jie, or take a Gùdōng-bound minibus. From Mǎzhàn town it's a 10-minute walk or take a motortricycle (Y5) to the volcano area. Alternatively, hire a van to take you there and back from Téngchōng for around Y150.

Sea of Heat 热海
Rè Hǎi

Rè Hǎi *(admission Y20 plus Y10 pool access)* is a cluster of hot springs, geysers and streams around 12km south-west of Téngchōng. In addition to the usual indoor baths, there is an outdoor hot spring and a nice warm-water swimming pool.

The site is a popular local resort and there are several hotels:

Rehai Grand Hotel (Rèhǎi Dàjiǔdiàn; ☎ *515 0366)* Main-/old-block doubles Y220/70. This three-star resort has its own swimming pool. The cheaper rooms are in the springs complex. *Mínzhū Dàjiǔdiàn* at the other end of the springs is similarly priced.

Jiāotōng Bīnguǎn Doubles Y100. To find this hotel, which is outside the main entrance, take the path up the hill to the left of the main gate.

Microbuses leave for the hot springs when full from the Huancheng Nanlu turnoff in the south of town. You can organise a van to the hot springs for around Y5 per person or Y25 for a whole van if you bargain.

Déhóng Prefecture

Déhóng Prefecture (Déhóng Lìsù) and Jǐngpō Autonomous Prefecture, like Xīshuāngbǎnnà, borders Myanmar and is heavily populated by distinctive minority groups, but hasn't captured travellers' imaginations as 'Bǎnnà' has. It's in the far west of Yúnnán and is definitely more off-the-beaten track than Xīshuāngbǎnnà.

Most Chinese tourists in Déhóng are here for the trade from Myanmar that comes through the towns of Ruìlì and Wǎndīng – Burmese jade is a popular commodity and countless other items are spirited over the border. The border with Myanmar is punctuated by many crossings, some of them almost imperceptible, so be careful if you go wandering too close.

The most obvious minority groups in Déhóng are the Burmese (normally dressed in their traditional sarong-like *longyi*), Dai and Jingpo (known in Myanmar as the Kachin, a minority long engaged in armed struggle against the Myanmar government). For information on etiquette for visiting temples in the region see the boxed text 'Etiquette in Dai Temples' in the Xīshuāngbǎnnà section earlier.

Throughout Déhóng there are signs in Chinese, Burmese, Dai and English. This is a border region getting rich on trade – in the markets you can see Indian jewellery, tinned fruits from Thailand, Burmese papier-mache furniture, young bloods with wads of foreign currency, and Chinese plain-clothes police.

MÁNGSHÌ (LÙXĪ) 芒市
☎ 0692

Mángshì is Déhóng's air link with the outside world. If you fly in from Kūnmíng there are minibuses running direct from the airport to Ruìlì and most people take this option. But Mángshì has a casual South-East Asian feel to it and there are a few sights in and around the town that make dallying here a day or so worthwhile.

Things to See

It's interesting just to take a wander round. There are a couple of markets in town and a number of temples in the vicinity of

Mángshì Bīnguǎn, including **Pútí Sì** (ad-mission Y2), **Wǔyún Sì** (Five Clouds Tem-ple) and **Fóguāng Sì**.

Halfway along Youyi Lu, tucked down a side street is the 200-year-old **Shùbāo Tǎ** (Embracing Tree Pagoda; admission Y2), so named because over the years it has fused with the surrounding tree. It's only worth a look from a distance, otherwise you'll be hit with an 'entrance' ticket.

Not far from the southern bus station is the **Nationalities Cultural Palace** (Mínzú

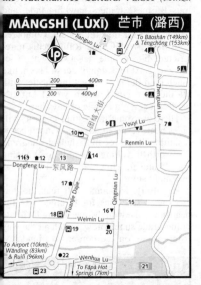

Wénhuà Gōng; Qingnian Lu; admission Y3), which is more like a large park/plaza full of elderly Chinese practising their tai chi. There are a few small exhibits on na-tionalities and a couple of reconstructed Dai buildings.

Around 7km south of town are the **Fǎpà Hot Springs** (Fǎpà Wēnquán), which get good reports from travellers.

Places to Stay & Eat

Mángshì Bīnguǎn (Zhenguan Lu) Doubles/triples with bath per person Y45/35, main-block doubles Y120-180. This is the most popular place to stay and it is peaceful, friendly and very well run. Rooms have TV and fan and are an excellent deal. There is a nice sitting area and surrounding gardens though lower-floor rooms are a little damp. It is set back a bit off the road (you have to go under a gate of sorts). To get here from the main road, head south down a bizarre-looking block completely redone in Miami Beach Art Deco pastels.

Nánjiāng Fàndiàn (☎ 212 1641, Tuanjie Dajie) Dorm beds Y20, doubles/triples from Y80/90. Situated on the main road, this place is nothing to rave about, but it's conveniently located if you're catching an early bus or booking plane tickets.

Mángshì Tángchǎng Dàjiǔjiā (cnr Weimin Lu & Qingnian Lu) Doubles with shared/private bath Y20/50. Good rooms and clean bathrooms make this place worth trying.

MÁNGSHÌ (LÙXĪ)

PLACES TO STAY & EAT
1 Jiànguó Fàndiàn
   建国饭店
7 Mángshì Bīnguǎn
   芒市宾馆
8 Měngzì Chuántǒng
   Guòqiáo Mǐxiàn
   蒙自传统过桥米线
12 Tàifēng Bīnguǎn
   泰丰宾馆
16 Restaurants
   餐厅
17 Nánjiāng Fàndiàn
   南疆饭店
20 Mángshì Tángchǎng
   Dàjiǔjiā
   芒市糖厂大酒家

OTHER
2 Market
   市场
3 Long-Distance
   Bus Station
   客运中心
4 Wǔyún Sì
   五云寺
5 Fóguāng Sì
   佛光寺
6 Pútí Sì
   菩提寺
9 Shùbāo Tǎ
   树包塔
10 Post Office
   邮局
11 Bank of China
   中国银行

13 Market
   市场
14 Minorities'
   Monument
15 Fruit market
   水果市场
18 Private Bus Station
   私人汽车站
19 Southern Bus Station
   客运南站
21 Nationalities
   Cultural Palace
   民族文化宫
22 Yunnan Airlines
   云南航空公司
23 Buses to Wǎndīng
   & Ruìlì
   到畹町和瑞
   丽的汽车

Jiànguó Fàndiàn (☎ 212 5642, Jianguo Lu) Doubles with bath Y80-140, triples with shared bath Y60. This is a comfortable place but it's a bit far from anywhere, on the north-eastern edge of town.

Tàifēng Bīnguǎn (☎ 211 5328, Dongfeng Lu) Doubles Y280. The rooms here can be discounted by 60%, making this a comfortable mid-range alternative.

Měngzì Chuántǒng Guòqiáo Mǐxiàn (Mengzi Traditional Across-the-Bridge Noodles; Youyi Lu) Noodles Y5-20. This is a basic but friendly place; for Y15 you get a huge bowl of noodles plus a side dish of herb-infused chicken.

There are several *point-and-choose restaurants* along Qingnian Lu, as well as a fruit market.

Getting There & Away

Air There are daily flights between Mángshì and Kūnmíng for Y530. Buses sometimes leave from Mángshì airport to the town centre 10kms away (Y2) but you might have no choice but to negotiate with the taxi sharks at the airport. The taxi fare into town should cost Y10, though many will try for Y20. A fleet of minibuses to Ruìlì (Y30, two hours) awaits incoming flights.

Buses leave the Mángshì Yunnan Airlines office for the airport around an hour before flight departures. It is possible to book or reconfirm flights here, or you could wait until you get to Ruìlì. The office is open 8.30am to 11.30am and 2pm to 5.30pm Monday to Friday.

Bus Mángshì has several private bus stations. The southern bus station is the most useful, though there are also plenty of departures from the long-distance bus station in the northern part of town. A bus stand a block south-west of the main bus stand has the most frequent departures to Wǎndīng (Y15) and Ruìlì (Y20). Minibuses leave when full so be prepared to wait.

The long-distance bus station has scheduled departures to Téngchōng (Y22, four hours) at 8am and 1pm and to Bǎoshān (Y25, five hours) at 7am, 8.30am and 9.30am. There are sleeper buses to Xiàguān (Y80, 12 hours) at 8pm and Kūnmíng (Y110, 20 hours) at 10.30am, 12.30pm and 6.30pm.

The southern and long-distance bus stations offer similar destinations and prices. If you don't find your bus at one, trudge to the other.

RUÌLÌ 瑞丽
☎ 0692

Ruìlì is without a doubt one of the more interesting towns in south-western China. It's just a few kilometres from Myanmar and it has a real border-town feel. There's a great mix of Han Chinese, minorities and ubiquitous Burmese traders hawking jade, and travellers tend to linger longer than they intended, just for the atmosphere. Compared with the rest of China, Ruìlì seems unrestricted, like people get away with a lot more here. At first sight it doesn't seem like much (and the place is getting dustier with all the new construction work) but it's worth spending a couple of days here.

There are some interesting minority villages nearby; the stupas are in much better condition than those in Xīshuāngbǎnnà, and it's worth travelling onwards to Wǎndīng and Mángshì, either as day trips or as overnight stops.

Hopefully, Myanmar will relax border-crossing restrictions for foreigners in the near future. New highways laid to facilitate border trade should now stretch all the way from Jiěgào, on the border, to Mandalay.

making what had been a horrible five-day journey much more sane. Chinese tour groups are already visiting north Myanmar and Ruìlì's travel agencies offer tantalising information on the sights. Soon, foreign travellers may be able to recreate the 'Southern Silk Route', of which Ruìlì and Mandalay were a part.

Information

The shop next to the reception area of Ruìlì Bīnguǎn has maps and a few brochures on Ruìlì, as does the travel agency next to Yǒngchāng Dàjiǔdiàn. The Xinhua Bookshop sells the useful *Ruili Tour Traffic Map,* published by the Ruili Tourism Bureau.

At the corner of Minzi Lu and Renmin Lu you'll find the post and telephone office, where you can make direct-dial international calls. Just around the corner, you can get Internet access at a China Telecom business centre. Access is pricey at Y18 per hour but this rate should fall over time. The office is open from 8am to 6pm Monday to Friday.

The speedy and efficient Bank of China is on Nanmao Jie. In case you're headed to Myanmar, the bank will let you cash travellers cheques for US dollars, which should come in handy across the border. The 2nd floor of the new Industrial & Commercial Bank of China (ICBC) will change cash and travellers cheques but cannot give cash advances on credit cards. Opening hours are

8am to 11.30am and 2.30pm to 5.30pm Monday to Friday.

The PSB is just up the road from Ruìlì Bīnguǎn.

Dangers & Annoyances You'll hear incessantly of Ruìlì's image problems, for which there is some empirical evidence. The town's pubs and discos – many simply fronts for an enormous prostitution industry – have always had a rough reputation. And though most of the populace are simple traders, a significant share of the local commerce is of the poppy-derived variety, Ruìlì being an entry point for Burmese opium headed to Hong Kong. This has resulted in a serious IV drug use problem in the Déhóng region, along with its pernicious sibling – HIV. The province, with Běijīng's help, has poured millions of yuán into anti-drug efforts along the border with Myanmar.

Myanmar Border Crossing The border crossing between China and Myanmar is open to travellers carrying permits for the region north of Lashio, though you can only legally cross the border in one direction – from Ruìlì into Myanmar via Mu-se in the northern Shan State. This only seems possible if you book a visa-and-transport package from Chinese travel agencies in Kūnmíng. Once across the border at Mu-se, you can continue on to Lashio on a good road, and farther south to Mandalay, Yangon and so on.

RUÌLÌ

PLACES TO STAY
- 2 Ruìlì Bīnguǎn
  瑞丽宾馆
- 11 Nányáng Bīnguǎn
  南洋宾馆
- 13 Yǒngchāng Dàjiǔdiàn
  永昌大酒店
- 20 Lìmín Bīnguǎn
  利民宾馆
- 22 Kaitong
  International Hotel
  凯通国际大酒店

PLACES TO EAT
- 5 Burmese & Cantonese
  Restaurants
  缅甸餐厅
  广东餐厅
- 6 Buffet Restaurants
  餐厅

- 10 Night Food Market
  夜市场
- 12 Jo Jo's Cold
  Drinks Shop
  觉觉冷饮店
- 19 Shěn Yāzi
  沈鸭子

OTHER
- 1 PSB
  公安局
- 3 Buses to Zhāngfèng
  往章凤的汽车
- 4 Jade Market
  珠宝街
- 7 Bank of China
  中国银行
- 8 Minibus Stand
  中巴车站

- 9 Long-Distance
  Bus Station
  长途汽车站
- 14 Yunnan Airlines
  云南航空公司
- 15 China Telecom
  Business Centre
  (Internet)
  电信营业厅
  (网吧)
- 16 Post and
  Telephone Office
  邮电大楼
- 17 Xinhua Bookshop
  新华书店
- 18 ICBC
- 21 Hospital
  医院
- 23 Market
  市场

Things to See

There is really not a lot to see in Ruìlì itself, although it's a great town to wander around, and is small enough that you can cover most of it in an hour or so. The **market** in the west of town is the most colourful by day, especially in the morning, when the stalls are lined with Burmese smokes, tofu wrapped in banana leaves, snack stalls and charcoal sellers. At the other end of town, Ruìlì's **jade market** is worth a visit for its Burmese faces and the fascinating surrounding warren of street stalls. Most of Ruìlì's sights are outside town, and you'll need a bicycle to get out and see them.

Nobody really comes to Ruìlì for the day life, though. Ruìlì doesn't even open a drowsy eye until 10pm, at which point it transforms itself into an entirely different city. Hundreds of sidewalk restaurants spring open, casino doors swing open and Chinese tourists get taken everywhere to look at cheap jade while their friends scream into karaoke microphones. The population of Ruìlì seems to triple at night. The market just around the corner from Ruìlì Bīnguǎn is the liveliest place to hang out. All this fun madness is, over the years, lasting until later and later; it still isn't a city that never sleeps, but it's getting there.

Places to Stay

Lìmín Bīnguǎn (Nanmao Jie) Doubles with bath & air-con Y80, triples with shared bath per person Y20. This well-run establishment is currently the most popular place with travellers. The staff are good – it's one of the few places in China where your floor attendant actually stays at the desk, meaning you, for once, won't be tracking them down to get into your room. Solo travellers can normally get the doubles with bathroom for Y50.

Ruìlì Bīnguǎn (Jianshe Jie) Beds Y20, doubles with bath Y80. This place takes foreigners and has dormitory accommodation. Being a bit farther away from the main strip, it offers refuge from the blaring discos and evil roadside karaoke stands. Beds are in basic quads and doubles. Bathrooms and showers are on the 1st floor. Doubles with bathroom are sometimes discounted to Y50, which is a good deal.

Yǒngchāng Dàjiǔdiàn (☎ 414 1808) Doubles with bath Y120-168. This hotel north of Nanmao Jie attracts fewer travellers but it is a comfortable and clean place to stay. Look at a few rooms.

Nányáng Bīnguǎn (☎ 414 1768, Nanmao Jie) Doubles Y90-120, discounted to Y50-80. On the main strip, this place doesn't look like much at first but some of the rooms aren't bad. It has the pluses of 24-hour hot water and a management amenable to price negotiation.

Kaitong International Hotel (Kǎitōng Guójì Dàjiǔdiàn; ☎ 414 9528, fax 414 9526, cnr Luchuan Lu & Biancheng Lu) Doubles from Y360. This three-star monster is currently the best hotel in town, though top-end resorts are being added all the time for wealthy Chinese holiday-makers. Facilities include a snooker hall and a nice pool.

Places to Eat

Reports concerning the existence of decent curries in Ruìlì are the result perhaps of wishful embellishment, but there is some good food available. Take a stroll up the market street in the evening and check out all the **snack stands** serving everything from hotpot to won tons and seafood.

For good Burmese food, there are several **restaurants** in a small alley off Jiegang Lu. The one at the top of the north-western corner is particularly good, and sees a lot of Burmese patrons. This is also the spot to go for Thai Mekong whisky, served Thai-style with soda water and ice. There are also lots of Cantonese restaurants here.

There are a couple of good **buffet restaurants** south of here on Jiegang Lu, where you choose a selection of pre-cooked food for around Y5.

Jo Jo's Cold Drinks Shop (Juéjué Lěngyǐndiàn; cnr Nanmao Jie & Baijiang Xiang) Try this shop for nice iced coffee and fruit juice drinks, or something stronger. Burmese ales cost Y10 a pop but they are twice the strength of Chinese beers. You can also get fried noodles or other basic dishes. A proliferation of other 'beer/coffee/tea/ice cream/juice' places – many actually incorporate all those in their names – have cropped up along the main and side drags.

Shěn Yāzi (cnr Nanmao Jie & Renmin Lu) For something different try the house speciality, roast duck (kǎoyā). A whole duck costs Y30 (Y15 for a half portion) which comes with hoisin sauce and shallots.

There is also a full menu of other cheap dishes. The outdoor seating is very pleasant.

Take the opportunity to try freshly squeezed lime juice from one of the numerous stands dotting the town. At Y5 a glass it costs a bit more than your average drink, but the taste is superb.

Entertainment

Ruìlì may only be a small town, but by Chinese standards it packs a lot of punch on the entertainment level. For the Chinese, Ruìlì has a reputation as one of *the* happening places in Yúnnán, and young people with money head down here just for a few nights out. But where discos used to be the venue of choice, now massage parlours have taken over. Prostitution is rampant in Ruìlì, and it's difficult to find a sleaze-free bar or dance hall. This is, of course, still China, and things are much tamer than Bangkok or Manila. Everything closes down around 1am to 2am, and you needn't worry about being flagged down in the street by pimps. Still, be aware if you get adventurous and duck into a dark bar for a drink.

The discos are still in action, although they tend to slow down even earlier, around midnight on a slow night. There is also a dance hall opposite the Burmese restaurants on Renmin Jie that has a live band playing most nights. There is usually an entrance fee of Y20 or so, depending on where you go, but it's worth it for an insight into China's jiving nightspots.

Getting There & Away

Air Ruìlì has daily flight connections to Kūnmíng via Mángshì, which is a two-hour drive away. See the Mángshì entry for details. Yunnan Airlines (☎ 414 8275) has an office next to Yǒngchāng Dàjiǔdiàn. Minibuses leave daily for the two-hour trip to the airport; check that day's flight schedule to see what time the buses leave. You can also use the ticket office to book and reconfirm return flights – do so early as this is an increasingly popular flight.

Bus It's still a long haul to Kūnmíng by bus. Sleeper buses to Kūnmíng (Y103, 24 hours, God willing) leave from the long-distance bus station 11 times daily from 6.20am to 4pm. Sleeper buses to Xiàguān (Dàlǐ) leave at 4pm, 6pm and 7pm (Y80, 10 hours).

There are eight buses to Bǎoshān between 6.30am and noon (Y40, sleeper Y50, eight hours). Work is progressing on a new highway linking Ruìlì and Bǎoshān.

Buses for Téngchōng leave twice daily at 6.30am and 7am (Y30, six hours). There are hourly buses for Yíngjiāng via Zhāngfēng (Lóngchuān) between 8am and 2.30pm (Y21, five hours on a good day). A new road is being built.

Buses leave for Mángshì frequently between 8am and 3pm from a driveway just east of the long-distance bus station (Y15 to Y20, two hours). Private entrepreneurs advertise destinations from just a few steps to the west of the bus station's ticket window, so check the signs for more convenient departures or prices.

If you're in the mood to rough it, private sleeper buses leave for Jǐnghóng in Xīshuāngbǎnnà at 6.30am and arrive sometime in the afternoon of the third day.

Minibuses and vans leave for more local destinations from opposite the long-distance bus station. Destinations include Wǎndīng (Y15, one hour), the border checkpoint at Jiěgào (Y4), and the village of Nóngdǎo (Y8). Buses to Zhāngfēng (Y10, one hour) leave from Xinjian Lu.

Getting Around

Ruìlì is easily seen on foot, but all the most interesting day trips require a bicycle. Lìmín Bīnguǎn rents bikes for Y10, with a Y200 deposit if you aren't staying at the hotel.

A flat rate for a taxi ride inside the city should be Y5, and up for negotiation from there. There are also cheaper motor and cycle rickshaws.

AROUND RUÌLÌ

Most of the sights around Ruìlì can be explored easily by bicycle. It's worth making frequent detours down the narrow paths leading off the main roads to visit minority villages. The people are friendly, and there are lots of photo opportunities. The *Ruili Tour Traffic Map* published by the Ruili Tourism Bureau shows the major roads and villages.

The shortest ride is to turn left at the corner north of the post office and continue out of the town proper into the little village of Měngmǎo. There are half a dozen Shan temples scattered about; the fun is in finding them.

Nóng'ān Jīnyā Tǎ 弄安金鸭塔
Golden Duck Pagoda
A short ride south-west of town, on the main road, Jīnyā Tǎ is an attractive stupa set in a temple courtyard. It was established to mark the arrival of a pair of golden ducks that brought good fortune to what was previously an uninhabited marshy area.

Jiěgào Border Checkpoint 姐告边检点
Continue straight ahead from Nóng'ān Jīnyā Tǎ, cross the Myanmar bridge over Ruìlì Jiāng and you will come to Jiěgào, about 7km from Ruìlì. It's a little thumb of land jutting into Myanmar that serves as the main checkpoint for a steady stream of cross-border traffic (see the Myanmar Border Crossing section earlier for more details). There's not a lot to see but you can still marvel at how laid-back everything seems on both sides of the – quite literally – bamboo curtain and indulge the perennial fascination with illicit borders. Wildly popular casinos and other dens of iniquity line the streets of both sides of the border, and in one case apparently right on the border.

Microbuses shuttle between the border and Ruìlì's long-distance bus station when full for Y4 or you can charter one for around Y20. Buses continue until late at night.

Temples
Just past Nóng'ān Jīnyā Tǎ is a crossroad and a small wooden temple. The road to the right (west) leads to the villages of Jiěxiàng and Nóngdǎo, and on the way are a number of small temples, villages and stupas. None is spectacular but the village life is interesting and there are often small markets near the temples.

The first major Dai temple is **Hánshā Zhuāng Sì**, a fine wooden structure with a few resident monks. It's set a little off the

road and a green tourism sign marks the turn-off. The surrounding Dai village is interesting.

Another 20 minutes or so down the road, look out for a white stupa on the hillside to the right. This is **Léizhuāngxiāng**, Ruìlì's oldest stupa, dating back to the middle of the Tang dynasty. There's a nunnery in the grounds of the stupa and fantastic views of the Ruìlì area. Once the stupa comes into view, take the next path to the right that cuts through the fields. There are blue signs in Chinese and Dai pointing the way through a couple of Dai villages. When you get to market crossroads at the centre of the main village take the right path. You'll need to push your bicycle for the last ascent to the stupa. In all, it takes about 50 minutes to cycle here from Nóng'ān Jīnyā Tǎ.

About 2km past the town of Jiěxiàng is **Dēnghánnóng Zhuāng Sì**, a wooden Dai temple with pleasant surroundings. Like the other temples in the area, the effect is spoiled by the corrugated tin roof.

It's possible to cycle all the way to Nóngdǎo, around 29km south-west of Ruìlì. There's a solitary hotel in town that has cheap doubles or you can return to Ruìlì on one of the frequent minibuses.

Golden Pagoda
Jiělè Jīntǎ 姐勒金塔
A few kilometres to the east of Ruìlì on the road to Wǎndīng is the Golden Pagoda, a fine structure that dates back 200 years.

Jiědōng 姐东
Another possible cycling route takes you west of Ruìlì, past the old town of Měngmǎo, now a suburb of Ruìlì. After 4km, just past the village of Jiědōng, a turn-off north leads to Bàngmǎhè village, a Jingpo settlement with a small waterfall nearby.

Sìchuān 四川

Capital: Chéngdū
Population: 109 million
Area: 488,000 sq km

The Chinese often refer to Sìchuān as the Heavenly Kingdom (Tiānfǔ Zhīguó), a reference to the province's abundance in natural resources and cultural heritage. Its name, 'Four Rivers', refers to four of the more than 80 mighty rivers spilling across the province, weaving their way down through the soaring mountains of the north-west and across the Chuānxī plain in the east.

Sìchuān is the largest province in the south-west, with a population displaying as much diversity as its landscape. While the east supports one of the densest rural populations in the world, the west rises in giant steps to the Tibetan plateau, where green tea becomes butter tea and Confucianism yields to Buddhism. These windswept grasslands and deep forests are home to the Qiang and Tibetans.

Sìchuān's mountainous terrain and fast rivers have kept it relatively isolated until the present era, with much of the western fringe still fairly remote. Such inaccessibility has given Sìchuān its own food, dialect and character and made it the site of various breakaway kingdoms throughout Chinese history. It was here that the Kingdom of Shu ruled as an independent state during the Three Kingdoms Period (AD 220–80) and the Kuomintang Party spent its last days before being vanquished and fleeing to Taiwan. The latest breakaway region is Chóngqìng, which split from Sìchuān in March 1997.

Sìchuān became famous during the Warring States period (475–221 BC), when a famed engineer, Li Bing, managed to harness Dū Hé on the Chūanxī plain with his weir system, allowing Sìchuān some 2200 continuous years of irrigation and prosperity.

Today the province continues to get rich, having played an active role in China's labouring economic reforms – most specifically as the site where the Communist Party first instituted its pioneering agricultural reforms. Plots of land were let out to individual farmers on the condition that a portion of the crops be sold back to the government. By 1984 this 'responsibility

Highlights

- Chéngdū, with fantastic backstreets, great teahouses, Sichuan opera and giant pandas

- Jiǔzhàigōu, a national park set in pristine alpine scenery with brightly coloured lakes

- Western Sìchuān, with soaring snow-capped peaks, grasslands, glaciers and a heavy Tibetan influence

- Grand Buddha, the world's largest Buddha statue, sitting in splendour across from the city of Lèshān

- Éméi Shān, one of China's four Buddhist sacred mountains, great for hiking and monastery-hopping

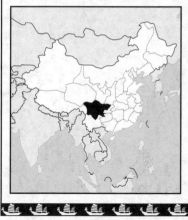

system' had spread throughout China and was later applied to the industrial sector.

While the fruits of these economic reforms are clearly evident in Chéngdū, one of the most prosperous, liberal and fashionable cities in the region, a less fortunate result has been soaring unemployment. With downsized bureaucracies, Sìchuān has the lion's share of China's 130 million-strong 'surplus labour force'.

Worlds away from the scenes of urban renewal and economic reform, the remote mountains of Sìchuān, bordering Gānsù and Qīnghǎi provinces, are the natural habitat of the giant panda. This shy animal is the one

SÌCHUĀN 四川

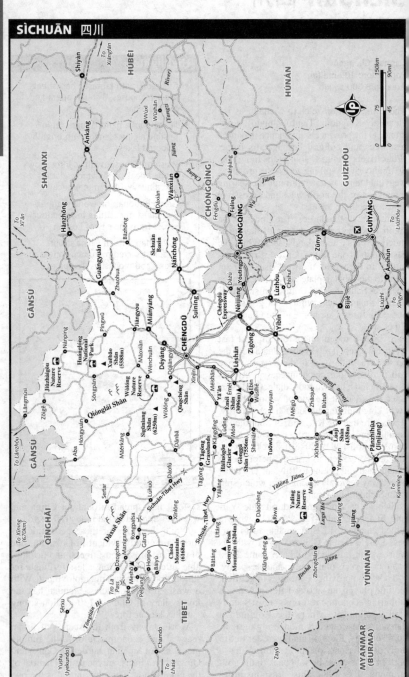

that Westerners are quick to associate with China, landing it a new job as 'little ambassador' for the Chinese government.

CHÉNGDŪ 成都

☎ 028 • pop 11.3 million z elevation 500m

For a capital city, Chéngdū is a manageable size and its abundance of greenery makes it an enjoyable place to wander on foot.

There are still many miles of bustling side streets to explore, where you'll stumble upon markets, commercial districts, underground shopping malls, countless tiny restaurants specialising in Sìchuān snacks, and old men walking their song birds or huddled over a game of go. You'll also encounter the city's artisans: small-time basket-weavers, cobblers, itinerant dentists, tailors, houseware merchants and snack hawkers who swarm the streets and contribute to Chéngdū's lively atmosphere. All up, you're looking at one of China's more intriguing cities.

Chéngdū also abounds with newfound affluence and is bent on modernising. Many of the city's older wooden buildings have been pushed aside and replaced with trendy, opulent department stores and high-rise commercial and residential blocks. This may well be a positive change for residents who associate the older buildings with the poverty of generations past and, despite the transformation, the city has surprisingly managed to retain much of its charm.

History

Built in 316 BC during the late Warring States period, when the Dūjiāngyàn dam and irrigation system was put into place, Chéngdū boasts a 2300-year history which is linked closely with the arts and crafts trades.

Running through Chéngdū is Jǐn Jiāng (Brocade River), a reminder of the city's silk brocade industry which thrived during the Eastern Han dynasty (AD 25–220). The city's name eventually shifted from Jǐnchéng (Brocade City) to 'Lotus City', still used today by locals. The name 'Chéngdū' means Perfect Metropolis and by the time of the Tang dynasty (AD 618–907) the city had become a cornerstone of Chinese society. Three hundred years later, during the Song dynasty, Chéngdū began to issue the world's first paper money.

Like other major Chinese cities, it has had its share of turmoil. First, it was devastated

Streetwise

Chéngdū is a true Asian city in its nonchalant disregard of systematic street numbering and naming. It's not unusual, when following street numbers in one direction, to meet another set coming the other way, leaving some places with five sets of numbers on their doors. Street names, also, seem to change every 100m or so – with very little apparent logic involved. Try to bear this in mind when you're looking for somewhere in particular, and rely more on nearby landmarks and relative locations on maps than on street numbers and names.

by the Mongols in retaliation for the fierce resistance put up by the Sichuanese. From 1644 to 1647 it was presided over by the rebel Zhang Xiangzhong, who set up an independent state in Sìchuān, ruling by terror and mass executions. Three centuries later the city became one of the last strongholds of the Kuomintang.

The original city was walled and surrounded with a moat. Gates were built at the four compass points with the Viceroy's Palace (14th century) at the city's heart. The remains of the city walls were demolished in the early 1960s and the Viceroy's Palace was blown up at the height of the Cultural Revolution. In its place was erected the Russian-style Sichuan Exhibition Centre with a massive Mao statue outside, waving merrily down Renmin Nanlu.

Orientation

Ring roads circle the outer city: Yihuan Lu (First Ring Rd), Erhuan Lu (Second Ring Rd) and Sanhuan Lu (Third Ring Rd). These are divided into numbered segments (duàn). The main boulevard that sweeps through the centre of everything is Renmin Lu – in its north (běi), central (zhōng) and south (nán) manifestations.

The nucleus of the city is the square that interrupts Renmin Lu, with administrative buildings, the Sichuan Exhibition Centre, a sports stadium and the colossal Mao.

The area where Renmin Nanlu crosses Jǐn Jiāng has become the city's backpacker ghetto. This is where you'll find many of the Western-style restaurants and coffee shops and, just south of here down Renmin Nanlu, a multiplying number of bars.

CHÉNGDŪ 城都

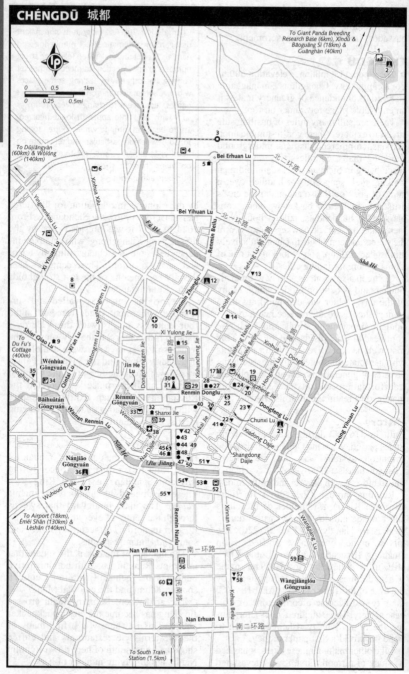

To Giant Panda Breeding
Research Base (6km), Xīndū &
Bǎoguāng Sì (18km) &
Guǎnghàn (40km)

To Dūjiāngyàn
(60km) & Wòlóng
(140km)

Bei Erhuan Lu 北二环路

Bei Yihuan Lu 北一环路

Yingmenkou Lu

Xinhua Xilu

Fǎ Hé

Xi Yihuan Lu

Jiefang Lu – 解放路

Renmin Beilu

Renmin Zhonglu

Caoshi Jie

Shà Hé

Shier Qiao Lu

To
Du Fu's
Cottage
(400m)

Qinghua Jie

Kuan Jie

Xiatongren Lu

Shaotongren Lu

Dongchengen Jie

Xi Yulong Jie

Jin He
Lu

Xishuncheng Jie

Taicheng Nanlu

Shuwa Beijie

Xinhua

Dong Yihuan Lu

Dongfeng Lu

Hongxing Lu

Dونglu

Huanwangcheng Lu

Wénhuà
Gōngyuán

Báihuātán
Gōngyuán

Rénmín
Gōngyuán

Renmin Donglu

Chunxi Lu

Xiadong Dajie

Shangdong
Dajie

Nánjiāo
Gōngyuán

Wenmiaohou Jie

Nán Dàjiē

Nan He

Jin Jiāng (Jīn Jiāng)

Wainan Renmin Lu

Wuhouci Dajie

Xinnan Lu

Renmin Nanlu

Jiangui Jie

Ximian Qiao Jie

To Airport (18km),
Éméi Shān (130km) &
Lèshān (140km)

Wangjiang Lu

Wàngjiānglóu
Gōngyuán

Nan Yihuan Lu 南一环路

Kehua Beilu

Nan Erhuan Lu 南二环路

To South Train
Station (1.5km)

CHÉNGDŪ

PLACES TO STAY

5　Chéngdū Dàjiǔdiàn
　成都大酒店
9　Chéngdū Bǎoyuán
　Táng Jiǔlóu; Chengdu
　College of Traditional
　Medicine Guesthouse
　成都保元堂酒楼; 成都
　中医药大学招待所
14　Jīndì Fàndiàn
　金地饭店
15　Sheraton Chengdu
　Lido Hotel
　天府丽都喜
　来登饭店
24　Holiday Inn Crowne
　Plaza; Sìchuān Bīnguǎn;
　Dragon Air
　总府皇冠假日酒店
28　Yinhe Dynasty Hotel
　银河王朝大酒店
32　Sam's Guesthouse;
　Róngchéng Fàndiàn
　蓉城饭店
46　Jǐnjiāng Bīnguǎn
　锦江宾馆
48　Mínshān Fàndiàn
　岷山饭店
53　Traffic Hotel
　交通饭店

PLACES TO EAT

13　Chén Mápó Dòufu
　陈麻婆豆腐
20　Shìměixuān Cāntīng
　市美轩餐厅
22　Lóngchāoshǒu
　Cāntīng
　龙抄手餐厅
23　Shìqiáo Shǒu Miàn
26　Chéngdū Cāntīng
　成都餐厅
35　Chén Mápó Dòufu
　陈麻婆豆腐
42　Hotpot Restaurants
　火锅
50　Bean's Cafe
51　Paul's Oasis
54　Carol's by the River
　卡罗西餐

55　Highfly Cafe
　高飞咖啡
57　Red Brick Cafe Pub &
　Pizzeria
　红砖西餐厅
58　Grandma's Kitchen
　祖母的厨房
61　Bǎguó Bùyī
　Fēngwèijiǔbù;
　Grandma's Sunflower
　Cafe
　巴国布衣风味酒部

OTHER

1　Chengdu Zoo
　成都动物园
2　Zhàojué Sì
　照觉寺
3　North Train Station
　火车北站
4　North Bus Station
　城北汽车客运中心
6　General Post
　Office/EMS
　市邮电局
7　Xīmén Bus Station
　西门汽车站
8　Tomb of Wang Jian
　王建墓
10　No 3 Hospital
　三医院
11　PSB
　公安局
12　Wénshū Temple
　文殊院
16　Municipal Sports
　Stadium
　市体育场
17　Cultural Palace
　文化宫
18　Main Post Office
　市电信局
19　Jǐnjiāng Theatre
　锦江剧场
21　Dàcí Sì
　大慈寺
25　Bank of China
　银行大厦
27　PICC Office
　中国人民保险公司

29　Telecommunications
　Business Centre
　电话电报大楼
30　Sichuan Exhibition
　Centre
　省展览馆
31　Mao Statue
　毛主席像
33　Post Office
　邮电局
34　Green Ram Temple
　青羊宫
36　Wǔhóu Temple
　武侯祠南郊公园
37　Tibetan Shops
　西藏专卖店
38　PSB (Foreign Affairs
　Section)
　省公安局外事科
39　Internet Cafes
　网吧
40　Advance Rail Booking
　Office
　火车站售票处
41　South-West Book
　Centre
　西南书城
43　Sichuan Airlines
　四川航空公司
44　China Southwest
　Airlines
　中国西南航空公司
45　Bank of China
　中国银行
47　CAAC; CITS
　中国民航;
　中国国际旅行社
49　Qīngshíqiáo Market
　青石桥市场
52　Xīnnánmén Bus Station
　新南门汽车站
56　Sichuan Provincial
　Museum
　省博物馆
59　Sichuan University
　Museum
　四大博物馆
60　Wild Goose Cafe;
　Seventh Sensation;
　Twelve Oaks

Maps The most useful map for foreigners is the English-language *Chengdu – the Latest Tourist Map*. Unfortunately it's not quite as recent as it claims.

City maps in Chinese can be found at train and bus stations, the Traffic Hotel, and the South West Book Centre and can be useful for tracing bus routes even if you can't read Chinese, though not even the best ones can hope to fully capture the insanity that is Chéngdū's street naming. Chinese maps also provide excellent detail of Sìchuān province and Chéngdū's surrounding areas.

Information

Tourist Offices Unless you're interested in joining a local or Tibet-bound tour group, there's no real point in bothering with China International Travel Service (CITS; Zhōngguó Guójì Lǚxíngshè). The main office (☎ 665 8731, e citsfit@sc.homeway .com.cn), on Renmin Nanlu, is open 8.30am to 5pm daily. Staff here are friendly enough but they can't book train tickets and don't have much information beyond their own tours.

More useful are the travel agencies in and around the Traffic Hotel (see Travel Agencies later in this section). Sam Yue of Sam's Guesthouse is also a great source of information on travel around Sìchuān.

Money Many of Chéngdū's hotels have foreign-exchange counters, although they aren't likely to offer the best rates. There are two useful branches of the Bank of China: one on Renmin Nanlu, and the other at the eastern end of Renmin Donglu. Both change money painlessly, have ATMs and offers cash advances on a credit cards. Banking hours are 8.30am to 11.30am and 2.30pm to 5pm Monday to Friday.

Post & Communications China Post's main office is on the corner of Huaxingzheng Jie and Shuwa Beijie, close to the Cultural Palace in the centre of town. It's open 8.30am to 6pm daily.

Numerous other little post offices are scattered throughout the city centre. For poste restante you will need to go to the general post office (the EMS building) on Shawan Lu, near the intersection of Bei Erhuan Lu. To get there, take bus No 48 from Xishuncheng Jie, east of Mao's statue.

More convenient might be the poste restante service at the Traffic Hotel, which holds letters and parcels for 15 days at the luggage-storage counter. Items should be mailed care of the Traffic Hotel, 77 Linjiang Lu, Xinnanmen, Chengdu 610041.

The best place in town for making reverse-charge (collect) calls is in the Telecommunications Business Centre (Diànxìn Shāngchéng), east of the Sichuan Exhibition Centre. You can also make direct-dial overseas calls and faxes from here. Public phones for home-country direct calls are along a wall to the left after entering.

The telecommunications service is supposed to be open 24 hours but don't count on it.

Chéngdū has countless Internet cafes offering access for Y3 per hour, some with faster servers than others. There are three offices across from Sam's Guesthouse and more around Bean's Cafe and Paul's Oasis. A number of restaurants (such as Grandma's Kitchen) also offer access although at slightly higher rates.

Travel Agencies There are several travel agencies and private entrepreneurs operating from within the compound of the Traffic Hotel and offering a wide range of useful services. A number of travellers have complained about the travel service within the hotel itself.

Commonly available tours include those to Hǎiluógōu Glacier Park, Wòlóng, Jiǔzhàigōu, Éméi Shān and Sōngpān. There are also day trips to the Giant Panda Breeding Research Centre, local operas and the Traditional Chinese Medicine Centre. Prices depend upon the number of travellers but are generally good value. Agencies can often arrange Cháng Jiāng (Yangzi River) cruise tickets, train and flight tickets and permits to Tibet.

You may also encounter Mr Lee who frequents the Rénmín Gōngyuán (People's Park) teahouse. In addition to providing free information to travellers, he can arrange tours of everything from artists' quarters to silk factories to kindergartens. For a visit to a local Sichuan opera, including a back stage tour, contact Mike (☎ 626 6510) after 8.30pm (see 'Entertainment' later in this section).

PSB The main Public Security Bureau (PSB; Gōngānjú) office is 1.5km north of the centre on Wenwu Lu, east of the intersection with Renmin Zhonglu. However, whether you're seeking visa extensions or reporting a theft, you'll probably do better at the Foreign Affairs section (☎ 630 1454), which is open 8am to 11am and 2.30pm to 5pm Monday to Friday, and 8.30am to 11am Sunday. It's a single-storey building at 40 Wenmiaohou Jie, off Nan Dajie. Some members of the staff here speak excellent English. Saturday hours here are hit-and-miss; some travellers have managed to badger guards into tracking down somebody official.

Dangers & Annoyances There have been several reports of foreigners becoming targets for rip-offs and theft in Chéngdū. In particular there have been a couple of incidents on the riverside pathway between Jǐnjiāng Bīnguǎn and the Traffic Hotel. Take care late at night – it's best not to walk alone.

To avoid being ripped off by pedicab drivers and restaurants, always get the price at the start. Check notice boards and notebooks in cafes and guesthouses for warnings from other travellers of particular tourist agencies to avoid. Pickpockets are common around bus and train stations and post offices; watch out for gangs who use razors to slit your bags on buses or crowded streets. If you want to play it safe with train tickets, make a note of the ticket numbers: if the tickets are stolen you'll be given replacements, providing you can supply the numbers of the old ones.

Wénshū Temple 文殊院
Wénshū Yuàn

Wénshū Temple (admission Y1; open 6am-8.30pm daily), a monastery which dates back to the Tang dynasty, is Chéngdū's largest and best-preserved Buddhist temple. Originally known as Xinxiang Temple, it was renamed after a Buddhist monk who lived there in the late 17th century.

Perhaps the best thing about the monastery is the bustling crowd of worshippers who flock to the place. Together with the exquisite relief carvings that decorate many of the buildings in the complex, they render the temple well worth a visit.

On the monastery grounds, check out the *teahouse*, one of the largest and most bustling in Chéngdū with what seems like acres of tables. If you want to join in, sit on the west side of the path, closest to the main temple, where tea costs Y1. The tea must be greener on the other side of the path where it costs Y10. The *vegetarian restaurant* next door to the teahouse has great food at good prices.

The alley off Renmin Zhonglu, on which Wénshū is located, is a curiosity in itself, filled with joss-stick vendors, foot-callus removers, blind fortune-tellers with bamboo spills, and flower and fireworks sellers.

Tomb of Wang Jian 王建墓
Wángjiàn Mù

In the north-west of town, the tomb of Wang Jian (admission Y3; open 8.30am-6pm daily) was, until 1942, thought to be Zhuge Liang's music pavilion (see Wǔhòu Temple in the following Temple Parks section). Wang Jian (AD 847–918) was a Tang general who established the Former Shu kingdom in the aftermath of the collapse of the Tang in 907.

The tomb in the central building is surrounded by statues of 24 musicians all playing different instruments, and is considered to be the best surviving record of a Tang dynasty musical troupe. Also featured are relics taken from the tomb itself, including a jade belt, mourning books and imperial seals.

Temple Parks

There are a couple of worthwhile temple parks in the city area.

West of the Mao statue is **Wénhuà Gōngyuán** (admission Y1.5; open 6am-8pm daily). This park is home to the **Green Ram Temple** (Qīngyáng Gōng; admission Y1; open 8am-5pm daily), the oldest and most extensive Taoist temple in the Chéngdū area. The story goes that Laotzu, the high priest of Taoism, asked a friend to meet him there. When the friend arrived he saw only a boy leading two goats on a leash – and in an impressive leap of lateral thinking realised the boy was Laotzu.

The goats are represented in bronze in the rear building on the temple grounds. If the one-horned goat looks slightly ungoat-like, it is because it combines features of all the Chinese zodiac animals. The other goat can vanquish life's troubles and pains if you stroke its flank.

In the centre of the temple grounds is an eight-sided pagoda, considered to be an architectural illustration of Taoist philosophy. There are no bolts or pegs holding the building together. Instead each piece fits into the next and the building balances as a whole.

Green Ram Temple can be combined with a visit to nearby **Du Fu's Cottage** (Dùfǔ Cǎotáng; admission grounds/cottage Y5/15; open 7am-11pm daily), erstwhile home of the celebrated Tang dynasty poet. Du Fu (AD 712–70) was born in Hénán but left his home province at the tender age of 20 to see China. After being captured by rebels following an uprising, he eventually fled to Chéngdū, where he lived for four years in a humble cottage. He penned more than 200 poems here on simple themes around the lives of the people who lived and worked nearby. From the time of his death in exile (in Húnán), Du Fu acquired a cult status, and his poems have been a major source of inspiration for many Chinese artists.

The present grounds – 20 hectares of leafy bamboo and luxuriant vegetation – are a much enlarged version of Du Fu's original poetic retreat. It's also the centre of the Chengdu Du Fu Study Society, and several halls display examples of the poet's work.

Next to **Nánjiāo Gōngyuán** (admission Y2; open 6am-10pm daily) is **Wǔhòu Temple** (Wǔhòu Cí; admission Y2; open 6.30am-10pm daily). Wǔhòu might be translated as 'Minister of War', the title given to Zhuge Liang, who was a famous military strategist of the Three Kingdoms period (AD 220–80) and immortalised in one of the classics of Chinese literature, *The Romance of the Three Kingdoms*.

Curiously, Zhuge Liang is not the main attraction of the temple. Instead, the front shrine is dedicated to Liu Bei, Zhuge Liang's emperor. Liu's temple, the Hanzhaolie Temple, was moved here and rebuilt during the Ming dynasty.

In the south-east of town, near Sichuan University, is **Wàngjiānglóu Gōngyuán** (River Viewing Pavilion Park; admission Y2; open 6am-9pm daily). The pavilion itself is a four-storey wooden Qing structure overlooking Jǐn Jiāng, and was built in memory of Xue Tao, a female Tang dynasty poet with a great love for bamboo. Nearby is a well where Xue Tao is believed to have drawn water to dye her writing paper.

The park is famous for its lush forests, boasting over 150 varieties of bamboo from China, Japan and South-East Asia. They range from bonsai-sized potted plants to towering giants, creating a shady retreat in the heat of summer and a cold, damp one in winter.

Rénmín Gōngyuán 人民公园
People's Park

To the south-west of the city centre, Rénmín Gōngyuán (admission Y2; open 6.30am-2am daily) is one Chinese park well worth visiting. The *teahouse* here is excellent (see Entertainment later in this section).

The park also holds a bonsai rockery, a playground, swimming pools, and the **Monument to the Martyrs of the Railway Protection Movement** (1911). This obelisk, decorated with shunting manoeuvres and railway tracks, marks an uprising of the people against officers who pocketed cash raised for the construction of the Chéngdū to Chóngqìng line. Since, at the time, Rénmín Gōngyuán was a private officer's garden, it was a fitting place to erect the structure.

Across the lake from the teahouse is the entry to an underground **museum/funhouse** (admission Y10) that must count as one of Chéngdū's weirder experiences. The entry fee buys you a tour through a converted air-raid shelter where, after finding your way through a maze of cafeterias and arcades, you can hop on a shuttle-train and travel through bizarre and aging scenes from the wild west, space, the dinosaur age and straight into the mouth of a shark.

Sichuan Provincial Museum
Sìchuān Shěng Bówùguǎn 四川省博物馆
This museum (admission Y10; open 9am-4pm Mon-Fri, 10am-4pm Sat & Sun) is the largest provincial museum in China's south-west, with more than 150,000 items, although not nearly that many are on display. For historians, the displays of tiled murals and frescoes taken from tombs are of great interest for their depiction of ancient daily activities. Be warned, however, that many tourists feel the admission not worth it.

The museum is down Renmin Nanlu in the direction of the south train station and within cycling distance of the city centre.

Sichuan University Museum
Sìchuān Dàxué Bówùguǎn 四川大学博物馆
Founded in 1914 by US scholar DS Dye, the Sichuan University Museum (admission Y10; open 8.30am-11.30am & 2.40pm-5.30pm Mon-Fri) underwent several closures and name changes before reopening under its current name in 1984. The four exhibition rooms display more than 40,000 items on a rotating basis; give yourself a minimum of an hour to have a look around.

The collection is particularly strong in the fields of ethnology, folklore and traditional arts. The ethnology room exhibits artefacts from the Yi, Qiang, Miao, Jingpo, Naxi and Tibetan cultures. The Chinese painting and calligraphy room displays works from the

Tang, Song, Yuan, Ming and Qing dynasties. Some exhibits have English captions.

From the university's main gate, enter and go straight until the road ends at a 'T' intersection. The museum is the first building on the right.

Chengdu Zoo 成都动物园
Chéngdū Dòngwùyuán

Although upstaged by the nearby Giant Panda Breeding Research Base, the Chengdu Zoo (admission Y3; open 7.30am-8pm daily) still has a respectable collection of six pandas. Nevertheless, Chinese zoos are generally a slightly depressing experience, and this one is no exception.

The zoo is about 6km north-east of Chéngdū city centre. Direct minibuses run here from the north train station. Cycling isn't advisable unless you don't mind arriving asphyxiated from riding along clogged motorways.

Zhàojué Sì 照觉寺
Zhàojué Sì (admission Y1; open 7am-7pm daily) is a Tang dynasty temple dating from the 7th century. During the early Qing dynasty, it underwent extensive reconstruction under the supervision of Po Shan, a famous Buddhist monk who established waterways and groves of trees around the temple. The temple has since served as a model for many Japanese and South-East Asian Buddhist temples.

The temple went through hard times during the Cultural Revolution and has only been restored during the last decade. There's a *vegetarian restaurant* on the grounds that serves lunch from 11am to 2pm and a *teahouse* next door.

Giant Panda Breeding Research Base 大熊猫繁殖研究中心
Dàxióngmāo Fánzhí Yánjiū Zhōngxīn

About 6km north of the zoo, this is a research station and breeding ground (admission Y10; open 8am-6pm daily) for giant and lesser pandas. The base has been in operation since 1990 and was first opened to the public in 1995.

About 10 to 12 giant pandas currently reside at the base, in quarters somewhat more humane than those at the zoo, although still fairly small. There is also a breeding area that has been partially opened and where

some of China's animal ambassadors are allowed to 'freely roam'. The result has been a number of baby pandas and if you visit in autumn, you may also have the opportunity to see tiny newborns in the 'nursery'.

Just past the entrance gate, the base museum has detailed exhibits on panda evolution, habits, habitats and conservation efforts, all with English captions.

Once the breeding area is completed and opened, the base will cover over 230 hectares. It's best to visit the base between 8.30am and 10am: feeding is around 9.30am and soon thereafter the pandas return to their other predominant pastime – sleeping.

Getting to the base is tricky. Cycling is not recommended, as you'll mainly be travelling along congested motorways. The base is not served by any bus routes, so your other options are to take a tour or to hire a taxi. The Traffic Hotel and Sam's Guesthouse offer tours for Y50 per person, including the entrance fee. This is cheaper than the taxi ride alone and definitely the best deal.

Places to Stay – Budget
There is some excellent, foreign-friendly budget accommodation in Chéngdū.

Many travellers head to the Chengdu College of Traditional Medicine, west of downtown, in search of a budget bed. While the ever-popular Sam's Guesthouse is no longer located here, there are two other guesthouses on the campus, although neither is particularly quiet and you'll probably need to bargain for a decent price.

Chéngdū Bǎoyuán Tāng Jiǔlóu (☎ 777 0511) Dorm beds/doubles with bath Y40/150. As you enter the college grounds off Shier Qiao Lu and walk straight up the drive, this guesthouse is on your left.

Chengdu College of Traditional Medicine Guesthouse (Chéngdū Zhōngyīyào Dàxué Zhāodàisuǒ; ☎ 775 3909) Dorm beds Y20-50, doubles 160. Take a left at Chéngdū Bǎoyuántāng Jiǔlóu and then a right. This second guesthouse is on your right. Rooms in both guesthouses are similarly bland and somewhat overpriced and dorm beds are hard to get your hands on.

Sam's Guesthouse (☎ 609 9022, e Sam tour@yahoo.com, 130 Shanxi Jie) Dorm beds Y20, doubles with bath Y80-120. Sam has moved to Róngchéng Fàndiàn where he leases a wing for Sam's Guesthouse. Clean, comfortable rooms overlook a garden and are surprisingly quiet considering the hotel is only a few steps away from the heart of downtown. Enter through the gate on the hotel's left, head into the building straight ahead and you'll find Sam's reception down the first hall on the left. You'll also find left luggage, a cafe, email, a travel service, laundry, bike rental, a book exchange and an information/notice board.

Traffic Hotel (*Jiāotōng Fàndiàn;* ☎ *555 1017, fax 558 2777, 77 Linjiang Lu)* Beds in triples Y40, doubles/triples with bath Y200/300. The Traffic Hotel has for a long time been the main hang-out for backpackers. It's clean and comfortable and has similar services to Sam's, including left luggage (Y1 per day) and a large array of tours. The cheaper rooms have satellite TV and fan, with showers and toilets down the hall. Rates

The Elusive Panda

Distributed almost entirely in the north and north-west of Sìchuān are the thousand or so giant pandas surviving in the wild. Living at high altitudes in mountainous regions, this endangered mammal is shrouded as much by mystery as by perpetual mist and cloud. Sightings are rare and our knowledge remains scant.

Some sources claim that the giant panda has existed for around 600,000 years while others date earliest remains of the panda back as far as the ice age, between one and three million years ago. Scientists have spent over a century debating whether pandas belong to the bear family, the raccoon family, or are a separate family of their own.

As good climbers and solitary animals, pandas are adept at evading observation. If you did manage to spot one in the wild, however, you'd quickly recognise it, with its black and white face having been popularised as the emblem of the World Wide Fund for Nature, as the logo on Chinese cigarettes, a common stuffed animal in zoo gift shops around the globe and once a popular present from the Chinese government to foreign governments. While Chinese literature has references to pandas (called *xióngmāo* or bear cats) going back over 3000 years, it wasn't until 1869 that the West found out about the panda, when a French missionary brought a pelt back with him to Paris. Now, in the 21st century, this stout, pigeon-toed animal is racing towards extinction.

An obvious factor in the depletion of the giant panda population is the encroachment of humans as China's massive population attempts to meet its land and resource needs. To counter this, the government has set up 11 reserves in the south-west for the panda. The Government has also attempted to deter panda hunting by imposing life sentences and public executions on convicted poachers.

Pandas are also threatened by their exclusive eating habits. They consume enormous amounts of food – up to 20kg a day each – with bamboo accounting for around 95% of their diet. They spend 10 to 16 hours a day munching on it, but will only eat around 20 of China's 300 species of bamboo. In the mid-70s more than 130 pandas starved to death when one of these favoured species flowered and withered in Mín Shān, Sìchuān.

Perhaps the greatest difficulty faced by conservationists is the panda's slow reproductive rate. Pandas remain solitary throughout the year, except during their short, three-month mating season each spring. Then pandas not only have a tricky time finding one another, they're also rather particular about who they'll mate with.

Females generally give birth to only one cub, weighing about as much as an apple. When two cubs are born, the mother tends to leave one behind or crush it in its sleep, unable to care for both. For the first month after birth, she carries the cub in one of her paws at all times, even as she sleeps and eats.

Conservationists have had low success rates with breeding pandas in captivity. Artificial insemination has even been attempted at Beijing Zoo. Chéngdū's Giant Panda Breeding Research Base has seen the birth of a number of pandas but still remains unable to multiply the population to the level hoped for.

With world attention on the survival of the panda, Chinese laws now strictly forbid locals to hunt, fell trees or make charcoal in the habitats of the panda. Peasants in these areas are offered rewards equivalent to double their annual salary if they save a starving panda. And despite a constant battle with budget deficits, China's central government maintains its funding to the Breeding Research Base, which continues in its struggle to preserve pandas and their habitats.

include breakfast. To get here from the north train station, take bus No 16 and get off past the bridge; from there it's a 10-minute walk east along the south bank of the river.

Places to Stay – Mid-Range

Chéngdū hasn't much in the way of mid-range options.

Jìndì Fàndiàn (☎ 691 5339 ext 281) Singles/doubles with bath & air-con Y160/230. This two-star hotel has bright, clean rooms with private safes.

Chéngdū Dàjiǔdiàn (☎ 317 3888 ext 3105) Standard doubles Y120-400. With clean, comfortable rooms conveniently located for early morning trains, this place is well worth seeing if it's offering a deal. At the time of writing, large, heated doubles with bath and minibar were offered at a 50% discount.

Róngchéng Fàndiàn (☎ 611 2933) Doubles Y240. This place used to be dirt-cheap but has endured an overhaul and now offers somewhat overpriced, mediocre rooms. A few travellers have reported nocturnal visitations by Mr Rat.

Places to Stay – Top End

With continuously growing competition, you may often get huge discounts (up to 40%) at top-end hotels during winter so it's worth shopping around. The prices listed are the posted rates and what you can expect to pay during high season.

Mínshān Fàndiàn (☎ 558 3333, e mhotel@swww.com.cn, Renmin Nanlu) Doubles or suites Y800-1400. This hotel has bright, four-star standard rooms, a couple of bars, a coffee shop and five restaurants. It's a popular option for tour groups.

Jǐnjiāng Bīnguǎn (☎ 558 2222, e ajjhsw @shell.scsti.ac.cn, 80 Renmin Nanlu) Old-wing singles/doubles Y788/960, new-wing rooms Y1180. The rooms in this five-star giant aren't half as nice as those at Mínshān Fàndiàn; however, they do offer the option of nonsmoking rooms. There are good views to be had from the rooftop Chinese restaurant here, but at a high price: beer and soft drinks are around Y30 each.

Holiday Inn Crowne Plaza (☎ 678 6666, fax 678 6599, 31 Zongfu Jie), *Yinhe Dynasty Hotel* (☎ 661 8888, e dynasty@mail.sc.cn info.net, 99 Xishancheng Jie) and *Sheraton Chengdu Lido Hotel* (☎ 676 8999, 15 Section 1, Renmin Zhonglu) all have standard doubles from US$140. All three of these sparkling hotels offer nothing short of luxury with five-star services and plush international restaurants and shops.

Sìchuān Bīnguǎn (☎ 675 9147, 31 Zongfu Lu) Singles/doubles Y580/800. This hotel is attached to the Holiday Inn and offers similar, although somewhat older rooms at a much better deal.

Places to Eat

Chinese Restaurants Places to sample Chinese cuisine include:

Chéngdū Cāntīng (134 Shangdong Dajie) This is one of Chéngdū's most famous and authentic Sichuanese restaurants. It has a good atmosphere, decent food and reasonable prices; downstairs serves set courses of appetisers, while full meals can be had upstairs. It's best to visit as a group as the more people in your party, the more dishes you get to sample. Arrive early: the place starts shutting down around 8.30pm.

Shìměixuān Cāntīng (Huaxingzheng Jie) Dishes Y10. For *guōbā ròupiàn* (crispy rice with meat), you can't beat this restaurant. Large plates overflowing with crispy rice in pork and lychee are plenty for two. The restaurant has lots of other great dishes.

Bāguó Bùyī Fēngweìjiǔbù (Renmin Nanlu) This place is named after the traditional cotton clothing worn by peasants in an ancient state of eastern Sìchuān. Best described as country Sìchuān, the food is prepared all over its two storeys; you wander and point. Be careful – it isn't cheap.

Snack Bars & Cheap Eats Many of Chéngdū's specialities originated as *xiǎo chī* (little eats). The snack bars are great fun and will cost you next to nothing. In fact, the offerings can be outdone in no other Chinese city – and if you line up several of these places you will get yourself a banquet. Unfortunately, many of the city's best-known snack places have fallen prey to the massive reconstruction work that is tearing down entire neighbourhoods.

Lóngchāoshǒu Cāntīng (Chunxi Lu) Set courses Y5-15. This is one little snack restaurant that is still going strong with sampler courses that allow you to dip into the whole gamut of the Chéngdū snack experience. The cheapest option gives you a range of sweet and savoury items, with each price bracket giving you the same deal on a grander and more filling scale. Unfortunately it hasn't much to offer vegetarians. The restaurant is near the corner of Shangdong Dajie.

Huǒguō (hotpot) is very popular in Chéngdū. You'll see lots of sidewalk hotpot operations in the older section of town, near the Chunxi Lu market. It's similar to a fondue affair: dip skewered meat and vegies into big woks filled with hot, spiced oil and then into little dishes of peanut oil and garlic. Skewers are around two to five *jiǎo* each and you can easily fill up for around Y5. Be forewarned – hotpot can be *very* hot; even many Sichuanese can't take it. If you want something a little more tame, try asking for *báiwèi*, the hotpot for wimps. Peanut milk, sold in tins, will also stop you from breathing fire.

Equally as popular as hotpot is *shāokǎo*, Sichuanese barbecue. Skewers of meat, vegies and smoked tofu are brushed with oil and chilli and grilled. Unlike hotpots, which generally don't appear until the sun goes down, shāokǎo is a popular lunchtime snack as well. You'll find roadside stalls all over the city as well as portable grills on bikes.

Shìqiǎo Shǒu Miàn (Hongxin Lu) Noodles Y2. This place serves up excellent bowls of filling noodles. You can watch noodles being made fresh on the premises and the friendly staff are happy to cater to vegetarians. Try a side plate of spicy radish pickles.

Chén Mápó Dòufu (*Pockmarked Grandma Chen's Bean Curd; Jiefang Lu*) Bowls Y3. *Mápó dòufu* is served here with a vengeance – soft, fresh bean curd with a fiery sauce of garlic, minced beef, salted soybean, chilli oil and nasty little peppercorns. Also served are spicy chicken, duck and plates of tripe.

The 2nd floor has been redone to look like a typical Chinese banquet hall and carries a Y5 'seating charge'. Sit downstairs instead; don't worry about the grotty decor – those spices should kill any lurking bugs. This place is no longer an unknown cubbyhole and has franchised, with a second, more pleasant version across from Wénhuà Gōngyuán.

Vegetarian A special treat for vegetarians is to head out to the *Wénshū Temple*, where there is an excellent vegetarian restaurant with an English menu.

Zhàojué Sì also serves up vegetarian dishes for lunch and if you're really keen, you might ride out to *Bǎoguāng Sì* (*Monastery of Divine Light*) in Xīndū, 18km north of Chéngdū, in time for lunch (11am to noon). For details of the bus service see Around Chéngdū later in this chapter.

Western Restaurants A number of Western restaurants are also on offer:

Grandma's Kitchen (*Zǔmǔ Dēchúfang;* ☎ 524 2835; 75 Kehau Lu*) Mains from Y40. Fill up here on baked macaroni and cheese, steak, pizza, salads, soup, fluffy pancakes and excellent desserts. At *Grandma's Sunflower Cafe* (*Renmin Nanlu*) you can choose from a more limited version of the same menu in front of a roaring log fire.

Red Brick Cafe Pub & Pizzeria (*Hóng Zhuān Xīcāntīng; Kehau Lu*) Set meals from Y38. This restaurant specialises in pizzas and pastas and also offers moderately priced appetisers, chicken dishes and even some pan-Asian and African dishes.

Paul's Oasis This is the most popular of the many backpacker-friendly Western-style cafes that have exploded all over Chéngdū. Here you can get fries, pizza and cheap, ice-cold beer. Paul's often sees travellers moving furniture outside and dancing into the morning.

Bean's Cafe Excellent, freshly ground coffees and a limited menu are offered at this cafe.

Carol's by the River (*Kǎluó Xīcān; Linjiang Lu*) This restaurant serves up tasty food with south-western US and Mexican overtones, and often shows Hollywood videos.

Highfly Cafe (*Gāofēi Kāfēi*) This is one of Chéngdū's longest-running cafes, famous for its fudge brownies.

Also try the small cafe at *Sam's Guesthouse* for an excellent vegetarian pizza.

Entertainment

Entertainment can be fruitful hunting in Chéngdū, but you will have to hunt. If you don't speak Chinese, ask around among the English-speaking staff at the Traffic Hotel or the travel outfits nearby.

If something strikes your fancy, get it written down in Chinese and get a good map location – these places are often hard to find, especially at night. If you have more time, try and get advance tickets if possible.

Opera Chéngdū is the home of Sichuan opera, which has a 200-year tradition and features slapstick, eyeglass-shattering songs, men dressed as women and occasional gymnastics. Several opera houses are scattered throughout the older sections of town.

If you are interested in seeing a local Sichuan opera, your best bet may be to contact a friendly, English-speaking local, Mike (☎ 626 6510) after 8:30pm. He'll take you to a small, local opera house hidden in the depths of a market. The cast, costume and make-up is all very professional. You'll also get a backstage tour, tea and a taxi to and from the opera for Y60 per person. The price is a little steep but all in all it is an entertaining and worthwhile experience. Try to go on the weekends when the performance is a combination of the highlights from a number of operas.

Local English-speaking tour guides around the Traffic Hotel as well as Sam's Guesthouse also organise backstage tours for around Y40 to Y50 per person, with tours leaving around 2pm.

If you'd rather go on your own, one of the easier Sichuan opera venues to find is the **Jinjiang Theatre** (*Jǐnjiāng Jùyuàn; Huaxingzheng Jie*), which is a combination teahouse, opera theatre and cinema. High-standard Sichuan opera performances are given here every Sunday afternoon.

Teahouses Chéngdū is renowned for its excellent teahouses and *Rénmín Teahouse* (*Rénmín Cháguǎn; Rénmín Gōngyuán*) s is one of its finest. A most pleasant afternoon can be spent here in relative anonymity over a bottomless cup of stone-flower tea.

Another charming indoor family type teahouse is in **Wénshū Temple**, with an amazingly crowded and steamy ambience. This is in addition to the huge tea garden outside (see Wénshū Temple earlier in this section). As well, try the teahouse in **Dàcí Sì** (*Temple of Mercy; admission Y1*). The temple itself doesn't offer much to see, however the grounds, with tables piled high with *mahjong* pieces and teacups, are a perfect place for a lazy afternoon in the sun.

Pubs & Bars South of the river on Renmin Nanlu is a strip of Western-style bars including the **Wild Goose Cafe**, **Seventh Sensation** and the **Twelve Oaks**, which regularly has live music. Most of these bars have similar prices with cocktails for Y25 to Y30 and beer for about Y15. You may also be served complimentary plates of fruit and seeds.

If you're looking for somewhere to go dancing, it's probably best to ask at Paul's Oasis for the current clubbing hotspot as it changes like the wind.

Shopping

The main downtown shopping area extends from the eastern end of Renmin Donglu south to Shangdong Dajie, and has taken on the look of most modern cities, with trendy clothing shops and department stores. If you delve into the narrow alleys between the main streets you'll find arcades of smaller shops and stalls selling similar items at cheaper prices.

Arts & Crafts Service Department Store (*Chéngdū Měishùpǐn Fúwùbù; 10 Chunxi Lu*) Located in Chunxi Commercial District, this shop deals in such Sichuanese specialities as lacquerware, silverwork and bamboo products.

Derentang Chemist (*Chunxi Lu*) At the southern end of Chunxi Commercial District look out for this place, the oldest and largest of all Chéngdū's Chinese pharmacies.

Qīngshíqiáo Market This large market is one of the most interesting and busiest places to wander in town. Shops and stalls sell brightly coloured seafood, flowers, cacti, birds, pets and a thousand dried foods. Although fairly frantic itself, it's a nice change of pace from the commercialism of the department stores.

Directly behind Mínshān Fàndiàn are a number of antique stores and in the evening, dozens of stalls appear and turn the street into an antique market. Across the street, Renmin Nanlu turns into an evening art gallery as street hawkers sell paintings, calendars and intricate paper cuts.

South of the river, on a street across from the entrance of the Wǔhòu Temple, is a small Tibetan neighbourhood. While it's not evident in the architecture, it is in the prayer papers, colourful scarves, beads and brass goods for sale. You won't find the variety of things (nor the bargains) that you'll find in the north-west of Sìchuān, but it still makes for an interesting wander.

Getting There & Away

Air Shangliu airport is 18km west of the city and currently undergoing renovations. Be prepared to pay a whopping Y90 departure tax.

Major internal destinations include Běijīng (Y1150, six days per week), Hāěrbīn (Y1820, five days per week), Shànghǎi (Y1290, daily), Kūnmíng (Y640, five days per week), Guǎngzhōu (Y1040, daily), Jǐ'nán (Y1090, three days per week), Xī'ān (Y500, four days per week), Dàlián (Y1450, five days per week) and Chóngqìng (Y190, three days per week). You can purchase tickets from the Civil Aviation Administration of China (CAAC; Zhōngguó Mínháng; ☎ 664 7163) on Renmin Nanlu. The office is open 8am to 7.30pm Monday to Friday and 8.30am to 7.30pm on Saturday and Sunday.

China Southwest (☎ 666 5911) has flights to Hong Kong (Y2550, daily), Bangkok (Y2480, four days per week), Singapore (Y3300, two days per week), Seoul (Y3480, two days per week) and Lhasa (Y1200, daily). Its office is a few doors south of the CAAC office on Renmin Nanlu.

Dragon Air (☎ 675 5555 ext 6105) has an office in Sìchuān Bīnguǎn, and offers flights to Tokyo (Y5200) and Osaka (Y4200) in Japan, via Hong Kong.

Tibet The most frequently asked question in Chéngdū must be 'Can I fly to Lhasa?'. If you're on your own without a permit, China Southwest's official answer is 'No'. To get around this, travel agents in the Traffic Hotel, Sam's Guesthouse and elsewhere can sign you onto a 'tour', which usually includes a one-way ticket to Lhasa, the transfer to Chéngdū airport and a Tibet Tourism Bureau permit which you will probably never see. At the height of summer, you may have to book the two-hour transfer from Gonggar airport to Lhasa. The fact that members of the tour group have never seen each other prior to the flight and split up immediately after, is overlooked by the authorities.

At the time of research these packages were priced at about Y2000 (the ticket alone costs Y1200) and were the most cost-effective way of getting into Tibet. CITS runs its own four-day tours for around Y3500 or will get you a one-way ticket and permit for Y2600.

If you can arrange for a permit from a travel agency, you can try picking up a ticket from one of the airlines yourself; regulations change and travellers occasionally – no, rarely – get lucky. Just make sure you have the cash on hand to buy the ticket before they change their mind. Another trick is to ask for a 1st-class ticket.

Sìchuān's land borders into Tibet are still closed to foreigners. Some travellers attempt to sneak across but the majority are turned back and fined heavily.

Bus Transport connections in Chéngdū are more comprehensive than in other parts of the south-west. High-speed expressways from Chéngdū to both Chóngqìng and Lèshān have cut down travel time to each of these cities to a mere two hours.

The main bus station is Xīnnánmén, next to the Traffic Hotel, with tickets to most destinations around Sìchuān. For northern destinations you will need to trek over to the Xīmén bus station in the north-west of the city and for eastern destinations such as Chóngqìng, your best bet is to try the north bus station, near the north train station.

Xīnnánmén Bus Station Regular buses head for Lèshān and Éméi from 7am. For Éméi you can get a seat for Y20 if you're willing to spend four or five hours on it or you can opt for the Y31 tickets and be there in two hours. Likewise, Lèshān has slow buses for Y26 or an express bus for Y46.

Between 7am and 10am there are about four departures to Dūjiāngyàn (Y18.5).

Early morning buses for Lúdíng (Y90) and Kāngdìng (Y110) only depart every other day while construction continues on the new tunnel through the once treacherous Èrláng Shān Pass. There is also a sleeper departing around 4pm (Y162). However, as the journey time has been sliced down to about seven or eight hours (depending on the queues for the tunnel), this bus will dump you off in the middle of the night.

Even if you have proof of PICC insurance, a couple of yuán insurance will likely be tacked onto tickets purchased at Xīnnánmén bus station. (See the boxed text 'Warning'.)

Xīmén Bus Station This station is for travellers heading up to Jiǔzhàigōu or taking the overland route to Xiàhé in Gānsù province by way of northern Sìchuān.

There is a daily departure from here to Sōngpān at 7am (Y46) and a sleeper leaving for Jiǔzhàigōu at 7.20am (Y86.5, 10 to 12 hours). Daily buses also run to Xiǎojīn (Y43, 6.30am) and Hóngyuán (Y67.5, 10.30am).

There are a number of departures each day to Dūjiāngyàn (Y11, 9.50am) from where you can change for Qīngchéng Shān or Wòlóng. There is also a direct bus to Wòlóng at 11.40am (Y20). One departure leaves daily for Lèshān (Y35, 3.30pm) although you'd be better off trying the Xīnnánmén Station.

North Bus Station Chéngdū's north bus station has seemingly constant minibuses to Chóngqìng between 6.30am and 9.30pm (Y112). There are also morning departures to Dàzú. Buses depart every 15 minutes for Dūjiāngyàn between 7am and 6pm (Y7.5), every half-hour to Bàogúo Sì at Éméi Shān between 7.30am and 3pm (Y25) and regularly to Lèshān from 6.30am to 6pm (Y25).

Train Getting train tickets out of Chéngdū is far easier today than in recent years and the advance-booking offices around town have become more user-friendly. While it's possible to reserve tickets, you'll need some intervention from the gods to make same-day reservations for hard-sleeper tickets to popular destinations such as Kūnmíng or Xī'ān.

Alternatively, you can spend an extra Y30 or so and get Sam's Guesthouse or the Traffic Hotel to arrange the tickets for you. You'll usually need to organise this a day and a half in advance and, while they're usually successful, it's not guaranteed – remember, everyone and their sister is trying to get to Xī'ān and Kūnmíng. Don't even bother with CITS.

Trains to Kūnmíng take either 19 hours (express) or 21½ hours, and cost Y222/338 for a hard/soft sleeper. An afternoon train departs at 1.57pm and arrives in Kūnmíng at 9.05am the following morning, and an evening train departs at 9.15pm, arriving at 5.48pm the next evening.

For Lìjiāng or Dàlǐ, take the train to Pānzhīhūa (Jinjiang) on the Chéngdū-Kūnmíng route, from where you can catch a bus or minibus to either destination. Trains depart at 6.12pm, 7.03pm and 8.27pm and

---

Warning

The question of whether or not you are required to purchase insurance from the People's Insurance Company of China (PICC) for bus travel to and around northern Sìchuān is open to great debate. If you ask the staff at PICC, their helpful response is, 'You require our insurance to travel anywhere in our country'.

You were once obliged to show PICC insurance before you could board most buses in Sìchuān. The requirement was originally introduced following a lawsuit brought upon the Chinese government by the family of a Japanese tourist who was killed in a bus crash in the Jiǔzhàigōu area. Nowadays, however, almost all bus stations factor the insurance cost into the ticket price, regardless of whether or not you've already purchased it. The only place you are likely to need it is in remote areas of the north that don't see many travellers, such as Zöigê. Unfortunately, you won't be able to buy any insurance once you're there and may well not be allowed on the bus without it, at least not without paying a huge surcharge. Don't bother telling them you have travel insurance already: non-PICC coverage is not recognised. If you're planning on travelling off the beaten path, it might be worth picking up some insurance while you're in Chéngdū.

The insurance costs around Y15 per week and is available from the PICC office (Zhōngguó Rénmín Bǎoxiǎn Gōngsī) at the eastern end of Renmin Donglu (Shudu Dadao), a few minutes' walk from Mao in central Chéngdū.

---

arrive in Pānzhīhūa about 12 hours later. Hard/soft sleepers for the 6.12pm departure cost Y112/182 or Y166/248 for the two later departures.

All trains headed for Kūnmíng or Pānzhīhūa stop in Éméi. Express trains take just under two hours, while fast trains take around three hours. A hard seat should cost Y9.

There are daily trains to Chóngqìng and Yóutíngpū (for Dàzú) but they take much longer than the buses that continuously plough down the new expressway (around 12 hours to Chóngqìng). The same is true for trains to Yíbīn and Zìgòng, cities now linked by expressways to Lèshān.

Other daily departures include Běijīng (28 to 34 hours) with hard sleepers ranging from Y241 to Y418, Shànghǎi (36 to 39½ hours) with hard sleepers from Y269 to Y499, Xī'ān (Y122, 16½ hours), Guǎngzhōu, Guìyáng, Lánzhōu and Ürümqi.

Getting Around

To/From the Airport Shuangliu airport is 18km west of the city. CAAC runs a bus every half-hour between the ticket office on Renmin Nanlu and Shuangliu airport. The fare is Y8. Taxi drivers will take you for Y10 per person (minimum two people) from outside the office. On the meter the ride is about Y40.

Bus The most useful bus is No 16, which runs from Chéngdū's north train station to the south train station along Renmin Nanlu. Regular buses cost Y1, while the double-deckers cost Y2. Bus No 81 runs from the Mao statue to Green Ram Temple and Bus No 12 circles the city along Yihuan Lu, starting and ending at the north train station.

Taxi Taxis have a flag fall of Y5 (Y6 at night), plus Y1.4 per kilometre. From the Traffic Hotel to the Xīmén bus station, the direct route should cost around Y15.

Bicycle Both Sam's Guesthouse and the Traffic Hotel rent bikes for about Y10 per day, plus around Y200 deposit. The bikes are in fairly good condition but the usual rules apply – check your bike before you cycle off and make an effort to park it in a designated parking area. Bicycle theft is a problem here as in most Chinese cities.

AROUND CHÉNGDŪ
Bǎoguāng Sì 宝光寺

Bǎoguāng Sì *(Monastery of Divine Light; open 8am-5.30pm daily)*, in the north of Xīndū county, is an active Buddhist temple with five halls and 16 courtyards surrounded by bamboo.

Founded in the 9th century, the monastery was destroyed and reconstructed in the 17th century. Among the treasures here are a white jade buddha from Myanmar (Burma), Ming and Qing paintings, calligraphy, a stone tablet engraved with 1000 Buddhist figures (AD 540) and ceremonial musical instruments. Unfortunately, most

of the more valuable items are locked away and require special permission to be viewed – you may be able to get this if you can find whoever's in charge.

The **Arhat Hall**, built in the 19th century, contains 500 2m-high clay figurines of Buddhist saints and disciples – well, not all of them: among this spaced-out lot are two earthlings, the emperors Kangxi and Qianlong. They're distinguishable by their royal costumes, beards, boots and capes.

About 1km from the monastery is **Osmanthus Lake** with its bamboo groves and Osmanthus trees. In the middle of the lake is a small memorial hall for the Ming scholar Yang Shengan.

Bǎoguāng Sì has an excellent *vegetarian restaurant (open 10am-3pm daily)* where a huge array of dishes is prepared by monastic chefs. It is best to be here around lunch time, when there are more dishes available.

Getting There & Away Xīndū is 18km north of Chéngdū. Buses run there from in front of the north train station and from the north bus station from around 6am to 6pm. The trip takes just under an hour.

On a Chinese bicycle, the round trip would be 40km, or at least four hours cycling time.

Qīngchéng Shān 青城山
Azure City Mountain

A holy Taoist mountain some 65km west of Chéngdū, with a summit of only 1600m, Qīngchéng Shān *(admission Y40 plus Y1 insurance)* is an excellent day trip into the subtropics. It offers beautiful trails lined with gingko, plum and palm trees, picturesque vistas and plenty of atmospheric sights along its four-hour return route. In nasty weather it's a good alternative to Éméi Shān as its somewhat sturdier steps are stone rather than slate (and therefore less slippery) and the views here are less likely to be obscured by mist and cloud.

Situated outside the entrance gate, **Jiànfú Temple** *(Jiànfú Gōng)* is the best preserved of the mountain's temples. Of the 500 or so Taoist monks resident here prior to liberation, there are still about 100 living here.

Further up the hill, both **Cháoyáng Cave** *(Cháoyáng Dòng)* and **Taoist Master Cave** *(Tiānshī Dòng)* are temples built into hollows in the side of the mountain. In the courtyard of Taoist Master Cave are ancient twin gingko trees planted during the Han dynasty over 1000 years ago. Only 500m from the mountain's summit is **Shàngqīng Temple** *(Shàngqīng Gōng)*, established in the Jin dynasty.

The most popular way of ascending Qīngchéng Shān is by gliding across **Yuèchéng Hú** on a small ferry (Y6) and then riding the chairlift up (Y25 one way, Y40 return) to within a 20-minute walk from Shàngqīng Temple. This removes most of the hard work and makes it very easy to fit Qīngchéng Shān into a day trip from Chéngdū. If you do walk only one way, the western trail past Cháoyáng Cave and Taoist Master Cave offers the most sights and views. At the southern end of this route is the lush **Chunxian Mountain Path**, created early in the 19th century by headmaster Chunxian Peng who had each visitor to the mountain plant a tree along the path.

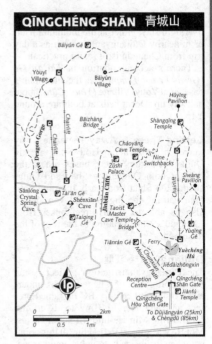

Places to Stay There are a few accommodation options:

Shàngqīng Gōng (Shàngqīng Temple) Doubles Y50. This temple offers clean, basic rooms and common balconies that look out over the surrounding forests. Staying at Shàngqīng Gōng means an easier walk to the summit for sunrise than from Tiānshī Dòng.

Tiānshī Dòng (Taoist Master Cave) Doubles Y50. This temple also offers basic rooms and shared balconies overlooking the forests. Tiānshī Dòng has loads of atmosphere, is likely to be quieter than Shàngqīng Gōng and also has slightly fancier doubles with bath available for Y80.

Jiēdaizhōngxīn Triples Y120. At the bottom of the hill, this hotel has damp, dingy, exorbitantly priced rooms. While you can bargain all the way down to a third the price, you're better off heading back into Dūjiāngyàn or Chéngdū.

On the road leading up to Qīngchéng Shān are a growing number of resort-style hotels.

Places to Eat You will likely be met at the base of the mountain by women keen to drag you to their restaurant, part-way up the mountain. These places are generally quite good although pricey.

There are a number of *restaurants* along Qīngchéng Shān's trails as well as *snack stands* at the top of the chairlift and noodles available inside Taoist Master Cave. You are also likely to find fruit and boiled eggs for sale along the way.

Getting There & Away To reach Qīngchéng Shān from Chéngdū, catch a bus from Xīmén station to Dūjiāngyàn (Y12, one hour). These run from 7am to 7pm. From Dūjiāngyàn, it's a 20-minute minibus ride (Y4) to the foot of the mountain. The last minibus returns from the mountain to Dūjiāngyàn at 6pm. During the high season there are likely to be buses running directly between Chéngdū's Xīmén station and Qīngchéng Shān.

Qīngchéng Hòu Shān 青城后山

In a bid to bolster tourism, the local authorities have opened up Qīngchéng Hòu Shān to trekkers. Its base lies about 15km northwest of the base of Qīngchéng Shān proper. With over 20km of hiking trails, this mountain offers a more natural environment than the temple-strewn slopes of Qīngchéng Shān, with **Five Dragon Gorge** *(Wǔlóng Gōu)* offering dramatic vistas. There is a cable car to help with part of the route, but climbing the mountain will still require an overnight stay, either at the mountain itself or in nearby Dūjiāngyàn: doing it as a day trip from Chéngdū isn't really practical.

There's accommodation in **Tài'ān Gé** (*Great Peace Temple*), at the mountain's base, or at **Yòuyī Village** (*Yòuyī Cūn*), about halfway up. Dorm beds at both are around Y15.

Getting There & Away The easiest way to reach Qīngchéng Hòu Shān is via Dūjiāngyàn from where buses run to the base of both Qīngchéng Shān and Qīngchéng Hòu Shān from early morning until 6pm. During the high season you should also be able to catch direct buses from Chéngdū's Xīmén station to the foot of the mountain.

Dūjiāngyàn 都江堰

The Dūjiāngyàn irrigation project, some 60km north-west of Chéngdū, was undertaken in the 3rd century BC by famed prefect and engineer Li Bing to divert the fast-flowing Mín Hé into irrigation canals. Mín Hé was subject to flooding at this point, yet when it subsided, droughts could ensue. A weir system was built to split the force of the river and a trunk canal was cut through a mountain to irrigate the Chéngdū plain.

Li Bing's most brilliant idea was to devise an annual maintenance plan to remove silt build-up. Thus the mighty Mín was tamed, with a temple erected in AD 168 to commemorate the occasion. Located in **Lídūī Gōngyuán** (*Solitude Park; admission park & temple Y4*), **Dragon-Subduing Temple** (*Fúlóng Guàn*) contains a tame gallery of prideful propaganda photographs.

The project is ongoing – it originally irrigated over a million hectares of land and since the Communists' rise to power (Liberation) this has expanded to three million hectares. Most of the present dams, reservoirs, pumping stations, hydroelectric works, bridgework and features are unsurprisingly modern. A good overall view of the outlay can be gained from **Èrwáng Miào** (*Two Kings Temple*), which dates from AD 494 and commemorates Li Bing and his son, Er Lang. Inside the temple is a statue of Li Bing, shockingly lifelike; in the rear hall is a standing figure of his son holding a dam tool.

A chairlift (cable car) runs from Lídūī Gōngyuán to Èrwáng Miào and on to **Yùlěi Shān Gōngyuán** (*Jade Wall Hall Park; open 8am-6pm daily*) and costs Y16 to Y25 per segment.

While the whole idea of visiting a mocha-coloured, massive irrigation project may not sound thrilling, Dūjiāngyàn is a friendly enough place to overnight and a visit to the teahouses lining the river around the funky south bridge is a pleasant way to while away the afternoon. You could also get lost for weeks in Yùlěi Shān Gōngyuán.

Places to Stay & Eat Dūjiāngyàn is an easy day trip from Chéngdū. Should you decide to stay overnight, to tackle Qīngchéng Shān the next day or en route to Wòlóng, there are a few accommodation options.

Shìkèyùn Zhōngxīn Zhāodàisuǒ (☎ 720 2300) Doubles with/without bath Y60/20. Attached to the bus station, this hotel has the cheapest beds in town; however, rooms are very basic, damp and rather drab.

Jīnqiǔ Bīnguǎn (☎ 711 5616, Jianshe Lu) Doubles with bath Y100-150. This is a good option, with clean, comfortable rooms, heating and friendly staff.

China Travel Service Hotel (*Zhōnglǚv Fàndiàn;* ☎ 713 1188, Jianshe Lu) Singles/doubles Y280/298. The most upmarket option in town, this brand-new hotel has plush rooms and caters to tour groups.

There isn't much to recommend for food in Dūjiāngyàn. You'll find the usual *barbecue stalls* along the streets in the evening, particularly on the western half of Jianshe Lu and along Taiping Jie. There are a few *restaurants* across from the bus station and, if you're looking for a pricey cup of coffee in comfy surroundings, try the *coffee house* next door to Jīnqiǔ Bīnguǎn.

Getting There & Away The bus station is inconveniently located south of town. To find downtown from here, turn left out of the station (towards the giant statue), and bear right onto what is eventually called Taiping Jie. Follow this north into town.

Buses run regularly (about once an hour) between Chéngdū and Dūjiāngyàn from 7am to 7pm (Y12, one hour). Buses to and from Qīngchéng Shān also run frequently until 6pm. One bus leaves daily for Wòlóng at 8am (Y13, 2½ hours).

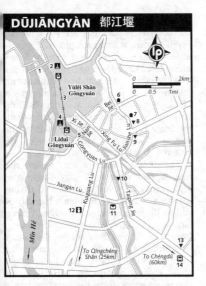

DŪJIĀNGYÀN 都江堰

DŪJIĀNGYÀN

PLACES TO STAY & EAT
6 China Travel Service Hotel
中旅饭店
7 Jīnqiú Bīnguǎn
金球宾馆
8 Coffee House
9 Barbecue Stalls
10 Barbecue Stalls
13 Restaurants

OTHER
1 Anlán Cable Bridge
安澜索桥
2 Èrwáng Miào
二王庙
3 Chairlift
索道
4 Dragon-Subduing Temple
伏龙观
5 South Bridge
南桥
11 Post Office
邮电大楼
12 Kuíguāng Pagoda
奎光塔
14 Bus Station; Shìkèyùn
Zhōngxīn Zhāodàisuǒ
汽车站；市客运中心招待所

Wòlóng Nature Reserve

Wòlóng Zìrán Bǎohùqū 卧龙自然保护区

Wòlóng Nature Reserve *(admission Y20)* lies 140km north-west of Chéngdū, about four hours by bus (via Dūjiāngyàn). It was set up in the late 1970s and is the largest of the 16 reserves set aside by the Chinese government for panda conservation. (Of these 16 reserves, 11 are in Sìchuān.) The United Nations has designated Wòlóng an International Biosphere Preserve.

The reserve is estimated to have some 3000 kinds of plants and covers an area of 200,000 hectares. To the north-west rises Sìgūniang Shān (6250m); to the east the reserve drops as low as 155m. Pandas like to dine on fang cane and fountain bamboo in the zone from 2300m to 3600m, ranging lower in winter. Other animals protected here are the golden monkey, golden langur, musk deer and snow leopard.

Before setting out for Wòlóng be forewarned: there is little chance of seeing a panda in the wild. The pandas have a hard enough time finding each other; in spring, the park is closed so that trekkers don't disturb the pandas' hunt for each other during their mating season.

The **China Research and Conservation Center for the Giant Panda** *(admission Y18)*, on the edge of the reserve, has about 30 pandas cooped up in small cages.

However, to see a live panda in something resembling its natural habitat, you'd be better off visiting the Giant Panda Breeding Research Base in Chéngdū.

If you're just out to commune with nature, Wòlóng can be pleasant. The rainy season, however, is a bad time to be here as leeches take over the park. Summer is the most popular time to visit, especially for Japanese tourists who are looking for the two rare types of azaleas that bloom here.

Trekking here is fairly tough and the trails are faint. The Park Administration Office in Wòlóng village (also called Shawan), at the centre of the reserve, can give information on hiking trails and researchers at the Conservation Centre (some of whom speak English) are good sources of info on conditions. Be sure to bring your own supplies, including warm clothing.

At the Conservation Centre, 6km from Wòlóng village, the ***Panda Inn*** *(doubles Y200)* has clean, comfortable doubles with hot showers and heaters. There is also a ***restaurant*** in the hotel and ***barbecue stalls*** across the road.

Getting There & Away

The opening of the Chéngdū's research base and improved access to northern Sìchuān has dampened demand for tours of the Wòlóng reserve. Though most travel outfits at the Traffic Hotel in Chéngdū have dropped this tour, one or two still offer overnight package tours. Sam's Guesthouse in Chéngdū will also organise a tour for you, tailored to your interests.

There is theoretically at least one bus a day from Chéngdū's Xīmén bus station to Wòlóng village at 11.40am (Y20). There are also a number of daily departures from Chéngdū to Dūjiāngyàn (Y12) – if you catch the first one at 7am you might just make it for the 8am connecting bus from Dūjiāngyàn to Wòlóng (Y13, 2½ hours). If you want to get dropped at the Conservation Centre, rather than Wòlóng village, be sure to tell the bus driver. You should see the sign on the left.

Onward buses continue on from Wòlóng village over the 4497m Bālǎngshān Pass to Rilong and Xiǎojīn, from where you can catch buses to Kāngdìng. Schedules on these routes are irregular.

ÉMÉI SHĀN 峨眉山
☎ 0842 • elevation 3099m

Éméi Shān *(admission Y60),* locked in a medieval time warp, is dotted with monasteries and temples, many of which have their histories posted for visitors both in English and in Chinese. If not, you are likely to encounter a friendly caretaker or monk to answer your questions.

The Éméi Shān climb is filled with hundreds of views of luxuriant scenery and seemingly millions of stairs. For the traveller itching to do something active, the Éméi climb is a good opportunity to observe post-1976 religious freedoms in action, with the chance to stay in the atmospheric monasteries along the trail.

Éméi Shān is one of the Middle Kingdom's four famous Buddhist mountains (the others are Pútuó Shān, Wǔtái Shān and Jiǔhuá Shān). The original temple structures dated from as long ago as the advent of Buddhism itself in China; by the 14th century, the estimated 100 or so holy structures housed several thousand monks. Unfortunately, Éméi Shān has little of its original temple-work left. Glittering Jīndǐng Sì, with

its brass tiling engraved with Tibetan script, was completely gutted by fire. A similar fate befell numerous other temples and monasteries on the mountain. War with the Japanese and Red Guard looting didn't help either.

After a Cultural Revolution hiatus, around 20 temples are now active, regaining traces of their original splendour. Since 1976 the remnants have been renovated, access to the mountain has been improved, hiking paths widened, lodgings added, and tourists permitted to climb to the sacred summit.

The pilgrims, tourists and hawkers that line the path on a sunny day during peak season may remove the chance of finding much solitude on the mountain but they do add to the atmosphere. The crowds hover largely around the monasteries; once away from them, the path is not lined so much with stalls as with the fir, pine and cedar trees that clothe the slopes. Lofty crags, cloud-kissing precipices, butterflies and azaleas together form a nature reserve of sorts. The mountain was added to Unesco's list of World Heritage Sites in 1996, joining Lèshān and Jiǔzhàigōu.

The major scenic goal of Chinese hikers is to witness a sunrise or sunset over the sea of clouds at the summit. On the rare afternoon there is also a phenomenon known as Buddha's Aureole where rainbow rings, produced by refraction of water particles, attach themselves to a person's shadow in a cloud bank below the summit. Devout Buddhists, thinking this was a call from yonder, used to jump off the Cliff of Self-Sacrifice in ecstasy, leading officials of the Ming and Qing dynasties to set up iron poles and chain railings to prevent suicides.

Tickets

The Éméi Shān entrance ticket is dated and so theoretically you can re-enter the grounds at different points throughout the day. You also get your mug shot scanned onto the ticket and can even have it laminated for Y1 – not a bad idea if it's raining. Entry to Bàoguó Sì and Fúhǔ Sì at the foot of the mountain do not require this ticket. They have tickets of their own (see later).

Climate

The best time to visit is from May to October. Winter is not impossible, but will present some trekking problems – iron soles

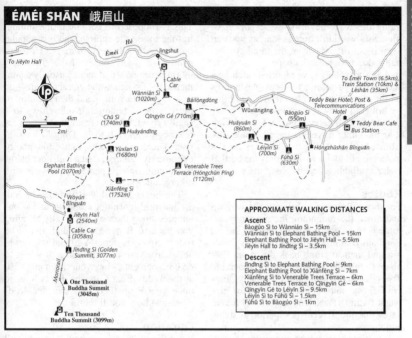

ÉMÉI SHĀN 峨眉山

To Jiēyìn Hall

Éméi   Hé   Jīngshuǐ

Cable Car

Wànnián Sì (1020m)   Báilóngdòng

Chù Sì (1740m)   Qīngyīn Gé (710m)

Huáyándǐng

Yùxiān Sì (1680m)

Elephant Bathing Pool (2070m)

Xiānfēng Sì (1752m)

Wòyún Bīnguǎn

Jiēyìn Hall (2540m)

Cable Car (3058m)

Jīndǐng Sì (Golden Summit, 3077m)

Monorail

One Thousand Buddha Summit (3045m)

Ten Thousand Buddha Summit (3099m)

Venerable Trees Terrace (Hóngchūn Píng) (1120m)

Wùxiāngāng

Huáyuán Sì (860m)

Léiyīn Sì (700m)

Fúhǔ Sì (630m)

Bàoguó Sì (550m)

To Éméi Town (6.5km), Train Station (10km) & Lèshān (35km)

Teddy Bear Hotel; Post & Telecommunications Hotel

Teddy Bear Cafe   Bus Station

Hóngzhūshān Bīnguǎn

0   2   4km
0   1   2mi

APPROXIMATE WALKING DISTANCES

Ascent
Bàoguó Sì to Wànnián Sì – 15km
Wànnián Sì to Elephant Bathing Pool – 15km
Elephant Bathing Pool to Jiēyìn Hall – 5.5km
Jiēyìn Hall to Jīndǐng Sì – 3.5km

Descent
Jīndǐng Sì to Elephant Bathing Pool – 9km
Elephant Bathing Pool to Xiānfēng Sì – 7km
Xiānfēng Sì to Venerable Trees Terrace – 6km
Venerable Trees Terrace to Qīngyīn Gé – 6km
Qīngyīn Gé to Léiyīn Sì – 9.5km
Léiyīn Sì to Fúhǔ Sì – 1.5km
Fúhǔ Sì to Bàoguó Sì – 1km

with spikes can be hired to deal with encrusted ice and snow on the trails. Snowfall generally starts around November on the upper slopes.

At the height of summer, which is scorching elsewhere in Sìchuān, Éméi Shān presents cool majesty. Temperate zones start at 1000m.

Cloud cover and mist are prevalent year-round and will most likely interfere with your view of the sunrise. If you're *very* lucky, you'll see Gònggā Shān to the west; if not, you'll have to settle for the Telecom tower and the meteorological station. Some average temperatures in degrees Celsius are:

	Jan	Apr	Jul	Oct
Éméi Town	7	21	26	17
Summit	-6	3	12	-1

What to Bring

Definitely not your entire pack. Nevertheless, Éméi Shān is a tall one at 3099m, so the weather is uncertain and it's best to prepare for sudden changes without weighing yourself down (steps can be steep). If

you're staying at the Teddy Bear Hotel, you can store your bags there for free. If not, staff will probably keep them for you anyway for a modest charge.

There is no heating or insulation in the monasteries, but blankets – albeit damp ones – are provided. A couple of places now even have electric blankets and you can also hire heavy overcoats at the top. Heavy rain can be a problem, as even a light mist can make the slate steps slippery and extremely treacherous. A good pair of rough-soled shoes or boots is a must. When it does rain, big, flimsy, plastic bags with hoods are sold by enterprising vendors on the slopes. They appear to do the trick, at least for a little while.

Strange hiking equipment as it may sound, a fixed-length umbrella would be most useful – for the rain and as a walking stick. You should be able to find one in Éméi town for Y30 to Y45. If you want to look even more authentic, you can buy yourself a handcrafted walking stick (very cheap), for sale along the way. A torch (flashlight) is important if you're spending the night or planning to hike at dawn. Food supplies are not necessary with food stalls along the way; nevertheless a pocket of munchies wouldn't hurt as long as you can keep it out of sight from the monkeys. Finally, don't forget toilet paper.

A few travellers have reported catching a serious case of conjunctivitis at guesthouses on the mountain. You can try to avoid this by bringing a towel or pillowcase to cover the pillow and then washing it before using it again. Other travellers have become sick from contaminated water supplies on the mountain; it's wise to drink only the bottled water available at stands along the way.

Routes

For those planning to hike all the way up and down the mountain, the most popular route is to ascend via Wànnián Sì, Chū Sì, Elephant Bathing Pool and on to the summit and then to climb back down via Elephant Bathing Pool, Xiānfēng Sì, Venerable Trees Terrace (Hóngchūn Píng) and Qīngyīn Gě. The paths converge just below Elephant Bathing Pool. The majority of hikers agree that the descent is superior in sights and views.

If you're short on time or energy, you can be carried up on the sturdy back of a porter. If this doesn't sound like your cup of tea, there is now a bus that runs up the mountain from the bus station in Bàoguó, next door to the Teddy Bear Cafe. You can either take a bus up to Wǔxiǎngǎng and begin your hike from there or continue on the bus up to the village of Jìngshuǐ where a cable car (Y30/20/45 up/down/return), open 6am to 6pm, awaits you for a lift up to Wànnián Sì. From the top of the cable car, you can pick up the route to the summit. Buses also run as far up the mountain as Jiēyǐn Hall (Jiēyǐn Diàn; two hours) from where it's a two-hour hike or five-minute cable car ride (Y40/30 up/down) to the top.

Bus routes and prices are posted at the Bàoguó bus station as well as at the stops en route. A ride to the top costs Y30, to Wǔxiǎngǎng costs Y15 and a return trip with a number of stops en route is Y60. Buses run from approximately 6am to 6pm but you don't want to cut it too close on the way down – if you miss the last bus, it's a 15km walk down from Wànnián Sì.

If for some reason you wish to conquer the whole mountain in one day, most hotels can book you on a bus leaving at 3.30am (!). This is supposed to get you to the summit in time to see the sunrise, and is a popular option with Chinese tourists. Unfortunately, so many buses make this early morning run now that there's usually an immense traffic jam at the entrance gate – up to a 45-minute wait – and then the clog of tourists up the mountainside slows to a snail's crawl, with the result that very, very few people make it to Jīn Dǐng Sì for sunrise. There's also only one good photo-opportunity vantage point a half-hour below the summit, and it's generally crowded with other shutterbugs.

The buses head down from Jiēyǐn Hall around mid-morning, stopping at various temples along the way and finally bringing you back to Bàoguó at around 5pm. The round trip costs about Y40 and will probably leave your head spinning. It's best to do it in segments – buy your ticket up (Y30) at the Teddy Bear Cafe the day before, so once you're up there you can decide if, when and how you'll return.

Duration

It's difficult to estimate how long you will need to make it up and back down Éméi Shān by foot. While you don't require any particular hiking skills, it is nonetheless a tough climb. You will be quoted wildly differing times by locals and other hikers. Many say that two days is enough time to make it to the summit from Wànnián Sì and back down to Bàoguó Sì, but this is only possible if you're able and willing to spend at least 10 hours hiking each day and are fortunate enough to have optimum conditions. Crowds and weather (heavy rainfall in particular) can dampen these plans. The altitude may also play havoc with your breathing and ascending too quickly will only increase this. Finally, you may well want to explore the many temples and monasteries en route and to enjoy the vistas. All up, it's wise to leave yourself three days for the trek.

The following will give you an idea of the distances involved (remember you are climbing a steep staircase). To get an idea of how long it's going to take you, time yourself on the first kilometre or two and then average out your own probable climbing duration.

Bàoguó Sì – 15km – Wànnián Sì – 15km – Elephant Bathing Pool – 5.5km – Jiēyǐn Hall – 3.5km – Jīndǐng Sì – 4km – Ten Thousand Buddha Summit – 4km – Jīndǐng Sì – 9km – Elephant Bathing Pool – 7km – Xiānfēng Sì – 6km – Venerable Trees Terrace – 6km – Qīngyīn Gé – 9.5km – Léiyīn Sì – 1.5km – Fúhǔ Sì – 1km – Bàoguó Sì

Bàoguó Sì 报国寺
Declare Nation Temple
Bàoguó Sì (admission Y8) was constructed in the 16th century, enlarged in the 17th century by Emperor Kangxi and recently renovated. Its 3.5m-high porcelain Buddha, made in 1415, is housed near the Sutra Library. To the left of the gate is a rockery for potted miniature trees and rare plants.

A **museum** (admission Y4) is diagonally across the road from the monastery, around the side of the knoll. It's unlikely that you'll find its taxidermy displays worth the entrance fee.

Fúhǔ Sì 伏虎寺
Crouching Tiger Monastery
The renovated Fúhǔ Sì (admission Y6) is sunk deep within the forest. Inside is a 7m-high copper pagoda inscribed with Buddhist images and texts.

Qīngyīn Gé 清音阁
Pure Sound Pavilion
Named after the sound effects produced by rapid waters coursing around its surrounding rock formations, this temple is built on an outcrop in the middle of a fast-flowing stream.

There are several small pavilions from which to observe the waterworks and appreciate the natural music. It's possible to swim here although the water is only likely to be warm enough during the summer months.

Wànnián Sì 万年寺
Long Life Monastery
This monastery is the oldest surviving Éméi temple (reconstructed in the 9th century). It's dedicated to the man on the white elephant, the Bodhisattva Puxian, who is the protector of the mountain. This 8.5m-high **statue** is dated from AD 980, cast in copper and bronze and weighs an estimated 62,000kg. If you can manage to rub the elephant's back, good luck will be cast upon you.

The statue is housed in Brick Hall, a domed building with small stupas on it. When the temple was damaged by fire in 1945, Brick Hall was the only building left unharmed. There is also a **graveyard** to the rear of the temple.

Xiānfēng Sì 仙峰寺
Magic Peak Monastery
Somewhat off the beaten track, this monastery is backed by rugged cliffs, surrounded by fantastic scenery and oozing with character. The nearby **Jiǔlǎo Cave** is inhabited by big bats.

Elephant Bathing Pool 洗象池
Xǐxiàng Chí
According to legend, Elephant Bathing Pool is the spot where Puxian flew his elephant in for a big scrub, but today there's not much of a pool to speak of. Being almost at the crossroads of both major trails, the temple here is something of a hang-out and often crowded with pilgrims.

Jīndǐng Sì 金顶寺
Golden Summit Temple
At the Golden Summit (Jīn Dǐng; 3077m), this magnificent temple is as far as most hikers make it. It has been entirely rebuilt

---

Monkey Etiquette

The monkeys have got it all figured out. If you come across a monkey 'tollgate', the standard procedure is to thrust open palms towards the outlaw to show you have no food. The Chinese find the monkeys an integral part of the Éméi trip, and many like to tease them.

The monkey forms an important part of Chinese mythology, and there is a saying in Chinese, 'With one monkey in the way, not even 10,000 men can pass' – which may be deeper than you think!

Some of these chimps are big, and staying cool when they look like they might make a leap at you is easier said than done. There is much debate as to whether it's better to give them something to eat or to fight them off.

One thing is certain, if you do throw them something, don't do it in too much moderation. They get annoyed very quickly if they think they are being undersold.

since being gutted by a fire several years ago. Covered with glazed tiles and surrounded by white marble balustrades, the temple now occupies 1695 sq metres. The original temple had a bronze-coated roof, which is how it got the name Jīn Dǐng (which can also mean 'Gold Top').

It's constantly overrun with tourists, pilgrims and monks, and you'll be continuously bumped and jostled. The sun rarely forces its way through the mists up here and the result is that it is usually impossible to see very far past your own nose.

From the Golden Summit it was once possible to hike to Ten Thousand Buddha Summit (Wànfó Dǐng) but pilgrims now take a monorail – a one-hour return ticket costs Y50.

Places to Stay & Eat

On the Mountain The old monasteries offer food, shelter and sights all rolled into one. While some travellers complain about the spartan and somewhat damp conditions, others find what may be as many as a thousand years of character a delightful change from the regular tourist hotels.

There are a number of *monastery guesthouses* – at Bàogúo Sì, Qīngyīn Gé, Wànnián Sì, Elephant Bathing Pool, Xiānfēng Sì, Venerable Trees Terrace, Fúhǔ Sì, Léiyīn Sì and Jīndǐng Sì. There's also a host of smaller lodgings at Chū Sì, Jiēyǐn Hall, Yùxiān Sì, Báilóngdòng and Huáyuán Sì, among others. The smaller places will accept you if the main monasteries are full. Failing those, if night is descending, you can kip virtually anywhere – a teahouse, a restaurant.

During peak season, be prepared to backtrack or advance under cover of darkness, as key points are often full of pilgrims.

You won't often find a reception desk at the monasteries. Instead, find a monk or caretaker and ask to be pointed in the right direction. A few of the monasteries at key junctions have posted prices but at others you may well have to bargain with the monks. You can expect to pay between Y15 and Y40 for a bed in a dorm room, with plumbing and electricity provided in those at the higher end of the scale. The following should give you an idea as to where to head for the cheapest beds, but, in the high season, expect to pay the top-end price:

Bàogúo Sì dorm beds Y20
Fúhǔ Sì dorm beds Y30
Qīngyīn Gè dorm beds Y15-20, doubles Y150
Wànnián Sì dorm beds Y10-40
Elephant Bathing Pool dorm beds Y30-40
Jīndǐng Sì dorm beds Y15-40

There are also a growing number of *guesthouses* cropping up on Éméi Shān. Many of the cheaper guesthouses do not accept foreigners. Others are closed during the off season. On average you can expect to pay between Y100 and Y250 for a room, depending on the availability of hot water and whether or not you opt for a private bath. The majority of these guesthouses are clumped behind Jīndǐng Sì, to the west.

Wòyún Bīnguǎn Doubles Y280-480. If you are in the mood for (relative) luxury, this hotel is located just under the cable-car station, and is the summit's only accommodation that can boast round-the-clock hot water and heating.

Vegetarian meals are included with the price of a bed at many of the monasteries. There is also often a small food stall or shop near the monastery grounds selling biscuits, instant noodles, peanuts and drinks – not to mention a wide variety of fungus.

You will also come across a large number of *food stalls* and *restaurants* along the route. Food becomes more expensive and less varied the higher you climb, due to cartage surcharges and difficulties. Be wary of teahouses or restaurants serving *shénshuǐ* (divine water), or any type of tea or food said to possess mystical healing qualities. Miracles are not guaranteed but the price of at least Y10 for the cup of water or tea is.

Around the Base The stretch of road leading up to Bàogúo Sì witnesses the rise and fall of many hotels. Most are nondescript and overpriced but will accept foreigners if you catch staff in the right mood. It's best to have a wander and check out a few options as prices and room conditions fluctuate.

Teddy Bear Hotel Beds Y30. This is the best and most popular deal in town. Rooms are basic and a bit damp but comfortable enough. The hotel is run from a wing of the Post and Telecommunications Hotel, directly across from the Teddy Bear Cafe.

Post and Telecommunications Hotel (☎ 559 3367) Rooms with bath Y238. Rooms here in the main hotel are plusher but overpriced.

Hóngzhūshān Bīnguǎn (☎ 652 3666, ext 3010) Doubles Y280. You might want to splurge on a room here. Doubles in building No 7 are the best deal and, while they may not appear particularly special, the tranquil setting of lush forests and the view on the edge of a pond easily make it feel like money well spent.

Teddy Bear Cafe This has long been a favoured haunt for backpackers. Friendly staff serve up Chinese and a few Western dishes, which you can order off an English menu. They can also help you with information on transport up the hill as well as with buses and trains further afield.

The street leading up to Bàoguó Sì is lined with *restaurants* including *huǒguō* (hotpot) and *shāokǎo* (barbecue) stalls which begin to appear as the evening approaches. There are also a large number of *shops* along here which stock food supplies for your trek up the mountain.

Getting There & Away

The hubs of the transport links to Éméi Shān are Bàoguó village and Éméi town. Éméi town itself is best skipped although it does have markets, some cheap hotels, restaurants and a long-distance bus station and train station.

Bus Éméi town lies 6.5km from Bàoguó village and the base of Éméi Shān. To Bàoguó from Éméi town, frequent microbuses (Y2) depart from the first intersection as you exit the bus station to the left. You can also try to negotiate a taxi for Y20.

Minibuses and taxis run back from Bàoguó to Éméi town for the same prices. You'll find them lurking around the bus station, next to the Teddy Bear Cafe. Also from the bus station at Bàoguó, hourly buses head to Chéngdū (Y35, two hours) from 6.30am to 6pm. You can also catch buses from here to Chóngqìng (Y95) at 7.30am and 4.30pm.

Buses from Éméi town to Chéngdū run frequently from the main bus terminal throughout the day. The trip takes two hours and tickets cost around Y30, depending on

the size and speed of the bus. While all of Chéngdū's bus stations have departures throughout the day for Éméi town, the Xīnnánmén station offers the most choice in times and prices. Buses departing from Chéngdū to Bàoguó leave from both the north and Xīmén bus stations in the mornings.

Buses run between Lèshān and Éméi town every half-hour (Y6, one hour) from 7am to 6.30pm. Buses to Yǎ'ān depart at 7.40am, 8.40am, 12.10pm, and 2.10pm and return between 7am and 4pm. This is the route you want for Móxī and Kāngdìng.

Train Éméi train station is on the Chéngdū-Kūnmíng line and lies 3.5km from the centre of Éméi town. Bus No 4 (Y0.5) runs between the train station and the long-distance bus station.

Morning trains bound for Chéngdū depart Éméi town at 7.40am and 11.18am and an evening train passes through at 7.40pm (Y9, three hours). To Kūnmíng trains leave at 12.50pm, 6.40pm and 7.30pm. To Wūshíhé (another route to Móxī and Kāngdìng) trains go at 11.14am and 9pm.

LÈSHĀN 乐山
☎ 0833 • pop 3.5 million

Once a sleepy counterpart to Éméi Shān, Lèshān has taken off as a popular tourist destination thanks to its main claim to fame – the towering Grand Buddha. Prospering from increasing droves of Chinese tourists, Lèshān has revamped many of its old quarters, levelling old residential districts to make way for new apartment towers and department stores. Nevertheless, the city has managed to retain a friendly, relaxed atmosphere and a wander through its markets and side streets will unearth some of its unique character, along with some excellent food.

Information

Money The efficient main branch of the Bank of China is on Renmin Nanlu, just past Yueertang Jie. There is also an ATM here which accepts Plus and Cirrus bank cards as well as major credit cards.

Post & Communications China Post's main office is on the corner of Yutang Jie and Fu Jie.

China Telecom runs an Internet service from the 3rd floor of the main post office (Y3 per hour). There is also a cafe here with sporadic opening hours.

Private Internet cafes are sprouting up throughout the city. The one on Baita Jie, just east of the PSB, offers access for Y2 per hour and is open until 11pm. There's another one on Binjiang Lu with similar rates.

Travel Agencies For a long time, Mr Yang of The Yangs' Restaurant (☎ 211 2046), 49 Baita Jie, has been the guru of travel information in Lèshān. While he can organise almost anything – a visit to a local doctor, a local family, a silk or tea factory, nearby villages – he has recently been getting mixed reviews from travellers who feel he has doled out dubious information in order to encourage them to patronise his services. Nevertheless, he's a great source of information and fantastic at arranging boat tickets along Cháng Jiāng (he can often get you tickets for one class higher than you pay).

PSB The PSB is at 29 Shanxi Jie, and is claimed by many travellers to be one of the best places in China to try for a visa extension.

Grand Buddha 大佛
Dà Fó

Carved into a cliff face overlooking the confluence of Dàdù Hé and Mín Hé, the Grand Buddha (admission Y40) measures an overwhelming 71m high. Qualifying as the largest buddha in the world, his ears are 7m long, his insteps 8.5m broad, and you could picnic on the nail of his big toe – the toe itself is 8.5m long.

This mammoth project was begun in AD 713, engineered by a Buddhist monk called Haitong who organised fund raising and hired workers; it was completed 90 years later, after the death of Haitong. Below the Grand Buddha was a hollow where boatmen used to vanish – Haitong hoped that the buddha's presence would subdue the swift currents and protect the boatmen. And the buddha has done a lot of good, as the surplus rocks from the sculpting filled the river hollow.

Inside the body, hidden from view, is a water-drainage system put into place to

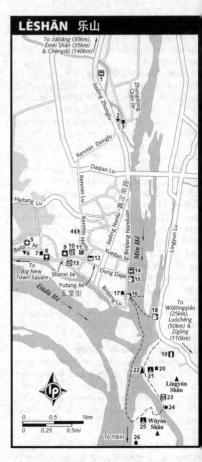

LÈSHĀN 乐山

prevent weathering, although the stone statue has had its fair share of it. A building once sheltered the giant statue, but it was destroyed during a Ming dynasty war.

Officials are worried about the possibility of collapse due to soil erosion; one suggestion that has not met with an enthusiastic response is to cover the buddha with a huge transparent shell.

It's worth looking at the Grand Buddha from several angles. While the easiest way to see him is to walk along the riverfront on Binjiang Lu (an especially attractive spectacle in the evening when the site is lit), you need to get closer to him to really appreciate his magnitude. You can go to the top, opposite the head, and then descend a short stairway to the feet for a Lilliputian perspective.

LÈSHĀN

PLACES TO STAY

3 Lèshān Jiàoyù
Bīnguǎn
乐山教育宾馆

7 Jiāzhōu Bīnguǎn
嘉州宾馆

17 Táoyuán Bīnguǎn
桃源宾馆

20 Nánlóu Bīnguǎn
南楼宾馆

26 Xiāndǎo Bīnguǎn
仙岛宾馆

PLACES TO EAT

2 Hotpot
Restaurant
火锅饭店

6 The Yangs'
Restaurant
杨家餐厅

OTHER

1 Long-Distance Bus
Station
长途汽车站

4 Bank of China
中国银行

5 Hospital
医院

8 Newcastle Arms Pub

9 PSB
公安局

10 Internet Cafe
网吧

11 Workers' Cultural Palace
劳动人民文化宫

12 Post Office
邮电局

13 Internet Cafe

14 Central Bus Station
省汽车客运中心站

15 Small Tour Boats &
Ticket Office
小旅游船及售票处

16 Ferry Ticket Office;
Ferry Dock
渡轮售票处; 渡轮码头

18 Ferry Dock
渡轮码头

19 Língbǎo Pagoda
灵宝塔

21 Dàfó Sì
大佛寺

22 Grand Buddha
大佛

23 Máhàoyá Tombs Museum
麻浩崖博物馆

24 Dōngfāng Fódū Gōngyuán
东方佛都公园

25 Wūyóu Sì
乌尤寺

Boat Tours Tour boats pass by for a frontal view of the Grand Buddha, which reveals two guardians in the cliff side, not visible from land.

To make a round tour that encompasses the many views of the Grand Buddha, take a boat from the dockside along Binjiangnan Lu. You currently have a choice of three types of boat. Best value is the ferry which charges the bargain fare of Y1 (plus an extra Y1 to sit on the top deck) and goes from just south of Táoyuán Bīnguǎn to Wūyóu, continues on to the Lèshān paper mill and its opposite bank and then returns by the same route. The only snag is that you don't get much time in front of the buddha – one shot with the camera and you've passed it. It helps to sit on the upper deck facing the dock, since the boat turns around when leaving.

The two other options are on a large tour boat (Y30) or a smaller speedboat for the same price. You won't see anything different on these boats but you will have more time to enjoy it, as the boats will hover for five to 10 minutes in front of the buddha, engines whirring madly against the current. Boats leave from north of the ferry dock approximately every 30 minutes from 7am to 5pm.

All the boats pass close by the Grand Buddha and then stop at **Wūyóu Sì** (admission Y5; open daily). Like the Grand Buddha, this monastery dates from the Tang dynasty with Ming and Qing renovations. It commands panoramic views and is a museum piece containing calligraphy, painting and artefacts, many with English captions.

Wūyóu Sì has a hall of 1000 terracotta arhat monks displaying an incredible variety of postures and facial expressions – no two are alike. The arhats are housed in the **Luohan Hall** which dates back to 1909. Inside is also a fantastic statue of **Avalokiteshvara**, the Goddess of Mercy (Guanyin in Chinese).

The temple's *vegetarian restaurant* is famed for its imitation meats dishes: spare ribs and beef strips that look like the real thing. The taste, however, is another matter, and you'll probably be better off with straight vegetables.

If you get off the boat at Wūyóu Sì, a visit through the temple will take you across Wūyóu Shān and down to a small bridge which crosses over to **Língyún Shān** (Towering Cloud Hill). Here you can visit **Dōngfāng Fódū Gōngyuán** (Oriental Buddha Park; admission Y25; open daily), a newly assembled collection of 3000 buddha statues and figurines from all around Asia. The park's centrepiece is a 170m-long reclining buddha, said to be the world's longest. Though touted by local tourist authorities as a major attraction, the park seems more of a hasty effort to cash in on buddha-mania – the Hong Kong and Chinese sculptors raced to knock off the reclining buddha in a mere two years. Still it makes for an interesting walk.

Next door is the **Máhàoyá Tombs Museum** *(Máhàoyámù Bówùguǎn; admission Y2; open daily)*, which has a modest collection of tombs and burial artefacts dating from the Eastern Han dynasty (AD 25–220).

Continuing past the Buddha Park and up Língyún Shān brings you to the entrance gate of **Dàfó Sì** *(admission Y40; open daily)*. This is where you can get right up close to the Grand Buddha, with views from a platform level with his head. You can also follow a narrow staircase down to reach his feet. Nearby is the **Língbǎo Pagoda**.

To return to Lèshān, there are local ferries (Y1) departing from the first dock north of the main exit. The service is sporadic and the last runs are awfully early – around mid-afternoon sometimes. Buses also run from the exit back to town.

This whole exercise can be done in less than 1½ hours from the Lèshān dock; however, it's worth making a day of it.

During winter you can get another angle on the Grand Buddha from the island in the middle of the two rivers' confluence. Boatmen ferry passengers onto the island, from where you can walk along the spit. In summer you should be careful of how far you wander, as river levels are generally higher. Get local advice before attempting this.

Thousand Buddha Cliffs
Jiājiāng Qiānfóyán 夹江千佛岩

About 30km north of Lèshān, 2.5km west of the train station at Jiājiāng, are the Thousand Buddha Cliffs *(admission Y30; open 8am-4.45pm daily)*. For once, the name is not an exaggeration: over 2400 buddhas dot the cliffs, dating from as early as the Eastern Han dynasty. The statues show a few signs of wear and tear but, considering their age, are in fairly good condition.

Set in a rather pretty location along a riverbank and on the edge of the countryside, this site takes something of an effort to reach. Catch one of the many buses from Lèshān's long-distance bus station down the bumpy road to Jiājiāng (Y5, one hour). From Jiājiāng bus station, take a pedicab (Y10) or taxi (Y15) to the site. The last bus returning to Lèshān leaves Jiājiāng at 6pm.

Other Sights
The boardwalk along Binjiang Lu follows Dàdù Hé from its confluence with Mín Hé,

up past Jiāzhōu Bīnguǎn. Popular for strolling in the evenings, if you follow it as far as Jiāzhōu Bīnguǎn, you'll see fan dancers practising in a square near the intersection with Baita Jie. You can also take bus No 6 out to the **Big New Town Square** where a 27m-high fountain attracts crowds of Leshanese in the evenings.

Travellers have recommended day trips to villages outside Lèshān, including **Luóchéng**, 50km south-east, famed for its old 'boathouse' architecture, and **Wǔtōngqiáo**, 25km south. Check with Mr Yang at The Yangs' Restaurant.

Places to Stay
Táoyuán Bīnguǎn (☎ 212 7784, fax 212 9904) Southern-bldg doubles Y50, northern-bldg doubles Y160-260. Located down by Lèshān's pier, this hotel has been receiving mixed reports, probably because it is housed in two separate buildings, practically next door to one another, with separate receptions and very different conditions. The building to the south offers cheap rooms that are somewhat grotty with reports of cockroaches living it up at night. Three doors north, the northern building offers comfortable, clean rooms which may be discounted to Y50 – excellent value for money.

Lèshān Jiàoyù Bīnguǎn (☎ 213 4257, 156 Liren Jie) Doubles Y100-180, triples Y180. Near the main bus station, this hotel was once a favourite haunt of backpackers. However, its hike in prices seems to have been matched with a plunge in quality. Rooms are damp and dingy. Business is unsurprisingly slow these days and it may be willing to slash prices in half.

Nánlóu Bīnguǎn Doubles/suites with bath & air-con Y120/180. This hotel is in Dàfó Sì, on the eastern side of the river. Perhaps due to the buddha's drainage system, the cliff around here is wet and the dampness can extend to the rooms. The rooms, however, are reasonable and the greatest bonus is that in the morning you can beat the rush to the Grand Buddha. To find the hotel simply walk through the temple to the last courtyard where you'll find the reception.

Xiāndǎo Bīnguǎn (☎ 230 1988) Rooms Y168. This hotel is near the sights and the rooms are clean, though somewhat pricey.

Jiāzhōu Bīnguǎn (☎ 213 9888, fax 213 3233, 19 Baita Lu) Doubles or triples Y360, suites Y600. This three-star hotel is Lèshān's fanciest accommodation. To get there from the bus station take the No 1 bus to the end of the line. Rates include breakfast.

Places to Eat

Tasty meals abound in Lèshān with the best food served up at the dozens of small cubby-hole restaurants and street stalls. Try Xue-dao Jie, just north of the pier, which is buzzing with activity and culinary delights. Be sure to check prices here before ordering.

The Yangs' Restaurant (49 Baita Jie) For a local, home-style meal and good conversation, try this small, wooden restaurant. It has an English menu and Chinese prices.

Also try the fantastically popular *hotpot restaurant* just north of the intersection at Jiading Zhonglu and Renmin Lu.

There are also dozens of *restaurants* overlooking the river at the bottom end of Binjiang Nanduan. If you're craving a more relaxed atmosphere or a pint of beer with your meal, try the *Newcastle Arms Pub* next door to Jiāzhōu Bīnguǎn.

Getting There & Away

Transportation links to Lèshān are both expanding and improving. The expressway from Chéngdū has reached Lèshān, cutting travel time down to a mere two hours. An expressway from Lèshān to Chóngqìng is also near completion, resulting in a triangular transportation conduit which is second to none in south-west China. Plans are also being finalised for an enormous new airport 20km outside Lèshān; when finished – no exact date for this yet – it will be larger than Chéngdū's.

Bus There are two bus stations in Lèshān. The main one for travellers is the Lèshān long-distance bus station, somewhat inconveniently located in the northern reaches of the city. The central bus station is closer to the centre of town, next to Mín Hé.

From the long-distance station, buses to Chéngdū leave every 10 to 20 minutes from 6.30am to 7pm (Y37, two hours). Watch out for the buses' Chéngdū destination. While most go to Xīnnánmén bus station next to the Traffic Hotel, several go to the north bus station or train station, which are inconveniently located for Chéngdū's budget accommodation.

Buses leave for Éméi town from both bus stations at least once every half-hour between 6.30am and 6pm (Y5.5, one hour). Those running from the central bus station seem to stop far more frequently than those departing from the long-distance bus station.

From the long-distance bus station, regular buses to Chóngqìng (Y84) depart hourly from 7.10am until 2.10pm and then at 3.30pm and 5pm. Buses for Yǎ'ān (for connections to Lúdìng and Kāngdìng) depart hourly from 7.10am to 10.10am and at 11.50am and 9pm (Y21, three hours). Note that connecting buses to Lúdìng only leave Yǎ'ān every other day.

Train It doesn't matter what anyone says, there simply is no train service to Lèshān. Ticket sellers in other cities will swear blind they can sell you a ticket to Lèshān but in reality they will only sell you a ticket to Éméi Shān, or more likely Jiājiāng, both about an hour away by bus.

Boat At one time there was a regular boat service between Lèshān and Yíbīn, with further services to Chóngqìng. River fluctuations and bad management doomed it and there were no services at the time of writing. The money poured into the new expressways has made bus travel faster, safer and understandably more popular. If you're lucky, you may find private high-speed boats to Yíbīn (Y80, 2½ hours) running from June to August.

Getting Around

Bus Nos 1 and 8 run the length of Jiading Lu and connect the pier area with the long-distance bus station. Buses runs from 6am to 6pm, at roughly 20-minute intervals.

On foot, it's about an hour's walk from one end of town to the other. A pedicab from the main long-distance bus station to Táoyuán Bīnguǎn should cost about Y5 and from the pier to Jiāzhōu Bīnguǎn about Y2. Pedicab operators in Lèshān all split up the fares, so don't be paranoid when one of them stops halfway and tells you to get on his buddy's pedicab. Just pay him half (or whatever) and pay the remainder when you arrive. Taxis in Lèshān start at a flat rate of Y3 for the first 3km.

Unfortunately there doesn't seem to be a bicycle hire in Lèshān – or many bicycles at all for that matter. But you probably wouldn't want to take them up and down the stairs at the Grand Buddha anyway.

Western Sìchuān & the Road to Tibet

The Sìchuān mountains to the north and west of Chéngdū rise above 5000m with deep valleys, vast grasslands and rapid rivers. To Tibetans, this area is part of the province of 'Kham' which covers the eastern third of the Tibetan Plateau. For travellers, it is an opportunity to visit Tibet without actually crossing the 'official' provincial border.

Tibetans and Tibetan-related peoples (Qiang) live here by herding yaks, sheep and goats on the high-altitude Kangba Plateau grasslands. The further out you go from Kāngdìng, the more evident the Tibetan customs and clothing become.

Towns in these areas experience cold temperatures, with up to 200 freezing days per year; summers are blistering by day and the high altitude invites particularly bad sunburn. Lightning storms are frequent from May to October, when cloud cover can shroud the scenic peaks.

The Sìchuān-Tibet Highway, begun in 1950 and finished in 1954, is one of the world's highest, roughest, most dangerous and most beautiful roads. It splits into northern and southern routes 70km west of Kāngdìng. Much of this area was only opened to foreigners in 1999 and, as yet, there isn't much in the way of tourist facilities. For more information on Kham, check out the Web site at Ⓦ www.khamaid.org.

If you're planning to attempt to cross into Tibet from Bātáng or Dégé, you may want to reconsider. The PSB in both of these towns keep a close eye on foreigners, and as truck drivers are levied hefty fines and lose their driving licence for carrying foreigners across the border, they're unlikely to give you a lift. Some travellers have managed to bribe their way in but at costs that make flying from Chéngdū more economical. If you do reach Lhasa, you'll likely be fined and sent back. However, if you're arriving from Tibet into Sìchuān, nobody seems to give a damn.

Be forewarned: at the time of writing it was not possible to change money or travellers cheques or to get advances on credit cards in Sìchuān's north-west. Bring your Renminbi with you.

KĀNGDÌNG (DARBO) 康定
☎ 0836 • elevation 2560m

Kāngdìng is a fairly large town nestled in a steep river valley at the confluence of the swift Zheduo and Yala rivers, known as the Dar and Tse in Tibetan. Kāngdìng is famous throughout China for a popular love song that the town's surrounding scenery inspired. If you're en route to western Sìchuān, chances are you'll end up overnighting here and it's worth staying for a day to take in the sights and check out some of this dreamy scenery. Towering above Kāngdìng is the mighty peak of Gōnggà Shān (7556m).

Arriving in Kāngdìng, there is a tangible sense that you've reached the end of the Chinese world and the beginning of the Tibetan. The town has been a trade centre between the two cultures for centuries with the exchange of yak hides, wool, Tibetan herbs and, especially, bricks of tea from Yǎ'ān wrapped in yak hide. It also served as an important staging post on the road to Lhasa, as indeed it does today. Kāngdìng was historically the capital of the local Tibetan kingdom of Chakla (or Chala) and later, from 1939 to 1951, the capital of the short-lived province of Xikang, when it was controlled by the opium-dealing warlord Liu Wenhui.

Today Kāngdìng is largely a Chinese town, though you'll still see plenty of Khambas down from the hills shopping or selling huge blocks of yak butter in the market. You'll also spot monks wandering around town in crimson robes.

Information
The PSB (☎ 281 1415 ext 6035) is on the 4th floor of a building five minutes' walk south-east of Gònggàshān Lǔshè. It processes visa extensions quickly and painlessly.

China Post and Telecom are next to the river on Yanhe Xilu. The Bank of China is next door but does not change money or provide any other service which might be useful for travellers.

Lí Jiāng, in Guǎngxī, is lined with towering limestone pinnacles.

Zhōngdiàn, in Yúnnán, is a winter wonderland in late November.

A criss-cross of rice fields below a rural village in Guìzhōu.

A spectacular gorge in Yúnnán.

This old bicycle in Guìzhōu has been around.

Limestone pillars of Shílín (Stone Forest), Yúnnán

Fixing fishing nets in Xīngpíng, Guǎngxī.

An elderly lady writes Buddhist scriptures in Xīshuāngbǎnnà, Yúnnán.

There is an Internet service in the China Telecom office though it's a little tricky to find. Enter through the back of the building through a doorway marked No 10. Climb up to the 3rd floor, turn left down the hall and the office is the first on the right, most noticeable for its red velvet curtain. Access costs Y3 per hour and the office closes when all of the customers have gone home.

There is also cheap Internet access available (Y3 to Y4) in the Internet cafes next door to Pǎomǎ Bīnguǎn.

Travel Agencies The Kangding Tour Service (Kāngdìng Lǚvyóu Fúwù Zhōngxīn; ☎ 283 4000, fax 283 1946, e js@ganzi .scst.ac.cn) offers information and tours of nearby sights including treks, horse tours and bus rides to Gònggà Shān. The Tibetan owner speaks English and seems happy to tailor tours for you.

Things to See & Do
There are several lamaseries in and around Kāngdìng. Just behind Gònggàshān Lǚshè, **Ānjué Sì** (Ngachu Gompa in Tibetan) is a fairly quiet temple with several monks and a few old prayer wheels.

Nánwù Sì is the most active lamasery in the area with around 80 lamas in residence. Set in the west of town on the northern bank of the river, it affords good views of Kāngdìng and the valley. Walk south along the main road, following its bend to the left for 2km. Cross the bridge at the southern end of town and continue on 300m. Next to a walled Han Chinese cemetery is a dirt path that follows a stream uphill to the lamasery.

You can also head up **Pǎomǎ Shān** for excellent views of Kāngdìng, the surrounding mountains and valleys and – if you're lucky – Gònggà Shān. The ascent takes you past oodles of prayer flags, several Buddhist temples and up to a white *chörten* (stupa). Take particular care when wandering around Pǎomǎ Shān and try to avoid hiking on your own. A British tourist was murdered here in the spring of 2000.

To reach the hill, bear left at the fork in the road just south of the bus station and walk about 10 minutes until you reach a lamasery on the left; a stairway leads up the hill from here. A second, more direct route, heads up the hill further south, beginning above the staircase on Dong Dajie.

About 5km north of Kāngdìng are the **Erdao Bridge Hot Springs** (*admission Y10*), where you can have a half-hour bath in slightly eggy-smelling, warm, sulphur water. You can go in on your own or get a larger bath for a group soak. Take your own towel. You can reach the hot springs by taxi for about Y8.

In town, the **market** on Dong Dajie is worth a look. The **Walking around the Mountain Festival** (*Zhuànshānjié*) takes place on Pǎomǎ Shān on the eighth day of the fourth lunar month to commemorate the birthday of the Historical Buddha, Sakyamuni. White-and-blue Tibetan tents cover the hillside and there's plenty of wrestling, horse racing and visitors from all over western Sìchuān, making it a good time to visit Kāngdìng.

Places to Stay
Gònggàshān Lǚshè (*Hei Zhanpeng Zhuse in Tibetan*) Beds in triples Y17-30. The basic rooms here are quiet and clean. Beds boast electric blankets. The toilets are relatively OK for this part of the world and washing facilities consist of the usual basin and heated water. The teahouse on the ground floor is the place to come to if you want to relax or meet other travellers.

Kāngdìng Bīnguǎn (☎ 282 3153) Beds with/without student card Y20/36. This chaotic place was once the best hotel in town. Rooms are now weary-looking and overpriced. Solo travellers are almost always overcharged and may have to bargain the price down to around Y50 or Y60 for a room. At least there's hot water at night, which comes on simultaneously with the rousing karaoke sessions.

Jīnlù Bīnguǎn (☎ 283 3216) Beds Y30. This hotel offers well-priced beds in spacious, clean rooms. Hot water in private bathrooms (with tubs!) is available 24 hours. To find the reception, walk through the gate and turn right.

Tàiníng Jiǔdiàn (☎ 282 4530) Beds in triples Y40. Conveniently located, this friendly place has clean rooms. Hot showers are down the hall.

Pǎomǎ Bīnguǎn (☎ 283 3110) Dorm beds in 4-bed rooms with/without student card Y35/70, doubles Y240. This is the place to come for more upmarket rooms, all with bath. It's amazingly expensive for this part of the world; however, if you have a student card you can get a cheaper dorm bed.

Places to Eat

For a rousing cup of yak butter tea, try the *teahouse* adjacent to Gònggàshān Lǔshè. It also carries a wide selection of other types of teas from around these parts but it's best to ask the price first. For inexpensive meals, the guesthouse will likely recommend the *restaurant* across the road.

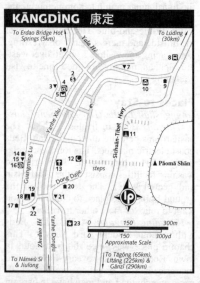

KĀNGDÌNG 康定

Jíxiáng Fàndiàn This small restaurant has an English menu and the friendly owners serve fantastic local cuisine at good prices. Try the potato pancake or the black bean fish.

At the Kangding Tour Service you'll also find a *teahouse* and *Tibetan restaurant* offering up such delicacies as Tibetan butter dumplings and *zanba* (roasted barley flour).

Pǎomǎsān Cāntīng All-you-can-eat Y38. This restaurant serves an all-you-can-eat hotpot extravaganza with oodles of exotic-looking vegies, fish, meat, prawns, squid and chicken feet.

Tàiníng Jiǔdiàn Dishes Y8-20. This hotel has a good restaurant with a large menu and surprisingly reasonable prices, considering its fancy decor.

There are also numerous point-and-choose *restaurants* near the bus station and a couple of noodle and *bāozi* (steamed stuffed buns) places in the market. In the evening, numerous covered *Sìchuān stalls* set up camp at the northern end of town with arguably the widest selection of skewered meat, vegies and fish in Sìchuān. There is also a late night *bakery* on the road behind the post office.

Getting There & Away

Improved roads have made Kāngdìng far more accessible. Services east only run every other day due to tunnel construction at the Èrláng Shān Pass. Once the tunnel is completed, daily travel should resume.

Buses leave every other day for Chéngdū from 6.20am to 8pm (Y107, seven to eight hours). From Chéngdū, early morning buses for Kāngdìng depart from the Xīnnánmén station. The 4pm sleeper will dump you off in Kāngdìng in the middle of the night.

To Lúdìng (for Móxī and Hǎiluógōu Glacier), shared taxis and minivans depart from a stand south of the bus station. Drivers will start bargaining high but you should be able to get a seat for around Y15.

Going west from Kāngdìng, a bus departs daily to Lǐtáng (Y84, seven hours) at 6.20am. There is a 6.40am bus for Gānzī (Y112) and a 7am bus for Bātáng (Y110, 11 hours). For Dégé there is a departure every other day at 7am.

There are also departures for Xiāngchéng (Y144) that depart at 7am every other day (or so) and overnight in Lǐtáng.

AROUND KĀNGDÌNG

About 110km north-west of Kāngdìng lie the **Tǎgōng Grasslands** (*Tǎgōng Cǎoyuán*), a vast expanse of green meadow surrounded by snow-capped peaks and dotted with Tibetan herdsmen and tents. An annual horse racing festival (*sàimǎhuì*) features thousands of local Tibetan herdsmen and Tibetan opera.

The small village of **Tǎgōng** is a fantastic place to visit if you want to get a taste of Sìchuān's Tibetan Wild West. In the village, **Tǎgōng Sì** blends Han Chinese and Tibetan styles and dates back to the Qing dynasty.

Local families will likely offer you cheap accommodation and meals. Ask in the small lamasery shop where a friendly monk may take you home to his folk's amazing little ornate guesthouse. If that fails, try *Tǎgōng Bīnguǎn* with dorm beds ranging from Y5 for a lumpy mattress to Y15 for something a bit more comfy. To find the hotel head south down the main street, away from the lamasery; it's on your right.

Buses to Tǎgōng village run every day from Kāngdìng (Y23, three hours) at 7.20am and drop you outside the lamasery. (During the horse festival there are likely to be more frequent departures.) If you're headed on to Gānzī, you can pick up the same bus the next day at about 10am as it passes through town. Returning to Kāngdìng, afternoon buses can be flagged down as they pass through Tǎgōng village. You can also catch a minibus on the main street that will take you to Yǎjiāng from where there are buses to Chéngdū or Lǐtáng.

There are several mountain lakes and hot springs in the vicinity of Kāngdìng. Lying 21km to the north of town up the Yala Valley, **Mùgécuò Hú** is one of the highest lakes in north-western Sìchuān, at 3700m. Locals also boast that it's one of the most beautiful. Trails around the lake lead to other smaller lakes such as the **Red Sea** (*Hóng Hǎi*). Also worth checking out is **Seven Colour Lake** (*Qīsè Hǎi*), which lies a few kilometres before Mùgécuò. It's best not to wander around these parts alone or to stray too far off the path. The area of 'Wild Men's Lake', as Mùgécuò means in Tibetan, is home to wolves and other wild beasts.

There are no buses running to Mùgécuò but idle taxi drivers will be more than pleased to shuttle you there and back for Y150 to Y200 (1½ hours). You can also talk to the Kangding Tour Service to see if it has any tours going there.

Mùgécuò Hú can easily be done as a day trip from Kāngdìng but if you choose to stay out there, both *Qísehai Bīnguǎn* and *Mùgécuò Bīnguǎn* have beds which you may be able to get for as low as Y30.

LÚDÌNG 泸定

Lúdìng is a small, bustling town about halfway between Kāngdìng and Móxī. As a major connection point for buses between western Sìchuān and Chéngdū, Lèshān and Móxī, you are likely to find yourself here. For those with a keen interest in China's Communist history, it may be worth a brief stop.

Lúdìng is famous throughout China as the site of what is often regarded as the most glorious moment of the Long March which took place on the **Lúdìng Bridge** (*Lúdìng Qiáo; admission Y5*), a 100m-long chain suspension bridge over Dàdù Hé.

On 29 May 1935 the Communist troops approached Lúdìng Bridge only to discover that Kuomintang troops had beat them to it, removed the planks from the bridge and had it covered with firepower. In response, 20 Communist troops crossed the bridge hand-over-hand armed with grenades and then proceeded to overcome the Kuomintang troops on the other side. This action allowed the Long March to continue before the main body of the Kuomintang forces could catch up with them.

The bridge is five minutes' walk south along the river from the northern bus station. The original bridge was first constructed in 1705 and was an important link in the Sìchuān-Tibet road.

On the main street in town you might also want to check out the **Luding Bridge Revolutionary Artefacts Museum** (*Lúdìng Qiáo Gémìng Wénwù Chénlièguǎn*), which houses a collection of some 150 items left behind by members of the Long March. You can also get a gander at some of Mao's calligraphy on a shelter near the Buddhist Temple on the hillside above town.

Places to Stay & Eat The hotel situation in Lúdìng is not very bright. As they gear up for the anticipated tourist boom in Móxī, hotel proprietors have inflated their prices but left the quality of rooms way behind in the dust – lots of dust.

Chēzhàn Lǚguǎn Beds in 3-bed dorms Y30. Across the street from the southern bus station, the rooms here are fairly drab and some are kind of stinky but they're the cheapest you'll find in town.

Yagudu Bīnguǎn Doubles with bath Y70. Rooms here are shabby and overpriced, with hot water kicking in after 9pm. To find it, turn right out of the south bus station and walk back to the highway. Look for 'Yagudu Restaurant' stencilled on the window.

Xiàn Zhāodàisuǒ Doubles with/without bath Y120/100. Between the Lúdìng Bridge and the north bus station, rooms at the County Government's guesthouse are cleaner and perhaps a bit brighter than elsewhere in town, but they're still overpriced. On the up side, there is 24-hour hot water.

Clustered around the southern bus station are a number of nondescript *restaurants* as well as a *teahouse* where you can while away your time until the next bus pulls into town.

Getting There & Away For some unknown reason, Lúdìng has two bus stations. Getting information out of staff at either station is excruciating. They'll claim there is only one bus each morning for every destination, despite buses pulling in and out all day. If you don't want to wait around, you can get shared taxis to Móxī and Kāngdìng for practically the same price as the bus or you can try flagging down through-buses as they pass by town.

The town itself is built up along two roads – the through highway to Kāngdìng which runs along the river and the more bustling main street of town which arcs in a half-moon shape, meeting the highway at each end.

On the highway, where it bends to cross the river, you'll find the north bus station. Here you can get the 7am bus to Móxī (Y15) or bargain a shared taxi down to Y20 per person (minimum four passengers). The trip takes two hours by bus or one hour by taxi. The bus to Chéngdū (Y90) leaves at 7am every other day. A bus for Kāngdìng (Y40) also leaves at 7am or you can bargain a taxi down to Y20 to Y30 for the trip (one hour).

At the other end of town, on the main street, is the southern bus station. It looks more like a parking lot than a bus station; you'll find the ticket office (which doubles as the reception for Chēzhàn Lǚguǎn across the street. One bus a day departs from here to Shímián (Y15) at 6am. The bus for Yǎ'ān (Y55) leaves every other day at 7am.

Lúdìng-Yǎ'ān-Lèshān

If you're travelling between Kāngdìng or Móxī and Éméi Shān or Lèshān, you may decide (or be forced) to break the journey in Yǎ'ān. Buses from Lèshān leave for Yǎ'ān (four hours) more or less hourly from 7.10am until 9pm. From Éméi Shān, buses go at 8.40am, 12.10pm and 2.10pm.

Buses between Yǎ'ān and Lúdìng (where you can change for Móxī or carry on to Kāngdìng) are somewhat more tricky. The Èrláng Shān Pass, renowned for its steep climb, blind corners and landslides, is being conquered by a new tunnel cutting through the mountainside. This and other road works have made the already narrow road even narrower. The result: the bus service runs in each direction only every other day – one day west from Yǎ'ān, the next day east from Lúdìng. Traffic must also wait on either side of the tunnel for designated times to pass through, making it best to head out of Yǎ'ān no later than 9.30am or risk facing a four- or five-hour wait. The trip from Yǎ'ān to Lúdìng is supposed to take four hours but due to queues it may well take closer to seven or eight.

Once road works are completed, it is likely that travel will resume daily from both directions. Nevertheless, you may still want to overnight in **Yă'ān**. A friendly town during the day, Yă'ān really comes to life at nightfall with its **Music Square**, Yă'ān's bat at tourism. Visit the square during the day and find it desolate. Return in the evening and find the entire town out, gathered around a huge, lit fountain and moving to the beat of Chinese and Euro dance music.

Be warned, however: as a foreigner, you may well become the object of interest to what can quickly become a frenzied mob of 12-year-olds, screaming for your signature on scraps of paper, their arms and T-shirts. To find the Music Square, turn right out of the bus station and cross the bridge.

Xīka Fàndiàn (☎ 0835-262 3583) Doubles Y40-80. If you're spending the night in Yă'ān, this place has clean rooms, varying in size and quality. As you exit the bus station, the hotel is on the left of the road directly ahead of you. The staff are friendly and will fill you in with information on bus schedules.

A second route between Éméi Shān and Lúdìng, without doubling back to Chéngdū, is south via Wūsīhé. There is usually one morning bus at 6am from Lúdìng to Wūsīhé (Y15) but if it doesn't appear, jump on a bus to Shímián from where there is frequent onward transport. Once you reach Wūsīhé you'll need to hop on a train to Éméi town. The train departs Wūsīhé in the afternoon meaning you shouldn't have to overnight here but should you need to, there are several cheap hotels around the train station. Coming from Éméi town, the train to Wūsīhé leaves at 11.14am or 9pm (Y10, 3½ hours). If you're headed south to Pānzhīhūa or Kūnmíng, be advised that you can only buy hard-seat tickets in Wūsīhé and very few onward trains stop here.

MÓXĪ 磨西
☎ 0836

Nestled in the mountains around 50km south-west of Lúdìng, this peaceful one-street village is the gateway to the Hǎiluógōu Glacier Park (see the following section). With lots of character, Móxī itself is also worth a visit.

Móxī's older, traditional wooden buildings are at the bottom of the village. Also at this end is a somewhat out-of-place, multi-coloured **Catholic church**. Boarded up and sprouting grass on its steeple, the church's principal claim to fame these days is that Mao camped out in it during the Long March.

From here, the village climbs its way up a hill. If you follow the dirt road up, about 200m past the main cross-road, on the right is **Guānyīnggǔ Gompa**, a 400-year-old Bön temple. In the courtyard is a mammoth, gnarled tree around which the temple has been built. Across the road from the temple is a small **pagoda** from where you can get a view of the surrounding scenery.

Places to Stay

Lǚyóu Fàndiàn Beds Y15. Next to the Catholic church, this small guesthouse has quiet, all-wood rooms in a building at the back of the courtyard. The rooms are simple, clean and good value. The friendly owner and his family can help with bus and transport information.

Up the hill about 300m from here is the *Hǎiluógōu Bīnguǎn* which is currently being rebuilt but promises to offer upmarket rooms and facilities.

Aurum Conch Guesthouse Dorm beds/doubles with bath Y30/120. Further uphill from the church than Hǎiluógōu Bīnguǎn, this place has OK rooms but is definitely not the best deal in town.

Hǎiluó Fàndiàn (☎ 326 6296) Doubles Y60. Directly next door to the Aurum Conch Guesthouse, this place is much better value. Rooms are extremely clean and comfortable with hot showers down the hall. There is also a rooftop terrace that offers views of the glacier should the weather be on your side.

Hǎiluógōu Bīnguǎn Dorm beds/doubles Y30/80. At the top of the hill, over the cross-road, is a second Hǎiluógōu Bīnguǎn. This is where buses and taxi drivers generally drop their passengers and then try their mightiest to convince them to stay. Rooms are bleak but the staff seem willing to bargain.

Shāhǎigōujīnxué Doubles with/without bath Y120/60. If you continue further uphill about 175m from the second Hǎiluógōu Bīnguǎn, you'll find this sparkling, brand-new hotel on the right. Showers here are hot and rooms are great value.

Places to Eat

Lǚyóu Fàndiàn will bring on a feast for you at very good prices. You'll also find a fair number of *restaurants* along the main road as well as *barbecue stalls*. Móxī's shops and fruit stands are well stocked if you need to buy some supplies for a trip to Hǎiluógōu.

Getting There & Away

From Móxī there is a 7am bus to Lúdìng (Y15, two hours) which can be flagged down outside Lǚyóu Fàndiàn. Change at Lúdìng for Chéngdū, Yǎ'ān and Kāngdìng. If you're headed to Shímián, get off the bus at Maoziping, on the other side of the bright orange Rainbow Bridge. From here you can flag down a southbound bus.

If your bus doesn't show up, catch one of the minibuses that come bumping down the road. Rates are similar to bus prices.

To reach Móxī, get off your bus in Lúdìng from where you can try to catch the 7am bus (Y15) or hunt down a minibus for the same price. You can also bargain a taxi down to about Y20 per person. If you're arriving from the south via Shímián, you can either carry on to Lúdìng and backtrack or get off at Maoziping and flag down a minicab to Móxī from there.

The main draw to Móxī is, of course, Hǎiluógōu Glacier Park. The entrance to the park is within easy walking distance from Móxī. Turn left at Móxī's main crossroads at the top of the hill and carry on to the ticket office, about 400m up the road.

HǍILUÓGŌU GLACIER PARK

Hǎiluógōu Bīngchuān Gōngyuán 海螺沟冰川公园
Magnificent Hǎiluógōu Glacier tumbles off the eastern slopes of Gònggā Shān to form the lowest glacier in Asia. **No 1 Glacier**, the main glacier, is 14km long and covers an area of 16 sq km. It's relatively young as glaciers go: around 1600 years.

The top of Hǎiluógōu can offer incredible vistas of Gònggā Shān and surrounding peaks, all above 6000m, but how much you actually see is entirely up to Mother Nature. Constantly framed with a backdrop of snowy peaks, the surrounding forests are also beautiful, with their ecosystems changing as you ascend the mountain.

The rainy season for this area spans July and August, although the locals say they get 200 days of rain a year. The best time to visit the Hǎiluógōu Glacier Park *(admission Y60)* is between late September and November, when skies are generally clear. Autumn colours are particularly beautiful at this time, though it can be cold up at Camp No 3.

Once a popular foot or pony trek, the park has fallen under the watchful eye of the government's tourism board. Today there is not a neigh to be heard for miles, the path is neglected and overgrown and a cable car should be up and running by the time you read this. The most popular way to ascend the mountain is now by minibus (Y50 return, 30 minutes one way), departing from the park entrance at 7.30am.

The atmosphere of Hǎiluógōu Glacier Park is quickly changing and will continue to do so with increased tour buses racing up and down the mountain and tourists hanging out of the cable cars above the glacier. If you're looking for a real getaway into the wilderness, this is no longer it. But if your main interest is seeing and even walking across a glacier, then the park is still worth a visit.

At the time of research, trekking to the top was still possible, but many trekkers have complained of finding the path difficult to follow as both use and maintenance fall away. Other parts of the route are now paved road used by the minibuses. You are also likely to be discouraged from walking (if not told flat out that you can't) by workers at the park entrance.

If you do plan to trek, come prepared with warm clothes and sunglasses. You'll also need to bring food and water, as you might not find much to buy en route until you reach Camp No 3 and its pricey restaurants. Maps of the park are available from the entrance gate; however, marked trails may be less than accurate and some may have disappeared. For information on specific camps en route, see the following Places to Stay & Eat section.

The entrance fee to the park includes a guide, compulsory for all tourists going out on the glacier and handy for keeping you away from deep crevices and melting points, as well as for pointing out wind tunnels and naming mountain peaks. Guides will not depart for the glacier from Camp No 3 after 2pm.

From Camp No 3, you have a 3km walk to the top of the road. From there you will eventually be able to take a cable car over the glacier or it's about an hour's walk up to the glacier's base. Although this walk is short, it affords some beautiful mountain views and takes you through some lovely forest. During summer, it is possible to hire horses to take you from Camp No 3 up to the base, from a stand just up the road from the hotels. During the low season you may be able to arrange this through the Golden Mountain Hotel.

En route to the base is the **Glacier Waterfall Viewing Platform** (*Bīngchuān Guānjǐngtái*) at 3000m. From here you can see the main glacier tongue, plus **Glacier No 2** and **Golden Peak** (6368m). Once at its base, you can walk up onto the glacier, although how far depends on the conditions and stability of the ice.

If you want to head back down the mountain the same day, your guide and driver will agree on a return time with you and the bus will wait for you at Camp No 3. If you spend the night, your return bus ticket remains valid until you use it.

Places to Stay & Eat
Cheap accommodation in the park is quickly becoming a thing of the past. *Camp No 1 (Yīhào Yíngdì)*, at 1940m, still offers budget dorm beds but conditions are damp and dirty. *Camp No 2 (Èrhào Yíngdì; beds Y150)* sits at 2620m and has overpriced beds although the price does include a dip into the hot springs. *Camp No 3* is the highest camp at 2940m and is taking on resort proportions.

The huge *Golden Mountain Hotel* (☎ 326 6433; doubles Y400-500) is all that's available at Camp No 3 although a second, even plusher hotel is about to open with doubles from Y350 to Y400.

The park authorities frown upon camping and there isn't a great deal in the way of flat ground on the way up, in any case.

The camps sell some food and drinks although, out of season, you can only count on this at Camp No 3. Mineral water, soft drinks, beer and instant noodles are usually available. Prices are naturally higher than in Móxī and rise with the altitude.

Getting There & Away
Hǎiluógōu is accessible via Móxī, which in turn can be reached by bus from Lúdìng (see the Lúdìng and Móxī Getting There & Away sections for details). A bus up the mountain departs from the park entrance gate at 7.30am. More buses are likely to race up and down during peak season.

SÌCHUĀN-TIBET HIGHWAY – NORTHERN ROUTE
Of the two routes to Tibet, this is the less heavily travelled. This may be because, at 2412km, it is 300km longer than the southern route, but it likely has more to do with the fact that it crosses Chola Mountain, the highest pass this side of Lhasa. The highway also crosses through the Tǎgōng Grasslands, with their blue-green rivers and velvety hills, studded with Tibetan prayer flags and watched over by gracefully soaring eagles.

For travellers, this highway leads to the border town of Dégé, with its internationally revered Printing Lamasery. It also takes you to the north where it is possible to work your way up to Qīnghǎi province via Sêrxu.

If you do come this way, be sure to bring some warm clothing; this area reaches high, frozen altitudes. Remember that bus service can be erratic – this is no place to be if you're in a hurry. It's also not possible to change money or travellers cheques up here so come prepared.

Gānzī 甘孜
The lively market town of Gānzī sits in a valley at 3800m, surrounded by the sleeping giants of Chola Mountain. Some 385km north-west of Kāngdìng, Gānzī is the capital of the Gānzī (Garzê) Autonomous Prefecture and is mostly populated by Tibetans and Khambas.

Now open to tourism, Gānzī sees a growing number of foreigners sojourning here as an intermediate stop between Sêrxu and Kāngdìng or on their way west to Dégé. It is a friendly place to spend a night and has a lamasery that is well worth a visit.

Gānzī Sì (Garzê Gompa in Tibetan) is a lamasery situated just north of the town's Tibetan quarter. Over 540 years old, it glimmers with blinding quantities of gold. Encased on the walls of the main hall are hundreds of small golden Sakyamunis. In a smaller hall just west of the main hall is an awe-inspiring statue of Jampa (Maitreya or Future Buddha), dressed in a giant silk robe.

To find the lamasery, take a left out of the bus station and head north for about 10 minutes until you reach the Tibetan neighbourhood. From there wind your way uphill, around the clay and wooden houses. You'll see the lamasery long before you reach it.

There are also a number of lamaseries that you might want to visit in neighbouring towns. **Beri Gompa** is about a half-hour drive west, on the road to Dégé. Also off this road, one hour from Gānzī, is **Dagei Gompa**. Set against white-capped mountains, this lamasery's *guesthouse* is a relaxing place to rest for a day or two. There are also hot springs here.

To reach Beri Gompa and Dagei Gompa, catch the morning bus to Dégé or one of the sporadic local buses heading west.

Places to Stay Accommodation options in Gānzī are limited.

Hóngyuèliàng (752 2676) Doubles Y60. This is the only hotel officially allowed to take foreigners. To find it, turn left out of the bus station, cross the main intersection, and continue on for about a block. There is no English sign outside but look for the hotel's telephone number on the lit-up blue, yellow and red sign on the left. With lots of hot water and fairly clean toilets, what this place lacks in character is made up for in friendliness and electric blankets.

A second option is a small, unmarked *guesthouse (beds Y4)* in a wooden Tibetan home. Beds are in clean, basic rooms. Ask for the toilets, however, and they'll direct you out onto the street. To find the guesthouse, take a left out of the bus station and then the first left. Follow this up behind the bus station and the guesthouse is on the right. Your best bet of finding it is to ask someone to point out the *zhāodàisuǒ*.

Places to Eat A number of small *restaurants* are located around the main intersection, just north of the bus station. On the north-eastern corner of these crossroads is a particularly tasty and popular restaurant serving excellent noodles, vegies and meat dishes.

If you head west, up the hill at the main intersection, you'll find *eateries* pumping out fresh Tibetan flatbread. Across from the bus station, dumplings are available in the early morning.

Getting There & Away Buses to Gānzī (Y112, 12 hours) leave Kāngdìng daily at 6.40am. From Gānzī, a bus leaves each morning at 6am for Kāngdìng. A rather decrepit bus leaves Gānzī every other morning at 7.30am for Dégé (Y50, 8 to 10 hours). Every third morning, there is also a Dégé-bound bus from Kāngdìng passing through Gānzī, but it's fairly difficult to get a seat on.

You can head north from Gānzī to Xīníng (Y76, 2½ days) in Qīnghǎi province via Sêrxu. Buses to Sêrxu originate in Kāngdìng every third day or so, overnight in Dàofú and stop over in Gānzī around 1pm before resuming their drive.

Dégé (Dêgê) 德格

Resting in a valley with Chola Mountain to the east and the Tibetan border to the west, Dégé is steeped in living tradition and sees little of the distant, outside world, other than the truckers and few travellers who pass through. While the Chinese influence is evident in the newer, tiled buildings, the village is mainly Tibetan and the military presence that you might expect so near to the Tibetan border is not prevalent in the town itself.

Getting to Dégé is a long haul. En route you'll see the towering snowy peaks of Chola Mountain stretching up 6168m, and the Xinhua Glacier which comes down almost to the road at 4100m. Chola Mountain itself was first scaled in 1988 and you might begin to wonder if your bus driver is attempting the same, as the bus grumbles and inches its way uphill to the top of the peaks. At the Tro La (Chola) Pass of nearly 6000m, Tibetans on board will throw coloured prayer papers out the window and chant something that you can only hope will carry your bus to safety.

While the views from here are phenomenal, conditions can be treacherous on this narrow, ice-encrusted dirt road and it's a toss up as to whether you'll be more frozen from the icy blasts or fear. Overturned buses are not uncommon – you'll see them from your window. Altitude sickness is also a *very* real possibility up here. Once you descend from the mountains on the other side of the pass, you can breathe a sigh of relief as the bus heads through a beautiful farmed valley and gorge and enters Dégé at 4000m, some eight to 10 hours after leaving Gānzī.

Bakong Scripture Printing Lamasery

At the heart of Dégé is this lamasery (admission Y25; open daily). While the present structure dates from 1744, the printing house has existed on this site for over 270 years with printing blocks dating from the early 18th century. The lamasery currently houses over 217,000 engraved blocks of Tibetan scriptures from the five Tibetan Buddhist sects, including Bön. Texts include ancient works on astronomy, geography, music, medicine and Buddhist classics. A history of Indian Buddhism, comprising 555 woodblock plates, is the only surviving copy in the world (written in Hindi, Sanskrit and Tibetan).

Built in the Qing dynasty by the 42nd prefect of Dégé, the lamasery is revered as one of the three most important Tibetan lamaseries (along with Sakya Monastery and Lhasa's Potala Palace) – not surprising when you consider that the material stored in Dégé makes up an estimated 70% of Tibet's literary heritage.

Within the lamasery, hundreds of workers hand-produce over 2500 prints each day. A visit will give you the opportunity to witness this rare sight as ink, paper and brushes fly through the workers' hands at lightning speed. Upstairs, an older crowd of printers produce larger prints of Tibetan gods on paper or coloured cloth that later find their way to hills and temples as prayer flags. If you catch them with a free moment, they'll print you one of your choice for Y10.

You can also examine storage chambers, paper cutting and binding rooms and the main hall of the lamasery itself. Protecting the monastery from fire and earthquake is a guardian Goddess, a green Avalokiteshvara (Guanyin).

The entrance fee to the lamasery includes a tour guide who is excellent at communicating through pictures if your Chinese isn't up to scratch. The lamasery is closed holidays.

There are three other lamaseries in town, including a large one just behind the printing house, which is over 1000 years old.

To reach the printing house, turn left out of the bus station and right over the bridge. Continue up this road to the southeast of town and it will bring you to the lamasery's front door. If you arrive in the morning, you may see the town's many devotees circling the building and spinning their prayer wheels.

Places to Stay & Eat There is only one place in town that is open to foreigners.

Dégé Bīnguǎn (☎ 822 2167) Beds in 3-bed dorms Y30, doubles Y50. This place is characterless but clean.

There are several point-and-choose *restaurants* around the bus station.

Getting There & Away Buses leave Gānzī for Dégé (Y50, 8 to 10 hours) every other day at 7.30am, returning from Dégé the next day at 6.30am. This is an old beast of a bus. More comfortable buses from Kāngdìng leave for Dégé every third day at 7am, overnight in Lúhuò and pass through Gānzī the following morning around 10am. Unfortunately, getting a seat on this bus in Gānzī is unlikely. These buses return from Dégé the morning after their arrival and take two days to reach Kāngdìng.

There is also a bus from Tibet headed for Gānzī (and on to Lúhuò) that passes through Dégé every other afternoon at 12.30pm. This bus overnights here en route to Gānzī and arrives around 11am the following morning.

SÌCHUĀN-TIBET HIGHWAY – SOUTHERN ROUTE

A journey along this 2140km route takes you through vast, open landscapes with horizons of majestic peaks. Tibetan homes dot the landscape like small stone castles. Huge vultures soar overhead while roaming yaks munch on frosty grass. Solitary Tibetans watch your bus pass from a distance and you may be miles down the road before you spot the black tents of these nomadic herdsmen. This area allows a view into Tibet for those not actually going that far west.

With roads and transport improving and restrictions for foreign visitors lifted, it is no wonder that the southern route of the Sìchuān-Tibet Highway is seeing a considerable rise in the number of foreign tourists. In particular, the route Kāngdìng-Lǐtáng-Xiāngchéng-Zhōngdiàn has become a popular back-door route into Yúnnán.

As with the rest of north-west Sìchuān, warm clothing is a must. Some travellers experience difficulties with the high altitudes here; be on the lookout for side effects (see Health in the Facts for the Visitor chapter) and if you're feeling unwell, head to somewhere lower. There are no money-changing facilities here.

Lǐtáng 理塘

Surrounded by snow-capped peaks and resting on open grassland at an altitude of 4680m, Lǐtáng will leave you breathless in more than one way. This is Sìchuān's Wild West, where tall fur hats and silver embossed knives are the on-going fashion rage and where neighbouring herdsmen can be seen kicking up a trail of dust at dawn. Tibetan culture abounds here. Markets are filled with yak-skin coats, wooden and silver teacups and brightly coloured woven cloth. 'Tashi delek', the Tibetan greeting, is more commonly used than 'Nǐ hǎo' and traditional stone and dirt homes fill the northern half of town.

Lǐtáng has a fantastically relaxed and friendly atmosphere. While there may not be much in the way of sights, this is an excellent small town to spend a few days hanging out with the local people under a blazing sun and starry night skies.

There are also some spectacular walks into the surrounding hills. Advice on where to go (ie, where isn't currently being used as grazing pastures or for sky burials; see the boxed text 'Sky Burial', later) should be sought from locals. Be sure to allow yourself time to acclimatise to the altitude before you set out.

If you do find yourself suffering from altitude sickness and can't get out of town, there is a local treatment consisting of medicated pills and re-hydration drinks. The woman running Xiānhè Bīnguǎn may be able to help you out; however, this shouldn't be considered a remedy and you should still descend to a lower altitude as soon as possible.

Information None of Lǐtáng's streets appears to be named but the town is small enough to find your way around regardless. China Post is on the main north-south street. Next door is China Telecom which has an Internet service for Y5 per hour, open until midnight.

Things to See At the northern end of town is **Chöde Gompa**, a Tibetan lamasery, built for the third Dalai Lama. Inside is a statue of Sakyamuni, which is believed to have been carried from Lhasa by foot. Tibetan homes lead up to the lamasery and you are likely to encounter friendly monks en route who may offer to give you a tour.

On the eastern edge of Lǐtáng is **Qūdēnggābù**, a newly erected chörten which active worshippers seem to be perpetually circling, reciting mantras and spinning prayer wheels. Dozens of smaller chörtens fill the courtyard which itself is edged with a corridor of prayer wheels.

Places to Stay A few accommodation options include:

Xiānhè Bīnguǎn Beds in 2-bed dorms Y25. The rooms here are impeccably clean with fresh sheets and electric blankets – a great deal. Toilets are across the courtyard and washing facilities consist of basins and all the boiling water you can stand. To find the hotel, take a left out of the bus station and head about 350m east into town. The hotel is not easily spotted; it's on the right side of the road and on the Chinese-only sign over the entrance is a painting of a bird (something like a heron).

Lǐtáng Zhāodàisuǒ (☎ 532 3089) Dorm beds Y25. Down the road, further east from Xiānhè Bīnguǎn, the rooms here are slightly grotty. Toilets and washing facilities are the same as at Xiānhè Bīnguǎn.

High City Hotel (Gāochéng Bīnguǎn) Dorm beds Y10. This is the cheapest option in town and it seems to have an abundance of rooms – or at least keys – but the conditions are something of a mystery as the staff were unable to unlock any of the doors when we last visited.

Places to Eat Lǐtáng has countless hole-in-the-wall *restaurants*, the majority of which are on the south side of the main road running east-west or over the road from the High City Hotel.

Lǎoqī Xiǎochī Serving plates of extremely tasty vegies and meat and huge, steaming bowls of noodles, this place is a popular little gathering place for local monks. You'll find it across the road from Lǐtáng Zhāodàisuǒ.

There are also lots of *barbecue stalls* grilling spicy potatoes, tofu and meat, and a *bakery* and *market* in town where you can stock up for long bus journeys.

Getting There & Away Lǐtáng's bus schedule is in something of a muddle (as are the staff at the station). Tickets are sold for buses that don't exist and oversold for those that do. When you attempt to buy a ticket in advance, you'll likely be told to go away and come back in the morning but don't give up, especially if you plan to travel on the weekend or a holiday when buying tickets for same-day travel is next to impossible.

The following times are best double-checked before you make your travel plans. All roads but that to Bātáng have been vastly improved in this area, reducing travel times immensely.

From Kāngdìng there is a daily departure for Lǐtáng at 6.20am and for Xiāngchéng (passing through Lǐtáng) at 7am.

At the time of writing there were buses leaving Lǐtáng for Kāngdìng daily at 8.30am as well as a Kāngdìng-bound bus or two passing through from Bātáng and Xiāngchéng.

Buses for Bātáng (Y60, 5½ hours) depart Lǐtáng daily at 7am and 7.30am and for Xiāngchéng (Y60, five hours) at 7am. If the bus to Xiāngchéng is full (or oversold), you may be able to hire a minivan to take you and a group of friends there for about Y600.

Lǐtáng to Zhōngdiàn – the Back Door to Yúnnán

As an alternative route to Yúnnán that takes you through 400km of spectacular scenery and Tibetan territory, the route from Lǐtáng to Zhōngdiàn has once again been opened up to foreigners.

Buses from Kāngdìng and Lǐtáng head for **Xiāngchéng** (see the Getting There & Away sections of Kāngdìng and Lǐtáng), where you'll have to spend the night. From Xiāngchéng you can catch an onward bus to Zhōngdiàn in Yúnnán province between 7am and 8am. Going the other way, buses from Xiāngchéng head back to Lǐtáng at around the same time. Try to buy your onward ticket on arrival in Xiāngchéng as the ticket seller may not show up in the morning before the bus departs. Be forewarned: the road between Xiāngchéng and Zhōngdiàn is sometimes closed in the dead of winter due to heavy snowfall. You'd be wise to check before heading out from Lǐtáng.

Xiāngchéng is a small border town that is quickly expanding with the usual tiled buildings and blaring horns. A hike up to the **Tibetan temple** offers views over the valley and what's left of the town's traditional square stone houses. This lamasery itself is being completely rebuilt by hand and is worth a visit to watch carvers and painters at work.

The lamasery is at the opposite end of town from the bus station. To find it, follow the dirt track up on the left as you reach the edge of town.

Bámùshān Bīnguǎn Dorm beds/doubles Y25/240. This is the only hotel in town with a permit to accept foreigners. Don't let its fancy exterior scare you – beds in clean, warm dorm rooms are a good deal. The hotel is the huge building on the right as you exit the muddy bus station.

Bātáng 八塘

Lying 32km from the Tibetan border and 5½ bumpy hours down a dirt track from Lǐtáng, Bātáng's strict security and remote location has kept it off the tourist route. The town is now open to foreigners; however, there's little to see or do here other than to contemplate the surrounding mountains from one of the many sidewalk teahouses. There is a definite Chinese presence in Bātáng and your attempts at Tibetan phrases may not always be well received.

Across the river from the town lie farmland, beautiful Tibetan homes and a chörten and is a pleasant place to stroll. The suspension bridge to cross the river is at the eastern end of town and is a little hairy. It's not high up, but it's missing more than a few planks.

Many travellers trying to sneak into Tibet by land have made their attempts from Bātáng. Unsurprisingly, the local PSB is suspicious of foreigners and may pay you a visit to suss you out. It might help to buy your return ticket upon arrival as proof that you don't intend to cross the border. It's also a good idea to double-check with the PSB in Chéngdū that Bātáng is still open to tourists, as penalties for crossing into ever-changing restricted zones can be high – up to Y400.

Places to Stay Two places to try are:

Kèyùn Fàndiàn Dorm beds Y10-15. The rooms here are dilapidated, the mattresses lumpy and the common toilets grotty. At least there's late-night karaoke on the ground floor should you get bored. Take a left out of the bus station and the hotel is in the first courtyard on the left.

Jīnhùi Bīnguǎn (☎ 562 2700) Doubles with/without bath Y70/50. If you head into town from the bus station and take the first right after the huge, hard-to-miss golden bird, you'll find this hotel about a block down on the left. Rooms are clean and comfortable.

Getting There & Away One bus heads east from Bātáng daily at 6.30am. It stops in Lǐtáng (Y60, 5½ hours) and Kāngdìng (Y140, 13 hours) en route to Chéngdū. Before reaching Kāngdìng, this bus overnights in Yǎjiāng where there is an unpleasant hotel in the bus compound or a better option in town, with doubles for Y50. To find the hotel, go right out of the station, take the stairs up on the left until you reach a main road and stay to the right when the road forks. The hotel is on the left.

From Kāngdìng, a bus leaves for Bātáng (Y110) each morning at 7am, overnighting in Lǐtáng. Buses from Lǐtáng to Bātáng leave daily at 7am and 7.30am. While you're attempting to ignore the plunging cliffs that the bus careens ever so close to between Lǐtáng and Bātáng, you can take in some stunning scenery.

Northern Sìchuān

With dense alpine forests and wide grasslands, northern Sìchuān is a great place to get out and commune with nature. Pony treks around Sōngpān and hiking in the stunning nature preserve of Jiǔzhàigōu have made this area increasingly popular with travellers.

Northern Sìchuān is home to the Ābà Tibetan and Qiāng Autonomous Prefecture. In the extreme north-west, the region around Zöigê and Lǎngmùsì is the territory of the Goloks, nomads who speak their own dialect of Tibetan, distinct from the local Amdo dialect. You'll see meadows speckled with their black and white tents and roaming yaks. While these Tibetan destinations are less visited, you can incorporate them into an alternative route into Gānsù.

Most of northern Sìchuān is between 2000m and 4000m in altitude so make sure you take warm clothing. The grassland plateau in the north-west averages more than 4000m and even in summer, temperatures can dip to 15°C at night. The rainy season lasts from June to August.

Beyond the Sōngpān-Jiǔzhàigōu route, roads in the region aren't always in the best condition. In worse condition are many of the buses. Roads are particularly hazardous in summer when heavy rains prompt frequent landslides; several foreigners were killed in the summer of 1995 when their bus got caught in a landslip and plunged into a river. You might want to think about planning this trip for the spring or autumn, when the weather is likely to be better.

As in the rest of Sìchuān, travellers are required to purchase Chinese PICC insurance for travel. The difference in this area is that you may actually need it. If you're coming from Chéngdū, the insurance will be included in the cost of the ticket. However, if you're in northern Sìchuān without insurance, you'll either be charged a huge surcharge or may not be allowed onto the onward or returning bus. You won't have an easy time purchasing insurance once you're up here either. This is the one area of Sìchuān where we actually felt that buying insurance in Chéngdū had paid off. (See the boxed text 'Warning' in the Chéngdū section.)

One thing you are bound to see in the north are the countless logging trucks that shuttle up and down the Mínjiāng Valley, stripping the area of its forest. Some sources estimate that up to 40% of the region's forests have been logged in the last half decade, causing erosion, landslides and increased levels of silt heading downstream, eventually flowing into Cháng Jiāng.

While you're getting prepared, bear in mind that there is nowhere to change money in this region, so bring sufficient cash Renminbi.

SŌNGPĀN 松潘
☎ 0837

Although largely viewed as a stopover point on the road to Jiǔzhàigōu or as a base for horse treks, it's worth having a wander around Sōngpān itself. While the bustling downtown is filled with modern tourist shops selling Tibetan wares (yak-skin coats are said to be cheaper here than elsewhere), old wooden buildings still line many of the side streets and residential areas. The ancient gates from Sōngpān's days as a walled city are also still intact and a couple of old wooden bridges cross over Mín Hé. On the far eastern side of the river is **Guānyīn Gé**. Walking up to it will take you through a village-like setting and the small temple offers views over Sōngpān.

On another note, be sure to bring a torch (flashlight) with you to Sōngpān, which is often plagued with faulty electricity.

Horse Treks

Several kilometres outside Sōngpān lie idyllic mountain forest and emerald-green lakes. One of the most popular ways to experience this is by joining up with a horse trek from Sōngpān. Guides can take you out from one to seven days through pristine, peaceful valleys and forests, all aboard a not-so-big, very tame horse. The treks usually cost Y60 per day.

There are two prominent horse trekking operators in Sōngpān. Don't worry about finding them – they'll find you. While some travellers find their sales pitch a little too hard to stomach, those who do go out on treks with either company return with raving reviews.

Shun Jiang Horse Treks (Shùnjiāng Lǚyóu Mǎduì) was the first trekking operation in Sōngpān catering to backpackers. *Happy Trails*, next door, is run by ex-guides of Shun Jiang and also has bikes for rent, laundry services and a book exchange. Employees of both are friendly and helpful.

Tours from both companies appear to be virtually identical. It's probably best to visit both offices and see which one takes your fancy or has room on a tour already organised. The basic three-day trip takes you to a series of mountain lakes and a hot spring, and then to the **Zhaga Waterfall**. If you're keen to go elsewhere, the guides are happy

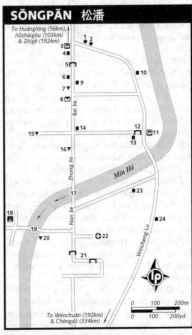

SŌNGPĀN 松潘

To Huánglóng (56km),
Jiǔzhàigōu (103km)
& Zōigé (152km)

To Wénchuān (192km)
& Chéngdū (334km)

0   100   200m
0   100   200yd

SŌNGPĀN

PLACES TO STAY
4	Tàiyáng Dàjiǔdiàn 太阳大酒店
6	Sōngzhōu Bīnguǎn 松州宾馆
9	Jīnyuán Bīnguǎn 县政府招待所
10	Línyè Bīnguǎn 林业宾馆
13	Gǔchéng Bīnguǎn 古城宾馆
14	Huánglóng Bīnguǎn 黄龙宾馆
23	Dájí Bīnguǎn 达吉宾馆
24	Sōngpān Bīnguǎn 松潘宾馆

PLACES TO EAT
7	Yùlán Fànguǎn 玉兰饭馆
15	Hotpot Restaurant
16	Muslim Restaurant 穆斯林餐厅
20	Teahouse 茶馆

OTHER
1	Happy Trails 快乐的小路 骑马旅游
2	Shun Jiang Horse Treks 顺江旅游马
3	North Bus Station 汽车北站
5	North Gate 北门
8	Post Office 邮局
11	East Bus Station 汽车站
12	East Gate; Teahouse 东门; 茶馆
17	Covered Bridge 古松桥
18	Guānyīn Gé 观音阁
19	Covered Bridge
21	South Gate 南门
22	Hospital 医院

to tailor a trip to suit you. Rates are very reasonable; you get you a horse, three meals a day, tents, bedding, warm jackets and raincoats. The guides take care of everything: you won't touch a tent pole or a cooking pot unless you want to. The only additional charge is entrance to the different sites (around Y30 each), but the tour companies will warn you of these before you set out.

As food consists mainly of green vegies, potatoes and bread, you may want to take along some extra snacks for variety.

Places to Stay
With Sōngpān's faulty electricity also comes a shortage of hot water (apparently the water pumps halt), something you might want to consider before splashing out on an expensive room with an en suite. If you're coming in from a horse trek, be prepared to stay grimy. If the hot water is flowing, there are two public bathhouses in town where you can take a steaming shower.

Līnyè Bīnguǎn Beds in 2-4-bed dorms Y15. This is one of two budget options in town. Rooms are basic and quiet. Washing facilities consist of a bowl and thermos of hot water, and there are common toilets.

Sōngzhōu Bīnguǎn Beds in 2-4-bed dorms Y15. This hotel is more or less identical to Līnyè Bīnguǎn; while it's a little cheerier, it's also a little noisier.

Jīnyuán Bīnguǎn (Songpan County Government Guesthouse) Doubles with bath Y100. Once a popular budget choice, this hotel appears to have been recently refurbished, with prices soaring way above the quality of the rooms.

Huánglóng Bīnguǎn Beds Y30. You'll find cheap beds at this hotel. However, the rooms are run-down and the rank toilets are outside.

Gǔchéng Bīnguǎn (☎ 723 2575) Beds Y50. The rooms here are clean and comfortable. Unfortunately, at the time of writing, the plumbing wasn't working and toilets consisted of a small bucket in each room.

Dájí Bīnguǎn (☎ 723 2080) Beds Y100. This sparkling new hotel is spotless and has friendly staff.

Taìyáng Dàjiūdiàn Doubles Y280. This is one of the most upmarket hotels in town. Its rooms are lovely if the electricity is working.

Sōngpān Bīnguǎn Doubles/triples Y260/360. This place is closed in the off season.

Places to Eat
Sōngpān has an excellent assortment of breads for sale, made and sold fresh all day at small stalls along Zhong Jie – big crusty loaves, dumplings, Tibetan flatbread and sweet breads.

There are also a huge number of restaurants along Zhong Jie including *hotpot* and *noodle shops*. Many have English signs and menus. There are numerous hole-in-the-wall *restaurants* on the eastern side of town, between Līnyè Bīnguǎn and the East Gate. These restaurants aren't likely to have a menu, much less an English one, but you can point out what you want. You'll find a large *hotpot restaurant* in what was once the town's cinema, before the advent of DVD. Head west from Huánglóng Bīnguǎn.

Yùlán Fànguǎn is a favourite hang-out for foreign travellers, serving pancakes, hot chocolate and tasty Chinese dishes. It has an English menu.

South of the intersection on Zhong Jie, is a recently refurbished *Muslim restaurant* with fantastic food. Prices are a bit high and there's no English menu, but you can easily pick out what you want in the kitchen. The *yúxiāng qiézi* (fish-flavoured eggplant) is particularly good.

Along Mín Hé, on the western edge of town, is a great outdoor *teahouse* where you can enjoy views of the covered wooden bridge, Guānyīn Gé and wooden houses. There is another teahouse atop the East Gate that is also a good place to relax.

Getting There & Away
Sōngpān has two bus stations. If you want to guarantee a seat, you need to buy your ticket from the station that your bus originates at. This is the north station for all destinations except Píngwǔ.

A bus to Chéngdū departs every morning at 6am (Y41.5, 10 hours). A Chéngdū-bound sleeper bus from Nánpíng also passes through town at around 9.30am, but you can't be guaranteed a bunk. From Chéngdū, a bus departs the Xīmén bus station at 7am (Y46, 10 hours).

Heading north to Jiǔzhàigōu, a bus leaves Sōngpān's north station at 7am (Y26, four

Sky Burial

The white cloth is removed from the body while those in attendance are bathed in the incense of the juniper fire. The *Tomden* sharpens his large knife on a nearby stone, circles around a small Buddhist monument while reciting mantras, and slices into the body lying before him on the stone slab. The flesh is cut into large chunks while the bones and brain are smashed and mixed with barley flour.

By this time, the smell of the flesh and the incense have drawn a large number of vultures who circle high above. The Tomden steps away and the huge birds descend into a feeding frenzy, devouring every bit of the body and carrying it up to the heavens, witnessed by the family of the deceased from a nearby hilltop.

This is sky burial *(tiānzàng)*, an ancient Buddhist-Tibetan burial tradition. While it may at first seem a gruesome affront to most Western sensibilities, in this corner of the world it makes sense both spiritually and practically. According to Buddhist beliefs, the body is merely a vehicle to carry you through this life; once a body dies, the spirit leaves it and the body is no longer of use. Giving one's body as food for the vultures is a final act of generosity to the living world and provides a link in the cycle of life. Vultures themselves are revered and believed to be a manifestation of the flesh-eating God Dakinis.

On a more practical note, sky burial provides an ecologically sound way to dispose of bodies in a terrain where wood is scarce and the ground is often too hard to dig into. Traditionally, only people of high status were cremated while those with smallpox or other infectious ailments were chopped up and disposed of as fish food through water burial, perhaps accounting for the unpopularity of fish in the Tibetan diet.

The Chinese banned sky burials in the 1960s and '70s and it wasn't until the '80s, as Tibetans regained limited religious rights, that the practice was once again legalised. Chinese officials continue to regard sky burial as a primitive practice. The fact that one Buddhist sect has been known to keep the tops of the skulls from the deceased to use as enlarged sacred teacups has often been touted as proof of Tibetan savagery.

In Lhasa, tourists require official permission to attend a sky burial; in the more remote areas of Sìchuān, however, you may well be told where and when the burials are to take place. Nevertheless, local Tibetans have been unsurprisingly offended by travellers who have turned these funerals into tourist outings. Common decency applies – if you aren't invited, don't go, and whatever you do, do not attempt to capture the moment on Kodak.

Korina Miller

hours) and continues on to Nánpíng. For Zöigê, a daily bus departs at 6am (Y31).

From the east bus station, a bus leaves each morning for Píngwǔ. This bus takes you within hiking/hitching distance of Huánglóng (Y40).

HUÁNGLÓNG 黄龙
Yellow Dragon Valley
Designated a national park in 1983, Huánglóng *(adult/student Y75/50)* is studded with waterfalls and terraced, coloured limestone ponds of blue, yellow, white and green. The most spectacular ponds are located behind **Huánglóng Sì**, located deep in the valley, 7.5km from the road. A round-trip along a footpath takes about four hours, with the trail returning through dense (and

dark) forest. While some people rave about the valley's beauty and love the peace and quiet here, others find it disappointing and prefer an extra day at Jiǔzhàigōu. If you do visit, there are no vendors, so bring some water and supplies.

A great time to visit is during the annual **Temple Fair** *(Miào Huì)*. Held here around the middle of the sixth lunar month (usually July), it attracts large numbers of traders from the Qiang minority.

In the national park there are several small **guesthouses** with cheap beds – no frills, just hard beds and maybe a coal burner in the winter. **Huánglóng Zhāodàisuǒ** has slightly more upmarket accommodation, with dorm beds in triples, and standard doubles.

Around 56km from Sōngpān, Huánglóng is almost always included on the itinerary of the seven-day Jiǔzhàigōu tours that run out of Chéngdū, as well as on the horse-trekking tours out of Sōngpān. Unfortunately, unless you've signed up on a tour, the valley can be difficult to reach. Buses from Sōngpān to Píngwǔ pass within hitching/hiking distance of the entrance but you may then be stuck for transport back. You might be able to jump on a tour bus setting out from either Sōngpān or Jiǔzhàigōu early in the morning, but drivers are often reluctant to take foreigners, citing the risk of insurance liability.

JIǓZHÀIGŌU 九寨沟

Just inside Sìchuān's northern border lies **Jiǔzhàigōu** *(adult/student Y153/113)*, a gorgeous alpine valley studded with dazzling lakes as clear and bright as gemstones. Heavily forested and surrounded by snowy peaks, Jiǔzhàigōu is a national nature reserve and home to the protected takins, golden monkeys and pandas. There are also a number of Tibetan villages here and the valley is lightly sprinkled with Bön prayer flags, chörtens and prayer wheels that spin anticlockwise, powered by the current of the rivers.

The park is in pristine condition; however, it has also been groomed for the rapidly increasing influx of tourists. Jiǔzhàigōu was first pinpointed for tourism in the 1970s. Judging by the number of new resort-style hotels being built along the highway leading up to the park entrance, the number of visitors is only expected to grow. Don't let this put you off, however, as most tourists only visit Jiǔzhàigōu for the day, hopping on and off the tourist bus and not venturing far from the roadside sights.

The scenery here is spectacular and extremely unique and you can easily spend three or four days hiking between the sites and beyond the tourist route. While autumn can plunge the park into icy temperatures, it's also quieter, with beautiful snowy scenes and colourful trees. Admission prices to the park include transport.

Things to See

Buses from Chéngdū and Sōngpān will drop you outside the park reception centre and ticket office, just north of the park entrance. If you can produce something remotely resembling a student card you'll be given a discount. The price includes entrance to all areas of the park and bus service within the park for as long as you're there (see Getting Around later in this section).

The first official site inside the park is Tibetan **Zārú Sì** (Zaru Gompa in Tibetan). The bus is unlikely to take you there, but it's only a short walk down the first fork off the main road.

If you continue on the main road, you'll follow **Zécháwā Hé** as it runs past **Héyè Stockade** *(Héyè Cūn)* to **Huǒhuā Hú** *(Sparkling Lake)*. This is the first in a series of lakes filled by the **Shùzhēng Waterfall** *(Shùzhēng Pùbù)*. Keep your eyes open for trees growing unexpectedly out of the middle of the river, lakes and waterfalls. This is caused by fertile pockets of calcium in the waterways which create impromptu flowerpots.

A walking trail begins north of Huǒhuā Hú and runs along the eastern edge of the river as far as **Shùzhēng Stockade**

JIǓZHÀIGŌU 九寨沟

To Sōngpān (103km) & Huánglóng (128km)
Jiǔzhàigōu Town
To Long-Distance Bus Station & Nánpíng (38km)
Jīnshòu Bīnguǎn
Bus Ticket Office
Yángdōng Bīnguǎn
Mùwū Bīnguǎn
Reception Centre & Tickets
Guìbīnlóu Bīnguǎn
Bus Station
Park Entrance Gate
Zārú Sì
Héyè Stockade
Zéchāwā Hé
0   2   4km
0   1   2mi
Huǒhuā Hú
Shùzhēng Stockade
Shùzhēng Waterfall
Tiger Lake
Mirror Lake
Rhinoceros Lake
Pearl Shoal Waterfall
Promising Bright Bay Waterfall
Multi-Coloured Lake
Nuorilang Bus Station
Zéchāwā Stockade
Panda Lake
Arrow Bamboo Lake
Rize Stockade
Rizé Hé
To Swan Lake (5km)
To Five-Coloured Pool & Long Lake (9km)

(Shùzhēng Zhài). Here it crosses back over, leading you to a number of water-powered prayer wheels. The trail then continues up to the Shùzhēng Waterfall.

South from here, just past **Promising Bright Bay Waterfall** *(Nuòrìlǎng Pùbù)*, the road branches in two, with the eastern road leading to **Long Lake** *(Cháng Hǎi)* and **Five-Coloured Pool** and the western road to **Swan Lake** *(Tiānè Hǎi)*. If you're looking to stretch your legs and clear your lungs, you'd be better off heading along the western route where there are a number of scattered sights and a quiet forest trail leading from **Mirror Lake** to **Panda Lake** *(Xióngmāo Hǎi)*. Views from this trail are particularly good, especially of **Pearl Shoal Waterfall** *(Zhēnzhūtán Pùbù)*. If you continue past Panda Lake, you will leave the majority of the traffic behind.

The eastern route is almost better done by bus as the narrow road sees a great deal of traffic from one end to the other. Nevertheless, the two lakes at the far end are both well worth a visit.

You can either base yourself at one village and bus out to different areas for walks each day or walk from one settlement to the next – an ambitious itinerary. From the park entrance to Promising Bright Bay Waterfall is about 14km. It's a further 17.5km along the western road to the primary forest and 18km down the eastern road to Long Lake.

Organised Tours

During summer, various companies in Chéngdū operate tours to Jiǔzhàigōu and the surrounding area. Most of the trips are advertised for a certain day, but the bus will only go if full. If you are unlucky you may have to spend days waiting so it's best to try to register first and then pay before departure.

A standard tour includes Huánglóng and Jiǔzhàigōu, lasts seven days and costs a minimum of Y250 to Y300 per person. Hotels, food and entry fees are not included in the price. There are longer tours that include visits to the Tibetan grassland areas of Mǎěrkāng and Zöigê. Chéngdū travel agencies in the Traffic Hotel, Sam's Guesthouse, the Xīmén bus station, Jǐnjiāng Bīnguǎn and CITS all offer tours. The latter two are the most expensive. Check around and compare prices.

A word of warning: several tour operators in Chéngdū have been blacklisted by travellers for lousy service, rip-offs and rudeness. Ask around among travellers to pinpoint a reliable agency and look in the travellers' notebooks in cafes such as Sam's Guesthouse or Paul's Oasis.

Places to Stay

Inside the Park Unless you're catching an early bus the next day, it's worth staying in the park amid the scenery. Lodging is found in three villages: Héyè Stockade, Shùzhēng Stockade and Zéchǎwā Stockade. During the high season your options will increase considerably with a choice between concrete block guesthouses or basic, wooden Tibetan-style rooms with the lingering scent of pine. The latter rooms are usually family run.

At all three villages you are meant to report to the 'central desk' – often located somewhere in the middle of the village. Here you'll be asked to choose a hotel from a number of outdated photographs. If you're not interested in the pricey rooms, the folks at the office are unlikely to be interested in you. It seems easiest to have a look around by yourself, and to deal directly with the guesthouse proprietors. You can find beds in the villages for Y15 to Y20.

Héyè Stockade is the place where the least travellers stay, since it's the furthest from the local sights (but closest to the park entrance). More popular is **Shùzhēng Stockade** where many of the rooms have beautiful views of turquoise pools. For cheap, comfortable rooms, check out the Tibetan *guesthouses* at the back of the village, up the hill.

On the northern edge of **Zéchǎwā Stockade** is a *guesthouse* (*beds/doubles Y15/50*) offering doubles with bath as well as beds in wooden rooms. Located in the middle of the park near the main junction, this is a great location for those planning to set out on long walks. The hotel is on the road to Long Lake, a five-minute walk south of the Nuorilang bus station. Look for the wooden building peeking out from behind a yellow-tiled building.

Outside the Park Accommodation options here include:

Jīnshòu Bīnguǎn (☎ 773 4129) Beds Y30. This is the cheapest option outside the park. Rooms are basic with private baths and heated blankets, although we've received reports of extremely dubious cleaning practices. The hotel is a 15-minute walk west of the park entrance.

Yángdòng Bīnguǎn (☎ 773 9770) Beds in doubles Y50. East from the park entrance, this hotel has clean, comfortable doubles with bath.

Mǔwū Bīnguǎn Doubles Y258. This is one of the many upmarket hotels outside the park entrance. Next to the park reception centre on the main road, it has wooden chalet-style rooms with showers and heaters.

Guìbīnlóu Bīnguǎn Doubles Y668. On the other side of the reception centre from Mǔwū Bīnguǎn, this hotel has plush doubles.

Places to Eat

While there are a number of small *restaurants* in the village outside and to the west of the park entrance, inside the park options are more limited, especially if you visit during the off season. You can also expect to pay slightly more for food inside the park.

On the northern edge of the main parking lot at Shùzhēng Stockade is a *restaurant* that serves up greasy Chinese dishes at lunch and dinner. At the other end of the parking lot is a tiny *shop* that will make you a cheap bowl of noodles at almost any time of day.

Further up the road at Nuorilang bus station is another *restaurant* that opens for an early lunch to cater to the tourists. A set price of Y30 gives you a number of dishes, rice and tea.

Getting Around

Included in your entrance fee is bus service within the park on minibuses that zip between the sights. Unfortunately, these buses are often commandeered by tour groups who hop off at each sight, take their obligatory photos and hop back on 15 minutes later to race to the next. This can become rather tedious if you're just trying to get from point A to B.

Buses run from about 7am until the sun begins to sink behind the mountains. They often don't go beyond Panda Lake. If you're wandering around in the afternoon, it's best to make sure you're within an easy walking distance of your base as buses seem to travel more by the whim of their tour group than by any sort of schedule or route.

Getting There & Away

Although local authorities are planning to build an airport, the local bus remains the best means of transport. It can be taken in one dose or as part of a bus/train combination.

Between October and April, snow often cuts off access to Jiǔzhàigōu for weeks on end. Even at the best of times, transport is not plentiful. Hitching to Jiǔzhàigōu on tour buses has supposedly happened, but it's a rare occurrence indeed.

With a new road from Sōngpān to Jiǔzhàigōu, the once horrid ride from Chéngdū can be done in 12 relatively painless hours; take the Nánpíng sleeper bus (Y86.5) at 7.20am from Chéngdū's Xīmén station. If you're coming from Gānsù via Zöigê, you'll have to go through Sōngpān. From Sōngpān to Jiǔzhàigōu (Y26, four hours), the road goes up and over some gorgeous scenery. Buses drop you outside the entrance of the park.

Bus/train combinations are more troublesome but can be done. The recommended option with the best connections is to take a train to Miányáng, north of Chéngdū. From there, you should be able to get a bus to Nánpíng, and then on to Jiǔzhàigōu. You can also get a train from Chéngdū to Jiāngyóu from where you can catch a bus to Píngwǔ. From there you can get a Sōngpān-bound bus and stop at Huánglóng, and then continue on to Sōngpān and Juǐzhàigōu.

Returning from Jiǔzhàigōu to Sōngpān or Chéngdū, you are more likely to get a seat by heading north to Nánpíng and purchasing your ticket there. As buses leave Nánpíng at the break of day, you will have to overnight there (see the following Nánpíng section). Minicabs run back and forth between Jiǔzhàigōu and Nánpíng (one hour). In a full van it should cost Y10 or Y15 per person.

If you do want to chance buying a ticket in Jiǔzhàigōu, you'll find the bus station a few kilometres east of the park, on the road to Nánpíng. In the high season, a bus ticket office is also open on the main road, across from the entrance to Jiǔzhàigōu, and you can attempt to purchase your onward tickets from there. Theoretically, this office has six berths reserved daily on the Nánpíng-Chéngdū sleeper. Even so, it's best to book your tickets in advance.

NÁNPÍNG 南坪
☎ 0837

East of Jiǔzhàigōu, Nánpíng doesn't see many foreign visitors except for those searching for a seat on a Chéngdū or Sōngpān-bound bus. If you do find yourself overnighting here, there isn't much to see or do but the town is bustling and pleasant enough to wander through.

Places to Stay & Eat
Jiǔzhài Bīnguǎn (☎ 773 0686) Doubles with bath Y150. Minibuses and taxis from Jiǔzhàigōu will drop you outside this hotel, across from the river at the northern edge of town. Clean, comfortable rooms with bathrooms and hot water may be offered for a 20% discount.

Jinsuí Bīnguǎn (☎ 773 3168) Doubles Y80. This is the closest thing Nánpíng has to budget accommodation. Rooms here are similar to Jiǔzhài Bīnguǎn, although slightly more run down. To find the hotel, continue up the street from Jiǔzhài Bīnguǎn, bearing to the right.

For something to eat, take the first right after Jiǔzhài Bīnguǎn into the centre of town where there are numerous *hotpot restaurants* and *barbecue stalls*. You'll also find well-stocked *fruit stalls* and *bakeries*. Across from Jinsuí Bīnguǎn is a small *shop* selling tasty, fresh flatbread.

Getting There & Away
Minibuses from Jiǔzhàigōu will drop you outside Jiǔzhài Bīnguǎn, attached to which is a small bus ticket office. Unfortunately it probably won't sell tickets to foreigners and, if it does, a nasty insurance charge will be added. Instead, you'll need to haul yourself uphill to the other side of town where the long-distance bus station is hidden.

To find the long-distance bus station, turn left out of Jiǔzhài Bīnguǎn, walk about 25m and take a left into a narrow pedestrian market street. Follow this all the way to the top of the hill, about 15 minutes' walk. At the top is the bus station.

A sleeper bus to Chéngdū leaves at a merciless 5.30am (Y45, 12 hours). In peak season you may also find a night bus on this route. There are two buses daily to Sōngpān at 7am and noon (Y25, four hours) and departures to Miányáng at 5.30am, 7.50am and 9.10am (Y50).

THE NORTH-WEST ROUTE TO GĀNSÙ

This journey through the extreme northwest of Sìchuān has emerged as a popular backdoor route into Gānsù province for many travellers. Even if you're not headed north beyond the Sìchuān border, this area offers an opportunity to explore more remote Tibetan towns and villages. At an average altitude of 3500m to 4000m, travel through this grassland bog is not recommended for those in a hurry – bus transport is slow and sporadic. If you plan to explore any of the towns or lamaseries on the way, you'll need a minimum of five days, more if you make a side trip to Jiǔzhàigōu.

In winter months, roads often become impassable and temperatures plummet way past the tolerance levels of most mere mortals. While still cold, early autumn sees little rain and many clear and sunny skies. If you are travelling in the autumn or winter, it's best to buy your onward tickets as soon as possible as, during these colder months, the nomadic Goloks stay closer to main roads and towns and do much of their travel by bus, leaving little room for you and your pack.

The first leg of this route is from Chéngdū to Sōngpān (see Getting There & Away in the Sōngpān section, earlier). Most travellers take a side trip from Sōngpān to Jiǔzhàigōu at this point. From Sōngpān you can travel 168km north-west to your next overnight stop in Zöigê, and from there it's worth heading to Lǎngmùsì, just inside the Sìchuān border, for a day or two before crossing into Gānsù.

Zöigê 若尔盖
A somewhat dusty town set amid the grasslands, Zöigê doesn't have much pull for travellers other than as a resting point en route to Lǎngmùsì (see the entry in the Gānsù chapter) and north to Gānsù province. It is easy enough to spend a day here sipping tea in the sun and at the north-eastern edge of town is a **gompa** with pleasant, peaceful grounds. While the town's Chinese name is Ruòěrgài, it is most commonly referred to by its Tibetan name, Zöigê.

The 'Foreigner's Registration Office' in town once charged travellers for a permit but thankfully no longer seems to be in business as Zöigê is officially open to foreigners.

Places to Stay & Eat There are a number of options:

Liyuán Bīnguǎn (☎ 299 1885) Beds Y15. Conveniently located across the road from the western bus station, the rooms here are fairly clean but rather bleak with toilets outside and central heating that isn't likely to be working. As the hotel serves as a guesthouse for truckers, it can be noisy through to the wee hours as these big rigs pull into town.

Pānchuān Bīnguǎn Beds Y15. This place isn't much better than Liyuán Bīnguǎn, but staff seem friendly and toilets and showers are indoors. Take a right out of the western bus station and the hotel is up the road on the right, just before the crossroads.

Liángjú Bīnguǎn (☎ 229 8360) Beds Y25. This is the best option in town. Beds are a bit more expensive but it's quieter, cleaner and more cheerful. And the central heating works! Head right as you come out of the western bus station, take the first left onto the main street and walk up about 15 minutes. This white-and-yellow hotel will be on your left. The small sign is in Chinese only but you can watch for the telephone number.

A couple of doors down from Liángjú Bīnguǎn, *Ruòěrgài Xiànzhèngfǔ Zhāodàisuǒ* has closed down and is being rebuilt in the courtyard behind the original dingy building. The new hotel looks like it'll be the plushest place in town.

Between Liángjú Bīnguǎn and the south-western end of the main street are a number of small restaurants including *hotpot* and *noodles shops*.

Gābāfǎngjiǎo Cháguǎn Across from the ever-popular pool tables in the centre of town, this is a teahouse where you can sit outside on the balcony, eat fresh bread and sip delicious eight-treasure tea.

There are also some small *restaurants* next to the western bus station that sell fresh bread and dumplings in the mornings.

Getting There & Away Zöigê has two bus stations, one at the western edge of town and the other, on the same road, in the south-east. The more conveniently located western bus station has services to all destinations while the south-eastern only has buses to Sōngpān. If you're heading to Sōngpān and can't get a ticket at the western station, it's worth trying at the south-eastern one.

Arriving in Zöigê, you are only likely to end up at the south-eastern station if you arrive from Sōngpān.

To Sōngpān there is a departure at 6.30am (Y62). Buses to Lǎngmùsì leave every other day at 6.30am (Y28, three to four hours). This bus carries on to Hézuò in Gānsù province which is only a few hours from Xiàhé. From Xiàhé you have the option of travelling on to Lánzhōu or taking the more unusual option of heading to Xīníng in Qīnghǎi province, via Tongren.

Chóngqìng 重庆

Population: 32.5 million
Area: 82,400 sq km

CHÓNGQÌNG CITY 重庆
☎ 0236 • pop 5.8 million • elevation 261m

Perched on steep hills overlooking the confluence of two rivers, Chóngqìng is one of China's more unusual cities. Dusty grey tenements and shining office towers cling to the precipitous hillsides that make up much of the city centre.

Chóngqìng is a pleasant city to stroll around and is popular with Chinese tourists as the site of the Kuomintang's wartime capital from 1938 to 1945. The bulk of Chóngqìng's sights are linked to this history.

Something immediately noticeable in Chóngqìng is the absence of bicycles. The hill climbs make it coronary country for any would-be rider. As a replacement, Chóngqìng is the largest producer of motorbikes in China. Despite this dependence on motor transport, you may also notice a certain silence on the city streets. In 1997 the city banned outright the use of car horns to reduce noise pollution on the congested peninsula.

Chóngqìng is a city with big plans, most of them connected with the hype surrounding the Three Gorges Dam. It already rates as the chief industrial city of south-western China, with its production equal to a quarter of the industrial output of neighbouring Sìchuān. Cheap electricity from the dam and faster communications with Wǔhàn and Shànghǎi are set to boost the city's industries even further and kick-start economic growth throughout the entire south-west. Either that or it will place the city right at the end of the largest toilet in China (see the boxed text 'The Damned Yangzi' later in this chapter).

With all this, the city long lobbied for a special status akin to that of Shànghǎi. In 1997 what it got was not quite provincial status, but the 30-odd million residents of the three-county area separated from Sìchuān and became a 'special' municipality directly under central government control. In many respects, Chóngqìng is now the largest city in China.

Highlights

- Dàzú, the site of some of China's most celebrated Buddhist cave sculptures and grotto art

- Cháng Jiāng (Yangzi River) cruises, departing from Chóngqìng city, offer an opportunity to view the famous Three Gorges before they are submerged

- Red Cliff Village, the WWll headquarters of the Communist representatives to the Kuomintang and now home to one of China's better revolutionary history museums

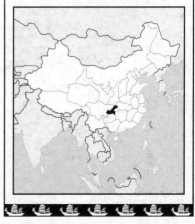

Within China, Chóngqìng is famous for its searing summers, when temperatures can exceed 40°C (104°F). This lovely climate has earned the city a place among the country's 'three furnaces', along with Wǔhàn and Nánjīng.

History

In 1996 stone tools unearthed along the Cháng Jiāng (Yangzi River) valleys showed that humans were found in this region two million years ago, a million years earlier than had been thought.

Chóngqìng (known in pre-pinyin China as 'Chungking') was opened as a treaty port in 1890, but not many foreigners made it up the river to this isolated outpost, and those who did had little impact.

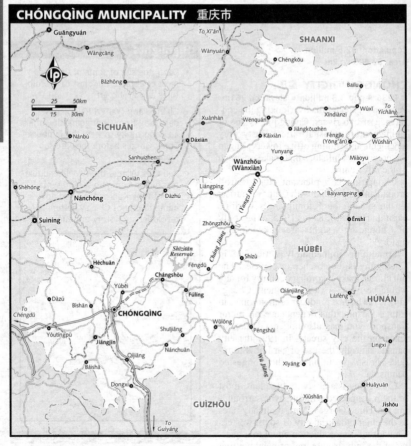

CHÓNGQÌNG MUNICIPALITY 重庆市

An industrialisation program got under way in 1928, but it was in the wake of the Japanese invasion that Chóngqìng really took off as a major centre, after the Kuomintang retreated to set up its wartime capital here. Refugees from all over China flooded in, swelling the population to over two million.

In a city overpopulated and overstrained, with its bomb-shattered houses, these wartime residents must have found the name of their new home somewhat ironic: Chóngqìng means something like 'double jubilation' or 'repeated good luck'. Originally named Gongzhou, Emperor Zhaodun of the Song dynasty renamed it in 1190 when he ascended the throne. As he had previously been made the prince of the city, he called it Chóngqìng in celebration of these two happy events.

It was in Chóngqìng, under the shadow of Kuomintang military leaders, that representatives of the CCP (including Zhou Enlai) acted as 'liaisons' between the Kuomintang and the Communists' headquarters at Yán'ān, in Shaanxi province. Repeated efforts to bring the two sides together in a unified front against the Japanese largely failed due to mutual distrust and Chiang Kaishek's obsession with wiping out the Communists, even at the cost of yielding Chinese territory to an invading army.

Orientation

The heart of Chóngqìng spreads across a hilly peninsula of land wedged between

Jiālíng Jiāng to the north and Cháng Jiāng to the south. The rivers meet at the tip of the peninsula at the eastern end of the city.

For most visitors, the central focus of this congested peninsula is the now neon-shrouded **Liberation Monument** *(Jiěfàng Bēi)*, which is within walking distance of most accommodation. Originally a wooden structure built to commemorate Sun Yat-sen's death, the monument was rebuilt in 1945 to celebrate the end of China's war with Japan.

Chóngqìng is easy to explore on foot. The distances are manageable, and there's always an interesting alley to duck into. Between the Liberation Monument and **Cháotiānmén Dock** *(Cháotiānmén Mǎtou)* are a number of steep, laddered alleyways, lined with little shops.

Maps Good maps in Chinese and much less detailed ones in English are available from street vendors around the Liberation Monument area as well as at the bus and train stations.

Information

Tourist Offices China International Travel Service (CITS; Zhōngguó Guójì Lǚxíngshè; ⓔ citscq@cq.col.com.cn), at 63 Zaoailanya Jie, is located near Rénmín Gōngyuán and can arrange tickets on tourist boats heading down the Yangzi.

Money The main Chóngqìng branch of the Bank of China is on Minzu Lu. Inside is an ATM. A few doors east is another ATM at the Huaxia Bank and a couple of doors west is a 24-hour ATM centre for Visa and Plus card holders. Many of the larger hotels also have exchange desks.

Post & Communications There is a China Post on Minzu Lu, within walking distance of the Chung King Hotel and Huìxiānlóu Bīnguǎn. It claims to have 24-hour service but we're sceptical. Most of the top-end hotels offer limited postal services.

At the time of writing, the Internet servers in Chóngqìng were painfully slow and searching or browsing online was next to impossible.

A huge Xinhua Bookshop has opened on Minsheng Lu with close to 100 computers on the 3rd floor where you can surf the net and

drink coffee, 24 hours a day. Access is Y3 an hour. Across the street, Intel offers the same services on the 3rd floor of a shopping mall, past the glitzy shops and table tennis tables.

Down an alley, behind the Marriott Hotel, is yet another Internet cafe, offering beer and slightly cheaper rates (Y2 per hour).

PSB The Public Security Bureau (PSB; Gōngānjú; ☎ 383 1830) is officially on Linjiang Lu, but the entrance is off Wusi Lu. You can apply for visa extensions here but if you're after anything more unusual, you'd be better off waiting until you get to Chéngdū.

Luóhàn Sì 罗汉寺
Arhat Temple

Built around 1000 years ago, Luóhàn Sì *(admission Y2; open 8am-5pm daily)* has since been sandwiched between the skyscrapers and apartments of the city. At its peak, this temple was home to 70 monks; there are only around 18 in residence these days. Nonetheless, the temple is still popular with local worshippers, who burn tonnes of fragrant incense, and it's worth a visit.

Luóhàn is the Chinese rendering of the Sanskrit *arhat*, which is a Buddhist term referring to people who have released themselves from the psychological bondage of greed, hate and delusion. Appropriately enough, there are 500 life-like, terracotta arhat sculptures inside the temple. You'll also find a large golden Buddha figure, behind which is an Indian-style *jataka* mural depicting Prince Siddhartha in the process of cutting his hair to renounce the world.

The temple's most remarkable feature is its long entrance flanked by rock carvings, many of which have survived the onslaught of time, the Cultural Revolution and the city's pollution amazingly well.

The *vegetarian restaurant* here has been spiffed up for tour groups and is pricey.

Red Cliff Village 红岩村
Hóngyán Cūn

During the tenuous Kuomintang-Communist alliance against the Japanese during WWII, Red Cliff Village, *(admission Y6; open 8am-5.30pm daily)*, outside Chóngqìng, was used as the offices and living quarters of the Communist representatives to the Kuomintang.

SOUTH-WEST CHINA

CHÓNGQÌNG CITY 重庆

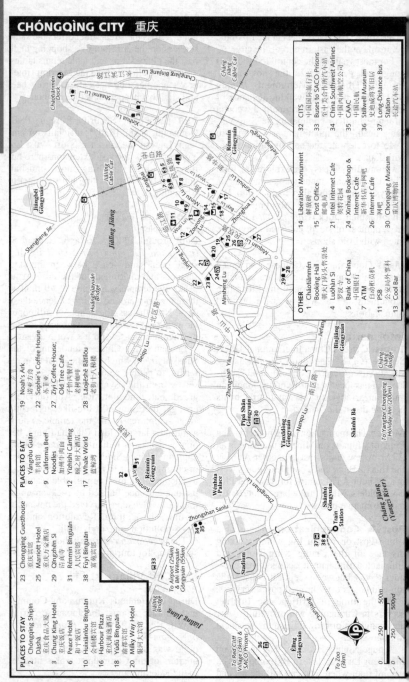

PLACES TO STAY
2 Chongqing Shipín
   重庆实馆
   Dàshà
3 Marriott Hotel
   重庆万豪酒店
6 Chung King Hotel
   重庆饭店
10 Peace Hotel
   和平饭店
16 Huixianlóu Bínguan
   会仙楼宾馆
18 Harbour Plaza
   重庆海逸酒店
20 Yùdú Bìnguan
   渝都宾馆
   Milky Way Hotel
   银河大饭店

23 Chongqing Guesthouse
   重庆宾馆
25 Marriott Hotel
   重庆万豪大酒店
29 Qingzhèn Sì
   清真寺
31 Renmín Bìnguan
   人民宾馆
38 Fúyì Bìnguan
   富艺宾馆

PLACES TO EAT
8 Yángròu Guan
   羊肉馆
9 California Beef
   Noodles
   加州牛肉面
12 Yìzhíshí Cantíng
   颐之时大酒店
17 Whale World
   蓝鲸湾

19 Noah's Ark
   诺亚方舟
22 Sophie's Coffee House
   苏菲屋
27 Zìyì Coffee House;
   Old Tree Cafe
   子衫咖啡厅;
   老树咖啡
28 Laoqiéshè Bàtílóu
   老街十八梯楼

OTHER
1 Chaotianmén
   Booking Hall
   朝天门码头售票处
4 Luóhàn Sì
   罗汉寺
5 Bank of China
   中国银行
7 ATM
   自动取款机
11 PSB
   公安局外事科
13 Cool Bar
   阳

14 Liberation Monument
   解放碑
15 Post Office
   邮电局
21 Intel Internet Cafe
   英特尔网吧
24 Xinhua Bookshop &
   Internet Cafe
   新华书店与网吧
26 Internet Cafe
   网吧
30 Chongqing Museum
   重庆博物馆

32 CITS
   中国国际旅行社
33 Buses to SACO Prisons
   至中美合作所汽车站
34 China Southwest Airlines
   中国西南航空公司
35 CAAC
   中国民航
36 Stillwell Museum
   史迪威将军旧居
37 Long-Distance Bus
   Station
   长途汽车站

Among others, Ye Jianying, Zhou Enlai and Zhou's wife, Deng Yingchao, lived in Red Cliff Village. After the Japanese surrender in 1945, Mao Zedong also arrived in Chóngqìng – at the instigation of US ambassador Patrick Hurley – to join in the peace negotiations with the Kuomintang. The talks lasted 42 days and resulted in a formal agreement which Mao described as 'words on paper'.

One of China's better revolutionary history museums now stands at the site and has a large collection of photos, although all of the captions are in Chinese only.

A short walk from the museum stands the old headquarters of the South Bureau of the Communist Party's Central Committee and the office of the representatives of the Eighth Route Army. There are only a few sparse furnishings and photographs to see.

To get to Red Cliff Village, take bus No 104 from its terminal on Beiqu Lu, just north of the Liberation Monument.

US-Chiang Kaishek Criminal Acts Exhibition Hall & SACO Prisons

Zhōngměi Hézuòsuǒ Jízhōngyíng Jiùzhǐ

In 1943 the USA and Chiang Kaishek signed a secret agreement to set up the Sino-American Cooperation Organisation (SACO) under which the USA helped to train and dispatch secret agents for the Kuomintang. As an extension of SACO, a number of prison camps were also built here. The chief of SACO was Tai Li, the notorious head of the Kuomintang military secret service; its deputy chief was a US Navy officer, Commodore ME Miles. Both an exhibition hall and the prisons (*admission Y2; open 8am-7pm daily*) have been opened to the public.

The Kuomintang never recognised the Communist Party as a legal political entity, although in theory it recognised its army as allies in the struggle against the Japanese invaders. Civilian Communists remained subject to repressive laws and hundreds were kept captive as political prisoners by the Kuomintang in these prisons and others. According to the Communists, many were also executed.

Unfortunately, the site has Chinese captions only, making it fairly uninteresting for non-Chinese-speaking visitors. The exhibition hall has lots of photos on display;

there are manacles and chains but nothing too ghoulish.

To get there take bus No 215 or 217 just south of Zhongshan Sanlu, not far from the Jiālíng Bridge. It's about a 45-minute ride. Make sure that the driver knows where you want to get off, as the place is not obvious. The SACO Prisons are an hour's walk from the hall.

Alternatively, if you are keen to see these sights, there are tour buses leaving from the Cháotiānmén Dock and train station areas. For a pricey Y60, the four-hour tour takes in both the hall and the prisons and throws in some other revolutionary sights as well.

Stillwell Museum

The Stillwell Museum (*admission Y5; open 9am-6pm daily Mar-Dec*) is something of a novelty in China, as it sheds a relatively positive light on the US involvement in WWII. The museum is housed in the former VIP Guesthouse of the Kuomintang and residence of General Stillwell, who was Commander of China-Burma-Indian Theatre and Chief of Staff to Chiang Kaishek in 1942. On display are mostly US-supplied photos, documents, articles and videos which may be of interest to American history buffs.

Parks

Chóngqìng's two temple parks are neglected by many visitors, but they are a pleasant enough way to while away an afternoon. At 345m, **Pípá Shān Gōngyuán** (*admission Y5, plus Y3 for temple; open 6am-10pm daily*) marks the highest point on the Chóngqìng peninsula. The Hongxing Pavilion at the top of the park provides good views of Chóngqìng.

Élíng Gōngyuán, at the neck of the peninsula, is more of a hike and not really worth a special trip. You can find the Liangjiang Pavilion here.

Along Cháng Jiāng, just east of the bus station, is **Shānhú Gōngyuán** (*Coral Park; admission Y10*), opened in 1997. Designed as a theme park, it has paths, palms and gardens inside. It's a pleasant place to wander or wait for your bus, if you're willing to shell out the steep entrance fee. In summer, musical performances are hosted here.

Bridges

As you tour around Chóngqìng, it's hard to miss the enormous Jiālíng and Cháng Jiāng bridges. The **Jiālíng Bridge** (*Jiālíng Qiáo*), which crosses the river west of central Chóngqìng, was built between 1963 and 1966. It is 150m long and 60m high and for 15 years was one of the few means of access to the rest of China. In 1981 the **Cháng Jiāng Bridge** (*Cháng Jiāng Qiáo*), to the south, was finished and in 1989 the **Shímén Bridge** (*Shímén Qiáo*) over Jiālíng Jiāng was completed.

Cable-Car Trips

Cable cars spanning both Jiālíng Jiāng and Cháng Jiāng carry you over the precipitously stacked housing and polluting industrial estates for a bird's-eye view of the murky waters. The ride over Cháng Jiāng links up to a series of lifts and Chiang Kaishek's old domicile. Both are within walking distance of the Liberation Monument, run from 6.30am to 9.30pm and cost Y1.

Chongqing Museum 重庆博物馆
Chóngqìng Bówùguǎn

The dinosaur skeletons on display at this museum (*admission Y10, plus Y10 for dinosaur exhibits; open 9am-5pm daily*) were unearthed at Zìgòng, Yangchuan and elsewhere in Sìchuān between 1974 and 1977. The museum is at the foot of Pípá Shān Gōngyuán in the south of town.

Běi Wēnquán Gōngyuán
Northern Hot Springs Park 北温泉公园

Fifty-five kilometres north-west of the city, at the foot of Jìnyún Shān and overlooking Jiālíng Jiāng, the Northern Hot Springs are in a large park that is also the site of a 5th-century Buddhist temple.

The springs have an Olympic-size swimming pool where you can bathe to an audience, or private rooms with big hot baths. Water temperature averages around 32°C. There are also gardens and a water slide that should be open by the time you read this. Swimsuits can be hired here – they're coloured red, symbolising happiness.

To get to the springs, take bus No 306 from the Liberation Monument.

Another group of springs 20km south of Chóngqìng has hotter waters, and may be quieter than the northern springs.

Places to Stay – Budget

If you're thinking of splurging, Chóngqìng is the place to do it as there is next to nothing in the way of budget accommodation here.

You will undoubtedly be met by touts at the bus/train station who will insist that foreign friends can stay at their cheap hotel (figure Y40 for the cheapest). Remember, however, that these folk only get paid to bring you to the hotel and aren't that interested in the rules. The hotel may well turn you away (although you might not mind as those we checked were grotty and unsafe).

Huìxiānlóu Bīnguǎn (☎ 384 5101, *Minzu Lu*) Dorm beds in 7-bed rooms Y50. This place offers the only dorms in the city centre. It's still fairly expensive, but well located and the remodelled air-con dorms are quite good. From the train station, walk up to Zhongshan Lu and take bus No 405 to the Liberation Monument.

Chóngqìng Shípǐn Dàshà (☎ 384 7300, *72 Shaanxi Lu*) Doubles Y150-200, triples Y180. This place has pleasant, clean rooms with bathroom and air-con as well as plusher 'deluxe' doubles. You can book boat and train tickets here.

Places to Stay – Mid-Range

Peace Hotel (*Hépíng Bīnguǎn*; ☎ 384 7800, *Minzu Lu*) Singles/doubles Y158/210. The refurbished comfortable rooms here are excellently located and a relatively good deal.

Qīngzhēn Sì (☎ 374 0018) Doubles Y190. Large doubles in this remodelled high-rise mosque have a view of the river below, but they're somewhat musty and frayed. (The mosque itself is now on the 18th floor.)

Fūyì Bīnguǎn (☎ 389 3994, *38 Caiyuan Ba*) Standard twins/triples Y160/180, deluxe twins Y220. This place is quite a haul out of town but is convenient for early morning buses and trains. Unfortunately, the standard rooms are inevitably full and you'll be shown to the deluxe twins instead.

Rénmín Bīnguǎn (☎ 385 1421, fax 385 2076, *Renmin Lu*) Doubles Y200-1700. This hotel appears to be a palace from the outside. Constructed in 1953, the hotel comprises three wings separated by an enormous 65m-high circular concert hall which seats 4000 people. Unfortunately, this grandeur only extends to the very top-end rooms inside. Nevertheless, competition is steep in the big city and you may land a good mid-range deal here. From the train station, head up to Zhongshan Lu and catch bus No 401 or 405 to the traffic circle and walk east down Renmin Lu.

Chung King Hotel (*Chóngqìng Fàndiàn;* ☎ *384 9301, fax 384 3085, Xinhua Lu*) Singles/doubles Y198/268. This three-star hotel has a small gift shop (with a few English titles), foreign exchange, post and telecommunications, taxi and clinic. The hotel has its own shuttle bus to and from the train station and the airport.

Milky Way Hotel (*Yínhé Dàbīnguǎn;* ☎ *380 8585, 49 Datong Lu*) Doubles Y298. Rooms here are comfortable and like new and prices are surprisingly low.

Places to Stay – Top End

There is definitely no shortage of top-end hotels in Chóngqìng. During the off season it's worth shopping around as you can find some excellent deals.

Chongqing Guesthouse (*Chóngqìng Bīnguǎn;* ☎ *384 5888, Minsheng Lu*) Singles/ doubles Y228/260, VIP-wing rooms Y435. This guesthouse has transformed itself into a four-star luxury hotel. The rooms in the old wing are comfortable but nothing special. The VIP wing, however, is an oasis – check here for bargains. The hotel has all amenities, including a pool.

Yúdū Bīnguǎn Doubles Y280. This hotel boasts a good location and relatively reasonable prices.

Harbour Plaza (*Chǒngxǐhǎiyì Jiǔdiàn;* ☎ *370 0888,* Ⓦ *www.harbour-plaza.com/ hpcq*) Rooms Y1330. This brand-new hotel has five-star facilities. Posted rates are high, but if you're lucky you may get these for as low as Y465.

Marriott Hotel (*Wànháo Jiǔdiàn;* ☎ *388 8888,* Ⓦ *www.marriott.com*) Not far away from the Harbour Plaza, this flashy international hotel has similar service, rates and deals.

Places to Eat

The central business district, in the eastern section of the city near the docks, abounds with small *restaurants* and *street vendors*. For tasty noodles and *bāozi* (steamed stuffed buns), check out Xinhua Lu and Shaanxi Lu towards Cháotiānmén Dock.

There are some good *night markets* behind Huìxiānlóu Bīnguǎn, in the vicinity of Luóhàn Sì and near Yúdū Bīnguǎn.

Chóngqìng's No 1 speciality is *huǒguō*, or hotpot. While it's usually cheap, it's a good idea to check prices as you go along. Although hotpot can be found wherever there are street vendors or small restaurants, Wuyi Lu has the greatest variety and is locally known as *huǒguō jiē*, or hotpot street. Bayi Lu is also a great street for snack hunting.

Yízhīshí Cāntīng (*Zourong Lu*) Sampler course Y25. Among the many larger, sit-down restaurants along Zourong Lu, this popular restaurant is an excellent place to feast on Sichuanese main courses. Sìchuān-style pastries are served in the morning and local specialities like tea-smoked duck and dry-stewed fish at lunch and dinner. The 2nd floor has full-course meals; go up to the 3rd floor for a sampler course of famous Chóngqìng snacks. Draught beer and special 'eight-treasure tea' (*bābǎochá*) do a fine job of washing it all down.

Yángròu Guǎn (*Lamb Restaurant*) The dishes here are spicy, but the kebabs aren't too punishing on the tongue. The surrounding neighbourhood is teeming with restaurants.

California Beef Noodles (*Wusi Lu*) Part of a national chain, the food here is pretty good, although the small, hole-in-the-wall restaurants along this street serve up more interesting noodles in clay pots.

Ziyi Coffee House (*Zīyìxī Cāntīng; Mi-quan Lu*) This restaurant has excellent pizzas, soups and pasta at reasonable prices. Just down the street, Qīngzhēn Sì runs a fairly busy *Muslim restaurant*.

Whale World (*Lánjīngwān; open 9am–1am daily*) Across from the Harbour Plaza, Whale World has a pan-Asian menu and a relaxed atmosphere.

The Harbour Plaza itself has a number of *restaurants* with a Western buffet breakfast/dinner for Y60/128.

Coffee & Tea Houses There are a number of coffee and tea houses that are worth a visit.

Old Tree Cafe (*Lǎosù Kāfēi*) Here you'll find a long menu of freshly ground coffees that you can order with flavoured syrups or liquors.

Lǎojiēshí Bǎfílǒu Down the street from the Old Tree Cafe, this is a beautiful teahouse with wooden and bamboo decor and old teapots, cups and photos on display. There's lots of tea to sample here and the cups are bottomless, although they're also fairly pricey (Y25).

Noah's Ark (*Nuòyà Fāngzhōu*) With four cosy floors, this cafe/bar has coffee, tea, popcorn, ice cream and an international collection of beer.

Sophie's Coffee House (*Sūfēiyà*) The keen staff here serve coffees, teas and snacks.

Entertainment

Bars come and go with great frequency in Chóngqìng. The *Cool Bar*, open at the time of writing, serves inexpensive beer in something akin to a Western bar. Your best bet, however, is to ask around.

The Harbour Plaza has a *coffeehouse/bar* on its ground floor with live Singaporean music in the evenings.

Getting There & Away

Air Chóngqìng's new Jiangbei airport is 25km north of the city. You can buy airline tickets at the Civil Aviation Administration of China (CAAC; Zhōngguó Mínháng; ☎ 360 3144) on Zhongshan Sanlu, in the west of the city. China Southwest Airlines (☎ 785 3191) has an office a couple of doors down and Dragonair (☎ 280 3380) has an office at the Yangtze Chongqing Holiday Inn, in the south of the city. You can also book flights at the Chung King Hotel and in numerous ticket offices around the Liberation Monument.

Connections within the south-west include Chéngdū (Y220, daily), Guìlín (Y670, daily), Guìyáng (Y420, Monday, Wednesday and Saturday), Kūnmíng (Y660, daily) and Nánníng (Y700, daily). Flights to other major cities include Běijīng (Y1400, daily), Guǎngzhōu (Y1080, daily), Lhasa (Y1300, Sunday), Shànghǎi (Y1340, daily), Ürümqi (Y1610, Wednesday and Saturday), Wǔhàn (Y720, daily) and Xī'ān (Y530, daily).

China Southwest and Dragonair also have flights to Hong Kong (Y2320, Thursday to Tuesday), Bangkok (Y2860, Friday) and Nagoya in Japan (Y3600, Tuesday and Friday).

Bus Transport between Chóngqìng, Chéngdū and Lèshān is much faster with the completion of the new expressways, creating a commerce-friendly triangle of transportation.

Buses from Chóngqìng depart from the two-storey long-distance bus terminal next to the train station. With two ticket halls, two waiting halls and dozens of gates, the station can process 800 to 1000 buses daily, or so the management claims.

To Chéngdū, there are buses running from 6.30am to 9.30pm (Y112, three to four hours). For Dàzú, most buses are of the micro variety, departing from 6am to 6pm (Y80, three hours). To Lèshān buses depart from 6.15am to 6pm (Y80).

You can also catch buses to Chéngdū (the speedy, plush, air-con type) in the mornings from in front of Cháotiānmén Dock.

Train While you're much better off taking the bus to Chéngdū than the 6.37am morning train (hard seat Y64, 11 hours), it might be worth taking the overnight train at 11.17pm (hard sleeper Y83) to save a night's pricey accommodation in Chóngqìng.

There are a couple of trains a day that stop at Dàzú, but the station is 30km from Dàzú town. The train is far more inconvenient and time-consuming than the buses that speed down the expressway.

A daily train to Shànghǎi (hard sleeper Y475, 43 hours), leaving at 6.12pm, takes in Guìyáng, before making a long haul through the sticks to Hángzhōu and on to Shànghǎi. There is another train to Guìyáng at 8.34pm (hard sleeper Y103, 10 hours).

There are two trains daily to Kūnmíng at 9.19am and 2.39pm (hard sleeper Y200, 23 hours). These trains pass through Chéngdū and Pānzhīhūa (for Lìjiāng or Dàlǐ).

There are three trains daily to Guǎngzhōu (40 hours) and two trains each day to Běijīng (30 hours). Daily trains also depart for Xī'ān (28 hours) and Zhèngzhōu (25 hours).

Boat It certainly seems that zillions of boats make the run from Chóngqìng down Cháng Jiāng to Wǔhàn. The ride is a popular tourist trip, a good way of getting away from the trains and an excellent way to get to Wǔhàn. Consider doing it before the Chinese government finishes its massive dam project and floods the Three Gorges (see 'The Damned

Yangzi' boxed text). For details, see the special section 'Cruising Downriver'.

Travelling upriver by boat from Chóngqìng is no longer a viable option ever since the government pulled its money out of the ferry business and put it all behind the expressway. You may find private boats selling tickets for Yíbīn or Lèshān in the summer; however, it's considered by locals to be a risky ride.

Getting Around
To/From the Airport CAAC runs shuttle buses between the airport and the ticket office (Y15), timed to coincide with flights. Buses to the airport leave 2½ hours before scheduled flight times.

Bus In Chóngqìng buses can be tediously slow, and since there are no bicycles they're even more crowded than in other Chinese cities. Useful routes include: No 401, which runs between the Cháotiānmén Dock and the intersection of Renmin Lu and Zhongshan Lu, near the CAAC office; No 405, running the length of Zhongshan Lu up to the Liberation Monument; and No 102, which connects the train station and Cháotiānmén Dock.

There are also minibuses running between the dock and the train station for Y1.

Taxi Nowadays, as in most other Chinese cities, flagging down a taxi is no problem. Flag fall is Y6, although it can be slightly higher depending on the size of the car. Expect to pay Y10 to Y15 from downtown to the bus station. Note that the plethora of one-way and 'no entrance' streets makes for some circuitous routing.

DÀZÚ COUNTY 大足县
The grotto art of Dàzú county, 160km north-west of Chóngqìng, is rated alongside China's other great Buddhist cave sculptures at Dūnhuáng, Luòyáng and Dàtóng.

Historical records for Dàzú are sketchy. The cliff carvings and statues (with Buddhist, Taoist and Confucian influences) amount to thousands of pieces, large and small, scattered over the county in some 40-odd places. The main groupings are at Běi Shān and the more interesting Bǎodǐng. They date from the Tang dynasty (9th century) to the Song (13th century).

The town of Dàzú is small and relatively unhurried. Despite the tour buses that visit the grottos in the summer, the town itself sees few tourists.

Běi Shān 北山
North Hill
According to inscriptions, the Běi Shān site (admission Y5, plus Y40 for sculptures; open 8am-5pm daily) was originally a military camp, with the earliest carvings commissioned by a general. The dark niches hold small statues, many in poor condition; only one or two really stand out.

Niche No 136 depicts Puxian, the patron saint (male) of Émeí Shān, riding a white elephant. The same niche has the androgynous Sun and Moon Guanyin. Niche 155 holds a bit more talent, the Peacock King.

Běi Shān is about a 30-minute hike from Dàzú town – aim straight for the pagoda visible from the bus station. From the top of the hill, there are good views.

Bǎodǐng Shān 宝顶山
Treasured Summit Hill
Fifteen kilometres north-east of Dàzú town, the sculptures at Bǎodǐng Shān (admission Y50, with Běi Shān Y80; open 8am-5pm daily) are definitely more interesting than those at Běi Shān. It is believed the sculptures were completed over 70 years, between 1179 and 1249. It's easy to spend a few hours wandering around this area.

The founding work is attributed to Zhao Zhifeng, a monk from an obscure Yoga sect of Tantric Buddhism. A monastery with nice woodwork and throngs of pilgrims sits atop a hill; on the lower section of the hill is a 125m horseshoe-shaped cliff sculptured with coloured figures, some of them up to 8m high.

The centrepiece is a 31m-long, 5m-high reclining Buddha, depicted entering nirvana, with the torso sunk into the cliff face. Next to the Buddha, with a temple built around her for protection, is a mesmerising, gold Avalokiteshvara (or Guanyin, the Goddess of Mercy). Her 1007 individual arms fan out around her, entwined and reaching for the skies. Each hand has an eye, the symbol of wisdom.

Statues around the rest of the horseshoe vary considerably: Buddhist preachers and sages, historical figures, realistic scenes (on

The Damned Yangzi

The Three Gorges Dam is China's biggest engineering project since the construction of the Great Wall. When completed in 2009, it will back Cháng Jiāng up for 550km, flood an area the size of Singapore and wash away the homes of up to two million people. It will rank as the world's largest dam – an epic show of Communist might, definitive proof of man's dominance of capricious nature and the 21st century symbol of a new superpower.

A cherished vision since the early years of Republican China, the dam proposal was only finally given government go-ahead in April 1992, despite having been originally proposed by Sun Yatsen in 1919 and enjoying the staunch support over the years of other political heavyweights such as Mao Zedong and, most recently, Premier Li Peng, himself a Moscow-trained engineer.

The colossal project involves the construction of a 2km-wide, 185m-high dam wall across Cháng Jiāng at Sandouping, 38km upstream from the existing Gēzhōu Dam. Cháng Jiāng has already been blocked and its water diverted; images of the final few boulders filling in the plug were broadcast simultaneously on all of China's TV channels in November 1997. Now that the riverbed is dry, 60,000 workers work round the clock on pouring the concrete for the main dam, construction of which will continue until 2003 when water levels are expected to rise significantly. Navigation currently travels along a diversion canal through a temporary lock.

The Three Gorges Dam is a cornerstone of government efforts to channel economic growth from the dynamic coastal provinces into what are considered the more backward western regions, somehow transforming hinterland into heartland. Cháng Jiāng is likened by enthusiastic officials to a dragon with its head in Shànghǎi and its tail in Chóngqìng, or to a crossbow shooting Shanghai's economic energy up into Chóngqìng and beyond. In between the two will be the 220-million-people-strong Yangzi Economic Region, stretched over nine provinces. The dam's hydroelectric production – the equivalent of 18 nuclear power plants and reckoned to equal almost one-fifth of China's current generating capacity – is intended to power this continuing industrialisation and relieve the region's environmentally damaging dependency on coal and other fossil fuels.

The dam will also improve navigation on Cháng Jiāng, which already transports 70% of the entire county's shipping. Although passing the dam itself will be an inconvenience (the dam will have five locks, raising boats over 100m), the navigability of upper Cháng Jiāng will be drastically improved by the widening of shipping lanes and the creation of a constant water level within the new lake. Inundation will also eliminate strong river currents, and obstacles dangerous to navigation such as sandbars, shoals and submerged rocks.

At least as important will be the dam's role in flood control. Cháng Jiāng is prone to repeated flooding (the most recent in 1998), often causing great loss of life. Catastrophic floods have been recorded for the past millennia and in the past 100 years alone more than one million lives have been claimed by them.

However the massive scale of the Three Gorges Dam project has caused disquiet among environmentalists and economists, arousing some of the most outspoken criticism of government policy in China since 1989. The official debate by the National Congress recorded the largest number of negative votes ever recorded against government policy. Free discussion has hardly been encouraged; Dai Qing's outspoken book *Yangzi! Yangzi!* earned her a 10-month spell in prison.

Construction of the dam is enormously expensive, and the initial estimates of US$20 to US$30 billion have now risen to as high as US$70 billion. The dam

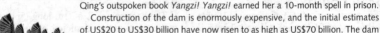

the rear of a postcard one is described as 'Pastureland – Cowboy at Rest') and delicate sculptures a few centimetres high. Some of them have been eroded by wind and rain, some have lost layers of paint, but overall there is a remarkable survival rate.

Bǎodǐng Shān differs from other grottoes in that it was based on a preconceived plan which incorporated some of the area's

natural features – a sculpture next to the reclining Buddha, for example, makes use of an underground spring.

Minibuses to Bǎodǐng Shān leave the Dàzú bus station about every 30 minutes (or as soon as they fill up). They start to thin out by about 4pm, with the last one at 6pm. The fare is Y2 to Y5. The trip takes anywhere from 30 to 45 minutes. For a much quicker

The Damned Yangzi

is a magnet for graft: in 2000 a local government official in Chóngqìng was executed for taking over US$1 million in bribes relating to the dam and another 96 officials were arrested. Economists both in China and abroad have warned that it may be imprudent for the government to concentrate so much investment into one single project and that epic dam constructions are simply an anachronism. The World Bank has refused to back the project. The US government has advised its companies not to get involved. Nevertheless, given the political and economic investment to date, work is most likely too far along to be halted.

The social implications of the dam are profound indeed. An estimated 1.5 million people living in inundated areas will need to be relocated and, more importantly, given a new livelihood. Compensation packages range from US$2000 to US$4000 and Chóngqìng municipality alone has to re-settle over one million people, the price it must pay for economic clout. That is, if the money is still there: government auditors estimate that US$52 million of resettlement funds is now unaccounted for, with other sources quoting figures as high as US$600 million.

Perhaps the greatest fears come from environmentalists. Friends of the Earth has described the dam as 'the most socially and environmentally destructive dam in history'. It is thought that as the river slows so will its ability to oxygenate. The untreated waste that pours into the river from over 40 towns and 400 factories, as well as the toxic materials and pollutants from the inundated industrial sites, could well create another world record for the dam; a 480km-long septic tank – the largest toilet in the world. The slowing of the river will also lead to more silt deposits, which in turn could block the turbines of the dam or silt up Chóngqìng's port. The dam will also disrupt the environments of such endangered species as the Yangzi River dolphin, Chinese sturgeon and Siberian crane. Some say that the massive waters could even induce a localised earthquake. The same experts suggest that a series of smaller dams further downstream would provide a far more effective and less damaging system of flood control.

The rising waters will cover countless cultural artefacts at over 8000 important archaeological sites in the Cháng Jiāng basin, many of which offer clues to China's early political development that have not yet been properly studied. Despite an ambitious plan of relocation and preservation, time is running out and archaeologists are racing smugglers to collect as much of the region's cultural heritage as time allows.

Some destruction of the natural and scenic splendour of the Three Gorges is certain, though how the dam will affect Cháng Jiāng tourism is uncertain. Boat trips of the Three Gorges are running overtime as local and foreign tourists rush to see one of China's most famous sights before the concrete slabs begin to spell the demise of a great river.

Fears about the project were also heightened when information was released about two dams that collapsed in Hénán province in 1975. After 20 years as a state secret, it is now apparent that as many as 230,000 people died in the catastrophe. If a similar accident was to happen on Cháng Jiāng, the population of nearby Yíchāng would be dead within an hour.

Planners insist that the Three Gorges Dam will be constructed according to safety regulations that would make such disasters impossible. Still, the collapse of the walls holding back the world's largest storage reservoir in one of the world's most densely populated pieces of real estate is a scenario that must keep even the most gung-ho supporters of the Three Gorges project awake at night.

---

ride, hop on the back of a motorcycle taxi, which you can bargain down to Y15.

As you pass by in the bus, keep an eye on the cliff faces for solo sculptures.

Places to Stay & Eat

Most hotels don't take foreigners, leaving you with only two options in Dàzú, neither of which is particularly cheap.

Běishān Bīnguǎn Doubles Y180. Near the base of Běi Shān, this hotel is musty, unkempt and horrendously overpriced. The only real reason to look in here is to make Dàzú Bīnguǎn seem like that much better a deal.

Dàzú Bīnguǎn Doubles Y180-489. Rooms here are clean and comfortable with good service and a Chinese breakfast included. The hotel also has new, fancier doubles with all amenities. To find the hotel, turn left out of the bus station, cross over the bridge and take the road branching to the right. This will bring you to one of the hotel's two main gates. This one may be locked but don't panic; walk around the left side to the back entrance.

Finding a bite to eat in Dàzú is no problem. Shizi Jie (the first right up from the roundabout) comes alive at night with dozens of *street stalls* serving noodles, dumplings, hotpot and wok-fried dishes. If you head straight up the main road from the roundabout, you'll come to a number of *restaurants* serving fresh noodles for Y2 a bowl.

Getting There & Away

Bus There are four departures for Chéngdū from Dàzú between 6.30am and 9.30am (Y51, four hours). There are also frequent departures to Chóngqìng between 6.30am and 5.30pm (Y29).

From Chóngqìng, buses leave the main bus terminal for Dàzú between 7am to 7pm. Morning departures leave Chéngdū's north bus station for Dàzú or you can catch a fast bus bound for Yóutíngpū, roughly halfway to Chóngqìng. Just north of the expressway here is a bustling crossroads bus station, and from here there are dozens of buses to Dàzú.

Train Travelling to Dàzú by train is impractical and time-consuming. You're much better off taking a bus down the new expressways.

To get to Dàzú by train, you need to get off the Chéngdū-Chóngqìng railway line at Yóutíngpū (five hours from Chóngqìng, seven hours from Chéngdū), which is the nearest stop to Dàzú. Despite the fact that the town is around 30km from Dàzú, train timetables refer to it as Dàzú station. There are frequent minibuses running from the train station to Dàzú.

Cháng Jiāng (Yangzi River) from Chóngqìng to Shànghǎi – cruise China's greatest river.

Cruising Downriver

MARTIN MOOS

MARTIN MOOS

Title page: Traditional Chinese pavilion above Wǔhàn, overlooking Cháng Jiāng and the start of Wǔ Gorge, the second gorge of the famous Three Gorges passage in Chóngqìng. (Photograph by Martin Moos.)

Top: Boats cruising along Cháng Jiāng in Sìchuān.

Bottom: A little boat travelling along Cháng Jiāng in Sìchuān, is dwarfed by the gorge.

CRUISING DOWNRIVER
Cháng Jiāng (Yangzi River) from Chóngqìng to Shànghǎi

The dramatic scenery and rushing waters of China's greatest river may have been inspirational to many of China's painters and poets, but there was very little in the way of inspiration for those charged with the task of negotiating the twists and turns of this dangerous stretch of water.

It was sheer hard work. A large boat pushing upstream needed hundreds of coolies (trackers) who lined the riverbanks and hauled the boat with long ropes against the surging waters. Even today smaller boats on branches of the river can be seen being pulled up the river by their crews.

Cháng Jiāng is China's longest river and at 6300km is the third longest in the world. Originating in snow-covered Tánggǔlǎ Shān in south-western Qīnghǎi, it cuts its way through Tibet and seven Chinese provinces before emptying into the East China Sea just north of Shànghǎi. Between the towns of Fēngjié, in Sìchuān, and Yíchāng, in Húběi, lie three great gorges, regarded as one of the great scenic attractions of China. Well, for now anyway: by 2009, when the mega-project Three Gorges Dam (Sānxiá Dàbà) is completed, the famed Three Gorges will become part of history, 1.5 million people will have been dislocated and south-western China will never be the same. See the boxed text 'The Damned Yangzi' in the Chóngqìng chapter for more information. For the moment, tour boats are running constantly to take care of tourists and their last-ditch efforts to see it all.

The boat ride from Chóngqìng to Wǔhàn is a popular tourist trip and the scenery is pleasant, but don't expect to be dwarfed by mile-high cliffs! Some people find the trip a bit of an anti-climax after their high expectations, while others are not disappointed. If you're in a rush, hydrofoils do the trip from Chóngqìng to Yíchāng in 11 hours for Y382. Alternatively, you could take a hydrofoil from Chóngqìng to Wànzhōu (Wànxiàn) in six hours (Y135) and try to hook up with a ferry there. From Yíchāng you can take direct trains to Běijīng, Wǔhàn, and Xī'ān or Huáihuà to connect to trains south. A few boats go beyond Wǔhàn, including one all the way to Shànghǎi, which is 2400km downriver – a week's journey.

Tickets

Try to book two or three days ahead of your intended date of departure, although an expansion in the number of cruise operators means tickets are usually ready for same day travel. CITS adds a service charge of Y50 to the ticket price. Budget travellers take note: if you book tickets with CITS, make sure you're not being put on one of the luxury boats reserved solely for foreigners – the price could blow your budget.

CITS (☎ 023-6385 1665, e citscq@public.cta.cq.cn) in Chongqing is at 120 Zaozi Gangya Zhengjie, just adjacent to Rénmín Bīnguǎn. Some of the staff speak English and are quite helpful.

Once you've boarded, a steward will exchange your ticket for a numbered, colour-coded tag that denotes your bed assignment. Hang on to the tag, since it must be exchanged for your ticket at the end of the voyage – without it they may not let you off the boat.

Classes

With the promise of an egalitarian China now shelved, most boats these days boast 1st-class cabins. These cabins come with two beds, a private bathroom, a television and air-con.

Second-class cabins have two to four berths, with soft beds, a small desk and chair, and a washbasin. Third class usually has from six to 12 beds depending on the boat. Fourth class usually has eight to 12, but on older vessels can have over 20 beds. Toilets and showers are shared, although you should be able to use the toilets and showers in 2nd class. In any event, upkeep on some boats is minimal and the toilets and washing facilities can get grotty.

Travellers have complained that access to the outside decks is often restricted depending on what class your ticket is, though it's usually possible to argue your way to the upper decks. Nevertheless, it can be very annoying; just don't expect to have access to the outside all the time.

There are also several vessels catering to foreign tour groups with higher standards (and deck chairs!). CITS and some of the independent booking agents around Chóngqìng's Cháotiānmén Dock area can arrange tickets for these luxury boats.

Fares

Shop around. Prices will be higher if you book through CITS or one of the independent brokers rather than buying directly from the Cháotiānmén boat ticket office. If you happen to be heading to Chóngqìng from Chéngdū, many travellers have got good deals from some of the budget travel agencies there.

Chóngqìng (downriver) to:	1st class (Y)	2nd class (Y)	3rd class (Y)	4th class (Y)
Yíchāng	929	482	225	160
Yuèyáng	1227	632	298	212
Wǔhàn (Hankou)	1369	704	330	237
Nánjīng	1837	978	459	329
Shànghǎi	2059	1109	519	372

Food

Restaurants and the quality of food vary from boat to boat, as do the prices. Most likely costs will be reasonable but it's a good idea to bring some of your own food with you. When the boat stops at a town for any length of time, passengers may disembark and eat at little restaurants near the pier.

The Route

Boats stop frequently during the cruise to visit cities, towns and a slew of tourist sights. If you buy your ticket from an agency they may insist you need to pay an extra Y360 for the tours visiting sights along the way. There's no need to because you can buy entry tickets right at the sights and you might choose not to visit them all. For the tour of the Little Three Gorges, however, it's a good idea to buy a ticket on the ferry rather than at the sight itself. See the Wànzhōu to Yíchāng section.

When the boat stops make sure you find out when it's leaving again; it won't wait for latecomers.

Chóngqìng to Wànzhōu For the first few hours the river is lined with factories, although this gives way to some pretty, green terraced countryside with the occasional small town.

One of the first stops is usually the town of **Fúlíng**. It overlooks the mouth of Wū Hé, which runs southwards into Guìzhōu and controls the river traffic between Guìzhōu and eastern Sìchuān.

Look for large white signs along the route indicating where the water level will rise to. By 2004 it's expected to rise 135m from the present level, and in 2009, with the dam's completion, it will rise to 175m.

The next major town is **Fēngdū**. Nearby is the **Abode of Ghosts** (Guǐchéng; ☎ 7061 9114; admission Y60; open 6am-6pm daily), which is said to be the place of devils. Numerous temples containing sculptures of demons and devils have been built since the Tang dynasty, with heartening names like 'Between the Living and the Dead', 'Bridge of Helplessness' and 'Palace of the King of Hell'. A cable car goes up to the temples (Y15) but you can also walk up. The boat then passes through the county of **Zhōngxiàn**.

Soon after comes the **Stone Treasure Stockade** (Shíbǎo Zhài; ☎ 5484 0174; admission Y15; open 8am-4pm daily) on the northern bank of the river. The Stone Treasure Stockade is a 12-storey 56m-high wooden temple built on a huge rock bluff which is supposed to look something like a stone seal. Construction began during the early years of Emperor Kangxi's reign (1662–1722) in the Qing dynasty. It houses a statue of Buddha and inscriptions which commemorate its construction. It will all become an island when the water level reaches its full height after the completion of the Three Gorges Dam.

Next is the large town of **Wànzhōu** (Wànxiàn), where most morning boats tie up for the night. It's a neat, hilly town and a great place to wander around for a few hours while the boat is in port.

Wànzhōu to Yíchāng Boats staying overnight at Wànzhōu generally depart before dawn. Before entering the gorges the boat passes by (and may stop at) the town of **Fēngjié** (Yǒng'ān). This ancient town was the capital of the state of Kui during the Spring and Autumn and Warring States periods from 722 to 221 BC.

The town overlooks Qútáng Gorge (Qútáng Xiá), the first of the three Cháng Jiāng gorges. At the entrance to Qútáng Gorge, just east of Fēngjié, is **White King Town** (Báidìchéng; ☎ 5673 1478; admission Y30; open 24 hours), which lies on the river's northern bank. It was here that the dying King of Shu, Liu Bei, entrusted his son and kingdom to Zhu Geliang, as chronicled in the classic Chinese novel Romance of the Three Kingdoms. Plaster mannequins on display depict this historic event inside one of the temples.

The spectacular **Three Gorges** (Sānxiá), Qútáng, Wū and Xīlíng, start just after Fēngjié and end near Yíchāng, a stretch of about 200km. The gorges vary from 300m at their widest to less than 100m at their narrowest. The seasonal difference in water level can be as much as 50m.

Qútáng Gorge is the smallest and shortest gorge (only 8km long), although the water flows most rapidly here. High on the northern bank is **Bellows Gorge** *(Fēngxiāng Xiá)*. Nine coffins were discovered high up in the cliffs, possibly put there by an ancient tribe whose custom was to place the coffins of their dead in high mountain caves. Some of the coffins contained bronze swords, armour and other artefacts, believed to date back as far as the Warring States period.

Wū Gorge *(Wū Xiá)* is about 40km in length and the cliffs on either side rise to just over 900m, topped by sharp, jagged peaks on the northern bank, including Goddess Peak (Shénnǚ Fēng) and Peak of the Immortals (Jíxiān Fēng). If it's misty, and it very often is, you get a good idea for the inspiration behind Chinese traditional painting. **Bādōng** is a town on the southern bank of the river within the gorge. It's a communications centre from which roads span out into western Húběi.

In between Qútáng and Wū gorges, most boats will stop for five or six hours so passengers can shift to smaller boats for tours of the **Little Three Gorges** *(Xiǎo Sānxiá)*. Flanking Dàníng Hé, these gorges are much narrower than their larger counterparts and, some travellers say, more dramatic. The tour usually costs Y100 to Y150 and it's a good idea to book it ahead on the ferry, otherwise the tour boats might be full when you get there. Though some travellers have complained of the cost, many enjoy the chance to get out and view the rock formations up close.

Xīlíng Gorge *(Xīlíng Xiá)*, at 80km, is the longest of the three gorges. Just before you get to the end, the massive Three Gorges Dam project looms up. At the end of the gorge everyone crowds out onto the deck to watch the boat pass through the locks of the huge **Gézhōu Dam** *(Gézhōu Bà)*.

The next stop is the industrial town of **Yíchāng**, which is regarded as the gateway to upper Cháng Jiāng and was once a walled city

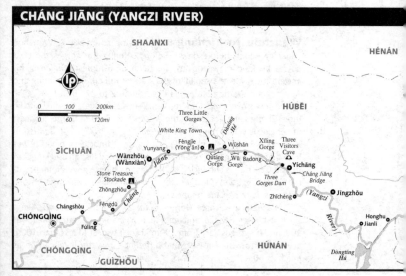

CHÁNG JIĀNG (YANGZI RIVER)

dating back at least as far as the Sui dynasty. Near Yíchāng's train station you can take bus No 10 to the **Three Visitors Cave** (Sānyóu Dòng; ☎ 0717-670 0715; admission Y15; open 8am-6pm daily) and walk through caverns with impressive stalactites and stalagmites. A cliff trail nearby overlooks Cháng Jiāng.

Yíchāng to Wǔhàn After leaving Yíchāng, the boat passes under the 1700m-long Yangzi River Bridge (Cháng Jiāng Qiáo) at the town of **Zhīchéng**. The next major place is **Jīngzhōu**, which is a light-industrial town. As early as the Tang dynasty, Jīngzhōu was a trading centre of some importance. The town enjoyed great prosperity during the Taiping Rebellion when trade lower down Cháng Jiāng was largely at a standstill. About 7.5km from here you will find **Jīngzhōu Ancient City** (Jīngzhōu Gǔchéng; ☎ 0716-846 8124; admission Y10; open 7.30am-7.30pm), the remains of the ancient town, which is open to visitors.

After Jīngzhōu there's not much to look at: you're out on the flat plains of central China, the river widens immensely and you can see little of the shore. The boat continues downriver to pass by (and possibly stop at) the town of **Chénglíngjī**, which lies at the confluence of Dòngtíng Hú and Cháng Jiāng.

East of Dòngtíng Hú is the town of **Yuèyáng**. Another nine hours will bring you to Wǔhàn, at which point most travellers are quite ready to part ways with their boat.

Wǔhàn to Shànghǎi Wǔhàn more or less marks the halfway point in the long navigable stretch of Cháng Jiāng from Chóngqìng down to Shànghǎi. The journey to the sea is far more mundane than the trip upriver to Chóngqìng; Cháng Jiāng broadens and most of the towns and cities are industrial.

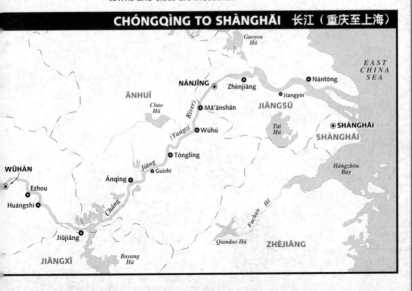

CHÓNGQÌNG TO SHÀNGHǍI 长江（重庆至上海）

Leaving Wǔhàn, you pass through **Huángshí** in eastern Húběi on the southern bank of the river. Nearby is an ancient mining tunnel dating back to the Spring and Autumn period, where numerous mining tools, including bronze axes, were discovered.

Near the border with Jiāngxī, on the northern bank, is the town of **Wùxué**, known for the production of bamboo goods.

The first major town you come to in Jiāngxī is **Jiǔjiāng**, the jumping-off point for nearby Lúshān. The mouth of Pōyáng Hú is situated here on Cháng Jiāng and on the southern bank of the river is **Shízhōng Shān** *(Stone Bell Mountain)*, noted for its numerous Tang-dynasty stone carvings.

Crossing into Ānhuī, you come to **Ānqìng**, on the northern bank, in the foothills of the **Dàbié Shān** range. Next comes the town of **Guìchí**, where you can get a bus to **Jiǔhuá Shān** *(Nine Brilliant Mountains)* and spectacular **Huáng Shān** *(Yellow Mountain)*.

The town of **Tónglíng** lies in a mountainous area in central **Ānhuī** on the southern bank. It's been a copper-mining centre for 2000 years and is still a source for the minting of coins. At the confluence of the Cháng and Qīngyì rivers is **Wúhú**, also a jumping-off point for Huáng Shān. Just before Ānhuī ends is the city of **Mǎ'ānshān**, the site of a large iron and steel complex.

In Jiāngsū the first large city you pass is **Nánjīng**, followed by **Zhènjiāng**, then the port of **Nántōng** at the confluence of the Yángtōng and Tōnglǔ canals. The ferry then proceeds along Cháng Jiāng and turns down **Huángpǔ Jiāng** to **Shànghǎi**, where Cháng Jiāng empties into the East China Sea.

Xīnjiāng 新疆

Capital: Ürümqi
Population: 19.1 million
Area: 1,600,000 sq km

In Xīnjiāng vast deserts and arid plains
stretch for thousands of kilometres before
ending abruptly at the foot of towering
mountain ranges. The ruins of Buddhist
cities pepper the deserts as reminders of the
past, while newer Islamic monuments point
the way to the future.

Xīnjiāng is a huge, geopolitically strategic
area, four times the size of Japan. It shares an
international border with eight other nations
and is the largest province in China, comprising 16% of the country's land surface.

The province was made an autonomous
region in 1955 and named after the majority Turkic-speaking Muslim Uyghurs at a
time when more than 90% of the population
was non-Chinese. The north has traditionally consisted of nomadic pastoralists, such
as the Kazakhs, while the Uyghurs are settled in the south in fertile oases scattered
along the ancient Silk Road. With the building of the railway from Lánzhōu to Ürümqi
and the development of industry in the region, the Han Chinese now form a majority
in the northern area, while the Uyghurs continue to predominate in the south.

For travellers, the region is one of the
most interesting in China, packed with history, archaeological remains, ethnic variety,
superb landscapes and a vibrant Central
Asian culture. Memories of cold Xīnjiāng
beer under the grape trellises of Turpan, of
wandering the bustling bazaars of Hotan or
Kashgar, and of the poplar-lined Uyghur
villages will remain long after the end of
most peoples' trips.

HISTORY

Han dynasty China had already pioneered its
new trade route (later named the Silk Road)
through this region by the 1st century BC.
The first Chinese conquest of Xīnjiāng, led
by the brilliant Chinese general Pan Zhao
(AD 32–102) was between AD 73 and 97. In
AD 138 the Chinese envoy Zhang Qian
passed through the region in his search for
potential allies against the Xiongnu tribes
who were ceaselessly harassing the Chinese

Highlights

- Heaven Pool, pretty alpine scenery
  that looks like a Swiss postcard

- Kashgar, the fabled oasis of the
  ancient Silk Road that still retains its
  exotic Eastern feel

- Travelling the Sino-Pakistani Karakoram Highway, one of the most
  beautiful road journeys in the world

- Turpan, a desert oasis, the lowest and
  hottest spot in China, graced with
  grape vines, mosques and abandoned
  ancient cities

- Hānàsī Hú, a beautiful lake surrounded by alpine wilderness and
  semi-nomadic Kazakhs

- The southern Silk Road, a necklace of
  old town markets, traditional artisans,
  and backstreet bazaars – not to
  mention a hard-core back door into
  Qīnghǎi

SILK ROAD

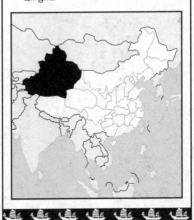

heartland. Despite the expenditure of vast resources in policing the 'Western Region', it
eventually succumbed to northern nomadic
warrior tribes, Mongols and later, Turks.

At the time that the Buddhist pilgrims Fa
Xian and Xuan Zang visited the region in
search of Buddhist scriptures, in AD 400 and
644 respectively, the region was a Buddhist
powerhouse. Ruined cities have revealed a
culture where red-haired Indo-European and

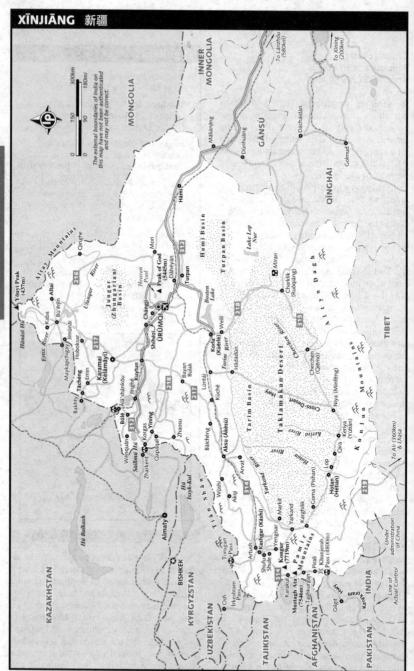

XĪNJIĀNG 新疆

The external boundaries of India on this map have not been authenticated and may not be correct.

Altaic peoples worshipped at Buddhist, Manichaeist or Nestorian Christian temples, expressing themselves in beautiful pieces of art that blended Kashmiri, Tibetan, Indian and even Greek styles.

Imperial power was not reasserted until the Tang dynasty in the 7th and 8th centuries and even this amounted to little more than an annual tribute of goods and envoys.

Tang control of Kashgaria came to an end about this time with the arrival of the Uyghur Turks, and the area was ruled by a succession of tribal kingdoms – Uyghur, Qarakhanid and Karakitay – for more than four centuries. It was during Qarakhanid rule in the 11th and 12th centuries that Islam took hold here. Qarakhanid tombs are still standing in Kashgar and nearby Artush.

Yīlí (Ili), Hotan and Kashgar fell to the Mongols in 1219, and Timur sacked Kashgar in the late 14th century. The area remained under the control of Timur's descendants or various Mongol tribes until the Manchu army marched into Kashgar in 1755.

The Manchus remained for a century, although resentment of their rule often boiled over in local revolts. In 1847 Hunza, then an independent Karakoram state, helped the Chinese quell a revolt in Yarkand. During the 1860s and 1870s a series of Muslim uprisings erupted across western China, and after Russian troops were withdrawn from a 10-year occupation of the Yīlí region in 1871, waves of Uyghurs, Chinese Muslims (Dungans) and Kazakhs fled into Kazakhstan and Kyrgyzstan.

In 1865 a Kokandi officer named Yaqub Beg seized Kashgaria, proclaimed an independent Turkestan and made diplomatic contacts with Britain and Russia. A few years later, however, a Manchu army returned, Beg committed suicide and Kashgaria was formally incorporated into China's newly created Xīnjiāng (New Dominions) province.

With the fall of the Qing in 1911, Xīnjiāng came under the rule of a succession of warlords, over whom the Kuomintang had very little control.

The only real attempt to establish an independent state was in the 1940s, when a Kazakh named Osman led a rebellion of Uyghurs, Kazakhs and Mongols. He took

SILK ROAD

The Beginning or the End?

Uyghurs have, with good reason, always viewed Han Chinese as invaders, and relations between the two nationalities have never been good. However, ties have become far more strained since the early 1950s, when Communist China began its policy of bolstering the Xīnjiāng population with Han settlers.

Although China has actually invested a fair amount of money in developing Xīnjiāng's economy and infrastructure, Uyghurs frequently argue that all the good jobs and business opportunities are dominated by Han Chinese. A look through Xīnjiāng's towns and cities shows little integration between the two nationalities, although there seems to be more Han-Uyghur interaction in the capital, Ürümqi. Even there, however, it's possible to detect the underlying tension.

This long simmering Uyghur resentment boiled over in February 1997 when Muslim separatists in the northern city of Yīníng started riots that led to a swift crackdown by Chinese security forces. At least nine people died and nearly 200 were injured, making the protest the most violent to date, according to Chinese media.

Some 30 Muslim residents were arrested for their roles in the riots: three were executed on the day of their trial, the rest were given life sentences. These arrests sparked several deadly responses. In late February separatists blew up three buses in Ürümqi, killing at least nine passengers and wounding many others.

The violence returned to Yīníng in April 1997, when a mob attacked prison vehicles transporting some of the convicted February rioters. Again, several people were killed or wounded. In 2001 Chinese secret police raided a number of Uyghur underground mosques in Korla; one prominent leader and a handful of others were tried and executed. Uyghurs in exile have vowed to continue the campaign of violent protest until Xīnjiāng gains its freedom from Běijīng. At the same time, Běijīng has clamped down heavily on separatist activities and is keeping a close watch on all of Xīnjiāng's Muslims. The question now is: were the February riots the start of a long march towards secession or the last gasp of a hopeless cause?

control of south-western Xīnjiāng and established an independent eastern Turkestan Republic in January 1945.

The Kuomintang convinced the Muslims to abolish their new republic in return for a pledge of real autonomy. This promise wasn't kept, but Chiang Kaishek's preoccupation with the civil war left him with little time to re-establish control over the region.

The Kuomintang eventually appointed a Muslim named Burhan as governor of the region in 1948, unaware that he was actually a Communist supporter.

A Muslim league opposed to Chinese rule was formed in Xīnjiāng, but in August 1949 a number of its most prominent leaders died in a mysterious plane crash on their way to Běijīng to hold talks with the new Communist leaders. Muslim opposition to Chinese rule collapsed, although the Kazakh Osman continued to fight until he was captured and executed by the Chinese Communists in early 1951.

Since 1949 Běijīng's main goal has been to keep a lid on minority separatism while flooding the region with Han settlers. Xīnjiāng's minorities, notably the Uyghurs, make little secret of their dislike of China's policies and have staged sporadic protests over the past decades, some of them violent.

ÜRÜMQI 乌鲁木齐
☎ 0991 • pop 1,100,600

The capital of Xīnjiāng, Ürümqi (Wūlǔmùqí) has little to distinguish itself other than the claim to being the farthest city in the world from the ocean (2250km).

The white-tile and concrete-block architecture has been imported lock, stock and barrel from eastern China, but Ürümqi essentially looks much different from the smokestack cities 2000km east. It's clean, noticeably efficient, and most folks are surprised at how easy it is to hang around here. An important crossroad, it is interesting for all the various nationalities you see on the streets: Uyghurs, Kazakhs, Pakistanis, Russians and Uzbeks.

Orientation
Most of the sights, tourist facilities and hotels are scattered across the city, although they're all easily reached on local buses.

The train and long-distance bus stations are in the south-western corner of the city.

The city centre revolves around Minzhu Lu, Zhongshan Lu and Jianshe Lu, where government offices, fancier hotels and department stores are located. In the north of town are Yǒuhǎo and Hóngshān, major intersections that are popular shopping areas; the latter is an important local transport hub.

Information
Consulates Kazakhstan has a consulate (Hāsàkèsītǎn Lǐngshìguǎn; ☎ 383 2324, 382 5564) just off Beijing Lu at 31 Kunming Lu. It issues a three-day transit visa to those who have an onward visa for a neighbouring country, not including China. The visa takes as little as three days (but a week isn't unheard of) to be issued and costs US$40. It is theoretically possible to obtain a three-day transit visa on arrival at Almaty airport, however Chinese customs won't let you on a plane without a Kazakhstan visa.

The visa section is open Monday to Thursday only, from 10.30am to 1.30pm. But get there much earlier to get your name on the list!

Ring ahead before you go to the consulate. A taxi there will cost about Y15.

Money The main Bank of China is at the corner of Jiefang Beilu and Minzhu Lu. Another branch is opposite the main post office at the Yǒuhǎo intersection. Both are open daily. Credit card cash advances are available here.

Post & Communications The main post office is in the north of the city at the Yǒuhǎo intersection. This is the only place that handles international parcels and is open daily from 10am to 8pm. There is also a post and telephone office on Zhongshan Lu, near the corner of Xinhua Nanlu.

The Galaxy 169 Internet Bar (Yínyǔ Diànnǎo Wǎngbā) is on Guangming Lu. The bar is on the 2nd floor and is open 24 hours a day. It charges a reasonable Y10 an hour for Internet access in a posh coffee shop, Y5 an hour in an adjacent room, usually filled with students.

Travel Agencies The Luyou Hotel is home to several tourist and travel agencies. On the ground floor is China International Travel Service (CITS; Zhōngguó Guójì Lǚxíngshè; ☎ 282 6719, fax 281 0689).

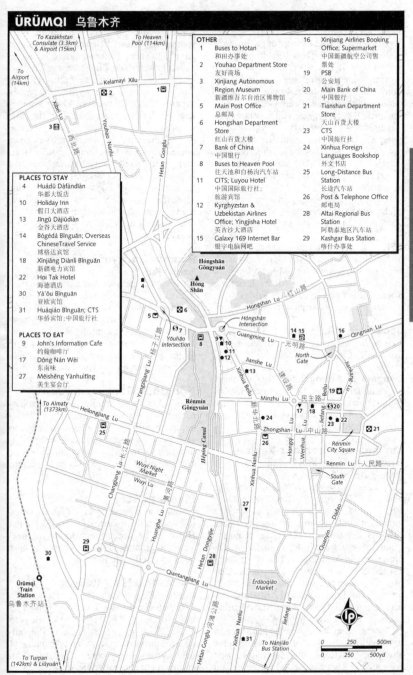

ÜRÜMQI 乌鲁木齐

OTHER

1 Buses to Hotan
   和田办事处
2 Youhao Department Store
   友好商场
3 Xinjiang Autonomous
   Region Museum
   新疆维吾尔自治区博物馆
5 Main Post Office
   总邮局
6 Hongshan Department
   Store
   红山百货大楼
7 Bank of China
   中国银行
8 Buses to Heaven Pool
   往天池和白杨沟汽车站
11 CITS; Luyou Hotel
   中国国际旅行社；
   旅游宾馆
12 Kyrghyzstan &
   Uzbekistan Airlines
   Office; Yingjisha Hotel
   英吉沙大酒店
15 Galaxy 169 Internet Bar
   银星电脑网吧

16 Xinjiang Airlines Booking
   Office; Supermarket
   中国新疆航空公司售
   票处
19 PSB
   公安局
20 Main Bank of China
   中国银行
21 Tianshan Department
   Store
   天山百货大楼
23 CTS
   中国旅行社
24 Xinhua Foreign
   Languages Bookshop
   外文书店
25 Long-Distance Bus
   Station
   长途汽车站
26 Post & Telephone Office
   邮电局
28 Altai Regional Bus
   Station
   阿勒泰地区汽车站
29 Kashgar Bus Station
   喀什办事处

PLACES TO STAY

4 Huádū Dàfàndiàn
   华都大饭店
10 Holiday Inn
   假日大酒店
13 Jīngǔ Dàjiǔdiàn
   金谷大酒店
14 Bógédá Bīnguǎn; Overseas
   ChineseTravel Service
   博格达宾馆
18 Xīnjiāng Diànlì Bīnguǎn
   新疆电力宾馆
22 Hoi Tak Hotel
   海德酒店
30 Yà'ōu Bīnguǎn
   亚欧宾馆
31 Huáqiáo Bīnguǎn; CTS
   华侨宾馆；中国旅行社

PLACES TO EAT

9 John's Information Cafe
   约翰咖啡厅
17 Dōng Nán Wèi
   东南味
27 Měishēng Yànhuìtīng
   美生宴会厅

A more useful place is the Overseas Chinese Travel Service (☎ 284 2624) on the 2nd floor of a building in the rear of the grounds of Bógédá Bīnguǎn. The staff is friendly and helpful here. Better, since they have lots of overseas Chinese from Singapore and Hong Kong, among other places, your chances of finding English speakers are pretty good.

China Travel Service (CTS; Zhōngguó Lǚxíngshè; ☎ 652 1440) is in the grounds of Huáqiáo Bīnguǎn but a smaller branch is just off Jiefang Beilu on a small street near the Hoi Tak Hotel. The travel agency of Yà'ōu Bīnguǎn has also been recommended by readers.

If you encounter any problems with the quality of tourism services in Xīnjiāng, there is a tourist complaint hotline (☎ 283 1902).

PSB The foreign affairs office of the Public Security Bureau (PSB; Gōngānjú) is on Jiankang Lu, just north of Minzhu Lu: look out for the sign that reads 'Aliens Reception Room'. It is open Monday to Friday from 9.30am to 2pm and from 4pm to 8pm.

Bookshops The Xinhua Foreign Languages Bookshop is along Xinhua Beilu, just south of Minzhu Lu.

Dangers & Annoyances Lots of backpack slashers lurk in the region of Bógédá Bīnguǎn near the North Gate (Běi Mén); locking yours even while you're wearing it wouldn't be too paranoid.

Xinjiang Autonomous Region Museum 新疆自治区博物馆
Xīnjiāng Zìzhìqū Bówùguǎn

This museum (☎ 453 6436, 132 Xibei Lu; admission Y25; open 9.30am-7.30pm Mon-Fri, 10am-4.30pm Sat & Sun) is worth a look as it contains some interesting visual exhibits relating to Xīnjiāng minority groups. There are at least 13 different ethnic groups in Xīnjiāng, and facets of daily existence of each group are on special display. There is a fascinating collection of minority clothing, musical instruments, textiles, jewellery, cooking and farming utensils, and tools for hunting.

Another wing of the museum has a section devoted to the history of early settlements along the Silk Road, which includes a fine collection of ceramics, tools, tapestries and bronze figures. Prime exhibits are the preserved bodies of nearly a dozen men, women and babies discovered in tombs in Xīnjiāng. These mummies are of note because they are Indo-European, not Chinese. One author has written an entire book on this interesting fact, even positing an intriguing Celtic connection! There are very few English explanations, but the museum's exhibits are a rich visual experience.

The museum is a distinctive green domed Soviet-style building, about 20 minutes' walk from Hóngshān intersection. From Hóngshān intersection take bus No 7 for four stops and ask to get off at the museum (bówùguǎn). Note that this place was being overhauled in a major fashion at the time of writing so lots of exhibits were packed away.

Rénmín Gōngyuán 人民公园
People's Park

This scenic, tree-shaded park (admission Y5; open 7.30am-10pm daily) is about 1km in length and can be entered from either the northern or southern gates. The best time to visit is early in the morning when many locals exercise here. There are plenty of birds in the park, a few pavilions and a lake where you can hire rowing boats.

Hóngshān Gōngyuán 洪山公园

This is Xīnjiāng's premier amusement park (admission Y3; open dawn-dusk daily), complete with a Ferris wheel, bumper cars and those swinging gondolas designed to bring up your lunch. Other attractions include an eight-storey pagoda and sweeping views of the city.

Places to Stay

Ürümqi has a good variety of hotels, offering, generally, reasonably priced rooms. However, be warned that during the peak summer months (June to October) most hotel rooms double in price.

Places to Stay – Budget

Bógédá Bīnguǎn (☎ 282 3910, fax 281 5769, 10 Guangming Lu) Dorm beds Y25, twins/triples Y144/154 low season, Y288/298 high season. This is the only cheap option downtown and virtually all backpackers head here. The dorms are cramped but generally OK; the doubles are somewhat overpriced in summer but still clean. Be nice to these people: this is the only game around and they do a reasonably efficient job given the traveller traffic. The travel agency here comes recommended.

Near the train station a number of cheap, formerly Chinese-only hotels have started at least considering foreigners. It's worth walking around and inquiring.

Yà'ōu Bīnguǎn (☎ 585 6699, fax 585 7619, Huoche Zhan) Dorm beds from Y20, beds in triples/quads with bath Y50/40, singles/twins Y130/158. This hotel is the best option. Its singles and twins are a little overpriced, but you should be able to bargain them down; you may or may not be let into the eight-person dorms. The other advantage to this hotel is that train tickets can be purchased for guests, free of service charge.

Huáqiáo Bīnguǎn (*Overseas Chinese Hotel;* ☎ 286 0793, fax 286 2279, 51 Xinhua Nanlu) Older rooms Y100, newer rooms Y158-300. For relatively cheap twins, this hotel has compact older rooms in a Russian-style building. Other twins are in a newer wing.

Places to Stay – Mid-Range

Xīnjiāng Diànlì Bīnguǎn (*Xinjiang Electricity Hotel;* ☎ 282 2911, fax 282 6031, 57 Minzhu Lu) Twins Y388-660. This is a pretty good and comfortable choice. The staff here collect and deliver guests to the airport and train station for free. Rates include breakfast.

Jīngǔ Dàjiǔdiàn (*Golden Valley Hotel;* ☎ 282 6788, fax 283 3613, 84 Xinhua Beilu) Singles or twins Y280-450. At the time of writing, this place had been renovated and was already bursting with tour groups – a good sign. Standard rooms are in solid shape here and service was fairly good considering how busy the place is. Rates include breakfast.

Huádū Dàfàndiàn (☎ 452 9922, fax 452 2708, 23 Youhao Nanlu) Twins Y418-665. Another renovation job took place at this huge hotel. Service is very attentive. Try for one of their larger twin rooms with a nice view of Hóngshān Gōngyuán.

Places to Stay – Top End

Hoi Tak Hotel (*Hǎidé Jiǔdiàn,* ☎ 232 2828, e hthxjbc@mail.wl.xj.cninfo.net, 1

Which Time Is It?

Xīnjiāng is several time zones removed from Běijīng, which prefers to ignore the fact. While all of China officially runs on Běijīng time (*shíjiān*), most of Xīnjiāng runs on an unofficial Xīnjiāng time, two hours behind Běijīng time. Thus 9am Běijīng time is 7am Xīnjiāng time. Almost all government-run services such as the bank, post office, bus station and Xinjiang Airlines run on Běijīng time. To cater for the time difference, government offices (including the post office and CITS) generally operate from 10am to 1.30pm and from 4pm to 8pm. Unless otherwise stated, we use Běijīng time in this book. To be sure, though, if you arrange a time with someone make sure you know which, as well as what, time.

Dongfeng Lu) Rooms Y1200-4180 plus 15% service charge & 3% tax. The Hoi Tak has five-star services and facilities. Even if you can't afford to stay here, it has great coffee and an excellent breakfast/lunch/dinner buffet. By the way, the name is Cantonese because its ownership group is from Hong Kong.

Holiday Inn (*Jiàrì Dàjiǔdiàn,* ☎ 281 8788, e holiday@mail.wl.xj.cn, Xinhua Beilu) Standard rooms Y710-935, singles Y620, plus 15% service charge. This is a popular choice with Western tour groups. There is a cake shop on the 1st floor that sells a good range of pastries and after 8pm everything is discounted by 25%. During the summer months it also offers a number of deals on the buffets and barbecues.

Places to Eat

Ürümqi is not a bad spot to try Uyghur foods, such as *náng* (shish kebab with flatbread). Another local speciality is *lāmiàn* (noodles with spicy vegetables, beef or lamb). The whole province eats *dàpánjī*, where a pressure-cooked chicken is cut up and fried in a spicy sauce with potatoes and vegies; the area around the Wuyi night market has restaurants with this signature dish. There is a row of restaurants on Jianshe Lu where you can sample these dishes as well as Han Chinese food.

Měishēng Yànhuìlíng (☎ 232 1118, 38 Xinhua Nanlu) Dishes from Y20. This is a large Uyghur restaurant that is popular with

Uyghur Food

Uyghur cuisine includes all the trusty Central Asian standbys such as kebabs, pilau *(plov)* and dumplings *(chuchura)*, but has benefited from Chinese influence to make it the most enjoyable region of Central Asia in which to eat.

Uyghurs boast endless varieties of laghman *(lāmiàn* in Chinese), though the usual topping is some combination of mutton, peppers, tomatoes, eggplant, green beans and garlic. *Suoman* are noodle squares fried with tomatoes, peppers, garlic and meat. *Suoman goshsiz* are the vegetarian variety. Suoman can be quite spicy so ask for *lazasiz* (without peppers) if you prefer a milder version.

Kebabs are another staple and are generally of a much better standard than the ropey shashlick of the Central Asian republics. *Jiger* (liver) kebabs are the low-fat variety. *Tonor kebabs* are larger and baked in an oven *tonor* – tandoori style.

Breads are a particular speciality, especially when straight out of the oven and sprinkled with poppy seeds, sesame seeds or fennel. They make a great plate for a round of kebabs. Uyghur bakers also make wonderful bagels *(girde nan)*.

Other snacks include *serik ash* (yellow meatless noodles), *nokot* (chickpeas with carrot), *pintang* (meat and vegetable soup) and *gangpen* (rice with fried vegetables and meat). Most travellers understandably steer clear of *opke*, a broth of bobbing goat's heads and coiled, stuffed intestines.

Samsas (baked envelopes of meat) are available everywhere but the meat-to-fat ratio varies wildly. Hotan and Kashgar offer huge meat pies called *daman* or *gosh girde*. You can even get *balyk* (fried fish).

For dessert you can try *maroji* (vanilla ice cream churned in iced wooden barrels), *matang* (walnut fruit loaf), *kharsen meghriz* (fried dough balls filled with sugar, raisins and walnuts) or *dogh* (sometimes known as *durap*), a delicious, though potentially deadly, mix of shaved ice, syrup, yoghurt and iced water. *Tangzaza* are triangles of glutinous rice wrapped in bamboo leaves covered with syrup.

Xīnjiāng is justly famous for its fruit, whether it be *uruk* (apricots), *uzum* (grapes), *tawuz* (watermelon), *khoghun* (sweet melon) or *yimish* (raisins). The best grapes come from Turpan; the sweetest melons from Hami.

 Meals are washed down with *kok chai* (green tea), often laced with nutmeg, or beer. Uyghur restaurants usually provide a miniature rubbish bin on the table in which to dispose of the waste tea after rinsing out the bowl.

---

the locals. Both Uyghur and Chinese food is on offer and there are traditional dancing and singing performances most nights, usually starting after 10pm. Most of the dishes are very generous, so you may prefer asking for an entree serving *(bàn pán)*.

Honqi Lu, in the city centre, is another good street to go restaurant hunting. It has lots of noodle and dumpling shops and other small eateries.

Dōng Nán Wèi *(Honqi Lu)* Dishes from Y5. This is one place that locals speak highly of. It's little more than a hole in the wall, but has a good reputation for its *huángyú* (fish) and *páigǔ* (spare rib) dishes. You'll happily find an English menu.

John's Information Cafe *(Hóngshān intersection)* Dishes from Y4. This cafe is inside the small park north of the Holiday Inn. It has Chinese food as well as some reasonably priced Western fare, all in an al fresco setting.

If you're craving Western food, then head for either the Hoi Tak Hotel or the Holiday Inn. The Holiday Inn's all-you-can-eat breakfast and lunch buffets may do the trick, but at more than Y100 per person you'd want to be hungry.

At night the sidewalk areas along Minzhu Lu and around the Youhao, North Gate and Hóngshān intersections become bustling night markets with fresh handmade noodle dishes, shish kebab skewers and a whole range of point-and-choose fried dishes. They're definitely worth a look around. The most thriving by far is the **Wuyi night market** *(Wuyi Lu);* bus No 902 runs nearby between the train station and Bógédá Bīnguǎn (get off at Huanghe Lu).

During July and August markets are packed with delicious fruit, both fresh and dried. The best market is the **Èrdàoqiáo Market** *(Èrdàoqiáo Shìchǎng)*, in the southern end of the city, not too far from the

Turpan bus station. There's a supermarket in the same building as the Xinjiang Airlines booking office; it has freshly baked goods and a sort of fast-food Chinese buffet.

Getting There & Away

Air Ürümqi is well served by domestic services and even has a few international flights, especially to neighbouring Central Asian countries. International departures include flights to Almaty (Kazakhstan), Bishkek (Kyrgyzstan), Islamabad (Pakistan), Novosibirsk (Russia) and Moscow. It's not uncommon for these flights to be suspended, especially during the winter months.

There are several international airline offices in town. Siberia Airlines (☎ 286 2326) has an office in Huáqiáo Bīnguǎn; Kazakhstan Airlines (☎ 382 5564) has an office next to the Kazakhstan consulate; Kyrghyzstan Airlines and Uzbekistan Airways (☎ 231 6333) share an office on the 1st floor of the Yingjisha Hotel.

Domestic flights connect Ürümqi with Běijīng (Y2380), Chéngdū (Y1670), Chóngqìng (Y1610), Lánzhōu (Y1210), Guǎngzhōu (Y2670), Hong Kong, Shànghǎi (Y2540), Xī'ān (Y1350) and most other major cities.

Within Xīnjiāng there are regular flights from Ürümqi to Aksu (Ākèsū), Hotan (Hétián), Karamai (Kèlāmǎyī), Kashgar (Kāshí), Korla (Kùěrlè), Tǎchéng and Yīníng. Information on some of these flights can be found in the Getting There & Away sections of the relevant destinations.

The Xinjiang Airlines booking office (☎ 264 1826) is at 2 Xinmin Lu, near the North Gate on the 1st floor of the China Construction Bank building.

It's also possible to purchase tickets through most hotels.

Bus The long-distance bus station is on Heilongjiang Lu. There are buses going to most cities in Xīnjiāng, the notable exception being Turpan and southern Xīnjiāng, and many destinations have their own bus station scattered across town.

Large public buses and more comfortable minibuses to Turpan (and southern and western Xīnjiāng) run from the Nánjiāo bus station (Nánjiāo kèyùnzhàn), in the southern part of the city. In fact, this newer station is probably a better place to start for most destinations now. The ride shouldn't cost more than Y10 to Y15 from anywhere within the city; bus No 1 has its terminus across the street, from where it runs to Bógédá Bīnguǎn.

If you're heading to Kashgar, you can get a sleeper bus from either the main station but start with the Nánjiāo station, which has more departures. There is, or was, a Kashgar bus station, just east of the train station but a massive downtown reconstruction plan had slowed departures to a trickle at last check.

Departure times and fares are listed in the Getting There & Away sections for the relevant destinations.

An interesting option is the Almaty (Ālāmùtú) bus service. The 1052km trip takes 24 hours with three stops for meals, and costs Y450.

At the time of writing buses to Almaty were leaving the long-distance bus station once daily (except Saturday) at 6pm; check at window No 8 for the latest on this service – it changes *often*. Alternately, take a sleeper bus to Yīníng and be prepared to line up. Crossing the border shouldn't really be a problem, but you should prepare yourself for possible bureaucratic delays.

Train To Lánzhōu there are many departures; the one shown in the following table is the best choice. The schedule of best-option daily departures from Ürümqi is as follows:

destination	train	departs	duration (hours)
Běijīng	T70	12.35pm	49
Chéngdū	1014	2.29pm	52
Lánzhōu	508	11.28pm	30½
Shànghǎi	T54	10.09am	51
Xī'ān	1044	5.14pm	44
Dūnhuáng	K860	11.58pm	14
Kashgar	K886	12.54pm	23
	5806	5.19pm	30

Getting tickets can still be a hassle; hard sleepers on special express trains to places like Běijīng and Shànghǎi sell out quickly, so it's good to book as far in advance as possible. The good news is that, though the lines are long, even one day ahead is often good enough (even same day for some places).

SILK ROAD

The new rail link between Ūrümqi and Kashgar via Kùchē began in 1999. The journey takes 23 to 30 hours and takes you through an interesting mix of desert and mountain scenery; sandstorms closing down the line are not uncommon.

There are trains running Monday and Saturday from Ūrümqi to Almaty, Kazakhstan. The journey takes a very slow 35 hours, eight of which is spent at both the Chinese and Kazakh customs, and the fare is Y409. At the Ūrümqi train station there's a special ticket window for these trains, inside the large waiting room in the main building. It's only open Monday, Thursday, Friday and Saturday, from 10am to 1pm and 3pm to 7pm. You will, of course, need a visa for Kazakhstan.

Getting Around
To/From the Airport Minibuses (Y8) head out to the airport half-hourly from 6am, departing from the Xinjiang Airlines office and passing through the Hóngshān intersection. The same minibuses also greet all incoming flights.

The airport is 16km from the Hóngshān intersection. A taxi should cost between Y40 and Y50. If you're in no hurry, bus No 51 runs between Hóngshān intersection and the airport gate, but takes about an hour.

Bus Some of the more useful bus routes include No 7, which runs up Xinhua Lu through the Hóngshān intersection to the Yǒuhǎo intersection, linking the city centre with the main post office; and No 2, which runs from the train station, past the main post office and way up along Beijing Lu, past the Kazakhstan consulate. No 1 goes from the Nánjiāobus station past Bógédá Bīnguǎn; from the train station take bus No 902 to get to Bógédá Bīnguǎn.

AROUND ŪRÜMQI
Heaven Pool 天池
Tiān Chí
Halfway up a mountain in the middle of a desert is Heaven Pool (admission Y60), a small, deep-blue lake surrounded by hills covered with fir trees and grazed by horses. Scattered around are the *yurts* (circular tents) of the Kazak people who inhabit the mountains; in the distance are the snow-covered peaks of **Tiān Shān** (*Heavenly*

Mountains), and you can climb the hills right up to the snow line. It's a heavily touristed spot, especially in the high season, but is beautiful nonetheless and once you climb into the hills, you'll be alone.

The lake is 115km east of Ūrümqi at an elevation of 1980m. Nearby is the 5445m **Peak of God** (*Bógédá Fēng*), which can be climbed by well-equipped mountaineers with permits (see CITS for information). The lake freezes over in Xīnjiāng's bitter winter and the roads up here are open only in the summer months.

The best way to spend your time is to hike around the lake and even up into the hills. The surrounding countryside is quite beautiful. Follow the track skirting the lake for about 4km to the far end where there is a small nursery and PSB office. From here you can just choose your valley. From personal experience, avoid trying a circuit of the lake as a day trip.

During the summer, Kazakhs set up yurts in this area for tourist accommodation (Y40 per person with three meals). This is not a bad option; during the day the area can get quite cramped with day-trippers, but you'll pretty much have the place to yourself after 4pm and in the morning. *Rashit's Yurt* is about half-way around the lake and has an English-speaking owner; this has been the most popular backpacker hang-out for a while. Some people have also brought their own tents and gear and camped here.

It is possible to hire horses for treks around the lake, a trip to the snow line costs about Y80. The return trek takes between eight and 10 hours, depending on where the snowline is.

Buses to Heaven Pool leave Ūrümqi from 9am to 9.30am from the north gate of Rénmín Gōngyuán and return between 5pm and 6pm. The return fare is between Y35 and Y50, depending on the size and quality of the bus. The trip takes about 2½ hours.

DÀHÉYÁN 大河沿
The jumping-off point for Turpan is a place on the train line signposted 'Turpan Zhan' (Tǔlǔfān Zhàn). In fact, you are actually in Dàhéyán, and the Turpan oasis is a 58km drive south-east across the desert. Dàhéyán is not really a place where you'll want to hang around.

The bus station is a five-minute walk from the train station. Walk up the road leading from the train station and turn right at the first main intersection; the bus station is a few minutes' walk ahead on the left-hand side of the road.

Minibuses run from here to Turpan (Y5, 1½ hours) about once every 30 minutes throughout the day starting at 6.30am.

Although Dàhéyán train station is rarely crowded, it can be difficult to get hard-sleeper tickets, as most of these will have already been sold from Ürümqi. The best option is to board the train and try your luck with an upgrade or find out when tickets for your train go on sale, then show up and fight for a ticket.

Most travellers are interested in trains heading east or west, since people going northwards from Turpan usually opt for the bus to Ürümqi, which is much faster than trekking up here to catch a train. There are daily trains to Běijīng, Chéngdū, Lánzhōu (30 hours), Xī'ān and Kashgar (29 hours). Trains also go to Liǔyuán (10 hours) and Jiāyùguān (16 hours).

TURPAN 吐鲁番
☎ 0995

East of Ürümqi Tiān Shān split into a southern and a northern range, and between the two lie the Hami and Turpan basins. Both basins are below sea level and receive practically no rain so summers are searingly hot.

Part of the Turpan Basin is 154m below sea level – it's the lowest spot in China and the second lowest depression in the world (after the Dead Sea).

Turpan (Tǔlǔfān) holds a special place in Uyghur history, since nearby Gāochāng was once the capital of the Uyghurs. It was an important staging post on the Silk Road and was a centre of Buddhism before being converted to Islam in the 8th century. During the Chinese occupation it served as a garrison town.

Turpan is also the hottest spot in China – the highest recorded temperature here was 49.6°C (121.3°F). Fortunately, the humidity is low – so low that your laundry is practically dry by the time you hang it out! To compensate, Turpan is famous for its grapes and is an important producer of sultanas and wine.

TURPAN 吐鲁番

PLACES TO STAY
3　Oasis Hotel;
　　CITS
　　绿洲宾馆；
　　中国国际旅行社
6　Jiāotōng
　　Bīnguǎn
　　交通宾馆
8　Liángmào
　　Bīnguǎn
　　粮贸宾馆

10　Tǔlǔfān
　　　Bīnguǎn
　　　吐鲁番宾馆

OTHER
1　Bank of
　　China
　　中国银行
2　Turpan
　　Museum
　　吐鲁番博物馆

4　Main Post
　　Office
　　邮局
5　Long-Distance
　　Bus Station
　　长途汽车站
7　Bank of China
　　中国银行
9　John's Infor-
　　mation Cafe
　　约翰中西餐厅

Turpan county is inhabited by about 240,000 people – just over half are Uyghurs and the rest mostly Han. The centre of the county is the Turpan oasis, a small city set in a vast tract of grain fields and grape vines. Despite the concrete-block architecture of the city centre, it's a pleasant, relaxing place. Some of the smaller streets have pavements covered with grapevine trellises, which are a godsend in the fierce heat of summer.

Moving farther out of town, the narrow streets are lined with mud-brick walls enclosing thatch-plaster houses. Open channels with flowing water run down the sides of the streets; the inhabitants draw water from these and use them to wash their clothes, dishes and themselves.

The living is relatively cheap, the food is good, the people friendly, and there are numerous interesting sights in Turpan to keep you occupied.

Orientation
The centre of Turpan is called the Old City (Lǎo Chéng) and the western part is called New City (Xīn Chéng). The Old City is where you'll find the tourist hotels, shops,

SILK ROAD

market, long-distance bus station and restaurants – all within easy walking distance. Most of the sights are scattered on the outskirts of the oasis or in the surrounding desert.

Information

The Bank of China has two branches that can change cash and travellers cheques. Both are open daily.

The main post office is west of the bus station and there is also a small post office inside the Oasis Hotel that handles parcels.

CITS (☎ 852 1352) has a branch on the grounds of the Oasis Hotel and can help book train and plane tickets, as well as arrange tours of local sights.

The PSB is on Gaochang Lu, in the north of downtown; they'd really rather you went to the capital for anything other than the most mundane requests.

Bazaar 市贸易市场
Shì Màoyì Shìchǎng

While this market is fun to poke around, it's nothing like its more exotic counterpart in Kashgar. At the front you'll find a few stalls selling brightly decorated knives, Muslim clothing and some other interesting items, but as you move towards the back it's mainly household goods and synthetic fabrics.

Qīngzhēn Sì 清真寺
City Mosque

There are several mosques in town. Qīngzhēn Sì, the most active of them, is on the western outskirts about 3km from the town centre. Take care not to disturb the worshippers. You can get here by bicycle.

Émǐn Tǎ & Sūgōng Tǎ 额敏塔
Émǐn Minaret & Sūgōng Mosque

This tower and adjoining mosque (admission Y30; open dawn-dusk), is just 3km from Turpan on the eastern edge of town. It's designed in a simple Afghani style and was built in 1777 by the local ruler, Emin Hoja.

The minaret is circular, 44m high and tapers towards the top. The temple is bare inside, but services are held every Friday and on holidays. The surrounding scenery is nice, and from the roof of the mosque you can get a good view of the Turpan oasis. You can't climb the minaret: it was closed off to tourists in 1989 to help preserve the structure.

You can walk or bicycle here.

Places to Stay

All hotels in Turpan increase their already inflated prices during the hot summer months. During this period the first thing you will probably be looking for, other than a pool, is air-con in working order.

Jiāotōng Bīnguǎn (☎ 853 1320, 125 Laocheng Lu) Dorm beds with fan Y15-24, with air-con Y22-30, twins with bath & air-con Y60-110. This hotel is pretty noisy, but is definitely the cheapest spot in town. Some rooms are actually pretty nice, so look at a few. Extensive renovations were planned so things may have changed.

Oasis Hotel (Lǚzhōu Bīnguǎn; ☎ 852 2491, e stos-tl@mail.xj.cninfo.net, w www .the-silk-road.com, 41 Qingnian Beilu) Twins Y280-680. Sadly, the dorms here are being phased out. Twins, which include an Uyghur-style room, get mixed reviews but some are quite cosy.

Tǔlǔfān Bīnguǎn (☎ 852 2301, e lfhan-tl @mailxj.cninfo.net, 2 Qingnian Lu) Dorm beds with fan or air-con Y22-27, triples/twins Y220/350. Most backpackers wind up here now. This hotel has a nice vine-trellised courtyard, a beer garden, quiet rooms and even a swimming pool. The twins here are over-priced (although CITS will book you into these for Y200).

Liángmào Bīnguǎn (Grain Trade Hotel; ☎ 852 4301, Munaer Lu) Twins/quads Y140/160. This is a friendly and clean place with the smell of industrial cleaners permeating. It should be easy to bargain them down here.

Places to Eat

There is a string of small restaurants along Laocheng Lu, and between Gaochang Lu and Qingnian Lu. Quite a few have English menus, and the food is generally good and reasonably priced. Most of the places serve Sìchuān and other Han-style dishes, but you can also get Uyghur food on request. Most locals partake of the lively night market action along many streets surrounding the public square; definitely the most fun way to eat.

John's Information Cafe Dishes from Y4. This is the only place in town that does good Western food, but there are Chinese meals available too. The menu is in English, prices are reasonable and you can even get cold drinks with ice (much appreciated in Turpan's heat!).

Entertainment

A traditional Uyghur music, song and dance show is staged at Tǔlǔfān Bīnguǎn in the courtyard under the trellises, almost nightly in the high season (tickets Y20). In the low season, performances take place on the 2nd floor of the hotel restaurant building. It's possible to order a decent meal here prior to the performance.

During the summer the shows are held almost every night from around 10pm. They're fun nights that usually end up with the front row of the audience being dragged out to dance with the performers.

Getting There & Away

The bus station is near the bazaar. Buses to Ürümqi (Y24, 2½ to three hours) via the new freeway leave between 7am and 7pm.

The nearest train station is at Dàhéyán, 58km north of Turpan (see the Dàhéyán section for information). Minibuses to Dàhéyán (Y6, 1½ hours) run approximately every 30 minutes between 7am and 6pm. If you don't want to shell out extra money for a ticket commission or fight the crowds here, consider sightseeing in Ürümqi first, where it's easy to buy tickets for westward destinations, even though this means doubling back.

Getting Around

Public transport around Turpan is by minibus, pedicab, bicycle or donkey cart. Bicycles are most convenient for the town itself. John's Information Cafe and Tǔlǔfān Bīnguǎn also have bicycle rental. Pedicab drivers usually hang around the hotel gates – negotiate the fare in advance. Donkey carts can be found around the market, but this mode of transport is gradually fading.

AROUND TURPAN

There are many sights in the countryside around Turpan, including the **Bezeklik Thousand Buddha Caves** (*Bózīkèlǐkè Qiānfó Dòng; admission Y20; open dawn-dusk daily*). However, these are in dreadful condition having been devastated by Muslims or robbed by all and sundry.

It requires at least a day to see everything of importance. The only way to see the sights is to join a tour or hire a minibus for a full day (about 10 hours). You won't have to look for them – the drivers will come looking for you. They will find other travellers to share the expense. Figure on paying between Y40 and Y60 (depending on your bargaining skills) each. Both the tours organised by the Oasis Hotel and Tǔlǔfān Bīnguǎn include an English guide and are cheap, reliable and recommended by readers. CITS will give you a vehicle for the day for Y200, regardless of how many people you have.

Make sure it's clearly understood which places you want to see. This is key because every site charges an arm and a leg to get in and it *adds up*. Few drivers speak English, but some speak fluent Japanese.

Don't underestimate the weather. The desert sun is hot – damn hot. Essential survival gear includes a water bottle, sunglasses and a straw hat. Some sunscreen and chapstick for your lips will prove useful.

Astana Graves 阿斯塔那古墓区

Āsītǎnà Gǔmùqū

These graves (*admission Y20; open dawn-dusk daily*), where the dead of Gāochāng are buried, lie north-west of the ancient city. Only three of the tombs are open to tourists, and each of these is approached by a short flight of steps that lead down to the burial chamber about 6m below ground level.

One tomb contains portraits of the deceased painted on the walls, while another

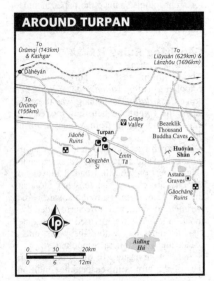

AROUND TURPAN

To Ürümqi (143km) & Kashgar

To Liǔyuán (629km) & Lánzhōu (1696km)

Dàhéyán

To Ürümqi (155km)

Grape Valley

Jiāohé Ruins

Turpan

Bezeklik Thousand Buddha Caves

Huǒyàn Shān

Qīngzhēn Sì

Émǐn Tǎ

Astana Graves

Gāochāng Ruins

Àidīng Hú

0   10   20km
0   6   12mi

SILK ROAD

Foreign Devils on the Silk Road

Adventurers on the road to Xīnjiāng might like to reflect on an earlier group of European adventurers who descended on Chinese Turkestan, as Xīnjiāng was then known, and carted off early Buddhist art treasures by the ton at the turn of the century.

The British first began to take an interest in the Central Asian region from their imperial base in India. They heard from oasis dwellers in the Taklamakan Desert of legendary ancient cities buried beneath the sands of the desert. In 1864 William Johnson was the first British official to sneak into the region, visiting one of these fabled lost cities in its tomb of sand close to Hotan. He was soon followed by Sir Douglas Forsyth, who made a report on his exploits: *On the Buried Cities in the Shifting Sands of the Great Desert of Gobi*. Not long afterwards, the race to unearth the treasures beneath the desert's 'shifting sands' was on.

By 1914, expeditions by Swedes, Hungarians, Germans, Russians, Japanese and French had all taken their share of the region's archaeological treasures. While these explorers were feted and lionised by adoring public at home, the Chinese today commonly see them as robbers who stripped the region of its past. Defenders point to the wide-scale destruction that took place during the Cultural Revolution and to the defacing of Buddhist artworks by Muslims who stumbled across them. Whatever the case, today most of Central Asia's finest archaeological finds are scattered across the museums of Europe.

has paintings of birds. The third tomb holds two well-preserved corpses like those in the museums at Ürümqi and Hángzhōu (one mummy from the original trio seems to have been removed to Turpan's museum).

Some of the artefacts date back as far as the Jin dynasty, from the 3rd to 5th centuries AD. The finds include silks, brocades, embroideries and many funerary objects, such as shoes, hats and sashes made of recycled paper. The last turned out to be quite special for archaeologists, since the paper included deeds, records of slave purchases, orders for silk and other everyday transactions.

Gāochāng Ruins 高昌故城
Gāochāng Gùchéng

About 46km east of Turpan are the Gāochāng ruins (*admission Y20; open dawn-dusk daily*). Gāochāng was the capital of the Uyghurs when they moved into the Xīnjiāng region from Mongolia in the 9th century.

The town was founded in the 7th century during the Tang dynasty and became a major staging post on the Silk Road. The walls of the city are clearly visible. They stood as thick as 12m, formed a rough square with a perimeter of 6km, and were surrounded by a moat. Gāochāng was divided into an outer city, an inner city within the walls, and a palace and government compound.

A large monastery in the south-western part of the city is in reasonable condition,

with some of its rooms, corridors and doorways still preserved.

Note that there's a good deal of walking here in the heat, so those less hale should consider a donkey-cart ride.

Huǒyàn Shān 火焰山
Flaming Mountains

North of Gāochāng lie aptly named Huǒyàn Shān – the mountains look like they're on fire in the midday sun. Purplish-brown in colour, they are 100km long and 10km wide. The minibus tours don't usually include a stop here, but they drive through on the way to Bezeklik Thousand Buddha Caves.

Huǒyàn Shān were made famous in Chinese literature by the classic novel *Journey to the West*. The story is about the monk Xuan Zang and his followers who travelled west in search of the Buddhist sutra. The mountains were a formidable barrier that they had to cross.

Grape Valley 葡萄沟
Pútao Gōu

This small paradise (*admission Y20*), a thick maze of vines and grape trellises, is surrounded by stark desert. Most of the minibus tours stop here for lunch (around Y15); the food isn't bad, and there are plenty of grapes in season (late August to early September is best).

There is a winery (*guójiǔchǎng*) near the valley and lots of well-ventilated brick buildings for drying grapes – wine and raisins are major exports of Turpan. CITS runs an annual 'grape festival' in August, featuring dancing, singing, wine-tasting and, of course, a lot of grape eating.

Tempting as it might be, don't pick the grapes here or anywhere else in Turpan. There is a Y15 fine if you do. Considerable effort goes into raising these grapes and the farmers don't appreciate tourists eating their profits.

Jiāohé Ruins 交河故城
Jiāohé Gùchéng

During the Han dynasty, Jiāohé (admission Y30; open dawn-dusk daily) was established by the Chinese as a garrison town to defend the borderlands. The city was decimated by Genghis Khan and there's little left to see.

The buildings are rather more obvious than the ruins of Gāochāng though, and you can walk through the old streets and along the roads. A main road cuts through the city, and at the end is a large monastery with figures of Buddha still visible.

The ruins are around 7km to 8km west of Turpan and stand on an island bound by two small rivers – thus the name Jiāohé, which means 'confluence of two rivers'. During the cooler months you can cycle out here without any problem.

Àidīng Hú 艾丁湖
Aydingkol Lake

At the very bottom of the Turpan depression is Àidīng Hú, 154m below sea level. The 'lake' usually has little water – it's a huge, muddy, evaporating pond with a surface of crystallised salt, but technically it's the second lowest lake in the world, surpassed only by the Dead Sea in Israel and Jordan.

Most tours don't stop here. If you want to see Àidīng Hú, tell your driver and expect to pay extra for the additional distance. And be forewarned that it's a pretty rough ride.

KÙCHĒ 库车
pop 63,500

The oasis town of Kùchē (Kuqa) was another key stop on the ancient Silk Road. Scattered around the area are eight **Thousand Buddha Caves** (*Qiānfó Dòng*), which rival those of Dūnhuáng, Dàtóng and Luòyáng. There are also at least four ancient ruined cities in the area.

Karez

The *karez* is a peculiarly Central Asian means of irrigation that can be found in Xīnjiāng, Afghanistan and Iran. Like many dry, arid countries Xīnjiāng has great underground reservoirs of water, which can transform otherwise barren stretches of land – if you can get the water up. This subterranean water is often so far underground that drilling or digging for it, with primitive equipment, is virtually impossible.

Long ago the Uyghurs devised a better way. They dig a karez, known as the 'head well', on higher ground, where snowmelt from the mountains collects (in Turpan's case the Bogda Mountains). A long underground tunnel is then dug to conduct this water down to the village farmland. A whole series of vertical wells, looking from above like giant anthills, are dug every 20m along the path of this tunnel to aid construction and provide access. The wells are fed entirely by gravity, thus eliminating the need for pumps. Furthermore, having the channels underground greatly reduces water loss from evaporation.

Digging a karez is skilled and dangerous work and the *karez-kans* are respected and highly paid workers. The cost of making and maintaining a karez was traditionally split between a whole village and the karez was communally owned.

The city of Turpan owes its existence to these vital wells and channels, some of which were constructed over 2000 years ago. There are over a thousand wells, and the total length of the channels runs to an incredible 5000km, all constructed by hand and without modern machinery or building materials.

The Buddhist cave paintings and ruined cities in the area are remains of a pre-Islamic Buddhist civilisation. When the 7th century Chinese monk Xuan Zang passed through Kùchē he recorded that the city's western gate was flanked by two enormous 30m-high Buddha statues, and that there were a number of monasteries in the area decorated with beautiful Buddhist frescoes; 1200 years later, the German archaeologist-adventurers Grünwedel and Le Coq removed many of these paintings and sculptures and took them to Berlin.

Sadly, modern-day Kùchē retains little, if any, of its former glory. There is still some traditional architecture remaining, and traffic jams of donkey-cart taxis add some appeal. But for most people, it's the sights outside the town that justify a stop here.

Orientation & Information

There is no real town centre as such, but the main thoroughfare is Renmin Lu, which connects the new and old parts of town. The bus station is in the east of town and the train station is an isolated 5km southeast of here.

CITS (☎ 712 2005) is located in Qiūcí Bīnguǎn, a hotel in the west of town on Tianshan Lu.

Qiūcí Ancient City Ruins
Qiūcí Gùchéng 龟兹古城

These 'ruins' are all that is left of the ancient capital of Qiūcí, one of several ancient feudal states in what was once loosely called the Western Region of China. The ruins are along the main road, about a 10-minute walk west of Qiūcí Bīnguǎn.

Bazaar & Great Mosque
Lǎochéng Bāzā & Qīngzhēn Dàsì 老城巴扎与清真大寺

Every Friday a large bazaar is held about 2.5km west of town, next to a bridge on Renmin Lu. Traders come in from around the countryside to ply their crafts, wares and foodstuffs. While the local tourism offices are trying to make it a sightseeing draw, the bazaar is thus far largely a local affair, and is worth a visit.

About 150m farther west from the bazaar is the Great Mosque, Kùchē's main centre for Muslim worship. Though large in size, the mosque is a fairly modest affair, but some of the carvings around the main gateway are quite elaborate.

Places to Stay & Eat

Jiāotōng Bīnguǎn (☎ 712 2682) Quads/twins Y20/30 per bed, twins with bath Y100. The cheapest place in town, without question, is this hotel next door to the bus station. There is usually hot water after 10pm. If you are staying in the dorms and need a shower, there are public showers next door for Y1 a wash. This place was being spruced up at last check, though it wasn't bad to start with.

Kùchē Bīnguǎn (☎ 712 2901, fax 712 9490, 76 Jiefang Lu) Quads without bath Y30 per bed, twins with bath Y80 per bed. This place offers nicer surroundings with a large courtyard. The rooms are simple and clean, but the doubles are overpriced at Y160. Hot showers are available in the evenings or on demand. The hotel is in the north-west of town; look for the small sign.

Kùchē Fàndiàn (☎ 712 0285, fax 713 1160, 8 Tianshan Lu) Twins/triples Y110/130. This hotel is a little out of town, but offers the best value accommodation. In addition to spacious and clean rooms, it also has a swimming pool, sauna, train ticket reservations, spa and a beauty salon the size of a cinema. Bus No 6 from the train station travels here, or it's a 15-minute walk east from the bus station.

The *restaurant* at Kùchē Fàndiàn serves tasty Chinese food, but the best place to get a bite to eat is at one of the stalls in the *market*. There are the usual kebabs, noodles and breads available for a few *yuán*.

Mùsīlín Cāntīng (Wenhua Lu) Dishes from Y5. If you prefer to eat indoors, then try this place near the corner of Jiefang Lu. It has cheap and tasty kebabs, lāmiàn noodles and cold beer.

Getting There & Away

Bus Most buses east and west just stop here so you can't be guaranteed a berth. One daily sleeper to Kashgar (Y84 to Y120) takes about 16 hours, barring breakdowns and sandstorms. From Kùchē there are five buses to Ürümqi (Y80 to Y129, 14 to 19 hours) daily. There is also one daily bus at 11am to Yīníng (Y78, 22 hours): a spectacular trip crossing Tiān Shān. All buses to Hotan go the long way around to the west instead of the cross-desert highway, so consider breaking up the trip.

Train The best way to visit Kùchē is by train from either Kashgar or Turpan. If you want to purchase sleeper tickets, then it would be best to get to the train station at least 10 minutes before it opens at 10.30am on the day of departure. Bus No 2 runs there. There is also a ticket office along Wenhua Lu that sells tickets for trains that depart for Korla and Ürümqi. Hard seat to Kashgar is Y51.

SILK ROAD

Getting Around

Taxi Kùchē's sights are scattered around the surrounding countryside, and the only way to see them is to hire a vehicle. CITS can arrange jeep or car hire for the day, however taxi drivers will offer better rates.

Within town, taxi rides are a standard Y10 per trip, while horse or donkey carts are generally Y2 to Y3, depending on the distance.

AROUND KÙCHĒ
Kizil Thousand Buddha Caves

Kèzīěr Qiānfó Dòng 克孜尔千佛洞

There are quite a lot of Thousand Buddha Caves around Kùchē, but the most important site is this one, 72km to the west of Kùchē in Bàichéng county. The caves *(admission Y25 per section, additional caves up to Y150; open 9.30am-8pm daily)* date back to the 3rd century AD and are believed to have taken over 500 years to complete.

Although there are more than 230 caves here, only 24 are generally open to the public. Sadly, most of the caves have been damaged by both religious attacks and the elements over the centuries. The caves are divided into eastern and western sections. In the eastern section the caves are more general in style and include many depictions of the Buddhist legends. The western caves contain paintings that depict the life of Sakyamuni (the 'Historical Buddha').

More caves are planned to be open to the public in the near future. If you visit during the summer months, you are compensated with delicious berries and grapes that can be freely picked from the orchard in front of the caves.

The easiest way to get to the caves is to hire a vehicle. CITS charges Y300 for the return trip, while private taxi drivers offer rates of around Y150 to Y200. It is also possible to catch the Bàichéng bus from Kùchē and get off at the turn-off to the caves. It is still another 11km along a dirt track, so you will need to hitch the rest of the way.

Other Buddhist cave sites around Kùchē include **Kumtura** and **Kizilgaha**. Kumtura is theoretically closed, but CITS can arrange exclusive visits. The catch: Y450 for the privilege of viewing the caves here. Considering that it takes most of the day to get there and back, most travellers opt to forgo this particular trip.

The one-way journey to Kèzīěr or Kazilgaha takes 1½ hours, and to Kumtura around four hours.

Ancient City Ruins 故城
Gùchéng

Aside from Qiūcí (in Kùchē itself), there are several other ruined cities in the region. Around 23km to the north-east of Kùchē is the ancient city of **Sūbāshí**. About 20km to the south of Kùchē is the ancient city of **Wushkat**.

About 60km south-west of Kùchē is **Tonggusibashi**, one of the largest and best preserved of the ruined cities. Again you'll need to hire a vehicle to get to these spots; rates are similar to those for the Kizil Thousand Buddha Caves.

South-West Xīnjiāng – Kashgaria

Kashgaria is the historical name for the western Tarim Basin. Despite its present isolation, Kashgaria was a major hub of the Silk Road and has bristled with activity for over 2000 years. A ring of oasis lined with poplar trees and centred around weekly bazaars remain a testament to the mercantile tradition. The region remains the heartland of the Uyghur.

KASHGAR 喀什
☎ 0998 • pop 189,900

Even in the 21st century, the name Kashgar (Kāshí) still sparks images of a remote desert oasis, the sole outpost of civilisation leading from the vast deserts of Xīnjiāng to the icy peaks of the Karakoram. Desert brigands, exotic bazaars and colourful silks spring to mind at the mention of China's westernmost city.

Kashgar is no longer so remote, and the modern age has certainly taken its toll (emphatically symbolised by the statue of Chairman Mao – one of the largest in China). Kashgar is only 1½ hours by plane from Ürümqi, or less than two days by sleeper bus. The old town walls have been torn down, flashy red taxis with blaring horns congest the pavements and Chinese super freeways encircle the beleaguered old town. In 1999 the railway link from Ürümqi was formally opened, sounding what many fear will be the death-knell for traditional Kashgar.

Even so, Kashgar retains an intoxicating air of the exotic, mainly due to its fascinating ethnic mix of Uyghurs (who comprise the majority of the population), Tajiks, Kyrgyz, Uzbeks and a growing number of Han Chinese. Some things haven't changed since medieval times – blacksmiths, carpenters and cobblers use hand tools in the old quarter and the Id Kah Mosque draws the town's faithful as it has since 1442. Markets with rows of shimmering silks, knives and jewellery vie for your attention and narrow backstreets lined with earthen-walled homes beckon for exploration.

Kashgar has been a Silk Road trading centre for two millennia and traders from Kazakhstan, Kyrgyzstan, Pakistan and even Russia (along with travellers from around the globe) continue to fuel the city with impromptu street-corner negotiations, perpetual bazaars, and hotel-room deals with Gilgit traders. Shifting geopolitics have reopened lines of communication and it's not hard to imagine a new high-tech Silk Road recrossing the Tarim Basin one day. Kashgar's future, it seems, lies firmly rooted in its past.

With all the trading activity, one couldn't call Kashgar 'laid-back', but it has a great atmosphere and it is a fine place to settle back for a week or so. The town is also a good launching pad for trips along the southern Silk Road to Hotan, over the Torugart Pass to Kyrgyzstan or south to beautiful Karakul Lake and the stunning Karakoram Highway to Pakistan.

Kashgar experiences blistering hot summers, although at 1290m above sea level it's cooler than Turpan, Kùchē and other stops along the Xīnjiāng section of the Silk Road.

Orientation

Official (Chinese) street names are given here. The town centre is a Tiānānmén-style square north of Rénmín Gōngyuán, dominated by a statue of Mao Zedong. The Uyghur old town lies just north of here, bisected by Jiefang Beilu. The budget travellers' enclave is on the west side. The grounds of the Sunday Market are on the east side.

Information

John's Cafe (☎/fax 255 1186, e Johncafe @public.qd.sd.cn) organises bookings, transport and excursions and can link you up with other budget-minded tourists to share costs.

At some point in your stay you are bound to bump in to Ablimit Ghopor (aka 'Elvis'). Elvis' main business is buying and selling carpets but he also takes tourists on offbeat tours of the old town to visit anything from a local *pir* or holy man, to a traditional Uyghur house or local teahouse, where he can act as translator and cultural interpreter. He'll also line up desert treks. He makes the rounds of cafes and has good reviews from travellers.

Money The central Bank of China, at 239 Renmin Xilu, can change travellers cheques and cash and can also give quick cash advances on major credit cards; ditto with a branch farther to the east. Bank summer hours are weekdays from 9.30am to 1.30pm and 4pm to 8pm, and weekends from 11am to 3pm. You can also sell yuán back into US dollars at the bank's foreign exchange desk if you have exchange receipts; a good idea if you are headed to Tashkurgan, where the bank hours are erratic.

Post & Communications The post office at 40 Renmin Xilu is open daily from 10am to 8pm. Across the road is the telephone office, open daily from 9.30am to 8pm.

The telephone office has an Internet bar with access for Y8 an hour; five minutes west is on the opposite side of the street is a hole-in-the-wall Internet bar with service for Y5 an hour.

Travel Agencies The main CITS office (☎ 282 8473, fax 282 3087) is up two flights of stairs in a building just outside the Chini Bagh Hotel. However, the more useful CITS Foreign Independent Traveller (FIT) branch is just inside the gate. CTS (☎ 283 2875, fax 282 2552) is up two more flights from CITS near the Chini Bagh Hotel, but it also has an independent office for small groups and individuals in the plaza facing Shengli Lu, outside the Chini Bagh gate. CTS is consistently cheaper than CITS.

KASHGAR 喀什

KASHGAR

PLACES TO STAY
3 Chini Bagh Hotel
其尼瓦克宾馆
4 Noor Bish Hotel
脑北西旅社
9 Sèmǎn Bīnguǎn
色满宾馆
11 Sèmǎn Bīnguǎn Block
No.3
色满宾馆第3号
28 Qiánhǎi Bīnguǎn
前海宾馆
33 Kashgar Hotel
喀什噶尔宾馆
37 Tiānnán Fàndiàn
天南饭店

PLACES TO EAT
8 Oasis Cafe
10 John's Cafe
约翰中西餐厅
12 Noor Look Kebab
House
烤肉大排挡
18 Night Food Market
夜市场
23 Lao Shāndōng Shuǐjiǎo
老山东水饺
25 Chinese Food Stalls

OTHER
1 International Bus
Station
际汽车站

2 Former British
Consulate
前英国领事馆
5 CITS FIT Branch
6 CITS & CTS
中国国际旅行社
7 Hospital of Traditional
Uyghur Medicine
13 Old Town Walls
14 PSB
公安局
15 Gold and Brass/
Coppersmiths Bazaar
16 Id Kah Mosque
艾提尕清真寺
17 Kashgar City
Traditional Minority
Handicraft & Souvenir
Shop
19 Ababekry Seley (Shop)
20 Post Office
邮局
21 Internet Cafe
网吧
22 Caohu Department
Store
草湖商场
24 Regional Bus Stop
26 Main Bank of China
中国银行
27 Huanjiang
Shangmaocheng
Department Store
环疆商贸城

29 Telephone Office;
Internet Cafe
电信局；网吧
30 Mao Statue
毛泽东塑像
31 PSB
公安局
32 Old Town Walls
34 Kashgar Regional
Museum
喀什地区博物馆
35 Long-Distance Bus
Station
长途汽车站
36 Ak Mazar
38 Bank of China
中国银行
39 Local & Regional Bus
Stand
40 Xinjiang Airlines
(CAAC)
中国新疆航空公司
售票处
41 Kashgar
Mountaineering
Association (KMA)
喀什登山协会
42 Tomb of Yusup Has
Hajip
玉素甫哈斯哈吉甫陵墓
43 Tomb of Ali Arslan
Khan
赛衣提艾里艾斯拉罕墓

The Kashgar Mountaineering Association (KMA; Takka Chkesh in Uyghur; Dēngshān Xiéhuì in Chinese) is a government liaison office for expeditions and group sports travel and will help individuals with guides or vehicles, though both are scarce in the high season. The office (☎ 282 3680, fax 282 2957) is far away at 45 Tiyu Lu, off Jiefang Nanlu beyond the Civil Aviation Administration of China (CAAC; Zhōngguó Mínháng).

PSB The PSB is at 111 Yunmulakexia Lu. A friendlier office is located at 67 Renmin Donglu, north-east of Rénmín Gōngyuán. Alien Travel Permits (Wàibīn Tōngxíng Zhèng), for areas not freely open to foreigners, cost Y50 a pop.

You can get a month-long visa extension here too; price depends on nationality. The office is open weekdays from 9.30am to 1.30pm and 4pm to 8pm.

Medical Services The main Chinese hospital is the People's Hospital (Rénmín Yīyuàn), located on Jiefang Beilu, north of the river. There's also a Hospital of Traditional Uyghur Medicine on Seman Lu about 500m east of Sèmǎn Bīnguǎn, though it is reportedly none too clean. A small clinic under the CITS building in the Chini Bagh compound can administer first aid and medicines. Some staff here speak English.

Dangers & Annoyances Travellers have lost money or passports to pickpockets at the Sunday Market, in the ticket scrum at the bus station, and even on local buses, so keep yours tucked away.

Some foreign women walking the streets alone have been sexually harassed, by locals and also by visiting Pakistanis. The Muslim Uyghur women dress in long skirts and heavy stockings like the Uyghur women in Ürümqi and Turpan, but here one sees more female faces hidden behind veils of brown gauze. It is wise for women travellers to dress as would be appropriate in any Muslim country, covering arms and legs. This should be second nature for travellers who have come from Pakistan but it may come as a surprise if you've come from Kyrgyzstan, Kazakhstan or eastern China.

Sunday Market 星期日市场
Xīngqīrì Shìchǎng

Once a week Kashgar's population swells by 50,000 as people stream in to the Sunday Market *(Aizilaiti Lu)* – surely the most mind-boggling bazaar in Asia, and not to be missed. By sunrise the roads east of town are a sea of pedestrians, horses, bikes, motorcycles, donkey carts, trucks and belching tuk-tuks, everyone shouting *boish-boish!* (coming through!).

In arenas off the livestock market, men 'test-drive' horses or peer into sheep's mouths. A wonderful assortment of people sit by their rugs and blankets, clothing and boots, hardware and junk, tapes and boomboxes – and, of course, hats. In fact the whole town turns into a bazaar, with hawkers everywhere. It's wonderfully photogenic so bring twice as much film as you think you might need and get there early to avoid the tour groups.

The grounds are a 30- or 40-minute walk from the Chini Bagh Hotel gate or Sèmǎn Bīnguǎn respectively. You can take a bike and park it in the bike-lot in front of the entrance to the carpet pavilion. Taxis are plentiful outside tourist hotels on market day, cost should be about Y10 from the Sèmǎn, less from Chini Bagh. You might catch a donkey cart outside the city centre, but negotiate a price beforehand. In July and August John Hu of John's Cafe offers a free one-way minibus shuttle from his cafe after breakfast.

If the tourist crush gets to you, try the Sunday market at Hotan (see the Southern Silk Road section) or even the Monday market in Upal (see entry, later).

Id Kah Mosque
Ài Tígǎ'ér Qīngzhēn Sì

The big yellow-tiled Id Kah Mosque *(admission Y3)* is one of the largest in China, with a courtyard and gardens that can hold 20,000 people during the annual Qurban Baiyram celebrations. It was built in 1442 as a smaller mosque on what was then the outskirts of town. During the Cultural Revolution Id Kah suffered heavy damage, but has since been restored. There are also more than 90 tiny neighbourhood mosques throughout the city.

It's acceptable for non-Muslims to go into Id Kah. Local women are rarely seen inside but Western women are usually ignored if they're modestly dressed (arms and legs covered and a scarf on the head). Take off your shoes if entering carpeted areas, and be discreet about photos. In front of the mosque is Id Kah Square, which on sunny days swarms with a diverse array of locals.

At night the square comes alive with exotic food vendors and blaring televisions surrounded by dozens of onlookers.

Other Tombs

There are numerous other interesting tombs in and around Kashgar, including: **Abakh Hoja Tomb** (*Xiāngfēi Mù*), **Tomb of Yusup Has Hajip** (*Yùsùfǔ Hāsī Hājífǔ Mù*), **Tomb of Ali Arslan Khan** (*Āiěrsīlánhàn Qīngzhēnsì*) and **Ak Mazar** (*Bái Mázā*).

Old Town 故城
Gǔchéng

Sprawling all around Id Kah are roads full of Uyghur shops and narrow passages lined with adobe houses that seem trapped in a time warp.

At the east end of Seman Lu stands a 10m-high section of the old town walls, at least 500 years old. Another rank of them are visible from Yunmulakexia Lu opposite the vegetable market. Construction around, on and in them makes access impossible, and there's clearly no interest in preserving them.

Kashgar Regional Museum
Kāshí Dìqū Bówùguǎn 喀什地区博物馆

This museum (*19 Tawuguzi Lu; admission Y6; open 7.30am-noon & 4pm-8pm daily*) is out on the eastern edge of Kashgar. Despite half-hearted attempts to liven up the exhibits here, most travellers come away underwhelmed.

Three Immortals Caves 三仙洞
Sānxiān Dòng

Twenty kilometres north of Kashgar is one of the area's few traces of the flowering of Buddhism, the Three Immortal Caves, three grottoes high on a sandstone cliff, one of which has some peeling frescoes. Unfortunately, the cliff is too sheer to climb. Watch for them if you enter Kashgar via the Torugart Pass.

Ha Noi Ruins & Mor Pagoda
Hànnuòyí Gùchéng & Mù'ěr Fótǎ

At the end of a jarring 35km drive northeast of town are the ruins of Ha Noi, a Tang dynasty town built in the 7th century and abandoned in the 12th century. Little remains except a great solid pyramid-like structure and the huge Mor Pagoda or stupa.

CITS will take you to Ha Noi for Y200 per Land Cruiser, or you can hire a car from the CTS for Y70 per person. John Hu, at John's Cafe, charges Y350 per car.

Places to Stay – Budget

Accommodation can be tighter on the days preceding the Sunday Market than afterward. Low season you may be able to coax out some discounts. High season prices are given here.

Chini Bagh Hotel (*Qíníwǎkè Bīnguǎn;* ☎ 284 2299, fax 282 3842, 93 Seman Lu) Triples/quads with hot shower Y30/25 per bed, main building doubles with hot shower Y260, Jingyuan annex singles or doubles with TV Y200. This is a five-storey tower where the British consulate's front gate used to be. Dorm rooms are spartan but clean and the carpeted doubles are very cosy. The complex has Chinese and Uyghur restaurants, souvenirs, travel agencies and a coffee shop.

Sèmǎn Bīnguǎn (☎ 255 2147, fax 255 2861, 170 Seman Lu) Dorm beds/doubles with shared bath Y15/30 per person, No 2/3 block doubles with private bath Y60/40 per person, No 1 block doubles Y290. This hotel dominates the courtyard of the old Russian consulate, and is probably the most popular place for backpackers, due more to the good amenities nearby than the quality of the shared bathrooms. The 500-bed complex has three buildings, a restaurant, money exchange, a laundry service, shady gardens and overpriced souvenir shops. The doubles with shared bathroom are actually quite nice, while some others are small, musty and overpriced. The only downside is the shared baths themselves: you'll find dirty showers that barely drizzle and toilet/wash areas that are an embarrassment to *hôtellerie*. No 1 block doubles are better. Be sure to lock your doors here to guard against theft.

Block No 3 is actually across the street above John's Cafe. The rooms here are compact but carpeted and have hot water. Standards vary, so check more than one room. The place is particularly popular with Pakistani traders.

SILK ROAD

Tiānnán Fàndiàn (☎ 282 4023, 49 Renmin Donglu) Beds in doubles Y38-90, beds in triples/quads with shared bath Y20/16. This place has a number of buildings. Showers are communal except for the most expensive doubles. Some travellers have liked this place; check more than one room since quality varies a lot. Some renovation is ongoing so changes may be afoot.

Noor Bish Hotel (Nǎoběixī Lǚshè; ☎ 282 3092) Rooms Y15-20. This is a small Uyghur guesthouse just off the road that connects the Chini Bagh to the Id Kah Square. The basic rooms are set around a pleasant courtyard. It's a friendly place very popular with Pakistani visitors. They may try to charge Westerners a bit more, but you can politely negotiate. Water can be spotty here though facilities are clean.

Places to Stay – Mid-Range

Kashgar Hotel (Kāshí Gáěr Bīnguǎn; ☎ 261 2367, fax 261 4679, 57 Tawaguzi Lu) Doubles with bath & phone Y160-200, with bath & TV Y250-400, triples/quads with bath & TV Y210/200. Also called the Kashgar Guesthouse, this place has seen better days. The spacious, dusty 200-room compound has Chinese and Uyghur restaurants and a beer garden. The quads here are better value than the doubles. The drawback is that it's 3km east of the centre, although taxis (about Y5 to the centre) linger at the gate. Bus No 10 goes to the Id Kah Mosque and Rénmín Gōngyuán, or you can rent a bike from the hotel for Y3 an hour.

Qiánhǎi Bīnguǎn (☎ 282 2922, fax 282 0644, 199 Renmin Xilu) Doubles with aircon Y240, suites Y500. Tucked back about 50m from the street, this hotel is in a great location for quietude; the staff is pretty friendly as well. Rooms can be plush but smoky, so look at a few. The hotel has two restaurants, a business centre, a meeting hall and some basic exercise facilities. Rooms even have refrigerators and coffeemakers.

Sèmǎn Bīnguǎn (see Places to Stay – Budget) Rooms/suites Y400/600. The former Russian consulate at the back of this hotel has been converted into five standard rooms and two suites. Nicely decorated and oozing atmosphere this is the must-stay choice of the well-heeled Great Game aficionado (see the boxed text 'Listening Posts of the Great Game').

Places to Eat

Uyghur Food The best way to sample Uyghur food is at the food stalls outside Id Kah Mosque. Vendors sell noodles, chickpeas, poached eggs, kebabs, breads, boiled goat heads, chicken and fried fish; bring your own fork. For desert you can try watermelon by the slice, vanilla ice cream, *tangzaza* (triangles of glutinous rice covered in syrup), *kharsen meghriz* (fried dough balls filled with sugar, raisins and walnuts), or just a glass of hot milk and a pastry. In local restaurants, recommended is the *suoman* (spicy noodles) or *suoman goshsiz* (spicy noodles without meat).

Noor Look Kebab House (Kǎoròu Dàpái; 285 Seman Lu) Dishes from Y2. Situated inside a cool courtyard, this place specialises in kebabs, but the staff will cook anything if you can explain it.

Chini Bagh Hotel, Sèmǎn Bīnguǎn and Kashgar Hotel each have clean Muslim dining halls where you can eat fixed Uyghur meals during limited hours.

Chinese Food Chinese fast food stalls serve oily but cheap lunches in an alley off Renmin Xilu, behind the Bank of China. This is a good option for vegetarians; just point and pay, a tray of ready-cooked food costs about Y5. Go at noon when the food is hot.

At night, tables are set up outside the Chinese restaurants on Yunmulakexia Lu, north of Renmin Xilu, selling beer and cheap snacks. Among the snails and chicken's feet are more appealing offerings such as *shāguō* (vegetables, tofu and mushroom broth in an earthenware pot), *shuǐjiǎo* (ravioli) and *húndun* (wonton soup).

Lǎo Shāndōng Shuǐjiǎo (Yunmulakexia Lu) Dishes Y6. This nearby restaurant is recommended for shuǐjiǎo – order by the bowl or the *jin* (500g is enough for two).

Both *John's Cafe* and the *Oasis Cafe* offer large quasi-Chinese menus in English, from which you can satisfy a raging hunger for under Y15.

Shopping

Souvenirs For serious shopping go to the old town; Sunday Market prices tend to be higher. The citizens of Kashgar have been selling things for 2000 years, so be ready to bargain.

Listening Posts of the Great Game

The British and Russian rivalry across the Pamir Range was matched by personal rivalries across town – for information, influence and even Silk Road antiquities. The Russian and British consulates in Kashgar quickly became listening posts on the front line of the Great Game. While opening up mountain routes and expanding trade, the consul-generals kept an anxious ear open for news of political alliances and military manoeuvres.

In 1890, 24-year old George Macartney arrived with Francis Younghusband to set up the British office (Chini Bagh) in Kashgar. Younghusband left a year later; Macartney remained for the next 28. Eventually George was joined by his wife Catherine, who gradually turned the Chini Bagh into an island of European civility, with cuttings from English gardens, exotic flowers, and pear and apple trees. Tabletennis tables were set up indoors and tennis courts were built nearby. Brahms records provided melodious lullabies and eventually a piano was shipped over the mountain passes. Explorers such as Aurel Stein and Albert Von le Coq called at the Chini Bagh on their way to the sandy wastes of the Taklamakan Desert, and Peter Fleming enjoyed his first bath and coffee there for over five months. Subsequent consuls included Percy Etherton, Clarmont Skrine (1922), George Gillan, Thompson Glover and Eric Shipton (1940–42 and 1946–48).

Across town the Russian consuls made similar attempts at introducing luxuries, vying for the company of passing Westerners and gaining the favour of information. The Russian consul Nikolai Petrovsky once gave Macartney a much-coveted pane of glass, only to demand it back (secured by his Cossack guard) after a sensitive issue involving a political cartoon. Following the incident the two didn't speak to each other for 2½ years. Subsequent Russian consuls included Mestchersky, who later fled the Bolshevik revolution in Russia and ended up in Paris, working as a waiter while his wife became a chambermaid. Ironically, the Russian consulate in Kashgar became a safe haven for White Russians, including Paul Nazarov, who sought refuge here for four years, until the Bolshiviks took the consulate in 1925.

Both consulates were closed in 1949, though the Chini Bagh functioned as a British representative office to India and Pakistan for a while. The consulates remain today as the Chini Bagh Hotel and Sèmǎn Bīnguǎn.

The Chini Bagh Hotel is built right smack in front of the old consulate, whose main floor is now a Chinese banquet hall. The upper three-room suite, finished in 1913, is awaiting renovation, but you may be able to talk your way upstairs to the living quarters and enjoy the view from the flat roof, where one consul's wife was shot through the shoulder during the Dungan rebellion of 1934.

The Russian consulate has fared better than the Chini Bagh and remains in the form of atmospheric suites in the courtyard behind Sèmǎn Bīnguǎn. The well-appointed suites are a must for Great Game buffs and romantics.

To recreate a flavour of these lost times try reading Diana Shipton's *The Antique Land* (Diana was Eric Shipton's wife) or Catherine Macartney's *An English Lady in Chinese Turkistan*.

Look for hats, teapot sets, copper/brass ware and handicrafts along the south side of Id Kah Mosque. A better place for hats is the bazaar. Uyghur knives, which have colourfully inlaid handles, are popular.

There are a couple of high-quality but pricey handicraft stores on the east side of the Id Kah Mosque. These and the bazaar have a depressing line-up of snow leopard pelts. Aside from the moral issues of buying the skins of endangered species, bear in mind that you may not be able to import such items into your own country.

Musical Instruments Beautiful longnecked stringed instruments run the gamut from junk to collector's items. They include the bulbous two-string *dutar,* larger threestring *khomuz,* small *tambur* and elaborately shaped *rabap,* which has five strings and a snake or lizard-skin sounding board. The small reed horn is a *sunai* or *surnai.* A *dab* is a type of tambourine.

Ababekry Seley This friendly shop is on the street north from the post office. It sells these instruments plus miniature tourist versions. Try to negotiate a carrying case if you buy one as this will greatly increase the chances of it getting home in one piece.

Gold An arcade of goldsmiths is just south-west of Id Kah Mosque. At the rear of some you can see young apprentices at work making jewellery. Typically heavy and ornate, the jewellery is designed for dowry pieces.

Carpets There are a few dealers in the bazaar and some bargains in small shops, but most have moved out to the Sunday Market pavilion. Do some carpet homework if you plan to buy one in Kashgar. Regionally, the best carpets are said to be in Hotan.

Kashgar City Traditional Minority Handicrafts & Souvenir Shop (Goldsmiths' Arcade) This carpet and handicraft shop is located north of the mosque near the bazaar. Many carpet vendors are planning their own bazaar; till then, the Sunday market is the place to find carpets.

Getting There & Away
Air The only place you can fly to/from Kashgar is Ürümqi (Y980/1220 low/high season; daily flights in summer, four flights weekly in winter). These flights are sometimes cancelled because of wind or sandstorms. If so, just show up for the next flight and you get priority; there's no need to change the ticket (but you must change any ticket for a connecting flight out of Ürümqi).

You should try to book at least a week ahead in summer. The China Xinjiang Airlines/CAAC ticket office (☎ 282 2113), at 95 Jiefang Nanlu on the ground floor of a blue four-storey building, opens daily from 10am to 1pm and 4.30pm to 8pm. You can buy tickets here for other domestic flights.

Bus to Kyrgyzstan There are public buses to Kyrgyzstan over the Torugart Pass but at the time of writing foreigners were not allowed to use these services.

For the record, a Chinese bus runs from the international bus station to Bishkek every Monday for US$50. Another Kyrgyz bus runs to Naryn every Friday for US$25. There are also services to Bishkek and Naryn from nearby Artux.

See the boxed text 'Over the Torugart Pass'.

Bus to Pakistan The terminus for buses to/from Sost (Y270 plus Y2 per bag, two days) in Pakistan is also the international bus station. From June to September it lays on as many buses as needed, so you needn't book very far ahead. Earlier or later in the season there may not be buses on some days. Landslides can cancel departures even in summer.

The bus leaves about noon Běijīng time. The 500km trip takes two days, with an overnight at Tashkurgan. Bring water and snacks and warm clothes as nights can be cold in any season. Sit on the left side for the best views.

Customs procedures are conducted at Tashkurgan. Drivers like luggage to go on the roof, though most people load up the back seats if there aren't too many passengers.

If buses have stopped for the season but you're desperate to cross the border, Pakistani traders may have space in a truck or chartered bus. You can also hire a 4WD; see Renting a 4WD in this section.

Bus to Ürümqi You can now make the 1480km trip to Ürümqi in a non-stop, soft-seat or sleeper coach in around 30 to 35 hours, for Y210 (upper berth) or Y240 (lower). Express luxury sleepers cost up to Y345. You can also go in a regular non-sleeper bus for Y153 though this is for hardcore penny-pinchers only.

These buses leave from the long-distance bus station (*aptoos biket*) and the international bus station. There are around 15 buses per day, between 7.30am and 8pm.

Other Bus Destinations Other buses use the long-distance bus station. There have been instances of theft at the bus station, especially in the early morning crush, sometimes with packs cut open, so keep a close watch on your bags.

Local buses to Tashkurgan leave daily except Sunday at 7.30am (Y45) and charge the full fare to drop you off in Karakul. There are also sleeper buses to Toksun (for Turpan) for Y188 to Y235.

Buses leave for Hotan (Y51, 10 hours) as frequently as every two hours between 7.30am and 6pm but it is more fun to stop off in Yengisar (Y7, 1½ hours), Yarkand

Over the Torugart Pass

Officially the Torugart Pass is a 'second grade' pass and therefore for local not international traffic. Except of course that it is. What you require on the Chinese side is a *xǔkězhèng* permit from the PSB entry-exit section in Ürümqi. Most agents in Kashgar can get this (CTS claim in two working days), though no-one will arrange a permit without transport (see the Renting a 4WD section for prices).

It's unclear whether you can get into Kyrgyzstan without booking Kyrgyz transport. Officially the Chinese won't let you leave the arch without onward transport into Kyrgyzstan and Chinese travel agencies are reluctant to take you without booking onward transport. But it looks likely that the Chinese guards will let you cross if you can find a lift from the arch to the Kyrgyz border post. If you do manage to get to the Kyrgyz border post you will need to find onward transport to Naryn or Bishkek. Taxi sharks may open the bidding at US$200 or more to Bishkek (and may lead you to think that's for the vehicle, then later tell you it's per person), though US$50 for the car is a more realistic amount.

There are public buses to Kyrgyzstan over the Torugart Pass, but at the time of writing foreigners were not allowed to take these services. Without a permit you'll most likely be thrown off the bus at the customs post. You must of course already have a Kyrgyzstan visa. There are local buses from Kashgar to the customs post but this doesn't help much.

(Y20, four hours) or Karghilik (Y25, five hours). Otherwise, buses to these last three towns run hourly or half-hourly.

Train Two daily trains to Ürümqi depart at 4pm and 9pm (Běijīng time) and take 23 and 30 hours respectively. Sleeper tickets cost Y198 to Y275.

Renting a 4WD You can hire 4WD Land Cruisers (four to six passengers) and minibuses (eight to 12 passengers) from the Kashgar Mountaineering Association, CTS, CITS or John Hu at John's Cafe. At the time of research a Land Cruiser to meet/ drop you off at Torugart was about Y1200, plus Y250 to Y300 per person to arrange the requisite permits. CTS was offering the cheapest rates, while John Hu was charging Y2000 for a car (up to four people). A Land Cruiser to Sost (Pakistan border) costs up to Y5000 depending on season and conditions (and bureaucracy). Food and lodging are extra, and the driver pays for his own. It's wise to book ahead, by a week or more in the high season.

Hitching You might be able to hitch a lift to Tashkurgan but from there to Pakistan you'll probably have to wait for an empty seat on the bus. There are plenty of goods trucks crossing the Torugart Pass to Kyrgyzstan but you'll it's likely that you will have problems getting past the customs post.

Getting Around
To/From the Airport A CAAC bus (Y4) leaves from the China Xinjiang Airlines/ CAAC ticket office, on Jiefang Nanlu, 2½ hours before all flight departures, and one bus meets all incoming flights. The airport is 12km north-east of the centre. A taxi there will cost Y30.

Bus A local bus stand at the west end of the square, opposite the Mao Statue, is the terminus for bus No 2 (to the airport), bus No 10 (to the Kashgar Hotel), bus No 20 (to the Abakh Hoja Tomb) and bus No 9 (to Sèmǎn Bīnguǎn, Chini Bagh gate, People's Hospital and Artush). Bus No 28 runs between the Mao Statue and the train station; a taxi would cost around Y20.

Taxis A new fleet of noisy, red taxis clog every street and alleyway, honking and congesting the city. About Y5 to Y10 should get you anywhere within the city.

Donkey-Carts The traditional Kashgar 'taxis' are getting scarce. They're not allowed in the centre in the daytime, so routes tend to be roundabout. If you hire your own, set the price and destination before you go. Don't pay until you get there, and make sure you have exact change.

Bicycle Rental A bike is the cheapest and most versatile way to get around Kashgar. One-gear clunkers can be hired by the hour (Y2) or the day at many hotels and John's Cafe. A deposit is required; don't leave your passport with them, as some ask you to do. You can negotiate a daily rate with most hotels.

KARAKORAM HIGHWAY 中巴公路

The Karakoram Highway (Zhōngbā Gōnglù) over the Khunjerab Pass (4800m) is the gateway to Pakistan. For centuries this route was used by caravans plodding down the Silk Road. Khunjerab means 'valley of blood', a reference to local bandits who took advantage of the terrain to plunder caravans and slaughter the merchants.

Nearly 20 years were required to plan, push, blast and level the present road between Islamabad and Kashgar and more than 400 road-builders died in the process. Facilities en route are being steadily improved, but take warm clothing, food and drink on board with you – once stowed on the roof of the bus your baggage will not be easily accessible.

Even if you don't wish to go to Pakistan, it's worth doing the trip to Tashkurgan from Kashgar – there's plenty to see. From Kashgar, you first cross the Pamir Plateau (3000m), passing the foothills of Kongur Mountain (Gōnggé'ér Shān), which is 7719m high, and nearby Muztagh-Ata Mountain (Mùshìtǎgé Shān) at 7546m. In between the two lies Karakul Lake, one of the most scenic spots on the Chinese side of the highway.

The journey continues through stunning scenery – high mountain pastures with grazing camels and yaks tended by Tajiks who live in yurts. The last major town on the Chinese side is Tashkurgan at 3600m.

Officially, the border opens 15 April and closes 31 October. However, the border can open late or close early depending on conditions at Khunjerab Pass. Travel formalities are performed at Sost, on the Pakistan border; the Chinese border post is at Tashkurgan.

At the time of writing travellers could get a seven-day Pakistan transit visa at the border, though it wouldn't be wise to plan your trip around the possibility of this happening. If you're coming in from Pakistan, make sure you have enough cash on hand

– the bank in Tashkurgan doesn't change travellers cheques.

Kashgar to Karakul Lake

This is becoming a popular short trip for those who aren't going into Pakistan. Karakul Lake is drop dead gorgeous and you can make it a two or three-day trip. There's superb hiking to be found in the surrounding hills; even circumnavigating this jewel of a lake makes for a lovely afternoon.

As you leave Kashgar the main attraction, rising up from the plain to the west, is the luminous rampart of the Pamir. An hour down the road is **Upal** village (Wùpàěr in Chinese), where the Kashgar-Sost bus normally stops for lunch. There's an interesting weekly market here every Monday. About 3km off the road from here is the small tomb of Mahmud al-Kashgari, an 11th century Uyghur scholar (born at Barskoön in Kyrgyzstan) famous for writing the first comparative dictionary of Turkic languages. Most settlements as far as Karakul are Kyrgyz.

Two hours from Kashgar you enter the canyon of the Ghez River (Ghez Darya in Uyghur), with wine-red sandstone walls at its lower end. **Ghez** itself is just a checkpost; photographing soldiers or buildings here can result in confiscated film. Upstream the road is cut into sheer walls or inches across huge boulder fields. At the top of this canyon, 3½ hours above the plain, is a huge wet plateau ringed with sand dunes, aptly called **Kumtagh** (Sand Mountain) by locals.

The bus will drop you off after five or six hours next to resplendent Karakul Lake, ringed by magnificent ice mountains. There's only one **hotel** that has yurts (Y40) and rooms. Camping is possible but not recommended. Travellers have warned of strong-arm tactics from local leaders who 'control' the area.

One bus daily (except Sunday) leaves the long-distance bus station at 7.30am, takes five to six hours and costs Y45. If you oversleep, the bus to Sost from the international station also passes by here, but it's more expensive. It's supposed to leave at 9.30am local time but never does (they have to overnight in Tashkurgan anyway so it does not matter when they leave) – you can often still get it around noon!

Southern Silk Road

The Silk Road east of Kashgar splits into two threads in the face of the huge Taklamakan Desert. The northern thread follows the course of the modern road and railway to Kùchē and Turpan. The southern road charts a more remote course between the desert sands and the huge Pamir and Kunlun ranges. The ancient route is marked by a ring of abandoned cities deserted by retreating rivers and encroaching sands. Some cities, like Niya, Miran and Yotkan, remain covered by sand, others, like Yarkand and Khotan, remain important Uyghur centres.

From Kashgar you can visit the southern towns as a multi-day trip from Kashgar, en route to Ürümqi or as part of a rugged backdoor route into China's Qīnghǎi or Gānsù provinces.

YENGISAR

The sleepy town of Yengisar (Yīngjíshā), 58km south of Kashgar, is synonymous with knife production. There are dozens of knife shops here (though prices are not much better than in Kashgar) and it's sometimes possible to visit the **knife factory** (*xiǎodāochǎng* in Chinese; *pichak chilik karakhana* in Uyghur) in the centre of town to see the knives actually being made. Each worker makes the blade, handle and inlays himself, using only the most basic of tools. There's a big sign saying 'No entrance' but some travellers have managed to get a quick look. Try not to visit between noon and 4pm when most workers head off for lunch. From the main highway walk east past Yīngjíshā Bīnguǎn then turn left to the bazaar. The factory is just west of the bazaar.

Places to Stay

Yīngjíshā Bīnguǎn (☎ 362 2390, 125 Jianguang Lu) Bldg No 1 triples/doubles with hot shower Y40/50 per bed, bldg No 2 quads/triples/doubles with hot water Y20/25/30. This is a pretty good choice; rooms are decent and the staff are nice. The rooms in building No 2 are more spartan. There's no English sign so look out for the 'Handicraft of National Store' at the entrance gate.

Getting There & Away

Buses pass through the town regularly en route to Yarkand (Y15, 2½ hours) and Kashgar (Y7, 1½ hours). Shared taxis wait at the main crossroads to speed passengers to the Kashgar bus station for Y10 per person, whenever there are three passengers or more.

YARKAND 莎车

Yarkand (Shāchē) is one of those Central Asian towns, like Samarkand and Kashgar, whose name still resonates deeply with Silk Road romance. At the end of a major trade route from British India, over the Karakorum Pass from Leh, Yarkand was for centuries an important caravan town and centre of Hindu tradesmen and moneylenders.

Today Yarkand is dominated by its **Chinese new town**, which is little more than a single street of department stores and Sichuanese restaurants. The **old town**, to the east, is of far more interest, and is an excellent place to explore traditional Uyghur life.

Things to See

Yarkand's main 'sight' is the **Altyn Mosque complex** (*admission Y10*). In the central courtyard of the mosque, near where worshippers carry out their pre-prayer ablutions, is the newly built **Tomb of Aman Isa Khan** (1526–60), musician, poetess and wife of the Khan of Yarkand. From here you can gain access to the **Tombs of the Kings of Yarkand**. Across from the mosque is the solitary gateway, or *orda darvaza*, all that remains of the former citadel.

The huge sprawling **cemetery** behind the mosque is a fascinating place to visit, especially at dawn when mourners are out in force. Amid the endless graves are the blue tilework and the **Yeti Sultan Mosque and Mazar** at the back of the cemetery. There should be no charge to visit the cemetery.

If you turn left out of the mosque and then left again after 30m, this road takes you down into the centre of the traditional old town and the back of **Wénhuà Gōngyuán**, where there is a small bazaar and several traditional Uyghur teahouses.

Other tombs out of town include **Hajiman Deng Mazar**, **Sud Pasha Mazar** and **Hayzi Terper Mazar**. There's plenty of scope here to take many interesting walks around the surrounding countryside.

Yarkand also has a large **Sunday Market**, untouristed but smaller than the markets at Kashgar or Hotan. The market is held a block north of the Altyn mosque.

Places to Stay & Eat
Finding a cheap place to stay can be a problem in Yarkand.

Shāchē Bīnguǎn (☎ 851 2365, 4 Xincheng Lu) Old-block rooms Y60-120, doubles/triples Y220/240. You should be able to get a room elsewhere, but if not, you'll be led here. This is particularly bad value for single travellers who must pay for all the beds in the room. Rooms in the old block are without a bathroom and are laughably overpriced. The other rooms are comfortable. The good news is that they're usually willing to bargain a lot.

Jiāotōng Bīnguǎn (☎ 851 6401, Wenhua Lu) Quads/triples/doubles Y15/20/35 per bed, doubles with bath Y80. This hotel is by the bus station. It takes foreigners and the rooms aren't that bad, especially the Y80 doubles. Some travellers have experienced an extra surcharge for being foreign.

There are Uyghur *foodstalls* in front of the bus station and on most street corners. For Chinese snacks there are several places just west of Shāchē Bīnguǎn.

Getting There & Around
Buses leave hourly for Kashgar (Y20, four hours) and Yengisar (Y14, 2½ hours) and every 30 minutes to Karghilik (Y6, one hour). Buses leave at 9.30am for Hotan (Y30, six hours) and three times daily to Ürümqi (Y208, 36 hours).

From the bus station it's about 1.5km to Shāchē Bīnguǎn and the same again to the start of the old town. Cycle rickshaws cost Y1 or Y2.

KARGHILIK 叶城
Karghilik (Yèchéng) is a convenient place to break the long trip to Hotan. There are decent places to stay and you could enjoyably spend several hours exploring the interesting Uyghur old town. Karghilik is also of importance to travellers as the springboard for the long overland trip to Tibet.

The main thing to see in town is the 15th-century **Friday Mosque** *(Jama Masjid)*. The mosque is surrounded by an interesting covered bazaar, while the traditional mud-walled backstreets of the old town spread south behind the mosque.

The town of Charbagh, 10 minutes' drive towards Yarkand has an interesting market on Tuesday.

Places to Stay & Eat
Jiāotōng Bīnguǎn (☎ 728 5540, 1 Jiaotong Lu) Quads Y30 per bed, doubles with bath Y80-100. Located right by the bus station, this is actually the best place in town. The rooms here are comfortable and carpeted. Hot water can be temperamental on the upper floors.

There are some busy 24-hour *food stalls* across the main road from the bus station and some good Uyghur places in front of the mosque.

Getting There & Away
There are four buses to Hotan (Y24, five hours) 9am to 4pm and to Yarkand/Kashgar every half hour until 8pm (Y6/24). There are also daily sleeper buses to Korla (Y155) and Ürümqi (Y216).

To Tibet The 1100km-long road to Ali, in western Tibet, branches off from the main Kashgar-Hotan road 6km east of Karghilik. There are no buses along this road so you'll have to hitch a ride with a truck. This is a very tough road with several passes over 5400m and several foreigners have died, either from exposure or in traffic accidents. You should come equipped with warm clothes and enough food for a week (though the trip to Ali can take as little as three days). In addition, the route is officially off-limits to foreigners and there are numerous checkpoints en route (though surprising numbers of travellers have been making it through in recent years). See Lonely Planet's *Tibet* guidebook for more details.

Getting Around
Pedicabs charge a flat Y1 anywhere in town.

HOTAN 和田
☎ 0903 • pop 96,000
About 1980km south-west of Ürümqi by road, dusty Hotan (Hétián), or Khotan, is one of the most remote parts of Xīnjiāng, sitting at the southern boundary of the Taklamakan Desert. It's still remarkably larger, cleaner and more bustling than one would expect.

The main reason to haul yourself all the way out here is to catch the fantastic **Sunday Market**, but Hotan is also renowned for its silk, carpets and jade, which are considered the finest in China. You can even see deposits of white jade along the Jade Dragon Kashgar River, which passes to the east of town. You can check out the local selection at the rows of stores and stalls along the town's main street.

For those setting off on the infrequently explored southern Silk Road, via Keriya (Yútián), Cherchen (Qiěmò), Charklik (Ruòqiāng) and on to Golmud, this is the last place to take care of important errands like changing money, stocking up on supplies or extending your visa.

Information

Hetian International Travel Service (Hétián Guójì Lǚxíngshè; ☎ 251 6090), in Yíyuàn Bīnguǎn, can arrange a car and guide to the ruins at Yuètègān and Málìkèwàtè for Y350 for three people, or to the Silk Factory for Y150. It also offers an adventurous (and expensive) week-long trip into the Mushi Mountains, 150km south of Hotan, and trips into the Yengi Eriq Desert to the north.

The Bank of China cashes travellers cheques and is open Monday to Friday from 9.30am to 1.30pm and 4pm to 8pm.

Sunday Market

Hotan's most popular attraction is its traditional weekly market, which rivals Kashgar's in both size and interest. The colourful market swamps the old town and reaches fever pitch between noon and 2pm Xīnjiāng time. The most interesting parts to head for are the *gillam* (carpet) bazaar, which also has a selection of *atlas* silks, the *doppi* (skullcap) bazaar, and the livestock bazaar.

Hotan Cultural Museum

Also known as the Historical Relics Ancient Corpses Exhibit, this small museum *(admission Y7; open 9am-2pm & 4pm-7pm daily)* is worth a brief visit. The main attractions are two mummies, a 10-year-old girl and 35-year-old man, both of whom are now over 1500 years old. The mummies here are of note as they are Indo-European, not Chinese. There's a useful map showing the location of the region's buried cities.

Ancient Cities

The deserts around Hotan are peppered with the faint ruins of abandoned cities. Ten kilometres to the west of town are the **Yotkan Ruins** *(Yuètègān Yízhǐ; admission Y5)*, the ancient capital of a pre-Islamic kingdom dating from the 3rd to 8th centuries AD. It's an additional Y5 to take photos.

The **Melikawat Ruins** *(Málìkèwàtè Gùchéng; admission Y5)* are 25km south of town, and there are some temples and pagoda-like buildings a further 10km to the south. Visiting any of these places will require hiring a taxi, which can be arranged at the hotels, through the museum, or with any taxi driver who knows the way. It's an additional Y5 to take photos.

Other ruins such as the Rawaq Pagoda and city of Niya (Endere) have been put off limits due to the high fees charged.

Silk and Carpet Factories

Jíyǎxiāng This small town north-east of Hotan, is a traditional centre for atlas silk production. Look around the small but fascinating workshop *(karakhana* in Uyghur) to see how the silk is spun, dyed and woven using traditional methods. A taxi from Hotan to the village costs Y10.

En route to the village, on the eastern bank of the Jade Dragon Kashgar River, is a small **carpet factory** *(gillam karakhana* in Uyghur), which is also worth a quick look. Take minibus No 2, which leaves from in front of Hétián Shì Bīnguǎn, a hotel at the main crossroads downtown, and then change to minibus No 3 or walk 20 minutes over the bridge.

Hotan Silk Factory *(Hétián Sīchóu Chǎng; open 9am-1.30pm & 3.30pm-7.30pm Mon-Fri)* uses a less traditional form of silk production, employing over 2000 workers. Staff at the office will give you a tour of the plant to see the boiling of cocoons and spinning, weaving, dyeing and printing of silk. If you don't speak at least some Chinese, you are better off arranging a visit through Hetian International Travel Service. No photos are allowed in the factory. To get there, take minibus No 1 from outside the bus station to the end of the line and then walk back 150m.

None of the aforementioned factories charges for a look around, though all have shops that you are expected to at least look in.

Places to Stay

Hétián Yíngbīnguǎn (☎ *202 2824, fax 202 3688, 4 Tanayi Beilu*) North-bldg quads/triples with shared bath Y20/25 per bed, doubles with hot shower Y45 per bed, new-block rooms from Y190. This is the cheapest reliable accommodation for foreigners; if you don't like this place, just about every hotel in town has cheapie options. Older rooms are comfortable; newer ones are more upmarket. Rates include a miserable breakfast and the service here can be a bit frosty.

Hétián Bīnguǎn (☎ *202 3564, fax 251 3570, 10 Urumqi Nanlu*) Dorm beds Y30, doubles/triples Y240/260. Located on the western edge of town, this hotel is somewhat fancier than Hétián Yíngbīnguǎn, with comfortable but smoky rooms. They offer beds in carpeted six-bed dorms – the bathrooms are grim but if you are the only foreigner you'll get the room to yourself.

Jiāotōng Bīnguǎn (☎ *203 2700, Guodao 315*) Doubles Y45 per bed. This hotel, right next to the bus station, has comfortable, carpeted rooms and if they give you the whole double for Y45, as they did us, it'll be the best value room you'll get in China!

Xìngfú Lǚshé (*Happy Hotel;* ☎ *202 4804, Guodao 315*) Beds Y30. This basic Uyghur-style alternative is a couple of minutes' walk to the right from the bus station. Rooms are a little grimy but there are hot showers.

Silk Town Guest House Beds Y5. This 100% Uyghur place also not far from the bus station is ultra-basic but ultra-cheap.

Places to Eat

There are plenty of standard Chinese restaurants in the new town and Uyghur restaurants in the old town, though few places speak English.

Getting There & Away

Air There are four flights weekly between Hotan and Ürümqi (Y1000). The CAAC/Xinjiang Airlines office (☎ 202 2178) is on Positan Nanlu. The airport is located 10km south of town and the taxi ride from town costs Y20.

Bus From Ürümqi to Hotan buses now travel along the recently opened Cross-Desert Highway, which spans 500km of almost completely deserted land between Luntai and Niya (Mínfēng). The roadway is actually built on a raised roadbed to help prevent sandstorms from building up dunes on the tarmac. Regular sleeper buses leave Hotan four times a day (Y250 to Y290, 30 hours), most in the morning. Express sleeper buses (Y340 to Y360, 24 hours) leave in the afternoon.

Note that if you're trying to get to Korla or Kucha, the express buses do not stop. You'll be placed on a rattletrap sleeper and taken the long way around via Yecheng, Yarkand, and Aksu. It can take up to 40 hours to get to Korla this way but it's the only option.

There are two daily morning buses between Hotan and Kashgar. The 530km trip takes around 10 hours and seats cost Y34 to Y48 for the regular bus, or Y55 for the 'luxury' bus. There are also several buses daily to Yarkand (Y32) via Yecheng (Y24 to Y28).

Getting Around

Donkey carts take you to and from the Sunday Market (Y0.5 a trip). Taxis cost a flat Y5; there are also three-wheeler motorbikes.

HOTAN TO GOLMUD 和田至格尔木

To continue along the southern Silk Road into China proper catch an early-morning bus to Qiěmò (Cherchen), 580km to the east. The trip generally takes two days and costs Y55 and goes via the Uyghur towns of Keriya (Yútián) and Niya (Mínfēng).

From Qiěmò buses continue another 320km east to Ruòqiāng (Charklik). The trip takes anywhere from 13 to 16 hours under good conditions, and tickets are around Y35. From Ruòqiāng you may be able to get a bus to Golmud, although some travellers have had to resort to private jeep services that take you the nine hours to the border with Qīnghǎi. From there you can reportedly take a series of buses on to Dachaidan in Qīnghǎi, and from there connect with buses to Golmud. This route requires a few overnight stops, and roads in this area are plagued by washouts and landslides, so don't try this route if you're in a hurry.

Northern Xīnjiāng

This part of Xīnjiāng is positively stunning; a land of thick evergreen forests, rushing rivers and lakes. The highlight of the area is beautiful Hānàsī Hú (Hanas Lake) and the surrounding mountainous valleys.

Until recently, the area was a quiet backwater of China's far north-west and closed off to foreigners due to the proximity of the Russian, Mongolian and Kazakhstan borders. The area is rich in ethnic minorities and despite constant Han migration, continues to remain predominantly Kazakh. Tourism and its related industries are just starting to take off and the region remains relatively untouched by pollution.

BÙ'ĚRJĪN 布尔津
☎ 0906 • pop 60,000

Bù'ěrjīn, meaning 'dark green water' in Mongolian, is named after the nearby river Bù'ěrjīn Hé, which is a tributary of the Ertix River. The Ertix is the only river in China to flow into the Arctic Ocean. Bù'ěrjīn, 620km north of Ürümqi, marks the end of the desert and the beginning of the grasslands and mountains to the north. The town's population is mainly Kazakh (57%), but there are also Han, Uyghurs, Tuwa Mongolians and Russians.

There isn't much to see in Bù'ěrjīn, especially on that *long* ride through the desert, but it is a convenient transit stop if your heading for Hānàsī Hú or Kaba.

Information
The PSB is on the corner of Xiangyang Lu and Xinfu Lu. This is where you come to pick up a permit for Hānàsī Hú.

There is nowhere to change travellers cheques in Bù'ěrjīn, but the local Industrial & Commercial Bank (ICBC) can change major currencies.

Places to Stay
Bù'ěrjīn Lǚyóu Bīnguǎn (☎ 652 1325, fax 652 1201, Huangcheng Nanlu) Twins/triples/quads Y65/30/20 per bed, singles Y95. This is a more pleasant and comfortable option though hot water is quite unreliable. The grounds are spacious and big enough to take a stroll.

Jiākèsī Jiǔdiàn (☎/fax 652 1716, 2 Xiangyang Nanlu) Dorm beds Y20, twins with bath Y60 per bed. This is another reasonable option, where the hot water is turned on from 10pm to 1am. The staff is very helpful.

Jiāotōng Bīnguǎn (Wenming Lu) Triples/quads Y20/10 per bed, singles Y70. The most convenient place to stay is this hotel at the bus station. The rooms are nothing special and there is often no hot water, but the staff is friendly. The PSB has some sort of beef with this place so they may not be able to take you.

Places to Eat
Duōwèi Kǎonángdiàn (Wenming Lu) Dishes from Y5. You will find the best freshly baked *nang* in Xīnjiāng at this place.

Yínchuān Huímín Fàndiàn (Wenming Lu) This place, which serves up a tasty bowl of spicy *niúròumiàn* noodles, is just next door.

Opposite Jiākèsī Jiǔdiàn is a great night market specialising in regional fresh fish grilled on skewers. You can also get good kebabs.

SILK ROAD

BÙ'ĚRJĪN 布尔津

PLACES TO STAY & EAT		11	Bù'ěrjīn Lǚyóu
1	Yínchuān Huímín Fàndiàn 银川回民饭店		Bīnguǎn 布尔津旅游宾馆
2	Duōwèi Kǎonángdiàn 多味烤馕店	**OTHER**	
3	Jiāotōng Bīnguǎn 交通宾馆	4	Bus Station 客运站
5	Nánqiáo Dìèr Huímín Shítáng 南桥第二回民食堂	6	PSB 公安局外事科
8	Jiākèsī Jiǔdiàn 嘉客思酒店	7	Post & Telephone Office 邮电局
10	Night Market 夜市	9	ICBC 中国工商银行

To Hānàsī Hú (150km)
To Altai (91km)
To Jeminay (75km)
To Ürümqi (560km)

Huangcheng Beilu
Huangcheng Nanlu
Xiangyang Lu
Shengli Lu
Wenming Lu
Xinfu Lu
Jianxin Lu

0   200   400m
0   200   400yd

Getting There & Away

Buses from Ürümqi leave in the evening and take around 15 hours to get to Bù'ěrjīn. Seats cost Y94 to Y110. Tickets can be bought at either the main bus station or the alternative bus station for the Altai region (Ālètài bànshìchǔ), which is on Hetan Dongyijie, just after the overpass and north of Qiantangjiang Lu. Heading back to Ürümqi there are departures at 4pm, 5pm and 6pm though any bus from the north will stop here and pick up passengers.

There are two daily buses to Chōnghū'ǎr (Y11, two hours) at 4am and 5pm. There are regular buses to Kaba (Y7, one hour) and to Jímǔnǎi (Y11, two hours).

HANAS LAKE NATURE RESERVE

Hānàsī Hú Zìrán Bǎohùqū哈纳斯湖自然保护区
The most splendid sight in the Altai region is Hānàsī Hú, an alpine lagoon surrounded by pines, boulders and mountains. In the autumn, the aspen and maple trees provide a scenic backdrop of riotous colour.

The whole area has a diverse range of flora and fauna. In addition to the camels, cattle, horses, sheep, and goats, there are also eagles, brown bears, lynx, snow leopards, black storks and lots of squirrels. The forests are dominated by spruce, birch, elm, poplar, Korean pine and Siberian larch.

The trip to Hānàsī Hú is stunning, with beautiful vistas that range from desert, to grasslands, to alpine wilderness. Along the way you pass hundreds of semi-nomadic Kazakhs, who are either on their way up or down the valley, depending on the season. The latter half of the road runs along the roaring Hānàsī Hé. As the road slowly winds its way up to Hānàsī Hú, 1370m elevation, there are many scenic spots along the road that are worth stopping at to take in the beauty.

There are many possibilities for hiking in and around the lake. In fact, there is even more incredible scenery in the neighbouring valley of **Hemu Hanas** (Hémù Kānàsī), and **Bai Kaba** (Báihābā) village. For those more content with day hikes, there are a couple of paths that lead out from the tourist village of Hānàsī.

A popular day walk is the trip to **Guānyú Pavilion** (Guānyú Tíng; 2030m), the peak on the other side of the lake. It's a 1½-hour walk from the river up the steps to the pavilion. From the top you are rewarded with panoramic views of the lake, the mountains and surrounding grasslands. It is possible to return to Hānàsī via a circuitous scenic route down the eastern slope by following the dirt road. The round walk takes a lazy five hours.

It's also possible to climb the mountains behind the tourist camp or even partly around the lake to some nearby rock paintings.

Boats also leave from the pier to **Shuāng Hú** (Twin Lakes) and up to the head waters of the lake (though this is pricey).

The area is really only easily accessible from June to early October, with ice and heavy snow closing the road between October and May. There isn't really any summer up here, more a gradual transition from autumn to spring, with the temperature remaining pleasant throughout.

During June and July a blanket of alpine flowers accentuates the beauty of the region. In August wild berries litter the ground. In September and October the first snow starts to fall and the forests begin to turn a brilliant red and yellow. Winter trips are also possible by trekking in on horseback, on skis or for the well endowed, snow jet skis.

Places to Stay

An accommodation construction boom is currently underway and no doubt the area will undergo some dramatic changes. Hopefully the impact on the environment can be minimised.

Officially, the only option for foreigners is the tourist bureau's cabins and yurts. Most of these are located in the northern section of the tourist village. Rates range from Y25 per person in a yurt to Y200 for a twin room with bathroom. Unofficially, we found locals willing to take us into their yurt for as little as Y15, with no meals. During the peak summer months, there are nightly barbecues around the yurts accompanied by Kazakh and Mongolian dancing and a roaring bonfire.

The best accommodation up here is either staying in a yurt with some Kazakhs and Mongolians, or bringing your tent with you and heading out into the great wilderness. Some of the best places for camping are actually along the route up to Hānàsī Hú after the town of Chōnghŭ'ăr. Chinese tourists are already doing this, but the officials are still a bit nervous about foreigners making their own plans. If you do head off, make sure you are equipped to deal with freezing temperatures and heavy rain, both of which are common throughout the year.

Getting There & Away

This is the hard part. The lake is a 145km stunning journey from Bù'ěrjīn. During July and August there should be tourist buses (Y50) that head up to the lake from Bù'ěrjīn's bus station. Unfortunately, they're becoming pretty scarce – we found none on a recent July visit – because almost all tourists come here with tour groups from Ürümqi. You could have a long wait, hoping for solo travellers to show up to split a taxi.

A more flexible option is to hire a 4WD (Y500/Y700 one way/return), which allows you to stop and take photos along the way. The drive takes about five to six hours.

You might also consider a tour. Travellers have recommended the four-day trip out of Ürümqi with the Overseas Chinese Travel Service (see the Ürümqi section, previously, for details) in Bógédá Bīnguăn. For Y900 you get a comfy air-con van ride, two nights in a comfy double room in Bù'ěrjīn, PSB permit, entrance ticket and one night's lodging at an inn at the lake. It saves a *lot* of slogging and is actually fairly economical when you break it down. Plus, the other travellers are often from Hong Kong or Singapore, so you'll likely be with English speakers.

The road from Bù'ěrjīn passes through Chōnghŭěr, Hāliútān, and Jìadè Dēngyù before reaching the tourist town of Hānàsī. All of these towns have restaurants and small supply stores. The main road is sealed to just past Chōnghŭ'ăr, but there are plans to widen and seal the road all the way to the lake. In fact, the tourist bureau also plans to construct a runway up here, but hopefully this will take a bit longer.

Entrance to the Hanas Lake Nature Reserve costs Y50, but foreigners are also expected to pay an extra Y6 per day to ensure the ongoing protection of the area.

Before you head up to Hānàsī Hú, drop into Bù'ěrjīn's PSB to arrange a permit. The permit costs Y52, plus an extra Y50 deposit, which the staff give back to you when you return from your trip. If you are interested in visiting other areas or villages, then make sure you include them on the permit. There are a number of checkpoints throughout the whole region, where you will be asked to hand over your permit and sometimes your passport. This regimentation will probably fade away as time goes on and more and more foreigners make their way up here.

Friendship Peak 友谊峰

Yŏuyì Fēng

At 4374m, this is the highest summit in this mountainous area. Standing on the glacier-covered summit allows you to be in three nations at once. Presumably you won't need a visa for each one, but you will need a climbing permit, a guide, an ice axe, crampons and other appropriate mountaineering paraphernalia.

JÍMŬNĂI 吉木乃

The only reason you would want to visit this little town is if you are heading for Kazakhstan. The border checkpoint is 18km from town. The border here has become more popular in recent years due to the irregularity of the crossing at Tăchéng, but border guards are still not used to foreigners and you should come armed with a plan B in case you don't get through. The first major town in Kazakhstan is Maykipchagay, from where you can catch a taxi to Zaysan and then a bus to Semey (12 hours).

There are a couple of buses that depart from the bus station and the main intersection for Ürümqi between 4pm and 5pm daily. The trip takes 14 hours and costs Y52 for a seat or Y100 for a sleeper, although prices are negotiable with the private operators. There are four daily buses that make the dusty trip to Bù'ěrjīn (Y11, two hours).

There is no reliable public transport to the border, but you can catch a taxi there for Y25. Coming the other way you can share a taxi to Jímŭnăi for Y5.

TĂCHÉNG 塔城

Located in a lonely corner of north-west Xīnjiāng, Tăchéng is a relatively obscure border crossing into neighbouring Kazakhstan. Life here is usually pretty slow and relaxed, but things have dropped a tempo in recent years due to the closure of the Kazakh side of the border. Locals report that the Kazakh customs are a little erratic in charging duties and were therefore shutdown. However, now and then the gates are opened and a rush of trade starts to flow through the main streets again. If you do make it here and discover the border closed, don't despair, Tǎchéng is a pleasant enough place to relax before catching a bus south to Alashankou or north to Jímǔnǎi.

Note that the city is open, but other parts of the region are closed to foreigners, so know where you're going.

Information

The post and telephone office in the centre of town, on the corner of Xinhua Lu and Ta'er Bahetai Lu. The PSB is on Jianshe Jie

The Bank of China is south of here on Guangming Lu and can handle both cash and travellers cheques.

Places to Stay & Eat

Tǎchéng Bīnguǎn (☎ 622 2093, *Youhao Jie*) Dorm beds with bath Y20/30, main hotel twins Y80-160. This hotel, tucked away in the north-west of town, offers beds in a Russian-style building. The rooms come complete with cracked ornate plaster, broken windows, peeling paint and wet carpet. The twins here are comfortable and the hotel has 24-hour hot water.

Tǎchéngshì Kèyùn Bīnguǎn (☎ 622 2544) Dorm beds with shared bath Y10-18, twins/triples Y25/50 per bed. This is the cheapest option in town. Twins here are simple and triples come with a large sofa. There is hot water from 10pm to 2am.

Yínxiáng Bīnguǎn (☎ 622 2222, *ext 2666*) Twins/suites Y124/188. The most upmarket option is this hotel. The suites come complete with living room and a large double bed. It has 24-hour hot water and can usually offer a bit of a discount on all rooms.

There is a great *night market* in front of the cinema on Xinhua Lu, just opposite Yínxiáng Bīnguǎn. It has an amazing array of dishes for all budgets and tastes.

Yuèliangchéng (*Ta'er Bahetai Lu*) Dishes from Y5. This restaurant has a good range of cheap and tasty Chinese dishes. It is adjacent to the post office; look for the pink characters on the window.

Getting There & Away

Air There are flights on Monday, Wednesday, Friday and Sunday between Ürümqi and Tǎchéng (Y310). Tickets can be purchased from CAAC (☎ 622 3428). The shuttle bus to the airport also departs from here.

Bus There is one daily bus to Tǎchéng (Y84, 12 to 15 hours) from Ürümqi, departing at 7pm. From Tǎchéng to Ürümqi the time and price are similar.

Getting Around

Taxi Tǎchéng is small enough to get around on foot. Taxis cost Y5 to get around town or Y20 if you want to head down to the border checkpoint. If you have come from Kazakhstan, then you can share a taxi for Y5 into town.

YĪNÍNG 伊宁
pop 216,600

Also known as Gulja, Yīníng lies close to the Kazakhstan border, about 390km west of Ürümqi. It is the centre of the Ili Kazak Autonomous Prefecture.

The Ili Valley (Yīlí Gǔ) has, in times past, been an easy access point for invaders, as well as for the northern route of the Silk Road. The Russian influence has probably been the most influential, not counting the obvious Han influence. Yīníng was occupied by Russian troops in 1872 during Yakub Beg's independent rule of Kashgaria. Five years later, the Chinese cracked down on Yakub Beg and Yīníng was handed back by the Russians. In 1962 there were major Sino-Soviet clashes along Yīlí Hé (Ili River).

Today Yīníng has little to show for this influence: a few faded remnants of Russian architecture and street names. Overall there's not much to the town itself, other than enjoying the surrounding scenery. The best of which can be seen along the roads from Ürümqi and Kùchē that pass through some spectacular desert, grassland and alpine landscapes.

More recently, Yīníng was the scene of violent riots started by Uyghur separatists, resulting in a number of deaths. Although the riots were swiftly quelled, underlying tension and resentment continues. Despite this, there is little trace today of a turbulent

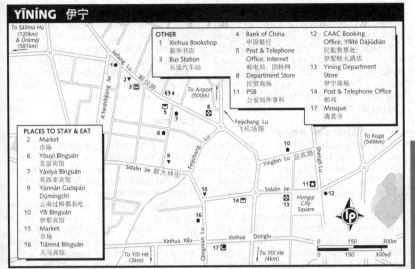

YĪNÍNG 伊宁

OTHER
1 Xinhua Bookshop 新华书店
3 Bus Station 长途汽车站

4 Bank of China 中国银行
5 Post & Telephone Office; Internet 邮电局; 因я网
8 Department Store 民贸商场
11 PSB 公安局外事科

12 CAAC Booking Office; Yīlitè Dàjiǔdiàn 民航售票处; 伊犁特大酒店
13 Yining Department Store 伊宁商场
14 Post & Telephone Office 邮局
17 Mosque 清真寺

PLACES TO STAY & EAT
2 Market 市场
6 Yǒuyì Bīnguǎn 友谊宾馆
7 Yàxīyà Bīnguǎn 亚西亚宾馆
9 Yúnnán Guòqiáo Dūmíngchī 云南过桥都名吃
10 Yīlí Bīnguǎn 伊犁宾馆
15 Market 市场
16 Tiānmǎ Bīnguǎn 天马宾馆

To Sàilmù Hú (120km) & Ūrūmqi (581km)

To Airport (500m)

Feijichang Lu 飞机场路

To Kuga (549km)

Sidalin Jie 斯大林街

Yingbin Lu 迎宾路

Shengli Lu

Sidalin Jie

Hongqi City Square

Xinhua Xilu

Xinhua Donglu

To Yīlí Hé (3km)

To Yīlí Hé (4km)

SILK ROAD

past. The people of Yīníng are a pretty friendly bunch and at night during the warmer months the streets are often bustling with night markets and small eateries.

Information

The PSB is opposite Yīlítè Dàjiǔdiàn (Yilite Grand Hotel) on Sidalin Jie. The Bank of China is opposite the post and telephone office, which is right on the big traffic circle in the centre of town. There is also another post and telephone office east of the bus station on Jiefang Lu. Internet access is available on the 2nd floor of this office. Xinhua Bookshop is about 500m west of the bus station, on the 2nd floor of the department store. You can pick up a city map here.

Things to See

Just to the south of town is **Yīlí Hé** (Ili River), a popular recreational area with the locals. Down by the river are some pleasant restaurants, teahouses and bars – it's a good place to relax and enjoy the river passing you by. To get there, hop on bus No 2 and get off at the last stop, just before the bridge over the river.

Places to Stay & Eat

Yǒuyì Bīnguǎn (Friendship Hotel; ☎ *802 3901, fax 802 4631, 73 Hang Sidalin Jie)* Triples Y40 per bed, singles/twins from Y100/120. Budget travellers can try this place. It isn't that easy to find – it's down an obscure side street and the only sign pointing the way is in Chinese. They're friendly here and the rooms are excellent value.

Yàxīyà Bīnguǎn (Asia Hotel; ☎ *803 1800, fax 803 6077, 119 Hang Sidalin Jie)* Twins/triples Y50/36 per bed, doubles Y110. This place is fine but not as good as Yǒuyì Bīnguǎn.

Tiānmǎ Bīnguǎn (☎ *802 2800, fax 802 2662, 10 Qingnian Lu)* Quads with shared bath Y22 per bed, twins Y80-116. Other than the cigarette burns in the carpet and the decrepit common areas, this nine-storey white tiled hotel is the cheapest in town and has rooms that are clean and good value – look at a few. Look out for the small English sign that reads 'Fixed Hotel for overseas visitors'.

Yīlí Bīnguǎn (☎ *802 3799, fax 802 4964, 8 Yingbin Lu)* Triples Y40 per bed, older-wing twins Y110-150, new-wing twins Y360. The triples here are clean and the new wing is three-star. It has very pleasant tree-shaded grounds, in fact you almost need a map to find your way around. If you are looking for some remnants of Soviet architecture, this is where you will find it, complete with a bust of Lenin at the entrance.

There are plenty of *street markets* that set up stalls in the evenings around town.

Yúnnán Guòqiáo Dūmíngchī (Yunnan Across-the-Bridge Noodle Capital; ☎ 803 5915, Sidalin Jie) Dishes from Y8. It is an unexpected surprise to find this famed southwest China standard fare here. You can get a variety of these noodles in which steaming water cooks the ingredients you choose as you wait; prices range from a basic bowl (Y8) to the super deluxe bowl (Y25).

Getting There & Away

Air There are daily flights between Ürümqi and Yīníng for Y590, usually late at night. There's a CAAC office inside Yīlítè Dàjiǔdiàn, opposite Hóngqí City Square (Hóngqí Guǎngchǎng). A taxi to the airport is Y7.

Bus Between 9am and 6pm buses leave every hour from Ürümqi. The 581km ride takes 12 to 16 hours. Departures from Yīníng start at around 8am. Sleepers cost Y100; there are also the occasional express air-con buses (Y125, nine hours). There is a spectacular bus ride to Kùchē in the south, which passes over Tiān Shān and through the small Mongolian village of Bayanbulak: a good place to break the journey. A daily bus leaves at 10.30am and seats costs Y59 for the 22-hour trip; a sleeper (Y117) also makes the run. Buses leave three times daily to Kashgar.

It is possible to travel by bus from Yīníng to Almaty in Kazakhstan. Buses leave Yīníng on Monday, Wednesday, Thursday and Saturday around 6.30am. The ticket office is in the main waiting hall, next to the customs office. Tickets cost US$30.

AROUND YĪNÍNG
Ili Valley 伊犁谷
Yīlí Gǔ

About 6km south of the town centre is a bridge over Yīlí Hé. The Ili Valley is pretty

– the roads are lined with tall birch trees and there are farms everywhere. This is dairy country and home to some 20,000 Xibe (Xībózú) people, who were dispatched to safeguard the region by the Manchus. They have proudly retained their own language and writing system and continue to live in a relatively closed community.

Sàilǐmù Hú 赛里木湖
Sayram Lake

Large and beautiful Sàilǐmù Hú is 120km north of Yīníng, and offers some nice hiking opportunities. The lake is especially colourful during June and July, when alpine flowers blanket the ground.

A village consisting mainly of yurts has sprung up on the main road to cater for the influx of tourists during July and August. The first signs of inadequate management are already revealing themselves in the form of scum along the shore of the lake. If you would prefer peace and tranquillity rather than *kok* (karaoke) and traffic, then just hop off the bus anywhere along the lake and set off. If you need a quick getaway then there are horses and speedboats for hire from the village.

If you want to spend some time exploring this alpine lake area, then bring a tent. There is food up here, but the selection is limited and prices expensive, so bring what you need. Otherwise there are plenty of Kazakh yurts (usually charging Y30 per night with meals) around the lake willing to take a boarder.

Buses from Yīníng to Sàilǐmù Hú take about three hours. From Kyutun it takes 6½ hours and costs Y30. All buses between Ürümqi and Yīníng pass by the lake, so just stand by the road and wave a passing bus down.

Gānsù 甘肃

Capital: Lánzhōu
Population: 24.7 million
Area: 450,000 sq km

A rugged, barren province consisting mostly of mountains and deserts, Gānsù has long been a poor and forgotten backwater controlled only loosely by Běijīng. Nonetheless it has played an important role in Chinese history. Threading its way through Gānsù was the famed Silk Road, the ancient highway along which camel caravans carried goods in and out of China.

Travellers and merchants from as far as the Roman Empire entered the Middle Kingdom via the Silk Road using a string of oasis towns as stepping-stones through the barren landscape. Buddhism was also carried into China along the Silk Road, and the Buddhist cave temples that are found all the way from Xīnjiāng through Gānsù and up through northern China are reminders of the influx of ideas that were made possible by the road. The Great Wall extended to here but much of it has crumbled in this region.

Traditionally the towns of Gānsù have been established in the oases along the major caravan route where agriculture is possible. With the arrival of modern transport, some industrial development and mining has taken place. The 1892km Lánzhōu-Ürümqi railway line, completed in 1963, was one of the greatest achievements of the early Communist regime, and it has done much to relieve the isolation of this region. Today, tourism is an important cash cow, especially in Lánzhōu, Dūnhuáng and Jiāyùguān.

Gānsù is home to a considerable variety of minority peoples, including the Hui, Mongols, Tibetans and Kazaks, although the Chinese Han are now in the vast majority.

LÁNZHŌU 兰州
☎ 0931 • pop 2,804,600
Gānsù's capital, Lánzhōu has been an important garrison town and transport centre since ancient times. Its development as an industrial centre began after the Communist

Highlights

- Bǐnglíng Sì, Buddhist grottoes carved into a splendid area of cliffs towering over a branch of Huáng Hé (Yellow River)

- Dūnhuáng, home of the stunning Mògāo Caves, set amid towering sand dunes

- The Tibetan monastery town of Xiàhé, a magnet for pilgrims and a tranquil break from the rigours of the road

- Píngliáng, site of Kōngtóng Shān, one of China's sacred Taoist mountains

- Màijī Shān – home to one of China's largest grotto and temple groups

victory and the city's subsequent integration into China's expanding national rail network. The city's population increased more than tenfold in little more than a generation. China's economic reform policies have spurred further growth, and office towers and new housing blocks are sprouting up throughout the city.

Although Lánzhōu is not a major tourist drawcard in itself, there are some interesting sights in the surrounding area. Lánzhōu's strategic location also makes it an important transport hub for travellers heading into western China.

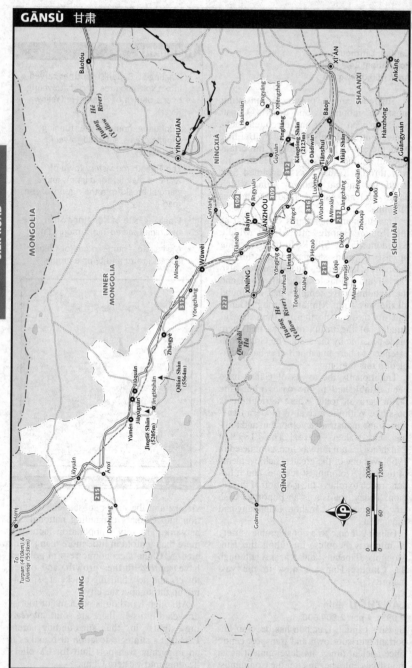

GĀNSÙ 甘肃

Orientation

Geography has conspired to make Lánzhōu a city of awkward design. At 1600m above sea level, the city is crammed into a narrow valley walled in by steep mountains, forcing it to develop westwards in a long, urban corridor that extends for more than 20km along the southern banks of Huáng Hé (Yellow River).

The valley is a perfect trap for exhaust fumes from motor vehicles and chimneys, often burying Lánzhōu in a perpetual haze of pollution. Nevertheless, the rugged topography does give the city a certain unique charm, which is augmented by the general friendliness of the locals.

Information

Money The main branch of the Bank of China is in a brand new tower on Tianshui Lu. Banking hours are 9.30am to noon and 2pm to 5pm Monday to Friday and 10am to 4pm Saturday. There is another branch on the southern side of Dōngfānghóng Square (Dōngfānghóng Guǎngchǎng).

Post & Communications The main post and telephone office is on the corner of Minzhu Lu and Pingliang Lu and is open daily from 8am to 7pm. There is also a post office across from Lánzhōu's main train station and another near the west bus station.

For Internet access, simply wander in any direction from the entrance of Lanzhou University along Tianshui Lu and you'll find an Internet bar (at last count there were five in a two-square block area). All charge Y3 per hour.

Travel Agencies China International Travel Service (CITS; Zhōngguó Guójì Lǚxíngshè; ☎/fax 881 3222) is on the 2nd floor of the Tourism Building on Nongmin Xiang, the street running behind Lánzhōu Fàndiàn (see Places to Stay later). You can also find a smaller office (☎ 840 0001) on the eastern side of Dōngfānghóng Square and another (☎ 872 1333) on Donggang Xilu just west of Tianshui Lu.

Heaps of travel agents cater to the foreign market, offering one-day and overnight tours to scenic spots in the vicinity of Lánzhōu.

One place worth checking out is the reliable Western Travel Service (☎ 841 6321 ext 8638, fax 841 8608), located in the west wing of Lánzhōu Fàndiàn. It readily gives out information regardless of whether you bring it business, and its prices for tours and ticket bookings are competitive.

PSB The Public Security Bureau (PSB; Gōngānjú; ☎ 882 7961 ext 4421) is at 38 Qingyang Lu, near the Dōngfānghóng Square. The office is on the left before you go through the main gate, look for the 'Reception Room' sign. It's open Monday to Friday 9am to 11.30am and 3pm to 5pm but it's closed Tuesday afternoons. Some travellers have been referred to another office a few minutes away on Wudu Lu.

Gansu Provincial Museum
Gānsù Shěng Bówùguǎn 甘博物馆

If you're into them, you should enjoy this museum (Xijin Xilu; admission Y25; open 9am-5pm Tues-Sun). The 'Cultural Relics of the Silk Road' exhibition features Neolithic painted pottery taken from a site 300km south-east of here at Dàdìwān. Dàdìwān culture existed at least 7000 years ago and is thought by some archaeologists to predate the better known Yangshao culture.

Exhibits from the Han dynasty include inscribed wooden tablets used to relay messages along the Silk Road and an outstanding 1.5m-high Tang-dynasty warrior made from glaze-coloured earthenware. Also interesting is a 2nd century BC gilded silver plate depicting Bacchus, the Greco-Roman God of Wine, from the eastern Roman Empire. It was unearthed in 1989 at Jīngyuán, 120km north-east of Lánzhōu, and is evidence of significant contact between the two ancient civilisations.

Lánshān Gōngyuán 兰山公园

The mountain range of Lán Shān rises steeply to the south of Lánzhōu. The temperature at its 2100m-high summit is normally a good 5°C cooler than in the valley, so it's a good retreat in summer.

The quickest and easiest way up is by chairlift (lánshān lǎnchē) from behind **Wǔquán Gōngyuán** (Five Springs Park; admission Y3; open 9am-10pm). The chairlift takes about 20 minutes to make the diagonal climb to the upper terminal. On the summit you'll find **Sāntái Gé**, refreshment

LÁNZHŌU 兰州

stands and a fun-park. A paved trail zigzags its way back down to Wǔquán Gōngyuán, although it's a long walk.

Getting here can take some effort. From the main train station take bus No 31 or 34 five stops to Wǔquán stop, get off and walk back until you reach Wuquan Lu. Turn right here and walk about 500m to the Wǔquán Gōngyuán ticket office. You can access the chairlift by going through the park. Otherwise, you can catch a taxi to the chairlift terminus. For foreigners, the chairlift costs Y10 for the ride up or Y18 return. During summer the locals usually head up to the peak of Lán Shān to enjoy the sunset and the city's night lights.

Báitǎ Shān 白塔山
White Pagoda Hill

This pleasant, well-managed park (admission Y6; open 6.30am-10pm summer) is on the northern bank of Huáng Hé, near the Zhōngshān Bridge. The steep slopes are terraced, with small walkways leading through the forest to pavilions, teahouses and a plant nursery on a secluded hillside. The chairlift costs Y12/16 one way/return.

On top of the hill is **Báitǎ Sì** (White Pagoda Temple), originally built during the Yuan dynasty (AD 1206–1368), from where you get a good view across the city. There are several mosques on the park periphery. It's possible to catch the chairlift across Huáng Hé to the park. The terminal is just to the west of Zhōngshān Bridge and the last chairlift departs at 7pm. Minibus No 101 comes here from in front of the train station on Tianshui Lu.

Places to Stay

Lánzhōu Dàshà (☎ 841 7210, fax 841 7177, 7-9 Tianshui Lu) Triples with/without bath Y25/24 per person, twins with bath Y82-120. The room prices here are not such a bad deal for Lánzhōu. The main advantage of staying here is its proximity to the station.

Lánshān Bīnguǎn (☎ 861 7211, fax 861 4475, 6 Tianshui Lu) Singles Y66, twins/triples/quads Y26/22/18 per bed. This is a very humble abode and the staff would prefer you took the whole room. The singles are good value. Hot water is available from 8pm to 11pm.

LÁNZHŌU

PLACES TO STAY

5 Yǒuyì Bīnguǎn
友谊宾馆

23 Lánzhōu Fàndiàn;
Western Travel Service
兰州饭店；西部旅行社

26 Lánzhōu Fēitiān
Dàjiǔdiàn
兰州飞天大酒店

33 Wànzhòng Dàshà
万众大厦

34 Lánshān Bīnguǎn
兰山宾馆

35 Lánzhōu Dàshà
兰州大厦

37 Xīnshìjì Jiǔdiàn
新世纪酒店

PLACES TO EAT

7 Snack Tents
帐篷

19 Nóngmín Xiàng
(Street Food Stalls)
农民巷

22 Bǎisùjī
百岁鸡

25 Bakery
面包店

32 Dingxi Nanlu Day
Market
定西南路市场

OTHER

1 Post & Telephone Office
邮电局

2 Huangjin Shopping Centre
黄金大厦

3 West Train Station
火车西站

4 Gansu Provincial Museum
省博物馆

6 West Bus Station
汽车西站

8 Báitǎ Sì
白塔寺

9 Asia-Europe Shopping
Centre
亚欧商厦

10 Jinda Shopping Centre
金达商厦

11 Department Store
民百大楼

12 PICC Office
中国人民保险公司

13 Telephone & Telegram
Office
电信大楼

14 PSB
公安局

15 PSB
公安局

16 Bank of China
中国银行

17 Dōngfānghóng Square
东方红广场

18 CITS
中国国际旅行社

20 CITS
中国国际旅行社

21 China Northwest
Airlines Booking Office
(CAAC)
中国西北航空公司售票
处

24 CITS
中国国际旅行社

27 Lanzhou University
兰州大学

28 Main Bank of China
中国银行

29 Xinhua Bookshop
新华书店

30 East Bus Station
汽车东站

31 Post & Telephone
Office
邮电局

36 Main Train
Station
火车总站

38 Post & Telephone
Office
邮电局

SILK ROAD

Wànzhòng Dàshà (☎ *863 8918, fax 861 9747, 50 Tianshui Lu*) Doubles Y120-168. This is a newer place and if these introductory prices hold, it'll be a steal. The rooms are clean and well-maintained.

Lánzhōu Fàndiàn (☎ *841 6321, fax 841 8608, 434 Donggang Xilu*) Triples with bath Y40 per bed, older-wing twins Y120-230, main-building twins Y480. This is a large, fully renovated Sino-Stalinist edifice, and a pleasant place to stay. It offers clean, comfortable triples at the higher end of the budget range, but they are decidedly worth it. The twins in the older wings are also a good price for Lánzhōu. The staff is usually open to a bit of friendly bargaining on most rooms. The hotel is a 20-minute walk from the main train station or you can take bus No 1 or 7 for two stops.

Xīnshìjì Jiǔdiàn (New Century Hotel; ☎ *861 5888, fax 861 9133, 109-1 Huochezhan Donglu*) Twins/suites from Y428/675. This hotel has upper mid-range prices and very comfortable rooms. It was offering 40% off these prices when we last checked. Rates include buffet breakfast.

Lánzhōu Fēitiān Dàjiǔdiàn (Lanzhou Legend Hotel; ☎ *888 2876*, ⓔ *legend@ public.lz.gs.cn, 599 Tianshui Lu*) Twins Y623-690. This four-star hotel is the most upmarket place in town, with discounted rates. Rates include a delicious buffet breakfast.

Yǒuyì Bīnguǎn (Friendship Hotel; ☎ *233 3051, fax 233 0304, 16 Xijin Xilu*) Old-wing doubles without bath Y64, 3-star doubles Y380. This is a fairly upmarket place on the western side of town. It's only handy if you're catching the early bus to Xiàhé from the west bus station or visiting the Gansu Provincial Museum.

Places to Eat

One of the best spots for street food is Nongmin Xiang. The street is lined with small restaurants and food stalls. At the east end, across from CITS, are a few good places that have tasty, inexpensive dishes.

Travel Insurance

A regulation requires that foreigners who travel by public bus in Gānsù must be insured with the People's Insurance Company of China (PICC), regardless of whether they have taken out their own travel insurance or not.

Some long-distance bus stations may refuse to sell you a ticket unless you can show them your PICC insurance, or else they will charge you double for an 'insurance fee' on the spot (no receipt issued though).

The requirement is currently being enforced mainly on routes in and out of Lánzhōu and in eastern Gānsù. Ironically, you couldn't actually collect anything from this insurance policy if you were involved in some sort of accident – it is there to insure the government bus company against lawsuits.

You can buy insurance at most bus stations throughout Gānsù. If they don't sell it, then they probably don't need to see it. It costs Y40 for 20 days; after that it's possible to renew it. CITS and some of the hotels charge an additional Y5 to Y10 commission. Sadly, it's worth buying the insurance, just to avoid further hassles on buses and at the bus station.

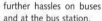

Both Dingxi Beilu and Dingxi Nanlu, just south of Lanzhou University, have rows of *restaurants* and *street stalls*. Prices here are a bit cheaper, to cater to the student clientele. Several typical Lánzhōu specialities are sold on the streets. One is called *ròujiābǐng*, which is lamb or pork fried with onion, capsicum and a dash of paprika, served inside a 'pocket' of flat bread.

Just 50m to the west of Lánzhōu Fàndiàn is *Bǎisùìjī* or literally '100-year-old chook', which is a chain of hotpot, spicy chicken restaurants. The chicken is cooked in a large wok at your table in a broth of carrots, zucchini, celery, onion, coriander and mushrooms. You will need a minimum of two people to finish the smallest serving *(xiǎo xiǎo guō)*. Try adding *tǔdòu* (potato), *dòufu* (tofu) and *fěntiáo* (noodles) and wash it all down with a cold draft beer (Y5).

Lánzhōu is famous for its *niúròumiàn* (beef noodles served in spicy soup) – if you don't want the chillies, say '*búyào làjiāo*'. There are a number of fine places to try this around town.

Down by Huáng Hé, near Zhōngshān Bridge, are dozens of *tents* serving tea, beer and snacks. It's possible to sit back in a banana chair and sink some beers, shoot some pool and watch the sun go down over the murky waters of China's No 2 river. For the more active, there are horse riding, speed boats and balloon shooting.

Just next to Lánzhōu Fēitiān Dàjiǔdiàn is a small *bakery* that makes a delicious banana cake loaf that is great for day hikes.

Getting There & Away

Air China Northwest Airlines has a booking office (☎ 882 1964) on Donggang Xilu. It's open from 8am to 9pm daily.

There are daily flights to Běijīng (Y1220), Chéngdū (Y860), Guǎngzhōu (Y1660), Ürümqi (Y1210) and Xī'ān (Y550). Other destinations include Kūnmíng, Shànghǎi, Shēnzhèn, Fúzhōu, Hángzhōu, Nánjīng, Qīngdǎo, Shěnyáng, Xiàmén and Wǔhàn.

Bus The west bus station (qìchē xīzhàn) on Xijin Xilu handles departures to Liújiāxiá, near Bǐnglíng Sì, Línxià, Xiàhé, Hézuò, Zhāngyè and Dūnhuáng. Foreigners have to purchase PICC insurance (see the boxed text 'Travel Insurance' for more details). For more information see the Getting There & Away section for the relevant destination.

Many travellers have reported that the private bus operators that tout at the bus station are unreliable and prone to ripping travellers off. Many claim to be going to Xiàhé, but instead terminate at Línxià or drop you off at the turn-off for Xiàhé. It's always best to purchase tickets from the ticket office inside, unless you are able to broker a reasonable deal in Chinese with a driver.

The east bus station on Pingliang Lu has departures for mainly eastern destinations. Staff here aren't as quick as their west station counterparts to check foreigners for insurance. There is one nightly sleeper to Xī'ān (Y138, 15 hours) and an evening bus for Yínchuān (Y75 sleeper, 10 hours) and Tiānshuǐ (Y41, Y64 sleeper, eight hours). There are buses every hour to Píngliáng (Y52 to Y70, seven hours) and one bus daily to Gùyuán (in Níngxià) leaving at 6.30am.

Train Trains run to: Ürümqi; Běijīng via Hohhot and Dàtóng; Golmud via Xīníng; Shànghǎi via Xī'ān and Zhèngzhōu; and

Běijīng via Xī'ān and Zhèngzhōu. You can also go south to Chéngdū. Heading west, it takes 10½ hours to reach Jiāyùguān, 20 hours to Liǔyuán, 30 hours to Turpan and 30½ hours to Ürümqi. The most popular route west is to Ürümqi (hard sleeper Y225), for which train No 2197 is probably best, and Xī'ān (hard sleeper Y175) to the east, for which train No K120 is good.

Now the bad news: Lánzhōu is notorious for getting travellers stranded, unable to land a train ticket, even if the train begins here. The earlier you buy, the better your chances. Tickets can be bought up to five days in advance, especially sleeper tickets for trains starting from Lánzhōu.

Getting Around

The airport is at Zhōngchuān, almost 90km north of the city. Airport buses (Y25, 1¼ hours) leave from the Civil Aviation Administration of China (CAAC; Zhōngguó Mínháng) office three hours before scheduled flight departures.

The most useful bus routes are Nos 1 and 31 running from the main train station to the west bus station and Yoǔyì Bīnguǎn. Bus Nos 7 and 10 run from the main train station up the length of Tianshui Lu before heading west and east, respectively. Public buses cost between Y0.3 and Y1.

AROUND LÁNZHŌU

Bǐnglíng Sì

Located 75km south-west of Lánzhōu, this set of Buddhist grottoes (admission Y20-30) carved into the cliffs of a 60m-high gorge is one of the more unusual sights in Gānsù. Isolated by the waters of the Liújiāxiá Reservoir (Liújiāxiá Shǐkù) on Huáng Hé, the grottoes were spared the vandalism of the Cultural Revolution.

The reservoir itself at one time actually threatened to inundate the caves, but a levy now protects the area from flooding during high-water periods.

Bǐnglíng Sì is also called the Thousand Buddha Caves (Qiān Fó Dòng), although in fact the total number of caves is only 183. The setting is spectacular, with soaring cliffs composed of eroded and porous rock with numerous natural cavities. The creators of these grottoes dangled from ropes while carving their masterpieces into the face of the cliffs.

The oldest caves have been repaired and added to on numerous occasions since they were built during the Western Qin dynasty. They contain 694 statues, 82 clay sculptures and a number of frescoes. Cave 169, containing a Buddha and two Bodhisattvas, is one of the oldest (AD 420) and best preserved in China. Most of the other caves were completed during the prosperous Tang dynasty. The star of the caves is the 27m-high seated statue of Maitreya, the Future Buddha (cave 172).

Depending on which caves you want to see, entry prices vary. The cheaper tickets are for the unlocked caves, while the Y300 ticket gives you a complete guided tour that includes the magnificent caves 169 and 172.

Getting There & Away From Lánzhōu to the caves is a 12-hour round trip – half of that time on a bus and half on a boat. The caves are inaccessible in winter because the water level in the river is too low and ice may also block the boats.

Western Travel Service (in Lánzhōu Bīnguǎn) and CITS all run tours to the caves whenever they have enough people; the usual tour price is Y250, which only includes transport. If there are two people, Western Travel and CITS charge Y300 per person.

If you're going on to Línxià or Xiàhé, you can avoid backtracking to Lánzhōu by catching a bus to Línxià. The trip from Liújiāxiá to Línxià takes about 4½ hours, via an interesting high route east of Huáng Hé through areas settled by the Dongxiang ethnic minority. Another alternative is the Western Travel tour where, instead of returning to the port of Liújiāxiā after visiting Bǐnglíng Sì, the staff drop passengers off at the small port of Lianhuatai. From there it is possible to catch a bus to Línxià (40 minutes) and then on to Xiàhé. You can also arrange this trip with the private boat operators at Liújiāxiá.

A bus from Lánzhōu to Liújiāxiá leaves the west bus station at 7.30am (Y7, one hour). It often arrives just in time to catch one of the boats to Bǐnglíng Sì. The last bus back to Lánzhōu from Liújiāxiá usually leaves between 5pm and 6pm, but if there are not enough passengers it waits until the next day.

SILK ROAD

The boat trip costs Y30 to Y50 and takes two to three hours each way; boats only stay at the caves for one hour, so don't mess about! Alternatively you could charter a speedboat for Y400, which gets there in one hour and carries up to eight people.

LÍNXIÀ 临夏
☎ 0930 • pop 88,400

Línxià was once an important stop on the Silk Road between Lánzhōu and the South Pass. The town has a decidedly Muslim Hui character, with a large mosque in the centre of town.

In the markets you'll see carved gourds, daggers, saddlery, carpets, wrought-iron goods and a thriving trade in spectacles made with ground crystal lenses and metal frames.

Línxià is also a regional centre for the Dongxiang minority. The Dongxiang minority speak their own Altaic language and are believed to be descendants of 13th-century immigrants from central Asia who were moved forcibly to China after Kublai Khan's conquest of the Middle East.

Place to Stay
Shuǐquán Bīnguǎn (☎ 621 4968, fax 621 4496, Sandao Qiao) Dorm beds Y15, twins with bath Y50-100. This friendly hotel is 50m along on your right as you leave the south bus station.

Getting There & Away
Buses to Línxià (Y20 to Y26, 2½ to four hours) leave Lánzhōu's west bus station every 30 minutes between 8am and 4pm. Private mini-buses also frequently make the trip and run until 6pm.

In the opposite direction, buses leave Línxià for Lánzhōu approximately every 20 minutes from 6.30am to 5pm.

From Línxià, buses to Xiàhé (Y13.5, two to three hours) leave approximately every 40 minutes between 7am and 4.40pm. Buses to Hézuò (Y9, 3½ hours) leave about every half hour from 6.30am to 5pm.

There are two long-distance bus stations in Línxià. For services to Qīnghǎi and Yǒngjìng as well as extra services to Xiàhé and Línxià, use the west bus station on Minzhu Xilu (bus No 6 runs between them). An interesting option is the buses to Xúnhuā and Dàhéjiā (Mèngdá Nature Reserve) in

Qīnghǎi. There are daily buses at 6am and 2pm to Xúnhuā (Y14, four hours) via Hanjie and Daowei. There is only one bus to Xīníng (Y38, 11 hours), at 5.40am, which runs via Yǒngjìng (Bǐnglíng Sì).

You can buy insurance at both of the long-distance bus stations.

XIÀHÉ 夏河
☎ 0941

Set in a beautiful mountain valley, Xiàhé is most definitely worth a visit, especially if you can't get to Tibet. It's the leading Tibetan monastery town outside of Lhasa and many Tibetans come here on pilgrimage dressed in their finest, most colourful clothing. Outside of town there are hiking opportunities in nearby grasslands and the surrounding mountains.

Religious activity centres on Lābǔléng Sì (Labrang Monastery), one of the six major Tibetan monasteries of the Gelukpa (Yellow Hat sect of Tibetan Buddhism). The others are Ganden, Sera and Drepung Monasteries in the Lhasa area; Tashilhunpo Monastery in Shigatse; and Tǎ'ěr Sì (Kumbum) near Xīníng, Qīnghǎi.

Walking through the warrens and alleys of this huge monastery, side by side with pilgrims and monks, feels like you've entered another world.

Xiàhé is a microcosm of south-western Gānsù, with the area's three principal ethnic groups represented. In rough terms, Xiàhé's population is 50% Tibetan, 40% Han and 10% Hui.

Orientation
At 2920m above sea level, Xià Hé flows for several kilometres along the valley of Dàxià Hé. Lābǔléng Sì is roughly halfway along, and marks the division between Xiàhé's mainly Han and Hui Chinese eastern quarter and the overwhelmingly Tibetan village to the west.

A 3km pilgrims' way, with long rows of prayer wheels (1174 of them!) and Buddhist shrines, encircles the monastery. There are some 40 smaller monasteries affiliated with Lābǔléng Sì in the surrounding mountains (as well as many others scattered across Tibet and China) and the area is a great place for hiking in clean, peaceful surroundings. Take warm clothing and rain gear.

You can follow the river up to Sāngkē or head up into the surrounding valleys, but carry a stick or a pocket full of rocks, as wild dogs can be a problem.

Information

It is possible to change US dollars at the banks, otherwise try some of the small antique shops along the main street, who will give you a reasonable rate.

The post and telephone office is in the east of town, near the bus station. Internet bars in the Chinese section of town open and close frequently; the Overseas Tibetan Hotel has two new dedicated Internet lines for Y8 for the first half-hour, Y4 per half-hour thereafter.

The PSB is just opposite Yǒuyì Bīnguǎn. You can no longer get a same-day visa extension (figure on a three-day wait).

Lābùléng Sì 拉卜楞寺

Labrang Monastery

This monastery (admission Y24; open 8am-12pm & 2pm-6pm daily) was built in 1709 by E'angzongzhe, the first-generation Jiamuyang (Living Buddha), who came from

the nearby town of Ganjia. It is home to six institutes (Institute of Esoteric Buddhism, Higher & Lower Institutes of Theology, Institute of Medicine, Institute of Astrology and Institute of Law). There are also numerous temple halls, 'Living Buddha' residences and living quarters for the monks.

At its peak the monastery housed nearly 4000 monks, but their ranks were decimated during the Cultural Revolution. The numbers are recovering, and there are about 1200 monks today, drawn from Qīnghǎi, Gānsù, Sìchuān and Inner Mongolia.

In April 1985 the main Prayer Hall of the Institute of Esoteric Buddhism was razed in a fire caused by faulty electrical wiring. The fire is said to have burnt for a week and destroyed some priceless relics. The hall's reconstruction was completed at great cost in mid-1990, but the monks remain reluctant to allow the use of electricity in most parts of the monastery.

Entry to the main temple is by tour only. Tours generally include the Institute of Medicine, the Ser Kung Golden Temple, the Prayer Hall and the museum. The ticket office and souvenir shop are on the right-hand

SILK ROAD

XIÀHÉ & LĀBŮLÉNG SÌ (LABRANG MONASTERY) 夏河、拉卜楞寺

XIÀHÉ & LĀBŮLÉNG SÌ

1	Lābùléng Bīnguǎn; CITS 拉卜楞宾馆； 中国国际旅行社	6	Snowland Restaurant 雪域餐厅	11	Mosque 清真寺
2	Nunnery 尼姑寺	7	Restaurant of the Labrang Monastery	12	Dàshà Bīnguǎn 大厦宾馆
3	Restaurant of the Labrang Monastery 拉卜楞寺饭店		拉卜楞寺饭店	13	Post & Telephone Office 邮电局
4	Monastery Ticket Office 售票处	8	Tara Guesthouse 卓玛旅社	14	Yǒuyì Bīnguǎn 友谊宾馆
5	Lābùléngsì Zhāodàisuǒ 拉卜楞寺招待所	9	Overseas Tibetan Hotel; Internet 华侨宾馆	15	PSB 公安局
		10	Everest Cafe	16	Bus Station 汽车站

side of the monastery car park. There are English tours of the monastery leaving the ticket office at around 11am though sometimes they might not run; an option is to show up at around 6am or 7am to be with the monks.

Access to the rest of the monastery area is free, and you can easily spend several hours just walking around and taking in the atmosphere. Try to make friends with a monk or two: they'll probably be happy to invite you into their living quarters, which always makes for an interesting house call. The opening hours are not set in stone.

Xiàhé also has two **nunneries** *(nígūsì)* with a total of some 110 nuns; they are sometimes amenable to visits. At one nunnery, the nuns are permitted to leave only twice a year!

Note that the **Display Terrace for Buddha Thangka** on the south side of Dàxià Hé is sacred and shouldn't be climbed; monks are tired of having to clamber up and bring travellers down. Also be cool (not aggressive) with your photography.

Festivals

These are important not only for the monks, but also for the nomads who stream into town in multicoloured splendour from the grasslands. Since the Tibetans use a lunar calendar, dates for individual festivals vary from year to year.

The Monlam (Great Prayer) Festival starts three days after the Tibetan New Year, which is usually in February or early March. On the 13th, 14th, 15th and 16th days of the month there are some spectacular ceremonies.

On the morning of the 13th a *thangka* (sacred painting on cloth) of Buddha, measuring over 30m by 20m, is unfurled from the hillside facing the monastery on the other side of Dàxià Hé. This event is accompanied by processions and prayer assemblies.

On the 14th there is an all-day session of Cham dances performed by 35 masked dancers, with Yama, the lord of death, playing the leading role. On the 15th there is an evening display of butter lanterns and sculptures. On the 16th the Maitreya statue is paraded around the monastery all day.

During the second month (usually starting in March or early April) there are several interesting festivals, especially those

held on the seventh and eighth days. Scriptural debates, lighting of butter lamps, collective prayers and blessings take place at other times during the year to commemorate Sakyamuni, Tsong Khapa or individual generations of the 'living Buddhas'.

Places to Stay

Overseas Tibetan Hotel (Huáqiáo Bīnguǎn; ☎ *712 2642,* ⓔ *othotel@public .lz.gs.cn, 77 Renmin Xijie)* Dorm beds Y20, twins Y80-200. This clean hotel is probably the best choice in the budget category. It has shared showers with hot water available all day. The Tibetan-style rooms are spiffy and have nice touches like decorations and paintings by local Tibetan artists. The staff is very helpful. It also has well-maintained bicycles for hire, a rooftop garden, and a laundry service.

Tara Guesthouse (Cáiràng Zhuōmǎ Lǚshè; ☎ *712 1274, 75 Renmin Jie)* Dorm beds Y25, twins with shared bath Y50. Most of the rooms are Tibetan style and are very clean and comfortable. The dorm beds are in cosy four-bed rooms. There is hot water from 6am to noon and again from 6pm to midnight.

Lābǔléngsì Zhāodàisuǒ (Labrang Monastery Guesthouse; Renmin Jie) Beds Y10. This is the cheapest option; this quiet place is nestled inside a small courtyard with authentic yak butter 'scented' beds. It doesn't have showers, but there's always plenty of hot water from the boiler.

Lābǔléng Bīnguǎn (Labrang Hotel; ☎ *712 1849, fax 712 1328)* Triples with bath Y20 per bed, twins Y120, main-building/ Tibetan-style twins Y280/380. The Lābǔléng is a comfortable option; it's by the river a few kilometres up the valley from the village. It's a friendly, tranquil place, where you can wake to the gentle sound of a rushing stream. The only drawback is the 'hot' water, which seems to only get lukewarm at best. The more basic rooms are in the rear building – both fairly good value for the money. The more expensive Tibetan-style twins are not such a good deal. Some of their more interesting rooms are being returned to the monastery who may turn them into a school. You can get there by motor-tricycle for about Y5, or walk there in 45 minutes. The hotel rents bicycles for Y5 per hour or Y15 per day.

In the Chinese quarter there are a few standard Chinese-style hotels that offer cheap rooms. Both Dàshà Bīnguǎn and Yǒuyì Bīnguǎn have hot water in the evening, generally after 9pm.

Dàshà Bīnguǎn (☎ 712 1546, Renmin Dongjie) Dorm beds from Y21, twins with bath Y102. This is a simple place, not bad in a pinch.

Yǒuyì Bīnguǎn (Friendship Hotel; ☎ 712 1593, Renmin Dongjie) Quads/triples Y12/18 per bed, twins Y80. The place is nearer to the bus station and is decent, too. All hotels in this area are usually empty so try polite bargaining.

Places to Eat

Just west of Tara Guesthouse are the two best Tibetan restaurants in town. Both have authentic Tibetan dishes such as yak-milk yoghurt and *tsampa*: a mixture of yak butter, cheese, barley and sugar mixed into a dough with the fingers and eaten uncooked. A bit bland, but worth trying at least once.

Restaurant of the Labrang Monastery (Lābǔléngsì Fàndiàn; Renmin Xilu) Dishes from Y3. It has a rear courtyard where tables are set up during the summer months.

Snowland Restaurant (Xuěyù Cāntīng; Renmin Xilu) Dishes from Y3. There are very good dishes served here and you'll find yourself dining with lots of local Tibetans.

Everest Cafe Dishes from around Y3. This place dishes up some surprisingly delicious Nepali vegetable, mutton or chicken curries.

For Chinese or Hui food, there is a row of small places east of the Tara Guesthouse along the main road.

Shopping

You can pick up some *Tibetan handicrafts* in the shops along the main street, including yak-butter pots, daggers, fur-lined boots, colourful Tibetan shawls, tiny silver teapots and Tibetan *lǎba* trumpets. Prices are sometimes negotiable, sometimes not.

Getting There & Away

Xiàhé is accessible only by bus. Some travellers arrive from Lánzhōu, while others come from Sìchuān – an interesting option is to travel through Qīnghǎi via Tóngrén (see the Qīnghǎi chapter). Bus schedules change wildly from year to year. A new airport is even being proposed.

From Lánzhōu, there are direct daily buses departing from the west bus station at 7.30am and 8.30am (Y32 to Y44). Other private operators lurk in front of the station but it's best to buy from the bus station. It's a six-hour ride, perhaps including a stop for lunch near Línxià. If you can't get a direct ticket from Lánzhōu to Xiàhé, then take a morning bus to Línxià and change there (see the Línxià section for more details).

From Xiàhé the direct buses to Lánzhōu leave from 6.30am to 2.30pm; turn up a bit earlier to get a good seat and store your luggage on the roof. Don't worry if this is too early as there are plenty of buses to Línxià, from where you can change to a Lánzhōu bus.

Buses to Línxià (Y13, 2½ to 3½ hours) run once or twice an hour between 6am and 6pm. The schedule is similar for buses to Hézuò (Y9, 2½ hours).

There are also two buses daily to Tóngrén, in Qīnghǎi (Y17, 4½ to six hours). From Tóngrén you can get a connecting bus to Xīníng or Xúnhuà.

You can buy insurance at the bus station.

Getting Around

Most hotels and restaurants rent bikes for about Y10 per day. Share taxis and the motor-tricycles cost about Y2 for a short trip.

AROUND XIÀHÉ
Sāngkē & Gānjiā Grasslands
桑科、甘加草原

Around and beyond the village of Sāngkē, 14km up the valley from Xiàhé, is a small lake surrounded by large expanses of open grassland, where the Tibetans graze their yak herds. In summer these rolling pastures are at their greenest and have numerous wildflowers. It's a lovely place for walking. Rumours of wild dogs abound; local officials vociferously deny it (trouble actually comes when travellers snoop around nomads' tents or dwellings). There is a Lower and an Upper Sāngkē; the latter is preferable.

Lābǔléng Bīnguǎn has some *yurt* (nomad-style tents) on the grasslands where you can stay overnight for around Y40 per bed. The road from Xiàhé rises gradually and you can cycle up in about one hour. You can also get there by taking a bus from Xiàhé to Sāngkē village (Sāngkē gōngshè) or hire a motor-tricycle for about Y20 return. Some travellers find the yurts cheesy and the horseback rides (Y20 per hour) not worth the money.

Around 34km outside Xiàhé, Gānjiā Grasslands (Gānjiā Cǎoyuán) feature rolling hills and even nicer views than Sāngkē. Buses pass by here; ask for Gānjiā Gōngshè. An additional half-hour by car from here is the **Takkar Grassland**, famed for its enormous rock formations. It's a great place to camp.

Tarzang Lake

Approximately 25km from Xiàhé towards Lánzhōu is this small sacred Tibetan lake. It makes for a lovely picnic; you can walk around it (clockwise as the Tibetans do) in about 20 minutes. You could also theoretically follow the stream that feeds it all the way to Ganjia Grassland (know before you go). You can cycle here or take a bus. When you see a white-on-blue sign above the road, take the next road up. It's a steep, rocky grade and will take up to an hour to get to the lake on foot.

HÉZUÒ 合作

This town is mainly used as a transit point for travellers plying the route between Gānsù and Sìchuān provinces. It's not too exciting, but certainly has some character – traders walk around with fur pelts slung over their shoulders, Tibetan monks make their way through narrow backstreets and white-capped Chinese Hui Muslims are busy running shops, restaurants and other small businesses.

About 2km from the bus station along the main road in the direction of Xiàhé is the **Ando Hezuo Mila Riba Palace** (Mǐlāerbā Fógé). Built in 1777, this 14-storey temple was razed by Red Guards during the Cultural Revolution and was rebuilt in 1988. The inside furnishings are quite elaborate and a climb to the top rewards you with views of the beautiful grasslands surrounding Hézuò.

Places to Stay

If you time your buses, you won't have to spend the night here. If not:

Jīndū Bīnguǎn (☎ 821 1132, 60 Renmin Jie) Triples with shared bath Y25 per bed, twins with bath Y45. This hotel is to the left as you exit the bus station, and 75m down

the road. Hot water is available from 8.30pm to 11pm.

Getting There & Away

There are two bus stations in Hézuò, one government-run, the other private, and their schedules are much the same. Buses from both stations often annoyingly roam the streets of Hézuò for an hour before they depart. The private bus station can be reached by walking east from the main bus station along Maqu Donglu for 10 minutes.

Hézuò is the place where buses from Zöigê (Sìchuān) and Xiàhé meet. There are frequent buses to Xiàhé (Y9, 2½ hours) and to Línxià (Y9, 3½ hours) from 7.30am to 5pm.

Going south is a different story. There is only one bus per day to Zöigê, leaving at 7.30am (Y30, nine hours). Buses to Lǎngmùsì leave between 6.30am and 10.50am (Y20, six hours).

You can buy insurance at the bus station.

LǍNGMÙSÌ 朗木寺

Lǎngmùsì (Namu) is a small, remote village nestled between alpine scenery to the west and grasslands to the east. It is home to a friendly population of Tibetans, Hui Muslims and Han Chinese. Surrounded by countless temples and with numerous possibilities for hikes and horse treks, it is easy to spend a few relaxing days here. The hills surrounding this area are also traditional sites for sky burials (see the boxed text 'Sky Burial' in the Sìchuān chapter).

On the north side of the village is a hill scattered with chörtens and gompas. In the west of the village is the **Dacheng Lamo Kerti Gompa** (admission Y10). Built in 1413, this lamasery is home to around 700 monks who study medicine, astrology and the sutras and tantrics. Also on the eastern side of the village is a **Hui mosque**.

If you follow the river beyond the western edge of the village, you will eventually come to a number of small caves, grottoes and Tibetan mantras carved into the foot of the hills, where monks give thanks for the village's water source.

In addition to hiking out on your own, there are two-day horse treks run by Lǎngmùsì Bīnguǎn. An English-speaking Tibetan guide takes you to nearby rivers, hot springs or simply out across the grasslands.

Places to Stay & Eat

Accommodation in Lǎngmùsì is basic.

Michael Hotel Dorm beds Y15. This hotel has comfortable beds in triple/quad rooms. The shower/toilet facilities are all brand new and clean.

Lǎngmùsì Bīnguǎn Dorm beds from Y15. This place is under the archway just around the corner from the Michael Hotel and has the added bonus of central heating and steaming hot common showers.

There are several small restaurants in town, including two with English signs and menus. The *restaurant* downstairs from Lǎngmùsì Bīnguǎn serves good pancakes and sandwiches as well as local dishes like fish and yak.

Lesha's Coffee Shop This tiny place is just past the hotels on the main road. Inside, Lesha whips up amazing fare including fresh apple pie, coffee (the real thing!), yak burgers and chips. Be warned – the servings are humungous!

Getting There & Away

Unless you take a direct bus to Lǎngmùsì from Hézuò, you can get here on one of the Hézuò/Xiàhé-Zöigê buses, which drop you off at an intersection about 4km from the village. Motor-tricycles that usually wait there will take you into town for Y2.

To get to Zöigê you'll need to catch one of the buses from Hézuò, which means catching a motor-tricycle out to the intersection with the main road to Sìchuān. Buses to Zöigê generally pass by between 11.30am and 2pm. From Lǎngmùsì there are two daily buses to Hézuò (Y19) departing at 6.30am and 8.30am. From Hézuò it is easy to travel on to Xiàhé, Línxià and Lánzhōu.

Hexi Corridor

JIĀYÙGUĀN 嘉峪关

☎ 0947 • pop 130,900

Jiāyùguān is an ancient Han Chinese outpost. The Great Wall once extended beyond here, but in 1372, during the first few years of the Ming dynasty, a fortress was built. From then on Jiāyùguān was considered both the western tip of the wall and the western boundary of the empire.

The city itself lacks soul. However it's not an unfriendly place, and the snow-capped mountains provide a dramatic backdrop when the weather is clear.

Although a mandatory stop for tour groups, Jiāyùguān and its surrounding sights are not so amazing as to merit a special visit. However, if you're moving east or west through the Hexi Corridor at a leisurely pace, a stop here should prove interesting enough.

Information

Money The main Bank of China, on Xinhua Nanlu, is the only place that changes travellers cheques and is open Monday to Friday 9.30am to 5.30pm, Saturday and Sunday 10am to 4pm.

Post & Communications The post and telephone office is open from 8.30am to 8pm daily. Just next door is China Telecom's Internet bar. It's open daily from 10am to 10pm and charges Y10 per hour.

PSB The PSB office is in the southern part of the city and has a roving foreign affairs officer who visits the hotels. Contact the front desk of your hotel.

Places to Stay

Xióngguān Bīnguǎn (☎ 622 5115, fax 622 5399, 1 Xinhua Nanlu) Dorm beds Y12-16, twins with bath Y120-200. This hotel is the best deal in town. The staff is friendly and speak a little English.

Jiāyùguān Bīnguǎn (☎ 622 6231, fax 628 7174, Xinhua Beilu) Twins from Y280. This upmarket place is on the traffic circle at the centre of town. The prices for the twin rooms can usually be bargained down. All the rooms are fairly reasonable value, given the facilities and service.

Places to Eat

Restaurants are few and far between in Jiāyùguān and tend to close by around 10pm.

For cheap and tasty food try the area in front of the Renmin department store, off Xinhua Beilu, or the night market, which is crammed with *stalls* selling *ròujiāmó* (grilled lamb and/or chicken skewers), *liáng miàn* (spicy cold noodles), yoghurt, and plenty of draft beer, which unfortunately tends to be rather flat.

Just opposite the bus station is a collection of competing restaurants.

Línyuàn Jiǔjiā (Lanxin Gonglu) Dishes from Y6. This is one of the most popular places here and does spicy Sìchuān food. It has a Romanised sign that says 'Linyuan Jiujia' and one or two of the staff speak a little English.

Getting There & Away

Air Jiāyùguān's airport only operates from July to the end of October, when it offers a flight five times per week to Dūnhuáng (Y420) and Lánzhōu (Y770) and a daily flight to Xī'ān. An Ürümqi flight is endlessly rumoured.

The CAAC booking office (☎ 622 6237) is on Xinhua Nanlu.

Bus There are three direct daily buses between Dūnhuáng and Jiāyùguān (Y45, five to six hours); an express bus leaves at 2.30pm. There are four departures to Lánzhōu (Y80 to Y129, 16 hours) in the afternoon, two of which are sleeper coaches. There are numerous buses to Zhāngyè (Y22 to Y44, 4½ to six hours).

The bus station may attempt to charge an extra foreigners' fee, regardless of whether you have PICC insurance or not, for all buses heading east to Zhāngyè and Lánzhōu. Take the staff up on the issue and they might back down.

Train Jiāyùguān lies on the Lánzhōu-Ürümqi railway line. From here it's five hours to Liǔyuán, less than four hours to Zhāngyè, 26 hours to Xī'ān, and 10½ hours to Lánzhōu. Sleeper tickets to Lánzhōu and to Ürümqi are sometimes available but don't count on it. Other destinations include Běijīng, Chéngdū, Zhōngwèi, Shànghǎi and Zhèngzhōu.

The train station is 5km south of the town centre. Minibuses run down Xinhua Nanlu to the station and charge Y1. A taxi there should cost no more than Y10.

Getting Around

To/From the Airport The airport is 13km north-east of the city and an airport bus (Y10) from the CAAC office meets all flights.

Taxi Motorbikes, taxis and minibuses congregate outside the main hotels and around the bus station. It is possible to hire a taxi and visit the Wei Jin Tombs, Jiāyù Pass Fort

and the Overhanging Great Wall in half a day, which should cost you no more than Y150 (see the Around Jiāyùguān section).

Bicycle Bikes are excellent for getting around town and to some of the surrounding attractions. Hypothetically, most of the hotels rent bicycles for Y2 per hour, however they rarely have ones in working order.

AROUND JIĀYÙGUĀN
Jiāyù Pass Fort 嘉峪关城楼
Jiāyùguān Chénglóu

This is Jiāyùguān's main tourist drawcard, thus it has taken on a sort of carnival atmosphere. The fort *(admission Y40; open 8am-8pm daily)* guards the pass that lies between snow-capped Qílián Shān peaks and **Hēi Shān** *(Black Mountain)* of the Mǎzōng Shān range.

Built in 1372, the fort was dubbed the 'Impregnable Defile Under Heaven'. Although the Chinese often controlled territory far beyond Jiāyùguān, this was the last major stronghold of the empire to the west.

At the eastern end of the fort is the **Gate of Enlightenment** *(Guānghuà Mén)* and in the west is the **Gate of Conciliation** *(Róuyuǎn Mén)*. Over each gate there stand 17m-high towers with upturned flying eaves. On the inside of each gate there are horse lanes leading up to the top of the wall. However, the entire complex has been renovated, which makes it a bit hard to get a feel for its history.

At the time of writing a **city museum** was also being relocated here so it should be ready by the time you read this.

The fort is 5km west of Jiāyùguān. It is possible to cycle out here in about half an hour, otherwise take a taxi.

Overhanging Great Wall
Xuánbì Chángchéng 悬壁长城

Linking Jiāyùguān with Hēi Shān, the wall is believed to have been constructed in 1539. It had since pretty much crumbled to dust, but was reconstructed in 1987.

From the upper tower high on a ridge you get a sweeping view of the desert, the oasis of Jiāyùguān and the glittering snow-capped peaks in the distance.

The wall is 6km north of Jiāyù Pass Fort via the shortest route (a rough dirt road leading north towards the mountains) or 10km on the surfaced road. A walk along the wall costs Y8.

Wei Jin Tombs
Xīnchéng Wèijìnmù
This place consists of ancient tombs with original wall paintings (admission Y30; open 8am-8pm daily). There are literally thousands of tombs in the desert 20km east of Jiāyùguān, but only one is currently open to visitors. The tombs date from approximately AD 220 to 420 (the Wei and Western Jin periods).

The brick-paintings vividly depict various social activities, including hunting, farming, fruit picking and banqueting. The contents of some of these tombs, including the wooden coffins, are held in an exhibition room opposite the ticket office.

July 1st Glacier 七一冰川
Qīyī Bīngchuān
The glacier sits at 4300m, high up in Qílián Shān. It is about 90km south-west of Jiāyùguān and is reached via the train to the iron-ore town of Jìngtiěshān, which departs from Jiāyùguān's Luhua train station at 8.30am. It's a scenic three-hour train trip to Jìngtiěshān, where you can hire a taxi to the glacier. It is a further 20km to the glacier and the return trip should cost about Y120. Hikers can walk a 5km trail alongside the glacier, but at that elevation it gets cold even in summer, so come prepared.

As the train schedule doesn't allow for a same-day return, you will need to stay the night in Jìngtiěshān in order to get to the glacier. This leaves you with enough time the next morning to hire a taxi (Y50 return) up to Tiān'é Hú and the Tibetan village Qíqīng. This same bumpy road eventually ends up in Qīnghǎi, but there is no public transport past Jìngtiěshān. There is a cheap and basic hostel (zhāodàisuǒ) in town.

ZHĀNGYÈ 张掖
☎ 0936
The next major town east of Jiāyùguān, Zhāngyè warrants a visit for Dàfó Sì (Great Buddha Temple; ☎ 821 9671; admission Y20; open 7.30am-6.30pm daily). It dates to 1098 (Western Xia dynasty) and contains the largest sleeping Buddha figure in China: the gilded wood and clay figure is 35m long

JIĀYÙGUĀN 嘉峪关

1 Night Market
   夜市
2 Jiāyùguān Bīnguǎn
   嘉峪关宾馆
3 China Telecom Internet Cafe
   网吧
4 Post & Telephone Office
   邮电局
5 CAAC
   民航售票处
6 Department Store
   百货商店
7 Renmin Department Store
   人民商城
8 Vegetable Market
   市场
9 Línyuàn Jiǔjiā
   林苑酒店
10 Bus Station
   汽车站
11 Xióngguān Bīnguǎn
   雄关宾馆
12 Bank of China
   中国银行

and 8m wide. Arhats and 530 square metres of murals surround the Buddha.

In the blocks surrounding the complex there are three other **temples** found in back alleys. It's good fun to poke around the older neighbourhoods. One block north you'll find a **mù tǎ** (wooden pagoda; admission Y5; open 7.30am-6.30pm daily), a brick and wooden structure that dates to AD 528. Its nine storeys make it the highest building in the city. A small temple sits to the rear. You can climb all the way to the top of the pagoda.

Places to Stay & Eat
Zhāngyè Bīnguǎn (☎ 821 2601, fax 821 3806, Xianfu Jie) Quads/triples Y14/18, doubles with bath Y90-480. This is the easiest place to stay; it's a few blocks from Dàfó Sì. The grounds are nice and there's a plethora of rooms – take a look at a few because standards vary. They may annoyingly charge you a foreigner surcharge.

Try this good spot for eats: two large blocks north of Zhāngyè Bīnguǎn look for an alley with colourful, wooden signs at the entrance. This historical pedestrian street has literally dozens of clean, friendly *restaurants*. All display their fare on large signs outside; there's no English so it's a perfect time to whip out the phrasebook and match up dishes (in most places the delighted staff will probably help!).

Getting There & Away

The city has two bus stations, one in the east and one in the west. Both have similar schedules and many buses stop at both. To Jiāyùguān (Y22 to Y44, 4½ to six hours) buses leave mostly from the west station.

LIǓYUÁN 柳园
☎ 0937

Liǔyuán, a forlorn little town found on the Lánzhōu–Ürümqi railway line, is the jumping-off point for Dūnhuáng, 130km and 2½ hours south by bus (train schedules say Dūnhuáng). Unless you're catching an early morning train, there should be no need to stay here.

Liǔyuán Bīnguǎn (☎ 557 2340) Dorm beds with/without shared bath Y25/15, twins Y80-120. If you must stay in town, this place has decent if musty rooms.

There are six trains daily in each direction. Going east, it takes five hours to reach Jiāyùguān and 20 hours to Lánzhōu. To the west, it's 12 hours to Turpan and 15 hours to Ürümqi. Train No K889 is a good option for Ürümqi as it originates here; it departs at 7.32pm and takes 13 hours.

Tickets can be purchased up to three days in advance, otherwise turn up in Liǔyuán a bit earlier on the day of departure. Tickets were readily available when we last checked but it always depends on how many tour groups book trains out further up the line. There are also daily departures to Běijīng, Chéngdū, Korla, Shànghǎi, Xī'ān and Zhèngzhōu.

Minibuses for Dūnhuáng depart from in front of the train station when trains arrive. If there are enough passengers you will leave immediately; if not be prepared to wait until the bus fills up. The one-way fare is Y10, plus Y5 for each bag placed on the roof, and the trip takes about 2½ hours. A share taxi is not a bad option if the bus isn't moving. They generally charge between Y25 and Y30 per person.

If you're coming back from Dūnhuáng to catch a train, check the weather: if sand storms are blowing, the ride could take as long as four hours.

On the way to Dūnhuáng, the road passes some crumbling remains of the Great Wall that were built during the Han dynasty. The sections are visible from the road between the 85km and 90km markers.

DŪNHUÁNG 敦煌
☎ 0937

After travelling for hours towards Dūnhuáng, the flat, barren desert landscape suddenly gives way to lush, green cultivated fields with mountainous rolling sand dunes as a backdrop. The area has a certain haunting beauty, especially at night under a star-studded sky. It's not so much the desert dunes and romantic nights that attract so many tourists to Dūnhuáng, but the superb Buddhist art at the nearby Mògāo Caves.

During the Han and Tang dynasties Dūnhuáng was a major point of interchange between China and the outside world – a stopping-off post for both incoming and outgoing trading caravans. Despite a surge in tourism-related development, the town still has a fairly relaxed feel to it, and it's easy to kick back here for a few days.

Information

Money A small branch of the Bank of China, on Yangguan Zhonglu, is open daily and can change cash and travellers cheques. The larger bank opposite doesn't close for lunch, but is closed on weekends.

Post & Communications The post and telephone office is on the north-western side of the main traffic circle. There is an Internet cafe just north-east of the post office. It charges Y4 per hour. A number of others are found throughout downtown and should all charge the same.

Travel Agencies CITS (☎ 882 3012) has a branch inside Dūnhuáng Bīnguǎn. There are other travel agents scattered about town, sequestered in various hotels. Most can book train and air tickets, as well as tours to surrounding sights such as the South Pass and the Jade Gate Pass.

PSB The PSB foreign affairs office is in the main PSB building on Yangguan Zhonglu, near the Bank of China. As of 2001 no visa extensions were being given here.

County Museum
Xiàn Bówùguǎn
This museum (☎ 882 2981, Yangguan Donglu; admission Y10; open 8am-12pm & 2.30pm-6pm daily) makes for a pleasant browse.

Exhibits include some of the Tibetan and Chinese scriptures unearthed from Cave No 17 at Mògāo, sacrificial objects from the Han to Tang dynasties, and relics such as silks, brocades and reed torches for the beacons from the South Pass and the Jade Gate Pass.

Places to Stay
Most hotels in Dūnhuáng vary the rates by season. The tourist season is from June to September and hotel rates rise by about 50% or more at that time. The rates quoted in this section are for the low season.

Places to Stay – Budget
Fēitiān Bīnguǎn (☎/fax 882 2337, Mingshan Lu) Dorm beds/twins from Y30/320. This two-star hotel offers a good location. Beds are in clean, multi-bed dorms and the twins are comfortable.

Wǔhuán Zhāodàisuǒ (Five Rings Olympic Hotel; ☎ 882 2620, Mingshan Lu) Dorm beds Y12-25, twins with bath Y80. This place has dicey shared facilities but it's dirt cheap and the rooms are clean. The staff is fairly friendly. To top things off, it has 24-hour hot water.

Yǒuhǎo Bīnguǎn (☎ 882 2678, Mingshan Lu) Dorm beds Y20, twins/triples with bath Y80/200. The rooms with a private bathroom are surprisingly good here, some with new renovations.

Míngshān Bīnguǎn (☎ 882 2122, Mingshan Lu) Quads from Y20 per bed, twins with bath Y80-220. This old-style place has comfortable twins, some of which have been recently spruced up. For the money it's not a bad deal and it's conveniently located.

There are two places in town calling themselves the 'Dunhuang Hotel' in English, but they have different Chinese names.

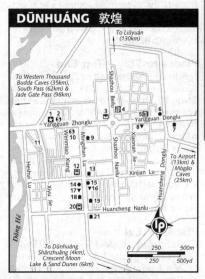

SILK ROAD

DŪNHUÁNG

PLACES TO STAY	PLACES TO EAT	5 County Museum 县博物馆
7 Dūnhuáng Bīnguǎn; CITS 敦煌宾馆; 中国国际旅行社	8 Night Market 敦煌夜市	6 CAAC Booking Office 民航售票处
9 Míngshān Bīnguǎn 鸣山宾馆	16 Charlie Johng's Cafe 风味餐馆	10 Bank of China 中国银行
13 Dūnhuáng Fàndiàn 敦煌饭店	17 Shirley's Cafe 风味餐馆	11 Day Market 农副市场
18 Wǔhuán Zhāodàisuǒ 五环招待所	**OTHER**	12 Minibus Stop 小公共汽车站
19 Fēitiān Bīnguǎn; John's Information Cafe 飞天宾馆	1 PSB 公安局	14 Bike Rental
21 Yǒuhǎo Bīnguǎn 友好宾馆	2 Bank of China 中国银行	15 China Northwest Airlines 西北航空公司
	3 Post & Telephone Office 邮电局	20 Long-Distance Bus Station 长途汽车站
	4 Internet Cafe 网吧	

Dūnhuáng Fàndiàn (☎ 882 2413, fax 882 2785, 16 Mingshan Lu) Quads/triples with shared bath Y20/25 per bed, twins with private bath Y160 per person, suites with air-con Y360. This place is the budget alternative, near the bus station.

Places to Stay – Mid-Range

Dūnhuáng Bīnguǎn (☎ 882 2415, fax 882 2309, 14 Yangguan Donglu) Twins with breakfast Y580-650. This larger hotel is a three-star place aimed at tour groups and visiting cadres. The staff is friendly and the gardens here are quite pleasant, but the catch is the overpriced rooms. The rooms are comfortable and come with a fridge. Although rates are negotiable, it still isn't really worth the money.

Places to Stay – Top End

Dūnhuáng Shānzhuāng (Silk Road Dunhuang Hotel; ☎ 888 2088, fax 888 2086) Twins from US$100, stylish suites from US$150. The twins here are nicely decorated and the suites are stylish. A 15% service charge is added to all rates. During the low season, prices drop by 50% to 80% and there is no service charge. Although expensive, this is a tastefully designed place and, being only a kilometre from the Míngshā Shān sand dunes, it enjoys great sunrise and sunset views. It is 4km south of town.

Places to Eat

Charlie Johng's Cafe (Mingshan Lu) Dishes from Y4. This place has good Western and Chinese food at cheap prices, plus an English menu and nice background music (you can bring your own tapes if you wish).

Shirley's Cafe (Mingshan Lu) Dishes from Y4. This cafe is also pretty good. Shirley is Charlie Johng's sister.

John's Information Cafe Dishes from Y4. This place inside the grounds of Fēitiān Bīnguǎn has a nice outdoor location (for those evening beers) and friendly staff who can also help with travel arrangements and information.

On this same block there are numerous Chinese restaurants – most have English menus, reasonable prices and are worth trying. A popular local dish speciality is *dàpánjī*, a whole chicken cut up and stir-fried with potatoes, herbs and vegetables, and served on a bed of noodles. It usually costs between

Y35 to Y50, but you'll need three people at the very least to finish the thing, so it's not that pricey and certainly worth a try.

Dūnhuáng's *night market* is an extremely lively scene and worth a visit. Mostly contained within a large courtyard off Yangguan Donglu, it houses scores of restaurants and small tables surrounded by lawn chairs and a drinking hostess. The tables are rented out by entrepreneurs, who charge fairly steep prices for beer, soft drinks, tea and the pourer. Instead, you might prefer a tasty *ròujiāmó*, delicious noodle-and-vegie *bāozì* (large fried dumpling), and yoghurt from one of the nearby barbecue vendors.

Getting There & Away

Air In the summer high season from June to September there are regular flights to Lánzhōu (Y940), Xī'ān (Y1340), Běijīng (Y1650) and Ürümqi (Y650). Flights to Jiāyùguān (Y420) only operate from July to September. Flight frequency is cut during the winter months to just Lánzhōu and Xī'ān. Seats can be booked at the CAAC office (☎ 882 2389) on Yangguan Donglu, which is open from 8.30am to 11.30am and 3pm to 6pm. China Northwest Airlines has a ticket office (☎ 882 9710) along Mingshan Lu.

Bus Minibuses to Liǔyuán depart from the bus station when full. The last bus usually leaves around 8pm. The fare is Y10 to Y21. The trip usually takes 2½ hours, but can take up to four hours if there's a sand storm blowing.

There are three or four buses to Jiāyùguān leaving between 6.30am and 1pm (Y45, up to seven hours). There is also a more comfortable air-con bus that departs at 2.30pm (Y66, five hours).

Departures to Lánzhōu are at 10.30am and 2.30pm each day. Regular buses cost Y135; sleepers Y214. The 1148km trip takes at least 22 hours.

The regular bus to Golmud (Y45) leaves at 8am, and takes 12 hours via a rugged but scenic route that crosses the snow-capped Altun Shān. There is also a sleeper bus (Y80) at 5.30pm. Arrive early enough to store your luggage on the roof. It's chilly up in the mountains, so keep some warm clothing handy regardless of how hot it may be in Dūnhuáng itself.

SILK ROAD

Other daily departures include buses to Xīníng, Hāmì and Ürümqi.

Train The closest station is at Liŭyuán, on the Lánzhōu–Ürümqi railway line (see the Liŭyuán section for more details).

Getting Around

Dūnhuáng's airport is 13km east of town. Aside from the CAAC bus (Y6), you can hire a minibus to the airport for about Y30.

Dūnhuáng is small enough that you can easily cover it on foot, but taxis and minivans can be chartered for trips to sights outside town. The minibus stop near Dūnhuáng Fàndiàn is the place to go to start the negotiations.

Fēitiān Bīnguǎn has modern and well-maintained bikes for a reasonable Y2 per hour. Otherwise, just across the street there are a number of stalls that rent bikes for Y1 per hour. A bit of exploratory pedalling around the oasis is fine, and getting to some outlying sights is also possible, although maybe not such a great idea during the height of summer.

AROUND DŪNHUÁNG
Crescent Moon Lake 月牙泉
Yuèyáquán

This lake (admission lake & dunes Y50) is 6km south of the centre of Dūnhuáng at **Míngshā Shān** (Singing Sand Mountains), where the oasis meets the desert. Spring water trickles into a depression between huge sand dunes, forming a small, crescent-shaped pond (not to be confused with the concrete storage pool nearby).

More impressive than the lake are the incredible sand dunes that tower above (the highest peak reaching 1715m). The climb to the top of the dunes is sweaty work, but the dramatic view across the rolling desert sands towards the oasis makes it worthwhile.

Out here the recreational activities include camel rides, 'dune surfing' (sand sliding) and paragliding (jumping off the top of high dunes with a chute on your back). There is also a tow-gliding operation closer to the entry gate: continue past it if you want to jump off a dune.

The admission fee to the lake and dunes area includes admission to **Dunhuang Folk Arts Museum**.

Most people head out to the dunes at around 5pm when the weather starts to cool down. You can ride a bike out to here in around 20 minutes. Minibuses cost Y3 and make the run whenever full. Taxis cost Y15 one way.

Mògāo Caves 莫高窟
Mògāo Kū

Most of Dūnhuáng's art dates from the Northern and Western Wei, Northern Zhou, Sui and Tang dynasties, although examples from the Five Dynasties, Northern Song, Western Xia and Yuan can also be found. The Northern Wei, Western Wei, Northern Zhou and Tang caves are in the best state of preservation.

The caves are generally rectangular or square with recessed, decorated ceilings. The focal point of each is a group of brightly painted statues representing Buddha and the Bodhisattvas.

The smaller statues are composed of terracotta coated with a kind of plaster surface so that intricate details could be etched into the surface.

The walls and ceilings were plastered with layers of cement and clay and then painted with watercolour. Large sections of the murals are made up of decorative patterns using motifs from nature, architecture or textiles.

Many of the caves have been touched up at one time or another.

Northern Wei, Western Wei & Northern Zhou Caves The Turkic-speaking Tuobas, who invaded and conquered the country in the 4th century, inhabited the region north of China and founded the Northern Wei dynasty around AD 386.

Friction between groups who wanted to maintain the traditional Tuoba lifestyle and those who wanted to assimilate with the Chinese eventually split the Tuoba empire in the middle of the 6th century.

The eastern part adopted the Chinese way of life and the rulers took the dynasty name of Northern Qi. The western part took the dynasty name of Northern Zhou and tried in vain to revert to Tuoba customs. By AD 567, however, they had managed to defeat the Qi to take control of all of northern China.

The fall of the Han dynasty in AD 220 sent Confucianism into decline. This, plus the turmoil of the Tuoba invasions, made Buddhism's teachings of nirvana and personal salvation highly appealing to many people. The religion spread rapidly and made a new and decisive impact on Chinese art, which can be seen in the Buddhist statues at Mògāo.

The art of this period is characterised by its attempt to depict the spirituality of those who had achieved enlightenment and transcended the material world through their asceticism. The Wei statues are slim, ethereal figures with finely chiselled features and comparatively large heads, and clearly show the influence of Indian Buddhist art and teachings.

Sui Caves The Sui dynasty began when a general of Chinese or mixed Chinese-Tuoba origin usurped the throne of the Northern Zhou dynasty. Prudently putting to death all the sons of the former emperor, he embarked on a series of wars which by AD 589 had reunited northern and southern China for the first time in 360 years.

The Tuobas simply disappeared from history, either mixing with other Turkic tribes from central Asia or assimilating with the Chinese.

The Sui dynasty was short-lived, and very much a transition between the Wei and Tang periods. This can be seen in the Sui caves: the graceful Indian curves in the Buddha and Bodhisattvas figures start to give way to the more rigid style of Chinese sculpture.

Tang Caves During the Tang dynasty (AD 618–907), China pushed its borders forcefully westward as far as Lake Balkhash in today's Kazakhstan. Trade expanded and foreign merchants and people of diverse religions streamed into the Tang capital of Chang'an.

Buddhism became prominent and Buddhist art reached its peak; the proud bearing of the Buddhist figures in Mògāo Caves reflects the feelings of the times, the prevailing image of the brave Tang warrior, and the strength and steadfastness of the empire.

This was also the high point of the cave art at Mògāo. Some 230 caves were carved, including two impressive grottoes containing enormous, seated Buddha figures. The statue residing in cave 96 is a towering 34.5m tall – a slightly shorter (26m) counterpart in cave 130 is no less impressive.

The portraits of Tang nobles are considerably larger than those of the Wei and Sui dynasties, and the figures tend to occupy important positions within the murals. In some cases the patrons are portrayed in the same scene as the Buddha.

Post-Tang Caves The Tang dynasty marked the ultimate development of the cave paintings. During later dynasties, the economy around Dūnhuáng went into decline and the luxury and vigour typical of Tang painting began to be replaced by simpler drawing techniques and flatter figures. However there were some masterpieces in the post-Tang era, notably the 16m-long reclining Buddha (cave 158), attended by rows of disciples, all bearing different expressions that show you how close they are to achieving the state of nirvana.

Admission A general entrance ticket costs Y80, which entails entrance to about 15 caves and a Chinese-speaking guide. For an extra Y5, you can visit the **museum** (highly recommended), and for an additional Y20 per person, you are provided with an English-speaking guide (best Y20 spent at Mògāo). It doesn't matter if you want one or not – the guide has the keys to doors protecting all of the caves you'll be seeing. Guides are usually available for French, Italian, Spanish, German, Korean and Japanese speakers. Paying the extra for the foreign language guide is rewarding. As the groups are much smaller, you can choose which caves you would like to visit (within reason), you have much more time to browse and you can ask more questions (the guides are usually very helpful and informative).

In addition to the 30 caves that are open to the public, it is possible to visit some of the 'closed' caves for an 'additional fee'. Some, like cave 465, contain Tantric art whose explicit sexual portrayals have been deemed too corrupting for the public to view. (However, you can check them out if you ask special permission and pay an extra Y60 to Y200.)

The grottoes are theoretically open from 8am to 5pm daily, but guides are generally only available between 8.30am and 10am and again at 2pm. The 15-cave tour usually takes between one hour (Chinese tours) and two hours or more (foreign tours).

Photography is strictly prohibited everywhere within the fenced-off caves area. Cameras and hand luggage must be deposited at an office near the entrance gate (for a fee of Y2).

Most caves are lit only by indirect sunlight from outside, often making it hard to see detail, particularly in the niches. Heavy but low-powered torches (flashlights) can be hired outside the gate (Y3); if you have your own, bring it.

Despite the high fee and the inconvenience of the guide system, don't be discouraged – entering your first cave will make it all seem worthwhile.

Getting There & Away The Mògāo Caves are 25km from Dūnhuáng – half an hour by bus. A bus leaves at around 8am from in front of Fēitiān Bīnguǎn. The one-way fare is Y5. If you miss this, you'll have to negotiate with minibus drivers who sit opposite Dūnhuáng Fàndiàn; you should get a seat for Y10.

At other times you can hire a whole minibus for around Y60 to Y80 return, depending on your bargaining skills. If you go in the afternoon, don't bother heading out before 2pm, as you won't be able to get in to see the caves until at least 2.30pm.

Some people ride out to the caves on a bicycle, but be warned that half the ride is through total desert – hot work in summer.

Western Thousand Buddha Caves
Xī Qiānfó Dòng 西千佛洞

These caves *(admission Y20),* 35km west of Dūnhuáng, are cut into the cliff face of the scenic Dǎng Hé gorge. Many travellers skip these caves due to the popularity of the impressive caves at Mògāo, however, the paintings are in fact in good condition and a visit is very rewarding.

There are currently 16 caves still intact here, 10 of which are open to the public. The earliest caves date back to the Northern Wei dynasty and the most recent were carved during the Tang dynasty. Many of the images and stories depicted in the paintings are similar to those at Mògāo. Unless you have a good knowledge of Buddhism, hiring a guide from Dūnhuáng is recommended.

The caves are best reached by hire vehicle and can be included in a day trip to the South Pass and the Jade Gate Pass. Alternatively catch a public bus from the intersection of Xiyu Jie and Yangguan Zhonglu (also known as Xi Dajie) in Dūnhuáng, which goes to Shāzǎoyuǎn. Just ask the driver to drop you off at the turn-off to the caves. It's a five-minute walk down to the caves. A return taxi fare is Y50.

South Pass & Jade Gate Pass
Yáng Guān & Yùmén Guān 阳关、玉门关

The South Pass is some 62km south-west of Dūnhuáng. Here, Han-dynasty beacon towers marked the caravan route westwards and warned of advancing invaders, but what remains has now largely disappeared under the shifting sands.

Nearby are the ruins of the ancient Han town of Shouchang. The Jade Gate Pass, 98km north-west of Dūnhuáng, is also known for its ancient ruins.

Caravans leaving China would travel the Hexi corridor to Dūnhuáng; the Jade Gate Pass was the starting point of the road which ran across the north of what is now Xīnjiāng; the South Pass was the start of the route that cut through the south of the region.

The road to the Jade Gate Pass is still to be completed and at the time of writing was not very good. An interesting day trip could include the two passes, a visit to the Western Thousand Buddha Caves, as well as a trip to the village of Shāzǎoyuǎn and the nearby Wowa Reservoir. To hire a Santana taxi for this sort of trip would cost between Y200 and Y300, but any taxi will negotiate a fare. There are also a couple of buses a day to Shāzǎoyuǎn that pass by the caves and the South Pass.

Eastern Gānsù

PÍNGLIÁNG 平凉
☎ 0912

Following the completion of the Bǎojī-Zhōngwèi railway line in 1996, Píngliáng has become a lot more accessible to the outside world. Despite this, it remains a quiet town tucked away in the foothills of Liùpán Shān and a good base for exploring nearby Taoist Kōngtóng Shān.

Orientation & Information

The train station is in the north-eastern part of town and the bus station in the far western part. The two stations are connected by Dajie, the main thoroughfare and home to the town's major hotels, restaurants and shops.

The Bank of China is on Dong Dajie in the eastern part of town. The PSB is on Xi Dajie, west of Xinmin Beilu, and the post and telephone office is opposite the PSB.

Places to Stay & Eat

Píngliáng Bīnguǎn (☎ 821 2921, 86 Xidajie) Twins/triples with shared bath Y22/20 per bed, twins with private bath Y63, doubles Y100. This place is in a central location and has clean rooms and friendly staff. The twins here are comfortable and the doubles are large. From either the bus or train station you can catch bus No 1 to the hotel or it will cost Y5 in a taxi.

Huámíng Diànlì Bīnguǎn (☎ 821 3922, 71 Xidajie) Triples or quads from Y25 per bed, singles/doubles/twins Y50/160/120. This is a clean place with a good range of inexpensive rooms; some of the larger doubles are actually suites. The hotel is adjacent to Píngliáng Bīnguǎn.

Huámíng Cāntīng (Xidajie) Dishes from Y5. This is a good place to eat and is surprisingly cheap. This restaurant is just next door to Huámíng Diànlì Bīnguǎn.

Getting There & Away

Bus From Xī'ān, there are half-hourly buses to Píngliáng leaving from 7am to 4pm (Y30, eight hours). Express buses (Y50) leave at 7.30am and 10.30am. Heading the other way, buses depart from Píngliáng at 6.20am, 6.40am, 7am and 7.40am. There is one daily bus to Yán'ān at 6am (15 hours) that passes through some pleasant rural countryside on the way.

There are regular buses to Gùyuán (Níngxià) throughout the day. Buses to Lánzhōu mostly leave in the morning (express buses all leave in the morning) and take eight hours.

Train The best way to visit Píngliáng is by train, although you do seem to miss most of the surrounding scenery. There is an overnight train to Lánzhōu (No K431) and trains to Xī'ān via Baòjī.

The ticket office at the station is reluctant to sell sleepers for trains that don't originate in Píngliáng. Instead, the staff send you to Kōngdòngshān Bīnguǎn, on Dong Dajie, where you can line up at 9am.

Getting Around

Bus No 1 runs from the train station to the bus station along Dajie. The town is small enough to walk to most destinations, otherwise hop in a taxi for Y5.

AROUND PÍNGLIÁNG
Kōngtóng Shān 崆峒山

Sitting on the border of Níngxià, in the range of Liùpán Shān, Kōngdóng Shān *(admission Y30)* is 11km to the west of Píngliáng. The highest peak is over 2100m and there are numerous small paths that lead to the dozens of temples and pagodas that are scattered across the mountain. Many of the buildings date back to the Tang dynasty and contain valuable frescoes.

There is simple accommodation and food available on the mountain.

Kōngtóng Shānzhuāng (☎ 860 0099) Quads Y20 per bed, triples/suites Y30/180. Showers are available here in the evening.

Getting There & Away

There are regular buses from Píngliáng that depart from opposite the bus station and head up to the base of the mountain (Y4) or up to the car park (Y8) near the summit. A taxi to the base costs Y20/40 one way/return, including waiting time. Try to head back early as there are not many buses after 5pm.

If you interested in exploring Liùpán Shān further, then there are a couple of buses that pass the main entrance heading for Jīngyuán in Níngxià. Jīngyuán is only 36km away and is a good base from which to explore the surrounding mountains.

MÀIJĪ SHĀN & TIĀNSHUǏ
☎ 0938 • pop (Tiānshuǐ) 3,253,800

Màijī Shān *(Haystack Mountain)*, a small mountain south of Tiānshuǐ town in southeastern Gānsù, is the site of some impressive Buddhist cave art.

The mountain bears some resemblance to a haystack, hence the name. The scenery is also quite nice: a lush valley dotted with fields and surrounded by green hills that offers some pleasant hiking opportunities.

The Karakul Lake area in Xīnjiāng is dotted with Mongolian yurts, homes of the local Tajiks.

Bridge at Wòlóng Nature Reserve, Sìchuān

Buddhist carving at Bǎodǐng Shān, Chóngqìng

Silhouetted against a temple, Éméi Shān, Sìchuān.

Reading the Koran in Kashgar, Xīnjiāng.

Afghani-style Érmǐn Tǎ and its adjoining mosque in Turpan, Xīnjiāng.

Camel trekking accross the desert dunes around Dūnhuáng in Gānsù.

Míngshā Shān, Gānsù

Orientation

Tiānshuǐ has two sections – the railhead, known as Běidào, and the main city area 16km to the east, known as Qínchéng. Bus Nos 1 and 6 run frequently between the two districts (Y2, 20 minutes). However, unless you have some business with CITS or need to catch a long-distance bus, there's no compelling reason to go to Qínchéng.

Màijī Shān is 35km south of Běidào. There are no direct public buses to Màijī Shān, but minibuses leave when full from in front of the train station (Y8 to Y10, 1½ hours). You can also hire a taxi for Y100 return.

Information

In Běidào you can change cash and travellers cheques at the Bank of China branch on Weihe Nanlu, about 500m south of the intersection with Weibin Beilu. There's also a branch on Minzhu Donglu in Qínchéng. Opening hours are 8.30am to noon and 2.30pm to 5.30pm.

CITS (☎ 821 3621) is in Qínchéng, south of the bus station, on Huancheng Nanlu; you'll also find a small office in Tiānshuǐ Bīnguǎn.

Haystack Mountain Grottoes
Màijī Shān Shíkū 麦积山石窟

These grottoes (*admission park & caves with/without guide Y50/40; open 9am-5pm daily*) are one of China's four largest temple groups; the others are at Dàtóng, Luòyáng and Dūnhuáng. The caves date back to the Northern Wei and Song dynasties and contain clay figures and wall paintings.

It's not certain just how the artists managed to clamber so high; one theory is that they piled up blocks of wood to the top of the mountain before moving down, gradually removing blocks of wood as they descended. Stone sculptures were evidently brought in from elsewhere, since the local rock is too soft for carving, as at Dūnhuáng.

SILK ROAD

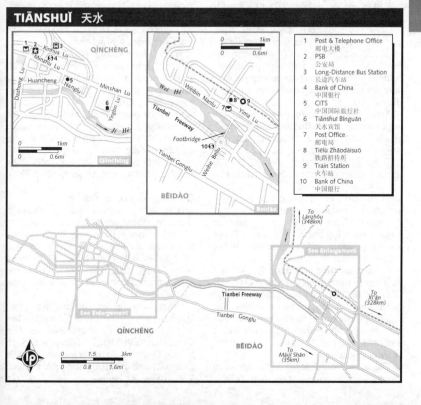

TIĀNSHUǏ 天水

1	Post & Telephone Office 邮电大楼
2	PSB 公安局
3	Long-Distance Bus Station 长途汽车站
4	Bank of China 中国银行
5	CITS 中国国际旅行社
6	Tiānshuǐ Bīnguǎn 天水宾馆
7	Post Office 邮电局
8	Tiělù Zhāodàisuǒ 铁路招待所
9	Train Station 火车站
10	Bank of China 中国银行

Words & Pictures

石窟 **Shíkū: grotto**
The top of the character *shí* (stone, rock) is like the corner of a rock or a cliff, whereas the bottom half is a cake of rock. The top of *kū* means a cave or an earth room. The bottom half sees someone bending to carry something into or out of the cave or room, which would usually have a very low ceiling.

Earthquakes have demolished many of the caves in the central section, while murals have tended to drop off due to damp or rain. Fire has also destroyed a large number of the wooden structures. Parts of the rock wall have now been stabilised with sprayed-on liquid cement.

Catwalks and steep spiral stairs have been built across the cliff face, so while the art is not as amazing as that at Dūnhuáng, getting to it is more fun. Most of the remaining 194 caves can only be seen through wire netting or barred doors – bring a torch (flashlight).

Apart from the **Qifo Pavilion** and the huge Buddha statues that are easily accessible, it's hard to get a rewarding peek into many of the caves unless you take a guide. CITS has English-speaking guides for Y100 (excluding transport and admission fees) – you'll need to go to CITS in Qínchéng to meet up before heading to the caves. There are guides available at Màijī Shān (ask at the ticket office) for a fee, but getting an English-speaking one at short notice is not always possible and a minimum of six people are needed.

The ticket office is about a five-minute walk uphill from where the bus lets you off. Cameras and bags may not be taken into the caves area – the office has a left-luggage section (Y2 per item) for this purpose. You may also get charged an Y11 'area fee' if you catch a taxi or the minibus stops at the outermost gateway.

The area behind Màijī Shān has been turned into a botanical garden (sēnlín gōngyuán). There are some nice hiking opportunities accessing the high ridge behind Màijī Shān, which offers fine views of the grottoes. To get to the park, take the stairs to the right just as the road turns sharply left towards Màijī Shān's ticket office and upper parking lot. If you come across the main entrance, there is a steep entrance fee of Y30.

Places to Stay & Eat
Tiělù Zhāodàisuǒ (☎ 273 5154, Yima Lu) Dorm beds Y10-45. This place has simple but cheap rooms. Showers are on the 1st floor and there is hot water between 8pm and 10.30pm. To get here, turn right as you leave the square in front of the train station and continue for about 50m. Any number of hotels in this area will have good, comfy doubles for Y100 to Y125.

Tiānshuǐ Bīnguǎn (☎ 821 4542, fax 821 2823, 5 Yingbin Lu) Twins/doubles/triples Y186/166/159 per person. This is a clean and friendly mid-range option in Qínchéng. Buses from the train station can drop you off at the corner just up from the hotel. The hotel's restaurant is not bad.

Màijī Shānzhuāng (☎ 272 2277 ext 2100) Triples/quads with shared bath Y31/26 per bed, twins/triples with private bath Y122/169. If you have some time on your hands, you could try this quiet, slightly worn-down place about 500m before the main car park to the grottoes. Staying here will give you a chance to do some hiking in the surrounding area. The hotel has a small *restaurant*, and there are also food *stalls* and cheap *restaurants* closer to Màijī Shān.

Getting There & Away
Bus From the long-distance bus station in Qínchéng there are four daily buses to Lánzhōu from 6.30am to noon, a regular bus at 6am and 8am (Y29, nine hours) and an express bus at 6.30pm (Y60, seven hours). There are also buses to Lánzhōu that depart at similar times from in front of the train station at Běidào.

Other long-distance destinations from Qínchéng's bus station include a 6.30am bus to Línxià (Y32, 13 hours) and an 8am sleeper bus to Níngchuān in Níngxià (Y85, 15 hours). There are also daily buses to Gùyuán (Níngxià) and Píngliáng (Kōngtóng Shān; Y36 to Y46, six hours).

Train Tiānshuǐ is on the Xī'ān-Lánzhōu railway line; there are dozens of daily trains in either direction, all of which stop here. If you arrive early you can visit Màijī Shān as a day trip, avoiding the need to stay overnight in Tiānshuǐ.

There are westbound departures approximately hourly from 7pm to 7am. Heading east, trains leave about once an hour between 12.45pm and 7pm and again from 11pm to 7am. From Tiānshuǐ it's about seven hours to either Lánzhōu or Xī'ān.

LUÒMÉN 洛门

In Wǔ Shān outside Luòmén, a small town 250km south-east of Lánzhōu, are the **Water Curtain Thousand Buddha Caves** *(Shuǐlián Dòng; admission Y5)*, which contain **Lāshāo Sì**. This temple is a quaint old building nestled in a shallow cave on the nearby forested mountainside. The temple, cave paintings and rock carvings date back to the early Northern Wei dynasty (AD 386–534). Carved onto a rock face is a remarkable 31m-high figure of Sakyamuni, made during the Northern Wei period.

The caves and Lāshāo Sì are in a remote and spectacular gorge, which is accessible in good weather via a 17km makeshift road up the dry riverbed. You can charter a minibus from Luòmén for around Y60 return. A ***hostel*** *(zhāodàisuǒ; dorm beds Y15)* is directly opposite the Luòmén train station.

Luòmén is on the Lánzhōu-Xī'ān railway line, but it's a small station and only a few trains stop here. If you're coming from Lánzhōu, most trains arrive in the afternoon, whereas from Tiānshuǐ they are mostly morning trains.

You can also get a bus to Luòmén from Tiānshuǐ; buses leave from in front of the train station throughout the morning (Y9, 3½ hours).

SILK ROAD

Níngxià 宁夏

Capital: Yínchuān
Population: 5.9 million
Area: 66,400 sq km

Níngxià is part of the arid north-west of China and much of its landscape suffers a harsh climate. Plummeting temperatures mean winters are hard, and blistering summers make irrigation a necessity. The province would be virtually uninhabitable if it were not for Huáng Hé (Yellow River), Níngxià's lifeline. Most of the population lives near the river or the irrigation channels that run off it. These channels were created in the Han dynasty, when the area was first settled by the Han Chinese in the 1st century BC.

About a third of Níngxià's people are Hui, living mostly in the south of the province, and the rest are Han Chinese. The Hui minority are descended from Arab and Iranian traders who travelled to China during the Tang dynasty. Immigrants from Central Asia increased their numbers during the Yuan dynasty. Apart from their continued adherence to Islam, the Hui have been largely assimilated into Han culture.

The completion of the Bāotóu-Lánzhōu railway in 1958 helped to relieve the area's isolation and develop industry in this otherwise almost exclusively agricultural region.

YÍNCHUĀN 银川
☎ 0951 • pop 928,300
Sheltered from the deserts of Mongolia by the high ranges of Hèlán Shān to its west and abundantly supplied with water from nearby Huáng Hé, Yínchuān occupies a favoured geographical position in otherwise harsh surroundings.

This city was once the capital of the Western Xia, a mysterious kingdom founded during the 11th century. Today it's one of China's more pleasant, relaxed provincial capitals, with a few interesting sights and a lively market atmosphere.

Orientation
Yínchuān is divided into two parts. The new industrialised section is close to the train station and is simply called New City (Xīn Chéng). The Old City (Lǎo Chéng) is

Highlights

- Yínchuān, the pleasant capital city of this remote province, and a jumping-off point for trips to Hèlán Shān and the Gobi Desert

- Zhōngwèi, where the eerie beauty of the sand dunes meets the greenbelt surrounding Huáng Hé (Yellow River)

- The isolated, fascinating set of grottoes at Xūmí Shān (Treasure Mountain)

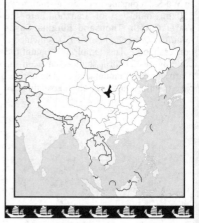

about 8km to the east and has most of the town's sights, hotels, restaurants and shops, as well as the long-distance bus station.

Information
Money The main branch of the Bank of China is on Jiefang Xijie and there is another branch on Xinhua Xijie, just west of Minzu Nanjie. Both can change cash and travellers cheques and are open Monday to Friday 8am to noon and 2.30pm to 5pm.

Post & Communications The post and telephone office is in the centre of town on Jiefang Xijie, next to Hóngqiáo Dàjiǔdiàn (see Places to Stay later). The telephone office is on the 2nd floor and is open daily from 8am to 6pm.

There are two China Telecom Internet cafes in town. One is on Zhongshan Beijie and the other is on the 5th floor of the

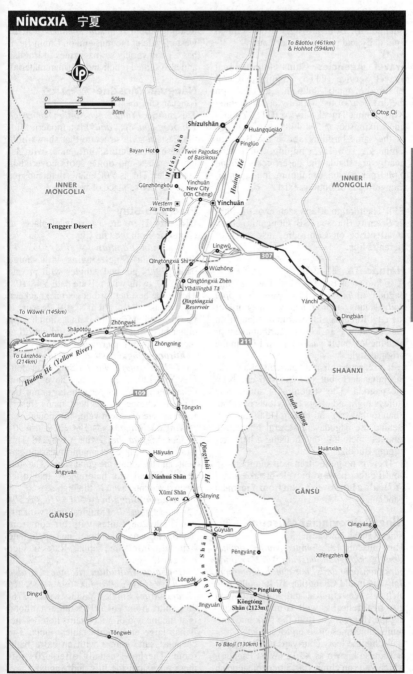

NÍNGXIÀ 宁夏

SILK ROAD

To Bāotóu (461km)
& Hohhot (594km)

Otog Qi

Shízuǐshān

Huángqúqiáo

Pínglúo

Bayan Hot

Twin Pagodas
of Baisikou

INNER
MONGOLIA

Gūnzhōngkǒu

Yínchuān
New City
(Xīn Chéng)

Yínchuān

Hèlán Shān

Huáng Hé

INNER
MONGOLIA

Western
Xia Tombs

Tengger Desert

Língwǔ

Qīngtóngxiá Shì

Wǔzhōng

Qīngtóngxiá Zhèn

Yìbǎilíngbā Tǎ

307

Yánchí

Dīngbiān

To Wǔwēi (145km)

Qīngtóngxiá
Reservoir

Gantang

Shāpōtóu

Zhōngwèi

Zhōngníng

211

SHAANXI

To Lánzhōu
(214km)

Huáng Hé (Yellow River)

Huán Jiāng

109

Tōngxīn

Húnxiàn

Qīngshuǐ Hé

Hǎiyuán

Jìngyuán

▲ Nánhuá Shān

Xūmí Shān
Cave

Sānyíng

GĀNSÙ

Qīngyáng

GĀNSÙ

Xījí

Gùyuán

Péngyáng

Xīfēngzhèn

Lóngdé

Lùpán Shān

Píngliáng

Dīngxī

Jìngyuán

Kōngtóng
Shān (2123m)

Tōngwèi

To Bǎojī (130km)

0 — 25 — 50km
0 — 15 — 30mi

Xīnhuá Department Store (Xīnhuá Bǎihuò Shāngdiàn). Both are open from 8am to 7pm daily and charge Y8 per hour.

Travel Agencies China International Travel Service (CITS; Zhōngguó Guójì Lǚxíngshè; ☎ 504 8006) has an office on the 3rd floor of the building at 116 Jiefang Xijie. China Travel Service (CTS; Zhōngguó Lǚxíngshè; ☎ 504 4485) has an office in the same building above the Bank of China. A two-day camping trip to the nearby grasslands and desert costs around Y600 per person (minimum four people) though loads of options exist.

PSB The foreign affairs section of the Public Security Bureau (PSB; Gōngānjú) is in a small office on Limin Jie, just south of Jiefang Xijie.

Hǎibǎo Tǎ 海宝塔

Also known as Běi Tǎ (North Pagoda), this pagoda (admission Y5; open 7am-6pm daily) stands out prominently in the north of the city. Records of the structure date from the 5th century. In 1739 an earthquake toppled the lot, but it was rebuilt in 1771 in the original style.

It's set in the pleasant gardens of a working monastery, but you can still climb up the pagoda. The structure is some nine storeys high and offers fine views of Hèlán Shān to the west and Huáng Hé to the east. Behind the pagoda are several interesting temples, including one housing a hefty reclining Buddha.

There is no public transport out there, so you'll either have to bicycle or take a taxi (Y7). It's a little over 3.5km from Yínchuān Fàndiàn.

Ningxia Provincial Museum
Níngxià Shěng Bówùguǎn

This museum (32 Jinning Nanjie; admission park/pagoda/museum Y2/3/5; open park 6am-6pm daily, museum 8.30am-6pm daily) is in old Chéngtiān Sì. Its collection includes Western Xia and Northern Zhou historical relics, as well as material covering the Hui culture. Both the park and museum sometimes close on Monday.

Within the leafy courtyard is **Chéngtiānsì Tǎ**, also known as Xī Tǎ (West Pagoda), which you can climb via 13 tiers of steepish

stairs. Perhaps of more interest is the small **Reading Room** (Cānkǎo Yuèlǎnshì) at the western gate of the museum on Limin Jie. It has a good variety of magazines in English and also some French and German material.

Nánguān Mosque 南关清真寺
Nánguān Qīngzhēnsì

This mosque (Yuhuangge Nanjie; admission Y8; open 8am-8pm daily) is a modern Middle Eastern-style structure that shows little Chinese architectural influence, with Islamic arches and dome roofs covered in green tiles. This is Yínchuān's main mosque and is an active place of worship.

Places to Stay
Old City There are a variety of places to choose from in the Old City.

Yínchuān Fàndiàn (☎ 602 3053, 17 Jiefang Xijie) Singles/twins with shared bath Y39/24 per bed, singles with private bath Y80, twins with private bath Y48-108. This is the best bet for budget backpackers. Upkeep is spotty but it's still decent. If you're coming from the train station hop on either bus No 1 or 11 (Y0.7) and get off at the post office stop (yóudiàn dàshà).

Fúróng Bīnguǎn (☎ 601 6688, fax 601 1411, 12 Yuxingge Nanjie) Singles or doubles Y92-220. The staff may have a group debate about whether you can stay or not, but if so, the cheaper rooms here, many freshly fixed up, are excellent value for money.

Níngxià Bīnguǎn (☎ 503 1229, fax 504 4338, Gongyuan Jie) Twins Y178-218. This is a peaceful place set among pleasant gardens, and the rooms are good value. The staff gets high marks for helpfulness; they offer steep discounts, even in the high season.

Zhōngyín Bīnguǎn (☎ 501 1918, fax 504 7545, 53 Funing Jie) Singles/twins with air-con Y200/268, suites with air-con from Y580. This very clean hotel, just off Jiefang Xijie, also offers free saunas. Rates include breakfast.

Hóngqiáo Dàjiǔdiàn (Rainbow Bridge Hotel; ☎ 691 8888, fax 691 8788, 16 Jiefang Xijie) Singles Y382, twins Y276-339, suites from Y615. This three-star hotel is at the top end of Yínchuān's hotel scene. It has large and comfortable rooms. The cheapest suite comes with an extra bathroom. The hotel usually offers 20% off these prices outside July and August.

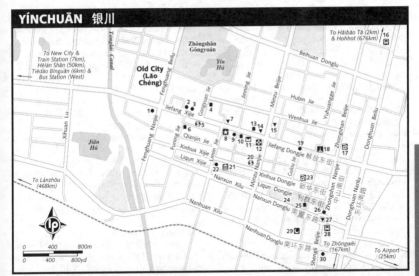

YÍNCHUĀN 银川

YÍNCHUĀN

PLACES TO STAY
4   Níngxià Bīnguǎn
    宁夏宾馆
6   Zhōngyín Bīnguǎn
    中银宾馆
10 Hóngqiáo Dàjiǔdiàn
    虹桥大酒店
13 Yínchuān Fàndiàn
    银川饭店
25 Fúróng Bīnguǎn
    芙蓉宾馆

PLACES TO EAT
7   Shāojīgōng
    烧鸡公
14 Yíngbīnlóu Qīngzhēn
    Fànzhuāng
    迎宾楼清真饭庄
15 Ālǐ Xībǐng
    A里西饼
27 Qīngzhēn
    Niúròu Lāmiàn
    清真牛肉拉面

OTHER
1   CITS; CTS
    中国国际旅行社；
    中国旅行社
2   Train Booking Office
    银川火车站售票处
3   Xinhua Bookshop
    新华书店
5   Bank of China
    中国银行
8   PSB
    公安局
9   Foreign Languages
    Bookshop
    外文书店
11 Post & Telephone Office
    邮电大楼
12 Yinchuan Department Store
    银川百货大楼
16 North Bus Station
    北门车站
17 China Telecom Internet
    Cafe
    网吧

18 Yùhuáng Gé
    玉皇阁
19 Drum Tower
    鼓楼
20 Main Bank of China
    中国银行
21 Ningxia Provincial
    Museum; Chéngtiānsì Tǎ
    宁夏省博物馆；承天寺塔
22 Reading Room
    参考阅览室
23 Internet Café; Xīnhuá
    Department Store
    网吧；新华百货商店
24 Indoor/Outdoor Market
    商城
26 Nánmén Tower
    南门楼
28 Long-Distance Bus Station
    银川汽车站
29 Nánguān Mosque
    南关清真寺
30 CAAC
    民航售票处

New City The new city is mostly sprawling development with little charm.

Tiědào Bīnguǎn (Railway Hotel; ☎ *306 9119, Xingzhou Lu)* Beds in quads with/without bath Y35/25, twins or triples with bath Y250. This is the most convenient place for making a quick getaway as it's just a short walk from the train station.

The staff are usually willing to take 20% off these prices.

Places to Eat

Good for street food are the *stalls* in the backstreets around the long-distance bus station or the *night market (Xinhua Dongjie)* nearby.

Yíngbīnlóu Qīngzhēn Fànzhuāng (Ying-binlou Islamic Restaurant) Dishes from Y5. This is a raucous spot, popular with the locals. The restaurant on the 2nd floor has some tasty dishes and the 1st floor offers yoghurt, ice cream and beer.

Qīngzhēn Niúròu Lāmiàn (Muslim Noodle Restaurant; Zhongshan Nanjie) Dishes Y2. You'll find cheap and tasty noodles here.

Shāojīgōng (Jiefang Xijie) Small dishes Y36. The speciality of this restaurant is a spicy chicken stew. You cook it yourself and you can add various vegetables and noodles to this tasty meal. A small serving is enough for two people.

Ālǐ Xībǐng (Aile Cakeshop; Minzu Beijie) Snacks Y2. This is a pleasant place to sit down and write a few postcards. It has basic cakes and instant coffee.

Over in the New City there is a lively *market*, just across from Tiědào Bīnguǎn, where you can warm your tummy with a bowl of spicy noodles.

Getting There & Away

Air The main ticket office of the Civil Aviation Administration of China (CAAC; Zhōngguó Mínháng; ☎ 691 3455) is south of the bus station on the corner of Nanhuan Donglu and Shengli Beijie. The office is open daily from 8am to 5.30pm. There are flights connecting Yínchuān with Běijīng (Y870), Chéngdū (Y810), Guǎngzhōu (Y1510), Shànghǎi (Y1080), Tàiyuán (Y590), Ürümqi (twice weekly), Xīníng, and Xī'ān (Y430) among many other national destinations.

Bus The long-distance bus station is in the south-eastern part of town on the square near the South Gate (Nán Mén). For some northern destinations you may get referred to the northern bus station (beǐmén zhàn); to get there from the long-distance bus station hop on a No 4 bus (Y1).

There are six buses to Zhōngwèi (Y16, four hours) that leave between 7am and 4.30pm. Buses to Gùyuán (Y30 to Y41, seven hours) leave every half-hour from 6am to 1pm. There are much faster expresses at 8am and 10am. There are four daily buses (Y122) leaving in the afternoon for the 17-hour trip to Xī'ān. There are two buses a day to Yán'ān (Shaanxi) at 6am and 6pm; the trip takes at least 13 hours and costs Y75.

Train Yínchuān is on the Lánzhōu-Běijīng railway line, which also runs via Bāotóu, Hohhot and Dàtóng. Express trains from Yínchuān take nine hours to Lánzhōu, 11 hours to Hohhot, 17 hours to Xī'ān and 21 hours to Běijīng. If you're heading for Lánzhōu or Xīníng, there is a convenient overnight tourist train (No K423). The train station is in the New City, about 9km west of the Old City centre.

There's a train booking office in the Old City, at 57 Jiefang Xijie, where tickets can be bought at least four days in advance. The office is on the ground floor at the eastern end of a five-storey building, opposite the China Construction Bank. It's open daily from 9.30am to noon and 2pm to 5pm.

Getting Around

The airport is 25km from town and a CAAC shuttle bus (Y15) meets all flights. A taxi to the airport will cost around Y40.

Bus No 1 runs from the bus station in the Old City, along Jiefang Jie and then on to the train station in the New City. The fare is just Y0.7. Minibuses cover the same route faster, but charge Y3.

Taxis are fairly cheap, with flag fall at Y5 to Y6 depending on the vehicle. A taxi between the train station and the Old City will cost around Y25.

AROUND YÍNCHUĀN
Hèlán Shān 贺兰山

The mountains of this range are clearly visible from Yínchuān. The range forms an important natural barrier against desert winds and invaders alike, with the highest peak reaching 3556m. Along the foothills of Hèlán Shān lie some interesting sights.

About 54km north-west of Yínchuān's New City is the historic pass village of **Gǔnzhōngkǒu**, where there are walking trails up into the surrounding hills. No buses travel here, the only way to reach it is by taxi or by hiring a vehicle through CITS or another travel agency.

North of Gǔnzhōngkǒu are the **Twin Pagodas of Baisikou** *(Báisìkǒu Shuāngtǎ)*, which are 13 and 14 storeys high and decorated with Buddha statuettes. These are accessible only by jeep, bicycle or on foot, so don't expect taxis to be able to get you here.

South of Gǔnzhōngkǒu lie the **Western Xia Tombs** *(Xīxià Wánglíng; admission*

Y20), the main tourist destination in this area. According to legend, the founder of the Western Xia kingdom, Li Yuanhao, built 72 tombs. One was for himself, others held relatives or were left empty. The Western Xia kingdom lasted for 190 years and 10 successive emperors, and had its own written language and a strong military.

Again, you'll need to cycle or hire a vehicle to get here. Hiring a minivan taxi for half a day should cost Y80 or Y150 for the full day. In half a day you could visit Hèlán Shān and the Western Xia Tombs. For a full day add the Twin Pagodas of Baisikou and Gǔnzhōngkǒu.

CITS asks considerably more, but it throws in an English-speaking guide for 'free'.

Yībǎilíngbā Tǎ 兰州
108 Dagobas
These mysterious Buddhist dagobas, or stupas (admission Y5), are 83km south of Yínchuān by Huáng Hé, near the town of Qīngtóngxiá Zhèn. The 12 rows of dagobas are arranged in a large triangular constellation on the banks of the Huáng Hé. The dagobas date from the Yuan dynasty and it's still not known why they were erected here. The white vase-like shape contrasts strikingly with the surrounding arid landscape. A visit to the Yībǎilíngbā Tǎ can be a very relaxing day trip from Yínchuān. You may even stumble across an isolated stretch of the Great Wall not far from the town.

It is possible to visit this site independently by catching a train or bus from Yínchuān. Only a few buses go directly to the smaller town of Qīngtóngxiá Zhèn, but you can catch a local bus or taxi from Qīngtóngxiá Shì to Yībǎilíngbā Tǎ. From town there are sometimes tourist buses; otherwise hire a taxi or even walk.

Bayan Hot 阿拉山左旗
Ālāshàn Zuòqí
Bayan Hot is a town just over the border with Inner Mongolia, some 105km from Yínchuān, and a worthy day trip. It lies surrounded by desert, just over Hèlán Shān from Yínchuān and has a real desert outpost feel to it. In town **Yánfú Sì** (admission Y2) is a small Mongolian temple that dates back over 300 years; once populated by 200 lamas, it now houses around 30. It was nearly destroyed in the Cultural Revolution but restoration work has been ongoing since 1984. You can see services here most mornings. From Bayan Hot ('Rich City' in Mongolian) there's lots to explore in the desert.

Halfway to Bayan Hot the road broaches crumbling, yet still mighty, remains of the Great Wall. It's a special experience to hop off and wander along the wall into the foothills of the mountains from which it descended – one of the few moments of solitude in China. Be very careful where you wander, there are military restricted zones all over the place and officials are very humourless about it. And try not to get stranded here, unless you want to sleep in a cave.

Getting There & Away Lots of buses leave the Yínchuān long-distance bus station for Bayan Hot (Y11 to Y19, two to three hours); they stop at the west bus station first. Buses return from the Bayan Hot bus station every 30 minutes throughout the day but they slow in frequency in late afternoon.

ZHŌNGWÈI 中卫
☎ 0953
Zhōngwèi lies 167km south-west of Yínchuān on the Lánzhōu-Bāotóu railway line, sandwiched between the sand dunes of the Tengger Desert (Tengger Shāmò) to the north and Huáng Hé to the south. In addition to its unusual setting, Zhōngwèi has a fairly relaxed pace – a nice change from the rush of most Chinese cities.

Information
Zhongwei Travel Service (☎ 701 2620), in the foyer of Yìxīng Dàjiǔdiàn, can arrange some interesting trips to sights out of town (see the Around Zhōngwèi section for details). Across from the Drum Tower (Gǔ Lóu) roundabout is the Bank of China, open Monday to Friday from 8am to noon and 2.30pm to 6pm. Next to the post office on Gulou Xijie is an Internet cafe that charges Y2 per hour.

Gāo Miào 高庙
The main attraction in town is Gāo Miào (Gulou Beijie; admission Y5; open 8am-6pm daily), an eclectic, multipurpose temple that serves Buddhism, Confucianism and Taoism, set in a nice park. Built during

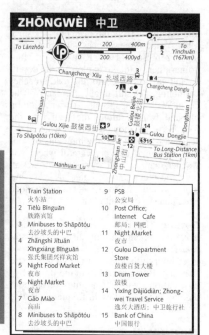

ZHŌNGWÈI 中卫

1 Train Station 火车站	9 PSB 公安局
2 Tiělù Bīnguǎn 铁路宾馆	10 Post Office; Internet Cafe 邮局；网吧
3 Minibuses to Shāpōtóu 去沙坡头的中巴	11 Night Market 夜市
4 Zhāngshì Jítuán Xīngxiáng Bīnguǎn 张氏集团兴祥宾馆	12 Gulou Department Store 鼓楼百货大楼
5 Night Food Market 夜市	13 Drum Tower 鼓楼
6 Night Market 夜市	14 Yìxīng Dàjiǔdiàn; Zhong- wei Travel Service
7 Gāo Miào 高庙	逸兴大酒店；中卫旅行社
8 Minibuses to Shāpōtóu 去沙坡头的中巴	15 Bank of China 中国银行

the 15th century and flattened by an earth-quake during the 18th century, it was later rebuilt and expanded several times until being virtually razed again by fire in 1942.

During the Cultural Revolution the temple's basement was converted into a bomb shelter. To try and rake in a bit more cash, the eerie shelter has now become a neon-light torture chamber hell, complete with patrons being sawn in half.

Places to Stay & Eat
Tiělù Bīnguǎn (Railway Hotel; ☎ 701 1441) Dorm beds Y15, beds in triples with shared bath Y25, singles/twins with bath Y66/70. This hotel is to the left as you exit the train station. The rooms are fairly comfortable and it is not a bad deal. Keep in mind that dorm beds are usually given to Chinese only; rates for dorms include breakfast.

Zhāngshì Jítuán Xīngxiáng Bīnguǎn (☎/fax 701 9970, 61 Changcheng Donglu) Dorm beds from Y18, singles or doubles with private bath Y100-150. This place rates a mention for its superb doubles with bathroom, which are spacious and spotless. A Y100 room can often be bargained to Y80

and with breakfast *delivered to your door,* it's the best deal around. The Chóngqìng-style *restaurant* is also excellent with a friendly staff; they're often willing to prepare smaller, cheaper versions of dishes for solo travellers. Look for the pictures of wedding models on the building's facade.

Yìxīng Dàjiǔdiàn (☎ *701 7666, fax 701 9993, 2 Gulou Beijie)* Triples/twins Y45/50 per bed, more comfortable triples/twins Y150/168, suites Y388. This is the most up-market place in town. Surprisingly, it has a good range of prices. Rates include breakfast.

There's a nice *guesthouse* at Shāpōtóu (20km from Zhōngwèi) that's worth considering as an alternative to staying in town (see the Around Zhōngwèi section for details).

In Zhōngwèi there are lots of small *restaurants* along Gulou Beijie. The best place in town is the *night market;* it's a happening spot with different types of local specialities. Two favourites are *ròujiāmó* (fried pork or beef stuffed in pita bread, sometimes with green peppers and cumin) and *shāguō* (mini-hotpot). Otherwise there are always kebabs (Y0.2 each) and draft beer (Y2.5).

Getting There & Away
Bus The long-distance bus station is about 1km east of the Drum Tower, on the southern side of Dong Dajie. Buses to Yínchuān (Y16, four hours) leave every half-hour from 6am to 5.30pm. No buses go to Lánzhōu from Zhōngwèi.

Train From Zhōngwèi you can catch trains heading north, south, west and south-east. In general, heading south and west you'll find convenient times, not so if you're heading to Yínchuān. By express it's 2½ hours to Yínchuān (No K44), six hours to Lánzhōu (No K43), 11 hours to Xī'ān (No 2987) and 23 hours to Ürümqi (No 1013). Other destinations include Běijīng, Chéngdū, Píngliáng, Shànghǎi and Hohhot.

AROUND ZHŌNGWÈI
The best thing about exploring this area is seeing the abrupt convergence of desert sand dunes and lush farm fields.

Shāpōtóu *(admission main area Y20, botanical gardens & desert Y5),* 10km west of Zhōngwèi, lies on the fringe of the Tenger Desert. It's based around the **Shapotou**

Desert Research Centre *(Shāpōtóu Shāmò Yánjiùsuǒ)*, which was founded in 1956 to find a way to keep drifting sand dunes from covering the railway line.

Shāpōtóu has become a bit of a Chinese playground, with camel rides, speed boats, a castle, cable cars, sheep skin rafts, sand sleds and desert walks. It is a scenic spot next to Huáng Hé and it's not a bad place to spend the night. There are two entrances to the area, one at the guesthouse and the other at the top of the sand dunes. From the top entrance it is possible to rent a sand sled and skid across the sand dunes almost all the way to the front gate of the guesthouse.

Water wheels *(shuǐ chē)* used to be a common sight in Níngxià. Mechanical pumps have now taken over, but there is still one operational water wheel upstream from Shāpōtóu at Beichangtai, a small mountain village some 70km south-west of Zhōngwèi. It's best reached by boat.

At Shāpōtóu you can also see some leather rafts *(yángpí fázi)* in action. A traditional mode of transport on Huáng Hé for centuries, the rafts are made from sheep or cattle skins soaked in oil and brine and then inflated. An average of 14 hides are tied together under a wooden framework to make a strong raft capable of carrying four people and four bikes. Touts at Shāpōtóu offer rides down to Shāhéyuàn (10km west of Zhōngwèi) for Y150 per person, including transport back to Shāpōtóu. For Y40 you can hop on a raft for a short stretch of the river, but you have to make your own way back.

To the north of Zhōngwèi in the Tengger Desert, there's a few scattered remains of the **Great Wall** dating from the Ming dynasty. There isn't much left of the wall, but getting there is quite interesting.

Organised Tours

Zhongwei Travel Service offers several interesting river and desert trips. Examples include a two-day journey into the Tengger Desert that features a visit to the Great Wall and camping in the dunes. Transport (including camels), guide and accommodation cost around Y200 per person per day, as long as there are at least three of you. Desert trips of up to seven days are available.

Another option is a one-day leather raft trip down Huáng Hé, starting at Shāpōtóu

The Wrath of Khan

According to legend, Genghis Khan saw the Xia kingdom as a potential vassal/ally, but the Xia baulked at the thought of bowing to another ruler.

Genghis Khan mounted six separate campaigns against the Xia, all of which failed. During the sixth campaign, Xia archers sneaked down to Khan's war camp, near present-day Gùyuán, and fatally wounded the military leader with poison-tipped arrows.

Enraged even at death's door, Genghis Khan gave his final order: the total annihilation of the Western Xia kingdom. Looking at the site today, one must conclude that Khan's subordinates carried out his command with a vengeance.

and ending at Zhōngwèi. With three people this should cost around Y150, including transport to Shāpōtóu from Zhōngwèi.

Place to Stay

Shāpō Shānzhuāng (☎ 768 1481) Twins/triples with bath Y50/90. A pleasant option would be a night or two at this guesthouse built around a garden courtyard on the bank of Huáng Hé. There's also a small *bar/restaurant* on the premises; however, cold beers are rare.

Getting There & Away

From Zhōngwèi there are regular minibuses to Shāpōtóu (Y4, one hour). Minibuses leave from inside a courtyard opposite the long-distance bus station, stop first at the intersection of Gulou Beijie and Changcheng Xilu, pause again at the corner of Gulou Xijie and Xihuan Lu, and then head off to Shāpōtóu.

The frequency increases during the peak tourist months of June, July and August, when buses run as often as every half-hour. At other times you may have to wait an hour or two. The first bus departs Zhōngwèi at 7am and the last bus departs from the Shāpōtóu main entrance, near Shāpō Shānzhuāng, at 6.30pm.

Trains heading for Wǔwēi stop at Shāpōtóu for half an hour after leaving Zhōngwèi at 3.15pm. You can also hire a motor-tricycle to take you there for Y30/40 one way/return.

SILK ROAD

GÙYUÁN 固原
☎ 0954

Gùyuán is located in the south of Níngxià, about 460km from Yínchuān. There is an interesting set of **Buddhist Grottoes** (*Shíkū*) at Xūmí Shān (Treasure Mountain), which is about 50km north-west of Gùyuán. Xūmí is the Chinese version of the Sanskrit word *sumeru*, which translates as 'treasure mountain'.

Cut into five adjacent peaks are 132 caves containing more than 300 Buddhist statues dating back 1400 years, from the Northern Wei to the Sui and Tang dynasties. The finest statues are in caves 14, 45, 46, 51, 67 and 70. Cave 5 contains the most famous statue on Xūmí Shān: a colossal Maitreya Buddha, standing 19m high. It remains remarkably well preserved even though the protective tower has long since collapsed and left it exposed and vulnerable to the elements.

There is no regular transport to the caves, but you can catch a bus from Gùyuán directly to Sānyíng. Sānyíng is on the main road 40km north of Gùyuán near the Xūmí Shān turn-off. From Sānyíng you can hop on a minibus to **Huángduóbǎo** and then a tractor (Y2) up to the caves. Or you can hire a taxi from Sānyíng for about Y50 return.

Places to Stay
Dōngyuè Bīnguǎn (☎ 203 4131) Dorm beds/singles/twins/triples Y20/80/35/30 per bed. This place is to the left as you exit the train station. The dorms here are good, but there are no common showers.

Gùyuán Bīnguǎn (☎ 203 2479, *Zhengfu Jie*) Twins Y136, triples with bath Y33 per bed. Located south-east of the bus station, the rooms here are nice.

Getting There & Away
Gùyuán is on the Zhōngwèi-Bǎojī railway line and is served by trains from Xī'ān (eight hours), Zhōngwèi (3½ hours) and Yínchuān (six hours).

Buses to Gùyuán (Y30, seven hours) leave every half-hour between 6am and 1pm from the Yínchuān long-distance bus station. There are buses running once daily from Lánzhōu (Y41, 11 hours) and Tiānshuǐ (Y29, seven hours) in Gānsù. There are also regular buses to Jīngyuán.

Inner Mongolia 内蒙古

Capital: Hohhot
Population: 24.4 million
Area: 1,183,000 sq km

For most foreigners, the big attractions of
Inner Mongolia (Nèi Ménggǔ) are the
grasslands, the horses and the Mongolian
way of life.

Just how much you can see of the Mongolian way of life in China is dubious, but
the grasslands are indeed perfect horse country, and horse-drawn carts seem to be a common form of transport on the communes (a
Hohhot tourist leaflet shows foreigners riding in a decorated camel cart with suspension
and truck tyres). However, the small Mongolian horse is being phased out – herders
can now purchase motorcycles (preferred
over bicycles because of strong winds), and
on some of the large state-run farms, helicopters and light aircrafts are used to round
up steers and spot grazing herds.

It's important to distinguish between
Inner Mongolia (the Chinese province) and
Mongolia, the independent country to the
north, formerly called Outer Mongolia. For
more information on the country of Mongolia, see Lonely Planet's *Mongolia* guide.

HISTORY
The nomadic tribes to the north of China
have always been a problem for China's
rulers. The first emperor of the Qin dynasty,
Qin Shihuang, started building the Great
Wall for the express purpose of keeping
them out.

Inner Mongolia is only one part of what
was originally the Mongol homeland, a vast
area that also encompassed all of Outer
Mongolia and a large slice of Siberia.

The Mongols endured a rough life as
shepherds and horse breeders in the grasslands beyond the Great Wall and the Gobi
Desert. They moved with the seasons in
search of pastures for their animals, living
in tents known as *yurt* (a Russian word) or
ger (the Mongolian word). The yurts were
made of animal hide usually supported by
wooden rods, and could be taken apart
quickly to pack onto wagons.

At the mercy of their environment, the
Mongols based their religion on the forces of

Highlights

- The grasslands, offering a glimpse of
  the rapidly vanishing traditional
  lifestyle of the nomads

- Mǎnzhōulǐ, the bordertown with
  Russia and gateway to splendid
  Hūlún Hú

- Bāotóu, the stage for Resonant Sand
  Gorge

- Dōngshèng, stop-off point for
  Ghenghis Khan's Mausoleum, where
  the great leader's bones are
  purportedly interred

nature: moon, sun and stars were all revered,
as were the rivers. The gods were virtually
infinite in number, signifying a universal supernatural presence. Mongol priests could
speak to the gods and communicate their orders to the tribal chief, the khan.

Mongol Empire
United by Genghis Khan and later led by
his grandson Kublai Khan, the Mongols
went on to conquer not only China but most
of the known world, founding an empire
that stretched from Vietnam to Hungary.

It was an empire won on horseback: the
entire Mongol army was cavalry and this
allowed rapid movement and deployment
of the armies. The Mongols excelled in
military science and were quick to adopt

INNER MONGOLIA

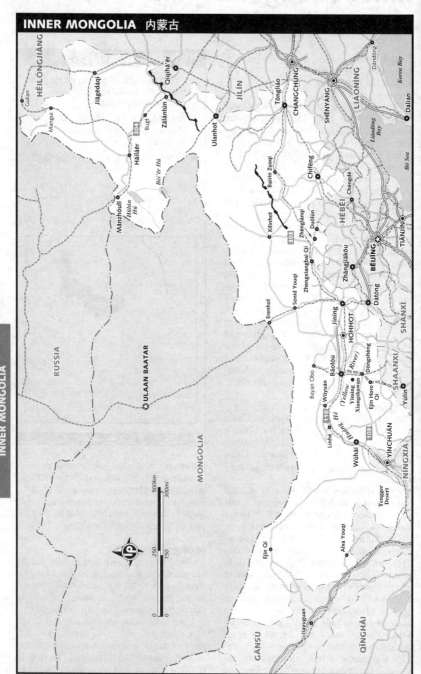

and improve on Persian and Chinese weaponry. But their cultural and scientific legacy was meagre.

Once they abandoned their policies of terror and destruction, they became patrons, but not practitioners, of science and art. Influenced by the people they had conquered, they also adopted the local religions – mainly Buddhism and Islam.

The Mongol conquest of China was slow, delayed by campaigns in the west and by internal strife. Secure behind their Great Wall, the Chinese rulers had little idea of the fury the Mongols would unleash in 1211, when the invasion began.

For two years the Great Wall held them back, but the Mongols eventually penetrated through a 27km gorge into the northern Chinese plains. In 1215 a Chinese general went over to the Mongols and led them into Běijīng. Nevertheless, the Chinese stubbornly held out, and the war in China was placed under the command of one of Genghis' generals so the Khan could turn his attention to the west.

Despite the death of Genghis Khan in 1227, the Mongols lost none of their vigour. Genghis had divided the empire into separate domains, each domain ruled by one of his sons or other descendants. Ogadai was given China and was also elected the Great Khan in 1229 by an assemblage of princes. Northern China was subdued, but the conquest of the south was delayed while Khan turned his attention to the invasion and subjugation of Russia. With the death of Ogadai in 1241, the invasion of Europe was cancelled and Mangu Khan, a grandson of Genghis, continued the conquest of China.

He sent his brother Kublai to attack the south of China, which was ruled by the Song emperors. Mangu died of dysentery while fighting in China in 1259 and Kublai was elected Great Khan. Once he had swept away a challenge to his rule by his brother Arik-Boko and opposition from his enemies in the 'Golden Horde' (the Mongol faction that controlled the far west of the empire), Kublai was able to complete the conquest of southern China by 1279. It was the first and only time that China had been ruled in its entirety by foreigners.

The Mongols established their capital at Běijīng, and Kublai Khan became the first emperor of the Yuan dynasty. Kublai's empire was the largest nation the world has ever known. The Mongols improved the road system linking China with Russia, promoted trade throughout the empire and with Europe, instituted a famine relief scheme and expanded the canal system, which brought food from the countryside to the cities. It was into this China that Marco Polo wandered, and his book *Description of the World* revealed the secrets of Asia to an amazed Europe.

Kublai died in 1294, the last Khan to rule over a united Mongol empire. He was followed by a series of weak and incompetent rulers who were unable to contain the revolts that spread all over China.

The entire Mongol Empire had disintegrated by the end of the 14th century, and the Mongol homeland returned to the way of life it knew before Genghis Khan. The Mongols once again became a loose collection of disorganised roaming tribes, warring among themselves and occasionally raiding China, until the Qing emperors finally gained control over them in the 18th century.

Mongolia Today

Mongolians make up only about 15% of the total population of Inner Mongolia – the other 85% are mostly Han Chinese with a smattering of minority Hui, Manchu, Daur and Ewenki.

Since 1949 the Chinese have done their best to assimilate the Mongolians, though the Mongolians have been permitted to keep their written and spoken language. Tibetan Buddhism, the traditional religion of the Mongolians, has not fared so well.

The Mongolians are scattered throughout China's north-eastern provinces, as well as through Qīnghǎi and Xīnjiāng. Altogether there are about 3.5 million of them living in China, and another half a million in Russia.

Today, the 'Inner Mongolia Autonomous Region' enjoys little or no autonomy at all. Since the break-up of the Soviet Union in 1991, Outer Mongolia has been free of Soviet control and is reasserting its nationalism. This has the Chinese worried – nationalistic movements like those in Tibet and Xīnjiāng do not please Běijīng. As a result, the PSB keeps a tight lid on potential real or imagined independence activists.

Much of the Inner Mongolia region comprises vast areas of natural grazing land. However, the far north is forested – the Greater Hinggan range contains about one-sixth of the country's forests and is an important source of timber and paper pulp. Inner Mongolia is also rich in minerals such as coal and iron ore, as you'll see if you visit Bāotóu.

The Mongolian climate tends towards extremes. Siberian blizzards and cold currents rake the plains in winter (from December to March) – forget it! In winter you'll even witness snow on the desert sand dunes. Summer (from June to August) brings pleasant temperatures, but it can get scorchingly hot during the day in the western areas.

From May to September is the recommended time to visit, but pack warm clothing for the Inner Mongolian spring or autumn.

HOHHOT 呼和浩特
☎ 0471 • pop 2,003,700

Hohhot (Hūhéhàotè) was founded in the 16th century and, like other towns, grew around its temples and lamaseries, which are now in ruins. It became the capital of Inner Mongolia in 1952.

Hohhot means Blue City in Mongolian, although many Chinese-speaking locals mistakenly claim it means 'green city'.

Hohhot is a relatively prosperous and cosmopolitan city that serves as the main entrance point for tours of the grasslands. Tour agencies can line you up a trip – from the grasslands tour to the equestrian displays at the horse racing ground. Horse racing, polo and stunt riding are put on for large tour groups, if you latch onto one; otherwise, they take place only on rare festive occasions. It's the same with song and dance soirees.

Information

Money The Bank of China is on Xinhua Dajie. There are also money changing facilities inside Nèi Ménggǔ Fàndiàn.

Post & Communications The main post and telephone office is on Zhongshan Xilu. There is an Internet bar on the 2nd floor of the telephone section. It costs Y8 an hour and drinks are available. There is a more convenient post office on the left-hand side of the square as you exit the train station.

The entrance closest to the station is the place to make long-distance phone calls.

Travel Agencies China Travel Service (CTS; Zhōngguó Lǚxíngshè; ☎ 696 4233 ext 8123) and China International Travel Service (CITS; Zhōngguó Guójì Lǚxíngshè) both have small offices at Nèi Ménggǔ Fàndiàn and can help you stake out the grasslands (this hotel was slated for renovation, so they may have moved). CTS also has an office in the Post Hotel, just west of the train station. China Youth Travel Service (CYTS; Zhōngguó Qīngnián Lǚxíngshè; ☎ 696 4969) is at 91 Zhongshan Donglu; this office is quite friendly and helpful.

PSB For visa extensions and other inquiries the Public Security Bureau (PSB; Gōngānjú; ☎ 696 8148) is at 30 Zhongshan Xilu. Go through a gate toward a building with an antenna on top and bear right to an adjacent building.

Inner Mongolia Museum
Nèi Ménggǔ Bówùguǎn 内蒙古博物馆

Well presented and definitely worth a visit, this museum (*Hulunbei'er Lu; admission Y8; open 9am-5pm Wed-Mon*) is the biggest attraction in town. The collection includes a large mammoth skeleton dug out of a coal mine near Mǎnzhōulǐ, dinosaur exhibits, a yurt and a fantastic array of Mongolian costumes, artefacts, archery equipment and saddles. The top floors of the museum are sometimes closed.

Xílètú Temple 席勒图召
Xílètú Zhào

This temple (*admission Y6*) is the stomping ground of the 11th Grand Living Buddha, who dresses in civvies and is apparently active. There's nothing special to see though. The original temple burned down and the present one was built in the 19th century; the Chinese-style building has a few Tibetan touches.

Great Mosque 清真大寺
Qīngzhēn Dàsì

North of Xílètú Temple is the Great Mosque (*Tongdao Jie*). Built in Chinese style, with the addition of a minaret, it dates from the Qing dynasty (with later expansions). It is an active place of worship for

INNER MONGOLIA

the Hohhot Muslim community, with prayers held five times a day. You can wander around, as long as you don't enter the prayer area. There is no entrance fee.

Naadam

The summer festival known as Naadam features traditional Mongolian sports such as competition archery, wrestling, horse racing and camel racing. Prizes vary from a goat to a fully equipped horse. The fair has its origins in the ancient Obo-Worshipping Festival (an *obo* is a pile of stones with a hollow space for offerings – a kind of shamanistic shrine).

The Mongolian clans make a beeline for the fairs on any form of transport they can muster, and create an impromptu yurt city. For foreigners, Hohhot is a good place to see the Naadam festivities. Horse racing, camel racing, wrestling and archery take place at the horse racing grounds *(sàimǎchǎng)* in the northern part of the city on bus route No 13.

The exact date of Naadam varies in China, but is usually between mid-July and mid-August. Apparently it depends on when the grass is at its greenest. It's worth knowing that Naadam is celebrated at a different time in Outer Mongolia – always from 11 to 13 July, which corresponds to the date of Mongolia's 1921 revolution.

Places to Stay

Běiyúan Fàndiàn (☎ 696 6211, fax 696 9153, 28 Chezhan Xijie) Singles/twins/ triples/quads with shared bath Y30/60/75/80,

twins with private bath Y120, suites Y180. This hotel is the best value in Hohhot and it's extremely convenient to both the bus and train station. The prices here are very reasonable but it fills up very early in the day and Chinese get preference for cheap beds. Rooms include breakfast.

Hūhéhàotè Tiělù Bīnguǎn (Hohhot Railway Hotel; ☎ 693 3377, fax 695 4746, 131 Xilin Guole Lu) Twins with shared bath Y54, with private bath Y116-420. If the Běiyúan is full, try this hotel which also has a gym, library and billiards room. Rates include breakfast and the staff is friendly.

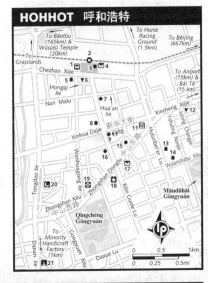

HOHHOT		
PLACES TO STAY	12 Mǎlāqìn Fàndiàn	11 Inner Mongolia Museum
5 Běiyúan Fàndiàn	马拉沁饭店	内蒙古博物馆
北原饭店		15 CYTS
8 Hūhéhàotè Tiělù	**OTHER**	中国青年旅行社
Bīnguǎn	1 Bus Station	16 CAAC
呼和浩特铁路宾馆	汽车站	中国民航
13 Xīnchéng Bīnguǎn	2 Train Station	17 Main Post Office;
新城宾馆	火车站	Telephone Office
14 Nèi Ménggǔ Fàndiàn;	3 Bike Rental	邮局；中国电信
CITS; CTS	4 Post Office	18 PSB
内蒙古饭店；中国国际	邮局	公安局外事科
旅行社；中国旅行社	7 Bike Rental	19 Minzu Department Store
	9 Foreign Language	民族商场
PLACES TO EAT	Bookshop	20 Great Mosque
6 Wángshì	外文书店	清真大寺
Huǒguōchéng	10 Bank of China	21 Xílètú Temple
王市火锅成	中国银行	席勒图召

Nèi Ménggǔ Fàndiàn (Inner Mongolia Hotel; ☎ *696 4233, fax 696 1479, Wulanchabu Xilu)* Twins Y280-340. This 14-storey high-rise was undergoing extensive renovations to finally make its three-star rating legitimate. It has a couple of travel agencies and a nice location.

Xīnchéng Bīnguǎn (☎ *629 2288,* W *www .xincheng-hotel.com.cn, 40 Hulun Nanlu)* Doubles, triples or quads Y120, standard doubles Y440-680. On spacious, well-treed grounds and once a homely guesthouse, this place has now become a sybaritic, five-star retreat. Amazingly, a few wings still have cheaper rooms. If you can get a cheaper double, it's excellent value, given the standards, amenities and service. There's no bus from the train station to the hotel. Bus No 20 stops near the hotel, but to catch this bus you must turn left as you exit the train station and walk a long block to Hulunbei'er Lu. A taxi ride (Y6) is recommended, as the hotel's reception is a long way from the bus stop.

Places to Eat

Wángshì Huǒguōchéng (Hongqi Jie) Dishes from Y4. This popular place is on the northern side of Hongqi Jie, a mall running west off Xilin Guole Lu. Tables are set up out the front where you can have your Sichuan hotpot and watch the crowds watch you. Food vendors also set up tables on summer nights at the corner in front of Zhāojūn Dàjiǔdiàn.

Mǎlāqìn Fàndiàn (Julong Changjie) Dishes from Y6. This place is recommended for Mongolian and Chinese food. Try the Mongolian hotpot, roasted lamb and kebab. Tasty vegetarian dishes include: *sùhézǐ* (an egg, spinach and noodle patty) and *chǎoxiānnǎi* (fried milk and egg with pine nuts). Prices are moderate and the friendly staff speak some English.

Shopping

Minority Handicraft Factory (Shiyangqiao Xilu) This factory is in the southern section of town on the bus No 1 route and has a retail outlet for tourists. It's on the southern side of the street, near the intersection with Nanchafang Jie. It only carries a limited selection of stock, but wares include inlaid knife and chopstick sets, saddles, daggers, boots, embroidered shoes, costumes, brassware, blankets and curios.

Mínzú Shāngchǎng (Nationality's Market; 2nd floor, Minzu Department Store, Zhongshan Xilu) You'll actually find a better selection and lower prices here. It's situated where the pedestrian bridge crosses the road. Other good buys in this section of the store are the very cheap silver earrings, necklaces and bracelets.

Many of the *souvenir shops* have selections of jewellery as well, and the small *shop* beside the Inner Mongolia Museum has some nice items.

Getting There & Away

Air Civil Aviation Administration of China (CAAC; *Zhōngguó Mínháng;* ☎ *696 4103)* has an office on Xilin Guole Lu. There are regular flights to Běijīng (Y460), Guǎngzhōu (Y1650), Shànghǎi (Y1230) and many other major cities.

There are also flights to Ulaan Baatar in Outer Mongolia five days a week with Mongolian Airlines (☎ 430 2026) or China Air for Y1000 one way.

Bus There are bus connections between Hohhot and Dàtóng (Y30 to Y40, 3½ to 5 hours). Buses and expresses to Bāotóu (Y16 to Y25, 1½ to 3 hours) leave about every 30 minutes. There are a half-dozen daily buses to Dōngshèng (Y25 to Y35, five to six hours), starting at 7.30am.

Train Hohhot is on the Běijīng-Lánzhōu railway line that cuts a long loop through Inner Mongolia. About 2½ hours out of Běijīng you'll pass the crumbled remains of the Great Wall (it looks like little more than a dirt embankment).

Express trains go to Běijīng (11 hours), Dàtóng (4½ hours), Bāotóu (2½ hours) and Yínchuān (11 hours).

You can use any window in the main office to buy advance tickets for all destinations except Baōtóu; you buy those tickets from a window behind the escalators near the main entrance. Otherwise many hotels and travel agencies sell sleepers for a service fee of Y30.

Getting Around

Hohhot airport is about 15km east of the city. The airport bus (Y5) leaves from the CAAC booking office or you can catch a taxi for around Y30.

Bus No 1 runs from the train station to the old part of the city in the south-western corner, via Zhongshan Xilu.

Hohhot is reasonably small and there are quite a few stalls hiring bicycles for a pittance.

There are two bike rental places near the train station. One is in the small rectangular building to the left as you exit the train station and the other is at the corner of Xilin Guole Lu and Hua'an Jie. Both are ridiculously cheap, about Y2 for the day.

Bicycle rental is also available at the Běiyuán, Xīnchéng and Nèi Ménggǔ hotels.

AROUND HOHHOT

About 20km west of Hohhot is the Sino-Tibetan **Wūsùtú Temple** *(Wūsùtú Zhào)*. It is hardly worth looking at, but the surrounding arid landscape is impressive. A taxi will cost about Y50 to take you there from the train station.

About 15km east of Hohhot, just past the airport, is the **Bái Tǎ** *(White Pagoda)*, a seven-storey octagonal tower. The pagoda can be reached by a 20-minute train ride on No 6055 that leaves at 10.40am; buy your tickets on the train. You'll probably have to get a taxi (Y25) back though, because the train only makes the return journey in the evening.

THE GRASSLANDS

The Grasslands (Cǎoyuán) is what most travellers come to see in Inner Mongolia, but if you are after a more authentic experience of the grasslands, consider a trip to Hǎilāěr or Mǎnzhōulǐ (or better still, the nation of Mongolia).

Organised Tours

Cashing in on the magic draw of 'Mongolia' is the name of the game here. As for visions of the descendants of the mighty Khan riding the endless plains, the herds of wild horses and the remnants of Xanadu, remember that this is China and most of the population is now Han Chinese. Nevertheless, CTS, CYTS and CITS are only too happy to organise tours to give you a glimpse of the traditional Mongolian lifestyle, which now seems to be an anachronism in Inner Mongolia.

The real country for seeing Mongolians in their own environment is Outer Mongolia,

but getting there is both expensive and difficult. Grasslands and yurt dwellings can be seen in other parts of China, such as Xīnjiāng. Remember that grass is only green in summer – the verdant pasturelands can turn a shrivelled shade of frost-coated brown from November to April. Make sure you take warm, windproof clothing – there's a considerable wind-chill factor even in the middle of summer.

There are three grasslands areas targeted by most tours: **Xilamuren** (two hours from Hohhot; Y840 for a two-day tour), **Gegentala** (2½ to three hours from Hohhot; Y960 for a two-day tour) and **Huitengxile** (three to 3½ hours from Hohhot; Y920 for a two-day tour), which is the most beautiful but least visited. Tour agencies can arrange one- to three-day camping tours to Xilamuren – there's a two-day minimum for the latter two.

There are some fledgling private travel agents who try to solicit business in the lobbies of the tourist hotels and all around the train station – you may want to talk to them and discuss prices. You can get to Xilamuren independently on one of the twice-daily buses to Zhaohe (Y11). Just ask the driver to drop you off at the grasslands. There are also taxi drivers around the train station who do self-styled grasslands tours for around Y300 per person (extra if you stay overnight). The trip may consist of staying in a yurt belonging to the driver's family. There is a general Grasslands management fee of Y30 for all designated areas.

The name of the game is 'bargain'. Be aware that these unofficial tours get very mixed reviews. One traveller was served a wretched meal in a yurt – cooked over a cow-dung fire – and got food poisoning. As you'll discover if you explore the Mongolian hinterland, sanitation is not a strong point, so watch what you eat and drink. Others have reported that the so-called 'Mongolians' are just Han dressed up in Mongolian costume. Also, if you're planning for a multi-day trip, remember that there are other things to see other than grass. Instead of lolling in grass for three or four days, consider a couple of days in the grasslands, then some place else (say, the desert). Travel agents will have lots of ideas.

INNER MONGOLIA

BĀOTÓU 包头
☎ 0472 • pop 1,989,200

Bāotóu lies on the bleak northernmost reaches of Huáng Hé (Yellow River), to the west of Hohhot. The name means 'land with deer' in Mongolian, and although there is still a deer farm outside of Bāotóu you are only likely to encounter these creatures on the dinner plate in some of the upmarket restaurants around town.

Previously set in an area of undeveloped semi-desert inhabited by Mongol herders, Bāotóu underwent a radical change when the Communists came to power in 1949. Over the next decade, a 1923 railway line linking the town with Běijīng was extended south-east to Yínchuān, and roads were constructed to facilitate access to the region's iron, coal and other mineral deposits.

Today, Bāotóu is an industrial community of about two million people. Despite the showcase street signs in Mongolian, nearly the entire population is Han Chinese. While West Bāotóu has undergone a major facelift, East Bāotóu remains an unpleasant urban area. Bāotóu is definitely a city for specialised interests – a couple of nearby monasteries, a steel mill, a steam locomotive museum, sand dunes and a mausoleum dedicated to Genghis Khan. Most of these sights are not in the city itself, but a couple of hours outside town.

Overall, Bāotóu is a useful transit point and you can keep yourself amused here for a day or so, but if you miss it, don't lose any sleep. The best thing we can say for the place is that the people are friendly.

Orientation

Bāotóu is a huge town – 20km of urban sprawl separate the eastern and western parts of the city. It's the eastern area that most travellers visit because it's useful as a transit hub – the western area has the steel mill and locomotive museum.

The station for the western area is Baotou train station (Bāotóu zhàn); for the eastern area it's Baotou east train station (Bāotóu dōng zhàn). The eastern district is called Dōnghé; the western area is subdivided into two districts – Qīngshān and Kūndūlún.

Information

Money In Dōnghé the Bank of China is on the left as you exit the train station. It only does currency exchange. To change travellers cheques you have to go to the branch in West Bāotóu.

Post & Communications In West Bāotóu there is a night-telephone office just next door to the main post and telephone office; there is an Internet cafe on the 2nd floor of this building.

Travel Agencies CITS (☎ 515 4615) is inconveniently located at 9 Qingnian Lu, in West Bāotóu. The offices are on the 4th floor. In East Baótóu CITS has an office (☎ 415 6235) in room 6106 at Dónghé Bīnguǎn. There is a friendly and more helpful

EAST BĀOTÓU (DŌNGHÉ)
包头东河区

To Wūdāng Monastery (67km)

Huancheng Lu 环城路

Gongye Beilu

To Měidài Monastery (50km)

0   250   500m
0   250   500yd

Bayan Tala Xidajie

To West Bāotóu (6km)

巴彦塔拉西大街

Nanmenwai Dajie 南门外大街

Bayan Tala Dajie

Gongye Lu

Zhanbei Lu 站北路

To Lánzhōu (996km)

To Běijīng (817km)

To Airport (2km)

PLACES TO STAY
2 Dōnghé Bīnguǎn;
   CAAC; CITS
   东河宾馆；中国民航；
   中国国际旅行社
3 Xīhú Fàndiàn
   西湖饭店
5 Jiāotōng Dàshà
   交通大厦

PLACE TO EAT
1 Pénglǎigé Cāntīng
   蓬莱阁餐厅
6 Dàdùzi Jiǎozi
   大肚子饺子

OTHER
4 Bank of China
   中国银行
7 Long-Distance Bus
   Station
   汽车站
8 Baotou East Train
   Station
   包头东站

WEST BĀOTÓU 包头西部

WEST BĀOTÓU

PLACES TO STAY & EAT
1 Tiānjīn Gǒubùlì Bāozidiàn
天津狗不里孢子店
5 Bāotóu Bīnguǎn; CYTS; CAAC
包头宾馆；中国青年旅行社；
中国民航
6 Xīngyuàn Dàjiǔdiàn
兴苑大酒店

OTHER
2 PSB
公安局
3 Post & Telephone
Office
邮电局
4 CITS
中国国际旅行社

7 Bank of China
中国银行
8 CAAC
中国民航
9 TV Tower
电视塔

CYTS (☎ 511 0920) on the 3rd floor of the west building in Bāotóu Bīnguǎn.

PSB The PSB is at 59 Gangtie Dajie, near the Baotou Department Store. The Foreign Affairs office is behind the main building; just follow the lane to the right.

Steam Locomotive Museum
Zhēngqì Huǒchē Bówùguǎn 蒸汽火车博物馆
The Steam Locomotive Museum is fairly small and tours have to be organised through CITS or CYTS. The latter is a bit cheaper and will do a tour for Y50, not including car hire.

Keep in mind that steam trains offer a more dramatic spectacle in the winter time. This is when most people visit the museum and it might be easier to hook up with a tour then.

Places to Stay
East Bāotóu Some places to try here are:

Jiāotōng Dàshà (☎ 417 2626) Dorm beds Y12, twins with bath Y48-112. This reasonably priced hotel is opposite the train station and seems willing to accept foreigners. It's basic but clean.

Dōnghé Bīnguǎn (☎ 417 2266, fax 417 2541, 14 Nanmenwai Dajie) Singles/

doubles with bath Y60/70, twins with bath Y70-90, rooms with bath Y50. This hotel is about 10 minutes' walk (or take bus No 5) from the Baotou east train station. The cheaper rooms are in the south building, but they were looking a little worse for wear at the time of writing. Rates include breakfast.

Xīhú Fàndiàn (West Lake Hotel; ☎ 417 2288, fax 416 8181, 15 Nanmenwai Jie) Dorm beds Y30, twins with bath Y116, suites with air-con Y418. This is a reasonably new Sino-US joint venture. The twins are basic but comfortable and clean, suites have a fridge and balcony, and dorm beds are in triples or quads. Try a bit of friendly bargaining on the standard rooms.

West Bāotóu Unfortunately, some of the hotels near the train station won't take foreigners though it's getting easier all the time.

Bāotóu Bīnguǎn (☎ 515 6655, fax 515 4641, 33 Gangtie Dajie) Beds from Y38, twins Y160. The best option for budget accommodation is this place. It has a range of rooms in three buildings, including a more comfortable, newer high-rise. If you're arriving by train, you should get off at Baotou train station. The station is 8km from the hotel – you can take bus No 1, a taxi or

INNER MONGOLIA

a motor-tricycle. If arriving by bus from Hohhot, you can ask the driver to drop you off right in front of the hotel.

Xīngyuàn Dàjiǔdiàn (☎ *512 8888, fax 513 6408, 28 Gangtie Dajie)* Twins or doubles Y298-368. This hotel with good rooms is just to the west of the Bank of China.

Places to Eat
Pénglǎigé Cāntīng (Gongye Beilu) Dishes from Y5. This is one of the most popular and serves a whole assortment of delicious food.

Dàdùzi Jiǎozi (Big Tummy Dumpling Restaurant; Huoche Zhan) Dishes from Y2. Just opposite the train station is this large canteen that serves a good range of staple Chinese breakfast dishes, like congee and buns. Its dumplings are not bad, but nothing worth writing home about.

If you're visiting in the summer, tables and foodstalls are set up for a lively **night market** just to the north of Dōnghé Bīnguǎn, at the intersection of Huancheng Lu and Nanmenwai Dajie.

Tiānjīn Gǒubùlì Bāozidiàn Dishes from Y3. In western Bāotóu, this restaurant is very popular with locals for reproducing the famous Tiānjīn dumplings. Just about everyone eats the dumplings, so ordering them is easy.

Shopping
The hotel *gift shops* offer a small selection of tourist-oriented minority handicrafts, but Hohhot is a better place to buy this stuff. As China's mineral capital, Bāotóu would be a good place to find bargains on iron ore, cobalt and lignite, in case you need to stock up.

Getting There & Away
Air The CAAC ticket office (☎ 513 5492) is at 26 Gangtie Dajie beside the Bank of China. Another is at Bāotóu Bīnguǎn; you can book tickets at Dōnghé Bīnguǎn and pick them up at the airport. There are flights connecting Bāotóu with Běijīng (Y540), Guǎngzhōu (Y1660), Wǔhàn (Y1110), Shànghǎi (Y1230) and Xī'ān (Y750).

Bus To Hohhot buses go from in front of the long-distance bus station for Y16 to Y25 and the trip takes three hours or 1½ hours via the freeway. Regular buses to

Dōngshèng leave every 17 minutes, take two to three hours and cost Y13 to Y17. There are also buses to Yúlín (Y50, 10 hours) and Yán'ān (Y87, 18 hours) in Shaanxi; note that the road into Shaanxi was being transformed into an expressway all the way to Dōngshèng so these times may all be different.

From West Bāotóu, buses leave from the intersection of Tuanjie Dajie and Baiyun E'bo Lu.

Train There are frequent trains to and from Hohhot to Bāotóu that stop in both the eastern and western sections. The journey takes just under two hours on the fast trains.

There are also trains to Běijīng (14 hours), Yínchuān (eight hours), Tàiyuán (14½ hours) and other major cities to the south.

Getting Around
While East Bāotóu is easy to get around on foot, West Bāotóu is a sprawling expanse of long boulevards, necessitating the use of public buses.

To/From the Airport The airport is 2km south of Baotou east train station. In spite of the short distance, taxis ask around Y20 for the one-way journey. If you are coming from west Bāotóu, an airport bus leaves from the CAAC ticket office; tickets are Y10.

Bus Close to the Bāotóu Bīnguǎn bus Nos 5 and 10 stop and take 45 minutes to shuttle between the western and eastern sections of Bāotóu. The double-decker buses are the most comfortable.

There are also minibuses *(zhōngbā),* which cost Y2.5 – you board these at the regular bus stops.

AROUND BĀOTÓU
Wǔdāng Monastery 五当召
Wǔdāng Zhào
The main tourist attraction near Bāotóu is this large monastery *(admission Y15; open 8am-6pm),* about 2½ hours from the city by bus.

This monastery of the Gelukpa (Yellow Hat) sect of Tibetan Buddhism was built around 1749 in typical Tibetan flat-roofed style. It once housed 1200 monks. The ashes of seven reincarnations of the monastery's 'living Buddha' are kept in a special hall and there is a collection of Buddhist wall paintings dating from the Qing dynasty. Today all religious activity is restricted to a handful of pilgrims and doorkeeper-monks who collect the admission fee.

The lighting is a bit dim so you might want to take a torch if you want to see anything inside the monastery.

The crowds of day-tripping, camera-clicking tourists make this no place for religion. Try to walk into the hills away from the pandemonium; the site has a peculiar strength in its secretive atmosphere.

Getting There & Away The monastery is 67km north-east of Bāotóu. Direct buses (Y7) leave from early morning to around noon – whenever they are full – from East Bāotóu's long-distance bus station.

Otherwise, bus No 7 (Y4, one hour), at the far left of the parking lot as you exit the long-distance bus station, goes to Shiguai, 40km north-west of Bāotóu. From Shiguai there are infrequent buses that can do the second leg of the journey. If your time is limited, you'd be better off hiring a taxi from Shiguai to the monastery and back for about Y70.

Měidài Monastery 美岱召
Měidài Zhào

This monastery (admission Y5) is much smaller than Wǔdāng Monastery and though easier to get to, is little visited. Měidài Monastery halfway between Bāotóu and Hohhot, a 10-minute walk north of the main highway. As long as they take the old highway and not the freeway, buses on the Bāotóu-Hohhot route can drop you off here. From Hohhot the fare is Y8 and from Bāotóu Y7. Like Wǔdāng Monastery, Měidài belongs to the Gelukpa sect.

Resonant Sand Gorge 伊盟响沙湾
Yīméng Xiǎngshāwān

The Gobi Desert starts just to the south of Bāotóu. Some 60km south of Bāotóu and a few kilometres west of the Bāotóu-Dōngshèng highway is a gorge filled to the brim with sand dunes.

Although the gorge has long been known to locals as a barren place to be avoided (no grass for the sheep), it has recently been turned into a money-spinner by CITS.

Japanese tour groups in particular come here to frolic in the sand. To spice up the romance of such frolicking, the area has been named Resonant Sand Gorge, a reference to the swooshing sound made by loose sand when you step on it. The highest dunes are about 90m high.

The Bāotóu-Dōngshèng bus passes by the turn-off to the new chairlift that shuttles visitors from the main road. It's a long trek from the highway in the hot sun and the planned new highway may bend farther west, away from the entrance. Make sure it's still walking distance.

Prior to the completion of the chairlift, entry to the sands was Y10. It is also possible to ride a camel (Y10) to the top of the dunes or you can try parasailing (Y20), if sliding around in the sand isn't enough for you.

DŌNGSHÈNG 东胜
☎ 0477

Dōngshèng lies south-west of Bāotóu and serves as the stage for Genghis Khan's Mausoleum. Dōngshèng itself is not blessed with scenic attractions, though it's smaller and more attractive than Bāotóu.

Of interest is the **Mínshēng Indoor Market** (Mínshēng Shìchǎng), where you can buy practical things such as clothing (not Mongolian style).

If you get an early start it's possible to reach Dōngshèng in the morning, visit Genghis Khan's Mausoleum, then return to Dōngshèng to spend the night, or even travel all the way back to Bāotóu the same day (though this would be exhausting).

Places to Stay & Eat
Jiàotóng Bīnguǎn (☎ 832 1575, Hangjin Beilu) Twins with/without bath Y28/Y18, singles/doubles with bath Y60/75. This hotel is adjacent to the long-distance bus station. It's improved greatly since previous editions but there are still one or two dumpy rooms to be found so look at a couple of rooms before you decide if you'll stay.

Dōngshèng Dàjiǔdiàn (☎ 832 7333, fax 832 3142, 1 Hangjin Lu) Twins/triples with bath Y122/138, new-building twins Y186-198. This is farther south from the bus station on the same side of the road. It claims three stars and maybe some of the rooms qualify, but the cheapies don't.

Otherwise, almost any hotel near the bus station will be very good (doubles roughly Y120) and staff are usually willing to negotiate.

For food, exit the bus station and walk south for about ten minutes on the right side of the road; look for a statue of a chicken. This will be the doorway to the great *Maìkěnī (Hangjin Beilu)*. This cacophonic place is a quasi-Chinese fast food place with excellent fare. You go in, wander about the buffet tables, and point – you pay by the dish and amount (average Y4). Vegetarians will find lots to eat here. This place is so popular it helps explain the odd dearth of restaurants in the city otherwise.

Getting There & Away

Bus Every fifteen minutes or so buses leave for Baòtóu; they take up to three hours and cost Y13 to Y17. There are three buses daily departing Dōngshèng for Hohhot, the last one leaving at 12.30pm; the 8.30am bus is an express (Y36).

If you wish to head into Shaanxi, buses to Yúlín (Y26, four to five hours) depart throughout the day. There is also a bus to Xī'ān (18 hours) from Dōngshèng, departing in the early afternoon and arriving late the next morning. Note that very heavy road construction along this road is ongoing.

AROUND DŌNGSHÈNG
Genghis Khan's Mausoleum

This mausoleum *(Chéngjí Sīhán Língyuán; admission Y25; open 24 hours)* is a bus trip away from Dōngshèng in the middle of nowhere. What are said to be the ashes of the Great Khan were brought back from Qīnghǎi (where they had been taken to prevent them from falling into the hands of the Japanese) in 1954, and a large Mongolian-style mausoleum was built near Ejin Horo Qi.

The Cultural Revolution did enough damage to keep the renovators busy for eight years. Since the collapse of Soviet domination in 1991, Mongolia has been whipping itself into a nationalistic fervour and Genghis Khan has been elevated to god-like status. As a result, holy pilgrimages to the mausoleum have become the sacred duty of both Inner and Outer Mongolians. If you would like to meet any true Mongolians, this is probably the best place in China to do it.

Ceremonies are held four times a year at the mausoleum to honour his memory. Butter lamps are lit, *khatas* (ritual scarves) presented and whole cooked sheep piled high before the Khan's stone statue while chanting is performed by Mongolian monks and specially chosen Daur elders. On the embankment beside the entrance there is an obo festooned with prayer flags in commemoration of Genghis Khan.

Inside are displays of the Khan's martial gear and a statue. Various yurts contain the biers of Genghis and his close relatives. The huge frescoes around the walls are rendered in cartoon style to depict important stages in the Khan's rise – all that's missing is bubble captions with 'pow' or 'zap'.

Buy your ticket at the booth to the right of the parking lot as you enter before you head up the steps to the mausoleum entrance, otherwise the staff will send you down again to buy a ticket.

After you've taken a look at the mausoleum you can visit the **temporary residence** of the Khan on the same ticket. It's 1km down the dirt road to the right of the parking lot (when facing the mausoleum).

Nearby is a **compound** *(open summer)* with nice grasslands, horses, cows, sheep and goats, plus some interesting buildings with traditional clothing, warrior outfits and riding equipment inside – all ready for the Naadam tourist carnival.

Places to Stay

Chéngjísīhán Bīnguǎn (Ghenghis Khan Hotel) Yurts Y20-35 per person, doubles Y120. This is a tourist yurt camping ground, with yurts *(měnggǔbāo)* to stay in at the right of the parking lot as you enter. However, most visitors elect to stay in Dōngshèng or Bāotóu and go to the mausoleum on a day trip.

Getting There & Away

Several buses depart from Dōngshèng each day heading towards the mausoleum; the first one leaves at 7am and the last one at 12.30pm though some leave later but this forces you to stay overnight at the mausoleum. Tickets cost Y7. The driver will let you off, but you won't be able to miss the blue-tiled dome of the museum as it comes into view. It's about a two-hour ride, but if the road is being repaired it can take up to four hours. Again, road construction may alter these instructions.

HǍILĀĔR 海拉尔
☎ 0470

The northernmost major town in Inner Mongolia, Hǎilāĕr has very little to offer visitors beyond being a useful transit point to nearby Mǎnzhōulǐ. In fact, unless you fly, there is no compelling reason to stop here as there are direct trains to Mǎnzhōulǐ.

You can visit the surrounding Hūlún-bèi'ĕr Grasslands from Hǎilāĕr though, and both CITS and CTS in Hǎilāĕr offer tours, but they are mainly geared towards larger tour groups and consist of tourist 'yurt camps' rather than places where Mongolians actually live.

Information

The main Bank of China branch is in the eastern section of town called Hédōng ('east of the river') at 5 Shengli Lu. It's about a five-minute walk north from the roundabout at Shengli Jie and is the only place to change travellers cheques.

The main post and telephone office is on Zhongyang Dajie, just north of the main square.

CITS (☎ 822 4017) is also located in Hédōng inside Běiyuàn Bīnguǎn on Shengli Jie. The PSB is opposite at 10 Shengli Jie.

Places to Stay & Eat

Mínzú Fàndiàn (☎ 833 0548, *Qiaotou Dajie*) Twins with bath Y25-40. This rather dilapidated but friendly place has a central location, just opposite the CAAC office. The rooms are OK, but the bathrooms are filthy. Rates include breakfast.

Yǒuyì Dàjiǔdiàn (*Friendship Hotel;* ☎ 833 1040, *Qiaotou Dajie*) Twins or triples with bath Y180. This is a good place to stay for mid-range prices. The entrance is on the right of the market lane, near the main intersection, and the reception desk is hidden on the 2nd floor. The hotel also sells train tickets for a Y5 commission. Rates include breakfast.

Hǎizhàn Dàjiǔdiàn Dorm beds/twins Y15/40. This is just behind the train station and offers reasonable and cheap beds. As you exit the train station turn left and cross the footbridge. The hotel is to the left just on the other side of the bridge.

Most of the hotels have decent *restaurants*, with the restaurant of the Yǒujì Dàjiǔdiàn winning the praise of the locals. There's also a night *food market* in front of the hotel.

Getting There & Away

Air CAAC (☎ 833 1010) is on Qiaotou Dajie beside the bridge. There are direct flights between Hǎilāĕr and Běijīng (Y1060) five times a week, and also three times a week to Hohhot (Y1200).

Bus The long-distance bus station is on Chezhan Jie, south-east of the train station. There are half-hourly buses to Mǎnzhōulǐ (four hours), but it's cheaper and easier to take the train.

Train You can reach Hǎilāĕr by train from Hāĕrbīn (12 hours), Qíqíhā'ĕr (nine hours) and Běijīng (27 hours). There are also four trains a day to Mǎnzhōulǐ (three hours), all in the morning. The station is in the north-western part of town. If you arrive by train, it's better to cross the train tracks using the footbridge to the left of the station as you exit and get a bus, taxi or motor-tricycle from there.

Getting Around

The airport bus leaves from the booking office; tickets are Y3. A taxi costs about Y20.

Bus No 1 runs from Hédōng to the train station, although all buses are marked No 3; best to ask first. In fact, it's just as easy to walk.

MǍNZHŌULǏ 满洲里
☎ 0470

The border town where the Trans-Siberian Railway crosses from China to Russia, Mǎnzhōulǐ was established in 1901 as a stop for the train, although the area has long been inhabited by Mongolians and other nomads. There are huge coal deposits in the vicinity, including the open-pit mine in nearby Zālàinuò'ĕr that was first developed by the Russians early in the 20th century. The Russians have played a major role in Mǎnzhōulǐ's history, as evidenced in the old buildings and log houses with their fili-gree windows dotting the town. Recently they've returned, crossing the border by bus and private car from Siberia to buy Chinese goods. The place feels more Russian than Chinese and there's a special kind of laissez-faire bordertown ambience that can make for some interesting encounters.

Orientation

Mǎnzhōulǐ is small enough to get around on foot and the grid layout of the streets makes this easier. The town centre sits between the train station in the south and Beihu Park in the north.

Information

The Bank of China is at 16 Erdao Jie. The post and telephone office is on the corner of Sidao Jie and Haiguan Jie. Xinhua Bookshop is on the corner of Sidao Jie and Xinhua Lu. It has Internet access and sells maps of Mǎnzhōulǐ.

CITS (☎ 622 4241) is next door to the Guójì Fàndiàn at 121 Erdao Jie on the 4th floor. If you're heading for Moscow you can purchase tickets here for the Trans-Siberian Railway. The PSB is also in this building, on the 2nd floor.

Places to Stay

Diànlì Bīnguǎn (☎ 622 2549, *cnr Sandao Jie & Shulin Lu*) Twins with bath Y35/45. This is one of the best-value places to stay with beds in pleasant and comfortable rooms. This intersection is in the eastern part of town.

Mǎnzhōulǐ Fàndiàn (☎ 622 4855, *cnr Sandao Jie & Zhongsu Lu*) Dorm beds/twins/doubles Y18/120/100. Another good option is this place where the clean rooms can be bargained down to Y100/70.

Míngzhū Fàndiàn (☎ 622 7418, *cnr Xinhua Lu & Yidao Jie*) Twins Y140-240. Most of the Russians stay at this comfortable place, which makes it lively. For entertainment you can't beat sitting in the lobby and watching the world go by.

Places to Eat

Mockba Neon Lights Dishes from Y5. There are many Russian restaurants around town, but by far the best place to eat is this one just east of Míngzhū Fàndiàn. Just look for the neon lights. It has a Russian menu and even Russian dancers: the action starts about 9pm or 10pm. Try the *sūbā tāng* with bread, a delicious vegetable-and-broth soup.

For breakfast, drop into the western restaurant at *Míngzhū Fàndiàn* (*see Places to Stay*), where it has Russian tea and *nǎibǐng* (pancakes) with cream and jam.

Shèngquàn Xiǎochī (*Shengquan Snacks; Shulin Lu*) Snacks Y5. This place, on the other side of town, opposite Diànlì Bīnguǎn, serves up some tasty local dishes.

The southern end of Haiguan Lu has several reasonable budget *Chinese restaurants*. There are also numerous *Mongolian* and *Korean barbecue restaurants* around town, just look out for the different scripts outside the restaurants.

Getting There & Away

The best way to reach Mǎnzhōulǐ is by train from Hǎilāěr (three hours), Hāěrbīn (15 hours) or Qíqíhāěr (11 hours); better yet, get off the Trans-Siberian.

Most of the Russians drive over the border, which is 9km from town, in private vehicles and you might be able to organise a lift across. A taxi to the checkpoint costs Y10. Naturally, you will need a Russian visa.

The train to Moscow from Běijīng passes through town early on Monday morning. It's possible to purchase tickets here for Moscow at CITS or otherwise if you want to make a stopover. Confirm it when you buy your ticket in Běijīng or Moscow.

If you arrive by train you can easily walk (10 minutes) to the town centre. Turn right as you exit the station and cross the foot-bridge.

Regular buses leave all day for Hǎilāěr (four hours) from the long-distance bus station on Yidao Jie, three blocks west of Míngzhū Fàndiàn.

AROUND MǍNZHŌULǏ

The main reason for visiting Mǎnzhōulǐ, other than to see the Russians, is **Hūlún Hú**, also known as Dálài Hú. One of the largest lakes in China, it unexpectedly pops out of the Mongolian grasslands like an enormous inland sea. It's a prime venue for fishing and bird watching. Slightly farther south is **Bèiěr Hú**, which straddles the border with Outer Mongolia.

The easiest way to get to Hūlún Hú is to hire a taxi (Y150; they'll wait up to four hours) or try to hitch a ride with one of the Russian or Chinese tour buses that are often parked on Xinhua Lu or in the parking lot by the CITS building. The lake is 39km south-east of Mǎnzhōulǐ and the return trip by taxi will cost about Y80. Entrance to the lake is Y3 and Y10 per vehicle.

The vast grasslands are another feature of Mǎnzhōulǐ and they surround the town in verdant splendour. If you're looking for big-sky country, this is the place to come. It's possible to arrange taxi or jeep excursions to the grasslands with overnight stops in yurts, tea-tasting and campfires. Should you chance upon a Mongolian living traditionally, you might get a cup of their milk tea. It's made of horse's milk and salt, and tastes revolting; it's also most impolite to refuse. CITS can also arrange a stay in a yurt with a Mongolian family, which can include horse-back riding and a Mongolian banquet.

The other big feature is for train buffs – the steam locomotive storage and repair yards in Zālàinuò'ěr are some of the more impressive in China, as is the mine that still uses steam engines to haul out the coal.

Unfortunately, to visit the steam train repair yards and open-pit mine at Zālàinuò'ěr you'll also need to go through CITS, but it's cheaper to hire your own taxi than use its transport.

XANADU 元上都
☎ 0479

About 320km north of Běijīng, tucked away near Duōlún in Inner Mongolia, are the remains of Xanadu (Yuánshàngdū), the great Kublai Khan's palace of legendary splendour. In the 19th century, Samuel Taylor Coleridge (who never went near the place) stoked his imagination with some opium and composed *Kubla Khan*, a glowing poem about Xanadu that has been on the set menu for students of English literature ever since.

Over the centuries the deserted palace has crumbled back to dust and the site has been visited by very few foreigners. Hardly anything remains of the ancient city.

Getting There & Away

Unfortunately, foreigners can only visit Xanadu legally by going on a very expensive CITS tour, but perhaps this might change in the future. Check with the PSB (☎ 696 8148) in Hohhot.

The best way to get there would be to bus directly to Duōlún or Zhènglánqí and proceed to Xanadu from there, but these areas are closed at present.

If you want to go, first you have to travel to Xilinhot and arrange it through the CITS office (☎ 822 4448), which is on the 3rd floor of Báimǎ Fàndiàn.

INNER MONGOLIA

Tibet 西藏

Capital: Lhasa
Population: 2.7 million
Area: 1,220,000 sq km

'Shangri-La', 'the Land of Snows', 'the Rooftop of the World': locked away in its mountain fortress of the Himalayas, Tibet (Xīzàng, the 'Western Treasure House' in Chinese) has long exercised a unique hold on the imagination of the West.

Until recently, few outsiders had laid eyes on the holy city of Lhasa and the other secrets of Tibet. It is more the pity that when Tibet finally opened to tourism in the mid-1980s, it was no longer the magical Buddhist kingdom that had so intoxicated early Western travellers.

Tibetans have never had it easy. Their environment is harsh, and human habitation has always been a precarious proposition. By necessity, Tibetans have become a tough and resilient people. Even in the face of the cultural attacks of the last fifty years, Tibetans have not only kept their culture and religion alive, but retained a remarkably cheerful outlook on life.

With a geographical area more than twice that of France, Tibet still manages only a total population of 2.7 million. There are, however, estimated to be some four million more Tibetans spread out over Qīnghǎi, Sìchuān, Gānsù and Yúnnán.

Most of Tibet is made up of an immense plateau that lies at an altitude of 4000m to 5000m. The cultural heartland of Tibet is the fertile Yarlung Tsangpo (Brahmaputra) valley. On the uplands surrounding this and other valleys, the inhabitants are mainly semi-nomadic pastoralists, known as drokpas, who raise sheep, yaks and horses. Western Tibet is higher still and its spiritual and geographical focal point is sacred Mt Kailash (Kang Rinpoche), in whose vicinity rise the sources of the Indus, Sutlej and Brahmaputra Rivers.

Since full-scale coverage of Tibetan regions would take a whole book, Lonely Planet has published a separate *Tibet* guide.

HISTORY

Recorded Tibetan history begins in the 7th century AD when the Tibetan armies were

considered as great a scourge to their neighbours as the Huns were to Europe. Under King Songtsen Gampo, the Tibetans occupied Nepal and collected tribute from parts of Yúnnán.

Shortly after the death of Gampo, the armies moved north and took control of the Silk Road, including the great city of Kashgar. Opposed by Chinese troops, who occupied all of Xīnjiāng under the Tang dynasty, the Tibetans responded by sacking the imperial city of Chang'an (present-day Xī'ān).

It was not until 842 that Tibetan expansion came to a sudden halt with the

TIBETAN PLATEAU

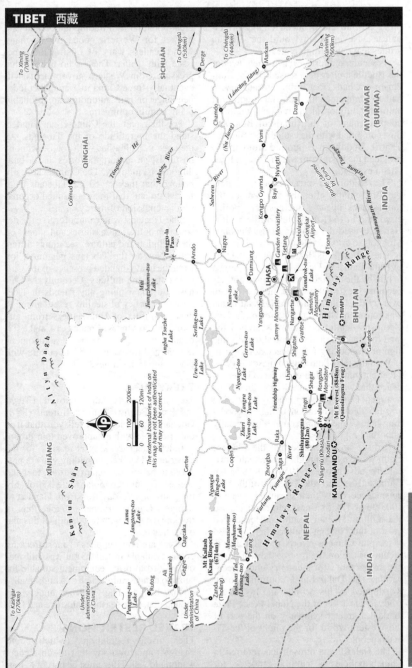

TIBET 西藏

assassination of the king, and the region broke up into independent feuding principalities. Never again would the Tibetan armies leave their high plateau.

As secular authority waned, the power of the Buddhist clergy increased. When Buddhism reached Tibet in the 3rd century, it had to compete with Bon, the traditional animistic religion of the region. Buddhism adopted many of the rituals of Bon, and this, combined with the esoteric practices of Tantric Buddhism (imported from India) provided the basis from which Tibetan Buddhism evolved.

The religion had spread through Tibet by the 7th century; after the 9th century the monasteries became increasingly politicised, and in 1641 the Gelukpa (the Yellow Hat sect) used the support of the Buddhist Mongols to crush the Red Hats, their rivals.

The Yellow Hats' leader adopted the title of Dalai Lama, or Ocean of Wisdom, given to him by the Mongols; religion and politics became inextricably entwined, presided over by the Dalai Lama. Each Dalai Lama was considered the reincarnation of the last. Upon his death, the monks searched the land for a newborn child who showed some sign of embodying his predecessor's spirit.

With the fall of the Qing dynasty in 1911, Tibet entered a period of de facto independence that was to last until 1950. In 1950 a resurgent China invaded Tibet (the invasion was labelled a 'liberation'), making good a long-held Chinese claim on the strategically important high plateau.

It made no difference that the Chinese claim was based on highly dubious historical grounds: between 1950 and 1970 the Chinese 'liberated' the Tibetans of their independence, drove their spiritual leader and 100,000 of Tibet's finest into exile, caused 1.2 million Tibetan deaths and destroyed most of the Tibetans' cultural heritage.

Despite Chinese efforts to paint a rosy picture of life on the roof of the world, the general picture is of a country under occupation. The Dalai Lama continues to be worshipped by his people, and his acceptance in late 1989 of the Nobel Peace Prize marked a greater sympathy on the part of the Western world for the plight of the Tibetan people.

The Dalai Lama himself has referred to China's policies as 'cultural genocide' for the Tibetan people. Unfortunately, China's great potential as a trading nation and as a market for Western goods makes many world leaders wary of raising the Tibet issue with China. Those who believe that pressure from Western governments will eventually force China to grant Tibet independence or true autonomy are probably being unduly optimistic.

For their part, the Chinese can't understand the ingratitude of the Tibetans. As they see it, China has built roads, schools, hospitals, an airport, factories and a budding tourist industry. The Chinese honestly believe that they saved the Tibetans from feudalism and that their continued occupation is a mission of mercy.

The Tibetans, who cannot forgive the destruction of their monasteries and attacks on their religion and culture, see things differently. Nor do the Tibetans get much joy from the heavy-handed presence of the Chinese police and military. Certainly the Chinese are not winning any friends in Tibet with their policy of stealthy resettlement. A massive influx of Han settlers from surrounding provinces threatens to make Tibetans a minority in their own 'autonomous region' and to swamp Tibetan culture with that of the Han Chinese.

TREKKING

Trekking is not officially approved in Tibet; the local Public Security Bureau (PSB; Gōngānjú) officials will tell you that it is only possible with an approved tour group.

Independent trekking is feasible for the experienced walker, providing you are prepared to be self-sufficient in food, fuel and shelter. The most popular route is probably the four- or five-day trek from Ganden to Samye. Lonely Planet's *Tibet* has a trekking chapter with full details of this and other treks.

There are now supplies of most trekking goods available in Lhasa, but it is still recommended to bring equipment suitable for subzero temperatures, such as a high-quality down sleeping bag, thermal underwear, ground mat, four-season tent, stove and fuel.

TRAVEL RESTRICTIONS

The current regulations (which could change tomorrow) say that all foreigners wanting to visit Tibet must be part of a 'tour group' (minimum of five people on a minimum three-day tour). In addition, every foreigner should have a Tibetan Tourism Bureau (TTB) permit, and a return ticket to either Kathmandu, Chéngdū or Golmud.

Travel agencies in Chéngdū organise packages to Lhasa for between Y2500 and Y3200 per person. This often includes a Y200 deposit, which either has to be used to arrange onward transport or is refunded when you leave Tibet. Buses from Golmud are arranged by the China International Travel Service (CITS; Zhōngguó Guójì Lǚxíngshè) and cost around Y1600 for the Y210 bus ticket alone! It is now possible to fly to Lhasa from Zhōngdiàn in Yúnnán by first arranging the ticket and permits through a travel agency in Kūnmíng. See the Chéngdū and Golmud entries for more details.

From Kathmandu, budget travel agencies offer various tours to Lhasa starting from around US$260 for a four-day overland trip to US$500 for an eight-day trip. As long as you have an Individual, not Group, Visa (these are currently available from the Chinese embassy in Kathmandu but regulations change with the wind) you can stay in Tibet as long as your visa is valid. Otherwise you are better off arriving in Nepal with a Chinese visa (available in Delhi), which is much easier than finding a way to split from a Group Visa. It is difficult to get a visa extension of more than a few days without booking a tour.

In reality, most people pay for a tour and then cancel or extend their return tickets when they arrive in Lhasa. On arrival in Lhasa these temporary 'groups' disband; there are no permit checks in Lhasa. A hardcore minority try to hitch in independently.

Once in Tibet, entry to anywhere outside of Lhasa prefecture and the cities of Shigatse and Tsetang (ie, to places such as Everest Base Camp, Samye, Sakya and Mt Kailash) requires you to procure a travel permit. To get a permit you have to be a member of a tour group arranged through an authorised travel agency. Permits cost Y50.

At time of writing only one government sponsored travel agency, known as Foreign Individual Traveller (FIT), was allowed to organise travel and permits for individual travellers, though this may well change.

It's worth bearing in mind that Tibet (much more than the rest of China) is effectively a police state, and political discussions with local Tibetans can have serious consequences. It is illegal to bring pictures of the Dalai Lama into Tibet. Incidentally, many of the secret police are ethnic Tibetans.

WHAT TO BRING

Figuring out what type of clothing to bring is tricky, due to the extremes of the climate. You can get warm clothing, trekking gear and most foodstuffs in Lhasa but it is advisable to bring sunscreen, books, deodorant, a water purification system and any medication you might need.

Food is no problem in Lhasa, but remote areas offer little to eat beyond instant noodles and beer. If you are considering a long journey then it would be wise to stock up before heading off.

There are several medications that are particularly useful in Tibet, and you should bring them from abroad rather than rely on local supplies. Drugs to consider carrying include Diomox, Tiniba and Flagyl. For more information see the Health section in the Facts for the Visitor chapter.

DANGERS & ANNOYANCES

The greatest dangers to travellers' health are acute mountain sickness (AMS) and giardiasis. For a full discussion of prevention and treatment, see the Health section in the Facts for the Visitor chapter.

Tibetans are among the friendliest, most hospitable people in the world but do not expect smiles all the way. Travellers who have poked their noses into Tibetan funerals and other personal matters have quite rightly received a very hostile reception. Stories abound of surly monks, of aggressive Tibetans at checkpoints and of rip-offs by Tibetan tour operators.

Tibetan dogs are even more xenophobic than the PSB, especially in the countryside. Keep your distance during the day, and watch your step in the dark.

FOOD

The staple diet in Tibet is *tsampa* (roasted barley meal) and *bö cha* (yak butter tea). Tibetans mix the two in their hands to create dough-like balls. *Momos* (dumplings filled with vegetables or yak meat) and *thukpa* (noodles with meat) are usually available at small restaurants. Tibetans consume large

TIBETAN PLATEAU

Visiting Monasteries and Temples

Most monasteries and temples extend a warm welcome to foreign guests and in remote areas will often offer a place to stay for the night. Please maintain this good faith by observing the following courtesies:

- Always circumambulate monasteries, chapels and other religious objects clockwise, thus keeping shrines and chörtens (stupas) to your right.
- Don't touch or remove anything on an altar.
- Don't take prayer flags or mani stones.
- Don't take photos during a prayer meeting. At other times always ask permission to take a photo, especially one using a flash. The larger monasteries charge photography fees, though some monks will allow you to take a quick picture for free. If they won't there's no point getting angry, you don't know what pressures they may be under.
- Don't wear shorts or short skirts in a monastery.
- Take your hat off when you go into a chapel.
- Don't smoke in a monastery.
- If you have a guide try to ensure that he or she is a Tibetan, as Chinese guides invariably know little about Tibetan Buddhism or monastery history.

quantities of *chang,* a tangy alcoholic drink derived from fermented barley. The other major beverage is sweet milky tea, known as *cha ngamo.*

GETTING THERE & AWAY

Although there are five major road routes to Lhasa, foreigners are officially allowed to use the Nepal and Qīnghǎi routes only.

Nepal Route The 920km road connecting Lhasa with Kathmandu is known as the Friendship Highway. It's a spectacular trip over high passes and across the Tibetan plateau, the highest point being Gyatso-la pass (5220m) outside of Lhatse.

If the weather's good, you'll get a fine view of Mt Everest (8848m) and Cho Oyu (8153m) from the Tibetan village of Tingri. Accommodation en route is generally basic with fairly reasonable prices (Y15 to Y25), and there's no great hardship involved, as long as you don't mind doing without luxuries such as a shower for the duration of your trip. The food situation has improved greatly in recent years.

By far the most popular option for the trip is renting a 4WD and driver through a travel agency in Lhasa; see the Lhasa, Getting There & Away section. A five-day 4WD trip from Lhasa to the Nepalese border, via Shigatse, Everest Base Camp and Tingri, will cost about Y1200 per person. It is possible to hitch along the Friendship

Highway if you have enough time. Public transport runs as far as Lhatse.

When travelling from Nepal to Lhasa, foreigners must arrange transport through tour agencies in Kathmandu (see Travel Restrictions earlier).

Qīnghǎi Route The 1754km road that connects Xīníng with Lhasa via Golmud crosses the desolate, barren and virtually uninhabited northern Tibetan Plateau. The highest point is the Tanggu-la pass (5180m), but despite the altitude, the surrounding scenery can be quite monotonous.

Reckon on anything from 30 to 50 hours from Golmud to Lhasa and remember to take warm clothing, food and water on the bus, since your luggage is often not accessible during the trip.

Other Routes Between Lhasa and Sìchuān, Yúnnán or Xīnjiāng provinces are some of the wildest, highest and most dangerous routes in the world. They are officially closed to foreigners, though increasing numbers of travellers are making it through.

The lack of public transport on these routes makes it necessary to hitch, but that is also prohibited. At the time of writing there were a few travellers hitching into Tibet from Kashgar, via Ali, with minimal hassles (see the Xīnjiāng chapter for more details). However, the authorities have

The Twin Pagodas of Baisikou in Níngxià.

Russian style in Mǎnzhōulǐ, Inner Mongolia.

Dumplings for sale in Hohhot, Inner Mongolia.

The bumpy road along Huáng Hé (Yellow River) between Xúnhuà and Dàhéjiā, Qīnghǎi.

The eastern face of Mt Kailash, Tibet's sacred peak.

A bicycle cart on the streets of Lhasa, Tibet.

A friendly wool and yarn salesman, Lhasa, Tibet.

Prayer flags fluttering on the Mt Kailash circuit.

Jamming with a homemade instrument, Lhasa.

come down very heavily on truck drivers giving lifts to foreigners, particularly on the Yúnnán and Sìchuān routes in or out of Tibet so don't expect to find a ride easily. A few travel companies in Yúnnán have started to organise overland trips from Lìjiāng or Zhōngdiàn to Lhasa. Prices are high but will probably drop over time.

GETTING AROUND

Transport can be a major hurdle if you want to explore the backwaters. The main types of vehicle are bus, minibus, truck and 4WD.

So-called public 'pilgrim buses' to monastery attractions have become more widespread in recent years, but are generally restricted to the major monastic sites in the Lhasa region.

Minibuses run around Lhasa prefecture and from Lhasa to the main towns of Shigatse, Tsetang and Gyantse. Land Cruisers are the most common form of transportation. They are pricey, but not impossible for non-budget travellers willing to split the cost among several people.

As for cycling – it is possible, but is not without its hazards. Aside from hassles with the PSB, cyclists in Tibet have died from road accidents, hypothermia and pneumonia. Tibet is not the place to learn the ins and outs of long-distance cycling – do your training elsewhere. Despite the odds, a number of experienced cyclists have individually travelled around Tibet without too many problems.

LHASA 拉萨

☎ 0891 • pop 200,000 • elevation 3700m
Lhasa (Lāsà) is the heart and soul of Tibet, the abode of the Dalai Lamas, and an object of devout pilgrimage. Despite the large-scale encroachments of Chinese influence, it is still a city of wonders.

As you enter the Kyi Chu Valley, either on the long haul from Golmud or from Gongkar airport, your first hint that Lhasa is close at hand is the sight of the Potala Palace, a vast white and ochre fortress soaring over one of the world's highest cities.

The Potala Palace dominates the Lhasa skyline. The home of the tombs of previous Dalai Lamas, it was once the seat of Tibetan government and the winter residence of the Dalai Lama. While the Potala Palace serves as a symbolic focus for Tibetan hopes for self-government, it is the

Jokhang Temple, some 2km to the east of the Potala Palace, that is the spiritual heart of the city.

The Jokhang, a curious mix of sombre darkness, wafting incense and prostrating pilgrims, is the most sacred and active of Tibet's temples. Encircling it is the Barkhor, the holiest of Lhasa's devotional circumambulation circuits. It is here that most visitors first fall in love with Tibet. The medieval push and shove of crowds, the street performers, the stalls hawking everything from prayer flags to jewel-encrusted yak skulls, and the devout tapping their foreheads to the ground at every step is an exotic brew that few newcomers can resist.

Orientation

Modern Lhasa divides clearly into a Chinese section in the west and a Tibetan old town in the east. For travellers who have arrived from other parts of China, the Chinese part of town harbours few surprises. Nestled at the foot of the Potala Palace and extending a couple of kilometres westward is an uninspired muddle of restaurants, karaoke bars, administrative blocks and department stores.

The Tibetan part of town, which begins west of the Jokhang Temple, is altogether more colourful and the better area to be based in.

Information

The best place for the latest on Tibetan individual travel these days is in the courtyards of one of the popular Tibetan hotels, or at a table in Tashi's restaurants. The information boards in some of the hotels can be very useful if you're looking for a travel partner or a used travel book.

Consulate The Nepalese consulate (☎ 682 2881, fax 683 6890) is on a side street just south of the Lhasa Hotel and north of the Norbulingka. Visa application hours are Monday to Friday 10am to 12.30pm. Visas are issued in 24 hours.

The fee for a 30-day visa is Y255, or Y425 if this is your second visit to Nepal within a year. Bring a visa photo. It is also possible to obtain visas for the same cost at Kodari, the Nepalese border town, although you'd be wise to use this for emergencies only.

TIBETAN PLATEAU

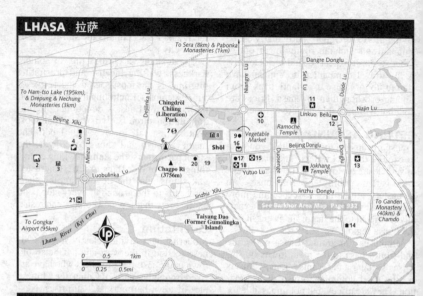

LHASA 拉萨

LHASA

PLACES TO STAY
1 Tibet Hotel
西藏宾馆
5 Lhasa Hotel
拉萨饭店
14 Himalaya Hotel
喜玛拉雅饭店

OTHER
2 Zoo
动物园
3 Norbulingka
罗布林卡
4 Nepalese
Consulate
尼泊尔领使馆
6 Yak Statues
牦牛像

7 Bank of China
(Main Branch)
中国银行
8 Potala Palace
布达拉宫
9 CAAC; Airport Bus
Departures
中国民航;
机场班车发车处
10 People's Hospital
人民医院
11 PSB (Visa Extension)
公安局外事科
12 Post Office;
Telephone Office
邮电局
13 PSB (Travel Permits)
公安局

15 New Century
Supermarket
新世界平价超市
16 Main Post Office;
Telephone Office
邮电局
17 Photographic Shops
18 Lhasa Department
Store
拉萨百货大楼
19 Potala Square
布达拉广场
20 North Col Outdoor
Equipment Shop
北坳登山徒装备总汇
21 Long-Distance Bus
Station
汽车站

Money The most convenient place for travellers is a branch of the Bank of China located between the Banak Shol and Kirey Hotels (open Monday to Friday 8.30am to 1.30pm and 3.30pm to 5.30pm.)

The main Bank of China is west of the Potala Palace – turn right at the yak statues and look for it on the left. Come here for credit card advances, bank transfers and foreign exchange on the weekends. Its opening hours are 9am to 6.30pm weekdays and 10am to 3pm weekends.

Post & Communications The main post office is east of the Potala Palace on Beijing Donglu. It is open 9am to 8pm Monday to Saturday, 10am to 6pm Sunday. Buy stamps from the counter in the far left corner as you walk through the main door. There is a telephone office next door, open 8am till midnight.

There is another post and telephone office located in the north-east of Lhasa on the corner of Linkuo Donglu and Linkuo Beilu.

IP phone cards are available in Lhasa but can be used only in Lhasa.

Internet access is available at many places around Tashi I, the Banak Shol Hotel and at the telephone office on Beijing Donglu for around Y5 per hour.

Travel Agencies If you want to do any official trekking or visit remote areas, you need to visit a travel agency in order to secure a permit, transport and (possibly) a guide.

At the time of writing, independent travel agencies had been outlawed by the Tibetan government and all independent travellers had to arrange travel with one of two FIT offices run by the TTB. These offices are located in the Snowlands Hotel and Banak Shol Hotel (☎ 634 4397, fax 681 5615).

Regulations change frequently so you may find that the old backpacker-oriented travel agencies have since resurfaced.

PSB There are two PSB offices in Lhasa, although it's doubtful that either will prove to be of much use. The one on the eastern end of Beijing Donglu issues travel permits, but the staff are unwilling to issue these to individual travellers and will instead refer you to a travel agency.

The PSB office on Linkuo Beilu has been more helpful with information and grants visa extensions of up to seven days. If you require a longer extension contact one of the travel agencies.

Medical Services In the case of an emergency you will probably be taken or directed to the People's Hospital on Linkuo Beilu. Expect minimal hygiene standards, but the staff are competent.

Barkhor 八角

The Barkhor (*Bājiǎo*) is essentially a pilgrim circuit (*kora*) that proceeds clockwise around the periphery of the Jokhang Temple. It is also a hive of market activity, an astounding pilgrim jamboree, and a wonderful introduction to Tibet.

All around the circuit are shops, stalls, teahouses and hawkers. There's a wide variety of items to gladden a Tibetan heart – prayer flags, block prints of holy scriptures, turquoise jewellery, Tibetan boots, Nepalese biscuits, yak butter and incense. Whether you buy from a shop or a hawker,

many of the Tibetan goods on sale have been imported from Nepal and many of the 'antiques' are not genuine. Be prepared to bargain hard.

People who roll up from remote parts of Tibet include Khambas from eastern Tibet, who braid their hair with red yarn and stride around with ornate swords or daggers. Goloks (Tibetan nomads) from the northeast wear ragged sheepskins. Golok women display incredibly ornate braids and coral headpieces.

Jokhang Temple 大昭寺

The golden-roofed Jokhang Temple (*Dàzhāo Sì; admission independent travellers with/without guide Y25/free; inner chapels open 8am-noon & sometimes 3pm-5.30pm daily*) is 1300 years old and is one of Tibet's holiest shrines. It was built to commemorate the marriage of the Tang princess Wencheng to King Songtsen Gampo, and houses a pure gold statue of the Buddha Sakyamuni brought to Tibet by the princess.

Follow the pilgrims through a labyrinth of shrines, halls and galleries containing some of the finest and oldest treasures of Tibetan art. Some originals were destroyed during the Cultural Revolution and have been replaced with duplicates.

The Jokhang Temple is best visited early in the morning; after noon you will have to enter via the side door to the right of the main entrance and interior chapels may be shut. There are often prayers led by monks on the roof around 6.30pm. The outer halls and the roof are effectively open daily from sunrise to sunset.

Potala Palace 布达拉宫

Lhasa's most imposing attraction is the Potala Palace (*Bùdálā Gōng; admission Y40; open 8.30am-3.30pm Mon, Wed & Fri, 9.30am-3.30pm Tues, Thur, Sat & Sun*), once the centre of the Tibetan government and the winter residence of the Dalai Lama. Each day a stream of chanting pilgrims files through this religious maze to offer *khata* (ceremonial scarves) or yak butter at the innumerable chapels and shrines.

One of the architectural wonders of the world, this immense construction is 13 storeys tall and contains thousands of rooms. Construction of the present structure began during the reign of the fifth Dalai Lama in 1645 and took more than 50 years to complete. The first recorded use of the site dates from the 7th century AD, when King Songtsen Gampo built a palace here.

The general layout of the Potala Palace includes the White Palace (the eastern part of the building), for the living quarters of the Dalai Lama, and the Red Palace (the central building rising above), for religious functions. The Red Palace contains many halls and chapels – the most stunning chapels house the jewel-bedecked tombs of previous Dalai Lamas. The apartments of the 13th and 14th Dalai Lamas, in the White Palace, offer an insight into court life. The roof gives marvellous views of Lhasa and around. There are extra charges to get access to the roof and an exhibition room, both Y10.

Queues at the Potala Palace are longer on Monday, Wednesday and Friday when pilgrims are admitted free of charge. Photography is not allowed inside the chapels. The long climb to the entrance is not recommended on your first day in town; do something relaxing at ground level until you acclimatise. English guides are available for Y50, and the last chapel closes at 4.30pm.

Norbulingka 罗布林卡

About 3km west of the Potala Palace is the Norbulingka (Luóbùlínkǎ; Jewel Park; admission Y25; open 9am-1pm & 2.30pm-6pm daily), the former summer residence of the Dalai Lama. The pleasant park contains several palaces and chapels, the highlight of which is the **New Summer Palace** (Takten Migyü Potrang). Avoid the awful zoo. The best time to visit is during festivals or on public holidays. Bus No 2 runs to the Norbulingka (Y2) from a block west of Barkhor Square.

Festivals

If possible, try and time your visit to Lhasa to coincide with one of the city's festivals. The Losar and Saga Dawa festivals are particularly exciting as thousands of pilgrims flood into town and the koras exude a party atmosphere.

Tibetan festivals are held according to the Tibetan lunar calendar, which usually lags at least a month behind the West's Gregorian calendar. The following are a brief selection of Lhasa's major festivals:

BARKHOR AREA 八角街

BARKHOR AREA

PLACES TO STAY
1   Yak Hotel
    亚客旅社
4   Banak Shol Hotel;
    Kailash Restaurant;
    FIT
    八郎学旅馆
6   Kirey Hotel;
    Tashi II Restaurant
    吉日旅馆
8   Dhood Gu Hotel
    敦固宾馆
12 Hotel Kyichu
    拉萨吉曲饭店
13 Pentoc Guesthouse
    攀多旅馆
14 Snowlands Hotel; FIT
    雪域旅馆

20 Mandala Hotel
    满斋酒店
23 Flora Hotel
    哈达花神旅馆

PLACES TO EAT
2   Dunya
9   Tashi Targyel Restaurant
10 Tashi I Restaurant
15 Snowlands Restaurant
    雪域饭馆
21 Makye Ame
    情人饭店

OTHER
3   Outlook Outdoor
    Equipment
    看风云变幻远景

5   Bank of China
    中国银行
7   Tromsikhang Market
11 Mount Green Trekking
16 Tibetan Hospital
    (Mentsikhang)
    藏医院
17 Minibus Stop
    小型车站
18 Minibuses to Drepung,
    Ganden, Samye &
    Tsetang
19 Jokhang Temple
    大昭寺
22 Main Mosque
    清真寺

Losar Festival (New Year Festival) Taking place in the first week of the first lunar month, Losar is a colourful week of activities. There are performances of Tibetan drama, pilgrims making incense offerings and the streets are thronged with Tibetans dressed in their finest.

Lantern Festival Held on the 15th day of the first lunar month; huge yak-butter sculptures are placed around Lhasa's Barkhor circuit.

Mönlam Also known as the Great Prayer Festival, this is held mid-way through the first lunar month (officially culminating on the 25th). An image of Maitreya from Lhasa's Jokhang Temple is borne around the Barkhor circuit, attracting enthusiastic crowds of locals and pilgrims.

Saga Dawa (Sakyamuni's Enlightenment) The 15th day of the fourth lunar month (full moon) is an occasion for outdoor operas and also sees large numbers of pilgrims at the Jokhang Temple and on the Barkhor circuit.

Worship of the Buddha During the second week of the fifth lunar month, the parks of Lhasa, in particular the Norbulingka, are crowded with picnickers.

Shötun Festival (Yoghurt Festival) This is held in the first week of the seventh lunar month. It starts at Drepung Monastery and moves down to the Norbulingka. Operas and masked dances are held, and locals use the occasion as another excuse for more picnics.

Palden Lhamo The 15th day of the 10th lunar month has a procession around the Barkhor bearing Palden Lhamo, protective deity of the Jokhang Temple.

Places to Stay – Budget

Banak Shol Hotel (Bālángxué Lǚguǎn; ☎ *632 3829, 143 Beijing Donglu)* Dorm beds/singles/doubles Y25/35/60, doubles with private bath Y120-150. This is a popular abode with a charming Tibetan-style courtyard, a free laundry service, a great restaurant, bicycles for hire and a good information board. The walls are paper thin, singles are pokey and some rooms face onto the noisy main road. The mid-range doubles are the best value in Lhasa.

Kirey Hotel (Jírì Lǚguǎn; ☎ *632 3462, 105 Beijing Donglu)* Dorm beds/doubles Y20/50. This is a quiet, comfortable place. It has reliable hot showers at the back, a free laundry service, Tashi II restaurant and super-friendly staff.

Yak Hotel (Yàkè Bīnguǎn; ☎ *632 3496, 100 Beijing Donglu)* Dorm beds Y20-25, doubles with shared bath Y50-60, twins with private bath Y260. This hotel has a range of options, from dark dorms to excellent twins with Tibetan-style decor. Hot showers are available in the morning and evening.

Snowlands Hotel (Xuěyù Lǚguǎn; ☎ *632 3687, 4 Zangyi Lu)* Dorm beds/doubles Y25/60, doubles with bath Y260-350. This place is now the least popular backpacker option, though you may have to stay here for a couple of nights as part of your 'tour' to get into Tibet. Toilets can be 'fragrant' and the hot water showers are unreliable.

Pentoc Guesthouse (Pānduō Lǚguǎn; ☎ *632 6686,* Ⓔ *pentoc@public.east.cn.net,* Ⓦ *www.pentoc.com, 5 Zangyi Lu)* Dorm beds/singles/doubles Y25/40/65. The Pentoc is friendly, clean and stylish, with nice touches like free videos every night at 8pm, print-outs of news reports and individual bed lights in the three-bed dorms. It has 24-hour hot showers.

Places to Stay – Mid-Range

During the last few years the backpacker hotels mentioned earlier have built carpeted mid-range rooms with private hot water bathroom which are far better value than staying at the more expensive hotels. The best options are currently the *Yak Hotel* and *Banak Shol Hotel*. Most other places are Chinese-style and cater to the growing numbers of Chinese tourists.

Hotel Kyichu (Lāsàjìqǔ Fàndiàn; ☎ *633 8824, fax 632 0234, 18 Beijing Zhonglu)* Singles/doubles/deluxe doubles Y180/260/320. This is a friendly and well-run place. Singles and doubles are carpeted and the other rooms are well-furnished.

Mandala Hotel (Mǎnzhài Jiǔdiàn; ☎ *633 8940, fax 632 4787, 31 South Barkhor)* Singles/doubles/triples with bath Y180/260/300. This new hotel has a great location just off the Barkhor. The rooms are clean and comfortable and there's a rooftop teahouse and Nepali-style restaurant.

Flora Hotel (Hādáhuāshén Lǚguǎn; ☎ *632 4491,* Ⓔ *flora@public.ls.xz.cn, Hobaling Lam)* Dorms Y35, doubles/triples with private bath Y250/350. The Flora is a well-run Nepali-owned hotel in the interesting Muslim quarter. There are nice touches like a minibar at local shop prices, a stock of foreign magazines and a laundry service. Decent three-bed dorms out the back offer a quiet alternative to Lhasa's backpacker hotels.

TIBETAN PLATEAU

Dhood Gu Hotel *(Dūngù Bīnguǎn;* ☎ *632 2555,* ⓔ *dhoodgu@public.ls.xz.cn)* Singles/doubles Y320/480. This stylish Nepali-run hotel has excellent Tibetan-style decoration. Rooms come with modern bathrooms and kettles, though some are cramped. Rates include breakfast.

Himalaya Hotel *(Xīmǎlāyǎ Fàndiàn;* ☎ *632 1111, fax 623 2675, 6 Linkuo Donglu)* Standard doubles/triples Y373/439, superior singles/doubles Y456/648, deluxe double Y747. Rooms in both the old and new blocks are overpriced and the location is awkward but trekking groups sometimes stay here because of travel agency connections.

Places to Stay – Top End

Lhasa Hotel *(Lāsà Fàndiàn;* ☎ *683 2221, fax 683 5796, 1 Minzu Lu)* Standard/superior doubles Y1020/1328, economy triples Y980, Tibetan suites from Y1555. Standards here have dropped considerably since the Holiday Inn pulled out in 1997 and a discount of 20% is common on all rooms.

Tibet Hotel *(Xīzàng Bīnguǎn;* ☎ *683 9999, fax 683 6787, 64 Beijing Xilu)* Doubles/triples Y880/980. A cheaper toption is this new four-star block opened in 2001.

Places to Eat

Lhasa offers a range of cuisine you won't find anywhere else in Tibet, including Chinese, Western, Tibetan, Nepalese and Indian, so enjoy it while you can.

Tashi I Restaurant *(cnr Zangyi Lu & Beijing Donglu)* Dishes Y8-15. This place deserves a special mention. It has been running for a while now, and despite increased competition continues to be a favourite. Special praise is reserved for the *bobis* (chapatti-like unleavened bread), which come with seasoned cream cheese and fried vegetables or meat. The Western dishes are less authentic and portions can be small. Tashi's cheesecakes (with chocolate and pineapple) are still to die for.

Tashi II *(*☎ *632 3462, Beijing Donglu, in Kirey Hotel)* This has the same menu and same food but friendlier service than Tashi I.

Kailash Restaurant *(*☎ *632 1895)* Dishes Y12-25. In the Banak Shol Hotel, this is probably the most popular place in town. Prices are definitely higher than at the Tashi restaurants but the chicken sizzler (Y20) could well be the best meal in Tibet.

Makye Ame Mains Y18-25. This cafe serves decent Italian, Nepalese and Tibetan cuisine and, voyeurism aside, has the best location in town in the south-eastern corner of the Barkhor circuit.

Snowlands Restaurant *(*☎ *632 3687)* Dishes Y25-35. This is a slightly more up-market place that serves a mixture of Tibetan and Nepalese food in civilised surroundings.

Dunya *(Beijing Donglu)* Dishes Y30-40. With sophisticated decor, excellent and wide-ranging food and interesting specials this foreign-run place feels like a 'real' restaurant. It's pricier than most other places in town but it's popular with groups and travellers who aren't on a shoestring.

Tashi Targyel Restaurant *(Zangyi Lu)* Dishes Y12-22. This is probably the pick of the Nepali restaurants and the place for all your Thamel favourites. Prices are low, service is impeccable and the food is good. The Chinese and Nepali dishes (try the *thali* for Y20) are the best bets.

Entertainment

Apart from the ubiquitous karaoke bars and video houses, entertainment is restricted to impromptu beers and tall tales at the *Kailash*, *Makye Ame*, and *Tashi's restaurants*.

Dunya *(Beijing Donglu)* The upstairs bar(bottled beer Y12) is popular with local expats and tour groups. Happy hour gives a Y2 discount between 7pm and 9.30pm.

Shopping

Whether it's prayer wheels, daggers, *thangkas* (Buddhist paintings) or muesli, you shouldn't have a problem finding it in Lhasa. The *Barkhor circuit* is especially good for buying souvenirs to fill up your pack, though you'll have to haggle hard for a sane price.

Lhasa Department Store *(Lāsà Bǎihuò Dàlóu)* is a good one-stop shop for most supplies, especially clothes, though it's a little more expensive than elsewhere.

Three shops in Lhasa rent and sell Gore-Tex jackets, fleeces, sleeping bags, stoves, tents, mats and so on. ***Outlook Outdoor Equipment*** *(*☎*/fax 634 5589, 11 Beijing Donglu)* is probably the best and most convenient place. ***Mount Green Trekking*** *(Beijing Donglu)* concentrates on Nepali-made products and ***North Col Outdoor Equipment***

Shop (☎ *681 6379*) offers mostly Chinese-made trekking equipment and mountaineering supplies.

It is still a good idea to come with your own film supplies, but slide film is now relatively easy to find in Lhasa. A profusion of *photographic shops* are clustered to the east of the Potala Square.

Getting There & Away

Air Lhasa has air connections to Kathmandu (Y2290) on Tuesday, Thursday and Saturday; to Chéngdū (Y1270) twice daily; to Zhōngdiàn (Y1250) and Kūnmíng (Y1720) weekly; to Chóngqìng (Y1400) weekly; to Xīníng (Y1390) four times a week. Flights connections to Xī'ān (Y1420), Běijīng (Y2040), Shànghǎi (Y2310) and Guǎngzhǒu (Y2100) require a change of aircraft. Flights between Kathmandu and Lhasa operate twice weekly in the low season (departing Tuesday and Saturday) and three times a week in the high season.

No matter where you fly in from, all tickets to Lhasa have to be purchased through a travel agency. At the time of writing, the cheapest tour from Kathmandu was a three-day tour for around US$360. This included the flight ticket (US$275), airport transfer to Kathmandu and Lhasa, TTB permits and dormitory accommodation for three nights in Lhasa.

Leaving Lhasa is a lot simpler, as tickets can be purchased from the Civil Aviation Administration of China (CAAC; Zhōngguó Mínháng; ☎ 633 3446) at 88 Niangre Lu. The CAAC is open daily from 9am until 8pm. If possible purchase your ticket several days in advance of your intended departure date.

Bus Tickets for buses from Lhasa to Golmud (Y210 sleeper bus, 30 to 50 hours) can be bought at the long-distance bus station in the south-west of town, near the Norbulingka. There are also sleeper buses that continue all the way to Xīníng (Y334), the capital of Qīnghǎi. Hard-core masochists might be attracted by the epic nonstop 3287km sleeper bus to Chéngdū (three days and four nights, via Golmud), though most sane people will take the plane. There are also three daily departures to Tsetang (Y30), daily departures to Shigatse (Y38), and departures to on alternate days (Y63).

Private minibuses to Shigatse (and sometimes Samye) depart from the junction of Ramoche Lu and Beijing Donglu from 7.30am, though some travellers have been turfed off these buses as they are not officially allowed to take foreigners. The easiest way to Gyantse is to change in Shigatse; there is no public transport via Yamdrok-tso.

Buses to Ganden (Y18 return, 6.30am), the Samye ferry crossing (Y25) and Tsetang (advertised as Shannan, the name of the county; Y30, 8am) leave every morning from the west side of Barkhor Square.

There are no longer buses to the Nepalese border at Zhāngmù, though the private agencies in the Tibetan quarter advertise occasional minibuses. Seats cost between Y250 and Y350 for the two-day trip.

Rented Vehicles The most popular way to get around Tibet in recent years is by rented vehicle. The most popular route is a leisurely and slightly circuitous journey down to Zhāngmù on the Tibetan-Nepalese border, taking in Yamdrok-tso Lake, Gyantse, Shigatse, Sakya, Tingri and Everest Base Camp on the way. A six- to seven-day trip of this sort in a 4WD costs around Y6000, including all necessary permits, driver, guide and car and can be divided between four (five at a pinch) passengers.

Other popular trips include Mt Kailash (17 to 21 days), Nam-tso Lake (three days) and various options to eastern Tibet.

At the time of writing, all Land Cruiser trips were supposed to be organised through FIT (see Travel Agencies section earlier), though for trips around Lhasa prefecture (which require no permits) there is nothing to stop you talking direct to a driver or other travel agency.

Getting Around

To/From the Airport Gongkar airport is 95km (1½ hours by bus) from Lhasa. Airport buses leave at 6am for the morning flights to Kathmandu and Chéngdū, and at 10am and 3pm, from the courtyard in front of the CAAC building. Tickets (Y25 to Y35) are sold on the bus, so show up early to guarantee yourself a seat. If you need to get to the airport more quickly, you could share a taxi for about Y25 per person, but this is usually a bit of a squeeze.

CAAC buses greet incoming flights (Y25).

Minibus Privately run minibuses are frequent on and around Beijing Lu. There is a flat Y2 charge. This is a quick and convenient way to get across town. Minibus No 2 runs to the Norbulingka and long-distance bus station. Minibus No 3 runs to Drepung Monastery and No 5 runs north to Sera Monastery.

From the minibus station near Barkhor Square there are more minibuses for Drepung and Sera Monasteries.

Taxi These are plentiful and charge a standard fare of Y10 to anywhere within the city. Few Chinese drivers know the Tibetan names for even the major sites.

Bicycle The best option is to hire a bike and peddle around yourself. They can be hired from the Banak Shol and Snowlands hotels for Y2 to Y3 per hour (Y20 to Y30 per day).

AROUND LHASA
Drepung Monastery 哲蚌寺
Drepung Monastery (*Zhébàng Sì; admission Y35; open 9am-4.30pm daily*), 7km west of Lhasa, dates back to the early 15th century. In its time it was the largest of Tibet's monastic towns and, some maintain, the largest monastery in the world. Drepung, Sera and Ganden Monasteries functioned as the three 'pillars of the Tibetan state'.

Prior to 1959 the number of monks in residence here was around 7000. During the Cultural Revolution there was a concerted effort to smash the influence of the major monasteries and much of the monastic population was wiped out. Today around 700 monks reside here and in nearby **Nechung Monastery**, a 10-minute walk downhill. Around 40% of the monastery's structures have been destroyed.

The best way to see the chapels is to follow a group of pilgrims. Try and catch the lunch break when the monks feast on tsampa and yak butter tea. Afternoons often see debating. There is an excellent 1½ hour long kora (pilgrim path) around the monastery.

Drepung Monastery is easily reached by bike, although most people take minibus No 3 (Y2) from the minibus stop near Barkhor Square. There is a Y20 charge per chapel for photography.

Sera Monastery 色拉寺
About 5km north of Lhasa, Sera Monastery (*Sèlā Sì; admission Y35; open 9am-5pm daily*) was founded in 1419 by a disciple of Tsongkhapa.

About 600 monks are now in residence, well down from an original population of around 5000. Debating takes place from 3.30pm in a garden next to the assembly hall in the centre of the monastery. Like Drepung, there's a fine kora path around the monastery. Minibus No 5 runs to Sera for Y2 or it's a 30-minute bicycle ride from the centre of town. There is a Y30 fee per chapel for photography, and it's Y850 for video.

From Sera Monastery it's possible to walk north-west for another hour to **Pabonka Monastery**. Built in the 7th century by King Songtsen Gampo, this is one of the most ancient Buddhist sites in the Lhasa region and is well worth the walk.

Ganden Monastery 甘丹寺
About 40km east of Lhasa, Ganden Monastery (*Gāndān Sì; elevation 4500m; admission Y25; open 9am-5pm daily*) was founded in 1417 by Tsongkhapa. During the Cultural Revolution the monastery was subjected to intense shelling, and monks were made to dismantle the remains.

Some 400 monks have now returned and extensive reconstruction work is taking place. The monastery is still well worth visiting and remains an active pilgrimage site. There is a Y20 per chapel fee for photography, and it's Y1500 for video.

Pilgrim buses leave for Ganden Monastery (Y18 return) at 6.30am from Barkhor Square. You can buy tickets on the bus.

Nam-tso Lake 纳木错
An overnight stay at Nam-tso Lake (*Nàmùcuò; admission Y35*), 195km north of Lhasa, has become a popular trip in recent years. The sacred, turquoise-blue lake is bordered to the north by the Tangula Mountain and to the south-east by 7111m Nyenchen Tanghla peak – the scenery is breathtaking.

Accommodation is available at **Tashi Dor Monastery** (elevation 4718m), which is on the edge of the lake, or you can camp nearby. There are two *guesthouses* with beds for Y25 to Y35. There are no toilets so bury your waste and burn all your toilet paper after use.

The closest public transport to Nam-tso Lake takes you to Damxung (Dāngxióng), a small town with a couple of **guesthouses** and **Sichuanese restaurants**, but the lake is still another 40km or more. The best option would be to organise a Land Cruiser in Lhasa, which should cost between Y1200 and Y1600 for a two- or three-day trip.

Permits and guides are not necessary for the area. Nam-tso is 1100m higher than Lhasa so it's best to have been in Tibet for at least a week to avoid AMS (see the Health section in the Facts for the Visitor chapter).

YARLUNG VALLEY 雅鲁流域
About 170km south-east of Lhasa, the Yarlung Valley (Yǎlǔ Liúyù) is considered to be the birthplace of Tibetan culture.

Samye Monastery
Located about 30km west of Tsetang, on the opposite bank of the Yarlung Tsangpo (Brahmaputra) River, Samye Monastery (Sāngyī Sì) was founded in AD 775 by King Trisong Detsen as the first monastery in Tibet. Getting there is quite complicated, but it commands a beautiful, secluded position.

To reach Samye, catch one of the morning buses from opposite the Kirey Hotel in Lhasa or from Barkhor Square. Buses leave at 7.30am, cost Y25 and drop you at the Samye ferry crossing. There is sometimes a police check at the ferry crossing for valid permits, though there was no such check during our last visit. Before you leave Lhasa, ask around about the current situation.

The ferry leaves when full. The crossing costs Y3 but foreigners are often charged Y10. From the far shore, a bumpy lift in the back of a truck or tractor (Y3) will carry you the 9km to Samye Monastery.

Simple accommodation is available at the **Monastery Guesthouse** (beds Y10-25) and there is a monastery restaurant, as well as a better private **restaurant** outside the monastery's east gate.

Tsetang 泽当
☎ 0893 • elevation 3550m
The rather uninteresting town of Tsetang (Zédāng), 183km from Lhasa, is mainly used as a jump off for exploration of the Yarlung Valley area. Officially you need to organise a permit for the surrounding area, which can only be done by arranging a Land Cruiser and guide. The Tsetang PSB can be particularly unfriendly, so avoid them like the plague. If you don't have a permit, keep a low profile and you might be able to avoid the PSB altogether.

Accommodation for foreigners is restricted to three expensive hotels:

Yóudiàn Gōngyù (☎ 782 1888, Naidong Lu) Dorms Y60, doubles with shared bath Y150, rooms with private bath Y280-300. This is the cheapest option but it's still grossly overpriced, especially as foreigners pay a 50% surcharge.

Shānnán Bīnguǎn (☎ 782 6168, Naidong Lu) Twins Y280 and Y380. This is a comfortable mid-range option, about a 15-minute walk south from the main round-about.

Tsetang Hotel (Zédāng Fàndiàn; ☎ 782 5666, fax 782 1855, Naidong Lu) Twins Y888. This is the town's premier lodging.

Getting There & Away Buses for Tsetang leave Lhasa early in the morning from the long-distance bus station and Barkhor Square. Buses heading back to Lhasa depart hourly from the roundabout in Tsetang until about 2pm (Y27 to Y40).

Yumbulagang
About 12km south-west of Tsetang on a dirt road, Yumbulagang (Yōngbùlākāng) is the legendary first building in Tibet. Although small in scale, it soars in recently renovated splendour above the valley and offers fine views. If you don't have your own Land Cruiser you'll have to hike and hitch on a tractor.

On your way to Yumbulagang it's well worth stopping at **Trandruk Monastery** (Chāngzhū Sì), one of Tibet's oldest Buddhist monasteries and a popular destination for pilgrims.

YAMDROK-TSO LAKE
On the old road between Gyantse and Lhasa, dazzling Yamdrok-tso Lake (4488m) can be seen from the summit of the Ganba-la pass (4794m). The lake lies several hundred metres below the road, and in clear weather is a fabulous shade of deep turquoise. Far in the distance is the huge massif of Mt Nojin Kangtsang (7191m).

TIBETAN PLATEAU

Nangartse, a small town along the way, has basic *accommodation* and a couple of *restaurants*.

A 20- to 30-minute drive or a two-hour walk from Nangartse brings you to **Samding Monastery** *(admission Y10)*, a charming place with scenic views of the surrounding area and lake.

GYANTSE 江孜
☎ 0892 • elevation 3950m

Gyantse (Jiāngzī) is one of the least Chinese-influenced towns in Tibet and is worth a visit for this reason alone. It's also one of southern Tibet's principal centres, although it's more like a small village.

Most people visit Gyantse as part of an organised tour down to the Nepali border, but it's also possible to visit independently. Three-day permits are sometimes available from Shigatse PSB (Y50, with a Y200 deposit), but many travellers risk going without one.

Things to See

The **Pelkhor Chöde Monastery** *(admission with/without government-produced souvenir CD Y40/30; open 9am-1pm & 3pm-7.30pm)*, founded in 1418, is notable for its superb **Kumbum Chörten** *(10,000 Images Stupa)*, which has nine tiers and, according to the Buddhist tradition, 108 chapels. Take a torch (flashlight) for the excellent murals.

Dzong *(Old Fort; admission Y25; open 8.30am to 8.30pm)* towers above Gyantse and has amazing views of the neighbouring sights and surrounding valley. Entry is via the large gate at the main intersection.

Places to Stay & Eat

Rooms are expensive in Gyantse, aggravated by the fact that officially only the Wutse, Cando and the expensive Gyantse hotels are allowed to host foreigners.

Hostel of Gyantse Town Furniture Factory (☎ 817 2254, Pelkor Rd) Rooms Y40 per person. This decent, although officially forbidden, place is on the main junction. The rooms are fairly clean and there are toilets and grubby showers. There's also a *Tibetan teahouse* next door, visible from the sitting area.

Wutse Hotel (☎ 817 2909, fax 817 2880, Yingxiong Nanlu) Dorms with TV Y40 per bed, singles/doubles with bath Y250/300.

The massive Kumbum Chörten, built in the 15th century, offers a glimpse of a lost era.

Most travellers stay in the comfy dorms of this new hotel. There are clean showers and a very pleasant grassed courtyard complete with a shady Tibetan-style tent.

Foodstuffs Hotel Singles/doubles Y40/60. Opposite Furniture Factory Hostel, this is a Chinese-style hotel but it's better than it looks from the outside. Again there are no showers but rooms have a basin and a TV – not bad for the money.

Canda Hotel (Yingxiong Nanlu) Doubles with bath Y150. The Canda is a spotless mid-range hotel that's good value.

Gyantse's dining options have improved immensely in recent years, largely due to Sichuanese and Muslim Chinese immigration. *Restaurants* are concentrated on the stretch of road opposite the Wutse Hotel.

Getting There & Away

A minibus from Lhasa direct to Gyantse leaves the bus station at around 6.30am on alternate days (Y63, eight to 12 hours). It returns the next day from Gyantse's main intersection at around 7am. If you'd prefer to get a permit in Shigatse first, you can catch a minibus from in front of Shigatse's main bus station between 10am and 6pm (Y25, two to three hours). Minibuses return to Shigatse between 8am and 9am from the main intersection in Gyantse.

SHIGATSE 日喀则宗
☎ 0892 • elevation 3900m

Shigatse (Rikāzé) is the second largest town in Tibet and the traditional capital of Tsang. Shigatse has long been an important trading town and administrative centre. The Tsang kings exercised their power from the once imposing heights of the Shigatse Fortress – the present ruins only hint at its former

SHIGATSE

PLACES TO STAY & EAT
3   Tenzin Hotel;
    Tenzin Restaurant
    天新旅馆；天富餐
10 Orchard Hotel
    果园旅馆
11 Tashi 1
16 Shigatse Hotel
    日喀则宾馆

OTHER
1   Shigatse Fortress
    日喀则宗

2   Market
    农贸市场
4   Minibuses to Lhasa
5   People's Hospital
    人民医院
6   Department Store
    商场
7   PSB
    公安局
8   Tashilhunpo
    Monastery
    扎什伦布寺
9   Minibuses to Lhatse

12 Telephone Office
    中国电信
13 Post Office
    邮局
14 China Telecom
    Internet Bar
    中国电信网巴
15 Bus Station
    汽车站
17 Bank of China
    中国银行
18 CITS
    中国国际旅行社

glory – and the fort later became the residence of the governor of Tsang. Since the Mongol sponsorship of the Gelukpa order, Shigatse has been the seat of the Panchen Lama, who is traditionally based in Tashilhunpo Monastery. The monastery is Shigatse's foremost attraction.

Information

The Bank of China is open weekdays 9am to 6pm, and weekends 10am to 3pm. Travellers cheques and cash in most currencies can be changed with a minimum of fuss but avoid lunchtime (1pm to 3.30pm).

The main post office is open 9am to noon and 4pm to 7pm. You can make international phone calls and send faxes from the telephone office, 100m west of the post office on Zhufeng Lu.

A good, fast Internet service is available at the China Telecom Internet Bar (Y10 per hour), open 24 hours. It's a few doors south of the main post office on Shandong Lu.

PSB Shigatse itself is an open town and so a permit is not required to visit. If you want to travel in the closed areas of Tsang without the cost of a tour and 4WD then you can ask for a permit at the Shigatse PSB. At the time of writing they were issuing seven-day permits for all towns along the Friendship Highway to the border (including Everest Base Camp). Three-day permits for Gyantse and Shalu Monastery were also available, but only with a Y200 deposit, reclaimable on your return to Shigatse. The cost of any permit is Y50 per person. However, many recent independent travellers have had great difficulty getting a permit so ask other travellers what the score is, as the rules change

like the wind. If you have trouble you could try asking for advice from Shigatse CITS (see the Rented Vehicles section later). They can book you a tour with all the necessary permits and they've even helped some travellers to get individual travel permits.

The PSB office does not have the power to extend your visa. You'll have to go to Lhasa to do this.

Tashilhunpo Monastery 扎十伦布寺

Shigatse's main attraction is this monastery (*Zhāshílúnbù Sì; admission Y45; open 9am-noon & 4pm-6pm*), the seat of the Panchen Lama. Built in 1447 by a nephew of Tsongkhapa, the monastery once housed over 4000 monks, but now there are only 600.

Apart from a giant statue of Maitreya Buddha (nearly 27m high) in the Temple of the Maitreya, the monastery is also famed for its Grand Hall, which houses the opulent tomb (containing 85kg of gold and masses of jewels) of the fourth Panchen Lama. Photography inside the monastic buildings costs a whopping Y75 for a full roll of film.

Shigatse Fortress

Little remains of the former Shigatse Fortress (Rìkāzé Zōng) but the ruins on the skyline are imposing all the same. It's possible to hike up to the fortress from the pilgrim circuit for good views of the town.

Places to Stay & Eat

Tenzin Hotel (Tiānxīn Lǚguǎn; ☎ 882 2018, 10 Bangjialin Lu) Dorm beds/singles Y25/50, doubles Y60-100. This is a friendly and busy place. The four-bed rooms here are nice and the modern doubles have a fine view of the fort. Hot water is usually available from 8pm to 10pm. You'll need ear plugs to sleep through the dogs' nocturnal howlings.

Orchard Hotel (Guǒyuán Lǚguǎn; ☎ 882 2282, 9 Zhufeng Lu) Dorm beds from Y15, doubles Y40 per person. This is a simple Chinese-style hotel run by the Tashilhunpo Monastery. The manager will usually open up one of the suites and let you use the hot shower there.

Hotel Manasarovar (☎ 883 2000, fax 882 8111, 20 Qingdao Lu) Dorm beds/ doubles with TV Y40/120. This new hotel is a bit of a hike from the action but is probably the best value for money in Shigatse. Rooms are spacious and spotless and the opulent shared bathrooms have 24-hour hot water. Prices may drop when they're not busy.

Shigatse Hotel (Rìkāzé Fàndiàn; ☎ 882 2525, fax 882 1900, 13 Jiefang Zhonglu) Doubles/triples with bath Y400/450, Tibetan/Chinese suites Y980/1540. This is a three-star palace in the south of town. The rooms are Chinese or Tibetan-style and have 24-hour hot water! Prices are reasonably negotiable.

Tenzin Restaurant (☎ 882 2018, Ground floor, Tenzin Hotel) Dishes Y8-30. This is the most convenient place to eat if you're staying at the Tenzin. It has a wide range of food, including Western-style breakfasts.

Tashi 1 (☎ 882 2516, Zhufeng Lu) Meals Y10-18. This friendly place has a full English menu and is a good place to stop for a break after visiting the monastery. Try the excellent home-style bean curd (Y12).

Getting There & Away

Bus Between Lhasa and Shigatse most travellers use the private minibuses. Minibuses for Lhasa (Y38, seven hours) leave between 7.30am and 8am from a crossroads at the eastern edge of town.

Buses to Gyantse (Y25, two hours) depart from the main bus station whenever full, from around 10am until 6pm. From outside the Tashilhunpo there are also minibuses every other day at 8am for Sakya (Y27). These return to Shigatse the next day so you get either an afternoon or 2½ days at Sakya – neither one ideal. An alternative is to take the daily bus to Lhatse, get off at the Sakya turn-off and hitch the remaining 25km. You'll most likely have to pay the full fare to Lhatse though. Private minibuses depart daily at around 8.30am to Lhatse (Y30) from outside the Tashilhunpo.

Those heading out to the Nepal border or Tingri have very few options. Hitching is one possibility, or you could inquire at the Tenzin Hotel for minibuses or Land Cruisers heading out to the border to pick up tour groups. Prices vary and the service is unreliable but you should get a lift for around Y250 to Y280.

Rented Vehicles This is more difficult in Shigatse than in Lhasa. CITS (☎ 882 9688) is the only official agent in town. Their office near the Shigatse Hotel is often closed, but you can track them down through the Tashi 1 restaurant.

CITS prices are not cheap but they can arrange permits for you. Sample prices are Y3400 per vehicle for a three-day round trip to Rongphu Monastery or Y5000 to Rongphu and on to the border. Permits are extra (Y50 per person for the PSB permit and Y65 per person for entry to the Everest region) but unlike the tours offered in Lhasa, the price includes the Y405 charge for vehicle entry to the Everest region.

You could also hire a Land Cruiser unofficially by talking to the drivers who park outside the Tenzin Hotel. Expect to pay around Y2500 to Y3000 for a trip to Rongphu and the border, but you'll have to arrange your own permits with the PSB and pay the entrance fees to Everest yourself.

SAKYA 萨迦
☎ 0892 • elevation 4280m

The monastic town of Sakya (Sàjiā) is one of Tsang's most important historical sights and, even more than Gyantse, is very Tibetan in character, making it an interesting place to spend a day or so. Sakya's principal attractions are its northern and southern monasteries on either side of the Trum Chu (Trum River). The fortress-like southern monastery is of most interest. The original, northern monastery has been mostly reduced to picturesque ruins, though restoration work is ongoing.

Places to Stay & Eat

Sakya Guesthouse (☎ 824 2233) Beds Y15-20. This guesthouse has basic rooms with no electricity but there's a certain timeless feel about the place.

Sakya Restaurant and Teahouse Meals Y10-15. Outside Sakya Guesthouse, this is a popular place with the standard menu of noodles and fried dishes.

Sakya Monastery Restaurant (☎ 824 2267) Dishes Y7-12. This restaurant belongs to the monastery and serves good-value Tibetan-style dishes.

Getting There & Away

Sakya is the last stop for foreigners using public transport. The bus leaves Shigatse every two days and is a slow journey. Buy your ticket the day before.

Most people arrange to see Sakya as an overnight stop when they hire a 4WD to the border or to the Everest Base Camp. It's also possible to hitch, as there is plenty of transport on the main road.

RONGPHU MONASTERY & EVEREST BASE CAMP

Before heading down to the border, many travellers doing the Lhasa-Kodari trip take in Rongphu Monastery and the Everest Base Camp (also known as Mt Qomolangma Base Camp).

The road to Rongphu Monastery was under massive reconstruction at the time of

writing and soon it will take only around two hours to get to Rongphu from the Chay checkpoint. Before you set off you'll need to stop in Shegar to pay the entrance fee of Y405 per vehicle, plus Y65 per passenger.

The walk from Rongphu Monastery to Everest Base Camp (5200m) takes about two hours, or 15 minutes in a 4WD. The route is obvious, past a glacial moraine and across a sandy plain. The site has a couple of permanent structures and there are usually tents belonging to various expeditions. Endowed with springs, Everest Base Camp was first used by the 1924 British Everest expedition.

There is a pricey *guesthouse* (dorm beds Y40) next to Rongphu Monastery with a *restaurant* that also sells simple supplies. There are *basic rooms* at the monastery for Y25 a bed.

TINGRI 定日
elevation 4390m

Tingri (Dìngrì) is a huddle of Tibetan homes that overlooks a sweeping plain bordered by the towering Himalaya Range. It's where most travellers spend their first or last night in Tibet en route to or from Nepal.

Ruins on the hill overlooking Tingri are all that remain of the **Tingri Fortress**. This fort was not blown up by Red Guards but rather destroyed in a late 18th-century Nepalese invasion. Many more ruins on the plains between Shegar and Tingri shared the same fate.

Everest View Hotel (*Lao Dhengre Haho Everest Veo Hotel & Restaurant*) Beds Y20. Most budget travellers passing through in rented vehicles stay in this shabby little place arranged around a compound. Basic food is available.

Everest Snow Leopard Hotel Beds Y90. This is the nicest place by far and is about 400m east of the other hotels. The all-brick rooms are spotlessly clean, very cosy and there are some nice touches like unsolicited buckets of hot and cold water and views of Cho Oyu from most of the rooms. There's also a nice restaurant and sitting area, which doubles as reception. The official rates normally crumble to around Y30 if you don't arrive in a flashy Land Cruiser.

From Tingri it's four or five spectacular hours to the border – up, up, up and then down, down, down.

ZHĀNGMÙ 樟木
☎ 0892 • elevation 2300m

Zhāngmù (Khasa in Nepali, Dram in Tibetan) is a remarkable town that hugs the rim of a seemingly never-ending succession of hairpin bends down to the customs area at the border with Nepal. After Tibet, it all seems incredibly green and luxuriant, the smells of curry and incense in the air are smells from the subcontinent and the babbling sound of fast-flowing streams that cut through the town is music to the ears.

Unless you're booked onto an organised tour, it's difficult to enter Tibet from Zhāngmù. The PSB (near the Gang Gyen Hotel) will only issue travel permits to travellers with a TTB permit, guide and transport, and there are checkpoints at both Zhāngmù and Nyalam, the next town north.

Gang Gyen Hotel (☎ *874 2188, fax 874 2413*) Dorm beds/doubles Y50/150. This hotel is just up from Chinese customs. The dorms are nice and spotlessly clean, though the communal bathrooms are a little grim. Hot showers are available on the roof if you arrange them in advance.

ZHĀNGMÙ TO KODARI

Access to Nepal is via the Friendship Bridge and Kodari, around 8km below Zhāngmù. Traffic on the stretch of no-man's land between the two countries has increased over the last couple of years and it has now become quite easy to hitch a lift, though you will probably have to pay.

Around Y20 should do the trick, but the amount depends entirely on who is giving the lift and the condition of the road. Frequent landslides mean that many travellers find themselves scrambling over debris in the places where vehicles can't pass.

If you decide to walk, it takes a couple of hours down to the bridge. There are porters at both customs points who will carry your pack for a few rupees or yuán. Look out for short cuts down between the hairpin bends of the road. They save quite a bit of time if you find them, though they put a real strain on the knees.

It is possible to get a Nepali visa at the border for the same price as in Lhasa (you'll need a passport photo) though it would be sensible to get one beforehand in Lhasa just in case. There are a few hotels that offer rooms on the Nepalese side. For those looking at continuing straight on to Kathmandu, there are a couple of buses a day from Kodari that leave whenever they are full. If you can't find a direct bus you'll have to change halfway at Barabise. The other option is to hire a vehicle. There are usually touts for vehicles to Kathmandu in front of the hotels on the Nepalese side. Most of the vehicles are private cars, and small ones at that; you will be hard pressed to fit more than three people into one, especially if you have big packs. Depending on the condition of the road, it should take around four to five hours from Kodari to Kathmandu.

Nepal is 2¼ hours behind Chinese time.

Qīnghǎi 青海

Capital: Xīníng
Population: 5.3 million
Area: 720,000 sq km

Qīnghǎi lies on the north-eastern border of Tibet and is one of the great cartographic constructions of our time. For centuries this was part of the Tibetan world; these days it's separated from the Tibetan Autonomous Region by nothing more than the colours on a Chinese-made map.

With the exception of the eastern area around the provincial capital Xīníng, Qīnghǎi (formerly known as Amdo) was not incorporated into the Chinese empire until the early 18th century. Since 1949 the province has served as a sort of Chinese Siberia, where common criminals, as well as political prisoners, have been incarcerated. These prisoners have included former Kuomintang army and police officers, 'rightists' arrested during the late 1950s harvesting of the Hundred Flowers, victims of the Cultural Revolution, former Red Guards arrested for their activities during the Cultural Revolution, supporters of the Gang of Four, and opponents of the present regime.

Eastern Qīnghǎi is a high grassy plateau rising between 2500m and 3000m above sea level, slashed by a series of mountain ranges with peaks rising up to 5000m. It's also the source of Huáng Hé (Yellow River).

Most of the agricultural regions are concentrated in the east around Xīníng, but the surrounding uplands and the regions west of Qīnghǎi Hú have good pasturelands for sheep, horses and cattle.

North-western Qīnghǎi is a great basin consisting mainly of barren desert surrounded by mountains. It's littered with salt marshes and saline lakes and afflicted by harsh, cold winters.

Southern Qīnghǎi is a high plateau sitting 3500m above sea level. It's separated from Tibet by the Tanggula Mountains, which have peaks rising to more than 6500m; both Cháng Jiāng (Yangzi River) and the Mekong River (Láncāng Jiāng) have their source here. Most of the region is grassland and the population is composed almost

Highlights

- Tǎ'ěr Sì, one of the six great monasteries of the Yellow Hat sect of Tibetan Buddhism
- Qīnghǎi Hú, China's largest lake, renowned for its breathtaking scenery and abundant birdlife
- The rough but stunning overland trip into Tibet via Golmud
- Mèngdá Nature Reserve, a beautiful place by Huáng Hé (Yellow River)
- Tóngrén, a quiet town with lovely temples and famed Tibetan painters

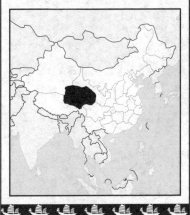

entirely of seminomadic Tibetan herders rearing goats, sheep and yaks.

The population of Qīnghǎi is a mixture of minorities, including the Kazakhs, Mongols and Hui (Chinese Muslims). Tibetans are found throughout the province and the Han settlers are concentrated around the area of Xīníng.

Although a train line stretching to Golmud has helped improve Qīnghǎi's economy, it still remains one of China's poorest provinces. Unemployment is high, and those who do have jobs often earn as little as Y300 per month. This situation is supposed to change with the proposed train line from Golmud to Lhasa (see the boxed text 'The Lhasa Express' later in this chapter).

TIBETAN PLATEAU

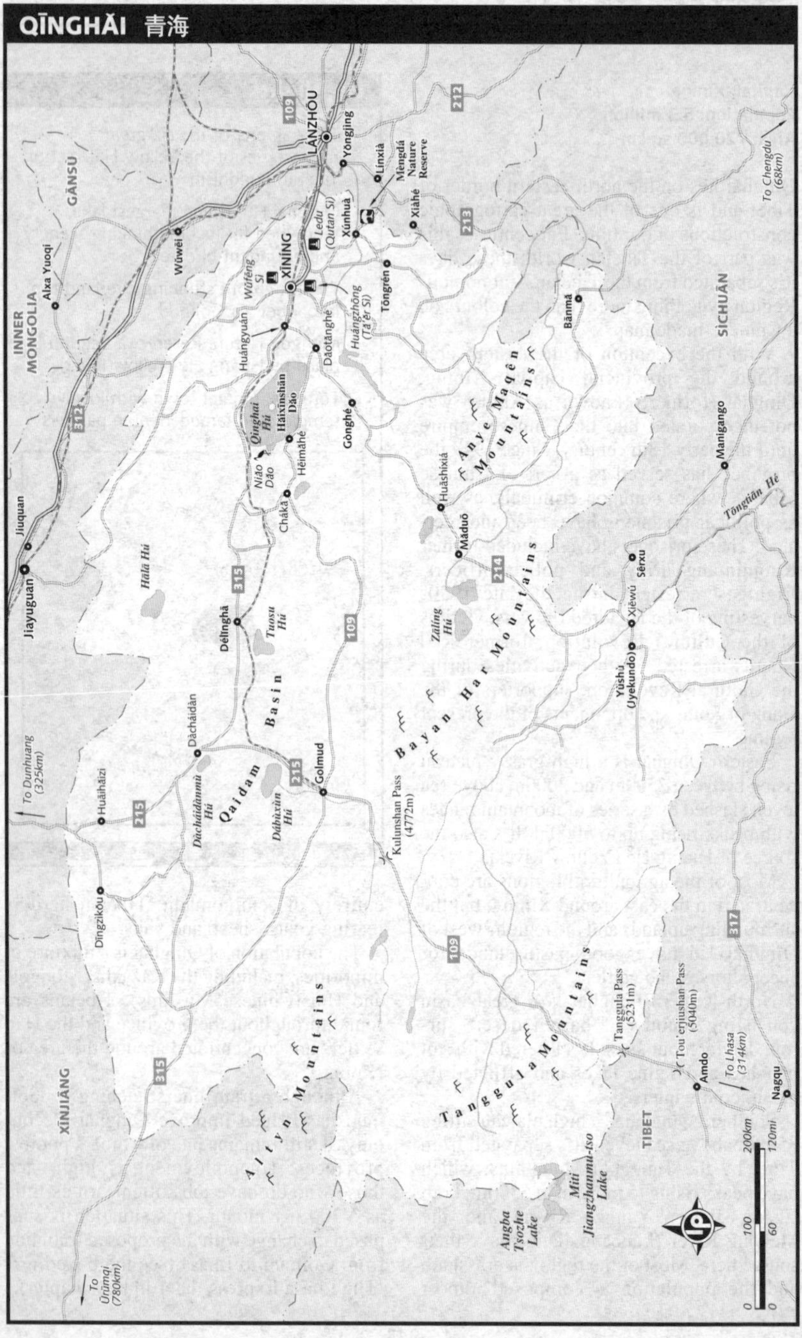

TIBETAN PLATEAU

XĪNÍNG 西宁
☎ 0971 • pop 1,112,600

Xīníng is the only large city in Qīnghǎi and is the capital of the province. Long established as a Chinese city, it's been a military garrison and trading centre since the 16th century.

Nowadays it's also a stopover for foreigners following the Qīnghǎi-Tibet route. Perched at an elevation of 2275m on the edge of the Tibetan plateau, the city itself is not the most aesthetic, but it is a convenient staging post for visiting Tǎ'ěr Sì, Mèngdá Nature Reserve and Qīnghǎi Hú.

Xīníng sits in an eroded desolate valley, but just one hour out of town there are lush green valleys with thick alpine forests. The city has a friendly feel and the streets are full of colourful markets and street stalls.

Information
Money The main Bank of China is on Dongguan Dajie. It is open from 8.30am to noon and 2.30pm to 6pm Monday to Friday and 9am to 4pm Saturday. The Bank of China opposite the main post office can also change cash and travellers cheques. There are money-changing facilities at both Qīnghǎi Bīnguǎn and Xīníng Bīnguǎn (see Places to Stay).

Post & Communications The main post office is in the centre of town and the telephones are on the 2nd floor. Internet access is available on the 2nd floor of the China Telecom building on Tongren Lu, which is just next door to the main telephone office on the corner. There are other Internet cafes located in a small alley south of the train station and along Dongguan Dajie. Expect to pay Y5 per hour.

Travel Agencies China International Travel Service (CITS; Zhōngguó Guójì Lǚxíngshè; ☎ 611 4037) is located in Qīnghǎi Bīnguǎn. The staff is quite friendly and helpful and has an extensive list of potential tours around Qīnghǎi. There is a branch of China Youth Travel Service (CYTS; Zhōngguó Qīngnián Lǚxíngshè; ☎ 813 3466) in a small booth at the front of the train station, which not only runs tours, but can also book discounted accommodation. China Travel Service (CTS; Zhōngguó Lǚxíngshè; ☎ 817 0923) has an office on the 2nd floor of Lóngyuán Bīnguǎn south of the train station, and has friendly, English-speaking staff.

PSB The Public Security Bureau (PSB; Gōngānjú) is at 35 Bei Dajie and is a good place to extend your visa. Bus No 14 goes right to the door.

Běishān Sì 北山寺
North Mountain Temple
The temple (admission Y6) is about a 45-minute walk up the mountainside northwest of Xīníng Bīnguǎn. The hike is pleasant and you'll be rewarded with a good view over the city.

Great Mosque 东关清真大寺
Qīngzhēn Dàsì
This mosque (30 Dongguan Dajie; admission Y5) is one of the largest in China's north-west and attracts large crowds of worshippers. You cannot actually enter the mosque but you can stroll the grounds. It was built during the late 14th century and was recently restored.

Shuǐjǐng Xiàng Market 水井巷商场
Shuǐjǐng Xiàng Shāngchǎng
This market is the most colourful in town and occupies several streets. It's an enjoyable place just to browse and watch the crowds watch you. There is a good supply of munchies here if you need to stock up. The market is near the West Gate (Xī Mén).

There are lots of other markets around town, including along Shangye Xiang and in the park on Nánchuān Hé (Nánchuān River).

Places to Stay
Yóuzhèng Gōngyù Bīnguǎn (☎ 814 9484 ext 2751, fax 817 1272, 138 Huzhu Lu) Dorm beds Y18-24, singles with bath Y50. This longtime budget bargain lies only a few minutes' walk south-east of the train station. It's a friendly place and fairly clean. One drawback is the noise; you have a choice of rooms, either with hooting cars or tooting trains.

Jiāngzhè Bīnguǎn (☎ 814 9385, fax 814 9386, Huoche Zhan) Doubles or triples Y90-200. This place only recently started taking foreigners and may have somebody to meet you at the train station. The rooms

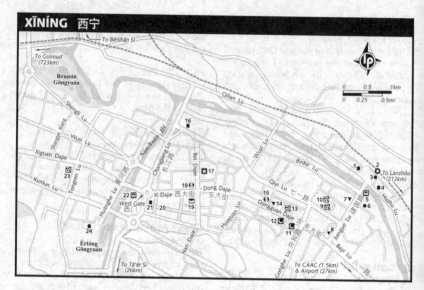

XÍNÍNG 西宁

are better than those at the Yóuzhèng and the staff are willing to negotiate on rates.

Jiànyín Bīnguǎn (☎ *826 1886, fax 826 1551, 55 Xi Dajie)* Twins Y218-298, doubles Y258. This is probably the fanciest hotel in town and has good, comfortable rooms with breakfast – more than one reader has highly complimented the place. There is a classy restaurant on the top floor, which serves both Western and Chinese food.

Xīníng Bīnguǎn (☎ *845 8701, fax 845 0798, 348 Qiyi Lu)* Twins with bath Y198-520, triples with bath per person Y30. Although not in a convenient location, this is a peaceful place set in nice gardens. It's a typical Chinese three-star operation, and the triples here are good value. The only drawback is that the hotel charges foreigners an extra 10%. The reception is in the building at the rear, behind the pleasant gardens where you can play golf and sip tea. Rates include breakfast. Take bus No 9 from opposite the train station and get off at the seventh stop.

Qīnghǎi Bīnguǎn (☎ *614 4888, fax 614 4145, 158 Huanghe Lu)* Twins from Y268. This towering pink monolith in the western part of town really wants to be Xīníng's most upmarket hotel, which is reflected in the rates, but the rooms don't always pass muster. Staying here is probably not worth the money, although staff do try to do their best.

Places to Eat

Xī'ān Mǎjiā Pàomó (Jianguo Lu) Dishes Y5-10. This great little restaurant serves heart-warming bowls of lamb *pàomó* (a soup dish that involves breaking bread into a bowl and adding a delicious stock). At this place, break up the bread yourself and then hand the bowl back, but remember your peg number.

The area around the train station and farther down Jianguo Lu has a good selection of *food tents* in the evening. Check out the kebab stalls and the places selling *shā guō* (a mini-hotpot of beef, mutton, vegetables, tofu and noodles), which is very filling and costs only Y5, including a bowl of rice.

Xiǎoyuánmén Shífǔ (188 Dongguan Dajie) This Muslim place – look for the hanging red lanterns – has a good reputation among locals.

There are also a number of excellent eating options near the Shuǐjǐng Xiàng Market.

Getting There & Away

Air There are flights from Xīníng to Běijīng (Y1630, daily), Chéngdū (Y1150, twice weekly), Guǎngzhōu (Y1950, twice weekly), Shànghǎi (Y1970, three times weekly), Ürümqi (Y1400, twice weekly) and Xī'ān (Y710, daily except Saturday).

There is also a twice-weekly flight from Xīníng to Lhasa for Y1300, but you'll still

XĪNÍNG

PLACES TO STAY

1 Jiāngzhè Bīnguǎn
江浙宾馆
4 Yóuzhèng Gōngyù
Bīnguǎn
邮政公寓宾馆
16 Xīníng Bīnguǎn
西宁宾馆
21 Jiànyín Bīnguǎn
建银宾馆
24 Qīnghǎi Bīnguǎn; CITS
青海宾馆;
中国国际旅行社

PLACES TO EAT

7 Xī'ān Mǎjiā Pàomó
西安马家泡馍
8 Food Tents
帐篷食摊
14 Xiǎoyuánmén Shífǔ
小圆门食府

OTHER

2 Train Station
火车站
3 CYTS
中国青年旅行社
5 Long-Distance Bus
Station
长途汽车站
6 CTS; Lóngyuán Bīnguǎn
中国旅行社;
龙源宾馆
9 Internet Cafe
网吧
10 Internet Cafe
网吧
11 Mosque
清真小寺
12 Great Mosque
东关清真大寺
13 Internet Cafe
网吧

15 Main Bank of
China
中国银行
17 PSB
公安局
18 Bank of China
中国银行
19 Main Post Office;
Telephone Office
邮电局; 邮政大楼
20 Shuǐjǐng Xiàng
Market
水井巷商场
22 Buses to
Huángzhōng
& Tǎ'ěr Sì
往湟中汽车,
塔尔寺
23 China Telecom
Internet Cafe
中国电信网吧

need to go through CITS to purchase your ticket. The same rules apply here, in that you have to wait for another five passengers before they will process the 'Tibet permit'. In Xīníng, it could take a while before another four people turn up. For interest's sake, the whole deal should cost about Y2000 per person (though you wouldn't believe the exhorbitant price quoted to us on a recent trip; you don't even want to know, trust us).

Civil Aviation Administration of China (CAAC; Zhōngguó Mínháng; ☎ 817 4616) has a booking office on the eastern edge of town at 34 Bayi Xilu, which is open from 8.30am to noon and 2pm to 5.30pm daily. To get there, take the eastbound bus No 9 from the corner of Jianguo Lu and Dongguan Dajie, get off at the second stop and walk east another 50m. Bus No 28 also runs there from the train station. You can also purchase tickets at almost any travel agency or hotel.

Bus The long-distance bus station serves all destinations except Tǎ'ěr Sì. Sleeper buses to Golmud (Y72, 20 hours) leave daily between 4pm and 6pm. Buses to Lánzhōu (Y31, five hours) leave every 20 minutes from 7am to 5pm. There is also a sleeper bus to Dūnhuáng (Y180, 20 hours plus) in Gānsù that leaves every second day at 10am.

Between 7.30am and 4pm there are buses every 30 minutes to Tóngrén (Y19 to Y23, five hours). From Tóngrén it is possible to take onward buses to Xiàhé in Gānsù. Heading towards Mèngdá Nature Reserve, there are three morning buses prior to 7am to Xúnhuà (Y17, four hours). There are also several buses to Hēimǎhé (Y19, four to five hours), near Qīnghǎi Hú (see Qīnghǎi Hú later in this chapter).

Some travellers looking for an off-beat Tibetan experience have made the journey from Xīníng to Chéngdū in Sìchuān by bus. The scenery is stunning and very Tibetan, but it's a rough trip that takes nearly a week. The route to Chéngdū is as follows: Xīníng to Mǎduō; Mǎduō to Xiēwú; Xiēwú to Sêrxu (Shíqú); Sêrxu to Kāngdìng; and Kāngdìng to Chéngdū.

Along the way there are cheap places to stay – the bus company will either put you up at its own hostels or direct you to another hotel. Another option would be to take a bus to Bānmǎ (two days), where you could then get a bus to Zöigê (one day), then to Sōngpān (eight hours) and on to Chéngdū (14 hours). The problem is, at last check, Bānmǎ had been closed to foreigners though the bus station seemed willing to sell us a ticket.

From Xīníng, buses to Mǎduō (Y73, 10 hours) leave three times daily between 9am and 1pm; those to Bānmǎ (1½ days) depart only on the 4th, 10th, 14th, 20th, 24th and 30th of each month.

Train Xīníng has frequent train connections to Lánzhōu (4½ hours). A special tourist train offers soft seats (Y42) and does the trip in a rapid 3½ hours. It leaves from Xīníng at 8am daily; coming from Lánzhōu the times aren't as good. Other cities connected by train include Běijīng, Shànghǎi, Qīngdǎo, Xī'ān and Golmud.

There are two trains to Golmud and the trip takes either 18 or 24 hours; these tickets are very easy to get.

Getting Around

To/From the Airport The airport is 27km east of the city. A CAAC shuttle bus meets all flights and costs Y10; a taxi fare there should be around Y50.

AROUND XĪNÍNG
Tǎ'ěr Sì 塔尔寺

One of the six great monasteries of the Yellow Hat sect of Tibetan Buddhism, Tǎ'ěr Sì (*admission Y21*), or Kumbum in Tibetan, is found in the town of Huángzhōng, a mere 26km south of Xīníng. It was built in 1577 on sacred ground – the birthplace of Tsong Khapa, founder of the Yellow Hat sect.

The monastery is noted for its extraordinary sculptures of human figures, animals and landscapes carved out of yak butter. The art of butter sculpture probably dates back 1300 years in Tibet and was taken up by the Tǎ'ěr Sì in the last years of the 16th century.

It's a pretty place and very popular with local tourists. An earthquake in 1990 and subsequent heavy snows threatened to destroy many of the buildings, and the Chinese government eventually forked out Y70 million for a major restoration project. Despite the damage, the place still maintains its historical atmosphere.

You can go hiking in the surrounding area or follow the pilgrims clockwise on a scenic circuit around the monastery. Six temples are open, with admission tickets sold at the building diagonally opposite the row of stupas. Photography is prohibited inside the temples.

Places to Stay & Eat *Tǎ'ěr Sì Bīnguǎn* (☎ 232 452) Twins with bath Y120-Y180,

triples per person Y35. This place is outside the monastery wall, opposite the ticket office.

Just behind the row of stupas is a sign saying 'Kumbun Motel', but at the time of research, the monastery was not taking guests. Instead, there's a small *restaurant* in the courtyard that serves a few Tibetan dishes and reasonably priced Chinese food.

For some variety, take a stroll down the hill towards town and sample some noodles at one of the many *Muslim restaurants*.

Getting There & Away If you are on a tour, you may visit the monastery as a stopover on the way to or from Qīnghǎi Hú. However, this probably means that your tour to Qīnghǎi Hú won't visit Niǎo Dǎo (Bird Island) – for details see Qīnghǎi Hú later in this chapter.

Minibuses and taxis to Huángzhōng (Y3, 45 minutes) leave every 10 to 20 minutes from the lane next to the Xining Sports Arena (Xīníng Tǐyùguǎn) near the West Gate. A minivan taxi costs Y30, which is not a bad option if there is a group of you.

Buses first stop at the Huángzhōng bus station, but most will continue on to the monastery.

Catch the return bus or minibus to Xīníng from the square in Huángzhōng; 500m down the road from the monastery. The last buses leave at around 8pm. To get to the Xining Sports Arena from the train station, take bus No 1 for seven stops to the West Gate.

Tóngrén

This town 107km west of Xiàhé (known as 'Repkong' in Tibetan) is actually in Qīnghǎi province. It makes for a nice way to enter/exit Qīnghǎi. The town is famed for its three **temples** and especially for its Tibetan *thangka* paintings, made by local artisans in an outlying village. Above the town is **Lóngwù Sì** (*Longwu Lamasery*), built in 1301 and now housing three colleges and assorted smaller lamaseries of the Red Hat sect. Some 10km outside of town toward Xiàhé is the village of Sāngkēshān; besides its legendary painters it also has Upper and Lower Wutong monasteries (around the 91km to 93km markers). This fascinating village's residents actually speak a mixture of Tibetan, Mongolian and other dialects.

If you have to stay overnight here, there's only one place:

Huángnán Bīnguǎn (☎ 722 2293, fax 722 6769, 18 Zhongshan Lu) Quads Y10, doubles up to Y178. This place is friendly enough, with dark but clean rooms.

To get to Tóngrén from Xiàhé, two buses (Y17, 4½ to six hours) leave in the morning. The return times to Xiàhé are similar. You pass through incredibly beautiful grasslands and cross over Qīnghǎi Pass along the way. The road should be sealed by the time you read this, so times should shorten. Buses to Xīníng (Y23, five hours) leave 12 times daily.

MÈNGDÁ NATURE RESERVE
Mèngdá Tiān Chí

This beautiful nature reserve (admission Y15) is situated by Huáng Hé, 190km south-east of Xīníng. The highlight of the reserve is **Heavenly Lake** (Tiān Chí), a sacred lake for both the local Sala Muslims and Tibetan Buddhists. It's a scenic 2½-hour walk up to the lake from Huáng Hé, along a dirt track through a lush valley of verdant alpine forest.

Once you reach the top it's possible to walk around the lake when the water level is low enough, or to head up to most of the surrounding peaks.

The bus will drop you off at the turn-off to Heavenly Lake, from where it is a 4km (one hour) walk to the ticket office. All the way up from the turn-off to the park entrance and office, people will try and offer you horses to ride and accommodation in their homes. From the ticket office, the road continues on for a couple more kilometres until the car park. From the car park it's a sweaty one-hour walk up to the lake.

Places to Stay & Eat
There is plenty of accommodation available on the way up and at the lake itself. Most people lodge at one of the two very basic hostels, the first by the lake and the other at the ticket office. They both charge Y15 for a dorm bed. Both hostels are reasonably clean, claim the owners, with rooms and sheets cleaned at least weekly!

There is a **Hui restaurant** by the lake, which serves some tasty mushroom and noodle dishes. The two hostels also serve a few basic meals.

In the nearby town of **Xúnhuà**, there are two basic accommodation options, both with hot water from 9pm.

Jiāotōng Bīnguǎn Dorm beds Y10-30, twins/suites Y90/130. This place is next door to the bus station and has good dorm rooms. Staff might try to charge you double, but be insistent and they'll probably back down. If not, turn left out the door and head down the road 500m until you get to a small market street, where you'll find the following alternative.

Zhèngfǔ Zhāodàisuǒ (Government Hostel) Dorm beds Y8-16, twins per person Y25. This hotel is in the building on the left-hand corner of the small market street.

Getting There & Away
Mèngdá Nature Reserve is 1½ hours by bus from Xúnhuà (27km) along a road cut into the cliffs of Huáng Hé. This is a spectacular drive along a precipitous cliff face. The road passes through a couple of peaceful rural towns as it slowly descends to Mèngdá, passing fields of barley, corn and wheat, while Huáng Hé slurps its way through the gorge below. There are four daily buses that pass Mèngdá Nature Reserve on their way to Dàhéjiā, from where it is possible to continue on to Línxià in Gānsù.

From Xúnhuà there are four daily buses to both Línxià (Y12, four hours) and Xīníng (Y17, four hours).

QĪNGHǍI HÚ 青海湖
Qīnghǎi Hú (Koko Nor), known as the Western Sea in ancient times, is a somewhat surreal-looking saline lake to the west of Xīníng. It's the largest lake in China and contains a huge number of fish.

The main attraction here is **Niǎo Dǎo** (Bird Island; admission Y55), located on the western side of the lake, and about 300km from Xīníng. It's a breeding ground for thousands of wild geese, gulls, cormorants, sandpipers, extremely rare black-necked cranes and many other bird species. Perhaps the most interesting are the bar-headed geese. These hardy birds migrate high over the Himalayas to spend winter on the Indian plains, and have been spotted flying at altitudes of 10,000m. You will see great numbers of birds only during the breeding season, which is between March and early June.

Despite its name, Niǎo Dǎo is not an island, but used to be before the lake shore receded and made it part of the mainland. There is one small island, Hǎixīnshān Dǎo, and for Y50 you can take a boat trip from Niǎo Dǎo around the lake to take in this and other sights.

It gets chilly at night so bring warm clothing. The lake water is too salty to drink, so be sure to carry a sufficient water supply if you intend to do any hiking. There are nomads living around the lake – most are friendly and may invite you in for a cup of tea in their tents.

Organised Tours

Between May and early September, tour buses run almost daily to Niǎo Dǎo. Xīníng has a plethora of travel agencies offering tours to the lake and most of them offer the same deals.

Both CITS and CYTS in Xīníng charge Y100 to Y120 (transport) for a very long day trip. The tour bus usually departs at around 6am and returns after 9pm, and much of the day is spent sitting in the bus. Therefore, it might be a better option to join the two-day tour (Y240), which includes an overnight stay at Niǎo Dǎo. Prices don't include accommodation, food or admission fees. These two tours often include trips to Tǎ'ěr Sì and a brief stop at **Sun Moon Mountain Pass** (*Rìyuè Shānkǒu*) for some photo opportunities. Most tours visit either Tǎ'ěr Sì or Niǎo Dǎo, but check with the operators first.

Places to Stay & Eat

Niǎo Dǎo Bīnguǎn Dorm beds Y20, twins from Y120. If you're not content with a day trip, you can stay here overnight. It's north of Hēimǎhé on the west side of the lake. Note that Chinese get first crack at the dorm beds. The restaurant in the hotel is surprisingly good.

Getting There & Away

Bus Unfortunately there are no public buses to Niǎo Dǎo. The closest you can get is to the small settlement of Hēimǎhé, 50km from Niǎo Dǎo. Getting from Hēimǎhé to Niǎo Dǎo will probably cost you another Y50 for a taxi, or less if you hitch. From Xīníng there are three departures to Hēimǎhé (Y19, four to five hours) between 7.30am and 9am, and the return schedule is similar.

GOLMUD 格尔木
☎ 0979

For travellers, the only reason to visit this forlorn outpost in the oblivion end of China is to continue into Tibet. While not a terrible place, you probably wouldn't want to stay around Golmud (Géěrmù) more than a day or two, and few visitors do. The town owes its existence to mining and oil drilling. It's inhabited mostly by Chinese, but there are a few Tibetans around.

The eerie moonscape of the Tibetan plateau can be an inhospitable place – come prepared! At 2800m elevation, summer days can be very warm, but the nights are always cool. The daytime sun is incredibly bright – sunglasses and sunblock lotion are *de rigueur*. Winters are brutally cold.

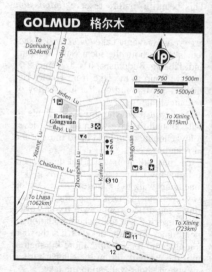

GOLMUD

1	Tibet Bus Station 西藏汽车站	7	Golmud Hotel; CITS 格尔木宾馆; 中国国际旅行社
2	Mosque 清真寺	8	Post Office 邮局
3	Nongken No 1 Department Store 农垦一商场	9	PSB 公安局
4	Bǎisuìjī 百岁鸡	10	Bank of China 中国银行
5	Market 格尔木集贸市场	11	Golmud Bus Station 长途汽车站
6	Bakery	12	Train Station 火车站

Information

CITS (☎/fax 413 003) has an office in the Golmud Hotel. If you're planning to go to Lhasa, according to the rules of the 'Tibet game', you'll almost certainly have to visit this office (see Getting to Tibet later in this chapter).

The PSB is on Chaidamu Lu, east of the post office. The Bank of China is on the corner of Kunlun Lu and Chaidamu Lu.

Places to Stay & Eat

Golmud Hotel (Géěrmù Bīnguǎn; ☎ 412 061, fax 416 484, 219 Kunlun Lu) Dorm beds in triples Y20, hotel singles/twins from Y60/100. This place has staff greeting foreigners at the train station. It's divided into two sections – the upmarket hotel (*bīnguǎn*) and the hostel (*zhāodàisuǒ*). Dorms have six beds and the hotel rooms are reasonable. Hot water is available 24 hours.

Bǎisuìjī (21 Zhongshan Lu) Dishes from Y5. If you're getting hungry waiting for that fifth person for the Tibet permit, head over to this place, with a name that literally means '100-year-old chook'. The restaurant specialises in a spicy chicken stew, cooked on the table in front of you. The chook is cooked in a broth of carrots, zucchini, celery, onion, coriander and mushrooms. You will need a minimum of two people to finish its smallest serving (*xiǎo xiǎo guō*). Try adding *tǔdòu* (potato) or *fěntiáo* (tofu and noodles) and wash it all down with a cold draught beer (Y5). This eatery is pretty easy to find – just look out for the green-uniformed staff loitering in the entrance.

North of the Golmud Hotel is a good *bakery* selling fresh breads and cakes. The *market* has lots of open-air food vendors; there's a large variety and you'll find lots of hot-fired clay pot stews.

Getting There & Away

Air Nobody actually flies to Golmud but if you want to, the city is connected by air with – besides Lhasa – Qīngdǎo (three times weekly), Xī'ān (three times weekly), Xīníng (daily), and a few other places.

Bus The Golmud bus station is opposite the train station. The journey from Golmud to Dūnhuáng is 524km (Y88, 11 to 13 hours) and there are two sleeper buses, one at 8am and another at 8pm. It's a scenic trip

The Lhasa Express

In 2001, after decades of dreams and indecision, the Chinese government proudly unveiled plans for its Herculean project: a 1118km-long, US$2.4 billion train line from Golmud (Qīnghǎi) to Lhasa (Tibet), and what they hope won't be a Sisyphean venture.

The scope – nay, 'megalomaniacal lunacy', spouted critics – of the project is hard to imagine. The government had sought international consultancy on numerous occasions, all of whom told them they were daft to attempt it; the Swiss, the world's best tunnel builders, said ice mountains made it impossible.

'Pish, pish' is apparently the answer. The planning committee announced all technical problems had been solved; yet, at the meeting, they gave no specifics. It is hoped that work will be finished before the 2008 Olympics.

Consider the downsides: four-fifths of the line will ride above 4000m (workers will have to work carefully timed shifts, and oxygen bars are planned for sleeper cars); over 60 medical clinics will need to be built to deal with altitude-sickness problems; engines for the harsh, ever-changing conditions will need to be designed; and more than half the distance will be atop permafrost while a radical Chinese-designed (but unproven) cooling system – questioned by many engineers – will be used for the rest of the way. Of perhaps most concern is that the line will encroach on six national protected zones, which are home to endangered species such as the Tibetan antelope and black-necked crane.

Culturally, there will also be an impact. The government proudly says that formerly 'destitute' Tibet will now be able to bring in supplies much more easily. This is true, but is this really a good thing? (*China Daily* reported that it would be wonderful when Tibetans could import and burn coal!) Tibetans fear an even more ambitious Han transmigration boom with the proposed eight trains daily running each way.

through the desert and mountains, but take a jacket as it can get cold at night.

There are also daily buses to Xīníng, but it makes little sense to go this way, as the train is smoother and faster.

Train Express trains (Nos K427 and 5701) on the Xīníng-Golmud route take just 13 to 18¼ hours, while the local trains chug along for 24 hours.

See the boxed text 'The Lhasa Express' on the plan to build a train track all the way from Golmud to Lhasa.

GETTING TO TIBET

CITS has an iron grip on foreign bus tickets from Golmud to Lhasa – all travellers must buy their tickets through the travel agency, and they pay dearly for it.

The situation is increasingly frustrating for travellers. CITS says it is required by the Tibet Tourism Bureau to ensure every foreigner has not only a Tibet Tourism Bureau permit (TTB), insurance and a minimum three-day tour, but also a return ticket to a choice of three destinations (Kathmandu, Chéngdū or back to Golmud). For all this, you will have the pleasure of handing over a minimum of Y1660, which includes the return bus fare to Golmud; this is the cheapest and most popular option. In comparison the Chinese pay either Y120 (seat) or Y160 (sleeper) for a ticket to Lhasa. If you would like to stay in Tibet for more than three days, then you have to pay an extra Y100 per day. In reality, most people either pay up and then throw their return ticket away when they arrive in Lhasa or they try one of the numerous touts offering lifts.

Of course travellers try to get around this by going directly to the Tibet bus station to purchase a ticket to Lhasa – the staff at the station politely tell them to go to CITS. Others try to hitch rides on trucks, but the local PSB are wise to this, and drivers have been cowed by the threat of a heavy fine if caught.

You won't have to go looking for the guys offering seats on a bus to Tibet; they will find you. They generally ask for between Y600 and Y1000 to Lhasa. It's assumed that this price includes a bribe to the PSB along the way. There is no way to guarantee that you will get to Lhasa or that you won't be fined and sent back. Some travellers have encountered problems, while others have made it to Lhasa hassle-free.

This scheme is crying out for reform and is only serving to reinforce foreign travellers' negative attitude towards Chinese bureaucracy.

If the situation doesn't improve and you're not willing to risk hitching, then the cheapest option is to buy your return ticket with a minimum three-day tour. When you purchase your ticket, make sure that CITS provides you with the ticket, not just a receipt. In Lhasa you should be able to extend the date of departure at either the bus office or CAAC office. Otherwise, cancel the ticket. Either way you'll probably lose 10% of the ticket price. Once you're in Lhasa there doesn't seem to be anyone telling foreigners to leave, although this could also change.

For those who wish to avoid this aggravating scenario, remember that there are many areas outside the Tibetan Autonomous Region (TAR) in Qīnghǎi, Gānsù, Sìchuān and Yúnnán, where foreigners are free to visit.

There are buses to Lhasa from the main bus station, as well as a number of private operators around town. CITS-approved buses for Lhasa leave from the Tibet bus station on Jinfen Lu at around 5pm. Foreigners are usually picked up at the Golmud Hotel and taken by CITS to the station. The road to Lhasa has vastly improved in recent years, and the trip can take anywhere from 26 to 60-odd hours. The latter time is usually a result of breakdowns or traffic holdups (both highly possible).

It would be wise to stock up on a few necessities for the trip. Toasty-warm People's Liberation Army (PLA) overcoats are available for around Y65 in town – consider getting one even if you wind up giving it away in Lhasa. It can easily get down to -10°C or lower in those mountain passes at night; although the buses are heated, you could be in serious trouble if you are ill equipped and there is a breakdown. Keep an eye on your possessions, as there have been a couple of reports of thieves on the buses. Some travellers were buying oxygen from the Golmud Hotel for Y30 a canister to try to avoid altitude sickness.

Language

Chinese

The official language of the PRC is the dialect spoken in Beijing. It is usually referred to in the west as 'Mandarin', but the Chinese call it Putonghua – common speech. Putonghua is variously referred to as *hànyǔ* (the Han language), *guóyǔ* (the national language) or *zhōngwén* or *zhōngguóhuà* (simply 'Chinese').

The Spoken Language

Dialects Discounting its ethnic minority languages, China has eight major dialect groups: Putonghua (Mandarin), Yue (Cantonese), Wu (Shanghainese), Minbei (Fuzhou), Minnan (Hokkien-Taiwanese), Xiang, Gan and Hakka. These dialects also divide into many more sub-dialects.

With the exception of the western and southernmost provinces, most of the population speaks Mandarin, although regional accents can make comprehension difficult.

The Written Language

Chinese is often referred to as a language of pictographs. Many of the basic Chinese characters are in fact highly stylised pictures of what they represent, but most Chinese characters (around 90%) are compounds of a 'meaning' element and a 'sound' element.

So just how many Chinese characters are there? It's possible to verify the existence of some 56,000 characters, but the vast majority of these are archaic. It is commonly felt that a well-educated, contemporary Chinese person might know and use between 6000 and 8000 characters. To read a Chinese newspaper you will need to know 2000 to 3000 characters, but 1200 to 1500 would be enough to get the gist.

Writing systems usually alter people's perception of a language, and this is certainly true of Chinese. Each Chinese character represents a spoken syllable, leading many people to declare that Chinese is a 'monosyllabic language.' Actually, it's more a case of having a monosyllabic writing system. While the building block of the Chinese language is indeed the

monosyllabic Chinese character, Chinese words are usually a combination of two or more characters. You could think of Chinese words as being compounds. The Chinese word for 'east' is composed of a single character *(dōng)*, but must be combined with the character for 'west' *(xī)* to form the word for 'thing' *(dōngxī)*. English has some compound words too (although not nearly as many as Chinese), examples being 'whitewash' and 'backslide'.

Theoretically, all Chinese dialects share the same written system. In practice, Cantonese adds about 3000 specialised characters of its own and many of the dialects don't have a written form at all.

Simplification In the interests of promoting universal literacy, the Committee for Reforming the Chinese Language was set up by the Beijing government in 1954. Around 2200 Chinese characters were simplified. Chinese communities outside China (notably Taiwan and Hong Kong), however, continue to use the traditional, full-form characters.

Over the past few years – probably as a result of large-scale investment by overseas Chinese and tourism – full-form or 'complex' characters have returned to China. These are mainly seen in advertising (where the traditional characters are considered more attractive) and on restaurant, hotel and shop signs.

Grammar

Chinese grammar is much simpler than that of European languages. There are no articles (a/the), no tenses and no plurals. The basic point to bear in mind is that, like English, Chinese word order is subject-verb-object. In other words, a basic English sentence like 'I (subject) love (verb) you (object)' is constructed in exactly the same way in Chinese. The catch is mastering the tones.

MANDARIN
Pinyin

In 1958 the Chinese adopted a system of writing their language using the Roman alphabet. It's known as *pīnyīn*. The original idea was to eventually do away with characters. However, tradition dies hard, and the idea has been abandoned.

Pinyin is often used on shop fronts, street signs and advertising billboards. Don't expect Chinese people to be able to use Pinyin, however. There are indications that the use of the Pinyin system is diminishing.

In the countryside and the smaller towns you may not see a single Pinyin sign anywhere, so unless you speak Chinese you'll need a phrasebook with Chinese characters.

Since 1979 all translated texts of Chinese diplomatic documents, as well as Chinese magazines published in foreign languages, have used the Pinyin system for spelling names and places. Pinyin replaces the old Wade-Giles and Lessing systems of Romanising Chinese script. Thus under Pinyin, 'Mao Tse-tung' becomes Mao Zedong; 'Chou En-lai' becomes Zhou Enlai; and 'Peking' becomes Beijing. The name of the country remains as it has been written most often: 'China' in English and German, and 'Chine' in French – in Pinyin it's Zhōngguó.

Now that Hong Kong (a Romanisation of Cantonese for 'fragrant harbour') has gone over to China, many think it will only be a matter of time before it gets renamed Xiānggǎng.

See the 'Pinyin' boxed text on the following page.

Pronunciation
Vowels

a	as in 'father'
ai	as in 'high'
ao	as the 'ow' in 'cow'
e	as the 'u' in 'fur'
ei	as the 'ei' in 'weigh'
i	as the 'ee' in 'meet' (or like the 'oo' in 'book' after c, ch, r, s, sh, z or zh)
ian	as in 'yen'
ie	as the English word 'yeah'
o	as in 'or', without the 'r' sound
ou	as the 'oa' in 'boat'
u	as in 'flute'
ui	as the word 'way'
uo	like a 'w' followed by 'o'
yu	as in the German 'ü' – pucker your lips and try saying 'ee'
ü	as the German 'ü'

Consonants

c	as the 'ts' in 'bits'
ch	as in 'chop', but with the tongue curled back
h	as in 'hay', but articulated from farther back in the throat
q	as the 'ch' in 'cheese'
r	as the 's' in 'pleasure'
sh	as in 'ship', but with the tongue curled back
x	as in 'ship'
z	as the 'dz' in 'suds'
zh	as the 'j' in 'judge' but with the tongue curled back

The only consonants that occur at the end of a syllable are n, ng and r.

In Pinyin, apostrophes are occasionally used to separate syllables in order to prevent ambiguity, eg, the word píng'ān can be written with an apostrophe after the 'g' to prevent it being pronounced as pín'gān.

Tones

Chinese is a language with a large number of words with the same pronunciation but a different meaning; what distinguishes these 'homophones' is their 'tonal' quality – the raising and lowering of pitch on certain syllables. Mandarin has four tones – high, rising, falling-rising and falling, plus a fifth 'neutral' tone which you can all but ignore. To illustrate, look at the word ma, which has four different meanings according to tone:

high tone	mā (mother)
rising tone	má (hemp, numb)
falling-rising tone	mǎ (horse)
falling tone	mà (scold, swear)

Mastering tones is tricky for newcomers to Mandarin, but with a little practice it can be done.

Gestures

Hand signs are frequently used in China. The 'thumbs-up' sign has a long tradition as an indication of excellence. An alternative way to indicate excellence is to gently pull your earlobe between your thumb and index finger.

The Chinese have a system for counting on their hands. If you can't speak the language, it would be worth your while at least to learn Chinese finger counting. One of the

Pinyin

While there are many dialects across China, the one thing all Chinese speakers have in common is their written language. Efforts have been made over the last 100 years to reform the written language, and a system called Pinyin (literally meaning 'spell sound') was invented last century as the standard for spelling Chinese characters. While Pinyin started life as a communist ploy to unite the peoples and popularise Mandarin within China, in its short life it has become the United Nations standard for 'spelling' Chinese characters, and for transliterating the names of people, places and scientific terms. Taiwan initially promulgated a different system of Romanisation, but recently announced that it was switching to the communist-designed Pinyin system, falling into line with the rest of the world.

Pinyin was not the first foray into spelling out Chinese characters. As early as the 17th century, foreign missionaries sought effective ways to spread the word and various spelling systems arose; even the Bible was reproduced in such scripts. In the late 19th century the Chinese themselves started to explore the issue of phonetic spelling systems. In 1933 the communists worked with a Russian and designed what they called Latinised New Script. This was based on Mandarin pronunciation and in 1958 the communist government implemented this as the official system, coinciding with its decision to adopt Mandarin as the official language of China. This new script came to be known as Pinyin. The government's prime purpose for adopting a Roman alphabet pronunciation of Chinese characters was to promote Mandarin throughout the nation. Although Mandarin was the the language of government, it had previously only enjoyed the same status as numerous other dialects spoken in China. A secondary purpose was to enable non-Chinese ethnic groups in China to create or reform their languages with a common base.

Another, less important, aim of Pinyin was to assist foreigners to learn Chinese. As foreign language learners will tell you, Pinyin is a fantastic tool, particularly at the beginning of a quest on the road to fluency. Unlike English, once you learn the Pinyin pronunciation system it is completely consistent. However, once the pronunciation system is learnt, problems start to arise: for one, Pinyin does not itself indicate tones (mandarin has four tones) and there may be dozens of characters represented by one Pinyin word: for example there are about 80 dictionary entries for the word pronounced and written *yi*. Luckily, context and grammatical structure, as well as the formation of compound words when *yi* combines with other sounds, usually give a few clues as to which of the 80 possibilities is meant. To assist travellers, this book has used tones throughout for towns, cities, sights, hotels, restaurants and entertainment venues.

Pinyin has permeated some groups in Chinese society, but most ordinary Chinese cannot use it very effectively, and some people argue that Pinyin is for foreigners. For those travelling in China using either this book or the Lonely Planet *Mandarin phrasebook*, the ability to use Pinyin and the government's regulation that all signs be in Pinyin and characters, will be a blessing.

Charles Qin

disadvantages of finger counting is that there are regional differences. The symbol for number 10 is to form a cross with the index fingers, but many Chinese just use a fist. (See the illustration on page 956).

Phrasebooks

Phrasebooks are invaluable, but it's a better idea to copy out the appropriate phrases in Chinese rather than show someone the book – otherwise they may take it and read every page! Reading place names or street signs isn't difficult, since the Chinese name is usually accompanied by the Pinyin form; if not, you'll soon learn lots of characters just

by repeated exposure. A small dictionary with English, Pinyin and Chinese characters is also useful for learning a few words.

Lonely Planet's *Mandarin phrasebook* includes script throughout and loads of useful phrases – it's also a very useful learning tool.

Pronouns

I
   wǒ   我
you
   nǐ   你
he, she, it
   tā   他/她/它

we, us
  wǒmen   我们
you (plural)
  nǐmen   你们
they, them
  tāmen   他们

Greetings & Civilities
Hello.
  nǐ hǎo   你好
Goodbye.
  zàijiàn   再见
Thank you.
  xièxie   谢谢
You're welcome.
  búkèqi   不客气
I'm sorry.
  duìbùqǐ   对不起

Small Talk
May I ask your name?
  nín guìxìng?   您贵姓？
My (sur)name is ...
  wǒ xìng ...   我姓 ...
No. (don't have)
  méi yǒu   没有
No. (not so)
  búshì   不是
I'm a foreign student.
  wǒ shì liúxuéshēng   我是留学生
What's to be done now?
  zěnme bàn?   怎么办？
It doesn't matter.
  méishì   没事
I want ...
  wǒ yào ...   我要...

No, I don't want it.
  búyào   不要
Where are you from?
  nǐ cōng nǎr lái?   你从 哪儿来？
I'm from ...
  wǒ shì cōng ... láide   我是从 ... 来的
Australia
  àodàliyà   澳大利亚
Canada
  jiānádà   加拿大
Denmark
  dānmài   丹麦
France
  fǎguó   法国
Germany
  déguó   德国
Netherlands
  hélán   荷兰
New Zealand
  xīnxīlán   新西兰
Spain
  xībānyá   西班牙
Sweden
  ruìdiǎn   瑞典
Switzerland
  ruìshì   瑞士
UK
  yīngguó   英国
USA
  měiguó   美国

Language Difficulties
I understand.
  wǒ tīngdedǒng   我听得懂

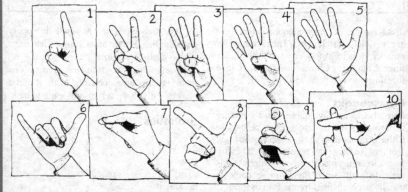

The Chinese system of finger counting

Chinese Sayings & Expressions

Chinese is an extremely rich idiomatic language. Many sayings are four-character phrases that combine a great balance of rhythm and tone with a clever play on the multiple meanings of similar-sounding characters. Perhaps most interesting is how many phrases have direct English equivalents.

缘木求鱼 *(yuánmù qiúyú)*
Like climbing a tree to catch fish (a waste of time)

问道于盲 *(wèndào yú máng)*
Like asking a blind man for directions (another waste of time)

同床异梦 *(tóngchuáng yìmèng)*
To sleep in the same bed but have different dreams

坐井观天 *(zuòjǐng guāntiān)*
Like looking at the sky from the bottom of a well (not seeing the whole picture)

水落石出 *(shuǐluò shíchū)*
When the tide goes out the rocks are revealed (the truth will out)

守株待兔 *(shǒuzhū dàitù)*
Like a hunter waiting for a rabbit to kill itself by running into a tree (trusting to dumb luck)

殊途同归 *(shūtú tóngguī)*
Different roads all reach the same end

临阵磨枪 *(línjūn móqiāng)*
To not sharpen your weapons until the battle is upon you (to do things at the last minute)

热锅上的蚂蚁 *(règuōshàng demǎyǐ)*
Like ants on top of a hot stove (full of worries)

新瓶装旧酒 *(xīnpíng zhuāng jiùjiǔ)*
A new bottle filled with old wine (a superficial change)

削足适履 *(xiāozú shìlǚ)*
Like trimming the foot to fit the shoe

种瓜得瓜 *(zhòngguā déguā)*
If a man plants melons, so will he reap melons

酒肉朋友 *(jiǔròu péngyou)*
An eating and drinking friend (fair-weather friend)

晴天霹雳 *(qíngtiān pīli)*
Like thunder from a blue sky (a bolt from the blue)

沐猴而冠 *(mù hóu ér guàn)*
A monkey dressed in a tall hat (a petty official)

燃眉之急 *(ránméi zhījí)*
A fire that is burning one's eyebrows (extremely urgent)

I don't understand.
　wǒ tīngbudǒng　　我听不懂
Do you understand?
　dǒng ma?　　懂吗？
Could you speak more slowly please?
　qīng nǐ shuō màn　　请你说慢
　yīdiǎn, hǎo ma?　　一点，好吗？

Toilets
Men/Women　　男/女
toilet (restroom)
　cèsuǒ?　　厕所
toilet paper
　wèishēng zhǐ　　卫生纸
bathroom (washroom)
　xǐshǒu jiān　　洗手间

Money
How much is it?
　duōshǎo qián?　　多少钱？
Is there anything cheaper?
　yǒu piányi yìdiǎn de ma?　　有便宜一点的吗？

That's too expensive.
　tài guìle　　太贵了
Bank of China
　zhōngguó yínháng　　中国银行
change money
　huàn qián　　换钱

Accommodation
Is there a room vacant?
　yǒu méiyǒu kōng fángjiān?　　有没有空房间？
Yes, there is/No, there isn't.
　yǒu/méiyǒu　　有/没有
Can I see the room?
　wǒ néng kànkan fángjiān ma?　　我能看看房间吗？
I don't like this room.
　wǒ bù xǐhuan zhèijiān fángjiān　　我不喜欢这间房
Are there any messages for me?
　yǒu méiyǒu liú huà?　　有没有留话？

May I have a hotel namecard?
yǒu méiyǒu lǚguǎn de míngpiàn?
有没有旅馆的名片？

Could I have these clothes washed, please?
qíng bǎ zhè xiē yīfu xǐ gānjìng,
hǎo ma?
请把这些衣服洗干净，好吗？

hotel
lǚguǎn 旅馆
tourist hotel
bīnguǎn/fàndiàn/ 宾馆/饭店/
jiǔdiàn 酒店
reception desk
zǒng fúwù tái 总服务台
dormitory
duōrénfáng 多人房
single room
dānrénfáng 单人房
twin room
shuāngrénfáng 双人房
bed
chuángwèi 床位
economy room
(no bath)
pǔtōngfáng 普通房
standard room
biāozhǔn fángjiān 标准房
deluxe suite
háohuá tàofáng 豪华套房

Visas & Documents
passport
hùzhào 护照
visa
qiānzhèng 签证
visa extension
yáncháng qiānzhèng 延长签证
Public Security
Bureau (PSB)
gōng'ān jú 公安局
Foreign Affairs Branch
wài shí kē 外事科

Post
post office
yúojú 邮局
letter
xìn 信
envelope
xìnfēng 信封
package
bāoguǒ 包裹
air mail
hángkōng xìn 航空信

surface mail
píngyóu 平邮
stamps
yóupiào 邮票
postcard
míngxìnpiàn 明信片
aerogramme
hángkōng xìnjiàn 航空邮件
poste restante
cúnjú hòulínglán 存局候领栏
express mail (EMS)
yóuzhèng tèkuài
zhuāndì 邮政特快专递
registered mail
guà hào 挂号

Telecommunications
telephone
diànhuà 电话
telephone office
diànxùn dàlóu 电讯大楼
telephone card
diànhuà kǎ 电话卡
international call
guójì diànhuà 国际电话
collect call
duìfāng fùqián
diànhuà 对方付费电话
direct-dial call
zhíbō diànhuà 直拨电话
fax
chuánzhēn 传真
computer
diànnǎo 电脑
email
diànzǐyóujiàn 电子邮件
(often called 'email')
internet
yīntè wǎng/ 因特网/
(hùlián wǎng) (互联网)
(more formal name)
online
shàng wǎng 上网
Where can I get
online?
wǒ zài nǎr kěyǐ 我在哪儿
shàng wǎng? 可以上网？

Directions
Where is the ...?
... zài nǎlǐ? ... 在哪里？
I'm lost.
wǒ mílùle 我迷路了
Turn right.
yòu zhuān 右转

Turn left.
zuǒ zhuǎn 左转
Go straight ahead.
yìzhí zǒu 一直走
Turn around.
wàng huí zǒu 往回走

alley
nòng 弄
boulevard
dàdào 大道
lane
xiàng, hútóng 巷\胡同
map
dìtú 地图
road
lù 路
section
duàn 段
street
jiē, dàjiē 街，大街
No 21
21 hào 21号

Time
What's the time?
jǐ diǎn? 几点？
... hour ... minute
... diǎn ... fēn ... 点 ... 分
3.05
sān diǎn wǔ fēn 3点5分
now
xiànzài 现在
today
jīntiān 今天
tomorrow
míngtiān 明天
day after tomorrow
hòutiān 后天
yesterday
zuótiān 昨天
Wait a moment.
děng yī xià 等一下

Transport
I want to go to ...
wǒ yào qù ... 我要去 ...
I want to get off.
wǒ yào xiàchē 我要下车
What time does it
depart/arrive?
jǐdiǎn kāi/dào? 几点开/到？
How long does the
trip take?
zhècì lǚxíng yào huā 这次旅行要花
duōcháng shíjiān? 多长时间？

Chinglish

Help!
Initially you might be puzzled by a sign in the bathroom that reads 'Please don't take the odds and ends put into the nightstool'. In fact this is a warning to resist sudden impulses to empty the contents of your pockets or backpack into the toilet. An apparently ambiguous sign with anarchic implications like the one in the Lhasa Bank of China that reads 'Question Authority' is really just an economical way of saying 'Please address your questions to one of the clerks'.

On the other hand, just to confuse things, a company name like the 'Risky Investment Co' means just what it says. An English-Chinese dictionary proudly proclaims in the preface that it is 'very useful for the using'. And a beloved sign in the Liangmao Hotel in Tài'ān proclaims:

Safety Needing Attention!
Be care of depending fire
Sweep away six injurious insect
Pay attention to civilisation

If this all sounds confusing, don't worry. It won't be long before you have a small armoury of Chinglish phrases of your own. Before you know it, you'll know without even thinking that 'Be careful not to be stolen' is a warning against thieves; that 'Shoplifters will be fined 10 times' means that shoplifting is not a good idea in China; that 'Do not stroke the works' (generally found in museums) means 'No touching'; and that you 'very like' something means that you 'like it very much'.

The best advice for travellers in China grappling with the complexities of a new language is not to set your sights too high. Bear in mind that it takes a minimum of 15 years of schooling in the Chinese language and a crash course in English to be able to write Chinglish with any fluency.

Please use the meter.
dǎ biǎo 打表
luggage
xíngli 行李
left-luggage room
jìcún chù 寄存处
one ticket
yìzhāng piào 一张票

two tickets
liǎngzhāng piào 两张票
buy a ticket
mǎi piào 买票
refund a ticket
tuì piào 退票
taxi
chūzū chē 出租车
microbus taxi
miànbāo chē, miǎndī 面包车、面的

Air

airport
fēijīchǎng 飞机场
charter flight
bāojī 包机
CAAC ticket office
zhōngguó mínháng 中国民航
shòupiào chù 售票处
one way ticket
dānchéng piào 单程票
return ticket
láihuí piào 来回票
boarding pass
dēngjì kǎ 登记卡
reconfirm
quèrèn 确认
cancel
qǔxiāo 取消
bonded baggage
cúnzhàn xínglǐ 存栈行李

Bus

bus
gōnggòng qìchē 公共汽车
minibus
xiǎo gōnggòng qìchē 小公共汽车
long-distance bus station
chángtú qìchē zhàn 长途汽车站

When is the first bus?
tóubān qìchē jǐdiǎn kāi?
头班汽车几点开？
When is the last bus?
mòbān qìchē jǐdiǎn kāi?
末班汽车几点开？
When is the next bus?
xià yìbān qìchē jǐdiǎn kāi?
下一班汽车几点开？

Train

train
huǒchē 火车
ticket office
shòupiào chù 售票处

Emergencies – Mandarin

Help!
jiùmìng a! 救命啊
Fire!
huǒ zāi! 火灾
Thief!
xiǎo tōu! 小偷
I'm sick.
wǒ shēng bìng 我生病
I'm injured.
wǒ shòushāng 我受伤
emergency
jǐnjí qíngkuàng 紧急情况
hospital
yīyuàn 医院
emergency room
jízhěn shì 急诊室
police
jǐngchá 警察
foreign affairs police
wàishì jǐngchá 外事警察
pickpocket
páshǒu 扒手
rapist
qiángjiānzhě 强奸者

---

train station
huǒchē zhàn 火车站
hard-seat
yìngxí, yìngzuò 硬席、硬座
soft-seat
ruǎnxí, ruǎnzuò 软席、软座
hard-sleeper
yìngwò 硬卧
soft-sleeper
ruǎnwò 软卧
platform ticket
zhàntái piào 站台票
Which platform?
dìjǐhào zhàntái? 第几号站台？
upgrade ticket (after boarding)
bǔpiào 补票
subway (underground)
dìxiàtiě 地下铁
subway station
dìtiě zhàn 地铁站

Bicycle

bicycle
zìxíngchē
自行车
I want to hire a bicycle.
wǒ yào zū yíliàng zìxíngchē
我要租一辆自行车

How much is it per day?
yìtiān duōshǎo qián?
一天多少钱？
How much is it per hour?
yíge xiǎo shí duōshǎo qián?
一个小时多少钱？
How much is the deposit?
yājīn duōshǎo qián?
押金多少钱？

Health
hospital
yīyuàn　医院
laxative
xièyào　泻药
anti-diarrhoea
medicine
zhǐxièyào　止泻药
rehydration salts
shūwéizhí dīnà　舒维质低钠
fā pàodìng　发泡锭
aspirin
āsīpǐlín　阿斯匹林
antibiotics
kàngjūnsù　抗菌素
condom
bìyùn tào　避孕套
tampon
wèishēng mián tiáo　卫生棉条
sanitary napkin (Kotex)
wèishēng mián　卫生棉
sunscreen (UV) lotion
fáng shài yóu　防晒油
mosquito coils
wénxiāng　蚊香
mosquito pads
diàn wénxiāng　电蚊香

Numbers
0	*líng*	零
1	*yī, yāo*	一、幺
2	*èr, liǎng*	二、两
3	*sān*	三
4	*sì*	四
5	*wǔ*	五
6	*liù*	六
7	*qī*	七
8	*bā*	八
9	*jiǔ*	九
10	*shí*	十
11	*shíyī*	十一
12	*shí'èr*	十二
20	*èrshí*	二十

21	*èrshíyī*	二十一
100	*yìbǎi*	一百
200	*liǎngbǎi*	两百
1000	*yìqiān*	一千
2000	*liǎngqiān*	两千
10,000	*yíwàn*	一万
20,000	*liǎngwàn*	两万
100,000	*shíwàn*	十万
200,000	*èrshíwàn*	二十万

CANTONESE
What a difference a border makes. Cantonese is still the most popular dialect in Hong Kong, Guǎngzhōu and the surrounding area. It differs from Mandarin as much as French differs from Spanish. Speakers of both dialects can read Chinese characters, but a Cantonese speaker will pronounce many of the characters differently from a Mandarin speaker. For example, when Mr Ng from Hong Kong goes to Beijing the Mandarin-speakers will call him Mr Wu. If Mr Wong goes from Hong Kong to Fújiàn the character for his name will be read as Mr Wee, and in Beijing he is Mr Huang.

Romanisation
Unfortunately, several competing systems of Romanisation of Cantonese script exist and no single one has emerged as an official standard. A number have come and gone, but at least three have survived and are currently used in Hong Kong: Meyer-Wempe, Sidney Lau and Yale. In this language guide we use the Yale system. It's the most phonetically accurate and the one generally preferred by foreign students.

Pronunciation
The following Romanisation system is a simplified version designed to help you pronounce the Cantonese words and phrases in this book as quickly and easily as possible. Note that the examples given reflect British pronunciation.

Vowels
a　as in 'father'
ai　as the 'i' in 'find', but shorter
au　as the 'ow' in 'cow'
e　as in 'let'
ei　as the 'a' in 'say', but without the 'y' sound

eu similar to the 'ur' in 'urn' with lips pursed, but without the 'r' sound
i as in 'marine'
iu similar to the word 'you'
o as in 'not'; as in 'no' when at the end of a word
oi as the 'oy' in 'boy'
oo as in 'soon'
ou as the word 'owe'
u as in 'put'
ue separate, as the 'u-e' in 'suet'
ui separate, as 'oo-ee'

Consonants In general, consonants are pronounced as in English. Three that may give you a little trouble are:

g as in 'go'
j as the 'ds' in 'suds'
ng as in 'sing'

Tones

Chinese languages are rich in homonyms (ie, words that sound alike) and much of their superstitious beliefs, poetry and humour is based on this wealth. The Cantonese word for 'silk', for example, sounds the same as the words for 'lion', 'private', 'poem', 'corpse' and 'teacher'. What distinguishes the meaning of each word are changes in a speaker's pitch or 'tone' and the context of the word within the sentence; say *mai dan* in a restaurant and everyone will know you're asking for 'the bill'. Say the same thing in a market and people will come up to ask how much the 'eggs' you are 'selling' cost. Cantonese has seven tones (although you can easily get by with six).

The Yale Romanisation system is designed to make pronunciation of Cantonese tones as simple as possible and may not necessarily reflect what you come across where official transliteration systems are used.

In the Yale system six basic tones are represented: three 'level' tones, which do not noticeably rise or fall in pitch (high, middle and low), and three 'moving' tones, which either rise or fall in pitch (high rising, low rising and low falling). Remember that it doesn't matter whether you have a high or low voice when speaking Cantonese as long as your intonation reflects relative changes in pitch. The following examples show the six basic tones. Note how important they can be to your intended meaning:

high tone: represented by a macron above a vowel, as in *fōo* (husband)
middle tone: represented by an unaccented vowel, as in *foo* (wealthy)
low tone: represented by the letter 'h' after a vowel, as in *fooh* (owe); note that 'h' is only pronounced if it occurs at the start of a word; elsewhere it signifies a low tone
middle tone rising: represented by an acute accent, as in *fóo* (tiger)
low falling tone: represented by a grave accent followed by the low tone letter 'h', as in *fòoh* (to lean)
low rising tone: represented by an acute accent and the low tone letter 'h', as in *fóoh* (woman)

Getting Started

The following list should help get you started. For a more detailed guide to Cantonese, with script throughout, loads of phrases, and information on grammar and pronunciation, get a copy of Lonely Planet's *Cantonese phrasebook*.

Pronouns

I	*ngóh*	我
you	*néhìh*	你
he/she/it	*kúhìh*	佢
we/us	*ngóh dēìh*	我哋
you (plural)	*néhìh dēìh*	你哋
they/them	*kúhìh dēìh*	佢哋

Greetings & Useful Phrases

Hello, how are you?
  néhìh hó ma?
  你好嗎?
Fine, and you?
  géìh hó, néhìh nē?
  幾好，你呢?
Good morning.
  jó sàhn
  早晨
Goodbye.
  bāàhìh baàhìh/joìh gin
  拜拜/再見
Thank you very much.
  dōh jē saàhìh/m gōìh saàhìh
  多謝哂/唔該哂
Thanks. (for a gift or special favour)
  dōh jē
  多謝
Thanks. (making a request or purchase)
  m gōìh
  唔該

You're welcome.
m sáih haàhk hēih
唔使客氣

Excuse me. (calling someone's attention)
m gōih
唔該

I'm sorry.
m hó yi si
唔好意思

What is your surname? (polite)
chéng mahn gwaìh sing?
請問貴姓？

My surname is ...
síuh sing ...
小姓 . . .

Is it OK to take a photo?
hóh m hóh yíh yíng séùhng a?
可唔可以影相呀？

Do you speak English?
néhìh sìk m sìk góng yìng mán a?
你識唔識講英文呀？

I don't understand.
ngóh m mìhng
我唔明

Getting Around

airport	*gēih chèhùhng*	機場
bus stop	*bā sí jahàhm*	巴士站
pier	*máh tàhùh*	碼頭
subway station	*dēih tit jahàhm*	地鐵站
north	*bāk*	北
south	*nàhàhm*	南
east	*dūng*	東
west	*sāih*	西

I'd like to go to ...
ngóh séùhng huìh ...
我想去 . . .

Where is the ...?
... háìh bìn doh a?
. . . 喺邊度呀？

Does this (bus, train etc) go to ...?
huìh m huìh ... a?
去唔去 . . . 呀？

How much is the fare?
géìh dōh chín a?
幾多錢呀？

Please write down the address for me.
m gōih sé goh dēih jí bêìh ngóh
唔該寫個地址俾我

Emergencies – Cantonese

Help!
gaùh mēng a! 救命呀！
I'm sick.
ngóh yáhùh bēng 我有病
I need a doctor.
ngóh yiùh táih yī sāng 我要睇醫生
Call an ambulance!
giùh gaùh sēùhng chē! 叫救傷車！
Call the police!
giùh gíng chaàht! 叫警察！
Watch out!
síuh sām! 小心！
Thief!
chéùhng yéh a! 搶嘢呀！

Accommodation & Food

Do you have any rooms available?
yáhùh mó fóng a?
有冇房呀？

I'd like a (single/double) room.
ngóh séùhng yiùh yāt gāàhn (dāàhn yàhn/sēùhng yàhn) fóng
我想要一間(單人/雙人)房？

How much per night?
géìh dōh chín yāt máhàhn a?
幾多錢一晚呀？

Can you recommend any dishes?
yáhùh māt yéh hó gaàhìh siùh a?
有乜嘢好介紹呀？

I'm a vegetarian.
ngóh sihk jāàhìh
我食齋

Shopping

How much is this?
nī goh géìh dōh chín a?
呢個幾多錢呀？

That's very expensive.
hó gwaìh
好貴

Can you reduce the price?
pèhng dī dāk m dāk a?
平啲得唔得呀？

I'm just looking.
ngóh sīn táih yāt táih
我先睇一睇

Numbers

0	*lìhng*	零
1	*yāt*	一
2	*yih (léhùhng)*	二(兩)

3	*sāàhm*	三
4	*sēìh*	四
5	*ng*	五
6	*luhk*	六
7	*chāt*	七
8	*baàht*	八
9	*gáùh*	九
10	*sahp*	十
11	*sahp yāt*	十一
12	*sahp yih*	十二
20	*yih sahp*	二十
21	*yih sahp yāt*	二十一
100	*yāt baàhk*	一百
101	*yāt baàhk lìhng yāt*	一百零一
110	*yāt baàhk yāt sahp*	一百一十
120	*yāt baàhk yih sahp*	一百二十
200	*yih baàhk*	二百
1000	*yāt chīn*	一千
10,000	*yāt mahàhn*	一萬
100,000	*sahp mahàhn*	十萬

one million
   yāt baàhk mahàhn   一百萬

Portuguese

Like French, Italian, Spanish and Romanian, Portuguese is a Romance language (one closely derived from Latin). It's spoken in Portugal, Brazil, several African states and Macau. Note that some words in Portuguese require different endings depending on the gender of the speaker, usually 'o' for masculine, 'a' for feminine. In this guide, these alternatives are shown separated by a slash (eg, *obrigado/a*, 'thank you').

Pronunciation

Pronunciation of Portuguese is a little tricky; like English, vowels and consonants have more than one possible sound depending on their position and word stress. Moreover, there are nasal vowels and diphthongs in Portuguese with no equivalents in English.

Vowels Single vowels shouldn't present too many problems. Nasalisation is represented by an 'n' or an 'm' after the vowel, or by a tilde (eg, **ã**) over it. The nasal 'i' exists in English as the 'ing' in 'sing'. For other nasal vowels, try to pronounce a long 'a', 'ah', 'e' or 'eh' while holding your nose, so that you sound as if you have a cold.

Vowel combinations (diphthongs) are relatively straightforward. For nasal diphthongs, try the same technique as for nasal vowels. To say *não*, pronounce 'now' through your nose.

Word Stress Many Portuguese words have a written accent above a vowel to indicate the syllable on which word stress falls.

Greetings & Civilities

Hello.	*Bom dia/Olá/Chao.*
Good morning.	*Bom dia.*
Good evening.	*Boa tarde.*
Goodbye.	*Adeus/Chao.*
See you later.	*Até logo.*
How are you?	*Como está?*
I'm fine, thanks.	*Bem, obrigado/a.*
Please.	*Se faz favor/Por favor.*
Thank you.	*Obrigado/a.*
You're welcome.	*De nada.*
Sorry. (forgive me)	*Desculpe.*
Yes.	*Sim.*
No.	*Não.*
Maybe.	*Talvez.*
What's your name?	*Como se chama?*
My name is …	*Chamo-me …*

Getting Around

What time does the (next) … leave/ arrive?	*A que horas parte/ chega o (próximo) …?*
boat	*barco*
bus (city)	*autocarro*
bus (intercity)	*camionete*

I want to go to …	*Quero ir a …*
Where is the bus stop?	*Onde é a paragem do autocarro*
Is this the bus to ...?	*E este o autocarro para … ?*
I'd like a one-way ticket.	*Queria um bilhete simples/de ida.*
I'd like a return ticket.	*Queria um bilhete de ida e volta.*
left-luggage office	*o depósito de bagagem*
platform	*cais*
timetable	*horário*

I'd like to hire …	*Queria alugar …*
a car	*um carro*
a motorcycle	*uma motocicleta*
a bicycle	*uma bicicleta*

Emergencies – Portuguese

Help!	*Socorro!*
Call a doctor!	*Chame um médico!*
Call the police!	*Chame a polícia!*
Where is a ...?	*Onde é um ...?*
hospital	*hospital*
medical clinic	*centro de saúde*
I'm allergic to ...	*Sou alérgica/o a ...*
antibiotics	*antibióticos*
penicillin	*penicilina*
Go away!	*Deixe-me em paz!*
I've been robbed.	*Fui roubado/a.*
I'm lost.	*Estou perdido/a.*

What ... is this?	*O que ... é esta?*
street/road	*rua/estrada*
town	*cidade/vila*
How do you get to (the) ...?	*Como se vai para (o/a) ...?*
north	*norte*
south	*sul*
east	*estee*
west	*oeste*

Around Town

Where is ...?	*Onde é ...?*
a bank	*um banco*
an exchange office	*um câmbio*
the city centre	*o centro da cidade/da baixa*
the hospital	*o hospital*
my hotel	*o meu hotel*
the post office	*o correio*
a public toilet	*uma casa de banho público*
the telephone centre	*da central de telefones*
the tourist office	*o posto de turismo*
What time does it open/close?	*A que horas abre/fecha?*
I'd like to make a telephone call.	*Quero usar o telefone.*
I'd like to change some money/ travellers cheques.	*Queria trocar dinheiro/ cheques de viagem.*

Accommodation

I'm looking for ...	*Procuro ...*
a guesthouse	*uma pensão*
a hotel	*um hotel*
a youth hostel	*uma pousada de juventude/ um albergue de juventude*
Do you have any rooms available?	*Tem quartos livres?*
I'd like to book ...	*Quero fazer uma reserva para ...*
a bed	*uma cama*
a single room	*um quarto individual*
a double room/ with twin beds	*um duplo/um quarto de casal*
a dormitory bed	*uma cama de dormitório*
May I see the room?	*Posso ver o quarto?*
How much is it per night/per person?	*Quanto é por noite/ por pessoa?*
Is breakfast included?	*O pequeno almoço está incluído?*
Where is the toilet?	*Onde ficam os lavabos?*

Time & Dates

What time is it?	*Que horas são?*
When?	*Quando?*
today	*hoje*
tonight	*hoje à noite*
tomorrow	*amanhã*
yesterday	*ontem*
morning	*manhã*
afternoon	*tarde*

Numbers

1	*um/uma*
2	*dois/duas*
3	*três*
4	*quatro*
5	*cinco*
6	*seis*
7	*sete*
8	*oito*
9	*nove*
10	*dez*
20	*vinte*
30	*trinta*
100	*cem*
1000	*mil*

LANGUAGE

Tibetan

Pronunciation

Like all foreign languages Tibetan has its fair share of tricky pronunciations. There are quite a few consonant clusters, and Tibetan is a language (like Korean and Thai) that makes an important distinction between aspirated and unaspirated consonants.

Naturally, the best way to approach these difficulties is to work through a phrasebook with a native speaker or with a tape. Lonely Planet's *Tibetan phrasebook* has script throughout and is an excellent tool for those wishing to learn the language in greater depth.

Vowels The following pronunciation guide is based on standard British pronunciation (North Americans beware).

a	as in 'father'
ay	as in 'play'
e	as in 'met'
ee	as in 'meet'
i	as in 'big'
o	as in 'go'
oo	as in 'soon'
ö	as the 'u' in 'fur', without the 'r' sound
ü	as in 'flute'

Consonants With the exception of those listed below, Tibetan consonants should be pronounced as in English. Where consonants are followed by an 'h', it means that the consonant is aspirated (ie, accompanied by a puff of air). An English example might be 'kettle', where the 'k' is aspirated and the 'tt' is unaspirated. The distinction is fairly important, but in simple Tibetan the context should make it clear what you're talking about even if you get the sounds muddled up a bit.

ky	as the 'kie' in 'Kiev'
ng	as the 'ng' in 'sing'
r	produced with a slight trill
ts	as the 'ts' in 'bits'

Pronouns

I	nga
you	kerang
he, she	khong
we	nga-tso
you all	kerang-tso
they	khong-tso

Useful Phrases

Hello.	tashi dele
Goodbye. (to person leaving)	kale phe
Goodbye. (by person leaving)	kale shoo
Thank you.	thoo jaychay
Yes, OK.	la ong
I'm sorry. (forgive me)	gonda
I want ...	nga la ... go
Do you speak English?	injeeke shing gi yö pe?
Do you understand?	ha ko song-ngey?
I understand.	ha ko song
I don't understand.	ha ko ma song
How much?	ka tsö ray?
It's expensive.	gong chenpo ray
What's your name?	kerang gi ming la kary zer gi yö?
My name is ...	ngai ... ming la
... and you?	... a ni kerang zer gi yö?
Where are you from?	kerang lungba ka-nay yin?
I'm from ...	nga ...-nay yin

Getting Around

I want to go to ...	nga ... la drondö yö
I'll get off here.	nga phap gi yin
What time do we leave?	ngatso chutsö katsö la dro gi yin?
What time do we arrive?	ngatso chutsö katsö la lep gi yin?
Where can I rent a bicycle?	kanggari kaba ragi ray?
How much per day?	nyima chik laja katsö ray?
Where is the ...?	... kaba yo ray?
I'm lost.	nga lam khag lag song

airport	namdrutang
bicycle	kanggari
bus	lamkhor
right	yeba
left	yönba
straight ahead	shar gya
north/south	chang/lo
east/west	shar/noop
porter	dopo khur khen
pack animal	skel semchen

Accommodation

guesthouse	dhön-khang
hotel	drü-khang/fan-dian

Do you have a room?	*kang mi yöpe?*
How much is it for one night?	*tsen chik la katsö ray?*
I'd like to stay with a Tibetan family.	*nga phöbe mitsang nyemdo dendö yö*

Geographical Terms

cave	*trapoo*
hot spring	*chuzay*
lake	*tso*
mountain	*ree*
river	*tsangpo*
road/trail	*lam*
valley	*loong shon*
waterfall	*papchu*

Health

I'm sick.	*nga bedo mindu*
Please call a doctor.	*amchi ke tongda*
altitude sickness	*lâdu na*
diarrhoea	*troko she*
fever	*tsawa*
hospital	*menkang*

Time

What's the time?	*chutsö katsö ray?*
hour/minute	*chutsö/karma*
When?	*kadü?*
now	*thanda*
today	*thiring*
tomorrow	*sangnyi*

yesterday	*kesa*
morning	*shogay*
afternoon	*nying gung gyab la*
evening/night	*gonta*

Numbers

Note: to form compound numbers, add the appropriate number for one to nine after the word in brackets, eg, 21 is *nyi shu tsa chig*, 32 is *sum shu so nyi*.

1	*chig*
2	*nyi*
3	*sum*
4	*shi*
5	*nga*
6	*troo*
7	*dün*
8	*gye*
9	*gu*
10	*chu*
11	*chu chig*
20	*nyi shu (tsa ...)*
30	*sum shu (so ...)*
40	*shi chu (shay ...)*
50	*nga chu (ngay ...)*
60	*doog chu (ray ...)*
70	*dun chu (don ...)*
80	*gye chu (gya ...)*
90	*gu chu (go ...)*
100	*chig gya*
1000	*chig tong*

Glossary

adetki mashina – (Uyghur) ordinary bus
ali mashina – (Uyghur) soft seat coach
amah – a servant who cleans houses and looks after the children
apsaras – Buddhist celestial beings, similar to angels
aptoos biket – (Uyghur) long-distance bus station
arhat – Buddhist, especially a monk who has achieved enlightenment and passes to nirvana at death

báijiŭ – literally 'white alcohol', a type of face-numbing rice wine served at banquets and get-togethers
bāozi – steamed savoury buns with tasty meat filling
běi – north. The other points of the compass are: *nán* (south), *dōng* (east) and *xī* (west)
bēicái – quarry
biānjiè – border
biéshù – villa
bīnguǎn – tourist hotel
Bodhisattva – one worthy of nirvana but who remains on earth to help others attain enlightenment
Bön – the pre-Buddhist indigenous faith of Tibet, pockets of which survive in western Sìchuān
bówùguǎn – museum

CAAC – Civil Aviation Administration of China
cadre – Chinese government bureaucrat
cāntīng – restaurant
cǎoyuán – grasslands
catty – unit of weight, one catty (*jīn*) equals 0.6kg
CCP – Chinese Communist Party, founded in Shànghǎi in 1921
chang – a Tibetan brew made from fermented barley
Chángchéng – the Great Wall
chau – (Cantonese) land mass, such as an island
cheongsam – (Cantonese) originating in Shànghǎi, a fashionable tight-fitting Chinese dress with a slit up the side.
chí – lake, pool
chim – (Cantonese) sticks used to divine the future. They're shaken out of a box onto the ground and then 'read'

chops – see name chops
chörten – Tibetan stupa, see *stupa*
CITS – China International Travel Service; deals with China's foreign tourists
CTS – China Travel Service; originally set up to handle tourists from Hong Kong, Macau, Taiwan and overseas Chinese
cūn – village
CYTS – China Youth Travel Service

dàdào – boulevard
dàfàndiàn – large hotel
dàjiē – avenue
dàjiŭdiàn – large hotel
dānwèi – work unit, the cornerstone of China's social structure
dǎo – island
dàpùbù – large waterfall
dàqiáo – large bridge
dàshà – hotel, building
dàshèngtǎ – pagoda
dàxué – university
dìtiě – subway
dōng – east. The other points of the compass are: *běi* (north), *nán* (south) and *xī* (west)
dòng – cave
dòngwùyuán – zoo

értóng – children

fàndiàn – a hotel or restaurant
fēng – peak
fēngjǐngqū – scenic area
fengshui – geomancy, literally 'wind and water', the art of using ancient principles to maximise the flow of 'qi', or universal energy
Fifth Generation – a generation of film directors who trained after the Cultural Revolution and whose political works revolutionised the film industry in the 1980s and 1990s
fó – a Buddha
Fourth Generation – a generation of film directors whose careers were suspended by the Cultural Revolution

gǎng – harbour
Gang of Four – members of a clique, headed by Mao's wife, Jiang Qing, who were blamed for the Cultural Revolution
gé – pavilion, temple

ger – (Inner Mongolia) the Mongolian word for a circular tent made with animal skin or felt; see yurt

godown – (Guǎngzhōu, Hong Kong) a warehouse, usually located on or near the waterfront

gompa – (Tibet) monastery

gōng – palace

gōngyuán – park

gōu – gorge, valley

gù – previous, earlier

gǔ – valley

guān – pass

guānxì – advantageous social or business connections

gùchéng – ruins

gùjū – house, home, residence

gwailo – (Cantonese) a foreigner; literally meaning 'ghost person' and interpreted as 'foreign devil'

hǎi – sea

hǎitān – beach

Hakka – a Chinese ethnic group

hé – river

hong – (Cantonese) a company, usually engaged in trade. Often refers to Hong Kong's original trading houses, such as Jardine Matheson or Swire

hú – lake

Hui – ethnic Chinese Muslims

húndùn – (Cantonese) wontons

huǒshānqún – volcano

hútòng – a narrow alleyway

jiāng – river

jiàotáng – church

jiǎozi – stuffed dumpling

jiē – street

jié – festival

jìniànbēi – memorial

jìniànguǎn – memorial hall

jìniàntǎ – monument

jiǔdiàn – hotel

jū – residence, home

junk – originally referred to Chinese fishing and war vessels with square sails. Now applies to various types of boating craft

kadimi shahr – (Uyghur) old part of towns

kaido – (Cantonese) a small to medium-sized ferry that makes short runs on the open sea, usually used for non-scheduled service between small islands and fishing villages

kǎoyādiàn – roast duck restaurant

karakhana – (Uyghur) workshop, factory

karst – denotes the characteristically eroded landscape of limestone regions, eg, the whimsical scenery of Guìlín and Yángshuò

KCR – Kowloon-Canton Railway

Kham – traditional name for eastern Tibet, encompassing western Sìchuān

kūnjù – a regional form of classical opera developed in the cities of Sūzhōu, Hángzhōu and Nánjīng

KMB – Kowloon Motor Bus

kuài – colloquial term for the currency, yuán

Kuomintang – Chiang Kaishek's Nationalist Party, the dominant political force after the fall of the Qing dynasty. Now Taiwan's major political party

laobaixing – common people, the masses

lama – a Buddhist priest of the Tantric or Lamaist school; a title bestowed on monks of particularly high spiritual attainment

lǎowài – foreigners

lín – forest

líng – tomb

lìshǐ – history

lóu – tower

luóhàn – see arhat

LRT – (Hong Kong) Light Rail Transit

lù – road

lǚguǎn – hotel

lúshēng – a reed pipe that features in many festivals in Guìzhōu

mahjong – popular Chinese card game for four people, played with engraved tiles

Mandate of Heaven – a political concept where heaven gives wise leaders a mandate to rule and removes power from those who are evil or corrupt

mánmányoū – motor taxi

máo – colloquial term for *jiǎo,* 10 of which equal one *kuài*

mǎtou – dock

mén – gate

Miao – ethnic group living in Guìzhōu

miào – temple

motor-tricycle – an enclosed three-wheeled vehicle with a small motorbike engine, a driver at the front and seats for two passengers in the back

MTR – (Hong Kong) Mass Transit Railway

mù – tomb

name chop – a carved name seal that acts as a signature

nán – south. The other points of the compass are: *běi* (north), *dōng* (east) and *xī* (west)

obo – (Inner Mongolia) a pile of stones with a hollow space for offerings, a kind of shaman shrine

oolong – (Cantonese) high-grade Chinese tea, partially fermented

pailou – traditional ornamental arches

pedicab – pedal-powered tricycle with a seat to carry passengers

piāolǔ – rafting trip

pingù – Beijing opera

Pinyin – the official system for transliterating Chinese script into roman characters

pípá – a plucked string instrument

PLA – People's Liberation Army

Politburo – the 25-member supreme policy-making authority of the CCP

PRC – People's Republic of China

PSB – Public Security Bureau/Police; the arm of the police force set up to deal with foreigners

pùbù – waterfall

Putonghua – the standard form of the Chinese language used since the beginning of this century, based on the dialect of Běijīng

qarvatlik mashina – (Uyghur) sleeper coach

qi – vital energy (life force) or cosmic currents manipulated in acupuncture and massage

qiáo – bridge

qigong – exercise that channels qi

qīngzhēnsì – mosque

quán – spring

rénmín – people, people's

Renminbi – literally 'people's money', the formal name for the currency of China. Shortened to RMB

ROC – Republic of China, also known as Taiwan

sampan – (Cantonese) a small motorised launch, too small for the open sea

SAR – Special Administrative Region

savdo dukoni – (Uyghur) commercial shops

shān – mountain

shāngdiàn – shop, store

shěng – province, provincial

shì – city

shí – rock

shìchǎng – market

shìjiè – world

shíkū – grotto

shuǐkù – reservoir

sì – temple, monastery

siheyuan – traditional courtyard house

special municipality – the name given to centrally administered regions such as Běijīng, Tiānjīn, Chóngqìng and Shànghǎi

stele – a stone slab or column decorated with figures or inscriptions

stupa – usually used as reliquaries for the cremated remains of important *lamas*

tǎ – pagoda

tael – unit of weight; one tael *(liang)* equals 37.5g; there are 16 taels to the *catty*

taijiquan – the graceful, flowing exercise that has its roots in China's martial arts. Also known as taichi

taipan – (Cantonese) boss of a large company

tán – pool

Tanka – a Chinese ethnic group who traditionally live on boats

tíng – pavilion

triads – secret societies. Originally founded to protect Chinese culture from the influence of usurping Manchurians, their modern-day members are little more than gangsters

tripitaka – Buddhist scriptures

walla walla – a motorised launch used as a water taxi and capable of short runs on the open sea

wān – bay

wēnquán – hot springs

xī – west. The other points of the compass are: *běi* (north), *nán* (south) and *dōng* (east)

xī – small stream or brook

xiá – gorge

xiàn – county

xiàng – statue

xuěshān – snow mountain

yá – cliff

yán – rock or crag

yangi shahr – (Uyghur) new part of towns, usually Han-dominated

yēlín – coconut plantation

yuán – the Chinese unit of currency; also referred to as RMB
yuán – garden
yurt – (Inner Mongolia) the Russian word for a circular tent made with animal skin or felt; see ger

zhāodàisuǒ – basic lodgings, a hotel or guesthouse
zhāpí – a pint (of beer)
zheng – a 13- or 14-stringed harp
zhíwùyuán – botanical gardens
zhong – middle
zìrán bǎohùqū – nature reserve
zǔjū – ancestral home

How to Use this Book

In the text and on the maps the following terms are written in Pinyin:

Pinyin	English
Hú	Lake
Shān	Mountain
Sì, Gé (Taoist), Miào	Temple
Tǎ	Pagoda
Gōngyuán	Park
Dǎo	Island
Jiāng, Hé	River, Creek

Street names are also given in Pinyin:
Lu, Jie, Dajie, Xiaojie (with prefix Xi, Dong, Nan, Bei and Zhong meaning West, East, South, North and Centre respectively)

Acknowledgements

THANKS

Many thanks to the travellers who used the last edition and wrote to us with helpful hints, useful advice and interesting anecdotes.

Mia Abrams, Gale Acuff, Philippe Adam, Cary Ader, Alex Ahlbom, Ovorkhangai Aimag, Ally Akbarzadeh, Shahida Akram, Marinka Albers, Patrick Alexander, Michael Allen, Rachel Allen, Lior Almaro, Victoria Almiroty, Lior Alon, Havard Altern, Jaime C Alvarez, Jorge Alves, Signe Andreassen, Mark Andrews, Alessia Angiolini, Joe Angulo, Alessandro Arduino, Hazel Armstrong, Luke Arnold, Mieke Arts, Lyndsay Atkinson, Majorie Atkinson, Simon Atkinson, Muneeza Aumir, Ruth Baetz, Murray Bailey, Thomas Bailey, Dougie Baird, Harry Baker, James Baldus, John Bament, Chris Barker, Daniel Barker, Margriet Barkhuysen, Charles Barnes, John Barnett, Lorenzo & Alessandra Barsi, Owen Barwick, Bonnie Baskin, Jeremy Bassan, Alison Battisson, Nick Baughan, Steve Baxa, Nathalie Beauval, Thaddeus Beebe, Jens Behrens, A Rafael Bejerano, Anonda Bell, Maria A Benavides, Jeff Bent, Michael Berg, Alexander Berghofen, Bill Bernhardt, Alex Berry, David Berry, Nadine Bertalli, Florian Beulich, Jan Bevan, Dr Ajit Bhalla, Hilary Bienstock, James Bierman, Susanne Bierschenk, Matthew Bird, Yvonne Bischofberger, Sara Biscioni, Signy Bjarnason, Rebecca Blackwell, Nathan Bland, Cindy & Maggie Blick, Susan Blick, Johan Bodin, Becky Boltz, Cees-Jan Booij, Ritsert Boonstra, Brandon Booth, Gary Booth, Michelle Bos-Lun, Michelle & Asian Studies Teacher Bos-Lun, Sander Bouten, Alison Boutland, Chris Bowling, Geoffrey Bowman, Wayne Brabin, Kathleen Brand, Bryan Brandsma, Marian Brandwijk, Jeremy Bray, Derek Brennan, Maureen Breslin, Ben Brice, Steve Brimson, Jorrit Britschgi, Joe Brock, Michael Broennimann, Edwin Bronsteede, David Broomfield, Kevin Brown, Liam Brown, Pat Brown, Xantha Bruso, Rod George Bryant, Helene Buckley, Richard Buckley, Hans J Buhrmester, Linda Burgin, Penny Burke, Brad Burkman, Lorie Burnett, John Burns, Robert H Burns, Amanda Buster, Di Butler, Majella Butler, Iliana Cacchione, Marcello Cafiero, Catherine Calver, Noel Cameron, Chris Campbell, Gregory G Campbell, Racheal Cann, Ben Capell, Jason Carpenter, Matt Carr, Guy Carrier, Margo Carter, Shelby Carter, Gisa Casarubea, John Cashman, Bernie Cavanagh, Thomas Chabrieres, Bradley Chait, Patra Chakshuvej, Clifford Chan, Emily Chan, Caroline Chandler, T K Chang, Shin-yi Chao, Flaminia Chapman, Charles Chase, J E Chase, Fritzie Chavez, Karen Cheung, Alex Chevrolle, Lawrence Chin, Kevin Cho, Patrick Chon, Chris Chong, Scott Chorna, Amy Chow, Lee-Peng Chow, Michelle Chow, Alam Chowdury, Louise Choy, Melinda Choy, Jennifer Christian, Danny Juul Christophersen, Hyeong Chu, Jonathan Chu, Dan Chugg, Louisa Chui, Leigh Churchill, Neil F Clancy, David Clark, Fiona Clarkson, Bahout Claude, Emma Claxton, Thierry Clerc, Simon Coffey, Alastor Coleby, Bill Coleman, Olivia Collas, Johan Collier, Cameron Collins, Cheryl Collins, Steven Collins, Herb Con, Zhang Cong, Edward Congdon, Maurice Conklin, Tom Cook, Anne Corbett, William Corr, Foster Corwith, Carissa Cosgrove, Carlos Costa, Theresa Costigan, Ventus Costin, Adrian Cotter, Heather Couch, Carl Court, Caitlin Cox, Steven Coxhead, E D Craig, Sarah Cramer, Stephani Cramer, Mike Crisp, Margaret Cronin, Neil Crookes, Tim & Marika Crosby, Kate Crossan, Ian Cruickshank, Chris Cummins, Ron & Anne Cummins, Ake Dahllof, Daniel Dahlmeier, Toby Dalton, Grant Daniel, Paul Daniels, Greg Daruda, Jo & Richard Darvill, Sarah Davey, U Davidsen, Keith Davies, Bob Davis, Colin Day, David Dayton, Ilse de Bass, Dylan de Lange, Robin Deal, Nynhe Deinema, Rosemarijn & Joost Dekker, Jim Demets, Laurens den Dulk, Wynia Derks, Julie Dessureault, Sarah Dettwiler, Kate Dewey, Jennifer Dickinson, Chris Dieckmann, Graham Dixon, Mary Dodd, Kylie Douglas-Hill, Lori Doyle, Peter Dryden, Matt Dukoff-Gordon, Mark Duncan, Frank Dutton, Vladi Dvoyris, Lawrence Earl, Roland W Earl, Randal Eastman, Martin Ebner, Linzi Edge, Thomas Edlund, Bo Edvinsson, John Edwards, Garth Eichel, Caroline Elgar, Pierre Elias, Raz Elmaleh, Monique en Ruud, Angie Eng, Jesse Engdahl, Digby Entwisle, Yang Er Che, Finn Erik Espegren, Francine Esterman, Marion Evans, Merry Ewing, Dana Eyde, Lola Fahrenholz, Bi Ji Fang, Martin Fecitt, Jono Feldman, Sona Felixova, Shaaron Feltis, Susan Feltus, Jonathon Fenby, Ann Feng, Xue Feng, Elspeth Ferguson, Molly Fergusson, Mauricio Fernandez, Melissa Ferrer, Rick Fijnaut, Richard Fish, Ben Fisher, Neil Fisher, Leonard Fitzpatrick, Hans & Anne Fix, Mike Fleming, Mike Flemming, Noel Flor, Jose Flores, Pauline Fong, Carol Forsett, Mike Forster, Doug Francis, Elke Franke, Dick Freed, David Fregona, Elina Freitag, Jennifer Fresco, Christian Frey, Mike Frey, Klaus & Sylivia Friedrichs, Bernd Friese, Laure Friscourt, Kate Frost, Tanya Frymersum, Dave Fuller, Jonathan Fursland, Jean-Baptiste Gagelin, Mario-Artur Galvao, Andrea Garrett, Louise Gaudry,

Adam Gault, Paul Gaylard, Jez Gidley, Sarie Gilbert, Adam Giles, Lisa Gill, Anthony Ginn, Paul W Gioffi, Louise Gjor, Yvonne Gluyas, Katie Glynn, A B Goldstein, Herb Goldstein, John Gould, Brigitte Graeser, M R Graham, Alistair J Grant, John Grant, Matthew Grant, John Graven, Richard Graves, Daniel Gray, Andrew Graybill, Timothy Green, Jennifer Gregory, Eiko Grieger, Jolanda Griens, Richard Groom, Yoran Guenegou, Jenny X Guo, Sanne Haaning, Minna Haapanen, Soelvi Haavik, Paul Hague, Uwe Haizmann, Jenny Hall, Leon Hamilton, Paul Hammond, Phil Hand, Nicola Handscomb, Jan Hanley, Paul Hannon, Eric Harbeson, Mandy Hardie, Bryon Hardie-Bays, Margaret Hardie-Bays, Wade & Helen Harlen, Nicky Harman, Will Harper, Jonathan Harris, Mark Harrison, Korey Hartwich, Chris Hauserman, Bianca Haushern, Jamie Hayward, Moritz J Heidbuechel, Sirkka Heiskanen, M Helmbrecht, Song Heng Mun, Jill Henry, Moritz Herrmann, C Hertogh, Emma Hetherington, Erin Hetrick, Sarah Heywood, Robert Hickey, Roz Hiebert, Muhammad Hikmat, Megan Ho, Jacqueline Hobbs, Graham Hodden, Zak Hofman, Alice Holden, Andy Holloway, Emma Holmbro, Phil Holmes, Joachim Holtz, Vanessa Hoppe, Bernard Horowitz, Chris Horton, Doug Horwich, Joakim Hovet, James Howard, Peter Hruska, David Hughes, Laura Hughes, Rhidian Hughes, Chiang Hsing Hui, Wolfgang Hutt, Lifon Huynh, Lars Hylander, Sam Iliffe, Alessandra Innocenti, Tony Ives, Peter Jacklyn, Jessica Jacobson, Susan Jacups, Rick Jali, Volkmar E Janicke, Vicky Janse de Jonge, James Jarvis, Debra Jason, Tony Jenkins, Brad Jennings, Patrik Jensch, Per Jensen, David Jinwei, Vladimir Jiras, Carol Johnson, Duncan Johnson, Ryan Y Johnson, Tess Johnston, Erica T Jolly, Debra Jones, Gary Jones, Morgan Jones, Rowan Jones, Stephen Jones, Steve Jones, Torsten Jonsson, Frank Jordans, Nena Joy, Chris Jules, Richard Juterbock, Elmer Jutte, Jean Kahe, Jean & Paul Kahe, Markus Kallander, Mikko Kallio, David Kanig, Thomas Kantz, Muira Katsuo, Masayoshi Kawaguchi, Geoffrey Keating, Fiona Kelcher, Sandra Kemp, Eldon Kendrew, Claire Kennedy, Des Kennedy, Justin Kennedy-Good, Thom Kenrick, Dayna Kesten, Dayna & Ezra Kesten, Silvia Kettelhut, Alexandra Kettle, Joerg Kilian, Heather Kimmel, Erica King, Wyona King, Richard Lee Eng Kit, Allyson Klein, Erwin Klein, Peter Klein, Otto Klepper, Alexandra Klier, Joshua & Sarah Knight, Jens Koch, Elaine Kochar, Ravit Kocshitzki, John Koehler, Sharon Koh, Alex Koh Wei Hiong, Jan Kok, Katie Koloseike, Arik Korman, Roshani Kothari, Gerhard Kotschenreuther, Erik Kramer, Klaudia Krammer, Peter Krebs, Juergen krenz, Maldelon Kuiper, Andrew Kwee, Michele Kwik, Joe Kwok, Leo Lacey, Andreas Laimboeck, Suzanne

Lamb, Guy-Anne Landry, Francis Lang, Erik Laridon, Bill Lawler, Pat Lawson, Greg Layda, Alix Lee, Hyung Lee, Jeffrey Lee, Kwan-por Lee, Mary A K Lee, Matt Lee, Jean Lennane, Cressida Lennox, Peter Lentz, Andrew Levy, Helen Lewis, Guo Zhao Li, Lily Li, David Liang, Ping Lim, Tang Lin, Kyle Linden, Aimee Linnett, Andy Lister, Andrew Liu, Adrian Lloyd, Deanne Lowe, Khai Lu, Dagmar Lukas, Franke Lutz, Smon Lynch, Stephan Maaskant, Summer Macdonald, Anne MacGregor, Christopher Machin, K Macknight, Marcel Maessen, Goncalo Magalhaes, Peter Mah, Jeffrey Mahn, Zhan Mai, Ryu Makoto, Allardyce Mallon, Phil Manson, Ato Mariano, Joe Marks, Cindy Marleau & family, A Marogna, Jessica Marteinson, Amanda Martin, Andre Martino, Daniel Massart, Lawrence Maxwell, Tim McCaffrey, Sally McCausland, Julia McCleave, Michele McCrystall, Chris McCullough, Marilyn McCullough, Gregory McElwain, Dudley McFadden, Nicole McGaffney-Lee, Nicola McGuigan, Rob McIlwaine, Angus McIntyre, Julienne McKay, Leah Mckeand, Ned McKerchar, John McKimmy, Gary McMurrain, Rachel Meakin, William Mee, Allan Meinhardt, Tan Meng Shern, Clare Mercer, Molly Merson, Dawn Metcalfe, Peter Micic, Lee Min, Thomas Ming, Chris Mitchell, Jesper Moensted, Jamie Moir, Britt Moller, Frederick Moller, Adeline Monike, Jongejan Monique, Brett Montgomery, Joanna Moore, Jose Moran, Margaret Moran, Natalia Moran, Andy Morentz, Luis Moreton Achsel, Helen Mortimer, Richard Morton, Patrick Mulkey, Patrick Mullen, Anton Mureau, Patrick Murphy, James Murray, Andrew Musgrave, Terry Nakazono, Alex Negen, Daniel & Judith Nehorai, Carol & Peter Nelson, Trent Nelson, Raquel Neto, David New, Irwin Ngeow, Joanne Nicel, Debbie Nicholson, Debbie & Andy Nicholson, Carmen & Robin Niethammer, Hugo M Nijhof, Ulrika Nilsson, Justin Nobbs, Johannes Nohl, Mike Nolan, Brian Nomi, Erin & Dan Noose, Jenny Norval, Kimberly Novak, Marlene Nylander, Diarmuid O Coimin, David Oates, Debbie O'Bray, Conor O'Brien, Roderick O'Brien, Eric Obuabang, Ben Oei, Kevin O'Grady, Jim O'Hagan, Sven-Olof & Yue Ohlsson, Kristen Olafson, Adam Oliver, Gezina Oorthuys, Dror Orell, Rupert Osborne, Kate O'Shaugnessy, Kate O'Shea, Christine O'Sullivan, Evan Owens, Paul Oxenham, Nanthana P, Lluis Pages, Elisa & Debora Paglerani, Daniel Pak, Zvi Paldi, Ray Palmer, Kyril Pamburg, Janine Parker, Robin Parker, Tom Parker, Vanessa Parkin, S Patel, Murphy Patrick, Adam John Patterson, Mark Patton, Elena Pavan, Krzysztof Pawlik, Geoff Payne, Maua Payne, Grant Pearse, Marion Penaud, Antoni Peris, Matt Perrement, Matthew Perrement, Piergiorgio Pescali, Ken Peter, Barry Peters, Brent Peters, Sheridan Pettiford, Terese

Piccoli, Row Pin, Hong Xiu Ping, Pierre-Manuel Plante, Julie Poirier, Andries Polman, Sofie Ponsaerts, Dan Pool, Kate Pope, Wendy Potter, Barbara Prevel, Paul Prowting, Suzanne Prymek, John Pryor, Joan Pryse, Paul Przibilla, Paul & Linda Przibilla, Toni Pudding, April Pulkrabek, David Pullman, Rick & Tanya Rabern, Karthig Rajakulendran, Tom Rasmussen, Douglas Raupach, Karen Rayle, Juan Recio, David Reece, Colin Rees, Chris Regester, Moira Rehmer, Dietrich Rehnert, Jill Remy, Sonja Rengel, Wolfram Reuter, Jo Reynolds, Peter Richards, Burt Richmond, Jennifer Richmond, Winfried Richter, Caroline Ringrow, Claudia Riquelme, Anita Ritchie, Dr J A G Roberts, Mike Roberts, Paul Robinson, Hendnk Rocholl, Barak Rodwell, John Ross, Gernot Roth, Bojan Rotovnik, Sara Rovira, Al Rowley, Charles Roy, G Roy, Guy & Iris Rozanes, Chris Rozendaal, Yoav Rubin, Claire Rudd, R F Rudderham, Jose Ruiz, Robert Ruprecht, Bruce Rusk, Mark Russell, Matthew Rutledge, Daniel Rutter, Rob Ryan, Eyal Sadeh, Suzi Saeki, Pat Sala, Lyle Sanda, Maria & Ross Sartori, Zac Savage, Xandra Savelkouls, Richard Savinson, Jane Sayers, Dirk Scharbatke, Johannes Schilli, Markus Schilling, Judith Scott, Sigrid Seel, Frank Seewald, John Sehn, Richard Selby, Eugene Semb, Liew Loy Seng, Ong Seow Chong, Jude Sequeira, Carlos Serra, Sean Seurin, Girish Shahane, Gary Shapcott, Danny Shaw, D J She, Lori Shemanski, Dawn Sheridan, Andrew Sherley-Dale, James Shields, Susan Shields, Rosana C Sialong, Itay Sidar, Greg Silas, Ben Silverman, Maria Siow, Anneke Sips, T J Smart, Anna Smith, David Smith, Jimmee Smith, Margot Smith, Nick Smith, Ria Smith, Sharon Smith, Lisa Smyth, Lene Jul Soerensen, Juned Sonido, Kim Sonnack, C Sorensen, Brian Souter, Mike Souter, David Speary, Bianca Spence, Jan Sperling, R Spreeuw, Jonatan Stanczak, Walter Stanish, Nikola Stankovic, Gavin Staton, Rachael Stead, E Steel, Larissa Steiner, Susan Steiner, John Steingraeber, Jenni Stenman, Tia Stephens, Sammie Stephenson, Jeremy Stevens, Linda Stevens, Donna Stewart, Ian Stone, Donald Stumpf, Trudy Sturkenboom, Eric Su, Beverly Suderman, Birgit Suhr, Mariana Sulaiman, Christie Sunwoo, Michelle Sutherland, Andrew Sutton, Jiap Suvansarang, E & J Swabey, Janet Sweeney, Shannon Sweeney, Hal Swindall, Teung Sze Wing, Nad Tabit, Don Tait, Ruud Takken, Clive Tan, Carlo Tardani, Eric Taylor, Nathalie te Rietstap, Gary Teeling, Henry Tenby, Lucrezia Terzi, Christobel Thomas, Ronan Tierney, David Tilley, Grace Tin, Robert Tissing, Henry To, Sandro Todeschini, Peter Toh, Michael Tom, Lars Tomren, Greg Tong, Duncan Touch, Genevieve & Piers Touzel, Sara Treadgold, Gail Tregear, Steve Trewin, Peter Tribe, Massimo Triberti, Ryan Trigg, Marion Trommsdorff, Steven P Tseng, Theofilos Tsoris, Andrew Turner, Audrey & Peter Turner, Emil Umetaliev, Maria Valeria Urbani, Bjorn Utgard, Sylvia Vaassen, Phillipa Vallely, Tom Sanpaworn Vamvanij, Caroline & Herman van den Wall Bake, Elzeline van der Neut, Linda van der Paauw, Saskia van der Zande, Mascha van der Zon, Lillian van Deurzen, J W J van Dorp, Barbara van Duynen Montijn, Jordi van Harlingen, Karin van Hout, Anneke van Kollenburg, Tim van Veen, Christien van Verseveld, Kevin Vans-Colina, Milli Vayrynen, Pim & Olga Vernooij, Elin Vigrestad, Dorothy Volk, Bettina von Reden, Renate Wagant, Matt Walker, Richard Wall, Rolf Walther, Jennifer Wang, Karen Wang, Qian Wang, Yau Wankong, Angus Wann, Duncan Ward, Jane Ward, Ann Warden, Whitney Watanabe, Monica Waterhouse, Alan Waters, Jim Waterson, Karen Watkins, Carolyn Watt, Rebecca Webb, Katherine Weedon, Wu Wei, Bill Weigand, Bill & Jerrine Weigand, Mike Weigh, Fan Weihong, Robert Wellwood, Philip Wharmby, Peter White, Richard White, Emma Whiteley, Lynda Wieloch, Jennifer Wiger, Nigel Wikeley, Olga Wikeley, Madine Wilburn, Becca Wiley, Huck Wilken, Laura Willemsen, Bruce Williams, Geordie Williamson, Paul Willis, Kristyn Wilson, Marge Wilson, Simon Wilson, Tim Windever, Bettina Winert, Leon R Withrington, Marcin Wodzinski, Fran Wong, Jeanette Wong, Lucille Wong, Mandy Wong, Pierre Wong, Roberta Wong Leung, Clayton Wood, Wyn Woods, Stephen Woodward, Tom Woodward, Chris Worsnop, Christopher Wortley, Stephen Wrage, C Wrentmore, Mary Lee Wu, Cynthia Wuu, Jon Wyler, Wang Xiaocong, George Xu, Guan Yang, Yael Yariv, Maria Yatano Roche, Eric Yau, Frank Yau, Su Ming Yeh, Tian Yi, Kin Yip, Lian Yi Yong, Qiu Yongyin, Elie Younes, Park Mi Young, Kim Young wan, Anson Yu, Lucia Yu, Daniel Yuen, Kent Zado, Giuseppe Zapelloni, Nils Zeeuwen, John Zhang, Maike Ziesemer, Felix Zimmermann, Oliver Zoellner, Alex Zogbi, Manja Zschuppe, Rob Zweerman

LONELY PLANET

You already know that Lonely Planet produces more than this one guidebook, but you might not be aware of the other products we have on this region. Here is a selection of titles which you may want to check out as well:

South-West China
ISBN 1 86450 370 X
US$21.99 • UK£13.99

Shanghai
ISBN 0 86442 507 4
US$15.99 • UK£9.99

Mandarin phrasebook
ISBN 0 86442 652 6
US$7.95 • UK£4.50

Beijing
ISBN 1 74059 281 6
US$15.99 • UK£9.99

Tibet
ISBN 1 86450 162 6
US$19.99 • UK£12.99

Cantonese phrasebook
ISBN 0 86442 645 3
US$6.95 • UK£4.50

Read this First: Asia & India
ISBN 1 86450 049 2
US$14.95 • UK£8.99

Hong Kong & Macau
ISBN 1 86450 230 4
US$16.99 • UK£10.99

World Food Hong Kong
ISBN 1 86450 288 6
US$13.99 • UK£8.99

Hong Kong City Map
ISBN 1 86450 007 7
US$5.95 • UK£3.99

Beijing City Map
ISBN 1 86450 255 X
US$5.99 • UK£3.99

Hong Kong Condensed
ISBN 1 86450 253 3
US$11.99 • UK£6.99

Available wherever books are sold.

LONELY PLANET

ON THE ROAD

Travel Guides explore cities, regions and countries, and supply information on transport, restaurants and accommodation, covering all budgets. They come with reliable, easy-to-use maps, practical advice, cultural and historical facts and a rundown on attractions both on and off the beaten track. There are over 200 titles in this classic series, covering nearly every country in the world.

 Lonely Planet Upgrades extend the shelf life of existing travel guides by detailing any changes that may affect travel in a region since a book has been published. Upgrades can be downloaded for free from **www.lonelyplanet.com/upgrades**

For travellers with more time than money, **Shoestring** guides offer dependable, first-hand information with hundreds of detailed maps, plus insider tips for stretching money as far as possible. Covering entire continents in most cases, the six-volume shoestring guides are known around the world as 'backpackers bibles'.

For the discerning short-term visitor, **Condensed** guides highlight the best a destination has to offer in a full-colour, pocket-sized format designed for quick access. They include everything from top sights and walking tours to opinionated reviews of where to eat, stay, shop and have fun.

CitySync lets travellers use their Palm™ or Visor™ hand-held computers to guide them through a city with handy tips on transport, history, cultural life, major sights, and shopping and entertainment options. It can also quickly search and sort hundreds of reviews of hotels, restaurants and attractions, and pinpoint their location on scrollable street maps. CitySync can be downloaded from **www.citysync.com**

MAPS & ATLASES

Lonely Planet's **City Maps** feature downtown and metropolitan maps, as well as transit routes and walking tours. The maps come complete with an index of streets, a listing of sights and a plastic coat for extra durability.

Road Atlases are an essential navigation tool for serious travellers. Cross-referenced with the guidebooks, they also feature distance and climate charts and a complete site index.

LONELY PLANET

ESSENTIALS

Read This First books help new travellers to hit the road with confidence. These invaluable predeparture guides give step-by-step advice on preparing for a trip, budgeting, arranging a visa, planning an itinerary and staying safe while still getting off the beaten track.

Healthy Travel pocket guides offer a regional rundown on disease hot spots and practical advice on predeparture health measures, staying well on the road and what to do in emergencies. The guides come with a user-friendly design and helpful diagrams and tables.

Lonely Planet's **Phrasebooks** cover the essential words and phrases travellers need when they're strangers in a strange land. They come in a pocket-sized format with colour tabs for quick reference, extensive vocabulary lists, easy-to-follow pronunciation keys and two-way dictionaries.

Miffed by blurry photos of the Taj Mahal? Tired of the classic 'top of the head cut off' shot? **Travel Photography: A Guide to Taking Better Pictures** will help you turn ordinary holiday snaps into striking images and give you the know-how to capture every scene, from frenetic festivals to peaceful beach sunrises.

Lonely Planet's **Travel Journal** is a lightweight but sturdy travel diary for jotting down all those on-the-road observations and significant travel moments. It comes with a handy time-zone wheel, a world map and useful travel information.

Lonely Planet's eKno is an all-in-one communication service developed especially for travellers. It offers low-cost international calls and free email and voicemail so that you can keep in touch while on the road. Check it out on **www.ekno.lonelyplanet.com**

FOOD & RESTAURANT GUIDES

Lonely Planet's **Out to Eat** guides recommend the brightest and best places to eat and drink in top international cities. These gourmet companions are arranged by neighbourhood, packed with dependable maps, garnished with scene-setting photos and served with quirky features.

For people who live to eat, drink and travel, **World Food** guides explore the culinary culture of each country. Entertaining and adventurous, each guide is packed with detail on staples and specialities, regional cuisine and local markets, as well as sumptuous recipes, comprehensive culinary dictionaries and lavish photos good enough to eat.

LONELY PLANET

OUTDOOR GUIDES

For those who believe the best way to see the world is on foot, Lonely Planet's **Walking Guides** detail everything from family strolls to difficult treks, with 'when to go and how to do it' advice supplemented by reliable maps and essential travel information.

Cycling Guides map a destination's best bike tours, long and short, in day-by-day detail. They contain all the information a cyclist needs, including advice on bike maintenance, places to eat and stay, innovative maps with detailed cues to the rides, and elevation charts.

The **Watching Wildlife** series is perfect for travellers who want authoritative information but don't want to tote a heavy field guide. Packed with advice on where, when and how to view a region's wildlife, each title features photos of over 300 species and contains engaging comments on the local flora and fauna.

With underwater colour photos throughout, **Pisces Books** explore the world's best diving and snorkelling areas. Each book contains listings of diving services and dive resorts, detailed information on depth, visibility and difficulty of dives, and a roundup of the marine life you're likely to see through your mask.

LONELY PLANET

OFF THE ROAD

Journeys, the travel literature series written by renowned travel authors, capture the spirit of a place or illuminate a culture with a journalist's attention to detail and a novelist's flair for words. These are tales to soak up while you're actually on the road or dip into as an at-home armchair indulgence.

The range of lavishly illustrated **Pictorial** books is just the ticket for both travellers and dreamers. Off-beat tales and vivid photographs bring the adventure of travel to your doorstep long before the journey begins and long after it is over.

Lonely Planet **Videos** encourage the same independent, tough-minded approach as the guidebooks. Currently airing throughout the world, this award-winning series features innovative footage and an original soundtrack.

Yes, we know, work is tough, so do a little bit of deskside dreaming with the spiral-bound Lonely Planet **Diary** or a Lonely Planet **Wall Calendar**, filled with great photos from around the world.

TRAVELLERS NETWORK

Lonely Planet Online. Lonely Planet's award-winning Web site has insider information on hundreds of destinations, from Amsterdam to Zimbabwe, complete with interactive maps and relevant links. The site also offers the latest travel news, recent reports from travellers on the road, guidebook upgrades, a travel links site, an online book-buying option and a lively travellers bulletin board. It can be viewed at **www.lonelyplanet.com** or AOL keyword: lp.

Comet, our free monthly email newsletter, is loaded with travel news, advice, dispatches from authors, raging debates, travel competitions and letters from readers. To subscribe, click on the newsletters link on the front page of our Web site or go to: **www.lonelyplanet.com/comet/**.

Planet Talk is a free quarterly print newsletter, full of travel advice, tips from fellow travellers, author articles, news about forthcoming Lonely Planet events and a complete list of Lonely Planet books and other products. It provides an antidote to the being-at-home blues and helps you dream about and plan your next trip. To join our mailing list contact any Lonely Planet office or email us at: talk2us@lonelyplanet.com.au.

Lonely Planet Guides by Region

Lonely Planet is known worldwide for publishing practical, reliable and no-nonsense travel information in our guides and on our Web site. The Lonely Planet list covers just about every accessible part of the world. Currently there are 16 series: Travel guides, Shoestring guides, Condensed guides, Phrasebooks, Read This First, Healthy Travel, Walking guides, Cycling guides, Watching Wildlife guides, Pisces Diving & Snorkeling guides, City Maps, Road Atlases, Out to Eat, World Food, Journeys travel literature and Pictorials.

AFRICA Africa on a shoestring • Botswana • Cairo • Cairo City Map • Cape Town • Cape Town City Map • East Africa • Egypt • Egyptian Arabic phrasebook • Ethiopia, Eritrea & Djibouti • Ethiopian Amharic phrasebook • The Gambia & Senegal • Healthy Travel Africa • Kenya • Malawi • Morocco • Moroccan Arabic phrasebook • Mozambique • Namibia • Read This First: Africa • South Africa, Lesotho & Swaziland • Southern Africa • Southern Africa Road Atlas • Swahili phrasebook • Tanzania, Zanzibar & Pemba • Trekking in East Africa • Tunisia • Watching Wildlife East Africa • Watching Wildlife Southern Africa • West Africa • World Food Morocco • Zambia • Zimbabwe, Botswana & Namibia
Travel Literature: Mali Blues: Traveling to an African Beat • The Rainbird: A Central African Journey • Songs to an African Sunset: A Zimbabwean Story

AUSTRALIA & THE PACIFIC Aboriginal Australia & the Torres Strait Islands •Auckland • Australia • Australian phrasebook • Australia Road Atlas • Cycling Australia • Cycling New Zealand • Fiji • Fijian phrasebook • Healthy Travel Australia, NZ & the Pacific • Islands of Australia's Great Barrier Reef • Melbourne • Melbourne City Map • Micronesia • New Caledonia • New South Wales • New Zealand • Northern Territory • Outback Australia • Out to Eat – Melbourne • Out to Eat – Sydney • Papua New Guinea • Pidgin phrasebook • Queensland • Rarotonga & the Cook Islands • Samoa • Solomon Islands • South Australia • South Pacific • South Pacific phrasebook • Sydney • Sydney City Map • Sydney Condensed • Tahiti & French Polynesia • Tasmania • Tonga • Tramping in New Zealand • Vanuatu • Victoria • Walking in Australia • Watching Wildlife Australia • Western Australia
Travel Literature: Islands in the Clouds: Travels in the Highlands of New Guinea • Kiwi Tracks: A New Zealand Journey • Sean & David's Long Drive

CENTRAL AMERICA & THE CARIBBEAN Bahamas, Turks & Caicos • Baja California • Belize, Guatemala & Yucatán • Bermuda • Central America on a shoestring • Costa Rica • Costa Rica Spanish phrasebook • Cuba • Cycling Cuba • Dominican Republic & Haiti • Eastern Caribbean • Guatemala • Havana • Healthy Travel Central & South America • Jamaica • Mexico • Mexico City • Panama • Puerto Rico • Read This First: Central & South America • Virgin Islands • World Food Caribbean • World Food Mexico • Yucatán
Travel Literature: Green Dreams: Travels in Central America

EUROPE Amsterdam • Amsterdam City Map • Amsterdam Condensed • Andalucía • Athens • Austria • Baltic States phrasebook • Barcelona • Barcelona City Map • Belgium & Luxembourg • Berlin • Berlin City Map • Britain • British phrasebook • Brussels, Bruges & Antwerp • Brussels City Map • Budapest • Budapest City Map • Canary Islands • Catalunya & the Costa Brava • Central Europe • Central Europe phrasebook • Copenhagen • Corfu & the Ionians • Corsica • Crete • Crete Condensed • Croatia • Cycling Britain • Cycling France • Cyprus • Czech & Slovak Republics • Czech phrasebook • Denmark • Dublin • Dublin City Map • Dublin Condensed • Eastern Europe • Eastern Europe phrasebook • Edinburgh • Edinburgh City Map • England • Estonia, Latvia & Lithuania • Europe on a shoestring • Europe phrasebook • Finland • Florence • Florence City Map • Frankfurt City Map • Frankfurt Condensed • French phrasebook • Georgia, Armenia & Azerbaijan • Germany • German phrasebook • Greece • Greek Islands • Greek phrasebook • Hungary • Iceland, Greenland & the Faroe Islands • Ireland • Italian phrasebook • Italy • Kraków • Lisbon • The Loire • London • London City Map • London Condensed • Madrid • Madrid City Map • Malta • Mediterranean Europe • Milan, Turin & Genoa • Moscow • Munich • Netherlands • Normandy • Norway • Out to Eat – London • Out to Eat – Paris • Paris • Paris City Map • Paris Condensed • Poland • Polish phrasebook • Portugal • Portuguese phrasebook • Prague • Prague City Map • Provence & the Côte d'Azur • Read This First: Europe • Rhodes & the Dodecanese • Romania & Moldova • Rome • Rome City Map • Rome Condensed • Russia, Ukraine & Belarus • Russian phrasebook • Scandinavian & Baltic Europe • Scandinavian phrasebook • Scotland • Sicily • Slovenia • South-West France • Spain • Spanish phrasebook • Stockholm • St Petersburg • St Petersburg City Map • Sweden • Switzerland • Tuscany • Ukrainian phrasebook • Venice • Vienna • Wales • Walking in Britain • Walking in France • Walking in Ireland • Walking in Italy • Walking in Scotland • Walking in Spain • Walking in Switzerland • Western Europe • World Food France • World Food Greece • World Food Ireland • World Food Italy • World Food Spain **Travel Literature:** After Yugoslavia • Love and War in the Apennines • The Olive Grove: Travels in Greece • On the Shores of the Mediterranean • Round Ireland in Low Gear • A Small Place in Italy

Lonely Planet Mail Order

onely Planet products are distributed worldwide. They are also available by mail order from Lonely Planet, so if you have difficulty finding a title please write to us. North and South American residents should write to 150 Linden St, Oakland, CA 94607, USA; European and African residents should write to 10a Spring Place, London NW5 3BH, UK; and residents of other countries to Locked Bag 1, Footscray, Victoria 3011, Australia.

INDIAN SUBCONTINENT & THE INDIAN OCEAN Bangladesh • Bengali phrasebook • Bhutan • Delhi • Goa • Healthy Travel Asia & India • Hindi & Urdu phrasebook • India • India & Bangladesh City Map • Indian Himalaya • Karakoram Highway • Kathmandu City Map • Kerala • Madagascar • Maldives • Mauritius, Réunion & Seychelles • Mumbai (Bombay) • Nepal • Nepali phrasebook • North India • Pakistan • Rajasthan • Read This First: Asia & India • South India • Sri Lanka • Sri Lanka phrasebook • Tibet • Tibetan phrasebook • Trekking in the Indian Himalaya • Trekking in the Karakoram & Hindukush • Trekking in the Nepal Himalaya • World Food India **Travel Literature:** The Age of Kali: Indian Travels and Encounters • Hello Goodnight: A Life of Goa • In Rajasthan • Maverick in Madagascar • A Season in Heaven: True Tales from the Road to Kathmandu • Shopping for Buddhas • A Short Walk in the Hindu Kush • Slowly Down the Ganges

MIDDLE EAST & CENTRAL ASIA Bahrain, Kuwait & Qatar • Central Asia • Central Asia phrasebook • Dubai • Farsi (Persian) phrasebook • Hebrew phrasebook • Iran • Israel & the Palestinian Territories • Istanbul • Istanbul City Map • Istanbul to Cairo • Istanbul to Kathmandu • Jerusalem • Jerusalem City Map • Jordan • Lebanon • Middle East • Oman & the United Arab Emirates • Syria • Turkey • Turkish phrasebook • World Food Turkey • Yemen **Travel Literature:** Black on Black: Iran Revisited • Breaking Ranks: Turbulent Travels in the Promised Land • The Gates of Damascus • Kingdom of the Film Stars: Journey into Jordan

NORTH AMERICA Alaska • Boston • Boston City Map • Boston Condensed • British Columbia • California & Nevada • California Condensed • Canada • Chicago • Chicago City Map • Chicago Condensed • Florida • Georgia & the Carolinas • Great Lakes • Hawaii • Hiking in Alaska • Hiking in the USA • Honolulu & Oahu City Map • Las Vegas • Los Angeles • Los Angeles City Map • Louisiana & the Deep South • Miami • Miami City Map • Montreal • New England • New Orleans • New Orleans City Map • New York City • New York City City Map • New York City Condensed • New York, New Jersey & Pennsylvania • Oahu • Out to Eat – San Francisco • Pacific Northwest • Rocky Mountains • San Diego & Tijuana • San Francisco • San Francisco City Map • Seattle • Seattle City Map • Southwest • Texas • Toronto • USA • USA phrasebook • Vancouver • Vancouver City Map • Virginia & the Capital Region • Washington, DC • Washington, DC City Map • World Food New Orleans **Travel Literature:** Caught Inside: A Surfer's Year on the California Coast • Drive Thru America

NORTH-EAST ASIA Beijing • Beijing City Map • Cantonese phrasebook • China • Hiking in Japan • Hong Kong & Macau • Hong Kong City Map • Hong Kong Condensed • Japan • Japanese phrasebook • Korea • Korean phrasebook • Kyoto • Mandarin phrasebook • Mongolia • Mongolian phrasebook • Seoul • Shanghai • South-West China • Taiwan • Tokyo • Tokyo Condensed • World Food Hong Kong • World Food Japan **Travel Literature:** In Xanadu: A Quest • Lost Japan

SOUTH AMERICA Argentina, Uruguay & Paraguay • Bolivia • Brazil • Brazilian phrasebook • Buenos Aires • Buenos Aires City Map • Chile & Easter Island • Colombia • Ecuador & the Galapagos Islands • Healthy Travel Central & South America • Latin American Spanish phrasebook • Peru • Quechua phrasebook • Read This First: Central & South America • Rio de Janeiro • Rio de Janeiro City Map • Santiago de Chile • South America on a shoestring • Trekking in the Patagonian Andes • Venezuela **Travel Literature:** Full Circle: A South American Journey

SOUTH-EAST ASIA Bali & Lombok • Bangkok • Bangkok City Map • Burmese phrasebook • Cambodia • Cycling Vietnam, Laos & Cambodia • East Timor phrasebook • Hanoi • Healthy Travel Asia & India • Hill Tribes phrasebook • Ho Chi Minh City (Saigon) • Indonesia • Indonesian phrasebook • Indonesia's Eastern Islands • Java • Lao phrasebook • Laos • Malay phrasebook • Malaysia, Singapore & Brunei • Myanmar (Burma) • Philippines • Pilipino (Tagalog) phrasebook • Read This First: Asia & India • Singapore • Singapore City Map • South-East Asia on a shoestring • South-East Asia phrasebook • Thailand • Thailand's Islands & Beaches • Thailand, Vietnam, Laos & Cambodia Road Atlas • Thai phrasebook • Vietnam • Vietnamese phrasebook • World Food Indonesia • World Food Thailand • World Food Vietnam

ALSO AVAILABLE: Antarctica • The Arctic • The Blue Man: Tales of Travel, Love and Coffee • Brief Encounters: Stories of Love, Sex & Travel • Buddhist Stupas in Asia: The Shape of Perfection • Chasing Rickshaws • The Last Grain Race • Lonely Planet ... On the Edge: Adventurous Escapades from Around the World • Lonely Planet Unpacked • Lonely Planet Unpacked Again • Not the Only Planet: Science Fiction Travel Stories • Ports of Call: A Journey by Sea • Sacred India • Travel Photography: A Guide to Taking Better Pictures • Travel with Children • Tuvalu: Portrait of an Island Nation

Index

Abbreviations

Text

Boxed Text

Bold indicates maps.

MAP LEGEND

CITY ROUTES

Freeway	Freeway
Highway	Primary Road
Road	Secondary Road
Street	Street
Lane	Lane
On/Off Ramp	

Unsealed Road	
One Way Street	
Pedestrian Street	
Stepped Street	
Tunnel	
Footbridge	

REGIONAL ROUTES

Tollway, Freeway
Primary Road
Secondary Road
Minor Road

BOUNDARIES

International
State
Disputed
Fortified Wall

HYDROGRAPHY

River, Creek
Canal
Lake

Dry Lake; Salt Lake
Spring; Rapids
Waterfalls

TRANSPORT ROUTES & STATIONS

Train
Underground Train
Metro
Tramway
Cable Car, Chairlift

Ferry
Walking Trail
Walking Tour
Path
Pier or Jetty

AREA FEATURES

Building
Park, Gardens

Market
Sports Ground

Beach
Cemetery

Campus
Plaza

POPULATION SYMBOLS

✪ CAPITAL	National Capital	● CITY	City	● Village	Village
◉ CAPITAL	State Capital	● Town	Town		Urban Area

MAP SYMBOLS

■	Place to Stay	▼	Place to Eat	●	Point of Interest
✈	Airport	Gate, Golf		National Park	Telephone
$	Bank	Hospital		Pagoda, Pass	Temple (Confucian)
	Border Crossing	Internet Cafe		Police Station	Temple (Other)
	Bus Terminal, Stop	Lookout, Lighthouse		Post Office	Temple (Taoist)
	Cave	Monument, Ruins		Pub or Bar	Tomb
	Church	Mosque		Shopping Centre	Tourist Information
	Cinema	Mountain, Range		Stately Home	Transport
	Embassy	Museum, Theatre		Swimming Pool	Zoo

Note: not all symbols displayed above appear in this book.
For a list of Chinese terms used on maps see the glossary.

LONELY PLANET OFFICES

Australia
Locked Bag 1, Footscray, Victoria 3011
☎ 03 8379 8000 fax 03 8379 8111
email: talk2us@lonelyplanet.com.au

USA
150 Linden St, Oakland, CA 94607
☎ 510 893 8555 TOLL FREE: 800 275 8555
fax 510 893 8572
email: info@lonelyplanet.com

UK
10a Spring Place, London NW5 3BH
☎ 020 7428 4800 fax 020 7428 4828
email: go@lonelyplanet.co.uk

France
1 rue du Dahomey, 75011 Paris
☎ 01 55 25 33 00 fax 01 55 25 33 01
email: bip@lonelyplanet.fr
www.lonelyplanet.fr

**World Wide Web: www.lonelyplanet.com *or* AOL keyword: lp
Lonely Planet Images: lpi@lonelyplanet.com.au**